Also from the Hound

VideoHound's® Golden Movie Retriever®

VideoHound's Epics:
Giants of the Big Screen

VideoHound's Horror Show:
999 Hair-Raising, Hellish, and Humorous Movies

VideoHound's Independent Film Guide, 2nd Edition

VideoHound's Vampires on Video

VideoHound's War Movies:
Classic Conflict on Film

VideoHound's World Cinema:
The Adventurer's Guide to Movie Watching

The St. James Film Directors Encyclopedia

The St. James Women Filmmakers Encyclopedia:
Women on the Other Side of the Camera

VideoHound's
DVD
GUIDE

"If you don't have a good story to tell, you're dead."

—John A. Alonzo, A.S.C.

VideoHound's DVD GUIDE

Mike Mayo

VISIBLE INK PRESS

AN IMPRINT OF THE GALE GROUP

DETROIT · NEW YORK · SAN FRANCISCO · LONDON · BOSTON · WOODBRIDGE, CT

VideoHound's DVD Guide

Copyright   © 2001 by Visible Ink Press

Published by   Visible Ink Press® , a division of Gale Group, Inc.

27500 Drake Rd.

Farmington Hills, MI 48331-3535

Visible Ink Press, *VideoHound,* the VideoHound logo, and A Cunning Canine Production are registered trademarks of Gale Group, Inc.

Gale Group and Design is a trademark used herein under license.

Most Visible Ink books are available at special quantity discounts when purchased in bulk by corporations, organizations, or groups. Customized printings, special imprints, messages, and excerpts can be produced to meet your needs. For more information, contact Special Markets Manager, Gale Group, 27500 Drake Rd., Farmington Hills, MI 48331-3535.

Art Direction   Pamela A.E. Galbreath

Library of Congress
Cataloging-in-Publication Data   Mayo, Mike, 1948–
     VideoHound's DVD Guide / Mike Mayo

                                                p.   cm.

     Includes bibliographical references and indexes.
     ISBN 1-57859-115-5 (softcover)
       1. Motion pictures—Catalogs. 2. DVD videodiscs—Catalogs
   I. Title.
   PPN 1998.M319   2001
   016.79143'75–dc21   00-043481
                                                  CIP

ISBN 1-57859-115-5   Printed in the United States of America

All rights reserved

10 9 8 7 6 5 4 3 2 1

A Cunning Canine Production®

Contents

Now that the new millennium has shepherded digital entertainment into the mainstream, a short reflection is in order.

by
Paul Culberg

DVD has enjoyed the fastest growth of any entertainment
format in the history of the world, with the exception, of
course, of humankind. The difference is that humankind
preys upon itself where DVD promises to build upon its basic
growth blocks (features) and continues to improve. A recent
stroll through an incredibly large DVD section in a well-known
entertainment retailer had my mind racing through the thousands of man- and woman-hours spent making DVD a cus-
tomer-friendly, highly useable entertainment.

It took eons, it seemed, to reach consensus on basic standards and compatibility issues—ratings, bar codes, regional
coding, and feature designations like 5.1 and full-screen
anamorphic. But despite the difficulties, there they were, filling
the shelves: the world's greatest movies, music videos, and
docu-everythings, all digitally reproduced and packed with information and anecdotal bits and pieces. Rewind? Never again!

All of this on a 5" disk that is easy to store and play in a
machine that is compact and attractive and delivers the
most remarkable sound. Sound, the most under-appreciated
feature of this format, is a very powerful part of the experience and anyone who neglects maximizing their entertainment space with the use of sound is missing out big time.
Several years ago I brought home the remastered and digitized version of *Das Boot* and marveled at how my dogs, not
fearful beasts in any way, tried to claw their way under the
couch to avoid the depth charges falling about the room in
5.1 Surround sound reproduction.

If I hadn't already been sold, that experience would have
done the job.

The promise has not been fulfilled, for the true promise of digital technology is that it will only continue to improve. The digital images will improve incrementally and the features will improve in a geometric manner. Those ubiquitous added-value snippets of outtakes and deleted scenes, story boards, and commentaries will soon be reworked into integrated supportive entertaining expository visions either independent of the movie and/or as stand-alone elements on each and every disk. The decoding power of chips integrated into players will create cable-ready, web-connected, PC-compatible, game-ready movie and music machines that will live in the entertainment center in the home. The amount of content that we will play on these machines will grow so that we will need a database market to ourselves just to help us decide what to watch. We will go to the store and we will go to the Net and to friends and to theatres and concerts and television and festivals to find our entertainment. No one delivery or access system will obliterate all of the rest. We, humankind, will determine how we want to access our entertainment by choosing the method of delivery. So, read this volume either on paper—my preference—or online, but use these tools to find and marvel at the depth and breadth of the creativity that defines us.

—Paul Culberg
July 2000

Paul Culberg spent more than 11 years with Columbia TriStar Home Video. Most recently, he was responsible for the company's online sales and marketing projects. During his tenure, he helped the division quadruple in size to exceed a billion dollar business. Before that, he was president of New World Video. He is now president of the DVD Entertainment Group, the trade organization of DVD manufacturers created to promote consumer awareness of the new medium. He is also executive vice president of VM Labs and chief operating officer of VM's NUON group, working with new areas of DVD performance and interactivity.

In the beginning, the acronym DVD stood for "Digital Video Disc." But things change quickly in today's world of competing and complementary technologies, and when the computer community expressed an interest, it was changed to "Digital Versatile Disc." What difference does it make to movie fans? None.

For the purposes of this book, DVD is simply the best form of home video. In almost every case—almost—a film seen and heard on DVD will be superior to VHS tape. It may even be better than a theatrical presentation. At least, that was the idea put forth by some directors at a 1999 panel on DVD who claimed that DVD was becoming their "medium of choice." More about that later.

For many years, the gold standard for home video was the laserdisc (LD). Laser delivers a sharper picture, and a disc may contain extra features related to the film. But LDs are big—as wide as LP (long playing) record albums—and heavy. Though image and sound were superior to VHS tape, the discs themselves were clumsy. Using analog information storage, they were incapable of holding an entire feature-length film on one side; and they were expensive. DVD corrects each of those shortcomings by switching from the analog technology of VHS and laser to digital. On DVD, the picture and sound are reduced to bits, or combinations of 1s and 0s, and then those bits are compressed. In his seminal book *Being Digital* (Knopf. 1995), Nick Negroponte defines compression as "looking at the bits over time, space, or both and removing the intrinsic redundancies and repetitions." From frame to frame, 95% of the information on a film stays the same and so doesn't need to be repeated. To put it another way: without compression, the visual and audio information on a DVD would fill up the hard drive of most home computers today.

For practical purposes, then, DVD combines the clarity and added features of laser disc (separate commentaries and other supplementary material) with the convenience of VHS tape at a price that's lower than either. In addition, every DVD player is also a CD player (though many people who own them seem not to realize that). What's lacking is recordability. For now, DVD technology is for playback only. That too will change, probably soon.

At its best, the DVD presentation of a film can have crystalline clarity that reveals intricate detail with a new depth to the image. Sound—particularly when experienced through multi-speaker Surround speakers—can add another new dimension that actually surpasses theatrical presentation. That's the ideal, although the medium does not always live up to it. If it did, there would be no need for this book. Still, digital disc is almost always an improvement over tape and, even when a DVD player is hooked up to an older television, it's going to deliver a significantly superior picture in almost every case.

Until now, most DVD reviews and guides have been aimed at "early adopters," those guys—they're almost all guys—who must have the newest toy. But DVD has grown beyond that audience with astonishing speed. *Entertainment Weekly* magazine (June 23, 2000) predicts DVD revenues will equal VHS tape by 2002. The medium has become mainstream, and that's the audience this book is aimed at: anyone who likes movies and wants to watch them at home in the finest and most convenient form possible.

The value of the book is threefold:

1) Virtually every film that was available on DVD by mid 2000 is listed here.

2) The important added features are noted in a separate section with each review.

3) With most titles, we're able to give some basis of comparison to other forms of home video—VHS tape and laser disc—and theatrical release.

In terms of image quality, the rule of thumb is that new big-budget films will look very good to excellent on DVD. The studios can make the digital transfer from a perfect original—"pre-print" is the term some reviewers use—that has never been run through a projector. The number of extra features on a disc is a measure of the film's financial and critical success. Big hits get the full treatment: deleted scenes, alternate endings, storyboards, production notes, "making of" documentaries, etc. Each is different. At a 1999 director's DVD panel, Robert Altman said that he doesn't like to include outtakes and deleted scenes on his discs out of a sense of "protection" for his actors. Director Werner Herzog, while happy that his older films are still appreciated on DVD, said that he doesn't want to spend too much of his own time revisiting that same work because, as he so elegantly put it, "a carpenter shouldn't sit on his shavings."

The most popular "extra" is the director's commentary track, sometimes solo, sometimes accompanied by creative collaborators. Those comments cover the full spectrum from genuine insights into the filmmaking process to fatuous flattery of everyone else the director has ever worked with. Generally, the observations of older directors are more worthwhile. Listening to Ken Russell describe what he was doing in the wonderful *Lair of the White Worm* brings new appreciation to an often-overlooked gem. Altman is always articulate and forthright with his opinions. On the other hand, some younger filmmakers reveal their ignorance and shallowness with embarrassing transparency.

With older films, the image transfer to DVD can be dicey. First, there's the condition of the original to be considered. Remember that interest in film preservation and restoration is a fairly recent development. Many excellent films have deteriorated horribly. It takes interest, work, and money to bring them up to something approaching the standard of presentation that today's audiences expect. It can be done, though, and when it's done right, the results are spectacular. Take a look at Buster Keaton's *The General, Man with a Camera,* the two versions of the restored *The Big Sleep,* or *The Third Man* to see just how good black-and-white full-frame film can look when it's transferred carefully to DVD. Without prohibitively expensive computer enhancement, DVD cannot improve a badly damaged original, but I'd still rather watch a banged-up, scratchy version of a good Sam Fuller film than an absolutely perfect copy of the newest Hollywood remake. And some wear and tear actually adds character to the best older films, such as George Clouzot's *Wages of Fear.* One caveat: when a title goes into public domain, anybody can slap it on disc. Some of those bargain-bin discs look pretty good; others are atrocious. *Two Women* immediately comes to mind in that regard.

The primary interest of the industry, though, is in new films, and many of the best and most innovative contain significant DVD additions that make them better on disc than they were in theaters. The most obvious recent examples are *L.A. Confidential, The Sixth Sense, Run Lola Run,* and *The Matrix.* Each of those terrific films contains useful extra features and an image transfer that's virtually flawless. Not all discs are so successful.

These are the main problems that can appear on DVD:

- Pixels: parts of the image coalesce into visible squares.

- Flashing patterns: often found in tweed clothes or background mini-blinds. When parallel lines are close together, they may flash stroboscopically or appear to pinwheel.

- Aliasing: diagonal lines break into a shallow stairstep pattern.

- Graininess increases in large areas of solid color.

- Digital sound can pop or "clip."

- Surround sound effects, which are meant to place the viewer in the middle of the audio, can be absent or minimal in action scenes.

- As is the case with CDs, surface scratches or blemishes on a disc can cause it to hang up or malfunction in a player.

Since this is a new technology, the terminology may be unfamiliar and difficult to define. One ultra-low-budget disc, *Caress of the Vampire,* contains such strange visual distortions that I really didn't know how to describe them.

Advances in DVD and other digital image technologies have increased audience awareness of image quality and raised their expectations. Recently I went to one of the first screenings of a big summer release—one of those movies that's supposed to make more than $100 million for its studio. I was there on a Friday afternoon for the first screening and was horrified by the condition of the print. Parts of it looked like someone had attacked the reels of film with a weed whacker! In the third or fourth week of release, after a print has been through the platter projection system a hundred times, then surface scratches, breaks, and nicks are to be expected. But to see such a shabby product on opening day is really unacceptable. And it's not just the picture; theatrical sound can suffer, too. A few weeks later, I went to the first matinee of another summer blockbuster. That time, the stereo effects started dropping out intermittently half way through. Such sloppy presentation cannot continue. People who are accustomed to seeing really sharp, clear DVD images at home are not going to put up with that kind of thing, no matter how good the popcorn is.

I predict that DVD is going to become a driving force behind the changes we will see in theatrical presentation as it goes digital. It's just starting to happen now, and the pressure is going to increase when the next generation of high-definition television monitors hits the stores. At about the same time, network broadcasts will be going digital, and people will be watching widescreen images at home without the expense, fuzziness, and physical space required to utilize projection systems. DVD is creating a new standard. This book is a snapshot of a medium that is just beginning to realize its capabilities. The directors on the DVD panel recognized that fact, too. Though they preferred full-sized theatrical presentation of their work, they realized the compromises that must be made in that line of distribution. Studio executives and the Motion Picture Association of America make demands for certain ratings. Theatre chains and exhibitors object to lengthy films that cannot be scheduled as often as shorter works. So, when it comes to putting everything that they wish to see on-screen—realizing their "artistic vision"—DVD is the medium of choice.

—Mike Mayo
Chatham, NJ

No book like this is the product of a single individual. Without the help of the following people, it would not have been possible.

Danielle Avazian made sure that New Line Home Video releases were included.

Martin Blythe worked with both Disney and Paramount films.

Sandi Bushnell and Dana Kornbluth of DKPR were particularly helpful in the earliest stages with WinStar and Fox Lorber titles.

Mike Canich, Greg Fichter, and Steve Bollinger provided critical input.

Bill Cubellis at Sony Electronics answered many technical questions.

Paul Culberg of both VM Labs and the DVD Entertainment Group wrote the Foreword.

Fritz Friedman, Jeff Kaplan, and Kavita Smith provided information and review discs for Columbia TriStar.

Rick Hale of Kim's Video in New York went out of his way to loan several rare titles at the last minute.

Liz Haggar held down the fort at Paramount.

Garrett Lee and Marc Walkow of Image Entertainment provided hundreds of review discs and helpful suggestions.

Jim Olenski, along with writing hundreds of reviews, was generous in loaning discs from the sales and rental sections of Thomas Video.

Sue Procko and Maral Kaloustian made sure that all the Anchor Bay releases were covered.

Rick Rhoades made sure that Fox films were made available.

John Soo facilitated review copies from Tai Seng Video Marketing.

Ralph Tribbey, editor of *The DVD Release Report,* provided reviews and valuable advice about the business.

To all, my most sincere thanks.

VideoHound's DVD Guide would not have been possible without the following talented people:

Editor

Mike Mayo (MM), editor in chief of Video-Hound's DVD Guide, is the author of Video-Hound's War Movies, VideoHound's Horror Show, and VideoHound's Video Premieres, and is a proud contributor to VideoHound's Complete Guide to Cult Flicks and Trash Pics and Sci-Fi Experience. He has written about film and video for the Roanoke Times and the Washington Post. Mike is also the co-host on the weekly syndicated radio program "The Movie Show on Radio."

Reviewers

Andrew BeDell (AB) lives in bucolic Mahwah, New Jersey, and is a freelance writer and editor who specializes in pop culture. For many years he wrote a syndicated column about TV (trying hard not to confuse fact with fiction); most recently he worked as a feature writer and pop music reviewer for the St. Louis Post-Dispatch, and contributed reviews to VideoHound's cousin, MusicHound.

Mike Brantley (MB) writes about film, television, and other media for the Mobile Register newspaper on the Gulf Coast of Alabama. He and his wife Cheryl are avid collectors of cinema in every format, including DVD, laserdisc, 16mm, and even Beta-max when they run across the rare garage sale find. Whenever he gets the chance, Mike rolls his own movies with a vintage Super 8 movie camera. He is webmaster of www.super8filmmaking.com, an Internet gathering place for small-gauge filmmakers.

Justine Elias (JE) is the only film critic to write for both Film Comment and Seventeen magazine within a single 30-day period. However, she is most notable for pioneering the Planet of the Apes Unified Film Theory, which holds that all movies—including those made decades before the 1968 classic—were actually influenced by or conceived as a reaction against it. She is now an editor at Entertainment Weekly Online.

When he is not designing and producing award-winning computer games, **Guido Henkel (GH)** spends most of his time working on www.DVDReview.com, one of the most popular DVD information websites on the Internet. He also writes for a variety of industry and consumer publications.

Jennifer Kramer (JK) and her husband Steve are proprietors of The Picture Palace (www.picpal.com).

Mike Long (ML) has a Bachelor's Degree in Film Studies from the University of North Carolina, where he began reviewing movies years ago. He also has a Master's Degree in Counseling from the University of North Carolina at Charlotte, and is a Licensed Professional Counselor. Mike has been reviewing films for DVDReview.com since March of 1999.

Jim Olenski (JO) is the owner of Thomas Video (www.thomasvideo.com) in Clawson, MI, a fabulous video store that specializes in hard-to-find, cult, foreign, independent, and classic film on VHS, DVD, and laserdisc. Jim is a frequent contributor to the *VideoHound*, and his column, "Videophile," appears weekly in *Real Detroit*. Jim's pseudo-elite and sometimes abrasive critical style spawned from the same punk ethic demonstrated in his 25 years as lead guitarist for the Detroit band Cinecyde. Jim is grateful for the opportunity to write for this book, because it gave him the excuse to buy a really expensive home theatre system.

In the dark days before home video, **Ralph Tribbey (RT)** brought *The Rocky Horror Picture Show* to weekly midnight screenings in a chain of small theatres that he owned and operated in Southern California. More recently, he has served in various capacities within the entertainment industry. On the publishing side of the business, he has served as managing editor for *American Video Monthly,* editor of *Video $ell Magazine,* and is currently editor and publisher of *The DVD Release Report.* On the manufacturing end of the business, he was senior vice president of marketing for West Coast Video Duplicating and is currently a consultant for Technicolor.

Michael J. Tyrkus (MJT) is an award-winning independent filmmaker, author, and editor. He has co-written and directed more than a dozen short films. As a writer and editor specializing in biographical and critical reference sources in literature and film, he has contributed to numerous references, including *The International Dictionary of Films and Filmmakers Vol 1: Films, Twentieth-Century Young Adult Writers,* and *The St. James Film Directors Encyclopedia,* edited by Andrew

Sarris. He is editor of *Gay & Lesbian Biography* and co-editor of *Outstanding Lives: Profiles of Lesbians and Gay Men.* He has also served as in-house project editor for and contributor to the *The St. James Women Filmmakers Encyclopedia.* He is co-founder of Lamb-Kiss Productions and founder of CityScene Productions.

Production Editors
Carol A. Schwartz and Diane Sawinski

Editor Without Whom Nothing Would Be Accomplished
Chris Tomassini

The VideoHound Litter
Michelle Banks, Erin Bealmer, Laura Berger, Joann Cerrito, Jim Craddock, Stephen Cusack, Miranda Ferrara, Kris Hart, Laura Kryhoski, Margaret Mazurkiewicz, and Mike Tyrkus

The Big Giant Hound Head
Peter Gareffa

Design Hound
Pamela A.E. Galbreath

Techno Hound
Wayne Fong

Proofreader and Former Hound
Beth Fhaner

Guy Who Spent a Lot of Time on the Phone Checking Facts
Jim Olenski

Production Hounds
Rita Wimberley, Evi Seoud, Mary Beth Trimper, and Dorothy Maki

Hype Hounds
Lauri Taylor, Kim Marich, Marilou Carlin, PJ Butland, and Betsy Rovegno

Special Hound Markets

Inez Torbert

Typesetting

Marco Di Vita of the Graphix Group

VideoHound Development

Christa Brelin, Julia Furtaw, and Martin Connors

And All the Hounds We've Loved Before

Shawn Brennan, Dean Dauphinais, Michelle DiMercurio, Diane Dupuis, Bob Elster, Barb Eschner, Judy Galens, Jeff Hermann, Roger Janecke, Mary Claire Krzewynski, Brad Morgan, Cyndi Naughton, Becky Nelson Ferguson, Leslie Norback Banks, Mary Alice Rattenbury, Tracey Rowens, Chris Scanlon, Terri Schell, Devra Sladics, Sue Stefani Wilkinson, Jenny Sweetland, Hilary Weber, and Julie Winklepleck

This book attempts to review every feature-length film that's available on DVD. The first discs were released in 1997; our deadline was mid-2000. The total number of movies that we had to work with was more than 3,000. Following the criteria used for the *VideoHound's Golden Movie Retriever,* we don't review works that are shorter than feature length (less than one hour, for practical purposes). We don't review music discs or adult films. We have included a few worthy TV shows and cartoon collections.

Each review begins with a brief plot synopsis and comment on the artistic quality of the film. Following that are remarks—some detailed, some cursory—on the technical details of image and sound. We then give each disc two ratings: one for content and one for presentation. That's something new for the VideoHound, but we—the editors, reviewers, and I—feel that the medium demands it. To explain: the content rating is based on the traditional 𝄢𝄢𝄢𝄢 to woof scale that judges the quality of the storytelling and filmmaking:

𝄢𝄢𝄢𝄢 Excellent: One of the best of its kind. Worth owning.

𝄢𝄢𝄢► Very good: Prime rental material. Perhaps worth owning.

𝄢𝄢𝄢 Good: Well worth watching.

𝄢𝄢 Average: For fans of the genre or star.

𝄢 Poor: Make sure the scan button is working properly.

woof You have been warned.

The technical rating refers to the quality of image, sound and extras:

𝄢𝄢𝄢𝄢 Excellent: Wow! The image approaches or even surpasses theatrical quality. Audio is equally spectacular.

𝄢𝄢𝄢► Very good: The image is noticeably sharper and brighter than videotape. The sound is crisp and clear.

𝄢𝄢𝄢 Good: Image and sound are somewhat better than tape but not really special.

𝄢𝄢 Average: Image and sound are not noticeably superior to VHS tape.

𝄢 Poor: Image and sound are substandard, due either to a poor original or transfer.

woof What *were* they thinking?

(Other half-bone ratings indicate the individual reviewer's mixed emotions, second and third thoughts, and free-floating equivocation.)

Each review ends with a listing of the extra features, if any, included on the disc. We also comment on those extras within the review when it's appropriate.

The various sound options available on many DVDs can be confusing and intimidating to those who are not familiar with the medium. This explanation, created by Image Entertainment and included with many discs, illustrates and explains the most popular systems (used with permission):

Dolby Digital Mono

This program features a mono soundtrack encoded to an AC-3 bitstream. When played through Dolby Digital equipment, sound will be heard from the center channel speaker only.

Dolby Digital Stereo

This program features a stereo soundtrack encoded to an AC-3 bitstream. When played through Dolby Digital equipment, sound will be heard from the front left and front right speakers only.

Dolby Digital Surround

This program features a matrixed Surround soundtrack encoded to an AC-3 bitstream. When played through Dolby Digital equipment, sound will be heard from all five system speakers. The Surround information will be discrete monophonic.

Dolby Digital 4.0

This program features a discrete four-channel soundtrack encoded to an AC-3 bitstream. When played through Dolby Digital equipment, sound will be heard from all five system speakers. The Surround information will be discrete monophonic.

Dolby Digital 5.0

This program features a discrete five-channel soundtrack encoded to an AC-3 bitstream. When played through Dolby Digital equipment, discrete sound will be heard from all five system speakers.

Dolby Digital 5.1

This program features a discrete 5.1-channel soundtrack encoded to an AC-3 bitstream. When played through Dolby Digital equipment, discrete sound will be heard from all five system speakers and a subwoofer.

PCM

This program features an uncompressed digital stereo soundtrack for improved fidelity. When played, discrete stereo sound will be heard from the front right and front left speakers.

DTS

This program features a discrete 5.1-channel soundtrack and must be played through DTS-capable equipment. When played through DTS equipment, sound will be heard from all five system speakers and a subwoofer.

The more advanced stereo Surround systems, which require extra equipment, add a dramatic dimension to newer films, but even without additional speakers and amplifiers, digital sound can be an improvement, particularly when heard through good headphones. (A headphone jack is available on many DVD players.) The soundtracks of some older films still contain static and hiss. Others have been cleaned up admirably.

Format and aspect ratios generally fall into three main categories: Full frame is the general dimensions of your TV screen (usually 1.33:1); if the original film was a different (usually wider) aspect ratio, this picture has probably been cropped or "panned and scanned." Letterboxed video offers a widescreen presentation, with black bands across the top and bottom of the picture, to better approximate the original aspect ratio of the theatrical presentation. The anamorphic format, like letterboxing, perserves the widescreen ratio, but with higher quality. In this book, the specific aspect ratios are provided when available.

While we address the technical questions with each title, we don't obsess over them.

This book is for people who like movies. Anyone who watches *Saving Private Ryan* and tries to find flaws in the black background when Capt. Miller and Sgt. Horvath talk at night in the church is missing the point.

Like videophiles everywhere, reviewers have different tastes, different equipment, different budgets, different living arrangements. It would be wonderful if all of us—reviewers and readers—could have state-of-the-art "reference" systems like the ones used by the writers at *Widescreen Review* magazine; true home theatres with widescreen monitors and Surround sound systems in rooms which could be darkened to the proper levels. But that's not the case, and so we do not presume to make definitive judgments. Having played many of the same discs on two different DVD players through the same monitor, I know that no two systems produce precisely the same image and sound.

When you watch a disc at home, your experience may not be the same as our reviewer's. You may see more flaws or fewer. If you enjoy a movie, you're likely to be forgiving. If you don't like it, the errors are going to jump off the screen at you.

In the end, we experience films in our minds. Yes, we use our eyes and ears, but intellect and emotion are just as important.

The various reviewers are identified by their initials at the end of each review. (Please see their thumbnail biographies on page xvii.) As a group, they are superbly qualified for the job. Each of them has written about film and video for other publications, and each brings different concerns to DVD. For example, JO, who belongs to a band, pays more attention to sound than most others. MB has a widescreen projection system and so he's often concerned with the difference between letterboxed and anamorphic image transfers. At the beginning of this project, JE had an old television set, and so when it came time to watch Shannon Whirry discs for review, she'd take her DVD player to the apartment across the hall and make her neighbor share his video monitor. (She then realized that "there are some things that'll make a man draw the line and fight for his turf, and there are some things that'll make a man realize that he is powerless to resist you. Shannon Whirry DVDs are such a thing.")

The one quality they share is a love of film.

Most of the entries were written from review copies of DVDs provided by the studios, but not all of them were willing to make their products available. Jim Olenski lent many discs from the rental and sales section of his store, Thomas Video, in Clawson, MI (www.thomasvideo.com). Other reviewers worked from their personal libraries, and, when necessary, we rented and bought discs wherever we could find them.

Readers should pay little attention to the prices listed here. They are the retail prices suggested by the distributors. DVDs are often put on sale and, after their initial release, catalogue titles are routinely marked down.

Finally, I must admit that we weren't able to get to everything. Since the beginning of the DVD business, production and distribution have been troublesome. Even though the industry is only a few years old, it is extremely difficult to find some titles. Several discs have gone out of print after having been released in small numbers. Others have been announced but never delivered.

As this book goes to press, the Criterion Collection version of John Woo's *The Killer* is so rare that copies fetch premium prices on Internet auction sites. By the time the book is in stores, a new WinStar edition should be available. The situation changes from week to week. We've done the best we could, but when we could not find and watch a title, we've included a brief plot review, as much technical information as we could find, and "NYR" (not yet reviewed) in place of a technical rating. We hope to fill in the gaps in the second edition.

—MM

Alphabetization

Titles are arranged on a word-by-word basis, including articles and prepositions. Leading articles (A, An, The) are ignored in English-language titles; the equivalent foreign articles are not ignored (because so many people—not you, of course—don't recognize them as articles); thus, *The Abyss* appears in the As, but *L'Enfer* appears in the Ls. Acronyms appear alphabetically as if regular words; for example, *D.O.A.* is alphabetized as "DOA." Common abbreviations in titles file as if they were spelled out, so *Dr. Strangelove* will be alphabetized as "Doctor Strangelove" and *Mr. Nice Guy* as "Mister Nice Guy." Movie titles with numbers, such as *2001: A Space Odyssey,* are alphabetized as if the number were spelled out—so Kubrick's classic would appear in the Ts as if it were "Two Thousand and One: A Space Odyssey." Proper names in titles are alphabetized beginning with the individual's first name; for instance, *Richard Pryor: Live on the Strip* is under "R;" *Stephen King's The Tommyknockers* is under "S."

Country of Origin Codes

The country of origin codes indicate the country or countries in which a film was produced or financed. A listing of films by country may also be found in the **Category Index** under the appropriate term below.

AT	Austrian	*IR*	Irish
AU	Australian	*IS*	Israeli
BE	Belgian	*IT*	Italian
BR	Brazilian	*JP*	Japanese
GB	British	*KO*	Korean
CA	Canadian	*MX*	Mexican
CH	Chinese	*NZ*	New Zealand
CU	Cuban	*NO*	Norwegian
CZ	Czech	*PL*	Polish
NL	Dutch	*PT*	Portuguese
PH	Filipino	*RU*	Russian
FR	French	*SA*	South African
GE	German	*SP*	Spanish
HK	Hong Kong	*SW*	Swedish
HU	Hungarian	*TW*	Taiwanese
IN	Indian	*YU*	Yugoslavian
IA	Iranian		

Abbreviations

No detailed technical explanations here, just a quick reference list (with a few literal definitions, for the really curious reader) for abbreviations and acronyms used in this book.

AC3	audio coding algorithm (that is, Dolby Digital)
AKA	also known as
B	black and white
B&W	black and white
C	color
CAP:	Closed captions:
Cat.	catalog (number)
CD	compact disc
CD-I	compact disc—interactive
CE	Collector's Edition
CGI	computer-generated image
CS	Collector's Series
D.P.	director of photography (cinematographer)
DC	Director's Cut
DD	Dolby Digital
DS	Dolby Surround
DTS	Digital Theater Systems (a surround audio system)
DVD	digital versatile disc
DVD-ROM	digital versatile disc—read only memory
f/x	effects
HDTV	high-definition television
LANG:	Language(s):
LD	laserdisc
min.	minute
mm.	millimeter
MPAA	Motion Picture Association of America
NOM:	Nominations:
NSL	no standard list (price)
NYR	not yet reviewed
PCM	pulse code modulation (a sound format)
RSDL	reverse spiral dual-layer
SE	Special Edition
sf	science fiction
SUB:	Subtitles:
THX	Tomlinson Holman experiment (an audio system certification)
UPC	Universal Product Code (number)
VHS	video helical scan (the predominate videotape format)

Sample Review

Each review contains up to 25 tidbits of information, as enumerated below. Please realize that we faked a bit of info in this review for demonstration purposes.

1. Title; some titles have the designation SE (Special Edition), CE (Collector's Edition), CS (Collector's Series), or DC (Director's Cut), as indicated by the distributor

2. Synopsis/review

3. Byline of reviewer; see **Contributors,** p. xvii

4. Alternative title (we faked it here)

5. Critical rating of the movie (🐾 to 🐾🐾🐾🐾 or woof, 🐾🐾🐾🐾 being the ultimate praise)

6. Technical rating of DVD image, sound, and extras (using the same scale); DVDs that were not yet available for review are noted "NYR"

7. Distributor of the DVD

8. Distributor catalog number

9. Distributor UPC

10. Format and aspect ratio (more than one option may be offered)

11. Sound (again, more than one are possible)

12. Price of DVD

13. Type of DVD case

14. Language(s)

15. Subtitle(s), if any

16. Closed captions, if any

17. Special added features of the DVD

18. Other information about the DVD

19. Year movie was released

20. MPAA rating

21. Length in minutes

22. Black and white (B) or Color (C)

23. Country of origin (if other than the U.S.); see previous page for codes

24. Credits, including cast, voice cast (**V:**), director (**D:**), screenwriter (**W:**), cinematographer (**C:**), and music composer/lyricist (**M:**)

25. Awards and nominations

---

① Clerks

② Day in the life of a bored convenience store clerk (O'Halloran) and his best friend Randal, who mans the video store next door. Nothing much actually happens—other than a constant parade of crazies, a hockey game on the roof, and even a little necrophilia. Lots of scuzzy fun and non-stop offensive (and hilarious) dialogue. First-time director Smith (Silent Bob in the movie) based this low-budget ($27,575) film on his four years of tormenting customers at the convenience store where he shot on location. The big plus is that the DVD offers all the extras that first appeared on the laserdisc, including the alternate ending and deleted scenes. Unfortunately the video itself looks far worse than the VHS tape. There's so much grain that on most movies it would be unbearable; but because the film's style is so deliberately rough, that's not too aggravating. The contrast and brightness levels are good (about the same as the laserdisc), and the sound is very good, in fact almost too good when the music cuts come in. The bottom line is that, despite the picture, this DVD is worth adding to your collection even if its just for the supplemental material. ③ —JO ④ AKA: Kevin Smith's Clerks.
⑤ Movie: 🐾🐾 ⑥ DVD: 🐾🐾
⑦ Miramax ⑧ (Cat # 17365, ⑨ UPC # 717951002716). ⑩ Widescreen (1.85:1) letterboxed. ⑪ Dolby Surround. ⑫ $34.98.
⑬ Keepcase. ⑭ LANG: English.
⑮ SUB: French, Spanish ⑯ CAP: English.
⑰ FEATURES: 18 chapter links · Theatrical trailer · Alternate ending · Deleted scenes · Commentary: director Smith and cast members · Soul Asylum music video. ⑱ Also available as part of a "Kevin Smith" two-pack boxed set.
⑲ 1995 ⑳ (R) ㉑ 89m/ ㉒ B
㉓ US ㉔ Brian O'Halloran, Jef Anderson, Marilyn Ghigliotti, Lisa Spoonhauer, Jason Mewes, Kevin Smith; D: Kevin Smith; W: Kevin Smith; C: David Klein; A: David Klein; M: Scott Angley. ㉕ Sundance Film Festival '94: Filmmakers Trophy; NOM: Independent Spirit AWARDS '95: Best First Feature, Debut Performance (Anderson), First Screenplay.

Abbott and Costello in the Foreign Legion

Wrestling promoters Jonesy (Abbott) and Max (Costello) trail their runaway fighter to Algiers where they're tricked into joining the French Foreign Legion. They have to cope with a sadistic sergeant and a sexy spy (Medina) to find their man. Most of the laughs come from Lou's wild desert mirages. The no-frills DVD reflects the spirit of this long-running but low-budget Universal series. As was almost always the case, the black-and-white photography is crisp and the familiar sets are well used. The only obvious visual flaw is some wild flashing on Lou's tie. —MM

Movie: ♫♫▶ **DVD:** ♫♫♫

Image Entertainment (Cat #ID4298USDVD, UPC #014381429824). Full frame. PCM Mono. $24.99. Snapper. *LANG:* English. *FEATURES:* 16 chapter links.

1950 80m/B Bud Abbott, Lou Costello, Walter Slezak, Patricia Medina, Douglass Dumbrille, Leon Belasco, Marc Lawrence, Tor Johnson; *D:* Charles Lamont; *W:* John Grant, Martin Ragaway, Leonard Stern; *C:* George Robinson.

About Last Night . . .

Semi-realistic comedy-drama explores the ups and downs of a couple's relationship. Mostly quality performances, especially Perkins and Delushi as friends of the young lovers. Based on David Mamet's play *Sexual Perversity in Chicago*, but considerably softened so that more people would buy tickets at the boxoffice, the film acts as a historical view of contemporary mating rituals before the onset of the AIDS crisis. This is a pretty so-so DVD. The sharpness is, for the most part, average, but in bright scenes the grain really picks up. The blacks are never really true and when they are dominant in a scene they lean towards gray/green and become grainy. The colors (mostly earthtones) are adequate and there is little bleed. The

sound is also average, with a touch too much mid-range, making it at times a little tinny. All in all, about the same quality as the VHS SP version. —JO

Movie: ♫♫▶ **DVD:** ♫♫▶

Columbia Tristar Home Video (Cat #07359, UPC #043396073593). Widescreen (1.85:1) letterboxed; full frame. Dolby Surround. NSL. Keepcase. *LANG:* English; Spanish; French. *SUB:* Spanish; French. *CAP:* English. *FEATURES:* 28 chapter links ➥ Theatrical trailers.

1986 (R) 113m/C Rob Lowe, Demi Moore, Elizabeth Perkins, James Belushi, George DiCenzo, Robin Thomas, Michael Alldredge; *D:* Edward Zwick; *W:* Tim Kazurinsky, Denise DeClue; *C:* Andrew Dintenfass; *M:* Miles Goodman.

Above the Law

Seagal makes his screen debut as a tough Chicago police detective planning a big drug bust of a most-wanted bad guy (and former associate) when the Feds order him to back off. Sure, like he'd listen to the FBI. The abundant action scenes are well choreographed with plenty of violence. Seagal's character is rumored to be based on his "mysterious" secret past when he was supposedly some sort of government operative. Before Seagal's wooden acting became unchangingly familiar, it almost seemed introspective and showed promise for the action genre— promises, promises. This DVD is very sharp and relatively grain-free. Blacks are true, as are the colors, which are vibrant and have no significant bleed. Contrast and brightness levels are excellent and consistent. The soundtrack is another strong point with good thumping low end, great dynamics and fidelity, and good Surround all the way through, even when just effects-free music. —JO

Movie: ♫♫▶ **DVD:** ♫♫♫▶

Warner Home Video, Inc. (Cat #11786, UPC #085391178620). Full frame; widescreen (1.85:1) letterboxed. Dolby Digital

5.1. $24.98. Snapper. *LANG:* English; Spanish. *SUB:* Spanish; French. *CAP:* English. *FEATURES:* 31 chapter links ➥ 8 theatrical trailers ➥ Production notes.

1988 (R) 99m/C Steven Seagal, Pam Grier, Henry Silva, Sharon Stone, Ron Dean, Daniel Faraldo, Chelcie Ross, Thalmus Rasulala, Michael Rooker; *D:* Andrew Davis; *W:* Andrew Davis, Steven Pressfield; *C:* Robert Steadman; *M:* David Michael Frank.

Abraxas: Guardian of the Universe

Actor-governor Jesse Ventura stars as good space cop Abraxas charged with the task of preventing planets from ecological destruction and senseless wars. His current mission is here on Earth where he must save the life of an alien kid while his ex-partner turned bad space cop Secundas (Ole-Thorsen) tries to obtain an anti-life power that can destroy the universe. The two exes duke it out, turning the Earth (or at least a town) into a low-budget special effects battleground. B-grade all the way, but entertaining nonetheless, especially the Guv, whose performance mirrors his former wrestling career. Fairly well-written trash. The first bad things you'll notice about this DVD are the digital artifacts that often blur the picture, which is actually pretty sharp most of the time. Grain is present but not too aggravating. The colors don't bleed much but are not saturated near enough. Brightness and contrast levels, though comfortable, could have used a little boost. The blacks are about average with occasional grain and leanings toward gray. You won't use this soundtrack to show off your system—it's pretty lifeless overall with even Ventura's booming voice needing a little more punch. —JO **AKA:** Abraxas.

Movie: ♫♫▶ **DVD:** ♫♫

Simitar Entertainment (Cat #7575, UPC #082551757527). Full frame. Dolby Digi-

tal 2.0. $14.98. Keepcase. *LANG:* English. *FEATURES:* 8 chapter links ▪ Cast and crew bios ▪ Production notes.
1990 (R) 90m/C Jesse Ventura, Sven-Ole Thorsen, Damian Lee, Marjorie Bransfield, Ken Quinn, Marilyn Lightstone, Moses Znaimer, Layne Coleman, Sonja Belliveau, James Belushi; *D:* Damian Lee; *W:* Damian Lee; *C:* Curtis Petersen.

Absence of Malice

High-minded story about the harm that the news media can inflict. Field is the earnest reporter who, after being fed some facts by an unscrupulous federal investigator, writes a story implicating Newman in a murder he didn't commit. Field hides behind journalistic confidentiality privilege to put off the outraged Newman, who loses a friend to suicide during the debacle. This is a very good DVD in almost every way. From the get go, the Dave Grusin orchestral score is great, a good full, dynamic sound, with the brassy sections punching through crisply. The picture is sharp and digital grain is almost nonexistent. Contrast and brightness levels are very good and consistent—the disc's biggest problem is some distortion along high-contrast lines. There are no noticeable artifacts or pixelation. Both colors and blacks are very close to true and there is very little color bleed, even among the reds. —*JO*
Movie: 🎵🎵🎵 *DVD:* 🎵🎵🎵
Columbia Tristar Home Video (Cat #26959, UPC #043396269590). Widescreen (1.85:1) letterboxed; full frame. NSL. Keepcase. *LANG:* English; Spanish; French. *SUB:* Spanish; French. *CAP:* English. *FEATURES:* 28 chapter links ▪ Theatrical trailer.
1981 (PG) 116m/C Paul Newman, Sally Field, Bob Balaban, Melinda Dillon, Luther Adler, Barry Primus, Josef Sommer, John Harkins, Don Hood, Wilford Brimley; *D:* Sydney Pollack; *W:* Kurt Luedtke; *C:* Owen Roizman; *M:* Dave Grusin. *AWARDS: NOM:* Academy Awards '81: Best Actor (Newman), Best Original Screenplay, Best Supporting Actress (Dillon).

Absolute Power

Eastwood is "In the Line of Fire" (against the very agents he previously glorified) as an expert thief being pursued by rogue Secret Service men in this fast-paced thriller. While looting a Washington official's place, Luther (Eastwood) inadvertently witnesses a murder committed by none other than U.S. President Richmond (Hackman) and his goons. Immediately, a cover-up is organized by his unbalanced chief-of-staff (Davis). Harris gives his usual solid performance as the homicide detective. Eastwood's simple directorial style maintains the suspense and propels the film forward, though the plot gets improbable near the end. The blacks are so true on this DVD that Clint's black shirt at the beginning of the film matches the black bars of the letterbox. You shouldn't

see any bleed in the colors, which are true to the theatrical release. The picture is crisp and sharp and the only time grain appears is in scenes that are near dark. The soundtrack features good Surround, very good dynamics and low end, and very good imaging and space on both the main and Surround tracks. A little brighter picture with a boost on the contrast would have helped a bit but this is still a very good-looking DVD. —*JO*
Movie: 🎵🎵🎵 *DVD:* 🎵🎵🎵
Warner Home Video, Inc. (Cat #C2508, UPC #01256925082). Widescreen (2.35:1) letterboxed; full frame. Dolby Digital 5.1. $24.98. Snapper. *LANG:* English. *SUB:* Spanish; French. *CAP:* English. *FEATURES:* 35 chapter links ▪ Production notes.
1997 (R) 120m/C Clint Eastwood, Gene Hackman, Ed Harris, Laura Linney, Judy Davis, Scott Glenn, Dennis Haysbert, E.G. Marshall, Melora Hardin; *D:* Clint Eastwood; *W:* William Goldman; *C:* Jack N. Green; *M:* Lennie Niehaus.

The Abyss (SE)

James Cameron's epic underwater sf adventure arrives on DVD as a two-disc set with every conceivable extra, including two separate versions of the film itself. One is the 140-minute theatrical release; the other is the "special edition" with roughly another 31 minutes of restored footage. It has been available on laser. The main difference here is the inclusion of both versions on one disc. All of the other extras are on the second. The package also includes a booklet that details the differences between the two versions. To some tastes, even the shorter version is too long and part of the on-screen commentary text is devoted to explanations of narrative uncertainties. (The extended story has to do with first contact with an alien race and World War III.) Needless to say, the DVD image is virtually perfect. It's actually much sharper than the scratched-up print I saw in the theatre. Sound is excellent, too. The choice of text rather than audio commentary is probably wise. It ranges from trivia about the supporting cast to details of the special effects and other aspects of the production. —*MM*
AKA: L'Oeuvre au Noir.
Movie: 🎵🎵🎵 *DVD:* 🎵🎵🎵🎵
Twentieth Century Fox Home Entertainment (Cat #2000119, UPC #024543001195). Widescreen (2.35:1) letterboxed. Dolby Digital Surround Stereo. $34.98. Keepcase. *LANG:* English; French. *SUB:* English; Spanish. *CAP:* English. *FEATURES:* 54 chapter links, special edition ▪ 45 chapter links, theatrical ▪ Text commentary track ▪ 60-minute "making of" featurette ▪ Screenplay ▪ Multi-angle presentation of pseudo-pod sequence ▪ DVD-ROM games, storyboard, and stills ▪ 12-page booklet.
1989 (PG-13) 140m/C Ed Harris, Mary Elizabeth Mastrantonio, Todd Graff, Michael Biehn, John Bedford Lloyd, J.C. Quinn, Leo Burmester, Kidd Brewer Jr., Kimberly Scott, Adam Nelson, George Robert Kirk, Chris Elliott, Jimmie Ray

Weeks; *D:* James Cameron; *W:* James Cameron; *C:* Mikael Salomon; *M:* Alan Silvestri. *AWARDS:* Academy Awards '89: Best Visual Effects; *NOM:* Academy Awards '89: Best Art Direction/Set Decoration, Best Cinematography, Best Sound.

Ace Ventura: Pet Detective

Shamelessly silly comedy casts human cartoon Carrey, he of the rubber limbs and spasmodic facial muscles, as Ace, the guy who'll find missing pets, big or small. When the Miami Dolphins' mascot Snowflake is kidnapped, he abandons his search for an albino pigeon to save the lost dolphin just in time for the Super Bowl. Full-throttled juvenile humor with the hyper-energetic Carrey and Young as the police chief with a secret. Critically trashed boxoffice smash catapulted Carrey into nearly instant stardom after seven seasons on *In Living Color*. From the moment you put this DVD on, the first thing you'll notice is the excessive grain in any of the darker colors; it starts right in the film company's logo and continues throughout. There is a lot more print damage than you would expect from a major title this recent. The picture is of average sharpness and during bright scenes the grain reaches unacceptable levels. Blacks are close to true most of the time but pick up a gray grain in the dimmer scenes. Everything else is pretty much average, including the colors, which bleed from time to time. The sound is thin and would definitely have been helped by a little boost on the low end. —*JO*
Movie: 🎵🎵▶ *DVD:* 🎵▶
Warner Home Video, Inc. (Cat #23000, UPC #085392300020). Full frame. Dolby Digital 5.1. $24.98. Snapper. *LANG:* English. *SUB:* Spanish; French. *CAP:* English. *FEATURES:* 31 chapter links ▪ Theatrical trailer ▪ Commentary: director Tom Shadyac ▪ Additional footage.
1993 (PG-13) 87m/C Jim Carrey, Dan Marino, Courteney Cox Arquette, Sean Young, Tone Loc; *D:* Tom Shadyac; *W:* Jim Carrey, Tom Shadyac, Jack Bernstein; *C:* Julio Macat; *M:* Ira Newborn. *AWARDS:* Blockbuster Entertainment Awards '95: Male Newcomer, Video (Carrey), Comedy Actor, Video (Carrey); *NOM:* MTV Movie Awards '94: Best Comedic Performance (Carrey).

Ace Ventura: When Nature Calls

Ace (Carrey) is back on the case as the pet dick ventures to Africa to restore peace among rival tribes by finding an albino bat that's M.I.A. Plot is secondary to multi-million dollar man Carrey's outrageous brand of physical comedy combined with his unique ability to deliver junior-high level lines with pseudo-suave savoir-faire, but the film contains only a handful of outstanding gags, the best with Carrey and a mechanical rhino. The low-brow humor runs a bit thin by the end. It figures that

the DVD of the weaker of the two *Ace Ventura* films would be far superior to the original. It's still lacking in the sharpness department but has colors that are true and very little grain—they bleed only on very intense reds. For the most part the blacks are dead-on and never overly grainy. The contrast and brightness levels consistently give the picture some punch, although there are a few times when the contrast lines are very distorted. Some needed guts have also been added to the soundtrack which is crisper, more dynamic, and has the low-end boost that would have greatly helped the first one. —*JO*
AKA: Ace Ventura Goes to Africa.
Movie: 🐾🐾 **DVD:** 🐾🐾🐾
Warner Home Video, Inc. (Cat #23500, UPC #085392350025). Widescreen (2.35:1) letterboxed; full frame. Dolby Digital 5.1; Dolby Surround. $24.98. Snapper. *LANG:* English (DDS5.1); Spanish (DS); French (DS). *SUB:* Spanish; French. *CAP:* English. *FEATURES:* 36 chapter links • Theatrical trailers • Production notes.
1995 (PG-13) 94m/C Jim Carrey, Ian McNeice, Simon Callow, Maynard Eziashi, Bob Gunton, Sophie Okonedo, Tommy Davidson; **D:** Steve Oedekerk; **W:** Steve Oedekerk; **C:** Donald E. Thorin; **M:** Robert Folk. *AWARDS:* MTV Movie Awards '96: Best Male Performance (Carrey), Best Comedic Performance (Carrey); Blockbuster Entertainment Awards '96: Comedy Actor, Theatrical (Carrey); *NOM:* MTV Movie Awards '96: Best Kiss (Jim Carrey/Sophie Okonedo).

Across the Moon

A good ensemble is cast adrift in a fitful comedy-drama about Carmen (Pena) and Kathy (Applegate), who follow their jailbird boyfriends (Fields and Berg) to the Mojave desert after said boyfriends' incarceration in a remote prison. Eccentric supporting characters (played by Remar, Meredith, and McKean) are introduced and abandoned pointlessly. The film is generally overacted and the actors look far too glamorous for their allegedly down-and-out characters. That goes for the locations, too. The bright DVD gives the desert exteriors and mobile home interiors the right feeling, and the sound is excellent. —*MM*
Movie: 🐾▶ **DVD:** 🐾🐾▶
Image Entertainment (Cat #ID5688PZDVD, UPC #014381568820). Full frame. Dolby Digital Surround. $14.99. Snapper. *LANG:* English. *FEATURES:* 14 chapter links.
1994 (R) 88m/C Elizabeth Pena, Christina Applegate, Tony Fields, Peter Berg, James Remar, Michael McKean, Burgess Meredith, Jack Nance; **D:** Lisa Gottlieb; **W:** Stephen Schneck; **C:** Andrzej Sekula; **M:** Christopher Tyng, Exene Cervenka.

Action Jackson

Power-hungry auto tycoon Nelson tries to frame rebellious black police sergeant Weathers for murder. Being a graduate of Harvard and a tough guy, the cop doesn't go for it. Nelson chews up the screen as the heavy with no redeeming qualities, while Weathers is tongue-in-cheek as the resourceful good guy who keeps running afoul of the law in spite of his best efforts. Lots of action, violence, and enough sexy women to keep things interesting. This is a Warner Bros. budget line DVD that actually looks pretty good. The biggest problem is that pseudo 3-D effect caused by the foregrounds being so much sharper than the backgrounds, which are sometimes incredibly foggy—you can almost see nonexistent matte lines. The colors are rich but there are times when bright reds (Jackson's red shirt two-thirds into the film) shimmy and shake out of their boundaries. Blacks range from dead-on to gray/green grainy. The stereo soundtrack is generally crisp and clean, with good dynamics. However, the low end sometimes has a digitized sound to it. All in all, well worth the $14.98. —*JO*
Movie: 🐾🐾▶ **DVD:** 🐾🐾▶
Warner Home Video, Inc. (Cat #816, UPC #012569081628). Full frame. Dolby Digital Stereo. $14.98. Snapper. *LANG:* English; French. *FEATURES:* 30 chapter links.
1988 (R) 96m/C Carl Weathers, Vanity, Craig T. Nelson, Sharon Stone; **D:** Craig R. Baxley; **W:** Robert Reneau; **C:** Matthew F. Leonetti; **M:** Herbie Hancock, Michael Kamen.

Adam's Rib

Classic war between the sexes finds Tracy and Hepburn cast as married attorneys on opposite sides of the courtroom in the trial of blonde bombshell Holliday who's charged with the attempted murder of her philandering husband's lover. The couple find it increasingly difficult to leave their work at the office as the courtroom battle escalates. Sharp, snappy dialogue by Gordon and Kanin with superb direction by Cukor. Perhaps the best of the nine movies pairing Tracy and Hepburn is another great-looking black-and-white DVD. The blacks are exceptionally true, the graytone range very broad, and both the contrast and brightness levels excellent. Grain is near nonexistent and the picture is very sharp. All this makes for a detailed image with a wonderful feeling of depth. There is occasional artifacting during a few sweeping camera pans but then the picture returns to excellent once again. The soundtrack is fine, within the limitations of a mono recording this old. —*JO*
Movie: 🐾🐾🐾🐾 **DVD:** 🐾🐾🐾▶
MGM Home Entertainment (Cat #906010, UPC #027616661029). Full frame. Dolby Digital Mono. $24.98. Snapper. *LANG:* English; French. *SUB:* English; Spanish; French. *FEATURES:* 28 chapter links.
1950 101m/B Spencer Tracy, Katharine Hepburn, Judy Holliday, Tom Ewell, David Wayne, Jean Hagen, Hope Emerson, Polly Moran, Marvin Kaplan, Paula Raymond, Tommy Noonan; **D:** George Cukor; **W:** Garson Kanin, Ruth Gordon; **C:** George J. Folsey; **M:** Miklos Rozsa. *AWARDS:* National Film Registry '92; *NOM:* Academy Awards '50: Best Story & Screenplay.

Addicted to Love

After they're both dumped, mild-mannered Sam (Broderick) and wild woman Maggie (Ryan) discover they have a lot in common. First of all, their exes Linda (Preston) and Anton (Karyo) are dating each other. Secondly, they're both stalkers! Yep, romantic comedy about stalking. Sam wants nothing more than to reclaim Linda as his own. Maggie wants nothing less than Anton's head on a plate. Interesting comedy wavers between dark and light moments. The DVD looks far better than the VHS but could have used some added punch to the picture, probably with a boost to both the sharpness and contrast, which are at least consistent. Within these levels the colors are above average and do not bleed and there are very few artifacts. The soundtrack is a little better than the picture and is crisp and full. —*JO*
Movie: 🐾🐾▶ **DVD:** 🐾🐾▶
Warner Home Video, Inc. (Cat #15252, UPC #085391525226). Widescreen (1.85:1) letterboxed; full frame. Dolby Digital 5.1; Dolby Digital Stereo. $24.98. Snapper. *LANG:* English (DD5.1); French (DS). *SUB:* English; Spanish; French. *CAP:* English. *FEATURES:* 32 chapter links • Theatrical trailer • Production notes.
1996 (R) 100m/C Meg Ryan, Matthew Broderick, Kelly Preston, Tcheky Karyo, Maureen Stapleton, Remak Ramsay, Nesbitt Blaisdell, Dominick Dunne; **D:** Griffin Dunne; **W:** Robert Gordon; **C:** Andrew Dunn; **M:** Rachel Portman.

Adventures in Babysitting

One of the truly great girls adventures deserves better treatment on DVD. When Chris Parker (Shue) is left in the lurch out in the ritzy Chicago 'burbs, she takes a last-minute babysitting job. Then her friend Brenda (Miller) calls for help; Chris and the kids are off on a wild ride that entails gangsters, chases, death-defying escapes, and a lesson in singing the blues. The lightweight action benefits from lively direction and an attractive, enthusiastic cast. Unfortunately, their efforts are undermined by a lackluster disc that appears to have been made from a less-than-perfect print. In conventional interiors, colors are faded and washed-out. Dark scenes are grainy. The stereo sound is acceptable but ought to be better than that in the Silver Dollar Room sequence with Albert Collins. —*MM*
Movie: 🐾🐾🐾 **DVD:** 🐾🐾
Buena Vista Home Entertainment (Cat #17593, UPC #717951003300). Widescreen (1.85:1) letterboxed. Dolby Digital Surround Stereo. $29.99. Keepcase. *LANG:* English; French. *CAP:* English. *FEATURES:* 22 chapter links.
1987 (PG-13) 102m/C Elisabeth Shue, Keith Coogan, Maia Brewton, Anthony Rapp, Calvin Levels, Vincent D'Onofrio, Penelope Ann Miller, George Newbern, John Ford Noonan, Lolita (David) Davidovich, Albert Collins; **D:** Chris Columbus;

W: David Simkins; **C:** Ric Waite; **M:** Michael Kamen.

The Adventures of Baron Munchausen

From the director of *Time Bandits, Brazil*, and *The Fisher King* comes an ambitious, imaginative, chaotic, and underappreciated marvel based on the tall (and often confused) tales of the Baron. Munchausen rides a cannonball, gets swallowed by a sea monster, and encounters the King of the Moon (and other odd characters) in what might be described as a circular narrative in which things are never what they seem to be. Wonderful special effects and visually stunning sets prove what Gilliam can do with a big budget. A good-looking DVD. All the components of the picture—sharpness, brightness, contrast—are very good. The blacks are near perfect as are the earthy colors, which show only a little bleed during a couple of scenes; this is pretty amazing since the film's dominant color is a reddish brown. Grain is near nonexistent as are artifacts. The sound doesn't disappoint with its quirky orchestral score, sound effects, and dialogue all very crisp and full-bodied. Performance-wise, the DVD stands up favorably to Criterion's laser version, though missing all the supplementals. —*JO*
Movie: 🎵🎵🎵▶ **DVD:** 🎵🎵🎵
Columbia Tristar Home Video (Cat #76989, UPC #043396769892). Widescreen (1.85:1) letterboxed. Dolby Surround. Keepcase. *LANG:* English (DS); Spanish (Mono); Portuguese (Mono). *SUB:* Spanish; Portuguese; Korean; Chinese; Thai. *CAP:* English. *FEATURES:* Dual-layered RSDL ▪ 28 chapter links ▪ Theatrical trailer.
1989 (PG) 126m/C *GB GE* John Neville, Eric Idle, Sarah Polley, Valentina Cortese, Oliver Reed, Uma Thurman, Sting, Jonathan Pryce, Bill Paterson, Peter Jeffrey, Alison Steadman, Charles McKeown, Winston Dennis, Jack Purvis, Don Henderson, Ray Cooper, Andrew MacLachlan; **Cameos:** Robin Williams; **D:** Terry Gilliam; **W:** Terry Gilliam, Charles McKeown; **C:** Giuseppe Rotunno; **M:** Michael Kamen. *AWARDS: NOM:* Academy Awards '89: Best Art Direction/Set Decoration, Best Costume Design, Best Makeup.

The Adventures of Elmo in Grouchland

Like Alice and Dorothy, Elmo takes a journey to a fantastic land. He's trying to find his beloved blanket after Oscar tosses it into his trash can. At the bottom, Elmo finds Grouchland where Huxley (Patinkin) claims to own everything he touches, including—you guessed it—the blue blankie. The infantile red guy must go to Huxley's castle on Mt. Pickanose to retrieve it. DVD makes the familiar Sesame Street locations and characters a bit unusual with the increased clarity, but that's certainly not going to bother the target audience of young fans. The catchy

tunes sound fine. Adults are not likely to become involved—the film lacks the anarchic humor of the more mature Muppets—but kids will watch it over and over. —*MM*
Movie: 🎵🎵🎵 **DVD:** 🎵🎵🎵
Columbia Tristar Home Video (Cat #04168, UPC #04339604168). Full frame. Dolby Digital 5.1 Surround Stereo; Dolby Digital Surround Stereo. $24.95. Keepcase. *LANG:* English. *CAP:* English. *FEATURES:* Introduction by Elmo and Bug ▪ "Making of" featurette ▪ Theatrical trailers ▪ 28 chapter links. Despite box copy, the disc contains no talent files or production notes.
1999 (G) 77m/C Mandy Patinkin, Vanessa L(ynne) Williams, Ruth Buzzi; **D:** Gary Halvorson; **W:** Joseph Mazzarino, Mitchell Kriegman; **C:** Alan Caso; **M:** John Debney; **V:** Kevin Clash, Carroll Spinney, Frank Oz, Steve Whitmire, Joseph Mazzarino.

The Adventures of Milo & Otis

Delightful Japanese children's film is about a farm-dwelling dog and cat and their odyssey after the cat is accidentally swept away on a river. It's notable that no humans appear in the film and the effects used later in *Babe* are not employed to humanize the critters. Dudley Moore narrates superbly. On DVD, the image is carefully detailed. On that level, this is not a children's film. It is as expertly photographed as any Hollywood production. The remastered sound is equally fine. Highly recommended to audiences of all ages. —*MM* **AKA:** Koneko Monogatari; The Adventures of Chatran.
Movie: 🎵🎵🎵▶ **DVD:** 🎵🎵🎵
Columbia Tristar Home Video (Cat #50149, UPC #043396501492). Full frame; widescreen (1.85:1) letterboxed. Dolby Digital Surround; Dolby Digital Mono. $24.95. Keepcase. *LANG:* English; Spanish. *SUB:* English; French; Spanish. *CAP:* English. *FEATURES:* 28 chapter links ▪ Theatrical trailer ▪ Crew and cast thumbnail biographies.
1989 (G) 76m/C *JP* **D:** Masanori Hata; **W:** Mark Saltzman; **C:** Hideo Fujii, Shinji Tomita; **M:** Michael Boddicker; **Nar:** Dudley Moore.

The Adventures of Pinocchio

Live-action version of Carlo Collodi's famous tale of woodcarver Gepetto (Landau) who carves himself a puppet son (Thomas) who longs to be a real boy. The adaptation differs from the Disney cartoon version in that it's a little darker and the cat, the fox, and the cricket have larger roles. Jim Henson's Creature Shop provided the animatronic magic to bring Pinocchio to life. His head alone was jammed with wiring and 18 tiny motors to give the "boy" a full range of facial expressions. It took as many as five puppeteers at a time to animate the character. So lifelike was the puppet that some of the crew actually spoke to it as they did the human actors.

On DVD, both video and audio transfers are adequate, although the picture does tend toward the murky side from time to time. That leads to a loss of color and some not-too-well-defined blacks during several lowlit scenes. The 5.1 soundtrack lacks any real blow-out-the-back-of-head dynamics. —*MJT* **AKA:** Pinocchio; Carlo Collodi's Pinocchio.
Movie: 🎵🎵▶ **DVD:** 🎵🎵🎵
New Line Home Video (Cat #N4438, UPC #794043443824). Widescreen (2.35:1) letterboxed; full frame. Dolby Digital 5.1 Surround Sound. $24.99. Snapper. *LANG:* English. *SUB:* English; Spanish. *FEATURES:* 20 chapter links ▪ Theatrical trailer ▪ Behind the scenes featurette ▪ Cast biographies and filmographies ▪ 2 original interactive games ▪ New Line's Family Line highlights.
1996 (G) 88m/C Martin Landau, Jonathan Taylor Thomas, Rob Schneider, Bebe Neuwirth, Udo Kier; **D:** Steven Barron; **W:** Steven Barron, Tom Benedek, Sherry Mills; **C:** Juan Ruiz-Anchia; **M:** Rachel Portman.

The Adventures of Priscilla, Queen of the Desert

Quirky down-under comedy follows two drag queens (Weaving and Pearce) and a transsexual (Stamp) across the Australian Outback on their way to a gig in a small resort town. They make the drive in a pink bus named Priscilla. Along the way, they encounter and perform for the usual unusual assortment of colorful characters. The finest moments occur on the bus or onstage, courtesy of Abba. The excellent performances are led by Stamp, as the widowed Bernadette. The characters rise above the cliches in what is basically a bitchy, cross-dressing road movie celebrating drag as art and the nonconformity of its heroes. The costumes and wigs by Lizzy Gardner and Tim Chappel are a lark. The photography's surreal and the soundtrack's fittingly campy. Unfortunately, the film does not do well on DVD. Heavy pixelation and other distortion are most evident in the wide desert landscapes and shots of the chrome trim on the bus. The bus's busy interior and the spangly showgirl outfits fare little better. Sound is nothing special. —*MM*
Movie: 🎵🎵🎵 **DVD:** 🎵▶
USA Home Entertainment (Cat #633713). Widescreen (2.35:1) letterboxed; full frame. Dolby Digital Stereo. $29.95. *LANG:* English; French. *SUB:* Spanish. *FEATURES:* 29 chapter links ▪ Trailers ▪ Cast and crew thumbnail bios.
1994 (R) 102m/C *AU* Terence Stamp, Hugo Weaving, Guy Pearce, Bill Hunter, Sarah Chadwick, Mark Holmes, Julia Cortez, Rebel Russell, June Marie Bennett, Alan Dargin, Al Clark, Margaret Pomeranz; **D:** Stephan Elliott; **W:** Stephan Elliott; **C:** Brian J. Breheny; **M:** Guy Gross. *AWARDS:* Academy Awards '94: Best Costume Design; Australian Film Institute '94: Best Costume Design; *NOM:* Australian Film

Institute '94: Best Actor (Stamp), Best Actor (Weaving), Best Cinematography, Best Director (Elliott), Best Film, Best Original Screenplay; Golden Globe Awards '95: Best Actor—Musical/Comedy (Stamp), Best Film—Musical/Comedy; Writers Guild of America '94: Best Original Screenplay.

Aelita: Queen of Mars

Despite the inspired title, this little-known silent Soviet sci-fi flick is destined to remain little known. After building a rocket to fly to Mars, a Russian engineer finds that it's no holiday on the red planet. (The locals are in the midst of a revolution.) But with the help of the title character, he leads the masses to a politically correct conclusion wherein the proletariat break their chains and take up the hammer and sickle. The Martian scenes benefit most from DVD, which shows off the sets and costume design in full nuttiness, but before anyone feels too superior to the dated look, remember that future viewers will think the same about contemporary sf. The monotonous piano accompaniment gains nothing on disc. —*MM* **AKA:** Aelita: The Revolt of the Robots.
Movie: ♫♫ *DVD:* ♫♫▶
Image Entertainment (Cat #ID5665SDVD, UPC #014381566529). Full frame. Dolby Digital Mono. $24.99. Snapper. *SUB:* English. *FEATURES:* 18 chapter links.
1924 113m/B *RU* Yulia Solntseva, Nikolai Batalov, Igor Illinski, Nikolai Tseretelli, Vera Orlova, Pavel Poi, Konstantin Eggert, Yuri Zavadski, Valentina Kuindzi, N. Tretyakova; *D:* Yakov Protazanov; *W:* Fedor Ozep, Aleksey Fajko; *C:* Yuri Zhelyabuzhsky, Emil Schoenemann.

Aeon Flux

DVD collects several episodes of the futuristic animated TV show onto one disc, with stories following the far-flung exploits of Aeon Flux, a leather-clad mercenary babe. Clearly inspired by Japanese anime, the program formerly seen on MTV delivers animated sci-fi for adults that isn't all sex and violence like many of the anime imports. Sexiness and violence are components of *Aeon Flux*, just not the whole point. The image looks good and the audio is acceptable, though certainly not state of the art. Extras? No extras here, not even a menu. —*MR*
Movie: ♫♫♫ *DVD:* ♫♫▶
Sony Music Video Enterprises (Cat #LDV49810, UPC #074644981094). Full frame. Dolby Digital 2.0. $24.99. Keepcase. *LANG:* English. *FEATURES:* 11 chapter links.
1997 120m/C *D:* Howard E. Baker, Peter Chung.

Affliction

A man is killed in snowy woods on the first day of hunting season in upstate New Hampshire. Small town cop Wade Whitehouse (Nolte) tries to use the incident to break out of the patterns of violence that his father (Oscar-winner Coburn) inflicted upon him and his brother (Dafoe) and that Wade is repeating with his ex-wife and daughter. Paul Schrader's film is more emotional drama than crime story. The plot is less important than the complex characters and the vivid sense of place. The DVD captures both in the bleak Canadian snowscapes, ultra-grainy flashbacks, and dim cold uncomfortable rooms where most of the important dramatic action takes place. Credit must be shared by Schrader and director of photography Paul Sarossy. The superb performances are the real key. If the voice-over narration takes itself too seriously, that's a small flaw. —*MM*
Movie: ♫♫♫▶ *DVD:* ♫♫♫▶
Universal Studios Home Video (Cat #20588, UPC #025192059920). Widescreen (1.85:1) letterboxed. Dolby Digital Surround Stereo. $29.98. Keepcase. *LANG:* English. *CAP:* English. *FEATURES:* 18 chapter links • Production notes • Cast and crew thumbnail biographies • Theatrical trailer • Universal web links.
1997 (R) 113m/C Nick Nolte, James Coburn, Sissy Spacek, Willem Dafoe, Mary Beth Hurt, Jim True, Marian Seldes, Brigid Tierney, Sean McCann, Wayne Robson, Holmes Osborne; *D:* Paul Schrader; *W:* Paul Schrader; *C:* Paul Sarossy; *M:* Michael Brook. *AWARDS:* Academy Awards '98: Best Supporting Actor (Coburn); New York Film Critics Awards '98: Best Actor (Nolte); National Society of Film Critics Awards '98: Best Actor (Nolte); *NOM:* Academy Awards '98: Best Actor (Nolte); Golden Globe Awards '99: Best Actor—Drama (Nolte); Independent Spirit Awards '99: Best Actor (Nolte), Best Cinematography, Best Director (Schrader), Best Film, Best Screenplay, Best Supporting Actor (Coburn); Screen Actors Guild Award '98: Best Actor (Nolte), Best Supporting Actor (Coburn).

AFI's 100 Years, 100 Movies

These 100 "greatest" American movies were chosen from 40,000 titles by assorted film historians, politicians, and generic celebrities who were selected by the American Film Institute. It's hard to argue with the "usual suspects" title choices, and the scenes taken from them are particularly illuminating. The most obvious problem with this made-for-TV special is the various guests who comment on the films. What qualifies Tommy LaSorda or Donald Trump to talk about movies? And many of the actors simply reveal how shallow and self-centered they are. So, pay no attention to them. Concentrate instead on the films themselves. Not surprisingly, the quality of the images varies. Overall, they are excellent, but the real value of the DVD lies in the indexing. With 24 chapters, it's easy to zip to your favorites. For my money, chapters 14, 16, and 19 are the tops. —*MM*
Movie: ♫♫♫ *DVD:* ♫♫▶
Image Entertainment (Cat #ID5775AFDVD, UPC #014381577525). Full frame; widescreen. Dolby Digital Stereo. $29.99. Snapper. *LANG:* English. *CAP:* English. *FEATURES:* 24 chapter links.
1998 145m/C *D:* Gary Smith; *W:* Gary Smith, Fred A. Rappaport, Marty Farrell.

After Dark, My Sweet

A troubled young man (Patric) in search of a little truth ends up in the sack with the sensuous Ward, at odds with Dern, and embroiled in a no-win kidnapping scheme. Somewhat muddled direction is overcome by above-average performances and gritty realism. Based on the novel by Jim Thompson. At first look, the DVD appears to be a little contrasty, but that's pretty much the way it was in the theatre. The picture is sharp and the grain level is low (although there is too much grain in the darkly lit climactic sex scene), but there are times where artifacts completely wipe out the sharpness. Colors are accurate and relatively bleed-free. The blacks lean towards gray during scene transitions but are otherwise very true. There is so little music or sound effects in this film that it's hard to really judge the soundtrack, but the dialogue is easy to understand. —*JO*
Movie: ♫♫♫ *DVD:* ♫♫▶
Artisan Entertainment (Cat #DVD68943, UPC #013023024090). Full frame. $24.98. Keepcase. *LANG:* English. *FEATURES:* 20 chapter links.
1990 (R) 114m/C Jason Patric, Rachel Ward, Bruce Dern, George Dickerson, James Cotton, Corey Carrier, Rocky Giordani; *D:* James Foley; *W:* Robert Redlin, James Foley; *C:* Mark Plummer; *M:* Maurice Jarre.

Air America

Give the doctors from *M*A*S*H* pilots licenses and put them in Laos in 1969 and they'd be the CIA fliers with the same hip, flip, cynical attitudes. The film begins as a fairly accurate look at a secret war, then almost becomes a buddy picture and finally arrives at a moralistic conclusion that undercuts all that's gone before. Gene Rydak (Gibson) is the veteran pilot who shows newcomer Billy Covington (Downey) the ropes. Gibson never seems fully engaged and leaves most of the heavy lifting to Downey. Character actor Lane Smith almost steals the show from them. On DVD, the Thai locations look all right, though they're not spectacular. Almost all diagonal lines flash irritatingly. The '60s score sounds fine. —*MM*
Movie: ♫♫▶ *DVD:* ♫♫▶
Artisan Entertainment (Cat #60471, UPC #012236047100). Widescreen letterboxed; full frame. Dolby Digital Surround Stereo. $29.98. Snapper. *LANG:* English. *SUB:* Spanish. *CAP:* English. *FEATURES:* 36 chapter links • Theatrical trailer • Cast and crew thumbnail biographies • Production notes.
1990 (R) 113m/C Mel Gibson, Robert Downey Jr., Marshall Bell, Nancy Travis, David Marshall Grant, Tim Thomerson, Lane Smith; *D:* Roger Spottiswoode; *W:*

Richard Rush; **C:** Roger Deakins; **M:** Charles Gross.

Air Bud

Buddy's a charming, photogenic, basket-ball-playing Golden Retriever who befriends lonely 12-year-old Josh (Zegers), the new kid in town, and teaches him the finer points of the lay-up, pick-and-roll, and fade-away jumper. No cliche goes unexploited, including Michael Jeter's overwrought performance as the bad guy who abandons the pooch and then demands him back. The bare-bones DVD exhibits the usual problems with grid patterns, clothes designs, and fast-panning shots, but those are not going to be a problem for young fans who will love this one. Buddy the dog, a favorite of the Video-Hound, is just terrific, a canine star with the potential of Old Yeller. *—MM*
Movie: 🎬🎬➤ **DVD:** 🎬🎬➤
Buena Vista Home Entertainment (Cat #13681, UPC #717951000163). Full frame. Dolby Digital Surround Stereo. $29.99. Keepcase. *LANG:* English. *CAP:* English. *FEATURES:* 16 chapter links.
1997 (PG) 92m/C Kevin Zegers, Michael Jeter, Bill Cobbs, Wendy Makkena, Eric Christmas, Brendan Fletcher, Jay Brazeau, Stephen E. Miller, Nicola Cavendish; **D:** Charles Martin Smith; **W:** Paul Tamasy, Aaron Mendelsohn; **C:** Mike Southon; **M:** Brahm Wenger.

Air Force One

Ford stars as tough-as-nails U.S. President James Marshall. Onboard Air Force One, his policy of not negotiating with terrorists is put to the test when he, his wife, and daughter are hijacked by Russian nationalists led by ice-cold Ivan (Oldman). Ford is in fine form as he kicks Commie butt while the first woman Veep (Close) holds the fort on the ground. Director Petersen *(Das Boot)* supplies nail-biting suspense and pulse-pounding action in this tour-de-force adventure. When *Air Force One* first hit DVD, it boasted the best sound yet heard on the format and is still no slouch in that department. The explosions almost knock you out of your seat, the dialogue is crisp and easy to understand, and the dynamics of Goldsmith's score come through unscathed. Visually, the transfer is a good one, featuring sharp colors, true blacks, clean details, and very little noticeable pixelation. Brightness and contrast levels are very good throughout. *—JO AKA:* AFO.
Movie: 🎬🎬🎬 **DVD:** 🎬🎬🎬➤
Columbia Tristar Home Video (Cat #71889, UPC #043396718890). Widescreen (2.35:1) letterboxed; full frame. Dolby Digital 5.1; Dolby Surround. Keepcase. *LANG:* English (DD5.1); English, Spanish, French (DS). *SUB:* English; Spanish; French. *FEATURES:* 35 chapter links • Theatrical trailer • Director's commentary.
1997 (R) 124m/C Harrison Ford, Gary Oldman, Glenn Close, Dean Stockwell,

William H. Macy, Wendy Crewson, Xander Berkeley, Paul Guilfoyle, Liesl Matthews, Bill Smitrovich, Elya Baskin, David Vadim, Tom Everett, Philip Baker Hall, Spencer Garrett, Donna Bullock; **Cameos:** Juergen Prochnow; **D:** Wolfgang Petersen; **W:** Andrew Marlowe; **C:** Michael Ballhaus; **M:** Jerry Goldsmith. *AWARDS: NOM:* Academy Awards '97: Best Film Editing, Best Sound; MTV Movie Awards '98: Best Villain (Oldman), Best Fight (Harrison Ford/Gary Oldman).

Airport

Old-fashioned disaster thriller is built around an all-star cast, a fairly moronic script, and an unavoidable accident during the flight of a passenger airliner. The box-office hit paved the way for many lesser disaster flicks (including its many sequels) detailing the reactions of the passengers and crew as they cope with impending doom. Considered to be the best of the *Airport* series; adapted from the Arthur Hailey novel. Usual so-so Goodtimes DVD quality—this one is not even letterboxed. Picture clarity is average with noticeable grain throughout. Blacks are fairly true. There is light shimmering along contrast lines and a little color bleed. Sound is average with good separation and clarity, but some background hiss. *—JO*
Movie: 🎬🎬➤ **DVD:** 🎬➤
Goodtimes Entertainment (Cat #05-81029, UPC #018713810298). Full frame. Dolby Surround. $19.98. Snapper. *LANG:* English. *SUB:* Spanish; French. *CAP:* English. *FEATURES:* 18 chapter links.
1970 (G) 137m/C Dean Martin, Burt Lancaster, Jean Seberg, Jacqueline Bisset, George Kennedy, Helen Hayes, Van Heflin, Maureen Stapleton, Barry Nelson, Lloyd Nolan, Dana Wynter, Barbara Hale, Gary Collins, Jessie Royce Landis; **D:** George Seaton; **W:** George Seaton; **C:** Ernest Laszlo; **M:** Alfred Newman. *AWARDS:* Academy Awards '70: Best Supporting Actress (Hayes); Golden Globe Awards '71: Best Supporting Actress (Stapleton); *NOM:* Academy Awards '70: Best Adapted Screenplay, Best Art Direction/Set Decoration, Best Cinematography, Best Costume Design, Best Film Editing, Best Picture, Best Sound, Best Supporting Actress (Stapleton), Best Original Score.

Airport '75

After a mid-air collision, a jumbo 747 is left pilotless and stewardess (hey, this is before the days of flight attendants) Black must fly da plane. She does her cross-eyed best in this absurd sequel to *Airport* built around a lesser "all-star cast." Safe on the ground, Heston tries to talk the airline hostess/pilot in to landing, before taking more drastic (and ridiculous) action. Grouchy Kennedy readies the foam for a crash landing. Slick attempt garnered enough boxoffice to lead to two more sequels. This inferior sequel's DVD is far superior to the original's DVD, which was not even letterboxed. In this case the pic-

ture is very sharp and, most of the time, free of grain. The colors are very good, vibrant and without much bleed. Most of the blacks are fairly true and are helped by good contrast and brightness levels. Unlike the first *Airport*, which at least had stereo sound, this one's mono with very limited fidelity and dynamics. *—JO*
Movie: 🎬🎬➤ **DVD:** 🎬🎬➤
Goodtimes Entertainment (Cat #05-81010, UPC #018713810106). Widescreen (2.35:1) letterboxed. Dolby Digital 1.0. $19.98. Snapper. *LANG:* English; Spanish; French. *SUB:* Spanish; French; English. *FEATURES:* 16 chapter links • Production notes.
1975 (PG) 107m/C Charlton Heston, Karen Black, George Kennedy, Gloria Swanson, Helen Reddy, Sid Caesar, Efrem Zimbalist Jr., Susan Clark, Dana Andrews, Linda Blair, Nancy Olson, Roy Thinnes, Myrna Loy, Ed Nelson, Larry Storch; **D:** Jack Smight; **W:** Don Ingalls; **C:** Philip Lathrop; **M:** John Cacavas.

The Alarmist

Tommy Hudler (Arquette) is the eager beaver new employee at the L.A. home-security company owned by slick super-salesman Heinrich Grigoris (Tucci). But Tommy's soon shocked to learn that Heinrich makes certain clients continue to need his services by breaking into their homes. Tommy makes his first sale to fortysomething widow Gale (Capshaw), who enjoys seducing the boyish innocent, and the two embark on a torrid affair. Tucci steals the show as Tommy's sleazy boss. A very good-looking DVD complements this subtly lit, well-photographed film. The sharpness is very good and grain is never a problem. The colors are dead-on and I didn't notice any bleed. Blacks are also true and grain-free. The contrast and brightness levels are very consistent, which helps to convey a great feeling of depth. On the audio side, the soundtrack is very full. The dialogue cuts through, and the music is full of dynamics with a healthy low end. *—JO AKA:* Life During Wartime.
Movie: 🎬🎬➤ **DVD:** 🎬🎬🎬
Columbia Tristar Home Video (Cat #03497, UPC #043396034976). Widescreen (1.85:1) letterboxed. Dolby Digital Stereo. NSL. Keepcase. *LANG:* English. *SUB:* Spanish; Portuguese; Chinese. *CAP:* English. *FEATURES:* 28 chapter links • Theatrical trailers • Cast bios and filmographies.
1998 93m/C Stanley Tucci, David Arquette, Kate Capshaw, Ryan Reynolds, Mary McCormack, Tricia Vessey; **D:** Evan Dunsky; **W:** Evan Dunsky; **C:** Alex Nepomniaschy; **M:** Christophe Beck.

Alaska: Spirit of the Wild

Like most other IMAX documentaries, this one is visually stunning and has an audio score that is both dynamic and stimulating. Most of the film is dedicated to showing off the tundra and miles and miles of

ice and snow. The abundant wildlife is also given its share of attention and all this is narrated by Charlton Heston. Also like most IMAX documentaries, the DVD is stunning. The picture is exceptionally sharp with very little grain. As you can imagine, with all the bright white images, both contrast and brightness is very important, and their levels are also excellent. The lush colors are accurate and the blacks true. The sound is superb. Crisp highs and rumbling lows are accented by exceptional Surround tracks. A great DVD for both attentive viewing or just as a background piece. —JO
Movie: 🎞🎞🎞▶ **DVD:** 🎞🎞🎞▶
SlingShot Entertainment (Cat #9837, UPC #01707898372). Full frame. Dolby Digital 5.1. $24.99. Expanded jewel case. *LANG:* English; Spanish; French; Swedish; Chinese; German; Japanese. *SUB:* English. *FEATURES:* 14 chapter links.
1996 40m/C

Albino Alligator
Actor Spacey's directorial debut is a fair crime drama. Three small-time crooks (Dillon, Sinise, Fichtner) bungle a job in New Orleans and run down a federal agent during their getaway. They go to ground in a picturesque bar, take the occupants hostage, and commence to arguing among themselves while the cops surround the place. A veritable who's-who supporting cast keeps the potentially claustrophobic material from imploding, though the action is never as gripping as it needs to be. On DVD, the film looks terrific with well-realized nocturnal exteriors. On the commentary track, Spacey and editor Jay Cassidy focus on the technical side of filmmaking—problems of budget, cast, and compromises. How, for example, do you film your establishing helicopter shot when you can't afford the right camera mount? Their insights are easily as interesting as the action itself. —MM
Movie: 🎞🎞▶ **DVD:** 🎞🎞🎞▶
Miramax Pictures Home Video (Cat #17101, UPC #717951002150). Widescreen (2.35:1) letterboxed. Dolby Digital Stereo. $29.99. Snapper. *LANG:* English. *CAP:* English. *FEATURES:* 16 chapter links ▪ "Making of" featurette ▪ Commentary: director Kevin Spacey and editor Jay Cassidy.
1996 (R) 94m/C Matt Dillon, Gary Sinise, Faye Dunaway, William Fichtner, Joe Mantegna, Viggo Mortensen, John Spencer, Skeet Ulrich, M. Emmet Walsh; *D:* Kevin Spacey; *W:* Christian Forte; *C:* Mark Plummer; *M:* Michael Brook. *AWARDS: NOM:* Golden Raspberry Awards '97: Worst Supporting Actress (Dunaway).

Alegria
Unlike most other circus-based films, this one uses the Cirque du Soleil as background and inspiration; it is not a filmed performance or a drama that stops cold for the various acts. The story has an archetypal simplicity reminiscent of Felli-

ni's *The Clowns*. Its approach is similar to the musical *Cats* with a few fine songs and stylized action. The story is told by Momo (Mako as an adult; Miano as a child), who is remembering his friendship with Frac (Bazinet) and Frac's infatuation with the lovely daughter (Cox) of a ringmaster (Langella). At the same time, Momo is trying to escape from the Faginesque Marcello (Williams). The film may be too intense for younger kids, and those who are fans of the live show may be put off by this unusual combination of drama and performance. I thought it was delightful. The dark scenes do not have the traditional DVD sparkle but that's the nature of the material. The 5.1 Surround track is excellent. In his commentary track, director Dragone talks about the story's extended evolution. —MM
Movie: 🎞🎞🎞🎞 **DVD:** 🎞🎞🎞▶
Image Entertainment (Cat #OVED6874 DVD, UPC #014381687422). Widescreen (1.85:1) letterboxed. Dolby Digital 5.1 Surround Stereo; Dolby Digital Stereo. $24.99. Snapper. *LANG:* English. *FEATURES:* 12 chapter links ▪ Commentary: director Franco Dragone ▪ "Making of" featurette ▪ Music video "Love Leaves Someone Behind" by Irene Marc ▪ Music montages "A Child in His Eyes," and "Let Them Live" ▪ Extended performance footage of "Hoops" and "Cube Act."
1998 (PG) 93m/C *CA* Rene Bazinet, Frank Langella, Mako, Julie Cox, Clipper Miano, Heathcote Williams, Whoopi Goldberg; *D:* Franco Dragone; *W:* Rudy Barcello; *C:* Pierre Mignot.

Alexander Nevsky
While the climactic conflict between the medieval Teutonic knights and the brave Russians on the frozen lake scene is still studied and imitated by filmmakers, Eisenstein's anti-Nazi epic lacks enthusiasm and life. Today, the story of a 13th-century invasion of Russia by Germany is most notable for its impressive battlefield orchestration, big crowd scenes, pneumatic heroines, and stiff-backed heroes. Actually, its most obvious successors are those stiff, lumbering historical epics that Hollywood cranked out in the 1950s. In fact, a young Troy Donahue in a blond Prince Valiant wig would have been perfect in the title role, and that's what the times called for. To judge the work as anything but propaganda misses the point. For DVD release, the opening credits have been translated into English and the white subtitles come from the 1982 edition. At times, the image bounces and it's obvious that the disc was made from a print that's flecked with white throughout and has suffered some breakage. Even so, it looks much better than many older tapes on the rental market, and even in monaural sound, Sergei Prokofiev's soundtrack is magnificent. Rob Edelman's scholarly liner notes provide a good introduction. —MM
Movie: 🎞🎞🎞 **DVD:** 🎞🎞🎞
Image Entertainment (Cat #ID4575CODVD, UPC #014381457520). Full frame. Dolby

Digital Mono. $24.99. Snapper. *LANG:* Russian. *SUB:* English. *FEATURES:* 16 chapter links.
1938 110m/B *RU* Nikolai Cherkasov, Nikolai P. Okhlopkov, Andrei Abrikosov, Alexandra Danilova, Dmitri Orlov, Vera Ivasheva, Sergei Blinnikov, Lev Fenin, Vladimir Yershov, Nikolai Arsky, Naum Rogozhin, Varvara O. Massalitinova, Vasili Novikov, Ivan Lagutin; *D:* Sergei Eisenstein; *W:* Sergei Eisenstein, Pyotr Pavlenko; *C:* Eduard Tisse; *M:* Sergei Prokofiev.

Alice in Wonderland
Hallmark Hall of Fame television production owes almost as much to *The Wizard of Oz* as to the real source material in this version of Lewis Carroll's story. It's all a little too precious, sophisticated, and scary for the youngest viewers. Teens and adults are more likely to appreciate the psychedelic elements. The creations of Jim Henson's Creature Shop overshadow the human actors. (The March Hare might have been a prototype for Jar-Jar Binks in *Phantom Menace*.) DVD is a fine medium for the subtle visual changes that differentiate levels of reality and fantasy. No serious flaws show up on the disc. Sound is fine, too, but overall, the admittedly impressive enterprise is not as satisfying as the Disney animated version. —MM
Movie: 🎞🎞🎞 **DVD:** 🎞🎞🎞▶
Artisan Entertainment (Cat #91021, UPC #707729102106). Full frame. Dolby Digital Stereo. $19.98. Keepcase. *LANG:* English. *CAP:* English. *FEATURES:* 34 chapter links ▪ Production notes ▪ Trailer ▪ Original illustrations.
1999 129m/C Tina Majorino, Martin Short, Miranda Richardson, Whoopi Goldberg, Ben Kingsley, Gene Wilder, Christopher Lloyd, Pete Postlethwaite, Peter Ustinov, George Wendt, Robbie Coltrane; *D:* Nick Willing; *W:* Peter Barnes; *C:* Giles Nuttgens; *M:* Richard Hartley.

Alice Sweet Alice
Though this psycho-horror has been hyped as the debut of a very young Brooke Shields, she has a tiny role. The film is really a complex indictment of Catholicism. Director Alfred Sole's use of middle-class New Jersey locations recalls the better work of George Romero, and he fills the screen with realistic grotesques that are every bit as frightening as walking corpses. He and cowriter Rosemary Ritvo create an interconnected series of bizarre conflicts involving Alice (Sheppard), her sister Karen (Shields), and their extended family, community, and church in the early 1960s. The film's influence on various slasher films, particularly the Italians, of following decades is obvious. (Here Sole admits that his main influence is Nicholas Roeg's *Don't Look Now*.) Despite a modest budget, it's aged better than many more expensive productions of the same era, and this restoration is far superior in sound and image to any of the several

tape editions available. The commentary track with Soles, editor Edward Salier, and film preservationist William Lustig deals mostly with the problems involved in low-budget independent film production, Sole's background as an architect, and the various actors and characters. The faded pale look is true to the '70s, and, as Lustig notes, Sole created some memorable images of beauty and violence. Though the film lacks recognition among mainstream audiences, it's always been a favorite of true horror fans and it deserves the respectful treatment it has gotten on DVD. —MM *AKA:* Holy Terror; Communion.
Movie: 🎬🎬🎬▶ *DVD:* 🎬🎬🎬🎬
Anchor Bay (Cat #DV10662, UPC #013131066296). Widescreen (1.85:1) letterboxed. Dolby Digital Mono. $24.98. Keepcase. *LANG:* English. *FEATURES:* Commentary: Alfred Sole, Edward Salier, William Lustig ▪ Biographies of Alfred Sole, Brooke Shields ▪ Stills gallery ▪ Alternate opening credit sequence ▪ 25 chapter links.
1976 (R) 112m/C Linda Miller, Paula Sheppard, Mildred Clinton, Niles McMaster, Jane Lowry, Rudolph Willrich, Brooke Shields, Alphonso de Noble, Gary Allen, Tom Signorelli, Lillian Roth; *D:* Alfred Sole; *W:* Alfred Sole, Rosemary Ritvo; *C:* John Friberg, Chuck Hall; *M:* Stephen Lawrence.

Alien

Terse direction, stunning sets and special effects, and a well-seasoned cast save this from being just another "Slimy Monster from Outer Space" story. Instead it's a grisly roller coaster of suspense. Intergalactic freighter's crew is invaded by an unstoppable carnivorous alien. While most of the cast awaits their imminent demise, Ripley (Weaver) goes toe to toe with the big ugly. Futuristic, in-the-belly-of-the-beast visual design by H.R. Giger creates a sense of claustrophobic doom. Writer O'Bannon's influences include Mario Bava's *Planet of the Vampires,* and *It, the Terror from Beyond Space.* This DVD proves that the format can handle dark scenes very well if authored correctly. While most of the film is low-light, the visuals are still extremely sharp and relatively grain-free (the DVD actually looks better than the CAV laserdisc). The colors are excellent, and the absence of bleed contributes to the sharpness. Contrast is very good, and the brightness levels are very consistent. The blacks are right on. As you would expect, the sound is also fine. Jerry Goldsmith's ominous score sounds great, as do the dialogue and effects. The highs and lows are all there and the separation is also fine. All the supplemental sections are worth going through, particularly the deleted scenes, during which director Scott explains why they were left out of the finished film. The *Alien* series was well worth the wait on DVD and Fox Home Video has done a great job on this fine DVD. —JO
Movie: 🎬🎬🎬🎬 *DVD:* 🎬🎬🎬🎬

20th Century Fox (Cat #4110430, UPC #086162000751). Widescreen (2.35:1) anamorphic. Dolby Digital 5.1; Dolby Surround. $34.98. Keepcase. *LANG:* English (DD5.1, DS); French (DS). *SUB:* English; Spanish. *FEATURES:* 20 chapter links ▪ Theatrical trailers ▪ Deleted scenes ▪ Commentary: Ridley Scott ▪ Original storyboards ▪ Artwork and photo galleries ▪ Isolated score ▪ Alternate music track ▪ Dual-layered RSDL. Also available as part of the "Alien Legacy" 4-pack ($109.95).
1979 (R) 116m/C *GB* Tom Skerritt, Sigourney Weaver, Veronica Cartwright, Yaphet Kotto, Harry Dean Stanton, Ian Holm, John Hurt, Bolaji Badejo; *D:* Ridley Scott; *W:* Dan O'Bannon; *C:* Derek Vanlint; *M:* Jerry Goldsmith; *V:* Helen Horton. *AWARDS:* Academy Awards '79: Best Visual Effects; *NOM:* Academy Awards '79: Best Art Direction/Set Decoration.

Alien Chaser

Alien android Zagarino, who crashed in the African desert thousands of years ago, returns to life thanks to the unwitting aid of archeologists Jensen and MacDonald. They literally hold the key to stopping his destruction of mankind. Good camera moves for a low-budget romp, but the DVD's pan-and-scan framing is a bit cramped and some effects shots are not convincing. No subtitles or other extras to speak of. —MB
Movie: 🎬🎬 *DVD:* 🎬🎬▶
Image Entertainment (Cat #ID 5763 UMDVD, UPC #014381576320). Full frame. Dolby Digital 2.0. $24.99. Snapper. *LANG:* English. *FEATURES:* 12 chapter links.
1996 (R) 95m/C Frank Zagarino, Todd Jensen, Jennifer MacDonald, Brian O'Shaughnessy; *D:* Mark Roper; *W:* B.J. Nelson; *C:* Rod Stewart; *M:* Robert O. Ragland.

Alien Seed

At best, this low-budget sf is no more far-fetched than Whitley Strieber's *Communion* or any of the other "alien abduction" tales that some people seem to take seriously. The tough heroine is well played by Heidi Paine. The plot is goofy from the first frame, but the flick delivers all the lively cheap thrills you want from an unpretentious, low-budget B-movie. The bargain basement production values show through strongly on DVD. —MM
Movie: 🎬🎬 *DVD:* 🎬🎬
Image Entertainment (Cat #ID5689PZDVD, UPC #014381568929). Full frame. Dolby Digital Mono. $24.99. Snapper. *LANG:* English. *FEATURES:* 16 chapter links.
1989 88m/C Erik Estrada, Heidi Paine, Steven Blade; *D:* Bob James.

Aliens (SE)

Popular sequel to *Alien* amounts to non-stop, ravaging combat in space. Fresh from deep-space sleep, Ripley and a slew

of pulsar-equipped marines return to confront the mother alien at her nest, which is also inhabited by a whole bunch of the nasty critters spewing for a fight. Ripley discovers maternal instincts lurking within her space suit while looking after a young girl, the lone survivor of the infested colony. DVD version is the "special edition" that was previously only available in the CAV laserdisc box set. The extra 17 minutes is well worth it, and even explains where the little girl came from. As with *Alien,* this DVD looks better than the laserdisc and has no problem with all the dark scenes in the film. Excellent blacks, contrast, and brightness levels combine with a near grain- and artifact-free picture to produce another stunning DVD. The sound is also great and the Surround and sub woofer get a real workout with the non-stop shoot-outs and explosions that make up the second half of the film. The mix is very good, and the crisp dialogue always manages to punch through, as does the creepy score by James Horner. Buy this one, too. —JO *AKA:* Alien 2.
Movie: 🎬🎬🎬▶ *DVD:* 🎬🎬🎬🎬
20th Century Fox (Cat #4110431, UPC #086162104312). Widescreen (1.85:1) anamorphic. Dolby Digital 5.1; Dolby Surround. $34.98. Keepcase. *LANG:* English (DD5.1; DS). *SUB:* Spanish. *CAP:* English. *FEATURES:* 34 chapter links ▪ Theatrical trailer ▪ Behind the scenes footage ▪ Photo gallery ▪ Interview with James Cameron. 154-minute version is 17 minutes longer than VHS.
1986 (R) 138m/C Sigourney Weaver, Michael Biehn, Lance Henriksen, Bill Paxton, Paul Reiser, Carrie Henn, Jenette Goldstein, William Hope, Al Matthews, Mark Rolston, Ricco Ross, Colette Hiller; *D:* James Cameron; *W:* James Cameron, Walter Hill; *C:* Adrian Biddle; *M:* James Horner. *AWARDS:* Academy Awards '86: Best Sound Effects Editing, Best Visual Effects; *NOM:* Academy Awards '86: Best Actress (Weaver), Best Art Direction/Set Decoration, Best Film Editing, Best Sound, Best Original Score.

Alien3

Directed by David Fincher (*Seven*), *Alien 3* is the darkest and most disturbing of the series. This one picks up where *Aliens* left off, as Ripley crashlands on Farina 161, a planet that serves as a penal colony for 25 celibate but horny men. After shaving her head (there is a lice problem in the prison), Ripley tries to survive on the cold planet until a rescue ship can arrive, but soon discovers that she has been implanted with an alien of her own. Intended as the final installment of the series. Another dimly lit entry in the *Alien* series and another DVD that has no problem with it. Pretty much the same technicals as the first two films. Everything is excellent: sharpness; little or no artifacting; contrast; brightness; blacks; both soundtracks (5.1 and Dolby Surround). Although the supplemental section is not as full as on *Alien* or *Aliens,* there is a documentary

on the making of the film. Most important-ly, another superb DVD. —JO
Movie: 🎬🎬🎬 **DVD:** 🎬🎬🎬🎬
20th Century Fox (Cat #4110432, UPC #086162104329). Widescreen (2.35:1) anamorphic. Dolby Digital 5.1, Dolby Sur-round. $34.98. Keepcase. *LANG:* English (DD5.1); DS); French (DS). *SUB:* English; Spanish. *FEATURES:* 29 chapter links • Theatrical trailer • "Making of" documen-tary.
1992 (R) 135m/C Sigourney Weaver, Charles S. Dutton, Charles Dance, Paul McGann, Brian Glover, Ralph Brown, Danny Webb, Christopher John Fields, Holt McCallany, Lance Henriksen; *D:* David Fincher; *C:* Alex Thomson; *M:* Elliot Gold-enthal. *AWARDS: NOM:* Academy Awards '92: Best Visual Effects.

Alive and Kicking
Tonio (Flemyng) is a handsome vain ballet dancer with AIDS who hides his emotions beneath his work and a witty facade. At a club, he meets older, equally driven Jack (Sher), an AIDS counselor, who pursues him. Though they become lovers, Tonio's obsession with his latest (and possibly last) dance role causes a rift between them. The subplot between Tonio and les-bian dancer Millie (Parish) is self-con-scious and Tonio's theatrics become annoying, but Flemyng and Sher do well with thin characters. The full-frame DVD is no better than VHS tape with a fairly grainy image and mediocre sound. —MM *AKA:* Indian Summer.
Movie: 🎬🎬 **DVD:** 🎬🎬
Image Entertainment (Cat #OVED6858 DVD, UPC #014381685824). Full frame. Dolby Digital Surround Stereo. $24.99. Snapper. *LANG:* English. *FEATURES:* 12 chapter links • 2 theatrical previews.
1996 (R) 100m/C *GB* Jason Flemyng, Anthony Sher, Dorothy Tutin, Anthony Hig-gins, Diane Parish; *D:* Nancy Meckler; *W:* Martin Sherman; *C:* Chris Seager; *M:* Peter Salem.

All About Ah Long
This Hong Kong version of *Kramer vs. Kramer* is notable mostly for an early per-formance by a very young Chow Yun-Fat. He's Ah Long, a construction worker with a troubled past, who's raising his young son. The DVD is not bad-looking, though it lacks the sparkle of the best. The occa-sional grubbiness of the image is appro-priate for a serious (though overly senti-mental to American tastes) family drama. The odd "hex errors" in translation are unintentionally comic. When our heroes are stuck in traffic, they yell to the other irate drivers, "Stop horning!" —MM
Movie: 🎬🎬🎬 **DVD:** 🎬🎬🎬
Tai Seng Video Marketing (Cat #5060). Widescreen letterboxed. Dolby Digital 5.1 Surround Stereo. $49.95. Keepcase. *LANG:* Cantonese; Mandarin. *SUB:* Eng-lish; Traditional Chinese; Simplified Chi-nese; Japanese; Bahasa (Indonesia); Thai; Korean; Vietnamese. *FEATURES:* 8 chapter

links • Theatrical trailers • Cast thumb-nail biographies.
1989 99m/C *CH* Sylvia Chang, Chow Yun-Fat, To Kai-Fung; *D:* To Kai-Fung; *W:* Cheng Chung Tai.

All About Eve
The archetypal Broadway story gets respectful but uncluttered treatment on DVD. It's the story of Eve Harrington (Bax-ter), who backstabs her way to the top over established star Margo Channing (Davis). The supporting cast, led by Oscar-winning Sanders as the caustic drama crit-ic, is superb. Mankiewicz's script is even better. The disc contains few extras. The monaural sound is fine for the sparkling nasty dialogue. The black-and-white cine-matography is very good, but not com-pletely sharp in every scene. Those flaws, negligible as they are, come from the origi-nal, not the digital transfer. The print dis-plays a few minor imperfections, but over-all it's fine. Even darker shades of black maintain a high level of detail. —MM
Movie: 🎬🎬🎬🎬 **DVD:** 🎬🎬🎬
20th Century Fox (Cat #4112621, UPC #086162126215). Full frame. $29.98. Keepcase. *LANG:* English; French. *SUB:* English; Spanish. *CAP:* English. *FEATURES:* 27 chapter links.
1950 138m/B Bette Davis, Anne Baxter, George Sanders, Celeste Holm, Gary Mer-rill, Thelma Ritter, Marilyn Monroe, Hugh Marlowe, Gregory Ratoff, Eddie Fisher; *D:* Joseph L. Mankiewicz; *W:* Joseph L. Mankiewicz; *C:* Milton Krasner; *M:* Alfred Newman. *AWARDS:* Academy Awards '50: Best Costume Design (B & W), Best Direc-tor (Mankiewicz), Best Picture, Best Screenplay, Best Sound, Best Supporting Actor (Sanders); American Film Institute (AFI) '98: Top 100; British Academy Awards '50: Best Film; Cannes Film Festi-val '51: Best Actress (Davis), Grand Jury Prize; Directors Guild of America Awards '50: Best Director (Mankiewicz); Golden Globe Awards '51: Best Screenplay, National Film Registry '90; New York Film Critics Awards '50: Best Actress (Davis), Best Director (Mankiewicz), Best Film; *NOM:* Academy Awards '50: Best Actress (Baxter), Best Actress (Davis), Best Art Direction/Set Decoration (B & W), Best Black-and-white Cinematography, Best Supporting Actress (Holm, Ritter), Best Original Dramatic Score.

All Dogs Christmas Carol
Curious direct-to-video sequel combines the characters and set-up from *All Dogs Go to Heaven* with a variation on Dickens's *Christmas Carol*. It's a silly hash of a story but that will not bother the young target audience. They'll appreciate the Saturday morning–simple animation and the songs. Some of them will also like the "sing-along" feature, which adds karoke-style subtitles to the musical numbers. That's the main attraction of the DVD. Otherwise, image and sound are nothing challenging.

There's not enough to the film for adults. —MM
Movie: 🎬🎬 **DVD:** 🎬🎬
MGM Home Entertainment (Cat #907034, UPC #027616703422). Full frame. Dolby Digital Surround Stereo. $24.98. Keep-case. *LANG:* English; French. *SUB:* English; French. *FEATURES:* 24 chapter links • "Sing-along" subtitles for songs.
1998 (G) 73m/C *D:* Paul Sabella; *W:* Jymn Magon; *M:* Mark Watters, Lorraine Feather; *V:* Steven Weber, Dom DeLuise, Sheena Easton, Ernest Borgnine, Charles Nelson Reilly, Bebe Neuwirth.

All of Me
Wealthy Edwina Cutwaters (Tomlin) dies and her guru accidentally transfers her soul into the right side of lawyer Roger Cobb's (Martin) body. This literal split per-sonality allows Martin to indulge in some inventive slapstick as Edwina tries to take control. For a full-frame version of a wide-screen film, the DVD is acceptable. Direc-tor Reiner does not make visually chal-lenging pictures. He's an old-fashioned comedy director who works with charac-ters and physical shtick. The sound is thin. —MM
Movie: 🎬🎬🎬 **DVD:** 🎬🎬
Trimark Home Video (Cat #7001D, UPC #031398700135). Full frame. $24.99. Keepcase. *LANG:* English. *SUB:* French; Spanish. *CAP:* English. *FEATURES:* 24 chapter links • Steve Martin, Lily Tomlin, Carl Reiner filmographies • Trailers.
1984 (PG) 93m/C Steve Martin, Lily Tom-lin, Victoria Tennant, Madolyn Smith, Richard Libertini, Dana Elcar, Selma Dia-mond, Jason Bernard, Eric Christmas, Peggy Feury; *D:* Carl Reiner; *W:* Phil Alden Robinson; *C:* Richard Kline; *M:* Patrick Williams. *AWARDS:* New York Film Critics Awards '84: Best Actor (Martin); National Society of Film Critics Awards '84: Best Actor (Martin).

All Quiet on the Western Front
Realistic anti-war epic based on the novel by Erich Maria Remarque centers on the experiences of young Paul Baumer, who changes from enthusiastic warrior to bat-tle-weary veteran in an emotionally exact performance by Ayres. Seven patriotic Ger-man youths go together from school to the battlefields of WWI. They experience the horrors of war firsthand, stuck in the trenches and facing gradual extermina-tion. Emotionally draining and startling with both graphic shots and haunting visu-al poetry. It's a little hard to give a techni-cal rating to a DVD of a film from this era since there can always be a lot of flaws attributed to the pre-print material. Video versions of this film have always been pretty grainy and the DVD seems to add some digital grain to it. The blacks are pretty true and the graytones are rich and varied so there is a good feeling of depth to the picture. There are a few nasty jumps in the film (along with the corre-

sponding missing bits of audio) and occasional white and black flecks, but nothing that you wouldn't expect from a film this old. The audio clips at times and is always on the tinny side—again, probably from the original. All in all this is still a disc worth adding to any videophile's collection. —*JO*

Movie: 🎬🎬🎬🎬 **DVD:** 🎬🎬▶

Universal Studios Home Video (Cat #20510, UPC #025192051029). Full frame. Dolby Digital Mono. $24.98. Keepcase. *LANG:* English. *SUB:* Spanish; French. *CAP:* English. *FEATURES:* Restored 140-min. version ▪ 18 chapter links ▪ Theatrical trailer ▪ Production notes ▪ Cast and filmmakers bios.

1930 103m/B Lew Ayres, Louis Wolheim, John Wray, Slim Summerville, Russell Gleason, Raymond Griffith, Ben Alexander, Beryl Mercer, Arnold Lucy, William "Billy" Bakewell, Scott Kolk, Owen Davis Jr., Walter Rodgers, Richard Alexander, Harold Goodwin, Pat Collins, Edmund Breese; *D:* Lewis Milestone; *W:* Maxwell Anderson, George Abbott, Del Andrews; *C:* Arthur Edeson, Karl Freund; *M:* David Broeckman. *AWARDS:* Academy Awards '30: Best Director (Milestone), Best Picture; American Film Institute (AFI) '98: Top 100, National Film Registry '90; *NOM:* Academy Awards '30: Best Cinematography, Best Writing.

All the President's Men

True story of the Watergate break-in that led to the political scandal that would not be topped until Ms. Lewinski opened her big mouth in the '90s. Intriguing, tense thriller is a nail biter even though the ending is no secret. Expertly paced by Pakula with standout performances by Hoffman and Redford as reporters Bernstein and Woodward who slowly uncover and connect the seemingly isolated facts that ultimately led to criminal indictments of the Nixon administration. Deep Throat Holbrook and Robards as executive editor Ben Bradlee lend authenticity to the endeavor. Warner delivers another excellent-looking under-$20 DVD. The picture is very sharp and very rarely is there any digital grain. The saturated colors are lush and very close to true, as are the blacks. Contrast and brightness levels are consistent, although the picture sometimes feels a little dark. This DVD also boasts one of the best mono soundtracks I've heard with good dynamic range and not bad fidelity, although the low end is lacking a bit. Excellent supplementary section. —*JO*

Movie: 🎬🎬🎬▶ **DVD:** 🎬🎬🎬▶

Warner Home Video, Inc. (Cat #1018, UPC #012569101821). Widescreen (1.85:1) letterboxed; full frame. Dolby Digital 2.0. $19.98. Snapper. *LANG:* English. *SUB:* Spanish; French. *CAP:* English. *FEATURES:* 32 chapter links ▪ Production notes.

1976 (PG) 135m/C Robert Redford, Dustin Hoffman, Jason Robards Jr., Martin Balsam, Jane Alexander, Hal Holbrook, F. Murray Abraham, Stephen Collins, Lindsay Crouse, Meredith Baxter, Ned Beatty, Penny Fuller; *D:* Alan J. Pakula; *W:* William Goldman; *C:* Gordon Willis; *M:* David Shire. *AWARDS:* Academy Awards '76: Best Adapted Screenplay, Best Art Direction/Set Decoration, Best Sound, Best Supporting Actor (Robards); National Board of Review Awards '76: Best Director (Pakula), Best Supporting Actor (Robards); New York Film Critics Awards '76: Best Director (Pakula), Best Film, Best Supporting Actor (Robards); National Society of Film Critics Awards '76: Best Film, Best Supporting Actor (Robards); Writers Guild of America '76: Best Adapted Screenplay; *NOM:* Academy Awards '76: Best Director (Pakula), Best Film Editing, Best Picture, Best Supporting Actress (Alexander).

The Alley Cats

Filmed in Berlin, this early Metzger exploitation tells the story of Leslie, who's treated shabbily by her sophisticated fiance Logan and then turns to the lovely Irena for solace. Virtually all of the sexual activity occurs off camera. In that regard, the film could almost be shown on network TV. The cocktail lounge music and "swinger" mindset are just terrific. In fact, many of the '60s conventions and attitudes that are parodied in *Austin Powers, International Man of Mystery* are treated with much more effective tongue-in-cheek satire here. Despite the box art, this is a black-and-white film and it does not fare well on DVD. Flecks, thin scratches, artifacts, and flashing along thin lines and grid patterns are visible throughout. It's still great fun as nostalgic comedy. —*MM*

Movie: 🎬🎬▶ **DVD:** 🎬🎬

Image Entertainment (Cat #ID5534FF DVD, UPC #014381553420). Widescreen (2.35:1) letterboxed. Dolby Digital Mono. $24.99. Keepcase. *LANG:* English. *FEATURES:* 17 chapter links ▪ Theatrical trailer.

1965 83m/B Anna Arthur, Sabrina Koch, Karen Field, Chaz Hickman, Harold Baerow, Uta Levka; *D:* Radley Metzger; *W:* Radley Metzger.

The Allnighter

This is bad. A college coed searches through the hypersexed beach-party milieu of her senior year for Mr. Right. Bangle Hoffs is directed by her mother, to no avail. You may not really care, but the DVD does allow the choice between letterboxed and pan-and-scan presentations. Quality is O.K., but not leagues better than the previous laserdisc issue. Ironically, this disc is loaded with extras. Much better movies have been treated far worse on DVD. —*MB*

Movie: 🎬 **DVD:** 🎬🎬🎬

Anchor Bay (Cat #DV10870, UPC #013131087093). Widescreen (1.85:1) letterboxed; full frame. Dolby Digital 2.0. $24.99. Keepcase. *LANG:* English. *FEATURES:* 25 chapter links ▪ Commentary: director Hoffs and daughter Susanna ▪ "The Haircut" featurette starring John Cassavetes ▪ Theatrical trailer ▪ Music

video "No TV No Phone" by Price-Sulton ▪ Talent biographies.

1987 (PG-13) 95m/C Susanna Hoffs, John Terlesky, Joan Cusack, Michael Ontkean; *D:* Tamar Simon Hoffs; *W:* Tamar Simon Hoffs; *C:* Joseph D. Urbanczyk; *M:* Charles Bernstein.

Allyson Is Watching

Allyson (Ambrose) goes to Hollywood seeking fame and fortune as an actress. She finds Bridget (Hammon), a working girl, in the apartment next door; a creepy building manager; aggressive photographer; arrogant acting coach. In the lead, Caroline Ambrose is fine but she overplays the wide-eyed Sandra Bullock sweet-young-thing routine. This is a Playboy production so the lighting and sets look fine in the important moments. The no-frills DVD gives skin tones the requisite warmth and soft focus. Sound is adequate. —*MM*

Movie: 🎬🎬 **DVD:** 🎬🎬

Image Entertainment (Cat #ID5844PLDVD, UPC #014381584424). Full frame. Dolby Digital Stereo. $24.99. Snapper. *LANG:* English. *FEATURES:* 12 chapter links.

1996 (R) 96m/C Caroline Ambrose, Jennifer Leigh Hammon, James Horan; *D:* Bob (Robert) Kubilos; *W:* David Keith Miller; *C:* Igor Meglic.

Aloha, Bobby and Rose

Bobby (LeMat) is a part-time mechanic and full-time screw-up; Rose (Hull) has a young son and limited prospects. After the proverbial crime that goes wrong, they find themselves on the run for Mexico. This little-known drama has the dusty, lived-in look of good '70s location movies and excellent characters. On DVD, William Fraker's cinematography is astonishing. He uses natural light for night exteriors and achieves similar results to Haskell Wexler's work on *American Graffiti*. Add in a terrific soundtrack and you've got a solid sleeper for fans of the period. —*MM*

Movie: 🎬🎬🎬▶ **DVD:** 🎬🎬🎬

Anchor Bay (Cat #DV11061, UPC #013131106190). Widescreen (1.85:1) letterboxed; full frame. Dolby Digital 5.1 Surround Stereo; Dolby Digital Surround Stereo. $24.98. Keepcase. *LANG:* English. *FEATURES:* 25 chapter links ▪ Paul LeMat thumbnail biography ▪ Theatrical trailer.

1974 (PG) 90m/C Paul LeMat, Dianne Hull, Robert Carradine, Tim McIntire, Noble Willingham, Leigh French; *D:* Floyd Mutrux; *W:* Floyd Mutrux; *C:* William A. Fraker.

Alphaville

Eddie Constantine plays pock-marked Lemmy Caution, the private dick hero of many a low-budget euro-thriller, this time in a science fiction mystery by the inimitable Godard. The P.I. searches for a missing scientist in a futuristic Paris run by robots led by a dictator. The technodependent

society must be upended so that true non-conformity can once again run amok (and to save the scientist). Surrealistic sci-fi makes good use of contemporary Parisian buildings for futuristic effect. Better production values than the typical Caution flick. This is not one of the better-looking Criterion DVDs, mostly due to the state of the preprint material which is at times very scratched and fleck-filled. There is, on occasion, substantial grain, and though it looks a tad better than the laserdisc, the picture is not that sharp. Where the DVD does shine is with its true blacks and very good graytones, which at least allow for depth details. The contrast and brightness are also above average. Even with the flaws, this DVD is the best way to see *Alphaville*. —*JO* *AKA:* Alphaville, a Strange Case of Lemmy Caution; Alphaville, Une Etrange Aventure de Lemmy Caution.
Movie: 🎵🎵🎵 **DVD:** 🎵🎵▸
Criterion Collection (Cat #25, UPC #037429130926). Full frame. Dolby Digital 1.0. $29.95. Keepcase. *LANG:* French. *SUB:* English. *FEATURES:* 20 chapter links ▪ Color bars.
1965 100m/B *FR* Eddie Constantine, Anna Karina, Akim Tamiroff, Howard Vernon, Laszlo Szabo, Michel Delahaye, Jean-Pierre Leaud; *D:* Jean-Luc Godard; *W:* Jean-Luc Godard; *C:* Raoul Coutard; *M:* Paul Misraki. *AWARDS:* Berlin International Film Festival '65: Golden Berlin Bear.

Altered States

Obsessed with the task of discovering the inner man, ambitious researcher Hurt ignores his family while consuming hallucinogenic drugs and floating in an immersion tank. He gets too deep inside, slipping way back through the evolutionary order and becoming a menace in the process. Great special effects are supported by the usual self-indulgent and provocative Russell direction. Hurt's a solemn hoot in his first starring role. A pretty good DVD to watch; the biggest problems are a couple of scenes when the backgrounds appear blatantly digitized. The colors are very good under all conditions, from vibrant to low-key earthtones, and there is rarely any bleed. The brightness and contrast levels are also very good and there is no added distortion along light/dark contrast lines. A full-sounding 5.1 remastered soundtrack complements the picture and allows full fidelity to the orchestral score without sacrificing and of the dialogue. One would think that Russell would have something mighty colorful to say about behind-the-scene goings on, but even the "production notes" in the limited supplemental section are very elementary. —*JO*
Movie: 🎵🎵🎵 **DVD:** 🎵🎵🎵
Warner Home Video, Inc. (Cat #11076, UPC #085391107620). Widescreen (1.85:1) letterboxed; full frame. Dolby Digital 5.1; Dolby Digital Stereo. $19.98. Snapper. *LANG:* English (DD5.1); French (stereo). *SUB:* French. *CAP:* English. *FEA-*

TURES: 31 chapter links ▪ 5 theatrical trailers ▪ 2 TV spots ▪ Production notes.
1980 (R) 103m/C William Hurt, Blair Brown, Bob Balaban, Charles Haid, Dori Brenner, Drew Barrymore, Miguel Godreau, Thaao Penghlis, Peter Brandon, Charles White Eagle, Meghan Jeffers, Jack Murdock, John Larroquette; *D:* Ken Russell; *W:* Paddy Chayefsky, Sidney Aaron; *C:* Jordan Cronenweth; *M:* John Corigliano. *AWARDS: NOM:* Academy Awards '80: Best Art Direction/Set Decoration, Best Original Score.

Alvarez Kelly

Offbeat western casts Holden as the Mexican-Irish Kelly, who has just sold a herd of cattle to the North during the Civil War. Confederate officer Widmark kidnaps him in an effort to have the cattle redirected to the South. Naturally, a beautiful woman (Rule) is involved, too, intensifying the fierce hatred that develops between the two. Based on a real incident, the script occasionally wanders far afield with the beef, who cleverly heighten the excitement by stampeding when things get slow. Holden's sleepy performance is counter-balanced by an intense Widmark.
Movie: 🎵🎵▸ **DVD:** NYR
Columbia Tristar Home Video (Cat #1199). Widescreen (2.35:1) letterboxed. Dolby Digital Mono. $24.95. Keepcase. *LANG:* English; Spanish. *SUB:* Chinese; Korean; Portuguese; Spanish; Thai. *FEATURES:* Cast and crew thumbnail biographies ▪ Trailer.
1966 109m/C William Holden, Richard Widmark, Janice Rule, Patrick O'Neal, Harry Carey Jr., Victoria Shaw, Roger C. Carmel; *D:* Edward Dmytryk; *W:* Elliott Arnold; *C:* Joe MacDonald; *M:* Johnny Green.

Always

Spielberg's loving remake of the Spencer Tracy vehicle *A Guy Named Joe* (one of his favorites) is filled with genuine warmth that somehow doesn't feel as manipulative as a lot of his other films. A hotshot pilot (Dreyfuss) crashes and burns only to find that he is to become the guardian angel of the rookie fire-fighting flyboy who steals his girl's heart. Goodman throws his usual energetic all into his performance and Hepburn appears as the angel who guides Dreyfuss. An old-fashioned tree burner romance that includes actual footage of the 1988 Yellowstone fire. The flying sequences are nothing short of spectacular. This is a great DVD. The picture is extremely sharp and grain-free. The colors are dead-on (with no noticeable bleed) and the blacks are true. There are no visible artifacts even when the screen is filled with frolicking flames. The soundtrack is excellent (although some will complain about the lack of 5.1) and is crisp and packs a lot of punch for the effects and music. —*JO*
Movie: 🎵🎵🎵 **DVD:** 🎵🎵🎵▸

Universal Studios Home Video (Cat #20556, UPC #025192055621). Widescreen (1.85:1) letterboxed. Dolby Digital 4.0; 2.0. $24.98. Keepcase. *LANG:* English (4.0); French (2.0). *SUB:* Spanish; French. *CAP:* English. *FEATURES:* 26 chapter links ▪ Theatrical trailer ▪ Production notes ▪ Cast bios.
1989 (PG) 123m/C Holly Hunter, Richard Dreyfuss, John Goodman, Audrey Hepburn, Brad Johnson, Marg Helgenberger, Keith David, Roberts Blossom, Dale Dye; *D:* Steven Spielberg; *W:* Jerry Belson; *C:* Mikael Salomon; *M:* John Williams.

Amadeus

Entertaining adaptation by writer Peter Shaffer of his play about the intense rivalry between 18th-century composers Antonio Salieri (Abraham) and Wolfgang Amadeus Mozart (Hulce). Mozart is an immature, boorish genius who remains unaffected and delighted by the beautiful music he creates while irking the hell out of everybody around him. Salieri, the emperor's court composer, is so jealous of Mozart's talents that he plots to destroy him. Terrific period piece filmed on location in Prague features beautiful sets, gorgeous costumes, and of course, great music including Neville Marriner's scoring of the Mozart and Salieri music. The soundtrack on the DVD is excellent. The dialogue is crisp, the ambiences all feel right, and the orchestrations sonicly spectacular. Visually the disc is very sharp and all the subtleties of the lighting come through. Contrast is very good and there is plenty of brightness (even in the dimly lit sequences). —*JO*
Movie: 🎵🎵🎵🎵 **DVD:** 🎵🎵🎵▸
Warner Home Video, Inc. (Cat #36218, UPC #085393621827). Widescreen (2.35:1) anamorphic. Dolby Digital 5.1; Dolby Surround Stereo. $24.98. Snapper. *LANG:* English (DD5.1); French (DS Stereo). *SUB:* English; French. *FEATURES:* 38 chapter links ▪ Theatrical trailer ▪ Alternative music-only track ▪ Production notes ▪ Cast and crew bios.
1984 (PG) 158m/C F. Murray Abraham, Tom Hulce, Elizabeth Berridge, Simon Callow, Roy Dotrice, Christine Ebersole, Jeffrey Jones, Kenny Baker, Cynthia Nixon, Vincent Schiavelli; *D:* Milos Forman; *W:* Peter Shaffer; *C:* Miroslav Ondricek; *M:* John Strauss. *AWARDS:* Academy Awards '84: Best Actor (Abraham), Best Adapted Screenplay, Best Art Direction/Set Decoration, Best Costume Design, Best Director (Forman), Best Makeup, Best Picture, Best Sound; American Film Institute (AFI) '98: Top 100; Cesar Awards '85: Best Foreign Film; Directors Guild of America Awards '84: Best Director (Forman); Golden Globe Awards '85: Best Actor—Drama (Abraham), Best Director (Forman), Best Film—Drama, Best Screenplay; Los Angeles Film Critics Association Awards '84: Best Director (Forman), Best Film, Best Screenplay; *NOM:* Academy Awards '84: Best Actor (Hulce), Best Cinematography, Best Film Editing; Los Angeles Film Critics Associa-

tion Awards '84: Best Actor (Abraham), Best Director (Forman), Best Screenplay.

Amarcord

Semi-autobiographical Fellini fantasy which takes place in the village of Rimini, his birthplace. The episodic film is made up of colorful slices of life as Fellini takes aim at religion, fascism, and family life in 1930's Italy. Although the focus is on Zanin's family, the film is filled with a plethora of amusing and eccentric characters. Visually ripe and filled with satire, burlesque, drama, and tragi-comedy. Considered one of Fellini's best and accessible to even his non-fans. The color on this DVD, which is so important to the film, is stunning and there are no problems with bleed. The contrast is just punchy enough and the brightness levels consistent and comfortable. Blacks are almost dead-on. The picture is very sharp and grain-free, allowing all of Fellini's subtle details to come through. The transfer was obviously done from a very pristine print with very little damage and even the sound is relatively glitch-free, if nothing more special than a mono soundtrack can be. —*JO* **AKA:** I Remember.
Movie: 🎞🎞🎞▶ ***DVD:*** 🎞🎞🎞▶
Criterion Collection (Cat #AMA060DV, UPC #037429121825). Widescreen (1.85:1) letterboxed. Mono. $39.95. Keepcase. *LANG:* Italian; English. *SUB:* English. *FEATURES:* 40 chapter links.
1974 (R) 124m/C *IT* Magali Noel, Bruno Zanin, Pupella Maggio, Armando Brancia; *D:* Federico Fellini; *W:* Federico Fellini, Tonino Guerra; *C:* Giuseppe Rotunno; *M:* Nino Rota. *AWARDS:* Academy Awards '74: Best Foreign Film; New York Film Critics Awards '74: Best Director (Fellini), Best Film; *NOM:* Academy Awards '75: Best Director (Fellini), Best Original Screenplay.

Amarilly of Clothesline Alley

This early Mary Pickford silent melodrama will show contemporary audiences just why she was such a huge star. Though the image is often dark and underlit, she shines forth as a plucky heroine with a particular kind of attractiveness that defies conventional standards of beauty. She's simply a person you like. Here, Amarilly is a blue-collar girl who sells cigarettes in a club and dates the bartender (Scott). Then a slumming socialite (Kerry) falls for her. The DVD was made from a print that has been knocked around and is moderately scratched up. The murkiness of the film—both on-screen and on disc—may put off some audiences but it reflects the standards of its day. The newly recorded score sounds very good. —*MM*
Movie: 🎞🎞🎞 ***DVD:*** 🎞🎞▶
Image Entertainment (Cat #ID5959MLSD-VD, UPC #014381595925). Full frame. Dolby Digital Stereo. $29.99. Snapper. *LANG:* Silent. *SUB:* English intertitles. *FEATURES:* 12 chapter links • Short 1911 film, "The Dream."

1918 77m/B Mary Pickford, William Scott, Norman Kerry, Ida Waterman, Kate Price, Margaret Landis; *D:* Marshall Neilan; *W:* Frances Marion; *C:* Walter Stradling.

The Amazing Transparent Man

Please see review of *Indestructible Man.*
Movie: woof
1960 58m/B Douglas Kennedy, Marguerite Chapman, James Griffith, Ivan Triesault, Red Morgan, Carmel Daniel, Jonathan Ledford, Norman Smith, Patrick Cranshaw, Kevin Kelly; *D:* Edgar G. Ulmer; *W:* Dr. Jack Lewis; *C:* Meredith Nicholson; *M:* Darrell Calker.

Amazon Women on the Moon

A plotless, irreverent media spoof, depicting the programming of a slipshod television station as it crams weird commercials and shorts around a comical '50s-style B-grade sci-fi film. Occasionally hilarious but often misses the mark resulting in many desperate and tedious attempts at humor. Produced by Landis, with the usual amount of in-joke cameos and allusions to his other works of art. In this case the DVD is definitely better than the film itself. The picture is sharp, with only occasional grain sneaking in. Blacks are above average with some leaning toward gray-green in a few scenes. Contrast and brightness levels are very good, as are the colors which seem accurate and bleed-free for the most part. The sound is mono and nothing special but it's good enough for this particular opus. —*JO* **AKA:** Cheeseburger Film Sandwich.
Movie: 🎞🎞 ***DVD:*** 🎞🎞🎞
Image Entertainment (Cat #ID4294US DVD, UPC #014381429428). Full frame. Mono. $24.99. Snapper. *LANG:* English. *FEATURES:* 24 chapter links.
1987 (R) 85m/C Rosanna Arquette, Steve Guttenberg, Steve Allen, B.B. King, Michelle Pfeiffer, Arsenio Hall, Andrew Dice Clay, Howard Hesseman, Lou Jacobi, Carrie Fisher, Griffin Dunne, Sybil Danning, Henny Youngman, Monique Gabrielle, Paul Bartel, Kelly Preston, Ralph Bellamy, Russ Meyer, Steve Forrest, Joey Travolta, Ed Begley Jr., Forrest J Ackerman, Archie Hahn, Phil Hartman, Peter Horton, Charlie Callas, T.K. Carter, Dick Miller, Roxie Roker; *D:* John Landis, Joe Dante, Carl Gottlieb, Peter Horton, Robert Weiss; *W:* Michael Barrie, Jim Mulholland; *C:* Daniel Pearl; *M:* Ira Newborn.

America

D.W. Griffith's attempt to use the American Revolution the same way he had used the Civil War in *The Birth of a Nation* is in some ways a better film. It lacks the blatant racism, excessive sentimentality, and religiosity. The important scenes are neatly built and suspenseful, but the film also lacks the scope and the energy of the

more famous epic, and, most importantly, it lacks the originality. Massachusetts patriot Nathan Holden (Hamilton) is torn between his political beliefs and his love for Nancy Montague (Dempster), daughter of a family of Virginia Tories. Meanwhile, evil Capt. Butler (Barrymore), leader of a band of murderous Mohawks, ruthlessly attacks the colonists and lusts after Nancy. On DVD, the film exhibits the expected nicks and scratches of a film its age, but the image is still superior to VHS, particularly in some of the tinted scenes which tend to be too dark on older rental tapes. —*MM*
Movie: 🎞🎞▶ ***DVD:*** 🎞🎞🎞
Image Entertainment (Cat #ID4726DSDVD, UPC #014381472622). Full frame. Dolby Digital Stereo. $24.99. Snapper. *LANG:* English. *FEATURES:* 29 chapter links.
1924 141m/B Neil Hamilton, Carol Dempster, Lionel Barrymore, Erville Alderson, Charles Bennett, Arthur Donaldson, Charles Mack, Frank McGlynn, Henry O'Neill, Ed Roseman, Harry Semels, Louis Wolheim, Hugh Baird, Lee Beggs, Downing Clarke, Sydney Deane, Arthur Dewey, Michael Donavan, Paul Doucet, John Dunton, Riley Hatch, Emil Hoch, Edwin Holland, W.W. Jones, William S. Rising, Frank Walsh; *D:* D.W. Griffith; *W:* Robert W. Chambers; *C:* Marcel Le Picard, Hendrik Sartov, Billy (G.W.) Bitzer.

An American Affair

District Attorney Sam Brady (Bersnen) falls for two women (D'Abo and Heitmeyer) who are best friends. He marries one and fools around with the other and gets exactly what he deserves for such idiocy. It's standard if underpowered stuff for the erotic video original market. On disc, the Canadian import generally looks better than it needs to with minimal flashing on patterned clothes. —*MM*
Movie: 🎞🎞 ***DVD:*** 🎞🎞▶
York Entertainment (Cat #YPD-1004, UPC #750723100425). Full frame. $24.98. Keepcase. *LANG:* English. *FEATURES:* 25 chapter links.
1999 90m/C *CA* Corbin Bernsen, Maryam D'Abo, Jayne Heitmeyer, Robert Vaughn; *D:* Sebastian Shah.

An American Christmas Carol

Dickens's famous story is shifted to Depression-era New Hampshire in this made-for-TV adaptation. The earnest effort gains little, though star Henry Winkler's makeup might have served as the model for *The Simpsons'* Mr. Burns. Both production values and acting are middle-of-the-road. The image on the no-frills DVD is good enough, but nothing more. —*MM*
Movie: 🎞🎞 ***DVD:*** 🎞🎞
Image Entertainment (Cat #ID6666ZFDVD, UPC #014381666625). Full frame. Dolby Digital Mono. $19.99. Snapper. *LANG:* English. *FEATURES:* 16 chapter links.

1979 98m/C Henry Winkler, David Wayne, Dorian Harewood; *D:* Eric Till; *M:* Hagood Hardy.

American Gigolo

Julian (Gere) is a high-class Los Angeles prostitute whose professional life is complicated when he's framed for a murder. At the same time, he begins a relationship with a woman (Hutton) who doesn't know what he does or who he is. Overall, the DVD looks good for a film of this age, though the image exhibits considerable grain in some exteriors. (If memory serves, that comes from the original.) Mannered performances in supporting roles arc more troublesome. Sound is O.K. —*MM*

Movie: 🎬🎬🎬 **DVD:** 🎬🎬🎬
Paramount Home Video (Cat #08989, UPC #097360898972). Widescreen anamorphic. Dolby Digital 5.1 Surround Stereo; Dolby Digital Surround; Mono. $29.99. Snapper. *LANG:* English; French. *SUB:* English. *FEATURES:* 27 chapter links ▪ Theatrical trailer.
1979 (R) 117m/C Richard Gere, Lauren Hutton, Hector Elizondo, Nina Van Pallandt, Bill Duke, K. Callan; *Cameos:* Paul Schrader; *D:* Paul Schrader; *W:* Paul Schrader; *C:* John Bailey; *M:* Giorgio Moroder.

American Graffiti

Atmospheric, episodic look at growing up in the innocence of America before the Kennedy assassination and the Vietnam War. It all takes place on one hectic but typical night in the life of recent California high school grads unsure of what the next big thing in life is. They spend their life cruising, listening to Wolfman Jack, and hanging out at the drive-in. The authentic soundtrack embellishes the intelligent script and consistently fine performances by the young cast. Catapulted Howard and Williams towards continued coming-of-age nirvana on *Happy Days.* Overall, the DVD is a little above average but not what this fine film deserves. The picture is of average sharpness and has a lot of problems with grain during darker sequences. Colors are a little better with only occasional bleed and the blacks are actually very true. Contrast and brightness are good enough except during those dimmer lit scenes. The sound is adequate and anything more spectacular might take away from the feel of the vintage music. The real highlight of the disc is the "making of" documentary, which features interviews and reflections from the cast and crew as well as insights into the early creativity of a pre-*Star Wars* Lucas. —*JO*

Movie: 🎬🎬🎬▶ **DVD:** 🎬🎬▶
Universal Studios Home Video (Cat #20272, UPC #025192027222). Widescreen (2.35:1) anamorphic. Dolby Digital 3.0; 2.0 Mono. $34.98. Keepcase. *LANG:* English; Spanish; French. *SUB:* Spanish. *CAP:* English. *FEATURES:* 49 chapter links (film) ▪ 7 chapter links (documentary) ▪

"Making of" featurette ▪ Cast screen tests ▪ Production photos ▪ Theatrical trailer.
1973 (PG) 112m/C Richard Dreyfuss, Ron Howard, Cindy Williams, MacKenzie Phillips, Paul LeMat, Charles Martin Smith, Suzanne Somers, Candy Clark, Harrison Ford, Bo Hopkins, Joe Spano, Kathleen Quinlan, Wolfman Jack; *D:* George Lucas; *W:* George Lucas, Gloria Katz, Willard Huyck; *C:* Jan D'Alquen, Ron Everslage. *AWARDS:* American Film Institute (AFI) '98: Top 100; Golden Globe Awards '74: Best Film—Musical/Comedy, National Film Registry '95; New York Film Critics Awards '73: Best Screenplay; National Society of Film Critics Awards '73: Best Screenplay; *NOM:* Academy Awards '73: Best Director (Lucas), Best Film Editing, Best Picture, Best Story & Screenplay, Best Supporting Actress (Clark).

American History X

Intense performances by Norton and Furlong make this film worth a look. Former skinhead Norton is released from prison after a three-year stint for killing two black teens. He returns home having renounced his neo-Nazi ideology and lifestyle, only to find that his kid brother (Furlong) is following in his footsteps. Controversial not only due to its subject matter and violence, but also because director Kaye demanded to have his name removed from the film. The DVD features three deleted scenes that, as is usually the case, were left out for good reason. The image is very sharp whether during the color or black-and-white (flashback) sections of the film. The same goes for the excellent contrast and brightness levels, and the very true blacks. There is little bleed in the colors and for the most part they are also true to the theatrical presentation. There is very little Surround but the dialogue is always crisp and the music features very good dynamics and excellent imaging. —*JO*

Movie: 🎬🎬🎬 **DVD:** 🎬🎬🎬
New Line Home Video (Cat #N4739, UPC #794043473920). Widescreen (1.85:1) anamorphic. Dolby Digital 5.1; Dolby Digital 2.0. $24.98. Snapper. *LANG:* English. *SUB:* English. *FEATURES:* 33 chapter links ▪ 3 deleted scenes ▪ Theatrical trailer ▪ Cast and crew bios.
1998 (R) 118m/C Edward Norton, Edward Furlong, Fairuza Balk, Beverly D'Angelo, Avery Brooks, Stacy Keach, Jennifer Lien, Elliott Gould, William Russ, Joe Cortese, Ethan Suplee, Guy Torry, Giuseppe Andrews, Jordan Marder, Anne Lambton, Paul LeMat; *D:* Tony Kaye; *W:* David McKenna; *C:* Tony Kaye; *M:* Anne Dudley. *AWARDS: NOM:* Academy Awards '98: Best Actor (Norton).

An American in Paris

Lavish, imaginative musical features a sweeping score, and knockout choreography by Kelly. Ex-G.I. Kelly stays on in Paris after the war to study painting, supported by rich American Foch, who hopes to

acquire a little extra attention. But Kelly loves the lovely Caron, unfortunately engaged to an older gent. Highlight is an astonishing 17-minute ballet, which holds the record as the longest movie dance number—and one of the most expensive, pegged at over half a million for a month of filming. This DVD delivers the film's magnificent colors the way they should be seen, rich and vibrant, looking very much like what you'd expect from one of these glorious MGM musicals. There are a few sequences where the colors are a little too strong, resulting in some bleed, but nothing to weaken the enjoyment of the film. For the most part the picture is quite sharp, with little grain, and brightness and contrast levels are very good, but there is some ghosting around some brighter images (this seems to occur mostly in black-and-white films). It would have nice to have been a punchier soundtrack, but overall it's very adequate, and I usually much prefer the original sound even if it is mono. —*JO*

Movie: 🎬🎬🎬▶ **DVD:** 🎬🎬🎬▶
MGM Home Entertainment (Cat #906273, UPC #027616627322). Full frame. Dolby Digital 1.0. $24.98. Keepcase. *LANG:* English; French. *SUB:* English; French. *FEATURES:* 32 chapter links ▪ Theatrical trailer ▪ 8-page booklet.
1951 113m/C Gene Kelly, Leslie Caron, Oscar Levant, Nina Foch, Georges Guetary; *D:* Vincente Minnelli; *W:* Alan Jay Lerner; *C:* John Alton; *M:* George Gershwin, Ira Gershwin. *AWARDS:* Academy Awards '51: Best Art Direction/Set Decoration (Color), Best Color Cinematography, Best Costume Design (Color), Best Picture, Best Story & Screenplay, Scoring of a Musical; American Film Institute (AFI) '98: Top 100; Golden Globe Awards '52: Best Film—Musical/Comedy, National Film Registry '93; *NOM:* Academy Awards '51: Best Director (Minnelli), Best Film Editing.

American Movie

If Ed Wood were reincarnated in Lake Wobegone and tried to make *The Blair Witch Project* there, he might be Mark Borchardt. Mark is the subject of this crowd-pleasing documentary, which has become a sleeper hit on the festival circuit and home video. The filmmakers follow him and his pal Mike Schank around as Mark tries to raise money to make a short film "Coven." (Mark pronounces it CO-ven because he doesn't want it to rhyme with "oven.") Also involved are other friends, family, girlfriend, ex-wife, kids, and significantly, Uncle Bill, who lives in a trailer park. In many ways, the relationship between Mark and Bill is at the center of the movie. At various times you'll feel superior to these people as they display their various weaknesses—alcohol most obviously but also gambling and harder drugs. Eventually though, you come to realize that Mark's film is the one ambitious thing that's holding them together and, each in his or her own way, buys into it. This really is "the stuff dreams are made of." The DVD is virtually identical to VHS tape in image and sound; the real difference is in the extras, including "Coven" and a commentary track by the key participants. Highly recommended. —*MM*

Movie: 🐾🐾🐾▶ **DVD:** 🐾🐾🐾
Columbia Tristar Home Video (Cat #04702, UPC #0433960474020). Full frame. Dolby Digital 5.1; Dolby 2-Channel. $27.95. Keepcase. *LANG:* English. *SUB:* English; Spanish. *FEATURES:* 20 chapter links • "Coven" • Trailers • Deleted scenes • Commentary: Smith, Price, Borchardt, Schank.
1999 (R) 104m/C Mike Schank, Mark Borchardt; *D:* Chris Smith; *C:* Chris Smith; *M:* Mike Schank.

American Pie (CE)

Four high school senior boys—Jim (Biggs), Stifler (Scott), Oz (Klein), and Finch (Thomas)—make a pact to lose their virginity on prom night. The realities of adolescent females, the possibilities of Internet embarrassment, and pastry provide most of the complications in this updated (but not necessarily improved) version of *Porky's.* The "unrated" DVD contains a few more moments of nudity and raunch, and a crowded commentary track with the filmmakers and cast members. Reflecting the film itself, the commentary has a frathouse, beerblast-quality of amateur enthusiasm. They laugh a lot. The Weitzs make the Farrelly brothers seem positively sophisticated. On DVD, the image is no better than it was in theatres, but what should anyone expect from a low-budget teen sex comedy? The disc also contains outtakes that are thoroughly unfunny. —*MM* *AKA:* East Great Falls High.

Movie: 🐾🐾 **DVD:** 🐾🐾
Universal Studios Home Video (Cat #20735, UPC #025192073526). Widescreen (1.85:1) anamorphic. Dolby Digital Surround Stereo; Dolby Digital 5.1 Surround Stereo. $26.98. Keepcase. *LANG:* English; French. *SUB:* Spanish. *CAP:* English. *FEATURES:* 18 chapter links • "Making of" featurette • Separate soundtrack presentation • Quotes • Commentary: Chris Weitz, Paul Weitz, Adam Herz • Commentary: Eddie Kaye Thomas, Jason Biggs, Seann William Scott • Outtakes.
1999 96m/C Jason Biggs, Thomas Ian Nicholas, Chris Owen, Chris Klein, Natasha Lyonne, Tara Reid, Mena Suvari, Alyson Hannigan, Shannon Elizabeth, Eugene Levy, Seann W. Scott, Jennifer Coolidge, Eddie Kaye Thomas, Lawrence Pressman; *D:* Chris Weitz, Paul Weitz; *W:* Adam Herz; *C:* Richard Crudo; *M:* David Lawrence.

American Pop

Ralph Bakshi's animated story of four generations of men is told in music. Immigrant Zalmie starts off in vaudeville and winds up in the mob; his pianist son Benny gets killed in WWII; Benny's son Tony winds up in the early psychedelic rock scene in Haight-Asbury; and Tony's son Little Pete becomes a rock star. The story seems a little weaker than it did 20 years ago, but Bakshi's stylized animation more than makes up for it. Even a Bakshi cartoon has a lot less in the way of subtle shading and details than a live-action film, so most look great on DVD. This one's no exception and is very sharp and grain-free, featuring strong vibrant colors that don't seem to bleed and very true blacks. Contrast and brightness levels are also very impressive. There is some film damage but nothing too distracting. The digital stereo Surround is top-notch and will give those sub woofers a good workout even without a discreet sub woofer track. —*JO*

Movie: 🐾🐾▶ **DVD:** 🐾🐾🐾▶
Columbia Tristar Home Video (Cat #19599, UPC #043396195998). Widescreen (1.85:1) anamorphic; full frame. Dolby Digital 3.0. NSL. Keepcase. *LANG:* English; Spanish. *SUB:* Spanish; French. *CAP:* English. *FEATURES:* 28 chapter links.
1981 (R) 95m/C *D:* Ralph Bakshi; *W:* Ronni Kern; *M:* Lee Holdridge; *V:* Ron Thompson, Marya Small, Lisa Jane Persky, Roz Kelly, Richard Singer, Jeffrey Lippa.

The American President

Widower President Andrew Shepherd (Douglas) decides it's time to get back into the dating game, but what woman wants to find her romance in the public eye? (Remember, this is a pre-Monica production.) Feisty environmentalist Sydney Wade (Bening) is right there, but the nasty opposition candidate, Bob Rumson (Dreyfuss), uses their relationship as political fodder. The glossy material is expertly handled by both director and cast, but it experiences some odd problems on DVD. Pixels show up in bright backgrounds; diagonal lines break up more than you'd expect (even Douglas's carefully groomed hair); and tie patterns flash. Sound is fine but not a major component of the film. —*MM*

Movie: 🐾🐾🐾 **DVD:** 🐾🐾▶
Warner Home Video, Inc. (Cat #2550, UPC #053939255027). Widescreen (2.35:1) letterboxed; full frame. Dolby Digital 5.1 Surround Stereo. $19.98. Snapper. *LANG:* English. *SUB:* English; French. *FEATURES:* Cast and crew thumbnail biographies • "Oval Office" notes on research • Trailer • 33 chapter links.
1995 (PG-13) 114m/C Michael Douglas, Annette Bening, Martin Sheen, Michael J. Fox, David Paymer, Samantha Mathis, John Mahoney, Anna Deavere Smith, Nina Siemaszko, Wendie Malick, Shawna Waldron, Richard Dreyfuss; *D:* Rob Reiner; *W:* Aaron Sorkin; *C:* John Seale; *M:* Marc Shaiman. *AWARDS: NOM:* Academy Awards '95: Best Original Score; Golden Globe Awards '96: Best Actor—Musical/Comedy (Douglas), Best Actress—Musical/Comedy (Bening), Best Director (Reiner), Best Film—Musical/Comedy, Best Screenplay; Writers Guild of America '95: Best Original Screenplay.

American Rampage

Early effort from prolific video-auteur Dave DeCoteau is a violent police revenge story set in L.A. From the shaky introductory helicopter shot to the final shootout, this cheapie doesn't look any better on DVD than it ever did. Reds bleed, the image is rough, and the disc appears to have been made from a print with a fair amount of scratches, nicks, and flakes. —*MM*

Movie: 🐾🐾 **DVD:** 🐾▶
Simitar Entertainment (Cat #7405, UPC #082551740529). Full frame. PCM Stereo. $14.98. Keepcase. *LANG:* English. *FEATURES:* 8 chapter links • Production factoids • Troy Donahue filmography.
1989 90m/C Troy Donahue, Tom Elliott, Kary J; *D:* David DeCoteau; *W:* David DeCoteau, Ross A. Perron.

American Strays

Episodic Tarantino wanna-be about various violent oddballs, most of whom cross paths at Kane's out-of-the-way roadside diner. The characters—a masochist who needs assistance in the suicide department, an unemployed family man who's about to lose it, a serial killer, and more—are quirky enough for a dark comedy, but the cast's over-the-top attempts just come off as overacting, and the writing at times just plain sucks. For a Simitar DVD, this one looks pretty good. The image is fairly sharp, and digital grain and pixelation, while present, is bearable. The colors are not really saturated, so there's not much bleed, but overall the hues look right. The blacks lean towards gray, and contrast and brightness levels are consistent, if a little weak. Imaging and separation on the soundtrack is nothing special and, though digital, it's overall kind of weak, lacking in low end and not as crisp as one would like. —*JO*

Movie: 🐾▶ **DVD:** 🐾🐾▶
Simitar Entertainment (Cat #731, UPC #082551734122). Full frame. Dolby Digital 2.0. $14.98. Keepcase. *LANG:* English. *FEATURES:* 8 chapter links • Cast bios.
1996 (R) 97m/C Carol Kane, Jennifer Tilly, Eric Roberts, John Savage, Luke Perry, Joe Viterelli, James Russo, Vonte Sweet, Sam Jones, Brion James, Toni Kalem, Melora Walters; *D:* Michael Covert; *W:* Michael Covert; *C:* Sead Mutarevic; *M:* John Graham.

American Streetfighter

Standard issue martial arts stuff: inexpensively produced with poor staging, pedestrian fight choreography, grainy light, and sets that are often filled with attractive cardboard boxes. The plot involves conflict between brothers (Daniels and Jacklin) and another rival martial artist—you know the drill. The disc makes the film look better than it does on tape, but the image still leaves much to be desired. —*MM*

Movie: 🐾🐾 **DVD:** 🐾🐾

Simitar Entertainment (Cat #7515, UPC #082551751525). Full frame. Dolby Digital Stereo. $19.98. Keepcase. *LANG:* English. *FEATURES:* 8 chapter links ● Production factoids.
1996 80m/C Gary Daniels, Ian Jacklin, Tracy Dali; *D:* Steve Austin.

American Streetfighter 2: The Full Impact

Non-sequel, actually filmed before the first *American Streetfighter*, concerns different characters and a serial killer. It's a notch or two lower in overall quality with poorly focused images and a leaden pace. The only attraction is personable star Daniels. —*MM*
Movie: 🦴▸ *DVD:* 🦴▸
Simitar Entertainment (Cat #7515, UPC #08255175152). Full frame. Dolby Digital Stereo. $19.98. Keepcase. *LANG:* English. *FEATURES:* 8 chapter links. Available on two-sided disc with *American Streetfighter.*
1997 90m/C Gary Daniels, Graciela Casillas; *D:* Marc Messenger.

An American Werewolf in London

Two American students (Naughton and Dunne) backpacking through Europe are viciously attacked by a werewolf one foggy night. Dunne is killed, but keeps appearing (in progressively decomposed form) before the seriously wounded Naughton, warning him of impending werewolfdom when the moon is full. (Dunne advises suicide.) Seat-jumping horror and gore, highlighted by intensive metamorphosis sequences by Rick Baker, are offset by wry humor. There is a lot of grain on this DVD, but don't be too scared off. At least it doesn't get any worse in the film's many dark sequences—the only scenes where it got nasty were the foggy ones. The sharpness is about average, and though the contrast is pretty good, a little more brightness would have made the DVD more comfortable to watch. Colors are good and blacks are true, and despite all the grain, there is very little color bleed. The vintage music is very important to the film, and the sound is fine when a song is playing, but is a little muddy overall. —*JO*
Movie: 🦴🦴🦴▸ *DVD:* 🦴🦴
Artisan Entertainment (Cat #60453, UPC #012236045304). Widescreen (1.85:1) letterboxed. Dolby Digital 5.1. $24.98. Snapper. *LANG:* English. *CAP:* English. *FEATURES:* 24 chapter links.
1981 (R) 97m/C *GB* David Naughton, Griffin Dunne, Jenny Agutter, Frank Oz, Brian Glover, Lila Kaye, David Schofield, John Woodvine, Don McKillop, Paul Kember, Colin Fernandes, Rik Mayall, Paddy Ryan; *D:* John Landis; *W:* John Landis; *C:* Robert Paynter; *M:* Elmer Bernstein. *AWARDS:* Academy Awards '81: Best Makeup.

An American Werewolf in Paris

Horror-comedy fails to live up to the wit and quirkiness of the original. Andy (Scott) is on a daredevil tour of Europe along with buddies Brad (Vieluf) and Chris (Buckman). As he bungees off the Eiffel Tower, he spots a French femme attempting a suicidal plunge nearby. He saves her and immediately falls in love. The girl (Delpy) warns him to stay away, but he keeps sniffing around, leading to a confrontation with a nasty batch of Nazi werewolves. Computerized werewolves look great at times and ridiculously digital at others. Doesn't it figure? The weaker of the two *American Werewolf* movies is the far superior DVD. This one is extremely sharp, so sharp that some of the CGI effects look even more fake than at the theatre. Digital grain is near nonexistent. Contrast is excellent and the brightness level is comfortably consistent, although the most noticeable flaw is that there is a shimmering along high-contrast lines. Colors are vibrant with no bleed and the blacks are dead-on. The sound is also top-notch all the way through, with good thumping low end during sound effects and music, great fidelity and dynamics, and very good Surround tracks. —*JO*
Movie: 🦴🦴 *DVD:* 🦴🦴🦴▸
Hollywood Pictures Home Video (Cat #14376, UPC #717591000477). Widescreen (1.85:1) letterboxed. Dolby Digital 5.1. $24.98. Keepcase. *LANG:* English (DD5.1); French. *CAP:* English. *FEATURES:* 15 chapter links ● Theatrical trailer.
1997 (R) 100m/C Anthony Waller, Julie Delpy, Tom Everett Scott, Julie Bowen, Pierre Cosso, Thierry Lhermitte, Vince Vieluf, Phil Buckman, Tom Novembre, Isabelle Constantini; *D:* Anthony Waller; *W:* Anthony Waller, Tim Burns, Tom Stern; *C:* Egon Werdin; *M:* Wilbert Hirsch. *AWARDS: NOM:* MTV Movie Awards '98: Best Song ("Mouth").

Amistad

Spielberg again creates an epic tale of human struggle, although not quite as effectively as he did in *Schindler's List*. In 1839, African captives aboard the slaveship *Amistad*, led by a Mende tribesman named Cinque (Hounsou), free themselves and stage a bloody mutiny. A property attorney (McConaughey) and former president John Quincy Adams (Hopkins) must prove in lengthy court proceedings that the Africans were rightfully freed individuals in the eyes of the law. A sequence depicting the Middle Passage, the slaves' horrific ocean journey to the Americas, is shocking and brutal, but too many sequences are undermined by heavy-handed musical orchestration. McConaughey is less laid-back than usual, but Morgan Freeman, as a freed slave turned abolitionist, is reduced to a cameo. With its attention to period detail and a superb performance by the dynamic Hounsou, the film rises above the clutches of melodrama, and is ultimately moving and eye-opening. Widescreen picture is first-rate, with rich golds and browns, which stay sharp and well defined even in nighttime scenes, and the sound quality is very good. DVD lacks commentary tracks, which would have been welcome. —*JE*
Movie: 🦴🦴🦴▸ *DVD:* 🦴🦴🦴▸
DreamWorks Home Entertainment (Cat #84162, UPC #6706841622). Widescreen (1.85:1) anamorphic. Dolby Digital Surround 5.1; Dolby 2.0 Surround. $34.98. Keepcase. *LANG:* English. *CAP:* English. *FEATURES:* 24 chapter links ● Theatrical trailer ● 25-minute "making of" featurette ● Production notes ● Cast and crew bios. Box lists only the Dolby 5.1 Surround option, but DVD menu offers the choice of second: Dolby 2.0 Surround.
1997 (R) 152m/C Djimon Hounsou, Anthony Hopkins, Matthew McConaughey, Morgan Freeman, Nigel Hawthorne, David Paymer, Pete Postlethwaite, Stellan Skarsgard, Anna Paquin, Austin Pendleton, Tomas Milian; *D:* Steven Spielberg; *W:* David Franzoni; *C:* Janusz Kaminski; *M:* John Williams. *AWARDS:* Broadcast Film Critics Association Awards '97: Best Supporting Actor (Hopkins); *NOM:* Academy Awards '97: Best Cinematography, Best Costume Design, Best Supporting Actor (Hopkins), Best Original Score; Directors Guild of America Awards '97: Best Director (Spielberg); Golden Globe Awards '98: Best Actor—Drama (Hounsou), Best Director (Spielberg), Best Film—Drama, Best Supporting Actor (Hopkins); Screen Actors Guild Award '97: Best Supporting Actor (Hopkins).

Anaconda

Snakes—lots and lots of snakes, including a couple of 40-footers that love to eat people and then vomit them up again. Voight gets to play yet another bad guy with a silly accent, this time guiding a documentary film crew along the Amazon River looking for a legendary Indian tribe. Plenty of cast members become appropriately horrified snake food. Lots of fun. Here's another case where the DVDs incredible sharpness exaggerates the phony look of a lot of the computer effects (and there are a lot of them). There is very little digital grain, no artifacts to speak of, and both the blacks and the near-bleedless colors are dead-on. Contrast and brightness are very good and very consistent. On the audio side, the dialogue is crisp, the music full, and the Surround really kicks in during any water or effects sequences. —*JO*
Movie: 🦴🦴▸ *DVD:* 🦴🦴🦴
Columbia Tristar Home Video (Cat #81759, UPC #043396817593). Widescreen (2.35:1) letterboxed; full frame. Dolby Digital 5.1; Stereo. NSL. Keepcase. *LANG:* English (DD5.1; Stereo); French (Stereo). *SUB:* Spanish; French. *CAP:* English. *FEATURES:* 34 chapter links.
1996 (PG-13) 90m/C Jon Voight, Jennifer Lopez, Ice Cube, Eric Stoltz, Owen C. Wilson, Kari Wuhrer, Jonathan Hyde, Vincent

Castellanos, Danny Trejo; **D:** Luis Llosa; **W:** Jim Cash, Jack Epps Jr., Hans Bauer; **C:** Bill Butler; **M:** Randy Edelman. *AWARDS: NOM:* Golden Raspberry Awards '97: Worst Picture, Worst Actor (Voight), Worst Director (Llosa), Worst Screenplay.

Analyze This

Anxiety-ridden mob boss Paul Vitti (De Niro) goes to suburban shrink Ben Sobel (Crystal) and is so pleased with the results that he strong-arms the doc into seeing him whenever he wants. Unfortunately for Ben and fiancee Laura (Kudrow), that usually happens when they're trying to get married. Palminteri is a rival gangster with whom Vitti "seeks closure." De Niro expertly winks at the mob genre, which he helped create, without losing the air of menace that surrounds the good fella character. On DVD, both image and sound are all that you'd expect from a big-budget, big-star comedy. Dark clothes look fine, even in dim interiors. —MM
Movie: ♫♫♫ **DVD:** ♫♫♫►
Warner Home Video, Inc. (Cat #16988). Full frame; widescreen (1.85:1) anamorphic. Dolby Digital 5.1 Surround Stereo. $24.98. Snapper. *LANG:* English. *SUB:* English. *FEATURES:* 35 chapter links • Commentary: Ramis • Commentary: De Niro and Crystal • Cast and crew thumbnail bios • Gag reel • Trailer.
1998 (R) 110m/C Robert De Niro, Billy Crystal, Lisa Kudrow, Chazz Palminteri, Joe Viterelli, Bill Macy, Leo Rossi, Rebecca Schull, Molly Shannon, Max Casella, Pat Cooper, Richard C. Castellano, Jimmie Ray Weeks, Elizabeth Bracco, Tony Darrow, Kyle Sabihy, Donnamarie Recco; **D:** Harold Ramis; **W:** Harold Ramis, Peter Tolan, Kenneth Lonergan; **C:** Stuart Dryburgh; **M:** Howard Shore. *AWARDS: NOM:* Golden Globe Awards '00: Best Actor—Musical/Comedy (De Niro), Best Film—Musical/Comedy.

Anastasia

No one should look to cartoons for historical accuracy, but this one still takes considerable liberties, blaming the Russian revolution on Rasputin. In any case, the film is beautifully drawn, if less successfully written. The obvious model is Disney's *Beauty and the Beast* with its strong heroine, big musical numbers, and intricate backgrounds. The voices are well chosen and the disc is loaded with extras aimed squarely at the younger set. Stereo sound is excellent and even the fast-moving action scenes and the slower ballroom sequences are handled flawlessly. Given the subject matter, this one will probably prove more popular with girls than with boys in the long run. Followed by *Bartok the Magnificent,* a video-premiere sequel. —MM
Movie: ♫♫♫ **DVD:** ♫♫♫►
20th Century Fox (Cat #4112601, UPC #086162126017). Widescreen (2.35:1) letterboxed; full frame. Dolby Digital Stereo; Dolby Digital 5.1 Surround Stereo.

$29.98. Keepcase. *LANG:* English; French; Spanish. *SUB:* English. *CAP:* English. *FEATURES:* 2 sing-along songs • 2 "making of" featurettes • 36 chapter links.
1997 (G) 90m/C D: Don Bluth, Gary Goldman; **W:** Bruce Graham, Susan Guathier, Bob Tzudiker, Noni White; **M:** David Newman; **V:** Meg Ryan, John Cusack, Kelsey Grammer, Angela Lansbury, Christopher Lloyd, Hank Azaria, Bernadette Peters, Kirsten Dunst. *AWARDS: NOM:* Academy Awards '97: Best Song ("Journey to the Past"), Best Original Musical/Comedy Score; Golden Globe Awards '98: Best Song ("Journey to the Past"), Best Song ("Once Upon a December").

And Now for Something Completely Different

Essentially, this is a "greatest hits" disc that compiles skits from the early years of the BBC's Monty Python's Flying Circus. Sketches include the "Dead Parrot," "Upper Class Twit of the Year," "The Townswomen's Guild Reconstruction of Pearl Harbour," and the unforgettable "Lumberjack Song." It's a great introduction to the Pythons for the uninitiated, or a chance for the converted to see their favorite bits again. Those who remember the original broadcasts on PBS will be surprised at the quality of the DVD. The film looks much better than many from the early '70s. Enough care was taken with the digital transfer that the DVD manages to handle the incredible mixed plaids of "Hell's Grannies" without a hitch. Sound is equally good. —MM
Movie: ♫♫♫► **DVD:** ♫♫♫
Columbia Tristar Home Video (Cat #1239, UPC #043396012394). Full frame; widescreen (1.85:1) anamorphic. Dolby Digital Mono. $24.95. Keepcase. *LANG:* English. *SUB:* English; French; Spanish. *FEATURES:* 28 chapter links • Cast and crew thumbnail biographies.
1972 (PG) 89m/C *GB* John Cleese, Michael Palin, Eric Idle, Graham Chapman, Terry Gilliam, Terry Jones, Carol Cleveland, Connie Booth; **D:** Ian McNaughton, Terry Gilliam; **W:** John Cleese, Michael Palin, Eric Idle, Graham Chapman, Terry Gilliam, Terry Jones; **C:** David Muir; **M:** Douglas Gamley.

And the Ship Sails On

In June 1914, a group of devoted opera lovers takes a luxury cruise on the *Gloria N* to pay respects to a recently deceased diva. Also on board is a group of fleeing Serbo-Croatian freedom fighters. The charming and absurd autumnal homage to life from the maestro was shot entirely on soundstages. The opening sequence, building slowly from silent sepia to sound color, is one of his most inspired and carefully controlled moments and it works beautifully on DVD. For the rest of the disc, some graininess is visible in the darker scenes and large groupings of char-

acters in black formal clothes lose detail. Those are quibbles. The film has never received wide distribution and so many fans have missed it. They ought to find it. Comparisons to *Amarcord* are not out of place. —MM *AKA:* El la Nave Va.
Movie: ♫♫♫► **DVD:** ♫♫♫♫
Criterion Collection (Cat #AND090, UPC #037429139028). Widescreen (1.85:1) letterboxed. Dolby Digital Mono. $39.95. Keepcase. *LANG:* Italian. *SUB:* English. *FEATURES:* 39 chapter links • Liner notes by Fellini from *I Fellini* by Charlotte Chandler.
1983 (PG) 130m/C *IT* Freddie Jones, Barbara Jefford, Janet Suzman, Peter Cellier, Philip Locke, Victor Poletti, Norma West; **D:** Federico Fellini; **W:** Federico Fellini, Tonino Guerra; **C:** Giuseppe Rotunno; **M:** Gianfranco Plenizio.

And Then There Were None

Based on an oft-filmed novel by Agatha Christie, this is a murder mystery in which ten strangers are lured to an island mansion by a mysterious host they don't know. Slowly one after the other is killed before they can leave the island. Who among them is the murderer? The DVD is showing signs of the film's age but looks unexpectedly good. The transfer exhibits some speckles and scratches, and some significant noise reduction has been applied to the transfer, giving it a rather soft look. The audio is a harsh sounding mono track that sounds aged and muffled but is understandable at any time. The noise floor is surprisingly low, leaving much of the moody ambience intact. —GH
Movie: ♫♫♫► **DVD:** ♫♫►
VCI Home Video (Cat #8209, UPC #089859820922). Full frame. Dolby Digital Mono. $19.99. Keepcase. *LANG:* English. *FEATURES:* Biographies.
1945 97m/B Louis Hayward, Barry Fitzgerald, Walter Huston, Roland Young, Sir C. Aubrey Smith, Judith Anderson, Mischa Auer, June Duprez; **D:** Rene Clair; **W:** Rene Clair, Dudley Nichols; **C:** Lucien N. Andriot; **M:** Mario Castelnuovo-Tedesco.

Andrei Rublev

A 15th-century Russian icon painter must decide whether to record history or participate in it as Tartar invaders make his life miserable. During the black-and-white portion, he becomes involved in a peasant uprising, killing a man in the process. After a bout of pessimism, and a vow of silence, he goes forth to create artistic beauty as the screen correspondingly blazes with color. Censored by Soviet authorities until 1971, this restored version is nothing short of amazing. Though the preprint has some scratches and flecks of white, the image is superb. There appears to be no digital grain or artifacts. In addition to its sharpness, the black and white (which comprised most of the film) has balanced graytones as well as excellent contrast and brightness levels. When the color comes in at end of the film, the image remains sharp and the colors true. The mono soundtrack is mostly free of clipping or other distortions and sounds as good as it probably can. Petric's commentary (essay) is not continuous but is labeled on the chapter guide. —*JO*

Movie: 🎵🎵🎵🎵 **DVD:** 🎵🎵🎵🎵

Criterion Collection (Cat #CC1550DVD, UPC #715515009928). Widescreen (2.35:1) letterboxed. Dolby Digital Mono. $39.98. Keepcase. *LANG:* Russian. *SUB:* English. *FEATURES:* 53 chapter links • Scene-specific audio essay by Vlada Petric • Tarkovsky interviews • Historical Russian timeline • Video essay on Tarkovsky • Dual-layered RSDL. Complete 205-min. version.

1966 205m/C *RU* Anatoli Solonitzin, Ivan Lapikov, Nikolai Grinko, Nikolai Sergeyev; **D:** Andrei Tarkovsky; **W:** Andrei Tarkovsky, Andrei Konchalovsky; **C:** Vadim Yusov; **M:** Vyacheslav Ovchinnikov.

The Andromeda Strain

A satellite falls back to Earth carrying a deadly bacteria that must be identified in time to save the population from extermination. A crack team of civilian scientists assembles at a secret underground laboratory to solve the crisis. Unfortunately, the bug keeps mutating. Though the technology is slightly dated, and the script a little too talky, the tension inherent in the Michael Crichton novel is kept intact due to the precision-paced work of director Robert Wise. There is a lot of grain on the DVD—even in the brighter sequences—and in the darker, redder scenes it is almost unbearable. The color is average, except when the reds bleed and overwhelm everything else on the screen. The brightness is fairly consistent, and the blacks at least a very dark gray, but the contrast is way too high. Sound is nothing spectacular but adequate and understandable. —*JO*

Movie: 🎵🎵🎵 **DVD:** 🎵

Image Entertainment (Cat #ID4220US DVD, UPC #014381422023). Widescreen (2.35:1) letterboxed. Mono. $29.99. Snapper. *LANG:* English. *CAP:* English. *FEATURES:* 20 chapter links.

1971 (G) 131m/C Arthur Hill, David Wayne, James Olson, Kate Reid, Paula Kelly, Ramon Bieri, George Mitchell; **D:** Robert Wise; **W:** Nelson Gidding; **C:** Richard H. Kline; **M:** Gil Melle. *AWARDS: NOM:* Academy Awards '71: Best Art Direction/Set Decoration, Best Film Editing.

Andy Warhol's Dracula

Sex and camp humor, as well as a large dose of blood, highlight Warhol's treatment of the tale. As Dracula can only subsist on the blood of pure, untouched maidens ("were-gins"), gardener Dallesandro rises to the occasion in order to make as many women as he can ineligible for Drac's pur-

poses. Very reminiscent of Warhol's *Frankenstein,* but with a bit more spoofery. Look for Roman Polanski in a cameo peek as a pub patron. I've always liked the music to this film, so the addition of a "suite" from Gizzi's score (in stereo) is great. The DVD has improved colors over the Criterion laserdisc and the picture is just about as sharp. The disc has no trouble with all the dark scenes and in the climax, details are more clearly visible than they were at the theatre. —*JO* *AKA:* Blood for Dracula; Young Dracula; Dracula Cerca Sangue di Vergine e...Mori de Sete; Dracula Vuole Vivere: Cerca Sangue de Vergina; Andy Warhol's Young Dracula.

Movie: 🎵🎵🎵 **DVD:** 🎵🎵🎵

Criterion Collection (Cat #CC1547DVD, UPC #715515009522). Widescreen (1.85:1) letterboxed. Dolby Digital Mono. $39.95. Keepcase. *LANG:* English. *FEATURES:* 28 chapter links • Commentary: Paul Morrissey, Udo Kier, Maurice Yacowar • Photo gallery • Excerpts from Claudio Gizzi's score.

1974 (R) 106m/C *IT FR* Udo Kier, Arno Juerging, Maxine McKendry, Joe Dallesandro, Vittorio De Sica, Milena Vukotic, Dominique Darel, Stefania Casini, Silvia Dionisio; **Cameos:** Roman Polanski; **D:** Paul Morrissey, Anthony (Antonio Margheriti) Dawson; **W:** Paul Morrissey; **C:** Luigi Kuveiller; **M:** Claudio Gizzi.

Andy Warhol's Frankenstein

Outrageous parody of Frankenstein features plenty of gore, sex, and bad taste in general. Baron von Frankenstein (Kier) derives sexual satisfaction from his corpses (he delivers a particularly thought-provoking philosophy on life as he lustfully fondles a gall bladder); his wife seeks her pleasure from the monster himself (Dallesandro). Originally made in 3-D, this is one of Warhol's campiest outings. This DVD is sharp and vibrant enough to actually make you feel that you are watching 3-D in some of the scenes. The carriage ride through the forest has nearly the same feeling of depth that the 3-D film had in the theatre—and you don't have to wear those damn glasses. The effect is there due to the sharp image and the vibrant contrasty colors. Like the Criterion's DVD edition of *Blood for Dracula,* this disc also has a stereo version of the score as a supplemental feature, which sounds great. The film itself is in mono and though the soundtrack is adequate, fidelity is nothing special and there is a level of distortion throughout the entire film, which can most likely be blamed on preprint material. —*JO* *AKA:* Flesh for Frankenstein; The Frankenstein Experiment; Up Frankenstein; The Devil and Dr. Frankenstein; Carne per Frankenstein; Frankenstein; Il Mostro e in Tavola...Barone Frankenstein.

Movie: 🎵🎵🎵 **DVD:** 🎵🎵🎵

Criterion Collection (Cat #CC1546D, UPC #715515009423). Widescreen (2.35:1) letterboxed. Dolby Digital Mono. $39.95. Keepcase. *LANG:* English. *FEATURES:* 30

chapter links • Commentary: Paul Morrissey • Photo gallery • Excerpts from the Claudio Gizzi score.

1974 (X) 95m/C *GE FR IT* Udo Kier, Monique Van Vooren, Joe Dallesandro, Dalia di Lazzaro, Arno Juerging, Srdjan Zelenovic, Nicoletta Elmi, Marco Liofredi, Cristina Gajoni, Carla Mancini, Liu Bozizio; **D:** Paul Morrissey; **W:** Paul Morrissey; **C:** Luigi Kuveiller; **M:** Claudio Gizzi.

Angel and the Badman

After the notorious gunslinger Quirt (Wayne) is wounded during a shoot-out, a pacifist family takes him in and nurses him back to health. Daughter Penelope (Russell) falls for him and begs him not to go back to his old ways, but a notorious gunslinger's gotta do what a notorious gunslinger's gotta do. The film is really one of Wayne's better mid-career westerns. He also produced and legendary stuntman Yakima Canutt was the second unit director. Unfortunately, this disc was made from a muddy original and so even the daylight exteriors look dark. —*MM*

Movie: 🎵🎵🎵 **DVD:** 🎵➤

Delta/Laserlight (Cat #82 027, UPC #018111998932). Full frame. $14.99. Keepcase. *LANG:* English. *SUB:* Spanish; Chinese; Japanese. *FEATURES:* 17 chapter links • Introduction by Tony Curtis • Documentary, *John Wayne on Film.*

1947 100m/B John Wayne, Gail Russell, Irene Rich, Harry Carey Sr., Bruce Cabot; **D:** James Edward Grant; **W:** James Edward Grant; **C:** Archie Stout; **M:** Richard Hageman.

Angel Heart

This is the film that featured ex-Huxtable Bonet shedding her nice-girl image (and her clothes) in the provocative mattress-thumping scene with Rourke beneath the bleeding ceiling. Director Parker's satanic thriller finds marginal PI Rourke hired by the devilish De Niro to find a missing big band singer who violated a "contract." The investigation leads to the bizarre world of the occult in New Orleans, where the blood drips to a different beat. Adapted from William Hjortsberg's *Falling Angel.* The DVD pretty much blows away the earlier laserdisc and VHS copies of the film. The picture is sharp: grain- and artifact-free, even with all the dark scenes. There is very little distortion or color bleed along high-contrast lines and the colors themselves are accurate, as are the blacks. The disc also boasts a fine dynamic soundtrack with crisp highs, resonant lows, just the right amount of mid-range, and good imaging—all without having been remastered to 5.1. —*JO*

Movie: 🎵🎵🎵➤ **DVD:** 🎵🎵🎵➤

Artisan Entertainment (Cat #6057, UPC #012236045700). Widescreen (1.85:1) anamorphic. Dolby Surround. $24.98. Keepcase. *LANG:* English. *SUB:* Spanish. *CAP:* English. *FEATURES:* 36 chapter links • Theatrical trailer • "Making of" featurette • Cast and crew bios • Production notes.

1987 (R) 112m/C Mickey Rourke, Robert De Niro, Lisa Bonet, Charlotte Rampling, Michael Higgins, Charles Gordone, Kathleen Wilhoite, Stocker Fontelieu, Brownie McGhee, Elizabeth Whitcraft, Eliott Keener, Dann Florek; **D:** Alan Parker; **W:** Alan Parker; **C:** Michael Seresin; **M:** Trevor Jones.

Angel Heart

Hong Kong soft-core eroticism is more emotional than most similar American products, though the copycat title is no accident. The plot deals with the rocky romance between ex-con Miao Wei and Wenny. The general level of image quality is good with careful lighting and photography. The credits are not translated into English. —*MM*

Movie: 🐾🐾🐾 **DVD:** 🐾🐾🐾
Tai Seng Video Marketing (Cat #GCA0002). Full frame. Dolby Digital Stereo. $49.95. Keepcase. *LANG:* Cantonese; Mandarin. *SUB:* Chinese; English. *FEATURES:* 6 chapter links.
1995 100m/C *HK*

Angel in Training

Twelve-year-old Dewey Brooker (Dagher) is dealing with the turmoil of adolescence when her cartoonist father's business is threatened with a hostile takeover. It takes heavenly intervention to save them. Many of the creative people behind this kid-vid have been active in the business for years, often making erotic video premieres. They handle the youth/supernatural/comedy formula with the same competence. Unfortunately, the corners they had to cut are all too apparent on DVD. The celestial scenes are filled with such heavy pixelation that it may have been intentional. Whatever the reason, it is difficult to watch. Sound is nondescript. —*MM*

Movie: 🐾 **DVD:** 🐾🐾
Image Entertainment (Cat #ID8796UM DVD, UPC #014381879629). Full frame. Dolby Digital Surround Stereo. $24.99. Snapper. *LANG:* English. *FEATURES:* 12 chapter links.
1999 (G) 89m/C Laila Dagher, Danielle Pessis, Veronica Allen, Gary Imhoff, Sally Truitt, Tracy Bassett; **D:** Gary Graver; **W:** Chick Vennera; **C:** Gary Graver; **M:** Charles Harrison.

Angel's Dance

Loopy riff on *Prizzi's Honor* is more fun than it ought to be. Young Tony (Chandler) has just been promoted to Mafia assassin by Uncle Vinnie (Polito). But before Tony can do his first job, he must serve a brief apprenticeship with Zen master Rosselini (Belushi) in California. To train Tony, they pick a name at random from the phone book. The theory: "If you can whack an innocent victim, you can whack anybody." But the intended, Angel Chaste (Lee), is no cupcake. Her transformation is the story of the film and it defies synopsis.

Writer-director Corley will keep you guessing and astonished all the way through to an unpredictable finish. On DVD, the film exhibits a few problems with flashing diagonal lines, but they're not a serious flaw. The image is generally excellent, but the real attractions here are the offbeat characters and a sense of humor that is both sly and cartoonish. Recommended. —*MM*

Movie: 🐾🐾🐾 **DVD:** 🐾🐾🐾
York Entertainment (Cat #YPD-1013, UPC #750723101323). Full frame. Dolby Digital 5.1 Surround Stereo. $24.98. Keepcase. *LANG:* English. *SUB:* Spanish. *FEATURES:* 30 chapter links • Theatrical trailer • Cast filmographies.
1999 (R) 102m/C James Belushi, Sheryl Lee, Kyle Chandler, Jon Polito, Ned Bellamy, Mac Davis, Frank John Hughes, Mark Carlton; **D:** David Corley; **W:** David Corley; **C:** Michael G. Wojciechowski.

Animal Crackers

The third and one of the funniest Marx Brothers films, this adapted George S. Kaufman play contains some of their finest moments. Capt. Spaulding (Groucho), the African explorer, is a guest at Mrs. Rittenhouse's (Dumont) Long Island estate. With the help of Chico, Harpo, and Zeppo, he does his best to destroy it. Complete with the Harry Ruby music score—including "Hooray for Capt. Spaulding," which eventually became the theme song of Groucho's TV show. (Show business rumor has it that the real Capt. Spaulding was a notorious cocaine dealer.) Great one-liners and general anarchy. DVD technology has little trouble handling the stage-bound action. The sound is thin and wavering in places, as is to be expected of films of the era. —*MM*

Movie: 🐾🐾🐾 **DVD:** 🐾🐾🐾
Image Entertainment (Cat #ID4272USDVD, UPC #014381427226). Full frame. Dolby Digital Mono. $29.99. Snapper. *LANG:* English. *FEATURES:* 16 chapter links.
1930 (G) 98m/B Groucho Marx, Chico Marx, Harpo Marx, Zeppo Marx, Lillian Roth, Margaret Dumont, Louis Sorin, Hal Thompson, Robert Greig, Margaret Irving, Edward Metcalf, Kathryn Reece; **D:** Victor Heerman; **W:** Morrie Ryskind; **C:** George J. Folsey; **M:** Bert Kalmar, Harry Ruby.

Animal Instincts

Joanne (Whirry) is a bored housewife whose husband (Caulfield), a cop, discovers that he gets turned on by watching her with other men. It's loosely based on the supermarket tabloid tale of the Florida call girl and her husband, who kept a list of names and videotapes of their encounters with the rich and politically connected in their little town. This one's the original video premiere "erotic thriller" and it's still one of the very best, because Shannon Whirry carries off her role with such intensity.

Movie: 🐾🐾🐾 **DVD:** NYR
Studio Home Entertainment (Cat #4020). Full frame. Dolby Digital Stereo. $24.95.

Keepcase. *FEATURES:* Cast and crew thumbnail biographies • Trailer.
1992 (R) 94m/C Maxwell Caulfield, Jan-Michael Vincent, Mitch Gaylord, Shannon Whirry, Delia Sheppard, John Saxon, David Carradine; **D:** Alexander Gregory (Gregory Dark) Hippolyte; **W:** Jon Robert Samsel, Georges des Esseintes; **C:** Paul Desatoff; **M:** Joseph Smith.

Animal Instincts 3: The Seductress

The glossy erotic series gets a tad studied in its third installment, minus original star Shannon Whirry. It's about Joanna Coles (Schumacher, who now works under the name Alexander Keith), a writer of dirty novels living with record producer Alex Savage (Matthew) who pretends to be blind so that he can "watch" her. Veteran producer-director Hippolyte (who's also Gregory Dark) tries some experimental visual techniques that translate well to DVD. He alternates black and white and color, and supersaturates colors in some scenes. The extra sharpness of the digital transfer also enhances the occasional graininess. More importantly for the film's purposes, flesh tones and textures are well rendered. —*MM*

Movie: 🐾🐾 **DVD:** 🐾🐾🐾
Image Entertainment (Cat #ID5764UM DVD, UPC #014381576429). Full frame. Dolby Digital Stereo. $24.99. Snapper. *LANG:* English. *FEATURES:* 12 chapter links.
1995 (R) 96m/C Wendy Schumacher, James Matthew, Marcus Graham, John Bates, Anthony Lesa; **D:** Alexander Gregory (Gregory Dark) Hippolyte; **W:** Selwyn Harris; **C:** Ernest Paul Roebuck.

Animal Room

Despite the title, this one has nothing to do with *Animal House*. Instead, the filmmakers do everything to remind viewers of *A Clockwork Orange*, but that resemblance is fleeting. The story, set in a near-future New Jersey, concerns youth violence. The Animal Room is a place in a high school basement where all of the problem students are kept segregated, including would-be droog Doug Van Housen (Lillard) and sensitive druggie Arnold Mosk (Harris). The violence is held within normal limits and the film does attempt something more than conventional exploitation. The DVD image is unusually bright and crisp for a low-budget picture. Sound is fair. —*MM*

Movie: 🐾🐾 **DVD:** 🐾🐾🐾
Vanguard International Cinema, Inc. (Cat #VF9938, UPC #658769993837). Widescreen (1.66:1) letterboxed. $29.95. Keepcase. *LANG:* English. *FEATURES:* 10 chapter links.
1995 98m/C Neil Patrick Harris, Matthew Lillard, Gabriel Olds, Catherine Hicks, Brian Vincent; **D:** Craig Singer.

Animaland

Animator David Hand is famous for his work with the Disney Studio. He also made a series of cute-animal cartoons in the 1940s. The nine on this disc are well restored, though a few film breaks are evident. As a group, they lack the detailed background and complex characterizations of contemporaneous Disney work, and they're not nearly as subversive as Warner Bros. Loony Tunes. Even so, kids who like animation will probably be entertained. The DVD color is a bit faded, and the image jumps slightly at times. The disc's main asset is the accessibility of individual cartoons. —*MM*
Movie: 🐾🐾▶ **DVD:** 🐾🐾🐾
Image Entertainment (Cat #ID4393CEDVD, UPC #014381439328). Full frame. Dolby Digital Mono. $24.99. Snapper. *LANG:* English. *FEATURES:* 10 chapter links.
1948 69m/C *GB D:* David Hand.

Animation Greats

Cartoons selected by the National Film Board of Canada.
Movie: 🐾🐾 **DVD:** NYR
Lumivision Corp. (Cat #4970). Full frame. Dolby Digital Stereo. $24.95. Keepcase.
1997 70m/C

Animation Legend: Winsor McCay

Collection of early short cartoons by the creator of "Gertie the Dinosaur."
Movie: 🐾🐾▶ **DVD:** NYR
Lumivision Corp. Full frame. $19.99. Keepcase.
1993 100m/C

Anna Karenina

Vivien Leigh stars in a stiff version of Tolstoy's passionate story of a married woman's illicit affair with a military officer (Richardson). In spite of the exquisite costumes and the talented leads, it's still tedious.
Movie: 🐾🐾▶ **DVD:** NYR
Madacy Entertainment (Cat #99021). Full frame. Dolby Digital Mono. $9.99. Keepcase. *FEATURES:* Cast and crew thumbnail biographies • Trivia questions • Production notes.
1948 123m/C *GB* Vivien Leigh, Ralph Richardson, Kieron Moore, Sally Ann Howes, Niall MacGinnis, Martita Hunt, Michael Gough; *D:* Julien Duvivier; *W:* Julien Duvivier; *C:* Henri Alekan; *M:* Constant Lambert.

Annie Hall

Widely acclaimed as Allen's best film, this wistful comedy is based in part on the life of its star and director. It's a light-hearted romantic comedy on top, but bubbling not too far from the surface is wonderfully right-on commentary about everything from love and loneliness to communicating and career goals. It has plenty of elements of drama, too, but so does life. Allen's story of a stand-up comedian and his lady love is as real as life, but no less entertaining for it. Keaton is superb in her Oscar-winning role, and the film deserves its Best Picture Academy Award. The soundtrack is mono, so it's no workout for your expensive audio gear. But the dialogue comes through clearly, and the letterboxed side of the DVD does relatively well by Gordon Willis's cinematography. Regrettably for viewers with widescreen sets, the picture was not enhanced for 16x9 displays. Extras are largely absent. —*MB*
Movie: 🐾🐾🐾🐾 **DVD:** 🐾🐾▶
MGM Home Entertainment (Cat #906559, UPC #027616655929). Widescreen (1.85:1) letterboxed; full frame. Dolby Digital 2.0. $25.98. Snapper. *LANG:* English; French. *SUB:* English; French; Spanish. *CAP:* English. *FEATURES:* Theatrical trailer • Booklet with cast and production notes.
1977 (PG) 94m/C Woody Allen, Diane Keaton, Tony Roberts, Carol Kane, Paul Simon, Colleen Dewhurst, Janet Margolin, Shelley Duvall, Christopher Walken, Marshall McLuhan, Dick Cavett, John Glover, Jeff Goldblum, Beverly D'Angelo; *D:* Woody Allen; *W:* Woody Allen, Marshall Brickman; *C:* Gordon Willis. *AWARDS:* Academy Awards '77: Best Actress (Keaton), Best Director (Allen), Best Original Screenplay, Best Picture; American Film Institute (AFI) '98: Top 100; British Academy Awards '77: Best Actress (Keaton), Best Director (Allen), Best Film, Best Screenplay; Directors Guild of America Awards '77: Best Director (Allen); Golden Globe Awards '78: Best Actress—Musical/Comedy (Keaton); Los Angeles Film Critics Association Awards '77: Best Screenplay; National Board of Review Awards '77: Best Supporting Actress (Keaton), National Film Registry '92; New York Film Critics Awards '77: Best Actress (Keaton), Best Director (Allen), Best Film, Best Screenplay; National Society of Film Critics Awards '77: Best Actress (Keaton), Best Film, Best Screenplay; Writers Guild of America '77: Best Original Screenplay; *NOM:* Academy Awards '77: Best Actor (Allen).

Another Day in Paradise

Tulsa teen junkies Bobbie (Kartheiser) and Rosie (Wagner) team up with older junkie couple Mel (Woods) and Sidney (Griffith) and things go from bad to worse. Mel's also a dealer and a thief and is glad to add two would-be partners in crime to Sidney's traveling roadshow to hell. Woods is all sly confidence while Griffith shows some seductive tough-chick grit. Based on the book by Eddie Little. This one's not for the faint of heart or queasy of stomach. It's no more than average-looking on DVD. There is way too much grain all the way through, and it only gets worse in darker scenes. For some reason it did seem to improve as the disc went on, but unfortunately artifacts were ever present. Color bleed is another problem, although the colors seem true to what they were in the theatre. The blacks are fine and at least the grain does not increase in them. Sound is above average and there is some nice ambience in the Surround tracks. —*JO*
Movie: 🐾▶ **DVD:** 🐾▶
Trimark Home Video (Cat #7030D, UPC #031398703037). Widescreen (1.85:1) letterboxed. Dolby Digital 5.1. $24.99. Keepcase. *LANG:* English. *SUB:* Spanish; French. *CAP:* English. *FEATURES:* 24 chapter links • Theatrical trailer • Commentary: director Larry Clark • Clarence Carter music video • Cast bios.
1998 (R) 101m/C James Woods, Melanie Griffith, Vincent Kartheiser, Natasha Gregson Wagner, Paul Hipp, Brent Briscoe, Lou Diamond Phillips; *D:* Larry Clark; *W:* Christopher Landon, Stephen Chin; *C:* Eric Alan Edwards.

Another 48 Hrs.

Continuing chemistry between Nolte and Murphy is one of the few worthwhile items in this stodgy rehash. Any innovation by Murphy seems tired and lost; the generic story could fit any cop thriller; and though violence and car chases abound, the result is pure tedium. Pointlessly energetic and occasionally fun only for the true devotee. If you've just gotta have every action movie ever made, then this DVD is worth owning. While not a showpiece, its performance is very good in every way. The image is grain-free and sharp with just a couple of scenes that appear hazy. Colors are accurate and vibrant with nary a hint of bleed. Brightness remains consistent and it's only in those aforementioned hazy shots that you would want more contrast. Those scenes are also the only ones where the black is a bit off. As expected, the sound is also better than this film deserves, lively and dynamic with great bottom and crisp highs, as well as a nice mix on the Surround tracks. —*JO*
Movie: 🐾▶ **DVD:** 🐾🐾🐾
Paramount Home Video (Cat #323867, UPC #097363238676). Widescreen (2.35:1) letterboxed. Dolby Digital 5.1; Dolby Surround. $29.98. Keepcase. *LANG:* English (DD5.1; DS); French (DS). *CAP:* English. *FEATURES:* 15 chapter links.
1990 (R) 98m/C Eddie Murphy, Nick Nolte, Brion James, Kevin Tighe, Bernie Casey, David Anthony Marshall, Ed O'Ross; *D:* Walter Hill; *W:* Jeb Stuart; *C:* Matthew F. Leonetti; *M:* James Horner.

Another Man's Poison

Bette's at her baddest in this British thriller. She's mystery novelist Janet Frobisher who is out to steal her secretary's (Williams) fiance (Steel), but first she must deal with George Bates (Merrill), partner of her inconvenient husband who's an escaped convict! Unfortunately, the execution of that febrile plot is not as spirited as it might have been. The first half is exceptionally dark and the DVD transfer is not able to let much extra light into the gloomy black-and-white photography. The monaural sound is completely adequate for the talky proceedings. On any medium, however, the drawing card is the star and even if this is not her finest vehicle, she is thoroughly enjoyable. —*MM*

Movie: 🎵🎵➤ **DVD:** 🎵🎵➤

Image Entertainment (Cat #ID6724CQDVD, UPC #014381672428). Full frame. Dolby Digital Mono. $24.99. Snapper. *LANG:* English. *FEATURES:* 12 chapter links.

1952 90m/B *GB* Bette Davis, Gary Merrill, Emlyn Williams, Anthony Steel, Barbara Murray, Reginald Beckwith, Edna Morris; *D:* Irving Rapper; *W:* Val Guest; *C:* Robert Krasker; *M:* Paul Sawtell.

Another 9 1/2 Weeks

Model Angie Everhart takes over as Lea Kello, a Paris fashion executive and old friend of Elizabeth McGraw, the character played by Kim Basinger in the first film. John Gray (a diffident Rourke) goes to Paris to find his long-lost sweetie-pie, but winds up with Lea instead. Judged as a sequel, this one's completely successful. It re-creates the original's polished look and utter lack of substance. The Paris locations, costumes, and sets are slick eye-candy. Director Anne Goursaud, who also made *Embrace of the Vampire* and *Poison Ivy II*, is much more restrained and coy here. Whenever the action heats up, she uses arty shadows and reflections in mirrors. And in the big love scene, when Mr. Rourke is smearing honey and wine and flower petals all over Ms. Everhart, you've got to wonder one thing. Who's going to clean all that up? The full-frame DVD image is only a negligible improvement over tape. —*MM*

Movie: 🎵🎵➤ **DVD:** 🎵🎵➤

Trimark Home Video (Cat #6772). Full frame. Dolby Digital Stereo. $24.99. Keepcase. *LANG:* English. *SUB:* French; Spanish. *FEATURES:* Trailer ➤ Cast thumbnail bios.

1996 (R) 104m/C Mickey Rourke, Angie Everhart, Steven Berkoff, Agathe de la Fontaine, Dougray Scott; *D:* Anne Goursaud; *W:* Michael Paul Davis; *C:* Robert Alazraki; *M:* Stephen Parsons, Francis Haines.

Antarctica

These IMAX creations are pretty much the best way to experience something or someplace without really doing anything about it. In this case, the rugged landscape of the Southern continent is presented in all its splendor. Some sequences go beyond exhilarating to downright nail-bitingly tense. The disc is another IMAX presentation on DVD that nicely shows off your system and makes for decent background at parties and such. The image is very sharp, has little grain (a bit shows up during some of the excessively bright scenes), and has a few, but not many artifacts. The colors are accurate, as are the blacks. Good and

consistent, the contrast and brightness levels prevent snow scenes from being washed-out and retain the detail. The 5.1 sound is also top-notch with good imaging, crisp highs, and a good solid and clean low end. —*JO*

Movie: 🎵🎵🎵 **DVD:** 🎵🎵🎵

SlingShot Entertainment (Cat #9810, UPC #724117029791). Full frame. Dolby Digital 5.1. $24.99. Expanded jewel case. *LANG:* English; Spanish; French. *SUB:* English. *FEATURES:* 6 chapter links.

1991 40m/C

Antonia's Line

Ninety-year-old Antonia (Van Ammelrooy) has decided that she is going to die today and so begins a 50-year-long flashback of her nonconformist life in a Dutch village. Her lesbian daughter Danielle (Dottermans) wants a child without bothering about a husband and Antonia obligingly arranges a brief interlude that produced child prodigy Therese (Van Overloop), who eventually has her own daughter Sarah (Ravesteijn). Lots of female bonding as the male characters are mostly shoved to the periphery, along with a slight tinge of magical realism. The widescreen DVD places a narrow band of black at the top of the screen and a much deeper bar at the bottom to accommodate the subtitles, keeping them completely out of the image. On the other hand, the colors of the menu make it virtually impossible to tell which chapter or choice has been highlighted. Some minor pixelation is visible in darker scenes but it is not at all serious. Sound is adequate. —*MM*

Movie: 🎵🎵➤ **DVD:** 🎵🎵➤

WinStar Home Entertainment (Cat #FLV5143, UPC #720917514321). Widescreen letterboxed. Dolby Digital Stereo. $29.98. Snapper. *LANG:* Dutch. *SUB:* English. *FEATURES:* 8 chapter links ➤ Cast and crew filmographies ➤ Production credits ➤ Theatrical trailer.

1995 (R) 102m/C *NL* Willeke Van Ammelrooy, Els Dottermans, Veerle Van Overloop, Thyrza Ravesteijn, Jan Decleir, Mil Seghers, Jan Steen, Marina De Graaf; *D:* Marleen Gorris; *W:* Marleen Gorris; *C:* Willy Stassen; *M:* Ilona Sekacz. *AWARDS:* Academy Awards '95: Best Foreign Film; *NOM:* British Academy Awards '96: Best Foreign Film.

Antz

Only the second feature film ever created entirely through computer animation (*Toy Story* being the first), this flick matches big-name voices with insect characters. Life is no picnic for Woody Allen as Z, a worker ant with an inferiority complex. Z switches places with a soldier ant (Stallone) and unwittingly winds up a hero. In the process, he wins the affections of beautiful (for an ant!) Princess Bala (Stone) and the ire of ruthless General Mandible (Hackman). Z and his future princess bride embark on a dangerous mission far from the colony as they search

for the mythical Insectopia. Along the way, they face dangers as diverse and bizarre as a giant wad of gum and a child with a magnifying glass! The computer-generated ants of this picture aren't as cutesy-cuddly as those of the similarly themed *A Bug's Life*, released the same year. But *Antz* delivers a story with more depth and thus may be more appreciated by adults. Nevertheless, it's a pleaser for the whole family. Parents of younger children need only worry about one scene, which depicts the horrific aftermath of a battle between ants and termites in a stylish, disturbing manner. An early Signature Selection DVD release from DreamWorks, the disc is loaded with extras. Would-be computer animators will most appreciate the behind-the-scenes stuff. The animated menus are entertaining all on their own. Audio and video quality are impeccable. —*MB*

Movie: 🎵🎵🎵➤ **DVD:** 🎵🎵🎵🎵

DreamWorks Home Entertainment (Cat #84199, UPC #6706841992). Widescreen (1.85:1) letterboxed. Dolby Digital 5.1. $34.98. Keepcase. *LANG:* English. *CAP:* English. *FEATURES:* 26 chapter links ➤ Commentary: directors Johnson and Darnell ➤ Production featurette ➤ Basics of computer animation and character design ➤ Production notes ➤ Cast and director biographies ➤ Theatrical trailer.

1998 (PG) 83m/C *D:* Eric Darnell, Tim Johnson; *W:* Chris Weitz, Paul Weitz, Todd Alcott; *M:* Harry Gregson-Williams, John Powell; *V:* Woody Allen, Sharon Stone, Sylvester Stallone, Anne Bancroft, Danny Glover, Christopher Walken, Jane Curtin, Jennifer Lopez, John Mahoney, Dan Aykroyd, Paul Mazursky, Gene Hackman.

Any Number Can Win

The best parts of this French caper flick are a superb performance by Jean Gabin as Charles, the professional thief just released from prison who decides to go for one last score, the support he gets from a youthful Alain Delon as his former cellmate, and a dynamite early '60s score by Michel Magne. The story of a casino heist is neatly spun out, but the location filming is just as enjoyable. The black-and-white photography owes more to the grittiness of Italian neo-realism than to the more stylized American studio approach. The DVD has a slightly muted look and some annoying hums are audible at times on the soundtrack. —*MM* *AKA:* Melodie en Sous-Sol; The Big Grab.

Movie: 🎵🎵🎵 **DVD:** 🎵🎵🎵

Image Entertainment (Cat #ID9084SIDVD, UPC #014381908428). Widescreen letterboxed. Dolby Digital Mono. $29.99. Snapper. *LANG:* French. *SUB:* English. *FEATURES:* 12 chapter links.

1963 118m/B *FR* Claude Cerval, Jean Gabin, Alain Delon, Viviane Romance, Maurice Biraud, Carla Marlier, Jose-Luis De Villalonga, Jean Carmet; *D:* Henri Verneuil; *W:* Henri Verneuil, Michel Audiard, Albert Simonin; *C:* Louis Page; *M:* Michel Magne.

Anywhere But Here

The flighty mom–serious daughter conflict was the subject of several big budget films in the late 1990s. Wayne Wang and Alvin Sargent's adaptation of Mona Simpson's novel is one of the best and certainly one of the most slickly made. Adele (Sarandon) drags teenaged daughter Ann (Portman) away from a happy life in small-town Wisconsin for the presumptive glamour and excitement in Beverly Hills. The performances are better than the plot. As usual, Wang works well with his cast. On DVD, both image and sound are excellent. Danny Elfman's score is terrific. Why, though, does the box art wipe 15 years off of Susan Sarandon's face, rendering her virtually unrecognizable? —MM

Movie: ♪♪♪ **DVD:** ♪♪♪
Twentieth Century Fox Home Entertainment (Cat #2000036, UPC #024543000 365). Widescreen (2.35:1) anamorphic. Dolby Digital 5.0 Surround Stereo; Dolby Digital Surround Stereo. $34.98. Keepcase. *LANG:* English; French. *SUB:* English; Spanish. *FEATURES:* 20 chapter links • Theatrical trailer • "Making of" featurette.
1999 (PG-13) 114m/C Susan Sarandon, Natalie Portman, Shawn Hatosy, Hart Bochner, Bonnie Bedelia, Eileen Ryan, Ray Baker, John Diehl, Caroline Aaron; *D:* Wayne Wang; *W:* Alvin Sargent; *C:* Roger Deakins; *M:* Danny Elfman. *AWARDS: NOM:* Golden Globe Awards '00: Best Supporting Actress (Portman).

The Apocalypse

Space pilot J.T. Wayne (Bernhard) teams up with salvage operator Suarez (McCoy) to retrieve a cargo ship lost in space for 25 years. Crewman Vendler (Zagarino) hijacks the cargo for himself but it turns out that the ship has been boobytrapped (by San Giacomo) and rigged to crash into Earth. This video premiere sf is slow, dark, and quirkily cast. The relative clarity of DVD makes the budgetary limitations all too obvious. —MM

Movie: ♪♪ **DVD:** ♪♪
Simitar Entertainment (Cat #7454, UPC #082551745425). Full frame. Dolby Digital Stereo. $14.98. Keepcase. *LANG:* English. *FEATURES:* 8 chapter links • Production factoids • Sandra Bernhard thumbnail biography.
1996 (R) 96m/C Sandra Bernhard, Laura San Giacomo, Cameron Dye, Frank Zagarino, Matt McCoy; *D:* Hubert de la Bouillerie; *C:* Greg Gardiner.

Apocalypse Now

Francis Ford Coppola's "other" masterpiece is a nightmare. The story, loosely based on Joseph Conrad's *Heart of Darkness,* weaves its way upriver through the illogical images of a dream. The surreal opening montage of jungle, dust, helicopters, and flame merges into the alcohol-drenched fever dream of Capt. Willard (Martin Sheen) staring at the ceiling fan in his Saigon hotel. "I wanted a mission," he says, "and for my sins, they gave me one."

Coppola captures the madness of that war, finding no easy answers, no clear-cut heroes and villains. Somehow, the more horrific it gets, the more sense it makes. The DVD is based on the restored laser edition that was created under the supervision of cinematographer Vittorio Storaro and sound genius Walter Murch. (Both won well-deserved Oscars for their original work on the film.) The DVD shares the same chapter breaks with the laser, but it adds the previously unavailable concluding air attack on Kurtz's compound. On a commentary track for that section only, Coppola explains that he was contractually obligated to destroy the set, so he decided to blow it up and to film it. That footage played with the limited 70mm release that contained no on-screen credits. (A program was handed out. It is reproduced on the DVD.) The only difference I could tell between the laser and DVD in a direct comparison is a slight enhancement of natural sounds over the musical score. Visually, the two are almost identical. —MM

Movie: ♪♪♪♪ **DVD:** ♪♪♪▶
Paramount Home Video (Cat #02306, UPC #097360230673). Widescreen (2.35:1) anamorphic. Dolby Digital 5.1 Surround Stereo; Dolby Digital Surround Stereo. $29.99. Keepcase. *LANG:* English; French. *SUB:* English; French. *FEATURES:* 20 chapter links • DVD production credits • Destruction of the compound sequence with Coppola commentary • Original theatrical premiere program • Theatrical trailer.
1979 (R) 153m/C Francis Ford Coppola, Marlon Brando, Martin Sheen, Robert Duvall, Frederic Forrest, Sam Bottoms, Scott Glenn, Albert Hall, Laurence "Larry" Fishburne, Harrison Ford, G.D. Spradlin, Dennis Hopper, Cynthia Wood, Colleen Camp, Linda Carpenter, Tom Mason, James Keane, Damien Leake, Jack Thibeau, R. Lee Ermey, Vittorio Storaro; *D:* Francis Ford Coppola; *W:* Francis Ford Coppola, John Milius, Michael Herr; *C:* Vittorio Storaro; *M:* Carmine Coppola. *AWARDS:* Academy Awards '79: Best Cinematography, Best Sound; American Film Institute (AFI) '98: Top 100; British Academy Awards '79: Best Director (Coppola), Best Supporting Actor (Duvall); Cannes Film Festival '79: Best Film; Golden Globe Awards '80: Best Director (Coppola), Best Supporting Actor (Duvall), Best Score; National Society of Film Critics Awards '79: Best Supporting Actor (Forrest); *NOM:* Academy Awards '79: Best Adapted Screenplay, Best Art Direction/Set Decoration, Best Director (Coppola), Best Film Editing, Best Picture, Best Supporting Actor (Duvall).

Apollo 13

By the time Apollo 13 blasted off for the moon in the spring of 1970, America had a severe case of "been-there-done-that." Few paid attention to the astronauts hurtling through space on their way to the third lunar landing. "Houston, we have a problem." The understatement of the decade following an explosion aboard the spacecraft put the Apollo program in the foreground again. Riveted to their TV screens, Americans watched with worry and anticipation as the astronauts and their colleagues on Earth fought long odds to bring the crew home. What could have become a NASA tragedy instead became another of the space agency's magnificent accomplishments. And this movie is a magnificent feat by actor-turned-director Howard. His biggest accomplishment is that he managed to turn this story into a nail-biter even though we all know the outcome. As astronaut Jim Lovell, Hanks portrays a bigger-than-life hero as a life-size human being. Quinlan plays wife Marilyn Lovell in a performance that embodies what was a nation's angst. Harris almost steals the movie as flight director Gene Kranz. The video and audio quality of this DVD has the right stuff, too. The thunderous launch of the Saturn V rocket carrying its precious payload into space is a showpiece for any well-equipped home theatre. A pair of audio commentary tracks and the other extras are icing on the cake. The director's track gives insight into how the film was made, but the more interesting track with the real Jim and Marilyn Lovell tells how heroes are made. —MB

Movie: ♪♪♪▶ **DVD:** ♪♪♪♪
Universal Studios Home Video (Cat #20153, UPC #02519201532). Widescreen (2.35:1) letterboxed. Dolby Digital 5.1. $34.98. Keepcase. *LANG:* English; French; Spanish. *SUB:* English; French; Spanish. *CAP:* English. *FEATURES:* 57 chapter links • Commentaries by director Howard and the real-life Lovells • "Lost Moon: The Triumph of Apollo 13" documentary • Theatrical trailer • Behind-the-scenes footage • Special effects artists explain sequences • Paxton's home movies of space school • Comparisons of NASA footage with movie sequences • Cast and crew biographies and filmographies • Production notes.
1995 (PG) 140m/C Tom Hanks, Kevin Bacon, Bill Paxton, Gary Sinise, Ed Harris, Kathleen Quinlan, Brett Cullen, Emily Ann Lloyd, Miko Hughes, Max Elliott Slade, Jean Speegle Howard, Tracy Reiner, Michelle Little, David Andrews, Mary Kate Schellhardt; *D:* Ron Howard; *W:* William Broyles Jr., Al Reinert; *C:* Dean Cundey; *M:* James Horner. *AWARDS:* Academy Awards '95: Best Film Editing, Best Sound; Directors Guild of America Awards '95: Best Director (Howard); Screen Actors Guild Award '95: Best Supporting Actor (Harris), Cast; Blockbuster Entertainment Awards '96: Drama Actor, Theatrical (Hanks); *NOM:* Academy Awards '95: Best Adapted Screenplay, Best Art Direction/Set Decoration, Best Picture, Best Supporting Actor (Harris), Best Supporting Actress (Quinlan), Best Original Dramatic Score; British Academy Awards '95: Best Cinematography; Golden Globe Awards '96: Best Director (Howard), Best Film—Drama, Best Supporting Actor (Harris), Best Supporting Actress (Quinlan); MTV Movie Awards '96:

Best Film, Best Male Performance (Hanks); Writers Guild of America '95: Best Adapted Screenplay.

The Apostle

No-holds-barred look at one man's search for religious redemption. Duvall is a devout, middle-aged Pentecostal preacher in Texas, with a true gift for inspiring his congregation. Unfortunately his wife (Fawcett) is cheating on him with a younger minister (Allen). Discovering the infidelity, Eulis smites the young preach with a bat, sending him into a coma. Forced to flee, Eulis sets up a new church, but rather than finding salvation, his past comes back to haunt him. Overall this is a good-looking DVD—it is also, as of this writing, out of print. The sharpness is very good and there is very little grain or artifacts. Colors are excellent and there is no bleed. A little boost to the contrast and brightness would have been nice, but their levels stay constant. The blacks range from true to leaning to gray/green in darker scenes. The soundtrack isn't going to be a showpiece in your collection, but everything is clear enough, and there is some very nice ambience in the numerous church meetings. —JO

Movie: 🎬🎬🎬▶ **DVD:** 🎬🎬🎬
Universal Studios Home Video (Cat #20321, UPC #025192032127). Widescreen (1.85:1) letterboxed. Dolby Surround. $34.98. Keepcase. *LANG:* English. *SUB:* Spanish; French. *CAP:* English. *FEATURES:* 34 chapter links (movie) ▪ 12 chapter links (documentary) ▪ Theatrical trailer ▪ "Making of" featurette ▪ Commentary: director Robert Duvall.
1997 (PG-13) 134m/C Robert Duvall, Miranda Richardson, Farrah Fawcett, John Beasley, Todd Allen, June Carter Cash, Billy Bob Thornton, Rick Dial, Walton Goggins, Billy Joe Shaver; *D:* Robert Duvall; *W:* Robert Duvall; *C:* Barry Markowitz; *M:* David Mansfield. *AWARDS:* Independent Spirit Awards '98: Best Actor (Duvall), Best Director (Duvall), Best Film; Los Angeles Film Critics Association Awards '97: Best Actor (Duvall); National Society of Film Critics Awards '97: Best Actor (Duvall); *NOM:* Academy Awards '97: Best Actor (Duvall); Independent Spirit Awards '98: Best Screenplay, Best Supporting Actress (Fawcett, Richardson); Screen Actors Guild Award '97: Best Actor (Duvall).

Apt Pupil

Stephen King's novella comes to the screen featuring a standout performance by Ian McKellen as an elderly Nazi war criminal residing in an upper–middle class neighborhood. His past catches the interest of a young honor student (Renfro). What starts out as friendship quickly disintegrates into a psychopathic mind game as the Nazi's tendencies begin to emerge and the student wants to know "what did it feel like?" The film's theatrical release was delayed when the parents of two boys

in a shower sequence sued to have their sons' performances removed. A good, sharp transfer with vibrant colors. Blacks, contrasts, and brightness levels are very good; only occasional grain in the darker scenes. Occasionally the foreground looks matted-in to the backgrounds, but overall there is a smooth flow between the two. Both audio tracks are excellent. The "making of" featurette is not much more than a chance for cast and director to praise each other and makes no mention of the controversy. —JO

Movie: 🎬🎬 **DVD:** 🎬🎬🎬
Columbia Tristar Home Video (Cat #22309, UPC #043396223097). Widescreen. Dolby Digital 5.1; Dolby Surround. Keepcase. *LANG:* English (DD 5.1); English (D Surround). *FEATURES:* 28 chapter links ▪ Theatrical trailer ▪ Cast and filmmaker bios ▪ "Making of" featurette.
1997 (R) 111m/C Ian McKellen, Brad Renfro, Jan Triska, Bruce Davison, Joe Morton, Elias Koteas, David Schwimmer, Michael Byrne, Heather McComb, Ann Dowd, Joshua Jackson; *D:* Bryan Singer; *W:* Brandon Boyce; *C:* Newton Thomas (Tom) Sigel; *M:* John Ottman.

Arabian Nights

The third of Pasolini's epic explicit adaptations of bawdy story collections features ten of the Scheherazade favorites and racy sexual scenes (both hetero- and homosexual). Filmed on Middle Eastern locations, the image is built around rough brown-gold earthtones. The lighting is dim in many of the night scenes and harsh in daylight exteriors. The DVD box copy admits as much in a disclaimer that states this version was put together from the best elements available to the New York City Museum of Modern Art. —MM
AKA: Il Fiore delle Mille e Una Notte; Flower of the Arabian Nights; A Thousand and One Nights.

Movie: 🎬🎬🎬 **DVD:** 🎬🎬▶
Image Entertainment (Cat #ID4417WB DVD, UPC #014381441727). Widescreen (1.75:1) letterboxed. Dolby Digital Mono. $24.99. Snapper. *LANG:* Italian. *SUB:* English. *FEATURES:* 15 chapter links.
1974 130m/C *IT* Ninetto Davoli, Franco Merli, Ines Pellegrini, Luigina Rocchi, Franco Citti; *D:* Pier Paolo Pasolini; *W:* Pier Paolo Pasolini; *C:* Giuseppe Ruzzolini; *M:* Ennio Morricone.

Arachnophobia

Big-budget big-bug horror story has a few funny moments as lots and lots of spiders wreak havoc in a white picket fence community somewhere off the beaten path. Lethal South American spider takes a vacation in sunny California, gets it on with local spiders, and rapidly multiplies. Utterly arachnophobic town doctor Daniels pairs with gung-ho exterminator Goodman to track down the culprits. Good, scary fun. Directorial debut for Marshall, a long-time friend and producer for Spielberg. With the 5.1 cranked up, the creepy

crawlers are even scarier than ever (and still fun). The separation makes you feel right in the middle of things, and there is plenty of bottom end to shake you up a little more. The picture is also very good—grain-free and sharp with few artifacts. Colors and blacks are very true and bleed is very minimal. The brightness and contrast levels are excellent and things remain comfortable and clear whether in the dark, brightly lit, or even on fire. The short featurette is more interesting than many full-blown documentaries included on other DVDs. —JO

Movie: 🎬🎬🎬 **DVD:** 🎬🎬🎬
Buena Vista Home Entertainment (Cat #17098, UPC #717951002129). Widescreen (1.85:1) letterboxed. Dolby Digital 5.1; Dolby Surround. $29.95. Keepcase. *LANG:* English. *CAP:* English. *FEATURES:* 9 chapter links ▪ Theatrical trailer ▪ "Making of" featurette.
1990 (PG-13) 109m/C Jeff Daniels, John Goodman, Harley Jane Kozak, Julian Sands, Roy Brocksmith, Stuart Pankin, Brian McNamara, Mark L. Taylor, Henry Jones, Peter Jason, James Handy; *D:* Frank Marshall; *W:* Wesley Strick, Don Jakoby; *C:* Mikael Salomon; *M:* Trevor Jones.

The Architecture of Doom

Peter Cohen shows how Nazism (National Socialism) used various artistic theories in an early 20th-century "culture war." His persuasive film uses documentary footage and other illustrative material to demonstrate how these cultural and artistic ideas were related to the political sphere. His approach is unusual and fascinating. On DVD, the image quality ranges between good new footage used to set the stage, and archival scenes that are generally of newsreel quality, giving the film an immediate and appropriately unpolished quality. Sound is thin in those sequences, too. —MM

Movie: 🎬🎬🎬▶ **DVD:** 🎬🎬🎬
First Run Features (Cat #FRF 90921 1D, UPC #720229909211). Full frame. Stereo. $29.95. Keepcase. *LANG:* English. *FEATURES:* 10 chapter links.
1991 119m/B *D:* Peter Cohen.

Aria

Ten directors were given carte blanche to interpret ten arias from well-known operas. Henry and D'Angelo star in Julian Temple's rendition of Verdi's *Rigoletto*. In Fonda's film debut, she and her lover travel to Las Vegas and eventually kill themselves in the bathtub, just like *Romeo & Juliet*. Jarman's piece (a highlight) shows an aged operatic star at her last performance remembering an early love affair. "I Pagliacci" is the one aria in which the director took his interpretation in a straightforward manner. The DVD looks fine, with an anamorphic transfer that should please widescreen set owners. Sound is quite acceptable, though certainly no workout for a big Surround system. —MB

Movie: 🎬🎬 **DVD:** 🎬🎬🎬
Image Entertainment (Cat #ID4701LYDVD, UPC #01438147012). Widescreen (1.85:1) anamorphic. Dolby Digital 2.0 Surround. $24.99. Snapper. *LANG:* English. *FEATURES:* 12 chapter links • Director filmographies.
1988 (R) 90m/C *GB* Theresa Russell, Anita Morris, Bridget Fonda, Beverly D'Angelo, Buck Henry, John Hurt; **D:** Ken Russell, Charles Sturridge, Robert Altman, Bill Bryden, Jean-Luc Godard, Bruce Beresford, Nicolas Roeg, Franc Roddam, Derek Jarman, Julien Temple; **W:** Ken Russell, Charles Sturridge, Robert Altman, Bill Bryden, Jean-Luc Godard, Bruce Beresford, Nicolas Roeg, Franc Roddam, Derek Jarman, Julien Temple; **C:** Caroline Champetier, Oliver Stapleton, Gale Tattersall.

Arlington Road

The tranquility of suburban life is shattered for college professor Faraday (Bridges) when he suspects that the picket fence and overly friendliness of new neighbor Lang (Robbins) is a cover for right-wing terrorism. When Faraday discovers more facts, his friends and colleagues begin to have suspicions about him. Impressive nail-biter contains several interesting twists and two rock solid performances. Much of the commentary track by director Pellington and Bridges is the expected puffery, but they also go into the film's real challenges, including an alternative ending that's not significantly different from the current one. The transfer to DVD was handled carefully and so the film has no serious visual or audio flaws. Perhaps because the thriller attempted to be something more serious, it did not find a receptive audience in theatrical release. It will fare better on home video. —MM

Movie: 🎬🎬🎬 **DVD:** 🎬🎬🎬
Columbia Tristar Home Video (Cat #03926, UPC #043396039261). Widescreen (2.35:1) letterboxed. Dolby Digital 5.1 Surround Stereo; Dolby Digital Surround Stereo. $25.95. Keepcase. *LANG:* English. *SUB:* English. *FEATURES:* 28 chapter links • "Making of" featurette • Cast and crew thumbnail biographies • Alternate ending • Commentary: Pellington and Bridges.
1999 (R) 119m/C Jeff Bridges, Tim Robbins, Joan Cusack, Hope Davis, Mason Gamble, Stanley Anderson, Robert Gossett, Spencer Treat Clark; **D:** Mark Pellington; **W:** Ehren Kruger; **C:** Bobby Bukowski; **M:** Angelo Badalamenti, Tomandandy.

Armageddon

This Hong Kong import is an *X-Files* imitation with a moody scientist, Dr. Ken (Andy Lau), who is somehow tied to a conspiracy. His police detective friend, Chiu Taipang (Anthony Wong) is on hand to protect him from the group. It's slow, talky, and too dependent on people running around in dim rooms with flashlights. The special

effects in the last reel are good but not great. The DVD image is the same. It handles some ambitious night exteriors well enough, though the "hex errors" in translation are intrusive. —MM *AKA:* Tian di xion xin.

Movie: 🎬🎬 **DVD:** 🎬🎬▶
Tai Seng Video Marketing (Cat #52774). Full frame. Dolby Digital Stereo. $49.95. Keepcase. *LANG:* Cantonese; Mandarin. *SUB:* English; Chinese. *FEATURES:* 12 chapter links.
1997 99m/C *HK* Andy Lau, Michelle Reis, Anthony Wong; **D:** Gordon Chan; **W:** Gordon Chan, Vincent Kok; **C:** Horace Wong.

Armageddon

Over-caffeinated end-of-the-world action thriller is wonderfully entertaining despite gaping narrative lapses that ought to sink it. As a Texas-sized asteroid hurtles past the moon toward Earth, oil driller Harry Stamper (Willis) and his crew of roughnecks blast off in a pair of shuttles. They're going to land on the rock, dig a hole to place a nuclear bomb, and save the world. Director Bay's background in commercials shows through in the jittery editing which attempts to paper over the ridiculous plot. The film benefits enormously from an attractive cast, strong support from Thornton as a sympathetic NASA executive, and an excellent underappreciated performance by Willis. On the special two-disc DVD set produced by Karen Stetler and supervised by Bay, the film gets royal treatment. The one noticeable visual glitch is occasional color flashing within narrow stripes. Otherwise, image and sound are flawless, even the many dark scenes in the second half. Still, such "big" special effects as the destruction of Paris and the Chrysler building and the complex nightmarish surface of the asteroid itself lose power on anything but the largest screen. Sound effects, however, remain particularly impressive through headphones. —MM

Movie: 🎬🎬🎬 **DVD:** 🎬🎬🎬▶
Criterion Collection (Cat #16720, UPC #715515010023). Widescreen (2.35:1) letterboxed. Disc 1: Dolby Digital 5.1 (English); Disc 2: Dolby Digital Stereo. $49.99. Keepcase. *LANG:* English. *FEATURES:* Commentary: Bay, Willis, Affleck, Bruckheimer • Commentary: NASA consultant, asteroid consultant • Bay's gag reel • Deleted scenes • Storyboards and production design drawings • Trailer, teaser, and TV spots • Aerosmith music video "I Don't Want to Miss a Thing" • Special effects analyses by visual effects supervisors • 31 chapter links. This is the 153-minute "director's cut" (the "PG-13" theatrical release runs 144 minutes).
1998 (PG-13) 150m/C Bruce Willis, Ben Affleck, Billy Bob Thornton, Steve Buscemi, Liv Tyler, Will Patton, Peter Stormare, Keith David, Owen C. Wilson, William Fichtner, Jessica Steen, Grayson McCouch, Jason Isaacs, Michael Clarke Duncan; **D:** Michael Bay; **W:** Jonathan Hensleigh, J.J. Abrams; **C:** John Schwartzman; **M:** Trevor

Rabin. *AWARDS:* MTV Movie Awards '99: Best Song ("I Don't Want to Miss a Thing"), Best Action Sequence; Golden Raspberry Awards '98: Worst Actor (Willis); *NOM:* Academy Awards '98: Best Song ("I Don't Want to Miss a Thing"), Best Sound, Best Sound Effects Editing, Best Visual Effects; MTV Movie Awards '99: Best Film, Best Male Performance (Affleck), Best Female Performance (Tyler), Best On-Screen Duo (Ben Affleck & Liv Tyler); Golden Raspberry Awards '98: Worst Picture, Worst Supporting Actress (Tyler), Worst Director (Bay), Worst Screenplay, Worst Song ("I Don't Want to Miss a Thing").

Armistead Maupin's More Tales of the City

Odd and risque adventures continue for the inhabitants of Barbary Lane (and the Blue Moon Lodge). The sequel picks up six weeks after the first installment. (It was filmed four years later; the reasons for that are covered in the commentary track.) In 1977 San Francisco, Mary Ann (Linney) and Michael (Hopkins) search for romance on a Mexican cruise. Mary Ann falls for handsome amnesiac Burke (Ferguson) while Michael is re-united with ex-lover Dr. Jon (Campbell). Meanwhile Mona (Siemaszko) searches for her roots, which leads to revelations from Mrs. Madrigal (Dukakis). Brian (Hubley) becomes a participatory voyeur and DeDe (Garrick) awaits the birth of twins, whose father is not her supercilious husband Beauchamp (Gibson). Since this miniseries was made for cable, the full frame image is fine but not exceptional. (Some of the more colorful patterns do create interesting pixels.) The most significant addition to the two-disc set is an extensive commentary track by Maupin and cast members. That focuses on the production and the controversy surrounding the original PBS series and its reincarnation on Showtime. A helpful six-page booklet outlines subjects and speakers. —MM *AKA:* More Tales of the City.

Movie: 🎬🎬🎬 **DVD:** 🎬🎬🎬▶
DVD International (Cat #DVD1 0717, UPC #783722700136). Full frame. $49.95. Keepcase. *LANG:* English. *FEATURES:* 145 chapter links, disc one; 57 chapter links, disc 2 • Commentary: Maupin, Linney, Dukakis, Garrick • Liner notes by Stephen McCauley.
1997 290m/C Laura Linney, Olympia Dukakis, Colin Ferguson, Bill Campbell, Paul Hopkins, Whip Hubley, Thomas Gibson, Barbara Garrick, Nina Siemaszko, Jackie Burroughs, Swoosie Kurtz, Francoise Robertson; *Cameos:* Parker Posey, Ed Asner, Paul Bartel, Brian Bedford, Sheila McCarthy, Scott Thompson; **D:** Pierre Gang; **W:** Nicholas Wright; **C:** Serge Ladouceur; **M:** Richard Gregoire.

Armitage 3: Polymatrix

Animated feature, based on a TV series, is set on Mars where Ross Sylibus (voice of

Sutherland) is the new cop on the beat. The title character (Berkley) is a robot police officer. They're caught up in a plot which, according to writer Konaka, borrows from H.P. Lovecraft's *The Dunwitch Horror*. It's easy to see why this franchise has developed a following; the characters actually have some depth. The DVD image is exceptionally sharp and sound is excellent. The overall level of animation is slightly superior to the general level of the genre, though the action still has a certain stiff quality. Particularly recommended to anime fans. —*MM*
Movie: 🎬🎬🎬 *DVD:* 🎬🎬🎬
Pioneer Entertainment (Cat #10000). Widescreen (1.85:1) letterboxed. Dolby Digital 5.1 Surround Stereo. $29.98. Slip-case. *LANG:* English. *SUB:* Japanese. *FEATURES:* 30 chapter links • Trailer • Writer and director biographies.
1994 90m/C *JP D:* Takuya Sato; *W:* Chiaki Konaka; *V:* Kiefer Sutherland, Elizabeth Berkley, Dan Woren, Wanda Nowicki.

Armstrong

Legendary B-movie producer Menacem Golan returns to the director's chair with a shoot-'em-up filmed in Russia. Navy SEAL Rob Armstrong (Zagarino) must stop a ruthless arms dealer (Lara) from selling warheads. The Moscow locations are a plus and Golan has come up with a plot twist that places his leading lady (Kates) in a wet transparent blouse and sends her on an extended chase through city streets. The no-extras DVD may look slightly better than VHS tape, but not much. Sound is equally nondescript. Lots of breaking glass and explosions. —*MM*
Movie: 🎬🎬 *DVD:* 🎬🎬
Image Entertainment (Cat #ID6227NG DVD, UPC #014381622720). Full frame. Dolby Digital Surround Stereo. $24.99. Snapper. *LANG:* English. *FEATURES:* 12 chapter links.
1999 99m/C Kimberley Kates, Frank Zagarino, Joe Lara, Richard Lynch; *D:* Menahem Golan; *W:* Menahem Golan, Jeno Hodi; *C:* Nickolai Lazarov.

Army of Darkness

Campbell returns for a third *Evil Dead* round as the square-jawed, none-too-bright hero Ash in this comic book extravaganza. He finds himself hurled back to the 14th century through the powers of an evil book. There he romances a babe, fights an army of skeletons, and generally causes all those Dark Age zombies a lot of grief, as he tries to get back to his own time. Raimi's technical exuberance is apparent and, as usual, the horror is graphic but still tongue-in-cheek. The DVD looks about as good as the letterboxed U.S. laserdisc but not as good as the Japanese import that featured the apocalyptic alternate ending and was somewhat sharper. On the review copy, several scene changes caused the picture to flicker or actually scrambled the video. The colors are vibrant and for the most part there

isn't much color bleed. A lot of grain shows up during dark scenes, and at the same time the brighter sequences seem a little contrasty, making the foregrounds appear pasted in at times. Brightness levels are good with a few exceptions. A slightly better-than-average DVD that'll do if you don't have a laserdisc player. —*JO*
AKA: Evil Dead 3; The Medieval Dead.
Movie: 🎬🎬🎬 *DVD:* 🎬🎬▶
Universal Studios Home Video (Cat #20322, UPC #025192032226). Widescreen (1.85:1) letterboxed. Dolby Surround. $24.98. Keepcase. *LANG:* English (DS); French (DS). *SUB:* Spanish. *CAP:* English. *FEATURES:* 16 chapter links • Theatrical trailer • Production notes • Cast and filmmaker bios.
1992 (R) 77m/C Bruce Campbell, Embeth Davidtz, Marcus Gilbert, Ian Abercrombie, Richard Grove, Michael Earl Reid, Tim Quill, Bridget Fonda, Patricia Tallman, Theodore (Ted) Raimi, Ivan Raimi, Donald Campbell, William Lustig, Josh Becker; *D:* Sam Raimi; *W:* Sam Raimi, Ivan Raimi; *C:* Bill Pope; *M:* Joseph LoDuca, Danny Elfman. *AWARDS:* VSDA DVD Festival '00: Best Audio Commentary.

Around the World in 80 Days

This TV adaptation of an oft-told tale by Jules Verne is notable for its who's who cast of British celebrities, UK and expatriate alike, headed by Pierce Brosnan as a dashing Phileas Fogg. The self-assured pace and tone smooth over any oddities, such as Eric Idle playing a Frenchman straight! The sheer length, over four and a half hours, allows its location scenes to go into details often dispensed with in a feature length work. The sound has that laundered quality typical of television productions, but is not in any way unsatisfactory. Video resolution is impressive. It renders natural white highlights and black formal attire with equal aplomb. Moreover, it gives justice to normally wretched-looking patterns in period costumes, like plaids and herringbone checks, set against dark woods and leathers. Any bits of alias are easily ignored. —*JK*
Movie: 🎬🎬▶ *DVD:* 🎬🎬🎬▶
Image Entertainment (Cat #ID48038FDVD, UPC #014381480320). Full frame. Dolby Digital Stereo. $29.99. Snapper. *LANG:* English. *FEATURES:* 32 chapter links • Scene access menus.
1989 270m/C Pierce Brosnan, Peter Ustinov, Eric Idle, Arielle Dombasle, Henry Gibson, John Hillerman, Jack Klugman, Christopher Lee, Patrick Macnee, Roddy McDowall, Darren McGavin, John Mills, Robert Morley, Lee Remick, Pernell Roberts, James B. Sikking, Jill St. John, Robert Wagner, Julia Nickson-Soul; *D:* Buzz Kulik.

The Arrival

Intense sf horror is driven by the same paranoia that made *The X-Files* such a hit, with some really creative special effects,

good characters, and an unpredictable story. Radio astronomer Zane Zaminski (Sheen) discovers a signal from another star and is immediately downsized by his boss Gordian (Silver). At the same time, environmental researcher Ilana Green (Crouse) can't believe some of the numbers she's seeing. In many respects writer-director David Twohy's first-contact story follows an established formula, but even its most familiar developments are handled with freshness, and no review should spoil the surprises. The well-chosen effects combine models, computer-generated creatures, some neat transformations and a deeply frightening scene involving scorpions. It's one of the most uncomfortable moments in modern horror. The DVD image ranges between good and very good with a brownish-tan tint to many scenes. Sound is fine. —*MM* *AKA:* Shockwave.
Movie: 🎬🎬🎬▶ *DVD:* 🎬🎬🎬
Artisan Entertainment (Cat #60446, UPC #012236044604). Widescreen letterboxed; full frame. Dolby Digital 5.1 Surround Stereo. $24.98. Snapper. *LANG:* English; French. *SUB:* English; French; Spanish. *FEATURES:* 41 chapter links (9 accessible from menu) • Cast and crew thumbnail bios. Title is also available with *Arrival II* (cat. #60761) for $29.98.
1996 (PG-13) 109m/C Charlie Sheen, Ron Silver, Lindsay Crouse, Teri Polo; *D:* David N. Twohy; *W:* David N. Twohy; *C:* Hiro Narita; *M:* Arthur Kempel.

Art and Jazz in Animation

Twelve animated films, ranging in length from 71 to 6 minutes, all revolve around jazz music and the experimental animation of Faith and John Hubley. Their work has a vaguely Impressionistic feel. The films tend to be non-linear narratives that depend more on style, atmosphere and, of course, music than on conventional plot. Musicians represented include Oscar Peterson, Ella Fitzgerald, Quincy Jones, Dizzy Gillespie, and Benny Carter. The films are "The Cosmic Eye," "Voyage to Next," "Of Men and Demons," "The Hole," "The Tender Game," "Eggs," "Harlem Wednesday," "The Adventures of *," "Of Stars and Men," "The Hat," and "Dig." Think *Yellow Submarine* but not so precious or druggy. Many of the films were nominated for various awards, including Oscars. "The Hole" won one. —*MM*
Movie: 🎬🎬🎬 *DVD:* 🎬🎬🎬
Image Entertainment (Cat #ID4709LYDVD, UPC #014381470925). Full frame. Dolby Digital Mono. $24.99. Snapper. *LANG:* English. *FEATURES:* 35 chapter links.
1985 245m/C *Nar:* Maureen Stapleton, Dudley Moore.

Arthur

Spoiled drunken billionaire Arthur Bach (Moore) stands to lose everything when he falls in love with a waitress (Minnelli). He must choose between wealth and a planned marriage on one hand, poverty and love on the other. Moore's hyperactive performance still has its moments though he can be irritating. As his dyspeptic valet, John Gielgud won a Supporting Actor Oscar and the years have made the intelligence of his performance shine even brighter. On DVD, the opening night scenes are extremely dark, but that's the way they have always been. The black streets and shadows are free of pixels. In general, the film has the sleek production values of a romantic comedy set among the ultra-wealthy of New York. —MM

Movie: ♪♪♪ **DVD:** ♪♪♪
Warner Home Video, Inc. (Cat #22020, UPC #085392202027). Full frame. Dolby Digital Mono. $19.98. Snapper. *LANG:* English; French. *SUB:* English; French. *CAP:* English. *FEATURES:* Thumbnail biographies of cast and crew ▪ Production notes ▪ 30 chapter links.
1981 (PG) 97m/C Dudley Moore, Liza Minnelli, John Gielgud, Geraldine Fitzgerald, Stephen Elliott, Jill Eikenberry, Lou Jacobi, Ted Ross, Barney Martin; **D:** Steve Gordon; **W:** Steve Gordon; **C:** Fred Schuler; **M:** Burt Bacharach. *AWARDS:* Academy Awards '81: Best Song ("Arthur's Theme"), Best Supporting Actor (Gielgud); Golden Globe Awards '82: Best Actor—Musical/Comedy (Moore), Best Film—Musical/Comedy, Best Song ("Arthur's Theme"), Best Supporting Actor (Gielgud); Los Angeles Film Critics Association Awards '81: Best Supporting Actor (Gielgud); New York Film Critics Awards '81: Best Supporting Actor (Gielgud); Writers Guild of America '81: Best Original Screenplay; *NOM:* Academy Awards '81: Best Actor (Moore), Best Original Screenplay.

As Good As It Gets

Entertaining and enjoyable outing from Brooks racked up an impressive list of Oscar noms (including Best Picture). Obsessive-compulsive romance novelist Nicholson is almost the meanest guy in New York City, liked by nobody and hating all. The only exception is single-mother/waitress Hunt, who puts up with his annoying habits at the local restaurant where he dines. Forced to look after gay neighbor Kinnear's fussy-but-cute dog, Nicholson falls into an improbable quest for love, friendship, and a life "as normal as it gets." Snappy dialogue and an easy-going, non stereotypical performance by Kinnear are highlights, almost overshadowing both Hunt's and Nicholson's Oscar-winning roles. This is a good-looking DVD whose best asset is the punchy and accurate color. The blacks are also dead-on. There is very little grain and no artifacting, which combined with how sharp the image is, makes for very pleasurable viewing. Both the contrast and brightness levels are near perfect. The 5.1 sound is full-bodied and very distinct, whether delivering music or dialogue. Most of the audio comes from the front speakers which makes sense due to the abundance of dialogue and lack of special effects. —JO
AKA: Old Friends.

Movie: ♪♪♪▸ **DVD:** ♪♪♪▸
Columbia Tristar Home Video (Cat #21709, UPC #043396217096). Widescreen (1.85:1) letterboxed; full frame. Dolby Digital 5.1; Dolby Digital 2.0. $28.95. Keepcase. *LANG:* English (DD5.1; 2.0); French (2.0). *SUB:* Spanish; French. *CAP:* English. *FEATURES:* 28 chapter links ▪ Commentary.
1997 (PG-13) 130m/C Jack Nicholson, Helen Hunt, Greg Kinnear, Cuba Gooding Jr., Skeet Ulrich, Shirley Knight, Yeardley Smith, Lupe Ontiveros, Bibi Osterwald, Brian Doyle-Murray, Randall Batinkoff, Shane Black, Tara Subkoff; **Cameos:** Danielle Brisebois, Lawrence Kasdan, Harold Ramis, Jimmy Workman, Todd Solondz, Tom McGowan; **D:** James L. Brooks; **W:** Mark Andrus, James L. Brooks; **C:** John Bailey; **M:** Hans Zimmer. *AWARDS:* Academy Awards '97: Best Actor (Nicholson), Best Actress (Hunt); Golden Globe Awards '98: Best Actor—Musical/Comedy (Nicholson), Best Actress—Musical/Comedy (Hunt), Best Film—Musical/Comedy; National Board of Review Awards '97: Best Actor (Nicholson), Best Supporting Actor (Kinnear); Screen Actors Guild Award '97: Best Actor (Nicholson), Best Actress (Hunt); Writers Guild of America '97: Best Original Screenplay; Broadcast Film Critics Association Awards '97: Best Actor (Nicholson); *NOM:* Academy Awards '97: Best Film Editing, Best Original Screenplay, Best Picture, Best Supporting Actor (Kinnear), Best Original Musical/Comedy Score; Directors Guild of America Awards '97: Best Director (Brooks); Golden Globe Awards '98: Best Director (Brooks), Best Screenplay; MTV Movie Awards '98: Best Female Performance (Hunt); Screen Actors Guild Award '97: Best Supporting Actor (Kinnear).

As You Like It

Rosalind (Bergner), daughter of a banished Duke, falls for Orlando (Olivier), second son of a courtier. She must disguise herself as a boy to get his attention. No, it's not that kind of movie; it's a Shakespearean comedy staged on lavish sets, but still not in the same league with Olivier's *Henry V, Hamlet,* or *Richard III*. David Lean edited the film. The DVD reproduces the black and white photography without any noticeable flaws. Still, it's recommended to fans of the period and the stars only. —MM

Movie: ♪♪▸ **DVD:** ♪♪♪
Image Entertainment (Cat #ID5666DSDVD, UPC #014381566628). Full frame. Dolby Digital Mono. $24.99. Snapper. *LANG:* English. *FEATURES:* 12 chapter links ▪ Extensive liner notes by Roy Hemming ▪ Filmographies of Paul Czinner, Laurence Olivier, Sophie Stewart.
1936 96m/B *GB* Elisabeth Bergner, Laurence Olivier, Henry Ainley, Felix Aylmer; **D:** Paul Czinner; **W:** J.M. Barrie, Robert Cullen; **C:** Jack Cardiff, Harold Rosson; **M:** William Walton.

The Asphyx

A 19th-century doctor (Stephens) is studying death when he discovers the Asphyx, an aura that surrounds a person just before he or she dies. He delves deeper into his research and finds the keys to immortality. However, his irresponsibility in unleashing the obscure supernatural power into the world brings a swarm of unforeseen and irreversible troubles. **AKA:** Spirit of the Dead.

Movie: ♪♪♪ **DVD:** NYR
Elite Entertainment, Inc. (Cat #97100001). Widescreen (2.35:1) letterboxed. Dolby Digital Mono. $24.99. Keepcase. *FEATURES:* Cast and crew thumbnail biographies.
1972 (PG) 98m/C *GB* Robert Stephens, Robert Powell, Jane Lapotaire, Alex Scott, Ralph Arliss, Fiona Walker, John Lawrence, Paul Bacon, Terry Scully; **D:** Peter Newbrook; **W:** Brian Comfort; **C:** Frederick A. (Freddie) Young; **M:** Bill McGuffie.

Assassin

Made-for-TV sf action flick brings us yet another mad scientist who creates a bionic killer to take over the world. Only retired CIA agent Robert Golen (Conrad) can stop him before he assassinates the president. On DVD, the slow-moving action is acceptably clear and detailed. —MM

Movie: ♪♪ **DVD:** ♪♪
Simitar Entertainment (Cat #7586, UPC #082551758623). Full frame. Dolby Digital Stereo. $14.98. Keepcase. *LANG:* English. *FEATURES:* 8 chapter links ▪ Production factoids ▪ Robert Conrad filmography.
1986 (PG-13) 94m/C Robert Conrad, Karen Austin, Richard Young, Jonathan Banks, Robert Webber; **D:** Sandor Stern; **W:** Sandor Stern; **C:** Chuck (Charles G.) Arnold; **M:** Anthony Guefen.

Assassins

Stallone gets to play elder statesman in the very deadly rivalry between two contract killers. Robert Rath (Stallone) is the man number one with a bullet whose reputation has caught up with him. Hot-headed Miguel Bain (the ever-smoldering Banderas) wants to off Rath and assume the position of top hitman. Caught in the middle of this macho posturing is surveillance expert and potential murderee Electra (Moore). It's Stallone to the rescue, but his character pays more attention to Pearl, Electra's pampered Persian cat, than to the lovely lady herself. Banderas is at his looney, over-the-top best and director Donner does know his action. The DVD for this wacky little action flick is pretty good. The picture is sharp and grain was only a problem during a few bright scenes and occasionally in some screen-filling blacks. Other than that, the blacks were true, as were the colors. The contrast was good and seemed to give enough definition to things, but was sometimes limited by too low a brightness level. The action scenes are sonically spectacular with great spa-

cious Surround and thundering low end. The dialogue and music are each crisply delivered. —*JO*
Movie: 🎬🎬🎬 **DVD:** 🎬🎬🎬
Warner Home Video, Inc. (Cat #13987, UPC #085391398721). Widescreen (1.85:1) letterboxed; full frame. Dolby Digital 5.1; Dolby Surround. $24.98. Snapper. *LANG:* English; French. *SUB:* English; Spanish; French. *FEATURES:* 37 chapter links ● Production notes.
1995 (R) 132m/C Sylvester Stallone, Antonio Banderas, Julianne Moore, Anatoly Davydov; *D:* Richard Donner; *W:* Brian Helgeland, Andy Wachowski, Larry Wachowski; *C:* Vilmos Zsigmond; *M:* Mark Mancina. *AWARDS: NOM:* Golden Raspberry Awards '95: Worst Actor (Stallone).

The Assault
Police detective Stacy Palermo (Randall) is forced to take a homicide witness to a women's halfway house only to find it under attack by the drug lord Blade (Dean). Director Wynorski, known for quick-and-dirty exploitation, takes a more enlightened approach here with a story that stresses action and strong female characters—it was written by costar Melissa Brasselle—over sex. On DVD, the image is surprisingly, even shockingly bright, without the cheap look that many low-budget video premieres have. —*MM*
Movie: 🎬🎬 **DVD:** 🎬🎬🎬
Image Entertainment (Cat #ID4758DRDVD, UPC #014381475821). Full frame. Dolby Digital Surround Stereo. $24.99. Snapper. *LANG:* English. *FEATURES:* 15 chapter links.
1997 83m/C Stacie Randall, Melissa Brasselle, Sandahl Bergman, Lydie Denier, Leo Rossi, Matt McCoy, Rick Dean; *D:* Jim Wynorski; *W:* Steve Jankowski, Melissa Brasselle; *M:* Andrew Keresztes.

Assault of the Killer Bimbos
A showgirl is framed for the murder of her boss and takes off for the border with a couple of girlfriends. On the way they are pursued by the expected dumb cops and meet up with horny, clean-cut hunks. In Mexico they encounter the villain and extract comic vengeance. Watchable mainly due to the likable female leads and pleasant, lightly camp execution, although it might prove too tame for most of its target audience. Overall, a nothing-special, but adequate DVD. The picture varies from so-so to good sharpness and there are occasional spots of grain and a few artifacts. The colors bleed a touch, but seem a little weak and it's hard to judge how accurate they are. In the blacks the grain picks up and contrast and brightness need a little tweaking. Unfortunately, the sound is on the same level as the disc. At times loud dialogue clips and the music, with its lack of fidelity and low end, is sometimes tinny. —*JO*
Movie: 🎬🎬 **DVD:** 🎬

Cult Video (Cat #8005, UPC #763843 800564). Full frame. Stereo. $24.98. Keepcase. *LANG:* English. *FEATURES:* 16 chapter links.
1988 (R) 85m/C Patti Astor, Christina Whitaker, Elizabeth Kaitan, Griffin O'Neal, Nick Cassavetes, Clayton Landey, Eddie Deezen, Arell Blanton, David Marsh, Tammara Souza, Jamie Bozian, Mike Muscat, Jeffrey Orman, John Quern, Jay O. Sanders; *D:* Anita Rosenberg; *W:* Ted Nicolaou; *C:* Thomas Callaway; *M:* Fred Lapides, Marc Ellis.

Assault on Precinct 13
Urban horror invades L.A. A sleepy police station is suddenly under siege from a violent youth gang. Paranoia abounds as the police are attacked from all sides and can see no way out. Carpenter's musical score adds much to the setting of this unique police exploitation story that somehow stands as Carpenter's adaptation of Howard Hawk's *Rio Bravo*. Semi-acclaimed and very gripping. Carpenter's commentary is worthwhile (not always the case). Though some may have wished it more humorously entertaining, it is packed full of facts that both fans and filmmakers should find of interest. This DVD, though not appearing as sharp as some major studio releases, is actually a very true representation of this low-budget gem. The colors are accurate and very rarely bleed. The blacks are true and both the contrast and brightness levels consistent and comfortable. Artifacts are minimal and despite the numerous dark sequences the same can be said for the grain. The sound is mono but very good, conveying the dialogue distinctly and Carpenter's minimal score very accurately. —*JO*
Movie: 🎬🎬🎬 **DVD:** 🎬🎬🎬
Image Entertainment (Cat #ID4161DKDVD, UPC #014381416121). Widescreen (2.35:1) letterboxed. Dolby Digital 1.0. $29.99. Snapper. *LANG:* English. *FEATURES:* 25 chapter links ● Theatrical trailer ● Commentary: John Carpenter.
1976 91m/C Austin Stoker, Darwin Joston, Martin West, Tony Burton, Nancy Loomis, Kim Richards, Henry (Kleinbach) Brandon, Laurie Zimmer, Charles Cyphers, Peter Bruni; *D:* John Carpenter; *W:* John Carpenter; *C:* Douglas Knapp; *M:* John Carpenter.

The Assignment
Infamous terrorist Carlos the Jackal (Quinn) is shown plying his trade in Europe under the nose of CIA counter-terrorism expert Jack Shaw (Sutherland). Later, in Israel, Mossad agent Amos (Kingsley) captures a man he thinks is Carlos, only it's his double—U.S. Naval officer Annibal Ramirez (Quinn again). Shaw and Amos turn Ramirez into the terrorist, making the Russians think that Carlos has betrayed them. More intense and thrilling than *The Jackal*, the Bruce Willis vehicle released the same year. Although this DVD is sharp

enough, the abundance of grain during bright sequences makes those scenes uncomfortable to watch. There is also some artifacting during quick motion or camera pans. Colors bleed very little and the contrast gives them a nice punch. The brightness at times feels a little low but is not a problem. The blacks are very true. The soundtrack is excellent in all areas with good crisp highs, clean low end, and better Surround than you'd expect from a film that had such a limited theatrical release. —*JO*
Movie: 🎬🎬 **DVD:** 🎬🎬
Columbia Tristar Home Video (Cat #28359, UPC #043396283596). Widescreen (1.85:1) letterboxed; full frame. Dolby Digital 5.1; Stereo. NSL. Keepcase. *LANG:* English (DD5.1; Stereo); French (Stereo). *SUB:* Spanish; French. *CAP:* English. *FEATURES:* 28 chapter links ● Theatrical trailer.
1997 (R) 115m/C *CA* Aidan Quinn, Donald Sutherland, Ben Kingsley, Liliana Komorowska, Claudia Ferri, Celine Bonnier, Vlasta Vrana, Von Flores, Al Waxman; *D:* Christian Duguay; *W:* Don Gordon, Sabi H. Shabtai; *C:* David Franco; *M:* Normand Corbeil.

The Associate
Laurel Ayres (Goldberg) is the most brilliant and savvy financial expert at her Wall Street firm, but her younger associate Frank (Daly) is promoted ahead of her. Why? First, because he's a sneaky rat who sabotages her deals, but mostly because he's a man. Enraged, Laurel resigns and starts her own company. But thickheaded men still refuse to take advice from a woman. Impulsively, Laurel invents a fictitious partner named Robert S. Cutty, and Fallon (Wallach) is hooked. The second half then turns into a dumbed-down variation of the none-too-bright *Mrs. Doubtfire*. The DVD is about as good as the film demands. Ms. Goldberg's bizarre Cutty makeup may actually look a little better on disc than it does on the big screen but diagonal lines tend to break up into shallow horizontal steps. Sound is adequate. —*MM*
Movie: 🎬🎬 **DVD:** 🎬🎬
Hollywood Pictures Home Video (Cat #17372, UPC #717951002761). Widescreen (1.85:1) letterboxed. Dolby Digital 5.1 Surround Stereo. $29.99. Snapper. *LANG:* English. *CAP:* English. *FEATURES:* 19 chapter links ● Theatrical trailer.
1996 (PG-13) 113m/C Whoopi Goldberg, Timothy Daly, Bebe Neuwirth, Dianne Wiest, Eli Wallach; *D:* Donald Petrie; *W:* Nick Thiel; *C:* Alex Nepomniaschy; *M:* Christopher Tyng.

Asteroid
Re-edited version of the TV miniseries emphasizes the special effects and action, which should help this routine disaster flick. Lily McKee (Sciorra) discovers that several giant asteroids are on a collision course with Kansas City. She contacts

FEMA and gets hotshot director Jack Wallace (Biehn) anxious to help out (and not just with the rock problem). Of course, the citizenry freaks when one asteroid hits, but there's an even bigger one on the way.
Movie: 🐶🐶 **DVD:** NYR
Pioneer Entertainment (Cat #10105). Full frame. Dolby Digital Stereo. $24.98. Keepcase.
1997 120m/C Michael Biehn, Annabella Sciorra, Don Franklin, Anne-Marie Johnson, Anthony Zerbe, Carlos Gomez, Jensen Daggett; **D:** Bradford May; **C:** David Hennings, Thomas Del Ruth; **M:** Shirley Walker.

The Astronaut's Wife

Astronaut Spencer Armacost (Depp) just isn't the same guy after a mysterious accident occurs outside the space shuttle. He and his wife Jillian (Theron) move from Florida to New York where she notices strange changes in behavior, such as listening to the TV test pattern and an old radio. Then she discovers that she's pregnant. In part, perhaps the film's lack of success in its theatrical release can be traced to the stars' matching ugly bottle-blond bleach jobs and atrocious haircuts. Both tonsorial disasters shine forth unfortunately on DVD, along with the superb sets. Image and sound are excellent, and even the menus are cool. —*MM*
Movie: 🐶🐶▶ **DVD:** 🐶🐶🐶
New Line Home Video (Cat #N4906, UPC #79043490620). Widescreen (2.35:1) anamorphic. Dolby Digital 5.1 Surround Stereo; Dolby Digital Surround Stereo. $24.98. Snapper. *LANG:* English. *SUB:* English. *FEATURES:* 19 chapter links • Theatrical trailer • Cast and crew filmographies • Extra DVD-ROM features.
1999 (R) 109m/C Johnny Depp, Charlize Theron, Joe Morton, Tom Noonan, Blair Brown, Nick Cassavetes, Clea DuVall, Donna Murphy, Samantha Eggar; **D:** Rand Ravich; **W:** Rand Ravich; **C:** Allen Daviau; **M:** George S. Clinton.

At First Sight

Slow-paced romantic drama stars Kilmer as Virgil, a blind masseur who falls for high-strung architect Amy (Sorvino). She persuades him to have an operation that restores his sight and he must adapt to a world he has never seen. Excellent supporting work by McGillis as Virgil's sister and Lane as the doctor who eases his transition. While Kilmer's performance is strong at times, he can't lose the habitual air of self-satisfaction he seems to bring to every role. The film's real strength is its lack of sentimentality, so rare in movies that center on a disability. The DVD looks fine with excellent visuals throughout. Voices are muffled in some scenes, though that sounds like it comes from the original dubbing, not the transfer. —*MM*
Movie: 🐶🐶▶ **DVD:** 🐶🐶
MGM Home Entertainment (Cat #907447, UPC #027616744722). Widescreen letterboxed; full frame. Dolby Digital 5.1 Sur-

round Stereo; Dolby Digital Surround Stereo. $24.98. Keepcase. *LANG:* English; French. *SUB:* English; French. *CAP:* English. *FEATURES:* 44 chapter links • Theatrical trailer.
1998 (PG-13) 128m/C Val Kilmer, Mira Sorvino, Kelly McGillis, Steven Weber, Bruce Davison, Nathan Lane, Ken Howard; **D:** Irwin Winkler; **W:** Steve Levitt; **C:** John Seale; **M:** Mark Isham.

At War with the Army

Martin and Lewis's debut as a comedy team is a serviceable service comedy based on a play by James Alardice. They're recruits who get mixed up in all sorts of wild situations at their Army base.
Movie: 🐶🐶 **DVD:** NYR
Digital Disc Entertainment (Cat #DDE573). Mono. $9.99. Keepcase.
1950 93m/B Dean Martin, Jerry Lewis, Polly Bergen, Mike Kellin; **D:** Hal Walker; **W:** Fred Finklehoffe; **C:** Stuart Thompson; **M:** Jerry Livingston.

Atomic Submarine

Futuristic sci-fi pits government agents against alien invaders. The battle, however, takes place in the ocean beneath the Arctic and is headed by an atomic-powered submarine clashing with a special alien underwater saucer. The acting is sometimes stilted, but the film is good fun for aficionados. Sometimes it seems a waste to put this type of film on DVD—it can't possibly make full use of the DVD's capabilities—but this one looks as good as it possibly could. By using an uncompressed PCM soundtrack, the sound makes the most of the original sources. The picture itself is crisp and the grain level stays low during most of the film (there is some film damage). The brightness and contrast are consistently comfortable, the blacks true, and the gray-tones very good. It would be fun if they could dig up some sort of supplementals (stills, props) from more of these B-level sci-fi flicks. —*JO*
Movie: 🐶🐶 **DVD:** 🐶🐶▶
Image Entertainment (Cat #ID4428GODVD, UPC #014381442823). Full frame. PCM Mono. $19.95. Snapper. *LANG:* English. *FEATURES:* 13 chapter links • Theatrical trailer.
1959 80m/C Arthur Franz, Dick Foran, Bob Steele, Brett Halsey, Joi Lansing, Tom Conway, Paul Dubov; **D:** Spencer Gordon Bennet; **W:** Orville H. Hampton; **C:** Gilbert Warrenton; **M:** Alexander Laszlo.

Atomic Train

This made-for-TV two-night mini series deliveries two adventures for the price of one. The first finds Rob Lowe desperately trying to stop a runaway train, which is roaring downhill out of the Rockies and bound for Denver. Derailing the train is not an option as it is full of dangerous chemicals and a contraband Soviet nuclear warhead. The second story covers Rob Lowe's

equally desperate attempts to save his family from nuclear annihilation when the train derails, the dangerous chemicals are spilled, and the resulting fire sets off the atomic warhead. Uneven disaster epic, with the first half delivering a fairly taut story that begins to unravel once the runaway train crashes and the focus shifts to the nuclear panic, run-for-your lives scenario. As a result of working with the source material there are virtually no flaws in this DVD presentation. It is clean and crisp, but clearly from a made-for-TV venue. —*RT*
Movie: 🐶🐶▶ **DVD:** 🐶🐶▶
Trimark Home Video (Cat #71670, UPC #031398716730). Full frame. AC3 - 2 Channel. $24.99. Keepcase. *LANG:* English. *SUB:* English; Spanish. *CAP:* English; Spanish. *FEATURES:* 28 chapters • Ten-minute "Making of" featurette (Side B) • Trimark Previews (Side A). DVD is a flipper (DVD-10), with part one on the Side A and part two on the Side B.
1999 (PG-13) 168m/C Rob Lowe, Kristen Davis, Esai Morales, John Finn, Mena Suvari, Sean Smith, Edward Herrmann, Erik King, Blu Mankuma; **D:** Dick Lowry, David Jackson; **C:** Steven Fierberg; **M:** Lee Holdridge.

Austin Powers: International Man of Mystery

Groovy '60s spy Austin Powers (Myers) discovers that his arch-enemy, Dr. Evil (Myers again), has frozen himself to elude capture, so the swingin' Brit does the same. They awaken 30 years later in the same state: woefully out of touch. While Dr. Evil attempts to blackmail the British government, Austin tries to "shag" every "groovy bird" he sees. A festival of crushed velvet, political incorrectness, and lethal breasts. All the psychedelic colors are a real challenge for any video format and this DVD does a good job with them. There is no bleed, hardly any artifacts, and very little grain with the result being a very sharp picture. The sound is excellent—crisp, dynamic, great highs and lows, no clipping, and the Surround is mixed perfectly. New Line has also loaded this DVD with more "shagadelic" extras than you can shake a Swedish penis pump at, including deleted scenes (you'll be glad they aren't in the film) and two alternate endings. —*JO*
Movie: 🐶🐶🐶 **DVD:** 🐶🐶🐶▶
New Line Home Video (Cat #N4577, UPC #794043457722). Widescreen (2.35:1) anamorphic; full frame. Dolby Digital 5.1; Dolby Surround. $24.98. Snapper. *LANG:* English (DD5.1, DS); French (DD Stereo). *SUB:* English; Spanish; French. *FEATURES:* 24 chapter links • Theatrical trailer • Commentary: Mike Myers and Jay Roach • Deleted scenes • Alternate endings • Cast and filmmaker bios • Star highlights • Cameo menu • Animated "Music to Shag By."
1997 (PG-13) 88m/C Mike Myers, Elizabeth Hurley, Michael York, Seth Green,

Mimi Rogers, Robert Wagner, Fabiana Udenio, Paul Dillon, Charles Napier, Will Ferrell, Mindy Sterling; *Cameos:* Tom Arnold, Carrie Fisher; *D:* Jay Roach; *W:* Mike Myers; *C:* Peter Deming; *M:* George S. Clinton. *AWARDS:* MTV Movie Awards '98: Best Villain (Myers), Best Dance Sequence (Mike Myers/Londoners); *NOM:* MTV Movie Awards '98: Best Film, Best Comedic Performance (Myers).

Austin Powers: The Spy Who Shagged Me

Mike Myers's sequel is actually funnier than the original. He and his fellow filmmakers have a better grasp on their material and seem to be enjoying themselves more. It's all more colorful and, well, shagadelic than the first. The plot shifts back in time to the 1960s where Dr. Evil (Myers) steals Austin's mojo. The DVD contains all of the expected New Line extras. On their commentary track, Myers, coproducer McCullers, and Roach have the self-assurance of guys who know that they've got a hit on their hands. Of course, both image and sound are exemplary. —*MM*

Movie: ♫♫♫ *DVD:* ♫♫♫♫
New Line Home Video (Cat #N4891, UPC #194043489129). Widescreen (2.35:1) letterboxed. Dolby Digital 5.1 Surround Stereo; Dolby Digital Surround Stereo. $24.98. Snapper. *LANG:* English. *SUB:* English. *FEATURES:* 30 chapter links • 10 deleted scenes • Cast and crew thumbnail biographies • 4 theatrical trailers • Music videos • Commentary: Myers, McCullers, and Roach • "Making of" featurette • Dr. Evil's "hidden" features page • Extra DVD-ROM features.
1999 (PG-13) 95m/C Muse Watson, Burt Bacharach, Elvis Costello, Mike Myers, Heather Graham, Elizabeth Hurley, Seth Green, Robert Wagner, Rob Lowe, Verne Troyer, Kristen Johnston, Mindy Sterling, Gia Carides, Clint Howard, Michael York, Will Ferrell, Woody Harrelson, Charles Napier, Willie Nelson, Tim Robbins, Jerry Springer, Fred Willard, Rebecca Romijn-Stamos, Jack Kehler; *D:* Jay Roach; *W:* Michael McCullers, Mike Myers; *C:* Ueli Steiger; *M:* George S. Clinton. *AWARDS:* *NOM:* Academy Awards '99: Best Makeup; Golden Globe Awards '00: Best Song ("Beautiful Stranger").

Autopsy

Rome is suffering from an epidemic of inexplicable suicides. A young pathologist (Farmer) and a priest (Primus), both wrestling demons of their own, try to find the reason. This is an archetypal Italian horror where plot details are less important than the collection of violent, grotesque images which might well have served as a partial inspiration for *Re-Animator.* According to the box copy (and other sources), the film was severely edited for American theatrical consumption and this is the first "complete" edition available in this country. Compared to

other films of the period, it looks very good, with bright exteriors and only a few underlit night scenes that are marred by excess grain. The monaural sound is fine for Ennio Morricone's effectively off-putting score. —*MM*

Movie: ♫♫▶ *DVD:* ♫♫♫
Anchor Bay (Cat #DV11071, UPC #013131107197). Widescreen (1.85:1) letterboxed. Dolby Digital Mono. $29.98. Keepcase. *LANG:* Italian; English. *FEATURES:* 29 chapter links.
1978 100m/C *IT* Mimsy Farmer, Barry Primus, Angela Goodwin, Ray Lovelock; *D:* Armando Crispino; *W:* Armando Crispino, Lucio Battistrada; *C:* Carlo Carlini; *M:* Ennio Morricone.

The Avengers

As an example of the changing social, sexual, and individual values of its era, this influential British TV series defines the 1960s better than any academic study could. Created at the peak of the spy craze, it turned the entire idea of the Bondish, testosterone-fueled secret-agent hero on its ear. The whimsical theme music is the tip-off. The two protagonists—sexy no-nonsense Mrs. Emma Peel (Rigg) and dapper John Steed (Macnee)—have become archetypes of a particular kind of originality and unconformity. Their effortless adventures often have a sci-fi element, but the stories were handled with such a deft touch that they really cannot be classified as espionage, either. Doubtless, part of the show's mystique stems from its lack of availability on home video for decades. Those who can remember watching the original shows on early color TVs will be astonished at the clarity of the images on DVD. Though the picture and sound may suffer when compared to today's action adventures, they have stood up well. Some of the colors look a little "off" but in most scenes, even the wildest sets, effects, and costumes are reproduced in all their frivolous glory. In the end, though, *The Avengers* was always about wit and that remains undiminished. Disk 1 (From Venus with Love, The Fear Merchants, Escape in Time), #AAE-70018, UPC 733961700183; Disc 2 (The See-Through Man, The Bird Who Knew Too Much, The Winged Avenger), #AAE-70019, UPC 733961700190; Disc 3 (The Living Dead, The Hidden Tiger, The Correct Way to Kill), #AAE-70020, UPC 733961700 206; Disc 4 (Never, Never Say Die; Epic; The Superlative Seven), #AAE-70021, UPC 733961700213; Disc 5 (A Funny Thing Happened on the Way to the Station, Something Nasty in the Nursery, The Joker), #AAE-70022, UPC 733961700 220; Disc 6 (Who's Who?, Return of the Cybernauts, Death's Door), #AAE-70023, UPC 733961700237; Disc 7 (The 50,000 Breakfast, Dead Man's Treasure, You Have Just Been Murdered), #AAE-70024, UPC 733961700244; Disc 8 (The Positive-Negative Man, Murdersville, The Forget-Me-Knot), #AAE-70025, UPC 733961700251. —*MM*

Movie: ♫♫♫♫ *DVD:* ♫♫♫
New Video Group. Full frame. Keepcase. *LANG:* English. *FEATURES:* Scene access (7–8 per episode) • Interactive menus • Production stills. The eight disks are sold in four two-volume sets.
1967 m/C Patrick Macnee, Diana Rigg; *M:* Laurie Johnson.

The Avengers

The fads and fashions of the swingin' '60s are overlaid with cool '90s culture all set in a surreal 1999 London. Scientist (and leather-girl) Mrs. Emma Peel (Thurman) teams up with dapper, bowler-wearing, umbrella-carrying secret agent John Steed (Fiennes) to defeat the maximum baddie, Sir August de Wynter (Connery), who takes his last name very seriously. Seems de Wynter has a machine that can manipulate the world's weather and he's not intending to do good deeds. What a waste—all that talent and the only thing you can say about this film is that it's got great colors. Ooooh pretty! If only the movie were as good as this DVD. The picture is so sharp that you might want to back the sharpness off on some monitors. Grain and artifacts are nonexistent. The colors are not just accurate, they're stunning, and never bleed no matter how vibrant they are. The picture's punch is brought up to an even higher level by the excellent contrast and brightness. During music, the sound is a little dull, but there is great imaging and track separation, highlighted when the Surround kicks in for the effects. Though this film seems a lot longer than its 89-minute running time, and I thought it sucked, the DVD is great to have around to impress the friends. —*JO*

Movie: ♫ *DVD:* ♫♫♫♫
Warner Home Video, Inc. (Cat #15873, UPC #085391587323). Widescreen (2.35:1) letterboxed; full frame. Dolby Digital 5.1. $24.98. Snapper. *LANG:* English; French. *SUB:* French. *CAP:* English. *FEATURES:* 31 chapter links • 6 theatrical trailers.
1998 (PG-13) 90m/C Ralph Fiennes, Uma Thurman, Sean Connery, Jim Broadbent, Fiona Shaw, Eileen Atkins, John Wood, Eddie Izzard, Carmen Ejogo, Keeley Hawes; *Cameos:* Patrick Macnee; *D:* Jeremiah S. Chechik; *W:* Don MacPherson; *C:* Roger Pratt; *M:* Joel McNeely. *AWARDS:* Golden Raspberry Awards '98: Worst Remake/Sequel; *NOM:* Golden Raspberry Awards '98: Worst Picture, Worst Actor (Fiennes), Worst Actress (Thurman), Worst Supporting Actor (Connery), Worst Director (Chechik), Worst Screenplay, Worst Song ("Storm").

Avenging Disco Godfather

Moore *(Dolomite)* parodies gangster and martial arts movies. *AKA:* Avenging Godfather; Disco Godfather.
Movie: ♫▶ *DVD:* NYR
Xenon Entertainment (Cat #1030). $19.95. Keepcase. *FEATURES:* Trailer.

1976 (R) 99m/C Rudy Ray Moore, Carol Speed, Jimmy Lynch, Jeny Jones, Lady Reeds, James H. Hawthorne, Frank Finn, Julius J. Carey III; **D:** J. Robert Wagoner; **W:** J. Robert Wagoner, Cliff Roquemore; **C:** Arledge Armenaki; **M:** Ernie Fields Jr.

Awakening of Gabriella

After she catches her boyfriend with another girl, Gabriella (Featherly) leaves the country for the big city where she becomes an exotic dancer and meets a wealthy older man (Ritter). It's typically polished soft-core fluff from Playboy. On disc, the skin tones are warm; the cast is attractive; the sets are luxurious. Plotting and acting leave more to be desired. —MM

Movie: 🎬🎬 **DVD:** 🎬🎬
Image Entertainment (Cat #ID5978PLDVD, UPC #014381597820). Full frame. Dolby Digital Stereo. $24.99. Snapper. *LANG:* English. *FEATURES:* 14 chapter links.
1999 93m/C Susan Featherly, Ron Galbraith, Mark Ritter, Anna Kaminskaia, Taimi Hannum; **D:** Carlton McRae; **W:** John Quinn.

Awakenings

Marshall's first dramatic effort is based on the true story of Dr. Oliver Sacks, from his book of the same title. It details the experimentation with the drug L-dopa, which inspired the "awakening" of a number of catatonic patients, some of whom had been "sleeping" for as long as 30 years. Occasionally over-sentimental, but still providing a poignant look at both the patients who find themselves confronted with lost opportunities and faded youth and at Sacks, who must watch their exquisite suffering as they slip away. De Niro's performance as the youngest of the group is heart-rending, while Williams offers a subdued, moving performance as the doctor. The soft picture on this DVD really brings its rating down. The thing is that there isn't much grain or many artifacts to detract, so one wonders if it could've been the preprint that was the problem. The colors bleed a little but are, for the most part, true, as are the blacks. Everything else—including the contrast and brightness—are also very good. If there is another flaw it would be the soundtrack, which is fairly lifeless, lacking a little on both crispness and low end. —JO

Movie: 🎬🎬🎬 **DVD:** 🎬🎬
Columbia Tristar Home Video (Cat #50569, UPC #043396505698). Widescreen (1.85:1) letterboxed. Dolby Surround. $25.95. Keepcase. *LANG:* English; Spanish; French. *SUB:* Spanish. *CAP:* English. *FEATURES:* 61 chapter links.
1990 (PG-13) 120m/C Robin Williams, Robert De Niro, John Heard, Julie Kavner, Penelope Ann Miller, Max von Sydow, Anne Meara; **D:** Penny Marshall; **W:** Steven Zaillian; **M:** Randy Newman. *AWARDS:* National Board of Review Awards '90: Best Actor (De Niro), Best Actor (Williams); National Society of Film Critics Awards '90: Best

Actor (De Niro); *NOM:* Academy Awards '90: Best Actor (De Niro), Best Adapted Screenplay, Best Picture.

Away All Boats

This is the true (well, mostly true) story of Capt. Hawks (Chandler), who leads a crew of misfits to victory aboard the transport *USS Belinda* during World War II in the Pacific. The battle scenes are well-done. Look for an early and brief appearance by Clint Eastwood.
Movie: 🎬🎬 **DVD:** NYR
Goodtimes Entertainment (Cat #81040). Full frame. Dolby Digital Mono. $24.95. Snapper. *SUB:* French; Spanish.
1956 114m/B Jeff Chandler, George Nader, Richard Boone, Julie Adams, Keith Andes, Lex Barker; **D:** Joseph Pevney; **W:** Ted Sherdeman.

Ayn Rand: A Sense of Life

This Oscar-nominated biography is very much an "authorized" look at the life of the famous author and philosopher. It tells her story through the usual combination of stills, film, and television interviews, and interviews with friends and fellow writers. Rand's ideas are presented without criticism and her interpretation of events is not questioned. It's obvious that filmmaker Michael Paxton is very fond of his subject, and so the film is really recommended to her fans only. The DVD generally looks good. The new interviews are first-rate, as is the sound. Naturally, the older footage varies in quality but it's watchable. —MM

Movie: 🎬🎬 **DVD:** 🎬🎬
Image Entertainment (Cat #ID5685DDVD, UPC #014381568523). Widescreen (1.85:1) letterboxed. Dolby Digital Stereo. $24.99. Snapper. *LANG:* English. *FEATURES:* 26 chapter links.
1998 143m/C D: Michael Paxton; **W:** Michael Paxton; **C:** Alik Sakharov; **M:** Jeff Britting; **Nar:** Sharon Gless.

Babe

This brilliant fantasy deserves to be ranked with *The Wizard of Oz* and *Snow White*. It's the story of a pig (voice of Cavanaugh) who learns to herd sheep after she is "adopted" by Fly, the sheepdog, on Farmer Hoggett's (Cromwell) place. Four different special effects houses were used to make the barnyard animals talk and walk, and their work holds up beautifully on DVD. The medium's clarity does not reveal any important defects in special effects, but those are—and should be—secondary to the superbly realized characters (both animal and human) and the intelligent humor. Adults who watch the film again will appreciate the sophistication of the filmmaking, most obviously in the whimsical set design and quick editing, while kids will simply dive into the story. If the film had been presented in both widescreen and full-frame

versions (as the sequel is), it would rate four bones in the technical department. As it is, both image and sound are as sharp as I remember them from the theatrical release. All that's missing is the original screen ratio. —MM *AKA:* Babe, the Gallant Pig.

Movie: 🎬🎬🎬🎬 **DVD:** 🎬🎬🎬
Universal Studios Home Video (Cat #20013, UPC #025192001321). Full frame. Dolby Digital 5.1 Surround sound. $29.98. Jewel case. *LANG:* English; French; Spanish. *SUB:* Spanish. *CAP:* English. *FEATURES:* 16 chapter links.
1995 (G) 91m/C *AU* James Cromwell, Magna Szubanski; **D:** Chris Noonan; **W:** Chris Noonan, George Miller; **C:** Andrew Lesnie; **M:** Nigel Westlake; **V:** Christine Cavanaugh, Miriam Margolyes, Danny Mann, Hugo Weaving; **Nar:** Roscoe Lee Browne. *AWARDS:* Academy Awards '95: Best Visual Effects; Golden Globe Awards '96: Best Film—Musical/Comedy; National Society of Film Critics Awards '95: Best Film; *NOM:* Academy Awards '95: Best Adapted Screenplay, Best Art Direction/Set Decoration, Best Director (Noonan), Best Film Editing, Best Picture, Best Supporting Actor (Cromwell); British Academy Awards '95: Best Adapted Screenplay, Best Film; Writers Guild of America '95: Best Adapted Screenplay.

Babe: Pig in the City

Ambitious sequel attempts to take the characters into new and darker territory and so it did not find a receptive audience in theatres. But DVD plays to the film's challenging visuals, and so it's recommended to anyone who missed it the first time around. After finding fame as a "sheep pig," Babe and Mrs. Hoggett (Szubanski) must go to the city to raise money to save the farm. There they find assorted animals who need their help, too, and they must overcome a host of problems before they can return. The set designs and visuals are just as carefully wrought as they were in the first film. Their sometimes ominous power may account for the film's lack of success. The film looks fine on disc, even the remarkable stuntwork in chapter 16. The disc is filled with extras. The only serious problem is a clunky menu that's a bit hard to navigate. —MM

Movie: 🎬🎬🎬 **DVD:** 🎬🎬🎬
Universal Studios Home Video (Cat #20527, UPC #025192052729). Full frame; widescreen (1.85:1) anamorphic. Dolby Digital 5.1 Surround Sound; Dolby Digital Surround Stereo. $29.98. Keepcase. *LANG:* English; French. *CAP:* English. *FEATURES:* 18 chapter links • Production notes • Cast and crew thumbnail biographies • Help menu • Product reel • "Making of" featurette • Interactive game • Theatrical trailers • Universal web links.
1998 (PG) 96m/C James Cromwell, Magna Szubanski, Mickey Rooney, Mary Stein, Julie Godfrey; **D:** George Miller; **W:** Judy Morris, Mark Lamprell; **C:** Andrew

Lesnie; **M:** Nigel Westlake; **V:** Elizabeth (E.G.) Daily, Danny Mann, Glenne Headly, Steven Wright, James Cosmo, Stanley Ralph Ross, Russi Taylor, Adam Goldberg, Roscoe Lee Browne, Nathan Kress, Myles Jeffrey. *AWARDS: NOM:* Academy Awards '98: Best Song ("That'll Do").

The Baby

Bizarre horror/thriller revolves around social worker Ann Gentry (Comer), who takes on the case of the Wadsworth family: alcoholic mom (Roman), good sister (Hill), bad sister (Zenor), and baby (Manzy), an adult male who wears diapers and lives in a crib. Before it's all been sorted out, cattle prods, butcher knives, and hatchets have come into play. On DVD, some reels are marred by a fine skein of scratches; others are completely clear. Throughout, lighting and sets are strictly low-budget material. The disc also contains a separate soundtrack of music and sound effects for those who prefer to dispense with dialogue altogether. —*MM*
Movie: 🎬🎬▸ **DVD:** 🎬🎬▸
Image Entertainment (Cat #ID6145TVDVD). Full frame. Dolby Digital Mono. $24.99. Snapper. *LANG:* English; Spanish. *FEATURES:* 14 chapter links.
1972 (PG) 85m/C Anjanette Comer, Ruth Roman, Marianna Hill, Suzanne Zenor, David Manzy, Michael Pataki, Erin O'Reilly, Virginia Vincent; **D:** Ted Post; **W:** Abe Polsky; **C:** Michael D. Margulies; **M:** Gerald Fried.

Baby Geniuses

The most irritating parts of *Look Who's Talking* resurface in this full-diaper misfire. Evil scientists (Lloyd and Turner) attempt to crack the secret language of babies using the infant experimental subjects they hold prisoner in their lab. Standing in their way are two nursery school operators (Cattrall and MacNicol) and an array of toddlers that spout inane dialogue via computer-generated effects. On DVD, the full-frame image exhibits a fair amount of grain, particularly in the special effects scenes. Sound is O.K. —*MM*
Movie: 🎬 **DVD:** 🎬🎬
Columbia Tristar Home Video (Cat #03711, UPC #043396037113). Full frame. Dolby Digital 5.1 Surround Stereo; Dolby Surround Stereo. $24.98. Keepcase. *LANG:* English. *CAP:* English. *FEATURES:* 28 chapter links • "Making of" featurette • Special effects featurette • Theatrical trailer • Cast and crew thumbnail biographies.
1998 (PG) 94m/C Kathleen Turner, Christopher Lloyd, Kim Cattrall, Peter Mac-Nicol, Dom DeLuise, Ruby Dee, Kyle Howard, Leo Fitzgerald, Myles Fitzgerald, Gerry Fitzgerald; **D:** Bob (Benjamin) Clark; **W:** Bob (Benjamin) Clark, Steven Paul, Francisca Matos, Robert Grasmere, Greg Michael; **C:** Stephen M. Katz; **M:** Paul Zaza.

The Babysitter's Seduction

Michelle (Russell) takes care of Bill's (Collins) children. After his wife's death, the teen seeks to upgrade her status within the family from hired help to significant other to... But is Bill a grieving widower or a cold-blooded psycho? Dating is always tough, isn't it? The made-for-TV fare gains nothing on DVD. Image, sound, and production values are standard. —*MM*
Movie: 🎬🎬 **DVD:** 🎬🎬
Simitar Entertainment (Cat #7591, UPC #082551759125). Full frame. Dolby Digital Stereo. $14.98. Keepcase. *LANG:* English. *FEATURES:* 8 chapter links.
1996 91m/C Keri Russell, Stephen Collins, Phylicia Rashad, Tobin Bell, John D'Aquino, Linda Kelsey; **D:** David Burton Morris; **W:** Shirley Tallman, Nancy Hersage; **M:** Jan Hammer.

The Bachelor

Loose remake of Buster Keaton's *Seven Chances* has an attractive cast that never quite generates the necessary cinematic chemistry for a romantic comedy. The laborious premise has bachelor Jimmy (O'Donnell) inheriting millions if he can just get married by 7:00 that evening. Is there any chance he'll get back together with ex-flame Ann (Zellweger)? On DVD, the action has the familiar glossiness associated with slickly produced Hollywood fluff. It sounds fine, too, but neither of those are enough for a recommendation. —*MM*
Movie: 🎬🎬 **DVD:** 🎬🎬🎬
New Line Home Video (Cat #N4994). Widescreen letterboxed; full frame. Dolby Digital 5.1 Surround Stereo; Dolby Digital Surround. $24.98. Snapper. *LANG:* English. *SUB:* English. *FEATURES:* 30 chapter links • Cast and crew thumbnail bios.
1999 (PG-13) 101m/C Chris O'Donnell, Renee Zellweger, Hal Holbrook, James Cromwell, Artie Lange, Ed Asner, Marley Shelton, Stacy Edwards, Rebecca Cross, Jennifer Esposito, Peter Ustinov, Mariah Carey, Brooke Shields; **D:** Gary Sinyor; **W:** Steve Cohen; **C:** Simon Archer; **M:** David A. Hughes, John Murphy.

Backdraft

High action story of Chicago firemen has some of the most stupendous incendiary special effects ever filmed. But then there's the B-movie plot about a mystery arsonist torching strategic parts of the community with the finesse of an expert, and a brother-against-brother conflict. Straightforward performances from most of the cast. Writer Widen wrote from experience—he used to be a fireman; real-life Chicago firefighters were reportedly very happy with the realistic and intense fire scenes, which are stupendous. There's a whole lot of flames-a-flickering in this film but this fine DVD has no problems handling the situation. In addition to the lack of artifacts, the grain level remains low

and the picture is very sharp. The colors are accurate and the contrast allows details to remain intact in both bright and dark situations. Blacks are true. The 5.1 mix helps to immerse you in the fire scenes as you can sometimes here (and feel) the flames and explosions around you. —*JO*
Movie: 🎬🎬🎬 **DVD:** 🎬🎬🎬▸
Universal Studios Home Video (Cat #20041, UPC #025192004124). Widescreen (2.35:1) letterboxed. Dolby Digital 5.1; Dolby Surround. $24.98. Keepcase. *LANG:* English; Spanish; French. *SUB:* Spanish. *CAP:* English. *FEATURES:* 16 chapter links • Production notes • Cast and filmmakers bios • Film highlights.
1991 (R) 135m/C Kurt Russell, William Baldwin, Robert De Niro, Donald Sutherland, Jennifer Jason Leigh, Scott Glenn, Rebecca DeMornay, Jason Gedrick, J.T. Walsh, Tony Mockus Sr., Clint Howard, David Crosby; **D:** Ron Howard; **W:** Gregory Widen; **C:** Mikael Salomon; **M:** Hans Zimmer. *AWARDS: NOM:* Academy Awards '91: Best Sound, Best Visual Effects.

Bad Boys

When a gang member's little brother is killed in a rumble, the teen responsible (Penn) is sent to a reformatory. Meanwhile, on the outside, his rival attacks his girlfriend (Sheedy, in her feature film debut), is incarcerated, and ends up in competition with Penn for control of the cellblock. With their mutual hatred and escalating inmate pressure, the two are pushed toward a violent confrontation. The film is not as graphic as it could be, and, to its credit, treats the situation seriously. The dark prison settings do not give DVD much to work with. In visual terms, the extras-free disc is not a significant improvement over VHS tape. The same goes for the sound. —*MM*
Movie: 🎬🎬🎬 **DVD:** 🎬🎬▸
Republic Pictures Home Video (Cat #39004). Widescreen (1.85:1) anamorphic. Dolby Digital Stereo. $24.98. Keepcase. *LANG:* English.
1983 (R) 104m/C Sean Penn, Esai Morales, Reni Santoni, Jim Moody, Eric Gurry, Ally Sheedy, Clancy Brown; **D:** Rick Rosenthal; **W:** Richard Dilello; **C:** Donald E. Thorin; **M:** Bill Conti.

Bad Boys

And you thought the old buddy-cop formula was played out. Well, Hollywood sticks with what works, and pairing the two television personalities definitely works at the minimalist level required. Mike (Smith) and Marcus (Lawrence) are Miami cops who must track down $100 million worth of heroin stolen from their evidence room before internal affairs shuts down the precinct. The case leads them to a vicious thief, as well as a beautiful female witness to his murderous handiwork. Plot lacks depth, but high energy and dazzling action sequences keep things moving. Feature film debut for director Bay. This

DVD handles all that you expect of an action film with very few problems. The colors are lush and accurate and the blacks true and grain-free. The picture is sharp and also has no problem with grain. Even when just-blown-up pieces and parts fly by there are no artifacts to be found. The sound is pretty good but lacking on the low end. The Surround mix is very good. —JO

Movie: 🎵🎵▶ **DVD:** 🎵🎵🎵
Columbia Tristar Home Video (Cat #10719, UPC #043396107199). Widescreen (1.85:1) letterboxed. Dolby Digital 5.1; Dolby Surround. $24.98. Keepcase. *LANG:* English; Spanish; French. *SUB:* Spanish; Korean. *CAP:* English. *FEATURES:* 55 chapter links.
1995 (R) 118m/C Martin Lawrence, Will Smith, Tcheky Karyo, Tea Leoni, Theresa Randle, Marg Helgenberger, Joe Pantoliano, John Salley; *D:* Michael Bay; *W:* Michael Barrie, Jim Mulholland; *C:* Howard Atherton; *M:* Mark Mancina. *AWARDS:* Blockbuster Entertainment Awards '96: Male Newcomer, Theatrical (Smith); *NOM:* MTV Movie Awards '96: Best On-Screen Duo (Martin Lawrence/Will Smith), Best Action Sequence.

Bad Lieutenant

Social chaos and degeneration characterize the story as well as the main character, a nameless loner police lieutenant (Keitel) who is as corrupt as they come. Assigned to a case involving a raped nun, he's confronted by his own lagging Catholic beliefs and the need for salvation by grace. Cult filmmaker Ferrara treated similar ideas in *Ms. 45* and this effort is filled with violence, drugs, and grotesque sexual situations. Like almost all of Ferrara's work, it's tense, grimy, and meant to be unsettling. Because he's so entranced with squalor, the image gains little on DVD. This movie's supposed to look nasty and it does on any medium. —MM

Movie: 🎵🎵🎵 **DVD:** 🎵🎵
Artisan Entertainment (Cat #60476). Widescreen anamorphic. Dolby Digital Stereo. $24.98. Keepcase. *LANG:* English. *SUB:* Spanish. *CAP:* English. *FEATURES:* Cast and crew thumbnail bios ● Production notes.
1992 (NC-17) 98m/C Harvey Keitel, Brian McElroy, Frankie Acciario, Peggy Gormley, Stella Keitel, Victor Argo, Paul Calderon, Leonard Thomas, Frankie Thorn; *D:* Abel Ferrara; *W:* Zoe Tamerlaine Lund, Abel Ferrara; *C:* Ken Kelsch; *M:* Joe Delia. *AWARDS:* Independent Spirit Awards '93: Best Actor (Keitel).

Bad Love

Gritty, naturalistic romance is the story of two losers searching for salvation in each other. Eloise (Gidley) is a secretary involved in a dead-end sexual relationship with her married boss (Dallesandro). Lenny (Sizemore) is a borderline alcoholic and dreamer who can't hold a job. They fall for each other immediately. Their rocky relationship is a search for love and employment. They're deeply flawed characters, and though there's an inevitability to their self-created predicaments, there's also something fascinating about them. Director Goldman makes their low-rent Southern California world an important part of the story. On DVD that aspect is even stronger than it is on tape. The entire production has a used-up look, heightened often with bruised yellowish light. What might be flaws on other discs are deliberate devices here. —MM

Movie: 🎵🎵🎵 **DVD:** 🎵🎵🎵
Image Entertainment (Cat #ID5765SUMD-VD, UPC #014381576528). Full frame. Dolby Digital Mono. $24.99. Snapper. *LANG:* English. *FEATURES:* 12 chapter links.
1995 (R) 93m/C Tom Sizemore, Pamela Gidley, Debi Mazar, Jennifer O'Neill, Margaux Hemingway, Richard Edson, Seymour Cassel, Joe Dallesandro; *D:* Jill Goldman; *C:* Gary Tieche; *M:* Rick Cox.

Bad Man's River

A Mexican revolutionary leader hires a gang of outlaws to blow up an arsenal used by the Army. That's the basis for a comic heist plot.
Movie: 🎵🎵 **DVD:** NYR
Parade (Cat #55286). Full frame. Dolby Digital Mono. $17.98. Keepcase. *SUB:* Japanese.
1972 92m/C *IT SP* Lee Van Cleef, James Mason, Gina Lollobrigida; *D:* Eugenio (Gene) Martin; *W:* Philip Yordan; *C:* Alejandro Ulloa; *M:* Waldo de los Rios.

Badlands

Based loosely on the Charlie Starkweather murders of the 1950s, this impressive movie debut by director Malick recounts a slow-thinking, unhinged misfit's murder of his 15-year-old girlfriend's parents and their subsequent killing spree across the Midwestern plains. Sheen and Spacek are disturbingly numb as the apathetic, ice cold duo. Watching this DVD makes you feel like you're looking through a piece of cheesecloth. Now, before you start thinking "it's just that arty Malick guy," this is not how the film looked in the theatre. The sharpness is a touch below average and there's just too darn much grain. The colors are saturated but the added grain and bleed is very unpleasant. To top it off there are just enough artifacts throughout to add a slight blur to rapid movement. Below average for Warner Bros. —JO

Movie: 🎵🎵🎵▶ **DVD:** 🎵▶
Warner Home Video, Inc. (Cat #16086, UPC #085391608022). Widescreen (1.85:1) anamorphic; full frame. Dolby Digital 5.1; Mono. $19.98. Snapper. *LANG:* English (DD5.1); French (Mono). *SUB:* French. *CAP:* English. *FEATURES:* 28 chapter links.
1974 (PG) 94m/C Martin Sheen, Sissy Spacek, Warren Oates, Ramon Bieri, Alan Vint, Gary Littlejohn, Charles Fitzpatrick, Howard Ragsdale, John Womack Jr., Dona

Baldwin; *Cameos:* Terrence Malick; *D:* Terrence Malick; *W:* Terrence Malick; *C:* Tak Fujimoto, Stevan Larner, Brian Probyn; *M:* Erik Satie, Carl Orff. *AWARDS:* National Film Registry '93.

Baker's Hawk

Not much to say about this DVD, but it's above-average family fare. A young boy (Montgomery) befriends recluse (Ives) and learns the meaning of family and caring from the old guy and a red-tailed hawk. The film boasts excellent location cinematography, but the disc is lacking in every way. The picture is soft and full of grain. Most scenes have at least some artifacts. Color seems faded and blacks are generally gray and grainy. The image is also on the dull side with not enough contrast or brightness. Unfortunately, the sound manages to keep the disc consistent and is nothing special at any point and clips at others. Well, I guess there was a lot to say. —JO

Movie: 🎵🎵▶ **DVD:** 🎵
UAV Entertainment (Cat #40095, UPC #084296400959). Full frame. Mono. $14.99. Snapper. *LANG:* English.
1976 98m/C Clint Walker, Diane Baker, Burl Ives, Lee Montgomery, Alan Young, Danny Bonaduce; *D:* Lyman Dayton; *W:* Dan Greer, Hal Harrison Jr.; *C:* Bernie Abramson; *M:* Lex de Azevedo.

Ball of Fire

A gang moll (Stanwyck) hides out with a group of ivory-tower professors led by Cooper in a version of "Snow White and the Seven Dwarfs" that might have been called "The Torch Singer and the Eight Intellectuals." The academics are busy compiling an encyclopedia and the brassy babe helps them out with the section on English language slang. Coop has his hands full when he falls for this damsel in distress and must fight when the gangsters try to take her. The chemistry between the leads, both in rather offbeat roles, simmers nicely, making this one of Hawks's best comedies. The DVD shows off Gregg Toland's superb black-and-white cinematography with wonderfully detailed interiors, particularly the busy Victorian room where the eggheads work. Sound is excellent, too. The disc appears to have been made from a pristine original. Any flaws are negligible. —MM

Movie: 🎵🎵🎵 **DVD:** 🎵🎵🎵
HBO Home Video (Cat #90750, UPC #026359075025). Full frame. Mono; Stereo. $24.98. Snapper. *LANG:* English; French; German; Italian; Spanish. *FEATURES:* Cast and crew thumbnail bios.
1941 111m/B Gary Cooper, Barbara Stanwyck, Dana Andrews, Gene Krupa, Oscar Homolka, Dan Duryea, S.Z. Sakall, Henry Travers; *D:* Howard Hawks; *W:* Billy Wilder, Charles Brackett; *C:* Gregg Toland; *M:* Alfred Newman. *AWARDS: NOM:* Academy Awards '41: Best Actress (Stanwyck), Best Sound, Best Story, Best Original Dramatic Score.

Baraka

According to the "making of" featurette, the filmmakers went around the world three times during the 13 months it took them to create this "nonverbal" look at the planet, its people, industry, and conflicts. They state that their subject is "humanity's relationship with the eternal." Though they also stress that their work is not a travelogue, it is a non-linear narrative aimed at hard-core National Geographic and Discovery Channel fans. Other audiences will either embrace this unconventional approach or they will turn it off within five minutes. In essence, the film is a series of images of nature and humanity that creates none-too-subtle connections among its subjects, be they newly hatched chicks, Japanese subway riders, or the oil well fires in Kuwait. It's a stunning work, filmed in 70mm and clearly meant for the largest theatre screen possible. It loses some power on anything smaller, but DVD adds the dimension of accessibility, and image and sound are both excellent. Also, the liner notes provide geographical information not available on-screen. Michael Stearns "world music" score is terrific. The title means "blessing" in several languages. —*MM*

Movie: 🦴🦴🦴 **DVD:** 🦴🦴🦴▸
MPI Home Video (Cat #DVD7060, UPC #030306706023). Widescreen letterboxed; full frame. Dolby Digital 5.1 Surround Stereo. $24.98. Keepcase. *FEATURES:* 22 chapter links • Behind-the-scenes featurette.
1993 104m/C *D:* Ron Fricke; *W:* Ron Fricke, Mark Magidson, Bob Green; *C:* Ron Fricke; *M:* Michael Stearns.

Barb Wire

Bizarre little hybrid is a comic book shoot-'em-up filled with pyrotechnic fight scenes, but the plot has been lifted from a more curious source: *Casablanca.* In this variation—set in Steel Harbor, the last free city in a fascist future America—Rick's Cafe is Hammerhead, a nightclub run by the motorcycle-riding blonde bombshell Barb Wire (Lee). The local corrupt policeman, Cmdr. Willis (Berkeley), takes over for Claude Rains's Capt. Renault. Ilsa is now Axel (Morrison), a man from Barb's past, and Victor Laszlo is Cora D (Rowell). Instead of letters of transit, they need "retinal lenses" to evade the evil Congressionals' security scanners. And Col. Pryzer (Railsback), filling in for Maj. Strasser, will do anything to stop them, etc., etc.
Movie: 🦴▸ **DVD:** NYR
USA Home Entertainment (Cat #639927). Widescreen (1.85:1) letterboxed. Dolby Digital 5.1 Surround Stereo; Dolby Digital Surround Stereo. $29.95. Keepcase. *LANG:* English; French. *CAP:* English. *FEATURES:* Deleted scenes • Cast and crew thumbnail biographies.
1996 (R) 98m/C Pamela Anderson, Temuera Morrison, Jack Noseworthy, Victoria Rowell, Xander Berkeley, Udo Kier, Steve Railsback, Clint Howard, Tony Bill; *D:* David Hogan; *W:* Chuck Pfarrer, Ilene

Chaiken; *C:* Rick Bota; *M:* Michel Colombier. *AWARDS:* Golden Raspberry Awards '96: Worst New Star (Anderson); *NOM:* MTV Movie Awards '97: Best Fight (Pamela Lee/A Guy); Golden Raspberry Awards '96: Worst Picture, Worst Screenplay, Worst Song ("Welcome to Planet Boom!").

Barbarella

Time change. 1960s' hot-and-heavy erotic sf is today's "PG"-rated exercise in nostalgia. Based on the popular French comic strip drawn by Jean-Claude Forest, this cult favorite details the bizarre adventures of the titular space babe (Fonda) as she encounters fantastic creatures, angels, and the like. Terry Southern contributed to the wide-eyed script. The opening credits built around Barbarella's stripping out of her plastic space suit and writhing around in her shag-carpeted spaceship remain the highlight. Even in mono, Charles Fox's score is a trip down memory lane. The digital image retains the good crisp colors and shows off the goofy sets in all their tackiness. —*MM* *AKA:* Barbarella, Queen of the Galaxy.
Movie: 🦴🦴▸ **DVD:** 🦴🦴🦴▸
Paramount Home Video (Cat #068127, UPC #097360681277). Widescreen. Dolby Digital Mono. $29.99. Keepcase. *LANG:* English; French. *FEATURES:* 19 chapter links • Theatrical trailer.
1968 (PG) 98m/C *FR IT* Jane Fonda, John Phillip Law, David Hemmings, Marcel Marceau, Anita Pallenberg, Milo O'Shea, Ugo Tognazzi, Veronique Vendell, Giancarlo Cobelli, Serge Marquand; *D:* Roger Vadim; *W:* Roger Vadim, Terry Southern, Vittorio Bonicelli, Claude Brule, Tudor Gates, Clement Biddle Wood, Brian Degas, Jean-Claude Forest; *C:* Claude Renoir; *M:* Charles Fox.

Barefoot in the Park

Neil Simon's hit play translates fairly well to the screen. Newlywed Corey (Fonda) tries to get uptight lawyer husband Paul (Redford) to loosen up in their fifth-floor walk-up. The two stars are impossibly young and attractive. They and the film are so cute that they're sometimes hard to take. It's really more enjoyable now as an illuminating glimpse at the sexual and social conventions of the mid-1960s. The DVD is exceptionally clear for a film of this age. The image contains only minimal flaws. Sound is not as strong, though most flaws can be traced to the original. The music is laid on very thick in some scenes and the voice dubbing has a detached sound at times. —*MM*
Movie: 🦴🦴▸ **DVD:** 🦴🦴🦴
Paramount Home Video (Cat #08027, UPC #097360802740). Widescreen anamorphic. Dolby Digital Mono. $29.99. Keepcase. *LANG:* English; French. *SUB:* English. *CAP:* English. *FEATURES:* 18 chapter links • Theatrical trailer.
1967 106m/C Robert Redford, Jane Fonda, Charles Boyer, Mildred Natwick; *D:*

Gene Saks; *W:* Neil Simon; *C:* Joseph LaShelle; *M:* Neal Hefti. *AWARDS: NOM:* Academy Awards '67: Best Supporting Actress (Natwick).

Barney's Great Adventure

First the bad news: That big purple dweebosaur made a movie and your three-year-old is going to make you buy the DVD. Now the good news: You can pop it into the player and run quickly from the room, safe in the knowledge that the small-fry will be entertained for 78 minutes. In this extravaganza of not-so-special effects, Barney and two little girls chase a magic egg around town and encounter a parade, a circus, and other allegedly wonderful things, all while trying to persuade the older Kyle that Barney is "cool." The full-frame DVD image handles the painfully bright colors with no problem. Sound is excellent. —*MM*
Movie: 🦴🦴 **DVD:** 🦴🦴🦴
USA Home Entertainment (Cat #55457, UPC #044005545722). Full frame. Dolby Digital 5.1 Surround Stereo; Dolby Digital Stereo. $19.95. Keepcase. *LANG:* English; French; Spanish. *CAP:* English. *FEATURES:* 19 chapter links • Theatrical trailers • *Barney's First Adventure* half-hour TV special.
1998 (G) 75m/C George Hearn, Shirley Douglas, Kyla Pratt, Trevor Morgan, Bob West, Renee Madeleine Le Guerrier; *D:* Steve Gomer; *W:* Stephen White; *C:* Sandi Sissel; *V:* Diana Rice, Julie Johnson. *AWARDS: NOM:* Golden Raspberry Awards '98: Worst Song ("Barney, The Song"), Worst New Star (Barney).

Barry Lyndon

Ravishing adaptation of the classic Thackeray novel about the adventures of an Irish gambler (O'Neal) moving from innocence to self-destructive arrogance in the aristocracy of 18th-century England. Excellent performances from all the actors, even O'Neal, who has never been better. Kubrick's usual visual opulence—every frame looks like an oil painting—and attention to detail, including the authentic music, is at times overwhelming. The film's graininess, like other Kubricks, is once again a slight problem for the DVD. However, the disc still looks very good and is by far the best way to see this amazing work. The colors are subtle where they're supposed to be and lush when needed. Bleed is minimal. Blacks, contrast, and brightness are all very good. The closest thing to artifacts are in the flicker of a candle's flame. The film's soundtrack, presented in its original mono, is very full-bodied. It clearly conveys dialogue, music, and even the sounds of battle. The DVD includes the intermission and allows the layer change to be as unobtrusive as possible. —*JO*
Movie: 🦴🦴🦴▸ **DVD:** 🦴🦴🦴▸
Warner Home Video, Inc. (Cat #17366, UPC #085391736622). Widescreen

(1.77:1) letterboxed. Dolby Digital Mono. $24.98. Snapper. *LANG:* English; French. *SUB:* French. *CAP:* English. *FEATURES:* Dual-layered RSDL ▪ 47 chapter links ▪ Theatrical trailer ▪ Production notes. Also available as part of the "Stanley Kubrick Collection" 7-DVD box set ($149.98).
1975 (PG) 185m/C Ryan O'Neal, Marisa Berenson, Patrick Magee, Hardy Kruger, Guy Hamilton; *D:* Stanley Kubrick; *W:* Stanley Kubrick; *C:* John Alcott. *AWARDS:* Academy Awards '75: Best Art Direction/Set Decoration, Best Cinematography, Best Costume Design, Original Song Score and/or Adaptation; British Academy Awards '75: Best Director (Kubrick); Los Angeles Film Critics Association Awards '75: Best Cinematography; National Board of Review Awards '75: Best Director (Kubrick); National Society of Film Critics Awards '75: Best Cinematography; *NOM:* Academy Awards '75: Best Adapted Screenplay, Best Director (Kubrick), Best Picture.

Bartok the Magnificent

Direct-to-video sequel to the theatrical hit *Anastasia* is not at all comparable in terms of animation or story. It does boast a sense of humor and first-rate voice talent. The story has to do with the sidekick from the original fighting the witch Baba Yaga for Prince Ivan. Overall, it's quickly paced and aimed squarely at the younger Saturday-morning cartoon fans. Visually, the DVD is nothing special. Only the extras and scene accessibility differentiate it from the videotape. —MM
Movie: ♫♫▶ **DVD:** ♫♫▶
20th Century Fox (Cat #4112600, UPC #086162126000). Full frame. Dolby Digital Surround Stereo. $29.98. Keepcase. *LANG:* English; French. *SUB:* English; Spanish. *CAP:* English. *FEATURES:* 16 chapter links ▪ 3 sing-along songs ▪ Theatrical trailers.
1999 (G) 68m/C D: Don Bluth, Gary Goldman; *W:* Jay Lacopo; *M:* Stephen Flaherty; *V:* Hank Azaria, Kelsey Grammer, Jennifer Tilly, Tim Curry, Catherine O'Hara.

The Base

Army Intelligence officer Maj. John Murphy (Dacascos) is sent undercover to Fort Tilman to investigate the murder of an army operations officer. Murphy is assigned to a border patrol unit and discovers his fellow soldiers are muscling in on the Mexican/American drug trade. When he learns who's behind the operation, his cover is blown.
Movie: ♫♫ **DVD:** NYR
Studio Home Entertainment (Cat #7245). Full frame. $24.95. Keepcase. *SUB:* Spanish. *FEATURES:* Cast and crew thumbnail biographies ▪ Commentary: Mark Lester ▪ Trailer.
1999 (R) 101m/C Mark Dacascos, Tim Abell, Paula Trickey, Noah Blake, Frederick Coffin; *D:* Mark L. Lester; *W:* Jeff Albert, William Martell; *C:* Jacques Haitkin; *M:* Paul Zaza.

BASEketball

Coop (Parker), Reamer (Stone), and Squeak (Bachar)—think *Dumb, Dumber, and Dumbest*—invent a combination of baseball and driveway basketball and become sports stars. The funniest bits come early with parodies of real professional sports. A Dallas Cowboys' end zone celebration escalates into a Rockettes routine. The rest is pretty much a misfire from the creators of *Airplane* and *South Park*. It's O.K. for fans of gross-out humor, though they have certainly seen grosser. The DVD image is fine, but like the film itself, unexceptional. The extras are equally limited. —MM
Movie: ♫♫ **DVD:** ♫♫▶
Universal Studios Home Video (Cat #20430, UPC #025192043024). Widescreen (1.85:1) letterboxed. Dolby Digital 5.1 Surround Stereo. $24.98. Keepcase. *LANG:* English. *SUB:* Spanish; French. *CAP:* English. *FEATURES:* Production notes ▪ 30 chapter links ▪ Cast and crew thumbnail biographies ▪ Universal web links ▪ Music video ▪ Theatrical trailer.
1998 (R) 103m/C Trey Parker, Matt Stone, Yasmine Bleeth, Jenny McCarthy, Ernest Borgnine, Dian Bachar, Robert Vaughn, Bob Costas, Al Michaels, Reggie Jackson, Robert Stack, Steve Garvey, Kareem Abdul-Jabbar; *D:* David Zucker; *W:* David Zucker, Robert Locash, Jeffrey Wright, Lewis Friedman; *C:* Steve Mason; *M:* Ira Newborn. *AWARDS: NOM:* Golden Raspberry Awards '98: Worst Actress (Bleeth), Worst Supporting Actress (McCarthy).

Basic Instinct

Whatever logical lapses this commercial hit suffers—and it's filled with gaping holes from one end to the other—star Sharon Stone makes her character, bisexual author Catherine Tramell, one of the screen's most powerful femmes fatale. She may be a psycho killer; San Francisco cop Nick Curran (Douglas) may not care. Stone's brassy, flashing, fearless performance turned her into a star overnight. Even so, some have dismissed the film as misogynist exploitation that denigrates women. Horror or suspense, feminism or homophobic trash, it's still a prime guilty pleasure. On DVD, the image looks about as good as it ever has, though it lacks the hot clarity of similar pictures made just a few years later. The disc is made from the "R"-rated version, not the even more explicitly violent unrated tape, and it also contains a Descriptive Video Service audio track which explains the action in steamy detail for the blind and visually impaired. —MM
Movie: ♫♫♫ **DVD:** ♫♫♫
Artisan Entertainment (Cat #60443, UPC #012236044307). Widescreen (2.35:1) letterboxed; full frame. Dolby Digital 5.1 Surround Stereo; Dolby Digital Surround Stereo. $24.99. Snapper. *LANG:* English; Spanish. *SUB:* English; French; Spanish. *CAP:* English. *FEATURES:* 50 chapter links ▪ Theatrical trailer ▪ Cast and crew

thumbnail biographies ▪ Production notes ▪ Descriptive Video Service.
1992 (R) 123m/C Michael Douglas, Sharon Stone, George Dzundza, Jeanne Tripplehorn, Denis Arndt, Leilani Sarelle Ferrer, Bruce A. Young, Chelcie Ross, Dorothy Malone, Wayne Knight, Stephen Tobolowsky; *D:* Paul Verhoeven; *W:* Joe Eszterhas; *C:* Jan De Bont; *M:* Jerry Goldsmith. *AWARDS:* MTV Movie Awards '93: Best Female Performance (Stone), Most Desirable Female (Stone); *NOM:* Academy Awards '92: Best Film Editing, Best Original Score.

Basket Case

One of the all-time great low-budget horrors is an ingeniously twisted original in every respect. After a bloody suburban opening, the scene shifts to a grainy, squalid Times Square where Duane (Kevin Van Hentenryck) carries a large wicker basket. He talks to the basket; he feeds it hamburgers and hotdogs. Inside is Belial, the amazing creation of Kevin Haney and John Caglione, who use stop-motion animation and models to transform the creature into one of the most grotesque and believable monsters you'll ever see. Writer-director-editor Frank Henenlotter's plot is too outrageous for words, and the actors handle it masterfully. The combination of strong atmosphere and total unpredictability gives this one an overall weirdness that few horror films even attempt. The DVD version looks much better than any tape, though the added clarity heightens Henenlotter's often harsh lighting. But then, this is not a movie that is supposed to look good. As the director would prove with the inferior sequels, bigger budgets do not mean better films. Though the reds in the opening credits are fuzzy, the colors remain sharp in the body of the film and Henenlotter uses red as visual punctuation. True fans will lament the lack of a commentary track. —MM
Movie: ♫♫♫ **DVD:** ♫♫♫
Image Entertainment (Cat #ID4785BCDVD, UPC #014381478525). Full frame. Dolby Digital Mono. $24.99. Snapper. *LANG:* English. *FEATURES:* 16 chapter links.
1982 89m/C Kevin Van Hentenryck, Terri Susan Smith, Beverly Bonner, Robert Vogel, Diana Browne, Lloyd Pace, Bill Freeman, Joe Clarke, Ruth Neuman, Richard Pierce, Dorothy Strongin; *D:* Frank Henenlotter; *W:* Frank Henenlotter; *C:* Bruce Torbet; *M:* Gus Russo.

The Basketball Diaries

DiCaprio is very good in this disappointing, self-conscious adaptation of underground writer-musician Jim Carroll's 1978 cult memoir. He's a teen athlete whose life disintegrates into drug addiction and hustling on the New York streets. Carroll and friends Mickey (Wahlberg), Neutron (McGaw), and Pedro (Madio) form the heart of the St. Vitus's hot hoopster team. But the defiant quartet really get their kicks from drugs, dares, and petty crime—leading to a downward spiral. The book takes place in the '60s, but the film can't decide which decade it's in. The picture tends to blur during some pans, but that's not completely inappropriate for the druggy distortions of the image. Sound is fine. —*MM*

Movie: ♫♫ **DVD:** ♫♫♫
Polygram (Cat #635899). Widescreen letterboxed. Dolby Digital 5.1 Surround Stereo. $29.95. Keepcase. *LANG:* English. *SUB:* English. *FEATURES:* 21 chapter links ⬝ Anti-drug trailer ⬝ Cast and crew interviews ⬝ TV spots.
1994 (R) 102m/C Leonardo DiCaprio, Mark Wahlberg, Patrick McGaw, James Madio, Bruno Kirby, Ernie Hudson, Lorraine Bracco, Juliette Lewis, Josh Mostel, Michael Rapaport, Michael Imperioli, Jim Carroll; *D:* Scott Kalvert; *W:* Bryan Goluboff; *C:* David Phillips; *M:* Graeme Revell.

Bastard out of Carolina

Huston's controversial directorial debut tells the story of young mom Anney (Leigh) who lives a hardscrabble life in 1950s Greenville, SC, with an illegitimate daughter nicknamed Bone (Malone). Working as a waitress, Anney succumbs to the charms of laborer Glen (Eldard), despite his nasty temper which only hints at darker emotions. The film, based on Dorothy Allison's autobiographical novel, was originally made for Ted Turner's TNT network but was released on the Showtime cable channel due to its graphic depiction of child abuse. Because the film was made for the small screen, neither image nor sound are strikingly sharp. On DVD, brick patterns flash and the color scheme emphasizes orange, peach, rust, and brown, with a softish focus. —*MM*

Movie: ♫♫ **DVD:** ♫♫▶
WinStar Home Entertainment (Cat #FLV5155, UPC #720917515526). Full frame. $24.98. Keepcase. *LANG:* English. *FEATURES:* 8 chapter links ⬝ Trailer ⬝ Cast and crew filmographies ⬝ Production credits.
1996 (R) 97m/C Jennifer Jason Leigh, Jena Malone, Ron Eldard, Glenne Headly, Lyle Lovett, Dermot Mulroney, Christina Ricci, Michael Rooker, Diana Scarwid, Susan Traylor, Grace Zabriskie; *D:* Anjelica Huston; *W:* Anne Meredith; *C:* Anthony B. Richmond; *M:* Van Dyke Parks. *AWARDS: NOM:* Independent Spirit Awards '97: Debut Performance (Malone).

The Bat

Oft-filmed plot, based on a Mary Robert Rinehart novel, revolves around a murderer called the Bat, who kills his victims by ripping out their throats when he isn't busy searching for a million dollars in securities stashed in the old house where he lives. The title is available as a double feature with the original 1958 edition of

The House on Haunted Hill (please see review).

Movie: ♫♫
Roan Group (Cat #2009). Full frame. Dolby Digital Mono. $29.95. Keepcase.
1959 80m/B Vincent Price, Agnes Moorehead, Gavin Gordon, John Sutton, Lenita Lane, Darla Hood; *D:* Crane Wilbur; *W:* Crane Wilbur; *C:* Joseph Biroc; *M:* Louis Forbes.

Bat 21

Hackman, an American officer, is stranded in the jungles of Vietnam after his plane is shot down. He must rely on himself and on Glover, with whom he has radio contact, to get him out. The stars give typically excellent performances in a fact-based story that has developed a strong following among war-film fans.

Movie: ♫♫▶ **DVD:** NYR
USA Home Entertainment (Cat #83495). $29.95.
1988 (R) 112m/C Gene Hackman, Danny Glover, Jerry Reed, David Marshall Grant, Clayton Rohner, Erich Anderson, Joe Dorsey; *D:* Peter Markle; *W:* Marc Norman, William C. Anderson; *C:* Mark Irwin; *M:* Christopher Young.

The Bat Whispers

The plot of this early sound comic mystery is nothing special. It retraces the elements already familiar from *The Old Dark House* and *The Cat and the Canary*. Instead, the film is notable as an early experiment with widescreen techniques. It was actually made in two separate versions with different cinematographers, one in 35mm, the other in 65mm. Both are included on the DVD. Generally, the film looks good on disc, though both versions display considerable "snow" throughout and the tiny flecks are all the more noticeable because the film is so dark. The extensive use of model buildings and cars is a delightfully quaint touch. In his extensive liner notes, Richard Valley describes the film's production and the controversy that later surrounded director West. —*MM*

Movie: ♫♫♫ **DVD:** ♫♫♫▶
Image Entertainment (Cat #ID5921MLSD-VD, UPC #014381592122). Full frame; widescreen (2.00:1) letterboxed. Dolby Digital Mono. $29.99. Snapper. *LANG:* English. *FEATURES:* 12 chapter links ⬝ Liner notes: Richard Valley of *Scarlet Street* magazine.
1930 82m/B Chester Morris, Chance Ward, Richard Tucker, Wilson Benge, DeWitt Jennings, Una Merkel, Spencer Charters; *D:* Roland West; *W:* Roland West; *C:* Ray June, Robert Planck.

Bataan

When this film was released in 1943, the fall of the Philippines following the attack on Pearl Harbor was a vivid, painful memory to American audiences. This rousing piece of propaganda is a successful

attempt to turn that military defeat into an emotional victory. The formula is the now-familiar "unit" picture where a bunch of scrappy soldiers, sailors, and fliers form a ragtag unit to hold a bridge and delay the Japanese advance while the rest of the American forces escape. The result is a movie that set new standards of explicit violence on-screen. The DVD appears to have been made from a near-perfect print with only a few inconsequential nicks marring Sidney Wagner's superb black-and-white cinematography. Monaural sound is just fine. Any war movie fan who has missed this one is in for a treat. —*MM*

Movie: ♫♫♫▶ **DVD:** ♫♫♫▶
MGM Home Entertainment (Cat #907662, UPC #027616766229). Full frame. Dolby Digital Mono. $24.98. Keepcase. *LANG:* English; French. *SUB:* English; French. *CAP:* English. *FEATURES:* 28 chapter links ⬝ Theatrical trailer.
1943 115m/B Robert Taylor, George Murphy, Thomas Mitchell, Desi Arnaz Sr., Lee Bowman, Lloyd Nolan, Robert Walker, Barry Nelson, Phillip Terry, Tom Dugan, Roque Espiritu, Kenneth Spencer, Alex Havier, Donald Curtis, Lynne Carver, Bud Geary, Dorothy Morris; *D:* Tay Garnett; *W:* Robert D. (Robert Hardy) Andrews; *C:* Sidney Wagner; *M:* Bronislau Kaper, Eric Zeisl.

Batman

This blockbuster fantasy epic renewed Hollywood's faith in media blitzing. The Caped Crusader is back in Gotham City, where even the criminals are afraid to walk the streets alone. There's a new breed of criminal in Gotham, led by the infamous Joker. The random attacks via acid-based makeup are just the beginning. Keaton is surprisingly good as the dual personality hero though Nicholson steals the show. Marvelously designed and shot. At first look, the DVD might appear a little dark and uncomfortable to watch. That's only because we're all used to the previous video versions where the blacks were a little off and the overall image brightened for more comfortable viewing. This DVD corrects all that and you can now see *Batman* the way it looked in the theatre. These blacks are perfect and the colors are accurate. There is almost no color bleed. The image is very sharp and there is less grain than in most brighter discs. The sound is nothing short of excellent. The bass will rattle the windows without being boomy, the highs are crisp, and the 5.1 Surround mix quite amazing. —*JO*

Movie: ♫♫♫▶ **DVD:** ♫♫♫♫
Warner Home Video, Inc. (Cat #12000, UPC #085391200024). Widescreen (1.85:1) letterboxed; full frame. Dolby Digital 5.1; Dolby Surround. $24.98. Snapper. *LANG:* English; French. *SUB:* Spanish; French. *CAP:* English. *FEATURES:* 31 chapter links ⬝ Production notes.
1989 (PG-13) 126m/C Michael Keaton, Jack Nicholson, Kim Basinger, Robert Wuhl, Tracey Walter, Billy Dee Williams, Pat Hingle, Michael Gough, Jack Palance, Jerry

Hall; **D:** Tim Burton; **W:** Sam Hamm, Warren Skaaren; **C:** Roger Pratt; **M:** Danny Elfman, Prince. *AWARDS:* Academy Awards '89: Best Art Direction/Set Decoration.

Batman and Robin

There's a lot of flash but not much substance in this fourth adventure, which features a less angst-ridden Caped Crusader in the charming persona of Clooney. O'Donnell, who apparently knows a good gig when he's got one, returns as Robin. They must battle evil industrialist Mr. Freeze (an impressively costumed Schwarzenegger), and his partner-with-the-deadly-kiss (but what a way to go), Poison Ivy (Thurman), who have plans to freeze Gotham City. Our heroes have some additional help in the person of Batgirl (Silverstone), who's now butler Alfred's (Gough) ward (she was Commissioner Gordon's daughter in the comics). Comic book hero's more fanatic fans complain about the film's camp and high-gloss tone. Although I prefer the Tim Burton *Batmans*, this is another amazing DVD. The film's neon colors are accurately vibrant, with the excellent contrast and brightness levels making them even more intense. The image is extremely sharp and grain is negligible, as are artifacts. Even though the film is so much brighter, the blacks are still dead-on. No great surprise, but the soundtrack is also killer, with dynamics from a whisper to a scream and good crisp highs accompanied by rumbling lows. The Surround mix is also top-notch. *—JO*
Movie: 🐾 **DVD:** 🐾🐾🐾🐾
Warner Home Video, Inc. (Cat #16500, UPC #085391650027). Widescreen (1.85:1) anamorphic. Dolby Digital 5.1. $24.98. Snapper. *LANG:* English; French. *SUB:* Spanish; French. *CAP:* English. *FEATURES:* 42 chapter links • Production notes.
1997 (PG-13) 125m/C George Clooney, Chris O'Donnell, Arnold Schwarzenegger, Uma Thurman, Alicia Silverstone, Michael Gough, Pat Hingle, John Glover, Elle Macpherson, Vivica A. Fox, Vendela Thommessen, Jeep Swenson; **D:** Joel Schumacher; **W:** Joel Schumacher, Akiva Goldsman; **C:** Stephen Goldblatt; **M:** Elliot Goldenthal. *AWARDS:* Golden Raspberry Awards '97: Worst Supporting Actress (Silverstone); *NOM:* Golden Raspberry Awards '97: Worst Picture, Worst Remake/Sequel, Worst Supporting Actor (O'Donnell, Schwarzenegger), Worst Supporting Actress (Thurman), Worst Director (Schumacher), Worst Screenplay, Worst Song ("The End is The Beginning is The End").

Batman Forever

Holy franchise, Batman! Third-time actioner considerably brightens up Tim Burton's dark vision for a more family-oriented Caped Crusader (now played by Kilmer, who fills out lip requirement nicely). The Boy Wonder also makes a first-time appearance in the bulked-up form of

O'Donnell, a street-smart Robin with revenge on his mind. Naturally the villains steal the show: Carrey as the Riddler, and the sartorially splendid Jones as Harvey "Two-Face" Dent. Rounding out this charismatic cast is Kidman's slinky psychologist Chase Meridian, who's eager to find the man inside the bat. Lots of splashy toys and awe-inspiring sets to show you where the money went. Another testimony to aggressive marketing: *Batman Forever* did $53 million for its opening weekend boxoffice. On the DVD, the image specs are still up there with the other *Batman* DVDs, but the soundtrack is a little lacking. Its main problem is delivering the different elements (music, effects, and dialogue) with their own individual clarity. The dialogue is buried most often, with some lines near inaudible even with the mix's excellent separation. The picture is very sharp and grain-free. The colors are bright and vibrant (just as in *Batman & Robin*) and the blacks are true. Brightness and contrast levels remain steady no matter the lighting and add even more to the color. Oh, what the hell, you may as well complete the set. *—JO*
Movie: 🐾🐾 **DVD:** 🐾🐾🐾
Warner Home Video, Inc. (Cat #15100, UPC #085391510024). Widescreen (1.85:1) anamorphic. Dolby Digital 5.1; Dolby Surround. $24.98. Snapper. *LANG:* English (DD5.1); French (DS). *SUB:* Spanish; French. *CAP:* English. *FEATURES:* 39 chapter links • Production notes.
1995 (PG-13) 121m/C Val Kilmer, Tommy Lee Jones, Jim Carrey, Chris O'Donnell, Nicole Kidman, Drew Barrymore, Debi Mazar, Michael Gough, Pat Hingle, Jon Favreau, George Wallace, Don "The Dragon" Wilson, Ed Begley Jr., Rene Auberjonois, Joe Grifasi, Jessica Tuck, Kimberly Scott; **D:** Joel Schumacher; **W:** Janet Scott Batchler, Akiva Goldsman, Lee Batchler; **C:** Stephen Goldblatt; **M:** Elliot Goldenthal. *AWARDS:* Blockbuster Entertainment Awards '96: Action Actress, Theatrical (Kidman); *NOM:* Academy Awards '95: Best Cinematography, Best Sound; Golden Globe Awards '96: Best Song ("Hold Me, Thrill Me, Kiss Me, Kill Me"); MTV Movie Awards '96: Most Desirable Male (Kilmer), Best Villain (Carrey, Jones), Best Song ("Kiss from a Rose", "Hold Me, Thrill Me, Kiss Me, Kill Me").

Batman Returns

More of the same from director Burton, with Keaton ably returning as the Caped Crusader, and another batch of provocative villains. DeVito is the cruelly misshapen Penguin who seeks to rule over Gotham City; Pfeiffer is the exotic and dangerous Catwoman who has more than a passing purr-sonal interest in Batman; Walken is the maniacal tycoon Max Schreck. Pfeiffer is the highlight in her wickedly sexy role and second-skin costume (complete with bullwhip). Weirder than the first, with great special effects and Burton's nightmarish settings. This grandiose sequel is of the love-it-or-leave-it

variety; personally, I loved it. Yes, yet another superb DVD in the *Batman* series. In this one, director Burton used a very grainy film stock, similar to ones that have wreaked havoc on some DVD transfers. But the disc looks just great with a super sharp picture and grainless (no added digital grain) handling of both light and dark sequences. The colors are exactly as in the theatre and do not bleed. Blacks are also true. The sound is very good, with distinct Surround separation, full body, and great low end. However, it would not have been a bad idea to boost the dialogue tracks for the home video release. *—JO*
Movie: 🐾🐾🐾 **DVD:** 🐾🐾🐾
Warner Home Video, Inc. (Cat #15000, UPC #085391500025). Widescreen (1.85:1) anamorphic. Dolby Digital 5.1; Dolby Surround. $24.98. Snapper. *LANG:* English (DD5.1); French (DS). *SUB:* Spanish; French. *CAP:* English. *FEATURES:* 39 chapter links • Production notes.
1992 (PG-13) 126m/C Michael Keaton, Danny DeVito, Michelle Pfeiffer, Christopher Walken, Michael Gough, Michael Murphy, Cristi Conaway, Pat Hingle, Vincent Schiavelli, Jan Hooks, Paul (Pee-wee Herman) Reubens, Andrew Bryniarski; **D:** Tim Burton; **W:** Daniel Waters; **C:** Stefan Czapsky; **M:** Danny Elfman. *AWARDS: NOM:* Academy Awards '92: Best Makeup, Best Visual Effects.

*batteries not included

As a real estate developer fights to demolish a New York tenement, the five remaining residents are aided by tiny metal visitors from outer space in their struggle to save their home. Each resident gains a renewed sense of life in this sentimental, wholesome family film produced by Spielberg. Cronyn and Tandy keep the schmaltz from getting out of hand and the little space critters are neat. This is a so-so DVD that makes you think they just transferred the VHS tape to a DVD. The picture is only of average sharpness and there is some grain and even a few artifacts. Colors appear a little washed-out and when they are a little more intense, they bleed quite a bit. Brightness is good but the disc could use a little more contrast—this might have helped the colors a little as well. The 5.1 sound, though an improvement over the VHS and the laserdisc, is no great shakes but adequate. *—JO*
Movie: 🐾🐾 **DVD:** 🐾🐾
Universal Studios Home Video (Cat #20520). Widescreen (1.85:1) anamorphic. Dolby Digital 5.1; Dolby Surround. $24.98. Keepcase. *LANG:* English (DD5.1); French (DS). *SUB:* English; Spanish. *FEATURES:* 19 chapter links • Theatrical trailer • Cast and filmmakers bios • Film highlights.
1987 (PG) 107m/C Hume Cronyn, Jessica Tandy, Frank McRae, Michael Carmine, Elizabeth Pena, Dennis Boutsikaris; **D:** Matthew Robbins; **W:** Matthew Robbins,

Brad Bird, Brent Maddock, S.S. Wilson; **C:** John McPherson; **M:** James Horner.

Battlecade: Extreme Fighting

"Extreme" fighting is an essentially unregulated form of public entertainment that has moved such luminaries as George Will to, yet again, predict the eminent collapse of western civilization as we know it. The disc is an accurate, unvarnished recording of bouts that took place in Wilmington, NC, in November 1995. For all the controversy, it's relatively tame. The fighters don't bite or gouge; no ripped ears. It's more like Olympic wrestling—not the hyperventilating professional madness—with submission holds. Considering the overall level of violence—both real and fictional—in society, the reaction to this particular form is overwrought. If the fights on these discs are representative, the potential for serious injury to the participants is less than it is for NFL linemen. The DVDs look better than you might expect for an essentially low-budget production with good lighting and sound and a welcome lack of extraneous pyrotechnics. —*MM*
Movie: 🎵🎵 **DVD:** 🎵🎵🎵
Image Entertainment (Cat #ID5583FMDVD, UPC #014381558324). Full frame. Dolby Digital Mono. $24.98. Snapper. *LANG:* English. *FEATURES:* 9 chapter links.
1995 120m/C

Battlecade: Extreme Fighting 2

This disc is a record of the second "extreme" fight that took place in 1996 on an Indian reservation outside Montreal. It's essentially the same as the first. —*MM*
Movie: 🎵🎵 **DVD:** 🎵🎵🎵
Image Entertainment (Cat #ID5584FM DVD, UPC #0143815584-25). Full frame. Dolby Digital Stereo. $24.99. Snapper. *LANG:* English. *FEATURES:* 15 chapter links.
1996 92m/C

The Battleship Potemkin

Eisenstein's best work documents the mutiny aboard the Russian battleship Potemkin in 1905, which led to a civilian uprising against the Czar in Odessan, and the resulting crackdown by troops loyal to the Czar. Beautiful cinematography, especially the use of montage sequences, changed filmmaking. In particular, a horrifying sequence depicting the slaughter of civilians on an Odessa beach by soldiers coming down the stairs is exceptional; many movies pay homage to this scene including *The Untouchables* and *Love and Death*. Viewers should overlook the obvious Marxist overtones and see the film for what it is: a masterpiece. The DVD features the mid-'70s restoration of this 1926 classic. The pre-print is flawed but

looks great for a film of this vintage, and is by far the best home video version. Although somewhat contrasty, the black-and-white image is sharp and there is very little of the ghosting around the edges of bright objects that is fairly common in these older films. The Shostakovich score sounds great even in mono. —*JO* **AKA:** Potemkin; Bronenosets Potemkin.
Movie: 🎵🎵🎵🎵 **DVD:** 🎵🎵🎵▶
Image Entertainment (Cat #ID4574COD-DVD, UPC #014381457421). Full frame. Mono. $24.98. Snapper. *LANG:* Russian. *SUB:* English. *FEATURES:* 12 chapter links.
1925 71m/B *RU* Alexander Antonov, Vladimir Barsky, Grigori Alexandrov, Mikhail Gomorov, Sergei Eisenstein, I. Brobov, Beatrice Vitoldi, N. Poltavseva, Alexandr Levshin, Repnikova, Korobei, Levchenko; **D:** Grigori Alexandrov, Sergei Eisenstein; **W:** Nina Agadzhanova Shutko, Sergei Eisenstein; **C:** Eduard Tisse; **M:** Dimitri Shostakovich.

Battlestar Galactica

Pilot episode of the TV series was released theatrically. Seen now on DVD, its appeal is mostly camp. Even fans will have to admit that it's made up of warmed-over elements from *Star Wars* and *Star Trek*. With the enhanced clarity of this medium, the shortcomings in special effects are perhaps more obvious than they have been either on conventional broadcast or on the big screen. At best, the production values do not rise above their made-for-TV roots and the effects shots are heavily grained. —*MM*
Movie: 🎵🎵 **DVD:** 🎵🎵
Universal Studios Home Video (Cat #20570, UPC #025192057021). Widescreen (1.85:1) letterboxed. Dolby Digital Mono. $24.98. Keepcase. *LANG:* English; French. *CAP:* English. *FEATURES:* 18 chapter links • Production notes • Cast and crew thumbnail biographies • Universal web links.
1978 (PG) 125m/C Lorne Greene, Dirk Benedict, Maren Jensen, Jane Seymour, Patrick Macnee, Terry Carter, John Colicos, Richard A. Colla, Laurette Spang, Richard Hatch; **D:** Richard A. Colla; **W:** Glen Larson, Richard A. Colla; **C:** Ben Colman; **M:** Stu Phillips.

Battling Butler

The three films on this disc—"Battling Butler," "The Haunted House," "The Frozen North"—are not Keaton's best, but they have their moments. In the first, director-star Keaton plays a wealthy young fop who impersonates a championship boxer to impress a girl. In the second, he's a bank teller. The third, taken from an incomplete print, is the roughest of the lot. All of them exhibit the flickering that comes with silent projection speed and, except "Frozen North," look pretty good. These are recommended mostly for Keaton's fans. —*MM*
Movie: 🎵🎵🎵 **DVD:** 🎵🎵▶

Image Entertainment (Cat #K128DVD, UPC #738329012823). Full frame. $29.99. Snapper. *FEATURES:* 22 chapter links.
1926 70m/B Buster Keaton, Sally O'Neil, Snitz Edwards, Francis McDonald, Mary O'Brien, Tom Wilson, Walter James; **D:** Buster Keaton; **W:** Al Boasberg, Lex Neal, Charles Henry Smith, Paul Girard Smith; **C:** Bert Haines, Devereaux Jennings.

Baywatch: Nightmare Bay / River of No Return

Two episodes of the popular syndicated television series about babes, hunks, and swimwear.
Movie: 🎵▶ **DVD:** NYR
Pioneer Entertainment (Cat #10242). Full frame. Dolby Digital Stereo. $29.98. Keepcase.
1994 178m/C David Hasselhoff.

Bean

Theatrical adaptation of rubber-faced Atkinson's Mr. Bean begins with our disaster-magnet hero working as a guard at London's Royal National Gallery. Circumstances find him assigned as an "expert" to accompany "Whistler's Mother" to a Los Angeles gallery. He stays with David (MacNicol), the American curator, and causes catastrophe after catastrophe from the moment he sets foot on the plane. Atkinson proves himself to be a master of the almost lost art of slapstick comedy. Perhaps the most valuable feature of the DVD is the choice of widescreen and full-frame images. The routines that focus most closely on Atkinson are actually more effective without the theatrical veneer. Others, including his inspired confrontation in LAX, need the widescreen. Since so much of Atkinson's comedy is accomplished without words, the sound is fine. —*MM*
Movie: 🎵🎵🎵 **DVD:** 🎵🎵🎵
USA Home Entertainment (Cat #440 046 913-2, UPC #044004691321). Full frame; widescreen (1.85:1) letterboxed. Dolby Digital 5.1 Surround Stereo; Dolby Digital Surround Stereo. $19.95. Keepcase. *LANG:* English; French. *SUB:* Spanish. *CAP:* English. *FEATURES:* 15 chapter links • Cast and crew thumbnail biographies • Teasers and trailers.
1997 (PG-13) 92m/C *GB* Rowan Atkinson, Peter MacNicol, Pamela Reed, Harris Yulin, Burt Reynolds, Larry Drake, Johnny Galecki, Richard Gant, Tom McGowan, Dakin Matthews, Peter Capaldi, Sandra Oh, Tricia Vessey, Peter Egan; **D:** Mel Smith; **W:** Richard Curtis, Robin Driscoll; **C:** Francis Kenny; **M:** Howard Goodall.

The Bears & I

Bob Leslie (Wayne), a Vietnam vet, helps Indians regain their land rights while he raises three bear cubs whose mother has been killed by evil hunters. This live-action Disney adventure was produced by Winston Hibler, who was also responsible for so many of the studio's nature films in the 1950s and '60s. On DVD, a few flecks are visible on the print, but they're nothing serious. The main attraction is the sanitized scenery and the cute furry woodland critter stuff. —MM

Movie: 🎬🎬 **DVD:** 🎬🎬🎬
Anchor Bay (Cat #DV10892, UPC #013131089295). Widescreen (1.85:1) letterboxed; full frame. Dolby Digital Mono. $24.98. Keepcase. *LANG:* English. *FEATURES:* 24 chapter links.
1974 (G) 89m/C Patrick Wayne, Chief Dan George, Andrew Duggan, Michael Ansara; **D:** Bernard McEveety; **W:** Jack Speirs, John Whedon; **C:** Ted D. Landon; **M:** Buddy (Norman Dale) Baker.

Beast Cops

Until the last quarter of the film, director Chan's *Beast Cops* is more of a buddy/buddy cop flick than a shoot 'em up. But don't worry, once it passes that point, the cops live up to their titular name and deliver a brutal slaughter worthy of the finest and/or vilest of Hong Kong action films. The near-romantic build-up makes the climax seem even all the more violent. Wong is excellent as the cop who loves the whoring and gambling that he uses to stay in touch with his mob contacts. The DVD is only slightly above average. The picture is a little harsh and at the same time soft. Grain and artifacts both take regular turns. Colors are faded and the contrast level is low. There is a little too much brightness. The 5.1 soundtrack provides some punch but also clips and distorts sporadically throughout the film. —JO *AKA:* Yeshou Xingjing.

Movie: 🎬🎬🎬 **DVD:** 🎬🎬
Media Asia (Cat #MS/DVD/036/98, UPC #489501700367). Widescreen (1.77:1) letterboxed. Dolby Digital 5.1. $29.95. Keepcase. *LANG:* Cantonese; Mandarin; English. *SUB:* Traditional & Simplified Chinese; English; Japanese; Korean; Bahasa Malaysia; Thai; Spanish. *FEATURES:* 9 chapter links • Production notes • 4 theatrical trailers.
1998 108m/C HK Anthony Wong, Michael Wong, Roy Cheung; **D:** Gordon Chan; **W:** Gordon Chan, Chan Hing-Kai.

Beat the Devil

Each person on a slow boat to Africa has a scheme to beat the other passengers to the uranium-rich land which they all hope to claim. This unusual black comedy did not fare well when released theatrically but over the years, it has become the epitome of spy spoofs. Also available with *Call It Murder.*

Movie: 🎬🎬🎬 **DVD:** NYR
Madacy Entertainment (Cat #99110). Dolby Digital Mono. $12.98. Keepcase.
1953 89m/C Humphrey Bogart, Gina Lollobrigida, Peter Lorre, Robert Morley, Jennifer Jones, Edward Underdown, Ivor Barnard, Bernard Lee, Marco Tulli; **D:** John

Huston; **W:** John Huston, Truman Capote; **C:** Oswald Morris; **M:** Franco Mannino.

The Beatles: The First U.S. Visit

About half of this black-and-white documentary is live (not lip-synched) performances of musical numbers shot on the *Ed Sullivan Show* and at a Washington, D.C., concert in the early months of 1964. The rest is unstaged footage of four incredibly young guys going through the prosaic side of rock stardom. Riding in taxis and trains, waiting in hotel rooms, mugging for photographers, plugging their stuff with DJs, generally fooling around and killing time. David and Albert Maysles tell the story without narration. Those who are younger may well wonder how and why such a few simple, catchy pop tunes generated such a global uproar, so perhaps a little explanation is in order. All of this took place less than four months after the assassination of President Kennedy. The world was just beginning to recover from a profound state of shock and "the four moptops," as they were called, offered something fresh and different. They were an innocent antidote, and, as they would show a year or so later in *A Hard Day's Night*—which is remarkably similar to this film—they refused to take themselves seriously. This film may not capture the sheer scope of hysteria that was "Beatlemania" but it does show those heady days as they were without any false sweetness. Because the film was made without the best lighting and sound systems, it is so rough that on DVD, the imperfections are heightened. One of the live numbers is almost painful to listen to in the opening bars. To have enhanced the sound digitally would have missed the point, and so the disc is filled with extras. —MM

Movie: 🎬🎬🎬 **DVD:** 🎬🎬🎬
MPI Home Video (Cat #DVD6218, UPC #030306621821). Full frame. Dolby Digital Mono. $24.98. Keepcase. *LANG:* English. *SUB:* English; French; Spanish. *FEATURES:* Thumbnail biographies of the Maysles and the Beatles • Numerous Beatles factoids, statistics, lists, and trivia • 15 chapter links.
1991 85m/B Paul McCartney, Ringo Starr, John Lennon, George Harrison, Ed Sullivan; **D:** Albert Maysles, David Maysles.

Beau Pere

This French import has become much more controversial in the years since its first release in 1981. The subject is the changing relationship between Remi (Dewaere), a 29-year-old man, and Marion (Besse), his 14-year-old stepdaughter, after the death of her mother. That's potentially explosive, exploitative material but director Blier handles it deftly. His main point is that maturity doesn't necessarily have much to do with age. Remi is never going to grow up and will always lean on the strongest emotional support. Marion may be inexperienced but she's

not stupid and knows what she wants. The film ends with an unusual but perfectly realistic and satisfying conclusion. On DVD, the image quality is slightly superior to the tape, though, like any film of its age, this one has a slightly faded look. The subtitles are particularly easy to read. The spare jazzy soundtrack sounds fine. —MM *AKA:* Stepfather.

Movie: 🎬🎬🎬 **DVD:** 🎬🎬
WinStar Home Entertainment (Cat #FLV5053, UPC #720917505329). Widescreen (2.35:1). $24.98. Keepcase. *LANG:* French. *SUB:* English. *FEATURES:* 9 chapter links • Filmographies • Production credits.
1981 125m/C FR Patrick Dewaere, Nathalie Baye, Ariel Besse, Maurice Ronet, Genevieve Mnich, Maurice Risch, Macha Meril, Rose Thiery; **D:** Bertrand Blier; **W:** Bertrand Blier; **C:** Sacha Vierny; **M:** Philippe Sarde.

Beautiful Girls

Slow but easy-going film highlights the differences between men and women in relationships. A 10-year high school reunion reunites buddies Tommy (Dillon), Kev (Perlich), Paul (Rappaport), Mo (Emmerich), and Willie (Hutton). They ice-fish, drink, and talk about women (about whom they haven't a clue). All are smitten by Andrea (Thurman), the gorgeous visiting cousin of another friend, and Willie becomes intrigued by Marty (Portman), his precociously tantalizing 13-year-old neighbor. The guys' whining gets annoying and the women are strictly secondary characters, but O'Donnell's tirade about fake femininity is refreshing. On this no-frills disc, neither sound nor image is an important improvement over VHS tape. —MM

Movie: 🎬🎬 **DVD:** 🎬🎬
Buena Vista Home Entertainment (Cat #16453). Widescreen (1.85:1) letterboxed. Dolby Digital Stereo. $29.99. Keepcase. *LANG:* English. *CAP:* English.
1996 (R) 110m/C Matt Dillon, Timothy Hutton, Michael Rapaport, Max Perlich, Noah Emmerich, Lauren Holly, Uma Thurman, Natalie Portman, Mira Sorvino, Martha Plimpton, Rosie O'Donnell, Annabeth Gish, Pruitt Taylor Vince, Sam Robards, David Arquette, Anne Bobby, Richard Bright; **D:** Ted Demme; **W:** Scott Rosenberg; **C:** Adam Kimmel; **M:** David A. Stewart.

Beauty and the Beast

Beautiful Belle, the daughter of a half-ruined merchant, goes to the castle of a half-man, half-beast creature to save her father, who has been sentenced to death by the frightening resident of the castle. But she finds the Beast is not so inhuman as he looks. The classic medieval fairy tale has been retold on the screen countless times, but this first cinematic telling is still the definitive *B&B*. Cocteau, the poet of the cinema, uses the film's famous set-pieces and clever special-effects trickery (for its day) to create a story of surreal beauty and lasting romanticism. High marks to Criterion for the extras, but especially for the digital restoration efforts, which make the DVD more than watchable. Thousands of bits of debris and tears were digitally removed from or repaired in the video image. It's still not pristine, but the film looks better than it has looked in years. —MB *AKA:* La Belle et la Bete.

Movie: ♫♫♫♫ **DVD:** ♫♫♫
Criterion Collection (Cat #BEA120, UPC #037429122020). Full frame. Dolby Digital Mono. $39.95. Keepcase. *LANG:* French. *SUB:* English. *FEATURES:* 32 chapter links • Documentary about the film and the fable • Original fable translated into English • Commentary: film historian Arthur Knight • Demonstration of restoration.
1946 90m/B *FR* Jean Marais, Josette Day, Marcel Andre, Mila Parely, Nane Germon, Michel Auclair; **D:** Jean Cocteau; **W:** Jean Cocteau; **C:** Henri Alekan; **M:** Georges Auric.

Beauty and the Beast: The Enchanted Christmas

Video premiere sequel to the popular Disney animated feature.
Movie: ♫♫ **DVD:** NYR
Buena Vista Home Entertainment (Cat #15282). Full frame. Dolby Digital 5.1. $34.99. Keepcase.
1997 89m/C **M:** Rachel Portman; **V:** Robby Benson, Angela Lansbury, Tim Curry, Bernadette Peters, Paige O'Hara, Jerry Orbach, David Ogden Stiers, Paul (Pee-wee Herman) Reubens, Haley Joel Osment.

Beauty Investigator

Two ditzy policewomen (Lee and Oshima) go undercover as nightclub hostesses to capture a rapist and soon find themselves in the middle of mob action. The martial arts, like the rest of the plot, are more silly than serious. The general level of the image is better than tape, but not much. The action blurs in fast-moving scenes. Black uniforms and clothes are solid, undifferentiated masses. —MM
Movie: ♫♫ **DVD:** ♫♫
Tai Seng Video Marketing (Cat #58614). Full frame. $19.95. Keepcase. *LANG:* English. *FEATURES:* 14 chapter links • Trailers.
1993 90m/C Moon Lee, Yukari Oshima, Sophia Crawford; **D:** Lee Jua Nan; **W:** Chung Jie Zang; **C:** Kwan Zhe Chin; **M:** Michael Fung.

Beavis and Butt-Head Do America

MTV's moronic metalheads go on the road in search of their stolen TV and are somehow mistaken for youthful hitmen. Writer-director-voice of B&B-H Mike Judge does-

n't change his creations for their first feature-length adventure. They're still perpetually horny and out of touch with everything else that is going on around them. The opening sequence, a parody of a '70s cop show, is hilarious and cool. Those who have come to understand Judge's humor and style through the TV series *King of the Hill* may be open to this one, too. Judge's simple, almost crude animation presents no problems for DVD, or for tape, so the only real difference is in accessibility. —MM
Movie: ♫♫♫ **DVD:** ♫♫►
Paramount Home Video (Cat #15561, UPC #097361556147). Widescreen anamorphic. Dolby Digital 5.1 Surround Stereo; Dolby Digital Surround Stereo. $29.99. Keepcase. *LANG:* English. *SUB:* English. *FEATURES:* 30 chapter links • 2 trailers.
1996 (PG-13) 82m/C **D:** Mike Judge; **W:** Mike Judge, Joe Stillman; **M:** John Frizzell; **V:** Mike Judge, Robert Stack, Cloris Leachman, Demi Moore, Eric Bogosian, Richard Linklater. *AWARDS:* NOM: MTV Movie Awards '97: Best On-Screen Duo (Beavis/Butt-head).

Bed and Board

Part four in Truffaut's Antoine series. *AKA:* Domicile Conjugal.
Movie: ♫♫ **DVD:** NYR
WinStar Home Entertainment (Cat #5122). $29.98. Keepcase. *LANG:* French. *SUB:* English. *FEATURES:* Cast and crew thumbnail biographies • Production notes • Trailer • Tribute to Jean-Pierre Leaud.
1970 100m/C *FR* Jean-Pierre Leaud, Claude Jade, Barbara Laage, Daniel Ceccaldi, Daniel Boulanger, Pierre Maguelon, Jacques Jouanneau, Jacques Rispal, Jacques Robiolles, Pierre Fabre, Billy Kearns, Hiroko Berghauer, Daniele Girard, Claire Duhamel, Sylvana Blasi, Claude Vega, Christian de Tiliere, Annick Asty, Marianne Piketi, Guy Pierauld, Marie Dedieu, Marie Irakane, Yvon Lec, Ernest Menzer, Christophe Vesque; **D:** Francois Truffaut; **W:** Francois Truffaut, Bernard Revon, Claude de Givray; **C:** Nestor Almendros; **M:** Antoine Duhamel.

Bed of Roses

Wistful romance finds workaholic investment banker Lisa Walker (Masterson) receiving lavish floral tributes from an unknown admirer. When Lisa tracks him down, it turns out to be lovestruck widowed florist Lewis Farrell (Slater). While walking late one night, he looked up to her apartment window and saw her crying. Is this guy too good to be true or what? Beyond the extras, the DVD is really not much better than VHS tape. The film's appeal on any medium lies in two very good performances from two very good actors. —MM *AKA:* Amelia and the King of Plants.
Movie: ♫♫♫ **DVD:** ♫♫♫
New Line Home Video (Cat #N4784, UPC #794043478420). Widescreen (1.85:1) anamorphic; full frame. Dolby Digital 5.1

Surround Stereo; Dolby Digital Surround Stereo. $24.98. Snapper. *LANG:* English. *CAP:* English. *FEATURES:* 19 chapter links • Cast and crew thumbnail biographies • Jann Arden "Insensitive" music video • Theatrical trailer.
1995 (PG) 88m/C Christian Slater, Mary Stuart Masterson, Pamela Segall, Josh Brolin, Ally Walker, Debra Monk; **D:** Michael Goldenberg; **W:** Michael Goldenberg; **C:** Adam Kimmel; **M:** Michael Convertino.

Beethoven

Sure-fire crowd-pleaser for the small set is a virtual live-action cartoon. It opens with our hero as an indescribably cute St. Bernard puppy. After a quick series of adventures, young B. finds himself in the Newton household. Dad (Grodin) is a strict disciplinarian who isn't about to have a dog in the home. But the rest of the family falls for the pup. The grown dog solves any problem that confronts the family, including nasty accountants and an evil vet (Jones).
Movie: ♫♫► **DVD:** NYR
Universal Studios Home Video (Cat #20027). $24.98. Keepcase. *LANG:* English; French; Spanish. *SUB:* Spanish.
1992 (PG) 89m/C Charles Grodin, Bonnie Hunt, Dean Jones, Oliver Platt, Stanley Tucci, Nicholle Tom, Christopher Castile, Sarah Rose Karr, David Duchovny, Patricia Heaton, Laurel Cronin; **D:** Brian Levant; **W:** John Hughes, Amy Holden Jones; **C:** Victor Kemper; **M:** Randy Edelman.

Beethoven's 2nd

Sequel has "awwww" factor going for it as new daddy Beethoven slobbers over four adorable and appealing St. Bernard pups and his new love Missy. Same basic evil subplot as the first, with wicked kidnappers replacing the evil vet. During the upheaval, the Newtons take care of the little yapping troublemakers, providing the backdrop for endless puppy mischief and exasperation on Grodin's part. Silly subplots and too many human moments tend to drag, but the kids will find the laughs. Considering this is a Universal Home Video release, this DVD is pretty bad (it's actually about average). The picture is not very sharp, although there is not that much grain or artifacting. Colors seem washed-out and appear to shift in hue intermittently. If they weren't so washed-out, there would be too much red and as it is there is a lot of pink. Blacks are almost true but have a tendency towards graininess. Sound is another non-event, lifeless and middy, with little low end, and very little Surround. —JO
Movie: ♫♫ **DVD:** ♫♫
Universal Studios Home Video (Cat #20270, UPC #02519202702). Widescreen (1.85:1) anamorphic. Dolby Surround. $24.98. Keepcase. *LANG:* English; Spanish; French. *SUB:* Spanish. *CAP:* English. *FEATURES:* 16 chapter links • The-

atrical trailer ▪ Production notes ▪ Cast and filmmakers bios ▪ Film highlights.

1993 (PG) 87m/C Charles Grodin, Bonnie Hunt, Nicholle Tom, Christopher Castile, Sarah Rose Karr, Debi Mazar, Christopher Penn, Ashley Hamilton; **D:** Rod Daniel; **W:** Len Blum; **C:** Bill Butler; **M:** Randy Edelman. *AWARDS: NOM:* Academy Awards '93: Best Song ("The Day I Fall in Love"); Golden Globe Awards '94: Best Song ("The Day I Fall in Love").

Beetlejuice

Here's a delightfully cheesy haunted-house farce in which the audience's sympathies are with the ghosts (Baldwin and Davis). They're ultra-nice and ultra-novice spirits whose post-living tranquility is disturbed by an obnoxious family that moves into their house. Unable to frighten away the interlopers on their own, they enlist the services of a maniacal poltergeist who promises to rid their house of trespassers. As it works out, they were better off without the help of Keaton, who contributes a wonderfully over-the-top performance as the demonic title character (though he spells it "Betelgeuse"). Other notable performances: Ryder is striking as the misunderstood teen with a death complex, while O'Hara is hilarious as the yuppie art poseur. The art direction is inventive and surreal, and it is rendered with crisp detail on the DVD not apparent on the earlier laserdisc. The audio is fun, too, thanks to Elfman's music, which also contributes much to Burton's other movies. After you watch the movie, groove to the music on the isolated score. —*MB*

Movie: ♪♪♪▶ **DVD:** ♪♪♪▶
Warner Home Video, Inc. (Cat #11785, UPC #085391178521). Widescreen (1.85:1) letterboxed; full frame. Dolby Digital 5.1. $24.98. Snapper. *LANG:* English; French; Spanish. *SUB:* English; French; Spanish. *CAP:* English. *FEATURES:* 28 chapter links ▪ Theatrical trailer ▪ Production Notes ▪ Isolated music score.

1988 (PG) 92m/C Michael Keaton, Geena Davis, Alec Baldwin, Sylvia Sidney, Catherine O'Hara, Winona Ryder, Jeffrey Jones, Dick Cavett, Glenn Shadix, Robert Goulet; **D:** Tim Burton; **W:** Michael McDowell, Warren Skaaren; **C:** Thomas Ackerman; **M:** Danny Elfman. *AWARDS:* Academy Awards '88: Best Makeup; National Society of Film Critics Awards '88: Best Actor (Keaton).

Before Sunrise

Light "getting-to-know-you" romance unfolds as two twentysomethings share an unlikely 14-hour date. Jesse (Hawke) and French beauty Delphy meet on the Eurail and he persuades her to join him in exploring Vienna (and their mutual attraction) before he heads back to the States in the morning. They exchange life stories and philosophies in typical Linklater conversational fashion, but the film stays away from the comical accounts of earlier works. Cinematographer Daniel captures

the Old World with finesse, particularly in the inevitable "first kiss" atop the Ferris wheel made famous in Orson Welles's *The Third Man*. The DVD image is slightly better than VHS tape, but this is not a particularly strong film visually. Sound is also an improvement, but performances and locations are the keys to the film. —*MM*

Movie: ♪♪♪ **DVD:** ♪♪♪
Warner Home Video, Inc. (Cat #2531). Full frame; widescreen letterboxed. $19.98. Snapper. *LANG:* English; French. *SUB:* English; French. *FEATURES:* 25 chapter links.

1994 (R) 101m/C Ethan Hawke, Julie Delpy; **D:** Richard Linklater; **W:** Richard Linklater, Kim Krizan; **C:** Lee Daniel. *AWARDS:* Berlin International Film Festival '94: Best Director (Linklater); *NOM:* MTV Movie Awards '95: Best Kiss (Ethan Hawke/Julie Delpy).

The Beguiled

During the Civil War a wounded Union soldier (Eastwood) is taken in by the women at a girl's school in the South. He manages to seduce both a student and a teacher, and jealousy and revenge ensue. Decidedly weird psychological melodrama from action vets Siegel and Eastwood, who had the guts to make a movie where one of the main themes was amputation. This is one of those DVDs that made me want to watch the full frame instead of the widescreen, which felt a little over-matted. Unfortunately, there is no full frame on the disc. Despite that, this is a good DVD with a sharp picture and crisp accurate colors. Blacks are handled well and the contrast and brightness levels are also very good. A few scenes had some slightly aggravating grain, but it didn't occur too often. The mono sound is full-bodied and crisp with no clipping or other distortion. —*JO*

Movie: ♪♪♪ **DVD:** ♪♪♪
Universal Studios Home Video (Cat #20238, UPC #025192023828). Widescreen (1.85:1) anamorphic. Dolby Digital 2.0 Mono. $24.98. Keepcase. *LANG:* English; French. *SUB:* Spanish. *CAP:* English. *FEATURES:* 16 chapter links ▪ Theatrical trailer ▪ Production notes ▪ Cast and filmmakers bios.

1970 (R) 109m/C Clint Eastwood, Geraldine Page, Elizabeth Hartman, Jo Ann Harris; **D:** Donald Siegel; **W:** Albert (John B. Sherry) Maltz, Irene (Grimes Grice) Kamp; **C:** Bruce Surtees; **M:** Lalo Schifrin.

Being John Malkovich

A puppeteer (Cusack) discovers a small door behind a filing cabinet. The door leads to a tunnel that takes him literally into the head of actor John Malkovich (playing himself). The rest of this comedy is just as off-center and original as the premise. The humor is certainly not for everyone, and director Spike Jonze's approach is equally original. The film is not particularly strong in visual terms, combining dim lighting with an independent-production look and many close-ups

of puppets. The strongest aspects of the DVD then are the numerous extras. Wisely, the producers elected to keep all of them, including Jonze's comments, separate from the film. —*MM*

Movie: ♪♪♪ **DVD:** ♪♪♪
USA Home Entertainment (Cat #0597572). Widescreen letterboxed. Dolby Digital 5.1 Surround Stereo. $24.95. Snapper. *LANG:* English. *SUB:* English; French; Spanish. *FEATURES:* 32 chapter links ▪ Trailer and TV spots ▪ 7 1/2 floor orientation film ▪ Malkovich featurette ▪ Puppeteering featurette ▪ Background driving featurette ▪ Spike Jonze interview and photo album ▪ Cast and crew thumbnail bios.

1999 (R) 112m/C John Cusack, Cameron Diaz, Catherine Keener, John Malkovich, Orson Bean, Mary Kay Place, Charlie Sheen; **D:** Spike Jonze; **W:** Charlie Kaufman; **C:** Lance Acord; **M:** Carter Burwell. *AWARDS:* British Academy Awards '99: Best Original Screenplay; Independent Spirit Awards '00: Best First Feature, First Screenplay; Los Angeles Film Critics Association Awards '99: Best Screenplay; MTV Movie Awards '00: Best New Filmmaker Award (Jonze); New York Film Critics Awards '99: Best Supporting Actor (Malkovich), Best Supporting Actress (Keener); National Society of Film Critics Awards '99: Best Film, Best Screenplay; *NOM:* Academy Awards '99: Best Director (Jonze), Best Original Screenplay, Best Supporting Actress (Keener); British Academy Awards '99: Best Film Editing, Best Supporting Actress (Diaz); Directors Guild of America Awards '99: Best Director (Jonze); Golden Globe Awards '00: Best Film—Musical/Comedy, Best Screenplay, Best Supporting Actress (Diaz, Keener); Independent Spirit Awards '00: Best Actor (Cusack); Screen Actors Guild Award '99: Best Supporting Actress (Diaz), Best Supporting Actress (Keener), Cast; Writers Guild of America '99: Best Original Screenplay.

Bell, Book and Candle

A young witch (Novak) makes up her mind to refrain from using her powers. When an interesting man (Stewart) moves into her building, she forgets her decision and enchants him with a spell. The transfer on this DVD is generally clean and without too many defects, but appears a little inconsistent in contrast and color. The anamorphic transfer is highly detailed with sharply defined edges but exhibits some grain, and the fact that colors appear washed-out in one shot, to be replaced by very vibrant tones in the next, makes the film appear aged and ripe for restoration. With its limited frequency response, the soundtrack sounds harsh and aged as well, due to the technical limitations of the time when the film was made. Despite these sonic insufficiencies, however, dialogue is always understandable and clear without overly noticeable noise. —*GH*

Movie: ♪♪▶ **DVD:** ♪♪♪

Columbia Tristar Home Video (Cat #01329, UPC #043396013292). Full frame; widescreen (1.85:1) anamorphic. Dolby Digital Mono. $25.95. Keepcase. *LANG:* English; Spanish. *SUB:* Spanish. *CAP:* English. *FEATURES:* 28 chapter links • Vintage advertising • Trailers • Talent files • Production notes.
1958 106m/C James Stewart, Kim Novak, Jack Lemmon, Elsa Lanchester, Ernie Kovacs, Hermione Gingold; *D:* Richard Quine; *W:* Daniel Taradash; *C:* James Wong Howe; *M:* George Duning. *AWARDS: NOM:* Academy Awards '58: Best Art Direction/Set Decoration, Best Costume Design.

Belle of the Nineties

Mae West struts her stuff as Ruby Carter, an 1890s singer involved with boxer Tiger Kid (Pryor). Her trademark sexual innuendos were already being censored but such lines as "It's better to be looked over than overlooked," done in West style, get the point across. So does her tight, slinky wardrobe. The creaky musical plot structure stops cold for songs. The quality of image and sound on the DVD are astonishing for a 1934 production, though the shadowy black-and-white photography and thin sound are less than perfect for a musical. Admittedly, Ms. West's voice was never the main attraction. —*MM* *AKA:* It Ain't No Sin.
Movie: ♫♫♪ *DVD:* ♫♫♫
Image Entertainment (Cat #ID4280USDVD, UPC #014381428025). Full frame. Uncompressed PCM Mono. $24.99. Snapper. *LANG:* English. *FEATURES:* 16 chapter links.
1934 73m/B Mae West, Roger Pryor, Johnny Mack Brown, John Miljan, Katherine DeMille, Harry Woods, Edward Gargan; *D:* Leo McCarey; *W:* Mae West; *C:* Karl Struss; *M:* Arthur Johnston.

The Bells / The Crazy Ray

The Bells is a silent ghost story that owes about as much to its source material (Poe's poem) as the Roger Corman drive-in movies of the early 1960s. Lionel Barrymore plays an innkeeper who resorts to murder to pay his debts. Boris Karloff makes a strong impression as the Mesmerist who might solve the crime. *The Crazy Ray* is a famous French sci-fi fantasy about a mad scientist who puts Paris to sleep. Part of it was shot on the Eiffel Tower. On DVD both films are remarkably clear with only a few fine scratches visible on the tinted images. The scores sound new. —*MM*
Movie: ♫♫♪ *DVD:* ♫♫♫
Image Entertainment (Cat #ID5832DSDVD, UPC #014381583229). Full frame. Dolby Digital Mono. $24.99. Snapper. *LANG:* Silent. *SUB:* English intertitles. *FEATURES: The Bells,* 12 chapter links • *The Crazy Ray,* 5 chapter links.
1926 67m/B Henri Rollan, Albert Prejean, Marcel Vallee, Madeleine Rodrigue, Lionel Barrymore, Boris Karloff, Gustav von Seyffertitz; *D:* James Young, Rene Clair; *W:* James Young; *C:* L.W. O'Connell.

The Bells of St. Mary's

Easy-going priest Father O'Malley (Crosby) finds himself in a subtle battle of wits with the Mother Superior (Bergman) over how the children of run-down St. Mary's school should be raised. It's the sequel to *Going My Way.* Songs include the title tune and "Aren't You Glad You're You?" The preprint used for the DVD transfer shows a little wear, but most of it (mainly some white flecks) just adds to the classic feel of the film. The black-and-white picture is very sharp, with excellent contrast and brightness levels. Graytones are also very good and the result is a lot of detail and depth on the screen. The crisp mono soundtrack is even cleaner than the picture. —*JO*
Movie: ♫♫♫♪ *DVD:* ♫♫♫
Republic Pictures Home Video (Cat #45506, UPC #017153550627). Full frame. Dolby Digital Mono. $24.98. Keepcase. *LANG:* English; Spanish; French. *SUB:* Spanish; French. *CAP:* English. *FEATURES:* 28 chapter links.
1945 126m/B Bing Crosby, Ingrid Bergman, Henry Travers; *D:* Leo McCarey; *W:* Dudley Nichols; *C:* George Barnes; *M:* Robert Emmett Dolan, Johnny Burke, James Van Heusen. *AWARDS:* Academy Awards '45: Best Sound; Golden Globe Awards '46: Best Actress—Drama (Bergman); New York Film Critics Awards '45: Best Actress (Bergman); *NOM:* Academy Awards '45: Best Actor (Crosby), Best Actress (Bergman), Best Director (McCarey), Best Film Editing, Best Picture, Best Song ("Aren't You Glad You're You"), Best Original Dramatic Score.

Belly

Toward the end of his commentary track, writer-producer-director Hype Williams whines that critics accused him of glorifying violence, drug use, and materialism for the first 90 minutes of his movie and then preaching against them for the last five minutes. The critics are right. He's wrong. That said, the story of two young criminal pals—Tommy (DMX) and Sincere (Nas)—whose careers take different paths is stylishly told. Williams uses his background in music videos to create some visually impressive scenes, though as he admits, he is less comfortable with physical action. For those not immersed in hip-hop, the final result is more bad than good. On DVD, the often-harsh lighting is re-created faithfully. Williams states that the dark murky shots are intentional. He doesn't mention the reflections of cameras and crews that intrude in one important scene. —*MM*
Movie: ♫♫ *DVD:* ♫♫♫
Artisan Entertainment (Cat #60738, UPC #012236073802). Widescreen (1.85:1) letterboxed. Dolby Digital 5.1 Surround Stereo. $29.98. Keepcase. *LANG:* English. *CAP:* English. *FEATURES:* 36 chapter links • Theatrical trailer • Cast and crew thumbnail biographies • Production notes • Commentary: Hype Williams.
1998 (R) 95m/C Nas, DMX, Taral Hicks, Tionne "T-Boz" Watkins, Method Man, Tyrin Turner, Hassan Johnson, Power, Louie Rankin, Minister Benjamin F. Muhammed; *D:* Hype Williams; *W:* Nas, Hype Williams, Anthony Bodden; *C:* Malik Hassan Sayeed; *M:* Stephen Cullo. *AWARDS: NOM:* Independent Spirit Awards '99: Best Cinematography.

Beloved

The Exorcist meets *The Color Purple* in an overlong adaptation of Toni Morrison's Pulitzer Prize–winning novel. In post–Civil War Ohio, Sethe (Winfrey) is haunted by the painful memories of slavery, both figuratively and literally in the form of a feral girl, Beloved (Newton). Paul D. (Glover) is another reminder of her past. Metaphors and symbols fill the screen as a connection is made between the girl and the child Sethe killed years before. Director Demme's experimental visuals—some questionable—may work slightly better on the small screen than in theatres, but the epic sense of the story doesn't translate as well. Again, that may be a positive; at three hours, the film has a sense of self-indulgence. On DVD, neither image nor sound display any real flaws. —*MM*
Movie: ♫♫♪ *DVD:* ♫♫♫
Buena Vista Home Entertainment (Cat #17243, UPC #717951002365). Widescreen (1.85:1) letterboxed. Dolby Digital 5.1 Surround Stereo. $29.99. Keepcase. *LANG:* English. *CAP:* English. *FEATURES:* 33 chapter links • Theatrical trailer • "Making of" featurette.
1998 (R) 172m/C Oprah Winfrey, Thandie Newton, Danny Glover, Kimberly Elise, Lisa Gay Hamilton, Beah Richards, Irma P. Hall, Albert Hall, Jason Robards Jr., Jude Ciccolella; *D:* Jonathan Demme; *W:* Akosua Busia, Richard LaGravenese, Adam Brooks; *C:* Tak Fujimoto; *M:* Rachel Portman. *AWARDS: NOM:* Academy Awards '98: Best Costume Design.

Beneath the 12–Mile Reef

Two rival groups of divers compete for sponge beds off the Key West coast. Lightweight entertainment notable for underwater photography and early Cinemascope production, as well as Moore in a bathing suit. The sharpness on this DVD is about average, with some grain appearing in very bright scenes. Considering the overall brightness, the contrast level is a little low, resulting in loss of detail. Colors are washed-out (preprint?) but judging from the fleshtones are fairly accurate. The sound is a little listless, with too little low end and too much mid range, which is too bad since the film features a fine score by Bernard Herrmann. —*JO*
Movie: ♫♫♪ *DVD:* ♫♫♪
Image Entertainment (Cat #ID9823DVD, UPC #017078982329). Widescreen

(2.35:1) letterboxed. Dolby Digital 2.0. $19.98. Snapper. *LANG:* English. *FEATURES:* 22 chapter links • Theatrical trailer.
1953 102m/C Robert Wagner, Terry Moore, Gilbert Roland, Richard Boone, Peter Graves, J. Carrol Naish; *D:* Robert D. Webb; *W:* A.I. Bezzerides; *C:* Edward Cronjager; *M:* Bernard Herrmann. *AWARDS: NOM:* Academy Awards '53: Best Color Cinematography.

Benji

In the loveable mutt's first feature-length movie, he falls in love with a female named Tiffany, and saves two young children from kidnappers. An immediate favorite with the short set, it was followed by sequels. Remarkably, the DVD looks much sharper and clearer than many more expensive productions from the mid-'70s. Despite the insipid theme, the film has always been one of the VideoHound's personal favs and in this new medium, it will probably find yet another generation of fans. —*MM*
Movie: 🎵🎵🎵 **DVD:** 🎵🎵🎵
Image Entertainment (Cat #ID48048BF DVD, UPC #0143814804-29). Full frame. Dolby Digital Mono. $24.99. Snapper. *LANG:* English. *FEATURES:* 14 chapter links.
1974 (G) 87m/C Benji, Peter Breck, Christopher Connelly, Patsy Garrett, Deborah Walley, Cynthia Smith; *D:* Joe Camp; *W:* Joe Camp; *C:* Don Reddy; *M:* Euel Box. *AWARDS:* Golden Globe Awards '75: Best Song ("I Feel Love"); *NOM:* Academy Awards '74: Best Song ("Benji's Theme (I Feel Love)").

Besieged

Fleeing bitter memories and political persecution in Africa, Shandurai (Newton) moves to Rome where she works as a housekeeper for Kinski (Thewlis), a pianist. The relationship between the two makes an oddly paced transition from the professional to the personal. In its best moments, the film is reminiscent of *The Unbearable Lightness of Being,* with a mature approach to eroticism. At many other times, though, the narrative is impenetrable. In their commentary track, director-cowriter Bertolucci and cowriter-associate producer Clare Peploe try to explain their reasons for the off-putting structure with its enigmatic editing. The film is told through muted colors that reflect the moody story. The technique also makes for a DVD that's less than spectacular in visual terms. The sound is fine, accenting the spare piano score. —*MM*
Movie: 🎵🎵▸ **DVD:** 🎵🎵🎵
New Line Home Video (Cat #N4859, UPC #794043485923). Widescreen (1.66:1) letterboxed; full frame. Dolby Digital Surround Stereo. $24.98. Snapper. *LANG:* English. *CAP:* English. *FEATURES:* 16 chapter links • Commentary: Bernardo Bertolucci and Clare Peploe • Reading of

short story "The Siege" by author James Lasdun.
1998 (R) 94m/C IT David Thewlis, Thandie Newton, Claudio Santamaria; *D:* Bernardo Bertolucci; *W:* Bernardo Bertolucci, Clare Peploe; *C:* Fabio Cianchetti; *M:* Alessio Vlad.

Best Laid Plans

The main problem with this fine little neo-noir is the box copy. Don't Read It! A key early plot point is revealed. The story involves three people—Nick (Nivola), a young man whose combination of intelligence, guile, and greed is enough to get him in trouble; his college pal Bryce (Brolin), who has recently moved to Tropico near Nick; and a young woman (Witherspoon), who calls herself Cathy. The three of them, and a few others, wrap themselves in a properly complex scheme that becomes uncomfortably threatening before it's over. On his commentary track, director Barker and assistant director Jeff Bayliss talk about the various revisions that were done to the story. It had three different endings—an alternative is included on the disc—and everyone will not be satisfied with the one that's here. Where traditional noir uses shades of black and dark gray, Barker plays with auburns, browns, and acid reds. They tend to give the action a soft focus, so the DVD is not particularly striking visually. Sound is equally unspectacular. The disc's main improvement over tape is in the extras—commentary and deleted scenes. Fans of *A Simple Plan* and *Very Bad Things* should give it a try. —*MM*
Movie: 🎵🎵🎵▸ **DVD:** 🎵🎵🎵▸
Twentieth Century Fox Home Entertainment (Cat #2000101, UPC #024543). Widescreen (1.85) anamorphic. Dolby Digital Surround Stereo; Dolby Digital 5.1 Surround Stereo. $34.98. Keepcase. *LANG:* English. *SUB:* English; Spanish. *CAP:* English. *FEATURES:* 17 chapter links • 9 deleted scenes • Commentary: Barker and assistant director Jeff Bayliss • Cast and crew thumbnail biographies.
1999 (R) 90m/C Alessandro Nivola, Josh Brolin, Reese Witherspoon, Rocky Carroll, Michael G. Hagerty, Jamie Marsh; *D:* Mike Barker; *W:* Ted Griffin; *C:* Ben Seresin; *M:* Craig Armstrong.

The Best Man

A collection of young good-looking actors plays a bunch of young successful, good-looking people. It's not much of a stretch. Harper Stewart (Diggs) is about to have his first novel featured as book of the month by *Oprah.* Problem number one: the novel chronicles his college life, and his friends'. Problem number two: Stewart is going to be the best man at his friend (and NFL star) Lance (Chestnut) and Mia's (Calhoun) wedding, and Stewart has seemingly dissed just about everyone he knows in the new book. The wedding party convenes; Stewart sweats; hilarity and trouble ensue; feelings are hurt; love blos-

soms; and everyone is handsome and beautiful. A predictable but very likable plot and charming cast. Long is especially lovely as Stewart's former flame. The picture is sharp and consistent, and the colors are vibrant. The sound is great with an outstanding musical soundtrack that does not overdo it when pushed to prominence. —*AB*
Movie: 🎵🎵🎵 **DVD:** 🎵🎵🎵▸
Universal Studios Home Video (Cat #20715, UPC #2519207152). Widescreen (1.85:1) anamorphic. Dolby Digital 5.1 Surround; DTS 5.1 Surround. Keepcase. *LANG:* English. *SUB:* English. *CAP:* English. *FEATURES:* 18 chapter links • Location feature • Production notes • Soundtrack presentation • Cast and filmmaker bios • Universal previews • Theatrical trailer • DVD-ROM capabilities.
1999 (R) 120m/C Taye Diggs, Monica Calhoun, Morris Chestnut, Nia Long, Melissa DeSousa, Harold Perrineau Jr., Terrence DaShon Howard, Sanaa Lathan, Victoria Dillard; *D:* Malcolm Lee; *W:* Malcolm Lee; *C:* Frank Prinzi; *M:* Stanley Clarke. *AWARDS: NOM:* Independent Spirit Awards '00: Best Supporting Actor (Howard).

The Best of British Cinema: Five Decades of Classic British Films

A showcase of some of the finest and most memorable feature films to be produced in major British studios during a 50-year period. This enjoyable five-episode documentary, first aired on British television, explores the richness and diversity of the British cinema, featuring a wide variety of genres and film types. The video transfer is admirable with, for the most part, fine colors and well-defined blacks. Some clips, however, seem to suffer from age deterioration. Consequently, several of the older scenes are extremely dark and feature muddied colors. The soundtrack is as crisp and impressive as a mono soundtrack can be. *MJT*
Movie: 🎵🎵▸ **DVD:** 🎵🎵▸
Image Entertainment (Cat #ID5951LFDVD, UPC #014381595123). Full frame. Dolby Digital Mono. $29.99. Snapper. *LANG:* English. *FEATURES:* 62 chapter links.
1988 120m/C GB *W:* Maurice Sellar, Lou Jones, Ashley Sidaway, Robert Sidaway; *Nar:* John Mills.

The Best of Times

Jack Dundee (Williams) thinks that everything in his life will change for the better if only he could relive his big high school football game and not drop the winning pass. Years later, he persuades his old teammates, including quarterback Reno Hightower (Russell), to challenge their longtime rival to a rematch. That's a thin premise. Writer Shelton handles sports material better in *Bull Durham* and *Tin Cup.* Aside from the few conventional extras, the DVD is identical to the VHS tape. —*MM*

Movie: 🎝🎝 **DVD:** 🎝🎝

Trimark Home Video (Cat #7000D, UPC #031398700036). Widescreen letterboxed. $24.99. English. *LANG:* English. *SUB:* French; Spanish. *CAP:* English. *FEATURES:* 30 chapter links • Robin Williams, Kurt Russell, Roger Spottiswoode filmographies • Trailers.

1986 (PG) 105m/C Robin Williams, Kurt Russell, M. Emmet Walsh, Pamela Reed, Holly Palance, Donald Moffat, Margaret Whitton, Kirk Cameron; *D:* Roger Spottiswoode; *W:* Ron Shelton; *C:* Charles F. Wheeler; *M:* Arthur B. Rubinstein.

The Best of Zagreb Film

This collection of short animated films from Yugoslavia owes nothing to Disney. These works are more experimental and do not follow conventional cartoon plots. They're definitely not for children; in fact, one of them, "Fisheye," is a horror story that is guaranteed to generate nightmares in any small fry who watch it. These are meant for adult fans of serious animation. Image is fine throughout. A bit of distortion is present but at least some of it appears to be intentional. Contents: Be Careful What You Wish For; Big Time; Curiosity; Musical Pig; Okay!; Elegy; The Fifth One; The Wall; Paranoia; The Ceremony; The Fly; Maxicat in the Hat, Lunch and Broom; Ersatz; Diary; Mask of the Red Death; Butterflies; Last Waltz in the Old Mill; Fisheye; Mass in A Minor. —*MM*

Movie: 🎝🎝▶ **DVD:** 🎝🎝🎝

Image Entertainment (Cat #ID9002ASDVD, UPC #014381900224). Full frame. Dolby Digital Mono. $24.99. Snapper. *FEATURES:* 19 chapter links.

? 114m/C *YU*

The Best Revenge

After his wife is tortured and murdered in El Salvador, Carlos (Riccelli) travels north and crosses the Mexican-American border illegally. He makes his way to Los Angeles and finds the location of the man he thinks responsible, a CIA advisor (Pine). That's when this suspense film begins to complicate itself. On DVD, neither sound nor image are particularly impressive; both are on a par with VHS tape. This is not a big-budget film. However, the story, approach, and seriousness are refreshingly different. —*MM*

Movie: 🎝🎝🎝 **DVD:** 🎝🎝

Image Entertainment (Cat #ID8906YODVD, UPC #014381890624). Full frame. Dolby Digital Stereo. $19.99. Snapper. *LANG:* English. *FEATURES:* 12 chapter links.

1996 88m/C Robert Pine, Carlos Alberto Riccelli; *D:* James Becket.

The Best Years of Our Lives

One of America's most honored films received the treatment it deserves on DVD. This edition has been restored to a clarity of sound and image that actually surpasses most theatrical releases. Since the film was made before the advent of widescreen processes, it fits onto a conventional TV screen with no loss, and good home video equipment will allow viewers to appreciate the complex "deep focus" that director Wyler and director of photography Toland were working with. The story revolves around three returning servicemen (March, Andrews, and Russell) after World War II. In a larger sense, though, the film is about a country trying to decide what to do with victory and with itself. The performances are superb, as is the restoration. Previous tape editions have looked pretty good, but the DVD is excellent. Notes in the extras section of the disc briefly explain how the film was cleaned up. My only reservation is a quibble; this is a two-sided disc that must be turned over midway through the film. Future editions may be made with a dual layer, which will eliminate the problem. —*MM*

Movie: 🎝🎝🎝🎝 **DVD:** 🎝🎝🎝🎝

HBO Home Video (Cat #90657, UPC #026359065729). Full frame. Dolby Digital Mono. $24.98. Snapper. *LANG:* English; French; Spanish. *CAP:* English. *FEATURES:* 34 chapter links • Trailer • Interviews with Virginia Mayo and Teresa Wright • Original poster • Awards • Notes on restoration • Cast and crew thumbnail biographies.

1946 170m/B Fredric March, Myrna Loy, Teresa Wright, Dana Andrews, Virginia Mayo, Harold Russell, Hoagy Carmichael, Gladys George, Roman Bohnen, Steve Cochran, Charles Halton, Cathy O'Donnell, Ray Collins, Victor Cutler, Minna Gombell, Walter Baldwin, Dorothy Adams, Don Beddoe, Ray Teal, Howland Chamberlain; *D:* William Wyler; *W:* Robert Sherwood; *C:* Gregg Toland; *M:* Hugo Friedhofer. *AWARDS:* Academy Awards '46: Best Actor (March), Best Director (Wyler), Best Film Editing, Best Picture, Best Screenplay, Best Supporting Actor (Russell), Best Original Dramatic Score; American Film Institute (AFI) '98: Top 100; British Academy Awards '47: Best Film; Golden Globe Awards '47: Best Film—Drama; National Board of Review Awards '46: Best Director (Wyler), National Film Registry '89; New York Film Critics Awards '46: Best Director (Wyler), Best Film; *NOM:* Academy Awards '46: Best Sound.

Betrayed by Innocence

Neglected by his attorney wife (Purcell), film director Nick DeLeon (Bostwick) is tempted into an affair with a mature-looking 16-year-old girl (Kauffman). Her father (Sorvino) takes serious objection. The made-for-TV drama looks fine on DVD but is nothing exceptional. —*MM*

Movie: 🎝🎝 **DVD:** 🎝🎝

Simitar Entertainment (Cat #7280, UPC #082551728022). Full frame. Dolby Digital Stereo. $14.98. Keepcase. *LANG:* English. *FEATURES:* 8 chapter links • Filmo-

graphies for Barry Bostwick and Paul Sorvino.

1986 94m/C Barry Bostwick, Lee Purcell, Paul Sorvino, Cristen Kauffman, Isaac Hayes, Susan Marie Snyder; *D:* Elliot Silverstein.

The Betsy

Typical Robbins pot-boiler about sex, greed, betrayal, and power in the automobile business. The main attraction is Olivier as a Henry Ford–type character with a curious Midwestern accent. The other members of the star-studded cast acquit themselves well enough, but somehow the movie isn't quite as trashy as it ought to be. If it were just a little bit worse, it would be a lot better. The no-frills DVD contains no noticeable flaws; it's an exceptionally clear version of a mediocre movie. —*MM*

AKA: Harold Robbins's The Betsy.

Movie: 🎝🎝 **DVD:** 🎝🎝▶

Warner Home Video, Inc. (Cat #864, UPC #012569086425). Full frame. Dolby Digital Mono. $14.98. Snapper. *LANG:* English; French. *CAP:* English. *FEATURES:* 33 chapter links.

1978 (R) 132m/C Laurence Olivier, Kathleen Beller, Robert Duvall, Lesley-Anne Down, Edward Herrmann, Tommy Lee Jones, Katharine Ross, Jane Alexander; *D:* Daniel Petrie; *W:* William Bast, Walter Bernstein; *C:* Mario Tosi; *M:* John Barry.

Better Than Chocolate

Sexy, sometimes funny coming-of-age story centers on young lesbian bohemian Maggie (Dwyer), who finds the woman of her dreams, an artist, Kim (Cox). Just as the two are setting up house, Maggie's wacky mother (Crewson) and brother (Mundy) show up. The four move in and share a loft with all the confusion and misunderstanding that accompanies. Maggie and Kim try to hide their relationship; Maggie's mom finds her own fulfillment while her brother experiences his own sexual awakening. Look for all the alternate lifestyle stereotypes: repressed lesbian bookshop owner, transvestite nightclub singer (with a heart of gold), biker chicks, and violent, hateful skinheads included. Made in Canada by director Anne Wheeler, the film looks good and sounds good. Since most of the scenes are interiors or at night in the rain, the DVD is rather dark, but the images are sharp, shots are well lit and all-around technically sound. Call it the independent film feel. —*AB*

Movie: 🎝🎝🎝▶ **DVD:** 🎝🎝🎝▶

Trimark Home Video (Cat #7253D, UPC #3139872533). Letterboxed. Dolby. $24.99. Keepcase. *LANG:* English. *SUB:* English; Spanish; French. *FEATURES:* Director's cut • 24 chapter links • Theatrical trailer • Commentary: director.

1999 (R) 101m/C *CA* Karyn Dwyer, Wendy Crewson, Christina Cox, Peter Outerbridge, Ann-Marie MacDonald, Kevin Mundy, Marya Delver, Jay Brazeau, Tony

Nappo; **D:** Anne Wheeler; **W:** Peggy Thompson; **C:** Gregory Middleton; **M:** Graeme Coleman.

A Better Tomorrow, Part 1

Two former hit men team up to bring down the mob boss who double-crossed them and sent one to prison and the other to the streets. One of them also has to protect his younger brother, a cop, from the gang. Considered one of the best of Woo's Hong Kong efforts; there's plenty of his hallmark balletic action and an interesting story. These Tai Seng DVDs aren't always the best, but they are consistently above average and watchable. Usually the problem seems to be the preprint and this one's no exception. Sharpness is above average, with a little grain sneaking in, usually during bright scenes. Colors are slightly washed-out, but bleed little and appear fairly true. Blacks are also close to true. Contrast is a little low and brightness is a little high. On the 5.1 soundtrack the gunfire overwhelms most everything else and the music is of average fidelity and lacking on the low end. —*JO* **AKA:** Ying Huang Boon Sik; Gangland Boss.

Movie: 🎬🎬🎬▶ **DVD:** 🎬🎬▶
Tai Seng Video Marketing (Cat #00664, UPC #060164300664). Widescreen (1.85:1) letterboxed. Dolby Digital 5.1. $29.98. Keepcase. *LANG:* Cantonese; Mandarin. *SUB:* English; Traditional & Simplified Chinese; Japanese; Korean; Malaysian; Indonesian; Thai. *FEATURES:* 9 chapter links • Theatrical trailers.
1986 95m/C *CH HK* Chow Yun-Fat, Leslie Cheung, Ti Lung, Emily Chu, Waise Lee, John Woo; **D:** John Woo; **W:** John Woo; **C:** Wing-hang Wong; **M:** Ka-Fai Koo.

A Better Tomorrow, Part 2

A smooth-talking gangster, who was killed in Part I, returns in Part II as the dead man's twin brother (unmentioned in Part I). He teams up with a cop and a reformed gangster to fight the forces of evil. Nobody combines sappy melodrama with stylized violence as well as Woo. The DVD is slightly improved in sharpness and color, which is much stronger and pretty accurate. Blacks are also truer and both the contrast and brightness levels are improved. Some of this is most likely due to better source material. The audio tracks are much the same as the first film, with average fidelity and just a light bit more low end. Gunfire once again dominates the Surround tracks, but overall the sound is pretty good. —*JO* **AKA:** Yinghung Bunsik 2.

Movie: 🎬🎬🎬 **DVD:** 🎬🎬🎬
Tai Seng Video Marketing (Cat #00674, UPC #060164300674). Widescreen (1.85:1) letterboxed. Dolby Digital 5.1. $29.98. Keepcase. *LANG:* Cantonese; Mandarin. *SUB:* English; Traditional & Simplified Chinese; Japanese; Korean;

Malaysian; Indonesian; Thai. *FEATURES:* 9 chapter links • Theatrical trailers.
1988 100m/C *HK* Chow Yun-Fat, Leslie Cheung; **D:** John Woo; **W:** John Woo; **M:** Joseph Koo.

Beverly Hills Ninja

Haru (Farley), a physically inept adopted son of a ninja is, nevertheless, sent to Beverly Hills on a rescue mission to break up a counterfeiting ring. Spoofy femme fatale Sheridan hires "the great white ninja" to follow her no-good boyfriend and becomes the object of Haru's desires. Farley's extraordinary gift for physical comedy is exploited to the hilt, and the increase in his tripping, stumbling (and in one harrowing scene, stripping) usually coincides with the fumbling of the plot. Rock's talents are squandered on a poorly conceived bellboy character. The film has a fairly soft focus throughout and so it gains little visually on DVD beyond the screen size options. Sound is adequate. —*MM*
Movie: 🎬▶ **DVD:** 🎬🎬▶
Columbia Tristar Home Video (Cat #3950, UPC #043396039506). Widescreen (1.85:1) letterboxed; full frame. Dolby Digital 5.1 Surround Stereo; Dolby Digital Surround Stereo. $24.95. Keepcase. *LANG:* English; Portuguese; Spanish. *SUB:* Korean; Portuguese; Spanish; Thai. *FEATURES:* 28 chapter links • Trailer • Cast and crew thumbnail biographies.
1996 (PG-13) 88m/C Chris Farley, Nicolette Sheridan, Robin Shou, Nathaniel Parker, Chris Rock, Soon-Teck Oh, Francois Chau, Keith Cooke Hirabayashi; **D:** Dennis Dugan; **W:** Mark Feldberg, Mitch Klebenoff; **C:** Arthur Albert; **M:** George S. Clinton. *AWARDS: NOM:* MTV Movie Awards '97: Best Comedic Performance (Farley).

Beware! Children at Play

Vile, lurid tale of cannibalistic children living in a Beowulf cult in the woods of New Jersey. An English literature professor and his son go missing on a camping trip. Years later the grown lad, who believes that he is Grendel (McClaughlin), kidnaps an ever-growing clan of local children to become his followers. Made in the spirit of legendary horror-trash filmmaker Herschell Gordon Lewis, this totally sub-par effort features among other things throat-cuttings, disembowelments, human sacrifice, and the climatic slaughter of the town's children by their parents. Troma has tried to make a silk purse out of this sow's ear by loading it up with a dozen or so extra features, most of which are juvenile amateurish home videos populated by Troma employees. —*RT*
Movie: 🎬 **DVD:** 🎬▶
Troma Team Video (Cat #9860, UPC #790357986033). Full frame. AC3 - 2 Channel. $24.98. Keepcase. *LANG:* English. *FEATURES:* 9 chapter markers • Tour of Troma • Troma Intelligence Test • 6 trailers.

1995 (R) 90m/C Michael Robinson, Eric Tonken, Jamie Krause, Mik Cribben, Danny McClaughlin; **D:** Mik Cribben; **C:** Mik Cribben.

Beyond Suspicion

Photographer Karen Reikhart (Kramer) takes pictures of corrupt cop Vince Morgan (Scalia) in action and promptly falls victim to amnesia. What are the two to do but begin a torrid affair? The curious thriller is exceptionally well photographed despite a modest budget. Night scenes are clearly lit and some of the close-ups reveal the texture of the stars' skin. Kramer and Scalia (and their body doubles) are actually better than the odd material, and doubtless this film is part of the reason both have developed genuine cult followings. The DVD sounds and looks better than many more expensive productions. Credit should be shared by director Paul Ziller and director of photography Bruce Worrall. —*MM*
Movie: 🎬🎬 **DVD:** 🎬🎬🎬
Image Entertainment (Cat #ID5861SVDVD, UPC #014381586121). Full frame. Dolby Digital Surround. $19.99. Snapper. *LANG:* English. *FEATURES:* 10 chapter links.
1994 102m/C Jack Scalia, Stephanie Kramer, Howard G.H. Dell; **D:** Paul Ziller; **W:** Simon Abbott; **C:** Bruce Worrall; **M:** Barron Abramovitch.

Beyond the Door 2

Mario Bava's story of psychic revenge and incestuous longings has nothing to do with the first *Beyond the Door*, though it was retitled as a sequel in this country apparently to capitalize on that film's inexplicable success. Young Marco (Colin Jr.) lusts for his mother Dora (Nicolodi) and tells her calmly that he's going to kill her. The final part of the three-character psycho-horror is Bruno (Steiner), her second husband. For once, Bava's vivid imagery and wild camerawork are used to describe complex emotional reality, not physical or narrative reality, and so his techniques are much more effective. Many fans consider this to be Bava's best and I agree, though *Black Sunday* is hard to top. Both image and sound are slightly soft but that quality comes from the original material. The film looks very good for a work of its age with virtually no significant flaws. —*MM* **AKA:** Shock; Shock (Transfer Suspense Hypnos); Suspense; Al 33 di Via Orologio fa Sempre Freddo.
Movie: 🎬🎬🎬 **DVD:** 🎬🎬🎬
Anchor Bay (Cat #DV11072, UPC #013131107296). Widescreen (1.85:1) anamorphic. Dolby Digital Mono. $24.98. Keepcase. *LANG:* English; French; Italian. *FEATURES:* 15 chapter links • Trailers and TV spots • Interview with assistant director Lamberto Bava.
1979 (R) 90m/C *IT* John Steiner, Daria Nicolodi, David Colin Jr., Ivan Rassimov, Nicola Salerno; **D:** Mario Bava; **W:** Lamberto Bava, Franco Barbieri, Dardano Sacchetti, Paolo Brigenti; **C:** Alberto Spagnoli.

The Bicycle Thief

De Sica's indisputable masterpiece is about Ricci (Maggiorani), a laborer who finds a job only to have someone steal the bike he must have to do the work. He and his son Bruno (Staiola) search Rome for it. The simple story seems to contain the whole of human experience. It's the acknowledged highpoint of Italian Neo-Realism. The only discernible flaw on the DVD is sound that wavers from time to time. The image captures the textured grays seen in so many post-war European films. The understated intensity has not aged a day. For those who dislike subtitles, the dialogue is available in either English or Italian. —*MM* **AKA:** Ladri di Biciclette.

Movie: ♪♪♪♪ **DVD:** ♪♪♪➧
Image Entertainment (Cat #ID4572CODVD, UPC #014381457223). Full frame. Dolby Digital Mono. $24.99. Snapper. *LANG:* Italian; English. *SUB:* English. *FEATURES:* 14 chapter links ● De Sica biography and filmography ● Liner notes by playwright Arthur Miller.
1948 90m/B *IT* Lamberto Maggiorani, Lianella Carell, Enzo Staiola, Elena Altieri, Vittorio Antonucci, Gino Saltamerenda, Fausto Guerzoni; *D:* Vittorio De Sica; *W:* Vittorio De Sica, Cesare Zavattini; *C:* Carlo Montuori; *M:* Alessandro Cicognini. *AWARDS:* Academy Awards '49: Best Foreign Film; British Academy Awards '49: Best Film; Golden Globe Awards '50: Best Foreign Film; National Board of Review Awards '49: Best Director (De Sica); New York Film Critics Awards '49: Best Foreign Film; *NOM:* Academy Awards '49: Best Screenplay.

Big

Twelve-year-old Josh Baskin makes a wish at a penny arcade fortune-teller and wakes up the next morning as an adult (Hanks). Though the film was made in the midst of a spate of child-adult transformation flicks, it rose above the pack. The reasons are easy to spot. First, Hanks's carefully shaded performance is brilliant. Second, director Marshall makes the human emotions much more important than the supernatural aspects of the plot. She and director of photography Michael Ballhaus give the proceedings a careful Hollywood sheen. On DVD, a few imperfections are visible in the carnival scene, but they're negligible. The stereo effects are fine and the widescreen transfer captures all of the action in the important toy store and party scenes. —*MM*

Movie: ♪♪♪ **DVD:** ♪♪♪
Twentieth Century Fox Home Entertainment (Cat #4112608, UPC #08616212 6086). Widescreen (1.85:1) letterboxed. Dolby Digital 2.0 Stereo. $29.98. Keepcase. *LANG:* English; French. *SUB:* Spanish. *CAP:* English. *FEATURES:* 24 chapter links ● Theatrical trailer.
1988 (PG) 98m/C Tom Hanks, Elizabeth Perkins, John Heard, Robert Loggia, Jared Rushton, David Moscow, Jon Lovitz, Mercedes Ruehl; *D:* Penny Marshall; *W:* Gary

Ross; *C:* Michael Ballhaus; *M:* Howard Shore. *AWARDS:* Golden Globe Awards '89: Best Actor—Musical/Comedy (Hanks); Los Angeles Film Critics Association Awards '88: Best Actor (Hanks); *NOM:* Academy Awards '88: Best Actor (Hanks), Best Original Screenplay.

Big Bad Mama

Tough and sexy machine-gun toting mother moves her two nubile daughters out of Texas during the Depression, and they all turn to robbing banks as a means of support while creating a sharp testosterone increase among the local men. Dickinson has a notable nude scene with Captain Kirk, making this a cult and cable favorite. The *Bonnie and Clyde* rip-off also features good B-movie gore. So-so DVD has at least barely respectable sharpness, but then the grain comes in and really messes things up. Colors are also dull (but still bleed) and blacks very often are even grainier and grayer. Brightness is adequate but the contrast needs a big boost. As you might expect, this low-budget effort was not a part of the film preservation project and there is substantial preprint damage. The mono sound is nothing special, but does the job. —*JO*

Movie: ♪♪ **DVD:** ♪➧
New Horizons Home Video (Cat #NH00136, UPC #736991413641). Full frame. Mono. $24.98. Keepcase. *LANG:* English. *FEATURES:* 24 chapter links ● Theatrical trailer ● Cast bios ● 8-page booklet ● Leonard Maltin interview of Roger Corman.
1974 (R) 83m/C Angie Dickinson, William Shatner, Tom Skerritt, Susan Sennett, Robbie Lee, Sally Kirkland, Noble Willingham, Royal Dano, Dick Miller, Joan Prather, Tom Signorelli; *D:* Steve Carver; *W:* William W. Norton Sr., Frances Doel; *C:* Bruce Logan; *M:* David Grisman.

The Big Brass Ring

Working from a script originally written by Orson Welles, F.X. Feeney and director George Hickenlooper spin out a complex, surprising political thriller. Blake Pellarin (Hurt) is close to winning the governor's race in Missouri when his mentor Mennaker (Hawthorne) shows up with old photographs that could ruin Pellarin's career. His equally ambitious wife (Richardson) and a curious reporter (Jacob) also play important parts. On their commentary track, Feeney and Hickenlooper talk briefly about the Hollywood business of getting their project off the ground, but they are more interested in Welles and the story's links to the work of Conrad and Twain. The DVD lacks bright clarity. Hickenlooper talks about the "monochromatic" look he was trying to achieve. The important scenes are all dimly lit and so the disc probably doesn't look much better than the VHS tape. The difference is in the extras. —*MM*

Movie: ♪♪♪ **DVD:** ♪♪♪

Columbia Tristar Home Video (Cat #04388, UPC #043396043886). Widescreen (1.77:1) letterboxed. Dolby Digital Surround Stereo. $27.95. Keepcase. *LANG:* English. *SUB:* English; French; Spanish. *CAP:* English. *FEATURES:* 28 chapter links ● Commentary: F.X. Feeney and George Hickenlooper ● Six deleted scenes ● Promotional trailers ● Cast and crew thumbnail biographies ● Production notes.
1999 (R) 104m/C William Hurt, Nigel Hawthorne, Miranda Richardson, Irene Jacob, Jefferson Mays, Ewan Stewart, Ron Livingston, Gregg Henry; *D:* George Hickenlooper; *W:* George Hickenlooper, F.X. Feeney; *C:* Kramer Morgenthau; *M:* Thomas Morse.

Big Bullet

Bill (Lau Ching Wan) is a cop who's demoted by an incompetent superior, but that doesn't stop him from getting into the middle of a *Die Hard* situation involving master criminals. If the film doesn't rise to the level of John Woo's inspired action pictures, it certainly moves quickly and Lau Ching Wan, like his countrymen Chow Yun-Fat and Anthony Wong, is a legitimate star. He's got a Lee Marvin mug of a face and a world-weary attitude to match. The overall quality of the image is very good, particularly in the big showy scenes. For the most part, the subtitles are colloquial, though the occasional "hex" error shows up in translation. —*MM*

Movie: ♪♪♪ **DVD:** ♪♪➧
Tai Seng Video Marketing (Cat #5021). Widescreen letterboxed. Dolby Digital 5.1 Surround Stereo. $49.95. Keepcase. *LANG:* Cantonese; Mandarin. *SUB:* Traditional Chinese; Simplified Chinese; English. *CAP:* English. *FEATURES:* 8 chapter links.
1996 90m/C Lau Ching Wan, Jordan Chan, Radium Cheung, Tat-Ming Cheung, Spencer Lam, Michael Ian Lambert; *D:* Benny Chan; *W:* Benny Chan, Suk-Yin Chan.

The Big Chill

Seven former '60s radicals, now coming upon middle age and affluence, reunite following a friend's suicide and use the occasion to examine their relationships and commitments. A beautifully acted, immensely entertaining and funny look at a generation and its problems. Kevin Costner is the dead man whose scenes did not make it to the theatrical screen. Even though this special edition DVD contains several deleted scenes, his were not among them. And, as is so often the case, the film really works better without those scenes. The disc with its remastered soundtrack looks as good as the theatrical release and probably sounds better. In a separate "retrospective documentary," director Kasdan, cowriter Barbara Benedek, other filmmakers and cast members take a fond look back at the work. It's a more effective way to comment on the film than a separate audio track running throughout. —MM

Movie: 🎵🎵🎵 **DVD:** 🎵🎵🎵▶

Columbia Tristar Home Video (Cat #02632, UPC #043396026322). Widescreen (1.85:1) letterboxed. Dolby Digital 5.1 Surround; Dolby Surround. $25.95. Snapper. LANG: English; French; Spanish. SUB: English; French; Spanish. FEATURES: 28 chapter links ▪ Retrospective documentary ▪ Deleted scenes ▪ Theatrical trailer.

1983 (R) 108m/C Tom Berenger, Glenn Close, Jeff Goldblum, William Hurt, Kevin Kline, Mary Kay Place, Meg Tilly, JoBeth Williams; **D:** Lawrence Kasdan; **W:** Lawrence Kasdan, Barbara Benedek; **C:** John Bailey. AWARDS: Writers Guild of America '83: Best Original Screenplay; NOM: Academy Awards '83: Best Original Screenplay, Best Picture, Best Supporting Actress (Close).

Big City Blues

Reynolds and Forsythe are assassins who become involved with a hooker.

Movie: 🎵🎵 **DVD:** NYR

Avalanche Entertainment (Cat #13996). Full frame. Dolby Digital Stereo. $24.95. Keepcase. SUB: Spanish. FEATURES: Cast and crew thumbnail biographies ▪ Trailer.

1999 (R) 94m/C Burt Reynolds, William Forsythe, Georgina Cates, Giancarlo Esposito, Roger Floyd, Balthazar Getty, Arye Gross, Donovan Leitch, Roxana Zal, Amy Lyndon, Jad Mager; **D:** Clive Fleury; **W:** Clive Fleury; **C:** David Bridges; **M:** Tomas San Miguel.

Big Combo

"First is first and second is nobody," snarls Mr. Brown (Conte), a maniacal gangster who always gets what he wants until the almost equally maniacal Lt. Diamond (Wilde) decides to clean up the mean streets. The object of both of their affections is Susan Lowell (Wallace), the original Suicide Blonde. Filling out the cast are Brown's lieutenant McClure (Donlevy), and two scene-stealing gunsels Fanty (Van Cleef) and Mingo (Holliman). As is so often the case with noir, the central story is less important than John Alton's first-rate black-and-white photography, and the overall nuttiness of the plotting. For 1955, the film is exceptionally violent. The DVD handles the often inky action with no visible flaws. The monaural sound is fine for David Raksin's brassy score. The main flaw is a low intermittent chatter that sounds like projector gears. It's an irritating but bearable intrusion in a rarely seen treat. —MM

Movie: 🎵🎵🎵 **DVD:** 🎵🎵🎵

Image Entertainment (Cat #ID6146TVDVD, UPC #014381614626). Full frame. Dolby Digital Mono. $24.99. Snapper. LANG: English. FEATURES: 16 chapter links.

1955 87m/B Cornel Wilde, Richard Conte, Jean Wallace, Brian Donlevy, Earl Holliman, Lee Van Cleef, Helen Walker; **D:**

Joseph H. Lewis; **W:** Philip Yordan; **C:** John Alton; **M:** David Raksin.

Big Daddy

To impress his ambitious girlfriend Vanessa (Swanson), underachieving Sonny (Sandler) becomes guardian to five-year-old Julian (Cole and Dylan Sprouse). Given that premise, Sandler's fans know pretty much what to expect, but they may be surprised by his comfortable performance. Though his phenomenally popular screen persona hasn't really changed, he seems to be evolving into a real actor. As is often the case with his comedies, the film has a grungy, lived-in look that probably isn't much clearer on DVD than it is on VHS tape. Sound is fine, though, and the disc contains the right number and kind of extras. —MM

Movie: 🎵🎵🎵 **DVD:** 🎵🎵▶

Columbia Tristar Home Video (Cat #03922, UPC #043396039223). Full frame; widescreen (1.85:1) letterboxed. Dolby Digital 5.1 Surround Stereo; Dolby Digital Surround Stereo. $25.95. Keepcase. LANG: English. SUB: English. FEATURES: 28 chapter links ▪ 2 music videos ▪ HBO "first look" featurette ▪ Cast and crew thumbnail biographies.

1999 (PG-13) 95m/C Adam Sandler, Cole Sprouse, Dylan Sprouse, Joey Lauren Adams, Jon Stewart, Leslie Mann, Josh Mostel, Rob Schneider, Kristy Swanson, Joseph Bologna, Steve Buscemi; **D:** Dennis Dugan; **W:** Steve Franks, Tim Herlihy, Adam Sandler; **C:** Theo van de Sande; **M:** Teddy Castellucci. AWARDS: Golden Raspberry Awards '99: Worst Actor (Sandler); NOM: Golden Raspberry Awards '99: Worst Picture, Worst Supporting Actor (Schneider), Worst Director (Dugan), Worst Screenplay.

The Big Doll House

Archetypal Philippine babes-behind-bars stars Pam Grier as one of a group of tormented female inmates who decide to break out. AKA: Women's Penitentiary 1; Women in Cages; Bamboo Dolls House.

Movie: 🎵🎵▶ **DVD:** NYR

New Horizons Home Video (Cat #20103). Full frame. $24.98. Keepcase. FEATURES: Roger Corman interview ▪ Cast and crew thumbnail biographies.

1971 (R) 93m/C Judy Brown, Roberta Collins, Pam Grier, Brooke Mills, Pat Woodell, Sid Haig, Christianne Schmidtmer, Kathryn Loder, Jerry Frank, Charles Davis; **D:** Jack Hill; **W:** Don Spencer; **C:** Fred Conde; **M:** Les Baxter, Hall Daniels.

The Big Easy

Uneven New Orleans thriller boasts a first-rate cast and a tricky plot with a few lapses. Remy McSwain (Quaid) uncovers a heroin-based mob war while romancing the uptight assistant D.A. (Barkin), who's investigating corruption within the police force. Quaid's Cajun accent wears thin quickly but the steamy bedroom scenes

he shares with Barkin have made the film an enduring audience favorite. The DVD image is an accurate re-creation of the theatrical release. It suffers mild pattern flash and the night exteriors are a bit harsh. Sound is a little flat, too. A bit better than VHS tape, perhaps, but not a lot. —MM

Movie: 🎵🎵▶ **DVD:** 🎵🎵▶

Trimark Home Video (Cat #7002D, UPC #031398700234). Widescreen letterboxed. Dolby Digital Mono. $24.99. Keepcase. LANG: English. SUB: English; French; Spanish. FEATURES: Trailer ▪ 30 chapter links ▪ Cast thumbnail bios.

1987 (R) 101m/C Dennis Quaid, Ellen Barkin, Ned Beatty, John Goodman, Ebbe Roe Smith, Charles Ludlam, Lisa Jane Persky, Tom O'Brien, Grace Zabriskie, Marc Lawrence; **D:** Jim McBride; **W:** Dan Petrie Jr.; **C:** Alfonso Beato; **M:** Brad Fiedel. AWARDS: Independent Spirit Awards '88: Best Actor (Quaid).

The Big Hit

Combustible mixture of extravagant stunts, cartoon violence, hip-hop soundtrack, and colorful young cast serves up an intermittently funny look at pretty-boy hitmen. When not working as assassins, Melvin, Cisco, Vince, and Crunch (Wahlberg, Phillips, Sabato Jr., and Woodbine) are regular working Joes with regular problems. For Melvin, financial and personal problems force him to partner with Cisco in the kidnapping of a Chinese heiress who turns out to be the goddaughter of their own crime boss. Hong Kong director Che-Kirk Wong brings flair to the action scenes and the film actually looks a little sharper on DVD than it did on theatre screens. Even so, it's still an air-weight piece of fluff. —MM

Movie: 🎵🎵▶ **DVD:** 🎵🎵🎵

Columbia Tristar Home Video (Cat #02606). Full frame; widescreen (1.85:1) letterboxed. Dolby Digital 5.1 Surround Stereo; Dolby Digital Surround. $28.95. Keepcase. LANG: English; French. SUB: English; French. FEATURES: 28 chapter links ▪ 3 deleted scenes ▪ Trailer ▪ Commentary: Che-Kirk Wong ▪ Commentary: writer and producer.

1998 (R) 91m/C Mark Wahlberg, Lou Diamond Phillips, Bokeem Woodbine, Antonio Sabato Jr., Christina Applegate, Avery Brooks, China Chow, Lainie Kazan, Elliott Gould, Lela Rochon, Sab Shimono; **D:** Kirk Wong; **W:** Ben Ramsey; **C:** Danny Nowak; **M:** Graeme Revell.

The Big Lebowski

Jeff Lebowski (Bridges) is a stuck-in-the-'70s stoner who insists on being called "the Dude" and loves to go bowling. Mistaken for a wheelchair-bound millionaire of the same name, he suffers a beating at the hands of thugs who are after money owed by the rich Lebowski's slutty wife. The Dude is drawn into a kidnapping, the attempted scamming of the payoff money, and more bowling. While this may not

seem like plot-a-plenty, it's mainly a showcase for the Coen Brothers' unique texturing of style and quirky-but-deep characters. Goodman is loud and funny as a Vietnam vet who takes any opportunity to pull a gun or explode into DI-like obscenities. Turturro steals his scenes as a pervert rival bowler who loves skintight lilac jumpsuits and polishing his ball. The showpiece is an amazing musical-bowling-fantasy sequence that would have made Busby Berkeley proud. One of my favorites; this film deserves a much better DVD presentation. The picture would have been sharp enough but for the bothersome grain that is in far too many scenes. Colors are hit or miss, ranging from dull to near spectacular, but don't bleed much. Brightness and contrast levels are good/very good with the more brightly lit scenes looking the best. The blacks are generally true (although there is an occasional increase in the grain). The 5.1 sound, however, is excellent, particularly the imaging on the Surround tracks. —JO
Movie: 𝄢𝄢𝄢▶ **DVD:** 𝄢𝄢
USA Home Entertainment (Cat #440 056 539-2, UPC #044005653922). Widescreen (1.77:1) anamorphic; full frame. Dolby Digital 5.1. $24.98. Keepcase. *LANG:* English. *SUB:* Spanish; French. *CAP:* English. *FEATURES:* 22 chapter links ▪ Teaser trailer ▪ Cohen Brothers interview ▪ Cast and filmmakers bios ▪ Dual-layered RSDL.
1997 (R) 117m/C Jeff Bridges, John Goodman, Steve Buscemi, Julianne Moore, Peter Stormare, David Huddleston, Philip Seymour Hoffman, Flea, Leon Russom, Sam Elliott, John Turturro, David Thewlis, Ben Gazzara, Tara Reid; *D:* Joel Coen; *W:* Joel Coen, Ethan Coen; *C:* Roger Deakins; *M:* Carter Burwell.

Big Night

Set in 1950s New Jersey, this film provides an Old World/New World look at Italian brothers Primo (Shalhoub) and Secondo (Tucci) Pilaggi and their elegant but failing restaurant. Primo is the perfectionist chef who hates compromise while Secondo wants to Americanize the place in an effort to make it a success. Secondo knows the customer is always right even if they can't appreciate Primo's exquisitely authentic Italian dishes. To get attention, Secondo arranges a special night in honor of jazz great Louis Prima, with Primo out to cook the feast of a lifetime if they can pull it off. This one's guaranteed to make you hungry. Sharpness is average at best, and there is some grain on the dimmer sequences. When the picture is brighter the colors tend to fog out and lose contrast. The blacks are also varied and range from gray to true. The Dolby Surround is actually very good and the soundtrack, made up of '50s tunes, is very punchy. —JO
Movie: 𝄢𝄢𝄢 **DVD:** 𝄢𝄢▶
Columbia Tristar Home Video (Cat #81019, UPC #04339681019). Widescreen (1.85:1) letterboxed. Dolby Sur-

round. NSL. Keepcase. *LANG:* English. *SUB:* Spanish. *CAP:* English. *FEATURES:* 33 chapter links ▪ Theatrical trailer.
1995 (R) 109m/C Tony Shalhoub, Stanley Tucci, Ian Holm, Minnie Driver, Campbell Scott, Isabella Rossellini, Marc Anthony, Allison Janney; *D:* Stanley Tucci, Campbell Scott; *W:* Stanley Tucci, Joseph Tropiano; *C:* Ken Kelsch. *AWARDS:* Independent Spirit Awards '97: First Screenplay; National Society of Film Critics Awards '96: Best Supporting Actor (Shalhoub); Sundance Film Festival '96: Best Screenplay; *NOM:* Independent Spirit Awards '97: Best First Feature, Best First Feature (Shalhoub, Tucci).

Big Red

Typical Disney fare revolves around an orphan boy (Payant), a prize-winning Irish Setter, and the dog's wealthy but unemotional owner (Pidgeon). The Quebec locations are nice, but this one's no *Old Yeller*. A few minor flecks are visible on the DVD image, but they're inconsequential for the target audience—kids who love dogs and dog stories. Sound is good. The disc's main asset is the inclusion of both widescreen and full-frame versions. —MM
Movie: 𝄢𝄢 **DVD:** 𝄢𝄢𝄢
Anchor Bay (Cat #DV11063, UPC #013131106398). Widescreen (1.85:1) letterboxed; full frame. Dolby Digital Mono. $24.98. Keepcase. *LANG:* English. *FEATURES:* 20 chapter links.
1962 89m/C Walter Pidgeon, Gilles Payant; *D:* Norman Tokar; *W:* Louis Pelletier; *C:* Edward Colman; *M:* Oliver Wallace, Richard M. Sherman, Robert B. Sherman.

The Big Red One

Fuller's harrowing semi-autobiographical account of the U.S. Army's famous First Infantry Division, "the Big Red One," is one of the finest war films ever made. The rifle squad (Hamill, Carradine, DiCicco, Ward) is led by the Sergeant (Marvin, in one of his finest roles) from North Africa through Sicily, Italy, then onto Omaha Beach on D-Day and into Europe where they confront the final horror of the war at a concentration camp. Fuller never lets the film's point of view rise above them. We see the war from their limited perspective and so even in the lighter, stranger moments, the film does not lose intensity. The DVD was made from a print that contains a few negligible scratches, but it looks fine. More importantly, the two-sided disc contains both the full-frame and widescreen versions of the film, though you learn that only by reading the fine print in the last lines of box copy. Reportedly, as much as 40% of the material that Fuller filmed was cut before its theatrical release. Many war movie fans have hoped that someday it would be restored on tape or disc, but to date that has not happened. —MM
Movie: 𝄢𝄢𝄢𝄢 **DVD:** 𝄢𝄢𝄢▶

Warner Home Video, Inc. (Cat #939, UPC #012569093928). Full frame; widescreen letterboxed. Dolby Digital Surround Stereo. $19.98. Snapper. *LANG:* English. *SUB:* English; French. *CAP:* English. *FEATURES:* 28 chapter links.
1980 (PG) 113m/C Lee Marvin, Robert Carradine, Mark Hamill, Stephane Audran, Bobby DiCicco, Perry Lang, Kelly Ward, Siegfried Rauch, Serge Marquand, Charles Macaulay, Alain Doutey, Maurice Marsac, Colin Gilbert, Joseph Clark, Ken Campbell, Doug Werner, Marthe Villalonga; *D:* Samuel Fuller; *W:* Samuel Fuller; *C:* Adam Greenberg; *M:* Dana Kaproff.

The Big Sleep

The DVD edition of one of Hollywood's seminal films noir shows just what the digital medium can accomplish. The disc contains two similar but significantly different versions of the film, along with supplemental material by Robert Gitt, Preservation Officer of the UCLA Film and Television Archives, detailing the changes and explaining the reasons behind them. Most fans are familiar with the inexplicably plotted mystery that detective Philip Marlowe (Bogart) must solve. Actually, the original 1945 version is a bit more explicably plotted, and anyone who hasn't discovered it is in for a rare treat. Beyond the extras, the DVD presentation shows off the studio black-and-white photography at its sharpest. Monaural sound is fine for Max Steiner's memorable Warner Bros. score. This disc belongs in every videophile's library, to learn who killed the chauffeur, if nothing else. —MM
Movie: 𝄢𝄢𝄢𝄢 **DVD:** 𝄢𝄢𝄢𝄢
Warner Home Video, Inc. (Cat #65026, UPC #012569502628). Full frame. Dolby Digital Mono. $19.98. Snapper. *LANG:* English. *SUB:* English; French. *CAP:* English. *FEATURES:* 32 chapter links ▪ Cast and crew thumbnail biographies ▪ Behind-the-scenes notes ▪ Explanatory material by Robert Gitt.
1946 114m/B Humphrey Bogart, Lauren Bacall, John Ridgely, Martha Vickers, Louis Jean Heydt, Regis Toomey, Peggy Knudsen, Dorothy Malone, Bob Steele, Elisha Cook Jr.; *D:* Howard Hawks; *W:* Jules Furthman, Leigh Brackett, William Faulkner; *C:* Sid Hickox; *M:* Max Steiner. *AWARDS:* National Film Registry '97.

The Big Squeeze

Engaging sleeper is the story of three men, two women, and one scam. Benny (Dobson) is a substandard conman. Henry (Bercovici) is an ex-baseball player who's found Jesus and lost his wife Tanya (Boyle). She tends bar where Jessie (Nucci), a shy gardener, is a regular. Her coworker Cece (Dispina) takes Benny in when he stops by to cadge a beer. Add in an impoverished church in desperate need of repairs and a $100,000 bank account ripe for the plucking, and everything's in place for a fine romantic comedy/caper movie. Writer-director De Leon maintains a

properly measured pace. Things move quickly enough to keep the conjob cooking but leisurely enough to let the characters reveal their quirky personalities. And these are interesting characters played by a talented ensemble cast. Throughout, the attitude is sexy, tricky, and irreverent in all the right ways. The DVD does not have the sparkle of some discs but that reflects the original. This one looks and sounds fine and the image is so clear that you can count Ms. Boyle's freckles. —MM
Movie: 🎬🎬🎬▶ **DVD:** 🎬🎬▶
WinStar Home Entertainment (Cat #FLV5167, UPC #720917516721). Full frame. Dolby Digital Stereo. $29.98. Keepcase. *LANG:* English. *FEATURES:* 12 chapter links • Production credits • Cast and crew filmographies.
1996 (R) 100m/C Lara Flynn Boyle, Peter Dobson, Luca Bercovici, Danny Nucci, Teresa Dispina, Sam Vlahos, Valente Rodriguez; **D:** Marcus De Leon; **W:** Marcus De Leon; **C:** Jacques Haitkin; **M:** Mark Mothersbaugh.

Big Wars

Man has colonized Mars, but he is not alone in the cosmos. An ancient race of alien beings, called The Gods, has been watching our progress. Now, these mysterious aliens have returned to put an end to mankind's expansion into space. Of course, you realize this means war! Mars and the solar system become battlegrounds, pitting humans against The Gods. The heroes are Captain Akuh and the crew of the Battleship Aoba. If his top-secret mission is successful, mankind will deal a decisive blow to its powerful enemy. Neither animation nor story is up to snuff compared to the best Japanese anime titles, but this tale is enjoyable enough. Colors are vibrant and image is sharp on the DVD, but there's nothing special about the soundtrack. No extras, either. —MB
Movie: 🎬🎬▶ **DVD:** 🎬🎬▶
Image Entertainment (Cat #ID4410CTDVD, UPC #014381441024). Widescreen (1.85:1) letterboxed. Dolby Digital 2.0. $24.99. Snapper. *LANG:* English; Japanese. *SUB:* English. *FEATURES:* 12 chapter links.
1993 110m/C JP

The Bikini Car Wash Company

No plot, but tons-o-babes in bikinis in Los Angeles. A young man is running his uncle's carwash when he meets a business major who persuades him to let her make over the business for a cut of the profits. She decides that a good gimmick would be to (un)dress all the female employees in the tiniest bikinis possible. The story is of course at best secondary to the amount of flesh on display, but occasionally the comedy works. An average DVD that could be sharper and have a lot less grain. There is also a fair amount of artifacts that blur the picture. The color is a little better and the fleshtones appear

to be very accurate. The disc is bright enough but needs more contrast and the blacks are never quite black. Topping it off is the sound, which is lame at best and distorted at its worst. —JO **AKA:** California Hot Wax.
Movie: 🎬 **DVD:** 🎬▶
Studio Home Entertainment (Cat #4005, UPC #065814940052). Full frame. Stereo. $24.98. Keepcase. *LANG:* English. *FEATURES:* 12 chapter links • Production notes.
1990 (R) 87m/C Joe Dusic, Neriah Napaul, Suzanne Browne, Kristie Ducati; **D:** Ed Hansen.

Bikini Hotel

How will Samantha (North) and friends save her inheritance, the Tiki Hotel, from the ruthless competition (Stevens)? Why not dress the staff up in bikinis! On DVD, the image of this latter-day beach picture is one short step up from your Uncle Bud's home movies, but that's somehow as it should be. The "making of" featurette accompanying the feature shows that the filmmakers shot most of the interiors in their own low-rent offices, and it proves that the sexy silliness came straight from the heart. These guys and girls were giving it their best shot. —MM
Movie: 🎬🎬 **DVD:** 🎬
Simitar Entertainment (Cat #7374, UPC #082551737420). Full frame. Dolby Digital Stereo. $14.98. Keepcase. *LANG:* English. *FEATURES:* 8 chapter links • Production factoids • "Making of" featurette • Julie Strain and Stella Stevens filmographies.
1997 95m/C J.J. North, Stella Stevens, Kareem Elseify; **D:** Jeff Frey.

Billy Jack

On an Arizona American Indian reservation, a half-breed ex–Green Beret (Laughlin) with pugnacious martial arts skills stands between a rural town and a school for runaways. The movie, the then-hit song "One Tin Soldier," and marketing by Laughlin inspired a "Billy Jack" cult phenomenon. It was followed by a sequel in 1974, *The Trial of Billy Jack,* which bombed; the best *Billy Jack* is the biker flick *Born Losers* (1967), which Laughlin likes to deny exists. Yet another great $14.98 DVD from Warner Bros. The colors are actually superior to what they were in the theatre and the picture is sharp, grain- and artifact-free, and packing a one–two punch of very good contrast and brightness. The blacks are good, though not perfect. The mono sound is lacking in low end but otherwise quite adequate. There are a few jumps in the film (and some scratches) due to preprint damage but it's all quite livable. —JO
Movie: 🎬🎬🎬 **DVD:** 🎬🎬🎬
Warner Home Video, Inc. (Cat #1040, UPC #012569104020). Full frame. Dolby Digital Mono. $14.98. Snapper. *LANG:* English. *FEATURES:* 36 chapter links.

1971 (PG) 112m/C Tom Laughlin, Delores Taylor, Clark Howat, Bert Freed, Julie Webb, Victor Izay, Teresa Kelly, Lynn Baker, Stan Rice, Howard Hesseman; **D:** Tom Laughlin; **W:** Tom Laughlin, Delores Taylor; **C:** Fred W. Koenekamp, John Stephens; **M:** Mundell Lowe.

Billy Madison

If an unholy genetic experiment were to combine DNA from Jerry Lewis and Pee Wee Herman, it would produce Billy Madison (Sandler). When his father (McGavin) is ready to retire, Billy decides to take over the family business, and vows to complete public school on his own, spending only two weeks in each class. His third grade teacher (Bridgette Wilson) is the blonde love interest. The rest of the film combines some sadistic physical humor with seamy, smirking sexual jokes—in an elementary school setting. Surprisingly, the DVD actually clarifies the cut-rate, grainy look that the film had in theatrical release. But is that really an improvement? —MM
Movie: 🎬 **DVD:** 🎬🎬
Universal Studios Home Video (Cat #20416, UPC #025192041624). Widescreen (1.85:1) letterboxed. Dolby Digital 5.1 Surround Stereo, Dolby Surround Stereo. $24.98. Keepcase. *LANG:* English; French; Spanish. *SUB:* Spanish. *CAP:* English. *FEATURES:* Production notes • Cast and filmmaker's thumbnail biographies • Film highlights • Theatrical trailer • Universal web links • 16 chapter links.
1994 (PG-13) 90m/C Adam Sandler, Darren McGavin, Bridgette Wilson, Bradley Whitford, Josh Mostel, Norm MacDonald, Mark Beltzman, Larry Hankin, Theresa Merritt, Chris Farley, Steve Buscemi; **D:** Tamra Davis; **W:** Adam Sandler; **C:** Victor Hammer; **M:** Randy Edelman. *AWARDS:* NOM: MTV Movie Awards '95: Best Comedic Performance (Sandler).

Billy's Hollywood Screen Kiss

Very gay Billy (Hayes) is an aspiring arts photographer in L.A. who's looking for romance. He thinks he's got a hot prospect in handsome-if-sexually-confused Gabriel (Rowe), a waiter/model. Billy's latest project is re-creating great film romantic scenes with drag queens and he hires Gabriel to play the male lover. Amusing feature film debut for director O'Haver always keeps things light and fluffy. Cult film director Bartel plays an old queen who attempts to exploit Gabe's good looks. The film's sweet and gentle nature is its biggest asset, along with its very likable cast. The colorful film has been very nicely rendered to DVD. The picture is sharp and the colors both lush and accurate. A nice boost to the color is given by very good brightness and contrast levels, which at the same time allow the blacks to remain true. The stereo sound is full-bodied with excellent space and imaging. —JO

Movie: 🎵🎵🎵 **DVD:** 🎵🎵🎵

Trimark Home Video (Cat #6900D, UPC #031398690030). Widescreen (2.35:1) letterboxed. Dolby Digital 2.0. $24.98. Keepcase. *LANG:* English. *SUB:* Spanish; French. *CAP:* English. *FEATURES:* 30 chapter links • Theatrical trailer • Commentary: director Tommy O'Haver.

1998 (R) 92m/C Sean P. Hayes, Brad Rowe, Richard Ganoung, Meredith Scott Lynn, Paul Bartel, Armando Valdes-Kennedy; *D:* Tommy O'Haver; *W:* Tommy O'Haver; *C:* Mark Mervis; *M:* Alan Ari Lazar.

Bird on a Wire

Rick (Gibson) is hiding in the Federal Witness Protection Program when he runs across old flame Marianne (Hawn) and the thug (Carradine) he's hiding from. A long comic chase ensues. Gibson wears a goofy-looking pony-tail; Hawn's character is irritating; and Carradine is plump. All involved have done much better. The DVD has problems, too. Noticeable flaws are revealed in a pan across the surface of a pond and a shake roof in one scene. The disc was made from a print marred by some flecks. —*MM*

Movie: 🎵🎵 **DVD:** 🎵🎵

Universal Studios Home Video (Cat #20318, UPC #025192031823). Widescreen (2.35:1) letterboxed. Dolby Digital Surround Stereo. $24.98. Keepcase. *LANG:* English; French. *SUB:* Spanish. *CAP:* English. *FEATURES:* Production notes • Cast and crew thumbnail biographies • Theatrical trailer • 16 chapter links.

1990 (PG-13) 110m/C Mel Gibson, Goldie Hawn, David Carradine, Bill Duke, Stephen Tobolowsky; *D:* John Badham; *W:* David Seltzer; *C:* Robert Primes; *M:* Hans Zimmer.

The Bird with the Crystal Plumage

An American writer (Musante) living in Rome witnesses a murder. He becomes more deeply involved when the alleged murderer is cleared because the woman believed to be his next victim is shown to be a psychopathic murderer herself. Of course it makes no sense; this is Argento. The DVD presents the unrated, 98-minute version of the film. Although generally clean and without distracting defects, the transfer unfortunately exhibits some problems that mostly result from the incorrectly set-up black level of the transfer; black never appears as true black but as dark grays throughout the presentation. As a result, the film's contrast is hampered, creating a washed-out, flat image without the depth of solid shadows. Due to the black level problem, the transfer exhibits signs of dot crawl and pixelation since much of the available bandwidth of the compression is spent coding/decoding redundant "black noise" rather than relevant picture information. —*GH* *AKA:* L'Ucello dalle Plume di Cristallo; The Phan-

tom of Terror; The Bird with the Glass Feathers; The Gallery Murders.

Movie: 🎵🎵► **DVD:** woof

VCI Home Video (Cat #8202, UPC #089859820229). Widescreen (2.35:1) anamorphic. Dolby Surround. $24.99. Keepcase. *LANG:* English. *FEATURES:* Original motion picture soundtrack • Theatrical trailer • Biographies.

1970 98m/C *IT GE* Tony Musante, Suzy Kendall, Eva Renzi, Enrico Maria Salerno, Mario Adorf, Renato Romano, Reggie Nalder, Werner Peters, Umberto Raho, Dario Argento; *D:* Dario Argento; *W:* Dario Argento; *C:* Vittorio Storaro; *M:* Ennio Morricone.

The Birdcage

Somewhat overlong but well-played remake of *La Cage aux Folles* features Williams suppressing his usual manic shtick to portray Armand, the subdued half of a longtime gay couple living in Miami. His partner is the ever-hysterical-but-loving drag queen Albert (Lane), whose presence provides a distinct challenge when Armand's son Val (Futterman) announces his engagement to the daughter of family-values, right-wing senator Kevin Keeley (Hackman). When the senator and family arrive for dinner, Armand tries to play it straight while Albert opts for a matronly mom impersonation (think Barbara Bush). The DVD delivers a crisp sharp picture with very little grain. During the nightclub sequences the colors are stunningly vibrant and just as in the theatre. What little bleed there is does not distract. The disc is very bright with excellent contrast and very good blacks. The music during the club scenes is also pretty spectacular sonically and the 5.1 track really kicks it out, with foot-tapping bass and screaming high end. —*JO* *AKA:* Birds of a Feather.

Movie: 🎵🎵🎵 **DVD:** 🎵🎵🎵►

MGM Home Entertainment (Cat #906033, UPC #027616603395). Widescreen (1.85:1) anamorphic; full frame. Dolby Digital 5.1; Stereo. $24.98. Snapper. *LANG:* English (DD5.1); Spanish (stereo); French (stereo). *SUB:* English; Spanish; French. *CAP:* English; Spanish; French. *FEATURES:* 24 chapter links • Theatrical trailer.

1995 (R) 120m/C Robin Williams, Nathan Lane, Gene Hackman, Dianne Wiest, Hank Azaria, Dan Futterman, Christine Baranski, Calista Flockhart, Tom McGowan; *D:* Mike Nichols; *W:* Elaine May; *C:* Emmanuel Lubezki; *M:* Mark Mothersbaugh, Jonathan Tunick. *AWARDS:* Screen Actors Guild Award '96: Cast; *NOM:* Academy Awards '96: Best Art Direction/Set Decoration; Golden Globe Awards '97: Best Actor—Musical/Comedy (Lane), Best Film—Musical/Comedy; MTV Movie Awards '97: Best On-Screen Duo (Robin Williams/Nathan Lane), Best Comedic Performance (Williams); Screen Actors Guild Award '96: Best Supporting Actor (Azaria), Best Supporting Actor (Lane); Writers Guild of America '96: Best Adapted Screenplay.

The Birds

Though incidents of avian attacks have been documented, Alfred Hitchcock has claimed that he views his most challenging horror film as "a speculation" with no connection to reality. In the book *Hitchcock Truffaut,* he says "With *The Birds* I made sure that the public would not be able to anticipate from one scene to another," and he certainly manages that. In the little town of Bodega Bay, flocks of birds inexplicably attack people. Non-love-birds Mitch Brenner (Taylor), an idealistic lawyer, and Melanie Daniels (Hedren), a flighty socialite, are inexorably drawn into and trapped by birds that attack without motivation or explanation. Reflecting the enigmatic plot, all of the personal relationships defy cinematic conventions, and, more importantly, so does the ending. In Laurent Bouuzeneau's fine documentary, *All About "The Birds,"* several people including writer Evan Hunter comment on that ending. (It's not the one he wrote. The original is included in storyboards and script pages.) That's probably the highlight of the extensive extras that come with the DVD. Virtually all of the surviving participants are interviewed. Their comments range from trivia—those are his own dogs that Hitch is walking in his cameo—to detailed discussion of the filmmaking process. If the image itself appears a bit rough by today's standards, the digital transfer is accurate. It's always looked that way and this is the finest version of the film available on home video. Sound is almost as important and it is first-rate, particularly through headphones which make the big scenes doubly effective. I had to take them off a couple of times. The dual-layer disc contains the entire film, the 79-minute documentary, and other extras on one side. —*MM*

Movie: 🎵🎵🎵🎵 **DVD:** 🎵🎵🎵🎵

Universal Studios Home Video (Cat #20275, UPC #025192027529). Widescreen (1.85:1) anamorphic. Dolby Digital Mono. $29.98. Keepcase. *LANG:* English; French. *CAP:* English. *FEATURES:* 20 chapter links • Deleted scene in script pages, storyboards and still photos • Original ending in script pages and storyboards • Tippi Hedren's screen test • 2 Universal promotional newsreels • *All About "The Birds"* documentary • Production notes and photos • Cast and crew thumbnail biographies • Universal web links • Storyboard sequence with drawings and stills.

1963 (PG-13) 120m/C Rod Taylor, Tippi Hedren, Jessica Tandy, Veronica Cartwright, Suzanne Pleshette, Ethel Griffies, Charles McGraw, Ruth McDevitt, Lonny (Loni) Chapman, Joe Mantell, Morgan Brittany, Alfred Hitchcock; *D:* Alfred Hitchcock; *W:* Evan Hunter; *C:* Robert Burks; *M:* Bernard Herrmann.

The Birth of a Nation

This lavish Civil War epic essentially created the feature film as we know it today. Griffith's poisonous racism and acceptance of KKK terrorism notwithstanding,

he still invented much of the grammar of film and this was the first time that all of his innovations came together in a long work. Early audiences were astonished and the film was the first blockbuster hit. When it was released, the standard cost of a movie ticket was 25 cents; for this one, the price was bumped to $2.00 and people came in droves. The story of Northern and Southern families divided by the war but united at the end of it has been copied many times since, and, as film historians Russell Merritt and David Shepard point out in their accompanying documentary, Griffith was not the first to tell it. They provide valuable background on the use of the Civil War in popular entertainment before Griffith's film. This version re-creates the tinted scenes—some of them quite striking—but the print does reveal inevitable wear in many places. What shows through are the performances by Lillian Gish and Henry Walthall, and the strong set pieces, like the assassination of Lincoln. With the re-recorded stereo score, DVD is the best medium to discover this archetypal flawed masterpiece. —MM **AKA:** The Clansman.
Movie: 𝄞𝄞𝄞▶ **DVD:** 𝄞𝄞𝄞
Image Entertainment (Cat #ID4674DSDVD, UPC #0143814674-20). Full frame. Dolby Digital Stereo. $29.99. Snapper. *FEATURES:* 32 chapter links (26 within the film; 6 within documentary) ▪ "The Making of 'The Birth of a Nation'" documentary ▪ Extensive liner notes by Russell Merritt.
1915 175m/B Lillian Gish, Mae Marsh, Henry B. Walthall, Ralph Lewis, Robert "Bobbie" Harron, George Siegmann, Joseph Henabery, Spottiswoode Aitken, George Beranger, Mary Alden, Josephine Crowell, Elmer Clifton, Walter Long, Howard Gaye, Miriam Cooper, John Ford, Sam De Grasse, Maxfield Stanley, Donald Crisp, Raoul Walsh, Erich von Stroheim, Eugene Pallette, Wallace Reid; **D:** D.W. Griffith; **W:** D.W. Griffith, Frank E. Woods; **C:** Billy (G.W.) Bitzer; **M:** D.W. Griffith. *AWARDS:* American Film Institute (AFI) '98: Top 100, National Film Registry '92.

The Bishop's Wife

Holiday favorite will make you feel good every time you put it on. It tells the tale of charming angel (Grant) who comes down to Earth at Christmas to help a young bishop save his church, his parishioners, and his marriage. Excellent performances by the cast make this an entertaining outing. It's a great-looking DVD (and one of the best when it comes to black and white), especially when you consider the age of the film. Sharpness is excellent and grain is hard to find. The brightness levels are consistent and comfortable. You can really feel the great depth of field in the cinematography thanks to excellent contrast and graytones. The blacks are also near-perfect. The mono soundtrack is as good as it can be, even though those who won't buy *Citizen Kane* because it doesn't have a 5.1 remix will have to pass on this one too. —JO

Movie: 𝄞𝄞𝄞 **DVD:** 𝄞𝄞𝄞▶
HBO Home Video (Cat #90658, UPC #026359065828). Full frame. Mono. $24.98. Snapper. *LANG:* English; Spanish; French; Italian. *CAP:* English. *FEATURES:* 21 chapter links ▪ Theatrical trailer.
1947 109m/B Cary Grant, Loretta Young, David Niven, Monty Woolley, Elsa Lanchester, James Gleason, Gladys Cooper, Regis Toomey; **D:** Henry Koster; **W:** Leonardo Bercovici, Robert Sherwood; **C:** Gregg Toland; **M:** Hugo Friedhofer. *AWARDS:* Academy Awards '47: Best Sound; *NOM:* Academy Awards '47: Best Director (Koster), Best Film Editing, Best Picture, Best Original Dramatic Score.

Black Cat

This low-budget Hong Kong *La Femme Nikita* rip-off is light on plot but filled with exhilarating cheap thrills. Bad girl Leung kills a cop and is "killed" by government assassins. When she comes to, she is trained as an assassin, aided by a computer chip that has been implanted in her head. The DVD seems way too dark, in this case at least too dark to be handled properly. The result is average picture sharpness and a whole lot of grain. When fast-moving action occurs, there are also artifacts. The colors are O.K. but bleed a little most of the time. The 5.1 sound is another one of those remixes that is basically stereo and, on this DVD, very crunchy. —JO **AKA:** Hak Mau.
Movie: 𝄞𝄞▶ **DVD:** 𝄞
Tai Seng Video Marketing (Cat #MSDVD05199, UPC #60164319916). Full frame. Dolby Digital 5.1. $29.95. Keepcase. *LANG:* Cantonese; Mandarin. *SUB:* English; Spanish; Japanese; Traditional & Simplified Chinese; Vietnamese; Bahasa; Thai. *CAP:* Cantonese; Mandarin. *FEATURES:* 9 chapter links ▪ Theatrical trailer ▪ Filmographies.
1991 91m/C HK Jade Leung, Simon Yam, Thomas Lam, Curtis Fraser; **D:** Stephen Shin; **W:** Wai-Lun Lam, Lam Tam Ping; **C:** Lee Kin Keung; **M:** Danny Chung.

Black Cat Run

Made-for-cable action flick has a mechanic (Muldoon) falsely accused and pursued by a deputy (Busey).
Movie: 𝄞𝄞 **DVD:** NYR
HBO Home Video (Cat #91481). Full frame. Dolby Digital Stereo. $24.98. Snapper. *LANG:* English; French; Spanish. *SUB:* Spanish. *FEATURES:* Cast and crew thumbnail biographies.
1998 (R) 88m/C Patrick Muldoon, Amelia Heinle, Russell Means, Kevin J. O'Connor, Peter Greene, Jake Busey; **D:** D.J. Caruso; **W:** Frank Darabont, Douglas Venturelli; **C:** Bing Sokolsky; **M:** Jeff Rona.

Black Circle Boys

Self-centered high schooler Kyle (Bairstow) is trying to fit into his new school when he becomes involved with the "Black Circle Boys," a clique of losers involved with drugs and the occult who are led by Shane (Mabius). They enjoy malicious pranks that come to repel Kyle. The allegedly fact-based story becomes increasingly silly as it goes along. The DVD is nothing special with pale, washed-out exteriors and overly dark night scenes. —MM
Movie: 𝄞▶ **DVD:** 𝄞
Image Entertainment (Cat #ID5897UM DVD, UPC #014381589726). Full frame. Dolby Digital Stereo. $24.99. Snapper. *LANG:* English. *FEATURES:* 14 chapter links.
1997 (R) 100m/C Scott Bairstow, Eric Mabius, Heath Lourwood, Chad Lindberg, Tara Subkoff, Dee Wallace Stone, Donnie Wahlberg, John Doe; **D:** Matthew Carnahan; **W:** Matthew Carnahan; **C:** Geary McLeod.

Black Death

Made-for-Canadian-TV disease-of-the-week medical thriller features that old favorite, bubonic plague. Dr. Nora Hart (Jackson) is the courageous public health officer who must save New York with the help of the handsome Dr. Prescott (Waxman) while the city suffers a garbage strike and prepares for the arrival of the Democratic National Convention. Casting, plotting, and pace are pretty much standard stuff for the genre, though director Larry does have a fair eye for detail. The DVD can do little to improve the film's mid-level production values. The disc is probably identical to the original broadcast in image and sound. —MM **AKA:** Quiet Killer.
Movie: 𝄞𝄞▶ **DVD:** 𝄞𝄞▶
Image Entertainment (Cat #ID5862SVDVD, UPC #014381586220). Full frame. Dolby Digital Stereo. $24.99. Snapper. *LANG:* English. *FEATURES:* 16 chapter links.
1991 92m/C CA Kate Jackson, Al Waxman, Jeffrey Nordling, Chip Zien, Barbara Williams, David Hewlett, Jerry Orbach, Howard Hesseman; **D:** Sheldon Larry; **W:** I.C. Rappaport; **C:** Ronald Orieux; **M:** Marty Simon.

Black Dog

Jack Crews (Swayze), who lost his license after an accident, is forced to get behind the wheel of an 18-wheeler to make an "off the books" run by his no good boss. The cargo is weapons; an FBI-ATF team (led by battling Dutton and Tobolowsky) is on his tail; Red (Meat Loaf) is trying to hijack the load and someone's helping him. Other parts of the plot are even sillier, but despite the many flaws and a poor theatrical run, this one is a fine guilty pleasure. Director Hooks gives the derivative material the same energy he brought to *Passenger 57* and the DVD could hardly look better. It's one of those surprising discs that seems to jump out of your set with a crisp, sharply focused image. A genuine sleeper, even though the stereo sound is occasionally muddy. —MM
Movie: 𝄞𝄞𝄞 **DVD:** 𝄞𝄞𝄞▶

Universal Studios Home Video (Cat #20391, UPC #025192039126). Widescreen (2.35:1) letterboxed. Dolby Digital 5.1 Surround Stereo; Dolby Digital Surround Stereo. $24.98. Keepcase. *LANG:* English; Spanish; French. *SUB:* Spanish. *CAP:* English. *FEATURES:* 26 chapter links • Cast and crew thumbnail biographies • Soundtrack videos • Theatrical trailer • Production notes.
1998 (PG-13) 88m/C Patrick Swayze, Randy Travis, Meat Loaf Aday, Gabriel Casseus, Graham Beckel, Stephen Tobolowsky, Charles S. Dutton, Brian Vincent, Brenda Strong, Erin Broderick; *D:* Kevin Hooks; *W:* William Mickelberry, Dan Vining; *C:* Buzz Feitshans IV; *M:* George S. Clinton.

Black Eagle

Pre-Glasnost anti-Soviet tale revolves around two high-kicking spies. CIA and KGB agents race to recover innovative equipment in the Mediterranean.
Movie: 🎬🎬 *DVD:* NYR
Studio Home Entertainment (Cat #4055). Full frame. Dolby Digital Mono. $24.95. Keepcase. *LANG:* English; Spanish. *FEATURES:* Cast and crew thumbnail biographies • Trailer.
1988 (R) 93m/C Bruce Doran, Jean-Claude Van Damme, Sho Kosugi; *D:* Eric Karson; *W:* Shimon Arama; *M:* Terry Plumeri.

The Black Hole

Disney attempt at *Star Wars* sf is set on a spaceship at the edge of a black hole. The ship is under the command of Reinhardt (Schell), your basic mad scientist. A competent cast of character actors plays second fiddle to some pretty good special effects which have been eclipsed by more recent advances in the field. Also worthy of note is John Barry's soaring score. On DVD, the graininess in the special effects scenes comes from the original. Sound is better. The widescreen edition contains an overture and is longer than the full-frame version on the flip side. —*MM*
Movie: 🎬🎬 *DVD:* 🎬🎬
Anchor Bay (Cat #DV10732, UPC #013131073294). Widescreen (2.35:1) letterboxed; full frame. Dolby Digital 5.1 Surround Stereo. $29.98. Keepcase. *LANG:* English. *FEATURES:* 18 chapter links, widescreen • 17 chapter links, full frame.
1979 (G) 97m/C Maximilian Schell, Anthony Perkins, Ernest Borgnine, Yvette Mimieux, Joseph Bottoms, Robert Forster; *D:* Gary Nelson; *W:* Gerry Day; *C:* Frank Phillips; *M:* John Barry. *AWARDS: NOM:* Academy Awards '79: Best Cinematography.

Black Mask

Action star Jet Li is Simon, a mild-mannered librarian who is really a biogenetically enhanced super warrior from the disbanded "701 Squad." Other members of the group are trying to take over the Hong Kong drug business. With the aid of his cop pal Rock (Lau Ching Wan), Simon becomes an avenging superhero who bears a strong resemblance to the Green Hornet's Kato. Fans of Hong Kong action films know what to expect—this one was dubbed into English for American release—wild gunplay, incredible stunts, gloriously unhinged fight choreography, violence that's more graphic than domestic fare. The disc looks very good compared to most similar imports. It's not quite as sharp as the best Hollywood can do. Sound is very good. Most fans will probably appreciate the extra which leads directly to the big fight scenes. —*MM* *AKA:* Hak Hap.
Movie: 🎬🎬▶ *DVD:* 🎬🎬🎬
Artisan Entertainment (Cat #10172, UPC #01223610172). Widescreen (1.85:1) letterboxed. Dolby Digital 5.1 Surround Stereo. $29.98. Keepcase. *LANG:* English. *CAP:* English. *FEATURES:* 26 chapter links • Trailer • TV spots • Separate links to action sequences.
1996 (R) 95m/C *HK* Jet Li, Karen Mok, Francoise Yip, Lau Ching Wan; *D:* Daniel Lee; *W:* Tsui Hark, Teddy Chen; *C:* Cheung Tung Leung; *M:* Ben Vaughn, Teddy Robin.

Black Orpheus

The myth of love and death unfolds against the blindingly colorful background of the carnival in Rio de Janeiro. In the black section of the city, Orpheus (Mello) is a streetcar conductor. Eurydice (Dawn) is a country girl fleeing from a man (Da Silva) sworn to kill her. Dancing, incredible samba music, and black magic add to the film's power. The DVD captures it without visible or audible flaws, despite a monaural soundtrack. Judged solely on the amount of color and motion on-screen in the big scenes, the film is a dizzying kaleidoscope. The bright colors appear to be as brilliant and intense as they were in 1958. —*MM AKA:* Orfeu Negro.
Movie: 🎬🎬🎬▶ *DVD:* 🎬🎬🎬▶
Criterion Collection (Cat #BLA070). Full frame. Dolby Digital Mono. $24.95. Keepcase. *LANG:* Portuguese; English. *SUB:* English. *FEATURES:* 17 chapter links • Liner notes by David Ehrenstein.
1958 103m/C *BR FR PT* Breno Mello, Marpessa Dawn, Lea Garcia, Fausto Guerzoni, Lourdes De Oliveira, Adhemar Da Silva, Alexandro Constantino, Waldetar De Souza; *D:* Marcel Camus; *W:* Vinitius De Moraes, Jacques Viot; *C:* Jean (Yves, Georges) Bourgoin; *M:* Antonio Carlos Jobim, Luis Bonfa. *AWARDS:* Academy Awards '59: Best Foreign Film; Cannes Film Festival '59: Best Film; Golden Globe Awards '60: Best Foreign Film.

The Black Pirate

A shipwrecked mariner vows revenge on the pirates who destroyed his father's ship, while at the same time attempting to rescue a princess. Quintessential Fairbanks, this film features astounding athletic feats and exciting swordplay. Filmed in early two-strip Technicolor, it's hard to really judge the accuracy of the colors on the DVD, but there are some reds that are reddish and most of the time the blacks are very close to true. The contrast seems a little high but that is not uncommon in a film from the 1920s. The preprint is in very good condition, especially when you consider the age of the film. The orchestral score written for the film is reproduced here with good fidelity on the stereo soundtracks, and is at times quite rousing. Don't ignore the supplementals, which include commentary and behind-the-scenes footage, that are very enlightening on film history. —*JO AKA:* Rage of the Buccaneers; The Black Buccaneer; Gordon il Pirata Nero.
Movie: 🎬🎬🎬 *DVD:* 🎬🎬🎬
Image Entertainment (Cat #K112DVD, UPC #738329011222). Full frame. Stereo. $29.98. Snapper. *LANG:* Silent. *SUB:* English. *FEATURES:* 18 chapter links • Outtakes • Photographs • Commentary: film historian Rudy Behlmer • Original orchestral score.
1926 122m/B *IT* Douglas Fairbanks Sr., Donald Crisp, Billie Dove; *D:* Albert Parker; *W:* Jack Cunningham, Douglas Fairbanks Sr.; *C:* Henry Sharp; *M:* Mortimer Wilson. *AWARDS:* National Film Registry '93.

Black Rain

Erstwhile Ozu assistant Imamura directs this powerful portrait of a Hiroshima family five years after the bombing. Yasuko (Tanaka) is a young woman who, having been caught in a shower of black rain (radioactive fallout) on an ill-timed visit to the city, returns to her village and finds that she's ostracized by her neighbors and no longer considered marriageable. Though the film's anti-nuclear politics are unmistakable, it's not a polemic. With some superb black-and-white photography, it would make a thoughtful companion piece to Ichikawa's *Fires on the Plain*. The film plays beautifully on DVD. The yellow subtitles, which cannot be turned off, are outlined in black and easy to read. Though a few exteriors lack sharp focus, the character-driven story depends on often-silent close-ups and those are powerful. —*MM AKA:* Kuroi Ame.
Movie: 🎬🎬🎬▶ *DVD:* 🎬🎬🎬
WinStar Home Entertainment (Cat #ID4305FLDVD, UPC #014381430523). Widescreen (1.85:1) letterboxed. Dolby Digital Mono. $29.98. Snapper. *LANG:* Japanese. *SUB:* English. *FEATURES:* 16 chapter links.
1988 123m/B *JP* Kazuo Kitamura, Yoshiko Tanaka, Etsuko Ichihara, Shoichi Ozawa, Norihei Miki, Keisuke Ishida; *D:* Shohei Imamura; *W:* Shohei Imamura, Toshiro Ishido; *C:* Takashi Kawamata; *M:* Toru Takemitsu.

Black Rain

Ruthless American cop (Douglas) teams up with a disciplined Japanese man-of-honor cop (the Japanese "Clint Eastwood," Ken Takakura) to chase a murder suspect through gang-controlled Tokyo. Loads of action and stunning visuals from the director who brought you *Blade Runner*. Conflict of cultures provides lots of tension between the two cops. Climax is an homage to Pollack's *Yakuza*. The DVD is a little grainier and not as sharp as the letterboxed laserdisc. The blacks are average but the color bleed is at times atrocious. Add to that the occasional artifacting and you might want to watch the laserdisc instead. If you can't, at least the sound is better on the DVD. With the 5.1, you actually feel like you're on the streets in Tokyo, especially when a bus rumbles by. —*JO*

Movie: 🎞🎞🎞 **DVD:** 🎞➤
Paramount Home Video (Cat #322207, UPC #097363222071). Widescreen (2.35:1) letterboxed. Dolby Digital 5.1; Dolby Surround. $29.99. Keepcase. *LANG:* English (DD5.1, DS); French (DS). *SUB:* English. *FEATURES:* 28 chapter links • Theatrical trailer.
1989 (R) 125m/C Michael Douglas, Andy Garcia, Kate Capshaw, Ken Takakura, Yusaku Matsuda, John Spencer, Shigeru Koyama; **D:** Ridley Scott; **W:** Craig Bolotin, Warren Lewis; **C:** Jan De Bont; **M:** Hans Zimmer. *AWARDS: NOM:* Academy Awards '89: Best Sound.

Black Robe

In 1634, a young Jesuit priest journeys across the North American wilderness to bring the word of God to Canada's Huron Indians. The winter journey is brutal and perilous. He begins to question his mission after seeing the strength of the Indians' native ways. Stunning cinematography, a good script, and fine acting combine to make this one superb. Indians are portrayed in a realistic manner, but Beresford presents white culture with few redeeming qualities and blames it for the Indians' downfall. Brian Moore adapted his novel for the screen.
Movie: 🎞🎞🎞➤ **DVD:** NYR
Trimark Home Video (Cat #6785). Widescreen letterboxed; full frame. Dolby Digital Stereo. $24.99. Keepcase. *LANG:* English. *SUB:* French; Spanish. *FEATURES:* Production notes • Trailers.
1991 (R) 101m/C *AU CA* Lothaire Bluteau, Aden Young, Sandrine Holt, August Schellenberg, Tantoo Cardinal, Billy Two Rivers, Lawrence Bayne, Harrison Liu; **D:** Bruce Beresford; **W:** Brian Moore; **C:** Peter James; **M:** Georges Delerue. *AWARDS:* Australian Film Institute '92: Best Cinematography; Genie Awards '91: Best Director (Beresford), Best Film.

The Black Stallion

The first half of this film is about as close to perfection as movies ever get. That's when young Alex (Reno) is shipwrecked on a Mediterranean island with a huge black horse. The storm and the scenes where the two come to trust each other are told

virtually without words in some powerfully composed scenes. In the second half, after they're rescued and return to America, the film is a more conventional kid's adventure, still very good but not as moving. Over the years, I've seen this one in theatres and on virtually every home video medium. The DVD is an improvement over the excellent laserdisc, in the sharpness of image, fullness of sound and, of course, convenience. If it suffers any flaws, I am blind to them. One of the best. —*MM*
Movie: 🎞🎞🎞➤ **DVD:** 🎞🎞🎞➤
MGM Home Entertainment (Cat #906269, UPC #027616626998). Widescreen letterboxed; full frame. Dolby Digital Surround Stereo. $24.98. Keepcase. *LANG:* English; French; Spanish. *SUB:* English; French; Spanish. *FEATURES:* 32 chapter links • 4-page booklet.
1979 (PG) 120m/C Kelly Reno, Mickey Rooney, Teri Garr, Clarence Muse; **D:** Carroll Ballard; **W:** William D. Wittliff, Melissa Mathison, Jeanne Rosenberg; **C:** Caleb Deschanel; **M:** Carmine Coppola. *AWARDS:* Academy Awards '79: Best Sound Effects Editing; Los Angeles Film Critics Association Awards '79: Best Cinematography; National Society of Film Critics Awards '79: Best Cinematography; *NOM:* Academy Awards '79: Best Film Editing, Best Supporting Actor (Rooney).

Black Sunday

Despite some dated dialogue, the key images in Mario Bava's masterpiece have lost none of their power. The resurrected revenge-seeking witch plot is familiar, but it's spun out at a lively pace with attention to detail. The stunning Barbara Steele is the Russian witch in question, and also her twin, who is a potential victim. The initial execution is still a frightening moment, even more shocking on DVD than it has been on existing tape version where the scene is slightly but significantly shortened. Her rebirth, complete with scorpions crawling out of empty eye sockets, is another nightmarish moment. The DVD faithfully reproduces Bava's inky black-and-white photography and fog-shrouded atmosphere. Beyond the image itself, the disc is filled with extras. Tim Lucas sounds like he is reading his commentary track, but he has filled it with fascinating trivia. This one belongs in every horror fan's library. —*MM* *AKA:* La Maschera del Demonio; The Demon's Mask; House of Fright; Revenge of the Vampire; Mask of Satan.
Movie: 🎞🎞🎞➤ **DVD:** 🎞🎞🎞🎞
Image Entertainment (Cat #ID5942AODVD, UPC #014381594225). Widescreen (1.66:1) anamorphic. Dolby Digital Mono. $24.99. Snapper. *LANG:* English. *FEATURES:* 15 chapter links • Photo and poster gallery • Bava thumbnail biography and filmography • Barbara Steele filmography • Commentary: film historian Tim Lucas • Explanation of the "extra" scene in the Italian theatrical release.

1960 83m/B *IT* Barbara Steele, John Richardson, Ivo Garrani, Andrea Checchi, Arturo Dominici, Antonio Pierfederici, Tino Bianchi, Clara Bindi, Enrico Oliveri, Germana Dominici; **D:** Mario Bava; **W:** Mario Bava, Ennio de Concini, Mario Serandrei; **C:** Mario Bava, Ubaldo Terzano; **M:** Les Baxter.

Black Tights

Chevalier introduces four stories told in dance by Roland Petit's Ballet de Paris company: "The Diamond Crusher," "Cyrano de Bergerac," "A Merry Mourning," and "Carmen." A keeper for dance fans. Shearer's Roxanne in "Cyrano" was her last performance before retirement. The DVD is visually compelling, scene to scene, with consistent color and crisp sound, although nothing spectacular. No sound information is given; it sounds like mono. —*AB AKA:* Un, Deux, Trois, Quatre!.
Movie: 🎞🎞🎞 **DVD:** 🎞🎞🎞
Kino on Video (Cat #K157, UPC #3832901572). Widescreen letterboxed. Keepcase. *LANG:* English. *FEATURES:* Original theatrical trailer • 5 chapter links.
1960 120m/C *FR* Cyd Charisse, Zizi Jeanmarie, Moira Shearer, Dirk Sanders, Roland Petit; **D:** Terence Young; **Nar:** Maurice Chevalier.

Blackjack

Action director John Woo (*Broken Arrow*, *Face/Off*, *Hard Boiled*, etc.) seems to have started out with two film scripts, neither of which seemed all that promising, so he combined them and settled for one. Dolph Lundgren stars as Jack "Blackjack" Devlin, a federal agent whose latest caper is to protect the daughter (Padraigin Murphy) of a casino owner from being kidnapped by the mob. About 15 minutes into the proceedings, this plot is abandoned in favor of Jack protecting a supermodel (Kam Haskin) from a former boyfriend with a sniper rifle and an itchy trigger finger. Strictly for John Woo fans, who fills in the plot holes with plenty of action, including a number of dance-like choreographed trademark gun-battles. DVD presentation is good, if uninspired, with the production's direct-to-video nature showing from time to time. —*MM*
Movie: 🎞🎞 **DVD:** 🎞🎞🎞
Buena Vista Home Entertainment (Cat #17759, UPC #717951003591). Full frame. AC3 - 2 channel. $29.99. Keepcase. *LANG:* English. *CAP:* English. *FEATURES:* 22 chapter links • Film recommendations (no trailers).
1997 (R) 113m/C *CA* Dolph Lundgren, Kam Haskin, Saul Rubinek, Fred Williamson, Phillip MacKenzie, Kate Vernon, Padraigin Murphy; **D:** John Woo; **W:** Peter Lance; **C:** Bill Wong; **M:** Micky Erbe.

Blade

Blade (Snipes) is a half-vampire/half-human vampire hunter who is intent on preventing evil vampire Frost (Dorff) from unleashing the blood tide upon humanity. Fighting at Blade's side is his friend and mentor Whistler (Kristofferson), and Dr. Karen Jansen (Wright), who is also trying to find the cure for vampirism. From its opening shower of blood in a Goth disco to its CGI effects–laden climax, *Blade* is non-stop, gory fun, with too many grisly demises to count. Snipes's physique and martial arts skill are both put to good use, but Dorff tries too hard (and might be too short) to be the ultimate evil. Adapted from the Marvel comic book. There are enough special features on this DVD to keep you busy for a couple of days. The transfer is very good with true blacks, and excellent contrast. Colors are crisp and vibrant with very little bleed—even when there are large amounts of red blood on the screen. Excellent sound and Surround effects throughout. —*JO*

Movie: 🎬🎬🎬 **DVD:** 🎬🎬🎬▶

New Line Home Video (Cat #N4709, UPC #794043470929). Widescreen (2.35:1) anamorphic. Dolby Digital 5.1; Dolby Surround. $24.98. Snapper. *LANG:* English. *CAP:* English. *FEATURES:* 38 chapter links ▪ Commentaries: Snipes, Dorff, writer, cinematographer, producer ▪ 4 featurettes ▪ Theatrical trailer ▪ Cast and crew bios ▪ Production sketches ▪ Vampire tribe notes ▪ Enhanced features for PC ▪ Isolated music score with commentary.

1998 (R) 91m/C Wesley Snipes, Stephen Dorff, Kris Kristofferson, N'Bushe Wright, Donal Logue, Udo Kier, Traci Lords, Tim Guinee, Arly Jover, Sanaa Lathan; **D:** Stephen Norrington; **W:** David S. Goyer; **C:** Theo van de Sande; **M:** Mark Isham. *AWARDS:* MTV Movie Awards '99: Best Villain (Dorff); *NOM:* MTV Movie Awards '99: Best Fight.

Blade Runner (DC)

Futuristic film noir set in 21st-century Los Angeles. World weary "blade runner" Rick Deckard (Ford) tracks down renegade replicants (synthetic humans) who are in the last phase of their programmed lifetimes and desperate to become human. Moody, beautifully photographed dark thriller features sets from an architect's dream. This supposed "director's cut" removes Ford's narration and the last scene of the film, which director Scott considered too "up," and inserts several scenes, including an implanted replicant dream. The problem is that the violence added into the original video release is missing from this cut, even though Scott wanted it included. The transfer of this dark and moody film is excellent, despite it being one of the earlier Warner DVD releases. There is virtually no grain or pixelation. The blacks are near perfect, and the brightness and contrast excellent as well. The sound is top-notch, despite the lack of 5.1 Surround, and the Vangelis score is a perfect match for the atmosphere of the film. Warner Bros. knew they

were working with a masterpiece and they had this one authored right. —*JO*

Movie: 🎬🎬🎬▶ **DVD:** 🎬🎬🎬🎬

Warner Home Video, Inc. (Cat #12682, UPC #085391268222). Widescreen (2.35:1) anamorphic; full frame. Dolby Surround. $24.98. Snapper. *LANG:* English. *SUB:* Spanish; French. *CAP:* English. *FEATURES:* 36 chapter links ▪ Cast and filmmaker bios.

1982 (R) 122m/C Harrison Ford, Rutger Hauer, Sean Young, Daryl Hannah, M. Emmet Walsh, Edward James Olmos, Joe Turkel, Brion James, Joanna Cassidy, William Sanderson; **D:** Ridley Scott; **W:** Hampton Fancher, David Peoples; **C:** Jordan Cronenweth; **M:** Vangelis. *AWARDS:* Los Angeles Film Critics Association Awards '82: Best Cinematography, National Film Registry '93; *NOM:* Academy Awards '82: Best Art Direction/Set Decoration.

The Blair Witch Project (SE)

The sleeper hit of the summer of 1999 became one of the first hits of DVD, too. Artisan Entertainment carefully orchestrated a digital release built on the film's success in festivals, on the Internet, and with larger movie-going audiences. On disc, the simple story of three students (Donahue, Williams, and Leonard) who go into the woods with a 16mm camera and a camcorder (and half a ton of batteries) is the central part of a larger work. The DVD combines more "newly discovered" footage, a "mockumentary" about the characters, and a more detailed explanation of the original Blair Witch and the "mysterious" events that have occurred over the years. Almost all of that material is meant to reinforce the illusion of the "truth" of the story, an illusion which, apparently, many gullible viewers have bought into. On their commentary track, however, the filmmakers drop the pretense and talk about the various compromises demanded by their low-budget approach. As for the film itself, it's as unapologetically rough as it ever was. The extras are the key to the disc and they make it an example of the possibilities of the medium. —*MM*

Movie: 🎬🎬🎬 **DVD:** 🎬🎬🎬▶

Artisan Entertainment (Cat #11266, UPC #012236112662). Full frame. Dolby Digital Surround Stereo. $39.98. Keepcase. *LANG:* English. *CAP:* English. *FEATURES:* 18 chapter links ▪ "Newly discovered" footage ▪ Theatrical teaser and trailers ▪ Production notes ▪ Cast and crew thumbnail biographies ▪ "Curse of the Blair Witch" featurette ▪ Mock documentary ▪ Commentary: Myrick, Sanchez, producers Cowie, Monello, Hale. More features accessible through computer DVD-ROM.

1999 (R) 87m/C Michael Williams, Heather Donahue, Joshua Leonard; **D:** Eduardo Sanchez, Daniel Myrick; **W:** Eduardo Sanchez, Daniel Myrick; **C:** Neal Fredericks; **M:** Tony Cora. *AWARDS: NOM:* Independent Spirit Awards '00: Best First

Feature; Golden Raspberry Awards '99: Worst Picture, Worst Supporting Actress (Donahue).

Blank Generation

Director Lommel's cult classic stars real-life punk icon Hell as Billy, a musician on the cusp of stardom. Throw in a gorgeous French TV journalist (Bouquet) as the love interest. Mix this in with Billy's musician inner demons and there's anxiety aplenty. Made on location in New York City's Lower East Side, the film captures the feel of the Punk life circa 1979 with all the excesses. Featured are a couple of entrancing live performances at the famed club CBGB by Hell and his band, the Voidoids. Included are the title track, "Blank Generation" (Hell's landmark record) and "Love Comes in Spurts," also from the album. Andy Warhol makes a priceless appearance, aping himself. Punk fans should delight in this release. The picture quality is very good and consistent, the sound is excellent. And even though the sound is mono, the live performances come through very well. —*AB*

Movie: 🎬🎬🎬 **DVD:** 🎬🎬🎬

Anchor Bay (Cat #DV11108, UPC #1313111089). Widescreen (1.66:1) anamorphic. Dolby Digital Mono. Keepcase. *LANG:* English. *FEATURES:* 19 chapter links.

1979 85m/C Richard Hell, Carole Bouquet, Andy Warhol, Suzanna Love, Ulli Lommel; **D:** Ulli Lommel; **W:** Ulli Lommel, Roger Deutsch; **M:** Elliot Goldenthal.

Blast from the Past

In 1962, mistaking a jet crash for an atomic bomb blast, scientist Calvin (Walken) and his pregnant wife (Spacek) lock themselves in their state-of-the-art bomb shelter. Thirty-five years later, they send their son Adam (Fraser) out for supplies and a wife. The gimmicky plot cannot sustain itself after Adam meets cute with Eve (Silverstone), a thoroughly modern woman with a low opinion of modern men. Even so, the cast is attractive and the film has its moments. The DVD is visually flawless, capturing the stylish look without a problem. And the menu is really cool. —*MM*

Movie: 🎬🎬▶ **DVD:** 🎬🎬🎬

New Line Home Video (Cat #N4751, UPC #794043475122). Widescreen (2.35:1) letterboxed; full frame. Dolby Digital 5.1 Surround Stereo. $24.98. Snapper. *LANG:* English. *SUB:* English. *FEATURES:* 24 chapter links ▪ Theatrical trailer ▪ Cast and crew thumbnail biographies.

1998 (PG-13) 106m/C Brendan Fraser, Alicia Silverstone, Christopher Walken, Sissy Spacek, Dave Foley, Joey Slotnick, Dale Raoul; **D:** Hugh Wilson; **W:** Hugh Wilson, Bill Kelly; **C:** Jose Luis Alcaine; **M:** Steve Dorff.

Blazing Saddles

Mel Brooks's masterpiece is one of Hollywood's truly great comedies, a film so irreverent and incorrect it could not be made in these sensitive days. The dizzy plot casts Little as Black Bart, a convict who is reprieved by the corrupt governor (Brooks) to run the residents out of a small town where the railroad is coming through. To reach the place, he has to ride through the desert right past the Count Basie Orchestra. Wilder is the Waco Kid, gunslinger and paramour of saloon singer Lili Von Shtupp (Kahn). Several writers, including Richard Pryor, had a hand in the wide-ranging script. The most famous moments are chapter 11, the "Beanfest," and chapter 23, the inspired "I Work for Mel Brooks" finale. In a separate 55-minute commentary, Brooks takes a funny and fanciful look at the genesis of the film. In general, the image is stunningly clear for a 1970s film. This disc belongs in every collection. —MM

Movie: 🎞🎞🎞🎞 **DVD:** 🎞🎞🎞▶
Warner Home Video, Inc. (Cat #1001, UPC #012569100121). Full frame; widescreen letterboxed. Dolby Digital Mono. $24.98. Snapper. *LANG:* English; French; Spanish. *SUB:* English; French; Spanish. *CAP:* English. *FEATURES:* Thumbnail biographies of cast and crew ▪ Production notes ▪ Theatrical trailer ▪ Mel Brooks interview ▪ 24 chapter links.
1974 (R) 90m/C Cleavon Little, Harvey Korman, Madeline Kahn, Gene Wilder, Mel Brooks, John Hillerman, Alex Karras, Dom DeLuise, Liam Dunn, Slim Pickens, David Huddleston, Burton Gilliam, Count Basie; *D:* Mel Brooks; *W:* Norman Steinberg, Andrew Bergman, Richard Pryor, Alan Uger, Mel Brooks; *C:* Joseph Biroc; *M:* John Morris. *AWARDS:* Writers Guild of America '74: Best Original Screenplay; *NOM:* Academy Awards '74: Best Film Editing, Best Song ("Blazing Saddles"), Best Supporting Actress (Kahn).

Blood and Sand

Young bullfighter Juan (Rydell) is on the verge of superstardom when he meets Dona Sol (Stone) and risks everything he has worked for. Will she destroy his one opportunity at fame? You'll be rooting for the bulls and Dona Sol.
Movie: 🎞🎞▶ **DVD:** NYR
Trimark Home Video (Cat #7045). Full frame. Stereo. $14.99. Keepcase. *SUB:* French; Spanish. *FEATURES:* Trailer.
1989 (R) 96m/C Christopher Rydell, Sharon Stone, Ana Torrent, Jose-Luis De Villalonga, Simon Andrew; *D:* Javier Elorrieta; *W:* Rafael Azcona, Ricardo Franco, Thomas Fucci; *C:* Antonio Rios; *M:* Jesus Gluck.

Blood Feast (SE)

Reportedly filmed for less than $70,000 in Miami, the first splatter movie is really a camp comedy. The silly writing and nonprofessional acting are actually part of the film's weird appeal. By today's standards, the gore effects in the story of an Egyptian caterer/killer (Arnold) are tame. But in 1963, no one showed lopped limbs or

scooped brains on the silver screen and, crude as they are, the effects still have the power to disgust. Producer-director Herschell Gordon Lewis creates a pornography of violence. Like conventional pornography, it's about limits, about crossing lines that cannot be crossed. Because of that, the film has undeniable historical value as a milestone in the genre and it receives properly respectful but light-hearted treatment in this "special edition." For fans, the most important extra is the commentary track with Lewis, producer Dave Friedman, and Something Weird staffer Mike Vraney. The old pals trot out all their favorite stories and trivia—the film was edited by Robert Sinise, father of actor-director Gary Sinise—and a few details are appropriately grotesque. On DVD, the film is surprisingly clear with a bright image that belies its age, budget, and concept. The disc is far superior to VHS tape. —MM *AKA:* Feast of Flesh.
Movie: 🎞🎞 **DVD:** 🎞🎞🎞
Something Weird Video (Cat #ID60125SWDVD, UPC #014381601220). Full frame. Dolby Digital Mono. $24.99. Snapper. *LANG:* English. *FEATURES:* 10 chapter links ▪ Commentary: Lewis, Friedman, and Vraney ▪ Theatrical trailer ▪ Outtakes ▪ "Carving Magic," short film with Harvey Korman and William Kerwin ▪ Stills gallery.
1963 70m/C Connie Mason, Thomas Wood, Mal Arnold, Scott H. Hall, Lyn Bolton, Toni Calvert, Gene Courtier, Ashlyn Martin, Jerome Eden, David Friedman; *D:* Herschell Gordon Lewis; *W:* Allison Louise Downe; *C:* Herschell Gordon Lewis; *M:* Herschell Gordon Lewis.

Blood, Guts, Bullets and Octane

Joe Carnahan tries to combine Tarantinian violence and editing with a couple of characters borrowed from David Mamet. Bob (Leis) and Sid (Carnahan) are fast-talking used car salesmen who have to look after a '63 Pontiac LeMans convertible for a few days. The payoff: $250,000. You know there's a catch, and the bodies pile up. The story is told in often-distorted images with fussy self-conscious direction. Given the artsy visuals, it's hard to make a meaningful judgment about the quality of the image. Sound is often curiously flat, and again that appears to be intentional. Recommended for the festival crowd only. —MM
Movie: 🎞🎞▶ **DVD:** 🎞🎞▶
Universal Studios Home Video (Cat #20729, UPC #025192072925). Widescreen (1.85:1) letterboxed. Dolby Digital Surround Stereo. $24.98. Keepcase. *LANG:* English. *CAP:* English. *FEATURES:* 18 chapter links ▪ Trailer.
1999 (R) 87m/C Joe Carnahan, Dan Leis, Ken Rudolph, James Salter, Dan Harlan; *D:* Joe Carnahan; *W:* Joe Carnahan; *C:* John A. Jimenez; *M:* Mark Priolo, Martin Burke.

Blood on the Sun

Newspaperman (Cagney) in Japan uncovers plans for world domination as propaganda, violence, and intrigue combine in this action adventure.
Movie: 🎞🎞▶ **DVD:** NYR
Parade (Cat #55086). Full frame. Dolby Digital Mono. $17.98. Keepcase. The title is also available from Madacy (cat. #990572) for $9.99.
1945 98m/B James Cagney, Sylvia Sidney, Robert Armstrong, Wallace Ford; *D:* Frank Lloyd; *W:* Lester Cole, Nathaniel Curtis, Frank Melford; *C:* Theodor Sparkuhl; *M:* Miklos Rozsa.

The Blood Oranges

Erotica with a literary bent follows in the footsteps of *The English Patient* and *Unbearable Lightness of Being*, but it was produced on a budget that was much less opulent. Cyril (Dance) and Fiona (Lee) are carefree expatriates open to sexual adventure when they meet Catherine (Robins) and Hugh (Lane), a married couple with family. Director Haas shifts back and forth in time to reveal the ramifications of the various relationships that develop. The DVD image handles the action with a combination of vivid landscapes—the film was made in Mexico—and evocative, rough-hewn interiors softened with warm orange light. The sound heightens Badalamenti's somniferous score. —MM
Movie: 🎞🎞▶ **DVD:** 🎞🎞🎞
Trimark Home Video (Cat #VM7086D, UPC #031398708636). Widescreen (1.66:1) letterboxed. Dolby Digital Surround Stereo. $24.99. Keepcase. *LANG:* English. *SUB:* English; French; Spanish. *CAP:* English. *FEATURES:* 30 chapter links ▪ Theatrical trailer.
1997 (R) 93m/C Charles Dance, Sheryl Lee, Colin Lane, Laila Robins, Rachael Bella; *D:* Philip Haas; *W:* Belinda Haas, Philip Haas; *C:* Bernard Zitzermann; *M:* Angelo Badalamenti.

The Blood Spattered Bride

Vicente Aranda mixes exploitation and fiery no-prisoners feminism in a strange evocative update of Sheridan LeFanu's *Carmilla*. Troubled newlyweds (Andreu and Martin) go to his lonely, lavish provincial estate and eventually are joined by a vampiric ghost (Bastedo), who has perhaps the weirdest introduction in the history of horror. Time has rendered some of the film's surrealistic touches and sexual notions dated and humorous. The somnambulant pace and striking locations have lost nothing, though. Simon Andreu's portrayal of the nameless self-centered husband is piggishly perfect. In theatrical release, the violent ending was severely reedited. The unrated disc is shocking. Of the three adaptations of the novel (the others are Vadim's *Blood and Roses* and *The Vampire Lovers*), this is by far the best. The DVD is a slight improvement over the excellent Anchor Bay VHS tape, retaining the slightly soft focus and bright vivid colors. Sound is nothing special. —MM **AKA:** Blood Castle; La Novia Esangrentada; Bloody Fiance; Till Death Us Do Part.

Movie: 🎞🎞🎞 **DVD:** 🎞🎞🎞

Anchor Bay (Cat #DV11115, UPC #013131111590). Widescreen (1.85:1) anamorphic. Dolby Digital Mono. $29.98. Keepcase. *LANG:* English. *FEATURES:* 24 chapter links • Liner notes by Michael Felsher.

1972 101m/C *SP* Simon Andreu, Maribel Martin, Alexandra Bastedo, Dean Selmier, Rosa Ma Rodriguez, Montserrat Julio, Angel Lombarte; *D:* Vicente Aranda; *W:* Vicente Aranda; *C:* Fernando Arribas.

Bloodstone

A couple (Stimely and Nicholas) honeymooning in India are caught up in an adventure when a fabulous ruby is stashed in their luggage. This is typically light-hearted fare from prolific producer Nico Mastorakis. On DVD the image is acceptable, with one seersucker suit that verges on the psychedelic in the right light. The Indian locations are captured well. —MM

Movie: 🎞🎞 **DVD:** 🎞🎞

Simitar Entertainment (Cat #7606, UPC #082551760626). Full frame. Dolby Digital Stereo. $14.98. Keepcase. *LANG:* English. *FEATURES:* 8 chapter links • Theatrical trailers • Thumbnail biography of Nico Mastorakis.

1988 (PG-13) 90m/C Charlie Brill, Christopher Neame, Jack Kehler, Brett Stimely, Anna Nicholas; *D:* Dwight Little; *W:* Nico Mastorakis, Curt Allen.

Bloodstorm: Subspecies 4

Fourth installment in the shot-on-location Transylvanian vampire series. Master vampire Radu Vladislas (Hove) has awakened with an agenda. He wants to reclaim his vast wealth and recapture fledgling vamp, Michelle (Duff). Meanwhile, Radu hangs around with former protege, Ash (Morris), and Michelle is taken in by a creepy doctor (Dinvale), who's after the bloodstone. If you liked the first three, this is just more of the same. **AKA:** Subspecies 4; Subspecies 4: Bloodstorm—The Master's Revenge.

Movie: 🎞➤ **DVD:** NYR

Full Moon Pictures (Cat #8010). Full frame; widescreen (1.85:1) letterboxed. Dolby Digital 5.1 Surround Stereo. $24.95. Jewel case. *LANG:* English; French. *SUB:* French; Spanish. *CAP:* English.

1998 (R) 90m/C Anders Hove, Denice Duff, Jonathan Morris, Mihai Dinvale, Floriella Grappini; *D:* Ted Nicolaou; *W:* Ted Nicolaou; *C:* Adolfo Bartoli; *M:* Richard Kosinski.

The Bloodsucker Leads the Dance

Another piece of Italian sleaze-horror where a group of people are invited to an ominous-looking gothic castle with gory and disastrous results. Luckily there's a lot of sex mixed in with beheadings to keep things lively. Like the other Image "Redemption" titles, the opening sequence (made for this series) is super sharp and colorful. Then the feature starts and things fade away, including the color. Since it really wouldn't hurt that this film's presentation is a little worn and weary, it'd be better if they just left the sexy but repetitive intros out. The film itself is fairly sharp, with colors that are both faded and a little off. Blacks are O.K. and grain is minimal. The sound is certainly up to par, and though scratchy at times, keeps well within the spirit of the film. Another cool vintage Eurosleaze score. —JO **AKA:** La Sanguisuga Conduce la Danza; Il Marchio di Santana; The Mark of Satan; The Passion of Evelyn.

Movie: 🎞🎞➤ **DVD:** 🎞🎞➤

Image Entertainment (Cat #ID4612SADVD, UPC #014381461220). Widescreen (1.85:1) letterboxed. Dolby Digital Mono. $24.99. Snapper. *LANG:* English. *FEATURES:* 19 chapter links.

1975 89m/C *IT* Femi Benussi, Giacomo "Jack" Rossi-Stuart, Krista Nell, Luciano Pigozzi, Patrizia Webley; *D:* Alfredo Rizzo; *W:* Alfredo Rizzo; *C:* Aldo Greci; *M:* Marcello Giombini.

Bloodsucking Freaks

Oh, how the VideoHound has trouble keeping his doggie chow down whenever this freak show is on the screen. The gross-out factor is off the charts as Reed keeps his camera trained on more straight-on scenes of torture, unabashed nudity, and eyeball-eating dwarfs than most hounds can stomach. O'Brien is Sardu, a sado-masochistic showman who tortures young women on stage for the amusement of his audience. Only Sardu, his dwarf assistant, and their victims realize it's all for real as the terrible twosome murders and maims the naked captives. There's little real humor, though the kidnapping and torture of a pompous theatre critic is a joke to be appreciated by every actor, director, and playwright who has suffered a negative review. It's all hard to look at, though admirers of seriously sicko cinema may find it hard to look away from. Most will think it intolerable. Such a no-budget piece of exploitation can only look and sound so good, but the DVD gets high technical marks for its extras and interactivity. It's easier to view the film with the commentary track covering the screams of Sardu's torture victims, and the rest of the extras are imaginative. —MB **AKA:** The Incredible Torture Show; The House of the Screaming Virgins.

Movie: woof **DVD:** 🎞🎞🎞

Troma Team Video (Cat #9830, UPC #790357983032). Full frame. Dolby Digi-

tal Mono. $24.98. Keepcase. *LANG:* English. *FEATURES:* Theatrical trailers • Commentary: blood-and-guts expert Eli Roth • Introduction by Troma chief Lloyd Kaufman • Interactive tour of Troma's studios • Interactive Troma intelligence test • Web links • Troma public service announcements • 9 chapter links.

1975 (R) 89m/C Seamus O'Brian, Niles McMaster, Viju Krim, Alan Dellay, Dan Fauci; *D:* Joel M. Reed; *W:* Joel M. Reed; *C:* Gerry Toll; *M:* Michael Sahl.

Blown Away

Boston Irish bomb-squad cop Jimmy Dove (Bridges) is after former compatriot Ryan Gaerity (Jones), an Irish radical who's taken his bombing expertise onto Jimmy's new turf. Meanwhile, Jimmy wants to keep his unsavory past from unsuspecting wife Amis. Real-life dad Lloyd plays Jeff's uncle. While Jones seems adequately obsessed with making things go boom and Bridges significantly concerned that they don't, this thriller moves on a predictable path toward an explosive climax. Special effects create the suspense, as everyday objects become lethal in Gaerity's knowledgeable hands. The final explosion was more than even the special effects coordinator desired—windows were unintentionally blown out in nearby buildings, and if you turn your home system up a touch, this DVD's 5.1 sound may have the same results. The mix is outstanding and the bass is supercharged, delivering plenty of guts to even a weaker subwoofer. The picture is also very sharp and colors detailed with plenty of contrast. —JO

Movie: 🎞🎞 **DVD:** 🎞🎞🎞➤

MGM Home Entertainment (Cat #906250, UPC #276166259900). Widescreen (2.35:1) letterboxed; full frame. Dolby Digital 5.1; Dolby Surround. $24.98. Keepcase. *LANG:* English (DD5.1); Spanish (DS); French (DD5.1). *SUB:* English; Spanish; French. *CAP:* English. *FEATURES:* 32 chapter links • Theatrical trailer.

1994 (R) 121m/C Jeff Bridges, Tommy Lee Jones, Suzy Amis, Lloyd Bridges, Forest Whitaker; *D:* Stephen Hopkins; *W:* Joe Batteer, John Rice; *C:* Gregory McClatchy; *M:* Alan Silvestri. *AWARDS: NOM:* MTV Movie Awards '95: Best Villain (Jones), Best Action Sequence.

Blue Collar

Facing financial pressures brought on by their families and their taste for wild drug-fueled parties, auto workers Jerry (Keitel), Smokey (Kotto), and Zeke (Pryor) hatch a scheme to rob their corrupt union local. Like so many '70s films, this one has never been a highly polished visual gem. Partly shot on location, it's as rough as its story and DVD does little to improve that. The real bonus here is a terrific commentary track by writer-director Paul Schrader with journalist Maitland McDonagh. Her questions lead the filmmaker to remember the incredible problems he went through with a cast that had such diametrically different working styles that he could seldom gather his three stars for more than one take in their scenes together. The personality conflicts, aggravated by on-set drug use, led to actual violence. Even so, the performances are excellent, and the disc does justice to a cult hit that's ready to be rediscovered by new audiences. —MM

Movie: 🎬🎬🎬 **DVD:** 🎬🎬🎬
Anchor Bay (Cat #DV10939, UPC #013131093995). Widescreen (1.85:1) letterboxed. Dolby Digital Mono. $24.98. Keepcase. *LANG:* English. *FEATURES:* 21 chapter links ● Theatrical trailer ● Commentary: Paul Schrader and Maitland McDonagh ● Cast and crew thumbnail biographies.
1978 (R) 114m/C Richard Pryor, Harvey Keitel, Yaphet Kotto, Ed Begley Jr., Lane Smith, Cliff DeYoung; *D:* Paul Schrader; *W:* Paul Schrader, Leonard Schrader; *C:* Bobby Byrne; *M:* Jack Nitzsche.

The Blue Gardenia

Seminal but rarely seen film noir makes a belated appearance on home video. Norah Larkin (Baxter) wakes up one morning in the apartment of womanizing lout Harry Prebble (Burr). He's dead and she's labeled "The Blue Gardenia" murderess by newspaper columnist Casey Mayo (Conte). The film also marks the debut of Nat "King" Cole's famous title song, arranged by Nelson Riddle. On DVD, the black-and-white photography ranges from good to very good to excellent. Sound is merely good. Both are accurate re-creations of the original. Required viewing for fans of vintage mysteries. —MM

Movie: 🎬🎬🎬 **DVD:** 🎬🎬🎬
Image Entertainment (Cat #ID9042AQ DVD, UPC #014381904222). Full frame. Dolby Digital Mono. $24.99. Snapper. *LANG:* English. *FEATURES:* 12 chapter links.
1953 88m/B Anne Baxter, Richard Conte, Ann Sothern, Raymond Burr, George Reeves, Nat King Cole; *D:* Fritz Lang; *W:* Charles Hoffman; *C:* Nicholas Musuraca; *M:* Raoul Kraushaar.

Blue Juice

"British surf movie" sounds like a contradiction in terms and a young cast is, for the most part, left waiting for a wave. JC (Pertwee), the big enchilada of the local Limey surfer set, has just recovered from a back injury. He'd rather go on safari with his pals (including McGregor) than make whoopee with his girl Chloe (Zeta-Jones). The few surfing scenes are the liveliest moments in the film. On DVD, their clarity and energy stand apart from the rest which is relatively unexceptional in image and sound. —MM

Movie: 🎬🎬 **DVD:** 🎬🎬
Trimark Home Video (Cat #7289D, UPC #03139872892). Widescreen letterboxed. Dolby Digital Surround Stereo. $24.99.

Keepcase. *LANG:* English. *SUB:* English; French; Spanish. *CAP:* English. *FEATURES:* 24 chapter links.
1995 (R) 90m/C *GB* Sean Pertwee, Catherine Zeta-Jones, Ewan McGregor, Steven Mackintosh, Peter Gunn, Heathcote Williams; *D:* Carl Prechezer; *W:* Carl Prechezer, Peter Salmi; *C:* Richard Greatrex; *M:* Simon Davison.

The Blue Lagoon

Useless remake of the 1949 film of the same name tells the story of an adolescent boy (Atkins) and girl (Shields) marooned on a tropical island where they discover demure sex without the restraints of society. The DVD looks pretty good for a film of its age, but it's hard to understand why so much effort was put into the presentation. Would anyone but the most dedicated Brooke-aphile want to go through her personal photo album? Why two commentary tracks? On any medium, this is an attractive, dopey movie. —MM

Movie: woof **DVD:** 🎬🎬▸
Columbia Tristar Home Video (Cat #01379, UPC #043396013797). Widescreen (1.85:1) letterboxed; full frame. Dolby Digital Surround Stereo; Dolby Digital Mono. $25.95. Keepcase. *LANG:* English; Spanish. *SUB:* English; Spanish; Portuguese; Chinese; Korean; Thai. *FEATURES:* 28 chapter links ● Commentary: Kleiser, Stewart, and Shields ● Commentary: Kleiser and Atkins ● Production notes ● Cast and crew thumbnail biographies ● "Making of" featurette.
1980 (R) 105m/C Brooke Shields, Christopher Atkins, Leo McKern, William Daniels; *D:* Randal Kleiser; *W:* Douglas Day Stewart; *C:* Nestor Almendros; *M:* Basil Poledouris. *AWARDS:* Golden Raspberry Awards '80: Worst Actress (Shields); *NOM:* Academy Awards '80: Best Cinematography.

The Blues Brothers (CE)

As an excuse to run rampant on the city of Chicago, Jake and Elwood Blues attempt to raise $5,000 for their childhood orphanage by putting their old band back together. Good music, quotable dialogue, lots of wrecked cars, plenty of cameos. A classic. The DVD looks pretty good and sounds even better. The musical numbers are extremely energized and all of the on-screen destruction properly thrashes your speakers to their limit. The bass is foot-stomping good. The picture could be sharper but colors are nicely detailed and excitedly vibrant. Watching the documentary not only fills in some details of the actual filmmaking, it also shows the passions of the filmmakers themselves, particularly Aykroyd. —JO

Movie: 🎬🎬🎬 **DVD:** 🎬🎬🎬
Universal Studios Home Video (Cat #20299, UPC #025192029929). Widescreen (1.85:1) anamorphic. Dolby Digital 5.1. $34.98. Keepcase. *LANG:* English.

SUB: Spanish; French. *CAP:* English. *FEATURES:* 7 chapter links ● Theatrical trailer ● "Making of" featurette ● Production notes ● Production photos ● Added footage.
1980 (R) 133m/C John Belushi, Dan Aykroyd, James Brown, Cab Calloway, Ray Charles, Henry Gibson, Aretha Franklin, Carrie Fisher, John Candy, Kathleen Freeman, Steven Williams, Charles Napier, Stephen Bishop; *Cameos:* Frank Oz, Steven Spielberg, Twiggy, Paul (Pee-wee Herman) Reubens, Steve Lawrence, John Lee Hooker, John Landis, Chaka Khan; *D:* John Landis; *W:* John Landis, Dan Aykroyd; *C:* Stephen M. Katz; *M:* Ira Newborn, Elmer Bernstein.

The Blues Brothers 2000

Eighteen years after the original caper, Landis, Aykroyd, and most of the original cast return to the scene of the crime. Jake's dead but Elwood gets the band back together, recruits a Blues cousin (Goodman), a half-foster brother (Morton), and an orphan (Bonifant) in need of mentoring, and heads for a battle of the bands between New Orleans and Chicago. Unfortunately, more than capturing the spirit of the original, this one comes off as a big-budget excuse to get a bunch of music superstars together. Watch the original... again. Most of the time the picture is very sharp on this DVD with very little digital grain. The colors are lush and bleed is minimal. Blacks are as true as anything I've seen and combine with very good contrast and brightness levels to make for very comfortable viewing. The biggest problem comes in on quick camera moves where the movement is not natural. The excellent 5.1 track really complements the music, delivering full fidelity, punchy dynamics, and very good low end. The Surround tracks kick in nicely during action sequences. —JO

Movie: 🎬🎬 **DVD:** 🎬🎬🎬▸
Universal Studios Home Video (Cat #20281, UPC #025192028120). Widescreen (1.85:1) anamorphic. Dolby Digital 5.1. $34.98. Keepcase. *LANG:* English; French. *SUB:* Spanish; French. *CAP:* English. *FEATURES:* 41 chapter links ● Theatrical trailer ● "Making of" featurette ● Production notes ● Production photos ● Cast bios ● Poster campaign.
1998 (PG-13) 123m/C Dan Aykroyd, John Goodman, Joe Morton, Evan Bonifant, Nia Peeples, Kathleen Freeman, Frank Oz, Steve Lawrence, Aretha Franklin, B.B. King, James Brown, Erykah Badu, Darrell Hammond; *D:* John Landis; *W:* John Landis, Dan Aykroyd; *C:* David Herrington; *M:* Paul Shaffer.

Body Armor

Special agent Conway (McColm) is recruited by an ex-girlfriend (Schofield) to find a missing scientist. That leads our hero to nutball virologist Dr. Krago (Perlman), who's using germ warfare for personal gain. For the action junkie who doesn't mind a little eye candy as well, the DVD looks pretty good. It's well photographed with a bright, sharp image and loud stereo in the right scenes. —*MM*

Movie: 🐾🐾 **DVD:** 🐾🐾▸
Simitar Entertainment (Cat #7429, UPC #082551742929). Full frame. Dolby Digital Stereo; Dolby Digital 5.1 Surround Stereo. $14.98. Keepcase. *LANG:* English. *FEATURES:* 8 chapter links ▪ Production factoids ▪ Matt McColm and Carol Alt filmographies.
1996 (R) 95m/C Matt McColm, Ron Perlman, Annabel Schofield, Carol Alt, Clint Howard, Morgan Brittany, Shauna O'Brien; *D:* Jack Gill; *W:* Jack Gill; *C:* Robert Hayes; *M:* Mark Holden.

Body Double

A voyeuristic unemployed actor peeps on a neighbor's nightly disrobing (choreographed by porn actress Annette Haven) and sees more than he wants to. A grisly murder leads him into an obsessive quest through the world of pornographic films. Director DePalma delivers another stylized Hitchcockian thriller, borrowing heavily from *Vertigo* and *Rear Window*, and then throws in his usual excesses. The film includes a music video–like segment done to the Frankie Goes to Hollywood song "Relax." Slightly below-average DVD has a little grain most of the time, and a lot during the dimly lit scenes. The colors bleed a little but are good and punchy, especially on the garish porn-set sequences. Blacks are close to true except during periods of excessive grain. The contrast is good and brightness a little low but consistent. The sound has good separation (comparable to the widescreen laserdisc) and O.K. bass, but it could be a little crisper on the high ends. Full-frame and anamorphic sides are very close in quality. —*JO*

Movie: 🐾🐾🐾 **DVD:** 🐾▸
Columbia Tristar Home Video (Cat #04119, UPC #043396041196). Widescreen (1.85:1) anamorphic; full frame. Dolby Surround. Keepcase. *LANG:* English (DS); French. *SUB:* English; French. *FEATURES:* 28 chapter links ▪ Theatrical trailer.
1984 (R) 114m/C Craig Wasson, Melanie Griffith, Gregg Henry, Deborah Shelton, Guy Boyd, Dennis Franz, David Haskell, Rebecca Stanley, Barbara Crampton; *D:* Brian DePalma; *W:* Brian DePalma, Robert J. Avrech; *C:* Stephen Burum; *M:* Pino Donaggio. *AWARDS:* National Society of Film Critics Awards '84: Best Supporting Actress (Griffith).

Body Heat

During a Florida heat wave, a none-too-bright lawyer becomes involved in a steamy love affair with a mysterious woman and then in a plot to kill her husband. Hurt and Turner (in her film debut) became stars under Kasdan's direction (the three would reunite for *The Accidental*

Tourist). Hot love scenes supplement a twisting mystery with a surprise ending. Rourke's arsonist and Danson's soft shoe shouldn't be missed. The smoldering image in this film is of the type that has wreaked havoc with several DVDs. In this case, however, the disc has no problems conveying the image accurately without the addition of digital grain or artifacts. Colors are sensual and vibrant. Contrast and brightness levels are very good. Blacks are perfect. The 5.1 sound is full and dynamic, but very little ambience or effects are offered by the Surround tracks. —*JO*

Movie: 🐾🐾🐾▸ **DVD:** 🐾🐾🐾▸
Warner Home Video, Inc. (Cat #20005, UPC #085392000524). Widescreen (1.85:1) anamorphic. Dolby Digital 5.1; Dolby Digital Mono. $24.98. Snapper. *LANG:* English (DD5.1); French (DDM). *SUB:* English; Spanish; French. *CAP:* English. *FEATURES:* 30 chapter links ▪ Theatrical trailers ▪ Production notes.
1981 (R) 113m/C William Hurt, Kathleen Turner, Richard Crenna, Ted Danson, Mickey Rourke, J.A. Preston, Kim Zimmer, Jane Hallaren; *D:* Lawrence Kasdan; *W:* Lawrence Kasdan; *C:* Richard H. Kline; *M:* John Barry.

Body of Influence 2

Dr. Benson (Anderson), a Beverly Hills psychiatrist with sexual problems of his own, is seduced by his patient Leza (Fisher), who has a jealous husband. For a direct-to-video erotic thriller, this one looks very good. It's well photographed with only minor pixelation in the nocturnal exteriors. Otherwise, the image is excellent. —*MM*

Movie: 🐾🐾▸ **DVD:** 🐾🐾▸
Simitar Entertainment (Cat #7450, UPC #082551745029). Full frame. Dolby Digital Stereo. $14.95. Keepcase. *LANG:* English. *FEATURES:* 8 chapter links ▪ Production factoids.
1996 (R) 88m/C Daniel Anderson, Jodie Fisher, Steve Poletti, Jonathan Goldstein, Pat Brennan; *D:* Brian J. Smith; *W:* Brian J. Smith; *C:* Azusa Ohno; *M:* Ron Sures.

Body Puzzle

Run-of-the-mill Italian horror has yet another serial killer making the rounds and taking one part of each victim. What does it all have to do with the lovely Tracey (Pacula)? This stuff has been done hundreds of times and director Lamberto Bava (son of Mario) really has nothing new to add. The dubbing is so-so; the image is little better, particularly in the rainy night scenes. —*MM AKA: Misteria.*

Movie: 🐾▸ **DVD:** 🐾🐾
Image Entertainment (Cat #ID5585FMDVD, UPC #014381558524). Full frame. Dolby Digital Mono. $14.99. Snapper. *LANG:* English. *FEATURES:* 14 chapter links.
1993 98m/C *IT* Joanna Pacula, Tom Aaron, Frank Quinn; *D:* Lamberto Bava; *W:* Bruce Martin; *C:* Lee Kraus.

Body Shot

Photographer Mickey Dane (Patrick) is so fascinated by rock star Chelsea that he roots through her garbage. That makes him a natural choice to shoot a series of suggestive pictures of a Chelsea lookalike (Johnson). When the original turns up dead, he's been framed. Robert Ian Strauss's script uses a noirish voice-over to good effect, and the presence of B-movie veterans Kenneth Tobey and Charles Napier doesn't hurt either. Director Logothetis shows a certain visual flair in some nicely composed shots, though he does overindulge in the circling camera cliche. Patrick is known best as Arnold Schwarzenegger's implacable antagonist in *T2,* and he brings the same intensity to this part. A tricky cut above the norm. On disc, the average production values are apparent. In the low-rent glitz nightclub scenes, blacks are solid masses, and many of the everyday interiors look washed-out and pale. Not much better than the tape as I remember it. —*MM*

Movie: 🐾🐾🐾 **DVD:** 🐾🐾▸
Image Entertainment (Cat #ID5586FM DVD, UPC #014381558623). Full frame. Dolby Digital Stereo. $24.99. Snapper. *LANG:* English. *FEATURES:* 12 chapter links.
1993 (R) 98m/C Robert Patrick, Michelle Johnson, Ray Wise, Jonathan Banks, Kim Miyori, Kenneth Tobey, Charles Napier; *D:* Dimitri Logothetis; *W:* Robert Strauss; *C:* Nicholas Josef von Sternberg; *M:* Cliff Magness.

Body Snatchers

For sheer paranoia, Abel Ferrara's take may not be as suspenseful as Don Siegel's original, but it's better than Philip Kaufman's 1978 remake. The inventive special effects are about as skin-crawly as any you'll see. They involve soft, gently probing little tendrils that do absolutely revolting things. Sullen teenaged Marti Malone (Anwar) hates everything about the new military base where her family has moved. She doesn't much care for her dad (Kinney), stepmom (Tilly), or little brother (Murphy) either. The only thing she likes is a handsome chopper pilot (Wirth). Of course, they're all potential pod fodder. Initially, Ferrara uses a funereal pace to turn the ordinary into the ominous, effectively building tension until the icky effects kick in. On the minus side, he overuses the shortcut of panning his camera through walls between rooms. It's a technique that rudely reminds viewers they're watching a movie when they should be suspending their disbelief. The DVD looks and sounds very good. Since this brilliant paranoid fable has had so many incarnations, commentary by Ferrara might have been interesting, but given a poor track record with such undertakings—his rambling semi-coherent remarks on *Driller Killer*—the disc is probably better without it. —*MM*

Movie: 🐾🐾🐾▸ **DVD:** 🐾🐾🐾

Warner Home Video, Inc. (Cat #13027, UPC #085391302728). Widescreen letterboxed; full frame. Dolby Digital Surround Stereo. $19.98. Snapper. *LANG:* English; French. *SUB:* English; French. *FEATURES:* 29 chapter links.
1993 (R) 87m/C Gabrielle Anwar, Meg Tilly, Terry Kinney, Forest Whitaker, Billy Wirth, R. Lee Ermey, Reilly Murphy; *D:* Abel Ferrara; *W:* Stuart Gordon, Dennis Paoli, Nicholas St. John; *C:* Bojan Bazelli; *M:* Joe Delia. —*MM*

Body Strokes

Blocked artist Leo (Johnston) tries to turn things around with two new models, Beth (Knittle) and Claire (Weber). The fantasies help to get his marriage back on track when his manager/wife Karen (Beck) becomes jealous. This erotic thriller is actually more serious than most with a genuine attempt at character development and plot. Unfortunately, on DVD, it's poorly focused with a rough edge to the colors. The sound is all right. Also available in an unrated version (catalog number 7471). —*MM* **AKA:** Siren's Kiss.
Movie: 🦴🦴 *DVD:* 🦴🦴
Simitar Entertainment (Cat #7448, UPC #082551744824). Full frame. PCM Stereo. $14.98. Keepcase. *LANG:* English. *FEATURES:* 8 chapter links • Production factoids.
1995 99m/C Bobby Johnston, Dixie Beck, Kristen Knittle, Catherine Weber; *D:* Edward Holzman; *W:* April Moskowitz; *C:* Kim Haun; *M:* Richard Bronskill.

The Bodyguard

Frank Farmer (Costner), a button-down ex–Secret Service agent with an extremely bad haircut, reluctantly takes on the job of protecting pop diva Rachel Marron (Houston). Both stars are fine in roles that might have been tailor-made for them in Lawrence Kasdan's script. (Actually, he wrote it with Steve McQueen in mind.) Though this one was universally panned by critics, it remains a proven crowd-pleaser. The DVD is another curiously mixed bag. The image is all right even in the big busy performance scenes; the sound is somewhat better. But that image is pan-and-scan and though the disc contains 38 chapter links, only 9 can be accessed from the index. —*MM*
Movie: 🦴🦴▸ *DVD:* 🦴🦴▸
Warner Home Video, Inc. (Cat #12591, UPC #085391259121). Full frame. Dolby Digital Surround 5.1; Dolby Surround. $24.98. Snapper. *LANG:* English; French. *SUB:* English; French; Spanish. *CAP:* English. *FEATURES:* 38 chapter links • Cast thumbnail biographies • Production notes.
1992 (R) 130m/C Kevin Costner, Whitney Houston, Gary Kemp, Bill Cobbs, Ralph Waite, Tomas Arana, Michele Lamar Richards, Mike Starr, Christopher Birt, DeVaughn Nixon, Charles Keating, Robert Wuhl; *Cameos:* Debbie Reynolds; *D:* Mick Jackson; *W:* Lawrence Kasdan; *C:* Andrew

Dunn; *M:* Alan Silvestri. *AWARDS:* MTV Movie Awards '93: Best Song ("I Will Always Love You"); *NOM:* Academy Awards '92: Best Song ("I Have Nothing"), Best Song ("Run to You").

Boiling Point

Darkly flavored action drama delves into the personalities of its two main characters before setting up a final showdown. Treasury agent Jimmy Mercer (Snipes) is trying to solve his partner's murder, relentlessly pursuing the killers in a cold, methodical fashion. Sleazy Red Diamond (Hopper), just out of prison, owes the mob and has one week to pay them back. A fine supporting cast helps, but the whole film is grim and clichéd. Interiors on this budget DVD look fine; some grain appears in bright backgrounds. Sound is O.K. —*MM*
Movie: 🦴🦴▸ *DVD:* 🦴🦴
Warner Home Video, Inc. (Cat #12976, UPC #085391297628). Full frame. Dolby Digital Surround Stereo. $14.98. Snapper. *LANG:* English. *CAP:* English. *FEATURES:* 24 chapter links.
1993 (R) 93m/C Wesley Snipes, Dennis Hopper, Lolita (David) Davidovich, Viggo Mortensen, Dan Hedaya, Valerie Perrine, Seymour Cassel, Jonathan Banks, Tony LoBianco, Christine Elise, James Tolkan, Paul Gleason; *D:* James B. Harris; *W:* James B. Harris; *C:* King Baggot; *M:* Cory Lerios, John D'Andrea.

The Bone Collector

Shamelessly ripping off *Silence of the Lambs, Seven,* and just about any other serial killer flick you care to name, director Phillip Noyce trots this genre piece through its paces professionally enough. He has a good cast to work with. Denzel Washington is the paralyzed police detective who must work with the rookie cop, played by Angelina Jolie, and they become the killer's targets, etc., etc. You know the drill. Both image and sound are exceptionally sharp. —*MM*
Movie: 🦴🦴🦴 *DVD:* 🦴🦴🦴▸
Universal Studios Home Video (Cat #20716, UPC #025192071621). Widescreen (2.35:1) anamorphic. DTS Stereo; Dolby Digital 5.1 Surround Stereo; Dolby Digital Surround. $26.98. Keepcase. *LANG:* English; French. *CAP:* English. *FEATURES:* 20 chapter links • Location featurette • Commentary: director Phillip Noyce • Production notes • Cast and crew thumbnail bios • DVD-ROM features.
1999 (R) 118m/C Denzel Washington, Angelina Jolie, Queen Latifah, Ed O'Neill, Michael Rooker, Mike McGlone, Leland Orser, Luis Guzman, John Benjamin Hickey, Bobby Cannavale; *D:* Phillip Noyce; *W:* Jeremy Iacone; *C:* Dean Semler; *M:* Craig Armstrong.

The Bonfire of the Vanities

Miscast and stripped of the novel's gutsy examination of the characters and

their world, this adaptation of Tom Wolfe's best-seller is a mess. It's not as big a mess as its most vocal critics claim, but it's still hard to take. On a trip to see his mistress (Griffith), wealthy Sherman McCoy (Hanks) is involved in a hit-and-run accident. Willis is the drunken journalist/narrator who tells the story. DePalma's direction is typically shallow and showy. On DVD, Vilmos Zsigmond's cinematography holds up nicely, but it can do little to save this overlong mediocrity. —*MM*
Movie: 🦴 *DVD:* 🦴🦴
Warner Home Video, Inc. (Cat #12048, UPC #085391204824). Widescreen letterboxed; full frame. Dolby Digital Surround Stereo. $19.98. Snapper. *LANG:* English; French. *CAP:* English. *FEATURES:* 35 chapter links.
1990 (R) 126m/C Tom Hanks, Melanie Griffith, Bruce Willis, Morgan Freeman, Alan King, Kim Cattrall, Saul Rubinek, Clifton James, Donald Moffat, Richard Libertini, Andre Gregory, Robert Stephens; *Cameos:* F. Murray Abraham; *D:* Brian DePalma; *W:* Michael Cristofer; *C:* Vilmos Zsigmond; *M:* Dave Grusin.

Bonnie & Clyde

In the Depression era, when any job—even an illegal one—was cherished, money, greed, and power created an unending cycle of violence and fury. Bonnie Parker (Dunaway) and Clyde Barrow (Beatty) roamed the Southwest robbing banks. With its pronounced bloodshed, the highly controversial and influential film spurred mainstream cinematic proliferation. Warner has done a fine job on this disc. It's a great DVD with excellent sharpness and nary a hint of digital grain. No artifacts either. Colors are rich and accurate with only occasional bleed on deep reds. During a couple of scenes I would have liked a boost on both the contrast and brightness, but for the most part the levels seem where they should be. Don't be fooled by that mono soundtrack—it's full-bodied and full of energy, without any hint of distortion. —*JO*
Movie: 🦴🦴🦴▸ *DVD:* 🦴🦴🦴▸
Warner Home Video, Inc. (Cat #17274, UPC #085391727422). Widescreen (1.85:1) anamorphic; full frame. Dolby Digital 2.0 Mono. $19.98. Snapper. *LANG:* English; French. *SUB:* Spanish; French. *CAP:* English. *FEATURES:* 35 chapter links • Theatrical trailer • Production notes.
1967 111m/C Warren Beatty, Faye Dunaway, Michael J. Pollard, Gene Hackman, Estelle Parsons, Denver Pyle, Gene Wilder, Dub Taylor, Evans Evans; *D:* Arthur Penn; *W:* David Newman, Robert Benton; *C:* Burnett Guffey; *M:* Charles Strouse. *AWARDS:* Academy Awards '67: Best Cinematography, Best Supporting Actress (Parsons); American Film Institute (AFI) '98: Top 100, National Film Registry '92; New York Film Critics Awards '67: Best Screenplay; National Society of Film Critics Awards '67: Best Screenplay, Best Supporting Actor (Hackman); Writers Guild of America

'67: Best Original Screenplay; *NOM:* Academy Awards '67: Best Actor (Beatty), Best Actress (Dunaway), Best Costume Design, Best Director (Penn), Best Picture, Best Story & Screenplay, Best Supporting Actor (Hackman, Pollard).

The Boogey Man

This whacked-out psycho/slasher flick has a cult following but its appeal has always eluded me. The central gimmick—a shard of broken mirror—is connected to a childhood murder witnessed by Lacey (Love) and committed by her brother. The rest of the plot defies synopsis, but the film looks terrific on DVD with a bright image that belies its low-budget regional roots and semi-professional acting. Followed by a lesser sequel. (Disc also includes director Lommel's *Devonsville Terror.*) *—MM*
Movie: 🐾🐾 ► ***DVD:*** 🐾🐾
Anchor Bay (Cat #DV10664, UPC #013131066494). Widescreen letterboxed. Dolby Digital Mono. $29.98. Keepcase. *LANG:* English. *FEATURES:* 29 chapter links • 2 TV spots.
1980 (R) 93m/C John Carradine, Suzanna Love, Ron James; *D:* Ulli Lommel; *W:* Ulli Lommel, Suzanna Love; *C:* Jochen Breitenstein, David Sperling; *M:* Tim Krog.

Boogie Nights

Jack Horner (Reynolds) is a hard-core pornography auteur who discovers young stud Eddie Adams (Wahlberg) and transforms him into X-rated movie superstar Dirk Diggler. Although Horner is in command as patriarch of a dysfunctional family of smutshow moviemakers who experience varying degrees of success moving from the late 1970s into a new decade, his young protege is the story's focal point. The 17-year-old former busboy leaves behind his uncaring real family for the support network of Horner's pseudo-family of pornographers. Director Anderson's aim seems to be for *Boogie Nights* to do for pornographers what Martin Scorsese's *Goodfellas* does for gangsters—make them seem real and more human. It's an ambitious production that spans the decadent disco-era '70s and the excess of the '80s, but it's not for all audiences. Chances are if you're offended by the many expletives that pepper director Anderson's commentary track, you won't care much for his movie either. Another DVD bonus is a collection of deleted scenes, but they are not particularly captivating. A picky viewer might complain about blotchiness in the backgrounds of a few shots, but most everyone else will admire the generally excellent video quality. Owing to the Dolby Digital mix, the collection of period tunes that comprise the soundtrack sound better than ever. *—MB*
Movie: 🐾🐾🐾 ► ***DVD:*** 🐾🐾🐾 ►
New Line Home Video (Cat #N4650, UPC #794043465024). Widescreen (2.35:1) letterboxed. Dolby Digital 5.1. $24.98.

Snapper. *LANG:* English; French. *SUB:* English; French; Spanish. *CAP:* English. *FEATURES:* 37 chapter links • Commentary: director Paul Thomas Anderson • Deleted scenes • Michael Penn "Try" music video • Cast and crew biographies and filmographies • Character biographies.
1997 (R) 155m/C Mark Wahlberg, Burt Reynolds, Julianne Moore, Don Cheadle, William H. Macy, Heather Graham, John C. Reilly, Luis Guzman, Philip Seymour Hoffman, Alfred Molina, Philip Baker Hall, Robert Ridgely, Joanna Gleason, Thomas Jane, Ricky Jay, Nicole Parker, Melora Walters, Nina Hartley, John Doe, Michael Jace, Laurel Holloman; *Cameos:* Michael Penn, Robert Downey; *D:* Paul Thomas Anderson; *W:* Paul Thomas Anderson; *C:* Robert Elswit; *M:* Michael Penn. *AWARDS:* Golden Globe Awards '98: Best Supporting Actor (Reynolds); Los Angeles Film Critics Association Awards '97: Best Supporting Actor (Reynolds), Best Supporting Actress (Moore); MTV Movie Awards '98: Breakthrough Performance (Graham); New York Film Critics Awards '97: Best Supporting Actor (Reynolds); National Society of Film Critics Awards '97: Best Supporting Actor (Reynolds), Best Supporting Actress (Moore); *NOM:* Academy Awards '97: Best Original Screenplay, Best Supporting Actor (Reynolds), Best Supporting Actress (Moore); British Academy Awards '97: Best Original Screenplay, Best Supporting Actor (Reynolds); Golden Globe Awards '98: Best Supporting Actor (Reynolds), Best Supporting Actress (Moore); MTV Movie Awards '98: Best Dance Sequence (Mark Wahlberg/cast); Screen Actors Guild Award '97: Best Supporting Actor (Reynolds), Best Supporting Actress (Moore), Cast; Writers Guild of America '97: Best Original Screenplay.

Booty Call

Reserved Rushon (Davidson) and conservative Nikki (Jones) have been dating for a couple of months and Rushon's decided they should consummate their relationship. Nikki's more ambivalent and first sets up a double date with her vivacious best friend Lysterine (Fox) and Rushon's bragging buddy Bunz (Foxx). The duos do pair up but since the "no glove, no love" rule prevails, first the guys have to find some condoms. Raunch rules, as might be expected, but it's an appealing cast. I first viewed this funny film on a VHS screener and, unfortunately, the picture was better than this DVD. The disc adds noticeable grain and is overall just not that sharp. The brightness level is high and contrast is a touch low. The sound is fine with nothing to add or detract from the viewing experience. *—JO*
Movie: 🐾🐾🐾 ***DVD:*** 🐾🐾
Columbia Tristar Home Video (Cat #94959, UPC #043396949591). Widescreen (1.85:1) anamorphic. Dolby Digital 5.1; Dolby Surround. NSL. Keepcase. *LANG:* English (DD5.1); Spanish (DS); French (DS). *SUB:* English; Spanish;

French. *FEATURES:* 28 chapter links • Theatrical trailer.
1996 (R) 120m/C Jamie Foxx, Tommy Davidson, Vivica A. Fox, Tamala Jones, Art Malik, Gedde Watanabe, Scott LaRose, Ammie Sin, Bernie Mac, David Hemblen; *D:* Jeff Pollack; *W:* Takashi Bufford; *C:* Ronald Orieux; *M:* Robert Folk.

Born in East L.A.

Marin brings his Bruce Springsteen–parody song to life as he plays a mistakenly deported illegal alien who struggles to return to the U.S. It's a surprisingly resolute effort by the usually self-exploiting Mexican-American. Stern is the American expatriate who helps him get back and Lopez is the love interest who stalls him. This DVD proves that Goodtimes can put out a good product. Colors are tremendously vibrant and the picture is sharp and grain-free. The DVD also features one of the more powerful mono soundtracks, which is actually packed with more energy than most Dolby Surround–encoded discs. *—JO*
Movie: 🐾🐾 ***DVD:*** 🐾🐾🐾 ►
Goodtimes Entertainment (Cat #05-81009, UPC #018713810090). Full frame. Dolby Digital Mono. $24.98. Snapper. *LANG:* English. *SUB:* Spanish; French. *CAP:* English. *FEATURES:* 18 chapter links.
1987 (R) 85m/C Richard "Cheech" Marin, Daniel Stern, Paul Rodriguez, Jan-Michael Vincent, Kamala Lopez, Tony Plana, Vic Trevino, A. Martinez; *D:* Richard "Cheech" Marin; *W:* Richard "Cheech" Marin; *C:* Alex Phillips Jr.; *M:* Lee Holdridge.

Born on the Fourth of July

A riveting meditation on American life affected by the Vietnam War, based on the real-life, best-selling experiences of Ron Kovic, though some facts are subtly changed. The film follows him as he develops from a naive recruit to an angry, wheelchair-bound paraplegic to an active antiwar protestor. Well-acted and generally lauded, Kovic cowrote the screenplay and appears as a war veteran in the opening parade sequence. Though the picture is very sharp, there are times when the color is oversaturated, resulting in some bleed and distortion. The colors are, however, accurate. Brightness and contrast levels are good and for the most part blacks are true. Director Stone usually makes good choices of music for his soundtracks and this is no exception. The disc's 5.1 tracks have no problems cranking out the tunes or placing the dialogue out front. The Surround is used to excellent effect conveying the ambience of both music and surroundings. *—JO*
Movie: 🐾🐾🐾 ► ***DVD:*** 🐾🐾 ►
Universal Studios Home Video (Cat #20208, UPC #025192020827). Widescreen (2.35:1) letterboxed. Dolby Digital 5.1. $26.98. Keepcase. *LANG:* English; French. *SUB:* Spanish. *CAP:* English. *FEA-*

TURES: 16 chapter links • Cast and filmmaker bios • Production notes • Film highlights.

1989 (R) 145m/C Tom Cruise, Kyra Sedgwick, Raymond J. Barry, Jerry Levine, Tom Berenger, Willem Dafoe, Frank Whaley, John Getz, Caroline Kava, Bryan Larkin, Abbie Hoffman, Stephen Baldwin, Josh Evans, Dale Dye, William Baldwin, Don "The Dragon" Wilson, Vivica A. Fox, Holly Marie Combs, Tom Sizemore, Daniel Baldwin, Ron Kovic; *Cameos:* Oliver Stone; *D:* Oliver Stone; *W:* Oliver Stone; *C:* Robert Richardson; *M:* John Williams. *AWARDS:* Academy Awards '89: Best Director (Stone), Best Film Editing; Directors Guild of America Awards '89: Best Director (Stone); Golden Globe Awards '90: Best Actor—Drama (Cruise), Best Director (Stone), Best Film—Drama, Best Screenplay; *NOM:* Academy Awards '89: Best Actor (Cruise), Best Adapted Screenplay, Best Cinematography, Best Picture, Best Sound, Best Original Score.

Born to Win

A New York hairdresser (Segal) with an expensive drug habit struggles through life in this well-made comedy drama. Excellent acting from a fine cast and interestingly photographed. The film was not well received in theatrical release, but it is worth a look. *AKA:* Addict.
Movie: ♪♪♪▶ *DVD:* NYR
Essex (Cat #1404). Full frame. Dolby Digital Mono. $19.95. Slipcase.
1971 (R) 90m/C George Segal, Karen Black, Paula Prentiss, Hector Elizondo, Robert De Niro, Jay Fletcher; *D:* Ivan Passer; *W:* Ivan Passer, David Scott Milton; *C:* Jack Priestley; *M:* William S. Fisher.

Born Yesterday

Ambitious junk dealer Harry Brock (Crawford) is in love with smart but uneducated Billie Dawn (Holliday). He hires newspaperman Paul Verrall (Holden) to teach her the finer points of etiquette. During their sessions, they fall in love and Billie realizes how she has been used by Brock. Retaliating against him, she delivers the now-famous line, "Do me a favor, drop dead." The source print on this DVD shows signs of age and wear, but it generally looks quite good without overly distracting problems, and I was genuinely surprised by the great quality of the movie on this disc. The DVD itself is very good without compression artifacts and a well-balanced contrast that ranges from deep blacks to good highlights. The mono track does contain some noise, but it is mostly limited and the track has been well restored to keep the dialogue intact without generating too much background noise. —*GH*
Movie: ♪♪♪▶ *DVD:* ♪♪♪▶
Columbia Tristar Home Video (Cat #10439, UPC #043396014398). Full frame. Dolby Digital Mono. $25.95. Keepcase. *LANG:* English. *SUB:* English; Spanish; Portuguese; Chinese; Korean; Thai. *CAP:* English. *FEATURES:* Production notes

• Vintage advertising • Theatrical trailer • Bonus trailers.
1950 103m/B Judy Holliday, Broderick Crawford, William Holden, Howard St. John, Frank Otto, Larry Oliver, Barbara Brown; *D:* George Cukor; *W:* Albert Mannheimer; *C:* Joseph Walker; *M:* Frederick "Friedrich" Hollander. *AWARDS:* Academy Awards '50: Best Actress (Holliday); Golden Globe Awards '51: Best Actress—Musical/Comedy (Holliday); *NOM:* Academy Awards '50: Best Costume Design (B & W), Best Director (Cukor), Best Picture, Best Screenplay.

The Borrowers

Charming big-budget tale of the little people who live under the floor is based on the children's books of Mary Norton. The Pod family—British, elfin, and about four inches tall—is headed by papa Pod (Broadbent). They live in the walls of the home of the normal-sized American Lenders and exist by "borrowing" objects from their humans' household. When an evil lawyer (Goodman) threatens their happiness, the Pods bond with young Peter Lender (Pierce) who volunteers to save their way of life. This remake focuses mainly on the impressive special effects, lending a modern look and appeal. Goodman is lovably evil in that wonderfully Snidely Whiplash way. The DVD re-creates the film's red-orange color scheme so faithfully that it may make some viewers a little bilious. Sound is very good. —*MM*
Movie: ♪♪▶ *DVD:* ♪♪♪
USA Home Entertainment (Cat #55125, UPC #044005512526). Widescreen anamorphic; full frame. Dolby Digital 5.1 Surround Stereo; Dolby Pro Logic Stereo. $19.95. Keepcase. *LANG:* English; French; Spanish. *FEATURES:* 14 chapter links • "Making of" featurette • Theatrical trailer • Cast and crew thumbnail biographies.
1997 (PG) 86m/C *GB* John Goodman, Hugh Laurie, Jim Broadbent, Mark Williams, Celia Imrie, Bradley Michael Pierce, Raymond Pickard, Aden Gillett, Ruby Wax, Flora Newbigin, Tom Felton, Doon Mackichan; *D:* Peter Hewitt; *W:* John Camps, Gavin Scott; *C:* John Fenner, Trevor Brooker; *M:* Harry Gregson-Williams. *AWARDS: NOM:* British Academy Awards '97: Best Film.

Boston Kickout

Phil (Simm) and three friends struggle to grow up in a bleak concrete town outside London. The title refers to a destructive game the guys play. Phil's hopes to find something more rest in his camera and his rocky relationship with Shona (McCourt), a bright energetic woman. Admittedly, this is familiar stuff, and nothing about the DVD's visuals will knock your eyes out. The film has that soft gray look that's found in so many films on British locations. Still, the characters ring true and the now-unknown cast shows promise, particularly the two leads. —*MM*
Movie: ♪♪▶ *DVD:* ♪♪▶

WinStar Home Entertainment (Cat #FLV5168, UPC #720917516820). Full frame. $24.98. Keepcase. *LANG:* English. *FEATURES:* 8 chapter links • Production credits • Filmographies • Weblink.
1995 105m/C *GB* John Simm, Andrew Lincoln, Richard Hanson, Nathan Valente, Emer McCourt, Marc Warren, Derek Martin, Vincent Phillips, Natalie Davies; *D:* Paul Hills; *W:* Paul Hills, Diane Whitley; *C:* Roger Bonnici; *M:* Robert Hartshorne.

The Bostonians

A faith healer's daughter (Redgrave) is forced to choose between the affections of a militant suffragette (Potter) and a young lawyer (Reeve) in 19th-century Boston. The combination of Merchant, Ivory, and James is stultifying. DVD can do nothing to improve the image with its dark gloomy interiors, pale washed-out colors, and echoing sounds. —*MM*
Movie: ♪▶ *DVD:* ♪♪
Rhino Home Video (Cat #2145). Full frame. Dolby Digital Mono. $24.98. Keepcase. *LANG:* English. *FEATURES:* 14 chapter links.
1984 (PG) 120m/C Christopher Reeve, Vanessa Redgrave, Madeleine Potter, Jessica Tandy, Nancy Marchand, Wesley Addy, Linda Hunt, Wallace Shawn; *D:* James Ivory; *W:* Ruth Prawer Jhabvala; *C:* Walter Lassally. *AWARDS:* National Society of Film Critics Awards '84: Best Actress (Redgrave); *NOM:* Academy Awards '84: Best Actress (Redgrave), Best Costume Design.

Bottle Rocket

This one's a failed-caper flick, a la *Reservoir Dogs,* but nice. After meeting small-time mobster Caan, a likable trio of aspiring criminals attempt to follow in his footsteps and make their mark in suburban Dallas. This smart ensemble piece, started off as a 13-minute black-and-white short, but after garnering producer James L. Brooks's attention at Sundance, received the backing to go feature length. Right off the bat the opening credits test the color performance by placing the saturated-red *Bottle Rocket* title on a true black background. Even with the high contrast, the bleed is minor. The picture is also very sharp and digital grain rarely makes an appearance. There is enough contrast to make the details come through, but the brightness is a little low. The sound is crisp and dynamic with good imaging and though there is not a lot of Surround, it does just fine when it kicks in. —*JO*
Movie: ♪♪♪ *DVD:* ♪♪♪
Columbia Tristar Home Video (Cat #11629, UPC #043396116290). Widescreen (1.85:1) letterboxed; full frame. Dolby Digital 5.1; 4.0. $24.98. Keepcase. *LANG:* English (DD5.1); Spanish (4.0). *SUB:* Spanish; French. *CAP:* English. *FEATURES:* 28 chapter links.

1995 (R) 91m/C Owen C. Wilson, Luke Wilson, Robert Musgrave, Lumi Cavazos, James Caan, Andrew Wilson, Jim Ponds; **D:** Wes Anderson; **W:** Wes Anderson, Owen C. Wilson; **C:** Robert Yeoman; **M:** Mark Mothersbaugh. *AWARDS:* MTV Movie Awards '96: Best New Filmmaker Award (Anderson).

Bound

The hot lesbian action between Gershon and Tilly will probably lead to more video rentals to the mainstream public than all this fine thriller's twists and quirks combined. (And the DVD contains a few extra moments of those sexual scenes that wouldn't pass MPAA muster for an "R" rating.) Ex-con Corky (Gershon) hooks up with sexy next-door neighbor Violet (Tilly). The two hatch a plan to steal two million freshly laundered dollars from Violet's boyfriend Caesar (Pantoliano), who goes ballistic when he discovers the theft. Flashy directorial debut for the brothers Wachowski. There are a lot of dark, contrasty scenes in this film and the DVD does a very good job with them. It doesn't hurt that the blacks are near perfect. The colors are also excellent and, for the most part, bleed-free. Most noticeable in the soundtrack is the full, clean low end. The fidelity is also excellent with good spatial imaging, especially when the Surround kicks in. —JO

Movie: 🎵🎵🎵 **DVD:** 🎵🎵🎵
Republic Pictures Home Video (Cat #46298, UPC #017153629828). Widescreen (1.85:1) letterboxed. Dolby Digital. $24.98. Keepcase. *LANG:* English; French. *SUB:* Spanish. *CAP:* English. *FEATURES:* 33 chapter links • Theatrical trailer • Commentary: the Wachowski Brothers.
1996 (R) 107m/C Gina Gershon, Jennifer Tilly, Joe Pantoliano, John P. Ryan, Barry Kivel, Christopher Meloni, Peter Spellos, Richard Sarafian, Mary Mara, Susie Bright, Ivan Kane, Kevin M. Richardson, Gene Borkan; **D:** Andy Wachowski, Larry Wachowski; **W:** Andy Wachowski, Larry Wachowski; **C:** Bill Pope; **M:** Don Davis. *AWARDS: NOM:* Independent Spirit Awards '97: Best Cinematography; MTV Movie Awards '97: Best Kiss (Jennifer Tilly/Gina Gershon).

Bound and Gagged: A Love Story

The box copy promises "not your average insane road movie," and it's not exaggerating. Instead, this indie/exploitation hybrid is a romantic comedy about attempted suicide, spouse abuse, lesbianism, and kidnapping, which may not sound like funny stuff, but can be. Leslie (Allen) is pretty much fed up with her loutish husband Steve (Mulkey). She has become involved in a relationship with Elizabeth (Saltarelli), a free spirit with a short fuse. Elizabeth thinks that she knows what's best for everyone, including her friend Cliff (Denton), who's tormented by memories of his own unfaithful wife (Ross). Without giv-

ing away the game, Elizabeth winds up heading west from Minneapolis in an aging Chrysler with a mute Cliff riding shotgun, Leslie (bound and gagged) in the back, and Steve in hot pursuit. For the most part, the film has the natural performances and spontaneous, unexpected quality that a good road movie needs. On DVD, the image is very good. Night scenes, often illuminated by splashy colored lights, hold up particularly well. For a mid- to low-budget production, the film looks terrific. —MM

Movie: 🎵🎵🎵 **DVD:** 🎵🎵🎵
Image Entertainment (Cat #ID5587FMDVD, UPC #014381558722). Full frame. Dolby Digital Stereo. $19.99. Snapper. *LANG:* English. *FEATURES:* 12 chapter links.
1993 (R) 96m/C Ginger Lynn Allen, Karen Black, Chris Denton, Elizabeth Saltarelli, Mary Ella Ross, Chris Mulkey; **D:** Daniel Appleby; **W:** Daniel Appleby; **C:** Dean Lent; **M:** William Murphy.

Bowfinger

Buddy Bowfinger (Martin), a struggling low-budget filmmaker, realizes that his last chance at a career lies in getting action star Kit Ramsey (Murphy) into his movie. When Kit refuses, Buddy comes up with a scheme to follow him around and secretly photograph the actor with his cast members. The ruse plays right into Kit's paranoia and leads to a rousing parody of the movie business that's filled with unsubtle parallels to reality. The DVD image is fine but the real value of the disc lies in the extras. First, two deleted scenes have some very funny stuff. Second, on his commentary track, director Frank Oz focuses on narrative changes that occurred between initial script and finished product; the mechanics of characterization; editing; pace; and the expected details of location work. Careful viewers will catch a continuity error concerning Buddy's ponytail. — MM *AKA:* Bowfinger's Big Thing.

Movie: 🎵🎵🎵 **DVD:** 🎵🎵🎵▶
Universal Studios Home Video (Cat #20576, UPC #025192057625). Widescreen (1.85:1) anamorphic. Dolby Digital 5.1 Surround Stereo; DTS Stereo. $26.98. Keepcase. *LANG:* English; French. *CAP:* English. *FEATURES:* 18 chapter links • "Making of" featurette • Outtakes • Commentary: Frank Oz • 2 deleted scenes • Theatrical trailer • Cast and crew thumbnail biographies.
1999 (PG-13) 96m/C Steve Martin, Eddie Murphy, Christine Baranski, Heather Graham, Terence Stamp, Jamie Kennedy, Robert Downey Jr., Barry Newman; **D:** Frank Oz; **W:** Steve Martin; **C:** Ueli Steiger; **M:** David Newman.

Box of Moonlight

Hard-working electrical systems engineer Al Fountain (Turturro) feels mysteriously compelled to play hookey from his family and career while on an out-of-town business trip. He meets up with the Kid, a quirky recluse played with energy and

appeal by Rockwell. Through a series of mix-ups, the two end up spending the Fourth of July weekend together. DiCillo's third feature was six years in the making and financed by the success of his second feature, *Living in Oblivion.* It's too bad that this great movie does not have a better DVD. Just about everything is average, including sharpness, color (there is considerable bleed), contrast, and brightness. Where the DVD is truly lacking is in its handling of blacks, which are sometimes perfect and at others very poor. In many instances background movement is digitally distorted. Sometimes, when you pick up a disc with so-so image quality, the soundtrack nearly makes up for it—not the case here. The sound is blah, with no crispness and too little low end. This DVD also has a very clunky menu. —JO

Movie: 🎵🎵🎵▶ **DVD:** 🎵🎵
Trimark Home Video (Cat #6838D, UPC #031398683834). Widescreen (2.35:1) letterboxed. Dolby Surround. $24.98. Keepcase. *LANG:* English. *SUB:* French. *CAP:* English. *FEATURES:* 30 chapter links • Theatrical trailer • Cast and crew bios.
1996 (R) 111m/C John Turturro, Sam Rockwell, Catherine Keener, Lisa Blount, Annie Corley, Dermot Mulroney, Alexander Goodwin; **D:** Tom DiCillo; **W:** Tom DiCillo; **C:** Paul Ryan; **M:** Jim Farmer. *AWARDS: NOM:* Independent Spirit Awards '98: Best Actor (Turturro).

The Boxer

Affecting, if predictable, romance set in Ulster, Northern Ireland. Having served 14 years in prison, Danny Flynn (Day-Lewis) wants nothing more to do with politics and violence. But his return to his old neighborhood—where he hopes to get back to his boxing career—finds him in the thick of both. Danny manages to persuade his ex-trainer, the alcoholic Ike (Stott), to help him re-open the local gym but resentment is high. Particularly from hard-liner Harry (McSorley), who doesn't like Danny's live-and-let-live attitude and is incensed that he's interested in rekindling his love for Maggie (Watson), the married daughter of IRA boss Joe (Cox). Things quickly turn ugly. A fine addition to the Universal Collector's Edition DVD line. The picture is very sharp and has no problem with grain or artifacts. Blacks are true and the colors are excellent. Good contrast and brightness levels allow the films realistically subtle lighting to come through. Excellent separation and dynamics on both the 5.1 and Dolby Surround, so whatever system you have, the music sounds good and the dialogue is distinct. When the Surround kicks in, the mix seems to be near perfect. Supplemental section is worth viewing (and listening to). —JO

Movie: 🎵🎵▶ **DVD:** 🎵🎵🎵🎵
Universal Studios Home Video (Cat #20240, UPC #025192024023). Widescreen (1.66:1) anamorphic. Dolby Digital 5.1; Dolby Surround. $34.98. Keepcase.

LANG: English (DD5.1, DS); French (DS). **SUB:** English; Spanish. **FEATURES:** 32 movies chapter links • 7 documentary chapter links • Theatrical trailer • Alternate ending • Deleted scenes • Cast and filmmaker bios • Production notes • "Making of" documentary • Commentary: Jim Sheridan • Film highlights • Dual-layered RSDL.
1997 (R) 113m/C *GB IR* Daniel Day-Lewis, Emily Watson, Brian Cox, Gerard McSorley, Ken Stott, Ciaran Fitzgerald, Kenneth Cranham; **Cameos:** Tom Bell; **D:** Jim Sheridan; **W:** Jim Sheridan, Terry George; **C:** Chris Menges; **M:** Gavin Friday, Maurice Seezer. **AWARDS: NOM:** Golden Globe Awards '98: Best Actor—Drama (Day-Lewis), Best Director (Sheridan), Best Film—Drama.

A Boy and His Dog

In the post-holocaust world of 2024, a young man (Johnson) and his telepathic canine cohort (McIntire supplies narration of the dog's thoughts) search for food and sex. They happen upon a community that drafts Johnson to repopulate their largely impotent race; Johnson is at first ready, willing, and able, until he discovers the mechanical methods they mean to employ. Based on a short story by Harlan Ellison. The dog was played by the late Tiger of *The Brady Bunch*. When the image is bright on this DVD, it is far superior to any of the previous video releases. But when it's dark, in comes the grain and out goes the sharpness. Colors seem weak for DVD, but because of the source, it's hard to judge if this is the best that could be done. The stereo sound has very little separation, way too much mid-range, and is lacking in bass. —*JO*
Movie: ♪♪▶ **DVD:** ♪♪▶
SlingShot Entertainment (Cat #9818, UPC #017078981827). Widescreen (2.35:1) letterboxed. Stereo. $29.99. Expanded jewel case. **LANG:** English. **FEATURES:** 22 chapter links • Theatrical re-issue trailer • Commentary: L.Q. Jones, John Morril, and Charles Champlin.
1975 (R) 87m/C Don Johnson, Susanne Benton, Jason Robards Jr., Charles McGraw, Alvy Moore, Helen Winston, Hal Baylor, L.Q. (Justus E. McQueen) Jones; **D:** L.Q. (Justus E. McQueen) Jones; **W:** L.Q. (Justus E. McQueen) Jones; **C:** John Morrill; **M:** Tim McIntire; **V:** Tim McIntire.

The Boy in the Plastic Bubble

This overachieving made-for-TV disease-of-the-week flick has become a solid audience favorite, doubtless because it stars a young John Travolta in the lead. He plays a young man who was born with immune deficiencies and must grow up in a specially controlled plastic environment.
Movie: ♪♪▶ **DVD:** NYR
Essex (Cat #1001). Full frame. Dolby Digital Mono. $10.97.
1976 100m/C John Travolta, Robert Reed, Glynnis O'Connor, Diana Hyland,

Ralph Bellamy, Anne Ramsey, Vernee Watson-Johnson, P.J. Soles, John Friedrich; **D:** Randal Kleiser; **W:** Douglas Day Stewart; **C:** Arch R. Dalzell; **M:** Paul Williams, Mark Snow.

Boyfriends & Girlfriends

Parisiennes Blanche (Chaulet) and Lea (Renoir) have just met and become friends. Lea is sort of living with her boyfriend Fabien (Viellard); Blanche is attracted to his handsome friend Alexandre (Gendron), even though everyone says they're wrong for each other. It takes nearly two mostly uneventful hours for these four to get their romantic attachments sorted out. Throughout, Rohmer's style is relaxed and confident, and so the film sneaks up on you. The characters are so likeable and real that it's easy to become involved with their situation. The story is told quietly, without a musical soundtrack, on starkly uncluttered sets and locations. The pace is appropriately languid for a summer story, and though it appears unfocused, the story builds to a fine conclusion, a cross-cut confrontation that neatly ties everything up. On disc, the image is not noticeably sharper than the tape, though the white subtitles outlined in black are easy on the eyes. Beyond that, the bare-bones presentation offers few extras. Again, that's fine for Rohmer's understated "Proverbs and Comedies" series. —*MM* **AKA:** My Girlfriend's Boyfriend; L'Ami de Mon Ami.
Movie: ♪♪♪▶ **DVD:** ♪♪▶
WinStar Home Entertainment (Cat #FLV5100, UPC #72091751002). Full frame. $24.98. Keepcase. **LANG:** French. **SUB:** English. **FEATURES:** 6 chapter links • Production credits • Filmographies and awards for Chaulet, Gendron, Meury, Renoir, Rohmer.
1988 (PG) 102m/C *FR* Emmanuelle Chaulet, Sophie Renoir, Eric Viellard, Francois-Eric Gendron, Anne-Laure Meury; **D:** Eric Rohmer; **W:** Eric Rohmer; **C:** Bernard Lutic; **M:** Jean-Louis Valero.

The Boys

French-Canadian comedy about ordinary guys who play amateur hockey has become a sleeper hit. "Les Boys" are sponsored by local tavern-owner Stan (Girard), who's in debt to a small-time mobster, Meo (Lebeau). Meo strikes a deal, pitting Stan's rag-tag team against his own thugs. If Stan's guys lose, Meo gets the bar. Dirty tricks abound on both sides. **AKA:** Les Boys.
Movie: ♪♪▶ **DVD:** NYR
Studio Home Entertainment (Cat #7165). Dolby Digital Stereo. $24.95. Keepcase. **LANG:** French; English.
1997 107m/C *CA* Remy Girard, Marc Messier, Patrick Huard, Serge Theriault, Yvan Ponton, Dominic Philie, Patrick Labbe, Roc Lafortune, Pierre Lebeau, Paul Houde; **D:** Louis Saia; **W:** Christian Fournier; **C:** Sylvain Brault; **M:** Normand

Corbeil. **AWARDS: NOM:** Genie Awards '98: Best Actor (Girard).

The Boys Club

Canadian teens-in-trouble film is given a tough core by first-time director Fawcett. Unhappy 14-year-olds Kyle (Zamprogna), Eric (Sawa), and Brad (Stone) spend their free time at an abandoned shack out in the woods until the day when they discover a wounded Luke Cooper (Penn) hiding there. He tells them he's a good cop who's been shot by bad cops. The boys buy into the story but Cooper is quick to show his psycho streak. The performances are excellent, particularly from Penn and Zamprogna. The DVD is a cut above average for a mid-budget production, too. Night scenes and the dark interior of the shack are handled well. Reds and oranges are overly bright. Sound is fine. —*MM*
Movie: ♪♪▶ **DVD:** ♪♪♪
Simitar Entertainment (Cat #7444, UPC #0082551744428). Full frame. Dolby Digital Stereo; Dolby Digital 5.1 Surround. $14.98. Keepcase. **LANG:** English. **FEATURES:** 8 chapter links • Production factoids • Christopher Penn filmography.
1996 (R) 92m/C *CA* Christopher Penn, Stuart Stone, Devon Sawa, Dominic Zamprogna, Nicholas Campbell, Jarred Blanchard; **D:** John Fawcett; **W:** Peter Wellington; **C:** Thom Best; **M:** Michael Timmins. **AWARDS: NOM:** Genie Awards '96: Best Actor (Penn), Best Art Direction/Set Decoration, Best Director (Fawcett), Best Film Editing, Best Original Screenplay.

Boys Don't Cry

Hilary Swank won an Oscar for her performance as Teena Brandon, a girl who passed as a boy under the name Brandon Teena. The fact-based film follows her/his various attempts at transformation and eventual murder. It has been criticized by various groups and individuals for its approach to the subject. On her commentary track, director Kimberly Peirce takes an explanatory approach. She's more careful than most filmmakers in talking about the choices she made, and her words are carefully edited. These are not the typical off-the-top-of-the-head remarks. Visually, the film is nothing special on DVD. It's an independent production that looks the way it was meant to look. Both the night exteriors and the honky-tonk interiors are very dim. Sound is good. But they are not the point; the performances—including Chloe Sevigny who was nominated for Supporting Actress—are the point. —*MM*
Movie: ♪♪▶ **DVD:** ♪♪♪
Twentieth Century Fox Home Entertainment (Cat #2000173, UPC #024543001737). Widescreen (1.85:1) anamorphic. Dolby Digital 5.1 Surround Stereo; Dolby Digital Surround Stereo. $34.98. Keepcase. **LANG:** English. **SUB:** English; Spanish. **FEATURES:** 24 chapter links • Theatrical

trailer and teaser ● 3 TV spots ● Commentary: director Kimberly Peirce.
1999 (R) 116m/C Hilary Swank, Chloe Sevigny, Peter Sarsgaard, Brendan Sexton III, Alison Folland, Alicia (Lecy) Goranson, Matt McGrath, Rob Campbell, Jeanetta Arnette; *D:* Kimberly Peirce; *W:* Kimberly Peirce, Andy Bienen; *C:* Jim Denault; *M:* Nathan Larsen. *AWARDS:* Academy Awards '99: Best Actress (Swank); Golden Globe Awards '00: Best Actress—Drama (Swank); Independent Spirit Awards '00: Best Actress (Swank), Best Supporting Actress (Sevigny); Los Angeles Film Critics Association Awards '99: Best Actress (Swank), Best Supporting Actress (Sevigny); New York Film Critics Awards '99: Best Actress (Swank); National Society of Film Critics Awards '99: Best Supporting Actress (Sevigny); Broadcast Film Critics Association Awards '99: Best Actress (Swank); *NOM:* Academy Awards '99: Best Supporting Actress (Sevigny); Golden Globe Awards '00: Best Supporting Actress (Sevigny); Independent Spirit Awards '00: Best First Feature, First Screenplay; MTV Movie Awards '00: Breakthrough Performance (Swank), Best Kiss (Hilary Swank/Chloe Sevigny); Screen Actors Guild Award '99: Best Actress (Swank), Best Supporting Actress (Sevigny).

Boys Life

Three shorts about gay teenagers coming-of-age. The best is the middle film, "A Friend of Dorothy," about a closeted NYU freshman Winston (O'Connell) looking for love in Greenwich Village, with the encouragement of a female pal. "Pool Days" has 17-year-old Justin (Weinstein) taking a summer job as a lifeguard at a health spa. Still confused about his sexual preferences, he's flustered when cruised by a charming male swimmer—but it does get him thinking. "The Disco Years," set in Southern California during the Nixon era, has a conflicted teenager Tom engaging in a clandestine romance by night, and participating in a gay bashing at school. The three short films had varying production values during their theatrical release, but the DVD transfer looks and sounds fine. "Pool Days" is slightly grainier than the other two films, and "Disco Years"—set in the '70s—has an appropriately faded color scheme. —*JE*
Movie: 🎵🎵▶ *DVD:* 🎵🎵▶
Image Entertainment (Cat #ID56865D DVD, UPC #01438156862). Full frame (1.33:1). Dolby Digital Mono. $24.99. Snapper. *LANG:* English. *FEATURES:* 24 chapter links.
1994 90m/C Josh Weinstein, Nick Poletti, Kimberly Flynn, Richard Salamanca, Raoul O'Connell, Kevin McClatchy, Greg Lauren, Anne Zupa, Matt Nolan, Russell Scott Lewis, Gwen Welles, Dennis Christopher; *D:* Robert Lee King, Brian Sloan, Raoul O'Connell; *W:* Robert Lee King, Brian Sloan, Raoul O'Connell; *C:* W. Mott Hupfel III, Jonathan Schell, Greg Gardiner.

Boys Life 2

Four shorts about gay life. "Must Be the Music" is a lightweight tale of four L.A. teenagers' trip to a dance club. The nighttime settings are shot with an oversaturated color scheme, and the DVD transfer, while sharp, has a slight bleed in reds. In "Nunzio's Second Cousin" (the best entry), a gay cop (D'Onofrio) exacts some darkly comic justice by forcing young gay basher (Perlich) to meet his mom (Brennan). This segment looks sharp, even in somber nighttime scenes. "Alkali, Iowa" is a tale of love and intolerance in a rural setting, while in "The Dadshuttle," an estranged father and son circle warily around a sensitive topic. Picture and sound are average in these two, but the sparseness of the settings and colors scheme come across well on disc. —*JE*
Movie: 🎵🎵▶ *DVD:* 🎵🎵▶
Image Entertainment (Cat #ID 567SDDVD, UPC #01438156872). Widescreen (1.85:1). Dolby Digital Mono. $24.99. Snapper. *LANG:* English. *FEATURES:* 24 chapter links.
1998 74m/C Justin Urich, Michael Saucedo, Travis Sher, Milo Ventimigilia, Vincent D'Onofrio, Eileen Brennan, Miles Perlich, Harry Walters Jr., John Dayton (J.D.) Cerna, Mary Beth Hurt, Kent Broadhurst, Ellen Hamilton-Latzen, Ed Seamon, Greg Villepique, Brett Barsky, Judy Kain, Stephen Tobolowsky, John Lizzi, Jonah Rooney, Allen Doraine; *D:* Tom DeCerchio, Mark Christopher, Nickolas Perry, Peggy Rajski; *W:* Tom DeCerchio, Mark Christopher, Nickolas Perry, James Lecesne; *C:* Steven Poster, Steve Adcock, Jami Silverstein, Marc Reshovsky; *M:* Robert Folk, Julian Harris, Danny Troob.

Boys on the Side

Unemployed lesbian singer Goldberg hooks up with real estate agent Parker for a road trip to California. The duo stop to pick up dizzy Barrymore who has just clubbed her abusive boyfriend with a baseball bat, hitting a fatal home run. The three run from the cops, become good buds, and set up house together. Big problems ensue, including pregnancy and AIDS. Director Ross elicits strong performances from the entire cast, particularly his leading ladies. This is a good-looking and good-sounding DVD. Sharpness is excellent and grain never a problem. Colors are lush and true with nary a trace of bleed. There are no artifacts. The blacks are very true and even in very dark scenes detail is very good due to excellent contrast and brightness levels. The stereo soundtrack has such good imaging and space that you don't really miss having Surround tracks. —*JO*
Movie: 🎵🎵▶ *DVD:* 🎵🎵🎵▶
Warner Home Video, Inc. (Cat #13570, UPC #085391357025). Widescreen (2.35:1) letterboxed; full frame. Dolby Digital Stereo. $19.98. Snapper. *LANG:* English; French. *SUB:* French. *CAP:* English. *FEATURES:* 38 chapter links.

1994 (R) 117m/C James Remar, Anita Gillette, Matthew McConaughey, Whoopi Goldberg, Mary-Louise Parker, Drew Barrymore; *D:* Herbert Ross; *W:* Don Roos; *C:* Donald E. Thorin; *M:* David Newman.

Boys Will Be Boys

With their parents (Travis and Hagerty) away at the company party, Matt (Williams) and Robbie (Winget) are "home alone" for the first time. The conventional chaos ensues when dad's business rival threatens them. On DVD, the image is completely clear. Judged as a mid-level kid flick, this one's fine. In some scenes, though, the clarity of the digital image reveals the wires that are used in the special effects. —*MM*
Movie: 🎵🎵▶ *DVD:* 🎵🎵
Simitar Entertainment (Cat #7463, UPC #082551746323). Full frame. Dolby Digital Stereo; Dolby 5.1 Surround Stereo. $14.98. Keepcase. *LANG:* English. *FEATURES:* 8 chapter links ● Filmographies and thumbnail biographies for Voight, Rooney, and Hagerty ● Production factoids.
1997 (PG) 89m/C Randy Travis, Julie Hagerty, Jon Voight, Michael DeLuise, Catherine Oxenberg, Mickey Rooney, Ruth Buzzi, Dom DeLuise, Charles Nelson Reilly, James Williams, Drew Winget; *D:* Dom DeLuise; *W:* Gregory Poppon, Mark Dubas; *C:* Leonard Schway; *M:* Kristopher Carter.

Boyz N the Hood

Singleton's debut is an astonishing picture of four black high school students with different backgrounds, aims, and abilities, trying to survive Los Angeles gangs and bigotry. Excellent acting throughout with special nods to Fishburne, Gooding Jr., and Ice Cube. It's often violent but the emotional conclusion is powerful.
Movie: 🎵🎵🎵▶ *DVD:* NYR
Columbia Tristar Home Video (Cat #50819). Widescreen (1.85:1) letterboxed. Dolby Digital Stereo. $29.95. Keepcase. *LANG:* English; French; Spanish. *SUB:* French; Spanish. *CAP:* English. *FEATURES:* Trailers.
1991 (R) 112m/C Laurence "Larry" Fishburne, Ice Cube, Cuba Gooding Jr., Nia Long, Morris Chestnut, Tyra Ferrell, Angela Bassett, Whitman Mayo; *D:* John Singleton; *W:* John Singleton; *C:* Charles Mills; *M:* Stanley Clarke. *AWARDS:* MTV Movie Awards '92: Best New Filmmaker Award (Singleton); *NOM:* Academy Awards '91: Best Director (Singleton), Best Original Screenplay.

Brain Damage

Henenlotter's second low-budget feature (after *Basket Case*) about a boy and his pet monster is also a visceral anti-drug horror-comedy. The critter is a grotesque little parasite that looks like a cross between a prune and a catfish. It feeds on brains (human or animal) and is capa-

ble of injecting its host with a highly addictive hallucinogen. This thing is called Aylmer, or Elmer, and in one of the film's strangest moments, it launches into an a cappella version of that old Glenn Miller favorite, "Elmer's Tune." Yes, Aylmer can sing and it can also talk; in fact, it can be quite persuasive. It comes into the possession of a young man, Brian (Herbst), and, as it begins to gain control of him, Aylmer argues that it's all right for him to kill people, as long as Brian isn't directly involved. Or, as he puts it, "Part of my talent, Brian, is to spare you any unpleasantness." And of course, there's plenty of unpleasantness to be spared. The violence is graphic (and often reminiscent of David Cronenberg's *Rabid*), outlandish, and comic. There's also a strong sexual element to the story, though it's played mostly for laughs and is even more excessive in this "unrated" edition. Beyond the Grand Guignol horror, the film has some serious things to say about addiction. The remastered DVD looks terrific. As Henenlotter notes on the commentary track, this one cost $600,000 to make compared to *Basket Case*'s $35,000. All the difference is on the screen. Despite the rough nature of this unrepentant B-movie, it's an imaginative, challenging work, far superior to any of the disappointing *Basket Case* sequels. —*MM*
Movie: 🎞🎞🎞 **DVD:** 🎞🎞🎞▶
Image Entertainment (Cat #SFD0005, UPC #654930300596). Widescreen. Dolby Digital Mono. $24.99. Keepcase. *LANG:* English. *FEATURES:* Commentary: Frank Henenlotter, Bob Martin, and Scooter McCray • Isolated music track • Director filmography • Theatrical trailer • 22 chapter links.
1988 (R) 89m/C Rick Herbst, Gordon MacDonald, Jennifer Lowry, Theo Barnes, Lucille Saint Peter; *Cameos:* Kevin Van Hentenryck, Beverly Bonner; *D:* Frank Henenlotter; *W:* Frank Henenlotter; *C:* Bruce Torbet; *M:* Gus Russo, Clutch Reiser; *V:* John Zacherle.

Brainstorm

Husband-and-wife scientific team (Walken and Wood) invents headphones that can record dreams, thoughts, and fantasies and allow other people to experience them by playing back the tape. Their marriage suffers when he becomes obsessed with pushing the limits of the technology. Then the government tries to exploit it. Natalie Wood died before work was completed; this is her last film.
Movie: 🎞🎞▶ **DVD:** NYR
Warner Home Video, Inc. (Cat #907045). $24.98. Keepcase. *LANG:* English; French. *SUB:* French; Spanish. *CAP:* English. *FEATURES:* Trailers.
1983 (PG) 106m/C Natalie Wood, Christopher Walken, Cliff Robertson, Louise Fletcher; *D:* Douglas Trumbull; *W:* Bruce Joel Rubin; *C:* Richard Yuricich; *M:* James Horner.

Bram Stoker's Shadowbuilder

Silly update that apparently takes the title of the Bram Stoker short story but not much else. Shadowbuilder (Jackson) is a demonic creature that wants to unleash hell's power upon the unsuspecting town of Grand River. But he needs 12-year-old Chris (Zegers) for your basic satanic ritual, which doesn't go over well with the local priest (Rooker) and sheriff (Thompson). *AKA:* Shadowbuilder.
Movie: 🎞🎞 **DVD:** NYR
Studio Home Entertainment (Cat #7045). Stereo. $24.95. Keepcase.
1998 (R) 101m/C Michael Rooker, Leslie Hope, Andrew Jackson, Kevin Zegers, Shawn Thompson, Tony Todd, Richard McMillan; *D:* Jamie Dixon; *W:* Michael Stokes; *C:* David Pelletier; *M:* Eckart Seeber.

Bram Stoker's Dracula

Please see *Dracula* (1992).

Branded to Kill

In *Branded to Kill*, "No. 3 Killer" wants to be number one, but finds himself being stalked by the latter. No. 3 is a wacky assassin who is sexually aroused by the smell of cooked rice. He also revels in finding unusual ways to dispatch his victims. One would think that, with its black-and-white photography, *Branded* would be a little tamer than Suzuki's other work, but it's not the case. He delivers another visual masterpiece, filled with brutality, humor, and even a little animation. Unfortunately, the Criterion laserdisc is a better way to view this film. The DVD is only pretty good. The sharpness is average and graininess shows up occasionally, possibly because of the harsh black and white. Still, the brightness and contrast are very good and consistent throughout the disc. The blacks are true and there aren't many artifacts to spoil the picture. If nothing special, the soundtrack is adequate and the subtitles are easy to read. Contains cool liner notes by musician John Zorn, who also supplied the posters for the supplemental section. —*JO AKA:* Koroshi no Rakuin.
Movie: 🎞🎞🎞 **DVD:** 🎞🎞▶
Criterion Collection (Cat #38, UPC #037429136225). Widescreen (2.35:1) letterboxed. Dolby Digital Mono. $29.95. Keepcase. *LANG:* Japanese. *SUB:* English. *FEATURES:* 27 chapter links • Interview with director Seijun Suzuki • Joe Shishido poster gallery.
1967 91m/B *JP* Joe Shishido, Mari Annu, Koji Nambara; *D:* Seijun Suzuki; *M:* Naozumi Yamamoto.

Brassed Off

Bittersweet tale of despair and hope is set in the fictional town of Grimly in Yorkshire, England, 1992, when sweeping closures of the coal mines devastated the popula-

tion of the area. The sole bright spot for the workers is playing in the pit's brass band, whose leader, Danny (Postlethwaite) dreams of winning a competition in Albert Hall. Gloria (Fitzgerald) is the girl who returns to her hometown and inspires the formerly all-male band, including her old flame (McGregor). Perhaps because the film was made with the participation of Britain's Channel Four, it appears completely at home on the small screen. Image and sound are both first-rate, though they're not so spectacular that you feel you're missing something. For fans of *Waking Ned Devine* and *The Full Monty*, it's a treat. —*MM*
Movie: 🎞🎞🎞 **DVD:** 🎞🎞🎞▶
Miramax Pictures Home Video (Cat #17252, UPC #717951002457). Widescreen (1.85:1) letterboxed. Dolby Digital Surround Stereo. $29.99. Keepcase. *LANG:* English. *CAP:* English. *FEATURES:* 12 chapter links • Theatrical trailer.
1996 (R) 100m/C *GB* Pete Postlethwaite, Ewan McGregor, Tara Fitzgerald, Jim Carter, Philip Jackson, Peter Martin, Stephen Tompkinson; *D:* Mark Herman; *W:* Mark Herman; *C:* Andy Collins; *M:* Trevor Jones. *AWARDS:* Cesar Awards '98: Best Foreign Film; *NOM:* British Academy Awards '96: Best Original Screenplay.

The Brave Frog

Combination of Japanese anime with Saturday morning cartoon simplicity will appeal to only the most undemanding young audience. The story of a big-eyed young frog's maturation is punctuated by an insipidly giggling girlfriend and rhymed couplet voice-overs that remind us, "Life is short and art is long and something's always going wrong." The DVD is flawlessly bright and colorful. Some kids will be entranced; others will wander away after five minutes. —*MM*
Movie: 🎞▶ **DVD:** 🎞🎞▶
Image Entertainment (Cat #ID5692PZDVD, UPC #014381569223). Full frame. Dolby Digital Mono. $24.99. Snapper. *LANG:* English. *FEATURES:* 13 chapter links.
1987 90m/C *D:* Michael Reynolds; *W:* Ilene Chase; *M:* Kathryn Nelligan, Randall Rumage.

The Brave One

This is a love story about a Spanish boy and the bull who saves his life. The animal is later carted off to the bull ring. The award-winning screenplay is credited to "Robert Rich," the then-blacklisted Dalton Trumbo.
Movie: 🎞🎞🎞 **DVD:** NYR
Lumivision Corp. (Cat #1697). Widescreen (2.35:1) letterboxed. Dolby Digital Stereo. $24.95. Keepcase. *CAP:* English. *FEATURES:* Trailer.
1956 100m/C Michel Ray, Rodolfo Hoyos, Joi Lansing; *D:* Irving Rapper; *W:* Dalton Trumbo; *C:* Jack Cardiff; *M:* Victor Young. *AWARDS:* Academy Awards '56: Best Story; *NOM:* Academy Awards '56: Best Film Editing, Best Sound.

Brazil

The Universal DVD of *Brazil* is basically just the U.S. theatrical release of the movie and the usual assortment of supplementals—chapter links, a trailer, bios, and notes. But if you don't care about the extras, or having Gilliam's "ultimate cut," this DVD will cost you less and is very close in quality to the Criterion release. —*JO*

Movie: 🎬🎬🎬▶ ***DVD:*** 🎬🎬🎬
Universal Studios Home Video (Cat #20168, UPC #025192016820). Widescreen (1.85:1) letterboxed. Dolby Surround. $24.98. Keepcase. *LANG:* English. *SUB:* French; Spanish. *CAP:* English. *FEATURES:* 16 chapter links ▪ Theatrical trailer ▪ Cast and filmmakers bios ▪ Production notes ▪ Film highlights.
1985 (R) 131m/C *GB* Jonathan Pryce, Robert De Niro, Michael Palin, Katherine Helmond, Kim Greist, Bob Hoskins, Ian Holm, Peter Vaughan, Ian Richardson; ***D:*** Terry Gilliam; ***W:*** Charles McKeown, Terry Gilliam, Tom Stoppard; ***C:*** Roger Pratt; ***M:*** Michael Kamen. *AWARDS:* Los Angeles Film Critics Association Awards '85: Best Director (Gilliam), Best Film, Best Screenplay; *NOM:* Academy Awards '85: Best Art Direction/Set Decoration, Best Original Screenplay.

Brazil (Criterion SE)

The acclaimed nightmare comedy about an Everyman trying to survive in a surreal paper-choked bureaucratic society. There are copious references to *1984* and *The Trial*, fantastic mergings of glorious fantasy and stark reality, and astounding visual design. The "director's cut" of the film, on disc one, is a superb DVD transfer that is so sharp it feels like looking out a window. Colors are terrific. This is one of the finest-looking DVDs out there, and that includes the darker scenes, where you would expect the quality to drop a little—but it doesn't. The supplemental section is probably the largest of any DVD, especially if you include the alternate cut of the film. Two documentaries, one produced by Criterion for their laserdisc edition, are included here. To effectively go through all the supplementals you should probably plan on a good ten hours (it's worth it). The Dolby Surround has as good imaging and separation as most 5.1 tracks and all the renditions of the title song are plenty lively. —*JO*

Movie: 🎬🎬🎬▶ ***DVD:*** 🎬🎬🎬🎬
Criterion Collection (Cat #BRA100, UPC #037429138526). Widescreen (1.85:1) letterboxed. Dolby Surround; Stereo. $59.95. Custom. *LANG:* English. *FEATURES:* 72 chapter links ▪ Theatrical trailer ▪ Ultimate 142-minute director's cut ▪ 94-minute "Love Conquers All" version of the film ▪ 2 documentaries ▪ Commentary: Terry Gilliam ▪ Storyboards ▪ Tom Stoppard and Charles McKeown discuss the script ▪ Special effects study ▪ Norman Garwood on *Brazil*'s look ▪ Michael Kamen on his score.
1985 (R) 131m/C *GB* Jonathan Pryce, Robert De Niro, Michael Palin, Katherine Helmond, Kim Greist, Bob Hoskins, Ian Holm, Peter Vaughan, Ian Richardson; ***D:*** Terry Gilliam; ***W:*** Charles McKeown, Terry Gilliam, Tom Stoppard; ***C:*** Roger Pratt; ***M:*** Michael Kamen. *AWARDS:* Los Angeles Film Critics Association Awards '85: Best Director (Gilliam), Best Film, Best Screenplay; *NOM:* Academy Awards '85: Best Art Direction/Set Decoration, Best Original Screenplay.

The Break Up

After a particularly brutal beating by her husband Frank (Bochner), Jimmy Dade (Fonda) wakes up in a hospital. Then Frank's wrecked car is found with a charred body inside. Detective John Box (Sutherland) thinks she might have killed him. Director Paul Marcus uses darkness to soften the rough edges of a trashy world of cheap motels and trailer parks. Because of that, the no-frills DVD is not much to look at. Sound is nothing special either. This one's an acceptable B-thriller. —*MM*

Movie: 🎬🎬▶ ***DVD:*** 🎬🎬▶
Buena Vista Home Entertainment (Cat #18156, UPC #717951004352). Widescreen (1.85:1) letterboxed. Dolby Digital Surround Stereo. $29.99. Keepcase. *LANG:* English. *CAP:* English. *FEATURES:* 23 chapter links.
1998 (R) 101m/C Bridget Fonda, Kiefer Sutherland, Penelope Ann Miller, Steven Weber, Hart Bochner, Tippi Hedren; ***D:*** Paul Marcus; ***W:*** Anne Amanda Opotowsky.

Breaker Morant

In 1901 South Africa, three Australian soldiers are put on trial for the murder of several prisoners. Based on a true story which was then turned into a play by Kenneth Ross, this riveting, popular antiwar statement and courtroom drama heralded Australia's film renaissance. Rich performances by Woodward and Waters. WinStar has so many great films that they really should get their DVD act together. For one thing, the sleeve lists nine chapter links but only three are accessible either from the menu or by doing a chapter skip. The picture is average at best and has grain during most of the film. Occasional artifacting only makes things worse. The colors are much better than the tape and the blacks are much truer. Contrast and brightness are acceptable. A mono soundtrack can do just fine, but this one is at times tinny, at times a little dull, and always lacking in the low-end department. —*JO*

Movie: 🎬🎬🎬▶ ***DVD:*** 🎬🎬
WinStar Home Entertainment (Cat #FLV5002, UPC #720917500225). Widescreen (1.85:1) letterboxed. Mono. $29.98. Keepcase. *LANG:* English. *FEATURES:* Several chapter links ▪ Theatrical trailer ▪ Production notes ▪ Cast and crew bios.
1980 (PG) 107m/C *AU* Edward Woodward, Jack Thompson, John Waters, Bryan Brown, Charles Tingwell, Terence Donovan, Vincent Ball, Ray Meagher, Chris Haywood, Lewis Fitz-Gerald, Rod Mullinar, Alan Cassell, Rob Steele; ***D:*** Bruce Beresford; ***W:*** Bruce Beresford, Jonathon Hardy, David Stevens; ***C:*** Donald McAlpine; ***M:*** Phil Cunneen. *AWARDS:* Australian Film Institute '80: Best Actor (Thompson), Best Film; *NOM:* Academy Awards '80: Best Adapted Screenplay.

Breakfast at Tiffany's

Truman Capote's amusing story of an endearingly eccentric New York City playgirl and her shaky romance with a young writer is now the stuff of cinematic legend. Hepburn lends Holly Golightly just the right combination of naivete and worldly wisdom with a dash of melancholy. Mickey Rooney's Japanese impersonation has not aged so comfortably. The DVD image takes a solid step up, particularly for those who have seen only the older, faded videotape. The colors are brighter and the entire film is well-preserved for a work of its age. Ms. Golightly's trademarked tiara and diamond necklace are a little overactive, but that's not a serious problem. The stereo soundtrack is fine for the justly famous Mancini score. —*MM*

Movie: 🎬🎬🎬▶ ***DVD:*** 🎬🎬🎬
Paramount Home Video (Cat #06505, UPC #097360650570). Widescreen anamorphic. Dolby Digital Surround Stereo; Dolby Digital 5.1 Surround Stereo. $29.99. Keepcase. *LANG:* English; French. *SUB:* English. *FEATURES:* 14 chapter links ▪ Theatrical trailer.
1961 114m/C Audrey Hepburn, George Peppard, Patricia Neal, Buddy Ebsen, Mickey Rooney, Martin Balsam, John McGiver; ***D:*** Blake Edwards; ***W:*** George Axelrod; ***C:*** Franz Planer; ***M:*** Henry Mancini. *AWARDS:* Academy Awards '61: Best Song ("Moon River"), Best Original Dramatic Score; *NOM:* Academy Awards '61: Best Actress (Hepburn), Best Adapted Screenplay, Best Art Direction/Set Decoration (Color).

The Breakfast Club

The Brat Pack play five students from different cliques at a Chicago suburban high school who spend a day together in detention in a rather well-done teenage culture study. These characters delve a little deeper than the standard adult view of adolescent stereotypes. Soundtrack features Simple Minds and Wang Chung. The music plays such an important role in this film that it's hard to believe they couldn't have at least come up with a stereo mix, although this mono track is reasonably full of energy. Picture quality is very good, with a clean sharp image mostly undisturbed by any excesses of grain or artifacts. Colors are very accurate and even the deeper hues have no problem with bleed. The DVD also seems to have much better contrast and brightness than the version that is aired on cable almost constantly. —*JO*

Movie: 🎬🎬🎬 ***DVD:*** 🎬🎬🎬

Universal Studios Home Video (Cat #20210, UPC #025192021022). Widescreen (1.85:1) letterboxed. Dolby Digital 2.0 Mono. $24.98. Keepcase. *LANG:* English; Spanish; French. *SUB:* Spanish. *CAP:* English. *FEATURES:* 16 chapter links • Cast and filmmaker bios • Production notes • Film highlights.
1985 (R) 97m/C Ally Sheedy, Molly Ringwald, Judd Nelson, Emilio Estevez, Anthony Michael Hall, Paul Gleason, John Kapelos; *D:* John Hughes; *W:* John Hughes; *C:* Thomas Del Ruth; *M:* Gary Chang, Keith Forsey.

Breeders

A meteorite crashes onto the campus of a women's college. Inside are an alien beastie on a mating mission and a cute brunette in a bustier (don't ask). The conventional shower scenes and stalking sequences ensue. Overall, the DVD doesn't look too bad for low-budget sf exploitation, but the exploitative elements are pretty weak and many scenes are intentionally shadowed to camouflage the pedestrian effects. —*MM*
Movie: 🎵 *DVD:* 🎵🎵
Simitar Entertainment (Cat #7425, UPC #082551742523). Full frame. Dolby Digital Stereo; Dolby Digital 5.1 Surround Stereo. $14.95. Keepcase. *LANG:* English. *FEATURES:* 8 chapter links • Production factoids.
1997 (R) 92m/C Todd Jensen, Samantha Janus, Kadamba Simmons, Oliver Tobias; *D:* Paul Matthews; *W:* Paul Matthews; *M:* Ben Heneghan.

Brenda Starr

Made in 1986, this stinker sneaked shamefully onto cassette some years later without a theatrical release, making it one of the most expensive video premieres in the history of Hollywood. The script is a hash of nonsensical elements that have nothing to do with each other. The part about the cartoonist (Peck) who's sucked into his own strip is particularly out of place. In the title role, Brooke Shields isn't that bad, but she has nothing to work with. The rest of the alleged plot has something to do with a mad scientist in the Amazon jungle. The producers might have made something of it if they'd stayed with a simple adventure storyline, but they aren't capable of the basic stuff of narrative filmmaking. Though the story is supposed to be set in 1948, it does not even attempt any historical detail, and in two shots you can see the rails of the track for the camera dolly. Despite all that, the DVD looks fine. Anchor Bay has given this dreck top-drawer treatment. Director of photography Freddie Francis makes the most of the hodgepodge of sets and settings he must work with, and he's particularly flattering to the star who has seldom been more striking. —*MM*
Movie: 🎵 *DVD:* 🎵🎵⯈

Anchor Bay (Cat #DV10927, UPC #013131092790). Widescreen (1.85:1); full frame. Dolby Digital Stereo. $24.98. Keepcase. *LANG:* English. *FEATURES:* 23 chapter links.
1986 (PG) 94m/C Brooke Shields, Timothy Dalton, Tony Peck, Diana Scarwid, Nestor Serrano, Jeffrey Tambor, June Gable, Charles Durning, Eddie Albert, Henry Gibson, Ed Nelson; *D:* Robert Ellis Miller; *W:* James David Buchanan; *C:* Freddie Francis; *M:* Johnny Mandel.

Brewster's Millions

An aging minor league baseball player (Pryor) must spend $30 million to collect an inheritance of $300 million. The catch—he cannot gain any assets. The seventh remake of the story looks very good on a no-frills DVD with a crisp widescreen image and good sound. —*MM*
Movie: 🎵⯈ *DVD:* 🎵🎵⯈
Goodtimes Entertainment (Cat #05-81011, UPC #018713810113). Widescreen (1.85:1) letterboxed. Dolby Digital Surround Stereo. $19.98. Snapper. *LANG:* English. *SUB:* English; French; Spanish. *FEATURES:* 18 chapter links.
1985 (PG) 101m/C Richard Pryor, John Candy, Lonette McKee, Stephen Collins, Jerry Orbach, Pat Hingle, Tovah Feldshuh, Hume Cronyn, Rick Moranis; *D:* Walter Hill; *W:* Timothy Harris, Herschel Weingrod; *C:* Ric Waite; *M:* Ry Cooder.

Bride of Chucky

Hong Kong director Ronny Yu and writer Don Mancini (cocreator of the original *Child's Play*) breathe fresh life into the used-up series with this surprisingly funny horror-comedy. Jennifer Tilly redefines trailer-park trash as Tiffany, the old flame who revives her serial killer beau trapped inside a doll's body. When she is likewise transmogrified, the two become pint-sized Natural Born Killers. The visual jokes are fast, funny, and bloody. The DVD captures them in all their tawdriness. The image is particularly good in the early going set during a rainy night. With the widescreen transfer, Yu's mobile camerawork gets its due. The commentary track with Tilly, Mancini, and Brad Dourif is offhand and light. Yu's track is more technical. Given the different approaches, it's good that the two are separate. The 3.5 bone rating is meant for horror fans. —*MM*
Movie: 🎵🎵🎵 *DVD:* 🎵🎵🎵⯈
Universal Studios Home Video (Cat #20521, UPC #025192052125). Widescreen (1.85:1) letterboxed. Dolby Digital 5.1 Surround Stereo; Dolby Digital Surround Stereo. $24.98. Keepcase. *LANG:* English; French. *SUB:* Spanish. *CAP:* English. *FEATURES:* Production notes • Jennifer Tilly's diary (taken from *Premiere* magazine) • Commentary: director Ronny Yu • Commentary: Jennifer Tilly, Don Mancini, Brad Dourif • History of Chucky • 18 chapter links • Location notes.
1998 (R) 89m/C Jennifer Tilly, Katherine Heigl, Nick Stabile, John Ritter, Alexis

Arquette, Gordon Michael Woolvett, Lawrence Dane, Michael Johnson, Kathy Najimy; *D:* Ronny Yu; *W:* Don Mancini; *C:* Peter Pau; *M:* Graeme Revell; *V:* Brad Dourif. *AWARDS: NOM:* MTV Movie Awards '99: Best Villain (Dourif).

The Bride of Frankenstein

In David Skal's excellent short documentary, "She's Alive! Creating the Bride of Frankenstein," the various experts he gathers tend to overpraise this seminal horror film, but if there were ever a place for fulsome compliments, this is it. The DVD is a gem. It presents the film itself with as much clarity as any 1935 production can attain today. It's still a bit murky in image and sound; that's all the technology would allow then. The extras make the disc. The documentary draws from excellent sources, including Boris Karloff's daughter; Bill Condon, director of *Gods and Monsters,* about James Whale; writer-director Clive Barker; and director Joe Dante. Their comments combine technical details with trivia—Elsa Lanchester based her famous hiss on swans—in the right amounts. The other extras are equally well chosen and make this one a valuable addition to any horror fan's library. —*MM*
Movie: 🎵🎵🎵 *DVD:* 🎵🎵🎵⯈
Universal Studios Home Video (Cat #20632, UPC #025192063220). Full frame. Dolby Digital Mono. $29.98. Keepcase. *LANG:* English. *SUB:* French. *CAP:* English. *FEATURES:* 18 chapter links • "She's Alive! Creating the Bride of Frankenstein" documentary • Commentary: film historian Scott MacQueen • Production notes • Theatrical trailer • Universal web links • Cast and crew thumbnail biographies • "The Bride of Frankenstein" Archive.
1935 75m/B Boris Karloff, Elsa Lanchester, Ernest Thesiger, Colin Clive, Una O'Connor, Valerie Hobson, Dwight Frye, John Carradine, E.E. Clive, O.P. Heggie, Gavin Gordon, Douglas Walton, Billy Barty, Walter Brennan; *D:* James Whale; *W:* John Lloyd Balderston, William Hurlbut; *C:* John Mescall; *M:* Franz Waxman. *AWARDS:* National Film Registry '98; *NOM:* Academy Awards '35: Best Sound.

Bride of Re-Animator

What a disappointment. Sequel to the cult masterpiece goes too far in all the wrong directions. Of course, the prosthetic special effects are graphic, but severed body parts have been so overused that they don't even have the power to shock anymore. The strong, flippant humor of the first film has become studied, though star Jeffrey Combs gives it his best. Worst of all, the filmmakers don't even pay attention to plot details from the original. Characters who were clearly dead and/or squashed are brought back without explanation. No, logic is not a prime consideration in cheap horror movies, but that kind

of unimaginative sloppiness is an insult to fans. *AKA:* Re-Animator 2.
Movie: woof *DVD:* NYR
Pioneer Entertainment (Cat #10317). Full frame. Dolby Digital Stereo. $29.98. Keepcase. *FEATURES:* Rehearsals, outtakes, deleted scenes, bloopers • Commentary: filmmakers.
1989 99m/C Bruce Abbott, Claude Earl Jones, Fabiana Udenio, Jeffrey Combs, Kathleen Kinmont, David Gale, Mel Stewart, Irene Forrest; *D:* Brian Yuzna; *W:* Brian Yuzna, Rick Fry, Woody Keith; *C:* Rick Fichter; *M:* Richard Band.

Bride of the Monster

Though *Plan 9 from Outer Space* is the auteur's alternative masterpiece, this one is arguably more inept. Made famous in Tim Burton's *Ed Wood*, it's a silly exercise notable for Lugosi's final starring appearance—he died during the filming of *Plan 9*—and the ridiculous immobile octopus monster with which several "victims" pretend to struggle. Even Woods's fans—and I am one—must admit that his films could be boring with long pointless scenes that are neither funny, suspenseful, nor goofy. They're simply slow and lifeless, and his *Bride* has far too many of them. That said, the DVD captures the black-and-white image (ignore the color box art) with real clarity. In some scenes, the photography is crisp and smooth. In others, the camera movement is jerky and focus is dicey. How appropriate. —*MM AKA:* Bride of the Atom.
Movie: ♫♫ *DVD:* ♫♫▶
Image Entertainment (Cat #ID8600CODVD, UPC #014381860023). Full frame. Dolby Digital Mono. $24.99. Snapper. *LANG:* English. *FEATURES:* 12 chapter links.
1955 68m/B Bela Lugosi, Tor Johnson, Loretta King, Tony McCoy, Harvey B. Dunn, George Becwar, Paul Marco, Billy (William) Benedict, Dolores Fuller, Don Nagel, Bud Osborne, Conrad Brooks; *D:* Edward D. Wood Jr.; *W:* Edward D. Wood Jr., Alex Gordon; *C:* William C. Thompson; *M:* Frank Worth.

The Bride with White Hair

One of the acknowledged masterpieces of Hong Kong cinema receives the treatment it's due on DVD. It's the magical tale of warring clans, one led by the young warrior prince Ye Hong (Leslie Cheung) who falls in love with his enemy, Wolf Girl (Bridgette Lin Ching Hsia). Their story mixes operatic overstatement with outsized emotions and Shakespearian plot turns all played out on stylized sets with soaring special effects. The stunt work owes more to dance than conventional martial arts. Ronny Yu's film is really meant to be seen on a theatre screen, but the DVD comes in a strong second. The widescreen image has more detail than the tape version, with some bleeding of reds; but in this kind of fantasy, that's a quibble. The night scenes, in particular, sparkle with silver moonlight.

For western audiences who may not be familiar with Chinese dramatic conventions, director Yu's commentary track provides some background. The bright subtitles might have been placed in the lower letterbox strip. Viewers who prefer English can dispense with them. Followed by an equally brilliant sequel. —*MM AKA:* Jiang-Hu: Between Love and Glory.
Movie: ♫♫♫♫ *DVD:* ♫♫♫♫
Tai Seng Video Marketing (Cat #45224, UPC #601643452241). Widescreen (2.35:1). Dolby Digital Stereo. $29.95. Keepcase. *LANG:* English; Cantonese; Mandarin. *SUB:* English. *FEATURES:* Interactive menu (see note) • 23 chapter links • Filmographies and biographies of stars and director • "Making of" featurette • Trailers • Commentary: Ronny Yu. On my DVD player, pressing the "Menu" button brings up the first six chapters. Hitting the "Back" arrow brings up the main menu.
1993 92m/C *HK* Leslie Cheung, Brigitte Lin Ching Hsia, Nam Kit-Ying, Frances Ng, Elaine Lui; *D:* Ronny Yu; *W:* Ronny Yu, David Wu, Lan Kei-Tou, Tseng Pik-Yin; *C:* Peter Pau; *M:* Richard Yuen.

The Bride with White Hair 2

Spectacular fantasy sequel is simpler than the original, as the white-haired witch (Bridgette Lin Ching Hsia) continues her revenge against the eight clans. A straightforward rescue-of-the-kidnapped-bride plot provides the basis for a no-holds-barred battle of the sexes fought on a cosmic scale—men against women, young against old, love against anger. Blood flies, passions and people soar, warriors are beheaded by hair. The story works with the stuff of myth and fairy tales. Bridgette Lin Ching Hsia and Leslie Cheung repeat their roles but most of the action is handled by younger cast members. As the fearless Moon, Christy Chung steals the film. On DVD, a few of the reds bleed, but blues and whites predominate in most scenes, and they gleam. Blacks are deep and sharp; the sound is fine. As is the case with the original, the DVD image is noticeably sharper and more detailed than the tape version. The subtitles are easy to read and English is available for those who prefer. Highly recommended. —*MM AKA:* Jiang-Hu: Between Love and Glory 2.
Movie: ♫♫♫♫ *DVD:* ♫♫♫♫
Tai Seng Video Marketing (Cat #45234, UPC #601643452340). Widescreen. Dolby Digital Stereo. $29.95. Keepcase. *LANG:* English; Cantonese; Mandarin. *SUB:* English. *FEATURES:* 20 chapter links • Filmographies and biographies of stars and director • Trailers. On my DVD player, pressing the "Menu" button brings up the first four chapters. Hitting the "Back" arrow brings up the main menu.
1993 80m/C *HK* Brigitte Lin Ching Hsia, Leslie Cheung, Christy Chung; *D:* David Wu, Ronny Yu; *W:* David Wu.

The Bridge of San Luis Rey

A priest investigates a bridge collapse in Peru which has left five people dead. The black-and-white film, based on Thornton Wilder's novel, looks good on DVD. The disc was made from a print that shows its age, but overall, the image is well preserved. —*MM*
Movie: ♫♫♫ *DVD:* ♫♫▶
Image Entertainment (Cat #5365). Full frame. Dolby Digital Mono. $24.99. Snapper. *LANG:* English.
1944 89m/B Lynn Bari, Francis Lederer, Louis Calhern, Akim Tamiroff, Donald Woods, Alla Nazimova, Blanche Yurka; *D:* Rowland V. Lee; *W:* Howard Estabrook, Herman Weissman; *C:* John Boyle; *M:* Dimitri Tiomkin. *AWARDS: NOM:* Academy Awards '44: Best Original Dramatic Score.

A Bridge Too Far

Richard Attenborough's underrated epic receives the respect it's due on DVD, though the letterboxing is so extreme that the film will suffer on smaller screens. The chapter selections help anyone who wants to cherry-pick among the all-star cast. Despite the film's reputation as one of the last of the dinosaurs, the mostly true story of a military disaster is accurate, long, engrossing, filled with sterling performances (led by Sir Laurence Olivier and Anthony Hopkins), demanding, and, well, long. Both image and sound are excellent compared to other films of the era. —*MM*
Movie: ♫♫♫▶ *DVD:* ♫♫♫♫▶
MGM Home Entertainment (Cat #906757, UPC #027616675729). Widescreen (2.35:1) letterboxed. Dolby Stereo Surround. $24.95. Keepcase. *LANG:* English; French. *SUB:* English. *CAP:* English. *FEATURES:* 32 chapter links • 8-page booklet • Theatrical trailer.
1977 (PG) 175m/C *GB* Sean Connery, Robert Redford, James Caan, Michael Caine, Elliott Gould, Gene Hackman, Laurence Olivier, Ryan O'Neal, Liv Ullmann, Dirk Bogarde, Hardy Kruger, Arthur Hill, Edward Fox, Anthony Hopkins, Maximilian Schell, Denholm Elliott, Wolfgang Preiss, Nicholas Campbell, Christopher Good, John Ratzenberger; *D:* Richard Attenborough; *W:* William Goldman; *C:* Geoffrey Unsworth; *M:* John Addison. *AWARDS:* British Academy Awards '77: Best Supporting Actor (Fox); National Society of Film Critics Awards '77: Best Supporting Actor (Fox).

The Bridges of Madison County

Leisurely pacing by director Eastwood combines with the low-key sexuality of actor Eastwood to make a thoroughly enjoyable adaptation of Robert James Waller's novel. While in Idaho to photograph Madison County's scenic bridges, Robert Kincaid (Eastwood) stops for directions at Francesca Johnson's (Streep) farm. The married farm gal and worldly camera guy are immediately attracted to each other and waste no time arranging a roll in the hay. Beautiful cinematography gets you through the somewhat slow beginning. Since the cinematography is the highlight here, a widescreen presentation would have been nice. Luckily the picture is a least very sharp and free from grain and artifact. The DVD is able to convey the subtle colors accurately and has no problem with bleed. Contrast is good and brightness is comfortable, but the blacks, though generally acceptable, at times lean towards gray-green. The soundtrack is very good and both the dialogue and the music are delivered with good fidelity and dynamics. —JO

Movie: 🐾🐾🐾 **DVD:** 🐾🐾🐾
Warner Home Video, Inc. (Cat #13772, UPC #085391377221). Full frame. Dolby Digital 5.1; Stereo. Snapper. *LANG:* English (DD5.1); French (Stereo). *SUB:* Spanish; French. *CAP:* English. *FEATURES:* 33 chapter links • Production notes.
1995 (PG-13) 135m/C Clint Eastwood, Meryl Streep, Victor Slezak, Annie Corley, Jim Haynie; *D:* Clint Eastwood; *W:* Richard LaGravenese; *C:* Jack N. Green; *M:* Lennie Niehaus. *AWARDS: NOM:* Academy Awards '95: Best Actress (Streep); Golden Globe Awards '96: Best Actress—Drama (Streep), Best Film—Drama; Screen Actors Guild Award '95: Best Actress (Streep).

Brigadoon

Two contemporary (mid-'50s) hunters (Kelly and Johnson) stumble upon the magical Scottish village that awakens once every hundred years. Like all of the MGM musicals, this one really ought to be seen on the theatrical screen. It loses a lot on anything smaller. That said, this one looks fine on DVD. The unreal brightness of the colors and the heavy areas of darkness fit the story, and they are an accurate reproduction of the original. The score is just as important and it sounds fine in stereo. —MM

Movie: 🐾🐾🐾 **DVD:** 🐾🐾🐾
MGM Home Entertainment (Cat #906560, UPC #027616656025). Widescreen letterboxed. Dolby Digital Surround Stereo. $24.95. Keepcase. *LANG:* English. *SUB:* English; French; Spanish. *FEATURES:* 28 chapter links • 4-page booklet with production notes.
1954 108m/C Gene Kelly, Van Johnson, Cyd Charisse; *D:* Vincente Minnelli; *W:* Alan Jay Lerner; *C:* Joseph Ruttenberg; *M:* Alan Jay Lerner, Frederick Loewe. *AWARDS: NOM:* Academy Awards '54: Best Art Direction/Set Decoration (Color), Best Costume Design (Color), Best Sound.

A Bright Shining Lie

Adaptation of Neil Sheehan's 1988 Pulitzer Prize–winning book views the Vietnam war through the eyes of Col. John Paul Vann (Paxton). The brash young officer ("Mark my words, gentlemen, Vietnam

is the war of the future.") arrives as a military adviser in 1962 and eventually leaves that post to become part of the State Department's Civilian Aid Program, where he exposes falsified battle reports and other deceptions to newsman Steven Burnett (Logue). Though the combat footage and the emotional impact do not equal *Apocalypse Now*, the film's historical accuracy makes it equally important. Since it was made for cable television, the image loses nothing in the full-frame presentation. On DVD, both image and sound are well above average, with only minor distractions in a few interiors. —MM

Movie: 🐾🐾🐾 **DVD:** 🐾🐾🐾
HBO Home Video (Cat #91220, UPC #026359122026). Full frame. Dolby Digital Surround Stereo. $19.98. Snapper. *LANG:* English; Spanish. *SUB:* English; French; Spanish. *FEATURES:* 14 chapter links • "Making of" featurette.
1998 (R) 118m/C Bill Paxton, Donal Logue, Kurtwood Smith, Eric Bogosian, Amy Madigan, Vivian Wu, Robert John Burke, James Rebhorn, Ed Lauter, Harve Presnell; *D:* Terry George; *W:* Terry George; *C:* Jack Conroy; *M:* Gary Chang.

Brighton Beach Memoirs

The film adaptation of the popular (and semi-autobiographical) Neil Simon play is a poignant comedy/drama about a young Jewish boy's coming-of-age in Depression-era Brooklyn. Followed by *Biloxi Blues* and *Broadway Bound*. This is a fairly average DVD transfer that neither enhances nor detracts from the viewing experience. Sharpness is above average and colors are reasonably good, but darker hues produce some bleed. —JO *AKA:* Neil Simon's Brighton Beach Memoirs.

Movie: 🐾🐾🐾 **DVD:** 🐾🐾▸
Image Entertainment (Cat #ID4295USDVD, UPC #014381429527). Full frame. Dolby Digital Mono. $24.95. Snapper. *LANG:* English. *FEATURES:* 16 chapter links.
1986 (PG-13) 108m/C Blythe Danner, Bob Dishy, Judith Ivey, Jonathan Silverman, Brian Drillinger, Stacey Glick, Lisa Waltz, Jason Alexander; *D:* Gene Saks; *W:* Neil Simon; *C:* John Bailey; *M:* Michael Small.

Broadcast News

Tom (Hurt) is the very model of a modern media superstar—handsome, empty-headed, great hair. Aaron (Brooks) is a smart reporter who yearns to be an anchorman. Jane (Hunter) is the driven producer who's caught between the two men, unsure of her feelings of friendship and/or love. They make an unusual romantic triangle and writer-director Brooks works out their problems—both personal and professional—with real wit intelligence and originality. Such erudite comedy-drama doesn't really depend on visual complexity, and so this is not the most impressive DVD on the shelf. Its flaws are minimal—some busyness in one dress, no-frills sound—but the performances are near perfect. —MM

Movie: 🐾🐾🐾 **DVD:** 🐾🐾🐾
Twentieth Century Fox Home Entertainment (Cat #4112893, UPC #08616212 8936). Widescreen (1.85:1) letterboxed. Dolby Digital Surround Stereo; Dolby Digital Stereo. $29.98. Keepcase. *LANG:* English; French. *SUB:* Spanish. *CAP:* English. *FEATURES:* 21 chapter links • Theatrical trailer.
1987 (R) 132m/C William Hurt, Albert Brooks, Holly Hunter, Jack Nicholson, Joan Cusack, Robert Prosky, Lois Chiles, John Cusack, Gennie James; *D:* James L. Brooks; *W:* James L. Brooks; *C:* Michael Ballhaus; *M:* Bill Conti, Michael Gore. *AWARDS:* Los Angeles Film Critics Association Awards '87: Best Actress (Hunter); National Board of Review Awards '87: Best Actress (Hunter); New York Film Critics Awards '87: Best Actress (Hunter), Best Director (Brooks), Best Film, Best Screenplay; *NOM:* Academy Awards '87: Best Actor (Hurt), Best Actress (Hunter), Best Cinematography, Best Film Editing, Best Original Screenplay, Best Picture, Best Supporting Actor (Brooks).

Brokedown Palace

After graduating high school, best buds Alice (Danes) and Darlene (Beckinsale) take a trip to Thailand where they wind up holding the bag during a drug smuggling deal. Trapped in the legal system, they find that Yankee Hank (Pullman), an expatriate lawyer, is their only hope. The DVD handles the exotic locales and the exceptionally busy backgrounds and patterns without trouble, save one set of venetian blinds. Actually, considering the subject matter and milieu, the image looks cleaner and sharper than it should. Sound is fine. —MM

Movie: 🐾🐾▸ **DVD:** 🐾🐾🐾
Twentieth Century Fox Home Entertainment (Cat #2000003, UPC #024543 000037). Widescreen (2.35:1) letterboxed. Dolby Digital 5.1 Surround Stereo; Dolby Digital Surround Stereo. $34.98. Keepcase. *LANG:* English. *SUB:* English; Spanish. *CAP:* English. *FEATURES:* 26 chapter links • Cast and crew thumbnail biographies • Theatrical trailer.
1999 (PG-13) 100m/C Claire Danes, Kate Beckinsale, Bill Pullman, Daniel Lapaine, Lou Diamond Phillips, Jacqueline Kim, Tom Amandes, Aimee Graham, John Doe; *D:* Jonathan Kaplan; *W:* David Arata; *C:* Newton Thomas (Tom) Sigel; *M:* David Newman.

Broken Arrow

Air Force pilot Vic Deakins (Travolta) rips off a couple of nuclear weapons during a routine exercise over the Utah desert. Deakins's ex-copilot Riley Hale (Slater), with help from spunky park ranger Terry Carmichael (Mathis), sets out to find and retrieve the warheads before the big bang. Hong Kong action king Woo once again tries his hand at the big-budget Hollywood action extravaganza, with mixed results. Triple script whammy of cheesy dialogue, continuity problems, and predictability undercuts—but doesn't obscure—his talent for choreographing mayhem. Travolta plays the All-American Boy as creepily charming psychotic to great effect. Well, this is far from the best John Woo film, but this DVD is one of the best there is. The picture is so sharp that it feels like looking through a window at something real. No grain. No artifacts. No color bleed even though they are amazingly vibrant. The blacks are never off and the contrast/brightness gives as much visual punch as I've seen on any video format. And the sound is just as amazing. The Surround puts you right in the center of things where the force of the subwoofer will knock you out of your seat. Right now, this is as good as video gets. —*JO*

Movie: ♫♫ **DVD:** ♫♫♫♫
20th Century Fox (Cat #4110420, UPC #086162104206). Widescreen (2.35:1) letterboxed. Dolby Digital 5.1; Stereo. $29.98. Keepcase. *LANG:* English (DD5.1); French (DS). *SUB:* Spanish. *CAP:* English. *FEATURES:* 22 chapter links ▪ Theatrical trailer.
1995 (R) 108m/C John Travolta, Christian Slater, Samantha Mathis, Delroy Lindo, Bob Gunton, Frank Whaley, Howie Long; *D:* John Woo; *W:* Graham Yost; *C:* Peter Levy; *M:* Hans Zimmer. *AWARDS: NOM:* MTV Movie Awards '96: Best Villain (Travolta), Best Action Sequence.

Broken Blossoms

One of Griffith's most widely acclaimed films revolves around a young Chinese man (Barthelmess) in London's squalid Limehouse district hoping to spread the peaceful philosophy of his Eastern religion. He befriends a pitiful street waif (Gish) who is mistreated by her brutal father (Crisp). The DVD was made from a slightly scratchy print but it still looks amazingly good for a film its age. The 1919 score by Louis Gottschalk doesn't fare as well. It sounds dated and thin, even though this character-driven material doesn't require thunderous accompaniment. (Griffith was trying to answer charges of racism that had been leveled in the wake of *The Birth of a Nation*.) A few of the more heavily tinted scenes are murky. —*MM*

Movie: ♫♫♫▪ **DVD:** ♫♫♫
Image Entertainment (Cat #ID4720SDVD, UPC #014381472028). Full frame. Dolby Digital Mono. $29.99. Snapper. *FEATURES:* 11 chapter links.
1919 89m/B Lillian Gish, Richard Barthelmess, Donald Crisp; *D:* D.W. Griffith; *W:* D.W. Griffith; *C:* Billy (G.W.) Bitzer; *M:* Louis F. Gottschalk. *AWARDS:* National Film Registry '96.

A Bronx Tale

Vivid snapshot of a young Italian-American boy growing up in the '60s among neighborhood small-time wiseguys. As a nine-year-old, Calogero witnesses mobster Sonny kill a man but doesn't rat to the police, so Sonny takes the kid under his wing. His upright bus-driving father Lorenzo doesn't approve but the kid is drawn to Sonny's apparent glamor and power. At 17, he's gotten both an education in school and on the streets, but he needs to make a choice. Good period detail and excellent performances mark De Niro's directorial debut. As long as there is enough light in a scene, this DVD looks great. When the light goes away, so does the image quality. More than any other DVD, this one looks like a different disc every time the lighting changes. Color also varies, looking good and contrasty when brightly lit, and dull when the lights go down. Dimness also brings in some artifacts and the grain level picks up, especially in the blacks. The 5.1 sound was so lifeless that I switched over to the stereo and found it not much different. —*JO*

Movie: ♫♫♫ **DVD:** ♫▶
HBO Home Video (Cat #9095, UPC #02635909529). Widescreen (1.85:1) letterboxed. Dolby Digital 5.1; Dolby Digital 2.0 Stereo; Mono. $24.98. Snapper. *LANG:* English (DD5.1); Spanish (Mono); French (stereo). *CAP:* English. *FEATURES:* 23 chapter links ▪ Theatrical trailer ▪ Cast bios.
1993 (R) 122m/C Robert De Niro, Chazz Palminteri, Lillo Brancato, Francis Capra, Taral Hicks, Kathrine Narducci, Clem Caserta, Alfred Saucheli Jr., Frank Pietrangolare, Joseph D'Onofrio; *Cameos:* Joe Pesci; *D:* Robert De Niro; *W:* Chazz Palminteri; *C:* Reynaldo Villalobos; *M:* Butch Barbella.

Brother, Can You Spare a Dime?

This curious documentary describes the Great Depression through a collection of clips from Hollywood films combined with newsreel footage and period music. The juxtaposition of such diverse images as John Dillinger's father, Huey Long, a young Orson Welles, and George Raft dancing a tango with Carol Lombard creates an unsettling emotional reaction. It's not an objective look at those years, but it is entertaining. The film certainly isn't to all tastes. (Director Mora went on to make *Communion* and *Howling 2: Your Sister Is a Werewolf*.) On DVD, the quality of the clips is excellent, for the most part, and the sound, which is so often the weakest element of 1930s films, isn't bad either. Perhaps the most useful part of the DVD is the extensive index which makes individual scenes easy to find. —*MM*

Movie: ♫♫♫▶ **DVD:** ♫♫♫▶
Image Entertainment (Cat #ID5889EUDVD, UPC #014381588927). Full frame. Dolby Digital Mono. $24.98. Snapper. *LANG:* English. *FEATURES:* 25 chapter links.
1975 112m/C

A Brother's Kiss

Growing up in an East Harlem neighborhood with an alcoholic mother (Moriarty), two brothers are set on diverging paths that strain their love for each other. Lex (Chinlund) is a never-was ex-basketball player with a bad marriage and an even worse drug habit. Mick (Raynor) is a tightly wound, obsessive cop. Both of their problems stem from a childhood trauma that neither is able or willing to discuss. Told in flashback, the film begins on a strong and abrasive note but the story, expanded from a one-act play, runs out of energy in the second half. The full-frame image is not a significant step up from VHS tape. The same goes for sound. —*MM*

Movie: ♫♫ **DVD:** ♫♫
WinStar Home Entertainment (Cat #FLV5146, UPC #720917515021). Full frame. Stereo. $24.98. Keepcase. *LANG:* English. *FEATURES:* 8 chapter links ▪ Theatrical trailer ▪ Cast and crew filmographies ▪ Production notes.
1997 (R) 92m/C Nicholas Chinlund, Michael Raynor, Justin Pierce, Cathy Moriarty, Rosie Perez, Marisa Tomei, Joshua Danowsky, John Leguizamo, Michael Rapaport, Frank Minucci, Adrian Pasdar; *D:* Seth Zvi Rosenfeld; *W:* Seth Zvi Rosenfeld; *C:* Fortunato Procopio; *M:* Frank London.

Brute Force

The influences of this seminal film noir can be seen in *Escape from Alcatraz, The Shawshank Redemption*, and almost any other prison movie made since 1950. Collins (Lancaster) leads the guys in his cell (one is a stoolie) in planning an escape when the coldly evil Capt. Munsey (Cronyn) tightens his grip on Westgate penitentiary. Short flashbacks reveal the weaknesses and mistakes that brought them all to the place. Both Jules Dassin's direction and Richard Brooks's script are tight and quick, if a bit blatant in their handling of bleak noir themes. The performances from an ensemble of first-rate character actors, including Charles Bickford, Whit Bissell, and Howard Duff, are excellent. The DVD captures William Daniels's black-and-white cinematography in all its subtle grittiness. At first Miklos Rozsa's score seems too big for the taut mid-budget drama but in the last reel, it fits perfectly. The overall look and sound of the disc are fine with no noticeable artifacts, even in the many dark scenes. Since the title is only recently arrived on home video in any form, it's highly recommended to Lancaster fans who may well have missed one of his best early roles. —*MM*

Movie: ♫♫♫▶ **DVD:** ♫♫♫▶
Image Entertainment (Cat #ID5745MK DVD, UPC #014381574524). Full frame. Dolby Digital Mono. $24.99. Snapper. *LANG:* English. *FEATURES:* 15 chapter links ▪ Filmographies for Lancaster, Cronyn, De Carlo, Dassin, and Brooks ▪ Stills and print ad illustrations.
1946 102m/B Burt Lancaster, Ann Blyth, Ella Raines, Yvonne De Carlo, Hume Cronyn, Charles Bickford, Whit Bissell, Howard Duff; *D:* Jules Dassin; *W:* Richard Brooks; *C:* William H. Daniels; *M:* Miklos Rozsa.

The Brute Man

A young man (Hatton) who had been disfigured by his school mates returns to take vengeance in this swiftly paced noirish horror. Veteran director Yarbrough makes the most of Rondo Hatton's unforgettable face and understated performance. Fine black-and-white photography is the perfect medium to capture him. Hatton was afflicted with acromegaly, a disease that produces an enlargement of the bones in the face, hands, and feet. He died several months before this film's release. On DVD, the film looks and sounds as crisp as it must have in theatres. Blacks and grays are sharply defined within the claustrophobic darkness of the overall setting. — *MM*

Movie: ♪♪♪ *DVD:* ♪♪♪➤
Image Entertainment (Cat #ID5366FWDVD, UPC #014381536621). Full frame. Dolby Digital Mono. $19.99. Snapper. *LANG:* English. *FEATURES:* 11 chapter links.
1946 62m/B Rondo Hatton, Tom Neal, Jane Adams, Donald McBride, Peter Whitney; *D:* Jean Yarbrough; *W:* George Bricker, M. Coates Webster; *C:* Maury Gertsman; *M:* Hans J. Salter.

The Bubble

The titular bubble is a force field, which traps the residents of a small town in a 3-D environment from which there is no escape. *AKA:* Fantastic Invasion of Planet Earth.
Movie: ♪➤ *DVD:* NYR
Rhino Home Video (Cat #5661). $19.95. Snapper.
1967 112m/C Michael Cole, Johnny Desmond, Deborah Walley; *D:* Arch Oboler; *W:* Arch Oboler; *C:* Charles F. Wheeler; *M:* Paul Sawtell, Bert Shefter.

Buck Privates

Abbott and Costello star as two dim-witted tie salesmen, running from the law, who become buck privates during WWII. The duo's first great success, and the film that established the formula for each subsequent film. Features the Andrews Sisters and their hit "Boogie Woogie Bugle Boy." This black-and-white transfer has none of the crisp details and deep graytones that make some classics really come to life on the TV screen. The image is O.K., but that's it. The sound is also a little lackluster, despite being PCM stereo, which can deliver plenty of fidelity and dynamics. — *JO AKA:* Rookies.
Movie: ♪♪➤ *DVD:* ♪♪
Image Entertainment (Cat #ID4267USDVD, UPC #014381426724). Full frame. PCM Stereo. $29.95. Snapper. *LANG:* English. *FEATURES:* 16 chapter links.
1941 84m/B Bud Abbott, Lou Costello, Shemp Howard, Lee Bowman, Alan Curtis, The Andrews Sisters; *D:* Arthur Lubin; *W:* Arthur T. Horman, John Grant; *C:* Milton Krasner; *M:* Charles Previn. *AWARDS: NOM:* Academy Awards '41: Best Song ("Boogie Woogie Bugle Boy of Company B"), Scoring of a Musical.

Buck Privates Come Home

Abbott and Costello return to their *Buck Privates* roles as two soldiers trying to adjust to civilian life after the war. They also try to help a French girl sneak into the United States. Funny antics culminate into a wild chase scene. This Image Entertainment transfer is far superior to the original *Buck Privates*. The picture is sharp, with good contrast and depth. The sound is also slightly improved, and the mono is much more energetic and full-bodied. —*JO AKA:* Rookies Come Home.
Movie: ♪♪♪ *DVD:* ♪♪♪
Image Entertainment (Cat #ID4285USDVD, UPC #014381428520). Full frame. Dolby Digital Mono. $29.95. Snapper. *LANG:* English. *FEATURES:* 16 chapter links.
1947 77m/B Bud Abbott, Lou Costello, Tom Brown, Joan Shawlee, Nat Pendleton, Beverly Simmons, Don Beddoe, Don Porter, Donald MacBride; *D:* Charles T. Barton; *W:* John Grant, Frederic Rinaldo, Robert Lees; *C:* Charles Van Enger; *M:* Walter Schumann.

Buddhist Fist

The main drawing card on this DVD is director Yuen Wo Ping, who staged the action sequences in *The Matrix*. This one is a fairly standard kung-fu tale about two friends (Tsui Siu Ming and Yuen Shun I) who are raised in a Buddhist monastery, are separated, then fight lots of bad guys before they are reunited. The fights are more like tumbling routines and emphasize athletic ability over bone-crunching violence. Even in this conventional genre piece, Yuen Wo Ping utilizes the third dimension more than most action filmmakers. Compared to other imports, the DVD looks fairly good. The image is bright but marred by surface scratches and heavy pixelation in night scenes. —*MM*
Movie: ♪♪♪ *DVD:* ♪♪➤
Tai Seng Video Marketing (Cat #75074, UPC #601643750743). Widescreen letterboxed. $19.95. Keepcase. *LANG:* Cantonese; Mandarin; English. *FEATURES:* 11 chapter links ➤ Yuen Wo Ping filmography.
1980 90m/C *HK* Tsui Siu Ming, Yuen Shun I; *D:* Yuen Woo Ping; *W:* Tsui Siu Ming, Lam Chi Ming, Wong Ching.

The Buddy Holly Story

First-rate biography of the famed '50s rock star (Busey) spans the short years between his meteoric career beginnings in Lubbock to his early death in the now famous plane crash. Don Stroud and Charles Martin Smith play the other members of his group. The film surges with the same energy that fueled those first days of rock music. On a commentary track recorded years after the film was made, director Steve Rash and star Busey take a long stroll down memory lane. They stress the low-budget "guerrilla" tactics they had to employ, and it is easy to see where they had to cut corners. But the immediacy is there, too, and that's what separates this bio-flick from the dozens that have followed. Busey performs Holly's hits himself. The disc looks and sounds terrific. Rave on. —*MM*
Movie: ♪♪♪➤ *DVD:* ♪♪♪➤
Columbia Tristar Home Video (Cat #08019, UPC #043396080195). Full frame; widescreen (1.85:1) letterboxed. Dolby Digital Surround; Dolby Digital Stereo. $25.98. Keepcase. *LANG:* English; French. *SUB:* English; French; Spanish. *CAP:* English. *FEATURES:* Commentary: Steve Rash and Gary Busey ➤ Theatrical trailer ➤ Cast and crew filmographies ➤ 28 chapter links.
1978 (PG) 113m/C Gary Busey, Don Stroud, Charles Martin Smith, Conrad Janis, William Jordan, Albert "Poppy" Popwell; *D:* Steve Rash; *W:* Robert Gittler; *C:* Stevan Larner; *M:* Joe Renzetti. *AWARDS:* Academy Awards '78: Original Song Score and/or Adaptation; National Society of Film Critics Awards '78: Best Actor (Busey); *NOM:* Academy Awards '78: Best Actor (Busey), Best Sound.

Buena Vista Social Club

In 1998 guitarist Ry Cooder and filmmaker Wim Wenders went to Havana and filmed an aging group of Cuban musicians. Cooder had recorded them earlier; Wenders wanted to make a "musicmentary" about them. This film is the result. The two wound up following these charming, canny guys (and one woman) on a journey that led to Europe and finally to Carnegie Hall. On DVD, or any medium, the visuals are much less important than the music, and it shines through just fine on disc, though the concerts and recording sessions have an unpolished quality that complements the image. Much of the film, after all, was made in a very poor country. Anyone who appreciates a more pure form of Latin jazz without the flashiness, will love this one. Others will be charmed by the subjects. —*MM*
Movie: ♪♪♪ *DVD:* ♪♪♪
Artisan Entertainment (Cat #10176). Widescreen letterboxed. Dolby Digital 5.1 Surround Stereo. $29.98. Snapper. *LANG:* English; Spanish. *SUB:* English. *FEATURES:* 30 chapter links ➤ Commentary: Wim Wenders ➤ 15 thumbnail bios of the musicians ➤ Trailer ➤ Filmmakers thumbnail bios ➤ Additional scenes.
1999 (G) 106m/C Ry Cooder; *D:* Wim Wenders. *AWARDS:* Los Angeles Film Critics Association Awards '99: Best Feature Documentary; National Board of Review Awards '99: Best Feature Documentary; New York Film Critics Awards '99: Best Feature Documentary; National Society of Film Critics Awards '99: Best Feature Documentary; *NOM:* Academy Awards '99: Best Feature Documentary; British Academy Awards '99: Best Foreign Film, Best Sound, Best Original Score.

Buffalo 66

Billy Brown (Gallo) is a loser of epic proportions. He's named after the Buffalo Bills, notorious losers of Super Bowls. After he loses $10,000 on one of the Super Bowls, he turns to a life of crime and lands in prison. He gets out of jail as a man with a mission. Stumbling into a dance studio, he kidnaps Layla (Ricci) and forces her to pose as his wife for a visit to his parents. He explains his five-year absence saying that he was on a mission for the CIA. Billy's father (Gazzara) barely hides his disdain, while Billy's mother (Huston) is too obsessed with the Bills to interact with him. Former artist and rock musician Gallo also directed, cowrote, and composed the music for the film. Don't be fooled by the disc's look; the grittiness is on purpose. Gallo shot the film using a reverse process, giving it a Super 8 feel and texture with professional-quality results. It works. —AB

Movie: 🎵🎵🎵 **DVD:** 🎵🎵🎵
Universal Studios Home Video (Cat #20648, UPC #2519206482). Widescreen (1.85:1) anamorphic. Dolby Digital; Dolby Surround. $24.98. Keepcase. *LANG:* English. *CAP:* English. *FEATURES:* Cast and filmmaker filmographies and bios • Production notes • Theatrical trailer.
1997 112m/C Vincent Gallo, Christina Ricci, Anjelica Huston, Ben Gazzara, Kevin Corrigan, Mickey Rourke, Rosanna Arquette, Jan-Michael Vincent; *D:* Vincent Gallo; *W:* Alison Bagnall, Vincent Gallo; *C:* Lance Acord; *M:* Vincent Gallo. *AWARDS:* National Board of Review Awards '98: Best Supporting Actress (Ricci); *NOM:* Independent Spirit Awards '99: Best First Feature.

Buffet Froid

Surreal black comedy about a group of bungling murderers is sometimes labeled the French *Blood Simple,* and with good reason. Depardieu loses his knife on the subway and shortly thereafter finds it imbedded in the chest of a mild-mannered man he had terrified earlier. The acting is all top-notch and director Blier is at his devilish best. The picture is sharper than a lot of Fox/Lorber DVDs, but still not where it should be. Grain is acceptable and at least the artifacts were sparse. The colors are a bit washed-out and lean to yellow, while the blacks are only about average. Adding some contrast and a touch of brightness made the disc a little more enjoyable to watch. The sound did clip mildly on occasion but was overall clean and crisp. —JO

Movie: 🎵🎵🎵 **DVD:** 🎵🎵
Fox/Lorber Home Video (Cat #FLV5031, UPC #720917503127). Widescreen (1.77:1) letterboxed. Mono. $29.98. Keepcase. *LANG:* French. *SUB:* English. *FEATURES:* 10 chapter links • Cast filmographies.
1979 95m/C *FR* Gerard Depardieu, Bernard Blier, Jean Carmet, Genevieve Page, Denise Gence, Carole Bouquet, Jean Benguigui, Michel Serrault; *D:* Bertrand Blier; *W:* Bertrand Blier; *C:* Jean Penzer;

M: Philippe Sarde. *AWARDS:* Cesar Awards '80: Best Writing.

Bug Buster

Generic bug-horror doesn't vary a whit from the formula. Big cockroaches created by pesticides, remote mountain town (Big Bear, CA), newly arrived young heroine (Heigl), regularly scheduled insect attacks, semi-comic exterminator (Quaid, in a variation of the role played by John Goodman in the far superior *Arachnophobia*), corrupt officials. Not much is done with an attractive, capable cast. Beyond the genuinely creepy opening scene with real bugs crawling over a bed, the effects tend to be silly. On DVD, the image is clear enough, though the blacks lack sharp definition. Overall, the film looks much better than low-budget horror needs to look. —MM

Movie: 🎵🎵 **DVD:** 🎵🎵 ➤
DMG Entertainment (Cat #DMG992G, UPC #640587990228). Full frame. Dolby Surround Stereo. Keepcase. *SUB:* Spanish. *FEATURES:* Synopsis • Trailer • Trailers for three other DMG releases • Star filmographies • 9 chapter links.
1999 (R) 93m/C Randy Quaid, Katherine Heigl, Meredith Salenger, Bernie Kopell, Anne Lockhart, George Takei, James Doohan, Ty O'Neal, Downtown Julie Brown, Brenda Doumani, David Lipper; *D:* Lorenzo Doumani; *W:* Malik Khoury; *C:* Hanania Baer; *M:* Sidney James.

A Bug's Life (CE)

Despite the expensive price-tag, this double-disc set really shows what the medium is capable of. The first disc contains both the full- and widescreen versions of the film, along with various extra audio tracks; the second disc has more than 100 minutes of extras, listed below. Since the film was created digitally, it has been transferred directly to DVD, without a celluloid generation. The result is a flawless image, which will delight fans of computer animation but will probably not convert diehard devotees of hand-drawn cartoons. On their commentary track, the filmmakers spend as much time talking about the characters and the story development as they do about the technical side of their work. When they do address the nuts-and-bolts of computer-generated animation, they stress the collaborative nature of their work at Pixar. Their discussion, taken with the extras on the second disc, is a tutorial on the state of computer art, which is changing daily. —MM

Movie: 🎵🎵🎵 **DVD:** 🎵🎵🎵🎵
Buena Vista Home Entertainment (Cat #17989, UPC #717951004024). Widescreen (1.85:1) letterboxed; full frame. Dolby Digital 5.1 Surround Stereo; Dolby Digital Surround Stereo. $49.99. Keepcase. *LANG:* English. *CAP:* English. *FEATURES:* Commentary: Lasseter, Stanton, supervising editor Lee Unkrich • Isolated music track for Randy Newman's score • Isolated sound effects track • 36 chapter links • "Making of" featurette

• Introduction and explanation by filmmakers • Early presentation reel, "Fleabie" • Original story treatment and pitch boards • Character designs, concept art, and color script • Storyboard-to-final-film split-screen comparison • Behind-the-scenes look at voice talent • Production progression demonstration with angle feature • Sound designer Gary Rydstrom's comments on sound effects • International and domestic trailers and posters • Behind-the-scenes look at home video presentation • Out-takes • Academy Award–winning short "Geri's Game."
1998 (G) 94m/C *D:* John Lasseter, Andrew Stanton; *W:* Donald McEnery, Bob Shaw, Andrew Stanton, Joe Ranft; *C:* Sharon Calahan; *M:* Randy Newman; *V:* Dave Foley, Kevin Spacey, Julia Louis-Dreyfus, Phyllis Diller, Richard Kind, David Hyde Pierce, Joe Ranft, Denis Leary, Jonathan Harris, Madeline Kahn, Bonnie Hunt, Michael McShane, John Ratzenberger, Brad Garrett, Roddy McDowall, Edie McClurg, Alex Rocco, David Ossman. *AWARDS: NOM:* Academy Awards '98: Best Original Musical/Comedy Score; Golden Globe Awards '99: Best Score.

Bugsy

Nearly perfect film tells the story of Benjamin "Bugsy" Siegel (Beatty), the '40s gangster who built the Flamingo Hotel in Las Vegas when it was still a virtual desert, before it became a gambling mecca. Bening is Bugsy's moll, Virginia Hill, who inspires him to carry out his dream of building the Flamingo (which was her nickname). Beatty and Bening heat up the screen. Adapted from the Dean Jennings novel *We Only Kill Each Other: The Life and Bad Times of Bugsy Siegel.* This DVD is as sharp as they come, with very little grain and no artifacts. Colors are lush, accurate, and bleed-free even when highly saturated. The contrast delivers plenty of punch to the image and the brightness levels are comfortable in all conditions. When it comes to sound, this DVD is no slouch there either. Loud or soft the tracks are full-bodied and crisp, whether the dialogue, the music, or the gunshots are in front. There is also a gutsy, but never boomy, low end. The Surround mix is also excellent adding ambience as well as effects. —JO

Movie: 🎵🎵🎵 ➤ **DVD:** 🎵🎵🎵🎵
Columbia Tristar Home Video (Cat #70679, UPC #043396706798). Widescreen (1.85:1) letterboxed; full frame. Dolby Surround. NSL. Keepcase. *LANG:* English; French. *SUB:* French. *CAP:* English. *FEATURES:* 28 chapter links • Theatrical trailers.
1991 (R) 135m/C Warren Beatty, Annette Bening, Harvey Keitel, Ben Kingsley, Elliott Gould, Joe Mantegna, Richard Sarafian, Bebe Neuwirth, Wendy Phillips, Robert Beltran, Bill Graham, Lewis Van Bergen, Debrah Farentino; *D:* Barry Levinson; *W:* James Toback; *C:* Allen Daviau; *M:* Ennio Morricone. *AWARDS:* Academy Awards

'91: Best Art Direction/Set Decoration, Best Costume Design; Golden Globe Awards '92: Best Film—Drama; Los Angeles Film Critics Association Awards '91: Best Director (Levinson), Best Film, Best Screenplay; National Board of Review Awards '91: Best Actor (Beatty); *NOM:* Academy Awards '91: Best Actor (Beatty), Best Cinematography, Best Director (Levinson), Best Original Screenplay, Best Picture, Best Supporting Actor (Keitel, Kingsley), Best Original Score.

Bull Durham

Lovable American romantic comedy deals with a very minor minor-league team and three of its current constituents: an aging baseball groupie (Sarandon) who beds one player each season; a cocky, foolish new pitcher (Robbins); and the older, weary catcher (Costner) brought in to wise the rookie up. The scene in which Sarandon tries poetry out on the banal rookie is a hoot and her love scenes with Costner smolder. The DVD transfer is great. No grain, no artifacts, and super, super sharp. The colors will stun you. Even the sound is given a good mix, with the Dolby Surround conveying as much life imaging as most 5.1 tracks. —JO
Movie: ♫♫♫▶ *DVD:* ♫♫♫♫
Image Entertainment (Cat #ID4078ORDVD, UPC #014381407822). Widescreen (1.85:1) anamorphic. Dolby Surround. $29.95. Snapper. *LANG:* English. *FEATURES:* 21 chapter links ▪ Commentary: Ron Shelton.
1988 (R) 107m/C Kevin Costner, Susan Sarandon, Tim Robbins, Trey Wilson, Robert Wuhl, Jenny Robertson; *D:* Ron Shelton; *W:* Ron Shelton; *C:* Bobby Byrne; *M:* Michael Convertino. *AWARDS:* Los Angeles Film Critics Association Awards '88: Best Screenplay; New York Film Critics Awards '88: Best Screenplay; National Society of Film Critics Awards '88: Best Screenplay; Writers Guild of America '88: Best Original Screenplay; *NOM:* Academy Awards '88: Best Original Screenplay.

A Bullet in the Head

Typically violent Woo tale of friendship finds Frank (Cheung), Ben (Leung), and Paul (Lee) heading out of 1967 Hong Kong for Saigon where they hope to make money selling contraband goods in the city. They wind up on the wrong side of the Vietnamese Army, steal a fortune, and become prisoners. Woo's familiar themes of honor, betrayal, death, and morality are combined with over-the-top violence. The DVD image is good but not as crisp as the best. The disc earns a more favorable rating compared to other Hong Kong imports, and it is the best home video version of the film available to the director's fans. — MM *AKA:* Die Xue Jie Tou.
Movie: ♫♫♫▶ *DVD:* ♫♫♫
Tai Seng Video Marketing (Cat #MS/DVD/021/98, UPC #4895017000 213). Widescreen letterboxed. Dolby Digital 5.1 Surround Stereo. $49.95. Keepcase.

LANG: Cantonese; Mandarin. *SUB:* Traditional Chinese; Simplified Chinese; English; Japanese; Korean; Bahasa Malaysia; Spanish. *FEATURES:* 9 chapter links ▪ Theatrical trailers ▪ Production notes.
1990 126m/C *HK* Tony Leung Chiu-Wai, Jacky Cheung, Waise Lee; *D:* John Woo; *W:* John Woo, Janet Chun, Patrick Leung; *C:* Wilson Chan, Ardy Lam, Chai Kittikum Som, Wing-hang Wong; *M:* Romeo Diaz, James Wong.

Bulletproof

Nary an ounce of originality is to be found anywhere here. From the cliched premise to the rigidly stereotyped characters to the no-surprises plot, it's a generic cop-buddy picture. But the stars work well together, generating a few real laughs, and cinematographer-turned-director Ernest Dickerson gives the action a funky off-center look. Keats (Wayans) is an L.A. undercover cop who's spent a year knocking around with Moses (Sandler), a flunky for Colton (Caan), a drug kingpin and used car magnate. When the big drug bust goes bad, Moses is enraged to learn that Keats has set him up. The chase is on.
Movie: ♫♫▶ *DVD:* NYR
Universal Studios Home Video Widescreen (2.35:1) letterboxed. $24.98. Keepcase. *LANG:* English; French. *SUB:* Spanish. *FEATURES:* Cast and crew thumbnail biographies ▪ Production notes ▪ Trailer.
1996 (R) 85m/C Damon Wayans, Adam Sandler, James Caan, Kristen Wilson, James Farentino, Bill Nunn, Mark Roberts, Xander Berkeley, Alan Covert, Jeep Swenson, Larry McCoy; *D:* Ernest R. Dickerson; *W:* Joe Gayton, Lewis Colick; *C:* Steven Bernstein; *M:* Elmer Bernstein. *AWARDS: NOM:* Golden Raspberry Awards '96: Worst Actor (Sandler).

Bullets over Broadway

Vintage Woody Allen is smart, funny, emotionally distant, and very New Yorkish; exactly the sort of film that his fans adore and everyone else ignores. As a comedy, it's more amusing than laugh-out-loud funny, and that's as it should be. This Prohibition-era comedy of actors and gangsters has a darker side. David Shayne (Cusack) is a passionate young playwright who initially refuses to compromise a single syllable of his new drama. But his agent Julian Marx (Warden) says he can't promote such a heavy piece. Then Julian runs across gangster Nick Valenti (Viterelli). Valenti has promised to make his ditzy girlfriend Olive Neal (Tilly) a star. He agrees to bankroll the play if she gets a good part. Shayne's compromises begin. Chazz Palminteri steals the show as her multi-talented bodyguard. The film's darker side is apparent throughout the DVD. Beyond a few daylight exteriors, most of the action is heavily shaded with amber-orange light on Art Deco sets. Moving shapes, such as black cars at night, tend to lose definition. Overall the film looks about the same as it

did in theatres, but it's still going to test the limits of your DVD player. —MM
Movie: ♫♫▶ *DVD:* ♫♫▶
Miramax Pictures Home Video (Cat #16789, UPC #717951001900). Widescreen (1.85:1) letterboxed. $29.99. Keepcase. *LANG:* English. *CAP:* English. *FEATURES:* 22 chapter links.
1994 (R) 106m/C Dianne Wiest, John Cusack, Jennifer Tilly, Rob Reiner, Chazz Palminteri, Tracey Ullman, Mary-Louise Parker, Joe Viterelli, Jack Warden, Jim Broadbent, Harvey Fierstein, Annie-Joe Edwards; *D:* Woody Allen; *W:* Woody Allen, Douglas McGrath; *C:* Carlo Di Palma. *AWARDS:* Academy Awards '94: Best Supporting Actress (Wiest); Golden Globe Awards '95: Best Supporting Actress (Wiest); Independent Spirit Awards '95: Best Supporting Actor (Palminteri), Best Supporting Actress (Wiest); Los Angeles Film Critics Association Awards '94: Best Supporting Actress (Wiest); New York Film Critics Awards '94: Best Supporting Actress (Wiest); National Society of Film Critics Awards '94: Best Supporting Actress (Wiest); Screen Actors Guild Award '94: Best Supporting Actress (Wiest); *NOM:* Academy Awards '94: Best Art Direction/Set Decoration, Best Costume Design, Best Director (Allen), Best Original Screenplay, Best Supporting Actor (Palminteri), Best Supporting Actress (Tilly); British Academy Awards '95: Best Original Screenplay; Independent Spirit Awards '95: Best Film, Best Screenplay; Writers Guild of America '94: Best Original Screenplay.

Bullitt

A detective assigned to protect a star witness for 48 hours senses danger; his worst fears are confirmed when his charge is murdered. Based on the novel *Mute Witness* by Robert L. Pike, and featuring one of filmdom's most famous car chases. And wait till you experience that chase on this DVD. The sound is really revved up and gives new throat to the supercharged engine roars. It does a great job on Shifrin's score as well. The image is commensurate with the audio and is sharper and more vibrant than ever. The included featurette, "Bullitt: Steve McQueen's Commitment to Reality," was produced in the '60s and shows the lengths McQueen and crew went through to capture the momentous and influential chase. —JO
Movie: ♫♫♫ *DVD:* ♫♫♫♫
Warner Home Video, Inc. (Cat #1029, UPC #012569102927). Widescreen (1.85:1) anamorphic. Dolby Surround; Dolby Digital Mono. $24.98. Snapper. *LANG:* English (DS); Spanish (DDM); French (DDM). *SUB:* English; Spanish; French. *CAP:* English. *FEATURES:* 22 chapter links ▪ "Making of" featurette ▪ Theatrical trailers ▪ Production notes.
1968 (PG) 105m/C Steve McQueen, Robert Vaughn, Jacqueline Bisset, Don Gordon, Jack Dukan, Norman Fell, Simon Oakland; *D:* Peter Yates; *W:* Alan R. Trustman; *C:* William A. Fraker; *M:* Lalo Schifrin. *AWARDS:* Academy Awards '68:

Best Film Editing; National Society of Film Critics Awards '68: Best Cinematography; *NOM:* Academy Awards '68: Best Sound.

Bulworth

Writer-director Beatty is on-screen as Sen. Jay Bulworth, a politician who has become disillusioned by dishonesty in the political arena. Ready to call it quits on life, he hires a contract on his own life. But before he can be assassinated, he rediscovers the truth by telling it. Everywhere he goes, he commits political suicide (in advance of the real deal) by calling things like he sees them. He drops the political double-talk and begins delivering his message to a rap beat. In the process, he becomes unexpectedly popular with constituents who admire his new straight-talking style, and he falls in love with a beautiful young black woman (Berry). The ending is unnecessarily ambiguous, which could leave a sour taste. But, on the whole, *Bulworth* is a daring and entertaining dish with a poignant political message. Too bad the image will disappoint picky viewers who won't put up with a soft picture lacking in detail. Simply, *Bulworth* is not nearly as crisp-looking as other DVDs. The soundtrack is fine, particularly the rap tunes. The price tag is high for a disc with few extras and a fuzzy picture. *—MB*
Movie: 🎬🎬🎬 ***DVD:*** 🎬►
20th Century Fox (Cat #41100398, UPC #086162103988). Widescreen (1.85:1) letterboxed. Dolby Digital 5.1. $34.98. Keepcase. *LANG:* English. *SUB:* English; Spanish. *CAP:* English. *FEATURES:* 20 chapter links ▪ Theatrical trailer ▪ Cast biographies and filmographies.
1998 (R) 107m/C Warren Beatty, Halle Berry, Oliver Platt, Paul Sorvino, Don Cheadle, Jack Warden, Christine Baranski, Isaiah Washington, Joshua Malina, Richard Sarafian, Amiri Baraka, Sean Astin, Laurie Metcalf, Wendell Pierce, Michele Morgan, Ariyan Johnson, Graham Beckel, Nora Dunn, Jackie Gayle; *D:* Warren Beatty; *W:* Jeremy Pikser, Warren Beatty; *C:* Vittorio Storaro; *M:* Ennio Morricone. *AWARDS:* Los Angeles Film Critics Association Awards '98: Best Screenplay; *NOM:* Academy Awards '98: Best Original Screenplay; Golden Globe Awards '99: Best Film—Musical/Comedy, Best Film—Musical/Comedy (Beatty), Best Screenplay; Writers Guild of America '98: Best Screenplay.

The 'Burbs

Dante's bizarre satire revolves around a group of suburbanites who believe that the new neighbors are murderers and possibly cannibals who bury the evidence in their basement. It's well designed and sharp with numerous homages thrown in for good measure. Jerry Goldsmith's score punctuates the humor perfectly and is well represented by the Dolby Surround sound on this DVD, which incorporates good space and imaging into the mix along with very good bass and balanced mids and highs. The picture is fairly sharp and picks

up only a little grain in the darker scenes (mainly in the basement). There is a very nice contrasty punch to the colors, which are rich and accurate. There are very few artifacts and the blacks are generally true. *—JO*
Movie: 🎬🎬 ***DVD:*** 🎬🎬🎬
Universal Studios Home Video (Cat #20528, UPC #025192052829). Widescreen (1.85:1) anamorphic. Dolby Surround. $24.98. Keepcase. *LANG:* English; French. *CAP:* English. *FEATURES:* 18 chapter links ▪ Theatrical trailer ▪ Cast and filmmakers bios ▪ Production notes ▪ Film highlights.
1989 (PG) 101m/C Tom Hanks, Carrie Fisher, Rick Ducommun, Corey Feldman, Brother Theodore, Bruce Dern, Gale Gordon, Courtney Gains; *D:* Joe Dante; *W:* Dana Olsen; *C:* Robert Stevens; *M:* Jerry Goldsmith.

Burglar

Mystery writer Lawrence Block's New York detective/thief Bernie Rhodenbarr becomes Bernice who lives in San Francisco in this disappointing adaptation mostly based on *Burglars Can't Be Choosers*. To be fair, Whoopi Goldberg does fairly effective work in the lead with Bobcat Goldthwait as her sometimes sidekick. The tricky plot isn't quite tricky enough. Director Hugh Wilson has had such diverse hits as *Police Academy* and *First Wives Club*. This is not the best effort for him or his cast. On DVD, the pan-and-scan image is fine, even in the rainy night scenes, and the sound is all right. *—MM*
Movie: 🎬🎬 ***DVD:*** 🎬🎬►
Warner Home Video, Inc. (Cat #11705, UPC #08539117052). Full frame. Dolby Digital Surround; Mono. $14.98. Snapper. *LANG:* English; French. *CAP:* English. *FEATURES:* 26 chapter links.
1987 (R) 103m/C Whoopi Goldberg, Bob(cat) Goldthwait, Lesley Ann Warren, John Goodman, G.W. Bailey, James Handy, Anne DeSalvo; *D:* Hugh Wilson; *W:* Hugh Wilson; *C:* William A. Fraker; *M:* Sylvester Levay, Bernard Edwards.

Bury Me in Niagara

Just your average comic ghost-gangster-doctor-road movie. Overprotective mom Mildred Malloy (Stapleton) dies while she's holding a magic stone that allows her "etheric double" to return and bother her son Martin (Davies), who's romancing his housekeeper Jean (D'Lyn) while Japanese mobsters try to steal Mom's body. It is every bit as senseless in execution as it sounds in synopsis. The production was made for television, so the image is acceptable but unspectacular. *—MM AKA:* Ghost Mom.
Movie: 🎬🎬► ***DVD:*** 🎬🎬►
Simitar Entertainment (Cat #7590, UPC #082551759026). Full frame. Dolby Digital Surround Stereo. $14.98. Keepcase. *LANG:* English. *FEATURES:* 8 chapter links ▪ Jean Stapleton thumbnail biography and filmography.

1993 96m/C Jean Stapleton, Geraint Wyn Davies, Shae D'Lyn, Denis Akiyama, Jayne Eastwood, Bernard Behrens, Zachary Bennett, Ed Sahely; *D:* David Thomas; *W:* Daniel J. Harris, Constantino Magnatta; *C:* Francois Protat; *M:* Ian Thomas.

Bustin' Loose

A teacher (Tyson) persuades a reluctant ex-con (Pryor) to drive a bus load of misplaced kids across the country to their school.
Movie: 🎬🎬► ***DVD:*** NYR
Goodtimes Entertainment (Cat #81047). Full frame. $14.99. Snapper.
1981 (R) 94m/C Richard Pryor, Cicely Tyson, Robert Christian, George Coe, Bill Quinn; *D:* Oz Scott; *W:* Lonnie Elder III, Richard Pryor; *C:* Dennis Dalzell; *M:* Roberta Flack, Mark Davis.

Butch Cassidy and the Sundance Kid

Two legendary turn-of-the-century outlaws (Newman and Redford) take it on the lam with a beautiful, willing ex-school teacher (Ross). With William Goldman's clever script, humanly fallible characters and warm witty dialogue, this film was destined to become a perennial favorite and it receives the treatment it deserves on this DVD. Virtually all of the key participants, including director Hill and composer Bacharach, either contribute to the commentary track or talk about their work in interviews recorded in 1994. The image is near perfect with no noticeable pixels or grain, even in the long telephoto shots of the "super posse" crossing the vast western landscapes. The monaural soundtrack is fine. Dialogue is clear and the dated "Raindrops" musical interlude is as bouncy as ever. *—MM*
Movie: 🎬🎬🎬🎬 ***DVD:*** 🎬🎬🎬🎬
20th Century Fox (Cat #2000043, UPC #024543000435). Widescreen (2.35:1) anamorphic. THX Mono. $34.98. Keepcase. *LANG:* English; French. *SUB:* English; Spanish. *FEATURES:* Commentary: Hill, David, Hall, associate producer Robert Crawford ▪ 1994 interviews with Neuman, Redford, Ross, Goldman, Bacharach ▪ 24 chapter links ▪ Trailer.
1969 (PG) 110m/C Paul Newman, Robert Redford, Katharine Ross, Jeff Corey, Strother Martin, Cloris Leachman, Kenneth Mars, Ted Cassidy, Henry Jones, George Furth, Sam Elliott; *D:* George Roy Hill; *W:* William Goldman; *C:* Conrad Hall; *M:* Burt Bacharach. *AWARDS:* Academy Awards '69: Best Cinematography, Best Song ("Raindrops Keep Fallin' on My Head"), Best Story & Screenplay, Best Original Score; American Film Institute (AFI) '98: Top 100; British Academy Awards '70: Best Actor (Redford), Best Actress (Ross), Best Director (Hill), Best Film, Best Screenplay; Golden Globe Awards '70: Best Score; Writers Guild of America '69: Best Adapted Screenplay; *NOM:* Academy Awards '69: Best Director (Hill), Best Picture, Best Sound.

Bye, Bye, Birdie

Sweet, energetic film version of the Broadway musical follows the visit of rock 'n' roll idol Conrad Birdie (Pearson doing Elvis) coming to a small town to see one of his fans (Ann-Margret) before he's drafted. The careful transfer to DVD makes for a visual presentation that's virtually perfect. The film hasn't looked this good since its theatrical release. The candy-colored pinks, aquas, and purples are there in all their cheesy splendor. Sound is not as bright. It never has been because the arrangements of these light bouncy songs have always seemed a little flat to me. —MM

Movie: 🎵🎵🎵 **DVD:** 🎵🎵🎵
Columbia Tristar Home Video (Cat #1509, UPC #043396015098). Widescreen (2.35:1) letterboxed; full frame. Dolby Digital 5.0 Surround Stereo; Dolby Digital Surround Stereo. $27.95. Keepcase. *LANG:* English. *SUB:* Korean; Mandarin; Portuguese; Spanish; Thai. *FEATURES:* 28 chapter links • Production notes booklet • Cast and crew filmographies • Theatrical trailer.
1963 112m/C Dick Van Dyke, Janet Leigh, Ann-Margret, Paul Lynde, Bobby Rydell, Maureen Stapleton, Ed Sullivan, Trudi Ames, Jesse Pearson; *D:* George Sidney; *W:* Irving Brecher; *C:* Joseph Biroc; *M:* Johnny Green. *AWARDS: NOM:* Academy Awards '63: Best Adapted Score, Best Sound.

Bye Bye Monkey

Film by Italian director Ferreri explores the disintegration of the traditional sex roles and decline of the nuclear family. Depardieu is Lafayette, a young lighting technician in New York who works for a feminist group of performers who abuse him for their own amusement. But one of his "tormentors" (Lawrence) falls in love with him. Lafayette's unencumbered life changes when he finds a baby chimpanzee—as well as his new girlfriend. Look closely, and you will see digital compression artifacts in the backgrounds of many scenes. Audio is a ho-hum monaural soundtrack. Don't look for the absent extras, but simple menu gets the job done. —MB

Movie: 🎵🎵🎵 **DVD:** 🎵🎵▶
Image Entertainment (Cat #ID4776SIDVD, UPC #014381477627). Widescreen (1.85:1) letterboxed. Dolby Digital 1.0. $24.99. Snapper. *LANG:* English. *FEATURES:* 14 chapter links.
1977 m/C *IT FR* Gerard Depardieu, Gail Lawrence; *D:* Marco Ferreri.

Cabaret

Hitler is rising to power, racism and anti-Semitism are growing, and the best place to hide from it all is the cabaret. With dancing girls, androgynous master of ceremonies Grey, and American expatriate Minnelli, you can laugh and drink and pretend tomorrow will never come. Minnelli does just that. Face-to-face with the increasing horrors of Nazism, she persists in the belief that the "show must go on." Impressive, with excellent direction and cinematography. *Cabaret* presents many challenges to the DVD format. Not only do the colors run the gamut from subtle to fully saturated, the lighting is just as varied. This DVD can handle it all. The picture is crisp all the way through. Colors are accurate to the film and there is no bleed. Consistent brightness and bold contrast levels combine with dead-on blacks to ensure that the details are distinct. *Cabaret* is a musical, and though the sound is only stereo, it is so dynamic that the songs still seem to leap off the screen. The "making of" featurette is the more interesting of the two documentaries on the disc and was filmed during the actual production. —JO

Movie: 🎵🎵🎵▶ **DVD:** 🎵🎵🎵🎵
Warner Home Video, Inc. (Cat #785, UPC #012569078529). Widescreen (1.85:1) letterboxed; full frame. Stereo. $24.98. Snapper. *LANG:* English. *SUB:* Spanish; French. *CAP:* English. *FEATURES:* 32 chapter links • Theatrical trailer • "Making of" featurette • Documentary • Photo gallery • Production notes.
1972 (PG) 119m/C Liza Minnelli, Joel Grey, Michael York, Marisa Berenson; *D:* Bob Fosse; *W:* Jay Presson Allen; *C:* Geoffrey Unsworth; *M:* Ralph Burns. *AWARDS:* Academy Awards '72: Best Actress (Minnelli), Best Art Direction/Set Decoration, Best Cinematography, Best Director (Fosse), Best Film Editing, Best Sound, Best Supporting Actor (Grey), Original Song Score and/or Adaptation; British Academy Awards '72: Best Actress (Minnelli), Best Director (Fosse), Best Film; Golden Globe Awards '73: Best Actress—Musical/Comedy (Minnelli), Best Film—Musical/Comedy, Best Supporting Actor (Grey); National Board of Review Awards '72: Best Director (Fosse), Best Supporting Actor (Grey), Best Supporting Actress (Berenson), National Film Registry '95; National Society of Film Critics Awards '72: Best Supporting Actor (Grey); Writers Guild of America '72: Best Adapted Screenplay; *NOM:* Academy Awards '72: Best Adapted Screenplay, Best Picture.

The Cabinet of Dr. Caligari

Pioneering film in the most extreme expressionistic style about a hypnotist in a carnival and a girl-snatching somnambulist was highly influential in its approach to lighting, composition, design, and acting. You have to forgive a few flaws when a film is 80 years old. The Image transfer is very good and shows that effort was made to camouflage film wear. There are still some scratches and white clicks. but overall the DVD looks great. The tint on the DVD is meant to reproduce the original theatrical showings, but I much prefer a crisp black-and-white image. The newly recorded score has a post-modern feel that keeps the character of the film nicely. —JO *AKA:* Das Cabinet des Dr. Caligari; Das Kabinett des Doktor Caligari.

Movie: 🎵🎵🎵🎵 **DVD:** 🎵🎵🎵▶
Image Entertainment (Cat #ID4099DSDVD, UPC #014381409925). Full frame. Stereo. $29.95. Snapper. *LANG:* English. *FEATURES:* 24 chapter links • Audio essay: Mike Budd.
1919 92m/B *GE* Conrad Veidt, Werner Krauss, Lil Dagover, Hans von Twardowski, Rudolf Klein-Rogge, Friedrich Feher, Rudolf Lettinger; *D:* Robert Wiene; *W:* Carl Mayer, Hans Janowitz; *C:* Willy Hameister.

The Cable Guy

Carrey's first $20 million paycheck finds cable subscriber Broderick in for a comedic nightmare when he accepts the offer of free movie channels. The overeager installer (Carrey, naturally) turns his life upside down. A little darker humor than Carrey fans may be used to. Director Stiller does a nice job of reining in his more manic impulses when necessary. Broderick holds his own as the reluctant pal. The DVD's sharpness is nothing special, but most of the other specs make up for it. There is very little grain and no artifacts. The colors are the standout here: rich, accurate, and bleed-free. Contrast and brightness levels are consistent and add even more to the vibrant colors. Blacks are very good. The imaging on the 5.1 tracks is excellent and the overall sound is very powerful, with clean, deep bass and crisp undistorted highs. —JO

Movie: 🎵🎵▶ **DVD:** 🎵🎵🎵
Columbia Tristar Home Video (Cat #82429, UPC #04339682494). Widescreen (2.35:1) anamorphic; full frame. Dolby Digital 5.1; Dolby Digital 2.0. $28.95. Keepcase. *LANG:* English (DD5.1); Spanish (DD2.0); French (DD2.0). *SUB:* Spanish; Korean. *CAP:* English. *FEATURES:* 42 chapter links.
1996 (PG-13) 95m/C Jim Carrey, Matthew Broderick, Leslie Mann, George Segal, Diane Baker, Jack Black, Janeane Garofalo, Andy Dick, Charles Napier; *D:* Ben Stiller; *W:* Judd Apatow, Lou Holtz Jr.; *C:* Robert Brinkmann; *M:* John Ottman. *AWARDS:* MTV Movie Awards '97: Best Villain (Carrey), Best Comedic Performance (Carrey); *NOM:* MTV Movie Awards '97: Best Fight (Jim Carrey/Matthew Broderick).

Cabo Blanco / U.S. Marshal

In *Cabo Blanco*, a bartender and a variety of other characters, including an ex-Nazi and a French woman searching for her lover, assemble in Peru after WWII. Nazi Robards controls police chief Rey, while American Bronson runs the local watering hole and eyes French woman Sanda. Hey, this sounds familiar! Everyone shares a common interest: finding a missing treasure of gold lost in a ship wreck. Remaking *Casablanca* via *The Treasure of the Sierra Madre* is never easy. In *U.S. Marshall* (an episode from a 1958 television series), Bronson plays a private in the army who, in a violent outbreak, decides to break away from military life. In a run that includes stealing a gun, shooting a sergeant, taking a girl hostage, and holding up a gas station, he tries to figure a way out of town, while the U.S. Marshall is hot on his heels. Whatever. Video and audio quality for both programs on this DVD are marginal at best. They appear to be mastered from a very poor copy of the original film, and it shows. The sound is incredibly muddy at times and better video has been seen on 3rd generation dubs. —MJT

Movie: ♬♬ **DVD:** ♬♬▶
Delta/Laserlight (Cat #82019, UPC #018111999533). Widescreen (1.66:1) letterboxed. Dolby Digital 2.0 Stereo. $14.99. Keepcase. *LANG:* English. *SUB:* Spanish; Chinese; Japanese. *FEATURES:* Cabo Blanco has 21 chapter links • U.S. Marshall has 10 chapter links • Trailer for The Great Escape • Introduction by Tony Curtis. Cabo Blanco is 92 minutes; U.S. Marshall is 26 minutes.
1981 (R) 112m/C Charles Bronson, Jason Robards Jr., Dominique Sanda, Fernando Rey, Gilbert Roland, Simon MacCorkindale; *D:* J. Lee Thompson; *W:* Morton S. Fine, Milton S. Gelman; *C:* Alex Phillips Jr.; *M:* Jerry Goldsmith.

Caddyshack

Inspired performances by Murray and Dangerfield drive this sublimely moronic comedy onto the green. The action takes place at Bushwood Country Club, where caddy O'Keefe is bucking to win the club's college scholarship. Characters involved in various sophomoric set pieces include obnoxious club president Knight, a playboy (Chase) who is too laid back to keep his score, a loud vulgar and extremely rich golfer (Dangerfield), and Murray as a filthy gopher-hunting groundskeeper. Moments of pure anarchy. Does for golf what *Major League* tries to do for baseball. The DVD actually does look a little better than a VHS tape, but hey, it's supposed to. As a DVD though, it's pretty poor. The picture is slightly sharper than the VHS, but there is a lot of grain in long shots and backgrounds. There are also a lot of artifacts during fast motion. The colors seem fairly accurate but bleed at least a little most of the time. There is also significant distortion along high-contrast lines. —JO

Movie: ♬♬♬ **DVD:** ♬♬
Warner Home Video, Inc. (Cat #2005, UPC #012569200524). Full frame. Dolby Digital 5.1. $24.98. Snapper. *LANG:* English; French. *SUB:* Spanish; French. *CAP:* English. *FEATURES:* 28 chapter links • Theatrical trailer • Production notes.
1980 (R) 99m/C Chevy Chase, Rodney Dangerfield, Ted Knight, Michael O'Keefe, Bill Murray, Sarah Holcomb, Brian Doyle-Murray, Cindy Morgan, Scott Colomby, Dan Resin, Henry Wilcoxon, Elaine Aiken; *D:* Harold Ramis; *W:* Harold Ramis, Doug Kenney, Brian Doyle-Murray; *C:* Stevan Larner; *M:* Johnny Mandel.

Caddyshack 2

Bill Murray opted to skip this obligatory sequel to *Caddyshack* but there are plenty of funny men in the cast to take up the slack. Unfortunately, the script sucks, and without the sure-handed comedic direction supplied by Ramis, the film seldom delivers the side-splitting laughs of the original. This time Mason is the star of the show as a crude self-made millionaire who tangles with the snobs at the country club. The collector who buys this disc probably won't care that this DVD is not widescreen and that its best asset is its sound, which on its own would rate four bones. Both the incidental orchestral music and the numerous rock songs sound great. The low end is excellent and does not detract at all from crisp high end or distinct dialogue tracks. The colors and blacks are very good although there is some color bleed—as are its contrast and brightness levels. Unfortunately, picture sharpness is only average and there is often substantial grain as well as occasional artifacts. —JO

Movie: ♬▶ **DVD:** ♬♬▶
Warner Home Video, Inc. (Cat #11791, UPC #085391179122). Full frame. Dolby Surround; Mono. $14.98. Snapper. *LANG:* English (DS); French (Mono). *CAP:* English. *FEATURES:* 31 chapter links.
1988 (PG) 103m/C Jackie Mason, Chevy Chase, Dan Aykroyd, Dyan Cannon, Robert Stack, Dina Merrill, Randy Quaid, Jessica Lundy, Jonathan Silverman, Chynna Phillips; *D:* Allan Arkush; *W:* Harold Ramis, Peter Torokvei; *C:* Harry Stradling Jr.; *M:* Ira Newborn. *AWARDS:* Golden Raspberry Awards '88: Worst Supporting Actor (Aykroyd), Worst Song ("Jack Fresh").

The Caine Mutiny

A group of naval officers on a mine sweeper revolt against a captain they consider mentally unfit. Bogart is masterful as Captain Queeg, obsessed with cleanliness and discipline on board and later a study in mental meltdown during the court-martial. The work remains one of Hollywood's most serious war films. The deep saturated tones of the "three-color" Technicolor process are undimmed on tape and DVD. Perhaps the main attraction of the disc is the widescreen transfer that captures the ocean-going exteriors and the cramped interiors of the ship much more successfully than the pan-and-scan version. If the image isn't quite as sharp as contemporary films, it looks fine. The carefully built plot, based on Herman Wouk's Pulitzer prize–winning novel, and the excellent ensemble acting are timeless. —MM

Movie: ♬♬♬ **DVD:** ♬♬♬▶
Columbia Tristar Home Video (Cat #79649, UPC #043396796492). Full frame; widescreen (1.85:1) letterboxed. $28.95. Keepcase. *LANG:* English; French. *SUB:* English; French; Spanish. *CAP:* English. *FEATURES:* Theatrical trailers • 28 chapter links.

1954 125m/C Humphrey Bogart, Jose Ferrer, Van Johnson, Fred MacMurray, Lee Marvin, Claude Akins, E.G. Marshall, Robert Francis, May Wynn, Tom Tully, Arthur Franz, Warner Anderson, Katherine Warren, Jerry Paris, Steve Brodie, Whit Bissell, Robert Bray, Ted Cooper; *D:* Edward Dmytryk; *W:* Stanley Roberts, Michael Blankfort; *C:* Franz Planer; *M:* Max Steiner. *AWARDS: NOM:* Academy Awards '54: Best Actor (Bogart), Best Film Editing, Best Picture, Best Screenplay, Best Sound, Best Supporting Actor (Tully), Best Original Dramatic Score.

Caligula

Infamous, expensive, extremely graphic, and sexually explicit adaptation of the life of the mad Roman emperor Caligula (McDowell) is perhaps one of the ugliest DVDs ever made. All the money spent on elaborate sets and the high-powered cast is wasted because the image is simply abominable. Even compared to films of its day, this one looks wretched with heavy grain, tenuous focus, and flat sound. The box copy claims that this 20th anniversary edition has been "digitally remastered and fully restored." Perhaps that's true because, if memory serves, the theatrical version was little better. Also available in a shorter (102 min.) "R"-rated version (catalog #ID8752GMDVD). —MM

Movie: woof **DVD:** woof
Image Entertainment (Cat #ID8753GM DVD, UPC #014381875324). Widescreen (1.85:1) letterboxed. Dolby Digital 5.1 Surround Stereo; Dolby Digital Stereo. $24.99. Snapper. *LANG:* English. *FEATURES:* "Making of" featurette • Cast filmographies.
1980 156m/C *IT* Malcolm McDowell, John Gielgud, Peter O'Toole, Helen Mirren, Theresa-Ann Savoy, John Steiner, Paolo Bonacelli, Adriana Asti; *D:* Tinto Brass; *W:* Gore Vidal; *C:* Tinto Brass, Silvano Ippoliti; *M:* Paul Clemente.

Call of the Wild

Charlton Heston stars in this adaptation of Jack London's famous novel of survival—by both men and dogs—in the Alaskan wilderness. Filmed in Finland.
Movie: ♬♬ **DVD:** NYR
Essex (Cat #1005). Full frame. Mono. $10.97. Slipcase.
1972 (PG) 105m/C Charlton Heston, Michele Mercier, George Eastman; *D:* Ken Annakin; *W:* Harry Alan Towers, Hubert Frank; *C:* John Cabrera; *M:* Carlo Rustichelli.

Camelot

The long-running Lerner and Loewe Broadway musical about King Arthur, Guinevere, and Lancelot was adapted from T.H. White's book, *The Once and Future King*. Redgrave and Nero have chemistry as the illicit lovers, and Harris is strong as the king struggling to hold together his dream, but muddled direction undermines the effort. The DVD tries hard but is overall a step down from Warner's own letterboxed laserdisc. The colors are fairly vibrant but image is not as sharp. There is also mild grain in a few darker scenes. The sound has been remastered to 5.1 but seems to lack both energy and guts and does not take advantage of the discreet separation of the rear channels. —JO

Movie: 🎵🎵 **DVD:** 🎵🎵▶
Warner Home Video, Inc. (Cat #12238, UPC #085391223825). Widescreen (2.35:1) anamorphic. Dolby Digital 5.1. $24.98. Snapper. *LANG:* English. *SUB:* English; Spanish; French. *CAP:* English. *FEATURES:* 36 chapter links • 5 theatrical trailers • 2 documentaries • Alternate music-only track • Production notes • Story of Camelot • Camelot World Premiere.
1967 150m/C Richard Harris, Vanessa Redgrave, David Hemmings, Franco Nero, Lionel Jeffries; *D:* Joshua Logan; *W:* Alan Jay Lerner; *C:* Richard H. Kline; *M:* Frederick Loewe, Alan Jay Lerner. *AWARDS:* Academy Awards '67: Best Adapted Score, Best Art Direction/Set Decoration, Best Costume Design; Golden Globe Awards '68: Best Actor—Musical/Comedy (Harris), Best Song ("If Ever I Should Leave You"), Best Score; *NOM:* Academy Awards '67: Best Cinematography, Best Sound.

Camille 2000

Translating the famous Dumas story into a soft-core skin flick is a dubious proposition, at best. Marguerite (Gaubert) is the object of Armand's (Castelnuovo) affections, but he does not know her tragic secret. Using late-'60s swinging jet-set Rome as a backdrop gives the action a nostalgic edge, but overall the film isn't as funny or as interesting as Metzger's other work of the period. Curiously, the DVD doesn't look as good as some of his older films, either. It seems to have been transferred from a scratchy print that isn't helped by the filmmaker's coy approach—demanded by the times—of shooting distorted reflections in mirrors. Many of the big scenes are notable for their ugly colors and gaudy light. Straight lines tend to break up during fast panning shots and night exteriors are far less than perfect. —MM

Movie: 🎵🎵▶ **DVD:** 🎵🎵▶
Image Entertainment (Cat #ID5535FFDVD, UPC #014381553529). Widescreen (2.35:1) letterboxed. Dolby Digital Mono. $24.99. Snapper. *LANG:* English. *FEATURES:* 13 chapter links.
1969 115m/C Daniele Gaubert, Nino Castelnuovo, Eleanora Rossi-Drago; *D:* Radley Metzger; *W:* Michael DeForrest; *C:* Ennio Guarnieri.

The Candidate

Realistic, satirical look at politics and political campaigning. A young, idealistic lawyer (Redford) is talked into trying for the Senate seat and learns the truth about running for office. Seeing this 1972

film on DVD, with its sharper image and stronger colors, made for a viewing experience as fresh as the first time through. The satire still remains topical despite its age, and would have made for an interesting comparative featurette, or at least an essay. Maybe on the special edition. —JO
Movie: 🎵🎵🎵 **DVD:** 🎵🎵🎵
Warner Home Video, Inc. (Cat #14577, UPC #0853914577200). Full frame. Dolby Surround. $24.98. Snapper. *LANG:* English. *SUB:* English; Spanish; French. *FEATURES:* 32 chapter links • Theatrical trailer • Production notes.
1972 (PG) 105m/C Robert Redford, Peter Boyle, Don Porter, Allen (Goorwitz) Garfield, Karen Carlson, Melvyn Douglas, Michael Lerner; *D:* Michael Ritchie; *W:* Jeremy Larner; *C:* John Korty, Victor Kemper; *M:* John Rubinstein. *AWARDS:* Academy Awards '72: Best Story & Screenplay; Writers Guild of America '72: Best Original Screenplay; *NOM:* Academy Awards '72: Best Sound.

Candleshoe

Conman Bundage (McKern) thinks that he can pass off L.A. street urchin Casey Brown (Foster) as Lady Gwendolyn's (Hayes) long-lost granddaughter, thereby planting an accomplice inside the Candleshoe estate. Together, they'll find the fortune in doubloons that are hidden there. But Bundage hasn't counted on the resourceful butler Priory (Niven). The high-powered cast is much stronger than the formulaic children's material, but the film is still recommended to older audiences. The daffy humor never becomes too sweet. The film looks good but not great on DVD. Minor flecks are visible throughout and since much of the action was shot on location, it lacks the high polish of some other live-action Disney productions of that era. The soundtrack appears to have been cleaned up to improve the voices, but it still has a flat quality. —MM
Movie: 🎵🎵🎵 **DVD:** 🎵🎵🎵
Anchor Bay (Cat #DV10894, UPC #013131089493). Widescreen (1.66:1) letterboxed; full frame. Dolby Digital Mono. $24.98. Keepcase. *LANG:* English. *FEATURES:* 19 chapter links • Liner notes.
1978 (G) 101m/C Vivian Pickles, Helen Hayes, David Niven, Jodie Foster, Leo McKern; *D:* Norman Tokar; *W:* Rosemary Anne Sisson, David Swift; *C:* Paul Beeson; *M:* Ronald Goodwin.

Candyman

On one level, this contradictory horror is your basic gore-fest. It's also visually sophisticated and well acted with a score by noted minimalist composer Philip Glass. More often than not, the two sides work well together. The title character (Todd) is a murderous hook-handed urban legend who dwells in Cabrini Green, the notorious Chicago housing project. Graduate student Helen Lyle (Madsen, excellent as always) leaves the groves of academe

to do some dangerous primary research into the myth. Writer-director Bernard Rose indulges his music-video taste for fast cutting in some key scenes. For the most part, though, he plays straight with the viewer and creates a palpable atmosphere of fear and dread. The conclusion is risky. Followed by lesser sequels. On DVD, the film retains the gritty look of the theatrical version with the right amount of graininess, blood, and garbage in the most intense moments. Glass's soundtrack works well, too. Not to all tastes, but recommended. —MM
Movie: 🎵🎵🎵 **DVD:** 🎵🎵🎵
Columbia Tristar Home Video (Cat #94369, UPC #043396946392). Full frame; widescreen (1.85:1) letterboxed. Dolby Digital Surround. $25.95. Keepcase. *LANG:* English; French. *SUB:* English; French. *CAP:* English. *FEATURES:* Theatrical trailer • 28 chapter links.
1992 (R) 98m/C Virginia Madsen, Tony Todd, Xander Berkeley, Kasi Lemmons, Vanessa Williams, DeJuan Guy, Michael Culkin, Gilbert Lewis, Stanley DeSantis; *D:* Bernard Rose; *W:* Bernard Rose; *C:* Anthony B. Richmond; *M:* Philip Glass.

Cannonball Run 2

Needless sequel receives a mediocre transfer to DVD and that's exactly what it deserves. The quality varies between exceptionally grainy road scenes—which ought to be the best moments—to crisp, carefully staged stunts. Has star Burt Reynolds ever smirked more in a single film or worn a more comical hairpiece? On the other hand, how many films have Shirley MacLaine and Jackie Chan in the supporting cast? —MM
Movie: 🎵 **DVD:** 🎵▶
Warner Home Video, Inc. (Cat #11377, UPC #085391137726). Full frame. Dolby Digital Mono. $14.98. Snapper. *LANG:* English. *CAP:* English. *FEATURES:* 32 chapter links.
1984 (PG) 109m/C Burt Reynolds, Dom DeLuise, Jamie Farr, Marilu Henner, Shirley MacLaine, Jim Nabors, Frank Sinatra, Sammy Davis Jr., Dean Martin, Telly Savalas, Susan Anton, Catherine Bach, Jack Elam, Sid Caesar, Ricardo Montalban, Charles Nelson Reilly, Henry Silva, Tim Conway, Don Knotts, Molly Picon, Jackie Chan; *D:* Hal Needham; *W:* Harvey Miller; *C:* Nick McLean; *M:* Steve Dorff.

Can't Hardly Wait

The John Hughes '80s teen-angst/party casserole has lost its flavor in this rehash. All of the expected high school cardboard cut-outs are here. Jock-jerk Mike (Facinelli) dumps teen queen Amanda (Hewitt) on the eve of the graduation blow-out. Shy sensitive Preston (Embry) decides this is his opportunity finally to tell her how he feels. Frolicking in the background are the other stereotypes. The film wavers unsuccessfully between the thoughtfulness of *American Graffiti* and the thoughtlessness of *Animal House.* On

their motor-mouthed audio commentary track, codirector-writers Kaplan and Elfont, producer Jenno Topping, and star Seth Green reveal themselves to be novice filmmakers who barely know what they're doing but never miss a chance to drop a name or to comment on Matt Damon's butt or Jennifer Love Hewitt's breasts. On DVD, the frivolous goings-on are visually flawless. —*MM* **AKA:** The Party.
Movie: 🎬🎬 **DVD:** 🎬🎬➤
Columbia Tristar Home Video (Cat #02714, UPC #043396027145). Full frame; widescreen (1.85:1) letterboxed. Dolby Digital Surround; Dolby Digital 5.1 Surround. $25.95. Keepcase. *LANG:* English; French; Spanish. *SUB:* English; French; Spanish. *CAP:* English. *FEATURES:* Stills gallery • 28 chapter links • Theatrical trailer • Smash Mouth video • Commentary: Elfont, Kaplan, Topping, Green.
1998 (PG-13) 101m/C Ethan (Randall) Embry, Jennifer Love Hewitt, Peter Facinelli, Charlie Korsmo, Seth Green, Jerry O'Connell, Lauren Ambrose, Jenna Elfman, Michelle Brookhurst, Erik Palladino; **D:** Harry Elfont, Deborah Kaplan; **W:** Harry Elfont, Deborah Kaplan; **C:** Lloyd Ahern; **M:** David Kitay, Matthew Sweet. *AWARDS: NOM:* MTV Movie Awards '99: Best Female Performance (Hewitt).

The Canterbury Tales
Four of Chaucer's tales—most notably "The Merchant's Tale" and "The Wife of Bath"—are recounted by travelers with director Pasolini as the poet himself. It's the second of Pasolini's medieval "Trilogy of Life," preceded by *The Decameron* and followed by *The Arabian Life.* All three films are rough-looking on DVD or any other medium, and the source material shows definite wear. Even so, for the director's admirers, this is probably the best version available on home video. —*MM* **AKA:** I Racconti di Canterbury.
Movie: 🎬🎬 **DVD:** 🎬🎬
Image Entertainment (Cat #4416). Widescreen (1.75:1) letterboxed. Dolby Digital Mono. $24.99. Snapper. *LANG:* Italian. *SUB:* English.
1971 109m/C *IT* Laura Betti, Ninetto Davoli, Pier Paolo Pasolini, Hugh Griffith, Josephine Chaplin, Michael Balfour, Jenny Runacre; **D:** Pier Paolo Pasolini; **W:** Pier Paolo Pasolini; **C:** Tonino Delli Colli; **M:** Ennio Morricone. *AWARDS:* Berlin International Film Festival '72: Golden Berlin Bear.

Capone
When FBI agent Michael Roarke (Carradine) puts a dent in Al Capone's (Sharkey) organization, the gangster goes after his wife (Atkinson) and kids. But the stronger threat turns out to be a seductive speakeasy waitress (Farentino). At its best, the film shows how morally ambiguous those times were, when everyone broke the law. On the street level, the cops and the crooks were less adversaries than guys who called each other by first names and

knew that they were playing the same game. Elliot Ness and J. Edgar Hoover are presented as self-promoting publicity seekers. Sharkey turns Capone into a rabid villain straight out of a *Batman* movie, but it's somehow appropriate to the story. Carradine, a severely underrated actor, plays Roarke as an ordinary man trying to do his job. On DVD, the film's limited budget is apparent in a dark image, slightly soft focus, and colors that are not quite true. The dubbing is off in some scenes and a few suits shimmer. —*MM* **AKA:** The Revenge of Al Capone.
Movie: 🎬🎬➤ **DVD:** 🎬🎬
Trimark Home Video (Cat #VM#7303D, UPC #031398730323). Full frame. Stereo. $34.99. Keepcase. *LANG:* English. *FEATURES:* Theatrical trailer • Previews for other Trimark films • 8 chapter links. Title is available for sale only as part of the "Mob Hits" four-pack.
1989 (R) 96m/C Ray Sharkey, Keith Carradine, Debrah Farentino, Jayne Atkinson, Bradford English, Marc Figueroa, Neil Giuntoli, Charles Haid, Nicholas Mele, Scott Paulin, Alan Rosenberg; **D:** Michael Pressman; **W:** Tracy Keenan Wynn; **C:** Tim Suhrstedt; **M:** Craig Safan.

Capricorn One
Under heavy political pressure, a NASA bigwig (Holbrook) decides to fake a mission to Mars rather than risk public failure. Three astronauts (Waterston, Brolin, and Simpson) are coerced into the project. Gould plays the reporter who tumbles to the scam. This post-Watergate thriller moves slowly for the first half or so. Things pick up later with some nice chases involving Telly Savalas as a biplane pilot and a couple of ominous choppers which might have been the inspiration for the oft-rumored "black helicopters" that have played such a prominent role in conspiracy fantasies of more recent years. On DVD, the image is acceptable with minor flashing lines. The sound is often thin. —*MM*
Movie: 🎬🎬➤ **DVD:** 🎬🎬➤
Artisan Entertainment (Cat #60475, UPC #012236047506). Widescreen (1.85:1) letterboxed. Dolby Digital Mono. $29.98. Snapper. *LANG:* English. *SUB:* Spanish. *CAP:* English. *FEATURES:* 36 chapter links • Teaser • Theatrical trailer • Cast and crew thumbnail biographies • Production notes.
1978 (R) 123m/C Elliott Gould, James Brolin, Brenda Vaccaro, O.J. Simpson, Hal Holbrook, Sam Waterston, Karen Black, Telly Savalas; **D:** Peter Hyams; **W:** Peter Hyams; **C:** Bill Butler; **M:** Jerry Goldsmith.

The Car
The story of a car from hell that terrorizes a New Mexico desert town has developed a strange reputation. Because it has been hard to find on home video, some fans have claimed that it's better than it actually is. In his DVD liner notes, Jim Knipfer goes a bit overboard in that direction, but

he also makes some valid points about the striking landscapes and the film's austere quality. On disc, those visuals are particularly strong. Director Elliot Silverstein combines the sensibility of his work on the original *Twilight Zone* series with the flashy style he brought to *A Man Called Horse.* He also got good performances from a capable cast, including James Brolin and Ronny Cox, but this is still a movie about a killer car, and the critics who noted the similarities to *Jaws* were not wrong. They might also have compared it to Steven Spielberg's first feature, *Duel.* The disc looks and sounds terrific, with only a few meaningless glitches—flashing between narrow lines of rock sediment, some scratchy lines on the print. Of the extras, the biographies contain useful, quirky information. —*MM*
Movie: 🎬🎬➤ **DVD:** 🎬🎬🎬
Anchor Bay (Cat #DV10866, UPC #013131086690). Full frame; widescreen. Dolby Digital 5.1; Surround 2.0. $24.98. Keepcase. *LANG:* English. *FEATURES:* Theatrical trailer • Biographies of Elliot Silverstein and James Brolin • 28 chapter links.
1977 (PG) 96m/C James Brolin, Kathleen Lloyd, John Marley, Ronny Cox, John Rubinstein, R.G. Armstrong, Elizabeth Thompson, Roy Jenson; **D:** Elliot Silverstein; **W:** Dennis Shryack, Michael Butler; **C:** Gerald Hirschfeld; **M:** Leonard Rosenman.

Car Wash
An L.A. car wash gives new meaning to the term soap-opera when it becomes the setting for a series of vaguely interrelated comic bits about the owners of dirty cars and the people who hose them down. Think *Grand Hotel* with disco and hot wax. The budget is small but the comic talent is huge, with Ajaye turning in particularly fine work.
Movie: 🎬🎬🎬 **DVD:** NYR
Goodtimes Entertainment (Cat #81008). Full frame. Dolby Digital Mono. $19.98. Keepcase.
1976 (PG) 97m/C Franklin Ajaye, Sully Boyer, Richard Brestoff, George Carlin, Richard Pryor, Melanie Mayron, Ivan Dixon, Antonio Fargas; **D:** Michael A. Schultz; **W:** Joel Schumacher; **C:** Frank Stanley; **M:** Norman Whitfield.

Career Opportunities
Jim Dodge (Whaley), widely known as "the town liar," winds up as the night janitor at the local Target department store. Locked in the building for the night, he finds that the town beauty, Josie McClellan (Connelly) is there with him. So are a couple of dim-witted would-be thieves. Producer John Hughes is trying to combine elements of his most successful films, *The Breakfast Club* and *Home Alone,* with poor results, even though Jennifer Connelly radiates goddess-like beauty. The DVD image is clear enough, but nothing spe-

cial, as it should be for a formula effort such as this. —*MM*
Movie: 🎵🎵 **DVD:** 🎵🎵
Universal Studios Home Video (Cat #20418, UPC #025192041822). Widescreen (2.35:1) letterboxed. Dolby Digital Surround Stereo. $24.98. Keepcase. *LANG:* English. *SUB:* Spanish; French. *CAP:* English. *FEATURES:* 19 chapter links • Production notes • Cast and crew thumbnail biographies • Universal web links • Theatrical trailer.
1991 (PG-13) 83m/C Frank Whaley, Jennifer Connelly, Dermot Mulroney, Kieran Mulroney, John M. Jackson, Jenny O'Hara, Noble Willingham, Barry Corbin, Denise Galik, William Forsythe, John Candy; *D:* Bryan Gordon; *W:* John Hughes; *C:* Donald McAlpine; *M:* Thomas Newman.

Caress of the Vampire (CE)

Ultra-low-budget erotic horrors were made on location in New Jersey. They feature semi-professional acting, bare-bones locations, and production values that are a short step above home movies. Many of the cast members are into tattoos and piercing. On DVD, both films demonstrate just about every visual flaw that plagues the medium, including harsh graininess and pixelation in dark scenes, and some visual distortions that I've never seen on other discs and cannot describe. The double feature includes the sequel, *Caress of the Vampire 2: Teenage Girl a Go-Go.* —*MM*
Movie: 🎵▶ **DVD:** 🎵
El Independent Cinema (Cat #7029, UPC #61238510092). Full frame. Mono. $19.98. Snapper. *LANG:* English. *FEATURES:* Cast and crew thumbnail bios • Deleted scenes.
1996 150m/C Paulina Monet, Jessica English, Darien Price, Joe Moeller; *D:* Frank Terranova.

Caress of the Vampire 2: Teenage Girl a Go-Go

See review above.
Movie: 🎵▶
1996 75m/C Matthew Ike Angel, William Hellfire, Ruby Honeycat, Mickey Ovum.

Carlito's Way

Puerto Rican crime czar Carlito Brigante (Pacino) has just gotten out of jail and wants to go straight. But his drug underworld cohorts don't believe he can do it. Penn (barely recognizable) is great as a sleazy coked-out lawyer who's way out of his league. Remarkably subdued violence given DePalma's previous rep—it's effective without being gratuitous, especially the final shootout set in Grand Central Station. Pacino's performance is equally subdued, with controlled tension and lots of eye contact rather than grandiose emotions. Based on the novels *Carlito's Way*

and *After Hours* by Edwin Torres. Pacino and DePalma previously teamed up for *Scarface.* There's not much improvement when going from the Universal letterboxed laserdisc to this DVD. Colors are much better though, and there is a slightly more detailed feel to the image. The sound has been beefed up with a driving bass track, but the Surround remains pretty much the same. —*JO*
Movie: 🎵🎵🎵 **DVD:** 🎵🎵🎵
Universal Studios Home Video (Cat #20222, UPC #025192022227). Widescreen (2.35:1) letterboxed. Dolby Digital 5.1; French Dolby Surround. $26.95. Keepcase. *LANG:* English (DD5.1); French (DS). *SUB:* Spanish. *CAP:* English. *FEATURES:* 16 chapter links • Theatrical trailer • Cast and filmmakers bios • Production notes • Film highlights • Dual-layered RSDL.
1993 (R) 145m/C Al Pacino, Sean Penn, Penelope Ann Miller, Luis Guzman, John Leguizamo, Ingrid Rogers, James Rebhorn, Viggo Mortensen, Jorge Porcel, Joseph Siravo, Adrian Pasdar; *D:* Brian DePalma; *W:* David Koepp; *C:* Stephen Burum; *M:* Patrick Doyle. *AWARDS: NOM:* Golden Globe Awards '94: Best Supporting Actor (Penn), Best Supporting Actress (Miller).

Carmen, Baby

Metzger's wonderfully dated skin-flick would hardly raise an eyebrow now. In this telling of the familiar tale, Carmen (Levka) is a Spanish prostitute who casts her spell on a young cop (Ringer). The DVD appears to have been made from a substandard print. The color values change so radically that in the opening scene, Carmen's sweater changes color from dirty orange to yellow. It's scratchy throughout. Many interiors have a muddy look with self-consciously symbolic reds that glow and bleed. —*MM*
Movie: 🎵🎵 **DVD:** 🎵
Image Entertainment (Cat #ID5536FFDVD, UPC #014381553628). Widescreen (2.35:1) letterboxed. Dolby Digital Mono. $24.99. Snapper. *LANG:* English. *FEATURES:* 18 chapter links.
1966 90m/C Uta Levka, Claus Ringer, Barbara Valentin, Walter Wilz; *D:* Radley Metzger; *W:* Jesse Vogel; *C:* Hans Jura; *M:* Daniel Hart.

Carnal Crimes

Well-made upscale soft-core follows a standard plot line. Rich neglected wife Elise (Carol) falls for sexy photographer Renny (Hewitt) and takes a walk on the wild side. Director Hippolyte tells the same story in several other video premieres. This early attempt is noticeably grainier and rougher than his more polished recent work. The extras-free DVD may be slightly sharper than the VHS tape, but not much. —*MM*
Movie: 🎵🎵 **DVD:** 🎵
Image Entertainment (Cat #ID5747MKDVD, UPC #014381574722). Full frame. Dolby Digital Mono. $24.99. Snapper. *LANG:* English. *FEATURES:* 12 chapter links.

1991 (R) 103m/C Martin Hewitt, Linda Carol, Rich Crater, Alex Kubik, Yvette Stefens, Paula Trickey; *D:* Alexander Gregory (Gregory Dark) Hippolyte; *W:* Jon Robert Samsel; *C:* Paul Desatoff; *M:* Matthew Ross, Jeff Fishman.

Carnival of Souls

Loose remake does not even come close to the hypnotic intensity of the original film. In this one, Alex Grant (Phillips) is plagued by visions of Louis Seagram (Miller) who killed her mother 20 years before. The structure leads to multiple it's-only-a-dream sequences; and that dim-witted device has been thoroughly overused in horror films good and bad. The DVD image is excellent, as is the sound. —*MM*
AKA: Wes Craven Presents Carnival of Souls.
Movie: 🎵🎵 **DVD:** 🎵🎵🎵
Trimark Home Video (Cat #VM6931D, UPC #031398693130). Widescreen letterboxed. Dolby Digital Surround Stereo. $24.98. Keepcase. *LANG:* English. *SUB:* English; French; Spanish. *CAP:* English. *FEATURES:* 30 chapter links • Trailer.
1998 (R) 87m/C Bobbie Phillips, Larry Miller, Paul Johansson, Cleavant Derricks, Sidney Berger, Shawnee Smith; *D:* Adam Grossman; *W:* Adam Grossman; *M:* Andrew Rose.

Carolina Skeletons

As a child in a small Southern town, Gossett watched as his brother was accused of a vicious double murder then quickly tried and executed. Thirty years later, the ex–Green Beret returns home to find the real killer and clear his brother's name. But there are those in the town who will do anything to stop their secrets from being revealed. Soft DVD video may reflect original cinematography's style, but the closely cropped pan-and-scan treatment surely was not intended. No extras, not even captions or a trailer. —*MB*
Movie: 🎵🎵▶ **DVD:** 🎵🎵
Image Entertainment (Cat #ID5588FMDVD, UPC #014381558821). Full frame. Dolby Digital 2.0. $24.99. Snapper. *LANG:* English. *FEATURES:* 20 chapter links.
1992 (R) 94m/C Louis Gossett Jr., Bruce Dern, Melissa Leo, Paul Roebling, G.D. Spradlin, Bill Cobbs, Henderson Forsythe, Clifton James; *D:* John Erman; *W:* Tracy Keenan Wynn; *C:* Tony Imi; *M:* John Morris.

Carousel

Much-loved Rodgers & Hammerstein musical based on Ferenc Molnar's play *Liliom* (filmed by Fritz Lang in 1935) about a swaggering carnival barker (MacRae) who tries to change his life after he falls in love with a good woman. Killed while attempting to foil a robbery he was supposed to help commit, he begs from his heavenly hosts for the chance to return to the mortal realm just long enough to set things straight with his teenage daughter. Now indisputably a classic, the film lost

$2 million when it was released. Fox Home Video continues to improve on their previous releases of their classic musicals with this DVD edition. The image is a touch sharper than the letterboxed laserdisc, and that's the only spec that's even close. The DVD's colors are stunningly vibrant and at times so punchy that they almost look cartoonish. They've also energized the sound, which is distortion-free and dynamic. —JO

Movie: 🦴🦴🦴 **DVD:** 🦴🦴🦴▶
20th Century Fox (Cat #4110866, UPC #086162001017). Widescreen (2.35:1) letterboxed. Stereo. $24.98. Keepcase. *LANG:* English. *FEATURES:* 27 chapter links ▪ Movietone News trailer.
1956 128m/C Gordon MacRae, Shirley Jones, Cameron Mitchell, Gene Lockhart, Barbara Ruick, Robert Rounseville, Richard Deacon, Tor Johnson; *D:* Henry King; *W:* Henry Ephron, Phoebe Ephron; *C:* Charles Clarke; *M:* Richard Rodgers, Oscar Hammerstein.

Cartel

Taylor (played by O'Keeffe doing his best squinty Clint Eastwood imitation) is framed for murder by a drug lord (Stroud), but then they wind up in the same cellblock. This rancid dope opera is slow moving and brutal. On DVD, moving diagonal lines tend to shimmer. Otherwise the image is average. —MM

Movie: 🦴 **DVD:** 🦴
Simitar Entertainment (Cat #7393, UPC #082551739325). Full frame. Dolby Digital Stereo. $14.98. Keepcase. *LANG:* English. *FEATURES:* 8 chapter links ▪ Production factoids ▪ Miles O'Keeffe filmography.
1990 (R) 106m/C Miles O'Keeffe, Don Stroud, Crystal Carson, William Smith; *D:* John Stewart; *W:* Moshe Hadar; *C:* Thomas Callaway; *M:* Rick Krizman.

Cartoon Crazys

The cartoons in these collections have been cleaned up nicely, but they're still likely to seem rough and primitive to young viewers brought up on contemporary computer animation. The appeal is mostly nostalgic for older viewers who may well remember seeing them first on local afternoon kids' TV shows way back when. The wartime cartoons also have genuine historical value. Where racial matters are concerned, the cartoons featuring black characters and caricatures reflect their times. These are some of the best from the 1930s, '40s, and early '50s by such pioneers as Max and Dave Fleischer, Bob Clampett, Chuck Jones, Friz Freleng, and Tex Avery, with many familiar characters: Bugs Bunny, Porky Pig, Popeye, Casper, Betty Boop, the Little King, Felix the Cat, and Superman among more. As the restoration demo shows, the originals were sometimes so dark as to be unwatchable. Those have been brightened with sound remixed for stereo. Though the first disc lacks many extras, the following volumes add more complex menus and

suggested reading lists. For adults, each cartoon is introduced with a synopsis and credits. Kids can go directly to the good stuff. That's the real advantage that DVD has over tape for this kind of compilation. It's easy to pick and choose among short works without having to watch all of them. A few of the individual cartoons are repeated on the discs. Contents: "Falling Hare," "Yankee Doodle Daffy," "Tale of Two Kitties," "Neptune Nonsense," "Crowing Pains," "Robin Hood Makes Good," "Fresh Hare," "Daffy the Commando," "Have You Got Any Castles," "Gabby Goes Fishing," "Corny Concerto." —MM

Movie: 🦴🦴 **DVD:** 🦴🦴▶
WinStar Home Entertainment (Cat #WHE73002, UPC #720917300221). Full frame. AC3-5.1; Dolby Digital Surround. Keepcase. *LANG:* English. *FEATURES:* 16 chapter links ▪ Production notes ▪ Scene access ▪ Synopsis, history, and credits for each cartoon ▪ Sound demo ▪ Previews ▪ Suggested reading list.
1997 100m/C

Cartoon Crazys 2

See review of *Cartoon Crazys*. Contents: "Doggone Tired," "To Duck or Not to Duck," "Inki and the Minah Bird," "It's a Greek Life," "The Wacky Wabbit," "The Goose That Laid the Golden Egg," "Egghead," "King for a Day," "The Wabbit Who Came to Dinner," "The Early Worm Gets the Bird," "Toonerville Trolley," "Fifth Column Mouse." —MM

Movie: 🦴🦴▶ **DVD:** 🦴🦴▶
WinStar Home Entertainment (Cat #WHE73009, UPC #720917300924). Full frame. Dolby Digital; Dolby Pro Logic; Stereo. $19.98. Keepcase. *LANG:* English. *FEATURES:* Production notes ▪ 17 chapter links ▪ Sound demo ▪ Previews.
1998 100m/C

Cartoon Crazys: And the Envelope, Please

See review of *Cartoon Crazys*. Contents: "Popeye the Sailor Meets Sinbad the Sailor," "Poor Cinderella," "Superman—The Mad Scientist," "Pigs in a Polka," "The Hole," "Superman—Mechanical Monsters," "The Dover Boys at Palmetto University," "MoonBird," "Hunky and Spunky," "SummerTime." —MM

Movie: 🦴🦴▶ **DVD:** 🦴🦴▶
WinStar Home Entertainment (Cat #WHE73045, UPC #720917304526). Full frame. Dolby Digital Stereo; Dolby Digital 5.1 Surround Stereo. $19.98. Keepcase. *LANG:* English. *FEATURES:* 13 chapter links ▪ Previews ▪ Restoration demonstration ▪ Synopses, credits, and histories for each cartoon.
1999 120m/C

Cartoon Crazys Christmas

See review of *Cartoon Crazys*. Contents: "Rudolf the Red-Nosed Reindeer," "A Waif's Christmas Welcome," "Fresh Hare,"

"The Christmas Circus," "The Pups Christmas," "Private Eye Popeye," "Santa's Surprise," "Hawaiian Birds Christmas," "Snow Foolings," "Christmas Comes but Once a Year," "Tarts and Flowers," "The Shanty Where Old Santy Claus Lives." —MM
Movie: 🦴🦴▶ **DVD:** 🦴🦴▶
WinStar Home Entertainment (Cat #WHE73017, UPC #720917301723). Full frame. Dolby Digital; Dolby Pro Logic; Stereo. $19.98. Keepcase. *LANG:* English. *FEATURES:* Production notes ▪ 16 chapter links ▪ Previews.
1998 100m/C

Cartoon Crazys Goes to War

See review of *Cartoon Crazys*. Contents: "Bugs Bunny Bond Rally," "Daffy the Commando," "Eleventh Hour," "Ding Dong Daddy," "Falling Hare," "Jurky Turky," "Tale of Two Kitties," "Jungle Drums," "Fifth Column Mouse," "Fony Fables," "Scrap Happy Daffy," "Hell Bent for Election," "Snafuperman," "Booby Traps," "Spies." —MM
Movie: 🦴🦴🦴 **DVD:** 🦴🦴▶
WinStar Home Entertainment (Cat #WHE73018, UPC #720917301822). Full frame. Dolby Digital; Dolby Pro Logic; Stereo. $19.98. Keepcase. *LANG:* English. *FEATURES:* Maps and diagrams ▪ Drawings and sketches ▪ Interactive menus ▪ 21 chapter links ▪ Production notes ▪ Previews.
1998 115m/C

Cartoon Crazys: Kids All-Time Favorites

See review of *Cartoon Crazys*. Contents: "Wakiki Rabbit," "Bars and Stripes Forever," "Daffy Duck and the Dinosaur," "Two for the Zoo," "The Dover Boys," "Bold King Cole," "Case of the Missing Hare," "Pigs in a Polka," "Boo Moon," "Barnyard Showdown," "Sports Chumpions," "Popeye Meets Ali Baba and the Forty Thieves." —MM
Movie: 🦴🦴▶ **DVD:** 🦴🦴▶
WinStar Home Entertainment (Cat #WHE73028, UPC #720917302829). Full frame. AC3-5.1; Dolby Digital Surround. $19.98. Keepcase. *LANG:* English. *FEATURES:* Production notes ▪ 14 chapter links ▪ Synopsis, history, and credits for each cartoon ▪ Sound demo ▪ Previews.
1999 110m/C

Cartoon Crazys Sci-Fi

See review of *Cartoon Crazys*. Contents: "Prest-O Change-O," "To Spring," "Arctic Giant," "Impatient Patient," "All's Fair at the Fair," "Cupid Gets His Man," "Dancing on the Moon," "Magnetic Telescope," "Sunshine Makers," "Cob Web Hotel," "Cooking with Gas," "House Cleaning Blues," "Crazy Inventions," "John Henry and the Inky Poo." —MM
Movie: 🦴🦴🦴 **DVD:** 🦴🦴▶

WinStar Home Entertainment (Cat #WHE73027, UPC #720917302720). Full frame. Dolby Digital; Dolby Pro Logic; Stereo. $19.98. Keepcase. *LANG:* English. *FEATURES:* 23 chapter links • History, synopsis, and credits for each cartoon • Sound demo.
1999 120m/C

Casablanca

Considered by many to be the best film ever made and one of the most quoted movies of all time, it rocketed Bogart from gangster roles to romantic leads as he and Bergman (who never looked lovelier) sizzle on-screen. Bogart runs a gin joint in Morocco during the Nazi occupation, and meets up with Bergman, an old flame; but romance and politics do not mix, especially in Nazi-occupied French Morocco. Greenstreet, Lorre, and Rains all create memorable characters, as does Wilson, the piano player to whom Bergman says the oft-misquoted, "Play it, Sam." Without a doubt, the best closing scene ever written; it was scripted on the fly during the end of shooting, and actually shot several ways. We've all got friends who refuse to watch classic films, especially if they're shot in black and white. Well, have them over and force—er—invite them to watch this DVD. It probably won't do any good, but this is an amazing disc to look at, and it's hard for me to believe that anyone could find a color picture more appealing. There is so much detail, and so much depth, that repeated viewings are required to capture it all. —*JO*
Movie: ♫♫♫♫ *DVD:* ♫♫♫♫
Warner Home Video, Inc. (Cat #906261, UPC #012569500822). Full frame. Dolby Digital Mono. $24.98. Snapper. *LANG:* English; French. *SUB:* English; French. *CAP:* English. *FEATURES:* 36 chapter links • Theatrical trailer • Documentary "You Must Remember This" • Intro by Lauren Bacall.
1942 (PG) 102m/B Humphrey Bogart, Ingrid Bergman, Paul Henreid, Claude Rains, Peter Lorre, Sydney Greenstreet, Conrad Veidt, S.Z. Sakall, Dooley Wilson, Marcel Dalio, John Qualen, Helmut Dantine, Madeleine LeBeau, Joy Page, Leonid Kinskey, Curt Bois, Oliver Blake, Monte Blue, Martin Garralaga, Ilka Gruning, Ludwig Stossel, Frank Puglia; *D:* Michael Curtiz; *W:* Julius J. Epstein, Philip G. Epstein, Howard Koch; *C:* Arthur Edeson; *M:* Max Steiner; *Technical Advisor:* Robert Aisner. *AWARDS:* Academy Awards '43: Best Director (Curtiz), Best Picture, Best Screenplay; American Film Institute (AFI) '98: Top 100, National Film Registry '89; *NOM:* Academy Awards '43: Best Actor (Bogart), Best Black-and-white Cinematography, Best Film Editing, Best Supporting Actor (Rains), Best Original Dramatic Score.

Casino

Scorsese's third cinematic trip into the underworld previously explored in *Mean Streets* and *Goodfellas* chronicles the rise

and fall of the mob's Las Vegas empire. Sin City circa 1973 is the setting in which casino boss Sam "Ace" Rothstein (De Niro), his ex-hustler wife Ginger (Stone), and lifelong buddy Nicky (Pesci) are the players in a high-stakes game of passion, ambition, and greed. Those are the ingredients in a lengthy, fictionalized account of how the mob lost Las Vegas in a haze of drugs, sex, and betrayal. Too bad the storyline too often becomes lost in this same maze of haze. Still, the jumbo-length and unflinchingly violent flick is a flashy visual feast with a killer soundtrack. Both are well preserved by a DVD edition that looks and sounds wonderful, and offers a minimal but acceptable (for the price) set of extras. What's more, the dual-layer disc fits the whole movie on a single side, which is better treatment than *Goodfellas* got with its first DVD. —*MB*
Movie: ♫♫♫ *DVD:* ♫♫♫▶
Universal Studios Home Video (Cat #20159, UPC #025192015922). Widescreen (2.35:1) letterboxed. Dolby Digital 5.1. $26.98. Keepcase. *LANG:* English; French. *SUB:* Spanish. *CAP:* English. *FEATURES:* 16 chapter links • Production notes • Cast and director biographies and filmographies.
1995 (R) 177m/C Robert De Niro, Joe Pesci, Sharon Stone, James Woods, Don Rickles, Alan King, Kevin Pollak, L.Q. (Justus E. McQueen) Jones, Dick Smothers, John (Joe Bob Briggs) Bloom, Frankie Avalon, Steve Allen, Jayne Meadows, Jerry Vale; *D:* Martin Scorsese; *W:* Nicholas Pileggi, Martin Scorsese; *C:* Robert Richardson. *AWARDS:* Golden Globe Awards '96: Best Actress—Drama (Stone); *NOM:* Academy Awards '95: Best Actress (Stone); Golden Globe Awards '96: Best Director (Scorsese); MTV Movie Awards '96: Best Female Performance (Stone), Best Villain (Pesci).

The Cassandra Crossing

European terrorists try to infest a luxury train with the plague. The proverbial all-star cast hangs in the balance.
Movie: ♫▶ *DVD:* NYR
Pioneer Entertainment (Cat #10305). Widescreen (1.85:1) letterboxed. Dolby Digital Stereo. $24.98. Keepcase.
1976 (R) 129m/C *GB* Sophia Loren, Richard Harris, Ava Gardner, Burt Lancaster, Martin Sheen, Ingrid Thulin, Lee Strasberg, John Phillip Law, Lionel Stander, O.J. Simpson, Ann Turkel, Alida Valli; *D:* George P. Cosmatos; *W:* George P. Cosmatos, Tom Mankiewicz; *C:* Ennio Guarnieri; *M:* Jerry Goldsmith.

The Castle

It's Daryl vs. Goliath when the Australian government tries to force a man to sell his house so that the nearby airport can expand. As leader of the Korrigan clan—the Aussie equivalent of *Dumb and Dumber*, with a dash of Yahoo Serious's lunacy—Daryl (Caton) loves his humble abode,

conveniently located between the runway and the power lines. Much of the cultural humor makes an uneasy transition to other countries, and visually the film is so weak that it really has little to offer on DVD. It's no better than most VHS tapes. —*MM*
Movie: ♫♫ *DVD:* ♫♫
Miramax Pictures Home Video (Cat #18155, UPC #717951004345). Widescreen (1.85:1) letterboxed. Dolby Digital 5.1 Surround Stereo. $29.99. Keepcase. *LANG:* English. *CAP:* English. *FEATURES:* 15 chapter links • Theatrical trailer.
1997 (R) 93m/C *AU* Michael Caton, Charles Tingwell, Sophie Lee, Robyn Nevin, Anne Tenney, Stephen Curry, Anthony Simcoe, Wayne Hope, Tiriel Mora, Eric Bana; *D:* Rob Sitch; *W:* Rob Sitch, Santo Cilauro, Tom Gleisner, Jane Kennedy; *C:* Miriana Marusic; *M:* Craig Harnath. *AWARDS:* Australian Film Institute '97: Best Original Screenplay; *NOM:* Australian Film Institute '97: Best Actor (Caton), Best Supporting Actor (Tingwell), Best Supporting Actress (Lee).

Castle Freak

Boasting the same director and lead actor as *Re-Animator*, this gothic tale leaves out the humor and concentrates on its dysfunctional characters who inherit an Italian castle, and the horror of it all. Something is living in the cellar of the castle, and it hasn't quite learned the social graces involved in not eating people. Not that you can blame him; he may have been the most abused child in movie history—to keep him away from the "evils of the flesh," mom even lopped off...well, take a guess. The DVD's picture is sharp enough to watch without straining the eyes, but is nothing special. Grain and artifacts are not too bothersome. Colors are more vibrant than the laserdisc and only rarely bleed. Blacks are fairly true. During scenes where there are no bright colors, some additional contrast would have brought out the details. The stereo sound is lively, full-bodied, with very good low end. Richard Band's excellent soundtrack sounds as good on this DVD as on its CD release. —*JO*
Movie: ♫♫ *DVD:* ♫♫▶
Full Moon Pictures (Cat #8002, UPC #728096800266). Full frame. Dolby Digital 2.0. $24.98. Keepcase. *LANG:* English. *FEATURES:* 14 chapter links.
1995 (R) 90m/C Jeffrey Combs, Barbara Crampton, Jonathan Fuller, Jessica Dollarhide; *D:* Stuart Gordon; *W:* Dennis Paoli; *C:* Mario Vulpiani; *M:* Richard Band.

Casual Sex?

Not a great movie, not even a good DVD. Supposedly a light-hearted comedy about safe sex, adapted from the play by Wendy Goldman and Judy Toll, this flick is limp in the morality and the humor departments. It's about two young women (Jackson and Thompson) looking for love and commitment, so they take a vacation at a posh resort only to be confronted by men with nothing on their minds but sex, casual or otherwise. The soundtrack is unimpressive, and the cramped, cropped image is a pan-and-scan throwback to the VHS era. No extras whatsoever—not even closed captions. —MB

Movie: 🎵🎵► **DVD:** 🎵
Image Entertainment (Cat #ID4299USDVD, UPC #014381429923). Full frame. Dolby Digital 2.0. $24.99. Snapper. *LANG:* English. *FEATURES:* 16 chapter links.
1988 (R) 87m/C Lea Thompson, Victoria Jackson, Stephen Shellen, Jerry Levine, Mary Gross, Andrew Dice Clay; *D:* Genevieve Robert; *W:* William Goldman, Judy Toll; *C:* Rolf Kestermann; *M:* Van Dyke Parks.

The Cat and the Canary

A breathless title card sets the scene: "On a lonely, pine-clad hill overlooking the Hudson, stood the grotesque mansion of an eccentric millionaire—" Director Paul Leni then uses a restlessly mobile camera to inject life into this adaptation of a play about the reading of a will 20 years after the death of the aforementioned eccentric millionaire. The story is as much comedy as horror with verbal and slapstick humor provided mostly by Creighton Hale, a lightweight Harold Lloyd–type leading man. Leni also distorts images and plays with extreme closeups and superimposed images. As a result, the style is much more enjoyable than the substance. The DVD version restores the bright color tinting and the original score, re-recorded in 1997. The print is also remarkably free of scratches; astonishingly so for a film of its age. Richard Peterson's extensive liner notes provide a good background for videophiles who are not familiar with the period. —MM

Movie: 🎵🎵🎵 **DVD:** 🎵🎵🎵►
Image Entertainment (Cat #ID4387DSDVD, UPC #014381438727). Full frame. Dolby Digital Stereo. $24.99. Snapper. *FEATURES:* Harold Lloyd short, "Haunted Spooks" ► 20 chapter links.
1927 81m/B Laura La Plante, Creighton Hale, Tully Marshall, Gertrude Astor, Arthur Edmund Carewe, Lucien Littlefield; *D:* Paul Leni; *W:* Robert F. "Bob" Hill, Alfred A. Cohn; *C:* Gilbert Warrenton.

Cat City

In this animated satire of politics, capitalism, and class struggle, times are tough for the mice living in Cat City. But they have a plan: A famous mouse scientist has created a powerful weapon to shrink the cats into mice-sized opponents! If they succeed, the balance of power will be forever shaken, and Cat City will become Mouseville. Unfortunately, the story is so hard to follow and ultimately hollow that what little charm the film had is lost. The video transfer fares better than the tinny soundtrack, but tragically lacks the vibrant colors and crisp definition that makes ani-

mation shine on DVD. —MJT **AKA:** Macskafogo.

Movie: 🎵🎵 **DVD:** 🎵🎵►
Image Entertainment (Cat #ID5694PZDVD, UPC #014381569421). Full frame. Dolby Digital Stereo. $24.99. Snapper. *LANG:* English. *FEATURES:* 12 chapter links.
1987 95m/C *D:* Bela Ternovsky; *W:* Joseph Nepp.

The Cat from Outer Space

One night, a glowing object lands near a remote farmhouse. The military immediately spirits the craft off to a lab but not before the pilot vanishes. And that pilot is a graceful Abyssinian cat (Jake) who can talk and manipulate objects with his mind. Given the seriousness with which this kind of stuff is now taken, the Disney children's comedy is more timely than it was when it was made. Though it's not likely to replace *The Shaggy Dog* as Disney's finest family pet–based sf, it is fun with an ensemble cast of faces familiar from TV. On DVD, the image is remarkably pristine. This low-budget fare looks as good as films made today costing ten times as much. The disc contains both wide and full-frame versions. —MM

Movie: 🎵🎵 **DVD:** 🎵🎵🎵
Anchor Bay (Cat #DV10733, UPC #013131073393). Full frame; widescreen (1.66:1) letterboxed. Dolby Digital Mono. $24.98. Keepcase. *LANG:* English. *FEATURES:* 14 chapter links.
1978 (G) 103m/C Ken Berry, Sandy Duncan, Harry (Henry) Morgan, Roddy McDowall, McLean Stevenson; *D:* Norman Tokar; *W:* Ted Key; *C:* Charles F. Wheeler; *M:* Lalo Schifrin.

Cat on a Hot Tin Roof

In this made-for-cable television adaptation of the Tennessee Williams play, fights over the family inheritance tear a family apart. Although this version restores racy material deleted from the 1958 film adaptation, the earlier movie and cast are the ones to watch. The video quality is poor, lower than a good prerecorded VHS tape. The PCM monaural soundtrack is muddy, at times rendering Williams's brilliant dialogue indistinct and difficult to hear. —MB

Movie: 🎵🎵 **DVD:** 🎵
Image Entertainment (Cat #ID4375DODVD, UPC #014381437522). Full frame. PCM Mono. $29.99. Snapper. *LANG:* English. *CAP:* English. *FEATURES:* 16 chapter links.
1984 122m/C Tommy Lee Jones, Jessica Lange, Rip Torn, Kim Stanley, David Dukes, Penny Fuller; *D:* Jack Hofsiss; *W:* Tennessee Williams.

Cat People

Paul Schrader's variation on Val Lewton's 1942 original may be the most sexually charged film in all horror. Where the first one is based on an ill-defined idea of original sin through female rebellion against male authority, this one works with more

overt themes—incest, bestiality, shape shifting—all boiling down to the basic conservative Christian notion that sex is evil. After a weirdly mythic introduction, the scene shifts to New Orleans where Irena (Kinski) arrives to stay with her bizarre older brother (McDowell). The keys are her feral, innocent, seductive performance and his much more threatening approach. They're backed up by Giorgio Moroder's spooky hypnotic score. The sensual seediness of the Big Easy has seldom been captured more effectively. Schrader carefully quotes the original without really turning his film into a remake. It's on the long side, but not indulgent. The director's expressionistic palette has been faithfully reproduced on DVD, even the tinted opening and the equally difficult shots of a black panther running at night. The sound is even more impressive through headphones, where those bass panther growls will make the hair on the back of your neck stand right up. A commentary track by Schrader would have been welcome, but that's a quibble. —MM

Movie: 🎵🎵🎵► **DVD:** 🎵🎵🎵►
Image Entertainment (Cat #ID4221USDVD, UPC #014381422122). Widescreen (1.85:1) letterboxed. Dolby Digital Surround. $24.99. Snapper. *LANG:* English. *FEATURES:* 34 chapter links.
1982 (R) 118m/C Nastassia Kinski, Malcolm McDowell, John Heard, Annette O'Toole, Ruby Dee, Ed Begley Jr., John Larroquette; *D:* Paul Schrader; *W:* Alan Ormsby; *C:* John Bailey; *M:* Giorgio Moroder.

Cats

Filmed version of the most successful stage musical in history is not quite a movie, not quite a play. It is a fairly accurate presentation of a performance of the mostly plotless production numbers. The music is actually more important and the stereo soundtrack is fine. Given the theatrical makeup and lighting, it is probably unfair to criticize the visual qualities of the DVD. —MM

Movie: 🎵🎵► **DVD:** 🎵🎵🎵
USA Home Entertainment (Cat #20682, UPC #044004799522). Widescreen (1.78:1) letterboxed. Dolby Digital Surround Stereo; Dolby Digital 5.1 Surround Stereo. $29.98. Keepcase. *LANG:* English. *CAP:* English. *FEATURES:* 21 chapter links ► "Making of" featurette.
1998 115m/C Elaine Page, Ken Page, John Mills; *D:* David Mallet, Trevor Nunn; *C:* Nicholas D. Knowland; *M:* Andrew Lloyd Webber.

Caught Up

After being an unwitting accomplice to a bank robbery and spending five years in jail, Daryl (Woodbine) meets Vanessa (Williams), a ringer for his lost girlfriend. She involves him in a plot with so many twists and reversals that it ought to fall apart completely, but somehow first-time director Scott keeps all the balls in the air. On the commentary track, he admits his

fondness for film noir and admits the influence of *Gun Crazy, Body Heat,* and *Taxi Driver* on his work. He and director of photography Tom Callaway also talk about the technical side. The DVD also boasts an exceptional image for a low-budget picture. This one really looks great. For mystery fans, it's one of the best sleepers in the video store. —*MM*
Movie: 🎞🎞🎞▸ **DVD:** 🎞🎞🎞▸
Artisan Entertainment (Cat #60470, UPC #012236047001). Widescreen (1.85:1) letterboxed; full frame. Dolby Digital 5.1 Surround. $29.98. Keepcase. *LANG:* English. *SUB:* Spanish. *CAP:* English. *FEATURES:* Theatrical trailer ▪ TV and radio spots ▪ Music videos ▪ Storyboards ▪ Cast and crew thumbnail biographies ▪ Production notes ▪ Commentary: Darin Scott, Bokeem Woodbine, Tom Callaway.
1998 (R) 95m/C Bokeem Woodbine, Cynda Williams, Snoop Doggy Dogg, Joseph Lindsey, Clifton Powell, Basil Wallace, Tony Todd, L.L. Cool J., Jeffrey Combs, Damon Saleem, Shedric Hunter Jr.; *D:* Darin Scott; *W:* Darin Scott; *C:* Thomas Callaway; *M:* Marc Bonilla.

Cause of Death
After the death of his brother, a stereotypical Colombian drug lord comes to L.A. to collect his money. On DVD, this leaden low-budgeteer is atrocious. Even ordinary interiors are grainy and other scenes are filled with abnormally heavy pixelation. Virtually unwatchable. —*MM*
Movie: 🎞▸ **DVD:** 🎞
Simitar Entertainment (Cat #7307, UPC #082551730728). Full frame. PCM Stereo. $14.98. Keepcase. *LANG:* English. *FEATURES:* 8 chapter links ▪ Production factoids.
1990 (R) 90m/C Michael Barak, Sydney Coale Phillips, Daniel Martine; *D:* Philip Jones.

Celebrity
Woody dissects the phenomenon of celebrity with his usual sarcastic and semi-autobiographical perspective. Lee Simon (Branagh) is a hack entertainment journalist who strives to enter the world of the famous people he writes about. Meanwhile, Simon's discarded wife (Davis) effortlessly achieves the fame he craves. DiCaprio steals his 15 minutes of screen time playing a hedonistic, hotel-trashing film star with amazing ease and conviction. Both Branagh and Allen seem to be engaged in a twitchy competition to out-Woody the director, and they, like the movie, become grating. On disc, the widescreen transfer sounds and looks sharp with good blacks and strong contrasts, but there are no bonus features. —*JE*
Movie: 🎞▸ **DVD:** 🎞🎞▸
Buena Vista Home Entertainment (Cat #17249, UPC #1795100242). Widescreen (1:85:1) letterboxed. Dolby Digital Mono. $29.99. Keepcase. *LANG:* English. *CAP:* English. *FEATURES:* 27 chapter links.

1998 (R) 113m/B Kenneth Branagh, Judy Davis, Hank Azaria, Leonardo DiCaprio, Joe Mantegna, Famke Janssen, Winona Ryder, Melanie Griffith, Michael Lerner, Charlize Theron, Bebe Neuwirth, Dylan Baker, Patti D'Arbanville, Kate Burton, Gretchen Mol, Allison Janney, Aida Turturro, Jeffrey Wright; *Cameos:* Greg Mottola, Isaac Mizrahi, Andre Gregory, Donald Trump; *D:* Woody Allen; *W:* Woody Allen; *C:* Sven Nykvist.

Center Stage
Maggie Cheung stars in an ambitious biography of actress Ruan Ling-yu, a star on the silent screen who committed suicide. The film opens with a prologue interview with Ms. Cheung about the subject and then intercuts dramatizations of Ruan Ling-yu's career with present-day footage. The technique made the film a hit on the festival circuit and will be just as successful with adventurous videophiles. This film is more serious than many imports that make it across the ocean, and it has strong production values equal to American historical dramas. Though the staging and lighting are non-realistic in many scenes, the transfer seems accurate with an emphasis on the colder blue end of the spectrum. Sound is fine; subtitles are easy to read in the lower part of the letterbox. —*MM* *AKA:* The Actress; Ruan Ling-Yu; The New China Woman.
Movie: 🎞🎞🎞▸ **DVD:** 🎞🎞🎞▸
Tai Seng Video Marketing (Cat #MS/DVD/025/98). Widescreen letterboxed. Dolby Digital 5.1 Surround Stereo. $49.95. Keepcase. *LANG:* Cantonese; Mandarin. *SUB:* Traditional Chinese; Simplified Chinese; English; Japanese; Korean; Bahasa Malaysia; Bahasa Indonesia; Thai; Spanish. *FEATURES:* 9 chapter links ▪ Production notes ▪ Theatrical trailers.
1991 121m/C *HK* Maggie Cheung, Tony Leung Chiu-Wai, Shin Hong, Carina Lau, Lawrence Ng, Waise Lee, Cheung Chung, Siu Sheung, Yip Sang; *D:* Stanley Kwan; *W:* Yau Tai On-Ping; *C:* Poon Hang-Seng.

Central Station
Dora (Montenegro) is a bitter, aging woman who makes her living writing letters for the illiterate at a stand in Rio de Janeiro's central railroad station. One of her customers sends letters to her nine-year-old son's Josue's (de Oliveira) father, who lives in northern Brazil and has never seen the boy. When Josue's mother is killed, Dora reluctantly takes him in and even more reluctantly decides they must locate his father. Their road trip is filled with surprises. This Oscar-nominee makes a smooth transition to DVD with an exceptionally clear, well-lighted, and well-photographed image. On the commentary track, Fernanda Montenegro seems sometimes uncomfortable with English but she makes her points. She and director Salles and producer Cohn are intelligent and perceptive. Fans of foreign films who missed

this one in theatres should give it a try. —*MM* *AKA:* Central Do Brasil.
Movie: 🎞🎞🎞▸ **DVD:** 🎞🎞🎞▸
Columbia Tristar Home Video (Cat #03833, UPC #043396038332). Widescreen (2.35:1) letterboxed. Dolby Digital Stereo. $28.95. Keepcase. *LANG:* Portuguese. *SUB:* English. *FEATURES:* 28 chapter links ▪ Commentary: Montenegro, Salles, Cohn ▪ Cast and crew thumbnail biographies ▪ Theatrical trailer.
1998 (R) 110m/C *BR* Fernanda Montenegro, Vinicius de Oliveira, Marilia Pera, Othon Bastos; *D:* Walter Salles; *W:* Joao Emmanuel Carneiro, Marcos Bernstein; *C:* Walter Carvalho; *M:* Antonio Pinto, Jaques Morelembaum. *AWARDS:* British Academy Awards '98: Best Foreign Film; Golden Globe Awards '99: Best Foreign Film; Los Angeles Film Critics Association Awards '98: Best Actress (Montenegro); National Board of Review Awards '98: Best Actress (Montenegro), Best Foreign Film; *NOM:* Academy Awards '98: Best Actress (Montenegro), Best Foreign Film; Golden Globe Awards '99: Best Actress—Drama (Montenegro); Independent Spirit Awards '99: Best Foreign Film.

C'est la Vie, Mon Cherie
Romantic melodrama is about a burnt-out jazzman (Lau Ching Wan) and a breezy street musician (Anita Yuen). The sentimentality that can be so strong in Hong Kong films is given full rein here. The no-frills (not even chapter breaks) DVD image is no better than good with faint white subtitles that are virtually impossible to read in some scenes. —*MM* *AKA:* Xin Buliao Qing.
Movie: 🎞🎞▸ **DVD:** 🎞▸
Tai Seng Video Marketing (Cat #DVD5008). Widescreen letterboxed. Dolby Digital Stereo. $49.95. Jewel case. *LANG:* Cantonese; Mandarin. *SUB:* English; Chinese.
1993 90m/C *HK* Lau Ching Wan, Anita Yuen, Sylvia Chang, Bo-Bo Fung, Carrie Ng; *D:* Yee Tung-shing; *W:* Yee Tung-shing; *C:* Tsi-wai Tam; *M:* Chris Babida, Stephen Chan.

Chairman of the Board
For fans who simply cannot get enough of comedian Carrot Top, he not only stars in this misfire, he talks about himself on the commentary track. Why, you ask, would someone who has never appeared in a movie before be asked to comment knowledgeably about it? Why was he given a movie in the first place? He impersonates surfer/inventor Edison whose Rube-Goldberg creations are failures. But then he meets and befriends CEO Armand McMillan (Warden). Armand dies, leaves his company to Edison, etc. About the best that can be said of the DVD is that the menu is kind of cool. The star brags that he's knocking back tequila during the recording of his commentary. You have been warned. —*MM*

Movie: 🎬 DVD: 🎬🎬
Trimark Home Video (Cat #6811D, UPC #031398681137). Widescreen letterboxed; full frame. Dolby Digital Stereo. $19.99. Keepcase. *LANG:* English. *SUB:* French; Spanish. *CAP:* English. *FEATURES:* 30 chapter links • Interview and commentary track by Carrot Top • Music video • Cast thumbnail biographies.
1997 (PG-13) 95m/C Carrot Top, Courtney Thorne-Smith, Larry Miller, Raquel Welch, Jack Warden, Estelle Harris, Bill Erwin, M. Emmet Walsh, Jack McGee, Glenn Shadix, Fred Stoller, Mystro Clark, Jack Plotnick; *D:* Alex Zamm; *W:* Al Septien, Turi Meyer, Alex Zamm; *C:* David Lewis; *M:* Chris Hajian. *AWARDS: NOM:* Golden Raspberry Awards '98: Worst Supporting Actress (Welch), Worst New Star.

The Challenge of Flight: Disc One

This evening's-worth of Military Channel compilations has striking menu design but an overall low-budget feel. Some of the source material is degraded of course, for which the producers blame the Department of Defense in their opening statement. The disc rattles in the machine and the image scans unevenly. The visual documentation, from official sources no average person has ever heard of, captures real pilots in moments of stress or crisis, and WWII dogfights between the U.S. and Axis gunners. Some items are less esoteric than others, like the unfortunate end of the very first F-22. The Japanese and German sequences are historic finds. The newly minted synth score often clashes with the clearly antique wartime footage. However, the narration and arrangement of segments presume a certain familiarity with aviation terminology and goes into often excruciating technological detail (Landings is followed by Landings Part 2). The real intended audience for this production are techno-junkies and fans of cinematic gadgetry. The style is reminiscent of Air Force recruitment featurettes, and the slightly muffled voice-over is the sort you hear on in-flight safety precaution recordings. —JK
Movie: 🎬 DVD: 🎬🎬🎬🎬
FOCUSfilm (Cat #FF7355, UPC #683070735524). Full frame. Dual-channel Mono. $19.99. Keepcase. *LANG:* English. *FEATURES:* 21 chapter links • Interactive menus • 2-color disc • Theatrical trailer.
19?? 90m/C *D:* Lee Joseph, Gary Evans; *W:* Tom Johnson; *M:* Network Projects Music.

The Chamber

Dull retelling of yet another John Grisham legal thriller fails to engross. White supremist Sam Cahill (Hackman) is on Mississippi's death row for killing two Jewish boys in a 1967 bombing. Young Chicago lawyer (O'Donnell), looking to find out more about his family's odious past, volunteers to work on his grandfather's case

and win a stay of execution. Hackman and Dunaway (as his alcoholic daughter) are their usual professional selves while the charming O'Donnell seems out of his depth. A very sharp picture with very little grain is complemented by accurate colors and very true blacks. Bleed is minimal except when Hackman is wearing his red prison garb—a lot of the time. The contrast is excellent, but the brightness level could have used an occasional boost. The 5.1 sound is very dynamic and has good low end. Dialogue is crisp. Ambience is nicely added by the Surround tracks which also kick in for the occasional effect. —JO
Movie: 🎬▶ DVD: 🎬🎬🎬▶
Universal Studios Home Video (Cat #20268, UPC #025192026829). Widescreen (2.35:1) anamorphic. Dolby Digital 5.1; Dolby Surround. $24.98. Keepcase. *LANG:* English (DD5.1); Spanish (DS); French (DS). *SUB:* Spanish. *CAP:* English. *FEATURES:* 16 chapter links • Theatrical trailer • Cast and filmmakers bios • Production notes.
1996 (R) 113m/C Gene Hackman, Chris O'Donnell, Faye Dunaway, Lela Rochon, Robert Prosky, Raymond J. Barry, Bo Jackson, David Marshall Grant, Millie Perkins; *D:* James Foley; *W:* Phil Alden Robinson, William Goldman; *C:* Ian Baker; *M:* Carter Burwell. *AWARDS: NOM:* Golden Raspberry Awards '96: Worst Supporting Actress (Dunaway).

Champions

The producers of this low-budget martial arts flick seem to have spent the bulk of their money on lighting and photography. The result is a no-surprises tournament story, loosely based on "extreme" fighting, that looks terrific on disc. The images are remarkably sharp with some interesting use of colored lights to distract the viewer from many other shortcomings in flashbacks and the like. —MM
Movie: 🎬 DVD: 🎬🎬▶
Simitar Entertainment (Cat #7433, UPC #082551743322). Full frame. Dolby Digital Stereo; Dolby Digital 5.1 Surround Stereo. $19.98. Keepcase. *LANG:* English. *FEATURES:* 8 chapter links • Production factoids.
1996 99m/C Louis Mandylor, Danny Trejo; *D:* Peter Gathings Bunche.

Chances Are

Nothing works right in this inept reincarnation romance. It's such a bad movie that it's often painful to watch on any medium. Apparently, it's meant to be a star vehicle for Cybill Shepherd but she's no better than anyone else connected with this stinker. When Washington lawyer Louie Jeffries (McDonald) is killed in 1964, he makes a big scene in heaven and they send him back right away, without the injection that will make him forget his previous life. Twenty-four years later, he's become Alex Finch (Downey Jr.). Alex knows nothing about Louie until he meets his widow, Corinne (Shepherd) in their old

Georgetown house. Then he begins to have visions of the past. The DVD captures the sugarcoated look of the film, but that's hardly a recommendation. —MM
Movie: woof DVD: 🎬🎬▶
Columbia Tristar Home Video (Cat #70159, UPC #043396701595). Full frame; widescreen (1.85:1) letterboxed. Dolby Surround Stereo. $28.95. Keepcase. *LANG:* English; French; Spanish. *SUB:* English; French; Spanish. *CAP:* English. *FEATURES:* 28 chapter links.
1989 (PG) 108m/C Cybill Shepherd, Robert Downey Jr., Ryan O'Neal, Mary Stuart Masterson, Josef Sommer, Christopher McDonald, Joe Grifasi, James Noble, Susan Ruttan, Fran Ryan; *D:* Emile Ardolino; *W:* Randy Howze, Perry Howze; *C:* William A. Fraker; *M:* Maurice Jarre. *AWARDS: NOM:* Academy Awards '89: Best Song ("After All").

Changing Habits

Starving artist Soosh (Kelly) moves into a nunnery to save money. She's so broke she has taken to stealing art supplies, but salesman Felix (Walsh) is more interested in romance than a shoplifting conviction. The attractive leads and a capable supporting cast are stuck with a dull dull script. The DVD only heightens the film's visual flaws: irritating soft focus, an overall dimness, and night scenes that lack detail. —MM
Movie: 🎬▶ DVD: 🎬▶
Simitar Entertainment (Cat #7449, UPC #082551744923). Full frame. Dolby Digital Stereo. $7.98. Keepcase. *LANG:* English. *FEATURES:* 8 chapter links • Filmographies of Christopher Lloyd and Moira Kelly.
1996 (R) 92m/C Moira Kelly, Christopher Lloyd, Teri Garr, Shelley Duvall, Dylan Walsh, Marissa Ribisi, Frances Bay, Bob Gunton, Anne Haney, Eileen Brennan; *D:* Lynn Roth; *W:* Scott Davis Jones; *C:* Mike Mayers; *M:* David McHugh.

Chaplin

The life and career of *The Little Tramp* are lovingly chronicled by director Attenborough and he's brilliantly portrayed by Downey Jr. A flashback format traces his life from its poverty-stricken Dickensian origins in the London slums through his directing and acting career, to his honorary Oscar in 1972. The film captures Chaplin's devotion to his art and also his penchant for jailbait. In a clever casting choice, Geraldine Chaplin, Chaplin's own daughter from his fourth marriage to Oona O'Neill, plays her own grandmother who goes mad. The menus on a lot of DVDs are pretty creative and this one's use of simulated film scratches is particularly fitting. The film itself looks great on DVD and is very sharp, having very little problem with grain or artifacting. Colors and blacks are very accurate and the contrast and brightness levels consistently excellent. This great DVD is topped off with crisp and dynamic sound that handles the full range of fidelity equally well. The movie, when combined with the supplementals on Chaplin's career and works, is an excellent way to get to know the work of the "little tramp." —JO

Movie: 𝄞𝄞𝄞► *DVD:* 𝄞𝄞𝄞►
Artisan Entertainment (Cat #60483, UPC #012236048305). Widescreen (1.77:1) letterboxed. Dolby Digital Stereo. $24.98. Snapper. *LANG:* English. *SUB:* Spanish. *CAP:* English. *FEATURES:* 36 chapter links • Theatrical trailer • "Making of" featurette • Cast and crew bios • Production notes.

1992 (PG-13) 135m/C *GB* Robert Downey Jr., Dan Aykroyd, Geraldine Chaplin, Kevin Dunn, Anthony Hopkins, Milla Jovovich, Moira Kelly, Kevin Kline, Diane Lane, Penelope Ann Miller, Paul Rhys, John Thaw, Marisa Tomei, Nancy Travis, James Woods, David Duchovny, Deborah Maria (Barrymore) Moore, Bill Paterson, John Standing, Robert Stephens, Peter Crook; *D:* Richard Attenborough; *W:* Bryan Forbes, William Boyd, William Goldman; *C:* Sven Nykvist; *M:* John Barry. *AWARDS:* British Academy Awards '92: Best Actor (Downey); *NOM:* Academy Awards '92: Best Actor (Downey), Best Art Direction/Set Decoration, Best Original Score.

The Chaplin Mutuals, Vol. 1

The two-reel comedies in this three-volume collection are some of the best that Charlie Chaplin made. They were produced in 1916–17, after his work with the Essanay Company. The famous "Little Tramp" character becomes more clearly defined and in all 12 films, it's easy to see Chaplin's growth as a comedian, actor, and director. My own favorite of the bunch is "Easy Street," though it's hard to argue with anyone who prefers "The Immigrant" or "One A.M." On DVD, the films have new scores and the original intertitle cards. The quality is generally good, but not excellent, reflecting the quality of film and equipment Chaplin had to work with. It's hard to imagine any version of these films looking much better. In this case, the primary attraction of DVD is the medium's quick access to particular titles. Films: "The Immigrant," "The Adventurer," "The Cure," "Easy Street." —MM

Movie: 𝄞𝄞𝄞► *DVD:* 𝄞𝄞𝄞
Image Entertainment (Cat #ID100DSDVD, UPC #014381410020). Full frame. $29.99. Snapper. FFEATURES: 22 chapter links • Liner notes by Sam Gill • Musical score by Michael Mortilla.

199? 100m/B Charlie Chaplin, Edna Purviance, Eric Campbell; *D:* Charlie Chaplin; *W:* Charlie Chaplin.

The Chaplin Mutuals, Vol. 2

Please see review of *The Chaplin Mutuals, Vol. 1*. Films: "The Count," "The Vagabond," "The Fireman," "Behind the Screen." —MM

Movie: 𝄞𝄞𝄞► *DVD:* 𝄞𝄞𝄞
Image Entertainment (Cat #ID4101DSDVD, UPC #014381410129). Full frame. $29.99. Snapper. *FEATURES:* 24 chapter links • Liner notes by Sam Gill • Musical score by Michael Mortilla.

199? 100m/B Charlie Chaplin, Edna Purviance, Eric Campbell; *D:* Charlie Chaplin; *W:* Charlie Chaplin.

The Chaplin Mutuals, Vol. 3

Please see review of *The Chaplin Mutuals, Vol. 1*. Films: "One A.M.," "The Pawn Shop," "The Floorwalker," "The Rink." —MM

Movie: 𝄞𝄞𝄞► *DVD:* 𝄞𝄞𝄞
Image Entertainment (Cat #ID4163DSDVD, UPC #014381416329). Full frame. $29.99. Snapper. *FEATURES:* 23 chapter links • Liner notes by Sam Gill • Musical score by Michael Mortilla.

199? 100m/B Charlie Chaplin, Edna Purviance, Eric Campbell; *D:* Charlie Chaplin; *W:* Charlie Chaplin.

Chaplin's Art of Comedy

Most of the clips in this appreciation come from the films found in *The Chaplin Mutuals* and *Chaplin's Essanay Comedies* DVD collections. They were made between 1915 and 1917. The narration and stock footage come straight from the mid-1960s and they give the entire film a double-edged nostalgia. Most younger viewers who are unfamiliar with Chaplin's work (or know it only from Robert Downey in *Chaplin*) will probably be put off by the preachy, didactic tone. The clips are well chosen and edited, and it's clear that producer Samuel Sherman loves his subject. Highly recommended for the Little Tramp's fans. Overall the quality of the DVD is as good as the source material. —MM

Movie: 𝄞𝄞𝄞 *DVD:* 𝄞𝄞𝄞
Image Entertainment (Cat #ID5546IIDVD, UPC #014381554625). Full frame. Dolby Digital Mono. $24.99. Snapper. *LANG:* English. *FEATURES:* 12 chapter links.

1966 82m/B Charlie Chaplin, Edna Purviance, Ben Turpin, "Broncho" Billy Anderson, Snub Pollard, Wesley Ruggles; *W:* Sam M. Sherman.

Chaplin's Essanay Comedies, Vol. 1

The short comedies in this collection were made in 1915 and so they're not as polished as the films Chaplin would make a year later for the Mutual Company, available on DVD as the three-volume *Chaplin Mutuals* set. Chaplin's talents as a performer are rougher. He had yet to fully understand his "Little Tramp" character and the basic tools of filmmaking were comparatively crude. Though obvious care was taken to restore these films for DVD, they're still filled with grainy speckles, visible breaks, and overall

scratchiness. Quality varies from shot to shot. Even so, they are watchable and are important early comedies, though probably of more interest to serious students of film than to the general viewer. Films: "His New Job," "A Night Out," "The Champion," "In the Park," "A Jitney Elopement." —MM

Movie: 𝄞𝄞𝄞 *DVD:* 𝄞𝄞𝄞
Image Entertainment (Cat #ID5413DSDVD, UPC #01438154132). Full frame. Dolby Digital Stereo. $24.99. Snapper. *FEATURES:* 24 chapter breaks • Extensive liner notes by Jeffrey Vance • Chaplin filmography.

199? 136m/C Charlie Chaplin, Edna Purviance, Ben Turpin; *D:* Charlie Chaplin; *W:* Charlie Chaplin.

Chaplin's Essanay Comedies, Vol. 2

Please see review of *Chaplin's Essanay Comedies, Vol. 1*. Films: "The Tramp," "By the Sea," "Work," "A Woman," "The Bank," "His Regeneration." —MM

Movie: 𝄞𝄞𝄞 *DVD:* 𝄞𝄞𝄞
Image Entertainment (Cat #ID5414DSDVD, UPC #014381541427). Full frame. Dolby Digital Stereo. $24.99. Snapper. *FEATURES:* 20 chapter breaks • Extensive liner notes by Jeffrey Vance • Chaplin filmography.

199? 135m/C Charlie Chaplin, Edna Purviance, Ben Turpin; *D:* Charlie Chaplin; *W:* Charlie Chaplin.

Chaplin's Essanay Comedies, Vol. 3

Please see review of *Chaplin's Essanay Comedies, Vol. 1*. Films: "Shanghaied," "A Night in the Show," "Police," "Burlesque on 'Carmen'," "Triple Trouble." —MM

Movie: 𝄞𝄞𝄞 *DVD:* 𝄞𝄞𝄞
Image Entertainment (Cat #ID5415DSDVD, UPC #014381541526). Full frame. Dolby Digital Stereo. $24.99. Snapper. *FEATURES:* 22 chapter breaks • Extensive liner notes by Jeffrey Vance • Chaplin filmography.

199? 131m/C Charlie Chaplin, Edna Purviance, Ben Turpin; *D:* Charlie Chaplin; *W:* Charlie Chaplin.

Chappaqua

Controversial and hypnotic mix of music and visuals is a semi-autobiographical psychodrama following an addict's journey from sickness to health, anguish to well-being. When Russel Harwick (Rooks), a young, well-to-do alcoholic and junkie, heads to Switzerland for the "Swiss Sleeping Cure," he enters a psychedelic world set not in reality, but in the explosive, delusional landscape of his mind. The video transfer is admirable, although the blend of color and black & white film does tend to bring the shortcomings of the source material to the foreground via some definition loss and an apparently abused negative. Likewise, the soundtrack is crisp and clear, except in more emotionally charged scenes where it becomes a bit hard to discern. But, having said all of this, these traits may have been done intentionally for dramatic effect. —MJT

Movie: 🎵🎵🎵 **DVD:** 🎵🎵🎵
Fox/Lorber Home Video (Cat #FLV5106, UPC #720917510620). Full frame. Dolby Digital Stereo. $29.98. Keepcase. *LANG:* English. *FEATURES:* 6 chapter links ● Filmographies and awards ● Production credits.
1966 82m/C Jean-Louis Barrault, William S. Burroughs, Ornette Coleman, Allen Ginsberg, Conrad Rooks, Ravi Shankar; *D:* Conrad Rooks; *W:* Conrad Rooks; *C:* Robert Frank.

Charade

One of the genuinely great romantic thrillers has had a rough career on home video. Several bargain-basement tape editions have appeared, and almost all of them have been substandard. This disc is by far the best the film has looked in decades. It's a terrific twisty tale of a young widow (Hepburn) in Paris, the shady stranger (Grant) who may know the truth behind her husband's death, and the others (Coburn, Kennedy, Matthau, Glass) who are far too interested in him. On DVD, the colors sparkle; the mono sound is completely clear and faithful to the original; and the filmmakers' commentary is chatty and intelligent. Even with its premium price, this one belongs in any collector's library. —MM

Movie: 🎵🎵🎵🎵 **DVD:** 🎵🎵🎵🎵
Criterion Collection (Cat #57, UPC #037429139424). Widescreen (1.85:1) letterboxed. Dolby Digital Mono. $39.95. Keepcase. *LANG:* English. *SUB:* English. *FEATURES:* 22 chapter links ● Commentary: Donen and Stone ● Thumbnail bios of Donen and Stone ● Liner notes by Bruce Eder ● Trailer.
1963 113m/C Cary Grant, Audrey Hepburn, Walter Matthau, James Coburn, George Kennedy; *D:* Stanley Donen; *W:* Peter Stone; *C:* Charles B(ryant) Lang; *M:* Henry Mancini. *AWARDS:* British Academy Awards '64: Best Actress (Hepburn); *NOM:* Academy Awards '63: Best Song ("Charade").

Chariots of Fire

A lush telling of the parallel stories of Harold Abraham (Cross) and Eric Liddell (Charleson), English runners who competed in the 1924 Olympics. One was compelled by a hatred of anti-Semitism, the other ran for the glory of God. Outstanding performances by the entire cast. The DVD actually looks sharper than the theatrical release, or the VHS tape. A few moments of slow-motion running are slightly distorted on the disc. Otherwise, it handles spectacular English landscapes, comfortable college interiors, and the dark textures of clothes and academic gowns with ease and clarity. A commentary track or separate chapter giving more of the historical

background would have been a welcome extra. —MM

Movie: 🎵🎵🎵► **DVD:** 🎵🎵🎵
Warner Home Video, Inc. (Cat #20004, UPC #085392000425). Full frame. Dolby Digital Surround Stereo. $24.98. Snapper. *LANG:* English; French; Spanish. *SUB:* English; French; Spanish. *CAP:* English. *FEATURES:* Cast and crew thumbnail biographies ● Awards ● Production notes ● Theatrical trailer ● 36 chapter links.
1981 (PG) 123m/C *GB* Ben Cross, Ian Charleson, Nigel Havers, Ian Holm, Alice Krige, Brad Davis, Dennis Christopher, Patrick Magee, Cheryl Campbell, John Gielgud, Lindsay Anderson, Nigel Davenport; *D:* Hugh Hudson; *W:* Colin Welland; *C:* David Watkin; *M:* Vangelis. *AWARDS:* Academy Awards '81: Best Costume Design, Best Original Screenplay, Best Picture, Best Original Score; British Academy Awards '81: Best Film, Best Supporting Actor (Holm); Golden Globe Awards '82: Best Foreign Film; New York Film Critics Awards '81: Best Cinematography; *NOM:* Academy Awards '81: Best Director (Hudson), Best Film Editing, Best Supporting Actor (Holm).

Charles Chaplin— A First National Collection

A collection of six restored classics— "Shoulder Arms" (1918); "Sunnyside," originally "Jack of All Trades" (1919); "A Day's Pleasure" (1919); "The Idle Class" (1921); "Pay Day" (1922); and "The Pilgrim" (1922)—is fun for the Chaplin fanatic and the newcomer alike. Each film has been digitally mastered with restored footage, the film speeds corrected to their intended style and pace. The movies attest to the genius of the man, as a director and an actor. The films have been restored beautifully, with great consistency. The accompanying soundtrack, as composed by Chaplin and re-created by Eric James, is well paced with great clarity. —AB

Movie: 🎵🎵🎵🎵 **DVD:** 🎵🎵🎵🎵
Image Entertainment (Cat #ID9177CUDVD, UPC #1438191772). Widescreen letterboxed. Dolby Digital Mono. $29.99. Keepcase. *LANG:* English. *SUB:* English. *FEATURES:* 48 chapter links ● A visit from Gen. Leonard Wood on the set of "Sunnyside" ● Home movie with Jackie Coogan, Lord and Lady Mountbatten, and Chaplin.
19?? ?m/B Charlie Chaplin, Edna Purviance, Henry Bergman, Allan Garcia; *D:* Charlie Chaplin; *C:* Roland H. Totheroh; *M:* Charlie Chaplin.

Charlie, the Lonesome Cougar

In the Pacific Northwest, forester Jess Bradley (Brown) adopts an orphan cougar kitten. A thin storyline is papered over nature footage and staged bits of business involving the full-sized feline. Perhaps because the action is so narratively

challenged, no director is listed in the credits. The DVD, however, looks just fine. It was produced from an excellent original and has no important flaws. Sound is O.K. —MM

Movie: 🎵🎵 **DVD:** 🎵🎵
Anchor Bay (Cat #DV11093, UPC #013131109399). Full frame. Dolby Digital Mono. $24.98. Keepcase. *LANG:* English. *FEATURES:* 16 chapter links.
1967 (G) 75m/C Linda Wallace, Jim Wilson, Ron Brown, Brian Russell, Clifford Peterson; *D:* Winston Hibler; *W:* Jack Speirs; *C:* William W. Bacon III, Lloyd Beebe; *M:* Franklyn Marks; *Nar:* Rex Allen.

Children of the Corn 666: Isaac's Return

The inexplicably long-lived series continues with an installment that's much more atmospheric than frightening, though the film has a few good moments. It begins with adopted teen Hannah Martin (Ramsey) going back to the hamlet of Gatlin to find her roots and to learn what really happened there. The sinister locals don't cotton to outsiders. Director Kari Skogland shows off insufferably with needless camera trickery, but she polishes the low-budget action with stylish visuals. The DVD captures the heavily textured sepia light. Sound is fine, too. —MM

Movie: 🎵🎵► **DVD:** 🎵🎵►
Buena Vista Home Entertainment (Cat #18149, UPC #717951004284). Widescreen (1.85:1) letterboxed. Dolby Digital 5.1 Surround Stereo. $29.99. Keepcase. *LANG:* English. *FEATURES:* 23 chapter links.
1999 (R) 82m/C Natalie Ramsey, John Franklin, Stacy Keach, Alix Koromzay, Nancy Allen; *D:* Keri Skogland.

Children Shouldn't Play with Dead Things

A band of foolhardy hippie filmmakers on an island cemetery skimp on special effects by using witchcraft to revive the dead. The plan works. Soon the crew has an island full of hungry ghouls to contend with. A late-night fave, sporting some excellent dead-rising-from-their-grave scenes as well as frequent yucks. Screenwriter-actor Ormsby went on to write the remake of *Cat People*, while director Clark would eventually helm *Porky's*. The DVD is limited by the source material of this low-budget gem. Everything is audible on the soundtrack, but there is hiss, clipping, and not much in the way of dynamics. The picture is soft but digital grain and artifacting are minimal. Considering that the whole film takes place in the dark, that's pretty amazing. Contrast and brightness levels vary from good to poor, again due to the source. Still, it's great to see films like this make it to DVD even if they can't possibly take advantage of the format's quality. —JO *AKA:* Revenge of the Living Dead.

Movie: ♫♫➤ **DVD:** ♫♫➤
VCI Home Video (Cat #8208, UPC #089859820823). Widescreen (1.85:1) letterboxed. Dolby Digital Mono. $24.99. Keepcase. *LANG:* English. *FEATURES:* 16 chapter links • Theatrical trailer • Photo gallery • Filmmaker bios.
1972 85m/C Alan Ormsby, Valerie Mamches, Jeff Gillen, Anya Ormsby, Paul Cronin, Jane Daly, Roy Engelman, Robert Philip, Bruce Solomon, Alecs Baird, Seth Sklarey; *D:* Bob (Benjamin) Clark; *W:* Bob (Benjamin) Clark, Alan Ormsby; *C:* Jack McGowan; *M:* Carl Zittrer.

Child's Play

Though the box art and premise make this look like a formula studio production, it's really much better. At death, the spirit of mad killer Charles Lee Ray (Dourif) is transported into a Good Guys doll named Chucky. A young boy (Vincent), his mother (Hicks), and a Chicago police detective (Sarandon) come to realize the truth, but not before the deranged toy has run amuck. The writing is well above average with inventive plotting and attention to character. The toy effects and Chicago locations are fine, too. Add in grim humor and an ending that just won't quit and you've got one of the best of recent years. On DVD, the full-frame image is not really much better than on VHS tape. The big effects shots are fine, but the whole thing lacks the clarity of the best discs. For comparative purposes, see *Bride of Chucky.* Sound is very good. —*MM*
Movie: ♫♫♫♫ **DVD:** ♫♫➤
MGM Home Entertainment (Cat #907504, UPC #027616750426). Full frame. Dolby Digital Surround Stereo. $24.98. Keepcase. *LANG:* English; French. *CAP:* English. *FEATURES:* 36 chapter links • Production notes booklet.
1988 (R) 95m/C Catherine Hicks, Alex Vincent, Chris Sarandon, Dinah Manoff, Brad Dourif, Tommy Swerdlow, Jack Colvin; *D:* Tom Holland; *W:* Don Mancini, John Lafia, Tom Holland; *C:* Bill Butler; *M:* Joe Renzetti.

Child's Play 2

Chucky lives. Basic doll-on-a-rampage story, a metaphor for the Reagan years, lives on in the sequel (you remember: somehow guy-doll Chucky made it past the quality control people with a highly inflammable temper). A little dotty from playing with dolls, young Vincent finds himself fostered by two new parents, and plagued by an obnoxious and very animated doll that fosters ill will toward all. What's worse is the doll is transmigratory, craving the boy's body as his next address. The DVD is very sharp and has no problem with either grain or artifacts. Just contrasty enough and with plenty of brightness, the disc also offers near flawless handling of its blacks. Colors are also very strong and vibrant, with only the deepest redtones

causing them to bleed a bit. There is not much in the way of Surround tracks, which ideally would have at least enhanced the ambience. But the tracks provide deep solid low end and crisp highs, delivering dialogue, music, and effects with equal clarity. —*JO*
Movie: ♫♫ **DVD:** ♫♫♫
MGM Home Entertainment (Cat #20522, UPC #025192052224). Widescreen (1.85:1) anamorphic. Dolby Surround. $24.98. Keepcase. *LANG:* English; French. *SUB:* Spanish. *CAP:* English. *FEATURES:* 18 chapter links • Theatrical trailer • Cast and filmmaker bios • Film highlights.
1990 (R) 84m/C Alex Vincent, Jenny Agutter, Gerrit Graham, Christine Elise, Grace Zabriskie; *D:* John Lafia; *W:* Don Mancini; *C:* Stefan Czapsky; *M:* Graeme Revell; *V:* Brad Dourif.

China O'Brien

Gorgeous police officer China (Rothrock) returns home for a little R&R and finds that she has to kick some major butt, instead. Typical martial arts action is handled with some style.
Movie: ♫♫ **DVD:** NYR
Studio Home Entertainment (Cat #4010). Full frame. $24.95. Keepcase. *LANG:* English; Spanish. *CAP:* English. *FEATURES:* Production notes • Trailer.
1988 (R) 90m/C Cynthia Rothrock, Richard Norton, Patrick Adamson, David Blackwell, Steven Kerby, Robert Tiller, Lainie Watts, Keith Cooke; *D:* Robert Clouse; *W:* Robert Clouse; *C:* Kent Wakeford; *M:* Paul Antonelli.

The China Syndrome

A somewhat unstable executive at a nuclear plant uncovers evidence of a concealed accident, and takes drastic steps to publicize the incident. Lemmon is excellent as the anxious exec, while Fonda and Douglas are scarcely less distinguished as a sympathetic TV journalist and camera operator, respectively. Tense, prophetic thriller that ironically preceded the Three Mile Island accident by just a few months. Columbia has done a good job on this DVD and the picture is the sharpest the film's ever had on home video. The vibrant colors are accurate and the blacks are true. Though only stereo, the sound on this disc is full-bodied and there is enough separation that the overall feel is very lively. —*JO*
Movie: ♫♫♫ **DVD:** ♫♫♫
Columbia Tristar Home Video (Cat #01599, UPC #043396015999). Widescreen (185:1) anamorphic; full frame. Stereo. $25.95. *LANG:* English; Spanish. *SUB:* English; Spanish; Portuguese; Chinese; Korean; Thai. *CAP:* English. *FEATURES:* 28 chapter links • Theatrical trailer • Production notes • Cast and filmmakers bios • Filmographies.
1979 (PG) 123m/C Jane Fonda, Jack Lemmon, Michael Douglas, Scott Brady,

James Hampton, Peter Donat, Wilford Brimley, James Karen; *D:* James Bridges; *W:* James Bridges, Mike Gray, T.S. Cook; *C:* James A. Crabe. *AWARDS:* British Academy Awards '79: Best Actor (Lemmon), Best Actress (Fonda); Cannes Film Festival '79: Best Actor (Lemmon); Writers Guild of America '79: Best Original Screenplay; *NOM:* Academy Awards '79: Best Actor (Lemmon), Best Actress (Fonda), Best Art Direction/Set Decoration, Best Original Screenplay.

Chinatown

In Roosevelt-era California, private detective Jake Gittes (Nicholson) finds himself overwhelmed in a case of staggering dimensions—both political and personal—involving the rich and powerful of Southern California. This masterpiece is gripping and atmospheric with superb plotting and memorable performances from Nicholson, Dunaway, and particularly Huston, as the embodiment of evil. Director Polanski has a significant cameo as a knife-wielding thug. In a separate retrospective interview, he explains precisely how that memorable bit of business was accomplished. Writer Towne talks about the origins of the title, and what it means. In visual terms, the DVD image is identical to the original theatrical release, and it's much much better than any of the several videotapes I have watched in the years since. Many of the stylistic devices of film noir—venetian blinds, patterned shadows, deco set design—can be problematic for DVD, but this one manages them well. The disc belongs in every library. —*MM*
Movie: ♫♫♫♫ **DVD:** ♫♫♫♫
Paramount Home Video (Cat #15516, UPC #097361551678). Widescreen anamorphic. Dolby Digital 5.1 Surround Stereo; Mono. $29.99. Keepcase. *LANG:* English; French. *SUB:* English. *FEATURES:* 16 chapter links • Retrospective interviews with Polanski, Towne, and Evans • Theatrical trailer.
1974 (R) 131m/C Jack Nicholson, Faye Dunaway, John Huston, Diane Ladd, John Hillerman, Burt Young, Perry Lopez, Darrell Zwerling, Roman Polanski; *D:* Roman Polanski; *W:* Robert Towne; *C:* John A. Alonzo; *M:* Jerry Goldsmith. *AWARDS:* Academy Awards '74: Best Original Screenplay; American Film Institute (AFI) '98: Top 100; British Academy Awards '74: Best Actor (Nicholson), Best Director (Polanski), Best Screenplay; Golden Globe Awards '75: Best Actor—Drama (Nicholson), Best Director (Polanski), Best Film—Drama, Best Screenplay, National Film Registry '91; New York Film Critics Awards '74: Best Actor (Nicholson); National Society of Film Critics Awards '74: Best Actor (Nicholson); Writers Guild of America '74: Best Original Screenplay; *NOM:* Academy Awards '74: Best Actor (Nicholson), Best Actress (Dunaway), Best Art Direction/Set Decoration, Best Cinematography, Best Costume Design, Best Director (Polanski), Best Film Editing, Best Picture, Best Sound, Best Original Dramatic Score.

Chinese Box

The complex story of John (Irons), a British journalist in Hong Kong, and Vivian (Li), a bartender, takes place before, during, and after the British handover of the city to the People's Republic of China. The combination of love, death, and history rivals *The English Patient* with its multiple layers of meaning, but somehow the film never caught on with audiences in theatres. On DVD, Wayne Wang's challenging visuals sparkle. Note the levels of dark detail that are revealed in the big New Year's Eve party and crowd scenes. Throughout, Wang commingles natural sounds with Graeme Revell's score and Irons's voice-over narration. The performances are brilliant; the relationships are complicated; the politics are sophisticated. If the film lacks the crowd-pleasing qualities of Wang's *The Joy Luck Club,* it is much more rewarding on other levels. —MM
Movie: 🎬🎬🎬▶ **DVD:** 🎬🎬🎬▶
Trimark Home Video (Cat #6859D, UPC #03139868937). Widescreen letterboxed. Dolby Digital Surround Stereo. $24.99. Keepcase. *LANG:* English; Mandarin. *SUB:* English; French; Spanish. *CAP:* English. *FEATURES:* 24 chapter links ▪ Cast and crew thumbnail biographies.
1997 109m/C *FR JP* Jeremy Irons, Gong Li, Maggie Cheung, Ruben Blades, Michael Hui; **D:** Wayne Wang; **W:** Wayne Wang, Jean-Claude Carriere, Larry Gross, Paul Theroux; **C:** Vilko Filac; **M:** Graeme Revell.

Chinese Connection

A martial arts expert (Lee) tracks down the thugs who killed his teacher. The going is slow between the action sequences that show off the star's superb martial arts skills. Despite some intermittent snowy flecks, the image is crisp, amazingly so, considering the film's age. The dubbing is as poor as it's ever been and the original language is not an option. Mono sound is mono sound. The film was loosely remade as *Fist of Legend* with Jet Li. —MM **AKA:** Fist of Fury; The Iron Hand; Jing Wu Men.
Movie: 🎬🎬▶ **DVD:** 🎬🎬▶
20th Century Fox (Cat #4112551). Widescreen letterboxed. Mono. $99.98. Box set. *LANG:* English. *SUB:* English. *FEATURES:* 22 chapter links. Title is available as part of "Bruce Lee The Master Collection."
1973 (R) 90m/C *HK* Bruce Lee, James Tien, Robert Baker; **D:** Lo Wei; **W:** Lo Wei; **C:** Chen Ching Chu; **M:** Fu-ling Wang.

A Chinese Ghost Story

This is a beautiful love story set in the older days in China. Ling Choi Sin is on his way to Kwok Pak Village when a rainstorm forces him to stay at the Lan Ro Temple for a night. He meets a beautiful lady ghost, Lit Siu Seen. They fall madly in love. However, Lit is controlled by Lau Lau, a true vampire. This DVD features a beautifully sharp and clean image. Although it shows signs of grain at times, the picture conveys plenty of detail and shows no sign of compression artifacts. The colors are rich and all the different hues and shades of the film's fascinating photography are perfectly transferred to this disc. You also find an engrossing 5.1 sound mix that is engaging and very well produced with good use of the Dolby Surround. —GH
Movie: 🎬🎬🎬▶ **DVD:** 🎬🎬🎬▶
Tai Seng Video Marketing (Cat #01324, UPC #164301324000). Widescreen letterboxed. Dolby Digital 5.1. $49.95. Keepcase. *LANG:* Cantonese; Mandarin. *SUB:* English; Japanese; Chinese; Korean; Bahasa; Thai. *FEATURES:* 9 chapter links ▪ Trailers.
1987 93m/C *HK* Leslie Cheung, Wong Tsu Hsien, Wu Ma, Joey Wong; **D:** Ching Siu Tung.

A Chinese Ghost Story II

Chinese horror-romance continues with Ning Tsai-shen (Leslie Cheung) and Nieh Hsiaotsing (Joey Wong) battling more inventive special effects.
Movie: 🎬🎬🎬 **DVD:** NYR
Tai Seng Video Marketing (Cat #19124). $49.95. Keepcase. *LANG:* Cantonese; Mandarin. *SUB:* Bahasa Malaysian & Indonesian; Chinese Simplified & Traditional; English; Japanese; Korean; Thai. *FEATURES:* Cast and crew thumbnail biographies ▪ Production notes ▪ Trailer.
1990 103m/C *HK* Leslie Cheung, Joey Wong, Wu Ma, Jacky Cheung, Michelle Reis, Waise Lee; **D:** Ching Siu Tung.

A Chinese Ghost Story III

A hundred years after the end of *Part 2*, a monk (Leung) and a ghost (Wong) fight supernatural forces.
Movie: 🎬🎬🎬 **DVD:** NYR
Tai Seng Video Marketing (Cat #24394). $49.95. Keepcase. *LANG:* Cantonese; Mandarin. *SUB:* English. *FEATURES:* Cast and crew thumbnail biographies ▪ Production notes ▪ Trailer.
1991 106m/C *HK* Joey Wong, Tony Leung Chiu-Wai, Jacky Cheung; **D:** Ching Siu Tung; **W:** Roy Szeto, Tsui Hark; **C:** Moon-Tong Lau.

Chinese Odyssey, Part One: Pandora's Box

This slapstick fantasy martial arts comedy doesn't translate well across cultural borders. It has to do with magic and characters, both human and divine, who are presumably familiar to Chinese audiences but who are merely silly to the uninitiated. The DVD image is acceptable but the "hex errors" in the subtitles ("Don't snap my pork!") are indicative of the overall humor. The disc contains no chapter links. Followed by a sequel. —MM
Movie: 🎬 **DVD:** 🎬🎬

Tai Seng Video Marketing (Cat #DVD-010). Widescreen letterboxed. Dolby Digital Stereo. $49.98. Keepcase. *LANG:* Cantonese; Mandarin. *SUB:* Chinese; English.
1994 87m/C *HK* Stephen Chow, Athene Chu, Karen Mok; **D:** Jeff Lau.

Chinese Odyssey, Part Two: Cinderalla

The silliness involving Monkey King and Spider Woman continues in a sequel with an identical cast. The funny makeup is even more exaggerated. Again, the use of colored lights and a modest budget keep the image from achieving the crispness that DVD is capable of. No chapter links. —MM
Movie: 🎬▶ **DVD:** 🎬▶
Tai Seng Video Marketing (Cat #DVD-011). Widescreen letterboxed. Dolby Digital Stereo. $49.95. Keepcase. *LANG:* Cantonese; Mandarin. *SUB:* English; Chinese.
1994 99m/C Stephen Chow, Athene Chu, Karen Mok; **D:** Jeff Lau.

Chino / Man with a Camera

Double feature of Bronson. In *Chino*, Bronson sets vengeance aside to play a soft-spoken half-Indian horse dealer who shelters a teenage runaway (Van Patten) and falls for a rival's sister (Ireland). Overall a poor-quality DVD transfer, made from a scratchy print whose colors have faded badly. Sound quality is muffled. *Man with a Camera*—the pilot for a should-have-stayed forgotten '50s black-and-white TV series—sees Bronson miscast as an arch, debonair leading man. Picture quality is faithful to the strange fisheye look of TV from the period, and sound quality is OK. Disc features a rambling yet spine-chilling introduction by Tony Curtis, who wears black gloves as though he plans to strangle somebody. During the movie, the "Delta" ID periodically appears on the lower right corner of the screen—like a TV network ID. Most annoying. It looks like *Man with a Camera* has not been previously available on home video, not that anyone would care. —JE **AKA:** Valdez Horses; The Valdez Horses; Man with a Camera.
Movie: 🎬🎬 **DVD:** 🎬
Delta/Laserlight (Cat #82020, UPC #1811199943). Full frame. $14.99. Keepcase. *LANG:* English; Spanish; Chinese; Japanese. *SUB:* Spanish; Chinese; Japanese. *FEATURES:* 34 chapter links total ▪ Introduction by Tony Curtis ▪ Trailer for *Kid Galahad,* featuring Bronson.
1975 (PG) 97m/C *IT* Charles Bronson, Jill Ireland, Vincent Van Patten; **D:** John Sturges; **W:** Massimo De Rita, Clair Huffaker, Arduino Maiuri; **C:** Armando Nannuzzi; **M:** Guido de Angelis, Maurizio de Angelis.

Chitty Chitty Bang Bang

An eccentric inventor (Van Dyke) spruces up an old car and, in fantasy, takes his children to a land where the evil rulers have forbidden children. Poor special effects and forgettable score stall the effort, which is loosely adapted by Roald Dahl and Hughes from an Ian Fleming story. Why MGM would release this Panavision film in full frame only is beyond me. This could be (and I guess is, except for the aspect ratio) a great DVD. The image is sharp and the colors accurate and vibrant. Grain and artifacts are hard to find. Blacks are true and both contrast and brightness levels are consistent and comfortable. The soundtrack is excellent. The Surround mix puts a lot of space in the effects and music tracks. Highs are well defined and lows are deep but never boomy. —JO

Movie: 🎵🎵 **DVD:** 🎵🎵🎵
MGM Home Entertainment (Cat #907032, UPC #027616703224). Full frame. Dolby Digital 5.1; Dolby Digital Stereo. $24.98. Keepcase. *LANG:* English (DD5.1); French (Stereo). *SUB:* French. *CAP:* English. *FEATURES:* 40 chapter links ▪ Theatrical trailer ▪ Production notes ▪ Sing-a-long.
1968 (G) **142m/C** *GB* Dick Van Dyke, Sally Ann Howes, Lionel Jeffries, Gert Frobe, Anna Quayle, Benny Hill; *D:* Ken Hughes; *W:* Ken Hughes, Roald Dahl; *C:* Christopher Challis; *M:* Richard M. Sherman, Robert B. Sherman. *AWARDS:* NOM: Academy Awards '68: Best Song ("Chitty Chitty Bang Bang").

Chloe in the Afternoon

A married man finds himself inexplicably drawn to an ungainly young woman. Sixth of the "Moral Tales" series is typical of director Rohmer's talky approach. Not for all tastes, but rewarding for those who are drawn to this sort of thing. Preprint material may be the problem with this DVD transfer. Sharpness is adequate and there is no more than the usual WinStar grain, but the colors appear faded and listless. Punching up the contrast would most likely have done the trick. Brightness is comfortable. The blacks are never quite right and are occasionally near gray in appearance. The mono sound is fairly faithful to the film's soundtrack, which is mainly dialogue, but certainly does nothing to enhance the overall feel. —JO *AKA:* L'Amour l'Apres-midi.

Movie: 🎵🎵🎵 **DVD:** 🎵🎵▶
WinStar Home Entertainment (Cat #FLV5018, UPC #720917501826). Full frame. Mono. $29.95. Keepcase. *LANG:* French. *SUB:* English. *FEATURES:* Cast filmographies ▪ 9 chapter links.
1972 (R) **97m/C** *FR* Bernard Verley, Zouzou, Francoise Verley, Daniel Ceccaldi, Malvina Penne, Babette Ferrier, Suzo Randall, Marie-Christine Barrault; *D:* Eric Rohmer; *W:* Eric Rohmer; *C:* Nestor Almendros; *M:* Arie Dzierlatka.

Choices

A deaf athlete (Carafotes) is alienated after being banned from the football team. The film is more noteworthy as the screen debut of Demi Moore in a supporting role.
Movie: 🎵▶ **DVD:** NYR
Essex (Cat #1002). Full frame. $10.97. Keepcase.
1981 90m/C Paul Carafotes, Victor French, Lelia Goldoni, Val Avery, Dennis Patrick, Demi Moore; *D:* Rami Alon; *W:* Rami Alon; *C:* Hanania Baer; *M:* Christopher Stone.

The Chosen One: Legend of the Raven

After her sister Emma (Sand) is murdered, McKenna (Electra) is guided by her shaman father and, at torturous length, becomes an avenging super-heroine. This is far from Troma's best but the plot is loopy. The DVD may be a bit better-looking than the VHS tape, but not much. On his commentary track, director Lanoff does not mention the parsimonious budget he was working with or Ms. Electra's use of a body double in her love scene. —MM
Movie: 🎵🎵 **DVD:** 🎵🎵
Troma Team Video (Cat #9840, UPC #790357984039). Full frame. $24.95. Keepcase. *LANG:* English. *FEATURES:* 9 chapter links ▪ Commentary: director Lawrence Lanoff ▪ Theatrical trailer ▪ Separate comments: producer India Allen ▪ Separate comments: Troma president Lloyd Kaufman ▪ Separate comments: Shauna Sand ▪ "Zebra Woman" publicity stunt ▪ Assorted aromatic extras.
1998 (R) **105m/C** Carmen Electra, Michael Stadvec, David Oliver, Shauna Sand; *D:* Lawrence Lanoff; *W:* Sam Rappaport, Khara Bromiley; *C:* Robert New; *M:* Keith Arem.

Christine

Under Carpenter's usual competent direction, Stephen King's automotive horror is engaging and well made, but not particularly frightening. Bookish teen Arnie (Gordon) becomes the proud owner of a '58 Chrysler that's bad to the bone, and he's changed by it. Dennis (Stockwell) is his friend and protector; Leigh (Paul) falls for the transformed Arnie. The effects are terrific, but the best part of King's novel is his understanding of teenagers and their changeable relationships. That's precisely the side of the story that's left out. The DVD image accurately reflects the theatrical release and so it's only slightly better than VHS tape. Choice of screen size is a more important feature. Sound is fine. —MM
Movie: 🎵🎵▶ **DVD:** 🎵🎵▶
Columbia Tristar Home Video (Cat #1619, UPC #043396016194). Widescreen (2.35:1) letterboxed; full frame. Dolby Digital Surround Stereo. $24.95. Keepcase. *LANG:* English; Portuguese; Spanish. *SUB:* Korean; Portuguese; Spanish; Thai. *CAP:*

English. *FEATURES:* 28 chapter links ▪ Cast and crew filmographies.
1984 (R) **110m/C** Keith Gordon, John Stockwell, Alexandra Paul, Robert Prosky, Harry Dean Stanton, Kelly Preston, Christine Belford, Roberts Blossom, William Ostrander, David Spielberg, Robert Darnell; *D:* John Carpenter; *W:* Bill Phillips; *C:* Donald M. Morgan; *M:* John Carpenter, Alan Howarth.

A Christmas Carol

The Alastair Sim version of the Dickens classic is considered the best by some. (Others prefer the 1984 George C. Scott.) *AKA:* Scrooge.
Movie: 🎵🎵🎵▶ **DVD:** NYR
VCI Home Video (Cat #8215). Full frame. Dolby Digital Mono. $19.99. Keepcase. *FEATURES:* Max Fleischer cartoon "Rudolph the Red-Nosed Reindeer" ▪ Intro by Patrick McNee ▪ Cast and crew thumbnail biographies ▪ Production notes. Title is also available in a colorized version (cat. #8201) for $29.99.
1951 86m/B *GB* Alastair Sim, Kathleen Harrison, Jack Warner, Michael Hordern, Patrick Macnee, Mervyn Johns, Hermione Baddeley, Clifford Mollison, George Cole, Carol Marsh, Miles Malleson, Ernest Thesiger, Hattie Jacques, Peter Bull, Hugh Dempster; *D:* Brian Desmond Hurst; *W:* Noel Langley; *C:* C.M. Pennington-Richards; *M:* Richard Addinsell.

A Christmas Carol

From the opening shot of a horse-drawn hearse, this version of Dickens's famous tale is a ghost story. George C. Scott is one of the screen's finest Scrooges, both the famous "Bah, Humbug!" character and his changed or reborn self. Director Clive Donner creates an almost palpable sense of place with the historic town of Shrewsbury, England. Filled with snow and coal smoke, the film captures that potent combination of horror and character revelation that makes the story so effective. For my money, this is the finest adaptation, and the DVD version is far better than any previous broadcast or tape. It captures Scrooge's gloomy office and his even gloomier bedroom, both dim and difficult to show in detail. Black clothes, so often a problem for this medium, lack some detail too, but that's appropriate for a story about that 3:00 a.m. darkness of the soul. The stereo sound is equally effective in the big scenes. The 3.5 technical rating would be a 4.0 if the disc came with a few more extras. Even so, highly recommended. —MM
Movie: 🎵🎵🎵🎵 **DVD:** 🎵🎵🎵▶
20th Century Fox (Cat #4112751). Full frame. Dolby Digital Surround Stereo. $24.98. Keepcase. *LANG:* English. *SUB:* Spanish. *CAP:* English. *FEATURES:* 22 chapter links.
1984 (PG) **100m/C** George C. Scott, Nigel Davenport, Edward Woodward, Frank Finlay, Lucy Gutteridge, Angela Pleasence, Roger Rees, David Warner, Susannah York;

D: Clive Donner; **W:** Roger O. Hirson; **C:** Tony Imi; **M:** Nick Bicat.

A Christmas Story

Unlikely but winning comedy of a boy's single-minded obsession to acquire a Red Ryder BB gun for Christmas has quickly become a seasonal favorite. One particularly great sequence involves an impatient department store Santa. Fun for everyone. The boy with his tongue stuck to the light pole is none other than Scotty Schwartz (*The Toy*), who has since gone on to be an adult film star. Based on *In God We Trust, All Others Pay Cash,* an autobiographical story by Shepperd. After owning this film on both VHS and laserdisc, it was great to get this DVD, which is a substantial improvement over both. The image is much sharper and no digital grain is added. Colors are both warmer and brighter and don't bleed no matter how deep the hue. The blacks have occasional problems but are overall very good. The mono soundtrack is full-bodied and clear. —*JO*
Movie: 🎵🎵🎵 **DVD:** 🎵🎵🎵▶
MGM Home Entertainment (Cat #906558, UPC #027616655820). Full frame. Dolby Digital Mono. $24.98. Snapper. *LANG:* English; Spanish; French. *SUB:* English; Spanish; French. *CAP:* English. *FEATURES:* 32 chapter links ▪ Theatrical trailer.
1983 (PG) 95m/C Peter Billingsley, Darren McGavin, Melinda Dillon, Ian Petrella; **D:** Bob (Benjamin) Clark; **W:** Bob (Benjamin) Clark, Leigh Brown, Jean Shepherd; **C:** Reginald Morris; **M:** Paul Zaza, Carl Zittrer. *AWARDS:* Genie Awards '84: Best Director (Clark).

Chronos

While no *Baraka* or *Koyaanisqatsi,* this film looks at many similar subjects, using similar filming techniques (including time-lapse and sped-up motion), all set to a New Age–like score. This is a fine Simitar DVD, featuring all kinds of lighting conditions, incredible fast motion, and shots with huge amounts of detail. The disc handles it all very well and the PCM stereo track conveys the accompanying music with equal energy. —*JO*
Movie: 🎵🎵🎵 **DVD:** 🎵🎵🎵▶
Simitar Entertainment (Cat #7323, UPC #082551732326). Full frame. PCM Stereo. $19.98. Snapper. *LANG:* English. *FEATURES:* 9 chapter links.
1987 40m/C D: Ron Fricke; **W:** Constantine Nicholas, Genevieve Nicholas; **C:** Ron Fricke; **M:** Michael Sterns.

Chushingura

Toshiro Mifune leads a group of samurai against the feudal lord who forced their master to commit suicide. The fact-based story is long on character development and intrigue, but short on martial arts action for those expecting the powerful physical action of a similar Kurosawa film. On DVD, this one looks pretty good, considering its age. (The title has not previously been available on tape.) —*MM*
Movie: 🎵🎵▶ **DVD:** 🎵🎵▶
Image Entertainment (Cat #4570). Widescreen (2.35:1) letterboxed. Dolby Digital Mono. $34.99. Snapper. *LANG:* Japanese. *SUB:* English.
1962 207m/C *JP* Toshiro Mifune, Yuzo Kayama, Koshiro Matsumoto, Chusha Ichikawa, Yoko Tsukasa, Setsuko Hara, Tatsuya Mihashi, Yosuke Natsuki; **D:** Hiroshi Inagaki; **W:** Toshio Yasumi; **C:** Kazuo Yamada; **M:** Akira Ifukube.

Cinderella

Disney's sparkling update of the Rodgers & Hammerstein telemusical is highlighted by winning performances, new songs, and multiracial casting. Singer Norwood is sweetly sincere in the title role, and Houston, who also produced, makes a show-stopping Fairy Godmother. Peters camps it up as the wicked stepmother, and Goldberg has a fresh take on the role of mother-of-the-groom (a handsome, charming Montalban). Alexander, as the prince's confidante, also surprises. The score has been augmented with more Rodgers tunes. The production's lavish, colorful sets and costumes transfer beautifully to DVD, and the musical performances sound lush and balanced. —*JE* *AKA:* Rodgers & Hammerstein's Cinderella.
Movie: 🎵🎵▶ **DVD:** 🎵🎵🎵
Buena Vista Home Entertainment (Cat #0788817809, UPC #1795100424). Full frame. Dolby Digital 5.1 Stereo. $29.99. Keepcase. *LANG:* English. *CAP:* English. *FEATURES:* 20 chapter links ▪ "Making of" featurette ▪ Theatrical trailer.
1997 88m/C Brandy Norwood, Whitney Houston, Paolo Montalban, Jason Alexander, Bernadette Peters, Whoopi Goldberg, Victor Garber; **D:** Robert Iscove; **W:** Robert Freedman; **M:** Richard Rodgers, Oscar Hammerstein.

Circle of Friends

Nostalgic Irish coming-of-age tale focuses on three friends (Driver, Burrows, O'Rawe), and the pressures they face when hearts and hormones conflict with a strict 1950s Catholic upbringing. As a priest says, "young girls' bodies are a garden for Jesus or a vessel for sin!" Benny (Driver) and her unsteady relationship with the hunky Jack Foley (O'Donnell) are at the heart of the story. Which will it be, garden or vessel? Despite a measured pace, the film never seems slow and it avoids the most blatantly manipulative aspects of the subject. A fine transfer to DVD makes the most of Irish locations and '50s nostalgia. Both image and sound are excellent. —*MM*
Movie: 🎵🎵🎵 **DVD:** 🎵🎵🎵
HBO Home Video (Cat #91214, UPC #026359121425). Widescreen (1.66:1) anamorphic. Dolby Digital 5.1 Surround Stereo; Dolby Digital Surround Stereo. $24.98. Keepcase. *LANG:* English; French; Spanish. *SUB:* English; French; Spanish.

FEATURES: 35 chapter links ▪ Theatrical trailer and TV spots ▪ Cast and crew thumbnail bios.
1994 (PG-13) 96m/C Chris O'Donnell, Minnie Driver, Geraldine O'Rawe, Saffron Burrows, Colin Firth, Alan Cumming, Aidan Gillen; **D:** Pat O'Connor; **W:** Andrew Davies; **C:** Kenneth Macmillan; **M:** Michael Kamen.

The Circus

One of Chaplin's greatest silent comedies finds the Little Tramp joining (and saving) a downtrodden traveling circus. Of course he falls for the daughter (Kennedy) of the nasty ringmaster (Garcia). The film contains some of the star's best physical comedy and it's less sentimental than many of his features. He won a special Academy Award for "versatility and genius in writing, acting, directing, and producing" for this one. Grand final scenes. Most of Chaplin's work has arrived on DVD in excellent shape but *The Circus* is particularly sharp. The image is near perfect—for once, the score matches it—and the disc contains a wealth of extras. Recommended. —*MM*
Movie: 🎵🎵🎵▶ **DVD:** 🎵🎵🎵▶
Image Entertainment (Cat #ID9180CUDVD, UPC #014381918021). Full frame. Dolby Digital Mono. $24.99. Snapper. *LANG:* Silent. *SUB:* English intertitles. *FEATURES:* 15 chapter links ▪ Notes on music ▪ Unused footage with commentary by David Shepard ▪ Production records and summary ▪ Sketches and press book.
1919 105m/B Charlie Chaplin, Merna Kennedy, Allan Garcia; **D:** Charlie Chaplin; **W:** Charlie Chaplin; **C:** Roland H. Totheroh; **M:** Charlie Chaplin. *AWARDS: NOM:* Academy Awards '28: Best Actor (Chaplin), Best Director (Chaplin).

City Hall

The first half of this film is a realistic look at contemporary big city politics. The second half is a disappointing crime story. The whole is less than the sum of the two parts. Al Pacino is John Pappas, the ambitious Democratic mayor of New York. John Cusack is his savvy young aide who tries to sort through a nasty bit of judicial corruption. Aiello is a Brooklyn boss; Franciosa is a publicity-shy mobster; Fonda is the obligatory love interest. The screenplay was originally conceived by Ken Lipper who was once deputy mayor under Ed Koch, but the involvement of three other writers causes considerable confusion. The DVD looks fine, even in the darker night exteriors, and it handles potential problems like narrow bamboo strip shades without a hitch. —*MM*
Movie: 🎵🎵🎵 **DVD:** 🎵🎵🎵
Warner Home Video, Inc. (Cat #C2523, UPC #053939252323). Full frame; widescreen letterboxed. Dolby Digital Surround Stereo. $19.98. Snapper. *LANG:* English; French. *SUB:* English; French. *CAP:* English. *FEATURES:* 30 chapter links.
1995 (R) 111m/C Al Pacino, John Cusack, Bridget Fonda, Danny Aiello, David

Paymer, Martin Landau, Anthony (Tony) Franciosa, Lindsay Duncan, Nestor Serrano, Mel Winkler, Richard Schiff; **D:** Harold Becker; **W:** Paul Schrader, Nicholas Pileggi, Bo Goldman, Ken Lipper; **C:** Michael Seresin; **M:** Jerry Goldsmith.

City Hunter

This cinematic comic book is so silly that it makes star Jackie Chan's *Rush Hour* look like *King Lear*. It's *Die Hard on a Ship* with Jackie as private eye Man Bor. The action is bright, fast, and frivolous and the DVD re-creates the candy-colored set pieces well enough, though reds tend to glow and there are a lot of reds. The special effects don't fare as well, most notably in a scene where Jackie and the bad guy become characters in the "Streetfighter" video game. —*MM*
Movie: 𝄢𝄢𝄢 **DVD:** 𝄢𝄢𝄢
Tai Seng Video Marketing (Cat #MS/DVD/062/99). Widescreen letterboxed. Dolby Digital 5.1 Surround Stereo. $49.95. Keepcase. *LANG:* Cantonese; Mandarin. *SUB:* Traditional Chinese; Simplified Chinese; English; Japanese; Bahasa Malaysia; Thai; Vietnamese; English. *FEATURES:* 9 chapter links • Cast and crew thumbnail biographies • Theatrical trailer • Production notes.
1992 95m/C Jackie Chan, Joey Want, Chingmy Yau, Gary Daniels, Leon Lai, Richard Norton; **D:** Wong Jing; **W:** Wong Jing; **C:** Le Chi Hang.

City Lights

Along with *Modern Times,* this is Chaplin's masterpiece, a silent film made at the dawn of the sound era (and re-released in 1950). The Little Tramp falls in love with a blind flower girl (Cherrill) and manages to finance the operation that will restore her sight. As always, the filmmaker is wearing his heart on his sleeve but he maintains the right balance of comedy, sentiment, and tragedy. Other Chaplin films on DVD have set a high standard, but, like *The Circus,* this one surpasses it. The clarity of the image is simply superb, and special attention has been paid to Chaplin's soundtrack. It's available in both the original version and a new version recorded in rich stereo by Carl Davis in 1989. (Switch between the two; the difference is astonishing.) Every serious student of film should have a copy. —*MM*
Movie: 𝄢𝄢𝄢𝄢 **DVD:** 𝄢𝄢𝄢𝄢
Image Entertainment (Cat #ID9181CUDVD, UPC #014381918120). Full frame. Dolby Digital Mono; PCM Stereo. $24.99. Snapper. *LANG:* Silent. *FEATURES:* 20 chapter links • Interview with conductor Carl Davis • Original story notes • Promotional material • Financial statements on production.
1931 86m/B Charlie Chaplin, Virginia Cherrill, Florence Lee, Hank Mann, Harry Myers, Henry Bergman, Jean Harlow; **D:** Charlie Chaplin; **W:** Charlie Chaplin; **C:** Roland H. Totheroh, Gordon Pollock; **M:** Alfred Newman, Charlie Chaplin. *AWARDS:*

American Film Institute (AFI) '98: Top 100, National Film Registry '91.

City of Angels

Weepy American remake of Wim Wenders's *Wings of Desire* finds guardian angel Seth (Cage) falling in love with heart surgeon Maggie (Ryan) and then trying to decide whether he wants to become mortal in order to join her. Subtle, it is not. Cage does his doe-eyed best to convey Seth's longing and innocence to earthly ways, and the chemistry with Ryan really clicks. Overly sappy and sentimental, especially near the end, but that won't stop the intended audience from loving it. Big Hollywood flick that wears its arthouse aspirations on its sleeve. The film is presented on one side of the DVD and the second side is taken up by an extensive supplemental section that is of more interest than the movie itself and provides many insights, especially when combined with the feature commentaries on the first side. The image is very sharp and detailed with very little grain or artifacts. Colors and blacks are accurate and the contrast levels work well in all lighting conditions. Unfortunately, the soundtrack is a little dull. While everything can be heard, a more ambient mix, combined with a lowering of the mids and tweaking of the highs, would have greatly improved things. —*JO*
Movie: 𝄢𝄢 **DVD:** 𝄢𝄢𝄢
Warner Home Video, Inc. (Cat #16320, UPC #085391632023). Widescreen letterboxed. Dolby Digital 5.1; Dolby Digital Stereo. $24.98. Snapper. *LANG:* English (DD5.1); French (Stereo). *SUB:* French. *CAP:* English. *FEATURES:* 40 chapter links • 5 theatrical trailers • Deleted scenes with commentaries • Multiple commentaries • "Making of" featurette; effects documentary • Music videos • Production notes.
1998 (PG-13) 117m/C Nicolas Cage, Meg Ryan, Andre Braugher, Dennis Franz, Colm Feore, Robin Bartlett, Joanna Merlin; **D:** Brad Silberling; **W:** Dana Stevens; **C:** John Seale; **M:** Gabriel Yared. *AWARDS: NOM:* Golden Globe Awards '99: Best Song ("Uninvited"); MTV Movie Awards '99: Best On-Screen Duo (Meg Ryan/Nicolas Cage), Best Song ("Iris").

The City of Lost Children

Profoundly weird and definitely not-for-the-kiddies fairytale finds crazed inventor Krank (Emilfork) setting his one-eyed minions, the appropriately named Cyclops, to kidnap children so that he can steal their dreams. (Krank himself is incapable of dreaming.) The latest victim is young Denree (Lucien), adopted brother of sideshow strongman One (Perlman), who single-mindedly pursues a way to get Denree back, aided by nine-year-old feral child Miette (Vittet) and a band of orphan thieves. On their commentary track, recorded six years after the fact, Perlman and the filmmakers admit that the film is

difficult to understand on a conventional narrative level, but that does not dim their enthusiasm. The DVD image is superb, capturing the incredible sets, which are reminiscent of an even more nightmarish version of Pleasure Island from *Pinocchio*. Both sub- and supertitles are employed for those who prefer the original French dialogue. Admittedly, such a visually ambitious film loses something on anything but a large theatre screen, but I could find no flaws with the widescreen presentation. Strongly recommended. —*MM* **AKA:** La Cite des Enfants Perdus.
Movie: 𝄢𝄢𝄢 **DVD:** 𝄢𝄢𝄢
Columbia Tristar Home Video (Cat #40019, UPC #043396400191). Widescreen (1.85:1) letterboxed; full frame. Dolby Digital Surround Stereo; Stereo. $28.95. Keepcase. *LANG:* French; English; Spanish. *SUB:* English; French; Spanish. *FEATURES:* 28 chapter links • Commentary track • Costume design gallery • Production sketch gallery • Cast and crew thumbnail biographies • Theatrical trailers.
1995 (R) 114m/C **FR** Ron Perlman, Daniel Emilfork, Joseph Lucien, Judith Vittet, Dominique Pinon, Jean Claude Dreyfus, Odile Mallet, Genevieve Brunet, Mireille Mosse; **D:** Jean-Pierre Jeunet, Marc Caro; **W:** Jean-Pierre Jeunet, Marc Caro, Gilles Adrien; **C:** Darius Khondji; **M:** Angelo Badalamenti; **V:** Jean-Louis Trintignant. *AWARDS:* Cesar Awards '96: Best Art Direction/Set Decoration; *NOM:* Cesar Awards '96: Best Cinematography, Best Costume Design, Best Score; Independent Spirit Awards '96: Best Foreign Film.

City on Fire

Hong Kong answer to *The French Connection* finds an undercover detective out to foil a jewel thievery syndicate. This is the movie that Quentin Tarantino borrowed heavily from for his brutal failed-caper flick *Reservoir Dogs*. It's one of the best of the Asian noirish crime films. Maybe someday *City on Fire* will get the DVD treatment it deserves. While very watchable, this DVD version is of only average sharpness, and the colors are generally pretty weak. There is some film damage, but not any more than the average Tai Seng release. The 5.1 sound is boisterous enough but lacking in the Surround department. —*JO*
Movie: 𝄢𝄢 **DVD:** 𝄢𝄢
Tai Seng Video Marketing (Cat #5061, UPC #164301364000). Widescreen (2.35:1) anamorphic. Dolby Digital 5.1. $49.95. Keepcase. *LANG:* Mandarin; Cantonese. *SUB:* English; Japanese; Chinese; Korean; Vietnamese; Bahasa; Thai. *CAP:* Mandarin; Cantonese. *FEATURES:* 9 chapter links.
1987 98m/C **HK** Chow Yun-Fat, Sun Yueh, Danny Lee, Carrie Ng, Roy Cheung; **D:** Ringo Lam; **W:** Tommy Sham; **C:** Andrew Lau; **M:** Teddy Robin Kwan.

City War

Fine performances by two leads elevate an otherwise unremarkable revenge-crime story. Chow Yun-Fat is a hair-trigger emotional cop; Ti Lung is a more thoughtful police negotiator. Both of them are targets of a gangster who has been released from prison. Director Sun Chung adds a slapstick element to John Woo–inspired action. The DVD image is good but not spectacular. The chemistry between the stars is the reason to watch this one. —MM

Movie: 🎬🎬🎬 **DVD:** 🎬🎬▶
Tai Seng Video Marketing (Cat #5144, UPC #601643014043). Widescreen letterboxed. Dolby Digital 5.1 Surround Stereo. $49.95. Keepcase. *LANG:* Cantonese; Mandarin. *SUB:* Traditional Chinese; Simplified Chinese; Japanese; Bahasa (Indonesia); Bahasa (Malaysia); Thai; Korean; English; Vietnamese. *CAP:* English. *FEATURES:* 8 chapter links ▪ Cast and crew thumbnail biographies ▪ Theatrical trailers.
1989 100m/C *CH* Chow Yun-Fat, Ti Lung, Tien Niu; *D:* Sun Chung; *W:* Tung Lu, Chung Kai Cheong, Leung Wai Ting; *C:* Lee Sun Yip.

A Civil Action

Low-keyed, slowly paced legal thriller doesn't contain many thrills. Jan Schlichtmann (Travolta) is a flashy personal injury lawyer whose defense of his profession is half-hearted at best. Approached by a grieving mother (Quinlan), he takes on an environmental case that drags on for years and threatens to destroy his small firm. Robert Duvall steals the show as the homespun Harvard lawyer representing one of the companies. The DVD handles the nonaction well enough in courtroom, boardroom, and hallway scenes. Black suits and overcoats lose some definition and diagonal lines break, but those are not a serious problem. The relative coolness of image and sound is appropriate. —MM

Movie: 🎬🎬▶ **DVD:** 🎬🎬🎬
Buena Vista Home Entertainment (Cat #16790, UPC #717951001917). Widescreen (1.85:1) letterboxed. Dolby Digital 5.1 Surround Stereo. $29.99. Snapper. *LANG:* English; French. *CAP:* English. *FEATURES:* 25 chapter links ▪ "Making of" featurette ▪ Theatrical trailer.
1998 (PG-13) 115m/C John Travolta, Robert Duvall, Kathleen Quinlan, Tony Shalhoub, Zeljko Ivanek, John Lithgow, William H. Macy, Bruce Norris, Sydney Pollack, Peter Jacobson; *D:* Steven Zaillian; *W:* Steven Zaillian; *C:* Conrad Hall; *M:* Danny Elfman. *AWARDS:* Screen Actors Guild Award '98: Best Supporting Actor (Duvall); *NOM:* Academy Awards '98: Best Cinematography, Best Supporting Actor (Duvall); Golden Globe Awards '99: Best Supporting Actor (Duvall); Writers Guild of America '98: Best Adapted Screenplay.

Claire's Knee

A diplomat (Brialy) about to be married goes on holiday in the Alps and develops a fixation on a young girl, particularly, on her knee. Fans of Rohmer know that his explorations of desire are talky and lan-

guidly paced, and this one is no exception. Some think it is his best. It's certainly one of his most scenic, making the most of Lake Geneva. The muted pastel colors and dim lighting are also typical of his "moral tales." DVD can do little to improve the image. The subtitles are exceptionally easy to read. —MM *AKA:* Le Genou de Claire.

Movie: 🎬🎬🎬▶ **DVD:** 🎬🎬▶
WinStar Home Entertainment (Cat #FLV5019, UPC #720917501925). Full frame. $29.98. Keepcase. *LANG:* French. *SUB:* English. *FEATURES:* 9 chapter links ▪ Cast and credits ▪ Filmographies and awards.
1971 105m/C *FR* Jean-Claude Brialy, Aurora Cornu, Beatrice Romand, Laurence De Monaghan, Gerard Falconetti; *D:* Eric Rohmer; *W:* Eric Rohmer; *C:* Nestor Almendros. *AWARDS:* National Society of Film Critics Awards '71: Best Film.

The Clan of the Cave Bear

A scrawny cavegirl (Hannah) is taken by Neanderthals after her parents are killed. Hannah is lifeless as the primitive gamine, and the film is similarly DOA. Despite a script by John Sayles, from Jean Auel's popular novel, it's ponderous and only unintentionally funny.

Movie: 🎬▶ **DVD:** NYR
Warner Home Video, Inc. (Cat #13753). Widescreen (2.35:1) letterboxed; full frame. $19.98. Snapper. *LANG:* English. *SUB:* French. *CAP:* English.
1986 (R) 100m/C Daryl Hannah, James Remar, Pamela Reed, John Doolittle, Thomas G. Waites; *D:* Michael Chapman; *W:* John Sayles; *C:* Jan De Bont; *M:* Alan Silvestri. *AWARDS: NOM:* Academy Awards '86: Best Makeup.

Class of Nuke 'Em High

Team Troma goes after the nuclear power industry with crazily violent results. Tromaville high school becomes a hotbed of mutants and maniacs after the power plant contaminates the water. Good teens Chrissy (Brady) and Warren (Brenton) go bad and that's only the beginning. Followed by two sequels to date. The DVD looks very good, presenting the low-budget craziness in its clearest form. Of course, the disc also contains all the bells and whistles. Codirector Lloyd Kaufman's commentary track is restrained but he makes his political points unambiguously. He also explains why he has worked under different names. Most of the time, though, he focuses on the making of the film. —MM

Movie: 🎬🎬🎬 **DVD:** 🎬🎬🎬
Troma Team Video (Cat #9200, UPC #790357920037). Full frame. $24.95. Keepcase. *LANG:* English. *FEATURES:* 9 chapter links ▪ Stills gallery ▪ Cast comments ▪ Commentary: director Lloyd Kaufman ▪ 7 "lost" scenes ▪ Several other humorous Troma-centric featurettes.

1986 (R) 84m/C Janelle Brady, Gilbert Brenton, Robert Prichard, R.L. Ryan, Theo Cohan, Diana De Vries, Brad Dunker, Gary Schneider; *D:* Richard W. Haines, Lloyd (Samuel Weil) Kaufman; *W:* Richard W. Haines, Lloyd (Samuel Weil) Kaufman, Mark Rudnitsky, Stuart Strutin.

Clay Pigeons

Bodies are piling up in a sleepy Montana town after cowboy trucker Lester (Vaughn) shows up. Clay Birdwell (Phoenix), who's not completely innocent, finds himself a prime suspect after a series of bizarre twists stemming from his affair with his recently deceased best friend's wife (Cates). Clay and Lester quickly become best buddies. Problem is, the FBI has shown up and Lester disappears, leaving Clay to take the heat. Outstanding performances all around, particularly from Vaughn who goes near, but never over the top. The DVD boasts a bright sharp image that makes the curious color scheme particularly bilious. Sound is fine. —MM

Movie: 🎬🎬▶ **DVD:** 🎬🎬🎬
USA Home Entertainment (Cat #440 056 531-2, UPC #044005653120). Widescreen letterboxed; full frame. Dolby Digital 5.1 Surround Stereo; Dolby Digital Surround Stereo. $19.95. Keepcase. *LANG:* English. *SUB:* French. *CAP:* English. *FEATURES:* 18 chapter links ▪ Trailer ▪ Cast and crew thumbnail bios.
1998 (R) 104m/C Vince Vaughn, Joaquin Rafael (Leaf) Phoenix, Janeane Garofalo, Scott Wilson, Georgina Cates, Phil Morris, Vince Vieluf, Nikki Arlyn, Monica Moench, Joseph D. Reitman, Gregory Sporleder; *D:* David Dobkin; *W:* Matthew Healy; *C:* Eric Alan Edwards; *M:* John Lurie.

Clean and Sober

A drug addict hides out at a rehabilitation clinic and actually undergoes treatment. This serious, subtle, and realistic look at the physical/emotional detoxification of an obnoxious, substance-abusing real estate broker is unpredictable and powerful without moralizing. Keaton is fine in the unsympathetic lead, with both Baker and Freeman excelling in lesser roles. Not for all tastes, but it's certainly a worthwhile work. Caron, creator of TV's *Moonlighting*, debuts here as director. There are exceptions, but a lot of these Warner $14.98 full-frame DVDs are overly grainy and not that sharp. This one is still viewable, but its image never rises above average. Colors are washed-out and blacks are gray and grainy. The sound is O.K. —JO

Movie: 🎬🎬🎬▶ **DVD:** 🎬▶
Warner Home Video, Inc. (Cat #11824, UPC #085391182429). Full frame. Dolby Surround. $14.98. Snapper. *LANG:* English. *CAP:* English. *FEATURES:* 3 chapter links.
1988 (R) 124m/C Michael Keaton, Kathy Baker, Morgan Freeman, M. Emmet Walsh, Claudia Christian, Pat Quinn, Ben Piazza, Brian Benben, Luca Bercovici, Tate Dono-

van, Henry Judd Baker, Mary Catherine Martin; **D:** Glenn Gordon Caron; **W:** Tod Carroll; **C:** Jan Kiesser; **M:** Gabriel Yared. *AWARDS:* National Society of Film Critics Awards '88: Best Actor (Keaton).

Clear and Present Danger

Ford returns for a second go at CIA agent Jack Ryan in the third installment of Tom Clancy's best-selling adventures. With the Cold War over, the U.S. government is the bad guy as Ryan discovers a link between a South American drug cartel and a Presidential advisor. Viewers will also finally get an answer to that nagging question at the end of *Patriot Games:* is it a boy or a girl? Archer's back as Ryan's annoying wife, and Birch and Jones also return. Keep alert for complex plot twists in lieu of tons of action, though there's enough to keep action fans happy. For a demonstration of what good sound can do to an action sequence, skip ahead to the roof-top rocket attack on the SUV caravan. The Surround is killer, the bass booming, and the sound harshly realistic overall. The rocket hits and crunching metal are terrifying. The DVD also has a very sharp picture and excellent color. —*JO*
Movie: ♫♫► ***DVD:*** ♫♫♫►
Paramount Home Video (Cat #324637, UPC #097363246374). Widescreen (2.35:1) letterboxed. Dolby Digital 5.1; Dolby Surround. $29.99. Keepcase. *LANG:* English; French. *SUB:* Spanish. *CAP:* English. *FEATURES:* 23 chapter links ● Theatrical trailer.
1994 (PG-13) 141m/C Harrison Ford, Anne Archer, James Earl Jones, Willem Dafoe, Thora Birch, Henry Czerny, Harris Yulin, Raymond Cruz, Joaquim de Almeida, Miguel Sandoval, Donald Moffat, Theodore (Ted) Raimi, Dean Jones; **D:** Phillip Noyce; **W:** John Milius, Donald Stewart, Steven Zaillian; **C:** Donald McAlpine; **M:** James Horner. *AWARDS:* Blockbuster Entertainment Awards '95: Action Actor, Theatrical (Ford); Blockbuster Entertainment Awards '96: Action Actor, Video (Ford); *NOM:* Academy Awards '94: Best Sound; MTV Movie Awards '95: Best Action Sequence.

Cleopatra

During its initial TV broadcast, this lavish miniseries about the Egyptian empress was famous for its sexy ad campaign, and, remarkably, the finished product lives up to it. Cleopatra (Varela) looks quite fetching in her various translucent cotton robes. The familiar story concerns the political and military machinations of Julius Caesar (Dalton) and Marc Anthony (Zane). By small-screen standards, it's a lush production, but it's certainly not going to make anyone forget the Taylor-Burton version. The few-extras DVD is a marginal improvement over VHS tape in image and sound, but that's all. —*MM*
Movie: ♫♫ ***DVD:*** ♫♫►
Hallmark Home Entertainment (Cat #10514). Full frame. Dolby Digital Stereo.

$19.98. Keepcase. *LANG:* English. *FEATURES:* Production notes ● Trailer ● Cast and crew thumbnail bios ● Cleopatra's Hidden Treasure game ● 25 chapter links.
1999 139m/C Leonor Varela, Timothy Dalton, Billy Zane, Rupert Graves, Art Malik, John Bowe, Nadim Sawalha, Owen Teale, Daragh O'Malley, Sean Pertwee, Bruce Payne, Caroline Langrishe; **D:** Franc Roddam; **W:** Stephen Harrigan, Anton Diether; **C:** David Connell; **M:** Trevor Jones.

Cleopatra Jones

Lean and lethal government agent with considerable martial arts prowess takes on a pack of loathsome drug lords run by Winters. Dobson is fetching as the butt-kicking lead in this fast-paced violent blaxploitation flick. This film did not look as good in the theatre as it does on this DVD, once again proving that even a cheap DVD can look great. The picture is very sharp and not hindered by either grain or artifacts. There is a little color bleed in a couple of spots, but overall the colors are lush and accurate. Blacks are true and complemented by balanced contrast and brightness levels. The power in this mono soundtrack should blow you away with its thumping bass and crisp high end. Surround is barely missed. —*JO*
Movie: ♫♫ ***DVD:*** ♫♫♫►
Warner Home Video, Inc. (Cat #11275, UPC #085391127529). Widescreen (2.35:1) anamorphic. Dolby Digital Mono. $14.98. Snapper. *LANG:* English. *CAP:* English. *FEATURES:* 28 chapter links.
1973 (PG) 89m/C Tamara Dobson, Shelley Winters, Bernie Casey, Brenda Sykes, Albert "Poppy" Popwell; **D:** Jack Starrett; **W:** Max Julien, Sheldon Keller; **C:** David M. Walsh; **M:** J.J. Johnson.

Clerks

Day in the life of a bored convenience store clerk (O'Halloran) and his best friend Randal, who mans the video store next door. Nothing much actually happens other than a constant parade of crazies, a hockey game on the roof, and even a little necrophilia. Lots of scuzzy fun and non-stop offensive (and hilarious) dialogue. First-time director Smith (Silent Bob in the movie) based this low-budget ($27,575) film on his four years of tormenting customers at the convenience store where he shot on location. The big plus is that the DVD offers all the extras that first appeared on the laserdisc, including the alternate ending and deleted scenes. Unfortunately, the video itself looks far worse than the VHS tape. There's so much grain that on most movies it would be unbearable; but because the film's style is so deliberately rough, that's not too aggravating. The contrast and brightness levels are good (about the same as the laserdisc), and the sound is very good, in fact almost too good when the music cuts come in. The bottom line is that, despite the picture, this DVD is worth

adding to your collection even if it's just for the supplemental material. —*JO*
Movie: ♫♫♫ ***DVD:*** ♫►
Miramax Pictures Home Video (Cat #17365, UPC #717951002716). Widescreen (1.85:1) letterboxed. Dolby Surround. $34.98. Keepcase. *LANG:* English. *CAP:* English. *FEATURES:* 19 chapter links ● Theatrical trailer ● Alternate ending ● Deleted scenes ● Commentary: director Smith and cast members ● Soul Asylum music video.
1994 (R) 89m/B Brian O'Halloran, Jeff Anderson, Marilyn Ghigliotti, Lisa Spoonhauer, Jason Mewes; **Cameos:** Kevin Smith; **D:** Kevin Smith; **W:** Kevin Smith; **C:** David Klein; **M:** Scott Angley. *AWARDS:* Sundance Film Festival '94: Filmmakers Trophy; *NOM:* Independent Spirit Awards '95: Best First Feature, Debut Performance (Anderson), First Screenplay.

The Client

Grisham thriller mixes well-drawn characters with flat stereotypes. The film begins with an intriguing premise and arrives at a comparatively weak conclusion; and it's about 15 minutes too long. Less-than-perfect attorney Reggie Love (Sarandon) is hired by Mark Sway (Renfro), an 11-year-old who has witnessed a murder. They've got vicious gangsters on one side, and an ambitious prosecutor (Jones) on the other. The big scenes—chases and confrontations—make the transition to DVD with ease, though they don't really generate much tension in any medium. Director Joel Schumacher stages them well enough but, like so many action sequences, they're illogical, and there's nothing fresh about them. The many night scenes are as clear on disc as they were in the theatrical release. In the end, the DVD is appropriate for a glossy, big-budget potboiler. —*MM*
Movie: ♫♫► ***DVD:*** ♫♫♫
Warner Home Video, Inc. (Cat #13233, UPC #085391323327). Widescreen letterboxed. Dolby Digital Surround Stereo. $24.98. Snapper. *LANG:* English; French; Spanish. *SUB:* English; French; Spanish. *CAP:* English. *FEATURES:* 47 chapter links ● Cast and crew thumbnail biographies ● Production notes ● Theatrical trailer.
1994 (PG-13) 121m/C Susan Sarandon, Tommy Lee Jones, Brad Renfro, Mary-Louise Parker, Anthony LaPaglia, Bradley Whitford, Anthony Edwards, Ossie Davis, Walter Olkewicz, J.T. Walsh, Will Patton, Anthony Heald, William H. Macy; **D:** Joel Schumacher; **W:** Robert Getchell, Akiva Goldsman; **C:** Tony Pierce-Roberts. *AWARDS:* British Academy Awards '94: Best Actress (Sarandon); *NOM:* Academy Awards '94: Best Actress (Sarandon); Screen Actors Guild Award '94: Best Actress (Sarandon).

Cliffhanger

In an action-packed thriller, expert climber Gabe Walker (Stallone) faces his greatest challenge when criminal mastermind Lithgow and his henchman appear on the scene. Turner plays fellow climber and love interest. Lithgow makes a particularly convincing, if not downright chilling, murderous thief. Filmed in the Italian Alps with a budget of $70 million–plus, the film boasts stunning cinematography and breathtaking footage of the Dolomite mountain range. Harlin's expert pacing and direction combine to produce maximum thrills and suspense. Finally, a DVD that features snow-cover mountaintops that aren't awash in digital grain. The picture is very sharp and distortion-free even along the almost constant high-contrast lines. Colors are rich and accurate, from the deep blue skies to the subtleties of a facial complexion. Excellent contrast levels accent details even when the entire screen is nearly filled with bright white snow. Blacks are near perfect. This much action has to be heard as well as seen, and the 5.1 sound gives its all. Explosions bounce around you as they echo through the mountain passes, avalanches rumble, and through the cacophony, the music remains boisterous, and the dialogue way out front. —*JO*

Movie: ♫♫♫ **DVD:** ♫♫♫▸
Columbia Tristar Home Video (Cat #52239, UPC #043396511398). Widescreen (2.35:1) anamorphic; full frame. Dolby Digital 5.1; Dolby Digital 2.0. $28.95. Keepcase. *LANG:* English. *CAP:* English. *FEATURES:* 51 chapter links.
1993 (R) 113m/C Sylvester Stallone, John Lithgow, Michael Rooker, Janine Turner, Rex Linn, Caroline Goodall, Leon, Paul Winfield, Ralph Waite, Craig Fairbrass, Michelle Joyner, Max Perlich; *D:* Renny Harlin; *W:* Sylvester Stallone, Michael France; *C:* Alex Thomson; *M:* Trevor Jones. *AWARDS: NOM:* Academy Awards '93: Best Sound, Best Sound Effects Editing, Best Visual Effects; MTV Movie Awards '94: Best Action Sequence.

The Climb

An indescribable opening scene introduces young Danny Himes (Smith), his single dad Earl (Strathairn), and their next door neighbor, Langer (Hurt), a grizzled chain-smoking whisky-soaked old coot who's getting ready to die. The setting is Baltimore, 1959. The subject is courage. Earl did not serve in Korea; Danny is trying to gather the guts to climb a 200-foot radio tower. Despite that offbeat premise, the family drama delivers the goods with superb performances in the leads, a fair evocation of the period as I remember it, and a well-constructed if predictable story. On DVD, the visuals are less impressive than the writing. The film has a rough-edged low-budget look, which is not inappropriate to the story. Sound is acceptable. —*MM*

Movie: ♫♫♫ **DVD:** ♫♫▸
Vanguard International Cinema, Inc. (UPC #658769993233). Full frame. $29.95. Keepcase. *LANG:* English. *FEATURES:* 8 chapter links.

1997 (PG-13) 94m/C *FR NZ* Gregory Smith, John Hurt, David Strathairn, Stephen McHattie, Seth Smith, Sarah Buxton; *D:* Bob Swaim; *W:* Vince McKewin; *C:* Allen Guilford; *M:* Greco Casadeus.

Clockers

Strike (Phifer), leader of a group of bottom-feeding drug dealers ("clockers"), engages in a power struggle with his boss (Lindo), his do-the-right-thing brother Victor (Washington), and his own conscience. He's also suspected of murder by relentless narcotics cop Rocco Klein (Keitel). Supported by an excellent cast, first-timer Phifer surprises with a fierce and powerful performance. Lindo, in particular, stands out as the paternally evil Rodney. Aggressively edited, with Turturro's performance mostly lost on the cutting room floor. Critically lauded cinematography is marred by the occasional boom shot. The poignant and compelling street drama is based on the Richard Price novel. Lee took over after Scorsese and De Niro dropped out to make *Casino*. The gritty feel is delivered intact on the DVD with good sharpness and excellent colors, as well as pretty good blacks. There are not a lot of gimmicky Surround effects, but the 5.1 sound keeps the environmental atmosphere pretty much in your face. —*JO*

Movie: ♫♫♫ **DVD:** ♫♫♫
Universal Studios Home Video (Cat #20016, UPC #025192001628). Widescreen (1.85:1) anamorphic. Dolby Digital 5.1. $24.98. Keepcase. *LANG:* English; French. *SUB:* Spanish. *CAP:* English. *FEATURES:* 18 chapter links • Theatrical trailer • Cast and filmmakers bios • Production notes.
1995 (R) 128m/C Mekhi Phifer, Harvey Keitel, Delroy Lindo, Isaiah Washington, John Turturro, Keith David; *D:* Spike Lee; *W:* Richard Price, Spike Lee; *C:* Malik Hassan Sayeed; *M:* Terence Blanchard.

A Clockwork Orange

In the Britain of the near future, a sadistic punk leads a gang on nightly rape and murder sprees, looking for "a bit of the ol' ultra violence." When captured, he becomes the subject of a grim experiment in behavior modification in this extraordinary adaptation of the controversial Anthony Burgess novel. The film is an exhilarating experience with an outstanding performance by McDowell as the funny, fierce psychopath. Many memorable, disturbing sequences, including a rape conducted while assailant McDowell belts "Singing in the Rain." With the exception of a few scenes, this is one of the best-looking DVDs in Warner Bros.' Stanley Kubrick collection. The picture is very sharp and the colors vibrant. A little bleed shows up in a couple of scenes, but nothing objectionable. Grain is minimal, which is unusual for a Kubrick DVD since his films are generally grainy (and hard for a DVD to handle) to start with. Artifacts are not a problem. Blacks are very good. The

brightness is consistent and even high-contrast shots are handled very well on the disc. Another excellent, though mono, soundtrack. The music, so important to this film, is always crisp and dynamic, whether orchestral or electronic. —*JO*

Movie: ♫♫♫♫ **DVD:** ♫♫♫▸
Warner Home Video, Inc. (Cat #17367, UPC #085391736721). Widescreen (1.77:1) letterboxed. Dolby Digital Mono. $24.98. Snapper. *LANG:* English; French. *SUB:* French. *CAP:* English. *FEATURES:* Dual-layered RSDL • 36 chapter links • Theatrical trailer • Production notes. Also available as part of the "Stanley Kubrick Collection" 7-DVD box set ($149.98).
1971 (R) 137m/C *GB* Malcolm McDowell, Patrick Magee, Adrienne Corri, Michael Bates, Warren Clarke, Aubrey Morris, James Marcus, Steven Berkoff, David Prowse, John Clive, Carl Duering, Miriam Karlin; *D:* Stanley Kubrick; *W:* Stanley Kubrick; *C:* John Alcott; *M:* Walter (Wendy) Carlos. *AWARDS:* American Film Institute (AFI) '98: Top 100; New York Film Critics Awards '71: Best Director (Kubrick), Best Film; *NOM:* Academy Awards '71: Best Adapted Screenplay, Best Director (Kubrick), Best Film Editing, Best Picture.

Closer and Closer

A serial killer is re-creating murders from wheelchair-bound novelist Kaitlin Sanders's (Delaney) best-seller. Made-for-TV thriller is thoroughly derivative and manipulative. On DVD, it looks fine with crisp clarity even in the night scenes, but this one's still nothing special. —*MM*

Movie: ♫♫ **DVD:** ♫♫
Simitar Entertainment (Cat #7589, UPC #082551758920). Full frame. Dolby Digital Stereo. $14.98. Keepcase. *LANG:* English. *FEATURES:* 8 chapter links • Filmography of Kim Delaney.
1996 93m/C Kim Delaney, John J. York, Peter Outerbridge, Peter MacNeill, Scott Craft, Anthony Sherwood; *D:* Fred Gerber; *W:* Matt Dorff.

Clueless

Ultra-rich but charming brat Cher (Silverstone) is out to make over all of her classmates and teachers, specifically flannel-shirted transfer student Tai (Murphy). The only person who can match her quick wits is her disapproving older stepbrother Josh (Rudd). The plot is loosely based on Jane Austen's *Emma,* but that should not dissuade anyone. The film is fast, bright, sexy, sweet, and genuinely funny. The best line is delivered by Cher's dad (Hedaya) to one of her boorish dates: "Anything happens to my daughter, I got a .45 and a shovel. I doubt anybody would miss you." The DVD handles the aggressively bright color scheme better than your eyes will. Sound is very good. —*MM* **AKA:** I Was a Teenage Teenager; No Worries.

Movie: ♫♫♫ **DVD:** ♫♫♫▸
Paramount Home Video (Cat #332157). Widescreen (1.85:1) letterboxed. Dolby Digital Stereo. $29.99. Keepcase. *LANG:*

English; French. *CAP:* English. *FEATURES:* 15 chapter links • Trailers.
1995 (PG-13) 113m/C Alicia Silverstone, Stacey Dash, Paul Rudd, Brittany Murphy, Donald Adeosun Faison, Julie Brown, Jeremy Sisto, Dan Hedaya, Wallace Shawn, Breckin Meyer, Elisa Donovan, Aida Linares; *D:* Amy Heckerling; *W:* Amy Heckerling; *C:* Bill Pope; *M:* David Kitay. *AWARDS:* MTV Movie Awards '96: Best Female Performance (Silverstone), Most Desirable Female (Silverstone); National Society of Film Critics Awards '95: Best Screenplay; Blockbuster Entertainment Awards '96: Female Newcomer, Theatrical (Silverstone); *NOM:* MTV Movie Awards '96: Best Film, Best Comedic Performance (Silverstone); Writers Guild of America '95: Best Original Screenplay.

Cobra

The titles of the "extras" chapters explain this brain-dead shoot-'em-up perfectly: "Weaponry," "Cobra's customized car," "Shooting in Los Angeles." The cop (Stallone) protects babe (Nielsen) plot was handled much better in *Fair Game* with Cindy Crawford. (Both are based on the same novel.) That said, the DVD is an excellent presentation of a bad movie with oodles of extras for those who are into a fetishistic relationship with firearms. —*MM*
Movie: ♫♫ *DVD:* ♫♫♫
Warner Home Video, Inc. (Cat #11594, UPC #085391159421). Widescreen anamorphic; full frame. Dolby Digital 5.1 Surround Stereo; Dolby Digital Surround Stereo; Mono. $24.98. Snapper. *LANG:* English; French; Spanish. *SUB:* English; French; Spanish. *FEATURES:* 26 chapter links • Commentary: director George Cosmatos • Behind-the-scenes documentary • Theatrical trailers • Weaponry • Shooting in Los Angeles • Cobra's customized car.
1986 (R) 87m/C Sylvester Stallone, Reni Santoni, Brigitte Nielsen, Andrew (Andy) Robinson; *D:* George P. Cosmatos; *W:* Sylvester Stallone; *C:* Ric Waite; *M:* Sylvester Levay.

The Cocoanuts

In their film debut, the Marx Brothers create their trademark, indescribable mayhem. Stagey, technically crude comedy nonetheless delights with zany, free-for-all exchanges and antics, including the famous "viaduct" exchange. Sadly, however, this disc is nothing special. The video transfer suffers not only from the age of the source material, but I noticed some strange shadows and a few bizarre flashes of light that I am at a loss to explain. As far as the black-and-white picture goes, it appears crisp in some scenes, yet is muddied in others (which might also be due to the age of the film). The soundtrack too, is a disappointment: I could only get the PCM Digital Stereo track to play from the left speaker (not exactly stereo,

eh?), which left everything somewhat muffled at times. —*MJT*
Movie: ♫♫ *DVD:* ♫♫
Image Entertainment (Cat #ID4279USDVD, UPC #014381427929). Full frame. PCM Digital Stereo. $29.99. Snapper. *LANG:* English. *FEATURES:* 16 chapter links.
1929 96m/B Groucho Marx, Chico Marx, Harpo Marx, Zeppo Marx, Margaret Dumont, Kay Francis, Oscar Shaw, Mary Eaton, Cyril Ring, Basil Ruysdael; *D:* Robert Florey, Joseph Santley; *W:* George S. Kaufman, Morrie Ryskind; *C:* George J. Folsey; *M:* Irving Berlin.

Cold Eyes of Fear

A man and his girlfriend are besieged by a raving convict whom his uncle, a judge, had put away years before. Shades of *Cape Fear* on a low budget. Quite a few twists and an excellent Morricone score make this one well worthwhile. This "Redemption" offering from Image Entertainment looks pretty good. Colors are much better that their usual Eurosleaze releases and the picture is actually sharp. In fact, if this DVD looked any better it might take away from the feel of the film. —*JO*
Movie: ♫♫ *DVD:* ♫♫♫
Image Entertainment (Cat #ID4611SADVD, UPC #014381461121). Widescreen (1.85:1) letterboxed. Dolby Digital Mono. $24.95. Snapper. *LANG:* English. *FEATURES:* 18 chapter links.
1970 88m/C Fernando Rey, Frank Wolfe, Karin Schubert; *D:* Enzo G. Castellari; *W:* Enzo G. Castellari, Tito Carpi, Leo Anchoriz; *C:* Antonio Ballesteros; *M:* Ennio Morricone.

Cold Harvest

Post-apocalyptic spaghetti western is derivative but handled with enough cheesy style to make it an enjoyable guilty pleasure. Roland Cheney (Daniels) is a bounty hunter who must save his sister-in-law (Crampton) after her husband (Daniels again) is killed by the evil Little Ray (Genesse). The martial arts action scenes are exaggerated to virtual cartoon violence. The junkyard sets are nothing new. On DVD, both image and sound are well above average for the modest demands of the genre. The film was made in South Africa. —*MM*
Movie: ♫♫ *DVD:* ♫♫
Image Entertainment (Cat #ID6260NGDVD, UPC #014381626025). Full frame. Dolby Digital Stereo. $24.99. Snapper. *LANG:* English. *FEATURES:* 18 chapter links.
1998 (R) 93m/C Gary Daniels, Barbara Crampton, Bryan Genesse; *D:* Isaac Florentine; *W:* Frank Dietz; *C:* David Varod; *M:* Steve Edwards.

Cold Sweat

A brutal drug trader (Bronson) takes violent revenge after his wife (Ireland) is captured by a drug boss's moronic henchmen. Typical Bronson flick boasts superior sup-

porting cast with Ullman and Mason, but mediocre writing and direction. *AKA:* L'Uomo Dalle Due Ombre; De la Part des Copains.
Movie: ♫♫ *DVD:* NYR
Essex (Cat #1006). Full frame. Dolby Digital Mono. $10.97. Slipcase.
1971 (PG) 94m/C *IT FR* Charles Bronson, Jill Ireland, Liv Ullmann, James Mason; *D:* Terence Young; *W:* Albert Simonin, Shimon Wincelberg; *C:* Jean Rabier; *M:* Michel Magne.

College

In one of his best, Keaton is a poor freshman who attempts to turn himself into a jock to win the hand of a lovely coed (Cornwall). The best routines involve an incredible shrinking suit, his work as a soda jerk, a short stint as a waiter in black-face, an appearance on the baseball diamond, a boat race, and a pole vault through a window. The DVD image is remarkably clear and sharp for a film of its age. Unfortunately, the other three shorter films on the disc—"The Electric House" (1922, 23 min.), "Hard Luck" (1921, 22 min.), and "The Blacksmith" (1922, 21 min.)—don't look nearly as good. They were made about five years before, and are so grainy they appear to be filled with snow. —*MM*
Movie: ♫♫♫ *DVD:* ♫♫♫
Kino on Video (Cat #K129DVD, UPC #738329012922). Full frame. $29.99. Snapper. *LANG:* Silent. *SUB:* English intertitles. *FEATURES:* 29 chapter links.
1927 60m/B Virginia Fox, Joe Roberts, Buster Keaton, Anne Cornwall, Harold Goodwin; *D:* Edward F. (Eddie) Cline, Malcolm St. Clair, Buster Keaton, James W. Horne; *W:* Brian Foy, Carl Harbaugh, Edward F. (Eddie) Cline, Malcolm St. Clair, Buster Keaton; *C:* Bert Haines; *M:* John Muri, Robert Israel.

The Colony

Aliens planning an Earth invasion decide to test humankind by abducting four people and observing their survival skills. Made for the Sci-Fi Channel.
Movie: ♫ *DVD:* NYR
Trimark Home Video (Cat #6892). Full frame. Dolby Digital Stereo. $24.99. Keepcase. *SUB:* French; Spanish. *FEATURES:* Trailer.
1998 (R) 94m/C Isabella Hoffman, Michael Weatherly, Cristi Conaway, Eric Allen Kramer, Jeff Kober, James Avery, Clara Salstrom; *D:* Peter Geiger; *W:* Peter Geiger, Richard Kletter; *C:* Zoltan David; *M:* Paul Rabjohns.

Color Me Blood Red

Goremeister H.G. Lewis's 1964 answer to Roger Corman's *Bucket of Blood* isn't as snappy or as sophisticated. (This is, of course, the only context in which *Bucket of Blood* could ever be called sophisticated.) Adam Sorg (Don Joseph) decides that he prefers blood to oils or tempera for the reds in his paintings, so he murders for art supplies. (Obviously, Adam's a man ahead of his time. Today he'd get a grant and be pilloried by Republicans.) It's all extremely silly with gore effects, faux hip humor, and several pointless scenes on water bicycles. The DVD is remarkably clear for a film made so cheaply and so long ago. Reds bleed, naturally, but they always have. On their avuncular commentary track, producer Friedman and Lewis reminisce about the Sarasota locations and their days as the kings of exploitation. —MM *AKA:* Model Massacre.

Movie: ♫♫ **DVD:** ♫♫
Something Weird Video (Cat #ID6013SW DVD, UPC #014381601329). Full frame. Dolby Digital Mono. $24.99. Snapper. *LANG:* English. *FEATURES:* 12 chapter links ● Outtakes ● Commentary: Friedman, Lewis, Mike Vraney, Jimmy Maslin ● Gallery of exploitation art ● Theatrical trailer.
1964 79m/C Don Joseph, Candi Conder, Elyn Warner, Scott H. Hall, Jerome Eden, Patricia Lee, James Jackel; *D:* Herschell Gordon Lewis; *W:* Herschell Gordon Lewis; *C:* Herschell Gordon Lewis.

The Color of Money

Flashy, gripping sequel to *The Hustler* finds Fast Eddie Felsen (Newman) coming back onto the pool circuit with Vincent (Cruise), a brilliant but temperamental young shark, under his wing. The performances are letter perfect all around, with strong support given by Shaver and Mastrantonio as the men's worldly girlfriends and Whitaker as a cheerful hustler. Much of the film has a deliberately harsh, nicotine-stained seediness and discordant rock soundtrack. DVD captures that side but the disc really shines in the extreme closeups of the game being played. (That's where the theatrical release was strongest, too.) The heavily shadowed pool halls contain no serious visual flaws that I could detect. A commentary track from any of the principals would have been a valuable extra. —MM
Movie: ♫♫♫▶ **DVD:** ♫♫♫▶
Buena Vista Home Entertainment (Cat #18148, UPC #717951004277). Widescreen (1.85:1) anamorphic. Dolby Digital 4.1 Surround Stereo. $29.99. Keepcase. *LANG:* English; French. *SUB:* English. *CAP:* English. *FEATURES:* 24 chapter links.
1986 (R) 119m/C Paul Newman, Tom Cruise, Mary Elizabeth Mastrantonio, Helen Shaver, John Turturro, Forest Whitaker; *D:* Martin Scorsese; *W:* Richard Price; *C:* Michael Ballhaus; *M:* Robbie Robertson. *AWARDS:* Academy Awards '86: Best Actor (Newman); National Board of Review Awards '86: Best Actor (Newman); *NOM:* Academy Awards '86: Best Adapted Screenplay, Best Art Direction/ Set Decoration, Best Supporting Actress (Mastrantonio).

Color of Night

Anyone who takes this wacky flick seriously will detest it. But those who see it as a parody of *Basic Instinct* thrillers will be wonderfully entertained. (The presence of B-veterans Henriksen and Dourif is the tip-off.) Willis plays a psychiatrist trying to solve the murder of a fellow shrink (Bakula) who was killed by one of his patients. The rest is a mix of racy sex scenes involving Rose (March), hammy overacting, and pop psychology. Only Ruben Blades, as a detective, seems to have understood how silly the material really is. The video version contains about 15 minutes more footage than the theatrical release. It shows a bit more skin—including blink-and-you'll-miss-it male nudity—and makes the already convoluted plot a little more so. Definitely not for kids, but a must for guilty-pleasure fans. The DVD captures the inventive staging and photography extremely well, particularly the first love scene which begins in a swimming pool, and nuttily shifts without transition to the kitchen, then a bedroom, then a dinner where he's dressed and she's not, and finally the shower. The big finish makes it equally demanding in visual terms, but the image is strong throughout. —MM
Movie: ♫♫▶ **DVD:** ♫♫♫
Hollywood Pictures Home Video (Cat #17633, UPC #717951003430). Widescreen (1.85:1) letterboxed. Dolby Surround. $29.99. Keepcase. *LANG:* English; French. *CAP:* English. *FEATURES:* 26 chapter links ● Theatrical trailer.
1994 (R) 151m/C Bruce Willis, Jane March, Scott Bakula, Ruben Blades, Lesley Ann Warren, Lance Henriksen, Kevin J. O'Connor, Andrew Lowery, Brad Dourif, Eriq La Salle, Jeff Corey, Shirley Knight, Kathleen Wilhoite; *D:* Richard Rush; *W:* Matthew Chapman, Billy Ray, Richard Rush; *C:* Dietrich Lohmann; *M:* Dominic Frontiere. *AWARDS:* Golden Raspberry Awards '94: Worst Picture; *NOM:* Golden Globe Awards '95: Best Song ("The Color of the Night"); Golden Raspberry Awards '94: Worst Actor (Willis).

The Color Purple

Celie (Goldberg) is a poor black girl who fights for her self-esteem when she is separated from her sister and forced into a brutal marriage with "Mr." (Glover). Spanning the years 1909 to 1947 in a small Georgia town, the movie is adapted from Alice Walker's acclaimed novel. It's also a remarkable double debut for Whoopi Goldberg and Oprah Winfrey. Though Spielberg gives some of the harrowing action a conventional Hollywood gloss, most of it works well. His picturesque visuals arrive on the screen intact but the DVD is far from perfect. It's a double-sided disc that must be flipped midway. The stereo sound is excellent. —MM
Movie: ♫♫▶ **DVD:** ♫♫▶
Warner Home Video, Inc. (Cat #11534, UPC #085391153429). Widescreen letterboxed. Dolby Digital 5.1 Surround; Dolby Digital Surround. $24.98. Snapper. *LANG:* English; French. *SUB:* English; French; Spanish. *CAP:* English. *FEATURES:* Cast

and crew thumbnail biographies ● Production notes ● Awards ● 37 chapter links.
1985 (PG-13) 154m/C Whoopi Goldberg, Danny Glover, Oprah Winfrey, Margaret Avery, Adolph Caesar, Rae Dawn Chong, Willard Pugh, Akosua Busia; *D:* Steven Spielberg; *W:* Menno Meyjes; *C:* Allen Daviau; *M:* Chris Boardman, Quincy Jones. *AWARDS:* Directors Guild of America Awards '85: Best Director (Spielberg); Golden Globe Awards '86: Best Actress— Drama (Goldberg); National Board of Review Awards '85: Best Actress (Goldberg); *NOM:* Academy Awards '85: Best Actress (Goldberg), Best Adapted Screenplay, Best Art Direction/Set Decoration, Best Cinematography, Best Costume Design, Best Makeup, Best Picture, Best Song ("Miss Celie's Blues (Sister)"), Best Supporting Actress (Avery, Winfrey), Best Original Score.

Coma

Young doctor Susan Wheeler (Bujold) discovers murder, corpse-napping, and worse at her Boston hospital. She defies her bosses (all men) and, with the help of Dr. Bellows (Douglas), sets out to discover what's going on before more patients die. Crichton (and novelist Robin Cook) essentially invented the modern medical thriller with this one. The creepy visuals in the sinister Jefferson Institute have a nightmare intensity. The DVD looks very good. Both image and monaural sound are exceptionally clear for a work of this age. A solid step up from VHS tape. —MM
Movie: ♫♫♫ **DVD:** ♫♫♫
Warner Home Video, Inc. (Cat #65046). Widescreen (1.85:1) letterboxed; full frame. Dolby Digital Mono. $19.98. Snapper. *LANG:* English; French. *SUB:* French. *CAP:* English. *FEATURES:* Theatrical trailer ● 35 chapter links.
1978 (PG) 113m/C Genevieve Bujold, Michael Douglas, Elizabeth Ashley, Rip Torn, Richard Widmark, Lois Chiles, Hari Rhodes, Tom Selleck, Ed Harris; *D:* Michael Crichton; *W:* Michael Crichton; *C:* Victor Kemper, Gerald Hirschfeld; *M:* Jerry Goldsmith.

Combat Shock

After being tortured in Vietnam, Frankie (Ricky Giovinazzo) cannot adjust to life in America. He lives in a squalid slum with his dispirited wife and their mutant baby, reminiscent of *Eraserhead*. He owes money to loan sharks and his only friend is a junkie. A day in his life is grimy stuff that makes *Taxi Driver* look like *The Sound of Music*. The DVD release is a "director's cut" that restores the bloody but not particularly convincing violence that has been edited out of other versions. Battles with the MPAA are detailed in an interview and introduction by Troma honcho Lloyd Kaufman. The image is so grainy that the stock footage from Vietnam is seamlessly blended with the film that was shot on Staten Island. The entire production is deliberately grubby and unpolished with muddy col-

ors which gain nothing on DVD. —*MM*
AKA: American Nightmares.
Movie: 🎬🎬 **DVD:** 🎬🎬▶
Troma Team Video (Cat #DVD9980, UPC #790357998036). Full frame. $24.95. Keepcase. *LANG:* English. *FEATURES:* Tour of Troma Studios • Troma Intelligence Test II • Commentary: director Buddy Giovinazzo and Jorg Buttgereit • Theatrical trailer • Comical "cooking" featurette • Troma public service announcements • Links to Troma website • Frames from Troma comic books • 9 chapter links.
1984 (R) 85m/C Ricky Giovinazzo, Nick Nasta, Veronica Stork, Mitch Maglio, Aspah Livni; *D:* Buddy Giovinazzo; *W:* Buddy Giovinazzo; *C:* Stella Varveris; *M:* Ricky Giovinazzo.

Come and Get It

Adaptation of the Edna Ferber novel about a lumber king battling his son for the love of a woman is Farmer's most important Hollywood role. **AKA:** Roaring Timber.
Movie: 🎬🎬🎬 **DVD:** NYR
HBO Home Video (Cat #00660). Full frame. Mono; Stereo. $24.98. Snapper. *LANG:* English; German; Italian. *SUB:* French; Spanish. *FEATURES:* Cast and crew thumbnail biographies • Trailer.
1936 99m/B Frances Farmer, Edward Arnold, Joel McCrea, Walter Brennan, Andrea Leeds, Charles Halton; *D:* William Wyler, Howard Hawks; *W:* Jules Furthman, Jane Murfin; *C:* Rudolph Mate, Gregg Toland; *M:* Alfred Newman. *AWARDS:* Academy Awards '36: Best Supporting Actor (Brennan); *NOM:* Academy Awards '36: Best Film Editing.

Comin' At Ya!

Three-D western follows a groom (Anthony) trying to rescue his kidnapped bride. The DVD offers terrible 3-D effects, and a grainy picture. —*JO*
Movie: 🎬▶ **DVD:** 🎬▶
Rhino Home Video (Cat #5660). Widescreen (2.35:1) letterboxed. $19.95. Snapper.
1981 91m/C Tony Anthony, Riccardo Palacio, Victoria Abril, Gene Quintano; *D:* Ferdinando Baldi; *W:* Lloyd Battista, Wolf Lowenthal; *C:* Fernando Arribas; *M:* Carlo Savina.

Coming to America

An African prince (Murphy) decides to go to America in search of a suitable bride. He lands in Queens, and quickly finds American women to be more confusing than he imagined. Sometimes overly cute entertainment is relieved by clever costume cameos by Murphy and Hall. A lawsuit resulted in columnist Art Buchwald being given credit for the story. Visually the DVD is very sharp. There is not much in the way of grain or artifacts. Colors are generally vibrant and natural except for a few scenes where they appear muted. The brightness levels are consistent, as is the contrast, although I would have liked a lit-

tle more edge to the picture. Blacks are very good. The 5.1 is strong, full-bodied with plenty of low end, but there's not much in the way of Surround. —*JO*
Movie: 🎬🎬🎬 **DVD:** 🎬🎬▶
Paramount Home Video (Cat #321577, UPC #097363215776). Widescreen (1.85:1) letterboxed. Dolby Digital 5.1; Dolby Surround. $29.99. Keepcase. *LANG:* English. *CAP:* English. *FEATURES:* 24 chapter links • Theatrical trailer.
1988 (R) 116m/C Eddie Murphy, Arsenio Hall, James Earl Jones, John Amos, Madge Sinclair, Shari Headley, Don Ameche, Louie Anderson, Paul Bates, Allison Dean, Eriq La Salle, Calvin Lockhart, Samuel L. Jackson, Cuba Gooding Jr., Vanessa Bell Calloway, Frankie Faison, Vondie Curtis-Hall; *D:* John Landis; *W:* David Sheffield, Barry W. Blaustein; *C:* Woody Omens; *M:* Nile Rodgers. *AWARDS:* *NOM:* Academy Awards '88: Best Costume Design.

Commando

An ex-commando leader's daughter is kidnapped in a blackmail scheme to make him depose a South American president. He fights instead, and proceeds to rescue his daughter amid a torrential flow of dying bad guys. It's all less exaggerated than Arnold's later flicks would become. Chong's character is the most unbelievable, but it doesn't detract from the fun of the film. Violent action and high body counts, spiced with throwaway deadpan comic lines. The picture is reasonably sharp with very little digital grain. Blacks are dead-on and the colors are both accurate and vibrant. Both contrast and brightness are punchy enough, while the blacks stay deep and true. The Dolby Surround is very dynamic with gutsy bass and screeching highs and the mix throws a lot to the rear speakers. —*JO*
Movie: 🎬🎬🎬 **DVD:** 🎬🎬🎬
20th Century Fox (Cat #4110424, UPC #08616210424). Widescreen (1.85:1) letterboxed. Dolby Surround; Stereo. $29.98. Keepcase. *LANG:* English (DS); French (Stereo). *SUB:* Spanish. *CAP:* English. *FEATURES:* 24 chapter links • Theatrical trailer.
1985 (R) 90m/C Arnold Schwarzenegger, Rae Dawn Chong, Dan Hedaya, Vernon Wells, James Olson, David Patrick Kelly, Alyssa Milano, Bill Duke; *D:* Mark L. Lester; *W:* Steven E. de Souza; *C:* Matthew F. Leonetti; *M:* James Horner.

The Commitments

Convinced that music is his ticket to success, hustler Jimmy Rabbitte (Arkins) gathers a group of working-class Dubliners to form a band and re-create the Motown sound. Alan Parker's high-energy production paints an unromanticized portrait of modern Ireland and rightly refuses to follow the conventional show business cliches. The film is really more about poverty than about music. The whimsical, poetically profane dialogue is delivered by a cast of relative unknowns. Large portions of

that dialogue are impossible for anyone unfamiliar with Irish accents and idioms to make out but the central emotions are unmistakable. Unfortunately, the DVD is something of a disappointment. It's pan-and-scan, not widescreen, and the stereo sound is no more than adequate. True, it would be wrong to digitally buff the image or to pump up the music. The film's appeal lies in its gritty honest evocation of a tough urban world. But no widescreen option? No commentary track? There's more to be done here. —*MM*
Movie: 🎬🎬🎬▶ **DVD:** 🎬🎬▶
Twentieth Century Fox Home Entertainment (Cat #4112892, UPC #086162128929). Full frame. Dolby Digital Surround Stereo. $29.98. Keepcase. *LANG:* English. *SUB:* English; Spanish. *CAP:* English. *FEATURES:* 35 chapter links • Theatrical trailer • Music video, "Treat Her Right" • Soundtrack sampler • "Making of" featurette.
1991 (R) 116m/C *IR* Andrew Strong, Bronagh Gallagher, Glen Hansard, Michael Aberne, Dick Massey, Ken McCluskey, Robert Arkins, Dave Finnegan, Johnny Murphy, Angeline Ball, Felim Gormley, Maria Doyle Kennedy, Colm Meaney; *D:* Alan Parker; *W:* Dick Clement, Roddy Doyle, Ian LaFrenais; *C:* Gale Tattersall; *M:* Paul Bushnell. *AWARDS:* British Academy Awards '91: Best Adapted Screenplay, Best Director (Parker), Best Film; *NOM:* Academy Awards '91: Best Film Editing.

The Complete Uncensored Private Snafu

Commissioned by the military during World War II, these propaganda cartoons were created by the famed animators at Warner Bros. and voiced by the legendary Blanc. This collection includes every Private Snafu cartoon ever released, chronicling an important piece of film history. The video transfer is quite good, with solid definition and crisp blacks. I did notice some warping in the borders of a few cartoons (though not enough to cause great concern). The audio is also impressive, especially when considering the age and type of the source material. —*MJT*
Movie: 🎬🎬🎬 **DVD:** 🎬🎬🎬
Image Entertainment (Cat #ID5533BKDVD, UPC #014381553321). Full frame. Dolby Digital Mono. $24.99. Snapper. *LANG:* English. *FEATURES:* 31 chapter links.
1946 135m/B *D:* Chuck Jones, Isadore "Friz" Freleng, Frank Tashlin, Bob Clampett, Osmond Evans, Zack Schwartz, George Gordon, Herman Ising; *V:* Mel Blanc.

Con Air

Big-budget guilty pleasure is idiotic in all the right ways. Unjustly jailed for manslaughter, ex–Army Ranger Cameron Poe (Cage) is paroled and sent home on a transport plane with America's worst criminals, including Cyrus "the Virus" (Malkovich) and other psychos. The feds on the ground are little better, but Marshall Larkin (Cusack) tries to help Poe after the cons take over the plane. Snappy one-liners and inventively staged action scenes zip right along. On DVD, the special effects are as clear as they were on the big screen, if not so oversized. The busy gridwork airplane interior is re-created without any noticeable problems. The Dolby sound adds considerably to the overall effect, but Cage's faux-Southern accent is as goofy as ever. —*MM*

Movie: ♫♫♫ **DVD:** ♫♫♫
Buena Vista Home Entertainment (Cat #13860, UPC #717951000262). Widescreen (2.35:1) letterboxed. Dolby Digital Stereo. $29.99. Keepcase. *LANG:* English; French. *SUB:* Spanish. *CAP:* English. *FEATURES:* 18 chapter links ▪ Theatrical trailers.
1997 (R) 105m/C Nicolas Cage, John Malkovich, John Cusack, Mykelti Williamson, Ving Rhames, Steve Buscemi, Colm Meaney, Rachel Ticotin, Dave Chappelle, M.C. Gainey, Danny Trejo, Nicholas Chinlund, Jesse Borrego, Angela Featherstone, Monica Potter, John Roselius, Renoly, Landry Allbright, Jose Zuniga; **D:** Simon West; **W:** Scott Rosenberg; **C:** David Tattersall; **M:** Mark Mancina, Trevor Rabin. *AWARDS: NOM:* Academy Awards '97: Best Song ("How Do I Live"), Best Sound; Golden Raspberry Awards '97: Worst Song ("How Do I Live").

The Con Artists

After conman Bang (Quinn) is sprung from prison, he and his protege Felix (Celentano) set up a sting against the elegant Belle Duke (Capucine). The film is neither clever nor witty enough for the caper to capture interest. On DVD, it looks about as good as a '70s Italian import could be expected to look, though the image, like the film, has a flat, lifeless feel. —*MM*
AKA: The Con Man. ►
Movie: ♫► **DVD:** ♫►
Simitar Entertainment (Cat #7250, UPC #082551725021). Full frame. PCM Stereo. $14.98. Keepcase. *LANG:* English. *FEATURES:* 8 chapter links ▪ Filmographies and bios on Quinn and Capucine.
1980 86m/C *IT* Anthony Quinn, Adriano Celentano, Capucine, Corinne Clery; **D:** Sergio Corbucci.

Conan the Barbarian

A fine sword-and-sorcery tale based on the character created by Robert E. Howard features brutality, excellent production values, and a rousing score. Conan's (Schwarzenegger) parents are killed and he's enslaved. But hardship makes him strong, so when he is set free he can avenge their murder and retrieve the sword bequeathed him by his father. Sandahl Bergman is great as the Queen of Thieves, and Schwarzenegger maintains an admirable sense of humor throughout. Jones is dandy, as always. The orchestral soundtrack has always been a highlight to this film, and initial disappointment over the use of mono sound proved, at least

partially, unfounded. The track is very strong, delivering full fidelity, with the brass accented by crisp highs and the low end strong and clean. The picture is a bit sharper than the laserdisc, and grain is minimal, appearing only in the darker scenes. The colors are vibrant, making the violent swordplay seem even more gory. The blacks were true except when they filled the entire screen, at which point they weakened, picking up a little grain and edging towards gray. Contrast and brightness are also improved over the earlier video releases. —*JO*
Movie: ♫♫♫ **DVD:** ♫♫♫
Universal Studios Home Video (Cat #20156, UPC #025192015625). Widescreen (2.35:1) letterboxed. Dolby Digital 2.0 Mono. $24.98. Keepcase. *LANG:* English. *SUB:* Spanish; French. *CAP:* English. *FEATURES:* 16 chapter links ▪ Theatrical trailer ▪ Cast and filmmaker bios ▪ Production notes.
1982 (R) 115m/C Arnold Schwarzenegger, James Earl Jones, Max von Sydow, Sandahl Bergman, Mako, Ben Davidson, Valerie Quennessen, Cassandra Gaviola, William Smith; **D:** John Milius; **W:** John Milius, Oliver Stone; **C:** Duke Callaghan; **M:** Basil Poledouris.

Conan the Destroyer

Where director John Milius made his Conan sword and fantasy epic for adults, Fleischer seems to have directed his towards a much younger audience, toning down the violence, the sex, and the attitude. Conan is manipulated by Queen Tamaris into searching for a treasure. In return, she'll bring Conan's love, Valeria, back to life. On his trip he meets Jones and Chamberlain, who later give him a hand. Jones is a natural. Excellent special effects, good humor, camp fun, somewhat silly finale. This Conan has much more of a soundstage look than the first, and on the DVD it is even more apparent. That's not knocking the disc—the colors are just more accurate than previous video releases and, combined with the improved contrast, the lighting textures are more obvious. The picture is reasonably sharp and the disc has very few problems with the numerous darker scenes, managing to keep the grain level down and the blacks mostly true. There were a couple moments of digital hesitation. The sound is once again monophonic but still strong enough to carry the film's clang-of-metal effects. —*JO*
Movie: ♫♫ **DVD:** ♫♫♫
Universal Studios Home Video (Cat #20172, UPC #02519201723). Widescreen (2.35:1) letterboxed. Dolby Digital 2.0 Mono. $24.98. Keepcase. *LANG:* English; French. *CAP:* English. *FEATURES:* 16 chapter links ▪ Theatrical trailer ▪ Cast and filmmaker bios ▪ Production notes ▪ Film highlights.
1984 (PG) 101m/C Arnold Schwarzenegger, Grace Jones, Wilt Chamberlain, Sarah Douglas, Mako, Jeff Corey, Olivia D'Abo, Tracey Walter; **D:** Richard Fleischer; **W:**

Stanley Mann; **C:** Jack Cardiff; **M:** Basil Poledouris. *AWARDS:* Golden Raspberry Awards '84: Worst New Star (D'Abo).

Condorman

Woody Wilkins (Crawford), an inventive comic book writer, adopts the identity of his own character, Condorman, to help a beautiful Russian spy (Carrera) defect. Lots of gadgetry akin to a James Bond adventure. Oliver Reed, as usual, makes a great villain. This Anchor Bay DVD doesn't pack the punch that most of their recent releases do. The picture is sharp enough, but dimly lit scenes pick up substantial grain, and the blacks are generally a dark gray. The colors are a little dull, even when compared to the old Disney VHS release. Contrast is a little low, as is the brightness. The artifacts become noticeable only in those dimmer scenes. The stereo sound is adequate but has so little separation it may as well be mono. —*JO*
Movie: ♫♫► **DVD:** ♫♫
Anchor Bay (Cat #DV0823, UPC #013131082395). Widescreen (2.35:1) letterboxed; full frame. Dolby Digital Stereo. $24.98. Keepcase. *LANG:* English. *FEATURES:* 17 chapter links.
1981 (PG) 90m/C Michael Crawford, Oliver Reed, Barbara Carrera, James Hampton, Jean-Pierre Kalfon, Dana Elcar; **D:** Charles Jarrott; **W:** Glenn Gordon Caron; **C:** Charles F. Wheeler; **M:** Henry Mancini.

The Confession

Courtroom drama about a client who refuses to defend himself.
Movie: ♫♫ **DVD:** NYR
Studio Home Entertainment (Cat #7255). Widescreen (1.85:1) letterboxed. Dolby Digital Stereo. $28.97. Keepcase. *LANG:* English. *SUB:* Spanish. *FEATURES:* Featurette ▪ Commentary: Jones, Black, Baldwin, Irving, Kingsley, Mann ▪ Trailer.
1998 (R) 114m/C Alec Baldwin, Ben Kingsley, Amy Irving, Jay O. Sanders, Kevin Conway, Anne Twomey, Christopher Lawford, Boyd Gaines, Christopher Noth; **D:** David Hugh Jones; **W:** David Black; **C:** Mike Fash; **M:** Mychael Danna.

Confidentially Yours

Truffaut's homage to Hitchcock is based on Charles William's noirish novel *The Long Saturday Night*. Small-town businessman Julien (Trintignant) is framed for murder. His secretary Barbara (Ardant), who is secretly in love with him, tries to clear his name. Truffaut's last film is stylish and entertaining. This restored DVD is first-rate in image and sound with new, easy-to-read subtitles (by Laurent Bouzereau) extended into the opening credits. Nestor Almendros's black-and-white photography captures the full range of grays with crisp focus. Some break-up of diagonal lines is the only visible flaw and it's a small one. Strongly recommended to anyone who is not completely put off by subtitles. —*MM*
AKA: Vivement Dimanche!; Finally, Sunday.

Movie: 🎵🎵🎵➤ **DVD:** 🎵🎵🎵➤
WinStar Home Entertainment (Cat #FLV5072, UPC #720917507224). Widescreen (1.66:1) letterboxed. $29.98. Keepcase. *LANG:* French. *SUB:* English. *FEATURES:* 6 chapter links.
1983 (PG) 110m/B *FR* Fanny Ardant, Jean-Louis Trintignant, Philippe Morier-Genoud, Philippe Laudenbach, Caroline Sihol; *D:* Francois Truffaut; *W:* Francois Truffaut, Suzanne Schiffman, Jean Aurel; *C:* Nestor Almendros; *M:* Georges Delerue.

Congo

Communications company exec (Linney) jets off to the African jungle with a primatologist (Walsh) to search for her missing coworkers who found a lost city complete with priceless diamonds. Monroe (Hudson) is the great black hunter who leads her band into the bush. Working from Michael Crichton's novel, writer Shanley *(Moonstruck)* and director Marshall *(Alive)* keep the pace quick and they never miss an opportunity to dust off a cliche—the lost city, hidden treasure, earthquakes, erupting volcanos, rivers of lava—or to create a new one—vicious killer hippos. Hudson, with a semi-British accent that makes him sound like a cross between Leslie Howard and George Sanders, steals the show. The disc maintains sharp images throughout, even holding details in the heavily shadowed scenes. Only the computer-generated lava looks suspect, though by the time it shows up, the sound effects have kicked in and they're fine. —*MM*
Movie: 🎵🎵➤ **DVD:** 🎵🎵🎵➤
Paramount Home Video (Cat #330387, UPC #097363303879). Widescreen. Dolby Digital 5.1; Dolby Surround. $29.99. Keepcase. *LANG:* English; French. *SUB:* English. *FEATURES:* Teaser trailer ⚬ Regular theatrical trailer ⚬ 13 chapter links.
1995 (PG-13) 109m/C Dylan Walsh, Laura Linney, Ernie Hudson, Tim Curry, Grant Heslov, Joe Don Baker; *D:* Frank Marshall; *W:* John Patrick Shanley; *C:* Allen Daviau; *M:* Jerry Goldsmith. *AWARDS: NOM:* Golden Raspberry Awards '95: Worst Picture.

The Conman

King (Lau) is a gambler who cheats at everything and winds up in jail. After he is released and is trying to put his life back together, he meets the ambitious young Dragon (Nick Cheung) and certain patterns re-emerge. The image quality is O.K. on the DVD, but it has a thin, almost transparent quality that probably comes from the original. This is an unapologetic B-movie—violent, lurid, and filmed with more imagination and style than money. —*MM*
Movie: 🎵🎵🎵➤ **DVD:** 🎵🎵➤
Tai Seng Video Marketing (Cat #56714, UPC #4890391102065). Widescreen letterboxed. Dolby Digital 5.1 Surround Stereo. $49.95. Keepcase. *LANG:* Cantonese; Mandarin. *SUB:* Simplified Chi-

nese; Traditional Chinese; English; Spanish; Thai; Malaysia Bahasa; Korean; Vietnamese; Japanese. *FEATURES:* 9 chapter links ⚬ Synopsis ⚬ Cast and crew thumbnail biographies.
1998 107m/C Andy Lau, Athene Chu, Nick Cheung, Angie Cheung; *D:* Wong Jing; *W:* Wong Jing.

The Conqueror

Wayne in pointed helmet and goatee is convincingly miscast as Genghis Khan in this woeful tale of the warlord's early life and involvement with the kidnapped daughter of a powerful enemy. Rife with stilted, unintentionally funny dialogue, the film was very expensive to make (with backing by Howard Hughes), and is now listed in the "Fifty Worst Films of All Time." No matter; it's surreal enough to enable viewers to approximate an out-of-body experience. Even those on the set suffered; filming took place near a nuclear test site in Utah and many members of the cast and crew eventually developed cancer. On the Goodtimes scale this is a fairly good-looking DVD. In fact, it would be a great-looking DVD except for some horrendous incidents of artifacting that totally distort the image. Other than that, the picture is sharp and the colors are very vibrant with only rare occasions of bleed. The sound is excellent with good body and effective imaging. —*JO AKA:* Conqueror of the Desert.
Movie: 🐾 **DVD:** 🎵🎵➤
Goodtimes Entertainment (Cat #05-81039, UPC #018713810397). Widescreen (2.35:1) letterboxed. Dolby Surround. $24.98. Snapper. *LANG:* English. *SUB:* Spanish; French. *CAP:* English. *FEATURES:* 18 chapter links.
1956 111m/C John Wayne, Susan Hayward, William Conrad, Agnes Moorehead, Lee Van Cleef, Pedro Armendariz Sr., Thomas Gomez, John Hoyt, Ted de Corsia, Leslie Bradley, Peter Mamakos; *D:* Dick Powell; *W:* Oscar Millard; *C:* Joseph LaShelle, William E. Snyder, Leo Tover, Harry Wild; *M:* Victor Young.

Conspiracy: The Trial of the Chicago Eight

Shot-on-tape courtroom drama focuses on the rambunctious trial of the radicals involved in the protests during the 1968 Democratic National Convention. Dramatized footage is mixed with interviews with the defendants. On DVD, the substandard production values defeat the filmmakers' obvious (and heavy-handed) passion for their subjects. The courtroom scenes are atrociously lit. —*MM*
Movie: 🎵 **DVD:** 🎵
Simitar Entertainment (Cat #7284, UPC #082551728428). Full frame. Dolby Digital Stereo. $14.98. Keepcase. *LANG:* English. *FEATURES:* 8 chapter links ⚬ Filmographies of Gould, Boyle, Loggia, Carradine, Sheen.
1987 118m/C Peter Boyle, Elliott Gould, Robert Carradine, Martin Sheen, David

Clennon, David Kagen, Michael Lembeck, Robert Loggia; *D:* Jeremy Paul Kagan.

Conspiracy Theory

Whacked-out New York cabbie Jerry Fletcher (Gibson) writes a newsletter on conspiracy theories, which he finds in every possible place and situation. Naturally, he doesn't keep his thoughts to himself and exasperated Justice Department attorney Alice Sutton (Roberts) is stuck listening to the love-struck fool. But as the saying goes, just because you're paranoid doesn't mean they're not out to get you. Sure enough, one of Jerry's conspiracies turns out to be true and suddenly he and Alice are being pursued by CIA shrink Dr. Jonas (Stewart), who's not what he seems to be either. Gibson's more geek than hero but appealing regardless, as is heroine Roberts. Another successful, enjoyable, and highly profitable teaming of Donner, Gibson, and producer Joel Silver. During the action scenes, the DVD's 5.1 sound really takes over and throws you right into the center of things with some excellent Surround effects and gut-shaking dynamics. The score sounds great too, as does the dialogue, which stays out front. The picture is also excellent. —*JO*
Movie: 🎵🎵🎵 **DVD:** 🎵🎵🎵➤
Warner Home Video, Inc. (Cat #15091, UPC #085391509127). Widescreen (2.35:1) anamorphic; full frame. Dolby Digital 5.1; Stereo. $24.98. Snapper. *LANG:* English (DD5.1); French (Stereo). *SUB:* English; Spanish; French. *CAP:* English. *FEATURES:* 33 chapter links ⚬ Theatrical trailer ⚬ Production notes.
1997 (R) 135m/C Mel Gibson, Julia Roberts, Patrick Stewart, Cylk Cozart; *D:* Richard Donner; *W:* Brian Helgeland; *C:* John Schwartzman; *M:* Carter Burwell.

Contact

Thought-provoking (if overlong) drama based on a novel by Carl Sagan is not really a sci-fi spectacular (though it has its fair share of special effects). Radio astronomer Dr. Ellie Arroway (Foster) discovers signals being transmitted from the distant star Vega. When they're deciphered, the signals turn out to be blueprints for a craft that will take its occupant into space and a first meeting with aliens. Ellie fights to become that first spokesperson for Earth's inhabitants. More philosophical than the usual alien encounter epic, but the excellent cast, led by Foster, pulls it off nicely. For the most part, it's an excellent DVD transfer. The picture is sharp with very little grain. There are a few scenes where artifacts are noticeable and the disc has an occasional problem with high detail. Colors are excellent—accurate, bright, and vibrant, and the blacks are true. Contrast and brightness are boosted over the VHS and laserdisc releases making the overall image much more appealing. The sound is superb with excellent fidelity across the spectrum, separation, and Surround. —JO

Movie: 🎬🎬 **DVD:** 🎬🎬🎬
Warner Home Video, Inc. (Cat #15041, UPC #08539150122). Widescreen (2.35:1) anamorphic; full frame. Dolby Digital 5.1; Dolby Surround. $24.98. Snapper. *LANG:* English (DD5.1); French (DS). *SUB:* Spanish; French. *CAP:* English. *FEATURES:* 43 chapter links • Theatrical trailer • 3 commentaries • Production notes • Design concepts and tests • Dual-layered RSDL.
1997 (PG) 150m/C Jodie Foster, Matthew McConaughey, James Woods, Tom Skerritt, Angela Bassett, John Hurt, David Morse, Rob Lowe, Jake Busey, William Fichtner, Geoffrey Blake, Jena Malone; *D:* Robert Zemeckis; *W:* Michael Goldenberg; *C:* Don Burgess; *M:* Alan Silvestri. *AWARDS:* VSDA DVD Festival '00: Best Use of Audio/Language Tracks (tie); *NOM:* Academy Awards '97: Best Sound; Golden Globe Awards '98: Best Actress—Drama (Foster).

Convict 762

Whenever a sexy, intergalactic crew makes an emergency landing at a barbaric prison, and discover two survivors of a brutal massacre, one of the two survivors is bound to be the killer (interesting, right?). The ordeal then becomes a lethal game of hide-and-seek, as well as a hodgepodge of every sci-fi/action cliché imaginable. The movie isn't helped by the often murky and dull video transfer. The soundtrack fares a bit better, but it isn't enough to redeem the project as a whole. —MJT

Movie: 🎬🎬 **DVD:** 🎬🎬
York Entertainment (Cat #YPD-1001, UPC #750723100128). Widescreen (1.85:1) letterboxed. Dolby Digital Stereo. $24.98. Keepcase. *LANG:* English. *SUB:* Spanish. *FEATURES:* 27 chapter links • Cast biographies • Theatrical trailer • Theatrical trailer for *Spoiler.*
1998 (R) 100m/C Frank Zagarino, Billy Drago, Shannon Sturges; *D:* Luca Bercovici; *W:* J. Reifel; *C:* Steven Wacks.

Cookie's Fortune

After eccentric, lonely matriarch "Cookie" Orcutt (Neal) is discovered dead, the local police (Beatty and O'Donnell) can't tell what happened. Murder or suicide? Her equally off-center nieces Camille (Close) and Cora (Moore) don't wait for an answer before they begin to move into the moldering family manse. A high-powered outside investigator (Vance) thinks that Cookie's friend Willis (Dutton) is somehow involved. Cora's prodigal daughter Emma (Tyler) doesn't believe it. Even though that synopsis only begins to describe the film, it moves at a languid, Southern pace and pays as much attention to place—Holly Springs, MS, a real small town—as it does to plot. In his commentary track, Altman takes the same approach. He focuses on the characters, their relation to the town, the location work, and the nuts and bolts of the collaborative creative process. Unlike so many younger filmmakers, he does not feel the need to fill every moment with his wisdom. On DVD, the film sparkles. The sound does justice both to David A. Stewart's jazz-blues soundtrack and to the small nuances of personality that are revealed in a muttered off-hand remark. If, in the end, the film is not as ambitious as *Nashville* or *The Player*, it belongs on the short list with Altman's best. —MM

Movie: 🎬🎬🎬 **DVD:** 🎬🎬🎬
USA Home Entertainment (Cat #440 044 993-2, UPC #044004499323). Widescreen (1.85:1) letterboxed; full frame. Dolby Digital 5.1 Surround Stereo; Dolby Surround Stereo. $24.95. Keepcase. *LANG:* English. *SUB:* French; Spanish. *CAP:* English. *FEATURES:* 17 chapter links • Cast and crew thumbnail biographies • Theatrical trailer • Commentary: Altman.
1999 (PG-13) 118m/C Charles S. Dutton, Glenn Close, Patricia Neal, Liv Tyler, Chris O'Donnell, Julianne Moore, Ned Beatty, Courtney B. Vance, Donald Moffat, Lyle Lovett, Matt Malloy, Rufus Thomas, Danny Darst, Randle Mell, Niecy Nash, Ruby Wilson, Preston Strobel; *D:* Robert Altman; *W:* Anne Rapp; *C:* Toyomichi Kurita; *M:* David A. Stewart. *AWARDS:* National Board of Review Awards '99: Best Supporting Actress (Moore); *NOM:* Independent Spirit Awards '00: Best Film, Best Supporting Actor (Dutton), First Screenplay.

Cool Hand Luke

One of the last great men-in-chains films. Luke (Newman), sentenced to sweat out a term on a prison farm, refuses to compromise with authority. Martin shines in his supporting role as the oily warden, uttering that now-famous phrase, "What we have here is a failure to communicate." Kennedy's performance as leader of the chain gang won him an Oscar. Based on the novel by Donn Pearce. The film's power is increased substantially by this fine DVD. Having only seen the film previously in a pan-and-scan version, I was finally able to appreciate the emotional highs and lows and was completely blown away by the end of the film. Judging by the fleshtones, the DVD's colors are dead-on and very vivid. Sharpness is right up there too. The sound is not noticeably improved over the earlier home video version, but is good enough. —JO

Movie: 🎬🎬🎬 **DVD:** 🎬🎬🎬
Warner Home Video, Inc. (Cat #11037, UPC #085391103723). Widescreen (2.35:1) anamorphic. Dolby Digital Mono. $24.98. Snapper. *LANG:* English; Spanish; French. *SUB:* English; Spanish; French. *CAP:* English. *FEATURES:* 37 chapter links • Theatrical trailer • Production notes.
1967 126m/C Paul Newman, George Kennedy, J.D. Cannon, Strother Martin, Dennis Hopper, Anthony Zerbe, Lou Antonio, Wayne Rogers, Harry Dean Stanton, Ralph Waite, Joe Don Baker, Richard Davalos, Jo Van Fleet, Robert Drivas, Clifton James, Morgan Woodward, Luke Askew, Robert Donner, Warren Finnerty, James Gammon, Rance Howard, Buck Kartalian, John McLiam, Charles Tyner, Donn Pearce, Marc Cavell, Charles Hicks, James Jeter, Robert Luster, John Pearce, Eddie Rosson; *D:* Stuart Rosenberg; *W:* Frank Pierson, Donn Pearce; *C:* Conrad Hall; *M:* Lalo Schifrin. *AWARDS:* Academy Awards '67: Best Supporting Actor (Kennedy); *NOM:* Academy Awards '66: Best Adapted Screenplay, Best Original Score; Academy Awards '67: Best Actor (Newman).

Cool Runnings

This bright, semi-slapstick comedy is loosely based on the true story of the 1988 Jamaican bobsled team's quest to enter the Winter Olympics in Calgary, Canada. John Candy is recruited to coach four unlikely athletes who don't quite exemplify the spirit of the Games. Their journey from four innocents who have never even seen a bobsled to a true team is the kind of story that's been told in hundreds, perhaps thousands of sports movies. Director John Turteltaub handles it with a light touch, and he gets a lot of help from Hans Zimmer's bouncy score. On disc, the Jamaican exteriors have a noticeable brown-orange cast and slightly soft focus that snaps into bright colors and icy sharpness when the action moves north. The stereo sound really kicks in nicely on the bobsled runs. —MM

Movie: 🎬🎬🎬 **DVD:** 🎬🎬🎬
Buena Vista Home Entertainment (Cat #17371, UPC #717951002754). Widescreen (1.85:1) letterboxed. Dolby Digital Surround Stereo. $29.99. Keepcase. *LANG:* English. *CAP:* English. *FEATURES:* Theatrical trailer • 20 chapter links.
1993 (PG) 98m/C Leon, Doug E. Doug, John Candy, Marco Brambilla, Malik Yoba, Rawle Lewis, Raymond J. Barry, Peter Outerbridge, Larry Gilman, Paul Coeur; *D:* Jon Turteltaub; *W:* Tommy Swerdlow, Lynn Siefert, Michael Goldberg; *C:* Phedon Papamichael; *M:* Hans Zimmer.

Cop and a Half

Home Alone meets *Lethal Weapon* minus the violence. Devon Butler (Golden) is a bright third-grader who loves to play policeman. One afternoon, he happens upon a drug bust by detective Nick McKenna (Reynolds), and notes down an important license plate number. That, in turn, leads him to witness a murder by a comic gangster (Sharkey). So we wind up with the cuter-than-cute little black kid teamed up with the gruff white cop who hates children. The characters are thin stereotypes; the plot contains no surprises or suspense. Overall, the film has a low-budget, almost made-for-TV look to it that is not improved on DVD. Still, it's acceptable entertainment for the short set. —MM

Movie: 🎬🎬 **DVD:** 🎬🎬
Universal Studios Home Video (Cat #20511, UPC #025192051128). Widescreen (1.85:1) letterboxed. Dolby Digital

Surround Stereo. $24.98. Keepcase. *LANG:* English; French; Spanish. *SUB:* Spanish. *CAP:* English. *FEATURES:* 18 chapter links ▪ Production notes ▪ Cast and crew thumbnail biographies ▪ Theatrical trailer ▪ Universal web links.
1993 (PG) 87m/C Norman D. Golden II, Burt Reynolds, Ruby Dee, Ray Sharkey, Holland Taylor, Frank Sivero, Marc Macaulay, Rocky Giordani, Sammy Hernandez; *D:* Henry Winkler; *W:* Arne Olsen; *C:* Bill Butler; *M:* Alan Silvestri. *AWARDS:* Golden Raspberry Awards '93: Worst Actor (Reynolds).

Cop Land
Partially deaf sheriff (Stallone), whose small New Jersey town is home to a number of New York cops, has divided loyalties when a criminal investigation could implicate his department and the cops he idolizes. Stallone wanted to put "actor" back on his resume, and made the ultimate sacrifice of his physique for the role by gaining some 35 pounds and letting his muscles go. Writer-director Mangold, who grew up in an upstate New York town populated by NYC cops and firemen, pairs his earnest morality tale with a western feel to provide the excellent, Method-Actors All-Star team cast a chance to do what they do best. The blacks on this DVD are as true as they get. The picture is very sharp, and remains grain-free under all lighting conditions. Colors are excellent featuring deep accurate hues with no bleed. Both the contrast and brightness levels are actually better than in the theatre. The 5.1 soundtrack needs a little more separation, but the high end is crisp without taking anything away from the gutsy lows. —JO
Movie: 🦴🦴🦴 *DVD:* 🦴🦴🦴▶
Buena Vista Home Entertainment (Cat #1257, UPC #717951000385). Widescreen (1.85:1) letterboxed. Dolby Digital. $29.99. Keepcase. *LANG:* English; French. *CAP:* English. *FEATURES:* 14 chapter links ▪ Theatrical trailer.
1997 (R) 105m/C Sylvester Stallone, Robert De Niro, Annabella Sciorra, Harvey Keitel, Peter Berg, Janeane Garofalo, Michael Rapaport, Ray Liotta, Cathy Moriarty, Robert Patrick, Noah Emmerich, John Spencer, Malik Yoba, Frank Vincent, Arthur J. Nascarelli, Edie Falco, Deborah Harry; *D:* James Mangold; *W:* James Mangold; *C:* Eric Alan Edwards; *M:* Howard Shore.

Copycat
Crowded serial killer genre yields crooner Connick as southern psychopath stuck on murder. Soon he's in jail, advising the police in their hunt for another serial killer who imitates the murders of other infamous serial killers. Agoraphobic boozing criminal psychologist Helen Hudson (Weaver), still suffering the after effects of an attack by sicko subject Darryl Lee Cullum (Connick), is enlisted to help detective M.J. Monahan (Hunter) catch the homage specialist. Weaver and Hunter bring sparks to the usually testosterone-laden formula,

helping mask the preponderance of serial killer cliches and giant holes in the script. Connick's turn as a nut-job killer won't make you forget Anthony Hopkins, or even Frank Sinatra. Exploitive and imitative, and always faithful to the formula. Viewing the DVD is a much more pleasurable experience than the theatre, due mostly to the Dolby Digital 5.1 sound, which makes excellent use of the atmospheric environmental nuances of the soundtrack. The picture can hold its own, too. Sharpness is very good and grain so minor that it is never a problem. There were some artifacts but only in the darkest sequences. Colors are accurate with rich bright hues. The contrast and brightness levels are fine for both light and dark scenes, and the blacks, though not dead-on, are more than respectably true. —JO
Movie: 🦴🦴 *DVD:* 🦴🦴🦴
Warner Home Video, Inc. (Cat #14168, UPC #05391416821). Widescreen anamorphic; full frame. Dolby Digital 5.1. $24.98. Snapper. *LANG:* English; French. *SUB:* Spanish; French. *CAP:* English. *FEATURES:* 29 chapter links ▪ Theatrical trailer ▪ Commentary: Jon Amiel ▪ Production notes.
1995 (R) 124m/C Sigourney Weaver, Holly Hunter, Dermot Mulroney, Harry Connick Jr., William McNamara, Will Patton, John Rothman, David Michael Silverman; *D:* Jon Amiel; *W:* Ann Biderman, David Madsen; *C:* Laszlo Kovacs; *M:* Christopher Young.

Corridors of Blood
A doctor in search of a viable anesthetic accidently becomes addicted to drugs, then turns to grave robbers to support his habit. Karloff plays his usual threatening doctor to perfection. The DVD delivers a fairly good black-and-white image that is sharp and has pretty good graytones. The film looks very fresh for its age, thanks to very good contrast and brightness levels. The sound is adequate; probably the best that could be done from the source materials. —JO *AKA:* The Doctor from Seven Dials.
Movie: 🦴🦴▶ *DVD:* 🦴🦴▶
Image Entertainment (Cat #ID4431GODVD, UPC #014381443127). Full frame. PCM Mono. $24.95. Snapper. *LANG:* English. *FEATURES:* 16 chapter links ▪ Theatrical trailer.
1958 86m/C *GB* Boris Karloff, Betta St. John, Finlay Currie, Christopher Lee, Francis Matthews, Adrienne Corri, Nigel Green; *D:* Robert Day; *W:* Jean Scott Rogers; *C:* Geoffrey Faithfull; *M:* Buxton Orr.

Corrina, Corrina
In the mid-'50s, recently widowed Manny Singer (Liotta) must find a maid to help take care of his young daughter Molly (Majorino). Enter Corrina Washington (Goldberg). The predictable romance that develops is unusual for its interracial element. At heart, though, it's a very well-made chick flick. The DVD image ranges between good and very good. The disc

faithfully re-creates Bruce Surtees's slightly nostalgic cinematography; the subdued jazzy soundtrack (with an appearance by Anita Baker) is excellent. —MM
Movie: 🦴🦴 *DVD:* 🦴🦴
New Line Home Video (Cat #N4892, UPC #794043489228). Widescreen (1.85:1) letterboxed; full frame. Dolby Digital Stereo; Dolby Digital 5.1 Surround Stereo. $24.98. Snapper. *LANG:* English. *CAP:* English. *FEATURES:* 26 chapter links ▪ Theatrical trailer ▪ Cast and crew thumbnail biographies.
1994 (PG) 115m/C Whoopi Goldberg, Ray Liotta, Don Ameche, Tina Majorino, Wendy Crewson, Jenifer Lewis, Larry Miller, Erica Yohn, Anita Baker; *D:* Jessie Nelson; *W:* Jessie Nelson; *C:* Bruce Surtees; *M:* Rick Cox, Thomas Newman.

The Corruptor
Slick, violent crime thriller stars Wahlberg as Danny, a young Caucasian cop assigned to New York's Chinatown precinct and partnered with shrewd veteran Chen (Chow Yun-Fat). The two are drawn into a maze of deception and betrayal as they try to stop a war between rival underground factions. Chow finally receives the Hollywood role that showcases the talents that made him an international star, and Wahlberg isn't bad either. The action sequences suffer in comparison to Chow's work with John Woo. On his somewhat defensive commentary track, director Foley claims (incredibly) never to have seen any of those before he made this film. The potentially difficult film makes a smooth transition to DVD, with busy cluttered sets maintaining detail and the big action set pieces arriving intact. Stereo sound is very strong. A delightful guilty pleasure. —MM
Movie: 🦴🦴🦴▶ *DVD:* 🦴🦴🦴▶
New Line Home Video (Cat #N4776, UPC #794043477621). Widescreen (2.35:1) anamorphic. Dolby Digital 5.1 Surround Stereo; Dolby Digital Surround Stereo. $24.98. Snapper. *LANG:* English. *SUB:* English. *FEATURES:* 23 chapter links ▪ Commentary: director Foley ▪ Music commentary: Carter Burrell and Mark Sansom ▪ Commentary track indices ▪ Music video ▪ Cast and crew thumbnail biographies ▪ "Making of" featurette ▪ DVD-ROM features.
1999 (R) 110m/C Chow Yun-Fat, Mark Wahlberg, Ric Young, Paul Ben-Victor, Brian Cox, Byron Mann, Kim Chan, Tovah Feldshuh, Jon Kit Lee, Andrew Pang, Elizabeth Lindsey, Bill MacDonald, Susie Trinh; *D:* James Foley; *W:* Robert Pucci; *C:* Juan Ruiz-Anchia; *M:* Carter Burwell.

Cost of Living
Billie (Falco) is a thief and conwoman who doesn't settle down in one place long enough for the law or her victims to catch up with her. But things go wrong when she gets involved in a Long Island scam. The performances and the realistic-seeming details of life on the wrong side of the law

(such as how to hide your money in a cheap hotel room) have a believably lived-in quality. On the other hand, this angsty, artsy, existential, low-budget road movie has every rough edge you've ever seen in an independent production. Throughout, the image is grainy and so poorly lit that all colors have a bilious tone. The box art plays up Edie Falco's more recent fame from *The Sopranos*. —MM

Movie: 🐾🐾 **DVD:** 🐾

Image Entertainment (Cat #ID8759SIDVD, UPC #014381875928). Widescreen letterboxed. Dolby Digital Stereo. $24.99. Snapper. *LANG:* English. *FEATURES:* 16 chapter links.

1997 104m/C Edie Falco, James Villemaire, Andrew Lowery, William Sage, Amy Horne, Caitlin Clarke, Steven Beach; **D:** Stan Schofield; **W:** Ed Schmidt, Stephen Schmidt; **C:** Larry Fong.

Court Jester

Swashbuckling musical comedy stars Danny Kaye as a former circus clown who teams up with a merry band of outlaws to dethrone a tyrant king. Kaye poses as the court jester to spy on the king, his henchman (Rathbone), and the princess (Lansbury), and to win the hand of his lady fair (Johns). Filled with songs and truly funny lines, the picture is Kaye's finest moment. On disc, the Technicolor looks as crisp as the day the first print was developed. It's brighter than many films half its age. For those who wish to zip to their favorite scenes, go to chapter 25 for Kaye's induction into knighthood; chapter 31 for the duel; and, of course, chapter 27 where the vessel with the pestle holds the brew that is true. Even though the soundtrack is mono, every lyric and line of dialogue is easily understood. If the staging of the musical numbers looks a little dated, this remains one of the best musical comedies for videophiles of all ages. —MM

Movie: 🐾🐾🐾▸ **DVD:** 🐾🐾🐾▸

Paramount Home Video (Cat #055127, UPC #097360551273). Widescreen (1.85:1) letterboxed. Dolby Digital Mono. $29.99. Keepcase. *LANG:* English; French. *FEATURES:* Theatrical trailer ▪ Interactive menus.

1956 101m/C Danny Kaye, Glynis Johns, Basil Rathbone, Angela Lansbury, Cecil Parker, John Carradine, Mildred Natwick, Robert Middleton; **D:** Melvin Frank, Norman Panama; **W:** Norman Panama; **C:** Ray June; **M:** Sammy Cahn, Sylvia Fine, Vic Schoen.

Cousin Bette

Nineteenth-century French realist novelist Honore de Balzac gets the art house treatment in this stylish, if somewhat sluggish tale of sexual intrigue, betrayal, and revenge among the Parisian upper crust. The sordid tale spins around the continued abuse of Bette (Lange), who was sacrificed in favor of her cousin Adelaide (deathbed bit part by Chaplin) because her family could only afford to groom one of the girls for society. Bette is then jilted by Ade-laide's husband (Laurie), who instead of marrying her, offers her the position of governess to his daughter, Hortense (Macdonald). The final straw comes when she nurses a starving artist (Young) back to health only to find him stolen from her by Hortense. If not complicated enough, throw in a theatre star of dubious singing talent, but endowed with other "virtues" (Shue), and the lust-filled lord mayor of Paris (Hoskins), and you have all the incidents necessary for a truly nasty, if too long in coming, day of retribution. An otherwise beautiful DVD presentation visually is coupled with only an adequate audio track. Another disappointment is the lack of an audio commentary from director Des McAnuff, something that would have been welcome in revealing the reasoning behind some of the choices he made in this production. —RT

Movie: 🐾🐾 **DVD:** 🐾🐾🐾

Twentieth Century Fox Home Entertainment (Cat #4110449, UPC #086162104497). Widescreen. AC3 - 2 Channel. $34.98. Keepcase. *LANG:* English. *SUB:* English; Spanish. *CAP:* English; Spanish. *FEATURES:* 25 chapter markers ▪ Theatrical trailer.

1997 (R) 112m/C Jessica Lange, Elisabeth Shue, Aden Young, Bob Hoskins, Kelly Macdonald, Hugh Laurie, Geraldine Chaplin, Toby Stephens, John Sessions; **D:** Des McAnuff; **W:** Lynn Siefert, Susan Tarr; **C:** Andrzej Sekula; **M:** Simon Boswell.

The Cowboy Way

A mess from start to finish made somewhat watchable by cowpoke charm of the leads and one good horse chase. Two rodeo stars (Harrelson and Sutherland) from New Mexico ride into New York City to avenge a buddy's death, with Hudson as a mounted NYC cop who always yearned to be a cowboy. Great premise is overcome by tasteless humor and a patched-up plot shot full of holes. The DVD, however, is not bad. Picture sharpness is good and digital grain is bothersome only in extremely bright sequences and even then is not too distracting. The color is accurate with strong hues bleeding a touch. Contrast is excellent and the brightness is just a slight bit high. Blacks stay close to true and graininess is rare. The dialogue is distinct on the soundtrack without harming any of the dynamics necessary to the music. Bass is deep and cleanly handled while the high end is very crisp and clear. —JO

Movie: 🐾▸ **DVD:** 🐾🐾🐾

Universal Studios Home Video (Cat #20446, UPC #02519204625). Widescreen (1.85:1) anamorphic. Dolby Digital 5.1; Dolby Surround. $24.98. Keepcase. *LANG:* English (DD5.1); Spanish (DS); Spanish (DD5.1). *SUB:* Spanish. *CAP:* English. *FEATURES:* 16 chapter links ▪ Theatrical trailer ▪ Cast and filmmaker bios ▪ Production notes.

1994 (PG-13) 106m/C Woody Harrelson, Kiefer Sutherland, Dylan McDermott, Ernie Hudson, Cara Buono, Marg Helgenberger, Tomas Milian, Joaquin Martinez; **Cameos:** Travis Tritt; **D:** Gregg Champion; **W:** William D. Wittliff, Rob Thompson; **C:** Dean Semler; **M:** David Newman.

The Cowboys

When his cowhands desert him to search for gold, rancher Will Anderson (Wayne) is forced to hire 11 schoolboys to drive his cattle 400 miles to market. This may be the Duke's most undervalued western—with echoes of *Red River* and *The Shootist*—and it receives well-deserved careful treatment on DVD. The disc is filled with extras aimed squarely at his fans. For the most part, image and sound are excellent. Some of the night scenes are a little murky, as they were in the theatrical release. The film is too long and indulgent with a separate Overture for John Williams's score and an intermission, but on home video, those are not a problem. Wayne's performance is one of his most emotional and the DVD captures it. —MM

Movie: 🐾🐾🐾🐾▸ **DVD:** 🐾🐾🐾🐾▸

Warner Home Video, Inc. (Cat #15183, UPC #085391518327). Widescreen (2.35:1) letterboxed. Dolby Digital 5.1 Surround; Dolby Digital Mono. $24.98. Snapper. *LANG:* English; French. *SUB:* English; French. *CAP:* English. *FEATURES:* 37 chapter links ▪ Cast and crew thumbnail biographies ▪ "Making of" featurette ▪ Theatrical trailers for 13 other John Wayne westerns ▪ Brief history of western films and cowboys.

1972 (PG) 128m/C John Wayne, Roscoe Lee Browne, A. Martinez, Bruce Dern, Colleen Dewhurst, Slim Pickens, Robert Carradine, Clay O'Brien, Nicolas Beauvy; **D:** Mark Rydell; **W:** Harriet Frank Jr., Irving Ravetch; **C:** Robert L. Surtees; **M:** John Williams.

Crackdown

Low-budget actioneer looks no better than it did at the drive-in, its natural element. It's a vigilante drug-revenge story set in the Philippines. (Vic Diaz, a familiar face in these productions for decades, shows up as one of the bad guys.) The DVD is rough, grainy, cheap-looking, and presented with no extras, not even chapter links. —MM

Movie: 🐾 **DVD:** 🐾

Image Entertainment (Cat #DVD103, UPC #066479101037). Full frame. $19.99. Keepcase. *LANG:* English.

1988 93m/C Chris De Rose, Seib Seibl, Tyke Caravelli; **D:** John Garwood.

The Craft

Call it *Heathers* with hexes. Troubled 17-year-old Sarah (Tunney) moves to L.A. and begins her senior year at St. Benedict's Academy. She takes up with three rebels—Nancy (Balk), Bonnie (Campbell), and Rochelle (True)—who like to dabble in witchcraft. Now, with the addition of would-be witch Sarah, these black magic women start slinging spells at their uppity classmates. The film works best when concentrating on the girls and their problems, but degenerates into a special effects barrage toward the end. Alas, no one is turned into a newt. The blacks aren't always on in this DVD presentation, but are generally pretty true and free of grain. The picture is of above-average sharpness and but for a couple of hesitant, jerky digital movements, has no artifact problem. Contrast and brightness levels are strong and give the image a lot of punch, more than the earlier laserdisc edition, which was not a bad disc. The sound is also very good and has excellent separation including good detail on the Surround tracks. They deliver a wallop and there is good dynamic range throughout the spectrum. —JO

Movie: 🦴🦴▶ **DVD:** 🦴🦴🦴

Columbia Tristar Home Video (Cat #84219, UPC #043396824195). Widescreen (1.85:1) letterboxed. Dolby Digital 5.1; Dolby Surround. $25.95. Keepcase. *LANG:* English (DD5.1); Spanish (DS); French (DS). *SUB:* Spanish; Korean. *CAP:* English. *FEATURES:* 45 chapter links.

1996 (R) 100m/C Robin Tunney, Fairuza Balk, Neve Campbell, Rachel True, Skeet Ulrich, Helen Shaver, Cliff DeYoung, Christine Taylor, Assumpta Serna; **D:** Andrew Fleming; **W:** Andrew Fleming, Peter Filardi; **C:** Alexander Grusynski; **M:** Graeme Revell. *AWARDS:* MTV Movie Awards '97: Best Fight (Fairuza Balk/Robin Tunney).

Crash

You can always expect surreal kinkiness from Cronenberg and this film, awarded a Special Jury Prize at Cannes for "daring, originality, and audacity," won't prove the exception. Based on J.G. Ballard's 1973 cult novel, it's "auto" erotica taken to the max, with car crashes and bodily injury turned into fetishes. James (Spader) lands in the hospital after an accident, which injured Helen (Hunter), a passenger in the other car. Helen and James's shared experience soon leads to a sexual relationship, which doesn't bother James's wife, Catherine (Unger). Then there's Vaughan (Koteas) and his group who like to reenact famous auto crashes (like those of James Dean and Jayne Mansfield). Oh yes, there's lots more sex (in various combinations). The DVD presents both the full uncut 100-minute version and the so-called "Director's 'R'-rated cut," which is pretty useless and was designed for rent in mainstream video stores. Having seen the Criterion laserdisc, it's safe to say that this is a substantial improvement. The picture is sharper (though there are still soft spots) and the DVD does not add much in the way of grain. Colors, subdued at times but generally rich, are a true representation of the theatrical release. Blacks are also true and even with the subtle increase in both contrast and brightness, do not edge towards gray. The sound is much stronger than the LD and a 5.1 remix is hardly mixed. The laserdisc contains an interest-

ing batch of supplementals that are not included on this DVD and would have been a welcome replacement for the lame "R"-rated version. —JO

Movie: 🦴🦴 **DVD:** 🦴🦴🦴

New Line Home Video (Cat #N4681, UPC #79404368124). Widescreen (1.78:1) anamorphic. Dolby Digital Stereo. $29.99. Snapper. *LANG:* English. *SUB:* Spanish; French. *CAP:* English. *FEATURES:* 21 chapter links • Theatrical trailer • Cast and crew bios. Includes both "NC-17" (100 mins.) and "R"-rated (90 mins.) versions.

1995 (NC-17) 98m/C CA James Spader, Holly Hunter, Elias Koteas, Deborah Kara Unger, Rosanna Arquette, Peter MacNeill; **D:** David Cronenberg; **C:** Peter Suschitzsky; **M:** Howard Shore. *AWARDS:* Cannes Film Festival '96: Special Jury Prize; Genie Awards '96: Best Adapted Screenplay, Best Cinematography, Best Director (Cronenberg), Best Film Editing; *NOM:* Genie Awards '96: Best Film, Best Sound.

The Crazy Ray

Please see review of *The Bells / The Crazy Ray*. **AKA:** Paris Qui Dort.

Movie: 🦴🦴🦴

1922 60m/B FR Henri Rollan, Albert Prejean, Marcel Vallee, Madeleine Rodrigue; **D:** Rene Clair.

Crazy Six

In the not-too-distant future, eastern Europe has become Crimeland, ruled by gangs. Crazy Six (Lowe) and Dirty Mao (Van Peebles) are trying to unseat Raul (Ice-T). Director Pyun is an old hand at these low-budget high-octane action flicks. His sometimes stylized violence and visuals arrive on DVD with no flaws worth noting. The image is somewhat sharper than VHS tape. Sound is about the same. —MM

Movie: 🦴🦴 **DVD:** 🦴🦴🦴

Studio Home Entertainment (Cat #7025, UPC #658149702523). Full frame. Dolby Digital Stereo. $24.95. Keepcase. *LANG:* English. *FEATURES:* 18 chapter links • Cast and crew thumbnail biographies • Theatrical trailer.

1998 (R) ?m/C Rob Lowe, Burt Reynolds, Ice-T, Mario Van Peebles; **D:** Albert Pyun.

Creator

A Frankenstein-like scientist plans to clone a being based on his wife, who died 30 years ago. As his experiments begin to show positive results, his romantic attention turns towards his beautiful lab assistant. O'Toole as the deranged scientist almost saves this one. The enjoyment of the film would have increased with a little better color, which is somewhat pale and occasionally pinkish. Overall the image is of slightly above-average sharpness and does have more grain than the laserdisc release, usually associated with warmer earthtone colors. —JO

Movie: 🦴🦴 **DVD:** 🦴🦴▶

Trimark Home Video (Cat #VM7038D, UPC #031398703839). Full frame. Stereo. $24.98. Keepcase. *LANG:* English. *SUB:* English; Spanish; French. *FEATURES:* 30 chapter links • Theatrical trailer.

1985 (R) 108m/C Peter O'Toole, Mariel Hemingway, Vincent Spano, Virginia Madsen, David Ogden Stiers, John Dehner, Karen Kopins, Jeff Corey; **D:** Ivan Passer; **W:** Jeremy Leven; **C:** Robbie Greenberg; **M:** Sylvester Levay.

Creepers

A young girl (Connelly) talks to bugs and gets them to follow her instructions, which comes in handy when she battles the lunatic who is killing her school chums. Argento weirdness—and graphic gore—may not be for all tastes. Formerly available only as the shorter American release. The DVD is not just longer than the older, shorter VHS release, it is also so far improved that there is no comparison. The picture is sharp and has only minor (and rare) occurrences of grain, even with the numerous dark scenes. Fleshtones are accurate and colors are vibrant, while detailed enough to reflect subtle shadings. Blacks are true. Contrast and brightness levels are both very good. The soundtrack is not objectionable, but at times sounds synthesized with too much of the music fed to the rear channels. Overall though, it sounds full and dynamic, and the added bass punch is well worth it. —JO **AKA:** Phenomena.

Movie: 🦴🦴▶ **DVD:** 🦴🦴▶

Anchor Bay (Cat #DV10726, UPC #01313082693). Widescreen (1.66:1) letterboxed. Dolby Digital 5.1; Mono. $29.98. Keepcase. *LANG:* English (DD5.1); French (mono). *FEATURES:* 20 chapter links • Theatrical trailer • Behind-the-scenes featurette • Commentary: Argento, Sergio Stivaletti, Claudio Simonetti, Loris Curci • Claudio Simonetti music video • Dario Argento interview by Joe Franklin.

1985 (R) 82m/C IT Jennifer Connelly, Donald Pleasence, Daria Nicolodi, Elenora Giorgi, Dalia di Lazzaro, Patrick Bauchau, Fiore Argento, Federica Mastroianni, Michele (Michael) Soavi, Gavin Friday; **D:** Dario Argento; **W:** Dario Argento, Franco Ferrini; **C:** Romano Albani; **M:** Simon Boswell.

The Creeps

Librarian Anna (Griffin) hires a detective (Lauer) to get back the original manuscript of Mary Shelley's *Frankenstein*, which has been stolen by a mildly mad scientist, Berber (Moynihan). He's using manuscripts and a crackpot lab to bring fictional monsters back to life. His experiment goes awry and the results are midget versions of Dracula (Fondacaro), Frankenstein's Monster (Wellington), the Werewolf (Simanton), and the Mummy (Smith). It's a

typical Full Moon production—low-budget, O.K. makeup, good effects, juvenile humor. *Movie:* 🎞🎞 *DVD:* NYR
Full Moon Pictures (Cat #8026). Full frame. $24.98. Keepcase. *FEATURES:* Cast and crew thumbnail biographies ▪ Blooper reel ▪ Trailers ▪ *Videozone* magazine "making of" featurette.
1997 (PG-13) 80m/C Phil Fondacaro, Rhonda Griffin, Justin Lauer, Bill Moynihan, Kristin Norton, Jon Simanton, Joe Smith, Thomas Wellington; *D:* Charles Band; *W:* Benjamin Carr; *C:* Adolfo Bartoli; *M:* Carl Dante.

Creepshow
Stephen King and George Romero pay affectionate and gory tribute to E.C. Comics with these five short films. With its use of split screens, animated frames, bright primary colors, live action that fades into and out of comic art, and even ads between the episodes, the collection is a true cinematic comic book. The best ones are "The Crate," with Adrienne Barbeau as a brassy shrew, and "Creeping Up on You," with E.G. Marshall as a cheerfully wicked millionaire. King himself plays "Jordy." Fans of blood-soaked silliness won't be disappointed. The main attraction of the DVD is the easy access it gives to the individual episodes. Visually, the night scenes are O.K. The red and blue light effects look like I remember them from the theatrical release. Overall, the disc is a distinct step up from the tape, particularly with both widescreen and full-frame versions. —*MM*
Movie: 🎞🎞🎞 *DVD:* 🎞🎞🎞
Warner Home Video, Inc. (Cat #16053, UPC #085391605324). Full frame; widescreen letterboxed. Dolby Digital Surround Stereo. $19.98. Snapper. *LANG:* English. *SUB:* French. *CAP:* English. *FEATURES:* 41 chapter links.
1982 (R) 120m/C Hal Holbrook, Adrienne Barbeau, Viveca Lindfors, E.G. Marshall, Stephen King, Leslie Nielsen, Carrie Nye, Fritz Weaver, Ted Danson, Ed Harris, John Amplas, Tom Savini; *D:* George A. Romero; *W:* Stephen King; *C:* Michael Gornick; *M:* John Harrison.

Crime Broker
Judge Holly McPhee (Bissett) experiences life on the other side of the law as the mastermind behind a series of robberies. When visiting criminologist Okazaki (Kato) uncovers her secret life, he wants in. This Australian variation on *The Thomas Crown Affair* is surprisingly enjoyable, particularly for Bissett fans. On DVD, the image is nothing exceptional with a slightly soft focus, too-heavy blacks, and colors that emphasize the red end of the spectrum. Sound is O.K. —*MM*
Movie: 🎞🎞▸ *DVD:* 🎞🎞
Simitar Entertainment (Cat #7317, UPC #082551731725). Full frame. PCM Stereo. $14.98. Keepcase. *LANG:* English. *FEATURES:* 8 chapter links ▪ Production

factoids ▪ Jacqueline Bissett thumbnail biography and filmography.
1994 93m/C Jacqueline Bisset, Massaya Kato, Gary Day; *D:* Ian Barry; *W:* Tony Morphett; *C:* Dan Burstall; *M:* Roger Mason.

Crimes & Misdemeanors
One of Allen's most mature films explores a range of moral ambiguities through the parallel and eventually interlocking stories of a nebbish filmmaker (Allen)—who agrees to make a profile of a smug Hollywood TV comic (Alda) and then sabotages it—and an esteemed opthamologist (Landau), who is being threatened with exposure by his neurotic mistress (Huston). Few directors could pull off the intriguing mix of drama and comedy. Look for Daryl Hannah in an unbilled cameo. Though Allen is not known as a visual stylist, this film looks very good on DVD with a nicely textured image. Some of the credit must go to director of photography Sven Nykvist. Sound is fine. —*MM*
Movie: 🎞🎞🎞 *DVD:* 🎞🎞🎞
Image Entertainment (Cat #4080, UPC #014381408027). Widescreen (1.85:1) letterboxed. Dolby Digital Stereo. $24.99. Snapper. *LANG:* English. *CAP:* English. *FEATURES:* 21 chapter links.
1989 (PG-13) 104m/C Martin Landau, Woody Allen, Alan Alda, Mia Farrow, Joanna Gleason, Anjelica Huston, Jerry Orbach, Sam Waterston, Claire Bloom, Jenny Nichols, Caroline Aaron, Daryl Hannah, Nora Ephron, Jerry Zaks; *D:* Woody Allen; *W:* Woody Allen; *C:* Sven Nykvist. *AWARDS:* National Board of Review Awards '89: Best Supporting Actor (Alda); New York Film Critics Awards '89: Best Supporting Actor (Alda); Writers Guild of America '89: Best Original Screenplay; *NOM:* Academy Awards '89: Best Director (Allen), Best Original Screenplay, Best Supporting Actor (Landau).

Crimes of Passion
Vintage whacked-out Russell revolves around a prim fashion designer (Turner) who transforms herself into a kinky prostitute at night. A disturbed street preacher (Perkins) makes her the heroine of his erotic fantasies. The dark vision of underground sexuality and moral hypocrisy is sexually explicit and violent with an extremely black comedic center. Turner's portrayal is honest and believable; Perkins overacts, but, for Russell's fans at least, it's all to good effect. The DVD image is slightly sharper than the unrated VHS tape, but given the subject matter, that's a mixed blessing. Sound is acceptable. —*MM*
Movie: 🎞🎞🎞 *DVD:* 🎞🎞🎞
Anchor Bay (Cat #10333). Widescreen (1.85:1) letterboxed. Dolby Digital Stereo. $24.98. Keepcase. *LANG:* English.
1984 101m/C Kathleen Turner, Anthony Perkins, Annie Potts, John Laughlin, Bruce Davison, Norman Burton; *D:* Ken Russell; *W:* Barry Sandler; *C:* Dick Bush; *M:* Rick

Wakeman. *AWARDS:* Los Angeles Film Critics Association Awards '84: Best Actress (Turner).

Criminal Act
Newspaper reporters chase stories and monsters. *AKA:* Tunnels.
Movie: NYR *DVD:* NYR
Digital Versatile Disc Ltd. (Cat #143). $19.95. Keepcase.
1988 94m/C Catherine Bach, Charlene Dallas, Nicholas Guest, John Saxon, Vic Tayback; *D:* Mark Byers.

Crimson Tide
Mutiny erupts aboard the submarine USS *Alabama* as Captain Ramsey (Hackman) and his Executive Officer Hunter (Washington) clash over the validity of orders to launch the sub's missiles. Ramsey, who wants to fire the missiles, and Hunter, who refuses to comply until the message is verified, battle for control of the sub. Suspenseful and well-paced thriller lets Hackman and Washington show off their considerable screen presence, while Bruckheimer, Simpson, and Scott show that they haven't lost any of their trademark big-budget, testosterone-laden flash. Original screenplay went under the knife of a number of script doctors, most notably Quentin Tarantino. The tints are off a bit on this DVD, which is fairly distracting since the color level itself is strong. The overall feel of the disc is a little dark and that further affects the colors representation. The contrast is a bit heavy but that is probably just because the brightness is low. The sound, however, is superb. Every effect and every bit of dialogue seems perfectly mixed and out front, and the Surround does its job by placing the viewer right aboard the sub. The rumbling of the bottom end never seems to mute the undistorted clarity of the orchestral score and effect tracks. —*JO*
Movie: 🎞🎞🎞 *DVD:* 🎞🎞▸
Buena Vista Home Entertainment (Cat #13679, UPC #717951000149). Widescreen (2.35:1) letterboxed. Dolby Digital 5.1. $29.99. Keepcase. *LANG:* English; French. *SUB:* Spanish. *CAP:* English. *FEATURES:* 32 chapter links.
1995 (R) 116m/C Gene Hackman, Denzel Washington, George Dzundza, Viggo Mortensen, James Gandolfini, Matt Craven, Lillo Brancato, Danny Nucci, Steve Zahn, Rick Schroder, Vanessa Bell Calloway, Rocky Carroll; *Cameos:* Jason Robards Jr.; *D:* Tony Scott; *W:* Michael Schiffer, Richard P. Henrick; *C:* Darius Wolski; *M:* Hans Zimmer. *AWARDS:* *NOM:* Academy Awards '95: Best Film Editing, Best Sound; MTV Movie Awards '96: Best Male Performance (Washington).

Crimson Wolf
The fate of the world rests in the ability of three untested warriors to defeat an unearthly army of darkness. Sorcery, martial arts, and an unrequited love spanning

the centuries play parts in this animated story. The image is generally good, and sound is O.K. but not great compared to the best anime titles. No extras to speak of, not even the expected subtitles. Anime purists who prefer to listen to the Japanese soundtrack and have English subtitles are out of luck. Not rated, but contains graphic depictions of violence and sex. —MB

Movie: ♫♫ **DVD:** ♫♫

Image Entertainment (Cat #ID4652SEDVD, UPC #014381465228). Full frame. Dolby Digital Stereo. $24.99. Snapper. *LANG:* English; Japanese. *FEATURES:* 14 chapter links.

1994 60m/C *JP D:* Shoichi Masuo; *W:* Shoichi Masuo.

Critical Care

Spader is a doctor in a high-tech intensive care unit who must deal with such ethical questions as euthanasia, insurance scams, and a drunken administrator (Brooks) whose only concern is hospital profits. Two sisters (Sedgwick and Martindale) fight over the fate of their terminally ill, near-vegetable father. Spader finds his career on the line after sleeping with Sedgwick and backing her attempts to pull the plug. Given the meatiness of the subject, Lumet could have made a much more scathing satire. Schwartz's script is lame even for a first-time effort.

Movie: ♫ **DVD:** NYR

Artisan Entertainment (Cat #60464). Widescreen (1.85:1) letterboxed; full frame. Dolby Digital 5.1 Surround Stereo. $29.98. Snapper. *LANG:* English. *SUB:* Spanish. *FEATURES:* Production notes ● Trailer.

1997 (R) 105m/C James Spader, Albert Brooks, Kyra Sedgwick, Helen Mirren, Margo Martindale, Jeffrey Wright, Wallace Shawn, Anne Bancroft, Philip Bosco, Edward Herrmann, Colm Feore, James Lally, Al Waxman, Harvey Atkin; *D:* Sidney Lumet; *W:* Steven S. Schwartz; *C:* David Watkin; *M:* Michael Convertino. *AWARDS: NOM:* Independent Spirit Awards '98: First Screenplay.

Crooklyn

Director Lee turns from the life of Malcolm X to the early lives of Generation X in this profile of an African-American middle-class family growing up in 1970s Brooklyn. Lee's least politically charged film to date is a joint effort between him and sibs Joie and Cinque, and profiles the coming-of-age of the only girl in a family of five children. Tender and real performances from all, especially newcomer Harris, propel the sometimes messy, music-laden trip to nostalgia land. This is a thoroughly enjoyable DVD, thanks in part to its excellent 5.1 mix. The song-oriented soundtrack is boisterous and nearly always there, while the dialogue remains crystal clear. The image is also very enjoyable with warm, vibrant colors, as well as true, grainless blacks and excellent contrast. —JO

Movie: ♫♫♫ **DVD:** ♫♫♫►

Universal Studios Home Video (Cat #20515, UPC #025192051524). Widescreen (1.85:1) letterboxed. Dolby Digital 5.1. $24.98. Keepcase. *LANG:* English; French. *SUB:* Spanish. *CAP:* English. *FEATURES:* 18 chapter links ● Production notes ● Cast and filmmakers bios ● Film highlights.

1994 (PG-13) 112m/C Alfre Woodard, Delroy Lindo, Zelda Harris, David Patrick Kelly, Carlton Williams, Sharif Rashed, Tse-March Washington, Christopher Knowings, Jose Zuniga, Isaiah Washington, Ivelka Reyes, N. Jeremi Duru, Frances Foster, Norman Matlock, Patriece Nelson, Joie Lee, Vondie Curtis-Hall, Tiasha Reyes, Spike Lee; *D:* Spike Lee; *W:* Joie Lee, Cinque Lee; *C:* Arthur Jaffa; *M:* Terence Blanchard.

Cross of Iron

Sam Peckinpah's embattled two-character study in contrasts sets Corporal Steiner (James Coburn) against a weaseling senior officer (Prussian aristocrat Captain Stransky, played by Maximilian Schell), who has just usurped Steiner's troops in a bloodthirsty, foolhardy attempt to win himself the Iron Cross. The director's only war film, a thinking man's dogfight of tight dramatic scope and deeply embittered humor, was lauded by Orson Welles as the best antiwar statement since *All Quiet on the Western Front*. The only existing print to work with on this project was not widescreen, and its original soundtrack was mono. The digital transfer has good and bad points. While there are moments of banding and aliasing on bright light sources and in sky and interior shots, the fire and dust explosions have a startlingly three-dimensional impact. Some may be disappointed, others relieved that the artillery cracks, whines, and booms on the soundtrack are more muted than intrusive. The slide show consists of a dozen German lobby cards. —JK *AKA:* Steiner—Das Eiserne Kreuz.

Movie: ♫♫► **DVD:** ♫♫♫►

Hen's Tooth Video (Cat #4065, UPC #759731406529). Full frame. Dolby Digital. $29.99. Keepcase. *LANG:* English. *FEATURES:* 12 chapter links ● Interactive menus ● Photo gallery.

1976 (R) 120m/C *GB GE* James Coburn, Maximilian Schell, James Mason, David Warner, Senta Berger, Klaus Lowitsch, Vadim Glowna, Roger Fritz, Dieter Schidor, Burkhard Driest, Fred Stillkrauth, Michael Nowka, Veronique Vendell, Arthur Brauss; *D:* Sam Peckinpah; *W:* Julius J. Epstein, Walter Kelley, James Hamilton; *C:* John Coquillon; *M:* Ernest Gold.

The Crossing Guard

Freddy (Nicholson) hangs out in strip joints, drinks too much, and is obsessed with revenge. His ex-wife Mary (Huston) goes to group therapy sessions and works through her grief. Then Booth (Morse), the drunk driver who killed their daughter, is released from prison. Freddy decides to

kill him. Those are the bare bones of writer-director Penn's story. At the film's best, Penn and Nicholson are able to make Freddy's dislocation, anger, and frustration seem absolutely real. As characters, Booth and Mary are almost as strong, but this underappreciated film belongs to Nicholson. He and Penn work well together and in his comments, Penn talks about his relationship with the actors. That commentary track, which he shares with other members of the cast, is a virtual textbook, much more informative and valuable than most of the self-congratulation that accompanies more financially successful films. It's particularly valuable on this DVD. Though the sound and image are fine, they're not nearly as important as the characters. These observations, which seem to have been taken from separate interviews, are focused on the creation of character and the decisions that the filmmakers made concerning them. —MM

Movie: ♫♫♫ **DVD:** ♫♫♫►

Miramax Pictures Home Video (Cat #17099, UPC #717951002136). Widescreen (1.85:1) letterboxed. Dolby Digital 5.1 Surround Stereo. $29.99. Keepcase. *LANG:* English. *CAP:* English. *FEATURES:* 30 chapter links ● Commentary: Penn, Huston, Morse, Zsigmond, Haller, Rabe.

1994 (R) 111m/C Jack Nicholson, Anjelica Huston, David Morse, Robin Wright Penn, Robbie Robertson, Piper Laurie, Richard Bradford, John Savage, Priscilla Barnes, Kari Wuhrer, Jennifer Leigh Warren, Richard Sarafian, Jeff Morris, Joe Viterelli, Eileen Ryan, Ryo Ishibashi, Michael Ryan, Nicky Blair, Gene Kirkwood, Jason Kristofer, Hadda Brooks; *D:* Sean Penn; *W:* Sean Penn; *C:* Vilmos Zsigmond; *M:* Jack Nitzsche. *AWARDS: NOM:* Golden Globe Awards '96: Best Supporting Actress (Huston); Independent Spirit Awards '96: Best Supporting Actor (Morse); Screen Actors Guild Award '95: Best Supporting Actress (Huston).

Crossworlds

All dimensions of the universe collide in the mystical valley of Crossworlds. When alien night riders attack Joe Talbot (Charles), he escapes with girlfriend Laura (Roth) and they meet up with mercenary A.T. (Hauer). Turns out the crystal pendant Joe's father left him is one of the keys that unlock the boundaries between worlds. Along with a scepter, they give the owner unlimited power. So the trio enter Crossworlds to fight a battle between good and evil. Since the picture is a little soft on this DVD, and there are some nasty artifacts at times, you'd expect a high level of digital grain. Surprisingly, there is a lot less than you find on DVDs with a much higher rating. Colors are accurate, with little bleed, and the blacks are true. The picture could have used a little more contrast and brightness. Though the sound has good low end, it is generally pretty listless with clips during loud dialogue or effects. —JO

Movie: ♫♫ **DVD:** ♫♫▶
Trimark Home Video (Cat #6770D, UPC #031398677031). Widescreen (1.85:1) letterboxed; full frame. Stereo. $24.98. Keepcase. *LANG:* English. *SUB:* Spanish. *CAP:* English. *FEATURES:* 30 chapter links ▪ Cast bios.
1996 (PG-13) 91m/C Rutger Hauer, Josh Charles, Andrea Roth, Stuart Wilson; *D:* Krishna Rao; *W:* Raman Rao, Krishna Rao; *C:* Chris Walling; *M:* Christophe Beck.

The Crow

In an unnamed, decaying inner city on Devil's Night (an excuse for arson before Halloween), Eric Draven (Lee) and his fiancee Shelly (Shinas) are murdered by four thugs. One year later, Eric rises out of the grave, literally, for revenge. Our young narrator Sarah (Davis) explains that his love was so strong that a crow has brought him back to this world for revenge. The main villain is a Byronic gangster, Top Dollar (Wincott), who lives incestuously with his half-sister Myca (Ling). Eric's only ally is an honest beat cop named Albrecht (Hudson). Virtually all of the action takes place at night on rainy streets or in grimy interiors. Director Proyas fills the screen with shiny blacks, deep grays, and red highlights. That dampens the film's violence while heightening the mood. The DVD handles the many shades and textures of darkness as well as the theatrical version. The stereo sound is equally sharp. The accidental death of Lee while making the film underscores its dark themes of resurrection and revenge. A commentary track on the computer effects that were used to complete Lee's work would have been a worthwhile addition. —MM
Movie: ♫♫♫ **DVD:** ♫♫♫
Miramax Pictures Home Video (Cat #13677, UPC #717951000125). Widescreen (1.85:1) letterboxed. Dolby Digital Stereo. $29.99. Keepcase. *LANG:* English; French. *CAP:* English. *FEATURES:* 18 chapter links.
1993 (R) 100m/C Brandon Lee, Ernie Hudson, Michael Wincott, David Patrick Kelly, Rochelle Davis, Angel David, Michael Massee, Bai Ling, Laurence Mason, Bill Raymond, Marco Rodriguez, Anna Thomson, Sofia Shinas, Jon Polito, Tony Todd; *D:* Alex Proyas; *W:* David J. Schow, John Shirley; *C:* Darius Wolski; *M:* Graeme Revell. *AWARDS:* MTV Movie Awards '95: Best Song ("Big Empty"); *NOM:* MTV Movie Awards '95: Best Film, Best Male Performance (Lee).

The Crow 2: City of Angels

James O'Barr's cult graphic-novel antihero returns in a new incarnation. It's eight years later (in film time) and the setting's changed form Detroit to L.A. But the horror remains. Ashe (Perez) and his young son witness a murder and are killed themselves by scumbags working for druglord Judah (Brooks). So the Crow brings back

Ashe to get revenge. Also involved is Sarah (Kirshner), who retains her role as story narrator but is now a grown-up tattoo artist who falls in love with Ashe. A good look, but not much substance. The highlight is the bad guy turn by punkster Iggy Pop. This dark-looking film actually appears a little better on the DVD than it did at the theatre. The colors are absolutely stunning and the contrast and brightness levels are intense without harming any of the hues or the perfect blacks. Most amazing is that, despite all the dimly lit scenes, there is no grain or artifacts. The 5.1 sound also delivers—pulsating bass, crisp highs, and state-of-the-art Surround. —JO
Movie: ♫♫▶ **DVD:** ♫♫♫♫
Miramax Pictures Home Video (Cat #13678, UPC #717951000132). Widescreen (1.85:1) letterboxed. Dolby Digital 5.1. $29.99. Keepcase. *LANG:* English. *SUB:* English; Spanish. *FEATURES:* 11 chapter links.
1996 (R) 93m/C Vincent Perez, Mia Kirshner, Iggy Pop, Richard Brooks, Ian Dury, Thuy Trang, Thomas Jane, Vincent Castellanos, Tracey Ellis; *D:* Tim Pope; *W:* David S. Goyer; *C:* Jean-Yves Escoffier; *M:* Graeme Revell.

Cruel Intentions

Fourth adaptation of the 1782 novel *Les Liasons Dangereuses* takes the tale of seduction and intrigue from 18th-century France to a modern Manhattan prep school. Think *I Know Who You Did Last Summer* with a cast of attractive vapid young stars and one genuine actress (Witherspoon). DVD retains the film's highly polished vision of wealth, but it can do little for the performances. The giddy commentary track by the filmmakers reinforces those flaws. It's clear that everyone involved was interested in style over substance and they got what they wanted. Both image and sound first-rate. The extras are extensive but uninspired. —MM
Movie: ♫♫▶ **DVD:** ♫♫♫▶
Columbia Tristar Home Video (Cat #03827, UPC #043396038271). Widescreen (1.85:1) letterboxed; full frame. Dolby Digital 5.1 Surround Stereo. $25.95. Keepcase. *LANG:* English. *SUB:* English. *FEATURES:* 28 chapter links ▪ "Making of" featurette ▪ Commentary: filmmakers ▪ 6 deleted scenes ▪ Theatrical trailer ▪ Cast and crew thumbnail biographies ▪ Music videos ▪ "Finding a visual style" featurette.
1998 (R) 95m/C Sarah Michelle Gellar, Ryan Phillippe, Reese Witherspoon, Selma Blair, Joshua Jackson, Eric Mabius, Louise Fletcher, Swoosie Kurtz, Christine Baranski, Sean Patrick Thomas; *D:* Roger Kumble; *W:* Roger Kumble; *C:* Theo van de Sande; *M:* Ed Shearmur.

Crumb

Once you've seen this documentary about legendary underground cartoon artist R. Crumb, you'll never worry about

your dysfunctional family (not that you've got one) and your psychotic episodes again. The most interesting thing is that Crumb himself is not the weird(est) one in his family, despite his reputation and art. *Crumb* is one of those films that finds the perfect way to present real-life material that is both offensive and tasteless, without forcing the viewer to assume responsibility. At the theatre, some parts of the film were fairly grainy and on the DVD that grain increases. Despite that, the picture is pretty sharp and the image is mostly free of artifacts. The colors seem natural and at times strong, and there is not much bleed. Contrast and brightness vary, but that may be due to the film itself. The film's original soundtrack has the feel of an early John Waters flick (scratchy records and all) and the DVD has no problem conveying it accurately (of course, neither would most cassette players). —JO
Movie: ♫♫♫ **DVD:** ♫♫▶
Columbia Tristar Home Video (Cat #10699, UPC #043396106994). Full frame. Dolby Surround. $28.95. Keepcase. *LANG:* English. *CAP:* English. *FEATURES:* 28 chapter links.
1994 (R) 119m/C *D:* Terry Zwigoff; *C:* Maryse Alberti. *AWARDS:* Directors Guild of America Awards '95: Best Feature Documentary (Zwigoff); National Society of Film Critics Awards '95: Best Feature Documentary; Sundance Film Festival '95: Best Cinematography, Grand Jury Prize.

Cry Freedom

Based-on-fact account of the death of South African activist Steve Biko (Washington) is earnest, long, and old-fashioned, like so much of director Attenborough's work (*A Bridge Too Far*, *Gandhi*). A large portion of the story is told through the eyes of editor Donald Woods (Kline), who worked to bring the facts of the case to the world's attention after Biko was murdered by the authorities. (The script is based on Woods's two books.) On DVD, the image ranges between good and very good, and the sound is a bit better. For such a large-scale production, the location is crucial—this one was made in Zimbabwe—and so it needs the full size of a theatre screen to pull the audience into that world. Despite heartfelt political convictions, the film loses a lot on home video. —MM
Movie: ♫♫▶ **DVD:** ♫♫♫
Universal Studios Home Video (Cat #20516, UPC #025192051623). Widescreen (2.35:1) letterboxed. Dolby Digital Surround Stereo. $26.98. Keepcase. *LANG:* English; French. *SUB:* Spanish. *CAP:* English. *FEATURES:* 18 chapter links ▪ Production notes ▪ Cast and crew thumbnail biographies ▪ Theatrical trailer ▪ Universal web links.
1987 (PG) 157m/C Kevin Kline, Denzel Washington, Penelope Wilton, Kevin McNally, John Thaw, Timothy West, John Hargreaves, Alec McCowen, Zakes Mokae, Ian Richardson, Juanita Waterman; *D:*

Richard Attenborough; **W:** John Briley; **C:** Ronnie Taylor; **M:** George Fenton, Jonas Gwangwa. *AWARDS: NOM:* Academy Awards '87: Best Song ("Cry Freedom"), Best Supporting Actor (Washington), Best Original Score.

Cry Uncle

Comedy follows a private eye who investigates a blackmailing case involving a film of orgies in which he participated. Even for Troma, this one's pretty strange.
Movie: 🐾 **DVD:** NYR
Troma Team Video (Cat #9950). Full frame. $24.95. Keepcase. *FEATURES:* Commentary: Avildsen, Odell, Garfield, Kaufman • The usual "Tromatic" extras.
1971 (R) 85m/C Allen (Goorwltz) Garfield, Paul Sorvino, Devin Goldenberg, Madeleine Le Roux; **D:** John G. Avildsen; **W:** David Odell; **C:** John G. Avildsen; **M:** Harper Mckay.

The Crying Game

PR lesson in how to launch a small movie into the hypersphere and ensure critical silence on salient characterization. Jordan's gritty drama is on par with his best, a complex blend of violence, love, betrayal, guilt, and redemption and is not about what it seems to be about much of the time. Wonderful performances by all, including Rea as the appealing, conscience-stricken Fergus; Richardson as the cold, violent IRA moll Jude; and Davidson, in a film debut, as the needy, charismatic Dil. Whitaker is terrific in his 15 minutes of intense screen time. Filled with definite surprises and unexpected pleasures. Title is taken from a top-5 British hit of 1964, three versions of which are heard. The DVD is reasonably sharp and has very little grain or artifacts. Colors are accurate to the theatre and the deep hues are accented by the disc's very good contrast and consistent brightness levels. Blacks are true with the exception of several dark scenes, which throw the blacks off as they seem to try and pull in some brightness. The audio needs a little punch but is O.K. for this dialogue-driven film. *—JO*
Movie: 🐾🐾🐾 **DVD:** 🐾🐾🐾
Artisan Entertainment (Cat #60463, UPC #012236046301). Widescreen (2.35:1) letterboxed; full frame. Dolby Digital 2.0. $24.98. Snapper. *LANG:* English. *CAP:* English. *FEATURES:* 30 chapter links • Theatrical trailer • Cast and crew bios • Production notes • Dual-layered RSDL.
1992 (R) 112m/C *IR* Stephen Rea, Jaye Davidson, Miranda Richardson, Forest Whitaker, Adrian Dunbar, Jim Broadbent, Ralph Brown, Breffini McKenna, Joe Savino, Birdy Sweeney, Andre Bernard; **D:** Neil Jordan; **W:** Neil Jordan; **C:** Ian Wilson; **M:** Anne Dudley. *AWARDS:* Academy Awards '92: Best Original Screenplay; Australian Film Institute '93: Best Foreign Film; Independent Spirit Awards '93: Best Foreign Film; Los Angeles Film Critics Association Awards '92: Best Foreign Film; New York

Film Critics Awards '92: Best Screenplay, Best Supporting Actress (Richardson); National Society of Film Critics Awards '92: Best Actor (Rea); Writers Guild of America '92: Best Original Screenplay; *NOM:* Academy Awards '92: Best Actor (Rea), Best Director (Jordan), Best Film Editing, Best Picture, Best Supporting Actor (Davidson).

Crystal Hunt

Low-budget Hong Kong action flick finds rich girl Lisa (Ng) and cops Wu (Hu) and Leung (Yen) hunting for a magic crystal that will cure Lisa's father. The martial arts scenes are fair; the dubbing and dialogue are straight from a spaghetti western. The DVD image is grainy and rough throughout. *—MM*
Movie: 🐾🐾 **DVD:** 🐾🐾
Tai Seng Video Marketing (Cat #45004, UPC #601643450049). Full frame. $19.95. Keepcase. *LANG:* English. *FEATURES:* 12 chapter links.
1992 90m/C *HK* Carrie Ng, Sibelle Hu, Donnie Yen; **D:** Tsui Pak Lam.

Cube

Claustrophobic sci-fi thriller about six people who inexplicably wake up chained together in a bare room attached to other bare rooms that are fiendishly booby-trapped is not as much fun as spending an hour and a half in a refrigerator box. The six are forced to work together in order to escape. The fact that the bizarro force holding these people hostage is never explained may escape you, since your senses will be dulled by the bad acting and lack of plot. The DVD transfer of this low-budget thriller is actually pretty good, although at first look, the picture is not as sharp as a major studio effort. Considering how dark the film is, there is surprising little grain. Colors are strong and accurate and fleshtones look very natural. Blacks are not quite true but close. The contrast could be higher but the brightness is fine. The most impressive stat of the DVD is the sound, which though only stereo is full-bodied and has very nice imaging. *—JO*
Movie: 🐾 **DVD:** 🐾🐾
Trimark Home Video (Cat #VM6914D, UPC #03139869133). Widescreen letterboxed. Stereo. $24.99. Keepcase. *LANG:* English. *SUB:* Spanish; French. *CAP:* English. *FEATURES:* 24 chapter links • Theatrical trailer • Deleted scenes • Storyboards • Production Design, Set Design, Effects Art with commentary.
1998 (R) 90m/C *CA* Maurice Dean Wint, Nikki DeBoer, David Hewlett, Wayne Robson, Andrew Miller, Nicky Guadagni, Julian Richings; **D:** Vincenzo Natali; **W:** Graeme Manson, Vincenzo Natali, Andre Bijelic; **C:** Derek Rogers; **M:** Mark Korven. *AWARDS: NOM:* Genie Awards '98: Best Art Direction/Set Decoration, Best Film Editing, Best Original Score.

The Cunning Little Vixen

A Czech opera by Leos Janacek, directed by Nicholas Hytner (*The Crucible*). The fanciful story follows the adventures of a clever vixen and her forest friends. The costumes and scenic design are boldly colorful, and the vocal performances strong, but the overall effect is somewhat static, given that this is a film of a stage production recorded in HDTV with particularly good, crisp reds and oranges. The white-and-black subtitles are sharp and easy to read. *—JE* *AKA:* Janacek: The Cunning Little Vixen.
Movie: 🐾🐾 **DVD:** 🐾🐾🐾
Image Entertainment (Cat #ID5783RADVD, UPC #01438157832). Widescreen (1.66:1) anamorphic. Dolby Digital Stereo. $24.99. Snapper. *LANG:* Czech. *SUB:* English; French. *FEATURES:* 19 chapter links.
1995 98m/C D: Nicholas Hytner; **M:** Leos Janacek.

Curse of the Puppet Master: The Human Experiment

The little guys have been taking a break since 1994's *Puppet Master 5* but they're baaaack. This time, they're trying to prevent their new master, evil Dr. Magrew, from transforming more victims into living dolls.
Movie: 🐾 **DVD:** NYR
Full Moon Pictures (Cat #8009). Full frame. $24.98. Jewel case. *FEATURES:* Trailer.
1998 (R) 90m/C George Peck, Emily Harrison, Michael Guerin, Robert Donovan; **D:** David DeCoteau; **W:** Benjamin Carr; **C:** Howard Wexler; **M:** Richard Band.

Curse of the Voodoo

Low-budget mid-'60s horror features oodles of stock footage and a casually racist attitude toward Africans made all too evident in the opening credits which roll over an offensive ritual "dance." But it's wrong to make much of that, because the rest of the film is a standard supernatural thriller, set in London. Cursed in Africa for killing a sacred lion, Mike Stacey (Haliday) goes back to England where he finds that he cannot escape. Fans know the drill. The black-and-white photography is surprisingly sharp and makes a fine transfer to DVD, even in the many night scenes. Sound is adequate. *—MM* *AKA:* The Curse of Simba.
Movie: 🐾🐾 **DVD:** 🐾🐾
Elite Entertainment, Inc. (Cat #EE8665, UPC #790594866525). Full frame. Mono. $24.95. Keepcase. *LANG:* English. *FEATURES:* 16 chapter links.
1964 77m/B Bryant Haliday, Dennis Price, Lisa Daniely, Mary Kerridge; **D:** Lindsay Shonteff; **W:** Tony O'Grady, Leigh Vance; **C:** Gerald Gibbs; **M:** Brian Fahey.

Curtain Call

Publisher Stevenson Lowe (Spader) and his girlfriend Julie (Walker) buy a brownstone that's haunted by the ghosts of actors Max (Caine) and Lily (Smith). Lowe can see and hear them; Julie can't, and moves out when he refuses to commit. Waiting in the wings is the Senator (Shepard), who's got eyes for her. Despite the first-rate cast, the usually sure-handed director Yates, and the participation of legendary cinematographer Nykvist, the lightweight material fizzles. First and most obviously on DVD, the image is so grainy and harsh that it lacks the polish necessary for this kind of romantic comedy. It's almost painful to watch, much worse than most VHS tapes. Sound is adequate. —MM

Movie: 🎬🎬 **DVD:** 🎬🎬
Image Entertainment (Cat #ID8804UM DVD, UPC #014381880427). Full frame. Dolby Digital Stereo. $24.99. Snapper. *LANG:* English. *FEATURES:* 6 chapter links ‑ Theatrical trailer.
1997 (PG-13) 94m/C James Spader, Polly Walker, Michael Caine, Maggie Smith, Buck Henry, Sam Shepard, Todd Alcott, Susan Berman, Marcia Gay Harden, Valerie Perrine, Frances Sternhagen, Frank Whaley; **D:** Peter Yates; **W:** Todd Alcott; **C:** Sven Nykvist; **M:** Richard Hartley.

The Curve

Think *Dead Man on Campus* since you've got basically the same premise. College roomies Tim (Lillard), Rand (Batinkoff), and Chris (Vartan) learn that the student myth is true at their small university. Should a roomie commit suicide, the survivors receive an automatic 4.0 for the semester. So Tim offs Rand and has Chris help him cover things up. Naturally nothing works out as expected, and it's not nearly as clever as it's trying to be. **AKA:** Dead Man's Curve.

Movie: 🎬🎬 **DVD:** NYR
Trimark Home Video (Cat #7092). Dolby Digital Stereo. $24.99. Keepcase. *FEATURES:* Trailer.
1997 (R) 90m/C Matthew Lillard, Michael Vartan, Randall Batinkoff, Keri Russell, Dana Delany, Tamara Craig Thomas, Anthony Griffin, Bo Dietle, Kevin Huff, Henry Stozier; **D:** Dan Rosen; **W:** Dan Rosen; **C:** Joey Forsyte.

Custer of the West

This retelling of Custer legend is most notable for the casting of Shaw, who looks pretty amazing in those long, curly, golden locks. The film does give some insight into the earlier political life of Custer, and the climactic massacre is portrayed with good energy and decent pathos. This Anchor Bay DVD is a huge improvement over the earlier Simitar release. The picture is pretty sharp and there is none of the outrageous artifacting that actually blurred the image on the previous issue. Colors are respectably strong and bleed is negligible. Contrast and brightness levels are increased, adding both detail and punch

to the picture. The stereo sound is also a big improvement, and although separation is limited, the fidelity is much better and there's a lot more guts on the bottom end. It certainly looks like Anchor Bay came up with much better preprint material than Simitar had to work with, and the resulting transfer shows it. —JO **AKA:** A Good Day for Fighting.

Movie: 🎬🎬 **DVD:** 🎬🎬
Anchor Bay (Cat #DV10693, UPC #013131069396). Widescreen (2.2:1) letterboxed; full frame. Dolby Digital Stereo. $24.98. Keepcase. *LANG:* English. *FEATURES:* 15 chapter links.
1967 (G) 143m/C Robert Shaw, Mary Ure, Jeffrey Hunter, Ty Hardin, Lawrence Tierney, Jack Cooper; **D:** Robert Siodmak; **W:** Bernard Gordon, Julian Halevy; **C:** Cecilio Paniagua; **M:** Bernardo Segall.

Cutthroat Island

Most don't like *Cutthroat Island*, but I think it delivers just what it promises: tons of noisy explosions, exaggerated stunts, plenty of swashbucklin', and the always appealing Davis as the exuberant pirate queen. Morgan Adams (Davis) is left part of a treasure map by her father and charms educated slave/thief William Shaw (Modine) to assist her. Her scurvy Uncle Dawg (despicably well played by Langella) also has a portion of the map and is willing to let Morgan find the treasure before taking it for himself. Nonstop action from start to finish. This is almost a great DVD, with the biggest problem being a slightly soft picture and a little too much grain. Still, it's not bad. The colors are lush and accurate with plenty of punch from the very good contrast and brightness levels. Artifacts are minimal. The 5.1 tracks deliver all those aforementioned explosions with plenty of guts that will crank up your subwoofer and rock your house. There are many Surround effects and they seem mixed to perfection. The dialogue is crisp and out front. —JO

Movie: 🎬🎬🎬 **DVD:** 🎬🎬🎬
Artisan Entertainment (Cat #60447, UPC #012236044703). Widescreen (2.35:1) letterboxed; full frame. Dolby Digital 5.1; Stereo. $24.98. Snapper. *LANG:* English (DD5.1); French (Stereo). *SUB:* Spanish; French. *CAP:* English. *FEATURES:* 30 chapter links ‑ Theatrical trailer ‑ Theatrical teaser ‑ Cast and crew bios ‑ Production notes.
1995 (PG-13) 123m/C Geena Davis, Matthew Modine, Frank Langella, Patrick Malahide, Stan Shaw, Maury Chaykin, Harris Yulin, George Murcell; **D:** Renny Harlin; **W:** Robert King, Marc Norman; **C:** Peter Levy; **M:** John Debney.

Cyber-Tracker

Terminator rip-off presents a future where androids hunt down criminals and execute them immediately. When Secret Service agent Eric Phillips (Wilson) is framed for murder, he's on their list and so joins the rebels.

Movie: 🎬🎬 **DVD:** NYR
Studio Home Entertainment (Cat #4050). Full frame. $24.95. Keepcase.
1993 (R) 91m/C Don "The Dragon" Wilson, Richard Norton, Joseph Ruskin, Abby Dalton, John Aprea; **D:** Richard Pepin; **W:** Jacobsen Hart; **C:** Ken Blakey; **M:** Bill Montei, Lisa Popeil.

Cybernator

Cybernetic assassins go after politicians and military officers in this ultra-low-budget sf action flick. The DVD is virtually unwatchable. It's slow, grainy, and in some scenes the pixelation is so heavy that it appears to be intentional. —MM

Movie: 🎬 **DVD:** woof
Simitar Entertainment (Cat #7514, UPC #082551751426). Full frame. PCM Stereo. $14.98. Keepcase. *LANG:* English. *FEATURES:* 8 chapter links ‑ Production factoids.
1991 (R) 85m/C Lonnie Schuyler, Christina Peralta, William Smith; **D:** Robert Rundle.

Cyborg

When a really bad movie plumbs the depths of its own badness and comes up smiling, it's called an alternative classic. This is just such a film. It is the *Mommie Dearest* of post-apocalyptic thrillers. From its redundant beginning to characters named for guitars to the cliched conclusion, it is filled with one glorious goof after another. Van Damme does his splits, etc.

Movie: 🎬🎬 **DVD:** NYR
MGM Home Entertainment (Cat #906561). Widescreen (1.85:1) letterboxed; full frame. Dolby Digital Stereo. $24.98. Slipcase. *LANG:* English; French. *SUB:* French; Spanish. *CAP:* English. *FEATURES:* Trailer.
1989 (R) 85m/C Jean-Claude Van Damme, Deborah Richter, Vincent Klyn, Dayle Haddon, Alex Daniels, Terrie Batson, Janice Graser, Jackson "Rock" Pinckney; **D:** Albert Pyun; **W:** Kitty Chalmers; **C:** Philip Alan Waters; **M:** Kevin Bassinson.

Daddy Long Legs

In both narrative and visual terms, this silent film is built on an unembarrassed sentimentality and that sweetness may well put off contemporary viewers. It is still an excellent vehicle for star Mary Pickford. She plays the plucky orphan Judy Abbott, who is befriended by a wealthy man she identifies as Daddy-Long-Legs. Her transformation from a girl through adolescence to young womanhood is a remarkable achievement. (She was 26 when the film was made.) The image is as dark as other films of its age, but the DVD was made from a well-preserved original. The only noteworthy visual flaws come from flickering light. The disc also includes a D.W. Griffith short, "What the Daisy Said," about a gypsy fortune teller. —MM

Movie: 🎬🎬🎬 **DVD:** 🎬🎬🎬

Image Entertainment (Cat #ID5923MLSD-VD, UPC #014381592320). Full frame. Dolby Digital Stereo. $29.99. Snapper. *FEATURES:* 18 chapter links.
1919 94m/B Mary Pickford, Milla Davenport, Mahlon Hamilton, Lillian Langdon, Marshall Neilan; *D:* Marshall Neilan; *W:* Agnes Christine Johnston; *C:* Charles Rosher, Henry Cronjager.

Damage
The elegant Irons portrays Stephen, a middle-aged, married British politician who has always been in complete control of his life, especially where his feelings are concerned. Then he meets Anna (Binoche), his son's less-than-innocent fiancee, and immediately begins an obsessive, wildly sexual affair with her. Stephen should have listened to Anna's warning about herself, "Damaged people are dangerous, they know they can survive," because their passion leads to betrayal and tragedy. Based on the novel by Josephine Hart, the film is a hypnotic exploration of passion. Highly accurate colors and deep true blacks give this DVD the sensuous feel that the film requires. The picture is very sharp, lacking grain and artifacts. Occasionally there is some slight bleed on a few of the deeper reds, but it's not too distracting. Even though there are not too many Surround effects, these often add a very nice ambience, and the incidental music sounds great. The dialogue is crisp, out front, and easy to understand. —*JO*
Movie: 🎭🎭🎭 *DVD:* 🎭🎭🎭▸
New Line Home Video (Cat #N4668, UPC #79404346682). Widescreen (1.85:1) anamorphic. Stereo. $24.98. Snapper. *LANG:* English. *SUB:* Spanish; French. *CAP:* English. *FEATURES:* 16 chapter links • Theatrical trailer • Interview with director Louis Malle • Behind-the-scenes footage • Cast and crew bios and filmographies. Contains both "R"-rated and unrated versions.
1992 (R) 111m/C *GB FR* Jeremy Irons, Juliette Binoche, Rupert Graves, Miranda Richardson, Ian Bannen, Leslie Caron, Peter Stormare, Gemma Clark, Julian Fellowes; *D:* Louis Malle; *W:* David Hare; *C:* Peter Biziou; *M:* Zbigniew Preisner. *AWARDS:* British Academy Awards '92: Best Supporting Actress (Richardson); Los Angeles Film Critics Association Awards '92: Best Score; *NOM:* Academy Awards '92: Best Supporting Actress (Richardson).

Dance with Me
Cuban emigre Rafael (Chayanne) goes to Houston where he teaches at the fading Excelsior Dance Studio. Fellow instructor and single mom Ruby (Williams) is looking for a partner who can help her into the world of competitive ballroom dance. She's not interested in love. Things change at the World Open Dance Championship in Las Vegas. Writer-choreographer Daryl Matthews gets zero points for originality in plotting but the music and the dancing are first-rate. On DVD, the image

is excellent with dance numbers staged on Cuban street corners and glittering ballrooms. The salsa-jazz score sounds terrific. —*MM* *AKA:* Shut Up and Dance.
Movie: 🎭🎭🎭 *DVD:* 🎭🎭🎭
Columbia Tristar Home Video (Cat #23949, UPC #043396239494). Full frame; widescreen (1.85:1) letterboxed. Dolby Digital Surround Stereo; widescreen; Dolby Digital 5.1 Surround. $25.95. Keepcase. *LANG:* English. *SUB:* English. *CAP:* English. *FEATURES:* 28 chapter links • Photo gallery • Theatrical trailer.
1998 (PG) 126m/C Vanessa L(ynne) Williams, Chayanne, Kris Kristofferson, Joan Plowright, Jane Krakowski, Beth Grant; *D:* Randa Haines; *W:* Daryl Matthews; *C:* Fred Murphy; *M:* Michael Convertino.

Dancer, Texas— Pop. 81
Four buds in the title town have to decide if they're going to fulfill the pact they made when they were 11—to leave the place upon graduating high school. Each has a reason to stay: Keller (Meyer) takes care of his widowed grandfather; Terrell Lee (Facinelli) is expected to join the family's oil business; Squirrel (Embry) thinks he should care for his alcoholic father; and John (Mills) is a natural at cattle ranching. The coming-of-age comedy deals in honest emotion and humor and never resorts to small-town stereotypes. Writer-director McCanlies's low-keyed debut is reminiscent of his fellow Texan Larry McMurtry. The image on the DVD is superb throughout, capturing the west Texas landscapes with originality and avoiding conventional locales and other contemporary western cliches. More importantly, the four young men are believable and winning. All that's missing is a commentary track. Even so, take a look. —*MM*
Movie: 🎭🎭🎭▸ *DVD:* 🎭🎭🎭▸
Columbia Tristar Home Video (Cat #02715, UPC #043396027152). Full frame; widescreen (1.85:1) letterboxed. Dolby Digital 5.1 Surround; Dolby Digital Surround. $28.95. Keepcase. *LANG:* English; French; Spanish. *SUB:* English; French; Spanish. *CAP:* English. *FEATURES:* 28 chapter links.
1998 (PG) 95m/C Breckin Meyer, Peter Facinelli, Eddie Mills, Ethan (Randall) Embry, Ashley Johnson, Patricia Wettig, Michael O'Neill; *D:* Tim McCanlies; *W:* Tim McCanlies; *C:* Andrew Dintenfass; *M:* Steve Dorff.

Dances with Wolves
Lt. John Dunbar (Costner) is rewarded for his heroism in the Civil War with his choice of assignments. He wants to see the western frontier before it disappears and so finds himself alone on the South Dakota prairie. Eventually, he comes to know and be accepted by a tribe of Dakota Sioux who are brought to life by a remarkable ensemble cast (most notably Greene, Grant, and McDonnell). Equally

impressive are the sweeping locations and John Barry's bold lyrical score. This is an archetypal big-screen western and the DVD captures the scope of the image as well as any home video format can. I could find no meaningful flaws in sound or picture. (Use headphones if possible.) The commentary track by director Costner and his coproducer Jim Wilson follows the expected conversational and congratulatory tone, but the two provide some useful information about the filmmaking process. They touch on the importance of casting, the use of locations, small details of character development, and their own tastes in movies. Unlike many "epics," this one has improved with age. —*MM*
Movie: 🎭🎭🎭▸ *DVD:* 🎭🎭🎭▸
Image Entertainment (Cat #ID4710ORDVD, UPC #014381471021). Widescreen (2.35:1) letterboxed. Dolby Surround; 5.1 Surround. $29.99. Snapper. *LANG:* English; Sioux. *SUB:* English. *FEATURES:* 25 chapter links • Commentary: Costner and Jim Wilson • Liner notes by Jeff Schwager • Filmographies of Costner, Wilson, Barry • Filmographies of Semler, McDonnell, Greene.
1990 (PG-13) 181m/C Kevin Costner, Mary McDonnell, Graham Greene, Rodney A. Grant, Floyd "Red Crow" Westerman, Tantoo Cardinal, Robert Pastorelli, Charles Rocket, Maury Chaykin, Jimmy Herman, Nathan Lee Chasing His Horse, Wes Studi; *D:* Kevin Costner; *W:* Michael Blake; *C:* Dean Semler; *M:* John Barry. *AWARDS:* Academy Awards '90: Best Adapted Screenplay, Best Cinematography, Best Director (Costner), Best Film Editing, Best Picture, Best Sound, Best Original Score; American Film Institute (AFI) '98: Top 100; Directors Guild of America Awards '90: Best Director (Costner); Golden Globe Awards '91: Best Director (Costner), Best Film—Drama, Best Screenplay; National Board of Review Awards '90: Best Director (Costner); Writers Guild of America '90: Best Adapted Screenplay; *NOM:* Academy Awards '90: Best Actor (Costner), Best Art Direction/Set Decoration, Best Costume Design, Best Supporting Actor (Greene), Best Supporting Actress (McDonnell).

Dancing at Lughnasa
Kate (Streep) is the eldest of five lonely unwed sisters living together on a farm in 1930s Ireland. Their brother Father Jack (Gambon) returns home, fresh from a stint as a missionary in Africa, and Gerry (Ifans), who fathered a son with sister Christina, turns up as well. The reunion and resulting emotions are the main elements in this anecdotal tale, but unfortunately most of the episodes are lacking energy and fun. Ifans delivers the only gusto as he readies to go to war in Spain. Adapted from the Tony Award–winning stage play by Brian Friels. The title refers to a pagan ritual the town engages in annually. This movie is often very dark and the DVD would have been improved if

some brightness was added to it. Overall, though, the contrast is very good and the brightness above average. The sharpness feels even better due to the lack (with rare exception) of grain and artifacts. The dark scenes are also a little softer. The sound on this DVD is pretty amazing even though it's only stereo. The fidelity is excellent, with crisp highs and deep low end; there is plenty of space making for great ambience. —JO

Movie: 🎵🎵 **DVD:** 🎵🎵▶

Columbia Tristar Home Video (Cat #02853, UPC #043396028531). Widescreen (1.85:1) letterboxed. Stereo. NSL. Keepcase. *LANG:* English. *SUB:* Spanish; French. *CAP:* English. *FEATURES:* 28 chapter links ▪ Theatrical trailers ▪ Cast and crew bios ▪ Filmographies.
1998 (PG-13) 92m/C *IR GB* Meryl Streep, Michael Gambon, Catherine McCormack, Rhys Ifans, Brid Brennan, Kathy Burke, Sophie Thompson, Lorcan Cranitch, Darrell Johnston, Peter Gowen, Dawn Bradfield, Marie Mullen; *D:* Pat O'Connor; *W:* Frank McGuinness; *C:* Kenneth Macmillan; *M:* Bill Whelan.

Dancing in the Dark

After Anna Forbes (Principal) is assaulted by her lecherous father-in-law (Vaughn at his creepiest), she becomes caught up in a treacherous maze of legal-psychiatric corruption. The made-for-TV woman-in-jeopardy movie doesn't look as sharp as many of its ilk on DVD. The loss of clarity in night scenes is particularly noticeable. Sound is nondescript. —MM

Movie: 🎵🎵 **DVD:** 🎵🎵

Simitar Entertainment (Cat #7588, UPC #082551758821). Full frame. Dolby Digital Stereo. $14.98. Keepcase. *LANG:* English. *FEATURES:* 8 chapter links ▪ Victoria Principal filmography ▪ Production factoids.
1995 93m/C Victoria Principal, Nicholas Campbell, Robert Vaughn, Geraint Wyn Davies; *D:* Bill Corcoran; *W:* Jacqueline Feather, David Seidler; *M:* Micky Erbe, Maribeth Solomon.

The Dandelion Crown

An allegorical film based on the music of Czech composer Leos Janacek, *The Dandelion Crown* shows how an insignificant member of society struggles to maintain her own individuality within an increasingly dictatorial society. Both picture and audio on this disc are quite good. The video boasts eye-popping colors and nicely defined blacks. The orchestral soundtrack is, likewise, crisp and clear. —MJT

Movie: 🎵🎵🎵 **DVD:** 🎵🎵🎵

Image Entertainment (Cat #ID5633CLDVD, UPC #014381565324). Full frame. PCM Digital Stereo. $19.99. Snapper. *FEATURES:* 9 chapter links.
1993 41m/C Miriam Stepanova, Jan Preucil; *D:* Klaas Rusticus; *W:* Klaas Rusticus; *M:* Leos Janacek.

Dangerous Beauty

In 16th-century Venice, poor but beautiful Veronica (McCormack) gains wealth and power by becoming a sought-after courtesan. The bewigged, bewitched, and bewildered heads of states fall as hard for the comely courtesan as victims to the plague that strikes Venice later in the film. The one man she wants, however, Marco (Sewell), comes from a wealthy family who look down on the common Veronica. Director Herskovitz mixes a strong feminist message with humor and a modern sensibility that sometimes makes you forget you're watching a period piece. Colors are deep, accurate, and bleed-free on this DVD. And the contrast and brightness levels, although not excellent, are very good. The blacks are also very true. Add to that a soundtrack that is full fidelity, dynamic, has good low end, and decent ambient Surround, and what have you got? Well, normally a pretty good DVD, but not in this case. Unfortunately, the picture is not very sharp and there is a lot of grain in both dim lighting and long shots that kind of ruin the whole thing. —JO *AKA:* The Honest Courtesan; Indiscretion; Venice; Courtesan.

Movie: 🎵🎵🎵 **DVD:** 🎵🎵🎵

Warner Home Video, Inc. (Cat #14775, UPC #085391477525). Widescreen (2.35:1) letterboxed; full frame. Dolby Digital 5.1. $19.98. Snapper. *LANG:* English; French. *SUB:* French. *FEATURES:* 34 chapter links ▪ Theatrical trailers ▪ Production notes.
1998 (R) 112m/C Catherine McCormack, Rufus Sewell, Moira Kelly, Jacqueline Bisset, Oliver Platt, Fred Ward, Naomi Watts, Jeroen Krabbe, Joanna Cassidy, Daniel Lapaine, Jake Weber, Simon Dutton, Michael Culkin, Peter Eyre; *D:* Marshall Herskovitz; *W:* Jeannine Dominy; *C:* Bojan Bazelli; *M:* George Fenton.

Dangerous Ground

Darrell Roodt is at best half successful in combining serious political and social commentary with a standard action plot. On the death of his father, Vusi (executive producer Ice Cube) returns to South Africa from San Francisco. That leads him on a search for his younger brother who has gone missing in the fleshpots of Johannesburg. Whenever the film is exploring the seductive dangers of drug use, it is frighteningly realistic and passionate. It's also heavy-handed at times. The anti-drug message is so strong that it doesn't need to be underlined. In the more slowly paced action scenes, Roodt can be more effective. One early carjacking is genuinely tense. The big finish, however, comes across as warmed-over John Woo, and the conclusion is simply wrong. DVD faithfully captures the theatrical release's harsh lighting and mixture of garish colors, dusty earthtones, and grainy black-and-white photography. Sound is good. —MM

Movie: 🎵🎵 **DVD:** 🎵🎵🎵

New Line Home Video (Cat #N4852, UPC #794043485220). Widescreen (1.85:1) anamorphic; full frame. Dolby Digital 5.1

Surround Stereo; Dolby Digital Surround Stereo. $24.98. Snapper. *LANG:* English. *SUB:* English. *FEATURES:* 16 chapter links ▪ Cast and crew thumbnail biographies ▪ Theatrical trailer.
1996 (R) 92m/C Ice Cube, Elizabeth Hurley, Ving Rhames, Eric Miyeni, Sechaba Morojele; *D:* Darrell Roodt; *W:* Darrell Roodt, Greg Latter; *C:* Paul Gilpin; *M:* Stanley Clarke.

Dangerous Liaisons

Stylish and absorbing, this adaptation of the Laclos novel and the Christopher Hampton play centers on the relationship of two decadent members of 18th-century French nobility. The two (Close and Malkovich) spend their time testing and manipulating the loves of others. They find love often has a will of its own. For an interesting comparison, view this one with director Milos Forman's version of the story, 1989's *Valmont.* On DVD the lighting had subtle shifts that caused a shimmering effect during many scenes. There is some grain in the picture and that increases dramatically in the blacks. The colors, though, are accurate and bleed little. Contrast and brightness levels are consistent but both are in need of a boost to make viewing comfortable. The sound is at least above average and features good fidelity and dynamics, good imaging, and a good solid low end to the music. —JO

Movie: 🎵🎵🎵▶ **DVD:** 🎵🎵▶

Warner Home Video, Inc. (Cat #11872, UPC #085391187226). Widescreen (1.85:1) letterboxed; full frame. Dolby Digital 5.1; Dolby Surround. $19.98. Snapper. *LANG:* English (DD5.1); French (DS). *SUB:* Spanish; French. *FEATURES:* 34 chapter links ▪ Production notes.
1988 (R) 120m/C John Malkovich, Glenn Close, Michelle Pfeiffer, Uma Thurman, Keanu Reeves, Swoosie Kurtz, Mildred Natwick, Peter Capaldi; *D:* Stephen Frears; *W:* Christopher Hampton; *C:* Philippe Rousselot; *M:* George Fenton. *AWARDS:* Academy Awards '88: Best Adapted Screenplay, Best Art Direction/ Set Decoration, Best Costume Design; British Academy Awards '89: Best Adapted Screenplay, Best Supporting Actress (Pfeiffer); Cesar Awards '90: Best Foreign Film; Writers Guild of America '88: Best Adapted Screenplay; *NOM:* Academy Awards '88: Best Actress (Close), Best Picture, Best Supporting Actress (Pfeiffer), Best Original Score.

Dangerous Minds

Unsurprising biopic is based on the experiences of LouAnne Johnson (Pfeiffer), a 10-year Marine turned inspirational inner-city high school English teacher. Of course, she has to take on the established education system to fight for her kids, etc., etc. The same story has been told in *To Sir with Love* and several other films. This version is nothing special. The DVD looks fine and makes the most of a catchy soundtrack, but it can't improve the famil-

iar material. —MM *AKA:* My Posse Don't Do Homework.
Movie: ♫♫⬗ *DVD:* ♫♫⬗
Hollywood Pictures Home Video (Cat #16794, UPC #717951001924). Widescreen (1.85:1) letterboxed. Dolby Digital 5.1 Surround Stereo; Dolby Digital Surround Stereo. $29.99. Snapper. *LANG:* English; French. *CAP:* English. *FEATURES:* 15 chapter links • "Gangsta's Paradise" music video by Coolio.
1995 (R) 99m/C Michelle Pfeiffer, George Dzundza, Courtney B. Vance, Robin Bartlett, Renoly Santiago, Lorraine Toussaint, John Neville; *D:* John N. Smith; *W:* Ronald Bass; *C:* Pierre Letarte. *AWARDS:* Blockbuster Entertainment Awards '96: Drama Actress, Theatrical (Pfeiffer); *NOM:* MTV Movie Awards '96: Best Film, Best Female Performance (Pfeiffer), Most Desirable Female (Pfeiffer), Best Song ("Gangsta's Paradise").

Daniella by Night

French model Daniella (Sommer) gets a contract to work for an Italian fashion house in Rome and she's soon attracting a lot of attention, including some that involves spies. It leads to a chase through a cabaret and a technical nude scene that's carefully staged behind a gauze curtain. DVD can do little to improve the murky black-and-white image. On its best day, this one didn't look that good. The disc was made from a pre-print marked by intermittent scratches and tears. The jazzy score by Charles Azanavour and Georges Garvarentz sounds very nice. —MM
Movie: ♫♫ *DVD:* ♫
First Run Features (Cat #FRF909259D, UPC #720229909259). Full frame. $29.95. Keepcase. *LANG:* French. *SUB:* English. *FEATURES:* 7 chapter links • Elke Sommer photo gallery • Theatrical trailer.
1961 83m/B *FR* Elke Sommer, Ivan Desny; *D:* Max Pecas; *W:* Grisha Dabat, Wolfgang Steinhardt; *C:* Andre Germain; *M:* Charles Aznavour, Georges Garvarentz.

Dante's Peak

Northwest volcano serves up a smorgasbord of molten disaster in the second most desirable town in the U.S.—the titular Dante's Peak. Brosnan is the intuitive scientist who comes to Washington to match wits with the conical adversary and joins forces with the town's tres femme mayor Wando (Hamilton). Ashes fall like snow in January, computer-generated lava flows profusely, poisonous gases leak out, and water turns to acid, all with desired nail-biting effect. Wando's two kids, dog, and grandma lend folksy charm and the requisite loved-ones-in-grave-danger, but this heated disaster flick is not exactly for the whole family. Cliched and predictable, it runs the Disaster Movie Playbook page by page as plot takes a backseat to nonstop action. With the superb image on this DVD, the movie's easier to take and its lack of plot just doesn't seem to matter. Just sit back

and let the great 5.1 sound immerse you in the incredibly sharp and colorful visuals. The documentary shows in detail how many of the effects were accomplished. —JO
Movie: ♫♫⬗ *DVD:* ♫♫♫⬗
Universal Studios Home Video (Cat #20149, UPC #025192014925). Widescreen (2.35:1) anamorphic. Dolby Digital 5.1; Dolby Surround. $34.98. Keepcase. *LANG:* English (DD5.1); Spanish (DS); French (DS). *SUB:* Spanish. *CAP:* English. *FEATURES:* 38 chapter links • Behind the scenes footage • "Making of" featurette • Cast interviews • Special effects • Commentary: Roger Donaldson and Dennis Washington.
1997 (PG-13) 112m/C Pierce Brosnan, Linda Hamilton, Charles Hallahan, Grant Heslov, Elizabeth Hoffman, Jaime Renee Smith, Arabella Field, Tzi Ma, Jeremy Foley, Brian Reddy, Kirk Trutner; *D:* Roger Donaldson; *W:* Leslie Bohem; *C:* Andrzej Bartkowiak; *M:* John Frizzell.

Dario Argento's World of Horror

A look at horror filmmaker Argento and his films *Suspiria, Demons, Creepers, Inferno,* and *Tenebrae.* Argento explains his style and technique with many film clips. This film has the interview where Argento basically says that it's a good thing he can make graphic horror films like this, or he might have to do it for real. It's too bad that this DVD is only average because, whether or not you like Argento's visions, most of them are stunningly beautiful, even while excessively violent. The picture is usually a little soft and colors are at times accurate and vibrant, and at others washed-out and pale. The sound is of least consequence, so it's adequate for the presentation. —JO
Movie: ♫♫♫ *DVD:* ♫♫⬗
Synapse (Cat #SFD0002, UPC #654930300299). Full frame. Dolby Digital Mono. $29.95. Keepcase. *LANG:* English. *FEATURES:* 20 chapter links • Filmography • Interviews.
1985 76m/C *D:* Dario Argento.

Dark City

Amnesiac John Murdoch (Sewell) wakes up naked in a bloody bathtub. A detective (Hurt) thinks he might be a serial killer; a creepy doctor (Sutherland) concurs; Murdoch's wife (Connelly) says no. But who are the creepy guys in long leather coats who can stop time? Murdoch finds that he is in a brooding sunless city whose skyline changes as its residents sleep. The place seems to belong to no specific era, looking at times like a neo-Goth music video, at others like a work of German expressionism, and at others like Cleveland. As in director Proyas's earlier work, *The Crow,* the look of the film is as important as the plot. Fans will see numerous references to it, along with *Blade Runner, Hell Raiser,* and *Seven.* The careful image transfer retains the dark

shadings from inky black to charcoal to light gray without excess pixelating or artifacts. The disc gets the usual careful New Line treatment, even admitting the mixed reviews and disappointing boxoffice that the film enjoyed. An interesting comparison can be made between this one and *The Matrix,* which came out about a year later. The films are remarkably similar in theme and plot but *The Matrix* uses the ideas to go to more violent direction with its special effects, while *Dark City* remains more thoughtful and, in its own way, more complex visually. —MM *AKA:* Dark Empire; Dark World.
Movie: ♫♫♫⬗ *DVD:* ♫♫♫⬗
New Line Home Video (Cat #N4657, UPC #794043465727). Widescreen (2.35:1) letterboxed; full frame. Dolby Surround 5.1. $24.98. Snapper. *LANG:* English; French. *SUB:* English; French; Spanish. *FEATURES:* Commentary: Roger Ebert • Commentary: Proyas, Dobbs, Groyer, Wolski, Tatopoulos • Illustrations and storyboard art from set designs • Comparisons to Fritz Lang's *Metropolis* • Theatrical trailer • "Find Shell Beach" interactive game • Cast and crew biographies, filmographies, star highlights • 16 chapter links.
1997 (R) 103m/C Kiefer Sutherland, William Hurt, Rufus Sewell, Richard O'Brien, Jennifer Connelly, Ian Richardson, Colin Friels, Frank Gallacher, Bruce Spence, John Bluthal, Mitchell Butel, Melissa George; *D:* Alex Proyas; *W:* Alex Proyas, Lem Dobbs, David S. Goyer; *C:* Darius Wolski; *M:* Trevor Jones.

The Dark Crystal

Jen and Kira, two of the last surviving Gelflings who are allied with the gentle three-handed Mystics, attempt to return a shard (discovered with the help of a sorceress) to the Dark Crystal which is in a castle guarded by the cruel reptilian Skeksis. The fantasy was designed by Brian Froud and Jim Henson, creator of the Muppets. The DVD handles the ornate color scheme emphasizing reds and purples well enough, but the combination of puppets and live action in the scenes that call for full movement makes for an uneven fantasy. Sound, too, is only good. —MM
Movie: ♫♫♫ *DVD:* ♫♫♫
Columbia Tristar Home Video (Cat #2849, UPC #043396028494). Widescreen (2.35:1) letterboxed. Dolby Digital 5.1 Surround Stereo; Dolby Digital Surround Stereo. $24.95. Keepcase. *LANG:* English. *SUB:* English; Spanish. *FEATURES:* "Making of" documentary • 2 deleted funeral scenes • Workprint sketches and character drawings • 28 chapter links • Cast and crew thumbnail biographies.
1982 (PG) 93m/C *D:* Jim Henson, Frank Oz; *W:* David Odell; *C:* Oswald Morris; *M:* Trevor Jones; *V:* Jim Henson, Frank Oz, Kathryn Mullen, Dave Goelz.

The Dark Half

Stephen King's relationship with his nom de plume Richard Bachman provides the basis for this variation on Jekyll and Hyde. When serious novelist Thad Beaumont (Hutton) tries to kill off George Stark, the name he uses for violent potboilers, Stark appears in the flesh. As the greasy-haired George, Hutton looks like he's about to morph into David Keith, but he's still good in both roles. He gets excellent support from Amy Madigan, as his wife, and Michael Rooker, as the local sheriff. As always, writer-director George Romero's cluttered middle-class world adds a strong note of realism to the fantastic story. He also gives new meaning to the term "pencil neck." Perhaps the film is a little too long, but the ending justifies the length. The DVD image is only slightly superior to VHS tape; same for sound. A commentary track by King and Romero might have been worthwhile, but all the extra information is in a short booklet and some of it is wrong. —*MM*

Movie: 🎜🎜🎜 *DVD:* 🎜🎜➤
MGM Home Entertainment (Cat #907866, UPC #027616786623). Full frame. Dolby Digital Surround Stereo. $24.98. Keepcase. *LANG:* English. *SUB:* English; French. *FEATURES:* 36 chapter links.
1991 (R) 122m/C Timothy Hutton, Amy Madigan, Michael Rooker, Julie Harris, Robert Joy, Kent Broadhurst, Beth Grant, Rutanya Alda, Tom Mardirosian, Chelsea Field, Royal Dano; *D:* George A. Romero; *W:* George A. Romero; *C:* Tony Pierce-Roberts; *M:* Christopher Young.

Dark Odyssey

Metzger's first feature tells the tragic tale of a young Greek seaman who jumps ship in New York to avenge his sister's rape. He finds himself conflicted between his masculine sense of family honor and love when he falls for a Greek-American woman. The film is certainly of its time: the black-and-white picture is grainy and the sound sometimes has a fluttering inconsistency. The flaws likely come from the original, not the transfer to DVD. A must for Metzger fans. —*AB*

Movie: 🎜🎜 *DVD:* 🎜🎜
Image Entertainment (Cat #ID5538FFDVD, UPC #1438155382). Full frame. Dolby Digital Mono. $24.99. Keepcase. *LANG:* English. *FEATURES:* 12 chapter links ● Theatrical trailer.
1957 85m/B David Hooks, Edward Brazier, Jeanne Jerrems; *D:* William Kyriakis, Radley Metzger; *W:* William Kyriakis, Radley Metzger; *C:* Peter Erik Winkler; *M:* Laurence Rosenthal.

Dark Planet

In 2638, after six world wars, a mission is sent to the "dark planet" inside a black hole. On DVD, the shortcomings of this low-budget sf are far too obvious. The computer-generated effects are flat, simple, and transparent. In almost all of the spaceship interiors, the backgrounds are completely black. When any set details are shown, the lighting is kept to a minimum, to hide more than it reveals. Sound is no better than the image. —*MM*

Movie: 🎜➤ *DVD:* 🎜➤
Simitar Entertainment (Cat #7461, UPC #082551746125). Full frame. Dolby Digital Stereo. $14.98. Keepcase. *LANG:* English. *FEATURES:* 8 chapter links ● Michael York filmography ● Production factoids.
1997 (R) 99m/C Paul Mercurio, Harley Jane Kozak, Michael York, Maria Ford, Ed O'Ross; *D:* Albert Magnoli; *W:* S.O. Lee; *C:* William MacCollum.

Dark Secrets

Straitlaced reporter Claire (Parent) wants to get a hot story on sex club mogul Justin (Carrol) and winds up falling prey to his "charms." Dominatrix Mauri (Strain) plays an important role in the loyalty tests he dreams up for Claire. In the last reel, the action gets about as steamy as it can without wandering into hard-core. And the truth is that some hard-core films look better than this one. Even on DVD, it's extremely grainy with bleached out colors that turn flesh tones into putty. The grubby look may be an intentional effort to add to the overall gaminess, but that doesn't make it any easier to watch. (Also available in "R"-rated version, catalog number 7447.) —*MM*

Movie: 🎜➤ *DVD:* 🎜➤
Simitar Entertainment (Cat #7468, UPC #082551746828). Full frame. PCM Stereo. $14.98. Keepcase. *LANG:* English. *FEATURES:* 8 chapter links ● Filmography and thumbnail biography of Julie Strain.
1995 99m/C Monique Parent, Julie Strain, Justin Carroll; *D:* John Bowen; *W:* Steve Tymon; *C:* Keith Holland; *M:* Efrem Bergman.

Dark Shadows (SE)

This curious DVD is a sort of combination documentary/appreciation/greatest-hits collection aimed squarely at fans of the Gothic soap opera. An introduction admits that though the series debuted in June 1966, it wasn't until almost a year later when the character of Barnabus Collins (Jonathan Frid) was introduced that the show became a hit. He, of course, was daytime TV's first vampire, and he is still a popular figure. In terms of image and sound, the DVD is little better than its mid-'60s source material. The technical rating is based on the large amount of material on the disc and the extras. —*MM*

Movie: 🎜🎜➤ *DVD:* 🎜🎜🎜
MPI Home Video (Cat #DVD7402, UPC #030306740225). Full frame. Dolby Digital Mono. $24.98. Keepcase. *LANG:* English. *SUB:* English; Spanish. *FEATURES:* 10 chapter links ● Spanish episode ● TV commercials ● Promotional spots ● Photo gallery and music montage ● Cast genre appearances ● Program history.
1999 210m/C

Dark Star

John Carpenter's directorial debut is a low-budget sf satire focused on a group of spacefarers whose mission is to destroy unstable planets. During their journey they battle their alien mascot (which resembles a walking beach ball), as well as a "sensitive" intelligent nuclear device which starts to question the meaning of its existence, giving new meaning to the then-unknown term "smart bomb." O'Bannon's script is very smart and funny. Visually, the disc is no great shakes, but it does offer two versions of the film, both the theatrical release version and the film as it was shown at the Filmex festival. The deleted scenes are included as a chapter; the viewer can choose which version to watch. Even though the film looks rough compared to today's sf, the DVD is a step up from older tapes, some of which are almost unwatchable. —*MM*

Movie: 🎜🎜🎜 *DVD:* 🎜🎜➤
VCI Home Video (Cat #8205, UPC #089859820526). Widescreen letterboxed. Dolby Digital 5.1 Surround Stereo. $29.95. Keepcase. *LANG:* English. *FEATURES:* 18 chapter links ● Cast and production notes ● Trailer.
1974 (G) 95m/C Dan O'Bannon, Brian Narelle, Dre Pahich, Cal Duniholm; *D:* John Carpenter; *W:* John Carpenter, Dan O'Bannon; *C:* Douglas Knapp; *M:* John Carpenter.

Dark Victory

Davis impressively seizes the part of the spoiled young heiress who discovers she is dying from a brain tumor. As she tries valiantly to pack a lifetime of parties into her few remaining months, she almost inevitably falls in love with her doctor. Davis is at the top of her game in the memorable final scene. Too bad Bogart, not in one of his better roles, sticks out like a sore thumb as he works not very hard at playing an Irish stable hand. Though the avid film buff will lament the lack of extras beyond the original theatrical trailer, most cinephiles will admire the deep, rich black-and-white imagery that isn't marred by noticeable artifacts other than the occasional blemish typical for a film of this vintage. The monaural soundtrack is clear and distinct. —*MB*

Movie: 🎜🎜🎜➤ *DVD:* 🎜🎜🎜
MGM Home Entertainment (Cat #906685, UPC #027616668523). Full frame. Dolby Digital 1.0. $24.98. Snapper. *LANG:* English. *SUB:* English; French; Spanish. *CAP:* English. *FEATURES:* 32 chapter links ● Theatrical trailer.
1939 106m/B Bette Davis, George Brent, Geraldine Fitzgerald, Humphrey Bogart, Ronald Reagan, Henry Travers; *D:* Edmund Goulding; *W:* Casey Robinson; *C:* Ernest Haller; *M:* Max Steiner. *AWARDS: NOM:* Academy Awards '39: Best Actress (Davis), Best Picture, Best Original Score.

Dark Waters

Traumatized by the death of her parents at sea and the ordeal she went through, heiress Leslie Cavan (Oberon) finds it difficult to recover. Then she learns that Aunt Emily (Bainter) and Uncle Norbert

(Mitchell) are right down the road in the bayou town of Belleville, LA. Do they have her best interests at heart? This noirish drama works well on DVD. Some of the black-and-white photography—from directors of photography Archie Stout and John Mescall—is a bit muddy, but most of it is so sharp that it reveals the grain of the wood in a painted board. Miklos Rozsa's score is too screechy in its louder moments, but it's still an effective evocation of the period. The fine cast carries the film through the weaker moments. —*MM*

Movie: 🎬🎬 **DVD:** 🎬🎬🎬
Image Entertainment (Cat #ID5367FWDVD, UPC #014381536730). Full frame. Dolby Digital Mono. $24.99. Snapper. *LANG:* English. *FEATURES:* 13 chapter links.
1944 93m/B Merle Oberon, Franchot Tone, Thomas Mitchell, Fay Bainter, Elisha Cook Jr., John Qualen, Rex Ingram; **D:** Andre de Toth; **W:** Joan Harrison, Marian Cockrell; **C:** Archie Stout, John Mescall; **M:** Miklos Rozsa.

Darkdrive

In the near future, the Zircon Corporation has created a virtual prison where the minds of criminals are held in isolation. Naturally, something's gone wrong and it's up to special operations officer Steven Falcon (Olandt) to risk his mind and solve the problem.

Movie: 🎬🎬 **DVD:** NYR
MTI Home Video (Cat #7003). Full frame. $24.95. Keepcase.
1998 (R) ?m/C Ken Olandt, Julie Benz, Claire Stansfield, Carlo Scandiuzzi; **D:** Phillip J. Roth; **W:** Alec Carlin; **C:** Andres Garreton; **M:** Jim Goodwin.

Darkman

Director Sam Raimi combines the unashamed cheesiness of the great Universal series of the 1940s with his own full-tilt energy to create one of the screen's great comic books. Dr. Peyton Westlake (Neeson) is on the verge of a major discovery involving skin replacement when the evil Durant (Drake) and his thugs break in and destroy the lab. Westlake is left disfigured and unhinged by his desire for revenge. The casting, including Frances McDormand, is inspired and, as he always does, Raimi keeps the pace zipping right along. On DVD, the film is not as crystalline as Raimi's *A Simple Plan*, but his attention to sharp focus in extreme close shots really benefits from the digital transfer. In the extended finale, some of the blue-screen special effects are made more obvious but the multiple cliff-hanger is still a kick in the pants. The sound effects and Danny Elfman's thundering score are impressive there, too. —*MM*

Movie: 🎬🎬🎬 **DVD:** 🎬🎬🎬
Universal Studios Home Video (Cat #20179, UPC #025192017926). Widescreen letterboxed. Dolby Digital Surround Stereo. $24.98. Keepcase. *LANG:* English; French. *SUB:* Spanish. *CAP:* English. *FEATURES:* 16 chapter links • Production

notes • Cast and crew thumbnail biographies • Theatrical trailer.
1990 (R) 96m/C Liam Neeson, Frances McDormand, Larry Drake, Colin Friels, Nelson Mashita, Jenny Agutter, Rafael H. Robledo, Nicholas Worth; **D:** Sam Raimi; **W:** Sam Raimi, Ivan Raimi, Daniel Goldin, Joshua Goldin, Chuck Pfarrer; **C:** Bill Pope; **M:** Danny Elfman.

Darkman 2: The Return of Durant

"I choose to live on as a creature of the shadows—as Darkman!" So says brilliant scientist Peyton Westlake in a sequel that recalls the great Universal horror series of the 1930s (particularly *The Invisible Man*). Evil villain Durant (Drake) has chosen to live on, too, even though he was turned to toast in the helicopter crash at the end of the first film. But good villains are hard to come by, so he miraculously survived and has been in a coma. Now, he's back and meaner than ever. Meanwhile, Westlake (Vosloo ably taking over for Liam Neeson) is still working on a formula for synthetic skin. Director-cinematographer Bradford May captures the energy, black humor, and comic book spirit of Sam Raimi's original, but this one lacks that extra spark, hard focus, and attention to small details that mark the best of Raimi's work. The shortcoming is particularly apparent on DVD, though the many night action scenes and deliberately dark interiors are free of artifacts. The sound is fine. —*MM*

Movie: 🎬🎬🎬 **DVD:** 🎬🎬🎬
Universal Studios Home Video (Cat #20323, UPC #025192032325). Widescreen letterboxed. Dolby Digital Surround Stereo. $24.98. Keepcase. *LANG:* English; French; Spanish. *SUB:* Spanish. *CAP:* English. *FEATURES:* 18 chapter links • Production notes • Cast and crew thumbnail biographies • Theatrical trailer • Universal web links.
1994 (R) 93m/C Arnold Vosloo, Larry Drake, Kim Delaney, Renee O'Connor, Rod Wilson; **D:** Bradford May; **W:** Steven McKay, Chuck Pfarrer; **C:** Bradford May; **M:** Randy Miller.

Darkroom

An unstable young man devises a scheme to photograph his father in bed with his mistress and then to use the pictures to blackmail dear old dad.
Movie: 🎬 **DVD:** NYR
Simitar Entertainment (Cat #7607). Full frame. Dolby Digital Stereo. $14.98. Keepcase.
1990 90m/C Jill Pierce, Jeffrey Allen Arbaugh, Sara Lee Wade, Aaron Teich; **D:** Terrence O'Hara.

Darkside Blues

Japanese animation presents yet another bleak vision of the near future.
Movie: NYR **DVD:** NYR
Central Park Media/U.S. Manga Corps (Cat #1827). Full frame. Dolby Digital Surround

Stereo. $26.97. Keepcase. *LANG:* Japanese. *SUB:* English. *CAP:* English.
1999 83m/C

Das Boot (DC)

Superb detailing of life in a German U-boat during WWII. Intense, claustrophobic atmosphere complemented by nail-biting action provides a realistic portrait of the stressful conditions that were endured on these submarines. Excellent performances, especially from Prochnow. Originally a six-hour special made for German television. This DVD substantially improves on all previous and current home video releases of either the theatrical or director's cut version. The film spends a lot of time in the dark, yet the picture remains sharp and detailed with super colors that look as good or better than they did in the theatre. The sound is also top-notch, and conveys torpedoes, depth charges, and a sub that dives too deep with incredible ambience and energy. The supplemental material is excellent, especially the commentary by Peterson, which is both personable and crammed full of information. —*JO* **AKA:** The Boat.

Movie: 🎬🎬🎬🎬 **DVD:** 🎬🎬🎬🎬
Columbia Tristar Home Video (Cat #22219, UPC #043396222199). Widescreen (1.85:1) letterboxed. Dolby Digital 5.1; Stereo. NSL. Keepcase. *LANG:* English; Spanish; German. *SUB:* English; Spanish; French. *CAP:* English. *FEATURES:* 66 chapter links • Commentary: Wolfgang Peterson • "Making of" featurette • Behind the-scenes featurette.
1981 (R) 210m/C GE Juergen Prochnow, Herbert Gronemeyer, Klaus Wennemann, Hubertus Bengsch, Martin Semmelrogge, Bernd Tauber, Erwin Leder, Martin May, Heinz Honig, Uwe Ochsenknecht, Claude-Oliver Rudolph, Jan Fedder, Ralph Richer, Joachim Bernhard, Oliver Stritzel, Konrad Becker, Lutz Schnell, Martin Hemme, Rita Cadillac; **D:** Wolfgang Petersen; **W:** Wolfgang Petersen; **C:** Jost Vacano; **M:** Klaus Doldinger. *AWARDS: NOM:* Academy Awards '82: Best Adapted Screenplay, Best Cinematography, Best Director (Petersen), Best Film Editing, Best Sound.

Daughters of Darkness

This is, without question, the most erotic lesbian vampire movie ever made. *The Hunger* pales in comparison. The opening shots establish a honeymooning couple, Stefan (Karlen) and Valerie (Ouimet), married only a few hours, but already being divided by dishonesty and tension. After an unplanned stop at a huge, empty seaside hotel, they meet the Countess (Seyrig) and her secretary Ilona (Rau), glamorous women languid as cats. The level of sexual uncertainty among the quartet rises steadily and largely without the expected conventions. The film is beautifully written and acted on a curiously conversational level. The filmmakers approach their subject from the edges. For

example, they delay the introduction of key characters and information, and they use color, pace, and camera angles to keep the viewer off balance. The DVD was made from the Anchor Bay "collector's edition" and runs the full 100 minutes, more than 12 important minutes longer than the U.S. theatrical release, in a beautifully restored widescreen image. Some of the darker moments have a curious textured quality. If it comes from any flaw in the digital transfer, it is appropriate to the film. The commentary conversation between star John Karlen and journalist David Del Valle is funny and affable. Of course, any fan who is discovering this cult hit on disc should watch it without interruption, but a second viewing with the talk is rewarding. —*MM* *AKA:* Le Rouge aux Levres; Blut an den Lippen; Erzebeth; The Promise of Red Lips; The Red Lips.
Movie: ♪♪♪➤ **DVD:** ♪♪♪➤
Anchor Bay (Cat #DV10494, UPC #013131049497). Widescreen (1.66:1) letterboxed. Dolby Digital Mono. $24.98. Keepcase. *LANG:* English. *FEATURES:* 13 chapter links ● Commentary: John Karlen and David Del Valle.
1971 (R) 100m/C *BE GE IT FR* Delphine Seyrig, John Karlen, Daniele Ouimet, Andrea Rau, Paul Esser, Georges Jamin, Joris Collet, Fons Rademakers; *D:* Harry Kumel; *W:* Harry Kumel, Pierre Drouot, Jean Ferry; *C:* Eddy van der Enden; *M:* Francois de Roubaix.

Dave

Regular guy Dave Kovic (Kline) is a dead ringer for the President, launching him into the White House after the prez suffers a stroke under embarrassing circumstances. Seamless comedy prompts lots of hearty laughs and the feel-good faith that despite the overwhelming odds, everything will turn out just fine. Political cameos abound: look for real-life Senators Alan Simpson, Paul Simon, Howard Metzenbaum, Tom Harkin, and Christopher Dodd, as well as the commentators from TV's *The McLaughlin Group,* and Oliver Stone, poking fun at himself on *Larry King Live.* This may sound stupid, but the thing that sticks with me about this DVD's performance is that the rain that occurs at the 52-minute point looks fake. There is also a lot of background grain, which could indicate a little heavy-handed digitizing (or something to that effect). That said, the picture is usually very sharp and both the colors and blacks are accurate. The contrast and brightness levels are comfortable if not punchy. The sound is definitely an asset: dynamic with good imaging, fidelity, and low end. —*JO*
Movie: ♪♪♪ **DVD:** ♪♪♪
Warner Home Video, Inc. (Cat #12962, UPC #085391296225). Widescreen (2.0:1) letterboxed; full frame. Dolby Surround. $24.98. Snapper. *LANG:* English; Spanish; French. *SUB:* English; Spanish; French. *CAP:* English. *FEATURES:* 27 chapter links ● Theatrical trailers ● "Making of" featurette ● Production notes.

1993 (PG-13) 110m/C Kevin Kline, Sigourney Weaver, Frank Langella, Kevin Dunn, Ving Rhames, Ben Kingsley, Charles Grodin, Faith Prince, Laura Linney, Bonnie Hunt, Parley Baer, Stefan Gierasch, Anna Deavere Smith, Bonnie Bartlett, Ben Stein; *Cameos:* Jay Leno, Larry King, Oliver Stone, Arnold Schwarzenegger; *D:* Ivan Reitman; *W:* Gary Ross; *C:* Adam Greenberg; *M:* James Newton Howard. *AWARDS:* NOM: Academy Awards '93: Best Original Screenplay; Golden Globe Awards '94: Best Actor—Musical/Comedy (Kline), Best Film—Musical/Comedy; Writers Guild of America '93: Best Original Screenplay.

David and Lisa

This early example of the '60s esthetic of aligning madness and alienation was a dark horse independent production. The story concerns two institutionalized teens and their highly charged platonic relationship. Performances, though sometimes violent, are never histrionic. At this late a stage, the real attraction is watching young leads who would soon be known almost exclusively for other performances. Kier Dullea (*2001*) is David, who fears being touched. Janet Margolin (*Take the Money and Run*) is the schizophrenic, compulsively rhyming Lisa. A pristine print means that highlights and even white on gray text show up plain as day. The serviceable mono mix alternates quiet moments with dramatically timed bursts of noise and music. —*JK*
Movie: ♪♪♪ **DVD:** ♪♪♪♪
Fox/Lorber Home Video (Cat #FLV5104, UPC #720917510422). Full frame. Dual-channel Mono. $29.98. Keepcase. *LANG:* English. *FEATURES:* 6 chapter links ● Interactive menus ● 2-color picture disc ● Star and director filmographies ● Production credits and award lists.
1962 94m/B Keir Dullea, Janet Margolin, Howard da Silva, Neva Patterson, Clifton James; *D:* Frank Perry; *W:* Eleanor Perry; *C:* Leonard Hirschfield; *M:* Mark Laurence. *AWARDS:* NOM: Academy Awards '62: Best Adapted Screenplay, Best Director (Perry).

Dawn of the Dead

Romero's gruesome sequel to his *Night of the Living Dead.* A mysterious plague causes the recently dead to rise from their graves and scour the countryside for living flesh. It's very violent, gory, graphic, and shocking, yet not without humor, and gives interesting consideration to the violence created by the living humans in their efforts to save themselves. Anchor Bay more often than not does a good job on their horror DVDs, and this is no exception. This disc is the 137-minute U.S. theatrical version, and it looks great. The preprint used has very little damage and the transfer to DVD is very sharp and the color is much stronger than any previous home video release. Even the sound is clearer, with a little more low end. —*JO*
AKA: Zombi; Zombie; Zombies.
Movie: ♪♪♪➤ **DVD:** ♪♪♪➤

Anchor Bay (Cat #DV10325, UPC #013131032598). Widescreen (1.66:1) letterboxed. Mono. $24.98. Keepcase. *LANG:* English. *FEATURES:* 9 chapter links ● Theatrical trailers.
1978 137m/C David Emge, Ken Foree, Gaylen Ross, Scott H. Reiniger, David Crawford, David Early, Daniel Dietrich, Richard France, Tom Savini, Howard K. Smith, George A. Romero; *D:* George A. Romero; *W:* George A. Romero; *C:* Michael Gornick; *M:* Dario Argento, The Goblins.

Day of the Animals

Nature goes wild when a depleted ozone layer has exposed them to radiation, turning Bambi and Bugs into ravaging beasts. Unaware of the transformation, backpackers trek into Sierras. Farfetched and silly. *AKA:* Something Is Out There.
Movie: ♪ **DVD:** NYR
Digital Versatile Disc Ltd. (Cat #144). $19.95.
1977 (PG) 95m/C Christopher George, Leslie Nielsen, Lynda Day George, Richard Jaeckel, Michael Ansara, Ruth Roman, Jon Cedar, Susan Backlinie, Andrew Stevens, Gil Lamb; *D:* William Girdler; *W:* William W. Norton Sr.; *C:* Robert Sorrentino; *M:* Lalo Schifrin.

Day of the Dead

The third (and probably the final) installment of George Romero's trilogy opens inside a bare cinderblock room where Sara (Cardille) stares at a calendar on the wall. Clearly, the original situation from *Night of the Living Dead,* where bodies rise up to devour the living, has deteriorated. A small group of scientists and soldiers is trapped inside an underground Florida missile installation. Do they study the living dead and possibly learn how to domesticate them? Or will the military types, under the command of a martinet, screw things up even more? Romero's social criticism is even stronger than it was in *Dawn of the Dead,* making for a slow first hour. The conclusion contains some of Tom Savini's most grotesque, detailed, and sophisticated gore effects. The DVD is a solid step up from older tapes, but, given the nature of the original material, it's only marginally better than the widescreen VHS edition which contains the same extras. (This is a two-sided disc with the feature on one side, extras on the other.) —*MM*
Movie: ♪♪♪ **DVD:** ♪♪♪
Anchor Bay (Cat #DV10602, UPC #013131060294). Widescreen (1.85:1) letterboxed. Dolby Digital Mono. $29.99. Keepcase. *LANG:* English. *FEATURES:* 12 chapter links ● Theatrical trailer ● Behind-the-scenes footage.
1985 91m/C Lori Cardille, Terry Alexander, Joe Pilato, Jarlath Conroy, Richard Liberty; *D:* George A. Romero; *W:* George A. Romero; *C:* Michael Gornick; *M:* John Harrison.

The Day of the Jackal

Frederick Forsyth's best-selling novel of political intrigue is splendidly brought to the screen by Zinnemann. A brilliant and ruthless assassin hired to kill Charles de Gaulle skirts the international intelligence pool, while intuitive police work to stop him. Tense, suspenseful, beautiful location photography. Excellent acting by Fox, Cusack, and Britton. The preprint used for the DVD transfer is showing its age and has a little wear, but nothing too bothersome. The transfer itself is pretty sharp and digital grain is limited to just a few scenes. Colors are very good, deep and accurate with only minor, occasional bleed. Contrast and brightness levels are much better than the earlier home video releases and more than make up for the aforementioned film damage. The mono sound is nothing special but is clear and distortion-free. —*JO*

Movie: ♫♫♫▶ *DVD:* ♫♫♫

Universal Studios Home Video (Cat #20261, UPC #025192026126). Widescreen (1.85:1) letterboxed. Mono. $24.95. Keepcase. *LANG:* English. *SUB:* Spanish; French. *CAP:* English. *FEATURES:* 16 chapter links • Theatrical trailer • Cast and filmmakers bios • Production notes • Film highlights.
1973 (PG) 142m/C Edward Fox, Alan Badel, Tony Britton, Derek Jacobi, Cyril Cusack, Olga Georges-Picot; *D:* Fred Zinnemann; *W:* Kenneth Ross; *M:* Georges Delerue. *AWARDS: NOM:* Academy Awards '73: Best Film Editing.

Daylight

After a massive explosion seals both ends of New York's Holland Tunnel, a small band of stock disaster-flick survivors are trapped under the waters of the Hudson River. Fortunately, a cab driver with a really square jaw who, conveniently, is an ex–emergency rescue worker AND who knows the entire layout of the tunnel, happens to be driving toward the tunnel at the exact moment of the disaster. Coincidence? Nope, just Hollywood. Kit Latura (Stallone) leads the survivors through cave-ins, floods, fire, rats, and poison gas only to discover to their dismay that they have emerged in New Jersey. Long on special effects but short on character development, this nod to the catastrophe movies of the '70s is still enjoyable for those who like to watch things go boom. And boy do things go boom on this DVD. The sound is spectacular! The subwoofer out is so pumped up, it'll rattle more than your window panes and the other dynamics of the 5.1 tracks follow suit. The separation and mix is as good as they come. The picture also holds its own and is very sharp, with well-defined colors that remain punchy and bright under all lighting conditions. Blacks are very true in all but a couple of scenes. Grain and artifacts are minimal. —*JO*

Movie: ♫♫ *DVD:* ♫♫♫▶

Universal Studios Home Video (Cat #20267, UPC #025192026720). Widescreen (1.85:1) anamorphic. Dolby Digital 5.1; Dolby Surround. $34.98. Keepcase. *LANG:* English (DD5.1); Spanish (DS); French (DS). *SUB:* Spanish. *CAP:* English. *FEATURES:* 43 chapter links (feature) • 11 chapter links ("The Making of 'Daylight'") • Theatrical trailer • 2 documentaries • "Whenever There Is Love" music video • Production notes.
1996 (PG-13) 109m/C Sylvester Stallone, Viggo Mortensen, Amy Brenneman, Stan Shaw, Claire Bloom, Renoly Santiago, Sage Stallone, Dan Hedaya, Jay O. Sanders, Karen Young, Vanessa Bell Calloway, Colin Fox, Danielle Harris, Jo Anderson, Mark Rolston, Rosemary Forsyth, Barry Newman; *D:* Rob Cohen; *W:* Leslie Bohem; *C:* David Eggby; *M:* Randy Edelman. *AWARDS: NOM:* Academy Awards '96: Best Sound Effects Editing; Golden Raspberry Awards '96: Worst Actor (Stallone), Worst Song ("Whenever There Is Love").

Days of Heaven

In 1916, Bill (Gere), his sister Linda (Manz), and Abby (Adams) go to work for a Texas farmer (Shepard). The love triangle that ensues has the dimensions of classical tragedy because director Malick sets it in a strongly realized natural world. The film has a sense of texture and depth that few others approach. Cinematographer Nestor Almendros (with contributions from Haskell Wexler) won an Academy Award for his work. The DVD captures it faithfully. The film looks identical to the original theatrical release as I remember it, and it sounds better, making Morricone's score (with contributions from guitarist Leo Kottke) even more magical. The sound also enhances Manz's voice-over narration, a key component that's often overlooked. In short, despite a lack of extras, the DVD does this masterpiece justice. —*MM*

Movie: ♫♫♫♫ *DVD:* ♫♫♫♫

Paramount Home Video (Cat #089427, UPC #097360894271). Widescreen letterboxed. Dolby Surround; 5.1 Surround. $29.98. Keepcase. *LANG:* English; French. *CAP:* English. *FEATURES:* 10 chapter links • Theatrical trailer.
1978 (PG) 95m/C Richard Gere, Brooke Adams, Sam Shepard, Linda Manz, Stuart Margolin; *D:* Terrence Malick; *W:* Terrence Malick; *C:* Nestor Almendros; *M:* Ennio Morricone. *AWARDS:* Academy Awards '78: Best Cinematography; Cannes Film Festival '79: Best Director (Malick); Los Angeles Film Critics Association Awards '78: Best Cinematography; New York Film Critics Awards '78: Best Director (Malick); National Society of Film Critics Awards '78: Best Cinematography, Best Director (Malick), Best Film; *NOM:* Academy Awards '78: Best Costume Design, Best Sound, Best Original Score.

Days of Thunder

Top Gun in racecars. That's the short review of this high-octane but empty star vehicle that lurches from unintentional humor—Cruise's first entrance on a motorcycle is one of his funniest moments—to loud stockcar scenes and almost every auto race cliche, including the beautiful doctor (Kidman). Actually, solid work by the supporting cast—Duvall, Rooker, Quaid—is the best part of the film. The DVD captures the artfully fancy visuals as well as any form of home video could. The rock video mix of music and sound effects in the races works well, but this is still a theme park ride of a movie and it loses something on anything but the largest theatre screen with full-bore stereo sound. —*MM*

Movie: ♫♫ *DVD:* ♫♫♫

Paramount Home Video (Cat #321237, UPC #097363212379). Widescreen (2.35:1) letterboxed. Dolby Digital Surround Stereo; Dolby Digital 5.1 Surround. $29.98. Keepcase. *LANG:* English; French. *CAP:* English. *FEATURES:* 23 chapter links • Theatrical trailer.
1990 (PG-13) 108m/C Tom Cruise, Robert Duvall, Randy Quaid, Nicole Kidman, Cary Elwes, Michael Rooker, Fred Dalton Thompson, John C. Reilly; *D:* Tony Scott; *W:* Tom Cruise, Robert Towne; *C:* Ward Russell; *M:* Hans Zimmer. *AWARDS: NOM:* Academy Awards '90: Best Sound.

Dazed and Confused

A day in the life of a bunch of high schoolers should prove to be a trip back in time for those who came of age in the 1970s. Eight seniors facing life after graduation have one last year-long hurrah, as they search for Aerosmith tickets and haze the incoming freshmen. Keen characterization by writer-director Linklater captures the spirit of a generation shaped by Watergate, feminism, and marijuana. Groovy soundtrack features Alice Cooper, Deep Purple, KISS, and Foghat. There's nothing special about the DVD image. The usual problems with bright diagonals are apparent and some cherry reds bleed a bit. Those who don't appreciate the music won't be impressed by the sound, either. —*MM*

Movie: ♫♫♫ *DVD:* ♫♫▶

Universal Studios Home Video (Cat #20277). Widescreen (1.85:1) letterboxed. Dolby Digital Surround Stereo. $24.98. Keepcase. *LANG:* English; French. *SUB:* Spanish. *FEATURES:* Cast and crew thumbnail bios • Production notes • Trailer • 16 chapter links.
1993 (R) 97m/C Jason London, Rory Cochrane, Sasha Jensen, Wiley Wiggins, Michelle Burke, Adam Goldberg, Anthony Rapp, Marissa Ribisi, Parker Posey, Joey Lauren Adams, Ben Affleck, Milla Jovovich, Cole Hauser, Matthew McConaughey, Kristin Hinojosa; *D:* Richard Linklater; *W:* Richard Linklater; *C:* Lee Daniel.

Dead Again

Kenneth Branagh shifted gears after *Henry V* and made this ambitious Gothic noir where he and then-wife Emma Thompson both play dual roles. In the black-and-white sections set in the late '40s, they're star musicians involved in suspected infidelity and murder. In the film's present, they're detective Mike Church and a woman who's suffering terrifying dreams of the past. A wonderful assortment of bizarre supporting characters keeps things moving throughout. The widescreen image is a definite step up from full-frame VHS tape, which, if my memory is correct, looks pretty good. The sound is fine and on his commentary track, Branagh sounds enthusiastic and happy to be revisiting a successful collaboration. —MM

Movie: ♫♫♫▶ **DVD:** ♫♫♫▶
Paramount Home Video Widescreen letterboxed. Dolby Digital 5.1 Surround Stereo; Dolby Digital Surround. $29.99. Keepcase. *LANG:* English; French. *SUB:* English. *FEATURES:* Trailer ▪ 14 chapter links ▪ Commentary: Kenneth Branagh ▪ Commentary: producer Lindsay Doran and writer Scott Frank.
1991 (R) 107m/C Kenneth Branagh, Emma Thompson, Andy Garcia, Lois Hall, Richard Easton, Derek Jacobi, Hanna Schygulla, Campbell Scott, Wayne Knight, Christine Ebersole; *Cameos:* Robin Williams; *D:* Kenneth Branagh; *W:* Scott Frank; *C:* Matthew F. Leonetti; *M:* Patrick Doyle.

Dead Alive

This outrageously over-the-top horror flick from New Zealand is a gore aficionado's delight (think *Evil Dead* movies for comparison). Set in 1957 and satirizing the bland times, the "plot" has the mom of a nerdy son getting bitten by an exotic monkey, which promptly turns her into a particularly nasty ghoul. This condition is apparently contagious (except for her son who tries to hide the fact mom is literally a monster) and calls for lots of spurting blood and body parts, which take on lives of their own. For those with strong stomachs and senses of humor, I was very disappointed in this DVD, one of my favorite sicko comedies. The picture is of only average sharpness and in many of the numerous dark scenes there is quite a bit of grain. The colors are also muted when compared to both the domestic laserdisc and the Japanese import LD, which also contains a seven-minute-longer cut of the film. Darker reds bleed a little. Contrast is somewhat low, as is the brightness level. Blacks range from true to grainy-gray. The sound was never a highlight of this low-budget wonder, and it seems that the tracks on the DVD accurately reflect the film's original soundtrack. —JO *AKA:* Braindead.

Movie: ♫♫♫ **DVD:** ♫♫▶
Trimark Home Video (Cat #VM6841D, UPC #031398684138). Widescreen (1.66:1) letterboxed. Stereo. $24.98. Keepcase. *LANG:* English. *SUB:* Spanish; French. *CAP:* English. *FEATURES:* 2 chapter links ▪ Theatrical trailer.
1993 97m/C NZ Timothy Balme, Elizabeth Moody, Diana Penalver, Ian Watkin, Breanda Kendall, Stuart Devenie; *D:* Peter Jackson; *W:* Peter Jackson, Frances

Walsh, Stephen Sinclair; *C:* Murray Milne; *M:* Peter Dasent.

Dead Bang

Jerry Beck (Johnson) is a divorced L.A. homicide detective who drinks too much, lives in a squalid apartment, drives a junker, and does things his own way; in short, a compendium of cliches. On Christmas Eve, he's assigned to the case of a murdered policeman. It leads him into an affair with the man's widow (Miller) and the discovery of a conspiracy of white supremacists. Director Frankenheimer handles the action scenes well enough, but they're nothing special and the conventional story isn't nearly as involving as his best work. On DVD, the film looks and sounds as clear as it did in theatres. The lack of extras is indicative of the overall level of quality. —MM

Movie: ♫♫▶ **DVD:** ♫♫♫
Warner Home Video, Inc. (Cat #658, UPC #01256906582). Full frame. Dolby Digital Stereo Surround. $14.98. Snapper. *LANG:* English; French. *CAP:* English. *FEATURES:* 31 chapter links.
1989 (R) 102m/C Don Johnson, Bob Balaban, William Forsythe, Penelope Ann Miller, Tim Reid, Frank Military, Michael Higgins, Michael Jeter, Evans Evans, Tate Donovan; *D:* John Frankenheimer; *W:* Robert Foster; *C:* Gerry Fisher; *M:* Gary Chang, Michael Kamen.

Dead Calm

Taut Australian thriller begins with a horrifying accident that results in the death of a child. The rest takes place at sea with three people: a married couple (Neill and Kidman) on a small yacht and the survivor (Zane) of a sinking ship. They take him on board and soon realize that he is profoundly dangerous. Fine performances and equally strong direction make up for other weaknesses. A no-frills DVD handles potentially difficult material without problems. From the dark beginning and heavily shadowed boat interiors to the extremely bright exteriors, the image is fine. Sound is adequate. —MM

Movie: ♫♫♫ **DVD:** ♫♫♫
Warner Home Video, Inc. (Cat #11870). Widescreen letterboxed; full frame. $19.98. Snapper. *LANG:* English; French. *SUB:* English; French. *FEATURES:* 36 chapter links ▪ Trailer.
1989 (R) 97m/C AU Sam Neill, Billy Zane, Nicole Kidman, Rod Mullinar; *D:* Phillip Noyce; *W:* Terry Hayes; *C:* Dean Semler; *M:* Graeme Revell.

Dead End

Police officer Henry "Smoke" Smovinski (Roberts) gains custody of his troubled 16-year-old son Adam (Tierney) after his ex-wife's death. But the death is being investigated as a murder and Adam is a prime suspect. Soon father and son are teamed up to find out what's happening. In a rare likeable role, Roberts is excel-

lent. (He almost always is.) On DVD, the Canadian film is fine, too. The image is sharply focused and extremely well photographed. From its vertiginous opening sequence to the end, it looks better than films that cost twice as much. —MM

Movie: ♫♫♫ **DVD:** ♫♫♫
Simitar Entertainment (Cat #7439, UPC #082551743926). Full frame. Dolby Digital Stereo; Dolby Digital 5.1 Surround Stereo. $19.98. Keepcase. *LANG:* English. *FEATURES:* 8 chapter links ▪ Production factoids ▪ Eric Roberts filmography.
1998 (R) 93m/C CA Eric Roberts, Jacob Tierney, Jayne Heitmeyer, Eliza Roberts, Jack Langedijk, Frank Schorpion; *D:* Douglas Jackson; *W:* Karl Schiffman; *C:* Georges Archambault; *M:* Milan Kymlicka.

Dead Man on Campus

Failing college freshmen Josh (Scott) and Cooper (Gosselaar) learn that if your roommate commits suicide, you get a straight-A average for the year. So they decide to find a new guy who's on the edge and then push him over. Anyone who's done time in the dorms has heard this urban legend, so it was only a matter of time before someone turned it into a screenplay. The one-joke premise can't sustain the movie, though the young cast is game and attractive, and the script has a few moments that approach the subversive humor of *Heathers*. Really, though, what should anyone expect from an MTV production? Scott is an appealing young actor who makes the most of the lead. This kind of comedy translates well to the small screen. On disc, some blacks lack sharpness, particularly in the night scenes. The sound is fine. —MM

Movie: ♫♫ **DVD:** ♫♫♫
Paramount Home Video (Cat #331747, UPC #097363317470). Widescreen. Dolby Digital Surround Stereo; Dolby Digital 5.1 Surround. Keepcase. *LANG:* English; French. *SUB:* English. *FEATURES:* Theatrical trailer ▪ Interactive menus ▪ Scene access.
1997 (R) 94m/C Tom Everett Scott, Mark Paul Gosselaar, Alyson Hannigan, Poppy Montgomery, Lochlyn Munro, Randy Pearlstein, Mari Morrow; *D:* Alan Cohn; *W:* Michael Traeger, Mike White; *C:* John Thomas; *M:* Mark Mothersbaugh.

Dead Men Walk / The Monster Maker

George Zucco plays the dual role of the good brother Lloyd and his evil twin Elwin who, with the aid of his assistant played by Dwight Frye, is reborn as a vampire. The low-budget effort is scratchy and dark on video. As the romantic lead David, Nedrick Young made a wise career change when he became a writer. Though he was blacklisted, he also won an Oscar for *The Defiant Ones. AKA:* Creatures of the Devil.
Movie: ♫♫ **DVD:** NYR
Roan Group (Cat #2023). Full frame. Dolby Digital Mono. $29.95. Keepcase.

1943 65m/B George Zucco, Mary Carlisle, Dwight Frye, Nedrick Young, Al "Fuzzy" St. John, Fern Emmett, Robert Strange; *D:* Sam Newfield; *W:* Fred Myton; *C:* Jack Greenhalgh; *M:* Leo Erdody.

Dead Poets Society

An idealistic English teacher inspires a group of boys in a 1950s prep school to pursue individuality and creative endeavor, resulting in clashes with school and parental authorities. Williams shows he can master the serious roles as well as the comic with his portrayal of the unorthodox educator. Big boxoffice hit scripted with an occasionally heavy hand in order to elevate the message. The ensemble cast is excellent. This is a dialogue-driven film, so you can sort of put up with the sound being only so-so (as long as you can understand it), but a film of this caliber deserves a much sharper image and certainly colors that are not washed-out. The laserdisc is superior and the VHS version is at least as good. —*JO*
Movie: ♪♪♪ *DVD:* ♪♪
Buena Vista Home Entertainment (Cat #15092, UPC #717951000682). Widescreen (1.85:1) letterboxed. Dolby Surround; Stereo. $29.99. Keepcase. *LANG:* English (DS); French (Stereo). *CAP:* English. *FEATURES:* 23 chapter links.
1989 (PG) 128m/C Robin Williams, Ethan Hawke, Robert Sean Leonard, Josh Charles, Gale Hansen, Kurtwood Smith, James Waterson, Dylan Kussman, Lara Flynn Boyle, Melora Hardin, Alexandra Powers; *D:* Peter Weir; *W:* Tom Schulman; *C:* John Seale; *M:* Maurice Jarre. *AWARDS:* Academy Awards '89: Best Original Screenplay; British Academy Awards '89: Best Film; Cesar Awards '91: Best Foreign Film; *NOM:* Academy Awards '89: Best Actor (Williams), Best Director (Weir), Best Picture.

Dead Presidents

Sophomore release for the Hughes brothers falls short of the impact of *Menace II Society*, but not for lack of ambition. Combination coming-of-age tale, war story, period piece, and caper film follows Anthony (*Menace*–veteran Tate) from his Bronx neighborhood in 1968 to Vietnam (for *Platoon* adventures in the wilds of Florida) and then back to the 'hood, where his life continues to spiral downward. Desperate to escape, he becomes involved in an armored car heist to grab some cash (the "dead presidents"). Supported by hard-edged and effective acting, the Hugheses continue to develop their control of cinematic imagery, displaying genius for staging violent, confrontational scenes. But the script, based on a story by the brothers, fails to live up to the vision, with characterization and dialogue lagging. Pounding period soundtrack with contributions by Curtis Mayfield, James Brown, and Marvin Gaye keeps things humming. This gritty film is also very colorful, with punchy contrasts. The DVD delivers it all with

stunning clarity. The film is also at times very dark and there is never any deterioration in the image quality or a loss of color details. The 5.1 sound is gutsy and dynamic, with good Surround during the action sequences. —*JO*
Movie: ♪♪♪ *DVD:* ♪♪♪
Buena Vista Home Entertainment (Cat #14258, UPC #717951000392). Widescreen (2.35:1) letterboxed. Dolby Digital 5.1; Dolby Surround. $29.99. Keepcase. *LANG:* English; French. *SUB:* Spanish. *FEATURES:* 20 chapter links.
1995 (R) 120m/C Larenz Tate, Keith David, Chris Tucker, Freddy Rodriguez, N'Bushe Wright, Bokeem Woodbine, Rose Jackson, Clifton Powell; *D:* Albert Hughes, Allen Hughes; *W:* Michael Henry Brown; *C:* Lisa Rinzler; *M:* Danny Elfman.

Dead Ringers

A stunning, unsettling chiller, based loosely on a real case and the best-seller by Bari Wood and Jack Geasland. Irons, in an excellent dual role, is effectively disturbing as the twin gynecologists who descend into madness when they can no longer handle the fame, fortune, drugs, and women in their lives. The acutely upsetting film is made all the more so by its graphic images and basis in fact. The reds in this film are just that—really red, and a true test of the colors on this DVD. For the most part the handling is very good and there is not much bleed. The picture is very sharp and a big improvement over the earlier DVD release. Contrast is exceptional and the brightness remains consistent throughout. The blacks are true enough to blend in with the letterboxing. If there is a disappointment, it is the stereo sound, which has occasional clipping and distortion and not much in the way of imaging or separation. The DVD does contain the excellent supplementals that were on the Criterion laser release. —*JO*
Movie: ♪♪♪ *DVD:* ♪♪♪
Criterion Collection (Cat #CC1541D, UPC #715515009249). Widescreen (1.66:1) letterboxed. Dolby Digital Stereo. $39.95. Keepcase. *LANG:* English. *FEATURES:* 42 chapter links ● Commentary: Cronenberg, Irons, Sanders, Spier, and Suschitzky ● Electronic press kit ● Photo gallery of design drawings ● Effects footage.
1988 (R) 117m/C *CA* Jeremy Irons, Genevieve Bujold, Heidi von Palleske, Barbara Gordon, Shirley Douglas, Stephen Lack, Nick Nichols; *D:* David Cronenberg; *W:* David Cronenberg, Norman Snider; *C:* Peter Suschitzky; *M:* Howard Shore. *AWARDS:* Genie Awards '89: Best Actor (Irons), Best Director (Cronenberg), Best Film; Los Angeles Film Critics Association Awards '88: Best Director (Cronenberg), Best Supporting Actress (Bujold); New York Film Critics Awards '88: Best Actor (Irons).

Deadfall

Father/son grifters plan an elaborate scam that goes wrong when son Joe

(Biehn) inadvertently kills dear old dad (Coburn). When Joe goes through his father's effects, he learns of an unknown twin uncle who's also a racketeer. Along with Uncle Lou's mistrustful henchman Eddie (Cage), they plan another con. Swindles and vendettas abound. The DVD image is generally dark with a slightly soft focus and some scratches. Brighter colors are slightly off. The film was made before Cage became so famous. Coburn and Fonda were between peaks of popularity. —*MM*
Movie: ♪♪ *DVD:* ♪♪
Trimark Home Video (Cat #VM#7303D, UPC #03139873032). Full frame. Stereo. $34.99. Keepcase. *LANG:* English. *FEATURES:* Theatrical trailer ● "Making of" featurette ● 8 chapter links. Title is available for sale only as part of the "Mob Hits" four-pack.
1993 (R) 99m/C Michael Biehn, Sarah Trigger, Nicolas Cage, James Coburn, Charlie Sheen, Peter Fonda; *D:* Christopher Coppola; *W:* Christopher Coppola, David Peoples; *C:* Maryse Alberti; *M:* Jim Fox.

Deadful Melody

Historical martial arts fantasy revolves around a magic lyre and the young woman, Snow (Bridget Lin), who uses it and her fighting skills to avenge her family who were murdered by the evil Six Cliques, etc., etc. The plot is nothing special. The sound and image are marginally better with soft pastel colors. No chapter links. —*MM*
Movie: ♪♪ *DVD:* ♪♪
Tai Seng Video Marketing (Cat #33254, UPC #601643332543). Widescreen letterboxed. Dolby Digital Stereo. $24.95. Jewel case. *LANG:* Cantonese; Mandarin. *SUB:* English.
1992 91m/C Brigitte Lin, Yuen Biao, Kam-Kong Tsui; *D:* Min Kun Ng.

Dean Koontz's Mr. Murder

Mini-series based on a particularly imaginative Koontz novel makes an excellent transition to DVD. The disc can boast truly striking clarity that many studio features would envy. Credit a careful image transfer, fine lighting, and photography (from Greg Gardiner). The wacky sf plot has to do with one of those evil government scientists (Coburn), whose experiment goes awry when blood samples are mixed up. He winds up creating a murderous doppelganger for writer Marty Stillwater (Baldwin). Though this is a two-sided disc and must be flipped over midway, that is not a serious problem with such a long work. — *MM* **AKA:** Mr. Murder.
Movie: ♪♪ *DVD:* ♪♪♪
Trimark Home Video (Cat #VM#7171D, UPC #031398717133). Full frame. $24.99. Keepcase. *LANG:* English. *SUB:* English; French; Spanish. *CAP:* English. *FEATURES:* 30 chapter links ● Animated menus.

1998 (R) 178m/C Stephen Baldwin, Thomas Haden Church, Julie Warner, Bill Smitrovich, James Coburn, Don Hood, Dan Lauria; **D:** Dick Lowry; **W:** Stephen Tolkin; **C:** Greg Gardiner; **M:** Louis Febre.

Dear Santa

Seasonal supernatural comedy.
DVD: NYR
Image Entertainment (Cat #8789). Full frame. Dolby Digital Stereo. $24.99. Snapper. *FEATURES:* Trailer.
1998 (G) 87m/C D.L. Green, Debra Rich, Harrison Myers.

Death Becomes Her

Aging actress Streep will do anything to stay young and beautiful, especially when childhood rival Hawn shows up, 200 pounds lighter and out to avenge the loss of her fiance, Streep's henpecked hubby. Doing anything arrives in the form of a potion that stops the aging process (and keeps her alive forever). Watch for the hilarious party filled with dead celebrities who all look as good as the day they died. Great special effects and fun performances by Streep and Hawn playing their glamour-girl roles to the hilt add merit to this biting commentary on Hollywood's obsession with beauty and youth. The DVD has considerable grain and is not very sharp. There are also artifacts when fast motion occurs in a darker scene. The picture is lacking in punch due to fairly blah color rendition and not enough contrast. Brightness levels are consistent and seem comfortable, but don't help the overall picture that much. The blacks come close to being true, but have additional grain. Well, at least the Dolby Surround sound is pretty good and the back channel kicks in during numerous key effect sequences. The best bet is to stick with the laserdisc if you can. —*JO*
Movie: 🎬🎬🎬 **DVD:** 🎬🎬
Universal Studios Home Video (Cat #20143, UPC #025192014321). Full frame. Dolby Surround. $29.99. Keepcase. *LANG:* English; Spanish; French. *SUB:* Spanish. *CAP:* English. *FEATURES:* 16 chapter links.
1992 (PG-13) 105m/C Meryl Streep, Bruce Willis, Goldie Hawn, Isabella Rossellini, Sydney Pollack, Michael Caine, Ian Ogilvy, Adam Storke, Nancy Fish, Alaina Reed Hall, Michelle Johnson, Mimi Kennedy, Jonathan Silverman; **Cameos:** Fabio Lanzoni; **D:** Robert Zemeckis; **W:** Martin Donovan, David Koepp; **C:** Dean Cundey; **M:** Alan Silvestri. *AWARDS:* Academy Awards '92: Best Visual Effects.

Death Race 2000

In the 21st century, five racing car contenders challenge the national champion (a leather-suited Carradine) of a cross-country race in which drivers score points by killing pedestrians. Sick and gory, filled with demented humor. Based on the 1956 story by Ib Melchior, and followed by *Deathsport.* This New Horizons DVD is far superior to the other DVD release issued by Digital Multimedia—unfortunately, that's not saying much. The picture is a little above average in sharpness, and does have varying degrees of grain throughout the film, appearing in darker scenes and longshots of the death-dealing autos on the road. There are some artifacts during the fast motion of action sequences. Colors are nothing special and have some bleed in the reds and earthtones. Contrast and brightness levels remain consistent, but a little low, and the blacks are most often a little grainy and grayish. There is also nothing special about the sound (it was never spectacular on any of the earlier VHS releases), but at least the dialogue can be understood. —*JO*
Movie: 🎬🎬 **DVD:** 🎬🎬
New Horizons Home Video (Cat #NH001, UPC #736991414440). Full frame. Mono. $24.98. Keepcase. *LANG:* English. *FEATURES:* 24 chapter links • Theatrical trailer • Cast bios • Leonard Maltin interview with Roger Ebert.
1975 (R) 80m/C David Carradine, Simone Griffeth, Sylvester Stallone, Mary Woronov, Roberta Collins, Martin Kove, Louisa Moritz, John Landis, Don Steele; **D:** Paul Bartel; **W:** Charles B. Griffith, Robert Thom; **C:** Tak Fujimoto; **M:** Paul Chihara.

Death Sentence

When a woman juror (Leachman) on a murder case finds out that the wrong man is on trial, she is stalked by the real killer in this made-for-TV movie. **AKA:** Murder One.
Movie: 🎬 **DVD:** NYR
Essex (Cat #1401). Full frame. Dolby Digital Mono. $10.97. Keepcase.
1974 74m/C Cloris Leachman, Laurence Luckinbill, Nick Nolte, William Schallert; **D:** E.W. Swackhamer; **M:** Laurence Rosenthal.

Death Wish 5: The Face of Death

Paul Kersey (Bronson) returns to vigilantism when his clothing manufacturer fiancee Olivia (Downs) has her business threatened by mobsters, one of whom turns out to be her sadistic ex (Parks). Bronson looks understandably bored with the rehashed material and grisly violence.
Movie: woof **DVD:** NYR
Trimark Home Video (Cat #6919). Full frame. $14.99. Keepcase. *SUB:* French; Spanish. *CAP:* English. *FEATURES:* Trailer.
1994 (R) 95m/C Charles Bronson, Lesley-Anne Down, Michael Parks, Kenneth Welsh; **D:** Allan Goldstein; **W:** Allan Goldstein; **C:** Curtis Petersen; **M:** Terry Plumeri.

Deathtrap

A creatively blocked playwright (Caine), his ailing rich wife (Cannon), and a former student (Reeve) who has written a surefire hit are the principals in Jay Presson Allen's adaptation of Ira Levin's stage play. The second act surprise is one of the all-time greats. On DVD, the image and sound are acceptable and that's all that's needed. The film depends on the performances and the viewers' willingness to accept the rules of the twisty game. —*MM*
Movie: 🎬🎬▶ **DVD:** 🎬🎬▶
Warner Home Video, Inc. (Cat #11256, UPC #085391125624). Full frame. Dolby Digital Mono. $14.98. Snapper. *LANG:* English; French. *SUB:* English; French. *CAP:* English. *FEATURES:* 31 chapter links.
1982 (PG) 118m/C Henry Jones, Michael Caine, Christopher Reeve, Dyan Cannon, Irene Worth; **D:** Sidney Lumet; **W:** Jay Presson Allen; **C:** Andrzej Bartkowiak; **M:** Johnny Mandel.

The Decalogue

Krzysztof Kieslowski's other masterpiece (beyond the *Three Colors* trilogy) is a ten-part examination of the Ten Commandments made for Polish television. The films, each a little less than an hour long, bear many similarities to the trilogy. Each work stands separately, though all are set in the same apartment complex and some characters overlap. Like all of Kieslowski's work, these are slow, without much action or movement, and certainly not aimed at the typical Hollywood audience. Though they contain a few humorous moments, they deal with the most serious subject matter that any work of art can attempt to handle. But I still recommend them without reservation to any viewer who really appreciates good film. Kieslowski was a brilliant filmmaker. He knew when to pay attention to the significant physical detail—often held for a moment in extreme close-up—and when to let his camera linger on characters. He could find sensitive, understated performances in a wide range of actors. These films were made before the trilogy and have never been distributed theatrically in this country. That's home video's gain, and, in this instance, DVD is far superior to VHS tape in the accessibility that it offers to individual films. The unsaturated color has a pale look that's appropriate to the subject. Despite the monaural soundtrack, Zbigniew Preisner's music is superb. —*MM*
Movie: 🎬🎬🎬🎬 **DVD:** 🎬🎬🎬🎬
Facets Multimedia, Inc. (Cat #ID9499FVDVD, UPC #014381949926). Full frame. Dolby Digital Mono. $79.99. Snapper. *LANG:* Polish. *SUB:* English. *FEATURES:* 80 chapter links. 2-disc boxed set.
1988 560m/C PL Krystyna Janda, Aleksander Bardini, Maja Komorowska, Daniel Olbrychski, Janusz Gajos, Maria Pakulnis, Jerzy Stuhr, Zbigniew Zamachowski, Boguslaw Linda, Artur Barcis, Henryk Baranowski; **D:** Krzysztof Kieslowski; **W:** Krzysztof Kieslowski, Krzysztof Piesiewicz; **C:** Wieslaw Zdort, Edward Klosinski, Krzysztof Pakulski, Slawomir Idziak, Witold Adamek, Witold Adamek, Dariusz Kuc, Andrzej Jaroszewicz, Piotr Sobocinski, Jacek Blawut; **M:** Zbigniew Preisner.

The Decameron

Pasolini's first epic pageant in his "Trilogy of Life" series is an acclaimed, sexually explicit adaptation of a handful of the Boccaccio tales. The image is rough, transferred from subpar film elements. The excessive grain in the film print used for the transfer obviously contributed to the digital artifacts apparent in some shots, and the whole film is peppered with little scratches, specks of dirt, and other blemishes that are not digital artifacts. Don't expect great sound either. The English subtitles are not optional and were optically burned into the film print used in the transfer. The white letters are sometimes difficult to read because of trash and other marks on the print. Unfortunately, this is the only way to view this classic film on DVD. —*MB* **AKA:** Il Decameron.
Movie: ♫♫♫▶ *DVD:* ♫

Image Entertainment (Cat #ID4419WB DVD, UPC #014381441925). Widescreen (1.85:1) letterboxed. Dolby Digital 1.0. $24.99. Snapper. *LANG:* Italian. *SUB:* English. *FEATURES:* 16 chapter links.
1970 (R) 111m/C FR IT GE Franco Citti, Ninetto Davoli, Angela Luce, Patrizia Capparelli, Jovan Jovanovich, Silvana Mangano, Pier Paolo Pasolini; *D:* Pier Paolo Pasolini; *W:* Pier Paolo Pasolini; *C:* Tonino Delli Colli; *M:* Ennio Morricone. *AWARDS:* Berlin International Film Festival '71: Silver Prize.

Deconstructing Harry

A writer's relationships with people in his life and characters in his books is given a post-modern stop-and-go treatment with the help of often irritating jump cuts and repetitions. Secondary or duplicate characters (Tucci and Benjamin and maybe Williams play alternate Harrys) do little more than dramatize what is essentially a monologue. This all implies a step backwards from Allen's earlier, more ambitious dramas. The dialogue is unnervingly foul-mouthed yet the storyline is only hesitantly pornographic. The fantasy sequence of Harry in hell presents what must be a first, as well as a new low, in Woody's movies—virtually naked women casually used as set dressing. Wistful throwbacks like stunt casting, odd moments of slapstick, and muted jazz only accentuate the film's basically unambitious aim. The disc sports well-recorded location sound and the full-frame visuals are actually preferable to the widescreen for the sake of detail. The menus are nicely laid out but the cast info is abbreviated. —*JK*
Movie: ♫♫▶ *DVD:* ♫♫♫▶

New Line Home Video (Cat #N4653, UPC #794043465321). Widescreen (1.85:1); full frame. Dolby Digital Stereo. $24.99. Snapper. *LANG:* English; French. *SUB:* English; French. *CAP:* English. *FEATURES:* 18 chapter links • Interactive menus • Star bios and filmographies • Coming attractions trailers.
1997 (R) 96m/C Woody Allen, Billy Crystal, Judy Davis, Elisabeth Shue, Kirstie Alley, Caroline Aaron, Bob Balaban,

Richard Benjamin, Eric Bogosian, Mariel Hemingway, Amy Irving, Julie Kavner, Eric Lloyd, Julia Louis-Dreyfus, Tobey Maguire, Demi Moore, Stanley Tucci, Robin Williams, Philip Bosco, Gene Saks, Hazelle Goodman; *D:* Woody Allen; *W:* Woody Allen; *C:* Carlo Di Palma. *AWARDS: NOM:* Academy Awards '97: Best Original Screenplay.

Dee Snider's Strangeland

Writer-producer-actor Snider stars as a pierced psycho who preys on young girls via the Internet. On the commentary track, Snider begins by trashing other horror films and then reveals his near total ignorance of the filmmaking process. At the same time, he revels in self-congratulation and shows a sadistic streak. As for the film itself, it's not so much frightening as unpleasant. The DVD looks fine but the most graphic violence and mutilation is carefully darkened. —*MM* **AKA:** Strangeland.
Movie: woof *DVD:* ♫♫

Artisan Entertainment (Cat #60498, UPC #012236049807). Widescreen (1.85:1) letterboxed. Dolby Digital Surround Stereo. $29.98. Keepcase. *LANG:* English. *CAP:* English. *FEATURES:* Soundtrack promo • Cast and crew thumbnail biographies • 36 chapter links • Theatrical trailer • Music video.
1998 (R) 90m/C Dee Snider, Kevin Gage, Brett Harrelson, Elizabeth Pena, Robert Englund, Amy Smart, Linda Cardellini; *D:* John Pieplow; *W:* Dee Snider; *C:* Goran Pavicevic; *M:* Anton Sanko.

The Deep

An innocent couple get involved in an underwater search for a shipwreck, and they quickly find themselves in over their heads. Gorgeous photography manages to keep this slow mover afloat. Famous for Bisset's wet T-shirt scene. The underwater sequences in this film are handled very nicely visually, but the soundtrack unfortunately doesn't add much in the way of ambience (in this case a 5.1 remix would really enhance the DVD). The picture is always very sharp and grain-free. Colors are vibrant and accurate without any noticeable bleed. The blacks are also true. The contrast level is excellent and for the most part so is the brightness—there were a couple of scenes that could have used a boost, though. In addition to that aforementioned lack of ambient Surround, the sound is lackluster overall. —*JO*
Movie: ♫♫ *DVD:* ♫♫♫

Columbia TriStar Home Video (Cat #10689, UPC #043396016897). Widescreen (2.35:1) letterboxed; full frame. Dolby Surround. $28.95. Keepcase. *LANG:* English; French. *SUB:* Spanish; French; Portuguese; Chinese; Korean; Thai. *CAP:* English. *FEATURES:* 28 chapter links.
1977 (PG) 123m/C Nick Nolte, Jacqueline Bisset, Robert Shaw, Louis Gossett

Jr., Eli Wallach; *D:* Peter Yates; *W:* Peter Benchley, Tracy Keenan Wynn; *C:* Christopher Challis; *M:* John Barry. *AWARDS: NOM:* Academy Awards '77: Best Sound.

Deep Blue Sea

Researchers led by science-babe Burrows are working on a cure for Alzheimer's Disease using material from shark brains. They're proving their work to their main backer, Franklin (Jackson), when everything goes wrong at their mid-ocean research station. The storm hits and they're trapped in the sinking facility. Outside are three giant genetically enhanced intelligent sharks who are, frankly, upset about the way they've been treated. The clarity of the DVD image makes the computer-generated effects even less realistic than they are on VHS tape, but that's not a serious flaw, considering the featherweight material. This is a well-made, absurdly entertaining shark-monster flick. Enjoy it as such or leave it on the shelf. —*MM*
Movie: ♫♫♫ *DVD:* ♫♫♫

Warner Home Video, Inc. (Cat #17242). Widescreen letterboxed. Dolby Digital 5.1 Surround Stereo. $24.98. Snapper. *LANG:* English. *SUB:* English. *FEATURES:* 34 chapter links • Commentary: Harlin and Jackson • Deleted scenes • "When Sharks Attack" • "Sharks of Deep Blue Sea" • Trailer • Stills gallery.
1999 (R) 105m/C Saffron Burrows, Samuel L. Jackson, Thomas Jane, L.L. Cool J., Jacqueline McKenzie, Michael Rapaport, Stellan Skarsgard, Aida Turturro; *D:* Renny Harlin; *W:* Duncan Kennedy, Donna Powers, Wayne Powers; *C:* Stephen Windon; *M:* Trevor Rabin.

Deep Cover

Russell Stevens Jr. (Fishburne) is a straight-arrow cop who infiltrates a Los Angeles cocaine cartel. While undercover, he becomes partner with drug-dealing lawyer David Jason (Goldblum) and undergoes an inner transformation until he realizes that he is betraying his own cause. The film is confusing and commercial, yet marked by a strong sense of morality. The DVD image is generally good, except for glowing reds, and director Duke uses the color regularly to highlight moments and emotions. Sound is fine. —*MM*
Movie: ♫♫▶ *DVD:* ♫♫▶

New Line Home Video (Cat #N4780, UPC #794043478024). Widescreen (1.85:1) anamorphic; full frame. Dolby Digital 5.1 Surround Stereo; Dolby Digital Surround Stereo. $24.98. Snapper. *LANG:* English. *SUB:* English. *FEATURES:* Cast and crew thumbnail biographies • 17 chapter links • Theatrical trailer.
1992 (R) 107m/C Laurence "Larry" Fishburne, Jeff Goldblum, Victoria Dillard, Charles Martin Smith, Sydney Lassick, Clarence Williams III, Gregory Sierra, Roger Guenveur Smith, Cory Curtis, Glynn Turman, Def Jef; *D:* Bill Duke; *W:* Michael

Tolkin, Henry Bean; **C:** Bojan Bazelli; **M:** Michel Colombier.

The Deep End of the Ocean

Beth (Pfeiffer) and husband Pat (Williams) live a stereotypically suburban life until their three-year-old son Ben is kidnapped in a hotel. The manipulative film follows the tortuous road of depression that Beth travels until, suddenly, nine years later, a boy shows up who might be her son. The conclusion is equally facile. The whole film looks and sounds like it was made for television with middle-of-the-road production values. Both colors and sounds have a dullness that is accentuated on DVD. —*MM*

Movie: ♪♪ **DVD:** ♪♪
Columbia Tristar Home Video (Cat #02851, UPC #043396028517). Widescreen (1.85:1) letterboxed; full frame. Dolby Digital 5.1 Surround Stereo; Dolby Digital Surround Stereo. $25.95. Keepcase. *LANG:* English. *SUB:* English. *FEATURES:* "Making of" featurette • 28 chapter links • Theatrical trailer.
1998 (PG-13) 105m/C Michelle Pfeiffer, Treat Williams, John Kapelos, Jonathan Jackson, Ryan Merriman, Whoopi Goldberg, Michael McGrady, Brenda Strong; **D:** Ulu Grosbard; **W:** Stephen Schiff; **C:** Stephen Goldblatt; **M:** Elmer Bernstein.

Deep Impact

Poor Morgan Freeman. He gets a chance to play the President of the United States only to have his term shortened by a dastardly comet the size of the Grand Canyon. Although his presidency would have been more interesting, the destruction's the star of this show, as well as the touchy-feely interaction of various two-dimensional characters. There are the astronauts (led by Duvall) sent into space to nuke the thing; ordinary teenager Leo (Wood), who initially discovered the rock; and career-conscious news anchor (Leoni), who first breaks the story. The all-star cast is underused, but lends the film a sense of gravity. The remaining stick figure characters evoke more yawns than tears. Good thing the comet comes along to—ironically—inject a little life into the flick. The special effects are the best in recent film history. The DVD features a very sharp image, rich in colors and virtually free of artifacts and grain. The colors are vibrant, accurate, and seldom bleed. Blacks are handled well and are true. The DVD's contrast and brightness levels are excellent and light and dark images are treated equally well, with the great colors getting most of the benefit. When it comes to the sound, the 5.1 track is incredible. Nicely used all the way through, it is very dynamic, with full fidelity and excellent imaging and separation. The ambience keeps the audience in the center of things. When the effects take over at the climax, the Surround tracks kick in and for the next 20 minutes, things are whizzing around and

by you, as the subwoofer shakes the house. —*JO*
Movie: ♪♪♪ **DVD:** ♪♪♪▶
Paramount Home Video (Cat #330827, UPC #097363308270). Widescreen (2.35:1) letterboxed. Dolby Digital 5.1; Dolby Surround. $29.99. Keepcase. *LANG:* English (DD5.1; DS); French (DS). *CAP:* English. *FEATURES:* 30 chapter links • 2 theatrical trailers.
1998 (PG-13) 120m/C Morgan Freeman, Robert Duvall, Tea Leoni, Elijah Wood, Vanessa Redgrave, Maximilian Schell, James Cromwell, Blair Underwood, Ron Eldard, Jon Favreau, Leelee Sobieski, Mary McCormack, Dougray Scott, Alexander Baluyev, Charles Martin Smith; **D:** Mimi Leder; **W:** Michael Tolkin, Bruce Joel Rubin; **C:** Dietrich Lohmann; **M:** James Horner.

Deep Red: Hatchet Murders

Argento's excesses tend to turn comic in translation and this slasher flick is no exception. At first. For American audiences, the presence of David Hemmings, as a pianist who witnesses the first murder, helps considerably. Yes, he did something similar in *Blow Up*, though that's where any useful comparison begins and ends. The interplay between him and Gianna (Nicolodi, Argento's wife), a reporter, adds the right intentional humor to the violent proceedings. Many of the visual and narrative devices are repeated in Argento's other work. His flowing style and relatively understandable plot make this one of his better efforts. The DVD looks very good and, with restored footage, is considerably longer than older tapes. Reds hold true throughout, and Argento's palette is filled with reds. For those who appreciate the synthesized score, the stereo sound is very good, too. —*MM* **AKA:** The Hatchet Murders; Profundo Rosso; Dripping Deep Red; The Sabre Tooth Tiger; Deep Red.
Movie: ♪♪▶ **DVD:** ♪♪♪
Anchor Bay (Cat #DV11069, UPC #013131106992). Widescreen (2.35:1) anamorphic. Dolby Digital 5.1 Surround Stereo. $29.98. Keepcase. *LANG:* English; Italian. *SUB:* English. *FEATURES:* 32 chapter links • Theatrical trailers • Cast and crew thumbnail biographies • 25th anniversary featurette.
1975 126m/C *IT* David Hemmings, Daria Nicolodi, Gabriele Lavia, Macha Meril, Eros Pagni, Guiliana Calandra, Erykah Badu, Clara Calamai, Nicoletta Elmi, Glauco Mauri; **D:** Dario Argento; **W:** Dario Argento, Barnardino Zapponi; **C:** Luigi Kuveiller; **M:** Girogio Gaslini, The Goblins.

Deep Rising

Giant worm-like creatures rise from the depths of the ocean to cause massive destruction to the cruise ship *Argonautica* and put major dinks in the plans of mercenaries who board the ship for greedy motives. Flick sticks to a reliable action-

horror formula with the good sense not to take its characters or slimy monsters too seriously. Sea critters have inventive ways of disposing of extraneous cast members, resulting in gore aplenty. Goofy chemistry between reluctant hero Williams and his slacker sidekick O'Connor injects the film with welcome B-movie campiness. This DVD gets a very good overall. The picture is sharp with very little grain, despite all the dimly lit sequences that you would expect in a horror film. Blacks are excellent, colors are true, and there is no perceivable bleed (not even in Janssen's bright red dress). Brightness and contrast are also very good. The 5.1 soundtrack is excellent with good separation and imaging, allowing the dialogue, sound effects, and Jerry Goldsmith's orchestral score to all be heard very clearly. One wonders why they bothered to give "bonus materials" its own spot on the main menu since all you get is one theatrical trailer and the cover art for three movie recommendations. —*JO*
Movie: ♪♪▶ **DVD:** ♪♪♪▶
Hollywood Pictures Home Video (Cat #14911, UPC #717951000651). Widescreen (2.35:1) letterboxed. Dolby Digital 5.1; Dolby Surround. $29.99. Keepcase. *LANG:* English (DD5.1; DS); French. *CAP:* English. *FEATURES:* 16 chapter links • Theatrical trailer.
1998 (R) 106m/C Treat Williams, Famke Janssen, Anthony Heald, Kevin J. O'Connor, Wes Studi, Derrick O'Connor, Jason Flemyng, Djimon Hounsou; **D:** Stephen Sommers; **W:** Stephen Sommers; **C:** Howard Atherton; **M:** Jerry Goldsmith.

The Deer Hunter

Powerful and vivid portrait of Middle America follows three steel-working friends who leave home to face the Vietnam War. Controversial, brutal sequences in Vietnam are among the most wrenching ever filmed; the rhythms and rituals of home are just as purely captured. The film is neither pro- nor anti-war, but rather the perfect evocation of how totally and forever altered these people are by the war. Emotionally shattering; not to be missed. Unfortunately, this is not a great DVD. The image is not sharp and there is considerable grain in a lot of long detailed shots. Although the film itself was not full of bright hues, the color on the DVD is much more drab than it should be. Even with the low color level, there is occasional bleed. The picture is also on the dull side, in grave need of a boost to the contrast. Brightness levels are O.K. Sometimes a so-so transfer can be saved by good sound. Not the case here, as the sound clips and distorts on a regular basis, and makes poor use of the Surround track. —*JO*
Movie: ♪♪♪♪ **DVD:** ♪♪
Universal Studios Home Video (Cat #20177, UPC #025192017728). Widescreen (2.35:1) letterboxed. Dolby Surround. $26.98. Keepcase. *LANG:* English. *SUB:* Spanish; French. *CAP:* English. *FEA-*

TURES: 16 chapter links • Theatrical trailer • Production notes • Cast and crew bios • Film highlights.
1978 (R) 183m/C Robert De Niro, Christopher Walken, Meryl Streep, John Savage, George Dzundza, John Cazale, Chuck Aspegren, Rutanya Alda, Shirley Stoler, Amy Wright, Mady Kaplan, Mary Ann Haenel, Richard Kuss, Pierre Segui, Joe Grifasi, Christopher Colombi Jr., Joe Strnad, Paul D'Amato; **D:** Michael Cimino; **W:** Michael Cimino, Deric Washburn, Louis Garfinkle; **C:** Vilmos Zsigmond; **M:** John Williams, Stanley Myers. **AWARDS:** Academy Awards '78: Best Director (Cimino), Best Film Editing, Best Picture, Best Sound, Best Supporting Actor (Walken); American Film Institute (AFI) '98: Top 100; Directors Guild of America Awards '78: Best Director (Cimino); Golden Globe Awards '79: Best Director (Cimino); Los Angeles Film Critics Association Awards '78: Best Director (Cimino), National Film Registry '96; New York Film Critics Awards '78: Best Film, Best Supporting Actor (Walken); National Society of Film Critics Awards '78: Best Supporting Actress (Streep); **NOM:** Academy Awards '78: Best Actor (De Niro), Best Cinematography, Best Original Screenplay, Best Supporting Actress (Streep).

Def by Temptation

From the beginnings of the horror film, the vampire story has been based on sexual attitudes, preconceptions, and stereotypes. And in the sexual stereotype department, few groups in America carry more baggage than black men. They're the subject of writer-director-producer-star James Bond III's impressive debut. The monster here is the Temptress (Cynthia Bond, no relation to JBIII), who "wants to remain in the fallen lustful state of existence...incarnate in the flesh." Her real prey is a young divinity student undergoing a crisis of faith. Bond makes several critical observations about male sexual irresponsibility. The best part of the story is its strong traditional moral sense, so conspicuously lacking in recent horror films. Also, fans will notice that the 1990 film eerily pre-dates *The X-Files* in its approach to the subject and in Bill Nunn's character. Visually, the film doesn't gain that much on DVD, though the transfer is excellent. Bond uses colored light and character development in place of splashy (and expensive) special effects, and so one suspects that cinematographer Ernest Dickerson (with help from Troma boss Lloyd Kaufman) was covering up as much as he was revealing with the camera. The disc comes with all the usual Troma extras, including perceptive expert commentary by *Fangoria* magazine editor Michael Gingold and yours truly. —MM
Movie: 🎞🎞🎞 **DVD:** 🎞🎞🎞
Troma Team Video (Cat #9800, UPC #790357980031). Full frame. $24.95. Keepcase. *LANG:* English. *FEATURES:* 9 chapter links • Introduction by Lloyd Kaufman • Commentary: Michael Gingold,

Mike Mayo • Production stills • Theatrical trailer • Troma Intelligence Test • Troma previews. DVD-ROM accesses Troma website.
1990 (R) 95m/C James Bond III, Kadeem Hardison, Bill Nunn, Samuel L. Jackson, Minnie Gentry, Rony Clanton, Cynthia Bond, John Canada Terrell; **D:** James Bond III; **W:** James Bond III; **C:** Ernest R. Dickerson; **M:** Paul Lawrence.

Def Jam's How to Be a Player

Dray (Bellamy) thinks that monogamy is a wood used to build furniture. Although he has a steady girlfriend, Lisa (Voorhies), he also has several ladies in waiting. In short, he is a player's player. (If only he had a screenplay.) His sister Jenny (Desselle), who has been hurt in love, cracks his numerical code and invites all of his harem to one party. The stand-up comedy roots of much of the cast translate into clunky performances and shapeless direction. The DVD actually looks very good with a careful transfer that captures busy, colorful sets and costumes with no serious problems. Sound is adequate. —MM
AKA: How to Be a Player.
Movie: 🎞🎞 **DVD:** 🎞🎞
USA Home Entertainment (Cat #440 055 955-2, UPC #044005595529). Widescreen (1.85:1) letterboxed; full frame. Dolby Digital 5.1 Surround Stereo. $19.95. Keepcase. *LANG:* English. *SUB:* French. *CAP:* English. *FEATURES:* 17 chapter links • Theatrical trailer • Cast and crew thumbnail biographies.
1997 (R) 93m/C Bill Bellamy, Natalie Desselle, Mari Morrow, Jermaine Hopkins, A.J. Johnson, Max Julien, Beverly Johnson, Gilbert Gottfried, Bernie Mac, Elise Neal, Amber Smith, Lark Voorhies; **D:** Lionel C. Martin; **W:** Mark Brown, Demetria Johnson; **M:** Darren Floyd.

Deliverance

John Boorman's adaptation of James Dickey's best-seller is a journey into a mythic wilderness where monsters dwell. Four suburbanites (Reynolds, Voight, Beatty, and Cox) head out for a weekend canoe trip on a river about to be dammed by the power company. They're attacked by predatory subhuman redneck sodomites in one of the most frightening and humiliating rape scenes ever put on film. The vicious act has been foreshadowed by images of inbred hillbillies and explosive large-scale destruction. A growing atmosphere of dread transforms the simple adventure into a real horror. The particulars of violent death have seldom been depicted more realistically, and the DVD is a solid step up from VHS, particularly those older tapes that have been rented hundreds if not thousands of times. Some pixels may be visible in the whitewater sequences, but those scenes have always been busy. The sound is enhanced by the stereo effects and so, for the first time—after several viewings

in theatres and on home video—I was able to make out the barely audible gunshot in one important scene. A commentary track is called for. —MM
Movie: 🎞🎞🎞🎞 **DVD:** 🎞🎞🎞
Warner Home Video, Inc. (Cat #15445, UPC #085391544524). Widescreen anamorphic; full frame. Dolby Digital 5.1 Surround Stereo; Mono. $19.98. Snapper. *LANG:* English; French. *SUB:* English; French. *FEATURES:* 31 chapter links • Behind-the-scenes featurette • "Making of" featurette • Theatrical trailer • Cast and crew thumbnail biographies.
1972 (R) 109m/C Jon Voight, Burt Reynolds, Ronny Cox, Ned Beatty, James Dickey, Bill McKinney, Ed O'Neill, Charley Boorman; **D:** John Boorman; **W:** James Dickey; **C:** Vilmos Zsigmond; **M:** Eric Weissburg. **AWARDS:** *NOM:* Academy Awards '72: Best Director (Boorman), Best Film Editing, Best Picture.

Dementia 13

Comparing Francis Ford Coppola's Gothic debut to the other low-budget Corman productions of the early 1960s, it's easy to see hints of the genius that would follow. Coppola tells a fairly simple story of ghosts and greed with pretty blonde Louise (Anders) trying to pry loose some of the Haloran family fortune from the possibly demented matriarch (Dunn). At least, that's the way things begin. It's obvious that Coppola is using Hitchcock's *Psycho* as his model. A key watery moment may be the first homage to the shower scene. More significantly, though, he shows a solid understanding of his medium—how to combine character, dialogue, sound, and image to tell a good story. And to scare an audience. Even if he'd never made another film, this one would have a following today. **AKA:** The Haunted and the Hunted.
Movie: 🎞🎞🎞 **DVD:** NYR
Madacy Entertainment (Cat #990602). Full frame. Dolby Digital Mono. $9.99. Keepcase. *FEATURES:* Cast and crew thumbnail biographies.
1963 75m/B William Campbell, Luana Anders, Bart Patton, Patrick Magee, Barbara Dowling, Ethne Dunn, Mary Mitchell, Karl Schanzer; **D:** Francis Ford Coppola; **W:** Francis Ford Coppola; **C:** Charles Hannawalt; **M:** Ronald Stein.

Demolition Man

No-brain sci-fier rests on the action skills of Stallone and Snipes. Psychovillain Snipes (sporting a Dennis Rodman 'do) is pursued by equally violent cop Stallone in the late 1990s. Then they're cryogenically frozen, defrosted in 2032, and back to their old tricks. One problem...this is not a fun future: virtual reality sex is the only kind allowed and puritan ethics and political correctness are enforced to the max. Cop and bad guy get to show this highly orderly society some really violent times. Implausible plot and minimal acting, but lots of action and violence for fans. The image on the DVD is pretty sharp and packs a lot of punch with vibrant and deep colors and just the right amount of contrast, to which the brightness levels are perfectly matched. Though a lot of the film takes place in the dark, there are few problems with grain or artifacts (even during fast action sequences). Colors don't bleed and the blacks are very true with only a couple of spots where they grain up a touch. The 5.1 mix is terrific with lots of Surround and good energy to both the music and the effects. Dynamics are excellent and the bass is properly pumped up. Dialogue is up front and Stallone's mouthful-o-slurs are never buried beneath the goings-on. —*JO*

Movie: 🎬🎬 **DVD:** 🎬🎬🎬▶
Warner Home Video, Inc. (Cat #12985, UPC #085391298526). Widescreen (2.35:1) anamorphic. Dolby Digital 5.1; Mono. $24.98. Snapper. *LANG:* English; Spanish. *SUB:* English; Spanish; French. *CAP:* English. *FEATURES:* 30 chapter links ● Theatrical trailer ● Production notes.
1993 (R) 115m/C Sylvester Stallone, Wesley Snipes, Sandra Bullock, Nigel Hawthorne, Benjamin Bratt, Bob Gunton, Glenn Shadix, Denis Leary; **D:** Marco Brambilla; **W:** Daniel Waters, Robert Reneau, Peter M. Lenkov; **C:** Alex Thomson; **M:** Elliot Goldenthal. *AWARDS: NOM:* MTV Movie Awards '94: Best Villain (Snipes).

The Demolitionist

Tough undercover cop Alyssa Lloyd (Eggert) is killed by crimelord Mad Dog Burne (Grieco) and then resurrected by scientist Jack Crowley (Abbott) as a hard-hitting futuristic superheroine who's out to save Metro City from evil. Good comic-book style action makes for great fun. The DVD's high point is the accuracy of its deep and vibrant colors. Unfortunately, they bleed a bit and consequently the overall picture sharpness suffers. The blacks also have some problems and vary from dark and true to grainy and slightly gray. The 5.1 sound is very good for a low budgeteer and packs good bass in with some nifty Surround effects. —*JO*

Movie: 🎬🎬 **DVD:** 🎬🎬▶
Simitar Entertainment (Cat #7431, UPC #082551743124). Full frame. Dolby Digital 5.1; Stereo. $14.98. Snapper. *LANG:* English. *FEATURES:* 8 chapter links ● "Making of" featurette.
1995 (R) 100m/C Nicole Eggert, Richard Grieco, Bruce Abbott, Susan Tyrrell, Peter Jason, Sarah Douglas, Andras Jones, Heather Langenkamp, David Anthony Marshall, Jack Nance, Tom Savini; **D:** Robert Kurtzman; **W:** Brian DiMuccio, Dino Vindeni; **C:** Marcus Hahn; **M:** Shawn Patterson.

Demon City Shinjuku

Japanese anime begins with two men battling against dark forces. One is killed, allowing his rival to turn Shinjuku into a city of monsters inhabited only by those

lawless enough to live among the remains of the dead, plus the occasional demon. When an official is kidnapped, his daughter Sayaka and martial arts student Kyoya go into the dark part of the city to save him and the world, as is so often the case in these movies.

Movie: 🎬🎬 **DVD:** NYR
Central Park Media/U.S. Manga Corps (Cat #1732). Full frame. Dolby Digital 5.1 Surround Stereo. $29.95. Keepcase. *LANG:* Japanese; English. *SUB:* English. *FEATURES:* Character notes ● Trailer.
1993 82m/C *JP* **D:** Yoshiaki Kawajiri; **W:** Kaori Okamura.

The Demoniacs

Vintage Rollin is a hallucinatory mix of misogyny, overacting, and oddly effective set pieces. On the coast of Normandy in the 19th century, "wreckers" lure ships onto the rocks, then they steal the goods that float ashore and kill any survivors. A gang of four rapes and murders two young girls who are resurrected to seek revenge. The story is told with Russ Meyer ferocity, but Rollin lacks Meyer's strong visual sense. The DVD was made from remastered elements and is remarkably sharp and detailed throughout. Sound is acceptable. As the villainous Tina, Joelle Coeur turns in a hyperventilating performance that is impossible to describe or to believe. She's the real star of the disc. —*MM*

Movie: 🎬🎬 **DVD:** 🎬🎬🎬
Image Entertainment (Cat #ID55575ADVD, UPC #014381555721). Widescreen (1.75:1) letterboxed. Dolby Digital Mono. $24.99. Snapper. *LANG:* French. *SUB:* English. *FEATURES:* 14 chapter links ● Director filmography ● Theatrical trailer ● Photo gallery ● Liner notes by Marc Morris.
1974 95m/C Joelle Coeur, Lieva Lone, Patricia Hermenier, John Rico, Willy Braque, Paul Bisciglia, Louise Dhour, Ben Zimet; **D:** Jean Rollin; **W:** Jean Rollin.

Demons

A horror film in a Berlin theatre is so involving that its viewers become the demons they are seeing. The new monsters turn on the other audience members. Virtually plotless, the film is most notable for its graphic gore, which is pretty much non-stop once the carnage begins and the rock soundtrack by Accept, Go West, Motley Crue, and others. Anchor Bay has done another top-notch job on this DVD. The picture surpasses the earlier VHS and laserdisc releases in every way. Sharpness is very good and the lack of grain in this very dark film is amazing. The colors are vibrant and even the deeper hues do not bleed. The blacks are near perfect and artifacts are never a factor. What's more, the picture has been given more contrast and is comfortably bright without sacrificing any of the atmosphere. The metal soundtrack has been really pumped up and although there's not much

in the way of Surround effects, the energy of the entire film is brought to new levels. —*JO AKA:* Demoni.

Movie: 🎬▶ **DVD:** 🎬🎬🎬▶
Anchor Bay (Cat #DV10728, UPC #013131072891). Widescreen (1.66:1) letterboxed. Dolby Digital 5.1. $29.98. Keepcase. *LANG:* English. *FEATURES:* 8 chapter links ● Theatrical trailer ● Commentary: Bava, Sergoi Stivaletti, Loris Curci ● Behind-the-scenes featurette.
1986 (R) 89m/C *IT* Urbano Barberini, Natasha Hovey, Paolo Cozza, Karl Zinny, Fiore Argento, Fabiola Toledo, Nicoletta Elmi, Michele (Michael) Soavi; **D:** Lamberto Bava; **W:** Lamberto Bava, Dario Argento, Franco Ferrini, Dardano Sacchetti; **C:** Gianlorenzo Battaglia; **M:** Claudio Simonetti.

Demons 2

The son of horror-meister Mario Bava, Lamberto, collaborated with Argento (who cowrote and produced) to create an inferior and improbable sequel to the monsters-amuck-in-the-theatre original. This time, they're coming out of televisions and other places in a high-rise—a sort of updated play-within-a-play ploy. True to the spirit of Italian horror, this one stresses blood, humor, and gore and never really tries to engage the viewer on a realistically emotional level. That said, the film looks fine on DVD. The transfer is visually flawless. Unfortunately, some of the extensive, gossipy commentary track by the filmmakers is difficult to hear and understand. Also, this is the full-length unrated 91-minute version, not the "R"-rated 88-minute theatrical release. —*MM*

Movie: 🎬🎬 **DVD:** 🎬🎬🎬
Anchor Bay (Cat #DV10729, UPC #013131072990). Widescreen (1.66:1) letterboxed. Dolby Digital 5.1 Surround Stereo; Dolby Digital Stereo. $29.98. Keepcase. *LANG:* English. *FEATURES:* 17 chapter links ● Theatrical trailer ● Commentary: Bava, Stivaletti, journalist Loris Curci ● Thumbnail biographies for cast and crew.
1987 91m/C *IT* David Knight, Nancy Brill, Coralina Cataldi Tassoni, Bobby Rhodes, Asia Argento, Virginia Bryant; **D:** Lamberto Bava; **W:** Dario Argento, Lamberto Bava; **C:** Gianlorenzo Battaglia; **M:** Simon Boswell.

The Dentist

After seeing this movie, you may never want to sit in that dental chair again. When his marriage falls apart, L.A. dental specialist Dr. Feinstone (Bernsen) takes to pill popping and psychotic behavior, including demonic drilling and particularly bloody oral surgery. The famous "Is it safe" scene in *Marathon Man* pales by comparison as this one feels like something Herschell Gordon Lewis might have done with a budget. This isn't a bad DVD, it's just nothing special (but I may be getting jaded). The picture is sharp enough to avoid giving you a headache and there's not much grain floating around. Artifacts are also minimal. The contrast and brightness levels are consistent and punchy enough to make the picture look a little more than it is. Colors are close to accurate and bleed is rarely a problem. The soundtrack is good enough that you would still squirm during those dental-destruction scenes even if you couldn't see the picture. —JO

Movie: 🎬🎬🎬 **DVD:** 🎬🎬🎬
Trimark Home Video (Cat #6886D, UPC #031398688631). Widescreen (1.85:1) anamorphic. Stereo. $24.99. Keepcase. *LANG:* English. *SUB:* French. *CAP:* English. *FEATURES:* 24 chapter links ▪ Trailer ▪ Cast bios.
1996 (R) 93m/C Corbin Bernsen, Ken Foree, Linda Hoffman, Michael Stadvec; *D:* Brian Yuzna; *W:* Charles Finch, Stuart Gordon, Dennis Paoli; *C:* Levie Isaacks; *M:* Alan Howarth.

The Dentist 2: Brace Yourself

Cable sequel to the first offers more of the gruesome same. Dr. Feinstone has escaped from the asylum to which he was sent in the first film. He's settled in a rural community and set up another practice. This DVD is very good all the way through. Picture sharpness is on a level with most 4.0 reviews and both the grain and artifact levels are low. Colors and blacks are both very accurate. The contrast and brightness levels are consistent and seem to have been boosted from where they were on the first film's DVD broadcast. As with the first film's DVD, the sound is also very good (though lacking Surround), and conveys every tooth-grinding, jaw-breaking, flesh-drilling scene with great intensity. —JO

Movie: 🎬🎬 **DVD:** 🎬🎬🎬
Trimark Home Video (Cat #7010D, UPC #031398701033). Widescreen (1.85:1) anamorphic. Stereo. $24.99. Keepcase. *LANG:* English. *SUB:* Spanish; French. *CAP:* English. *FEATURES:* 24 chapter links ▪ Trailer ▪ Cast and crew bios.
1998 (R) 99m/C Corbin Bernsen, Jillian McWhirter, Linda Hoffman; *D:* Richard Smith; *W:* Richard Smith; *C:* Jurgen Baum; *M:* Alan Howarth.

The Descendant of Wing Chun

The martial arts equivalent of a spaghetti western, this sequel should not be compared to the original *Wing Chun* on any level. The DVD was obviously made from an inferior print. Colors fade in and out within the same frame. Dark scenes are murky. For fans of alternative kung fu only. —MM

Movie: 🎬 **DVD:** 🎬
Tai Seng Video Marketing (Cat #44454, UPC #601643444543). Widescreen letterboxed. $19.95. Keepcase. *LANG:* English.
1978 92m/C Hsu Shao Chiang, Huang Chin Shen; *D:* Wang Ha.

Desecration

Give filmmaker Dante Tomaselli credit for trying to do something different with low-budget horror. He tells the story of a teenager's psychic reactions to a harsh Catholic upbringing with some flair. There's nothing fancy here, but he avoids the cliches and overdependence on graphic special effects that are so prevalent. On this no-frills DVD, the image is no better than you'd expect, though Tomaselli uses red tints to good effect early on. Sound is fine. —MM

Movie: 🎬🎬🎬 **DVD:** 🎬🎬
Image Entertainment (Cat #ID9150LDDVD, UPC #014381915020). Widescreen (1.85:1) letterboxed. Dolby Digital Stereo. $24.99. Snapper. *LANG:* English. *FEATURES:* 10 chapter links.
1999 88m/C Danny Lopes, Irma St. Paule, Christie Sanford, Salvatore Paul Piro, Vincent Lamberti; *D:* Dante Tomaselli; *W:* Dante Tomaselli.

Desert Blue

The only attraction in the little town of Baxter, CA (pop. 87), is a giant ice cream cone. Cable TV star Skye (Hudson) and her flaky dad (Heard) are there to see it when a chemical spill strands them. Blue (Sexton) is a local guy. There is no reason for them to fall for each other. The other small-town oddballs are Ely (Ricci), who's too fond of explosives; Pete (Affleck), who wants to win an All Terrain Vehicle race; Sandy (Gilbert), who sells ice cream cones; and Cale (Suplee), who ought to be sheriff. As a portrait of the conflicting pressures of youth and the pace of backwater life, this festival hit is not as successful as *Dancer, Texas*, but it is enjoyable. The DVD is not spectacular; it's not supposed to be. Baxter (actually Goldfield, NV) is presented as a soot-stained, cold, overcast place and so the digital image is effectively grim. Sound is equally restrained. —MM

Movie: 🎬🎬🎬 **DVD:** 🎬🎬🎬
Columbia Tristar Home Video (Cat #04389, UPC #043396043893). Widescreen (1.85:1) letterboxed. Dolby Digital Surround Stereo. $24.95. Keepcase. *LANG:* English. *SUB:* English; French; Spanish. *CAP:* English. *FEATURES:* 28 chapter links ▪ Music video, "The Frug" ▪ Cast and crew thumbnail biographies ▪ Theatrical trailers.
1998 (R) 87m/C Brendan Sexton III, Kate Hudson, John Heard, Christina Ricci, Casey Affleck, Sara Gilbert, Ethan Suplee, Lucinda Jenney; *D:* Morgan J. Freeman; *W:* Morgan J. Freeman; *C:* Enrique Chediak; *M:* Vytas Nagisetty.

Desert Heat

Disposable Van Damme vehicle casts him as a loner who helps the locals in a desert town stand up to a motorcycle gang. Guns, muscles, and explosions look fine on DVD, though the locations are by far the strongest part of the film. The star

coproduced. —MM *AKA:* Inferno; Coyote Moon.

Movie: 🎬🎬 **DVD:** 🎬🎬🎬
Columbia Tristar Home Video (Cat #04226, UPC #043396042261). Widescreen (1.85:1) letterboxed; full frame. Dolby Digital 5.1 Surround Stereo; Dolby Digital Surround Stereo. $25.95. Keepcase. *LANG:* English. *SUB:* English; French; Spanish. *FEATURES:* 28 chapter links ▪ Jean-Claude Van Damme featurette and thumbnail biography ▪ Theatrical trailer.
1999 (R) 95m/C Jean-Claude Van Damme, Noriyuki "Pat" Morita, Danny Trejo, Gabrielle Fitzpatrick, Larry Drake, Vincent Schiavelli; *D:* Danny Mulroon; *W:* Tom O'Rourke; *C:* Ross A. Maehl; *M:* Bill Conti.

The Designated Mourner

Movies are supposed to move and the three people in this anti-movie don't even stand up. Adapted from Wallace Shawn's play, the film laments the passing of the class of people who "appreciate the poetry of John Donne" and other forms of high art and, presumably, the film itself. The set, meant to represent an unnamed politically repressive country, is several tables with metallic tiled walls as a backdrop. Nichols plays the eponymous mourner Jack, a journalist who once ran with the literary crowd but betrayed their ideals for survival. Richardson plays his wife Judy, daughter of the final talking head Howard (de Keyser), a humanist poet who doesn't like people. If you need a lecture on culture written by a man who was in *My Favorite Martian* and *Mom and Dad Save the World*, then this is your movie. To quote the author, "Inconceivable!" There's little DVD can do to improve this flapdoodle which should have stayed on the stage. —MM

Movie: 🎬 **DVD:** 🎬🎬
Image Entertainment (Cat #0VED6875 DVD, UPC #014381687521). Full frame. Dolby Digital Stereo. $24.99. Snapper. *LANG:* English. *FEATURES:* 12 chapter links ▪ Commentary: Wallace Shawn and Michael Strago.
1997 (R) 94m/C *GB* Mike Nichols, Miranda Richardson, David de Keyser; *D:* David Hare; *W:* Wallace Shawn; *C:* Oliver Stapleton; *M:* Richard Hartley.

Desolation Angels

Nick Adams (Rodrick) returns to New York after a month spent caring for his mother and finds that his girlfriend Mary (Thomas) has been raped by his best friend Sid (Bassett). At least that's how Nick interprets the situation after an unwilling Mary admits that they had sex. Director McCann handles the difficult material with sensitivity and real understanding for the characters. Beyond the extras, which include deleted scenes, the DVD probably doesn't look much better than VHS tape. It's a low-budget production with slightly muted colors and sounds, more depen-

dent on performances and setting than on visuals. —*MM*
Movie: 🎵🎵 **DVD:** 🎵🎵
WinStar Home Entertainment (Cat #FLV5112, UPC #720917511221). Full frame. $29.98. Keepcase. *LANG:* English. *FEATURES:* 6 chapter links • Production credits • Filmographies and awards • Theatrical trailer • Deleted scenes.
1995 90m/C Michael Rodrick, Peter Bassett, Jennifer Thomas; *D:* Tim McCann; *W:* Tim McCann; *C:* Matt Howe.

Desperado

Rodriguez's nameless guitar player-turned-gunman returns—this time in the persona of heartthrob Banderas. The director also has a studio budget to play with (a sizable increase over the $7000 for *El Mariachi*), so the action's on a bigger, more violent scale (you'll quickly lose count of flying bodies and bullets) as El Mariachi tracks infamous drug lord Bucho (de Almeida). Gringo Buscemi provides assistance, beautiful bookstore owner Carolina (Hayek) offers solace, and Tarantino meets his well-deserved cameo demise. You'll also find original Mariachi, Gallardo, in a cameo role as a musician/gunslinger amigo of the hero. Though this is the original DVD release of *Desperado*, and not the one included on the double feature disc with *El Mariachi*, the image quality is very sharp and the slick picture is free of digital grain. The colors are vibrant with good contrast and brightness levels, and bleed is rare. The blacks remain true throughout the film. Most disappointing is the 5.1 sound, which though adequate, is lacking the energy that the film's music delivered in the theatre. A boost in the bass would help as would more defined separation on the tracks. —*JO* *AKA:* El Mariachi 2.
Movie: 🎵🎵🎵 **DVD:** 🎵🎵🎵
Columbia Tristar Home Video (Cat #11659, UPC #043396116597). Widescreen (1.85:1) letterboxed. Dolby Surround. NSL. Keepcase. *LANG:* English; Spanish; French. *SUB:* Spanish; Korean. *CAP:* English. *FEATURES:* 37 chapter links.
1995 (R) 103m/C Antonio Banderas, Salma Hayek, Joaquim de Almeida, Steve Buscemi, Richard "Cheech" Marin, Carlos Gomez; *Cameos:* Quentin Tarantino, Carlos Gallardo; *D:* Robert Rodriguez; *W:* Robert Rodriguez; *C:* Guillermo Navarro. *AWARDS: NOM:* MTV Movie Awards '96: Most Desirable Male (Banderas), Best Kiss (Antonio Banderas/Salma Hayek).

Desperado / El Mariachi

This digital double feature is great stuff for fans of director Rodriguez. *El Mariachi* is the legendary action film that he made for a ridiculously low budget in Mexico and then sold to Hollywood where he made the sequel *Desperado* with a lot more money. The original is essentially a reworking of *Yojimbo*. Our nameless hero (Gallardo) is a traveling musician who lives by his wits and his guitar. He has the bad luck to wan-

der into a desolate little town where two gangsters have just renewed a long feud. He's caught in the middle and blasts his way out in some dynamic action sequences. Flashes of that same unrefined energy show up in the sequel where Banderas takes over in the lead with Hayek as his love interest. The two stars play up the Latin lover stereotypes to a fare-thee-well. For my money, the second is weaker. In his commentary track, Rodriguez explains his filmmaking techniques. That's the real appeal of the disc because this kind of unpolished work really doesn't benefit from the added clarity of DVD. Sound is fine, but again, nothing special. —*MM*
Movie: 🎵🎵🎵 **DVD:** 🎵🎵🎵
Columbia Tristar Home Video (Cat #1969). Widescreen anamorphic. Dolby Digital 5.1 Surround Stereo; Dolby Digital Stereo. $41.95. Keepcase. *LANG:* English; French; Spanish. *SUB:* English; French; Spanish. *FEATURES:* Commentary: Robert Rodriguez • Short film, "Bedhead" • "Ten Minute Film School" featurette • "Ten More Minutes" featurette.
1995 (R) 103m/C Antonio Banderas, Salma Hayek, Joaquim de Almeida, Steve Buscemi, Richard "Cheech" Marin, Carlos Gomez; *Cameos:* Quentin Tarantino, Carlos Gallardo; *D:* Robert Rodriguez; *W:* Robert Rodriguez; *C:* Guillermo Navarro; *M:* Los Lobos. *AWARDS: NOM:* MTV Movie Awards '96: Most Desirable Male (Banderas), Best Kiss (Antonio Banderas/Salma Hayek).

Desperate Crimes

Larry (Quattro) goes to Genoa, Italy, in search of his sweetie (Kaitan) and finds himself in the middle of a war between two gangs. On DVD, the low-budget, poorly made action flick has an impoverished look. Even the daylight scenes are dim and the nocturnal interiors look like they were lit with a birthday candle. But, so what? Perhaps unsuspecting potential viewers should be glad that the haggard cast is not more clearly revealed. —*MM*
AKA: Mafia Docks.
Movie: 🎵 **DVD:** 🎵
Image Entertainment (Cat #ID6462JBDVD, UPC #014381646221). Full frame. Dolby Digital Stereo. $24.99. Snapper. *LANG:* English. *FEATURES:* 15 chapter links.
1993 103m/C Traci Lords, Denise Crosby, Franco (Columbo) Columbu, Van Quattro, Rena Niehaus, Nicoletta Boris, Elizabeth Kaitan, Randi Ingerman; *D:* Andreas Marfori; *W:* Andreas Marfori; *C:* Marco Isoli.

Desperate Measures

Police officer Frank Connor (Garcia) desperately searches for a bone marrow donor for his dying son. Turns out the only match is vicious murderer Pete McCabe (Keaton), who seizes the opportunity to unleash an elaborate and violent escape attempt from a San Francisco hospital. Anyone who can accept that baroque premise is in for a treat. Director Schroed-

er spins a dark atmospheric thriller told in heavy blacks and blues with exaggerated Dutch angles. Keaton is excellent in a fine, complex role. On DVD, the image is superior to VHS tape and the claustrophobic story, told virtually without exteriors, plays well on the small screen. A commentary track by Schroeder would have been worthwhile. —*MM*
Movie: 🎵🎵🎵 **DVD:** 🎵🎵🎵
Columbia Tristar Home Video (Cat #21759, UPC #043396217591). Full frame; widescreen (1.85:1) letterboxed. Dolby Digital 5.1 Surround; Dolby Digital Surround. $28.95. Keepcase. *LANG:* English; French; Spanish. *SUB:* English; French; Spanish. *CAP:* English. *FEATURES:* 28 chapter links.
1998 (R) 100m/C Andy Garcia, Michael Keaton, Marcia Gay Harden, Brian Cox; *D:* Barbet Schroeder; *W:* David Klass, Neal Jimenez, Henry Bean; *C:* Luciano Tovoli; *M:* Trevor Jones.

Destination Moon

This George Pal production was one of the first films to treat space travel seriously and it won an Academy Award for special effects. Today, it's more enjoyable as a glimpse at Cold War attitudes with its suspicions of sabotage and foreign propaganda against space travel. The script is based on Robert Heinlein's novel *Rocketship Galileo*. The background art by Chesley Bonestell is still delightful. The DVD looks pretty good, despite some surface scratches. The graininess and dark colors are typical of early '50s films. (Tuxedos are virtual black holes, absolutely solid and without any detail.) Tom Weaver's liner notes detail the film's rocky road from script to production. —*MM*
Movie: 🎵🎵🎵 **DVD:** 🎵🎵🎵
Image Entertainment (Cat #ID8754CODVD, UPC #014381875423). Full frame. Dolby Digital Mono. $24.99. Snapper. *LANG:* English. *FEATURES:* 15 chapter links • Liner notes by Tom Weaver.
1950 91m/C Warner Anderson, Tom Powers, Dick Wesson, Erin O'Brien-Moore; *D:* Irving Pichel; *W:* Rip Van Ronkel, Robert Heinlein, James O'Hanlon; *C:* Lionel Lindon; *M:* Leith Stevens. *AWARDS: NOM:* Academy Awards '50: Best Art Direction/Set Decoration (Color).

Detention

Urban drama about black teens and their teacher.
Movie: NYR **DVD:** NYR
MTI Home Video (Cat #54033). Full frame. $24.95.
1998 83m/C Justin Black, Charisse Brown, Reginald Davis, John Hall, Keisha Harvin, Kiatenai, Darryl Wharton; *D:* Darryl Wharton; *W:* Darryl Wharton; *C:* Boots Shelton; *M:* Camara Kambon.

Detroit Rock City

In 1978, four young KISS fans (Furlong, Andrews, De Bello, Huntington) will go to any lengths to get to the sold-out Detroit concert. Director Rifkin (whose name is occasionally misspelled in the DVD extras section) actually re-created the 1978 Kiss Love Gun Show with the band performing in Hamilton, Ontario. As a teen comedy, this one is only fitfully successful. The DVD is filled with extras—dozens upon dozens of extras—in a vain attempt to distract viewers from the film itself. In visual terms, the image is an accurate re-creation of a theatrical presentation that's as ugly as the '70s themselves. On the audio side, it contains all the sophistication of KISS. Further muddying the digital waters, the menu contains audio commands that make it virtually impossible to navigate. Only the most demented, er, dedicated metalheads will be able to make it through the entire experience. (There may be more extras than those listed below, but I couldn't figure out how to find them.) —MM

Movie: ♪♪ **DVD:** ♪♪♪
New Line Home Video (Cat #N4899, UPC #794043489921). Widescreen. Dolby Digital 5.1 Surround Stereo. $24.98. Snapper. *LANG:* English. *SUB:* English. *FEATURES:* 23 chapter links • Multi-angle "Detroit Rock City" concert footage • Deleted scenes • Commentary: KISS • Commentary: director Adam Rifkin • Commentary: cast and crew • DVD-ROM features.
1999 (R) 95m/C Edward Furlong, Sam Huntington, Giuseppe Andrews, Lin Shaye, James De Bello, Natasha Lyonne, Gene Simmons, Paul Stanley, Ace Frehley, Peter Criss; *D:* Adam Rifkin; *W:* Carl DuPre; *C:* John R. Leonetti; *M:* J. Peter Robinson.

The Devil Bat's Daughter

Hoping to avoid her batty father's fate, Nina (former Miss America Rosemary La Planche) consults a psychiatrist when she begins to have violent nightmares. Is she a vampiric murderess or is she being framed? During the opening credits, the music is virtually unlistenable. It improves during the body of the film, but this one looks and sounds like a low-budget 1940s horror flick. That's all it is and there is little that DVD can do to improve the look or sound of it. The film is not nearly as clear or polished as comparable Universal work of the period. —MM

Movie: ♪♪ **DVD:** ♪♪
Image Entertainment (Cat #ID5368FWDVD, UPC #014381536829). Full frame. Dolby Digital Mono. $19.99. Snapper. *LANG:* English.
1946 66m/B Rosemary La Planche, Michael Hale, John James, Molly Lamont; *D:* Frank Wisbar; *W:* Griffin Jay; *C:* James S. Brown Jr.

Devil in a Blue Dress

Down-on-his-luck Easy Rawlins (Washington) is an unemployed aircraft worker in 1948 L.A. He's hired to find mystery woman Daphne (Beals) by a shady businessman (Sizemore). What he finds are the usual noir staples: government corrup-

tion backed by thugs who want him to mind his own business. Easy and Daphne's torrid romance featured in the Walter Mosley novel is missing but the racism and violence are intact. Realism and accuracy in period detail enhance a solid performance by Washington, though the deliberate, literary pace is at times lulling. Cheadle takes over whenever he shows up as Mouse, Rawlins's loyal friend and muscle. The DVD transfer is excellent, led by a very sharp picture. The contrast and brightness allow for a lot of detail and all the subtleties of the lighting remain intact. Colors are accurate and bleed is not ever a factor. Blacks are handled perfectly and never grain up. The sound is not of the spectacular variety but is pretty good on all fronts, never sacrificing the dialogue though giving great dynamics and fidelity to all the other elements. The Surround is mainly used for ambience. —JO

Movie: ♪♪♪ **DVD:** ♪♪♪▶
Columbia Tristar Home Video (Cat #51349, UPC #043396513495). Widescreen (1.85:1) letterboxed; full frame. Dolby Digital 5.1. $28.95. Keepcase. *LANG:* English; Spanish; Portuguese. *SUB:* Spanish; Portugese. *CAP:* English. *FEATURES:* 28 chapter links • Theatrical trailer • Commentary: Carl Franklin • Don Cheadle's screen test.
1995 (R) 102m/C Denzel Washington, Jennifer Beals, Don Cheadle, Tom Sizemore, Maury Chaykin, Terry Kinney, Mel Winkler, Albert Hall; *D:* Carl Franklin; *W:* Carl Franklin; *C:* Tak Fujimoto; *M:* Elmer Bernstein. *AWARDS:* Los Angeles Film Critics Association Awards '95: Best Supporting Actor (Cheadle); National Society of Film Critics Awards '95: Best Cinematography, Best Supporting Actor (Cheadle); *NOM:* Screen Actors Guild Award '95: Best Supporting Actor (Cheadle).

Devil in the Flesh

Psycho teen Debbie Strand (McGowan) falls for teacher Peter Rinaldi (McArthur) and lets nothing stand in her way—not grandma, not grandma's dog, nothing! Despite the derivative nature of the story, it's handled with intelligent humor and energetically photographed. Fine acting, too. On DVD, the film looks terrific, but it's clear in one scene, when the essential action takes place off camera, that the image should have been presented in widescreen. An underrated effort from director Steve Cohen, a veteran who has been in the business in many capacities for some time. —MM

Movie: ♪♪ **DVD:** ♪♪♪
Simitar Entertainment (Cat #7442, UPC #082551744220). Full frame. Dolby Digital Stereo. $14.98. Keepcase. *LANG:* English. *FEATURES:* 8 chapter links • Production factoids.
1998 (R) 92m/C Rose McGowan, Alex McArthur, Sherrie Rose, Phil Morris, Robert Silver; *D:* Steve Cohen.

The Devil's Advocate

Forget the actors, this film belongs to cinematographer Bartkowiak and production designer Bruno Rubeo, who offer a lush rich look that's very enticing. And it's all about enticement—young Florida lawyer Kevin Lomax (Reeves) is seduced by the power and money of a position at an influential New York law firm run by the mysterious John Milton (Pacino). But soon Kevin's beautiful wife Mary Ann (Theron) is having a breakdown, his religious mother (Ivey) is prophesizing doom, and Kevin learns the boss is Satan—literally. Reeves is earnest, Pacino relishes his showy role, and the visual effects provide some much-needed jolts. The quality on even the early Warner DVD releases is generally very good and this is no exception—I take that back, this one's superb. The picture is super sharp and there's no grain or artifacts. The colors could not be better, accurate to the theatre and rich with no visible bleed. Blacks are dead-on and both contrast and brightness levels are consistent and punchy. The sound is also excellent with plenty of bass, super crisp highs, and plenty of space and separation on the tracks. Surround is used to good effect, even when just for ambience. —JO

Movie: ♪♪▶ **DVD:** ♪♪♪♪
Warner Home Video, Inc. (Cat #15090, UPC #085391509028). Widescreen (2.35:1) anamorphic; full frame. Dolby Digital 5.1. $24.98. Snapper. *LANG:* English; French. *SUB:* Spanish; French. *CAP:* English. *FEATURES:* 43 chapter links • 30 mins. of deleted scenes • 5 theatrical trailers • 2 TV spots • Commentary: Hackford • Dual-layered RSDL.
1997 (R) 144m/C Al Pacino, Keanu Reeves, Charlize Theron, Judith Ivey, Craig T. Nelson, Jeffrey Jones, Connie Nielsen, Ruben Santiago-Hudson, Debra Monk, Tamara Tunie, Vyto Ruginis, Laura Harrington, Pamela Gray, Heather Matarazzo, Delroy Lindo; *D:* Taylor Hackford; *W:* Tony Gilroy, Jonathan Lemkin; *C:* Andrzej Bartkowiak; *M:* James Newton Howard. *AWARDS: NOM:* MTV Movie Awards '98: Best Villain (Pacino).

The Devil's Nightmare

A woman leads seven tourists (representing the seven deadly sins) on a tour of a medieval European castle. There they experience demonic tortures. Lots of creepy moments. Horror/sex star Blanc is fantastic in this otherwise mediocre production. Maybe this is one of the weaker films in Image Entertainment's "Redemption" line of Eurosleaze, but the DVD holds up to the usual standard with an image that is fairly sharp and colors that are a little weak but probably the best that can be done with the preprint. There is also some grain; blacks are hit or miss. Despite that, the DVD holds up reasonably well for this sort of film. —JO *AKA:* Succubus; The Devil Walks at Midnight.
Movie: ♪▶ **DVD:** ♪♪▶

Image Entertainment (Cat #ID4684SADVD, UPC #014381468427). Widescreen (1.85:1) letterboxed. Dolby Digital Mono. $24.95. Snapper. *LANG:* English. *FEATURES:* 18 chapter links.
1971 (R) 88m/C *BE IT* Erika Blanc, Jean Servais, Daniel Emilfork, Lucien Raimbourg, Jacques Monseau, Colette Emmanuelle, Ivana Novak, Shirley Corrigan, Frederique Hender; *D:* Jean Brismee; *W:* Patrice Rhomm, Vertunnio De Angelis, Charles Lecocq; *C:* Andre Goeffers; *M:* Alessandro Alessandroni.

The Devil's Own

New York cop Tom O'Meara (Ford) and wife Shiela (Colin) take charming Irish emigre Rory Devaney (Pitt) into their home. But Rory's an IRA terrorist fleeing a botched job in Belfast and up to no good in America. The two men develop a strong friendship until Tom learns the truth. The film is more easily enjoyed as a low-keyed character study than as a political thriller. The cast is very good. Like the theatrical release, the DVD captures a gritty, realistic look with a muted, yellowish cast to the modest interiors. Those who are real fans of the cast will probably want to view the full-frame version. —MM
Movie: 🎬🎬🎬 *DVD:* 🎬🎬🎬
Columbia Tristar Home Video (Cat #82469, UPC #043396824690). Widescreen (2.35:1) letterboxed; full frame. Dolby Digital 5.1 Surround Stereo; Dolby Digital Surround Stereo. $25.95. Keepcase. *LANG:* English; French; Spanish. *SUB:* English; French; Spanish. *FEATURES:* 35 chapter links ▪ Theatrical trailer.
1996 (R) 110m/C Harrison Ford, Brad Pitt, Margaret Colin, Ruben Blades, Treat Williams, George Hearn, Natascha McElhone, Mitchell Ryan, Simon Jones, Paul Ronan; *D:* Alan J. Pakula; *W:* Kevin Jarre, David Aaron Cohen, Vincent Patrick; *C:* Gordon Willis; *M:* James Horner.

Devil's Rain

When first released, the finale of this film was touted as "the most horrifying of any motion picture ever." That may not quite be the case, but the cast alone makes this one worth seeing, and the ending isn't bad either. After three centuries, satanist Jonathan Corbis seeks revenge on the Preston family, who have kept the "book of souls" out of Corbis's hands for years, preventing him from completing his pact with Satan. The first thing one notices on the DVD is a lot of hiss on the soundtrack, and although you can hear everything, the music suffers greatly during quiet parts. The picture is a little too contrasty and at times darker than the laserdisc. Despite that, the blacks are fairly true. Color bleed is minimal but there is some grain throughout, making the sharpness a little below average. There were also several very nasty pops in the sound at a couple of scene changes. —JO
Movie: 🎬🎬 *DVD:* 🎬▸

VCI Home Video (Cat #8204, UPC #089859820427). Widescreen (2.35:1) letterboxed. Dolby Digital Stereo. $24.99. Keepcase. *LANG:* English. *FEATURES:* 19 chapter links ▪ Theatrical trailer ▪ Photo gallery.
1975 (PG) 85m/C Ernest Borgnine, Ida Lupino, William Shatner, Eddie Albert, Keenan Wynn, Tom Skerritt, Joan Prather, Claudio Brook, John Travolta, Anton La Vey; *D:* Robert Fuest; *W:* James Ashton, Gabe Essoe, Gerald Hopman; *C:* Alex Phillips Jr.; *M:* Al De Lory.

Devonsville Terror

Low-budget witchcraft story is told with a bit more inventiveness and wit than most, despite a cliche-ridden structure. Three hundred years ago the town fathers of Devonsville, in upstate New York (actually Wisconsin), brutally killed three women accused of being witches. In the present, the men's ancestors are cursed and still haven't changed their patriarchal attitudes. Enter the new teacher (Love, wife of writer-director Lommel). Donald Pleasence plays his familiar role with one bizarre and disgusting twist. The acting's uneven; some of the effects are O.K.; the rural atmosphere is strong. The DVD image is only slightly superior to VHS tape with high-contrast colors and extremely dark night scenes, both exterior and interior. (The title is available on disc as a double feature with Lommel's *The Boogey Man*.) —MM
Movie: 🎬🎬 *DVD:* 🎬🎬
Anchor Bay (Cat #DV10664, UPC #013131066494). Widescreen (1.85:1) letterboxed. Dolby Digital Mono. $29.98. Keepcase. *LANG:* English. *FEATURES:* 30 chapter links.
1983 (R) 97m/C Suzanna Love, Donald Pleasence, Deanna Haas, Mary Walden, Robert Walker Jr., Paul Wilson; *D:* Ulli Lommel; *W:* Ulli Lommel; *C:* Ulli Lommel; *M:* Ray Colcord.

Diabolique

The mistress and the wife of a sadistic schoolmaster conspire to murder the man, carry it out, and then begin to wonder if they have covered their tracks effectively. Plot twists and double-crosses abound. The basic premise has since been used time and again for both lowbrow and high-concept thrillers. Criterion has improved upon even their own laserdisc release, which at the time was, by far, the best thing available. The DVD has an excellent black-and-white picture with superb contrast and excellent graytones. The finely composed details of the film are even more evident and the subtitles are also improved. The mono sound is a little stronger but still has some distortion on the high end. —JO *AKA:* Les Diabolique.
Movie: 🎬🎬🎬▸ *DVD:* 🎬🎬🎬▸
Criterion Collection (Cat #DIA050, UPC #037429135020). Full frame. Dolby Digital Mono. $29.95. Keepcase. *LANG:*

French. *SUB:* English. *FEATURES:* 24 chapter links.
1955 107m/B *FR* Simone Signoret, Vera Clouzot, Paul Meurisse, Charles Vanel, Michel Serrault, Georges Chamarat, Robert Dalban, Therese Dorny, Camille Guerini; *D:* Henri-Georges Clouzot; *W:* Henri-Georges Clouzot, Frederic Grendel, Jerome Geronimi, Rene Masson; *C:* Armand Thirard; *M:* Georges Van Parys. *AWARDS:* New York Film Critics Awards '55: Best Foreign Film.

Diamondbacks

Futuristic thriller in which a militia group, led by O'Keefe, takes over a remote NASA station in order to reprogram a government weapons satellite for evil. And it's up to engineer Lottimer to stop them. Lots of action in a no-brainer adventure.
Movie: 🎬▸ *DVD:* NYR
York Entertainment (Cat #1008). Full frame. Dolby Digital 5.1 Surround Stereo. $24.98. Keepcase. *SUB:* Spanish. *FEATURES:* Cast and crew thumbnail biographies ▪ Trailer.
1999 90m/C Miles O'Keeffe, Chris Mitchum, Timothy Bottoms, Eb Lottimer; *D:* Bernard Salzman.

Diary of a Serial Killer

Down-on-his-luck journalist Nelson Keece (Busey) witnesses a murder and then is invited by the killer, Stefan (Vosloo), to conduct an exclusive interview. Stefan keeps killing and Nelson keeps writing, but the cops come to think that Nelson is the killer. Then Stefan targets Nelson's girlfriend Juliette (Campbell).
Movie: 🎬🎬 *DVD:* NYR
Simitar Entertainment (Cat #7424). Full frame. Dolby Digital 5.1 Surround Stereo. $14.98. Keepcase. *FEATURES:* Cast and crew thumbnail biographies.
1997 (R) 92m/C Gary Busey, Arnold Vosloo, Michael Madsen, Julia Campbell; *D:* Alan Jacobs; *W:* Jennifer Badham-Stewart; *C:* Keith Smith; *M:* Steve Edwards.

Die Hard

High-voltage action thriller pits a lone New York cop against a band of ruthless high-stakes terrorists who attack and hold hostage the employees of a large corporation as they celebrate Christmas in a new L.A. high rise. It's just as unbelievable as it sounds, but you'll love it anyway. Rickman, who later charmed audiences as the villain in *Robin Hood: Prince of Thieves,* turns in a marvelous performance as the chief bad guy. This is the way an action movie should look and sound on DVD—and the two sequels even manage to take it a step further. The image is very sharp with no grain or artifacts. Colors are vibrant and for the most part accurate, although the tint seems to shift in a few places. Fox has had no trouble with the blacks on most of their DVDs and that's true of this one; the blacks are true and grainless. Contrast and brightness levels

are high without having any adverse effect on colors, blacks, or dark scenes. The 5.1 sound is terrific and power-packed. The Surround tracks are used almost constantly, either for ambience, the music mix, or slam-bang effects. There is good crisp highs and loads of clean low end. This is a near-flawless DVD and, for the *Die Hard* trilogy, it just gets better. —*JO*
Movie: 𝒥𝒥𝒥 **DVD:** 𝒥𝒥𝒥▸
20th Century Fox (Cat #4110399, UPC #086162130995). Widescreen (2.35:1) letterboxed. Dolby Digital 5.1; Dolby Surround. $29.98. Keepcase. *LANG:* English; French. *SUB:* English; Spanish. *CAP:* English. *FEATURES:* 30 chapter links • Theatrical trailer • "Making of" featurette. Also available as part of the *Die Hard Trilogy* (cat. #FOX4110414) for $79.98.
1988 (R) 114m/C Bruce Willis, Bonnie Bedelia, Alan Rickman, Alexander Godunov, Paul Gleason, William Atherton, Reginald Vel Johnson, Hart Bochner, James Shigeta, Mary Ellen Trainor, De'voreaux White, Robert Davi, Rick Ducommun; *D:* John McTiernan; *W:* Jeb Stuart, Steven E. de Souza; *C:* Jan De Bont; *M:* Michael Kamen. *AWARDS: NOM:* Academy Awards '88: Best Film Editing, Best Sound.

Die Hard 2: Die Harder

Fast, well-done sequel brings another impossible situation before the wisecracking, tough-cookie cop. Our hero tangles with a group of terrorists at an airport under siege, while his wife remains in a plane circling above as its fuel dwindles. Obviously a repeat of the plot and action of the first *Die Hard,* with references to the former in the script. While the bad guys lack the fiendishness of their predecessors, this installment features energetic and finely acted performances. Fairly gory, especially the icicle-in-the-eyeball scene. *Die Hard 2*'s DVD is even sharper than the first, and seems to have somewhat improved upon the already top-notch blacks on the first. No grain or artifacts; colors are bright, punchy, and accurate (the DVD for *Die Hard* had a few shifts in hue) and never bleed. Contrast and brightness levels have once again been tweaked to perfection. The 5.1 sound is energized to ensure you get the most out of your system, and is packed full of gut-shaking bass and near glass-shattering highs. The Surround tracks are also used to the fullest. —*JO*
Movie: 𝒥𝒥𝒥 **DVD:** 𝒥𝒥𝒥𝒥
20th Century Fox (Cat #4110412, UPC #086162104121). Widescreen (2.35:1) letterboxed. Dolby Digital 5.1; Dolby Surround. $29.98. Keepcase. *LANG:* English; French. *SUB:* English; Spanish. *CAP:* English. *FEATURES:* 28 chapter links • Theatrical trailer • "Making of" featurette. Also available as part of the *Die Hard Trilogy* (cat. #Fox 4110414) for $79.98.
1990 (R) 124m/C Bruce Willis, William Atherton, Franco Nero, Bonnie Bedelia, John Amos, Reginald Vel Johnson, Dennis Franz, Art Evans, Fred Dalton Thompson,

William Sadler, Sheila McCarthy, Robert Patrick, John Leguizamo, Robert Costanzo, Tom Verica, Don Harvey, Tony Ganios, Vondie Curtis-Hall, Colm Meaney; *D:* Renny Harlin; *W:* Doug Richardson, Steven E. de Souza; *C:* Oliver Wood; *M:* Michael Kamen.

Die Hard: With a Vengeance

Third time is not a charm in the *Die Hard* series. McClane (Willis) is back home in the Big Apple and having another bad day. More Eurotrash terrorists, led by the brilliant and vengeful Simon (Irons), are out to blow things up, snag some gold, and make life miserable for McClane and his reluctant partner, Zeus Carver (Jackson). The claustrophobic settings of the first two outings have been replaced by the exhausting expanse of New York City, to good effect, but frenetic action scenes and good chemistry between Willis and Jackson don't quite compensate for a lackluster script and more cartoony feel. Jackson brings a fresh perspective and vitality to what will probably be the last ride of John McClane. Just when you thought a DVD couldn't get any better than *Die Hard 2*...throw this one in the player and hold on. When "A/B-ing" this one with the second installment, it seems even sharper. Again, no grain or artifacts; the colors are dead accurate and with the excellent contrast and brightness, they seem to jump off the screen. Blacks are also grain-free and true. The 5.1 sound is, of course, super. The mix doesn't take as much advantage of the Surround as the previous two DVDs. It is, however, still incredibly energy-packed and has enough dynamics and heavy bass to keep things moving. —*JO* *AKA:* Die Hard 3.
Movie: 𝒥𝒥▸ **DVD:** 𝒥𝒥𝒥𝒥
20th Century Fox (Cat #4110417, UPC #086162104176). Widescreen (2.35:1) letterboxed. Dolby Digital 5.1; Dolby Surround. $29.98. Keepcase. *LANG:* English; French. *SUB:* English; Spanish *CAP:* English. *FEATURES:* 26 chapter links • Theatrical trailer • "Making of" featurette. Also available as part of the *Die Hard Trilogy* (cat. #Fox 4110414) for $79.98.
1995 (R) 131m/C Bruce Willis, Samuel L. Jackson, Jeremy Irons, Graham Greene, Colleen Camp, Larry Bryggman, Tony Peck, Nick Wyman, Sam Phillips; *D:* John McTiernan; *W:* Jonathan Hensleigh; *C:* Peter Menzies Jr.; *M:* Michael Kamen. *AWARDS: NOM:* MTV Movie Awards '96: Best Action Sequence.

Die Watching

Sleazy erotic thriller focuses a video director (Atkins) who not only likes to film hot Hollywood babes but may also like to kill them as well. His latest discovery could be the next victim. Image quality is below par, apparently due to a so-so videotape master, but there aren't any easily discernible compression artifacts from the

DVD transfer. The sound is a so-so monaural track. No extras. —*MB*
Movie: 𝒥▸ **DVD:** 𝒥▸
Image Entertainment (Cat #ID5590FMDVD, UPC #014381559026). Full frame. Dolby Digital 2.0 Mono. $19.99. Snapper. *LANG:* English. *FEATURES:* 16 chapter links.
1993 (R) 92m/C Christopher Atkins, Vali Ashton, Tim Thomerson, Carlos Palomino, Mike Jacobs Jr.; *D:* Charles Davis; *W:* Kenneth J. Hall; *C:* Howard Wexler; *M:* Scott Roewe.

Digging to China

Hutton's directorial debut is a sentimental '60s story of a sweet friendship between misfits—precocious 10-year-old Harriet (Wood) and mentally handicapped 30-year-old Ricky (Bacon). Harriet's alcoholic mom (Moriarty) runs a motel in rural New Hampshire with Harriet's slutty older sister Gwen (Masterson). Ricky winds up at the motel with his dying mother Leah (Seldes), who is taking him to an institution when her car breaks down.
Movie: 𝒥𝒥▸ **DVD:** NYR
WinStar Home Entertainment (Cat #5140). Dolby Digital Surround Stereo. $24.98. Keepcase.
1998 (PG) 98m/C Evan Rachel Wood, Kevin Bacon, Mary Stuart Masterson, Cathy Moriarty, Marian Seldes; *D:* Timothy Hutton; *W:* Karen Janszen; *C:* Jorgen Persson; *M:* Cynthia Miller.

Dirty Dancing

An innocent 17-year-old (Grey) is vacationing with her parents in the Catskills in 1963. Falling for the hotel's sexy dance instructor (Swayze), she discovers love, sex, and rock and roll dancing. Grey and Swayze are appealing, the dance sequences fun, and the music great. Swayze, classically trained in ballet, performs one of the songs. With the addition of a 5.1 soundtrack, DVD is the way to see this music-driven film (this DVD was originally released by Live Home Video; see subsequent review of the "Collector's Edition"). The soundtrack is crisp and dynamic with a good thumping bass in the music. It also adds quite a bit of ambience to the numerous musical numbers and crowd scenes. Overall the picture is very good: sharp, with little grain or artifacts. The exception is just before the climatic number when the pic is a little soft and there are some artifacts. Color is very good with hardly any bleed and the blacks are excellent. Contrast and brightness levels consistently match the cinematography. —*JO*
Movie: 𝒥𝒥𝒥 **DVD:** 𝒥𝒥𝒥
Artisan Entertainment (Cat #60444, UPC #012236044406). Widescreen (1.85:1) letterboxed; full frame. Dolby Digital 5.1; Dolby Digital Stereo; Dolby Digital Mono. $24.98. Snapper. *LANG:* English (DD5.1); Spanish (DD1); French (DD2). *SUB:* English; Spanish; French. *FEATURES:* 44 chapter links • Theatrical trailer • Production notes • Cast and crew bios.

1987 (PG-13) 97m/C Patrick Swayze, Jennifer Grey, Cynthia Rhodes, Jerry Orbach, Jack Weston, Jane Brucker, Kelly Bishop, Lonny Price, Charles "Honi" Coles, Bruce Morrow; **D:** Emile Ardolino; **W:** Eleanor Bergstein; **C:** Jeffrey Jur; **M:** John Morris. *AWARDS:* Academy Awards '87: Best Song ("(I've Had) the Time of My Life"); Golden Globe Awards '88: Best Song ("(I've Had) the Time of My Life"); Independent Spirit Awards '88: Best First Feature.

Dirty Dancing (CE)

At a Catskills resort in the summer of '63, young Baby (Grey) discovers love, sex, and rock 'n' roll with a dance instructor (Swayze). The sleeper hit makes a smooth transition to DVD with a crisp image in most scenes and more moody dramatic effects in the big dance numbers. The early '60s soundtrack (and newer numbers that sound like they came from the era) is fine. For the film's most devoted fans, though, the real draw of this "collector's edition" is writer-producer Eleanor Bergstein's commentary track. She essentially tells a heartfelt story of her own ten-year effort to get the film produced. In the nascent business of DVD commentary, it's unusual for a writer-producer to be doing the talking, and it's also unusual for a woman. Her explanations of the production's location work in North Carolina and Virginia and its feminine perspective are well taken. —*MM*
Movie: ♪♪♪ **DVD:** ♪♪♪▶
Artisan Entertainment (Cat #10002, UPC #012236100027). Widescreen (1.85:1) letterboxed. Dolby Digital 5.1 Surround Stereo. $24.98. Snapper. *LANG:* English. *CAP:* English. *FEATURES:* 44 chapter links ▸ 3 music videos ▸ "Making of" featurette ▸ Commentary: writer-producer Eleanor Bergstein.
1987 (PG-13) 97m/C Patrick Swayze, Jennifer Grey, Cynthia Rhodes, Jerry Orbach, Jack Weston, Jane Brucker, Kelly Bishop, Lonny Price, Charles "Honi" Coles, Bruce Morrow; **D:** Emile Ardolino; **W:** Eleanor Bergstein; **C:** Jeffrey Jur; **M:** John Morris. *AWARDS:* Academy Awards '87: Best Song ("(I've Had) the Time of My Life"); Golden Globe Awards '88: Best Song ("(I've Had) the Time of My Life"); Independent Spirit Awards '88: Best First Feature.

The Dirty Dozen

Director Robert Aldrich combines a '40s look with '60s politics to create one of the most entertaining war/action movies ever made. The mix of nostalgia, anti-establishment rebellion, and graphic violence was a huge hit in 1967 and has remained popular on all forms of home video ever since. The DVD is the best-looking version I've seen since the first theatrical release. There is a certain roughness to the image and the colors are garish in some scenes, but those are as they should be. A few minor flecks are inconsequential. Sound

---

is fine. The "making of" featurette is a trip back in time to the swinging '60s. One to own. —*MM*
Movie: ♪♪♪♪ **DVD:** ♪♪♪
MGM Home Entertainment (Cat #906563, UPC #027616656322). Widescreen letterboxed. Dolby Digital Surround Stereo. $24.98. Keepcase. *LANG:* English; French. *SUB:* English; French; Spanish. *FEATURES:* 32 chapter links ▸ "Making of" featurette ▸ Theatrical trailer.
1967 (PG) 149m/C Lee Marvin, Ernest Borgnine, Charles Bronson, Jim Brown, George Kennedy, John Cassavetes, Clint Walker, Donald Sutherland, Telly Savalas, Robert Ryan, Ralph Meeker, Richard Jaeckel, Trini Lopez, Robert Webber, Stuart Cooper, Robert Phillips, Al Mancini; **D:** Robert Aldrich; **W:** Nunnally Johnson, Lukas Heller; **C:** Edward Scaife; **M:** Frank DeVol. *AWARDS:* Academy Awards '67: Best Sound Effects Editing; *NOM:* Academy Awards '67: Best Film Editing, Best Sound, Best Supporting Actor (Cassavetes).

The Dirty Girls

In 1964 America, this French import was pretty hot stuff. Today it remains a nostalgic treat for those who can remember when sex was really really dirty and seldom appeared on-screen in any form. This heavy-breathing story follows two prostitutes, Garance (Roland) in Paris and Monique (Rohan) in Munich, as they entertain customers. The leering voice-over promises more illicit thrills than the film delivers. The deleted footage, in a separate chapter, contains more nudity than the rest of the film, but the sexual activity is suggested, not explicit. On DVD, one plaid jacket and some black tiles flash like crazy. Otherwise, the black-and-white photography ranges from excellent to so-so in the underlit night exteriors. —*MM*
Movie: ♪♪▶ **DVD:** ♪♪▶
Image Entertainment (Cat #ID5539FFDVD, UPC #014381553925). Widescreen (2.35:1) letterboxed. Dolby Digital Mono. $24.99. Snapper. *LANG:* English. *FEATURES:* 12 chapter links ▸ Deleted scenes.
1964 82m/B Reine Rohan, Denise Roland, Marlene Sherter, Peter Parten, Lionel Bernier; **D:** Radley Metzger; **W:** Peter Fernandez.

Dirty Harry

Rock-hard cop Harry Callahan attempts to track down a psychopathic rooftop killer before a kidnapped girl dies. Harry abuses the murderer's civil rights, however, forcing the police to return him to the streets. The only answer seems to be cold-blooded violence, and Harry is just the man to do it. Taut, suspenseful direction by Siegel, who thoroughly understands Eastwood's on-screen character. Callahan's famous "Do you feel lucky?" line is the precursor to his "Go ahead, make my day." This DVD is overall of slightly lesser quality than the

---

Warner letterboxed laserdisc. The picture is a touch softer; colors are fairly strong but have tint problems intermittently throughout. The sound is improved a bit with much better bass and an overall crisper feel. —*JO*
Movie: ♪♪♪▶ **DVD:** ♪♪▶
Warner Home Video, Inc. (Cat #1019, UPC #012569101920). Widescreen (2.2:1) anamorphic. Dolby Digital 5.1. $24.98. Snapper. *LANG:* English; Spanish; French. *SUB:* English; Spanish; French. *CAP:* English. *FEATURES:* 22 chapter links ▸ Theatrical trailers ▸ Production notes.
1971 (R) 103m/C Clint Eastwood, Harry Guardino, John Larch, Andrew (Andy) Robinson, Reni Santoni, John Vernon, Albert "Poppy" Popwell; **D:** Donald Siegel; **W:** Dean Riesner, Harry Julian Fink, Rita M. Fink; **C:** Bruce Surtees; **M:** Lalo Schifrin.

Dirty Rotten Scoundrels

In this remake of the 1964 *Bedtime Story*, two conmen, Freddy Benson (Martin) and Lawrence Jamison (Caine), try to rip off detergent heiress Janet Colgate (Headly) on the French Riviera. The two leads are terrific—Martin has some of his best physical comedy—and Headly is charming as the prey who's always one step ahead of them. Director Oz, who also brought us the voice of Yoda, is in fine form. The widescreen image is very good. The only flaw, and it's hardly worth mentioning, is the way that the brightest reds glow. Otherwise the luxurious settings look sumptuous. —*MM*
Movie: ♪♪♪ **DVD:** ♪♪▶
Image Entertainment (Cat #ID4085ORDVD, UPC #014381408522). Widescreen (1.85:1) letterboxed. Dolby Digital Surround Stereo. $29.99. Snapper. *LANG:* English. *FEATURES:* 16 chapter links.
1988 (PG) 112m/C Steve Martin, Michael Caine, Glenne Headly, Anton Rodgers, Barbara Harris, Dana Ivey; **D:** Frank Oz; **W:** Dale Launer, Stanley Shapiro; **C:** Michael Ballhaus; **M:** Miles Goodman.

Dirty Work

You'll notice that star and ex-SNL newsguy MacDonald isn't even trying to act here; he's just doing his deadpan routine with a different name. His delivery and attitude, however, are about the only funny things in this tale of Mitch (MacDonald) and Sam (Lange), two losers who can't keep a job but have a talent for petty revenge. When Sam's father (Warden) has a heart attack, the boys decide to open a business specializing in dirty deeds done dirt cheap to pay for a transplant. Although the premise is good, the tricks are mostly of the junior high variety and don't seem quite dirty enough. Look for several unbilled cameos including Adam Sandler, John Goodman, and the late Chris Farley.
Movie: ♪▶ **DVD:** NYR

MGM Home Entertainment (Cat #907248). Widescreen (1.85:1) anamorphic. Dolby Digital 5.1 Surround Stereo. $24.98. Keepcase. *LANG:* English; French. *SUB:* French. *CAP:* English. *FEATURES:* Trailer.
1997 (PG-13) 81m/C Norm MacDonald, Artie Lange, Chevy Chase, Don Rickles, Jack Warden, Traylor Howard, Christopher McDonald; *Cameos:* Chris Farley, Gary Coleman, Ken Norton, John Goodman, Adam Sandler; *D:* Bob Saget; *W:* Fred Wolf; *C:* Arthur Albert; *M:* Richard Gibbs.

Disclosure

Likable, responsible executive and family man (Douglas) finds himself sexually harassed by his ex-lover turned dragon-lady boss (Moore). But when he rejects her lusty come-on, she points the finger at him. One-dimensional characters and hollow material turn sexual harassment into a trivial issue. High-tech saga of corporate politics, while flashy, is nothing we haven't seen before. Douglas just can't pass up these "Regular Joe meets beautiful, horny babe/bad things happen" roles, can he? While this excellent DVD doesn't make up for the plot, it does reveal far more of the cinematic details and makes for a more enjoyable viewing than previous video versions did. Even the goofy virtual effects are more interesting to look at. The 5.1 sound is also super and adds some nifty Surround effects. —*JO*
Movie: 🐾🐾 **DVD:** 🐾🐾🐾▶
Warner Home Video, Inc. (Cat #13575, UPC #085391357520). Widescreen (2.35:1) anamorphic. Dolby Digital 5.1; Dolby Surround. $24.98. Snapper. *LANG:* English; French. *SUB:* English; Spanish; French. *CAP:* English. *FEATURES:* 4 chapter links • Production notes.
1994 (R) 129m/C Michael Douglas, Demi Moore, Donald Sutherland, Caroline Goodall, Dylan Baker, Dennis Miller, Rosemary Forsyth, Roma Maffia; *D:* Barry Levinson; *W:* Paul Attanasio; *C:* Tony Pierce-Roberts; *M:* Ennio Morricone. *AWARDS:* Blockbuster Entertainment Awards '95: Drama Actress, Theatrical (Moore); Blockbuster Entertainment Awards '96: Drama Actress, Video (Moore); *NOM:* MTV Movie Awards '95: Most Desirable Female (Moore), Best Villain (Moore).

The Disenchanted

Seventeen-year-old Beth (Godreche) is having a rough time growing up. She's forced to look after her bedridden mother and younger brother and their survival depends on the generosity of her mother's ex-lover, who's now taking a more personal interest in the beautiful teenager. Meanwhile, Beth's arrogant boyfriend decides Beth should prove her love for him by sleeping with the ugliest man she can find. The image transfer is fine, although scenes that appear naturally lit do lean towards a bland, washed-out look. The soundtrack is crisp and clear, with no noticeable distortions or crackling though it does remain at a constant level through-

out, creating little or no excitement. —*MJT*
AKA: La Desenchantee.
Movie: 🐾🐾▶ **DVD:** 🐾🐾▶
First Run Features (Cat #FRF909198D, UPC #720229909198). Widescreen (1.85:1) letterboxed. Dolby Stereo. $29.95. Keepcase. *LANG:* French. *SUB:* English. *FEATURES:* 8 chapter links.
1990 78m/C *FR* Judith Godreche, Ivan Desny, Therese Liotard, Malcolm Conrath, Marcel Bozonnet; *D:* Benoit Jacquot; *W:* Benoit Jacquot; *C:* Caroline Champetier; *M:* Jorge Arriagada.

The Distinguished Gentleman

Eddie Murphy attempts to prove Will Rogers's famous observation that Congress is America's only native criminal class. Murphy plays Florida conman Jeff Johnson who scams his way into the House of Representatives when the incumbent of the same name (Garner) dies right before the election. The supporting cast is fine, but director Lynn keeps the camera on his star who seems to have fun with a larcenous hero. The few-frills disc equals the theatrical release with acceptable image and sound, though one loud plaid sportcoat will challenge your DVD player. —*MM*
Movie: 🐾🐾▶ **DVD:** 🐾🐾▶
Buena Vista Home Entertainment (Cat #17493, UPC #717951003119). Widescreen (1.85:1) letterboxed. Dolby Digital Stereo. $29.99. Keepcase. *LANG:* English; French. *CAP:* English. *FEATURES:* 17 chapter links • Theatrical trailer.
1992 (R) 122m/C Eddie Murphy, Lane Smith, Sheryl Lee Ralph, Joe Don Baker, Victoria Rowell, Grant Shaud, Kevin McCarthy, Charles S. Dutton, James Garner; *D:* Jonathan Lynn; *W:* Marty Kaplan; *C:* Gabriel Beristain; *M:* Randy Edelman.

Disturbing Behavior

Gavin (Stahl) welcomes new kid in town Steve (Marsden) by pointing out the social castes of Cradle Bay High School. Along with the standard computer geeks, auto shop rates, and punkers, are the goody-goody Blue Ribbons, an excessively straitlaced and perky group of athletes and cheerleaders. Along with fellow outcasts Rachel (Holmes) and U.V. (Donnella) they joke about a possible conspiracy, but when Gavin shows up with a crewcut and an inordinate love of pep rallies and bake sales, his friends know something is up. They discover that parents have allowed school shrink Dr. Caldicott (Greenwood) to use drugs to tinker with the brains of the Blue Ribbons. They also discover that the Stepford Teen's vanilla lives are topped with sprinkles of homicidal fury. Director Nutter, whose background includes episodes of *The X-Files*, creates just the right creepy and paranoid mood in his movie debut. The DVD is of adequate but not great sharpness. There's not any real problem with grain or artifacts, but sometimes deep colors

tend to fuzz out and bleed. For that matter the colors don't seem quite right. The blacks are true and contrast and brightness consistent but a touch low, and there is occasional distortion along high-contrast lines. There is a 5.1 soundtrack, and the Surround is put to good use, but the overall energy level is a little low and in need of some fine tuning on the equalization. —*JO*
Movie: 🐾🐾▶ **DVD:** 🐾🐾▶
MGM Home Entertainment (Cat #907432, UPC #027616743220). Widescreen anamorphic; full frame. Dolby Digital 5.1; Dolby Digital Stereo. $24.98. Keepcase. *LANG:* English (DD5.1); French (Stereo). *SUB:* French. *CAP:* English. *FEATURES:* 36 chapter links • Theatrical trailer • 11 additional scenes • Alternate ending • "Got You (Where I Want You)" music video • Commentary: director Nutter • Booklet.
1998 (R) 84m/C James Marsden, Nick Stahl, Katie Holmes, Bruce Greenwood, William Sadler, Chad E. Donella, Ethan (Randall) Embry, Steve Railsback; *D:* David Nutter; *W:* Scott Rosenberg; *C:* John Bartley; *M:* Mark Snow. *AWARDS:* MTV Movie Awards '99: Breakthrough Performance (Holmes).

Diva

While at a concert given by his favorite star, a young French courier secretly tapes a soprano who has refused to record. The film follows the young man through Paris as he flees from two Japanese recording pirates, and a couple of crooked undercover police who are trying to cover up for the chief, who not only has a mistress but runs a prostitution ring. Brilliant and dazzling photography complement the eclectic soundtrack. The DVD transfer is not too bad, but the remastered laserdisc of a few years ago was a little more impressive. The picture here is of average sharpness and some grain shows up here and there. The colors do look very good. They're deep and appear accurate to the theatrical release. Bleed is negligible. Blacks are mostly true with occasional grain. Contrast and brightness are maybe a touch better than the laserdisc, so the DVD does have a little more punch. The sound is nothing special, which is too bad since the soundtrack (both operatic and incidental) was a very big part of this film. —*JO*
Movie: 🐾🐾🐾▶ **DVD:** 🐾🐾▶
Fox/Lorber Home Video (Cat #FLV5000, UPC #720917500027). Widescreen (1.66:1) letterboxed. Dolby Digital Mono. $29.98. Keepcase. *LANG:* French. *SUB:* English. *FEATURES:* 9 chapter links • Production notes.
1982 (R) 123m/C *FR* Frederic Andrei, Roland Bertin, Richard Bohringer, Gerard Darmon, Jacques Fabbri, Wilhemenia Wiggins Fernandez, Dominique Pinon; *D:* Jean-Jacques Beineix; *W:* Jean-Jacques Beineix; *C:* Philippe Rousselot; *M:* Vladimir Cosma. *AWARDS:* Cesar Awards '82: Best Cinematography, Best Sound,

Best Score; National Society of Film Critics Awards '82: Best Cinematography.

Divine Madness

The Band got Martin Scorsese to direct their *The Last Waltz* so Bette Midler gets Michael Ritchie to do her concert film. Most likely no connection, but the point is that in both cases, the director's choice of scene composition and camera angles add excitement to the performance. The movie contains Midler at her best, belting them out, telling stories, flirting with the audience, and changing costumes more than Liberace. Probably of interest only to a true fan, but well-done nonetheless. I have not seen this one theatrically, so some aspects of the DVD may or may not have been elements of the original film. The most noticeable of them is the grain content, which could be a result of film stock, and is not really of much aggravation. There is also a lot of ghosting on the brighter stage images. The picture does seem very sharp and the colors are also natural in appearance, with very little bleed. The Dolby Surround is not spectacular but still conveys most of the energy of the performance. —*JO*

Movie: 🎵🎵🎵 **DVD:** 🎵🎵▶

Warner Home Video, Inc. (Cat #20001, UPC #085392000128). Widescreen (1.85:1) letterboxed. Dolby Surround. $14.98. Snapper. *LANG:* English. *CAP:* English. *FEATURES:* 22 chapter links.

1980 (R) 87m/C Bette Midler; **D:** Michael Ritchie; **W:** Bette Midler, Jerry Blatt.

Django

The Django series may have been the most popular of the spaghetti westerns made in the wake of the Man With No Name films. It was certainly one of the most prolific, with dozens of films featuring the character, though only two starred Franco Nero. In the original, he's a taciturn stranger who trudges into town with an anachronistic machine gun in a coffin. Director Sergio Corbucci creates an almost anti-western milieu that's cold, muddy, wet, and gray. The two groups of bad guys are Confederates and Mexicans, who spend most of their time fighting over the local brothel. It's energetic and psychotic but still derivative. For a film of its age, the DVD looks fine with well-preserved colors and only minor scratches on the print. The extras, including an interview with Franco Nero, are helpful for those who aren't familiar with these baroque exercises in escapism. The sound is only fair, though with the typical dubbing of the era, that's to be expected. —*MM*

Movie: 🎵🎵🎵 **DVD:** 🎵🎵🎵

Anchor Bay (Cat #DV10935, UPC #013131093599). Widescreen (1.66:1) letterboxed. Dolby Digital Mono. $39.98. Keepcase. *LANG:* English. *FEATURES:* 15 chapter links ▪ Theatrical trailers ▪ Franco Nero interview ▪ Cast and crew thumbnail biographies ▪ Django game ▪ Book-

let by Mach, Lamaj, Grimm, and Wahl. Available in double-disc set with *Django Strikes Again*.

1968 (PG) 90m/C Franco Nero, Loredana Nusciak, Angel Alvarez, Jose Bodalo, Eduardo Fajardo, Simon Arriaga, Ivan Scratuglia; **D:** Sergio Corbucci; **W:** Sergio Corbucci, Bruno Corbucci, Jose Maesso, Piero Vivarelli, Franco (Fred Gardner) Rossetti; **C:** Enzo Barboni; **M:** Luis Bacalov.

Django Strikes Again

This sequel was made more than 20 years after the original. As the accompanying booklet explains, in those years, more than 50 films were made featuring the character, though none had the participation of the original director or star. This one, made in Colombia, is barely a western at all. It's more a Felliniesque political period piece set in Mexico. After a fuzzily focused introduction, we learn that Django has put away his machine gun and taken up the prayer book. He's a monk until he learns that he has a daughter and she has been enslaved by the evil Olofsky (Connelly). Thousands of gunshots and explosions follow. The DVD looks and sounds pretty good, making the most of exotic locations and bizarre characters. For spaghetti western fans, it's grand stuff—never released theatrically in America—but it's so outlandish that it's not likely to be a hit with a larger audience. —*MM*

AKA: *Django 2: Il Grande Ritorno.*

Movie: 🎵🎵🎵 **DVD:** 🎵🎵🎵

Anchor Bay (Cat #DV10935, UPC #013131093599). Widescreen (1.66:1) letterboxed. Dolby Digital 2.0 Surround Stereo. $39.98. Keepcase. *LANG:* English; Italian. *SUB:* English. *FEATURES:* 23 chapter links ▪ Theatrical trailer ▪ Franco Nero interview ▪ Cast and crew thumbnail biographies ▪ Booklet by Mach, Lamaj, Grimm, and Wahl. Available in double-disc set with *Django.*

1987 96m/C *SP* Franco Nero, Donald Pleasence, Rodrigo Obregon, Christopher Connelly, William Berger; **D:** Nello (Ted Archer) Rossati; **W:** Nello (Ted Archer) Rossati; **M:** Gianfranco Plenizio.

Do the Right Thing

An uncompromising, brutal comedy about the racial tensions surrounding a white-owned pizzeria in the Bed-Stuy section of Brooklyn on the hottest day of the summer, and the violence that eventually erupts. Lee's coming-of-age is ambivalent and, for the most part, hilarious. His incredibly vivid images are all the more powerful on this DVD, which even improves upon the Criterion special edition laserdisc. The colors are accurate and convey the charging emotional intensities as things heat up and the violence escalates. The Dolby sound has great fidelity and dynamics and is used sparingly, but effectively, for Surround. —*JO*

Movie: 🎵🎵🎵▶ **DVD:** 🎵🎵🎵▶

Universal Studios Home Video (Cat #20242, UPC #025192024221). Widescreen (1.66:1) letterboxed. Dolby Surround. $24.98. Keepcase. *LANG:* English; French. *SUB:* Spanish. *CAP:* English. *FEATURES:* 16 chapter links ▪ Theatrical trailer ▪ Production notes ▪ Cast and filmmakers bios ▪ Film highlights.

1989 (R) 120m/C Spike Lee, Danny Aiello, Richard Edson, Ruby Dee, Ossie Davis, Giancarlo Esposito, Bill Nunn, John Turturro, John Savage, Rosie Perez, Frankie Faison; **D:** Spike Lee; **W:** Spike Lee; **C:** Ernest R. Dickerson; **M:** Bill Lee. *AWARDS:* Los Angeles Film Critics Association Awards '89: Best Director (Lee), Best Film, Best Supporting Actor (Aiello), National Film Registry '99; New York Film Critics Awards '89: Best Cinematography; *NOM:* Academy Awards '89: Best Original Screenplay, Best Supporting Actor (Aiello).

D.O.A.

On a wild vacation in San Francisco, Los Angeles accountant Frank Bigelow (O'Brien) is given a lethal slow-acting poison. He's got 48 hours to find out who's responsible, why he was targeted, and to do something about it. This seminal film noir gets the tough, no-frills treatment it deserves on DVD. The image, restored from the producer's negative, is as dark and moody as it's supposed to be. Cinematographer Ernest Laszlo's hallucinatory night sequences haven't looked this good in years. The Tiomkin score sounds fine, even in mono. A must for fans of late'40s/early '50s thrillers. —*MM*

Movie: 🎵🎵🎵▶ **DVD:** 🎵🎵🎵▶

Image Entertainment (Cat #ID8592CODVD, UPC #014381859225). Full frame. Dolby Digital Mono. $19.99. Snapper. *LANG:* English. *FEATURES:* 15 chapter links.

1949 83m/B Edmond O'Brien, Pamela Britton, Luther Adler, Neville Brand, Beverly Garland, Lynne Baggett, William Ching, Henry Hart, Laurette Luez, Virginia Lee, Jess Kirkpatrick, Cay Forrester, Michael Ross; **D:** Rudolph Mate; **W:** Russell Rouse, Clarence Green; **C:** Ernest Laszlo; **M:** Dimitri Tiomkin.

Doc Hollywood

Hotshot Dr. Ben Stone (Fox) is on his way to a lucrative California practice when he's stranded in Grady, SC. Will the pleasantly colorful locals persuade the sophisticated physician to stay? No surprises in plot or DVD. The so-so full frame image is no better than VHS tape. Sound might be a bit sharper, but not much. —*MM*

Movie: 🎵🎵▶ **DVD:** 🎵🎵

Warner Home Video, Inc. (Cat #12222, UPC #085391222224). Full frame. Dolby Digital Surround Stereo. $14.98. Snapper. *LANG:* English. *FEATURES:* 31 chapter links.

1991 (PG-13) 104m/C Michael J. Fox, Julie Warner, Woody Harrelson, Barnard Hughes, David Ogden Stiers, Frances Sternhagen, Bridget Fonda, George Hamilton, Roberts Blossom, Helen Martin,

Macon McCalman, Barry Sobel; **D:** Michael Caton-Jones; **W:** Daniel Pyne, Jeffrey Price, Peter S. Seaman; **C:** Michael Chapman; **M:** Carter Burwell.

Dr. Dolittle

Loose non-musical adaptation of the Hugh Loftin book and the 1967 movie casts Eddie Murphy as John Doolittle, successful physician whose re-found ability to understand animals is a mixed blessing. He plays straight man to a bunch of wise-cracking critters including, among others, a sick tiger (voice of Brooks), a snappy hamster (Rock), worried pigeons (Kavner and Shandling), and a faithful mutt (MacDonald). Dr. Weller (Platt) and Calloway (Boyle) are shallow villains in a subplot involving the corporate takeover of Doolittle's practice. The bathroom humor may be too much for some family tastes, but it stays within the expected bounds of a "PG-13" rating. On DVD, the film looks fine, particularly the special effects work by Jim Henson's Creature Shop on the animals. Sharp-eyed viewers will catch a Push-Me-Pull-You crossing in the background of one circus scene. —*MM*
Movie: 🎞️🎞️🎞️ **DVD:** 🎞️🎞️🎞️
Twentieth Century Fox Home Entertainment (Cat #4112491, UPC #086162124914). Widescreen (1.85:1) letterboxed. Dolby Digital 5.1 Surround; Surround. $34.98. Keepcase. *LANG:* English; French. *SUB:* English; Spanish. *CAP:* English. *FEATURES:* 22 chapter links.
1998 (PG-13) 85m/C Eddie Murphy, Oliver Platt, Peter Boyle, Jeffrey Tambor, Ossie Davis, Richard Schiff, Kyla Pratt, Raven-Symone, Steven Gilborn; **D:** Betty Thomas; **W:** Nat Mauldin, Larry Levin; **C:** Russell Boyd; **M:** Richard Gibbs; **V:** Julie Kavner, Albert Brooks, Chris Rock, John Leguizamo, Garry Shandling, Norm MacDonald, Paul (Pee-wee Herman) Reubens, Jean Stapleton, Dennis Franz, Gilbert Gottfried. *AWARDS: NOM:* MTV Movie Awards '99: Best Song ("Are You That Somebody?").

Dr. Giggles

A cast of allegedly young characters lifted from a dead teenager–slasher flick is transplanted to an escaped-lunatic plot. Dr. Rendell (Drake) is said wacko who goes back to his hometown after the breakout to reopen his practice, killing the locals with medical devices, including a giant Band Aid. The jokes are grisly and grim. Director Coto makes a limited budget look extravagant. Even though this one made its debut on video, it's solidly in the Universal tradition of slickly made, energetic horror. The good doctor deserves a place at the table with the Wolfman, Dracula, et al.
Movie: 🎞️🎞️🎞️ **DVD:** NYR
Goodtimes Entertainment (Cat #81024). Full frame. Dolby Digital Surround Stereo. $19.98. Snapper. *SUB:* French; Spanish. *FEATURES:* Production notes.

1992 (R) 96m/C Larry Drake, Holly Marie Combs, Glenn Quinn, Keith Diamond, Cliff DeYoung; **D:** Manny Coto; **W:** Manny Coto, Graeme Whifler; **C:** Rob Draper; **M:** Brian May.

Dr. Jekyll and Mr. Hyde

Perhaps its simple-minded notions of women as frail vessels and men as depraved beasts have kept this silent version of the famous story from exerting much influence on the others that have followed. By keeping the two sides of the Jekyll character completely separate, the film never addresses the real conflict. To be fair, John Barrymore's vampiric Hyde has effective moments. In one brief shot, he creates the elongated face without makeup, and the appearance of Hyde in another scene as a huge spider is shocking. On DVD, the flaws in the carefully restored print can be traced to the original. The image is dark and tends to waver. The organ score will not add much for younger fans. The disc also includes a clip from a 1911 Nickelodeon version of the story. It's the transformation scene, starring James Cruz. —*MM*
Movie: 🎞️🎞️ **DVD:** 🎞️🎞️🎞️
Image Entertainment (Cat #ID4667DSDVD, UPC #014381466720). Full frame. Dolby Digital Mono. $24.99. Snapper. *FEATURES:* 14 chapter links • Clip from 1911 version of film.
1920 96m/B John Barrymore, Martha Mansfield, Brandon Hurst, Charles Lane, J. Malcolm Dunn, Nita Naldi, Louis Wolheim; **D:** John S. Robertson; **W:** Clara Beranger; **C:** Karl Struss, Roy F. Overbaugh.

Dr. No (SE)

The world is introduced to British secret agent 007, James Bond, when it is discovered that a mad scientist is sabotaging rocket launchings from his hideout in Jamaica. The first 007 film is far less glitzy than any of its successors but boasts the sexiest "Bond girl" of them all in Andress, and promptly made stars of her and Connery. The first Bond is given a splendid transfer to DVD. The image is very sharp and the color has been greatly improved over both the MGM and Criterion laserdisc releases. Some contrast has also been added, which in itself helps deepen the colors. Digital grain, artifacts, and color bleed are not problematic. The additional contrast seems to have also helped the blacks which are very close to true. The mono sound, though nothing special, is a true representation of the film's soundtrack. —*JO*
Movie: 🎞️🎞️🎞️ **DVD:** 🎞️🎞️🎞️▶
MGM Home Entertainment (Cat #908123, UPC #027616812322). Widescreen (1.77:1) anamorphic. Dolby Digital Mono. $34.98. Keepcase. *LANG:* English; Spanish; French. *SUB:* Spanish; French. *CAP:* English. *FEATURES:* 32 chapter links • Theatrical trailers • "Inside Dr. No" docu-

mentary • Commentary: Young, cast, and crew • "Terence Young Bond Vivant" documentary • Bond featurette • TV and radio spots • Photo gallery.
1962 (PG) 111m/C *GB* Sean Connery, Ursula Andress, Joseph Wiseman, Jack Lord, Zena Marshall, Eunice Gayson, Margaret LeWars, John Kitzmiller, Lois Maxwell, Bernard Lee, Anthony Dawson; **D:** Terence Young; **W:** Johanna Harwood, Richard Maibaum, Berkely Mather; **C:** Ted Moore; **M:** John Barry.

Dr. Strangelove, or: How I Learned to Stop Worrying and Love the Bomb

Sellers plays a tour-de-force triple role in Kubrick's classic black anti war comedy. While a U.S. President (Sellers) deals with the Russian situation, a crazed general (Hayden) implements a plan to drop the A-bomb on the Soviets. Famous for Pickens's wild ride on the bomb, Haydens's character's "purity of essence" philosophy, Scott's gum-chewing militarist, and countless other scenes. The usual grain exaggeration shows up on another Kubrick DVD. In this case, occasional ghosting is visible in the high-contrast scenes of this black-and-white film, so overall the Criterion laserdisc and even the Columbia VHS tape looks a bit sharper. Like the laser, the DVD does preserve both aspect ratios that Kubrick utilized (the 1.33:1 filling up the entire screen and the 1.66:1 being very slightly letterboxed). Blacks are true. Contrast and brightness levels are comfortable, with the aforementioned ghosting being the only problem. The mono sound is full-bodied and clear, with no clipping. —*JO*
Movie: 🎞️🎞️🎞️🎞️ **DVD:** 🎞️🎞️
Columbia Tristar Home Video (Cat #04093, UPC #043396040939). Widescreen (1.66:1/1.33:1) letterboxed. Mono. $24.98. Snapper. *LANG:* English; French; Spanish. *SUB:* French. *CAP:* English. *FEATURES:* 29 chapter links. Also available as part of the "Stanley Kubrick Collection" 7-DVD box set ($149.98).
1964 93m/B *GB* Peter Sellers, George C. Scott, Sterling Hayden, Keenan Wynn, Slim Pickens, James Earl Jones, Peter Bull, Tracy Reed, Shane Rimmer, Glenn Beck, Gordon Tanner, Frank Berry, Jack Creley; **D:** Stanley Kubrick; **W:** Stanley Kubrick, Terry Southern, Peter George; **C:** Gilbert Taylor; **M:** Laurie Johnson. *AWARDS:* American Film Institute (AFI) '98: Top 100; British Academy Awards '64: Best Film, National Film Registry '89; New York Film Critics Awards '64: Best Director (Kubrick); *NOM:* Academy Awards '64: Best Actor (Sellers), Best Adapted Screenplay, Best Director (Kubrick), Best Picture.

Dodsworth

The lives of a self-made American tycoon and his wife are drastically changed when they take a tour of Europe. The success of their marriage seems questionable as they re-evaluate their lives. Huston excels as does the rest of the cast in this film, based upon the Sinclair Lewis novel. The age of the film is obvious as there is a lot of surface damage and it's easy to tell where the original reel changes were. The black and white, however, is very sharp and detailed with little grain and only minor artifacts. Blacks are true and gray-tones subtly varied, giving the film great depth. There is also minor ghosting in some high-contrast scenes, but it's rare. HBO has remastered the mono sound to Dolby Surround and it sounds quite good; in fact, it's far better than one can expect from a '30s vintage film. —*JO*

Movie: 🎜🎜🎜➤ **DVD:** 🎜🎜🎜
HBO Home Video (Cat #90659, UPC #026359065927). Full frame. Dolby Surround; Mono. $24.98. Snapper. *LANG:* English; Spanish; French; Italian; German. *CAP:* English. *FEATURES:* 18 chapter links • Cast bios.
1936 101m/B Walter Huston, David Niven, Paul Lukas, John Payne, Mary Astor, Ruth Chatterton, Maria Ouspenskaya, Charles Halton; *D:* William Wyler; *W:* Sidney Howard; *C:* Rudolph Maté; *M:* Alfred Newman. *AWARDS:* National Film Registry '90; New York Film Critics Awards '36: Best Actor (Huston); *NOM:* Academy Awards '36: Best Actor (Huston), Best Director (Wyler), Best Picture, Best Screenplay, Best Sound, Best Supporting Actress (Ouspenskaya).

Dog Day Afternoon

Based on a true story, this taut yet fantastic thriller centers on a bisexual and his slow-witted buddy, who rob a bank to obtain money to fund a sex change operation for the ringleader's lover. Pacino is breathtaking in his role as the frustrated robber, caught in a trap of his own devising. Very controversial for its language and subject matter when released, it nevertheless became a huge success. Director Lumet keeps up the pace, fills the screen with pathos without gross sentiment. Having just recently seen this film on cable, I was disappointed that the DVD's colors were a little weak in comparison. The image is very sharp, and overall the DVD is preferable to earlier home video editions. Grain and artifact levels are very low and blacks are true in most scenes. Contrast seems a little low, and the brightness feels a little high. The sound is more than adequate for the film that features very little in the way of effects or music and is basically all dialogue. —*JO*

Movie: 🎜🎜🎜➤ **DVD:** 🎜🎜➤
Warner Home Video, Inc. (Cat #1024, UPC #012569102422). Widescreen (1.85:1) letterboxed; full frame. Dolby Digital Mono. $19.98. Snapper. *LANG:* English. *SUB:* English; French; Spanish. *CAP:* English. *FEATURES:* 29 chapter links • Production notes.
1975 (R) 124m/C Al Pacino, John Cazale, Charles Durning, James Broderick, Chris Sarandon, Carol Kane, Lance Henriksen, Dick Williams; *D:* Sidney Lumet; *W:* Frank Pierson; *C:* Victor Kemper. *AWARDS:* Academy Awards '75: Best Original Screenplay; British Academy Awards '75: Best Actor (Pacino); National Board of Review Awards '75: Best Supporting Actor (Durning); Writers Guild of America '75: Best Original Screenplay; *NOM:* Academy Awards '75: Best Actor (Pacino), Best Director (Lumet), Best Film Editing, Best Picture, Best Supporting Actor (Sarandon).

Dolemite

Dolemite (Moore) is released from prison to settle the score with the guys who framed him. He gathers a band of kung-fu fightin' femmes to help. The mixture of action and comedy is very strange. This is perhaps the cheapest and most amateurish of the original blaxploitation movies. The quality of the DVD is much better than the acting or the low-voltage fight scenes. It captures the '70s outfits in all of their insurmountable excess. Sound is only O.K. —*MM*

Movie: 🎜🎜 **DVD:** 🎜🎜🎜
Xenon Entertainment (Cat #XE XX-1006DVD, UPC #000799100622). Full frame. $19.95. Keepcase. *LANG:* English. *FEATURES:* 24 chapter links • Documentary • Trailers • Song lyrics • Rudy Ray Moore thumbnail biography • DVD credits.
1975 (R) 88m/C Rudy Ray Moore, Jerry Jones, D'Urville Martin, Lady Reeds; *D:* D'Urville Martin; *W:* Jerry Jones; *C:* Nicholas Josef von Sternberg; *M:* Arthur Wright.

Dolores Claiborne

One of the best and most handsomely produced adaptations of Stephen King's work is powered by three excellent performances and unusual conflicts. Kathy Bates is Dolores, a hardbitten Maine woman accused of murdering her employer (Parfitt). Det. John Mackey (Plummer) is sure that she also killed her husband (Strathairn) years before. Her troubled daughter Selena (Leigh) isn't sure what she believes when she comes back to the island where she grew up. Director Taylor Hackford turns the curious tale into his most satisfying work since *An Officer and a Gentleman*. Kathy Bates isn't as commanding as she was in *Misery*, but Dolores is a much more complex character. Curiously, the film never caught on in theatres, so it's a first-rate sleeper on video. The DVD takes a solid step up from the VHS tape. It reproduces the blue cast of the film faithfully and shows off the Nova Scotia locations in their cold bleak beauty. On his commentary track, made from memory four years later, Hackford is, of course, complimentary to everyone. He stays focused mostly on the filming itself, his ideas about the characters and his work with the actors. —*MM*

Movie: 🎜🎜🎜➤ **DVD:** 🎜🎜🎜➤
Warner Home Video, Inc. (Cat #C2548, UPC #053939254822). Widescreen letter-boxed. Dolby Digital Stereo; Dolby Surround Stereo. $19.98. Snapper. *LANG:* English; French. *SUB:* English; French. *CAP:* English. *FEATURES:* Cast and crew thumbnail biographies • Notes on the re-creation of a solar eclipse on film • Commentary: director • 32 chapter links.
1994 (R) 132m/C Kathy Bates, Jennifer Jason Leigh, Christopher Plummer, Judy Parfitt, David Strathairn, John C. Reilly; *D:* Taylor Hackford; *W:* Tony Gilroy; *C:* Gabriel Beristain; *M:* Danny Elfman.

Dominion Tank Police

Masamune Shirow, creator of the characters in this four-episode mini-series (originally produced for Japanese television), is now much better known for the crossover hit film *Ghost in the Shell*. This title was a groundbreaker in its day as well. In the dystopian future of A.D. 2010, bands of "tank police" protect those remaining citizens who hide from the poisoned air and the criminal element. The squad commander has his hands full with his new recruit Leona and civil society's arch-enemies, twin gangsters called the "Cat Sisters." The DVD's sound mix is limited but effective. There is speckling, evidently on the image track source, and linear aspects of the animation break up into artifacting. The "meet the cast" section shows clips as well as stills. The "director's comments" is a still page with three lines of text. The "coming attractions" section is a direct sales solicitation. English subtitles are yellow. —*JK*

Movie: 🎜🎜🎜 **DVD:** 🎜🎜➤
Central Park Media/U.S. Manga Corps (Cat #USMD1779, UPC #719987177925). Full frame. Dolby Digital Stereo. $34.99. Keepcase. *LANG:* English; Japanese. *SUB:* English; Japanese. *FEATURES:* 12 chapter links • Interactive menus • Character gallery • Commentary: director • Web links.
1989 160m/C *JP D:* Takaaki Ishiyama; *W:* Dai Kono, Koichi Mashimo.

Don Juan DeMarco

Burned-out clinical psychiatrist Dr. Jack Meckler (Brando) is romantically inspired by a cape-wearing, suicidal man-child from Queens (Depp), who thinks he's legendary lover Don Juan. Delusional Depp recounts, in a convincing Castilian accent, thousands of conquests as the sympathetic shrink decides it's time to bring some spice to his own ho-hum life and marriage (to Dunaway). Depp turns in a sincere, engaging performance that avoids the huge potential for melodrama and compensates for inconsistent pacing. Brando and Dunaway make a charmingly quirky couple. Watch for slain Tejano queen Selena in a musical interlude. The DVD is not at all bad but has colors that appear a little weak. Overall sharpness is good, although there are occasions of grain and seemingly overly digitized backgrounds. The 5.1 sound is rich and full with enough ambient imaging processed through the rear channels. —*JO*

Movie: 🎬🎬➤ **DVD:** 🎬🎬🎬
New Line Home Video (Cat #N636, UPC #79404346362). Widescreen (1.85:1) letterboxed; full frame. Dolby Digital 5.1; Stereo. $24.95. Snapper. *LANG:* English (DD5.1); French (stereo). *SUB:* English; Spanish; French. *FEATURES:* 22 chapter links • Domestic and international theatrical trailers • Bryan Adams music video • Cast and filmmakers bios • Isolated music track.
1994 (PG-13) 92m/C Marlon Brando, Johnny Depp, Faye Dunaway, Geraldine Pailhas, Rachel Ticotin, Bob Dishy, Talisa Soto; **D:** Jeremy Leven; **W:** Jeremy Leven; **C:** Ralf Bode; **M:** Michael Kamen. *AWARDS: NOM:* Academy Awards '95: Best Song ("Have You Ever Really Loved a Woman?"); Golden Globe Awards '96: Best Song ("Have You Ever Really Loved a Woman?"), Best Score.

Donnie Brasco

Excellent look at the unglamourous working end of the mob and an undercover operation. In the late '70s, FBI agent Joe Piston (Depp) infiltrates the New York Bonanno crime family, under the alias Donnie Brasco, where he's mentored by aging low-level hood Lefty (Pacino). As Joe/Donnie gets deeper into the wiseguy life, Lefty takes a fatherly pride in his protege and the agent also becomes enamored by his new identity—to the possible detriment of both feds and family. Terrific lead performances. The picture on the DVD is very sharp and the grain level very low. Colors are deep and only the darkest of earthtones show any evidence of bleed. The contrast and brightness levels are up a bit from the VHS release resulting in a more gutsy image. The 5.1 sound is very good and the Surround adds nice ambience throughout. Music and dialogue are delivered with no distortion with crisp high end detail and smooth bass. *—JO*
Movie: 🎬🎬🎬 **DVD:** 🎬🎬🎬➤
Columbia Tristar Home Video (Cat #82519, UPC #043396825192). Widescreen (2.35:1) letterboxed; full frame. Dolby Digital 5.1; Dolby Digital 2.0. $28.95. Keepcase. *LANG:* English (DD); French (DD2.0). *SUB:* Spanish; French. *CAP:* English. *FEATURES:* 35 chapter links • Theatrical trailer.
1996 (R) 126m/C Johnny Depp, Al Pacino, Anne Heche, Michael Madsen, Bruno Kirby, James Russo, Zeljko Ivanek, Gerry Becker, Zach Grenier, Robert Miano; **D:** Mike Newell; **W:** Paul Attanasio; **C:** Peter Sova; **M:** Patrick Doyle. *AWARDS:* National Board of Review Awards '97: Best Supporting Actress (Heche); *NOM:* Academy Awards '97: Best Adapted Screenplay; Writers Guild of America '97: Best Adapted Screenplay.

Don's Party

Real political life mixes with kitchen sink drama in this period piece, featuring news footage of the Australian Prime Minister during the 1969 general election. Some left-leaning suburban neighbors congregate to watch what they hope will be an upset labor victory. Guests soon split off into viciously gossipy male and female camps, meeting only to have sex—or try—or start drunken fights. The visual track stands up well enough against murky location situations which could have degenerated into blobby or streaky colors, but sound fares a bit worse. The irritating center-speaker track means, for instance, the skritch of towels on skin competes with heavily accented whining when some of the guys are done skinny-dipping. *—JK*
Movie: 🎬🎬🎬 **DVD:** 🎬🎬🎬
Fox/Lorber Home Video (Cat #FLV5111, UPC #720917511122). Full frame. Stereo. $29.99. Keepcase. *LANG:* English. *FEATURES:* 6 chapter links • Interactive menus • Full-color picture disc • Production credits and filmographies • Trailer.
1976 90m/C *AU* Pat Bishop, Graham Kennedy, Candy Raymond, Veronica Lang, John Hargreaves, Ray Barrett, Claire Binney, Graeme Blundell, Jeanie Drynan; **D:** Bruce Beresford; **W:** David Williamson; **C:** Donald McAlpine; **M:** Leos Janacek. *AWARDS:* Australian Film Institute '77: Best Actress (Bishop).

Don't Answer the Phone

Deeply troubled photographer stalks and attacks the patients of a beautiful psychologist talk-show host. **AKA:** The Hollywood Strangler.
Movie: 🎬 **DVD:** NYR
Rhino Home Video (Cat #5740). Full frame. $14.95. Snapper. *FEATURES:* Cast and crew thumbnail biographies.
1980 (R) 94m/C James Westmoreland, Flo Gerrish, Ben Frank; **D:** Robert Hammer; **W:** Robert Hammer, Michael Castle; **C:** James L. Carter; **M:** Byron Allred.

Don't Be a Menace to South Central While Drinking Your Juice in the Hood

Parody of "life in the hood" movies pokes fun at the attitudes and characters that are quickly becoming cliches in the genre. Shawn Wayans plays G-next-door Ashtray, sent by his mother to discover "what it is to be a man" from his father in South Central L.A. He hooks up with his homey Loc Dog (Marlon Wayans), a gun-crazed beer-swilling gangsta who packs a nuclear warhead. As the title implies, almost every major black film in recent memory is given the Wayans's drive-by treatment, with a majority of the plot lifted from *Boyz N the Hood*. Fans of the TV series *In Living Color* will love this twisted look at ghetto life, but others may be offended. The sound on this DVD is only Dolby Surround, but the mix, including what's fed to the rear channels, is excellent. There is also plenty of low end and dynamics to give the film more energy than it seemed to have in the theatre. The image is sharp, with rich colors that are beefed up even further by the excellent contrast. Brightness levels are comfortable and the blacks respond nicely and rarely show any gain in grain. *—JO*
Movie: 🎬🎬➤ **DVD:** 🎬🎬🎬➤
Buena Vista Home Entertainment (Cat #15863, UPC #717951000989). Widescreen (1.85:1) letterboxed. Dolby Surround. $29.99. Keepcase. *LANG:* English. *CAP:* English. *FEATURES:* 13 chapter links.
1995 (R) 88m/C Shawn Wayans, Marlon Wayans, Tracey Cherelle Jones, Chris Spencer, Suli McCullough, Darrell Heath, Helen Martin, Isaiah Barnes, Lahmard Tate; *Cameos:* Keenen Ivory Wayans; **D:** Paris Barclay; **W:** Shawn Wayans, Marlon Wayans, Phil Beauman; **C:** Russ Brandt; **M:** John Barnes.

Don't Do It

Ensemble cast takes a realistic, funny look at love in the mid-1990s. Waitress Alicia (Trigger) is pregnant. Her current live-in beau Robert (Marshall) might be the father, or it might be former flame Dodger (LeGros), who is tentatively involved with Suzanna (Graham), who's carrying a torch for Charles (Morales) who, at that very moment, is putting some serious moves on Michelle (Lee), who hasn't gotten over Robert yet. Got that? Actually, writer-director Hess holds it all together pretty well. Even though most of the action consists of couples sitting around talking, there are enough two-timing lies and hanky-panky for six weeks of soap opera, plus a clever ending. Compared to VHS, the DVD looks to be a bit more sharply focused and clear, though this kind of character-based drama-comedy doesn't really depend on top-notch visuals. Sound is equally adequate *—MM*
Movie: 🎬🎬🎬 **DVD:** 🎬🎬🎬
Image Entertainment (Cat #ID5591FMDVD, UPC #014381559125). Full frame. Dolby Digital Stereo. $24.99. Snapper. *LANG:* English. *FEATURES:* 16 chapter links.
1994 (PG-13) 90m/C James Marshall, James LeGros, Sheryl Lee, Esai Morales, Alexis Arquette, Balthazar Getty, Sarah Trigger, Heather Graham; **D:** Eugene Hess; **W:** Eugene Hess; **C:** Ian Fox.

Don't Go in the House

Long-dormant psychosis is brought to life by the death of a young man's mother.
Movie: 🎬 **DVD:** NYR
Digital Versatile Disc Ltd. (Cat #147). Full frame. Dolby Digital Surround Stereo. $19.95. Keepcase.
1980 (R) 90m/C Dan Grimaldi, Robert Osth, Ruth Dardick; **D:** Joseph Ellison; **W:** Joseph Ellison, Ellen Hammill; **C:** Oliver Wood; **M:** Richard Einhorn.

Don't Look in the Basement

Things get out of hand at an isolated asylum and a pretty young nurse is caught between the inmates and the equally

deranged staff. There is little that the DVD image or sound can do to improve this low-budget wonder that was always destined for the drive-in screen and that tinny speaker that hung on the window. —*MM*
Movie: ♪♫ **DVD:** ♪♫
VCI Home Video (Cat #8214, UPC #089859821424). Full frame. Dolby Digital Mono. $19.99. Keepcase. *LANG:* English. *FEATURES:* 24 chapter links ▪ Production factoids ▪ Previews.
1973 (R) 95m/C Rosie Holotik, Anne MacAdams, William Bill McGhee, Rhea MacAdams, Gene Ross, Betty Chandler, Camilla Carr, Robert Dracup, Jessie Kirby, Hugh Feagin, Harryete Warren, Jessie Lee Fulton, Michael Harvey; *D:* S.F. Brownrigg; *W:* Tim Pope, Tom Pope; *M:* Robert Farrar.

Don't Touch the White Woman!
French surrealistic comedy retelling the Battle of Little Bighorn—with Mastroianni as Custer!—in a 1960s Parisian setting is every bit as nutty as you'd expect. To say that it's not to all tastes is a massive understatement. The DVD looks rough and pale, as is to be expected of such a low-budget experimental work. —*MM* *AKA:* Touche Pas a la Femme.
Movie: ♪ **DVD:** ♪♫
Image Entertainment (Cat #4777). Full frame. Dolby Digital Mono. $24.99. Snapper. *LANG:* French. *SUB:* English.
1974 110m/C *FR* Marcello Mastroianni, Catherine Deneuve, Michel Piccoli, Philippe Noiret, Ugo Tognazzi, Alain Cuny, Serge Reggiani; *Cameos:* Marco Ferreri; *D:* Marco Ferreri; *W:* Rafael Azcona; *C:* Etienne Becker; *M:* Philippe Sarde.

The Doors
Stone approached Jim Morrison with an early incarnation of this docudrama, but it's hard to believe even the Lizard King could play himself with any more convincing abandon than Kilmer, in a great performance. Trouble is, the story—one of drugs, abuse, and abject self-indulgence—grows tiresome, and the audience, with the exception of die-hard fans, may lose sight of any sympathy they might have had. Ryan is forgettable as Morrison's hippie-chick wife, MacLachlan sports a funny wig and dabbles on the keyboards as Ray Manszarek, and Quinlan is atypically cast as a sado-masochistic journalist paramour. The performance scenes are a highlight to the film and the DVD's 5.1 sound make it even better. The bass track is pumped up, too, and the highs literally scream at times (I mean that in a good way). The Surround creates concert-like ambience and is mixed to perfection. The picture isn't too bad either and is pretty sharp. There is a little grain but nothing too distracting. Colors are vibrant and accurate and blacks are mostly true. Some scenes have to have too much brightness, but generally the levels are pretty good along with the contrast. —*JO*

Movie: ♪♫ **DVD:** ♪♫♪
Artisan Entertainment (Cat #60451, UPC #012236045106). Widescreen (2.35:1) letterboxed. Dolby Digital 5.1. $24.99. Snapper. *LANG:* English. *SUB:* English; Spanish; French. *CAP:* English. *FEATURES:* 36 chapter links ▪ Theatrical trailer ▪ Cast and crew bios ▪ Production notes.
1991 (R) 138m/C Val Kilmer, Meg Ryan, Kevin Dillon, Kyle MacLachlan, Frank Whaley, Michael Madsen, Kathleen Quinlan, Crispin Glover, Josh Evans, John Densmore, William Jordan, Mimi Rogers, Paul Williams, Bill Graham, Billy Vera, William Kunstler, Wes Studi, Costas Mandylor, Billy Idol, Michael Wincott, Dennis Burkley; *D:* Oliver Stone; *W:* Oliver Stone, Ralph Thomas, Randy Johnson, J. Randall Johnson; *C:* Robert Richardson.

Double Dragon
Generally harmless brain candy based on the videogame finds orphaned brothers Jimmy (Dacascos) and Billy (Wolf) living in the rubble of post-earthquake L.A., circa 2007. They have half of a mystical dragon amulet. Obsessed mogul Koga Shuko (Patrick), who has the other half, is after them. Seems he needs the whole thing to control its vast power. Non-stop action will keep the kiddies amused.
Movie: ♪♫♪ **DVD:** NYR
Goodtimes Entertainment (Cat #81032). Widescreen (1.66:1) letterboxed. Dolby Digital 5.1 Surround Stereo. $19.98. Snapper. *LANG:* English. *SUB:* French; Spanish. *CAP:* English.
1994 (PG-13) 96m/C Scott Wolf, Mark Dacascos, Robert Patrick, Alyssa Milano, Kristina Malandro Wagner, Julia Nickson-Soul; *D:* Jim Yukich; *W:* Michael Paul Davis, Peter Gould; *C:* Gary B. Kibbe; *M:* Jay Ferguson.

Double Indemnity
MacMurray plays insurance man Walter Neff who abandons a life on the straight and narrow when he allows anklet-wearing Stanwyck to seduce him into killing her husband so they can collect the insurance money. Trouble is, boss Robinson is on to them. Wilder paints this tasty portrait of greed and self-destruction in tones of light and shadow. MacMurray's first-person narration is no cliche in this classic film noir (based on the James M. Cain novel) by which all others are measured. Bow-wow and boo-hiss to the DVD producers for failing to provide any extras whatsoever for this important movie. At least the picture and sound are good for a film of its vintage. —*MB*
Movie: ♪♫♪♪ **DVD:** ♪♫
Image Entertainment (Cat #ID4222USDVD, UPC #014381422221). Full frame. Dolby Digital Mono. $29.98. Snapper. *LANG:* English. *CAP:* English. *FEATURES:* 12 chapter links.
1944 107m/B Fred MacMurray, Barbara Stanwyck, Edward G. Robinson, Tom Powers, Porter Hall, Jean Heather, Byron Barr,

Fortunio Bonanova; *D:* Billy Wilder; *W:* Raymond Chandler, Billy Wilder; *C:* John Seitz; *M:* Miklos Rozsa. *AWARDS:* American Film Institute (AFI) '98: Top 100, National Film Registry '92; *NOM:* Academy Awards '44: Best Actress (Stanwyck), Best Black-and-white Cinematography, Best Director (Wilder), Best Picture, Best Screenplay, Best Sound, Best Original Dramatic Score.

Double Jeopardy
A high-powered cast and capable direction manage to save this abysmally written thriller, but it's a near thing. Libby Parsons (Judd) seems to have it all until her rat of a husband (Greenwood) fakes his own death, frames her for the murder, and takes off with her best friend (Gish) and son. Libby is convicted of the murder and after a breezily brief incarceration, is released to the care of parole officer Travis Lehman (Jones). Since she's already served her time, Libby is free to kill hubby if she can find him. The widescreen DVD image is a minor improvement over the full-frame tape, but on any medium, this is nothing more than frivolous nonsense. —*MM*
Movie: ♪♫ **DVD:** ♪♫
Paramount Home Video (Cat #333154). Widescreen letterboxed. Dolby Digital 5.1 Surround Stereo. $29.99. Snapper. *LANG:* English; French. *SUB:* English. *FEATURES:* 16 chapter links ▪ Behind-the-scenes featurette.
1999 (R) 105m/C Ashley Judd, Tommy Lee Jones, Bruce Greenwood, Annabeth Gish, Roma Maffia, Jay Brazeau, Gillian Barber, Davenia McFadden, Spencer Treat Clark; *D:* Bruce Beresford; *W:* David Weisberg, Douglas S. Cook; *C:* Peter James; *M:* Normand Corbeil. *AWARDS: NOM:* MTV Movie Awards '00: Best Female Performance (Judd).

Double Team
Counter-terrorist Jack Quinn (Van Damme) teams up with weapons guy Yaz (Rodman in his film debut) to take down international terrorist Stavros (Rourke). Several plot twists and many explosions later, Stavros kidnaps Quinn's wife and son. Quinn and Yaz ride to the rescue. Hong Kong action director Tsui Hark keeps the action loud, fast, and foolish. He employs lots of flashy lighting effects, fancy sets, excessive stunts, and egregious product placement. On disc, the image looks pristine throughout without setting any standards for the medium. Ditto sound. —*MM*
Movie: ♪♫ **DVD:** ♪♫♪
Columbia Tristar Home Video (Cat #83239, UPC #043396832398). Full frame; widescreen (1.85:1) letterboxed. Dolby Digital 5.1 Surround Stereo; Dolby Surround Stereo. $25.95. Keepcase. *LANG:* English; French; Spanish. *SUB:* English; French; Spanish. *CAP:* English. *FEATURES:* 28 chapter links ▪ Theatrical trailer.
1997 (R) 93m/C Jean-Claude Van Damme, Dennis Rodman, Mickey Rourke,

Natasha Lindinger, Paul Freeman, Valeria Cavalli, Jay Benedict; **D:** Tsui Hark; **W:** Paul Mones, Don Jakoby; **C:** Peter Pau; **M:** Gary Chang. *AWARDS:* Golden Raspberry Awards '97: Worst Supporting Actor (Rodman), Worst New Star (Rodman).

Down in the Delta

Matriarch Rosa Lynn (Alice) tries to prevent her jobless, single-mom daughter Loretta (Woodard) from succumbing to drugs, alcohol, and hopelessness in Chicago tenements. She sends Loretta and her two children to her brother Earl's (Freeman) home in the Mississippi delta for the summer, hoping that they'll rediscover the stability of family. Poet-novelist Angelou's first outing as director often verges on preachiness but its sentiments are heartfelt and it winds up being interesting and enjoyable in spite of its best intentions. The main reason is Freeman's near-perfect performance and another winning turn from Ms. Woodard. The DVD image ranges between good and very good. Often troublesome fabric patterns and blinds are not a problem. Sound is fine. *—MM*

Movie: 🎬🎬🎬 **DVD:** 🎬🎬🎬

Miramax Pictures Home Video (Cat #17440, UPC #717951002907). Widescreen (1.85:1) letterboxed. Dolby Digital 5.1 Surround Stereo. $29.99. Keepcase. *LANG:* English. *CAP:* English. *FEATURES:* 25 chapter links.

1998 (PG-13) 111m/C Alfre Woodard, Al Freeman Jr., Mary Alice, Wesley Snipes, Esther Rolle, Loretta Devine, Anne-Marie Johnson, Mpho Koaho, Kulani Hassen, Richard Blackburn; **D:** Maya Angelou; **W:** Myron Goble; **C:** William Wages; **M:** Stanley Clarke. *AWARDS: NOM:* Independent Spirit Awards '99: Best Actress (Woodard).

Dracula

The real value in this DVD of the great horror film lies not in the image transfer, though that's fine, but in the inspired extras. First among them is the inclusion of the Spanish-language version, which was made at the same time as the English. A new score by Philip Glass and the Kronos Quartet replacing the familiar borrowed music is well-chosen, and, as always, David Skal's documentary and commentary are excellent. Aces all around. *—MM*

Movie: 🎬🎬🎬🎬 **DVD:** 🎬🎬🎬

Columbia TriStar Home Video (Cat #20324, UPC #025192032424). Full frame. Dolby Digital Mono. *LANG:* English; Spanish; French. *SUB:* French. *CAP:* English. Keepcase. $29.98. *FEATURES:* "The Road to Dracula" documentary • New score by Philip Glass and the Kronos Quartet • Spanish-language version • Cast and crew thumbnail bios • Production notes.

1931 75m/B Bela Lugosi, David Manners, Dwight Frye, Helen Chandler, Edward Van Sloan, Frances Dade, Herbert Bunston; **D:** Tod Browning; **W:** Garrett Fort; **C:** Karl Freund.

Dracula

Frank Langella's Dracula isn't as menacing as Lugosi's or as powerful as Lee's. He and director John Badham interpret the Count as a Gothic hero. We see him dancing, riding a black horse with his cape flowing in the breeze, emerging dramatically from the fog, and seated for dinner surrounded by thousands of candles. Stoker's plot has been compressed and altered considerably, downplaying Van Helsing (Olivier). This version is as much a romance as pure horror, and that's certainly a valid approach. Peter Murton's sets, particularly Carfax Abbey, and John Williams's score make this one of Hollywood's most handsome interpretations of the story. The DVD captures that lush quality with only a few noticeable flaws. Wide angle shots of the ocean shiver; misty night scenes are heavily grained and the red light effects meant to represent soaring passion, which weren't that good to begin with, are still less than wonderful. Even so, this version is better than its reputation. *—MM*

Movie: 🎬🎬▶ **DVD:** 🎬🎬🎬

Image Entertainment (Cat #ID4227USDVD, UPC #014381427721). Widescreen (2.35:1) letterboxed. Dolby Digital Surround. $24.99. Snapper. *LANG:* English. *CAP:* English. *FEATURES:* 16 chapter links.

1979 (R) 109m/C Frank Langella, Laurence Olivier, Kate Nelligan, Donald Pleasence, Janine Duvitsky, Trevor Eve, Tony Haygarth; **D:** John Badham; **W:** W.D. Richter; **C:** Gilbert Taylor; **M:** John Williams.

Dracula

Combine the all-time classic vampire story, a world-class director, and a lead actor who holds nothing back, and you get...well, not exactly the best-ever vampire movie. The old-style special effects are a breath of fresh air in an age of sterile, computer-generated showmanship. Shot almost entirely on soundstages, the film has an oddly surreal feel, but on the whole it's a piece of old-fashioned filmmaking you can sink your teeth into. The picture is DVD sharp, revealing nuances not visible on even the best laserdisc edition. The Dolby Digital tracks showcase the award-winning audio. All that's missing are the extras. *—MB* **AKA:** Bram Stoker's Dracula.

Movie: 🎬🎬🎬 **DVD:** 🎬🎬🎬

Columbia Tristar Home Video (Cat #51419, UPC #043396514195). Widescreen (1.85:1) letterboxed; full frame. Dolby Digital 5.1. $27.98. Keepcase. *LANG:* English; French; Spanish. *SUB:* Spanish; Korean. *CAP:* English. *FEATURES:* 52 chapter links.

1992 (R) 128m/C Gary Oldman, Winona Ryder, Anthony Hopkins, Keanu Reeves, Richard E. Grant, Cary Elwes, Bill Campbell, Sadie Frost, Tom Waits; **D:** Francis Ford Coppola; **W:** Jim V. Hart; **C:** Michael Ballhaus. *AWARDS:* Academy Awards '92: Best Cos-

tume Design, Best Makeup, Best Sound Effects Editing; *NOM:* Academy Awards '92: Best Art Direction/Set Direction.

Dracula, Prince of Darkness

The second film in Hammer's successful series begins with the ending of the first, wherein the Count is reduced to a shoebox full of ashes. Flash forward ten years—about as long as it took the producers to coax Christopher Lee back into the cape. The rest follows one of the studio's favorite formulas with two couples innocently wandering into the monster's lair. An energetic abbot, Father Sandor (Keir) takes over the Van Helsing role as head vampire hunter. The best moments are the reconstitution and the imaginative ending. The small cast is excellent. The women are classy and about as sexy as the 1965 screen would allow. Barbara Shelley's transformation from a proper Victorian lady into a red-hot vampire mama is a delight. Lee's silent performance is one of his strongest. On the commentary track, he and costars Barbara Shelley, Francis Matthews, and Suzan Farmer sound like old friends sharing garrulous memories of the production. Of course, the DVD image and sound are first-rate. The two-sided disc puts all the extras, except the commentary track, on the second side. *—MM* **AKA:** The Bloody Scream of Dracula; Disciple of Dracula; Revenge of Dracula.

Movie: 🎬🎬🎬 **DVD:** 🎬🎬🎬🎬

Anchor Bay (Cat #DV10502, UPC #013131050295). Widescreen (2.35:1) letterboxed. Dolby Digital Mono. $29.98. Keepcase. *LANG:* English; French. *FEATURES:* Commentary: Lee, Shelley, Matthews, Farmer • Home movie shot during production with commentary by stars • Theatrical trailers • *World of Hammer* episode, "Dracula and the Undead."

1966 90m/C *GB* Christopher Lee, Barbara Shelley, Andrew Keir, Francis Matthews, Suzan Farmer, Charles Tingwell, Thorley Walters, Philip Latham; **D:** Terence Fisher; **W:** John Sansom, John (Anthony Hinds) Elder; **C:** Michael Reed; **M:** James Bernard.

Dragnet

Semi-parody of the vintage 1960s television cop show. Sgt. Joe Friday's straitlaced nephew (Aykroyd) and his sloppy partner (Hanks) take on the seamy crime life of Los Angeles. Neither Aykroyd nor Hanks can save this big-budget but lackluster spoof that's full of holes. Mismatch of sharpness between foregrounds and backgrounds lower the rating on this DVD substantially. At times the difference seems so great that you feel like you're playing a videogame, not watching a movie. The quality does appear to get a little better past the half-way point of the disc. Blacks are good but the color bleeds adding to the lack of clarity. The Dolby Surround has good separation, crisp highs, and average low end. —JO

Movie: 🎬🎬 **DVD:** 🎬▶

Universal Studios Home Video (Cat #20392, UPC #025192039225). Widescreen (1.77:1) anamorphic. Dolby Surround. $24.98. Keepcase. *LANG:* English (DS); Spanish (DS); French (DS). *SUB:* Spanish. *CAP:* English. *FEATURES:* 16 chapter links • Theatrical trailer • Cast and filmmaker bios • Production notes • Web links.

1987 (PG-13) 106m/C Dan Aykroyd, Tom Hanks, Christopher Plummer, Harry (Henry) Morgan, Elizabeth Ashley, Dabney Coleman, Alexandra Paul, Kathleen Freeman, Jack O'Halloran; *D:* Tom Mankiewicz; *W:* Tom Mankiewicz, Alan Zweibel, Dan Aykroyd; *C:* Matthew F. Leonetti; *M:* Ira Newborn.

The Dragon Fist

Early Jackie Chan entry is standard martial arts with an historical Chinese setting. Jackie is Juan, who must avenge his master's death at the hands of another master, etc., etc. The fights are static and unimaginative with only a few flashes of the acrobatic brilliance that has made Jackie Chan an international star. Overall, the disc looks better than some Hong Kong imports but the image is pale with deeply shadowed interiors. No concluding outtakes. Actually the short interview with Jackie is more interesting than the film itself. —MM

Movie: 🎬🎬 **DVD:** 🎬🎬

Simitar Entertainment (Cat #7258, UPC #082551725823). Full frame. Dolby Digital Stereo. $14.98. Keepcase. *LANG:* English; Cantonese. *FEATURES:* 8 chapter links • Jackie Chan interview, filmography, and thumbnail bio.

1980 77m/C Jackie Chan, Nora Miao, James Tien, Henry Zhou; *D:* Lo Wei; *W:* Tang Pakee; *C:* Shek Hak; *M:* Steven Ganji.

Dragon from Shaolin

Young Little Dragon (Sik Siu Loong) is sent from the monastery to find Buddha in the real world. He meets a street urchin (Fok Siu Man) and they have many grand adventures. Yes, it's kid fu. Adult star Yuen Biao isn't upstaged too often. The DVD image blurs during medium-fast pans, but otherwise is acceptable for a mid-budget martial arts flick. Children are the target audience. —MM

Movie: 🎬🎬 **DVD:** 🎬🎬

Tai Seng Video Marketing (Cat #60504, UPC #601643605043). Widescreen letterboxed. $29.95. Keepcase. *LANG:* Cantonese; Mandarin; English. *SUB:* English.

1996 89m/C Yuen Biao, Sik Siu Loong, Fok Siu Man; *D:* Ha Sau Hin.

Dragon: The Bruce Lee Story

Entertaining, inspiring account of the life of Chinese-American martial arts legend Bruce Lee. Jason Scott Lee (no relation) is great as the talented artist, exuding his joy of life and gentle spirit, before his mysterious brain disorder death at the age of 32. Ironically, this release coincided with son Brandon's accidental death on a movie set. The martial arts sequences in *Dragon* are extraordinary, but there's also romance as Lee meets and marries his wife (Holly, who acquits herself well). This DVD has an excellent supplemental section filled with facts about both the film and its subject, Bruce Lee. The transfer is adequate, but isn't as impressive than the earlier laserdisc release. The picture remains fairly sharp throughout and there's not a lot of grain. Colors are very good, deep and vibrant with only a little bleed during a screenful of red. Contrast levels are not bad and the brightness is at all times easy on the eyes. The sound has been slightly improved from the laserdisc, giving a boost to the deep clean bass that drives many of the action sequences. —JO

Movie: 🎬🎬🎬 **DVD:** 🎬🎬🎬

Universal Studios Home Video (Cat #20224, UPC #025192022425). Widescreen (2.35:1) letterboxed. Dolby Surround. $34.98. Keepcase. *LANG:* English; French. *SUB:* Spanish. *CAP:* English. *FEATURES:* 33 chapter links • Theatrical trailers • Cast and filmmaker bios • Production notes • 5 sets of storyboards • Jason Scott Lee screen test • Featurette • Production and Bruce Lee Photos • Bruce Lee interview • Promotional materials.

1993 (PG-13) 121m/C Jason Scott Lee, Lauren Holly, Robert Wagner, Michael Learned, Nancy Kwan, Kay Tong Lim, Sterling Macer, Ric Young, Sven-Ole Thorsen; *D:* Rob Cohen; *W:* Edward Khmara, John Raffo, Rob Cohen; *C:* David Eggby; *M:* Randy Edelman. *AWARDS: NOM:* MTV Movie Awards '94: Breakthrough Performance (Lee).

Dragonheart (SE)

O.K., get past the fact that Connery's Scottish burr is coming out of the teeth-filled mouth of an 18-foot tall, 43-foot long dragon and you'll be well on your way to enjoying this 10th-century fantasy. Knightly Bowen (Quaid) is the one-time mentor of evil-hearted King Einon (Thewlis) and it's up to him, Draco the dragon, feisty Kim (Meyer), and some peasants to band together to free themselves from the king. There are some slow spots but Bowen and Draco make for an amusing pairing and even with the enhanced clarity of DVD, the dragon effects look real. Sound is very good. —MM

Movie: 🎬🎬▶ **DVD:** 🎬🎬🎬

Universal Studios Home Video (Cat #20161). Widescreen (2.35:1) anamorphic. Dolby Digital 5.1 Surround Stereo. $34.98. Keepcase. *LANG:* English; French; Spanish. *SUB:* Spanish. *CAP:* English. *FEATURES:* Commentary: Rob Cohen • "Making of" featurette • Production notes • Trailer.

1996 (PG-13) 103m/C Dennis Quaid, David Thewlis, Pete Postlethwaite, Dina Meyer, Julie Christie, Jason Isaacs, Brian Thompson, Wolf Christian, Terry O'Neill; *D:* Rob Cohen; *W:* Charles Edward Pogue; *C:* David Eggby; *M:* Randy Edelman; *V:* Sean Connery, John Gielgud. *AWARDS: NOM:* Academy Awards '96: Best Visual Effects.

Dragons Forever

A big-time lawyer (Chan) is persuaded to work against a gangster (Yuen Wah) who wants to take over a site used by local fishermen. Complications arise when Jackie falls for the beautiful cousin (Pauline Yeung) of his client. A comic fight involving the three heroes—Chan, Biao, and director Hung—is the big finish. This is one of the best films that Chan made before he became an international star, and the violence in some moments may be a bit too strong for some of his newer fans. On DVD, some heavy grain is visible in dim, yellowish interiors. Overall, the stars are better than the image. The sound is good. —MM *AKA:* Dragon Forever.

Movie: 🎬🎬🎬 **DVD:** 🎬🎬▶

Tai Seng Video Marketing (Cat #5095, UPC #4895024900544). Widescreen letterboxed. Dolby Digital 5.1 Surround Stereo. $49.95. Keepcase. *LANG:* Cantonese; Mandarin. *SUB:* Traditional & Simplified Chinese; English; Bahasa Indonesian & Malaysian; Thai; Korean; Vietnamese. *FEATURES:* 8 chapter links • Thumbnail biographies of Chan, Hung, and Biao • Theatrical trailer.

1988 88m/C *CH* Jackie Chan, Yuen Biao, Sammo Hung, Pauline Yeung, Yuen Wah; *D:* Sammo Hung, Corey Yuen; *W:* Roy Szeto, Gordon Chan.

Dragons of the Orient

This curious hybrid is essentially a documentary about the history of Chinese martial arts and their various incarnations on-screen. It visits key historical sites but relies on footage of star Jet Li practicing, and an alleged 100-year-old kung fu master giving a demonstration. Throughout, the image is dim and grainy, not comparable to the best Asian imports. —MM

Movie: 🎬🎬▶ **DVD:** 🎬🎬

Tai Seng Video Marketing (Cat #34494, UPC #601643344942). Widescreen letterboxed. $49.95. Keepcase. *LANG:* English. *FEATURES:* 12 chapter links • Trailers for seven Jet Li films.

1988 88m/C Jet Li, Terry Fan, Yang Ching, Wang Chun; *D:* Rocky Law.

The Draughtsman's Contract

In England, 1694, an artist named Neville (Higgins) is hired to draw pictures of a nobleman's estate. A curious relationship develops with the man's wife (Suzman), but that doesn't begin to describe this perverse, surreal period piece. It also involves murder and a living statue. Setting and historical detail are carefully maintained. On DVD, the dark, heavy clothes are unusually well detailed, but many of the interiors are deliberately under-illuminated with candles and so the film has a softened focus in those scenes. The disc is an intriguing introduction to Greenaway, a challenging director. —*MM*

Movie: 🦴🦴🦴 **DVD:** 🦴🦴▶

WinStar Home Entertainment (Cat #FLV5196). Widescreen (1.66:1) letterboxed. Mono. $29.98. Keepcase. *LANG:* English. *FEATURES:* 9 chapter links. **1982 (R) 103m/C** *GB* Anthony Higgins, Janet Suzman, Anne Louise Lambert, Hugh Fraser; **D:** Peter Greenaway; **W:** Peter Greenaway; **C:** Sacha Vierny; **M:** Michael Nyman.

Dream Lover

Divorced architect Ray (Spader) meets and marries Lena (Amick), beautiful and seemingly perfect, who nonetheless warns him that she's just your average mixed-up gal. That's quite an understatement and the revelation of its dimensions are the basis for a fine mystery that's really much better than your run-of-the-mill "erotic thriller" video premiere. Cast is excellent and the story will keep you guessing.

Movie: 🦴🦴🦴 **DVD:** NYR

USA Home Entertainment (Cat #633113). Dolby Digital Surround Stereo. $29.95. **1993 (R) 103m/C** James Spader, Madchen Amick, Frederic Lehne, Bess Armstrong, Larry Miller, Kathleen York, Blair Tefkin, Scott Coffey, William Shockley, Clyde Kusatsu; **D:** Nicholas Kazan; **W:** Nicholas Kazan; **C:** Jean-Yves Escoffier; **M:** Christopher Young.

Dream Lovers

The familiar theme of reincarnated lovers gets the Hong Kong treatment. Song Yu (Chow Yun-Fat) is an orchestra leader who cannot understand the seizures that overpower him. At an art exhibit he meets Yuet-Heung (Brigitte Lin) and they connect with their past lives. But what about her husband and his girlfriend (Cher Yeung)? The DVD image is slightly faint throughout with grainy night scenes and some bleeding reds. Sound is adequate. —*MM AKA:* Meng zhong ren.

Movie: 🦴🦴 **DVD:** 🦴🦴

Tai Seng Video Marketing (Cat #MS/DVD/054/99, UPC #4895017000 541). Widescreen letterboxed. Dolby Digital 5.1 Surround Stereo. $49.95. Keepcase. *LANG:* Cantonese; Mandarin. *SUB:* Traditional & Simplified Chinese; English; Thai; Vietnamese; Spanish. *FEATURES:* 9 chapter links ▪ Synopsis ▪ Theatrical trailers. **1986 95m/C** *CH* Cher Yeung, Chow Yun-Fat, Lin Ching-hsai, Brigitte Lin; **D:** Tony Au; **W:** Yau Da Ah-Pin, Manfred Wong; **C:** Bill Wong.

The Dreamlife of Angels

Deceptively simple debut of director Zonca follows the friendship between two opportunistic working class French women,

Marie (Regnier) and Isa (Bouchez). Tensions arise between the two when Marie becomes involved with brutal nightclub owner Chriss (Colin). Zonca had his female leads live together during filming to create the realistic bickering. The DVD image is fine, but the character-driven story does not depend on complex visuals, so the disc is probably not that much better than VHS tape. —*MM AKA:* La Vie Revee des Anges.

Movie: 🦴🦴🦴 **DVD:** 🦴🦴🦴

Columbia Tristar Home Video (Cat #04012, UPC #043396040120). Widescreen (1.87:1) letterboxed. Dolby Digital Stereo. $28.95. Keepcase. *LANG:* French. *SUB:* English; French; Spanish. *FEATURES:* 28 chapter links ▪ Production notes. **1998 113m/C** *FR* Elodie Bouchez, Natacha Regnier, Gregoire Colin, Jo Prestia, Patrick Mercado; **D:** Erick Zonca; **W:** Erick Zonca, Roger Bohbot; **C:** Agnes Godard; **M:** Yann Thiersen. *AWARDS:* Cesar Awards '99: Best Actress (Bouchez), Best Film.

Dreams of Gold: The Mel Fisher Story

The story of real-life treasure hunter Fisher (Robertson) and his search for the Spanish galleon *Atocha* looks like it was made for television with carefully limited production values. The tone is more akin to a sitcom with breezy conflicts and a light banter. The underwater scenes are brightly lit and clear. The overall DVD image quality is fine but the film itself is nothing special. —*MM*

Movie: 🦴🦴 **DVD:** 🦴🦴▶

Simitar Entertainment (Cat #7278, UPC #082551727827). Full frame. PCM Stereo. $7.98. Keepcase. *LANG:* English. *FEATURES:* 8 chapter links ▪ Filmographies of Cliff Robertson and Loretta Swit ▪ Production factoids. **1986 (PG) 87m/C** Cliff Robertson, Loretta Swit, Ed O'Ross, Scott Paulin, Jennifer Runyon; **D:** James Goldstone; **W:** Stanford Whitmore; **C:** Eric Van Haren Noman; **M:** Ernest Gold.

Dreamscape (SE)

When a doctor teaches a young psychic (Quaid) how to enter into other people's dreams in order to end their nightmares, a corrupt, high-ranking government official (Plummer) wants to use the psychic for evil purposes. The special effects are far more convincing than the one-man-saves-the-country-with-his-psychic-powers plot. Somebody must really like this movie, however, because the DVD is fully loaded—and then some. First, the anamorphic video transfer is hampered only by defects in the original source materials. Look close and you'll see dirt, debris, and other blemishes present on the film element used for the video transfer. But the anamorphic treatment ensures plenty of lines of resolution for widescreen owners. Dolby Digital, Dolby ProLogic, and DTS Surround enthusiasts all will appreciate the soundtrack options.

The extras on this "special edition" are plentiful—more bountiful, in fact, than found on so-called special editions of some of the best movies. Just look at how fancy and cool the animated menus are. —*MB*

Movie: 🦴🦴▶ **DVD:** 🦴🦴🦴▶

Image Entertainment (Cat #ID6745CQDVD, UPC #014381674521). Widescreen (1.85:1) anamorphic. Dolby Digital 5.1; Dolby Digital 2.0; DTS 5.1. $24.99. Snapper. *LANG:* English. *FEATURES:* 20 chapter links ▪ Commentary: producer, writer, and effects artist ▪ Production stills ▪ Special effects makeup test footage. **1984 (PG-13) 99m/C** Dennis Quaid, Max von Sydow, Christopher Plummer, Eddie Albert, Kate Capshaw, David Patrick Kelly, George Wendt, Jana Taylor; **D:** Joseph Ruben; **W:** Chuck Russell; **C:** Brian Tufano; **M:** Maurice Jarre.

Driller Killer

Frustrated artist goes insane and kills off Manhattan residents with a carpenter's drill. In his rambling, confused commentary track, director Ferrara admits that the film was made on weekends in 1977 and 1978 with breaks in the production. The ultra-low budget horror is oppressively dark, dirty, and poorly lit, and so it looks no better on DVD than it ever has. Apparently, the ending of this "collector's edition"—where the screen turns red over the characters' dialogue—is incorrect because Ferrara simply curses and ends his pointless chatter. —*MM*

Movie: woof **DVD:** woof

Cult Epics (Cat #DVD004, UPC #0063390010042). Full frame. $34.95. Keepcase. *LANG:* English. *SUB:* Spanish; French; Dutch. *FEATURES:* Theatrical trailer ▪ Commentary: director Abel Ferrara ▪ Director's cut (long version) ▪ Director filmography. **1974 (R) 78m/C** Abel Ferrara, Jimmy (Abel Ferrara) Laine, Carolyn Marz, Bob DeFrank, Peter Yellen, Baybi Day, Harry Schultz; **D:** Abel Ferrara; **W:** Nicholas St. John; **C:** Ken Kelsch; **M:** Joe Delia.

Drive

Toby Wong (Dacascos) is a technologically enhanced martial artist on the run from biotech corporate hitmen. Malik (Hardison) is a would-be song writer who winds up driving him from San Francisco to Los Angeles. The stunt work and action scenes are handled with comic-book exaggeration. The image looks fine on DVD, though the predominance of black clothing on the generic bad guys gives the whole film a low-rent, imitative feeling. —*MM*

Movie: 🦴🦴▶ **DVD:** 🦴🦴▶

Simitar Entertainment (Cat #7240, UPC #082551724024). Full frame. Dolby Digital Stereo; Dolby Digital 5.1 Surround Stereo. $19.98. Keepcase. *LANG:* English. *FEATURES:* 8 chapter links ▪ Production factoids.

1996 (R) 99m/C Mark Dacascos, Kadeem Hardison, Brittany Murphy, John Pyper-Ferguson, Tracey Walter, James Shigeta, Massaya Kato; **D:** Steve Wang.

Driving Miss Daisy

Tender and sincere portrayal of a 25-year friendship between an aging Jewish woman (Tandy) and the black chauffeur (Freeman) forced upon her by her son. Humorous, thought provoking, skillfully acted and directed, it subtly explores the effects of prejudice in the South. The development of Aykroyd as a top-notch character actor is further evidenced here. Part of the fun is watching the changes in fashion and auto design. The image quality of this DVD varies, depending on the amount of detail and level of brightness on the screen. Though the picture starts out relatively grain-free, it seems to pick up as you get deeper into the film. For the most part the colors are accurate but there is considerable red bleed. Contrast and brightness levels are good. The soundtrack has excellent fidelity and dynamics along with crisp highs and deep, clean lows. Surround tracks contribute little more than occasional ambience. —*JO*
Movie: ♪♪♪ **DVD:** ♪♪▶
Warner Home Video, Inc. (Cat #11931, UPC #085391193128). Full frame. Dolby Surround. $19.98. Snapper. *LANG:* English; French. *SUB:* Spanish; French. *CAP:* English. *FEATURES:* 18 chapter links • Theatrical trailer • Production notes.
1989 (PG) 99m/C Jessica Tandy, Morgan Freeman, Dan Aykroyd, Esther Rolle, Patti LuPone; **D:** Bruce Beresford; **W:** Alfred Uhry; **C:** Peter James; **M:** Hans Zimmer. *AWARDS:* Academy Awards '89: Best Actress (Tandy), Best Adapted Screenplay, Best Makeup, Best Picture; British Academy Awards '90: Best Actress (Tandy); Golden Globe Awards '90: Best Actor—Musical/Comedy (Freeman), Best Actress—Musical/Comedy (Tandy), Best Film—Musical/Comedy; National Board of Review Awards '89: Best Actor (Freeman); Writers Guild of America '89: Best Adapted Screenplay; *NOM:* Academy Awards '89: Best Actor (Freeman), Best Art Direction/Set Decoration, Best Costume Design, Best Film Editing, Best Supporting Actor (Aykroyd).

Drop Dead Gorgeous

Gladys (Alley) is determined that her daughter (Richards) will win the Sarah Rose Cosmetics American Teen Princess Pageant in Mount Rose, MN (pop. 5,076). Other contestants are mysteriously eliminated, leaving Amber (Dunst) the main competition. When her mom (Barkin) is injured in a trailer-park explosion, Amber presses on. Using a mock-documentary framework, director Jann takes a broad, parodic approach to material that has been handled with much sharper wit on the big screen in *Smile*, and on the small screen by *The Simpsons*. The DVD faithfully captures the film's condescending attitude toward middle-class life in the hinter-

lands—the bright, off-putting colors; the cluttered rooms; and beauty contest tackiness. —*MM* **AKA:** Dairy Queens.
Movie: ♪♪ **DVD:** ♪♪♪
New Line Home Video (Cat #N4927, UPC #794043492723). Widescreen (1.85:1) letterboxed; full frame. Dolby Digital 5.1 Surround Stereo; Dolby Digital Stereo. $24.98. Snapper. *LANG:* English. *CAP:* English. *FEATURES:* 22 chapter links • Cast and crew thumbnail biographies • Theatrical trailer.
1999 (PG-13) 97m/C Denise Richards, Kirsten Dunst, Kirstie Alley, Ellen Barkin, Allison Janney, Sam McMurray, Mindy Sterling, Amy Adams, Tara Redepenning, Sara Stewart, Shannon Nelson, Matt Malloy, Michael McShane, Brooke Bushman, Will Sasso; **Cameos:** Adam West; **D:** Michael Patrick Jann; **W:** Lona Williams; **C:** Michael Spiller; **M:** Mark Mothersbaugh.

Drop Dead Rock

Rock-crime-comedy with Adam Ant.
Movie: NYR **DVD:** NYR
Pioneer Entertainment (Cat #10293). Full frame. Dolby Digital Surround Stereo. $24.98. Keepcase.
1995 93m/C Adam Ant, Deborah Harry, Soshana Ami, Eddie Brill, Ian Maynard; **D:** Adam Dubin; **W:** Adam Dubin, Ric Menello; **C:** David Hausen; **M:** John Hill.

DROP Squad

Buford Jamison Jr. (La Salle) is a black adman whose commercials are based on grotesque racial stereotypes. His sister thinks that he has strayed so far from his roots that she calls upon the DROP (Deprogramming and Restoration of Pride) Squad to kidnap him and show him the error of his ways. The provocative premise never quite delivers the goods, but considering that Spike Lee, whose work for Nike has been criticized along similar lines, is executive producer, perhaps that is inevitable. On DVD, the image is clear but not spectacular, and it shouldn't be. This is a mid-budget production made on location in Atlanta and so it doesn't need a glossy polish. Sound is acceptable. —*MM*
Movie: ♪♪ **DVD:** ♪♪▶
Universal Studios Home Video (Cat #20517, UPC #025192051722). Widescreen letterboxed. Dolby Digital Surround Stereo. $24.98. Keepcase. *LANG:* English. *SUB:* French; Spanish. *CAP:* English. *FEATURES:* 18 chapter links • Production notes • Theatrical trailer • Cast and crew thumbnail biographies.
1994 (R) 88m/C Eriq La Salle, Vondie Curtis-Hall, Ving Rhames, Kasi Lemmons, Vanessa Williams, Nicole Powell, Afemo Omilami, Spike Lee; **D:** David Johnson; **W:** David Johnson, Butch Robinson, David Taylor; **C:** Ken Kelsch; **M:** Michael Bearden.

Drop Zone

Routine action-thriller finds U.S. Marshal Pete Nessip (Snipes) and his brother Terry (Warner) assigned to protect drug cartel

snitch Earl Leedy (Jeter). Their plane is hijacked by Moncrief (Busey) who parachutes off with Leedy. Nessip must go undercover in the world of sky-diving with the aid of ex-con cutie Jessie (Butler). The plot holes would accommodate a 747 but the stunts are good and Snipes is never less than professional.
Movie: ♪♪▶ **DVD:** NYR
Paramount Home Video (Cat #327347). Widescreen (2.35:1) letterboxed. Dolby Digital 5.1 Surround Stereo; Dolby Digital Surround Stereo. $29.99. Keepcase. *LANG:* English; French.
1994 (R) 101m/C Wesley Snipes, Gary Busey, Yancy Butler, Michael Jeter, Corin "Corky" Nemec, Kyle Secor, Luca Bercovici, Malcolm Jamal Warner, Rex Linn, Grace Zabriskie, Sam Hennings, Claire Stansfield, Mickey Jones, Andy Romano; **D:** John Badham; **W:** John Bishop, Peter Barsocchini; **C:** Roy Wagner; **M:** Hans Zimmer.

Drugstore Cowboy

Gus Van Sant takes a grim, uncompromising look at a pack of early '70s drugstore-robbing junkies as they look to score. Brushes with the law and tragedy encourage them to change their ways but the trap seems impossible to shake. The well-crafted work reflects the "me generation" era though some will see it as a glamorization of drug use.
Movie: ♪♪♪▶ **DVD:** NYR
Artisan Entertainment (Cat #60497). Widescreen (1.85:1) letterboxed. Dolby Digital Stereo. $29.98. *FEATURES:* Commentary: Van Sant and Dillon • Theatrical trailers • Production notes.
1989 (R) 100m/C Matt Dillon, Kelly Lynch, James Remar, James LeGros, Heather Graham, William S. Burroughs, Beah Richards, Grace Zabriskie, Max Perlich; **D:** Gus Van Sant; **W:** Gus Van Sant, Daniel Yost; **C:** Robert Yeoman; **M:** Elliot Goldenthal. *AWARDS:* Independent Spirit Awards '90: Best Actor (Dillon), Best Cinematography, Best Screenplay, Best Supporting Actor (Perlich); Los Angeles Film Critics Association Awards '89: Best Screenplay; New York Film Critics Awards '89: Best Screenplay; National Society of Film Critics Awards '89: Best Director (Van Sant), Best Film, Best Screenplay.

Drunks

Ensemble pity-party may be an accurate representation of an Alcoholics Anonymous meeting, but it's boring drama. Jim (Lewis) has gone on a bender after the death of his wife; Rachel's (Wiest) an overworked doctor; Becky (Dunaway) is a divorcee with problem kids; Brenda (Hamilton) is an HIV-positive addict; Joseph (Rollins) is haunted by his son's death. There's more and everyone gets a chance to ham it up in the spotlight. That's also where the film's roots in the stage play *Blackout* are most apparent. On DVD, their monologues are delivered with adequate clarity of image and sound. The few exteriors are more troublesome.

In an introductory pan across a busy New York street, moving vehicles almost dissolve. On the big screen, tape or disc, this is simply a bad movie. —*MM*
Movie: 🎞 **DVD:** 🎞🎞
WinStar Home Entertainment (Cat #FLV5152, UPC #72091751522). Widescreen (1.85:1) letterboxed. Stereo. $24.98. Keepcase. *LANG:* English. *FEATURES:* 8 chapter links • Theatrical trailer • Production notes and credits • Filmographies. DVD-ROM contains a weblink.
1996 (R) 88m/C Richard Lewis, Faye Dunaway, Dianne Wiest, Lisa Gay Hamilton, Howard E. Rollins Jr., Parker Posey, Spalding Gray, Amanda Plummer, Calista Flockhart, George Martin, Anna Thomson; **D:** Peter Cohn; **W:** Gary Lennon; **C:** Peter Hawkins; **M:** Joe Delia.

Duck Soup
The Marx Brothers' satiric masterpiece, which failed at the boxoffice in its initial release, has found millions of fans over the decades. Rufus T. Firefly (Groucho) becomes the leader of Freedonia, "land of the free and brave!" and hires Harpo and Chico as spies. Zeppo plays the love-sick tenor in this, his last film with his brothers. The whole picture is packed with anarchic irreverence and the targets—government, war, fascism, patriotism—certainly deserve the treatment. On DVD, chapter 11, which finds Chico and Harpo disguised as Groucho, may be their funniest moment. Yes, that's the famous mirror scene but the rest is wonderful, too. Overall, the film looks fine, but the real improvement comes in the sound. Even in mono, the dialogue is completely crisp and understandable. One of the true greats. —*MM*
Movie: 🎞🎞🎞🎞 **DVD:** 🎞🎞🎞🎞
Image Entertainment (Cat #ID4223USDVD, UPC #014381422320). Full frame. Dolby Digital Mono. $29.99. Snapper. *LANG:* English. *FEATURES:* 16 chapter links.
1933 70m/B Groucho Marx, Chico Marx, Harpo Marx, Zeppo Marx, Louis Calhern, Margaret Dumont, Edgar Kennedy, Raquel Torres, Leonid Kinskey, Charles Middleton; **D:** Leo McCarey; **W:** Harry Ruby, Nat Perrin, Bert Kalmar, Arthur Sheekman; **C:** Henry Sharp; **M:** Harry Ruby, Bert Kalmar. *AWARDS:* American Film Institute (AFI) '98: Top 100, National Film Registry '90.

Dudley Do-Right
Lightning does not strike twice when Brendan Fraser tries another of Jay Ward's cartoon characters. (The first was *George of the Jungle*.) He simply doesn't have as much to work with in physical terms as the straitlaced Mountie. The same could be said of Sarah Jessica Parker's Nell Fenwick. Only Alfred Molina is able to plumb the depths of Snidely Whiplash's comic villain. Individual bits, such as the Indian "Riverdance" routine and cameos by Regis and Kathy Lee, are funny but the whole thing just doesn't work. Visually, the DVD is about the same as a VHS tape. —*MM*

Movie: 🎞🎞▸ **DVD:** 🎞🎞▸
Universal Studios Home Video (Cat #20707, UPC #025192070723). Widescreen (2.35:1) letterboxed; full frame. Dolby Digital 5.1 Surround Stereo; Dolby Surround Stereo; DTS. $24.98. Keepcase. *LANG:* English; French. *CAP:* English. *FEATURES:* 18 chapter links • Production notes • Cast and crew thumbnail biographies • Theatrical trailer • Fractured Fairy Tale, "The Phox, the Box and the Lox" • Extra DVD-ROM features.
1999 (PG) 75m/C Brendan Fraser, Sarah Jessica Parker, Alfred Molina, Robert Prosky, Eric Idle, Alex Rocco, Jack Kehler, Louis Mustillo, Regis Philbin, Kathie Lee Gifford; **D:** Hugh Wilson; **W:** Hugh Wilson; **C:** Donald E. Thorin; **M:** Steve Dorff; **Nar:** Corey Burton.

Duel in the Sun
David O. Selznick production overinflates a minor western story about Pearl (Jones), a vivacious half-breed Indian girl who lives on a powerful dynastic ranch and comes between two brothers (Peck and Cotten). Though ridiculed as *Lust in the Dust* at the time of its initial release, the film has aged agreeably. On DVD, the bright colors are so vivid that they appear too thick by today's standards. The no-frills disc boasts a fine image transfer. —*MM*
Movie: 🎞🎞🎞 **DVD:** 🎞🎞🎞
Anchor Bay (Cat #DV1065, UPC #013131065695). Full frame. Dolby Digital Stereo. $24.99. Keepcase. *LANG:* English. *FEATURES:* 17 chapter links.
1946 130m/C Gregory Peck, Jennifer Jones, Joseph Cotten, Lionel Barrymore, Lillian Gish, Butterfly McQueen, Harry Carey Sr., Walter Huston, Charles Bickford, Herbert Marshall; **D:** King Vidor; **W:** Oliver H.P. Garrett, David O. Selznick; **M:** Dimitri Tiomkin; **C:** Ray Rennahan. *AWARDS: NOM:* Academy Awards '46: Best Actress (Jones), Best Supporting Actress (Gish).

Dumb & Dumber
Moronic limo driver Lloyd (Carrey) and his equally dense pal Harry (Daniels), who has converted his van into a weirdly hilarious dog-mobile, go from Providence, Rhode Island, to Aspen to return a briefcase full of cash to the beautiful socialite (Holly) Lloyd has fallen for. First problem: Where's Aspen? Either California or France, they think, but hit the road anyway with bumbling bad guys in pursuit. The humor is either slapstick or gross-out, with bathrooms and bodily functions featured prominently. This brand of comedy is Carrey's stock and trade; Daniels is equally unrestrained, for better or worse. Since the Farrelly brothers admit that they hardly know which end of the camera to point, the DVD is not particularly strong visually. For a road picture, the landscapes have a muddy quality, though the image appears sharper on disc than it did in theatres. This kind of movie depends on the cast and with both full and widescreen versions

available, fans can choose which suits their home system. —*MM*
Movie: 🎞🎞▸ **DVD:** 🎞🎞🎞
New Line Home Video (Cat #N4036, UPC #794043403620). Full frame; widescreen (1.85:1) letterboxed. Dolby Surround 5.1 (English); Dolby Stereo (French). $25.00. Snapper. *LANG:* English; French. *SUB:* English; French; Spanish. *CAP:* English. *FEATURES:* 24 chapter links • Domestic and international trailers • Background profiles on stars • Photo gallery.
1994 (PG-13) 110m/C Jim Carrey, Jeff Daniels, Lauren Holly, Teri Garr, Karen Duffy, Mike Starr, Charles Rocket, Victoria Rowell, Felton Perry, Harland Williams; **D:** Peter Farrelly; **W:** Peter Farrelly, Bennett Yellin, Bobby Farrelly; **C:** Mark Irwin; **M:** Todd Rundgren. *AWARDS:* MTV Movie Awards '95: Best Comedic Performance (Carrey), Best Kiss (Jim Carrey/Lauren Holly); Blockbuster Entertainment Awards '96: Comedy Actor, Video (Carrey); *NOM:* MTV Movie Awards '95: Best On-Screen Duo (Jim Carrey/Jeff Daniels).

Dumb Luck in Vegas
A legitimate contender for worst-movie-ever-made richly deserves the no-extras treatment it receives on DVD. The vanity project from Joey Travolta concerns a tacky lounge singer involved with mobsters. It's poorly lit and unfunny, lacking even the most basic features, such as chapters. And why should it have them? —*MM*
Movie: woof **DVD:** woof
Simitar Entertainment (Cat #7214, UPC #082551721429). Full frame. PCM Stereo. $7.98. Keepcase. *LANG:* English.
1997 98m/C Joey Travolta, Jeff Conaway, Frank Sivero, David Proval, Robert Gallo, Kelly Emberg, John Landis; **D:** Joey Travolta, Raymond Martino; **W:** Joey Travolta, Rich Dillon.

Dune
Even those who are not *Dune* fans had hoped that someday a full-length version of David Lynch's film would arrive on home video. Reportedly, his original version of Frank Herbert's massive novel was too long for theatrical release and was seriously edited. When it was re-edited in a longer version for broadcast television, Lynch was so dissatisfied with the result that he had his name removed. DVD would be the perfect medium to restore his original intention, but that hasn't happened yet. Looking at this screw-loose space opera again, the humorous aspects have become even stronger, perhaps because we're more familiar with Lynch's wry tone. (Since Lynch is such an articulate filmmaker, a commentary track would have been welcome.) Visually, the disc is fine. The intricacies of the sets, props, costumes, and bizarre makeup are clearly revealed, even in the darker moments. Some of the effects are a little dated, but given the film's operatic excesses, that's hardly a flaw. The thunderous sound is fine, too. —*MM*

Movie: ♫♫♫ **DVD:** ♫♫♫
Universal Studios Home Video (Cat #20184, UPC #025192018428). Widescreen (2.35:1) letterboxed. Dolby Digital 5.1 Surround Stereo; Dolby Surround Stereo. $24.98. Keepcase. *LANG:* English; French; Spanish. *SUB:* Spanish. *CAP:* English. *FEATURES:* 16 chapter links ▪ Production notes ▪ Cast and crew thumbnail biographies ▪ Theatrical trailer.
1984 (PG-13) 137m/C Kyle MacLachlan, Francesca Annis, Jose Ferrer, Sting, Max von Sydow, Juergen Prochnow, Linda Hunt, Freddie Jones, Dean Stockwell, Virginia Madsen, Brad Dourif, Kenneth McMillan, Silvana Mangano, Jack Nance, Sian Phillips, Paul Smith, Richard Jordan, Everett McGill, Sean Young, Patrick Stewart; *D:* David Lynch; *W:* David Lynch; *C:* Freddie Francis; *M:* Brian Eno. *AWARDS: NOM:* Academy Awards '84: Best Sound.

Earth Girls Are Easy

Valley girl Valerie is having a bad week: first she catches her fiance with another woman, then she breaks a nail, then furry aliens land in her swimming pool. When the aliens are temporarily stranded, she decides to make amends by giving them a head-to-toe makeover. Devoid of their excessive hairiness, the handsome trio of fun-loving extraterrestrials set out to experience the Southern California lifestyle. Sometimes hilarious sci-fi/musical featuring bouncy shtick and a gleeful dismantling of modern culture. There's lots of color on this DVD and it all looks great. The colors are vibrant and bleed-free. The picture is very sharp and neither grain nor artifacts are of any concern. Contrast is excellent, the brightness level is comfortable, and the blacks are true. The only flaw on this visually near-perfect DVD is an occasional herringbone pattern. The Dolby Surround is very good with crisp, clear highs, and a good low end that gives great backbone to the music. —*JO*
Movie: ♫♫♫ **DVD:** ♫♫♫▪
Artisan Entertainment (Cat #60480, UPC #01223604808). Widescreen (2.35:1) anamorphic. Dolby Surround. $24.98. Keepcase. *LANG:* English. *FEATURES:* 36 chapter links ▪ Theatrical trailer ▪ Production notes ▪ Deleted scenes ▪ Cast and crew bios ▪ Karaoke ▪ Earth Girls TV.
1989 (PG) 100m/C *GB* Geena Davis, Jeff Goldblum, Charles Rocket, Julie Brown, Jim Carrey, Damon Wayans, Michael McKean, Angelyne, Larry Linville, Rick Overton, Diane Stilwell, Terrance McNally; *D:* Julien Temple; *W:* Charlie Coffey, Julie Brown, Terrance McNally; *C:* Oliver Stapleton; *M:* Nile Rodgers.

Earthly Possessions

Sarandon can't really pass for a drab housewife but she does her best in this made-for-cable adaptation of Anne Tyler's novel. She's Charlotte Emory, the very sheltered wife of a small-town minister (Sanders), who longs for a break from her

tedious routine. She gets her chance when she's taken hostage by would-be bank robber Jake Simms Jr. (Dorff), who suffers from impulse control problems and continual bad luck. Their fortunes change when he forces her to go on the road with him (he wants to see his pregnant girlfriend) and they form an increasingly close bond.
Movie: ♫♫▪ **DVD:** NYR
HBO Home Video (Cat #91475). Full frame. Dolby Digital Stereo. $24.98. Snapper. *LANG:* English; French. *SUB:* French; Spanish. *CAP:* English. *FEATURES:* Cast and crew thumbnail biographies.
1999 (R) 120m/C Susan Sarandon, Stephen Dorff, Jay O. Sanders, Elissabeth Moss, Margo Martindale; *D:* James Lapine; *W:* Steven Rogers; *C:* David Franco; *M:* Stephen Endelman.

Earthquake

Less-than-mediocre drama centers on a major earthquake in Los Angeles and its effects on an engineer, his spoiled wife, his mistress, his father-in-law, and a suspended policeman. Filmed in much-hyped Sensurround—a technique intended to shake up the theatre a bit. Some good special effects are not enough to make up for the lackluster script. This Goodtimes DVD is nowhere near as sharp as the Universal letterboxed laserdisc (using a single layer DVD for a movie over two hours long doesn't help). There are too many digital artifacts and grain, and some shimmering and color bleed along contrast lines, but surprisingly the blacks are about average. The Dolby Surround is fine with very little clipping and good separation and clarity, and there are actually a few good rumbles during the quake sequences. —*JO*
Movie: ♫▪ **DVD:** ♫▪
Goodtimes Entertainment (Cat #0581027, UPC #018713810274). Widescreen (2.35:1) letterboxed. Dolby Surround. $19.98. Snapper. *LANG:* English. *SUB:* Spanish; French. *CAP:* English. *FEATURES:* 18 chapter links ▪ Production notes.
1974 (PG) 123m/C Charlton Heston, Ava Gardner, George Kennedy, Lorne Greene, Genevieve Bujold, Richard Roundtree, Marjoe Gortner, Barry Sullivan, Victoria Principal, Lloyd Nolan, Walter Matthau, Scott Hylands; *D:* Mark Robson; *W:* Mario Puzo; *C:* Philip Lathrop; *M:* John Williams. *AWARDS:* Academy Awards '74: Best Sound, Best Visual Effects; *NOM:* Academy Awards '74: Best Art Direction/Set Decoration, Best Cinematography, Best Film Editing.

Eastern Condors

At the end of the Vietnam war, a band of Chinese convicts are recruited by the U.S. Army (and promised their freedom) if they can destroy an ammunition dump before the North Vietnamese can make use of it. This Hong Kong remake of *The Dirty Dozen* has the requisite levels of high energy and violence.

Movie: ♫♫ **DVD:** NYR
Tai Seng Video Marketing (Cat #2104). Dolby Digital 5.1 Surround Stereo. $49.95. Keepcase. *LANG:* Cantonese; Mandarin. *SUB:* Bahasia Malaysian & Indonesian; Simplified & Traditional Chinese; English; Japanese; Korean; Vietnamese; Thai. *FEATURES:* Cast and crew thumbnail biographies ▪ Trailer.
1987 94m/C *HK* Sammo Hung, Joyce Godenzi, Yuen Biao, Haing S. Ngor; *D:* Sammo Hung.

Easy Rider

The low-budget biker movie that defined a generation (and changed the movie industry) looks very good on DVD. In fact, this is the best-looking version I've seen on home video, with a superb image that appears to have been made from a pristine original. The stereo sound is excellent, too, and the extras, while not overwhelming, are just fine. Hopper's commentary track is restrained and to the point, but more animated than many of his similar efforts. This is an important film—certainly his best—but he doesn't overstate that importance. —*MM*
Movie: ♫♫♫▪ **DVD:** ♫♫♫▪
Columbia Tristar Home Video (Cat #01749). Widescreen letterboxed. Dolby Digital 5.1 Surround Stereo; Dolby Digital Surround Stereo. $25.98. *LANG:* English. *SUB:* English; Spanish; Portuguese; Chinese; Korean; Thai. *FEATURES:* "Making of" documentary ▪ 32 chapter links ▪ Cast and crew thumbnail bios ▪ Commentary: director Dennis Hopper.
1969 (R) 94m/C Peter Fonda, Dennis Hopper, Jack Nicholson, Karen Black, Toni Basil, Robert Walker Jr., Luana Anders, Luke Askew, Warren Finnerty, Mac Mashorian, Antonio Mendoza, Sabrina Scharf, Phil Spector; *D:* Dennis Hopper; *W:* Terry Southern, Peter Fonda, Dennis Hopper; *C:* Laszlo Kovacs. *AWARDS:* American Film Institute (AFI) '98: Top 100, National Film Registry '98; New York Film Critics Awards '69: Best Supporting Actor (Nicholson); National Society of Film Critics Awards '69: Best Supporting Actor (Nicholson); *NOM:* Academy Awards '69: Best Story & Screenplay, Best Supporting Actor (Nicholson).

Eat My Dust

Teenage son of a California sheriff steals the best stock cars from a race track to take the town's heartthrob for a joyride. Subsequently he leads everyone on a wild car chase. Brainless and fast-paced. The Corman interview is short but sweet on this DVD, whose biggest problem is an excessive amount of bleed on its reds. Other than that the colors are actually pretty good. However, picture sharpness is at best average and the grain and artifact levels pretty high. Blacks are average with some grain, while the contrast and brightness levels are better than this disc deserves. The mono sound is almost low-fi and tinny. —*JO*

Movie: 🎬🎬 **DVD:** 🎬🎬
New Horizons Home Video (Cat #NH00157, UPC #736991215740). Full frame. Mono. $24.98. Keepcase. *LANG:* English. *FEATURES:* 24 chapter links • Theatrical trailers • Cast bios • Roger Corman interview by Leonard Maltin.
1976 (PG) 89m/C Ron Howard, Christopher Norris, Warren Kemmerling, Dave Madden, Robert Broyles, Jessica Potter, Don Brodie, Evelyn Russell, Clint Howard, Paul Bartel, Rance Howard, Corbin Bernsen; **D:** Charles B. Griffith; **W:** Charles B. Griffith; **C:** Eric Saarinen; **M:** David Grisman.

Eat Your Heart Out
Romantic comedy about cooking and food.
Movie: NYR **DVD:** NYR
Pioneer Entertainment (Cat #10234). Full frame. Stereo. $19.98. Keepcase.
1996 (R) 96m/C Christian Oliver, Laura San Giacomo, Pamela Segall, Linda Hunt; **D:** Felix Adlon; **W:** Felix Adlon; **C:** Judy Irola; **M:** Alex Wurman.

Eaten Alive
This film has been so unsellable over the years that it has had five different titles, to no effect. Tobe Hooper tried to recycle some elements from his underground hit *The Texas Chainsaw Massacre* by using that film's cowriter and one of its pretty leads (Marilyn Burns). They just couldn't gel with the bizarre cast including Carolyn "Tish" Jones, Mel Ferrer, and Stuart Whitman. Neville Brand miraculously keeps his dignity as the lead character, bayou bed & breakfast operator Judd, even while brandishing a scythe and bounding upstairs after frightened women and children. Brand was one of those quintessentially American character actors, grizzled types like Warren Oates or Jack Elam, who circumvented the Hollywood cult of personality by putting their stamp on action genre films. It's so unusual to see him patting one of his captive's tears away, such a detail is more upsetting than anything the script delegates to the big rubber alligator lurking near the porch. Robert Englund, who plays a particularly unhappy, half-naked camper here, would later exact his revenge as Freddy Krueger by making other young and stupid characters suffer needlessly. DVD menus are blotchy and the film follows suit, a lost battle against International Film Lab (who?) processing. The included trailer sells the film as another *Jaws! —JK AKA:* Death Trap; Starlight Slaughter; Legend of the Bayou; Horror Hotel Massacre.
Movie: 🎬🎬 **DVD:** 🎬🎬🎬
Elite Entertainment, Inc. (Cat #E3181, UPC #790594318123). Widescreen (1.85:1) letterboxed. Dual-channel Mono. $24.99. Keepcase. *LANG:* English. *FEATURES:* 10 chapter links • Interactive menus • Theatrical trailer • 2-color picture disc.
1976 (R) 96m/C Neville Brand, Mel Ferrer, Carolyn Jones, Marilyn Burns, Stuart Whitman, Robert Englund, William Finley,

Roberta Collins, Kyle Richards, Janus Blythe; **D:** Tobe Hooper; **W:** Marti Rustam, Alvin L. Fast, Kim Henkel; **C:** Robert Caramico; **M:** Wayne Bell.

Ed McBain's 87 Precinct
You'd expect *The Simpsons* or the old SCTV series to cook up this kind of plot in one of their parodies, but yes, that's Randy Quaid as Steve Carella. He folds up the collar on his trench and chases a serial killer who specializes in female track stars, who have all apparently wound up in this gumshoe's backyard. Then, after a hard day's sleuthing, he comes home to his deaf-mute wife for a snack and a little slap and tickle. This is standard cable fare done by the book (it's not called Ed McBain's Whatnot for nothing), but it allows some gifted actors nice moments in two-character scenes. —*JK AKA:* Lightning.
Movie: 🎬🎬 **DVD:** 🎬🎬▶
Simitar Entertainment (Cat #7595, UPC #082551759521). Full frame. Dolby AC-3 Stereo. $14.99. Keepcase. *LANG:* English. *FEATURES:* 8 chapter links • Interactive menus • Randy Quaid bio • Theatrical trailer.
1996 96m/C Randy Quaid, Alex McArthur, Ving Rhames; **D:** Bruce Paltrow; **W:** Mike Krohn, Daniel Levine; **C:** Kenneth Zunder; **M:** Peter Bernstein.

Eddie
Edwina Franklin (Goldberg), limousine driver and New York Knicks fan, is made coach-for-a-night by Billy Burgess (Langella), the team's flamboyant new owner. He then hires her full-time. Can she turn the selfish losers into a winning team? Nobody needs three guesses. The stars handle this overly familiar material with more energy and humor than it deserves. On DVD, the interiors are all right, but the night exteriors and the basketball scenes filmed in Madison Square Garden have a rough texture. The main attraction for basketball fans lies in spotting such stars as Rick Fox and Brad Daugherty in cameos. —*MM*
Movie: 🎬🎬 **DVD:** 🎬🎬
Buena Vista Home Entertainment (Cat #17253, UPC #717951002464). Widescreen (1.85:1) letterboxed. Dolby Digital 5.1 Surround Stereo. $29.99. Keepcase. *LANG:* English; French. *CAP:* English. *FEATURES:* 13 chapter links • Theatrical trailer.
1996 (PG-13) 100m/C Whoopi Goldberg, Frank Langella, Dennis Farina, Richard Jenkins, Lisa Ann Walter, John Benjamin Hickey, John Salley; **D:** Steve Rash; **W:** Jon Connolly, David Loucka, Eric Champnella, Keith Mitchell, Steve Zacharias, Jeff Buhai; **C:** Victor Kemper; **M:** Stanley Clarke. *AWARDS: NOM:* Golden Raspberry Awards '96: Worst Actress (Goldberg).

Eden
Frustrated, Multiple Sclerosis–afflicted housewife Helen (Going) deals with the physical and emotional limitations of her life with dreams of astral projection. Husband Bill (Walsh) is a prep school teacher who doesn't want her to work even though she reaches one of his problem students (Flanery) more effectively than he does. First-time director Goldberg won a Sundance competition for his screenplay, but can't quite deliver on its promise. A tight budget and too many unanswered questions keep this one on the intriguing but ultimately disappointing level.
Movie: 🎬🎬 **DVD:** NYR
WinStar Home Entertainment (Cat #5135). Full frame. Dolby Digital Stereo. $29.98. Keepcase.
1998 (R) 106m/C Joanna Going, Dylan Walsh, Sean Patrick Flanery; **D:** Howard Goldberg; **W:** Howard Goldberg; **C:** Hubert Taczanowski; **M:** Brad Fiedel.

The Edge
Wealthy Hopkins suspects that his fashion-model wife Macpherson and photographer Baldwin are out to kill him. The two men end up depending on each other for survival when their plane crashes in the Alaskan wilderness. To compound their problems, they must do battle with a stalking killer bear. Screenplay by David Mamet delivers the usual cutting dialogue and mind games. Hopkins and Baldwin give intense performances—as does Bart the bear. The Alaskan scenery is breathtaking. If you ignore the intricacies of the plot, this is a great man-eating bear movie. The DVD transfer is very good; the picture stays sharp in both light and dark scenes (no noticeable grain). I didn't see any artifacts. There is very little color bleed and the colors are intense when they need to be. Contrast is good and the brightness levels consistent, whether the scene is in the sunlight, by the campfire, or in the snow. Both Surround tracks are very good: the dialogue is crisp, the music is full-bodied, and Bart's roars are scary as hell. —*JO AKA:* Bookworm.
Movie: 🎬🎬▶ **DVD:** 🎬🎬🎬
20th Century Fox (Cat #4110426, UPC #086162104268). Widescreen (2.35:1) anamorphic. Dolby Digital 5.1; Dolby Surround. $29.98. Keepcase. *LANG:* English (DD5.1; DS); French (DS). *SUB:* English; Spanish. *FEATURES:* 23 chapter links • Theatrical trailer • Cast bios • Dual-layered RSDL.
1997 (R) 120m/C Anthony Hopkins, Alec Baldwin, Elle Macpherson, Harold Perrineau Jr., L.Q. (Justus E. McQueen) Jones; **D:** Lee Tamahori; **W:** David Mamet; **C:** Donald McAlpine; **M:** Jerry Goldsmith.

EDtv
Ed (McConaughey) is a scruffy redneck video clerk who agrees to have his life broadcast 24/7 for a reality show produced by DeGeneres. The show becomes a hit and an entire nation watches breath-

lessly as Ed steals his brother's (Harrelson) girlfriend (Elfman), restocks shelves, and goes to the bathroom with the door open. Further revelations about friends and family ensue. In theatrical release, the film fared poorly commercially and critically when compared to *The Truman Show*. It should do better on video. The DVD transfer captures the smooth transitions within levels of film and video realities. The disc also contains two commentary tracks, one from director Howard, who brings a lifetime of direct experience to the film, and one from writers Lowell Ganz and Babaloo Mandel. Fans of the filmmakers and the cast are the target audience. —*MM*
Movie: 𝄞𝄞▶ **DVD:** 𝄞𝄞𝄞
Universal Studios Home Video (Cat #20560, UPC #025192056024). Widescreen (1.85:1) anamorphic. Dolby Digital 5.1 Surround Stereo; Dolby Digital Surround Stereo. $34.98. Keepcase. *LANG:* English; French. *CAP:* English. *FEATURES:* 18 chapter links • Commentary: director Ron Howard • Commentary: writers Lowell Ganz and Babaloo Mandel • "Making of" featurette • Soundtrack presentation with direct access to songs • Music videos • Deleted scenes • Theatrical trailer.
1999 (PG-13) 122m/C Ellen DeGeneres, Sally Kirkland, Martin Landau, Elizabeth Hurley, Rob Reiner, Dennis Hopper, Adam Goldberg, Viveka Davis, Clint Howard, Matthew McConaughey, Jenna Elfman, Woody Harrelson; *D:* Ron Howard; *W:* Lowell Ganz, Babaloo Mandel; *C:* John Schwartzman; *M:* Randy Edelman.

The Eiger Sanction

An art teacher (Eastwood) is forced to return to the CII (a fictionalized version of the CIA) and to assassinate the killers of an American agent. In the process, he finds himself climbing the Eiger. Beautiful Swiss Alps scenery fails to compensate for several dreary lapses. For a major studio release, this DVD is atrocious. The picture is not sharp at all and whenever there is any detail, flickering is added to the equation. In bright sequences (and there are a lot of snow-covered mountaintop scenes) the grain becomes unbearable. Colors are faded, but hey, at least they don't bleed. Blacks are hit and miss while the contrast and brightness never feel quite right. Unlikely as it may seem, the mono soundtrack is the best feature of the DVD, and has better fidelity and dynamics than a lot of stereo tracks. —*JO*
Movie: 𝄞𝄞 **DVD:** 𝄞▶
Universal Studios Home Video (Cat #20442, UPC #025192044229). Widescreen (2.35:1) letterboxed. Mono. $24.98. Keepcase. *LANG:* English. *SUB:* Spanish; French. *CAP:* English. *FEATURES:* 16 chapter links • Theatrical trailer • Cast and filmmaker's bios • Production notes.
1975 (R) 125m/C Clint Eastwood, George Kennedy, Vonetta McGee, Jack Cassidy, Thayer David; *D:* Clint Eastwood; *W:* Hal

Dresner, Warren B. Murphy, Rod Whitaker; *C:* Frank Stanley; *M:* John Williams.

8 Man

When Tokyo plainclothes cop Dakota is killed by vicious gangsters, his partner (and our narrator) Tanaka (Takahashi) takes him to a scientist who transforms the remains into a cyborg, 8 Man (Shishido). The character bears a certain resemblance to Robocop, though the box copy claims that this Japanese comic book character came first. Whatever, it's pretty much the same old ultra-violence tricked out with some interesting visuals. The DVD handles those fast-motion effects fairly well. The silly story is well filmed, too, and it was adapted into English with some care. —*MM*
Movie: 𝄞𝄞▶ **DVD:** 𝄞𝄞𝄞
Image Entertainment (Cat #ID4663FLDVD, UPC #014381466324). Full frame. Dolby Digital Stereo. $24.99. Snapper. *LANG:* English. *FEATURES:* 15 chapter links.
1992 83m/C *JP* Kai Shishido, Etsushi Takahashi, Sachiko Ayase; *D:* Yasuhiro Horiuchi, Carl Macek; *W:* Junko Suzuki; *C:* Junichi Baba; *M:* Mike Kennedy.

8 Man After: The Perfect Collection

Animated thriller features more perils of superhero 8 Man. This adventure finds him battling Tony Gleck and the cyberjunkies after they have kidnapped Sachiko to draw 8 Man to their hideout. See what happens when 8 Man faces the dilemma of choosing between Sachiko's safety and Tony's defeat. Also Sachiko learns more about the true identity of the "new" 8 Man. Sharper than the VHS, the DVD also has excellent colors. Like most animation on DVD there is no problem with bleed or grain. Since this film has been assembled from several episodes of *8 Man After*, it doesn't seem like this should really be called the perfect collection, but it's a pretty good DVD. —*JO*
Movie: 𝄞𝄞𝄞 **DVD:** 𝄞𝄞𝄞
Image Entertainment (Cat #ID4650SEDVD, UPC #014381465020). Full frame. Stereo. $24.95. Snapper. *LANG:* English. *FEATURES:* 16 chapter links.
1993 104m/C

8 Seconds

Though director John Avildsen attempts to pump this well-meaning little bio-pic up to *Rocky* heights, there's just not enough to it. The main characters—rodeo bull rider Lane Frost (Perry) and his wife Kellie (Geary)—are pleasant enough but their conflicts are fairly common. In the bullriding scenes, Avildsen does manage to capture the violence and brutal action of the sport. Again, though, for the uninitiated, the idea of trying to sit on top of several hundred pounds of angry bovine for eight seconds is hard to accept or understand. The DVD image is just as sharp as the theatrical release, but the entire film is

infused with a heroic, nostalgic glow that softens all hard edges. —*MM* *AKA:* The Lane Frost Story.
Movie: 𝄞𝄞 **DVD:** 𝄞𝄞▶
New Line Home Video (Cat #N4783, UPC #794043478321). Widescreen (1.85:1) letterboxed; full frame. Dolby Digital Stereo; Dolby Digital 5.1 Surround Stereo. $24.98. Snapper. *LANG:* English. *SUB:* English. *CAP:* English. *FEATURES:* 22 chapter links • Cast and crew thumbnail biographies • Theatrical trailer.
1994 (PG-13) 104m/C Luke Perry, Cynthia Geary, Stephen Baldwin, James Rebhorn, Carrie Snodgress, Red Mitchell, Ronnie Clair Edwards; *D:* John G. Avildsen; *W:* Monte Merrick; *C:* Victor Hammer; *M:* Bill Conti.

8mm

Surveillance expert Tom Welles (Cage) leads a normal family life until he is hired by Mrs. Christian (Carter) to identify a young girl who appears to be killed in a "snuff film" which was found in her late husband's safe. As Welles goes deep into the sick side of the porn business, he meets sleazeballs with names like Max California (Phoenix) and Dino Velvet (Storemare), and is both fascinated and disgusted by what he sees. Perhaps the gamy subject matter kept the film from finding much of an audience in its theatrical release. On his commentary track, director Schumacher offers up a strong, articulate defense of the film and the choices he made. The DVD looks remarkably good, despite the challenging nature of the original. Visually, thematically, stylistically, this is a very dark work, or, as Schumacher puts it, "existentially bleak." Even so, the image is clear, if dim in places, and such traditional problems as background mini-blinds are fine. The disc's main shortcoming is the menu. Though the liner notes claim that the film has 28 chapter links, I could access only the first four from the menu. —*MM*
Movie: 𝄞𝄞𝄞 **DVD:** 𝄞𝄞
Columbia Tristar Home Video (Cat #02854, UPC #043396028548). Widescreen (2.35:1) letterboxed; full frame. Dolby Digital 5.1 Surround Stereo; Dolby Digital Surround Stereo. $25.95. Keepcase. *LANG:* English. *SUB:* English. *FEATURES:* 28 chapter links • Commentary: Joel Schumacher • "Making of" featurette • Cast and crew thumbnail biographies • Theatrical trailer.
1998 (R) 123m/C Nicolas Cage, Joaquin Rafael (Leaf) Phoenix, James Gandolfini, Peter Stormare, Anthony Heald, Myra Carter; *D:* Joel Schumacher; *W:* Andrew Kevin Walker; *C:* Robert Elswit; *M:* Mychael Danna.

El Mariachi

See review of *Desperado / El Mariachi*.
Movie: 𝄞𝄞𝄞
1993 (R) 81m/C *MX* Carlos Gallardo, Consuelo Gomez, Peter Marquardt, Jaime de Hoyos, Reinol Martinez, Ramiro Gomez;

D: Robert Rodriguez; **W:** Robert Rodriguez, Carlos Gallardo; **C:** Robert Rodriguez; **M:** Eric Guthrie. *AWARDS:* Independent Spirit Awards '94: Best First Feature; Sundance Film Festival '93: Audience Award; *NOM:* Independent Spirit Awards '94: Best Director (Rodriguez).

Election

Writer-director Payne uses a high school student council election to skewer the American political system in general and the election process in particular. Smart comedy has wildly ambitious Tracy Flick (Witherspoon) running for council president unopposed until dedicated but flawed civics teacher Mr. McAllister (Broderick) decides she must be stopped and recruits likeable but dim jock Paul (Klein) to run against her. Everyone's foibles and hypocrisy are shown to great effect. The performances by Witherspoon and Broderick are among their very best. Payne's sure grasp of the material is obvious from the opening moment. The DVD image transfer is fine but, for fans, the best thing on the disc is Payne's intelligent commentary. Unlike so many filmmakers, he spends time explaining the things he tried to do that did not work. This film did well with critics but not so well with audiences in theatrical release. It's one of the best sleepers in your video store. —*MM*
Movie: 🦴🦴🦴🦴 **DVD:** 🦴🦴🦴🦴
Paramount Home Video (Cat #33403, UPC #097363340379). Widescreen letterboxed. Dolby Digital 5.1 Surround Stereo; Dolby Digital Surround Stereo. $29.99. Keepcase. *LANG:* English. *FEATURES:* 18 chapter links ● Commentary: director Alexander Payne.
1999 (R) 105m/C Matthew Broderick, Reese Witherspoon, Chris Klein, Jessica Campbell, Mark Harelik, Molly Hagan, Colleen Camp, Frankie Ingrassia, Matt Malloy, Holmes Osborne, Phil Reeves, Delaney Driscoll, Jeanine Jackson; **D:** Alexander Payne; **W:** Alexander Payne, Jim Taylor; **C:** James Glennon; **M:** Rolfe Kent. *AWARDS:* Independent Spirit Awards '00: Best Director (Payne), Best Film, Best Screenplay; New York Film Critics Awards '99: Best Screenplay; National Society of Film Critics Awards '99: Best Actress (Witherspoon); Writers Guild of America '99: Best Adapted Screenplay; *NOM:* Academy Awards '99: Best Adapted Screenplay; Golden Globe Awards '00: Best Actress—Musical/Comedy (Witherspoon); Independent Spirit Awards '00: Best Actress (Witherspoon), Debut Performance (Campbell).

The Electric Horseman

Journalist Fonda sets out to discover the reason behind the kidnapping of a prized horse by an ex–rodeo star. The alcoholic cowboy has taken the horse to return it to its native environment, away from the clutches of corporate greed. As Fonda investigates the story, she falls in love with rebel Redford. Excellent Las Vegas and remote western settings. The image quality generally is better than VHS, but it's not exceptional for DVD. The sound is mono, and other DVD niceties are limited to a few chapter stops and a nice-looking menu screen with still pictures for each chapter. —*MB*
Movie: 🦴🦴▶ **DVD:** 🦴🦴▶
Image Entertainment (Cat #ID4276USDVD, UPC #014381427622). Widescreen (2.35:1) letterboxed. Dolby Digital 1.0. $29.99. Snapper. *LANG:* English. *CAP:* English. *FEATURES:* 16 chapter links.
1979 (PG) 120m/C Robert Redford, Jane Fonda, John Saxon, Willie Nelson, Valerie Perrine, Wilford Brimley, Nicolas Coster, James B. Sikking; **D:** Sydney Pollack; **W:** Robert Garland; **C:** Owen Roizman; **M:** Dave Grusin. *AWARDS: NOM:* Academy Awards '79: Best Sound.

Elizabeth

Indian director Kapur takes a look at the turbulent life of Queen Elizabeth I (a brilliant Blanchett) from her uncertain days as a besieged Protestant Princess to her ascension to the English throne and the machinations surrounding her early reign. Elizabeth indeed proves to be her father's daughter as she must keep her head (literally) while dealing with religion, war, assassination, and the vexing question of a political marriage. This DVD deserves its rating just for the colors alone, which reflect all the subtleties and richness of the many colorful costumes. The picture is also superb with not a trace of grain or artifacts. Blacks are dead-on and image is further enhanced by excellent contrast and brightness levels. The 5.1 sound is not put to optimum use—there's not much on the Surround tracks, ambience or otherwise—but at least the front tracks deliver full, dynamic sound without a hint of distortion, and the dialogue is always up-front. —*JO*
Movie: 🦴🦴🦴 **DVD:** 🦴🦴🦴▶
USA Home Entertainment (Cat #4400582 732, UPC #044005827323). Widescreen (1.85:1) anamorphic. Dolby Digital 5.1; Dolby Surround. $34.95. Keepcase. *LANG:* English. *SUB:* Spanish; French. *CAP:* English. *FEATURES:* 20 chapter links ● Theatrical trailer and teaser ● "Making of" featurette ● Cast and crew bios ● Photo gallery.
1998 (R) 124m/C *GB* Cate Blanchett, Geoffrey Rush, Joseph Fiennes, Christopher Eccleston, Richard Attenborough, Fanny Ardant, Vincent Cassel, Daniel Craig, Kathy Burke, James Frain, Edward Hardwicke, Eric Cantona, John Gielgud, Emily Mortimer; **D:** Shekhar Kapur; **W:** Michael Hirst; **C:** Remi Adefarasin; **M:** David Hirschfelder. *AWARDS:* Academy Awards '98: Best Makeup; British Academy Awards '98: Best Actress (Blanchett), Best Cinematography, Best Film, Best Score; Golden Globe Awards '99: Best Actress—Drama (Blanchett); National Board of Review Awards '98: Best Director (Kapur); Broadcast Film Critics Association Awards '98: Best Actress (Blanchett); *NOM:* Academy Awards '98: Best Actress (Blanchett), Best Art Direction/Set Decoration, Best Cinematography, Best Costume Design, Best Picture, Best Original Dramatic Score; Australian Film Institute '99: Best Foreign Film; British Academy Awards '98: Best Costume Design, Best Director (Kapur), Best Film Editing, Best Original Screenplay, Best Supporting Actor (Rush); Golden Globe Awards '99: Best Director (Kapur), Best Film—Drama; MTV Movie Awards '99: Breakthrough Performance (Blanchett); Screen Actors Guild Award '98: Best Actress (Blanchett).

The Elm-Chanted Forest

Cute-animal animated musical is essentially a long-form Saturday morning cartoon. Painter Peter Palette finds inspiration and more from a magic elm tree. On DVD, it's bright, colorful, fast-moving and undemanding. Same for the songs. Smaller kids are probably the target audience. The DVD will allow those who find favorite moments in the film to get to them quickly. —*MM*
Movie: 🦴🦴 **DVD:** 🦴🦴▶
Image Entertainment (Cat #ID5697PZDVD, UPC #014381569728). Full frame. Dolby Digital Mono. $24.99. Snapper. *LANG:* English. *FEATURES:* 16 chapter links.
1997 ?m/C D: Milan Blazekovic; **W:** Fred P. Sharkey; **M:** Dennis Leogrande.

Elvira Madigan

Beautiful production, based on a true incident, chronicles the passionate 19th-century Swedish romance between a young officer and a beautiful circus tight-rope walker. Exceptional direction and photography supports the box notes' claim that the film is "visually breathtaking." The digital image isn't the sharpest, though, nor has it been anamorphically enhanced for widescreen sets, but the style of cinematography apparently relies on soft focus and softening filters. The DVD transfer reveals nicks and dirt on film element used to make the video master. The Swedish soundtrack is monaural. —*MB*
Movie: 🦴🦴🦴 **DVD:** 🦴🦴▶
WinStar Home Entertainment (Cat #FLV5065, UPC #720917506524). Widescreen (1.66:1) letterboxed. Dolby Digital Mono. $29.98. Keepcase. *LANG:* Swedish. *SUB:* English. *FEATURES:* 8 chapter links ● Production credits ● Filmographies and awards lists.
1967 (PG) 90m/C *SW* Pia Degermark, Thommy Berggren, Lennart Malmer, Nina Widerberg, Cleo Jensen; **D:** Bo Widerberg; **W:** Johan Lindstroem Saxon, Bo Widerberg; **C:** Jorgen Persson; **M:** Ulf Bjorlin. *AWARDS:* Cannes Film Festival '67: Best Actress (Degermark).

Embrace of the Vampire

Virginal college student Charlotte (Milano) is pursued by a vampire (Kemp). For reasons never fully explained, he needs her to charge his batteries. Director Goursaud certainly knows how to steam things up. Her approach ranges from bodice-ripper romanticism to Hollywood stereotypes to artfully posed eroticism. DVD plays to the strongest suits of this video premiere, capturing the soft-focus action with a shade more clarity than VHS tape. The disc also contains both widescreen and full-frame versions of both the unrated and "R"-rated versions of the film. —MM

Movie: 🎬🎬⯈ **DVD:** 🎬🎬🎬
New Line Home Video (Cat #N4849, UPC #794043484926). Widescreen (1.85:1) letterboxed; full frame. Dolby Digital 5.1 Surround Stereo; Dolby Digital Surround Stereo. $24.98. Snapper. *LANG:* English. *SUB:* English. *FEATURES:* 19 chapter links • Cast and crew thumbnail biographies.
1995 (R) 92m/C Alyssa Milano, Martin Kemp, Harrison Pruett, Charlotte Lewis, Jordan Ladd, Rachel True, Jennifer Tilly; **D:** Anne Goursaud; **W:** Halle Eaton, Nicole Coady, Rick Bitzelberger; **C:** Suki Medencevic; **M:** Joseph Williams.

Embrace the Darkness

Galen (Spirtas) and Miranda (High), two contemporary vampires, move to Los Angeles where he falls for his muse, Jennifer (Clark), a dancer. The erotic vampire story has become something of a staple in the world of video premieres. This Playboy production is one of the better attempts. Director Cauthen uses some simple tricks effectively in the opening reels. Her love scenes are well choreographed with Nicholas Rivera's score. Considering the constraints of the budget and genre expectations, this no-frills disc looks terrific with crisp photography and careful use of colored light for texture. Fair sound. —MM

Movie: 🎬🎬🎬 **DVD:** 🎬🎬🎬
Image Entertainment (Cat #ID5976PLDVD, UPC #014381597622). Full frame. Dolby Digital Stereo. $24.99. Snapper. *LANG:* English. *FEATURES:* 16 chapter links.
1998 104m/C Kevin Blair Spirtas, Madison Clark, Angelia High, Brad Bartram, Colleen McDermott; **D:** Kelley Cauthen; **W:** Rick Bitzelberger; **C:** Maximo Munzi; **M:** Nicholas Rivera.

Embryo

Average sci-fi drama about a scientist (Hudson) who uses raw genetic material to produce a beautiful woman (Carrera) with ghastly results. **AKA:** Created to Kill.
Movie: 🎬🎬 **DVD:** NYR
Passport International Productions (Cat #710). Full frame. $14.99. Keepcase. *FEATURES:* Trailer.
1976 (PG) 108m/C Rock Hudson, Barbara Carrera, Diane Ladd, Roddy McDowall, Ann Schedeen, John Elerick, Dr. Joyce Brothers; **D:** Ralph Nelson; **W:** Anita Doohan, Jack W. Thomas; **C:** Fred W. Koenekamp; **M:** Gil Melle.

Emma

Wealthy 21-year-old Emma Woodhouse (Paltrow) makes it her goal to "fix" the lives of all her friends, while ignoring her own problems (the modern adaptation was *Clueless*). Emma focuses much of her attention on Harriet Smith (Collette), a simple young woman whom Emma believes is in need of the perfect mate. Meanwhile, Emma neglects to notice the attractive, and exasperated, Mr. Knightley (Northam). MacGrath's screenplay makes Emma and Knightley more likable than they are in the book, but otherwise remains true. This DVD looks good but the image often feels darker than it did in the theatre. Sharpness is good with very little grain and no artifacts. Colors are accurate, with very good contrast levels making up for the somewhat low brightness levels. Blacks are excellent. The orchestral soundtrack is nicely handled by the Dolby Surround and features clean (if not excessive) low end and crisp highs. There is not much in the way of Surround effects, so that track is used mainly for ambience. —JO

Movie: 🎬🎬🎬 **DVD:** 🎬🎬🎬
Buena Vista Home Entertainment (Cat #15862, UPC #717951000972). Widescreen (1.85:1) letterboxed. Dolby Surround. $29.99. Keepcase. *LANG:* English. *CAP:* English. *FEATURES:* 16 chapter links • Theatrical trailer.
1996 (PG) 120m/C Gwyneth Paltrow, Jeremy Northam, Greta Scacchi, Toni Collette, Alan Cumming, Juliet Stevenson, Polly Walker, Ewan McGregor, James Cosmo, Sophie Thompson, Phyllida Law; **D:** Douglas McGrath; **W:** Douglas McGrath; **C:** Ian Wilson; **M:** Rachel Portman. *AWARDS:* Academy Awards '96: Best Original Score; *NOM:* Academy Awards '96: Best Costume Design; Writers Guild of America '96: Best Adapted Screenplay.

Emmanuelle

The mother of all soft-core skin flicks has aged gracefully. Filmed in Bangkok, it is the story of a young woman (Kristel) who is introduced to an uninhibited world of sensuality by her husband, by her friends, by people she meets on airplanes, by...you know the plot. It has been repeated in literally dozens of sequels and imitations. The star brings the right combination of curiosity and awareness to the role. Director Jaeckin gives the film a gauzy, soft-focused look that does not play to the strengths of DVD. Even so, the image is clear enough to reveal flaws in the print or negative it was made from. Fans will notice a distinct difference on disc between the visuals in this film and the one that was made immediately after it. This DVD contains no commentaries; it would be interesting to hear what Ms. Kristel thinks of the film now. By the way, the real Emmanuelle Arsan, author of the original novel, appears in the film *The Sand Pebbles* as Marayat Andriane, and one of the later sequels, *Forever Emmanuelle*. —MM

Movie: 🎬🎬⯈ **DVD:** 🎬🎬🎬
WinStar Home Entertainment (Cat #FLV5021, UPC #720917502120). Widescreen, nominal letterboxing. $29.98. Keepcase. *LANG:* English; French. *FEATURES:* Filmographies • Production credits • 6 chapter links.
1974 92m/C *FR* Sylvia Kristel, Alain Cuny, Marika Green, Daniel Sarky; **D:** Just Jaeckin; **W:** Jean-Louis Richard; **C:** Richard Suzuki; **M:** Pierre Bachelet.

Emmanuelle: Queen of the Desert

After completing an assassination mission, seven commandos are trapped in a sun-blasted countryside (actually Cyprus) where they rape, pillage, and attack each other until they meet a temptress (Gemser) who takes revenge. It's standard exploitation stuff with a strangely existential edge. The DVD looks about as rough as most early '80s drive-in fare. The night scenes suffer from heavy pixelation. The day-for-nights are not much better and the bright exteriors have an orange tint. —MM
AKA: The Dirty Seven.
Movie: 🎬🎬⯈ **DVD:** 🎬🎬
Simitar Entertainment (Cat #7658, UPC #082551765829). Widescreen (1.66:1) letterboxed. Dolby Digital 5.1 Stereo. $14.98. Keepcase. *LANG:* English. *FEATURES:* 8 chapter links • Production factoids.
1993 (R) 92m/C Laura Gemser, Angelo Infanti, Gabriele Tinti; **D:** Bruno (Roger Fontaine) Fontana; **W:** Bruno (Roger Fontaine) Fontana; **C:** Nino Celeste.

Emmanuelle, the Joys of a Woman

With the second film, the basic elements of the series are established: romantic, soft-core sexual scenes; exotic locations (here Hong Kong, Bangkok, and Bali); an attractive multiracial cast; and superior production values. This one also introduces Laura Gemser, who would take over in many later episodes as the eponymous heroine. On DVD, the film is much clearer than the first with a full widescreen transfer. For those who prefer the original French dialogue, the yellow subtitles are conveniently located in the lower black strip of the letterbox. As for the print itself, some scratches and flecks are visible throughout. —MM **AKA:** Emmanuelle l'Antivierge; Emmanuelle's 7th Heaven; Emmanuelle 2.
Movie: 🎬🎬⯈ **DVD:** 🎬🎬🎬
WinStar Home Entertainment (Cat #FLV5032, UPC #720917503226). Widescreen. $29.98. Keepcase. *LANG:* English; French. *SUB:* English. *FEATURES:* Sylvia Kristel biography and filmography • 6 chapter links.
1976 92m/C *FR* Sylvia Kristel, Umberto Orsini, Catherine Rivet, Frederic Lagache, Laura Gemser, Henri Czarniak, Tom Clark, Caroline Laurence; **D:** Francis Giacobetti; **W:** Francis Giacobetti, Jean-Marc Vasseur; **C:** Robert Fraisse; **M:** Pierre Bachelet, Francis Lai.

The Emperor's Shadow

This epic costume drama was intended for the theatre screen and anything less diminishes the film's ambitious, Shakespearean scope. With that qualification in mind, the DVD version is sumptuous. The story revolves around the formation of the first dynasty in 210 B.C. It begins with the aging emperor Ying Zheng (Jiang Wen) on his death bed. He remembers his childhood friend, the musician Gao Jianli (Ge You), his own daughter the Princess Yueyang (Xu Qing), and their forbidden affair. The film works beautifully in both the big, sweeping scenes and the smaller human moments. The performances are keyed toward a western style of acting and so the film presents no problems to those who don't mind clear subtitles. Enough care was taken with the image transfer so that potentially troublesome scenes, such as one set inside a room bordered by blinds made of thin reeds, cause no problems. For my money, this one's comparable to Kurosawa's *Ran* and far more enjoyable than *The Last Emperor*. —*MM* **AKA:** Qin Song.
Movie: ♫♫♫ *DVD:* ♫♫♫♫
WinStar Home Entertainment (Cat #FLV5124, UPC #720917512426). Widescreen (1.85:1) letterboxed. $29.98. Keepcase. *LANG:* Mandarin. *SUB:* English. *FEATURES:* Cast and crew filmographies ● 8 chapter links ● Theatrical trailer ● Production credits.
1996 123m/C *CH* Ge You, Jiang Wen, Xu Qing; *D:* Zhou Xiaowen; *W:* Wei Lu; *C:* Lu Gengxin; *M:* Jiping Zhao.

Encino Man

Prototypical "dumb" teen comedy has nerdy Dave (Astin) and Stoney (Shore) finding frozen a Cro-Magnon man (Fraser) in the back yard during a swimming pool excavation. For reasons that are never really clear, they pass off Link ("missing link," get it?) as an exchange student from Estonia ("stone age," get it?). They think that if they dress him up in retro '60s clothes, they'll become popular. The moronic "message" conclusion is the final insult. On DVD, the film looks as good as it did on theatre screens, for better and for worse. —*MM* **AKA:** California Man.
Movie: ♫ *DVD:* ♫♫
Hollywood Pictures Home Video (Cat #17601, UPC #717951003379). Widescreen (1.85:1) letterboxed. Dolby Digital Stereo. $29.99. Keepcase. *LANG:* English; French. *CAP:* English. *FEATURES:* "Making of" featurette ● Theatrical trailer ● 12 chapter links.
1992 (PG) 88m/C Sean Astin, Brendan Fraser, Pauly Shore, Megan Ward, Robin Tunney, Rick Ducommun, Mariette Hartley, Richard Masur, Michael DeLuise; *D:* Les Mayfield; *W:* Shawn Schepps; *C:* Robert Brinkmann. *AWARDS:* Golden Raspberry Awards '92: Worst New Star (Shore).

End of Days

In the last days of 1999, New York security guard Jericho (Schwarzenegger) must keep Satan (Byrne) from impregnating Christine (Tunney). If Old Scratch gets lucky, it's the end of the world, etc., etc. Having seen the *Omen* movies, we all know the pseudo-biblical drill by now. Once again, Peter Hyams proves himself to be a fine director of photography and a so-so director. Both image and sound are impressive, re-creating the big-budget special effects without noticeable flaws. The best parts of the extra material explain how the various effects were accomplished. The menus are pretty cool, too. —*MM*
Movie: ♫♫♫ *DVD:* ♫♫♫
Universal Studios Home Video (Cat #20721). Widescreen (2.35:1) letterboxed. Dolby Digital 5.1 Surround Stereo; Dolby Digital Surround. $26.99. Keepcase. *LANG:* English; French. *CAP:* English. *FEATURES:* 20 chapter links ● Commentary: Peter Hyams ● "Making of" documentary ● Thumbnail synopsis of the book of Revelation ● Explanation of special effects scenes.
1999 (R) 123m/C Arnold Schwarzenegger, Gabriel Byrne, Robin Tunney, Kevin Pollak, CCH Pounder, Rod Steiger, Derrick O'Connor, Miriam Margolyes, Udo Kier; *D:* Peter Hyams; *W:* Andrew Marlowe; *C:* Peter Hyams; *M:* John Debney. *AWARDS:* NOM: Golden Raspberry Awards '99: Worst Actor (Schwarzenegger), Worst Supporting Actor (Byrne), Worst Director (Hyams).

The Endless Summer

Classic surfing documentary captures the freedom and sense of adventure that the sport symbolizes. Director Brown follows two young surfers around the world in search of the perfect wave. Besides the excellent surfing photography, Big Kahuna Brown provides the amusing tongue-in-cheek narrative. Considered by many to be the best surf movie ever. The film elements used for the video transfer exhibit the occasional blemish, but the colors are vibrant and saturated. You'll spot the infrequent digital compression artifact in the grainy areas and in the surf foam, but you'll have to be looking close. The monaural soundtrack is O.K. Nothing dynamic, but free of distortion and excessive hardness. Extras? Bummer, but there aren't any. —*MB*
Movie: ♫♫♫ *DVD:* ♫♫
Image Entertainment (Cat #ID8790OTDVD, UPC #014381879025). Full frame. Dolby Digital 1.0. $24.99. Snapper. *LANG:* English. *FEATURES:* 20 chapter links.
1966 90m/C Mike Hynson, Robert August; *D:* Bruce Brown; *W:* Bruce Brown; *Nar:* Bruce Brown.

Enemy of the State

Paranoid thriller loosely reworks and amplifies ideas found in *The Conversation*. After a friend slips him a videocassette without his knowledge, Washington lawyer Robert Dean (Smith) is targeted by a surveillance-and-gizmo-happy government agency headed by the sinister Reynolds (Voight). They hound Dean, cutting him off from everything and everyone he holds dear, finally forcing him underground. He finds help in Brill (Hackman), a remorseful ex-agent who helped to create the cyber-surveillance monster. They make a likeable pair of heroes. The DVD handles director Scott's stylized visuals, often unrealistic color scheme, and experimental use of sound without a problem. If anything, the image is a bit brighter than it was in theatres. —*MM*
Movie: ♫♫♫ *DVD:* ♫♫♫
Buena Vista Home Entertainment (Cat #16537, UPC #717951001634). Widescreen (2.35:1) letterboxed. Dolby Digital 5.1 Surround Stereo. $29.99. Keepcase. *LANG:* English; French. *SUB:* English. *FEATURES:* Trailers ● 2 "making of" featurettes ● 29 chapter links.
1998 (R) 132m/C Will Smith, Gene Hackman, Jon Voight, Jason Lee, Regina King, Gabriel Byrne, Barry Pepper, Scott Caan, Loren Dean, Jake Busey, Lisa Bonet, Stuart Wilson, Tom Sizemore, James LeGros, Ian Hurt, Daniel Butler, Jamie Kennedy, Rebeca Silva, Jason Robards Jr., Bobby Boriello, Anna Gunn, Seth Green, Philip Baker Hall, Lillo Brancato, John Capodice; *D:* Tony Scott; *W:* David Marconi; *C:* Dan Mindel; *M:* Trevor Rabin, Harry Gregson-Williams. *AWARDS:* NOM: MTV Movie Awards '99: Best Male Performance (Smith).

The English Patient

During World War II in Tuscany, American allies care for dying burn victim Almasy (Fiennes), who was rescued from a fiery plane crash. The scarred-and-blistered English patient is concealed beneath bandages for the most part, but the methodically paced tale eventually takes the wraps off the dangerous secrets of his past. Binoche effectively portrays the strength and fragility of his chief caretaker, French-Canadian nurse Hana. It isn't long before the patient and nurse are joined by thief-turned-spy Caravaggio (Dafoe), who has a private score to settle, and British bomb disposal experts Sgt. Hardy (Whately) and Kip (Andrews). The latter falls in love with Hana. Based on Michael Ondaatje's novel, much of the story is told in flashback, revealing Almasy's illicit love affair with Katharine (Scott Thomas), wife of fellow cartographer Geoffrey (Firth), as they map the North African dessert. There is ample moral food for thought to please the thinking audience for which the film is intended. This filling fare for the mind is an equally bountiful meal for the eyes and ears, thanks to exquisite cinematography and a lush soundtrack. Regrettably, widescreen viewers must suffer softer-than-desired images because this DVD lacks a transfer enhanced for their displays. But the letterboxed picture looks fine on standard-shaped TV sets. The extras are nonexistent—a major bummer for the top Oscar winner of its year. There's nothing wrong with the audio at least. —*MB*

Movie: ♪♪♪♪ **DVD:** ♪♪▶
Miramax Pictures Home Video (Cat #14175, UPC #717951000286). Widescreen (1.85:1) letterboxed. Dolby Digital 5.1. $29.98. Keepcase. *LANG:* English. *SUB:* Spanish. *CAP:* English. *FEATURES:* 32 chapter links.
1996 (R) 162m/C Ralph Fiennes, Kristin Scott Thomas, Juliette Binoche, Willem Dafoe, Naveen Andrews, Colin Firth, Julian Wadham, Juergen Prochnow, Kevin Whately, Clive Merrison, Nino Castelnuovo; *D:* Anthony Minghella; *W:* Anthony Minghella; *C:* John Seale; *M:* Gabriel Yared. *AWARDS:* Academy Awards '96: Best Art Direction/Set Decoration, Best Cinematography, Best Costume Design, Best Director (Minghella), Best Film Editing, Best Picture, Best Sound, Best Supporting Actress (Binoche), Best Original Dramatic Score; British Academy Awards '96: Best Adapted Screenplay, Best Cinematography, Best Film, Best Supporting Actress (Binoche), Best Score; Directors Guild of America Awards '96: Best Director (Minghella); Golden Globe Awards '97: Best Film—Drama, Best Score; Los Angeles Film Critics Association Awards '96: Best Cinematography; National Board of Review Awards '96: Best Supporting Actress (Binoche), Best Supporting Actress (Scott Thomas); Broadcast Film Critics Association Awards '96: Best Director (Minghella), Best Screenplay; *NOM:* Academy Awards '96: Best Actor (Fiennes), Best Actress (Scott Thomas), Best Adapted Screenplay, Best Sound Effects Editing; British Academy Awards '96: Best Actor (Fiennes), Best Actress (Scott Thomas), Best Director (Minghella); Golden Globe Awards '97: Best Actor—Drama (Fiennes), Best Actress—Drama (Scott Thomas), Best Director (Minghella), Best Screenplay, Best Supporting Actress (Binoche); Screen Actors Guild Award '96: Best Actor (Fiennes), Best Actress (Scott Thomas), Best Supporting Actress (Binoche), Cast; Writers Guild of America '96: Best Adapted Screenplay.

The Englishman Who Went up a Hill But Came down a Mountain

Charming but slight tale of local pride is based on writer-director Monger's family stories. In 1917 two English cartographers—pompous George (McNeice) and naive Reginald (Grant)—travel to Wales to measure the height of Ffynnon Garw (a running gag concerns the surveyors struggling with the Welsh language). To the proud townspeople, it is the first mountain in Wales and without that designation, they might as well redraw the maps and be part of England—God forbid. But to be designated a mountain, the peak must be 1,000 feet high and she measures only 984. Grant stammers boyishly as the Eng-

lishman who is captivated by the village and by the spirited Betty (Fitzgerald). Meaney slyly shines as innkeeper Morgan the Goat, leading the townful of colorful characters. Wales is shown to great advantage on the DVD, but other aspects of the film do not fare as well. Shingles, a windowpane plaid, a tie pattern, and diagonal car trim all display flaws. The sound is good, but the first printing of the disc suffered from errors that ground it to a halt in the second half. The problem was corrected. —*MM*

Movie: ♪♪♪ **DVD:** ♪♪▶
Miramax Pictures Home Video (Cat #17591, UPC #717951003287). Widescreen (2.35:1) letterboxed. Dolby Digital Surround Stereo. $29.99. Keepcase. *LANG:* English. *CAP:* English. *FEATURES:* 22 chapter links ▪ Theatrical trailer.
1995 (PG) 96m/C *GB* Hugh Grant, Tara Fitzgerald, Colm Meaney, Ian McNeice, Ian Hart, Kenneth Griffith; *D:* Christopher Monger; *W:* Christopher Monger; *C:* Vernon Layton; *M:* Stephen Endelman.

Enter the Dragon (SE)

The American film that broke Bruce Lee worldwide combines Asian conventions with 007 thrills. Spectacular fighting sequences including Karate, Judo, Tae Kwon Do, and Tai Chi Chaun are featured as Lee is recruited by the British to search for opium smugglers in Hong Kong during a martial arts tournament. Saxon is at his macho best. The sound on this DVD is close to amazing. Remastered in Dolby Digital 5.1, it's dynamic; Lalo Schifrin's jazz score has plenty of crisp highs and good low end, and the exaggerated fight sounds let you feel each blow—all without sacrificing the dialogue's clarity. The picture is a little above average with some grain and color bleed throughout the film (mainly the reds in the credits and final showdown). The blacks are very close to true, and the contrast consistent, but a little more brightness would make viewing more comfortable. The DVD is the restored version, with three minutes of footage not in the original American theatrical release. Lee fans should find the two included documentaries alone worth the price of the disc. —*JO* *AKA:* The Deadly Three.

Movie: ♪♪♪ **DVD:** ♪♪▶
Warner Home Video, Inc. (Cat #15921, UPC #085391592129). Widescreen (2.35:1) anamorphic. Dolby Digital 5.1. $24.98. Snapper. *LANG:* English. *SUB:* French; Spanish. *CAP:* English. *FEATURES:* 29 chapter links ▪ Theatrical trailers ▪ 1973 behind-the-scenes documentary; new documentary ▪ Commentary: producer Paul Heller and screenwriter Michael Allin ▪ Intro by Linda Lee Cadwell ▪ Production notes ▪ Cast and crew bios ▪ Other related notes: Jackie Chan, Hong Kong films, martial arts. Includes many other similar features.
1973 (R) 102m/C Bruce Lee, John Saxon, Jim Kelly, Ahna Capri, Shih Kien, Bob Wall, Angela Mao, Betty Chung, Jackie

Chan, Tony Liu, Chuck Norris; *D:* Robert Clouse; *W:* Michael Allin; *C:* Gil Hubbs; *M:* Lalo Schifrin.

Entrapment

Mac (Connery) is a master cat burglar. Gin (Zeta-Jones) is an insurance investigator with a bit of larceny in her heart. They go through the expected romantic dalliances as they plot a short series of increasingly improbable capers. The supporting cast is fine, but the entire enterprise comes across as slick, soulless, and superficial. Director Amiel and writer Bass have done much, much better work. The DVD looks fine, even in the complex, darkly lit heist sequences. The stereo sound is particularly effective in the same scenes. With the added clarity of the digital transfer in the brighter final scenes, the difference in age between the two stars is alarmingly apparent. —*MM*

Movie: ♪♪▶ **DVD:** ♪♪♪
20th Century Fox (Cat #4112309, UPC #NA). Widescreen letterboxed. Dolby Digital 5.1 Surround Stereo; Dolby Digital Surround Stereo. $34.98. Keepcase. *LANG:* English. *SUB:* Spanish. *CAP:* English. *FEATURES:* 24 chapter links ▪ Trailers for *Entrapment* and *Rising Sun*.
1999 (PG-13) 112m/C Sean Connery, Catherine Zeta-Jones, Ving Rhames, Will Patton, Maury Chaykin; *D:* Jon Amiel; *W:* Ronald Bass, William Broyles Jr.; *C:* Phil Meheux; *M:* Christopher Young. *AWARDS: NOM:* Golden Raspberry Awards '99: Worst Actress (Zeta-Jones).

Entre-Nous

Two attractive young French mothers (Miou-Miou and Huppert) find in each other the fulfillment their husbands cannot provide. One was confined in a concentration camp during World War II; the other is a disaffected artist. Writer-director Kurys based the story on her own family and she tells it at a leisurely pace. On DVD, the film is astonishingly clear. Most imports of this age do not look half as good. Both image and sound are excellent. White subtitles are located in the lower letterbox bar. —*MM* *AKA:* Between Us; Coup de Foudre; At First Sight.

Movie: ♪♪♪ **DVD:** ♪♪♪▶
WinStar Home Entertainment (Cat #FLV5049, UPC #720917504926). Widescreen letterboxed. $29.98. Keepcase. *LANG:* French. *SUB:* English. *FEATURES:* 6 chapter links ▪ Production credits ▪ Filmographies and awards.
1983 (PG) 112m/C *FR* Jean-Pierre Bacri, Patrick Bauchau, Jacqueline Doyen, Isabelle Huppert, Miou-Miou, Guy Marchand; *D:* Diane Kurys; *W:* Alain Henry, Diane Kurys; *C:* Bernard Lutic; *M:* Luis Bacalov. *AWARDS: NOM:* Academy Awards '83: Best Foreign Film.

Eraser

Arnold returns to familiar big-budget action territory and looks right at home. He plays

elite U.S. Marshal John Kruger, who protects federal witnesses by "erasing" their previous identities. When a beautiful witness uncovers a high-level conspiracy, the two go on the run to stay alive long enough to expose the truth. Fans of the big-bang Schwarzenegger of yore will not be disappointed. Rumors of production delays and budget overruns, not to mention difficulties between director Russell and producer Kopelson, brought up the specter of *Waterworld,* but the final result is more reminiscent of the success of *True Lies.* The picture on this DVD is so sharp that the computer-animated crocodiles look even more fake than they did on the big screen. There is no grain and artifacts make an appearance only a couple of times. Colors are vibrant with no bleed and the blacks are black enough to blend in with the letterboxing. Contrast and brightness levels are excellent. The 5.1 soundtrack more than keeps up—excellent Surround punctuates the action sequences and both the music and dialogue are crisp and defined. Excellent imaging and low end. —*JO*
Movie: ♫♫▶ DVD: ♫♫♫♫
Warner Home Video, Inc. (Cat #214202, UPC #085391420224). Widescreen (2.35:1) letterboxed; full frame. Dolby Digital 5.1. $24.98. Snapper. *LANG:* English; French. *SUB:* Spanish; French. *CAP:* English. *FEATURES:* 44 chapter links ▪ Theatrical trailer ▪ Cast and filmmaker's bios.
1996 (R) 115m/C Arnold Schwarzenegger, Vanessa L(ynne) Williams, James Caan, James Coburn, Robert Pastorelli, Andy Romano, James Cromwell, Danny Nucci, Nicholas Chinlund, Mark Rolston, Gerry Becker; **D:** Chuck Russell; **W:** Walon Green, Tony Puryear; **C:** Adam Greenberg; **M:** Alan Silvestri. *AWARDS: NOM:* MTV Movie Awards '97: Best Action Sequence.

The Eric Rohmer Collection: The Moral Tales

In "The Girl at the Monceau Bakery," a young man becomes infatuated with a girl he sees on the street, but after several days without seeing her again sets his sights on a girl in the local bakery. Eventually he has to choose between the two when he arranges dates with them both on the same day. "Suzanne's Career" examines the relationship between two friends when they both become interested in the same girl. The video transfer is a solid one; blacks are crisp and the sharpness of the overall image tends not to fluctuate as it does in most foreign films of this age. Likewise, the soundtrack is clear and discernable. —*MJT*
Movie: ♫♫♫ DVD: ♫♫▶
Fox/Lorber Home Video (Cat #FLV5204, UPC #720917520421). Full frame. Dolby Digital Stereo. $29.98. Keepcase. *LANG:* French. *SUB:* English. *FEATURES:* 12 chapter links ▪ Production credits ▪ Filmographies and awards ▪ Weblinks.
1962 78m/B *FR* Claudine Soubrier, Catherine See, Philippe Beuzen, Christian

Charriere, Diane Wilkinson; **D:** Eric Rohmer; **W:** Eric Rohmer; **C:** Daniel Lacambre, Barbet Schroeder, Michele Girardon, Bruno Barbey, Jean-Michel Meurice.

Erotic Ghost Story

A young scholar who's actually a demon seduces three supernatural sisters (one of whom is the cult star Amy Yip) and eventually gets some sort of comeuppance, but it's difficult for western fans who are not familiar with the conventions of Chinese comedy and horror to keep track of the soft-core action. Plot, however, is the least important part of the film. The DVD looks terrific with reds that are mostly true and well-defined. The same goes for the bright neon-colored outfits that the sisters wear and do not wear. Subtitles are white outlined in black and are exceptionally easy to read. —*MM*
Movie: ♫♫▶ DVD: ♫♫♫
Tai Seng Video Marketing (Cat #5097, UPC #4895024901565). Widescreen letterboxed. Dolby Digital Mono. $49.95. Keepcase. *LANG:* Mandarin. *SUB:* Traditional & Simplified Chinese; English. *FEATURES:* 8 chapter links ▪ Trailers ▪ Amy Yip thumbnail biography.
1990 89m/C *HK* Amy Yip, Leslie Cheung; **D:** Ngai Kai Lam.

Erotic Ghost Story: Perfect Match

Frivolous supernatural soft-core import is nothing special in the genre. The story has to do with three female spirits who are rabbits in heaven but beautiful women on Earth where they trick mortal men. The film was made with an overexposed, blurry focus, and an overreliance on colored light in dark scenes, so the image gains little on DVD. It is probably not much different from VHS tape. —*MM*
Movie: ♫♫ DVD: ♫♫
Tai Seng Video Marketing (Cat #5228, UPC #4895024901596). Full frame. Dolby Digital Mono. $49.95. Keepcase. *LANG:* Cantonese; Mandarin. *SUB:* Traditional Chinese; Simplified Chinese; English. *FEATURES:* 8 chapter links ▪ Thumbnail biographies of Elvis Tsui and Diana Pang ▪ Theatrical trailers.
1997 92m/C *CH* Elvis Tsui, Diana Pang, Kung Ka Ling, Wong Lei; **D:** Lam Yee Hung; **C:** Pang Chun Wai.

Escape from Alcatraz

Low-keyed, intense prison-break film is an overlooked masterpiece of the genre. Director Siegel tells the story without frills or fancy tricks; often without dialogue. The introduction of Alcatraz Island (where much of the action was shot) on a rainy night is virtually wordless. It's 1960, and the arriving con is Frank Morris (Eastwood). Once the situation has been established, Siegel, writer Tuggle, and cinematographer Bruce Surtees essentially let the fact-based story tell itself. After Morris

decides to escape, the plan and its execution are shown, not explained. The viewer gets the information through the images, not through descriptions or voice-overs. It's an exceptionally involving way to bring the viewer into the proceedings. Even on disc, the film retains the rough shot-on-location look of a good '70s picture. Some of the night scenes are hard to make out. They're supposed to be, but there's no pixelation even in the darkest moments. The mono sound is sharp and crisp. Any Eastwood fan who has missed this one is in for a treat. It's one of his very best. Somehow the no-frills DVD package is appropriate. —*MM*
Movie: ♫♫♫ DVD: ♫♫♫
Paramount Home Video (Cat #012567, UPC #0973601235672). Widescreen. Dolby Digital Mono. Keepcase. *LANG:* English; French. *CAP:* English. *FEATURES:* Interactive menus ▪ Scene access.
1979 (PG) 112m/C Clint Eastwood, Patrick McGoohan, Roberts Blossom, Fred Ward, Danny Glover; **D:** Donald Siegel; **W:** Richard Tuggle; **C:** Bruce Surtees; **M:** Jerry Fielding.

Escape from L.A.

Well, Snake Plissken is back (Russell once again) and so's Carpenter, who did the original *Escape from New York* saga, and technology's advanced a lot in 15 years, so sit back and enjoy the action. In 2013, L.A.'s been turned into a gang-infested island, thanks to a 9.6 earthquake. That's where Snake is forced to find a doomsday weapon in just 10 hours. Seems he's been injected with a virus that will kill him unless he can complete his job and escape to get the antidote. I never thought I'd say it, but this DVD might have a little too much contrast, resulting in an unreal, fake 3-D–look to the disc. However, the picture is very sharp, and even with the added contrast, there is no problem with distortion along the high-contrast lines. Colors are vibrant and only very rarely bleed. The brightness stays very consistent and the blacks are deep and true. Your Surround speakers will get a real workout with this one as there's always plenty routed to them during any of the action sequences. The sound is also very energetic and pumped full of good clean bass as well as crisp highs. —*JO AKA:* John Carpenter's Escape from L.A.
Movie: ♫♫▶ DVD: ♫♫♫
Paramount Home Video (Cat #332497, UPC #097363324973). Widescreen (2.35:1) letterboxed. Dolby Digital 5.1; Dolby Surround. $29.99. Keepcase. *LANG:* English (DD5.1; DS); French (DS). *SUB:* Spanish. *CAP:* English. *FEATURES:* 27 chapter links ▪ Theatrical trailer.
1996 (R) 101m/C Kurt Russell, Georges Corraface, Stacy Keach, Peter Fonda, Steve Buscemi, Pam Grier, Valeria Golino, Cliff Robertson, Michelle Forbes, Bruce Campbell, A.J. Langer; **D:** John Carpenter; **W:** Kurt Russell, John Carpenter, Debra Hill; **C:** Gary B. Kibbe; **M:** John Carpenter, Shirley Walker.

The Eternal Kiss of the Mummy

Despite the breathless title (which appears to have been extended from *The Eternal* for video), this curiosity is essentially a Gothic horror told in the oblique manner of an independent production. High-living socialites Nora (Elliott) and Jim (Harris) are introduced in New York, but the scene quickly shifts to Ireland where they go to reconnect with her family, including Uncle Bill (Walken), who lives in a gloomy mansion. On DVD, the cool greens, grays, and blues of the rainy Irish countryside are clear and evocative. Interiors are warmer and equally well realized. Overall, the film looks fine, but it is such an unusual exercise that it's not going to appeal to all audiences. —*MM* **AKA:** The Eternal Kiss of the Mummy.
Movie: 🦴🦴 **DVD:** 🦴🦴▶
Trimark Home Video (Cat #VM7065D, UPC #03139870653). Widescreen letterboxed. Dolby Digital Stereo. $24.99. Keepcase. *LANG:* English. *SUB:* English; French; Spanish. *CAP:* English. *FEATURES:* 30 chapter links ▪ Cast and crew filmographies.
1999 (R) 95m/C Alison Elliott, Jared Harris, Christopher Walken, Lois Smith, Karl Geary; *D:* Michael Almereyda; *W:* Michael Almereyda; *C:* Jim Denault; *M:* Simon Fisher-Turner.

Eternal Evil

A bored television director is taught how to have out-of-body experiences by his devil-worshipping girlfriend, but when he leaves the body, it runs around and kills people. On DVD, this nonsense is almost painful to watch. The pixelation in the darker scenes is extraordinary. Throughout the image is dim and grainy with a yellowish cast. The sound is poor, too. —*MM*
Movie: 🦴 **DVD:** woof
Simitar Entertainment (Cat #7303, UPC #082551730322). Full frame. PCM Stereo. $14.98. Keepcase. *LANG:* English. *FEATURES:* 8 chapter links ▪ Production factoids ▪ Karen Black filmography.
1987 (R) 85m/C Karen Black, Winston Rekert, Lois Maxwell; *D:* George Mihalka; *W:* Robert Geoffrion; *C:* Paul Van der Linden.

Even Dwarfs Started Small

Director Werner Herzog's companion piece to *The Terror of Tiny Town* (the all-midget western) is about tiny inmates who take over their asylum. Yes, movie fans, this one came from the 1960s, and it's a political allegory with chickens and little people. Actually, I cannot imagine why anyone would watch this thing voluntarily, though there was a time in my youth when I might well have found it terribly profound. On DVD, the smudgy black-and-white image appears to have been preserved or restored to its original condition. Sound is deliberately harsh. —*MM* **AKA:** Auch Zwerge Haben Klein Angefangen.
Movie: 🦴🦴 **DVD:** 🦴🦴🦴

Anchor Bay (Cat #DV10985, UPC #013131098594). Full frame. Dolby Digital Mono. $29.98. Keepcase. *LANG:* German. *SUB:* English. *FEATURES:* Commentary: Werner Herzog, Crispin Glover, Norman Hill ▪ 17 chapter links ▪ Herzog thumbnail bio.
1969 96m/B *GE D:* Werner Herzog; *W:* Werner Herzog; *C:* Thomas Mauch; *M:* Werner Herzog.

Event Horizon

Big-budget sci-fi combines elements of *Alien*, *The Shining*, and *Hellraiser* with predictably mixed results. Fishburne and Neill head an overachieving ensemble cast on a rescue mission to a mysteriously reappeared derelict spacecraft thought destroyed years before. Their own ship is attacked by spirits (or something). As high-quality eyecandy, the film mostly succeeds. On DVD, some of the fast-moving space exteriors are more than the medium can handle, with lines and shapes that lose their true form, and black objects that become featureless. The busy spaceship interiors tend to flash in places. Other computer-generated effects have the characteristic bright translucency that's impressive but obvious. Overall, this one's on a visual par with *Armageddon* and *Lost in Space*. —*MM*
Movie: 🦴🦴🦴 **DVD:** 🦴🦴🦴
Paramount Home Video (Cat #334827, UPC #097363348276). Widescreen letterboxed. Dolby 5.1 (English); Dolby Surround; Dolby Surround (French). $29.99. Keepcase. *LANG:* English; French. *SUB:* Spanish. *CAP:* English. *FEATURES:* 17 chapter links ▪ Theatrical trailer.
1997 (R) 97m/C Laurence "Larry" Fishburne, Sam Neill, Kathleen Quinlan, Joely Richardson, Richard T. Jones, Jack Noseworthy, Sean Pertwee, Jason Isaacs; *D:* Paul Anderson; *W:* Philip Eisner; *C:* Adrian Biddle; *M:* Michael Kamen.

Ever After: A Cinderella Story

The adorable Barrymore takes on Cinderella, renamed Danielle, and is very capable in this not-so-fairytale version set in 16th-century France. Huston is the peeved stepmother, Rodmilla, who reduces Danielle to the servant role in her own home after her beloved father (Krabbe) dies. Danielle still falls for handsome Prince Henry (Scott), though she is not above trying to change him about his privileged upbringing. Artist/genius Leonardo da Vinci (Godfrey) is the prince's confidante and there's still a lovely ball and a shoe to be lost (and found). The studio gave this DVD its all and it shows. The picture looks great, with zippy color and brightness and clean sound. Close to a theatrical experience. —*AB*
Movie: 🦴🦴🦴 **DVD:** 🦴🦴🦴🦴
Twentieth Century Fox Home Entertainment (Cat #4110381, UPC #8616210 381). Widescreen (2.35:1) letterboxed. Dolby Digital 5.1 Surround Stereo; Dolby Digital Surround. $34.98. Keepcase. *LANG:* Eng-

lish. *SUB:* English; Spanish. *FEATURES:* 30 chapter links ▪ Original theatrical trailer.
1998 (PG-13) 122m/C Drew Barrymore, Anjelica Huston, Dougray Scott, Patrick Godfrey, Megan Dodds, Melanie Lynskey, Timothy West, Judy Parfitt, Jeroen Krabbe; *Cameos:* Jeanne Moreau; *D:* Andy Tennant; *W:* Andy Tennant, Susannah Grant, Rick Parks; *C:* Andrew Dunn; *M:* George Fenton.

Everyone Says I Love You

Woody sings! Granted, he doesn't sing very well, but who else could twist a story of love among the neurotic rich with lavish production numbers from the golden age of movie musicals? The excellent cast (who weren't told that they were in a musical until after they'd all signed on) proves that as singers, they're pretty good actors. The plot centers on the wandering love lives of Steffi (Hawn), her husband Bob (Alda), her ex-husband Joe (Allen), and their assorted children—especially the preppy Skylar (Barrymore) and her fiance Holden (Norton). Some of the musical productions are shaky (Allen's duet with Julia Roberts is straight out of Tin Alley), but the feeling behind them is genuine. Besides, where else are you going to find Groucho's "Hurray for Captain Spaulding" sung in French or a chorus of pregnant women singing "Makin' Whoopee"? The DVD looks to be a minimal effort by Miramax/Disney, with no trailer, no anamorphic enhancement, not even production notes. Still, the image is sharper than VHS, and the dialogue—usually the most important audio element in a film by Allen—is clear and distinct on the 2.0 monaural soundtrack. Anyway, state-of-the-art Surround sound probably wouldn't have done much for the singing. —*MB*
Movie: 🦴🦴🦴 **DVD:** 🦴🦴▶
Miramax Pictures Home Video (Cat #17504, UPC #717951003225). Widescreen (1.85:1) letterboxed. Dolby Digital 2.0 Mono. $29.99. Keepcase. *LANG:* English. *CAP:* English. *FEATURES:* 15 chapter links.
1996 (R) 105m/C Woody Allen, Alan Alda, Drew Barrymore, Goldie Hawn, Gaby Hoffman, Edward Norton, Natalie Portman, Julia Roberts, Tim Roth, Natasha Lyonne, Lukas Haas, David Ogden Stiers; *D:* Woody Allen; *W:* Woody Allen; *C:* Carlo Di Palma; *M:* Dick Hyman. *AWARDS:* Los Angeles Film Critics Association Awards '96: Best Supporting Actor (Norton); National Board of Review Awards '96: Best Supporting Actor (Norton); *NOM:* Golden Globe Awards '97: Best Film—Musical/Comedy.

Eve's Bayou

In 1962 Louisiana, young Eve (Smollett) comes from the upper–middle class Batiste family that seems almost perfect on the outside. Secrets and lies slowly surface when she mistakenly catches her doctor father (Jackson) doing more than a routine checkup with a female patient. The discovery soon affects her emotionally strained mother Roz (Whitfield) and adolescent tease older sister Cisely (Good). Told in flashback, the film presents a mesmerizing, complex story with haunting visuals beautifully captured on DVD. Both image and sound are carefully detailed and exceptionally clear. Recommended. —MM

Movie: 🎬🎬🎬 **DVD:** 🎬🎬🎬▷
Trimark Home Video (Cat #6741). Widescreen anamorphic. Dolby Digital Stereo. $24.99. Keepcase. *LANG:* English; French; Spanish. *FEATURES:* Short film, "Dr. Hugo" • Filmmakers' commentary track • "Making of" soundtrack featurette • Cast and crew thumbnail bios • Trailer.
1997 (R) 109m/C Samuel L. Jackson, Lynn Whitfield, Debbi Morgan, Diahann Carroll, Jurnee Smollett, Meagan Good, Vondie Curtis-Hall, Lisa Nicole Carson, Jake Smollett, Ethel Ayler; **W:** Kasi Lemmons; **C:** Amy Vincent; **M:** Terence Blanchard; **Nar:** Tamara Tunie. *AWARDS:* Independent Spirit Awards '98: Best First Feature, Best Supporting Actress (Morgan).

Evil Dead

Five college students, vacationing in the Tennessee mountains, unwittingly resurrect demons that transform the students into evil monsters. Director Raimi keeps tensions flowing and gives the world its first chance to see his energetic and inventive camera moves. Exuberantly gory low-budgeter followed by two sequels. Elite's DVD transfer is identical to the theatrical presentation, with perhaps better contrast. The image is sharp and most of the grain is from the original preprint. Colors are accurate and the added contrast makes them a little more vibrant, without being harsher, than they were in the theatre. Blacks are very good and the brightness level is also improved. The remastered 5.1 is a little gutsier than the original, even if the additional channels are synthesized and gimmicky. —JO

Movie: 🎬🎬🎬▷ **DVD:** 🎬🎬🎬
Elite Entertainment, Inc. (Cat #EE7265, UPC #790594726522). Full frame. Dolby Digital 5.1; Stereo. $34.95. Keepcase. *LANG:* English. *FEATURES:* 16 chapter links • Audio commentary • Still photo gallery • Alternate takes and behind-the-scenes footage • Theatrical trailer.
1983 (NC-17) 85m/C Bruce Campbell, Ellen Sandweiss, Betsy Baker, Hal Delrich, Sarah York, Theodore (Ted) Raimi, Sam Raimi, Scott Spiegel; **D:** Sam Raimi; **W:** Sam Raimi; **C:** Tim Philo; **M:** Joseph LoDuca.

Evil Dead 2:
Dead by Dawn

Rare sequel is actually superior to the original in some senses. Sam Raimi creates a special effects tour de force using

stop-motion animation, prosthetics, reverse motion, and long dizzying tracking shots. Bruce Campbell (also a producer) being attacked by his own hand is a grand moment. The graphic violence is so removed from any reality that it has no emotional content and that heightens the film's strong humor. On DVD, the clarity of the images rivals theatrical projection, and somehow, the smaller size accentuates Raimi's comic intentions while de-emphasizing the power of the gory effects. Sound is fine. One quibble: Wouldn't a commentary track with director and star have been fun? —MM

Movie: 🎬🎬🎬 **DVD:** 🎬🎬🎬
Anchor Bay (Cat #DV10504, UPC #013131050493). Widescreen (1.85:1) letterboxed. Dolby Digital Stereo. $29.98. Keepcase. *LANG:* English. *FEATURES:* 12 chapter links • Theatrical trailer.
1987 (R) 84m/C Bruce Campbell, Sarah Berry, Dan Hicks, Kassie Wesley, Theodore (Ted) Raimi, Denise Bixler, Richard Domeier, Scott Spiegel, Josh Becker, Lou Hancock; **Cameos:** Sam Raimi; **D:** Sam Raimi; **W:** Sam Raimi, Scott Spiegel; **C:** Peter Deming; **M:** Joseph LoDuca.

Evil Ed

A strong stomach is required to watch this tale of formerly mild-mannered film editor Ed (Ruebeck). He becomes obsessed with the horror series he's working on, goes off the deep end, and embarks upon a series of killings that mimic the ones from the films. The result: Buckets of splatter. The packaging describes the gorefest as "Splatterific," so let that assessment guide you, as if the gross-out box art doesn't do the trick on its own. The letterboxing preserves the theatrical framing, and sound and picture are acceptable considering the content, though visual noise in the darker scenes is problematic. Extras are absent. —MB

Movie: 🎬▷ **DVD:** 🎬🎬
Image Entertainment (Cat #ID4656APDVD, UPC #014381465624). Widescreen (1.66:1) letterboxed. Dolby Digital 2.0. $24.98. Snapper. *LANG:* English. *FEATURES:* 12 chapter links.
1996 (R) 90m/C SW Johan Ruebeck, Olof Rhodin, Pete Lofbergh; **D:** Anders Jacobsson; **W:** Anders Jacobsson; **C:** Anders Jacobsson; **M:** Goran Lundstrom.

Evita

Webber/Rice rock opera about the life and death of Eva Peron finally comes to the screen with all its extravaganza intact. Madonna's in the title role (in fine voice, lavishly costumed but unflatteringly lit) of an ambitious poor girl willing to do anything to make her mark—in this version by sleeping her way up the ladder of power to Argentine strongman Juan Peron (Pryce as wax dummy). Evita becomes a would-be champion of the people, even as the government ruthlessly suppresses their freedoms. The surprisingly strong-voiced Banderas (perhaps his emphatic

enunciation is to make his English as clear as possible) is everyman narrator Che (changed from the stage version's revolutionary Che Guevera). The highlight is still Madonna's balcony scene, singing "Don't Cry for Me, Argentina," but some of the other songs are drowned out by loud orchestration. Director Parker has a cameo as a frustrated film director trying to work with Evita. The 5.1 sound is a little wasted here; it is of average fidelity and doesn't make much use of the Surround channels, even for ambience. Good bass, dynamics, and fidelity come through on the musical numbers. Picture sharpness is above average and both grain and artifacts are minimal. Colors are very good, accurate and vibrant, and there is little bleed. The contrast is excellent and brightness both comfortable and consistent. Blacks are true with no grain added. —JO

Movie: 🎬🎬▷ **DVD:** 🎬🎬🎬
Buena Vista Home Entertainment (Cat #13849, UPC #717951000200). Widescreen (2.35:1) letterboxed. Dolby Digital 5.1. $29.99. Keepcase. *LANG:* English. *SUB:* Spanish. *CAP:* English. *FEATURES:* 33 chapter links.
1996 (PG) 133m/C Madonna, Antonio Banderas, Jonathan Pryce, Jimmy Nail, Victoria Sus, Julian Littman, Olga Meediz, Laura Pallas, Julia Worsley; **Cameos:** Alan Parker; **D:** Alan Parker; **W:** Oliver Stone, Alan Parker; **C:** Darius Khondji; **M:** Andrew Lloyd Webber, Tim Rice. *AWARDS:* Academy Awards '96: Best Song ("You Must Love Me"); Golden Globe Awards '97: Best Actress—Musical/Comedy (Madonna), Best Film—Musical/Comedy, Best Song ("You Must Love Me"); *NOM:* Academy Awards '96: Best Art Direction/Set Decoration, Best Cinematography, Best Film Editing, Best Sound; British Academy Awards '96: Best Adapted Screenplay; Golden Globe Awards '97: Best Actor—Musical/Comedy (Banderas), Best Director (Parker); MTV Movie Awards '97: Best Female Performance (Madonna), Best Song ("Don't Cry for Me Argentina").

Evolver

Teenaged Kyle Baxter (Randall) wins a robot patterned after a video arcade game but the machine has a secret military weapon's program hidden in its circuitry. It threatens Kyle and his fellow game-player Jamie (Rae). DVD can do nothing to elevate this low-budget material. All the usual problems—flashing lines, grainy darkness—are apparent. —MM

Movie: 🎬▷ **DVD:** 🎬▷
Trimark Home Video (Cat #7056D). Full frame. Dolby Digital Surround Stereo. $14.99. Keepcase. *LANG:* English. *FEATURES:* 11 chapter links.
1994 (R) 90m/C Ethan (Randall) Embry, John de Lancie, Cassidy Rae, Cindy Pickett, Paul Dooley; **D:** Mark Rosman; **W:** Mark Rosman; **C:** Jacques Haitkin; **V:** William H. Macy.

Excalibur

John Boorman's retelling of the Arthurian legends begins with Uther (Byrne) receiving the sword from Merlin (Williamson) and follows it through the quest for the grail to the tragic conclusion. Though some may object to Boorman's choices, he captures the essence of the myth and he's never boring. Though this is definitely a big-screen film, it fares well on DVD. Boorman's expressive use of glowing greens is particularly strong. The director's commentary track touches on technical trivia, his interpretation of the material, the problems involved in bringing it to the screen, casting, and locations. Though he claims that he had no problems directing his own daughter in a nude rape scene, he sounds uncomfortable. The film is still one of the very best of its kind. —*MM*
Movie: 🦴🦴🦴► **DVD:** 🦴🦴🦴►
Warner Home Video, Inc. (Cat #22018, UPC #085392201822). Widescreen letterboxed. Dolby Digital 5.1 Surround; Dolby Digital Mono. $19.98. Snapper. *LANG:* English; French. *SUB:* English; French. *CAP:* English. *FEATURES:* 45 chapter links • Commentary: director Boorman.
1981 (R) 140m/C Nigel Terry, Nicol Williamson, Nicholas Clay, Helen Mirren, Cherie Lunghi, Paul Geoffrey, Gabriel Byrne, Liam Neeson, Patrick Stewart, Charley Boorman, Corin Redgrave; *D:* John Boorman; *W:* Rospo Pallenberg, John Boorman; *C:* Alex Thomson; *M:* Trevor Jones. *AWARDS: NOM:* Academy Awards '81: Best Cinematography.

Excess Baggage

Attention-seeking rich girl Emily (Silverstone) fakes her own kidnapping to get back at dear old dad, involving car thief Vincent Roche (del Toro) in the crime. Things get out of control when her creepy "Uncle" Ray (Walken), who's an ex-CIA assassin, is hired by Emily's father to get her back. Silverstone's character is alternately whiny and pouting, you'll wonder why dad would want her back and why Vincent hangs on at all. This above-average DVD has decent sharpness and very little grain. Colors are fairly strong and bleed is never a problem. Blacks are true unless they engulf the whole screen, which causes them to seek a little brightness and turn a little gray. This is one of those films where you wonder if it really needed a 5.1 track. The bass is a little more defined and has more balls, but there is hardly anything in the way of Surround, even musically. —*JO*
Movie: 🦴► **DVD:** 🦴🦴►
Columbia Tristar Home Video (Cat #82309, UPC #043396823099). Widescreen (1.85:1) letterboxed; full frame. Dolby Digital 5.1; Dolby Digital 2.0. $29.95. Keepcase. *LANG:* English; French; Spanish. *SUB:* English; French; Spanish. *CAP:* English. *FEATURES:* 36 chapter links • Theatrical trailer.

1996 (PG-13) 101m/C Alicia Silverstone, Benicio Del Toro, Christopher Walken, Harry Connick Jr., Jack Thompson, Nicholas Turturro, Michael Bowen, Leland Orser, Robert Wisden, Sally Kirkland; *D:* Marco Brambilla; *W:* Mikhaila Max Adams, Dick Clement, Ian LaFrenais; *C:* Jean-Yves Escoffier; *M:* John Lurie. *AWARDS: NOM:* Golden Raspberry Awards '97: Worst Actress (Silverstone).

Exclusive

TV reporter Marcy (Somers) investigates a murder and is caught between a new ratings-obsessed station owner and her professor husband (Nouri) who's a suspect. The made-for-TV thriller is absolutely average in plot and acting. On DVD, the same can be said of the picture and sound quality, though the night exteriors are noticeably weak. —*MM*
Movie: 🦴► **DVD:** 🦴►
Simitar Entertainment (Cat #7582, UPC #082551758227). Full frame. Dolby Digital Stereo. $14.98. Keepcase. *LANG:* English. *FEATURES:* 8 chapter links • Suzanne Somers filmography.
1982 91m/C Suzanne Somers, Ed Begley Jr., Joe Cortese, Scott Bryce, Kelly Rowan, Jerry Adler, Michael Nouri; *D:* Alan Metzger; *W:* Mimi Rothman Schapiro, Bill Wells.

The Executioners

When a nuclear explosion contaminates most of the city's drinking water, the remainder falls under the harsh control of the Black Knight. Now, it's up to the Heroic Trio to defeat their nemesis. Sequel to *The Heroic Trio* is grimmer and not quite as good, but still enjoyable. The DVD for the earlier movie was just O.K., but this one loses a little bit of sharpness. The colors are strong enough, and although there is the usual Tai Seng preprint damage, this disc is also at least acceptable to view. Like the first film, the sound is still blah, and with this kind of action-fantasy, Surround tracks are missed. —*JO*
Movie: 🦴► **DVD:** 🦴🦴
Tai Seng Video Marketing (Cat #44614, UPC #601643446161). Widescreen (1.77:1) letterboxed. Stereo. $29.95. Keepcase. *LANG:* English; Mandarin; Cantonese. *SUB:* English; Chinese. *FEATURES:* 9 chapter links • Trailers.
1993 100m/C *HK* Anita Mui, Michelle Yeoh, Maggie Cheung; *D:* Ching Siu Tung; *W:* Susanne Chan; *C:* Poon Hang-Seng; *M:* Cacine Wong.

Executive Decision

Those wacky terrorists are at it again. You would think that after getting their butts kicked in almost every action picture since 1980 that they would learn. But here they are, hijacking a 747, cutting off communications, and affixing a nerve gas bomb to the plane. This time a group of high-tech commandos, led by Russell and (briefly)

Seagal, must sneak onto the plane and generally mess up the bad guys' plans. Brave stewardess Berry helps tango with the central casting mad dog terrorists. The title refers to the President's decision on whether or not to blow the plane up. Or maybe "Die Hard: Ad Nauseum" wasn't available. With the 5.1 sound there are some pretty big bangs in the air. The picture is fairly good, too, although the colors lose a little of their strength, and the sharpness trails off as well, in the darker scenes. It seems strange, but even then the blacks stay mostly true, and on the whole the disc looks pretty good. —*JO*
Movie: 🦴🦴► **DVD:** 🦴🦴🦴
Warner Home Video, Inc. (Cat #14211, UPC #085391421122). Widescreen (2.35:1) anamorphic. Dolby Digital 5.1. $24.98. Snapper. *LANG:* English. *SUB:* English; Spanish; French. *CAP:* English. *FEATURES:* 37 chapter links • Production notes.
1996 (R) 132m/C Kurt Russell, Halle Berry, Oliver Platt, John Leguizamo, Steven Seagal, Joe Morton, David Suchet, B.D. Wong, Len Cariou, Whip Hubley, J.T. Walsh; *D:* Stuart Baird; *W:* Jim Thomas, John Thomas; *C:* Alex Thomson; *M:* Jerry Goldsmith. *AWARDS: NOM:* Golden Raspberry Awards '96: Worst Supporting Actor (Seagal).

eXistenZ

Given the timing of its release (1999) and subject matter (levels of subjective reality), it was inevitable that David Cronenberg's film would be compared to *Dark World* and *The Matrix*. The three are similar, but Cronenberg continues to explore ideas and visual motifs that can be traced back to *Videodrome* and *Naked Lunch*. Here computer game designer Allegra Geller (Leigh) and P.R. guy Ted Pikul (Law) are on the run from assassins who may be real or may be part of her newest game, *eXistenZ*, which is played through "bioports" drilled directly into the players' spines. Cronenberg's approach to the subject is slow and deliberately stylized. The DVD captures his often off-putting visual effects, and the uniformly fine ensemble performances. Sound is fine but not overpowering. Visual quality is about the same because the image lacks a certain brightness. Anyone expecting the somber atmospherics and dazzling kinetic action of the other two films will be disappointed. Cronenberg's fans know what to expect. —*MM*
Movie: 🦴🦴🦴 **DVD:** 🦴🦴🦴
Buena Vista Home Entertainment (Cat #18326, UPC #717951005120). Widescreen (1.77:1) letterboxed. Dolby Digital Surround Stereo. $39.99. Keepcase. *LANG:* English. *CAP:* English. *FEATURES:* Theatrical trailer • 26 chapter links.
1999 (R) 97m/C *CA* Jennifer Jason Leigh, Jude Law, Ian Holm, Willem Dafoe, Sarah Polley, Christopher Eccleston, Don McKellar, Callum Keith Rennie; *D:* David Cronenberg; *W:* David Cronenberg; *C:* Peter Suschitzsky; *M:* Howard Shore.

The Exorcist (SE)

Truly terrifying story of a young girl who is possessed by a malevolent spirit. Brilliantly directed by Friedkin, with underlying themes of the workings and nature of fate. Impeccable casting and unforgettable, thought-provoking performances. A rare film that remains startling and engrossing with every viewing, it spawned countless imitations and changed the way horror films were made. Not for the squeamish. The image on the original DVD release of the film was sharp enough but lacked contrast and colors were hindered by the high level of the brightness. The "Special Edition" has a sharper picture, even less grain, and much richer colors. The contrast has also been boosted and brightness is down a bit. Blacks are grainless and true. The re-done 5.1 sound is also much preferred with better low end, and while the highs are still there, they have been smoothed considerably. Some nice ambience and Surround effects have also been added to liven up the mix. —*JO*
Movie: *♫♫♫►* **DVD:** *♫♫♫►*
Warner Home Video, Inc. (Cat #16176, UPC #085391617624). Widescreen (1.85:1) letterboxed. Dolby Digital 5.1; Dolby Surround; Mono. $24.98. Snapper. *LANG:* English (DD5.1; DS); French (mono). *SUB:* English; French. *CAP:* English. *FEATURES:* 47 chapter links ▪ Exclusive documentary (23 chapter links) ▪ Audio commentary ▪ Behind-the-scenes footage ▪ Production notes ▪ 8 theatrical trailers ▪ 6 TV spots.
1973 (R) 120m/C Ellen Burstyn, Linda Blair, Jason Miller, Max von Sydow, Jack MacGowran, Lee J. Cobb, Kitty Winn, Barton Heyman, Peter Masterson; *D:* William Friedkin; *W:* William Peter Blatty; *C:* Owen Roizman, Billy Williams; *M:* Jack Nitzsche; *V:* Mercedes McCambridge. *AWARDS:* Academy Awards '73: Best Adapted Screenplay, Best Sound; Golden Globe Awards '74: Best Director (Friedkin), Best Film—Drama, Best Screenplay, Best Supporting Actress (Blair); *NOM:* Academy Awards '73: Best Actress (Burstyn), Best Art Direction/Set Decoration, Best Cinematography, Best Director (Friedkin), Best Film Editing, Best Picture, Best Supporting Actor (Miller), Best Supporting Actress (Blair).

Exotica

Egoyan's meditation on loss and loneliness takes Leonard Cohen's haunted "Everybody Knows" as its musical theme. The film is also a mystery where motivations and intentions are not at all what they first appear to be. The central character is Christina (Kirshner), a dancer at Exotica, a relatively classy Toronto strip club. Her most devoted customer is Francis (Greenwood), a tax auditor whose single-minded obsession doesn't seem to bother her as much as it ought to be. Eric (Koteas), the club's DJ, is more upset and, in his own way, equally obsessed. Exotica's very pregnant owner, Zoe (Khanjian), is starting to worry about him. While Fran-

cis spends his nights at the club, during the day he goes over the books at a pet store owned by Thomas (McKellar), a gay man who has reasons to be worried about a tax audit. That synopsis only begins to describe the levels of complexity that are revealed. Surprisingly, the difficult interiors are rendered faithfully on DVD. Dark, curiously illuminated material can be difficult for a digital medium, but the disc contains no serious visual flaws. A commentary track by Egoyan would have been a real asset. —*MM*
Movie: *♫♫♫►* **DVD:** *♫♫♫*
Miramax Pictures Home Video (Cat #17506, UPC #71795100324). Widescreen (1.66:1) letterboxed. Dolby Digital Stereo. $29.99. Keepcase. *LANG:* English. *CAP:* English. *FEATURES:* 26 chapter links.
1994 (R) 104m/C *CA* Mia Kirshner, Elias Koteas, Bruce Greenwood, Don McKellar, Victor Garber, Arsinee Khanjian, Sarah Polley, Calvin Green, David Hemblen; *D:* Atom Egoyan; *W:* Atom Egoyan; *C:* Paul Sarossy; *M:* Mychael Danna. *AWARDS:* Genie Awards '94: Best Art Direction/Set Decoration, Best Cinematography, Best Costume Design, Best Director (Egoyan), Best Film, Best Original Screenplay, Best Supporting Actor (McKellar), Best Score; Toronto-City Award '94: Best Canadian Feature Film; *NOM:* Genie Awards '94: Best Actor (Greenwood), Best Actor (Koteas); Independent Spirit Awards '96: Best Foreign Film.

Expect the Unexpected

This tricky, fast-moving action flick begins with a robbery-gone-bad that leads to the discovery of much more serious crimes. The main players are a particularly vicious gang and the cops of the Organized Crime Bureau led by Capt. Chung Kin (Yam). Though the film was made with unusually high production values, the DVD suffers from a host of visual flaws. Busy background shapes often break up during fast and medium pans—and director Patrick Yau seldom lets his camera stay still—bright diagonal lines break up and miniblinds pinwheel. The stereo is remarkably good, emphasizing street sounds, and other natural effects. Though Yau does not choreograph his action scenes with the artfulness of John Woo, his work is just as viscerally violent. In many respects this one is similar to Michael Mann's *Heat.* —*MM*
Movie: *♫♫♫* **DVD:** *♫♫►*
Tai Seng Video Marketing (Cat #5199, UPC #4895024900650). Widescreen letterboxed. Dolby Digital 5.1 Surround Stereo. $49.95. Keepcase. *LANG:* Cantonese; Mandarin. *SUB:* Traditional Chinese; Simplified Chinese; English. *FEATURES:* 8 chapter links ▪ Cast thumbnail biographies and print interviews ▪ Outtakes ▪ Footage of the theatrical premiere.
1998 87m/C *HK* Lau Ching Wan, Simon Yam, Ruby Wong, Yo Yo Wong, Raymond Wong, Hui Siu Hung; *D:* Patrick Yau; *W:*

Szeto Kam Yuen, Yau Nai Hoi, Taurus Chow; *C:* Ko Chiu Lam.

Expert Weapon

It's an ultra-low-budget male version of *La Femme Nikita* with Adam Collins (Jacklin), an imprisoned cop killer recruited as an assassin by Janson (Jones) for his ultra-secret government organization. The sets are cheap; the fights are slow and amateurish. On DVD, the daylight exteriors look washed-out and the sound is poor. —*MM*
Movie: *♫►* **DVD:** *♫*
Simitar Entertainment (Cat #7484, UPC #082551748426). Full frame. Dolby Digital Stereo. $14.98. Keepcase. *LANG:* English. *FEATURES:* 8 chapter links ▪ Sam Jones filmography.
1993 90m/C Ian Jacklin, Sam Jones, Mel Novak, Judy Landers, Joe Estevez; *D:* Steve Austin.

Exterminator

There's nothing about the plot of this archetypal revenge flick—Vietnam vet John Eastland (Ginty) gets even with the street gang that attacks his best bud and fellow vet. What's interesting now is the undeniable influence it has had on the action films that have come since. Director Glickenhaus steadily ratchets up the violence from a graphic beginning. At the time of the film's theatrical release, it was labeled as sadistic by critics and became a huge cult hit. This DVD actually looks better and brighter than the theatrical version of the film that I reviewed in 1980, and it's longer. Significant cuts were made, though the liner notes are unclear as to who demanded them, citing only unnamed "censors," which do not exist in this country and did not in 1980 either. Apparently the difference between this unrated version and the "R"-rated tape is three minutes. —*MM*
Movie: *♫♫♫* **DVD:** *♫♫♫*
Anchor Bay (Cat #DV10336, UPC #013131033694). Widescreen. Dolby Digital Mono. $24.99. Keepcase. *LANG:* English. *FEATURES:* 18 chapter links.
1980 104m/C Christopher George, Samantha Eggar, Robert Ginty, Steve James, Tony DiBenedetto, Dick Boccelli, Patrick Farrelly, Michele Harrell, Stan Getz, Roger Grimsby; *D:* James Glickenhaus; *W:* James Glickenhaus; *C:* Robert M "Bob" Baldwin Jr.; *M:* Joe Renzetti.

Extramarital

A magazine editor (Fahey) assigns a reporter (Lords) to investigate a woman whose affair with a mystery man turns deadly.
Movie: *♫♫* **DVD:** NYR
Sunland Studios (Cat #281). Full frame. $24.99. Keepcase.
1998 (R) 90m/C Jeff Fahey, Traci Lords, Brian Bloom, Maria Diaz; *D:* Yael Russcol.

Extreme Justice

Generic title is fitting for a violent expose of the Special Investigations Section of the LAPD, a real undercover squad of cops that dealt harshly with repeat offenders. They were accused of stalking their prey until they committed crimes and then killing them. In this fictionalized version, Phillips is the young cop who is brought in to the unit run by Glenn and Kotto. Originally a theatrical release that was pulled in the wake of the Rodney King verdict. Usually reliable B-director Mark L. Lester handles the action well enough, but the entire production is a bit stale. The DVD transfer reflects the level of quality. The chapter links are unlabeled. Even in daylight scenes, dark shapes lose definition and detail. —MM

Movie: ♫♫ **DVD:** ♫♫
Trimark Home Video (Cat #7052D, UPC #031398704331). Full frame. Dolby Digital Surround. $34.99. Keepcase. LANG: English. FEATURES: 11 chapter links. The title is available for sale only as a part of "The Best of Action" 4-pack.
1993 (R) 96m/C Lou Diamond Phillips, Scott Glenn, Yaphet Kotto, Ed Lauter, Chelsea Field; **D:** Mark L. Lester; **W:** Robert Boris; **C:** Mark Irwin; **M:** David Michael Frank.

An Extremely Goofy Movie

When his son Max (voice of Marsden) goes off to college, Goofy (Farmer) decides it's time for him to get a degree, too, much to the embarrassment of the boy and his pals. The quality of the animation and the writing is much closer to Saturday morning TV fare than the studio's feature-length work, but it's still bright and funny enough to entertain young viewers who have been weaned on Rugrats and other high-energy fare, though their folks will probably get just as big a kick out of Goofy in an ice-cream suit getting down with "Shake Your Groove Thing." —MM

Movie: ♫♫▸ **DVD:** ♫♫▸
Buena Vista Home Entertainment (Cat #19146, UPC #717951007100). Widescreen (1.66:1) letterboxed. Dolby Digital 5.1 Surround Stereo. $29.99. Keepcase. LANG: English. FEATURES: 21 chapter links • Trivia game • "Me and My Dad" read-along • "Right Back Where We Started From" music video • DVD-ROM features • Kid's goofiest jokes.
1999 76m/C D: Douglas McCarthy; **W:** Scott Gorden, Hillary Carlip; **M:** Steve Bartek; **V:** Bill Farmer, Jason Marsden, Bebe Neuwirth, Kellie Martin, Wallace Shawn, Jo Anne Worley, Pauly Shore.

Eye of the Serpent

Semi-tongue-in-cheek sword and sorcery rounds up the usual suspects—brave warrior, sorceress, brave female warrior, princess, ultimate evil (with a bucket on his head)—and puts them through their paces. The image is acceptable on DVD, though soft focus and scenes tinted with colored lights hardly test the limits of the medium. —MM

Movie: ♫♫ **DVD:** ♫▸
Simitar Entertainment (Cat #7309, UPC #082551730926). Full frame. PCM Stereo. $14.98. Keepcase. LANG: English. FEATURES: 12 chapter links • Production factoids.
1992 (R) 85m/C Diana Frank, Lenore Andriel, Tom Schultz, Lisa Toothman; **D:** Ricardo Jacques Gale.

Eyes Wide Shut

When Dr. William Harford (Cruise) learns that his wife Alice (Kidman) once considered having an affair with another man, he sets off on a long, tortuous search for extra-marital adventure. In typical Kubrick fashion, the characters are not so much fully human as pieces in the director's bag of tricks, only marginally more important than set decoration and the symbolic use of color. (Film students of the future will write long papers on his use of Christmas trees here.) The image is often striking—the scenes at the opening party are reminiscent of the best parts of The Shining—but the monotonous one-note score will drive you nuts and the pace is lethargic. Perhaps the film's lack of boxoffice success and length led Warner Bros. to release it in full frame only, and without removing the computer-generated figures that hide the action during the low-octane gold-tinted orgy. Those same shots are dark, grainy, and filled with pixels, too. (Reportedly, Kubrick had intended for the film to be released on home video in a conventional full-frame ratio and photographed it that way.) —MM

Movie: ♫♫▸ **DVD:** ♫♫♫
Warner Home Video, Inc. (Cat #17655). Full frame. $24.98. Snapper. LANG: English. FEATURES: 38 chapter links • Interviews with Cruise, Kidman, Steven Spielberg • TV spots • Trailers.
1999 (R) 159m/C Tom Cruise, Nicole Kidman, Sydney Pollack, Marie Richardson, Vinessa Shaw, Todd Field, Rade Serbedzija, Leelee Sobieski, Alan Cumming, Thomas Gibson, Sky Dumont, Fay Masterson; **D:** Stanley Kubrick; **W:** Stanley Kubrick; **C:** Larry Smith; **M:** Jocelyn Pook. AWARDS: NOM: Golden Globe Awards '00: Best Original Score.

The Fabulous Baker Boys

Two brothers, Jack and Frank Baker (Bridges and Bridges), have been performing a tired act as nightclub pianists for 15 years in Seattle. When they hire sultry vocalist Suzie Diamond (Pfeiffer) to revitalize the routine, her presence triggers long-hidden hostilities between the "boys." It's a bit predictable but the characters and the performances are first-rate. The DVD image is exceptionally strong; so is the sound, but the disc's best feature is the commentary track by director of photography Michael Ballhaus. He takes a more technical approach than most filmmakers, but he's perceptive and he makes excellent points. —MM

Movie: ♫♫♫ **DVD:** ♫♫♫▸
Artisan Entertainment (Cat #60485, UPC #012236048503). Widescreen letterboxed; full frame. Dolby Digital Surround Stereo. $24.98. Snapper. LANG: English. SUB: Spanish. CAP: English. FEATURES: Cast and crew thumbnail biographies • Production notes • Trailers • 36 chapter links • Commentary: Michael Ballhaus.
1989 (R) 116m/C Michelle Pfeiffer, Jeff Bridges, Beau Bridges, Elie Raab, Jennifer Tilly; **D:** Steven Kloves; **W:** Steven Kloves; **C:** Michael Ballhaus; **M:** Dave Grusin. AWARDS: Golden Globe Awards '90: Best Actress—Drama (Pfeiffer); Los Angeles Film Critics Association Awards '89: Best Actress (Pfeiffer), Best Cinematography; National Board of Review Awards '89: Best Actress (Pfeiffer); New York Film Critics Awards '89: Best Actress (Pfeiffer); National Society of Film Critics Awards '89: Best Actress (Pfeiffer), Best Cinematography, Best Supporting Actor (Bridges); NOM: Academy Awards '89: Best Actress (Pfeiffer), Best Cinematography, Best Film Editing, Best Original Score.

Face/Off

Woo returns to his blood-soaked, violence-as-poetry-in-motion roots with the story of a fed who assumes the identity of the presumed-dead terrorist who killed his son. When the master criminal wakes up, he "steals" the cop's identity, Woo's Hong Kong efforts have always explored the blurry lines between the good guys and the bad guys, and with Cage and Travolta, he has the perfect actors to display his findings. Woo cultists will welcome the return to his old style. This is a very good DVD in every way, but the only added feature is the theatrical trailer. Blacks are true, and the contrast and brightness levels are as good as when it was when projected in the theatre. Grain is very minimal, whether the scene is light or dark and there are very few artifacts (some showed up on a couple of very quick camera pans). Colors are excellent, with bleed pretty much nonexistent. On the DVD the final showdown is a real show stopper, featuring great color saturation, and heart-pounding sound both on the Dolby Digital and Dolby Surround tracks. —JO

Movie: ♫♫♫▸ **DVD:** ♫♫♫▸
Paramount Home Video (Cat #154957, UPC #097361549576). Widescreen (2.35:1) anamorphic. Dolby Digital 5.1; Dolby Surround. $29.95. Keepcase. LANG: English (DD5.1; DS); French (DS). SUB: French. CAP: English. FEATURES: Dual-layered RSDL • 40 chapter links • Theatrical trailer.
1997 (R) 140m/C John Travolta, Nicolas Cage, Joan Allen, Alessandro Nivola, Gina Gershon, Nick Cassavetes, Dominique Swain, Harve Presnell, Margaret Cho, CCH

Pounder, Colm Feore, John Carroll Lynch, Matt Ross; **D:** John Woo; **W:** Mike Werb, Michael Colleary; **C:** Oliver Wood; **M:** John Powell. AWARDS: MTV Movie Awards '98: Best On-Screen Duo (John Travolta/Nicolas Cage), Best Action Sequence; NOM: Academy Awards '97: Best Sound Effects Editing; MTV Movie Awards '98: Best Film, Best Male Performance (Cage, Travolta), Best Villain (John Travolta/Nicolas Cage).

Face the Evil

Fans of video premieres know that Shannon Tweed and Lance Henriksen are two of the most reliable actors in the business. They're in fine form in this quirky thriller. She plays a TV actress taken hostage in an art gallery where her gang wants to retrieve a shipment of nerve gas hidden in one of the works. Yes, it's pretty silly but they pull it off. On DVD, the image is clear throughout and the sound is adequate. —MM

Movie: 🎞️🎞️🎞️ **DVD:** 🎞️🎞️🎞️
Simitar Entertainment (Cat #7458, UPC #082551745821). Full frame. Dolby Digital Stereo; Dolby Digital 5.1 Surround. $14.98. Keepcase. LANG: English. FEATURES: 8 chapter links • Filmographies for Lance Henriksen and Shannon Tweed.
1997 (R) 92m/C Shannon Tweed, Lance Henriksen, Bruce Payne, Jayne Heitmeyer; **D:** Paul Lynch; **W:** Richard Beattie; **C:** Barry Gravelle; **M:** Paul Zaza.

Faces of Death

First an admission: I skipped and scanned my way through this disc as quickly as I could. As most videophiles probably know, the infamous, controversial title is a compilation of film clips of allegedly "real" deaths, atrocities, and brutal events. Some footage, such as the slaughterhouse, is probably real. Other parts are cheap obvious fakes. None of it is very interesting. The image quality is poor. —MM

Movie: 🎞️ **DVD:** 🎞️
Gorgon Video (Cat #DVD2200, UPC #742107220027). Full frame. Dolby Digital Mono. $24.98. Keepcase. LANG: English. SUB: English; Spanish. FEATURES: 24 chapter links.
1978 88m/C D: Conan LeClaire; **W:** Alan Black; **Nar:** Frances B. Gross.

The Faculty

High school students make a terrifying discovery that ultimately confirms their worst suspicions—their teachers really are from another planet! With this knowledge, they are forced to band together to save their school and town from alien domination. This DVD offers great picture and sound, but no bonus features. No compression or bending of the frame is visible and the color balancing is accurate. The picture is very clear, having obviously been struck from a pristine master print. The DVD's Dolby Digital 5.1 soundtrack is put to great use, especially in the scenes involv-

ing creepy alien sound effects. The quality presentation of the disc actually enhances the film. —ML

Movie: 🎞️🎞️ **DVD:** 🎞️🎞️
Buena Vista Home Entertainment (Cat #17224, UPC #717951002280). Widescreen (1.85:1) letterboxed. Dolby Digital 5.1 Surround. $29.99. Keepcase. LANG: English. CAP: English. FEATURES: 31 chapter links • Trailer.
1998 (R) 102m/C Elijah Wood, Robert Patrick, Bebe Neuwirth, Salma Hayek, Jon Stewart, Piper Laurie, Famke Janssen, Christopher McDonald, Jordana Brewster, Clea DuVall, Laura Harris, Josh Hartnett, Usher Raymond; **D:** Robert Rodriguez; **W:** Kevin Williamson; **C:** Enrique Chediak; **M:** Marco Beltrami.

Fade to Black

Undervalued character study can almost be seen as a west coast Taxi Driver with Hollywood Blvd. standing in for the mean streets of New York. Toss in strong nods to Targets and Whatever Happened to Baby Jane. Eric Binford (Christopher) is a delivery boy who has trouble separating his encyclopedic knowledge of old movies with everyday reality. A young Marilyn wanna-be (Kerridge) further blurs his perceptual problems until Eric begins to take on his favorite screen identities—Dracula, the Mummy, Cody Jarrett from White Heat—to get even with an uncaring world. The attractions are Christopher's flamboyant but believable performance and dozens of clips and quotes from old films. The visual and audio quality of the DVD are flawless. The film looks as good as or better than it did in theatres. Don't miss the trivia-rich liner notes covering the curious careers of cast and crew. —MM

Movie: 🎞️🎞️🎞️ **DVD:** 🎞️🎞️🎞️
Anchor Bay (Cat #DV10864, UPC #0131311086492). Widescreen (1.85:1) letterboxed. Dolby Digital Mono. $24.98. Keepcase. LANG: English. FEATURES: 28 chapter links • Liner notes.
1980 (R) 100m/C Dennis Christopher, Tim Thomerson, Linda Kerridge, Mickey Rourke, Melinda Fee, Gwynne Gilford, Norman Burton, Morgan Paull, James Luisi, John Steadman, Marcie Barkin, Eve Brent Ashe; **D:** Vernon Zimmerman; **W:** Vernon Zimmerman; **C:** Alex Phillips Jr.; **M:** Craig Safan.

Fahrenheit 451

In a chilling adaptation of the Ray Bradbury novel, a futuristic society has banned all reading material. Firemen keep the fires at 451 degrees: the temperature at which paper burns. Werner is a fireman who begins to question the rightness of his actions when he meets the book-loving Christie—who also plays the dual role of Werner's TV-absorbed wife. Truffaut's first color and English-language film. Most people probably focus on the fascist and Big Brother-like politics when they think of this film, but the cinematography is both beautiful and emotionally affecting. The

DVD gives the movie the treatment it deserves, with an image that is rich and finely detailed. The sound remains mono, but much more powerful, thanks to a Dolby Digital 2.0 mono remix. —JO

Movie: 🎞️🎞️🎞️ **DVD:** 🎞️🎞️🎞️
Image Entertainment (Cat #ID4231USDVD, UPC #014381423129). Widescreen (1.85:1) letterboxed. Dolby Digital Mono. $29.95. Snapper. LANG: English. FEATURES: 16 chapter links.
1966 112m/C FR GB Oskar Werner, Julie Christie, Cyril Cusack, Anton Diffring, Alex Scott, Anna Palk, Ann Bell, Mark Lester; **D:** Francois Truffaut; **W:** Francois Truffaut, Ray Bradbury, Jean-Louis Richard, David Rudkin; **C:** Nicolas Roeg; **M:** Bernard Herrmann.

Fair Game

Any movie that finds so many excuses to display the world's most popular covergirl in tight, sweaty tanktops has something going for it. Cindy Crawford plays Kate McQuean, a hotshot Miami lawyer—don't laugh!—who's being pursued by high-tech Russian assassins who can, as one character puts it, "reach into your living room and pick your nose." They're after Kate and Max (Baldwin), a Miami detective for reasons too ridiculous to mention. On DVD, the action scenes work well enough. As a group, they are as ridiculous as the rest of the film, and lit in imaginative ways. The pan-and-scan image is really not noticeably worse than the original widescreen. An acceptable no-frills disc. —MM

Movie: 🎞️🎞️ **DVD:** 🎞️🎞️
Warner Home Video, Inc. (Cat #14072, UPC #085391407225). Full frame. Dolby Digital 5.1 Surround. $14.98. LANG: English; French. CAP: English. FEATURES: 27 chapter links.
1995 (R) 91m/C William Baldwin, Cindy Crawford, Miguel Sandoval, Christopher McDonald, Johann Carlo, Salma Hayek, John Bedford Lloyd, Jenette Goldstein; **D:** Andrew Sipes; **W:** Charlie Fletcher; **C:** Richard Bowen; **M:** Mark Mancina. AWARDS: NOM: Golden Raspberry Awards '95: Worst New Star (Crawford).

The Falcon and the Snowman

In 1977, Daulton Lee (Penn) and Christopher Boyce (Hutton) are childhood friends who, almost accidentally, sell American secrets to the KGB. The stars are excellent in a fact-based story that avoids cliches of the genre and sticks with strong characterizations. The DVD image is of average brightness with no serious flaws. The production values are typical of a film of this vintage. The disc appears to have been made from a well-preserved or restored original. Particularly recommended to fans of the cast. —MM

Movie: 🎞️🎞️🎞️ **DVD:** 🎞️🎞️🎞️
MGM Home Entertainment (Cat #907792). Widescreen letterboxed. Dolby Digital Surround Stereo. $24.98. Keepcase. LANG:

English. *SUB:* English; French. *FEATURES:*
40 chapter links.
1985 (R) 110m/C Sean Penn, Timothy
Hutton, Lori Singer, Pat Hingle, Dorian
Harewood, Richard Dysart, David Suchet,
Jennifer Runyon, Priscilla Pointer, Nicholas
Pryor, Joyce Van Patten, Mady Kaplan,
Michael Ironside; *D:* John Schlesinger; *W:*
Steven Zaillian; *C:* Allen Daviau; *M:* Lyle
Mays, Pat Metheny.

Fall Time

Offbeat crime drama is set in small-town
Minnesota, circa 1957. Three high schoolers set in motion a prank that turns bad
when they pull up in front of the local
bank. David (Arquette), Joe (Blechman), and
Tim (London) intend to stage a mock
robbery—but a real robbery is in progress
and the teens wind up hostages of creepy
criminals Florence (Rourke) and Leon
(Baldwin). *AKA:* Falltime.
Movie: 🎵🎵▶ *DVD:* NYR
Pioneer Entertainment (Cat #10267). Full
frame. Dolby Digital Stereo. $24.98. Keep-
case. *FEATURES:* Trailer.
1994 (R) 88m/C Mickey Rourke, Stephen
Baldwin, Jason London, David Arquette,
Jonah Blechman, Sheryl Lee; *D:* Paul
Warner; *W:* Steve Alden, Paul Skemp; *C:*
Mark J. Gordon; *M:* Hummie Mann.

Fallen

Take a police-story suspense thriller, add
the occult and a big dose of the supernatural, stir in a heaping helping of philosophy, a dash of a wrong-man subplot, shake
vigorously, and out pours the bitter *Fallen.*
After the execution of serial killer Edgar
Reese (Koteas), crack cop Hobbes (Washington) is soon chasing down copycat
killings springing up everywhere. The real
culprit is not Reese, but a fallen angel who
inhabits body after body, creating new
killers with each new host. Washington
manages to hold his own as the pic gets
messy and overly complicated. Goodman's
character provides needed earthbound
common sense when the banter gets a bit
too lofty, debating things like the meaning
of life, existence of God, and other issues
that don't belong here. Hoblit's second
feature tries to take on way too much in
its already lengthy span. With a mish-
mash of conflicting film styles and dicey
dialogue, film manages to land on the
careers of an otherwise talented cast and
crew. *Fallen* is another very darkly lit
thriller that challenges the DVD format to
retain details and avoid excess grain, yet
preserve the lighting conditions and shadings of the original film. The DVD has no
problem and remains sharp throughout
with strong colors and true blacks. The
5.1 mix is excellent with plenty of atmospheric ambience, particularly from the rear
channels. —*JO*
Movie: 🎵🎵▶ *DVD:* 🎵🎵🎵▶
Warner Home Video, Inc. (Cat #T6434, UPC
#053939643428). Widescreen (2.35:1)
anamorphic; full frame. Dolby Digital 5.1;
Dolby Surround. $24.98. Snapper. *LANG:*

English; French. *SUB:* English; French;
Spanish. *CAP:* English. *FEATURES:* 32
chapter links • Commentary: Gregory
Hoblit, Nicholas Kazan, and Charles Roven
• Theatrical trailer • 3 TV spots • Pro-
duction notes.
1997 (R) 124m/C Denzel Washington,
Donald Sutherland, John Goodman, Elias
Koteas, Embeth Davidtz, James Gandolfi-
ni, Robert Joy, Gabriel Casseus; *D:* Grego-
ry Hoblit; *W:* Nicholas Kazan; *C:* Newton
Thomas (Tom) Sigel; *M:* Tan Dun.

Fallen Angels

Contract killer Wong Chi-Ming (Lai) has
been getting his assignments from a
nameless female agent (Reis) who's fallen
for him. Wong wants to retire, which
upsets her. Then there's mute ex-con He
Zhiwo (Kaneshiro), who becomes involved
with a strange woman named Cherry
(Young) who still loves her ex-boyfriend.
The subplot about a son and his father is
perhaps the most engrossing part of the
picture. The disjointed narrative proves a
challenge in what director Kar-Wai originally intended to be a third story for his film
Chunking Express. Still, the film has a go-
for-broke look all its own thanks to dynamic cinematography, editing, and a generous
deployment of wide-angle lenses. The
nighttime streets of Hong Kong come alive
with visuals loaded with neon and humanity. The look is marred somewhat by a sub-
par video transfer hurt by what is obviously damaged original film elements. No
state-of-the-art soundtrack here, but you'll
probably be reading the subtitles anyway.
—*MB AKA:* Duoluo Tianshi.
Movie: 🎵🎵▶ *DVD:* 🎵▶
Image Entertainment (Cat #K120DVD, UPC
#738329012021). Widescreen (1.66:1)
letterboxed. Dolby Digital 1.0. $29.99.
Snapper. *LANG:* Cantonese. *SUB:* English.
FEATURES: 12 chapter links • Theatrical
trailer.
1995 97m/C *HK* Leon Lai, Michelle Reis,
Takeshi Kaneshiro, Charlie Young, Karen
Mok; *D:* Wong Kar-Wai; *W:* Wong Kar-Wai;
C: Christopher Doyle; *M:* Frankie Chan.

Falling Down

Douglas is "DFENS" (taken from his
license plate), a normally law-abiding
white-collar geek who snaps while stuck in
a traffic jam on a hot day in L.A. Like
Charles Bronson in *Death Wish,* he
decides to take matters into his own
hands. Unlike Bronson, he is not avenging
an attack by a specific criminal, but raging
against whomever gets in his way. Duvall
is a detective on his last day before retirement; Hershey has the thankless role of
Douglas's ex. Essentially a revenge fantasy that was vilified by some for catering to
the baser emotions. It wouldn't have
taken much more to make this a four-bone
DVD. There are just a few flawed scenes
where the detail seems to create a shimmering in the otherwise extremely sharp
picture. There is also some grain in a few
long shots. The colors are accurate and

even deep hues do not bleed. The blacks
are as good as any DVD I've seen and the
contrast and brightness levels seemed
close to perfection. Some would argue
that the lack of 5.1 sound should also cut
the rating, but the stereo tracks deliver
with fat but clean bass frequencies tied
into crisp high end. —*JO*
Movie: 🎵🎵🎵 *DVD:* 🎵🎵🎵▶
Warner Home Video, Inc. (Cat #12648,
UPC #085391264828). Widescreen
(2.35:1) anamorphic; full frame. Stereo.
$19.98. Snapper. *LANG:* English; French.
SUB: French. *CAP:* English. *FEATURES:* 33
chapter links • Theatrical trailer.
1993 (R) 112m/C Michael Douglas,
Robert Duvall, Barbara Hershey, Rachel
Ticotin, Tuesday Weld, Frederic Forrest,
Lois Smith, D.W. Moffett, Dedee Pfeiffer,
Vondie Curtis-Hall, Michael Paul Chan,
Raymond J. Barry, Jack Kehoe, John Diehl;
D: Joel Schumacher; *W:* Ebbe Roe Smith;
C: Andrzej Bartkowiak; *M:* James Newton
Howard.

Falling in Love Again

Romantic comedy focuses on middle-aged
dreamer Harry (Gould), his realistic wife
(York), and their trip from Los Angeles to
New York for his high school reunion.
There Harry is attacked by nostalgia vibes
for his youth, seen in countless flashbacks, and prominently featuring Pfeiffer,
notable in her film debut. Overall, though,
it's like watching a home movie about people you don't really care about. On DVD,
the film looks and sounds dated and fuzzy,
though, admittedly, that comes with the
territory in this kind of story. Still, it's not
nearly as sharp as it needs to be for
those who do not share the filmmakers'
fondness for the early '40s. —*MM AKA:*
In Love.
Movie: 🎵▶ *DVD:* 🎵▶
Simitar Entertainment (Cat #7355, UPC
#082551735525). Full frame. PCM
Stereo. $14.98. Keepcase. *LANG:* English.
FEATURES: 8 chapter links • Production
factoids • Elliot Gould, Michelle Pfeiffer,
Susanna York filmographies.
1980 (PG) 103m/C Elliott Gould, Susan-
nah York, Michelle Pfeiffer; *D:* Steven
Paul; *W:* Ted Allan; *C:* Michael Mileham;
M: Michel Legrand.

Family of Cops

Trouble comes to Inspector Paul Fein's
(Bronson) close-knit Milwaukee (actually
Toronto) family when his party-hearty
daughter Jackie (Featherstone) comes
home to visit. She's accused of murdering
the wealthy businessman she picked up in
a drunken stupor and her cop kin take
over the investigation. The film's made-for-
TV production values and acting standards
translate with ease to DVD, and so it looks
fine throughout, though the content is
such generic fare—the chapters are identified only by number—that there's little to
recommend the disc. —*MM*
Movie: 🎵🎵 *DVD:* 🎵🎵▶

Trimark Home Video (Cat #7050D, UPC #031398704331). Full frame. Stereo. $34.99. Keepcase. *LANG:* English. *FEATURES:* 10 unlabelled chapter links. Title is available for sale only as part of "Best of Action" 4-pack.
1995 (PG-13) 90m/C Charles Bronson, Daniel Baldwin, Angela Featherstone, Sebastian Spence, Lesley-Anne Down, Barbara Williams, Simon MacCorkindale; *D:* Ted Kotcheff; *W:* Joel Basberg.

Family Reunion

Low-budget horror is notable for its strong ghost-town setting and below-average acting. The Andrews family finds itself mysteriously drawn to and then trapped in Sutterville, NV, while a weird fellow with psychic powers is being held by the local cops. On DVD, image and sound are strictly on the drive-in level. —*MM*
Movie: 🦴 *DVD:* 🦴
Image Entertainment (Cat #OVED6836DVD, UPC #014381683622). Full frame. Dolby Digital Stereo. $24.99. Snapper. *LANG:* English. *FEATURES:* 10 chapter links.
1979 88m/C Mel Novak, John Andes, A.J. Woods, Kaylin Cool, Pam Phillips, Mark McTague; *D:* Michael Hawes; *W:* Michael Hawes; *C:* Jack Anderson.

The Fan

Knife salesman and obsessed baseball fan Gil Renard (De Niro) stalks his favorite player Bobby Rayburn (Snipes) who has just signed a big contract with the hometown San Francisco Giants. When Rayburn goes into a slump, Renard figures he can help his idol—by any means necessary. De Niro does the psycho thing with practiced aplomb while Snipes is persuasive in another jock role. On DVD, Scott's sumptuous visuals get the royal treatment. Virtually every shot is artfully framed and tinted to perfection. If only the substance equaled the style. —*MM*
Movie: 🦴🦴 *DVD:* 🦴🦴🦴
Columbia Tristar Home Video (Cat #82479, UPC #043396824799). Full frame; widescreen (1.85:1) letterboxed. Dolby Digital 5.1 Surround Stereo; Dolby Digital Surround. $25.95. Keepcase. *LANG:* English; French; Spanish. *SUB:* English; Spanish. *CAP:* English. *FEATURES:* 36 chapter links.
1996 (R) 117m/C Robert De Niro, Wesley Snipes, Ellen Barkin, John Leguizamo, Benicio Del Toro, Patti D'Arbanville; *D:* Tony Scott; *W:* Phoef Sutton; *C:* Darius Wolski; *M:* Hans Zimmer. *AWARDS: NOM:* MTV Movie Awards '97: Best Villain (De Niro).

Fando and Lis

Felliniesque fantasy caused quite the uproar when it was shown at the Acapulco Film Festival in 1968. Seen today, it's very much a product of its time, a surrealistic odyssey—not unlike *Fellini Satyricon* which was made three years later—about two young people searching for the truth in a series of bizarre, unrealistic encoun-

ters. It paves the way for Jodorowsky's *El Topo* and *Santa Sangre*. (Not surprisingly, it is much more similar to the former, lacking the polish and technical expertise of the latter.) This one features such non-shocking images as a jazz combo playing in a junkyard with a flaming piano. Still, for fans of the filmmaker, it's a fascinating trip down memory lane, one that looks about as good as could be expected on DVD. The disc's real strength is the extras, including a feature-length 1995 documentary, *La Constellation Jodorowsky*. —*MM*
Movie: 🦴🦴🦴 *DVD:* 🦴🦴🦴
Fantoma (Cat #FAN7010, UPC #695026701026). Widescreen (1.66:1) letterboxed. Mono. $39.95. Keepcase. *LANG:* Spanish. *SUB:* English; French. *FEATURES:* 32 chapter links (16 in feature; 16 in documentary) • Reproduction of 8-page handbill distributed at Acapulco Film Festival • Liner notes.
1968 96m/B *MX* Maria Teresa Rivas, Tamara Garina, Juan Jose Arreola, Rene Rebetez; *D:* Alejandro Jodorowsky; *W:* Alejandro Jodorowsky, Arrabal Jodorowsky; *C:* Reynoso y Corkidi.

The Fantastic Night

Considering that this film was made in France during the Nazi occupation, it is a remarkably clear work. It's a fantasy about Denis (Gravet), who is visited by a beautiful woman (Presle) as he sleeps and then follows her through a series of adventures. According to the box copy, the star was working with the Resistance while he was making the film. On DVD, the focus is appropriately dreamy. The image is marred by a few flecks and marks, and one long scratch right down the middle in the final reel, but those are not serious flaws. Sound is fine. —*MM AKA:* La Nuit Fantastique.
Movie: 🦴🦴🦴 *DVD:* 🦴🦴🦴
Image Entertainment (Cat #ID9082SIDVD, UPC #014381908220). Full frame. Dolby Digital Mono. $24.99. Snapper. *LANG:* French. *SUB:* English. *FEATURES:* 12 chapter links.
1942 90m/B *FR* Fernand Gravet, Micheline Presle, Marcel Levesque, Christiane Nere; *D:* Marcel L'Herbier; *W:* Louis Chavance, Marcel L'Herbier; *M:* Maurice Thiriet.

Fantastic Planet

Critically acclaimed French animated film is based on the drawings of Roland Topor. A race of humans is enslaved and exploited by a race of blue giants on a savage planet, until one of the small creatures manages to unite his people to fight for equality. Stylistically, the film is slightly similar to *Yellow Submarine* but without the drug references. The animation makes an easy transition to DVD. The main differences between disc and tape are the choices of language and the inclusion of three of codirector Laloux's early shorts, "Les Dents du Singe" (Monkey's Teeth, 1960), "Les Temps Morts" (Dead Times, 1964), "Les Escargots" (The Snails,

1965). —*MM AKA:* La Planete Sauvage; Planet of Incredible Creatures; The Savage Planet.
Movie: 🦴🦴🦴 *DVD:* 🦴🦴🦴
Anchor Bay (Cat #DV10702, UPC #013131070293). Widescreen (1.66:1) letterboxed. Dolby Digital Mono. $29.98. Keepcase. *LANG:* French; English. *SUB:* English. *FEATURES:* 32 chapter links.
1973 (PG) 72m/C *FR D:* Roland Topor, Rene Laloux; *W:* Roland Topor, Steve Hayes, Rene Laloux; *C:* Boris Baromykin, Lubomir Rejthar; *M:* Alain Goraguer; *V:* Barry Bostwick.

Far and Away

Meandering old-fashioned epic about immigrants, romance, and settling the American West. In the 1890s, Joseph Donelly (Cruise) is forced to flee his Irish homeland after threatening the life of his landlord, and emigrates to America in the company of the landlord's daughter, feisty Shannon Christie (Kidman). Particularly brutal scenes of Cruise earning his living as a bare-knuckled boxer contrast with the expansiveness of the land rush ending. Overall, it's slow, spotty, and a little too slick for its own good. Filmed in 70mm Panavision in Ireland and Montana. Some preprint damage detracts from this otherwise fine DVD presentation. Sharpness is excellent and free of both grain and artifacts. The lush colors never bleed and are on the money. Blacks are true throughout and are complemented by contrast and brightness levels that are punchy and consistent. The 5.1 mix puts the dialogue out front, while retaining good low end and great dynamics for music and Surround effects. —*JO*
Movie: 🦴🦴 *DVD:* 🦴🦴🦴
Universal Studios Home Video (Cat #20212, UPC #025192021220). Widescreen (2.20:1) anamorphic. Dolby Digital 5.1; Dolby Surround. $26.98. Keepcase. *LANG:* English (DD5.1); Spanish (DS); French (DS). *SUB:* Spanish. *FEATURES:* 16 chapter links • Theatrical trailer • Cast and filmmaker's bios • Production notes.
1992 (PG-13) 140m/C Tom Cruise, Nicole Kidman, Thomas Gibson, Robert Prosky, Barbara Babcock, Colm Meaney, Eileen Pollock, Michelle Johnson, Cyril Cusack, Clint Howard, Rance Howard; *D:* Ron Howard; *W:* Bob Dolman; *C:* Mikael Salomon; *M:* John Williams.

Farewell My Concubine

Dickensian epic ranges over more than 50 years of Chinese cultural, political, and sexual history. The main characters are Shitou (played by Fengyi as an adult and by Yang as a child) and Douzi (Cheung and Mingwei), who meet as boys when they're forced to work in the Peking Opera. As their country undergoes massive changes, Juxian (Li), a prostitute, comes between the two. Director Kaige adopts the languid pace and heroic staging of an old-fash-

ioned epic. Much of the action takes place within huge, nearly empty structures. Following a subtle sepia introduction, Kaige and director of photography Changwei repeatedly heighten scenes with smoky light and tints of orange and honey. Though this kind of large-scale film loses something on anything smaller than a theatrical screen, the DVD faithfully re-creates those striking images. Sound is equally acceptable. —*MM AKA:* Bawang Bie Ji.
Movie: 🦴🦴🦴 *DVD:* 🦴🦴🦴
Buena Vista Home Entertainment (Cat #17368, UPC #717951002723). Widescreen (1.85:1) letterboxed. Dolby Digital 2.0 Surround Stereo. $29.99. Keepcase. *LANG:* Chinese. *SUB:* English. *CAP:* English. *FEATURES:* 21 chapter links.
1993 (R) 157m/C *HK* Leslie Cheung, Zhang Fengyi, Gong Li, Lu Qi, Ying Da, Ge You, Fei Yang, Ma Mingwei; *D:* Chen Kaige; *W:* Lilian Lee, Lu Wei; *C:* Gu Changwei; *M:* Zhao Jiping. *AWARDS:* British Academy Awards '93: Best Foreign Film; Cannes Film Festival '93: Best Film; Golden Globe Awards '94: Best Foreign Film; Los Angeles Film Critics Association Awards '93: Best Foreign Film; National Board of Review Awards '93: Best Foreign Film; New York Film Critics Awards '93: Best Foreign Film, Best Supporting Actress (Li); *NOM:* Academy Awards '93: Best Cinematography, Best Foreign Film.

Farewell, My Lovely

Robert Mitchum turns in one of his best performances as Phillip Marlowe in this remake of the 1944 Chandler mystery *Murder, My Sweet.* The production overrelies on some genre cliches, but they're cliches that we love. This time out, Marlowe is trying to find an ex-con's (O'Halloran) missing fiancee (Rampling). Though some might criticize the soft DVD image, the film looks just like it has always looked. The grain in the night scenes comes from the original. So do the blurry neon blues and reds in John Alonzo's photography. If the sound lacks the power of more recent productions, it's fine for David Shire's underappreciated score. All in all, this is a terrific mystery that will always find an audience. —*MM*
Movie: 🦴🦴🦴 *DVD:* 🦴🦴🦴▸
Pioneer Entertainment (Cat #10270). Full frame. Dolby Digital Stereo. $24.98. Keepcase. *LANG:* English. *FEATURES:* 16 chapter links.
1975 (R) 95m/C *GB* Robert Mitchum, Charlotte Rampling, Sylvia Miles, John Ireland, Anthony Zerbe, Jack O'Halloran, Harry Dean Stanton, Sylvester Stallone, Cheryl "Rainbeaux" Smith; *D:* Dick Richards; *W:* David Zelag Goodman; *C:* John A. Alonzo; *M:* David Shire. *AWARDS: NOM:* Academy Awards '75: Best Supporting Actress (Miles).

Fargo

Another malicious, extra-dark comedy from the Coen brothers. Car salesman Jerry Lundegaard (Macy) hires a couple of losers to kidnap his wife so he can swindle the ransom money out of his father-in-law. Naturally, the scheme begins to unravel and the very pregnant police chief Marge Gunderson (McDormand) treks through the frozen tundra of Minnesota to put the pieces of the puzzle together. McDormand's performance as the chatty competent chief is first-rate. The DVD improves the colors over the laserdisc, but is not as sharp. There is also some grain that appears in the long snowy shots that was not on the LD. Color are better though, and at times they are vibrant enough to give preference to the DVD. Blacks tend to pick up a little grain, but are close enough to true to be acceptable. The sound is a little muffled and is at the same time lacking some low end causing it to be a little thin. The Surround is not used to any great degree and even just a little ambient background would have livened things up a bit. A disappointment. —*JO*
Movie: 🦴🦴🦴 *DVD:* 🦴🦴
Polygram (Cat #8006386932, UPC #780063869324). Widescreen (1.85:1) letterboxed; full frame. Dolby Surround. $29.95. Expanded jewel case. *LANG:* English. *SUB:* English; French; Spanish. *FEATURES:* 17 chapter links • Cast and filmmakers bios.
1996 (R) 97m/C William H. Macy, Frances McDormand, Steve Buscemi, Peter Stormare, Harve Presnell, Steve Reevis, John Carroll Lynch, Kristin Rudrud, Steve Park; *Cameos:* Jose Feliciano; *D:* Joel Coen; *W:* Ethan Coen, Joel Coen; *C:* Roger Deakins; *M:* Carter Burwell. *AWARDS:* Academy Awards '96: Best Actress (McDormand), Best Original Screenplay; American Film Institute (AFI) '98: Top 100; Australian Film Institute '96: Best Foreign Film; British Academy Awards '96: Best Director (Coen); Cannes Film Festival '96: Best Director (Coen); Independent Spirit Awards '97: Best Actor (Macy), Best Actress (McDormand), Best Cinematography, Best Director (Coen), Best Film, Best Screenplay; National Board of Review Awards '96: Best Actress (McDormand), Best Director (Coen); New York Film Critics Awards '96: Best Film; Screen Actors Guild Award '96: Best Actress (McDormand); Writers Guild of America '96: Best Original Screenplay; Broadcast Film Critics Association Awards '96: Best Actress (McDormand), Best Film; *NOM:* Academy Awards '96: Best Cinematography, Best Director (Coen), Best Film Editing, Best Picture, Best Supporting Actor (Macy); British Academy Awards '96: Best Actress (McDormand), Best Film, Best Original Screenplay; Cesar Awards '97: Best Foreign Film; Directors Guild of America Awards '96: Best Director (Coen); Golden Globe Awards '97: Best Actress—Musical/Comedy (McDormand), Best Director (Coen), Best Film—Musical/Comedy, Best Screenplay; MTV Movie Awards '97: Best On-Screen Duo (Peter Stormare/Steve Buscemi); Screen Actors Guild Award '96: Best Supporting Actor (Macy).

The Farmer's Wife

Samuel Sweetland (Thomas), a recently widowed farmer, searches for a new wife in this silent British comedy. His lovely housekeeper Araminta (Hall-Davis) would be the perfect candidate. Director Hitchcock handles the story (based on Eden Philpott's play) with his usual sure hand but this material is not his forte. The DVD image is acceptable and the musical soundtrack is scratchy. Recommended to those who must have a complete Hitchcock collection. —*MM*
Movie: 🦴🦴▸ *DVD:* 🦴🦴
Delta/Laserlight (Cat #82038, UPC #018111997232). Full frame. $14.99. Keepcase. *SUB:* English; Spanish; Chinese; Japanese. *FEATURES:* 20 chapter links.
1928 97m/B *GB* Jameson Thomas, Lillian Hall-Davis, Gordon Harker; *D:* Alfred Hitchcock; *W:* Alfred Hitchcock; *C:* Jack Cox.

Fascination

In 1916, two well-to-do Frenchwomen (Mai and Lahaie) meet at a slaughterhouse to drink bull's blood for their health. They're up to something else, too. When a small-time thief (Lemaire), who has betrayed his gang, takes up refuge in their chateau, he thinks he's in charge. The first half is essentially soft-core exploitation that turns to fairly graphic violence in the second, while playing with some interesting ideas about sexual power. Rollin's work—one of his best—compares favorably to American low-budget work of the same era, though it would be better if Lemaire were able to project a stronger screen presence. The DVD image is clear with only a few signs of wear. The second half takes place at night and becomes grainier. Even so, the disc looks and sounds much better than the tape versions of the film that have been available on the gray market. —*MM*
Movie: 🦴🦴🦴 *DVD:* 🦴🦴🦴
Image Entertainment (Cat #ID5633SADVD, UPC #014381563320). Widescreen (1.66:1) letterboxed. Dolby Digital Mono. $24.99. Snapper. *LANG:* French. *SUB:* English. *FEATURES:* 15 chapter links • Liner notes by Marc Morris.
1979 80m/C *FR* Franca Mai, Brigitte Lahaie, Jean-Marie Lemaire, Fanny Magier, Muriel Montosse, Alain Plumey; *D:* Jean Rollin; *W:* Jean Rollin; *C:* Georges Fromentin.

The Fatal Image

While on vacation in Paris, Pauline (Lee) and her daughter Glinda (Bateman) videotape an international mob hit, making themselves the target of ruthless assassins. Parisian locations are the main attraction in this made-for-TV thriller. On DVD, such potentially difficult moments as the patterns of rails and girders in the Eiffel Tower are handled without a hitch. The sound is fine. —*MM*
Movie: 🦴🦴▸ *DVD:* 🦴🦴▸

Simitar Entertainment (Cat #7579, UPC #082551757923). Full frame. Dolby Digital Stereo. $14.98. Keepcase. *LANG:* English. *FEATURES:* 8 chapter links ☛ Michele Lee filmography.
1990 96m/C Michele Lee, Justine Bateman, Francois Dunoyer, Jean-Pierre Cassel, Sonia Petrovna; *D:* Thomas J. Wright; *C:* Jean-Yves Le Mener.

Fatal Pursuit

International jewel heists have never looked so dull as New Orleans private eye (Brown) teams up with a British insurance investigator (Whirry) to recover stolen diamonds. The usually sensitive and sensual Whirry, sporting an unconvincing British accent, seems morose and put-upon during her one obligatory nude scene, while Brown, the nominal hero, is creepy and lewd. The image quality is substandard, varying in clarity from wan interiors to grainy, dark exteriors. Sound quality is poor, with some dialogue inaudible. —*JE*
Movie: woof *DVD:* ♪
Image Entertainment (Cat #4759DR, UPC #1438147592). Full frame. Dolby Digital Stereo. $24.99. Snapper. *LANG:* English. *FEATURES:* 12 chapter links.
1998 (R) 103m/C Shannon Whirry, Malcolm McDowell, Robert Z'Dar, Charles Napier, L.P. Brown III; *D:* Eric Louzil; *W:* Chuck Conaway; *C:* Ron Chapman.

Father of the Bride

Remake of the 1950 comedy classic portrays one of the most overextravagant weddings in recent film history, but falls short of the original. Predictable plot and characters don't hide any surprises, but nothing detracts from the purpose of the film: to be a nice, charming movie. Martin is fine as the reluctant dad but Keaton is little more than window dressing as the bride's mom; Short is annoying as a pretentious wedding coordinator. Williams pulls off a nice film debut—and was almost immediately cast in a TV ad as a young-bride-to-be calling her dad long distance to tell him she's engaged. This DVD is a pleasure to watch. It's very sharp with little grain and no artifacts. Colors are vastly improved over previous video versions and are both vibrant and accurate, with only a touch of bleed on some of the deeper hues. Blacks are very good, as are the contrast and brightness levels, which are also very consistent. The sound is also very good and both the dialogue and music are very dynamic. The Surround is used sparingly, but does just fine where it's required. —*JO*
Movie: ♪♪☛ *DVD:* ♪♪♪☛
Buena Vista Home Entertainment (Cat #16322, UPC #717951001405). Widescreen (1.85:1) letterboxed. Dolby Surround. $29.99. Keepcase. *LANG:* English; French. *CAP:* English. *FEATURES:* 20 chapter links ☛ Theatrical trailer.
1991 (PG) 105m/C Steve Martin, Diane Keaton, Kimberly Williams, Kieran Culkin, George Newbern, Martin Short, B.D. Wong,

Peter Michael Goetz, Kate McGregor Stewart, Martha Gehman; *Cameos:* Eugene Levy; *D:* Charles Shyer; *W:* Charles Shyer, Nancy Meyers; *C:* John Lindley; *M:* Alan Silvestri.

Father's Day

The comedy team of Williams and Crystal makes its feature film debut in this affable take on fatherhood. Freelance writer Putley (Williams) unites with attorney Lawrence (Crystal) to help their mutual ex-girlfriend Kinski search for her runaway son (she's led each man to believe he's the father). Their quest leads to some inevitable sticky situations, but the erratic, adolescent Williams is wonderfully balanced by the calm, upstanding Crystal. Who needs a son when you have to deal with Williams? Together, they're fun to watch and almost make you forget the contrived plot. Almost. Remake of the 1984 French film *Les Comperes*. I still couldn't get into this movie, but the DVD looks so good it was worth giving it a shot. Colors are vibrant and accurate with sharpness that seemed better than the theatre. Part of the problem may have been the muted and lifeless sound that often made me think I had cotton in my ears. —*JO*
Movie: ♪♪☛ *DVD:* ♪♪♪
Warner Home Video, Inc. (Cat #15386, UPC #085391538622). Widescreen (1.85:1) anamorphic. Dolby Digital 5.1. $24.98. Snapper. *LANG:* English. *SUB:* English; Spanish; French. *CAP:* English. *FEATURES:* 34 chapter links ☛ Theatrical trailer ☛ Production notes.
1996 (PG-13) 98m/C Robin Williams, Billy Crystal, Nastassia Kinski, Julia Louis-Dreyfus, Charlie Hofheimer, Bruce Greenwood, Jared Harris, Patti D'Arbanville, Charles Rocket, Dennis Burkley; *D:* Ivan Reitman; *W:* Lowell Ganz, Babaloo Mandel; *C:* Stephen Burum; *M:* James Newton Howard. *AWARDS: NOM:* Golden Raspberry Awards '97: Worst Supporting Actress (Louis-Dreyfus).

Father's Little Dividend

Tracy expects a little peace and quiet now that he has successfully married off daughter Taylor in this charming sequel to *Father of the Bride*. However, he's quickly disillusioned by the news that he'll soon be a grandfather—a prospect that causes nothing but dismay.
Movie: ♪♪♪ *DVD:* NYR
Madacy Entertainment (Cat #99014). Full frame. Dolby Digital Mono. $9.99. Keepcase. *FEATURES:* Cast and crew thumbnail biographies ☛ Production credits.
1951 82m/B Spencer Tracy, Joan Bennett, Elizabeth Taylor, Don Taylor, Billie Burke, Russ Tamblyn, Moroni Olsen; *D:* Vincente Minnelli; *W:* Frances Goodrich, Albert Hackett; *C:* John Alton; *M:* Albert Sendry.

The Fear

A psychology student (Bowz) takes a group to a cabin in the woods to explore their fears for his thesis. After the expected false scares, they're picked off one by one and it seems that Morty (Weiss), a guy in a wood-grained rubber suit, is responsible. Connect-the-dots horror is never particularly frightening. On DVD, the dark scenes are too heavily shaded. The pixelation becomes heavier and more irritating in the last reels. Followed by a sequel. Wes Craven appears in a cameo as Dr. Arnold. —*MM*
Movie: ♪☛ *DVD:* ♪☛
Simitar Entertainment (Cat #7316, UPC #082551731626). Full frame. PCM Stereo. $14.98. Keepcase. *LANG:* English. *FEATURES:* 8 chapter links ☛ Production factoids ☛ Vince Edwards filmography.
1994 (R) 98m/C Eddie Bowz, Darin Heames, Anna Karin, Leland Hayward, Monique Mannen, Heather Medway, Antonio Todd, Erick Weiss, Vince Edwards, Ann Turkel, Wes Craven; *D:* Vincent Robert; *W:* Ron Ford; *C:* Bernd Heinl; *M:* Robert O. Ragland.

Fear

Ham-fisted variation on the *Fatal Attraction–Hand That Rocks the Cradle* formula is at best half successful. In those films, a beautiful insane woman menaces a middle-class family. This time out, Mark Wahlberg is psycho-boy David. His chilling performance is undercut by formulaic plot twists. Immature teen Nicole (Witherspoon) falls for David the moment she sees him. He's a cute sociopath who says all the right things to her parents (Petersen and Brenneman). The DVD improves somewhat on the image of the theatrical release, particularly in the night scenes of the third act, which is borrowed from *Straw Dogs*. Sound is fine throughout, particularly in one long party sequence. —*MM AKA:* No Fear.
Movie: ♪ *DVD:* ♪♪☛
Universal Studios Home Video (Cat #20393, UPC #025192039324). Widescreen (2.35:1) letterboxed. Dolby Digital 5.1 Surround Stereo; Dolby Surround Stereo. $24.98. Keepcase. *LANG:* English; French. *SUB:* Spanish. *CAP:* English. *FEATURES:* 16 chapter links ☛ Cast and crew thumbnail biographies ☛ Theatrical trailer ☛ Production notes ☛ Universal web links.
1996 (R) 96m/C Reese Witherspoon, Mark Wahlberg, William L. Petersen, Amy Brenneman, Alyssa Milano, Tracy Fraim, Christopher Gray, Todd Caldecott; *D:* James Foley; *W:* Christopher Crowe; *C:* Thomas Kloss; *M:* Carter Burwell. *AWARDS:* MTV Movie Awards '97: Best Song ("Machinehead"); *NOM:* MTV Movie Awards '97: Best Villain (Wahlberg).

Fear and Loathing in Las Vegas

Hunter S. Thompson's screen alter-ego Duke (Depp) packs his caddy with illicit drugs and his equally wasted lawyer (Del Toro), and heads for Vegas to cover a drug enforcement conference. Depp does a great job as Thompson and Del Toro pukes a lot in the sidekick role. Director Gilliam has no problem conveying all the excesses in Thompson's 1971 cult memoir. The DVD's stunning color helps to portray this one-of-a-kind trip. Reds predominate but there is no bleeding of the colors. The blacks, contrast, and brightness are excellent. The picture is sharp all the way through and you won't see any grain, even if you look for it in the blacks. Too bad the sound isn't 5.1. However, the Dolby Surround does just fine, especially when it kicks in for some of the freak-out sequences. The sound is crisp, with good high and low ends, and very good dynamics. A great trip. —JO

Movie: 🎬🎬🎬 **DVD:** 🎬🎬🎬▶
Universal Studios Home Video (Cat #20339, UPC #025192033926). Widescreen (2.35:1) anamorphic. Dolby Surround. $26.98. Keepcase. *LANG:* English. *SUB:* Spanish; French. *CAP:* English. *FEATURES:* 18 chapter links.
1998 (R) 119m/C Johnny Depp, Benicio Del Toro, Christina Ricci, Gary Busey, Craig Bierko, Ellen Barkin, Cameron Diaz, Flea, Mark Harmon, Katherine Helmond, Michael Jeter, Penn Jillette, Lyle Lovett, Tobey Maguire, Harry Dean Stanton, Tim Thomerson; *D:* Terry Gilliam; *W:* Terry Gilliam, Alex Cox, Tony Grisoni, Tod Davies; *C:* Nicola Pecorini.

The Fear: Halloween Night

Improbably, Morty, the monster who looks like a tree, is back in a sequel that makes even less sense and is even less frightening than the low-powered original. Another group of young people come out to a remote house. To nobody's surprise, they're picked off one by one in imaginative ways. Considering the excesses of the genre, blood and gore are kept to acceptable levels. On DVD, the film looks somewhat better than the first. That is not a recommendation. —MM **AKA:** Fear 2; Fear: Resurrection.

Movie: 🎬▶ **DVD:** 🎬🎬
Image Entertainment (Cat #ID8756UM DVD, UPC #014381875621). Full frame. Dolby Digital Stereo. $24.99. Snapper. *LANG:* English. *FEATURES:* 16 chapter links.
1999 (R) 87m/C Gordon Currie, Stacy Grant, Brendan Beiser, Betsy Palmer, Emmanuelle Vaugier, Rachel Hayward, Larry Pennell, Phillip Rhys, Myc Agnew, Kelly Benson; *D:* Chris Angel; *W:* Kevin Richards.

Fearless

Two plane crash survivors reach out to each other as they cope with everyday life. Bridges is riveting as the transformed Max, and Perez compelling as the sorrowful Carla. Hulce provides dead-on amusement as a casualty lawyer who knows

he's slime but can't help himself. Opening sequences of smoke in the corn fields are haunting as are flashbacks of the crash itself. Weir provides an engrossing look at facing death, both psychological and spiritual, but the ending is something of a letdown in its sappiness. O.K., we know this is one of those Warner budget DVDs, but how in the hell do they rationalize releasing a Peter Weir film full frame? That means it's best to stick with the widescreen laserdisc, which also has the edge on image quality. The DVD is of average sharpness and has some grain, and some of the dark scenes have minor artifacts. Color is also not an improvement over the DVD and, though they are fairly accurate, they are not as saturated as they should be. There is some bleed. Blacks are also in the average range with some grain in darker scenes. On the plus side, the Dolby Surround track is very good, and the excellent choice of music is delivered with great fidelity and solid dynamics. Some of the music is channeled to the back channel and the effect is sometimes quite mesmerizing, particularly the use of the Gorecki's 3rd Symphony for the climax. —JO

Movie: 🎬🎬🎬 **DVD:** 🎬🎬▶
Warner Home Video, Inc. (Cat #12986, UPC #085391298625). Full frame. Dolby Surround. $14.98. Snapper. *LANG:* English; French. *CAP:* English. *FEATURES:* 32 chapter links.
1993 (R) 122m/C Jeff Bridges, Isabella Rossellini, Rosie Perez, Tom Hulce, John Turturro, Benicio Del Toro, Deirdre O'Connell, John de Lancie; *D:* Peter Weir; *W:* Rafael Yglesias; *C:* Allen Daviau; *M:* Maurice Jarre. *AWARDS:* Los Angeles Film Critics Association Awards '93: Best Supporting Actress (Perez); *NOM:* Academy Awards '93: Best Supporting Actress (Perez); Golden Globe Awards '94: Best Supporting Actress (Perez).

Fearless Hyena

Early Jackie Chan (called Jacky Chan in on-screen credits) is a conventional Hong Kong martial arts flick. The first fights are so stylized they'll probably provoke laughter in western audiences. Later, the film acquires a Stoogian sense of humor. On DVD, the image is acceptable. Actually, it's pretty good for a film of its age and it compares favorably to many similar imports. The sound is only fair, but given the silly dubbing and phony sound effects, that's unimportant. —MM

Movie: 🎬🎬 **DVD:** 🎬🎬
Simitar Entertainment (Cat #7237, UPC #082551723720). Full frame. $14.98. Keepcase. *LANG:* English; Cantonese. *FEATURES:* 12 chapter links • Jackie Chan filmography and interview. The film is also available on a disc with *Fearless Hyena: Part 2,* catalog number 7488.
1979 (PG) 96m/C Jackie Chan; *D:* Jackie Chan; *W:* Jackie Chan; *C:* Chen Yung Shu.

Fearless Hyena: Part 2

Sequel in title only is another standard-issue Hong Kong martial arts movie with a historical setting. Jackie (billed as Jackie Chen in on-screen credits) must face a gang with supernatural kung-fu powers which allow them to zip around in fast-motion that most viewers will find hysterically funny. That appears to be unintentional but Jackie's work displays the light touch that would make him so famous. On disc, the image ranges from fair to good; same for the sound. —MM

Movie: 🎬🎬 **DVD:** 🎬🎬
Simitar Entertainment (Cat #7238, UPC #082551723829). Full frame. $14.98. Keepcase. *LANG:* English; Cantonese. *FEATURES:* 8 chapter links • Production factoids • Jackie Chan interview and filmography. The film is also available with *Fearless Hyena,* catalog number 7488.
1983 (PG) 91m/C Jackie Chan; *D:* Chuen Chan.

Feeling Minnesota

The cast will be enough to attract some viewers to this dark bizarre comedy. Incompetent criminal Jjaks (Reeves) shows up at his sleazy older brother's (D'Onofrio) wedding and falls for Freddie (Diaz), the bride who's being forced into the marriage by mobster Red (Lindo). Off they go on the run. The DVD is a depressingly accurate reproduction of the bleak theatrical image. Sound is acceptable. —MM

Movie: 🎬 **DVD:** 🎬🎬▶
New Line Home Video (Cat #N4853). Widescreen (1.85:1) anamorphic; full frame. Dolby Digital 5.1 Surround Stereo; Dolby Digital Surround Stereo. $24.98. Snapper. *LANG:* English. *SUB:* English. *FEATURES:* 23 chapter links • Cast and crew thumbnail biographies • Theatrical trailer.
1996 (R) 96m/C Keanu Reeves, Cameron Diaz, Vincent D'Onofrio, Delroy Lindo, Dan Aykroyd, Courtney Love, Tuesday Weld, Levon Helm; *D:* Steven Baigelman; *W:* Steven Baigelman; *C:* Walt Lloyd.

Felicia's Journey

Felicia (Cassidy) is an Irish girl on her own in England. Hilditch (Hoskins) is a kindly stranger. Or is he a serial murderer? As is always the case in Egoyan's films, the situation and the questions that arise from it are densely complicated. For his fans, the disc is well worth owning. Both image and sound are excellent, though flashy visuals and room-rattling sound are not the point. The extras are numerous and intelligent, particularly Egoyan's commentary track. —MM

Movie: 🎬🎬🎬▶ **DVD:** 🎬🎬🎬▶
Artisan Entertainment (Cat #10134). Widescreen (16:9) letterboxed. Dolby Digital 5.1 Surround Stereo. $24.98. Snapper. *LANG:* English. *FEATURES:* 32 chapter links • Isolated music track • Commentary: director Atom Egoyan • Hilditch's video collection • Gala's cooking show • "Making of" featurette • Trailers and TV

spots • Cast and crew thumbnail bios • Production notes.

1999 (PG-13) 111m/C CA GB Bob Hoskins, Elaine Cassidy, Arsinee Khanjian, Peter McDonald, Gerard McSorley, Brid Brennan, Claire Benedict; **D:** Atom Egoyan; **W:** Atom Egoyan; **C:** Paul Sarossy; **M:** Mychael Danna. *AWARDS:* Genie Awards '99: Best Actor (Hoskins), Best Adapted Screenplay, Best Cinematography, Best Original Score; *NOM:* Genie Awards '99: Best Actress (Cassidy), Best Director (Egoyan), Best Film.

Femalien

A strange alien being, composed of pure light energy, travels to Earth and assumes corporal form (Taylor) so she can once again experience sexual pleasure. She sure does, in some enthusiastic soft-core scenes.

Movie: ♪♪ **DVD:** NYR
Full Moon Pictures (Cat #8007). Full frame. $24.98.
1996 (R) 90m/C Vanessa Taylor, Jacqueline Lovell, Matt Schue; **D:** Cybil Richards; **W:** Cybil Richards.

The Fence

The recording quality on this disc is on par with the film's plot—dispassionate and unambitious. It sets out its limited scope of drab urban settings, hits its marks, gets the job done and gets out. Too bad its hero, the young jailbird Terry Griff (Wirth), doesn't have it so cut and dried. He's 29 and up for early release, but crosses paths with a dishonest parole officer. His girlfriend Jackie (Erica Gimpel of TV's *Fame*) has promised to wait, but how long? It's obvious what you're in for when not only the title and the box cover illustration but a number of scenes, including the very last, prominently use—you guessed it—a chain link fence. —*JK*
Movie: ♪♪▸ **DVD:** ♪♪♪
Image Entertainment (Cat #ID5592FMDVD, UPC #014381559224). Full frame. Dolby Digital Stereo. $24.99. Snapper. *LANG:* English. *FEATURES:* 15 chapter links • Scene access menu.
1994 90m/C Billy Wirth, Erica Gimpel, Marc Alaimo, Paul Benjamin, Lorenzo Clemons; **D:** Peter Pistor; **W:** Peter Fedorenko; **C:** John Newby; **M:** Jeff Beal.

Ferris Bueller's Day Off

It's almost graduation and Ferris (Broderick) wants one more sick day. He talks his best friend (Ruck) into sneaking out with his dad's vintage Ferrari and his girlfriend (Sara), for fun in Chicago. Out to get him are his jealous sister (Grey) and the officious principal (Jones). Of course, the DVD transfer of this hit comedy is flawless in visuals and audio, though the material doesn't exactly challenge the medium. Director Hughes's commentary is confident and low-keyed. The disc is sharper

than tape, but the difference between the two is not immense. —*MM*
Movie: ♪♪♪ **DVD:** ♪♪♪
Paramount Home Video (Cat #01890, UPC #097360189025). Widescreen letterboxed. Dolby Digital 5.1 Surround Stereo; Dolby Digital Surround Stereo. $29.99. Keepcase. *LANG:* English; French. *SUB:* English. *FEATURES:* 14 chapter links • Commentary: John Hughes.
1986 (PG-13) 103m/C Matthew Broderick, Mia Sara, Alan Ruck, Jeffrey Jones, Jennifer Grey, Cindy Pickett, Edie McClurg, Charlie Sheen, Del Close, Virginia Capers, Max Perlich, Louie Anderson, Richard Edson, Lyman Ward, Kristy Swanson, Larry "Flash" Jenkins, Ben Stein; **D:** John Hughes; **W:** John Hughes; **C:** Tak Fujimoto; **M:** Ira Newborn.

Fetishes

Documentarian Nick Broomfield (*Heidi Fleiss: Hollywood Madame*) spent several weeks in a New York S&M club, Pandora's Box, and gained the trust of both the women who work there and their patrons. It's a gamy subject, presented in all its tawdriness on DVD. The image is rough, and it ought to be. —*MM*
Movie: ♪♪♪ **DVD:** ♪♪▸
Simitar Entertainment (Cat #7412, UPC #082551741229). Full frame. $19.98. Keepcase. *LANG:* English.
1996 87m/C D: Nick Broomfield.

A Few Good Men

Strong performances by Cruise and Nicholson carry this story of a peacetime military cover-up. Cruise is a smart aleck Navy lawyer sleepwalking through his comfortable career in D.C. He's ready to write off two soldiers accused of the murder of their cohort until he interviews their commanding officer, Nicholson. Cruise smells a rat, but Nicholson practically dares him to prove it. Moore is another military lawyer assigned to the case, though her function seems to be holding Cruise's hand throughout the judicial process (there's no actual romance between the two). Well worth it for the incredible fireworks between Cruise and Nicholson in the courtroom. Based on the play by Sorkin, who also wrote the screenplay. The image transfer suffers from an abundance of brown and very diffused blacks (which are particularly prevalent in the courtroom scenes so they may very well have been intended as such). Likewise, the soundtrack suffers from not being re-mixed in Dolby 5.1 as the dialogue is often muddied and sound effects are less than awe-inspiring. —*MJT*
Movie: ♪♪♪ **DVD:** ♪♪▸
Columbia Tristar Home Video (Cat #27899, UPC #043396278998). Full frame; widescreen (2.35:1) letterboxed. Dolby Surround. $27.95. Keepcase. *LANG:* English; Spanish; French. *SUB:* Spanish; Korean. *FEATURES:* 51 chapter links.
1992 (R) 138m/C Tom Cruise, Jack Nicholson, Demi Moore, Kevin Bacon,

Kevin Pollak, Kiefer Sutherland, James Marshall, J.T. Walsh, Christopher Guest, J.A. Preston, Matt Craven, Wolfgang Bodison, Xander Berkeley, Cuba Gooding Jr., Noah Wyle; **D:** Rob Reiner; **W:** Aaron Sorkin; **C:** Robert Richardson; **M:** Marc Shaiman. *AWARDS:* MTV Movie Awards '93: Best Film; National Board of Review Awards '92: Best Supporting Actor (Nicholson); *NOM:* Academy Awards '92: Best Film Editing, Best Picture, Best Sound, Best Supporting Actor (Nicholson).

Fiddler on the Roof

Adaptation of the long-running Broadway musical tells the poignant story of Tevye, a poor Jewish milkman at the turn of the century in a small Ukrainian village, and his five dowryless daughters, his lame horse, his wife, and his companionable relationship with God. Topol, an Israeli who played the role in London, is charming, if not quite as wonderful as Zero Mostel, the Broadway star. Finely detailed set decoration and choreography, and strong performances from the entire cast create a sense of intimacy in spite of near epic proportions of the production. This is a very good DVD with interesting commentary that reveals both historic and cinematic details. The picture is sharp and has little grain despite the earthtone colors that some DVDs have trouble with. The colors are not particularly vibrant but are accurate to the film's actual coloring. Contrast and brightness are fine, making for comfortable viewing and not altering the look of the film. Blacks are deep and true. The 5.1 track is much improved from previous home video edition and is very full-bodied. Separation and imaging is excellent. —*JO*
Movie: ♪♪♪▸ **DVD:** ♪♪♪▸
MGM Home Entertainment (Cat #906728, UPC #027616672827). Widescreen (2.35:1) anamorphic. Dolby Digital 5.1. $24.95. Keepcase. *LANG:* English. *SUB:* English; Spanish; French. *CAP:* English. *FEATURES:* 36 chapter links • Commentary: Norman Jewison and Topol • Theatrical trailer • 8-page booklet.
1971 (G) 184m/C Chaim Topol, Norma Crane, Leonard Frey, Molly Picon, Paul Mann, Rosalind Harris, Michele Marsh, Neva Small, Paul Michael Glaser, Ray Lovelock; **D:** Norman Jewison; **W:** Joseph Stein; **C:** Oswald Morris; **M:** John Williams. *AWARDS:* Academy Awards '71: Best Cinematography, Best Sound, Original Song Score and/or Adaptation; Golden Globe Awards '72: Best Actor—Musical/Comedy (Topol), Best Film—Musical/Comedy; *NOM:* Academy Awards '71: Best Actor (Topol), Best Art Direction/Set Decoration, Best Director (Jewison), Best Picture, Best Supporting Actor (Frey).

The Field

After an absence from the big screen, intense and nearly over-the-top Harris won acclaim as an iron-willed peasant fighting to retain a patch of Irish land he has tended all his life, now offered for sale to a wealthy American. His uncompromising stand divides his community in this glowing adaptation of John B. Keane's play, an allegory of Ireland's internal problems. **Movie:** 🐾🐾🐾▶ **DVD:** NYR Pioneer Entertainment (Cat #10113). Full frame. $24.98. Keepcase. **1990 (PG-13) 113m/C** *GB* Richard Harris, Tom Berenger, John Hurt, Sean Bean, Brenda Fricker, Frances Tomelty, John Cowley, Sean McGinley, Jenny Conroy; **D:** Jim Sheridan; **W:** Jim Sheridan; **C:** Jack Conroy; **M:** Elmer Bernstein. *AWARDS: NOM: Academy Awards '90: Best Actor (Harris).*

Fierce Creatures

This not-really-a-sequel features the same cast as *A Fish Called Wanda* and was jokingly known as "Death Fish II" until a more appropriate title was thought of. A failing London zoo gets a new lease on life—and officious new manager Rollo Lee (Cleese)—by stocking only man-eating predators. This plan has kindly, insect house manager Bugsy (Palin) tongue-tied at the thought of destroying the zoo's cuddly current occupants. Kline is again in fine form with his dastardly dual role of zoo's Aussie owner Rod McCain and his idiot son, Vince. Curtis displays her obvious talents as Willa Weston, Vince's more sympathetic partner. Despite inspired moments, flick's not as tightly told or as wickedly funny as *Fish* (an admittedly tough act to follow). A family-friendlier attitude has effectively declawed this *Creature*. Many scenes were reshot after unfavorable advance screenings, necessitating a new director and the recall of the actors from far and wide. Well, if that's not enough to make you stay away from this DVD, just take a look at the image quality. The sound is good, though, and actually a little souped-up from the laserdisc release, which basically blows away this DVD. —JO **Movie:** 🐾🐾 **DVD:** 🐾🐾 Universal Studios Home Video (Cat #20144, UPC #025912014420). Full frame. Dolby Digital 5.1; Dolby Surround. $24.98. Keepcase. *LANG:* English (DD5.1); Spanish (DS); French (DS). *SUB:* Spanish. *CAP:* English. *FEATURES:* 16 chapter links. **1996 (PG-13) 93m/C** John Cleese, Jamie Lee Curtis, Kevin Kline, Michael Palin, Ronnie Corbett, Robert Lindsay, Carey Lowell, Bille Brown, Derek Griffiths, Cynthia Cleese; **D:** Robert M. Young, Fred Schepisi; **W:** John Cleese, Iain Johnstone; **C:** Adrian Biddle, Ian Baker; **M:** Jerry Goldsmith.

Fifth Day of Peace

In the last days of World War II, two Wehrmacht deserters are court-martialed by their commandant in a prisoner-of-war camp, even though the Allies have forbidden German military trials. An interesting plot, based on a true story, is marred by too many obvious twists. The DVD suffers even more. The image is so poor—with lots of static, blurring, and jittery scenes—

that it might have been made from a second-generation duplicate. —MM **Movie:** 🐾🐾 **DVD:** 🐾 Simitar Entertainment (Cat #7236, UPC #082551723621). Full frame. PCM Stereo. $14.98. Keepcase. *LANG:* English. *FEATURES:* 8 chapter links • Production factoids • Richard Johnson, Franco Nero bios and filmographies. **1972 (PG) 95m/C** *IT* Richard Johnson, Franco Nero, Larry Aubrey, Helmut Schneider; **D:** Giuliano Montaldo.

The Fifth Element

Besson's view of the future is colorful, loud, and fashionable. Dressed in costumes by Jean Paul Gaultier, Willis (in a blonde dye job) is New York City cab driver turned unwilling hero Korban Dallas, who must save Earth from destruction at the hands of evil arms dealer Zorg (Oldman). Bruce is up to the old heroics that made him a household name, and takes time to romance orange-haired nymph Jovovich, who holds the key to all the madness going on. Oldman is over-the-top as the icy villain with a distinct southern accent, which makes him more of a bad gag than a bad guy. Jumbled story fortunately takes a backseat to weird aliens and stunning visuals that make this an eye-catching (albeit confusing) sci-fi trip. The film's comic book-like colors are captured perfectly by this DVD and the result is a visually stunning disc that will be a showpiece in your collection. The colors are incredibly bright and seem to have no bleed at all. Contrast is exceptionally punchy and brightness levels are matched to perfection. The image is extremely sharp and detailed with no visible digital grain or artifacts. Blacks are well handled and true. The 5.1 sound itself is as explosive as the climactic shoot-'em-up blow-'em-up finale. The lows are rumbling, but not boomy, and the highs crisp and clear. Surround effects are frequent and energized. —JO **Movie:** 🐾🐾▶ **DVD:** 🐾🐾🐾🐾 Columbia Tristar Home Video (Cat #82409, UPC #043396824096). Widescreen (2.35:1) anamorphic; full frame. Dolby Digital 5.1; Stereo. $27.95. Keepcase. *LANG:* English (DD5.1; DS); Spanish (DS). *SUB:* English; Spanish. *CAP:* English. *FEATURES:* 36 chapter links. **1997 (PG-13) 125m/C** Bruce Willis, Gary Oldman, Ian Holm, Milla Jovovich, Luke Perry, Lee Evans, Chris Tucker, Brion James, Tommy (Tiny) Lister, John Neville, John Bluthal, Maiwenn Le Besco, Mathieu Kassovitz; **D:** Luc Besson; **W:** Luc Besson; **C:** Thierry Arbogast; **M:** Eric Serra. *AWARDS:* British Academy Awards '97: Best Visual Effects; Cesar Awards '98: Best Art Direction/Set Decoration, Best Cinematography, Best Director (Besson); *NOM:* Academy Awards '97: Best Sound Effects Editing; MTV Movie Awards '98: Best Fight (Milla Jovovich/aliens); Golden Raspberry Awards '97: Worst Supporting Actress (Jovovich), Worst New Star (Tucker).

54

Disco, drugs and '70s style hedonism return in this look back at Manhattan's infamous Studio 54. Myers portrays coked-out club owner Steve Rubell, while Phillippe plays a gorgeous, naive Jersey boy Shane O'Shea who starts off as a bartender and descends into debauchery. Others hitting the dance floor are an ambitious soap star (Campbell), a coat-check girl/would-be diva (Hayek) and her bus boy husband (Meyer). Shane's a pouty bore, but Myers is effective—and unrecognizable—in a rare dramatic performance. Despite some resemblance to *Boogie Nights,* film is meandering and strangely tame, considering the setting. The dusk-to-dawn glitter ball lifestyle comes across a bit murkier on DVD. Dialogue remains impressively audible even over the thumping disco score, which sounds great. —JE **Movie:** 🐾 **DVD:** 🐾🐾 Miramax Pictures Home Video (Cat #16700, UPC #1795100183). Widescreen (1.85:1) letterboxed. Dolby Digital 5.1 Audio. $29.99. Keepcase. *LANG:* English. *CAP:* English. *FEATURES:* 36 chapter links • Chapter search • "If You Could Read My Mind" music video performed by Stars on 45. **1998 (R) 92m/C** Mike Myers, Ryan Phillippe, Breckin Meyer, Salma Hayek, Neve Campbell, Sela Ward, Sherry Stringfield, Ellen A. Dow, Heather Matarazzo, Skipp Sudduth; **Cameos:** Lauren Hutton, Michael York; **D:** Mark Christopher; **W:** Mark Christopher; **C:** Alexander Grusynski. *AWARDS: NOM:* Golden Raspberry Awards '98: Worst Actor (Phillippe), Worst Supporting Actress (Dow).

Fight Club

Director Fincher continues the "distressed" look that he gave to *Seven* in a mock FBI Warning at the beginning of this DVD. He looks to the dark side of masculinity in an adaptation of Chuck Palahniuk's novel. Tyler Durden (Pitt) is a self-styled anarchist; Jack (Norton) is an insomniac dissatisfied materialist. They wind up sharing a mouldering house, strongly reminiscent of Norman Bates's place up on the hill in *Psycho,* and founding underground fight clubs which become a countrywide phenomenon and lead to something more. Helena Bonham Carter plays a kinky, suicidal woman both men fancy. It's hardly heartthrob territory but the two-bit nihilism is leavened by sharp intelligent humor. Fox gave the film royal treatment on DVD. It's a two-disc set with most extras on the second, and the film and four separate commentary tracks on the first. For better or for worse, Fincher's dirty, acid-washed visuals are translated faithfully. Because the film is so deliberately unsettling, it's somehow easier to take on home video than it was in theatres where it did not live up to critical expectations. —MM **Movie:** 🐾🐾🐾 **DVD:** 🐾🐾🐾🐾 20th Century Fox (Cat #2000035). Widescreen. Dolby Digital 5.1 Surround Stereo;

Dolby Digital Surround Stereo. $39.98. Box set. *LANG:* English. *SUB:* Spanish. *CAP:* English. *FEATURES:* 36 chapter links • Commentary: David Fincher • Commentary: Fincher, Pitt, Norton, and Bonham Carter • Commentary: Palahniuk, Jim Uhls • Commentary: McDowell, Cronenworth, Kaplan, Haug • Behind-the-scenes footage • Deleted scenes • Extensive publicity material • Storyboards and other art • Extensive liner notes.
1999 (R) 139m/C Brad Pitt, Edward Norton, Helena Bonham Carter, Meat Loaf Aday, Jared Leto, Eion Bailey; *D:* David Fincher; *W:* Jim Uhls; *C:* Jeff Cronenweth; *M:* Howard Shore.

The Fighting Sullivans

Unalloyed propaganda is best known today as the partial inspiration for *Saving Private Ryan*. The five Sullivan brothers were all killed when their ship, the Juneau, was sunk off Guadalcanal. The family's loss was so extreme that the armed services decided that brothers would never again be assigned to the same ship or unit. This film is really more about their upbringing than their fate. As shown here, their parents (Mitchell and Royle) raised them in a *Little Rascals* world. When the kids grow up, the youngest (Ryan) courts and marries Katherine Mary (Baxter). On this few-frills DVD, the image is very good, but not much better than VHS tape. The patriotic commentary track has no real bearing on the film and should be listened to separately, since the film's soundtrack is eliminated. Though the box copy lists titles for 21 chapter links, they cannot be accessed through the menu. —*MM* **AKA:** The Sullivans.
Movie: 🎬🎬🎬 *DVD:* 🎬🎬
Roan Group (Cat #AED-2000, UPC #785604200024). Full frame. Dolby Digital Mono. $29.95. Keepcase. *LANG:* English. *FEATURES:* Commentary: Jack Bilello.
1942 110m/B Anne Baxter, Thomas Mitchell, Selena Royle, Eddie Ryan, Trudy Marshall, James B. Cardwell, Roy Roberts, Ward Bond, Mary McCarty, Bobby Driscoll, Addison Richards, Selmer Jackson, Mae Marsh, Harry Strang, Barbara Brown, George Offerman Jr., John Campbell, John Alvin, Patrick Curtis, Nancy June Robinson, Marvin Davis; *D:* Lloyd Bacon; *W:* Edward Doherty, Mary C. McCall, Jules Schermer; *C:* Lucien N. Andriot; *M:* Cyril Mockridge, Alfred Newman.

Final Analysis

Glossy thriller starring Gere as a San Francisco psychiatrist who falls for the glamorous sister of one of his patients. Basinger plays the femme fatale and Thurman is Gere's sexually neurotic patient. Although heavily influenced by *Vertigo*, this film never comes close to attaining the depth of Hitchcock's cinematic masterpiece. Roberts gives the most gripping performance in this slick suspense movie as Basinger's sleazy gangster husband.

The DVD is pretty good, and most of its problems occur during the darker sequences, of which there are many. In stronger lighting, the picture is sharp and grain is low. Grain picks up when the lights go down and the image goes soft. Colors are fairly accurate but bleed and pick up some grain when they're deep, and in those dimmer scenes. Blacks fare the same and are true in the light and so-so in the dark. Contrast could be a little higher, but brightness levels are adequate. There's nothing at all special about the sound, but it'll do. —*JO*
Movie: 🎬🎬 *DVD:* 🎬🎬
Warner Home Video, Inc. (Cat #12243, UPC #085391224327). Full frame. Dolby Surround. $14.98. Snapper. *LANG:* English; French. *CAP:* English. *FEATURES:* 37 chapter links.
1992 (R) 125m/C Richard Gere, Kim Basinger, Uma Thurman, Eric Roberts, Paul Guilfoyle, Keith David, Robert Harper, Jolyon Baker, Harris Yulin, Agustin Rodriguez; *D:* Phil Joanou; *W:* Wesley Strick, Robert Berger; *C:* Jordan Cronenweth; *M:* George Fenton.

Final Justice

A loosy-goosy plot sends Texas deputy sheriff Thomas Jefferson Geronimo (Baker) to Italy with mob boss Anthony Palermo (Venantini) who promptly escapes. A series of chases and shootouts ensues. This violent exploitation looks no better on DVD than it did on the drive-in screen, which is its natural element. The disc lacks any features, including chapters. —*MM*
Movie: 🎬 *DVD:* 🎬
Digital Versatile Disc Ltd. (Cat #DVD 106, UPC #066479101068). Full frame. $19.95. Keepcase.
1984 (R) 90m/C Joe Don Baker, Rossano Brazzi, Patrizia Pellegrino, Venantino Venantini; *D:* Greydon Clark; *W:* Greydon Clark; *C:* Nicholas Josef von Sternberg; *M:* David Bell.

Finding Graceland

Compilation of pop culture cliches finds Byron (Schaech) driving a banged-up Cadillac convertible across the desert where he meets a guy (Keitel) who thinks he's Elvis and a Marilyn Monroe look-alike (Fonda). Guess where they all decide to go. Perhaps those who love all things Elvisian will be entertained by this claptrap, but even the presence of the always-reliable Keitel is not enough. That said, the DVD looks and sounds terrific. Its evocation of the road is excellent. Winkler's commentary track is a virtual Filmmaking 101. —*MM*
Movie: 🎬🎬 *DVD:* 🎬🎬🎬
Columbia Tristar Home Video (Cat #04038, UPC #043396040380). Widescreen (2.35:1) letterboxed. Dolby Digital Surround Stereo. $25.95. Keepcase. *LANG:* English; Spanish. *SUB:* English; French; Spanish. *FEATURES:* 28 chapter links • 2 deleted scenes • Trailers • Cast and crew thumbnail biographies.

1998 (PG-13) 97m/C Johnathon Schaech, Harvey Keitel, Bridget Fonda, Gretchen Mol; *D:* David Winkler; *W:* Jason Horwitch; *C:* Elliot Davis; *M:* Stephen Endelman.

Finding North

A *Hollywood Reporter* blurb on the box cover compares this independent to the bisexual broadcast sitcom *Will and Grace*, indicating not only its budget and subject, but its marketing difficulties as well. Rhonda (Makkena) is a Brooklyn gal fending off middle age by ordering a strip-o-gram guy with "puppy dog eyes" and "class." What she gets by mistake is a rapidly unfolding yet frustratingly platonic relationship with a suicidal gay man named Travis (Hickey). They take off on a series of cross-country hijinx, often—much to Travis's consternation—in matching hats. In case you miss anything, Rhonda stops midway through the film to recap the plot. She retells it as a fairy tale to a little girl she just met! Considering the film is dedicated to two deceased people, you can understand why its comedy is often more bitter or morose than chipper. However, it takes some effort to indulge lines like, "It's a good thing I don't have my period today or you'd be in big trouble." Despite being shot in two different states, it remains too cramped to be a fully hell-bent screwball comedy. Pallid interior lighting is often very much along sitcom lines, though exteriors and Denton, TX, location shots fare much better on the Eastmancolor stock. Images are heavily though evenly artifact-laden, and the bottom half of the screen is thick with wavering bands throughout. The sound emanates nicely enough through the center speaker, but left and right ones just give off static except when the theme music appears. The commentators lean into their mike and sometimes drift into self-indulgence, but they pick up on the right details. —*JK*
Movie: 🎬🎬🎬 *DVD:* 🎬🎬
Wolfe Video (Cat #WOL3239DVD, UPC #754703761507). Widescreen. Dual-channel Mono. $24.99. Keepcase. *LANG:* English. *FEATURES:* 8 chapter links • Interactive menus • 4-color disc • Commentary: director and producer • Theatrical trailer • 5 video trailers.
1997 96m/C Wendy Makkena, John Benjamin Hickey, Angela Pietropinto, Freddie Roman, Molly McClure; *D:* Tanya Wexler; *W:* Kim Powers; *C:* Michael Barrett; *V:* Jonathan Walker.

Fire Down Below

Seagal comes armed with his trademark ponytail, martial arts expertise, big leather jackets, and environment-friendly message to the Appalachians in this hoedown showdown. As undercover (yeah, he blends right in) EPA agent Jack Taggart, Seagal must stop evil industrialist Hanner (Kristofferson) from dumping toxic waste. Of course, the company town sends the usual band of thugs (thoughtfully attacking one at a time) to make him go away. He finds allies in the local outcasts (Helgenberger and Stanton) en route to the final confrontation. Seagal at his worst. The usually impressive fight scenes become tedious after a while. At least he didn't try to direct this one, which was originally conceived as a Bruce Willis project at Columbia. Fair is fair and this nothing-special film is given a nothing-special DVD. The picture is fairly sharp and grain is minimal. There are some artifacts in the unnaturally fast-moving action sequences. Colors are saturated but the tint is usually a touch off. Blacks range from O.K. to true, depending on lighting conditions. The disc's 5.1 sound is fine with some good Surround effects and separation with energized dynamics enhanced by the somewhat pumped low end. —JO

Movie: 🎵▶ **DVD:** 🎵🎵▶
Warner Home Video, Inc. (Cat #14914, UPC #085391491422). Widescreen (2.35:1) anamorphic; full frame. Dolby Digital 5.1; Stereo. $24.98. Snapper. *LANG:* English; French. *SUB:* English; Spanish; French. *CAP:* English. *FEATURES:* 32 chapter links • 8 theatrical trailers • Production notes.
1997 (R) 105m/C Steven Seagal, Marg Helgenberger, Kris Kristofferson, Harry Dean Stanton, Stephen Lang, Levon Helm, Brad Hunt, Richard Masur, Ed Bruce, Randy Travis, Mark Collie, Alex Harvey; **D:** Feliz Alcala; **W:** Jeb Stuart; **C:** Tom Houghton; **M:** Nick Glennie-Smith. *AWARDS: NOM:* Golden Raspberry Awards '97: Worst Picture, Worst Actor (Seagal), Worst Song ("Fire Down Below").

Fire on the Amazon

Roger Corman's answer to *Salvador* even includes a costar, Juan Fernandez, who was also featured in that Oliver Stone picture. Estimates range as to exactly when this was filmed on location along the Amazon, anywhere from 1990 to 1993, but the print's copyright is 1998. Ungainly, creepily nosy investigative photographer R.J. (Sheffer) is just lucky that uptight rainforest preservationist Alyssa (Bullock) springs him from jail as "harmless." Once they're finally kidnapped by Bolivian natives and share a drug-induced (and perhaps selectively pixelated) night of passion, they more resemble the carefully draped moptops from *The Blue Lagoon* than hard-bitten adventurers. Moreover, they respond to this emotional breakthrough by immediately going back to carping about each other's political commitments. The image is grainy but otherwise clean, except for smoky bar scenes, and scans well. Too bad no one could smooth over the lumpy, B-movie bones of the script or the television series quality of the film's makeup and sets. The stereo is neatly separated, and unleashes a rush of affected, politicized balladeering at crucial points. An enclosed eight-page booklet cryptically describes the fate of Corman's 1994

live-action *The Fantastic Four* (partners bought him out at the last minute) and offers other curious tidbits from his long and loopy career. Plus, it identifies the background photos in its timeline layouts. That's more than you can usually expect from such fluffy promo items. The review copy contained only the film and a "play movie" menu. Spanish subtitles are promised to be optional. —JK

Movie: 🎵🎵 **DVD:** 🎵🎵
New Horizons Home Video (Cat #NH20355D, UPC #73699143554X). Full frame. Stereo. $19.99. Keepcase. *LANG:* English. *SUB:* Spanish. *FEATURES:* 1 chapter link • Interactive menu • Cast biographies • Theatrical trailer • "A History of Roger Corman and New Horizons" booklet.
1993 (R) 81m/C Sandra Bullock, Craig Sheffer, Judith Chapman, Juan Fernandez; **D:** Luis Llosa; **W:** Catherine Cyran, Jane Gray; **C:** Pili Flores-Guerra; **M:** Roy J. Ravio.

Fire Over England

Young naval officer volunteers to spy at the Spanish court to learn the plans for the invasion of his native England and to identify the traitors among the English nobility. He arouses the romantic interest of his queen, Elizabeth I, one of her ladies, and a Spanish noblewoman who helps with his mission. Later he leads the fleet to victory over the huge Spanish armada. The first of many on-screen pairings of Olivier and Leigh is just one of the many virtues of this entertaining period drama.
Movie: 🎵🎵🎵 **DVD:** NYR
Lumivision Corp. (Cat #298). Full frame. Mono. $19.95. Keepcase.
1937 81m/B *GB* Flora Robson, Raymond Massey, Laurence Olivier, Vivien Leigh, Leslie Banks, James Mason; **D:** William K. Howard; **W:** Clemence Dane, Sergei Nolbandov; **C:** James Wong Howe; **M:** Richard Addinsell.

Firehouse

In the style of *Police Academy* (but made on a much smaller budget), three nubile firefighting recruits klutz up an already helpless urban firehouse. There's little sex in this soft-core comedy. Actually, the Jersey City locations are more important. On DVD, the film doesn't look much better than it did on the drive-in screen where it really belongs. —MM
Movie: 🎵▶ **DVD:** 🎵▶
Simitar Entertainment (Cat #7396, UPC #082551739622). Full frame. Dolby Digital Stereo. $14.98. Keepcase. *LANG:* English. *FEATURES:* 8 chapter links • Production factoids.
1987 (R) 91m/C Barrett Hopkins, Shannon Murphy, Violet Brown, John Anderson, Julia Roberts; **D:** J. Christian Ingvordsen; **W:** J. Christian Ingvordsen, Steven Kaman, Rick Marx; **C:** Steven Kaman; **M:** Michael Montes.

Firestarter

Stephen King's story of psychic powers, government spooks, and violent effects is comparable to *The Fury*, but it's much more enjoyable. The difference—veteran B-movie director Mark L. Lester *(Truck Stop Women)* understands the pulp roots of the material about a little girl (Barrymore) who can cause people and objects to burst into flame, and so he doesn't try to make the film more than it is. He keeps the plot moving swiftly, but gives the believably middle-class protagonists time to develop. No matter what has happened since, Drew Barrymore certainly was a cute chubby-cheeked little rascal, even when she flames feds, turning them into shish kebabs in suits. Scott and Sheen are good villains, too. On disc, one scene with mini-blinds in the background is almost painful to watch and some detail is lost in night scenes. Otherwise, the transfer is fine and the widescreen treatment captures the full range of the ambitious pyrotechnics. —MM

Movie: 🎵🎵▶ **DVD:** 🎵🎵🎵
Image Entertainment (Cat #ID427USDVD, UPC #014381427424). Widescreen (2.35:1) letterboxed. Dolby Digital Mono. $29.99. Snapper. *LANG:* English. *FEATURES:* 16 chapter links.
1984 (R) 115m/C David Keith, Drew Barrymore, Freddie Jones, Martin Sheen, George C. Scott, Heather Locklear, Louise Fletcher, Moses Gunn, Art Carney, Antonio Fargas, Drew Snyder; **D:** Mark L. Lester; **W:** Stanley Mann; **C:** Giuseppe Ruzzolini; **M:** Tangerine Dream.

Firestorm

In his first starring role, ex-NFL tough guy Long plays Jesse Graves, a parachuting firefighter with a really square head. Jesse and his "smoke jumping" mentor Wynt (Glenn) must drop into a raging Wyoming forest fire to save a group of trapped firemen. Except they aren't real firemen, they're convicts in disguise who have escaped through a hole in the plot. Ringleader Shaye (Forsythe) had his lawyer set the fire so that he could use the volunteer murderer/fire fighter release program to escape and find the $37 million he has hidden. Happens all the time. The smoky chain gang also stumbles across beautiful bird-watcher Jennifer (Amis) and takes her hostage. Jesse must foil the bad guys, save the girl, and douse the fire; all the while lugging around his humongous chin and speaking in monotone. Fire effects were enhanced by computer-generated graphics. The disc has a nice crisp transfer, replete with the vibrant colors you would expect with a movie about fire. The 5.1 soundtrack is also quite impressive, but the technical worth of the disc is overshadowed by the awfulness of the film itself. —MJT
Movie: 🎵▶ **DVD:** 🎵🎵🎵
Twentieth Century Fox Home Entertainment (Cat #4110427, UPC #086162104 275). Widescreen (2.35:1) letterboxed. Dolby Digital 5.1; Dolby Surround. $29.98. Keep-

case. *LANG:* English; French. *SUB:* English; Spanish. *FEATURES:* 16 chapter links • Theatrical trailer • Cast and crew mini bios.
1997 (R) 89m/C Howie Long, Scott Glenn, William Forsythe, Suzy Amis, Christianne Hirt, Garwin Sanford, Sebastian Spence, Michael Greyeyes, Benjamin Ratner, Barry Pepper, Vladimir Kulich, Tom McBeath; *D:* Dean Semler; *W:* Chris Soth; *C:* Stephen Windon; *M:* J. Peter Robinson.

The Firing Line

A Central American government hires a mercenary rebel-buster (Brown) to squash insurgents. Everything's great until he agrees with the rebels' cause and trains them to fight.
Movie: 🎕🎕 *DVD:* NYR
Tapeworm Video Distributors (Cat #313). Full frame. $19.95. Keepcase.
1991 93m/C Reb Brown, Shannon Tweed, Michael Monty, Kathlena Marie, Melvin Davidson, Carl Terry, Andy Jacobson; *D:* John Gale; *W:* John Gale, Sonny Sanders; *C:* Carl Sommers; *M:* Martia Manuel.

The Firm

Top-flight cast promises a good time, and the script based on John Grisham's bestseller delivers. Ambitious, idealistic law school grad Mitch McDeere (Cruise) accepts a great offer with a small but wealthy Memphis law firm, which turns out to be more than it appears. Fine performances from all concerned, particularly Cruise, Hackman and Hunter. Though the DVD lacks extras, the transfer of image and sound is all that a big-budget Hollywood thriller deserves. Both are flawless. —*MM*
Movie: 🎕🎕🎕 *DVD:* 🎕🎕🎕
Paramount Home Video (Cat #32523, UPC #097363252375). Widescreen anamorphic. Dolby Digital 5.1 Surround Stereo; Dolby Surround Stereo. $29.99. Snapper. *LANG:* English; French. *SUB:* English. *FEATURES:* 19 chapter links • 2 theatrical trailers.
1993 (R) 154m/C Tom Cruise, Jeanne Tripplehorn, Gene Hackman, Hal Holbrook, Terry Kinney, Wilford Brimley, Ed Harris, Holly Hunter, David Strathairn, Gary Busey, Steven Hill, Tobin Bell, Barbara Garrick, Jerry Hardin, Karina Lombard, John Beal; *Cameos:* Paul Sorvino; *D:* Sydney Pollack; *W:* Robert Towne, David Rayfiel; *C:* John Seale; *M:* Dave Grusin. *AWARDS:* NOM. Academy Awards '93: Best Supporting Actress (Hunter), Best Original Score; British Academy Awards '93: Best Supporting Actress (Hunter); MTV Movie Awards '94: Best Male Performance (Cruise), Most Desirable Male (Cruise).

First Blood

Sylvester Stallone's portrayal of a heroic Vietnam vet sealed his status as a major star and this film changed the rules for action movies. David Morrell, who wrote the novel, notes those facts in his com-

mentary track. He also talks about the development of the main characters—Rambo's based on Audie Murphy—and the historical context that bridges the gap between the novel's roots in the late 1960s and its filming in the early '80s. Since he had nothing to do with the production, he brings an odd combination of objectivity and intimacy to his work. He talks about director Ted Kotcheff's under-appreciated work, the valuable contribution made by composer Jerry Goldsmith, and the incredible stuntwork. The remastered image looks fine on DVD, though it's not perfect. A few flaws are visible on the print, and the film has always had a grainy quality. —*MM*
Movie: 🎕🎕🎕 *DVD:* 🎕🎕🎕
Artisan Entertainment (Cat #60465, UPC #012236046509). Widescreen (2.35:1) letterboxed. Dolby Digital Surround Stereo. $24.98. Keepcase. *LANG:* English. *SUB:* Spanish. *CAP:* English. *FEATURES:* 30 chapter links • Cast and crew thumbnail biographies • Production notes • Documentary, *First Blood: A Look Back* • Trivia game • Teaser • Theatrical trailer • Sylvester Stallone featurette • Commentary: novelist David Morrell.
1982 (R) 96m/C Sylvester Stallone, Richard Crenna, Brian Dennehy, Jack Starrett, David Caruso; *D:* Ted Kotcheff; *W:* Sylvester Stallone; *C:* Andrew Laszlo; *M:* Jerry Goldsmith.

The First Deadly Sin

NYPD detective Francis X. Delaney (Sinatra) investigates a series of motiveless murders while dealing with his imminent retirement and the serious illness of his wife (Dunaway). With the passage of time, Sinatra's last film appearance has aged with dignity. His scenes with Dunaway are honestly moving. But considering the source material—Lawrence Sanders's book is one of the great American crime novels—the film could have been much more suspenseful. The brightness seems to change during several scenes on this DVD and overall it feels darker than it should be. More contrast would have made for more comfortable viewing. Sharpness is average and there is more grain than you'd see on a Warner Bros. DVD. Artifacts appear during numerous scenes. That said, the color is very good with only a little bleed along lines of high contrast, and the blacks are usually true. The mono soundtrack is average in every way, and a little tinny on the highs and lacking lows. This DVD looked comparatively better than the VHS tape, so if you like the film, buy it. In the end, it's an adequate pan-and-scan digital transfer of a fair film. —*JO/MM*
Movie: 🎕🎕🎕 *DVD:* 🎕🎕
Warner Home Video, Inc. (Cat #11368, UPC #085391136828). Full frame. Dolby Digital Mono. $14.98. Snapper. *LANG:* English. *CAP:* English. *FEATURES:* 35 chapter links.
1980 (R) 112m/C Frank Sinatra, Faye Dunaway, David Dukes, Brenda Vaccaro,

James Whitmore; *D:* Brian G. Hutton; *W:* Mann Rubin; *C:* Jack Priestley; *M:* Gordon Jenkins.

First Knight

King Arthur/Camelot legend comes to life again, but isn't worth the time it takes to watch. Wandering swordsman Lancelot (Gere) saves beautiful Guinevere (Ormond), soon to be Arthur's (Connery) queen, from evil renegade knight Malagant. They yearn, they gaze, they kiss—you gag. Written like a Harlequin romance, the dialogue (especially when uttered by Gere) is unintentionally funny, and the plot will cause much eye-rolling. This movie has lighting conditions that run the gamut from very dark (castle and forest scenes) to very bright (other outdoor sequences) and the DVD handles them all with no problem. The picture is extremely sharp with no grain or artifacts. The colors remain true and bleedless, and are very vibrant. Contrast and brightness levels are excellent. Blacks are true. The 5.1 sound is also superb, with lively and crisp highs as well as gut-shaking low end. The Surround tracks add plenty of ambience and really kick in nicely during the action sequences. —*JO*
Movie: 🎕 *DVD:* 🎕🎕🎕🎕
Columbia Tristar Home Video (Cat #71179, UPC #043396711792). Widescreen (1.85:1) letterboxed; full frame. Dolby Digital 5.1; Dolby Surround. $28.95. Keepcase. *LANG:* English (DD5.1; DS); Spanish (DS); French (DS). *SUB:* Spanish; Korean. *CAP:* English. *FEATURES:* 46 chapter links.
1995 (PG-13) 134m/C Sean Connery, Richard Gere, Julia Ormond, Ben Cross, John Gielgud, Liam Cunningham, Christopher Villiers, Valentine Pelka; *D:* Jerry Zucker; *W:* William Nicholson; *C:* Adam Greenberg; *M:* Jerry Goldsmith.

First Man into Space

An astronaut returns to Earth after being bombarded by cosmic rays and space dust. He has an organism growing inside him that slowly turns him into a hideous (well, semi-hideous) monster who feeds on human blood. Actually, he could be a prototype for Troma's "Toxic Avenger," and he spends most of his time lumbering around a plot that follows the genre's formula to the letter. The biggest flaw in this DVD is the incredible amount of grain that shows up, particularly in the faces of the cast. It could be that the original film print that was used is the same, but it doesn't make the DVD any more pleasing to watch. Along with the grain, the sharpness is only average, as are the brightness levels and contrast. The blacks are close to true. The mono soundtrack is crisp, and the dialogue can be easily understood, but as expected from a B-film of this era there are no dynamics to speak of. —*JO/MM*
AKA: Satellite of Blood.
Movie: 🎕🎕 *DVD:* 🎕🎕🎕

Image Entertainment (Cat #ID4429GODVD, UPC #014381442922). Full frame. PCM uncompressed mono. $24.99. Keepcase. *LANG:* English. *FEATURES:* 15 chapter links ● Theatrical trailer.
1959 78m/B Marshall Thompson, Marla Landi, Bill Edwards; *D:* Robert Day; *W:* John C. Cooper, Lance Z. Hargreaves; *C:* Geoffrey Faithfull; *M:* Buxton Orr.

First Name: Carmen

Although posing as an aspiring filmmaker, Carmen (Detmers) is really a bank robber and terrorist. She's also a femme fatale who, in mid-heist, seduces a cop (Bonnaffe) and runs off with him. Director Godard, who casts himself as Carmen's funny uncle Jean, intercuts their story with footage of a string quartet playing Beethoven. On DVD, the sound is really more impressive than the image, where black shadows and clothes tend to melt into solid blobs. But then, standards of Hollywood visual perfection are antithetical to Godard's purposes, and it's wrong to criticize his work on those grounds. — *MM* **AKA:** Prenom: Carmen.
Movie: 🐾🐾🐾 *DVD:* 🐾🐾
WinStar Home Entertainment (Cat #FLV5064, UPC #720917506425). Widescreen (2.33:1) letterboxed. $29.98. Keepcase. *LANG:* French. *SUB:* English. *FEATURES:* 8 chapter links ● Godard filmography and awards.
1983 95m/C *FR* Maruschka Detmers, Jacques Bonaffe, Jean-Luc Godard, Myriem Roussel, Christophe Odent; *D:* Jean-Luc Godard; *W:* Anne-Marie Mieville; *C:* Raoul Coutard.

The First 9 1/2 Weeks

Prequel to *9 1/2 Weeks* finds investor Matt Wade trying to close the biggest deal of his career with eccentric New Orleans businessman Francois Dubois. But Dubois's wife starts raising Wade's temperature even more than steamy New Orleans.
Movie: woof *DVD:* NYR
Studio Home Entertainment (Cat #7085). Full frame. Dolby Digital Stereo. $24.95. Keepcase. *SUB:* Spanish. *FEATURES:* Production notes ● Trailer.
1998 (R) 99m/C Paul Mercurio, Clara Bellar, Malcolm McDowell, Frederic Forrest, Dennis Burkley, James Black, Anna Jacyszyn, William Keane, Richard Durden; *D:* Alexander Wright; *W:* Alexander Wright; *C:* John Tarver; *M:* Norman Orenstein.

First Option

In Hong Kong, the Special Duty Unit is the equivalent of a SWAT team. They like to dress up in tight black T-shirts and masks that match their automatic weapons. They're led by Mike Stone (Wong), who learns that his newest opponents are his old military pals. This action film is the familiar mix of bulging biceps and gunfights. The DVD image and sound (with a

Terminator-inspired score) are excellent, easily the equal of comparable American productions. —*MM*
Movie: 🐾🐾 ► *DVD:* 🐾🐾🐾
Tai Seng Video Marketing (Cat #MS/DVD/044/98, UPC #4895017000442). Widescreen letterboxed. Dolby Digital 5.1 Surround Stereo. $49.95. Keepcase. *LANG:* Cantonese; Mandarin; English. *SUB:* Traditional & Simplified Chinese; English; Japanese; Korean; Bahasa Malaysia; Thai; Vietnamese; Spanish. *FEATURES:* 9 chapter links ● Production credits ● Theatrical trailers ● 3 "making of" featurettes.
1996 86m/C *HK* Michael Wong, Gigi Leung; *D:* Gordon Chan; *W:* Gordon Chan, Chan Hing-Kai; *C:* Horace Wong.

The First Wives Club

As the first Mrs. Trump, who makes a most appropriate cameo, so wisely puts it, "Don't get mad, get everything." But to the three rich, middle aged friends who are dumped by their husbands so the guys can marry younger "trophy" wives, there's just nothing like revenge. Comedy begins in 1969 with the young and idealistic Annie (Keaton), Brenda (Midler), Elise (Hawn), and Cynthia (Channing) graduating college, then moves to the present with the wronged Cynthia ledge-diving from her swanky Manhattan apartment because her husband left her. The remaining mistreated trio goes into action, using their exes' own money, businesses, power, and various mistresses against them. This film's appeal and success had Hollywood tongues wagging, predicting the dawn of new roles for older actresses. The DVD image is pretty sharp with only a little grain cropping up during the dimmer scenes. Colors are accurate, with no bleed and are fairly punchy despite the overall need for both a brightness and contrast boost. Blacks are good. The audio does its job to convey the dialogue crisply and the music with nice fidelity and ambience. —*JO*
Movie: 🐾🐾 ► *DVD:* 🐾🐾 ►
Paramount Home Video (Cat #326127, UPC #097363261270). Widescreen (1.85:1) letterboxed. Dolby Digital 5.1; Dolby Surround. $29.99. Keepcase. *LANG:* English. *SUB:* Spanish. *CAP:* English. *FEATURES:* 36 chapter links ● Theatrical trailer.
1996 (PG) 104m/C Goldie Hawn, Diane Keaton, Bette Midler, Sarah Jessica Parker, Heather Locklear, Marcia Gay Harden, Elizabeth Berkley, Victor Garber, Dan Hedaya, Stephen Collins, Maggie Smith, Stockard Channing, Bronson Pinchot, Jennie Dundas, Eileen Heckart, Philip Bosco, Rob Reiner, James Naughton; *D:* Hugh Wilson; *W:* Robert Harling; *C:* Donald E. Thorin; *M:* Marc Shaiman. *AWARDS:* NOM: Academy Awards '96: Best Original Score.

A Fish Called Wanda

Absurd, high-speed farce about four criminals trying to retrieve $20 million they've

stolen from a safety deposit box—and each other. Meanwhile, barrister Cleese falls in love with the female thief (Curtis). Some sick, but tastelessly funny humor involves Palin's problem with stuttering and some very dead doggies. Written by Monty Python alum Cleese and director Crichton, who understand that silence is sometimes funnier than speech, and that timing is everything. The DVD's picture is sharper than the laserdisc and grain level is very low. Artifacts are seldom. Though the opposite usually is true, the DVD has colors that are a little weaker than the LD. Contrast is also a little low, as is the brightness level. Blacks are very close to true. Although only mono, the soundtrack does have very good fidelity and dynamics, and is lacking only a little in bass. —*JO*
Movie: 🐾🐾🐾 *DVD:* 🐾🐾🐾
MGM Home Entertainment (Cat #906266, UPC #027616626622). Widescreen (1.85:1) letterboxed; full frame. Mono. $24.98. Keepcase. *LANG:* English; French. *SUB:* English; French. *CAP:* English. *FEATURES:* 32 chapter links ● Theatrical trailer.
1988 (R) 98m/C John Cleese, Kevin Kline, Jamie Lee Curtis, Michael Palin, Tom Georgeson, Maria Aitken, Patricia Hayes, Geoffrey Palmer, Andrew MacLachlan; *D:* Charles Crichton; *W:* Charles Crichton, John Cleese; *C:* Alan Hume; *M:* John Du Prez. *AWARDS:* Academy Awards '88: Best Supporting Actor (Kline); British Academy Awards '88: Best Actor (Cleese), Best Supporting Actor (Palin); *NOM:* Academy Awards '88: Best Director (Crichton), Best Original Screenplay.

Fist of Legend

Chen Zuen (Li) is a student and martial artist studying abroad in Japan on the eve of World War II. He returns to China at the death of his teacher but cannot avoid the international conflicts at the heart of the story. The film is a tribute to Bruce Lee's *The Chinese Connection*, and for anyone who has wondered if Jet Li deserves all the attention he has received, this is the answer. True, much of the credit must go to Yuen Woo Ping's fight choreography, but Li has the screen presence of a real star. Also, those who are accustomed to the often substandard imports will be happily surprised by the high production values here and the sparklingly clear DVD image. The film looks as sharp as big-budget Hollywood productions. Both the fast-moving fight scenes and bright reflective colors of costumes and sets are handled without any visual flaws. —*MM*
Movie: 🐾🐾🐾 *DVD:* 🐾🐾🐾 ►
Buena Vista Home Entertainment (Cat #18329, UPC #717951005151). Widescreen (1.85:1) letterboxed. Dolby Digital Surround Stereo. $24.99. Keepcase. *LANG:* English. *CAP:* English. *FEATURES:* 18 chapter links.
1994 (R) 92m/C *HK* Jet Li, Yasuka Kurata; *D:* Woo-ping Yuen, Gordon Chan; *M:* Joseph Koo.

Fist of the North Star

Animated post-apocalyptic martial-arts science-fiction is too violent for kids and too childish for adults. The plot, such as it is, revolves around the competition between the Fist of the South Star, Chin, and the Fist of the North Star, Ken, who both want Julia. The animation is static and stylized and the entire film is told in an odd elliptical style. This one is not nearly as enjoyable as the live-action version, though both are based on the same comic book. —MM **AKA:** Hokuto No Ken.
Movie: 🐾▶ **DVD:** 🐾🐾
Image Entertainment (Cat #ID4661SEDVD, UPC #014381466126). Full frame. Dolby Digital Stereo. $24.99. Snapper. *LANG:* English. *FEATURES:* 25 chapter links.
1986 110m/C *JP* **D:** Toyoo Ashida; **W:** Susumu Takahisa; **M:** Katsuhisa Hattori.

Fist of the North Star

Legendary warrior Kenshiro (Daniels) returns from the grave to avenge the death of his father (McDowell) and restore his North Star clan. He must battle the evil Lord Shin (Mandylor) and his henchmen in a post-apocalyptic future. This is the live-action version of an animated feature, both based on the comic book.
Movie: 🐾🐾▶ **DVD:** NYR
WinStar Home Entertainment (Cat #5139). Full frame. Dolby Digital Surround Stereo. $24.98. Keepcase.
1995 (R) 90m/C Gary Daniels, Costas Mandylor, Christopher Penn, Julie Brown, Malcolm McDowell, Melvin Van Peebles, Isako Washio; **D:** Tony Randel; **W:** Tony Randel; **C:** Jacques Haitkin; **M:** Christopher Stone.

A Fistful of Dollars

The first "spaghetti western" to achieve worldwide popularity pits Eastwood as "the man with no name" against two outlaw families. Actually, the story is a remake of Kurosawa's *Yojimbo.* The DVD was made from the 1998 restoration that adds several minutes of footage not seen theatrically. One of those scenes gives the character a name. The DVD is a nice transfer, with good color saturation and a sharp image. —JO
Movie: 🐾🐾🐾 **DVD:** 🐾🐾🐾
MGM Home Entertainment (Cat #907858). Widescreen letterboxed; full frame. Dolby Digital Mono. $24.98. Keepcase. *LANG:* English. *SUB:* English; French. *FEATURES:* 32 chapter links.
1964 (R) 101m/C *IT* Clint Eastwood, Gian Maria Volonte, Marianne Koch; **D:** Sergio Leone; **W:** Sergio Leone, Victor Andres Catena, Duccio Tessari, G. Schock; **C:** Massimo Dallamano, Federico G. Larraya; **M:** Ennio Morricone.

Fists of Fury

Bruce Lee stars in this violent but charming martial arts adventure in which he must break a solemn vow of nonviolence to avenge the murder of his teacher by drug smugglers. The violence ranges between graphic and silly—a character knocked through the side of a building leaves an outline of his body in the wall. The mono sound is just right for the dubbing and the wild score. Considering the original film's lack of sophistication, this DVD version is about as sharp and detailed as any you're likely to see on home video. Some patterns flash but heavy blacks remain true in the final reels. The widescreen version is available as part of the boxed set *Bruce Lee: The Master Collection.* —MM **AKA:** The Big Boss; Tang Shan da Xiong.
Movie: 🐾🐾🐾 **DVD:** 🐾🐾▶
20th Century Fox (Cat #4112551). Widescreen. Mono. $99.98. Snapper. *LANG:* English. *SUB:* English. *CAP:* English. *FEATURES:* 24 chapter links. Title is also available from United American Video and Madacy.
1973 (R) 102m/C Bruce Lee, Maria Yi; **D:** Lo Wei; **W:** Lo Wei, Bruce Lee; **C:** Chen Ching Chu; **M:** Fu-ling Wang.

Fitzcarraldo

Although he failed to build a railroad across South America, Fitzcarraldo is determined to build an opera house in the middle of the Amazon jungle and to have Enrico Caruso sing there. Based on a true story of a charismatic Irishman's impossible quest at the turn of the century. It is interesting to note that no special effects were used in this film; everything you see actually occurred during filming, including the hauling of a large boat over a mountain. In short, this disc is an absolute masterpiece. The image transfer is superb with crisp colors and solid blacks. The numerous audio tracks are also excellent (although I would steer clear from the English language dubbed version—something is definitely lost in the translation). But what really makes the disc worthwhile are the supplements, the most impressive of which is the audio commentary featuring director Herzog. —MJT
Movie: 🐾🐾🐾🐾 **DVD:** 🐾🐾🐾🐾
Anchor Bay (Cat #DV10938, UPC #013131093896). Widescreen (1.85:1) anamorphic. Dolby Digital 5.1. $34.98. Keepcase. *LANG:* English; German. *SUB:* English. *FEATURES:* 23 chapter links • Commentary: Herzog, producer Lucki Stipetic, Norman Hill • Theatrical trailer • Still gallery • Cast and crew biographies.
1982 (PG) 157m/C *GE* Klaus Kinski, Claudia Cardinale, Jose Lewgoy, Miguel Angel Fuentes, Paul Hittscher; **D:** Werner Herzog; **W:** Werner Herzog; **C:** Thomas Mauch; **M:** Popul Vuh. *AWARDS:* Cannes Film Festival '82: Best Director (Herzog).

Five Corners

Coming-of-age sleeper is set in the Bronx, 1964, and it features an ensemble cast on the cusp of fame. John Turturro plays a recently paroled psychotic criminal; Jodie Foster is the girl he tried to rape years before; Tim Robbins is her none-too-well-equipped protector. Writer Shanley is also responsible for *Moonstruck.* Unfortunately, this DVD is one of the absolute worst in distribution. Filled with background pixels, the image is so grainy and pale it might have been made from a third-generation dupe. —MM
Movie: 🐾🐾🐾▶ **DVD:** woof
St. Mulus (Cat #40096, UPC #084296400966). Full frame. Dolby Digital Stereo. $9.99. Snapper. *LANG:* English. *FEATURES:* 9 chapter links. Title is also available from Universal Home Video for $19.99.
1988 (R) 92m/C Jodie Foster, John Turturro, Todd Graff, Tim Robbins, Elizabeth Berridge, Rose Gregorio, Gregory Rozakis, Rodney Harvey, John Seitz; **D:** Tony Bill; **W:** John Patrick Shanley; **C:** Fred Murphy; **M:** James Newton Howard. *AWARDS:* Independent Spirit Awards '89: Best Actress (Foster).

The Flamingo Kid

In the summer of '63, Jeffrey Willis (Dillon) works as a cabana boy at the El Flamingo Beach Club on Long Island. He also plays gin there and falls for Carla (Jones), who's visiting from California. Though Garry Marshall's film lacks the sparkle of more recent '60s period pieces, it's honest nostalgia, without a hint of false sweetness. It tells a complex coming-of-age story and never loses sight of a large cast of believably flawed but fascinating characters. For some of us, the shot of Janet Jones in that white swimming suit (chapter three) is worth the price of the disc. It looks fine throughout, though eye-popping visuals would be counter-productive to Marshall's shot-on-location re-creation of that place and time. The oldies score sounds fine. —MM
Movie: 🐾🐾🐾▶ **DVD:** 🐾🐾🐾▶
Anchor Bay (Cat #DV11059, UPC #013131015995). Widescreen (1.85:1) letterboxed; full frame. Dolby Digital Mono. $24.98. Keepcase. *LANG:* English. *FEATURES:* 18 chapter links • Liner notes by Michael Felsher.
1984 (PG-13) 100m/C Matt Dillon, Hector Elizondo, Molly McCarthy, Martha Gehman, Richard Crenna, Jessica Walter, Carole Davis, Janet Jones, Fisher Stevens, Bronson Pinchot; **D:** Garry Marshall; **W:** Garry Marshall, Neil Marshall; **C:** James A. Contner; **M:** Curt Sobel.

Flash Gordon

Camp feature based on the serial (and on *Barbarella* and *Star Wars*) has aged well with its humor intact. This time Flash (Jones) and Dale Arden (Anderson) are forced by Dr. Zarkov (Topol) to accompany him on a mission to the planet Mongo ruled by Ming the Merciless (von Sydow), who threatens to destroy the Earth. The pace is quick, the women are sexy, the guys are dense hunks, the acting is wonky. The entire production design employs more bright reds and glittering golds than you normally find in a Chinese restaurant, but the DVD still looks good. If the garish colors vibrate and if Flash's bottle-blond hair sometimes looks a little green, neither are inappropriate. The stereo separation is fine and Queen's soundtrack strikes the right mock heroic tone. —*MM*

Movie: 𝄞𝄞𝄞 **DVD:** 𝄞𝄞𝄞
Image Entertainment (Cat #ID4630USDVD, UPC #014381463026). Widescreen (2.35:1) letterboxed. Dolby Digital Surround. $24.99. Snapper. *LANG:* English. *FEATURES:* 16 chapter links.
1980 (PG) 111m/C Sam Jones, Melody Anderson, Chaim Topol, Max von Sydow, Ornella Muti, Timothy Dalton, Brian Blessed; **D:** Mike Hodges; **W:** Lorenzo Semple Jr.; **C:** Gilbert Taylor; **M:** Howard Blake.

Flashfire

The torching of an apartment building and the murder of a cop seem unrelated until troubled detective Jack Flinder (Zane) becomes involved. Soon, he and murder witness Lisa (Minter) are on the run from the arsonists and crooked police.

Movie: 𝄞𝄞 **DVD:** NYR
Trimark Home Video (Cat #7047). Full frame. Stereo. $14.99. Keepcase. *FEATURES:* Trailer.
1994 (R) 88m/C Billy Zane, Kristin Minter, Louis Gossett Jr.; **D:** Elliot Silverstein; **W:** John Warren, Dan York; **C:** Albert J. Dunk; **M:** Sylvester Levay.

Flatliners

A group of medical students (Sutherland, Roberts, Bacon, Baldwin, Platt) attempt after-hours experimentation with death and out-of-body experiences. DVD captures the ambitious visuals that director Schumacher, director of photography De Bont, and production designer Zanetti use to tell the story. The film looks and sounds terrific. Fans of the effects should choose the widescreen option; fans of the attractive young cast can go full frame. —*MM*

Movie: 𝄞𝄞𝄞 **DVD:** 𝄞𝄞𝄞
Columbia Tristar Home Video (Cat #50389, UPC #043396503892). Widescreen (2.35:1) letterboxed; full frame. Dolby Digital Surround Stereo. $28.95. Keepcase. *LANG:* English; French; Spanish. *SUB:* English; Korean; Spanish. *FEATURES:* 35 chapter links ▪ Liner notes.
1990 (R) 111m/C Kiefer Sutherland, Julia Roberts, William Baldwin, Oliver Platt, Kevin Bacon, Kimberly Scott, Joshua Rudoy, Aeryk Egan; **D:** Joel Schumacher; **W:** Peter Filardi; **C:** Jan De Bont; **M:** James Newton Howard.

Fled

Charles Piper (Fishburne) and Luke Dodge (Baldwin) are combative prison escapees who need to find a stash of cash in Atlanta and a computer disk that could save them from both the Cuban mob and the cops. Bombshell Cora (Hayek) decides to help the duo and tries to get steamy

with Piper. Lost of chases and shooting; not much sense. The climactic battle takes place in a sightseeing gondola at Georgia's Stone Mountain.

Movie: 𝄞𝄞 **DVD:** NYR
MGM Home Entertainment (Cat #906278). Widescreen anamorphic. Dolby Digital 5.1 Surround Stereo. $24.98. Keepcase. *LANG:* English; French. *SUB:* French. *FEATURES:* Trailer.
1996 (R) 98m/C Laurence "Larry" Fishburne, Stephen Baldwin, Salma Hayek, Will Patton, Robert John Burke; **D:** Kevin Hooks; **W:** Preston A. Whitmore II; **C:** Matthew F. Leonetti; **M:** Graeme Revell.

Flesh

Andy Warhol–produced seedy urban farce is about a bisexual street hustler who meets a variety of drug-addicted, deformed, and sexually deviant people. Dallesandro fans will enjoy his extensive exposure (literally). Since the film never had a high-quality Hollywood look, it's pretty safe to say that the DVD delivers it near perfectly, flaws intact. Of course, it doesn't matter, and too slick a look would totally ruin things. The first time I saw this film, sometime in the mid-'70s, that print had more scratches and damage than the source material for the DVD. —*JO* *AKA:* Andy Warhol's Flesh.

Movie: 𝄞𝄞𝄞 **DVD:** 𝄞𝄞𝄞
Image Entertainment (Cat #ID4731PYDVD, UPC #014381472332). Full frame. Dolby Digital Mono. $24.95. Snapper. *LANG:* English. *FEATURES:* 12 chapter links.
1968 90m/C Joe Dallesandro, Geraldine Smith, Patti D'Arbanville, Candy Darling, Jackie Curtis, Geri Miller, Barry Brown; **D:** Paul Morrissey; **W:** Paul Morrissey; **C:** Paul Morrissey.

Flesh Gordon

The '70s weren't so open-minded as people might now believe, as the story behind this sci-fi serial parody shows. Pals Flesh (Williams) and Flexi (Hudgins), accompanied by damsel Dale, battle a dastardly "sex ray" emanating from the planet Porno. Their adventures mimic the most fantastic Harryhausen effects sequences (very well, thanks to a design team including such future Hollywood hotshots as Rick Baker). However, each fantasy obstacle or enemy has a kink to call its own! The film may seem coy now, but it was much more daring and dangerous, never mind more fun, than some give it credit for being. Darker, smokier scenes threaten to go runny as cheese, but really the aged DeLuxe processing and hand-painted watercolor credit sequences look surprisingly good, all told. Well-recorded music by a soloist balances the sometimes muted, low-budget dramatic vocals. You can't pick the audio commentary from the main menu, but you can access it with the audio button on a remote. Ziehm reads from a prepared script that sometimes addresses things more generally. Some stories are so sad they clash

with the freewheeling slapstick onscreen. Some bits of info are priceless, though, like how he paid Oingo Boingo a hundred bucks to play at the premiere party. The cover drawing is gorgeous; technically adept but with all the flair of fan art. —*JK*

Movie: 𝄞𝄞▸ **DVD:** 𝄞𝄞𝄞
Hen's Tooth Video (Cat #HTVM4048, UPC #759731404822). Widescreen. Dolby Digital. $29.99. Keepcase. *LANG:* English. *FEATURES:* 8 chapter links ▪ Interactive menus ▪ 15 mins. of restored footage ▪ Star bios and filmographies ▪ Original theatrical trailers ▪ Commentary: director Howard Ziehm.
1972 90m/C Jason Williams, Suzanne Fields, Joseph Hudgins, John Hoyt, Howard Zieff, Michael Benveniste; **Cameos:** Candy Samples; **D:** Howard Ziehm, Michael Benveniste; **W:** Michael Benveniste; **C:** Howard Ziehm; **M:** Ralph Ferraro; **V:** Craig T. Nelson.

Fletch

Somewhat charming comedy. When newspaper journalist Fletch (Chase) goes undercover to get the scoop on the local drug scene, a wealthy young businessman enlists his help in dying. Something's rotten in Denmark when the man's doctor knows nothing of the illness and Fletch comes closer to the drug scene than he realizes. Throughout the entire film, Chevy Chase assumes a multitude of flippant comic characters to discover the truth. Based on Gregory McDonald's novel. On the DVD, the image is soft and occasionally grainy. This is another case where the overall appearance is better on the laserdisc, although colors and contrasts are stronger here on the DVD. The Dolby Surround has enough power going for it but the dialogue definitely could have used a boost. —*JO*

Movie: 𝄞𝄞▸ **DVD:** 𝄞𝄞▸
Universal Studios Home Video (Cat #20285, UPC #025192028526). Widescreen (1.85:1) anamorphic. Dolby Surround. $24.98. Keepcase. *LANG:* English; French. *SUB:* Spanish. *CAP:* English. *FEATURES:* 16 chapter links ▪ Theatrical trailer ▪ Production notes ▪ Cast and filmmakers bios ▪ Film highlights.
1985 (PG) 98m/C Chevy Chase, Tim Matheson, Joe Don Baker, Dana Wheeler-Nicholson, M. Emmet Walsh, Kenneth Mars, Geena Davis, Richard Libertini, George Wendt, Kareem Abdul-Jabbar, Alison La Placa, George Wyner, Tony Longo, James Avery, William Sanderson, Beau Starr, Ralph Seymour, Larry "Flash" Jenkins; **D:** Michael Ritchie; **W:** Andrew Bergman; **C:** Fred Schuler; **M:** Harold Faltermeyer.

The Flintstones (CE)

Preceded by massive hype, popular '60s cartoon comes to life thanks to a huge budget and creative sets and props. Seems that Fred's being set up by evil corporate types MacLachlan and Berry to take the fall for their embezzling scheme. Soon he gives up dining at RocDonald's for Cavern on the Green and cans best buddy Barney (Moranis). Forget the lame plot (32 writers took a shot at it) and sit back and enjoy the spectacle. Goodman's an amazingly true-to-type Fred, O'Donnell has Betty's giggle down pat, and Perkins looks a lot like Wilma. Wilma's original voice, Vander Pyl, has a cameo; listen for Korman's voice as the Dictabird. The DVD does a good job in bringing this colorful and cartoon-like film to the home theatre. The picture is very sharp, with little in the way of grain or artifacts. Colors are excellent, being both accurate and vibrant. Blacks are true. The contrast and brightness levels seem right where they should be and the picture packs a lot of punch. The sound comes close to matching the image quality with good low end and crisp clears highs all mixed nicely with the Surround tracks, which although underused, keep the soundtrack lively. —JO

Movie: 🎵🎵▶ **DVD:** 🎵🎵🎵▶
Universal Studios Home Video (Cat #20274, UPC #025192027420). Widescreen (1.85:1) anamorphic. Dolby Digital 5.1; Dolby Surround. $34.98. Keepcase. *LANG:* English (DD5.1; DS); Spanish; French (DD5.1; DS). *SUB:* Spanish. *CAP:* English. *FEATURES:* 12 chapters for documentary • Feature commentary • Original documentary • Theatrical and teaser trailer • MCA soundtrack presentation • Production photos • Art Department concept sketches.
1994 (PG) 92m/C John Goodman, Rick Moranis, Elizabeth Perkins, Rosie O'Donnell, Elizabeth Taylor, Kyle MacLachlan, Halle Berry, Jonathan Winters, Richard Moll, Irwin Keyes, Dann Florek; **Cameos:** Laraine Newman, Jean Vander Pyl, Jay Leno; *D:* Brian Levant; *W:* Tom S. Parker, Jim Jennewein, Steven E. de Souza; *C:* Dean Cundey; *M:* David Newman; *V:* Harvey Korman. *AWARDS:* Golden Raspberry Awards '94: Worst Supporting Actress (O'Donnell), Worst Screenplay; *NOM:* MTV Movie Awards '95: Most Desirable Female (Berry); Golden Raspberry Awards '94: Worst Remake/Sequel, Worst Supporting Actress (Taylor).

Flirting with Disaster

Mel Coplin (Stiller) is your average neurotic New York entomologist searching for his birth parents so he can finally name his four-month-old child and make love to his wife. Tagging along on his bumpy ride are his wife Nancy (Arquette), a beautiful quirky adoption agency shrink (Leoni), and a pair of bisexual FBI agents. The excellent cast also features Moore as Mel's bra-baring adoptive mother, Segal as his weirdly paranoid adoptive father, and Alda and Tomlin as hilarious send-ups of ex-hippie mentality. As events spin madly out of control, every type of relationship is satirized, and every character is left in underwear. This is director Russell's first big-budget movie, and is as close to a vintage screwball comedy as you'll see. The Dolby Surround sound is perfect for this kind of dialogue-driven film with minimal effects. It often seems that the engineers try for more energy and Surround that will work with this style of filmmaking when they master to 5.1. As it is, the rear track is used minimally and the concentration is on the dialogue and some ambience. The picture is pretty sharp with only a little grain and artifacts. Colors are accurate and fairly detailed, while blacks are true and mostly clean. Contrast and brightness are good and in need of just a slight boost. —JO

Movie: 🎵🎵🎵 **DVD:** 🎵🎵🎵
Miramax Pictures Home Video (Cat #17250, UPC #717951002433). Widescreen (1.85:1) letterboxed. Dolby Surround. $29.99. Keepcase. *LANG:* English. *CAP:* English. *FEATURES:* 16 chapter links.
1995 (R) 92m/C Ben Stiller, Patricia Arquette, Tea Leoni, Alan Alda, Mary Tyler Moore, George Segal, Lily Tomlin, Josh Brolin, Richard Jenkins, Celia Weston, Glenn Fitzgerald, Beth Ostrosky, Cynthia Lamontagne, David Patrick Kelly, John Ford Noonan, Charles Oberly; *D:* David O. Russell; *W:* David O. Russell; *C:* Eric Alan Edwards; *M:* Stephen Endelman. *AWARDS: NOM:* Independent Spirit Awards '97: Best Director (Russell), Best Screenplay, Best Supporting Actor (Jenkins), Best Supporting Actress (Tomlin).

Floundering

Semi-focused, politically naïve satire uses the 1992 L.A. riots as a backdrop to the disastrous life of unemployed James Boyz (LeGros). He owes money to the IRS; his brother (Hawke) has skipped out of detox; his girlfriend (Zane) is casually unfaithful. James drags himself among the city's downtrodden as he fantasizes. About half of writer-director McCarthy's experiments work. Don't miss all of the appearances and cameos by pre-famous stars from Cusack to Piven. On DVD, the film has a slightly soft focus that's appropriate to its surreal approach. Sound is slightly superior to the tape version. Some commentary by McCarthy might have been worthwhile. —MM

Movie: 🎵🎵▶ **DVD:** 🎵🎵▶
Simitar Entertainment (Cat #7338, UPC #082551733828). Full frame. PCM Stereo. $14.98. Keepcase. *LANG:* English. *FEATURES:* 8 chapter links • Production factoids • Buscemi, Cusack, Hawke, Thornton filmographies.
1994 (R) 97m/C James LeGros, Ethan Hawke, Steve Buscemi, John Cusack, Lisa Zane, Sy Richardson, Jeremy Piven, Billy Bob Thornton; *D:* Peter McCarthy; *W:* Peter McCarthy; *C:* Denis Maloney.

Flubber

Bland remake of Disney's *The Absent-Minded Professor* casts Williams as the brilliant but befuddled Prof. Brainard. Putting his wedding on the back Bunsen burner, much to the dismay of his fiancee Sara Jean (Harden), Brainard invents a bouncy, flying green slime named "flubber." As the substance becomes the cure-all for romantic turmoil and the fledgling school basketball team, it also attracts the attention of a corrupt businessman and his moronic henchmen. With all the dull subplots, both kids and adults will be disappointed that the cute green goo doesn't have more screen time. Somehow the whole thing is not quite as mature and insightful as the original. That said, the DVD re-creates the special effects with astonishing clarity and no flaws worth mentioning. Sound is very good. —MM

Movie: 🎵🎵 **DVD:** 🎵🎵🎵
Buena Vista Home Entertainment (Cat #14249, UPC #717951000309). Widescreen (1.85:1) letterboxed. Dolby Digital 5.1 Surround Stereo. $29.99. Keepcase. *LANG:* English; French; Spanish. *SUB:* Spanish. *CAP:* English. *FEATURES:* 18 chapter links • Theatrical trailer.
1997 (PG) 93m/C Robin Williams, Marcia Gay Harden, Christopher McDonald, Raymond J. Barry, Clancy Brown, Ted Levine, Wil Wheaton, Edie McClurg; *D:* Les Mayfield; *W:* John Hughes; *C:* Dean Cundey; *M:* Danny Elfman.

Fly Away Home

Does for geese what *Babe* did for pigs. Young Amy (Paquin) withdraws when she loses her mother in a car crash and is forced to live with her estranged father, Thomas (Daniels), a scruffy sculptor/inventor in rural Ontario. Still dealing with her mother's death, Amy suddenly becomes a mother herself to a tiny gaggle of goslings when she happens upon a nest of uprooted eggs. Extraordinary technical achievements make up for some unnecessary melodrama in the second half as the geese head South, led by Amy, in a glider built by her father. Touching but unsentimental, mostly well scripted and acted, and extraordinarily well shot. Based on the true story of inventor Bill Lishman, who led domesticated geese on a winter migration from Toronto, Canada, to North Carolina, leading the formation in his motor-powered glider. On the DVD, some long shots have a little grain, but other than that, the picture is sharp and detailed. Colors are vibrant and accurate as are the blacks. The DVD does a nice job of keeping the contrast and brightness levels consistent with the enormous lighting changes when scenes shift from Earth to the sky. The 5.1 mix has a lot of ambience going on in the rear channels and the overall sound is very lively with a lot of crisp highs and more than sufficient bass. —JO *AKA:* Father Goose; Flying Wild.

Movie: 🎵🎵🎵 **DVD:** 🎵🎵🎵▶
Columbia Tristar Home Video (Cat #82439, UPC #043396824393). Full frame. Dolby Digital 5.1; Dolby Surround. $29.95. Keepcase. *LANG:* English (DD5.1; DS); French (DS); Spanish (DS). *SUB:* Spanish. *CAP:* English. *FEATURES:* 58 chapter links.
1996 (PG) 107m/C Jeff Daniels, Anna Paquin, Dana Delany, Terry Kinney, Jeremy Ratchford; *D:* Carroll Ballard; *W:* Robert

Rodat, Vince McKewin; **C:** Caleb Deschanel; **M:** Mark Isham. *AWARDS: NOM:* Academy Awards '96: Best Cinematography.

The Flying Deuces / Utopia

Ollie's broken heart lands Laurel and Hardy in the Foreign Legion. The comic pair escape a firing squad only to suffer a plane crash that results in Hardy's reincarnation as a horse. The musical interlude with a Laurel soft shoe while Hardy sings "Shine On, Harvest Moon" is one of the film's highlights. **AKA:** Flying Aces.
Movie: 🐾🐾🐾 **DVD:** NYR
Madacy Entertainment (Cat #99113). Full frame. Dolby Digital Stereo. $12.98. Keepcase. *FEATURES:* Cast and crew thumbnail biographies.
1939 65m/B Stan Laurel, Oliver Hardy, Jean Parker, Reginald Gardiner, James Finlayson; **D:** Edward Sutherland; **W:** Ralph Spence, Charles R. Rogers, Harry Langdon, Alfred Schiller; **C:** Elmer Dyer, Art Lloyd; **M:** Leo Shuken, John Leopold.

The Flying Serpent

Fans of campy, low-budget, black-and-white '50s horror are the target audience for this rarely seen gem, making its home video debut on DVD. Professor Forbes (Zucco) is the self-appointed custodian of a fabulous (well, semi-fabulous) Aztec treasure that's hidden in the New Mexico mountains and guarded by Quetzacoatl, the titular beastie which Forbes sics on anyone who happens by. Prolific B-movie director Newfield keeps the pace popping right along for 58 fun-filled minutes. The disc was made from a scratchy, chewed-up print, which is probably a blessing for the shoestring special effects. Even in its distressed condition, this one would make a fine double feature with Larry Cohen's *Q (The Winged Serpent).* —*MM*
Movie: 🐾🐾🐾 **DVD:** 🐾🐾
Image Entertainment (Cat #ID5370FWDWV, UPC #014381537024). Full frame. Dolby Digital Mono. $19.99. Snapper. *LANG:* English. *FEATURES:* 10 chapter links.
1955 58m/B George Zucco, Ralph Lewis, Hope Kramer, Eddie Acuff, Budd Buster, Wheaton Chambers, Terry Frost, Henry Hall; **D:** Sam Newfield; **W:** John Thomas Neville; **C:** Jack Greenhalgh; **M:** Leo Erdody.

FM

The uncredited inspiration for the TV series *WKRP in Cincinnati* and, apparently, much of what goes on with the current generation of "shock jocks" is a trip down memory lane. The guys and gals at QSKY in Los Angeles have to put up with corporate owners, sex-crazed fans, prima donnas, and all the rest. Martin Mull makes an inspired debut. The roughness of the image comes from the original material, but this is one case where image is definitely subordinate to sound. A commen-

tary track from cinematographer-turned-director John A. Alonzo might have been fascinating. He is an articulate commentator on many aspects of filmmaking. —*MM*
AKA: Citizen's Band.
Movie: 🐾🐾🐾 **DVD:** 🐾🐾🐾
Anchor Bay (Cat #DV19044, UPC #013131094497). Widescreen (2.35:1) anamorphic; full frame. Dolby Digital 5.1 Surround Stereo; Dolby Digital Surround Stereo. $24.98. Keepcase. *LANG:* English. *FEATURES:* 24 chapter links ● Theatrical trailer.
1978 (PG-13) 104m/C Eileen Brennan, Alex Karras, Cleavon Little, Martin Mull, Cassie Yates, Linda Ronstadt, Jimmy Buffett; **D:** John A. Alonzo; **W:** Ezra Sacks; **C:** David Myers.

Follow Your Heart

After promising her dying mother that she would marry for love, Taylor (Doumani) is forced to choose between wealthy handsome hunk Scott (Scalia) and not-so-wealthy but equally hunkish Jimmy (Ted McGinley). The film has the highly polished look of a big-budget Hollywood romance, and if the cast doesn't equal Doris Day and Rock Hudson in star power, they're certainly as attractive and they handle the fluffy formula with a light touch. It's great stuff for the fans of cult fave Scalia, who, along with McGinley is listed as a coproducer. Brenda Doumani, from TV's *The Young and the Restless,* is married to the producer-writer-director. The film appears to have been made for the small screen but with above-average production values, so the DVD image is superb. There are no important visual flaws and the sound is fine.—*MM*
Movie: 🐾🐾▶ **DVD:** 🐾🐾🐾
DMG Entertainment (Cat #DMG981D, UPC #640587990129). Full frame. Dolby Digital Surround Stereo. $24.98. Keepcase. *SUB:* Spanish. *FEATURES:* Previews ● 8 chapter links ● Synopsis ● Filmographies of stars ● "If You Believe" music video.
1998 98m/C Brenda Doumani, Ted McGinley, Jack Scalia, Leah Remini, Brian Keith, Bernie Kopell; **D:** Lorenzo Doumani; **W:** Lorenzo Doumani; **C:** Hanania Baer.

Fong Sai Yuk

In this historical martial arts flick (with some comic scenes), Jet Li plays the legendary hero Fong Sai Yuk. The star's strong screen presence and energetic pacing are the only reasons to watch the disc. It's an absolutely no-frills presentation (not even chapters). The image is pale and grainy, even in night scenes. The subtitles are small and difficult to read, and they often slip partially beneath the lower edge of the frame. —*MM* **AKA:** The Legend; The Legend of Fong Sai-Yuk; Fong Shi Yu.
Movie: 🐾🐾 **DVD:** 🐾▶
Tai Seng Video Marketing (Cat #DVD5006). Widescreen letterboxed. Dolby Digital

Stereo. $49.95. Keepcase. *LANG:* Cantonese; Mandarin. *SUB:* English; Chinese.
1993 100m/C *HK* Jet Li, Michelle Reis, Adam Cheng, Chu Kong, Josephine Siao; **D:** Corey Yuen; **W:** Kung-Yung Chai, Jiang-Chung Change; **C:** Jingle Ma; **M:** Romeo Diaz.

Foolish

Eddie Griffin stars as the title character, a struggling young comic, in an allegedly autobiographical comedy. Rapper and writer Master P plays his brother. Not a single genuine laugh surfaces in the entire film, though those who think that profanity is funny will bust a gut. Director Dave Meyers's semi-coherent commentary track is filled with stumbles, half-formed ideas, and bad grammar—When "cast" is used as a verb, the past tense is not "casted."—but that's not really inappropriate for such a slapdash picture. Because both the budget and shooting schedule were tight, the film may look better on DVD than it did in theatres. The comedy club interiors have a suitably claustrophobic feeling. Sound is adequate. —*MM*
Movie: woof **DVD:** 🐾🐾
Artisan Entertainment (Cat #10169, UPC #012236101697). Widescreen (16:9) letterboxed. Dolby Digital 5.1 Surround Stereo. $29.98. Keepcase. *LANG:* English. *CAP:* English. *FEATURES:* 24 chapter links ● Unfunny deleted stand-up routines ● Theatrical trailer ● Cast and crew thumbnail biographies.
1999 (R) 96m/C Eddie Griffin, Master P, Frank Sivero, Amy Petersen, Jonathan Banks, Andrew Dice Clay, Marla Gibbs, Daphnee Lynn Duplaix, Sven-Ole Thorsen, Bill Nunn, Bill Duke; **D:** Dave Meyers; **W:** Master P; **C:** Steve Gainer; **M:** Wendy Melvoin, Lisa Coleman.

Fools Rush In

Workaholic executive Alex Whitman (Perry) meets beautiful Latina casino worker Isabel Fuentes (Hayek) in Las Vegas. They spend the night together; three months later she shows up at his New York front door to announce that she's pregnant and will keep the baby. Movie cliches commingle with movie stereotypes when they marry and find that the relationship suffers under vast ethnic and cultural differences. But, the leads are undeniably attractive and that will be enough for some viewers. On DVD, the film is essentially flawless. Both sound and visuals have all the polished slickness of a solid Hollywood formula production. —*MM*
Movie: 🐾🐾▶ **DVD:** 🐾🐾🐾
Columbia Tristar Home Video (Cat #94949, UPC #043396949492). Widescreen (1.85:1) letterboxed; full frame. Dolby Digital 5.1 Surround Stereo; Dolby Digital Surround Stereo. $28.95. Keepcase. *LANG:* English; French; Spanish. *SUB:* English; French; Spanish. *FEATURES:* 35 chapter links ● Theatrical trailer.

1997 (PG-13) 110m/C Matthew Perry, Salma Hayek, Jon Tenney, Carlos Gomez, Tomas Milian, John Bennett Perry, Jill Clayburgh, Stanley DeSantis, Anne Betancourt; **D:** Andy Tennant; **W:** Katherine Reback; **C:** Robbie Greenberg; **M:** Alan Silvestri.

For a Few Dollars More

The Man with No Name returns as a bounty hunter who teams up with a gunslinger/rival to track down the sadistic leader of a gang of bandits. The violent sequel to *A Fistful of Dollars* (1964) was followed by *The Good, the Bad, and the Ugly*. We were all so excited when the Eastwood/Leone trilogy finally came out letterboxed on laserdisc. Now the DVD takes it to the next level with a much sharper image and truer colors that show just how masterful the scene composition is in these films. There is an occasional fleck or two around reel changes, but other than that the preprint is very good. In addition to being accurate, the colors are deep and have very little problem with bleed. Blacks are true and the combination of very good contrast and brightness levels gives the DVD far more punch than the LD ever had. The mono soundtrack sounds better than ever, and works very well with the limitations of the original film. —JO

Movie: 🎵🎵🎵 **DVD:** 🎵🎵🎵➤

MGM Home Entertainment (Cat #906271, UPC #027616627124). Widescreen (2.35:1) letterboxed. Dolby Digital Mono. $24.98. Keepcase. *LANG:* English; French. *SUB:* English; French; Spanish. *CAP:* English. *FEATURES:* 32 chapter links • Theatrical trailer • 8-page booklet.

1965 (PG) 127m/C *IT* Clint Eastwood, Lee Van Cleef, Klaus Kinski, Gian Maria Volonte; **D:** Sergio Leone; **W:** Sergio Leone, Luciano Vincenzoni; **C:** Massimo Dallamano; **M:** Ennio Morricone.

For Hire

Suffering from cancer and with a pregnant wife, Chicago cabbie Mitch Lawrence (Lowe) is desperate for money. So, he agrees to kill an associate of famous writer Louis Webber (Mantegna) for $50,000. When the job is done, Mitch learns just why he was chosen to do the deed.

Movie: 🎵🎵➤ **DVD:** NYR

Pioneer Entertainment (Cat #10249). Full frame. Dolby Digital Surround Stereo. $19.98. Keepcase.

1998 96m/C Rob Lowe, Joe Mantegna, Dominic Philie, Bronwen Black; **D:** Jean Pellerin; **M:** Alan Reeves.

For Love of a Child

Treacly story of a child's death and its religious consequences is pretty hard to stomach on any level. The sugarcoated score matches the simple-minded script, the soft-focus photography, and the kitschy postcard settings. DVD does nothing to improve the made-for-TV material. —MM **AKA:** *Casey's Gift: For Love of a Child.*

Movie: 🎵 **DVD:** 🎵

Simitar Entertainment (Cat #7272, UPC #082551727223). Full frame. PCM Stereo. $7.98. Keepcase. *LANG:* English. *FEATURES:* 8 chapter links • Kevin Dobson filmography.

1990 93m/C Kevin J. Dobson, Michael Tucker, Belinda J. Montgomery, Karen Austin, Olivia Burnette, Staci Keanan, Bradley Michael Pierce; **D:** Kevin J. Dobson; **W:** Allan Sloane, Phil Penningroth.

For Richer or Poorer

On their tenth anniversary, stereotypical New York greedheads Brad (Allen) and Caroline (Alley) Sexton take it on the lam after their accountant fleeces them. They wind up hiding out from the IRS in Pennsylvania Amish country. How? They trick a farm family into believing they're visiting relatives. Nothing else in this flapdoodle comedy rises above the level of the strained premise. The DVD image re-creates the phony Hollywood gloss of both the ritzy New York scenes and the bucolic countryside. Even the black clothes have a degree of detail that's unusual for the medium. —MM

Movie: 🎵➤ **DVD:** 🎵🎵➤

Universal Studios Home Video (Cat #20265, UPC #025192026522). Widescreen (2.35:1) letterboxed. Dolby Digital 5.1 Surround Stereo; Dolby Surround Stereo. $24.98. Keepcase. *LANG:* English; French. *SUB:* Spanish. *CAP:* English. *FEATURES:* 32 chapter links • Production notes • Cast and crew thumbnail biographies • Theatrical trailer.

1997 (PG-13) 122m/C Tim Allen, Kirstie Alley, Wayne Knight, Larry Miller, Jay O. Sanders, Michael Lerner, Miguel Nunez, Megan Cavanagh, John Pyper-Ferguson, June Claman, Katie Moore; **D:** Bryan Spicer; **W:** Jana Howington, Steve Lukanic; **C:** Buzz Feitshans IV; **M:** Randy Edelman.

For the Love of Benji

In his second outing, Benji, everyone's favorite cinematic mutt, accompanies his canine squeeze Tiffany and his human family to Greece. Kidnapped by spies and used as a courier for a secret code, he escapes to have another series of adventures. Some of the complicated plotting and unsubtitled Greek dialogue may cause younger viewers to ask questions of the grown-ups, but they'll be able to follow things well enough. The remastered DVD looks fine for a 1977 production, but it lacks the remarkable clarity of the first one. Unfortunately, it has another theme song that's as gooey as the original. —MM

Movie: 🎵🎵➤ **DVD:** 🎵🎵➤

Image Entertainment (Cat #ID4805BFDVD, UPC #14381480528). Full frame. Dolby Digital Mono. $24.99. Snapper. *LANG:* English; Greek. *FEATURES:* 10 chapter links.

1977 (G) 85m/C Benji, Patsy Garrett, Cynthia Smith, Allen Finzat, Ed Nelson; **D:** Joe Camp; **W:** Joe Camp; **C:** Don Reddy; **M:** Euel Box.

For Whom the Bell Tolls

Hemingway novel, gorgeously translated to the big screen, features a star-crossed romantic tale of derring-do. American schoolteacher Robert Jordan (Cooper) decides to join the Spanish Civil War and fight the fascists. He's ordered to rendezvous with peasant guerillas to aid in blowing up a bridge, and in the rebel camp Jordan meets the beautiful Maria (Bergman). Lots of heroics (and some romance under the stars). Both leads were personally selected by the author. It was great to see the restored 156-minute version of this film, which was also available on laserdisc. The DVD image is not as sharp as the laser but both color and contrast is much stronger, making the DVD much preferable. The Dolby Digital sound is a little thin but is full enough to make the overture and exit music very enjoyable. —JO

Movie: 🎵🎵🎵➤ **DVD:** 🎵🎵🎵

Universal Studios Home Video (Cat #20423, UPC #025192042324). Full frame. Dolby Digital 2.0 Mono. $26.98. Keepcase. *LANG:* English. *SUB:* French; Spanish. *CAP:* English. *FEATURES:* 48 chapter links • Theatrical trailer • Cast and filmakers bios • Production notes • Film highlights.

1943 156m/C Gary Cooper, Ingrid Bergman, Akim Tamiroff, Katina Paxinou, Arturo de Cordova, Vladimir Sokoloff, Mikhail Rasumny, Fortunio Bonanova, Victor Varconi, Joseph Calleia, Alexander Granach, Yakima Canutt, George Coulouris, Yvonne De Carlo, Martin Garralaga, Soledad Jiminez, Duncan Renaldo, Tito Renaldo, Pedro de Cordoba, Frank Puglia, John Mylong, Eric Feldary, Lilo Yarson, Leo Bugakov, Antonio Molina; **D:** Sam Wood; **W:** Dudley Nichols; **C:** Ray Rennahan; **M:** Victor Young. *AWARDS:* Academy Awards '43: Best Supporting Actress (Paxinou); *NOM:* Academy Awards '43: Best Actor (Cooper), Best Actress (Bergman), Best Color Cinematography, Best Film Editing, Best Picture, Best Supporting Actor (Tamiroff), Best Original Dramatic Score.

For Your Eyes Only (SE)

In this James Bond entry, 007 must keep the Soviets from getting hold of a valuable instrument aboard a sunken British spy ship. Much of the gadgetry of the 1970s is replaced with spectacular stunt work, along with the usual beautiful girls and exotic locales. Second-unit director Glen made his debut here. On the exceptionally well-produced commentary track, he talks about the excitement of being given the job and the challenges it presented. Like all the Bond DVDs, this one comes with every extra bell and whistle imaginable. —MM

Movie: 🎬🎬🎬 **DVD:** 🎬🎬🎬
MGM Home Entertainment (Cat #907027, UPC #027616702722). Widescreen letterboxed. Dolby Digital 5.1 Surround Stereo; Dolby Digital Surround Stereo. $34.98. Keepcase. *LANG:* English; French. *SUB:* English; French. *FEATURES:* 56 chapter links • 4 trailers • 2 radio spots • "Making of" featurette • Commentary: director John Glen • Commentary: executive producer Michael Wilson and crew members • Music video by Sheena Easton • Animated storyboard sequences • Stills gallery • "Making of" booklet.
1981 (PG) 136m/C *GB* Roger Moore, Carole Bouquet, Chaim Topol, Lynn-Holly Johnson, Julian Glover, Cassandra Harris, Jill Bennett, Michael Gothard, John Wyman, Jack Hedley, Lois Maxwell, Desmond Llewelyn, Geoffrey Keen, Walter Gotell, Charles Dance; *D:* John Glen; *W:* Michael G. Wilson; *C:* Alan Hume; *M:* Bill Conti. *AWARDS: NOM:* Academy Awards '81: Best Song ("For Your Eyes Only").

Forbidden Planet

Sci-fi version of Shakespeare's *The Tempest* is set in A.D. 2200 when a space cruiser visits the planet Altair-4 to uncover the fate of a previous mission of space colonists. They are greeted by Robby the Robot and discover the only survivors of the Earth colony, which has been preyed upon by a terrible space monster. The overall rating on this DVD had to be knocked down a notch just because it comes from MGM and their own letterboxed laserdisc was far superior. The picture is of average sharpness at best and the colors are far weaker than the LD. Some bleed adds to the overall softness and the grain level is a little high. Blacks are close to true but have occasional problems with grain. Contrast and brightness are a little low and adding to the lackluster image. The Surround is not any better and sounds dull at best and a little distorted when turned up. —JO

Movie: 🎬🎬🎬 **DVD:** 🎬
MGM Home Entertainment (Cat #906565, UPC #027616656520). Widescreen (2.35:1) letterboxed; full frame. Dolby Surround; Mono. $24.98. Snapper. *LANG:* English; French; Spanish. *SUB:* English; French; Spanish. *CAP:* English. *FEATURES:* 30 chapter links • Theatrical trailer.
1956 98m/C Walter Pidgeon, Anne Francis, Leslie Nielsen, Warren Stevens, Jack Kelly, Richard Anderson, Earl Holliman, George D. Wallace, Robert Dix, Frankie Darro; *D:* Fred M. Wilcox; *W:* Cyril Hume; *C:* George J. Folsey; *M:* Bebe Barron, Louis Barron; *V:* Marvin Miller; *Nar:* Les Tremayne.

Forces of Nature

Lightweight screwball comedy has straitlaced copywriter Ben (Affleck) trying to get to Savannah in time for his wedding with Tierney. When his plane skids off the run-

way in New York, he hitches a ride with a free-spirited stranger Sara (Bullock) on an obstacle-filled trip down south. Some stunning weather-related mishaps and unusually sharp characterizations are undone by sluggish pace and a distinct lack of chemistry between the stars. Enjoyment of the conclusion depends on your opinion of romantic comedy conventions. The movie's bright, super-saturated primary color scheme tends to bleed around the edges: nighttime scenes are murky, and Bullock's kohl-rimmed eyes are often invisible. Deft sound design—which captures every rumble of highway, bus, and plane travel—comes across well. —JE

Movie: 🎬🎬 **DVD:** 🎬
DreamWorks Home Entertainment (Cat #84662, UPC #6706846622). Widescreen (1.85:1) anamorphic. Dolby Digital 5.1 Surround; Dolby Digital 2.0 Surround. $29.99. Keepcase. *LANG:* English. *CAP:* English. *FEATURES:* 20 chapter links • Production notes • Cast and filmmakers biographies • Theatrical trailer • Behind-the-scenes featurette • 4 deleted scenes, including alternate ending.
1999 (PG-13) 104m/C Sandra Bullock, Ben Affleck, Maura Tierney, Steve Zahn, Blythe Danner, Ronny Cox, Michael Fairman, Janet Carroll, Richard Schiff, Meredith Scott Lynn, George D. Wallace, John Doe, Steve Hytner, David Strickland; *D:* Bronwen Hughes; *W:* Marc Lawrence; *C:* Elliot Davis; *M:* John Powell.

Forever and a Day

Tremendous salute to British history revolves around a London manor originally built by an English admiral during the Napoleonic era and the exploits of succeeding generations. The WWII blitz is used as a framing device for the various stories that come from a virtual who's-who of 1940s writers, filmmakers, and actors. That may have been the high-water mark of Anglo-American relations and the film is appropriately shameless propaganda. It's also entertaining. On DVD, many of the wartime scenes are dark and murky, and again, that's probably an appropriate reflection of the circumstances. The comic scenes are bright. A chapter index that identified the stars by scene would have been more helpful than this conventional organization. —MM

Movie: 🎬🎬🎬 **DVD:** 🎬🎬🎬
Image Entertainment (Cat #ID4533JFDVD, UPC #014381453324). Full frame. Dolby Digital Mono. $24.99. Snapper. *LANG:* English. *FEATURES:* 16 chapter links.
1943 104m/B Brian Aherne, Robert Cummings, Ida Lupino, Charles Laughton, Herbert Marshall, Ray Milland, Anna Neagle, Merle Oberon, Claude Rains, Victor McLaglen, Buster Keaton, Jessie Matthews, Roland Young, Sir C. Aubrey Smith, Edward Everett Horton, Elsa Lanchester, Edmund Gwenn; *D:* Rene Clair, Edmund Goulding, Cedric Hardwicke, Frank Lloyd, Victor Saville, Robert Stevenson, Herbert Wilcox, Kent Smith; *W:* Christopher Isherwood, Gene Lockhart, Donald Ogden Stewart,

Charles Bennett, Michael Hogan, Peter Godfrey; *C:* Robert De Grasse, Lee Garmes, Russell Metty, Nicholas Musuraca; *M:* Anthony Collins.

Forever Young

In 1939, test pilot Daniel McCormick's (Gibson) fiancee (Glasser) is hit by a car and lapses into a coma. He agrees to be cryogenically frozen for one year, but—Oops!—he's left in the machine for 50 years. When he's finally thawed out by a couple of kids, he's off to find his true love. The schmaltz is laid on thicker than thick and it's all meant for fans of the softer side of the star. The DVD gives the period details the right slightly sepia-toned nostalgic warmth. The central California locations look fine and the flying scenes aren't bad either. —MM

Movie: 🎬🎬 **DVD:** 🎬🎬🎬
Warner Home Video, Inc. (Cat #12571, UPC #085391257127). Full frame. Dolby Digital Surround Stereo. $19.98. Snapper. *LANG:* English; French; Spanish. *SUB:* English; French; Spanish. *CAP:* English. *FEATURES:* Cast and crew thumbnail biographies • Production notes • Theatrical trailer • 29 chapter links.
1992 (PG) 102m/C Mel Gibson, Jamie Lee Curtis, Elijah Wood, Isabel Glasser, George Wendt, Joe Morton, Nicolas Surovy, David Marshall Grant, Art LaFleur, John David (J.D.) Cullum; *D:* Steve Miner; *W:* Jeffrey Abrams; *C:* Russell Boyd; *M:* Jerry Goldsmith.

Forgotten City

When his brother is threatened by thugs in Costa Rica, James Wheeler (Patrick) agrees to bring a pre-Columbian artifact to him. But James arrives to find his brother dead and millionaire Drew Fallon (Ward) intensely interested in buying the thingy. According to the local expert Katerina Carrera (Caselli), it contains the location of a gold-filled city. A few chases later, they're off to the jungle where more adventures ensue. Overall, the quality of writing, acting, image, and sound are a bit better than you'd expect for a B-movie. The DVD has the clarity and depth of detail usually associated with bigger-budgeted productions. The location work is just as important as any other aspect of the film. —MM

Movie: 🎬🎬 **DVD:** 🎬🎬
York Entertainment (Cat #YPD-1025, UPC #750723102528). Full frame. Dolby Digital 5.1 Surround Stereo. $24.99. Keepcase. *LANG:* English. *SUB:* Spanish. *FEATURES:* 28 chapter links • Filmographies of Patrick, Ward, Caselli.
1999 (R) 96m/C Robert Patrick, Fred Ward, Chiara Caselli; *D:* H. Gordon Boos; *W:* Denne Bart Petitclerc, Arthur Sellers; *C:* Fabrizio Lucci.

The 47 Ronin, Parts 1 & 2

Turn of the 18th-century epic chronicles the samurai legend. The warriors of Lord

Asano set out to avenge their leader, tricked into committing a forced seppuku, or hara-kiri. The photography is generously laden with views of 18th-century gardens as well as panoramic vistas. This is the largest and most popular film of the Kabuki version of the story by Seika Mayama. This DVD doesn't look great, due to extensive preprint damage. This is probably the best print available and in any case, the DVD still looks better than the VHS edition. The sound is in very bad shape with parts that are muted, and others that warble. Even so, *The 47 Ronin* is such an important film that fans of the Japanese cinema will still want to add it to their collection. —*JO* **AKA:** The Loyal 47 Ronin; 47 Samurai.

Movie: 🎬🎬🎬 **DVD:** 🎬🎬▶
Image Entertainment (Cat #ID4541JFDVD, UPC #014381454123). Full frame. Dolby Digital Mono. $34.95. Snapper. *LANG:* Japanese. *SUB:* English. *FEATURES:* 20 chapter links.
1942 214m/C *JP* Yoshisaburo Arashi, Chojuro Kawarazaki, Kunitaro Kawarazaki, Utaemon Ichikawa, Mantoyo Mimasu, Mieko Takamine; **D:** Kenji Mizoguchi; **W:** Yoshikata Yoda, Kenchiro Hara; **C:** Kohei Sugiyama; **M:** Shiro Fukai.

The 400 Blows

French movie critic-turned-director Truffaut based his first film on his own troubled childhood, and thus *The 400 Blows (Les Quatre Cents Coups)* is rightly labeled his most personal film. The start of his career-long Antoine Doinel series, it's one of the greatest and most influential of films. The director's on-screen alter ego is 13-year-old Antoine, who turns to a life of small-time crime to escape the abuse of his parents and teachers. When Antoine skips school to see movies, it presumably is just one way Truffaut's film is autobiographical. Because this is a vintage title, the image is marred by blemishes in places and the sound isn't state of the art, but credit Criterion for its digital restoration work that resulted in the cleanest-ever video edition. The French soundtrack is intelligible enough to see the actors' lips are not in perfect synch, which is the result of Truffaut's guerilla production technique of shooting with a silent camera and dubbing dialogue later. Unfortunately, the video is not enhanced for widescreen displays. The shot-by-shot audio essay by Professor Brian Stonehill is revealing. Regrettably, this well-conceived Criterion edition is out of print at the time of this writing. It is a collectible well worth seeking out. For casual collectors, the current (but inferior) WinStar DVD, reviewed below, is an easier find. —*MB* **AKA:** Les Quatre Cents Coups.

Movie: 🎬🎬🎬🎬 **DVD:** 🎬🎬🎬
Criterion Collection (Cat #FOU060, UPC #037429122228). Widescreen (2.35:1) letterboxed. Dolby Digital Mono. $39.95. Keepcase. *LANG:* French. *SUB:* English. *FEATURES:* 23 chapter links • Commentary: Stonehill, Robert Lachenay, cowriter

Marcel Moussey • Theatrical trailer • Animated menus.
1959 97m/B *FR* Francois Truffaut, Jean-Pierre Leaud, Claire Maurier, Albert Remy, Guy Decomble, Georges Flament, Patrick Auffay, Jeanne Moreau, Jean-Claude Brialy, Jacques Demy, Robert Beauvais; **D:** Francois Truffaut; **W:** Francois Truffaut, Marcel Moussey; **C:** Henri Decae; **M:** Jean Constantin. *AWARDS:* Cannes Film Festival '59: Best Director (Truffaut); New York Film Critics Awards '59: Best Foreign Film; *NOM:* Academy Awards '59: Best Story & Screenplay.

The 400 Blows (WinStar Edition)

The WinStar DVD edition of Truffaut's famous debut suffers some typical visual and aural flaws. Diagonal lines disintegrate in fast pans; tweeds flash; the score sounds tinny. Balancing those, the disc boasts new, easy-to-read subtitles and an informative commentary track by *Premiere* magazine critic Glenn Kenny. He aims his observations at the interested fan, not specifically at the cineaste. —*MM*

Movie: 🎬🎬🎬🎬 **DVD:** 🎬🎬▶
WinStar Home Entertainment (Cat #FLV5078, UPC #720917507828). Widescreen (2.35:l) letterboxed. Keepcase. *LANG:* French. *SUB:* English. *FEATURES:* 6 chapter links • Filmographies and awards • Theatrical trailers • Commentary: critic Glenn Kenny.
1959 97m/B

The Four Musketeers

Continuation of *The Three Musketeers*, filmed at the same time, is a lavish swashbuckler that jaunts from France to England to Italy, following the adventures of D'Artagnan (York) and cohorts (Reed, Finlay, Chamberlain). Both pictures give an amusing depiction of 17th-century Europe as envisioned by director Lester and writer-historian Fraser. **AKA:** The Revenge of Milady.

Movie: 🎬🎬🎬 **DVD:** NYR
WinStar Home Entertainment (Cat #5030). Widescreen (1.66:1) letterboxed. Dolby Digital Mono. $29.98. Keepcase. *FEATURES:* Cast and crew thumbnail biographies • Production notes.
1975 (PG) 108m/C Michael York, Oliver Reed, Richard Chamberlain, Frank Finlay, Raquel Welch, Christopher Lee, Faye Dunaway, Jean-Pierre Cassel, Geraldine Chaplin, Simon Ward, Charlton Heston, Roy Kinnear, Nicole Calfan; **D:** Richard Lester; **W:** George MacDonald Fraser; **C:** David Watkin; **M:** Lalo Schifrin. *AWARDS: NOM:* Academy Awards '75: Best Costume Design.

Four Rooms

Four stories by four hot indie filmers set in the same L.A. hotel on New Year's Eve are tied together by bellboy Roth, stumbling around in a Jerry/Carrey-like stupor. Leading off is Anders's roomful of witches try-

ing to resurrect spirit of '50s stripper DeCadenet. After this disappointing start is Rockwell's bland look at infidelity, with wife Beals tied and gagged by her husband (Proval) over an alleged fling with Roth. Banderas heads the best seg as a mobster who leaves his demonic children in Roth's hands. Tarantino is the anchor man with his take on Hitchcock, dealing with a macabre bet involving the removal of body parts. Altogether disjointed and uninspired. It's easy to check out the color accuracy on this DVD—just scan into that nekkid witch sequence and there's plenty of fleshtones to compare. Well, the colors are accurate, and while not the punchiest, certainly vibrant enough. The picture is also sharp and the grain level stays low throughout. Blacks are true and contrast very good. Brightness levels are consistent. The Dolby Surround mix is lively and full-bodied. —*JO*

Movie: 🎬🎬 **DVD:** 🎬🎬🎬
Buena Vista Home Entertainment (Cat #16786, UPC #717951000894). Widescreen (1.85:1) letterboxed. Dolby Surround. $29.99. Keepcase. *LANG:* English. *CAP:* English. *FEATURES:* 21 chapter links.
1995 (R) 98m/C Tim Roth, Antonio Banderas, Jennifer Beals, Paul Calderon, Sammi Davis, Valeria Golino, Madonna, Ione Skye, Marisa Tomei, Tamlyn Tomita, Bruce Willis, David Proval, Lili Taylor, Alicia Witt, Amanda DeCadenet, Danny Verduzco, Lana McKissack, Quentin Tarantino; **Cameos:** Salma Hayek; **D:** Quentin Tarantino, Alexandre Rockwell, Robert Rodriguez, Allison Anders; **W:** Quentin Tarantino, Alexandre Rockwell, Robert Rodriguez, Allison Anders; **C:** Phil Parmet, Guillermo Navarro, Andrzej Sekula, Rodrigo Garcia; **M:** Combustible Edison, Esquivel. *AWARDS:* Golden Raspberry Awards '95: Worst Supporting Actress (Madonna).

Four Weddings and a Funeral

The refreshing, intelligent comedy follows the fortunes and misfortunes of Charles (Grant) and company as they look for true love while tending to life and attending, well, four weddings and a funeral. Bachelor Brit Charles witnesses his share of nuptials, but he manages to avoid taking the matrimonial plunge himself before falling hard for Carrie (MacDowell), an American who seems just out of his reach. Loaded with sophisticated wit, the film turns solemn for one occasion—the funeral, of course—but quickly regains its love-and-laughs outlook. While Grant makes this a star turn as the romantic bumbler, MacDowell charms without seeming particularly needed. Supporting characters are superb all the way around, especially Coleman as the flirty Scarlett and Atkinson as a new minister. Though an early DVD issue, the image is pleasing, with a minimal of digital artifacts probably not noticed by most. Sorry 5.1 buffs, but the soundtrack is encoded in two-channel Dolby Digital. But you'll have no problem hearing the witty dialogue and the tunes on an enjoyably musical soundtrack. More typical of early DVD releases, letterbox and pan-and-scan versions are on the disc. —MB

Movie: ♫♫♫ **DVD:** ♫♫►
MGM Home Entertainment (Cat #907850, UPC #2761678502). Widescreen letterboxed (1.85:1); full frame. Dolby Digital 2.0. $24.98. Keepcase. *LANG:* English; French. *SUB:* Spanish. *CAP:* English. *FEATURES:* 20 chapter links ● Theatrical trailer ● "Love Is All Around" music video ● Biographies and filmographies for cast and filmmakers.
1994 (R) 118m/C *GB* Hugh Grant, Andie MacDowell, Simon Callow, Kristin Scott Thomas, James Fleet, John Hannah, Charlotte Coleman, David Bower, Corin Redgrave, Rowan Atkinson, Rosalie Crutchley, Kenneth Griffith, Jeremy Kemp, Sophie Thompson; *D:* Mike Newell; *W:* Richard Curtis; *C:* Michael Coulter; *M:* Richard Rodney Bennett. *AWARDS:* Australian Film Institute '94: Best Foreign Film; British Academy Awards '94: Best Actor (Grant), Best Director (Newell), Best Film, Best Supporting Actress (Scott Thomas); Golden Globe Awards '95: Best Actor—Musical/Comedy (Grant); Writers Guild of America '94: Best Original Screenplay; *NOM:* Academy Awards '94: Best Original Screenplay, Best Picture; Directors Guild of America Awards '94: Best Director (Newell); Golden Globe Awards '95: Best Actress—Musical/Comedy (MacDowell), Best Film—Musical/Comedy, Best Screenplay; MTV Movie Awards '95: Breakthrough Performance (Grant).

The 4D Man
A physicist makes two fateful discoveries while working on a special project that quickly gets out of control, leaving him able to pass through matter and see around corners. (O.K., so it's not the greatest super power in the world). He also finds that his touch brings instant death. Cheap but effective sci-fi film with nice 1950s feel. Young Duke has a small part. The video transfer showcases the film's age with a weathered image (although it looks as good as most movies of the era). Where the disc really comes up short is in the tinny and often muddied mono soundtrack (which is noticeably poor when the score plays over and under dialogue). —MJT
Movie: ♫♫► **DVD:** ♫♫
Image Entertainment (Cat #ID6599WE DVD, UPC #014381659924). Full frame. Dolby Digital Mono. $24.99. Snapper. *LANG:* English. *FEATURES:* 18 chapter links.
1959 85m/C Robert Lansing, Lee Meriwether, James Congdon, Guy Raymond, Robert Strauss, Patty Duke; *D:* Irvin S. Yeaworth Jr.; *W:* Theodore Simonson, Cy Chermack; *C:* Theodore J. Pahle; *M:* Ralph Carmichael.

Fractured Follies
For a comedy aimed at an adult audience, this one is ridiculously silly, though, admit-

tedly, cultural differences present difficulties for humor. Joe (Chow Yun-Fat) is a cabbie who believes that he caused injuries that crippled May (Joi Wang), though she was born with a bad leg. The main source of amusement for American audiences is in the near-continual "hex" errors in the subtitles. When May is really really mad at a bad guy, she yells "Good Damn You!" Overall, the DVD looks and sounds no better than a VHS tape of comparable low-budget domestic fare. —MM
Movie: ♫► **DVD:** ♫►
Tai Seng Marketing (Cat #5111, UPC #4895024902616). Widescreen letterboxed. Dolby Digital Mono. $24.98. Keepcase. *LANG:* Cantonese; Mandarin. *SUB:* Traditional & Simplified Chinese; English; Japanese; Bahasa Indonesia; Korean; French. *FEATURES:* 8 chapter links ● Chow Yun-Fat thumbnail biography ● 4 theatrical trailers.
1988 93m/C *CH* Chow Yun-Fat, Joi Wang, Nina Li, James Wong, Wong Ching; *D:* Chung Wong; *C:* Chan Hau Ming.

Frances
Frances Farmer (Lange) is the beautiful and talented screen actress of the 1930s and '40s who was driven to a mental breakdown by bad luck, drug and alcohol abuse, a neurotic domineering mother, despicable mental health care, and her own stubbornness. The film isn't nearly as bleak as it sounds in synopsis because Lange understands the character from the inside out and never allows her to become melodramatic or weak.
Movie: ♫♫♫ **DVD:** NYR
Republic Pictures Home Video (Cat #11189). $24.98.
1982 134m/C Jessica Lange, Kim Stanley, Sam Shepard, Jeffrey DeMunn, Gerald S. O'Loughlin, Chris Pennock, John Randolph, Lane Smith; *D:* Graeme Clifford; *W:* Christopher DeVore, Nicholas Kazan, Eric Bergren; *C:* Laszlo Kovacs; *M:* John Barry. *AWARDS: NOM:* Academy Awards '82: Best Actress (Lange), Best Supporting Actress (Stanley).

Francesco
Thirteenth-century Italy is the setting for this depiction of the life of St. Francis of Assisi. Follows the pleasure-loving son of a wealthy merchant through his religious awakening, and the founding of the Franciscan order of monks. Rourke, in a definite change-of-pace role, is actually believable, while Bonham Carter offers fine support as a devoted disciple. *Francesco* looked great on laserdisc and even on VHS, but this DVD has almost constant artifacts, which increase when the scene is darker. The picture is never sharp and colors are faded. The sound is of similar quality with the seeming fidelity of a poor cassette player. —JO
Movie: ♫♫♫ **DVD:** ♫
Simitar Entertainment (Cat #7378, UPC #082551737826). Full frame. Stereo.

$19.95. Keepcase. *LANG:* English. *FEATURES:* 8 chapter links ● Filmography.
1989 (PG-13) 119m/C Mickey Rourke, Helena Bonham Carter, Paolo Bonacelli, Andrea Ferreol, Hanns Zischler, Peter Berling; *D:* Liliana Cavani; *W:* Liliana Cavani; *C:* Giuseppe Lanci, Ennio Guarnieri; *M:* Vangelis.

Frank and Jesse
Another revisionist western finds outlaw Jesse James (Lowe) brooding about his violent existence while brother Frank (Paxton) keeps the gang together and they all try to avoid capture by the vengeful Alan Pinkerton (Atherton) and his detective agency.
Movie: ♫♫► **DVD:** NYR
Trimark Home Video (Cat #7395). Widescreen anamorphic. Dolby Digital Stereo. $14.98. Keepcase. *SUB:* French; Spanish. *CAP:* English. *FEATURES:* Cast and crew thumbnail biographies ● Trailer.
1994 (R) 106m/C Rob Lowe, Bill Paxton, Randy Travis, William Atherton, Alexis Arquette; *D:* Robert Boris; *W:* Robert Boris; *C:* Walt Lloyd; *M:* Mark McKenzie.

Frankenstein
This DVD may be the finest version of James Whale's masterpiece that's been available since the initial theatrical release. In some ways, it's better with sound that's been cleaned up to make one crucial line of dialogue—"Now I know what it feels like to be God!"—completely clear. (On tape and on theatrical prints, it is muffled by thunder.) The image has an equally fresh-scrubbed look, though the focus is a little rough in spots, reflecting the technology of 1931. The extensive extras are well chosen, particularly Donald Skal's short documentary, *The Frankenstein Files*. It focuses on background information, earlier stage adaptations, the cast, and makeup, through interviews with several film historians and technical experts. In short, this is the first disc that any horror fan should buy for the library. —MM
Movie: ♫♫♫♫ **DVD:** ♫♫♫♫
Universal Studios Home Video (Cat #20325, UPC #025192032523). Full frame. Dolby Digital Mono. $29.98. Keepcase. *LANG:* English. *SUB:* French. *CAP:* English. *FEATURES: The Frankenstein Files* documentary by David Skal ● Commentary: Rudy Behlmer ● Ads and stills ● "Boo!" a Universal short film ● Production notes ● Cast and crew thumbnail biographies ● Theatrical trailer ● Universal web links.
1931 71m/B Boris Karloff, Colin Clive, Mae Clarke, John Boles, Dwight Frye, Edward Van Sloan, Frederick Kerr, Lionel Belmore, Arletta Duncan; *D:* James Whale; *W:* Garrett Fort, John Lloyd Balderston, Robert Florey, Francis Edwards Faragoh; *C:* Arthur Edeson; *M:* David Broeckman. *AWARDS:* American Film Institute (AFI) '98: Top 100, National Film Registry '91.

Frantic

In Paris, an American surgeon's wife is kidnapped after she inadvertently picks up the wrong suitcase. Her kidnappers want their hidden treasure returned, which forces the husband into the criminal underground and unexpected heroism when he seeks to rescue her. Contrived ending weakens on the whole, but Polanski is still master of the dark film thriller. The DVD review could be very short: Keep your VHS or laserdisc copy. The picture is soft and very grainy. There are artifacts in most darker scenes. Colors are dull and faded. Blacks only get close to true occasionally. There should be more contrast and it seems that the brightness is sometimes too low and sometimes too high. The sound is a little better and has good fidelity and good low end, with adequate use of the Surround channel. —JO

Movie: ♪♪♪ **DVD:** ♪
Warner Home Video, Inc. (Cat #11787, UPC #085391178729). Full frame. Dolby Surround. $14.98. Snapper. *LANG:* English. *CAP:* English. *FEATURES:* 32 chapter links.
1988 (R) 120m/C Harrison Ford, Betty Buckley, John Mahoney, Emmanuelle Seigner, Jimmie Ray Weeks, Yorgo Voyagis, David Huddleston, Gerard Klein; *D:* Roman Polanski; *W:* Roman Polanski, Gerard Brach; *C:* Witold Sobocinski; *M:* Ennio Morricone.

Fraternity Demon

The guys at Sigma Upsilon Xi are ready for the year's biggest party when a professor inadvertently calls up a sexy spirit (Bowie) from the underworld. The ultra-low-budget production scrapes the bottom of the T&A barrel. On DVD, the image is poor, the sound is worse, and given the quality of the acting, nobody should complain. —MM

Movie: ♪▶ **DVD:** ♪▶
Simitar Entertainment (Cat #7311, UPC #082551731121). Full frame. PCM Stereo. $14.98. Keepcase. *LANG:* English. *FEATURES:* 8 chapter links ▪ Production factoids.
1992 (R) 85m/C Trixxie Bowie, Charles Laulette, Deborah Carlin, Al Darrouch, Michael McKay, Brenda Holiday; *D:* C.B. Rubin; *W:* Steve Tymon; *C:* Richard C. Glouner.

Freddy's Dead: The Final Nightmare

If nothing else, this unnumbered 6 proves that women can make horror sequels just as poorly as men. Director Rachel Talalay quotes the *Twilight Zone*'s "Nightmare at 10,000 Feet" and *The Wizard of Oz* early on, and her substantial budget allows for a barrelful of crackerjack visual effects. So what? The rest of more of the same bad acting from another bland young cast. In Ms. Talalay's favor, it should be noted that the violence is handled with cartoonish exaggeration and so it's not particularly sadistic. Also, DVD is able to reproduce the 3-D effects and they look very good. (Glasses are included with the boxed set.) Sound is fine. —MM *AKA:* Nightmare on Elm Street 6: Freddy's Dead.

Movie: ♪♪ **DVD:** ♪♪♪▶
New Line Home Video (Cat #N4824, UPC #794043478826). Widescreen (1.85:1) letterboxed. Dolby Digital 5.1 Surround Stereo; Stereo. $24.98. Snapper. *LANG:* English. *SUB:* English. *FEATURES:* 23 chapter links ▪ "Jump to Nightmare" screen navigation ▪ Original 3-D sequence ▪ DVD-ROM extras ▪ Cast and crew thumbnail biographies. Also available as part of "The Nightmare on Elm Street Collection" boxed set ($129.98, catalog #N4788.
1991 (R) 96m/C Robert Englund, Lisa Zane, Shon Greenblatt, Leslie Deane, Ricky Dean Logan, Breckin Majer, Yaphet Kotto, Elinor Donahue, Roseanne, Johnny Depp, Alice Cooper, Tom Arnold; *D:* Rachel Talalay; *W:* Michael De Luca; *C:* Declan Quinn.

Free Enterprise

Robert (Weigel) and Mark (McCormack), two Hollywood hopefuls, finally meet their idol (and fantasy mentor) William Shatner and discover that he's not at all what they think he is. That sounds like a thin and obvious premise, but the filmmakers take it in interesting directions. Think *Swingers* with a touch of *Being John Malkovich*. They reel off so many pop culture references that a separate subtitle track is used to identify them, and those who, like me, have never seen *The Brady Bunch* will need all the help they can get. The extensive extras are the disc's primary feature. Visually, it's fine most of the time, but mini-blinds have seldom flashed quite so crazily and one patterned sport coat is almost as irritating. —MM

Movie: ♪♪♪ **DVD:** ♪♪♪▶
Pioneer Entertainment (Cat #PEAD-009, UPC #013023032798). Widescreen letterboxed. Dolby Digital Stereo. $29.98. Keepcase. *LANG:* English. *SUB:* English. *FEATURES:* 25 chapter links ▪ Many deleted scenes ▪ "Ebionics" glossary ▪ "Making of" documentary ▪ Filmmakers' stat sheets ▪ Trivia subtitles ▪ Music video ▪ Commentary: Burnett and Altman.
1998 (R) 114m/C Eric McCormack, Rafer Weigel, William Shatner, Audie England, Patrick Van Horn, Jonathan Slavin, Phil LaMarr, Deborah Van Valkenburgh; *D:* Robert Meyer Burnett; *W:* Robert Meyer Burnett, Mark Altman; *C:* Charles L. Barbee; *M:* Scott Spock.

Free Willy

Inexcusable juvenile crap has become a perennial favorite among the short set. Go figure. It's the tender but idiotic story of a spoiled kid (Richter) who learns important life lessons from a killer whale (Keiko) in an aquarium. They're abetted by one-dimensional villains and Hollywood's idea of American Indian mysticism. Neither image nor sound is particularly striking. At best, the picture is good but heavy pixelation dots the surface of the water under some lighting conditions. The special effects don't look bad, however. —MM

Movie: ♪♪ **DVD:** ♪♪▶
Warner Home Video, Inc. (Cat #18000). Widescreen (2.35:1) letterboxed; full frame. Dolby Digital 5.1 Surround Stereo. $24.98. Snapper. *LANG:* English; French; Spanish. *SUB:* French; Spanish. *CAP:* English. *FEATURES:* 35 chapter links ▪ Cast and crew thumbnail bios ▪ Production notes ▪ Trailers.
1993 (PG) 112m/C Jason James Richter, Lori Petty, Jayne Atkinson, August Schellenberg, Michael Madsen; *D:* Simon Wincer; *W:* Keith A. Walker, Corey Blechman; *C:* Robbie Greenberg; *M:* Basil Poledouris. *AWARDS:* MTV Movie Awards '94: Best Song ("Will You Be There"); *NOM:* MTV Movie Awards '94: Breakthrough Performance (Richter), Best Kiss (Jason James Richter/Willy).

Freedom Strike

On a covert United Nations strike mission—a United Nations "strike mission"?—Navy pilot Stone (Dudikoff) is sent to sabotage an Iraqi nuclear reactor before terrorists can use it. A microchip is the McGuffin in this so-so military action flick. Curiously, the image of this mid- to low-budget production is exemplary. The interiors are so subtly lit that skin tones and facial features are absolutely clear, and director Jacobs uses lots of close-ups to divert attention from his less-than-convincing sets. The action scenes are not quite as sharp but the sound is fine. —MM

Movie: ♪♪ **DVD:** ♪♪♪
Simitar Entertainment (Cat #7436, UPC #082551743629). Full frame. Dolby Digital Stereo; Dolby Digital 5.1 Surround. $19.95. Keepcase. *LANG:* English. *FEATURES:* 8 chapter links ▪ Production factoids.
1998 (R) 93m/C Michael Dudikoff, Tone Loc, Felicity Waterman; *D:* Jerry P. Jacobs.

French Kiss

Kate (Ryan) has a fear of flying but she's more afraid of losing her fiance (Hutton) to a newly met French "goddess" (Anbeh). She jets off to Paris and on the way meets dashing, nicotine-stained French rogue Luc (Kline). Their ensuing romance is so slowly paced that it will appeal mostly to Ryan's fans. (She also produced.) Reno, as a cop, is very good and so is Spielvogel as a stereotypically rude French hotel concierge. Both image and sound are first-rate. The careful digital transfer is essentially flawless, retaining the film's careful production values. —MM

Movie: ♪♪▶ **DVD:** ♪♪♪
Twentieth Century Fox Home Entertainment (Cat #2000004, UPC #024543000 044). Widescreen (2.35:1) letterboxed. Dolby Digital 5.1 Surround Stereo; Dolby Surround Stereo. $24.99. Keepcase. *LANG:* English; French. *SUB:* English; Span-

ish. *FEATURES:* 22 chapter links • Theatrical trailers.
1995 (PG-13) 111m/C Meg Ryan, Kevin Kline, Timothy Hutton, Jean Reno, Francois Cluzet, Renee Humphrey, Michael Riley, Susan Anbeh, Laurent Spielvogel; *D:* Lawrence Kasdan; *W:* Adam Brooks; *C:* Owen Roizman; *M:* James Newton Howard.

The Freshman

Brando, in an incredible parody of his Don Corleone character, makes this work. Broderick is a college student in need of fast cash, and innocent enough to believe that any work is honest. A good supporting cast and a twisty plot keep things interesting. Sometimes heavy-handed with its sight gags, but Broderick and Brando push the movie to hilarious conclusion. Don't miss Bert Parks's musical extravaganza. The DVD transfer is solid and features both sharp visuals and a nicely mixed Dolby Surround soundtrack. There is very little grain to the picture and the artifact level is low. Colors are pretty vibrant and well defined, and the blacks are accurate. Contrast and brightness levels are excellent throughout. The sound is lively and full-bodied, with good separation and imaging. *—JO*
Movie: 🎞🎞▶ **DVD:** 🎞🎞🎞
Columbia Tristar Home Video (Cat #70299, UPC #043396702998). Widescreen (1.85:1) anamorphic; full frame. Dolby Surround. $29.95. Keepcase. *LANG:* English; Spanish; French. *SUB:* English; Spanish; French. *CAP:* English. *FEATURES:* 28 chapter links • Theatrical trailer.
1990 (PG) 102m/C Marlon Brando, Matthew Broderick, Penelope Ann Miller, Maximilian Schell, Bruno Kirby, Frank Whaley, Jon Polito, Paul Benedict, Richard Gant, B.D. Wong, Bert Parks; *D:* Andrew Bergman; *W:* Andrew Bergman; *C:* William A. Fraker; *M:* David Newman.

Friday

It's *Boyz N the Hood* meets *Good Times.* Ice Cube wrote and stars as Craig in this humorous look into life in the 'hood. Craig's just lost his job and spends his time sitting on the porch with his pot-smoking sidekick Smokey (Tucker), with the two getting mixed up in a variety of crazy antics involving their kooky neighbors. The laughs come at the expense of overworn cliches and stereotypical characters, but there's originality in the movie's energy and boldness (i.e. the local dope dealer is also the neighborhood ice cream man). To some, this *Friday* could be something to look forward to. The whole package is pretty good on this DVD. The image itself is sharp, colors and blacks are good, and the sound, though not spectacular, is acceptable. The supplementals on this DVD are worth a look and the deleted scenes are funny and not just thrown on in order to make the claim special-edition. *—JO*
Movie: 🎞🎞🎞 **DVD:** 🎞🎞🎞▶

New Line Home Video (Cat #N4680, UPC #794943468025). Widescreen (1.85:1) letterboxed. Dolby Surround. $24.98. Snapper. *LANG:* English. *SUB:* English; Spanish; French. *FEATURES:* 27 chapter links • Theatrical trailers • 7 deleted scenes • Interviews • 2 music videos • Cast and filmmakers bios • Filmographies.
1995 (R) 91m/C Ice Cube, Chris Tucker, Bernie Mac, John Witherspoon, Regina King, Nia Long, Tommy (Tiny) Lister; *D:* F. Gary Gray; *W:* DJ Pooh, Ice Cube; *C:* Gerry Lively; *M:* Frank Fitzpatrick. *AWARDS: NOM:* MTV Movie Awards '96: Breakthrough Performance (Tucker), Best On-Screen Duo (Chris Tucker/Ice Cube), Best Comedic Performance (Tucker).

Friday the 13th

The first entry in one of the genre's most successful franchises is a long variation on that old campfire favorite, The Hook. Judged as a low-budget horror flick, it's not bad, and not particularly original, either. The plot and direction rip off *Halloween,* and the score rips off Bernard Herrmann. Tom Savini's bloody effects are well-done and have been repeated many many times since. So has the story of camp counselors being preyed on by a slasher. Though this low-budget overachiever has never been that polished, the DVD image is a step up from VHS tape, particularly those rental tapes that have been circulated hundreds of times. The heavy black nocturnal scenes are free of artifacts. Monaural sound is very good. *—MM*
Movie: 🎞🎞 **DVD:** 🎞🎞▶
Paramount Home Video (Cat #13957, UPC #097360139570). Widescreen anamorphic. Dolby Digital Mono. $29.99. Keepcase. *LANG:* English; French. *SUB:* English. *FEATURES:* Trailers • 15 chapter links.
1980 (R) 95m/C Betsy Palmer, Adrienne King, Harry Crosby, Laurie Bartram, Mark Nelson, Kevin Bacon, Jeannine Taylor, Robbi Morgan, Peter Brouwer, Walt Gorney; *D:* Sean S. Cunningham; *W:* Victor Miller; *C:* Barry Abrams; *M:* Harry Manfredini.

Friday the 13th, Part 2

The series really doesn't get started until this entry, which establishes the ground rules. Like *Halloween*'s Michael Myers and all the Universal studio monsters before him, Jason is an unstoppable monster of ill-defined superpowers. Shoot him, stab him, burn him, blow him up—it doesn't matter. Every time you're really truly absolutely positively sure that he's dead, he pops back up for more. Sex is the trigger; violent death is the result. That's the ongoing message of the films. In both image and sound, this DVD is comparable to the original. *—MM*
Movie: 🎞🎞 **DVD:** 🎞🎞▶
Paramount Home Video (Cat #14577, UPC #097360145779). Widescreen (1.85:1) anamorphic. Dolby Digital 5.1 Surround Stereo. $29.99. Keepcase. *LANG:* English; French. *SUB:* English. *FEATURES:* Theatrical trailer • 14 chapter links.

1981 (R) 87m/C Amy Steel, John Furey, Adrienne King, Betsy Palmer, Kirsten Baker, Stu Charno, Warrington Gillette, Walt Gorney, Marta Kober, Bill Randolph, Jack Marks; *D:* Steve Miner; *W:* Ron Kurz; *C:* Peter Stein; *M:* Harry Manfredini.

Fried Green Tomatoes

Two stories about four women, love, friendship, Southern charm, and eccentricity are untidily held together by wonderful performances. Unhappy, middle-aged Evelyn (Bates) meets the talkative 83-year-old Ninny Threadgoode (Tandy). Ninny reminisces about her Depression-era life in the town of Whistle Stop, AL, and the two women, Idgie (Masterson) and Ruth (Parker), who ran the local cafe. Back-and-forth narrative as it tracks multiple storylines is occasionally confusing, though strong character development holds interest. Surprising boxoffice hit was adapted by Fannie Flagg from her novel *Fried Green Tomatoes at the Whistle Stop Cafe.* This is a very good color transfer. Not only are the colors accurate, they are vibrant with subtle hue variations that all captured perfectly on the DVD. The picture is sharp and grain is never a problem. Blacks are also handled nicely and there is sufficient contrast teamed with excellent brightness levels. The Dolby Surround sound does just fine and has very good low end and crisp, undistorted highs, although it makes very little use of the rear Surround. *—JO*
Movie: 🎞🎞🎞 **DVD:** 🎞🎞🎞▶
Universal Studios Home Video (Cat #2024, UPC #0251920229). Widescreen (1.85:1) anamorphic. Dolby Surround. $29.98. Keepcase. *LANG:* English. *SUB:* Spanish; French. *CAP:* English. *FEATURES:* 57 chapter links • Theatrical trailer • Commentary: Jon Avnet • Documentary "Moments of Discovery" • Production photos • Poster campaign • Longer version (adds 7 mins.).
1991 (PG-13) 130m/C Kathy Bates, Jessica Tandy, Mary Stuart Masterson, Mary-Louise Parker, Cicely Tyson, Chris O'Donnell, Stan Shaw, Gailard Sartain, Timothy Scott, Gary Basaraba, Lois Smith, Grace Zabriskie; *D:* Jon Avnet; *W:* Fannie Flagg, Carol Sobieski; *C:* Geoffrey Simpson; *M:* Thomas Newman. *AWARDS: NOM:* Academy Awards '91: Best Adapted Screenplay, Best Supporting Actress (Tandy).

Friend of the Family

Soft-core fluff finds sexy Elke (O'Brien) as a houseguest to a dysfunctional family of ultra-rich Californians. Acting as a combination of Ann Landers and the Happy Hooker, she helps each of them—from spoiled daughter (Boyle) to long-suffering dad (Miller) and stepmother (Drew)—overcome their sexual problems and accept themselves for who they are. Like all Andrew Garroni productions it's highly polished and the people are pretty, even if

their acting abilities are limited. That's not exactly the point. The DVD looks no better than VHS tape with harsh bright daylight scenes and tinny sound. —*MM AKA:* Elke.
Movie: 🎬🎬▶ **DVD:** 🎬🎬
Image Entertainment (Cat #ID5593FMDVD, UPC #014381559323). Full frame. Dolby Digital Stereo. $24.99. Snapper. *LANG:* English. *FEATURES:* 16 chapter links.
1995 98m/C Shauna O'Brien, C.T. Miller, Griffin Drew, Lisa Boyle; *D:* Edward Holzman; *W:* Edward Holzman, April Moskowitz; *C:* Kim Haun; *M:* Richard Bronskill.

Friend of the Family 2
Sequel-in-title-only finds star O'Brien cast as psycho-babe Jill who follows Jack (Robinson) to San Francisco after they have passionate fling in New Orleans. In familiar *Fatal Attraction* fashion, she insinuates herself into his family and sets out to destroy him. In the end, the film is less than successful both as a thriller and as soft-core eroticism. The image looks about as grainy and rough on DVD as it does on tape. Nothing special. —*MM*
Movie: 🎬🎬 **DVD:** 🎬🎬
Image Entertainment (Cat #ID5594FMDVD, UPC #014381559422). Full frame. Dolby Digital Stereo. $24.99. Snapper. *LANG:* English. *FEATURES:* 12 chapter links.
1996 (R) 90m/C Shauna O'Brien, Paul Michael Robinson, Jenna Bodnar, Jeff Rector; *D:* Fred Olen Ray; *W:* Henry Krinkle; *C:* Gary Graver.

The Frighteners
Con man Frank Bannister (Fox) has a unique scam—he works with a group of ghosts who haunt a home until Frank comes along to drive them out, for the right price. But the small town of Fairwater is plagued by a serial killer's evil spirit and Frank and his spiritual cronies face the challenge of getting rid of the ghost before the police decide to get rid of Frank. Interesting horror-comedy takes a lot of twists and turns to get where it's going, but the payoff in gore and humor is worth it for fans of the genre. New Zealand helmer Jackson makes his American directorial debut. The definitive way to own *The Frighteners* is still the laserdisc box, which contains a "making of" documentary that is as enjoyable as the film itself. But this DVD looks good, and even if you own a laserdisc player, very few of the boxes were produced. The picture is comparable to the LD and the 5.1 sound seems a little more energized. —*JO*
Movie: 🎬🎬🎬 **DVD:** 🎬🎬🎬
Universal Studios Home Video (Cat #20286, UPC #025192028625). Widescreen (2.35:1) anamorphic. Dolby Digital 5.1; Dolby Surround. $24.98. Keepcase. *LANG:* English; French. *SUB:* Spanish. *CAP:* English. *FEATURES:* 16 chapter links • Theatrical trailer • Production notes • Cast and filmmakers bios • Film highlights.
1996 (R) 106m/C Michael J. Fox, Trini Alvarado, Peter Dobson, Dee Wallace

Stone, John Astin, Jeffrey Combs, Troy Evans, Chi McBride, Jake Busey, R. Lee Ermey, Jim Fyfe; *D:* Peter Jackson; *W:* Peter Jackson, Frances Walsh; *C:* Alun Bollinger, John Blick; *M:* Danny Elfman.

From Dusk Till Dawn
Escaped cons Seth and Richie Gecko (Clooney and Tarantino) pick up an ex-preacher (Keitel) and his two kids (Lewis and Liu) as hostages en route to their Mexican rendezvous spot, a raunchy biker joint run (unbeknownst to them) by vampires. Feels like two movies in one, as Rodriguez's and Tarantino's styles don't necessarily mesh as much as they coexist. The first half features Tarantino's gift for snappy dialogue and somewhat sympathetic scumbags while the barroom finale shows off Rodriguez's mastery of the go-for-broke action set piece. Clooney proves the jump from TV to movies can be made successfully. Penned by Tarantino in 1990 during his video store days, he used the fee to get *Reservoir Dogs* off the ground. This testosterone-filled and juicy action/gore flick had a great-looking laserdisc and the DVD is even a touch better. There is a lot of fast action in dark scenes and, despite that, the picture is sharp with little grain or artifacts. Colors are accurate to the theatrical release and generally very vibrant. Blacks are usually dead-on and always very close. Contrast and brightness are both a bit punchier than the LD. The 5.1 sound is loud and energized and has no problem shaking things up a bit, accenting gunshots, exploding (or disintegrating) bodies or even a noisy Los Lobos rocker equally well. Good lows, crisp highs, super Surround. —*JO*
Movie: 🎬🎬🎬 **DVD:** 🎬🎬🎬▶
Buena Vista Home Entertainment (Cat #14373, UPC #717951000446). Widescreen (1.85:1) letterboxed. Dolby Digital 5.1. $29.99. Keepcase. *LANG:* English. *SUB:* English; Spanish. *CAP:* English. *FEATURES:* 26 chapter links • Theatrical trailer and teaser trailer.
1995 (R) 108m/C George Clooney, Quentin Tarantino, Harvey Keitel, Juliette Lewis, Ernest Liu, Fred Williamson, Richard "Cheech" Marin, Salma Hayek, Michael Parks, Tom Savini, Kelly Preston, John Saxon, Danny Trejo; *D:* Robert Rodriguez; *W:* Quentin Tarantino; *C:* Guillermo Navarro; *M:* Graeme Revell. *AWARDS:* MTV Movie Awards '96: Breakthrough Performance (Clooney); *NOM:* Golden Raspberry Awards '96: Worst Supporting Actor (Tarantino).

From Dusk Till Dawn 2: Texas Blood Money
Buck (Patrick) and escaped con Luther (Whitaker) gather a gang and plan a bank job in Mexico but they run into the bat vampires of the Titty Twister Bar. (The film is set two weeks after the first.) Director Spiegel jazzes up the action with ultra-fancy camera work and oddball points-of-

view. He also overplays the humor with perhaps the nuttiest *Psycho* shower scene since Mel Brooks's parody in *High Anxiety*. Patrick, an underrated actor, is fine in the lead. Several scenes are tinted in shades of red and auburn, and they tend to lose some definition on DVD. That's not a serious visual flaw, though. Other scenes are deliberately darkened to heighten or to hide special effects. For a direct-to-video sequel, this one looks and sounds fine. —*MM AKA:* Texas Blood Money.
Movie: 🎬🎬🎬 **DVD:** 🎬🎬🎬
Buena Vista Home Entertainment (Cat #17497, UPC #717951003157). Widescreen (1.85:1) letterboxed. Dolby Digital Surround Stereo. $29.99. Keepcase. *LANG:* English. *CAP:* English. *FEATURES:* 22 chapter links.
1998 (R) 88m/C Robert Patrick, Bo Hopkins, Muse Watson, Duane Whitaker, Raymond Cruz, Tiffani-Amber Thiessen, Brett Harrelson, Danny Trejo, Bruce Campbell; *D:* Scott Spiegel; *W:* Duane Whitaker, Scott Spiegel; *C:* Philip Lee; *M:* Joseph Williams.

From Dusk Till Dawn 3: The Hangman's Daughter
Third time's the charm with a sequel that's as energetic as the original and even more enjoyable in many ways. It begins in Mexico, 1914, where writer Ambrose Bierce (Parks) faces a firing squad. Taking the structure of Bierce's "Occurrence at Owl Creek Bridge," the rest is flashback. The first act quotes *The Wild Bunch* and *The Good, the Bad, and the Ugly* as the principals are introduced: the title character Esmeralda (Celi); her outlaw lover (Leonardi); her enraged father (Morrison). Director Pesce tints some scenes with dusty red. Others sparkle with unnatural clarity. The DVD captures his visual flair with no real flaws. A genuine sleeper. —*MM*
Movie: 🎬🎬🎬 **DVD:** 🎬🎬🎬
Buena Vista Home Entertainment (Cat #18271, UPC #717951004642). Widescreen (1.85:1) letterboxed. Dolby Digital 5.1 Surround Stereo. $29.99. Keepcase. *LANG:* English. *CAP:* English. *FEATURES:* 15 chapter links • Deleted scene.
1999 (R) 94m/C Michael Parks, Sonia Braga, Marco Leonardi, Rebecca Gayheart, Temuera Morrison, Lenny Y. Loftin, Danny Trejo, Ara Celi; *D:* P.J. Pesce.

From Russia with Love
Bond's second outing is right up there with *Goldfinger* as the best in the long-running series. The formula had not been locked in yet and so there's a freshness and energy to the film that's lost in later entries. Connery is at his best; the locations are excellent and the supporting work by Armendariz, Lenya, and particularly Shaw as the coldly efficient villain could not be better. This title hasn't yet been

given the full extras package, but that's fine. The DVD looks terrific for a film of its age and the mono sound is adequate. —MM

Movie: 🎬🎬🎬🎬 **DVD:** 🎬🎬🎬▶
MGM Home Entertainment (Cat #906725). Widescreen anamorphic; full frame. Dolby Digital Mono. $24.98. Snapper. *LANG:* English; French; Spanish. *SUB:* English; French; Spanish. *FEATURES:* 32 chapter links • Trailer • Bond villains featurette.
1963 (PG) 125m/C *GB* Sean Connery, Daniela Bianchi, Pedro Armendariz Sr., Lotte Lenya, Robert Shaw, Eunice Gayson, Walter Gotell, Lois Maxwell, Bernard Lee, Desmond Llewelyn, Nadja Regin, Alizia Gur, Martine Beswick, Leila; *D:* Terence Young; *W:* Johanna Harwood, Richard Maibaum; *C:* Ted Moore; *M:* John Barry.

From the Earth to the Moon

Executive producer Tom Hanks shows off his fascination with the space program in this 12-part series covering the Apollo space program through the 1960s and '70s. It covers behind-the-scenes action at NASA, the heroics of the astronauts and their missions, and the families that are left behind to wait and worry. The effects are great and most of the episodes are very entertaining. This DVD set is worth owning just for the supplementary material, which is all on one densely packed disc of its own, and features such things as a tour of the solar system, a look at the creation of the excellent special effects, and a loaded DVD-ROM section. The overall image is excellent: very sharp and full of vibrant well-defined colors. The 5.1 sound is superb and would give most theatrical films a run for their money. —JO

Movie: 🎬🎬🎬 **DVD:** 🎬🎬🎬▶
HBO Home Video (Cat #99363, UPC #026359936326). Full frame. Dolby Digital 5.1; Dolby Digital Mono. $99.98. Special with slipcase. *LANG:* English; Spanish. *SUB:* English; Spanish; French. *FEATURES:* 12 chapter links • HBO "First Look" featurette • Special effects featurette • 13 TV spots • Virtual solar system • 3-D ship models • Mission objectives • Kennedy speech • Timeline of space missions • Mission objectives • Dual-layered RSDL.
1998 720m/C David Andrews, Bryan Cranston, Timothy Daly, Al Franken, Tony Goldwyn, Chris Isaak, Cary Elwes, Brett Cullen, Robert John Burke, Peter Scolari, Nick Searcy, Lane Smith, Dan Lauria, Mark Rolston, Mason Adams, Ronny Cox, Dakin Matthews, Kevin Pollak, Ben Marley, Joe Spano, Daniel Hugh-Kelly, Stephen Root, Dann Florek, John Slattery, Ted Levine, Ann Cusack, Jo Anderson, James Rebhorn, Mark Harmon, Rita Wilson; *D:* Tom Hanks, David Frankel, Lili Fini Zanuck, Graham Yost, Frank Marshall, Jon Turteltaub, Gary Fleder, David Carson, Sally Field, Jonathan Mostow; *W:* Tom Hanks, Graham Yost, Stephen Katz, Remi Aubuchon, Al Reinert, Andy Wolk, Jeffrey Alladin Fiskin, Karen

Janszen; *C:* Gale Tattersall; *M:* Michael Kamen, Mark Mancina.

From the Journals of Jean Seberg

An imaginary look at the life of the ill-fated actress, who began her career as a 17-year-old, miscast in Otto Preminger's *Saint Joan*, achieved fame in Godard's *Breathless*, and killed herself at age 40 in 1979. Viewing film clips, Seberg (Hurt) coolly narrates her story and dissects her difficult career as she goes from naive Iowa teenager to would-be star, through abusive marriages, political activism, and FBI harassment. Though the DVD transfer is sharp, the story relies on stock film clips, which vary in quality from fair to extremely grainy and faded, with some white subtitles that are sometimes difficult to read. —JE

Movie: 🎬🎬🎬 **DVD:** 🎬🎬
Image Entertainment (Cat #ID5107WB DVD, UPC #1438151072). Full frame. Dolby Digital Mono. $24.99. Snapper. *LANG:* English; French. *SUB:* English. *FEATURES:* 16 chapter links.
1995 97m/C Mary Beth Hurt; *D:* Mark Rappaport; *W:* Mark Rappaport; *C:* Mark Daniels.

The Front Page

Billy Wilder's remake of the famous Hecht-MacArthur play is generally underrated, but this lackluster DVD will do little to improve its reputation. Lemmon is Hildy Johnson, the ace reporter who wants to get married (to Sarandon); Matthau is his overbearing editor Walter Burns who wants a story about a hanging. This full-frame image is no better than fair with constant grain and mediocre sound. That's a shame because the film really does deserve better. —MM

Movie: 🎬🎬🎬 **DVD:** 🎬🎬
Goodtimes Entertainment (Cat #05-81020, UPC #018713810205). Full frame. Dolby Digital Mono. $19.98. Snapper. *LANG:* English. *SUB:* English; French; Spanish. *FEATURES:* 18 chapter links • Production notes.
1974 (PG) 105m/C Jack Lemmon, Walter Matthau, Carol Burnett, Austin Pendleton, Vincent Gardenia, Charles Durning, Susan Sarandon; *D:* Billy Wilder; *W:* I.A.L. Diamond, Billy Wilder; *C:* Jordan Cronenweth; *M:* Billy May.

Frozen

It's difficult to know exactly what to make of this film. The pseudonymous director (Wu Ming means "no name") claims that this story of a Bejing art student who stages his suicide as a work of performance art is based on fact. The work certainly looks like a product of guerrilla filmmaking with some images that are little better than surveillance camera footage. Natural sounds intrude on the material. Even in the more polished scenes, light is unflattering. All of the challenging visual

elements appear to come from the original, not the transfer to DVD. —MM

Movie: 🎬🎬▶ **DVD:** 🎬▶
WinStar Home Entertainment (Cat #FLV5200, UPC #720917520025). Full frame. $29.98. Keepcase. *LANG:* Mandarin. *SUB:* English. *FEATURES:* 8 chapter links • Filmographies • Production credits.
1998 90m/C *CH* Jia Hongshen, Ma Xiaoqing, Bai Yu, Li Geng, Wei Ye; *D:* Wu Ming; *W:* Wu Ming, Pang Ming; *C:* Yang Shu; *M:* Roeland Dol.

The Fruit Is Swelling

Import takes the premise of *Big* and turns it into a soft-core skin T&A comedy. This time, though, the child who grows up over night is an eight-year-old girl and that gives this frivolous material an unsavory edge. The DVD looks and sounds about the same as a VHS tape of a low-budget original. —MM *AKA:* Mi Tao Cheng Shu Shi.

Movie: woof **DVD:** 🎬
Tai Seng Video Marketing (Cat #DVD-018, UPC #601643524146). Widescreen letterboxed. Dolby Digital Mono. $29.98. Jewel case. *LANG:* Cantonese; Mandarin. *SUB:* Chinese; English; Japanese; Korean; Bahasa. *FEATURES:* 19 chapter links.
1997 90m/C *HK* Elvis Tsui, Chung Chun, Wong She Key.

The Fugitive

Exciting big-screen version of the '60s TV series has the same basic storyline: Dr. Richard Kimble's (Ford) wife is murdered and he's implicated. He goes on the lam to find the real killer, the mysterious one-armed man. Lots of mystery and action, particularly a spectacular train/bus crash sequence, keep the tension high. Due to illness, Richard Jordan was replaced by Krabbe after production had begun. Alec Baldwin was originally slated to star as Kimble, but backed out and Ford was cast. Sound familiar? Ford also replaced Baldwin as Jack Ryan in *Patriot Games*. A lot of DVD fans ended up with this disc as a free item when they purchased their player. It's a good one to have in the collection, and can be used to show off your entire system to its fullest. The colors and blacks are super accurate and the contrast seems to be as intense as it can be without adding harshness. The sound is also terrific and there is plenty going on throughout the film on the rear channels, as well as a loud bass track, which is also very deep and very clean. —JO

Movie: 🎬🎬🎬▶ **DVD:** 🎬🎬🎬🎬
Warner Home Video, Inc. (Cat #21000, UPC #085391210026). Widescreen (1.85) anamorphic. Dolby Digital 5.1; Stereo. $24.98. Snapper. *LANG:* English; French. *SUB:* English; Spanish; French. *CAP:* English. *FEATURES:* 2 chapter links • Production notes.
1993 (PG-13) 127m/C Harrison Ford, Tommy Lee Jones, Jeroen Krabbe, Julianne Moore, Sela Ward, Joe Pantoliano, Andreas Katsulas, Daniel Roebuck; *D:* Andrew Davis; *W:* David N. Twohy, Jeb Stuart; *C:*

Michael Chapman; *M:* James Newton Howard. *AWARDS:* Academy Awards '93: Best Supporting Actor (Jones); Golden Globe Awards '94: Best Supporting Actor (Jones); Los Angeles Film Critics Association Awards '93: Best Supporting Actor (Jones); MTV Movie Awards '94: Best On-Screen Duo (Harrison Ford/Tommy Lee Jones), Best Action Sequence; Blockbuster Entertainment Awards '95: Action Actor, Video (Ford); *NOM:* Academy Awards '93: Best Cinematography, Best Film Editing, Best Picture, Best Sound, Best Sound Effects Editing, Best Original Score; British Academy Awards '93: Best Supporting Actor (Jones); Directors Guild of America Awards '93: Best Director (Davis); Golden Globe Awards '94: Best Actor—Drama (Ford), Best Director (Davis); MTV Movie Awards '94: Best Film, Best Male Performance (Ford); Writers Guild of America '93: Best Adapted Screenplay.

Full Contact

For American audiences new to Hong Kong cinema, Ringo Lam's noir-adventure is one of the great discoveries. While it lacks the polish of John Woo's *The Killer* and *Hard Boiled,* its bubbling energy makes up for technical flaws. The real attraction, though, is a brilliant early performance by Chow Yun-Fat, It's not an exaggeration to say that he's reminiscent of a young Robert Mitchum with that same cocky spontaneity. Here, he's Jeff, a nightclub bouncer and leader of a group that's forced into an uneasy alliance with Judge (Simon Yam), a flamboyantly gay villain, and his equally colorful henchpersons Virgin (Bonnie Fu) and Deano (Franklin Chin). The immediate goal is an armored car heist, but that's just the beginning. Lam mixes several high-octane action sequences with highly stylized visuals, and never lets the pace lag. Like so many other Hong Kong imports, the film is really concerned with complex questions of loyalty, betrayal, and the responsibilities that both entail. The DVD is a distinct step up from VHS tape though the film is filled with flecks and nicks. So what? The film is dark, rough, and grainy, just as it's meant to be. —*MM*
Movie: 𝄢𝄢𝄢𝄢 *DVD:* 𝄢𝄢𝄢
Tai Seng Video Marketing (Cat #DVD-222, UPC #4890391102225). Widescreen. Dolby Digital 5.1 Surround Stereo. $49.95. Keepcase. *LANG:* Cantonese; Mandarin. *SUB:* Simplified & Traditional Chinese; English; Korean; Japanese; Bahasa Indonesia & Malaysia; Thai; Vietnamese. *FEATURES:* 9 chapter links • Synopsis • Cast and crew thumbnail biographies • 3 trailers.
1992 99m/C *HK* Chow Yun-Fat, Anthony Wong, Simon Yam, Bonnie Fu, Franklin Chin, Ann Bridgewater, Chan Chi Leung; *D:* Ringo Lam.

Full Metal Jacket

Savage Vietnam War epic follows a group of young men as they pass through Marine basic training and then fight at the onset of the Tet offensive. First half of the film is the most realistic bootcamp sequence ever filmed. Ermey is riveting as the brutal D.I. who turns men into killers. Episodic and unfocused but extremely powerful, the film is based on the novel by Gustav Hasford, who also coscripted. DVD exaggerates Kubrick's grainy film stock, but is still very sharp. The blacks are true and there is actually less grain in the darker areas. Artifacts are minimal. Colors are also very good with only slight red bleed. Contrast and brightness levels are good. There's no Surround, but the mono track is clear and its realistic sound at times gives Kubrick's elaborate cinematography a semi-documentary feel. Far better than the VHS tape and at least a small step above the laserdisc. —*JO*
Movie: 𝄢𝄢𝄢► *DVD:* 𝄢𝄢►
Warner Home Video, Inc. (Cat #17371, UPC #085391737124). Full frame. Mono. $24.98. Snapper. *LANG:* English; French. *SUB:* French. *CAP:* English. *FEATURES:* Dual-layered RSDL • 39 chapter links • Theatrical trailer. Also available as part of the "Stanley Kubrick Collection" 7-DVD box set ($149.98).
1987 (R) 116m/C Matthew Modine, R. Lee Ermey, Vincent D'Onofrio, Adam Baldwin, Dorian Harewood, Arliss Howard, Kevyn Major Howard, Ed O'Ross, John Terry, Jon Stafford, Marcus D'Amico, Kieron Jecchinis, Bruce Boa, Kirk Taylor, Tim Colceri, Ian Tyler, Gary Landon Mills, Sal Lopez, Ngoc Le, Peter Edmund, Tan Hung Francione, Leanne Hong, Costas Dino Chimona; *D:* Stanley Kubrick; *W:* Stanley Kubrick, Michael Herr, Gustav Hasford; *C:* Doug Milsome; *M:* Abigail Mead. *AWARDS: NOM:* Academy Awards '87: Best Adapted Screenplay.

The Full Monty

Unemployed Yorkshire steel workers decide to earn some money by transforming themselves into male strippers. When Gaz (Carlyle) notices the local women lining up to see the Chippendale dancers, he persuades his middle-aged, overweight, pallid pals to join in. Throughout, the humor is sharp and fueled with subtle social criticism. The film is as concerned with economics as it is with sex, though solid performances from the ensemble cast keep the commentary from becoming preachy. Compared to VHS tape, the DVD image brings perhaps a bit more sharpness to details and more brightness to color. Differences between the U.K. and U.S. English soundtracks are not significant in most scenes. —*MM*
Movie: 𝄢𝄢𝄢 *DVD:* 𝄢𝄢𝄢
Twentieth Century Fox Home Entertainment (Cat #4111851, UPC #0861262118 517). Widescreen (1.85:1) letterboxed. Dolby Digital Surround Stereo. $29.98. Keepcase. *LANG:* English (U.S. theatrical version); English; French. *SUB:* English U.S.; English U.K.; Spanish. *CAP: FEATURES:* 22 chapter links • Theatrical trailer • Cast and crew thumbnail biographies in liner notes.

1996 (R) 90m/C *GB* Robert Carlyle, Tom Wilkinson, Mark Addy, Steve Huison, William Snape, Paul Barber, Hugo Speer, Lesley Sharp, Emily Woof, Deirdre Costello; *D:* Peter Cattaneo; *W:* Simon Beaufoy; *C:* John de Borman; *M:* Anne Dudley. *AWARDS:* Academy Awards '97: Best Original Musical/Comedy Score; British Academy Awards '97: Best Actor (Carlyle), Best Film, Best Supporting Actor (Wilkinson); Screen Actors Guild Award '97: Cast; *NOM:* Academy Awards '97: Best Director (Cattaneo), Best Original Screenplay, Best Picture; Australian Film Institute '98: Best Foreign Film; British Academy Awards '97: Best Director (Cattaneo), Best Film Editing, Best Original Screenplay, Best Sound, Best Supporting Actor (Addy), Best Supporting Actress (Sharp), Best Score; Golden Globe Awards '98: Best Film—Musical/Comedy; MTV Movie Awards '98: Best Dance Sequence (Cast); Writers Guild of America '97: Best Original Screenplay.

Full Moon in Paris

Louise (Ogier) moves out of her lover's (Karyo) apartment to experience the freedom of Paris. Through a series of random encounters, she finds that what she hoped for is not what she really wanted. Rohmer directs this installment of his "comedies and proverbs" series with typically understated wit and perception. Ogier is a sexy, gamine-faced heroine. With all of Rohmer's work, the focus is on a few middle-class characters and their everyday world so flashy visuals are not the DVD's primary appeal. On this one, the picture is sharp, particularly in the nocturnal interiors, with occasionally fuzzy reds prominent in some costumes. Sound is all right. —*MM AKA:* Les Nuits de la Pleine.
Movie: 𝄢𝄢𝄢 *DVD:* 𝄢𝄢𝄢
20th Century Fox (Cat #FLV5099, UPC #720917509921). Full frame. Keepcase. *LANG:* French. *SUB:* English. *FEATURES:* 6 chapter links • Production credits • Filmographies and awards for Ogier, Karyo, Luchini, Rohmer.
1984 (R) 101m/C *FR* Pascale Ogier, Tcheky Karyo, Fabrice Luchini; *D:* Eric Rohmer; *W:* Eric Rohmer; *C:* Renato Berta. *AWARDS:* Venice Film Festival '84: Best Actress (Ogier).

Full Throttle

Curious coming-of-age import is set in the world of motorcycle racing. Joe (Andy Lau) loves to ride but an accident forces him to reconsider that and to think more seriously about his girlfriend Yee (Gigi Leung). At the same time, his friend David (David Ng) is becoming more successful on the circuit. Director Derek Yee Tung Sing gives the nighttime road races a bracing sense of immediacy. Though the DVD image suffers in those long scenes, the grainy yellow light is entirely appropriate. Sound is particularly strong there, too. The pace flags in the domestic scenes, but the film avoids many of the genre's cliches. The no-frills disc lacks even chapter breaks. —*MM*

Movie: 🎬🎬▶ **DVD:** 🎬🎬
Tai Seng Video Marketing (Cat #DVD-004). Widescreen letterboxed. Dolby Digital Surround Stereo. $49.95. Jewel case. *LANG:* Cantonese; Mandarin. *SUB:* English.
1996 108m/C *HK* Andy Lau, Gigi Leung, David Ng; *D:* Yee Tung-shing; *W:* Yee Tung-shing, Law Chi Leung; *C:* Chung Chi Man; *M:* Frankie Chan, Roel A. Garcia.

The Funeral

It's difficult for a comedy to begin with an excruciatingly realistic heart attack, but this one manages it. Wabisuke (Yamazaki) narrates the story of the death of his father-in-law, and the effect that it has on his wife Chizuko (Miyamoto) and her family. The patriarch's funeral is the focus for a conflict between traditional and modern cultures in Japan. Though some references may be lost in translation, the comedy cuts across national borders. On DVD, the sound and full-frame image are fine; nothing spectacular but more than adequate for a modest character-based comedy. —*MM* *AKA:* Funeral Rites; Ososhiki.
Movie: 🎬🎬🎬▶ **DVD:** 🎬🎬▶
WinStar Home Entertainment (Cat #FLV5109, UPC #72091751092). Full frame. $29.98. Keepcase. *LANG:* Japanese. *SUB:* English. *FEATURES:* 6 chapter links • Cast and crew filmographies • Theatrical trailer.
1984 112m/C *JP* Tsutomu Yamazaki, Nobuko Miyamoto, Kin Sugai, Ichiro Zaitsu, Nekohachi Edoya, Shoji Otake; *D:* Juzo Itami; *W:* Juzo Itami; *C:* Yonezo Maeda; *M:* Joji Yuasa.

The Funhouse

Tobe Hooper pays tribute to some of horror's best with this original and grimly funny tale. Fans will catch references to *Psycho, Halloween,* and, significantly, James Whale's *Frankenstein.* The premise traps four young people (Berridge, Huckabee, Woodruff, and Davis) in a carnival funhouse with a hideously deformed freak (Doba) and his father (Conway). But...who are the good guys and who are the bad guys? That's the point of Larry Block's script. John Beal's music and makeup by Rick Baker and Craig Reardon add a lot. No, it's not as intense as *Texas Chainsaw*—few movies are—but it does just about everything you could ask of a good fright flick. The picture is clear, but quite dark at times. (We learn from the Production Notes that Hooper shot some of the interiors using only flashlights.) While there is a lot of Surround action from the 2-channel mix, the sound is uneven, going from loud to soft without warning. —*MM/ML*
Movie: 🎬🎬🎬 **DVD:** 🎬🎬▶
Goodtimes Entertainment (Cat #81043, UPC #018713810434). Widescreen (2.35:1) letterboxed. Dolby Digital Stereo. $14.99. Keepcase. *LANG:* English. *SUB:* French; Spanish. *CAP:* English. *FEATURES:* Production notes.

1981 (R) 96m/C Elizabeth Berridge, Shawn Carson, Cooper Huckabee, Largo Woodruff, Sylvia Miles, Miles Chapin, Kevin Conway, William Finley, Wayne Doba; *D:* Tobe Hooper; *W:* Larry Block; *C:* Andrew Laszlo; *M:* John Beal.

Funny Farm

New York sportswriter Andy Farmer (Chase) quits his job and heads to Vermont with wife Elizabeth (Smith) in tow. Hoping to become a best-selling novelist, Andy soon finds that life in the country is not quite what he envisioned: the mailman's a wacko, the neighbors aren't much better, and at the local restaurant, parts is parts. The comedy is uneven throughout, with the best scenes coming at the end. The DVD improves on the VHS copy, but only a little. The picture is adequate when brightly lit and close to unacceptable in the darker sequences, where grain also becomes a problem. Colors are reasonably accurate and bleed is minor. Contrast is only a little low, but the brightness levels are O.K. Blacks are true in the brighter scenes and pick up some grain in the dark. Not much use is made of the Surround, but it adds some life to the front speaker mix, and both dialogue and music are crisp sounding with not bad low end. —*JO*
Movie: 🎬🎬 **DVD:** 🎬🎬
Warner Home Video, Inc. (Cat #11809, UPC #085391180920). Full frame. Dolby Surround. $14.98. Snapper. *LANG:* English; French. *CAP:* English. *FEATURES:* 30 chapter links.
1988 (PG) 101m/C Chevy Chase, Madolyn Smith, Joseph Maher, Jack Gilpin, Brad Sullivan, MacIntyre Dixon; *D:* George Roy Hill; *W:* Jeffrey Boam; *C:* Miroslav Ondricek; *M:* Elmer Bernstein.

Funny Games

Working some of the same ground as George Sluizer's *The Vanishing,* this Austrian import is a true chiller. Georg (Muhe), his wife Anna (Lothar), and their young son Georgie (Clapczynski) are vacationing at their lakeside cottage when their peace is invaded by psycho Paul (Frisch) and his sniveling partner Frank (Giering). The family is forced to play humiliating games with the amoral killers. Most of the physical violence occurs offscreen and the overpowering atmosphere of dread is all the stronger for it. In the end, this is one of those rare horrors that scares you days after you've seen it. The DVD makes the most of director Michael Haneke's sharp focus. Even in the night scenes, dark shapes are detailed. Both interiors and exteriors on the lake are exceptionally crisp. —*MM*
Movie: 🎬🎬🎬 **DVD:** 🎬🎬🎬▶
WinStar Home Entertainment (Cat #FLV5055, UPC #720917505527). Widescreen (1.66:1) letterboxed. $29.98. Keepcase. *LANG:* German. *SUB:* English. *FEATURES:* 8 chapter links • Filmographies

and awards for Lothar, Muhe, Giering, Frisch, Haneke • Theatrical trailer.
1997 103m/C *AT* Susanne Lothar, Ulrich Muhe, Frank Giering, Arno Frisch, Stefan Clapczynski; *D:* Michael Haneke; *W:* Michael Haneke; *C:* Jurgen Jurges.

Futuresport

In 2025, Futuresport—a combination of skateboarding, basketball, and hockey, lifted from *Rollerball*—has replaced football. On the day of the national championship, Hawaiian separatist terrorists take the star player, Tre Ramsey (Cain) hostage. Director Dickerson handles the action well enough, but the whole film is derivative. Amazingly, the DVD is able to handle the swoopy skateboarding camera movements without any bothersome flaws. That side of the film is much more convincing than the computer-generated backdrops and effects. Sound is acceptable. —*MM*
Movie: 🎬🎬 **DVD:** 🎬🎬▶
Columbia Tristar Home Video (Cat #03302, UPC #043396033023). Widescreen (1.85:1) anamorphic; full frame. Dolby Digital Stereo. $19.95. Keepcase. *LANG:* English. *SUB:* English; Spanish; Portuguese; Chinese; Korean; Thai. *FEATURES:* 28 chapter links • Theatrical trailers.
1998 (R) 89m/C Dean Cain, Vanessa L(ynne) Williams, Wesley Snipes, Bill Smitrovich, Francoise Yip; *D:* Ernest R. Dickerson; *W:* Robert Hewitt Wolfe.

Gallipoli

Before *Platoon,* before *Saving Private Ryan,* Peter Weir established the key themes and tone of the contemporary war film. His approach here is unflinchingly anti-war. In the end, he says, appeals to duty and glory are empty; destruction, waste, and futility are real. The main characters are Frank (Gibson) and Archy (Lee), Huck and Tom down under, who become comrades in arms at the Australian army's ill-conceived attack on the Turks in World War I. Superbly filmed (by director of photography Russell Boyd) with a haunting score. On DVD, the image lacks the vivid clarity of some newer films, but the widescreen presentation looks much better than the tape edition, and the emotional truth of the story is as strong as it ever was. In a 1999 interview, Weir talks briefly about the production, location work, and script problems, noting how the key to the entire film was the discovery of the famous final shot. —*MM*
Movie: 🎬🎬🎬🎬 **DVD:** 🎬🎬🎬▶
Paramount Home Video (Cat #015047, UPC #097360150476). Widescreen letterboxed. Dolby 5.1 Surround, Dolby Surround (English); Mono (French). $29.99. Keepcase. *LANG:* English; French. *FEATURES:* 15 chapter links • Theatrical trailer • Interview with Peter Weir.
1981 (PG) 111m/C *AU* Mel Gibson, Mark Lee, Bill Kerr, David Argue, Tim McKenzie, Robert Grubb, Graham Dow, Stan Green, Heath Harris, Harold Hopkins, Charles Yunupingu, Ronny Graham, Gerda Nicol-

son; **D:** Peter Weir; **W:** Peter Weir, David Williamson; **C:** Russell Boyd; **M:** Brian May. *AWARDS:* Australian Film Institute '81: Best Actor (Gibson), Best Film.

The Game

Investment banker Nicholas Van Orton (Douglas) is an uptight corporate control freak. He receives a dangerous birthday present from his blacksheep younger brother, Conrad (Penn). It's a subscription to Consumer Recreation Services, a real life-and-death version of a roleplaying game that is designed to tap the hidden emotional and physical resources of the client. His life is overrun with an escalating series of traps and terrors, with the game reaching into every facet of his life. Dark nearly all the way through, *The Game* still looks incredible on this DVD. The picture is extremely sharp and grain and artifact levels very low. Colors are accurate to the theatrical release, and may in fact be a little deeper and brighter, thanks to punchy contrast and brightness levels. Blacks are for the most part excellent with only a couple of sequences allowing a little grain to sneak in. The sound is very lively with incredible ambience and Surround effects. The bass is loud and rumbling without being boomy and the balance between it and the crisp high end seems just right. The dialogue is out front and easy to understand and the music (particularly the "White Rabbit" sequence) is energy packed. —*JO*
Movie: 🎞🎞🎞 **DVD:** 🎞🎞🎞▶
Polygram (Cat #0478532, UPC #044004 783521). Widescreen (2.35:1) letterboxed; full frame. Dolby Digital 5.1; Dolby Surround. $29.95. Keepcase. *LANG:* English (DD5.1; DS); French (DS). *SUB:* Spanish. *CAP:* English. *FEATURES:* 19 chapter links ▪ Talent biographies.
1997 (R) 128m/C Michael Douglas, Sean Penn, Deborah Kara Unger, Armin Mueller-Stahl, James Rebhorn, Peter Donat, Carroll Baker, Anna Katarina; **D:** David Fincher; **W:** John Brancato, Michael Ferris; **C:** Harris Savides; **M:** Howard Shore.

Gargoyles

When it was produced in 1972, this was considered one of the finest films made for television, and it has held up remarkably well. It's a simple horror tale about Dr. Mercer Boley (Wilde) and his teenaged daughter (Salt), who go out into the desert and discover a race of gargoyles bent on conquering the world (etc., etc.). Bernie Casey plays their leader and he has a magnificent rubber monster suit, created by Stan Winston and Milt Rice. A few expected visual flaws are apparent—distortion of a shingle roof and automobile chrome trim—but overall, the DVD looks fine. The box copy claims that it was mastered from a European theatrical version. —*MM*
Movie: 🎞🎞🎞 **DVD:** 🎞🎞🎞
VCI Home Video (Cat #8207, UPC #089859820724). Full frame. Dolby Digi-

tal Surround Stereo. $24.99. Keepcase. *LANG:* English. *FEATURES:* 24 chapter links ▪ VCI previews ▪ Cast and crew thumbnail biographies.
1972 74m/C Cornel Wilde, Jennifer Salt, Bernie Casey, Scott Glenn, Richard Moll; **D:** Bill W.L. Norton; **W:** Stephen Karpf, Elinor Karpf; **C:** Earl Rath; **M:** Robert Prince.

Gattaca

It's a future world where genetic tinkering allows parents to tweak their children's DNA before birth and a caste system of "perfect" humans exists. Vincent (Hawke) dreams of employment with the aerospace corporation Gattaca, so he assumes the identity of the genetically superior Jerome (Law). Soon Vincent is falling for icy coworker Thurman and getting involved in a murder investigation, which could uncover his true identity. Thinking man's sci-fi (read: no spaceships or explosions) along the lines of George Lucas's *THX-1138*. Many lighting effects are used during the film and the DVD responds well under all conditions. The picture is sharp and grain is minimal. Colors are accurate and also punchy when required. There is very little bleed. Contrast is excellent and the brightness levels are very consistent. The 5.1 sound uses its Surround mainly for ambience, which works fine in this intelligent, dialogue-driven film. There is good fidelity and dynamics along with full-range frequency response, enabling both music and dialogue to shine. —*JO*
Movie: 🎞🎞🎞 **DVD:** 🎞🎞🎞▶
Columbia Tristar Home Video (Cat #82469, UPC #043396826496). Widescreen (2.35:1) letterboxed; full frame. Dolby Digital 5.1; Stereo. $29.95. Keepcase. *LANG:* English; Spanish; French. *SUB:* English; Spanish; French. *CAP:* English. *FEATURES:* 28 chapter links ▪ Deleted scenes ▪ Theatrical trailers.
1997 (PG-13) 112m/C Ethan Hawke, Uma Thurman, Jude Law, Gore Vidal, Alan Arkin, Loren Dean, Jayne Brook, Elias Koteas, Tony Shalhoub, Ernest Borgnine; **D:** Andrew Niccol; **W:** Andrew Niccol; **C:** Slawomir Idziak; **M:** Michael Nyman. *AWARDS:* NOM: Academy Awards '97: Best Art Direction/Set Decoration; Golden Globe Awards '98: Best Score.

The Gauntlet

Phoenix cop Ben Shockley (Eastwood) has to escort Gus Mally (Locke), a hooker who's a witness in a case, from Las Vegas, but everybody including fellow lawmen and gangsters is trying to stop them. The violence reaches surreal, almost cartoonish heights. Many of the daytime desert exteriors look rough and grainy, as they always have, most notably in the fast-moving action scenes. Some of the night scenes are so dark you can see little or nothing of what's going on. That's simply the way Eastwood made the film; it's not the fault of the transfer to DVD. For a '70s action movie, it looks good and sounds very good. —*MM*

Movie: 🎞🎞▶ **DVD:** 🎞🎞▶
Warner Home Video, Inc. (Cat #11083, UPC #085391108320). Widescreen letterboxed. Dolby Digital 5.1 Surround; Dolby Digital Mono. $19.98. Snapper. *LANG:* English; French. *SUB:* English; French. *CAP:* English. *FEATURES:* 34 chapter links ▪ Eastwood filmography.
1977 (R) 111m/C Clint Eastwood, Sondra Locke, Pat Hingle, Bill McKinney; **D:** Clint Eastwood; **W:** Michael Butler; **C:** Rexford Metz; **M:** Jerry Fielding.

The General

Keaton's masterpiece is one of the great American films. In plot, execution, pace, humor, and philosophy, its value is undimmed by the years. Keaton is Johnnie Gray, a Southern railroad engineer who, at the outbreak of the war, loves Annabelle Lee (Mack) and his steam engine, the General. A series of misunderstandings leads everyone, including Johnnie, to think that he's unfit to serve the Confederacy, so he's stuck in his civilian job. That leads him into an extended railway chase when Yankee spies steal the General and Annabelle Lee. It's simply some of the most inventive physical comedy that has ever been put onscreen, and, like Jackie Chan, Keaton does all of his own stunts. The DVD looks good but not great with some marks and stains throughout. In visual terms, this is about as good a version as you'll find, but the film is still a prime candidate for a full restoration. Robert Israel's score, written in 1995, is appropriate. The disc also contains two shorter Keaton films, *The Playhouse* (1921), featuring the star in multiple roles, and *Cops* (1922), another chase picture. —*MM*
Movie: 🎞🎞🎞🎞 **DVD:** 🎞🎞🎞
Image Entertainment (Cat #K131DVD, UPC #738329013127). Full frame. $29.99. Snapper. *SUB:* English. *FEATURES:* 29 chapter links.
1926 78m/B Buster Keaton, Marion Mack, Glen Cavender, Jim Farley, Joe Keaton, Frederick Vroom, Charles Smith, Frank Barnes, Mike Donlin; **D:** Clyde Bruckman, Buster Keaton; **W:** Clyde Bruckman, Al Boasberg, Charles Henry Smith, Buster Keaton; **C:** Bert Haines, Devereaux Jennings. *AWARDS:* National Film Registry '89.

The General

Biopic of maverick Dublin crime lord Martin Cahill (Gleeson), nicknamed "The General" for his planning abilities, is one long flashback beginning with his 1994 assassination. Cahill supports his family through various burglaries, making a mockery of the local cops including Ned Kenny (Voight). But Cahill's rise from petty criminal to mobster is noted by the IRA who want part of his take. The performances by the two leads are superb, but the most curious aspect of the film on DVD is the choice of color. It was released theatrically in black and white, and on disc, that version is razor sharp. But for those who demand something more, the film is also available in extremely desaturated color, which really adds nothing to Boorman's (and director of photography Seamus Deasy's) depiction of Ireland. Sound is very good. —*MM*

Movie: 🎵🎵🎵▶ *DVD:* 🎵🎵🎵▶

Columbia Tristar Home Video (Cat #03726, UPC #043396037267). Widescreen (2.35:1) letterboxed. Dolby Digital Surround Stereo. $29.95. Keepcase. *LANG:* English; French. *SUB:* English; French. *FEATURES:* 28 chapter links ⚫ Cast and crew thumbnail biographies ⚫ Desaturated color version.

1998 (R) 123m/B *IR GB* Brendan Gleeson, Adrian Dunbar, Sean McGinley, Jon Voight, Maria Doyle Kennedy, Angeline Ball, Ciaran Fitzgerald, Eamonn Owens; *D:* John Boorman; *W:* John Boorman; *C:* Seamus Deasy; *M:* Richie Buckley. *AWARDS:* Cannes Film Festival '98: Best Director (Boorman); *NOM:* Independent Spirit Awards '99: Best Foreign Film.

The General's Daughter

Military investigator Paul Brenner (Travolta) looks into the rape-murder of an Army captain (Stefanson) whose father is a general (Cromwell) with political ambitions. William Goldman's script tightens up Nelson DeMille's 1992 thriller and director Simon West gives the proceedings the burnished look of Hollywood's best escapism. The DVD is virtually perfect in image and sound. In fact, it looks a bit too good for a story that's set almost entirely on a military base. West's commentary track is dry. —*MM*

Movie: 🎵🎵▶ *DVD:* 🎵🎵🎵

Paramount Home Video (Cat #32903, UPC #097363290377). Widescreen anamorphic. Dolby Digital 5.1 Surround Stereo; Dolby Digital Surround Stereo. $29.99. Keepcase. *LANG:* English; French. *SUB:* English. *FEATURES:* 17 chapter links ⚫ 4 deleted scenes ⚫ Commentary: Simon West ⚫ "Making of" featurette ⚫ Trailers.

1999 (R) 116m/C John Travolta, Madeleine Stowe, James Cromwell, Timothy Hutton, James Woods, Leslie Stefanson, Clarence Williams III, Daniel von Bargen, Boyd Kestner, Mark Boone Jr., John Beasley, Peter Weireter, John Benjamin Hickey, Rick Dial, Brad Beyer; *D:* Simon West; *W:* William Goldman, Christopher Bertolini; *C:* Peter Menzies Jr.; *M:* Carter Burwell.

Gentleman's Agreement

Newly arrived in New York, magazine writer Phil Green (Peck) researches an article on anti-Semitism by pretending to be Jewish. The impersonation affects his life in unexpected ways, threatening personal relationships. Controversial in its day, the film was one of Hollywood's first attempts to deal with social issues. Now its stiffness is most apparent in the story structure. In visual terms, though, the DVD shows off some of the best black-and-white photography that studios could achieve when they used it for "serious" subjects. It has a rich texture that color film of the time could not touch. The monaural sound is fine. —*MM*

Movie: 🎵🎵🎵 *DVD:* 🎵🎵🎵

Twentieth Century Fox Home Entertainment (Cat #4112748, UPC #086162127 489). Full frame. $29.98. Keepcase. *LANG:* English; French. *SUB:* Spanish. *CAP:* English. *FEATURES:* 13 chapter links ⚫ Theatrical trailer ⚫ Theatrical trailer for *All About Eve*.

1947 118m/B Gregory Peck, Dorothy McGuire, John Garfield, Celeste Holm, Anne Revere, June Havoc, Albert Dekker, Jane Wyatt, Dean Stockwell, Nicholas Joy; *D:* Elia Kazan; *W:* Moss Hart; *C:* Arthur C. Miller; *M:* Alfred Newman. *AWARDS:* Academy Awards '47: Best Director (Kazan), Best Picture, Best Supporting Actress (Holm); Golden Globe Awards '48: Best Director (Kazan), Best Film—Drama, Best Supporting Actress (Holm); New York Film Critics Awards '47: Best Director (Kazan), Best Film; *NOM:* Academy Awards '47: Best Actor (Peck), Best Actress (McGuire), Best Film Editing, Best Screenplay, Best Supporting Actress (Revere).

George Balanchine's The Nutcracker

The filmed version of the New York City Ballet stage production is dreary stuff. In the opening credits, the camera moves through a pop-up proscenium arch, warning viewers that the film is never going to leave the theatre. It's the worst of both media. The immediacy of a live presentation is lost, and the camera is trapped in the narrow limits of the stage. Worse still, the entire production appears to have been lit by one 25-watt bulb. Somehow, the DVD seems slightly brighter than the theatrical presentation, but even so, the medium cannot improve what isn't there. —*MM* *AKA:* The Nutcracker.

Movie: woof *DVD:* woof

Warner Home Video, Inc. (Cat #13000, UPC #085391300021). Full frame; widescreen letterboxed. Dolby Digital Surround; Dolby Digital Mono. $24.98. Snapper. *LANG:* English; French; Spanish. *SUB:* English; French; Spanish. *CAP:* English. *FEATURES:* Cast and crew thumbnail biographies ⚫ Production notes ⚫ Theatrical trailer ⚫ 30 chapter links.

1993 (G) 93m/C Macaulay Culkin, Jessica Lynn Cohen, Bart Robinson Cook, Darci Kistler, Damian Woetzel, Kyra Nichols, Wendy Whelan, Gen Horiuchi, Margaret Tracey; *D:* Emile Ardolino; *W:* Susan Cooper; *C:* Ralf Bode; *Nar:* Kevin Kline.

George of the Jungle

The '60s cartoon hero makes a hugely successful transition to live-action with Fraser starring as the clumsy jungle hero. While on safari, socialite Ursula (Mann) falls in love with George and takes him back to San Francisco, leaving behind obnoxious fiance Lyle (Church). But when poachers capture George's "brother" Ape (voice of Cleese), he returns to save the day. Fraser is an appealing lead and the script is sweetly funny while retaining creator Ward's smart subversive edge. The stunts and effects are more impressive than you'd expect from a cartoon adaptation. The DVD image is perfectly clear and the sound is strong, but why no widescreen, even as an option? —*MM*

Movie: 🎵🎵🎵 *DVD:* 🎵🎵🎵

Buena Vista Home Entertainment (Cat #13213). Full frame. Dolby Digital Stereo. $29.99. Clamshell. *LANG:* English; French; Spanish. *SUB:* English; French; Spanish. *CAP:* English. *FEATURES:* Theatrical trailers ⚫ 19 chapter links.

1997 (PG) 91m/C Brendan Fraser, Leslie Mann, Thomas Haden Church, Holland Taylor, Richard Roundtree, Greg Cruttwell, Abraham Benrubi, John Bennett Perry, Kelly Miller; *D:* Sam Weisman; *W:* Dana Olson, Audrey Wells; *C:* Thomas Ackerman; *M:* Marc Shaiman; *V:* John Cleese; *Nar:* Keith Scott.

Georgia

Of all the challenging, unattractive roles she has played, Sadie may be Ms. Leigh's most irritating. She's a raccoon-eyed drunken drug-addled no-talent singer who must live in the shadow of her more successful and conventional sister Georgia (Winningham). Director Grosbard aims for a gritty, naturalistic look in image and sound, and the DVD re-creates it accurately, down to the last gob of mascara. Even with the widescreen transfer, most interiors are claustrophobic. Both women do their own singing. (Screenwriter Turner is Leigh's mother.) —*MM*

Movie: 🎵🎵🎵 *DVD:* 🎵🎵▶

Buena Vista Home Entertainment (Cat #17600, UPC #717951003362). Widescreen (1.85:1) letterboxed. Dolby Digital Surround Stereo. $29.99. Keepcase. *LANG:* English; French. *CAP:* English. *FEATURES:* 20 chapter links.

1995 (R) 117m/C Jennifer Jason Leigh, Mare Winningham, Ted Levine, Max Perlich, John Doe, John C. Reilly, Jimmy Witherspoon; *D:* Ulu Grosbard; *W:* Barbara Turner; *C:* Jan Kiesser. *AWARDS:* Independent Spirit Awards '96: Best Supporting Actress (Winningham); Montreal World Film Festival '95: Best Actress (Leigh), Best Film; New York Film Critics Awards '95: Best Actress (Leigh); *NOM:* Academy Awards '95: Best Supporting Actress (Winningham); Independent Spirit Awards '96: Best Actress (Leigh), Best Director (Grosbard), Best Supporting Actor (Perlich); Screen Actors Guild Award '95: Best Supporting Actress (Winningham).

Geronimo: An American Legend

Well-intentioned revisionist history is slow, stodgy, and emotionally flat. The narrator is young Army officer Gatewood (Patric), whose division is to round up the renegade Apaches led by Geronimo (Studi), whom, naturally, Gatewood comes to admire. The movie stops about every ten minutes for one character to say how much he respects another. As a General and a wily scout, Hackman and Duvall steal any scene they're in. The DVD accurately re-creates director Hill's curious visual choices of deep sepia and ochre tints. His heavy-handed use of music is equally blatant on disc. —MM

Movie: 🎞🎞▶ **DVD:** 🎞🎞
Columbia Tristar Home Video (Cat #58709, UPC #043396587090). Widescreen (2.35:1) letterboxed; full frame. Dolby Digital 5.1 Surround Stereo; Dolby Digital Stereo. $28.95. Keepcase. *LANG:* English; French. *SUB:* English; French. *FEATURES:* 28 chapter links ▪ Theatrical trailer.
1993 (PG-13) 115m/C Wes Studi, Jason Patric, Robert Duvall, Gene Hackman, Matt Damon, Rodney A. Grant, Kevin Tighe, Carlos Palomino, Stephen McHattie; **D:** Walter Hill; **W:** John Milius, Larry Gross; **C:** Lloyd Ahern; **M:** Ry Cooder. *AWARDS: NOM:* Academy Awards '93: Best Sound.

Get Shorty

Low-level Miami loan shark and film buff Chili Palmer (Travolta) heads to Hollywood via Las Vegas, looking for a deadbeat drycleaner (Paymer) and a grade-Z movie producer (Hackman) who owes Vegas $150,000. Aided by a B-movie scream-queen (Russo), Palmer is pitted against a variety of shady Hollywood-types, including an egomaniacal star (DeVito), while trying to get into showbiz himself. Snappy scripting and performances finally do screen justice to an Elmore Leonard novel. DeVito, with the smaller title role, was originally cast as Chili Palmer, a role Travolta twice turned down until the ubiquitous Quentin Tarantino advised him to take it. The DVD is an improvement over the previous laserdisc and VHS editions. The picture is very sharp and has no problem with grain or artifacts. Colors are accurate and strong with practically no bleed. Contrast is excellent and the image stands out with a good feeling of depth. Brightness is also excellent. Blacks are true with no grain. The sound is very good and there is much in the way of ambience on the Surround tracks. Imaging and space are very good and the mix very lively. —JO

Movie: 🎞🎞🎞 **DVD:** 🎞🎞🎞▶
MGM Home Entertainment (Cat #906036, UPC #027616603692). Widescreen (1.85:1) anamorphic; full frame. Dolby Digital 5.1; Dolby Surround. $24.98. Snapper. *LANG:* English; French; Spanish. *SUB:* English; French; Spanish. *CAP:* English. *FEATURES:* 46 chapter links.
1995 (R) 105m/C John Travolta, Gene Hackman, Danny DeVito, Rene Russo, Dennis Farina, Delroy Lindo, David Paymer, James Gandolfini; *Cameos:* Bette Midler, Harvey Keitel, Penny Marshall; **D:** Barry Sonnenfeld; **W:** Scott Frank; **C:** Don Peterman; **M:** John Lurie. *AWARDS:* Golden Globe Awards '96: Best Actor—Musical/Comedy (Travolta); *NOM:* Golden Globe Awards '96: Best Film—Musical/Comedy,

Best Screenplay; Screen Actors Guild Award '95: Cast; Writers Guild of America '95: Best Adapted Screenplay.

The Getaway

McQueen plays a thief released on a parole arranged by his wife (McGraw) only to learn that a corrupt politician wants him to rob a bank. After the successful holdup, McQueen finds out his cohorts are in the politician's pocket and trying to double-cross him. McQueen and McGraw are forced into a feverish chase across Texas to the Mexican border, pursued by the politician's henchmen and the state police. Completely amoral depiction of crime and violence with McQueen taciturn as always and McGraw again showing a complete lack of acting skills. (McQueen and McGraw had a romance during filming and later married.) There is some grain added in this DVD transfer, but still, this is the best the film has looked on home video. The picture is sharp and artifacts are never high enough to distort. Flesh-tones are accurate and the colors are both vibrant and bleed-free. Contrast is very good, giving the film more oomph than earlier editions. Brightness levels are comfortable and blacks are mostly true. The Dolby Digital mono sound is pretty good and delivers both the music and the shotgun blasts with equal intensity, even without the added bass boost even a synthesized 5.1 mix might have brought. —JO

Movie: 🎞🎞 **DVD:** 🎞🎞🎞
Warner Home Video, Inc. (Cat #11122, UPC #085391112228). Widescreen (2.35:1) anamorphic; full frame. Dolby Digital Mono; Mono. $24.98. Snapper. *LANG:* English; French. *SUB:* English; French; Spanish. *CAP:* English. *FEATURES:* 33 chapter links ▪ Production notes ▪ Theatrical trailer.
1972 (PG) 123m/C Steve McQueen, Ali MacGraw, Ben Johnson, Sally Struthers, Al Lettieri, Slim Pickens, Jack Dodson, Dub Taylor, Bo Hopkins; **D:** Sam Peckinpah; **W:** Walter Hill; **C:** Lucien Ballard; **M:** Quincy Jones.

The Getaway

It was a bad movie in 1972 and the remake hasn't improved the situation. Doc and Carol are husband and wife crooks (played by marrieds Basinger and Baldwin). Doc gets doublecrossed and winds up in a Mexican jail; Carol gets a well-connected crook (Woods) to spring her hubby—by sleeping with him and promising Doc will pull off another heist. The robbery's botched, there are double-crosses galore, and the couple go on the run. The stars are pretty but everything's predictable. This is a very nice transfer to DVD with a sharp picture and very little grain. Colors are deep, vibrant, accurate, and free of bleed. The contrast is punchy and the brightness feels comfortable. Blacks are true. The 5.1 sound is energy-packed with excellent low end that combines with the Surround tracks to give

incredible and earthshaking life to all the gunfire. The dialogue is crisp and the score is delivered with good fidelity. —JO

Movie: 🎞▶ **DVD:** 🎞🎞🎞
Universal Studios Home Video (Cat #20269, UPC #025192026928). Widescreen (2.35:1) letterboxed. Dolby Digital 5.1; Dolby Surround. $24.98. Keepcase. *LANG:* English (DD5.1; DS); French (DS). *SUB:* Spanish. *CAP:* English. *FEATURES:* 16 chapter links ▪ Production notes ▪ Cast and filmmaker bios ▪ Film highlights ▪ Theatrical trailer.
1993 (R) 110m/C Alec Baldwin, Kim Basinger, James Woods, Michael Madsen, Jennifer Tilly, David Morse; **D:** Roger Donaldson; **W:** Walter Hill, Amy Holden Jones; **C:** Peter Menzies Jr.; **M:** Mark Isham. *AWARDS: NOM:* MTV Movie Awards '94: Most Desirable Female (Basinger).

The Ghost and the Darkness

Based on the true story of two man-eating lions who killed 130 people and nearly derailed the building of the East African railroad in 1896. Engineer John Patterson (Kilmer) is sent to build a bridge over the Tsavo river, but as African liaison Samuel (Kani) informs him, Tsavo prophetically means "place of slaughter." The workers become convinced the lions, nicknamed "The Ghost" and "The Darkness," are actually demons and, try as he might, Patterson has little luck killing the beasts. Then, legendary big game hunter Remington (Douglas) is called in—but the lions still seem to have the advantage. Lots of crunching bones, slurping blood, and quick cut editing is used to depict the lions' attacks. The DVD presentation is so good that it is almost preferable to the theatrical showing (depending on how many talkers you get to punch out). Colors are vibrant with great contrast and the image is very sharp. The sound is even better with almost constant ambience and good solid bass. The sound is so real that if you close your eyes and just listen to the lions roar, it should scare the hell out of you. —JO

Movie: 🎞🎞▶ **DVD:** 🎞🎞🎞▶
Paramount Home Video (Cat #323507, UPC #097363235071). Widescreen (1.85:1) letterboxed. Dolby Digital 5.1; Dolby Surround. $29.99. Keepcase. *LANG:* English; French. *SUB:* Spanish. *CAP:* English. *FEATURES:* 15 chapter links ▪ Theatrical trailer.
1996 (R) 110m/C Val Kilmer, Michael Douglas, John Kani, Bernard Hill, Om Puri, Brian McCardie, Tom Wilkinson, Emily Mortimer, Henry Cele; **D:** Stephen Hopkins; **W:** William Goldman; **C:** Vilmos Zsigmond; **M:** Jerry Goldsmith. *AWARDS:* Academy Awards '96: Best Sound Effects Editing; *NOM:* Golden Raspberry Awards '96: Worst Supporting Actor (Kilmer).

The Ghost Goes Gear

At the height of the British invasion of the 1960s, virtually every rock group made a movie. If memory serves, this one was never released in this country, and probably wouldn't appear now if it weren't for the popularity of the *Austin Powers* spoofs. The band in question is the Spencer Davis Group, who perform a few non-hits and go to a haunted manor. About the best that can be said is that the DVD image is sparklingly clear. The box copy claims that the disc was made from "the only uncut print known to exist" and it appears never to have been through a projector. For those who remember those days, the film doesn't measure up to *Mrs. Brown, You've Got a Lovely Daughter*. —MM

Movie: ♫♫ **DVD:** ♫♫♫
Anchor Bay (Cat #DV10940, UPC #013131094091). Widescreen (1.66:1) letterboxed. Dolby Digital Mono. $24.98. Keepcase. *LANG:* English. *FEATURES:* 27 chapter links ● Commentary: Spencer Davis and humorist Martin Lewis ● Cast thumbnail biographies.
1966 79m/C *GB* Spencer Davis Group, Steve Winwood, Nicholas Parson, Jack Haig, Arthur Howard, Joan Ingram, Tony Sympson, Sheila White; *D:* Hugh Gladwish; *W:* Roger Dunton, Hugh Gladwish.

Ghost in the Shell

Set in a heavily stylized rendition of the future, this *Blade Runner* of Japanese anime offers a philosophically dense sci-fi story encased in an exciting plot. The animation is breathtaking, so this will be a show-off disc for anime fans. In the year 2029, the evil Puppet Master is able to make almost anyone his unwitting pawn because nearly everyone has been cybernetically enhanced. Hot on his trail is Major Motoko Kusanagi of the Security Police Station 9, a heroine conflicted because all that remains of her original body is a small slice of brain. In a world where the only humanity some people have are their ghosts (souls), where they may or may not be within the shells (or bodies) they were born with, what happens when a ghost exists where it should not? Based on the story by Masamune Shirow, this flick will get you thinking about such matters even as it raises the hair on your neck. The DVD is top-notch, with beautifully rendered video and a powerful soundtrack. Choose to listen to the original Japanese vocals or English, with or without subtitles. The DVD is a substantial improvement of the fuzzy VHS issue from a few years ago. —MB *AKA:* Koukaku Kidoutai.

Movie: ♫♫♫ **DVD:** ♫♫♫♫
Rykodisc USA (Cat #800 635 529-2, UPC #780063552929). Widescreen (1.85:1) letterboxed. Dolby Digital 5.1. $34.98. Keepcase. *LANG:* English; Japanese. *SUB:* English. *CAP:* English. *FEATURES:* 15 chapter links ● "Making of" documentary ● Movie production report.
1995 82m/C *JP* **D:** Mamoru Oshii.

Ghost Story

Though it's generally dismissed by critics for the "stunt" casting of veterans Fred Astaire, Melvyn Douglas, John Houseman, and Douglas Fairbanks Jr., this unconventional adaptation of Peter Straub's novel has built a strong following. It's about four old men who have formed "The Chowder Society," where they frighten themselves with spooky tales. The tales are meant to distract them from the memory of the worst thing that ever happened to them. That was 50 years in the past and now its supernatural consequences are being played out in the present. Besides the presence of four canny pros and Alice Krige's complex, sexy performance, the evocation of small-town New England in winter is so strong that it makes up for the flaws. Most of the literary re-creations in Peter Straub's novel are missing. Curiously, the setting makes for a difficult but successful translation to DVD. The dark rooms filled with heavy leather furniture and lit by small glowing fireplaces are contrasted with bright winter exteriors and other busier scenes of falling snow and moving water. Some detail is lost in the heaviest shadows but that's how I remember the theatrical release. This version is certainly clearer than tape. —MM

Movie: ♫♫♫ **DVD:** ♫♫♫▶
Image Entertainment (Cat #ID4228USDVD, UPC #014381422825). Widescreen (1.85:1) letterboxed. Dolby Digital Mono. $29.99. Snapper. *LANG:* English. *CAP:* English. *FEATURES:* 28 chapter links.
1981 (R) 110m/C Fred Astaire, Melvyn Douglas, Douglas Fairbanks Jr., John Houseman, Craig Wasson, Alice Krige, Patricia Neal; *D:* John Irvin; *W:* Lawrence D. Cohen; *C:* Jack Cardiff; *M:* Philippe Sarde.

Ghostbusters

After losing their scholastic funding, a group of "para-normal" investigators decide to go into business for themselves, aiding New York citizens in the removal of ghosts, goblins, and other annoying spirits. Comedy-thriller about Manhattan being overrun by ghosts contains great special effects, zany characters, and some of the best laughs of the decade. The big gimmick on this DVD is the feature that allows the viewer to hear the commentary by Ramis, Reitman, and producer Medjuck, while viewing silhouettes of them a la *Mystery Science Theater*. The supplemental section is packed with much more, but the gimmick works, for at least a one-time viewing. The image is very sharp (even sharper than the Criterion laserdiscs) and the colors are vibrant. There is no grain and artifacts are rare. Blacks are true and the contrast and brightness levels are excellent. The 5.1 mix also adds a lot when compared to the earlier video edition, featuring more powerful bass, and clean crisp highs. Surround use is not excessive, but it does fine when called upon. —JO

Movie: ♫♫♫ **DVD:** ♫♫♫▶
Columbia Tristar Home Video (Cat #04139, UPC #043396041394). Widescreen (2.35:1) letterboxed. Dolby Digital 5.1. $29.95. Keepcase. *LANG:* English. *CAP:* English. *FEATURES:* 28 chapter links ● Audio commentary ● Deleted scenes ● DVD-ROM and web links ● Storyboards and production photos ● Featurette and trailers ● SFX documentary ● Theatrical trailer.
1984 (PG) 103m/C Bill Murray, Dan Aykroyd, Harold Ramis, Rick Moranis, Sigourney Weaver, Annie Potts, Ernie Hudson, William Atherton, David Margulies, Steven Tash, Reginald Vel Johnson, Timothy Carhart; *D:* Ivan Reitman; *W:* Dan Aykroyd, Harold Ramis; *C:* Laszlo Kovacs; *M:* Elmer Bernstein. *AWARDS:* VSDA DVD Festival '00: Best Use of Menu Features. *NOM:* Academy Awards '84: Best Song ("Ghostbusters").

Ghostbusters 2

After being sued by the city for the damage they caused in the original *Ghostbusters*, the boys in khaki are doing kiddie shows at birthday parties. When a river of evil slime is discovered running beneath the city, the Ghostbusters are called back into action. They must do battle with a wicked spirit or the entire world, or at least Manhattan, will fall prey to its ravaging whims. There's not too much grain on this DVD, but for some reason the picture seems a little soft. The colors, although very rich, do bleed a bit and there are occasional motion problems. Contrast and brightness are very good with some of the effects shots almost blinding. Both the Dolby Surround and the 5.1 tracks are excellent. The Surround on some of the spectral encounters is great even if you don't have 5.1, and overall the sound is very crisp while retaining a good low end. —JO

Movie: ♫♫▶ **DVD:** ♫♫▶
Columbia Tristar Home Video (Cat #50169, UPC #043396501690). Widescreen (2.35:1) letterboxed; full frame. Dolby Digital 5.1; 2 channel; Stereo; Mono. Keepcase. *LANG:* English (DD5.1, 2 channel); Spanish (Stereo); Portuguese (Mono). *SUB:* English; Spanish; Portuguese; Mandarin; Cantonese; Korean; Thai. *FEATURES:* 28 chapter links ● Theatrical trailers ● Cast and crew bios and filmographies ● Production notes.
1989 (PG) 102m/C Bill Murray, Dan Aykroyd, Sigourney Weaver, Harold Ramis, Rick Moranis, Ernie Hudson, Peter MacNicol, David Margulies, Wilhelm von Homburg, Harris Yulin, Annie Potts, Ben Stein, Richard "Cheech" Marin, Brian Doyle-Murray, Janet Margolin; *D:* Ivan Reitman; *W:* Dan Aykroyd, Harold Ramis; *C:* Michael Chapman; *M:* Randy Edelman.

G.I. Jane

The feminist slant is as bald as Demi Moore's head in this flimsy propaganda. Beyond the questionable title—*G.I.* typically refers to a soldier in the Army; the plot concerns Navy SEALs—the film is showily overdirected to a fault. To satisfy a senator's (Bancroft) political ambitions, Lt. Jordan O'Neil (Moore) tries to become the first woman SEAL, despite the best efforts of the misogynistic brass, most notably Chief (Mortensen). At two hours plus, the film affords director Scott many opportunities to indulge his taste for dramatic landscapes, often tinted with odd metallic colors. The DVD handles the visuals with no problems, making it an accurate version of a mediocre movie. Sound could be stronger. —*MM* **AKA:** In Pursuit of Honor; Navy Cross.

Movie: 🎜🎜➤ **DVD:** 🎜🎜🎜
Hollywood Pictures Home Video (Cat #14250, UPC #717951000316). Widescreen (2.35:1) letterboxed. Dolby Digital Stereo. $29.99. Keepcase. *LANG:* English; French. *SUB:* Spanish. *CAP:* English. *FEATURES:* 23 chapter links ● Theatrical trailer.
1997 (R) 124m/C Demi Moore, Viggo Mortensen, Anne Bancroft, Jason Beghe, Scott Wilson, Morris Chestnut, Lucinda Jenney, James Caviezel; *D:* Ridley Scott; *W:* David N. Twohy, Danielle Alexandra; *C:* Hugh Johnson; *M:* Trevor Jones. *AWARDS:* Golden Raspberry Awards '97: Worst Actress (Moore); *NOM:* MTV Movie Awards '98: Best Fight (Demi Moore/Viggo Mortensen).

Gigi

A young Parisian girl (Caron) is trained to become a courtesan to the wealthy Gaston (Jourdan). But he finds out he prefers her to be his wife rather than his mistress. Chevalier is Gaston's roguish uncle, who casts an always admiring eye on the ladies. Gingold is Gigi's grandmother and former Chevalier flame, and Gabor amuses as Gaston's current, and vapid, mistress. One of the first MGM movies to be shot on location, this extravaganza features some of the best tributes to the French lifestyle ever filmed. Score includes memorable classics. When a DVD transfer is done right, the color can be incredible, and this is one of those DVDs. The colors are bright and accurate without a hint of bleed. The picture is also very sharp and neither grain nor artifacts are ever a problem. The contrast and brightness levels are perfectly matched to enhance the color, allowing plenty of details to the subtle shadings. Blacks are also dead-on. There appears to be absolutely no Surround on the Dolby Surround track but the sound is excellent with good dynamics in the music as well as good imaging on the basically stereo mix. —*JO*

Movie: 🎜🎜🎜🎜 **DVD:** 🎜🎜🎜🎜
MGM Home Entertainment (Cat #907482, UPC #027616748225). Widescreen (2.35:1) anamorphic; full frame. Dolby Surround; Mono. $24.98. Keepcase. *LANG:* English (DS); French (mono). *SUB:* English; French. *CAP:* English. *FEATURES:* 36 chapter links ● Theatrical trailer.
1958 119m/C Leslie Caron, Louis Jourdan, Maurice Chevalier, Hermione Gingold,

Eva Gabor, Isabel Jeans, Jacques Bergerac; *D:* Vincente Minnelli; *W:* Alan Jay Lerner; *C:* Joseph Ruttenberg; *M:* Frederick Loewe. *AWARDS:* Academy Awards '58: Best Adapted Screenplay, Best Art Direction/Set Decoration, Best Color Cinematography, Best Costume Design, Best Director (Minnelli), Best Film Editing, Best Picture, Best Song ("Gigi"), Scoring of a Musical; Directors Guild of America Awards '58: Best Director (Minnelli); Golden Globe Awards '59: Best Director (Minnelli), Best Film—Musical/Comedy, Best Supporting Actress (Gingold), National Film Registry '91.

The Gingerbread Man

Savannah lawyer Rick Macgruder (Branagh) falls for a scheming femme (Davidtz) who hires him to have her deranged, stalker father (Duvall) committed. It becomes clear that nothing is clear and plot takes on noirish twists and turns of intrigue and suspense before the cigarette smoke clears. Shakespeare savant Branagh proves he can also master a Southern accent. Hannah, as Rick's mousy partner, surprises with an unusually good performance. Grisham's first original screenplay. Studio Polygram disliked Altman's original cut, replaced his editor, and recut the movie to its own specifications, angering Altman who threatened to remove his name from the film. Though not an Altman masterpiece, sly thriller doesn't fail to entice. The DVD retains all the subtleties of Altman's lighting and excellent use of muted colors. The image is sharp, even in the many dark scenes, and there is no problem with grain and very few artifacts. The colors are accurate to the theatrical release and are well defined with no bleed. Contrast is very good, allowing details to be visible in shadows or extremely dark scenes. The brightness level is very comfortable. The 5.1 sound is also very good with plenty of low end to drive the music and good use of the Surround tracks for environmental ambience and the occasional effect. —*JO*

Movie: 🎜🎜➤ **DVD:** 🎜🎜🎜
Polygram (Cat #4400850492, UPC #044008504924). Widescreen (1.85:1) letterboxed; full frame. Dolby Digital 5.1. $29.95. Keepcase. *LANG:* English. *SUB:* French; Spanish. *CAP:* English. *FEATURES:* 15 chapter links ● Film and cast bios ● Theatrical trailer ● Commentary: Robert Altman.
1997 (R) 114m/C Kenneth Branagh, Embeth Davidtz, Robert Duvall, Tom Berenger, Daryl Hannah, Robert Downey Jr., Famke Janssen, Mae Whitman, Jesse James Jr.; *D:* Robert Altman; *W:* John Grisham, Al Hayes; *C:* Gu Changwei; *M:* Mark Isham.

Girl Hunters

Mickey Spillane does a remarkably effective job of portraying his most famous creation, Mike Hammer, in this rarely seen

mystery. Since he was so involved with the film—he also cowrote and -produced—it's more faithful to the spirit and tone of the novels than any other adaptation. The plot has to do with communist spies, wicked women, and Hammer's missing secretary Velda. The reason the film has been so hard to find is that it really stinks. Mike spends far too much time putting on and taking off his trench coat, and that porkpie hat appears to have been surgically attached to his head. There's very little physical action; it's mostly about people sitting in offices and bars, and talking. At one point when something does happen, Mike leaves New York in a Ford and arrives at his destination in a Thunderbird without explanation. For the most part, the DVD looks sharp, handling the noir-tinged black-and-white action well. It runs into the usual problems with one pin-striped shirt and tweed jacket that sizzle in close-ups. The mono sound is fine. It's a shame the Mick couldn't have provided a commentary track, but then, he probably knows better. —*MM*

Movie: 🎜➤ **DVD:** 🎜🎜🎜
Image Entertainment (Cat #ID6776CQDVD, UPC #014381677621). Widescreen (2.35:1) letterboxed. Dolby Digital Mono. $24.99. Snapper. *LANG:* English. *FEATURES:* 16 chapter links.
1963 103m/B Mickey Spillane, Lloyd Nolan, Shirley Eaton, Hy Gardner, Scott Peters; *D:* Roy Rowland; *W:* Roy Rowland, Robert Fellows; *C:* Ken Talbot; *M:* Philip Green.

The Girl on a Motorcycle

On his commentary track, director Jack Cardiff talks about the hatchet job his film suffered when it was recut for American distribution in 1968. In those days, the story of bored wife Danielle (Faithfull) riding her Harley to see her lover Daniel (Delon) was too hot for stateside theatre screens. Today it would have trouble scaring up a "PG-13" rating, despite the subject matter. The clarity of the print on DVD actually accentuates the film's central problem: The star couldn't ride a motorcycle and the inserts of Ms. Faithfull holding handlebars are completely at odds with the superb helicopter tracking shots of the big bike on European roads. The monaural soundtrack is perfect for Les Reed's delightfully dated score. —*MM* **AKA:** Naked under Leather; La Motocyclette.

Movie: 🎜🎜 **DVD:** 🎜🎜➤
Anchor Bay (Cat #DV10671, UPC #013131067194). Widescreen (1.66:1) letterboxed. Dolby Digital Mono. $29.98. Keepcase. *LANG:* English. *FEATURES:* 20 chapter links ● Commentary: director Jack Cardiff ● Theatrical trailer ● Commercial ● Cast and crew thumbnail biographies ● Stills gallery.
1968 91m/C *GB* Alain Delon, Marianne Faithfull, Roger Mutton; *D:* Jack Cardiff; *W:* Gillian Freeman, Ronald Duncan; *C:* Jack Cardiff; *M:* Les Reed.

Girls of the White Orchid

Naive American Carol Heath (Leigh) thinks she's getting a job singing in a Japanese nightclub, but it turns out to be a front for prostitution run by the Yakuza. Veteran showgirl Marilyn (Jillian) tries to wise her up. Made-for-TV movie has a few steamy scenes that probably didn't make it to prime time. The whole thing is a step up from the Filipino drive-in exploitation of the '60s and '70s, but only a short step. On DVD, vertical lines, noticeable in a stand of bamboo, lose their edges in slow pans. The image ranges from sharp to grainy in the night scenes. —MM AKA: Death Ride to Osaka.

Movie: 🎬🎬 **DVD:** 🎬🎬
Simitar Entertainment (Cat #7581, UPC #082551758128). Full frame. Dolby Digital Stereo. $14.98. Keepcase. LANG: English. FEATURES: 8 chapter links • Filmographies and thumbnail bios of Leigh and Jillian • Production factoids.
1985 96m/C Thomas Jefferson Byrd, Carolyn Seymour, Mako, Ann Jillian, Jennifer Jason Leigh; **D:** Jonathan Kaplan; **C:** John Lindley; **M:** Brad Fiedel.

Girls School Screamers

Seven young women and a nun are assigned to go to the Wells's mansion to catalog the contents after the place is willed to the Trinity school. Séance, ghost, showers, murders—you know the drill. This Philadelphia production has the semi-professional quality found in many low-budget horrors and so it gains nothing in sound or appearance on DVD. —MM
Movie: 🎬🎬 **DVD:** 🎬🎬
Troma Team Video (Cat #DVD9910, UPC #790357991020). Full frame. $24.95. Keepcase. LANG: English. FEATURES: 9 chapter links • Stills gallery • Humorous Troma shorts.
1986 (R) 85m/C Mollie O'Mara, Sharon Christopher, Vera Gallagher; **D:** John P. Finegan; **W:** John P. Finegan; **C:** Albert R. Jordan; **M:** John Hodian.

Girls Unbuttoned

Soft-core Hong Kong fluff follows the romantic adventures of three young women who cannot seem to find Mr. Right.
Movie: 🎬🎬 **DVD:** NYR
Tai Seng Video Marketing (Cat #35344). $49.95.
1993 ?m/C HK Loletta Lee, Yu Lan Hong, Mia Oyi Wu, Yu Mei Yan; **D:** Tai Loy Wong.

Glen or Glenda?

Directorial debut of Wood (who pseudonymously plays the lead) is one of the phenomenally bad films of the 20th century, an integral part of the auteur's alternative canon. It's a quasi-documentary about transvestism interspersed with meaningless stock footage, inept dream sequences, and long static scenes of Lugosi sitting in a chair and rambling semi-coherently. Curiously, the DVD looks fine and it probably sounds about as good as could be expected. (The production is the subject of Tim Burton's Ed Wood.) —MM AKA: He or She; I Changed My Sex; I Led Two Lives; The Transvestite; Glen or Glenda: The Confessions of Ed Wood.
Movie: 🎬 **DVD:** 🎬🎬🎬
Image Entertainment (Cat #ID8578CODVD, UPC #014381857825). Full frame. Dolby Digital Mono. $24.99. Snapper. LANG: English. FEATURES: 16 chapter links.
1953 67m/B Edward D. Wood Jr., Bela Lugosi, Lyle Talbot, Timothy Farrell, Dolores Fuller, Charles Crafts, Tommy Haynes, Captain DeZita, Evelyn Wood, Shirley Speril, Conrad Brooks, Henry Bederski, William C. Thompson, Mr. Walter, Harry Thomas, George Weiss; **D:** Edward D. Wood Jr.; **W:** Edward D. Wood Jr.; **C:** William C. Thompson.

The Glimmer Man

When a vicious L.A. serial killer starts dispatching whole families, N.Y. detective Jack Cole (Seagal) is teamed with local homicide detective Jim Campbell (Wayans). However, since this is a Seagal movie, things have to be a little different. Cole, for example, is an ex-CIA operative who has been convinced by a Buddhist monk to stop killing people and start wearing goofy Nehru jackets and prayer beads. Campbell is a couch potato who cries over old movies (or perhaps he was watching the dailies from this one). After Cole's ex-wife is killed, he's implicated; and then somehow the Russian Mafia and the CIA are brought into the mix. Cole uses his unique brand of non-violence to slash, chop, and impale his way to justice. Predictable when it's not being unbelievable, this could have been called "Hard to Watch." The film would have been a lot more bearable if they just skipped the plot altogether and left in the mayhem. The DVD makes that even more true, as the action scenes are souped-up by the DVD's punchy image and great slam-bang soundtrack. Rent it and hit the right chapter links and you'll keep yourself entertained for 45 minutes or so. —JO
Movie: 🎬 **DVD:** 🎬🎬🎬
Warner Home Video, Inc. (Cat #14479, UPC #085391447924). Widescreen (1.85:1) anamorphic. Dolby Digital 5.1. $24.98. Snapper. LANG: English; French. SUB: English; Spanish; French. CAP: English. FEATURES: 33 chapter links • Theatrical trailer • Production notes.
1996 (R) 92m/C Steven Seagal, Keenen Ivory Wayans, Michelle Johnson, Brian Cox, Bob Gunton, Stephen Tobolowsky, John Strong, Ryan Cutrona; **D:** John Gray; **W:** Kevin Brodbin; **C:** Rick Bota; **M:** Trevor Rabin.

Glitch!

Bonehead burglars Egan and Donmyer break into producer Gautier's mansion, but before they can abscond with his TV, they learn that a hundred starlets are on their way to take screen tests for roles in the upcoming epic, Sex and Violence. Should they take what's behind Door Number Three, or hang around and pass themselves off as Hollywood bigshots? What follows is accurately described by Nickson-Soul as "tasteless, exploitative, full of adolescent humor and sleazily preoccupied with T&A." It ends with a sharp send-up of the "legitimate" movie business, and the closing credits contain lots of Pythonesque bits. On DVD, the image is average, at best, with some graininess noticeable throughout. Sound is acceptable. —MM
Movie: 🎬🎬▶ **DVD:** 🎬🎬
Simitar Entertainment (Cat #7608, UPC #082551760824). Full frame. Dolby Digital 5.1 Surround Stereo. $14.98. Keepcase. LANG: English. FEATURES: 8 chapter links • Filmographies of Dick Gautier and Nico Mastorakis.
1988 (R) 88m/C Julia Nickson-Soul, Will Egan, Steve Donmyer, Dan Speaker, Dallas Cole, Ji Tu Cumbuka, Dick Gautier, Ted Lange, Teri Weigel, Fernando Carzon, John Kreng, Lindsay Carr; **D:** Nico Mastorakis; **W:** Nico Mastorakis; **C:** Peter C. Jensen; **M:** Tom Marolda.

Gloria

Remake of the 1980 film casts Stone as the title character, a gangland moll who reluctantly becomes guardian of a boy whose parents are killed by her low-life boyfriend Kevin (Northam). Most interiors are fine and well-detailed on DVD. Pixels and other distortion are visible in fast-motion scenes. Sound is adequate. Overall, the disc is only a marginal improvement over VHS tape. —MM
Movie: 🎬🎬 **DVD:** 🎬🎬▶
Columbia Tristar Home Video (Cat #2846). Widescreen (1.85:1) letterboxed; full frame. Dolby Digital 5.1 Surround Stereo; Dolby Digital Surround Stereo. $24.95. LANG: English. SUB: English. FEATURES: 28 chapter links • Trailers for both versions • "Making of" featurette.
1998 (R) 108m/C Sharon Stone, Jeremy Northam, Cathy Moriarty, George C. Scott, Mike Starr, Don Billett, Tony DiBenedetto, Bonnie Bedelia, Jean-Luke Figueroa, Barry McEvoy, Jerry Dean, Teddy Atlas; **D:** Sidney Lumet; **W:** Steve Antin; **C:** David Watkin; **M:** Howard Shore. AWARDS: NOM: Golden Raspberry Awards '99: Worst Actress (Stone).

Glory

A rich, historical spectacle chronicling the 54th Massachusetts, the first black volunteer infantry unit in the Civil War. The film manages to artfully focus on both the 54th and their white commander, Robert Gould Shaw. Based on Shaw's letters, the film uses thousands of accurately costumed "living historians" (re-enactors) as extras in this panoramic production. A haunting, bittersweet musical score pervades what finally becomes an anti-war statement. Stunning performances throughout, with exceptional work from Freeman and Washington. The battlefield makes a great subject for a good 5.1 soundtrack, and this one is great. The tracks put you right in the heat of battle, with the chaos all around. The gunfire is realistic and the canons give a workout to both the Surround tracks and the subwoofer. The impressive cinematography is beautiful to look at and the DVD conveys it flawlessly with stunning colors and detailed sharpness. —JO

Movie: ♫♫♫▶ **DVD:** ♫♫♫▶
Columbia Tristar Home Video (Cat #70289, UPC #043396702899). Widescreen (1.85:1) letterboxed; full frame. Dolby Digital 5.1; Stereo. $29.95. Keepcase. *LANG:* English; French; Spanish. *SUB:* English; French; Spanish. *CAP:* English. *FEATURES:* 34 chapter links.

1989 (R) 122m/C Matthew Broderick, Morgan Freeman, Denzel Washington, Cary Elwes, Jihmi Kennedy, Andre Braugher, John Finn, Donovan Leitch, John David (J.D.) Cullum, Bob Gunton, Jane Alexander, Raymond St. Jacques, Cliff DeYoung, Alan North, Jay O. Sanders, Richard Riehle, Ethan Phillips, RonReaco Lee, Peter Michael Goetz; *D:* Edward Zwick; *W:* Kevin Jarre, Marshall Herskovitz; *C:* Freddie Francis; *M:* James Horner. *AWARDS:* Academy Awards '89: Best Cinematography, Best Sound, Best Supporting Actor (Washington); Golden Globe Awards '90: Best Supporting Actor (Washington); *NOM:* Academy Awards '89: Best Art Direction/Set Decoration, Best Film Editing.

Go

At Christmas, a group of young Los Angelenos go out on a wild night of interrelated adventures on the fringes of the law. While Simon (Askew) goes to Vegas, his fellow grocery store clerks Ronna (Polley), Manny (Bexton), and Clair (Holmes) decide to buy some Ecstacy from dealer Todd (Olyphant) and sell it to Adam (Wolf) and Zach (Mohr), but is their creepy pal Burke (Fichtner) a narc who's setting them all up? That is only the beginning of a premise that proves director Liman's first feature *Swingers* was no fluke. Though the influence of Tarantino is clear, this one's an original—fast paced, consistently funny, and unpredictable. It's the kind of movie that plays beautifully on DVD, where the confused can go back to check out key plot details in earlier chapters. Image and sound are top of the line and the disc is filled with extras. You'll want to watch this one more than once. —MM

Movie: ♫♫♫▶ **DVD:** ♫♫♫▶
Columbia Tristar Home Video (Cat #3826). Widescreen letterboxed. Dolby Digital Stereo; Dolby Digital 5.1 Surround. $25.95. Keepcase. *LANG:* English. *SUB:* English. *FEATURES:* 28 chapter links ▪ Commentary: director and editor ▪ Music videos ▪ Deleted scenes ▪ "Making of" featurette ▪ Trailer ▪ Cast and crew thumbnail biographies.

1999 (R) 103m/C Sarah Polley, Katie Holmes, Scott Wolf, Jay Mohr, Desmond Askew, Taye Diggs, William Fichtner, Breckin Meyer, Jane Krakowski, Timothy Olyphant, J.E. Freeman, James Duval, Nathan Bexton, Jay Paulson, Jimmy Shubert; *D:* Doug Liman; *W:* John August; *C:* Doug Liman. *AWARDS: NOM:* Independent Spirit Awards '00: Best Director (Liman), Best Supporting Actress (Polley).

Go West

The Keaton films on DVD vary in quality from excellent to acceptable. These three are some of the best, apparently made from near-perfect originals. In "Go West" (1925, 69 minutes), Keaton plays an unusually poignant character, Friendless, who heeds Horace Greeley's advice and heads for the frontier to find work as a cowboy—literally. Brown Eyes becomes his favorite cow. In "The Scarecrow" (1920, 19 minutes), Buster and his roommate are in love with the same girl. The film contains some inventive mechanical gags and several fast chases. In "The Paleface" (1921, 20 minutes), he's a bumbling butterfly catcher who wanders onto an Indian reservation while evil capitalists are trying to steal the oil rights. A few of the exteriors are slightly over-exposed, but that's not a serious problem. The disc is a fine addition to the Keaton collection. —MM

Movie: ♫♫♫ **DVD:** ♫♫♫
Kino on Video (Cat #K132DVD, UPC #738329013226). Full frame. $29.99. Snapper. *SUB:* English intertitles. *FEATURES:* 26 chapter links.
1925 69m/B

God.com

Hong Kong thriller pits policeman Chan (Koo Tin Lok) against a charismatic Christ-like religious leader whose followers wear a tattoo of a ram and tend to end up dead in mysterious circumstances. The story contains enough bizarre twists to satisfy exploitation fans, and the presence of crafty character actor Anthony Wong is a big help. The DVD is probably not much better than VHS tape because the film was made with the misty focus typical of low-budget imports. Sound is adequate. —MM

Movie: ♫♫ **DVD:** ♫♫
Tai Seng Video Marketing (Cat #DVD-192, UPC #4890391101921). Widescreen letterboxed. Dolby Digital Surround Stereo. $49.95. Keepcase. *LANG:* Cantonese; Mandarin. *SUB:* Simplified Chinese; Traditional Chinese; English. *FEATURES:* 9 chapter links.
1999 87m/C *HK* Koo Tin Lok, Lam Nga Sze, Andrew Lin, Mak Cheung Chin, Emily Kwan; *D:* Ivan Lai; *W:* Lai Kai Keun; *C:* Kwan Chi Kun; *M:* Danny Chun.

God of Cookery

Thoroughly offbeat comedy is largely based on grotesque food and other fun

stuff that's equally off-putting. The God of Cookery (director Stephen Chow) rules the culinary world of Hong Kong and is merciless with all who are beneath him. Of course, he is unseated and finds that his only ally is a disfigured street vendor (Karen Mok) who loves him. The sense of humor seems to be slightly reminiscent of Yahoo Serious, but much of the comedy doesn't cross cultural boundaries. (At least, it didn't for me.) The DVD is generally good with lots of glittering gold sets and backgrounds. Sound is equally bright and sharp. —MM

Movie: ♫♫ **DVD:** ♫♫
Tai Seng Video Marketing (Cat #5024). Widescreen letterboxed. Dolby Digital 5.1 Surround Stereo. $49.95. Keepcase. *LANG:* Cantonese; Mandarin. *SUB:* Traditional Chinese; Simplified Chinese; English. *FEATURES:* 8 chapter links ▪ Cast and crew thumbnail biographies ▪ Previews.
1996 95m/C *HK* Stephen Chow, Karen Mok; *D:* Stephen Chow; *W:* Stephen Chow, Kenneth Tsang.

God of Gamblers

Chow Yun-Fat is Ko Chun, the titular "god" of Hong Kong gamblers and master of all he surveys, until he's hit on the head and suffers amnesia that reduces him to childish innocence. The curious mix of drama and comedy is difficult for many western audiences to appreciate. Further complicating the issue here is a full-frame DVD image made from an original that has seen some wear. The burned-in subtitles sometimes creep partially below the frame. Still, when Chow Yun-Fat turns it on, he's fantastic. Sound is O.K. —MM
AKA: Du Shen.

Movie: ♫♫▶ **DVD:** ♫♫
Tai Seng Video Marketing (Cat #3084). Full frame. Dolby Digital 5.1 Surround Stereo. $49.95. Keepcase. *LANG:* Cantonese; Mandarin. *SUB:* Chinese; English. *FEATURES:* Trailer ▪ 9 chapter links.
1989 126m/C *HK* Chow Yun-Fat, Fui-On Shing, Cheung Man, Charles Heung; *D:* Jing Wong.

God of Gambler's Return

Virtually senseless sequel—Chow Yun-Fat played the title character in the original 1990 film but had nothing to do with *2* and *3* which followed—is a James Bondish mish-mash of elements. Revenge for murdered wife, slapstick, and spaghetti-western gunplay all have their moments. The plot, such as it is, pits the God of Gamblers against the Devil of Gamblers (Wu Hsin Kuo). Hilarious "hex" errors abound in the subtitles. The DVD appears to have been made from a worn print. It's grainy, pale, and dinged up throughout. Sound is nondescript. —MM

Movie: ♫ **DVD:** ♫
Tai Seng Video Marketing (Cat #DVD-176). Widescreen. Dolby Digital Stereo. $49.95. Keepcase. *LANG:* Cantonese; Mandarin.

SUB: English; Chinese. *FEATURES:* 9 chapter links.

1994 124m/C *HK* Chow Yun-Fat, Wu Hsin Kuo, Cheung Man; *D:* Wong Ching.

Godmoney

Nathan (Rodney) is a New York street kid who tries to clean up his life of drugs and crime by moving to the Los Angeles suburbs where he is recruited by Matthew (Field), a dealer who tries to get him back into his old ways. Director Doane's debut made an impression on the festival circuit, and it deserves its reputation. Despite a background in music videos, he is able to tell a coherent story about interesting characters without letting style overpower substance. On his occasionally hesitant commentary track, he reveals himself to have more enthusiasm than experience or expertise. The main visual flaw on the DVD is a set of blinds that create distracting semi-circular patterns in several scenes. Some shots are intentionally out of focus and distorted, but most of the film looks better than its shoestring budget would suggest. —*MM*

Movie: 🎬🎬 *DVD:* 🎬🎬🎬
Image Entertainment (Cat #OVED6868 DVD, UPC #014381686821). Widescreen (1.85:1) letterboxed. Dolby Digital Surround Stereo. $24.99. Snapper. *LANG:* English. *FEATURES:* 18 chapter links • Commentary: Darren Doane • Spoof commentary track by Doane and producer Ken Daurio • 3 deleted scenes • 4 music videos • "Making of" featurette • Gag reel • Location walk-through with Doane • First 12 minutes of original filming attempt • Theatrical trailer.

1999 (R) 99m/C Rick Rodney, Bobby Field, Christi Allen; *D:* Darren Doane; *W:* Darren Doane, Sean Atkins, Sean Nelson; *M:* Nicholas Rivera.

Gods and Monsters

Although British director James Whale (McKellen) had a varied (if short) Hollywood career in the '30s and '40s, his name rested on his Universal horror films: *The Invisible Man, Frankenstein,* and *The Bride of Frankenstein.* Now long-retired and suffering from ill-health, the openly gay Whale lives quietly in L.A. with his protective housekeeper, Hanna (Redgrave). Whale does enjoy the company of his new gardener—hunky, hetero ex-Marine Clayton Boone (Fraser)—but a stroke has left the director with a confusing sense of reality—returning him to his soldiering days in WWI and *Frankenstein* re-creations. Brilliant performance from McKellen, with solid support from Fraser and Redgrave. The DVD transfer is pretty good with decent sharpness and not much grain. It handles blacks very well and even in some flashback scenes where lighting flashes, the blacks remain true and the high-contrast lines are detailed and undistorted. Colors are accurate and bleed rarely enters the picture. The Dolby Surround is excellent, with clean full fidelity, and good dynamics featuring crisp highs and nicely handled bass tones. The Surround track itself is very limited. I very rarely make it through a commentary all in one sitting, but this one is an exception. Condon speaks both intelligently and enthusiastically, having no problem holding your interest. —*JO*

Movie: 🎬🎬🎬 *DVD:* 🎬🎬🎬
Universal Studios Home Video (Cat #20584, UPC #025192058424). Widescreen (2.35:1) anamorphic. Dolby Surround. $34.98. Keepcase. *LANG:* English. *CAP:* English. *FEATURES:* 18 chapter links • Commentary: Bill Condon • Theatrical trailer • Cast and filmmakers bios • Production notes • "The World of Gods and Monsters: A Journey with James Whale" • Dual-layered RSDL.

1998 105m/C Ian McKellen, Brendan Fraser, Lynn Redgrave, Lolita (David) Davidovich, David Dukes, Kevin J. O'Connor, Brandon Kleyla, Jack Plotnick, Rosalind Ayres, Arthur Dignam, Jack Betts, Martin Ferrero; *D:* Bill Condon; *W:* Bill Condon; *C:* Stephen M. Katz; *M:* Carter Burwell. *AWARDS:* Academy Awards '98: Best Adapted Screenplay; Golden Globe Awards '99: Best Supporting Actress (Redgrave); Independent Spirit Awards '99: Best Actor (McKellen), Best Film, Best Supporting Actress (Redgrave); Los Angeles Film Critics Association Awards '98: Best Actor (McKellen); National Board of Review Awards '98: Best Actor (McKellen), Best Film; Broadcast Film Critics Association Awards '98: Best Actor (McKellen); *NOM:* Academy Awards '98: Best Actor (McKellen), Best Supporting Actress (Redgrave); British Academy Awards '98: Best Supporting Actress (Redgrave); Golden Globe Awards '98: Best Actor—Drama (McKellen); Golden Globe Awards '99: Best Film—Drama; Independent Spirit Awards '99: Best Screenplay; Screen Actors Guild Award '98: Best Actor (McKellen), Best Supporting Actress (Redgrave); Writers Guild of America '98: Best Adapted Screenplay.

Godzilla

On DVD, this overhyped movie is actually more enjoyable than it was as an "event." It's still a silly monster flick—that's all it has ever been—but disc preserves the carefully detailed special effects without the expectations generated by a no-prisoners ad campaign. Nuclear testing in France has created a giant mutant lizard who destroys all boats, piers, people, buildings, and cities that get in his way. Biologist Nick Tatopoulos (Broderick) is hired to get a fix on the critter, only to realize that the big boy has chosen New York to give birth to his brood. Reno is the French agent out to kill the monster. On disc, all of the big scenes appear intact, even the dark, rainy ones. Sound is fine, too. The film certainly doesn't deserve a place in every horror fan's video library, but it's an enjoyable evening's rental. —*MM*

Movie: 🎬🎬🎬 *DVD:* 🎬🎬🎬
Columbia Tristar Home Video (Cat #23129, UPC #043396231290). Widescreen (2.35:1) letterboxed; full frame. Dolby Digital 5.1 Surround Stereo; Dolby Digital Surround Stereo. $25.95. Keepcase. *LANG:* English. *SUB:* English. *FEATURES:* 28 chapter links • Theatrical trailers • Publicity materials • Commentary: special effects supervisors • Cast and crew thumbnail biographies • "Making of" featurette • Before and after stills • Music video • Photo gallery.

1998 (PG-13) 138m/C Matthew Broderick, Jean Reno, Maria Pitillo, Hank Azaria, Kevin Dunn, Michael Lerner, Harry Shearer, Arabella Field, Vicki Lewis, Doug Savant, Malcolm Danare; *D:* Roland Emmerich; *W:* Roland Emmerich, Dean Devlin; *C:* Ueli Steiger; *M:* David Arnold. *AWARDS:* Golden Raspberry Awards '98: Worst Remake/Sequel, Worst Supporting Actress (Pitillo); *NOM:* Golden Raspberry Awards '98: Worst Picture, Worst Remake/Sequel, Worst Director (Emmerich), Worst Screenplay.

Godzilla, King of the Monsters

A prehistoric reptile emerges from the depths to terrorize Tokyo after he is awakened by atomic testing. In the American version, scenes with Raymond Burr, as correspondent Steve Martin, are inserted into the Japanese action. The premise was borrowed blatantly from Ray Harryhausen's *The Beast from 20,000 Fathoms,* though the effects don't even come close. Still, the film has spawned a series of sequels that range in quality from ridiculous to indescribable, and the famous 1998 big-budget Hollywood remake. This DVD contains just about everything that a fan could want. The print is a bit scratchy and some night scenes are murky, but those are to be expected of any 1950s film. In general, image and sound are excellent and the two-sided disc contains both widescreen and full-frame versions of the film, along with a generous helping of extras. —*MM*

AKA: Gojira.

Movie: 🎬🎬🎬 *DVD:* 🎬🎬🎬
Simitar Entertainment (Cat #7473, UPC #082551747320). Full frame; widescreen letterboxed. Dolby Digital Mono; Dolby 5.1 Surround Stereo. $19.98. Keepcase. *LANG:* English. *FEATURES:* 8 chapter links per film • Trivia game • Art Gallery • Theatrical trailers • '50s movie monster documentary. Also available as part of "Godzilla" 5-pack boxed set (catalog #7603). DVD-ROM features: screen savers, Godzilla website links, printable art.

1956 80m/B *JP* Raymond Burr, Takashi Shimura, Akira Takarada, Akihiko Hirata, Momoko Kochi, Sachio Sakai, Fuyuki Murakami, Ren Yamamoto; *D:* Inoshiro Honda, Terry Morse; *W:* Inoshiro Honda, Takeo Murata; *C:* Masao Tamai, Guy Roe; *M:* Akira Ifukube.

Godzilla vs. Monster Zero

In many ways, this virtually unknown entry is the most impressive of the original series. Writer Shinichi Sekizawa's unhinged plot begins with astronauts

Glenn (Adams) and Fuji (Takarada) rocketing off to the newly discovered Planet X where they find that the inhabitants are struggling against Monster Zero, known to Earthlings as Ghidra, and so Godzilla and Rodan are brought in to fight it, but the treacherous aliens really have other plans. Director Inoshiro Hondo, also in charge of the original, keeps the action moving at a frantic page. On DVD, the color photography is sharp and remarkably clear, revealing the sets and effects in all their '60s splendor. The two-sided disc contains both full- and widescreen versions and abundant extras. —*MM* **AKA:** Monster Zero; Battle of the Astros; Invasion of the Astro-Monsters; Invasion of the Astros; Invasion of Planet X; Kaiju Daisenso; The Great Monster War; War of the Monsters.
Movie: 🦴🦴🦴➤ **DVD:** 🦴🦴🦴➤
Simitar Entertainment (Cat #7477, UPC #082551747726). Full frame; widescreen (2.35:1) letterboxed. Dolby Digital Mono; Dolby Digital 5.1 Surround Stereo. $19.98. Keepcase. *LANG:* English. *FEATURES:* 8 chapter links per film ● Trivia Game ● Art Gallery. Also available as part of "Godzilla" 5-pack boxed set (catalog #7603). DVD-ROM has Godzilla website links, printable art, screensavers.
1968 (G) 93m/C *JP* Akira Takarada, Nick Adams, Kumi Mizuno, Jun Tazaki, Akira Kubo, Keiko Sawai, Yoshio Tsuchiya, Noriko Sengoku, Fuyuki Murakami; **D:** Inoshiro Honda; **W:** Shinichi Sekizawa; **C:** Hajime Koizumi; **M:** Akira Ifukube.

Godzilla vs. Mothra

Mighty Mothra is called in to save the populace from a rampaging Godzilla. Mothra is aided by two juniors who hatch in the nick of time. The hesitant monster moth avoids the fire-breathing saurian until succumbing to the pleadings of the two diminutive Peanut Sisters. On DVD, the special effects and models are even more distinct than they are on tape or on-screen, and that, somehow, adds to the fun of these goofy flicks. The artifacts in night scenes don't really detract. —*MM* **AKA:** Godzilla vs. the Thing; Godzilla vs. the Giant Moth; Godzilla Fights the Giant Moth; Mothra vs. Godzilla; Mosura Tai Gojira.
Movie: 🦴🦴🦴 **DVD:** 🦴🦴🦴
Simitar Entertainment (Cat #7474, UPC #082551747429). Full frame; widescreen letterboxed. Dolby Digital Mono; Dolby Digital 5.1 Surround Stereo. $19.98. Keepcase. *LANG:* English. *FEATURES:* 8 chapter links ● Trivia game ● Art Gallery ● Theatrical trailers. Also available as part of "Godzilla" 5-pack boxed set (catalog #7603). DVD-ROM has Godzilla website links, printable art, screen savers.
1964 88m/C *JP* Akira Takarada, Yuriko Hoshi, Hiroshi Koizumi, Emi Ito, Yumi Ito, Yoshifumi Tajima, Kenji Sahara, Yu Fujiki; **D:** Inoshiro Honda; **W:** Shinichi Sekizawa; **C:** Hajime Koizumi; **M:** Akira Ifukube.

Godzilla's Revenge

A young boy who is having problems with bullies and school escapes to Monster Island where he is befriended by Minya, Godzilla's son. This may be the most overtly juvenile film of the bunch and the effects are equally childish. On DVD, they look fine, however, and the '60s score sounds great. Like the other discs in this series, it comes with many extras. —*MM* **AKA:** Oru Kaiju Daishingeki.
Movie: 🦴🦴➤ **DVD:** 🦴🦴🦴
Simitar Entertainment (Cat #7475, UPC #082551747528). Full frame; widescreen letterboxed. Dolby Digital Mono; Dolby Digital 5.1 Surround Stereo. $19.98. Keepcase. *LANG:* English. *FEATURES:* 8 chapter links ● Trivia game ● Art gallery ● Theatrical trailers. Also available as part of "Godzilla" 5-pack boxed set (catalog #7603). DVD-ROM has Godzilla website links, printable art, screen savers.
1969 70m/C *JP* Kenji Sahara, Tomonori Yazaki, Machiko Naka, Sachio Sakai, Chotaro Togin, Yoshifumi Tajima, Eisei Amamoto, Ikio Sawamura; **D:** Inoshiro Honda; **W:** Shinichi Sekizawa; **C:** Sokei Tomioka; **M:** Kunio Miyauchi.

Going My Way / Holiday Inn

In the first film on this double-feature disc, Bing Crosby plays a progressive young priest assigned to a downtrodden parish. He works to get the church out of debt but clashes with his elderly curate (Fitzgerald) who's set in his ways. In *Holiday Inn* (see separate entry for credits) Bing is teamed up with Fred Astaire and Virginia Dale. The two guys turn a Connecticut farm into an inn that's open only on holidays. On DVD, both look about as good as could be expected for movies of their age. The black-and-white images range from good to very good with only a few surface scratches. Sound, however, varies between fair and good, particularly on *Going My Way*, which has annoyingly noticeable hiss and scratchiness on the soundtrack. —*MM*
Movie: 🦴🦴🦴 **DVD:** 🦴🦴➤
Universal Studios Home Video (Cat #20394, UPC #025192039423). Full frame. Dolby Digital Mono. $29.98. Keepcase. *LANG:* English. *SUB:* English; French. *FEATURES:* 18 chapter links each ● Production notes ● Trailer ● Universal web links.
1944 126m/B Bing Crosby, Barry Fitzgerald, Rise Stevens, Frank McHugh, Gene Lockhart, Porter Hall; **D:** Leo McCarey; **W:** Frank Butler, Frank Cavett, Leo McCarey; **C:** Lionel Lindon. *AWARDS:* Academy Awards '44: Best Actor (Crosby), Best Director (McCarey), Best Picture, Best Screenplay, Best Song ("Swinging on a Star"), Best Story, Best Supporting Actor (Fitzgerald); Golden Globe Awards '45: Best Director (McCarey), Best Film—Drama, Best Supporting Actor (Fitzgerald); New York Film Critics Awards '44: Best Actor (Fitzgerald), Best Director (McCarey),

Best Film; *NOM:* Academy Awards '44: Best Actor (Fitzgerald), Best Black-and-white Cinematography, Best Film Editing.

Going Overboard

Sandler's big screen debut shows just how far he has come. In the opening scene, he admits that "this is a no-budget flick" that he and his pals made because they had access to a cruise ship and several moderately attractive women. The occasional plot concerns waiter Shecky Moskowitz (Sandler) who dreams of becoming a stand-up comic. He often drops the character and speaks directly to the camera. DVD image and sound are correspondingly lackluster. —*MM* **AKA:** Babes Ahoy.
Movie: woof **DVD:** 🦴
Trimark Home Video (Cat #VM7071D, UPC #03139870173). Full frame. Dolby Digital Surround Stereo. $19.98. Keepcase. *LANG:* English. *SUB:* English; French; Spanish. *CAP:* English. *FEATURES:* 24 chapter links.
1989 (R) 99m/C Adam Sandler, Burt Young, Billy Zane, Peter Berg; **D:** Valerie Breiman.

The Gold Rush

Chaplin's most critically acclaimed film may be the best definition of his simple approach to film form; adept maneuvering of visual pathos. The Little Tramp searches for gold and romance in the Klondike in the mid-1800s. Among his obstacles: a blizzard, a bear, a killer, a rogue, a crazed gold miner, and even gravity. Includes the dance of the rolls, pantomime sequence of eating the shoe, and Chaplin's lovely music. The film looks and sounds great for its vintage. Of course, there are imperfections in every frame, but Chaplin's masterpiece has never looked better on video. Print used for the DVD is from the 1942 re-release, with music and narration by Chaplin that wasn't present upon its initial release as a silent feature. Bonus materials will be appreciated by historical cinema buffs. —*MB*
Movie: 🦴🦴🦴🦴 **DVD:** 🦴🦴🦴
Image Entertainment (Cat #ID9179CUDVD, UPC #014381917925). Full frame. Dolby Digital 1.0. $29.99. Snapper. *LANG:* English. *FEATURES:* 15 chapter links ● Interview with Lita Grey Chaplin ● Production photographs ● Production summary ● Chaplin's original scenario, "The Lucky Strike—A Play in Two Scenes."
1925 85m/B Charlie Chaplin, Mack Swain, Tom Murray, Georgia Hale; **D:** Charlie Chaplin; **W:** Charlie Chaplin; **C:** Roland H. Totheroh, Jack Wilson; **M:** Charlie Chaplin. *AWARDS:* American Film Institute (AFI) '98: Top 100, National Film Registry '92.

The Golden Child

When a Tibetan child "whose destiny is to save the world" is kidnapped and transported to Los Angeles, Chandler (Murphy), a professional "finder of lost children," must come to the rescue. The search takes him through Chinatown in a hunt that visits every cliché from the Oriental swashbucklers. The digital transfer to DVD handles the image well, though the effects have been eclipsed by more recent efforts. Murphy is his usual engaging self—though this is not his finest vehicle—and he's the real point, anyway. —MM

Movie: 🎬🎬 **DVD:** 🎬🎬🎬
Paramount Home Video (Cat #019307, UPC #097360193077). Widescreen letterboxed. Dolby Surround Stereo, Dolby Digital 5.1 Surround (English); Dolby Mono. $29.99. Keepcase. *LANG:* English; French (Dolby Mono). *CAP:* English. *FEATURES:* 21 chapter links • Theatrical trailer.
1986 (PG-13) 94m/C Eddie Murphy, Charlotte Lewis, Charles Dance, Victor Wong, Randall "Tex" Cobb, James Hong; *D:* Michael Ritchie; *W:* Dennis Feldman; *C:* Donald E. Thorin; *M:* Michel Colombier.

Goldeneye

James Bond was out of commission for an excruciating six years before *Goldeneye* renewed the British secret agent's license to kill and introduced Brosnan as a dashing new 007. During Timothy Dalton's relatively short turn as Bond in the late 1980s, the owners of the franchise wrongly attempted to update the Cold War hero and lady-killer by making him politically correct. This new Bond who battled drug lords and organized crime bosses rather than Soviet spies and crazed scientists wasn't as appealing as predecessors Sean Connery and Roger Moore, even though he was more respectful of women. It seemed for a while that Bond might be retired. But then *Goldeneye*—though far from the best 007 outing—made a huge step toward setting things straight. It put the series back on its decadent, entertaining path and proves that Russia remains fertile ground for escapist adventure stories, even if the Cold War's end played havoc on the genre. Bond must settle for the villainy of the Russian Mafia conspiring to use stolen weapons against the free world. Many of the action scenes run too long, but a spectacularly impossible stunt sequence begins the fun in high style. A sometimes shaky story is adequately propped up by generous amounts of eye-popping stunts, international intrigue, and sexy women with suggestive names such as Onatopp. The DVD's picture and sound are excellent, but the extras are minimal in this standard edition. Serious Bond fans will prefer the $34.98 Special Edition disc loaded with behind-the-scenes features. Still, the less expensive DVD offers the advantage of widescreen and pan-and-scan versions of the film on dual layers. —MB

Movie: 🎬🎬🎬 **DVD:** 🎬🎬🎬
MGM Home Entertainment (Cat #906035, UPC #027616660359). Widescreen letterboxed (2.35:1); full frame. Dolby Digital 5.1. $24.98. Snapper. *LANG:* English; French; Spanish. *SUB:* English; French;

Spanish. *CAP:* English. *FEATURES:* 49 chapter links • Theatrical trailer.
1995 (PG-13) 130m/C Pierce Brosnan, Famke Janssen, Sean Bean, Izabela Scorupco, Joe Don Baker, Robbie Coltrane, Judi Dench, Tcheky Karyo, Gottfried John, Alan Cumming, Desmond Llewelyn, Michael Kitchen, Serena Gordon, Samantha Bond, Minnie Driver; *D:* Martin Campbell; *W:* Jeffrey Caine, Michael France; *C:* Phil Meheux; *M:* Eric Serra. *AWARDS:* Blockbuster Entertainment Awards '96: Action Actor, Theatrical (Brosnan).

Goldfinger

Ian Fleming's James Bond, Agent 007, attempts to prevent international gold smuggler Goldfinger and his pilot Pussy Galore from robbing Fort Knox. Features villainous assistant Oddjob and his deadly bowler hat. The third in the series is perhaps the most popular. Shirley Bassey sings the theme song. The DVD transfer gives *Goldfinger* a far fresher look than it has ever had and is superior to both the Criterion and the MGM laserdisc releases. The picture is sharp and has no added digital grain, although there is some from the film itself, mainly in detailed long shots. Colors are vibrant and accurate with virtually no bleed. Blacks are perfectly true and free of grain. The image is punchier than ever thanks to the excellent contrast and brightness levels. The sound has never been a high point on any of the video versions, and there isn't much of a change here. Although it can't be called muffled, nothing really cuts through. It really doesn't hinder the viewing of the film, however. —JO

Movie: 🎬🎬🎬 **DVD:** 🎬🎬🎬
MGM Home Entertainment (Cat #906726, UPC #027616672629). Widescreen (1.77:1) letterboxed. Dolby Digital Mono. $24.98. Snapper. *LANG:* English; French; Spanish. *SUB:* English; French; Spanish. *CAP:* English. *FEATURES:* 32 chapter links • Film trivia • Featurette.
1964 (PG) 117m/C *GB* Sean Connery, Honor Blackman, Gert Frobe, Shirley Eaton, Tania Mallet, Harold Sakata, Cec Linder, Bernard Lee, Lois Maxwell, Desmond Llewelyn, Nadja Regin; *D:* Guy Hamilton; *W:* Paul Dehn, Richard Maibaum; *C:* Ted Moore; *M:* John Barry. *AWARDS:* Academy Awards '64: Best Sound Effects Editing.

Gone with the Wind

America's most popular (and overrated) epic looks very good on DVD. Of course, it looks good on tape and conventional broadcast, too. The film has been restored and re-released so often that it ought to be in excellent shape. Compared to VHS, that bright Technicolor is perhaps a bit richer with more depth. The background grain comes from the original and is most noticeable in the big special effects shots. The mono sound is fine.

This is a two-sided disc that must be turned over at the Intermission. —MM

Movie: 🎬🎬🎬 **DVD:** 🎬🎬🎬
MGM Home Entertainment (Cat #906331, UPC #027616611121). Full frame. Dolby Digital 5.1 Surround Stereo; Mono. $26.98. Keepcase. *LANG:* English. *SUB:* English; French. *FEATURES:* 56 chapter links • Trailer.
1939 231m/C Clark Gable, Vivien Leigh, Olivia de Havilland, Leslie Howard, Thomas Mitchell, Hattie McDaniel, Butterfly McQueen, Evelyn Keyes, Harry Davenport, Jane Darwell, Ona Munson, Barbara O'Neil, William "Billy" Bakewell, Rand Brooks, Ward Bond, Laura Hope Crews, Yakima Canutt, George Reeves, Marjorie Reynolds, Ann Rutherford, Victor Jory, Carroll Nye, Paul Hurst, Isabel Jewell, Cliff Edwards, Eddie Anderson, Oscar Polk, Eric Linden, Violet Kemble-Cooper, Fred Crane, Howard Hickman, Leona Roberts, Cammie King, Mary Anderson, Frank Faylen; *D:* Victor Fleming; *W:* Sidney Howard; *C:* Ray Rennahan; *M:* Max Steiner. *AWARDS:* Academy Awards '39: Best Actress (Leigh), Best Color Cinematography, Best Director (Fleming), Best Film Editing, Best Picture, Best Screenplay, Best Supporting Actress (McDaniel); American Film Institute (AFI) '98: Top 100, National Film Registry '89; New York Film Critics Awards '39: Best Actress (Leigh); *NOM:* Academy Awards '39: Best Actor (Gable), Best Sound, Best Supporting Actress (de Havilland), Best Original Score.

Good Luck

Inspirational buddy picture manages to avoid the worst sentimental excesses. Football player Tony Olezniak (D'Onofrio) is blinded in a game injury. He's on a downward spiral and winds up in jail where paraplegic Bernard Lemley (Hines), once Tony's tutor, finds him. Bernard wants to enter a rigorous whitewater raft race and needs Tony's strength to do it. The emotional payoff comes as the two bicker and bond, not from the challenge of the race, which in itself is a change of pace. The DVD looks fine with the expected crisp interiors and exteriors that do justice to the excellent Oregon scenery. Sound is good, too. —MM

Movie: 🎬🎬 **DVD:** 🎬🎬🎬
Simitar Entertainment (Cat #7427, UPC #082551742721). Full frame. Dolby Digital Stereo. $14.98. Keepcase. *LANG:* English. *CAP:* English. *FEATURES:* 8 chapter links • Production factoids • Gregory Hines filmography.
1996 (R) 95m/C Vincent D'Onofrio, Gregory Hines, Max Gail, James Earl Jones, Sarah Trigger, Joe Thiesman; *D:* Richard LaBrie; *W:* Bob Comfort; *C:* Maximo Munzi; *M:* Tim Truman.

The Good, the Bad and the Ugly

Eastwood returns for the final and finest of the spaghetti western trilogy featuring The Man with No Name. Set during the

Civil War, Leone's grandiloquent epic follows the seemingly endless adventures of a trio of dirtbags in search of a cache of gold buried in a nameless grave. The first-ever three-way gunfight depicted on-screen is a thrilling high point. Carefully considered compositions demonstrate why the movie should never, ever be viewed in other than its native widescreen state. From the long-shot expanses of Italian terrain doubling as the American West to enormous close-ups of the actors' faces, every inch of the screen earns its right to be seen. The close-ups are so big and so tight, in fact, that only two eyes and the bridge of a nose fill the frame in the most dramatic shots. Morricone's exciting music is the perfect mate to the visuals and is frequently parodied in contemporary films and TV shows. The score sounds bright, but not shrill, on the DVD—about as good as it's ever sounded on home video. Although the mono soundtrack is adequate, it suffers from a lack of fidelity during canon fire and explosions that are sometimes muffled and too frequently distorted. But that's to be expected from a film of this vintage and doesn't reflect badly on the DVD transfer. Likewise, the beautifully sharp image is marred by the occasional flash or speck that no doubt was present on the film element used for the transfer. That's OK, too, because the movie hasn't looked or sounded this good in decades. The DVD betters the most recent laserdisc by a measurable margin. The bonus footage of deleted scenes is nice to have, but it is not integrated into the film—probably wise since no English soundtrack was ever created for these scenes. —MB
Movie: ♪♪♪▶ **DVD:** ♪♪♪
MGM Home Entertainment (Cat #906729, UPC #027616672926). Widescreen (2.35:1) letterboxed. Dolby Digital Mono. $24.98. Keepcase. *LANG:* English; French; Spanish. *SUB:* English; French; Spanish. *CAP:* English. *FEATURES:* 64 chapter links ● 14 minutes of footage previously unreleased in the U.S. ● Production notes ● Theatrical trailer.
1967 161m/C *IT* Clint Eastwood, Eli Wallach, Lee Van Cleef, Chelo Alonso, Luigi Pistilli, Rada Rassimov, Livio Lorenzon, Mario Brega; *D:* Sergio Leone; *W:* Sergio Leone, Sergio Donati, Furio Scarpelli, Luciano Vincenzoni, Agenore Incrocci; *C:* Tonino Delli Colli; *M:* Ennio Morricone.

Good Will Hunting

Oscar-winning debut effort from screenwriting actors Damon and Affleck gets the full treatment on DVD. Troubled young Will Hunting (Damon) is a janitor at MIT who's also an undiscovered mathematical genius. He is found out by big-shot Professor Lambeau (Skarsgard), who must vouch for Will with the parole board by giving him weekly math sessions and taking him to a therapist to work on his anger. Equally troubled shrink Sean Maguire (Williams) takes on the task and tries to help Will rise above his working-class

roots. But Will does not want to break the ties he has to his friends, including Affleck. On disc, the only blatant visual problem is flashing within narrow stripes on one article of clothing. Beyond that, the South Boston locations are displayed with such sharp clarity that each crumbling shingle and paint-peeling board is distinct. The often claustrophobic interiors are equally authentic-looking and well realized. On the commentary track, director Van Sant and writer-stars Affleck and Damon are relaxed. They mostly stay focused on the production process itself—costume choices, writing changes, acting, technical details, editing choices, the help they received from mathematicians and teachers. (They do not mention the continuity glitches with the blackboard in the opening scene.) They're quick to point out their friends and family who fill the background in many scenes. Damon explains that they actually bought the title from a friend who makes an appearance, and Affleck admits a comic homage to *Menace II Society*. The dialogue is muted almost entirely under their commentary, so you've got to watch the 11 deleted scenes twice to get the sense of them. For anyone seriously interested in the filmmaking process, those are particularly instructive. —MM
Movie: ♪♪♪ **DVD:** ♪♪♪▶
Miramax Pictures Home Video (Cat #14888, UPC #717951000552). Widescreen (1.85:1) letterboxed. Dolby Digital 5.1. $29.99. Keepcase. *LANG:* English. *CAP:* English. *FEATURES:* Commentary: Gus Van Sant, Ben Affleck, Matt Damon ● 11 deleted scenes with commentary ● Production featurette ● Theatrical trailer ● TV spots ● Academy Award Best Picture montage ● Behind-the-scenes footage ● "Miss Misery" music video ● 21 chapter links.
1997 (R) 126m/C Matt Damon, Robin Williams, Ben Affleck, Stellan Skarsgard, Minnie Driver, Casey Affleck, Cole Hauser; *D:* Gus Van Sant; *W:* Matt Damon, Ben Affleck; *C:* Jean-Yves Escoffier; *M:* Danny Elfman. *AWARDS:* Academy Awards '97: Best Original Screenplay, Best Supporting Actor (Williams); Golden Globe Awards '98: Best Screenplay; Screen Actors Guild Award '97: Best Supporting Actor (Williams); Broadcast Film Critics Association Awards '97: Breakthrough Performance (Damon), Best Original Screenplay; *NOM:* Academy Awards '97: Best Actor (Damon), Best Director (Van Sant), Best Film Editing, Best Picture, Best Song ("Miss Misery"), Best Supporting Actress (Driver), Best Original Score; Directors Guild of America Awards '97: Best Director (Van Sant); Golden Globe Awards '98: Best Actor—Drama (Damon), Best Film—Drama, Best Supporting Actor (Williams); MTV Movie Awards '98: Best Film, Best Male Performance (Damon), Best On-Screen Duo (Matt Damon/Ben Affleck), Best Kiss (Matt Damon/Minnie Driver); Screen Actors Guild Award '97: Best Actor (Damon), Best Supporting Actress (Driver), Cast; Writers Guild of America '97: Best Original Screenplay.

Goodbye, Lover

Sandra (Arquette) and Ben (Johnson) are hot 'n' heavy lovers. Jake (Mulroney) is husband to one, brother to the other. Peggy (Parker) has eyes for Ben and works with Jake. Since this is a faux-noir comedy, it's filled with plot twists, betrayal, blackmail, murder, and a fortune in insurance. Two cops (DeGeneres and McKinnon) try to piece it all together. All of the excesses make the result more silly than funny, but it still looks great on DVD. Director Joffe uses bold shapes and colored light to create an almost cartoon-like atmosphere. Sound is fine, too. Recommended for fans of the offbeat. (Joel Coen had a hand in the script.) —MM
Movie: ♪♪▶ **DVD:** ♪♪♪▶
Warner Home Video, Inc. (Cat #15092, UPC #085391509226). Widescreen anamorphic; full frame. Dolby Digital 5.1 Surround Stereo. $19.98. Snapper. *LANG:* English; French. *SUB:* English; French. *FEATURES:* 33 chapter links ● Cast and crew thumbnail biographies ● "Making of" featurette ● Theatrical trailer.
1999 (R) 104m/C Don Johnson, Patricia Arquette, Dermot Mulroney, Ellen DeGeneres, Mary-Louise Parker, Ray McKinnon, Alex Rocco, Andre Gregory, John Neville, Nina Siemaszko, David Brisbin, Lisa Eichhorn, George Furth, Barry Newman, Max Perlich, Frances Bay; *D:* Roland Joffe; *W:* Joel Cohen, Alec Sokolow, Ron Peer; *C:* Dante Spinotti; *M:* John Ottman.

Goodfellas

Scorsese's brilliant look at "wiseguys" is at turns both violent and funny. Henry Hill (Liotta) grows up in the mob, works hard to advance himself through the ranks, and enjoys the life of the rich and violent, oblivious to the horror of his world. Cocaine addiction and hubris ultimately lead to his fall from the heights, but the journey is dazzling from the introduction of Henry's mob pals (De Niro, Pesci)—accomplished by long, impressive shots in and around nightclubs by Scorsese and cinematographer Ballhaus—to the nightmarish conclusion. Oscar-quality acting from the three leads. Watch for Scorsese's mom as Pesci's mom. Many of the themes and cast members were reunited in the HBO series *The Sopranos*. Though the DVD lacks filmmakers' commentary, the image transfer ranges from good to very good. The intense rock soundtrack is stronger in Dolby stereo. Overall, the DVD is probably as sharp as any video version of the film could be, but this is one of Scorsese's best, made for the theatrical screen. The courtroom conclusion loses power on the small screen. As DVD technology improves, a one-sided disc will probably become available. (This one must be flipped over midway through.) —MM
Movie: ♪♪♪♪ **DVD:** ♪♪♪
Warner Home Video, Inc. (Cat #12039, UPC #085391203926). Widescreen (1.85:1) letterboxed. Dolby Surround 5.1 (English); Dolby Surround Stereo (French).

$24.98. Snapper. *LANG:* English; French. *SUB:* English; French; Spanish. *FEATURES:* 32 chapter links ● Production notes ● Cast biographies and filmographies ● 2 theatrical trailers.
1990 (R) 146m/C Robert De Niro, Ray Liotta, Joe Pesci, Paul Sorvino, Lorraine Bracco, Frank Sivero, Mike Starr, Frank Vincent, Samuel L. Jackson, Tony Darrow, Chuck Low, Frank DiLeo, Christopher Serrone, Illeana Douglas, Debi Mazar, Michael Imperioli, Peter Onorati, Beau Starr, Angela Pietropinto, Joseph D'Onofrio, Jerry Vale, Henny Youngman, Catherine Scorsese; *D:* Martin Scorsese; *W:* Nicholas Pileggi, Martin Scorsese; *C:* Michael Ballhaus. *AWARDS:* Academy Awards '90: Best Supporting Actor (Pesci); American Film Institute (AFI) '98: Top 100; British Academy Awards '90: Best Adapted Screenplay, Best Director (Scorsese), Best Film; Los Angeles Film Critics Association Awards '90: Best Cinematography, Best Director (Scorsese), Best Film, Best Supporting Actor (Pesci), Best Supporting Actress (Bracco); National Board of Review Awards '90: Best Supporting Actor (Pesci); New York Film Critics Awards '90: Best Actor (De Niro), Best Director (Scorsese), Best Film; National Society of Film Critics Awards '90: Best Director (Scorsese), Best Film; *NOM:* Academy Awards '90: Best Adapted Screenplay, Best Director (Scorsese), Best Film Editing, Best Picture, Best Supporting Actress (Bracco); Golden Globe Awards '90: Best Director (Scorsese), Best Film—Drama, Best Screenplay, Best Supporting Actor (Pesci), Best Supporting Actress (Bracco).

Gorillas in the Mist

Film follows the life of Dian Fossey, animal rights activist and world-renowned expert on the African gorilla, from her pioneering contact with mountain gorillas to her murder at the hands of poachers. Weaver is totally appropriate as the increasingly obsessed Fossey, but the character moves away from us, just as we need to see and understand more about her. Excellent special effects. As you might imagine, there are a lot of jungle scenes, some of which are very dark, and many of which are full of shadows and contrasty bright areas. The DVD does a great job in delivering the image to video. The picture is sharp and near-grainless throughout. The contrast and brightness levels are important in making sure that all the subtle lighting and different color hues remain distinct, and they do their job. Colors and blacks are true. The dialogue is crisp and out front and the music full and dynamic. The excellent Surround mix enables the viewer to be right in the middle of the jungle by adding enormous environmental ambience. —*JO*
Movie: ♪♪♪ **DVD:** ♪♪♪▶
Universal Studios Home Video (Cat #20421, UPC #025192042126). Widescreen (1.85:1) anamorphic. Dolby Digital 5.1; Dolby Surround. $26.98. Keepcase. *LANG:* English (DD5.1); French (DS). *CAP:*

English. *FEATURES:* 18 chapter links ● Production notes ● Talent biographies ● Theatrical trailer ● Web links.
1988 (PG-13) 117m/C Sigourney Weaver, Bryan Brown, Julie Harris, Iain Cuthbertson, John Omirah Miluwi, Constantin Alexandrov, Waigwa Wachira; *D:* Michael Apted; *W:* Anna Hamilton Phelan; *C:* John Seale; *M:* Maurice Jarre. *AWARDS:* Golden Globe Awards '88: Best Actress—Drama (Weaver); Golden Globe Awards '89: Best Score; *NOM:* Academy Awards '88: Best Actress (Weaver), Best Adapted Screenplay, Best Film Editing, Best Sound, Best Original Score.

The Gospel According to St. Matthew

Perhaps Pasolini's greatest film retells the story of Christ in gritty, neo-realistic tones and portrays the man less as a divine presence than as a political revolutionary, while remaining faithful to the source material. It is still the yardstick against which all other cinematic depictions of the life of Jesus must be judged. Though the box copy on the DVD contains a disclaimer, admitting that this transfer made from less-than-perfect elements owned by New York's Museum of Modern Art, the film is fine. True, some dim interiors lack sharpness and the contrast is too high in some exteriors, but the print is not too scratchy or marred. Overall, it looks as good as any film of its budget and era could be expected to look. The sound is the same; subtitles are clear and easy to read. —*MM* **AKA:** Il Vangelo Secondo Matteo; L'Evangile Selon Saint-Matthieu.
Movie: ♪♪♪♪ **DVD:** ♪♪♪
Image Entertainment (Cat #ID5108WB DVD, UPC #014381510829). Widescreen (1.85:1) letterboxed. Dolby Digital Mono. $29.99. Snapper. *LANG:* Italian. *SUB:* English. *FEATURES:* 10 chapter links.
1964 142m/B *IT* Enrique Irazoqui, Susanna Pasolini, Margherita Caruso, Marcello Morante, Mario Socrate; *D:* Pier Paolo Pasolini; *W:* Pier Paolo Pasolini; *C:* Tonino Delli Colli; *M:* Luis Bacalov. *AWARDS:* *NOM:* Academy Awards '66: Best Adapted Score, Best Art Direction/Set Decoration (B & W), Best Costume Design (B & W).

The Governess

Rosina da Silva (Driver) is a young Jewish woman living in 1840s London. After her doting father dies, she changes her name to Mary Blackchurch to pass as a Gentile and secure a position as a governess with the Cavendish family in remote Scotland. Among her charges are the randy teenager Henry (Rhys Myers) and the spoiled brat Clementina (Hoath). Rosina's free spirit entrances stodgy father Charles (Wilkinson) whom she aids in his obsession with the new art of photography. With a dark room and chemistry, more than photos are bound to develop and soon Mr. Cavendish comes up with a fixation of his own. What begins as a story of a woman adapting to

different surroundings ends up as a history of the first girly pictures. In the end, Rosina's Jewishness isn't that big a deal, leaving that portion of the story a dead end. On DVD, the film looks very good. Black clothes and oppressive dimly lit interiors of period pieces can pose difficult problems for the medium but they're clearly detailed here. Sound is very good. —*MM*
Movie: ♪♪▶ **DVD:** ♪♪♪
Columbia Tristar Home Video (Cat #2845, UPC #043396028456). Widescreen (2.35:1) anamorphic; full frame. Dolby Digital Stereo. $29.95. Keepcase. *LANG:* English; French. *SUB:* French. *CAP:* English. *FEATURES:* 28 chapter links.
1998 (R) 114m/C Minnie Driver, Tom Wilkinson, Harriet Walter, Florence Hoath, Jonathan Rhys Meyers, Arlene Cockburn, Emma Bird, Adam Levy, Bruce Meyers; *D:* Sandra Goldbacher; *W:* Sandra Goldbacher; *C:* Ashley Rowe; *M:* Ed Shearmur.

Grace of My Heart (CE)

Engaging ensemble pop melodrama appears to have been loosely patterned on the career of Carole King. In 1958, wealthy young Edna Buxton (Douglas) defies her domineering mother and heads to New York to become a singer. That doesn't work out, but she changes her name to Denise Waverly and becomes a pop songwriter. Over the next dozen or so years, she's part of just about every major development in rock music and hooks up with a succession of wrong men. Douglas does a fine job (her singing's dubbed by Kristen Vigard), and keeps the whole thing from dissolving into a puddle of showbiz kitsch. Both image and sound are first-rate. This "collector's edition" disc is filled with extras, including a commentary track where director Anders takes an unusually personal approach to the film. —*MM*
Movie: ♪♪♪ **DVD:** ♪♪♪▶
Universal Studios Home Video (Cat #20438, UPC #025192043826). Widescreen (1.85:1) letterboxed. Dolby Digital 5.1 Surround Stereo; Dolby Digital Surround Stereo. $34.98. Keepcase. *LANG:* English; French. *CAP:* English. *FEATURES:* 18 chapter links ● Commentary: writer-director Anders ● Deleted scenes ● "Making of" featurette ● Cast and crew thumbnail biographies ● Theatrical trailer.
1996 (R) 116m/C Illeana Douglas, John Turturro, Matt Dillon, Eric Stoltz, Bruce Davison, Patsy Kensit, Bridget Fonda, Jennifer Leigh Warren, Chris Isaak; *D:* Allison Anders; *W:* Allison Anders; *C:* Jean-Yves Escoffier; *M:* Larry Klein; *V:* Peter Fonda.

Grambling's White Tiger

Made-for-TV based-on-fact story of the first white man to play at Grambling College's all-black football team. As Jim Gregory, Olympian Jenner's a little too old but in his TV-acting debut, Belafonte is fine as legendary coach Eddie Robinson. Given the limited production values and age, the DVD doesn't look bad, but it's nothing special either. Ditto sound. For fans of the cast. —*MM*

Movie: 🎵🎵▶ **DVD:** 🎵🎵

Simitar Entertainment (Cat #7275, UPC #082551727520). Full frame. PCM Stereo. $14.98. Keepcase. *LANG:* English. *FEATURES:* 8 chapter links • Production factoids • Harry Belafonte, LeVar Burton, Bruce Jenner filmographies.

1981 98m/C Bruce Jenner, Harry Belafonte, LeVar Burton, Ray Vitte, Byron Stewart; *D:* Georg Stanford Brown; *M:* John D'Andrea.

Grand Illusion

Jean Renoir's humanistic masterpiece of World War I has not looked this sharp in decades. This restoration is so impressive that it received a limited theatrical release in 1999. A demonstration chapter on the disc shows the steps of the process. For the viewer, though, the proof is in the image and the disc is much better than any tape, particularly older ones that have been around the block a few times. (I wish the DVD had been available when I was writing *VideoHound's War Movies*.) This new image is so detailed that you can now make out the texture of Erich von Stroheim's leather flying suit. Any visual flaws are negligible. Film historian Peter Cowie's commentary is a knowledgeable, carefully written explanation of many of the period details. It has nothing to do with the often frivolous filmmaker's comments that come with most contemporary movies. On DVD, the newly translated subtitles are easy to read. With all the other extras, this disc earns a solid recommendation to any library. One of the very best. —*MM* *AKA:* La Grande Illusion.

Movie: 🎵🎵🎵🎵 **DVD:** 🎵🎵🎵🎵

Criterion Collection (Cat #GRA070, UPC #037429121914). Full frame. $39.95. Keepcase. *LANG:* French. *SUB:* English. *FEATURES:* 17 chapter links • Theatrical trailer • Commentary: film historian Peter Cowie • Press book excerpts • Restoration demonstration.

1937 111m/B *FR* Jean Gabin, Erich von Stroheim, Pierre Fresnay, Marcel Dalio, Julien Carette, Gaston Modot, Jean Daste, Dita Parlo, Georges Peclet, Werner Florian, Sylvain Itkine, Jacques Becker; *D:* Jean Renoir; *W:* Jean Renoir, Charles Spaak; *C:* Christian Matras; *M:* Joseph Kosma. *AWARDS:* New York Film Critics Awards '38: Best Foreign Film; *NOM:* Academy Awards '38: Best Picture.

Grandma's House

As the title indicates, this horror film has a solid premise based on the primal fears that give fairy tales their power. After the loss of their parents, a brother and sister David (Foster) and Lynn (Valentine) go to live with their grandparents in a rural California town. When odd things happen in

and around the house, they suspect that the two older people are hiding something. Loose ends abound and the story won't stand up to any serious examination. The pace is so quick that the clichés and flaws aren't too obvious, and it's suspenseful without being overly violent. When the protagonists are children, that's a significant distinction. Judged as low-budget horror, the DVD is acceptable with images that have a slightly washed-out look in brightly lit scenes. Darker moments suffer. —*MM* *AKA:* Grandmother's House.

Movie: 🎵🎵🎵 **DVD:** 🎵🎵▶

Simitar Entertainment (Cat #7609, UPC #082551760923). Full frame. Dolby Digital 5.1 Surround Stereo. $14.98. Keepcase. *LANG:* English. *FEATURES:* 8 chapter links • Nico Mastorakis thumbnail biography and filmography.

1988 (R) 90m/C Eric Foster, Kim Valentine, Brinke Stevens, Ida Lee, Len Lesser; *D:* Peter Rader; *W:* Peter C. Jensen; *C:* Peter C. Jensen.

Gray's Anatomy

Even at 80 minutes, this monologue has a padded feeling. Soderbergh's adaptation of Gray's performance piece about his eye problems is introduced by other people's tales of vision woes, much of it presented in deliberately distressed black and white. It looks and sounds fine, but it's still essentially about one man sitting and talking. —*MM*

Movie: 🎵🎵 **DVD:** 🎵🎵▶

WinStar Home Entertainment (Cat #FLV5108, UPC #720917510828). Widescreen letterboxed. $29.98. Keepcase. *LANG:* English. *FEATURFS:* 6 chapter link • Cast and crew thumbnail biographies • Theatrical trailer • Production credits.

1996 80m/C Spalding Gray; *D:* Steven Soderbergh.

The Great Conqueror's Concubine

Mock epic brings the sensibility of a cheap martial arts flick to a historical setting and the proverbial cast of thousands. To anyone not familiar with the genre, it's often unintentionally funny, particularly in the wacko action scenes. Unfortunately, the ravishing costars Rosamund Kwan and Gong Li are wasted. The DVD image is cheap-looking throughout, certainly no better than most widescreen VHS tapes and the bare bones disc lacks even menu and chapter links. —*MM*

Movie: 🎵🎵 **DVD:** 🎵

Tai Seng Video Marketing (Cat #TDVD0002). Widescreen letterboxed. Dolby Digital Stereo. $49.95. Jewel case. *LANG:* Chinese. *SUB:* English; Chinese.

1994 177m/C *HK* Ray Liu, Rosamund Kwan, Gong Li, Shang Feng Yi; *D:* Stephen Shin; *W:* Stephen Shin, Liu Heng, Ziao He, Shi Yang Ping; *C:* Zheng Shao Qiang.

The Great Conqueror's Concubine, Part 2

This costume drama set in 203 B.C. is a ponderous affair with marching armies, castles under siege, palace intrigue, and martial arts violence. Since none of the credits are translated into English, it is difficult for those unfamiliar with the genre to know what to make of it. On DVD, the image is slightly muddy, even in the best moments, and so it doesn't begin to live up to the "epic" scope of the production. Director Stephen Shin is better known for such exploitation films as *Black Cat*. —*MM*

Movie: 🎵🎵▶ **DVD:** 🎵🎵▶

Tai Seng Video Marketing (Cat #38894). Widescreen letterboxed. Dolby Digital Stereo. $49.95. Jewel case. *LANG:* Mandarin; Cantonese. *SUB:* English; Chinese. *FEATURES:* 12 chapter links.

1994 94m/C *HK* Ray Liu, Rosamund Kwan, Gong Li, Zhang Yi; *D:* Stephen Shin; *W:* Stephen Shin, Liu Heng, Ziao He, Shi Yang Ping.

A Great Day in Harlem / The Spitball Story

In August 1958, in front of a Harlem brownstone, photographer Art Kane assembled 57 of the greatest jazz stars of all time and snapped a picture that would live forever. This Academy Award–nominated documentary examines the lives of the musicians in that photograph through interviews, home movies, and archival performance footage. Also included on the disc is the short film "The Spitball Story" (1997, 21 mins.). The video transfer is exceptional with solid colors and crisp blacks; even the archival footage (which could have really looked horrible) looks great. The audio is also solid with no hissing or thin-sounding dialogue. —*MJT*

Movie: 🎵🎵🎵 **DVD:** 🎵🎵▶

Image Entertainment (Cat #ID5567BVDVD, UPC #014381556728). Full frame. Dolby Digital Stereo. $24.99. Snapper. *LANG:* English. *FEATURES:* 15 chapter links for *A Great Day in Harlem* • 5 chapter links for "The Spitball Story."

1994 60m/C *W:* Jean Bach, Susan Peehl, Matthew Seig; *C:* Steve Petropoulos; *Nar:* Quincy Jones.

The Great Dictator

Chaplin's parody of Nazism is a mixed bag, at best. Inspired moments are surrounded by strained scenes that simply do not work. And when Nazi henchman says "We've just discovered the most wonderful, the most marvelous poison gas. It'll kill everybody!" who can laugh? Chaplin plays both a hapless Jewish barber and dictator Adenoid Hynkel. His famous dance with a balloon globe, chapter 7, is the film's highpoint. The DVD, complete with a raft of extras, looks much better than older VHS tapes. The black and white is crisp throughout with almost no surface scratches. Sound is adequate. —*MM*

Movie: 🐾🐾▶ **DVD:** 🐾🐾🐾▶
Image Entertainment (Cat #ID9183CUDVD, UPC #014381918328). Full frame. Dolby Digital Mono. $29.99. Snapper. *LANG:* English. *FEATURES:* 26 chapter links (17 feature and 9 supplemental material) ▪ 7-minute sequence from 1918 film *Sunnyside* ▪ 1933 Fox Movietone Newsreel about Adolf Hitler ▪ Story notes, script drafts, production records, etc. ▪ Premiere program ▪ Liner notes.
1940 126m/B Charlie Chaplin, Paulette Goddard, Jack Oakie, Billy Gilbert, Reginald Gardiner, Henry Daniell, Maurice Moscovich, Emma Dunn, Bernard Gorcey, Paul Weigel, Chester Conklin, Grace Hayle, Carter DeHaven; *D:* Charlie Chaplin; *W:* Charlie Chaplin; *C:* Roland H. Totheroh, Karl Struss; *M:* Meredith Willson. *AWARDS:* National Film Registry '97; New York Film Critics Awards '40: Best Actor (Chaplin); *NOM:* Academy Awards '40: Best Actor (Chaplin), Best Original Screenplay, Best Picture, Best Supporting Actor (Oakie), Best Original Score.

The Great Escape

For decades, novelists and screenwriters have mined WWII for its seemingly countless legacy of rousing true stories of heroism. Here's another, an exciting story about a group of troublesome POWs who join forces to break free of an allegedly escape-proof prison camp. One of the classic war movies. McQueen, who performed many of his own stunts over the objections of director Sturges, is widely regarded as the star. Truth be told, he's part of a great ensemble, notably featuring strong contributions by Garner, Attenborough, and the others. A true story based on the book by Paul Brickhill. The DVD looks and sounds great considering the movie's age, and benefits from the dual-layer format that fits the film's nearly 3 hours on one disc. The documentary, production notes, and trailer are welcome, but the excellent commentary track and 250+ production photos on the earlier laserdisc edition are missed. —*MB*

Movie: 🐾🐾🐾▶ **DVD:** 🐾🐾🐾
MGM Home Entertainment (Cat #906680, UPC #027616668028). Widescreen (2.35:1) letterboxed. Dolby Digital 2.0. $24.98. Keepcase. *LANG:* English; French. *SUB:* English; French; Spanish. *CAP:* English. *FEATURES:* 32 chapter links ▪ 24-min. documentary ▪ Trivia ▪ Production notes ▪ Theatrical trailer.
1963 170m/C Steve McQueen, James Garner, Richard Attenborough, Charles Bronson, James Coburn, Donald Pleasence, David McCallum, James Donald, Gordon Jackson, Hannes Messemer, John Leyton, Nigel Stock, Jud Taylor, Hans Reiser, Robert Freitag, Karl Otto Alberty, Angus Lennie, Robert Graf, Harry Riebauer; *D:* John Sturges; *W:* James Clavell, W.R. Burnett; *C:* Daniel F. Fapp; *M:* Elmer Bernstein. *AWARDS:* *NOM:* Academy Awards '63: Best Film Editing.

Great Expectations

Lean's adaptation of the Dickens novel in which an English orphan (Mills) is graced by a mysterious benefactor and becomes a well-heeled gentleman is moody and magisterial. Though the acting style seems a bit forced and dated, the characters are some of the most memorable in all English literature and the cast is equal to them. Guy Green's black-and-white photography emphasizes the Gothic elements of the tale, none of them more memorable than designer John Bryan's creation of Miss Havisham's house. My only complaint is the ending, but then that has always given people problems. On DVD, the film is superb. Since Lean was not working for the widescreen, the image fits a conventional video monitor. I find no flaws in the image and think that the mono sound is fine, even in the spooky, windswept opening. Both the novel and the film are wasted on school kids. One of the best from post-war England. —*MM*

Movie: 🐾🐾🐾▶ **DVD:** 🐾🐾🐾🐾
Criterion Collection (Cat #31, UPC #037429128022). Full frame. Dolby Digital Mono. $39.95. Keepcase. *LANG:* English. *CAP:* English. *FEATURES:* 36 chapters ▪ Theatrical trailer.
1946 118m/B *GB* John Mills, Valerie Hobson, Anthony Wager, Alec Guinness, Finlay Currie, Jean Simmons, Bernard Miles, Francis L. Sullivan, Martita Hunt, Freda Jackson, Torin Thatcher, Hay Petrie, Eileen Erskine, George "Gabby" Hayes, Everley Gregg, O.B. Clarence; *D:* David Lean; *W:* David Lean, Ronald Neame; *C:* Guy Green; *M:* Walter Goeher. *AWARDS:* Academy Awards '47: Best Art Direction/Set Decoration (B & W), Best Black-and-white Cinematography; *NOM:* Academy Awards '47: Best Director (Lean), Best Picture, Best Screenplay.

Great Expectations

Expecting *Great Expectations?* The title and basic storyline are about all the filmmakers took for their contemporary updating of Dickens's story. The artistic, orphaned Finn (Hawke) is living a meager existence with his trashy sister and his "uncle" Joe in a Florida fishing town. His destiny is intertwined with an escaped convict (De Niro) whom he aids, the rich and loony Ms. Dinsmoor (Bancroft), and Dinsmoor's beautiful niece, Estella (Paltrow). After being spurned by Estella as a teen, Finn quits painting and drawing entirely. Years later, a mysterious art dealer offers him a one-man show in New York if he will move there and start creating again. Estella inevitably reappears in his life, providing more than a little inspiration. More style than substance. Although the visuals are stunning, the director should have learned that beauty on the surface isn't all it's cracked up to be from, say, hmm...*Great Expectations* by Charles Dickens maybe? The image on this disc is at times very murky, with muddied blacks and wasted shadows; brighter colors, how-

ever, are represented a bit more impressive (though they are still nothing to strike up the band over). The soundtrack fares better, with crisp dialogue and some nicely recorded sound effects. —*MJT*

Movie: 🐾🐾 **DVD:** 🐾🐾▶
Twentieth Century Fox Home Entertainment (Cat #2000005, UPC #024543000 051). Widescreen (2.35:1) letterboxed. Dolby Digital 5.1; Dolby Surround. $29.98. Keepcase. *LANG:* English; French. *SUB:* English; Spanish. *FEATURES:* 22 chapter links ▪ Theatrical trailer ▪ Film recommendations.
1997 (R) 112m/C Ethan Hawke, Robert De Niro, Gwyneth Paltrow, Hank Azaria, Anne Bancroft, Chris Cooper, Josh Mostel, Kim Dickens, Nell Campbell, Stephen Spinella; *D:* Alfonso Cuaron; *W:* Mitch Glazer; *C:* Emmanuel Lubezki; *M:* Patrick Doyle.

The Great Locomotive Chase

During the Civil War, Union spy Jack Andrews (Parker) leads a band of Yankee soldiers behind Confederate lines where they steal a locomotive and sabotage the railroad and communications in a bold raid. Southern engineer William Fuller (Hunter) gives chase. This true story is also the basis for Buster Keaton's masterpiece, *The General.* If this version isn't quite as successful, it's still a lot of fun. (I loved it when I was eight years old and though my enthusiasm has tempered somewhat, I'm still a fan.) The DVD looks good with bright, deeply saturated Technicolor and only minor surface snow in a few scenes. The breakup of bright diagonals and flashing stripes is more bothersome. Sound is fine. —*MM* **AKA:** Andrews' Raiders.

Movie: 🐾🐾▶ **DVD:** 🐾🐾🐾
Anchor Bay (Cat #DV11097, UPC #013131109795). Widescreen (2.35:1) letterboxed; full frame. Dolby Digital Mono. $24.98. Keepcase. *LANG:* English. *FEATURES:* 22 chapter links ▪ Liner notes by Michael Felsher.
1956 85m/C Fess Parker, Jeffrey Hunter, Kenneth Tobey; *D:* Francis D. Lyon; *W:* Lawrence Edward Watkin; *C:* Charles P. Boyle; *M:* Paul J. Smith.

The Great Outdoors

Good cast is mostly wasted in another John Hughes's tale of vacation gone bad. A family's peaceful summer by the lake is disturbed by their uninvited, trouble-making relatives. Aykroyd and Candy are two funny guys done in by a lame script that awkwardly examines friendship and coming-of-age, and throws in a giant bear when things get unbearably slow. May be fun for small fry. An average disc for a kinda average movie delivers a soft picture that picks up grain in almost all darker scenes. The Dolby Surround does nothing to enhance things by avoiding the use of the rear channel almost entirely and not even offering much in the way of separation up front. —*JO*

Movie: 🐾🐾➤ *DVD:* 🐾🐾
Universal Studios Home Video (Cat #20228, UPC #025192022821). Widescreen (1.85:1) letterboxed. Dolby Surround. $24.98. Keepcase. *LANG:* English; French. *SUB:* Spanish. *CAP:* English. *FEATURES:* 16 chapter links • Theatrical trailer • Production notes • Cast and filmmakers bios • Film highlights.
1988 (PG) 91m/C Dan Aykroyd, John Candy, Stephanie Faracy, Annette Bening, Chris Young, Lucy Deakins, John Bloom; *D:* Howard Deutch; *W:* John Hughes; *C:* Ric Waite; *M:* Thomas Newman.

The Great Rupert

Mr. Amendola (Durante) and his family of unemployed vaudevillians are befriended by a helpful trained squirrel during the Depression. The box copy makes the dubious claim that 1950 audiences thought that Rupert the squirrel was real. The stop-motion animation simply is not that good. It doesn't hold a candle to *King Kong* and it's only a preview to the work that producer George Pal would go on to do in *The War of the Worlds* and *The Seven Faces of Dr. Lao.* On DVD, at least, the scenes with models and real squirrels are easily distinguishable. Kids and older viewers who remember star Durante fondly will probably enjoy this one. —*MM*
Movie: 🐾🐾🐾 *DVD:* 🐾🐾🐾
Image Entertainment (Cat #ID5506ALDVD, UPC #014381550627). Full frame. Dolby Digital Mono. $24.99. Snapper. *LANG:* English. *FEATURES:* 16 chapter links.
1950 86m/B Jimmy Durante, Terry Moore, Tom Drake, Frank Orth, Sara Haden, Queenie Smith; *D:* Irving Pichel; *W:* Laszlo Vadnay; *C:* Lionel Lindon.

The Great Santini

Lt. Col. Bull Meechum (Duvall), the "Great Santini," is a Marine fighter pilot stationed stateside. He fights a war involving his frustrated career goals, repressed emotions, and family. His wife (Danner) and son (O'Keefe) become his company of Marines, as he abuses them in the name of discipline because he has no other way to show affection. With a standout performance from Duvall, the film successfully blends warm humor and tenderness with harsh cruelty. The DVD is little better than VHS tape, with unspectacular sound and a full-frame image. The graininess of the image comes from the original, not the transfer. —*MM AKA:* Ace.
Movie: 🐾🐾🐾 *DVD:* 🐾🐾➤
Warner Home Video, Inc. (Cat #16374, UPC #085391637424). Full frame. Dolby Digital Mono. $19.98. Snapper. *LANG:* English. *SUB:* English; French. *FEATURES:* 42 chapter links.
1980 (PG) 118m/C Robert Duvall, Blythe Danner, Michael O'Keefe, Julie Ann Haddock, Lisa Jane Persky, David Keith; *D:* Lewis John Carlino; *W:* Lewis John Carlino; *C:* Ralph Woolsey; *M:* Elmer Bernstein. *AWARDS:* Montreal World Film Festival '80: Best Actor (Duvall); *NOM:* Academy Awards '80: Best Actor (Duvall), Best Supporting Actor (O'Keefe).

The Great Train Robbery

In 1855, dapper thief Edward Pierce (Connery) arranges to steal gold bullion from the Folkstone Express. It's the first heist from a moving train. Writer-director Crichton keeps the pace quick enough to make the robbery fun, but not so fast that we don't have time to appreciate the period details. On his intelligent, offhand commentary track, Crichton sounds a bit nostalgic about the entire enterprise. The choice of what he calls the "gold motif" in set decoration makes for a production that has aged well and looks very good on DVD when compared to other films of its era. The desaturated colors and smoky light are just right for this depiction of 19th-century England (actually Ireland). Sound is fine. This one's worth another look, and not just for Connery fans. —*MM*
AKA: The First Great Train Robbery.
Movie: 🐾🐾🐾 *DVD:* 🐾🐾🐾➤
MGM Home Entertainment (Cat #907149, UPC #027616714923). Widescreen letterboxed. Dolby Digital 5.1 Surround Stereo. $24.98. Keepcase. *LANG:* English; French. *SUB:* English; French. *FEATURES:* 28 chapter links • Commentary: Michael Crichton • Theatrical trailer • Booklet.
1979 (PG) 111m/C *GB* Sean Connery, Donald Sutherland, Lesley-Anne Down, Alan Webb; *D:* Michael Crichton; *W:* Michael Crichton; *C:* Geoffrey Unsworth; *M:* Jerry Goldsmith.

Greedy

Aging scrap metal tycoon Joe McTeague (Douglas) is surrounded by a host of greedy nieces and nephews, played with understated comic zest by a fine ensemble. (Director Lynn almost steals the show as a tart tongued butler.) They spend their time fighting with each other until Molly (D'Abo), a sexy pizza girl, moves in with Joe. To find out what she's up to, they entice Uncle Joe's favorite nephew Daniel (Michael J. Fox) back into the fold. The rapport between Fox and Douglas is the most enjoyable part of the slow-moving comedy. On DVD, image and sound are completely adequate, though the film is not visually challenging on any medium. —*MM*
Movie: 🐾🐾➤ *DVD:* 🐾🐾➤
Universal Studios Home Video (Cat #20429, UPC #025192049228). Widescreen (1.85:1) letterboxed. Dolby Digital 5.1 Surround Stereo. $24.98. Keepcase. *LANG:* English; French. *SUB:* Spanish. *CAP:* English. *FEATURES:* 18 chapter links • Production notes • Cast and crew thumbnail biographies • Universal web links.
1994 (PG-13) 109m/C Kirk Douglas, Michael J. Fox, Olivia D'Abo, Phil Hartman, Nancy Travis, Ed Begley Jr., Bob Balaban, Colleen Camp, Jere Burns, Khandi Alexander, Jonathan Lynn; *D:* Jonathan Lynn; *W:* Lowell Ganz, Babaloo Mandel; *C:* Gabriel Beristain; *M:* Randy Edelman.

The Green Berets

Arguably John Wayne's worst film is marred by a slow pace, political posturing, and a few cheapjack special effects that would not have been out of place in an Ed Wood Jr. horror movie. Pay special attention to chapter 5, side B, when the toy helicopter catches fire, and the model observation tower (complete with clay dolls) collapses. And then, of course, there is the famous ending where the sun slowly sets in the east. On DVD, the night action scenes fare particularly poorly. They're no easier to make out than they are on tape. The extras are really all that the two-sided DVD has to offer to Wayne's many fans. —*MM*
Movie: 🐾 *DVD:* 🐾➤
Warner Home Video, Inc. (Cat #1002, UPC #012569100220). Widescreen letterboxed. Dolby Digital Mono. $19.98. Snapper. *LANG:* English; French; Spanish. *SUB:* English; French; Spanish. *CAP:* English. *FEATURES:* 37 chapter links • Thumbnail biographies of cast and crew • "Making of" featurette • Theatrical trailers.
1968 (G) 135m/C John Wayne, David Janssen, Jim Hutton, Aldo Ray, George Takei, Raymond St. Jacques, Bruce Cabot, Jack Soo, Patrick Wayne, Luke Askew, Irene Tsu, Edward Faulkner, Jason Evers, Mike Henry, Chuck Roberson, Eddy Donno; *D:* John Wayne; *W:* James Lee Barrett; *C:* Winton C. Hoch; *M:* Miklos Rozsa.

The Green Mile

Frank Darabont's second adaptation of Stephen King may not equal *The Shawshank Redemption,* but it is sure-handed entertainment. In pre–World War II South, John Coffey (Duncan) is convicted of the brutal murder of two little girls. The Green Mile is Death Row, the cellblock run by Paul Edgecomb (Hanks). Incredible supernatural events power the story and they're handled through some restrained special effects that lose nothing on DVD. The film's image is very sharp. Even dark uniforms in dim interiors retain texture and detail. Sound is fine, too. The film was a hit in theatres, but even so, the overwhelming public response that greeted its release on home video—both in DVD sales and tape rentals—surprised even veteran observers of the industry. —*MM*
Movie: 🐾🐾🐾➤ *DVD:* 🐾🐾🐾➤
Warner Home Video, Inc. Widescreen anamorphic. Dolby Digital 5.1 Surround Stereo. $24.98. Snapper. *LANG:* English. *SUB:* English; French. *FEATURES:* Cast and crew thumbnail bios • Trailer • Behind-the-scenes documentary • 54 chapter links.
1999 (R) 187m/C Tom Hanks, Michael Clarke Duncan, David Morse, Bonnie Hunt, Michael Jeter, Sam Rockwell, James Cromwell, Patricia Clarkson, Graham Greene, Barry Pepper, Doug Hutchison, Jeffrey DeMunn, Harry Dean Stanton,

Dabbs Greer, Eve Brent, William Sadler, Gary Sinise; *D:* Frank Darabont; *W:* Frank Darabont; *C:* David Tattersall; *M:* Thomas Newman. *AWARDS:* Broadcast Film Critics Association Awards '99: Best Adapted Screenplay, Best Supporting Actor (Duncan); *NOM:* Academy Awards '99: Best Adapted Screenplay, Best Film, Best Sound, Best Supporting Actor (Duncan); Directors Guild of America Awards '99: Best Director (Darabont); Golden Globe Awards '00: Best Supporting Actor (Duncan); MTV Movie Awards '00: Breakthrough Performance (Duncan); Screen Actors Guild Award '99: Best Supporting Actor (Duncan), Cast.

Gremlins

Comedy horror has a deft satiric edge. Fumbling gadget salesman Rand Peltzer (Axton) is looking for something really special to get his son Billy. He finds it in a small store in Chinatown. The wise shopkeeper is reluctant to sell him the adorable "mogwai," but relents after fully warning him "Don't expose him to bright light, don't ever get him wet, and don't ever, ever feed him after midnight." Naturally, this all happens and the result is a gang of nasty gremlins who decide to tear up the town on Christmas Eve. The DVD is superior in every way to the previous home video releases. The picture is extremely sharp and the colors vibrant and distinct. Even when the pesky little critters are rapidly skittering about and the scene is dark, there is very little grain or artifacts. Bleed is minimal. Contrast is excellent, as is the brightness. Blacks are true and have no problem with additional grain. The 5.1 makes excellent use of the Surround tracks, and does it often, keeping things lively with good ambience during those rare times when there isn't much action going on. Dialogue is crisp and easy to understand and the music full-bodied. —*JO*
Movie: 🎜🎜🎜 *DVD:* 🎜🎜🎜▶
Warner Home Video, Inc. (Cat #11388, UPC #085391138822). Widescreen (1.85:1) letterboxed. Dolby Digital 5.1; Dolby Surround. $24.98. Snapper. *LANG:* English (DS5.1); French (DS); Spanish (DS). *SUB:* English; French; Spanish. *CAP:* English. *FEATURES:* 27 chapter links • Production notes • Theatrical trailer.
1984 (PG) 106m/C Zach Galligan, Phoebe Cates, Hoyt Axton, Polly Holliday, Frances Lee McCain, Keye Luke, Dick Miller, Corey Feldman, Judge Reinhold, Glynn Turman, Scott Brady, Jackie Joseph; *D:* Joe Dante; *W:* Chris Columbus; *C:* John Hora; *M:* Jerry Goldsmith; *V:* Howie Mandel.

Gridlock'd

Junkies and sometime-musicians Spoon (Shakur) and Stretch (Roth) decide to kick the habit after their singer Cookie (Newton) overdoses and slips into a coma. The hapless pair are thrown into the switches of social services programs and government offices where they shuffle endlessly but nothing happens. Think *Waiting for Godot* meets "Waiting for the Man." Meanwhile, their dealer is murdered and they're the prime suspects, pursued by the cops and the actual killers, who believe that they've stolen said dealer's stash. Shakur shows flashes of the brilliance-that-might-have-been as the more sensitive and sane of the pair, while Roth complements him perfectly as his bug-crazy shortsighted partner. Fellow actor Curtis-Hall's directorial debut. The DVD's picture is of only average sharpness, with occasional grain and a few spots of artifacting. Colors seem accurate and at times even vibrant, with only rare occurrences of bleed. I would have preferred a little more contrast and brightness but the levels are not uncomfortable. Blacks are pretty good with a little grain here and there. There is not much in the way of Surround on this disc, but overall the soundtrack has both good frequency response and decent energy. —*JO*
Movie: 🎜🎜🎜 *DVD:* 🎜🎜▶
Polygram (Cat #0549872, UPC #044005498721). Widescreen (1.85:1) letterboxed; full frame. Dolby Surround. $19.95. Expanded jewel case. *LANG:* English; French. *SUB:* Spanish. *CAP:* English. *FEATURES:* 17 chapter links • Talent biographies.
1996 (R) 91m/C Tim Roth, Tupac Shakur, Thandie Newton, Charles Fleischer, Howard Hesseman, James Pickens Jr., John Sayles, Tom Towles, Eric Payne; *Cameos:* Vondie Curtis-Hall; *D:* Vondie Curtis-Hall; *W:* Vondie Curtis-Hall; *C:* Bill Pope; *M:* Stewart Copeland.

The Grifters

Evocative rendering of a terrifying sub-culture. Huston, Cusak, and Bening are con artists, struggling to stay on top in a world where violence, money, and lust are the prizes. Bening and Huston fight for Cusak's soul, while he's determined to decide for himself. Seamless performances and dazzling atmosphere, along with director Frears's superb pacing, make for a provocative film. Writer Donald Westlake based the script on a novel by Jim Thompson. Several acquaintances have said that *The Grifters* is their all-time favorite film. It certainly is a great one, and one where the DVD was anxiously awaited. Unfortunately, this release from HBO is a big disappointment. Not only does a decent VHS transfer look better, most EP VHS tapes look as good. Just about everything is a little off, and the biggest aggravation is the soft, and usually grainy image. The 5.1 sound is O.K., but since this isn't an audio book, it hardly makes this one worth owning. —*JO*
Movie: 🎜🎜🎜🎜 *DVD:* 🎜
HBO Home Video (Cat #90545, UPC #02635905525). Full frame. Dolby Digital 5.1. $24.98. Snapper. *LANG:* English. *CAP:* English. *FEATURES:* 22 chapter links • Cast and filmmakers bios.
1990 (R) 114m/C Anjelica Huston, John Cusack, Annette Bening, Pat Hingle, J.T. Walsh, Charles Napier, Henry Jones, Gailard Sartain, Jeremy Piven; *D:* Stephen Frears; *W:* Donald E. Westlake; *C:* Oliver Stapleton; *M:* Elmer Bernstein. *AWARDS:* Independent Spirit Awards '91: Best Actress (Huston), Best Film; Los Angeles Film Critics Association Awards '90: Best Actress (Huston); National Society of Film Critics Awards '90: Best Actress (Huston), Best Supporting Actress (Bening); *NOM:* Academy Awards '90: Best Actress (Huston), Best Adapted Screenplay, Best Director (Frears), Best Supporting Actress (Bening).

Grim

Average low-budget horror suffers from a ludicrous premise and a soundtrack filled with melodramatic organ music. The title character, a guy in silly monster suit, lives in caverns beneath a new subdivision and communicates telepathically—or something to that effect—with certain residents before he chops them up and worships the devil. The characters have no depth, and the whole thing becomes far too gory for my taste. Again, though, it's too ridiculous to be offensive. The DVD image is just as dark and grain-filled as the substandard VHS tape. —*MM*
Movie: 🎜 *DVD:* 🎜
Image Entertainment (Cat #4657). Full frame. Mono. $24.99. Snapper. *LANG:* English.
1995 (R) 86m/C Emmanuel Xuereb, Tres Handley, Peter Tregloan; *D:* Paul Matthews; *W:* Paul Matthews; *C:* Alan M. Trow; *M:* Dennis Michael Tenney.

Grizzly

A giant, killer grizzly terrorizes a state park in this blatant (and boring) *Jaws* rip-off. From the same folks that gave us *Abby,* a blatant *Exorcist* rip-off. Filmed in Georgia, and that's the highlight. It's hard to believe, but the DVD is even more of a disappointment than the film. If, however, you insist on buying or renting this one (an old VHS tape will look better), here goes. This DVD has more color bleed than any I've seen this far. What sharpness there is can't really be called sharpness, and the grain is almost as bad as the aforementioned bleed. The blacks were no worse—but no better—and with all these flaws you really can't get a feel for what the contrast and bright levels are like. The sound is not worth mentioning. To put that 0.5 technical rating into words, this DVD sucks. —*JO AKA:* Killer Grizzly.
Movie: 🎜 *DVD:* 🎜
Digital Versatile Disc Ltd. (Cat #DVD 149, UPC #066479101495). Full frame. Mono. $19.95. Keepcase. *LANG:* English.
1976 (PG) 92m/C Christopher George, Richard Jaeckel, Andrew Prine, Victoria (Vicki) Johnson, Charles Kissinger; *D:* William Girdler; *W:* Harvey Flaxman, David Sheldon; *M:* Robert O. Ragland.

Grosse Pointe Blank

Combine one part Quentin Tarantino with one part Woody Allen, one part John Cusack; season with a dash of John Woo, and stir lightly. The result is a hip action-comedy. Coproducer-writer Cusack stars as a hitman suffering career burnout who goes back to his tenth high school reunion and the girl (Driver) he stood up at the prom. He can't get away from his work, though. The action-comedy has the off-center sensibility of an independent production and the gaudier pleasures of a studio shoot-'em-up. The DVD is an absolutely faithful re-creation of the theatrical release as I remember it, with no visual flaws worth mentioning. —*MM*
Movie: ♫♫♫ **DVD:** ♫♫♫
Hollywood Pictures Home Video (Cat #14259). Widescreen (1.85:1) letterboxed. Dolby Digital 5.1 Surround Stereo. $29.99. Keepcase. *LANG:* English; French. *SUB:* Spanish. *CAP:* English. *FEATURES:* Trailer.
1997 (R) 107m/C John Cusack, Minnie Driver, Dan Aykroyd, Alan Arkin, Joan Cusack, Jeremy Piven, Mitchell Ryan, Hank Azaria, Michael Cudlitz, Benny "The Jet" Urquidez, Barbara Harris, Ann Cusack, K. Todd Freeman; *D:* George Armitage; *W:* Tom Jankiewicz, D.V. DeVincentis, Steve Pink, John Cusack; *C:* Jamie Anderson; *M:* Joe Strummer.

Ground Control

Jack Harris (Sutherland) is a former air traffic controller who retired after a fatal plane crash. Five years later, an old friend (McGill) begs him to help out at the Phoenix airport on a short-staffed busy night. You do not need three guesses to predict what will happen. The complexity of *Pushing Tin* is conspicuously absent. A top-notch cast can't quite overcome the cliché-ridden script and mediocre production values. On DVD, the many dark backgrounds and computer-created aerial effects make it all too obvious where the producers had to cut corners. —*MM*
Movie: ♫♫ **DVD:** ♫♫
Trimark Home Video (Cat #VM7014D, UPC #031398701439). Full frame. Stereo. $24.99. Keepcase. *LANG:* English. *SUB:* English; French; Spanish. *CAP:* English. *FEATURES:* 24 chapter links • Cast thumbnail biographies.
1998 (PG-13) 98m/C Kiefer Sutherland, Robert Sean Leonard, Kelly McGillis, Henry Winkler, Michael Gross, Margaret Cho, Charles Fleischer, Farrah Forke, Bruce McGill, Kristy Swanson; *D:* Richard Howard.

Groundhog Day

Phil (Murray), an obnoxious weatherman, is in Punxatawney, PA, to cover the annual emergence of the famous rodent from its hole. After he's caught in a blizzard that he didn't predict, he finds himself trapped in a time warp, doomed to relive the same day over and over again until he gets it right. Lighthearted romantic comedy manages to carry it

through to the end. Murray has fun with the role, although he did get bitten by the groundhog during the scene when they're driving. Elliott, who has been missed since his days as the man under the seats on *Late Night with David Letterman* is perfectly cast as a smart-mouthed cameraman. The DVD is sharp and the stronger colors, combined with boosted contrast and brightness, makes for much more enjoyable viewing than the laserdisc (which was not bad at all). The colors are also accurate and finely detailed with little bleed. Blacks are also very good. The DVD sounds good, too, with a fairly good if limited mix (not much Surround) that keeps the dialogue in front and the music dynamic and full-bodied. —*JO*
Movie: ♫♫♫ **DVD:** ♫♫♫
Columbia Tristar Home Video (Cat #52299, UPC #043396522992). Widescreen (1.85:1) letterboxed. Dolby Surround. $29.95. Keepcase. *LANG:* English; French; Spanish. *SUB:* English; French; Spanish. *CAP:* English. *FEATURES:* 33 chapter links.
1993 (PG) 103m/C Bill Murray, Andie MacDowell, Chris Elliott, Stephen Tobolowsky, Brian Doyle-Murray, Marita Geraghty, Angela Paton; *D:* Harold Ramis; *W:* Harold Ramis, Daniel F. Rubin; *C:* John Bailey; *M:* George Fenton. *AWARDS:* British Academy Awards '93: Best Original Screenplay.

Grumpier Old Men

Max (Matthau) and John (Lemmon) are back at each other's throats, but with John happily married to Ariel (Ann Margret), he's not much of an adversary. Enter Maria (Loren), who wants to turn the boys' favorite bait shop into an Italian restaurant. In a twist that should surprise no one, Max soon falls for the beautiful Maria, and she with him. Jokes are similar but more adolescent than in the first, and subplots involving John and Max's kids' wedding and Grandpa's (Meredith) romantic interests are forced. Suffers the standard sequel fate of not measuring up to the original. As with the original's DVD, this one is also not letterboxed, but the image is very sharp and grain levels low. Colors are strong enough but seem a little off a lot of the time. Bleed is minimal. The blacks are true most of the time and supported by good contrast and a consistently comfortable brightness levels. The 5.1 sound has as much energy as you can expect in a non-action film and is crisp and full-bodied, with deep, clean bass. Surround is pretty much ambience only, but more than adequate. —*JO*
Movie: ♫♫ **DVD:** ♫♫♫
Warner Home Video, Inc. (Cat #14191, UPC #085391419129). Full frame. Dolby Digital 5.1; Dolby Surround. $24.98. Snapper. *LANG:* English (DD5.1); French (DD5.1); Spanish (DS). *SUB:* English; French; Spanish. *CAP:* English. *FEATURES:* 31 chapter links • Production notes • Theatrical trailers.
1995 (PG-13) 101m/C Jack Lemmon, Walter Matthau, Ann-Margret, Sophia

Loren, Kevin Pollak, Burgess Meredith, Daryl Hannah, Ann Guilbert; *D:* Howard Deutch; *W:* Mark Steven Johnson; *C:* Tak Fujimoto; *M:* Alan Silvestri.

Grumpy Old Men

Lemmon and Matthau team up for their seventh movie, in parts that seem written just for them. Boyhood friends and retired neighbors, they have been feuding for so long that neither of them can remember why. Doesn't matter much, when it provides a reason for them to spout off at each other every morning and play nasty practical jokes every night. This, and ice-fishing, is life as they know it, until feisty younger woman Ann-Margret moves into the neighborhood and lights some long-dormant fires. Eighty-three-year-old Meredith is a special treat playing Lemmon's 90 something father. The image is very sharp on the DVD and, though there is a little grain here and there, it's not too bothersome. Artifacts are also rare. Colors are close to accurate and bleed is minimal. Contrast and brightness levels remain consistent and are not bad, but just a touch of boost to both would have made the image just punchy enough. Blacks are good. The sound is not extraordinary, but does deliver the dialogue crisply and the music with good fullness and not bad energy. The Surround is used sparingly. —*JO*
Movie: ♫♫♫ **DVD:** ♫♫♫
Warner Home Video, Inc. (Cat #13050, UPC #085391305026). Full frame. Dolby Surround. $24.98. Snapper. *LANG:* English (DS); French (DS). *SUB:* English; French; Spanish. *CAP:* English. *FEATURES:* 33 chapter links • Production notes • Theatrical trailer.
1993 (PG-13) 104m/C Jack Lemmon, Walter Matthau, Ann-Margret, Burgess Meredith, Daryl Hannah, Kevin Pollak, Ossie Davis, Buck Henry, Christopher McDonald; *D:* Donald Petrie; *W:* Mark Steven Johnson; *C:* Johnny E. Jensen; *M:* Alan Silvestri.

The Guardian

If Stephen King and Mel Brooks teamed up to make a version of *Three Men and a Baby* they couldn't come up with as many real laughs as the unintentional variety generated in this misfire. Actually, director Friedkin begins well, with an eerie dream-like evocation of the archetypal stuff of fairy tales: abandonment by parents, the loss of children, ancient secrets hidden deep in the forest. That mood soon evaporates when Phil (Brown) and Kate (Lowell) move to L.A. and hire Camilla (Seagrove), the nanny who's too good to be true. The laughs start when Phil dreams that a tree is growing in his living room, and the film never recovers. On disc, the film looks much better than it needs to, re-creating the dark special effects with excellent clarity. On the commentary track, interviewer Dennis Bartok of American Cinemateque is respectful and flattering to Friedkin, who spends much of his time talking about

other films and ideas. He also puts forth several dubious opinions, most notably the notion that the rise of Nazism was caused by "demonic possession on a mass scale." —*MM*
Movie: ♫ **DVD:** ♫♫♫▶
Anchor Bay (Cat #DV10868, UPC #013131086898). Widescreen (1.85: 1) letterboxed; full frame. Dolby Digital 5.1 Surround Stereo. $24.98. Keepcase. *FEATURES:* 20 chapter links • Theatrical trailer • Cast and crew thumbnail biographies • Commentary: Dennis Bartok and William Friedkin.
1990 (R) 92m/C Jenny Seagrove, Dwier Brown, Carey Lowell, Brad Hall, Miguel Ferrer, Natalija Nogulich, Pamela Brull, Gary Swanson; *D:* William Friedkin; *W:* William Friedkin, Stephen Volk, Dan Greenberg; *C:* John A. Alonzo; *M:* Jack Hues.

Guarding Tess

Long-suffering Secret Service agent Doug Chesnic (Cage) is nearing the end of his three-year assignment to crotchety widowed First Lady Tess Carlisle (MacLaine) when the Prez extends his tour of duty. This odd couple is not unlike *Driving Miss Daisy* with a 9mm in a shoulder holster. The curious chemistry between the stars generates more sparks than you'd expect, and the DVD's image and sound are equally sharp. Curiously, this is one film that is at least as good in the full-frame version on disc as it is in widescreen. The stars do very good work with these characters. Keep them center stage. —*MM*
Movie: ♫♫♫ **DVD:** ♫♫♫
Columbia Tristar Home Video (Cat #78709, UPC #043396787094). Widescreen (1.85:1) letterboxed; full frame. Dolby Digital 5.1 Surround Stereo; Dolby Digital Surround Stereo. $29.95. Keepcase. *LANG:* English; French; Spanish. *SUB:* English; French; Spanish. *FEATURES:* Theatrical trailer • 28 chapter links.
1994 (PG-13) 98m/C Shirley MacLaine, Nicolas Cage, Austin Pendleton, Edward Albert, Richard Griffiths, Dale Dye; *D:* Hugh Wilson; *W:* Hugh Wilson, Peter Torokvei; *C:* Brian Reynolds; *M:* Michael Convertino. *AWARDS: NOM:* Golden Globe Awards '95: Best Actress—Musical/Comedy (MacLaine).

Guess Who's Coming to Dinner

Controversial in its day, this romantic drama seems innocent now. A young white woman (Houghton) brings her black fiance (Poitier) home to meet her parents (Tracy and Hepburn) in San Francisco. The situation tests their open-mindedness and understanding. Hepburn and Tracy (in his last film appearance) are wonderful and their performances are undimmed. Houghton is the real-life niece of Hepburn. On DVD, image and sound are fine for a film of this age, but it is still most enjoyable for fans of the two stars. —*MM*
Movie: ♫♫♫ **DVD:** ♫♫♫

Columbia Tristar Home Video (Cat #05419, UPC #043396054196). Widescreen (1.85:1) letterboxed; full frame. Dolby Digital 3-channel; Dolby Digital Stereo; Dolby Digital Mono. $28.95. Keepcase. *LANG:* English; French. *SUB:* English; French. *FEATURES:* 28 chapter links • Theatrical trailer.
1967 108m/C Katharine Hepburn, Spencer Tracy, Sidney Poitier, Katharine Houghton, Cecil Kellaway; *D:* Stanley Kramer; *W:* William Rose; *C:* Sam Leavitt; *M:* Frank DeVol. *AWARDS:* Academy Awards '67: Best Actress (Hepburn), Best Story & Screenplay; American Film Institute (AFI) '98: Top 100; British Academy Awards '68: Best Actor (Tracy), Best Actress (Hepburn); *NOM:* Academy Awards '67: Best Actor (Tracy), Best Adapted Score, Best Art Direction/Set Decoration, Best Director (Kramer), Best Film Editing, Best Picture, Best Supporting Actor (Kellaway), Best Supporting Actress (Richards).

Guilty by Suspicion

Examination of the 1950s McCarthy investigation by the House Un-American Activities Committee comes off like a bland history lesson. De Niro plays a director who attended a Communist party meeting in the '30s but who otherwise doesn't have any red connections. He takes the moral high ground and refuses to incriminate his buddy (Wendt) to get off the hook and finds himself blacklisted. Characterized by average performances (except Wettig, who goes overboard) and a lightweight script. The film uses a lot of soft focus and at times appears hazy, which can create problems for a DVD. This one's not bad, though, and the picture is sharp and doesn't appear to have much more grain than in the theatre. Colors are both accurate and deep with only rare occurrences of bleed. Brightness and contrast levels are both consistent and comfortable without taking away any of the texture of the film. The sound is also very faithful to the theatre, featuring little in the way of Surround effects or even ambience, but nonetheless of full fidelity and decent separation. —*JO*
Movie: ♫♫▶ **DVD:** ♫♫♫
Warner Home Video, Inc. (Cat #12053, UPC #085391205326). Full frame. Dolby Digital Surround. $14.98. Snapper. *LANG:* English. *CAP:* English. *FEATURES:* 28 chapter links.
1991 (PG-13) 105m/C Robert De Niro, Annette Bening, George Wendt, Patricia Wettig, Sam Wanamaker, Chris Cooper, Ben Piazza, Martin Scorsese, Barry Primus, Gailard Sartain, Stuart Margolin, Barry Tubb, Roxann Biggs-Dawson, Robin Gammell, Brad Sullivan, Luke Edwards, Adam Baldwin; *D:* Irwin Winkler; *W:* Irwin Winkler; *C:* Michael Ballhaus; *M:* James Newton Howard.

Guinevere

Feminist revision of the Arthurian legends isn't going to make anyone forget *Excal-*

ibur. In this made-for-TV effort, Guinevere (Lee) is the much put-upon princess who marries the no-good cheating Arthur (Flanery) while she truly loves her childhood pal Lancelot (Wyle). (They met while she was in princess school.) On DVD, the image is somewhat transparent. Its crispness cannot overcome the limited sets and props. —*MM*
Movie: ♫▶ **DVD:** ♫▶
Simitar Entertainment (Cat #7594, UPC #082551759422). Full frame. Dolby Digital Stereo. $14.98. Keepcase. *LANG:* English. *FEATURES:* 8 chapter links • Sheryl Lee filmography.
1993 93m/C Sheryl Lee, Noah Wyle, Sean Patrick Flanery, Brid Brennan, James Faulkner, Donald Pleasence; *D:* Jud Taylor; *W:* Ronni Kern.

Guinevere

Harper (Polley) is an uncertain, inexperienced 20-year-old in San Francisco who ditches family responsibilities at her sister's wedding reception in order to talk to fortysomething photographer Connie (Rea). Worldly-wise and a natural charmer, Connie soon recruits Harper as his latest "Guinevere," the innocent young women he beds and nurtures until they outgrow the need for his so-called guidance. Harper certainly doesn't seem to have much personality on her own, but Connie also needs something of a lifeline as his drinking increases while his job prospects decline. Polished production with compelling performances by both Polley and Rea. The video transfer is crisp and features bright colors and solid blacks. The audio transfer is also quite good, with nice, clear dialogue and a lush musical score and soundtrack. —*MJT*
Movie: ♫♫♫ **DVD:** ♫♫♫
Miramax Pictures Home Video (Cat #18789, UPC #717951005885). Widescreen (1.85:1) anamorphic. Dolby Digital 5.1. $29.99. Keepcase. *LANG:* English. *CAP:* English. *FEATURES:* 29 chapter links.
1999 (R) 104m/C Stephen Rea, Sarah Polley, Jean Smart, Gina Gershon, Paul Dooley, Francis Guinan, Jasmine Guy, Sandra Oh, Emily Procter, Gedde Watanabe; *D:* Audrey Wells; *W:* Audrey Wells; *C:* Charles Minsky; *M:* Christophe Beck. *AWARDS:* Sundance Film Festival '99: Best Screenplay; *NOM:* Independent Spirit Awards '00: Best Screenplay, Best Supporting Actress (Smart).

Gulliver's Travels

Despite ambitious and successful efforts at restoration, this feature-length cartoon from animation's "Golden Age" should not be compared to the best work of the Disney studio, or even Warner Bros. Dave Fleischer's version of Swift's satire is a nicely done kid flick that combines silly comic characters with more stately rotoscoped work (where animators draw a character over film of a live actor). On DVD, the film looks and sounds much brighter than it has on tape, but still, when

seen alongside *Snow White and the Seven Dwarfs,* made two years earlier, it suffers. Will kids care about that? Some won't, but others who have been weaned on the fast-paced razzle dazzle of today's animation are likely to become bored. The disc also includes two other short cartoons, "King for a Day" and "Swing Cleaning." —*MM*
Movie: ♫♫♫ **DVD:** ♫♫♫
WinStar Home Entertainment (Cat #WHE73044, UPC #720917304427). Full frame. Dolby Digital Stereo; Dolby Digital 5.1 Surround Stereo. $19.98. Keepcase. *LANG:* English. *FEATURES:* Restoration demonstration • Documentary on the Fleischer studios • Previews • Production credits • Picture Gallery • 7 chapter links.
1939 110m/C D: Dave Fleischer; **W:** Dan Gordon, Tedd Pierce, Edmond Seward, Izzy Sparber; **C:** Charles Schettler; **V:** Lanny Ross, Jessica Dragonette. *AWARDS: NOM:* Academy Awards '39: Best Song ("Faithful Forever"), Best Original Score.

The Guns of Navarone

One of the all-time great World War II adventures receives the treatment it's due on DVD. This impossible-mission-behind-enemy-lines yarn was an expensive production when it was made in 1959, and this bright widescreen image captures the dusty, lived-in look of Geoffrey Drake's production design. Sound is particularly good in the 14-minute storm sequence. The night scenes have never been particularly clear and they're no better here, but that's a quibble. A required addition to the video library of any war movie fan. —*MM*
Movie: ♫♫♫♫ **DVD:** ♫♫♫►
Columbia Tristar Home Video (Cat #72129). Widescreen letterboxed. Dolby Digital 5.1 Surround Stereo. $25.95. Keepcase. *LANG:* English; French; Spanish. *SUB:* English; French; Spanish; Portuguese; Korean; Thai. *FEATURES:* Trailers • Documentary "Memories of Navarone" • Commentary: director J. Lee Thompson • Cast and crew thumbnail bios • Featurettes • "Message from Carl Foreman" • 28 chapter links.
1961 159m/C Gregory Peck, David Niven, Anthony Quinn, Richard Harris, Stanley Baker, Anthony Quayle, James Darren, Irene Papas, Gia Scala, James Robertson Justice, Bryan Forbes, Allan Cuthbertson, Michael Trubshawe, Percy Herbert, Walter Gotell, Tutte Lemkow; **D:** J. Lee Thompson; **W:** Carl Foreman; **C:** Oswald Morris; **M:** Dimitri Tiomkin. *AWARDS:* Golden Globe Awards '62: Best Film—Drama, Best Score; *NOM:* Academy Awards '61: Best Adapted Screenplay, Best Director (Thompson), Best Film Editing, Best Picture, Best Sound, Best Original Dramatic Score.

Gustav Mahler: To Live, I Will Die

Director Lesowsky uses many of the same techniques that Ken Burns employs in his American documentaries to touch upon the high spots of composer Gustav Mahler's life. A voice-over narrator describes key events. Some of them are shown in real photographs and then re-created by actors; other scenes are completely fictional. More often, Mahler's music is played over empty pastoral landscapes to create a mood that is, well, Germanic. On DVD, interiors are generally dark and brooding; exteriors are more inviting and bright. The music is superb. —*MM*
Movie: ♫► **DVD:** ♫
Image Entertainment (Cat #ID5750CHDVD, UPC #014381575026). Widescreen (1.66: 1) letterboxed. Uncompressed PCM Stereo. $24.99. Snapper. *LANG:* German. *SUB:* English. *FEATURES:* 16 chapter links.
1987 93m/C Erika Mottl, Dana Gillespie, Corrine Hochwarter, Reinhard Mauser; **D:** Wolfgang Lesowsky.

GWAR: Phallus in Wonderland

GWAR, a Midwest multimedia band that can only be insufficiently described as a cross between Kiss and Devo, make the world safe for sex, drugs, and rock and roll with this strange homebrew of music video, social satire, and outlandish costumes. The bizarre story involves a kidnapped sex organ, an obscenity trial, a secret hideout in the Antarctic, a Godzilla-sized monster named Gor-Gor, and a host of other characters, of whom "Beefcake the Mighty" and "Dr. D. Bill Attaited" are the least offensively named. Yet the real hero of the piece, perhaps even its sole survivor, is the lead singer's um, piece—really the hand puppet that plays it! Hybrid film and video footage is inconsistently letterboxed and often intentionally over processed. The cheerfully evil-minded power punk score grinds out of the center speaker while forcing the left and right ones into slavery as extra-huge sub-woofers! —*JK*
Movie: ♫♫♫► **DVD:** ♫♫♫
Music Video Distributors (Cat #34002DVD, UPC #022891340027). Full frame. Stereo. $24.95. Keepcase. *LANG:* English. *FEATURES:* 22 chapter links • 6 song links • Interactive menus • 2-color picture disc • Curtain call cast list photos.
1992 56m/C D: Distortion Wells, Judas Bullhorn; **W:** Slave Pit, Inc.; **C:** Merrick Von Libel, Mel Mandl; **M:** GWAR.

Habit

Sam (Fessenden) has problems with alcohol and relationships when he meets Anna (Snaider), an enigmatic woman who comes and goes elusively, but after an intense sexual encounter that leaves him unconscious and bleeding, he becomes obsessed with her. Writer-editor-director Fessenden's presentation of the gritty side of New York City is first-rate, making the film a hit with festival audiences and fans of independent productions. That low-budget look doesn't gain much on DVD. Reds still bleed; they're supposed to. Night scenes are rough edged. But the disc contains several extras, including Fessenden's commentary, where he talks about the film's history, production, and his own efforts "looking for new truths in old cliches." Several features have tried to use horror as a metaphor for more serious ideas recently. This is one of the best. —*MM*
Movie: ♫♫♫ **DVD:** ♫♫♫
WinStar Home Entertainment (Cat #FLV5132, UPC #720917513225). Full frame. $24.98. Keepcase. *LANG:* English. *FEATURES:* 8 chapter links • 6-chapter commentary on the making of *Habit* • Music video, "Save You from Yourself" by Just Desserts • Theatrical trailer • Cast and crew thumbnail biographies. PC DVD-ROM can access weblinks.
1997 112m/C Larry Fessenden, Meredith Snaider, Aaron Beall, Heather Woodbury, Patricia Coleman; **D:** Larry Fessenden; **W:** Larry Fessenden; **C:** Frank DeMarco; **M:** Geoffrey Kidde. *AWARDS: NOM:* Independent Spirit Awards '98: Best Cinematography, Best Director (Fessenden).

Habitat

Despite a half-baked stereotyped premise and an uneven script, this offbeat sf/eco-horror is really ambitious and more successful than not. In a near future when the ozone layer has disappeared, Hank Symes (Karyo), a renegade mad scientist who's madder than most, turns the interior of his house into a fertile Garden of Eden. In the middle of a sun-blasted suburban wasteland it's a lush jungle where everything grows. His not-quite-so-mad wife Clarissa (Krige) thinks it's neat. Their teenaged son Andreas (Getty) is horribly embarrassed. That conflict between the freaky parents and the kid who wants to fit in is the most interesting part of the film, along with the computer effects. The cardboard villains and the less-than-successful sets get in the way. Some of the one-with-nature dialogue comes off as bad Walt Whitman—"I swim with the plankton and frolic with the sperm!"—but the intentional comic touches are welcome. The DVD captures the weird glowing interiors and imaginative effects better than VHS tape. The tinted exteriors are also more vivid on disc. My only real criticism is the lack of a commentary track. Daalder, who also made the cult hit *Massacre at Central High,* might have much to add. —*MM*
Movie: ♫♫♫ **DVD:** ♫♫
Simitar Entertainment (Cat #7428, UPC #082551742820). Full frame. Dolby Digital Stereo; Dolby Digital 5.1 Surround Stereo. $14.98. Keepcase. *LANG:* English. *FEATURES:* 8 chapter links • Production factoids.
1997 (R) 103m/C Alice Krige, Balthazar Getty, Tcheky Karyo, Kenneth Welsh, Lara Harris; **D:** Renee Daalder; **W:** Renee Daalder; **C:** Jean Lepine; **M:** Ralph Grierson.

Hackers

Teenaged computer cyber-geeks surf the Net and become the prime suspects in an industrial conspiracy when hacker Dade (Miller) breaks into the computer at Ellingson Oil Company. It's really an inside job but just try getting anyone (read "adult") to believe him. So the techno whiz kids band together, with cops and security all wanting to shut them down. This is an above-average DVD that never quite hits spectacular, but is consistently enjoyable to watch. The colors are very good, with strong vibrant hues, complemented by good contrast and brightness levels. Blacks are also very good. The image is very sharp and grain is always tolerable and most-times nonexistent. The 5.1 sound gives more life to the mix than the previous laserdisc or VHS editions did. There is plenty of bass and very crisp highs. The rear channels add some additional energy and are used well for ambience and the occasional effect. —JO

Movie: 🎬🎬 **DVD:** 🎬🎬🎬
MGM Home Entertainment (Cat #907169, UPC #027616716927). Widescreen (1.85:1) anamorphic. Dolby Digital Surround 5.1; Dolby Surround. $24.98. Keepcase. *LANG:* English (DD5.1); French (DS). *SUB:* English; French; Spanish. *CAP:* English. *FEATURES:* 32 chapter links • Theatrical trailer • 8-page booklet.
1995 (PG-13) 105m/C Jonny Lee Miller, Angelina Jolie, Fisher Stevens, Lorraine Bracco, Jesse Bradford, Wendell Pierce, Alberta Watson, Laurence Mason, Renoly Santiago, Matthew Lillard, Penn Jillette; *D:* Iain Softley; *W:* Rafael Moreu; *C:* Andrzej Sekula; *M:* Simon Boswell.

Hair

Film version of the explosive 1960s Broadway musical about the carefree life of the flower children and the shadow of the Vietnam War that hangs over them boasts great music, as well as wonderful choreography by Twyla Tharp, that help portray the surprisingly sensitive evocation of the period so long after the fact. Director Forman has an uncanny knack for understanding the textures of American life. Watch for a thinner Nell Carter. This DVD gives the film that extra boost it needs to be entertaining. Color rendition is accurate; so are the punchy contrast and brightness levels. Blacks are true as well. The picture is very sharp and grain and artifacts rare. The 5.1 sound is another big plus (although the Surround is used rarely) and the musical numbers sound as lively as the CD. The bass is loud and digitally clean. Highs are crisp and undistorted. —JO

Movie: 🎬🎬🎬 **DVD:** 🎬🎬🎬
MGM Home Entertainment (Cat #907641, UPC #027616764126). Widescreen (1.85:1) letterboxed; full frame. Dolby Digital 5.1; Dolby Digital Mono. $24.98. Keepcase. *LANG:* English; French. *SUB:* English; French. *FEATURES:* 44 chapter links • Theatrical trailer • Poster gallery • 8-page booklet.

1979 (PG) 122m/C Treat Williams, John Savage, Beverly D'Angelo, Annie Golden, Nicholas Ray, Nell Carter; *D:* Milos Forman; *W:* Michael Weller; *C:* Miroslav Ondricek; *M:* Galt MacDermot.

Half a Loaf of Kung Fu

The worthy bodyguards of Sem Chuan are called upon to deliver a valuable jade statue. Thwarted again and again by ruthless robbers, they falter. Only Chan carries on, meeting the enemy alone. Fast action, good story, with the trademarked Chan humor. The DVD image is not perceptively better than on previous VHS editions; that is, it's not very good. Picture is soft, with plenty of visible scars on the original film element used for the transfer. Audio is fair, occasionally distorted. Of the extras, the video interview with Chan is revealing but production values are low (off-camera interviewer is heard, but barely audible). The expected subtitles aren't present, so English-speaking audiences are stuck with the dubbed soundtrack if they want to follow the action. —MB *AKA:* Dian Zhi Gong Fu Gan Chian Chan.

Movie: 🎬🎬 **DVD:** 🎬
Simitar Entertainment (Cat #7259, UPC #08255172592). Full frame. Dolby Digital 2.0. $14.98. Keepcase. *LANG:* English; Cantonese. *FEATURES:* 10 chapter links • Movie factoids • Biography/filmography • Interview with Chan.
1985 98m/C *HK* Jackie Chan, James Tien.

Half-Baked

Four seedy roommates whose problems stem from their love of marijuana float through life with loser jobs that give them just enough money to buy their next bag. When Kenny (H. Williams) is arrested for killing a diabetic police horse during a munchies run, the three remaining friends must put their resinated brains together and come up with a way to bail him out. Thurgood (Chappelle), a custodian for a pharmaceutical company, decides to steal some high-grade grass from the lab; and along with Brian (Breuer, doing a very convincing stoned) and Scarface (Diaz), he begins dealing. This puts them afoul of the law as well as local drug lord Samson Simpson (C. Williams). Just say no. Trust me, dude, this stuff is bogus and it won't get you off. The colors on this DVD are at times so intense that they don't quite look real. That's all right. though, because the cartoon-like look works fine with the pothead humor. The movie would have been helped at least a little with a more souped-up sound. —JO

Movie: 🎬 **DVD:** 🎬🎬🎬
Universal Studios Home Video (Cat #20246, UPC #025192024627). Widescreen (1.85:1) anamorphic. Dolby Digital 5.1. $24.98. Keepcase. *LANG:* English. *SUB:* French; Spanish. *CAP:* English. *FEATURES:* 16 chapter links • Theatrical trailer • Cast and filmmakers bios • Production notes • Film highlights.

1997 (R) 83m/C Harland Williams, Dave Chappelle, Jim Breuer, Guillermo Diaz, Rachel True, Clarence Williams III, Thomas Chong, Jon Stewart, Stephen Baldwin, Willie Nelson, Janeane Garofalo, Steven Wright, Laura Silverman, Snoop Doggy Dogg; *D:* Tamra Davis; *W:* Neal Brennan, Dave Chappelle; *C:* Steven Bernstein; *M:* Alf Clausen.

Halloween

John Carpenter's horror classic has been acclaimed "the most successful independent motion picture of all time." A deranged youth returns to his hometown with murderous intent after 15 years in an asylum. Very, very scary—you feel this movie more than you see it. This is one of the earlier Anchor Bay DVD releases and should not be confused with their two THX editions, which are completely restored and re-mastered, and contain the documentary "Halloween Unmasked 2000." This DVD has both widescreen and full-frame sides and are similar in quality. Most of the film is very dark and, in the case of the DVD, very grainy. Artifacts appear at times. From the opening credits (red letters on black background) on there is a lot of color bleed. Overall, the Anchor Bay VHS tape would be a better addition to your collection, and their THX DVDs, the best way to go. —JO

Movie: 🎬🎬🎬 **DVD:** 🎬➤
Anchor Bay (Cat #DV10324, UPC #013131032499). Widescreen (2.35:1) letterboxed; full frame. Dolby Digital Mono. $24.98. Keepcase. *LANG:* English. *FEATURES:* 9 chapter links • Theatrical trailer.
1978 (R) 90m/C Jamie Lee Curtis, Donald Pleasence, Nancy Loomis, P.J. Soles, Charles Cyphers, Kyle Richards, Brian Andrews, John Michael Graham, Nancy Stephens, Arthur Malet, Mickey Yablans, Brent Le Page, Adam Hollander, Robert Phalen, Sandy Johnson, David Kyle, Nick Castle; *D:* John Carpenter; *W:* John Carpenter, Debra Hill; *C:* Dean Cundey; *M:* John Carpenter.

Halloween 2: The Nightmare Isn't Over!

Trying to pick up where *Halloween* left off, the sequel begins with the escape of vicious killer Michael, who continues to murder and terrorize the community of Haddonfield, IL. Lacking the innovative intentions of its predecessor, it relies on old-fashioned buckets of blood. No chills, just trauma. Coscripted by Carpenter, director of the original. After watching (and trashing) numerous Goodtimes releases, this was a pleasant surprise. This DVD is very sharp, and has very little grain to it. Like most horror films, this one contains many dark scenes, but the disc handles them with no problem. Not only are the brightness and contrast levels consistent, they are also comfortable to watch. The blacks are so good that at times they blend right into the letterbox bars. There are a couple of times when the reds bleed a little, but overall the picture still gets a very good rating. The sound is no slouch either, and although not 5.1 Surround, it is crisp, clean, has enough low end and dynamics, and the pro-logic is there when it's supposed to be. —*JO*

Movie: 🎬🎬 **DVD:** 🎬🎬🎬
Goodtimes Entertainment (Cat #05-81022, UPC #018713810229). Widescreen (2.35:1) letterboxed. Dolby Surround. $19.95. Snapper. *LANG:* English. *SUB:* English; French; Spanish. *FEATURES:* 18 chapter links • Production notes.
1981 (R) 92m/C Jamie Lee Curtis, Donald Pleasence, Jeffrey Kramer, Charles Cyphers, Lance Guest; ***D:*** Rick Rosenthal; ***W:*** John Carpenter, Debra Hill; ***C:*** Dean Cundey; ***M:*** John Carpenter.

Halloween 3: Season of the Witch

Unusual sequel has nothing to do with the others in the series. Instead it's a town-with-a-secret story that borrows freely from *Invasion of the Bodysnatchers, Stepford Wives,* and even *Alien.* Dr. Challis (Atkins) and Ellie (Nelkin) try to find out what happened to her father in the little town of Santa Mira—yes, that's the home of the pod people—but something else is going on there at the Silver Shamrock Novelty Company. Unfortunately, the script by director Tommy Lee Wallace works itself into a corner and can't find its way out. Reportedly, writer Nigel Kneale *(Quatermass and the Pit)* had his name removed. The effects are bloody and imaginative. Surprisingly, both image and sound are a little sharper than I remember from the original theatrical release. —*MM*

Movie: 🎬🎬 **DVD:** 🎬🎬
Goodtimes Entertainment (Cat #81023). Widescreen (2.35:1) letterboxed. Dolby Digital Mono. $19.98. Snapper. *LANG:* English; French; Spanish. *SUB:* French; Spanish. *FEATURES:* 18 chapter links.
1982 (R) 98m/C Tom Atkins, Stacey Nelkin, Dan O'Herlihy, Ralph Strait, Michael Currie; ***D:*** Tommy Lee Wallace; ***W:*** Tommy Lee Wallace; ***C:*** Dean Cundey; ***M:*** John Carpenter.

Halloween 4: The Return of Michael Myers

Eagle-eyed viewers will remember that at the end of *2,* Michael Myers isn't merely dead, he's really most sincerely dead—morally, ethically, spiritually, physically, positively, absolutely, undeniably, and reliably DEAD. But, sensing a profit, accountants decreed that he lives, hence this connect-the-dots installment. The plot contains nothing new but several scenes have the supernatural psychopath stalking a young child (Danielle Harris) and that's offensive. On DVD, this unfortunate dreck looks good and sounds very good. —*MM*
Movie: woof **DVD:** 🎬🎬🎬

Anchor Bay (Cat #DV10537, UPC #013131053791). Widescreen (1.85:1) letterboxed. Dolby Digital 5.1 Surround Stereo; Dolby Digital Surround Stereo. $24.98. Keepcase. *LANG:* English. *FEATURES:* 24 chapter links • Theatrical trailers.
1988 (R) 88m/C Donald Pleasence, Ellie Cornell, Danielle Harris, Michael Pataki, George P. Wilbur, Beau Starr, Kathleen Kinmont, Sasha Jenson, Gene Ross; ***D:*** Dwight Little; ***W:*** Alan B. McElroy; ***C:*** Peter Collister; ***M:*** Alan Howarth, John Carpenter.

Halloween: H2O

After changing her name and moving to California, Laurie Strode (Curtis) still hasn't got over the traumatic events of her past. Twenty years later, her brother Michael finds the private school where she works. Toss in four romantically inclined teens, a boyfriend (Arkin), and a security guard (Cool J), and all the elements are in place for the final (probably) entry in the uneven series. This is one of the better efforts with strong performances, a fair if unsurprising script, and competent direction. On DVD, the film looks fine, handling the dark conclusion without a problem. This kind of horror, which is not dependent on flashy computer-generated effects, actually works as well on the small screen as it does in theatres. Home video—particularly a crisp image like this—adds an element of intimacy. (By the way, fans who listen carefully in chapter seven will catch a brief quote of Bernard Herrmann's *Psycho* score when Janet Leigh is standing in front of a familiar Ford.) —*MM* *AKA:* Halloween: H20 (Twenty Years Later); Halloween 7.
Movie: 🎬🎬🎬 **DVD:** 🎬🎬🎬
Buena Vista Home Entertainment (Cat #16785, UPC #717951001887). Widescreen (2.35:1) letterboxed. Dolby Digital 5.1 Surround Stereo. $39.99. Keepcase. *LANG:* English. *CAP:* English. *FEATURES:* "Unmasking the Horror," featurette on the *Halloween* series • Music video • Trivia game • 13 chapter links.
1998 (R) 86m/C Jamie Lee Curtis, Adam Arkin, Josh Hartnett, Michelle Williams, Adam Hann-Byrd, Jodi Lyn O'Keefe, Janet Leigh, L.L. Cool J., Joseph Gordon-Levitt, Nancy Stephens, Branden Williams, Chris Durand; ***D:*** Steve Miner; ***W:*** Matt Greenberg, Robert Zappia; ***C:*** Daryn Okada; ***M:*** John Ottman, John Carpenter. *AWARDS: NOM:* MTV Movie Awards '99: Breakthrough Performance (Hartnett).

Hamburger Hill

Despite its claims of historical accuracy, this Vietnam film boasts the prettiest ensemble of young Hollywood actors ever assembled. At the first possible moment, they strip to the waist to show off their abs and pecs and yet once the action begins, they turn into a bunch of right-wing crybabies who complain that their girlfriends have been deluded by liberals. The

combat scenes are well paced and unusually graphic with exploding heads, shredded organs, and severed limbs created by in-your-face special effects. On DVD, both image and sound are crisp and sharply focused, but that clarity actually undercuts any feeling of authenticity, which can be captured more effectively with shaky handheld cameras and grainy, dirty images. —*MM*

Movie: 🎬🎬 **DVD:** 🎬🎬
Artisan Entertainment (Cat #60495, UPC #01223604950). Widescreen (1.85:1) letterboxed. Dolby 5.1 Stereo. $24.98. Keepcase. *FEATURES:* Theatrical trailer • 36 chapter links.
1987 (R) 104m/C Michael Dolan, Daniel O'Shea, Dylan McDermott, Tommy Swerdlow, Courtney B. Vance, Anthony Barille, Michael Boatman, Don Cheadle, Tim Quill, Don James, Michael A. Nickles, Harry O'Reilly, Steven Weber, Tegan West, Kieu Chinh, Doug Goodman, J.C. Palmore; ***D:*** John Irvin; ***W:*** Jim Carabatsos; ***C:*** Peter Macdonald; ***M:*** Philip Glass.

Hand Gun

Wounded in a shoot-out after a robbery, Jack McCallister (Cassel) gets away with half a million in cash. His two sons, the violent George (Williams) and con-man Michael (Schulzie), want a cut of the loot. Parts of this crime drama have a realistic feel, but the action scenes are static. The DVD does justice to the low-budget look and sound of the film, but, as the generic title suggests, there's really not enough to it to earn a strong recommendation. —*MM*
Movie: 🎬🎬 **DVD:** 🎬🎬
Image Entertainment (Cat #ID5595FMDVD, UPC #014381559521). Full frame. Dolby Digital Stereo. $19.99. Snapper. *LANG:* English. *FEATURES:* 12 chapter links.
1993 (R) 90m/C Seymour Cassel, Treat Williams, Paul Schulzie, Michael Rapaport; ***D:*** Whitney Ransick; ***W:*** Whitney Ransick; ***C:*** Michael Spiller; ***M:*** Douglas J. Cuomo.

The Hand that Rocks the Cradle

Rebecca DeMornay is at her eye-rolling best as Peyton Flanders, the vengeful widow who attempts to destroy a suburban family. Along with *Fatal Attraction,* the film established the "female-from-hell" thriller. Claire Bartel (Sciorra) is the target of her madness. Ernie Hudson turns what could have been a cliched supporting role into something more. The DVD contains no significant flaws. It looks and sounds fine with a clarity that rivals the theatrical release. Suspense films with this kind of domestic setting seem to gain something when they're brought to the small screen properly. —*MM*
Movie: 🎬🎬🎬 **DVD:** 🎬🎬🎬
Hollywood Pictures Home Video (Cat #15283, UPC #717951000774). Widescreen (1.85:1) letterboxed. Dolby Digital Surround Stereo. $29.99. Keepcase. *LANG:*

English; French. CAP: English. FEATURES: 15 chapter links • Theatrical trailer.

1992 (R) 110m/C Annabella Sciorra, Rebecca DeMornay, Matt McCoy, Ernie Hudson, Julianne Moore, Madeline Zima, John de Lancie, Mitchell Laurance; **D:** Curtis Hanson; **W:** Amanda Silver; **C:** Robert Elswit; **M:** Graeme Revell. AWARDS: MTV Movie Awards '92: Best Villain (DeMornay).

Hang 'Em High

A cowboy is saved from a lynching and vows to hunt down the gang that nearly killed him in this American-made spaghetti western. Eastwood's first major vehicle made outside of Europe tries hard but is no substitution for the real thing. It's best to just skip this DVD and buy the Eastwood/Leone films. The disc is as lackluster as the film itself. The laser looked a touch better and the VHS even seemed to be a little sharper, although the colors on the DVD are much stronger and don't bleed much. Grain is also not too bad. Contrast and brightness are adequate, but the blacks range from average to occasionally true. The mono sound just doesn't cut it, sounding very thin and desperate for a big bass boost. —JO

Movie: ♪♪➤ **DVD:** ♪➤
MGM Home Entertainment (Cat #906730, UPC #027616673022). Widescreen (1.85:1) anamorphic; full frame. Mono. $24.98. Snapper. LANG: English; French. SUB: English; Spanish; French. CAP: English. FEATURES: 32 chapter links • Theatrical trailer.

1967 (PG-13) 114m/C Clint Eastwood, Inger Stevens, Ed Begley Sr., Pat Hingle, James MacArthur; **D:** Ted Post; **W:** Leonard Freeman, Mel Goldberg; **C:** Richard H. Kline, Leonard J. South; **M:** Dominic Frontiere.

Hangmen

Rogue CIA agents and Vietnam vets battle it out on the East side of New York. Amazingly, Sandra Bullock's career survived this early micro-budget disaster. It's extremely violent with semi-professional acting in many roles and a fetishist attitude toward weapons. The DVD is barely watchable with heavily grained shadows. Throughout, the film is dark, poorly lit, and cold-looking. —MM

Movie: ♪ **DVD:** ♪
Simitar Entertainment (Cat #7394, UPC #082551739424). Full frame. Dolby Digital Stereo. $14.98. Keepcase. LANG: English. FEATURES: 8 chapter links • Sandra Bullock filmography.

1987 (R) 88m/C Jake La Motta, Rick Washburne, Doug Thomas, Sandra Bullock; **D:** J. Christian Ingvordsen; **W:** J. Christian Ingvordsen, Steven Kaman; **C:** Steven Kaman; **M:** Michael Montes.

Hans Christian Andersen

Sentimental story of Hans Christian Andersen (Kaye) is an admitted "fairy tale," not a biography. The fanciful sets and overly sweet acting style are both dated now. On DVD, the bright, rich Technicolor images emphasize the red end of the spectrum. Sound is adequate. —MM

Movie: ♪♪ **DVD:** ♪♪➤
HBO Home Video (Cat #90650, UPC #026359065026). Full frame. Dolby Digital Stereo; Mono. $24.98. Snapper. LANG: English; French; Spanish; Italian; German. SUB: English; French; Spanish. FEATURES: 22 chapter links • Cast and crew thumbnail biographies • Theatrical trailer.

1952 112m/C Danny Kaye, Farley Granger, Zizi Jeanmarie, Joey Walsh; **D:** Charles Vidor; **W:** Moss Hart; **C:** Harry Stradling; **M:** Frank Loesser. AWARDS: NOM: Academy Awards '52: Best Art Direction/Set Decoration (Color), Best Color Cinematography, Best Costume Design (Color), Best Song ("Thumbelina"), Best Sound, Scoring of a Musical.

The Happiest Millionaire

A Disney film about a newly immigrated lad (Steele) who finds a job as butler in the home of an eccentric millionaire (MacMurray). Based on the book My Philadelphia Father by Kyle Crichton and reminiscent of Mary Poppins–era Disney, but without the charm and appeal. This disc is definitely the finest version of this film that is currently available. On DVD, the colors are vibrant, crisp, and really announce themselves throughout the film. The audio, however, would benefit from additional remastering. The nearly 80 minutes of musical sequences sound good enough, but dialogue is occasionally muddled and hard to understand. —MJT

Movie: ♪♪ **DVD:** ♪♪♪
Anchor Bay (Cat #DV10827, UPC #013131082791). Widescreen (1.66:1) letterboxed. Dolby Digital Stereo. $29.90. Keepcase. FEATURES: 27 chapter links • Theatrical overture • Intermission • Road show presentation. Features 46 minutes added to previously available 118-minute version.

1967 164m/C Fred MacMurray, Tommy Steele, Greer Garson, Geraldine Page, Lesley Ann Warren, John Davidson; **D:** Norman Tokar; **W:** A.J. Carothers; **C:** Edward Colman; **M:** Richard M. Sherman, Robert B. Sherman. AWARDS: NOM: Academy Awards '67: Best Costume Design.

Happiness

Very disturbing film defines the "love it or hate it" category. The story revolves around three middle-class New Jersey sisters—perky housewife Trish (Stevenson), underachieving Joy (Adams), and glamourous writer Helen (Boyle). Trish is married to shrink Bill (Baker) and they have an 11-year-old son, Billy (Read), who's getting curious about sex. His dad is the wrong person to ask since he's a pedophile who abuses his son's friends. Then there's Allen (Hoffman), one of Bill's patients. He makes obscene phone calls to Helen, who turns out to be turned on by the dirty talk. Suburban hell, indeed. Some riveting performances, especially Baker and Hoffman. Director Solondz creates a morally skewed universe that is both depressing and hilarious (you should feel guilty for laughing at so much human misery). A blacker-than-black comedy. The DVD has a softer look than expected due to many sequences that are digitally smeared by artifacts. When that's not going on, the picture is sharp and the grain level is low. Colors are excellent—accurate, with strong deep hues and only minor bleed. Blacks are generally true. Contrast is very good and brightness always comfortable. The Dolby Surround works very well in supplying ambience and is no slouch in delivering a fairly lively mix, including bright high end and smooth deep bass. —JO

Movie: ♪♪♪ **DVD:** ♪♪♪
Trimark Home Video (Cat #VM7023D, UPC #031498702337). Widescreen (1.85:1) letterboxed. Dolby Surround. $24.99. Keepcase. LANG: English. SUB: English; Spanish; French. FEATURES: 36 chapter links • Cast and crew bios.

1998 139m/C Dylan Baker, Cynthia Stevenson, Lara Flynn Boyle, Jane Adams, Philip Seymour Hoffman, Ben Gazzara, Louise Lasser, Rufus Read, Jared Harris, Jon Lovitz, Camryn Manheim, Elizabeth Ashley, Marla Maples; **D:** Todd Solondz; **W:** Todd Solondz; **C:** Maryse Alberti; **M:** Robbie Kondor. AWARDS: NOM: Golden Globe Awards '99: Best Screenplay; Independent Spirit Awards '99: Best Actor (Baker), Best Director (Solondz), Best Supporting Actor (Hoffman).

Happy Gilmore

Skating-impaired hockey player Gilmore (Sandler) translates his slap shot into a 400-yard tee shot and joins the pro golf tour. His unique style brings a new, less refined breed of fan to the game and upsets the reigning tour hotshot (McDonald). Sandler improves on Billy Madison, which isn't saying much. There's still plenty of ammo for his many detractors, but the laughs are more frequent and consistent. Replacing bathroom humor with abusive behavior, the misnamed Happy swears at or beats up about 90% of the supporting cast, including Bob Barker (it's about time someone did the job) in a charity pro-am. The image is very sharp and free of grain. Artifacts are also not a problem. The colors definitely rate four bones and are extremely vibrant and accurate to the theatre. Bleed is rare. Blacks are true and the contrast and brightness levels seem just right to both retain picture accuracy while giving the image real punch. The 5.1 sound is excellent with plenty of space in the mix and good solid bass to go along with the crisp highs that give both music and dialogue great presence. —JO

Movie: ♪♪➤ **DVD:** ♪♪♪➤
Universal Studios Home Video (Cat #20151, UPC #025192015120). Full frame. Dolby Digital 5.1; Dolby Surround.

$24.98. Keepcase. *LANG:* English (DD5.1); French (DS). *SUB:* Spanish. *CAP:* English. *FEATURES:* 16 chapter links • Theatrical trailer • Cast and filmmakers bios • Production notes • Film highlights.
1996 (PG-13) 92m/C Adam Sandler, Christopher McDonald, Carl Weathers, Julie Bowen, Frances Bay, Ben Stiller, Richard Kiel, Joe Flaherty, Kevin Nealon, Alan Covert, Robert Smigel, Bob Barker, Dennis Dugan; *D:* Dennis Dugan; *W:* Adam Sandler, Tim Herlihy; *C:* Arthur Albert; *M:* Mark Mothersbaugh. *AWARDS:* MTV Movie Awards '96: Best Fight (Adam Sandler/Bob Barker); *NOM:* MTV Movie Awards '96: Best Comedic Performance (Sandler); Golden Raspberry Awards '96: Worst Actor (Sandler).

Happy, Texas

Not-exactly-hardened criminals Harry (Northam) and Wayne (Zahn) accidentally escape from a chain gang and wind up in a stolen RV in the little town of Happy, TX, where they are mistaken for gay beauty pageant producers. Said producers have been brought in to coach the town's prepubescent cherubs in the "Miss Fresh-Squeezed Pre-Teen" contest. The two guys decide to continue the impersonation long enough to rob the local bank, which is run by Joe (Walker). Also on hand are Ms. Shaefer (Douglas) and Sheriff Chappy (Macy). The comedy avoids most stereotypes and focuses on small-town values and strongly written characters. Much of the film was made on location (in a small California town) and so neither image nor sound gain much on DVD, though both are fine. The extras are more important here. In their comments, Illsley and Stone explain why the second half is so loosely plotted, and how the film rose from its low-budget beginnings. As usual, it's not difficult to see why the deleted scenes were deleted. The shift in the two levels of the dual-layers of information causes a brief digital hiccup. —MM
Movie: ♫♫♫ *DVD:* ♫♫♫
Miramax Pictures Home Video (Cat #18298, UPC #717951004833). Widescreen (1.85:1) anamorphic. Dolby Digital Surround Stereo. $39.99. Keepcase. *LANG:* English; French. *SUB:* Spanish. *FEATURES:* 33 chapter links • Commentary: Mark Illsley and Ed Stone • Deleted scenes • "Making of" featurette • Interview with Illsley and Stone • 2 music videos.
1999 (PG-13) 104m/C Steve Zahn, Jeremy Northam, Ally Walker, Illeana Douglas, William H. Macy, M.C. Gainey, Ron Perlman, Michael Hitchcock, Paul Dooley; *D:* Mark Illsley; *W:* Phil Reeves, Ed Stone, Mark Illsley; *C:* Bruce Douglas Johnson; *M:* Peter Harris. *AWARDS:* Independent Spirit Awards '00: Best Supporting Actor (Zahn).

Happy Together

Lovers Lai Yiu-Fai (Leung) and Ho Po-Wing (Cheung) travel to Argentina from Hong Kong looking for adventure but soon go their separate ways. Lai is working as a doorman at a tango bar when a badly beaten Ho unexpectedly re-enters his life. Lai looks after the self-destructive Ho but restlessness causes him to desert Lai once again, even as Lai befriends young Taiwanese Chang (Chen). After Chang returns to Taipei, Lai begins to suffer from depression and serious homesickness, as well as still worrying about Ho. Edgy visuals and playful performances belie a serious nature. Kino has delivered a fine DVD with this release. The picture is as sharp as most big-budget mainstream releases and there are no grain or artifacts to get in the way. The colors are rich, and the contrast and brightness levels ensure that shading details remain intact under all lighting conditions. Even the soundtrack, which is only stereo, features good dynamics and excellent imaging and separation. —JO *AKA:* Cheun Gwong Tsa Sit.
Movie: ♫♫♫ *DVD:* ♫♫♫ ▶
Kino on Video (Cat #K119DVD, UPC #738329011925). Widescreen (1.85:1) letterboxed. Stereo. $29.95. Snapper. *LANG:* Chinese. *SUB:* English. *FEATURES:* 13 chapters.
1996 92m/C *HK* Leslie Cheung, Tony Leung Chiu-Wai, Chang Chen; *D:* Wong Kar-Wai; *W:* Wong Kar-Wai; *C:* Christopher Doyle; *M:* Danny Chung. *AWARDS:* Cannes Film Festival '97: Best Director (Kar-Wai); *NOM:* Independent Spirit Awards '98: Best Foreign Film.

Hard-Boiled

Made by the Hong Kong filmmaker credited for mastering violence as visual poetry, Woo's crime action-drama tells the story of Yuen, a jaded police inspector played by Woo regular Yun-Fat. The violence here is far more brutal and far less stylized than in earlier Woo movies, but it delivers with flourish the point that America's Dirty Harry Callahan can learn a thing or two about excessive force from "Tequila" Yuen. While investigating an organized crime syndicate and a group of gun smugglers who killed his partner, Yuen joins forces with Tony, an undercover cop who's working as a gangster hitman. Of course there's lots of gunplay and betrayals among all the participants, with the usual Woo way with violence and action sequences—along with a dash of dark humor—helping to sustain a somewhat contrived plot. The climactic action sequence in the hospital is unforgettable. Given the typically better-than-competent treatment from Criterion, the film has never looked or sounded better on video than it does on the DVD. After the end credits roll off the screen, spend some time with the abundant supplements. —MB *AKA:* Lashou Shentan.
Movie: ♫♫♫ *DVD:* ♫♫♫ ▶
Criterion Collection (Cat #CC1516D, UPC #715515009041). Widescreen (1.85:1) letterboxed. Dolby Digital Mono. $39.98. Keepcase. *LANG:* Cantonese; English. *SUB:* English. *FEATURES:* 45 chapter links • Commentary: Woo, Terence Chang, Roger Avary, Dave Kehr • Theatrical trailers for 11 of Woo's Hong Kong films • A student film by Woo • Essays on *Hard Boiled* and Hong Kong crime films by David Chute.
1992 126m/C *HK* Chow Yun-Fat, Tony Leung Chiu-Wai, Philip Chan, Anthony Wong, Teresa Mo, Bowie Lam, Hoi-Shan Kwan, Philip Kwok, John Woo; *D:* John Woo; *W:* Barry Wong, John Woo; *C:* Wing-Heng Wang; *M:* Michael Gibbs.

Hard Bounty

While the feminist western *Bad Girls* was a critical and popular fiasco, this one's not bad. The plot's more or less identical; the acting is certainly no worse and the humor is intentional. It's obvious from beginning to end that this story of prostitutes rebelling against patronizing patriarchs is the stuff of a B-movie. That's what *Bad Girls* was supposed to be, but somewhere in the filmmaking process, it tried to become "a major motion picture." Director Wynorski, who has a reputation for working fast and cheap, avoided such delusions and came up with a completely serviceable little sagebrush and silicone time-waster. On DVD, the flaws—so-so production values, less than perfect focus—are more evident than they are on tape. —MM
Movie: ♫♫ *DVD:* ♫♫
Image Entertainment (Cat #ID5596FMDVD, UPC #014381559620). Full frame. Dolby Digital Stereo. $24.99. Snapper. *LANG:* English. *FEATURES:* 12 chapter links.
1994 (R) 90m/C Matt McCoy, Kelly Le Brock, Rochelle Swanson, Felicity Waterman, Kimberly Kelley; *D:* Jim Wynorski; *W:* Karen Kelly; *C:* Zoran Hochstatter; *M:* Taj.

A Hard Day's Night

Peer in on an average "day in the life" of the Fab Four with the Beatles' first film, a riotous black-and-white musical romp released at the height of Beatlemania. More than 35 years after it was made, it remains joyous, funny, and fresh. Shot in a pseudo-documentary style with great flair by Lester and noted as the first music video. The story is thin—the foursome are mobbed by fans beyond the verge of hysterics as they travel from Liverpool to London for a TV appearance—but the musicians, their music, and plenty of comic turns make up for it. Now a collectors' item among Beatlephiles and DVD buffs, this currently out-of-print disc sports a handsome B&W video transfer and nice, old-fashioned stereo sound. The extras are great fun, too. —MB
Movie: ♫♫♫ ▶ *DVD:* ♫♫♫ ▶
MPI Home Video (Cat #DVD7082, UPC #030306708225). Full frame. Dolby Digital 2.0 Stereo. $24.98. Keepcase. *LANG:* English; French; Spanish. *SUB:* English; French; Spanish. *FEATURES:* 29 chapter links • Rarely seen additional footage • Newsreel footage • Theatrical trailer for the 1982 re-release • Interview with

director Lester • Short film, "The Running, Jumping Standing Still," with Peter Sellers.
1964 90m/B *GB* John Lennon, Paul McCartney, George Harrison, Ringo Starr, Wilfrid Brambell, Norman Rossington, John Junkin, Victor Spinetti, Anna Quayle, Deryck Guyler, Richard Vernon, Lionel Blair, Eddie Malin, Robin Ray, Alison Seebohm, David Saxon, Patti Boyd; *D:* Richard Lester; *W:* Alun Owen; *C:* Gilbert Taylor; *M:* George Martin, John Lennon, Paul McCartney. *AWARDS: NOM:* Academy Awards '64: Best Adapted Score, Best Story & Screenplay (Owen).

Hard Drive

Produced in the early days of Internet popularity, this video premiere is marketed as an erotic thriller (hence the silly title) about Jack (Damian) and Delilah's (Fulton) online sexual fantasies. In reality, it's an exceptionally clever and often funny noirish thriller. Writer-director Merendino's story turns around on itself about every ten minutes or so. All of the computer stuff is dated now but the film holds up well with solid supporting performances from McCoy, Albert, and other B-movie veterans. The DVD looks and sounds very good (with a fine jazz score by Nels Cline). In one scene, a set of mini-blinds pinwheels. Otherwise, the heavy blacks and grays of the sets and costumes are fine. A true sleeper. —*MM*
Movie: ♫♫♫ *DVD:* ♫♫♫
Image Entertainment (Cat #ID5597FMDVD, UPC #014381559729). Full frame. Dolby Digital Stereo. $24.99. Snapper. *LANG:* English. *FEATURES:* 20 chapter links.
1994 92m/C Matt McCoy, Christina Fulton, Edward Albert, Leo Damian, Stella Stevens; *D:* James Merendino; *W:* James Merendino; *C:* Sead Muhtarevic; *M:* Nels Cline.

Hard Rain

Armored car guards Tom (Slater) and uncle Charlie (Asner) are transporting millions to high ground during a flood in a small Indiana town. When their truck is submerged, a band of jet ski–riding thieves led by Jim (Freeman) show up, and then the local sheriff (Quaid) decides that he wants to take a cut of the loot, too. Toss in Karen (Driver), a comely church restorer, and a cast of colorful supporting characters, and you've got an energetic if soggy adventure. Two things that give many DVDs problems are dark scenes and moving water. This one is set at night in a flood, but it handles both elements with ease. Director Salomon, who filmed much of the action in a huge tank in Palmdale, CA, must share credit with production designer J. Michael Riva and director of photography Peter Menzies Jr., whose exemplary work shines through. —*MM AKA:* Flood.
Movie: ♫♫♫ *DVD:* ♫♫♫
Paramount Home Video (Cat #332137, UPC #097363321378). Widescreen letterboxed. Dolby Digital 5.1 Surround; Surround Stereo; Dolby Stereo. $29.99. Keepcase. *LANG:* English (DD5.1); French (DS). *SUB:* Spanish. *CAP:* English. *FEATURES:* 26 chapter links • Theatrical trailer.
1997 (R) 96m/C Morgan Freeman, Christian Slater, Randy Quaid, Minnie Driver, Ed Asner, Richard Dysart, Betty White, Mark Rolston, Peter Murnik, Dann Florek, Wayne Duvall, Michael Goorjian; *D:* Mikael Salomon; *W:* Graham Yost; *C:* Peter Menzies Jr.; *M:* Christopher Young.

Hard Target

Van Damme continues his action-hero ways as Chance Boudreaux, a Cajun (which explains the accent) merchant seaman, who comes to the rescue of Natasha (Butler), albeit with lots of violence. Brimley provides the humor as Chance's bayou uncle. It's another variation of "The Most Dangerous Game" story but it moves. American directorial debut of over-the-top Hong Kong action director Woo, who had to tone down his usual stylistic effects and reportedly cut some of the more violent scenes to earn an "R" rating. Woo's preferred cut was available on Japanese laserdisc, but it's not here on the DVD. His cut is not much more violent but somehow feels more powerful, thanks to some editing tweaks here and there. The DVD looks good, though, and Woo's slick look is presented in fine detail with excellent colors, and a good 5.1 "action" mix that features excellent bass and nice use of the Surround channels. —*JO*
Movie: ♫♫♫ *DVD:* ♫♫♫
Universal Studios Home Video (Cat #20230, UPC #025192023026). Widescreen (1.85:1) anamorphic. Dolby Digital 5.1; Dolby Surround. $24.98. Keepcase. *LANG:* English (DD5.1); French (DS). *SUB:* Spanish. *CAP:* English. *FEATURES:* 16 chapter links • Theatrical trailer • Production notes • Cast and filmmakers bios • Film highlights.
1993 (R) 97m/C Jean-Claude Van Damme, Lance Henriksen, Yancy Butler, Arnold Vosloo, Wilford Brimley, Kasi Lemmons, Eliott Keener, Theodore (Ted) Raimi, Chuck Pfarrer; *D:* John Woo; *W:* Chuck Pfarrer; *C:* Russell Carpenter; *M:* Graeme Revell. *AWARDS: NOM:* MTV Movie Awards '94: Most Desirable Male (Van Damme), Best Action Sequence.

Hard Times

Depression-era drifter Chaney (Bronson) becomes a bare-knuckle prize fighter with the assistance of the gambler Speed (Coburn). This sleeper hit is one of the finest efforts for all concerned. Director Hill has seldom been in such control of the material. The two stars underplay their roles to perfection. On DVD, the film still looks great. A few scratches and a little grain only add character to a film that already has plenty of character. The sound, which fades at odd moments, is not as strong, but Barry DeVorzon's score is excellent. —*MM*
Movie: ♫♫♫ *DVD:* ♫♫♫

Columbia Tristar Home Video (Cat #03063, UPC #043396030633). Widescreen (2.35:1) letterboxed; full frame. Dolby Digital Mono. $25.95. Keepcase. *LANG:* English; Portuguese. *SUB:* English; Spanish; Portuguese; Chinese; Korean; Thai. *FEATURES:* 28 chapter links • Theatrical trailers.
1975 (PG) 92m/C Charles Bronson, James Coburn, Jill Ireland, Strother Martin; *D:* Walter Hill; *W:* Walter Hill, Bryan Gindoff, Bruce Henstell; *C:* Philip Lathrop; *M:* Barry DeVorzon.

Hard to Kill

Policeman Seagal is shot and left for dead in his bedroom, but survives against the odds, though his wife does not. After seven years, he is well enough to consider evening the score with his assailants. He hides while training in martial arts for the final battle. Strong outing from Seagal, with good supporting cast. No better way to see Segal throw his body around (when he still managed to move during martial arts scenes) than on this DVD. The image remains sharp during all lighting conditions and all degrees of motion. No artifacts or grain. Colors and blacks are true. The separation and effects are excellent on the 5.1 soundtrack and the boisterous bass keeps the action flowing. —*JO*
Movie: ♫♫ *DVD:* ♫♫♫
Warner Home Video, Inc. (Cat #11914, UPC #085931191421). Widescreen (1.85:1) anamorphic. Dolby Digital 5.1; Dolby Digital Mono; Dolby Surround. $24.98. Snapper. *LANG:* English; Spanish; French. *SUB:* English; Spanish; French. *CAP:* English. *FEATURES:* 26 chapter links • 8 theatrical trailers • Production notes.
1989 (R) 96m/C Steven Seagal, Kelly Le Brock, William Sadler, Frederick Coffin, Bonnie Burroughs, Zachary Rosencrantz, Dean Norris; *D:* Bruce Malmuth; *W:* Steven McKay; *C:* Matthew F. Leonetti; *M:* Charles Fox.

Hard Vice

Las Vegas cops Owens (Jones) and Thompson (Tweed) have their work cut out for them when too many high rollers turn up dead. All the clues point to a psycho-hooker. The DVD image is clear enough, but it lacks the depth of detail that the best examples of the medium display. Fast pans blur and one plaid coat flashes. In general, it's slightly better than the generic direct-to-video title would lead you to expect. —*MM*
Movie: ♫♫ *DVD:* ♫♫
Simitar Entertainment (Cat #7315, UPC #082551731527). Full frame. PCM Stereo. $14.98. Keepcase. *LANG:* English. *FEATURES:* 8 links • Production factoids • Sam Jones and Shannon Tweed thumbnail bios and filmographies. The box copy gives the film an "R" rating. The production factoids list it as "PG-13." Contents suggest the latter.

1994 (R) 86m/C Shannon Tweed, Sam Jones, James Gammon, Rebecca Ferratti; *D:* Joey Travolta; *W:* Joey Travolta; *C:* F. Smith Martin; *M:* Jeff Lass.

The Hard Way

Tough New York cop John Moss (Woods) is on the trail of another of those pesky serial killers when Hollywood star Nick Lang (Fox) decides that he'll tag along with Moss to research a role and change his big-screen image. The chemistry between the two stars, along with nice cameo work from Penny Marshall, is enough to overcome the overly familiar plot elements. The DVD manages to look good, even in some difficult scenes, including nocturnal city street exteriors and splashy dance clubs. The image doesn't have the bright sparkle of the best discs, but it's fine for the story. —*MM*

Movie: 🎯🎯🎯 **DVD:** 🎯🎯➤
Universal Studios Home Video (Cat #20434, UPC #025192043420). Widescreen (2.35:1) letterboxed. Dolby Digital Surround Stereo. $24.98. *LANG:* English; French. *SUB:* Spanish. *CAP:* English. *FEATURES:* 16 chapter links • "Making of" featurette • Music video • Production notes • Cast and crew thumbnail biographies • Theatrical trailer • Universal web links.
1991 (R) 91m/C James Woods, Michael J. Fox, Annabella Sciorra, Stephen Lang, Penny Marshall, L.L. Cool J., John Capodice, Christina Ricci, Karen Gorney, Luis Guzman; *D:* John Badham; *W:* Daniel Pyne, Lem Dobbs; *C:* Robert Primes; *M:* Arthur B. Rubinstein.

The Haunted Strangler

Mid-level Karloff horror opens with a rowdy Dickensian execution scene at Newgate Prison, 1860. Flash forward 20 years. Novelist John Rankin (Karloff) attempts to reopen the investigation of the murder of a character named Martha Stewart by a mysterious one-armed man. He sees a miscarriage of justice. As it unfolds, the odd but finally archetypal story deserves more complex treatment. It's padded with Folies Bergere–style dance numbers when it ought to be more deeply involved with the characters. The black-and-white photography looks very good on DVD with only a few artifacts in large areas of solid black. Even with that reservation, the disc still looks better than older tapes. —*MM* *AKA:* The Grip of the Strangler.
Movie: 🎯🎯➤ **DVD:** 🎯🎯🎯
Image Entertainment (Cat #ID4430GODVD, UPC #014381443028). Full frame. Dolby Digital Mono. $24.99. Snapper. *LANG:* English. *FEATURES:* Theatrical trailer • 16 chapter links.
1958 78m/B *GB* Boris Karloff, Anthony Dawson, Elizabeth Allan, Timothy Turner, Diane Aubrey, Dorothy Gordon, Jean Kent, Vera Day; *D:* Robert Day; *W:* John C. Cooper, Jan Read; *C:* Lionel Banes; *M:* Buxton Orr.

The Haunting

Dr. Marrow (Neeson) introduces three naive subjects—Theo (Zeta-Jones), Luke (Wilson), and Nell (Taylor)—to the paranormal world when the four stay at an allegedly haunted house to investigate reports of ghosts. De Bont's remake of the famous understated horror overrelies on big special effects and incredible set design for its scares. Both of those lose some of their power on anything smaller than a theatre screen, but on DVD, they're still impressive. The cathedral-like interiors of the mansion (created by production designer Eugenio Zanetti) are almost humorous in their magnificence. The importance of the technical aspects of the film accentuate the idea that the whole thing is a gaudy box with nothing inside. —*MM* *AKA:* The Haunting of Hill House.
Movie: 🎯🎯 **DVD:** 🎯🎯➤
DreamWorks Home Entertainment (Cat #84820, UPC #667068482027). Widescreen (2.35:1) letterboxed. Dolby Digital 5.1 Surround Stereo; Dolby Digital Surround Stereo. $29.99. Keepcase. *LANG:* English. *SUB:* English. *FEATURES:* 24 chapter links • Theatrical trailers • "Making of" featurette • Cast and crew thumbnail biographies.
1999 (PG-13) 114m/C Lili Taylor, Liam Neeson, Catherine Zeta-Jones, Owen C. Wilson, Bruce Dern, Marian Seldes, Virginia Madsen, Todd Field, Alix Koromzay; *D:* Jan De Bont; *W:* David Self; *C:* Caleb Deschanel; *M:* Jerry Goldsmith. *AWARDS: NOM:* Golden Raspberry Awards '99: Worst Picture, Worst Actress (Zeta-Jones), Worst Director (De Bont), Worst Screenplay.

Havana

In 1958, on the eve of revolution, gambler Jack Weil (Redford) goes to Cuba in search of high-stakes poker. On the boat he meets Roberta (Olin), wife of Arturo (Julia), and becomes involved in the island's politics. Though the film didn't catch on in theatrical release, it looks fine on disc. Visually, director Pollack is working with darker shades, even in bright sunny tropic scenes. More garish nightclub dives are handled well, too, and the sound is fine, doing justice to Dave Grusin's terrific jazz score. —*MM*
Movie: 🎯🎯🎯 **DVD:** 🎯🎯🎯
Universal Studios Home Video (Cat #20414, UPC #025192041426). Widescreen (1.85:1) letterboxed. Dolby Digital 5.1 Surround Stereo; Dolby Digital Surround Stereo. $26.98. Keepcase. *LANG:* English; French; Spanish. *SUB:* Spanish. *CAP:* English. *FEATURES:* 21 chapter links • "Making of" featurette • Production notes • Cast and crew thumbnail biographies • Universal web links.
1990 (R) 145m/C Robert Redford, Lena Olin, Alan Arkin, Raul Julia, Tomas Milian, Tony Plana, Betsy Brantley, Lise Cutter, Richard Farnsworth, Mark Rydell, Daniel Davis; *D:* Sydney Pollack; *W:* Judith Rascoe, David Rayfiel; *C:* Owen Roizman; *M:* Dave Grusin. *AWARDS: NOM:* Academy Awards '90: Best Original Score.

Hawaiian Rainbow

An examination of Hawaii's traditional chants, percussion, ukulele, slack key and steel guitar, male and female falsetto, and lush vocal harmonics; all of them accompanied by authentic Hawaiian hula. Featured performers include a veritable who's who of Hawaiian artists and Hawaiian culture scholars. The video transfer is quite good, with vibrant colors and crisp, clear blacks; although some faults with the source material (i.e. scratches and hairs) do surface from time to time. The soundtrack is also nicely done with no noticeable distortion. —*MJT*
Movie: 🎯🎯➤ **DVD:** 🎯🎯🎯
WinStar Home Entertainment (Cat #WHE73032, UPC #720917303222). Full frame. Dolby Digital Stereo. $24.98. Keepcase. *LANG:* English. *FEATURES:* 6 chapter links • Audio track by the Sam Bernard Trio • Audio track by Billy Hew Len and the Genoa Keawe Group • Photo gallery • DVD-ROM, Discography • DVD-ROM, Production notes • DVD-ROM, Musical listing.
1987 85m/C *D:* Robert Mugge; *C:* Lawrence McConkey.

He Got Game

Spike Lee tries to tell two stories. High school basketball great Jesus Shuttlesworth (newcomer and NBA player Allen) must decide between college and a lucrative pro contract. Then up pops incarcerated dad Jake (Washington) to pressure him to choose his warden's alma mater, which turns the film into a questionable examination of the father-son relationship. Many of the details of illicit recruiting practices were first dealt with in *Blue Chips*. The performances are generally stronger than the scattershot script. Lee's aggressive choice of acid colors and lighting that often leaves scenes in deep shadow can be tough for DVD. Even his bright daylight sequences can have a palpable heaviness, but all of those make the transition to DVD with admirable accuracy. Sound is excellent, too. —*MM*
Movie: 🎯🎯🎯 **DVD:** 🎯🎯🎯
Buena Vista Home Entertainment (Cat #15281, UPC #717951000750). Widescreen (1.85:1) letterboxed. Dolby Digital 5.1 Surround Stereo. $29.99. Keepcase. *LANG:* English. *FEATURES:* 16 chapter links • Trailer.
1998 (R) 134m/C Denzel Washington, Ray Allen, Milla Jovovich, Rosario Dawson, Hill Harper, Zelda Harris, Jim Brown, Ned Beatty, Lonette McKee, John Turturro, Michele Shay, Bill Nunn, Thomas Jefferson Byrd; *D:* Spike Lee; *W:* Spike Lee; *C:* Malik Hassan Sayeed. *AWARDS: NOM:* MTV Movie Awards '99: Breakthrough Performance (Allen).

He Walked by Night

Los Angeles homicide investigators track down cop killer Ray Morgan (Basehart) in this excellent production that served as partial inspiration of Jack Webb's *Dragnet*. The final chase takes place in the L.A. County Flood Control System, consisting of some 700 miles of underground tunnels.

Movie: 🎵🎵🎵▸ **DVD:** NYR

Kino on Video (Cat #AED2002). Full frame. $39.95. Title is available as part of the two-disc set "The Film Noir of Anthony Mann" with *T-Men* and *Raw Deal*.

1948 80m/B Richard Basehart, Scott Brady, Roy Roberts, Jack Webb, Whit Bissell; **D:** Alfred Werker, Anthony Mann; **W:** John C. Higgins; **C:** John Alton; **M:** Leonid Raab.

Heart and Souls

Pay no attention to the contrived premise of this romantic sleeper. An excellent ensemble overcomes it. In 1959 when Thomas Reilly (Downey) is born, four disparate individuals (Woodard, Grodin, Sedgwick, and Sizemore) are killed in a bus accident. They become young Thomas's guardian angels. He can hear and see them until, for reasons best left unexplained, they choose to disappear. When Thomas grows up to become a hard-charging young executive, the four spirits return. They're destined to finish their lives' work through him before they're carried off to wherever. Yes, it's schmaltzy, overdone, derivative and...terrific. It works well on DVD, too, though the early dark scenes are less than completely perfect. The effects are very good. On any medium, this is a sleeper waiting to be discovered. —*MM*

Movie: 🎵🎵🎵▸ **DVD:** 🎵🎵🎵

Universal Studios Home Video (Cat #20433, UPC #025192043321). Widescreen (2.35:1) letterboxed. Dolby Digital 5.1 Surround Stereo. $24.98. Keepcase. *LANG:* English; French. *SUB:* Spanish. *CAP:* English. *FEATURES:* 16 chapter links • Production notes • Cast and crew thumbnail biographies • Universal web links.

1993 (PG-13) 104m/C Robert Downey Jr., Charles Grodin, Tom Sizemore, Alfre Woodard, Kyra Sedgwick, Elisabeth Shue, David Paymer; **D:** Ron Underwood; **W:** Erik Hansen, Brent Maddock, S.S. Wilson, Gregory Hansen; **C:** Michael Watkins; **M:** Marc Shaiman.

Heart of Dragon

A police officer (Chan) takes care of his mentally retarded brother (Hung), who is mistaken for a robbery suspect. After tracking down the real crooks, Jackie finishes things up with a bravura 20-minute fight scene. DVD is a definite step up from the VHS tapes that have been in distribution, but image and sound are still not quite equal to Chan's (or Hung's) best work in this country. —*MM*

Movie: 🎵🎵▸ **DVD:** 🎵🎵▸

Tai Seng Video Marketing (Cat #5086). Widescreen letterboxed. Dolby Digital 5.1 Surround Stereo. $49.95. Keepcase. *LANG:* Cantonese; Mandarin. *SUB:* Traditional & Simplified Chinese; English; Japanese; Bahasa Malaysia; Thai; Korean; Vietnamese. *FEATURES:* 8 chapter links • Star thumbnail biographies • Theatrical trailer.

1985 85m/C *HK* Jackie Chan, Sammo Hung, Emily Chu; **D:** Sammo Hung; **W:** Barry Wong; **C:** Arthur Wong; **M:** Man Yee Lam.

The Heartbreak Kid

Director May's comic examination of love and hypocrisy. Grodin embroils himself in a triangle with his new bride and a woman he can't have, an absolutely gorgeous and totally unloving woman he shouldn't want. Based on Bruce Jay Friedman's story, the film walks the fine line between tragedy and comedy, with an exceptional performance from Berlin. Unfortunately, the video transfer is often muddied and washed-out; it even switches contrasts between shot in the same scene (oh, the horror!). The soundtrack doesn't fare much better; it is tinny and, at times, sounds as if it were recorded with the microphone sitting in the cameraman's coat pocket. —*MJT*

Movie: 🎵🎵🎵 **DVD:** 🎵🎵▸

Anchor Bay (Cat #DV10408, UPC #013131040890). Full frame. Dolby Digital Mono. $24.95. Keepcase. *LANG:* English. *FEATURES:* 9 chapter links.

1972 (PG) 106m/C Charles Grodin, Cybill Shepherd, Eddie Albert, Jeannie Berlin, Audra Lindley, Art Metrano; **D:** Elaine May; **W:** Neil Simon; **C:** Owen Roizman; **M:** Garry Sherman, Cy Coleman, Sheldon Harnick. *AWARDS:* New York Film Critics Awards '72: Best Supporting Actress (Berlin); National Society of Film Critics Awards '72: Best Supporting Actor (Albert), Best Supporting Actress (Berlin); *NOM:* Academy Awards '72: Best Supporting Actor (Albert), Best Supporting Actress (Berlin).

Heat

Another Andy Warhol–produced journey into drug-addled urban seediness features a former child actor/junkie and a has-been movie star barely surviving in a run-down motel. This is one of Warhol's better film productions; even non-fans may enjoy it. The DVD is pretty similar in quality to the other Morrissey/Warhol Image transfers, and though the picture may be so-so, it's the fault of the original source material and not the disc. Like *Flesh* and *Trash,* the lack of quality may actually enhance the feel of the film. —*JO* *AKA:* Andy Warhol's Heat.

Movie: 🎵🎵🎵 **DVD:** 🎵🎵▸

Image Entertainment (Cat #ID4730PYDVD, UPC #014381473025). Full frame. Dolby Digital Mono. $24.98. Snapper. *LANG:* English. *FEATURES:* 16 chapter links.

1972 102m/C Joe Dallesandro, Sylvia Miles, Pat Ast, Andrea Feldman, Ray Vestal; **D:** Paul Morrissey; **W:** Paul Morrissey; **C:** Paul Morrissey; **M:** John Cale.

Heat

Obsessive master thief McCauley (De Niro) leads a crack crew on various military-style heists across Los Angeles while equally obsessive detective Hanna (Pacino) tracks him. Each man recognizes and respects the other's ability and dedication, even as they express the willingness to kill each other if necessary. Excellent script provides all the fireworks you'd expect, as well as a surprising look into emotional and personal sacrifice. Fine cinematography shows off the industrial landscape to great effect and that's captured well on DVD. The image is fine, even in the low-light scenes; sound is very good but not great. —*MM*

Movie: 🎵🎵🎵▸ **DVD:** 🎵🎵🎵

Warner Home Video, Inc. (Cat #14192). Widescreen (2.35:1) anamorphic. Dolby Digital 5.1 Surround Stereo. $19.98. Snapper. *LANG:* English; French. *SUB:* English; French. *FEATURES:* Trailers • 53 chapter links.

1995 (R) 171m/C Robert De Niro, Al Pacino, Val Kilmer, Jon Voight, Diane Venora, Ashley Judd, Wes Studi, Tom Sizemore, Mykelti Williamson, Amy Brenneman, Ted Levine, Dennis Haysbert, William Fichtner, Natalie Portman, Hank Azaria, Henry Rollins, Kevin Gage; **Cameos:** Tone Loc, Bud Cort, Jeremy Piven; **D:** Michael Mann; **W:** Michael Mann; **C:** Dante Spinotti; **M:** Elliot Goldenthal.

Heathers

Clique of stuck-up girls named Heather rule the high school social scene until the newest member (not a Heather) decides that enough is enough. She and her outlaw boyfriend embark (accidentally on her part, intentionally on his) on a murder spree disguised as a rash of teen suicides. Dense, take-no-prisoners black comedy is fueled by buckets of potent slang, satire, and unforgiving hostility. Humor this dark is rare; sharply observed and acted, though the end is out of place. Slater does his best Nicholson impression. The picture on the DVD is very good and it's almost a toss up when choosing between it and the special edition laserdisc. Overall, the image is very sharp and there are only occasional problems with grain. Artifacts are minimal and don't distract. The colors are accurate and a little more vibrant than the laser. Contrast and brightness are consistently comfortable. The DVD also has one of those mono soundtracks that is far more impressive than expected, having both a lot of energy and good fidelity. —*JO*

Movie: 🎵🎵🎵▸ **DVD:** 🎵🎵🎵

Anchor Bay (Cat #DV10672, UPC #013131067293). Widescreen (1.85:1) letterboxed. Dolby Digital Stereo. $24.98. Keepcase. *LANG:* English. *FEATURES:* 26

chapter links ● Theatrical trailer ● Featurette/interviews.
1989 (R) 102m/C Winona Ryder, Christian Slater, Kim Walker, Shannen Doherty, Lisanne Falk, Penelope Milford, Glenn Shadix, Lance Fenton, Patrick Laborteaux, Jeremy Applegate, Renee Estevez; *D:* Michael Lehmann; *W:* Daniel Waters; *C:* Francis Kenny; *M:* David Newman. *AWARDS:* Independent Spirit Awards '90: Best First Feature.

Heaven

This strange supernatural thriller from New Zealand works with some of the splintered time first seen in *Pulp Fiction.* It also attempts a squalid walk on the wild side that's never fully authentic. Gambling addict architect Robert (Donovan) spends most of his time at a strip joint run by his pal Stenner (Schiff), while his soon-to-be-ex-wife (Going) is messing around with her psychiatrist (Malahide), who is also treating Heaven (Edwards), a psychic stripper who can see Robert's troubled future. It's all every bit as nuttily crazed as it sounds, but all involved try to treat it seriously. The tightly limited sets and locations are handled competently enough on DVD, though much of the dialogue is difficult to understand. —*MM*
Movie: ♫♫ *DVD:* ♫♫➤
Miramax Pictures Home Video (Cat #18154, UPC #717951004338). Widescreen (2.35:1) letterboxed. Dolby Digital Stereo. $29.99. Keepcase. *LANG:* English. *CAP:* English. *FEATURES:* 37 chapter links.
1999 (R) 103m/C *NZ* Martin Donovan, Joanna Going, Patrick Malahide, Danny Edwards, Richard Schiff; *D:* Scott Reynolds; *W:* Scott Reynolds; *C:* Simon Raby; *M:* Victoria Kelly.

Heaven Can Wait

Remake of 1941's *Here Comes Mr. Jordan* is one of the comic gems of the 1970s. Joe Pendleton (cowriter-director Beatty) is about to make his first start at quarterback for the Los Angeles Rams when he is mistakenly whisked up to a heavenly waystation by a novice angel (codirector Henry). Installed in a new body, he finds that his wife (Cannon) and her lover (Grodin) are trying to kill him. On DVD, the image looks fine, though this is not the kind of film that tests the medium's limits. This sparkling transfer does make the most of Beatty's easygoing, engaging performance. Though he lost the Best-Actor Oscar to Jon Voight (for *Coming Home*), his work has become much better with age. Overall, the film looks and sounds (even in mono) much better than many of its contemporaries. —*MM*
Movie: ♫♫♫➤ *DVD:* ♫♫♫➤
Paramount Home Video (Cat #011097, UPC #097360110975). Widescreen anamorphic. Dolby Digital Mono. $29.99. Keepcase. *LANG:* English; French. *SUB:* English. *FEATURES:* 22 chapter links ● Theatrical trailer.

1978 (PG) 101m/C Warren Beatty, Julie Christie, Charles Grodin, Dyan Cannon, James Mason, Jack Warden, Buck Henry; *D:* Warren Beatty, Buck Henry; *W:* Elaine May, Warren Beatty; *C:* William A. Fraker; *M:* Dave Grusin. *AWARDS:* Academy Awards '78: Best Art Direction/Set Decoration; Golden Globe Awards '79: Best Actor—Musical/Comedy (Beatty), Best Film—Musical/Comedy, Best Supporting Actress (Cannon); Writers Guild of America '78: Best Adapted Screenplay; *NOM:* Academy Awards '78: Best Actor (Beatty), Best Adapted Screenplay, Best Cinematography, Best Director (Beatty, Henry), Best Picture, Best Supporting Actor (Warden), Best Supporting Actress (Cannon), Best Original Score.

Heavy Metal

Collection of fantasy and science-fiction stories inspired by the titular magazine encompasses the theme of good vs. evil in a glowing green ball. The artistic styles vary considerably. The soundtrack features many metal artists and Bernstein's score with the London Philharmonic. A three-minute transitional segment called "Neverwhere Land" that was cut from the theatrical release has been restored in sketch form along with a different unused framing device. The extras are the only significant difference between the DVD and a widescreen VHS tape, and that's to be expected with animation of this vintage. It looks and sounds fine but does not challenge the limits of the medium. —*MM*
Movie: ♫♫♫ *DVD:* ♫♫➤
Columbia Tristar Home Video (Cat #3929). Widescreen (1.85:1) letterboxed. Dolby Digital 5.1 Surround Stereo; Dolby Digital Surround Stereo. $27.95. Keepcase. *LANG:* English. *SUB:* Spanish; Portuguese. *FEATURES:* Carl Macek reading "Heavy Metal: The Movie" ● Deleted scenes ● Photo gallery ● Documentary "Imagining Heavy Metal" ● *Heavy Metal* magazine cover art gallery ● Art work from film ● 24 chapter links.
1981 (R) 90m/C *CA D:* Gerald Potterton; *W:* Dan Goldberg, Len Blum; *C:* Brian Tufano; *M:* Elmer Bernstein; *V:* John Candy, Joe Flaherty, Don Francks, Eugene Levy, Rodger Bumpass, Jackie Burroughs, Harold Ramis, Richard Romanus, Doug Kenney.

Hell in the Pacific

Conrad Hall's splendid cinematography gets its full due in the widescreen version of this curious cult favorite. Perhaps more importantly, the disc also includes an alternative ending that's much more satisfying than the abrupt, unsatisfying conclusion that viewers have seen until now. It's still a properly enigmatic finish to an unusual character study. The story concerns an American pilot (Marvin) and a Japanese soldier (Mifune) who are cast away on a Pacific island in 1944. Their transit from conflict to cooperation to

something else is an elliptical story—neither understands the other's language—that leaves many gaps. On DVD, the image is virtually flawless, capturing the power of the ocean and the intricate jungle backdrop. The sound is excellent if unspectacular stereo. The only real flaw is one of omission; a commentary track by John Boorman could have been a real asset. (By the way, unless you're really familiar with the film, don't watch the alternative ending on its own.) —*MM*
Movie: ♫♫♫➤ *DVD:* ♫♫♫➤
Anchor Bay (Cat #DV10982, UPC #013131098297). Widescreen (2.35:1); full frame. Dolby Digital Stereo. $24.98. Keepcase. *LANG:* English. *FEATURES:* 12 chapter links ● Alternative ending.
1969 (PG) 101m/C Lee Marvin, Toshiro Mifune; *D:* John Boorman; *W:* Eric Bercovici, Alexander Jacobs; *C:* Conrad Hall; *M:* Lalo Schifrin; *Technical Advisor:* Masaaki Asukai.

Hell Night

Four college pledges, including Marti (Blair), must spend the night in haunted Garth Manor for their initiation. Their friends mean to scare them but the ghostly murderer may still be alive. Cast, plot, and setting make this one a combination of *The Exorcist, Halloween,* and *Animal House.* Actually, the setting is strong and the film is one of the better dead-teen flicks, coming as it does near the beginning of the cycle. On DVD, it looks very good for a film of its budget and age. On their commentary track, neither filmmakers nor star try to make much of this lightweight. —*MM*
Movie: ♫♫ *DVD:* ♫♫♫
Anchor Bay (Cat #DV10863, UPC #013131086393). Widescreen (1.85:1) letterboxed. Dolby Digital Mono. $24.98. Keepcase. *LANG:* English. *FEATURES:* 22 chapter links ● Theatrical trailer ● TV spots ● Commentary: Blair, DeSimone, producers Yablans and Curtis ● Cast and crew thumbnail biographies.
1981 (R) 100m/C Linda Blair, Vincent Van Patten, Kevin Brophy, Peter Barton, Jenny Neumann; *D:* Tom De Simone; *W:* Randy Feldman; *C:* Mac Ahlberg; *M:* Danny Wyman.

Hellbound: Hellraiser 2

In this, the first sequel to Clive Barker's inter-dimensional nightmare, the traumatized daughter from the first film is pulled into the Cenobites' universe. Far funnier and more surrealistic than the original, the unrated version has several hard-to-take images right out of the gate. Gore and weird imagery abound. The overall picture on the DVD seems pretty sharp but there is a lot of grain with some artifacts also mixed in. Colors are fairly vibrant but seem a touch off. However, blacks are deep and true. Contrast is good enough to allow detail in the dark scenes, which make up the entire last third of the film

and the brightness level is very comfortable. The stereo sound is nothing special, but allows adequate delivery of the dialogue and music. —JO AKA: Hellraiser 2.
Movie: 🎬🎬 **DVD:** 🎬🎬▶
Anchor Bay (Cat #DV10331, UPC #013131033199). Widescreen (1.85:1) letterboxed. Stereo. $24.98. Keepcase. LANG: English. FEATURES: 9 chapter links.
1988 96m/C GB Ashley Laurence, Clare Higgins, Kenneth Cranham, Imogen Boorman, William Hope, Oliver Smith, Sean Chapman, Doug Bradley; **D:** Tony Randel; **W:** Peter Atkins; **C:** Robin Vidgeon; **M:** Christopher Young.

Hellfighters

When a young whippersnapper (Hutton) marries the daughter of a fellow oil well firefighter (Wayne), things take a slightly sappy turn. There are some good inferno effects (for the time). The DVD is a big improvement over the tape and the LD, with far more vibrant and accurate colors. The picture is sharp and stays that way, with very little in the way of artifacts or distortion, even when the dancing edges of the hellfire. The sound mix is fairly conventional but pleasing and manages to throw a little more intensity into the fires. —JO
Movie: 🎬🎬 **DVD:** 🎬🎬🎬
Universal Studios Home Video (Cat #20512, UPC #025192051227). Widescreen (2.35:1) letterboxed. Dolby Surround; Dolby Digital Mono. $24.98. Keepcase. LANG: English; Spanish. SUB: Spanish; French. CAP: English. FEATURES: 18 chapter links ● Production notes ● Cast and filmmakers bios ● Film highlights.
1968 (G) 121m/C John Wayne, Katharine Ross, Jim Hutton, Vera Miles, Bruce Cabot, Jay C. Flippen; **D:** Andrew V. McLaglen; **W:** Clair Huffaker; **C:** William Clothier; **M:** Leonard Rosenman.

Hellraiser

Graphic horror fantasy about a woman who is manipulated by the monstrous spirit of her husband's dead brother. (He was also her lover.) To bring the man back to life, she must lure and kill human prey for his sustenance. Grisly and inventive scenes keep the action fast-paced; not for the faint-hearted. Unfortunately, the DVD is not the ultimate way to own this great horror flick—that would be the limited edition laserdisc set—but the transfer is still pretty good. Though the laser is sharper, the color is comparable on both and the DVD's blacks are near perfect. The stereo mix is not the best, but likely no worse than the original film. Included on the disc are a few TV spots, which are fairly creepy without being too graphic. —JO
Movie: 🎬🎬🎬▶ **DVD:** 🎬🎬🎬
Anchor Bay (Cat #DV10330, UPC #013131033090). Widescreen (1.85:1) letterboxed. Stereo. $24.98. Keepcase. LANG: English. FEATURES: 9 chapter links ● Theatrical trailer ● TV spots.

1987 (R) 94m/C GB Andrew (Andy) Robinson, Clare Higgins, Ashley Laurence, Sean Chapman, Oliver Smith, Robert Hines, Doug Bradley, Nicholas Vince, Dave Atkins; **D:** Clive Barker; **W:** Clive Barker; **C:** Robin Vidgeon; **M:** Christopher Young.

Help!

Ringo's ruby ring, sent to him by an adoring teenaged fan, is the object of a search by a comical Kali-worshipping cult, led by a wonderful McKern, who will stop at nothing to retrieve the bauble. But like women everywhere in the mid-'60s, his assistant, Ahme (Bron), has fallen for the lads. The lively chase leads from London to the Alps to the Bahamas with regular stops for musical numbers. Because the film is so completely frivolous and breezy, it has aged beautifully. Some of that "timeless" quality must be credited to the loving 1996 restoration that is the basis for the DVD. The image is crisply focused with bright colors in the interiors, and a strong sense of the damp cold in the English and Alpine exteriors. The songs are some of the best early Beatles and they still sound just fine, too. The disc is loaded with extras, making it a nostalgia-filled treat. —MM AKA: Eight Arms to Hold You.
Movie: 🎬🎬🎬🎬 **DVD:** 🎬🎬🎬🎬
MPI Home Video (Cat #DVD7081, UPC #030306708126). Full frame. Dolby Digital Stereo. $24.98. Keepcase. LANG: English; French; Spanish. SUB: English; French; Spanish. FEATURES: Biographies of filmmakers and supporting cast ● Previews for A Hard Day's Night and other Beatles films ● Newsreels ● Film set promo footage ● Still photos, posters, original radio ads, radio interview with Beatles ● Theatrical trailer ● 17 chapter links ● Interactive menus.
1965 (G) 90m/C GB John Lennon, Paul McCartney, Ringo Starr, George Harrison, Leo McKern, Eleanor Bron, Victor Spinetti, Roy Kinnear, John Bluthal, Patrick Cargill, Alfie Bass, Warren Mitchell, Peter Copley, Bruce Lacey; **D:** Richard Lester; **W:** Charles Wood, Marc Behm; **C:** David Watkin; **M:** George Martin, Ken Thorne, John Lennon, Paul McCartney, Ringo Starr, George Harrison.

Henry & June

The diaries of writer Anais Nin chronicle her triangular relationship with author Henry Miller and his wife June, a relationship that provided the erotic backdrop to Miller's Tropic of Capricorn. Set in Paris in the early '30s, the setting moves between the impecunious expatriate's cheap room on the Left Bank—filled with artists, circus performers, prostitutes, and gypsies—to the conservative, well-appointed home of Nin and her husband. The film captures the heady atmosphere of Miller's gay Paris; no one plays an American better than Ward (who replaced Alec Baldwin). Notable for having prompted the creation of an "NC-17" rating

because of its adult theme. An excellent transfer to DVD retains all the subtle lighting and beautifully framed composition of the theatrical presentation. The image is very sharp and even in the many darker sequences there is practically no grain or artifacts. The colors are accurate and have no bleed. Contrast and brightness levels consistently ensure that the detailed composure is viewable no matter what the shading. The Dolby Surround is more than adequate and quite full-bodied as well as supplying good ambience (theatrically the film did not have much in the way of Surround effects) through the rear channel. —JO
Movie: 🎬🎬🎬 **DVD:** 🎬🎬🎬▶
Universal Studios Home Video (Cat #20518, UPC #025192051821). Widescreen (1.66:1) letterboxed. Dolby Digital Surround. $26.98. Keepcase. LANG: English; French. SUB: Spanish. CAP: English. FEATURES: 16 chapter links ● Theatrical trailer ● Cast and filmmakers bios ● Production notes ● Film highlights ● Web links.
1990 (NC-17) 136m/C Fred Ward, Uma Thurman, Maria De Medeiros, Richard E. Grant, Kevin Spacey; **D:** Philip Kaufman; **W:** Philip Kaufman; **C:** Philippe Rousselot; **M:** Mark Adler. AWARDS: NOM: Academy Awards '90: Best Cinematography.

Henry: Portrait of a Serial Killer

John McNaughton's fact-based chiller is simply one of the most disturbing and frightening horror films anyone has ever made. Henry (grimly underplayed by Michael Rooker) is an illiterate drifter who moves from job to job, and kills at random. Though Henry claims to have been abused as a child, that doesn't explain him. Neither does the sexual element that some of the murders contain. Killing is simply something he does without emotion or pleasure. McNaughton tells the story in a flat, documentary style: stark naturalistic lighting and acting, Midwest locations, grainy color, limited music. The film was rated "X" for violence and subject matter, but has been released on home video without a rating. It is definitely not for kids, and older audiences looking for titillating violence or elaborate effects will be disappointed. In terms of on-screen acts of violence, it contains only a tiny fraction of the average Friday the 13th or Elm St. flick. But this is a real nightmare and these suggested horrors—including an unexpected ending—are much more terrifying than graphic cinematic schlock. Followed by a lesser 1996 sequel. On DVD, the lack of polish cannot be ignored but that rough texture is part of the film's power. In a conversational interview, separate from the feature, McNaughton talks about his background and Chicago upbringing, his hesitant entry into the film business, and the curious genesis of Henry. It's as useful as an accompanying commentary, though not as detailed as some. —MM

Movie: ♪♪♪➤ **DVD:** ♪♪♪➤

MPI Home Video (Cat #DVD7382, UPC #030306738222). Full frame. Dolby Digital Stereo. $24.98. Keepcase. *LANG:* English. *SUB:* English; Spanish; French. *FEATURES:* 16 chapter links • Interview with John McNaughton • Filmographies of Rooker, Tom Towles, Tracy Arnold, McNaughton • Trailers for *Henry* and *Henry 2* • 5 factoids.
1990 90m/C Michael Rooker, Tom Towles, Tracy Arnold, David Katz; **D:** John McNaughton; **W:** John McNaughton, Richard Fire; **C:** Charlie Lieberman; **M:** Robert F. McNaughton.

Henry: Portrait of a Serial Killer 2: Mask of Sanity

In *Henry: Portrait of a Serial Killer,* Michael Rooker gave a chilling performance as serial killer Henry but, in part 2, Giuntoli is merely dull. A sullen drifter, Henry manages to get a job and fellow worker Kai (Komenich) invites him to crash at his place. Turns out Kai is a part-time arsonist for hire and Henry helps him out—also introducing Kai to the pleasures of casual murder. The gore is actually limited to a few bloody scenes (usually more is heard than shown) but the whole project is too incomparably boring for anything to redeem it. The transfer is very grainy and seems rather blurry in some parts. The stereo mix is nothing special either. (It's hard to be blown away by repeated close-ups of someone acting crazy.) There are, however, over 15 minutes of behind-the-scenes footage featuring interviews with the cast and crew. But, then again, why would you care who made this movie and why? —*MJT* *AKA:* Henry 2: Portrait of a Serial Killer.
Movie: ♪ **DVD:** ♪♪

MPI Home Video (Cat #DVD7343, UPC #030306734323). Full frame. Dolby Digital Stereo. $24.98. Keepcase. *LANG:* English. *SUB:* English; Spanish; French. *FEATURES:* Behind-the-scenes notes and interviews • Theatrical trailers for *Henry 1* and *Henry 2* • Filmographies • 16 chapter links.
1996 (R) 84m/C Neil Giuntoli, Rich Komenich, Katherine Walsh, Carri Levinson, Penelope Milford; **D:** Chuck Parello; **W:** Chuck Parello; **C:** Michael Kohnhurst; **M:** Robert F. McNaughton.

Henry V

Masterful wartime adaptation of Shakespeare's history is Olivier's first directorial effort (though he took the job only after William Wyler turned it down). From an experimental introduction to the battle of Agincourt, it is a true triumph. The DVD was created from virtually pristine elements and and so it contains only a few specks and nicks. Some detail is lost in the night scenes, but that's due more to the filmmaking techniques of the time than to the digital transfer. The critical scenes in chapter 29, "A little touch of Harry in the night," are properly dark and meditative, as they need to be if they're going to set up chapter 30, the famous St. Crispin's Day stemwinder. All in all, this DVD does an important film justice. —*MM*
Movie: ♪♪♪♪ **DVD:** ♪♪♪♪

Criterion Collection (Cat #HEN030, UPC #037429128527). Full frame. Dolby Digital Mono. $39.95. Keepcase. *LANG:* English. *SUB:* English. *FEATURES:* 42 chapter links • Liner notes and commentary track by Bruce Eder • Brief historical background • *Book of Hours* visual references • Theatrical trailer • Production photos.
1944 136m/C *GB* Laurence Olivier, Robert Newton, Leslie Banks, Esmond Knight, Renee Asherson, Leo Genn, George Robey, Ernest Thesiger, Felix Aylmer, Ralph Truman, Harcourt Williams, Max Adrian, Valentine Dyall, Russell Thorndike, Roy Emerton, Robert Helpmann, Freda Jackson, Griffith Jones, John Laurie, Niall MacGinnis, Michael Shepley; **D:** Laurence Olivier; **W:** Alan Dent, Dallas Bower, Laurence Olivier; **C:** Robert Krasker; **M:** William Walton. *AWARDS:* National Board of Review Awards '46: Best Actor (Olivier); New York Film Critics Awards '46: Best Actor (Olivier); *NOM:* Academy Awards '46: Best Actor (Olivier), Best Picture, Best Original Dramatic Score.

Her Alibi

When mystery novelist Phil Blackwood (Selleck) runs out of ideas, he seeks inspiration in a criminal courtroom where he discovers Nina (Porizkova), a beautiful Romanian immigrant accused of murder. He springs her by providing an alibi and then ensconces her in his digs. Who are the guys who are following her and is she guilty? Blackwood provides faux-tough voice-over narration. The entire production is slick escapism. The pan-and-scan DVD faithfully captures the superficial glamour with an image that's bright, crisp, and empty. —*MM*
Movie: ♪♪ **DVD:** ♪♪

Warner Home Video, Inc. (Cat #11835, UPC #085391183525). Full frame. Dolby Digital Surround Stereo. $14.98. Snapper. *LANG:* English. *CAP:* English. *FEATURES:* 29 chapter links.
1988 (PG) 95m/C Tom Selleck, Paulina Porizkova, William Daniels, James Farentino, Hurd Hatfield, Patrick Wayne, Tess Harper, Joan Copeland; **D:** Bruce Beresford; **W:** Charlie Peters; **C:** Freddie Francis, **M:** George Delerue.

Hercules

The Disney animators take an adventurous approach to Greek myths. Both the artistic style of the animation and the script are breezy, bright, and sharp with a satiric edge that adults will appreciate more than kids will. Attempting a hostile takeover of Mt. Olympus, the god Hades (wonderfully voiced by Woods) kidnaps Zeus's son Hercules and turns him into a mortal. When the teenaged Herc learns the true story, he sets out to prove himself. The highly exaggerated characters make a smooth transition to DVD. The Underworld scenes, which might have been too much for tykes on the big screen, are easier to handle here. Overall, both image and sound are up to the studio's high standards. Though the film did not do as well as some Disney animation in its theatrical release, it will have a long and popular run on home video. —*MM*
Movie: ♪♪♪➤ **DVD:** ♪♪♪➤

Buena Vista Home Entertainment (Cat #18010, UPC #717951004062). Widescreen (1.66:1) letterboxed. Dolby Digital 5.1 Surround Stereo. $39.99. Keepcase. *LANG:* English; French; Spanish. *CAP:* English. *FEATURES:* 32 chapter links • "Go the Distance" music video • "Making of" featurette.
1997 (G) 92m/C D: John Musker, Ron Clements; **W:** John Musker, Ron Clements, Bob Shaw, Donald McEnery, Irene Mecchi; **M:** Alan Menken, David Zippel; **V:** Tate Donovan, James Woods, Danny DeVito, Matt Frewer, Bob(cat) Goldthwait, Susan Egan, Rip Torn, Samantha Eggar, Paul Shaffer, Barbara Barrie, Hal Holbrook, Amanda Plummer, Carol Shelley; **Nar:** Charlton Heston. *AWARDS: NOM:* Academy Awards '97: Best Song ("Go the Distance"); Golden Globe Awards '98: Best Song ("Go the Distance").

Hero

Interesting twist on the Cinderella fable and modern media satire has television reporter Gale Gayley (Davis) looking for the man (Hoffman), who saved her life in a plane crash. She expects a genuine hero and accepts without question the one who fits her vision. Though the film did poorly in theatrical release, Garcia and Hoffman make a great team and Davis is fine, as usual. On DVD, the image is good, but probably not much better than a widescreen VHS tape. Sound is fine. —*MM*
Movie: ♪♪♪ **DVD:** ♪♪➤

Columbia TriStar Home Video (Cat #51569, UPC #043396515697). Widescreen (1.85:1) letterboxed; full frame. Dolby Digital Surround Stereo. $25.95. Keepcase. *LANG:* English; Spanish; Portuguese. *SUB:* English; Spanish; Portuguese; Chinese; Korean; Thai. *FEATURES:* 28 chapter links • Liner notes • Theatrical trailers.
1992 (PG-13) 116m/C Geena Davis, Dustin Hoffman, Andy Garcia, Joan Cusack, Kevin J. O'Connor, Chevy Chase, Maury Chaykin, Stephen Tobolowsky, Christian Clemenson, Tom Arnold, Warren Berlinger, Susie Cusack, James Madio, Richard Riehle, Don Yesso, Darrell Larson; **D:** Stephen Frears; **W:** David Peoples; **C:** Oliver Stapleton; **M:** George Fenton.

A Hero Never Dies

Jack (Leon Lai) and Martin (Lau Ching Wan) are lieutenants in rival gangs. They bond over bullets and burgundy, but then are betrayed by their bosses. In style and clarity of image, this one is roughly comparable to the DVD of Ringo Lam's *Full Contact*. Both are grainy and gritty and they're powered by a crazy spaghetti-western approach to action. Both share a soft, sometimes overexposed focus and both make extensive use of colored light that further diminishes sharpness. Sound is acceptable. —*MM*

Movie: 🎬🎬🎬 **DVD:** 🎬🎬▶

Tai Seng Video Marketing (Cat #5217, UPC #489502490166). Widescreen letterboxed. Dolby Digital 5.1 Surround Stereo. $49.95. Keepcase. *LANG:* Cantonese; Mandarin. *SUB:* Traditional Chinese; Simplified Chinese; English. *FEATURES:* 8 chapter links ● Cast and crew thumbnail biographies ● Yoyo Mong interview.

1998 98m/C *HK* Leon Lai, Lau Ching Wan, Fiona Leung, Yoyo Mong; *D:* Johnny To; *W:* Nai-Hoi Yau; *C:* Cheng Siu Keung.

The Heroic Trio

Three superheroines battle the Lord of the Underground to prevent him from stealing any more human babies. Lots of airborne martial arts and semi-gory supernatural action. Demon kung-fu at its best. The Tai Seng DVD is much better than the one they put together for the film's sequel, *Executioners*. The colors are much stronger, the image sharper, and there is a lot less damage to the source material. The soundtrack has pretty good energy whether you listen to the English dubbing or the original Chinese. —*JO*

Movie: 🎬🎬▶ **DVD:** 🎬🎬🎬

Tai Seng Video Marketing (Cat #30294, UPC #601643302942). Full frame. Stereo. $29.95. Keepcase. *LANG:* English; Chinese. *SUB:* English. *FEATURES:* 9 chapter links ● Trailers ● Cast and filmmakers bios and filmographies.

1993 87m/C *HK* Michelle Yeoh, Maggie Cheung, Anita Mui, Anthony Wong; *D:* Ching Siu Tung, Johnny To; *W:* Sandy Shaw; *C:* Poon Hang-Seng, Tom Lau; *M:* William Hu.

The Hidden

A seasoned cop (Nouri) and a benign alien posing as an FBI agent (MacLachlan) team up to track down and destroy a hyper-violent alien lifeform that lives for fast cars and loud rock music. The creature survives by invading the bodies of humans, causing them to go on murderous rampages. In its initial release, the film was coolly received by many as a *Terminator-Robocop* rip-off. It's still violent, but the humor, high-velocity action, and fine performances all around have earned the film a substantial cult following. Its influence on other sf films like *Men in Black* is undeniable. The DVD is even sharper than the laserdisc release and the stereo sound is much better. —*MM*

Movie: 🎬🎬🎬 **DVD:** 🎬🎬🎬▶

New Line Home Video (Cat #N4909, UPC #794043490927). Widescreen (1.85:1) anamorphic; full frame. Dolby Digital 5.1 Surround Stereo. Mono. $24.98. Snapper. *LANG:* English. *SUB:* English. *FEATURES:*

21 chapter links ● Special effects "creature" footage ● Theatrical trailer ● Cast and crew thumbnail biographies ● Commentary: Jack Sholder and Tim Hunter.

1987 (R) 98m/C Kyle MacLachlan, Michael Nouri, Clu Gulager, Ed O'Ross, Claudia Christian, Clarence Felder, Richard Brooks, William Boyett, Chris Mulkey; *D:* Jack Sholder; *W:* Bob Hunt, Jim Kouf; *C:* Jacques Haitkin; *M:* Michael Convertino.

Hide and Seek

A desperate, childless, and completely wacko couple kidnap a pregnant woman (Hannah) and lead her husband to believe she is dead. Tilly, as one of Hannah's nutty kidnappers, gets the best role, and her all-out performance is the reason to watch. Poor pacing, preposterous situations, and too much repetition are reasons against it. Too many escapes and recaptures become monotonous. The DVD looks and sounds good, with the letterboxed image working well, particularly with the exterior shots of the remote farmhouse where Hannah and her unborn baby are held captive. The cast and crew interviews are too short and aren't very revealing. —*MB* **AKA:** Cord.

Movie: 🎬🎬 **DVD:** 🎬🎬🎬

Trimark Home Video (Cat #7333D, UPC #031398733324). Widescreen (1.85:1) letterboxed. Dolby Digital. $24.98. Keepcase. *LANG:* English. *SUB:* English; French; Spanish. *CAP:* English. *FEATURES:* 12 chapter links ● Cast and crew interviews ● Theatrical trailer.

2000 (R) 100m/C Daryl Hannah, Jennifer Tilly, Vincent Gallo, Bruce Greenwood, Johanna Black; *D:* Sidney J. Furie; *W:* Joel Hladecek, Yas Takata; *M:* Robert Carli.

Hideous Kinky

Free-spirited single mom Julie (Winslet) takes her two young daughters to live in Morocco, 1972. She gets by on the sale of homemade dolls and the occasional check from the girls' father. She moves in with a charismatic juggler, Bilal (Taghmaoui) and thinks about converting to Sufi mysticism. Winslet plays the character's mixture of naivete and motherly concern well and she looks good doing it, as does the whole movie. The Moroccan locales are brilliantly displayed on DVD with pale, sun-washed exteriors and evocative, colorful interiors. The sound is almost as good, with a score filled with fine oldies. —*MM*

Movie: 🎬🎬▶ **DVD:** 🎬🎬🎬

Columbia Tristar Home Video (Cat #03740, UPC #043396037403). Widescreen (2.35:1) letterboxed. Dolby Digital Stereo. $28.95. Keepcase. *LANG:* English. *SUB:* English; French; Spanish. *FEATURES:* 28 chapter links ● Production notes.

1999 (R) 97m/C *GB FR* Kate Winslet, Said Taghmaoui, Bella Riza, Carrie Mullan, Pierre Clementi, Abigail Cruttenden, Sira Stampe; *D:* Gilles Mackinnon; *W:* Billy Mackinnon; *C:* John de Borman; *M:* John Keane.

Hideous Sun Demon

Archetypal monster-created-by-nuclear-radiation story begins with this ominous voice-over narration: "Immediately after the launching of U.S. satellites number one and number three into outer space, newspaper headlines across the country told the world of a new radiation hazard from the sun, far more deadly than cosmic rays. An obscure scientist, my colleague Dr. Gilbert MacKenna, had already discovered this danger form the sun. This is his story." The unlucky doctor (producer-director Robert Clarke) is exposed to a new isotope and comes to realize that every time he goes out in the sun, he turns into the title character and commits unspeakable acts. Does Gil put up the convertible top on his MG? This low-budget wonder looks just fine on DVD with very few visual flaws, not that a few scratches would be completely out of place. The no-frills disc is slightly better than VHS tape. —*MM* **AKA:** Blood on His Lips; Terror from the Sun; The Sun Demon.

Movie: 🎬🎬🎬 **DVD:** 🎬🎬🎬

Image Entertainment (Cat #ID8586CODVD, UPC #014381858624). Full frame. Dolby Digital Mono. $24.99. Snapper. *LANG:* English. *FEATURES:* 12 chapter links.

1959 75m/B Robert Clarke, Patricia Manning, Nan Peterson, Patrick Whyte, Peter Similuk, Fred La Porte, Robert Garry, Del Courtney; *D:* Thomas Bontross, Robert Clarke; *W:* Doane R. Hoag, E. S. Seeley Jr.; *C:* Vilis Lapenieks, John Morrill, Stan Follis; *M:* John Seeley.

High & Low

Fine Japanese film noir about a wealthy businessman who is being blackmailed by kidnappers claiming to have his son. When he discovers that they have mistakenly taken his chauffeur's son, he must decide whether to face financial ruin or risk the life of a young boy. Based on an Ed McBain novel. The Criterion folk did a very good job on this one and have improved the quality over their laserdisc release. The black-and-white picture is super sharp and has excellent graytones. The blacks themselves are very dark and true. The sound is also improved over the LD; it has more low end, making everything fuller, and there appears to be a little less high-end distortion. —*JO* **AKA:** Tengoku To Jigoku.

Movie: 🎬🎬🎬 **DVD:** 🎬🎬🎬▶

Criterion Collection (Cat #HIG050, UPC #003729130322). Widescreen (2.35:1) letterboxed. Dolby Digital Mono. $39.95. Keepcase. *LANG:* French. *SUB:* English. *FEATURES:* 23 chapter links.

1962 (R) 143m/B *JP* Toshiro Mifune, Tatsuya Mihashi, Tatsuya Nakadai; *D:* Akira Kurosawa; *W:* Evan Hunter, Ryuzo Kikushima, Hideo Oguni, Akira Kurosawa; *C:* Asakazu Nakai, Takao Saito; *M:* Masaru Sato.

High Noon

One of Hollywood's great westerns receives the treatment it's due on DVD.

Gary Cooper is at his taciturn best as retiring Marshal Will Kane who must defy his new wife (Kelly) and the entire town of Hadleyville when four outlaws come gunning for him. Most of the film is a careful study of group and individual psychology with a superb supporting cast. The last reel is a long, beautifully paced showdown. The accompanying "making of" documentary contains comments by most of the important participants. On disc, the black-and-white cinematography is rendered in clear detail with only minor flaws—a flashing vest, broken diagonal lines. The remastered sound captures all of the dialogue and Dimitri Tiomkin's famous score. —MM

Movie: 🎵🎵🎵▶ **DVD:** 🎵🎵🎵▶
Republic Pictures Home Video (Cat #43486, UPC #017153348620). Full frame. THX Digital. $24.98. Keepcase. *LANG:* English; French; Spanish. *SUB:* French; Spanish. *CAP:* English. *FEATURES:* 24 chapter links ● "Making of" with Leonard Maltin, Bridges, Zinnemann, Kramer ● Theatrical trailer.
1952 85m/B Gary Cooper, Grace Kelly, Lloyd Bridges, Lon Chaney Jr., Thomas Mitchell, Otto Kruger, Katy Jurado, Lee Van Cleef, Harry (Henry) Morgan, Robert J. Wilke, Sheb Wooley; *D:* Fred Zinnemann; *W:* Leonardo Bercovici, Carl Foreman; *C:* Floyd Crosby; *M:* Dimitri Tiomkin. *AWARDS:* Academy Awards '52: Best Actor (Cooper), Best Film Editing, Best Song ("High Noon (Do Not Forsake Me, Oh My Darlin')"), Best Original Dramatic Score; American Film Institute (AFI) '98: Top 100; Golden Globe Awards '53: Best Actor—Drama (Cooper), Best Supporting Actress (Jurado), Best Score, National Film Registry '89; New York Film Critics Awards '52: Best Director (Zinnemann), Best Film; *NOM:* Academy Awards '52: Best Director (Zinnemann), Best Picture, Best Screenplay.

High Plains Drifter

A violent, surreal, western ghost story focuses on a mysterious stranger (Eastwood), who appears out of the heat waves in the desert. When he rides into the town of Lago, he immediately commences to kill and rape, while dream sequences and flashbacks reveal his true identity and purpose. The townspeople offer him "anything he wants" to protect them from three gunmen who are about to be released from prison. Eastwood's second film as director owes its style to his "Man with No Name" days with Italian director Sergio Leone. The DVD offers a widescreen version only, preserving Eastwood's excellent framing. For the most part, the DVD looks much better than the letterboxed laserdisc (mainly due to less color bleed), but the film's many dark sequences range from fairly sharp to grainy and slightly blurred. The blacks are very close to true and the contrast is consistently above average. The mono soundtrack is crisp. —JO
Movie: 🎵🎵🎵 **DVD:** 🎵🎵▶

Universal Studios Home Video (Cat #20152, UPC #025192015229). Widescreen (2.35:1) letterboxed. Dolby Digital Mono. $24.98. Keepcase. *LANG:* English; French. *SUB:* Spanish. *CAP:* English. *FEATURES:* 16 chapter links ● Production notes ● Theatrical trailer ● Cast and filmmakers bios.
1973 (R) 105m/C Clint Eastwood, Verna Bloom, Mitchell Ryan, Marianna Hill, Jack Ging, Stefan Gierasch; *D:* Clint Eastwood; *W:* Ernest Tidyman; *C:* Bruce Surtees; *M:* Dee Barton.

High Risk

Apparently producer-director Wong Jing has a score to settle with Jackie Chan. This action/comedy revolves around a drunken action star called Frankie (Jacky Cheung) who claims to do all of his own stunts but uses a team of stuntmen, including Kit Li (Jet Li), whose wife and son were killed in a particularly ridiculous opening sequence. It's virtually impossible for western audiences to figure out where the action ends and the comedy begins. The DVD image is slightly better than VHS tape, but not by much. Sound is identical. —MM
Movie: 🎵🎵 **DVD:** 🎵🎵▶
Tai Seng Video Marketing (Cat #5018, UPC #4895024904191). Widescreen letterboxed. Dolby Digital Mono. $29.95. Keepcase. *LANG:* Cantonese; Mandarin. *SUB:* Chinese; English.
1995 100m/C *HK* Jet Li, Jacky Cheung, Chingmy Yau, Valerie Chow, Charlie Yoeh; *D:* Wong Jing; *W:* Wong Jing.

High Voltage

Tough guy Johnny Clay (Sabato) and his dim-witted gang wind up in hot water when they try to knock over a bank that launders money for the Asian mob. The big boss (Cheung) decides to teach them a lesson. Director Florentine is no John Woo, though his direct-to-video film is surprisingly sharp and clean on DVD. Beyond a little blurring of bright reds, the image quality is first-rate. —MM
Movie: 🎵🎵 **DVD:** 🎵🎵▶
Simitar Entertainment (Cat #7620, UPC #082551762026). Full frame. AC3 Prologic; AC3 Stereo. $14.98. Keepcase. *LANG:* English. *FEATURES:* 8 chapter links ● Production factolds ● Sabato filmography and thumbnail biography.
1998 (R) 92m/C Antonio Sabato Jr., Lochlan Monroe, William Zabka, George Kee Cheung, Amy Smart, James Lew, Antonio Sabato, Shannon Lee; *D:* Isaac Florentine; *W:* Mike Mains; *C:* Philip D. Schwartz; *M:* Steve Edwards.

Highlander (DC)

A strange tale about an immortal 16th-century Scottish warrior who has had to battle his evil immortal enemy through the centuries. The feud comes to blows in modern-day Manhattan. Connery makes a memorable appearance as the good war-

rior's mentor. Spectacular battle and death scenes. The cult favorite has spawned weak sequels and a television series. This is the six minute–longer director's cut of the film. The image is much sharper than earlier home video editions and, though there is some grain, it has been reduced to a more than acceptable level. The colors are also much stronger, at times very vibrant, and appear much more accurate. There is very little bleed. The contrast is much punchier than it has been, and the brightness levels remain fairly consistent even within varying lighting conditions. Blacks are mostly true. The 5.1 sound is improved enough that there is no comparison to the older editions. The subwoofer track is pretty incredible, delivering loud and deep bass with no artificial digital interference. The Surround itself is also pretty amazing and there's a lot of explosive swirling going on during any of the quickenings. —JO
Movie: 🎵🎵🎵 **DVD:** 🎵🎵🎵▶
Republic Pictures Home Video (Cat #45895, UPC #017153589528). Widescreen (2.35:1) letterboxed. Dolby Digital 5.1. $24.98. Keepcase. *LANG:* English. *SUB:* Spanish. *CAP:* English. *FEATURES:* 30 chapter links ● Photo, publicity, and production stills ● Theatrical trailer ● Deleted scenes ● Audio commentary.
1986 (R) 110m/C Christopher Lambert, Sean Connery, Clancy Brown, Roxanne Hart, Beatie Edney, Alan North, Sheila Gish, Jon Polito; *D:* Russell Mulcahy; *W:* Gregory Widen, Peter Bellwood, Larry Ferguson; *C:* Gerry Fisher; *M:* Michael Kamen.

Highlander 2: The Quickening

The saga of Connor MacLeod and Juan Villa-Lobos continues in this sequel set in the year 2024. An energy shield designed to block out the sun's harmful ultraviolet rays has left planet Earth in perpetual darkness, but there is evidence that the ozone layer has repaired itself. An environmental terrorist and her group begin a sabotage effort and are joined by MacLeod and Villa-Lobos in their quest to save Earth. Stunning visual effects don't make up for the lack of substance. Although this DVD looks good most of the time, there are some nasty bits of artifacting in several of the darker sequences, and for that reason alone, I prefer the laserdisc version. Other than that, the picture is generally pretty sharp and doesn't have a lot of digital grain. The color is actually much more vibrant than the laser though there is only a touch of bleed in the reddish hues. Blacks are fairly true and have the occasional problem in those dimmer scenes. Brightness is good and contrast is even better. The 5.1 track is no slouch and delivers some crunching low end and crisp highs. The Surround kicks in mainly in the big action scenes (and there are a lot) but does supply some ambience as well. —JO *AKA:* Highlander 2: Renegade Version.

Movie: 🎬▶ *DVD:* 🎬🎬
Republic Pictures Home Video (Cat #45900, UPC #017153590029). Widescreen (2.35:1) anamorphic. Dolby Digital 5.1. $24.98. Keepcase. *LANG:* English. *SUB:* Spanish. *CAP:* English. *FEATURES:* 33 chapter links ⬝ Commentary: Russell Mulcahy, Bill Panzer, Peter Davis ⬝ Photos, sketches ⬝ Documentary.
1991 (R) 90m/C Christopher Lambert, Sean Connery, Virginia Madsen, Michael Ironside, John C. McGinley; *D:* Russell Mulcahy; *W:* Peter Bellwood; *C:* Phil Meheux; *M:* Stewart Copeland.

Highway Hitcher

In the middle of a divorce he doesn't want, Charles Duprey (Forsythe) heads to Reno for a gambling vacation. On a lonely stretch of road, he comes across Hunter (LeGros) whose car has died. Charles, "the world's oldest boy scout," offers a ride and learns that Hunter has killed a woman. The rest is a road/suspense film that works fairly well though the acting and the pace are both a bit lethargic at times. On DVD, the well-lit and photographed image could hardly look better. Director Voss favors the cool blue end of the spectrum and gives the action a glossy finish that belies a modest budget. —*MM* *AKA:* The Pass.
Movie: 🎬🎬🎬 *DVD:* 🎬🎬🎬
York Entertainment (Cat #YPD-1012, UPC #750723101224). Full frame. Dolby Digital 5.1 Surround Stereo. $24.98. Keepcase. *LANG:* English; French. *SUB:* Spanish. *FEATURES:* 22 chapter links ⬝ Trailer ⬝ Filmographies for Forsythe, LeGros, Pena.
1998 100m/C William Forsythe, James LeGros, Elizabeth Pena, Jamie Kennedy, Nancy Allen, Michael McKean, Jaason Simmons, John Doe; *D:* Kurt Voss; *W:* Kurt Voss; *C:* Denis Maloney; *M:* Vinnie Golia.

Hilary and Jackie

Cover girl cellist Jacqueline Du Pre (Watson) has a complex relationship with her sister Hilary (Griffiths) in this fact-based film. As Jackie takes the world of classical music by storm, Hilary gives up her musical ambitions and marries conductor Kiffer (Morrissey). The film shifts perspective between the two women, with the second half focusing on Jackie's decline and the sisters' mutual bonds. The DVD image reflects the choices that director Tucker makes involving some harshly saturated colors to illustrate the characters' inner turmoil. Fire-lit interiors, for example, are reduced to amber shapes and dense shadows. The bucolic exteriors suffer somewhat on the small screen. Sound, of course, is excellent. —*MM*
Movie: 🎬🎬🎬 *DVD:* 🎬🎬▶
USA Home Entertainment (Cat #440 044 243-2, UPC #044004424325). Widescreen (2.35:1) letterboxed; full frame. Dolby Digital 5.1 Surround Stereo; Dolby Digital Surround Stereo. $24.95. Keep-

case. *LANG:* English. *SUB:* French. *FEATURES:* 20 chapter links ⬝ Cast and crew thumbnail biographies ⬝ "Making of" featurette.
1998 (R) 124m/C GB Emily Watson, Rachel Griffiths, James Frain, David Morrissey, Charles Dance, Celia Imrie, Rupert Penry-Jones, Nyree Dawn Porter, Bill Paterson, Vernon Dobtcheff, Auriol Evans, Keeley Flanders; *D:* Anand Tucker; *W:* Frank Cottrell-Boyce; *C:* David Johnson; *M:* Barrington Pheloung. *AWARDS: NOM:* Academy Awards '98: Best Actress (Watson), Best Supporting Actress (Griffiths); British Academy Awards '98: Best Actress (Watson), Best Adapted Screenplay, Best Film, Best Sound, Best Score; Golden Globe Awards '98: Best Actress—Drama (Watson); Screen Actors Guild Award '98: Best Actress (Watson), Best Supporting Actress (Griffiths).

The Hindenburg

A dramatization of what might have happened on the fateful night the Hindenburg exploded. Scott plays an investigator who is aware that something is up, and has numerous suspects to interrogate. The plot doesn't matter, there's just something romantically special about a super-luxurious dirigible. The DVD looks pretty good and generally the picture is sharp. There is some grain but nothing excessive. Colors are fairly deep and the contrast and brightness levels stay good; they don't seem to have any problems, even during the flaming climax, where film stocks and lighting condition are extremely varied. If the movie were to be made now, the sound would have to be spectacular, but it's not on this one, and there doesn't seem to have been much effort put into a remix, which would have helped quite a bit. —*JO*
Movie: 🎬🎬 *DVD:* 🎬🎬🎬
Universal Studios Home Video (Cat #20413, UPC #025192041327). Widescreen (2.35:1) letterboxed. Dolby Surround. $24.98. Keepcase. *LANG:* English. *SUB:* Spanish; French. *CAP:* English. *FEATURES:* 16 chapter links ⬝ Cast and filmmakers bios ⬝ Production notes ⬝ Film highlights.
1975 (PG) 126m/C George C. Scott, Anne Bancroft, William Atherton, Roy Thinnes, Gig Young, Burgess Meredith, Charles Durning, Richard Dysart; *D:* Robert Wise; *W:* Nelson Gidding, Richard Levinson, William Link; *C:* Robert L. Surtees; *M:* David Shire. *AWARDS:* Academy Awards '75: Best Sound Effects Editing, Best Visual Effects; *NOM:* Academy Awards '75: Best Art Direction/Set Decoration, Best Cinematography, Best Sound.

His Girl Friday

Classic, unrelentingly hilarious war-between-the-sexes comedy in which a reporter (Russell) and her ex-husband editor (Grant) help a condemned man escape the law—while at the same time furthering their own ends as they try to get the big

scoop on political corruption in the town. One of Hawks's most furious and inventive screen combats in which women are given uniquely equal (for Hollywood) footing, with staccato dialogue and wonderful performances. Based on the Hecht-MacArthur play *The Front Page*, which was originally filmed in 1931. Remade again in 1974 as *The Front Page*, and in 1988 as *Switching Channels*. The disc succeeds admirably with a very crisp transfer that provides a really sharp black-and-white image, although in some scenes high-definition detail (such as patterns on suits) appear smeared just a bit. The soundtrack is good enough, though some scenes are a bit muddled. The 30-minute "Cary Grant on Film: A Biography" adds to the value of the disc although it is little more than a collection of stills and clips presided over by a narrator. —*MJT*
Movie: 🎬🎬🎬🎬 *DVD:* 🎬🎬🎬
Delta/Laserlight (Cat #82040, UPC #018111997034). Full frame. Dolby Digital. $14.99. Keepcase. *LANG:* English. *SUB:* Spanish; Chinese; Japanese. *FEATURES:* 18 chapter links ⬝ Includes "Cary Grant on Film: A Biography" documentary ⬝ Introduction by Tony Curtis ⬝ Theatrical trailer for *Gunga Din*. The disc lists title as "Special Edition—Double Feature," but it hardly seems accurate when the one feature is merely 30 minutes long.
1940 92m/B Cary Grant, Rosalind Russell, Ralph Bellamy, Gene Lockhart, John Qualen, Porter Hall, Roscoe Karns, Abner Biberman, Cliff Edwards, Billy Gilbert, Helen Mack, Ernest Truex, Clarence Kolb, Frank Jenks; *D:* Howard Hawks; *W:* Charles Lederer; *C:* Joseph Walker; *M:* Morris Stoloff. *AWARDS:* National Film Registry '93.

History of the World: Part 1

Mel Brooks's wonderfully incorrect comedy is certainly too broad for some tastes, but, sadly, not for mine. For my money, the raunchier the Brooks, the better, and he's at his bawdy best in Ancient Rome and other places. Most famous line: "It's good to be king." Most inspired moment: the Spanish Inquisition as an Esther Williams production number. On DVD, the image looks just as sharp as it did in theatres; much sharper than VHS tape. Mono sound is acceptable. A commentary track of some kind would have been welcome. —*MM*
Movie: 🎬🎬🎬 *DVD:* 🎬🎬🎬
Twentieth Century Fox Home Entertainment (Cat #4112890, UPC #086162128 905). Widescreen (2.35:1) letterboxed. Mono. $29.98. Keepcase. *LANG:* English; French. *SUB:* English; Spanish. *FEATURES:* 19 chapter links.
1981 (R) 90m/C Mel Brooks, Dom DeLuise, Madeline Kahn, Harvey Korman, Cloris Leachman, Gregory Hines, Pamela Stephenson, Paul Mazursky, Beatrice Arthur, Fritz Feld, John Hurt, Jack Carter, John Hillerman, John Gavin, Barry Levinson, Ron Carey, Howard Morris, Sid Caesar, Jackie Mason, Charlie Callas, Henny Youngman,

Hugh Hefner; **D:** Mel Brooks; **W:** Mel Brooks; **C:** John Morris, Woody Omens; **M:** Shecky Greene; **Nar:** Orson Welles.

Hitman

Fu (Li) is a reluctant assassin who can never quite complete a job. He stumbles into a multimillion dollar operation that puts him against "The King of Killers." The star's strong screen presence is the only recommendation this disc gets. Though the film is well photographed, the image lacks the depth of the best Hong Kong or American action pictures. Sound is good. —MM

Movie: 🎜🎜 **DVD:** 🎜🎜
Tai Seng Video Marketing (Cat #DVD-126). Widescreen letterboxed. Dolby Digital 5.1 Surround Stereo. $49.95. Keepcase. *LANG:* Cantonese; Mandarin. *SUB:* Chinese; English. *FEATURES:* 9 chapter links • Theatrical trailer.
1998 104m/C *HK* Jet Li, Eric Tsang.

Holiday Inn

Please see review of *Going My Way.*
Movie: 🎜🎜🎜
1942 101m/B Bing Crosby, Fred Astaire, Marjorie Reynolds, Walter Abel, Virginia Dale; **D:** Mark Sandrich. *AWARDS:* Academy Awards '42: Best Song ("White Christmas"); *NOM:* Academy Awards '42: Best Story, Scoring of a Musical.

Hollywood Christmas

Created for the Starz! cable channel, this compilation of clips from Christmas movies is an understandably mixed bag. The oldest one—a two-minute English film—dates back to 1898. Also included is a 1905 Thomas Edison version of *The Night Before Christmas.* The rest cover fairly familiar territory from Shirley Temple and the World War II era to *Home Alone.* Jane Seymour's saccharine narration will have most viewers muttering "Humbug." The image quality varies somewhat, but on DVD, even the oldest footage looks pretty good. Sound isn't quite as crisp. —MM

Movie: 🎜🎜▸ **DVD:** 🎜🎜🎜
Image Entertainment (Cat #ID8768FSDVD, UPC #014381876826). Full frame. Dolby Digital Stereo. $19.99. Keepcase. *LANG:* English. *FEATURES:* 11 chapter links • "Making of" featurette.
1996 90m/C **D:** Kevin Burns; **W:** Kevin Burns; **Nar:** Jane Seymour.

Holy Man

Murphy tries to play against type as G, a serene wise man who is used by Ricky Hayman (Goldblum) and Kate Newell (Preston), two shallow greedy cable shopping channel executives. Cable shopping is such an easy target that the satiric barbs carry little sting, and the plot follows the Hollywood formula without varying a whit. Overall, though, the performances are not bad. On DVD, the film looks terrific. Image is superb and sound is good. Since the subject is television, the ultra-widescreen ratio is often pointless. —MM

Movie: 🎜🎜 **DVD:** 🎜🎜🎜
Buena Vista Home Entertainment (Cat #16536, UPC #717951001627). Widescreen (2.35:1) letterboxed. Dolby Digital 5.1 Surround Stereo. $29.99. Keepcase. *LANG:* English. *CAP:* English. *FEATURES:* 23 chapter links.
1998 (PG) 113m/C Eddie Murphy, Jeff Goldblum, Kelly Preston, Robert Loggia, Jon Cryer, Eric McCormack, Marc Macaulay, Sam Kitchin, Robert Small, Morgan Fairchild; **D:** Stephen Herek; **W:** Tom Schulman; **C:** Adrian Biddle; **M:** Alan Silvestri.

Home Alone

The megahit that created a pint-sized star overnight makes a smooth transition to DVD. Eight-year-old Kevin (Culkin) is left behind in his Chicago suburban home when his family goes on Christmas vacation to France. Set upon by comic burglars (Pesci and Stern), he defends the family manse in elaborately staged sequences of full-bore slapstick. Though the disc contains no important extras, it looks fine. The busy interiors, crammed to bursting with props, clashing patterns, and miscellaneous stuff are every bit as clear as they need to be. Not surprisingly, the focus is intentionally softened in many scenes. The sound adds the right dimension to the comic pratfalls and keeps them from becoming too painful. —MM

Movie: 🎜🎜▸ **DVD:** 🎜🎜🎜
Twentieth Century Fox Home Entertainment (Cat #4112753, UPC #0861620015 98). Widescreen (1.85:1) letterboxed. Dolby Digital Surround Stereo. $34.98. Keepcase. *LANG:* English; French; Spanish. *SUB:* English. *FEATURES:* 24 chapter links • Theatrical trailer. Also available as part of the "Home Alone" boxed set (catalog #4112760) $79.98.
1990 (PG) 105m/C Macaulay Culkin, Catherine O'Hara, Joe Pesci, Daniel Stern, John Heard, Roberts Blossom, John Candy, Billie Bird, Angela Goethals, Devin Ratray, Kieran Culkin; **D:** Chris Columbus; **W:** John Hughes; **C:** Julio Macat; **M:** John Williams. *AWARDS: NOM:* Academy Awards '90: Best Song ("Somewhere in My Memory"), Best Original Score.

Home Alone 2: Lost in New York

When the McCallister family flies off for a Florida vacation, Kevin (Culkin) gets on the wrong plane and winds up in New York, where he meets the escaped cons (Pesci and Stern) he hammered in the first film. In most respects, the film is more a recapitulation of the original than a sequel. The set-ups are identical and despite the different locations, the action looks exactly like *HA1.* If you put the DVDs in a multi-disc player and shuffled between scenes from the two films, you'd probably have trouble telling them apart. Depending on your opinion of the series, that is either a plus or a minus. —MM

Movie: 🎜🎜▸ **DVD:** 🎜🎜▸
Twentieth Century Fox Home Entertainment (Cat #4112754, UPC #086162127 540). Widescreen (1.85:1) letterboxed. Dolby Digital Surround Stereo. $34.98. Keepcase. *LANG:* English; French; Spanish. *SUB:* English. *FEATURES:* 29 chapter links • Theatrical trailers for all three *Home Alone* films. Also available as part of the "Home Alone" boxed set (catalog #4112760) $79.98.
1992 (PG) 120m/C Macaulay Culkin, Joe Pesci, Daniel Stern, Catherine O'Hara, John Heard, Tim Curry, Brenda Fricker, Devin Ratray, Hillary Wolf, Eddie Bracken, Dana Ivey, Rob Schneider, Kieran Culkin, Gerry Bamman, Donald Trump; **D:** Chris Columbus; **W:** John Hughes; **C:** Julio Macat; **M:** John Williams.

Home Alone 3

Only writer-producer Hughes returns from the first two films, but the essential idea remains the same. International bad guys who are looking for the missing missile computer chip go after young Alex Pruitt (Linz) in the Chicago 'burbs. The gizmo has been hidden in one of his toys. The cartoon violence is easily the equal of the previous pictures, but on DVD, the image is a bit slicker than the first two. Sound is about the same. Linz may not be cuter than Culkin but he is certainly more cherubic. —MM

Movie: 🎜🎜 **DVD:** 🎜🎜▸
Twentieth Century Fox Home Entertainment (Cat #4109065, UPC #086162090 653). Widescreen (1.85:1) letterboxed. Dolby Digital 5.1 Surround Stereo; Dolby Digital Surround Stereo. $34.98. Keepcase. *LANG:* English; French; Spanish. *SUB:* English. *CAP:* English. *FEATURES:* 21 chapter links • Theatrical trailer. Also available as part of the "Home Alone" boxed set (catalog #4112760) $79.98.
1997 (PG) 102m/C Alex D. Linz, Kevin Kilner, Olek Krupa, Rya Kihlstedt, Lenny Von Dohlen, David Thornton, Haviland Morris, Marian Seldes, Scarlett Johansson, Christopher Curry, Baxter Harris, Seth Smith; **D:** Raja Gosnell; **W:** John Hughes; **C:** Julio Macat; **M:** Nick Glennie-Smith. *AWARDS: NOM:* Golden Raspberry Awards '97: Worst Remake/Sequel.

Home Fries

Things go from bad to worse for pregnant fast-food cashier, Sally (Barrymore), as she learns that the father of her child is not only married, but dead! The catch is that the philanderer's stepsons are responsible for his demise and believe that Sally may have overheard their dastardly deed on her drive-through headset. Brother Dorian (Wilson) takes a job at the Burger-Matic to find out just what Sally knows, but predictably falls in love with her instead. The film tries to be a quirky dark comedy in a sweet love story, but the result is a bad mix of bleak humor and saccharine-sweet puppy love. Barrymore's cute and convincing performance manages to keep the whole thing from spoiling. Unfortunately, first-time director Parisot leaves the audience thinking, "this isn't what I ordered." The DVD has a sharp image that is free of both grain and artifacts. Colors are accurate and have no problem at all with bleed, possibly helped by the film's lack of deep tints. The blacks are true and contrast is very good with possibly just a touch too much brightness. The sound is 5.1 and that seems like more than required for this film. However, there is very good fidelity and plenty of energy resulting from the sporadic ambient use of the Surround. —JO

Movie: 🎵🎵 **DVD:** 🎵🎵🎵
Warner Home Video, Inc. (Cat #15169, UPC #085391516927). Widescreen (1.85:1) letterboxed; full frame. Dolby Digital 5.1. $19.98. Snapper. *LANG:* English; French. *SUB:* English; French. *CAP:* English. *FEATURES:* Theatrical trailer • Production notes • Filmographies.
1998 (PG-13) 94m/C Drew Barrymore, Luke Wilson, Catherine O'Hara, Jake Busey, Shelley Duvall, Kim Robillard, Darryl (Chill) Mitchell, Lanny Flaherty, Christopher Ellis, Blue Deckert; **D:** Dean Parisot; **W:** Vince Gilligan; **C:** Jerzy Zielinski; **M:** Rachel Portman.

Homeward Bound: The Incredible Journey

Remake of Disney's 1963 *The Incredible Journey* is an animal tale told without the computer effects used more recently to humanize critters and to approximate mouth movements for dialogue. Even so, kids will still get into the plight of the bulldog Chance (voice of Fox), the cat Sassy (Field), and Shadow (Ameche) the golden retriever, who must wander through forests and mountains to find their way back to their family. Great stuff for the short set. The DVD probably isn't that much better than VHS tape in terms of image and sound—both are excellent—but given the way children like to rewatch their favorites so often, the disc might last longer. —MM

Movie: 🎵🎵🎵 **DVD:** 🎵🎵▶
Buena Vista Home Entertainment (Cat #13079, UPC #717951000071). Full frame. Dolby Digital Surround Stereo. $29.99. Clamshell. *LANG:* English; French; Spanish. *CAP:* English. *FEATURES:* 17 chapter links • Theatrical trailer.
1993 (G) 85m/C Robert Hays, Kim Greist, Jean Smart, Benj Thall, Veronica Lauren, Kevin Timothy Chevalia; **D:** Duwayne Dunham; **W:** Linda Woolverton, Carolyn Thompson; **C:** Reed Smoot; **M:** Bruce Broughton; **V:** Don Ameche, Michael J. Fox, Sally Field.

Honeymoon in Vegas

Romantic comedy turns frantic after Jack Singer (Cage) loses his fiancee Betsy (Parker) to gangster Tommy Korman (Caan) in a poker game. Cage displays a

real talent for comedy as the distraught young groom-to-be who must overcome countless obstacles including hundreds of Elvis impersonators on his way to the altar. Neither image nor sound on this full-frame DVD are significantly better than VHS tape. —MM

Movie: 🎵🎵 **DVD:** 🎵🎵
MGM Home Entertainment (Cat #908094, UPC #027616809421). Full frame. Dolby Digital Surround Stereo. $29.95. Keepcase. *LANG:* English. *SUB:* French; Spanish. *FEATURES:* 32 chapter links • Trailer.
1992 (PG-13) 95m/C James Caan, Nicolas Cage, Sarah Jessica Parker, Noriyuki "Pat" Morita, John Capodice, Robert Costanzo, Anne Bancroft, Peter Boyle, Seymour Cassel, Tony Shalhoub, Ben Stein, Angela Pietropinto; **D:** Andrew Bergman; **W:** Andrew Bergman; **C:** William A. Fraker; **M:** David Newman.

Hong Kong 1941

Hong Kong version of *Casablanca* is a wonderful sleeper. On the eve of the Japanese invasion of the city, two friends, Yip Kim Fay (Chow Yun-Fat) and Wong Hak Keung (Alex Man) fall in love with Ah Nam (Cecilia Yip), whose wealthy father is trying to force her into a hasty marriage. Personal problems merge with the political situation as they sort things out. The image has a slightly faded tone. It's a solid step up from VHS tape, though still not up to the best DVD. Sound is fine. Those criticisms are quibbles. This is a terrific movie, particularly recommended to Chow Yun-Fat's many fans. —MM

Movie: 🎵🎵🎵▶ **DVD:** 🎵🎵
Tai Seng Video Marketing (Cat #5113). Widescreen letterboxed. Dolby Digital 5.1 Surround Stereo. $34.95. Keepcase. *LANG:* Cantonese; Mandarin. *SUB:* Traditional & Simplified Chinese; English; Japanese; Bahasa Malaysia & Indonesia; Thai; Korean; Vietnamese.
1984 118m/C *HK* Cecilia Yip, Alex Man, Chow Yun-Fat; **D:** Po-Chi Leung; **W:** Koon-Chung Chan.

Honor Among Thieves

Two former mercenaries (Bronson and Delon) reteam for a robbery that doesn't come off as planned. Not as swiftly paced as others in the Bronson canon. *AKA:* Farewell, Friend.

Movie: 🎵▶ **DVD:** NYR
Essex (Cat #1403). Full frame. Dolby Digital Stereo. $10.97. Slipcase.
1968 (R) 115m/C *FR IT* Charles Bronson, Alain Delon, Brigitte Fossey, Olga Georges-Picot, Bernard Fresson; **D:** Jean Herman; **W:** Sebastien Japrisot; **C:** Jean-Jacques Tarbes; **M:** Francois de Roubaix.

The Hoodlum

A criminal does his best to rehabilitate and, with a little help from his brother, is able to hold a steady job. However, the

crime bug dies hard and when he spots an armored car, he just can't resist the temptation. Tierney's real brother, Edward, plays his screen brother. The DVD is not as sharp as one would expect but, given the low key colors and extensive use of dimly lit scenes, it's not bad. There is some grain but nothing too distracting and artifacts are minimal. The colors are accurate despite the fact that both contrast and brightness seem a little higher than on the big screen, and make the DVD more enjoyable to view. Blacks are handled very well and remain true. The 5.1 sound makes sure you can actually feel when someone pulls the trigger (which happens quite a bit) and while the music is appropriately dynamic and full-bodied, it never steps on the dialogue. Highs, lows, and mids are excellent, as are the Surround effects. —JO

Movie: 🎵🎵 **DVD:** 🎵🎵🎵
MGM Home Entertainment (Cat #906995, UPC #027616699527). Widescreen (1.85:1) anamorphic; full frame. Dolby Digital 5.1; Dolby Surround. $24.98. Keepcase. *LANG:* English (DD5.1); French (DS). *SUB:* English; Spanish; French. *CAP:* English. *FEATURES:* 32 chapter links • Theatrical trailer • Production notes and trivia (booklet).
1951 61m/B Lawrence Tierney, Allene Roberts, Marjorie Riordan, Lisa Golm, Edward Tierney; **D:** Max Nosseck.

Hooper

Lightweight behind-the-scenes satire about the world of movie stuntmen. Reynolds is a top stuntman who becomes involved in a rivalry with an up-and-coming young man out to surpass him. Dated good-ole-boy shenanigans. The DVD features an O.K. transfer that is fairly sharp and grain-free for full frame. Colors are also fairly good, with accurate fleshtones and only occasional bleed. Blacks are handled pretty well except in a few spots where some grain sneaks in. Contrast and brightness levels are adequate although a little low for my taste. The sound is of the nothing-special variety, but more than up to the rest of the disc's specs. —JO

Movie: 🎵🎵 **DVD:** 🎵🎵▶
Warner Home Video, Inc. (Cat #16881, UPC #085391768128). Full frame. Stereo. $14.98. Snapper. *LANG:* English. *CAP:* English. *FEATURES:* 30 chapter links.
1978 (PG) 94m/C Burt Reynolds, Jan-Michael Vincent, Robert Klein, Sally Field, Brian Keith, John Marley, Adam West; **D:** Hal Needham; **W:** Bill Kerby, Tom Rickman; **C:** Bobby Byrne; **M:** Bill Justis. *AWARDS: NOM:* Academy Awards '78: Best Sound.

Hoosiers

In Indiana of the 1950s, high school basketball is THE sport. One small town gets a new but surprisingly experienced coach in Norman Dale (Hackman). The story is based on the real 1954 championship team of Milan, IN, but the film really rings

true in Hackman's complex and sensitive performance, supported by Hopper's touching portrait of his alcoholic assistant. On DVD, the widescreen version captures those flat lonely Midwestern landscapes. With either version, the nostalgic image is excellent. So is the sound. —*MM*
Movie: 🎬🎬🎬 **DVD:** 🎬🎬🎬
MGM Home Entertainment (Cat #908018, UPC #027616801821). Widescreen letterboxed; full frame. Dolby Digital 5.1 Surround Stereo; Mono. $24.98. Keepcase. *LANG:* English; French; Spanish. *SUB:* French; Spanish. *CAP:* English. *FEATURES:* 36 chapter links • Trailer • Production notes booklet.
1986 (PG) 115m/C Gene Hackman, Barbara Hershey, Dennis Hopper, David Neidorf, Sheb Wooley, Fern Parsons, Brad Boyle, Steve Hollar, Brad Long; *D:* David Anspaugh; *W:* Angelo Pizzo; *C:* Fred Murphy; *M:* Jerry Goldsmith. *AWARDS:* Los Angeles Film Critics Association Awards '86: Best Supporting Actor (Hopper); *NOM:* Academy Awards '86: Best Supporting Actor (Hopper), Best Original Score.

Hope Floats

Lifeless tale of a small-town girl (Bullock) returning home after her marriage goes south. On paper this must have seemed like a good idea, teaming perky Sandra Bullock with crooner Harry Connick Jr. in a romantic comedy, but there's no chemistry, no fire, not even a spark. Gena Rowlands (*A Woman under the Influence*) gets the thankless task of playing Bullock's off-center mother, while Michael Pare (*Streets of Fire*) wanders through the story as Bullock's wayward husband. The DVD presentation is first class, with both French and English language tracks, English and Spanish subtitles, and a classy widescreen transfer from superb source material. —*RT*
Movie: 🎬🎬 **DVD:** 🎬🎬🎬
Twentieth Century Fox Home Entertainment (Cat #4109063, UPC #086162090639). Widescreen. AC3 - 5.1 Dolby Digital Surround; AC3 - 2 Channel (French). $34.98. Keepcase. *LANG:* English; French. *SUB:* English; Spanish. *CAP:* English. *FEATURES:* 21 chapter links • Theatrical trailer • Cast biographies.
1998 (PG-13) 114m/C Sandra Bullock, Harry Connick Jr., Gena Rowlands, Mae Whitman, Cameron Finley, Michael Pare, Rosanna Arquette, Kathy Najimy, Bill Cobbs; *D:* Forest Whitaker; *W:* Steven Rogers; *C:* Caleb Deschanel; *M:* Dave Grusin.

Horror Express

Spanish production set in pre-Revolutionary Russia is *The Thing* on the trans-Siberian Express. Professor Saxton (Lee), an archeologist, finds a critter frozen in the ice and takes it to England to study. His rival Dr. Wells (Cushing) is jealous and wants to find out what's happening, but said critter has no intention of going to England or anywhere else. Then toss in a mad monk and Savalas as a crazed Cossack. The railway setting works well, making this one classy fun with a slight satiric edge. On DVD, the image varies in clarity from grainy exteriors to sharper interiors, mostly in the gaudy passenger cars. Overall, the colors have faded. —*MM AKA:* Panic on the Trans-Siberian Express; Panico en el Transiberiano; Panic in the Trans-Siberian Train.
Movie: 🎬🎬🎬 **DVD:** 🎬🎬
Simitar Entertainment (Cat #7225, UPC #082551722525). Full frame. Dolby Digital. $7.98. Keepcase. *LANG:* English. *FEATURES:* Biographies of Lee, Cushing, and Savalas • Film factoids • 8 chapter links.
1972 (R) 88m/C *SP GB* Christopher Lee, Peter Cushing, Telly Savalas, Alberto De Mendoza, Sylvia Tortosa, Julio Pena, Angel Del Pozo, Helga Line, Jorge Rigaud, Jose Jaspe; *D:* Eugenio (Gene) Martin; *W:* Julian Zimet, Arnaud d'Usseau; *C:* Alejandro Ulloa.

Horror Express (Image Entertainment)

For any serious horror fan, this Image Entertainment edition is the preferred version of the Lee-Cushing film. Beyond the widescreen image, the image is much brighter and the sound is noticeably sharper. Also, Marc Walkow's liner notes are a wealth of production trivia. —*MM*
Movie: 🎬🎬🎬 **DVD:** 🎬🎬🎬
Image Entertainment (Cat #ID6158TVDVD, UPC #014381615821). Widescreen (1.66:1) letterboxed. Dolby Digital Mono. $24.99. Snapper. *LANG:* English; Spanish. *FEATURES:* 18 chapter links • Cast filmographies • Isolated sound and music track • Liner notes by Marc Walkow.
1984 m/C

Horror Hospital

Patients are turned into zombies by Doctor Storm (Gough), a mad scientist who uses his Rolls Royce to decapitate escapees from his rural retreat. Frederick (Martin) is the evil dwarf. Long-haired Jason (Askwith) and Judy (Shaw) are the newest visitors. This is an exceptionally silly British sex/horror flick. On DVD, the sharpness of the image is truly remarkable for a film of this age. It's virtually flawless. Sound is unremarkable. —*MM AKA:* Computer Killers; Doctor Blood Bath.
Movie: 🎬🎬 **DVD:** 🎬🎬🎬
Elite Entertainment, Inc. (Cat #EE4677, UPC #790594467722). Widescreen (1.85:1) letterboxed. $24.95. Keepcase. *LANG:* English. *FEATURES:* 21 chapter links.
1973 (R) 91m/C *GB* Michael Gough, Robin Askwith, Vanessa Shaw, Ellen Pollock, Skip Martin, Dennis Price; *D:* Antony Balch; *W:* Antony Balch, Alan Watson; *C:* David McDonald.

Horror Planet

Vile, repulsive, dim-witted imitation of *Alien* manages to disgust and bore in almost equal measures. On an archeological expedition to a distant planet, archeo-astronaut Judy Geeson is impregnated by a creature with glowing green liquid. As her stomach swells, bumps off her dim-witted companions. In any given situation, if there's something stupid that these one-dimensional characters can do, rest assured they will. The special effects aren't special, and the general level of sets and props is marked by the motorcycle helmets meant to pass for space helmets. *AKA:* Inseminoid.
Movie: woof **DVD:** NYR
Elite Entertainment, Inc. (Cat #4674). Full frame; widescreen (2.35:1) letterboxed. Dolby Digital Stereo. $24.95. Keepcase.
1980 (R) 93m/C *GB* Robin Clarke, Jennifer Ashley, Stephanie Beacham, Judy Geeson, Stephen Grives, Victoria Tennant; *D:* Norman J. Warren; *W:* Gloria Maley, Nick Maley; *C:* John Metcalfe; *M:* John Scott.

Horse Feathers

This, the fourth film by the brothers Marx, sets up Groucho as a college president, Zeppo as his no-goodnik son, and Harpo and Chico as wanna-be goons ("Get tough with both of them. Tougher!"). Everyone has their fave bit, from Swordfish to "tie on the bed, rope out the window," to musical numbers you don't need to scan through impatiently. The real question is, why this print is the same we've seen on television all these years? It may be all anyone will ever have. The flow is consequently hobbled at times by unintentional jump cuts, especially the apartment scene (chapter 7, "The Iceman Cometh and Goeth"). The "uncompressed" sound seems to have had little done to it as well. The saving grace of having the thing digitized is a chance to see Thelma Todd's trompe l'oeil gowns in newly eye-popping detail. Yowza! —*JK*
Movie: 🎬🎬🎬 **DVD:** 🎬🎬🎬
Universal Studios Home Video (Cat #ID4289USDVD, UPC #01438142892). Full frame. Dual-channel mono uncompressed PCM soundtrack. $24.99. Snapper. *LANG:* English. *FEATURES:* 16 chapter links • Scene access menu.
1932 67m/B Groucho Marx, Chico Marx, Harpo Marx, Zeppo Marx, Thelma Todd, David Landau, Nat Pendleton; *D:* Norman Z. McLeod; *W:* Bert Kalmar, S.J. Perelman, Harry Ruby; *C:* Ray June; *M:* Harry Ruby.

The Horse Whisperer

After her teenaged daughter Grace (Johansson) is injured in a frightening riding accident, Annie (Thomas) takes the girl and the horse to Montana. That's where "horse whisperer" or healer Tom Booker (Redford) will try to work his magic on both equine and family. The performances are first-rate throughout, though on the small screen, the impressive landscapes are less so. But the film still works well on DVD. Redford is a more stylish director than he is given credit for. Like *Quiz Show*, this film has a distinctive, highly polished look and a steady pace, though at almost three hours, it may be a bit too unhurried for some. In the important moments, sound is almost as important as image. No important flaws are to be found in either. Even those who tend to avoid adaptations of popular best-sellers—it's based on Nicholas Evans's novel—may find this one to their taste. —*MM*

Movie: 🎬🎬🎬 **DVD:** 🎬🎬🎬
Buena Vista Home Entertainment (Cat #15640, UPC #717951000859). Widescreen (2.35:1) letterboxed. Dolby Digital 5.1 Surround Stereo. $29.99. Keepcase. *LANG:* English; French. *CAP:* English. *FEATURES:* 22 chapter links • Theatrical trailer.
1997 (PG-13) 168m/C Robert Redford, Kristin Scott Thomas, Scarlett Johansson, Sam Neill, Chris Cooper, Dianne Wiest, Cherry Jones, Jeanette Nolan, Don Edwards, Ty Hillman, Catherine Bosworth, Steve Frye; *D:* Robert Redford; *W:* Eric Roth, Richard LaGravenese; *C:* Robert Richardson; *M:* Thomas Newman. *AWARDS: NOM:* Academy Awards '98: Best Song ("A Soft Place to Fall"); Golden Globe Awards '98: Best Film—Drama; Golden Globe Awards '99: Best Director (Redford).

Horton Foote's Alone

John Webb (Cronyn) is an elderly Texas farmer who's feeling lost after the death of his wife of 52 years. His nephews (Forrest and Cooper) want him to sell his land to an interested oil company; his daughters (Miles and Hart) want to cry on his shoulder. The only person he can really talk to is Grey (Jones), a tenant farmer of his generation. The film's made-for-cable production values translate to DVD with no perceptible gain or loss. Foote's typically languid pace and lack of intense physical action present no visual problems. Sound is O.K. Overall, the disc is not much better than tape. —*MM AKA:* Alone.
Movie: 🎬🎬▸ **DVD:** 🎬🎬▸
WinStar Home Entertainment (Cat #FLV5212, UPC #720917521220). Full frame. $29.98. Keepcase. *LANG:* English. *FEATURES:* 8 chapter links • Cast and crew filmographies • Production credits • Weblink.
1997 107m/C Hume Cronyn, James Earl Jones, Chris Cooper, Frederic Forrest, Joanna Miles, Roxanne Hart, Shelley Duvall, Hallie Foote, Ed Begley Jr., David Selby, Piper Laurie; *D:* Michael Lindsay-Hogg; *W:* Horton Foote; *C:* Jeffrey Jur; *M:* David Shire.

Hot Blooded

This is your basic story of an Ohio State freshman (Winters) and his road adventures on his way home during Thanksgiv-ing break. A nine-hour drive turns into a multi-day trek filled with sex, guns, booze, and car chases when he picks up a dominatrix hooker (Wuhrer), who is being pursued by her molester, truck-driving father (Young). The plot, which seems to be operating in some sort of a time warp, is quite beside the point as this direct-to-video production is strictly a vehicle for the sexual escapades of Kari Salin-Wuhrer. David Keith drifts through the final ten minutes as the young lad's father. DVD presentation is adequate, with the chief advantage over its VHS counterpart being the ability to freeze frame Wuhrer in various stages of undress. —*RT AKA:* Hit & Run; Red Blooded American Girl 2.
Movie: 🎬▸ **DVD:** 🎬🎬
Image Entertainment (Cat #4760, UPC #014381476026). Full frame. AC3 - 2 Channel. $24.99. Snapper. *LANG:* English. *FEATURES:* 12 chapters.
1998 (R) 95m/C Kari Wuhrer, Kristoffer Ryan Winters, David Keith, Burt Young; *D:* David Blyth; *W:* Nicolas Stiliadis; *C:* Edgar Egger; *M:* Paul Zaza.

The Hot Spot

Buried deep inside this little wanna-be, there's a fine sleazy film noir struggling to get out. The movie has all the right elements: greedy, lustful characters; a sleepy small town filled with secrets; a bank full of money; an older, wealthy husband; and an assortment of crimes including blackmail, arson, robbery, and murder. Unfortunately, director Dennis Hopper gave free rein to his taste for excess and forgot that noir is supposed to be fast, sharp, and lean. At two hours plus, this one is slow, indulgent, and flabby. It also lacks the visual sharpness of the best noir. Both image and sound are soft throughout; voice synchronization is even slightly off in a few scenes. Most of the flaws come from the original, though some of them might have been corrected with a careful digital transfer. —*MM*
Movie: 🎬🎬🎬 **DVD:** 🎬🎬▸
MGM Home Entertainment (Cat #908170, UPC #027616817020). Widescreen letterboxed. Dolby Digital Surround Stereo; Mono. $19.98. Keepcase. *LANG:* English; Spanish. *SUB:* French; Spanish. *CAP:* English. *FEATURES:* 32 chapter links • Trailer.
1990 (R) 120m/C Don Johnson, Virginia Madsen, Jennifer Connelly, Charles Martin Smith, William Sadler, Jerry Hardin, Barry Corbin, Leon Rippy, Jack Nance; *D:* Dennis Hopper; *W:* Charles Williams, Nona Tyson; *C:* Ueli Steiger; *M:* Jack Nitzsche.

Hot War

Big-budget Hong Kong sci-fi adventure suffers from a heavy dose of MTV-influenced style. The opening scenes flit from Belfast, Northern Ireland, to Chicago to Miami with black trenchcoated bad guys knocking off everyone in sight. It all has to do with virtual reality and mind control and the three attractive protagonists—Blue (Kelly Chan), Tango (Ekin Cheng), and C.S. (Jordan Chan)—and a synopsis-proof plot. (Jackie Chan produced.) On DVD, both image and sound vary from scene to scene, with some absolutely clear and bright, others muddy or faded. Sound is the same. —*MM*
Movie: 🎬🎬▸ **DVD:** 🎬🎬
Tai Seng Video Marketing (Cat #5247, UPC #4895024901954). Widescreen letterboxed. Dolby Digital 5.1 Surround Stereo. $24.95. Keepcase. *LANG:* Cantonese; Mandarin. *SUB:* Traditional Chinese; Simplified Chinese; English. *FEATURES:* 8 chapter links • "Making of" featurette • Music video.
1998 93m/C *HK* Ekin Cheng, Jordan Chan, Kelly Chan, Terence Lin, Vanessa Yeung; *D:* Jingle Ma; *W:* Po-Chi Leung, Calvin Poon, Chow Siu Man; *C:* Chan Chi Ying.

The Hound of the Baskervilles

Made-for-television remake is one of the better and more faithful adaptations of Sir Arthur Conan Doyle's most famous novel. Ian Richardson is a coolly restrained Holmes. Donald Churchill's Watson is closer to the original character than Nigel Bruce's comic interpretation. If the production values are not the most lavish, they're certainly adequate to the story both at 221B Baker St. and out on the moors where the Hound lurks. The film makes an easy transition to DVD. The night scenes are clear, and even black clothing is properly lit so that they have visible texture and shape. —*MM*
Movie: 🎬🎬🎬 **DVD:** 🎬🎬🎬
Image Entertainment (Cat #ID6627ZFDVD, UPC #014381662726). Full frame. Dolby Digital Mono. $19.99. Snapper. *LANG:* English. *FEATURES:* 18 chapter links.
1983 100m/C *GB* Ian Richardson, Donald Churchill, Martin Shaw, Nicholas Clay, Denholm Elliott, Brian Blessed, Ronald Lacey; *D:* Douglas Hickox; *W:* Charles Edward Pogue; *C:* Ronnie Taylor; *M:* Michael Lewis.

House of Whipcord

A tongue-in-cheek preface ("This film is dedicated to those who are disturbed by today's lax moral codes and who eagerly await the return of corporal punishment...") sets the tone for a grim, oppressively dark British variation on *The Story of O* with torture (mostly offscreen) replacing sex. The plot revolves around a French model who's kidnapped and locked up in a private prison run by feeble, demented aristocracy. The reasons why are too silly to mention. Producer-director Pete Walker is more interested in a blunt-object attack on the ruling power structure—"the establishment" as it was called at the time—with more anger than subtlety. On DVD, the film is just as dim and difficult to make out as it is on tape. Fault the original production, not the transfer. This is one of those movies that uses darkness to hide its many shortcomings. It's never going to be a silk purse in any medium. More to the point, it doesn't deliver the sleaze that it promises. —MM

Movie: ♫♪ **DVD:** ♫♪

Image Entertainment (Cat #ID5892EUDVD, UPC #014381589221). Full frame. Dolby Digital Mono. $24.99. Snapper. *LANG:* English. *FEATURES:* 16 chapter links.
1975 102m/C *GB* Barbara Markham, Patrick Barr, Ray Brooks, Penny Irving, Anne Michelle, Ivor Salter, Robert Tayman; **D:** Pete Walker; **W:** David McGillivray; **C:** Peter Jessop; **M:** Stanley Myers.

The House of Yes

Arch black comedy is never far from its origins on the stage. At Thanksgiving, Marty (Hamilton) brings his fiancee Lesley (Spelling) back to his Virginia family home to meet the relatives who range from his eccentric mother (Bujold) to his twin sister Jackie-O (Posey), who has morphed into a bizarre reincarnation of Jacqueline Kennedy as she was on the day her husband was assassinated, complete in every detail, right down to the pink Chanel suit. That's only the beginning of the dark-and-stormy night revelation of family secrets. The tone swings between extremes of hysterics and tastelessness. Since virtually all of the action takes place indoors and at night on darkened sets with occasional archival film and video footage tossed in, the DVD image is unspectacular, though striking visuals are certainly not the point. Sound is acceptable. Overall, the no-frills disc is little different from VHS tape. —MM

Movie: ♫♪ **DVD:** ♫♪

Miramax Pictures Home Video (Cat #17595, UPC #717951003324). Widescreen (1.85:1) letterboxed. Dolby Digital 2.0 Surround Stereo. $29.99. Keepcase. *LANG:* English. *CAP:* English. *FEATURES:* 16 chapter links.
1997 (R) 90m/C Parker Posey, Josh Hamilton, Tori Spelling, Freddie Prinze Jr., Genevieve Bujold, Rachael Leigh Cook; **D:** Mark Waters; **W:** Mark Waters; **C:** Michael Spiller; **M:** Jeff Rona. *AWARDS: NOM:* Golden Raspberry Awards '97: Worst New Star (Spelling).

House on Haunted Hill

Secret passages, the vat of acid in the basement, walking skeletons, ghosts in the hallway, even the proverbial dark and stormy night—they're all part of William Castle's good-natured collection of cliches. Eccentric millionaire Vincent Price offers a disparate group—test pilot, shop girl, columnist, doctor—$10,000 apiece to spend the night in a house where gruesome murders have been committed. You don't need three guesses to figure out the rest, and you get the feeling, right or wrong, that everybody had fun on the sets of Castle productions. This is unapologetic cinematic popcorn with lots of salt and butter. For those who don't know, Cas-

tle was affectionately spoofed in *Matinee*. The title is available as a double feature with *The Bat*. (Please see review.) The DVD transfer is very clean and without overly noticeable noise or grain beyond the opening credits sequence. Although some signs of age are evident in the black-and-white transfer, the image is very sharp and well defined. Compression is superb, without pixelation or other compression artifacts. The disc contains a monaural audio track in Dolby Digital that is well preserved, but contains a few audible distortions. Nonetheless, the presentation is excellent if not surprising, given the film's actual age. —MM/GH

Movie: ♫♫♪ **DVD:** ♫♫♪

Warner Home Video, Inc. (Cat #2009, UPC #012569091320). Widescreen (1.85:1) anamorphic; full frame. Dolby Digital Mono. $29.95. Snapper. *LANG:* English. *SUB:* English; French. *CAP:* English. *FEATURES:* 24 chapter links • Theatrical trailer.
1958 75m/B Vincent Price, Carol Ohmart, Richard Long, Alan Marshal, Carolyn Craig, Elisha Cook Jr., Julie Mitchum, Howard Hoffman; **D:** William Castle; **W:** Robb White; **C:** Carl Guthrie; **M:** Von Dexter.

House on Haunted Hill

Lively intelligent remake captures the cheesy spirit of the original and gives the special effects a substantial upgrade. Geoffrey Rush (cast with real inspiration) takes over the Vincent Price role as Steven Price, the eccentric who invites a disparate group of strangers to celebrate his wife's birthday in a deco mansion that once housed an insane asylum where a massacre took place. On DVD, many of the CGI effects are perhaps more obvious than they are on tape, but given the nature of the material, that's hardly a serious flaw. Sound is excellent. Both the extra features and the menu are imaginative. Great stuff for horror fans. I'm a fan of the original and think that this one is better. —MM

Movie: ♫♫♪ **DVD:** ♫♫♪

Warner Home Video, Inc. (Cat #18018). Widescreen (1.85:1) letterboxed. $24.98. Snapper. *LANG:* English. *SUB:* English; French. *FEATURES:* 30 chapter links • Commentary: director William Malone • Trailers • Cast and crew thumbnail bios • Clips from Malone's 1985 *Creature* • Deleted scenes • "Tale of Two Houses" featurette • Behind-the-scenes effects explanations.
1999 (R) 96m/C Geoffrey Rush, Famke Janssen, Taye Diggs, Peter Gallagher, Chris Kattan, Ali Larter, Bridgette Wilson, Max Perlich, Jeffrey Combs; **D:** William Malone; **W:** Dick Beebe; **C:** Rick Bota; **M:** Don Davis.

How Stella Got Her Groove Back

Angela Bassett brings the heroine of Terry McMillan's novel to life. Stella is an executive supermom whose biggest weakness

is that she has yet to realize she deserves better. A Jamaican vacation she can't afford to take, and the soul-searching young man she meets on the island, cause her much friction and eventually force her to adjust her attitudes towards her life, family, and future. Yes, sweeping, romantic grandstanding is finally unleashed in the last scene. That does not make this any more "hollow" than those spectacular confections from the height of Hollywood's studio days, when female star vehicles revolved around the likes of Joan Crawford or Rosalind Russell or Ava Gardner. If anyone in film today deserves to seem bigger and more perfect than life, it's Bassett. The technical quality is singular, a true-blue justification of DVD as a medium. Though celluloid was historically never calibrated with black skin in mind, somehow this film makes everyone from its glamorously clothed stars to the most common-looking extras look fabulous. The featurette promised on the box did not appear in the review copy. —JK

Movie: ♫♫♪ **DVD:** ♫♫♫

20th Century Fox (Cat #4109660, UPC #086162000775). Widescreen (1.85:1) letterboxed. Dolby Digital Stereo Surround 5.1. $34.99. Keepcase. *LANG:* English. *SUB:* Spanish; English. *CAP:* English. *FEATURES:* 35 chapter links • Featurette • Animated interactive menus • Full-color picture disc • Cast and director mini-bios • Original theatrical trailers.
1998 (R) 124m/C Angela Bassett, Whoopi Goldberg, Taye Diggs, Regina King, Suzanne Douglas, Richard Lawson, Michael J. Pagan, Barry (Shabaka) Henley, Sicily; **D:** Kevin Rodney Sullivan; **W:** Ronald Bass, Terry McMillan; **C:** Jeffrey Jur; **M:** Michel Colombier.

How the West Was Won

DVD highlights all of the flaws in this sprawling panorama of America's westward expansion. The film was made in the Cinerama process that employed three cameras and three projectors to display an extra-wide image on curved screens in theatres. The technique is so faithfully reproduced here that two vertical lines neatly divide the image into three separate sections. In some scenes, the image actually bends at those lines. In others—most noticeable in landscapes with a bright blue sky—the difference in color values is obvious (and annoying) between the center and side screens. For my money, the disc is essentially unwatchable. If the film and the subject appeal, find an older full-frame tape. —MM

Movie: ♫♪ **DVD:** ♫

Twentieth Century Fox Home Entertainment (Cat #906292, UPC #027616629227). Widescreen letterboxed. Dolby Digital Surround Stereo. $24.98. Keepcase. *LANG:* English; French. *SUB:* English; French; Spanish. *FEATURES:* 32 chapter links • Theatrical trailer • Booklet • Behind-the-scenes featurette.

1963 (G) 165m/C John Wayne, Carroll Baker, Lee J. Cobb, Spencer Tracy, Gregory Peck, Karl Malden, Robert Preston, Eli Wallach, Henry Fonda, George Peppard, Debbie Reynolds, Carolyn Jones, Richard Widmark, James Stewart, Walter Brennan, Andy Devine, Raymond Massey, Agnes Moorehead, Harry (Henry) Morgan, Thelma Ritter, Russ Tamblyn; **D:** John Ford, Henry Hathaway, George Marshall; **W:** James R. Webb; **C:** Milton Krasner, Charles B(ryant) Lang. *AWARDS:* Academy Awards '63: Best Film Editing, Best Sound, Best Story & Screenplay, National Film Registry '97; *NOM:* Academy Awards '63: Best Art Direction/Set Decoration (Color), Best Color Cinematography, Best Costume Design (Color), Best Picture, Best Original Score.

How to Be a Woman and Not Die in the Attempt

Witty comedy about the stresses of being a modern woman. Topics range from marital relationship to dealing with sexual harassment and gender discrimination in the workplace. As usual, Maura is excellent. The video transfer is quite good, complete with well-defined colors that refrain from bleeding and nice sharp blacks. Surprisingly, the mono soundtrack is also rather decent. For the most part, dialogue is clear and understandable (though it does get a bit muddied in a few instances, but those are easily overlooked). —*MJT* **AKA:** How to Be a Woman and Not Die Trying; Como ser Mujer y No Morir en El.
Movie: 🎬🎬🎬 **DVD:** 🎬🎬➤
Image Entertainment (Cat #OVED6876 DVD, UPC #014381687620). Full frame. Dolby Digital Mono. $24.99. Snapper. *LANG:* Spanish. *SUB:* English. *FEATURES:* 12 chapter links ➤ Theatrical trailer.
1991 96m/C *SP* Carmen Maura, Antonio Resines; **D:** Ana Belen; **W:** Carmen Rico Godoy; **C:** Juan Amoros.

How to Make an American Quilt

Slow-moving take on female friendship and marriage revolves around perennial grad student Finn (the mopey Ryder), who is frantic to both finish her third attempted thesis and to answer a marriage proposal from practically perfect beau Sam (Mulroney). She takes a summer refuge with her grandmother (Burstyn), where a variety of family friends work on her wedding quilt as they tell stories of loves lost and won. Lots of (somewhat overextended) flashbacks and with so many characters, naturally some get the short end of the script. Based on the novel by Whitney Otto. The film has a muted-color look to it that gives a very nice feeling of warmth. On the DVD they haven't messed with that: the colors are accurate, and the feel remains. The picture is also very sharp. There isn't much going on with sound effects, but the

5.1 stereo conveys the music and environment very nicely, without attempting to bury the dialogue. —*JO*
Movie: 🎬🎬➤ **DVD:** 🎬🎬🎬➤
Universal Studios Home Video (Cat #20018, UPC #025192001826). Widescreen (1.77:1) letterboxed. Dolby Digital 5.1; Dolby Surround. $24.98. Keepcase. *LANG:* English; Spanish; French. *SUB:* Spanish. *CAP:* English. *FEATURES:* 30 chapter links ➤ Production notes ➤ Cast and filmmakers bios ➤ Film highlights.
1995 (PG-13) 109m/C Winona Ryder, Ellen Burstyn, Anne Bancroft, Lois Smith, Jean Simmons, Kate Nelligan, Maya Angelou, Alfre Woodard, Dermot Mulroney, Kate Capshaw, Rip Torn, Derrick O'Connor, Loren Dean, Samantha Mathis, Joanna Going, Tim Guinee, Johnathon Schaech, Claire Danes, Jared Leto, Esther Rolle, Melinda Dillon, Alicia (Lecy) Goranson, Maria Celedonio, Mykelti Williamson; **D:** Jocelyn Moorhouse; **W:** Jane Anderson; **C:** Janusz Kaminski; **M:** Thomas Newman. *AWARDS: NOM:* MTV Movie Awards '96: Best Kiss (Winona Ryder/Dermot Mulroney); Screen Actors Guild Award '95: Cast.

Howard's End

E.M. Forster's 1910 novel about property, privilege, class differences, and Edwardian society is brought to enchanting life by the Merchant Ivory team. A tragic series of events occurs after two impulsive sisters become involved with a working class couple and a wealthy family. Tragedy aside, this is a visually beautiful effort with subtle performances where a glance or a gesture says as much as any dialogue. Thompson is especially notable as the compassionate Margaret, while Hopkins plays the repressed English gentleman brilliantly. Much of the lighting is subtle in this visually stimulating film and this DVD seems to handle all of it very well, without uncomfortable changes in the brightness or contrast levels. The colors also fare very well throughout the disc, and remain extremely accurate, as do the blacks. Grain is very seldom a problem and artifacts even less noticeable. The Dolby Surround is full and seems to supply almost as much ambience as a 5.1 mix, with very nice imaging and separation throughout. —*JO*
Movie: 🎬🎬🎬🎬 **DVD:** 🎬🎬🎬➤
Columbia Tristar Home Video (Cat #26779, UPC #043396267794). Widescreen (2.35:1) anamorphic. Dolby Surround. NSL. Keepcase. *LANG:* English; French. *SUB:* English; French. *CAP:* English. *FEATURES:* 28 chapter links ➤ 3 theatrical trailers.
1992 (PG) 143m/C *GB* Anthony Hopkins, Emma Thompson, Helena Bonham Carter, Vanessa Redgrave, James Wilby, Samuel West, Jemma Redgrave, Nicola Duffett, Prunella Scales, Joseph Bennett; **Cameos:** Simon Callow; **D:** James Ivory; **W:** Ruth Prawer Jhabvala; **C:** Tony Pierce-Roberts. *AWARDS:* Academy Awards '92: Best Actress (Thompson), Best Adapted Screenplay, Best Art Direction/Set Decoration;

British Academy Awards '92: Best Actress (Thompson); Golden Globe Awards '93: Best Actress—Drama (Thompson); Los Angeles Film Critics Association Awards '92: Best Actress (Thompson); National Board of Review Awards '92: Best Actress (Thompson), Best Director (Ivory), Best Film; New York Film Critics Awards '92: Best Actress (Thompson); National Society of Film Critics Awards '92: Best Actress (Thompson); *NOM:* Academy Awards '92: Best Cinematography, Best Costume Design, Best Director (Ivory), Best Picture, Best Supporting Actress (Redgrave), Best Original Score.

The Hubley Collection: Everybody Rides the Carousel

Please see review of *The Hubley Collection, Vol. 1*. Contents: "Everybody Rides the Carousel" (1975), "A Doonesbury Special" (1977), and "My Universe Inside Out" (1975). —*MM*
Movie: 🎬🎬🎬 **DVD:** 🎬🎬🎬
Image Entertainment (Cat #ID5845PIDVD, UPC #014381585421). Full frame. Dolby Digital Mono; Stereo. $24.99. Snapper. *LANG:* English. *FEATURES:* 26 chapter links.
199? 123m/C D: John Hubley, Faith Hubley.

The Hubley Collection, Vol. 1

The animated films in this three-volume collection from Faith and John Hubley are not to be confused with conventional cartoons from the studios. These are more abstract and serious, though they are definitely aimed at audiences of all ages. Made between 1959 and 1995, they cover a wide range of subjects and artistic styles. You'll see influences of Joan Miro, various Impressionists, and Garry Trudeau. At their worst, the films seem preachy liberal political positions; at their best, they capture the essence of humanity. Much of their fine children's work is created around semi-scripted conversations between real kids, sometimes their own. On these DVDs, some of the older films are not sharply focused and quick movement can present a problem. DVD also makes the individual works much more easily accessible. For more of the Hubleys' work, see *Art and Jazz in Animation: The Cosmic Eye*. Contents: "Enter Life," (1981), "Upside Down" (1991), "Who Am I?" (1989), "Blake Ball" (1988), "Time of the Angels" (1987), "W.O.W. (Women of the World)" (1975), "People, People, People" (1975), "Amazonia" (1989), "Yes We Can" (1988), "Moonbird" (1959), "Tall Time Tales" (1992), "Windy Day" (1967), and "Cloudland" (1993). —*MM*
Movie: 🎬🎬🎬 **DVD:** 🎬🎬➤
Image Entertainment (Cat #ID5855PIDVD, UPC #014381585520). Full frame. Dolby Digital Mono. $24.99. Snapper. *LANG:* English. *FEATURES:* 13 chapter links.

1992 118m/C D: Faith Hubley, Emily Hubley.

The Hubley Collection, Vol. 2

Please see review of *The Hubley Collection, Vol. 1.* Contents: "Seers and Clowns" (1994), "Sky Dance" (1979), "Cockaboody" (1973), "Hello" (1984), "Step by Step" (1978), "Rainbows of Hawai'i" (1995), "The Big Bang and Other Creation Myths" (1981), "Zuckerkandl!" (1968), "Whither Weather" (1977), and "Her Grandmother's Gift" (1995). —*MM*
Movie: 🎬🎬🎬 **DVD:** 🎬🎬🎬
Image Entertainment (Cat #ID5856PIDVD, UPC #014381585629). Full frame. Dolby Digital Stereo. $24.99. Snapper. *LANG:* English. *FEATURES:* 10 chapter links.
199? 99m/C D: Faith Hubley, John Hubley.

Hudson Hawk

In a big-budget, broad, and goofy star vehicle, Willis plays the titular master burglar released from prison, only to find himself trapped by the CIA into one last theft— Leonardo DaVinci's secret method of converting lead into gold, which rich thrill seekers Grant and Bernhard want for themselves. The caper leads to Rome where a charming Vatican spy steals Hudson's heart. The DVD has occasional excessive grain and bleeding of the reds, but looks pretty good overall. The grain tends to show up in flesh and earthtones, but not very often. Other than that the picture sharpness is a little above average. Blacks are pretty good but lean to blue at times. Contrast and brightness are good, but artifacts appear during contrasty scenes with fast movement. The sound is better than the picture—crisp, with a lot of presence and good dynamics. A clear step above the VHS copy but slightly below the laserdisc. —*JO*
Movie: 🎬🎬▸ **DVD:** 🎬🎬▸
Columbia Tristar Home Video (Cat #70599, UPC #043396705999). Widescreen (1.85:1) letterboxed; full frame. Dolby Surround. $25.95. Keepcase. *LANG:* English; French. *SUB:* French. *CAP:* English. *FEATURES:* Dual-layered RSDL ▪ 28 chapter links ▪ Theatrical trailers ▪ Commentary: director Michael Lehmann.
1991 (R) 95m/C D: Bruce Willis, Danny Aiello, Andie MacDowell, James Coburn, Sandra Bernhard, Richard E. Grant, Frank Stallone; **D:** Michael Lehmann; **W:** Steven E. de Souza, Daniel Waters; **C:** Dante Spinotti; **M:** Michael Kamen, Robert Kraft. *AWARDS:* Golden Raspberry Awards '91: Worst Picture, Worst Director (Lehmann), Worst Screenplay.

The Hudsucker Proxy

In an effort to scare off would-be investors in a public stock offering, dim-bulb mailboy Robbins is installed as the Prez of Hudsucker Industries (in 1958) by Board Director Newman after corporate magnate Hud-

sucker (Durning) takes a swan dive from the 44th floor. First truly mainstream effort from the maverick Coen brothers is peppered with obscure references to numerous points on the historical map of cinematic style, and trots out an equally old but instantly recognizable story. Will delight Coen fans, but may be too dark for others. Destined to keep art history profs busy for decades. The Coens' unique visual style is retained on the DVD and the image is sharp and slick, with natural fleshtones and overall accurate colors. Blacks are also dead-on and remain that way, even during an effects sequence when almost all color drops out. The Dolby Surround is excellent and conveys the lively score with great fidelity and dynamics. —*JO*
Movie: 🎬🎬🎬 **DVD:** 🎬🎬🎬🎬▸
Warner Home Video, Inc. (Cat #13166, UPC #085391316626). Widescreen (1.85:1) letterboxed; full frame. Dolby Surround. $19.98. Snapper. *LANG:* English; French. *SUB:* English; French. *CAP:* English. *FEATURES:* 37 chapter links.
1993 (PG) 115m/C Tim Robbins, Paul Newman, Jennifer Jason Leigh, Charles Durning, John Mahoney, Jim True, Bill Cobbs, Bruce Campbell, Steve Buscemi; **Cameos:** Peter Gallagher; **D:** Joel Coen; **W:** Ethan Coen, Joel Coen, Sam Raimi; **C:** Roger Deakins; **M:** Carter Burwell.

Hugo Pool

Hugo Dugay (Milano) cleans the pools of 44 backyard eccentrics. She must enlist the aid of her gambler mom (Moriarty) and drug addict dad (McDowell, who appears to be doing a Popeye imitation). Bizarre L.A. characters abound, including Downey Jr. overacting with a Hungarian accent that changes with each line. Most interesting is Dempsey as ALS-afflicted Floyd Galen. The romance between Floyd and Hugo supplies the most sensitive and well-acted sequences. In the end, though, this is a disappointing outing from Downey Sr. *(Putney Swope)* who shared writing duties with wife Laura, who died of ALS in 1994. Despite a modest budget, the film has solid production values and so the DVD sparkles in every scene. The mostly static action does not challenge the limitations of the medium. —*MM*
Movie: 🎬🎬 **DVD:** 🎬🎬▸
WinStar Home Entertainment (Cat #FLV5129, UPC #720917512921). Full frame. $24.98. Keepcase. *LANG:* English. *FEATURES:* 8 chapter links.
1997 (R) 92m/C Alyssa Milano, Patrick Dempsey, Robert Downey Jr., Malcolm McDowell, Cathy Moriarty, Sean Penn, Richard Lewis, Chuck Barris; **D:** Robert Downey; **W:** Laura Downey; **C:** Joe Montgomery; **M:** Danilo Perez.

Hum Dil De Chuke Sanam

Euro-Indian music student Sameer (Khan) proposes to his teacher's willfully vivacious daughter Nandini (newcomer and former model Rai). Pundit Darbar

(Gokhale) cancels Sameer's scholarship and returns him to Hungary. Nandini's marriage is arranged, but her groom Vanraj (Devgan) soon discovers she grieves for a lost love. The unhappy couple embark on a fateful, nearly fatal attempt to track down Sameer and allow Nandini to choose between her two suitors. Studio hacks should hang their heads in shame before this new gold standard for musicals Hollywood no longer makes. The innovative staging of *On the Town,* the delicate coloring of *The Umbrellas of Cherbourg,* the sheer length (188 minutes) of *The Sound of Music,* even the assured comedic touch of *Singin' in the Rain* are combined with the emotional sophistication of *High Society* and a unique, subtly multicultural score. Writer-director-producer Bhansali dedicated his effort, sometimes coarsely droll yet ultimately concerned with maturity and genuine family loyalty, to his father with the words "come hold me just once." Minor glitches, like sometimes out of sync subtitling or untranslated lyrics and intermittently cloudy blacks in the few dimly lit scenes, only render its visual and sonic glories all the more precious. —*JK* **AKA:** Straight from the Heart.
Movie: 🎬🎬🎬🎬 **DVD:** 🎬🎬🎬🎬
Video Sound (Cat #VSMD1299-DVD62, UPC #677565006299). Widescreen. Dolby Digital 5.1 Surround Stereo. $29.95. Keepcase. *LANG:* Hindi; English. *SUB:* English. *FEATURES:* 20 chapter links ▪ Animated interactive menus ▪ "Select a Song" menu of 12 songs ▪ Full-frame "making of" documentary covering major aspects of production. All regions coding.
1999 (PG) 188m/C IN Salman Khan, Aishwarya Rai, Ajay Devgan, Vikram Gokhale; **D:** Sanjay Leela Bhansali; **W:** Sanjay Leela Bhansali, Kenneth Phillips; **C:** Anil Mehta; **M:** Ismail Darbar, Mehboob, Anjan Biswas.

The Human Condition: No Greater Love

In the first of a three-part series of films, a pacifist is called into military service and subsequently sent to run a military mining camp. A gripping look at one man's attempt to retain his humanity in the face of war. Image has gotten a fine print to work from for the release of this very fine, but older, Japanese film. There is very little film damage. The black-and-white image is crisp, deep, and detailed. Both contrast and graytones are very good. There is very little of the ghosting around high-contrast lines that is fairly common in older black-and-white prints. The sound is at times a little scratchy, but is overall very acceptable. —*JO*
Movie: 🎬🎬🎬▸ **DVD:** 🎬🎬🎬
Image Entertainment (Cat #ID4550JFDVD). Widescreen (2.2:1) letterboxed. Dolby Digital Mono. $29.95. Snapper. *LANG:* Japanese. *SUB:* English. *FEATURES:* 17 chapter links.

1958 200m/B *JP* Tatsuya Nakadai, Michiyo Aratama, So Yamamura, Eitaro Ozawa, Akira Ishihama, Chikage Awashima, Ineko Arima, Keiji Sada, Shinji Nambara, Seiji Miyaguchi, Toru Abe, Masao Mishima, Eijiro Tono, Yasushi Nagata, Yoshio Kosugi; *D:* Masaki Kobayashi; *W:* Masaki Kobayashi, Zenzo Matsuyama; *C:* Yoshio Miyajima; *M:* Chuji Kinoshita.

The Human Condition: Road to Eternity

In the second volume of his autobiographical trilogy, writer-director Masaki Kobayashi tells the story of Kaji (Nakadai), a pacifist drafted into the Japanese army and stationed in Manchuria, where some of the most unspeakable atrocities of the war occurred. Kaji's attempts to maintain his humanity are detailed with horrifying clarity. The DVD looks very good for a 1950s Japanese black-and-white film, though the image suffers from some slippage, as if the film were not completely steady in the projector gate. The usual surface flecks and soundtrack pops are also evident. The subtitles are displayed in the lower bar of the deep letterbox. —*MM AKA:* No Greater Love; Ningen No Joken.
Movie: 🎵🎵🎵 *DVD:* 🎵🎵🎵
Image Entertainment (Cat #ID4551JFDVD, UPC #014381455120). Widescreen (2.20:1) letterboxed. Dolby Digital Mono. $29.99. Snapper. *LANG:* Japanese. *SUB:* English. *FEATURES:* 17 chapter links.
1959 180m/B *JP* Tatsuya Nakadai, Michiyo Aratama, Kokinji Katsura, Jun Tatara, Michio Minami, Keiji Sada, Minoru Chiaki, Ryohei Uchida, Kan Yanagidani, Kenjiro Uemura, Yusuke Kawazu, Susumu Fujita; *D:* Masaki Kobayashi; *W:* Masaki Kobayashi, Zenzo Matsuyama; *C:* Yoshio Miyajima; *M:* Chuji Kinoshita.

Humanoids from the Deep

Mutated salmon-like monsters rise from the depths of the ocean and decide to chomp on some bikinied babes. Violent and bloody fun features an early score by James Horner. Like most of the New Horizon–released Corman DVDs, the picture is very soft and colors are generally a little dull. Blacks are frequently grainy and contrast is a little low. Artifacts arise during darker moments—pretty much any reptilian attack scene. The sound is tolerable but nothing special. Also like the others, the disc contains an interview with Corman. —*JO AKA:* Monster.
Movie: 🎵🎵▶ *DVD:* 🎵▶
New Horizons Home Video (Cat #NH00200, UPC #736991420045). Full frame. Stereo. $24.98. Keepcase. *LANG:* English. *FEATURES:* Theatrical trailers ● Cast and filmmakers bios ● Roger Corman interview ● 8-page booklet.
1980 (R) 81m/C Doug McClure, Ann Turkel, Vic Morrow, Cindy Weintraub,

Anthony Penya, Denise Balik, Hoke Howell, Meegan King, Rob Bottin; *D:* Barbara Peeters; *W:* Frank Arnold, Frederick James, Martin B. Cohen; *C:* Daniel Lacambre; *M:* James Horner.

The Hunchback of Notre Dame

Today, the anti-fascist propaganda aspects of this masterpiece are obvious—and what's wrong with that? Even if Charles Laughton's makeup doesn't equal Lon Chaney's, he's such a marvelous actor that he's a more sympathetic and moving Quasimodo, though the technical shortcomings are heightened by the extra clarity of DVD. Teaming him with Maureen O'Hara's Esmeralda is the magical chemistry that Hollywood creates every decade or so. (If you don't mist up when she gives him water and then when he stumbles back into the cathedral, something's wrong.) Hardwicke's Claude Frollo is a complex and sinister villain. The gigantic cathedral facade, the bell tower sets, and the proverbial cast of thousands are just terrific. Also, since the black-and-white film was made for a conventional-sized screen, it looks grand on disc, with only the expected amount of graininess. The big finish, complete with molten lead spewing from the mouths of gargoyles, is about as good as it gets. Sound is fine. This one belongs in every video library. —*MM*
Movie: 🎵🎵🎵🎵 *DVD:* 🎵🎵🎵🎵
Warner Home Video, Inc. (Cat #T2058, UPC #053939205824). Full frame. Dolby Digital Mono. $24.98. Snapper. *LANG:* English; Spanish. *SUB:* English; French; Spanish. *FEATURES:* 31 chapter links ● Behind-the-scenes featurette ● "Making of" featurette ● Production and historical factoids ● Cast and crew thumbnail biographies ● Theatrical trailer.
1939 117m/B Charles Laughton, Maureen O'Hara, Edmond O'Brien, Cedric Hardwicke, Thomas Mitchell, George Zucco, Alan Marshal, Walter Hampden, Harry Davenport, Curt Bois, George Tobias, Rod La Rocque; *D:* William Dieterle; *W:* Sonya Levien, Bruno Frank; *C:* Joseph August; *M:* Alfred Newman. *AWARDS: NOM:* Academy Awards '39: Best Sound, Best Score.

The Hunt for Red October

Adaptation of Tom Clancy's blockbuster novel is a high-tech Cold War yarn about a Soviet nuclear sub turning rogue and heading straight for U.S. waters, as both the U.S. and the U.S.S.R. try to stop it. Complicated, ill-plotted potboiler that succeeds breathlessly due to the cast and McTiernan's tommy-gun direction. The film also introduces the character of CIA analyst Jack Ryan, who returns in *Patriot Games* in the guise of Harrison Ford. Submarine movies usually make for good Surround and overall sound, and this is no exception. In fact, even when the camera is not aboard the subs, there is still plenty

of ambient Surround and effects that make use of the entire mix. Highs and lows are equally good and the overall feel is very lively. The image is also very good, with very good sharpness and only minor grain, despite all the dark interior shots in the film. There are occasional artifacts. Colors are vibrant and highly detailed with detailed shading. Contrast is good and the DVD is a little brighter than other video formats. The blacks are also true and have only occasional problems with grain. —*JO*
Movie: 🎵🎵🎵 *DVD:* 🎵🎵🎵
Paramount Home Video (Cat #320207, UPC #097363202073). Widescreen (2.35:1) letterboxed. Dolby Digital 5.1; Dolby Surround. $29.99. Keepcase. *LANG:* English (DD5.1; DS) French (DS). *SUB:* Spanish. *CAP:* English. *FEATURES:* 13 chapter links ● Theatrical trailer.
1990 (PG) 137m/C Sean Connery, Alec Baldwin, Richard Jordan, Scott Glenn, Joss Ackland, Sam Neill, James Earl Jones, Peter Firth, Tim Curry, Courtney B. Vance, Jeffrey Jones, Fred Dalton Thompson; *D:* John McTiernan; *W:* Larry Ferguson, Donald Stewart; *C:* Jan De Bont; *M:* Basil Poledouris. *AWARDS:* Academy Awards '90: Best Sound Effects Editing; *NOM:* Academy Awards '90: Best Film Editing, Best Sound.

The Hunted

American businessman in Japan meets, beds, and witnesses the assassination of a mysterious woman and is forced on the run by the modern-day ninja clan that committed the crime. Only a notch above the low-budget, badly dubbed martial arts flicks of the '70s, this shameless bloodfest features unintentionally campy performances by Lambert and Lone and lots of silly dialogue. Beware—the cliches pile up as quickly as the bodies. The DVD makes the film much more enjoyable by allowing its principle asset—the cinematography—to be viewed as photographed. The image is sharp and without much grain, even in dark scenes. Artifacts rarely intrude. The color is super and is always lush and accurate, with very little bleed. Contrast and brightness levels are up from earlier home video editions. The 5.1 sound is very lively and benefits from excellent channel separation and full-bodied frequency response, though the Surround is utilized almost exclusively for environmental ambience. —*JO*
Movie: 🎵🎵 *DVD:* 🎵🎵🎵▶
Universal Studios Home Video (Cat #20443, UPC #025192044328). Widescreen (1.85:1) anamorphic. Dolby Digital 5.1; Dolby Surround. $24.98. Keepcase. *LANG:* English (DD5.1); French (DS). *SUB:* Spanish. *CAP:* English. *FEATURES:* 18 chapter links ● Theatrical trailer ● Cast and filmmakers bios ● Film highlights.
1994 (R) 110m/C Christopher Lambert, John Lone, Joan Chen, Yoshio Harada, Yoko Shimada, Mari Natsuki, Tak Kubota; *D:* Jonathan Lawton; *W:* Jonathan Lawton; *C:* Jack Conroy; *M:* Motofumi Yamaguchi.

Hunter's Moon

World War I veteran Turner (Carradine) wanders into a backwoods community where he falls for the lovely Flo Samuels (Du Mond) and runs afoul of her tyrannical father Clayton (Reynolds), whose foul mood can probably be traced to his unspeakable shoulder-length white wig. Actually, the Depression-era setting is rather nicely evoked with muted colors and an autumnal feeling. The DVD image is slightly better than VHS tape. Sound suffers from brief breaks. —*MM*

Movie: 𝄞𝄞▶ ***DVD:*** 𝄞𝄞▶

Monarch Home Video (Cat #7547, UPC #723952075475). Full frame. $19.95. Keepcase. *LANG:* English. *FEATURES:* 14 chapter links.

1997 (R) 104m/C Burt Reynolds, Keith Carradine, Hayley Du Mond, Ann Wedgeworth, Pat Hingle, Brion James, Charles Napier; ***D:*** Richard Weinman; ***W:*** Richard Weinman, L. Ford Neale, John Huff, William Kemper; ***C:*** Suki Medencevic.

The Hurricane

A couple (Hall and Lamour) on the run from the law (Massey) are aided by a hurricane to build a new life for themselves on a tropical island. Ford made the picture two years before the Academy's special effects award was created, but his film still displays some of the best effects of the decade. Like the other process shots, though, they suffer from excess graininess and the clarity of DVD only makes that more apparent. Sound is fine. —*MM*

Movie: 𝄞𝄞𝄞 ***DVD:*** 𝄞𝄞▶

HBO Home Video (Cat #90756, UPC #026359075629). Full frame. Chase Stereo; Mono. $24.98. Snapper. *LANG:* English; French; Spanish; Italian; German. *SUB:* English; French; Spanish. *FEATURES:* 20 chapter links • Cast and crew thumbnail biographies • Theatrical trailer.

1937 102m/B Jon Hall, Dorothy Lamour, Mary Astor, Sir C. Aubrey Smith, Raymond Massey, Thomas Mitchell, John Carradine; ***D:*** John Ford; ***W:*** Oliver H.P. Garrett, Dudley Nichols; ***C:*** Bert Glennon, Paul Eagler, Archie Stout; ***M:*** Alfred Newman. *AWARDS:* Academy Awards '37: Best Sound; *NOM:* Academy Awards '37: Best Supporting Actor (Mitchell), Best Score.

Hush

Stink-bomb thriller stars Paltrow as a working-class girl (yeah, right) who marries wealthy dreamboat Jackson (Schaech) and moves into his family's Kentucky estate. There smother-in-law Lange camps it up as she turns psycho on the pregnant bride while coming on to her son who doesn't have a clue. Neither, apparently, did filmmaker Darby, whose film was held from release for two years. On disc, the image is flawless, making it that much easier to see the awkward cut between the nude body double and Ms. Paltrow in one key early scene. —*MM* *AKA:* Kilronan; Bloodline.

Movie: woof ***DVD:*** 𝄞𝄞𝄞

Columbia Tristar Home Video (Cat #02356, UPC #043396023567). Widescreen (1.85:1) letterboxed; full frame. Dolby Digital 5.1 Surround Stereo; Dolby Digital Surround Stereo. $25.95. Keepcase. *LANG:* English; French. *SUB:* French. *FEATURES:* 28 chapter links • Theatrical trailer.

1998 (PG-13) 96m/C Gwyneth Paltrow, Jessica Lange, Johnathon Schaech, Nina Foch, Debi Mazar, Kaiulani Lee, David Thornton, Hal Holbrook; ***D:*** Jonathan Darby; ***W:*** Jonathan Darby, Jane Rusconi; ***C:*** Andrew Dunn; ***M:*** Christopher Young. *AWARDS: NOM:* Golden Raspberry Awards '98: Worst Actress (Lange).

Hush Little Baby

Susan Nolan (Meldrum), with a husband and family of her own, is shocked when the biological mother she had thought was dead tries to contact her. Turns out that Edie Landers (Ladd) is another of those female psychos who were so popular in suspense films of the late '80s and 1990s. This made-for-TV variation connects the dots competently enough. On disc, it's brightly lit and sharp with strong colors. The image suffers the usual problems with Venetian blinds, but the night scenes are fine. —*MM*

Movie: 𝄞▶ ***DVD:*** 𝄞𝄞

Simitar Entertainment (Cat #7593, UPC #082551759323). Full frame. Dolby Digital Stereo. $14.98. Keepcase. *LANG:* English. *FEATURES:* 8 chapter links • Diane Ladd filmography.

1993 91m/C Diane Ladd, Wendel Meldrum, Geraint Wyn Davies, Illya Woloshyn, Ingrid Veninger; ***D:*** Jorge Montesi.

Hyper Space

Six people awaken from cryogenic sleep to discover that their spaceship has become marooned light years from Earth and only a single-passenger shuttle is available to get someone back home. DVD technology heightens the flaws of this bargain basement sf—poor focus, slow action, tacky effects, grainy color. —*MM* *AKA:* Black Forest: Rage in Space.

Movie: 𝄞𝄞 ***DVD:*** 𝄞

Simitar Entertainment (Cat #7514, UPC #082551751426). Full frame. Dolby Digital Stereo. $14.98. Keepcase. *LANG:* English. *FEATURES:* 8 chapter links • Production footoids.

1989 90m/C Richard Norton, Don Stroud, Lynn-Holly Johnson, James Van Patten, Ron O'Neal, Rebecca Cruz; ***D:*** David Huey; ***W:*** Richard Dominguez; ***C:*** Roger Olkowski.

I, a Woman

In the early stages of the mid-'60s sexual revolution, this Swedish import was pretty hot stuff, so for videophiles of a certain age, the wish-fulfillment fantasy does have a nostalgia value. Siv (Persson) is a young nurse who hops into the sack with virtually every man she meets. On DVD, the film is barely watchable. It was created from a

scratchy print of an original that was filmed in grainy black and white with lighting that ranges from extremes of darkness and overexposure with little middle ground. The sound wavers and the opening bars of the screeching violin score will probably send dogs howling from the TV room. —*MM* *AKA:* Jag, en Kvinna.

Movie: 𝄞𝄞 ***DVD:*** 𝄞𝄞

Image Entertainment (Cat #ID5752FFDVD, UPC #014381575224). Full frame. Dolby Digital Mono. $19.99. Snapper. *LANG:* English. *FEATURES:* 14 chapter links.

1966 90m/B *SW* Essy Persson, Jorgen Reenberg, Preben Mahrt; ***D:*** Mac Ahlberg; ***W:*** Peer Guldbrandsen; ***C:*** Mac Ahlberg.

I Am Cuba

Agit-prop Russian-Cuban coproduction illustrates the different aspects of the Cuban revolution, from the toppling of Batista and the decadence of Havana to the idealistic students, soldiers, and peasants of the revolution. Lots of over-the-top oratory and artificiality; but that's part of the beauty of the film. That, and cinematographer Urusevsky's amazing high-contrast B&W photography. With the billing "Presented by Francis Ford Coppola and Martin Scorsese," you can bet that this DVD is as close to the original print as possible. The B&W photography is certainly dramatic, and the sound clear. —*AB* *AKA:* Soy Cuba; Ja Cuba.

Movie: 𝄞𝄞 ***DVD:*** 𝄞𝄞𝄞

Image Entertainment (Cat #ID5925MLSDVD, UPC #1438159252). Full frame. Dolby Digital Mono. $29.99. Keepcase. *LANG:* Russian; Spanish. *SUB:* English. *FEATURES:* 37 chapter links • Theatrical trailer.

1964 141m/B *CU RU* Luz Maria Collazo, Jose Gallardo, Sergio Corrieri, Jean Bouise, Raul Garcia, Celia Rodriguez; ***D:*** Mikhail Kalatozov; ***W:*** Yevgeny Yevtushenko, Enrique Pineda Barnet; ***C:*** Sergei Urusevsky; ***M:*** Carlos Farinas. *AWARDS: NOM:* Independent Spirit Awards '96: Best Foreign Film.

I Know What You Did Last Summer

Writer Kevin Williamson's follow-up to *Scream* is loosely based on Lois Duncan's young adult novel. The small-town quarterback (Phillippe), the beauty queen (Gellar), the brainy girl (Hewitt), and the ambitious poor boy (Prinze Jr.) are the protagonists of the self-aware horror. In the middle of their last summer of irresponsibility after they've graduated from high school, they're involved in an accident, perhaps a murder. They cover it up, but a year later, it's not over. Yes, there's more than a little Hitchcock in the premise, and, for a time, Williamson and Scottish director Jim Gillespie follow the master's lead with a tricky, unpredictable tale. The second half becomes more conventional stalker stuff. The young characters are attractive, though the girls are in constant danger of falling out of their Wonderbras. What the film really lacks is a convincing sense of place. In North Carolina, the mountains and the beach are opposite ends of the state. The DVD may look slightly better than the VHS tape, but the only real difference is in the commentary track. Fans of the cast will probably want to watch the full-frame version. —*MM*

Movie: 🐾🐾▶ **DVD:** 🐾🐾▶
Columbia Tristar Home Video (Cat #23925). Widescreen (2.35:1) letterboxed; full frame. Dolby Digital 5.1 Surround Stereo. $29.95. Jewel case. *LANG:* English; French. *SUB:* French; Spanish. *CAP:* English. *FEATURES:* 28 chapter links • Commentary: Gillespie and editor Steve Berkovich. Title is also available on double-feature disc with *I Still Know What You Did Last Summer* (cat. #4213).
1997 (R) 100m/C Jennifer Love Hewitt, Sarah Michelle Gellar, Ryan Phillippe, Freddie Prinze Jr., Muse Watson, Anne Heche, Bridgette Wilson, Johnny Galecki, Dan Albright; **D:** Jim Gillespie; **W:** Kevin Williamson; **C:** Denis Crossan; **M:** John Debney. *AWARDS: NOM:* MTV Movie Awards '98: Breakthrough Performance (Gellar).

I Like to Play Games

Michael (Steadman) is looking for a woman who enjoys sexual games. He thinks he has found the perfect partner in Suzanne (Boyle), but it turns out that her ideas are even kinkier than his. On DVD, this Playboy production generally looks O.K., though one striped shirt flashes so strongly that it will hurt your eyes. An unrated version (catalog #7466) is also available. —*MM*

Movie: 🐾🐾▶ **DVD:** 🐾🐾
Simitar Entertainment (Cat #7423, UPC #082551746620). Full frame. PCM Stereo. $14.98. Keepcase. *LANG:* English. *FEATURES:* 8 chapter links • Lisa Boyle filmography.
1995 (R) 95m/C Lisa Boyle, Ken Steadman; **D:** Moctezuma Lobato; **W:** David Keith Miller; **C:** Kim Haun; **M:** Herman Beeftink.

I Love Maria

Maria (Sally Yeh) is the leader of a gang of criminals who rob banks with giant robots in this Hong Kong sci-fi/action/comedy. A reporter and a scientist who have been left holding the bag by the cops manage to recruit a beautiful robot (Sally Yeh again) to turn the tables. The action is fast and silly. On DVD, though, the high-contrast image is no better than good. Some of the sound effects editing is extremely poor. Marginally superior to VHS tape. —*MM*
AKA: Roboforce.
Movie: 🐾🐾▶ **DVD:** 🐾🐾▶
Tai Seng Video Marketing (Cat #5148, UPC #4895024901855). Widescreen letterboxed. Dolby Digital 5.1 Surround Stereo. $24.95. Keepcase. *LANG:* Cantonese; Mandarin. *SUB:* Traditional Chinese; Simplified Chinese; English; Bahasa (Indonesia). *FEATURES:* 8 chapter links • Cast and crew thumbnail biographies.

1988 96m/C *HK* Sally Yeh, Tsui Hark, Tony Leung Chiu-Wai, John Shum; **D:** David Chung; **C:** Law Wan Shing.

I Love Trouble

Dueling reporters for rival Chicago newspapers, Sabrina Peterson (Roberts) and Peter Brackett (Nolte) put aside their competitive instincts long enough to find romance and solve a murder mystery. An enjoyable comedy-thriller is undermined by a lack of chemistry between Roberts and Nolte. DVD is visually clean and crisp, with a 5.1 Dolby Digital Surround audio track supporting the overall presentation. —*RT*
Movie: 🐾🐾▶ **DVD:** 🐾🐾🐾
Buena Vista Home Entertainment (Cat #17494, UPC #717951003126). Widescreen. Dolby Digital 5.1 Surround (English); Dolby Digital Stereo (French). $29.99. Keepcase. *LANG:* English; French. *SUB:* English. *CAP:* English. *FEATURES:* 27 chapter links • Theatrical trailer.
1994 (PG) 123m/C Julia Roberts, Nick Nolte, Saul Rubinek, Robert Loggia, James Rebhorn; **D:** Charles Shyer; **W:** Nancy Myers, Charles Shyer; **C:** John Lindley; **M:** David Newman.

I Love You, I Love You Not

The Holocaust becomes a metaphor for one teen's first painful romance. Daisy (Danes) is a Jewish student at a snobby and anti-Semitic prep school where she falls in love with Ethan (Law), the ultimate Gentile. Daisy spends her weekends with her grandmother Nana (Moreau), a Holocaust survivor, and the two share their stories. Danes also plays Nana as a young girl, and both actresses are excellent. Unfortunately, the handling of the serious subject matter is given less dramatic weight than Daisy's romance. (The similar *Scent of a Woman* suffered the same lack of balance.) Hopkins, an established casting director, makes his feature debut. Overall, the full-frame DVD image and sound are passable. Some stripes flash and dark clothes and shadowed sets lose detail, but those don't overly detract from the performances and the attractive cast. —*MM*
Movie: 🐾🐾▶ **DVD:** 🐾🐾▶
Miramax Pictures Home Video (Cat #17762, UPC #717951003614). Full frame. Dolby Digital Surround Stereo. $29.99. Keepcase. *LANG:* English. *FEATURES:* 20 chapter links.
1997 (PG-13) 92m/C *FR GE GB* Claire Danes, Jeanne Moreau, Jude Law, James Van Der Beek, Robert Sean Leonard, Kris Park, Lauren Fox, Emily Burkes-Nossiter, Carrie Slaza; **D:** Billy Hopkins; **W:** Wendy Kesselman; **C:** Maryse Alberti; **M:** Gil Goldstein.

I Saw What You Did

Left without parental supervision one night, teens Kitt (Lane) and Liby (Garrett) make prank calls, telling unsuspecting

adults "I saw what you did and I know who you are." As luck would have it, one them is Steve Marak (Ireland), who just murdered his wife. But his next door neighbor Amy (Crawford) doesn't care; she loves the big lug anyway. The rest piles one ridiculous plot twist upon another, but so what? This black-and-white Castle comic thriller was made with television production values—perhaps the most enjoyable of them being Van Alexander's bouncy score—and so it might have been subtitled "Ozzie and Harriet and Norman Bates" but with a few genuine scares. Ireland is a sort of quizzical psycho. Perhaps he's wondering why Joan Crawford is wearing 20 pounds of costume jewelry around her neck. Given the film's modest roots, it gains little on DVD, and that's reflected in the skimpy extras. Both image and sound are exemplary, nonetheless. —*MM*
Movie: 🐾🐾🐾 **DVD:** 🐾🐾
Anchor Bay (Cat #DV10867, UPC #013131086799). Widescreen (1.78:1) letterboxed. Dolby Digital Mono. $24.98. Keepcase. *LANG:* English. *FEATURES:* Bios of Crawford and Castle • Theatrical trailers • 20 chapter links.
1965 82m/C Joan Crawford, John Ireland, Leif Erickson, Sarah Lane, Andi Garrett, Sharyl Locke; **D:** William Castle; **W:** William McGivern; **M:** Van Alexander.

I Spit on Your Grave

Woman vacationing at a Connecticut lake house (on the Housatonic River) is brutally attacked and raped by four men. Left for dead, she recovers and seeks gory revenge, usually involving genital mutilation. The film is actually very well photographed, and has been both criticized as over-the-top exploitation of a very serious subject, as well as hailed as a feminist anthem. The DVD does the best it can with the preprint used and the result is a fairly sharp image with only smatterings of grain and artifacts. Colors and blacks are true. The DVD is contrasty, but not any more than the low-budget film itself. Brightness is comfortable. The mono sound is O.K. but seems muffled when compared to the earlier laserdisc release. —*JO AKA:* Day of the Woman.
Movie: woof **DVD:** 🐾🐾
Elite Entertainment, Inc. (Cat #EE7749, UPC #790594774929). Widescreen (1.85:1) anamorphic. Mono. $29.95. Keepcase. *LANG:* English. *FEATURES:* 21 chapter links • Theatrical trailer.
1977 (R) 98m/C Camille Keaton, Eron Tabor, Richard Pace, Anthony Nichols, Gunter Kleeman, Alexis Magnotti; **D:** Mier Zarchi; **W:** Mier Zarchi; **C:** Yuri Haviv.

I Still Know What You Did Last Summer

Perky survivor Julie James (Hewitt) and new best friend Karla (Brandy) win a vacation to the Bahamas and take boyfriends Tyrell (Phifer) and Will (Sattle) along for some fun in the monsoon. Along with the hurricane, the kids must cope with the

return of Ben Willis, the fishstick guy with the slicker and hook. The scares come at such regular intervals and are based on such a lame premise—lame even for a wretched sequel—that the film has no emotional punch. That doesn't mean that it's not well produced. This one looks fine with a DVD image that captures all the goofy lighting, boomy sound effects, tricky camerawork, and artful stunts that are employed in place of a real plot. At least we are spared the embarrassment of a commentary track. —MM
Movie: 🦴🦴 **DVD:** 🦴🦴▶
Columbia Tristar Home Video (Cat #39789, UPC #043396397897). Widescreen (2.35:1) letterboxed; full frame. Dolby Digital 5.1 Surround Stereo; Dolby Digital Surround Stereo. $24.95. Keepcase. *LANG:* English. *CAP:* English. *FEATURES:* 28 chapter links ▪ "Making of" featurette ▪ Theatrical trailers ▪ Music video.
1998 (R) 100m/C Jennifer Love Hewitt, Freddie Prinze Jr., Brandy, Mekhi Phifer, Muse Watson, Matthew Sattle, Bill Cobbs, Jeffrey Combs, John Hawkes, Jennifer Esposito; *D:* Danny Cannon; *W:* Trey Callaway; *C:* Vernon Layton; *M:* John Frizzell. *AWARDS: NOM:* MTV Movie Awards '99: Breakthrough Performance.

I Was a Teenage Zombie

Awful spoof of high school horror films features a good zombie against a drug-pushing zombie. Forget the story (if you can) and listen to the music by Los Lobos, the Fleshtones, the Waitresses, Dream Syndicate, and the Violent Femmes. The audio and video transfers on this disc are absolutely horrid. The video, which looks like it was taken from a damaged Super 8 original, features bleeding and undefined colors. Likewise, the audio is incomprehensible and is often downright annoying. —MJT
Movie: 🦴 **DVD:** 🦴▶
Image Entertainment (Cat #ID549JFDVD, UPC #014381454925). Full frame. Dolby Digital Mono. $24.99. Snapper. *LANG:* English. *FEATURES:* 12 chapter links.
1987 92m/C Michael Rubin, Steve McCoy, Cassie Madden, Allen Rickman; *D:* John E. Michalakis; *W:* Steve McCoy, George Seminara; *C:* Peter Lewnes; *M:* Jonathan Roberts, Craig Seeman.

An Ideal Husband

Oscar Wilde's drawing room comedy makes a splendid transition from the stage to the screen, and it even gains subtle but important dimensions on DVD. In 1895, Sir Robert Chilton (Northam) is a rising young member of Parliament. But the lovely and duplicitous Lady Cheveley (Moore) knows a guilty secret in his past that could ruin him. Also involved in the intrigues are his wife Gertrud (Blanchett), sister Mabel (Driver), and friend Lord Goring (Everett). Though this is not the kind of material that traditionally lends itself to the strengths of DVD, it is actually better

on disc than it was in theatres. The image, not strikingly sharp to begin with, is well suited to the smaller screen and the relative intimacy of home video. With the added sharpness of the digital sound and image, the viewer can see every small gesture and expression, and can hear every syllable of the delicious epigrammatic dialogue ("To love one's self is the beginning of a lifelong romance."). Think *Masterpiece Theatre* with an even sharper wit, an extra layer of complexity, and a letter-perfect ensemble cast. A commentary track by director Parker might have been a welcome addition. —MM
Movie: 🦴🦴🦴 **DVD:** 🦴🦴🦴
Miramax Pictures Home Video (Cat #18269, UPC #717951004628). Widescreen (1.85:1) letterboxed. Dolby Digital 5.1 Surround Stereo. $29.99. Keepcase. *LANG:* English. *CAP:* English. *FEATURES:* 28 chapter links ▪ "Making of" featurette.
1999 (PG-13) 96m/C *GB* Cate Blanchett, Jeremy Northam, Minnie Driver, Rupert Everett, Julianne Moore, Jeroen Krabbe, Lindsay Duncan, Peter Vaughan, John Wood, Marsha Fitzalan, Benjamin Pullen; *D:* Oliver Parker; *W:* Oliver Parker; *C:* David Johnson; *M:* Charlie Mole. *AWARDS:* National Board of Review Awards '99: Best Supporting Actress (Moore); *NOM:* British Academy Awards '99: Best Adapted Screenplay, Best Costume Design, Best Makeup; Golden Globe Awards '00: Best Actor—Musical/Comedy (Everett), Best Actress—Musical/Comedy (Moore).

Igor & the Lunatics

Tasteless Troma (O.K., that is redundant) tale of a cannibal cult leader who's released from prison and picks up where he left off. Even by the studio's alternative standards, this one looks raw. The relative clarity of DVD makes the amateurish nature of the special effects even more obvious and so the film's gross-out level is diminished. Without that, little is left beyond the usual bells and whistles. —MM
Movie: 🦴🦴 **DVD:** 🦴🦴▶
Troma Team Video (Cat #9900, UPC #790357990023). Full frame. $24.95. Keepcase. *LANG:* English. *FEATURES:* 9 chapter links ▪ Tour of Troma and Troma Intelligence Test ▪ Theatrical trailer ▪ Production stills. PC DVD-ROM drive links to Troma website.
1985 (R) 79m/C Joseph Eero, Joe Niola, T.J. Michaels; *D:* Billy Parolini.

I'll Be Home for Christmas

Snotty college kid Jake (Thomas) wants to teach his dad a lesson by boycotting Christmas and stealing away to Mexico with his girlfriend (Biel)? Why? Jake thinks his dad remarried too soon after the death of his mother. But Jake is bribed home with pop's prized Porsche (now there's a lesson for the kiddies) if he can arrive for Christmas Eve dinner. A series of absurd mishaps ensue (almost all of which occur

because Jake is a lying, cheating jerk) and he makes his way cross-country while glued inside a Santa suit. The characters are superficial and annoying in this run-of-the-mill holiday stinker.
Movie: 🦴▶ **DVD:** NYR
Buena Vista Home Entertainment (Cat #17596). Widescreen (1.85:1) letterboxed. Dolby Digital 5.1 Surround Stereo. $29.99. Keepcase. *LANG:* English; French. *CAP:* English. *FEATURES:* Theatrical trailer.
1998 (PG) 86m/C Jonathan Taylor Thomas, Jessica Biel, Adam LaVorgna, Gary Cole, Eve Gordon, Sean O'Bryan, Andrew Lauer; *D:* Arlene Sanford; *W:* Harris Goldberg, Tom Nursall; *C:* Hiro Narita; *M:* John Debney.

Ill-Gotten Gains

Black historical drama.
Movie: NYR **DVD:** NYR
Xenon Entertainment (Cat #4071). Full frame. $19.95. Keepcase. *FEATURES:* Radio interview with director Joel Ben Marsden ▪ Separate soundtrack ▪ Theatrical trailer.
1997 (R) 106m/B Djimon Hounsou, Akosua Busia, De'Aundre Bonds, Reg E. Cathey; *D:* Joel B. Marsden; *W:* Joel B. Marsden; *C:* Ben Kufrin; *M:* Keith Bilderbeck, Mike Baum, Tina Meeks; *V:* Eartha Kitt.

I'm Losing You

Confusing story with too many shocks and no point of view, which wastes a good cast. TV producer Perry Krohn (Langella) learns that he is dying of cancer. His wife, Diantha (Jens), takes the news badly, as do his wayward children Bertie (McCarthy) and Rachel (Arquette). But it seems everyone has a doom-laden revelation to deal with. Wagner adapts from his own novel.
Movie: 🦴🦴 **DVD:** NYR
Studio Home Entertainment (Cat #7325). Widescreen (1.85:1) letterboxed. Dolby Digital Surround Stereo. $24.95. Keepcase. *LANG:* English. *SUB:* Spanish. *FEATURES:* Cast and crew thumbnail bios ▪ Commentary: Wagner and Arquette.
1998 (R) 102m/C Frank Langella, Salome Jens, Rosanna Arquette, Andrew McCarthy, Amanda Donohoe, Elizabeth Perkins, Gina Gershon, Buck Henry, Ed Begley Jr.; *D:* Bruce Wagner; *W:* Bruce Wagner; *C:* Rob Sweeney; *M:* Daniel Catan.

I'm No Angel

This vehicle takes its place in movie history as an expression of female star power not seen again until the Madonna-dominated '80s. West asked for and got the unusual screen credit "Story, Screen Play and All Dialogue by Mae West" followed by, in much smaller print, "with suggestions by Lowell Brentano." She plays Tira, who sings honky tonk for circus sideshow suckers (hey, that's what she calls them) who chew with their mouths open—agape, really. She soon lands a jazzier gig as a lion tamer. Her subsequent fame brings

Jack (Cary Grant) into her circle. He falls under her spell and vice versa, but her ex (an ex-con) has other plans. The image is a little grainy and worn but with a smooth range of grays. That and a brassy soundtrack frame West in all her bespangled and sonorous glory. —JK

Movie: 🎵🎵🎵 **DVD:** 🎵🎵🎵

Universal Studios Home Video (Cat #ID4230USDVD, UPC #014381423020). Full frame. Dolby Digital Mono. $29.99. Snapper. *LANG:* English. *CAP:* English. *FEATURES:* 26 chapter links ▪ Scene access menu ▪ Colorized gatefold cover with photo montage.

1933 88m/B Mae West, Cary Grant, Gregory Ratoff, Edward Arnold, Ralf Harolde, Kent Taylor, Gertrude Michael, Russell Hopton, Dorothy Peterson, William B. Davidson, Gertrude Howard, Hattie McDaniel; *D:* Wesley Ruggles; *W:* Lowell Brentano, Mae West; *C:* Leo Tover; *M:* Harvey Brooks.

Image of an Assassination: A New Look at the Zapruder Film

This disc offers a digitally enhanced look at the Zapruder film, which captures the moments of President Kennedy's assassination. The new clarity makes the horrifying moment as terrifying as it was when first viewed. The presentation also chronicles the history of the film from November 22, 1963, through the painstaking digital replication process. The quality of the DVD's image is varied, as one might expect. It does appear though that the transfer is very true to the various elements and techniques used. The image is usually crisper than expected and any grain seems to be from the original source. Both the contrast and brightness levels appear tweaked to provide the clearest presentation of details. The sound is nothing special but delivers the narration very clearly. —JO

Movie: 🎵🎵▶ **DVD:** 🎵🎵🎵

MPI Home Video (Cat #DVD7282, UPC #030306728223). Full frame. Stereo. $24.98. Keepcase. *LANG:* English. *SUB:* English; Spanish; French; German. *FEATURES:* 6 chapter links ▪ 4 versions of film ▪ Additional footage ▪ Cast and filmmaker bios.

1998 60m/C

Immortal Combat

A ninja army seems to have immortal powers. Can our two violent heroes find an equally destructive way to stop them? Both Piper and Chiba have done better work. On DVD, this action flick has a rough look throughout. It becomes exceptionally poor during the many night scenes. Box copy and disc art claims an "R" rating. On-screen intro says "PG-13." The level of violence is probably "R." —MM

Movie: 🎵▶ **DVD:** 🎵▶

Simitar Entertainment (Cat #7314, UPC #082551731428). Full frame. PCM Stereo. $14.98. Keepcase. *LANG:* English. *FEATURES:* 8 chapter links.

1994 (R) 109m/C Roddy Piper, Sonny Chiba, Tommy (Tiny) Lister, Meg Foster; *D:* Daniel Neira; *W:* Robert Crabtree, Daniel Neira; *C:* Henner Hofmann.

Impact

Hard-driving industrialist Walter Williams (Donlevy) has only one weakness—his beautiful young wife (Walker). She's got a murderous lover (Barrett) and an eye for Walter's millions. This little-known noirish (but not true noir) thriller works through a twisty plot, excellent San Francisco locations, a top-notch performance by the star, and a supporting cast that's filled with familiar faces. On DVD, the black-and-white photography is very good but not as finely detailed as Hollywood's best. That's a quibble, though, because the period look and feel of the film are so strong. Recommended. —MM

Movie: 🎵🎵🎵 **DVD:** 🎵🎵🎵

Image Entertainment (Cat #ID8595CODVD, UPC #014381859522). Full frame. Dolby Digital Mono. $19.99. Snapper. *LANG:* English.

1949 111m/B Brian Donlevy, Ella Raines, Charles Coburn, Helen Walker, Anna May Wong, Philip Ahn, Art Baker, Tony Barrett, Harry Cheshire, Lucius Cooke, Sheilah Graham, Tom Greenway, Hans Herbert, Linda Johnson, Joe Kirk, Clarence Kolb, Mary Landa, Mae Marsh; *D:* Arthur Lubin; *W:* Dorothy Reid, Jay Dratler; *C:* Ernest Laszlo; *M:* Michel Michelet.

The Impossible Spy

Elie Cohen (Shea) was an unassuming Israeli who was also a top-level spy in Syria during the 1960s. Elie became so close to Syria's president that he was nominated to become the Deputy Minister of Defense before his double life was exposed. Fact-based, made-for-cable spy thriller is well acted and worth a look for espionage fans.

Movie: 🎵🎵🎵 **DVD:** NYR

E-Realbiz.com (Cat #9856). Full frame. Dolby Digital 5.1 Surround Stereo. $19.99. Keepcase.

1987 96m/C *GB* John Shea, Eli Wallach, Michal Bat-Adam, Rami Danon, Sasson Gabray, Chaim Girafi; *D:* Jim Goddard; *M:* Richard Hartley.

The Imposters

In the 1930s, Arthur (Tucci) and Maurice (Platt) are out-of-work third-rate actors. A chance encounter with a boorish star (Molina) forces them to stow away on an ocean liner that's populated by an ensemble of not-very-funny comic types: the fascist steward (Scott), the helpful entertainment director (Taylor), the suicidal singer (Buscemi), the anarchist bomber (Shalhoub), the deposed queen (Rossellini), the gay Scottish wrestler (Connolly). They all

don an assortment of costumes and rip through the scenery like a colony of starving beavers. Unfortunately, the pace begins at a crawl—it takes ten minutes before the plot kicks in—and then abruptly zooms into overdrive. Neither extreme is funny. On DVD, the glossy art deco sets are shown off in the most flattering light and they're often more interesting than the characters. Only the final ambitious shot really pushes the digital envelope and, unfortunately, the closing credits roll over it. The perceptive touch that makes *Big Night* so enjoyable is absent. —MM

AKA: Ship of Fools.

Movie: 🎵🎵 **DVD:** 🎵🎵▶

Twentieth Century Fox Home Entertainment (Cat #4110383, UPC #086162000 744). Widescreen (2.35:1) letterboxed. Dolby Surround Stereo. $29.98. Keepcase. *LANG:* English; French. *SUB:* English; Spanish. *FEATURES:* 20 chapter links ▪ Theatrical trailer.

1998 (R) 101m/C Stanley Tucci, Oliver Platt, Elizabeth Bracco, Steve Buscemi, Billy Connolly, Allan Corduner, Hope Davis, Dana Ivey, Allison Janney, Richard Jenkins, Matt McGrath, Alfred Molina, Isabella Rossellini, Campbell Scott, Tony Shalhoub, Lili Taylor, Lewis J. Stadlen, Woody Allen; *D:* Stanley Tucci; *W:* Stanley Tucci; *C:* Ken Kelsch; *M:* Gary DeMichele.

Impulse

Small town residents can't control their impulses, all because of government toxic waste in their milk (yeah, like that could happen). A woman worried about her mother's mental health returns to town with her doctor boyfriend to discover most of the inhabitants are quite mad. The plot starts strong, but quickly descends into bad, B-movie schlock. The disc looks good in some places. For the most part, however, it appears washed-out and has a pastel quality. The audio transfer is better and features clear dialogue and very little distortion. —MJT

Movie: 🎵🎵 **DVD:** 🎵🎵▶

Anchor Bay (Cat #DV10608, UPC #013131060898). Full frame. Dolby Digital Stereo. $19.99. Keepcase. *LANG:* English. *FEATURES:* 14 chapter links.

1984 (R) 95m/C Tim Matheson, Meg Tilly, Hume Cronyn, John Karlen, Bill Paxton, Amy Stryker, Claude Earl Jones, Sherri Stoner; *D:* Graham Baker; *W:* Bart Davis; *C:* Thomas Del Ruth; *M:* Paul Chihara.

In and Out

See what an Oscar can do? When Tom Hanks thanked, and inadvertently outed, his high school drama teacher during his Academy Awards speech (for *Philadelphia*), it lead to this feature. Popular high school English teacher Howard Brackett (Kline) has his sexuality come into question on the eve of his wedding thanks to a former-student-turned-movie-star (Dillon). As a media circus converges on the small town, Howard is forced to examine his sexuality by openly gay reporter Selleck (out to prove Howard's gay), his mother Reynolds (who wants the wedding to go on regardless of his orientation), and his tightly wound fiancee Cusack (who wants to put a serious hurtin' on Barbra Striesand). All-around excellent performances, especially by Kline and Cusack. The DVD transfer is sharp, without grain or artifacts. The colors are not particularly vibrant, but based on the fleshtones, appear to be accurate. Bleed is minimal. Blacks are true and grainless. Contrast and brightness are consistent and comfortable. The 5.1 sound is wasted on the film's soundtrack, which features very little in the way of Surround effects, with the same being true of dynamic auditory moments. The sound is, however, clear and full-bodied, and both the incidental music and dialogue are accented properly in the mix. —JO

Movie: 🎧🎧🎧 **DVD:** 🎧🎧🎧
Paramount Home Video (Cat #329877, UPC #097363298779). Widescreen (1.85:1) anamorphic. Dolby Digital 5.1; Dolby Surround. $29.99. Keepcase. *LANG:* English (DD5.1; DS); French (DS). *SUB:* Spanish. *CAP:* English. *FEATURES:* 28 chapter links • Theatrical trailer.
1997 (PG-13) 92m/C Kevin Kline, Joan Cusack, Matt Dillon, Debbie Reynolds, Wilford Brimley, Bob Newhart, Tom Selleck, Deborah Rush, Lewis J. Stadlen, J. Smith-Cameron, Zak Orth, Gregory Jbara, Shalom Harlow, Kate McGregor-Stewart, Shawn Hatosy, Lauren Ambrose, Alexandra Holden; *D:* Frank Oz; *W:* Paul Rudnick; *C:* Rob Hahn; *M:* Marc Shaiman. *AWARDS:* New York Film Critics Awards '97: Best Supporting Actress (Cusack); Broadcast Film Critics Association Awards '97: Best Supporting Actress (Cusack); *NOM:* Academy Awards '97: Best Supporting Actress (Cusack); Golden Globe Awards '98: Best Actor—Musical/Comedy (Kline), Best Supporting Actress (Cusack); MTV Movie Awards '98: Best Kiss (Kevin Kline/Tom Selleck).

In Country
A Kentucky high school student (Lloyd) searches for her father, killed in Vietnam. Willis plays her uncle, a veteran still struggling to accept his own survival and crippled with memories.
Movie: 🎧🎧▸ **DVD:** NYR
Warner Home Video, Inc. (Cat #11888). Full frame. $19.98. Snapper. *LANG:* English. *CAP:* English.
1989 (R) 116m/C Bruce Willis, Emily Lloyd, Joan Allen, Kevin Anderson, Richard Hamilton, Judith Ivey, Peggy Rea, John Terry, Patricia Richardson, Jim Beaver; *D:* Norman Jewison; *W:* Frank Pierson, Cynthia Cidre; *C:* Russell Boyd; *M:* James Horner.

In Dreams
Bening is a small-town wife and mother with a psychic connection to twisted child killer Downey, causing her to dream of his gruesome crimes before he commits

them. After she dreams that her daughter is killed, her life begins to unravel, causing those around her to suspect her of insanity. The film draws its chills from a more cerebral standpoint, so fans of big action may want to pass. The unnerving dream sequences are suitably murky and ominous thanks to cinematographer Darius Khondji, who also filmed *Seven*. Unfortunately, the video transfer is also rather murky, with blacks that bleed into insurmountable shadows, making it frequently impossible to identify what is actually on the screen (not too effective when trying to create dramatic tension). The 5.1 soundtrack, however, is an improvement and features solid dialogue and a very effective special effects track. —MJT
AKA: Blue Vision.
Movie: 🎧🎧▸ **DVD:** 🎧🎧▸
DreamWorks Home Entertainment (Cat #84665, UPC #667068466522). Widescreen (1.85:1) anamorphic. Dolby Digital 5.1; Dolby 2.0 Surround. $29.99. Keepcase. *LANG:* English. *SUB:* English. *FEATURES:* 21 chapter links • Production notes • Cast and filmmakers biographies • Theatrical trailer.
1998 (R) 99m/C Annette Bening, Robert Downey Jr., Aidan Quinn, Stephen Rea, Paul Guilfoyle, Dennis Boutsikaris, Pamela Payton-Wright, Margo Martindale, Prudence Wright Holmes, Katie Sagona, Krystal Benn; *D:* Neil Jordan; *W:* Neil Jordan, Bruce Robinson; *C:* Darius Khondji; *M:* Elliot Goldenthal.

In God's Hands
Three surfers (Dorian, George, and Liu) travel the world in search of the perfect wave. Disjointed, plot-deprived, but beautifully shot flick has the trio busting out of prison (why they're there to begin with is never explained) to begin their quest from Madagascar to Bali to Hawaii. One finds love with a girl from Ipanema; another contracts malaria; the third succumbs to the surf. What happens to whom doesn't much matter because as actors, these guys are great surfers. Besides, the story is just connective tissue for the surfing scenes. Gnarly.
Movie: 🎧🎧 **DVD:** NYR
Columbia Tristar Home Video (Cat #21749). Full frame; widescreen (2.35) anamorphic. Dolby Digital Surround Stereo. $29.95. Keepcase. *LANG:* English; French. *SUB:* French. *FEATURES:* Trailer.
1998 (PG-13) 98m/C Patrick Shane Dorian, Matt George, Matty Liu, Brion James, Shaun Thompson, Maylin Pultar, Bret Michaels, Brian L. Keaulana, Darrick Doerner; *D:* Zalman King; *W:* Zalman King, Matt George; *C:* John Aronson.

In Love and War
Adapted from *Hemingway in Love and War: The Lost Diary of Agnes Von Kurowsky* by Henry Villard and James Nagel, this World War I romance is a fizzle. Ernie (O'Donnell) volunteers to go to Italy to work for the American Red Cross. Agnes (Bullock) is a

worldly 26-year-old nurse. Ernie's a 20-year-old pup so eager to see some action that he bicycles to the front lines at the first opportunity. And promptly finds himself in Agnes's hospital. Villard (Astin), an old college pal and also a patient there, becomes a rival as Ernie falls for his nurse. Then there's Dr. Caracciolo (Bonucci), who's also attracted to Agnes. The doctor is too old for her, but he's distinguished and rich; Ernest is too young, but he's passionate. What's a dedicated health care professional to do? The main problem is a complete lack of chemistry between the two stars, who are attractively photographed. Director Attenborough's use of smoky focus doesn't play to the strengths of DVD, particularly in the dark scenes, though the image remains viewable and the colors are distinct. —MM
Movie: 🎧▸ **DVD:** 🎧🎧🎧
New Line Home Video (Cat #N4785, UPC #794043478529). Full frame; widescreen (2.35:1) letterboxed. Dolby Digital 5.1 Surround (English); Dolby Surround Stereo (French). $24.98. Snapper. *LANG:* English; French. *SUB:* English. *FEATURES:* Biographies of Sandra Bullock, Chris O'Donnell, Richard Attenborough • 24 chapter links • Original theatrical trailer.
1996 (PG-13) 115m/C Chris O'Donnell, Sandra Bullock, MacKenzie Astin, Ingrid Lacey, Emilio Bonucci, Margot Steinberg, Colin Stinton, Ian Kelly, Richard Blackburn; *D:* Richard Attenborough; *W:* Allan Scott, Anna Hamilton Phelan, Clancy Sigal, Dimitri Villard; *C:* Roger Pratt; *M:* George Fenton.

In Search of Dracula
This documentary features Christopher Lee as narrator and as the title character in clips from his appearances in Hammer films. It mixes fact and fiction and generally keeps them separate. For hard-core horror fans, the film covers familiar territory, but it is a good introduction to the character and his thousands of appearances in fiction, on the stage and on film. It will make them want to take another look at the Hammer horrors. On DVD, both image and sound are acceptable, but not spectacular. —MM
Movie: 🎧🎧▸ **DVD:** 🎧🎧
Image Entertainment (Cat #ID5547IIDVD, UPC #014381554724). Full frame. Dolby Digital Mono. $24.99. Snapper. *LANG:* English. *FEATURES:* 10 chapter links.
1976 82m/C *D:* Calvin Floyd; *W:* Yvonne Floyd; *Nar:* Christopher Lee.

In the Company of Men
A couple of dissatisfied Yuppies, Chad (Eckhart) and Howard (Malloy), are sent on a six-week job out of town by their home office. Grumbling about the lack of control in their lives (and blaming it on women), Chad formulates a nasty plan (to which Howard eventually agrees)—they'll deliberately get involved with the same girl, sec-

retary Christine (Edwards), string her along, and then abandon her when their job is done. But Chad actually has his own agenda and bigger corporate ideas in mind. Think misogynistic satire. The DVD is very average, and in need of a little sharpness, although grain and artifact levels are low. Colors are pretty tame and fleshtones drift off at times. The contrast level is low, while the brightness level appears a shade too high. Blacks range from good to slightly grainy in the dimmer scenes. The Dolby Surround sound is adequate for the film, but lacks anything in the way of Surround, and has occasional clipping on the highs. —JO

Movie: 🎬🎬 **DVD:** 🎬🎬▸
Columbia Tristar Home Video (Cat #26019, UPC #043396260191). Widescreen (1.85:1) anamorphic; full frame. Dolby Surround. $29.95. Keepcase. *LANG:* English. *SUB:* English; French; Spanish. *CAP:* English. *FEATURES:* 28 chapter links ▪ Commentary: director and cast ▪ Theatrical trailer.
1996 (R) 93m/C Matt Malloy, Aaron Eckhart, Stacy Edwards, Mark Rector, Jason Dixie, Emily Cline, Michael Martin, Chris Hayes; *D:* Neil LaBute; *W:* Neil LaBute; *C:* Anthony P. Hettinger; *M:* Ken Williams. *AWARDS:* Independent Spirit Awards '98: Debut Performance (Eckhart); Independent Spirit Awards '99: First Screenplay; Sundance Film Festival '97: Filmmakers Trophy; *NOM:* Independent Spirit Awards '98: Best Actress (Edwards), Best First Feature.

In the Line of Duty 3

A young Hong Kong policewoman (Cynthia Khan) has trouble proving her capabilities to her superiors but finally is given the chance to take out a gang of jewel thieves, with the help of a Japanese cop (Fujioka). This long-running action series is roughly similar to the *Lethal Weapon* films but with a more prominent comic edge and a decidedly smaller budget. The DVD image is better than most tapes, but still not very good. Reds glow and the sound effects are sometimes a microsecond off. —MM

Movie: 🎬🎬▸ **DVD:** 🎬🎬▸
Tai Seng Video Marketing (Cat #5182, UPC #4895024901695). Widescreen letterboxed. Dolby Digital 5.1 Surround Stereo. $49.95. Keepcase. *LANG:* Cantonese; Mandarin. *SUB:* Traditional Chinese; Simplified Chinese; English. *FEATURES:* 8 chapter links ▪ Cast and crew thumbnail biographies.
1988 88m/C *HK* Cynthia Khan, Hiroshi Fujioka, Stuart Ong, Nishiwaki Michiko; *D:* Anthony Wong, Brandy Yuen; *W:* Chan Kui Ying, Law Tai Man; *C:* Jimmy Au, Wong Bo Man.

In the Line of Duty 4

Generally, the image and sound quality of this disc are identical to *3*. The difference here is almost continuous "hex" errors in the English subtitles that render the

action incomprehensible. Early on, our heroine (Cynthia Khan) and an American cop are observing drugs being offloaded from a freighter. She says, "Let me see anything…incorrect or not," and he answers, "The into you provided us is much valuable." Context provides little help. I have no idea what either statement means. —MM

Movie: 🎬🎬 **DVD:** 🎬🎬
Tai Seng Video Marketing (Cat #5184, UPC #4895024901701). Widescreen letterboxed. Dolby Digital 5.1 Surround Stereo. $49.95. Keepcase. *LANG:* Cantonese; Mandarin. *SUB:* Traditional & Simplified Chinese; English; Japanese; Indonesia & Malaysia Bahasa; Thai; Korean; Vietnamese. *FEATURES:* 8 chapter links ▪ Cast and crew thumbnail biographies.
1989 93m/C *HK* Cynthia Khan, Donnie Yen, Michael Wong; *D:* Yuen Woo Ping; *W:* Cheung Chi Shing, Wong Wing Fai; *C:* Ma Kwun Wah.

In the Line of Duty 5

Our heroine (Khan) is now Inspector Yeung. Her cousin and his friend, both in the U.S. Navy, get into trouble over marijuana, and they're spies, too. On DVD, the image looks even more faded than other entries in the series. Sound is no better than average and the "hex" errors in translation continue. —MM

Movie: 🎬🎬 **DVD:** 🎬🎬
Tai Seng Video Marketing (Cat #5187, UPC #895024901718). Widescreen letterboxed. Dolby Digital 5.1 Surround Stereo. $49.95. Keepcase. *LANG:* Cantonese; Mandarin. *SUB:* Traditional & Simplified Chinese; English; Japanese; Malaysia & Indonesia Bahasa; Thai; Korean; Vietnamese. *FEATURES:* 8 chapter links ▪ Cast and crew thumbnail biographies.
1990 96m/C *HK* Cynthia Khan, David Wu, Kong Yan Yin; *D:* Cha Chuen Yee; *W:* Kim Ip, Leung Hung Wah, Patrick Yuen; *C:* Cheng Siu Keung.

In the Line of Fire

Aging Secret Service agent Frank Horrigan (Eastwood) meets his match in a spooky caller (Malkovich) who threatens his professionalism and the president in an exciting, fast-paced cat and mouse game. The two leads are terrific and they get fine support by Russo. Eerie special effects add to the mood. The Secret Service cooperated and most scenes are believable with only a few Hollywood exceptions, including an exciting chase across the rooftops of Washington. The DVD image is very good, particularly in dark detailed scenes, but not great. Same for sound. —MM

Movie: 🎬🎬🎬 **DVD:** 🎬🎬🎬
Columbia Tristar Home Video (Cat #52315). Widescreen (2.35:1) letterboxed. Dolby Digital 5.1 Surround Stereo; Dolby Digital Surround. $27.95. Jewel case. *LANG:* English; French. *SUB:* Korean; Spanish. *CAP:* English. *FEATURES:* 61 chapter links.

1993 (R) 128m/C Clint Eastwood, John Malkovich, Rene Russo, Dylan McDermott, Gary Cole, Fred Dalton Thompson, John Mahoney, Gregory Alan Williams; *D:* Wolfgang Petersen; *W:* Jeff Maguire; *C:* John Bailey; *M:* Ennio Morricone. *AWARDS: NOM:* Academy Awards '93: Best Film Editing, Best Original Screenplay, Best Supporting Actor (Malkovich); British Academy Awards '93: Best Original Screenplay, Best Supporting Actor (Malkovich); Golden Globe Awards '94: Best Supporting Actor (Malkovich); MTV Movie Awards '94: Best Villain (Malkovich); Writers Guild of America '93: Best Original Screenplay.

In the Mouth of Madness

Like *Wes Craven's New Nightmare*, this is a horror film about imagination, the source of all horror. But writer Michael De Luca and director Carpenter are telling a more traditional story that's firmly rooted in the H.P. Lovecraft mythos. As no-nonsense investigator John Trent (Neill) searches for missing horror author Sutter Cane (Prochnow), he finds that the writer's novels have an odd effect on him. Be patient with the complex structure. This is a well-made film with some genuinely creepy moments. Sam Neill is a fine hero. The subtle special effects created by Industrial Light and Magic and KNB EFX Group are excellent, and the whole film receives the treatment it's due on DVD with a nice sharp image and impressive sound. On their commentary track, Carpenter and cinematographer Gary B. Kibbe understandably emphasize the technical aspects of their work. —MM

Movie: 🎬🎬🎬▸ **DVD:** 🎬🎬🎬▸
New Line Home Video (Cat #N4907, UPC #794043490729). Widescreen (2.35:1) anamorphic; full frame. Dolby Digital 5.1 Surround Stereo; Dolby Digital Surround Stereo. $24.98. Snapper. *LANG:* English. *SUB:* English. *FEATURES:* 28 chapter links ▪ Cast and crew thumbnail biographies ▪ Commentary: Carpenter and Kibbe.
1995 (R) 95m/C Sam Neill, Juergen Prochnow, Julie Carmen, Charlton Heston, David Warner, John Glover, Bernie Casey, Peter Jason, Frances Bay; *D:* John Carpenter; *W:* Michael De Luca; *C:* Gary B. Kibbe; *M:* John Carpenter, Jim Lang.

In the Name of the Father

The compelling story of Gerry Conlon (Day-Lewis) is mostly based on truth, but the film takes enough liberties to give serious viewers reason to question that authenticity. Conlon and his father (Postlethwaite) are jailed after a horrible IRA bombing near London. Politics and family life in a prison cell share the focus in the film's strongest moments. Late in the story, a lawyer, Gareth Peirce (Thompson), takes the Conlons' case and forces a re-examination of the evidence. Then, briefly, the film becomes a sharp courtroom drama with a rousing conclusion. Though the filmmakers are careful to show the violence of the IRA, the conclusions are not as clear-cut as they appear. Overall, the DVD is only a small step up from a widescreen VHS tape. Image and sound are acceptable, but nothing more. —MM

Movie: 🎬🎬🎬 **DVD:** 🎬🎬🎬

Universal Studios Home Video (Cat #20248). Widescreen (1.85:1) letterboxed. Dolby Digital Stereo. $24.98. Keepcase. *LANG:* English; French; Spanish. *SUB:* Spanish. *CAP:* English. *FEATURES:* 16 chapter links ▪ Production notes ▪ Cast and crew thumbnail bios.

1993 (R) 127m/C GB IR Daniel Day-Lewis, Pete Postlethwaite, Emma Thompson, John Lynch, Corin Redgrave, Beatie Edney, John Benfield, Paterson Joseph, Marie Jones, Gerard McSorley, Frank Harper, Mark Sheppard, Don Baker, Britta Smith, Aidan Grennell, Daniel Massey, Bosco Hogan; *D:* Jim Sheridan; *W:* Jim Sheridan, Terry George; *C:* Peter Biziou; *M:* Trevor Jones, Bono, Sinead O'Connor. *AWARDS:* Berlin International Film Festival '94: Golden Berlin Bear; *NOM:* Academy Awards '93: Best Actor (Day-Lewis), Best Adapted Screenplay, Best Director (Sheridan), Best Film Editing, Best Picture, Best Supporting Actor (Postlethwaite), Best Supporting Actress (Thompson); British Academy Awards '93: Best Actor (Day-Lewis), Best Adapted Screenplay; Golden Globe Awards '94: Best Actor—Drama (Day-Lewis), Best Film—Drama, Best Song ("(You Made Me the) Thief of Your Heart"), Best Supporting Actress (Thompson); Writers Guild of America '93: Best Adapted Screenplay.

In the Navy

Singer, heartthrob, and radio star Dick Powell turns his back on the big time to join the Navy. There he finds his quest for anonymity tossed out the window when he meets up with career sailors Lou Costello and his straight-man sidekick Bud Abbott in this pre-war comedy-musical. Although the Andrews Sisters are around for plenty of screen time, and deliver several snappy musical numbers, *In the Navy* remains one of the boy's weaker films, plagued by too much formula plotting. DVD production is acceptable, but really cries out for supporting materials to complement the feature presentation. —RT *AKA:* Abbott and Costello in the Navy.

Movie: 🎬🎬 **DVD:** 🎬🎬▪

Image Entertainment (Cat #4296, UPC #014381429626). Full frame. AC3 - 2 Channel. $24.99. Snapper. *LANG:* English. *FEATURES:* 16 chapters.

1941 85m/B Lou Costello, Bud Abbott, Dick Powell, The Andrews Sisters; *D:* Arthur Lubin; *W:* Arthur T. Horman, John Grant; *C:* Joseph Valentine.

In the Realm of Passion

Toyoji (Tatsuya Fuji), a laze-about veteran, seduces Seki (Kazuko Yoshiyuki), the wife of rickshaw driver Gisaburo (Takahiro

---

Tamura). The lovers kill him, dump the body in an abandoned well, and then must deal with their guilt and/or his ghost. Though plot and title are similar to director Nagisa Oshima's *In the Realm of the Senses,* he is much more restrained here, focusing more on the emotional side of the action than on the physical. DVD provides only a slight improvement in sound and image over VHS tape. On any medium, colors are muted and interiors are exceptionally dark, with intermittent snowy flecks. The yellow subtitles are large, bright, and easy to read. —MM *AKA:* Empire of Passion; Ai No Borei.

Movie: 🎬🎬 **DVD:** 🎬🎬▪

WinStar Home Entertainment (Cat #FLV5207, UPC #720917520728). Full frame. $29.98. Snapper. *LANG:* Japanese. *SUB:* English. *FEATURES:* 8 chapter links ▪ Production credits ▪ Filmographies and awards. DVD-ROM access to weblinks.

1980 (R) 108m/C Kazuko Yoshiyuki, Takahiro Tamura, Tatsuya Fuji; *D:* Nagisa Oshima; *W:* Nagisa Oshima; *C:* Yoshio Miyajima; *M:* Toru Takemitsu.

In the Realm of the Senses

Famous (some would say notorious) Japanese film about violent sexual obsession is such an intense, graphic, and disturbing experience that it was banned at the 1976 New York Film Festival. Based on incidents that occurred in Tokyo in 1936, it is the story of the sexual relationship that develops between a young businessman, Kichi-San (Eiko Matsuda), and Sada (Tatsuya Fuji), an ex-prostitute. Their affair moves from simple sex to a virtual exchange of identities and finally to a sort of mutual death wish. It is difficult to describe the intense atmosphere that director Nagisa Oshima creates. The film contains such graphic sexual acts and explicit violence that it becomes a sensual horror show. The foreign setting—white-painted geishas, the droning atonal music that sounds so harsh to western tastes, the flowing robes and stark sets—gives the story a vivid, nightmarish surrealism. For all the excesses and successful attempts to shock, the film is too long. By the end, what was once outrageous has become tedious. Compared to VHS tape, the DVD has a greater degree of clarity. Some scenes are overly grainy and lack focus, but the intense reds and occasional lack of focus are part of the point. This is a story of excess; any sort of perfection would defeat the point. —MM *AKA:* Ai No Corrida.

Movie: 🎬🎬🎬 **DVD:** 🎬🎬🎬

Image Entertainment (Cat #FLV5037, UPC #720917503721). Full frame. $24.98. Keepcase. *LANG:* Japanese. *SUB:* English. *FEATURES:* 8 chapter links ▪ Director filmography.

1976 (NC-17) 105m/C JP FR Tatsuya Fuji, Eiko Matsuda, Aio Nakajima, Meika Seri; *D:* Nagisa Oshima; *W:* Nagisa Oshima; *C:* Hideo Ito; *M:* Minoru Miki.

In the Shadows

Slow-moving tale about an odd love triangle set against the backdrop of the Pacific Northwest. Lovely, lonely, and wealthy Eleanor (Richardson), who is dying of cancer, hires Cynthia (Parker), a drifter, to be her companion during her final days. Before long, boyfriend Buck (Young) shows up and is passed off as Cynthia's half-brother and landscaper. A plan is soon hatched whereby Buck will tend the gardens, romance the dying Eleanor, marry her, and inherit the grand estate. Although this could have been played as a dark tale of intrigue, greed, and betrayal, writer-director Richman chose a more genteel approach. A doomed love affair blooms and lives are changed. DVD presentation lacks the visual pop one would expect from the Seattle locations, which include a magnificent mansion, splendid gardens, lakes, and side trips into the nearby woods. —RT *AKA:* Under Heaven.

Movie: 🎬🎬 **DVD:** 🎬🎬

Image Entertainment (Cat #5899, UPC #014381589924). Full frame. AC3 - 2 Channel. $24.99. Snapper. *LANG:* English. *FEATURES:* 15 chapter links ▪ Trailer.

1998 (R) 115m/C Joely Richardson, Molly Parker, Aden Young; *D:* Meg Richman; *W:* Meg Richman; *C:* Claudio Rocha; *M:* Marc Olsen. *AWARDS: NOM:* Independent Spirit Awards '99: Best Supporting Actress (Richardson).

In Too Deep

Epps plays a young, gung-ho Cincinnati cop who goes undercover to infiltrate a drug ring. LL Cool J. is convincing as the menacing drug lord Epps seeks to bust. (Enough with the rappers playing thugs). Epps gets sucked deeper and deeper into the underworld, finally losing touch with his stereotyped detective captain boss (Tucci). Typical plot, plenty of suspense, and a decent soundtrack. Look for Grier as a passable hard-nose detective and Nia Long as Epp's love interest. Another film that gives a kind of seedy glamour to the strife of the inner-city. The picture is sharp and consistent, while the sound is borderline superb, with the music tracks getting a little too much punch. —AB

Movie: 🎬🎬▪ **DVD:** 🎬🎬🎬▪

Buena Vista Home Entertainment (Cat #18284, UPC #1795100474). Widescreen (2.35:1) anamorphic. Dolby Digital Stereo; 5.1 Surround. Keepcase. *LANG:* English. *CAP:* English. *FEATURES:* 13 chapter links ▪ Music video by Jagged Edge ▪ Theatrical trailer.

1999 (R) 104m/C Omar Epps, Stanley Tucci, L.L. Cool J., Pam Grier, Veronica Webb, Nia Long, David Patrick Kelly, Hill Harper; *D:* Michael Rymer; *W:* Paul Aaron, Michael Henry Brown; *C:* Ellery Ryan; *M:* Christopher Young.

Incognito

Art forger Harry Donovan (Patric) is approached by a couple of British art dealers and a Japanese broker to make a

Rembrandt for a Japanese client. He checks out the painter's style by traveling to Amsterdam and Paris, where he falls for art expert Marieke (Jacob). Harry forges the painting and then gets double-crossed and caught up in murder. Convoluted plot; lots of cliches. Original director Peter Weller was replaced by Badham after two weeks of filming. The DVD looks good with the exception of the darker sequences, where the picture softens and grain appears. During those scenes, the color also loses some detail. The excellent supplemental section features informative commentary and interviews, which should be of special interest to young actors. —JO

Movie: 🎬🎬 **DVD:** 🎬🎬➤
Warner Home Video, Inc. (Cat #14538, UPC #085391453826). Widescreen (1.85:1) anamorphic. Dolby Digital 5.1. $24.98. Snapper. *LANG:* English; French. *SUB:* English; Spanish; French. *FEATURES:* 18 chapter links ➤ Theatrical trailers ➤ Cast and filmmakers bios and filmographies ➤ Interactive interviews ➤ Commentary: John Badham, Jordan Katz, and John Ottman ➤ Interviews with Rod Steiger, Irene Jacob, and John Badham ➤ Production notes ➤ Slideshow.
1997 (R) 107m/C Jason Patric, Irene Jacob, Rod Steiger, Thomas Lockyer, Simon Chandler, Michael Cochrane, Ian Richardson, Pip Torrens, Togo Igawa; *D:* John Badham; *W:* Jordan Katz; *C:* Denis Crossan; *M:* John Ottman.

Independence Day

Producers Emmerich and Devlin shamelessly steal elements from virtually every other alien invasion story (*Buck Rogers, V,* etc.) and whip up a corking crowd-pleaser. An armada of giant saucers descends upon the planet. The fate of the world rests in the hands of an unlikely band of Earthlings led by President Whitmore (Pullman), a computer expert (Goldblum), a Marine fighter pilot (Smith), and a drunken crop duster (Quaid). This two-disc set contains both the original theatrical release of the film and a slightly longer (nine-minute) special edition. The main differences between the two are some pointless business involving Quaid's family and one nice scene in an alien fighter with Goldblum and Smith. The films are on one disc along with two commentary tracks; the multitudinous extras, including a unintentionally hilarious "bi-plane" ending (which was wisely ditched), are on the second. Naturally, both image and sound are absolutely first-rate, but the truth is that this kind of sf really depends on the sheer size of a theatrical screen and an enthusiastic audience for maximum effect. On DVD though, many of the nutball effects where people outrun explosions are every bit as silly as they were on the big screen. —MM

Movie: 🎬🎬🎬 **DVD:** 🎬🎬🎬🎬
20th Century Fox (Cat #2000045, UPC #024543000457). Widescreen. Dolby Digital 5.1 Surround Stereo; Dolby Digital 2.0

Surround Stereo. $34.98. Keepcase. *LANG:* English; French. *SUB:* English; Spanish. *FEATURES:* Theatrical and special edition versions ➤ 56 chapter links in special edition; 54 in theatrical release ➤ Link to internet space combat game ➤ Disc-based game ➤ HBO "making of" documentary ➤ Mockumentary "ID4 Invasion" ➤ "Creating Reality" behind-the-scenes documentary ➤ Commentary: Devlin and Emmerich ➤ Commentary: special effects supervisors Engel and Smith ➤ Storyboards, artwork, production stills ➤ Theatrical trailer and TV spots ➤ Original bi-plane ending.
1996 (PG-13) 135m/C Bill Pullman, Will Smith, Jeff Goldblum, Judd Hirsch, Margaret Colin, Randy Quaid, Mary McDonnell, Robert Loggia, Brent Spiner, James Rebhorn, Vivica A. Fox, James Duval, Harry Connick Jr., Harvey Fierstein; *D:* Roland Emmerich; *W:* Dean Devlin, Roland Emmerich; *C:* Karl Walter Lindenlaub; *M:* David Arnold. *AWARDS:* Academy Awards '96: Best Visual Effects; MTV Movie Awards '97: Best Kiss (Vivica A. Fox/Will Smith); *NOM:* Academy Awards '96: Best Sound; MTV Movie Awards '97: Best Film, Best Male Performance (Smith), Breakthrough Performance (Fox), Best Action Sequence.

The Indestructible Man / The Amazing Transparent Man

Near the end of his career, an alcoholic Chaney gamely made his way through this low-budget horror as a gangster who is electrocuted and brought back to life. The second feature is a lesser work from cult-fav director Edward James Ulmer, made at the Texas State Fair.
Movie: 🎬➤ **DVD:** NYR
Roan Group (Cat #2007). Full frame. $29.95. Keepcase.
1956 70m/B Ross Elliott, Ken Terrell, Robert Shayne, Lon Chaney Jr., Marian Carr, Max (Casey Adams) Showalter; *D:* Jack Pollexfen; *W:* Sue Bradford, Vy Russell; *C:* John L. Russell; *M:* Albert Glasser.

Indomitable Teddy Roosevelt

Entertaining mix of newsreel footage and staged re-enactments with Bob Boyd as TR, traces the career of the feisty president. George C. Scott provides narration and John Philip Souza provides the music. On DVD, the quality of the historical footage varies radically. The scenes of Roosevelt shaking hands with supporters are extremely clear and capture the man's swaggering walk and presence. Other historical film is almost unwatchable and the new color footage is mediocre. The night scenes are filled with abundant artifacts. Even so, it's a fine introduction to the man. —MM
Movie: 🎬🎬➤ **DVD:** 🎬🎬➤
Image Entertainment (Cat #ID5709SFDVD, UPC #014381570922). Full frame. Dolby Digital Surround Stereo. $24.99. Snapper.

LANG: English. *FEATURES:* 22 chapter links.
1983 93m/C Bob Boyd; *D:* Harrison Engle; *W:* Theodore Strauss; *Nar:* George C. Scott.

Inferno

Typically uneven Argento occult horror contains some of his most imaginative work. Rose (Miracle) discovers the secret of the demonic "Three Mothers" in a surreal underwater scene that takes place beneath a house in New York. Her brother Mark (McCloskey) comes in to investigate. Overall, the image is softer than it is in other Argento films on DVD. He uses more colored light than usual here. Sound is very good, especially in that underwater sequence. Also, the DVD version is significantly longer than older tapes. —MM
Movie: 🎬🎬➤ **DVD:** 🎬🎬🎬
Anchor Bay (Cat #DV11068, UPC #013131106893). Widescreen (1.85:1) anamorphic. Dolby Digital 5.1 Surround Stereo; Dolby Digital Surround Stereo. $29.98. Keepcase. *LANG:* English. *FEATURES:* 20 chapter links ➤ Argento interview ➤ Trailer ➤ Cast and crew thumbnail biographies ➤ Stills gallery ➤ Liner interview with Leigh McCloskey.
1980 (R) 106m/C *IT* Leigh McCloskey, Elenora Giorgi, Irene Miracle, Sacha Pitoeff; *D:* Dario Argento; *W:* Dario Argento; *C:* Romano Albani; *M:* Keith Emerson.

Infinity

Actor Matthew Broderick makes an accomplished but somewhat understated directorial debut. He also stars. Based on physicist Richard Feynman's autobiographical writings, the film is about the first years of his marriage to Arline Greenbaum (Arquette). It's also a slowly paced coming-of-age story set against his college days at Princeton and his work with the Manhattan Project at Los Alamos, NM. The two leads do some of their best work—and that's very good indeed—with equally good support from Peter Riegert as Richard's father. The first half or so is done in golden nostalgic light, and, throughout, the focus is never particularly sharp. Sound is very good. The menus are really neat. A solid sleeper. —MM
Movie: 🎬🎬🎬 **DVD:** 🎬🎬🎬
WinStar Home Entertainment (Cat #FLV 5170, UPC #720917517025). Widescreen. $24.98. Keepcase. *LANG:* English. *FEATURES:* 12 chapter links ➤ Thumbnail biographies of Broderick, Arquette, Feynman.
1996 (PG) 119m/C Matthew Broderick, Patricia Arquette, James LeGros, Peter Riegert, Dori Brenner, Peter Michael Goetz, Zeljko Ivanek; *D:* Matthew Broderick; *W:* Patricia Broderick; *C:* Toyomichi Kurita; *M:* Bruce Broughton.

The Inheritance

Wealthy, grouchy patriarch (Quinn) retired from the flour business becomes sexually

involved with his scheming daughter-in-law (Sanda) in turn-of-the-century Rome. The tawdry tale is nonetheless engaging on a guilty-pleasure level. The DVD image vacillates between too-dark and too-pale, not surprising for an import of this age. Some of director Bolognini's stagings are influenced by early Impressionists, but his work is poorly served by a haphazard pan-and-scan transfer of a scratchy print. —MM **AKA:** L'Eredita Ferramonti.
Movie: 🐕🐕▶ **DVD:** 🐕🐕
Simitar Entertainment (Cat #7235, UPC #082551723522). Full frame. PCM Stereo. $14.98. Keepcase. *LANG:* English. *FEATURES:* 8 chapter links ▪ Production factoids ▪ Bios and filmographies for Dominique Sanda and Anthony Quinn.
1976 (R) 121m/C *IT* Anthony Quinn, Fabio Testi, Dominique Sanda; **D:** Mauro Bolognini; **W:** Sergio Bazzini; **C:** Ennio Guarnieri; **M:** Ennio Morricone. *AWARDS:* Cannes Film Festival '76: Best Actress (Sanda).

Innocent Blood

John Landis's guilty-pleasure might have been called "A French Vampire in Pittsburgh." Undead Marie (Parillaud) finds herself in the middle of a Mafia gang war and decides to indulge in a little Italian food. Joe Gennaro (LaPaglia) is a cop who has infiltrated Sal Macelli's (Loggia) family. Don Rickles has a nice cameo as a mob lawyer. Fans will also spot genre luminaries Forrest J. Ackerman, Dario Argento, and Sam Raimi in bit parts. Landis is trying to be as irreverent and provocative as possible, and he's generally successful. Even in the many dark scenes, the pan-and-scan image looks about as good as it did in theatres. Landis is not a strong visual stylist and so the story and some tongue-in-cheek performances are the main attractions. —MM ▶
Movie: 🐕🐕🐕 **DVD:** 🐕🐕▶
Warner Home Video, Inc. (Cat #12570, UPC #085391257028). Full frame. Dolby Digital Surround Stereo. $14.98. Snapper. *LANG:* English; French. *CAP:* English. *FEATURES:* 31 links.
1992 (R) 112m/C Anne Parillaud, Anthony LaPaglia, Robert Loggia, David Proval, Don Rickles, Rocco Sisto, Kim Coates, Chazz Palminteri, Angela Bassett, Tom Savini, Frank Oz, Forrest J Ackerman, Sam Raimi, Dario Argento, Linnea Quigley; **D:** John Landis; **W:** Michael Wolk; **C:** Mac Ahlberg; **M:** Ira Newborn.

The Inside Man

Double agents struggle to find a submarine-detecting laser device. The Swedish film is based on true incidents in which a Soviet sub ran aground in Sweden.
Movie: 🐕🐕▶ **DVD:** NYR
Essex (Cat #1010). Full frame. $10.97. Slipcase.
1984 90m/C *SW* Dennis Hopper, Hardy Kruger, Gosta Ekman, David Wilson; **D:** Tom Clegg; **C:** Jorgen Persson; **M:** Stefan Nilsson.

The Insider

The story of Dr. Jeffrey Wigand's (Crowe) decision to tell what he knew about the tobacco industry to *60 Minutes* is as problematic on DVD as it was in theatres. The critically lauded film (seven Oscar nominations) is serious, well made, slow, often boring, and like so many "based on a true story" Hollywood productions, open to charges of manipulation. That said, the parallels between Wigand's struggles and those faced by *60 Minutes* producer Lowell Bergman (Pacino) do make for a complex drama. But because so little of the action is physical, director Mann uses all sorts of tricks—some obvious, some subtle—to give the film visual tension. First, he often bathes the screen in blue, to provide emotional coolness. He's also fond of highlighting the characters' eyeglasses, and to note differences in perspective and focus. Perhaps his most irritating device, however, is a musical score that adds a celestial benediction from a choir at significant moments, hammering home the idea that THIS IS A SERIOUS FILM. The DVD captures both the visual flourishes and the sound without any serious problems. On disc, the film is as complex and distant as it has ever been. The single interesting extra underscores that cold objectivity. It's an analysis of one short important scene through the script and production notes by Mann. His attention to detail is amazing. —MM
Movie: 🐕🐕🐕 **DVD:** 🐕🐕🐕
Buena Vista Home Entertainment (Cat #19298, UPC #717951007391). Widescreen (2.35:1) anamorphic. Dolby Digital 5.1 Stereo. $32.99. Keepcase. *LANG:* English; French. *SUB:* English. *FEATURES:* 30 chapter links ▪ Theatrical trailer ▪ "Making of" featurette ▪ Inside a scene, notes, and script.
1999 (R) 157m/C Russell Crowe, Al Pacino, Christopher Plummer, Gina Gershon, Philip Baker Hall, Diane Venora, Lindsay Crouse, Debi Mazar, Stephen Tobolowsky, Colm Feore, Bruce McGill, Michael Gambon, Rip Torn, Lynne Thigpen, Hallie Kate Eisenberg, Michael Paul Chan, Wings Hauser, Pete Hamill, Nestor Serrano, Michael Moore; **D:** Michael Mann; **W:** Michael Mann, Eric Roth; **C:** Dante Spinotti; **M:** Graeme Revell. *AWARDS:* Los Angeles Film Critics Association Awards '99: Best Actor (Crowe), Best Cinematography, Best Film, Best Supporting Actor (Plummer); National Board of Review Awards '99: Best Actor (Crowe); National Society of Film Critics Awards '99: Best Actor (Crowe), Best Supporting Actor (Plummer); Broadcast Film Critics Association Awards '99: Best Actor (Crowe); *NOM:* Academy Awards '99: Best Actor (Crowe), Best Adapted Screenplay, Best Cinematography, Best Director (Mann), Best Film, Best Film Editing, Best Sound; British Academy Awards '99: Best Actor (Crowe); Directors Guild of America Awards '99: Best Director (Mann); Golden Globe Awards '00: Best Actor—Drama (Crowe), Best Director (Mann), Best Film—Drama, Best Screenplay, Best Original Score; Screen Actors

Guild Award '99: Best Actor (Crowe); Writers Guild of America '99: Best Adapted Screenplay.

Insomnia

After a young woman is murdered in northern Norway, Oslow detectives Engstrom (Skarsgard) and Vik (Ousdal) are called in to investigate, with the aid of a local cop, Hilde (Armand). Another killing ensues, leading one of the cops to try to cover up one death while solving another. The constant sunlight leads to insomnia that manifests a moral breakdown. In this impressive debut, director Skjoldbjaerg uses color as a dramatic tool. He tells the story in neutral shades of light gray and white that lend a certain *Twin Peaks* quality to the combination of police procedural and psychological thriller. The DVD faithfully captures the image with crystalline clarity and superb stereo sound. This kind of work is certainly not to all tastes, but it deserves the careful treatment it receives on this Criterion disc. —MM
Movie: 🐕🐕🐕 **DVD:** 🐕🐕🐕▶
Criterion Collection (Cat #INS030, UPC #037429138229). Widescreen (1.85:1) letterboxed. Dolby Digital Surround Stereo. $29.95. Keepcase. *LANG:* Norwegian; Swedish. *SUB:* English. *FEATURES:* 21 chapter links ▪ Liner notes by Peter Cowie ▪ Norwegian theatrical trailer and TV spot.
1997 97m/C *NO* Stellan Skarsgard, Sverre Anker Ousdal, Maria Bonnevie, Bjorn Floberg, Gisken Armand, Marianne O. Ulrichsen, Maria Mathiesen; **D:** Erik Skjoldbjaerg; **W:** Nikolaj Frobenius; **C:** Erling Thurmann-Andersen; **M:** Geir Jenssen.

Inspector Gadget

Security guard John Brown (Broderick) is injured in an explosion when the evil Claw (Everett) steals one of Dr. Brenda Bradford's (Fisher) inventions. After an operation, he becomes the mechanically enhanced titular character. With its emphasis on large patches of primary colors and silly special effects (courtesy of Richard Hoover and Stan Winston), this live-action cartoon presents no problems for DVD. It's still too slight—with as much product placement as plot—to recommend to most grown-up audiences. —MM
Movie: 🐕🐕▶ **DVD:** 🐕🐕▶
Buena Vista Home Entertainment (Cat #18325, UPC #717951005113). Widescreen (1.85:1) letterboxed. Dolby Digital 5.1 Surround Stereo. $29.99. Keepcase. *LANG:* English; French. *CAP:* English. *FEATURES:* 13 chapter links ▪ Theatrical trailer ▪ Promotional featurette ▪ Youngstown music video.
1999 (PG) 77m/C Matthew Broderick, Rupert Everett, Joely Fisher, Michelle Trachtenberg, Dabney Coleman, Andy Dick, Michael G. Hagerty, Rene Auberjonois, Frances Bay; **D:** David Kellogg; **W:** Kerry Ehrin, Zak Penn; **C:** Adam Greenberg; **M:** John Debney; **V:** Don Adams, D.L. Hughley.

Inspector Wears Skirts

After kicking some serious butt against terrorists, Miss Wu (Hu) is appointed to form and train an all-woman police squad. Like so many Hong Kong action pictures, this one has a fair-to-good high-contrast image on DVD. Sound, however, is much better, and the stunt work is grand. Jackie Chan produced and, according to some sources, directed. —*MM*

Movie: 🎬🎬 *DVD:* 🎬🎬
Tai Seng Video Marketing (Cat #5129, UPC #895024902487). Widescreen letterboxed. Dolby Digital 5.1 Surround Stereo. $49.95. Keepcase. *LANG:* Cantonese; Mandarin. *SUB:* Simplified Chinese & Traditional Chinese; Japanese; Bahasa (Indonesia); English. *FEATURES:* 8 chapter links • Cast and crew thumbnail biographies.
1988 93m/C *HK* Sibelle Hu, Cynthia Rothrock, Ellen Chan, Kara Hui, Jade Kan, Alex To; *D:* Wellson Chin; *W:* Abe Kwong Man Wai; *C:* Lau Wai-Keung.

Instinct

Ambitious young psychiatrist Theo Caulder (Gooding) examines anthropologist Ethan Powell (Hopkins), accused of multiple murders in Africa where he was studying gorillas. Is the bearded doctor a variation on Hannibal Lecter, or on Dian Fossey? Actually, it's some of both, and the combination is less than wholly satisfactory. The DVD image is excellent. It handles both hospital wards and jungle exteriors without any significant flaws. Sound is very good, too. —*MM*

Movie: 🎬🎬➤ *DVD:* 🎬🎬🎬➤
Buena Vista Home Entertainment (Cat #18152, UPC #717951004314). Widescreen (2.35:1) letterboxed. Dolby Digital 5.1 Surround Stereo. $29.99. Keepcase. *LANG:* English; French. *SUB:* English. *FEATURES:* 21 chapter links • Theatrical trailer.
1999 (R) 123m/C Anthony Hopkins, Cuba Gooding Jr., Donald Sutherland, George Dzundza, Maura Tierney, John Ashton, Paul Bates, John Aylward; *D:* Jon Turteltaub; *W:* Gerald Di Pega; *C:* Philippe Rousselot; *M:* Danny Elfman.

Interceptor

Aerial thriller with sf elements is notable for its slow pace and preposterous plot. Terrorists led by Phillips (Prochnow) decide to steal two Stealth fighters from a C5-A transport plane while it's in flight. Capt. Winfield (Divoff) is the brave, cardboard fighter jock. Jane Morgan (Morehead) is the transport pilot. The most far-fetched moments are two murders by Perrier and toilet flush, and the hijacking itself. The flying scenes, which seem to have been done largely with models and computer effects, are much better, but on DVD they exhibit noticeable pixelation in the brighter moments. —*MM*

Movie: 🎬 *DVD:* 🎬➤

Trimark Home Video (Cat #VM6883D, UPC #031398688334). Widescreen letterboxed. Stereo. $24.99. Keepcase. *LANG:* English. *SUB:* Spanish; French. *CAP:* English. *FEATURES:* 24 chapter links • Juergen Prochnow and Andrew Divoff filmographies.
1992 (R) 92m/C Juergen Prochnow, Andrew Divoff, Elizabeth Morehead; *D:* Michael Cohn; *W:* John Brancato; *M:* Rick Marvin.

Interlocked

The inevitable evolution of the murderous femme introduced in *Fatal Attraction* continues with psycho-cyberbabe Eva (Harrison) who can't handle it when her online flirtation with Michael (Trachta, also coproducer) crashes on the rocks of reality. He's married and has a pregnant wife (Ferguson). Actually, the film is several cuts above average for the genre. The DVD image is excellent, particularly in the sweaty sexual fantasies. (If the film really is rated "R" as the box copy states, the folks at the MPAA ratings board must have been asleep at the switch the day it came through.) The over-the-top suspense elements actually work well, too. Harrison and Trachta previously worked together on the TV soap, *The Bold and the Beautiful*. —*MM* *AKA:* A Bold Affair.

Movie: 🎬🎬🎬 *DVD:* 🎬🎬🎬
Simitar Entertainment (Cat #7440, UPC #082551744022). Full frame. Dolby Digital Stereo; Dolby Digital 5.1 Surround. $19.98. Keepcase. *LANG:* English. *FEATURES:* 8 chapter links • Production factoids.
1998 (R) 94m/C Jeff Trachta, Schae Harrison, Sandra Ferguson, George Alvarez, Bruce Kirby; *D:* Rick Jacobson; *W:* Al Sophianopoulos; *C:* Jesse Weathington.

Intermezzo

Married violinist Ekman meets pianist Bergman and they fall in love. He deserts his family to tour with her but the feelings for his wife and children become too much. One of the great grab-your-hanky melodramas. (The 1939 English remake is Bergman's American debut.) On DVD, the Swedish film is not as polished as the best black and white that Hollywood could produce in '36. Bergman's radiant youthful beauty still shines through and that has always been the main attraction. Even without stereo, the soundtrack is good, capturing the simple score, mostly violin solos. The subtitles are exceptionally clear and easy to read. —*MM* *AKA:* Interlude.

Movie: 🎬🎬🎬 *DVD:* 🎬🎬
WinStar Home Entertainment (Cat #FLV 5059, UPC #720917505923). Full frame. $29.98. Keepcase. *LANG:* Swedish. *SUB:* English. *FEATURES:* 6 chapter links • Production credits • Filmographies, biographies, and awards.
1936 88m/B *SW* Gosta Ekman, Inga Tidblad, Ingrid Bergman, Erik "Bullen" Berglund, Anders Henrikson, Hasse (Hans) Ekman, Britt Hagman, Hugo Bjorne; *D:* Gustaf Molander; *W:* Gustaf Molander,

Gosta Stevens; *C:* Ake Dahlqvist; *M:* Heinz Provost.

Internal Affairs

Wild, sexually charged action piece follows an LAPD Internal Affairs officer (Garcia) who becomes obsessed with uncovering a sleazy, corrupt street cop (Gere). It all becomes pretty illogical before it's over, but the performances and bizarre humor are terrific. Gere's creepy degenerate is one of his best and strangest roles.

Movie: 🎬🎬➤ *DVD:* NYR
Paramount Home Video (Cat #322457). Widescreen (1.85:1) letterboxed. Dolby Digital 5.1 Surround Stereo; Dolby Digital Surround Stereo. $29.99. Keepcase. *LANG:* English; French. *CAP:* English.
1990 (R) 114m/C Richard Gere, Andy Garcia, Laurie Metcalf, Ron Vawter, Marco Rodriguez, Nancy Travis, William Baldwin, Richard Bradford, Annabella Sciorra, Michael Beach; *D:* Mike Figgis; *W:* Henry Bean; *C:* John A. Alonzo; *M:* Brian Banks, Mike Figgis.

Interview with the Vampire

The Anne Rice–Neil Jordan adaptation of her famous novel is the *Gone with the Wind* of vampire movies. Like *GwtW*, it's long, romantic, and wildly overstated. Unlike *GwtW*, it's gruesomely bloody, disgusting and, at the right times, very funny. Louis (Pitt), a centuries-old undead, recounts his story to a writer (Slater), telling how he was transformed in 18th-century New Orleans by Lestat (Cruise), and came to transform young Claudia (Dunst). Director Jordan lets the tone tack between opulence and outright horror without ever losing control of the story. He also generates the intensity that any real horror film needs. The gay subtext, so important to Rice's work, is remarkably strong for a mainstream film. Her script is talky and often poetic, and the cast is up to it, though Cruise's fey performance is initially off-putting. Stan Winston's effects are among his best. For home video purposes, the DVD is a solid step up from VHS tape. The image is more detailed, revealing subtler colors and patterns in the pale makeup. Virtually all of the action takes place at night with reddish tinges to the lighting that reveals everything of importance in the ornate sets and costumes. The sound is fine, too, and the two-sided disc contains both the widescreen and pan-and-scan versions of the film. —*MM*

Movie: 🎬🎬🎬 *DVD:* 🎬🎬🎬➤
Warner Home Video, Inc. (Cat #13176, UPC #085391317623). Full frame; widescreen letterboxed. Dolby Digital 5.1 Surround. $24.98. Snapper. *LANG:* English; French. *SUB:* English; French; Spanish. *CAP:* English. *FEATURES:* 34 chapter links • Cast and crew thumbnail biographies • Production notes.
1994 (R) 123m/C Tom Cruise, Brad Pitt, Kirsten Dunst, Christian Slater, Antonio Banderas, Stephen Rea, Domiziana Gior-

dano; *D:* Neil Jordan; *W:* Anne Rice; *C:* Philippe Rousselot; *M:* Elliot Goldenthal. *AWARDS:* MTV Movie Awards '95: Best Male Performance (Pitt), Breakthrough Performance (Dunst), Most Desirable Male (Pitt); *NOM:* Academy Awards '94: Best Art Direction/Set Decoration, Best Original Score; Golden Globe Awards '95: Best Supporting Actress (Dunst), Best Score; MTV Movie Awards '95: Best Film, Most Desirable Male (Slater, Cruise), Best On-Screen Duo (Tom Cruise/Brad Pitt), Best Villain (Cruise).

Into the Woods
American Playhouse version of Stephen Sondheim's Tony-winning musical fusion of fairy tales, featuring the original Broadway cast, in this tale of a husband and wife that must venture into the woods to find a cow, a red cape, a pair of golden slippers, and magic beans in order to lift the curse that has left them childless.
Movie: 🎵🎵🎵 *DVD:* NYR
Image Entertainment (Cat #3951). Full frame. Dolby Digital Stereo. $34.99. Snapper.
1990 150m/C Bernadette Peters, Joanna Gleason, Chip Zien, Tom Aldredge, Kim Crosby, Ben Wright, Barbara Byrne; *D:* James Lapine; *W:* James Lapine; *M:* Stephen Sondheim.

Intolerance
Though this DVD was made from the best existing elements of D.W. Griffith's ambitious follow-up to *Birth of a Nation*, the screen is filled with scratches, flecks, and scenes that are almost too dark to make out. The supplemental material claims that the original tinting and toning have been re-created as faithfully as possible. Gaylord Carter's organ score further heightens the period feel. Though some claim that the film is a masterpiece of the silent era—and the shots of the great gate of Babylon are impressive, even on a small screen—this is a long, unwieldy work that will appeal only to serious students. —MM
Movie: 🎵🎵🎵 *DVD:* 🎵🎵🎵
Image Entertainment (Cat #ID839DSDVD, UPC #014381583922). Full frame. Dolby Digital Stereo. $29.99. Snapper. *SUB:* English intertitles. *FEATURES:* 36 chapter links • Separate cast and credit screens for the four stories • Extra footage from various release prints • Publicity materials • Liner notes by DVD producer David Shepard • Production photographs.
1916 175m/B Lillian Gish, Mae Marsh, Constance Talmadge, Bessie Love, Elmer Clifton, Erich von Stroheim, Eugene Pallette, Seena Owen, Alfred Paget; *D:* D.W. Griffith; *W:* D.W. Griffith, Tod Browning; *C:* Billy (G.W.) Bitzer, Karl Brown. *AWARDS:* National Film Registry '89.

Invaders from Mars
A young boy (Hunt) cries "Martian!" in this sf cheapie classic. He can't convince the townspeople of this invasion because they've already been possessed by alien beings, his parents being among the first to succumb. Amid all the campy foolishness, the moments of child abuse still have the power to shock. The DVD image is very grainy with scratches and marks throughout and a constant hiss on the soundtrack. The disc may be a bit brighter than VHS tape, but the edge is very slight. —MM
Movie: 🎵🎵➤ *DVD:* 🎵🎵
UAV Entertainment (Cat #40085, UPC #084296400850). Full frame. Dolby Digital Stereo. $14.99. Snapper. *LANG:* English. *FEATURES:* 9 chapter links • Trailer.
1953 78m/C Helena Carter, Arthur Franz, Jimmy Hunt, Leif Erickson, Hillary Brooke, Morris Ankrum, Lock Martin; *D:* William Cameron Menzies; *W:* Richard Blake, John Tucker Battle; *C:* John Seitz; *M:* Raoul Kraushaar.

Invaders from Mars
Big-budget (well, bigger-budget) remake of the classic (well, semi-classic) 1953 original tells the story of a young boy (Carson) who's the only person who realizes that the Martians have invaded and are taking over the population one by one. A sympathetic school nurse (Black, Carson's real mother) is little help. The filmmakers realize that they're dealing with campy material and so they treat the story as a comic book with bug-eyed monsters and ornate sets meant to be the Martians' underground lair. The DVD is nothing special. Virtually all reds glow brightly, and red is the predominate color. Overall the image has a pale but grainy look. Despite good stereo separation, sound is flat. —MM
Movie: 🎵🎵 *DVD:* 🎵🎵
Anchor Bay (Cat #DV10328, UPC #013131032895). Widescreen (2.35:1) letterboxed. Dolby Digital Stereo. $24.99. Keepcase. *LANG:* English. *FEATURES:* 9 chapter links • Theatrical trailer.
1986 (PG) 102m/C Hunter Carson, Karen Black, Louise Fletcher, Laraine Newman, Timothy Bottoms, Bud Cort, Dale Dye; *D:* Tobe Hooper; *W:* Dan O'Bannon, Don Jakoby; *C:* Daniel Pearl; *M:* Sylvester Levay, David Storrs, Christopher Young.

Invasion of the Body Snatchers
"In my practice I've seen how people have allowed their humanity to drain away— only it happens slowly, instead of all at once. They didn't seem to mind." That's how Dr. Miles Bennell (Kevin McCarthy) describes the strange things that are going on in the little town of Santa Mira. How he comes to that understanding is one of the most suspenseful and frightening movies ever made. The Daniel Mainwaring–Don Siegel film works so well on so many levels that its power as a pure thriller is often overlooked. It's beautifully constructed—steadily, inexorably ratcheting up the pressure. Notice how Siegel changes the lighting from bright sun to tightening shadows that reflect the characters' growing awareness. McCarthy's performance builds from blase self-satisfaction to raving dementia without a false move. (By the way, that is director Sam Peckinpah—who helped with the script—as Charlie, the gas man.) Even those with small monitors should choose the widescreen edition. Siegel uses the whole frame and the missing action is all too obvious on the pan-and-scan version. Background grain is noticeable in large areas of solid grays, and solid lines tend to break in panning shots, but neither is particularly serious. This DVD is an excellent version of a great film. —MM
Movie: 🎵🎵🎵 *DVD:* 🎵🎵🎵
Republic Pictures Home Video (Cat #42018). Widescreen (2.35:1) letterboxed; full frame. Dolby Digital Mono. $24.98. Keepcase. *LANG:* English; Italian; Spanish. *SUB:* French; Spanish. *CAP:* English. *FEATURES:* Trailers • Interview with Kevin McCarthy • 25 chapter links.
1956 80m/B Kevin McCarthy, Dana Wynter, Carolyn Jones, King Donovan, Larry Gates, Jean Willes, Whit Bissell, Richard Deacon, Pat O'Malley, Sam Peckinpah, Donald Siegel; *D:* Donald Siegel; *W:* Daniel Mainwaring, Sam Peckinpah; *C:* Ellsworth Fredericks; *M:* Carmen Dragon. *AWARDS:* National Film Registry '94.

Invasion of the Body Snatchers
One of the few instances where a remake is an improvement on the original, which was itself a classic. This time, the "pod people" are infesting San Francisco, with only a small group of people aware of the invasion. A ceaselessly inventive, creepy version of the alien-takeover paradigm, with an intense and winning performance by Sutherland. Features cameos by Don Siegel and Kevin McCarthy from the original, as well as an uncredited appearance by Robert Duvall. This disc is lacking in two of the most important specs for a DVD: the picture is not sharp enough, and colors are weak with a drifting tint. There is surprisingly little grain and artifacts for an image this soft. Blacks also have some grain, but it's hard to tell if it's an increase overall. Contrast and brightness levels are pretty good. The Dolby Surround sends very little to the rear and is lacking in both fidelity and dynamics. —JO
Movie: 🎵🎵🎵➤ *DVD:* 🎵🎵➤
MGM Home Entertainment (Cat #906274, UPC #027616627421). Widescreen (1.85:1) letterboxed; full frame. Dolby Surround. $24.98. Keepcase. *LANG:* English (DS); French (mono). *SUB:* English; French; Spanish. *CAP:* English. *FEATURES:* 32 chapter links • Commentary: director • Theatrical trailer.
1978 (PG) 115m/C Donald Sutherland, Brooke Adams, Veronica Cartwright, Leonard Nimoy, Jeff Goldblum, Kevin McCarthy, Donald Siegel, Art Hindle, Robert Duvall; *D:* Philip Kaufman; *W:* W.D. Richter; *C:* Michael Chapman.

The Invisible Strangler

A death-row murderer who can meditate himself into invisibility rubs out the witnesses who helped put him away. The action is sleazy and violent, but it's too inept to be offensive. On DVD, the entire film looks like it was shot through a layer of gauze so it's pointless to comment on the image. Actually, the incredible clothes and other period details are the only fun to be had. —*MM* **AKA:** The Astral Factor.
Movie: *♪♪* **DVD:** *♪*
Simitar Entertainment (Cat #7304, UPC #082551730421). Full frame. PCM Stereo. $14.98. Keepcase. *LANG:* English. *FEATURES:* 8 chapter links • Production factoids • Robert Foxworth, Stefanie Powers, Elke Sommer filmographies.
1976 (PG) 85m/C Robert Foxworth, Stefanie Powers, Elke Sommer, Sue Lyon, Leslie Parrish, Marianna Hill; *D:* John Florea; *W:* Arthur C. Pierce; *C:* Alan Stenvold; *M:* Richard Hieronymous, Alan Oldfield.

The Ipcress File

In their commentary track, director Sidney Furie and editor Peter Hunt state that this thriller was always meant to be the opposite of a James Bond film. Even though it was made at the height of the spy craze, it really owes as much to *The Third Man* and *The Manchurian Candidate* as it does to the razzle-dazzle escapism of its day. It's a relatively simple story of government agent Harry Palmer (Caine) who has to figure out which of his two superiors, Dolby (Green) or Ross (Doleman) is the traitor who's selling out British scientists to the highest bidder. The real beauty of this DVD is in its retention of the entire widescreen ratio, which is so important to Furie's inventive camera work. He fills the screen with unusual compositions, Dutch angles, and match cuts. Most of them are lost in conventional pan-and-scan transfers. Those not familiar with '60s movies may complain that the locations are too dark, but none of the action is lost. In their talk, Furie and Hunt (editor of the best Bond films and director of *On Her Majesty's Secret Service*) come across as two solid craftsmen reminiscing about a particularly satisfying collaboration. They do not comment on many of the more interesting shots and though they drop some tantalizing hints, they do not go into the juiciest gossip, either. A separate track for John Barry's haunting score would have been welcome, too, but those are quibbles. This is one of my own all-time favorite films. On disc, it looks better than it has in decades. —*MM*
Movie: *♪♪♪♪* **DVD:** *♪♪♪♪*
Anchor Bay (Cat #DV10925, UPC #131310925926). Widescreen (2.35:1) letterboxed. Dolby Digital Stereo. $24.98. Keepcase. *LANG:* English. *FEATURES:* 22 chapter links • Commentary: director Sidney J. Furie and editor Peter Hunt • The-

atrical trailer • Thumbnail biographies of Michael Caine, Furie, and Hunt • Stills gallery.
1965 108m/C *GB* Michael Caine, Nigel Green, Guy Doleman, Sue Lloyd; *D:* Sidney J. Furie; *W:* Bill Canaway, James Doran; *C:* Otto Heller; *M:* John Barry. *AWARDS:* British Academy Awards '65: Best Film.

Irma Vep

Satiric tweaking of French filmmaking begins with has-been director Rene Vidal (Leaud) hiring Hong Kong star Maggie Cheung to take the lead role of Irma Vep in a remake of the 1915 silent French classic *Les Vampires*. But from the moment the actress arrives in Paris, it's one disaster after another. Cheung has trouble with the language barrier, Vidal is having a breakdown, lesbian costumer Zoe (Richard) is instantly smitten by Cheung and has her interest humiliatingly conveyed to everyone on the production. Then there's Jose Murano (Castel), a snobbish auteur who replaces Vidal and believes the Chinese actress can't play a French thief, not knowing that Cheung has become obsessed with her role and is practicing stealing from other hotel guests. Here's another Fox/Lorber DVD that does not improve upon the VHS tape. The picture is not very sharp and the grain is nasty at times. Colors are fairly weak and occasionally the tint drifts towards the reds. Even with the low color level, there are still instances of bleed. Blacks also vary, ranging from O.K. to poor. Contrast and brightness levels seem to work well with what they're given. The stereo sound is a little lame with not much low end, or high end, and only so-so separation. —*JO*
Movie: *♪♪* **DVD:** *♪♪*
Fox/Lorber Home Video (Cat #FLV5015, UPC #720917501529). Widescreen (1.66:1) letterboxed. Stereo. $29.98. Keepcase. *LANG:* French. *SUB:* English. *FEATURES:* 6 chapter links • Filmographies • Theatrical trailer.
1996 96m/C *FR* Maggie Cheung, Jean-Pierre Leaud, Nathalie Richard, Bulle Ogier, Lou Castel, Antoine Basler, Nathalie Boutefeu, Arsinee Khanjian, Alex Descas; *D:* Olivier Assayas; *W:* Olivier Assayas; *C:* Eric Gautier.

Iron Eagle 4

By the fourth installment, this inexplicable series has gotten very old, though Lou Gossett Jr. gives the material a much better performance than it deserves. As Gen. Chappy Sinclair, he and pilot Doug Masters (Cadieux) are running the Iron Eagle Flight School, a training center/holding cell for troubled teens. They and their charges discover sinister goings-on at the nearby Air Force base, leading to a dog-fight between state-of-the-art jet fighters and World War II–era T-4 trainers. The full-frame image is mediocre. Beyond a few extras, the DVD is not really much better than VHS tape. —*MM*

Movie: *♪* **DVD:** *♪►*
Trimark Home Video (Cat #6926D, UPC #031398692638). Full frame. Dolby Digital Stereo. $24.99. Keepcase. *LANG:* English. *SUB:* French; Spanish. *FEATURES:* 30 chapter links • Cast and crew thumbnail biographies • Theatrical trailer.
1995 (PG-13) 95m/C *CA* Louis Gossett Jr., Jason Cadieux, Al Waxman, Joanne Vannicola, Rachel Blanchard, Sean McCann, Ross Hill, Karen Gayle; *D:* Sidney J. Furie; *W:* Michael Stokes; *C:* Curtis Petersen; *M:* Paul Zaza.

Iron Giant

At the height of the Cold War in 1957, something crashes into the ocean near the coastal town of Rockwell, ME. Enthusiastic young Hogarth Hughes (voice of Eli Marienthal) goes out into the woods and finds the title character, a huge robot (Diesel). But he can't let his single mom (Aniston) or a self-important FBI agent (McDonald) find out. The story, based on poet Ted Hughes's book, touches on various forms of paranoia and misunderstanding. Director Brad Bird gives the film the style and sensibility of the great Warner Bros. cartoons of the '40s and '50s. DVD is an excellent medium for the bold primary colors, towering shapes, and innovative sound that Bird employs. Though the film was something of a disappointment at the theatrical boxoffice, it is going to become a staple of children's home entertainment. (Adults will like it just as much.) —*MM*
Movie: *♪♪♪►* **DVD:** *♪♪♪►*
Warner Home Video, Inc. Widescreen letterboxed; full frame. Dolby Digital Stereo. $24.98. Snapper. *LANG:* English. *CAP:* English. *FEATURES:* 30 chapter links • Theatrical trailer • "Making of" featurette • "Cha-Hua-Hua" music video by Eddie Platt • Cast and crew thumbnail biographies.
1999 (PG) 86m/C *D:* Brad Bird; *W:* Tim McCanlies; *M:* Michael Kamen; *V:* Vin Diesel, Eli Marienthal, Jennifer Aniston, Harry Connick Jr., John Mahoney, M. Emmet Walsh, Cloris Leachman, James Gammon, Christopher McDonald.

Iron Maze

A fascinating notion forms the center of this dramatic scrapheap: the classic Japanese *Rashomon* plot shifted to the rusting Pennsylvania steel town of Corinth. That's where Tokyo businessman Sugita (Hiroaki Murakami) is found bludgeoned. Initially it appears that Barry (Fahey) is the guilty party—he was having an affair with Sugita's American-born wife (Fonda)—but in a series of flashbacks, the sheriff (Walsh) eventually finds the truth. If the DVD image is less than perfect, its graininess is not inappropriate for the setting and story. The disc is a slight improvement over VHS tape. Sound is fine. —*MM*
Movie: *♪♪►* **DVD:** *♪♪►*
Image Entertainment (Cat #ID6797CQDVD, UPC #014381679724). Full frame. Dolby

Digital Stereo. $24.99. Snapper. *LANG:* English. *FEATURES:* 12 chapter links. **1991 (R) 102m/C** Jeff Fahey, Bridget Fonda, Hiroaki Murakami, J.T. Walsh, Gabriel Damon, John Randolph, Peter Allas; *D:* Hiroaki Yoshida; *W:* Tim Metcalfe; *C:* Morio Saegusa; *M:* Stanley Myers.

Iron Monkey

Historical fantasy martial arts is built around the Iron Monkey (Rongguang Yu), a Robin-Hood figure who defeats whole armies of opponents and can leap tall buildings in a single bound. The numerous comic "hex" errors in English translation somehow add to the overall merriment. The DVD image ranges between fair and good with some daylight exteriors having a washed-out look. Night scenes are fine. Sound Is very good. —*MM AKA:* Siunin Wong Fei-hung Tsi Titmalau.
Movie: 🎬🎬 *DVD:* 🎬🎬
Tai Seng Video Marketing (Cat #MS/DVD/064/99, UPC #895017000640). Widescreen letterboxed. Dolby Digital 5.1 Surround Stereo; Dolby Digital Stereo. $19.95. Keepcase. *LANG:* Cantonese; Mandarin; English. *SUB:* Traditional & Simplified Chinese; English; Japanese; Bahasa Malaysia; Thai; Vietnamese; Spanish. *FEATURES:* 9 chapter links • Cast and crew thumbnail biographies.
1993 87m/C *HK* Rongguang Yu, Donnie Yen, Yam Sai-kun, Tsing-ying Wong; *D:* Woo-ping Yuen; *W:* Tseng Pik-Yin, Tsui Hark, Tai-Muk Lau, Cheung Tan, Pik-yin Tang; *C:* Arthur Wong.

The Island at the Top of the World

A rich Englishman, in search of his missing son, travels to the Arctic Circle in 1908. The rescue party includes an American archeologist, a French astronaut, and an Eskimo guide (no, that isn't the start of a joke). Astonishingly, they discover an unknown, "lost" Viking kingdom. This Jules Verne–style adventure doesn't quite measure up, but the kids should like it. The image transfer is surprisingly good, with crisp, vibrant colors and solid blacks. The soundtrack, however, sounds as if it were recorded with a microphone shielded by a cardboard box. —*MJT*
Movie: 🎬🎬▶ *DVD:* 🎬🎬▶
Anchor Bay (Cat #DV10825, UPC #013131082593). Widescreen (1.66:1) letterboxed; full frame. Dolby Digital. $24.98. Keepcase. *LANG:* English. *FEATURES:* 25 chapter links.
1974 (G) 93m/C David Hartman, Donald Sinden, Jacques Marin, Mako, David Gwillim; *D:* Robert Stevenson; *W:* John Whedon; *C:* Frank Phillips; *M:* Maurice Jarre. *AWARDS: NOM:* Academy Awards '74: Best Art Direction/Set Decoration.

The Island of Dr. Moreau

Seen strictly as a horror-comedy, this one's hard to top. Marlon Brando's mountainous Moreau is the *Mad Magazine* version of his Col. Kurtz from *Apocalypse Now*. He makes his first entrance wearing white makeup, an umbrella hat, and riding in a Popemobile. He also adopts a lisping Boris Karloff British accent and later appears with a small trashcan on his head. Val Kilmer, as his assistant Montgomery, and David Thewlis, as the castaway Douglas, give their characters a curious gay spin. (The fact that top-billed Kilmer plays a supporting role and character actor Thewlis is the protagonist says a lot about the unbalanced dramatic weight.) Director Frankenheimer (who took over from writer Richard Stanley after the traditional "creative differences") keeps the story of animal experimentation moving quickly. Some of Stan Winston's make-up effects are excellent, but the overall tone is unstable. Still, the entire production is so bizarre that it deserves a look for curiosity value, if nothing else. On DVD, the images range from sparkling clarity to extra-grainy night scenes and dark interiors. (The opening credits are real eye-zappers, so flashy that they're hard to watch.) This "unrated director's cut" appears to contain nine extra minutes of fairly graphic violence. —*MM*
Movie: 🎬🎬🎬 *DVD:* 🎬🎬🎬
New Line Home Video (Cat #N4444, UPC #794043444425). Full frame; widescreen (2.35:1) letterboxed. Dolby Digital 5.1 Surround (English); Dolby Digital Stereo (French). $24.98. Snapper. *LANG:* English; French. *SUB:* English; French. *CAP:* English. *FFATURES:* Behind-the-scenes featurette • 25 chapter links • Cast biographies and filmographies • 2 theatrical trailers • Scenes from stars' other New Line films.
1996 91m/C Marlon Brando, Val Kilmer, David Thewlis, Fairuza Balk, Marco Hofschneider, Temuera Morrison, Ron Perlman; *D:* John Frankenheimer; *W:* Richard Stanley, Ron Hutchinson; *C:* William A. Fraker; *M:* Gary Chang. *AWARDS: NOM:* Golden Raspberry Awards '96: Worst Picture, Worst Supporting Actor (Kilmer, Brando), Worst Director (Frankenheimer), Worst Screenplay.

Island of Greed

The island of the title is Taiwan. The story concerns the attempts of a mobster to buy his way into elected office, with complications provided by gambling, corruption, and long action sequences. On DVD, casino interiors, with their gaudy red lighting and busy backgrounds lose detail. Other exteriors are much better and the sound is good throughout. —*MM AKA:* Hak Gam.
Movie: 🎬🎬▶ *DVD:* 🎬🎬▶
Tai Seng Video Marketing (Cat #DVD-111). Widescreen letterboxed. Dolby Digital 5.1 Surround Stereo. $49.95. Keepcase. *LANG:* Cantonese; Mandarin. *SUB:* English; Chinese. *FEATURES:* 9 chapter links • Cast and crew thumbnail biographies.
1997 125m/C *HK* Winston Chao, Paulyn Sun, Annie Wu, Kathie Kuo; *D:* Michael Mak; *W:* Johnnie Mak; *C:* Jingle Ma, Cheung Tung Leung.

It Happened Here

Kevin Brownlow and Andrew Mollo's "what if" alternative history is based on a Nazi invasion and occupation of England following the retreat from Dunkirk. The story is told as a mock documentary and so it looks exactly like combat footage from World War II. The plot follows an English nurse (Murray) who goes to work for the Germans and comes to realize what they are really up to. On DVD, the visual imperfections—scratches, poor focus, muddy audio, hand-held camera, artless lighting—are part of the film's power, its sense of verisimilitude. Some of the most shocking images of violence might have been the inspiration for similar moments in Spielberg's *Schindler's List*. This astonishing film is even more astonishing when you realize that the filmmakers were teenagers when they made it. A commentary track might have been illuminating. —*MM*
Movie: 🎬🎬🎬▶ *DVD:* 🎬🎬🎬▶
Image Entertainment (Cat #ID5926MLSDVD, UPC #014381592627). Full frame. Dolby Digital Mono. $24.99. Snapper. *LANG:* English; German. *SUB:* English. *FEATURES:* 16 chapter links.
1965 (PG) 93m/B *GB* Sebastian Shaw, Pauline Murray, Bart Allison, Nicolette Bernard; *D:* Kevin Brownlow, Andrew Mollo; *W:* Kevin Brownlow, Andrew Mollo; *C:* Kevin Brownlow, Peter Suschitzky; *M:* Jack Beaver, Anton Bruckner.

It Happened One Night

The prototypical screwball comedy begins when heiress Ellie Andrews (Colbert) runs off to marry a playboy but meets reporter Peter Warne (Gable) on the bus to New York. It's one of Frank Capra's most easygoing films. On the commentary track, his son lovingly remembers the tortuous path that the original short story took en route to the screen. He's suitably complimentary to all involved, and he covers much of the same territory in a separate "making of" featurette. In visual terms, the disc is near perfect, capturing the black-and-white cinematography through the full range of grays, and Claudette Colbert's diagonally striped blouse is never a problem. Some of the special effects process shots are grainy, but that's the nature of the original. The remastered sound is excellent throughout, capturing all of the rapid-fire dialogue. Like so much of Capra's work, this one does not depend on a big-screen presentation. It's about likeable, fully realized characters and these are two of the best. —*MM*
Movie: 🎬🎬🎬🎬 *DVD:* 🎬🎬🎬🎬
Columbia Tristar Home Video (Cat #03949, UPC #043396039490). Full frame. Dolby Digital Mono. $25.95. Keepcase. *LANG:* English; Spanish. *SUB:* English; Spanish; Portuguese; Chinese; Korean; Thai. *CAP:*

English. *FEATURES:* 28 chapter links • "Making of" featurette, "Frank Capra Jr. Remembers " • Original live radio broadcast • Cast and crew thumbnail biographies • Original advertising • Theatrical trailers.
1934 105m/B Clark Gable, Claudette Colbert, Roscoe Karns, Walter Connolly, Alan Hale, Ward Bond; **D:** Frank Capra; **W:** Robert Riskin; **C:** Joseph Walker. *AWARDS:* Academy Awards '34: Best Actor (Gable), Best Actress (Colbert), Best Adapted Screenplay, Best Director (Capra), Best Picture; American Film Institute (AFI) '98: Top 100, National Film Registry '93.

It's a Wonderful Life

Capra's classic fantasy is corny but inspirational and heartwarming with fine performances in all of the key roles. Jimmy Stewart is at his best as George Bailey, the man who is given a chance by an angel (Travers) to see what the world would have been like without his presence. Though the film was a commercial flop in its initial release, it has become an enduring audience favorite and now receives a sterling incarnation on DVD. Both image and sound are flawless. Actually, the soundtrack has been enhanced so that it is better than older tapes—particularly the cheaper editions created when the title went into the public domain. The black-and-white photography is superb; this disc is better than some theatrical presentations I've seen. The extras (on the B-side of the two-sided disc) are well chosen. It's worth owning for the swimming pool scene (chapter 8) if nothing else. —*MM*
Movie: ♫♫♫♫ **DVD:** ♫♫♫♫
Republic Pictures Home Video (Cat #42071, UPC #017153207125). Full frame. Dolby Digital Mono; THX Mastered. $24.98. Keepcase. *LANG:* English; French; Spanish. *SUB:* French; Spanish. *CAP:* English. *FEATURES:* 28 chapter links • "Making of" featurette • 1991 remembrance by Frank Capra Jr. and Jimmy Stewart.
1946 125m/B James Stewart, Donna Reed, Henry Travers, Thomas Mitchell, Lionel Barrymore, Samuel S. Hinds, Frank Faylen, Gloria Grahame, H.B. Warner, Ellen Corby, Sheldon Leonard, Beulah Bondi, Ward Bond, Frank Albertson, Todd Karns, Mary Treen, Charles Halton; **D:** Frank Capra; **W:** Frances Goodrich, Albert Hackett, Jo Swerling; **C:** Joseph Biroc, Joseph Walker; **M:** Dimitri Tiomkin. *AWARDS:* American Film Institute (AFI) '98: Top 100; Golden Globe Awards '47: Best Director (Capra), National Film Registry '90; *NOM:* Academy Awards '46: Best Actor (Stewart), Best Director (Capra), Best Film Editing, Best Picture, Best Sound.

Ivan the Terrible, Part 1

Sergei Eisenstein's epic has aged oddly. Today, the acting style, exaggerated costumes, and grim black-and-white interiors will certainly put off most younger viewers.

The target audience of those more familiar with early Soviet and European films will be much more enthusiastic. In the first film Ivan (Cherkasov) marries and then faces the Mongol invaders. *Part II* focuses more on court intrigues. Again, the score by Prokofiev is impressive. Nikolai Cherkasov, who also had the lead in *Alexander Nevsky*, has to wear even more strange wigs here. On DVD, the image looks superior to many films of its time. (The film was made while the Soviet Union was still at war with Germany.) Rob Edelman's extensive liner notes provide excellent background to both films, which were meant to be the first two volumes of a trilogy. —*MM* **AKA:** Ivan Groznyi.
Movie: ♫♫♫ **DVD:** ♫♫♫
Image Entertainment (Cat #ID4577CODVD, UPC #014381457728). Full frame. Uncompressed PCM soundtrack. $24.99. Snapper. *LANG:* Russian. *SUB:* English. *FEATURES:* 15 chapter links • Liner notes by Rob Edelman.
1944 100m/B *RU* Nikolai Cherkasov, Ludmila Tselikovskaya, Serafina Birman, Piotr Kadochnikev; **D:** Sergei Eisenstein; **W:** Sergei Eisenstein; **C:** Eduard Tisse; **M:** Sergei Prokofiev.

Ivan the Terrible, Part 2

Landed gentry conspire to dethrone the czar (Cherkasov) in this continuation of the innovative epic. More stunning imagery from Eisenstein, the early master. In technical terms, the DVD is identical to the first film. —*MM* **AKA:** Ivan the Terrible, Part 2: The Boyars' Plot; Ivan Groznyi 2.
Movie: ♫♫♫ **DVD:** ♫♫♫
Image Entertainment (Cat #ID4578CODVD, UPC #014381457827). Full frame. Uncompressed PCM soundtrack. $24.99. Snapper. *LANG:* Russian. *SUB:* English. *FEATURES:* 14 chapter links • Liner notes by Rob Edelman.
1946 87m/B *RU* Nikolai Cherkasov, Ludmila Tselikovskaya, Serafina Birman, Piotr Kadochnikev; **D:** Sergei Eisenstein; **W:** Sergei Eisenstein; **C:** Eduard Tisse, Andrei Moskvin; **M:** Sergei Prokofiev.

I've Been Waiting for You

California teen Sarah (Chalke), who has an interest in the occult, moves with her mom (Post) to a New England town. Her fellow teens begin to believe she's a witch out for revenge on the descendants of the townspeople who burned another witch who had the same name. The film is based on a novel by Lois Duncan who knows her audience well. Unfortunately, this made-for-TV attempt is mired in substandard production values made more glaring by DVD. Even simple shapes tend to dissolve in fast pans; dark areas are heavily pixelated. If anything, the no-frills disc may be a bit worse than VHS tape. —*MM*
Movie: ♫♫ **DVD:** ♫

Sunland Studios (Cat #PM 366-D, UPC #757449336633). Full frame. $24.95. Keepcase. *LANG:* English. *CAP:* English. *FEATURES:* 6 chapter links.
1998 (PG-13) 90m/C Sarah Chalke, Soleil Moon Frye, Markie Post, Christian Campbell, Tom Dugan; **D:** Christopher Leitch; **W:** Duane Poole.

Jack & the Beanstalk

While baby-sitting, Lou falls asleep and dreams he's Jack in this spoof of the famous fairy tale.
Movie: ♫♫ **DVD:** NYR
Digital Disc Entertainment (Cat #514). Full frame. Dolby Digital Mono. $9.99. Keepcase. *FEATURES:* Cast bios • Trivia.
1952 78m/C Bud Abbott, Lou Costello, Buddy Baer, Dorothy Ford, Barbara Brown, William Farnum; **D:** Jean Yarbrough; **W:** Nathaniel Curtis; **C:** George Robinson; **M:** Heinz Roemheld.

Jack Be Nimble

New Zealand Gothic horror has been properly compared to Stephen King's work and to Peter Jackson's *Heavenly Creatures,* though it's much darker and more frightening. Jack (Arquette) and his sister Dora (Smuts-Kennedy) are taken from their parents as children and raised in separate homes. She goes to middle-class suburbia; he winds up in a rural hellhole. His tortured upbringing there turns him into a rebellious, unstable young man who's driven to find his lost sister. By then she has begun an affair with Teddy (Lawrence), who understands her on an unusually sympathetic level. And that is all anyone should know about the plot. Writer-director Maxwell is an imaginative filmmaker who really knows what he's doing with grim, grainy images that gain little on DVD. And they should not. The bleak visual aspects are just right for a story set in the darker corners of the imagination. Despite its obviously limited budget, the film is strong stuff, building to an unpredictable finish that's not for everyone. Recommended on tape or disc. Image and sound are virtually identical on either. —*MM*
Movie: ♫♫♫ **DVD:** ♫♫♫
Image Entertainment (Cat #ID5598FMDVD, UPC #014381559828). Full frame. Dolby Digital Surround. $24.99. Snapper. *LANG:* English. *FEATURES:* 16 chapter links.
1994 (R) 93m/C *NZ* Alexis Arquette, Sarah Kennedy, Bruno Lawrence; **D:** Garth Maxwell; **W:** Garth Maxwell; **C:** Donald Duncan; **M:** Chris Neal.

The Jack Bull

Cusack's father adapted a 19th-century German novel, *Michael Kohlhaas,* by Heinrich Von Kleist, into an American western set in Wyoming. Myrl Redding (Cusack) is a peaceful horse trader who demands justice when Ballard (Jones), a wealthy landowner, beats two of Redding's horses and his Indian caretaker. Since Ballard has the local law in his pocket, Redding gets no satisfaction and turns to vigilante tactics.

Movie: ♫♫➤ **DVD:** NYR
HBO Home Video (Cat #91574). Dolby Digital Stereo. $24.98. Snapper. *LANG:* English; Spanish. *SUB:* French; Spanish. *CAP:* English. *FEATURES:* Cast and crew thumbnail bios ➾ "Making of" featurette.
1999 (R) 120m/C John Cusack, L.Q. (Justus E. McQueen) Jones, John Goodman, Rodney A. Grant, Miranda Otto, John C. McGinley, John Savage, Jay O. Sanders, Scott Wilson, Drake Bell, Glenn Morshower, Ken Pogue; *D:* John Badham; *W:* Dick Cusack; *C:* Gale Tattersall; *M:* Lennie Niehaus.

Jack Frost

Convicted serial killer Jack Frost (McDonald) mutates after exposure to experimental liquid DNA. He becomes a killer snowman in a town preparing for—you guessed it—the annual Snowman festival. The horror comedy actually has a nicely nasty sense of humor. On DVD, it looks remarkably good for a low-budget B-movie, at least better than the silly formula suggests. For fans of cheap horror only. —*MM*

Movie: ♫♫ **DVD:** ♫♫➤
Simitar Entertainment (Cat #7422, UPC #082551742226). Widescreen letterboxed. Dolby Digital Stereo; Dolby Digital 5.1 Surround Stereo. $14.98. Keepcase. *LANG:* English. *FEATURES:* 8 chapter links ➾ Production factoids.
1997 (R) 89m/C Scott McDonald, Christopher Allport, F. William Parker; *D:* Michael Cooney; *W:* Michael Cooney; *C:* Dean Lent.

Jack Frost

Formula feel-good flick is as emotionally honest as a plastic snowflake. Jack Frost (Keaton) is a struggling musician who spends too much time away from wife (Preston) and son (Cross), and then is killed in an accident trying to get back to them for Christmas. A year later, the kid makes a snowman, dresses it in deceased dad's duds, blows a mournful note on dad's harmonica and, SHAZAM!, Jack's back as a creepy special-effects snowman. Additional warning: Keaton sings. DVD handles all of the saccharine action with lamentable clarity. Sound is excellent, too. —*MM*

Movie: ♫ **DVD:** ♫♫➤
Warner Home Video, Inc. (Cat #17227, UPC #085391722724). Widescreen anamorphic; full frame. Dolby Digital 5.1 Surround Stereo. $24.98. Snapper. *LANG:* English; French. *SUB:* Spanish. *CAP:* English. *FEATURES:* 27 chapter links ➾ Cast and crew thumbnail biographies ➾ Behind-the-scenes featurette ➾ Theatrical trailer.
1998 (PG) 95m/C Michael Keaton, Kelly Preston, Joseph Cross, Mark Addy, Eli Marienthal, Dweezil Zappa, Henry Rollins, Andy Lawrence, Ahmet Zappa, Jeff Cesario; *D:* Troy Miller; *W:* Mark Steven Johnson, Steven L. Bloom, Jonathan

Roberts, Jeff Cesario; *C:* Laszlo Kovacs; *M:* Trevor Rabin.

Jack-O

The equivalent of a suburban Halloween spook house is a low-budget horror comedy emphasizing laughs over scares. Like any good spook house, it's also a loving evocation of the season. The opening nursery rhyme, "Mr. Jack will break your back and cut off your head with a whack, whack, whack," sets the tone. The bloody effects that follow are about the least realistic you'll ever see, and the hoary plot revolves around a warlock who's resurrected as a pumpkin-headed slasher. Young Ryan Latshaw is fine as the trick-or-treating hero. He shares the screen with a host of horror veterans who ham it up happily. If it weren't for one shower scene, this one would be recommended for kids. Instead, it's aimed more at nostalgic drive-in fans, and they will not mind the threadbare production values. The many visual shortcomings are actually more obvious on DVD. The disc is not substantially better than VHS tape. —*MM*

Movie: ♫♫➤ **DVD:** ♫♫
Image Entertainment (Cat #ID5599FMDVD, UPC #014381559927). Full frame. Dolby Digital Stereo. $24.99. Snapper. *LANG:* English. *FEATURES:* 12 chapter links.
1995 (R) 90m/C Linnea Quigley, Ryan Latshaw, Cameron Mitchell, John Carradine, Dawn Wildsmith, Brinke Stevens; *D:* Steve Latshaw; *W:* Patrick Moran; *C:* Maxwell J. Beck; *M:* Jeff Walton.

The Jackal (CE)

Remake of Fred Zinneman's *Day of the Jackal* completely lacks the element that makes the original so compelling—realism. The original story of an attempt by French army officers to have Charles DeGaulle assassinated is closely based on fact. This updated version is typical Hollywood hokum about Russian gangsters buying a hit on an American official. Willis phones in his performance as the killer. What could anyone expect of Richard Gere as an IRA gunman hired by the Feds to find oh, never mind. The plot is an embarrassment to all concerned. The DVD looks and sounds excellent in every regard, and director Michael Caton-Jones mounts a brave but futile defense of his film on the commentary track. —*MM*

Movie: woof **DVD:** ♫♫
Universal Studios Home Video (Cat #20262, UPC #025192026225). Widescreen (2.35:1) letterboxed. Dolby Digital 5.1 Surround Stereo; Dolby Digital Surround Stereo. $34.98. Keepcase. *LANG:* English; French. *SUB:* Spanish. *CAP:* English. *FEATURES:* 31 chapter links ➾ "Making of" featurette ➾ Commentary: Michael Caton-Jones ➾ Production notes ➾ Cast and crew thumbnail biographies ➾ Theatrical trailer.
1997 (R) 124m/C Bruce Willis, Richard Gere, Sidney Poitier, Diane Venora, Mathilda May, Stephen Spinella, John Cunning-

ham, J.K. Simmons, Tess Harper, Richard Lineback, Jack Black, David Hayman, Steve Bassett; *D:* Michael Caton-Jones; *W:* Chuck Pfarrer; *C:* Karl Walter Lindenlaub; *M:* Carter Burwell.

Jackie Chan: My Story

To make this video biography, the filmmakers followed Jackie Chan around for several months. They make extensive use of clips from his films, and whenever possible, they go wild with camera movement. The quality of the image varies with the material, of course. The original footage is first-rate. The rest ranges between fair and very good. Also, this is a double-sided disc with narrator David Wu and the star speaking in English on one side, Mandarin on the other. Appropriately, Jackie introduces the disc with a quote from Buster Keaton. —*MM*

Movie: ♫♫♫ **DVD:** ♫♫♫
Tai Seng Video Marketing (Cat #MS/DVD/037/98, UPC #8950170003 74). Widescreen letterboxed. Dolby Digital Surround Stereo. $29.95. Keepcase. *LANG:* Mandarin; English. *SUB:* Traditional & Simplified Chinese; English; Korean; Indonesian & Malaysia Bahasa; Thai; Malaysian; Japanese. *FEATURES:* 9 chapter links ➾ Jackie Chan thumbnail biography ➾ Select filmography ➾ "Making of" essay.
1997 74m/C *W:* Jackie Chan, Chien Wen Lung, Tony White, Bey Logan, Richard J. Havis; *Nar:* David Wu.

Jackie Chan: My Stunts

Companion disc to *Jackie Chan: My Story* focuses on Chan's work behind the camera. It contains enough of his big action sequences, but he's more interested in explaining how they're done and what makes his work unique. Amazingly, he's able to do that without coming across as a raging egomaniac. Instead, he's letting you in on the joke. He emphasizes the theatricality of his approach and the importance of dance to his martial arts. He doesn't ignore editing, camera placement, and lenses, either, but none of this gets too technical. Of course, image quality varies, but the new footage is excellent. So is the sound. The two-sided disc has the English version on one side, Mandarin on the other. —*MM*

Movie: ♫♫♫ **DVD:** ♫♫♫
Tai Seng Video Marketing (Cat #MS/DVD/048/98). Widescreen letterboxed. Dolby Digital 5.1 Surround Stereo. $49.95. Keepcase. *LANG:* Mandarin; English. *SUB:* Traditional & Simplified Chinese; English; Japanese; Bahasa Malaysian; Thai; Vietnamese; Spanish. *FEATURES:* 9 chapter links ➾ "Making of" essay.
1998 97m/C Jackie Chan; *D:* Jackie Chan; *W:* Bey Logan; *Nar:* Michael Brown.

Jackie Chan's First Strike

Once again, Chan plays a Hong Kong cop known simply as Jackie. This time he's on the trail of spies from Hong Kong to the Ukraine to Australia. The big scenes are set on snowmobiles, in a big aquarium, and at a funeral. Though the pace is a little slow at first, the film ends with long, involving chase sequences. Chan has been quick to admit the influence of Buster Keaton and Harold Lloyd on his work. He's playing essentially the same character they invented—the little guy who's surrounded by larger enemies and who survives with self-deprecating wit, fast moves, and humor. And like those early screen clowns, Jackie Chan does his own stunts. This film contains some of his most inventive creations. He can do amazing things with such simple props as a folding table, a piece of scaffolding, or a stepladder. Working with director-stunt coordinator Stanley Tong, Chan has choreographed the physical action into fluid dance routines. If my memory is at all accurate, the crisp DVD image actually looks better than the theatrical release. Even extremely bright snow scenes contain no visible flaws. —*MM* **AKA:** First Strike; Police Story 4.

Movie: 🎬🎬🎬 **DVD:** 🎬🎬🎬➤
New Line Home Video (Cat #N4669, UPC #794043466922). Full frame; widescreen (2.35:1) letterboxed. Dolby Surround 5.1 (English); Dolby Surround (French). $24.98. Snapper. *LANG:* English; French. *SUB:* English; French; Spanish. *FEATURES:* 21 chapter links • Theatrical trailer • Cast and crew biographies and filmographies.
1996 (PG-13) 87m/C *HK* Jackie Chan, Bill Tung, Jackson Lou, Chen Chun (Annie) Wu, Jouri (Yuri) Petrov, Grishajeva Nonna; **D:** Stanley Tong; **W:** Stanley Tong, Greg Mellott, Nick Tramontane, Elliot Tong; **C:** Jingle Ma; **M:** J. Peter Robinson. *AWARDS:* NOM: MTV Movie Awards '97: Best Fight (Jackie Chan/A ladder).

Jackie Chan's Who Am I

Jackie (Chan) is recruited by the CIA to join a team of commandos on a raid on a secret weapons research lab in South Africa. The good guys are betrayed by their leader. Only Jackie survives and he's got amnesia. Our hero zips through a globe-hopping plot with assassins on his trail. The action scenes are up to the star's high standards but the DVD image lacks the brightness and sharp focus of his best American work. The concluding outtakes are O.K. —*MM* **AKA:** Who Am I; Ngo Hai Sui.

Movie: 🎬🎬🎬 **DVD:** 🎬🎬🎬
Columbia Tristar Home Video (Cat #02717, UPC #043396027176). Widescreen (1.85:1) letterboxed; full frame. Dolby Digital 5.1 Surround Stereo; Dolby Digital Surround Stereo. $24.95. Keepcase. *LANG:* English; French. *SUB:* English;

French. *FEATURES:* 28 chapter links • Theatrical trailer.
1998 (PG-13) 108m/C *HK* Jackie Chan, Ed Nelson, Ron Smerczak, Michelle Ferre, Mirai Yamamoto; **D:** Jackie Chan, Benny Chan; **W:** Jackie Chan, Lee Reynolds, Susan Chan; **C:** Hang-Sang Poon; **M:** Nathan Wang.

Jacob's Ladder

A man struggles with events he experienced while serving in Vietnam. Gradually, he becomes unable to separate reality from the strange, psychotic world into which he increasingly lapses. His friends and family try to help him before he's lost forever. Great story potential is flawed by too many flashbacks, leaving the viewer more confused than the characters. The DVD transfer is of average sharpness and has some minor grain sporadically in earthtones. There are some artifacts but they don't distract. Colors seem natural and have no real problems with bleed, although they might have benefitted from a boost in contrast. Brightness levels are consistent and comfortable. Blacks are close to true. There is not a lot going on in the 5.1 track (Surround wise), but overall the music sounds rich and the dialogue is crisp. —*JO*

Movie: 🎬🎬➤ **DVD:** 🎬🎬🎬
Artisan Entertainment (Cat #60458, UPC #012236045809). Widescreen (1.85:1) anamorphic. Dolby Digital 5.1. $24.98. Keepcase. *LANG:* English. *SUB:* Spanish. *CAP:* English. *FEATURES:* 36 chapter links • Theatrical trailer • Commentary: Adrian Lynne • "Making of" documentary • Production notes • Cast and crew bios • Dual-layered RSDL.
1990 (R) 116m/C Tim Robbins, Elizabeth Pena, Danny Aiello, Matt Craven, Pruitt Taylor Vince, Jason Alexander, Patricia Kalember, Eriq La Salle, Ving Rhames, Macaulay Culkin; **D:** Adrian Lyne; **W:** Bruce Joel Rubin; **C:** Jeffrey L. Kimball; **M:** Maurice Jarre.

Jade

Sleazy whodunnit scraped from the bottom of the Eszterhas barrel (and it's a deep one) has hot-shot San Francisco Assistant D.A. David Corelli (Caruso) tracking a trail of pubic hairs across San Francisco. Seems he's caught up in the murder of a millionaire that points to his ex-lover, psychologist Katrina Gavin (Fiorentino), as the killer. Oh yeah, she's also a kinky call girl of choice to California's rich and famous, and happens to be married to Corelli's best friend (Palminteri). Psycho-thriller with little of either injects lots of lurid details (and a car chase scene that Friedkin has done much better elsewhere) in an attempt to curtail boredom; it doesn't work. Combine it with *Showgirls* for the No Self-Respect Film Festival, then go to confession. From the opening sequence, which features a long searching tracking shot set to music by Loreena McKennitt, it's obvious that

this will be a very enjoyable DVD to watch. The 5.1 sound is very ambient and has incredibly clean, punchy bass tones and crisp highs. There are also many Surround effects and imaging and separation are both excellent. The picture is very sharp and grain is never bothersome. Colors are strong and accurately present the subtle changes and shadings of the lush and stylized cinematography. The contrast and brightness levels ensure proper detail without loss of changes in lighting conditions. —*JO*

Movie: 🎬➤ **DVD:** 🎬🎬🎬➤
Paramount Home Video (Cat #329867, UPC #097363298670). Full frame. Dolby Digital 5.1; Dolby Surround. $29.99. Keepcase. *LANG:* English. *CAP:* English. *FEATURES:* 16 chapter links • Theatrical trailer.
1995 (R) 94m/C David Caruso, Linda Fiorentino, Chazz Palminteri, Michael Biehn, Richard Crenna, Kenneth King, Angie Everhart; **D:** William Friedkin; **W:** Joe Eszterhas; **C:** Andrzej Bartkowiak; **M:** James Horner.

Jail Bait

Early Wood crime drama focuses on a group of small-time crooks who are always in trouble with the law and so blackmail a plastic surgeon. The title refers to a handgun. On DVD, the image is fine, unusually so. Of course the sound, the acting, the pace, and the ludicrous "comic relief" including a long black-face routine, are as lousy as they've always been. —*MM* **AKA:** Hidden Face.

Movie: 🎬➤ **DVD:** 🎬🎬🎬
Image Entertainment (Cat #ID8601CODVD, UPC #014381860122). Full frame. Dolby Digital Mono. $24.99. Snapper. *LANG:* English. *FEATURES:* 12 chapter links.
1954 80m/B Timothy Farrell, Clancy Malone, Lyle Talbot, Steve Reeves, Herbert Rawlinson, Dolores Fuller, Theodora Thurman, Conrad Brooks, Mona McKinnon; **D:** Edward D. Wood Jr.; **W:** Edward D. Wood Jr., Alex Gordon; **C:** William C. Thompson.

Jailhouse Rock

While serving time for manslaughter, Vince Everett (Presley) learns to play the guitar. After his release, he becomes a top recording star. The Pandro S. Berman production may be the best of the early films to capture the presence of a star in the making. For everyone else, the black-and-white action is dated. The image presents no problems for DVD. Sound is noticeably lacking. —*MM*

Movie: 🎬🎬➤ **DVD:** 🎬🎬➤
MGM Home Entertainment (Cat #906611, UPC #027616661128). Widescreen anamorphic; full frame. Dolby Digital Mono. $24.98. Snapper. *LANG:* English; French; Spanish. *SUB:* English; French; Spanish. *FEATURES:* 28 chapter links • Theatrical trailer.
1957 (G) 96m/B Elvis Presley, Judy Tyler, Vaughn Taylor, Dean Jones, Mickey Shaughnessy, William Forrest, Glenn

Strange, Jennifer Holden, Anne Neyland; *D:* Richard Thorpe; *W:* Guy Troper; *C:* Robert J. Bronner; *M:* Jeff Alexander.

Jakob the Liar

After the success of *Life Is Beautiful,* this similar story (actually a remake of a 1974 film) was delayed from theatrical release. In Nazi-occupied Poland, Jewish cafe owner Jakob Heym (Williams, who also served as executive producer) claims to have a radio and invents stories to keep up the spirits of his daughter and fellow ghetto residents. As is almost always the case with stories attempting to deal with this difficult subject, the results are mixed. For my money, the clarity of the DVD image is something of a flaw, as it sanitizes the action. Sound is fine, too. —*MM*
Movie: 🐾🐾▶ *DVD:* 🐾🐾🐾
Columbia Tristar Home Video (Cat #02844, UPC #043396028449). Widescreen (1.85:1) letterboxed; full frame. Dolby Digital 5.1 Surround Stereo. $28.95. Keepcase. *LANG:* English. *SUB:* English. *FEATURES:* 28 chapter links ● Commentary: Peter Kassovitz ● "Making of" featurette ● Production notes ● Cast and crew thumbnail biographies.
1999 (PG-13) 114m/C Robin Williams, Armin Mueller-Stahl, Alan Arkin, Bob Balaban, Michael Jeter, Liev Schreiber, Hannah Taylor Gordon, Nina Siemaszko, Mathieu Kassovitz, Mark Margolis; *D:* Peter Kassovitz; *W:* Peter Kassovitz, Didier Decoin; *C:* Elemer Ragalyi; *M:* Ed Shearmur. *AWARDS: NOM:* Golden Raspberry Awards '99: Worst Actor (Williams).

Jamaica Inn

In old Cornwall, an orphan girl (O'Hara) becomes involved with smugglers led by the local squire (Laughton). Though this period piece is not as involving as Hitchcock's later suspense films, it does provide a nice showcase for Laughton, who has a wonderful time with a villainous role, and for a young Maureen O'Hara at her loveliest. Overall, the DVD looks remarkably good even in the dark-and-stormy-night scenes. The sound is noticeably thin by today's standards. —*MM*
Movie: 🐾🐾▶ *DVD:* 🐾🐾🐾
Delta/Laserlight (Cat #82 032, UPC #018111997836). Full frame. $14.99. Keepcase. *LANG:* English. *SUB:* Spanish; Japanese; Chinese. *FEATURES:* Introduction by Tony Curtis ● Hitchcock promo for *The Birds* ● 24 chapter links.
1939 98m/B *GB* Charles Laughton, Maureen O'Hara, Leslie Banks, Robert Newton; *D:* Alfred Hitchcock; *W:* Sidney Gilliat, Joan Harrison; *C:* Harry Stradling; *M:* Eric Fenby.

Jamaica Inn (Image)

This DVD claims to have been made from a 35mm archive print and it does have a slightly brighter look and sound when com-

pared to the lower-priced LaserLight edition. —*MM*
Movie: 🐾🐾▶ *DVD:* 🐾🐾🐾
Image Entertainment (Cat #K105, UPC #738329010522). Full frame. $29.98. Snapper. *LANG:* English. *FEATURES:* 12 chapter links ● Liner notes by Elliott Stein.
1939 98m/B

James Dean Double Feature: Hill Number One / I Am a Fool

This DVD is made of two early '50s James Dean television appearances. He has a small part as John, in *Hill Number One,* a religious show combining a contemporary combat story with the resurrection of Christ. In *I Am a Fool,* he's a poor boy who falls for rich girl Natalie Wood. Ronald Reagan provides the introduction. The quality of both is very poor, with all shortcomings due to the original material, not the transfer. The image is muddy; sound nondescript. —*MM AKA:* Hill Number One; I Am a Fool.
Movie: 🐾▶ *DVD:* 🐾🐾
Delta/Laserlight (Cat #82014, UPC #018111999830). Full frame. $14.99. Keepcase. *LANG:* English. *SUB:* Spanish; Japanese; Chinese. *FEATURES:* 19 chapter links ● Introduction by Tony Curtis ● Theatrical trailer for *Giant.*
1951 120m/B James Dean, Michael Ansara, Leif Erickson, Ruth Hussey, Roddy McDowall, Natalie Wood; *D:* Arthur Presson, Don Medford.

James Dean Story

Robert Altman produced this early video biography of James Dean using film clips and photographs. The footage includes outtakes from *East of Eden,* the Hollywood premiere of *Giant,* and the infamous Highway Public Safety message that Dean made for television. The image throughout is murky and that appears to have been a deliberate choice by the producers who emphasize the moody, tragic side of the Dean mythos. Sound is adequate. The three-bone technical rating does not apply to "The Bells of Cockaigne," a one-hour Armstrong Circle drama that has the ghostly look of old TV, which is included on the disc. —*MM*
Movie: 🐾🐾🐾 *DVD:* 🐾🐾🐾
Delta/Laserlight (Cat #82013, UPC #018111999939). Full frame. $14.99. Keepcase. *LANG:* English. *SUB:* Spanish; Chinese; Japanese. *FEATURES:* 39 chapter links ● Introduction by Tony Curtis ● Theatrical trailer for *Rebel without a Cause.*
1957 140m/B James Dean; *D:* George W. George, Robert Altman; *W:* Stewart Stern; *M:* Leith Stevens; *Nar:* Martin Gabel.

Jan Svankmajer's Faust

Svankmajer's long-awaited follow-up to his acclaimed *Alice* is an equally astounding

version of the myth of Dr. Faustus. By merging live action with stop-motion and claymation animation, Svankmajer has created an unsettling universe presided over by diabolic life-size marionettes and haunted by skulking human messengers from hell. The disc's video and audio transfers are quite well-done. The video features strong, vivid colors though shadows and blacks are occasionally muddied (some occasional blotches also occurred on the screen while viewing). The audio is crisp and clear, with no thin sounds or tinny dialogue. —*MJT AKA:* Faust.
Movie: 🐾🐾🐾 *DVD:* 🐾🐾▶
Image Entertainment (Cat #K122DVD, UPC #738329012229). Full frame. Dolby Digital Stereo. $29.99. Snapper. *LANG:* English. *FEATURES:* 12 chapter links.
1994 97m/C *CZ GB D:* Jan Svankmajer, Ernst Gossner; *W:* Jan Svankmajer; *C:* Svatopluk Maly; *V:* Petr Cepek.

Jane Doe

This award-winning (Best Feature, New York International Independent Film and Video Festival) independent is a low-budget, distaff answer to *Leaving Las Vegas,* set partially in Atlantic City. Calista Flockhart sheds her uptight television personality of Ally McBeal to play a wild, drug-addicted waif who likes role playing and the attentions of a struggling writer named Horace (Peditto). The punchy, Latin-laced pop score is fashion forward. On the downside, the punky, jagged '80s style of the film and interactive screens only looks like a run-through for a video effects sequence—patchy and garish. The two trailers are almost identical; one is a bit racier than the other. —*JK AKA:* Pictures of Baby Jane Doe.
Movie: 🐾🐾 *DVD:* 🐾🐾▶
A-PIX Entertainment Inc. (Cat #ID5895UMDVD, UPC #014381589528). Widescreen (1.85:1). Dolby Digital Stereo. $24.99. Snapper. *LANG:* English. *FEATURES:* 15 chapter links ● Interactive menus ● 2 theatrical trailers.
1996 (R) 92m/C Calista Flockhart, Elina Lowensohn, Joe Ragno, Christopher Peditto; *D:* Paul Peditto; *W:* Paul Peditto.

Jane Street

Freshly installed in a new city, new apartment, and new job, Kim (Hoffman) enters into an ill-advised affair with her boss (Kelly). At the same time she experiences plumbing problems and visions of a dark-haired woman's death. This is a Playboy production so the working out of the complications is less important than the softcore love scenes. Though the film was made on a strict budget, the DVD looks pretty good. Blinds do not flash, though dark areas tend to lose detail and one red dress glows. The disc is a slight improvement over VHS tape. —*MM*
Movie: 🐾🐾 *DVD:* 🐾🐾▶
Image Entertainment (Cat #ID5842PLDVD, UPC #014381584226). Full frame. Dolby

Digital Stereo. $19.99. Snapper. *LANG:* English. *FEATURES:* 16 chapter links.
1996 91m/C Linda Hoffman, D.K. Kelly, Carrie Stevens, Robert Gant; *D:* Vicangelo Bulluck; *W:* Chris Chisholm; *C:* Geza Sinkovics; *M:* K. Alexander Wilkinson.

Jason and the Argonauts

Jason, son of the King of Thessaly, sails on the Argo to the land of Colchis, where the Golden Fleece is guarded by a seven-headed Hydra. Superb special effects and multitudes of mythological creatures, as well as an army of skeletons grown from the teeth of the slain Hydra. Fun for the whole family. Features another superb Bernard Herrmann score. This DVD is better looking than all the previous home video releases, including the Criterion Collection version. The picture is sharper and the colors much stronger. The original film always had additional grain during the effects sequences, and the DVD may add a little to it, but still looks great. If there are artifacts, they blend in perfectly with the blurring effects of the stop-motion animation and don't detract in the least. Even with the more vibrant colors, the blacks are still very true. Contrast and brightness levels are also better than earlier editions and seem to accent details. The sound is mono and a little flat sounding, but again improves upon its predecessors. —*JO*
Movie: 🎦🎦🎦 *DVD:* 🎦🎦🎦
Columbia Tristar Home Video (Cat #00259, UPC #043396002593). Widescreen (1:85.1) letterboxed; full frame. Mono. $28.95. Keepcase. *LANG:* English; Spanish; French. *SUB:* English; Spanish; French. *CAP:* English. *FEATURES:* 28 chapter links • Theatrical trailer • Interview with Ray Harryhausen.
1963 (G) 104m/C *GB* Todd Armstrong, Nancy Kovack, Gary Raymond, Laurence Naismith, Nigel Green, Michael Gwynn, Honor Blackman, Niall MacGinnis, Douglas Wilmer, Jack Gwillim; *D:* Don Chaffey; *W:* Jan Read, Beverley Cross; *C:* Wilkie Cooper; *M:* Bernard Herrmann.

Jawbreaker

Writer-director Stein steals the plot from *Heathers* and adds a dash of S&M to this black comedy about high school clique queens. Courtney (McGowan) is the leader of a group of glam princesses who accidentally kill one of their own during a mock kidnapping. Fellow beauties Julie (Gayheart) and Marcie (Benz) help her cover up, but class nerd Fern (Greer) is a witness. Further complicating things are nosy detective Vera Cruz (Grier) and the upcoming prom, which provides a *Carrie*-style finale. Although the movie treads familiar ground, McGowan's performance keeps it interesting. Cameo by shock rocker Marilyn Manson, billed as Brian Warner. On DVD, the surreal colors—particularly the pallid skin tones and the slightly off

reds favored by Courtney—are all too accurate. Sound is fine. —*MM*
Movie: 🎦🎦 *DVD:* 🎦🎦🎦
Columbia Tristar Home Video (Cat #3615). Full frame; widescreen (1.85:1) letterboxed. Dolby Digital Surround Stereo; Dolby Digital 5.1 Surround Stereo. $24.95. Keepcase. *LANG:* English. *SUB:* English. *FEATURES:* Commentary: Darren Stein • Cast and crew thumbnail bios • Trailers • 28 chapter links.
1998 (R) 87m/C Rose McGowan, Rebecca Gayheart, Julie Benz, Charlotte Roldan, Judy Greer, Chad Christ, Carol Kane, Pam Grier, William Katt, P.J. Soles, Jeff Conaway, Ethan Erickson; *D:* Darren Stein; *W:* Darren Stein; *C:* Amy Vincent. *AWARDS: NOM:* MTV Movie Awards '99: Best Villain (McGowan).

Jaws: The Revenge

Third sequel finds Mrs. Brody (Gary) pursued the world over by a seemingly personally motivated Great White. The home video version includes footage not seen in the theatrical release. Another altogether inferior entry in the downwardly spiraling series.
Movie: 🎦 *DVD:* NYR
Goodtimes Entertainment (Cat #81030). Widescreen (1.85:1) letterboxed. Dolby Digital Stereo. $19.98. Snapper. *LANG:* English. *SUB:* French; Spanish. *CAP:* English.
1987 (PG-13) 87m/C Lorraine Gary, Lance Guest, Karen Young, Mario Van Peebles, Michael Caine, Judith Barsi, Lynn Whitfield; *D:* Joseph Sargent; *W:* Michael deGuzman; *C:* John McPherson; *M:* Michael Small.

The Jazz Singer

Though this Neil Diamond star vehicle has been roundly ridiculed, it's an interesting artifact of the late 1970s. The New York locations are well filmed and the concert scenes shine forth with true tackiness. Yes, the acting and the rags-to-riches story have many moments of unintentional humor, and they're all here on the DVD. The image is rough throughout and the sound is nothing special. The main attraction of the disc for Diamond's fans is a separate jump-to-song index. Look for Ernie Hudson as a nightclub heckler. —*MM*
Movie: 🎦🎦▸ *DVD:* 🎦🎦▸
Artisan Entertainment (Cat #33334, UPC #017153333428). Widescreen (1.85:1) letterboxed. Dolby Digital Surround Stereo. $24.98. Keepcase. *LANG:* English. *CAP:* English. *FEATURES:* 36 chapter links • Jump-to-song index.
1980 (PG) 115m/C Neil Diamond, Laurence Olivier, Lucie Arnaz, Catlin Adams, Franklin Ajaye, Ernie Hudson; *D:* Richard Fleischer; *W:* Herbert Baker, Stephen H. Foreman; *C:* Isidore Mankofsky; *M:* Leonard Rosenman, Neil Diamond. *AWARDS:* Golden Raspberry Awards '80: Worst Actor (Diamond), Worst Supporting Actor (Olivier).

Jeremiah Johnson

Johnson (Redford) turns his back on civilization, circa 1850, heads for the hills, and learns a new code of survival in a brutal land of isolated mountains populated with hostile Indians. In the process, he becomes part of the mountains and their wildlife. A notable and picturesque film based on the life of "liver eating" Johnson. This DVD handles all the extremes of lighting conditions—indoor earthtones, bright-blue skies, even brighter snow scenes—equally well. The image is very sharp, with little grain, and no noticeable artifacts. As the scenes shift from bright to dim, the contrast and brightness levels remain consistent. Colors are at times stunning; bleed is almost nonexistent. They've given the DVD a 5.1 soundtrack, and although there's not a ton of Surround, it more than fills the room with crisp, dynamic music and effects, while not hindering the dialogue. Well worth owning. —*JO*
Movie: 🎦🎦🎦 *DVD:* 🎦🎦🎦
Warner Home Video, Inc. (Cat #11061, UPC #085391106128). Widescreen (1.85:1) letterboxed; full frame. Dolby Digital 5.1; Dolby Digital Mono. $24.98. Snapper. *LANG:* English (DD5.1); French (DDM). *SUB:* French; Spanish. *CAP:* English. *FEATURES:* 29 chapter links • Theatrical trailer • Production notes • Featurette: "The Saga of Jeremiah Johnson" • Historical notes.
1972 (PG) 107m/C Robert Redford, Will Geer; *D:* Sydney Pollack; *W:* John Milius, Edward Anhalt; *C:* Duke Callaghan; *M:* John Rubinstein.

The Jerk

A jerk tells his rags-to-riches-to-rags story in comedic flashbacks, from "I was born a poor Black child," through his entrepreneurial success in his invention of the "Optigrab," to his inevitable decline. Only film in history with a dog named "Shithead." This was Martin's first starring role, back in his wild and crazy days. His ridiculous misadventures pay tribute to Jerry Lewis movies of the late '60s. Now, the DVD...not too much more could be wrong with a DVD, and there is certainly no excuse for a major studio to release a disc of this quality. The picture is soft and grainy, with colors that lean too far to the red. Contrast and brightness are also not optimized, and there are many scenes that lose color and image details. The sound is O.K., though, and is more dynamic than either the VHS or the laserdisc. —*JO*
Movie: 🎦🎦🎦 *DVD:* 🎦
Universal Studios Home Video (Cat #20214, UPC #025192021428). Full frame. Dolby Digital Mono. $24.98. Keepcase. *LANG:* English; French. *SUB:* Spanish. *CAP:* English. *FEATURES:* 16 chapter links • Theatrical trailer • Cast and filmmakers bios • Production notes • Film highlights.
1979 (R) 94m/C Carl Gottlieb, Steve Martin, Bernadette Peters, Catlin Adams, Bill

Macy, Jackie Mason, Mabel King, Richard Ward, M. Emmet Walsh, Dick O'Neill, Maurice Evans, Pepe Serna, Trinidad Silva; **Cameos:** Carl Reiner, Rob Reiner; **D:** Carl Reiner; **W:** Carl Gottlieb, Michael Elias, Steve Martin; **C:** Victor Kemper; **M:** Jack Elliott.

Jerry Maguire

Who knew the off-field action in high-stakes professional sports could be so exciting? Apparently writer-director Crowe did, because he made the sports agent the hero here—definitely risky business in a time of strikes, lockouts, and outrageous salaries. Cruise is the shark-like agent who learns to live like a dolphin when he suddenly discovers his scruples—and loses his job in the process. He's left with only the loyalty of one obnoxious client (Gooding Jr., who made "Show me the money!" the catch phrase of 1996) and an adoring, idealistic young colleague (Zellweger) with a cute son (Lipnicki) and a heart meant for breaking. The disc gets high marks for its pristine picture—one of the best from early DVD issues, and definitely helped by the anamorphic transfer most appreciated by owners of widescreen sets. The sound is superb, and does justice both to the football action sequences and the well-written, expertly delivered dialogue. A caveat: For some reason, Dolby Digital 5.1 is not selected as default, so check the settings before getting cozy in your couch. Stealing a bit more from the technical rating is the poor menu interface and lack of extras. —*MB*
Movie: 🦴🦴🦴▸ **DVD:** 🦴🦴🦴
Columbia Tristar Home Video (Cat #82539, UPC #043396825390). Widescreen (1.85:1) letterboxed. Dolby Digital 5.1. $27.98. Keepcase. *LANG:* English; French; Spanish. *SUB:* Spanish. *CAP:* English. *FEATURES:* 63 chapter links.
1996 (R) *135m/C* Tom Cruise, Cuba Gooding Jr., Renee Zellweger, Kelly Preston, Bonnie Hunt, Jerry O'Connell, Jay Mohr, Regina King, Glenn Frey, Jonathan Lipnicki, Todd Louiso, Mark Pellington; **Cameos:** Eric Stoltz; **D:** Cameron Crowe; **W:** Cameron Crowe; **C:** Janusz Kaminski; **M:** Nancy Wilson. *AWARDS:* Academy Awards '96: Best Supporting Actor (Gooding); Golden Globe Awards '97: Best Actor—Musical/Comedy (Cruise); MTV Movie Awards '97: Best Male Performance (Cruise); National Board of Review Awards '96: Best Actor (Cruise); Screen Actors Guild Award '96: Best Supporting Actor (Gooding); Broadcast Film Critics Association Awards '96: Breakthrough Performance (Gooding); *NOM:* Academy Awards '96: Best Actor (Cruise), Best Film Editing, Best Original Screenplay, Best Picture; Directors Guild of America Awards '96: Best Director (Crowe); Golden Globe Awards '97: Best Actor—Musical/Comedy (Cruise), Best Film—Musical/Comedy, Best Supporting Actor (Gooding); MTV Movie Awards '97: Best Film, Break-

through Performance (Zellweger); Screen Actors Guild Award '96: Best Actor (Cruise), Best Supporting Actress (Zellweger); Writers Guild of America '96: Best Original Screenplay.

Jessica: A Love Story

Horror film about lost loves.
Movie: NYR **DVD:** NYR
Simitar Entertainment (Cat #7610). Full frame. Dolby Digital 5.1 Surround Stereo. $14.98. Keepcase. *FEATURES:* Trailer.
1992 *95m/C* Karen Trumbo; **D:** Richard Lowry; **W:** Richard Lowry.

Jesus Christ, Superstar

Rock opera portrays the last seven days in the earthly life of Christ, as reenacted by young tourists in Israel. An outstanding musical score is the key to the success of the stage play by Tim Rice and Andrew Lloyd Webber. The film is sometimes stirring, and often abstract, while exhibiting the usual heavy-handed Jewison approach. There is a little grain in both the brightly lit desert scenes as well as some very dim scenes, but not enough to ruin the excellent transfer to DVD. The image is crisp and the colors are both vibrant and accurate. Contrast and brightness levels are very good and have no problem making sure that details are retained in those bright scenes. Blacks are for the most part true. Neither artifacts nor color bleed are a problem. The 5.0 sound is basically the Dolby Surround with a subwoofer track and discreet feeds of the mono rear channel to both left and right speakers. It results in much better imaging and a punchier sound as well as cleaner and gutsier handling of the bass, and sounds great. —*JO*
Movie: 🦴🦴🦴 **DVD:** 🦴🦴🦴
Universal Studios Home Video (Cat #20524, UPC #025192052422). Widescreen (2.35:1) letterboxed. Dolby Digital Surround 5.0; Dolby Surround. $24.98. Keepcase. *LANG:* English (DS 5.0); French (DS). *SUB:* Spanish. *CAP:* English. *FEATURES:* 24 chapter links • Theatrical trailer • Cast and filmmakers bios • Production notes • Film highlights • Web links.
1973 (G) *108m/C* Ted Neeley, Carl Anderson, Yvonne Elliman, Josh Mostel; **D:** Norman Jewison; **W:** Melvyn Bragg; **C:** Douglas Slocombe; **M:** Andrew Lloyd Webber, Andre Previn, Herbert W. Spencer. *AWARDS: NOM:* Academy Awards '73: Original Song Score and/or Adaptation.

Jet Li's The Enforcer

Offbeat Hong Kong import attempts to combine a cop/action plot with a more serious look at the relationship between a father and his son. Kung Wei (Jet Li) is an undercover cop who'd rather spend time with his young son (Xie Miao), a budding martial artist. Also involved are his ailing wife and a sympathetic fellow officer (Anita Mui). The fight scenes are typically

overblown (and overdirected) and the stickiness of the emotions may strike Americans as excessive, but Jet Li is a genuine star and he's terrific here. With its thin sound and washed-out image, the DVD does him few favors, but I still recommend the film to his fans. —*MM* **AKA:** The Enforcer; My Father Is a Hero; Letter to Daddy; Gei Ba Ba de Xin.
Movie: 🦴🦴▸ **DVD:** 🦴🦴▸
Tai Seng Video Marketing (Cat #DVD138). Widescreen letterboxed. Dolby Digital 5.1 Surround Stereo. $49.95. Keepcase. *LANG:* Cantonese; Mandarin. *SUB:* Chinese; English. *FEATURES:* 9 chapter links • Trailers.
1995 *100m/C* *HK* Jet Li, Anita Mui, Damian Lau, Tse Miu, Rongguang Yu, Ngai Sing; **D:** Corey Yuen.

Jezebel

Davis is a willful Southern belle who loses fiance Fonda through her selfish and spiteful ways in this pre–Civil War drama. When he becomes ill, she realizes her cruelty and rushes to nurse him back to health. Davis's role won her an Oscar for Best Actress, and certainly provided Scarlett O'Hara with a rival for most memorable female character of all time. The DVD transfer preserves the detailed and "glorious" black-and-white photography. The picture is very sharp and grain is never an issue, nor are artifacts. Graytones are excellent and the various shadings give the image great depth. Blacks are true and though the contrast is high it never distorts or ghosts. The mono sound is stronger than I've ever heard it and has decent low end as well as overall fidelity. Sound distortion is very low for this age of film. —*JO*
Movie: 🦴🦴🦴▸ **DVD:** 🦴🦴🦴▸
MGM Home Entertainment (Cat #906677, UPC #027616667724). Full frame. Dolby Digital Mono. $24.98. Snapper. *LANG:* English; Spanish. *SUB:* English; French; Spanish. *CAP:* English. *FEATURES:* 32 chapter links • Theatrical trailer.
1938 *105m/B* Bette Davis, George Brent, Henry Fonda, Margaret Lindsay, Fay Bainter, Donald Crisp, Spring Byington, Eddie Anderson; **D:** William Wyler; **W:** Clements Ripley, Abem Finkel, John Huston, Robert Buckner; **C:** Ernest Haller; **M:** Max Steiner. *AWARDS:* Academy Awards '38: Best Actress (Davis), Best Supporting Actress (Bainter); *NOM:* Academy Awards '38: Best Cinematography, Best Picture, Best Score.

JFK

Stone spins a highly controversial examination of President John F. Kennedy's 1963 assassination, from the viewpoint of New Orleans district attorney Jim Garrison (Costner). Hotly debated because of the director's conspiracy theories, it sparked new calls to open the sealed government records from the 1977 House Select Committee on Assassinations investigation. Considered by some to be a cinematic masterpiece for the outstanding performances from all-star principal and supporting casts, stunning cinematography, and excellent editing. Others see it as revisionist history that should be taken with a grain of salt. With all the different film stocks and effects used in this film, it's really hard to tell if any grain is added by the DVD, but overall the transfer appears very good. The picture is sharp and detailed but there are some intermittent artifacts. Colors and blacks are both accurate partially due to the brightness and contrast, which handles all the different film looks very well. This is the 206-minute Director's Cut of the film and it uses both sides of the DVD, which is not dual layered. The Dolby Surround has good fidelity and decent low end but is lacking in separation and Surround, as well as dynamic punch. —JO

Movie: 🐾🐾 **DVD:** 🐾🐾🐾
Warner Home Video, Inc. (Cat #1261, UPC #085391261421). Widescreen (2.35:1) letterboxed. Dolby Surround. $24.98. Snapper. LANG: English. SUB: English; Spanish; French. CAP: English. FEATURES: 88 chapter links ● Production notes.
1991 (R) 206m/C Dale Dye, Kevin Costner, Sissy Spacek, Kevin Bacon, Tommy Lee Jones, Laurie Metcalf, Gary Oldman, Michael Rooker, Jay O. Sanders, Beata Pozniak, Joe Pesci, Donald Sutherland, John Candy, Jack Lemmon, Walter Matthau, Ed Asner, Vincent D'Onofrio, Sally Kirkland, Brian Doyle-Murray, Wayne Knight, Tony Plana, Tomas Milian, Sean Stone; *Cameos:* Lolita (David) Davidovich, Frank Whaley, Jim Garrison; *D:* Oliver Stone; *W:* Oliver Stone, Zachary Sklar; *C:* Robert Richardson; *M:* John Williams. AWARDS: Academy Awards '91: Best Cinematography, Best Film Editing; Golden Globe Awards '92: Best Director (Stone); NOM: Academy Awards '91: Best Adapted Screenplay, Best Director (Stone), Best Picture, Best Sound, Best Supporting Actor (Jones), Best Original Score.

Jingle All the Way

Producer Chris Columbus grabs the reins of the slapstick and sentiment sleigh from mentor John Hughes in this farce of holiday capitalism. Any parent who has searched frantically for the Mighty Morphin Cabbage Elmo will understand hapless Howard Langston (Schwarzenegger), a workaholic dad who was supposed to secure the coveted Turbo Man action figure for his son Jamie (Lloyd). Unfortunately, it slips his mind until Christmas Eve and all the Turbo Men have blasted off with more mindful parents. In his panic-stricken quest for the toy, he is confronted by a crazed postman (Sinbad) hunting Turbo Man, a pack of sleazy Santas, and a vicious reindeer attack. Meanwhile, Howard's slimy neighbor Ted (Hartman) is attempting to get into his wife Liz's (Wilson) stockings with great care. Although aimed at a younger audience, there's a definite lack of kids, which leaves it too grown-up for the kids and too childish for

the adults. There is some satisfaction in seeing the Mall of America torn to shreds, however. A great transfer to DVD accents the vibrant accurate colors without adding any bleed and allows the picture to remain extremely sharp. The contrast is punchy and the brightness levels are excellent. Blacks remain true, though there are very few dark scenes to test them with. The 5.1 sound is very lively and the Surround tracks really kick in for the climactic airborn showdown. Fidelity is excellent and the low end is gutsy and clean. —JO

Movie: 🐾🐾 **DVD:** 🐾🐾🐾
20th Century Fox (Cat #4109066, UPC #086162090660). Widescreen (1.85:1) letterboxed. Dolby Digital 5.1; Dolby Surround; Stereo. $29.98. Keepcase. LANG: English (5.1; DS); Spanish (Stereo); French (Stereo). SUB: English; French. CAP: English. FEATURES: 23 chapter links ● Theatrical trailer.
1996 (PG) 88m/C Arnold Schwarzenegger, Phil Hartman, Sinbad, Rita Wilson, James Belushi, Robert Conrad, Martin Mull, Jake Lloyd, Harvey Korman, Laraine Newman; *D:* Brian Levant; *W:* Randy Kornfield; *C:* Victor Kemper; *M:* David Newman. AWARDS: NOM: Golden Raspberry Awards '96: Worst Director (Levant).

Joan of Arc

Flamboyant mini-series looks fine on DVD. The European locations are properly cold, muddy, and grim. Even the battle scenes are fairly impressive. In the title role, fresh-faced young Leelee Sobieski looks like she'd be more at home in the mall than in 15th-century France, but what can you expect from a version of the story that begins with a reference to Merlin? Production values are well above average for a television production. Both image and sound are excellent; writing and acting are less so. —MM

Movie: 🐾🐾 **DVD:** 🐾🐾🐾
Artisan Entertainment (Cat #10232, UPC #012236102328). Widescreen anamorphic. Dolby Digital Surround Stereo. $19.98. Keepcase. LANG: English. CAP: English. FEATURES: 36 chapter links.
1999 240m/C Leelee Sobieski, Neil Patrick Harris, Peter O'Toole, Robert Loggia, Jacqueline Bisset, Powers Boothe, Shirley MacLaine, Olympia Dukakis, Maury Chaykin, Jonathan Hyde, Maximilian Schell, Peter Strauss; *D:* Christian Duguay; *W:* Ronald Parker, Michael Miller; *C:* Pierre Gill; *M:* Asher Ettinger, Tony Kosinec.

Joe Kidd

A land war breaks out in New Mexico between Mexican natives and American land barons. Eastwood, once again portraying the "mysterious stranger," must decide with whom he should side, all the while falling in love with Garcia. Lackluster direction results in a surprisingly tedious western, in spite of the cast. One of Eastwood's lowest money grossers. Some catalogue titles released by Universal on DVD

are absolutely atrocious (take a look at *The Eiger Sanction*) and some are absolutely great. This one falls in to the latter category. The picture is extremely sharp and both grain and artifacts seem nonexistent. Colors are tremendous—accurate and vibrant with not a trace of bleed. Blacks are deep, true, and grain-free. Contrast is high, yet smooth, and the brightness level remains consistent whether during dimmer indoor scenes or in the naturally bright outdoors. The Dolby Digital mono is full-bodied, and lack of 5.1 sound shouldn't deter you from acquiring this disc for your collection. —JO

Movie: 🐾🐾 **DVD:** 🐾🐾🐾
Universal Studios Home Video (Cat #20288, UPC #025192028823). Widescreen (2.35:1) letterboxed. Dolby Digital Mono 2.0. $24.98. Keepcase. LANG: English; Spanish; French. SUB: Spanish. CAP: English. FEATURES: 16 chapter links ● Theatrical trailer ● Cast and filmmakers bios ● Production notes ● Film highlights.
1972 (PG) 88m/C Clint Eastwood, Robert Duvall, John Saxon, Don Stroud, Stella Garcia, James Wainwright, Paul Koslo, Gregory Walcott, Dick Van Patten, Lynn Marta; *D:* John Sturges; *W:* Elmore Leonard; *C:* Bruce Surtees; *M:* Lalo Schifrin.

Joe the King

One is immediately reminded of *The Outsiders* or *Stand by Me*, but probably closer to the mark is the Jean-Pierre Leaud character of Antoine, first introduced to us in Francois Truffaut's *The 400 Blows*. Frank Whaley, best known for his turn-the-tables nemesis role opposite Kevin Spacey in *Swimming with Sharks*, tackles both the writing and directorial honors here in a semi-autobiographical tale of unrelenting childhood misery. Noah Fleiss is nothing short of brilliant as the title character Joe, a 14-year-old youth from a broken and troubled home, complete with an alcoholic father (Val Kilmer) and a "see-no-evil-hear-no-evil" mother (Karen Young). School is wretched, home is hellish, and everything in between is some strange nightmare land known only to children without a moral compass or adult guidance. This is one of those little "gems" that we all love to ferret out and call our own—an "actor's actor" movie peppered with superb performances all around, including Ethan Hawke and John Leguizamo as well-meaning, if ineffectual adult figures in young Joe's life. The DVD presentation is deceptively effective in its overall delivery. This 1999 Sundance Film Festival winner features an audio commentary from director Whaley, which is a real treat once we discover that his childhood is the source for much of the material covered on-screen. —RT

Movie: 🐾🐾🐾 **DVD:** 🐾🐾🐾
Trimark Home Video (Cat #VM7245D, UPC #031398724537). Widescreen. AC3 - 2 Channel. $24.99. Keepcase. LANG: English. SUB: English; French; Spanish. CAP: English; French; Spanish. FEATURES: 24

chapter links ◆ Theatrical trailer ◆ Commentary: director-writer Frank Whaley ◆ Featurette: "Anatomy of a Scene" (6 mins.). **1999 (R) 101m/C** Noah Fleiss, Val Kilmer, Ethan Hawke, Karen Young, John Leguizamo, Austin Pendleton, Max Ligosh, James Costa; *D:* Frank Whaley; *W:* Frank Whaley; *C:* Mike Mayers; *M:* Robert Whaley, Anthony Grimaldi. *AWARDS:* Sundance Film Festival '99: Best Screenplay.

Joe's Apartment

Fresh-from-Iowa Joe (O'Connell) comes to New York, finds a squalid apartment, and then discovers its other occupants are hordes of singing, joking cockroaches. Luckily for Joe, his unwelcome roommates are on his side, even helping out with his love life, when necessary. Gross but interesting; throw in Vaughn as a panty-wearing politician and you've got yourself a potential cult-movie favorite. Neat freaks probably won't enjoy it much. Flick took three years to finish as computer-animated roaches had to do all the dancing and singing. Feature directorial debut for writer Payson, who created the original 1992 live-action/animation MTV short. The DVD transfer is very good, delivering a sharp image and vibrant colors accurately captured in all lighting conditions. Blacks are true and contrast is excellent. The brightness levels are also very good and stay consistent. The Dolby Surround is lovely and there's plenty channeled to the rear speakers in the way of both ambience and effects. —*JO*
Movie: 🎵🎵 **DVD:** 🎵🎵🎵▶
Warner Home Video, Inc. (Cat #14042, UPC #08539104224). Full frame. Dolby Surround. $14.98. Snapper. *LANG:* English; French. *CAP:* English. *FEATURES:* 24 chapter links.
1996 (PG-13) 82m/C Jerry O'Connell, Megan Ward, Robert Vaughn, Jim Turner, Don Ho, Sandra "Pepa" Denton, Shiek Mahmud-Bey; *D:* John Payson; *W:* John Payson; *C:* Peter Deming; *V:* Billy West, Reginald Hudlin.

John Carpenter's Vampires

Carpenter directed this vampire flick with Sam Peckinpah's eye—and composed the score with Ry Cooder's ear—giving it more the feeling of a gritty western than a typical horror film. Don't worry, there's still plenty of bloodsucking, gore, and fiends roasting alive in the sunlight when a group of mercenary vampire hunters (on the Vatican's payroll), led by Woods, hunt down master vampire Valek (Griffith). Visually, the widescreen side is very good; the resolution drops off a touch on the full-frame side. The blacks are good, as are the brightness levels and contrast. There is very little grain, despite all the dark scenes you'd expect in a vampire film. Artifacts are barely noticeable, even during the films action-packed motel massacre scene, which is a montage of dissolves layered over each other. The sound is excellent and both

Dolby tracks (5.1 and Surround) feature excellent separation and dynamic range. —*JO* *AKA:* Vampires.
Movie: 🎵🎵🎵 **DVD:** 🎵🎵🎵▶
Columbia Tristar Home Video (Cat #03064, UPC #043396030640). Widescreen (2.35:1) anamorphic; full frame. Dolby Digital 5.1; Dolby Surround. Keepcase. *LANG:* English (DD5.1; DS); French. *SUB:* English; French. *FEATURES:* 28 chapter links ◆ Theatrical trailer ◆ Photo gallery ◆ Commentary: John Carpenter.
1997 (R) 108m/C James Woods, Thomas Ian Griffith, Sheryl Lee, Daniel Baldwin, Tim Guinee, Maximilian Schell, Cary-Hiroyuki Tagawa, Mark Boone Jr., Tom Rosales; *D:* John Carpenter; *W:* John Carpenter, Don Jacoby; *C:* Gary B. Kibbe; *M:* John Carpenter.

John Grisham's The Rainmaker

Rudy Baylor (Damon) is an idealistic lawyer whose first work is for Memphis's sleaziest lawyer, "Bruiser" Stone (Rourke at his funniest). Later Baylor is partnered with Deck Shifflet (DeVito), "almost a lawyer," in an insurance case that pits them against a high-powered team led by Voight. Several other subplots fill out the two hours–plus of a well-paced courtroom thriller that's handled competently if not brilliantly by director Coppola. Even so, Coppola at less than 100% is far more enjoyable than most directors on their best day. Curiously, this DVD is hampered by the busy, cluttered world that he creates. Virtually every shot, interior and exterior, is filled with objects and clashing patterns of clothing in the background. Many of those tend to vibrate, particularly the Venetian blinds, which again figure prominently in almost every office. The same digital technology that has trouble with the overactive visuals makes the dialogue sound crisp and clear. —*MM AKA:* The Rainmaker.
Movie: 🎵🎵▶ **DVD:** 🎵🎵
Paramount Home Video (Cat #335037, UPC #097363350378). Widescreen letterboxed. Dolby Digital Surround Stereo; Dolby Digital 5.1 Surround. $29.98. Keepcase. *LANG:* English; French. *SUB:* Spanish. *CAP:* English. *FEATURES:* 33 chapter links.
1997 (PG-13) 137m/C Matt Damon, Claire Danes, Danny DeVito, Jon Voight, Danny Glover, Virginia Madsen, Mary Kay Place, Mickey Rourke, Johnny Whitworth, Teresa Wright, Dean Stockwell, Red West, Roy Scheider, Randy Travis, Andrew Shue; *D:* Francis Ford Coppola; *W:* Francis Ford Coppola, Michael Herr; *C:* John Toll; *M:* Elmer Bernstein. *AWARDS: NOM:* Golden Globe Awards '98: Best Supporting Actor (Voight).

Johnny Mnemonic

Robo-yuppie data courier Johnny (Reeves) has overextended the storage capacity in his head and must download his latest job before his brain turns to applesauce. Aided by an implant-enhanced bodyguard

(Meyer), underground hacker rebels called LoTeks, and a former doctor (Rollins) battling a technology-induced epidemic, Johnny is on the run from the corporation that wants his head (literally). Freshman director Longo can't seem to get a handle on the plot and doesn't get much help from writer Gibson, who combined characters and scenarios from his other books. Action sequences and computer effects are appropriately spiffy, preventing a total system crash. The DVD transfer, though not worthy of being called a showpiece, is excellent. *Mnemonic* is a very dark film and the disc is still sharp with hardly any grain or artifacts. Colors are vibrant and even deep rich reds do not bleed. Contrast and brightness levels are excellent and allow the blacks to remain true whether filling the screen or surrounded by bright colors. The 5.1 sound really delivers. There is plenty of Surround, mixed equally well for both effects and music. The bass provides plenty of power and is handled very cleanly. —*JO*
Movie: 🎵🎵 **DVD:** 🎵🎵🎵▶
Columbia Tristar Home Video (Cat #73479, UPC #04379704791). Widescreen (1.85:1) letterboxed; full frame. Dolby Digital 5.1; Stereo. NSL. Keepcase. *LANG:* English (DD5.1; Stereo); Spanish (Stereo); French (Stereo). *SUB:* English; Spanish. *CAP:* English. *FEATURES:* 36 chapter links.
1995 (R) 98m/C Keanu Reeves, Dina Meyer, Ice-T, Takeshi "Beat" Kitano, Dolph Lundgren, Henry Rollins, Udo Kier, Barbara Sukowa, Denis Akiyama; *D:* Robert Longo; *W:* William Gibson; *C:* Francois Protat; *M:* Brad Fiedel.

Johnny 2.0

Contrived thriller finds genetic scientist Johnny Dalton (Fahey) awakening from a 15-year coma to discover that his memory has been transplanted into a clone, Johnny 2.0. Now he has six days to find his duplicate before the Corporation, the group behind the procedure, decides on termination.
Movie: 🎵▶ **DVD:** NYR
York Entertainment (Cat #1000). Full frame. Stereo. $24.98.
1999 (PG-13) 95m/C Jeff Fahey, Michael Ironside, Tahnee Welch; *D:* Neill Fearnley.

The Johnsons

This Dutch horror film has a well-earned cult reputation. It's intelligent, surprising, and frightening. The complex story revolves around a photographer (Van De Ven), her teenage daughter (De La Bretoniere), an anthropology professor (Herdigein), and the Mahxitu Indians. To describe it much more would spoil the film's curious twists. Despite the constant use of the color red for both symbolic and narrative purposes, the film looks fine on DVD with sharply defined images, even in dream sequences. On their commentary track, writers Roy Frumkes and Rocco Simonelli and director Rudolf Van Den

Berg talk about how an unapologetic genre piece written specifically for a New York City setting came to be moved to Holland, and how it almost starred Glenda Jackson and Oliver Reed. Overall, their approach to the business of discussing a film is one of the more useful and lucid, particularly for horror fans. Recommended. —MM

Movie: 🎬🎬🎬 **DVD:** 🎬🎬🎬▶

Image Entertainment (Cat #DV10673, UPC #013131067392). Widescreen (1.85:1) letterboxed. Dolby Digital Surround Stereo. $24.98. Keepcase. *LANG:* Dutch; English. *SUB:* English. *FEATURES:* 23 chapter links • Theatrical trailer • Writer and director thumbnail biographies • Commentary: Van Den Berg, Frumkes, and Simonelli.

1992 98m/C *NL* Monique Van De Ven, Esmee De La Bretoniere, Kenneth Herdigein; *D:* Rudolf Van Den Berg; *W:* Roy Frumkes, Rocco Simonelli, Leon de Winter; *C:* Theo Bierkes; *M:* Patrick Seymour.

Journey to the Far Side of the Sun

Underrated sci-fi adventure from the creators of the TV puppet shows *Thunderbirds* and *Supercar*. Chaos erupts in the Earth's scientific community when it is discovered that a second mirror-image Earth is hidden in a parallel orbit on the opposite side of the sun. Astronaut Roy Thinnes *(The Invaders)* is sent on an exploratory mission to the heretofore undiscovered planet. Cool special effects (for its time) and a good twist ending make this a journey well worth taking. A slightly below-average DVD with too much grain (especially in contrasty scenes near the beginning of the disc), although there is very little color bleed and the colors are good overall. The blacks are good and the brightness levels consistent. Some noticeable artifacts at times produce unnatural motion. PCM Mono soundtrack is adequate, but nothing special. —JO *AKA:* Doppelganger.

Movie: 🎬🎬▶ **DVD:** 🎬🎬

Image Entertainment (Cat #ID4297USDVD, UPC #014381429725). Widescreen (1.85:1) letterboxed. PCM Mono. $24.99. Snapper. *LANG:* English. *CAP:* English. *FEATURES:* 16 chapter links.

1969 (G) 92m/C *GB* Roy Thinnes, Ian Hendry, Lynn Loring, Patrick Wymark, Loni von Friedl, Herbert Lom, Ed Bishop; *D:* Robert Parrish; *W:* Gerry Anderson; *C:* John Read; *M:* Barry Gray.

Ju Dou

An aging factory worker searches for an heir in this breathtaking Oscar nominee (best foreign language film). He takes a third wife (Gong Li) but she finds caring in the arms of another man when her husband's brutality proves too much. Beautiful color cinematography, excellent acting, epic story. The DVD's colors seem oversaturated, with chalky blacks. —JO

Movie: 🎬🎬🎬🎬 **DVD:** 🎬🎬▶

Pioneer Entertainment (Cat #10269). Full frame. Dolby Digital Stereo. $24.95. Keepcase. *LANG:* Chinese. *SUB:* English.

1990 (PG-13) 98m/C *CH* Gong Li, Li Bao-Tian, Li Wei, Zhang Yi, Zheng Jian; *D:* Zhang Yimou; *W:* Liu Heng; *C:* Gu Changwei, Yang Lun; *M:* Xia Ru-jin, Jiping Zhao. *AWARDS: NOM:* Academy Awards '90: Best Foreign Film.

Judge & Jury

Joey Meeker (Keith) is another of those cinematic mad killers who is resurrected after he's electrocuted. Or are his various incarnations (some involving orange hair and black nail polish that are particularly virulent on DVD) a product of Michael's (Kove) imagination because he was involved with Joey's wife's death? The derivative material is handled with more wit and style than it really deserves. The key participants—Keith, Kove, and veteran video director Eyres—are old hands with this level of low-budget *Elm St.* material. Since the visuals are purposefully off-putting, they gain nothing on DVD. It's essentially identical to VHS tape. This one is recommended to fans of the cast only. —MM

Movie: 🎬🎬 **DVD:** 🎬🎬

Image Entertainment (Cat #ID5767UM DVD, UPC #014381576726). Full frame. Dolby Digital Stereo. $24.99. Snapper. *LANG:* English. *FEATURES:* 16 chapter links.

1996 (R) 98m/C David Keith, Martin Kove, Laura Johnson, Thomas Ian Nicholas, Paul Koslo; *D:* John Eyres; *W:* John Eyres, John Cianetti, Amanda I. Kirpaul; *C:* Bob Paone; *M:* Johnathon Flood.

Judge Dredd

Futuristic lawman Dredd (Stallone), who acts as cop, judge, jury, and executioner, is framed for murder by ex-judge/arch-criminal Rico (Assante), who loves to kill and knows some dark Dredded family secret. Banished from Mega City One with nothing but comic relief in the form of Schneider, Dredd must face the Angel family, most notably the psychotic-mental misfit, Mean Machine, who just happens to have a dial on his head to crank up the ol' nastiness. Highlights include an opening aerial tour of Mega City One that goes one up on *Blade Runner*, and a high-speed, high-altitude motorcycle chase with lots-o'-bullets and tons-o'-neon. The source comic book *2000 AD* has been a cult favorite for decades. *Judge Dredd* was great on laserdisc and this DVD is even better. Extremely sharp, this disc has no problem at all with grain or artifacts. The comic book colors are vibrant, accurate, and free of bleed. Blacks are near perfect and strongly supported by excellent contrast and brightness levels. The 5.1 sound is obnoxiously loud when it needs to be, with plenty of effects peppering the Surround channels. Music is full-bodied and the dialogue is crisp. Not everyone likes this movie, but you gotta love this DVD. —JO

Movie: 🎬🎬🎬 **DVD:** 🎬🎬🎬▶

Buena Vista Home Entertainment (Cat #14899, UPC #717951000644). Widescreen (2.35:1) letterboxed. Dolby Digital 5.1; Stereo. $29.99. Keepcase. *LANG:* English (DD5.1); French (Stereo). *CAP:* English. *FEATURES:* 17 chapter links • Theatrical trailer.

1995 (R) 96m/C Sylvester Stallone, Armand Assante, Diane Lane, Rob Schneider, Joan Chen, Juergen Prochnow, Max von Sydow; *D:* Danny Cannon; *W:* Steven E. de Souza, Michael De Luca, William Wisher; *C:* Adrian Biddle; *M:* Alan Silvestri. *AWARDS: NOM:* Golden Raspberry Awards '95: Worst Actor (Stallone).

Judgment Night

Four macho buddies on their way to a boxing match detour a highway traffic jam via surface streets and find themselves witness to a murder. The rest of their guys-night-out is spent trying to escape a gloomy ghetto and determined killer (played convincingly by Leary). Lots of action and oomph. Based on a story by Lewis Colick and Jere Cunningham. Considering that most of this film takes place in the dark, this is a pretty good DVD. The contrast is good and the brightness levels are very consistent. If you look hard you can find a little artifacting, but nothing too distracting. The blacks are on par with the rest of the specs and there is only occasional grain. On a few gunshots the Dolby Surround appeared to clip, but for the most part, the sound quality is good, and the music punches through with plenty of dynamics. —JO

Movie: 🎬🎬 **DVD:** 🎬🎬▶

Goodtimes Entertainment (Cat #0581005, UPC #018713810052). Widescreen (1.78:1) anamorphic. Dolby Surround. $19.98. Snapper. *LANG:* English. *SUB:* Spanish; French. *CAP:* English. *FEATURES:* 18 chapter links • Production notes.

1993 (R) 109m/C Emilio Estevez, Cuba Gooding Jr., Stephen Dorff, Denis Leary, Jeremy Piven, Peter Greene; *D:* Stephen Hopkins; *W:* Lewis Colick; *C:* Peter Levy; *M:* Alan Silvestri.

Juliet of the Spirits

Fellini uses the spare story of a middle-aged woman (Masina, his real-life wife) deliberating her husband's possible infidelity to create a wild, phantasmagoric, surrealistic journey through her memories, dreams, and visions. The mix of comedy and introspection is pure Fellini, though it is impossible to overestimate the contributions of his star and the music of his long-time collaborator, Nino Rota. Many older tapes have a muddy, scratchy look. The DVD is pristine, with a clarity that recalls the first time I saw the film decades ago. The maestro's collection of grotesques, clashing colors, and funny hats has never looked so gorgeous on home video. —MM *AKA:* Giulietta Degli Spiriti.

Movie: 🎬🎬🎬🎬 **DVD:** 🎬🎬🎬▶

Image Entertainment (Cat #ID477815SI DVD, UPC, #014381477825). Widescreen (1.66:1) letterboxed. Dolby Digital Mono. $24.99. Snapper. *LANG:* Italian. *SUB:* English. *FEATURES:* 18 chapter links • Filmographies for Fellini and Giulietta Masina.

1965 142m/C IT Giulietta Masina, Valentina Cortese, Sylva Koscina, Mario Pisu, Sandra Milo, Caterina Boratto, Valeska Gert; *D:* Federico Fellini; *W:* Federico Fellini, Tullio Pinelli, Ennio Flaiano, Brunello Rondi; *C:* Gianni Di Venanzo; *M:* Nino Rota. *AWARDS:* New York Film Critics Awards '65: Best Foreign Film; *NOM:* Academy Awards '66: Best Art Direction/Set Decoration (Color), Best Costume Design (Color).

Jumanji (CS)

This fast-paced fantasy is actually more successful on DVD than it was on the theatrical screen. The combination of smaller image size with increased clarity makes the integration of live-action and special effects more persuasive. No adult is going to believe that those are real elephants and rhinos crashing through the walls of a suburban home, but on disc, the lines between the film's "reality" and "fantasy" are less obvious than they have been. After a long introduction that begins in 1869 and then moves up 100 years, young Alan Parrish (Hann-Byrd) discovers a buried board game called Jumanji that literally sucks him in. Fast-forward 26 years. Young Judy (Dunst) and Peter (Pierce) move into the same house and find the same game. When they play, out pops the grown-up Alan (Williams) followed by many other creatures, animal, vegetable, and mineral. On the commentary track, several members of the special effects team discuss the problems they had in creating the animatronic and computer-generated creatures. Their focus is technical and not of much interest to the casual viewer. Visually, the disc is a solid step up from VHS tape with an image that sparkles in every frame. Even with a conventional video sound system, the stereo is superb, both in the effects—ominous drum beats, lion's roar—and in the isolated track for James Horner's fine score. Viewers who were troubled by the film's combination of violence with a children's story ought to give it another look on DVD. —MM

Movie: 🦴🦴🦴▸ *DVD:* 🦴🦴🦴▸
Columbia Tristar Home Video (Cat #11742, UPC #043396117426). Widescreen (1.85:1) letterboxed. Dolby Digital 5.1 Surround Stereo; Dolby Digital Surround Stereo. $27.95. Keepcase. *LANG:* English. *SUB:* English. *CAP:* English. *FEATURES:* 28 chapter links • Isolated music score • Commentary: special effects crew • Storyboards • Photo galleries • Cast and crew thumbnail biographies • Theatrical trailers • "Making of" featurette • Special effects featurette.

1995 (PG) 104m/C Robin Williams, Kirsten Dunst, Bonnie Hunt, Bradley Michael Pierce, Bebe Neuwirth, Jonathan Hyde, David Alan Grier, Adam Hann-Byrd; *D:* Joe Johnston; *W:* Jonathan Hensleigh; *C:* Thomas Ackerman; *M:* James Horner.

June Night

Kerstin (Bergman), who was victimized by a shooting incident, cannot escape the public eye due to her previous promiscuous behavior. After making this one, Ingrid Bergman moved to Hollywood and starred in *Casablanca* and the rest is cinematic history. Here, she is absolutely lovely and the superb black-and-white transfer on this DVD makes the most of her presence. As should be expected of any film from 1940, some night scenes are too dark but all of the action is easy to follow. Most of the film is remarkably sharp. Sound, typical of the era, is nothing special. —MM
AKA: Juninatten.

Movie: 🦴🦴 *DVD:* 🦴🦴🦴
WinStar Home Entertainment (Cat #FLV5060, UPC #720917506029). Full frame. $29.98. Keepcase. *LANG:* Swedish. *SUB:* English. *FEATURES:* 8 chapter links • Production credits • Filmographies and awards.

1940 90m/C SW Ingrid Bergman, Marianne Lofgren, Gunnar Sjoberg, Olaf Widgren; *D:* Per Lindberg; *W:* Ragnar Hylten-Cavalius; *C:* Ake Dahlqvist; *M:* Jules Sylvain.

The Jungle Book

Perennial favorite in theatrical re-release and on home video, this was the last of the Disney animated features to be overseen by Uncle Walt himself. Despite the memorable catchy tunes, it is certainly not the studio's finest effort. The animation looks almost crude compared to what had been done before and what has come since. But why quibble? Kids love the film and it looks virtually flawless on DVD. Sound is excellent, and the thorough indexing will make it easy for the small-fry to zip to their favorite numbers. Songs: "Col. Hathi's March," "The Bare Necessities," "I Wan'na Be Like You," "Trust in Me," "That's What Friends Are For," "My Own Home." —MM

Movie: 🦴🦴🦴 *DVD:* 🦴🦴🦴
Buena Vista Home Entertainment (Cat #18788, UPC #717951005878). Full frame. Dolby Digital Surround Stereo. $39.99. Keepcase. *LANG:* English; French; Spanish. *CAP:* English. *FEATURES:* 24 chapter links.

1967 78m/C D: Wolfgang Reitherman; *M:* George Bruns; *V:* Phil Harris, Sebastian Cabot, Louis Prima, George Sanders, Sterling Holloway, J. Pat O'Malley, Verna Felton, Darlene Carr. *AWARDS: NOM:* Academy Awards '67: Best Song ("The Bare Necessities").

Jungle Boy

After being lost in the jungles of India, Manling (Seth) is raised by a monkey and an elephant. Able to communicate with the animals, this junior-grade Mowgli uses his talents to defeat the poacher Hook (Roberts) who's out to steal a sacred statue. Combining a modest number of the effects used in *Babe* with a solid adventure story, this DVD is a real surprise for kids. The image is simply superb. Some exteriors lose a bit of quality, but the brilliant clarity belies a low budget. Sound is excellent, too. —MM

Movie: 🦴🦴▸ *DVD:* 🦴🦴🦴
Simitar Entertainment (Cat #7443, UPC #082551744329). Full frame. Dolby Digital Stereo; Dolby Digital 5.1 Surround Stereo. $19.95. Keepcase. *LANG:* English. *FEATURES:* 8 chapter links • Production factoids.

1996 (PG) 88m/C Asif Mohammed Seth, Jeremy Roberts, Lea Moreno; *D:* Allan Goldstein; *W:* Allan Goldstein, John Howard Lawson, Damian Lee; *C:* Nicholas Josef von Sternberg.

Jungle Fever

A married black architect's affair with his white secretary provides the backdrop for a cold look at interracial love. The story focuses more on the discomfort of friends and families than with the intense world created by the lovers for themselves. It provides the quota of humor and fresh insight we expect from Lee, but none of the joyous sexuality experienced by the lovers in *She's Gotta Have It*. In fact, Lee tells viewers that interracial love is unnatural, never more than skin deep, never more than a blind obsession with the allure of the opposite race. That idea may be hard to take if you disagree with Lee, but this is a fine film nonetheless. However, just about all the subtleties of the cinematography are totally lost on this poor DVD transfer. The picture can never be called sharp and colors never quite accurate. Brightness is too high and contrast too low. If you're going to bother watching this disc (the LD or VHS would be a better choice), the sound is fine, with O.K. bass and at least ambient use of the Surround. —JO

Movie: 🦴🦴🦴▸ *DVD:* 🦴▸
Universal Studios Home Video (Cat #2028, UPC #025192042829). Widescreen (1.85:1) anamorphic. Dolby Surround. $24.95. Keepcase. *LANG:* English; Spanish; French. *SUB:* Spanish; French. *CAP:* English. *FEATURES:* 19 chapter links • Theatrical trailers • "Making of" featurette • Production notes • Cast and filmmakers bios.

1991 (R) 131m/C Wesley Snipes, Annabella Sciorra, John Turturro, Samuel L. Jackson, Ossie Davis, Ruby Dee, Lonette McKee, Anthony Quinn, Spike Lee, Halle Berry, Tyra Ferrell, Veronica Webb, Frank Vincent, Tim Robbins, Brad Dourif, Richard Edson; *D:* Spike Lee; *W:* Spike Lee; *C:* Ernest R. Dickerson; *M:* Terence Blanchard. *AWARDS:* New York Film Critics Awards '91: Best Supporting Actor (Jackson).

Jungleground

Lt. Jake Cornel (Piper) is a cop who's forced by a drug gang to make his way across an urban wasteland before dawn. If he doesn't, they kill his girlfriend (Higginson). It's a variation on Walter Hill's fine action film, *The Warriors*, with inventiveness, colorful characters, and humor. Even in the quieter moments, Piper seems at ease—that's a trick that other action stars, such as Arnold and Jean-Claude haven't completely mastered—and in one nice bit of comic business, he even manages a fine Elmer Fudd imitation. In the DVD's darkest scenes, large areas of blackness tend to solidify, but that's less of a problem than you might think in a film that's set largely at night. Most of the action is clearly defined in this Canadian production. —*MM*

Movie: 🎬🎬🎬 **DVD:** 🎬🎬🎬

Image Entertainment (Cat #ID5600MDVD, UPC #014381560022). Full frame. Dolby Digital Stereo. $24.99. Snapper. *LANG:* English. *FEATURES:* 16 chapter links.

1995 (R) 90m/C *CA* Roddy Piper, Torri Higginson, Peter Williams; *D:* Don Allan; *W:* Michael Stokes; *C:* Gilles Corbeil; *M:* Varouje.

Junior

Out of the way, women! Schwarzenegger trades the war room for the delivery room to experience the miracle of birth. As scientists, he and DeVito take a dip in the gene pool once again to test an anti-miscarriage drug. Thompson provides the egg and some surprisingly good physical comedy as the klutzy cryogenics expert who moves into their university digs. Every pregnancy cliche is explored as Schwarzenegger and DeVito bring the concept to term. Sorry, action fans...nothing blows up except Arnold. It's unusual to see this on a major studio–released DVD, but the picture sharpness actually fluctuates. There is also an increase in grain and minor artifacts in the darker scenes. The colors are pretty accurate and bleed is minimal. Contrast and brightness levels are consistent, but the blacks range from very true to dark grays. The 5.1 Surround is wasted on this DVD and is very flat, with very little in the way of sound effects. (It does successfully add some needed ambience at times.) —*JO*

Movie: 🎬🎬 **DVD:** 🎬🎬▶

Universal Studios Home Video (Cat #20338, UPC #025192033827). Widescreen (1.85:1) anamorphic. Dolby Digital 5.1; Dolby Surround. $24.98. Keepcase. *LANG:* English (DD5.1); Spanish (DS); French (DS). *SUB:* Spanish. *CAP:* English. *FEATURES:* 18 chapter links ▪ Theatrical trailer ▪ Cast and filmmakers bios ▪ Production notes.

1994 (PG-13) 109m/C Arnold Schwarzenegger, Danny DeVito, Emma Thompson, Frank Langella, Pamela Reed, Judy Collins, James Eckhouse, Aida Turturro; *D:* Ivan Reitman; *W:* Kevin Wade, Chris Conrad; *C:* Adam Greenberg; *M:* James Newton Howard. *AWARDS: NOM:* Academy Awards '94: Best Song ("Look What Love Has Done"); Golden Globe Awards '95: Best Actor—Musical/Comedy (Schwarzenegger), Best Actress—Musical/Comedy (Thompson), Best Song ("Look What Love Has Done").

Junior Bonner

Modern-day western is yet another story of a free spirit who has outlived his time. Junior Bonner (McQueen) is a rodeo star who can't seem to ride a bull named Sunshine. That's the least of his problems as his brother (Baker) is a hustling land developer; his father (Preston) is ailing and his mother (Lupino) can't hold the family together. Though Peckinpah and McQueen were much more successful with *The Getaway*, the director had a sterling cast to work with in this low-keyed story and they are superb. Compared to other films made on location in the early 1970s, this one looks very good. The DVD image is much sharper and brighter than the one I saw at a drive-in all those years ago. Sound is not quite as good. The dual-sided disc has the full-frame version on one side, widescreen on the other. —*MM*

Movie: 🎬🎬🎬 **DVD:** 🎬🎬🎬

Anchor Bay (Cat #DV10730, UPC #013131073096). Widescreen (2.35:1) letterboxed; full frame. Dolby Digital Mono. $24.98. Keepcase. *LANG:* English. *FEATURES:* 12 chapter links.

1972 (PG) 100m/C Steve McQueen, Robert Preston, Ida Lupino, Ben Johnson, Joe Don Baker, Barbara Leigh; *D:* Sam Peckinpah; *W:* Jeb Rosebrook; *C:* Lucien Ballard; *M:* Jerry Fielding.

Junior's Groove

Disjointed, unfocused, and often uneven in its presentation, but populated with some fine individual performances and some impressive dramatic moments. Life on the streets of Toronto unfolds around the "planet" of Junior Brown (original title was *The Planet of Junior Brown*), an obese young man (played by Martin Villafana) who spends much of his time playing a piano whose strings have been cut by his mother (Lynn Whitfield—*Eve's Bayou*, *Thin Line Between Love and Hate*) and hanging out with the homeless street people in the neighborhood. He has tremendous talent, but his diabetic mother discourages him, and his friends are, well, street people with emotional problems of their own. DVD is a film-only presentation with minimal chapter links. No director (Clement Virgo—*Rude*) audio commentary, or information about the rather diverse cast members. In addition to the marquee value of Lynn Whitfield, Margot Kidder does a turn as a truly nutty piano teacher, and Sarah Polley (*Sweet Hereafter*) is an all-too-preppie street person. —*RT* *AKA:* The Planet of Junior Brown.

Movie: 🎬🎬▶ **DVD:** 🎬🎬▶

Image Entertainment (Cat #8799UM, UPC #014381879926). Full frame. AC3 - 2 Channel. $24.99. Snapper. *LANG:* English. *FEATURES:* 12 chapter links.

1997 (R) 91m/C Lynn Whitfield, Clark Johnson, Margot Kidder, Sarah Polley, Martin Villafana; *D:* Clement Virgo; *W:* Clement Virgo, Cameron Bailey; *C:* Jonathan Freeman; *M:* Christopher Dedrick.

The Juror

Plucky single mom Annie (Moore) volunteers to be on the jury at the trial of a powerful mobster and draws the attention of a hitman (Baldwin) and his henchman (Gandolfini), who want her to provide the right verdict. Despite an impressive cast and attention to physical details, the rest is formulaic stuff with a predictably dopey ending. The DVD sound and image are aces, proving just how worthy Ms. Moore was of her 1996 Golden Raspberry Worst Actress Award. —*MM*

Movie: 🎬▶ **DVD:** 🎬🎬🎬

Columbia Tristar Home Video (Cat #11609, UPC #043396116092). Widescreen (2.35:1) letterboxed; full frame. Dolby Digital 5.1 Surround Stereo; Dolby Digital Surround Stereo. $28.95. Keepcase. *LANG:* English; Spanish; French. *SUB:* English; Spanish; French. *FEATURES:* 28 chapter links ▪ Theatrical trailers.

1996 (R) 107m/C Demi Moore, Alec Baldwin, Joseph Gordon-Levitt, Anne Heche, James Gandolfini, Lindsay Crouse, Tony LoBianco, Michael Constantine, Matt Craven; *D:* Brian Gibson; *W:* Ted Tally; *C:* Jamie Anderson; *M:* James Newton Howard. *AWARDS: NOM:* Golden Raspberry Awards '96: Worst Actress (Moore).

Just a Little Harmless Sex

Heavy-handed romantic comedy-drama is an ensemble effort that does nobody any favors. After Chuey (Larriva) is caught with a prostitute—it was all a mistake, he swears—his wife Laura (Eastwood) tosses him out. He and two pals hang out and commiserate while she does the same with two of her friends. Over the course of a long night, they all get together, sort of. The no-frills full-frame DVD is not significantly better than VHS tape, but it does justice to Bruce Surtees's first-rate photography. —*MM*

Movie: 🎬▶ **DVD:** 🎬🎬

Sunland Studios (Cat #367). Full frame. $24.99. Keepcase. *LANG:* English. *FEATURES:* 6 chapter links.

1999 (R) 98m/C Robert Mailhouse, Alison Eastwood, Jonathan Silverman, William Ragsdale, Lauren Hutton, Kimberly Williams, Jessica Lundy, Rachel Hunter, Michael Ontkean, Tito Larriva; *D:* Rick Rosenthal; *W:* Roger Miller, Marti Noxon; *C:* Bruce Surtees; *M:* Tito Larriva.

Just Cause

Incoherent mystery/thriller is set in the Florida Everglades. Retired attorney Paul Armstrong (Connery), now a Harvard law professor, decides to defend Bobby Earl (Underwood), on death row for the murder of a white girl. As Armstrong investigates the case, he discovers that the arresting officer, Tanny Brown (Fishburne), is corrupt and tortured the confession out of Bobby. Starts off promising with the electricity of Connery's and Fishburne's presence and a frightening cameo by Ed Harris as an incarcerated serial killer, but once the barrage of plot twists start, creating gator size holes in the plot, the movie drifts into a murky swamp of absurdity. This DVD has colors that run the gamut from lushly vibrant, to subtle earthtones that are dimly lit with finely detailed shading. They are consistently accurate and the transfer has nothing in the way of aggravating color bleed. The picture also stays sharp and free of grain with nothing in the way of noticeable artifacts. Contrast levels are very good with more than adequate brightness in both indoor and outdoor scenes. The stereo sound has very good imaging between the channels and at times feels like there is some Surround mixed in. Fidelity and dynamics are also very good. —JO

Movie: 🎬🎬 **DVD:** 🎬🎬🎬➤
Warner Home Video, Inc. (Cat #13623, UPC #085391362326). Widescreen (1.85:1) anamorphic. Dolby Digital Stereo. $14.98. Snapper. *LANG:* English; French. *CAP:* English. *FEATURES:* 30 chapter links.
1994 (R) 102m/C Sean Connery, Laurence "Larry" Fishburne, Kate Capshaw, Blair Underwood, Ruby Dee, Daniel J. Travanti, Ned Beatty, Lynne Thigpen, George Plimpton, Chris Sarandon, Kevin McCarthy, Ed Harris; *D:* Arne Glimcher; *W:* Jeb Stuart, Robert Stone; *C:* Lajos Koltai; *M:* James Newton Howard.

Just the Ticket

Romantic comedy set in the seedy world of ticket scalpers should have skipped over the trite love story and centered on the business side. Gary (Garcia) is a fast-talking huckster who's trying to win back his ex-girlfriend Linda (MacDowell). He's also hoping for that ever-popular last big score before he goes legit. The opportunity arrives with the Pope's visit to Yankee stadium. The reason for the film's spectacular lack of success at the boxoffice can be found in the extras section of the DVD. That's where you can find a total of 18 deleted scenes taken from two different cuts of the film. Obviously, director Wenk had ambitious ideas, but he could not quite figure out how to put them together. DVD image and sound are virtually flawless, capturing subtle textures in the darkness of a confessional and the buzz of activity on Park Avenue. Sound is fine, too. (By the way, Garcia wrote many of the Salsa-flavored songs in the soundtrack.) —MM

Movie: 🎬🎬 **DVD:** 🎬🎬🎬➤
MGM Home Entertainment (Cat #907453, UPC #027616745323). Widescreen anamorphic. Dolby Digital 5.1 Surround Stereo. $24.98. Keepcase. *LANG:* English;

French. *SUB:* English; French. *FEATURES:* 42 chapter links • Commentary: Richard Wenk and Andy Garcia • "Making of" booklet • Theatrical trailer • Original "Scalper" test footage.
1998 (R) 115m/C Andy Garcia, Andie MacDowell, Richard Bradford, Laura Harris, Andre B. Blake, Elizabeth Ashley, Patrick Breen, Ron Leibman, Chris Lemmon, Don Novello, Abe Vigoda, Bill Irwin, Ronald Guttman, Donna Hanover, Irene Worth, Fred Asparagus, Louis Mustillo, Paunita Nichols, Joe Frazier; *D:* Richard Wenk; *W:* Richard Wenk; *C:* Ellen Kuras; *M:* Rick Marotta.

Just Write

Sweet, slight romantic comedy finds Harold (Piven), a Hollywood tour bus driver, mistaken for a hotshot screenwriter by rising star Amanda (Fenn) who happens to have a script that needs work. She's also got a jealous boyfriend (Mandylor) and an agent (Williams) who's not so sure about Harold. This exceptionally well-crafted independent production is a real find on DVD. Both image and sound overachieve, and since the film arrives in stores without an avalanche of hype, it's a happy discovery. Fans of the cast will not be disappointed. —MM

Movie: 🎬🎬🎬 **DVD:** 🎬🎬🎬
WinStar Home Entertainment (Cat #FLV5161, UPC #720917516127). Widescreen letterboxed. Dolby Digital Stereo. $24.98. Keepcase. *LANG:* English. *FEATURES:* 8 chapter links • Production credits • Filmographies and awards • Trailer.
1997 (PG-13) 95m/C Jeremy Piven, Sherilyn Fenn, JoBeth Williams, Alex Rocco, Jeffrey D. Sams, Wallace Shawn, Costas Mandylor, Yeardley Smith, Holland Taylor; *Cameos:* Nancy McKeon, Ed McMahon; *D:* Andrew Gallerani; *W:* Stan Williamson; *C:* Michael Brown; *M:* Leland Bond.

K-9

After having his car destroyed by a drug dealer, "I work alone" Belushi is forced to take on a partner—a German Shepherd. Together they work to round up the bad guys and maybe chew on their shoes a little. Sometimes amusing one-joke comedy done in by a paper-thin script. Both the dog and Belushi are good, however. Followed by K-911. There is plenty of sharpness on this DVD, and little in the way of grain or artifacts to detract from it. Colors are also good with plenty of punch added by very good contrast and brightness levels. Blacks are also true, with only a scene or two where they hedged towards gray. The Dolby Surround sounds good on the music and the mix keeps dialogue out front, but there is virtually nothing going on in the rear, or even between the front channels for that matter. —JO

Movie: 🎬🎬 **DVD:** 🎬🎬🎬
Universal Studios Home Video (Cat #20585, UPC #025192058523). Widescreen (1.85:1) anamorphic. Dolby Surround. $24.98. Keepcase. *LANG:* English;

French. *SUB:* French. *CAP:* English. *FEATURES:* 18 chapter links • Theatrical trailer • Cast and filmmakers bios • Production notes • Film highlights.
1989 (PG-13) 111m/C James Belushi, Mel Harris, Kevin Tighe, Ed O'Neill, Cotter Smith, James Handy, Jerry Lee; *D:* Rod Daniel; *W:* Steven Siegel, Scott Myers; *C:* Dean Semler; *M:* Miles Goodman.

Kalifornia

Badlands meets the '90s in a road trip with the hitchhikers from hell. Early Grayce (Pitt) is your average slimeball who murders his landlord and hops a ride with his waifish girlfriend Adele (Lewis) from Kentucky to California with Brian (Duchovny), a yuppie writer interested in mass murderers, and his sultry photographer girlfriend Carrie (Forbes). Pitt and Lewis were still an item when they made this. Pitt reportedly wanted to play against type, and as pretty boy gone homicidal, he succeeds. Extremely violent and disturbing. Picture sharpness is above average and there is some minor grain in a few scenes. Colors, however, are excellent with a lot of depth and very little bleed. Blacks are right on. Brightness levels are consistent and contrast is good, although I would have liked a very small boost on booth. Even without the discreet subwoofer track, the low end is powerful and clean on the Dolby Surround sound, which is very lively and overall full-bodied. —JO

Movie: 🎬🎬➤ **DVD:** 🎬🎬🎬
Polygram (Cat #4400432992, UPC #044004329927). Widescreen (2.35:1) letterboxed; full frame. Dolby Surround. $29.95. Expanded jewel case. *LANG:* English; French. *SUB:* Spanish. *CAP:* English. *FEATURES:* 21 chapter links • Behind the scenes footage • Cast and filmmakers bios • "R"-rated and unrated versions.
1993 (R) 117m/C Brad Pitt, Juliette Lewis, David Duchovny, Michelle Forbes, Sierra Pecheur, Lois Hall, Gregory Mars Martin; *D:* Dominic Sena; *W:* Tim Metcalfe; *C:* Bojan Bazelli; *M:* Carter Burwell.

Kama Sutra: A Tale of Love

Erotic but flawed fantasy covering the sexual and political wiles of palace life in 16th-century India. Princess Tara (Choudhury) and girlhood friend/servant Maya (Varma) are close, until the princess becomes jealous of the even more beautiful Maya. In revenge for public humiliation, Maya seduces Tara's dissolute fiance, Raj Singh (Andrews), and is banished from the palace after the wedding. She becomes involved with handsome royal sculptor Jai Kumar (Tikaram) and later learns the sexual arts of the Kama Sutra, becoming the chief courtesan to the Raj. Messy, somewhat overwrought plot vs. extremely attractive cast. The most important aspects of this film are the beautiful scene composition and the rich, luxurious colors. The DVD's image is sharp enough, but where it really shines is with its colors, which are vibrant and highly detailed. The colors are so good that *Kama Sutra* becomes one of those movies, which, despite a slow-moving plot, warrants repeated viewings. The DVD blows away both the laserdisc and the VHS editions. —*JO*

Movie: 🎞🎞▶ **DVD:** 🎞🎞🎞
Trimark Home Video (Cat #VM6771D, UPC #031398677130). Full frame. Dolby Surround. $24.95. Keepcase. *LANG:* English. *CAP:* English. *FEATURES:* 36 chapter links • Theatrical trailer • Commentary: director • Filmography.
1996 117m/C IN Indira Varma, Sarita Choudhury, Ramon Tikaram, Naveen Andrews, Devi Rekha; **D:** Mira Nair; **W:** Mira Nair, Helena Kriel; **C:** Declan Quinn; **M:** Mychael Danna. *AWARDS:* Independent Spirit Awards '98: Best Cinematography.

Kentucky Fried Movie

Inspired send-up of various media—from educational films to the nightly news to kung-fu flicks—has been copied so many times that it's easy to forget how fresh it once was, and how funny it still is. In these more "correct" days, many groups can find something to be offended at, and that's the point. My own favorites are Henry Gibson's United Appeal for the Dead and the 11:00 News. There's not much that DVD can (or should) do to improve the low-budget look and sound. The image is as fuzzy as it's always been. The value of the disc lies in the extras, choice of screen size, and the accessibility of the various episodes. —*MM*

Movie: 🎞🎞🎞 **DVD:** 🎞🎞🎞
Anchor Bay (Cat #DV11117, UPC #013131 111798). Widescreen (1.85:1) anamorphic; full frame. Dolby Digital Mono. $24.98. Keepcase. *LANG:* English. *FEATURES:* 24 chapter links • Trailer • Cast and crew thumbnail bios • Behind-the-scenes stills gallery • Commentary: Landis, Zucker, Zucker, Abrahams, and producer Weiss.
1977 (R) 85m/C Bill Bixby, Jerry Zucker, Jim Abrahams, David Zucker, Donald Sutherland, Henry Gibson, George Lazenby, Tony Dow, Uschi Digart, Rick Baker, Marilyn Joi, Forrest J Ackerman; **D:** John Landis; **W:** Jerry Zucker, Jim Abrahams, David Zucker; **C:** Stephen M. Katz.

Key to Sex

When a Hollywood producer leaves his assistant Simon (Carson) in charge of his mansion for the weekend, it's time to party and make some career moves with the boss's girlfriend (Ford) and any other babes who happen by. This Playboy production is probably not much sharper on a no-frills DVD than it is on tape. It is well photographed with lighting that emphasizes the pink and orange range of the spectrum to flatter the cast's skin tones. Sound is adequate —*MM*

Movie: 🎞🎞▶ **DVD:** 🎞🎞▶
Image Entertainment (Cat #ID5969PLDVD, UPC #014381596922). Full frame. Dolby

Digital Stereo. $24.99. Snapper. *LANG:* English. *FEATURES:* 13 chapter links.
1998 95m/C Maria Ford, Monique Parent, Jacqueline Lovell, Scott Carson, Jeannie Millar; **D:** John Quinn; **W:** Christopher Byrne; **C:** Harris Done.

Keys to Tulsa

After losing his job as a movie reviewer (gasp!), Richter Bourdreau (Stoltz), the blacksheep son of a wealthy Tulsa family, is lured into a blackmail scheme by ex-flame Vicky (Unger) and her perpetually stoned husband Ronnie (Spader). When the tables are turned, Richter gets up off his slacker butt for some revenge. Excellent cast includes Moore as his flinty mother and Coburn as a wealthy redneck patriarch. Stoltz's performance holds the spiraling story of class distinction, murder, and deceit together, and Spader's Elvis-helmeted loser is fun to watch.

Movie: 🎞🎞🎞 **DVD:** NYR
USA Home Entertainment (Cat #638255). Full frame. Stereo. $29.95. Keepcase.
1996 (R) 112m/C Eric Stoltz, James Spader, Mary Tyler Moore, Joanna Going, Cameron Diaz, James Coburn, Michael Rooker, Peter Strauss, Deborah Kara Unger; **D:** Leslie Greif; **W:** Harley Peyton; **C:** Robert Fraisse; **M:** Stephen Endelman.

Khamoshi the Musical

The idea behind this script and its innovative production make it one of a kind. What a shame the storyline is developed so melodramatically that just watching everyone suffer in between musical numbers is punishing up to the very end. The film is set and was shot on India's island of Goa, an unusually self-contained Christian community. The main character Annie (Koirala) is born to an embattled, impoverished deaf-mute couple (the startlingly true Patekar and Biswas) who deny her love of music. Annie grows up to be romanced, in a graveyard and convent no less, by a musician named Raj (Khan). Together they fight to overcome the bitterness and fear of Annie's parents and the reticence of Raj's Hindu family. Writer-director Bhansali consulted with a government agency to portray the world of a deaf person sensitively. The seaside photography unavoidably renders a few scenes as harshly backlit. The score is bass-heavy for a reason, since deaf-mutes "listen" to music through its vibrations. If you can allow for these DVD-unfriendly technical realities, sit down prepared with a big box of tissues! —*JK* *AKA:* Silence.

Movie: 🎞🎞🎞▶ **DVD:** 🎞🎞🎞
Video Sound (Cat #VSDM0100-DVD122, UPC #677565012290). Widescreen. Dolby Digital 5.1 Surround Sound AC-3. $29.95. Keepcase. *LANG:* Hindi, English, Sign. *SUB:* English; Japanese; Chinese. *FEATURES:* 21 chapter links including 9 songs • Animated interactive menus • Autoqueue songs to play as an uninterrupted sequence •

Coming attractions trailers. All regions coding.
1996 167m/C IN Salman Khan, Manisha Koirala, Nana Patekar, Helen, Seema Biswas; **D:** Sanjay Leela Bhansali; **W:** Sanjay Leela Bhansali; **C:** Anil Mehta; **M:** Jatin-Lalit, Majrooh Sultanpuri.

Kickboxer

The brother (Van Damme) of a permanently crippled kickboxing champ trains for a revenge match.
Movie: 🎞▶ **DVD:** NYR
HBO Home Video (Cat #90233). Full frame. Dolby Digital Stereo. $24.98. Snapper. *LANG:* English; French. *SUB:* French; Spanish. *FEATURES:* Cast and crew thumbnail bios.
1989 (R) 97m/C Jean-Claude Van Damme, Rochelle Ashana, Dennis Chan, Dennis Alexio; **D:** Mark DiSalle; **W:** Jean-Claude Van Damme, Mark DiSalle, Glenn A. Bruce; **C:** Jon Kranhouse; **M:** Paul Hertzog.

The Kid / A Dog's Life

A Dog's Life is Chaplin's first long (three-reel) film, and his famous Little Tramp shares the screen with Mut, a wonderful mongrel pup. He took another chance, and was just as successful three years later with *The Kid*, where he made Jackie Coogan a star. Here, the youngster combines Shirley Temple cuteness with the knockabout charm of the Li'l Rascals. The two films are among Chaplin's best early efforts, though both rely on the naked sentimentality and religiosity of their time. Despite the age of the works, the DVD images are extraordinarily clean and unblemished with only minor imperfections. The disc belongs in the collection of any serious student of silent film. —*MM*

Movie: 🎞🎞🎞▶ **DVD:** 🎞🎞🎞▶
Image Entertainment (Cat #ID9178CUDVD, UPC #014381917826). Full frame. Dolby Digital Mono. $24.99. Snapper. *LANG:* Silent. *SUB:* English intertitles. *FEATURES:* 27 chapter links • Original contract between Chaplin & First National Exhibitor's Circuit • Home movies of the construction of Chaplin's studio.
1921 103m/B Charlie Chaplin, Jackie Coogan, Edna Purviance; **D:** Charlie Chaplin; **W:** Charlie Chaplin.

A Kid Called Danger

Adolescent adventure at its most marginal. A cop's son, 13-year-old "Danger" McGuire (Taylor), is on the lookout for trouble. He comes across the case involving stolen jewels that even the police can't seem to solve. With the help of his buddies, Danger sets traps, plans stakeouts, and engages in all kinds of "DANGEROUS" activities. Lots of low-impact action for the kids and only kids. Throughout, the lighting and picture are consistent, the color vivid. Sound quality is fine, except at times of extreme DANGER it really cranks. —*AB*

Image Entertainment (Cat #ID8809UM DVD, UPC #1438188092). Full frame. Dolby Digital Stereo. Keepcase. *LANG:* English. *SUB:* English. *FEATURES:* 12 chapter links • Theatrical trailer.
1999 (PG) 87m/C Clayton Taylor, Devin Gardner, John Armstrong, Mace Melonas, Randi-Lynn Strong; *D:* Eric Hendershot; *W:* Eric Hendershot; *C:* T.C. Christensen; *M:* Geoff Levin.

A Kid in Aladdin's Palace

In a sequel to *A Kid in King Arthur's Court*, young Calvin (Nicholas) is transported by a smart-aleck genie (Negron) to save Aladdin (Ipale) from his nefarious brother (Faulkner). The comely Scheherazade (Mitra) also figures prominently. The limited special effects are not all that special, but judged as a kid's video premiere, this one fills the bill adequately. The DVD may be slightly brighter than VHS tape, but the difference is probably not significant. —*MM*
Movie: 🎬🎬🎬 *DVD:* 🎬🎬
Trimark Home Video (Cat #VM6805D, UPC #031398680536). Full frame. Dolby Digital Stereo. $19.99. Keepcase. *LANG:* English; Spanish. *SUB:* French; Spanish. *CAP:* English. *FEATURES:* 24 chapter links • Trailer.
1997 (PG) 89m/C Thomas Ian Nicholas, Rhona Mitra, Taylor Negron, James Faulkner, Aharon Ipale; *D:* Robert L. Levy; *W:* Michael Part; *C:* Wally Pfister; *M:* David Michael Frank.

Kids

Very controversial docudrama examines 24 hours in the lives of some aimless New York teenagers. The sullen Telly (Fitzpatrick) enjoys bragging about his skill in deflowering virgins but his promiscuity has lead Jennie (Sevigny) to test HIV positive—something Telly is as yet unaware of. Telly'd rather hang around with best friend Casper (Pierce) anyway, out on the streets, being generally profane and obnoxious. Can either be regarded as a brutally realistic look at teen life today or a lot of fuss about nothing. Korine was 19 when he wrote the screenplay. The MPAA rated the film "NC-17"; after a protest the distributors chose to release it unrated. The DVD conveys the film almost exactly as it played in theatres. The picture is crisp and detailed and the contrast and brightness retain the realistic feel of the images. Colors and blacks are accurate. The Dolby Surround doesn't sound like much, but it is also a true representation of the theatrical release, which was a little flat and lacking both space and Surround effects. —*JO*
Movie: 🎬🎬 *DVD:* 🎬🎬🎬
Trimark Home Video (Cat #LDVM6311D, UPC #013023000995). Widescreen (1.85:1) letterboxed; full frame. Dolby Digital 5.1; Dolby Surround. $24.98. Keep-

case. *LANG:* English. *CAP:* English. *FEATURES:* 12 chapter links.
1995 90m/C Leo Fitzpatrick, Justin Pierce, Chloe Sevigny, Rosario Dawson, Sarah Henderson, Harold Hunter, Yakira Peguero, Joseph Knafelmacher; *D:* Larry Clark; *W:* Harmony Korine; *C:* Eric Alan Edwards; *M:* Louis Barlow. *AWARDS:* Independent Spirit Awards '96: Debut Performance (Pierce); *NOM:* Independent Spirit Awards '96: Best First Feature, Best Supporting Actress (Sevigny), First Screenplay.

Kika

Director Pedro Almodovar (*Women on the Verge of a Nervous Breakdown, Tie Me Up! Tie Me Down!*) serves up an amateurish, unfocused bit of pretentious movie trash that pretends to be film art. Since the French and Italians tend to dominate the foreign language market domestically, anything coming from Spain must be important. This is clearly not the case here. Veronica Forque draws the role of Kika, a "beautician" who excels at preparing the dead, sleeps around, and is raped by a porno star fresh from prison, but the film really isn't about her. Victoria Abril is on hand as a "journalist" who dresses as a dominatrix, rides a motorcycle, and wears a head-mounted camera so she won't miss any of the important stories. If the film is a satire on the media, then Almodovar doesn't make that clear either—throw in a couple of murders and you begin to suspect that *Kika* is really nothing more than a muddled mess. The DVD presentation serves up only the basics, with the English subtitles burned into the source print material. There's no commentary or other supporting material that defines the DVD experience. —*RT*
Movie: 🎬🎬 *DVD:* 🎬🎬
Image Entertainment (Cat #4189OC, UPC #014381418927). Widescreen. AC3 - 2 Channel. $29.99. Snapper. *LANG:* Spanish. *SUB:* English. *FEATURES:* 24 chapter links.
1994 115m/C *SP* Veronica Forque, Peter Coyote, Victoria Abril, Alex Casanovas, Rossy de Palma; *D:* Pedro Almodovar; *W:* Pedro Almodovar; *C:* Alfredo Mayo; *M:* Enrique Granados.

Kill and Kill Again

A martial arts champion attempts to rescue a kidnapped Nobel Prize–winning chemist who has developed a high-yield synthetic fuel. The action is colorful and tongue-in-cheek, so it can be fun even for those unfamiliar with the genre. DVD presentations don't get much worse, however. The pan-and-scan image is fuzzier than the typical homespun VHS tape recording of late-night cable fare. The image breaks into large pixelated blocks at times. The soundtrack is in stereo, but it's fuzzy and distorted, and the dialogue can be difficult to understand. Only two chapter stops? Why did they bother? No need for a menu, since there would be little to select on one anyway. —*MB*

Movie: 🎬🎬 *DVD:* 🎬
Digital Versatile Disc Ltd. (Cat #DVD104, UPC #06647910104). Full frame. Dolby Digital 2.0. $19.95. Keepcase. *LANG:* English. *FEATURES:* 2 chapter links.
1981 (PG) 100m/C James Ryan, Anneline Kriel, Stan Schmidt, Bill Flynn, Norman Robinson, Ken Gampu, John Ramsbottom; *D:* Ivan Hall; *W:* John Crowther; *C:* Tai Krige.

Kill, Baby, Kill

A small Transylvanian town is haunted by the ghost of a seven-year-old witchcraft victim, and the town's suicides all seem to have hearts of gold (coins, that is). Lots of style and atmosphere in this tale from horror tongue-in-cheekster Bava. It's considered by some genre connoisseurs to be one of his finest, though it bears early symptoms of the director's infatuation with zoom lenses. *AKA:* Curse of the Living Dead; Operacione Paura.
Movie: 🎬🎬🎬 *DVD:* NYR
VCI Home Video (Cat #8217). Full frame. Dolby Digital Stereo. $24.99. Keepcase. *LANG:* English. *FEATURES:* Cast and crew thumbnail bios.
1966 83m/C *IT* Erika Blanc, Giacomo "Jack" Rossi-Stuart, Fabienne Dali, Giana Vivaldi; *D:* Mario Bava; *W:* Mario Bava; *C:* Antonio Rinaldi; *M:* Carlo Rustichelli.

The Killer

Jeffrey Chow is a gangster gunman who wants out. He's hired by his best friend to perform one last killing, but it doesn't go as smoothly as he wanted. He's almost caught by "Eagle" Lee, a detective who vows to hunt him down using Jennie, a singer blinded by Chow in crossfire. The film works with stylized action and elaborately choreographed gunfights, but it's also pretty sappy and sentimental. Still, it's a good introduction to the Chinese gangster-flick genre. Like other out-of-print Criterion DVDs, *The Killer* fetches incredible amounts on internet auction sites. The transfer is not bad, but is not as sharp as Criterion's widescreen laserdisc. Like the laserdisc, there is some preprint damage that is at times irritating, but also common on many Hong Kong releases. Colors are O.K. and maybe a touch stronger than the LD. Blacks are deep and for the most part free of grain. The image is also contrasty, again traceable to the preprint. The biggest improvement on the DVD is the subtitles, which are much easier to read. Woo's commentary is very pleasant (he sounds like such a nice guy) and provides some pretty detailed information about the actual production. —*JO AKA:* Die Xue Shuang Xiong.
Movie: 🎬🎬🎬 *DVD:* 🎬🎬🎬
Criterion Collection (Cat #CC1515D, UPC #715515008976). Widescreen (1.85:1) letterboxed. Mono. $39.95. Keepcase. *LANG:* Cantonese. *SUB:* English. *FEATURES:* 41 chapter links • Commentary:

John Woo, Terence Chang • Deleted scenes • Theatrical trailer.
1990 (R) 110m/C *HK* Chow Yun-Fat, Sally Yeh, Danny Lee, Kenneth Tsang, Chu Kong, Fui-On Shing; *D:* John Woo; *W:* John Woo; *C:* Wing-hang Wong, Peter Pau; *M:* Lowell Lo.

Killer: A Journal of Murder

Young, idealistic Jewish guard Henry Lesser (Leonard) befriends prisoner Carl Panzram (Woods) and encourages the man to write his life story. Then he must deal with the consequences of discovering the brutality behind Panzram's murderous crimes. The leads are fine, but there's nothing new in a story inspired by true events and set in the 1920s. All in all this is an average DVD. The picture is O.K.; some minor grain pops in on occasion. Artifacts exist but are minimal. Colors are fairly accurate but have occasional bleed on reds and earthtones. Contrast and brightness levels are consistent, but just a hair low. The blacks vary a bit but are generally handled acceptably well. The sound is also nothing special and is in need of some equalization, both on the high and low ends. —*JO*
Movie: 🎬🎬 *DVD:* 🎬🎬➤
Artisan Entertainment (Cat #46294, UPC #017153629422). Widescreen (1.85:1) letterboxed. Stereo. $24.98. Keepcase. *LANG:* English. *SUB:* English; Spanish. *CAP:* English. *FEATURES:* 46 chapter links • Commentary • Theatrical trailer.
1995 (R) 91m/C James Woods, Robert Sean Leonard, Ellen Greene, Cara Buono, Robert John Burke, Steve Forrest, John Bedford Lloyd, Harold Gould; *D:* Tim Metcalfe; *W:* Tim Metcalfe; *C:* Ken Kelsch; *M:* Graeme Revell.

Killer Condom

Deadpan humor, gore, and severed flesh—all based on a Ralf Konig comic book that's definitely for adults. The killer condoms are jellyfish-like creatures with piranha-like teeth who have taken to feeding on the male sexual organs of the unfortunates who frequent Times Square's sleazy Hotel Quickie. Gay cop Luigi Macaroni (Semel) is determined to prevent any more emasculations. This disc is a below-average transfer of the film. The transfer is dark and grainy and there are several obvious flaws in the source print. At times, the transfer is sub-VHS quality. The film's English subtitles are a pale white, and are often hard to read. —*ML* *AKA:* Kondom des Grauens.
Movie: 🎬🎬 *DVD:* 🎬
Troma Team Video (Cat #9984, UPC #790357998432). Widescreen (1.45:1) letterboxed. Dolby Digital Mono. $24.95. Keepcase. *LANG:* German. *SUB:* English. *FEATURES:* Commentary: director Martin Walz, Jorg Buttgereit • Bonus trailers • Troma studio tour • Photo Gallery.
1995 108m/C *GE* Udo Semel, Peter Lohmeyer, Marc Richter, Leonard Lansink;

D: Martin Walz; *W:* Martin Walz, Ralf Konig; *C:* Alexander Honisch.

The Killer Elite

Two professional assassins begin as friends but end up stalking each other when they are double-crossed. This minor Peckinpah effort is murky and doesn't have a clear resolution, but is plenty bloody. Lots of Dobermans roam through this picture, too. Any Peckinpah film deserves better treatment than this DVD gives. The picture is sharper than previous video releases, but still not great, and there are considerable grain and some artifacting at times. Colors are acceptable but not quite as vibrant as in the theatre. Contrast and brightness are also just O.K.; a boost to the contrast might have improved both the colors and the blacks, which are also average. The sound conveys the dialogue in an understandable manner but is lacking in dynamics and low end. —*JO*
Movie: 🎬🎬➤ *DVD:* 🎬🎬➤
MGM Home Entertainment (Cat #907443, UPC #027616744326). Widescreen (2.35:1) letterboxed. Dolby Digital Mono. $24.98. Keepcase. *LANG:* English. *SUB:* English; French. *CAP:* English. *FEATURES:* 32 chapter links • Theatrical trailer • 8-page booklet.
1975 (PG) 120m/C James Caan, Robert Duvall, Arthur Hill, Gig Young, Burt Young, Mako, Bo Hopkins, Helmut Dantine; *D:* Sam Peckinpah; *W:* Marc Norman, Stirling Silliphant; *C:* Peter Lathrop; *M:* Jerry Fielding.

The Killer inside Me

Deputy Lou Ford (Keach) knows that Central City, MT, is corrupt, and that the mine owner (Wynn) runs things, but Ford works within the system to change it and to keep the peace. As the film unfolds, we come to understand that Ford is troubled and, as seen through flashbacks, the dimensions of his illness keep growing. Keach is an underrated actor and this is one of his most effective and controlled performances. On disc, the film looks about as good as any low-budget mid-'70s production could reasonably be expected to look. It lacks sharp focus and memorable production values, and DVD does not improve the original. As is the case with most adaptations of cult favorite Jim Thompson's work, the inventive plotting, vivid characters, and attitude are the important parts. For his fans, this is one of the best. —*MM*
Movie: 🎬🎬🎬 *DVD:* 🎬🎬➤
Simitar Entertainment (Cat #7296, UPC #082551729623). Full frame. Dolby Digital. $9.98. Keepcase. *LANG:* English. *FEATURES:* Brief film facts • Stacy Keach filmography • 8 chapter links.
1976 37m/C Stacy Keach, Susan Tyrrell, Tisha Sterling, Keenan Wynn, John Dehner, John Carradine, Don Stroud, Charles McGraw, Julie Adams, Royal Dano; *D:* Burt Kennedy; *W:* Robert Chandlee; *C:*

William A. Fraker; *M:* Tim McIntire, John Rubinstein.

The Killer Meteors

Chan as the villain? Yep, and he tries really hard to thwart the Killer Meteor from solving the theft of palace treasures and obtaining an antidote for the poison slowly consuming the immortal Wa. Whatever you do, don't take the flesh-decomposing drug! Image and audio on this DVD are terrible, with visual artifacts in nearly every scene and audio distortion on much of the disc. Picture is soft, with plenty of visible scars on the original film element used for the transfer. Pan-and-scan treatment is confining, and some shots appear severely squeezed rather than cropped. To see how wide this movie is supposed to be, look at the extreme letterboxing of the opening titles. The separate interview with Chan is revealing but production values are low (off-camera interviewer is heard, but barely audible). Subtitles aren't present, so English-speaking audiences are stuck with the dubbed soundtrack if they want to follow the action. —*MB* *AKA:* Feng Yu Shuang Liu Xing.
Movie: 🎬 *DVD:* 🎬
Simitar Entertainment (Cat #7254, UPC #082551725427). Full frame. Dolby Digital 2.0. $14.98. Keepcase. *LANG:* English; Cantonese. *FEATURES:* 14 chapter links • Movie factoids • Biography/filmography • Interview with Chan.
1987 ?m/C *HK* Jackie Chan; *D:* Lo Wei.

Killers

Drug crime adventure.
Movie: NYR *DVD:* NYR
MTI Home Video (Cat #229). Dolby Digital 5.1 Surround Stereo. $29.99. Keepcase. *FEATURES:* Commentary: director David Michael Latt • Cast and crew thumbnail bios • Trailers.
1997 (R) 86m/C Kim Little, Scott Carson, Anastasia Martino; *D:* David Michael Latt.

Killer's Kiss

A boxer and a dancer set out to start a new life together after he saves her from an attempted rape. Gritty second feature from Kubrick was financed by family and friends and shows signs of his budding talent.
Movie: 🎬🎬➤ *DVD:* NYR
MGM Home Entertainment (Cat #907707). Full frame. Dolby Digital Mono. $24.98. Keepcase. *FEATURES:* Theatrical trailer.
1955 67m/C Frank Silvera, Jamie Smith, Irene Kane, Jerry Jarret; *D:* Stanley Kubrick; *W:* Stanley Kubrick; *C:* Stanley Kubrick; *M:* Gerald Fried.

Killer's Romance

In London, Jeff (Yam) is a revenge-seeking assassin. Joey Wang is a girl who witnesses one of his hits. The standard Hong Kong action is virtually unwatchable in many scenes. One car chase is so over-exposed that it disappears in white-out. Many of the interiors go to the other extreme in darkness. —MM

Movie: ♪ **DVD:** ♪
Tai Seng Video Marketing (Cat #44544, UPC #601643445441). Full frame. $49.95. Keepcase. *LANG:* English. *FEATURES:* 10 chapter links.
1990 91m/C *HK* Simon Yam, Joey Wang; **D:** Philip Ko.

The Killing

An ex-con (Hayden) engineers the complex heist of a racetrack, but matters go awry in this brilliantly directed and edited effort that was years ahead of its time stylistically. Kubrick made a couple of small films first, but *The Killing* established the director as a talent on the rise. What he accomplished so early in his career is a nearly perfect, unconventionally told caper story about an elaborate racetrack robbery. Hayden and Gray lead a large cast of actors who play out their parts on-screen in a seemingly out-of-sequence fashion similar to the nonlinear approach used more recently by director Quentin Tarantino in his *Pulp Fiction*. Scripted by Kubrick himself, the film is adapted from Lionel White's novel *Clean Break*. Famous B&W cinematographer Lucien Ballard's expertise gives the film a striking visual style that is preserved by this good-looking disc. In terms of quality of presentation, this film actually fares better than some of Kubrick's later works on DVD. The mono soundtrack is quite acceptable for low-budget films of its period. Extras are minimal, and the "production notes" are printed rather than presented on-screen. —MB

Movie: ♪♪♪ **DVD:** ♪♪♪
MGM Home Entertainment (Cat #907706, UPC #027616770622). Full frame. Dolby Digital 1.0. $24.98. Keepcase. *LANG:* English. *SUB:* English; French. *CAP:* English. *FEATURES:* 32 chapter links • 4-page booklet.
1956 83m/B Sterling Hayden, Marie Windsor, Elisha Cook Jr., Jay C. Flippen, Vince Edwards, Timothy Carey, Coleen Gray, Joseph (Joe) Sawyer, Ted de Corsia, James Edwards, Jay Adler, Kola Kwarian, Joe Turkel; **D:** Stanley Kubrick; **W:** Stanley Kubrick, Jim Thompson; **C:** Lucien Ballard; **M:** Gerald Fried.

The Killing Grounds

No, it's not death by espresso; it's a rough rehash of *A Simple Plan*. Killers Vince (Gains) and Art (Hall) are searching the mountains for a missing plane that carried $3 million in gold. But it's been found by a group of hikers (Rocket, Barnes, and Geary) and their guide (Grant). Many mid- to low-budget DVDs suffer when they attempt to deal with rugged outdoor settings. This one doesn't; the image is absolutely solid. Sound is good, too, and the cast is effective in this sometimes

too-tricky but nonetheless enjoyable thriller. —MM

Movie: ♪♪♪ **DVD:** ♪♪♪
Simitar Entertainment (Cat #7441, UPC #082551744121). Full frame. Dolby Digital Stereo; Dolby Digital 5.1 Surround Stereo. $19.95. Keepcase. *LANG:* English. *FEATURES:* 8 chapter links • Production factoids • Anthony Michael Hall and Priscilla Barnes filmographies.
1997 (R) 93m/C Anthony Michael Hall, Courtney Gains, Priscilla Barnes, Charles Rocket, Rodney A. Grant, Cynthia Geary; **D:** Kurt Anderson; **W:** Thomas Ritz.

Killing Hour

Early serial killer thriller revolves around a psychic painter (Kemp) who finds that the visions in her pictures come true in a string of New York murders. Her ability interests a TV reporter (King) and a detective (Parker). Many familiar faces fill the supporting cast. This is one of those low-budget films that has benefitted tremendously from digital restoration. The image has probably never looked better, and, given the problems the film has had with the MPAA-detailed in the commentary track with director Mastroianni and preservationist William Lustig—it has never been shown in its full length. (The ratings board demanded cuts in a particularly brutal sex scene, which is included here.) Sound is very good. —MM **AKA:** The Clairvoyant.

Movie: ♪♪♪ **DVD:** ♪♪♪
Anchor Bay (Cat #DV11078, UPC #013131107890). Widescreen (1.85:1) anamorphic. Dolby Digital 5.1 Surround Stereo. $24.98. Keepcase. *LANG:* English. *FEATURES:* 24 chapter links • Mastroianni thumbnail biography • Theatrical trailer • Deleted scenes.
1984 97m/C Elizabeth Kemp, Perry King, Norman Parker, Kenneth McMillan; **D:** Armand Mastroianni; **W:** Armand Mastroianni; **M:** Alexander Peskanov.

The Killing Jar

Michael Sanford (Cullen) brings his pregnant wife Diane (Tomita) back to the California wine country to take over the failing family vineyard. Is it a coincidence that a series of vicious murders begins then? Hypnosis brings up Michael's repressed memories and he becomes a suspect. This woozy thriller is, at best, fitfully entertaining for viewers who are able to accept its crackpot psychological premises. The superb supporting cast is filled with D-movie veterans. On DVD, the image ranges from fair to good with one sweater that flashes annoyingly. The sound is O.K., but, again, nothing special. The disc is only a marginal improvement over VHS tape. —MM

Movie: ♪♪ **DVD:** ♪♪
Simitar Entertainment (Cat #7302, UPC #082551730223). Full frame. Dolby Digital Stereo; Dolby Digital 5.1 Surround Stereo. $14.98. Keepcase. *LANG:* English. *FEATURES:* 8 chapter links • Production factoids.

1996 (R) 101m/C Brett Cullen, Tamlyn Tomita, Wes Studi, Brion James, M. Emmet Walsh, Tom Bower, Xander Berkeley; **D:** Evan Crooke; **W:** Mark Mullin; **C:** Michael G. Wojciechowski; **M:** David Williams.

The Killing Man

Harlin Garrett (Wincott) is a mob enforcer who gets a new face, courtesy of a shadowy government agency run by Mr. Green (Ironside). He then runs into a fresh set of problems. For a low-budget martial arts thriller, this one has a relatively involving plot and it looks surprisingly good on DVD. It's well filmed, though the lighting in some of the nocturnal fight scenes is less than perfect. Fans have seen much worse. —MM

Movie: ♪♪ **DVD:** ♪♪
Simitar Entertainment (Cat #7339, UPC #082551733927). Full frame. PCM Stereo. $14.98. Keepcase. *LANG:* English. *FEATURES:* 8 chapter links • Production factoids • Jeff Wincott and Michael Ironside filmographies.
1994 (R) 91m/C Jeff Wincott, Terri Hawkes, Michael Ironside, David Bolt, Jeff Pustil; **D:** David Mitchell; **W:** David Mitchell, Damian Lee; **C:** David Pelletier.

Killing Obsession

Albert (Savage) has been locked in the Parkview State Psychiatric Facility for 20 years, ever since he murdered 11-year-old Annie's mother. The little girl is his obsession and when he is released—despite the strenuous objections of Dr. Sachs (Saxon)—he goes looking for her. Bodies do pile up, but this one does try to do something beyond the normal slasher/stalker stuff. Producer-director Paul Leder also made the infamously titled *I Dismember Mama*. This one looks and sounds much the same on DVD as it does on tape. That's true of most low-budget horrors. —MM

Movie: ♪♪ **DVD:** ♪♪
Image Entertainment (Cat #ID5601FMDVD, UPC #014381560121). Full frame. Dolby Digital Mono. $19.99. Snapper. *LANG:* English. *FEATURES:* 12 chapter links.
1994 95m/C John Savage, Kimberly Chase, John Saxon, Bernie White; **D:** Paul Leder; **W:** Paul Leder; **C:** Francis Grumman; **M:** Dana Walden.

The Killing of Sister George

The sexual content of this lesbian drama was revolutionary in a mainstream movie when it was made in the late 1960s. Today, it remains emotionally strong but the film never completely breaks free of its roots as a stage play. June Buckridge (Reid) is sure that Sister George, the character she plays on a popular British soap opera, is going to be killed. Her professional worries compound her suspicions about her lover "Childie" (York). The third point of the triangle is BBC executive Mercy Croft (Browne). Director Aldrich, who also made *Whatever Happened to Baby Jane?*, spins a slow-moving show-business tale of jealousy, alcoholism, and insecurity with some funny moments. On DVD, the image is excellent for a film of the period. The only recurring flaw is the kaleidoscope pattern that appears on June's tweed coat in medium shots. —*MM*

Movie: 🐾🐾▶ **DVD:** 🐾🐾▶
Anchor Bay (Cat #DV10980, UPC #013131098099). Widescreen (1.85:1) letterboxed. Dolby Digital Mono. $29.98. Keepcase. *LANG:* English. *FEATURES:* 25 chapter links.
1969 (R) 138m/C Beryl Reid, Susannah York, Coral Browne, Ronald Fraser, Patricia Medina, Hugh Paddick, Cyril Delevanti, Brandan Dillon, Sivi Aberg, William Beckley, Elaine Church, Mike Freeman, Maggie Paige, Jack Raine, Dolly Taylor; *D:* Robert Aldrich; *W:* Lukas Heller, Frank Marcus; *C:* Joseph Biroc; *M:* Gerald Fried.

Kindergarten Cop

Undercover cop Kimble (Schwarzenegger) stalks criminal Crisp (Tyson) by locating the drug lord's ex and six-year-old son. When his partner (Reed) succumbs to a nasty bout of food poisoning, Kimble is forced to take her place as a kindergarten teacher in the drowsy Pacific Northwest village where mother and son are living incognito. The action-comedy may be too strong for younger viewers, but it shows that the star can handle lighter material fairly well. The full-frame DVD is not really any better than VHS tape in either image or sound. —*MM*

Movie: 🐾🐾▶ **DVD:** 🐾🐾
Universal Studios Home Video (Cat #20145, UPC #025192014529). Full frame. Dolby Digital Surround Stereo. $24.98. Keepcase. *LANG:* English; French. *SUB:* Spanish. *CAP:* English. *FEATURES:* 16 chapter links ◆ Production notes ◆ Cast and crew thumbnail biographies ◆ Trailer.
1990 (PG-13) 111m/C Arnold Schwarzenegger, Penelope Ann Miller, Pamela Reed, Linda Hunt, Richard Tyson, Carroll Baker, Cathy Moriarty, Park Overall, Richard Portnow, Jayne Brook; *D:* Ivan Reitman; *W:* Murray Salem, Herschel Weingrod, Timothy Harris; *C:* Michael Chapman; *M:* Randy Edelman.

The King and I

English governess Kerr is hired to teach the King (Brynner) of Siam's many children and to help him bring them and the country into the 20th century. The cultural and personal conflicts that arise may be familiar stuff, but this is a film that continues to delight on repeated viewings, primarily because it features one of Rodgers and Hammerstein's best scores. Kerr's singing voice is dubbed by Marni Nixon, who did the same for *West Side Story* and *The Sound of Music*. The DVD looks and sounds terrific. It appears to have been made from a pristine original and even

without the Surround elements, the stereo soundtrack is fine. —*MM*

Movie: 🐾🐾🐾🐾 **DVD:** 🐾🐾🐾🐾
Twentieth Century Fox Home Entertainment (Cat #4110826). Widescreen (2.35:1) letterboxed. Dolby Digital Stereo; Dolby Digital 5.1 Surround Stereo. $24.98. Keepcase. *LANG:* English; French. *SUB:* Spanish. *FEATURES:* Production notes ◆ Trailer ◆ Movietone news featurettes ◆ Cast and crew thumbnail bios.
1956 133m/C Deborah Kerr, Yul Brynner, Rita Moreno, Martin Benson, Terry Saunders, Rex Thompson, Alan Mowbray, Carlos Rivas; *D:* Walter Lang; *W:* Ernest Lehman; *C:* Leon Shamroy; *M:* Richard Rodgers, Oscar Hammerstein. *AWARDS:* Academy Awards '56: Best Actor (Brynner), Best Art Direction/Set Decoration (Color), Best Costume Design (Color), Best Sound, Scoring of a Musical; Golden Globe Awards '57: Best Actress—Musical/Comedy (Kerr), Best Film—Musical/Comedy; *NOM:* Academy Awards '56: Best Actress (Kerr), Best Color Cinematography, Best Director (Lang), Best Picture.

The King and I

Animated musical compresses the plot of the famous Rodgers and Hammerstein play and adds a conventional one-dimension villain and typically insipid comic critters. The result will appeal to kids who like and understand feature-length cartoons and will send most adults screaming into the TV room. The DVD image is really nothing special with colors that bleed beyond their boundaries, but that probably comes from the original, which is overly bright, masking the transitions between computer-generated images and conventional drawing. The full slate of extras will be more appealing to the target audience, though navigating parts of the menu is difficult, again due to the pastel colors which make it difficult to tell which item is highlighted. —*MM*

Movie: 🐾🐾▶ **DVD:** 🐾🐾🐾
Warner Home Video, Inc. (Cat #17468, UPC #085391746829). Widescreen anamorphic. Dolby Digital 5.1 Surround Stereo; Dolby Digital Stereo. $29.98. Snapper. *LANG:* English; French; Spanish. *SUB:* English; French; Spanish. *FEATURES:* "Making of" featurette ◆ Character sketches ◆ "Sizzle" featurette ◆ Trailers and spots ◆ Karaoke sing-alongs ◆ "How to use this disc" tutorial ◆ Interactivity center for kids.
1999 (G) 87m/C *D:* Richard Rich; *W:* Jacqueline Feather, David Seidler, Peter Bakalian; *V:* Miranda Richardson, Martin Vidnovic, Ian Richardson, Darrell Hammond, Allen D. Hong, Armi Arabe, Adam Wylie, Sean Smith.

King Cobra

When a team of scientists led by Dr. Irwin Burns (Ruskin), tests a drug that increases aggression in animals and humans, their experiment results in a mutated nightmare. Half African King Cobra and

half Eastern Diamondback Rattlesnake, Seth (that's the killer snake, in case you're having trouble following me) is pure evil (er, I mean camp). The video transfer is excellent. The audio transfer, however, is often too quiet and requires constant manipulation of the volume control. Overall though, it is a solid effort. —*MJT*

Movie: 🐾🐾▶ **DVD:** 🐾🐾▶
Trimark Home Video (Cat #VM7125D, UPC #03139871253). Widescreen (1.85:1) letterboxed. Dolby Digital Surround. $24.99. Keepcase. *LANG:* English; French; Spanish. *SUB:* English; French; Spanish. *FEATURES:* 30 chapter links ◆ Making of *King Cobra* documentary ◆ Commentary: directors David Hillenbrand, Scott Hillenbrand ◆ Theatrical trailer.
1998 (PG-13) 93m/C Noriyuki "Pat" Morita, Hoyt Axton, Kasey Fallo, Scott Brandon, Joseph Ruskin, Courtney Gains; *D:* David Hillenbrand, Scott Hillenbrand; *W:* David Hillenbrand, Scott Hillenbrand; *C:* Philip D. Schwartz.

A King in New York / A Woman in Paris

Double-feature DVD holds Chaplin's last starring performance, in *A King in New York,* plus his 1923 film *A Woman in Paris,* which he wrote and directed but in which he did not star. In the former, Chaplin plays the deposed king of a European mini-monarchy who comes to the United States in hope of making a new life. While Chaplin's *The Great Dictator* pokes fun at fascism, this film does the same thing to societal problems in the 1950s. It looks critically at American life of the time, including Cold War paranoia and over reliance on technology. Perhaps that's why it wasn't released in the U.S. until 1973. The latter picture, a nice bonus, is Chaplin's legendary silent movie about manners, mores, and morals. Extras are abundant, and the material looks and sounds O.K. for its age, though minor compression artifacts are evident in some of the grainier parts of the picture. Smart menu design. —*MB*

Movie: 🐾🐾▶ **DVD:** 🐾🐾🐾
Image Entertainment (Cat #ID9186CUDVD, UPC #014381918625). Full frame. Dolby Digital 1.0. $29.99. Snapper. *LANG:* English. *FEATURES:* 18 chapter links ◆ 7 minutes restored to *King* that was cut after premiere ◆ Corrected running speed and restored footage for *Woman* ◆ Theatrical trailers for both films ◆ Footage of Chaplin conducting *King* recording session.
1957 105m/B *GB* Charlie Chaplin, Dawn Addams, Michael Chaplin, Oliver Johnston, Maxine Audley, Harry Green; *D:* Charlie Chaplin; *W:* Charlie Chaplin; *C:* Georges Perinal; *M:* Charlie Chaplin.

King Kong

In 1976, the ads proclaimed "There is only one King Kong!" They were right and this isn't it. Campy touches aren't enough to make the remake even remotely comparable to the original. The special effects, particularly those used to create King Kong, are much less authentic-looking than Willis O'Brien's stop-motion animation. Oil company official (Grodin) travels to a remote island to discover it inhabited by a huge gorilla. Ape meets girl (Lange), ape loses girl, ape gets girl back, ape climbs World Trade Center. Watch for Joe Piscopo and briefly for Corbin Bernsen as a reporter. The widescreen DVD magnifies the occasionally primitive effects. In close-ups, Kong's face can be expressive but his movements are more human than simian. Overall, the quality of the image is fine, even in the night scenes, but the Oscar-nominated sound is much better. Kong's roars are really impressive through headphones, and John Barry's underrated score is terrific. It's so good that it deserves a separate track. —MM

Movie: 🎬🎬 **DVD:** 🎬🎬🎬
Paramount Home Video (Cat #088727, UPC #097360887273). Widescreen anamorphic. Dolby Surround, 5.1 Surround (English); Dolby Mono (French). $29.98. Keepcase. *LANG:* English; French. *SUB:* English. *FEATURES:* 28 chapter links • Theatrical trailer.
1976 (PG) 135m/C Jeff Bridges, Charles Grodin, Jessica Lange, Rene Auberjonois, John Randolph, Ed Lauter, Jack O'Halloran, Dennis Fimple, John Agar, Rick Baker, Joe Piscopo, Corbin Bernsen; *D:* John Guillermin; *W:* Lorenzo Semple Jr.; *C:* Richard Kline; *M:* John Barry. *AWARDS:* Academy Awards '76: Best Visual Effects; *NOM:* Academy Awards '76: Best Cinematography, Best Sound.

King of Beggars

This historical martial arts comedy is so silly that it makes little sense to western audiences not familiar with Chinese culture. It has to do with a doltish young man (Chow) who leaves his wealthy family and becomes the title character. The gauzy image is pale throughout but clear. Overall, it looks better than most import tapes, but it's not up to the best DVDs. —MM

Movie: 🎬🎬 **DVD:** 🎬🎬
Tai Seng Video Marketing (Cat #MS/DVD/038/98). Widescreen letterboxed. Dolby Digital 5.1 Surround Stereo. $49.95. Keepcase. *LANG:* Cantonese; Mandarin. *SUB:* Traditional & Simplified Chinese; English; Korean; Japanese; Bahasa Malaysia; Thai; Vietnamese; Spanish. *FEATURES:* 9 chapter links • Cast and credits • Synopsis • Trailers
1992 96m/C *HK* Stephen (Chiau) Chow, Cheung Man, Man-Tat Ng; *D:* Gordon Chan; *W:* Gordon Chan, Kin-Chung Chan; *C:* David Chung.

King of the Zombies

Mad scientist (Victor) creates his own zombies without souls to fight in World War II. The use of childlike black characters for comic relief will strike viewers as racist. The rest is zombie nonsense. The image is no better than you'd expect from a very old very low-budget horror. It's dark

and grainy with particularly heavy pixels in special effects shots of a miniature airplane. The menu does not contain a chapter list. —MM

Movie: 🐶 **DVD:** 🎬
Roan Group (Cat #AED-2020, UPC #785604202028). Full frame. $29.95. Keepcase. *LANG:* English. *FEATURES:* Cast credits • Film background • 17 chapter links. Title is available as part of a double-feature disc with *Revolt of the Zombies*.
1941 67m/B John Archer, Dick Purcell, Mantan Moreland, Henry Victor, Joan Woodbury; *D:* Jean Yarbrough; *W:* Edmond Kelso; *C:* Mack Stengler. *AWARDS: NOM:* Academy Awards '41: Best Original Dramatic Score.

King Ralph

When the rest of the royal family is killed in a freak accident, lounge lizard Ralph Jones (Goodman) ascends to the throne of England. O'Toole is the long-suffering valet and private secretary who must prepare the commoner for his new duties; Coduri is the non-stripping stripper Ralph falls for. Goodman's always affable performance is the film's one shining virtue. The full-frame, no-extras DVD is really no better than tape in either image or sound. —MM

Movie: 🎬🎬 **DVD:** 🎬🎬
Goodtimes Entertainment (Cat #05-81016, UPC #018713810168). Full frame. Dolby Digital Surround Stereo. $19.98. Snapper. *LANG:* English. *SUB:* English; French; Spanish. *FEATURES:* 18 chapter links.
1991 (PG) 96m/C John Goodman, Peter O'Toole, Camille Coduri, Joely Richardson, John Hurt; *D:* David S. Ward; *W:* David S. Ward; *C:* Kenneth Macmillan; *M:* James Newton Howard.

Kingpin

Bowling epic serves up social satire and bad hair. Roy Munson (a very bald Harrelson) is a former bowling champ who, thanks to a hustle gone bad, lost his hand and is reduced to selling bowling supplies while wearing a crude rubber prosthesis. That is, until he meets innocent Amish phenomenon Ishmael (Quaid), whom he persuades to hit the road to a big money tournament in Reno, where Roy can confront an old nemesis (Murray). Cowritten and directed by the outrageous Farrelly brothers, who followed with *There's Something about Mary*. Highlight of the DVD is the ten extra minutes that earned a re-rated "R." Other than that, the disc is very average and has some problems with both red color bleed and noticeable grain in the low light scenes—so the sharpness could be better. There don't seem to be many true blacks; most of the time they look more like a dark charcoal. No problems with artifacts, and the DVD isn't hard to watch, it's just not anything special. Commentary is informative but not as entertaining as you would expect from the Farrellys. —JO

Movie: 🎬🎬🎬 **DVD:** 🎬🎬

MGM Home Entertainment (Cat #906275, UPC #027616627520). Widescreen (2.35:1) anamorphic. Dolby Digital 5.1. $24.98. Keepcase. *LANG:* English. *SUB:* French. *CAP:* English. *FEATURES:* 28 chapter links • Theatrical trailer • Commentary: directors Peter and Bobby Farrelly.
1996 (R) 117m/C Woody Harrelson, Randy Quaid, Vanessa Angel, Bill Murray, Chris Elliott; *D:* Peter Farrelly, Bobby Farrelly; *W:* Bobby Farrelly, Mort Nathan; *C:* Mark Irwin; *M:* Freedy Johnston.

Kiss Me Monster

This is '70s Eurosleaze at its best delivered by Franco with miniskirts aplenty, fast convertibles, super-cool trash music, and not much plot to distract. Two sexy musician/spies must prevent a mad scientist from using his race of evil supermen for world conquest. The DVD is nothing special, possibly because of the lack of good preprint material. There are quite a few scratches and other types of damage. The image is moderately sharp and does have occasional grain and artifacts. Colors are generally a little weak and both contrast and brightness levels are in the O.K. range, but comfortable enough to view. Deep blacks have some grain and are sometimes grayish green. The sound is mono and a little thin but somehow seems more than adequate (and maybe preferred) for this film. —JO *AKA:* Besame Monstruo.

Movie: 🎬🎬🎬 **DVD:** 🎬🎬
Anchor Bay (Cat #DV10600, UPC #013131060096). Widescreen (1.66:1) letterboxed. Dolby Digital Mono. $29.99. Keepcase. *LANG:* English. *FEATURES:* 12 chapter links • Theatrical trailer.
1969 80m/C *SP* Janine Reynaud, Rossana Yanni, Adrian Hoven, Michel Lemoine, Chris Howland; *D:* Jess (Jesus) Franco.

Kiss of the Vampire

Newlywed couple is stranded in Bavaria near a villa of vampires and are invited in by its charming evil owner. Fortunately, hubby manages to escape and finds a knowledgeable professor who unleashes a horde of bats to rout the bloodsuckers. Properly creepy Hammer fare; producer Hinds used the pseudonym John Elder for his screenplay. The first thing to say about this DVD is that although the packaging gives an aspect ratio of 1.66:1, it's actually 1.85:1. Next, it's great that these Hammer classics from the '60s are making it to DVD. The disc itself is a little above average with the main complaint being a little too much grain. The colors are vibrant enough, but do bleed a little. The blacks are O.K., as is the contrast and brightness. Occasionally the sound clips (mainly on loud music passages), but overall the PCM Mono track is probably as good as the original film could offer. —JO *AKA:* Kiss of Evil.

Movie: 🎬🎬 **DVD:** 🎬🎬

Image Entertainment (Cat #ID4286USDVD, UPC #014381428629). Widescreen (1.85:1) letterboxed. PCM Mono. $24.98. Snapper. *LANG:* English. *FEATURES:* 15 chapter links.

1962 88m/C *GB* Clifford Evans, Noel Willman, Edward De Souza, Jennifer Daniel, Barry Warren, Jacqueline Wallis, Peter Madden, Isobel Black, Vera Cook, Olga Dickie; *D:* Don Sharp; *W:* Anthony (John Elder) Hinds; *C:* Alan Hume; *M:* James Bernard.

Kiss Shot

Goldberg is a struggling single mom who loses her job but still must make the mortgage payments. She becomes a waitress but realizes it isn't going to pay enough so she tries her hand as a pool hustler. Frantz is the promoter who finances her; Harewood is the pool-shooting playboy whose romantic advances are destroying her concentration.
Movie: ♫♫ *DVD:* NYR
Studio Home Entertainment (Cat #4065). Full frame. $24.95. Keepcase.
1989 88m/C Whoopi Goldberg, Dennis Franz, Dorian Harewood, David Marciano, Teddy Wilson; *D:* Jerry London; *M:* Chuy Elizondo; *M:* Steve Dorff.

Kiss the Girls

After his niece is abducted, forensic psychologist Alex Cross (Freeman) joins the hunt for a lunatic who's kidnapping and collecting successful young women. Doctor Kate McTiernan (Judd), who also happens to be a kickboxer, escapes the sicko's love dungeon and helps Cross track him down. Borrowing heavily from *Silence of the Lambs* and *Seven,* this psycho-killer thriller falls far short of both. All the specs on this DVD run from very good to excellent, with the sound being the most impressive feature, with dynamics as good as anything yet reviewed, and strong deep bass. The different lighting conditions seem to have no effect on the quality of the image as it stays sharp and grain-free throughout, with lush accurate colors and very true blacks. The contrast and brightness levels consistently keep details visible and comfort high. Grain and artifact levels also stay consistent in both light and dark scenes. *—JO*
Movie: ♫♫ *DVD:* ♫♫♫▶
Paramount Home Video (Cat #331887, UPC #097363318873). Widescreen (2.35:1) anamorphic. Dolby Digital 5.1; Dolby Surround. $29.99. Keepcase. *LANG:* English (DD5.1; DS); French (DS). *SUB:* Spanish. *CAP:* English. *FEATURES:* 26 chapter links ▶ Theatrical trailer.
1997 (R) 117m/C Morgan Freeman, Ashley Judd, Cary Elwes, Tony Goldwyn, Jay O. Sanders, Bill Nunn, Brian Cox, Alex McArthur, Richard T. Jones, Jeremy Piven, William Converse-Roberts, Gina Ravera, Roma Maffia; *D:* Gary Fleder; *W:* David Klass; *C:* Aaron Schneider; *M:* Mark Isham.

Kissing a Fool

At Samantha's (Avital) wedding, her boss Linda (Hunt) explains to two guests how she introduced the bride and groom. The question is: Who's the groom? Is it obnoxious Chicago sportscaster Max (Schwimmer) or his pal Jay (Lee), a novelist? That less-than-compelling premise takes an hour and a half to work out. On DVD, the film looks about as good as any of the big-screen vehicles for a TV star is supposed to look. No significant flaws, but it's nothing special in any department. *—MM*
Movie: ♫▶ *DVD:* ♫♫▶
Universal Studios Home Video (Cat #20320, UPC #025192032028). Widescreen (1.85) letterboxed. Dolby Digital 5.1 Surround Stereo. $24.98. Keepcase. *LANG:* English. *SUB:* Spanish; French. *CAP:* English. *FEATURES:* 16 chapter links ▶ Production notes ▶ Case and crew thumbnail biographies ▶ Theatrical trailer.
1998 (R) 93m/C David Schwimmer, Jason Lee, Mili Avital, Bonnie Hunt, Vanessa Angel, Kari Wuhrer, Frank Medrano, Bitty Schram, Judy Greer; *D:* Doug Ellin; *W:* Doug Ellin, James Frey; *C:* Thomas Del Ruth; *M:* Joseph Vitarelli.

Klash

Caribbean crime drama.
Movie: NYR *DVD:* NYR
Xenon Entertainment (Cat #4073). Full frame. $19.95.
1995 (R) 90m/C Carl Bradshaw, Paul Campbell, Giancarlo Esposito, Jasmine Guy, Stafford Ashani, Lucien Chen, Cedella Marley; *D:* Bill Parker; *W:* Bill Parker, Peter Allen; *C:* Bill Parker.

Klondike Annie

On the lam from San Francisco for murdering her Chinese lover—it was self defense—Rose Carlton (West) heads for the Alaskan Gold Rush aboard Capt. Bull Brackett's (McLaglen) ship. He falls for her right away and helps her with a scam to pass herself off as a missionary. It's vintage West material; she wrote the script. The DVD image varies between fair and good with imperfections that come from the original, not the transfer. The night scenes are often too dark by contemporary standards. The rinky-tink sound is typical of the '30s. *—MM*
Movie: ♫♫▶ *DVD:* ♫♫▶
Image Entertainment (Cat #ID4283USDVD, UPC #014381428322). Full frame. Uncompressed PCM Mono. $24.99. Snapper. *LANG:* English. *FEATURES:* 16 chapter links.
1936 77m/B Mae West, Victor McLaglen, Philip Reed, Helen Jerome Eddy, Harry Beresford, Harold Huber, Conway Tearle, Esther Howard; *D:* Raoul Walsh; *W:* Mae West; *C:* George T. Clemens.

Knock Off

For those who care about the plot, it concerns Hong Kong jeans makers Marcus (Van Damme) and Tommy (Schneider), who

are not what they seem and are trying to stop the sale of bombs to terrorists. Action director Tsui Hark keeps things zipping along at a breakneck pace with flashy special effects and mad action sequences that don't know when to stop. The DVD handles all of these visual excesses without flaws. It's a dazzling version of a featherweight movie. *—MM*
Movie: ♫♫♫ *DVD:* ♫♫♫
Columbia Tristar Home Video (Cat #25889, UPC #043396258891). Widescreen (2.35:1) letterboxed; full frame. Dolby Digital 5.1 Surround Stereo; Dolby Digital Stereo. $25.95. Keepcase. *LANG:* English. *SUB:* English. *FEATURES:* 28 chapter links ▶ Photo gallery ▶ Trailers.
1998 (R) 91m/C Jean-Claude Van Damme, Rob Schneider, Lela Rochon, Paul Sorvino, Michael Wong, Carmen Lee, Wyman Wong; *D:* Tsui Hark; *W:* Steven E. de Souza; *C:* Arthur Wong; *M:* Ron Mael, Russell Mael.

Koyla

It's big, sweaty, and garish. Think of a Sly Stallone movie redone as an Elvis musical, plus the supernaturally mythic overtones of an Eastwood western. That's the vaulting outline of what promises to be a melodrama of simple peasants in a coal town. This particular mining operation, however, is set among the imposing cliffs of an Indian mountain range. The villagers are Shankar (Khan) and Gauri (Dixit), manipulated by the gangster "saab" Raja (Puri). Raja tricks Gauri into marrying him, but his bullying ways soon come to light. Raja terrorizes the girl, her family, and her true love. Shankar is apparently thrown to his death, but only then does the Rajasaab begin to get his comeuppance. Is our young hero exacting revenge from beyond the grave? Or just beyond belief? The equally intense doses of fire and flood (well, waterfall) sound as breathtaking as they look, even without the aid of a subwoofer. *—JK* *AKA:* Coal.
Movie: ♫♫♫▶ *DVD:* ♫♫♫♫
Video Sound (Cat #SDM98-DVD105). Widescreen. Dolby Digital AC-3 Surround 5.1. $29.95. Keepcase. *LANG:* Hindi; English. *SUB:* English; Japanese; Chinese. *FEATURES:* 31 chapter links including 6 songs ▶ Animated interactive menus ▶ Auto-queue songs to play as an uninterrupted sequence ▶ Star bios and filmographies ▶ Coming attractions trailers. All regions coding.
1998 167m/C *IN* Madhuri Dixit, Shah Rukh Khan, Amrish Puri, Salim Ghouse; *D:* Rakesh Roshan.

Krakatoa East of Java

On DVD, the two versions of this oversized disaster epic are a textbook example of the choices that a viewer faces. The 1966 film was produced in Cinerama, an ultra-widescreen process that utilized three projectors. The picture immediately became the butt of jokes when people realized that

the volcano Krakatoa had been west of Java. The plot is filled with potentially intriguing elements—sunken treasure, hot air balloons, erupting volcano, tidal wave—but they're never compelling. The film fared poorly in its initial theatrical run and was shortened for wider distribution in conventional theatres. (Even so, it can be seen as a precursor to the early '70s disaster pictures which were built on the same combination of all-star casts and splashy special effects.) The Anchor Bay disc came from the original 131-minute version. The Simitar disc is 106 minutes. Anchor Bay contains both widescreen and full-frame versions. Simitar is widescreen only. The Anchor Bay disc contains 21 chapter links; the Simitar has eight. The Anchor Bay disc costs about $25; the Simitar is $20. Besides the extra length, the image of the Anchor Bay print is clearly superior with sharper focus, extra brightness, and fuller sound. Because it looks so much better, the special effects are even more dated. In short, Anchor Bay has produced a superior version of a film that isn't very good. —MM
Movie: 🎬🎬 **DVD:** 🎬🎬🎬
Anchor Bay (Cat #DV10983, UPC #013131098396). Full frame; widescreen (2.35:1) letterboxed. Dolby Digital Stereo. $24.98. Keepcase. *LANG:* English. *FEATURES:* 21 chapter links.
1966 (G) 131m/C Maximilian Schell, Diane Baker, Brian Keith, Barbara Werle, John Leyton, Rossano Brazzi, Sal Mineo; *D:* Bernard L. Kowalski; *W:* Bernard Gordon, Clifford Gould; *M:* Frank DeVol.

Krakatoa East of Java (Simitar)

Please see review of Anchor Bay edition of *Krakatoa East of Java.* —MM
Movie: 🎬🎬 **DVD:** 🎬🎬
Simitar Entertainment (Cat #7224, UPC #082551722426). Widescreen (2.35:1) letterboxed. Dolby Digital Stereo. $19.98. Keepcase. *LANG:* English. *FEATURES:* 8 chapter links • Production factolds • Diane Baker and Maximilian Schell filmographies.
1966 (G) 108m/C

Kull the Conqueror

Sorbo goes from TV's heroic Hercules to action-fantasy hero Kull, a slave who becomes the warrior king of a mythic land. Overthrown by a corrupt nobility, Kull begins a perilous journey to find the one weapon that will destroy the she-demon Akivasha (Carrere) and save the land of Valusia. Lots of action, although the "PG-13" rating keeps some of the mayhem less bloody than might be expected. (It's based on the '30s character created by pulp writer Robert E. Howard, who also originated *Conan the Barbarian.*) The image on this DVD is very sharp, with little in the way of artifacts or added grain. Color is a different story, leaning to red, and having some occasional problems

with bleed. Contrast and brightness levels are high enough to give the picture some needed punch and the blacks range from good to true. The best feature of the disc is the 5.1 sound, which adds enough guts to the film to make up for the average picture quality. There are plenty of effects and enough ambience sent to the Surround channels. —JO
Movie: 🎬🎬 **DVD:** 🎬🎬🎬
Universal Studios Home Video (Cat #20154, UPC #025192015427). Widescreen (2.35:1) anamorphic. Dolby Digital 5.1; Dolby Surround. $24.98. Keepcase. *LANG:* English (DD5.1); French (DS). *SUB:* Spanish. *CAP:* English. *FEATURES:* 16 chapter links • Production notes • Cast and crew bios • Theatrical trailer • Film highlights.
1997 (PG-13) 96m/C Kevin Sorbo, Tia Carrere, Thomas Ian Griffith, Karina Lombard, Litefoot, Harvey Fierstein, Roy Brocksmith, Douglas Henshall, Sven-Ole Thorsen, Terry O'Neill; *D:* John Nicolella; *W:* Charles Edward Pogue; *C:* Rodney Charters; *M:* Joel Goldsmith.

Kuma Hula: Keepers of the Culture

Many of Hawaii's finest kuma hula reveal ancient traditions which have survived and flourished there for hundreds of years in this film, shot at exotic locations throughout the islands. This is Hawaiian culture as few outsiders have ever seen it: rich, expressive, colorful, and totally unique. The video transfer is exceptional with vibrant and crisp, clear colors. The soundtrack is also quite solid, with no noticeable distortion. —MJT
Movie: 🎬🎬 **DVD:** 🎬🎬🎬
WinStar Home Entertainment (Cat #WHE73033, UPC #720917303321). Full frame. Dolby Digital Stereo. $24.98. Keepcase. *LANG:* English. *FEATURES:* 6 chapter links • Audio tracks by Raymond Kane, Led Kaapana, and George Kuo • Photo gallery • DVD-ROM, Production notes • DVD-ROM, The "making of" essay.
1989 85m/C *D:* Robert Mugge.

Kundun

Scorsese presents a cinematic portrait of the life of the young 14th Dalai Lama from 1937 through 1959, when he was forced to flee Chinese-occupied Tibet and live in exile in India. The incredibly detailed and sumptuous Tibetan journey begins with the discovery of the young boy as the Buddha reborn and uses different actors to portray him through young adulthood. Dramatic depiction of the Chairman Mao–ordered slaughter of Tibetan nuns and monks around the young Kundun illustrates the dilemmas facing a nonviolent man in an increasingly violent world. The adult Dalai Lama's (Tsarong) meeting with cartoonishly evil incarnate Chairman Mao Zedong (Lin) mars an otherwise realistic and honest portrayal. Made with the cooperation of the 14th Dalai Lama, the story reflects

the director's yen for accuracy and integrity. Scorsese's gamble on using a cast of non-professional Tibetan refugees pays off. Beautiful scenery and dreamy Philip Glass score set the proper mood. This beautiful film is also a gorgeous DVD. Sharpness is very good, thanks to low grain levels and no artifacting. Colors are lush, accurate, and bleed-free, and the blacks even more true. Brightness is comfortable and the contrast punchier than both previous video releases and the theatre. The 5.1 sound is tremendous and although the Surround only kicks in for the occasional effect, the ambience it supplies is spectacular. —JO
Movie: 🎬🎬🎬 **DVD:** 🎬🎬🎬
Buena Vista Home Entertainment (Cat #14890, UPC #717951000576). Widescreen (2.35:1) letterboxed. Dolby Digital 5.1. $29.99. Keepcase. *LANG:* English. *CAP:* English. *FEATURES:* 18 chapter links • Theatrical trailer.
1997 (PG-13) 134m/C Tanzin Thuthob Tsarong, Robert Lin; *D:* Martin Scorsese; *W:* Melissa Mathison; *C:* Roger Deakins; *M:* Philip Glass. *AWARDS:* New York Film Critics Awards '97: Best Cinematography; National Society of Film Critics Awards '97: Best Cinematography; *NOM:* Academy Awards '97: Best Art Direction/Set Decoration, Best Cinematography, Best Costume Design, Best Original Score; Australian Film Institute '98: Best Foreign Film; Golden Globe Awards '98: Best Score.

La Bamba

Romanticized biopic focuses on the short and not particularly dramatic life of Ritchie Valens (Phillips), who became a star in the early days of rock. He has a stormy relationship with his half-brother (Morales), a WASP girlfriend (von Zerneck), and a career cut short with the crash of Buddy Holly's airplane. The music is the point of the film and it makes a fine transition from the big screen to DVD. The stereo sound is excellent and so are the concert scenes, though they have always lacked the maniacal spark that the best rock groups generate. —MM
Movie: 🎬🎬 **DVD:** 🎬🎬🎬
Columbia Tristar Home Video (Cat #08549, UPC #043396085497). Widescreen (1.85:1) letterboxed. Dolby Digital 5.1 Surround Stereo; Dolby Digital Surround Stereo. $28.95. Keepcase. *LANG:* English; Spanish. *SUB:* English; Spanish; Portuguese; Chinese; Korean; Thai. *FEATURES:* 28 chapter links • Commentary: producer, director, and cast • Commentary: Taylor Hackford, Daniel Valdez • Music videos • "Remembering Ritchie" featurette • Theatrical trailer • Cast and crew thumbnail biographies.
1987 (PG-13) 99m/C Lou Diamond Phillips, Esai Morales, Danielle von Zerneck, Joe Pantoliano, Brian Setzer, Marshall Crenshaw, Howard Huntsberry, Rosana De Soto, Elizabeth Pena, Rick Dees; *D:* Luis Valdez; *W:* Luis Valdez; *C:* Adam Greenberg; *M:* Miles Goodman, Carlos Santana.

La Collectionneuse

The third of Rohmer's "moral tales" finds an artist (Bauchau) and an antiques dealer (Pommereulle) vacationing in St. Tropez with a beautiful young woman (Politoff) who picks a different man to sleep with every night. Both resist—with faltering degrees of rigor—the temptations of being added to her "collection." On DVD, the film shows minimal wear and tear for a work of its age. By American standards, the image is underlit and dim, even in bright daylight scenes. But with Rohmer, brilliant visuals are secondary to characters and their voluminous talk. Audio is actually a bit sharper, emphasizing the natural sounds of rural summer. —*MM* **AKA:** The Gentleman Tramp.

Movie: 🎵🎵🎵 *DVD:* 🎵🎵▶
WinStar Home Entertainment (Cat #FLV5205, UPC #720917520520). Full frame. $29.98. Keepcase. *LANG:* French. *SUB:* English. *FEATURES:* 12 chapter links ▪ Production credits ▪ Filmographies and awards ▪ Weblinks.
1967 88m/C *FR* Patrick Bauchau, Daniel Pommereulle, Haydee Politoff, Alain Jouffroy; *D:* Eric Rohmer; *W:* Eric Rohmer; *C:* Nestor Almendros.

L.A. Confidential

Hard-boiled, complicated crime drama is based on James Ellroy's even more complex novel. Fifties Hollywood is ripe with corruption in many forms—politics, police, business, gangsters, racial tensions, and journalistic sleaze in the persona of Sid Hudgeons (DeVito), editor of tabloid rag *Hush-Hush*. Sid's police contact is celebrity Sgt. Jack Vincennes (Spacey), who serves as an advisor to a TV cop show (think *Dragnet*). There's a bloodbath murder case that involves brutal-yet-tender cop Bud White (Crowe); the ruthlessly ambitious, college-educated neophyte Ed Exley (Pearce); and their veteran boss, Capt. Dudley Smith (Cromwell). There's also wealthy pimp/businessman Pierce Patchett (Strathairn) and his movie-star look-alike hookers, including world-weary Lynn (Basinger), who gets involved with Bud, who.... Well, let's just say that director Hanson does a masterful job tying up all the loose ends and still leaving you wanting more. This is one of those DVDs that makes the film as (or more) enjoyable than the theatre, depending on how many talkers you've gotta punch at the bijou. The colors and blacks are superb. The picture is extremely sharp and the grain level extremely low. This is all true no matter what lighting conditions the DVD has to handle. Contrast and brightness are consistent at comfortably high levels without altering the look of the film. The DVD also boasts one of the finest 5.1 soundtracks around, full-bodied, with those crisp highs (and dialogue) and gutsy low end. The Surround sounds great whether you're hearing effects, music, or just ambient enhancements. The climactic shootout at the end demonstrates the importance of sound in the film. —*JO*

Movie: 🎵🎵🎵🎵 *DVD:* 🎵🎵🎵🎵
Warner Home Video, Inc. (Cat #14913, UPC #085391491323). Widescreen anamorphic. Dolby Digital 5.1. $24.98. Snapper. *LANG:* English; French. *SUB:* English; Spanish; French. *CAP:* English. *FEATURES:* 40 chapter links ▪ 3 behind-the-scenes documentaries ▪ Music-only 5.1 track ▪ Theatrical trailer ▪ 3 TV spots ▪ Production notes ▪ Dual-layered RSDL.
1997 (R) 136m/C Kevin Spacey, Russell Crowe, Guy Pearce, Danny DeVito, Kim Basinger, James Cromwell, David Strathairn, Ron Rifkin, Graham Beckel, Matt McCoy, Simon Baker, Paul Guilfoyle, Amber Smith, John Mahon, Paolo Seganti, Gwenda Deacon; *D:* Curtis Hanson; *W:* Brian Helgeland; *C:* Dante Spinotti; *M:* Jerry Goldsmith. *AWARDS:* Academy Awards '97: Best Adapted Screenplay, Best Supporting Actress (Basinger); Australian Film Institute '98: Best Foreign Film; British Academy Awards '97: Best Film Editing, Best Sound; Golden Globe Awards '98: Best Supporting Actress (Basinger); Los Angeles Film Critics Association Awards '97: Best Cinematography, Best Director (Hanson), Best Film, Best Screenplay; National Board of Review Awards '97: Best Director (Hanson), Best Film; New York Film Critics Awards '97: Best Director (Hanson), Best Film, Best Screenplay; National Society of Film Critics Awards '97: Best Director (Hanson), Best Film, Best Screenplay; Screen Actors Guild Award '97: Best Supporting Actress (Basinger); Writers Guild of America '97: Best Adapted Screenplay; Broadcast Film Critics Association Awards '97: Best Adapted Screenplay, Best Film; *NOM:* Academy Awards '97: Best Art Direction/Set Decoration, Best Cinematography, Best Director (Hanson), Best Film Editing, Best Picture, Best Sound, Best Original Score; British Academy Awards '97: Best Actor (Spacey), Best Actress (Basinger), Best Adapted Screenplay, Best Cinematography, Best Costume Design, Best Director (Hanson), Best Film, Best Score; Directors Guild of America Awards '97: Best Director (Hanson); Golden Globe Awards '98: Best Director (Hanson), Best Film—Drama, Best Screenplay, Best Score; Screen Actors Guild Award '97: Cast.

La Femme Nikita

Stylish French noir version of *Pygmalion*. Having killed a cop during a drugstore theft gone awry, young French sociopath Nikita (Parillaud) is reprieved from a death sentence to enroll in a government finishing school, of sorts. Trained in etiquette and assassination, she's released after three years, and starts a new life with a new beau, all the while carrying out agency-mandated assassinations. Parillaud is excellent as the once-amoral street urchin transformed into a woman of depth and sensitivity—a bitterly ironic moral evolution of a contract killer. Remade as the not-as-good American film *Point of No Return*. The DVD is best experienced with the default French soundtrack chosen, not only for authenticity, but because the Eng-

lish soundtrack offers only a matrixed mix. Optional English captions can be turned on. The video quality is uneven—at times richly beautiful, but in places giving away the sometimes substandard source videotape used for the DVD transfer. The letterboxed image is not anamorphically enhanced for widescreen sets. Don't look for the expected extras; they aren't there. —*MB*

Movie: 🎵🎵🎵 *DVD:* 🎵🎵▶
Trimark Home Video (Cat #LDVM5471-D, UPC #013023000193). Widescreen (2.35:1) letterboxed. Dolby Digital 4.0. $24.98. Keepcase. *LANG:* French; English. *SUB:* English. *CAP:* English. *FEATURES:* 20 chapter links.
1991 (R) 117m/C *FR* Anne Parillaud, Jean-Hugues Anglade, Tcheky Karyo, Jeanne Moreau, Jean Reno, Jean Bouise; *D:* Luc Besson; *W:* Luc Besson; *C:* Thierry Arbogast; *M:* Eric Serra. *AWARDS:* Cesar Awards '91: Best Actress (Parillaud).

La Sentinelle

Morose Mathias (Salinger) is traveling by train from Germany to France to attend medical school. The sinister Bleicher (Richard), who seems to be a customs official, grills Mathias but lets him go. In his hotel, Mathias finds a strange package in his luggage and discovers it contains the shrunken head of a man. He keeps his discovery a secret but tests samples of the head in the school laboratory on a quest to figure out who the man was. May sound like a thriller but it's too talky and paced too slowly to hold complete interest. **AKA:** The Sentinel.

Movie: 🎵🎵🎵 *DVD:* NYR
WinStar Home Entertainment (Cat #5116). Full frame. $29.98. Keepcase. *LANG:* French. *SUB:* English. *FEATURES:* Production notes ▪ Cast and crew thumbnail bios.
1992 144m/C *FR* Emmanuel Salinger, Jean-Louis Richard, Thibault de Montalembert, Valerie Dreville, Marianne Denicourt, Bruno Todeschini, Jean-Luc Boutte; *D:* Arnaud Desplechin; *W:* Arnaud Desplechin; *C:* Caroline Champetier; *M:* Marc Oliver Sommer.

La Separation

Pierre (Auteuil) and Anne (Huppert) share a long-term relationship and a 15-month-old son. What they no longer seem to have is any passion for each other as they go through their daily routine. Anne decides to have an affair—but doesn't see any reason it should break up her household. However, the increasingly miserable Pierre doesn't share her belief. Based on the 1991 novel *Separation* by Franck.

Movie: 🎵🎵🎵 *DVD:* NYR
WinStar Home Entertainment (Cat #5123). Widescreen (1.85:1) letterboxed. $29.98. Keepcase. *LANG:* French. *SUB:* English. *FEATURES:* Cast and crew thumbnail bios ▪ Production notes ▪ Trailer.

1998 85m/C *FR* Daniel Auteuil, Isabelle Huppert, Karin Viard, Jerome Deschamps; *D:* Christian Vincent; *W:* Christian Vincent, Dan Franck; *C:* Denis Lenoir.

L.A. Story

Livin' ain't easy in the city of angels. Harris K. Telemacher (Martin), a weatherman in a place where the weather never changes, wrestles with the meaning of life and love while consorting with beautiful people, distancing from Significant Other Henner, cavorting with Valley Girl Parker, and falling for newswoman Tennant (then Martin's real-life wife). Written by the comedian, the story's full of keen insights into the everyday problems and ironies of living in the Big Tangerine. (It's no wonder the script's full of so much thoughtful detail: Martin is said to have worked on it intermittently for seven years.) It's a charming, fault-forgiving but not fault-ignoring portrait. The DVD's quality is a bit sporadic when it comes to sharpness and color. When you average it out, both those specs are just that—average, although they have moments of near greatness. The same can be said for the blacks, which have some trouble with changing lighting conditions. Some of these lackings are made up for by the contrast and brightness levels which do add some punch to the picture. Unfortunately, the disc's sound is also average with very little Surround, so-so fidelity, and a need for some low-end boost. —*JO*
Movie: ♫♫♫ *DVD:* ♫♫▶
Artisan Entertainment (Cat #60478, UPC #12236047803). Widescreen (1.85:1) letterboxed. Dolby Surround. $24.98. Snapper. *LANG:* English. *SUB:* Spanish. *CAP:* English. *FEATURES:* 36 chapter links ▪ Theatrical trailer ▪ Production notes ▪ Cast and crew bios.
1991 (PG-13) 98m/C Steve Martin, Victoria Tennant, Richard E. Grant, Marilu Henner, Sarah Jessica Parker, Sam McMurray, Patrick Stewart, Iman, Kevin Pollak; *D:* Mick Jackson; *W:* Steve Martin; *C:* Andrew Dunn; *M:* Peter Melnick.

La Traviata

Film version of Giuseppe Verdi's opera classic, based on *La Dame aux Camelias* by Alexandre Dumas, tells the tale of a tragic romance in the 19th century. By far, this DVD is the best version of *La Traviata* released to home video to date, but there are still a couple of problems. The picture is very sharp most of the time. But during scenes that are soft-focus, the disc seems to add a kind of grainy haze to the image. Believe it or not, the picture still looks very good. The color is vastly improved from the earlier versions and has no bleed problems even when fully saturated. Blacks could be better, drifting a little during those aforementioned hazy sequences. Both the contrast and the brightness are very good and very consistent. Soundwise, this DVD is like listening to a good CD. The music is full and

dynamic with good highs supported by clean balanced lows. —*JO*
Movie: ♫♫♫ *DVD:* ♫♫♫
Universal Studios Home Video (Cat #20326, UPC #025192032622). Widescreen (1.66:1) anamorphic. Dolby Surround. $24.98. Keepcase. *LANG:* Italian. *SUB:* French. *CAP:* English. *FEATURES:* 26 chapter links ▪ Theatrical trailer ▪ Cast and filmmakers bios ▪ Production notes ▪ Film highlights.
1982 105m/C *IT* Teresa Stratas, Placido Domingo, Cornell MacNeil, Alan Monk, Axelle Gall, Pina Cei; *D:* Franco Zeffirelli; *W:* Franco Zeffirelli; *C:* Ennio Guarnieri; *M:* Giuseppe Verdi. AWARDS: NOM: Academy Awards '82: Best Art Direction/Set Decoration, Best Art Direction/Set Decoration, Best Costume Design.

Labyrinth

When self-centered Sarah (Connelly) foolishly invites the King of the Goblins (Bowie) to take the little brother she has to babysit, he accepts. Her suburban neighborhood is then transformed into a labyrinth filled with magical creatures. She has 13 hours to find a castle at the center and to rescue the tot. Director Jim Henson quotes Salvadore Dali, Walt Disney, Maurice Sendak, and M.C. Escher in the creation of his frightening, gritty wonderland. In this world of fairy tales, beauty and wonder are never far from ugliness, and they are often all part of the same thing. In the end, the story is about growing up, maturing, accepting responsibility—in short, all of the things that most movies, even those aimed at kids, are not about. The DVD reflects that rough quality with an image that is seldom better than good. The same goes for sound. Both are not much better than VHS tape and are identical to the theatrical release as I remember it. —*MM*
Movie: ♫♫♫ *DVD:* ♫♫▶
Columbia Tristar Home Video (Cat #43459, UPC #043396434592). Widescreen (2.35:1) letterboxed. Dolby Digital Surround Stereo. $24.95. Keepcase. *LANG:* English. *SUB:* English; Spanish. *FEATURES:* "Making of" featurette ▪ Trailers ▪ 28 chapter links ▪ Cast and crew thumbnail biographies.
1986 (PG) 90m/C David Bowie, Jennifer Connelly, Toby Froud, Shelley Thompson, Dave Goelz, Karen Prell, Steve Whitmire; *D:* Jim Henson; *W:* Jim Henson, Terry Jones; *C:* Alex Thomson; *M:* Trevor Jones, David Bowie.

Lady and the Tramp

Disney's great animated canine romance has not looked this good since it first hit theatre screens. The story of wily mongrel and his pedigreed enamorata is one of the studio's finest moments. The widescreen transfer captures the stylized mid-'50s combination of kitsch and sweet characters with crystalline clarity. To quibble about the use of ethnic and racial stereotypes is pointless. In this case, the anima-

tors and writers came up with a solid story and a memorable idealized 19th-century American setting that has been a hit with generations of children and will continue to be. The DVD looks noticeably sharper than tape versions of the film, though younger viewers probably won't care much about that. They're more likely to want to jump to their favorite songs and moments. —*MM*
Movie: ♫♫♫♫ *DVD:* ♫♫♫
Buena Vista Home Entertainment (Cat #17975, UPC #717951003997). Widescreen (2.35:1) letterboxed. Dolby Digital Mono. $39.99. Keepcase. *LANG:* English; French; Spanish. *CAP:* English. *FEATURES:* 22 chapter links.
1955 (G) 76m/C *D:* Hamilton Luske; *M:* Peggy Lee, Sonny Burke; *V:* Larry Roberts, Peggy Lee, Barbara Luddy, Stan Freberg, Alan Reed, Bill Thompson, Bill Baucon, Verna Felton, George Givot, Dallas McKennon, Lee Millar.

Lady Dragon

A woman (Rothrock) and her husband are viciously attacked and only she survives. Found by an old man, she learns a number of martial arts tricks and sets out for revenge.
Movie: ♫♫ *DVD:* NYR
Studio Home Entertainment (Cat #4070). Full frame. $24.95. Keepcase. *LANG:* English. *FEATURES:* Cast and crew thumbnail bios ▪ Trailer.
1992 (R) 89m/C Cynthia Rothrock, Richard Norton, Robert Ginty, Bella Esperance, Hengko Tornando; *D:* David Worth; *W:* David Worth; *C:* David Worth; *M:* Jim West.

The Lady in White

Small-town ghost story begins when young Haas is locked in school one night and is visited by the ghost of a little girl who wants his help in solving her murder. Well-developed characters, interesting style, and a suspenseful plot make for an exceptional horror film.
Movie: ♫♫♫ *DVD:* NYR
Elite Entertainment, Inc. (Cat #5240). Widescreen (1.85:1) letterboxed. Dolby Digital 5.1 Surround Stereo. $29.95. Keepcase. *FEATURES:* Deleted scenes ▪ Commentary: director-writer Frank Laloggia ▪ Soundtrack with notes ▪ "Making of" featurette ▪ Trailer and promotional material.
1988 (PG-13) 92m/C Lukas Haas, Len Cariou, Alex Rocco, Katherine Helmond, Jason Presson, Renata Vanni, Angelo Bertolini, Jared Rushton, Joelle Jacob; *D:* Frank Laloggia; *W:* Frank Laloggia; *C:* Russell Carpenter; *M:* Frank Laloggia.

Lady Macbeth of Mtsensk

Fiddler on the Roof it's not, nor is it *Doctor Zhivago*, and for the uninitiated it is a bit of work to get through, but it does have its moments. Based on Russian composer Dimitri Shostakovich's adaptation of Kikolai Leskov's earlier literary work, director Petr Weigl delivers a visceral, well-crafted cinematic telling of lust, infidelity, and murder played out against the backdrop of the Russian Revolution. The once-banned opera has been lifted from its stage-bound settings and translated to the screen as a tragic operatic musical complete with barren and bleak landscapes, well-endowed peasant women, and non-stop singing. DVD presentation features English subtitles—an absolute necessity to untangle the proceedings—but that's the extent of the features associated with this release. —RT

Movie: 🎬🎬➤ **DVD:** 🎬🎬➤

Image Entertainment (Cat #5655, UPC #014381565522). Full frame. AC3 - 2 Channel. $24.99. Snapper. *LANG:* Russian. *SUB:* English. *CAP:* English. *FEATURES:* 16 chapter markers.

1992 ?m/C Michal Dlouhy, Marketa Hrubesova; *D:* Petr Weigl.

Lady of the Lake

A young artist living beside a lake is visited by a ghostly woman at night and is drawn into a supernatural affair. The plot of this independently produced Canadian horror is standard stuff, and it was made with more enthusiasm and imagination than money and expertise. That said, it's still recommended to fans of the genre. DVD treats the material seriously with all of the extras normally found on more polished Hollywood fare. Given the budget, neither image nor sound is particularly sharp, but that's not needed. Most fans are never going to see this kind of film in theatres, so home video becomes the primary medium. This DVD is a solid step up from tape. —MM

Movie: 🎬🎬➤ **DVD:** 🎬🎬➤

MTI Home Video (Cat #50027, UPC #619935402737). Widescreen (1.66:1) letterboxed. $24.98. Keepcase. *LANG:* English. *FEATURES:* Behind-the-scenes featurette • 20 chapter links • Cast and crew thumbnail bios • Trailer • Commentary: director Maurice Devereaux.

1998 (R) 82m/C Tennyson Loeh, Emidio Michetti, Erik Rutherford, Christopher Piggins, Marty Daniels; *D:* Maurice Devereaux; *W:* Maurice Devereaux; *C:* Denis-Noel Mostert, Richard Labelle; *M:* Martin Gauthier.

The Lady Vanishes

When a kindly old lady (Whitty) disappears from a fast-moving train, her young friend (Lockwood) finds an imposter in her place and a spiraling mystery to solve. Along with *The 39 Steps*, this is one of Hitchcock's first real winners, a wit-drenched British thriller that precipitated his move to Hollywood. The opening shot created with models is particularly cute. The DVD image and sound are clear but not great—really no better or worse than most other 1939 films. —MM

Movie: 🎬🎬🎬🎬 **DVD:** 🎬🎬➤

Delta/Laserlight (Cat #82021, UPC #018111202138). Full frame. Stereo. $14.99. Keepcase. *LANG:* English. *FEATURES:* 18 chapter links • Introduction by Tony Curtis • Trailer for Hitchcock's *Shadow of a Doubt*.

1938 99m/B *GB* Margaret Lockwood, Paul Lukas, Michael Redgrave, May Whitty, Googie Withers, Basil Radford, Naunton Wayne, Cecil Parker, Linden Travers, Catherine Lacey; *Cameos:* Alfred Hitchcock; *D:* Alfred Hitchcock; *W:* Sidney Gilliat, Frank Launder; *C:* Jack Cox; *M:* Louis Levy. *AWARDS:* New York Film Critics Awards '38: Best Director (Hitchcock).

Ladyhawke

In medieval times, a youthful pickpocket befriends a strange knight who is on a mysterious quest. This unlikely duo, accompanied by a watchful hawk, are enveloped in a magical adventure. The image is reasonably sharp and free of digital grain most of the time. However, on some long or detailed shots, the quality steps down a notch, particularly when the background is light—the hawk against the sky, for instance. Colors are fairly true but are a little duller than the theatre, with only a touch of bleed. Contrast and brightness are somewhat above average, and the blacks are very true. Here and there the print looks a little rough. Soundwise, the DVD is not bad, with good highs and mids, and excellent bass. —JO

Movie: 🎬🎬➤ **DVD:** 🎬🎬🎬

Warner Home Video, Inc. (Cat #11464, UPC #085391146421). Widescreen (2.35:1) letterboxed; full frame. Dolby Digital 5.1; Dolby Surround; Mono. $19.98. Snapper. *LANG:* English; Spanish; French. *SUB:* English; Spanish; French. *CAP:* English. *FEATURES:* 31 chapter links • Theatrical trailer • Production notes.

1985 (PG-13) 121m/C Matthew Broderick, Rutger Hauer, Michelle Pfeiffer, John Wood, Leo McKern, Alfred Molina, Ken Hutchison; *D:* Richard Donner; *W:* Edward Khmara, Michael Thomas, Tom Mankiewicz; *C:* Vittorio Storaro; *M:* Andrew Powell. *AWARDS:* NOM: Academy Awards '85: Best Sound.

The Lair of the White Worm

Ken Russell pits paganism (in the form of snake worship) against Christianity in a wonderfully screwy adaptation of Bram Stoker's last novel, AKA *The Garden of Evil*. When Lady Sylvia (Donohoe), "the fanged princess of darkness," arrives in contemporary England, no boy scout is safe. Our four heroes are the Trent sisters (Oxenberg and Davis), whose parents disappeared a year before, archeologist Angus Flint (Capaldi), who finds a huge skull in their backyard, and Lord James (Grant), the local Pooh-Bah who's still investigating the disappearances. The plot quickly succumbs to Russell's trademark flamboyance, and he's equally cheeky on his low-keyed commentary

track. "I was hypnotized by an adder as a child," he deadpans. Both image and sound are excellent, emphasizing the highly stylized lighting and effects that Russell uses throughout. This one's a real treat for any horror fan who has somehow missed it. —MM

Movie: 🎬🎬🎬 **DVD:** 🎬🎬🎬➤

Pioneer Entertainment (Cat #DVD5282-WS, UPC #013023011298). Widescreen letterboxed. Dolby Digital Stereo. $24.98. Keepcase. *LANG:* English. *FEATURES:* 12 chapter links • Production notes and photographs • Trailers • TV commercials • Commentary: Ken Russell.

1988 (R) 93m/C *GB* Amanda Donohoe, Sammi Davis, Catherine Oxenberg, Hugh Grant, Peter Capaldi, Stratford Johns, Paul Brooke, Christopher Gable; *D:* Ken Russell; *W:* Ken Russell; *C:* Dick Bush; *M:* Stanislas Syrewicz.

Lake Placid

Writer-producer David E. Kelley and director Steve Miner add a layer of hip humor to a standard '50s monster flick formula. The principal characters are unapologetic stereotypes. A New York museum sends out science babe Kelly Scott (Fonda) after a diver is chopped in half in a Maine lake. The local cop, Jack Wells (Pullman), actually from the fish and wildlife service, is in charge, but the arrival of Hector Cyr (Platt), a rich eccentric, changes everything. The monster is a giant crocodile, created through studio computer effects from Stan Winston's studio. Its appearances are timed to shock, but the overall result is still more comic than frightening and that's the filmmakers' goal. On DVD, the lightweight fluff really looks better than it needs to. The combination of "real" footage with computer-generated images is fairly seamless, and that's where the medium is most likely to reveal flaws in this kind of horror movie. Sound is serviceable. —MM

Movie: 🎬🎬🎬 **DVD:** 🎬🎬🎬

20th Century Fox (Cat #2000002, UPC #024543000020). Widescreen (2.35:1) letterboxed. Dolby Digital 5.1 Surround Stereo; Dolby Surround Stereo. $34.98. Keepcase. *LANG:* English; French. *SUB:* Spanish. *CAP:* English. *FEATURES:* 24 chapter links • "Making of" featurette • TV spots • Theatrical trailer.

1999 (R) 82m/C Bridget Fonda, Bill Pullman, Oliver Platt, Brendan Gleeson, Mariska Hargitay, Meredith Salenger, Betty White, David Lewis; *D:* Steve Miner; *W:* David E. Kelley; *C:* Daryn Okada; *M:* John Ottman.

The Land Before Time

Lushly animated children's film follows five orphaned baby dinosaurs who band together to find the Great Valley, a paradise where they might live safely. It works with the same parental separation theme as Bluth's *American Tail*. Followed by a series of video premiere sequels.

Movie: 🎬🎬🎬 **DVD:** NYR
Universal Studios Home Video (Cat #20278). $24.98. *LANG:* English; French; Spanish.
1988 (G) 67m/C **D:** Don Bluth; **W:** Stu Krieger; **M:** James Horner; **V:** Pat Hingle, Helen Shaver, Gabriel Damon, Candice Houston, Burke Barnes, Judith Barsi, Will Ryan.

The Landlady

When she catches her hubby fooling around with a floozy, Melanie (Shire), who's already a little unhinged, goes nuts and kills him. As luck would have it, she has just inherited a Los Angeles apartment building, so she moves in and sets out to find the perfect man. A strong sense of humor sets this one apart from most psycho-femme thrillers. The DVD image is nice and sharp, but probably not much better than the VHS tape. The film was made on a limited budget and it shows. —*MM*
Movie: 🎬🎬▸ **DVD:** 🎬🎬▸
Trimark Home Video (Cat #VM6897D, UPC #031398689737). Full frame. Stereo. $14.99. Keepcase. *LANG:* English. *SUB:* French; Spanish. *CAP:* English. *FEATURES:* 24 chapter links • Talia Shire, Jack Coleman, Melissa Behr filmographies • Trailers.
1998 (R) 98m/C Talia Shire, Jack Coleman, Bruce Weitz, Melissa Behr, Susie Singer, Bette Ford; **D:** Rob Malenfant; **W:** Frank Rehwaldt, George Saunders; **C:** Darko Suvak; **M:** Eric Lundmark.

Landmarks of Early Film

An uneven collection of early filmmaking efforts (1877–1913), this DVD presentation of 40 different silent film productions (shorts), as drawn from the Blackhawk Films Collection, cries out for an expert audio commentary describing the historical significance of each of these unique works. Included in the collection are George Melies's "A Trip to the Moon" (1902), Edwin Porter's "The Great Train Robbery" (1903), and D.W. Griffith's "The Girl and Her Trust" (1912). DVD presentation offers the film student or historian the chance to review each of the 40 examples on a frame-by-frame basis to study composition, style, and diverse techniques. —*RT*
Movie: 🎬🎬▸ **DVD:** 🎬🎬
Image Entertainment (Cat #4103, UPC #014381410327). Full frame. AC3 - 2 Channel. $29.99. Snapper. *LANG:* Silent, with some English commentary. *FEATURES:* 40 chapter links.
1994 117m/C

Landmarks of Early Film, Vol. 2: The Magic of Melies

Although billed as *Landmarks of Early Film, Volume 2*, this is actually a repositioning of a 1978 production from the Blackhawk Films Collection featuring early French filmmaker Georges Melies. It matters little the source, since the overall presentation is quite good as an historical film resource. Included are 16 of Melies's classic "magical" silent short subjects (1904–1907), which are in remarkably good condition considering the age. Georges Melies's style is that of a screen magician, specializing in special effects to tell his stories of amazing adventures, "The Impossible Voyage" (1904), or the simply fanciful, "The Hilarous Posters" (1905) or "The Living Playing Cards" (1905). The DVD presentation, while of good quality when you consider the age of the material, would have been greatly improved with the inclusion of an audio commentary describing the historical and production significance of each short film. —*RT*
Movie: 🎬🎬🎬 **DVD:** 🎬🎬▸
Image Entertainment (Cat #4668, UPC #014381466829). Full frame. AC3 - 2 Channel. $24.99. Snapper. *LANG:* Silent, with some English commentary during the introduction. *FEATURES:* 19 chapter links.
1994 102m/C

Lap Dancing

With the critical and commercial failure of *Showgirls*, fans wondered if they would ever see a sensitive and perceptive portrayal of topless dancing on DVD. The answer is a resounding "Yes!" Angie Parker (McComas) comes to Hollywood looking for a career in movies, but instead finds a job as a lap dancer. Tane McClure is the seasoned pro who shows her the ropes, as it were. This video original has all the sex and sleaze of its big-budget counterpart plus a sense of humor. Unfortunately, the disc also highlights the production's shortcomings with dark scenes that tend toward the impenetrable. Because the DVD is sharper, it's somehow less than the VHS tape. —*MM*
Movie: 🎬🎬🎬 **DVD:** 🎬🎬
Image Entertainment (Cat #ID602FMDVD, UPC #014381560220). Full frame. Dolby Digital Stereo. $24.99. Snapper. *LANG:* English. *FEATURES:* 12 chapter links.
1995 (R) 90m/C Lorissa McComas, Tane McClure, C.T. Miller; **D:** Mike Sedan; **W:** K.C. Martin; **C:** Carlos Montaner; **M:** Ron Allen, Todd Schroeder.

Laser Mission

When it is discovered that the Soviets have laser weapon capabilities, an agent (Lee) is given the task of destroying the thingy but he is kidnapped by the scientist (Borgnine) who developed it.
Movie: 🎬🎬▸ **DVD:** NYR
Diamond Entertainment Corporation (Cat #98002). Full frame. Dolby Digital Stereo. $6.99. Keepcase.
1990 83m/C Brandon Lee, Debi Monahan, Ernest Borgnine, Werner Pochat, Graham Clarke, Maureen Lahoud, Pierre Knoessen; **D:** Beau Davis; **M:** David Knopfler.

Laser Moon

After a promising beginning, this generic B-movie contains no real surprises. Traci Lords is less than convincing as yet another cop on the trail of yet another serial killer. This one uses a laser and is hooked up with a radio talk show host. Fans have seen the same thing done with more intelligence and style elsewhere. The DVD image is clear throughout, even in the night scenes, belying the film's low-budget roots. Sound is so-so. —*MM*
Movie: 🎬▸ **DVD:** 🎬🎬🎬
Image Entertainment (Cat #ID5700PZDVD, UPC #014381570021). Full frame. Dolby Digital Stereo. $24.99. Snapper. *LANG:* English. *FEATURES:* 12 chapter links.
1992 90m/C Traci Lords, Crystal Shaw, Harrison Leduke, Bruce Carter; **D:** Douglas K. Grimm.

Laserblast

Frustrated teen Billy (Milford) happens upon a laser weapon lost near his desert home by aliens—critters created by fair stop-motion animation—and uses it to exact revenge on everyone who's ever been mean to him. Downside: the device mutates him. Even the presence of the always delightful Cheryl "Rainbeaux" Smith as his girlfriend is not enough to salvage this refugee from the drive-in. It's always been a cheap sf flick and on DVD it's not noticeably superior to either VHS tape or the theatrical release, as I remember it. It's rough-looking throughout, with excessively heavy grain and accompanying pixelation in the stop-motion scenes. The color choices make the menu difficult to navigate. —*MM*
Movie: 🎬 **DVD:** 🎬
Cult Video (Cat #8016, UPC #763843801660). Widescreen letterboxed. $24.95. Keepcase. *LANG:* English. *FEATURES:* 26 chapter links • Cult Video trailers • Theatrical trailer • Cast thumbnail biographies.
1978 (PG) 87m/C Kim Milford, Cheryl "Rainbeaux" Smith, Keenan Wynn, Roddy McDowall; **D:** Michael Raeburn; **W:** Frank Ray Perilli, Franne Schacht; **C:** Terry Bowen; **M:** Richard Band, Joel Goldsmith.

Laserhawk

Young Zach Raymond (Richter) fakes an encounter with a UFO and then winds up leading the forces of Earth against the Arachtoids who are bent on galactic conquest. This is fairly standard sf with some above-average special effects. About half of those effects are cheap and lame, and half are cheap and cool. Perhaps in an effort to integrate the models and computer-generated images into the "real" footage, the producers have made the DVD image a bit too bright in all scenes. Some normal scenes seem to glow. Sound is good, too. —*MM*
Movie: 🎬🎬🎬 **DVD:** 🎬🎬🎬
York Entertainment (Cat #YPD 1026, UPC #750723102627). Full frame. Dolby Digital 5.1 Surround Stereo. $24.98. Keep-

case. *LANG:* English. *SUB:* Spanish. *FEATURES:* 30 chapter links ▪ Filmographies of Hamill, Richter, Currie, Galianos.

1999 (PG-13) 102m/C Mark Hamill, Jason James Richter, Gordon Currie, Melissa Galianos; *D:* Jean Pellerin; *W:* John A. Curtis.

Last Action Hero

Young Danny Madigan (O'Brien) finds himself in a movie with his favorite character Jack Slater (Schwarzenegger), the kind of guy who never loses a fight and is impervious to gunfire and explosions. (Of course, he's got a cool convertible and a really big pistol.) The plot moves back and forth between the film and the film-within-the-film where Danny tries to prove to the people that they are fictional characters. Though director McTiernan treats most of the violence as slapstick comedy, it's still too strong for younger viewers. The DVD, like the theatrical release, makes a clear distinction between the dark grimness of Danny's "real" world and the glittering polish of the "fantasy" world. Any action fan who was dissuaded from this one by the initial critical response might want to take a look. The movie's certainly not great on any medium, but it is worth a look and the DVD image and sound are pretty good. —*MM*

Movie: 🐕🐕▶ **DVD:** 🐕🐕▶
Columbia Tristar Home Video (Cat #27939, UPC #043396279391). Widescreen (2.35:1) letterboxed; full frame. Dolby Digital 5.1 Surround Stereo; Dolby Digital Stereo. $29.95. Keepcase. *LANG:* English; French; Spanish. *SUB:* Spanish; Korean. *FEATURES:* 55 chapter links.

1993 (PG-13) 131m/C Arnold Schwarzenegger, Austin O'Brien, Mercedes Ruehl, F. Murray Abraham, Charles Dance, Anthony Quinn, Robert Prosky, Tom Noonan, Frank McRae, Art Carney, Bridgette Wilson; *Cameos:* Sharon Stone, Hammer, Chevy Chase, Jean-Claude Van Damme, Tori Spelling, Joan Plowright, Adam Ant, James Belushi, James Cameron, Tony Curtis, Timothy Dalton, Tony Danza, Edward Furlong, Little Richard, Damon Wayans, Robert Patrick; *D:* John McTiernan; *W:* David Arnott, Shane Black; *C:* Dean Semler; *M:* Michael Kamen.

The Last Assassins

Ex-CIA hitwoman Anne Bishop (Allen) is persuaded to reunite with former commander McBride (Henriksen) for another mission. To ensure her cooperation he kidnaps her daughter. For a mid-budget video premiere, this one looks very good on DVD. Even the dark scenes are adequately lit, but the real appeal, as it almost always is with Henriksen films, comes from watching him work wonders with a cliched role and delivering potentially ludicrous lines with icy venom. Example: "All this child-in-jeopardy crap is souring my stomach." —*MM* *AKA:* Dusting Cliff Seven.
Movie: 🐕🐕▶ **DVD:** 🐕🐕▶

Simitar Entertainment (Cat #7435, UPC #082551743520). Full frame. Dolby Digital Stereo; Dolby Digital 5.1 Surround Stereo. $14.98. Keepcase. *LANG:* English. *FEATURES:* 8 chapter links ▪ Production factoids ▪ Nancy Allen filmography.

1996 (R) 90m/C Lance Henriksen, Nancy Allen, Floyd "Red Crow" Westerman, Dean Scofield; *D:* William H. Molina; *W:* William H. Molina, Jim Menza, Charles Philip Moore, Justin Stanley; *C:* William H. Molina; *M:* David Wurst, Eric Wurst.

The Last Boy Scout

Are you ready for some gunplay? Formula thriller stars Willis as a private eye and Wayans as an ex-quarterback teaming up against a football team owner who will stop at nothing to get political backing for a bill promoting legalized gambling on sports. Another variation of the violent buddy-picture by *Lethal Weapon*-screenwriter Black. I didn't see this one at the theatre so I don't know if it was shot on grainy film stock. But this DVD is intermittently grainy, though it has that look of a DVD exaggerating existing graininess. Another problem, one that only occurred a couple of times, was some artificial motion—some spinning helicopter blades, for instance. The colors are very good and bleed only slightly and rarely. Blacks are very close to true. Contrast and brightness levels are consistent. The 5.1 sound has great bottom and good dynamics and fidelity. The Surround does the job when needed. —*JO*

Movie: 🐕🐕 **DVD:** 🐕🐕▶
Warner Home Video, Inc. (Cat #12217, UPC #085391221722). Widescreen (2.35:1) anamorphic; full frame. Dolby Digital 5.1; Stereo. $24.98. Snapper. *LANG:* English (DD5.1; Stereo); French (Stereo). *SUB:* English; Spanish; French. *CAP:* English. *FEATURES:* 29 chapter links ▪ Theatrical trailer ▪ Production notes.

1991 (R) 105m/C Bruce Willis, Damon Wayans, Halle Berry, Chelsea Field, Noble Willingham, Taylor Negron, Danielle Harris, Chelcie Ross, Bruce McGill; *D:* Tony Scott; *W:* Shane Black; *C:* Ward Russell; *M:* Michael Kamen.

Last Breath

Martin (Perry) is obsessively devoted to his dying wife Chrystie (Swift) who needs a double lung transplant to live. When he strikes up a relationship with the lovely Gail (Carides), he has more than romance on his mind. Curious thriller looks very good on DVD. It's well photographed with unusually deep colors. The sound isn't bad either. —*MM* *AKA:* Lifebreath.
Movie: 🐕🐕 **DVD:** 🐕🐕▶

Simitar Entertainment (Cat #7267, UPC #082551726721). Full frame. Dolby Digital Stereo; Dolby Digital 5.1 Surround Stereo. $14.98. Keepcase. *LANG:* English. *FEATURES:* 8 chapter links ▪ Luke Perry filmography.

1996 (R) 90m/C Luke Perry, Gia Carides, Francie Swift, David Margulies, Lisa Gay Hamilton, Jack Gilpin, Matt McGrath, Hillary Bailey Smith; *D:* P.J. Posner; *W:* P.J. Posner, Joel Posner; *C:* Oliver Bokelberg; *M:* Michael Kessler.

The Last Broadcast

Festival hit—and the first film to be digitally distributed to theatres—predates *The Blair Witch Project* in telling the story of a group of young people who go into the woods with video cameras and meet a grisly fate. But this one is much more complicated and ambitious. Directors Steven Avalos and Lance Weiler play public access cable TV show hosts who take a sound man (Clabbers) and a psychic (Seward) into the Pine Barrens for a live broadcast of their search for the legendary Jersey Devil. Only one comes out. A year later, a documentary filmmaker (Beard) and a video editor (Pulaski) try to find the truth of the matter. In the background material accompanying the film on disc, the filmmakers discuss their use of consumer electronic equipment and home computers. Many important scenes have an intentionally distorted or distressed look, but the filmmakers are able to present strikingly clear images when they want to, and so the film works well on DVD. The sound is fine, too. In ways that may not be apparent to viewers in the early days of digital entertainment, this film is a genuine landmark. —*MM*

Movie: 🐕🐕🐕 **DVD:** 🐕🐕🐕▶
Wavelength Releasing/Ventura Distribution (Cat #WR-10182, UPC #634991101820). Full frame. $19.95. Keepcase. *LANG:* English. *SUB:* English. *FEATURES:* 18 chapter links ▪ 4 shorts on the Jersey Devil, production, post-production, distribution ▪ Commentary: directors Avalos and Weiler and cast members ▪ Theatrical trailers.

1998 87m/C Stefan Avalos, Lance Weiler, David Beard, Rein Clabbers, Michele Pulaski; *D:* Stefan Avalos, Lance Weiler; *W:* Stefan Avalos, Lance Weiler; *C:* Lance Weiler; *M:* Stefan Avalos.

The Last Days of Disco

A handful of yuppies-in-waiting are stuck between the '70s and '80s, the club circuit and the unemployment line. Triple-threat Stillman orchestrates the proceeding along the lines of his earlier *Metropolitan*, just with an almost imperceptibly more outre style. The flashy layout of the box and interactive features is heavy on hot pink. The technical specs are geared towards widescreen snobs but you are given a full-frame option on the flip side. Even the full-frame version, which may have been digitized differently from the widescreen one, handles difficult lighting situations well. Too bad the whole film isn't as loose and fun as its final "love train" joke. —*JK*
Movie: 🐕🐕🐕 **DVD:** 🐕🐕🐕🐕
Polygram (Cat #PV058267, UPC #044005826722). Widescreen (1.85:1); full frame. Dolby Digital AC-3 Surround 5.1; Dolby Pro Logic 2.0. $29.99. Keepcase.

LANG: English. *SUB:* French. *CAP:* English. *FEATURES:* 23 chapter links • Interactive menus • Dual-sided disc • Fold-out picture insert • Cast and crew bios and filmographies.
1998 (R) 113m/C Chloe Sevigny, Kate Beckinsale, Christopher Eigeman, MacKenzie Astin, Robert Sean Leonard, Matt Keeslar, Tara Subkoff, Jennifer Beals, David Thornton, Michael Weatherly, Burr Steers; *D:* Whit Stillman; *W:* Whit Stillman; *C:* John Thomas; *M:* Mark Suozzo.

The Last Detail

Petty officers "Bad-Ass" Buddusky (Nicholson) and "Mule" Mullhall (Young) are assigned to take Meadows (Quaid), a petty thief, from Virginia to the brig in New Hampshire. When they learn how troubled and innocent the young man really is, they decide to give him some experiences to remember before he's locked up. Nicholson's complete understanding of his character (and his now familiar profane outbursts) won an Oscar nomination. (Towne's script and Quaid were also nominated.) On DVD, Hal Ashby's location work in Washington, New York, and Boston looks and sounds as rough as it always has, though the disc was made from a print that's cleaner than many of the older tapes that are still in distribution. The lack of conventional Hollywood polish is intentional and so the film is a snapshot of east-coast America in the early 1970s. Required viewing for all Nicholson fans. —*MM*
Movie: 🎬🎬🎬🎬 *DVD:* 🎬🎬🎬
Columbia Tristar Home Video (Cat #00349, UPC #043396003491). Widescreen (1.85:1) letterboxed; full frame. Dolby Digital Mono. $25.95. Keepcase. *LANG:* English. *SUB:* English; Spanish; Portuguese; Chinese; Korean; Thai. *CAP:* English. *FEATURES:* 28 chapter links • Production notes • Cast and crew thumbnail biographies • Theatrical trailers.
1973 (R) 104m/C Jack Nicholson, Otis Young, Randy Quaid, Clifton James, Michael Moriarty, Carol Kane, Nancy Allen, Gilda Radner; *D:* Hal Ashby; *W:* Robert Towne; *C:* Michael Chapman; *M:* Johnny Mandel. *AWARDS:* British Academy Awards '74: Best Actor (Nicholson), Best Screenplay; Cannes Film Festival '74: Best Actor (Nicholson); New York Film Critics Awards '74: Best Actor (Nicholson); National Society of Film Critics Awards '74: Best Actor (Nicholson); *NOM:* Academy Awards '73: Best Actor (Nicholson), Best Adapted Screenplay, Best Supporting Actor (Quaid).

The Last Don

Double-sided disc contains the full four-hours-plus of the gangland mini series. Beginning in 1964, Don Clericuzio (Aiello) is the ruthless patriarch who wipes out rivals, even when it damages his own family. Pippi (Mantegna) is an enforcer who falls for Vegas showgirl Nalene (Miller). Their son Cross (Gedrick) carries the action into the next generation. This is very familiar territory for Puzo and his

fans. The filmmakers attempt to re-create the lighting and atmosphere of the original *Godfather.* The DVD rewards their efforts. It looks and sounds fine, particularly when compared to other made-for-TV fare. —*MM*
MM AKA: Mario Puzo's The Last Don.
Movie: 🎬🎬 *DVD:* 🎬🎬
Trimark Home Video (Cat #VM6907D, UPC #031398690733). Full frame. Dolby Digital Stereo. $34.99. Keepcase. *LANG:* English. *SUB:* French; Spanish. *CAP:* English. *FEATURES:* 30 chapters • "Making of" featurette.
1997 (R) 262m/C Danny Aiello, Joe Mantegna, Jason Gedrick, Rory Cochrane, Penelope Ann Miller, Daryl Hannah, Kirstie Alley, Michelle Rene Thomas, David Marciano, Robert Wuhl, k.d. lang, John Colicos, Cliff DeYoung, Michael Massee; *D:* Graeme Clifford; *W:* Joyce Eliason; *C:* Gordon C. Lonsdale; *M:* Angelo Badalamenti, Roger Bellon.

The Last Emperor

Deeply ironic epic detailing life of Pu Yi—crowned at the age of three as the last emperor of China before the onset of communism—follows him from childhood to manhood (sequestered away in the Forbidden City) to fugitive to puppet-ruler to party proletariat. O'Toole portrays the sympathetic Scot tutor who educates the adult Pu Yi (Lone) in the ways of the western world after he abdicates power in 1912. Shot on location inside the People's Republic of China with a cast of thousands and authentic costumes, this is a rich, visually stunning movie. The Talking Heads' David Byrne contributed to the score. This beautiful film is much better on this DVD than the older (and shorter) video releases, but still deserves better treatment. Colors look good most of the time and may be assumed accurate due to the disclaimer on the cover relating to altered color. The picture packs a little less punch than the theatrical release, and could have had both contrast and brightness levels kicked up a notch or two. It is, however, very sharp, and has little problem with grain or artifacts even in the many dimly lit sequences. The main audio on the film is Byrne's soundtrack and it is presented with fairly good imaging and fidelity. The Surround is used almost exclusively for ambience only. —*JO*
Movie: 🎬🎬🎬🎬 *DVD:* 🎬🎬🎬
Artisan Entertainment (Cat #60496, UPC #012236049609). Widescreen (2.35:1) letterboxed. Dolby Surround. $29.98. Keepcase. *LANG:* English. *CAP:* English. *FEATURES:* 36 chapter links • Theatrical trailer • Production notes • Cast and crew bios • Dual-layered RSDL • 218-minute version.
1987 (PG-13) 218m/C *IT* John Lone, Peter O'Toole, Joan Chen, Victor Wong, Ryuichi Sakamoto, Dennis Dun, Maggie Han, Ying Ruocheng, Ric Young; *D:* Bernardo Bertolucci; *W:* Mark Peploe, Bernardo Bertolucci; *C:* Vittorio Storaro; *M:* Ryuichi

Sakamoto, David Byrne. *AWARDS:* Academy Awards '87: Best Adapted Screenplay, Best Art Direction/Set Decoration, Best Cinematography, Best Costume Design, Best Director (Bertolucci), Best Film Editing, Best Picture, Best Sound, Best Original Score; British Academy Awards '88: Best Film; Cesar Awards '88: Best Foreign Film; Directors Guild of America Awards '87: Best Director (Bertolucci); Golden Globe Awards '88: Best Director (Bertolucci), Best Film—Drama, Best Screenplay, Best Score; Los Angeles Film Critics Association Awards '87: Best Cinematography; New York Film Critics Awards '87: Best Cinematography.

The Last Flight of Noah's Ark

Disney adventure concerns a high-living pilot (Gould), a prim missionary (Bujold), two stowaway orphans (Schroder and Lauren), and a shipment of animals who must plot their way off a deserted Pacific island following the crash of their vintage B-29 bomber. The critters are cute; the theme song is insipid; the kids are insufferable and so is Gould. The story comes from veteran aviation writer Ernest K. Gann. On DVD, the sharp image is really better than the mid-budget production deserves. The sound is only so-so. By the way, there's nothing wrong with the DVD or your player; the title and opening credits do not appear until 17 minutes into the movie. —*MM*
Movie: 🎬🎬 *DVD:* 🎬🎬🎬
Anchor Bay (Cat #DV10831, UPC #013131083194). Full frame; widescreen (1.85:1) letterboxed. Dolby Digital. $24.98. Keepcase. *FEATURES:* 18 chapter links.
1980 (G) 97m/C Elliott Gould, Genevieve Bujold, Rick Schroder, Vincent Gardenia, Tammy Lauren; *D:* Charles Jarrott; *W:* Steven W. Carabatsos, George Arthur Bloom; *C:* Charles F. Wheeler; *M:* Maurice Jarre.

The Last Game

Wholesome family drama—the film literally has the Good Housekeeping seal of approval—revolves around hearing-impaired Christina (Neville) who joins the high school basketball team, then struggles to be accepted by her teammates. She also has to deal with her father's (Travolta) health problems. The action is well-meaning but amateurish. The DVD looks fine, with made-for-TV production values, but the disc is a bare-bones presentation with no chapter links or extras. —*MM*
Movie: 🎬🎬 *DVD:* 🎬
Simitar Entertainment (Cat #7209, UPC #082551720927), Full frame. PCM Stereo. $7.98. Keepcase. *LANG:* English.
1995 75m/C *AU* Joey Travolta, Shearan Neville; *D:* Tom Parrish; *W:* Dean H. Crook.

Last Hurrah

Underrated Ford drama is based on Edwin O'Connor's novel, which in turn was based on Boston mayor James Curley. Frank

Skeffington (Tracy) is running for his fifth term as mayor of "a New England city," and battling challengers on all sides. The DVD image may be the best black and white that Ford ever filmed this side of Monument Valley. It's crisp and sharply focused, giving Spencer Tracy's fine performance the treatment it deserves. Mono sound is fine. —MM

Movie: 🎵🎵🎵 **DVD:** 🎵🎵🎵▶
Columbia Tristar Home Video (Cat #09229, UPC #043396092297). Widescreen (1.85:1) letterboxed; full frame. Dolby Digital Mono. $28.95. Keepcase. LANG: English. SUB: English; Spanish. FEATURES: 28 chapter links • Theatrical trailers • Production notes.
1958 121m/B Spencer Tracy, Basil Rathbone, John Carradine, Jeffrey Hunter, Dianne Foster, Pat O'Brien, Edward Brophy, James Gleason, Donald Crisp, Ricardo Cortez, Wallace Ford, Frank McHugh, Jane Darwell; **D:** John Ford; **W:** Frank Nugent; **C:** Charles Lawton Jr. AWARDS: National Board of Review Awards '58: Best Actor (Tracy), Best Director (Ford).

Last Man Standing

Engaging, but not terribly original gangster/western features a plot taken from Clint Eastwood's career-making *Fistful of Dollars* (in turn, an adaptation of Akira Kurosawa's *Yojimbo*). The producers and credits claim lineage directly from the Kurosawa film, but this story's been around for a while, folks. (Read Dashiell Hammett's *Red Harvest*.) In the small 1930s border town of Jericho, TX, Willis—under the pseudonym John Smith—hires himself out to both sides of a bootlegging war in an effort to make some quick cash. Bigger roles for Walken, the flinty trigger man for Irish boss Doyle (Kelly), and Dern, the town sheriff on the mob payroll, could have perked things up a little. Willis nicely injects his smirking brand of wit into a film that may have benefitted from more of the dark *Yojimbo* humor. Hill provides his trademark visually exciting action sequences. The reddish earthtones of the film create some problems for the DVD, which is less distinct and more grainy than the laserdisc release. Colors are dull, but that is pretty much how they were theatrically. Brightness and contrast levels are adequate and do not add or take away from the picture. The 5.1 sound is power packed and the plentiful gunshots are gutsy and nicely represented by the Surround channels. There is plenty of bass and the rest of the sound is crisp and punchy. —JO AKA: Welcome to Jericho.
Movie: 🎵🎵▶ **DVD:** 🎵🎵▶
New Line Home Video (Cat #N4507, UPC #794043450723). Widescreen (2.35:1) anamorphic; full frame. Dolby Digital Surround 5.1; Dolby Digital Stereo. $24.98. Snapper. LANG: English (DD5.1); French (Stereo). CAP: English. FEATURES: 28 chapter links • Theatrical trailer • "Star highlights" • Cast bios and filmographies.
1996 (R) 101m/C Bruce Willis, Bruce Dern, Christopher Walken, Karina Lom-

bard, William Sanderson, David Patrick Kelly, Alexandra Powers, Leslie Mann, Michael Imperioli, R.D. Call, Ken Jenkins, Ned Eisenberg; **D:** Walter Hill; **W:** Walter Hill; **C:** Lloyd Ahern; **M:** Ry Cooder.

The Last Metro

The delicate touch that characterizes so much of Truffaut's work is evident in his one war film, a subtle complex study of the effects of Nazi occupation on a Paris theatre company. In 1942 Jewish director Lucas Steiner (Bennent) is forced to turn the running of his company over to his wife (Deneuve, as stunning as ever) who must contend with a fascist critic (Richard) and her attraction to a new leading man (Depardieu). Though the image has a slightly faded, orange cast, the film looks much better on disc than many of the older tapes that are in circulation. Also, the improved subtitles, which begin in the opening credits, are unusually easy to read. Recommended. —MM AKA: Le Dernier Metro.
Movie: 🎵🎵🎵▶ **DVD:** 🎵🎵🎵▶
WinStar Home Entertainment (Cat #FLV5074, UPC #720917507422). Widescreen (1.66:1) letterboxed. $29.90. Keepcase. LANG: French. SUB: English. FEATURES: 6 chapter links • Production credits • Filmographies and awards • Vintage Truffaut trailer collection.
1980 (PG) 135m/C FR Catherine Deneuve, Gerard Depardieu, Heinz Bennent, Jean-Louis Richard, Jean Poiret, Andrea Ferreol, Paulette Dubost, Sabine Haudepin, Maurice Risch, Jean-Pierre Klein, Martine Simonet, Franck Pasquier, Jean-Jose Richer, Laszlo Szabo, Jessica Zucman; **D:** Francois Truffaut; **W:** Francois Truffaut, Suzanne Schiffman, Jean-Claude Grumberg; **C:** Nestor Almendros; **M:** Georges Delerue. AWARDS: Cesar Awards '81: Best Actor (Depardieu), Best Actress (Deneuve), Best Art Direction/Set Decoration, Best Cinematography, Best Director (Truffaut), Best Film, Best Sound, Best Writing, Best Score; NOM: Academy Awards '80: Best Foreign Film.

Last Night

It's 6 p.m. in Toronto and the world is going to end in six hours. No one's going to save the day so all concerned must decide how they're going to spend their final minutes. Patrick (McKellar) goes to see his folks but is drawn into Sandra's (Oh) predicament. She's stuck across town from her husband. Patrick's friend Craig is trying to finish things off in bed with a series of partners, perhaps including their high school French teacher, Mrs. Carlton (Bujold). Other supporting characters take equally low-keyed paths to the hereafter. McKellar's humor, somewhat reminiscent of Albert Brooks, will not appeal to all tastes. (This one was a hit on the festival circuit but couldn't catch on in wide release.) DVD does the film few favors. With so-so lighting, the full-frame image is often harsh and in imperfect

focus. Sound is about the same, but viewers' reaction to the characters is more important than the visuals. —MM
Movie: 🎵🎵🎵 **DVD:** 🎵🎵▶
Universal Studios Home Video (Cat #20709, UPC #025192070921). Full frame. Dolby Digital Stereo. $24.98. Keepcase. LANG: English. CAP: English. FEATURES: 20 chapter links • Theatrical trailer.
1998 (R) 94m/C CA Don McKellar, Sandra Oh, Callum Keith Rennie, Sarah Polley, David Cronenberg, Genevieve Bujold, Tracy Wright, Roberta Maxwell, Robin Gammell, Karen Glave, Jackie Burroughs; **D:** Don McKellar; **W:** Don McKellar; **C:** Douglas Koch; **M:** Alexina Louie, Alex Pauk. AWARDS: Genie Awards '98: Best Actress (Oh), Best Supporting Actor (Rennie); NOM: Genie Awards '98: Best Art Direction/Set Decoration, Best Cinematography, Best Director (McKellar), Best Film, Best Film Editing, Best Supporting Actress (Bujold), Best Original Score.

The Last Starfighter

A young man who becomes an expert at a video game is recruited to fight in an intergalactic war. Listless adventure explains where all those video games come from. Watch for O'Herlihy disguised as a lizard. Preston displays his usual charms. This is an extremely sharp DVD with a very low grain level and hardly any artifacts. Colors are usually pretty punchy, but the tint seems to drift a bit and a few sequences seemed a little faded. Bleed is controlled even during moments of deeper color. Contrast and brightness levels are both very good and consistent, and the blacks are pretty much perfect. That's true even in the space scenes where a good portion of the screen is black. The 5.1 tracks sound good, but overall it's in need of some bass boost, and the Surround seems underused. —JO
Movie: 🎵🎵 **DVD:** 🎵🎵▶
Universal Studios Home Video (Cat #20519, UPC #025192051920). Widescreen (2.35:1) anamorphic. Dolby Digital 5.1. $34.98. Keepcase. LANG: English. SUB: French. CAP: English. FEATURES: 18 chapter links • Theatrical trailer and teaser • "Making of" featurette • Commentary: Nick Castle and Ron Cobb • Cast and filmmakers bios • Production notes • Photos.
1984 (PG) 100m/C Lance Guest, Robert Preston, Barbara Bosson, Dan O'Herlihy, Catherine Mary Stewart, Cameron Dye, Kimberly Ross, Wil Wheaton; **D:** Nick Castle; **W:** Jonathan Betuel; **C:** King Baggot; **M:** Craig Safan.

Last Tango in Paris

Brando plays a middle-aged American who meets a French girl and tries to forget his wife's suicide with a short, extremely steamy affair. Bertolucci proves to be a master; Brando gives one of his best performances. Very controversial when made, still quite explicit, it's visually stunning.

Wow! This DVD not only looks better than the MGM laserdisc and VHS releases, it's even a step up from the Criterion LD, although there is more preprint damage than I remember on that Criterion edition. The only other problem is that the sound is mono and a little weak, but may be due to the original print. Other than that, the DVD is as sharp as they come and has colors that are rich, accurate, and defined. Blacks are true enough to blend into the letterboxing. The contrast and brightness levels give the disc plenty of punch and have no trouble keeping up with the various lighting conditions. —*JO* **AKA:** L'Ultimo Tango a Parigi; Le Dernier Tango a Paris.

Movie: ♪♪♪➤ **DVD:** ♪♪♪➤
MGM Home Entertainment (Cat #906570). Widescreen (1.85:1) letterboxed. Mono. $24.98. Keepcase. *LANG:* English. *SUB:* English; French. *CAP:* English. *FEATURES:* 32 chapter links • Theatrical trailer • 8-page booklet.
1973 (R) **126m/C** *IT FR* Marlon Brando, Maria Schneider, Jean-Pierre Leaud, Maria Michi, Massimo Girotti, Catherine Allegret; **D:** Bernardo Bertolucci; **W:** Bernardo Bertolucci; **C:** Vittorio Storaro; **M:** Gato Barbieri. *AWARDS:* New York Film Critics Awards '73: Best Actor (Brando); National Society of Film Critics Awards '73: Best Actor (Brando); *NOM:* Academy Awards '73: Best Actor (Brando), Best Director (Bertolucci).

The Last Time I Saw Paris

A successful writer reminisces about his love affair with a wealthy American girl in post–World War II Paris.
Movie: ♪♪➤ **DVD:** NYR
Madacy Entertainment (Cat #99028). Full frame. Dolby Digital Mono. $9.99. Keepcase. *FEATURES:* Cast and crew thumbnail bios • Trivia.
1954 116m/C Elizabeth Taylor, Van Johnson, Walter Pidgeon, Roger Moore, Donna Reed, Eva Gabor; **D:** Richard Brooks; **W:** Richard Brooks, Julius J. Epstein, Philip C. Epstein; **C:** Joseph Ruttenberg; **M:** Conrad Salinger.

The Last Valley

A scholar tries to protect a pristine 17th-century Swiss valley, untouched by the Thirty Years War, from marauding soldiers. Historical action with an intellectual twist.
Movie: ♪♪ **DVD:** NYR
Anchor Bay (Cat #10984). Widescreen (2.21:1) letterboxed. Dolby Digital Stereo. $24.98. Keepcase.
1971 (PG) **128m/C** Michael Caine, Omar Sharif, Florinda Bolkan, Nigel Davenport, Per Oscarsson, Arthur O'Connell; **D:** James Clavell; **W:** James Clavell; **C:** John Wilcox; **M:** John Barry.

The Last Word

Detroit newspaper columnist Martin (Hutton) hangs out with gangsters (Palminteri) and strippers until one of his books becomes a best-seller. Then he and his pal Doc (Pantoliano) head west for Hollywood and fame. But to get it, Martin may have to betray his paramour Caprice (Burke). The main attraction here is the astonishing number of cameo appearances. The DVD is not a significant improvement over VHS tape. Both image and sound are at best fair. —*MM*
Movie: ♪♪➤ **DVD:** ♪♪
Trimark Home Video (Cat #VM#7305D, UPC #031398730521). Full frame. Stereo. $34.99. Keepcase. *LANG:* English. *FEATURES:* 8 chapter links • Theatrical trailer • Previews of other Trimark titles. Title is available for sale only as part of the "Mob Hits" four-pack.
1995 (R) **95m/C** Timothy Hutton, Joe Pantoliano, Michelle Burke, Chazz Palminteri, Tony Goldwyn, Richard Dreyfuss, Cybill Shepherd, Jimmy Smits; **D:** Tony Spiridakis; **W:** Tony Spiridakis; **C:** Zoltan David; **M:** Paul Buckmaster.

Last Year at Marienbad

Dense, difficult-to-embrace archetypical example of style over substance from French auteur director Alain Resnais *(Hiroshima, Mon Amour, Je T'Aime, Je T'Aime)*. A must for film students, but if you're looking for a night's entertainment, complete with snappy dialogue, a well-conceived storyline, and actors with a pulse, then *Last Year at Marienbad* will not be a satisfying experience. The core of the story has "X" (Albertazzi), confronting "A" (Delphine Seyrig—*Stolen Kisses, The Discreet Charm of the Bourgeoisie*) with the notion that they met the previous year at the resort of Marienbad, where she promised to leave "M" (Pitoeff) if given one year to do so. What is true, and what is imagined remain a mystery throughout. The DVD presentation, while a worthy effort in delivering the basics, really cries out for additional supporting materials such as a theatrical trailer and an audio commentary from a recognized film historian to decipher the meaning of Resnais's work. —*RT* **AKA:** L'Anee Derniere a Marienbad.
Movie: ♪♪➤ **DVD:** ♪♪➤
Fox/Lorber Home Video (Cat #5061, UPC #720917506128). Widescreen letterboxed. AC3 - 2 Channel. $29.98. Keepcase. *LANG:* French. *SUB:* English. *FEATURES:* 8 chapter links.
1961 93m/B *FR IT* Delphine Seyrig, Giorgia Albertazzi, Sacha Pitoeff, Luce Garcia-Ville; **D:** Alain Resnais; **W:** Alain Resnais, Alain Robbe-Grillet; **C:** Sacha Vierny; **M:** Francis Seyrig. *AWARDS: NOM:* Academy Awards '62: Best Story & Screenplay.

Lauderdale

Two college schmoes hit the beach looking for beer and babes. Few laughs for the sober and mature. Surf's down in this woofer. **AKA:** Spring Fever USA; Spring Break USA.
Movie: woof **DVD:** NYR
Simitar Entertainment (Cat #7617). Full frame. Dolby Digital 5.1 Surround Stereo. $14.98. Keepcase.
1989 (R) **91m/C** Darrel Gilbeau, Michelle Kemp, Jeff Greenman, Lara Belmonte; **D:** Bill Milling; **W:** Bill Milling.

Laurel and Hardy and Friends

Collection of short comedy classics includes Laurel and Hardy's "Be Big!," the Little Rascals/Our Gang's "School's Out," "Bear Shooters," and "Our Gang Follies of 1938," as well as "Whispering Whoopee" with Charley Chase and Thelma Todd. Picture and sound are uneven and can be quite poor, as should be expected from such antique film elements. These are mastered from surviving 35mm original material; some from the original nitrate camera negatives. Menu interface is clunky, but serviceable. —*MB*
Movie: ♪♪♪ **DVD:** ♪
Image Entertainment (Cat #HRS4800, UPC #014381480023). Full frame. Dolby Digital Mono. $29.98. Snapper. *LANG:* English. *FEATURES:* 6 chapter links • Printed descriptions for each title • Printed images of original posters.
199? ?m/B Stan Laurel, Oliver Hardy, Charley Chase, Thelma Todd.

Lav Kush

This film's mythic plot is taken from Bharat Milap, a section of the religious mainstay known as the Uttar Ramayan. Lord Rama is crowned king in the opening scene, and soon warned of personal crises he must endure for the sake of his subjects. His endangered Queen Sita is spirited away in the woods, giving birth to twins named Lav and Kush during her exile. The boys grow to be skilled in fine and martial arts alike. Their estrangement from their father leads to a civil war only Queen Sita can stop. The production is as lavish as the Dieterle and Reinhardt version of *A Midsummer Night's Dream* and just as obscure to those unfamiliar with the source material. Stereophonic junkies will want to pop this in just for the trippy computerized opening credit sequence, set to the sound of a million monks chanting. The visuals do not fare as well, however, breaking up whenever overloaded by glittering jewels or a quickly panning camera. —*JK*
Movie: ♪♪♪ **DVD:** ♪♪♪➤
Indo American Video Corp. (Cat #SDVD-IA-135, UPC #671373013524). Widescreen. Dolby Digital 2 Channel. $29.95. Keepcase. *LANG:* Hindi. *SUB:* English; French; Spanish. *FEATURES:* 12 song links (no scene chapter stops) • Coming attractions trailers. All regions coding. Packaging includes religious artwork insert.
1997 166m/C *IN* Jeetendra, Jayapradha, Pran, Dara Singh, Arun Govil, Beena, Jayashree Gadkar, Tiku Talsania, Isha Gupta, Churni Banerji Aditi Chatterjee; **D:**

V. Madhusudan Rao; *C:* K.S. Prakash; *M:* Ram Laxman, Dev Kohli, Bhring Tupkari.

The Law

Wildly overheated melodrama concerns Enrico (Mastroianni), an engineer who comes to an Italian fishing village and meets Marietta (Lollobrigida), the sexiest woman who is lusted after by all the males. The black-and-white photography is not nearly as sharp and well defined as other works of that time. Blacks predominate. The DVD image seems true to the original. The most interesting visual flaw is found in the tight striped dress that Ms. Lollobrigida wears. It creates odd kaleidoscope patterns whenever she wriggles around in it, and that, after all, is the point. —*MM AKA:* La Legge; La Loi; Where the Hot Wind Blows.
Movie: 🐾🐾▶ *DVD:* 🐾🐾▶
Image Entertainment (Cat #ID9065SIDVD, UPC #014381906523). Full frame. Dolby Digital Mono. $24.99. Snapper. *LANG:* French. *SUB:* English. *FEATURES:* 14 chapter links.
1959 120m/C *FR IT* Gina Lollobrigida, Marcello Mastroianni, Yves Montand, Melina Mercouri, Paolo Stoppa, Pierre Brasseur; *D:* Jules Dassin; *W:* Jules Dassin, Francoise Giroud; *C:* Otello Martelli.

Lawn Dogs

After moving into a gated community, Morton (McDonald) and Clare (Quinlan) want their young daughter to mix with the social elite. Instead, the imaginative Devon (Barton) strikes up a friendship with Trent (Rockwell), an outsider who mows lawns in the sterile neighborhood. Their relationship, of course, leads to trouble, and it's interlaced with the Russian fairy tale of Baba Yaga. The climax is unlikely and suffers a bit under the hard clarity of DVD. Still, fans of director Duigan's *Sirens* and *The Year My Voice Broke* should give this one a try. —*MM*
Movie: 🐾🐾🐾 *DVD:* 🐾🐾🐾
Trimark Home Video (Cat #VM6893D, UPC #031398689331). Widescreen letterboxed. Dolby Digital Surround Stereo. $24.99. Keepcase. *LANG:* English. *SUB:* French; Spanish. *CAP:* English. *FEATURES:* Cast and crew thumbnail bios ● Trailer ● 30 chapter links.
1996 101m/C *GB* Sam Rockwell, Mischa Barton, Kathleen Quinlan, Christopher McDonald, Bruce McGill, David Barry Gray, Eric Mabius, Tom Aldredge, Beth Grant; *D:* John Duigan; *W:* Naomi Wallace; *C:* Elliot Davis; *M:* Trevor Jones.

The Lawnmower Man

The central story here is a loose retelling of *Frankenstein*. Jobe (Fahey) is a slow-witted handyman whose brain power is boosted by exposure to Dr. Angelo's (Brosnan) experiments in virtual reality. The plot has almost nothing to do with King's short story—he had his name removed from the

title—but the tone is faithful to his fictional territory of small towns, bullies, kids, cruelty, abuse, ominous government agencies and, of course, a big pyrotechnic finale. Curiously, the film reflects the history of home video. The first VHS version is 30 minutes longer than the theatrical release with more special effects and a fully developed, coherent story. On tape, it was so successful with viewers that the film, which had fared poorly in theatres, rose beyond cult status to become a solid mainstream hit. The double-sided DVD takes the process a step farther. The full version of the film with commentary is on one side. Oddly, in one scene, director Leonard describes the difficulties in a special effects scene where a chair is "levitated." With the clarity of DVD, one wire is clearly visible. (Most of the commentary is evenly divided between the technical and the creative.) The second side contains the extras, including deleted scenes. —*MM*
Movie: 🐾🐾🐾 *DVD:* 🐾🐾🐾▶
New Line Home Video (Cat #N4092, UPC #794045409226). Widescreen (1.85:1) letterboxed. Dolby Digital Surround 5.1. $29.98. Snapper. *LANG:* English. *SUB:* English; Spanish. *FEATURES:* 24 chapter links within the film ● 16 chapter links for extras ● Commentary: director Brett Leonard, writer-producer Gimel Everett ● Interviews ● Animated sequences ● Theatrical trailer ● Star highlights of Brosnan ● Storyboard comparison ● Cast biographies and filmographies.
1992 (R) 108m/C Jeff Fahey, Pierce Brosnan, Jenny Wright, Mark Bringleson, Geoffrey Lewis, Jeremy Slate, Dean Norris, Troy Evans, John Laughlin; *D:* Brett Leonard; *W:* Brett Leonard, Gimel Everett; *C:* Russell Carpenter; *M:* Danny Wyman.

Lawyer Lawyer

Extremely silly historical (1899) slapstick comedy has to do with a fatuous young man who wears clownish outfits, his servant, and their romantic adventures. The bathroom humor is so juvenile that it's not particularly offensive. The DVD image is little better than tape with pale subtitles that are difficult to read. —*MM*
Movie: 🐾🐾 *DVD:* 🐾🐾
Tai Seng Video Marketing (Cat #DVD-056). Widescreen (1.66:1) letterboxed. Dolby Digital Stereo. $49.95. Jewel case. *LANG:* Cantonese; Mandarin. *SUB:* English; Chinese. *FEATURES:* 17 chapter links.
1997 85m/C *HK* Stephen (Chiau) Chow, Chingmy Yau, Karen Mok, Erik Kol; *D:* Joe Ma; *W:* Joe Ma.

Le Beau Mariage

Mention the name Beatrice Romand and you immediately think of prolific French director Eric Rohmer. She has been doing films with him for years and years—*Claire's Knee, Chloe in the Afternoon, Summer,* and *Autumn Tale,* among others. As with all of Rohmer's films, it is about subtleties and nuance, not about grand things and

action—John Woo he is not. Here, Romand announces to her friend Arielle Dombasle (*Pauline at the Beach*) that she is tired of sleeping with a married man (Feodor Atkine) and wants to get married. Her plan of catching some unsuspecting man (Andre Dussollier, *Same Old Song*) and marrying him goes hopelessly awry. Indeed, she comes across as something of a stalker; possibly demented, but the mood is kept light throughout, with the opening and closing scenes offering hope for the frustrated Romand. The DVD presentation is something of a disappointment in that there are no on/off options for the subtitle function—the captions are burned into the print. The visuals are classic Rohmer, very pastel in nature with natural light used throughout, all of which has been translated fairly well to this disc. —*RT AKA:* A Good Marriage; The Well-Made Marriage.
Movie: 🐾🐾🐾 *DVD:* 🐾🐾🐾▶
WinStar Home Entertainment (Cat #FLV5101, UPC #720917510125). Full frame. AC3 - 2 Channel. $29.98. Keepcase. *LANG:* French. *SUB:* English. *CAP:* English. *FEATURES:* 6 chapter links ● Actor/director filmographies.
1982 (R) 97m/C *FR* Beatrice Romand, Arielle Dombasle, Andre Dussollier, Feodor Atkine, Pascal Greggory, Sophie Renoir; *D:* Eric Rohmer; *W:* Eric Rohmer; *C:* Bernard Lutic; *M:* Ronan Girre, Simon des Innocents. *AWARDS:* Venice Film Festival '82: Best Actress (Romand).

The Leading Man

Bon Jovi's charming in the title role as American movie star Robin Grange who has come to London to act on stage in playwright Felix Webb's (Wilson) prestigious *The Hitman*. But Felix would also like Robin to help him out of a jam. Seems Mrs. Webb (Galiena) has found out about his mistress Hilary Rule (Newton), who just happens to be costarring in the play. If Robin could just seduce Felix's wife, it would make things so much easier. Nothing, of course, goes as planned. The film's often muddy interiors have a grim, grainy look on DVD. The wardrobe emphasizes blacks, browns, and reds, adding to the murkiness. Sound is nothing special either. —*MM*
Movie: 🐾🐾▶ *DVD:* 🐾🐾
WinStar Home Entertainment (Cat #FLV5162, UPC #720917516226). Full frame. Dolby Digital 5.1 Surround Stereo; Dolby Digital Surround Stereo. $24.98. Keepcase. *LANG:* English. *FEATURES:* 8 chapter links ● Filmographies and awards ● Theatrical trailer.
1996 (R) 96m/C *GB* Lambert Wilson, Jon Bon Jovi, Anna Galiena, Thandie Newton, David Warner, Barry Humphries, Patricia Hodge, Diana Quick, Nicole Kidman; *D:* John Duigan; *W:* John Duigan; *C:* Jean-Francois Robin; *M:* Ed Shearmur.

A League of Their Own

Charming look at sports history follows the Rockford Peaches, one of the teams in

the real-life All American Girls Professional Baseball League, formed in the '40s when the men were off at war. Main focus is on sibling rivalry between Davis, the beautiful, crackerjack catcher, and Petty, the younger, insecure pitcher. Boozy coach Hanks is wonderful as he reluctantly leads the team; he also gets credit for the classic "There's no crying in baseball" scene. Great cast of supporting characters, including sarcastic talent scout Lovitz; opinionated, sleazy taxi dancer Madonna; loud-mouthed O'Donnell; and shy, homely Cavanagh. Lots of baseball for the sports fan. There are no major problems with the DVD, though overall it is just average. Sharpness is fine and there is not much in the way of grain or artifacts. The colors are very good, both accurate and vibrant, with little bleed. Contrast and brightness levels are above average and remain consistent throughout. Blacks are just a touch off and generally very good. The Dolby Surround is pretty good when it comes to dynamics and fidelity, but the Surround could have been better used to convey ambiences, particularly during the many outdoor sequences. —JO
Movie: ♪♪♪ **DVD:** ♪♪▶
Columbia Tristar Home Video (Cat #51229, UPC #043396512290). Widescreen (2.35:1) letterboxed. Dolby Surround. $28.95. Keepcase. LANG: English; Spanish; French. SUB: Spanish; Korean. CAP: English. FEATURES: 51 chapter links.
1992 (PG) 127m/C Geena Davis, Tom Hanks, Lori Petty, Madonna, Rosie O'Donnell, Megan Cavanagh, Tracy Reiner, Bitty Schram, Jon Lovitz, David Strathairn, Garry Marshall, Bill Pullman, Ann Cusack, Anne Elizabeth Ramsay, Freddie Simpson, Renee Coleman, Tea Leoni, Joey Slotnick, Mark Holton, Gregory Sporleder, David Lander; **D:** Penny Marshall; **W:** Lowell Ganz, Babaloo Mandel; **C:** Miroslav Ondricek; **M:** Hans Zimmer; **V:** Harry Shearer.

Lean on Me

The romanticized version of the career of Joe Clark, a tough New Jersey teacher who became the principal of the state's toughest, worst school and, through controversial hard-line tactics, turned it around. Warner once again proves that a good DVD doesn't have to be an expensive one. This one is very pleasing to the eye, although the sound is a little weaker than the VHS edition. The picture, though, is of above-average sharpness, colors accurate, and blacks are free of grain and true. —JO
Movie: ♪♪♪ **DVD:** ♪♪♪
Warner Home Video, Inc. (Cat #11875, UPC #085391197523). Full frame. Dolby Surround. $14.98. Snapper. LANG: English. CAP: English. FEATURES: 32 chapter links.
1989 (PG-13) 109m/C Morgan Freeman, Robert Guillaume, Beverly Todd, Alan North, Lynne Thigpen, Robin Bartlett, Michael Beach, Ethan Phillips, Regina Taylor; **D:** John G. Avildsen; **W:** Michael Schiffer; **C:** Victor Hammer; **M:** Bill Conti.

Leave It to Beaver

Gee, Mrs. Cleaver, that's an awful nice updating of an old TV favorite you have there. Cut the crap, Eddie. The "let's plop a lovable sitcom family into the dysfunctional '90s" bit has had its run. This time the victims are the Cleavers: wise dad Ward (McDonald), perfect mom June (Turner), popular older brother Wally (von Detten)...and newcomer Cameron Finley as the Beaver. Unlike the Bradys, the modern world has made some impact here. Beav has an African-American friend while Mom wears jeans and owns a business. Gosh Wally, do you really think America was anxiously awaiting the return of the impossible-to-live-up-to clan? Don't be such a little dope. This is one of the better-looking full-frame transfers to DVD. The picture is sharp and free of both grain and artifacts. Colors are vibrant and near perfect in their accuracy. Blacks are dead-on most of the time and very true the rest. The picture is good and contrasty, with plenty of brightness but no deterioration of the blacks or the color hues. The 5.1 sound is nothing special and needs some more low end as well as an overall dynamic boost. It also wouldn't have hurt to have livened things up with a little more Surround. —JO
Movie: ♪♪ **DVD:** ♪♪♪▶
Universal Studios Home Video (Cat #20150, UPC #025192015021). Full frame. Dolby Digital 5.1; Dolby Surround. $24.98. Keepcase. LANG: English (DD5.1); Spanish (DS); French (DS). SUB: Spanish. CAP: English. FEATURES: 16 chapter links • Theatrical trailer • Cast and filmmakers bios • Production notes • Film highlights.
1997 (PG) 88m/C Christopher McDonald, Janine Turner, Erik von Detten, Cameron Finley, Barbara Billingsley, Ken Osmond, Adam Zolotin, Alan Rachins; **D:** Andy Cardiff; **W:** Brian Levant; **C:** Thomas Del Ruth; **M:** Randy Edelman.

Leaving Las Vegas

Ben Sanderson (Cage) is a hopeless alcoholic who goes to Vegas to drink himself to death and meets Sera (Shue), a lonely hooker who loves him enough not to stop him. Definitely as depressing as it sounds, the film still manages to have both a subtle sense of humor and compassion. Cage tops his best work and Shue proves she deserves better than the lightweight roles she's had in the past. Not for everyone, but worth the effort for those who like to see honest emotion and hate Hollywood's insistence on happy endings. Based on the semi-autobiographical novel by John O'Brien, who committed suicide shortly before pre-production began. The DVD presents the same unrated version that made its first appearance on laserdisc. When compared to other MGM DVDs, the image is a little grainy, but when compared to the MGM letterboxed LD, the image is improved, suggesting that the source material is the contributing factor. The picture is sharp enough, and the colors are very vibrant when showing the

strip or other lit-up areas of Vegas. Figgis composed the jazz score himself and it sounds great on the 5.1 sound. —JO
Movie: ♪♪♪▶ **DVD:** ♪♪♪▶
MGM Home Entertainment (Cat #906997, UPC #027616699725). Widescreen (1.85:1) anamorphic; full frame. Dolby Digital 5.1. $24.98. Keepcase. LANG: English. SUB: English; Spanish; French. CAP: English. FEATURES: 32 chapter links • Theatrical trailer • Production notes • Trivia • Uncut version • Dual-layered RSDL.
1995 120m/C Nicolas Cage, Elisabeth Shue, Julian Sands, Laurie Metcalf, David Brisbin, Richard Lewis, Valeria Golino, Steven Weber, Mariska Hargitay, Julian Lennon, Carey Lowell, Lucinda Jenney, Ed Lauter, R. Lee Ermey; **D:** Mike Figgis; **W:** Mike Figgis; **C:** Declan Quinn; **M:** Mike Figgis. AWARDS: Academy Awards '95: Best Actor (Cage); Golden Globe Awards '96: Best Actor—Drama (Cage); Independent Spirit Awards '96: Best Actress (Shue), Best Cinematography, Best Director (Figgis), Best Film; Los Angeles Film Critics Association Awards '95: Best Actor (Cage), Best Actress (Shue), Best Director (Figgis), Best Film; National Board of Review Awards '95: Best Actor (Cage); New York Film Critics Awards '95: Best Actor (Cage); National Society of Film Critics Awards '95: Best Actor (Cage), Best Actress (Shue), Best Director (Figgis); Screen Actors Guild Award '95: Best Actor (Cage); NOM: Academy Awards '95: Best Actress (Shue), Best Adapted Screenplay, Best Director (Figgis); British Academy Awards '95: Best Actor (Cage), Best Actress (Shue), Best Adapted Screenplay; Directors Guild of America Awards '95: Best Director (Figgis); Golden Globe Awards '96: Best Actress—Drama (Shue), Best Director (Figgis), Best Film—Drama; Independent Spirit Awards '96: Best Actor (Cage), Best Screenplay; Screen Actors Guild Award '95: Best Actress (Shue); Writers Guild of America '95: Best Adapted Screenplay.

Leaving Scars

Diane (Boyle) and Michael (Downs) are on the run from drug dealers and pornographers. That could be the one-sentence synopsis of any number of low-budget thrillers, but this one is actually built around relatively realistic characters. The DVD is an equally curious enterprise. On a separate commentary track, director Brad Jacques and writer-producer Marc Johnson deliver a full-length running commentary on the action, much of it filmed in their native Boston. Lest anyone mistake them for serious filmmakers, they brought in a pizza for this job and munch away noisily throughout. One of them even belches loud and wet right in the middle of the big love scene. So, true DVD fanatics can run this one on a double bill with Good Will Hunting and listen to four of Beantown's more adventurous auteurs discussing their work. —MM
Movie: ♪♪ **DVD:** ♪♪

Vista Street Entertainment (Cat #9707, UPC #743383970729). Full frame. Dolby Digital Stereo. $24.99. Keepcase. *LANG:* English. *FEATURES:* 7 chapter links • Theatrical trailer • "Behide (sic) The Scenes" photo gallery.
1997 90m/C Lisa Boyle, Robin Downs, Jonathon Slater, Charlie Broderick; *D:* Brad Jacques; *W:* Marc Johnson.

Lee Rock

In 1949, Hong Kong police rookie Lee Rock (Lau) hits the streets as a vice detective. The subjects are police corruption and his rough marriage to a local Mafia princess (Man). The no-frills (not even chapters) DVD is only slightly superior to tape. The subtitles are burned in; the image is nicked and grainy; the credits are not translated. —*MM*
Movie: 🐾🐾 **DVD:** 🐾🐾
Tai Seng Video Marketing (Cat #DVD-002). Full frame. Dolby Digital Stereo. $49.95. Jewel case. *LANG:* Cantonese; Mandarin. *SUB:* English; Chinese.
1991 130m/C *HK* Andy Lau, Cheung Man; *D:* Larry Lau; *W:* Clifton Cole, Raymond Fung; *C:* Jimmy Bosco; *M:* Richard Krant.

Legacy of Rage

Brandon (Lee), a waiter, befriends young mobster Michael (Wong), who turns out to be in love with Brandon's fiancee May (Kent). Michael frames Brandon for a murder, has him thrown in jail, and goes after May. When Brandon gets out, he really cuts loose. The image of Lee's only Hong Kong film is better than import tapes, but not up to the best DVDs. It's grainy with moderate snow. The problems come from a worn print, not the transition to disc. —*MM*
Movie: 🐾🐾▸ **DVD:** 🐾🐾▸
Tai Seng Video Marketing (Cat #5176, UPC #895024900551). Widescreen letterboxed. Dolby Digital 5.1 Surround Stereo. $29.95. Keepcase. *LANG:* Cantonese; Mandarin. *SUB:* Traditional & Simplified Chinese; Japanese; Bahasa Malaysia; English; Thai; Korean; Vietnamese. *FEATURES:* 8 chapter links • Cast and crew thumbnail biographies.
1986 86m/C *HK* Brandon Lee, Michael Wong, Bolo Yeung, Regina Kent; *D:* Ronny Yu.

Legal Eagles

Clever, romantic caper-comedy from writer-director Ivan Reitman (*Ghostbusters*) is populated with a cast of beautiful people. Daryl Hannah (*Splash*), accused of theft and murder, is defended by Debra Winger and prosecuted by assistant DA Robert Redford, with character actor Steven Hill (*Law and Order*) doing a turn as Redford's boss, the New York district attorney. (Sound familiar?) The whodunit moves along at a nice clip, with plenty of twists and turns, red herrings, a seduction, warehouse explosion, and several nasty vil-

lains. Strong DVD production values, with a crisp, clean image presented in its original widescreen format. Extras such as trailers and possible behind-the-scenes footage would have been welcomed. —*RT*
Movie: 🐾🐾🐾 **DVD:** 🐾🐾🐾
Image Entertainment (Cat #5134, UPC #014381513424). Widescreen. AC3 - 2 Channel. $24.99. Snapper. *LANG:* English. *FEATURES:* 16 chapters.
1986 (PG) 116m/C Robert Redford, Debra Winger, Daryl Hannah, Brian Dennehy, Terence Stamp, Steven Hill, David Clennon, Roscoe Lee Browne, John McMartin, Jennie Dundas, Ivan Reitman; *D:* Ivan Reitman; *W:* Jack Epps Jr., Jim Cash; *C:* Laszlo Kovacs; *M:* Elmer Bernstein.

Legend of the Drunken Tiger

The gimmick behind this historical kung-fu flick is that the hero, San (Wai Ying Hung) is a great fighter when he's blotto. The rest of the action is far too talky, and the endless scenes of San swilling down booze are overplayed as broad slapstick. The martial arts action is fairly well choreographed, though fans won't find anything really new. On disc, the faded image is clear enough, but not spectacular. It's on a par with the English dubbing. (No subtitles are available.) —*MM*
Movie: 🐾🐾 **DVD:** 🐾🐾
Tai Seng Video Marketing (Cat #27564, UPC #61643275642). Full frame. $19.95. Keepcase. *LANG:* English. *FEATURES:* 6 chapter links • Interactive menu.
1992 98m/C Wai Ying Hung; *D:* Robert Tai; *C:* Tommy Tong.

The Legend of the 7 Golden Vampires

The marriage of a Hammer horror with a Shaw Brothers martial arts flick is a consummation devoutly to be deplored. It begins in 1804 with a Chinese monk visiting Transylvania to ask the help of Dracula (Forbes-Robertson). Flash forward 100 years to find Prof. Van Helsing (Cushing) lecturing at a Hong Kong University. The resulting action scenes are pretty tame stuff; the horrors are warmed over "Blind Dead" routines with silly makeup and bats on strings. The DVD image reflects the quality of the original material. In his first scene, Dracula's bright red lipstick seems to wander around his face and chin. Later, skin tones are too pink. The dual-sided disc contains the full-length version on one side, and the abbreviated U.S. release, under the title *The Seven Brothers Meet Dracula*, on the other. —*MM*
AKA: The Seven Brothers Meet Dracula; Dracula and the Seven Golden Vampires.
Movie: 🐾 **DVD:** 🐾▸
Anchor Bay (Cat #DV10560, UPC #013131056099). Widescreen (2.35:1) letterboxed. Dolby Digital Mono. $29.99. Keepcase. *LANG:* English; Chinese. *SUB:* English. *FEATURES:* 9 chapter links •

Peter Cushing "narrative" about vampires • Theatrical trailer.
1973 89m/C *GB* Peter Cushing, David Chang, Robin Stewart, Julie Ege, John Forbes-Robertson; *D:* Roy Ward Baker; *W:* Don Houghton; *C:* Roy Ford, John Wilcox; *M:* James Bernard.

Legends of the Fall

Meandering, would-be epic depends on spectacular Montana mountain setting (actually Alberta, Canada), and the appeal of star Brad Pitt having a very good hair day. Patriarch William Ludlow (Hopkins), a retired Indian fighter, is raising three sons: reserved Alfred (Quinn), idealistic Samuel (Thomas), and wildman Tristan (Pitt). They must deal with World War I and Samuel's wife Susannah (Ormond), whom the other brothers lust after. Director Zwick's fondness for dramatic landscapes loses a lot on DVD, even with a pristine image. The star, however, is at his photogenic best, and that will probably be enough for his fans, who might have preferred a full-frame image transfer. Sound is acceptable. —*MM*
Movie: 🐾🐾 **DVD:** 🐾🐾🐾
Columbia Tristar Home Video (Cat #78729, UPC #043396787292). Widescreen (1.85:1) letterboxed. Dolby Digital 5.1 Surround Stereo; Dolby Digital Surround Stereo. $25.95. Keepcase. *LANG:* English; French; Spanish. *SUB:* Spanish; Korean. *FEATURES:* 61 chapter links.
1994 (R) 134m/C Brad Pitt, Aidan Quinn, Julia Ormond, Anthony Hopkins, Henry Thomas, Gordon Tootoosis, Tantoo Cardinal, Karina Lombard, Paul Desmond, Kenneth Welsh; *D:* Edward Zwick; *W:* Susan Shilliday, William D. Wittliff; *C:* John Toll; *M:* James Horner. *AWARDS:* Academy Awards '94: Best Cinematography; *NOM:* Academy Awards '94: Best Art Direction/Set Decoration, Best Sound; Golden Globe Awards '95: Best Actor—Drama (Pitt), Best Director (Zwick), Best Film—Drama, Best Score.

Legionnaire

In 1925, boxer Alain Lefevre (Van Damme) enlists in the French Foreign Legion and is stationed in Morocco. Training and desert warfare follow. This surprisingly enjoyable feature went straight to video. It's one of Van Damme's best, both for his acting and for the well-told story. The DVD contains a wealth of extras, befitting the excellent image and sound. Writer-executive producer Sheldon Lettich provides a straightforward commentary track. All in all, this is one of the better sleepers in the video store. —*MM*
Movie: 🐾🐾🐾 **DVD:** 🐾🐾🐾▸
Studio Home Entertainment (Cat #7145, UPC #658149714526). Widescreen (2.35:1) letterboxed. Dolby Digital Surround Stereo. $14.95. Keepcase. *LANG:* English. *SUB:* Spanish. *FEATURES:* 24 chapter links • Background featurettes on the Foreign Legion • Theatrical trailers • "Making of" featurette • Trivia game •

Commentary: Sheldon Lettich ◆ DVD-ROM features.
1998 (R) 99m/C Jean-Claude Van Damme, Nicholas Farrell, Steven Berkoff, Jim Carter, Adewale Akinnuoye-Agbaje; *D:* Peter Macdonald; *W:* Sheldon Lettich, Rebecca Morrison; *C:* Doug Milsome; *M:* John Altman.

L'Enfer

Claustrophobic thriller chronicles the descent into madness of hotel owner Paul (Cluzet), who is convinced that his wife Nelly (Beart) is having an affair. Intriguing plot points that blur appearances and reality lead to an ambiguous ending. Clouzot himself began filming his screenplay in 1964, but a heart attack forced him to abandon the project. Unfortunately, the film was made in such harsh colors that the DVD image is far less than perfect. It's rough and grainy, emphasizing deep reds. Some dark scenes become so black that they are indecipherable. Sound is O.K. — *MM AKA:* Jealousy; Torment.
Movie: 🐾🐾🐾 *DVD:* 🐾🐾
WinStar Home Entertainment (Cat #FLV5026, UPC #720917502625). Widescreen (1.66:1) letterboxed. $29.98. Keepcase. *LANG:* French. *SUB:* English. *FEATURES:* 9 chapter links.
1993 103m/C *FR* Emmanuelle Beart, Francois Cluzet, Nathalie Cardone, Andre Wilms, Marc Lavoine; *D:* Claude Chabrol; *W:* Claude Chabrol, Henri-Georges Clouzot, Jose-Andre Lacour; *C:* Bernard Zitzermann; *M:* Matthieu Chabrol.

Leonard Bernstein: Reaching for the Note

Produced for Public Television's "American Masters" series, this video biography is a fine introduction to the man who came to represent serious music for a generation of Americans. The film begins in standard fashion with Bernstein's funeral and then goes back to examine his unlikely introduction to music and the meteoric rise of his professional career. Filmmakers Susan Lacy and Margaret Smilow accentuate the positive, de-emphasize the negative and don't mess with Mr. In-Between, not that there was much of that in Bernstein's life. DVD is a fine medium for this kind of program. The extras feature additional interviews with his family and colleagues. The quality of the archival photographs and film and videotape varies, of course. The original footage sparkles. The sound is fine but not spectacular. Highly recommended to anyone interested in the subject. —*MM*
Movie: 🐾🐾🐾 *DVD:* 🐾🐾🐾
WinStar Home Entertainment (Cat #WHE73019, UPC #720917301921). Full frame. $34.98. Snapper. *LANG:* English. *FEATURES:* 12 chapter links ◆ 4 additional interviews ◆ Brief biography ◆ Selected discography, with links to performances in program.

1998 117m/C *D:* Susan Lacy; *W:* Susan Lacy; *C:* Terry Hopkins.

Leprechaun

Formulaic little video premiere has spawned an unlikely series of low-budget horrors. The poorly written story lurches into gear with a clumsy introduction and then moves to a back-lot North Dakota setting. The main attraction is the presence of cute-as-a-Junebug Jennifer Aniston as Tori, the California teeny-babe trapped for the summer up there in the Northern Tier. As the title character, Warwick Davis is a nasty-looking thing. The gore is played mostly for attempted laughs; the pace is fast and fitful; and what's this shoe fetish that the little gremlin has? In image and sound, the DVD is not substantially different from VHS tape. —*MM*
Movie: 🐾▸ *DVD:* 🐾🐾
Trimark Home Video (Cat #VM6840D, UPC #031398684039). Full frame. Dolby Digital Surround Stereo. $14.99. Keepcase. *LANG:* English. *SUB:* French; Spanish. *CAP:* English. *FEATURES:* 24 chapter links.
1993 (R) 92m/C Warwick Davis, Jennifer Aniston, Ken Olandt, Mark Holton, John Sanderford, Robert Gorman, Shay Duffin, John Voldstad; *D:* Mark Jones; *W:* Mark Jones; *C:* Levie Isaacks.

Leprechaun 2

Low-budget sequel is a definite step down from this none-too-wonderful original. On his 2,000th birthday, the grody little critter (Davis) gets "to claim his bride" if she sneezes three times. L.A. babe Bridget (Durkin) is the lucky gal. The nasty makeup and the ridiculous fake Irish legends are the same; the sadistic sexual angle is new and unneeded. One scene directly quotes Tod Browning's *Freaks*.
Movie: 🐾 *DVD:* NYR
Trimark Home Video (Cat #6918). Dolby Digital Stereo. $14.99. Keepcase. *SUB:* French; Spanish.
1994 (R) 85m/C Warwick Davis, Sandy Baron, Adam Biesk, James Lancaster, Clint Howard, Kimmy Robertson, Charlie Heath, Shevonne Durkin; *D:* Rodman Flender; *W:* Turi Meyer, Al Septien; *C:* Jane Castle; *M:* Jonathan Elias.

Les Miserables

Yet another adaptation of the Victor Hugo novel. Paroled convict Jean Valjean (Neeson) is chased by police inspector Javert (Rush) while factory worker Fantine (Thurman) turns to prostitution to survive. August chooses to begin this tale after Valjean's trial and imprisonment for petty theft and until the final third of the film, he doesn't really deal with the political upheaval of the time. It's not as sweeping or grand as other versions, but what this one lacks in scope, it makes up for with top-notch performances (especially by Neeson and Rush) and more careful study of the characters themselves.
Movie: 🐾🐾🐾 *DVD:* NYR

Columbia Tristar Home Video (Cat #23999). Widescreen (2.35:1) letterboxed. Dolby Digital 5.1 Surround Stereo. $29.95. Keepcase. *LANG:* English; French. *SUB:* French. *FEATURES:* Trailer.
1997 (PG-13) 134m/C Liam Neeson, Geoffrey Rush, Uma Thurman, Claire Danes, Paris Vaughan, Reine Brynolfsson, Hans Matheson, Mimi Newman; *D:* Bille August; *W:* Rafael Yglesias; *C:* Jorgen Persson; *M:* Basil Poledouris.

Lethal Weapon

In Los Angeles, a cop nearing retirement (Glover) unwillingly begins work with a new partner (Gibson), a suicidal, semi-crazed risk-taker who seems determined to get the duo killed. Both Vietnam vets, the pair uncover a vicious heroin smuggling ring run by ruthless ex–Special Forces personnel. It's packed with plenty of action, violence, and humorous undertones. Clapton's contributions to the musical score are an added bonus. Gibson and Glover work well together and give this movie extra punch. Followed by three sequels. As you would expect, Warner Bros. made sure to not screw up one of their biggest franchises, even in the earlier days of DVD. This disc has a very good image that is sharp and detailed with only the rare bit of grain. There are, however, artifacts during some scenes with fast motion in them. Colors are accurate and clean. Blacks are also very good, even though this is one of the earlier DVD releases. Contrast and brightness levels are consistent. Sound is dynamic, with plenty of high end, and good thumping bass. Excellent use is made of the Surround tracks, mainly for effects. —*JO*
Movie: 🐾🐾🐾 *DVD:* 🐾🐾🐾
Warner Home Video, Inc. (Cat #11709, UPC #085391170921). Widescreen (1.85:1) anamorphic; full frame. Dolby Digital 5.1; Dolby Surround. $24.98. Snapper. *LANG:* English (DD5.1); French (DS). *SUB:* English; Spanish; French. *CAP:* English. *FEATURES:* 23 chapter links ◆ Theatrical trailer ◆ Production notes.
1987 (R) 110m/C Mel Gibson, Danny Glover, Gary Busey, Mitchell Ryan, Tom Atkins, Darlene Love, Traci Wolfe, Steve Kahan, Jackie Swanson, Damon Hines, Lycia Naff, Mary Ellen Trainor, Jack Thibeau, Ed O'Ross, Gustav Vintas, Al Leong, Joan Severance; *D:* Richard Donner; *W:* Shane Black; *C:* Stephen Goldblatt; *M:* Michael Kamen, Eric Clapton. *AWARDS:* NOM: Academy Awards '87: Best Sound.

Lethal Weapon 2

This sequel to the popular cop adventure finds Gibson and Glover taking on a variety of blond South African "diplomats" who try to use their diplomatic immunity status to thwart the duo's efforts to crack their smuggling ring. Gibson finally finds romance, and viewers learn the truth about his late wife's accident. This installment also features the introduction of obnoxious, fast-talking con artist Leo ("O.K., O.K.") Getz, adeptly played by Pesci, who becomes a third wheel to the crime-fighting team. The DVD is of similar quality to *Lethal Weapon,* except that Warner seems to have solved the artifact problem (for the most part). The picture is still very sharp and has very little grain. The colors are accurate and punchy, making good use of the brightness and contrast levels. Blacks are true. Also as the original, this one has excellent sound and Surround. There is plenty of good clean bass and bright clear high end to liven things up. Dialogue is mixed up front. —*JO*

Movie: 🎬🎬🎬➤ **DVD:** 🎬🎬🎬➤
Warner Home Video, Inc. (Cat #11876, UPC #0853911876222). Widescreen (2.35:1) anamorphic. Dolby Digital 5.1; Dolby Surround. $24.98. Snapper. *LANG:* English (DD5.1); French (DS). *SUB:* English; Spanish; French. *CAP:* English. *FEATURES:* 39 chapter links • Theatrical trailer • Behind-the-scenes featurette • Production notes.
1989 (R) 114m/C Mel Gibson, Danny Glover, Joe Pesci, Joss Ackland, Derrick O'Connor, Patsy Kensit, Darlene Love, Traci Wolfe, Steve Kahan, Mary Ellen Trainor; *D:* Richard Donner; *W:* Jeffrey Boam; *C:* Stephen Goldblatt; *M:* Michael Kamen, Eric Clapton, David Sanborn.

Lethal Weapon 3

Murtaugh and Riggs return for more action in another slam-bang adventure. Murtaugh hopes his last week before retirement will be a peaceful one, but partner Riggs isn't about to let him go quietly. Not many changes from the successful formula with bickering buddies, lots of adventure, exploding buildings, a little comic relief from Pesci, and the addition of Russo as an Internal Affairs cop who proves to be more than a match for Riggs. Another excellent DVD transfer delivers the weakest in the series with true near-stunning flair. The image is sharp and the colors superb. No grain or artifacts. The usual boisterous 5.1 sound accompanies the picture and it'll please just as the others, with high-energy bass and finely tuned Surround that puts you where the action is. —*JO*

Movie: 🎬🎬➤ **DVD:** 🎬🎬🎬➤
Warner Home Video, Inc. (Cat #12475, UPC #085391247524). Widescreen (2.35:1) anamorphic. Dolby Digital 5.1; Dolby Surround. $24.98. Snapper. *LANG:* English (DD5.1); French (DS). *SUB:* English; Spanish; French. *CAP:* English. *FEATURES:* 31 chapter links • 2 theatrical trailers • Production notes.
1992 (R) 118m/C Mel Gibson, Danny Glover, Joe Pesci, Rene Russo, Stuart Wilson, Steve Kahan, Darlene Love, Traci Wolfe, Gregory Millar, Jason Meshover-Iorg, Delores Hall; *D:* Richard Donner; *W:* Jeffrey Boam, Robert Mark Kamen; *C:* Jan De Bont; *M:* Michael Kamen, Eric Clapton, David Sanborn. *AWARDS:* MTV Movie

Awards '93: Best On-Screen Duo (Mel Gibson/Danny Glover), Best Action Sequence.

Lethal Weapon 4

It's old home week as Gibson, Glover, Pesci, and Russo all reunite for one more escapade, six years after 1992's *Lethal Weapon 3.* Rock joins the veterans as junior detective Lee Butters, who has some unexpected ties to Murtaugh. They're investigating Asian crimelord Wah Sing Ku (Chinese action star Li), who's involved in smuggling and counterfeiting and has no problem with violence, including kicking the bejeezus out of Riggs on more than one occasion. Russo had to do her action sequences with a prosthetic belly since her character, Lorna Cole, and Riggs are about to become parents. It's the same old same-old but it's still a good time. If you've got the other three, you'll want to buy this one just for the supplemental section, which includes deleted scenes, bloopers, and more from the entire series. Like the other three, this is also a very good DVD with consistently excellent specs across the board. The disc is extremely sharp and grain-free, with only a few action sequences that have artifacts. Colors don't bleed and are both vibrant and accurate. Blacks are consistently dead-on and the excellent brightness and contrast levels complete the visuals. There is plenty of Surround (effects and ambience) in the 5.1 mix, which has excellent dynamics and plenty of gutsy, pile-driving bass. —*JO*

Movie: 🎬🎬➤ **DVD:** 🎬🎬🎬➤
Warner Home Video, Inc. (Cat #16075, UPC #085391607526). Widescreen (2.35:1) anamorphic. Dolby Digital 5.1. $24.98. Snapper. *LANG:* English; French. *SUB:* English; French. *CAP:* English. *FEATURES:* 45 chapter links • Theatrical trailers • Commentary: Richard Donner • Behind-the-scenes documentary • Deleted scenes from first 3 *Lethal Weapons* • Cast and crew bios • Production notes.
1998 (R) 125m/C Mel Gibson, Danny Glover, Joe Pesci, Rene Russo, Chris Rock, Jet Li, Steve Kahan, Darlene Love; *D:* Richard Donner; *W:* Channing Gibson; *C:* Andrzej Bartkowiak; *M:* Michael Kamen, Eric Clapton, David Sanborn. *AWARDS:* NOM: MTV Movie Awards '99: Breakthrough Performance (Rock), Best Villain (Li), Best Comedic Performance (Rock), Best Action Sequence; Golden Raspberry Awards '98: Worst Supporting Actor (Pesci).

Leviathan

A motley crew of ocean-floor miners are trapped when they are accidentally exposed to a failed Soviet experiment that turns humans into insatiable, regenerating fish-creatures. The film would be much improved with a 5.1 remix that punched up the bass a notch and filled the room with underwater ambience during lulls in the action. The picture, though, is as sharp as almost any DVD I've seen, and

the colors are contrasty and bright, while remaining totally accurate. And don't let that sound thing turn you off too much; this disc sounds as good as most Dolby Surround-encoded DVDs do. —*JO*

Movie: 🎬🎬➤ **DVD:** 🎬🎬🎬➤
MGM Home Entertainment (Cat #907044, UPC #027616704429). Widescreen (2.35:1) letterboxed. Dolby Surround. $24.98. Keepcase. *LANG:* English; French. *SUB:* English; French. *CAP:* English. *FEATURES:* 32 chapter links • Theatrical trailer.
1989 (R) 98m/C Peter Weller, Ernie Hudson, Hector Elizondo, Amanda Pays, Richard Crenna, Daniel Stern, Lisa Eilbacher, Michael Carmine, Meg Foster; *D:* George P. Cosmatos; *W:* David Peoples, Jeb Stuart; *C:* Alex Thomson; *M:* Jerry Goldsmith.

Liar Liar

Carrey takes on one of his less manic but still appealing personas as a compulsive liar and attorney. A constant disappointment to his ex-wife and son, he is forced to tell the truth for 24 hours, thanks to his son's supernatural birthday wish. This puts a crimp in his legal practice, especially as he tries to defend brazen would-be divorcee Tilly. It's all kind of sappy, but Carrey can carry almost any situation. The DVD is above average, and features good colors (in one or two scenes, there is a little bleed that doesn't detract too much) and true blacks. Contrast and brightness levels are consistent and very comfortable. Grain visits only occasionally during courtroom sequences. The audio is excellent—crisp, dynamically full, and featuring plenty of low end and good Surround for a film that doesn't have a lot of things blowing up. Oh yeah, to top it off, the picture is very sharp. —*JO*

Movie: 🎬🎬➤ **DVD:** 🎬🎬🎬➤
Universal Studios Home Video (Cat #20146, UPC #025192014628). Full frame. Dolby Digital 5.1; Dolby Surround. Keepcase. *LANG:* English (DD5.1); Spanish (DS); French (DS). *SUB:* Spanish. *CAP:* English. *FEATURES:* 16 chapter links • Theatrical trailer • Production notes • Cast and filmmaker bios.
1996 (PG-13) 87m/C Jim Carrey, Jennifer Tilly, Maura Tierney, Amanda Donohoe, Swoosie Kurtz, Justin Cooper, Jason Bernard, Mitchell Ryan, Anne Haney, Chip Mayer, Randall "Tex" Cobb, Cary Elwes; *D:* Tom Shadyac; *W:* Paul Guay, Steve Mazur; *C:* Russell Boyd; *M:* John Debney. *AWARDS:* MTV Movie Awards '98: Best Comedic Performance (Carrey); *NOM:* Golden Globe Awards '98: Best Actor—Musical/Comedy (Carrey).

License to Kill

Dalton's second Bond effort has improved with age. Its toughness and action sequences have less to do with the smarminess that had given the series a self-satisfied feeling. On DVD, the Florida Keys and Mexican settings look fine.

Unfortunately, the bright tropic light means that bright diagonal lines are even more prone to aliasing than they normally are. As with the other entries in the series, the extras are numerous, well chosen, and carefully produced, particularly the two commentary tracks. —*MM*

Movie: 🎬🎬🎬 **DVD:** 🎬🎬▶

MGM Home Entertainment (Cat #907708, UPC #027616770820). Widescreen letterboxed. Dolby Digital 5.1 Surround Stereo; Dolby Digital Surround Stereo. $34.98. Keepcase. *LANG:* English; French. *SUB:* English; French. *FEATURES:* 56 chapter links • Booklet • 2 commentary tracks with filmmakers and cast • "Making of" documentary • 2 music videos • Stills gallery • Theatrical trailers • Promotional featurette • Publicity footage.
1989 (PG-13) 133m/C *GB* Timothy Dalton, Carey Lowell, Robert Davi, Frank McRae, Talisa Soto, David Hedison, Anthony Zerbe, Everett McGill, Wayne Newton, Benicio Del Toro, Desmond Llewelyn, Priscilla Barnes; *D:* John Glen; *W:* Michael G. Wilson, Richard Maibaum; *C:* Alec Mills; *M:* Michael Kamen.

The Lickerish Quartet

Perhaps Metzger's best film, this one is also one of the most well-preserved. It's the story of a kinky family—Dad (Wolff), Mom (Remberg), and son (Turco)—who watch a skin flick at their mountain villa. Growing bored with the scratchy black-and-white images, they go into town to see a carnival daredevil show where they recognize a beautiful blonde cyclist (Venturelli) as a participant in their movie. They invite her back. The rest contains some of Metzger's most inventive erotic sequences, particularly the famous library scene. The DVD must have been made from a superior print or master. Colors are bright and vivid, and the focus is fairly sharp. Sound is fine. (By the way, the film was released in Italy under the hyperventilating title, *Erotica, Exotica, Psychotica, Fab!*) —*MM*
Movie: 🎬🎬▶ **DVD:** 🎬🎬▶
Image Entertainment (Cat #ID5541FFDVD, UPC #014381554120). Widescreen (1.85:1) letterboxed. Dolby Digital Mono. $24.98. Snapper. *LANG:* English. *FEATURES:* 12 chapter links.
1970 (R) 90m/C Silvana Venturelli, Frank Wolff, Erika Remberg, Paolo Turco; *D:* Radley Metzger; *W:* Michael DeForrest; *C:* Hans Jura.

Life

In 1932, conman Ray (Murphy) and straight-arrow Claude (Lawrence) are forced to go from Harlem to Mississippi to bring back a load of moonshine. Trumped up charges land them in a prison farm. The two leads make a remarkably effective comic duo and they're surrounded by an excellent supporting cast. It's really unfair to criticize such a light picture for its sanitized view of racial issues in the Deep South. The DVD captures director Ted Demme's careful staging well, though

soft-focus period pieces don't play to the strengths of the medium. He emphasizes browns, burgundies, and careful skin tones and so the image has a rich, textured patina. Audio is also excellent, highlighting a fine soundtrack. —*MM*
Movie: 🎬🎬🎬 **DVD:** 🎬🎬🎬▶
Universal Studios Home Video (Cat #20559, UPC #025192055928). Widescreen (1.85:1) letterboxed. Dolby Digital 5.1 Surround Stereo; Dolby Digital Surround Stereo. $29.98. Keepcase. *LANG:* English; French. *FEATURES:* 18 chapter links • "Making of" featurette • 2 deleted scenes with director's commentary • Separate audio commentary by director Ted Demme • Music highlights and videos • Cast and crew thumbnail biographies • Theatrical trailer • Production notes • DVD-ROM extras • Universal previews.
1999 (R) 108m/C Eddie Murphy, Martin Lawrence, Ned Beatty, Cicely Tyson, Clarence Williams III, Obba Babatunde, Bernie Mac, Michael "Bear" Taliferro, Miguel Nunez, Bokeem Woodbine, Barry (Shakaba) Henley, Brent Jennings, Guy Torry, Lisa Nicole Carson, O'Neal Compton, Poppy Montgomery, Ned Vaughn, R. Lee Ermey, Nick Cassavetes, Noah Emmerich, Anthony Anderson, Rick James; *D:* Ted Demme; *W:* Robert Ramsey, Matthew Stone; *C:* Geoffrey Simpson; *M:* Wyclef Jean. *AWARDS: NOM:* Academy Awards '99: Best Makeup.

Life Is Beautiful

The main attraction of this DVD is the language selection it offers. Those who simply cannot abide subtitled movies can experience the comedy-drama with translated dialogue that's remarkably well dubbed. That dubbing probably will not convert those who are put off by Oscar-winning writer-director-star Roberto Benigni's excessive enthusiasm. His tale of love, romance, and sacrifice in the Italian Holocaust has been a surprise hit with audiences. On disc, the film looks every bit as good as it does on the big screen, both in the lyrical first half focused on Guido's (Benigni) courtship of the lovely Dora (Braschi) and in the darker conclusion when they and their son (Cantarini) are taken to a concentration camp. The addition of the English language track will certainly make it accessible to an even larger audience on home video. The yellow subtitles are easy to read. —*MM* *AKA:* La Vita E Bella.
Movie: 🎬🎬🎬 **DVD:** 🎬🎬🎬▶
Miramax Pictures Home Video (Cat #17490, UPC #0788816209). Widescreen (1.85:1) letterboxed. Dolby Digital 5.1 Surround Stereo. $39.99. Keepcase. *LANG:* English; Italian. *SUB:* English. *CAP:* English. *FEATURES:* Theatrical trailer • "Making of" featurette • TV spots • Academy Award TV commercials • 27 chapter links.
1998 (PG-13) 122m/C *IT* Roberto Benigni, Nicoletta Braschi, Giustino Durano, Sergio Bustric, Horst Buchholz, Giorgio Cantarini, Marisa Paredes, Lidia Alfonsi,

Giuliana Lojodice; *D:* Roberto Benigni; *W:* Vincenzo Cerami, Roberto Benigni; *C:* Tonino Delli Colli; *M:* Nicola Piovani. *AWARDS:* Academy Awards '98: Best Actor (Benigni), Best Foreign Film, Best Original Dramatic Score; Australian Film Institute '99: Best Foreign Film; British Academy Awards '98: Best Actor (Benigni); Cannes Film Festival '98: Grand Jury Prize; Cesar Awards '99: Best Foreign Film; Screen Actors Guild Award '98: Best Actor (Benigni); Broadcast Film Critics Association Awards '98: Best Foreign Film; *NOM:* Academy Awards '98: Best Director (Benigni), Best Film Editing, Best Original Screenplay, Best Picture; British Academy Awards '98: Best Foreign Film, Best Original Screenplay; Directors Guild of America Awards '98: Best Director (Benigni); Screen Actors Guild Award '98: Cast.

A Life Less Ordinary

Third outing from the U.K. team of Boyle/Hodge/Macdonald, who made *Shallow Grave* and *Trainspotting*, is a magnificent-looking misfire. Hapless janitor Robert (McGregor), who's lost his job, girlfriend, and home, retaliates by kidnapping the boss's daughter Celine (Diaz), who's more upset by Robert's blundering than anything else. Meanwhile, two angels (Hunter and Lindo) are dispatched from heaven to make the mismatched pair fall in love. Confused? You should be. Script is a surreal wedding of *It Happened One Night*, *Stairway to Heaven*, and a Road Runner cartoon. The DVD lacks extra features, like a director's commentary that might have shed some light on the genesis of this strange project, but it has a spectacular visual transfer that captures every brilliant hue and gorgeous widescreen composition. Sound quality is good, though the extreme loud/soft transitions from scene to scene can be jarring. —*JE*
Movie: 🎬🎬▶ **DVD:** 🎬🎬🎬▶
Twentieth Century Fox Home Entertainment (Cat #4112301, UPC #08616212 3016). Widescreen (2.35:1) letterboxed. Dolby Digital Stereo. $29.98. Keepcase. *LANG:* English; French. *SUB:* English; Spanish. *FEATURES:* 22 chapter links • Theatrical trailer.
1997 (R) 103m/C Ewan McGregor, Cameron Diaz, Holly Hunter, Delroy Lindo, Ian Holm, Ian McNeice, Stanley Tucci, Dan Hedaya, Tony Shalhoub, Maury Chaykin, Judith Ivey, K.K. Dodds; *D:* Danny Boyle; *W:* John Hodge; *C:* Brian Tufano; *M:* David Arnold. *AWARDS: NOM:* MTV Movie Awards '98: Best Song ("Deadweight"), Best Dance Sequence (Cameron Diaz/Ewan McGregor).

Life of a Gigolo

When her editor at *Shimmer* magazine requests an article about sex, freelance writer Danielle (Hays) decides to observe a gigolo at work. The more she sees of Gage (Ritter), the more interested she becomes. This is standard soft-core fluff done with the polish that Playboy is known for. The DVD image and sound are probably a bit better than VHS tape, but this kind of indoor action doesn't test the limits of either medium. —MM

Movie: 🦴🦴 **DVD:** 🦴🦴
Image Entertainment (Cat #ID5971PLDVD, UPC #014381597127). Full frame. Dolby Digital Stereo. $24.99. Snapper. *LANG:* English. *FEATURES:* 12 chapter links.
1998 (R) ?m/C Mark Ritter, Lauren Hays; **D:** Leland Price.

The Life of Jesus

Small-town boredom and despair—French style. Twenty-year-old Freddy (Douche) is an unemployed epileptic who lives with his mother. He spends his time with girlfriend Marie (Cottreel) or riding his moped with his equally disenfranchised buddies. When Kader (Chaatouf), a young Arab, shows an interest in Marie (and it's reciprocated), Freddie and pals beat him up. Apparently the title is a reference to the spiritual suffering Freddy feels, even if he doesn't know exactly how to articulate his emotions. *AKA:* La Vie de Jesus.

Movie: 🦴🦴 **DVD:** NYR
WinStar Home Entertainment (Cat #5071). $29.98. Keepcase. *LANG:* French. *SUB:* English.
1996 96m/C FR David Douche, Marjorie Cottreel, Kader Chaatouf, Samuel Boidin, Genevieve Cottreel; **D:** Bruno Dumont; **W:** Bruno Dumont; **C:** Philippe Van Leeuw; **M:** Richard Cuvillier.

Life with Father

Based on the writings of Clarence Day Jr., this is the story of his childhood in 1880s New York City. It's a delightful saga of a stern but loving father (Powell) and his relationship with his knowing wife (Dunne) and four sons.

Movie: 🦴🦴🦴 **DVD:** NYR
Madacy Entertainment (Cat #99013). Full frame. Dolby Digital Mono. $9.99. Keepcase. *FEATURES:* Production notes • Trivia • Cast and crew thumbnail bios.
1947 118m/C William Powell, Irene Dunne, Elizabeth Taylor, Edmund Gwenn, ZaSu Pitts, Jimmy Lydon, Martin Milner; **D:** Michael Curtiz; **W:** Donald Ogden Stewart; **C:** William V. Skall, J. Peverell Marley; **M:** Max Steiner. *AWARDS:* Golden Globe Awards '48: Best Score; New York Film Critics Awards '47: Best Actor (Powell); *NOM:* Academy Awards '47: Best Actor (Powell), Best Art Direction/Set Decoration (Color), Best Color Cinematography, Best Original Dramatic Score.

Lifeforce

A beautiful female energy-sucking vampire from outer space drains Londoners of their souls and before long, the city is filled with disintegrating zombies. Everything you'd ever want in a sci-fi/horror film is here. Haley's comet, the space shuttle, a gigantic spaceship, exploding bodies, apocalyptic zombie mob scenes, weird sex with Matilda May showing herself off in her first film, and Steve "Manson" Railsback ranting and raving as only he can. Screenwriters Dan O'Bannon and Don Jakoby adapted the story from Colin Wilson's novel *The Space Vampires*. Great score by Henry Mancini ends with quirky march during the credits and is exhilarating on its own. The DVD features the longer European cut that was first released on laserdisc. The extra footage is mainly story and really helps in this non-stop film, which moved just a little too fast before the added scenes. The picture is very good with crisp, sharp colors and good detail. There is very little grain in the darker sequences and the blacks are fairly true. Contrast is also good and there is very little color bleed. The Dolby Digital 5.1 is excellent and adds even more punch to this already exciting film. —JO

Movie: 🦴🦴🦴 **DVD:** 🦴🦴🦴
MGM Home Entertainment (Cat #907017, UPC #027616701725). Widescreen (2.35:1) letterboxed. Dolby Digital 5.1. $24.98. Keepcase. *LANG:* English (DD5.1). *SUB:* Spanish; French. *CAP:* English. *FEATURES:* 32 chapter links • Theatrical trailer.
1985 100m/C Steve Railsback, Peter Firth, Frank Finlay, Patrick Stewart, Michael Gothard, Nicholas Ball, Aubrey Morris, Nancy Paul, Mathilda May, John Hallam; **D:** Tobe Hooper; **W:** Dan O'Bannon, Don Jakoby; **C:** Alan Hume; **M:** Henry Mancini, Michael Kamen.

Light Sleeper

Schrader takes a moody look at upscale drug dealers in New York. Dafoe is John LaTour, a 40-year-old drug courier to the club scene. Since his boss (Sarandon) is giving up the drug business for the safer world of natural cosmetics, John must look to his own future. His life becomes even more complicated when he runs into a bitter ex-flame (Delany) and finds the attraction is still overpowering. Cynical, contemplative, and menacing. If the film had been shot using a grainy film stock, that certainly would have fit the atmosphere. But the grain on the DVD is that digital garbage and it just about ruins the disc...no, it does ruin the disc. The picture is dull and lacking detail, while the drab colors are not true to either the theatrical release or VHS tape. The soundtrack is O.K. but seems muted in the high end. —JO

Movie: 🦴🦴 **DVD:** 🦴
Pioneer Entertainment (Cat #DVD69006, UPC #013023011496). Full frame. Stereo. $24.98. Keepcase. *LANG:* English. *FEATURES:* 19 chapter links.
1992 (R) 103m/C Willem Dafoe, Susan Sarandon, Dana Delany, David Clennon, Mary Beth Hurt; **D:** Paul Schrader; **W:** Paul Schrader; **C:** Edward Lachman; **M:** Michael Been.

Like It Is

Young boxer Craig (Bell) can't decide where he is, sexually speaking. One night outside of a Blackpool, England, gay nightclub, he meets Matt (Rose), an ambitious record producer. Their relationship is predictably rocky. Roger Daltrey almost steals the film as Matt's boss. The bare-bones DVD is no great shakes visually. The film was largely made on location and the limits of the budget are apparent in the imperfect lighting. Some of the accents are so thick that English subtitles would be welcome. —MM

Movie: 🦴🦴➤ **DVD:** 🦴🦴
First Run Features (Cat #908887, UPC #720229908887). Widescreen (1.66:1) letterboxed. $29.95. Keepcase. *LANG:* English. *FEATURES:* 8 chapter links • "Making of" featurette.
1998 95m/C GB Steve Bell, Ian Rose, Dani Behr, Roger Daltrey; **D:** Paul Oremland; **W:** Robert Cray; **C:** Alistair Cameron; **M:** Don McGlashan.

Like Water for Chocolate

In northern Mexico, 1910, domineering mother Elena (Torne) declares that her youngest daughter Tita (Cavazos) shall remain unmarried and will always care for her. As a child, Tita knuckles under. But as she matures and becomes a more accomplished cook under the guidance of Nacha (Carrasco), she realizes her real power. Whenever Tita is in the grip of a strong emotion, the essence of that feeling is transferred to others through the food she prepares. The details of that story would sound silly in synopsis. There are no conventional heroes and villains. Instead it's a story of dreams fulfilled, dreams abandoned, and dreams never forgotten. The film succeeds because it creates a strong, haunted atmosphere; a softly lit sense of love, desire, and dinner. It ends with a conclusion as perfect as any you'll ever see. The DVD mirrors the laserdisc edition of the film. Chapters are the same; image is somewhat better; sound is markedly better. The English dubbing is not bad, but it's not nearly as expressive as the Spanish. Unless you really hate subtitles, go with the original dialogue and narration. —MM *AKA:* Como Agua para Chocolate.

Movie: 🦴🦴🦴➤ **DVD:** 🦴🦴🦴➤
Miramax Pictures Home Video (Cat #17369, UPC #717951002730). Widescreen (1.85:1) letterboxed. Dolby Digital Surround Stereo. $29.99. Keepcase. *LANG:* Spanish; English. *SUB:* English. *FEATURES:* 19 chapter links.
1993 (R) 105m/C MX Lumi Cavazos, Marco Leonardi, Regina Torne, Mario Ivan Martinez, Ada Carrasco, Yareli Arizmendi, Claudette Maille, Pilar Aranda; **D:** Alfonso Arau; **W:** Laura Esquivel; **C:** Steven Bernstein; **M:** Leo Brower. *AWARDS:* *NOM:* British Academy Awards '93: Best Foreign Film; Independent Spirit Awards '94: Best Foreign Film.

Lilies

Strange revenge fantasy is set in a northern Quebec men's prison in 1952. A bishop (Sabourin) goes to hear the confession of a dying convict and is taken hostage in the chapel by the prison's homosexual population. There, he is forced to watch a play that re-creates a 40-year-old incident in his own life. As the prison walls fade away, the actor/prisoners turn into students Simon (Cadieux) and Vallier (Gilmore), who take the lovers' roles in the pageant about the martyrdom of St. Sebastien too seriously for comfort. The female roles are played by men. *AKA*: Les Feluettes.

Movie: 🎬🎬 *DVD*: NYR
Wolfe Video (Cat #5195). Dolby Digital Stereo. $24.95. Keepcase. *LANG*: English; French.
1996 (R) 95m/C *CA* Marcel Sabourin, Jason Cadieux, Danny Gilmore, Brent Carver, Matthew Ferguson, Alexander Chapman, Aubert Pallascio; *D*: John Greyson; *W*: Michel Marc Bouchard; *C*: Daniel Jobin; *M*: Mychael Danna. *AWARDS*: Genie Awards '96: Best Art Direction/Set Decoration, Best Costume Design, Best Film, Best Sound; *NOM*: Genie Awards '96: Best Actor (Cadieux), Best Actor (Ferguson, Gilmore), Best Adapted Screenplay, Best Cinematography, Best Director (Greyson), Best Film Editing, Best Supporting Actor (Chapman), Best Score.

Limbo

In Port Henry, Alaska, Joe Gastineau (Strathairn) finds himself involved with Donna de Angelo (Mastrantonio), an emotionally immature singer, and her troubled daughter Noelle (Martinez). The changing Alaskan culture and economy are important parts of the enigmatic turns that their relationship takes. Though Sayles is not particularly interested in striking visuals for their own sake, this DVD looks very good. Note the opening shots that shift from video to 35mm film. Throughout the film, he creates a memorably realized sense of place (Juneau), both the natural world and less scenic fish processing plants where people work on the "slime line." In his commentary track, Sayles is, as usual, articulate and focused mostly on the finer details of filmmaking. It's fascinating stuff, from the problems of photographing rain to the recording of two female voices in a noisy car. He talks about the collaborative process and is complimentary to his cast or his crew—particularly cinematographer Haskell Wexler and camera operator Scott Sakamoto—but he's never flattering. Perhaps of more interest to viewers, he explains the film's enigmatic ending. —MM

Movie: 🎬🎬🎬 *DVD*: 🎬🎬🎬
Columbia Tristar Home Video (Cat #4094). Widescreen letterboxed. Dolby Digital Stereo; Dolby Digital 5.1 Surround Stereo. $28.95. Keepcase. *LANG*: English. *SUB*: English. *FEATURES*: 28 chapter links • Isolated music soundtrack • Commen-

tary: writer-producer-editor John Sayles • Theatrical trailers.
1999 (R) 126m/C David Strathairn, Mary Elizabeth Mastrantonio, Vanessa Martinez, Casey Siemaszko, Kris Kristofferson, Kathryn Grody, Rita Taggart, Leo Burmester, Michael Laskin; *D*: John Sayles; *W*: John Sayles; *C*: Haskell Wexler; *M*: Mason Daring. *AWARDS*: *NOM*: Independent Spirit Awards '00: Best Actor (Strathairn), Best Supporting Actress (Martinez).

Limelight

In London, 1914, Calvero (Chaplin), a nearly washed up alcoholic clown, finds redemption when he saves the life of Terry (Bloom), a ballerina who believes she is paralyzed. The subtle, if somewhat self-indulgent story is admittedly autobiographical, but it does show that, despite the political and personal problems that Chaplin had been experiencing, he still knew what he was about. For many fans, the real treat of the DVD is in chapter 15 when he shares the screen, all too briefly, with Buster Keaton. The disc was made from a nearly flawless original and so it is pristine with fine black-and-white photography. —MM

Movie: 🎬🎬🎬 *DVD*: 🎬🎬🎬
Image Entertainment (Cat #ID9185CUDVD, UPC #014381918526). Full frame. Dolby Digital Mono. $29.99. Snapper. *LANG*: English. *FEATURES*: 16 chapter links • Production summary • Segments from Chaplin's novel *Footlights* • Flea Circus scene from *The Professor* • Deleted footage.
1952 120m/B Charlie Chaplin, Claire Bloom, Buster Keaton, Nigel Bruce, Sydney Chaplin; *D*: Charlie Chaplin; *W*: Charlie Chaplin; *C*: Karl Struss; *M*: Charlie Chaplin.

The Limey

It's easy to spot the antecedents of Steven Soderbergh's polished crime film—*Point Blank*, *Get Shorty*, even *Easy Rider*—but it's a solid original. Actually, its originality kept it from finding the audience it deserves in theatrical release. On DVD, it is a rare treat. Wilson (Stamp) is the Limey of the title, an ex-con who comes to L.A. to find out how his daughter died. The girl's friends, Edward (Guzman) and Elaine (Warren) help him. On the other side are Terry Valentine (Fonda), a '60s leftover who's become a wealthy record producer, and Avery (Newman), his security chief. The workings of the plot are not particularly innovative; Soderbergh's elliptical approach to the material is. He uses challenging editing techniques—breaking one scene up to stretch it across several minutes, for example—and curious lighting techniques. L.A. smog seems to provide the base for his desaturated color. All of that can keep viewers off balance, but they work wonderfully on home video. Though both of the commentary tracks are interesting, don't listen to them until you've watched the

film on its own. The extras-intensive disc is worth owning. —MM

Movie: 🎬🎬🎬▸ *DVD*: 🎬🎬🎬▸
Artisan Entertainment (Cat #60750, UPC #012236607502). Widescreen (1.85:1) anamorphic. Dolby Digital 5.1 Surround Stereo; Dolby Digital Surround Stereo. $29.98. Keepcase. *LANG*: English. *FEATURES*: 28 chapter links • Trailers • Cast and crew thumbnail biographies • Isolated music score • Technical information on DVD transfer • Commentary: Soderbergh and Dobbs • 1960s "Documentary": Stamp, Fonda, Warren, Newman, Dallesandro.
1999 (R) 90m/C Terence Stamp, Peter Fonda, Lesley Ann Warren, Luis Guzman, Barry Newman, Joe Dallesandro, Nicky Katt, Amelia Heinle, Melissa George; *D*: Steven Soderbergh; *W*: Lem Dobbs; *C*: Edward Lachman; *M*: Cliff Martinez. *AWARDS*: *NOM*: Independent Spirit Awards '00: Best Actor (Stamp), Best Director (Soderbergh), Best Film, Best Screenplay, Best Supporting Actor (Guzman).

The Lion King: Simba's Pride

Kiara (voice of Neve Campbell), daughter of Simba (Broderick), follows in her father's footsteps when she goes looking for adventure in the Outlands and meets Kovu (Marsden), a lion who is tempted by the dark side of the force, if that's the right pop culture cliche to use in this case. Though this sequel doesn't come close to the masterful first film in terms of animation, music, or story, it is far better than most video premieres. The ambitious scope of the original has been whittled down to a more modest effort, but it is executed with the polish that the Disney studio is famous for. On DVD, both image and sound are first-rate. The disc lacks the extensive extras that come with some Disney features. It's still recommended for young fans of the first film. —MM

Movie: 🎬🎬🎬 *DVD*: 🎬🎬🎬
Buena Vista Home Entertainment (Cat #17976, UPC #717951004000). Widescreen (1.66:l) letterboxed. Dolby Digital 5.1 Surround Stereo. $39.99. Keepcase. *LANG*: English; French; Spanish. *CAP*: English. *FEATURES*: 21 chapter links • Trailer • "Love Will Find a Way" music video.
1998 75m/C *D*: Darrell Rooney, Rob LaDuca; *W*: Flip Kobler, Cindy Marcus; *V*: Matthew Broderick, James Earl Jones, Nathan Lane, Ernie Sabella, Robert Guillaume, Andy Dick, Neve Campbell, Suzanne Pleshette, Jason Marsden.

Lion of the Desert

Bedouin horse militias face-off against Mussolini's armored terror in this epic historical drama. Omar Muktar (Quinn as the "Desert Lion") and his Libyan guerrilla patriots kept the Italian troops of Mussolini (Steiger) at bay for 20 years. Outstanding performances are enhanced by the desert backdrop in this British-Libyan coproduction. The lush, vibrant colors of

the film are reproduced extraordinarily well by the video transfer. Blacks are solid and crisp (although some of the more dimly lit scenes do suffer from a loss of definition of dark colors). The soundtrack is also quite good, devoid of any crackling or other distortion. The documentary on the making of the film puts the disc over the bar. —*MJT* **AKA:** Omar Mukhtar.
Movie: ♫♫♫ **DVD:** ♫♫♫
Anchor Bay (Cat #DV10483, UPC #013131048391). Widescreen (1.85:1) letterboxed. Dolby Digital Stereo. $29.98. Keepcase. *LANG:* English. *FEATURES:* 18 chapter links • Documentary "The Making of an Epic" • Theatrical trailers • Still gallery • Director profile.
1981 (PG) 162m/C *GB* Anthony Quinn, Oliver Reed, Irene Papas, Rod Steiger, Raf Vallone, John Gielgud; *D:* Moustapha Akkad; *W:* H.A.L. Craig; *C:* Jack Hildyard; *M:* Maurice Jarre.

Lionheart

Van Damme deserts the foreign legion and hits the streets when he learns his brother has been hassled. Many fights ensue, most related to no-holds-barred money tournaments, until you fall asleep. Less plot than the average Van Damme results in a film of little interest even to die-hard fans. Well, when you combine the quality of the image with the lackluster movie itself, there's absolutely no reason whatsoever to buy this DVD. The picture has a lot of grain and is nowhere near as sharp as the better Universal DVDs are. Colors are fairly strong, but their occasional bleed just makes the image seem even grainier. Blacks are O.K. but never totally true. The picture also feels a little dark and could have used some more contrast and brightness. The soundtrack is at least distortion-free and fairly full-bodied, although the Surround is used very sparingly, and a bass boost is needed. —*JO*
AKA: A.W.O.L.; Wrong Bet.
Movie: ♫ **DVD:** ♫♫
Universal Studios Home Video (Cat #20388, UPC #025192038822). Full frame. Dolby Surround. $24.98. Keepcase. *LANG:* English. *SUB:* Spanish; French. *CAP:* English. *FEATURES:* 16 chapter links • Theatrical trailer • Cast and filmmakers bios • Production notes • Film highlights.
1990 (R) 105m/C Jean-Claude Van Damme, Harrison Page, Deborah Rennard, Lisa Pelikan, Brian Thompson; *D:* Sheldon Lettich; *W:* Sheldon Lettich, Jean-Claude Van Damme; *C:* Robert New; *M:* John Scott.

Lips of Blood

Rollin whips up a typically festive mix of sex, horror, and hallucination in what some have dubbed his best film. A young man (Philippe) has visions of a woman (Briand, AKA Annie Belle) he met as a child in an abandoned castle. When he sees her again, she persuades him to unleash a couple of female vampires. Do not expect anything more in the way of

narrative. (Rollin's surrealism is not to my taste.) Like other Image releases of Rollin's work, this DVD was made from his own inter-negatives. It's an essentially flawless re-creation of a well-made low-budget French horror movie. For the most part, it looks better than similar American films of the same period, the mid '70s. —*MM* **AKA:** Levres de Sang.
Movie: ♫♫▶ **DVD:** ♫♫▶
Image Entertainment (Cat #ID56345ADVD, UPC #014381563429). Widescreen letterboxed. Dolby Digital Mono. $24.99. Snapper. *LANG:* French. *SUB:* English. *FEATURES:* 14 chapter links • Marc Morris liner notes • Photo gallery • Director filmography.
1975 88m/C *FR* Jean-Loup Philippe, Annie Belle; *D:* Jean Rollin.

Lipstick Camera

Ambitious young Omy (Keats) wants to be a TV news photographer. Her idol is cynical cameraman Flynn Dailey (Wimmer). To impress him, she borrows a tiny "lipstick camera" from her friend Joule (Feldman) and the three of them are caught up in a possible murder with a mysterious German (O'Quinn) and a woman (Bergman) who claims to be his wife. Though the mechanics of the plot take up too much time, the main characters are handled remarkably well. Corey Feldman turns what could have been a so-so supporting role into a believable and sympathetic character. Ele Keats does a lot with the lead, too, making Omy a complex character, one with more depth than you usually see in a protagonist, male or female. For a low-budget video premiere, the film looks astonishingly good on DVD. Director Mike Bonifer and D.P. M. David Mullen give the film a glossy sheen that more expensive productions would envy. Mono sound is fine. —*MM*
Movie: ♫♫♫ **DVD:** ♫♫♫▶
Image Entertainment (Cat #ID5604FMDVD, UPC #014381560428). Full frame. Dolby Digital Mono. $24.99. Snapper. *LANG:* English. *FEATURES:* 12 chapter links.
1993 (R) 93m/C Ele Keats, Brian Wimmer, Corey Feldman, Sandahl Bergman, Terry O'Quinn; *D:* Mike Bonifer; *W:* Mike Bonifer; *C:* M. David Mullen; *M:* Jeff Rona.

Lisa and the Devil / The House of Exorcism

Lisa Reiner (Sommer), a tourist in Toledo, Spain, sees a medieval fresco of a bald devil. Moments later in an antique store, she meets Savalas. They're the same guy! A long dark night of discovery at an ornate mansion ensues, and Mario Bava's action takes on a finely tuned surrealistic edge. As Tim Lucas writes in the liner notes, producer Alfredo Leone was unable to sell the film in 1973, and so he shot new "possession" footage and re-edited Bava's work to cash in on the popularity of The Exorcist, and retitled it The House of Exorcism. This disc contains both films, and for the most dedicated horror fan, they

make for an intriguing comparison. Sound and image are about the same in each. The graininess is not inappropriate for an import of this age, though it is heavy, particularly toward the end. Dialogue and music are muffled throughout. Even so, *Lisa* is one of Bava's best works. (The four-bone rating applies to *Lisa*; *House* would rate two bones.) —*MM* **AKA:** The House of Exorcism; La Casa Dell'Exorcismo; The Devil and the Dead; The Devil in the House of Exorcism; El Diablo se Lleva a los Muertos; Il Diavolo e i Morti; Lisa e il Diavolo.
Movie: ♫♫♫♫ **DVD:** ♫♫♫▶
Image Entertainment (Cat #ID8996AODVD, UPC #01438189962). Widescreen (1.85:1) letterboxed. Dolby Digital Mono. $39.99. Snapper. *LANG:* English. *FEATURES:* 14 chapter links in each film • Commentary: Elke Sommer and producer Alfredo Leone • Bava biography and liner notes by Tim Lucas • Cast and crew filmographies • Photo and poster gallery • Trailers.
1975 (R) 93m/C *IT SP* Telly Savalas, Elke Sommer, Sylva Koscina, Robert Alda, Alessio Orano, Gabriele Tinti, Eduardo Fajardo, Espartaco Santoni, Alida Valli; *D:* Mario Bava; *W:* Mario Bava, Alfred Leone; *C:* Cecilio Paniagua; *M:* Carlo Savina.

Little Buddha

Tibetan Lama Norbu informs the Seattle Konrad family that their 10-year-old son Jesse may be the reincarnation of a respected monk. He wants to take the boy back to Tibet to find out and, with some apparently minor doubts, the family head off on their spiritual quest. In an effort to instruct Jesse in Buddhism, this journey is interspersed with the story of Prince Siddhartha, who will leave behind his worldly ways to follow the path towards enlightenment and become the Buddha. The two stories are an ill fit, the acting awkward (with the exception of Ruocheng as the wise Norbu) but, boy, does the film look good (from cinematographer Vittorio Storaro). Filmed on location in Nepal and Bhutan. Sakamoto's score may be reason enough to buy this DVD, and the Dolby Surround presents it with full-bodied presence, giving just the right ambience on the Surround track. The imaging is tremendous. The picture is also stunning, extremely sharp and with rich, vibrant colors that are accurate and show no bleed even when fully saturated. Grain and artifacts are never a problem. The blacks are true and the brightness and contrast levels are as punchy as you'll find. —*JO*
Movie: ♫♫ **DVD:** ♫♫♫▶
Buena Vista Home Entertainment (Cat #17375, UPC #717951002792). Widescreen (2.35:1) letterboxed. Dolby Surround. $29.99. Keepcase. *LANG:* English. *CAP:* English. *FEATURES:* 25 chapter links.
1993 (PG) 123m/C Keanu Reeves, Alex Wiesendanger, Ying Ruocheng, Chris Isaak, Bridget Fonda; *D:* Bernardo Bertolucci; *W:* Mark Peploe, Rudy Wurl-

itzer; *C:* Vittorio Storaro; *M:* Ryuichi Sakamoto.

The Little Foxes

A vicious Southern woman will destroy everyone around her to satisfy her desire for wealth and power in a story filled with corrupt characters who commit numerous revolting deeds. The vicious matriarch is a part tailored for Davis, and she makes the most of it. Lillian Hellman wrote the script from her play. People who insist that a movie must be color and a DVD must have 5.1 sound don't know what they're missing. The picture on this disc is amazing. The sharpness is superb. Gain is low. Artifacts are near nonexistent. Contrast and brightness are both excellent without causing any ghosting. Graytones are subtle and full. Both detail and depth of field are far better than most color films. The DVD includes the original mono soundtrack and a synthesized stereo soundtrack that is a little beefier. —*JO*
Movie: 🎵🎵🎵▶ **DVD:** 🎵🎵🎵▶
HBO Home Video (Cat #9075, UPC #026359075421). Full frame. Stereo; Mono. $24.98. Snapper. *LANG:* English; Spanish; Italian; German. *SUB:* English; Spanish; French. *CAP:* English. *FEATURES:* 27 chapter links • Theatrical trailer • Cast bios.
1941 116m/B Bette Davis, Herbert Marshall, Dan Duryea, Teresa Wright, Charles Dingle, Richard Carlson; *D:* William Wyler; *W:* Lillian Hellman; *C:* Gregg Toland; *M:* Meredith Willson. *AWARDS: NOM:* Academy Awards '41: Best Actress (Davis), Best Director (Wyler), Best Film Editing, Best Picture, Best Screenplay, Best Supporting Actress (Collinge, Wright), Best Original Dramatic Score.

The Little Mermaid

The animation here may lack the complexity and computer enhancements of more recent features, but this is the film that began the resurgence of the Disney studio's work in the field and it is still hugely entertaining. The writing/directing team of John Musker and Ron Clements have taken considerable liberties with Hans Christian Andersen's tragic original and turned it into a traditional Disney story. In this version, the mermaid princess Ariel (voice of Benson) is a rebellious, somewhat thoughtless 16-year-old. She's fascinated by the world above the ocean's surface, much to the distress of her father Triton (Mars). He orders the crab Sebastian (Wright) to keep her in line. But once Ariel gets a look at prince Eric (Barnes), there's nothing Sebastian can do. She's so deeply in love that she enters into a Faustian deal with the evil witch Ursula (Carroll) to turn her into a human. As is almost always the case with the studio's animated work, the DVD is visually flawless. The stereo sound is almost as good, doing justice to the Oscar-winning score. —*MM*
Movie: 🎵🎵🎵🎵 **DVD:** 🎵🎵🎵▶

Buena Vista Home Entertainment (Cat #18787, UPC #717951005861). Widescreen (1.66:1) letterboxed. Dolby Digital 5.1 Surround Stereo. $39.99. Keepcase. *LANG:* English; French; Spanish. *CAP:* English. *FEATURES:* 27 chapter links.
1989 (G) 82m/C *D:* John Musker, Ron Clements; *W:* John Musker, Ron Clements; *M:* Alan Menken, Howard Ashman; *V:* Jodi Benson, Christopher Daniel Barnes, Pat Carroll, Rene Auberjonois, Samuel E. Wright, Buddy Hackett, Jason Marin, Edie McClurg, Kenneth Mars, Nancy Cartwright. *AWARDS:* Academy Awards '89: Best Song ("Under the Sea"), Best Original Score; Golden Globe Awards '90: Best Song ("Under the Sea"), Best Score; *NOM:* Academy Awards '89: Best Song ("Kiss the Girl").

Little Mother

Purportedly the story of Argentina's Eva Peron, Metzger's mildly racy, meandering melodrama traces Evita's rise from poverty to the heights of political power. On DVD, the film's attempt to create a historical setting is undermined by dark, muddy images, distorted colors, and often murky sound quality. —*JE*
Movie: 🎵▶ **DVD:** 🎵
Image Entertainment (Cat #ID5542FFDVD, UPC #01438155422). Widescreen (1.85:1) letterboxed. Dolby Digital Mono. $24.99. Snapper. *LANG:* English. *FEATURES:* 12 chapter links.
1971 95m/C Christiane Kruger, Ivan Desny, Anton Diffring; *D:* Radley Metzger; *W:* Brian Phelan; *C:* Hans Jura.

A Little Princess

Compelling fantasy, based on the children's book by Frances Hodgson Burnett, has until now been known best for the 1939 Shirley Temple incarnation. Sara (Matthews) has been raised in India by her widowed father (Cunningham). When he's called up to fight in WWI, Sara is taken to New York to be educated at stern Miss Michin's (Bron) school, where her money makes her a favored boarder. However, the irrepressible Sara suffers a severe reversal of fortune when her father is reported killed and Miss Michin promptly makes her a servant to pay her way. But Sara's charm has made her some true friends who become her allies under trying circumstances. Lively script, dazzling visuals, and a welcome lack of sappiness create a classic-in-the-making. The picture on the DVD is near excellent—very sharp and grain-free. Artifacts never intrude. Colors are accurate to the theatrical release and bleed is never a problem. The image is at times a little contrasty, resulting in a few scenes that feel too dark, but overall the picture brightness makes for comfortable viewing. The 5.1 sound is very lively and full-bodied. Though there are not many Surround effects, the rear channels add nice ambience to the music. Dialogue is crisp and out front. —*JO*
Movie: 🎵🎵🎵▶ **DVD:** 🎵🎵🎵▶

Warner Home Video, Inc. (Cat #19100, UPC #085391910022). Widescreen (1.85:1) anamorphic; full frame. Dolby Digital Surround 5.1; Dolby Surround Stereo. $19.98. Snapper. *LANG:* English (DS 5.1); French (DS 5.1); Spanish (DS Stereo). *SUB:* English; French; Spanish. *CAP:* English. *FEATURES:* 31 chapter links • 3 theatrical trailers • Production notes.
1995 (G) 97m/C Liesl Matthews, Eleanor Bron, Liam Cunningham, Rusty Schwimmer, Arthur Malet, Vanessa Lee Chester, Errol Sitahal, Heather DeLoach, Taylor Fry; *D:* Alfonso Cuaron; *W:* Richard LaGravenese; *C:* Emmanuel Lubezki; *M:* Patrick Doyle. *AWARDS: NOM:* Academy Awards '95: Best Art Direction/Set Decoration, Best Cinematography.

The Little Rascals

Alfalfa runs afoul of the membership requirements for the "He-Man Womun Haters Club" when he starts to fall for Darla. Charming remake of the short film series, now set in suburban L.A., from Spheeris, who also redid another television favorite, *The Beverly Hillbillies.* The DVD is sharp, and features excellent colors that are rich, vibrant, and have no aggravating bleed. Contrast and brightness levels are excellent and the picture packs quite a punch. Blacks are true. The 5.0 soundtrack is a big improvement over the Dolby Surround of the VHS and laserdisc releases, and is very dynamic with good bass and very lively imaging. —*JO*
Movie: 🎵🎵▶ **DVD:** 🎵🎵🎵
Universal Studios Home Video (Cat #20034, UPC #025192003424). Widescreen (1.85:1) anamorphic. Dolby Digital 5.0; Dolby Surround. $24.98. Keepcase. *LANG:* English (DS 5.0); Spanish (DS); French (DS). *SUB:* Spanish. *CAP:* English. *FEATURES:* 42 chapter links • Theatrical trailer • Production notes • Cast and crew bios • Film highlights • Web links.
1994 (PG) 83m/C Daryl Hannah, Courtland Mead, Travis Tedford, Brittany Ashton Holmes, Bug Hall, Zachary Mabry, Kevin Jamal Woods, Ross Bagley, Sam Saletta, Blake Collins, Jordan Warkol, Blake Ewing, Juliette Brewer, Heather Karasek; *Cameos:* Whoopi Goldberg; *D:* Penelope Spheeris; *W:* Penelope Spheeris, Paul Guay, Steve Mazur; *C:* Richard Bowen; *M:* David Foster, Linda Thompson.

Little Shop of Horrors

During a solar eclipse, Seymour (Moranis) buys an unusual plant and takes it back to the flower shop where he works. The plant, Audrey 2, becomes a town attraction as it grows at an unusual rate, but Seymour learns that he must feed Audrey fresh human blood to keep her growing. Soon, Audrey is giving the orders ("Feed me") and timid Seymour must find "deserving" victims. Martin's performance as the masochistic dentist is alone worth the price. Song, dance, gore, and more prevail in this outrageous musical comedy. Four Tops Levi Stubbs is the commanding

voice of Audrey 2. Based on the Off-Broadway play, which was based on Roger Corman's 1960 horror spoof. This is the original DVD release of *Little Shop of Horrors*, which included an alternate Godzilla-style ending that more properly fits the mood of the film. It was recalled before it hit most store shelves. This ending appears to be from a workprint, is poor quality black and white, and is lacking sound effects and has dubbed in music. Nonetheless, it's very cool. The quality of the film itself is no great shakes either, although the colors are at least vibrant. The picture quality is of average sharpness with some grain (actually some foreground subjects are too sharp for the rest of the image). The biggest problems are the backgrounds, which at times appear digitized to the point that human beings in motion look like video game characters. Contrast and brightness are good but blacks are inconsistent. The 5.1 sound is much more gutsy than previous release. Worth it just for the alternate ending. —*JO*
Movie: 🎟🎟🎟 **DVD:** 🎟🎟
Warner Home Video, Inc. (Cat #11702, UPC #085391170228). Widescreen letterboxed. Dolby Digital 5.1; Dolby Surround; Mono. $24.98. Snapper. *LANG:* English (DD5.1); Spanish (Mono); French (DS). *SUB:* English; Spanish; French. *CAP:* English. *FEATURES:* 21 chapter links • 2 theatrical trailers • Commentary: Frank Oz • Original ending • Outtakes • Production notes.
1986 (PG-13) 94m/C Rick Moranis, Ellen Greene, Vincent Gardenia, Steve Martin, James Belushi, Christopher Guest, Bill Murray, John Candy, Tisha Campbell, Tichina Arnold, Michelle Weeks; *D:* Frank Oz; *W:* Howard Ashman; *C:* Robert Paynter; *M:* Miles Goodman, Alan Menken, Howard Ashman; *V:* Levi Stubbs Jr. *AWARDS: NOM:* Academy Awards '86: Best Song ("Mean Green Mother from Outer Space").

Little Voice

Little Voice (Horrocks) misses her dead father so much that she refuses to speak and communicates only by singing along with the records Dad loved: Shirley Bassey, Judy Garland, Piaf. "LV" can match the voice precisely. When her mom's (Blethyn) sleazy talent-agent boyfriend (Caine) hears her, he sees his ticket to the big time. "LV" will not sing for an audience, but he books her at the weasely Mr. Boo's (Broadbent) club where a London talent scout will show up. Will she sing? All of the performances are superb, including MacGregor as a guy who's almost as shy as "LV," but the show belongs to Horrocks. The stage play was written to take advantage of her unique vocal talents. Not surprisingly then, on DVD, sound is just as important as image, and the captions come in a close second because some of the British slang is so difficult on American ears. The disc contains no serious visual flaws. For Anglophiles, a true sleeper. —*MM*
Movie: 🎟🎟🎟 **DVD:** 🎟🎟🎟

Miramax Pictures Home Video (Cat #17377, UPC #717951002815). Widescreen (1.85:1) letterboxed. Dolby Digital 5.1 Surround Stereo. $29.99. Keepcase. *LANG:* English. *CAP:* English. *FEATURES:* 24 chapter links.
1998 (R) 97m/C *GB* Jane Horrocks, Michael Caine, Ewan McGregor, Brenda Blethyn, Jim Broadbent, Annette Badland, Philip Jackson; *D:* Mark Herman; *W:* Mark Herman; *C:* Andy Collins; *M:* John Altman. *AWARDS:* Golden Globe Awards '99: Best Actor—Musical/Comedy (Caine); *NOM:* Academy Awards '98: Best Supporting Actress (Blethyn); British Academy Awards '98: Best Actor (Caine), Best Actress (Horrocks), Best Adapted Screenplay, Best Film, Best Sound, Best Supporting Actress (Blethyn); Golden Globe Awards '99: Best Actress—Musical/Comedy (Horrocks), Best Supporting Actress (Blethyn); Screen Actors Guild Award '98: Best Actress (Horrocks), Best Supporting Actress (Blethyn), Cast.

Little Witches

Rejected group of seniors at Catholic girls' high school are transformed into a witches coven, thanks to a book of spells. A rip-off of *The Craft*. This DVD is a cudda-been. It could have been at least a good (but not great) disc if only the sharpness had been as consistently good as it is some of the time. Of course, to go along with that, the grain would have to be cut a bit and the colors not only perked up, but also more defined (less bleed). The blacks are very rarely true and lean toward gray, and extra grain adds insult to injury. There are also some artifacts in the darker scenes. The stereo sound is lacking in bass, and of generally so-so fidelity. —*JO*
Movie: 🎟🎟 **DVD:** 🎟🎟
Image Entertainment (Cat #ID4658APDVD, UPC #014381465811). Full frame. Stereo. $24.99. Snapper. *LANG:* English. *FEATURES:* 18 chapter links.
1996 (R) 91m/C Mimi Reichmeister, Jack Nance, Jennifer Rubin, Sheeri Rappaport, Melissa Taub, Zoe Alexander, Zelda Rubinstein, Eric Pierpont; *D:* Jane Simpson; *W:* Brian DiMuccio, Dino Vindeni; *C:* Ron Turowski; *M:* Nicholas Rivera.

Little Women

Beloved story of the March women is beautifully portrayed in a solid production that blends a seamless screenplay with an excellent cast, authentic period costumes, and lovely cinematography and music. Ryder, perfectly cast as the unconventional Jo, is also the strongest of the sisters: domestically inclined Meg (Alvarado), the fragile Beth (Danes), and the youngest, mischievous Amy (the delightful Dunst), who grows up into a sedate young lady (Mathis). Charming adaptation remains faithful to the spirit of the Alcott classic while adding contemporary touches by producer Denise Di Novi, writer-coproducer Swicord, and director Armstrong. The image on the DVD is not as

sharp as it should be and there is a problem with grain in the darker sequences. The color is a little dull and has occasional bleed, usually in those darker scenes. Brightness and contrast boosts might have helped the picture considerably. The sound is full-bodied enough but lacking in space, which would have been helped by some ambience on the Surround track. —*JO*
Movie: 🎟🎟🎟🎟 **DVD:** 🎟🎟
Columbia Tristar Home Video (Cat #01029, UPC #043396010291). Widescreen (1.85:1) letterboxed. Dolby Digital Surround. $28.95. Keepcase. *LANG:* English; Spanish; French. *SUB:* Spanish. *CAP:* English. *FEATURES:* 55 chapter links.
1994 (PG) 118m/C Winona Ryder, Gabriel Byrne, Trini Alvarado, Samantha Mathis, Kirsten Dunst, Claire Danes, Christian Bale, Eric Stoltz, John Neville, Mary Wickes, Susan Sarandon; *D:* Gillian Armstrong; *W:* Robin Swicord; *C:* Geoffrey Simpson; *M:* Thomas Newman. *AWARDS: NOM:* Academy Awards '94: Best Actress (Ryder), Best Costume Design, Best Original Score; Writers Guild of America '94: Best Adapted Screenplay.

The Littlest Horse Thieves

Director Charles Jarrott, perhaps best known for his soapish mini-series based on the works of Jackie Collins, Danielle Steel, and Sidney Sheldon, delivered some interesting and diverse theatrical offerings during the '70s and early '80s. Chief among them is this story-driven period piece originally produced and distributed by the Walt Disney company. Set in one of Yorkshire, England's, coal mines in 1909, the story revolves around the rescue of the mine's pit ponies by two young sons of a miner killed in an earlier disaster and the daughter of the mine's stuffy manager. The ponies are to be replaced by machinery and slaughtered, which is pretty weighty stuff for a Disney film. Couple that with some class-warfare and the tragic death of one of the ponies and you have a family film with a slightly sharper edge. Although delivered with the option of either a full-frame or widescreen presentation, the production is movie-only, and the source material is beginning to show its age with the result being a less-than-stellar DVD visually. —*RT* *AKA:* Escape from the Dark.
Movie: 🎟🎟 **DVD:** 🎟🎟
Anchor Bay (Cat #18030, UPC #01313108 3095). Widescreen; full frame. AC3 - 2 Channel. $24.98. Keepcase. *LANG:* English. *FEATURES:* 22 chapter markers.
1976 (G) 109m/C Maurice Colbourne, Susan Tebbs, Andrew Harrison, Chloe Franks, Alastair Sim, Peter Barkworth; *D:* Charles Jarrott; *W:* Rosemary Anne Sisson; *C:* Paul Beeson; *M:* Ronald Goodwin.

Live and Let Die

Agent 007 (Moore, for the first time) is out to thwart Dr. Kananga (Kotto), a black

mastermind who's out to control the western world with voodoo and hard drugs. This lesser Bond adventure receives the red carpet treatment on DVD. The image compares favorably to other films of the early '70s, but suffers next to more recent entries in the series. The same goes for the monaural sound. The multitudinous extras, however, are first-rate. —*MM*
Movie: 🎞🎞 ***DVD:*** 🎞🎞🎞➤
MGM Home Entertainment (Cat #907026, UPC #027616702623). Widescreen anamorphic. Dolby Digital Mono. $34.98. Keepcase. *LANG:* English; French. *FEATURES:* 48 chapter links • Commentary: director Guy Hamilton and cast • Commentary: writer Tom Mankiewicz • "Making of" featurette • Stills gallery • 2 TV spots • 2 radio spots • UK Milk Board commercial • Behind-the-scenes footage • Booklet.
1973 (PG) 131m/C *GB* Roger Moore, Jane Seymour, Yaphet Kotto, Clifton James, Julius W. Harris, Geoffrey Holder, David Hedison, Gloria Hendry, Bernard Lee, Lois Maxwell, Madeleine Smith; ***D:*** Guy Hamilton; ***W:*** Tom Mankiewicz; ***C:*** Ted Moore; ***M:*** George Martin. *AWARDS:* NOM: Academy Awards '73: Best Song ("Live and Let Die").

The Living Dead Girl

Workers illegally trying to dispose of hazardous chemical wastes in a cellar make the mistake of indulging in a bit of grave robbing at the next-door crypt. A 55-gallon drum cracks open; the stuff hits an open coffin and a blonde (Blanchard) with long sharp fingernails and a taste for blood is reanimated. It's another sex-and-gore fest from the prolific Rollin, though this is one of his more polished productions. The DVD image is remarkably sharp and clear, and if the liner notes are to be believed, the film has seldom been distributed in its full-length form. It's virtually flawless here because the disc was made from the director's own materials. Mono sound is fine. —*MM AKA:* La Morte Vivante.
Movie: 🎞🎞➤ ***DVD:*** 🎞🎞
Image Entertainment (Cat #ID5556SADVD, UPC #014381555622). Widescreen (1.85:1) letterboxed. Dolby Digital Mono. $24.99. Snapper. *LANG:* French; English. *SUB:* English. *FEATURES:* 17 chapter links • Stills gallery • Theatrical trailer • Director filmography • Liner notes by Marc Morris.
1982 91m/C *FR* Marina Pierro, Francoise Blanchard, Mike Marshall, Carina Barone, Fanny Magier; ***D:*** Jean Rollin; ***W:*** Jean Rollin.

Living Out Loud

Judith (Hunter) is dumped by her cardiologist husband for a younger woman. While spiraling downward, she finally notices the elevator operator (DeVito) in her building and the two consider an unlikely relationship. This quirky tale works well on disc, though the extras are the significant difference from VHS tape. The film has a soft,

dark, intimate look that plays well on home video but isn't keyed to the relative clarity of DVD. Sound is excellent, particularly on Queen Latifah's confident interpretation of Billy Strayhorn's "Lush Life." The full-length version of the scene is included in the deleted scenes section. —*MM*
Movie: 🎞🎞🎞 ***DVD:*** 🎞🎞🎞
New Line Home Video (Cat #N4726, UPC #794043472626). Widescreen (2.35:1) anamorphic. Dolby Digital 5.1 Surround Stereo; Dolby Digital Surround Stereo. $24.98. Snapper. *LANG:* English. *CAP:* English. *FEATURES:* 29 chapter links • Commentary: writer-director LaGravenese • Readings of two Chekhov stories, "Misery" and "The Kiss" • 5 deleted scenes.
1998 (R) 102m/C Holly Hunter, Danny DeVito, Queen Latifah, Martin Donovan, Elias Koteas, Richard Schiff; ***D:*** Richard LaGravenese; ***W:*** Richard LaGravenese; ***C:*** John Bailey; ***M:*** George Fenton.

Lock, Stock and 2 Smoking Barrels

Plot twist–laden British caper comedy plays like Tarantino and crumpets. Four dim hoods—Bacon (Statham), Soap (Fletcher), Eddy (Moran), and Tom (Flemyng)—pool their ill-gotten gains so that Eddy can play in a high-stakes card game. They don't know that the game is fixed and they wind up owing gambler Hatchet Harry (Moriarty) 500,000 pounds. They then plan to rob a drug-dealing neighbor who's also planning a robbery of his own. Throw in a wandering pair of antique shotguns and you have the recipe for a cap-poppin' good time. Rock star Sting appears as the pub-owning father of one of the lads.
Movie: 🎞🎞🎞 ***DVD:*** NYR
USA Home Entertainment (Cat #59391). Full frame; widescreen (1.85:1) letterboxed. Dolby Digital 5.1 Surround Stereo. $24.95. Keepcase. *LANG:* English. *SUB:* French; Spanish. *FEATURES:* Cast and crew thumbnail bios • Trailers.
1998 (R) 105m/C *GB* Jason Flemyng, Dexter Fletcher, Nick Moran, Jason Statham, Steven Mackintosh, Vinnie Jones, Sting, Lenny McLean, P. H. Moriarty, Steve Sweeney, Frank Harper, Stephen Marcus; ***D:*** Guy Ritchie; ***W:*** Guy Ritchie; ***C:*** Tim Maurice-Jones; ***M:*** David A. Hughes, John Murphy. *AWARDS:* MTV Movie Awards '99: Best New Filmmaker Award (Ritchie); *NOM:* British Academy Awards '98: Best Film, Best Film Editing.

Lock Up

Senselessly violent prison fantasy is filled with unintentional humor and egregious overacting from all concerned. Stallone plays the noble prisoner Frank Leone who has only six months to go; Donald Sutherland is the evil Warden Drumgoole who's out to get him. Curiously, journeyman director John Flynn does not handle the action scenes very well. With its heavy shadows and smoky light, the film could present problems for DVD, but visually, the

disc is fine. So are the loud sound effects and ominous score. —*MM*
Movie: 🎞➤ ***DVD:*** 🎞🎞➤
Artisan Entertainment (Cat #60469, UPC #01223604690). Widescreen (1.85:1) letterboxed. Dolby Digital Surround Stereo. $24.98. Keepcase. *LANG:* English. *SUB:* Spanish. *CAP:* English. *FEATURES:* 36 chapter links • "Making of" featurette • Stallone featurette • Theatrical trailer.
1989 (R) 115m/C Sylvester Stallone, Donald Sutherland, Sonny Landham, John Amos, Darlanne Fluegel, Frank McRae; ***D:*** John Flynn; ***W:*** Jeb Stuart; ***C:*** Donald E. Thorin; ***M:*** Bill Conti.

The Lodger

Please see review of *Sabotage*. *AKA:* The Case of Jonathan Drew; The Lodger: A Case of London Fog.
Movie: 🎞🎞🎞
1926 91m/B *GB* Ivor Novello, Marie Ault, Arthur Chesney, Malcolm Keen, June; *Cameos:* Alfred Hitchcock; ***D:*** Alfred Hitchcock; ***W:*** Alfred Hitchcock, Eliot Stannard.

Logan's Run

In the 23rd century, a hedonistic society exists in a large bubble and people are only allowed to live to the age of 30, at which point they are expected to participate in a ritual public suicide. York plays a "Sandman" whose job is to track down an enclave of "Runners" who have escaped their fate. Intriguing concepts and great futuristic sets prevail here, but the plot tends to wander all over the place. Ustinov plays the oldest man in the world. Based on the novel by William Nolan and George Clayton. The DVD handles colors very well with little bleed, even with all the reds in the suicide ritual near the beginning of the movie. Unfortunately, that same sequence features some horrible motion problems as the masses take their seats. That aside, this is a pretty good DVD; the main problem is the occasionally scratchy print that it was made from. Good contrast and brightness levels combine with true blacks to make viewing very comfortable. The new 5.1 soundtrack provides good dynamic range and separation, particularly on Jerry Goldsmith's score, which ranges from orchestral to electronic. —*JO*
Movie: 🎞🎞 ***DVD:*** 🎞🎞➤
MGM Home Entertainment (Cat #907029, UPC #027616702920). Widescreen (2.35:1) anamorphic. Dolby Digital 5.1; Mono. $24.99. Keepcase. *LANG:* English (DD5.1); French (Mono). *SUB:* English, French. *FEATURES:* 32 chapter links • Theatrical trailer • Behind-the-scenes featurette • Commentary: Michael Anderson, Michael York, Bill Thomas • Essay by Michael Anderson • 8-page booklet.
1976 120m/C Michael York, Jenny Agutter, Richard Jordan, Roscoe Lee Browne, Farrah Fawcett, Peter Ustinov, Camilla Carr, Ann Ford; ***D:*** Michael Anderson Sr.; ***W:*** David Zelag Goodman; ***C:*** Ernest Laszlo; ***M:*** Jerry Goldsmith. *AWARDS:* Academy Awards '76: Best Visual Effects; *NOM:*

Academy Awards '76: Best Art Direction/Set Decoration, Best Cinematography.

Lola Montes

Adapted from an unpublished novel by Cecil Saint-Laurent, Ophuls's final masterpiece (and his only film in color) recounts the life and sins of the famous courtesan, mistress of Franz Liszt and the King of Bavaria. It was ignored upon release, but hailed later by the French as a cinematic landmark. This great film is better represented by the VHS release, which has much better colors and a slightly sharper image. On the DVD, there is a halo effect around high-contrast lines that is very bothersome, particularly when combined with the dull colors. Blacks are average and generally contain grain. The mono soundtrack clips a bit and is very thin. —JO

Movie: 🐾🐾🐾🐾 **DVD:** 🐾▶
Fox/Lorber Home Video (Cat #FLV5050, UPC #720917505022). Widescreen (2.35:1) letterboxed. Mono. $29.98. Keepcase. *LANG:* French. *SUB:* English. *FEATURES:* 6 chapter links ● Filmographies.
1955 110m/C *FR* Martine Carol, Peter Ustinov, Anton Walbrook, Ivan Desny, Oskar Werner; *D:* Max Ophuls; *W:* Max Ophuls; *C:* Christian Matras; *M:* Georges Auric.

Lolida 2000

In the future, all sexual activity is prohibited (bummer). Lolida (Lovell) works for an organization that destroys sexual material, but three particular stories get her all hot and bothered. The title was changed from *Lolita 2000*, as if anyone would find a meaningful connection to Vladimir Nabokov. *AKA:* Lolita 2000.
Movie: 🐾 **DVD:** NYR
Full Moon Pictures (Cat #8011). Full frame. $24.95.
1997 90m/C Jacqueline Lovell, Gabriella Hall, Eric Acsell; *D:* Sybil Richards.

Lolita

Middle-aged professor Humbert Humbert (Mason) weds Charlotte (Winters), but is consumed by his lust for her teenage-nymphet daughter Lolita (Lyon). Sellers is Claire Quilty, rival for Lolita's affections, in this strange film considered daring in its time. Based on Vladimir Nabokov's novel. Watch for Winters's terrific portrayal as the sex-starved Charlotte. This is a gorgeous black-and-white film and, for the most part, the DVD delivers the goods. The picture is sharp, the blacks are true, with very good graytones. Contrast and brightness levels are close to excellent, and artifacts are near non-existent. The only problems are found in sequences where the film stock's grain is heavy, and the DVD seems to amplify it—luckily, those spots are not too frequent. The mono sound is more than adequate with very little hiss, good clarity, and no clipping, with

good dynamics on the music. Enjoyable to watch. —JO
Movie: 🐾🐾🐾🐾 **DVD:** 🐾🐾🐾
Warner Home Video, Inc. (Cat #65004, UPC #012569500426). Widescreen (1.66:1) letterboxed. Mono. $24.98. Snapper. *LANG:* English; French. *SUB:* French. *CAP:* English. *FEATURES:* Dual-layered RSDL ● 42 chapter links ● Theatrical trailer ● Production notes. Also available as part of the "Stanley Kubrick Collection" 7-DVD box set ($149.98).
1962 152m/B *GB* James Mason, Shelley Winters, Peter Sellers, Sue Lyon, Gary Cockrell, Jerry Stovin, Diana Decker, Lois Maxwell, Cec Linder, Bill Greene, Shirley Douglas, Marianne Stone, Marion Mathie, James Dyrenforth, C. Denier Warren, Terence Kilburn, John Harrison; *D:* Stanley Kubrick; *W:* Vladimir Nabokov; *C:* Oswald Morris; *M:* Nelson Riddle. *AWARDS: NOM:* Academy Awards '62: Best Adapted Screenplay.

The Lonely Guy

Martin is a jilted writer who writes a best-selling book about being a lonely guy and finds stardom does have its rewards. Based on *The Lonely Guy's Book of Life* by Bruce Jay Friedman. This very average DVD is pretty good in the sharpness department and has only moderate problems with a little grain and a few artifacts. The colors are weak, though, and seem like they might bleed if boosted. Contrast and brightness are adequate but the blacks are a little light and have some grain. The mono sound does have some body and presence and does not distort. —JO
Movie: 🐾🐾▶ **DVD:** 🐾🐾
Universal Studios Home Video (Cat #20422, UPC #025192042225). Widescreen (1.85:1) letterboxed. Dolby Digital Mono 2.0. $24.98. Keepcase. *LANG:* English. *SUB:* Spanish; French. *CAP:* English. *FEATURES:* 16 chapter links ● Theatrical trailer ● Cast and filmmakers bios ● Production notes ● Film highlights.
1984 (R) 91m/C Steve Martin, Charles Grodin, Judith Ivey, Steve Lawrence, Robyn Douglass, Merv Griffin, Dr. Joyce Brothers; *D:* Arthur Hiller; *W:* Stan Daniels; *C:* Victor Kemper; *M:* Jerry Goldsmith.

Long Arm of the Law

Mainland Chinese jewel robbers go to Hong Kong and find themselves embroiled in the familiar job-that-goes-wrong. This is a nicely gritty crime flick, filmed to look like a documentary. The DVD is exceptionally grainy and pale, and the disc was made from a slightly damaged print with considerable snow in places. The English subtitles are legible but the background information that is supplied through superimposed text is not translated. —MM
Movie: 🐾🐾🐾 **DVD:** 🐾🐾🐾
Tai Seng Video Marketing (Cat #MS/DVD/060/99, UPC #4895017000602). Widescreen letterboxed. Dolby Digital 5.1 Surround Stereo. $49.95. Keepcase. *LANG:*

Cantonese; Mandarin. *SUB:* Traditional & Simplified Chinese; English; Thai; Vietnamese; Spanish. *FEATURES:* 9 chapter links ● Synopsis ● Cast and crew thumbnail biographies ● Trailers.
1984 101m/C *HK* Lam Wai, Shum Wai, Keen Wong, King Chan; *D:* Johnnie Mak; *W:* Philip Chan.

Long Arm of the Law II

This sequel, made by the first director's brother, is a much more polished production. It takes the first film's premise in another direction with a variation on a standard police plot: undercover cops infiltrating Mainland Chinese gangs. It's crisply handled and the acting is excellent. The image bears no resemblance to the first film. It's generally as sharp and clear as comparable American fare. —MM
Movie: 🐾🐾▶ **DVD:** 🐾🐾▶
Tai Seng Video Marketing (Cat #MS/DVD/061/99, UPC #4895017000619). Widescreen letterboxed. Dolby Digital 5.1 Surround Stereo. $49.95. Keepcase. *LANG:* Cantonese; Mandarin. *SUB:* Traditional & Simplified Chinese; English; Thai; Vietnamese; Spanish. *FEATURES:* 9 chapter links ● Synopsis ● Cast and crew thumbnail biographies ● Trailers.
1987 86m/C *HK* Alex Man, Pauline Wong, Xiu Jim Jiang, Kwok Bun Lam; *D:* Michael Mak; *W:* Philip Chan.

The Long Good Friday

One of the all-time great gangster films receives the treatment it's due on this DVD. Though the package lacks extras, the image is even sharper than I remember from the original theatrical release and the monaural sound is crisp and clear. Harold Shand (Hoskins) is at the top of the heap of the London underworld when everything goes wrong for him. Someone's blowing up his buildings and killing his key people. They even make an attempt on his mother! The only person he can trust is razor-sharp moll Victoria (Mirren). Their energetic performances are worth the price of the disc, but the film's relentless pace is almost as wonderful. One of the greats. —MM
Movie: 🐾🐾🐾▶ **DVD:** 🐾🐾🐾▶
Criterion Collection (Cat #26, UPC #71551009621). Widescreen (1.77:1) letterboxed. Dolby Digital Mono. $29.95. Keepcase. *LANG:* English. *FEATURES:* 21 chapter links ● Liner notes by Michael Sragow.
1980 109m/C *GB* Bob Hoskins, Helen Mirren, Dave King, Bryan Marshall, George Coulouris, Pierce Brosnan, Derek Thompson, Eddie Constantine, Brian Hall, Stephen Davies, P. H. Moriarty, Paul Freeman, Charles Cork, Paul Barber, Patti Love, Ruby Head, Dexter Fletcher, Roy Alon; *D:* John MacKenzie; *W:* Barrie Keefe; *C:* Phil Meheux; *M:* Francis Monkman.

The Long Kiss Goodnight

Audience-pleasing, blood-soaked, foul-mouthed, and action-packed flick casts Davis in dual role. As mild-mannered, brown-haired Samantha Caine, she's a schoolteacher with an eight-year-old daughter, Caitlin (Zima), a nice boyfriend, Hal (Amandes), and amnesia. Sam begins having flashbacks to her past—and what a past it turns out to be. With the help of seedy PI Mitch Henessey (Jackson), she discovers her name is Charly Baltimore and she's a highly trained and very deadly CIA assassin. And the now bleached-blonde, beyond-tough Charly must match her quickly regained lethal abilities with ruthless former nemesis Timothy (Bierko). The body count's high, the blood flows freely, and there are some spectacular stunts. If you're not squeamish it's a guar-anteed wild ride. Black got $4 million for his script. This DVD is the way to see this fast-moving film. The picture is extremely sharp and grain-free, with only a hint of artifacts during some action sequences. Colors are vibrant and accurate and rarely bleed. The image is very punchy with con-sistently good contrast and brightness lev-els that no doubt assist the blacks in remaining true and grainless. The 5.1 sound is just what you want for an action film. There are plenty of Surround effects and ambience. The bass pounds out con-sistently with heart-throbbing intensity. The music is full-bodied and the dialogue crisp. —JO

Movie: ♪♪▶ **DVD:** ♪♪♪▶
New Line Home Video (Cat #N4446, UPC #794043444623). Widescreen (2.35·1) letterboxed. Dolby Surround 5.1; Dolby Digi-tal Stereo. $24.98. Snapper. *LANG:* English (DS 5.1); French (DD Stereo). *SUB:* English; French; Spanish. *CAP:* English. *FEATURES:* 29 chapter links ▪ Theatrical trailer ▪ Cast bios.
1996 (R) 120m/C Geena Davis, Samuel L. Jackson, Craig Bierko, Patrick Malahide, Brian Cox, David Morse, Yvonne Zima, Tom Amandes, Melina Kanakaredes, G.D. Spradlin; *D:* Renny Harlin; *W:* Shane Black; *C:* Guillermo Navarro; *M:* Alan Sil-vestri.

The Long Shadow

Gabor (York), a Hungarian actor, learns that the father he never knew has died. He goes to Israel to find out something about him and meets the man's second wife, Katrina (Ullman). He learns that his dad was a famous archeologist and a film is being made about his life. Cinematogra-pher-turned-director Vilmos Zsigmond han-dles the static material fairly well. On DVD, the colors tend to be muted. They often are in serious European films and this one was made for Hungarian television with the participation of the Israeli government. The night scenes show some grain. Exotic locations are well chosen. Sound is fine. —MM

Movie: ♪♪▶ **DVD:** ♪♪▶

Simitar Entertainment (Cat #7298, UPC #082551729821). Full frame. PCM Stereo. $7.98. Keepcase. *LANG:* English. *FEATURES:* 8 chapter links ▪ Liv Ullman and Michael York filmographies.
1992 90m/C *HU IS* Michael York, Liv Ull-mann; *D:* Vilmos Zsigmond; *W:* Paul Sala-mon, Janos Edelenyi; *C:* Gabor Szabo.

The Longest Day

The story of the D-Day landings at Nor-mandy as seen through the eyes of many participants—English, American, French, German—is very much a product of the late '50s and early '60s. It's long, enter-taining, poorly focused, and leaves many of its big-name ensemble cast members with little to do. If the violence is not as horrify-ing as it has been portrayed in more recent depictions of the attack, it was considered realistic in its day. Many of the details are accurate, and some scenes are still really impressive. Don't miss the incredible long helicopter shot during the attack on the casino in chapter 9. The widescreen trans-fer captures all of the action well. English subtitles for the German and French are placed in the lower black strip. The black-and-white cinematography makes the tran-sition to DVD with no significant flaws, though the image is not noticeably superi-or to recent widescreen tapes. The sound is a step up. —MM

Movie: ♪♪♪ **DVD:** ♪♪♪▶
Twentieth Century Fox Home Entertainment Widescreen letterboxed. Dolby Surround, 5.0 Surround (English); Dolby Surround (French). $29.98. *LANG:* English; French; German. *SUB:* Spanish; English. *CAP:* Eng-lish. *FEATURES:* 12 chapter links.
1962 179m/C John Wayne, Richard Bur-ton, Red Buttons, Robert Mitchum, Henry Fonda, Robert Ryan, Paul Anka, Mel Fer-rer, Edmond O'Brien, Fabian, Sean Con-nery, Roddy McDowall, Arletty, Curt Jur-gens, Rod Steiger, Jean-Louis Barrault, Peter Lawford, Robert Wagner, Sal Mineo, Leo Genn, Richard Beymer, Jeffrey Hunter, Stuart Whitman, Eddie Albert, Tom Tryon, Alexander Knox, Ray Danton, Kenneth More, Richard Todd, Gert Frobe, Christo-pher Lee; *D:* Bernhard Wicki, Ken Annakin, Andrew Marton, Darryl F. Zanuck, Gerd Oswald; *W:* James Jones, David Pur-sall, Jack Seddon, Romain Gary; *C:* Jean (Yves, Georges) Bourgoin, Pierre Levent, Henri Persin, Walter Wottitz; *M:* Maurice Jarre. *AWARDS:* Academy Awards '62: Best Black-and-white Cinematography; *NOM:* Academy Awards '62: Best Art Direction/Set Decoration (B & W), Best Film Editing, Best Picture.

The Longest Nite

Hong Kong action flick revolves around two Macau gang bosses who are trying to end a feud and unite so that they won't be kicked out by their overboss. This one's grittier than most Asian imports and it's told with a spaghetti western sensibility, a sadistic streak and occasional continuity errors. The DVD is little better than a wide-

screen VHS tape with so-so image and sound. —MM

Movie: ♪♪▶ **DVD:** ♪♪▶
Tai Seng Video Marketing (Cat #5052, UPC #895024900575). Widescreen letter-boxed. Dolby Digital Mono. $49.95. Keep-case. *LANG:* Cantonese; Mandarin. *SUB:* Traditional & Simplified Chinese; English. *FEATURES:* 8 chapter links ▪ Trailer ▪ Featurettes.
1992 84m/C *HK* Tony Leung Chiu-Wai, Lau Ching Wan, Maggie Siu; *D:* Patrick Yau; *W:* Nai-Hoi Yau; *C:* Chiu-lam Ko; *M:* Ying-wah Wong.

Look Who's Talking

The ultimate cute-baby picture is only fit-fully entertaining. Mollie (Alley) is a single mom who's searching for the perfect dad for little Mikey (voice of Willis). James (Tra-volta) is his taxi-driver/babysitter. The DVD is no real improvement over VHS tape in either image or sound. —MM

Movie: ♪♪ **DVD:** ♪♪
Columbia Tristar Home Video (Cat #79109, UPC #04339679109). Widescreen (1.85:1) letterboxed; full frame. Dolby Digi-tal Surround Stereo. $29.95. Keepcase. *LANG:* English; French. *SUB:* English; French. *FEATURES:* 35 chapter links.
1989 (PG-13) 90m/C John Travolta, Kirstie Alley, Olympia Dukakis, George Segal, Abe Vigoda; *D:* Amy Heckerling; *W:* Amy Hecker-ling; *M:* David Kitay; *V:* Bruce Willis.

Looking for Lola

Dreadful, uninspired romantic comedy from prolific filmmaker Boaz Davidson. Whipped up to take advantage of the short-lived Macarena craze (original title was, you guessed it, *Macarena*). We labori-ously follow the misadventures of Lola (Ara Celi—*From Dusk Till Dawn 2*) and Mike (Mark Kassen); both have deceived the other into believing that each one is fabulously rich, which they are not. Their mutual web of deceit leads to predicable results, capped by a *Flashdance*-inspired ending, with neither the talent nor inspira-tion in place to carry it off. DVD is strictly by the numbers, no extras, save for a made-for-cable trailer. Only plus, if you can call it that, is several musical interludes featuring the Macarena. —RT *AKA:* Macarena.

Movie: ♪▶ **DVD:** ♪♪
Image Entertainment (Cat #6271NG, UPC #014381627121). Full frame. AC3 - 2 Channel. $24.99. Snapper. *LANG:* English. *FEATURES:* 20 chapter links ▪ Trailer.
1998 (PG) ?m/C *SP* Ara Celi, Mark Kassen, Armin Shimerman; *D:* Boaz David-son.

Lord of Illusions

New York P.I. Harry D'Amour (Bakula), who has an affinity for the occult, becomes involved with Dorothea (Janssen), the sup-

posed widow of magician Philip Swann (O'Connor). As Harry investigates, he discovers some terrifying secrets, including resurrected cult leader Nix (Von Bargen). Gruesome effects are more important than excessive gore, but you'll feel like you've been dropped in the middle of a plot without a clear idea of what's happening. Bakula's Harry obviously has more stories to tell but Janssen's Dorothea, while attractive, is just around to cower. Barker directs from his own short story "The Last Illusion." The DVD features the same cut as the laserdisc but improves upon its quality. The picture is about the same, sharpness-wise, but colors are more vibrant. The disc has no grain problems in the numerous dark sequences, where the contrast and brightness levels also remain good. The soundtrack conveys the excellent score very dynamically with a proper mix given to low and highs. Barker's commentary is not very informative but is at least delivered with enthusiasm. —JO **AKA:** Clive Barker's Lord of Illusions.
Movie: 🐾🐾🐾 **DVD:** 🐾🐾🐾▶
MGM Home Entertainment (Cat #906294, UPC #027616629425). Widescreen (1.85:1) anamorphic. Dolby Digital 5.1. $24.98. Keepcase. *LANG:* English. *SUB:* English; French. *CAP:* English. *FEATURES:* 32 chapter links ▪ Theatrical trailer ▪ Added footage ▪ Commentary: Clive Barker ▪ Isolated musical score ▪ 8-page booklet.
1995 (R) 109m/C Scott Bakula, Famke Janssen, Kevin J. O'Connor, Daniel von Bargen, Joel Swetow, Barry Sherman, Jordan Marder, Joseph Latimore, Vincent Schiavelli; *D:* Clive Barker; *W:* Clive Barker; *C:* Ronn Schmidt; *M:* Simon Boswell.

Lost and Found
The only, repeat ONLY, reason to see this movie is the lovely Sophie Marceau. Spade, in a bold bit of casting, plays Dylan, a sniveling pipsqueak taken with his new French neighbor (the aforementioned and still lovely Marceau). In a sick attempt to win her love, he kidnaps her dog in order to "find" him a few days later. When the pooch swallows an anniversary ring, several tasteless dog poo jokes ensue. (The VideoHound hates that.) Discounting the lame plot, the DVD looks and sounds as slick as any competent Hollywood romantic comedy with no serious technical flaws. —MM
Movie: 🐾 **DVD:** 🐾🐾🐾
Warner Home Video, Inc. (Cat #17563, UPC #085391756323). Widescreen anamorphic; full frame. Dolby Digital 5.1 Surround Stereo. $19.98. Snapper. *LANG:* English; French. *SUB:* English; French. *FEATURES:* 29 chapter links ▪ Cast and crew thumbnail bios.
1999 (PG-13) 97m/C David Spade, Sophie Marceau, Artie Lange, Martin Sheen, Patrick Bruel, Jon Lovitz, Mitchell Whitfield, Carole Cook, Estelle Harris, Marla Gibbs, Natalie Barish, Phil Leeds, Christian Clemenson, Daphnee Lynn

Duplaix; *D:* Jeff Pollack; *W:* J.B. Cook, Marc Meeks, David Spade; *C:* Paul Elliott; *M:* John Debney.

The Lost Boys
Teens Michael (Patric) and Sam (Haim) move with their divorced mom (Wiest) to Santa Carla, CA, "the murder capital of the world," and discover a gang of undead adolescents led by David (Sutherland) and the sexy Star (Gertz). Director Schumacher and D.P. Michael Chapman make the flimsy material look much better than it actually is with some dandy visual tricks which have been copied countless times in the rash of teen vampire movies and TV shows that have followed. The story relies so much on Hollywood conventions that it's easy to predict what's going to happen, and the big finish is equally stereotyped stuff. The DVD looks fine, particularly in the gaudy amusement park where much of the first part is set. The film has never been more than eye candy; on digital disc it is superior eye candy. —MM
Movie: 🐾🐾 **DVD:** 🐾🐾🐾
Warner Home Video, Inc. (Cat #11748, UPC #085391174820). Full frame; widescreen letterboxed. Dolby Digital 5.1 Surround. $24.98. Snapper. *LANG:* English. *SUB:* English; French; Spanish. *CAP:* English. *FEATURES:* 32 chapter links ▪ Case and crew thumbnail biographies ▪ Production notes.
1987 (R) 97m/C Jason Patric, Kiefer Sutherland, Corey Haim, Jami Gertz, Dianne Wiest, Corey Feldman, Barnard Hughes, Edward Herrmann, Billy Wirth, Jamison Newlander, Brooke McCarter, Alex Winter; *D:* Joel Schumacher; *W:* Jeffrey Boam, Janice Fischer, James Jeremias; *C:* Michael Chapman; *M:* Thomas Newman.

Lost Continent
Hammer's most bizarre production begins with a wildly inappropriate theme song and electric organ score that could have come from Happy Hour at a motel cocktail lounge. That introduces a group of characters from a Graham Greene novel inexplicably transplanted into a seagoing Edgar Rice Burroughs plot. A leaky freighter is en route to Caracas with a dangerous explosive cargo, five desperate passengers with secrets of their own, a troubled cynical captain (Eric Porter), and a mutinous crew. On the horizon lie a hurricane, religious persecution, giant mollusks, and carnivorous kelp. The whole thing is every bit as strange, screwy, and wonderful as it sounds. The sharp transfer to DVD is a mixed blessing. The tank shots of a model ship are even more obvious than they were on the tape version and the image seems to degrade a bit in the second half when tinted light is used to keep the "monsters" from being too clearly revealed. Some interiors then are not as sharp as they might have been. Also, like the tape, the disc contains eight minutes

that were too "adult" for American audiences in 1968. —MM
Movie: 🐾🐾🐾🐾 **DVD:** 🐾🐾🐾▶
Anchor Bay (Cat #DV10675, UPC #013131067590). Widescreen (1.77:1) letterboxed. Dolby Digital Mono. $29.98. Keepcase. *LANG:* English. *FEATURES:* 30 chapter links ▪ TV spots ▪ Theatrical trailer ▪ World of Hammer episode, "Lands before Time."
1968 97m/C Eric Porter, Hildegarde Knef, Suzanna Leigh, Tony Beckley, Nigel Stock, Neil McCallum, Ben Carruthers, Jimmy Hanley, Dana Gillespie; *D:* Michael Carreras; *W:* Michael Nash; *C:* Paul Beeson.

The Lost Films of Laurel and Hardy, Vol. 1
DVD collects six early classic comic adventures: "Do Detectives Think?" (1927), "Call of the Cuckoo" (1927), "The Finishing Touch" (1928), "Big Business" (1929), plus two Stan Laurel solo shorts, "Hustling for Health" (1919) and "On the Front Page" (1926). On all the discs in this series (including "Laurel and Hardy and Friends"), picture and sound are uneven and can be quite poor, as should be expected from such antique film elements. But these comic gems, mastered from surviving 35mm original material, have never looked better on home video, so no need to complain. *Big Business* was mastered from the original nitrate camera negative. Menu interface is clunky but serviceable. —MB
Movie: 🐾🐾🐾 **DVD:** 🐾▶
Image Entertainment (Cat #HRS4791, UPC #014381479126). Full frame. Dolby Digital Mono. $29.98. Snapper. *LANG:* English. *FEATURES:* 6 chapter links ▪ Printed descriptions for each title ▪ Printed images of original posters.
199? ?m/B Stan Laurel, Oliver Hardy.

The Lost Films of Laurel and Hardy, Vol. 2
Contents: "Sugar Daddies" (1927), "Early to Bed" (1928), "Double Whoopie" (1929), "Angora Love" (1929), plus two Stan Laurel solo shorts, "Oranges & Lemons" (1920) and "Roughest Africa" (1923). Please see review of *Vol.1*. —MB
Movie: 🐾🐾🐾 **DVD:** 🐾▶
Image Entertainment (Cat #HRS4792, UPC #014381479225). Full frame. Dolby Digital Mono. $29.98. Snapper. *LANG:* English. *FEATURES:* 6 chapter links ▪ Printed descriptions for each title ▪ Printed images of original posters.
199? ?m/B Stan Laurel, Oliver Hardy.

The Lost Films of Laurel and Hardy, Vol. 3
Contents: "Liberty" (1929), "We Faw Down" (1928), "A Lucky Dog" (1922), "Love 'Em and Weep" (1927), the Oliver

Hardy solo short "Along Came Auntie" (1926), and the Charley Chase short "Bromo and Juliet" (1926). Please see review of *Vol.1*. —MB

Movie: 𝄢𝄢𝄢 ***DVD:*** 𝄢

Image Entertainment (Cat #HRS4793, UPC #014381479324). Full frame. Dolby Digital Mono. $29.98. Snapper. *LANG:* English. *FEATURES:* 6 chapter links ▪ Printed descriptions for each title ▪ Printed images of original posters.

199? ?m/B Stan Laurel, Oliver Hardy, Charley Chase.

The Lost Films of Laurel and Hardy, Vol. 5

The main attraction on this volume of the "lost" collection is the debut of the famous screen duo, "Duck Soup," thought lost until a print surfaced in 1974. It is exceptionally grainy and rough, much more than the others on the disc. In terms of image quality, it's really comparable to the contemporaneous work of Keaton and Chaplin, which tends to be much more polished, technically and comedically. That said, the films look as good as could be expected on DVD, with careful transfers of image and soundtracks, in some cases utilizing Vitaphone soundtracks for music and effects. Contents: "Wrong Again" (1929), "Habeas Corpus" (1929), "Duck Soup" (1927), "Fluttering Hearts" (1927), "Leave 'Em Laughing" (1928), and "Short Kilts" (1924). (Laurel does not appear in "Fluttering Hearts" and Hardy does not appear in "Short Kilts.") —MM

Movie: 𝄢𝄢 ***DVD:*** 𝄢𝄢𝄢

Image Entertainment (Cat #HRS4795, UPC #014381479522). Full frame. $29.99. Snapper. *LANG:* Silent. *SUB:* English intertitles. *FEATURES:* 6 chapter links.

1999 124m/C Stan Laurel, Oliver Hardy.

The Lost Films of Laurel and Hardy, Vol. 6

Like the other discs in this series, the quality of image and sound ranges between poor and good. There's considerable hiss and popping on the soundtrack—which contains music and, in some cases, sound effects—and the image suffers similar visual flaws with scratches, surface snow and some poorly focused footage. Contents: "That's My Wife" (1929), "Flying Elephants" (1928), "Putting Pants on Philip" (1928), "Crazy Like a Fox" (1926), "The Soilers" (1923), and "45 Minutes from Hollywood" (1926). —MM

Movie: 𝄢𝄢 ***DVD:*** 𝄢𝄢

Image Entertainment (Cat #HRS4796, UPC #014381479621). Full frame. $29.99. Snapper. *LANG:* Silent. *SUB:* English intertitles. *FEATURES:* 6 chapter links ▪ Liner notes.

1999 122m/C Stan Laurel, Oliver Hardy.

Lost Horizon

The appalling deterioration of one of Hollywood's finest achievements led directly to the preservation and restoration movement that is so active today. On their commentary track, critic Charles Champlin and restoration expert Robert Gitt talk about the incredible efforts that were put forth by many people to return Frank Capra's film to something approaching its original 1937 condition. (They also explain how the film came to be in such bad shape.) It's the story of a group of people who are fleeing revolution in China and find an ageless paradise in the Himalayas. Compared to other films of its time, this one has stretches that look as good as the best, while other footage is poorly focused and rough-looking. In simple terms of image and sound, the DVD probably isn't that much better than the VHS tape made from the same original materials. The disc does contain the right extras. —MM

Movie: 𝄢𝄢𝄢𝄢 ***DVD:*** 𝄢𝄢𝄢

Columbia Tristar Home Video (Cat #07639, UPC #043396076396). Full frame. Dolby Digital Mono. $27.95. Keepcase. *LANG:* English. *SUB:* English; Spanish; Portuguese; Chinese; Korean; Thai. *FEATURES:* 28 chapter links ▪ Restoration commentary by Charles Champlin and Robert Gitt ▪ Production notes ▪ Alternative ending ▪ Restoration before-and-after comparison ▪ 3 deleted scenes ▪ Photo documentary narrated by Kendall Miller ▪ Theatrical trailer.

1937 132m/B Ronald Colman, Jane Wyatt, H.B. Warner, Sam Jaffe, Thomas Mitchell, Edward Everett Horton, Isabel Jewell, John Howard, Margo; *D:* Frank Capra; *W:* Robert Riskin; *C:* Joseph Walker; *M:* Dimitri Tiomkin. *AWARDS:* Academy Awards '37: Best Film Editing; *NOM:* Academy Awards '37: Best Picture, Best Sound, Best Supporting Actor (Warner), Best Score.

Lost in Space

Big-screen remake of the cheesy '60s TV show retains the basic premise but jettisons the camp. In 2058, the Robinson family and space fighter jock West (LeBlanc) are chosen to pioneer the first colonizing of a distant world. The evil Dr. Smith (an underused Oldman) sabotages the mission but is stuck on board. The rest is a collection of the usual suspects—giant mechanical spiders, robots, deserted spaceships, time warps—in a cliched script from the usually entertaining Goldsman, who also produced. Overall, the acting isn't much better, but who cares? On disc, this is some of the tastiest eye candy you'll ever see. Tremendous sets and effects reproduced with great care. From the big computer-generated futuristic cityscapes to the spaceship interiors, it looks great with dark textures and a full slate of extras. —MM

Movie: 𝄢𝄢 ***DVD:*** 𝄢𝄢𝄢𝄢

New Line Home Video (Cat #N4667, UPC #794045466724). Widescreen (2.35:1) letterboxed. Dolby Digital 5.1. $24.98.

Snapper. *LANG:* English. *SUB:* English. *CAP:* English. *FEATURES:* Cast and crew biographies ▪ Commentary: director Stephen Hopkins and writer-producer Akiva Goldsman ▪ Technical commentary track ▪ Production design illustrations ▪ TV series complete episode synopsis ▪ Original cast biographies ▪ Original cast Q&A ▪ "Future of Space Travel" featurette with Jeff Hohensee ▪ Music video with Apollo Four Forty ▪ Deleted scenes ▪ Theatrical trailer ▪ Interactive game ▪ 24 chapter links. For PC DVD-ROM, five interactive games; original screenplay with direct links to film; website access.

1998 (PG-13) 131m/C William Hurt, Mimi Rogers, Gary Oldman, Heather Graham, Matt LeBlanc, Lacey Chabert, Jack Johnson, Lennie James, Jared Harris, Mark Goddard, Edward Fox, Adam Sims; *Cameos:* June Lockhart, Marta Kristen, Angela Cartwright; *D:* Stephen Hopkins; *W:* Akiva Goldsman; *C:* Peter Levy; *M:* Bruce Broughton; *V:* Dick Tufeld. *AWARDS: NOM:* Golden Raspberry Awards '98: Worst Remake/Sequel.

The Lost World

A zoology professor leads a group on a South American expedition in search of the "lost world" where dinosaurs roam, in this silent film based on a novel by Sir Arthur Conan Doyle. Virtually all of the cinematic dinosaur cliches made their first appearances here, including everybody's favorite—the beast roaming the streets of a modern metropolis at the end. One of the first great stop-motion special effects efforts looks pretty good on DVD. The print is scratchy and damaged in many places, but on balance, the image is very good for a film of this age. The tinting is bright and the silent film is accompanied by a period score and added sound effects. —MM

Movie: 𝄢𝄢 ***DVD:*** 𝄢𝄢

SlingShot Entertainment (Cat #DVD9819). Full frame. $19.99. Keepcase. *LANG:* Silent. *SUB:* English intertitles. *FEATURES:* 12 chapter links ▪ Photo gallery.

1925 62m/B Wallace Beery, Lewis Stone, Bessie Love, Lloyd Hughes; *D:* Harry Hoyt; *W:* Marion Fairfax; *C:* Arthur Edeson. *AWARDS:* National Film Registry '98.

Lotto Land

Black and Hispanic characters in a Brooklyn neighborhood are brought together by a $27 million lottery ticket. Ambitious high school grad Hank (Gilliard Jr.) stocks shelves at the local liquor store for Flo (Costallos), who has raised his girlfriend Joy (Gonzalez). Her biological dad sells crack. Clearly, with this kind of story, sparkling visuals are counter-productive. The DVD image has shot-on-location, street-level grit. The characters are the point and these are some of the most believable you'll see. The no-frills disc is a solid sleeper. —MM

Movie: 𝄢𝄢𝄢 ***DVD:*** 𝄢𝄢

WinStar Home Entertainment (Cat #FLV5164, UPC #720917516424). Full frame. $24.98. Keepcase. *LANG:* English. *FEATURES:* 6 chapter links.
1995 90m/C Larry Gilliard Jr., Barbara Gonzalez, Suzanne Costallos, Wendell Holmes, Jamie Tirelli, Luis Guzman, Paul Calderon; *D:* John Rubino; *W:* John Rubino; *C:* Rufus Standefer; *M:* Sherman Holmes, Wendell Holmes.

Love Affair

Multi-hankie weeper has inspired countless romantic dreams of true love atop the Empire State Building. Dunn and Boyer fall in love on board a ship bound for NYC, but they're both involved. They agree to meet later—guess where—to see if their feelings hold true but tragedy intervenes. Excellent comedy-drama is witty at first, more subdued later, with plenty of romance and melodrama.
Movie: 🎬🎬🎬▶ *DVD:* NYR
Madacy Entertainment (Cat #99017). Full frame. Dolby Digital Mono. $9.99. Keepcase. *FEATURES:* Production notes.
1939 87m/B Irene Dunne, Charles Boyer, Maria Ouspenskaya, Lee Bowman, Astrid Allwyn, Maurice Moscovich, Scotty Beckett, Joan Leslie, Gerald Mohr, Dell Henderson, Carol Hughes; *D:* Leo McCarey; *W:* Leo McCarey, Delmer Daves, Donald Ogden Stewart; *C:* Rudolph Mate; *M:* Roy Webb. *AWARDS: NOM:* Academy Awards '39: Best Actress (Dunne), Best Picture, Best Song ("Wishing"), Best Story, Best Supporting Actress (Ouspenskaya).

Love After Love

Look at sex and relationships among thirtysomething professionals in Paris. Lola (Huppert), a successful romance novelist, is suffering a crisis in both her career and love life. She's involved with two men who, in turn, are involved with different women who happen to have borne them children. The movie starts off with so much mate switching and secret sexual rendezvous that by the second half you don't really care who Lola winds up with. *AKA:* Apres l'Amour.
Movie: 🎬🎬 *DVD:* NYR
WinStar Home Entertainment (Cat #5114). Full frame. $29.98. Keepcase. *LANG:* French. *SUB:* English. *FEATURES:* Cast and crew thumbnail bios ▪ Production notes.
1994 104m/C *FR* Isabelle Huppert, Hippolyte Girardot, Lio; *D:* Diane Kurys; *W:* Diane Kurys, Antoine Lacomblez; *C:* Fabio Conversi; *M:* Yves Simon, Serge Perathone, Jannick Top.

Love and a .45

Satirical and violent road movie finds petty career criminal Watty Watts (Bellows) living in a Texas trailer park with gal Starlene (Zellweger), for whom he's just purchased an expensive engagement ring. But he's borrowed the money from some crazed gangster types who want the loan repaid in timely fashion. Soon, the dippy duo are on the run to Mexico with a trail of dead bodies behind them and the media just delighted to make them the next tabloid darlings. The picture on the DVD is only average, and the laserdisc is overall the preferable way to go. In addition to lacking sharpness, the image is grainy with some artifacts. Colors are a bit faded and there is some bleed. The sound is as good as the LD, but doesn't seem any better. Both have very few Surround effects and are a little thin, though clarity is pretty good. —*JO*
Movie: 🎬🎬🎬 *DVD:* 🎬🎬
Trimark Home Video (Cat #VM7082D, UPC #031398708230). Full frame. Dolby Surround. $24.98. Keepcase. *LANG:* English. *SUB:* English; Spanish; French. *FEATURES:* 30 chapter links ▪ Theatrical trailer ▪ Music video ▪ Deleted scenes ▪ Storyboards.
1994 (R) 101m/C Gil Bellows, Renee Zellweger, Rory Cochrane, Ann Wedgeworth, Peter Fonda, Jeffrey Combs, Jace Alexander; *D:* C.M. Talkington; *W:* C.M. Talkington; *C:* Tom Richmond; *M:* Tom Verlaine. *AWARDS: NOM:* Independent Spirit Awards '95: Debut Performance (Zellweger).

Love and Anarchy

Director Lina Wertmuller was one hot filmmaker in the 1970s, with hit after hit— *The Seduction of Mimi, Swept Away, Seven Beauties, All Screwed Up*—and this prewar tale of brothel politics, sexual power, and the rise of Fascism. And then, the magic slipped away. Here, Wertmuller is at the top of her form, clicking on all cylinders with her personal actor-collaborator Giancarlo Giannini, who is on an ill-fated mission to assassinate Mussolini. He takes refuge in a Rome brothel run by Mariangela Melato while awaiting his opportunity to carry out his plan, but slowly slips into a web of sexual misadventures that ultimately lead to his own personal destruction. The DVD presentation features source material that is in generally good condition. An expert or filmmaker commentary would have been a nice touch as this is an important film from Wertmuller, a Fellini protege. —*RT AKA:* Film d'Amore et d'Anarchia.
Movie: 🎬🎬🎬 *DVD:* 🎬🎬▶
WinStar Home Entertainment (Cat #5044, UPC #720917504421). Widescreen. AC3 - 2 Channel. $29.98. Keepcase. *LANG:* Italian. *SUB:* English. *CAP:* English. *FEATURES:* 9 chapter links ▪ Cast biographies.
1973 108m/C *IT* Giancarlo Giannini, Mariangela Melato; *D:* Lina Wertmuller; *W:* Lina Wertmuller; *C:* Giuseppe Rotunno; *M:* Nino Rota. *AWARDS:* Cannes Film Festival '73: Best Actor (Giannini).

Love and Death on Long Island

Reclusive English author Giles De'Ath (Hurt), barely on speaking terms with the 20th century, wanders into the wrong theatre where a teen exploitation flick is playing and becomes obsessed with star Ronnie Bostock (Priestley). His passion leads to the discovery of fan magazines, TV, and video. It also takes the older man to Bostock's home on Long Island. Hurt, always excellent, really shines as De'Ath tries to reconcile his dignity and increasingly irrational behavior. Priestley does a fine job of lampooning his own image, while not exactly dispelling it. All of the characters are interesting and original, and they have real depth. The DVD image is equally sharp. Though this is not a particularly challenging film, both image and sound range between good and excellent. —*MM*
Movie: 🎬🎬▶ *DVD:* 🎬🎬🎬
Universal Studios Home Video (Cat #20728, UPC #025192072826). Widescreen (1.85:1) letterboxed. Dolby Digital Surround Stereo. $24.98. Keepcase. *LANG:* English. *CAP:* English. *FEATURES:* 18 chapter links ▪ Theatrical trailer.
1997 (PG-13) 93m/C *GB CA* John Hurt, Jason Priestley, Fiona Loewi, Sheila Hancock, Maury Chaykin, Gawn Grainger, Elizabeth Quinn; *D:* Richard Kwietniowski; *W:* Richard Kwietniowski; *C:* Oliver Curtis; *M:* Richard Grassby-Lewis.

Love, etc.

A tragic, outlandish tale begins innocently enough—as Marie meets Benoit through a personal ad. It's on the day they marry, however, that best friend Pierre realizes he too is in love with Marie. So Benoit and Pierre proceed to make the woman they love miserable. Expertly photographed movie is presented in a letterbox format, but regrettably the very wide image has not been anamorphically enhanced for widescreen TVs. Compression artifacts are apparent in some scenes. Soundtrack is in French, and the English subtitles are burned in, so there's no turning them off. —*MB*
Movie: 🎬🎬🎬 *DVD:* 🎬🎬
Fox/Lorber Home Video (Cat #FLV52090, UPC #720917520926). Widescreen (2.35:1) letterboxed. Dolby Digital Stereo. $29.98. Keepcase. *LANG:* French. *SUB:* English. *FEATURES:* 12 chapter links ▪ Filmographies ▪ Production credits.
1996 105m/C *FR* Charlotte Gainsbourg, Yvan Attal, Charles Berling; *D:* Marion Vernoux; *W:* Marion Vernoux, Dodine Herry; *C:* Eric Gautier; *M:* Leonard Cohen, Alexandre Desplat.

The Love Goddesses

This 60-year examination of some of the most beautiful women to grace the silver screen is an excellent introduction to the general treatment of sex in the movies, reflecting with extraordinary accuracy the customs, manners, and mores of the various times. The footage is uniformly well chosen and the quality of the older footage from turn-of-the-century peepshows to the 1930s is remarkable in many cases. The DVD is no better than that source material, in the worst cases,

but most of the clips look and sound fine. Writer-producers Saul J. Turell and Graeme Ferguson do more than round up the usual female suspects here. They try to show how some women are able to create such indelible impressions in front of the camera. Of secondary importance but still worth mentioning is the extensive use of chapter links so that fans can go straight to their favs from Lillian Gish to Sophia Loren. The film was released theatrically in 1972. A sequel is long overdue. —MM
Movie: ♪♪♪▶ **DVD:** ♪♪♪
Image Entertainment (Cat #ID4546JFDVD, UPC #014381454628). Widescreen (2:20:1) letterboxed. Dolby Digital Mono. $24.99. Snapper. *LANG:* English. *FEATURES:* 38 chapter links.
1965 83m/B Marlene Dietrich, Greta Garbo, Jean Harlow, Gloria Swanson, Mae West, Betty Grable, Rita Hayworth, Elizabeth Taylor, Marilyn Monroe, Theda Bara, Claudette Colbert, Dorothy Lamour, Lillian Gish, Sophia Loren; *D:* Saul J. Turell; *W:* Saul J. Turell, Graeme Ferguson; *Nar:* Carl King.

Love Jones

The Sanctuary nightclub is a gathering place for middle-class black Chicagoans looking for romance. Would be writer-poet Darius (Tate) performs provocative verse to beautiful photographer Nina (Long), who's not happy with men at the moment. (She's just been dumped.) But they make a connection, with both protesting a little too much that it's just a "sex thing." Witcher's directorial debut features fine performances from the leads. The DVD handles nocturnal exteriors, black clothing, and the dark nightclub scenes, with potentially difficult lighting, very well. The stereo sound has an intimate quality. —MM
Movie: ♪♪♪ **DVD:** ♪♪♪
New Line Home Video (Cat #N4786, UPC #794043478628). Widescreen (1.85:1) letterboxed; full frame. Dolby Digital 5.1 Surround Stereo; Dolby Digital Surround Stereo. $24.98. Snapper. *LANG:* English. *SUB:* English. *FEATURES:* 25 chapter links • Music video • Theatrical trailer • Cast and crew thumbnail biographies.
1996 (R) 105m/C Larenz Tate, Nia Long, Isaiah Washington, Lisa Nicole Carson, Khalil Kain, Bill Bellamy, Leonard Roberts, Bernadette L. Clarke; *D:* Theodore Witcher; *W:* Theodore Witcher; *C:* Ernest Holzman; *M:* Darryl Jones. *AWARDS:* Sundance Film Festival '97: Audience Award.

The Love Letter

Fortysomething bookstore owner Helen (Capshaw) receives an anonymous love letter in her shop's mail. Is it for her? Who sent it? Could it be Johnny (Scott), the college student who has a crush on her? Or George (Selleck), an old friend? The cast is the most interesting part of this fairly predictable romance. It's a quirky character-driven film that looks much the same on either VHS tape or DVD. The only

important difference is found in the extras, which do not add that much. —MM
Movie: ♪♪ **DVD:** ♪♪
DreamWorks Home Entertainment (Cat #85302, UPC #667068530223). Widescreen anamorphic. Dolby Digital 5.1 Surround Stereo. $29.98. Keepcase. *LANG:* English. *SUB:* English. *FEATURES:* 20 chapter links • 11 deleted scenes • Cast and crew thumbnail biographies • Theatrical trailer • Production notes.
1999 (PG-13) 88m/C Kate Capshaw, Tom Everett Scott, Tom Selleck, Ellen DeGeneres, Blythe Danner, Gloria Stuart, Geraldine McEwan, Alice Drummond; *D:* Peter Chan; *W:* Maria Maggenti; *C:* Tami Reiker; *M:* Luis Bacalov.

Love to Kill

Moe (Danza) is a low-level arms dealer who falls for Elizabeth (Barondes), a gal who likes guns. But their road to romance is rocked by dead bodies, dirty cops, and double-crosses. A surprisingly good cast is given a script filled with bizarre black humor and they make the most of it. This one's a genuine sleeper. On DVD, some pixelation is noticeable in the heaviest areas of darkness in the night scenes. Otherwise the picture quality and sound are first-rate. —MM *AKA:* The Girl Gets Moe.
Movie: ♪♪♪ **DVD:** ♪♪▶
Simitar Entertainment (Cat #7434, UPC #082551743421). Full frame. Dolby Digital Stereo; Dolby Digital 5.1 Surround Stereo. $14.98. Keepcase. *LANG:* English. *FEATURES:* 8 chapter links • Production factoids • Tony Danza filmography.
1997 (R) 102m/C Tony Danza, Michael Madsen, James Russo, Elizabeth Barondes, Louise Fletcher, Amy Locane, Richmond Arquette, Rustam Branaman; *D:* James Bruce; *W:* Monica Clemens, Rustam Branaman; *C:* Keith Smith; *M:* Barry Coffing.

Loveblind

Sarah (Yates) thinks that she's happy with her fiance, but when she begins to work with a photographer and his new model Chani (Larranaga), her fantasies intensify. For a Playboy production, this one looks very good on DVD. With soft, sophisticated lighting, the clarity of image and sound are exceptional, belying an obviously limited budget. —MM
Movie: ♪♪ **DVD:** ♪♪♪
Image Entertainment (Cat #ID5973PLDVD, UPC #014381597325). Full frame. Dolby Digital Stereo. $24.99. Snapper. *LANG:* English. *FEATURES:* 16 chapter links.
1998 100m/C Catalina Larranaga, Bobby Johnston, Eric Acsell, Kim Yates; *D:* C.B. Harding; *W:* Giorgio Serafini; *C:* Ben Kurfin; *M:* Carl Schurtz.

Lover of the Last Empress

In this Hong Kong variation on the Lancelot-Guinevere legend, Yu-lan (Yau) is a young woman who is raised by her family

to be a concubine to the emperor. On the way to see him for the first time, she meets and falls in love with his nephew Prince Kung (Leung). The rest of this opulent period piece follows their relationship and her progress in the royal court. The direction ranges between effective and heavy-handed. The main attraction is the lovely Chingmy Yau in her transformation from innocent to empress. Compared to other imports, the DVD image is fairly good, though it isn't equal to comparably budgeted and themed American films. Hex errors in the subtitles are frequent. —MM
AKA: Ci Xi Mi Mi Sheng Huo.
Movie: ♪♪▶ **DVD:** ♪♪▶
Tai Seng Video Marketing (Cat #DVD-148). Widescreen letterboxed. Dolby Digital Stereo. $24.95. Keepcase. *LANG:* Cantonese; Mandarin. *SUB:* English; Chinese. *FEATURES:* 9 chapter links • Trailer.
1995 99m/C *HK* Chingmy Yau, Tony Leung Chiu-Wai, Valerie Chow; *D:* Wai Keung Lau.

Lovers and Liars

A romantic adventure in Rome turns into a symphony of mishaps when the man (Giancarlo Giannini) forgets to tell the woman (Hawn) that he is married. *AKA:* Travels with Anita; A Trip with Anita.
Movie: ♪♪ **DVD:** NYR
Tapeworm Video Distributors (Cat #1735). Full frame. $19.95. Keepcase.
1981 (R) 93m/C *IT* Goldie Hawn, Giancarlo Giannini, Laura Betti; *D:* Mario Monicelli; *W:* Mario Monicelli, Paul Zimmerman; *C:* Tonino Delli Colli; *M:* Ennio Morricone.

Lovesick

A very-married New York psychiatrist (Moore) goes against his own best judgment when he falls in love with one of his patients (McGovern). Guiness is delightful as Moore's imaginary analyst, Sigmund Freud. The DVD is a big disappointment, having both soft focus and weak colors (which are also reddish). There is artifacting in dark scenes. The best thing going for the DVD is sound, which although mono and a little flat, is on a par with other video versions. —JO
Movie: ♪♪ **DVD:** ♪
Warner Home Video, Inc. (Cat #20011, UPC #085392001125). Full frame. Dolby Digital Mono. $14.98. Snapper. *LANG:* English. *FEATURES:* 28 chapter links.
1983 (PG) 98m/C Dudley Moore, Elizabeth McGovern, Alec Guinness, John Huston, Ron Silver; *D:* Marshall Brickman; *W:* Marshall Brickman; *C:* Gerry Fisher; *M:* Philippe Sarde.

Lucky Luke

Luke (Hill), the fastest gun in the West, brings law and order to the newly established hamlet of Daisy Town. He's aided by his horse Jolly Jumper (voice of Roger Miller) in this amiable spoof of westerns, both spaghetti and conventional. This one's even sillier than most of Hill's comedies. The DVD image could hardly look better. It's bright and clear—fine for the kiddies. —MM

Movie: 🎞🎞▶ **DVD:** 🎞🎞🎞
Simitar Entertainment (Cat #7361, UPC #082551736126). Full frame. PCM Stereo. $14.98. Keepcase. *LANG:* English. *FEATURES:* 8 chapter links • Production factoids • Terrence Hill filmography.
1994 (PG) 91m/C Terence Hill, Nancy Morgan, Ron Carey; *D:* Terence Hill; *W:* Morris, Rene Goscinny; *C:* Carlo Tafani, Gianfranco Transunto; *M:* David Grover, Aaron Schroeder; *V:* Roger Miller.

Lucky Texan

Please see review of *Winds of the Wasteland.*
Movie: 🎞▶
1934 61m/B John Wayne, George "Gabby" Hayes, Yakima Canutt; *D:* Robert North Bradbury; *W:* Robert North Bradbury; *C:* Archie Stout.

Lulu on the Bridge

This story is such a shaggy dog you wind up having to read credits like "Lou Reed As Not Lou Reed" to fulfill the questionable promise of the film's opening visual joke. It involves a men's room wall covered with glam shots of actresses you will eventually see in the film playing characters. Just in case you don't pick up on that right away, the writer-director makes sure to point out that it's coming up in his audio commentary. Izzy (Keitel) is a sax player caught in a crossfire, who embarks upon a mythopoetic adventure involving a dead body, a magic stone (since there's never such a thing as a magic rock in such movies, is there), and Mira Sorvino. Interspersed are philosophical arguments, both apparently casual and clearly staged, with the eclectic likes of Mandy Patinkin and Vanessa Redgrave—people who can make any amount of malarkey sound powerfully true. Self-reference rules, however, over this near-death experience. The film keeps to the music video standard of look and sound for those fusion fans who should appreciate its hip cameos, as well. As a new twist for value-added disc editions, this one's audio comment track is prefaced by a legal disclaimer usually reserved for talk and TV news shows! —JK

Movie: 🎞🎞🎞 **DVD:** 🎞🎞🎞▶
Trimark Home Video (Cat #7188D, UPC #031398718833). Full frame. Dolby 2.0 Surround. $24.99. Keepcase. *LANG:* English. *SUB:* Spanish; English; French. *CAP:* English. *FEATURES:* 24 chapter links • Interactive menus • Commentary: Paul Auster • Theatrical trailer • Previously unseen footage.
1998 (PG-13) 104m/C Harvey Keitel, Mira Sorvino, Willem Dafoe, Gina Gershon, Mandy Patinkin, Vanessa Redgrave, Victor Argo, Kevin Corrigan, Richard Edson; *D:* Paul Auster; *W:* Paul Auster; *C:* Alik Sakharov; *M:* Graeme Revell.

Lumiere and Company

To celebrate the 100th anniversary of the Lumiere Brothers' first films, 40 world-renowned film directors each produce a silent short film using the original Cinematographe camera. The Lumiere Brothers' invention held 17 meters of film, yielding approximately 50 seconds of silent film footage. An eclectic mix of mainly auteur directors (David Lynch, Spike Lee, Costa-Gavras, Wim Wenders, Claude LeLouch, etc.) are shown in a brief video presentation setting up their short film, which is followed by the film itself. DVD presentation is wildly uneven, with much of the connecting links nothing more than amateur home videos. The real focus is on the 40 different Lumiere-style silent shorts, which range from the inventive to the banal. —RT
AKA: *Lumiere et Compagnie.*
Movie: 🎞🎞▶ **DVD:** 🎞🎞
WinStar Home Entertainment (Cat #5013, UPC #720917050135). Full frame. AC3 - 2 Channel. $24.98. Keepcase. *LANG:* Silent, with both French and English commentary. *CAP:* English. *FEATURES:* 40 chapter markers, sorted by director • Trailer • Production credits.
1996 88m/C

The Lumiere Brothers' First Films

Historical presentation of 85 separate examples of the work of pioneer filmmakers Louis and Auguste Lumiere. Their invention, the Cinematographe, could hold 17 meters of film and deliver approximately 50 seconds of footage. For film buffs and historians, this collection of the brothers' work (1895–1905) comes with two separate commentaries—one in English (Bertrand Tavernier) and one in French (Thierry Fremaux). Virtually all of the examples presented are static shots of trains arriving at stations, people at work or what can best be described as home movies. The DVD presentation draws from source material that is uneven at times, but when considering the age of the 85 short films included in this compilation, the final result works quite well, with some of the examples crystal clear, remarkable in their detail and depth of field. —RT
Movie: 🎞🎞▶ **DVD:** 🎞🎞▶
Image Entertainment (Cat #K-106, UPC #738329010621). Full frame. AC3 - 2 Channel. $39.99. Snapper. *LANG:* Silent, with separate English and French audio commentaries. *FEATURES:* 10 chapters • Isolated music track • Separate English and French commentary tracks.
1997 62m/C

Lupin III: The Mystery of Mamo

This volume of a series about a vaguely supernatural adventurer is generally defect-free, puckish fun. The episodic story of capers involving fairly interchangeable magical objects is a crazy quilt of camp, sort of anime for *Night Stalker* fans.

Even the music seems right out of a '70s TV movie of the week. The translation leaves a lot to be desired, with cliche-ridden dialogue like, "deader than a doornail, there wasn't a shadow of a doubt." The drawing style, reminiscent of "Spy vs. Spy," leans much more towards animated manga (comic books) than true animation. The sound mix actually avoids the "bathroom acoustics" associated with dubbed Japanese animation. Oddly pretty moments are stumbled across like visual "Easter eggs" and a number of the backgrounds are parodies of famous paintings. —JK

Movie: 🎞🎞🎞 **DVD:** 🎞🎞🎞
Image Entertainment (Cat #ID4653SEDVD, UPC #014381465327). Widescreen (1.66:1) letterboxed. Dolby Digital Stereo. $24.99. Snapper. *LANG:* English. *CAP:* English. *FEATURES:* 18 chapter links • Interactive menus.
1978 102m/C *JP D:* Yasuo Ootsuka; *W:* Atsushi Yamotoya, Soji Yoshikawa.

M

With a fact-based story, Fritz Lang set the formula for the serial killer crime-horror film in 1931. Franz Beckert (Lorre) is a compulsive child murderer whose crimes paralyze a city. When the cops clamp down on the local underworld, the crooks decide to catch the killer themselves. Lang tells the story by intercutting between the various forces involved, but at the horrific heart of the story is Lorre's brilliant performance as a human monster. Though the film was released in the same year as Lugosi's *Dracula,* it's by far the more frightening of the two today. Lorre embodies many of the evils that Lugosi symbolizes. At the beginning, Lang uses starkly simple images—a ball, a balloon, an empty dinner plate—to convey the enormity of the crimes. Then things turn around with Lorre's haunted confession. At the end, when various parties comment on the terrible crimes they frame a debate that's still going on today. *M* is simply one of the world's great films, still suspenseful and entertaining. This DVD appears to have been made from the 1997 restoration. The image is very good with almost continuous faint vertical lines and a few other light marks. They're not serious flaws. The disc is notably brighter and sharper than older tapes. It's only marginally better than the Home Vision Cinema VHS tape. —MM

Movie: 🎞🎞🎞🎞 **DVD:** 🎞🎞🎞▶
Criterion Collection (Cat #30, UPC #037429126523). Full frame. $24.99. Keepcase. *LANG:* German. *SUB:* English. *FEATURES:* 18 chapter links • Liner notes by Stanley Kauffmann.
1931 111m/B *GE* Peter Lorre, Ellen Widmann, Inge Landgut, Gustav Grundgens, Otto Wernicke, Ernest Stahl-Nachbaur, Franz Stein, Theodore Loos, Fritz Gnass, Fritz Odemar, Paul Kemp, Theo Lingen, Georg John, Karl Platen, Rosa Valetti, Hertha von Walther, Rudolf Blumner; *D:* Fritz Lang; *W:* Fritz Lang, Thea von Harbou;

C: Fritz Arno Wagner, Gustav Rathje; **M:** Edvard Grieg.

Ma Saison Preferee

The relationship between middle-aged Antoine (Auteuil) and his sister Emilie (Deneuve, in one of her best performances) becomes more intense and complicated when their elderly mother Berthe (Villalonga) collapses and must move in with one of them. That's the catalyst that forces the two estranged siblings to reconnect, and tests the limits of Emilie's marriage. The film and the DVD are divided into four sections, each corresponding with a season. Director Techine gives his exteriors a pastel lightness that makes a smooth transition to disc. His night scenes are equally clear. Beyond a small amount of normal wear to the print, the image is flawless, but the yellow subtitles, outlined in black, are not on the lower bar of the letterbox. —*MM* **AKA:** My Favorite Season.
Movie: ♪♪♪ **DVD:** ♪♪♪
WinStar Home Entertainment (Cat #FLV5010, UPC #720917050102). Widescreen letterboxed. $29.98. Snapper. *LANG:* French. *SUB:* English. *FEATURES:* 4 chapter links.
1993 124m/C *FR* Daniel Auteuil, Catherine Deneuve, Marthe Villalonga, Jean-Pierre Bouvier, Chiara Mastroianni, Anthony Prada, Carmen Chaplin; **D:** Andre Techine; **W:** Andre Techine; **C:** Thierry Arbogast; **M:** Philippe Sarde.

Mad City

Out-of-work security guard Sam Baily (Travolta) goes postal, taking hostages in a museum while has-been journalist Max Brackett (Hoffman) manages to exploit Baily and hype the situation into a massive broadcast news event. The media circus that ensues provides social commentary on the questionable state of journalism. The relationship between Max and Sam carries most interest in Costa-Gravas's intense drama, while uneven tone and script inadequacies hold back satisfying story development. Talented supporting cast (Alda, Danner, Kirshner, Prosky) have little to do. Though improving on the VHS version, this DVD is of only average sharpness, and does have a few instances where the grain level seems a little high. Artifacts are there, but rare. Colors are very good, appearing both accurate and deep, with little bleed. Blacks are good. The 5.1 sound seems almost wasted on this dialogue-driven film that has very little in the way of Surround effects and is not heavy on its bass mix. —*JO*
Movie: ♪♪► **DVD:** ♪♪►
Warner Home Video, Inc. (Cat #15433, UPC #085391543329). Widescreen (2.35:1) anamorphic; full frame. Dolby Digital 5.1; Dolby Surround. $24.98. Snapper. *LANG:* English (DD5.1); French (DS). *SUB:* English; French; Spanish. *CAP:* English.

FEATURES: 32 chapter links • Production notes • Theatrical trailer and TV spots.
1997 (PG-13) 114m/C John Travolta, Dustin Hoffman, Mia Kirshner, Alan Alda, Blythe Danner, Robert Prosky, William Atherton, Ted Levine, Bill Nunn; **D:** Constantin Costa-Gavras; **W:** Tom Matthews; **C:** Patrick Blossier; **M:** Thomas Newman.

Mad Dog and Glory

Cast against type, Murray and De Niro play each other's straight man in this dark romantic comedy. Meek "Mad Dog" (De Niro) is an off-duty police photographer who happens upon a convenience store robbery and manages to save the life of Frank (Murray), obnoxious gangster by day, obnoxious stand-up comic by night. To settle up, Frank offers him Glory (Thurman) for a week. Eventually, Frank wants Glory back, forcing wimpy Mad Dog to either confront or surrender. Directed by McNaughton, who established himself with *Henry: Portrait of a Serial Killer*, the film is uneven and not of the knee-slapper ilk. But the performances are tight, including *NYPD Blue* Caruso as a cop buddy of De Niro's. For a no-frills disc, the video and audio transfer are surprisingly good. The picture is crisp, although some colors tend to be a bit washed-out (this might be an artistic choice, however). The soundtrack too, is also quite good, but it would benefit from a 5.1 remix. —*MJT*
Movie: ♪♪♪ **DVD:** ♪♪►
Image Entertainment (Cat #ID4278USDVD, UPC #014381427820). Widescreen (1.85:1) letterboxed. Dolby Digital Surround Sound. $29.99. Snapper. *FEATURES:* 16 chapter links.
1993 (R) 97m/C Robert De Niro, Uma Thurman, Bill Murray, David Caruso, Mike Starr, Tom Towles, Kathy Baker, Derek Anunciation, J.J. Johnston, Richard Belzer; **D:** John McNaughton; **W:** Richard Price; **C:** Robby Muller; **M:** Elmer Bernstein.

Mad Love

Even their most devoted fans will have to admit that Chris O'Donnell and Drew Barrymore have seldom been more smirky than they are in this dippy romance. He's solid student Matt; she's the free-spirited Casey. The filmmakers become a little uncomfortable when her free spirits are revealed to be serious mental illness, but that doesn't stop them from charging straight ahead. The disc looks and sounds fine, making good use of western landscapes in the second half and a fair rock music background. Even so, the bare-bones DVD is strictly for fans of the cast. —*MM*
Movie: ♪► **DVD:** ♪♪
Buena Vista Home Entertainment (Cat #17254, UPC #717951002471). Widescreen (1.85:1) letterboxed. Dolby Digital Surround Stereo. $29.99. Keepcase. *LANG:* English; French. *CAP:* English. *FEATURES:* 21 chapter links.
1995 (PG-13) 95m/C Chris O'Donnell, Drew Barrymore, Joan Allen, Kevin Dunn,

Jude Ciccolella, Amy Sakasitz, T.J. Lowther; **D:** Antonia Bird; **W:** Paula Milne; **C:** Fred Tammes.

Mad Max

Set on the stark highways of the post-apocalyptic near-future, the mother of the modern action film follows ex-cop Max (Gibson), who's seeking personal vengeance against the vicious outlaw Toecutter (Keays-Byrne) who killed his wife and child. The non-stop car chases are some of the best ever put on-screen, regardless of budget. But the budget was low and so the image is (and always has been) exceptionally grainy. Added to that, on DVD reds glow and moving diagonal lines break up regularly. The dubbing of American voices is even more apparent on DVD than it has been on tape. —*MM*
Movie: ♪♪♪► **DVD:** ♪♪
Image Entertainment (Cat #ID4082ORDVD, UPC #014381408225). Widescreen (2.35:1) letterboxed. $29.99. Snapper. *LANG:* English. *FEATURES:* 26 chapter links.
1980 (R) 93m/C *AU* Mel Gibson, Joanne Samuel, Hugh Keays-Byrne, Steve Bisley, Tim Burns, Roger Ward, Vincent Gil; **D:** George Miller; **W:** George Miller; **C:** David Eggby; **M:** Brian May.

Mad Max: Beyond Thunderdome

Bushwhacked in the post-apocalyptic wilderness, Max (Gibson) wanders into Bartertown ruled by Auntie (Turner). He becomes a gladiator in Thunderdome and finally encounters a band of feral children. The third film in the trilogy repeats themes from the first two and is the most visually sophisticated of them all, but it's also the least involving. (Part 2, *The Road Warrior*, is by far the best.) On DVD, the darkest subterranean scenes are grainy, but the widescreen transfer does justice to some impressive outdoor scenery. The sound is fine. —*MM*
Movie: ♪♪► **DVD:** ♪♪♪
Warner Home Video, Inc. (Cat #11519, UPC #085391151920). Full frame; widescreen letterboxed. Dolby Digital 5.1 Surround; Dolby Digital Surround. $24.98. Snapper. *LANG:* English; French. *SUB:* English; French; Spanish. *CAP:* English. *FEATURES:* 30 chapter links • Cast and crew thumbnail biographies • Production notes • Theatrical trailer.
1985 (PG-13) 107m/C *AU* Mel Gibson, Tina Turner, Helen Buday, Frank Thring Jr., Bruce Spence, Robert Grubb, Angelo Rossitto, Angry Anderson, George Spartels, Rod Zuanic; **D:** George Miller, George Ogilvie; **W:** Terry Hayes, George Miller; **C:** Dean Semler; **M:** Maurice Jarre.

Made for Each Other

A young lawyer and his bride find their honeymoon cancelled when the groom is urgently needed back at the office. Then their troubles really begin, leading to the near breakup of their burgeoning family.

The two perennially likeable stars (Stewart and Lombard) always knew how to make folks laugh or cry. Here they get to do both in a basically sappy film that got good reviews in its day. The delicately preserved Selznick melodrama is accompanied by a trailer for *Shop around the Corner*—though who knows why. The visuals on the 1939 films are constantly ever so slightly blurred, and the sound is as good as might be expected from a public domain product at a bargain bin price. Includes a companion documentary by Jerome Stern, "James Stewart on Film: A Biography" (1999), which is of much more recent vintage and tighter quality control, and packed with dreamy publicity shots and covers all the basics. The main menu has a nice "resume" option that actually picks up where you left off when you press it, which isn't always the case on DVDs. —*JK*
Movie: ♪♪♪ **DVD:** ♪♪♪
Delta/Laserlight (Cat #82006, UPC #018111998239). Full frame. Dual-channel Mono. $14.95. Keepcase. *LANG:* English; Spanish; Chinese; Japanese. *SUB:* Spanish; Chinese; Japanese. *FEATURES:* 24/10 chapter links • Interactive menus • 2-color picture disc • Intro by Tony Curtis • Theatrical trailer.
1939 94m/B James Stewart, Carole Lombard, Charles Coburn, Lucile Watson; **D:** John Cromwell; **W:** Jo Swerling; **C:** Leon Shamroy; **M:** Louis Forbes.

Made in America

High-energy, lightweight comedy stars Whoopi as a single mom whose daughter Long discovers her birth was the result of artificial insemination. More surprising is her biological dad: white, obnoxious, country-western car dealer Danson. Overwrought with obvious gags, basically a one-joke movie. Nonetheless, Goldberg and Danson chemically connect on-screen (and for a short time offscreen as well) while supporting actor Smith grabs comedic attention as Teacake, Long's best friend. Both Goldberg and Danson deserve better material. The DVD is a full-frame transfer, despite the fact that Warner had previously issued a widescreen laserdisc. The picture is not as sharp as the LD, but the color is more vibrant and the fresher image of the DVD is more appealing. —*JO*
Movie: ♪♪ **DVD:** ♪♪♪
Warner Home Video, Inc. (Cat #12652, UPC #085391265221). Full frame. Dolby Surround. $14.98. Snapper. *LANG:* English. *FEATURES:* 23 chapter links.
1993 (PG-13) 111m/C Whoopi Goldberg, Ted Danson, Will Smith, Nia Long, Paul Rodriguez, Jennifer Tilly, Peggy Rea, Clyde Kusatsu; **D:** Richard Benjamin; **W:** Holly Goldberg Sloan; **C:** Ralf Bode; **M:** Mark Isham.

Made Men

Bill Minuchi (Belushi) is hiding out with the Witness Protection Program in Harmony, OK (actually Utah), when four Chicago gangsters descend upon his farmhouse. The sheriff (Dalton) is crooked and the local meth dealer (Railsback) wants a piece of the action. All of them are after the $12 million that Bill claims to have taken from the mob. Then one of the gangsters (Beach) claims to be a fed. Director Morneau borrows some of his flashy visuals from the Wachowski brothers' *Bound*, and the story will remind viewers of *Reservoir Dogs* and *The Usual Suspects*. As the body count rises, the film wavers between comic violence and serious violence and finally almost becomes parody. On the commentary track, Morneau and Belushi (who also worked together on *Retroactive*) claim that much of the humor was improvised during the 24-day shooting schedule. In visual terms, the DVD has an expressive look that belies a low-powered budget, and a film that was made completely on location. Morneau uses rose and amber tints throughout. The stereo effects take full advantage of recurring train sounds. Despite a certain familiarity, this one's fun for fans of the genre. —*MM*
Movie: ♪♪♪ **DVD:** ♪♪♪
Columbia Tristar Home Video (Cat #04569, UPC #043396045699). Widescreen (1.78:1) letterboxed. Dolby Digital 5.1 Surround Stereo; Dolby Digital Surround Stereo. $28.95. Keepcase. *LANG:* English; Spanish. *SUB:* Spanish; English. *CAP:* English. *FEATURES:* 28 chapter links • Outtakes reel • Commentary: director Louis Morneau and James Belushi • Trailer and TV spot.
1999 (R) 90m/C James Belushi, Michael Beach, Timothy Dalton, Vanessa Angel, Steve Railsback; **D:** Louis Morneau; **C:** George Mooradian; **M:** Stewart Copeland.

Madigan

Realistic and exciting, this one is among the best of the behind-the-scenes urban police thrillers. Hardened NYC detectives (Widmark and Guardino) lose their guns to a sadistic killer and are given 72 hours to track him down. Fonda is the police chief none too pleased with their performance. DVD delivers the film pretty much as it looked in the theatre. The image is very sharp and what grain there is appears film-related. Artifacts are not a problem. The colors are accurate to the theatre, though some may feel they're weak. There is little bleed. Contrast is harsh, but again it feels right for the film and brightness levels stay consistent. Blacks are for the most part true. The mono sound is unspectacular, but more than adequate, and is also in line with the theatrical feel of the film. True film fans will want to read the production notes. —*JO*
Movie: ♪♪♪ **DVD:** ♪♪♪►
Universal Studios Home Video (Cat #20525, UPC #025192052521). Widescreen (2.35:1) letterboxed. Mono. $24.98. Keepcase. *LANG:* English; French. *SUB:* Spanish. *CAP:* English. *FEATURES:* 22 chapter links • Production notes • Talent bios • Theatrical trailer.
1968 101m/C Richard Widmark, Henry Fonda, Inger Stevens, Harry Guardino, James Whitmore, Susan Clark, Michael Dunn, Don Stroud; **D:** Donald Siegel; **W:** Abraham Polonsky; **C:** Russell Metty; **M:** Don Costa.

The Magic Voyage

Animated tale of a friendly bookworm named Pico who journeys with Columbus (voice of DeLuise) to the new world and convinces him that the world is round, not square, as the Navigator had theorized. Later, the magical firefly Marilyn (Cara) helps them bring gold back to Spain. This feature is bright, colorful, and silly enough for undemanding kids. More sophisticated animation fans—of any age—will not have the patience for it. On DVD, reds glow slightly though there is really nothing remarkable about the artwork or the forgettable songs. —*MM*
Movie: ♪♪ **DVD:** ♪♪
Image Entertainment (Cat #ID5701PZDVD, UPC #014381570120). Full frame. Dolby Digital Stereo. $14.99. Snapper. *LANG:* English. *FEATURES:* 12 chapter links.
1993 (G) 82m/C D: Michael Schoemann; **V:** Dom DeLuise, Mickey Rooney, Corey Feldman, Irene Cara, Dan Haggerty, Samantha Eggar.

Magical Mystery Tour

On the road with an oddball assortment of people, the Beatles take a fantasy bus tour across the English countryside. As the brief history accompanying this short film admits, it was originally intended to be a full-length feature, but the chaotic circumstances the band found itself in at the time made that impossible. In visual and conceptual terms, the film is often little more than a home movie. The big production numbers might have stood alone. This DVD was made from a 1988 restoration. The musical numbers sound terrific (particularly through headphones). Along with the extras, they make the disc a worthy addition to any Beatles fan's library. —*MM*
Movie: ♪♪♪ **DVD:** ♪♪♪►
MPI Home Video (Cat #DVD1538, UPC #030306153827). Full frame. Dolby Digital Stereo. $24.98. Keepcase. *LANG:* English. *SUB:* English; French; Spanish. *FEATURES:* 21 chapter links • Brief history of the film • Newsreels of Beatles.
1967 55m/C *GB* John Lennon, George Harrison, Ringo Starr, Paul McCartney, Victor Spinetti, Neil Innes, Jessie Robbins; **D:** John Lennon, George Harrison, Ringo Starr, Paul McCartney; **C:** Daniel Lacambre; **M:** John Lennon, George Harrison, Ringo Starr, Paul McCartney.

The Magnificent Seven

Western remake of Kurosawa's masterpiece *The Seven Samurai* places the action in a Mexican village. The seven gunfighters were mostly unknown at the time, but not for long. Followed by lesser sequels.

Movie: 🎬🎬🎬🎬 **DVD:** NYR
MGM Home Entertainment (Cat #906264). $24.99. Keepcase. *LANG:* English. *SUB:* French; Spanish. *CAP:* English.
1960 126m/C Yul Brynner, Steve McQueen, Robert Vaughn, James Coburn, Charles Bronson, Horst Buchholz, Eli Wallach, Brad Dexter; *D:* John Sturges; *W:* William Roberts; *C:* Charles B(ryant) Lang; *M:* Elmer Bernstein. *AWARDS: NOM:* Academy Awards '60: Best Original Dramatic Score.

Magnificent Warriors

Michelle Yeoh does an Indiana Jones turn as a dashing aviatrix in 1938 China. She battles the occupying Japanese and anyone else who tries to do her wrong. In one scene, she really looks like she's enjoying herself when she mows down a host of enemies with a .30 caliber machine gun. The DVD image has the pale cast you see in so many Hong Kong imports. Sound is thin and occasionally distorted. —*MM*
AKA: Zhong Hua Zhan Shi.

Movie: 🎬🎬▶ **DVD:** 🎬🎬
Tai Seng Video Marketing (Cat #5067). Widescreen letterboxed. Dolby Digital 5.1 Surround Stereo. $29.95. Keepcase. *LANG:* Cantonese; Mandarin. *SUB:* Traditional & Simplified Chinese; English; Japanese; Bahasa Indonesia & Malaysia; Thai; Korean; Vietnamese. *FEATURES:* 8 chapter links ▪ Cast thumbnail bios.
1987 88m/C *HK* Michelle Yeoh, Richard Ng, Lowell Lo, Derek Yee; *D:* David Chung; *W:* Tsang Kan Cheong; *C:* Ma Kwun Wah, Law Wan Shing.

Mah Jong Dragon

Hong Kong import revolves around gamblers, ex-cons, and revenge. It combines fairly graphic (but unconvincing) violence with silly comedy. This is a bare-bones DVD without chapter links. The sound is thin; the subtitles are burned in and very difficult to read. —*MM AKA:* Ma Qiao Fei Long; Mahjong Dragon.

Movie: 🎬 **DVD:** 🎬
Tai Seng Video Marketing (Cat #DVD-045). Widescreen letterboxed. Dolby Digital Mono. $49.95. Jewel case. *LANG:* Cantonese; Mandarin. *SUB:* English; Chinese.
1997 96m/C *HK* Josephine Siao, Ken Zhuo Zhao, Desiree Law, Sandra Ng; *D:* Corey Yuen, David (Dai Wei) Lai; *W:* Gee An.

Mahler

Typically strange Russell effort on the life of the great composer Mahler (Powell) begins with strong images that may leave some viewers wondering if they haven't stumbled across outtakes from *Lair of the White Worm*, which the director made more than a decade later. Strong acting and a genuine appreciation for the music counterbalance the narrative excesses.

On DVD, the film sounds better than it looks. Despite sumptuous sets and costumes, the image generally lacks brightness and sharp focus. Most noticeably in the interiors, deep browns, maroons, and blacks tend to blend together into undifferentiated dark masses. Recommended to the most dedicated fans of both Mahler and Russell only. —*MM*

Movie: 🎬🎬🎬 **DVD:** 🎬🎬▶
Image Entertainment (Cat #ID4528JFDVD, UPC #014381582822). Full frame. Dolby Digital Stereo. $24.99. Snapper. *LANG:* English. *FEATURES:* 16 chapter links.
1974 (PG) 110m/C Robert Powell, Georgina Hale, Richard Morant, Lee Montague, Terry O'Quinn; *D:* Ken Russell; *W:* Ken Russell; *C:* Dick Bush.

Major Payne

When the Marines have no more use for killing-machine Major Payne (Wayans), he reluctantly agrees to train the inept junior ROTC cadets at academically challenged Madison Academy. The misfit brigade contains the usual assortment of stock loser-types who follow the predictable "outcasts get even" plot to the letter. Wayans shows flashes of comic genius, but not nearly enough to make up for the one-dimensional characters and indifferent writing. Most of the showcase jokes involve the humiliation and degradation of the kids, always a laugh-riot. O.K., so this is another DVD that is far more than its film deserves. The picture is very sharp with low grain and artifact content. Colors are vibrant and accurate with little in the way of bleed. Blacks are true. The picture is also punchy thanks to the excellent contrast and brightness levels which stay comfortable throughout the film. The 5.1 sound adds lively energy though Surround effects are limited. Separation is very good as are fidelity and dynamics. —*JO*

Movie: 🎬 **DVD:** 🎬🎬🎬▶
Universal Studios Home Video (Cat #20513, UPC #025192051326). Widescreen (1.85:1) anamorphic. Dolby Digital 5.1; Dolby Surround (DS). $24.98. Keepcase. *LANG:* English (DD5.1); French (DS). *SUB:* Spanish. *CAP:* English. *FEATURES:* 18 chapter links ▪ Production notes ▪ Cast and filmmaker bios ▪ Theatrical trailer.
1995 (PG-13) 97m/C Damon Wayans, Karyn Parsons, William Hickey, Albert Hall, Steven Martini, Andrew Harrison Leeds, Scott "Bam Bam" Bigelow; *D:* Nick Castle; *W:* Dean Lorey, Gary Rosen, Damon Wayans; *C:* Richard Bowen; *M:* Craig Safan.

Male and Female

A group of British aristocrats are shipwrecked on an island and must allow their efficient butler (Meighan) to take command for their survival. Swanson is the spoiled rich girl who falls for her social inferior. Their rescue provides a return to the rigid British class system. The picture is based on the play *The Admirable Crichton* by James M. Barrie. This is quite

frankly one of the best transfers of an 80+-year-old film that I have yet seen. The blacks are crisp and do not bleed at all. Even the color tinting littered throughout the film does nothing to detract from the sharpness of the presentation. The stereo musical score is also an entertaining and well-recorded piece. —*MJT*

Movie: 🎬🎬🎬🎬 **DVD:** 🎬🎬🎬
Image Entertainment (Cat #ID5667DSDVD, UPC #014381566727). Full frame. Dolby Digital Stereo. $24.99. Snapper. *LANG:* Silent. *SUB:* English intertitles. *FEATURES:* 23 chapter links.
1919 110m/B Gloria Swanson, Thomas Meighan, Lila Lee, Raymond Hatton, Bebe Daniels; *D:* Cecil B. DeMille; *W:* Jeanie Macpherson; *C:* Alvin Wyckoff.

Malice

In a sleepy little college town, strange things sure do happen. Too bad rumpled college dean Andy Safian (Pullman) didn't see *Pacific Heights*. If he had, he would know that sometimes roommates are more trouble than they're worth, even if renovation on that old Victorian is getting expensive. Routine thriller throws out an inventive twist to keep things moving, but manages to be fairly predictable anyway. A fine DVD transfer delivers the goods with very good sharpness and low grain or artifacts even in darkly lit scenes. Colors are excellent, vibrant when they need to be and still able to differentiate between subtle hue changes. Contrast is excellent, and even heavily shadowed scenes have no distortion along the high-contrast lines. Brightness is also excellent. The music comes across very full-bodied and the Dolby Surround track delivers adequate ambience. The mix always puts the dialogue out front. —*JO*

Movie: 🎬🎬▶ **DVD:** 🎬🎬🎬
Polygram (Cat #8006336452, UPC #780063364522). Full frame. Dolby Surround. $29.95. Keepcase. *LANG:* English. *SUB:* French. *CAP:* English. *FEATURES:* 19 chapter links ▪ Theatrical trailer ▪ Cast and crew filmographies.
1993 (R) 107m/C Alec Baldwin, Nicole Kidman, Bill Pullman, Bebe Neuwirth, Anne Bancroft, George C. Scott, Peter Gallagher, Josef Sommer; *D:* Harold Becker; *W:* Aaron Sorkin, Scott Frank; *C:* Gordon Willis; *M:* Jerry Goldsmith.

Mallrats

Smith's better-financed but commercially disappointing follow-up to *Clerks* follows Jersey slackers T.S. (London) and Brodie (Lee) to the mall where they intend to wallow in food-court cookies and reclaim their girlfriends, who have recently dumped them. While wandering the stores in low-key and confused pursuit of their women, they encounter the usual band of bizarre inhabitants. Dialogue and sight gags are director-writer Smith's strong points; moving the plot along is not high on his list. The irreverent and honest commentary track details the problems that the production faced in its torturous journey from script to screen, and more than an hour of deleted scenes provides proof. Even with a larger budget, strong visuals are not the point and so the DVD is most valuable for all of the extras it contains, including footage of the commentary panel. Great stuff for fans of the filmmakers. —*MM*

Movie: ♪♪♪ **DVD:** ♪♪♪►

Universal Studios Home Video (Cat #20019, UPC #025192001925). Widescreen (1.85:1) anamorphic. Dolby Digital 5.1 Surround Stereo; Dolby Digital Surround Stereo. $34.98. Keepcase. *LANG:* English; French. *CAP:* English. *FEATURES:* 18 chapter links • Commentary: Smith, Affleck, Lee, Mews, Mosier, Pereira • Footage from commentary session • "Making of" featurette • Theatrical trailer • Music video "Build Me Up Buttercup" • Deleted scenes • Production stills.
1995 (R) 95m/C Priscilla Barnes, Stan Lee, Art James, Shannen Doherty, Jeremy London, Jason Lee, Claire Forlani, Michael Rooker, Renee Humphrey, Ben Affleck, Joey Lauren Adams, Jason Mewes, Brian O'Halloran, David Brinkley, Kevin Smith; *D:* Kevin Smith; *W:* Kevin Smith; *C:* David Klein; *M:* Ira Newborn.

Man from Utah / Sagebrush Trail

The Duke tangles with the crooked sponsor of some rodeo events in the first film. On the second half of this double bill—his second western—he's wrongly accused of killing a man and has to bust out of the hoosegow to clear his name. Stuntwork by the great Yakima Canutt.
Movie: ♪♪ **DVD:** NYR

Madacy Entertainment (Cat #990031). Full frame. Dolby Digital Mono. $9.99. Keepcase.
1934 55m/B John Wayne, George "Gabby" Hayes, Polly Ann Young, Yakima Canutt, Lafe (Lafayette) McKee; *D:* Robert North Bradbury; *W:* Lindsley Parsons; *C:* Archie Stout.

The Man in the Iron Mask

Lavish retelling of Alexandre Dumas's classic story boasts a stellar cast with teen heartthrob DiCaprio in a dual role. Tyrannical Louis XIV's (bad Leo) lust for women leads to a reunion of the retired Musketeers (Irons, Malkovich, Depardieu) bent on replacing Louis with his sensitive twin brother Phillippe (good Leo), a prisoner in the Bastille who is forced to wear a ghastly mask. D'Artagnan (Byrne), captain of the King's guards, must decide which side he's on, and his situation is further complicated by his forbidden love for the Queen Mother (Parillaud). First-time director Wallace, writer of *Braveheart,* allows the lushness of the production to overpower the swashbuckling. The widescreen version captures the well-chosen French locations, ornate costumes, and opulence of the royal court, including one sumptuous

masked ball where the many shades of gold and gilt positively shimmer on the screen. Those with smaller sets will want to view the full-frame version, to get the most out of Leo and his costars' many closeups. Like *Titanic,* this is an updated version of familiar escapist formulas, and it needs to be seen with the sharpest image possible. —*MM*

Movie: ♪♪♪ **DVD:** ♪♪♪

MGM Home Entertainment (Cat #906293, UPC #027616629326). Full frame; widescreen letterboxed. Dolby 5.1 Surround Stereo; Dolby Stereo Surround. $24.99. Keepcase. *LANG:* English (5.1); French (DSS). *SUB:* English; French; Spanish. *FEATURES:* Commentary: writer-director Randall Wallace • Alternate mask prototypes and drawings • 8-page booklet with trivia, production notes, etc. • 36 chapter links • Original theatrical trailer.
1998 (PG-13) 132m/C Leonardo DiCaprio, Gabriel Byrne, Jeremy Irons, John Malkovich, Gerard Depardieu, Anne Parillaud, Judith Godreche, Edward Atterton, Peter Sarsgaard, Hugh Laurie; *D:* Randall Wallace; *W:* Randall Wallace; *C:* Peter Suschitzsky; *M:* Nick Glennie-Smith.

A Man in Uniform

A look at the making of a sociopath. Henry (McCamus) is a quiet bank employee who moonlights as an actor. Then he gets his big break in the role of a self-righteous cop in a TV series. Only the lines between his make-believe cop and the real world begin to blur and Henry's intensity turns to violence. Fine performances lead to an unsatisfying film conclusion. Simitar's DVD does nothing to add to the enjoyment of this quirky little film. But, for Simitar, the sharpness is pretty good. Colors are off a bit, though, and the blacks lean toward gray with occasional grain. The stereo sound is thin on the bass end and somewhat muddy on the highs. —*JO* **AKA:** I Love a Man in Uniform.
Movie: ♪♪► **DVD:** ♪►

Simitar Entertainment (Cat #730, UPC #08255173023). Full frame. PCM Stereo. $24.95. Slipcase. *LANG:* English.
1993 (R) 99m/C *CA* Tom McCamus, Brigitte Bako, Kevin Tighe, David Hemblen, Alex Karzis, Graham McPherson, Richard Blackburn; *D:* David Wellington; *W:* David Wellington; *C:* David Franco; *M:* Ron Sures. *AWARDS:* Genie Awards '93: Best Actor (McCamus), Best Supporting Actor (Tighe).

Man of a Thousand Faces

A tasteful and touching portrayal of actor Lon Chaney, from his childhood with his deaf and mute parents to his success as a screen star, re-creates some of his most famous roles including the Phantom of the Opera and Quasimodo in *The Hunchback of Notre Dame.* Cagney is magnificent as the long-suffering film star who was a genius with makeup and mime. The DVD has some ghosting along contrast lines,

but other than that is a very good transfer of this 1957 B&W film. Overall the picture is very sharp, with blacks and graytones that convey a good feeling of depth. Brightness levels are consistent and except for that occasional ghosting, the contrast is also very good. The mono soundtrack doesn't have many dynamics, but there is no clipping and everything is fairly audible. —*JO*

Movie: ♪♪♪► **DVD:** ♪♪♪

Image Entertainment (Cat #ID4290USDVD, UPC #014381429022). Widescreen (2.35:1) letterboxed. Mono. $24.99. Snapper. *LANG:* English. *CAP:* English.
1957 122m/B James Cagney, Dorothy Malone, Jane Greer, Marjorie Rambeau, Jim Backus, Roger Smith, Robert Evans; *D:* Joseph Pevney; *W:* Ivan Goff; *C:* Russell Metty; *M:* Frank Skinner. *AWARDS:* *NOM:* Academy Awards '57: Best Story & Screenplay.

Man of the Year

Writer-director-star Dirk Shafer's autobiographical comedy is a quirky "mockumentary" about his 15 minutes of fame as *Playgirl* magazine's Man of the Year in 1992, but the real subject is his personal life and the eventual revelation of his homosexuality. The combination of non-fiction and drama is not completely successful. Though much of the story is genuinely funny, it lacks the surprise of really good documentaries. The acting is uneven with much overstatement but a strong performance by Vivian Paxton, and the film has a strong sense of condescension toward many of the female characters. Given the modest budget and the talking-heads format, it doesn't gain much on disc, but it is still extremely funny in places and provides some perceptive insights into sexual roles, the media, and celebrity in America. —*MM*

Movie: ♪♪► **DVD:** ♪♪►

WinStar Home Entertainment (Cat #FLV5063, UPC #720917506326). Widescreen, nominal letterboxing. $29.98. Keepcase. *FEATURES:* 8 chapter links.
1995 85m/C Dirk Shafer, Vivian Paxton, Claudette Sutherland, Michael Ornstein; *D:* Dirk Shafer; *W:* Dirk Shafer; *C:* Stephen Timberlake; *M:* Peitor Angell.

Man on the Moon

In some ways, Jim Carrey's portrayal of comedian Andy Kaufman is more effective on home video than it was in theatres. Kaufman was a TV star and his story seems more natural on the small screen. But the DVD is still an opportunity missed, because two of the deleted scenes, which are included as extras, should have been incorporated into the body of the film. They go a long way toward fleshing out the elliptical, somehow incomplete portrait of the man that was shown in the theatrical release. Overall, image and sound are no more than good. —*MM*

Movie: ♪♪♪ **DVD:** ♪♪►

Universal Studios Home Video Widescreen (2.35:1) anamorphic. Dolby Digital Stereo. $24.99. Keepcase. *LANG:* English. *FEATURES:* 20 chapter links • "Spotlight on location" featurette • Deleted scenes • Soundtrack presentation • Thumbnail biography of Kaufman.
1999 (R) 118m/C Jim Carrey, Courtney Love, Danny DeVito, Paul Giamatti, Vincent Schiavelli, Peter Bonerz, Marilu Henner, Judd Hirsch; *D:* Milos Forman; *W:* Scott Alexander, Larry Karaszewski; *C:* Terry Michos. *AWARDS:* Golden Globe Awards '00: Best Actor—Musical/Comedy (Carrey); *NOM:* Golden Globe Awards '00: Best Film—Musical/Comedy; MTV Movie Awards '00: Best Male Performance (Carrey); Screen Actors Guild Award '99: Best Actor (Carrey).

Man Wanted

Jack (Yam) is an undercover cop who becomes too friendly with Bill (Rongguang), the gangster whose organization he has infiltrated. Further complicating things, Jack is attracted to Penny (Chung), the girlfriend Bill treats with casual contempt. It's fairly standard stuff for a Hong Kong crime picture but it's handled energetically by the cast and director Chan. On DVD, the image and dubbing are acceptable for an import. Overall, this one looks about as good as comparable mid-level American movies, though it lacks the sparkle and the substance of *Hard Boiled* and *Organized Crime and Triad Bureau.* Brighter reds bleed throughout. —MM
AKA: Wang Jiao de Tian Kong.
Movie: 🎬🎬➤ *DVD:* 🎬🎬➤
Tai Seng Video Marketing (Cat #40054, UPC #601643400549). Widescreen letterboxed. Dolby Digital Stereo. $19.95. Keepcase. *LANG:* English; Cantonese; Mandarin. *SUB:* English. *FEATURES:* 17 chapter links • Cast and crew filmographies.
1994 92m/C *HK* Simon Yam, Christy Chung, Rongguang Yu; *D:* Benny Chan.

The Man Who Fell to Earth

Entertaining and technically adept cult classic about a man from another planet (Bowie, in a bit of typecasting) who ventures to Earth in hopes of finding water to save his family and drought-stricken planet. Instead he becomes a successful inventor and businessman, along the way discovering the human vices of booze, sex, and television. The DVD is the uncut 140-minute version of the film, which was deemed too long for the short attention span of American audiences. Picture sharpness varies on this Fox/Lorber DVD, as does the grain level and amount of color bleed. When a scene is brightly lit, everything is a little better, though never great. The colors seem accurate but are somewhat weak. Contrast and brightness levels are low, sometimes to the point of being uncomfortable. Blacks are also O.K. during bright scenes and then edge towards gray-green when dimmer. The

DVD's best feature may be its sound, which is only mono, but is fairly full and crisp enough to be enjoyable. —JO
Movie: 🎬🎬🎬➤ *DVD:* 🎬🎬
Fox/Lorber Home Video (Cat #FLV5039, UPC #720917503929). Widescreen (2.35:1) letterboxed. Mono. $29.98. Keepcase. *LANG:* English. *FEATURES:* Production notes • 9 chapter links • Filmographies.
1976 (R) 140m/C *GB* David Bowie, Candy Clark, Rip Torn, Buck Henry, Bernie Casey, Jackson D. Kane, Rick Riccardo, Tony Mascia; *D:* Nicolas Roeg; *W:* Paul Mayersberg; *C:* Anthony B. Richmond; *M:* John Phillips.

The Man Who Knew Too Little

Amiable parody of late-'50s Hitchcock would be more fun if it didn't wink at itself so constantly. Still, it's recommended for fans of the period. Midwestern video store manager Wallace Ritchie (Murray) goes to England to surprise his brother James (Gallagher). To keep Wallace out of the way during a big business dinner, James signs him up for an evening of participatory street theatre. Wallace blunders into an assassination scheme and, thinking it's part of the performance, heads off on a wild night's jaunt across London. Joanne Whalley is Lori, the professional spy who falls for the hapless amateur. Dodging bullets and eluding pursuers while never quite figuring out what's going on, Wallace is somewhere between James Bond and Inspector Clouseau. The film works surprisingly well on DVD, re-creating what director Jon Amiel calls "a slightly magical London." His comments are light and chatty, in the spirit of the film. No significant flaws show up in the nocturnal exteriors. Sound is fine. —MM
AKA: Watch That Man.
Movie: 🎬🎬🎬 *DVD:* 🎬🎬🎬
Warner Home Video, Inc. (Cat #15626, UPC #085391562627). Full frame; widescreen letterboxed. Dolby Digital 5.1 Surround. $24.98. Snapper. *LANG:* English; French. *SUB:* English; French; Spanish. *CAP:* English. *FEATURES:* 32 chapter links • Cast and crew thumbnail biographies • Theatrical trailer and TV spots • Commentary: director Jon Amiel.
1997 (PG) 94m/C Bill Murray, Peter Gallagher, Joanne Whalley, Alfred Molina, Richard Wilson, Geraldine James, John Standing, Anna Chancellor, Nicholas Woodeson, Simon Chandler; *D:* Jon Amiel; *W:* Howard Franklin, Robert Harrar; *C:* Robert Stevens; *M:* Chris Young.

The Man Who Knew Too Much

Hitchcock's first international hit established the storyline that he would exploit with such success in the decades that followed—an innocent caught between the villains and the authorities, who must save himself. This time, he also has to save his family. In the leads, Leslie Banks and Edna Best have the glittery sophisti-

cation of Nick and Nora Charles (from *The Thin Man,* made the same year), as a married couple on vacation in Switzerland. Hitch remade the film with Jimmy Stewart and Doris Day. This DVD version is made from a less-than-perfect print marred by scratches and flecks and a static-filled soundtrack. Even so, it's one of the Master's early best. —MM
Movie: 🎬🎬🎬 *DVD:* 🎬🎬➤
Delta/Laserlight (Cat #82023, UPC #018111202336). Full frame. $14.99. Keepcase. *LANG:* English. *SUB:* Spanish; Chinese; Japanese. *FEATURES:* 17 chapter links • Introduction by Tony Curtis • Theatrical trailer for *Saboteur.*
1934 75m/B *GB* Leslie Banks, Edna Best, Peter Lorre, Nova Pilbeam, Pierre Fresnay, Frank Vosper, Hugh Wakefield, Cicely Oates, D. A. Clarke-Smith, George Curzon, Henry Oscar, Wilfrid Hyde-White; *D:* Alfred Hitchcock; *W:* Emlyn Williams, Charles Bennett, A.H. Rawlinson, Edwin Greenwood, D. B. Wyndham-Lewis; *C:* Curt Courant.

The Man Who Would Be King

Grand, old-fashioned adventure is based on the classic story by Rudyard Kipling about two mercenary soldiers who travel from India to Kafiristan and set themselves up as kings. Splendid characterizations by Connery and Caine, and Huston's royal directorial treatment provides it with adventure, majestic sweep, and well-developed characters. This is a mighty fine transfer of a mighty fine adventure film. The DVD is very sharp with low grain and artifact levels. Colors are accurate and bleed-free even though they are subdued and detailed. Contrast supplies just enough punch to be enjoyable, but retain the film's original shadings. Brightness is consistent and comfortable, while the blacks are true. The sound packs considerable wallop, though only mono, and is both distinct and enjoyable. —JO
Movie: 🎬🎬🎬🎬 *DVD:* 🎬🎬🎬➤
Warner Home Video, Inc. (Cat #858, UPC #012569085824). Widescreen (2.35:1) anamorphic. Dolby Digital 2.0 Mono. $24.98. Snapper. *LANG:* English. *SUB:* English; French; Spanish. *CAP:* English. *FEATURES:* 36 chapter links • Production notes • 8 theatrical trailers • "Making of" featurette.
1975 (PG) 129m/C Sean Connery, Michael Caine, Christopher Plummer, Saeed Jaffrey, Shakira Caine; *D:* John Huston; *W:* Gladys Hill, John Huston; *C:* Oswald Morris; *M:* Maurice Jarre. *AWARDS:* *NOM:* Academy Awards '75: Best Adapted Screenplay, Best Art Direction/Set Decoration, Best Costume Design, Best Film Editing.

The Man with the Movie Camera

Dziga Vertov's 1929 experimental film can be seen as the first long-form music video, particularly with the addition of an adapted score as performed by the Alloy Orchestra. Vertov and his cameraman Mikhail Kaufman filmed ordinary people at work and play, awake and asleep, in Moscow, Kiev, and Odessa. The footage was then edited into an impressionistic "day-in-the-life" mosaic. It's absolutely fascinating both as an historical snapshot and as entertainment. The film is a textbook example of the power and importance of editing. Vertov's cutting rearranges time and motion and even viewers' relation to the film they're seeing. Echoes of his work can be seen in music videos. Though the DVD was not made from a perfect print, it's in excellent shape for a film of its age. The soundtrack is fine and the percussive score, reminiscent of Nino Rota's work, adds a crucial dimension. Unfortunately, that dimension is eliminated for those who choose to listen to Yuri Tsivian's commentary track. It's informative, dry, and professorial. Listen to it only after you've heard the score. Vertov's film would make an interesting double feature with Chaplin's *Modern Times*. —*MM* **AKA:** Chelovek s Kinoapparatom. **Movie:** 𝄢𝄢𝄢𝄢 **DVD:** 𝄢𝄢𝄢▶ Image Entertainment (Cat #ID4589DSDVD, UPC #014381458923). Full frame. Dolby Digital Stereo. $24.99. Snapper. *SUB:* English. *FEATURES:* 12 chapter links • Commentary track and liner notes by Yuri Tsivian. Produced for video by David Shepard. **1929 69m/B RU D:** Dziga Vertov; **W:** Dziga Vertov; **C:** Mikhail Kaufman; **M:** Pierre Henry.

The Man with Two Brains

Did you hear the one about the brilliant neuro-surgeon who falls in love with a woman in his laboratory? He only has two problems: dealing with his covetous wife and finding a body for his cerebral lover. There are plenty of laughs in this spoof of mad scientist movies that is redeemed from potential idiocy by the cast's titillating performances. Listen closely and you'll recognize the voice of Spacek as the brain-in-the-jar of Martin's dreams. This is one of the Warner budget DVDs that doesn't quite hack it. The picture is very soft, something that seems to be the case on a large number of full-frame transfers. There is some grain and artifacting as well, but nothing so aggravating as the lack of sharpness. Colors are a little weak, but not bad, and the minor bleed is tolerable. Contrast and brightness are in need of a boost and blacks are inconsistent. The mono sound is O.K. and certainly more than the DVD's picture quality deserves. —*JO* **Movie:** 𝄢𝄢𝄢 **DVD:** 𝄢▶ Warner Home Video, Inc. (Cat #16375, UPC #085391637523). Full frame. Mono. $14.98. Snapper. *LANG:* English. *CAP:* English. *FEATURES:* 28 chapter links. **1983 (R) 91m/C** Steve Martin, Kathleen Turner, David Warner, Paul Benedict, James Cromwell, Frank McCarthy, George Furth, Randi Brooks, Bernard Behrens, Stephanie Kramer; **Cameos:** Merv Griffin;

D: Carl Reiner; **W:** Carl Reiner, George Gipe, Steve Martin; **C:** Michael Chapman; **M:** Joel Goldsmith; **V:** Sissy Spacek.

The Manchurian Candidate

Political thriller about an American Korean War vet (Sinatra) who suspects that he and his platoon may have been brainwashed during the war, with his highly decorated, heroic friend (Harvey) programmed by commies to be an operational assassin. This influential thriller, based on Richard Condon's brilliant novel, is loaded with shocks, conspiracy, inventive visual imagery, and bitter political satire of naivete and machinations of the left and right. Excellent performances by an all-star cast, with Lansbury and Gregory particularly frightening. The black-and-white transfer is very sharp and detailed with no problems with grain of artifacts. Contrast is excellent, making the picture even crisper with just the right brightness. Good graytones and true blacks combine with that sharpness to enhance the depth. The mono sound is pretty good, and though lacking a little crispness, is definitely better than the VHS release. The interview with Sinatra and Frankenheimer deifies the star. —*JO* **Movie:** 𝄢𝄢𝄢𝄢 **DVD:** 𝄢𝄢𝄢▶ MGM Home Entertainment (Cat #90713, UPC #027616701329). Widescreen (1.85:1) letterboxed; full frame. Mono. $24.98. Keepcase. *LANG:* English; French; Spanish. *SUB:* English; French; Spanish. *CAP:* English. *FEATURES:* 36 chapter links • Cast and filmmaker interviews • Commentary: John Frankenheimer • Theatrical trailer. **1962 126m/B** Frank Sinatra, Laurence Harvey, Angela Lansbury, Janet Leigh, James Gregory, Leslie Parrish, John McGiver, Henry Silva, Khigh Deigh, James Edwards, Douglas Henderson, Albert Paulsen, Barry Kelley, Lloyd Corrigan, Whit Bissell, Joe Adams, Madame Spivy, Mimi Dillard, John Lawrence, Tom Lowell; **D:** John Frankenheimer; **W:** John Frankenheimer, George Axelrod; **C:** Lionel Lindon; **M:** David Amram. *AWARDS:* American Film Institute (AFI) '98: Top 100; Golden Globe Awards '63: Best Supporting Actress (Lansbury); National Board of Review Awards '62: Best Supporting Actress (Lansbury), National Film Registry '94; *NOM:* Academy Awards '62: Best Film Editing, Best Supporting Actress (Lansbury).

Mandragora

The director is an expatriate Pole. His third film is a stylized elaboration on his two previous documentaries about child exploitation in the post–Soviet Bloc world. This state-subsidized thriller about a throwaway delinquent strongly resembles a Central European *Hardcore*, featuring teen star Caslavka as a male Season Hubley. The title refers to a mythical plant that feeds on the emissions of men hanged at the gallows. Real street kids

contributed to the script and the cast mainly consists of non-professionals, acknowledged in the end credits by the statement, "We would like to thank all the parents and families, who agreed for (sic) their children to participate in this film." Svengali-like pimp Honza (Skripaz) bullies Marek (Caslavka) into prostitution, but Marek's smart young stablemate David (Svec) goads him into breaking away. Marek's dad finally comes searching for him in Prague's crime-infested red light district, once the trail has turned cold. The challenge the photographic original presented for those who digitized it becomes apparent from the first shot, of a dreary townscape at dusk interrupted by a bright display window getting smashed in and looted. Any reds, especially in the credit text, buzz a bit but don't bleed, though high-contrast backlighting washes out a shot here and there. Background surfaces display some artifacts, but foregrounds are fine and numerous dramatically lit club shots and demented boudoir scenes pull off quite well. A chapter three reel change introduces some distorted bass notes into the soundtrack that reappear momentarily from then on. Subtitles are white but in a large font. There is no main menu. —*JK* **Movie:** 𝄢𝄢𝄢▶ **DVD:** 𝄢𝄢𝄢 Water Bearer Films (Cat #WB4003, UPC #759259140035). Widescreen. Dolby Stereo. $29.99. Keepcase. *LANG:* Czech; English. *SUB:* English; Czech. *FEATURES:* 7 chapter links • Interactive menus • Full-color picture disc • *A Very Natural Thing* trailer. **1997 133m/C CZ** Miroslav Caslavka, David Svec, Miroslav Breu, Pavel Skripaz; **D:** Wiktor Grodecki; **W:** Wiktor Grodecki, David Svec; **C:** Vladimir Holomek; **M:** Wolfgang Hammerschmid.

Manhattan Murder Mystery

Larry and Carol Lipton (Allen and Keaton) are New Yorkers who become involved in a mystery when their neighbor dies under strange circumstances. The light, entertaining comedy steers clear of some of Allen's more irritating preoccupations and keeps the viewer engaged throughout. He has always worked better with Keaton than with any of his other leading ladies and if this isn't another *Annie Hall,* it's well worth another look. With the exception of the choice of image size (on the dual-sided disc), the DVD really is not much better than VHS tape. That's due to Allen's choice of a softish focus and unobtrusive lighting that tends to bathe nocturnal interiors in warm browns. —*MM* **Movie:** 𝄢𝄢𝄢 **DVD:** 𝄢𝄢 Columbia Tristar Home Video (Cat #71399, UPC #043396713994). Widescreen (1.85:1) letterboxed; full frame. $29.95. Keepcase. *LANG:* English; French. *SUB:* English; French. *CAP:* English. *FEATURES:* 28 chapter links. **1993 (PG) 105m/C** Woody Allen, Diane Keaton, Anjelica Huston, Alan Alda, Jerry

Adler, Ron Rifkin, Joy Behar, Lynn Cohen, Melanie Norris; **D:** Woody Allen; **W:** Woody Allen, Marshall Brickman; **C:** Carlo Di Palma. *AWARDS: NOM:* Golden Globe Awards '94: Best Actress—Musical/Comedy (Keaton).

Maniac

Director William Lustig collaborated with writer-star Joe Spinell and effects wizard Tom Savini in the production of this above-average psycho-killer tale. The plot is loosely based, in part, on the New York Son of Sam murders. Frank Zito (Spinell) is a fat, pathetic loner who murders and scalps women. Some of the physical details of his life and crimes ring true, but the psychological side is a collection of pop cliches, all based on another bad mommy. In the end, it's one of the best examples of a limited and distasteful genre. Spinell and costar Caroline Munro would play similar characters in *The Last Horror Movie*.
Movie: ♪♪➤ **DVD:** NYR
Elite Entertainment, Inc. (Cat #1981). Widescreen (1.85:1) letterboxed. Dolby Digital Surround Stereo; Dolby Digital 5.1 Surround Stereo. $29.95. Keepcase. *FEATURES:* Commentary: Lustig, Marinell, Luke Walker, Tom Savini ✦ Deleted scene ✦ Promotional reel for unproduced sequel.
1980 91m/C Joe Spinell, Caroline Munro, Gail Lawrence, Kelly Piper, Tom Savini, Rita Montone, Hyla Marrow, William Lustig, Sharon Mitchell; **D:** William Lustig; **W:** C.A. Rosenberg, Joe Spinell; **C:** Robert Lindsay; **M:** Jay Chattaway.

Maniac / Narcotic

These "education" films were the first widely distributed exploitation of the sound era. Despite the undeniable loosening of societal strictures against the depiction of certain subjects, they're still enjoyable guilty pleasures. In *Maniac*, a mad doctor attempts to raise the dead and has visions of hell; showgirls strut around in their underwear; eyeballs are eaten. You get the idea. *Narcotic* describes the moral collapse of a medical student who dabbles in drug use. Again, the story is punctuated with stock footage that has nothing to do with the story but complements director Esper's perverse predilections. On his commentary track, author Bret Wood (*Forbidden Fruit: The Golden Age of the Exploitation Film*) is knowledgeable. He appreciates these films for what they are and doesn't try to make them anything more than that. The DVD image is marred by near continuous scratches and lines, but these low-budget flicks have never been known for striking visuals, so the shadowy flickers and semi-audible sound are part of their charm. —*MM* **AKA:** Narcotic.
Movie: ♪♪♪ **DVD:** ♪♪➤
Kino on Video (Cat #K142, UPC #738329014223). Full frame. $29.95. Keepcase. *LANG:* English. *FEATURES:* 33 chapter links ✦ Original theatrical trailer

for *Maniac* ✦ Commentary: Bret Wood ✦ Censorship records ✦ Photo gallery ✦ Excerpt from the screenplay of *Maniac* ✦ Video clip from *Maciste in Hell*, featured in *Maniac*. *Maniac* runs 67 minutes; *Narcotic*, 52 minutes.
1934 119m/B Bill Woods, Horace Carpenter, Ted Edwards, Thea Ramsey, Jennie Dark, Marcel Andre, Celia McGann; **D:** Dwain Esper; **W:** Hildegarde Stadie; **C:** William C. Thompson.

Maniac Cop

Great action/horror film from director Lustig and writer Cohen features a strong urban feel, thanks to its New York locations, an incredible B-movie cast, and better-than-B stunt work. Hacked, slashed, and left for dead, officer Matt Cordell returns as an unhinged killer. Features a cameo by *Evil Dead* director Sam Raimi as a TV reporter. Followed by two sequels. Elite's DVD transfer is pretty good; the main problem is a little grain and color bleed, maybe due to slight oversaturation of colors, which are at times very vibrant. Blacks are very good, as are the contrast and brightness levels. The stereo soundtrack is crisp, and while lacking real Surround, the imaging and separation is excellent, adding a lot of punch during the action sequences. Menu selection (especially chapter search) is a little slow and clunky and the additional footage from Japanese TV is extremely soft. —*JO*
Movie: ♪♪♪ **DVD:** ♪♪
Elite Entertainment, Inc. (Cat #EE 3426, UPC #790594342623). Widescreen (1.85:1) letterboxed. Dolby Digital Stereo. $29.95. Keepcase. *LANG:* English. *SUB:* English. *FEATURES:* 31 chapter links ✦ Theatrical trailers and TV spots (foreign and domestic) ✦ Additional scenes for Japanese television ✦ Commentary: Lustig, Cohen, Chattaway, and Campbell.
1988 (R) 92m/C Tom Atkins, Bruce Campbell, Laurene Landon, Richard Roundtree, William Smith, Robert Z'Dar, Sheree North, Sam Raimi; **D:** William Lustig; **W:** Larry Cohen; **C:** Vincent Rabe.

The Manxman

Hitchcock's final silent film is a romantic melodrama about ambition and infidelity on the Isle of Man. Fisherman Pete (Brisson) and lawyer Philip (Keen) both love Kate (Ondra). While Pete is at sea, the other two have an affair. Marriage and complications follow. On DVD, the image is dim and dark, and the musical soundtrack is buzzy. Extras are minimal. —*MM*
Movie: ♪♪ **DVD:** ♪
Delta/Laserlight (Cat #82039, UPC #018111997133). Full frame. $14.99. Keepcase. *LANG:* English intertitles. *SUB:* Spanish; Japanese; Chinese. *FEATURES:* 21 chapter links.
1929 129m/B *GB* Carl Brisson, Anny Ondra, Malcolm Keen, Randle Ayrton; **D:** Alfred Hitchcock; **W:** Hall Caine, Eliot Stannard; **C:** Jack Cox.

Marat/Sade

The infamous Marquis de Sade, confined to an asylum, directs the other inmates in a surrealistic re-enactment of the bloody assassination of French revolutionary Jean-Paul Marat. The video transfer features bright colors, but falls short with muddied and poorly defined blacks. The video also shows some signs of aging and deterioration. The audio transfer is very unimpressive and features tinny dialogue and harsh sound effects. —*MJT* **AKA:** Persecution and Assassination of Jean-Paul Marat as Performed by the Inmates of the Asylum of Charenton under the Direction of the Marquis De Sade.
Movie: ♪♪➤ **DVD:** ♪♪
Image Entertainment (Cat #ID4523WB DVD, UPC #014381452327). Full frame. Dolby Digital Stereo. $24.99. Snapper. *LANG:* English. *FEATURES:* 16 chapter links.
1966 (R) 115m/C *GB* Patrick Magee, Clifford Rose, Glenda Jackson, Ian Richardson, Brenda Kempner, Ruth Baker, Michael Williams; **D:** Peter Brook; **C:** David Watkin; **M:** Richard Peaslee.

Marcello Mastroianni: I Remember

With an abundance of charm, wit, and thoughtful introspection, Mastroianni looks back and reminisces about his life and work. While disavowing the myth of the Latin lover, he brings vivacity, intelligence, and modesty to this delightful memoir directed by Anna Maria Tato (his companion since 1977). Also included are rarely seen screen tests and film clips. Although long and tedious at times, it is ultimately rewarding. The video transfer is very muddied; blacks tend to bleed and lose their distinction. Similarly, the soundtrack is a bit muffled at times, but dialogue is understandable for the most part. —*MJT*
Movie: ♪♪♪ **DVD:** ♪♪➤
Fox/Lorber Home Video (Cat #FLV5206, UPC #720917520629). Full frame. Dolby Digital Stereo. $29.98. Keepcase. *LANG:* Italian. *SUB:* English. *FEATURES:* 18 chapter links ✦ Production credits ✦ Filmographies and awards ✦ Theatrical trailers ✦ Weblinks.
1997 199m/C *IT* Marcello Mastroianni; **D:** Anna Maria Tato; **C:** Giuseppe Rotunno.

March of the Wooden Soldiers

The Mother Goose tale about the secret life of Christmas toys stars Laurel and Hardy as Santa's helpers who must save Toyland from the wicked Barnaby. **AKA:** Babes in Toyland.
Movie: ♪♪♪ **DVD:** NYR
Goodtimes Entertainment (Cat #81056). Full frame. $14.99. Snapper. *FEATURES:* Colorized.
1934 73m/B Stan Laurel, Oliver Hardy, Charlotte Henry, Henry (Kleinbach) Bran-

don, Felix Knight, Jean Darling, Johnny Downs, Marie Wilson; **D:** Charles R. Rogers, Gus Meins; **W:** Frank Butler, Nick Grinde; **C:** Art Lloyd, Francis Corby.

Maria Stuarda

This curious made-for-TV production combines elements of Donizetti's opera and Friedrich Schiller's stage play to tell the story of the conflicts between Queen Elizabeth (played by Kamila Magalova, sung by Huguette Tourangeau) of England and Mary Stuart (played by Magdalena Vasaryova, sung by Joan Sutherland). Some scenes are spoken and some are sung. The production is set on historical locations and natural exteriors. Luciano Pavarotti sings the role of the Earl of Leicester. Obviously, this kind of hybrid is not going to appeal to all viewers but it ought to find an audience somewhere in the cross section of fans shared by *Masterpiece Theatre* and the Metropolitan Opera. On DVD, the costumes, ornate makeup, and sets look fine and the sound is excellent, though I must admit here that I am not an opera fan. —*MM*
Movie: 🎜🎜 **DVD:** 🎜🎜🎜
Image Entertainment (Cat #ID5656CLDVD, UPC #014381565621). Full frame. Uncompressed PCM Stereo. $24.99. Snapper. *LANG:* German. *SUB:* English. *FEATURES:* 16 chapter links.
1988 ?m/C Kamila Magalova, Magdalena Vasaryova; **D:** Petr Weigl; **V:** Joan Sutherland, Luciano Pavarotti, Huguette Tourangeau.

Mark of the Devil

German historical exploitation, set in Austria 1770, is infamous for its prolonged scenes of torture aimed mostly at women. Pock-faced Reggie Nalder, known best as the assassin in Hitchcock's *The Man Who Knew Too Much*, is fine as the rapacious witchfinder Albino. Though the script is said to be based on true stories, the film is slow and talky between gore scenes. The incongruous soundtrack adds nothing, and the violence is handled with such relish that the film leaves a bad taste in the mouth. The Anchor Bay DVD, like the VHS tape, has been restored to remarkable, if lamentable clarity. The high-contrast colors and heavy blacks come from the original, not the transfer. —*MM* **AKA:** Burn, Witch, Burn; Brenn, Hexe, Brenn; Austria 1700; Satan; Hexen bis aufs Blut Gequaelt.
Movie: 🎜🎜 **DVD:** 🎜🎜
Image Entertainment (Cat #DV10601, UPC #013131060195). Widescreen (1.66:1) letterboxed. Dolby Digital Stereo. $29.99. Keepcase. *LANG:* English. *FEATURES:* 12 chapter links.
1969 97m/C GB GE Herbert Lom, Olivera Vuco, Udo Kier, Reggie Nalder, Herbert Fux, Michael Maien, Ingeborg Schoener, Johannes Buzalski, Gaby Fuchs, Adrian Hoven; **D:** Michael Armstrong; **W:** Sergio Casstner, Adrian Hoven; **C:** Ernst W. Kalinke; **M:** Michael Holm.

Mark of Zorro

The silent version of the oft-filmed story may not be the best, but the sense of athletic fun that star Douglas Fairbanks brings is still enjoyable. As both the fey aristocrat Don Diego and his black-masked alter ego Zorro, he is a delight. The acting conventions of the time are delightfully dated now. The same cannot be said of the print that the DVD was made from. It's so nicked up—with a dark stain prominent in an early scene—that the producers have actually added scratches to the main menu to give it a comparably distressed look. In most other scenes, the sepia and blue tinting is clear enough. If the organ score is true to the original, it's hard to take for the full running time. —*MM*
Movie: 🎜🎜🎜 **DVD:** 🎜🎜
Image Entertainment (Cat #ID4727DSDVD, UPC #014381472721). Full frame. Dolby Digital Stereo. $24.99. Snapper. *FEATURES:* 15 chapter links.
1920 80m/B Douglas Fairbanks Sr., Marguerite de la Motte, Noah Beery Sr.; **D:** Fred Niblo; **W:** Douglas Fairbanks Sr.; **C:** William McGann, Harris (Harry) Thorpe.

Marked for Death

Having killed a prostitute, DEA agent Seagal decides it's time to roll out the white picket fence in the 'burbs with the little woman and brood. Trouble is, a bunch of guys with dreadlocks don't approve of his early retirement, and the Jamaican gangsters plan to send him and his family to the great Rasta playground in the sky. Whereupon the Stevester kicks and punches and wags his ponytail. Much blood flows with a decent twist near the end. Tunes by Jimmy Cliff. This good-looking DVD has plenty of sharpness and low grain even in the numerous darker scenes. The colors are very good; accurate with very little bleed. Contrast and brightness levels are very good and the blacks stay true under all lighting conditions. The 5.1 sound contains a good mix of Surround effects and is energy packed, with plenty of bass and crisp highs. —*JO* **AKA:** Screwface.
Movie: 🎜 **DVD:** 🎜🎜🎜
20th Century Fox (Cat #4109067, UPC #086162090677). Widescreen (1.85:1) letterboxed. Dolby Digital 5.1; Stereo. $29.98. Keepcase. *LANG:* English (DD5.1); French (stereo). *SUB:* English; Spanish. *CAP:* English. *FEATURES:* 10 chapter links • Theatrical trailer.
1990 (R) 93m/C Steven Seagal, Joanna Pacula, Basil Wallace, Keith David, Danielle Harris, Arlen Dean Snyder, Teri Weigel; **D:** Dwight Little; **W:** Mark Victor, Michael Grais; **C:** Ric Waite; **M:** James Newton Howard.

Mars Attacks!

Only director Burton could make a movie based on a series of 1960s trading cards. Intentionally tacky, this huge-scale epic spoof of monster, sci-fi, and disaster flicks finds moronic President Dale (Nicholson), his frigid wife (Close), and a cast of thousands battling the greenskinned invaders. Jack's back for a second role as Vegas hotel developer Art Land, who tries to cash in on the opportunities the invasion brings. Plot is relatively nonexistent and zig-zags wildly throughout but the gist is that the aliens are bent on destroying the population, and have little trouble battling the bumbling humans. The DVD transfer is very sharp, but not quite as sharp as the Warner letterboxed laserdisc release. Grain and artifact levels are low. Where the DVD really shines, however, is the way it delivers the incredible colors that Burton has packed this film with. Those colors are accurate and very, very vibrant, without a hint of bleed. The blacks are also true and the punchy contrast and brightness levels are just right for this film. The 5.1 sound does a good job with the music, which is full-bodied and dynamic. Elman's score is so interesting that utilizing the isolated music track, without the dialogue, gives the film a whole new twist and is great at parties. The rest of the sound is good with decent separation, but not as many Surround effects as you'd expect. —*JO*
Movie: 🎜🎜 **DVD:** 🎜🎜🎜
Warner Home Video, Inc. (Cat #14480, UPC #085391448020). Widescreen (2.35:1) anamorphic; full frame. Dolby Digital 5.1; Dolby Surround. $24.98. Snapper. *LANG:* English (DD5.1; DS); French (DD5.1; DS); Spanish (DS). *SUB:* English; French; Spanish. *CAP:* English. *FEATURES:* 38 chapter links • Isolated music score • Production notes • 2 theatrical trailers.
1996 (PG-13) 106m/C Jack Nicholson, Glenn Close, Martin Short, Pierce Brosnan, Lukas Haas, Sarah Jessica Parker, Michael J. Fox, Natalie Portman, Rod Steiger, Paul Winfield, Annette Bening, Sylvia Sidney, Danny DeVito, Joe Don Baker, Pam Grier, Jim Brown, Lisa Marie; **Cameos:** Tom Jones; **D:** Tim Burton; **W:** Jonathan Gems; **C:** Peter Suschitzky; **M:** Danny Elfman. *AWARDS: NOM:* MTV Movie Awards '97: Best Fight (Jim Brown/A Martian).

Marvin's Room

Overqualified cast never really connects with weepy material. Sensitive Bessie (Keaton) is living in Orlando where she's been caring for both her bedridden father (Cronyn) who's been dying for 20 years and her eccentric aunt Ruth (Verdon). Then her doctor (De Niro) gives her bad news. Bessie has leukemia and needs a bone marrow donor, so she must call on her estranged sister Lee (Streep). Talk about timing: Lee's rebellious son Hank (DiCaprio) has just burned down their house. The DVD image is O.K., but like the theatrical release, it's often dark, and so the disc is not markedly better than VHS tape. Sound, however, is excellent. —*MM*
Movie: 🎜🎜 **DVD:** 🎜🎜
Miramax Pictures Home Video (Cat #16325, UPC #717951001429). Widescreen (1.85:1) letterboxed. Dolby Digital

Surround Stereo. $29.99. Keepcase. *LANG:* English. *CAP:* English. *FEATURES:* 19 chapter links.
1996 (PG-13) 98m/C Diane Keaton, Meryl Streep, Leonardo DiCaprio, Hume Cronyn, Gwen Verdon, Hal Scardino, Robert De Niro, Dan Hedaya, Margo Martindale, Cynthia Nixon; *D:* Jerry Zaks; *W:* Scott McPherson; *C:* Piotr Sobocinski; *M:* Rachel Portman. *AWARDS: NOM:* Academy Awards '96: Best Actress (Keaton); Golden Globe Awards '97: Best Actress—Drama (Streep); Screen Actors Guild Award '96: Best Actress (Keaton), Best Supporting Actress (Verdon), Cast.

Mary Poppins

Magical English nanny (Andrews, in her screen debut) arrives one day on the East Wind and takes over the household of a very proper London banker. She introduces her two charges to her friends and family, including Bert the chimney sweep (Van Dyke), and eccentric Uncle Albert (Wynn). She also changes the lives of everyone in the family. From her they learn that life can always be happy and joyous if you take the proper perspective. A Disney classic that hasn't lost any of its magic. Look for the wonderful sequence where Van Dyke dances with animated penguins. I first saw *Mary Poppins* on an Easter Sunday in my yoot, and despite my recent leanings towards more sinister and off-the-wall forms of cinema, I still love this film. The DVD is so sharp and colorful that it even surpasses the fine Disney Archive laserdisc of a few years back. The 5.1 sound is an excellent remix of the audio elements and the film has never looked or sounded better. —*JO*
Movie: 🎵🎵🎵▶ *DVD:* 🎵🎵🎵🎵
Buena Vista Home Entertainment (Cat #13854, UPC #717951000255). Widescreen (1.85:1) letterboxed. Dolby Digital 5.1. $29.99. Keepcase. *LANG:* English. *CAP:* English. *FEATURES:* 25 chapter links.
1964 139m/C Julie Andrews, Dick Van Dyke, Ed Wynn, Hermione Baddeley, David Tomlinson, Glynis Johns, Karen Dotrice, Matthew Garber; *D:* Robert Stevenson; *W:* Bill Walsh, Whip Wilson; *C:* Edward Colman; *M:* Richard M. Sherman, Robert B. Sherman. *AWARDS:* Academy Awards '64: Best Actress (Andrews), Best Film Editing, Best Song ("Chim Chim Cheree"), Best Visual Effects, Best Original Score; Golden Globe Awards '65: Best Actress—Musical/Comedy (Andrews); *NOM:* Academy Awards '64: Best Adapted Screenplay, Best Art Direction/Set Decoration (Color), Best Color Cinematography, Best Costume Design (Color), Best Director (Stevenson), Best Picture, Best Sound, Best Original Score.

Mary Shelley's Frankenstein

Director-star Branagh's take on the famous novel is a glorious mess of a movie—energetic to a fault, handsomely produced, and often visually astonishing.

A stilted, creaky script and an unsteady pace lie at the heart of the film's problems. Victor's (Branagh) childhood and family life are laboriously detailed. The centerpiece lab scenes (chapters 9 and 10) are real lulus involving assorted fluids, industrial-strength acupuncture, and a Rube Goldberg contraption that looks like an old-fashioned copper bathtub. The result is the Creature (De Niro), scarred, innocent, frightened, and strong. Some of the early scenes are staged on huge but virtually empty sets that leave the viewer wondering where all the furniture is. In the middle section, where several important events take place, the pace is so hurried that the plot makes virtually no sense. As both actor and director, Branagh seems barely under control. He and Helena Bonham Carter, who were having a well-publicized affair at the time, might have found their characters on the cover of a paperback bodice-ripper. The relative clarity of DVD over tape only magnifies the film's many flaws. Both image and sound equal the theatrical release. —*MM* *AKA:* Frankenstein.
Movie: 🎵🎵▶ *DVD:* 🎵🎵🎵
Columbia Tristar Home Video (Cat #78719, UPC #043396787193). Widescreen (1.85:1) letterboxed; full frame. Dolby Digital 5.1 Surround Stereo; Dolby Digital Stereo. $29.95. Keepcase. *LANG:* English; French; Spanish. *SUB:* English; French; Spanish. *FEATURES:* 28 chapter links • Theatrical trailers.
1994 (R) 123m/C Kenneth Branagh, Robert De Niro, Helena Bonham Carter, Tom Hulce, Aidan Quinn, John Cleese, Ian Holm, Richard Briers, Robert Hardy, Cherie Lunghi, Celia Imrie, Trevyn McDowell; *D:* Kenneth Branagh; *W:* Frank Darabont, Steph Lady; *C:* Roger Pratt; *M:* Patrick Doyle. *AWARDS: NOM:* Academy Awards '94: Best Makeup.

Mask

Based-on-a-true-story tearjerker shows us the life of Rocky Dennis (Stoltz), afflicted with Craniodiaphyseal Dysplasia (the same disease as the legendary "Elephant Man"), a teen who manages to make every minute count with an unflagging, upbeat spirit. It's a curious choice of a film project for director Peter Bogdanovich (*The Last Picture Show*), who nevertheless manages to skirt the maudlin melodrama that lies within, and pulls strong performances from both Cher and Eric Stoltz, who plays the entire film buried under pounds of prosthetic makeup devices. A DVD opportunity missed as this presentation delivers a solid video image, but nothing more. The audio is pedestrian, and this film begs for a behind-the-scenes look at the preparation that went into Stoltz's incredible makeup. A commentary track featuring Bogdanovich and Stoltz, at the very least, would have been a welcome addition. —*RT*
Movie: 🎵🎵▶ *DVD:* 🎵🎵▶
Image Entertainment (Cat #4293US, UPC #014381429329). Widescreen letter-

boxed. Dolby Digital Mono. $24.99. Snapper. *LANG:* English. *FEATURES:* 16 chapter markers • Director and actor's filmographies.
1985 (PG-13) 120m/C Cher, Sam Elliott, Eric Stoltz, Estelle Getty, Richard Dysart, Laura Dern, Harry Carey Jr., Lawrence Monoson, Marsha Warfield, Barry Tubb, Andrew (Andy) Robinson, Alexandra Powers; *D:* Peter Bogdanovich; *W:* Anna Hamilton Phelan; *C:* Laszlo Kovacs. *AWARDS:* Academy Awards '85: Best Makeup; Cannes Film Festival '85: Best Actress (Cher).

The Mask

Adolescent supernatural comedy with lollapalooza special effects is Carrey's follow-up to *Ace Ventura*. Mild-mannered bank clerk Carrey discovers an ancient mask that has supernatural powers. Upon putting on the mask, he turns into one truly animated guy. He falls for a dame mixed up with gangsters and from there on, our hero deals not only with the incredible powers of the mask, but with hormones and bad guys as well. It's based on the Dark Horse comic book series and was originally conceived as a horror flick. But director Russell, who gave Freddy Krueger a sense of humor, recast this one as a hellzapoppin' cartoon-action black comedy. Carrey's rubber face is an asset magnified by the breakthrough special effects courtesy of Industrial Light and Magic. With an almost flawless color transfer, this is a near-showpiece DVD that is exceptionally sharp and has no trouble in presenting the film's incredible colors both vibrantly and pretty much without any bleed. The contrast and brightness levels are excellent and when combined with the colors have no problem in maintaining the film's cartoon-like appearance as in the theatre. Blacks are dead-on as well. The energetic 5.1 sound has a beefed-up subwoofer track that sends the bass through with power to spare. The highs and mids are also excellent and the Surround mix is cranking almost constantly. Basically, everything sounds and looks great. —*JO*
Movie: 🎵🎵🎵 *DVD:* 🎵🎵🎵🎵
New Line Home Video (Cat #N4011, UPC #794043401121). Widescreen (1.85:1) letterboxed; full frame. Dolby Digital 5.1; Stereo. $24.98. Snapper. *LANG:* English (DD5.1); French (Stereo). *SUB:* English; French; Spanish. *CAP:* English. *FEATURES:* 31 chapter links • Deleted scenes • Commentary: director • Theatrical trailer.
1994 (PG-13) 100m/C Jim Carrey, Cameron Diaz, Peter Greene, Peter Riegert, Amy Yasbeck, Orestes Matacena, Richard Jeni, Ben Stein; *D:* Chuck Russell; *W:* Mike Werb; *C:* John R. Leonetti; *M:* Randy Edelman. *AWARDS:* Blockbuster Entertainment Awards '95: Comedy Actor, Theatrical (Carrey), Female Newcomer, Theatrical (Diaz); Blockbuster Entertainment Awards '96: Comedy Actor, Video (Carrey); *NOM:* Academy Awards '94: Best Visual Effects; Golden Globe Awards '95:

Best Actor—Musical/Comedy (Carrey); MTV Movie Awards '95: Breakthrough Performance (Diaz), Most Desirable Female (Diaz), Best Comedic Performance (Carrey), Best Dance Sequence (Jim Carrey/Cameron Diaz).

The Mask of Diijon

No, this one has nothing to do with mustard. This Diijon (von Stroheim) is a cranky magician who stumbles across a hypnotism gimmick and uses it on his wife (Bates) whom he suspects is unfaithful. It's similar in style to the formula horror-suspense B-pictures that Universal was cranking out in the '40s and '50s. Unfortunately, the disc was made from a substandard print that has obviously been around the block more than once. The thin sound is barely audible in some scenes and the image looks like it's been sandpapered. The main attraction is the star, but von Stroheim—"the man you love to hate," as he was called—can't really do much with this frail vehicle. —*MM*
Movie: ♫♫▶ **DVD:** ♫♫
Image Entertainment (Cat ID5372FWDVD, UPC #014381537222). Full frame. Dolby Digital Mono. $24.99. Snapper. *LANG:* English. *FEATURES:* 9 chapter links ● Erich von Stroheim filmography.
1946 73m/B Erich von Stroheim, Jeanne Bates, William Wright, Edward Van Sloan, Denise Vernac; *D:* Lew (Louis Friedlander) Landers; *W:* Griffin Jay, Arthur St. Claire; *C:* Jack Greenhalgh; *M:* Lee Zahler.

The Mask of Zorro

The dashing masked swordsman, who first made an appearance in a 1919 newspaper comic, returns to the big screen. Aging Zorro (Hopkins) escapes from 20 years in prison when he discovers his mortal enemy Montero (Wilson) is looking to establish an independent republic of California. But he needs some help and picks bandit Alejandro (Banderas), who needs a lot of training. Caught in the middle is Elena (Zeta-Jones), a spirited beauty who was raised by Montero (Wilson) and doesn't know she's really Zorro's daughter. She wields quite a mean sword herself as Alejandro learns before any romancing can begin. A little long but swashbuckling fun. There's not much to find wrong on this DVD. The picture is grainless and sharp, with nothing in the way of distracting artifacts. Colors are intense and accurate with no bleed. There are deep blacks in virtually every scene and they remain true throughout. Contrast is punchy and brightness is comfortable. The image remains detailed in light or dark scenes. The soundtrack is also spectacular and you'd better hang on to something if you crank it up. The bass track is super and really shakes things during explosions and other effects, and even occasionally on the music (which is one of the better James Horner scores). The Surround supplies a lot of ambience as well as effects, and is

working almost constantly—the overall mix is terrific. —*JO* **AKA:** Zorro.
Movie: ♫♫♫ **DVD:** ♫♫♫▶
Columbia Tristar Home Video (Cat #21699, UPC #043396216990). Widescreen (2.35:1) anamorphic. Dolby Digital 5.1; Dolby Surround. $28.95. Keepcase. *LANG:* English (DD5.1; DS). *SUB:* English. *CAP:* English. *FEATURES:* 28 chapter links ● Theatrical trailer ● Photo gallery ● "Making of" featurette.
1998 (PG-13) 136m/C Antonio Banderas, Anthony Hopkins, Catherine Zeta-Jones, Stuart Wilson, Matt Letscher, Maury Chaykin, Tony Amendola, Pedro Armendariz Jr., L.Q. (Justus E. McQueen) Jones; *D:* Martin Campbell; *W:* Ted Elliott, Terry Rossio, John Eskow; *C:* Phil Meheux; *M:* James Horner. *AWARDS:* NOM: Academy Awards '98: Best Sound, Best Sound Effects Editing; British Academy Awards '98: Best Costume Design; Golden Globe Awards '98: Best Actor—Musical/Comedy (Banderas), Best Film—Musical/Comedy; MTV Movie Awards '99: Breakthrough Performance (Zeta-Jones), Best Fight.

Mass Extinctions

Four short bargain-basement *National Geographic*–type TV shows have been combined to form this documentary look at prehistoric mass extinctions. Extremely complicated scientific evidence and theories are presented in simple terms. Interviews with scientists, nature photography, and drawings are not up to the best work seen on public television and the various non-fiction cable channels. The images don't gain much on DVD, either, though the production is not exploitative, as the box art might lead some to believe. —*MM*
Movie: ♫♫ **DVD:** ♫♫
Simitar Entertainment (Cat #7653, UPC #082551765324). Full frame. Dolby Digital Stereo. $14.98. Keepcase. *LANG:* English. *FEATURES:* 8 chapter links ● Production factoids.
1993 ?m/C

Masseuse

When Kristy's (Drew) dirty rotten no-good two-timing fiance Jack (Abell) tries to swindle her, she gets all the revenge she wants and then some. Most of the action is strictly within the limits of the soft-core genre. What sets this one apart is its humor and spirited feminist attitude. Fans, look for a cameo by Brinke Stevens. Unfortunately, the microscopic budget and corresponding production values show through on the DVD. It's really no better than the tape, though it's still a cut above the norm for video erotic thrillers. Followed by sequels. —*MM*
Movie: ♫♫▶ **DVD:** ♫♫
Image Entertainment (Cat #ID5610FMDVD, UPC #014381561029). Full frame. Dolby Digital Stereo. $24.99. Snapper. *LANG:* English. *FEATURES:* 12 chapter links.
1995 (R) 90m/C Griffin Drew, Monique Parent, Tim Abell, Brinke Stevens; *D:*

Daniel Peters; *W:* Steve Armogida; *C:* Gary Graver; *M:* Paul Di Franco.

The Master

Typical low-budget martial arts flick is notable for American locations, and a fair performance from star Jet Li. He's a guy from Hong Kong who comes to San Francisco and then avenges an attack on his kung-fu master by a creepy guy who has a bad haircut and atrocious taste in clothes. The thin sound is fine for the abominable dubbing; some of the dialogue is in English. The image is slightly better but not really any better than VHS tape. The pan-and-scan transfer misses considerable action in the wildly exaggerated fight scenes. —*MM*
Movie: ♫▶ **DVD:** ♫▶
Tai Seng Video Marketing (Cat #5096, UPC #4895024900858). Full frame. Dolby Digital 5.1 Surround Stereo. $49.95. Keepcase. *LANG:* Cantonese; Mandarin; English. *SUB:* Traditional & Simplified Chinese; English; Japanese; Bahasa Indonesia & Malaysia; Thai; Korean; Vietnamese. *FEATURES:* 8 chapter links ● Trailer ● Cast and crew thumbnail bios.
1992 93m/C *HK* Jet Li, Yuen Wah, Jerry Trimble, Crystal Kwok; *D:* Tsui Hark; *W:* Tai-Muk Lau, Kei To Lam; *C:* Henry Chan; *M:* Yee Tat Lam.

Masters of Russian Animation, Vol. 1

As a group, these Russian short films from the 1960s are more stylized, serious, intelligent, and challenging than the animation Americans are used to. They range in length from one to 20 minutes and there's no single theme. Dinosaurs, art, music, and film itself are subjects. Image is fine though these cartoons tend toward soft colors, restrained plotting, and subtle drawing. The true value of the DVD over tape is the accessibility of the individual works. Contents: Story of One Crime, Fyodor Khitruk (1962); Man in the Frame, Khitruk (1966); My Green Crocodile, Vadim Kurchevsky (1966); There Lives Kozyavin, Andrei Khrjanovsky (1966); Moutain of Dinosaurs, Rasa Strautmane (1967); Passion of Spies, Yefin Gamburg (1967); Glass Harmonica, Khrjanovsky (1968); Ball of Wool, Nikolai Serebryakov (1968); Singing Teacher, Anatoly Petrov (1968); Film Film Film, Fyodor Khitruk (1968). —*MM*
Movie: ♫♫♫ **DVD:** ♫♫♫
Image Entertainment (Cat #ID5525FJDVD, UPC #014381552522). Full frame. Dolby Digital Stereo. $24.99. Snapper. *LANG:* Russian. *SUB:* English. *FEATURES:* 10 chapter links ● Historical liner notes by Oleg Vidov ● Biographical liner notes by Joan Borsten.
1997 ?m/C *RU*

The Matchmaker

To help Sen. McGlory's flagging campaign, aide Marcy Tizard (Garofalo) heads to a

wee quaint Irish burgh to find up-close-and-personal anecdotes about his family. Instead, she lands in the middle of the annual matchmaking festival and becomes the target of a marriage broker (O'Shea). Will the razor-sharp, no-nonsense city girl succumb to the blarney or to Sean (O'Hara), her laconic suitor? Garofalo's intelligent screen presence is the key to the film. Unfortunately, it fares poorly on DVD. Close lines and diagonals vibrate throughout. Sound is adequate. —*MM*
Movie: 🎵🎵🎵 ***DVD:*** 🎵🎵
USA Home Entertainment (Cat #440 047 837-2, UPC #044004783729). Widescreen letterboxed; full frame. Dolby Digital Stereo. $19.95. Keepcase. *LANG:* English. *SUB:* French; Spanish. *CAP:* English. *FEATURES:* 16 chapter links • Cast and crew thumbnail biographies.
1997 (R) 97m/C Janeane Garofalo, Milo O'Shea, David O'Hara, Denis Leary, Jay O. Sanders, Rosaleen Linehan, Maria Doyle Kennedy, Saffron Burrows, Paul Hickey, Jimmy Keogh; ***D:*** Mark Joffe; ***W:*** Louis Nowra, Karen Janszen, Graham Linehan, Greg Dinner; ***C:*** Ellery Ryan; ***M:*** John Altman.

Matilda

Intelligent child Matilda Wormwood (Wilson) is oppressed by both her monstrous parents (DeVito and Perlman) and awful school principal, Trunchbull (Ferris). However, her first grade teacher, appropriately named Miss Honey (Davidtz), believes in her, which is enough to make Matilda plot an appropriate fate for the miserable people in her life. Excellent adaptation of a typically subversive book by Roald Dahl. Director DeVito, who wanted to create the illusion of a live-action cartoon, built, among other things, a "Carrot-cam" to capture the flying food of a food fight. The look of *Matilda* is very dependent on an accurate transfer of colors, and the DVD gets it just right. The crisp image also has just the right amount of contrast to ensure that the colors are vibrant under all lighting conditions. There are surprisingly few Surround effects, when you consider the subject matter and attitude of the film, but overall, the 5.1 sound is very good. —*JO*
Movie: 🎵🎵🎵 ***DVD:*** 🎵🎵🎵➤
Columbia Tristar Home Video (Cat #86869, UPC #043396868694). Full frame. Dolby Digital 5.1; Dolby Surround. NSL. Keepcase. *LANG:* English; Spanish; French. *SUB:* Spanish. *CAP:* English. *FEATURES:* 49 chapter links.
1996 (PG) 93m/C Mara Wilson, Danny DeVito, Rhea Perlman, Embeth Davidtz, Pam Ferris, Paul (Pee-wee Herman) Reubens, Tracey Walter; ***D:*** Danny DeVito; ***W:*** Robin Swicord, Nicholas Kazan; ***C:*** Stefan Czapsky; ***M:*** David Newman.

Matinee

"MANT: Half-man, Half-ant, All Terror!" screams from the movie marquee after Lawrence Woolsey (Goodman), promoter extraordinaire, and Ruth Corday (Moriarty), his leading lady, roll into Key West at the height of the Cuban missile crisis in 1962. Meanwhile, teen Gene Loomis (Fenton) listens to his girlfriend question the meaning of life while he worries about his dad stationed in Cuba. Director Joe Dante builds sly parallels between real life and movie horror by juxtaposing Woolsey (based on B-movie king William Castle) hyping his schlock—shown in "Atomo-Vision"—against JFK solemnly announcing the Russians' approach. Don't miss his explanation in chapter 6 of the evolution of horror. Goodman's performance is one of his most winning and this film has always deserved a larger audience. On disc, the tropical exteriors shimmer while the interiors look terrific with bright candy colors. Somehow, it seems even sharper than it did in the theatre. The black-and-white scenes from the film-within-the-film are equally clear. My only reservation is the lack of a commentary track by Dante. —*MM*
Movie: 🎵🎵🎵➤ ***DVD:*** 🎵🎵🎵
Image Entertainment (Cat #ID4288USDVD, UPC #014381428827). Widescreen (1.66:1) letterboxed. Dolby Digital Surround. $24.99. Snapper. *LANG:* English. *FEATURES:* 16 chapter links • Filmographies for cast and crew.
1992 (PG) 98m/C John Goodman, Cathy Moriarty, Simon Fenton, Omri Katz, Lisa Jakub, Kellie Martin, Jesse Lee, Lucinda Jenney, James Villemaire, Robert Picardo, Dick Miller, John Sayles, Mark McCracken, Jesse White, David Clennon, Luke Halpin, Robert Cornthwaite, Kevin McCarthy, William Schallert; ***D:*** Joe Dante; ***W:*** Charles Haas, Jerico (Weingrod) Stone; ***C:*** John Hora; ***M:*** Jerry Goldsmith.

The Matrix

One of the first major hits on DVD is also one of several alternate reality "cyberpunk" sf films to come out of the late 1990s. But compared to *Dark City* and *eXistenZ*, it is more visually ambitious, and it certainly made more of an impression at the boxoffice. Computer nerd Neo (Reeves) learns that Morpheus (Fishburne), Trinity (Moss), and their renegade pals are trying to save humanity from the false "reality" that has been created by machines, or something to that effect. The plot is wildly convoluted and the dazzling action-oriented effects mirror that byzantine mindset. The Wachowski Brothers take a quantum leap from the cinematic playfulness they displayed in *Bound* to create a series of "how-did-they-do-that?" stunts. The DVD explains how they did it in several technically oriented short films about the creation of *The Matrix*. Those who haven't already seen the film should not watch those first, nor should they listen to the audio track describing the Australian production's rough road to completion. Instead, they can enjoy those effects, which have a clarity on disc that rivals a full theatrical screen in the crispness of detail. Sound, naturally, is exemplary. For the most dedicated fans, though, the real attraction of the DVD lies in the wealth of extras that cannot be found anywhere else. This is one of the first discs to tap into the medium's potential for explanatory background material. It contains much more than most people will want to know. —*MM*
Movie: 🎵🎵🎵 ***DVD:*** 🎵🎵🎵🎵
Warner Home Video, Inc. (Cat #17737, UPC #085391773726). Widescreen letterboxed. Dolby Digital 5.1 Surround. $24.98. Snapper. *LANG:* English. *SUB:* English. *CAP:* English. *FEATURES:* 38 chapter links • Music-only track with commentary by composer Don Davis • Commentary: Moss, Staenberg, and Gaeta • HBO behind-the-scenes documentary • "Take the Red Pills" links to special effects explanations • "Follow the White Rabbit" to alternate angles. DVD-ROM can access several other features, including storyboards, screenplay, and websites.
1999 (R) 136m/C Keanu Reeves, Carrie-Anne Moss, Laurence "Larry" Fishburne, Joe Pantoliano, Hugo Weaving, Gloria Foster, Marcus Chong, Paul Goddard, Robert Taylor, Julian (Sonny) Arahanga, Matt Doran, Belinda McClory, Anthony Ray Parker; ***D:*** Andy Wachowski, Larry Wachowski; ***W:*** Andy Wachowski, Larry Wachowski; ***C:*** Bill Pope; ***M:*** Don Davis. *AWARDS:* Academy Awards '99: Best Film Editing, Best Sound, Best Visual Effects; VSDA DVD Festival '00: Best Supplementary Material, Best Use of DVD-ROM Features, Best of Show. *NOM:* British Academy Awards '99: Best Art Direction/Set Decoration, Best Cinematography, Best Film Editing, Best Sound.

Maverick

Entertaining remake of the popular western series is cute; both amusing-funny cute, and smirky-sticky cute. For most viewers, the balance will be determined by their reaction to the stars. Mel Gibson, Jodie Foster, and James Garner tapdance their way through fluffy material with apparently effortless ease. For Gibson and Garner, it's a familiar turn. Though Jodie Foster has been associated with more serious work, she's every bit as comfortable as her costars, and she's nothing less than drop-dead gorgeous. Still, even with such a classy leading lady, two full hours of unrelieved cuteness is a lot to take. Look for cameos from country singers, old-time western actors, and an unbilled appearance by Danny Glover. The digital transfer is fine, but this is a big-screen movie. Western fans should go for the widescreen version; fans of the cast—and those who will always associate *Maverick* with TV—will prefer the full-frame display. —*MM*
Movie: 🎵🎵➤ ***DVD:*** 🎵🎵➤
Warner Home Video, Inc. (Cat #13374, UPC #085391337423). Widescreen (2.35:1) letterboxed; full frame. Dolby Digital Stereo. $24.98. Snapper. *LANG:* English; French. *SUB:* French; Spanish. *CAP:* English. *FEATURES:* 41 chapter links • Cast and crew thumbnail bios • Production notes.

1994 (PG) 127m/C Mel Gibson, Jodie Foster, James Garner, Graham Greene, James Coburn, Alfred Molina, Paul Smith, Geoffrey Lewis, Max Perlich; *Cameos:* Dub Taylor, Dan Hedaya, Robert Fuller, Doug McClure, Bert Remsen, Denver Pyle, Will Hutchins, Waylon Jennings, Kathy Mattea, Danny Glover, Clint Black; *D:* Richard Donner; *W:* William Goldman; *C:* Vilmos Zsigmond; *M:* Randy Newman. *AWARDS:* Blockbuster Entertainment Awards '95: Comedy Actress, Theatrical (Foster); *NOM:* Academy Awards '94: Best Costume Design.

McLintock!

Rowdy western stars Wayne as the titular cattle baron whose refined wife (O'Hara) returns home after a two-year separation. She wants a divorce and custody of their 17-year-old daughter (Powers) who's been away at school. In the meantime, the Duke has hired a housekeeper (De Carlo) whose teenage son (real-life son Patrick) promptly falls for Powers. Other Wayne family members were involved with the production, too. The result is typically broad stuff, bordering on self-parody, that's fun for those who never tire of watching Wayne be Wayne. But it's no *Quiet Man* and it doesn't play particularly well on DVD. The heavily saturated colors are virulent; roofing shingles flash; fine vertical scratches are visible at intervals; and the image ranges between poor and good with a wavering focus. —*MM*
Movie: 🎬🎬▶ *DVD:* 🎬🎬
Goodtimes Entertainment (Cat #05-81003, UPC #018713810038). Full frame. Dolby Digital Mono. $19.99. Snapper. *LANG:* English. *CAP:* English. *FEATURES:* 12 chapter links.
1963 127m/C John Wayne, Maureen O'Hara, Yvonne De Carlo, Patrick Wayne, Stefanie Powers, Jack Kruschen, Chill Wills, Jerry Van Dyke, Edgar Buchanan, Bruce Cabot, Perry Lopez, Michael Pate, Strother Martin, Gordon Jones; *D:* Andrew V. McLaglen; *W:* James Edward Grant; *C:* William Clothier.

MD Geist (DC)

Unexceptional ultra-violent apocalyptic Japanese animation revolves around the usual giant robots, bomb-blasted landscapes, mouldering skeletons, and exaggerated weapons. This two-part story is set on a planet called Jerra. The title character, whose initials stand for "Most Dangerous," is a super warrior. Movements are flat and jerky without the fluidity of the best anime, and so the many beheadings and eviscerations are not as grotesque as they might have been. Focus and colors are noticeably sharper in the second volume. —*MM*
Movie: 🎬🎬 *DVD:* 🎬🎬
Image Entertainment (Cat #ID4412CTDVD, UPC #014381441222). Full frame. Dolby Digital Stereo. $24.99. Snapper. *LANG:* English; Japanese. *SUB:* English. *FEATURES:* 20 chapter links.
1986 91m/C *JP D:* Hayato Ikeda, Koichi Ohata.

Me & Will

Jane (Rose) and Will (Behr) are two drugged-up LA party dolls who meet in rehab and decide to set off on a quest to find the motorcycle that Peter Fonda rode in *Easy Rider*. The result is a road movie that never veers into exploitation but instead is a buddy flick. The stars wrote, produced, and directed, and they filled the supporting cast with familiar faces. The best thing about the film is its comfortable familiarity with the biker world. The two women do most if not all of their own riding and they're right at home with their tough-minded characters. DVD does nothing to hide the film's low budget. The often unflattering lighting emphasizes the garishness of the sets and the western landscapes are never as sharply focused as they could be. Sound is adequate. —*MM*
Movie: 🎬🎬▶ *DVD:* 🎬🎬
MTI Home Video (Cat #1055DVD, UPC #039414510553). Full frame. $24.95. Keepcase. *LANG:* English. *SUB:* Spanish. *FEATURES:* 20 chapter links • Theatrical trailer • 3 trailers for other MTI releases.
1999 (R) 93m/C Sherrie Rose, Melissa Behr, Patrick Dempsey, Seymour Cassel, Grace Zabriskie, M. Emmet Walsh, Steve Railsback, Traci Lords, Billy Wirth; *D:* Sherrie Rose, Melissa Behr; *W:* Sherrie Rose, Melissa Behr; *C:* Joey Forsyte.

Mean Guns

Lots of mayhem will redeem this silly plot for the action fan. Moon (Ice-T) lures 100 assassins to an abandoned prison with the promise of $10 million for the last three men standing. Lou (Lambert) and Marcus (Halsey) are his rivals.
Movie: 🎬🎬 *DVD:* NYR
Trimark Home Video (Cat #6839). Full frame. Dolby Digital Surround Stereo. $24.99. Keepcase. *LANG:* English. *SUB:* French; Spanish. *CAP:* English. *FEATURES:* Trailer.
1997 (R) 90m/C Ice-T, Christopher Lambert, Michael Halsey, Deborah Van Valkenburgh, Tina Cote, Yuji Okumoto; *D:* Albert Pyun; *W:* Andrew Witham, Nat Whitcomb; *C:* George Mooradian; *M:* Tony Riparetti.

Mean Streets

A grimy slice of street life in Little Italy among lower echelon Mafiosos, unbalanced punks, and petty criminals. A riveting, free-form feature film, marking the formal debut by Scorsese (five years earlier he had completed a student film, *Who's That Knocking at My Door?*). Unorthodox camera movement and gritty performances by De Niro and Keitel, with underlying Catholic guilt providing the moral conflict. Excellent early '60s soundtrack. *Mean Streets* has never looked really good on home video. This DVD changes that. The low-light sequences that feature a lot of red are no longer a problem. The picture stays sharp throughout and the colors are vibrant and have no bleed. There is very little grain or artifacts. Blacks stay pretty true and the contrast

gives the entire film a lot more zip. Brightness levels are very good. The Dolby Digital 2.0 mono track is also an improvement over the previous versions and has good fidelity and adequate dynamics. —*JO*
Movie: 🎬🎬🎬🎬 *DVD:* 🎬🎬🎬▶
Warner Home Video, Inc. (Cat #15240, UPC #085391524021). Widescreen (1.85:1) letterboxed; full frame. Dolby Digital 2.0 Mono. $24.98. Snapper. *LANG:* English. *SUB:* French. *CAP:* English. *FEATURES:* 33 chapter links • Production notes • Theatrical trailer.
1973 (R) 112m/C Harvey Keitel, Robert De Niro, David Proval, Amy Robinson, Richard Romanus, David Carradine, Robert Carradine, Cesare Danova, George Memmoli; *D:* Martin Scorsese; *W:* Martin Scorsese, Mardik Martin; *C:* Kent Wakeford. *AWARDS:* National Film Registry '97; National Society of Film Critics Awards '73: Best Supporting Actor (De Niro).

The Meanest Men in the West

Two criminal half-brothers (Bronson and Marvin) battle frontier law and each other.
Movie: 🎬 *DVD:* NYR
Goodtimes Entertainment (Cat #81017). Full frame. $19.98. Snapper. *LANG:* English. *SUB:* French; Spanish. *CAP:* English.
1976 (PG) 92m/C Charles Bronson, Lee Marvin, Lee J. Cobb, James Drury, Albert Salmi, Charles Grodin; *D:* Samuel Fuller; *W:* Charles S. Dubin; *C:* Lionel Lindon, Alric Edens; *M:* Hal Mooney.

Meantime

Such an early British collaboration between director Leigh and stars Oldman and Roth, who have gone on to international success, is of some interest. Unfortunately both subject and style make it almost impenetrably provincial. Colin and Mark (Roth and Daniels) are unemployed siblings, still sharing a room in the family flat though they can hardly fit into their boyhood cots. Colin, who's either slow, bored, or some numbing combination of both, tags after a local skinhead named Coxy (Oldman). The otherwise bickering family members band together, even as their walls, doors, and windows fall apart around them, to keep Colin out of gang life. Scattershot, often mumbled dialogue gets lost in the cracker box locations, in which nearly everyone seems backlit by a dreary window or door. Neither element makes compelling DVD content. The trailer, clearly made for the American video release, punches things up to seem much more antic and laced with physical humor than it really is. —*JK*
Movie: 🎬🎬 *DVD:* 🎬🎬
Fox/Lorber Home Video (Cat #FLV5056, UPC #720917505626). Full frame. Stereo. $29.99. Keepcase. *LANG:* English. *FEATURES:* 8 chapter links • Interactive menus • Full-color picture disc • Production credits and filmographies • Trailer.
1981 90m/C *GB* Tim Roth, Gary Oldman, Phil Daniels, Alfred Molina, Pam Ferris; *D:*

Mike Leigh; **C:** Roger Pratt; **M:** Andrew Dickson.

Meatballs

Tripper (Murray) is the Activities Director at Camp North Star. He runs a typically loose ship and turned this low-budget comedy into a major hit. Along with *Stripes*, it was instrumental in launching both Murray and director Reitman into the top rank of Hollywood. The image is no better on DVD than it is on tape or a theatre screen. The best moment is the stirring stem-winder speech, "It Just Doesn't Matter!" in chapter 18. —*MM*
Movie: 🦴🦴🦴 **DVD:** 🦴🦴➤
HBO Home Video (Cat #90612, UPC #026359061226). Widescreen letterboxed. Stereo; Mono. $24.98. Snapper. *LANG:* English; Spanish; French. *SUB:* English; Spanish; French. *FEATURES:* 21 chapter links • Trailer • Cast and crew thumbnail biographies.
1979 (PG) 92m/C *CA* Bill Murray, Harvey Atkin, Kate Lynch; **D:** Ivan Reitman; **W:** Len Blum, Harold Ramis, Janis Allen; **C:** Donald Wilder; **M:** Elmer Bernstein. *AWARDS:* Genie Awards '80: Best Actress (Lynch).

Medicine Man

Connery's usual commanding presence is the only real recommendation in this tame effort from director McTiernan. Dr. Robert Campbell (Connery) is a biochemist working in the Amazon rain forest. Dr. Rae Crane (Bracco) is sent to check on him by the institute sponsoring his research. Although she's uptight and he's gruff, they follow the stereotypical pattern and fall in love, but generate no real chemistry. The other side of the story revolves around the cancer cure he has discovered and lost. The jungle scenery which was so spectacular on the big screen fares poorly on DVD. It's often reduced to blurry background wallpaper here. The crowded jungle lab interiors suffer the same fate. Sound is adequate. —*MM*
Movie: 🦴🦴 **DVD:** 🦴🦴➤
Buena Vista Home Entertainment (Cat #17500, UPC #717951003188). Widescreen (2.35:1) letterboxed. Dolby Digital Surround Stereo. $29.99. Keepcase. *LANG:* English; French. *CAP:* English. *FEATURES:* 13 chapter links • "Making of" featurette • Theatrical trailer.
1992 (PG-13) 105m/C Sean Connery, Lorraine Bracco, Jose Wilker, Rodolfo de Alexandra, Francisco Tsirene Tsere Rereme, Elias Monteiro da Silva; **D:** John McTiernan; **W:** Tom Schulman; **C:** Donald McAlpine; **M:** Jerry Goldsmith.

Meet Joe Black

Remake of *Death Takes a Holiday* casts Pitt as Joe Black, Death incarnate, who's come to visit billionaire Bill Parrish (Hopkins). But he'll put off Bill's demise if Bill will show him around. Then he falls for Bill's daughter Susan (Forlani). On DVD, the image is just all right, not as highly polished as the ultra-rich setting and sumptuous sets would suggest. The sound is weak, too, particularly in an important scene set in a helicopter. While Hopkins and Pitt manage to make their characters interesting, Forlani is weak. Overall, the film is far too long with a plodding pace. —*MM*
Movie: 🦴🦴 **DVD:** 🦴🦴➤
Universal Studios Home Video (Cat #20531, UPC #025192053122). Widescreen (1.85:1) letterboxed. Dolby Digital 5.1 Surround Stereo; Dolby Digital Surround Stereo. $26.98. Keepcase. *LANG:* English; French. *CAP:* English. *FEATURES:* 18 chapter links • "Making of" featurette • Production notes • Cast and crew thumbnail biographies • Theatrical trailer • Universal web links.
1998 (PG-13) 180m/C Brad Pitt, Anthony Hopkins, Claire Forlani, Marcia Gay Harden, Jeffrey Tambor, Jake Weber; **D:** Martin Brest; **W:** Ron Osborn, Jeff Reno, Kevin Wade, Bo Goldman; **C:** Emmanuel Lubezki; **M:** Thomas Newman. *AWARDS: NOM:* Golden Raspberry Awards '98: Worst Remake/Sequel.

Meet John Doe

Capra's social commentary revolves around an unemployed, down-and-out man (Cooper) selected to be the face of a political goodwill campaign. Honest and trusting, he eventually realizes he is being used to further the careers of corrupt politicians. Strong performances from Cooper, Stanwyck, and Brennan, among others in smaller roles. The VideoHound hates it when a favorite flick gets shabby video treatment, and that is what has happened again and again with *Meet John Doe*. On this budget DVD, the picture is as fuzzy as it has been in other video releases, and the soundtrack isn't any better. Give an E for effort to Madacy for adding token extras, but they really aren't meaningful to the serious cinephile. —*MB*
Movie: 🦴🦴🦴 **DVD:** 🦴
Madacy Entertainment (Cat #DVD99019, UPC #056775005597). Full frame. Dolby Digital 1.0. $9.98. Keepcase. *LANG:* English. *FEATURES:* 9 chapter links • Lobby poster • Cooper biography • Interactive trivia questions and answers • Movie credits.
1941 123m/B Gary Cooper, Barbara Stanwyck, Edward Arnold, James Gleason, Walter Brennan, Spring Byington, Gene Lockhart, Regis Toomey, Ann Doran, Rod La Rocque; **D:** Frank Capra; **W:** Robert Riskin; **C:** George Barnes; **M:** Dimitri Tiomkin. *AWARDS: NOM:* Academy Awards '41: Best Story.

Meet Wally Sparks

No-brow *Man Who Came to Dinner* revolves around smutty TV talk show host Sparks (Dangerfield) who's given one week to save his gig when producer Reynolds (under one of his worst wigs) puts him on notice. At the governor's mansion to interview the conservative head honcho (Stiers), he falls victim to an accident with a drunken horse and cannot be moved. He makes himself at home and turns the gubernatorial digs into a TV studio. Dangerfield's one-liners provide the only energy. The low-budget production was so dark and grainy in theatres that there is really nothing that DVD can do to improve it. —*MM*
Movie: 🦴🦴 **DVD:** 🦴🦴
Trimark Home Video (Cat #6784). Widescreen letterboxed; full frame. Dolby Stereo. $19.99. Keepcase. *LANG:* English. *SUB:* French; Spanish. *CAP:* English. *FEATURES:* Cast and crew thumbnail bios • Production notes • Trailers.
1997 (R) 107m/C Rodney Dangerfield, David Ogden Stiers, Burt Reynolds, Debi Mazar, Cindy Williams, Alan Rachins; **D:** Peter Baldwin; **W:** Rodney Dangerfield, Harry Basil; **C:** Richard Kline; **M:** Michel Colombier.

Megazone 23 Part 1

Early feature-length Japanese anime is built around the themes and images that continue to be popular in the genre—exotic motorcycles, big weapons, a little sex, sf. The story concerns Shogo and Huey, two young people who discover a conspiracy that begins with the government and television and goes even farther. The animation is stylized and stiff with static unmoving backgrounds. Very 1980s outfits and hair styles. —*MM*
Movie: 🦴🦴 **DVD:** 🦴🦴
Image Entertainment (Cat #ID5550SEDVD, UPC #014381555028). Full frame. Dolby Digital Surround Stereo. $24.99. Snapper. *LANG:* English; Japanese. *SUB:* English. *FEATURES:* 13 chapter links.
1985 81m/C D: Carl Macek, Noboru Ishiguro; **W:** Hiroyuki Hoshiyama, Greg Snegoff.

Melvin and Howard

On the commentary track, director Jonathan Demme flatly states that he made this film with full belief that Melvin Dummar's (LeMat) incredible story of meeting reclusive billionaire Howard Hughes (Robards) out in the Nevada desert was completely true. Anyone who accepts that premise is in for a treat. True or not, this comedy is a portrait of life in America in the late 1970s. The film doesn't have the sparkle of some DVDs, because the best American films of the period weren't supposed to be polished. Demme is accompanied on the commentary track by production designer Toby Rafelson and their warm, chatty reminiscences focus on the sense of realism they brought to the picture. Perfection was never their goal. They wanted a lived-in, worked-in look. Their memories are generally flattering to all concerned—Mary Steenburgen who won an Oscar for her work—and sometime surprising. Demme's first choice to play Hughes was cult favorite Roberts

Blossom. (The real Dummar shows up as a counterman in a bus station.) The years have been kind to this one. It's one of Demme's best, somehow even better the second time around. —MM

Movie: 🎬🎬🎬▶ **DVD:** 🎬🎬🎬▶

Anchor Bay (Cat #DV10923, UPC #013131092394). Widescreen (1.85:1) letterboxed. Dolby Digital Mono. $24.98. Keepcase. *LANG:* English. *FEATURES:* 22 chapter links • Theatrical trailer • Cast and crew thumbnail biographies • Commentary: Jonathan Demme, production designer Toby Rafelson.
1980 (R) 95m/C Paul LeMat, Jason Robards Jr., Mary Steenburgen, Michael J. Pollard, Dabney Coleman, Elizabeth Cheshire, Pamela Reed, Cheryl "Rainbeaux" Smith; **D:** Jonathan Demme; **W:** Bo Goldman; **C:** Tak Fujimoto; **M:** Bruce Langhorne. *AWARDS:* Academy Awards '80: Best Original Screenplay, Best Supporting Actress (Steenburgen); Golden Globe Awards '81: Best Supporting Actress (Steenburgen); Los Angeles Film Critics Association Awards '80: Best Supporting Actress (Steenburgen); New York Film Critics Awards '80: Best Director (Demme), Best Screenplay, Best Supporting Actress (Steenburgen); National Society of Film Critics Awards '80: Best Film, Best Screenplay, Best Supporting Actress (Steenburgen); Writers Guild of America '80: Best Original Screenplay; *NOM:* Academy Awards '80: Best Supporting Actor (Robards).

Memphis Belle

Satisfactory fictionalization of William Wyler's fine documentary captures the story of the final mission of a B-17 bomber stationed in England during World War II. The crew of the *Memphis Belle* was the first to complete 25 missions. The fine ensemble cast is made of attractive young actors. Lithgow has a nice turn as a PR guy who's determined to exploit their boyish good looks on the homefront. Since Caton-Jones attempted to use 1940s film techniques—along with some spectacular effects and airplane models—the color has a desaturated look that does not make the most of DVD's clarity. Still, it looks and sounds fine, but don't even think about comparing it to the original. —MM

Movie: 🎬🎬▶ **DVD:** 🎬🎬🎬

Warner Home Video, Inc. (Cat #12040). Widescreen letterboxed; full frame. Dolby Digital 5.1 Surround Stereo; Mono. $24.98. Snapper. *LANG:* English; French; Spanish. *SUB:* French; Spanish. *CAP:* English. *FEATURES:* Production notes • Cast and crew thumbnail bios • Trailer • "Making of" featurette.
1990 (PG-13) 107m/C Matthew Modine, John Lithgow, Eric Stoltz, Sean Astin, Harry Connick Jr., Reed Edward Diamond, Tate Donovan, D.B. Sweeney, Billy Zane, David Strathairn, Jane Horrocks, Courtney Gains, Neil Giuntoli; **D:** Michael Caton-Jones; **W:** Monte Merrick; **C:** David Watkin; **M:** George Fenton.

Men

Chef Stella (Young) is encouraged by her drunken best friend Teo (Walsh) to leave New York for L.A. to find love, though Stella picks up guys wherever she meets them and hops in the sack. She promptly lands a job and a romance with George (Heard), a restaurant owner. But then there's cute Frank (Hillman), a photographer, and then there's.... On DVD, the film looks very good, though early on, director Clarke-Williams lets an equipment shadow intrude. A shirt flashes annoyingly and one complex night scene is problematic. Otherwise, the image is excellent and the sound is good. —MM

Movie: 🎬🎬 **DVD:** 🎬🎬🎬

Simitar Entertainment (Cat #7572, UPC #082551757220). Full frame. Dolby Digital Stereo; Dolby Digital 5.1 Surround Stereo. $14.98. Keepcase. *LANG:* English. *FEATURES:* 8 chapter links • Production factoids • Filmographies of Sean Young and Karen Black.
1997 (R) 93m/C Sean Young, John Heard, Dylan Walsh, Richard Hillman, Karen Black; **D:** Zoe Clarke-Williams; **W:** Zoe Clarke-Williams, Karen Black; **C:** Susan Emerson; **M:** Mark Mothersbaugh.

Men in War

Anthony Mann's Korean War film is a grim piece of work. Lt. Benson's (Ryan) patrol is lost and without transportation. Sgt. Montana (Ray) has a Jeep that he's using to get his shell shocked Colonel (Keith) back to safety. The conflict between the two men is at the center of the film. Details of combat are less certain. Mann and cinematographer Ernest Haller create some of the bleakest black-and-white landscapes you'll ever see on-screen. DVD reproduces their work flawlessly. The image is crisp and sharp throughout. Sound is acceptable. This is one of the best "lost" American war films, worth watching on any medium. —MM

Movie: 🎬🎬🎬▶ **DVD:** 🎬🎬🎬

MasterTone Multimedia, Inc. (Cat #DVD 5504, UPC #714151550467). Full frame. $17.98. Slide case. *LANG:* English. *FEATURES:* 13 chapter links • Cast and crew thumbnail biographies • Critical comments.
1957 100m/B Robert Ryan, Robert Keith, Aldo Ray, Vic Morrow, Phillip Pine, Nehemiah Persoff, James Edwards, L.Q. (Justus E. McQueen) Jones, Scott Marlowe, Adam Kennedy, Race Gentry, Walter Kelley, Anthony Ray, Robert Normand, Michael Miller, Victor Sen Yung; **D:** Anthony Mann; **W:** Philip Yordan, Ben Maddow; **C:** Ernest Haller; **M:** Elmer Bernstein.

Menace II Society

Portrayal of black teens lost in inner-city hell is realistically captured by twin directors Hughes in their feature debut. The opening scene deals with so many racial stereotypes, most notably the character of O-Dog (Tate), that it could be a recruiting tool for the KKK, but the filmmakers take

viewers into the heart of their characters. Caine (Turner) lives with his grandparents and peddles drugs from an equally spending cash on the eve of his high school graduation—and his possible escape from south-central L.A. to Atlanta. Bleak and troubled, with some of the most unsettling violence ever shown in a commercial film, this one isn't easy in any sense. If it's not entertaining, it is engrossing and frightening. And that's the point. The careful DVD transfer has a crisper, more detailed look than the film had on theatre screens. Particular care appears to have been taken to capture varying skin tones and textures. In their "making of" featurette, the Hughes brothers admit their inexperience and state that their influences are Scorsese, DePalma, and Spielberg. Their plot structure is based on *Goodfellas,* and they claim to be pure Hollywood filmmakers interested in making money with violent entertainment. —MM

Movie: 🎬🎬🎬 **DVD:** 🎬🎬🎬▶

New Line Home Video (Cat #N4156, UPC #794043416521). Full frame; widescreen (1.85:1). Dolby 5.1 (English); Dolby Stereo (French). $24.95. Snapper. *LANG:* English; French. *SUB:* English; French; Spanish. *FEATURES:* Hughes brothers interview • "Star highlights" showing scenes with the stars in five other films • Cast biographies and filmographies • Original theatrical trailer • 19 chapter links.
1993 (R) 104m/C Tyrin Turner, Larenz Tate, Samuel L. Jackson, Glenn Plummer, Julian Roy Doster, Bill Duke, Charles S. Dutton, Jada Pinkett Smith, Vonte Sweet, Ryan Williams; **D:** Allen Hughes, Albert Hughes; **W:** Tyger Williams; **C:** Lisa Rinzler. *AWARDS:* Independent Spirit Awards '94: Best Cinematography; MTV Movie Awards '94: Best Film; *NOM:* Independent Spirit Awards '94: Best Actor (Turner), Best First Feature.

Mercury Rising

Renegade FBI agent Art Jeffries (Willis) must protect an autistic child who has inadvertently cracked a secret government code. Together, they dodge bullets from evil government forces headed by Nicholas Kudrow (Baldwin), who insists on having the innocent boy killed rather than change the code. That glaring logic aside, Willis does more than grunt here, showing moments of tenderness as he bonds with the orphaned boy in between nailing bad guys and amassing an assortment of cuts and bruises. Baldwin is effective as the snake who truly believes killing a child will benefit national security. When action time isn't being sacrificed for Jeffries's paternal aspirations, film rises slightly above tepid to provide substantial thrills. The DVD's picture is very sharp and features excellent handling of both the blacks and the colors. There is very little grain, no artifacts, and the colors never bleed. Contrast and brightness levels are also very good, giving the DVD more visual punch than the film itself has. The 5.1 Surround tracks are very good with all the action punctuated and ambience added to both music and the environment. Highs are crisp, the lows rumble appropriately, and none of it covers up the dialogue. —JO

Movie: 🎬🎬 **DVD:** 🎬🎬🎬▸
Universal Studios Home Video (Cat #20333, UPC #025192033322). Widescreen (2.35:1) anamorphic. Dolby Digital 5.1; Dolby Surround. $24.98. Keepcase. *LANG:* English (DD5.1; DS); Spanish (DS); French (DS). *SUB:* Spanish. *CAP:* English. *FEATURES:* 33 chapter links • Production notes • Cast and crew bios • Theatrical trailer.
1998 (R) 112m/C Bruce Willis, Alec Baldwin, Miko Hughes, Kim Dickens, Chi McBride, Robert Stanton, Peter Stormare, Kevin Conway; *D:* Harold Becker; *W:* Larry Konner, Mark Rosenthal; *C:* Michael Seresin; *M:* John Barry. *AWARDS:* Golden Raspberry Awards '98: Worst Actor (Willis).

Merlin
Legend of Camelot and Arthur's mentor is brought to the small screen with fine performances and equally impressive special effects. Merlin is conceived through the magic of evil Queen Mab (Richardson) to bring Britain back to its pagan roots. But Merlin doesn't really like magic and grows up to be (in the commanding persona of Neill) a most reluctant sorcerer. Still, he teaches Arthur (Curran) and continues to battle Mab, who works with Arthur's half sister Morgan Le Fey (Bonham Carter) to destroy Camelot. Merlin also pursues a long-time romance with Nimue (Rossellini), who falls victim to Mab's treachery. The DVD actually looks better than the original television broadcast. The image is so sharp that some of the CGI effects lose a little impact, and there is no aggravating grain or artifacts. The colors are accurate and both deep and vibrant with very little bleed. Contrast is excellent and the brightness much the same. The sound is lacking just a bit but it seems only in the Surround mix as music, dialogue, and effects, all seem dynamic enough. —JO

Movie: 🎬🎬🎬 **DVD:** 🎬🎬🎬
Artisan Entertainment (Cat #96531, UPC #707729653103). Full frame. Dolby Surround. $24.98. Keepcase. *LANG:* English (DS). *SUB:* Spanish. *CAP:* English. *FEATURES:* 36 chapter links • "Making of" featurette • Production notes • Cast and crew info • Dual-layered RSDL.
1998 140m/C Sam Neill, Miranda Richardson, Isabella Rossellini, Martin Short, Helena Bonham Carter, Rutger Hauer, Paul Curran, Billie Whitelaw, Lena Headey, Jason Done, Mark Jax, John McEnery, Nicholas Clay, Sebastien Roche, Jeremy Sheffield; *Cameos:* John Gielgud; *D:* Steven Barron; *W:* David Stevens, Edward Khmara; *C:* Sergei Koslov; *M:* Trevor Jones; *V:* James Earl Jones.

A Merry War
Gordon Comstock (Grant) is a frustrated ad man in London, circa 1935. He believes that his comfortable middle-class life is stifling his creativity. Convinced that slumming is the only way to tap into his supposed poetic talent, he quits his job and moves into a shabby apartment to augment his misery, despite the doubts of his girlfriend Rosemary (Carter). The film is based on George Orwell's only comedy, which fictionalizes his own experiences and so it has the biting social commentary we now call "Orwellian." *AKA:* Keep the Aspidistra Flying.

Movie: 🎬🎬🎬 **DVD:** NYR
Digital Disc Entertainment (Cat #720). Widescreen (1.85:1) letterboxed. Dolby Digital Stereo. $29.95. Keepcase. *FEATURES:* Commentary: Bierman and Plater • Trailer.
1997 101m/C Richard E. Grant, Helena Bonham Carter, Julian Wadham, Jim Carter, Harriet Walter, Liz Smith, Barbara Leigh-Hunt; *D:* Robert Bierman; *W:* Alan Plater; *C:* Giles Nuttgens; *M:* Mike Batt.

Mesmer
Bio-flick tells the story of 18th-century Viennese physician Franz Anton Mesmer (Rickman), who used unorthodox healing practices based on his outlandish theory of "animal magnetism." Reviled by his contemporaries, he is exiled from Vienna only to become the toast of Paris. Was he a charlatan, a fraud, or a genius? The film makes no conclusions, though you may give Mesmer the benefit of the doubt based solely on Rickman's strong performance. Unfortunately, he is supported by a comparatively weak cast of costars. The DVD offers barely more than a minimum set of features, with a trailer and nothing more in the way of extras. Digital compression artifacts dance in the backgrounds of many scenes, and the soundtrack is acceptable but not exceptional. —MB

Movie: 🎬🎬▸ **DVD:** 🎬🎬▸
Image Entertainment (Cat #OVED9029 DVD, UPC #014381902921). Full frame. Dolby Digital Surround. $24.99. Snapper. *LANG:* English. *FEATURES:* 15 chapter links • Theatrical trailer.
1994 107m/C *GB* Alan Rickman, Donal Donnelly, Peter Dvorsky, David Hemblen, Simon McBurney, Gillian Barge, Jan Rubes; *D:* Roger Spottiswoode; *W:* Dennis Potter; *C:* Elemer Ragalyi; *M:* Michael Nyman.

Mesmerized
Based on the work by Jerzy Skolimowski, the film dramatizes the Victoria Thompson murder case in 1880s New Zealand. A teenaged orphan girl marries an older man and decides after years of abuse to kill him through hypnosis. The story is unengaging, though the lovely New Zealand landscape serves as a fitting contrast to the ominous tone. *AKA:* Shocked.

Movie: 🎬🎬 **DVD:** NYR
Tapeworm Video Distributors (Cat #2732). Full frame. $19.95. Keepcase.
1984 90m/C *GB NZ AU* John Lithgow, Jodie Foster, Michael Murphy, Dan Shor,

Harry Andrews; *D:* Michael Laughlin; *W:* Michael Laughlin; *C:* Louis Horvath; *M:* Georges Delerue.

The Message
This sprawling historical epic (almost 4 hours long) has to work around a curious (to American audiences) obstacle. The subject is the prophet Mohammad and the founding of Islam in 7th-century Arabia. But Islam forbids images of the man, so he does not appear in the film. Instead, he often provides the camera's point of view. Hamza the Berber (Quinn) leads the fight to spread the faith. The action scenes are few and not particularly exciting, but then the film's purposes are more serious and openly partisan. Seen simply as entertainment, it's as stiff and dated as most costume dramas of that era. The DVD image is very good throughout. The disc was obviously made from excellent original elements. Sound is acceptable. The two-sided disc must be turned over midway. —MM *AKA:* Mohammad: Messenger of God; Al-Ris-Alah.

Movie: 🎬🎬 **DVD:** 🎬🎬▸
Anchor Bay (Cat #DV10482, UPC #013131048292). Widescreen (2.35:1) letterboxed. Dolby Digital Stereo. $29.98. Keepcase. *LANG:* English. *FEATURES:* 18 chapter links • "Making of" documentary • English and Arabic theatrical trailer • Stills gallery.
1977 (PG) 220m/C *GB* Damien Thomas, Anthony Quinn, Irene Papas, Michael Ansara, Johnny Sekka, Michael Forest, Neville Jason; *D:* Moustapha Akkad; *W:* H.A.L. Craig; *C:* Jack Hildyard; *M:* Maurice Jarre. *AWARDS: NOM:* Academy Awards '77: Best Original Score.

Message in a Bottle
Romantic drama is paced slower than the method of mail delivery in the title. Wright Penn is a divorced mother who finds a love note written to a mystery man's lost love floating in the Atlantic. She tracks the note to strong silent guy Costner, still grieving for his dead wife. She tries to get him to open up and move on with his life (with her preferably), but this takes a mind-numbingly long time. The two are destined to be together, but half of those watching are destined to be asleep by the time it happens. The sole reason to watch this movie is to see old pro Paul Newman steal every scene he's in as Costner's father. The DVD transfer is pleasing enough but nothing spectacular. The picture is sharp and detail are not clouded by much in the way of grain or artifacts. Color is accurate and bleed slightly in only a couple of scenes. Blacks are true and contrast and brightness also above average. The 5.1 is probably punchier than this film needs even though the Surround is used mainly for ambience. The music does come through very full-bodied and the dialogue is always on top of things. —JO

Movie: 🐾🐾 **DVD:** 🐾🐾🐾
Warner Home Video, Inc. (Cat #16989, UPC #085391698920). Widescreen (2.35:1) anamorphic. Dolby Digital 5.1. $24.98. Snapper. *LANG:* English. *SUB:* English. *CAP:* English. *FEATURES:* 35 chapter links • Audio commentary • Deleted scenes • Documentary • Theatrical trailer.
1998 (PG-13) 132m/C Kevin Costner, Robin Wright Penn, Paul Newman, John Savage, Illeana Douglas, Robbie Coltrane, Jesse James Jr., Bethel Leslie, Tom Aldredge, Viveka Davis, Raphael Sbarge, Richard Hamilton, Rosemary Murphy, Stephen Eckholdt; *D:* Luis Mandoki; *W:* Gerald DiPego; *C:* Caleb Deschanel; *M:* Gabriel Yared. *AWARDS: NOM:* Golden Raspberry Awards '99: Worst Actor (Costner).

Metro

Murphy has now officially made this exact movie one kajillion times. He plays fast-talking, fast-shooting cop Axel Fo... er... Scott Roper, who's forced to accept a partner that he doesn't want, played by Nick.... um... Judge... uh... Michael Rapaport! When a villain kills his best friend, he vows revenge. He and his sidekick are involved in car chases, shoot-outs, and a tense situation where his girlfriend is taken hostage. Any of this ring a bell? Maybe it was in that *Another 48 Beverly Hills Cop Movies.* Even so-so movies (especially action-based) are helped by a good DVD, and this one does the trick with very good sharpness and colors that are punchy even if they are not always accurate. Grain, artifacts, and bleed do not intrude and the blacks are fairly true. The brightness and contrast levels are very good. What really gives the film some needed kick is the 5.1 sound, which boosts the energy level in all the action sequences and includes some excellent separation and Surround effects, as good crispness on the dialogue and excellent full-bodied dynamics on the music. —*JO*
Movie: 🐾▶ **DVD:** 🐾🐾🐾
Buena Vista Home Entertainment (Cat #13853, UPC #717951000248). Widescreen (2.35:1) letterboxed. Dolby Digital 5.1. $29.99. Keepcase. *LANG:* English; French. *SUB:* Spanish. *CAP:* English. *FEATURES:* 17 chapter links • Theatrical trailer.
1996 (R) 117m/C Eddie Murphy, Michael Rapaport, Michael Wincott, Carmen Ejogo, Denis Arndt, Art Evans, Donal Logue, Paul Ben-Victor, Kim Miyori, David Michael Silverman; *D:* Thomas Carter; *W:* Randy Feldman; *C:* Fred Murphy; *M:* Steve Porcaro.

Metroland

The title refers to bourgeois suburban boredom. The setting is England, 1977, where Chris (Bale) and Marion (Watson) have settled down with steady job, Volvo, child, mortgage, etc. Then old friend Toni (Ross) shows up. He's still a bachelor, still enjoying the wild life. His presence brings

back memories of a Parisian affair Chris enjoyed. Based on Julian Barnes's novel, the familiar story has some fine moments. The full-frame, no-frills DVD looks fine, though the image is unexceptional. Mark Knopfler's score is better. —*MM*
Movie: 🐾🐾🐾 **DVD:** 🐾🐾▶
Universal Studios Home Video (Cat #20726, UPC #025192072628). Full frame. Dolby Digital Surround Stereo. $24.98. Keepcase. *LANG:* English. *CAP:* English. *FEATURES:* 18 chapter links • Theatrical trailer.
1997 (R) 105m/C *GB FR* Christian Bale, Emily Watson, Lee Ross, Elsa Zylberstein, Ifan Meredith, Rufus, Amanda Ryan; *D:* Philip Saville; *W:* Adrian Hodges; *C:* Jean-Francois Robin; *M:* Mark Knopfler.

Metropolis

Though dismissed by many in its initial release, this meditation on futuristic technology and mass mentality has gained a following over the years. Original set design and special effects make this an innovative film whose influence can be seen in much of the sci-fi that has come since, but you wouldn't know it from this DVD. The fuzzy opening credits introduce a scratchy, muddy print. Some of the print on the title cards runs off the screen. The irritating soundtrack is no help. Other versions of the film exist on tape. Find them. —*MM*
Movie: 🐾🐾🐾 **DVD:** 🐾
Madacy Entertainment (Cat #DVD-9-9007, UPC #056775004392). Full frame. Dolby Digital. $9.95. Keepcase. *FEATURES:* Brief Brigitte Helm biography • Trivia quiz • Scene access • Interactive menu.
1926 115m/B *GE* Brigitte Helm, Alfred Abel, Gustav Froehlich, Rudolf Klein-Rogge, Fritz Rasp, Heinrich George, Theodore Loos, Erwin Biswanger, Olaf Storm, Hans Leo Reich, Heinrich Gotho, Fritz Alberti, Max Dietze; *D:* Fritz Lang; *W:* Fritz Lang, Thea von Harbou; *C:* Karl Freund, Gunther Rittau, Eugene Schufftan; *M:* Gottfried Huppertz.

Miami Rhapsody

Woody Allen-ish comedy focuses on copywriter Gwen (Parker), who becomes disillusioned with the idea of marriage as she learns that everyone in her family is having an affair. Perhaps it was not the best time for Matt (Bellows) to pop the question. Many of the characters come across as self-absorbed neurotics, but director Frankel keeps the tone light and charming throughout. Banderas is particularly good as the nurse who's taking care of Gwen's grandmother and having a fling with her mom (Farrow). On DVD, the film looks terrific. The soft focus that Frankel gives to the Miami locations comes from the original. Sound is very good. —*MM*
Movie: 🐾🐾🐾 **DVD:** 🐾🐾🐾
Hollywood Pictures Home Video (Cat #17637, UPC #717951003478). Widescreen (1.85:1) letterboxed. Dolby Digital

4.0 Surround Stereo. $29.99. Keepcase. *LANG:* English; French. *CAP:* English. *FEATURES:* 24 chapter links.
1995 (PG-13) 95m/C Sarah Jessica Parker, Gil Bellows, Antonio Banderas, Mia Farrow, Paul Mazursky, Kevin Pollak, Barbara Garrick, Carla Gugino, Bo Eason, Naomi Campbell, Jeremy Piven, Kelly Bishop, Ben Stein; *D:* David Frankel; *W:* David Frankel; *C:* Jack Wallner; *M:* Mark Isham.

Michael

Michael (Travolta) is an offbeat archangel with molting wings, and appetites for Schlitz, sugar, and women. He lives in a rural Iowa motel with Pansy (Stapleton) until he reveals himself to three tabloid reporters (Hurt, MacDowell, and Pastorelli). The now-standard Travolta dance sequence takes place in a bar to the tune of "Chain of Fools." Travolta shines; Hurt mopes; MacDowell is irritating. As usual director Ephron works mostly through close-ups and the DVD handles them easily, revealing pores and the textures of carefully maintained faces. The pan-and-scan transfer is adequate to the story. —*MM*
Movie: 🐾🐾▶ **DVD:** 🐾🐾🐾
Warner Home Video, Inc. (Cat #DT6306, UPC #NA). Full frame. Dolby Digital 5.1 Surround; Dolby Surround. $24.98. Snapper. *LANG:* English; French; Spanish. *SUB:* English; French; Spanish. *CAP:* English. *FEATURES:* Cast and crew thumbnail biographies • Theatrical trailer • 31 chapter links • Production notes.
1996 (PG) 105m/C John Travolta, William Hurt, Andie MacDowell, Bob Hoskins, Robert Pastorelli, Jean Stapleton, Teri Garr; *D:* Nora Ephron; *W:* Nora Ephron, Delia Ephron, Pete Dexter; *C:* John Lindley; *M:* Randy Newman.

Michael Collins

Writer-director Neil Jordan has clearly based his Irish epic on *Lawrence of Arabia.* Both are stories of historical figures who fought and "won" complex wars, but then found that peace was even more difficult to handle. Michael Collins (Liam Neeson) fought in Ireland in the early years of the 20th century, and people there are still struggling with the same issues. The film carefully avoids any contemporary political bias, and so it lacks the simple emotional appeal of most cinematic escapism. (Even so, various historians have attacked its accuracy.) Neeson's passionate performance holds it together. Jordan fills the screen with muted greens, blues, and grays that are a cool contrast to the violent action, and they're captured faithfully on DVD. The main problem with the two-sided disc is in its curious index. It allows full access to chapters on the B-side, but to only nine chapters out of 37 on the A-side. —*MM*
Movie: 🐾🐾🐾 **DVD:** 🐾🐾▶
Warner Home Video, Inc. (Cat #14205, UPC #085391420521). Widescreen letterboxed. Dolby Digital Surround 5.1; Dolby Digital Surround. $24.98. Snapper. *LANG:*

English; French. *SUB:* English; French; Spanish. *CAP:* English. *FEATURES:* Cast and crew thumbnails • *The South Bank Show* documentary • 49 chapter links. Two-sided disc must be turned over midway through. **1996 (R) 117m/C** Liam Neeson, Aidan Quinn, Alan Rickman, Stephen Rea, Julia Roberts, Ian Hart, Sean McGinley, Gerard McSorley, Stuart Graham, Brendan Gleeson, Charles Dance, Jonathan Rhys Meyers; *D:* Neil Jordan; *W:* Neil Jordan; *C:* Chris Menges; *M:* Elliot Goldenthal. *AWARDS:* Los Angeles Film Critics Association Awards '96: Best Cinematography; Venice Film Festival '96: Golden Lion, Best Actor (Neeson); *NOM:* Academy Awards '96: Best Cinematography, Best Original Dramatic Score; British Academy Awards '96: Best Supporting Actor (Rickman); Golden Globe Awards '97: Best Actor—Drama (Neeson), Best Score.

Mickey's Once upon a Christmas

These three cartoons are fine fare for younger videophiles. The first, a variation on *Groundhog Day,* finds Donald and his nephews repeating Christmas over and over. The second might have been titled, "Yes, Goofy, There Is a Santa Claus." The third casts Mickey and Minnie in O. Henry's famous story "Gift of the Magi." On DVD, the sound and image are better than the normal Saturday morning cartoon fare, but not in the same league with the studio's theatrical animation. —*MM* *Movie:* 🐾🐾➤ *DVD:* 🐾🐾🐾 Buena Vista Home Entertainment (Cat #18153, UPC #717951004321). Full frame. Dolby Digital Stereo. $39.99. Keepcase. *LANG:* English. *CAP:* English. *FEATURES:* 18 chapter links. **1999 (G) 70m/C V:** Kelsey Grammer.

Midaq Alley

Episodic drama set in Mexico City. *AKA:* The Alley of Miracles; El Callejon de los Milagros. *DVD:* NYR WinStar Home Entertainment (Cat #5142). Full frame. $29.98. Keepcase. *LANG:* Spanish. *SUB:* English. **1995 (R) 140m/C MX** Ernesto Cruz, Maria Rojo, Salma Hayek, Bruno Bichir, Claudio Obregon, Delia Casanova, Margarita Sanz, Juan Manuel Bernal, Luis Felipe Tovar, Daniel Gimenez Cacho; *D:* Jorge Fons; *W:* Vicente Lenero; *C:* Carlos Marcovich; *M:* Lucia Alvarez.

Midnight

A jury foreman's daughter is romantically involved with a gangster who's interested in a particular case before it appears in court. The foreman, who sentenced a girl to death, faces a dilemma when his own daughter is arrested for the same crime. An early Bogart appearance in a supporting role led to a re-release of the film as *Call It Murder* after he made it big. Weak melodrama. *AKA:* Call It Murder. *Movie:* 🐾🐾➤ *DVD:* NYR Madacy Entertainment (Cat #990571). Full frame. Dolby Digital Mono. $9.99. Keepcase. *FEATURES:* Cast and crew thumbnail bios. **1934 74m/B** Humphrey Bogart, Sidney Fox, O.P. Heggie, Henry Hull, Richard Whorf, Margaret Wycherly, Lynne Overman; *D:* Chester Erskine; *W:* Chester Erskine.

Midnight Confessions

Provocative night-time DJ Vannesse (Hoyt) lures her listeners into revealing their sexual fantasies. But when an obsessed fan begins killing women, her involvement is questioned. *Movie:* 🐾 *DVD:* NYR Digital Versatile Disc Ltd. (Cat #705). Full frame. $24.95. Keepcase. **1995 (R) 98m/C** Carol Hoyt, Julie Strain, Monique Parent, Richard Lynch; *D:* Allan Shustak; *W:* Jake Jacobs, Allan Shustak, Marc Cushman, Timothy O'Rawe; *C:* Tom Frazier; *M:* Scott Singer.

Midnight Cowboy

Drama about the relationship between a naive Texan hustler (Voight) and a seedy derelict (Hoffman) is set in the underbelly of New York City. Graphic and emotional character study is brilliantly acted and engaging. Shocking and considered quite risque at the time of its release, this originally "X"-rated film now carries an "R" rating. (It is the only "X"-rated film ever to win the Best Picture Oscar.) *Midnight Cowboy* has never looked better than on this DVD, which, despite some preprint flaws, is very sharp with detailed, accurate colors. Blacks are true with added punch given by the very good contrast. The brightness levels are far better than on earlier home video releases and viewing is far more comfortable. The sound has also been improved substantially and has both much better frequency response, imaging, and dynamics on the music, while making the dialogue easier to understand. —*JO* *Movie:* 🐾🐾🐾🐾 *DVD:* 🐾🐾🐾🐾 MGM Home Entertainment (Cat #906038, UPC #027616603890). Widescreen (1.85:1) letterboxed; full frame. Dolby Surround. $24.98. Snapper. *LANG:* English (DS); French (Mono). *SUB:* English; French; Spanish. *CAP:* English; French; Spanish. *FEATURES:* 31 chapter links • Theatrical trailer. **1969 (R) 113m/C** Dustin Hoffman, Jon Voight, Sylvia Miles, Brenda Vaccaro, John McGiver, Bob Balaban, Barnard Hughes; *D:* John Schlesinger; *W:* Waldo Salt; *C:* Adam Holender; *M:* John Barry. *AWARDS:* Academy Awards '69: Best Adapted Screenplay, Best Director (Schlesinger), Best Picture; American Film Institute (AFI) '98: Top 100; British Academy Awards '69: Best Actor (Hoffman), Best Director (Schlesinger), Best Film, Best Screenplay; Directors Guild of America Awards '69: Best Director (Schlesinger), National Film Registry '94; New York Film Critics Awards '69: Best Actor (Voight); National Society of Film Critics Awards '69: Best Actor (Voight); Writers Guild of America '69: Best Adapted Screenplay; *NOM:* Academy Awards '69: Best Actor (Hoffman), Best Actor (Voight), Best Film Editing, Best Supporting Actress (Miles).

Midnight Express

Gripping and powerful film based on the true story of Billy Hayes. Davis plays Hayes as a young American in Turkey who is busted trying to smuggle hashish. He is sentenced to a brutal and nightmarish prison for life. After enduring tremendous mental and physical torture, he seeks escape along the "Midnight Express." It's not always easy to watch, but the overall effect is riveting and unforgettable. This depressing film features a lot of subdued lighting, which helps convey the mood of the prison. Even in those sequences, the DVD remains sharp, with a very low grain level, and no shimmering in the blacks, which stay fairly true. Colors vary a little, sometimes looking like the preprint was gathered from several different sources, but are generally accurate. The dark scenes do not seem to generate any extra grain or color bleed. Contrast and brightness levels stay consistent and also work well with the differences in the lighting. The Dolby Digital 2.0 mono is almost always stronger than other mono tracks, and this one is pretty amazing. The mix gives the track very good imaging through the speakers and the sound itself is very full-bodied. —*JO* *Movie:* 🐾🐾🐾 *DVD:* 🐾🐾🐾 Columbia Tristar Home Video (Cat #00549, UPC #043396005495). Widescreen (1.85:1) letterboxed; full frame. Dolby Digital 2.0 Mono. $28.95. Keepcase. *LANG:* English; French. *SUB:* English; French. *CAP:* English. *FEATURES:* 28 chapter links • "Making of" featurette • Theatrical trailer. **1978 (R) 120m/C** John Hurt, Randy Quaid, Brad Davis, Paul Smith, Bo Hopkins, Oliver Stone; *D:* Alan Parker; *W:* Oliver Stone; *C:* Michael Seresin; *M:* Giorgio Moroder. *AWARDS:* Academy Awards '78: Best Adapted Screenplay, Best Original Score; British Academy Awards '78: Best Director (Parker), Best Supporting Actor (Hurt); Golden Globe Awards '79: Best Film—Drama, Best Screenplay, Best Supporting Actor (Hurt), Best Score; Writers Guild of America '78: Best Adapted Screenplay; *NOM:* Academy Awards '78: Best Director (Parker), Best Film Editing, Best Picture, Best Supporting Actor (Hurt).

Midnight in the Garden of Good and Evil (SE)

An all-star cast can't save Eastwood's grossly mishandled adaptation of John Berendt's best-selling book on the eccentric citizens and lush scenery of Savannah. New York journalist John Kelso

(Cusack) is sent on assignment to report on the glamourous Christmas parties of famed citizen and ham Jim Williams (Spacey, oozing his usual silky charm), only to be detoured by Williams shooting his male, live-in companion. Was it cold-blooded murder or self defense? With Eastwood's clumsy direction, a dragging running time, an overabundance of characters taken verbatim from the book (including drag queen Lady Chablis playing herself, unfortunately), and a dull romance between Kelso and local flower Mandy (Eastwood's daughter), the rich subject which made the book a top-seller for four years is all but lost and the answer to the above question is moot. *Midnight* has the star power for greatness, but looks certainly are deceiving. Overall the DVD transfer is sharp and grain-free, with good handling of details. Colors are also very good and appear accurate to the theatre. There is occasional color bleed, but nothing to worry about. Contrast and brightness are good, and although the picture feels like it could have used a boost to both, it might have taken away some of the subtleties of the cinematography. The 5.1 sound has good highs and lows, and is fairly dynamic but lacking in the use of the Surround tracks which fail to deliver much, even in the way of ambience. —*JO*
Movie: 🐾🐾🐾 **DVD:** 🐾🐾🐾
Warner Home Video, Inc. (Cat #14776, UPC #085391477624). Widescreen (1.85:1) anamorphic. Dolby Digital 5.1. $24.98. Snapper. *LANG:* English; French. *SUB:* English; French; Spanish. *CAP:* English. *FEATURES:* 43 chapter links • Interactive bonus footage • Production notes • Theatrical trailer.
1997 (R) 155m/C Kevin Spacey, John Cusack, Jack Thompson, Alison Eastwood, The Lady Chablis, Irma P. Hall, Paul Hipp, Jude Law, Dorothy Loudon, Anne Haney, Kim Hunter, Geoffrey Lewis; *D:* Clint Eastwood; *W:* John Lee Hancock; *C:* Jack N. Green; *M:* Lennie Niehaus.

Midnight Run

Grodin's character is in a world of trouble. The accountant has embezzled $15 million from the Mob, given the money to charity, and jumped bail. Now the law is after him, the Mob wants him, too, and De Niro—playing an ex-cop and bounty hunter—wants the reward for capturing him in New York and bringing him back to Los Angeles. Soon, the bounty hunter finds his task will be more trying than he first thought. The friction between the two leads is fun to watch, and the script finds the proper balance between action and comedy. The DVD is a bare-bones affair, with no extras whatsoever not even captions or subtitles. The letterboxed image looks good, but the picture is not anamorphically enhanced for wide TV sets. The soundtrack is a plain-Jane 2.0 Surround mix. —*MB*
Movie: 🐾🐾🐾 **DVD:** 🐾🐾
Image Entertainment (Cat #ID4271USDVD, UPC #014381427127). Widescreen

(1.85:1) letterboxed. Dolby Digital 2.0. $24.99. Snapper. *LANG:* English. *FEATURES:* 16 chapter links.
1988 (R) 125m/C Robert De Niro, Charles Grodin, Yaphet Kotto, John Ashton, Dennis Farina, Joe Pantoliano, Richard Foronjy, Wendy Phillips; *D:* Martin Brest; *W:* George Gallo; *C:* Donald E. Thorin; *M:* Danny Elfman.

Midway

The conventional all-star cast is saddled with perhaps the most ponderous and stilted dialogue ever written for a World War II epic. Virtually everything remotely enjoyable about the film has been done better elsewhere. (See *Tora! Tora! Tora!, Wake Island,* or even John Ford's short documentary "The Battle of Midway.") In this case, DVD actually heightens the film's many flaws. First, the difference between archival footage and studio re-creations is jarringly obvious in the combat and aerial scenes. Throughout, diagonal lines, tile patterns, and Venetian blinds flash. The dubbing of Paul Frees's rich bass voice for Toshiro Mifune's character is even more startling. Otherwise, the sound is only so-so, despite the fact that the film was released theatrically in the short-lived "Sensurround" sound process. —*MM*
Movie: 🐾🐾🐾 **DVD:** 🐾🐾
Image Entertainment (Cat #ID4292USDVD, UPC #014381429220). Widescreen (2.35:1) letterboxed. Dolby Digital Mono. $24.99. Snapper. *LANG:* English. *CAP:* English. *FEATURES:* 20 chapter links.
1976 (PG) 132m/C Charlton Heston, Henry Fonda, James Coburn, Glenn Ford, Hal Holbrook, Robert Mitchum, Cliff Robertson, Robert Wagner, Kevin Dobson, Christopher George, Toshiro Mifune, Tom Selleck; *D:* Jack Smight; *W:* Donald S. Sanford; *C:* Harry Stradling Jr.; *M:* John Williams.

The Mighty

Kevin (Culkin) suffers from crippling Morquio's syndrome. He moves next door to Max, who's huge and L.D. ("learning disabled"). It takes them some time to discover how strong they are together, but once that happens, they decide to emulate King Arthur and his knights and to fight injustice wherever they see it. Performances all around—particularly Stone as Kevin's down-to-earth mom—could not be better. The film never found much of an audience at the theatres. That is home video's gain because on DVD, it is excellent with a crisp sharp image and very good sound. Based on Rodman Philbrick's novel *Freak the Mighty,* it's a companion piece to Terry Gilliam's *Fisher King* and *October Sky.* Highly recommended. —*MM*
Movie: 🐾🐾🐾 **DVD:** 🐾🐾🐾
Miramax Pictures Home Video (Cat #17092, UPC #717951002068). Widescreen (1.85:1) letterboxed. Dolby Digital 5.1 Surround Stereo. $29.99. Keepcase. *LANG:* English. *CAP:* English. *FEATURES:*

19 chapter links • "Making of" featurette • "Making of" music video featurette.
1998 (PG-13) 100m/C Kieran Culkin, Elden Henson, Sharon Stone, Gillian Anderson, Harry Dean Stanton, Gena Rowlands, James Gandolfini, Joe Perrino, Meat Loaf Aday, Jenifer Lewis; *D:* Peter Chelsom; *W:* Charles Leavitt; *C:* John de Borman; *M:* Trevor Jones. *AWARDS: NOM:* Golden Globe Awards '99: Best Song ("The Mighty"), Best Supporting Actress (Stone).

Mighty Aphrodite

Neurotic (Surprise!) New York sportswriter Lenny Weinrib (Allen) is trapped in an unhappy marriage to art dealer Amanda (Bonham Carter), who talks him into adopting a child. Film comes alive when Lenny tracks down his son's biological mother, consummate dumb blond and hooker/porno actress Linda, played with over-the-top (in a good way) gusto by Sorvino. Lenny attempts to reform his son's real mother while a Greek chorus (including Abraham and Dukakis) provide a running commentary on the tragedy/ comedy of Lenny's predicaments. Allen's 31st film treads into familiar Woodman waters but falls short of his past comic genius. The DVD seems to be a truer representation of the theatrical release than previous home video versions, although the color appears to be unusual in most of the dimmer scenes. At times the colors are quite vibrant, and even the deeper hues bleed very little. Sharpness is good and those darker sequences only pick up a touch of grain. Contrast is very good and the brightness stays consistent from light to dark scenes. The sound is nothing special but the dialogue is always given enough boost in the mix to be clear and easy to understand. —*JO*
Movie: 🐾🐾▶ **DVD:** 🐾🐾🐾
Miramax Pictures Home Video (Cat #16451, UPC #71795100159). Widescreen (1.85:1) letterboxed. Mono. $29.99. Keepcase. *LANG:* English. *CAP:* English. *FEATURES:* 22 chapter links.
1995 (R) 95m/C Woody Allen, Helena Bonham Carter, Mira Sorvino, F. Murray Abraham, Michael Rapaport, Jack Warden, Olympia Dukakis, Peter Weller, Claire Bloom, David Ogden Stiers; *D:* Woody Allen; *W:* Woody Allen; *C:* Carlo Di Palma; *M:* Dick Hyman. *AWARDS:* Academy Awards '95: Best Supporting Actress (Sorvino); Golden Globe Awards '96: Best Supporting Actress (Sorvino); National Board of Review Awards '95: Best Supporting Actress (Sorvino); New York Film Critics Awards '95: Best Supporting Actress (Sorvino); Broadcast Film Critics Association Awards '95: Best Supporting Actress (Sorvino); *NOM:* Academy Awards '95: Best Original Screenplay; British Academy Awards '95: Best Supporting Actress (Sorvino); Screen Actors Guild Award '95: Best Supporting Actress (Sorvino); Writers Guild of America '95: Best Original Screenplay.

The Mighty Ducks

Emilio Estevez plays Gordon Bombay, a character named after two brands of gin. He's a cynical lawyer who's arrested for D.U.I. and sentenced to do his community service by coaching a pee-wee league hockey team. He bonds with the cute, latter-day Li'l Rascals kids, overcomes the hockey-related trauma in his past and though he tells the kids that winning doesn't matter, guess what happens at the end of the big game? The DVD image is no better than fair, reflecting the rough quality of the original. —MM
Movie: ♪♪▶ **DVD:** ♪♪
Buena Vista Home Entertainment (Cat #18151). Widescreen letterboxed. Dolby Digital Stereo. $29.99. *LANG:* English; French; Spanish. *CAP:* English. *FEATURES:* 24 chapter links.
1992 (PG) 114m/C Emilio Estevez, Joss Ackland, Lane Smith, Heidi Kling, Josef Sommer, Matt Doherty, Steven Brill, Joshua Jackson, Elden Ratliff, Shaun Weiss; **D:** Stephen Herek; **W:** Steven Brill, Brian Hohlfield; **C:** Thomas Del Ruth; **M:** David Newman.

Mighty Joe Young

The special effects collaboration of Rick Baker, Dream Quest Images and Hoyt Yeatman is responsible for seamless visuals that make a 15-foot-tall, 2,000-pound brown-eyed gorilla seem absolutely real and loveable. In this loose remake of the 1949 film—made by special effects genius Ray Harryhausen, who appears in a party scene—the big guy dwarfs his human costars in more ways than one. The story is strictly formula stuff from the Disney factory, but it's handled with such energy that the film is a wholesome winner. The stereo effects kick in nicely during the action scenes. —MM
Movie: ♪♪♪ **DVD:** ♪♪♪
Buena Vista Home Entertainment (Cat #16538, UPC #717951001641). Widescreen (1.85:1) letterboxed. Dolby Digital 5.1 Surround Stereo. $29.99. Keepcase. *LANG:* English. *CAP:* English. *FEATURES:* 16 chapter links • Theatrical trailer • "Making of" featurette.
1998 (PG) 114m/C Bill Paxton, Charlize Theron, David Paymer, Regina King, Rade Serbedzija, Peter Firth, Lawrence Pressman, Linda Purl, Ray Harryhausen; **D:** Ron Underwood; **W:** Mark Rosenthal, Larry Konner; **C:** Don Peterman, Oliver Wood; **M:** James Horner. *AWARDS: NOM:* Academy Awards '98: Best Visual Effects.

Mikey

In the evil-child sub-genre, this is a relatively weak but expensively staged entry. It lacks the emotional power of *The Other* and the strong performance of Patty McCormack in *The Bad Seed*. Even though he's offed his entire family before the first ten minutes, Mikey (Bonsall) isn't believably threatening. He's a troubled,

manipulative psychoboy who's a young version of *The Stepfather*. The adult cast of character actors do well with the unsurprising script.
Movie: ♪ **DVD:** NYR
Studio Home Entertainment (Cat #4045). $24.95.
1992 (R) 92m/C Brian Bonsall, John Diehl, Lyman Ward, Josie Bissett, Ashley Laurence, Mimi Craven, Whitby Hertford; **D:** Dennis Dimster; **W:** Jonathan Glassner; **C:** Thomas Jewett; **M:** Tim Truman.

Milk and Money

Robert Petkoff is a medical student in New York City who suddenly chucks it all and sets out on a series of meandering adventures with various screw-loose women. He finally settles upon Calista Flockhart, the mistress of wealthy businessman Robert Vaughn, and the story comes to an end. What must have started out on paper as a kooky bit of whimsy, populated by offbeat characters and "screwball" situations, comes across on film as dull, flat, and ultimately pointless. DVD presentation is a movie-only offering, with O.K. sound and picture quality, whose existence appears to be for die-hard Flockhart fans only. —RT
Movie: ♪▶ **DVD:** ♪♪
Image Entertainment (Cat #ID58790K, UPC #014381587920). Full frame. AC3 - 2 Channel. $19.99. Snapper. *LANG:* English. *FEATURES:* 14 chapter links.
1997 86m/C Robert Petkoff, Calista Flockhart, Robert Vaughn, Peter Boyle, Margaret Colin, Olympia Dukakis; **D:** Michael Bergmann; **C:** Irek Hartowicz.

Millennium

The Earth of the future is running out of time. The people are sterile and the air is terrible. To keep the planet viable, Louise Baltimore (Ladd) and company must go back in time and "rescue" certain people. Kristofferson is the investigator who falls for the mystery woman. The effects aren't bad and the plot is complex, if less than completely coherent, making the film more enjoyable than it really ought to be. The DVD image is a little on the soft side, with harsh explosion and pyrotechnic effects, but I think that's the way the theatrical release looked, too. The alternative ending is accessed through the "Special Features" section. —MM
Movie: ♪♪▶ **DVD:** ♪♪
Artisan Entertainment (Cat #60491, UPC #01223604910). Widescreen (1.85:1) anamorphic. Dolby Digital Surround Stereo. $24.98. Keepcase. *LANG:* English. *SUB:* Spanish. *FEATURES:* 36 chapter links • Cast and crew thumbnail bios • Production notes • Alternative ending.
1989 (PG-13) 108m/C Kris Kristofferson, Cheryl Ladd, Daniel J. Travanti, Lloyd Bochner, Robert Joy, Brent Carver, Maury Chaykin, David McIlwraith, Al Waxman; **D:** Michael Anderson Sr.; **W:** John Varley; **C:** Rene Ohashi; **M:** Eric N. Robertson.

The Millionaire's Express

Hung returns to his village and hopes to save it with a plan to derail the local train, which carries a large number of wealthy passengers. *AKA:* Shanghai Express; Fu Gui Lie Che.
Movie: ♪♪ **DVD:** NYR
Tai Seng Video Marketing (Cat #5374). Dolby Digital 5.1 Surround Stereo. $49.95. Keepcase. *LANG:* Cantonese; Mandarin. *SUB:* Bahasa Indonesian & Malaysian; Chinese Simplified & Traditional; English; Japanese; Korean; Thai; Vietnamese.
1986 107m/C *HK* Sammo Hung, Yuen Biao, Cynthia Rothrock, Richard Norton, Yukari Oshima; **D:** Sammo Hung; **W:** Sammo Hung.

The Millionairess

Though the film is a British version of a 1950s big-budget Hollywood romance, and so does not give famous cinematographer Jack Hildyard the most challenging raw material to work with, this one does feature a young Sophia Loren at her most drop-dead gorgeous, which may be as drop-dead gorgeous as any woman has ever been in the history of the planet and so that's more than enough to recommend the disc. She plays an incredibly wealthy woman who has ended a bad marriage and feels that the only thing she still needs to fulfill her life is a good husband. Enter Sellers, as a humble doctor from India. (His accent has been copied by a generation of actors.) The DVD image and sound are fine for a film of this age. The disc appears to have been made from a near-perfect original with exceptionally bright colors and only a minimum of flecks and scratches. —MM
Movie: ♪♪▶ **DVD:** ♪♪♪
Fox/Lorber Home Video (Cat #FLV5105, UPC #720917510521). Full frame. $29.98. Keepcase. *FEATURES:* 8 chapter links • Filmographies.
1960 90m/C *GB* Sophia Loren, Peter Sellers, Alastair Sim, Vittorio De Sica, Dennis Price; **D:** Anthony Asquith; **C:** Jack Hildyard.

Milo

Psychological crime drama. Four young girls are lured to the home of creepy kid Milo where they witness the murder of one of their friends. Sixteen years later, the girls are reunited for a wedding and Milo returns as well.
Movie: ♪♪ **DVD:** NYR
Studio Home Entertainment (Cat #7075). Full frame. Dolby Digital Stereo. $24.95. Keepcase. *LANG:* English. *SUB:* Spanish. *FEATURES:* Cast and crew thumbnail bios • Trailer.
1998 (R) 94m/C Jennifer Jostyn, Maya McLaughlin, Asher Metchik, Paula Cale, Vincent Schiavelli, Antonio Fargas, Rae'ven Kelly, Walter Olkewicz; **D:** Pascal Franchot; **W:** Craig Mitchell; **C:** Yuri Neyman; **M:** Kevin Manthei.

Mimic

Married biotech scientists Sorvino and Northam upset the balance of nature when they cure a plague only to have their insectoid concoction unleashed in the New York subways. This causes giant cockroaches to mimic—and kill—humans. Far-fetched story is forgiven with a unique script (both John Sayles and Steven Soderbergh made additions) and original kills and thrills. Plenty of gore also makes it a worthy addition to the horror genre. *Mimic* is incredibly dark, but the image is usually very sharp and grain level very low. There are some artifacts in the dark action scenes, but the DVD is still preferable to both the VHS and laserdisc copies. Colors and blacks stay accurate in the different lighting conditions. The contrast is usually able to pull the details out of these darker scenes and the brightness level is mostly very comfortable. The 5.1 Surround tracks really come in for the last third of the movie, which is pretty much nonstop chaos filled with action galore. The score also sounds very good with crisp highs and decent (if not rumbling) low end. —*JO*

Movie: 🐾🐾🐾▶ *DVD:* 🐾🐾🐾
Buena Vista Home Entertainment (Cat #14251, UPC #717951000323). Widescreen (1.85:1) letterboxed. Dolby Digital. $29.99. Keepcase. *LANG:* English. *CAP:* English. *FEATURES:* 14 chapter links • Theatrical trailer.
1997 (R) 105m/C Jeremy Northam, Mira Sorvino, Josh Brolin, Charles S. Dutton, Giancarlo Giannini, F. Murray Abraham, Alexander Goodwin; *D:* Guillermo del Toro; *W:* John Sayles, Steven Soderbergh, Matthew Robbins; *C:* Dan Laustsen; *M:* Marco Beltrami.

Minnie and Moskowitz

On their commentary track, stars Seymour Cassel and Gena Rowlands take a trip down memory lane. They admit up front that they haven't seen the film in years and the rest of their free association conversation mirrors director Cassavetes's shot-on-the-fly quality. The movie's a love story about a mismatched couple. Minnie Moore (Rowlands) is a museum curator. Seymour Moskowitz (Cassel) is an unreconstructed hippie who works as a parking lot attendant. Like so many '70s movies, the low-budget character-driven story does not depend on slick visuals, and DVD technology does nothing to change that. Appreciate it for the stars' performance and don't miss Tim Carey's inspired (and probably extemporaneous) monologue in a New York diner. —*MM*
Movie: 🐾🐾🐾▶ *DVD:* 🐾🐾🐾
Anchor Bay (Cat #DV10987, UPC #013131098792). Widescreen (1.85:1) anamorphic. Dolby Digital Mono. $24.98. Keepcase. *LANG:* English. *FEATURES:* 22 chapter links • Thumbnail biographies of Rowlands, Cassel, and Cassavetes • Theatrical trailer.

1971 114m/C Gena Rowlands, Seymour Cassel, Val Avery, Timothy Carey, Holly Near, Katherine Cassavetes, Mary Allen "Lady" Rowlands, David Rowlands, Elizabeth Deering, Elsie Adams, John Cassavetes; *D:* John Cassavetes; *W:* John Cassavetes; *C:* Arthur Ornitz.

Miracle on 34th Street

One of the all-time favorite Christmas films has aged gracefully with its use of sentimentality as a seasoning, not the main ingredient. The real Kris Kringle (Gwenn) fills in as Santa Claus in the Macy's Thanksgiving parade. Eventually, he must prove his identity in court and to young Susan (Wood). On DVD, the image suffers a few odd flaws—the first close-up of Gwenn seems to swim, but that might be due to window glass—but the rest contains some of Hollywood's better black-and-white cinematography, particularly in the New York exteriors. The monaural sound is fine. —*MM* *AKA:* The Big Heart.
Movie: 🐾🐾🐾▶ *DVD:* 🐾🐾🐾
20th Century Fox (Cat #4112755, UPC #086162127557). Full frame. Mono. $29.98. Keepcase. *LANG:* English; French. *SUB:* Spanish. *CAP:* English. *FEATURES:* 21 chapter links • Theatrical trailer • TV spot • Cast and crew filmographies.
1947 97m/B Maureen O'Hara, John Payne, Edmund Gwenn, Natalie Wood, William Frawley, Porter Hall, Gene Lockhart, Thelma Ritter, Jack Albertson; *D:* George Seaton; *W:* George Seaton; *C:* Lloyd Ahern, Charles Clarke; *M:* Cyril Mockridge. *AWARDS:* Academy Awards '47: Best Screenplay, Best Story, Best Supporting Actor (Gwenn); Golden Globe Awards '48: Best Screenplay, Best Supporting Actor (Gwenn); *NOM:* Academy Awards '47: Best Picture.

Miracles

In this wonderful sleeper, Jackie Chan plays a down-on-his-luck young man in pre–World War II Hong Kong who mistakenly becomes the head of one of the city's largest gangs. Of course, his innate good humor changes everything. Chan directed the big-budget production, and if it doesn't quite have the sparkle and polish of comparably ambitious American works, it looks just fine on DVD. The image is overly bright throughout and some patterns flash, but those are minor flaws. The fight routines are some of his most energetic and imaginative, and that Chan charm makes up for a lot. The English subtitles are placed in the lower bar of the letterbox. All in all, this is terrific for fans who are familiar only with Chan's more recent work. —*MM*
Movie: 🐾🐾🐾▶ *DVD:* 🐾🐾🐾
Tai Seng Video Marketing (Cat #MS/DVD/043/98). Widescreen (2.35:1) letterboxed. Dolby Digital 5.1 Surround Stereo. $49.95. Keepcase. *LANG:* Cantonese; Mandarin. *SUB:* Traditional & Simplified Chinese; English; Japanese; Bahasa Indonesia & Malaysia; Thai; Korean; Viet-

namese. *FEATURES:* 9 chapter links • Trailer • Cast and crew thumbnail bios.
1989 122m/C *HK* Jackie Chan, Anita Mui, Richard Ng, Yuen Biao; *D:* Jackie Chan; *W:* Edward Tong; *C:* Siu-Tin Lei.

The Mirror Has Two Faces

Producer-director-star Streisand's film isn't the complete disaster that many of her critics had predicted. But it's still a heavy-handed vanity piece that plods along at an elephantine pace. For a serious drama, that might not be a problem, but it's supposed to be a romantic comedy about two charming, oddball Columbia University professors (Streisand and Bridges)—she an ugly duckling, he a flustered hunk. It's makeover time for her. The bare-bones DVD is no improvement over VHS tape because both necessarily retain the slightly misty focus of the original theatrical release. Sound is fine. —*MM*
Movie: 🐾▶ *DVD:* 🐾🐾
Columbia Tristar Home Video (Cat #82529, UPC #043396825291). Widescreen (1.85:1) letterboxed; full frame. Dolby Digital 5.1 Surround Stereo; Dolby Digital Surround Stereo. $29.95. Keepcase. *LANG:* English; French; Spanish. *SUB:* Spanish; Korean. *FEATURES:* 57 chapter links.
1996 (PG-13) 127m/C Barbra Streisand, Jeff Bridges, Pierce Brosnan, Mimi Rogers, Lauren Bacall, Brenda Vaccaro, Austin Pendleton, George Segal, Elle Macpherson; *D:* Barbra Streisand; *W:* Richard LaGravenese; *C:* Dante Spinotti, Andrzej Bartkowiak; *M:* Barbra Streisand, Marvin Hamlisch. *AWARDS:* Golden Globe Awards '97: Best Supporting Actress (Bacall); Screen Actors Guild Award '96: Best Supporting Actress (Bacall); *NOM:* Academy Awards '96: Best Song ("I've Finally Found Someone"), Best Supporting Actress (Bacall); British Academy Awards '96: Best Supporting Actress (Bacall); Golden Globe Awards '97: Best Actress—Musical/Comedy (Streisand), Best Song ("I've Finally Found Someone"), Best Score.

Mischievous

Jeff (Jeffery) reconnects with his old flame Angela (Burton) at his high school reunion and learns that she has become something of a sexual adventuress, who dares him to more extreme encounters. It's standard stuff for erotic video thrillers and even on DVD, this one has an appropriately sordid look. The exterior night scenes are exceptionally grainy and even the conventional interiors have a rough texture that appears to be deliberate. —*MM*
Movie: 🐾🐾 *DVD:* 🐾🐾
Image Entertainment (Cat #ID4761DRDVD, UPC #014381476125). Full frame. Dolby Digital Stereo. $24.99. Snapper. *LANG:* English. *FEATURES:* 12 chapter links.
1996 95m/C Jennifer Burton, Doug Jeffery, Christopher Abraham, Cordell Conway; *D:* Mike Sedan; *W:* Helen Haxton; *C:* Henri Carboni.

Misery Brothers Y2K

Forgettable comedy brings together a host of second- and third-tier celebrities for an unapologetic knock-off of the "stupid" school of low-brow humor, with most of the jokes based on breasts. Debbe Dunning appears as lawyer Ima Barrister in a low-cut red dress. The titular brothers (coproducer Leo Rossi and writer-producer-director Lorenzo Doumani) wear clothes that are even harder on the eyes than the screaming wardrobe seen in *Dumb and Dumber*. The fact that the clashing clothes are faithfully reproduced on the DVD version is hardly a recommendation. The truth is that the film looks terrific on disc. But is that a good thing? By the way, "Y2K" was added to the title for no reason. —*MM*

Movie: 𝅘𝅥𝅘𝅥▶ **DVD:** 𝅘𝅥𝅘𝅥
DMG Entertainment (Cat #DMG993D, UPC #640587990327). Full frame. Dolby Digital Surround. $24.98. Snapper. *LANG:* English. *CAP:* English. *FEATURES:* 9 chapter links ▪ Trailers for *Misery Bros.* and three other DMG releases ▪ Plot synopsis.
1995 ?m/C Lorenzo Doumani, Leo Rossi, Debbe Dunning, Sherman Hemsley, Noriyuki "Pat" Morita, Abe Vigoda; *D:* Lorenzo Doumani; *W:* Lorenzo Doumani.

Mission: Impossible

Director DePalma updates the popular '60s TV series. Cruise is Ethan Hunt, pointman extraordinaire of the IMF team headed by Jim Phelps (Voight). Their team is sent to recover a computer disk with devastating information from a Russian spy. Mind-boggling plot twists abound. Alluring European locales, tight pacing, and tension-inducing special effects team up with solid acting talent, including French favorite Jean Reno. Most Paramount DVDs are above average, and this is no exception. The most amazing thing is that even during the dark, foggy street scenes, there are very few artifacts. The disc is very good in most aspects—contrast, brightness, blacks—and moves very close to excellent in sharpness, grain, and color. Reds bleed here and there, but they seldom interfere with the enjoyment of the disc. The audio matches the picture quality with full dynamics, crisp highs, booming (not boomy) lows, and great Surround, both 4.0 and 5.1. —*JO*

Movie: 𝅘𝅥𝅘𝅥𝅘𝅥 **DVD:** 𝅘𝅥𝅘𝅥𝅘𝅥▶
Paramount Home Video (Cat #154077, UPC #097361549774). Widescreen (2.35:1) letterboxed; full frame. Dolby Digital 5.1; Dolby Surround. $29.95. Keepcase. *LANG:* English (DD5.1, DDS); French (DDS). *SUB:* Spanish. *CAP:* English. *FEATURES:* Dual-layered RSDL ▪ 13 chapter links ▪ Theatrical trailer.
1996 (PG-13) 110m/C Tom Cruise, Jon Voight, Emmanuelle Beart, Ving Rhames, Henry Czerny, Emilio Estevez, Vanessa Redgrave, Jean Reno, Dale Dye; *D:* Brian DePalma; *W:* Robert Towne, David Koepp; *C:* Stephen Burum; *M:* Danny Elfman. *AWARDS: NOM:* MTV Movie Awards '97: Best Action Sequence.

Mississippi Burning

Director Alan Parker's hard-edged social drama revolves around the civil rights movement in Mississippi in 1964. Three activists are murdered on their way home. When the bodies turn up missing, racial hatred explodes into violence. FBI agents Ruppert Anderson (Hackman) and Alan Ward (Dafoe) are sent to head up the investigation, and use their own brand of intimidation to solve the case. Standout performance by McDormand garnered an Academy Award nomination. The film also received nominations for Best Picture, Best Director, and Best Actor (Hackman). A hard-hitting and controversial film based on true events. The DVD case says the digital transfer was approved by Parker, and it's a good one. From the opening murders (a very dark sequence) on through, the picture is sharp with very little grain or artifacts. Blacks are excellent, as are contrast and brightness levels. Colors are excellent and there is good depth throughout. The only thing missing is a 5.1 soundtrack but the Dolby Surround is so good, you shouldn't miss it at all. A great DVD. —*JO*

Movie: 𝅘𝅥𝅘𝅥𝅘𝅥▶ **DVD:** 𝅘𝅥𝅘𝅥𝅘𝅥𝅘𝅥
Image Entertainment (Cat #ID4081ORDVD, UPC #01438148126). Widescreen (1.85:1) letterboxed. Dolby Surround. $29.99. Snapper. *LANG:* English. *CAP:* English. *FEATURES:* 44 chapter links ▪ Theatrical trailer ▪ Commentary: Alan Parker.
1988 (R) 127m/C Gene Hackman, Willem Dafoe, Frances McDormand, Brad Dourif, R. Lee Ermey, Gailard Sartain, Stephen Tobolowsky, Michael Rooker, Pruitt Taylor Vince, Badja Djola, Kevin Dunn, Frankie Faison, Tom Mason, Park Overall; *D:* Alan Parker; *W:* Chris Gerolmo; *C:* Peter Biziou; *M:* Trevor Jones. *AWARDS:* Academy Awards '88: Best Cinematography; Berlin International Film Festival '88: Best Actor (Hackman); National Board of Review Awards '88: Best Actor (Hackman), Best Director (Parker), Best Supporting Actress (McDormand); *NOM:* Academy Awards '88: Best Actor (Hackman), Best Director (Parker), Best Film Editing, Best Picture, Best Sound, Best Supporting Actress (McDormand).

Mrs. Brown

Unusual drama about friendship finds Queen Victoria (Dench) suffering "unfettered morbidity" after the death of her husband and withdrawing from public life to her Scottish retreat at Balmoral. There she's looked after by coarse highlander John Brown (Connolly), who is ostensibly on hand to care for her pony. As he becomes more overprotective, whispers of an affair are bruited about. The Prince of Wales (Westhead) and the oily Prime Minister Disraeli (Sher) then must persuade Brown to withdraw to preserve her reputation. On DVD, the film has a definite dark cast with substantial graininess in the image. It's appropriate to the setting and story, though, and director Madden compensates by sharpening sounds. Natural noises are enhanced to help define the action, but at the center of the film is Dame Dench's commanding performance. —*MM*

Movie: 𝅘𝅥𝅘𝅥𝅘𝅥 **DVD:** 𝅘𝅥𝅘𝅥▶
Miramax Pictures Home Video (Cat #17251, UPC #717951002440). Widescreen (1.85:1) letterboxed. Dolby Digital Surround Stereo. $29.99. Keepcase. *LANG:* English. *CAP:* English. *FEATURES:* 15 chapter links ▪ Theatrical trailer.
1997 (PG) 103m/C *GB* Judi Dench, Billy Connolly, Geoffrey Palmer, Anthony Sher, Richard Pasco, Gerard Butler, David Westhead; *D:* John Madden; *W:* Jeremy Brock; *C:* Richard Greatrex; *M:* Stephen Warbeck. *AWARDS:* British Academy Awards '97: Best Actress (Dench), Best Costume Design; Golden Globe Awards '98: Best Actress—Drama (Dench); *NOM:* Academy Awards '97: Best Actress (Dench), Best Makeup; British Academy Awards '97: Best Actor (Connolly), Best Film, Best Original Screenplay; Screen Actors Guild Award '97: Best Actress (Dench), Best Supporting Actor (Connolly).

Mrs. Dalloway

Mannered adaptation of the Virginia Woolf novel has a radiant performance by Redgrave in the title role. Wealthy, middle-aged, and long married to boring politician Richard (Standing), Clarissa Dalloway is making preparations for her latest soiree in 1923 London. The past rudely intrudes when old flame Peter Walsh (Kitchen) returns from India and causes Clarissa to consider the choices she has made. Her encounter with a shell-shocked veteran (Graves) further roils her psychological waters. The action is slow, but the story is fascinating and the ensemble acting could not be better. The DVD image is clear and unmarred; sound is equally crisp. Recommended. —*MM*

Movie: 𝅘𝅥𝅘𝅥𝅘𝅥 **DVD:** 𝅘𝅥𝅘𝅥𝅘𝅥
WinStar Home Entertainment (Cat #FLV5144, UPC #720917514420). Widescreen letterboxed. Dolby Digital Surround Stereo. $29.98. Keepcase. *LANG:* English. *FEATURES:* 6 chapter links ▪ Trailer ▪ Production credits ▪ Filmographies and awards.
1997 (PG-13) 97m/C *GB* Vanessa Redgrave, Michael Kitchen, John Standing, Rupert Graves, Natascha McElhone, Alan Cox, Sarah Badel, Lena Headey, Robert Portal, Amelia Bullmore, Margaret Tyzack, Robert Hardy; *D:* Marleen Gorris; *W:* Eileen Atkins; *C:* Sue Gibson; *M:* Ilona Sekacz.

Mrs. Doubtfire

Daniel Hilliard (Williams) is an unemployed and immature actor who transforms himself into Mrs. Doubtfire, the perfect British nanny. He's so persuasive that he fools his ex-wife (Field) into hiring him so that he can spend more time with his kids. Director Columbus's approach to the material is manipulative and the entire story too sweet. Balanced against those flaws are another rambunctious performance by the star and some bawdy humor. The disc looks and sounds fine, making the San Francisco setting as picturesque and flawless as it was on the theatre screen. Though the liner notes claim a commentary track by the director, it's not on the menu. —*MM*

Movie: 🐕🐕▶ **DVD:** 🐕🐕🐕
20th Century Fox (Cat #4112577, UPC #086162125775). Widescreen (2.35:1) letterboxed. Dolby Digital 5.0 Surround Stereo; Dolby Digital Surround Stereo. $29.98. Keepcase. *LANG:* English; French; Spanish. *SUB:* English; Spanish. *CAP:* English. *FEATURES:* 23 chapter links • Cast interviews • Chuck Jones's comments on the animated sequence • Pencil test for animation.
1993 (PG-13) 120m/C Robin Williams, Sally Field, Pierce Brosnan, Harvey Fierstein, Robert Prosky, Mara Wilson; *D:* Chris Columbus; *W:* Leslie Dixon, Randi Mayem Singer; *C:* Donald McAlpine; *M:* Howard Shore. *AWARDS:* Academy Awards '93: Best Makeup; Golden Globe Awards '94: Best Actor—Musical/Comedy (Williams); Best Film—Musical/Comedy; MTV Movie Awards '94: Best Comedic Performance (Williams); *NOM:* MTV Movie Awards '94: Best Male Performance (Williams).

Mr. Ace

Director Edwin L. Marin's *(Johnny Angel, A Study in Scarlet)* leisurely and mushy look at sex and corruption in politics is backed by sumptuous sets and stylish deep-focus camera work. While the post-war cinema was delivering film noir, Marin elected a melodramatic approach for his subject, complete with rolling thunder and lightning flashes to emphasize the crisis, mood, or conflict of the moment. We find a scheming Sylvia Sidney as a congresswoman who decides to run for governor of a big eastern establishment state, while George Raft is in place as the kingpin of the political machine and her key to winning. Will it be sex, corruption, and business as usual, or will honor and idealism prevail? DVD is strictly by the numbers with no extras, but the transfer is from fairly good source material, although more attention could have been paid to the audio presentation. —*RT*

Movie: 🐕🐕 **DVD:** 🐕🐕▶
Image Entertainment (Cat #5373FW, UPC #014381537321). Full frame. AC3 - 2 Channel. $24.99. Snapper. *LANG:* English. *FEATURES:* 17 chapter links • Actor biographies.
1946 85m/B George Raft, Sylvia Sidney, Sara Haden, Stanley Ridges; *D:* Edwin L. Marin; *W:* Fred Finklehoffe; *C:* Karl Struss; *M:* Heinz Roemheld.

Mr. Baseball

Washed-up American baseball player tries to revive his career by playing in Japan and experiences cultures clashing under the ballpark lights. Semi-charmer swings and misses often enough to warrant return to minors. Film drew controversy during production when Universal was bought by the Japanese Matsushita organization and claims of both Japan- and America-bashing were thrown about. The baseball scenes themselves are the highlight of the film, and the on-the-field atmosphere is greatly enhanced by the Dolby Surround sound, which adds much to the realistic play-ball feel. The image is crisp, colors are rich, and there are very few of the problems that are sometimes found on a Goodtimes DVD. —*JO*

Movie: 🐕🐕 **DVD:** 🐕🐕🐕
Goodtimes Entertainment (Cat #05-81036, UPC #018713810366). Widescreen (2.35:1) letterboxed. Dolby Surround. $24.98. Snapper. *LANG:* English. *CAP:* English. *FEATURES:* 18 chapter links.
1992 (PG-13) 109m/C Tom Selleck, Ken Takakura, Toshi Shioya, Dennis Haysbert, Aya Takanashi; *D:* Fred Schepisi; *W:* Gary Ross, Kevin Wade, Monte Merrick; *C:* Ian Baker; *M:* Jerry Goldsmith.

Mr. Holland's Opus

Well-done Disney tearjerker begins in 1965 as musician Glenn Holland (Dreyfuss) takes a teaching job to get himself off the wedding reception circuit and help support his wife, Iris (Headly), and their deaf son. The story spans three decades, with actual newsreel footage thrown in to highlight time passing. Holland sets aside his dream of composing a great symphony and finds his true calling—mentoring and inspiring young minds. Holland's son being deaf might have proved corny, but their rocky relationship is deeply rooted to the storyline. Dreyfuss turns in his most vibrant performance in years and, while sentimental buttons are definitely pushed, director Herek avoids falling into sappiness. The 5.1 Surround on this DVD adds a lot of ambience to the various school environments in the film and delivers the band music with a lot of crisp high-end punch, while never sacrificing the clean, deep low end. The picture is sharp with only very minor grain, and very rarely, at that. Colors are accurate and detailed with very little bleed. Blacks are good. The brightness levels stay consistent and the contrast assists the blacks nicely while adding overall punch to the picture. —*JO*

Movie: 🐕🐕🐕 **DVD:** 🐕🐕🐕
Buena Vista Home Entertainment (Cat #17491, UPC #717951003096). Widescreen (2.35:1) letterboxed. Dolby Digital 5.1. $29.99. Keepcase. *LANG:* English (DD5.1); French. *CAP:* English. *FEATURES:* 25 chapter links • Production featurette.
1995 (PG) 142m/C Richard Dreyfuss, Glenne Headly, Jay Thomas, Olympia Dukakis, William H. Macy, Alicia Witt, Jean Louisa Kelly, Anthony Natale; *D:* Stephen Herek; *W:* Patrick Sheane Duncan; *C:* Oliver Wood; *M:* Michael Kamen. *AWARDS:* *NOM:* Academy Awards '95: Best Actor (Dreyfuss); Golden Globe Awards '95: Best Actor—Drama (Dreyfuss), Best Screenplay.

Mr. Jealousy

When Lester Grimm (Stoltz) was 15, he chickened out on a good night kiss from his girl, and later spied her necking with another boy. Ever since then, he's had this thing about infidelity and he trashes his every relationship because of his suspicions. It's no different when he meets the vivacious Ramona (Sciorra), who has recently broken up with arrogant author Dashiell (Eigeman). Lester joins Dashiell's therapy group to spy on his possible competition. Writer-director Baumbach stretches this thin material by making the characters interesting and the dialogue funny. Fonda's role is a cameo as Dashiell's stuttering girlfriend. The video transfer features some very nice color definition, although some dimly lit scenes are a bit murky and hard to discern. The soundtrack is also quite good, replete with clear sounding dialogue and no discernable distortion. —*MJT*

Movie: 🐕🐕▶ **DVD:** 🐕🐕🐕
Fox/Lorber Home Video (Cat #FLV5165, UPC #720917516523). Widescreen (1.85:1) letterboxed. Dolby Digital Stereo. $24.98. Keepcase. *LANG:* English. *FEATURES:* 8 chapter links • Filmographies and awards • Production credits • Theatrical trailer • Weblink access.
1998 (R) 105m/C Eric Stoltz, Annabella Sciorra, Christopher Eigeman, Carlos Jacott, Marianne Jean-Baptiste, Brian Kerwin, Peter Bogdanovich; *Cameos:* Bridget Fonda; *D:* Noah Baumbach; *W:* Noah Baumbach; *C:* Steven Bernstein; *M:* Robert Een, Luna.

Mister Johnson

In 1923 Africa, an educated black man working for the British magistrate constantly finds himself in trouble, thanks to backfiring schemes. The highly enjoyable film from the director of *Driving Miss Daisy* suffers only from the underdevelopment of the intriguing lead character. Based on the novel by Joyce Cary.

Movie: 🐕🐕🐕 **DVD:** NYR
Universal Studios Home Video (Cat #40099). Full frame. Dolby Digital Stereo. $19.99. Snapper.
1991 (PG-13) 105m/C Pierce Brosnan, Edward Woodward, Maynard Eziashi, Beatie Edney, Denis Quilley, Nick Reding; *D:* Bruce Beresford; *W:* Bruce Beresford, William Boyd; *C:* Peter James; *M:* Georges Delerue.

Mr. Magoo

Ah Magoo, we wish you wouldn't have done it again! Live-action version of the cartoon character popular in the '50s and '60s. Elderly myopic millionaire Quincy Magoo (Nielsen) unwittingly comes into possession of a stolen gem that he gives to his bulldog Angus as a toy. Bumbling government agents and evil arch-criminals are after the gem and Magoo, but he avoids them through luck and bad plot devices. Meanwhile, Magoo is mistaking a mummy's sarcophagus for a phone booth,

a riverboat paddle wheel for an escalator and...well, you get the idea. Nielsen puts a *Naked Gun* spin on Magoo, and that routine is getting a bit stale. Although criticized by some blind groups as an inaccurate portrayal of the visually challenged, after a very brief run in the theatres, no one was able to see it. Opening and closing sequences include animated Magoo bits. At least with the DVD you get good vibrant colors and a very sharp picture that can't make the film any worse, but unfortunately don't help enough. The film still sucks, but the disc is great. The high-contrast levels combine with the colors and the feel is more cartoony than the VHS or laserdisc release. Brightness levels are consistent and blacks are true. Good use of the 5.1 Surround tracks may have helped keep things moving, but unfortunately there's not much there. Fidelity is fine though and, also unfortunately, the dialogue is very understandable. —*JO*
Movie: 🎬 **DVD:** 🎬🎬🎬▶
Buena Vista Home Entertainment (Cat #14255). Widescreen (1.85:1) letterboxed. Dolby Digital 5.1. $29.99. Keepcase. *LANG:* English. *SUB:* Spanish. *CAP:* English.
1997 (PG) 87m/C Leslie Nielsen, Kelly Lynch, Matt Keeslar, Nicholas Chinlund, Ernie Hudson, Malcolm McDowell, Stephen Tobolowsky, Jennifer Garner, Miguel Ferrer; **D:** Stanley Tong; **W:** Pat Proft, Tom Sherohman; **C:** Jingle Ma; **M:** Michael Tavera.

Mr. Nice Guy

TV cook Jackie (Chan) gets into hot water when he saves a female reporter (Fitzpatrick), who has videotaped a drug deal between two semi-comic gangs. Jackie winds up with the tape and so reptilian bad guy Giancarlo (Norton) sends his men in their poorly tailored suits to get it back and to kidnap Jackie's girlfriend Miki (Lee). The rest is essentially chase and fight, fight and chase, ending up with a huge earth-moving machine and a grandly destructive conclusion. Director Sammo Hung, who appears in the movie as a bicyclist, never lets the pace flag and jazzes things up with unusual camera angles. The Australian/Hong Kong film has the production values of a comparable American action movie, and even though this is Chan's first effort to be filmed primarily in English, his familiar character is a completely comfortable combination of Bruce Lee and Buster Keaton. The DVD lacks many of the "extras" that Chan's more recent discs have included. The film itself is crisp, with a few inconsequential visual flaws—colors flashing within gridwork patterns, for example—and clear yellow subtitles for the few conversations in Chinese. —*MM* *AKA:* Yatgo Ho Yan.
Movie: 🎬🎬🎬 **DVD:** 🎬🎬🎬▶
New Line Home Video (Cat #N4662, UPC #794043466229). Full frame; widescreen (2.35:1). Dolby Digital 5.1. $24.98. Snapper. *LANG:* English; French. *SUB:* English;

French; Spanish. *FEATURES:* 20 chapter links ▪ Jackie Chan filmography and biography ▪ Action scenes from *First Strike* ▪ Action scenes from *Rumble in the Bronx* ▪ Action scenes from *Police Story* ▪ Theatrical trailer.
1998 (PG-13) 90m/C *HK* Jackie Chan, Richard Norton, Gabrielle Fitzpatrick, Miki Lee, Karen McLymont, Vince Poletto, Barry Otto, Sammo Hung; **D:** Sammo Hung; **W:** Edward Tang, Fibe Ma; **C:** Raymond Lam; **M:** J. Peter Robinson.

Mister Roberts

Crew of a Navy cargo freighter in the South Pacific during WWII relieves the boredom of duty with a series of practical jokes, mostly at the expense of the long-suffering and slightly crazy captain (Cagney), who then determines that he will get even. Mr. Roberts (Fonda) longs to be transferred to a fighting vessel and see some action. It was first a hit Broadway play (based on the novel by Thomas Heggen), which also featured Fonda in the title role, and was followed in 1964 by *Ensign Pulver*, and later a short-lived TV series. The DVD itself is above average, and better than both the laserdisc and the VHS re-issue. Overall sharpness is good and the grain is not too noticeable whether in a ship's cabin or in a brightly lit on-deck scene. Good brightness and contrast levels are also consistent in any type of lighting. Blacks are very good. Color is very good and bleed almost non-existent. Only a couple of scenes had any artifacts at all. A fine supplemental section (the second side of the DVD) tops off the presentation—if only Warner Bros. would knock off the multiple theatrical trailer tag on a lot of their packaging; there's only one for *Mister Roberts* and eight for other miscellaneous movies. —*JO*
Movie: 🎬🎬🎬▶ **DVD:** 🎬🎬🎬
Warner Home Video, Inc. (Cat #16692, UPC #085391669227). Widescreen (2.35:1) anamorphic. Dolby Digital 5.1. $24.98. Snapper. *LANG:* English. *SUB:* French. *CAP:* English. *FEATURES:* 33 chapter links ▪ Theatrical trailer ▪ 8 additional trailers ▪ Production notes ▪ Commentary: Jack Lemmon ▪ Documentary excerpts.
1955 120m/C Henry Fonda, James Cagney, Jack Lemmon, William Powell, Betsy Palmer, Ward Bond, Harry Carey Jr., Nick Adams, Phil Carey, Ken Curtis, Martin Milner, Jack Pennick, Perry Lopez, Patrick Wayne, Tige Andrews, William Henry; **D:** John Ford, Mervyn LeRoy; **W:** Frank Nugent, Joshua Logan, Thomas Heggen; **C:** Winton C. Hoch; **M:** Franz Waxman. *AWARDS:* Academy Awards '55: Best Supporting Actor (Lemmon); *NOM:* Academy Awards '55: Best Picture, Best Sound.

Mr. Saturday Night

Crystal, in his directorial debut, stars as Buddy Young Jr., a self-destructive comedian whose career spans five decades. His nasty one-liners and witty jokes combine

with poignancy in this satisfying comedy/drama. Paymer is excellent as Young's long-suffering, faithful brother and manager. Watch for Lewis in a cameo role. Expectations were very high and the boxoffice results were disappointing, but fans of Crystal shouldn't miss this one. The video also includes additional footage and outtakes selected and hosted by Crystal. This is an average DVD that is not much of an improvement over the VHS tape. There is some grain as well as minor artifacting that don't do much to assist the already so-so sharpness. Colors are a bit dull and the whole picture could have used boosts to both the contrast and brightness levels. Blacks are O.K. Surprisingly, the Dolby Surround complements much of the film very nicely, with some very good imaging and ambience. —*JO*
Movie: 🎬🎬▶ **DVD:** 🎬🎬▶
Polygram (Cat #4400582092, UPC #044005820928). Full frame. Dolby Surround 2.0. $29.95. Keepcase. *LANG:* English. *SUB:* French. *CAP:* English. *FEATURES:* 27 chapter links ▪ Filmographies ▪ Theatrical trailer.
1992 (R) 118m/C Billy Crystal, David Paymer, Julie Warner, Helen Hunt, Mary Mara, Jerry Orbach, Ron Silver, Sage Allen, Jackie Gayle, Carl Ballantine, Slappy (Melvin) White, Conrad Janis; *Cameos:* Jerry Lewis; **D:** Billy Crystal; **W:** Billy Crystal, Babaloo Mandel, Lowell Ganz; **C:** Don Peterman; **M:** Marc Shaiman. *AWARDS:* *NOM:* Academy Awards '92: Best Supporting Actor (Paymer).

Mr. Vampire

This Hong Kong horror comedy is so outrageous that American fans unfamiliar with the conventions of the genre will be happily baffled by it. Supernatural expert Kou (Lam Ching Ying) is unable to keep a vampire from escaping from its coffin. In the guise of a beautiful woman, the creature finally attacks his young friend and they do battle in a scene that features flying heads. The DVD image is acceptable for this kind of low-budget work, but nothing about the film recommends it to those who are not already into berserk horror. —*MM*
Movie: 🎬🎬▶ **DVD:** 🎬🎬▶
Tai Seng Video Marketing (Cat #MS/DVD/075/99, UPC #4895017000756). Widescreen letterboxed. Dolby Digital 5.1 Surround Stereo. $49.95. Keepcase. *LANG:* Cantonese; Mandarin. *SUB:* Traditional & Simplified Chinese; English; Thai; Vietnamese; Spanish. *FEATURES:* 9 chapter links ▪ Trailers ▪ Cast and crew thumbnail bios.
1986 99m/C *HK* Moon Lee, Lam Ching Ying, Ricky Hui, Pauline Wong; **D:** Ricky Lau; **W:** Roy Szeto; **C:** Peter Ngor.

Mr. Wonderful

Bittersweet look at love and romance begins with divorced Con Edison worker Gus (Dillon) hard up for cash and trying to marry off his ex-wife Lee (Sciorra). He wants to use the alimony money he's been paying her to invest in a bowling alley with his buddies. But as soon as it looks like he is succeeding, he falls in love with her again. Director Minghella made this sophomore effort between his cult hit debut, *Truly, Madly, Deeply*, and *The English Patient.*

Movie: 🦴🦴▶ **DVD:** NYR

Warner Home Video, Inc. (Cat #12988). Widescreen (1.85:1) letterboxed; full frame. Dolby Digital Stereo. $19.98. Snapper. *SUB:* French. *CAP:* English. **1993 (PG-13) 99m/C** Matt Dillon, Annabella Sciorra, William Hurt, Mary-Louise Parker, Luis Guzman, Dan Hedaya, Vincent D'Onofrio; **D:** Anthony Minghella; **W:** Amy Schor, Vicki Polon; **C:** Geoffrey Simpson; **M:** Michael Gore.

Mistress

A weak script does in a formidable cast in a behind-the-scenes look at moviemaking. Wuhl plays Marvin Landisman, a failed writer-director who's approached by has-been producer Jack Roth (Landau), who says he's found a backer to finance a movie from one of Marvin's old scripts. It turns out that Roth has three men (De Niro, Aiello, and Wallach) ready to finance the project as long as each of their mistresses, who all have acting ambitions, gets the starring role. Double-dealing at a bargain-basement level sets up the rest of this listless comedy.

Movie: 🦴🦴 **DVD:** NYR

Pioneer Entertainment (Cat #DVD9864). Full frame. Dolby Digital Stereo. $24.98. Keepcase. *LANG:* English. *CAP:* English. **1991 (R) 100m/C** Robert Wuhl, Martin Landau, Robert De Niro, Eli Wallach, Danny Aiello, Sheryl Lee Ralph, Jean Smart, Tuesday Weld, Jace Alexander, Laurie Metcalf; **Cameos:** Christopher Walken, Ernest Borgnine; **D:** Barry Primus; **W:** J.F. Lawton, Barry Primus; **C:** Sven Kirsten; **M:** Galt MacDermot.

Mob Story

Don Luciano (Vernon) is a big-wig mob boss on the run from the government and a few of his "closest" friends. He plans to disappear in Winnipeg, Canada, but if his girl (Kidder) and best pal (Waxman) find him first, he'll be traveling in a body bag. Very silly but fitfully fun for those who can put up with a substandard picture. On DVD, the dimly illuminated picture ranges from poor to fair. Nothing special in any department. —*MM*

Movie: 🦴▶ **DVD:** 🦴▶

Simitar Entertainment (Cat #7391, UPC #082551739127). Full frame. Dolby Digital Stereo. $14.98. Keepcase. *LANG:* English. *FEATURES:* 8 chapter links • Production factoids • Margot Kidder filmography. **1990 (R) 98m/C** John Vernon, Margot Kidder, Al Waxman, Kate Vernon; **D:** Gabriel Markiw, Jancarlo Markiw.

Mob War

A war breaks out between the head of New York's underworld and a media genius. After deciding to become partners, the "family" tries to take over. Boxer Jake La Motta, the subject of *Raging Bull*, appears as godfather Don Ricci. The film is so poorly lit that even daylight exteriors are filled with impenetrable shadows. The interiors are just as bad and the "jungle" scenes are inexplicably tinted in orange. The flaws appear to come from the original, not the transfer to DVD. —*MM*

Movie: 🦴▶ **DVD:** 🦴

Simitar Entertainment (Cat #7392, UPC #082551739226). Full frame. Dolby Digital Stereo. $14.98. Keepcase. *LANG:* English. *FEATURES:* 8 chapter links • Production factoids. **1988 (R) 96m/C** John Christian, David Henry Keller, Jake La Motta, Johnny Stumper; **D:** J. Christian Ingvordsen; **W:** J. Christian Ingvordsen, John Weiner; **C:** Steven Kaman.

Moby Dick

TV adaptation of Herman Melville's 1851 novel stars a mesmerizing Stewart as the obsessive peg-legged Captain Ahab. Novice seaman Ishmael (Thomas) signs aboard the whaling ship Pequod, making friends with Polynesian native, harpooner Queequeg (Waretini). Soon enough Ishmael learns about the great white whale who claimed the captain's leg, and Ahab's determination to seek revenge on the beast, no matter what the cost to himself, his crew, or the ship. Peck, who starred as Ahab in the 1956 movie version, takes on the role of Jonah-and-the-whale sermonizing Father Mapple. Shipboard scenes are somewhat grainy, as the DVD has trouble with any earthtone colors. Brightly lit scenes are pretty good-looking, though, but the image is sharp enough that the CGI whale (particularly a tail-fin shot that repeats) looks a little faker than on the VHS edition. The sound is weak by today's Surround standards, but music and dialogue are fine. —*JO*

Movie: 🦴🦴▶ **DVD:** 🦴🦴▶

Artisan Entertainment (Cat #96536, UPC #707729653608). Full frame. Dolby Surround. $19.98. Keepcase. *LANG:* English. *SUB:* Spanish. *CAP:* English. *FEATURES:* 36 chapter links • Cast and filmmakers bios • Production notes • Dual-layered RSDL. **1998 (PG) 145m/C** Patrick Stewart, Henry Thomas, Ted Levine, Piripi Waretini, Gregory Peck, Bill Hunter, Hugh Keays-Byrne, Norman D. Golden II, Bruce Spence; **D:** Franc Roddam; **W:** Franc Roddam, Anton Diether; **C:** David Connell; **M:** Christopher Gordon.

The Mod Squad

Tangled rehash of the '60s series tries very hard to be cool (and to look cool) but ends up as hip as a two-dollar haircut. Overaged teen criminals turned cops Pete (Ribisi), Linc (Epps), and Julie (Danes) merely look like they're guilty of making

unwise career decisions. They glower sullenly as they try to crack a convoluted case involving drugs, prostitution, and their dead boss Capt. Greer (Farina). Presumably the DVD is an accurate re-creation of the theatrical release and so it is difficult to judge. The image is dark and stylized throughout (or maybe the photo lab got their chemicals wrong) with a palette that's skewed to acid blues, browns, and blacks. Sound is O.K. —*MM*

Movie: 🦴 **DVD:** 🦴

MGM Home Entertainment (Cat #907450, UPC #027616745026). Widescreen anamorphic; full frame. Dolby Digital 5.1 Surround Stereo. $24.98. Keepcase. *LANG:* English; French. *SUB:* English; French. *FEATURES:* 44 chapter links • Booklet containing "cool insider info" • Theatrical trailer. **1999 (R) 94m/C** Claire Danes, Giovanni Ribisi, Omar Epps, Dennis Farina, Josh Brolin, Richard Jenkins, Larry Brandenburg, Steve Harris, Sam McMurray, Michael Lerner; **D:** Scott Silver; **W:** Scott Silver, Stephen Kay, Kate Lanier; **C:** Ellen Kuras; **M:** B.C. Smith. *AWARDS:* NOM: Golden Raspberry Awards '99: Worst Screenplay.

Modern Times

This "mostly silent" film finds Chaplin playing a factory worker who goes crazy from his repetitious job on an assembly line and his boss' demands for greater speed and efficiency. Ultimately encompassing the tyranny of machine over man, this cinematic masterpiece is as relevant as it ever was, and on DVD, it looks as good as it ever has. Beyond a few surface scratches—certainly no more than you could reasonably expect to see in a current theatrical release—the image is perfect, and since it was made for a conventional screen, nothing is lost in the full-frame presentation. Many consider this to be Chaplin's finest moment and it's hard to argue with them. The extras are few but well chosen. —*MM*

Movie: 🦴🦴🦴🦴 **DVD:** 🦴🦴🦴🦴

Image Entertainment (Cat #ID9182CUDVD, UPC #014381918229). Full frame. Dolby Digital Mono. $29.99. Snapper. *LANG:* Silent. *SUB:* English intertitles. *FEATURES:* 19 chapter links • Interview with music arranger David Raskin • Story notes • Script segments • Advertising, publicity, and promotional materials • Production reports on "feeding machine" sequence. **1936 87m/B** Charlie Chaplin, Paulette Goddard, Henry Bergman, Stanley Sandford, Gloria De Haven, Chester Conklin; **D:** Charlie Chaplin; **W:** Charlie Chaplin; **C:** Ira Morgan, Roland H. Totheroh; **M:** Charlie Chaplin. *AWARDS:* American Film Institute (AFI) '98: Top 100, National Film Registry '89.

Modern Vampires

If Russ Meyer directed an episode of *Buffy, the Vampire Slayer,* he'd doubtless come up with something like this horror-

comedy. Dallas (Van Dien) is a free-wheeling undead dude who blows into contemporary L.A. to see his friend Erica (Cattrall, doing a fine Zsa Zsa imitation). He's one step ahead of Dr. Van Helsing (Steiger). A vampire babe (Wagner) is working as a lethal prostitute, though The Count (Pastorelli) wants to get rid of her. Before it's over, director Elfman has indulged in about every incorrect excess imaginable; sexual, racial, and supernatural. Both the violence and the humor are too grotesque for a mainstream audience. Horror fans are the target audience. The DVD image is excellent, even in the exceptionally dark action scenes. Sound is O.K. Elfman and Van Dien are chatty on the commentary track. —*MM* **AKA:** Revenant.
Movie: 🐾🐾🐾 **DVD:** 🐾🐾🐾
Studio Home Entertainment (Cat #7345, UPC #658149734524). Full frame. Dolby Digital Surround Stereo. $24.95. Keepcase. *LANG:* English. *SUB:* Spanish. *FEATURES:* 20 animated chapter links • "Making of" featurette • Trailers • Commentary: Elfman and Van Dien • Cast and crew thumbnail biographies and filmographies.
1998 (R) 95m/C Casper Van Dien, Natasha Gregson Wagner, Rod Steiger, Robert Pastorelli, Kim Cattrall, Natasha Andreichenko, Gabriel Casseus, Udo Kier, Natasha Lyonne; **D:** Richard Elfman; **W:** Matthew Bright; **M:** Danny Elfman, Michael Wandmacher.

Mohawk

A cowboy and an Indian woman try to stop a war between Indian tribes and fanatical landowners.
Movie: 🐾 **DVD:** NYR
Parade (Cat #55156). Full frame. Dolby Digital Mono. $17.98. Keepcase. *LANG:* English. *SUB:* Japanese.
1956 80m/C Rita Gam, Neville Brand, Scott Brady, Lori Nelson; **D:** Kurt Neumann; **W:** Maurice Geraghty, Milton Krims; **C:** Karl Struss; **M:** Edward L. Alperson Jr.

Moll Flanders

Rousing, bawdy retelling of Daniel Defoe's 1722 novel about the wickedly seductive Moll Flanders (Kingston) was originally broadcast as a *Masterpiece Theatre* miniseries. Born in London's Newgate prison, Moll becomes a house servant, embarks on her first marriage, is soon widowed, and decides to make her own way (and fortune). She becomes a thief, a whore, marries several more times, and winds up back in prison and a candidate for the gallows. The DVD image is passable, but not as sharp as one might think. Interiors appear murky at times, and the outdoor settings look soft and at times washed-out. The sound, however, is outstanding. —*AB* **AKA:** The Fortunes and Misfortunes of Moll Flanders.
Movie: 🐾🐾🐾 **DVD:** 🐾🐾🐾
Anchor Bay (Cat #DV10332, UPC #1313103329). Full frame. Dolby Digital

Stereo. $29.99. Keepcase. *LANG:* English. *SUB:* English. *FEATURES:* 18 chapter links.
1996 210m/C *GB* Alex Kingston, Daniel Craig, Diana Rigg, Colin Buchanan, Christopher Fulford, James Fleet, Ian Driver, Tom Ward; **D:** David Attwood; **W:** Andrew Davies; **C:** Ivan Strasburg; **M:** Jim Parker.

Mommy

Schoolteacher is stalked by a murderous mom (McCormack) who'll do anything for her daughter. McCormack is best known for her starring role in *The Bad Seed*. Filmed in Muscatine, IA.
Movie: 🐾🐾 **DVD:** NYR
Roan Group (Cat #2013). Dolby Digital Stereo. $19.95. Keepcase. *FEATURES:* Commentary: Collins, McCormack and Lemieux.
1995 89m/C Patty McCormack, Majel Barrett, Jason Miller, Brinke Stevens, Rachel Lemieux, Mickey Spillane, Michael Cornelison, Sarah Jane Miller; **D:** Max Allan Collins; **W:** Max Allan Collins; **C:** Phillip W. Dingeldein; **M:** Richard Lowry.

Mommy 2: Mommy's Day

Murderous Mommy (McCormack) returns, as does her beloved daughter (now rebellious teen) Jessica Ann (Lemieux). Mom's on death row awaiting execution after her killing spree but the Mommy-style murders continue. Shot on location in Muscatine, IA, the film seldom rises above its minimal production values, but fans of the genre will be astonished by the cast. The impoverished lighting gives many of the interiors a yellowish cast, which seems to make reds glow even more than normal. The real difference between the disc and VHS tape is not in image quality but in the commentary track with Collins, McCormack, Lemieux, editor and director of photography Phillip Dingeldein, and sound man Greg Ballard, who discuss the details of ultra-low budget filmmaking. Chapters cannot be accessed from the menu. —*MM*
Movie: 🐾🐾 **DVD:** 🐾🐾
Roan Group (Cat #2014, UPC #785604201427). Full frame. Dolby Digital Stereo. $19.95. Keepcase. *LANG:* English. *FEATURES:* Commentary: Collins, McCormack, Lemieux, Dingeldein, Ballard • Trailer • Interview with Patty McCormack • 20 chapter links.
1996 89m/C Patty McCormack, Rachel Lemieux, Brinke Stevens, Michael Cornelison, Sarah Jane Miller, Gary Sandy, Paul Petersen, Arlen Dean Snyder, Todd Eastland, Del Close; **D:** Max Allan Collins; **W:** Max Allan Collins; **C:** Phillip W. Dingeldein; **M:** Richard Lowry.

Money Kings

Slow-starter is worth the time it takes to get the story moving. Soft-hearted Vinnie Glenn (Falk) runs a Boston bar and serves as a small-time bookie for some backroom gambling. Then the local wiseguys decide

that he needs an assistant to take care of bad debts and they send in hot-headed, eager young puppy Anthony (Prinze). Also involved are Frankie (Hutton), who owes more than he can pay, and his wife (Holly). The cast is excellent and the story rises above the stereotyped nature of the characters and situation. The DVD image lacks sharp focus and is not significantly superior to VHS tape. Same for sound. —*MM* **AKA:** Vig.
Movie: 🐾🐾 **DVD:** 🐾🐾
Studio Home Entertainment (Cat #7215, UPC #658149721524). Widescreen letterboxed. Dolby Digital Stereo. $24.95. Keepcase. *LANG:* English. *SUB:* Spanish. *FEATURES:* 18 chapter links • Cast and crew thumbnail biographies.
1998 (R) 96m/C Peter Falk, Freddie Prinze Jr., Lauren Holly, Timothy Hutton, Tyne Daly; **D:** Graham Theakston.

Money Train

Snipes and Harrelson team up again, this time as New York City transit cops (and foster brothers) who decide to rob the money train—a subway car that collects all the cash accrued from the transit system each day. To complicate matters, they're both in love with their new Latina partner (Lopez). Lame attempt to cash in on the Snipes and Harrelson chemistry leaves out one important ingredient—a competent script. The movie is almost over before the train actually becomes part of the plotline. Film came under criticism when it was blamed for a series of "copycat" arsons in which a New York City subway clerk was killed. The DVD is very sharp and has no problem with the many shadows and darkly lit scenes of the subway. Grain is minimal and artifacts are rare. Colors are accurate and vibrant with little bleed. Blacks are true and complemented by the excellent contrast and brightness levels. The image packs a lot of punch and so does the 5.1 sound. The Surround effects are great and the low end has plenty of guts to it. Even so, there is plenty of crisp high end and the music is very full-bodied with good dynamics. —*JO*
Movie: 🐾 **DVD:** 🐾🐾
Columbia Tristar Home Video (Cat #11079, UPC #043396110793). Widescreen (2.35:1) letterboxed. Full frame. Dolby Digital 5.1. $25.95. Keepcase. *LANG:* English; Spanish; French. *SUB:* English; Spanish; French. *CAP:* English. *FEATURES:* 28 chapter links • Theatrical trailer.
1995 (R) 110m/C Woody Harrelson, Wesley Snipes, Jennifer Lopez, Robert (Bobby) Blake, Chris Cooper, Joe Grifasi; **D:** Joseph Ruben; **W:** Doug Richardson, David Loughery; **C:** John Lindley; **M:** Mark Mancina.

Monkey Business

The Marx Brothers (Groucho, Harpo, Chico, and Zeppo) are stowaways on a luxury liner bound for New York. Throw in a couple of gangsters, a gangster's moll (Todd), and a debutante love-interest for

Zeppo and you have all the plot elements necessary for a Marx Brothers' movie. Groucho, with his puns, double-entendre wit, and outrageous shenanigans, along with the zany antics of Harpo and Chico, are more than enough to carry the day. Nearly 70 years after its initial release (1931), *Monkey Business* remains a laugh-filled feast, waiting to be rediscovered by yet another generation of new Marx Brothers' fans. The DVD presentation is an uninspired transfer from only fair source material and without any extras—the Marx Brothers deserve more than this. —RT

Movie: 🎞🎞🎞 **DVD:** 🎞🎞
Image Entertainment (Cat #4284US, UPC #014281428421). Full frame. PCM - 1 Channel. $24.99. Snapper. *LANG:* English. *FEATURES:* 16 chapter markers.
1931 77m/B Groucho Marx, Harpo Marx, Chico Marx, Zeppo Marx, Thelma Todd, Ruth Hall, Harry Woods, Tom Kennedy, Rockliffe Fellowes, Maxine Castle; **D:** Norman Z. McLeod; **W:** S.J. Perelman, Arthur Sheekman; **C:** Arthur L. Todd.

Monsieur Verdoux

A prim and proper bank cashier in Paris marries and murders rich women to support his real wife and family. On the shelf for years after it initially bombed, this well-executed, though somewhat dated tale is a favorite among some Chaplin devotees. It's a Chaplin production through and through; he produced it, directed it, wrote it, scored it, and starred in it. Though one murderer is the focus, the film delivers an anti-war message in that, according to Verdoux, warfare is nothing more than mass murder legalized, celebrated, and paraded. The complex film is not without flaws and does not always hold up to the passage of time, but it is rightfully admired for its strengths. Based upon a suggestion by Orson Welles, which is chronicled in the DVD supplements. There are other extras, too, and the picture and sound quality will do, considering the year the film was made and its limited availability for years afterward. In fact, film has never looked better on home video. —MB

Movie: 🎞🎞🎞 **DVD:** 🎞🎞🎞
Image Entertainment (Cat #ID9184CUDVD, UPC #014381918427). Full frame. Dolby Digital 1.0. $29.99. Snapper. *LANG:* English. *FEATURES:* 16 chapter links • Original script segments before censoring • Production sketches and photographs • Publicity materials • Production notes.
1947 123m/B Charlie Chaplin, Martha Raye, Isobel Elsom, Mady Correll, Marilyn Nash, Irving Bacon, William Frawley, Allison Roddan, Robert Lewis; **D:** Charlie Chaplin; **W:** Charlie Chaplin; **C:** Curt Courant, Roland H. Totheroh; **M:** Charlie Chaplin. *AWARDS: NOM:* Academy Awards '47: Best Original Screenplay.

Monsoon

Erotic thriller from prolific director Mundra.
Movie: NYR **DVD:** NYR

Tapeworm Video Distributors (Cat #1232). Full frame. Dolby Digital 5.1 Surround Stereo. $24.95. Keepcase. *LANG:* English; Hindi. *SUB:* Spanish. *FEATURES:* Trailer.
1997 96m/C Richard Tyson, Matt McCoy, Gulsham Grover, Jenny McShane, Doug Jeffery, Helen Brodie; **D:** Jag Mundhra; **C:** Blain Brown.

The Monster

Many American audiences discovered Roberto Benigni with this grand slapstick comedy. He's a petty criminal whom the police mistakenly suspect is a serial killer. Undercover cop Jessica (Braschi) is sent to tempt him into striking again. The physical humor is much stronger, and for my money more inspired than it is in *Life Is Beautiful*. The best bits involve our hapless hero hanging onto an out-of-control chainsaw and trying to deal with a lit cigarette down his pants. On DVD, the crisp image is, for practical purposes, flawless, but the disc's most useful features are the choice of image size, language, and subtitles. I recommend the original Italian and subtitles even for those who don't normally choose them because so much of Benigni's personality and humor are in his voice. —MM **AKA:** Il Monstro; Le Monstre.

Movie: 🎞🎞🎞 **DVD:** 🎞🎞🎞
Columbia Tristar Home Video (Cat #04322, UPC #043396043220). Widescreen (1.85:1) letterboxed; full frame. Dolby Digital Surround Stereo. $24.95. Keepcase. *LANG:* Italian; English. *SUB:* English; French; Spanish. *FEATURES:* 28 chapter links • Roberto Benigni thumbnail biography.
1996 (R) 110m/C *IT* Roberto Benigni, Nicoletta Braschi, Michel Blanc, Dominque Lavanant, Jean-Claude Brialy, Ivano Marescotti, Laurent Spielvogel, Massimo Girotti, Franco Mescolini; **D:** Roberto Benigni; **W:** Roberto Benigni, Vincenzo Cerami; **C:** Carlo Di Palma; **M:** Evan Lurie.

Monster in the Closet

Silly horror spoof is one of the more enjoyable for fans because the filmmakers really understand and appreciate the genre. The voice-over introduction sets just the right parodic tone and the rest has a strong Ed Wood Jr. feel, though director Bob Dahlin moves the action along much more quickly than the alternative master normally did. The titular critter is a grand rubber-suit creation, but perhaps the most surprising thing about it is the number of fine character actors in the cast. Nobody expects much in visual terms from Troma films, but this one looks as good as it needs to look with visible pixels in the fades to black between scenes. Sound is acceptable, too. —MM

Movie: 🎞🎞 **DVD:** 🎞🎞
Troma Team Video (Cat #9890, UPC #790357989027). Full frame. $19.98. Keepcase. *LANG:* English. *FEATURES:* 9 chapter links • Troma Intelligence Test • *Toxic Avengers* TV show episode • Theatri-

cal trailer • Production stills. DVD-ROM can access Troma website.
1986 (PG) 87m/C Paul Dooley, Donald Grant, Claude Akins, Denise DuBarry, Stella Stevens, Howard Duff, Henry Gibson, Jesse White, John Carradine; **D:** Bob Dahlin; **W:** Bob Dahlin; **C:** Ronald W. McLeish; **M:** Barrie Guard.

The Monster Maker

Please see review of *Dead Men Walk*.
Movie: 🎞🎞
1944 65m/B J. Carrol Naish, Ralph Morgan, Wanda McKay, Terry Frost; **D:** Sam Newfield; **W:** Martin Mooney, Pierre Gendron; **C:** Robert C. Cline; **M:** Albert Glasser.

Montenegro

Offbeat, bawdy comedy details experiences of a bored, possibly mad housewife who lands in a coarse, uninhibited ethnic community. To its credit, this film remains unpredictable to the end. And Anspach, an intriguing, resourceful—and attractive—actress, delivers what is perhaps her greatest performance. The DVD is very true to the theatrical feel of the film. That's not to say that it's anywhere near perfect. The biggest problem is the sharpness and an increase in grain. The colors are accurate, even though they may appear to wander. There is a little bleed, and also some errant artifacts from time to time. Blacks are average, and both contrast and brightness levels could have used a boost. Most everything can be heard on the mono soundtrack but there is some clipping on louder dialogue and music. —JO **AKA:** Montenegro—Or Pigs and Pearls.

Movie: 🎞🎞🎞▶ **DVD:** 🎞🎞▶
Fox/Lorber Home Video (Cat #5017). Widescreen (1.66:1) letterboxed. Mono. $29.99. Keepcase. *LANG:* English. *FEATURES:* Theatrical trailer • Cast filmographies.
1981 97m/C *SW* Susan Anspach, Erland Josephson; **D:** Dusan Makavejev; **W:** Dusan Makavejev; **C:** Tomislav Pinter; **M:** Kornell Kovac.

Monty Python's Life of Brian

The famous comic troupe's take on Christianity is their most conventionally plotted feature and certainly one of their most irreverent, though to some fans (including this one) it doesn't scale the heights of innovation that their sketch comedy does. But it's still a fine work, almost guaranteed to offend the devout. Since the Pythons have never been interested in creating carefully wrought visuals, the main attractions of this DVD edition are in the wealth of extras, including not one but two commentary tracks which take distinctly different approaches with background stories and memories—they were able to reuse sets and props that had been created for Franco Zefferilli's *Jesus of Nazareth*—but with a shared Pythonesque

sensibility. The five deleted scenes are a particular treat for the dedicated fan. —MM *AKA:* Life of Brian.
Movie: 𝄞𝄞𝄞 **DVD:** 𝄞𝄞𝄞
Criterion Collection (Cat #CC1554D, UPC #715515010320). Widescreen (1.85:1) letterboxed. Dolby Digital Surround Stereo. $39.95. Keepcase. *LANG:* English. *SUB:* English. *FEATURES:* Commentary: Terry Gilliam, Eric Idle, and Terry Jones • Commentary: John Cleese and Michael Palin • Theatrical trailer • 4 British radio ads • 5 deleted scenes with commentary • Documentary made during the production of *Life of Brian* • 19 chapter links • Liner notes by George Perry.
1979 (R) 94m/C *GB* Graham Chapman, John Cleese, Terry Gilliam, Eric Idle, Michael Palin, George Harrison, Terry Jones, Kenneth Colley, Spike Milligan, Carol Cleveland, Neil Innes, Andrew MacLachlan; *D:* Terry Jones; *W:* Graham Chapman, John Cleese, Terry Gilliam, Eric Idle, Michael Palin, Terry Jones; *C:* Peter Biziou; *M:* Geoffrey Burgon.

Monty Python's Life of Brian (Anchor Bay)
Visually, the Anchor Bay edition of the Python's religious comedy is essentially identical to the Criterion version. Neither is particularly striking. The differences are to be found in the extensive extras and higher price on the Criterion. —MM
Movie: 𝄞𝄞𝄞 **DVD:** 𝄞𝄞𝄞
Anchor Bay (Cat #DV10674, UPC #01313106749). Widescreen (1.85:1) letterboxed. Dolby Digital Stereo. $24.98. Keepcase. *LANG:* English. *FEATURES:* 31 chapter links.
1979 (R) 94m/C

Monty Python's The Meaning of Life
Funny, technically impressive film conducts various inquiries into the most profound questions confronting humanity. Notable among the sketches here are a live sex enactment performed before bored schoolboys, a student-faculty rugby game that turns quite violent, and an encounter between a physician and a reluctant, untimely organ donor. Another sketch provides a memorable portrait of a glutton prone to nausea. And at film's end, the meaning of life is actually revealed. This DVD seems like one of those that used the existing laser transfer, and is not much of an improvement over the LD, although substantially better than the VHS versions. Colors are pretty strong but the overall sharpness is a little low with occasional grain and minor artifacts. The picture is a bit lackluster and would have been helped by a contrast and corresponding brightness boost. Blacks are a little better than average. The Dolby Surround is very full on the opening sequence, but is sometimes a little thin. There are a few instances where the back channel kicks in but not many. —JO
Movie: 𝄞𝄞𝄞 **DVD:** 𝄞𝄞

Image Entertainment (Cat #ID4226USDVD, UPC #014381422627). Widescreen (1.85:1) letterboxed. Dolby Surround. $29.99. Snapper. *LANG:* English. *CAP:* English.
1983 (R) 107m/C *GB* Graham Chapman, John Cleese, Terry Gilliam, Eric Idle, Terry Jones, Michael Palin, Carol Cleveland, Matt Frewer, Simon Jones, Patricia Quinn, Andrew MacLachlan; *D:* Terry Gilliam, Terry Jones; *W:* Graham Chapman, John Cleese, Terry Gilliam, Eric Idle, Terry Jones, Michael Palin; *C:* Peter Hannan; *M:* John Du Prez, Graham Chapman, John Cleese, Eric Idle, Terry Jones, Michael Palin. *AWARDS:* Cannes Film Festival '83: Grand Jury Prize.

Monument Ave.
Updated Irish-American version of Scorsese's *Mean Streets* focuses on a group of petty thieves from Boston's mostly Irish Charleston neighborhood. The hoods, led by Bobby O'Grady (Leary), pass time stealing cars, snorting cocaine, and waxing poetic about their dead-end lives. But when a recently paroled member of their gang is murdered by neighborhood drug kingpin Jackie O' (Meaney), Bobby must decide between upholding the gang's code of silence and avenging his pal's death. The DVD image is excellent—noticeably better than the VHS release. The transfer is free of blemishes and the compression on this disc is without artifacts. Colors are rich, vivid, and natural. The Dolby Surround track found on the disc is also impressive, creating a very active Surround experience. Especially the music score features a noticeable depth that is much better than that found in most other Dolby Surround tracks. —GH *AKA:* Snitch.
Movie: 𝄞𝄞 **DVD:** 𝄞𝄞𝄞
Miramax Pictures Home Video (Cat #17093, UPC #717951002075). Widescreen (1.85:1) letterboxed. Dolby Surround. $29.99. Keepcase. *LANG:* English. *CAP:* English. *FEATURES:* 27 chapter links.
1998 90m/C Denis Leary, Billy Crudup, Famke Janssen, Colm Meaney, Martin Sheen, Jeanne Tripplehorn, Ian Hart, Jason Barry, John Diehl, Noah Emmerich, Greg Dulli; *D:* Ted Demme; *W:* Mike Armstrong; *C:* Adam Kimmel; *M:* Amanda Scheer-Demme.

The Moon Warriors
Historical fantasy follows simple peasant Phillip (Lau) who becomes involved with royal intrigue and must kick some serious butt. Characters fly when necessary and laugh off mortal wounds. The image is usually either too pale or too dark. The burned-in subtitles are sometimes illegible. —MM *AKA:* Zhan Shen Chuan Shu.
Movie: 𝄞𝄞 **DVD:** 𝄞𝄞
Tai Seng Video Marketing (Cat #5040, UPC #895024907543). Widescreen letterboxed. Dolby Digital Mono. $24.95. Keepcase. *LANG:* Cantonese; Mandarin. *SUB:* Traditional Chinese; English. *FEATURES:* 8 chapter links.

1992 91m/C *HK* Andy Lau, Anita Mui, Maggie Cheung, Kenny Chung; *D:* Sammo Hung; *W:* Law Kai Yui.

Moonlighting
The pilot episode to the hit 1980s series establishes the characters of two battling lovers—model Maddie Hayes (Shepherd) and David Addison (Willis), the private detective who works for her. It's bright, sophisticated, and funny. Visually, the crystalline DVD presentation belies the made-for-TV production values, but the real attraction of the disc lies in the separate audio track by writer-producer Glenn Gordon Caron and star Bruce Willis. In contrast to most commentaries that are either serious or nostalgic, these two guys are chummy, bawdy, and profane. —MM
Movie: 𝄞𝄞𝄞 **DVD:** 𝄞𝄞𝄞
Anchor Bay (Cat #DV10998, UPC #013131099898). Full frame. Dolby Digital Surround Stereo. $24.99. Keepcase. *LANG:* English. *FEATURES:* 16 chapter links • Bruce Willis's screen test • Commentary: Willis and Caron.
1985 93m/C Cybill Shepherd, Bruce Willis, Allyce Beasley; *D:* Robert Butler; *W:* Glenn Gordon Caron; *C:* Michael D. Margulies; *M:* Lee Holdridge.

Moonraker (SE)
Uninspired Bond fare has 007 unraveling intergalactic hijinks. Bond is aided by a female CIA agent, assaulted by a giant with jaws of steel, and captured by Amazons when he sets out to save the human race. Moore, Chiles, and Lonsdale all seem to be going through the motions only. The DVD has all the usual extras that we've come to expect on these Bond special editions. The two documentaries included are done well enough, but after a while the Bond docs begin to seem formulaic, even if the information included is unique to a particular film. The film transfer itself is excellent and the image is extremely sharp, almost like looking through a window. Colors are stunning and blacks are dead-on. The Dolby Surround is superb and has both excellent separation and Surround. The music sounds great. —JO
Movie: 𝄞𝄞 **DVD:** 𝄞𝄞𝄞𝄞
MGM Home Entertainment (Cat #908125, UPC #027616812520). Widescreen (2.35:1) anamorphic. Dolby Surround. $34.95. Keepcase. *LANG:* English; French. *SUB:* Spanish; French. *CAP:* English. *FEATURES:* 32 chapter links • Theatrical trailer • Commentary: Lewis Gilbert • 2 documentaries • Photo gallery • Collectible booklet.
1979 (PG) 136m/C *GB* Roger Moore, Lois Chiles, Richard Kiel, Michael (Michel) Lonsdale, Corinne Clery, Geoffrey Keen, Emily Bolton, Walter Gotell, Bernard Lee, Lois Maxwell, Desmond Llewelyn; *D:* Lewis Gilbert; *W:* Christopher Wood; *C:* Jean Tournier; *M:* John Barry.

Moonstruck

Winning romantic comedy about a widow engaged to one man but falling in love with his younger brother in Little Italy. Excellent performances all around, with Cher particularly fetching as an attractive, hapless widow. Unlikely casting of the usually dominating Aiello as an unassuming mama's boy also works well, and Cage is at his best as a tormented one-handed opera lover/baker. The romantic atmosphere of the film is conveyed perfectly by the DVD's accurate transfer of the deep, warm colors, which have no noticeable bleed. The picture is also very sharp and even the many dimly lit scenes are grain- and artifact-free. Blacks are true, the contrast punchy, and the comfortable brightness levels do nothing to harm the warmth of the image. The 5.1 sound is very full and contains crisp, clear highs as well as deep clean bass. Although the Surround is used almost exclusively for ambience, it's very effective and enhances the overall effect. —JO

Movie: ♫♫► **DVD:** ♫♫♫►

MGM Home Entertainment (Cat #906265, UPC #027616626523). Full frame. Dolby Digital 5.1; Dolby Stereo Surround. $24.98. Keepcase. *LANG:* English (DD5.1); French (DS). *SUB:* English; French; Spanish. *CAP:* English. *FEATURES:* Audio commentary ► Theatrical trailer.

1987 (PG-13) 103m/C Cher, Nicolas Cage, Olympia Dukakis, Danny Aiello, Vincent Gardenia, Julie Bovasso, Louis Guss, Anita Gillette, Feodor Chaliapin Jr., John Mahoney; **D:** Norman Jewison; **W:** John Patrick Shanley; **C:** David Watkin; **M:** Dick Hyman. *AWARDS:* Academy Awards '87: Best Actress (Cher), Best Original Screenplay, Best Supporting Actress (Dukakis); Berlin International Film Festival '87: Best Director (Jewison); Golden Globe Awards '88: Best Actress—Musical/Comedy (Cher), Best Supporting Actress (Dukakis); Los Angeles Film Critics Association Awards '87: Best Supporting Actress (Dukakis); National Board of Review Awards '87: Best Supporting Actress (Dukakis); Writers Guild of America '87: Best Original Screenplay; *NOM:* Academy Awards '87: Best Director (Jewison), Best Picture, Best Supporting Actor (Gardenia).

Mortal Kombat 1: The Movie

Inevitable film version of mega popular arcade game is shameless nirvana for younguns with permanent joystick scars on their hands. Grown-ups forced to sit through it may get into some of the eye-popping special effects and nifty martial arts sequences if they can block out the contrived plot, lame acting, and Lambert's presence as Thunder God. When you watch this DVD it's not just the on-screen characters who get pummeled. The 5.1 sound is so loud, the bass so crunching, and the Surround effects so abundant, that you get a beating of your own (it doesn't hurt too much). The picture isn't so bad either: fairly sharp and not much of a problem with all the dark scenes punctuated by bright flashes and explosions. Grain doesn't increase, and the contrast and brightness remain steady and comfortable. Colors and blacks are both accurate and both are detailed no matter how dark or rich the tone. —JO

Movie: ♫♫ **DVD:** ♫♫♫►

New Line Home Video (Cat #N4310, UPC #794043431029). Widescreen (1.85:1) letterboxed; full frame. Dolby Digital 5.1; Stereo. $24.98. Snapper. *LANG:* English (DD5.1); French (stereo). *SUB:* English; French; Spanish. *CAP:* English. *FEATURES:* 27 chapter links.

1995 (PG-13) 101m/C Christopher Lambert, Talisa Soto, Cary-Hiroyuki Tagawa, Bridgette Wilson; **D:** Paul Anderson; **W:** Kevin Droney; **C:** John R. Leonetti; **M:** George S. Clinton.

Mortal Kombat 2: Annihilation

Even though they were defeated and banished in the first film, the forces of video-game evil manage to rip the fabric of the universe and invade Earth. Liu Kang (Robin Shou) and his buds are on hand with cornball dialogue derring-do to save humanity. The filmmakers make no real attempt at "reality." They're trying to reproduce a game with obvious visual effects, the most blatant being star James Remar's white wig. The mostly bloodless fight choreography is handled with an equally breezy disregard for the laws of physics. Some of the creatures are imaginative enough but the anime-influenced big finish has nothing on the best stop-motion work of Ray Harryhausen. On DVD, the human characters are often surrounded by a slight halo that separates them from the computer-generated backgrounds and sets. The loud sound and techno-metal music are aimed directly at games-players. Martial arts action fans have seen much better action. —MM

Movie: ♫♫► **DVD:** ♫♫♫

New Line Home Video (Cat #N4652). Widescreen (1.85:1) letterboxed. Dolby Surround 5.1. $24.98. Snapper. *LANG:* English; French. *SUB:* English; French. *FEATURES:* Kombatant biographies ► 3-D computer models ► Character sketches ► Set designs ► Separate "jump to" fight index ► Preview scenes within the chapter index ► 16 chapter links.

1997 (PG-13) 98m/C James Remar, Robin Shou, Talisa Soto, Daron McBee, Sandra Hess, Brian Thompson, Reiner Schoene, Musetta Vander, Marjean Holden, Litefoot, Lynn Red Williams, Irina Pantaeva; **D:** John R. Leonetti; **W:** Brent Friedman, Bruce Zabel; **C:** Matthew F. Leonetti; **M:** George S. Clinton.

Mortal Thoughts

Best friends find their relationship tested when the brutal husband of one of them is murdered. Moore and Headly are exceptional, capturing the perfect inflections and attitudes of the hard-working New Jersey beauticians sure of their friendship. Excellent pacing, fine supporting cast, with Keitel and Willis stand-outs. The DVD transfer is sharp with crisp accurate colors that aptly convey the subtleties of the lighting. Contrast is very good and brightness follows suit, both at the proper levels to accent the nuances and details of the cinematography. The Dolby Surround is more than adequate in conveying the dynamics of both dialogue and music, with good imaging and separation. Surround is used sparingly and mainly for environmental ambience. —JO

Movie: ♫♫► **DVD:** ♫♫♫

Columbia Tristar Home Video (Cat #50749, UPC #043396507494). Widescreen (1.85:1) letterboxed; full frame. Dolby Surround. $28.95. Keepcase. *LANG:* English; Spanish; French. *SUB:* English; Spanish; French. *CAP:* English. *FEATURES:* 28 chapter links ► Theatrical trailers.

1991 (R) 104m/C Demi Moore, Bruce Willis, Glenne Headly, Harvey Keitel, John Pankow, Billie Neal; **D:** Alan Rudolph; **W:** William Reilly, Claude Kerven; **C:** Elliot Davis; **M:** Mark Isham. *AWARDS:* National Society of Film Critics Awards '91: Best Supporting Actor (Keitel).

Mosquito

Mutant mosquitoes from outer space are bigger than buzzards. Following the formula right down the line, they attack a campground filled with semi-professional actors. The redneck comedy is broad, dim, and aimed at horror fans. Gunnar Hansen, the original "Leatherface," has a major chainsaw scene. The special effects are a mix of real insects, models, and computer creations. All of them are even more obvious, silly, and non-frightening on DVD than they are on tape. Otherwise, the image of this low-budgeteer is grainy, gross, and unashamed, particularly in the night scenes. —MM

Movie: ♫♫► **DVD:** ♫♫►

Image Entertainment (Cat #ID5702PZDVD, UPC #014381570229). Full frame. Dolby Digital Stereo. $24.99. Snapper. *LANG:* English. *FEATURES:* 15 chapter links.

1995 (R) 92m/C Gunnar Hansen, Ron Asheton, Steve Dixon, Rachel Loiselle, Tim Loveface; **D:** Gary Jones; **W:** Gary Jones, Steve Hodge, Tom Chaney; **C:** Tom Chaney; **M:** Allen Lynch, Randall Lynch.

The Most Dangerous Game

Perhaps more adventure than horror, this Gothic is a companion piece to *King Kong*, made by the same people on some of the same sets with overlapping casts and similar atmosphere. The famous plot involves a hunter (McCrea) who becomes the hunted when he's shipwrecked on Count Zaroff's (Banks) South Pacific island. Robert Armstrong's comic drunk has nothing to do with his Carl Denham character from *Kong*, but Fay Wray's sexy heroine is

in the Ann Darrow mold. Zaroff is a properly Satanic villain, and the zippy pace makes this a particularly entertaining version of the oft-filmed story. On disc, the 1932 special effects hold up well, even if they're not of Titanic proportions. The focus is a little soft throughout, but the film looks fine on DVD, even in the busy, stylized jungle scenes. Far superior to many older rental tapes that are on the market. —MM **AKA:** The Hounds of Zaroff. **Movie:** 🎬🎬🎬▶ **DVD:** 🎬🎬🎬▶
Criterion Collection (Cat #46, UPC #037429137321). Full frame. Dolby Digital Mono. $24.95. Keepcase. *LANG:* English. *SUB:* English. *FEATURES:* Commentary: film historian Bruce Eder • Liner notes by professor Bruce Kawin • 20 chapter links.
1932 78m/B Joel McCrea, Fay Wray, Leslie Banks, Robert Armstrong, Noble Johnson; **D:** Ernest B. Schoedsack, Irving Pichel; **W:** James A. Creelman; **C:** Henry W. Gerrard; **M:** Max Steiner.

Most Wanted
Already scheduled for execution, Marine Sgt. James Dunn (Wayans) is sprung by a half-mad general (Voight) and then framed for an assassination. Then Dunn's on the run in L.A. from the CIA, FBI, LAPD, and the bad guys, with only a doctor (Hennessey) on his side, and she doesn't completely believe his wild story. Viewers expecting the machine gun pace of Con Air or the tightly coiled twists of Enemy of the State will be disappointed, but those looking for an overachieving B-movie will have lots of fun. Wayans is fine, though his own script gives him little to work with. With a baroque Southern accent, Voight feasts on the scenery. On disc, the film looks and sounds excellent, with well-defined dark scenes and only a little flashing in a set of mini-blinds. —MM
Movie: 🎬🎬▶ **DVD:** 🎬🎬🎬
New Line Home Video (Cat #N4653, UPC #794043463525). Widescreen (2.35:1) letterboxed; full frame. Dolby Digital 5.1 (English); Stereo (French). $24.98. Snapper. *LANG:* English; French. *SUB:* English; French; Spanish. *CAP:* English. *FEATURES:* Star highlights • Theatrical trailer • Separate audio track for film score • Cast biographies • 24 chapter links • Previews.
1997 (R) 99m/C Keenen Ivory Wayans, Jon Voight, Jill Hennessey, Eric Roberts, Paul Sorvino, Robert Culp, Wolfgang Bodison, Simon Baker, **D:** David Hogan; **W:** Keenen Ivory Wayans; **C:** Marc Reshovsky; **M:** Paul Bruckmaster. *AWARDS:* NOM: Golden Raspberry Awards '97: Worst Supporting Actor (Voight).

Motel Blue
Department of Defense agent Kyle Rivers (Frye) conducts a security clearance investigation on scientist Lana Hawking (Young) and uncovers some kinky corners of the woman's life and, perhaps, of her own. The low-budget thriller mostly works pretty

well with the help of a solid supporting cast. The DVD is probably not markedly superior to VHS tape because so much of the film is illuminated in shades of blue, giving the action a soft gauzy focus. Sound is acceptable. —MM
Movie: 🎬🎬▶ **DVD:** 🎬🎬▶
MTI Home Video (Cat #MTI50029DVD, UPC #619935402935). Full frame. $24.95. Keepcase. *LANG:* English. *SUB:* Spanish. *FEATURES:* 20 chapter links • Cast thumbnail biographies • Trailers for other MTI releases • Theatrical trailer.
1998 (R) 96m/C Sean Young, Soleil Moon Frye, Seymour Cassel, Robert Vaughn, Robert Stewart, Lou Rawls, Spencer Rochfort; **D:** Sam Firstenberg; **W:** Marianne S. Wibberly, Cormac Wibberly; **C:** Moshe Levin.

Mother
Innovative classic about a family shattered by the uprising in 1905 is the masterpiece of Russian cinema that established Pudovkin, who is rivaled only by Eisenstein for supremacy in montage, poetic imagery, and propagandistic ideals. Based on Maxim Gorky's great novel, it's one of cinematic history's seminal works. Striking cinematography and stunning use of montage for which the director was so famous make this one important. The video transfer of this film to DVD is surprisingly good, especially when considering what condition the source material must have been in. For the most part, it is very dark and muddied (it is rarely crisp and clear). But, then again, at least the film has been preserved in some form. The soundtrack seems designed to sound just as if you were watching the film when it was originally released, complete with volume reductions and sudden stops. —MJT
Movie: 🎬🎬🎬🎬▶ **DVD:** 🎬🎬🎬
Image Entertainment (Cat #ID4579CODVD, UPC #014381457926). Full frame. Dolby Digital Stereo. $29.99. Snapper. *LANG:* Silent. *SUB:* English intertitles. *FEATURES:* 10 chapter links.
1926 70m/B *RU* Vera Baranovskaya, Nikolai Batalov; **D:** Vsevolod Pudovkin.

Mother's Boys
Estranged mother Curtis attempts to reunite with the family she abandoned only to be snubbed, inspiring in her a ruthless effort to win back the children and to oust father Gallagher's now live-in girlfriend Whalley-Kilmer. With an almost psychotic devotion, she terrorizes everyone in the family. Familiar stuff.
Movie: 🎬🎬 **DVD:** NYR
Buena Vista Home Entertainment (Cat #16450). $29.99.
1994 (R) 96m/C Jamie Lee Curtis, Peter Gallagher, Joanne Whalley, Luke Edwards, Vanessa Redgrave, Colin Ward, Joss Ackland, Paul Guilfoyle, John C. McGinley, J.E. Freeman, Ken Lerner, Lorraine Toussaint, Joey Zimmerman, Jill Freedman; **D:** Yves Simoneau; **W:** Richard Hawley, Barry

Schneider; **C:** Elliot Davis; **M:** George S. Clinton.

Mountains of the Moon
Sprawling adventure details the obsessive search for the source of the Nile conducted by famed Victorian rogue/explorer Sir Richard Burton and cohort John Hanning Speke in the late 1800s. Director Rafelson, better known for more personal films such as Five Easy Pieces and The King of Marvin Gardens, shows considerable skill with the spectacular scenery and epic images.
Movie: 🎬🎬🎬▶ **DVD:** NYR
Pioneer Entertainment (Cat #DVD68915 WS). Widescreen letterboxed. Stereo. $24.98. Keepcase.
1990 (R) 140m/C Patrick Bergin, Iain Glen, Fiona Shaw, Richard E. Grant, Peter Vaughan, Roger Rees, Bernard Hill, Anna Massey, Leslie Phillips, John Savident, James Villiers, Delroy Lindo, Roshan Seth; **D:** Bob Rafelson; **W:** Bob Rafelson; **C:** Roger Deakins; **M:** Michael Small.

Mouse Hunt
This Gothic slapstick can't match Tim Burton's best work but it is certainly an impressively filmed work. In terms of set design, special effects, and photography, it is often astonishing. The story doesn't work as well. It concerns Lars (Lane) and Emile (Evans) Smuntz, two brothers who must evict a mouse from the mouldering mansion they have inherited before they can unload it. Walken makes the most of his cameo as a creepy exterminator. Virtually the entire film is staged on sets that emphasize muddy browns and dark grays. Though they make a faithful transition to DVD, they do not play to the strengths of the medium. The image intentionally lacks brightness. Of the extras, the deleted scenes are the most notable and it's easy to see why they were deleted. (Also available with DTS sound, catalog #84673.) —MM
Movie: 🎬🎬▶ **DVD:** 🎬🎬🎬
DreamWorks Home Entertainment (Cat #84159, UPC #667068415926). Widescreen (1.85:1) letterboxed; full frame. Dolby Digital 5.1 Surround Stereo; Dolby Digital Surround Stereo. $29.99. Keepcase. *LANG:* English; French; Spanish. *SUB:* Spanish. *CAP:* English. *FEATURES:* 20 chapter links • Theatrical trailer • Teaser • Deleted scenes • Cast and crew thumbnail biographies • Production notes.
1997 (PG) 97m/C Nathan Lane, Lee Evans, Christopher Walken, William Hickey, Vicki Lewis, Maury Chaykin, Eric Christmas, Michael Jeter, Debra Christofferson, Camilla Soeberg; **D:** Gore Verbinski; **W:** Adam Rifkin; **C:** Phedon Papamichael; **M:** Alan Silvestri.

Moving Target
Virtual sequel to Steve McQueen's The Hunter concerns bounty hunter Sonny

McClean (Dudikoff), whose latest job has him framed for murder and caught between trigger happy cops and dueling mobsters. The profession, the clothing, even the situation with McClean's pregnant wife (Johnson) come straight from the McQueen film. The DVD earns high marks for a sharp image that belies a modest budget. The snow-covered Canadian locations (filling in for New York) have the right cold, sooty look. A sleeper. —*MM*
Movie: 🐾🐾▶ *DVD:* 🐾🐾🐾
Simitar Entertainment (Cat #7462, UPC #082551746224). Full frame. Dolby Digital Stereo. $14.98. Keepcase. *LANG:* English. *FEATURES:* 8 chapter links ● Production factoids ● Billy Dee Williams filmography.
1996 (R) 106m/C *CA* Michael Dudikoff, Billy Dee Williams, Michelle Johnson, Aaron Bess, Tom Harvey, Len Doncheff, Noam Jenkins; *D:* Damian Lee; *W:* Mark Sevi, Kevin Mcarthy; *C:* David Pelletier; *M:* David Lawrence.

Ms. 45

Legendary cult hit arrives on DVD with a brilliantly sharp image that looks much better than older VHS tapes that have been around the block a time or two. Sound is not markedly superior but the picture is crystalline. Thana (Tamerlis) is a mute seamstress who is brutally raped twice one evening and then spends the rest of the film exacting revenge on almost any male who crosses her path. The deranged story has lost none of its power though the violent effects look pretty tame compared to those that have been developed since. —*MM* *AKA:* Angel of Vengeance.
Movie: 🐾🐾🐾 *DVD:* 🐾🐾🐾
Image Entertainment (Cat #ID9086CXDVD, UPC #014381908626). Widescreen (1.78:1) letterboxed. Dolby Digital Mono. $24.99. Snapper. *LANG:* English. *FEATURES:* 12 chapter links.
1981 (R) 84m/C Abel Ferrara, Zoe Tamerlis, Steve Singer, Jack Thibeau, Peter Yellen, Darlene Stuto, Editta Sherman, Albert Sinkys; *D:* Abel Ferrara; *W:* Nicholas St. John; *C:* James (James Lemmo) Momel, James Lemmo; *M:* Joe Delia.

Much Ado about Nothing

Shakespeare for the masses details romance between two sets of would-be lovers—the battling Beatrice and Benedick (Thompson and Branagh) and the ingenuous Hero and Claudio (Beckinsale and Leonard). Branagh brings passion to his quest of making Shakespeare more approachable. Filmed on location in Tuscany, Italy, the film is sunlit, lusty, and revealing about the vagaries of love. The locations make this a very bright movie and the DVD benefits from the lack of dark scenes (and grain), and has very little contrast problems, even along the actual contrast lines. Blacks are also very good.

The only problem with the picture is the occasional background appearing a little too soft and artificial. The Dolby Surround is very good, and the orchestral music full of dynamics while the dialogue is very crisp. However, if you use the Spanish or French tracks, the music sounds a little muffled, but acceptable. —*JO*
Movie: 🐾🐾🐾 *DVD:* 🐾🐾🐾
Columbia Tristar Home Video (Cat #71759, UPC #043396717596). Widescreen (1.85:1) anamorphic; full frame. Dolby Surround; Dolby Digital Stereo. $28.95. Keepcase. *LANG:* English (DS); Spanish (Stereo); French (Stereo). *SUB:* English; Spanish; French. *FEATURES:* 35 chapter links ● Theatrical trailer.
1993 (PG-13) 110m/C *GB* Kenneth Branagh, Emma Thompson, Robert Sean Leonard, Kate Beckinsale, Denzel Washington, Keanu Reeves, Michael Keaton, Brian Blessed, Phyllida Law, Imelda Staunton, Gerard Horan, Jimmy Yuill, Richard Clifford, Ben Elton, Richard Briers; *D:* Kenneth Branagh; *W:* Kenneth Branagh; *C:* Roger Lanser; *M:* Patrick Doyle. *AWARDS: NOM:* Golden Globe Awards '94: Best Film—Musical/Comedy; Independent Spirit Awards '94: Best Actress (Thompson), Best Film.

Mulan

This stylized, spare animation may not measure up to the standards set by *Snow White* or *Beauty and the Beast* or even *The Little Mermaid*, but it's cut from the same cloth. Like them, it's a loose adaptation of a well-known story with fairy-tale elements. Mulan (voice of Wen) is a young woman who lives in a mythic China that's being invaded by Shan-Yu (Ferrer) and his Huns. She's trying, unsuccessfully, to prepare herself for marriage when her family learns of the threat to their country. Her father, a wounded veteran, cannot serve, so she disguises herself as a man and goes off to war. She has the dubious assistance of Mushu (Murphy), the somewhat-magic dragon who is sent by her ancestors. The comic name "Mushu" gives you a good idea of the film's cultural sensitivity. Centuries-old Chinese traditions can be Disneyfied as easily as European ones. On DVD, the full-frame version of the film is not significantly different from the VHS version, so the real value of the disc lies in the widescreen option and the extras. —*MM*
Movie: 🐾🐾🐾▶ *DVD:* 🐾🐾🐾
Buena Vista Home Entertainment (Cat #17225, UPC #717951002297). Widescreen (1.85:1) letterboxed; full frame. Dolby Digital 5.1 Surround Stereo, THX-certified. $39.99. Keepcase. *LANG:* English; French; Spanish. *CAP:* English. *FEATURES:* 31 chapter links ● "Reflection" and "True to Your Heart" music videos ● Theatrical trailer.
1998 (G) 87m/C *D:* Barry Cook, Tony Bancroft; *W:* Philip LaZebnik, Raymond Singer, Rita Hsiao, Christopher Sanders, Eugenia Bostwick-Singer; *M:* Matthew Wilder, Jerry Goldsmith, David Zippel; *V:*

Matthew Wilder, Ming Na, Eddie Murphy, B.D. Wong, Miguel Ferrer, Soon-Teck Oh, Noriyuki "Pat" Morita, Harvey Fierstein, Gedde Watanabe, James Hong, Freda Foh Shen, June Foray, Marni Nixon, George Takei, Miriam Margolyes, James Shigeta, Frank Welker, Lea Salonga, Donny Osmond, Jerry S. Tondo. *AWARDS: NOM:* Academy Awards '98: Best Original Musical/Comedy Score; Golden Globe Awards '99: Best Song ("Reflection"), Best Score.

Multiplicity

With too many business and personal responsibilities, construction supervisor Doug Kinney (Keaton) is a prime candidate for Dr. Leeds's (Yulin) cloning experiments. Since the process hasn't been perfected, each duplicate winds up with a different dominant personality trait—hard charger, Mr. Mom, slacker. Confusion reigns with wife Laura (MacDowell). Pleasant comedy shows that Keaton can still be funny given the right material. Not surprisingly given the material, the focus is something less than diamond-hard. Sound is equally adequate. Overall, this one's not radically superior to VHS tape. —*MM*
Movie: 🐾🐾▶ *DVD:* 🐾🐾▶
Columbia Tristar Home Video (Cat #82449, UPC #043396824492). Widescreen (2.35:1) letterboxed; full frame. Dolby Digital 5.1 Surround Stereo; Dolby Digital Surround Stereo. $29.95. Keepcase. *LANG:* English; French; Spanish. *SUB:* English; French; Spanish. *FEATURES:* 28 chapter links ● Theatrical trailer.
1996 (PG-13) 117m/C Michael Keaton, Andie MacDowell, Harris Yulin, Richard Masur, Eugene Levy, Obba Babatunde, Ann Cusack, Brian Doyle-Murray, Julie Bowen; *D:* Harold Ramis; *W:* Harold Ramis, Chris Miller, Lowell Ganz, Babaloo Mandel, Mary Hale; *C:* Laszlo Kovacs; *M:* George Fenton.

Mumford

Mumford (Dean) is the new shrink in town. Mumford is also the name of the town. Something is up, but what? Part of writer-director Kasdan's purpose was to show that a good film could be made for a fraction of the multi-millions that Hollywood studios traditionally spend on their features. Consequently, the focus is on well-written, funny, quirky characters, not special effects or big name stars. Kasdan was successful and the film may eventually find a receptive audience on home video. The no-frills DVD looks and sounds fine, but it's not a huge step up from a widescreen VHS tape. —*MM*
Movie: 🐾🐾🐾 *DVD:* 🐾🐾🐾
Buena Vista Home Entertainment (Cat #18299). Widescreen letterboxed. Dolby Digital Stereo. $32.99. Keepcase. *LANG:* English. *FEATURES:* 30 chapter links ● "Making of" featurette.
1999 (R) 112m/C Loren Dean, Alfre Woodard, Hope Davis, Jason Lee, Mary McDonnell, Pruitt Taylor Vince, Zooey

Deschanel, Martin Short, David Paymer, Jane Adams, Dana Ivey, Kevin Tighe, Ted Danson, Jason Ritter, Elissabeth Moss, Robert Stack; **D:** Lawrence Kasdan; **W:** Lawrence Kasdan; **C:** Ericson Core; **M:** James Newton Howard.

Mumia: A Case for Reasonable Doubt?

The answer to the question posed in the subtitle is a resounding "No." As the jury said, in 1981, Mumia Abu-Jamal murdered Philadelphia policeman Daniel Faulkner. But Mumia is a photogenic figure with a smooth line, and he has made himself a cause celebre for death-penalty activists. In telling his story, the filmmakers ignore or discount the overwhelming evidence of his guilt and focus on less reliable testimony and the contradictions which can be found in almost any investigation. It's clear from the opening that they are solidly on Abu-Jamal's side. They choose to use repeated shots of chainlink fence and razor wire to set the scene, and those devices don't fare particularly well on DVD. Panning shots across the fence might induce migraines. The nighttime re-creation scenes are deliberately harshly lit and grainy. —*MM*
Movie: 🎵 *DVD:* 🎵🎵
WinStar Home Entertainment (Cat #FLV5058, UPC #720917505824). Full frame. $24.98. Snapper. *LANG:* English. *FEATURES:* 8 chapter links.
1996 74m/C **D:** John Edginton; **C:** Bestor Cram; **Nar:** Marlene Sanders.

The Mummy

Universal has done its usual excellent job with the third of its original horror hits. If the film itself doesn't have the scares of *Dracula* or *Frankenstein*, it does feature one of Karloff's best performances, a sleek art-deco look, and some memorable sets, which would be reused often in the following years. Both image and sound are first-rate, with less wear than you'd expect to see in a film of this age. The extras are comparable to the others in the "Classic Monster Collection." —*MM*
Movie: 🎵🎵🎵▶ *DVD:* 🎵🎵🎵🎵
Universal Studios Home Video (Cat #20327, UPC #025192032721). Full frame. Dolby Digital 2.0. *LANG:* English. *SUB:* French. Snapper. $29.98. *FEATURES:* Production notes ▪ Cast and crew thumbnail bios ▪ Web links ▪ "Mummy Dearest" documentary by David Skal ▪ Commentary: film historian Paul M. Jensen ▪ Original theatrical trailer ▪ The Mummy Archives.
1932 72m/B Boris Karloff, Zita Johann, David Manners, Edward Van Sloan, Arthur Byron, Bramwell Fletcher, Noble Johnson, Leonard Mudie, Henry Victor; **D:** Karl Freund; **W:** John Lloyd Balderston; **C:** Charles Stumar.

The Mummy

Grade-A hokum in the tradition of Saturday matinees bears virtually no resemblance to the 1932 Boris Karloff film. It's really closer to the Hammer films of the 1960s with a strong influence of *Raiders of the Lost Ark*. In the 1920s, American adventurer O'Connell (Fraser) is hired by British librarian Evelyn (Weisz) and her would-be Egyptologist brother (Hannah) to lead them to the ancient City of the Dead where they resurrect the semi-mummified priest Imhotep (Vosloo), who wants to bring back his ancient sweetie (Velasquez). You know the drill. The pace is jazzed up with non-stop action and inventive special effects. On DVD, the widescreen edition of the film looks fine, but rather than offering both wide and full-frame versions on the same disc, Universal has created two separate versions. (Unless your TV is tiny, go with the widescreen version.) The easy-going commentary track by director Sommers and his friend and editor Bob Ducsay focuses on the technical side of their work. The rest of the extensive bells and whistles are fine. —*MM*
Movie: 🎵🎵🎵 *DVD:* 🎵🎵🎵
Universal Studios Home Video (Cat #20327). Widescreen (2.35:1) anamorphic; full frame. Dolby 5.1 Surround (English); Dolby Surround (French). $29.98. Keepcase. *LANG:* English; French. *CAP:* English. *FEATURES:* 18 chapter links ▪ Commentary: director Stephen Sommers and editor Bob Ducsay ▪ "Building a Better Mummy, " 40-minute documentary ▪ Explanation of special effects by visual effects supervisor John Burton ▪ Separate audio track of Jerry Goldsmith score ▪ Egyptology 101 (factoids) ▪ Universal previews ▪ Cast and crew biographies and filmographies ▪ Production notes (press kit) ▪ 3 deleted scenes. DVD-ROM features include "The Mummy Game," screensavers, Universal web links.
1999 (PG-13) 124m/C Brendan Fraser, Rachel Weisz, Arnold Vosloo, John Hannah, Kevin J. O'Connor, Jonathan Hyde, Oded Fehr, Erik Avari, Tuc Watkins, Stephen Dunham, Corey Johnson, Bernard Fox, Aharon Ipale, Omid Djalili, Patricia Velasquez; **D:** Stephen Sommers; **W:** Stephen Sommers; **C:** Adrian Biddle; **M:** Jerry Goldsmith. *AWARDS: NOM:* Academy Awards '99: Best Sound.

Munster, Go Home!

Feature film based on TV series.
Movie: NYR *DVD:* NYR
Goodtimes Entertainment (Cat #81041). Full frame. $14.99. Snapper.
1966 96m/C Fred Gwynne, Yvonne De Carlo, Al Lewis, Butch Patrick, Debbie Watson, Terry-Thomas, Hermione Gingold, Robert Pine, John Carradine, Bernard Fox, Richard Dawson, Arthur Malet; **D:** Earl Bellamy; **W:** Joe Connelly, Bob Mosher, George Tibbles; **C:** Benjamin (Ben H.) Kline; **M:** Jack Marshall.

Muppets from Space

Gonzo and buddy Rizzo search for Gonzo's real family and discover that they are aliens from a distant planet. Gonzo announces his findings on Miss Piggy's talk show and soon government operative K. Edgar Singer (Tambor) is after him. The Muppets satirize the current acceptance of UFO credulity with their customary anarchic wit. On DVD, sound and image probably are not that much better than they are on VHS tape. The best feature is the commentary track by director Hill, Kermit, and Gonzo. It's done *MST3K* style with their silhouettes at the bottom of the screen and is as much fun as the movie. —*MM*
Movie: 🎵🎵🎵 *DVD:* 🎵🎵🎵
Columbia Tristar Home Video (Cat #03932, UPC #043396039322). Widescreen (1.85:1) letterboxed; full frame. Dolby Digital 5.1 Surround Stereo; Dolby Digital Surround Stereo. $24.95. Keepcase. *LANG:* English. *SUB:* French. *CAP:* English. *FEATURES:* 28 chapter links ▪ Music video ▪ Commentary: Hill, Kermit, and Gonzo ▪ 7 outtakes ▪ Theatrical trailers ▪ Cast and crew thumbnail biographies.
1999 (G) 88m/C Jeffrey Tambor, F. Murray Abraham, David Arquette, Ray Liotta, Andie MacDowell, Rob Schneider, Josh Charles, Kathy Griffin, Pat Hingle; **D:** Timothy Hill; **W:** Jerry Juhl, Joseph Mazzarino; **C:** Alan Caso; **V:** Frank Oz, Dave Goelz, Steve Whitmire.

Murder

Young actress Diana Baring (Baring) was found by the body of the murder victim with the weapon, and amnesia. Only jurist Sir John Menier (Marshall) can organize the pieces of the crime to save her. This early Hitchcock effort is not his finest effort, and DVD can do little to help this print. The image is scratched and the soundtrack contains an almost continuous hiss. —*MM*
Movie: 🎵🎵🎵 *DVD:* 🎵▶
Delta/Laserlight (Cat #82033, UPC #018111997737). Full frame. $14.99. Keepcase. *LANG:* English. *SUB:* Spanish; Chinese; Japanese. *FEATURES:* 21 chapter links ▪ Preview to *Rope* ▪ Introduction by Tony Curtis.
1930 92m/B *GB* Herbert Marshall, Nora Baring, Phyllis Konstam, Miles Mander; **D:** Alfred Hitchcock; **W:** Alfred Hitchcock; **C:** Jack Cox; **M:** John Reynders.

Murder at 1600

Jaded D.C. detective Harlan Regis (Snipes) is called to investigate the murder of Carla Town (Moore), a secretary found dead in a White House bathroom. He's reluctantly assisted by hard-boiled Secret Service agent Chance (Lane), while head of security Nick Spikings (Benzali) wants the whole matter wrapped up quickly and quietly—justice not being his main concern. Cliche-fest script gives stereotypical characters a little more development than you may be used to seeing, but doesn't give them anything new or interesting to say or do. Snipes and Lane make a good team, however, and Miller fulfills his usual wise-cracking sidekick role effortlessly. From the very beginning there are a lot of dark shots, and the DVD stays sharp and the colors detailed and accurate. Grain and artifacts are hardly worth mentioning. Overall, a good-looking and sounding disc. —*JO*

Movie: 🎬🎬 **DVD:** 🎬🎬🎬▶

Warner Home Video, Inc. (Cat #14915, UPC #085391491521). Widescreen (1.85:1) anamorphic. Dolby Digital 5.1; Dolby Surround. $24.98. Snapper. *LANG:* English; French. *SUB:* English; Spanish; French. *CAP:* English. *FEATURES:* 37 chapter links ● Theatrical trailers ● Production notes.

1997 (R) 107m/C Wesley Snipes, Diane Lane, Daniel Benzali, Dennis Miller, Alan Alda, Ronny Cox, Tate Donovan, Diane Baker, Mary Moore, Harris Yulin, Richard Blackburn; **D:** Dwight Little; **W:** Wayne Beach, David Hodgin; **C:** Steven Bernstein; **M:** Christopher Young.

A Murder of Crows

Both Tom Berenger and Cuba Gooding Jr. are splendid actors often forced to settle for sub-par material. Here they must together endure a would-be Hitchcockian thriller. The plot is hobbled from the get-go with unconvincing preliminaries. Virtuous but recently disbarred New Orleans attorney Lawson Russell (Gooding) puts his name on a best-seller he didn't write. It is actually handed to him by a stranger who conveniently drops dead. (What a shame the author's "old man" makeup is so obvious!) Lawson's daring, desperate subterfuge comes to light when the novel turns out to be a thinly veiled account of real murders. Detective Clifford Dubose (Berenger) and the FBI are on Lawson's case, but can he prove he's only guilty of plagiarism? The review copy included little more than the film. There are no extras as listed here except the theatrical trailer, full of lightning flash cuts that made the TV screen flip. —*JK*

Movie: 🎬🎬▶ **DVD:** 🎬🎬▶

Studio Home Entertainment (Cat #STHE7265, UPC #65814972652X). Widescreen (1.85:1). Dolby Stereo Surround. $14.99. Snapper. *LANG:* English. *SUB:* Spanish. *FEATURES:* 24 chapter links ● Animated interactive menus ● Commentary: Herrington, producer Broes ● Commentary: Berenger, Pelligrino ● Star bios and filmographies ● Coming attractions trailers and theatrical trailer ● Featurette with makeup artist Mike Maddi ● "Legalese" trivia game ● Photo gallery.

1999 (R) 102m/C Cuba Gooding Jr., Tom Berenger, Marianne Jean-Baptiste, Eric Stoltz; **D:** Rowdy Herrington; **W:** Rowdy Herrington.

The Muse

L.A. screenwriter Steven Phillips (director Brooks) is desperate to regain his "edge" after he's dropped by his studio. Fellow writer Bridges introduces him to the real-life daughter of the Greek god Zeus, Sharon Stone. The screen is filled with movie in-jokes and cameos by many actors

and directors. Like all of Brooks's films, this one works (or doesn't work) through him as writer and performer, so DVD doesn't add much. The image is fine; so is the sound. Extras are minimal. —*MM*

Movie: 🎬🎬🎬 **DVD:** 🎬🎬🎬

USA Home Entertainment (Cat #44999). Widescreen. Dolby Digital 5.0 Surround Stereo; Dolby Digital Surround Stereo. $24.95. Keepcase. *LANG:* English; French; Spanish. *FEATURES:* 25 chapter links ● Trailers ● "Making of" featurette ● Cast and crew thumbnail bios.

1999 (PG-13) 97m/C Albert Brooks, Sharon Stone, Jeff Bridges, Andie MacDowell, Steven Wright, Mark Feuerstein, Bradley Whitford, Dakin Matthews, Concetta Tomei; *Cameos:* James Cameron, Rob Reiner, Martin Scorsese, Jennifer Tilly, Lorenzo Lamas; **D:** Albert Brooks; **W:** Albert Brooks, Monica Johnson; **C:** Thomas Ackerman; **M:** Elton John. *AWARDS: NOM:* Golden Globe Awards '00: Best Actress—Musical/Comedy (Stone).

The Music Man

Con man in the guise of a traveling salesman gets off the train in River City, IA. He convinces the River Cityzens to cancel plans for a new pool hall (a "gateway to hell" for the town's young males) and to finance a wholesome children's marching band. Before he can take the money and run he meets and falls for Marian the librarian (Jones). Acting and singing are terrific "with a capital 'T' and that rhymes with 'P' and that stands for" Preston, who steals the show as the charismatic huckster. Out of print for years, this DVD was released at the same time as the new VHS edition. There is a little too much grain and some color bleed, so the disc is not as sharp as it could be. At times the foreground is a little too sharp for the background. But the colors are vibrant, the contrast is very good, and the brightness is comfortable all the way through. The new Dolby Digital 5.1 soundtrack is excellent and all the music, whether orchestral, vocal, or brassy marching band, is crisp and stirring. The Surround itself is very good. Included is the documentary "Right Here in River City," which is also very entertaining. —*JO*

Movie: 🎬🎬🎬🎬 **DVD:** 🎬🎬▶

Warner Home Video, Inc. (Cat #16768, UPC #085391676829). Widescreen (1.85:1) letterboxed (dual layered). Dolby Digital 5.1. $24.98. Keepcase. *LANG:* English. *SUB:* French. *CAP:* English. *FEATURES:* 45 chapter links ● Theatrical trailers ● Production notes ● "Making of" documentary ● Intro by Shirley Jones.

1962 (G) 151m/C Robert Preston, Shirley Jones, Buddy Hackett, Hermione Gingold, Paul Ford, Pert Kelton, Ron Howard; **D:** Morton DaCosta; **W:** Marion Hargrove; **C:** Robert Burks; **M:** Meredith Willson, Ray Heindorf. *AWARDS:* Academy Awards '62: Best Adapted Score; Golden Globe Awards '63: Best Film—Musical/Comedy; *NOM:* Academy Awards '62: Best Art Direction/Set Decoration (Color), Best

Costume Design (Color), Best Film Editing, Best Picture, Best Sound.

My Best Friend's Wedding

Yes, it's a romantic comedy but like director Hodge's previous effort, *Muriel's Wedding*, it delivers some snap among the laughs. Restaurant critic Julianne (Roberts) and sports writer Michael (Mulroney) are best friends who have vowed to marry at 28 if they haven't found anyone else by that time. When Michael falls for sweet, wealthy Kimmy (Diaz), Julianne realizes that she's in love with him and decides to sabotage the nuptials, and enlists her gay friend George (Everett), posing as her new beau, to help. The DVD image is excellent; sound is very good. Both are all that this exceptionally slick star vehicle needs. —*MM*

Movie: 🎬🎬🎬 **DVD:** 🎬🎬🎬

Columbia Tristar Home Video (Cat #82729, UPC #04339682729). Widescreen (2.35:1) letterboxed; full frame. Dolby Digital 5.1 Surround Stereo; Dolby Digital Surround Stereo. $29.95. Keepcase. *LANG:* English; French; Spanish. *SUB:* English; French; Spanish. *FEATURES:* 17 chapter links ● Cast and crew thumbnail biographies ● Theatrical trailer.

1997 (PG-13) 105m/C Julia Roberts, Dermot Mulroney, Cameron Diaz, Rupert Everett, Philip Bosco, M. Emmet Walsh, Rachel Griffiths, Susan Sullivan, Paul Giamatti; **D:** P.J. Hogan; **W:** Ronald Bass; **C:** Laszlo Kovacs; **M:** James Newton Howard. *AWARDS: NOM:* Academy Awards '97: Best Original Musical/Comedy Score; British Academy Awards '97: Best Supporting Actor (Everett); Golden Globe Awards '98: Best Actress—Musical/Comedy (Roberts), Best Film—Musical/Comedy, Best Supporting Actor (Everett); MTV Movie Awards '98: Best Female Performance (Roberts), Breakthrough Performance (Everett), Best Comedic Performance (Everett).

My Best Girl

Shop girl Maggie Johnson (Pickford) falls in love with Joe Grant (Rogers) not knowing that he is the scion of the family that owns the department store where she works. Comic tastes and conventions have dated much of the film, but Mary Pickford's charming screen presence is still radiant. It's easy to understand why she was such a popular star in Hollywood's early days. Almost all of this DVD looks and sounds terrific with a new symphonic score and limited sound effects. It's marred by only a few sprocket tears and dings. Otherwise, the print is in remarkable shape with nice tinting and sharp focus. —*MM*

Movie: 🎬🎬🎬 **DVD:** 🎬🎬🎬

Image Entertainment (Cat #ID5927MLSDVD, UPC #014381592726). Full frame. Dolby Digital Stereo. $29.99. Snapper. *FEATURES:* 14 chapter links ● Home

movie/newsreel footage of Pickford and Rogers.
1927 88m/B Mary Pickford, Charles "Buddy" Rogers, Lucien Littlefield, Carmelita Geraghty, Sunshine Hart, Hobart Bosworth; **D:** Sam Taylor; **W:** Hope Loring, Tim Whelan, Allen McNeil; **C:** Charles Rosher, David Keeson. *AWARDS: NOM:* Academy Awards '28: Best Cinematography.

My Blue Heaven

After agreeing to rat on the Mafia, Martin is dropped into suburbia as part of the witness protection program. Moranis plays the FBI agent assigned to help the former mobster become an upstanding citizen. Adjusting to life in the slow lane isn't easy for an ex-con who has grown accustomed to the big time. Not the typical role for Martin, who plays a brunette with a New York accent and is handcuffed by bad writing. The picture is very sharp and has very little grain—what there is appears in the shadows or in out-and-out dimly lit scenes. Colors are vibrant and free of bleed, but the tint seems to change in a few scenes, and sometimes you can tell they're not quite right. Blacks perform similarly and range from true to slightly gray with a little grain. The sound has some guts to it and pretty good separation for a Dolby Surround mix. Music is full and the dialogue crisp. —JO
Movie: 🎬🎬 *DVD:* 🎬🎬
Warner Home Video, Inc. (Cat #12003, UPC #085391200321). Full frame. Dolby Surround. $14.98. Snapper. *LANG:* English; French. *CAP:* English. *FEATURES:* 30 chapter links.
1990 (PG-13) 96m/C Steve Martin, Rick Moranis, Joan Cusack, Melanie Mayron, Carol Kane, Bill Irwin, William Hickey, Daniel Stern; **D:** Herbert Ross; **W:** Nora Ephron; **C:** John Bailey; **M:** Ira Newborn.

My Dinner with Andre

Wallace Shawn and Andre Gregory play versions of themselves in this talky dull movie which has developed a cult of fans. Essentially, the title tells it all as they have dinner in a New York restaurant and lightly skip over all sorts of topics from the state of the theatre to their most profound beliefs. The DVD is exceptionally rough-looking with a grainy image and unexceptional sound. Beyond the modest extras, it is no improvement over VHS tape. —MM
Movie: 🎬🎬 *DVD:* 🎬🎬
WinStar Home Entertainment (Cat #FLV5043, UPC #720917504322). Full frame. $29.98. Keepcase. *LANG:* English. *FEATURES:* 9 chapter links • Filmographies and awards.
1981 110m/C Andre Gregory, Wallace Shawn, Roy Butler, Jean Lenauer; **D:** Louis Malle; **W:** Andre Gregory, Wallace Shawn; **C:** Jeri Sopanen; **M:** Allen Shawn.

My Fair Lady

Colorful production of Lerner and Loewe's musical version of *Pygmalion*, about an ill-mannered cockney girl who is plucked from her job as a flower girl by Professor Henry Higgins. Higgins makes a bet with a colleague that he can turn this rough diamond into a "lady." Winner of eight Academy Awards. Hepburn's singing voice is dubbed by Marni Nixon, who was also responsible for the singing in *The King and I* and *West Side Story*; the dubbing may have undermined her chance at an Oscar nomination. Typecasting role for Harrison as the crusty, egocentric Higgins. The DVD format's color capabilities make it an ideal medium for big-budget musicals, and *My Fair Lady* fits the bill perfectly. When you watch the DVD it's like seeing the film anew, with stronger, deeper colors and contrast that accents both color and details. The sound is also excellent and feels much more high energy, even if, as with most older films, Surround and imaging is a little weak. But don't worry about the fact that Arnold's new movie is loaded with slam-bang Surround and *My Fair Lady* isn't; just relax and enjoy the film like never before. —JO
Movie: 🎬🎬🎬 *DVD:* 🎬🎬🎬
Warner Home Video, Inc. (Cat #16668, UPC #085391666820). Widescreen (2.35:1) anamorphic. Dolby Digital 5.1; Dolby Surround; Mono. $24.98. Snapper. *LANG:* English; French. *SUB:* English; French. *CAP:* English. *FEATURES:* 50 chapter links • Audio commentary • Behind-the-scenes documentary • Production notes • 4 theatrical trailers.
1964 (G) 170m/C Audrey Hepburn, Rex Harrison, Stanley Holloway, Wilfrid Hyde-White, Theodore Bikel, Mona Washbourne, Jeremy Brett, Robert Coote, Gladys Cooper; **D:** George Cukor; **W:** Alan Jay Lerner; **C:** Harry Stradling; **M:** Frederick Loewe, Alan Jay Lerner. *AWARDS:* Academy Awards '64: Best Actor (Harrison), Best Adapted Score, Best Art Direction/Set Decoration (Color), Best Color Cinematography, Best Costume Design (Color), Best Director (Cukor), Best Picture, Best Sound; American Film Institute (AFI) '98: Top 100; British Academy Awards '65: Best Film; Directors Guild of America Awards '64: Best Director (Cukor); Golden Globe Awards '65: Best Actor—Musical/Comedy (Harrison), Best Director (Cukor), Best Film—Musical/Comedy; New York Film Critics Awards '64: Best Actor (Harrison), Best Film; *NOM:* Academy Awards '64: Best Adapted Screenplay, Best Film Editing, Best Supporting Actor (Holloway), Best Supporting Actress (Cooper).

My Favorite Martian

Semi-awful retread of the semi-successful '60s sitcom, in which TV producer Tim (Daniels) is cajoled into hiding "Uncle Martin" (Lloyd), who is actually a marooned space alien. Numerous animated and computer morphed sight gags, including a horny, wisecracking space suit, take the place of a plot. Undiscriminating children

may enjoy it. Others will note the slightly dimmed image quality. —JE
Movie: 🎬 *DVD:* 🎬🎬
Buena Vista Home Entertainment (Cat #0-78881646-2, UPC #1795100284). Widescreen (1.85:1). Dolby Digital 5.1. $29.99. Snapper. *LANG:* English; French. *CAP:* English. *FEATURES:* 20 chapter links • "Making of" featurette • Trailer.
1998 (PG) 93m/C Jeff Daniels, Christopher Lloyd, Elizabeth Hurley, Daryl Hannah, Wallace Shawn, Christine Ebersole, Ray Walston, Michael Lerner; **D:** Donald Petrie; **W:** Sherri Stoner, Deanna Oliver; **C:** Thomas Ackerman; **M:** John Debney.

My Fellow Americans

Political "Odd Couple" pits cantankerous conservative Kramer (Lemmon) against womanizing liberal Douglas (Garner) when current President Aykroyd frames his two predecessors for a White House scandal. The age-old adversaries must set aside their differences long enough to clear their names by reaching Kramer's presidential library, where he has vindicating papers. Along the way, they encounter adventure, danger, and "the people," the average Americans they used to work for. *Grumpy Old Men*–veteran Lemmon is plenty cranky while Garners's charisma is a suitable foil. The ironic "charm" of the coarse banter from the mouths of two ex-presidents carries much of the humor. This DVD, however, isn't up to Warner's usual par. The picture seems like it would be pretty sharp but there are quite a bit of artifacts that distort the image. There is also some grain in the darker scenes. Colors are pretty accurate and the contrast tries to give the picture a little life. Unfortunately, the artifacts ensure that the VHS tape would be a better choice for viewing this film. —JO
Movie: 🎬🎬🎬 *DVD:* 🎬
Warner Home Video, Inc. (Cat #14535, UPC #085391453529). Full frame. Dolby Digital 5.1; Dolby Surround; Dolby Digital Mono. $24.98. Snapper. *LANG:* English; Spanish; French. *SUB:* English; Spanish; French. *CAP:* English. *FEATURES:* 36 chapter links • Theatrical trailer • Production notes • Bloopers.
1996 (PG-13) 96m/C Dan Aykroyd, James Garner, Jack Lemmon, John Heard, Sela Ward, Wilford Brimley, Everett McGill, Bradley Whitford, Lauren Bacall, James Rebhorn, Esther Rolle, Conchata Ferrell, Jack Kehler, Tom Everett, Jeff Yagher; **D:** Peter Segal; **W:** E. Jack Kaplan, Richard Chapman, Peter Tolan; **C:** Julio Macat; **M:** William Ross.

My Giant

Billy Crystal plays a short, annoying, Hollywood-type guy and Romanian-born NBA player Gheorghe Muresan plays a really tall Romanian guy, so you know there's not exactly an Olivier thing happening here. Crystal is the brutish showbiz agent Sammy, who accidently stumbles onto Muresan's Max. The gentle Max is at peace in his monastery; but Sammy, being an agent, quickly finds a way to make money off of him. Max is talked into a movie career so he can be reunited with his childhood crush Lillianna (Pacula). The odd couple shtick is milked until bone dry, and then the sentimentality floodgates open when it's discovered that Max has a serious medical condition. If you are going to watch this film, you may as well throw this DVD into the machine—maybe the good-quality image will ease your suffering a little. The grain- and artifact-free image is sharp, and colors are strong and vibrant with very little bleed. The 5.1 sound is a bit of a waste, with little Surround or even much in the way of stereo effects. The fidelity is fine, though, and there is a decent amount of bass to go along with the crisp and clean high-end. —*JO*

Movie: ♫♫ ► **DVD:** ♫♫♫

Warner Home Video, Inc. (Cat #C2535, UPC #053939253528). Widescreen (1.85) anamorphic. Dolby Digital 5.1. $19.98. Snapper. *LANG:* English. *SUB:* English; French. *CAP:* English. *FEATURES:* 34 chapter links • 6 Theatrical trailers • Production notes.

1998 (PG) 103m/C Billy Crystal, Gheorghe Muresan, Kathleen Quinlan, Joanna Pacula, Rider Strong, Harold Gould, Doris Roberts, Philip Sterling, Heather Thomas, Zane Carney; *Cameos:* Steven Seagal; *D:* Michael Lehmann; *W:* David Seltzer; *C:* Michael Coulter; *M:* Marc Shaiman.

My Girl

Chlumsky is delightful in her film debut as an 11-year-old tomboy who must come to grips with the realities of life. Culkin plays her best friend Thomas, who understands her better than anyone else, including her father, a mortician, and his girlfriend, the makeup artist at the funeral parlor. Some reviewers questioned whether young children would be able to deal with some unhappy occurrences in the film, but most seemed to classify it as a movie the whole family would enjoy. The DVD transfer could be a little sharper but holds up pretty well. There is some increase in the grain in darker sequences. Colors are mostly accurate but the more intense ones bleed a little. Blacks fare about the same and are true most of the time. Contrast and brightness levels are comfortable and consistent. The Dolby Surround doesn't add much to the film; there's not much, and even the front tracks are both lifeless and a little thin. —*JO*

Movie: ♫♫ ► **DVD:** ♫♫ ►

Columbia Tristar Home Video (Cat #50999, UPC #043396509993). Full frame. Dolby Surround. $28.95. Keepcase. *LANG:* English; Spanish; French. *SUB:* English; Spanish; French. *CAP:* English. *FEATURES:* 20 chapter links • Theatrical trailer.

1991 (PG) 102m/C Dan Aykroyd, Jamie Lee Curtis, Macaulay Culkin, Anna Chlumsky, Griffin Dunne, Raymond Buktenica, Richard Masur, Ann Nelson, Peter Michael Goetz, Tom Villard; *D:* Howard Zieff; *W:* Laurice Elehwany; *C:* Paul Elliott; *M:* James Newton Howard. *AWARDS:* MTV

Movie Awards '92: Best Kiss (Macaulay Culkin/Anna Chlumsky).

My Left Foot

Gritty, unsentimental drama is based on the autobiography of cerebral-palsy victim Christy Brown (Day-Lewis). He is considered an imbecile by everyone but his mother (Fricker, in a stunning award-winning performance) until he teaches himself to write. He survives his impoverished Irish roots to become a painter and writer using his left foot, the only appendage over which he has control. The star is astounding and the supporting cast, especially Shaw and Cusack, match him measure for measure. The image is good to very good, a bit better than VHS tape but not a lot. A few light flecks are visible in the high-contrast color but they're hardly worth noting and do not detract from the strong story and cast. Sound is fine. —*MM*

Movie: ♫♫♫ ► **DVD:** ♫♫♫

HBO Home Video (Cat #90373, UPC #026539037320). Full frame. Dolby Digital Mono. $24.98. Snapper. *LANG:* English. *SUB:* English; French; Spanish. *FEATURES:* 17 chapter links • Cast and crew thumbnail biographies • Theatrical trailer.

1989 (R) 103m/C *IR* Daniel Day-Lewis, Brenda Fricker, Ray McAnally, Cyril Cusack, Fiona Shaw, Hugh O'Conor, Adrian Dunbar, Ruth McCabe, Alison Whelan; *D:* Jim Sheridan; *W:* Shane Connaughton, Jim Sheridan; *C:* Jack Conroy; *M:* Elmer Bernstein. *AWARDS:* Academy Awards '89: Best Actor (Day-Lewis), Best Supporting Actress (Fricker); British Academy Awards '89: Best Actor (Day-Lewis), Best Supporting Actor (McAnally); Independent Spirit Awards '90: Best Foreign Film; Los Angeles Film Critics Association Awards '89: Best Actor (Day-Lewis), Best Supporting Actress (Fricker); Montreal World Film Festival '89: Best Actor (Day-Lewis); New York Film Critics Awards '89: Best Actor (Day-Lewis), Best Film; National Society of Film Critics Awards '89: Best Actor (Day-Lewis); *NOM:* Academy Awards '89: Best Adapted Screenplay, Best Director (Sheridan), Best Picture.

My Life As a Dog

A troublesome boy is separated from his brother and sent to live with relatives in the country when his mother is taken ill. Unhappy and confused, he struggles to understand sexuality and love and tries to find security and acceptance. The usual Fox/Lorber fare. A soft and grainy picture, with somewhat dull colors, and blacks that never seem to quite get there. The sound is also a little thin and there is slight distortion occasionally on the high end. The film itself, however, is great. —*JO* *AKA:* Mitt Liv Som Hund.

Movie: ♫♫♫♫ **DVD:** ♫♫

Fox/Lorber Home Video (Cat #FLV5051, UPC #720917505121). Full frame. Stereo. $24.98. Keepcase. *LANG:* Swedish; English. *SUB:* English. *FEATURES:* 8 chapter links.

1985 101m/C *SW* Anton Glanzelius, Tomas Van Bromssen, Anki Liden, Melinda

Kinnaman, Kicki Rundgren, Ing-mari Carlsson; *D:* Lasse Hallstrom; *W:* Lasse Hallstrom, Per (Pelle) Berglund, Brasse Brannstrom; *C:* Jorgen Persson, Rolf Lindstrom; *M:* Bjorn Isfalt. *AWARDS:* Golden Globe Awards '88: Best Foreign Film; Independent Spirit Awards '88: Best Foreign Film; New York Film Critics Awards '87: Best Foreign Film; *NOM:* Academy Awards '87: Best Adapted Screenplay, Best Director (Hallstrom).

My Life So Far

In a lovingly photographed Argyll, Scotland, in the early 1930s, young Fraser Pettigrew (Norman) discovers the mysteries of sex with the arrival of his French aunt Heloise (Jacob). The household is headed up by his inventor dad (Firth) and mother (Mastrantonio). The action may be a bit too sweet and charming for some audiences, but anyone who appreciates the less serious *Masterpiece Theatre* entries and such imports as *Waking Ned Devine* should give it a try. The DVD has no serious flaws, though the exotic locales lose something on the small screen. Sound is excellent. —*MM*

Movie: ♫♫♫ **DVD:** ♫♫♫

Miramax Pictures Home Video (Cat #18270, UPC #717951004635). Widescreen (1.85:1) anamorphic. Dolby Digital 5.1 Surround Stereo. $29.99. Keepcase. *LANG:* English. *CAP:* English. *FEATURES:* 16 chapter links.

1998 (PG-13) 93m/C *GB* Colin Firth, Mary Elizabeth Mastrantonio, Irene Jacob, Malcolm McDowell, Rosemary Harris, Tcheky Karyo, Robert Norman, Kelly Macdonald; *D:* Hugh Hudson; *W:* Simon Donald; *C:* Bernard Lutic; *M:* Howard Blake.

My Life to Live

Godard showcased his then-wife Anna Karina in a quick yet intimate epic. Nana, an impressionable young wife and mother, abandons her family for an acting career but is soon enough made a martyr to the streets. Cinema has as little to offer the creature as society; she goes nowhere fast in "douze tableaux." The soundtrack, true to Godardian form, intermittently blares or goes dead silent. The digitally remastered image track is speckled, with "rain-streak" aliasing. French students can disable the subtitles with a menu option. —*JK* *AKA:* Vivre Sa Vie; It's My Life.

Movie: ♫♫♫♫ **DVD:** ♫♫ ►

WinStar Home Entertainment (Cat #FLV5035, UPC #720917503523). Full frame. Dolby Digital AC-3 Surround 5.1. $29.98. Keepcase. *LANG:* French. *SUB:* English. *FEATURES:* 12 chapter links • Interactive menus • 2-color picture disc • Production credits • Filmographies and awards lists.

1962 85m/B *FR* Anna Karina, Sady Rebbot, Andre S. Labarthe, Guylaine Schlumberger; *D:* Jean-Luc Godard; *W:* Jean-Luc Godard; *C:* Raoul Coutard; *M:* Michel Legrand. *AWARDS:* Venice Film Festival '62: Special Jury Prize.

My Lucky Stars

Muscles (Chan) and Ricky (Yuen Biao) are Hong Kong cops chasing bad guys in Japan. After an extended chase/fight that goes from subway to amusement park, they have to call in Kidstuff (Sammo Hung) and his pals for help. The DVD looks good and bright, but in fast, swervy chases and pans, some shapes tend to dissolve. The sound is thin throughout, but those don't matter. The stuntwork is imaginative and brilliant. Great for Chan fans. —MM

Movie: 𝄇𝄇𝄇 **DVD:** 𝄇𝄇𝄇
Tai Seng Video Marketing (Cat #5094, UPC #4895024900582). Widescreen letter-boxed. Dolby Digital 5.1 Surround Stereo. $49.95. Keepcase. LANG: Cantonese; Mandarin. SUB: Traditional & Simplified Chinese; Japanese; Indonesia & Malaysia Bahasa; Thai; Korean; Vietnamese. FEATURES: 8 chapter links • Cast and crew thumbnail biographies.
1985 96m/C HK Jackie Chan, Richard Ng, Sammo Hung, Yuen Biao, Sibelle Hu; **D:** Sammo Hung; **W:** Barry Wong, Szeto Cheuk Hon; **C:** Peter Ngor.

My Man Godfrey

A spoiled rich girl picks up someone she assumes is a bum—or "forgotten man" as the script puts it—as part of a scavenger hunt and decides to keep him as her butler. In the process, he teaches her about life, money, and happiness. Top-notch screwball comedy defines the genre. Lombard is a stunner alongside the equally charming Powell. Watch for Jane Wyman as an extra in a party scene. It's difficult to tell where the flaws on this disc come from. The dark opening credits are filled with heavy grain and pixels. The body of the film is better but still far from exemplary; sound is thin throughout. On the other side, both acting and writing are brilliant. Powell is at his best and that is very good, indeed. —MM

Movie: 𝄇𝄇𝄇𝄇 **DVD:** 𝄇𝄇
Madacy Entertainment (Cat #99022). Full frame. Dolby Digital Mono. $9.99. Keepcase. LANG: English. FEATURES: 9 chapter links • William Powell biography • Credits.
1936 95m/B William Powell, Carole Lombard, Gail Patrick, Alice Brady, Mischa Auer, Eugene Pallette, Alan Mowbray, Franklin Pangborn, Jane Wyman; **D:** Gregory La Cava; **W:** Gregory La Cava, Morrie Ryskind; **C:** Ted Tetzlaff; **M:** Charles Previn. AWARDS: National Film Registry '99; NOM: Academy Awards '36: Best Actor (Powell), Best Actress (Lombard), Best Director (La Cava), Best Screenplay, Best Supporting Actor (Auer), Best Supporting Actress (Brady).

My Mom's a Werewolf

An average suburban mother gets involved with a dashing stranger and soon, to her terror, begins to turn into a werewolf. Her daughter and companion must come up with a plan to regain dear sweet mom.
Movie: 𝄇 **DVD:** NYR

Rhino Home Video (Cat #5741). Full frame. $14.95. Snapper.
1989 (PG) 90m/C Susan Blakely, John Saxon, John Schuck, Katrina Caspary, Ruth Buzzi, Marilyn McCoo, Marcia Wallace, Diana Barrows; **D:** Michael Fischa; **W:** Mark Pirro; **C:** Bryan England; **M:** Dana Walden, Barry Fasman.

My Night at Maud's

Typically subtle Rohmer entry concerns the quandary of upright Jean-Louis (Trintignant) who is in love with the beautiful Francoise (Barrault), but finds himself attracted to the more free-spirited Maud (Fabian). It's an understated tale of love, religious faith, and logic. The DVD is an accurate reproduction of an acceptable original. The black-and-white photography is not particularly crisp and there's little that the disc can do to improve it or the spare sound. The "enhanced" subtitles are large and easy to read. —MM AKA: My Night with Maud; Ma Nuit Chez Maud.
Movie: 𝄇𝄇𝄇 **DVD:** 𝄇𝄇
WinStar Home Entertainment (Cat #FLV5007, UPC #720917050072). Full frame. $29.98. Keepcase. LANG: French. SUB: English. FEATURES: 9 chapter links • Filmographies of Rohmer and Trintignant • Production credits.
1969 111m/B FR Jean-Louis Trintignant, Francoise Fabian, Marie-Christine Barrault, Antoine Vitez; **D:** Eric Rohmer; **W:** Eric Rohmer; **C:** Nestor Almendros. AWARDS: New York Film Critics Awards '70: Best Screenplay; National Society of Film Critics Awards '70: Best Cinematography, Best Screenplay; NOM: Academy Awards '70: Best Foreign Film, Best Story & Screenplay.

My Science Project

Teenager Stockwell stumbles across a crystal sphere with a funky light. Unaware that it is an alien time-travel device, he takes it to school to use as a science project in a last-ditch effort to avoid failing his class. Chaos follows and Stockwell and his chums find themselves battling gladiators, mutants, and dinosaurs. Plenty of special effects and a likeable enough, dumb teenage flick. The DVD transfer is a touch soft and colors seem a little dull. Contrast could be higher, and blacks add some grain to the mix. During some special effects, there is some added distortion along contrast lines. —JO
Movie: 𝄇 **DVD:** 𝄇𝄇
Anchor Bay (Cat #DV10824, UPC #013131082494). Widescreen (2.35:1) letterboxed; full frame. Stereo. $24.98. Keepcase. LANG: English. FEATURES: 19 chapter links.
1985 (PG) 94m/C John Stockwell, Danielle von Zerneck, Fisher Stevens, Raphael Sbarge, Richard Masur, Barry Corbin, Ann Wedgeworth, Dennis Hopper, Candace Silvers, Beau Dremann, Pat Simmons, Pamela Springsteen; **D:** Jonathan Betuel; **W:** Jonathan Betuel; **C:** David M. Walsh; **M:** Peter Bernstein.

My Son the Fanatic

Pakistani-born cabbie Parvez (Puri) works hard in England, and deals with tough problems involving his job and family. Primary among them is Bettina (Griffiths), a young prostitute he tries to help. The immigrant story has been told often enough. Writer Kureishi and director Prasad bring conviction and beautifully drawn characters to their contribution. The DVD handles bright colors, dim night scenes, and potentially troublesome intricate fabric patterns without a hitch. Sound is fine. A serious sleeper. —MM

Movie: 𝄇𝄇𝄇 **DVD:** 𝄇𝄇𝄇
Miramax Pictures Home Video (Cat #18327, UPC #717951005137). Widescreen (1.85:1) anamorphic. Dolby Digital Surround Stereo. $29.99. Keepcase. LANG: English. CAP: English. FEATURES: 17 chapter links.
1997 (R) 86m/C GB Om Puri, Rachel Griffiths, Stellan Skarsgard, Akbar Kurtha; **D:** Udayan Prasad; **W:** Hanif Kureishi; **C:** Alan Almond; **M:** Stephen Warbeck. AWARDS: NOM: Independent Spirit Awards '00: Best Foreign Film.

My Stepmother Is an Alien

When eccentric physicist Aykroyd sends a message beam to another galaxy on a stormy night, the last thing he expects is a visit from beautiful alien Basinger. Unfortunately, he does not realize that this gorgeous blond is an alien and continues to court her despite her rather odd habits. Only his daughter seems to notice the strange goings-on, but dad ignores her warnings, enabling Basinger's evil sidekick to continue in its plot to take over the Earth. The first kiss is the film's highlight. Some may say that the DVD looks better than this film deserves. Sharpness is good and there is very little grain. Blacks are true, colors very good, and color bleed is minimal (the worst is in Basinger's bright red dress when she first appears). Brightness is consistent and the contrast is good. However, early in the film, during some laboratory sequences, lightning flashes in the movie caused distortion in the black bars of the letterboxing—very aggravating. You shouldn't see any artifacts. Excellent sound. —JO
Movie: 𝄇𝄇 **DVD:** 𝄇𝄇
Columbia Tristar Home Video (Cat #61029, UPC #043396610293). Widescreen (1.85:1) letterboxed; full frame. Dolby Surround. Keepcase. LANG: English; French; Spanish. SUB: French; Spanish. CAP: English. FEATURES: 28 chapter links • Theatrical trailer.
1988 (PG-13) 108m/C Dan Aykroyd, Kim Basinger, Jon Lovitz, Alyson Hannigan, Joseph Maher, Seth Green, Wesley Mann, Adrian Sparks, Juliette Lewis, Tanya Fenmore; **D:** Richard Benjamin; **W:** Jerico Weingrod, Herschel Weingrod, Timothy Harris, Jonathan Reynolds; **C:** Richard H. Kline; **M:** Alan Silvestri.

My Teacher's Wife

Updated version of *My Tutor* with younger boy/older woman romance. High-schooler London has big college plans, which won't get anywhere if he doesn't pass math. So he asks Carrere to tutor him, only the problems they study become more personal. **Movie:** 🎵🎵▸ **DVD:** NYR
Trimark Home Video (Cat #6911). Stereo. $24.99. *LANG:* English. *CAP:* English.
1995 (R) 90m/C Tia Carrere, Jason London, Christopher McDonald, Leslie Lyles, Zak Orth, Jeffrey Tambor, Randy Pearlstein; **D:** Bruce Leddy; **W:** Bruce Leddy, Seth Greenland; **C:** Zoltan David; **M:** Kevin Gilbert.

Mystery Men

Complete comic misfire pits seven inept superheroes with such powers as fork-throwing and flatulence against the evil Casanova Frankenstein (Rush) after Captain Amazing (Kinnear) is kidnapped. The soaring backdrops and sets will remind viewers of Tim Burton's big-budget work, but his wit is absent. In its place, we have a strong disco subtext. Director Kinka Usher's semi-coherent commentary track is no better than the film itself. He says that, like, you know, everybody who worked with him was like pretty much totally awesome or whatever, you know. —*MM*
Movie: WOOF **DVD:** 🎵🎵▸
Universal Studios Home Video (Cat #20688, UPC #025192068829). Widescreen (1.85:1) letterboxed. Dolby Digital 5.1 Surround Stereo; Dolby Digital Surround Stereo. $29.98. Keepcase. *LANG:* English; French. *CAP:* English. *FEATURES:* 18 chapter links ◦ "Making of" featurette ◦ Commentary: director Kinka Usher ◦ Soundtrack presentation ◦ Music highlights ◦ Production notes ◦ Theatrical trailer ◦ Origin of the "Mystery Men" comic book characters. Includes extra features for computer DVD-ROM.
1999 (PG-13) 120m/C Ben Stiller, Hank Azaria, William H. Macy, Paul (Pee-wee Herman) Reubens, Claire Forlani, Wes Studi, Janeane Garofalo, Kel Mitchell, Geoffrey Rush, Lena Olin, Greg Kinnear, Tom Waits, Eddie Izzard, Ricky Jay, Louise Lasser; **D:** Kinka Usher; **W:** Neil Cuthbert; **C:** Stephen Burum; **M:** Stephen Warbeck.

Mystery Science Theater 3000: The Movie

Somehow, giving the long-lived cable TV series the polish of a big-screen Hollywood production and then enhancing it on DVD, goes against the grain of everything *MST3K* stands for. Our protagonists are trapped on the Satellite of Love (which is a collection of cheesy detritus) and forced to watch really bad cheap-looking movies. This time out, they've got a fairly respectable subject, *This Island Earth*, and their jokes seem to lack the zip and the machine-gun pace of the best television episodes. The no-frills DVD looks

about the same as a widescreen edition of the VHS tape. —*MM*
Movie: 🎵🎵▸ **DVD:** 🎵🎵▸
Image Entertainment (Cat #ID4282USDVD, UPC #014381428223). Widescreen (1.85:1) letterboxed. Uncompressed PCM Stereo. $24.99. Snapper. *LANG:* English. *CAP:* English. *FEATURES:* 16 chapter links.
1996 (PG-13) 73m/C Trace Beaulieu, James Mallon, Michael J. Nelson, Kevin Murphy, John Brady; **D:** James Mallon; **W:** Trace Beaulieu, James Mallon, Michael J. Nelson, Kevin Murphy, Mary Jo Pehl, Paul Chaplin, Bridget Jones; **C:** Jeff Stonehouse; **M:** Billy Barber.

The Naked City

The use of voice-over narration to explain on-screen action seems dated now, but the semi-documentary techniques (including extensive use of New York locations) were unusual for crime films in 1948. Despite a far-fetched plot, this one helped to define the police procedural. After a playgirl is murdered, detectives Muldoon (Fitzgerald) and Hallran (Taylor) are left without clues. They're finally led to a playboy (Duff) and a spectacular ending on the Brooklyn Bridge. The film served as the impetus for the TV show of the same name where Hellinger's postscript became the famous tagline: "There are eight million stories in the naked city; this has been one of them." DVD can do little to improve the quality of the original black-and-white footage which exhibits all the shortcomings of location work. Exteriors range between vague muddiness and high contrast. Overall, though, the disc looks as good as any VHS tape. Sound is fine. —*MM*
Movie: 🎵🎵🎵 **DVD:** 🎵🎵▸
Image Entertainment (Cat #ID5746MK DVD, UPC #014381574623). Full frame. Dolby Digital Mono. $24.99. Snapper. *LANG:* English. *FEATURES:* 16 chapter links ◦ Cast and crew filmographies and awards.
1948 96m/B Barry Fitzgerald, Don Taylor, Howard Duff, Ted de Corsia, Dorothy Hart; **D:** Jules Dassin; **W:** Albert (John B. Sherry) Maltz; **C:** William H. Daniels; **M:** Miklos Rozsa; **Nar:** Mark Hellinger. *AWARDS:* Academy Awards '48: Best Black-and-white Cinematography, Best Film Editing; *NOM:* Academy Awards '48: Best Story.

Naked Killer

Kitty (Ching) turns to a female assassin to learn the art of killing so that she can avenge her father's death. When her teacher is unceremoniously murdered, Kitty and her policeman boyfriend (Yam) have two scores to settle.
Movie: 🎵 **DVD:** NYR
Tai Seng Video Marketing (Cat #57974). Dolby Digital 5.1 Surround Stereo. $49.95. Keepcase. *LANG:* Cantonese; Mandarin. *SUB:* Chinese; English; Spanish; Thai; Vietnamese. *FEATURES:* Trailer.
1992 86m/C *HK* My Yau Ching, Simon Yam; **D:** Clarence Fok Yiu Leung; **W:** Jing

Wong; **C:** Peter Pau, William Yim; **M:** Lowell Lo.

Naked Kiss

The lurid title is appropriate for Fuller's most savage and hysterical film noir. A brutalized prostitute escapes her pimp and tries to find a place in respectable small-town society. But the people she meets there are little different from the ones she left. The DVD is a virtually flawless re-creation of the black-and-white image. The mono sound is fine. —*MM*
AKA: The Iron Kiss.
Movie: 🎵🎵▸ **DVD:** 🎵🎵🎵
Home Vision Cinema (Cat #1258). Widescreen (1.66:1) letterboxed. Dolby Digital Mono. $29.95. Keepcase. *LANG:* English.
1964 92m/B Constance Towers, Anthony Eisley, Michael Dante, Virginia Grey, Patsy Kelly, Betty Bronson, Edy Williams, Marie Devereux, Karen Conrad, Linda Francis, Barbara Perry, Walter Matthews, Betty Robinson; **D:** Samuel Fuller; **W:** Samuel Fuller; **C:** Stanley Cortez; **M:** Paul Dunlap.

The Naked Truth

Airplane-inspired comedy is about Frank (Caso) and Frank (Schon) who go to Hollywood to become stars but wind up in drag in a beauty pageant. The silliness leaves room for a handful of quirky cameos from the likes of Zsa Zsa Gabor and Little Richard. The image is generally snappy and bright, so bright that reds glow and Venetian blinds flash even more strongly than normal. —*MM*
Movie: 🎵🎵 **DVD:** 🎵🎵🎵
Simitar Entertainment (Cat #7612, UPC #082551761227). Full frame. Dolby Digital Stereo. $14.98. Keepcase. *LANG:* English. *FEATURES:* 8 chapter links ◦ Theatrical trailers ◦ Cast and crew thumbnail biographies ◦ Production factoids ◦ Stills gallery.
1992 93m/C Robert Caso, Kevin Schon, Courtney Gibbs, Herb Edelman, Brian Thompson, M. Emmet Walsh, Billy Barty, David Birney, Yvonne De Carlo, Alex Cord, Erik Estrada, Norman Fell, Lou Ferrigno, Zsa Zsa Gabor, Dick Gautier, Ted Lange, Bubba Smith, Shannon Tweed, John Vernon, Little Richard; **D:** Nico Mastorakis; **W:** Nico Mastorakis; **C:** Andreas Bellis.

Naked Warriors

Ancient Romans capture beautiful women from around the world and force them to compete in gladiatorial games. This exploitation gem features a mostly Italian cast, including Bay, who had starred in *Lady Frankenstein* the year before, but none of them can upstage the magnificent Pam Grier. **AKA:** The Arena.
Movie: 🎵🎵▸ **DVD:** NYR
New Horizons Home Video (Cat #20129). Full frame. $24.98.
1973 (R) 75m/C Margaret Markov, Pam Grier, Lucretia Love, Paul Muller, Daniel Vargas, Marie Louise, Mary Count, Rosalba (Sara Bay) Neri, Vic Karis, Sid

Lawrence, Peter Cester, Anna Melita; *D:* Steve Carver; *W:* John W. Corrington, Joyce H. Corrington; *C:* Joe D'Amato; *M:* Francesco De Masi.

Napoleon and Samantha

After his grandfather (Geer) dies, young Napoleon (Whitaker) is befriended by Danny (Douglas), an unemployed college student who's spending the summer as a goat herder. They're joined by Samantha (Foster) and Major, an elderly lion. The main attractions are a fine cast—this is the cherubic, prepubescent Foster's screen debut—and some spectacular Northwest mountain scenery. For a film of its age, the image is exceptional on DVD with crystalline nature photography. That's to be expected; the film was produced by Winston Hibler, also responsible for the Disney studio's live-action nature films of earlier decades. —*MM*
Movie: 🐾🐾🐾 *DVD:* 🐾🐾🐾
Anchor Bay (Cat #DV10893, UPC #013131089394). Widescreen (1.85:1) letterboxed; full frame. Dolby Digital Mono. $24.98. Keepcase. *LANG:* English. *FEATURES:* 22 chapter links.
1972 91m/C Jodie Foster, Johnny Whitaker, Michael Douglas, Will Geer, Henry Jones; *D:* Bernard McEveety; *W:* Stewart Raffill; *C:* Monroe Askins; *M:* Buddy (Norman Dale) Baker. *AWARDS: NOM:* Academy Awards '72: Best Original Dramatic Score.

National Lampoon's Animal House

Classic vehicle for Belushi running amuck. Set in 1962 and responsible for launching Otis Day and the Knights and defining food fights. Every college tradition from fraternity rush week to the homecoming pageant is irreverently and relentlessly mocked in this wild comedy about Delta House, a fraternity on the edge. Sophomoric, but very funny, with a host of young stars who went on to more serious work. This first DVD issue of *Animal House* is not as good as the Collectors Edition, but is overall at least an improvement over all the previous home video releases. The picture is fairly sharp with only occasional grain, and very few artifacts. There isn't much bleed on the colors, which unfortunately are not very true. The blacks are relatively true, however both the contrast and the brightness levels should have been punched up a touch. The sound is mono but still sound fairly good, certainly good (and bad) enough to keep the spirit of the film. —*JO*
Movie: 🐾🐾🐾 *DVD:* 🐾🐾🐾
Universal Studios Home Video (Cat #20158, UPC #02519201583). Full frame. Dolby Digital 2.0 Mono. $24.98. Keepcase. *LANG:* English; Spanish; French. *SUB:* Spanish; French. *CAP:* English. *FEATURES:* 16 chapter links • Theatrical trailer • Cast and filmmakers bios • Production notes • Film highlights.

1978 (R) 109m/C John Belushi, Tim Matheson, John Vernon, Donald Sutherland, Peter Riegert, Stephen Furst, Bruce McGill, Mark Metcalf, Verna Bloom, Karen Allen, Tom Hulce, Mary Louise Weller, James Widdoes, Kevin Bacon, Doug Kenney, Martha Smith, Cesare Danova, Stephen Bishop, Sarah Holcomb; *D:* John Landis; *W:* Harold Ramis, Chris Miller, Doug Kenney; *C:* Charles Correll; *M:* Elmer Bernstein.

National Lampoon's Christmas Vacation

The third vacation for the Griswold family finds them hosting repulsive relatives for Yuletide. The sight gags, although predictable, are sometimes on the mark. Quaid is a standout as the slovenly cousin. This *Vacation* should have more vibrant colors than the first two films in the series. Unfortunately, on the DVD, that's not the case. The tint wanders a bit and is generally a little reddish. The widescreen laserdisc is still the best version to own. —*JO AKA:* Christmas Vacation.
Movie: 🐾🐾▶ *DVD:* 🐾🐾
Warner Home Video, Inc. (Cat #11889, UPC #085391188926). Full frame. Dolby Surround; Dolby Digital Mono. $24.98. Snapper. *LANG:* English (DS); Spanish (DDM); French (DDM). *SUB:* English; Spanish; French. *CAP:* English. *FEATURES:* 29 chapter links • Theatrical trailers • Production notes.
1989 (PG-13) 93m/C Chevy Chase, Beverly D'Angelo, Randy Quaid, Diane Ladd, John Randolph, E.G. Marshall, Doris Roberts, Julia Louis-Dreyfus, Mae Questel, William Hickey, Brian Doyle-Murray, Juliette Lewis, Johnny Galecki, Nicholas Guest, Miriam Flynn; *D:* Jeremiah S. Chechik; *W:* John Hughes; *C:* Thomas Ackerman; *M:* Angelo Badalamenti.

National Lampoon's Class Reunion

The magazine's third foray into the movie business is a grubby-looking slasher parody. At the ten-year reunion of the class of '72 from Lizzie Borden High School, one grad seeks vengeance for a sexual prank that was played on him years before. A few bright moments flicker to life but most of the attempted humor is flat, and the psycho-with-a-blade stuff has been done so many times that it is simply boring. The improved clarity of the DVD image does the cheapjack visuals no favors. —*MM*
AKA: Class Reunion.
Movie: 🐾 *DVD:* 🐾🐾
Anchor Bay (Cat #DV1060, UPC #01313110609). Widescreen (1.85:1) letterboxed. Dolby Digital Stereo. $24.98. Keepcase. *LANG:* English. *FEATURES:* 19 chapter links • Liner notes by Michael Felsher.
1982 (R) 85m/C Shelley Smith, Gerrit Graham, Michael Lerner; *D:* Michael Miller; *W:* John Hughes; *C:* Philip Lathrop; *M:* Peter Bernstein.

National Lampoon's Golf Punks

Innocuous comedy finds luckless former golf pro Al Oliver (Arnold) in desperate need of cash to pay off his gambling debts—so he becomes an instructor to a bunch of teen misfits and decides to enter the uncoordinated group in a prestigious tournament.
Movie: 🐾▶ *DVD:* NYR
Avalanche Entertainment (Cat #13978). Full frame. Dolby Digital Stereo. $24.95. Keepcase. *LANG:* English. *SUB:* Spanish.
1999 (PG) 92m/C *CA* Tom Arnold, James Kirk; *D:* Harvey Frost.

National Lampoon's Loaded Weapon 1

Send-up of the *Lethal Weapon* series (and other crime genres) hits all the right notes, though the attempts at verbal wit are lame. L.A. cops Colt (Estevez) and Luger (Jackson) embody all the clichés—imminent retirement, big hair, dead partner, lost love—in a plot that revolves around cocaine-laced Wilderness Girl cookies. Curry and Shatner ham it up shamelessly as the villains; F. Murray Abraham turns in a deft parody of Anthony Hopkins's Hannibal Lecter. Curiously, the DVD is strong visually with a bright, sharp image. The widescreen version catches many of the gags—one involving Mr. Potato-Head—that take place in the background. Sound is adequate. To date, the *1* in the title has been an empty threat. —*MM AKA:* Loaded Weapon 1.
Movie: 🐾🐾▶ *DVD:* 🐾🐾🐾
New Line Home Video (Cat #N4893, UPC #794043489327). Widescreen (1.85:1) letterboxed; full frame. Dolby Digital Stereo; Dolby Digital 5.1 Surround Stereo. $24.98. Snapper. *LANG:* English. *SUB:* English. *CAP:* English. *FEATURES:* 23 chapter links • Theatrical trailer • Cast and crew thumbnail biographies.
1993 (PG-13) 83m/C Emilio Estevez, Samuel L. Jackson, Jon Lovitz, Tim Curry, Kathy Ireland, William Shatner, Dr. Joyce Brothers, James Doohan, Richard Moll, F. Murray Abraham, Denis Leary, Corey Feldman, Phil Hartman, J.T. Walsh, Erik Estrada, Larry Wilcox, Allyce Beasley, Charlie Sheen; *D:* Gene Quintano; *W:* Don Holley, Gene Quintano; *C:* Peter Deming; *M:* Robert Folk.

National Lampoon's Vacation

The Clark Griswold (Chase) family of suburban Chicago embarks on a westward cross-country vacation via car to the renowned "Wally World." Their ridiculous and hysterical misadventures include a falling asleep at the wheel sequence and the untimely death of Aunt Edna. This DVD looks better than a lot of the other Warner catalog comedy titles. Either they started off with better preprint, or spent more on the authoring because they felt the film was of more value. (Of course, they did set the suggested retail price at their usual maximum of $24.98, instead of the budget $14.98.) The image is fairly sharp and colors seem accurate, if a touch pale. The Dolby Surround has a little more guts than the sound on the previous video editions. —*JO* **AKA:** Vacation.

Movie: 🎵🎵🎵 ***DVD:*** 🎵🎵🎵
Warner Home Video, Inc. (Cat #11315, UPC #085391131526). Full frame. Dolby Surround. $24.98. Snapper. *LANG:* English. *SUB:* English; Spanish; French. *CAP:* English. *FEATURES:* 33 chapter links • Theatrical trailer • Production notes.
1983 (R) 98m/C Chevy Chase, Beverly D'Angelo, Imogene Coca, Randy Quaid, Christie Brinkley, James Keach, Anthony Michael Hall, John Candy, Eddie Bracken, Brian Doyle-Murray, Eugene Levy, Dana Barron, Jane Krakowski, Miriam Flynn, Frank McRae, John Diehl, Mickey Jones; ***D:*** Harold Ramis; ***W:*** John Hughes, Harold Ramis; ***C:*** Victor Kemper; ***M:*** Ralph Burns.

National Velvet

A young English girl wins a horse in a raffle and is determined to train it to compete in the famed Grand National race. Taylor, only 12 at the time, is superb in her first starring role. Rooney also gives a fine performance. Filmed with a loving eye on lushly decorated sets, this is a masterpiece version of the story of affection between a girl and her pet. Based on the novel by Enid Bagnold and followed by *International Velvet* in 1978. The DVD looks very good and has a slightly sharper picture than the VHS and much deeper color. There is very little grain and the same for artifacts. Blacks are very good and good contrast helps show off the vibrant colors. The Digital mono sound is very strong for a 1940s film. —*JO*

Movie: 🎵🎵🎵🎵 ***DVD:*** 🎵🎵🎵
MGM Home Entertainment (Cat #906618, UPC #027616661921). Full frame. Dolby Digital Mono. $24.98. Snapper. *LANG:* English; French. *SUB:* English; Spanish; French. *CAP:* English. *FEATURES:* 32 chapter links.
1944 (G) 124m/C Elizabeth Taylor, Mickey Rooney, Arthur Treacher, Donald Crisp, Anne Revere, Angela Lansbury, Reginald Owen, Norma Varden, Jackie "Butch" Jenkins, Terence Kilburn; ***D:*** Clarence Brown; ***W:*** Theodore Reeves, Helen Deutsch; ***C:*** Leonard Smith; ***M:*** Herbert Stothart. *AWARDS:* Academy Awards '45: Best Film Editing, Best Supporting Actress (Revere); *NOM:* Academy Awards '45: Best Color Cinematography, Best Director (Brown).

The Navigator

Ever the quick thinker, Keaton actually bought a steamer headed for the scrap heap and used it as a stage for a brilliant string of sight gags. Rejected by his socialite sweetie (McGuire), Rollo Treadway (Keaton) finds himself alone with her on "The Navigator" adrift in the Pacific. The diving suit routines are grand. The only discordant note is the treatment of

black characters, which will strike some contemporary viewers as racist. The DVD image is excellent—clear and generally undamaged, though this is not the most well-photographed of Keaton's work. The other two films on the disc—*The Boat* (1921) and *The Love Nest* (1923)—are much rougher looking. —*MM*

Movie: 🎵🎵🎵 ***DVD:*** 🎵🎵🎵
Kino on Video (Cat #K124DVD, UPC #738329012427). Full frame. $29.99. Snapper. *LANG:* English intertitles. *FEATURES:* 20 chapter links.
1924 60m/B Buster Keaton, Kathryn McGuire, Frederick Vroom, Noble Johnson, Clarence Burton, H. M. Clugston; ***D:*** Donald Crisp, Buster Keaton; ***W:*** Clyde Bruckman, Jean C. Havez, Joseph A. Mitchell; ***C:*** Byron Houck, Elgin Lessley.

Navy SEALS

A group of macho Navy commandos, whose regular work is to rescue hostages from Middle-Eastern underground organizations, finds a stash of deadly weapons. They spend the balance of the movie attempting to destroy the arsenal. Sheen chews the scenery as a crazy member of the commando team. Lots of action and violence, but simplistic good guys–bad guys philosophy and plot weaknesses keep this from being more than below average. This DVD's Dolby Surround gives as much bang for your buck as most 5.1 tracks do. Gunfire is throaty and explosions are full and reverberating. When the action dies out, the soundtrack has a much harder time delivering the music and dialogue, both of which seem a little flat. The picture holds up well and retains its sharpness and good color detail, despite the fact that a lot of the action takes place in the dark. —*JO*

Movie: 🎵▶ ***DVD:*** 🎵🎵🎵
Image Entertainment (Cat #ID4079ORDVD, UPC #014381407921). Widescreen (1.85:1) letterboxed. Dolby Surround. $29.95. Snapper. *LANG:* English. *FEATURES:* 2 chapter links.
1990 (R) 113m/C Charlie Sheen, Michael Biehn, Joanne Whalley, Rick Rossovich, Cyril O'Reilly, Bill Paxton, Dennis Haysbert, Paul Sanchez, Ron Joseph, Nicholas Kadi; ***D:*** Lewis Teague; ***W:*** Gary Goldman; ***C:*** John A. Alonzo; ***M:*** Sylvester Levay.

Needful Things

In style and appearance, this Stephen King adaptation is similar to Kubrick's *The Shining*. Both are handsomely staged, slow moving, and brightened by mordant, dry wit. Neither is particularly frightening. The devil (von Sydow) opens an antique store in Castle Rock, ME, and touches the townspeople's deepest desires. Writer W.D. Richter does a good job of compressing the long novel, but some of the subplots may not make sense to those who haven't read it. Director Heston gets journeyman work from a cast of first-rate character actors (Harris, Bedelia, Plummer,

Walsh) but the film belongs to von Sydow's affable, persuasive Satan. On DVD, neither image nor sound are different from VHS tape. —*MM*

Movie: 🎵🎵▶ ***DVD:*** 🎵🎵
USA Home Entertainment (Cat #440 056 471-2, UPC #044005647129). Full frame. Dolby Digital 2.0 Surround Stereo. $29.95. Keepcase. *LANG:* English. *SUB:* French. *CAP:* English. *FEATURES:* 21 chapter links • Theatrical trailer • Cast and crew filmographies.
1993 (R) 120m/C Ed Harris, Bonnie Bedelia, Max von Sydow, Amanda Plummer, J.T. Walsh; ***D:*** Fraser Heston; ***W:*** W.D. Richter; ***C:*** Tony Westman; ***M:*** Patrick Doyle.

The Negotiator

Police hostage negotiator Danny Roman (Jackson) has had his life destroyed by false accusations of theft and murder. So he decides to go after his accusers by taking the Chicago Internal Affairs Bureau staff (what else?) hostage. Chris Sabian (Spacey), a negotiator from another precinct, is Roman's only hope to save himself and find the real culprits. Jackson and Spacey are excellent in their scenes together, and the supporting cast does a fine job. Nice action sequences and suspenseful storyline make for a thrilling ride, as long as you don't contemplate the details for too long. This excellent disc is super sharp and has no problems with grain or artifacts even in the darker scenes. The colors accurately reflect the theatrical release and bleed is never a problem. Blacks are excellent and the contrast gives the film a little more punch than it had theatrically. Brightness levels are consistent and very comfortable. The 5.1 sound also seems better than the theatre and is full fidelity, with solid bass and crisp highs. There is also very good imaging and separation with plenty of Surround effects, particularly in the numerous action sequences. —*JO*

Movie: 🎵🎵🎵 ***DVD:*** 🎵🎵🎵🎵
Warner Home Video, Inc. (Cat #16750, UPC #085391675020). Widescreen (2.35:1) anamorphic. Dolby Digital 5.1. $24.98. Snapper. *LANG:* English; French. *SUB:* English; French. *CAP:* English. *FEATURES:* 39 chapter links • 5 theatrical trailers • Documentary: "The 11th Hour: Stories from Real Negotiators" • Behind-the-scenes featurette • Production notes.
1998 (R) 115m/C Samuel L. Jackson, Kevin Spacey, David Morse, Ron Rifkin, John Spencer, Regina Taylor, J.T. Walsh, Siobhan Fallon, Paul Giamatti, Paul Guilfoyle, Carlos Gomez, Nestor Serrano; ***D:*** F. Gary Gray; ***W:*** James De Monaco, Kevin Fox; ***C:*** Russell Carpenter; ***M:*** Graeme Revell.

Neil Simon's The Odd Couple 2

Felix (Lemmon) and Oscar (Matthau) are reunited decades later at the California wedding of their grandchildren. The result is about what most people would expect from a sequel made 30 years after the original, with the added baggage of the long-running TV series. A certain staleness and a sense of going-through-the-motions are inevitable despite the stars' on-screen chemistry. One-liners like Oscar's "I hate a woman who talks like Muhammed Ali" are the point, not flashy visuals, and so the DVD is only marginally superior to the tape. —*MM* **AKA:** The Odd Couple 2.

Movie: 🎵🎵 **DVD:** 🎵🎵▸

Paramount Home Video (Cat #335787, UPC #097363357872). Widescreen letterboxed. Dolby Surround; Dolby 5.1 Surround; Dolby Surround Stereo. $29.98. Keepcase. *LANG:* English (DS, DS5.1); French (DSS). *SUB:* Spanish. *CAP:* English. *FEATURES:* 24 chapter links ▪ Theatrical trailer.

1998 (PG-13) 96m/C Jack Lemmon, Walter Matthau, Jonathan Silverman, Lisa Waltz, Christine Baranski, Jean Smart, Barnard Hughes, Doris Belack, Ellen Geer, Jay O. Sanders, Rex Linn, Mary Beth Peil, Alice Ghostley, Rebecca Schull, Florence Stanley, Lou Cutell; *D:* Howard Deutch; *W:* Neil Simon; *C:* Jamie Anderson; *M:* Alan Silvestri.

Nemesis

Futuristic thriller combines cybernetics and cyborgs in post-nuclear Los Angeles. Gruner plays a human (although he's mostly composed of mechanical replacement parts) in a world overwrought with system cowboys, information terrorists, bio-enhanced gangsters, and cyborg outlaws. Film's biggest flaw is the extremely confusing script that makes no attempt at logic whatsoever. Special effects are good despite the obviously low f/x budget. This action DVD from Sterling has a pretty entertaining soundtrack that uses hit-you-in-the-face separation effects and a mix that is extremely lively. The picture is only average with colors that drift a little and appear faded, even when compared to the VHS edition. There are both grain and artifacts, but not as excessive as the worst Sterling DVD releases. —*JO*

Movie: 🎵▸ **DVD:** 🎵🎵

Studio Home Entertainment (Cat #4000, UPC #658149400023). Full frame. Stereo. $24.95. Keepcase. *LANG:* English. *SUB:* Spanish; French. *CAP:* English. *FEATURES:* 18 chapter links ▪ Theatrical trailer ▪ Production notes ▪ Television spots ▪ "Making of" documentary.

1993 (R) 95m/C Olivier Gruner, Tim Thomerson, Cary-Hiroyuki Tagawa, Merele Kennedy, Yuji Okumoto, Marjorie Monaghan, Nicholas Guest, Vincent Klyn; *D:* Albert Pyun; *W:* Rebecca Charles; *C:* George Mooradian; *M:* Michael Rubini.

The Net

The ever-spunky Bullock gets stuck behind a computer screen rather than the wheel of a bus as reclusive computer systems analyst Angela Bennett. She's puzzled by a mysterious Internet program, which can easily access highly classified databases. It's soon apparent that someone knows she knows because every record of her identity has been erased and the conspirators decide to take care of one last detail by eliminating her as well. Miller's the ex she turns to for help and Northam's the seductive British hacker. Techno paranoia. The DVD picture is not as sharp as the laserdisc but is still acceptable, especially when you take into account the improved color performance. The colors are strong and accurate, and have only a hint of bleed in a few shots. Blacks are mostly true and contrast and brightness levels adequate. The 5.1 sound doesn't make that much use of the Surround tracks, but fidelity and dynamics are good and separation up front is excellent. —*JO*

Movie: 🎵🎵▸ **DVD:** 🎵🎵▸

Columbia Tristar Home Video (Cat #11619, UPC #043396116191). Widescreen (1.85:1) anamorphic; full frame. Dolby Digital 5.1; Dolby Surround. NSL. Keepcase. *LANG:* English; Spanish; French. *SUB:* English; Spanish; Korean. *CAP:* English. *FEATURES:* 6 chapter links.

1995 (PG-13) 114m/C Sandra Bullock, Jeremy Northam, Dennis Miller, Diane Baker, Ken Howard, Wendy Gazelle, Ray McKinnon; *D:* Irwin Winkler; *W:* John Brancato, Michael Ferris; *C:* Jack N. Green; *M:* Mark Isham.

Network

Scathing indictment of the television industry and its propensity towards self-prostitution is as timely now as it was then. A television newscaster's mental breakdown turns him into a celebrity when the network tries to profit from his illness. The individual characters are startlingly realistic and the acting is excellent, but this is an unusually poor DVD from MGM. The picture is not that sharp to start with, and it gets worse in the darker scenes, with grain and loss of detail coming into play. Colors are weak, and even then, there is bleed added to the equation. The sound is lackluster at best. —*JO*

Movie: 🎵🎵🎵▸ **DVD:** 🎵▸

MGM Home Entertainment (Cat #906720, UPC #027616672025). Widescreen (1.85:1) anamorphic; full frame. Stereo. $24.98. Keepcase. *LANG:* English. *SUB:* English; French; Spanish. *CAP:* English. *FEATURES:* 32 chapter links ▪ Theatrical trailer ▪ Interactive quiz game ▪ "Hidden menu page" ▪ Trivia and production notes.

1976 (R) 121m/C Faye Dunaway, Peter Finch, William Holden, Robert Duvall, Wesley Addy, Ned Beatty, Beatrice Straight; *D:* Sidney Lumet; *W:* Paddy Chayefsky; *C:* Owen Roizman. *AWARDS:* Academy Awards '76: Best Actor (Finch), Best Actress (Dunaway), Best Original Screenplay, Best Supporting Actress (Straight); American Film Institute (AFI) '98: Top 100; British Academy Awards '77: Best Actor (Finch); Golden Globe Awards '77: Best Actor—Drama (Finch), Best Actress—Drama (Dunaway), Best Director (Lumet), Best Screenplay; Los Angeles Film Critics Association Awards '76: Best Director (Lumet), Best Film; New York Film Critics Awards '76: Best Screenplay; Writers Guild of America '76: Best Original Screenplay; *NOM:* Academy Awards '76: Best Actor (Holden), Best Cinematography, Best Director (Lumet), Best Film Editing, Best Picture, Best Supporting Actor (Beatty).

Never Been Kissed

Lightweight and logic-defying, Barrymore's producing debut idiotically postulates that people who were unpopular in high school want another chance at it. Still-nerdy Chicago copy editor Josie (Barrymore) goes undercover as a student to write about high school life. She sees it as a chance to become a big-time journalist and one of the "cool" kids. When it turns out that nothing has changed for her, she enlists the help of her brother (Arquette) and a coworker (Shannon) and eventually falls for sensitive teacher Sam (Vartan). The star isn't particularly believable as either the ugly duckling or the swan. At their best, neither she nor the script are nearly as cute as they think they are. On the other hand, this slight material looks terrific on DVD. Such traditionally tricky devices as Venetian blinds are not a problem. Sound is very good. Fans may well be more enthusiastic. —*MM*

Movie: 🎵🎵 **DVD:** 🎵🎵🎵

Twentieth Century Fox Home Entertainment (Cat #4112307, UPC #086162123078). Widescreen (2.35:1) letterboxed. Dolby Digital 5.1 Surround Stereo; Dolby Digital Stereo. $34.98. Keepcase. *LANG:* English. *SUB:* English; Spanish. *FEATURES:* 30 chapter links ▪ Theatrical trailer.

1999 (PG-13) 107m/C Drew Barrymore, David Arquette, Leelee Sobieski, Michael Vartan, Molly Shannon, John C. Reilly, Garry Marshall, Sean Whalen, Jeremy Jordan, Marley Shelton, Jordan Ladd, Jessica Alba; *D:* Raja Gosnell; *W:* Abby Kohn, Marc Silverstein; *C:* Alex Nepomniaschy; *M:* David Newman. *AWARDS: NOM:* MTV Movie Awards '00: Best Female Performance (Barrymore), Best Kiss (Drew Barrymore/Michael Vartan).

Never Talk to Strangers

Dr. Sarah Taylor (DeMornay) is a shrink who's none too tightly wrapped herself. Tony Ramirez (Banderas) is the handsome stranger who picks her up one night in the wine section of the grocery store. But who's trying to frighten her? Her drunken dad (Cariou); the incarcerated murder suspect (Stanton) she's interviewing; the jealous neighbor (Miller)? Or Tony? And why? Nobody will worry too much over the answers in this silly thriller. The only real advantage DVD has over tape with this lightweight material is the choice of screen size and language. Visually, it's only a marginal improvement. —*MM*

Movie: 🎬🎬 **DVD:** 🎬🎬
Columbia Tristar Home Video (Cat #11809, UPC #043396118096). Widescreen (1.85:1) letterboxed; full frame. Dolby Digital 5.1 Surround Stereo; Dolby Digital Stereo. $27.95. Keepcase. *LANG:* English; Spanish; Portuguese. *SUB:* English; Spanish; Portuguese; Chinese; Korean; Thai. *FEATURES:* 28 chapter links • Cast and crew thumbnail biographies • Theatrical trailer.
1995 (R) 86m/C Rebecca DeMornay, Antonio Banderas, Harry Dean Stanton, Dennis Miller, Len Cariou, Beau Starr; *D:* Peter Hall; *W:* Lewis Green, Jordan Rush; *C:* Elemer Ragalyi; *M:* Pino Donaggio.

New Fist of Fury

During WWII, a former pickpocket (Chan) becomes a martial arts whiz with assistance of his fiancee, and fights the entire Imperial Army. Picture is very soft. Audio is frequently distorted. Current-day video interview with Chan (same as on several other Chan DVDs) is revealing but production values are low (off-camera interviewer is heard, but barely audible). No subtitles, so English-speaking audiences are stuck with the dubbed soundtrack. —*MB* **AKA:** Xin Ching-wu Men.

Movie: 🎬 **DVD:** 🎬
Simitar Entertainment (Cat #7260, UPC #08255172602). Full frame. Dolby Digital 2.0. $14.98. Keepcase. *LANG:* English; Mandarin. *FEATURES:* 10 chapter links • Movie factoids • Biography/filmography • Interview with Chan.
1976 120m/C Jackie Chan; *D:* Lo Wei; *W:* Lo Wei.

New Jack City

Just-say-no ghetto melodrama boasts a powerful performance by Snipes as the wealthy Harlem drug lord sought by rebel cops Ice-T and Nelson. Music by Johnny Gill, 2 Live Crew, Ice-T, and others. This is another instance where the sound is as important as the visuals, and both elements are excellent. The image is sharp and copes well with the various lighting conditions. Colors have nicely detailed shadings and are very vibrant. The blacks never stray from true, and contrast and brightness levels are very good. The 5.1 mix is as forceful as the music tracks chosen for the soundtrack, and has plenty piped through to the rear channels. Even so, the dialogue is never buried. —*JO*

Movie: 🎬🎬🎬 **DVD:** 🎬🎬🎬▶
Warner Home Video, Inc. (Cat #12073, UPC #085391207320). Widescreen (1.85:1) anamorphic. Dolby Digital 5.1; Dolby Surround. $19.98. Snapper. *LANG:* English; French. *SUB:* English; French. *CAP:* English. *FEATURES:* 34 chapter links • Theatrical trailer • Production notes.
1991 (R) 101m/C Wesley Snipes, Ice-T, Mario Van Peebles, Chris Rock, Judd Nelson, Tracy C. Johns, Allen Payne, Kim Park,

Vanessa Williams, Nick Ashford, Thalmus Rasulala, Michael Michele, Bill Nunn, Russell Wong; *D:* Mario Van Peebles; *W:* Keith Critchlow, Barry Michael Cooper; *C:* Francis Kenny; *M:* Roger Bourland, Michel Colombier.

New Jersey Drive

Jason (Corley) has dreams of life outside the mean streets of Newark but he jeopardizes his future by stealing cars and joyriding with his friends. Alleged realism, provided by credible actors (particularly Corley, a former gang member), mumbled profane dialogue, and location filming in the projects of Brooklyn and Queens are neutralized by stereotypical characters (particularly the lily-white sadistic cops) and lack of a sympathetic point of view. The film is loosely based on a series of articles by Michel Mariott, a reporter for *The New York Times*. The image is excellent, even in the scenes of nocturnal car chases. Sound is only so-so. —*MM*

Movie: 🎬🎬 **DVD:** 🎬🎬🎬
Goodtimes Entertainment (Cat #81031). Widescreen (1.85:1) letterboxed. Dolby Digital Stereo. $19.98. Snapper. *LANG:* English. *SUB:* French; Spanish. *CAP:* English. *FEATURES:* 18 chapter links.
1995 (R) 98m/C Sharron Corley, Gabriel Casseus, Saul Stein, Andre Moore, Donald Adeosun Faison, Conrad Meertin Jr., Deven Eggleston, Gwen McGee, Koran C. Thomas, Samantha Brown, Christine Baranski, Robert Jason Jackson, Roscoe Orman, Dwight Errington Myers, Gary DeWitt Marshall; *D:* Nick Gomez; *W:* Nick Gomez, Michel Marriott; *C:* Adam Kimmel; *M:* Wendy Blackstone. *AWARDS: NOM:* Independent Spirit Awards '96: Debut Performance (Casseus).

New Orleans

The great legends of jazz re-enact its birth in this song-filled tribute to the town where it all began. When the proprietor (de Cordova) of a Bourbon Street gambling joint (and haven for musicians) falls for an opera-singing socialite, he realizes that only through music will he gain responsibility. He begins a campaign to bring jazz to the highbrow American stage. The video transfer offers a very dark and muddied image. The quality is definitely telling of its age. The soundtrack is a bit better than the video, but it too shows signs of wear, showcased in very muffled and hard to discern dialogue. —*MJT*

Movie: 🎬🎬▶ **DVD:** 🎬🎬▶
Kino on Video (Cat #K159DVD, UPC #738329015923). Full frame. Dolby Digital Mono. $29.95. Keepcase. *LANG:* English. *FEATURES:* 19 chapter links • "A Rhapsody in Black and Blue," a 1932 short film with Louis Armstrong • "Symphony in Black," a 1935 short film with Billie Holiday • Essay on the making of *New Orleans*.
1947 90m/B Arturo de Cordova, Dorothy Patrick, Louis Armstrong, Billie Holiday, Woody Herman, Richard Hageman; *D:*

Arthur Lubin; *W:* Elliot Paul, Dick Irving Hyland; *C:* Lucien N. Andriot.

New Rose Hotel

Dependably loopy director Ferrara spins out another tale of sexual obsession, but considering the amount of potential weirdness from all involved, the result is pretty tame. Corporate bigwig Fox (Walken) wants his associate Mr. X (Dafoe) to enlist Sandii (Argento), a prostitute, in their efforts to seduce a man they're interested in. But X is entranced by Sandii's tattooed belly and falls for her. The DVD does an adequate job of handling Ferrara's tortured color scheme and distorted visuals. Whenever the image is dark and hard to make out, it's supposed to be. Sound is unremarkable. —*MM*

Movie: 🎬🎬 **DVD:** 🎬▶
Studio Home Entertainment (Cat #7315). Widescreen letterboxed. Dolby Digital 5.1 Surround Stereo; Dolby Digital Surround Stereo. $28.97. Keepcase. *LANG:* English. *SUB:* Spanish. *FEATURES:* 24 chapter links • Commentary: writer Christ Zois • Photo gallery • Trailer gallery • Trivia game.
1998 (R) 92m/C Christopher Walken, Willem Dafoe, Asia Argento, Yoshitaka Amano, Annabella Sciorra, Gretchen Mol, John Lurie, Ryuichi Sakamoto; *D:* Abel Ferrara; *W:* Abel Ferrara, Chris Zois; *C:* Ken Kelsch.

New World Disorder

Action thriller combines familiar elements of the formula with high-tech computer jargon. A gang of thieves led by the bestudded Bishop (McCarthy) blasts into a computer chip company and steals the Rosetta encryption program. Young computer-savvy FBI agent Paddock (Fitzgerald) winds up working with old-fashioned local cop Marx (Hauer) to catch the bad guys. The action scenes are fairly ambitious for a video premiere and the DVD image is exceptionally sharp—so sharp that it's easy to see the reflections of crew and equipment in a passing car window in one scene. Sound is fine. —*MM*

Movie: 🎬🎬 **DVD:** 🎬🎬🎬
York Entertainment (Cat #YPD-1029, UPC #750723102924). Full frame. Dolby Digital 5.1 Surround Stereo. $24.98. Keepcase. *LANG:* English. *SUB:* Spanish. *FEATURES:* 30 chapter links • Trailer • Cast thumbnail biographies.
1999 (R) 94m/C Rutger Hauer, Andrew McCarthy, Tara Fitzgerald; *D:* Richard Spence; *W:* Ehren Kruger, Jeffrey Smith; *C:* Ivan Strasburg; *M:* Gast Waltzing.

New York Ripper

Writer-director Lucio Fulci brings a crazed Italian sensibility to an American setting in a piece of gamy exploitation. The title says it all with a serial killer slashing young women and one cop (Hedley) trying to stop him. As is so often the case in this kind of stalker/slasher horror, the unhinged plot is merely an excuse to string together a series of increasingly graphic scenes of sex, violence, and torture. On DVD, early '80s Times Square looks particularly seedy. The dubbing is spotty and all of the colors are garishly exaggerated, particularly in the rough night scenes. In many of the key scenes, Fulci means for the image to be ugly and he succeeds. —*MM* **AKA:** *Lo Squartatore de New York; The Ripper.*

Movie: 🎵🎵▶ **DVD:** 🎵🎵▶
Anchor Bay (Cat #DV10897, UPC #013131089790). Widescreen (2.35:1) letterboxed. Dolby Digital Mono. $29.98. Keepcase. *LANG:* English. *FEATURES:* 25 chapter links ▪ Theatrical trailer ▪ Lucio Fulci biography.
1982 88m/C *IT* Jack Hedley, Antonella Interlenghi, Howard (Renato Rossini) Ross, Andrea Occhipinti, Alessandra Delli Colli, Paolo Malco; *D:* Lucio Fulci; *W:* Lucio Fulci, Gianfranco Clerici, Vincenzo Mannino, Dardano Sacchetti; *C:* Luigi Kuveiller; *M:* Francesco DeMasi.

The Newton Boys

Independent filmmaker Richard Linklater (*Dazed and Confused, Slacker*) takes a step-up in cast and budget, but one gets the uneasy feeling throughout that the results play more like a made-for-TV movie than a big theatrical production. Matthew McConaughey, Ethan Hawke, Skeet Ulrich, and Vincent D'Onofrio star as the real-life Newton Brothers, a post–World War I bank-robbing clan. Julianna Margulies is on hand as the love interest in this affable retelling of the brother's larcenous exploits. DVD shines with an excellent visual transfer and superb audio presentation. —*RT*

Movie: 🎵🎵▶ **DVD:** 🎵🎵🎵▶
Twentieth Century Fox Home Entertainment (Cat #4110428, UPC #086162104 282). Widescreen. Dolby Digital 5.1 Surround Stereo; Dolby Digital Surround Stereo. $29.98. Keepcase. *LANG:* English; French. *SUB:* English; Spanish. *CAP:* English. *FEATURES:* 19 chapter links ▪ Theatrical trailer ▪ Cast biographies.
1997 (PG-13) 122m/C Matthew McConaughey, Skeet Ulrich, Ethan Hawke, Vincent D'Onofrio, Julianna Margulies, Dwight Yoakam, Gail Cronauer, Chloe Webb, Charles Gunning, Becket Gremmels, Richard Jones; *D:* Richard Linklater; *W:* Claude Stanush, Clark Lee Walker; *C:* Peter James; *M:* Edward D. Barnes.

Next of Kin

A Chicago cop returns to his Kentucky home to avenge his brother's brutal murder. Swayze's return to action films after his success in *Dirty Dancing* is unimpressive, but then-unknown supporting cast gives its all. The DVD is as average as the film itself and suffers from both grain and occasional artifacts. Both show up mainly in darker scenes but are nonetheless dis-

tracting and aggravating. Colors are dull and the redder hues tend to bleed. The contrast lacks punch and brightness is so-so. Blacks become grainy and grayish at times (again mainly in the darker sequences). The Dolby Stereo is at least O.K. and has both body and awesome energy, although lacking in the Surround department. —*JO*

Movie: 🎵🎵 **DVD:** 🎵🎵
Warner Home Video, Inc. (Cat #670, UPC #012569067028). Full frame. Dolby Surround. $14.98. Snapper. *LANG:* English. *CAP:* English. *FEATURES:* 33 chapter links.
1989 (R) 108m/C Patrick Swayze, Adam Baldwin, Bill Paxton, Helen Hunt, Andreas Katsulas, Ben Stiller, Michael J. Pollard, Liam Neeson; *D:* John Irvin; *C:* Steven Poster; *M:* Jack Nitzsche.

Nicholas and Alexandra

Slow-moving epic chronicles the final years of Tsar Nicholas II (Jayston), Empress Alexandra (Suzman), and their children. Their life of luxury gives way to the tumultuous events of the revolution. The beautiful but overlong costume drama loses steam in the second half, but not the scenes of Rasputin's (Baker) assassination. The DVD image is not as crisp as some, but the film has been restored with care and it looks remarkably good compared to others of its time. —*MM*

Movie: 🎵🎵▶ **DVD:** 🎵🎵🎵
Columbia Tristar Home Video (Cat #03295, UPC #043396032958). Widescreen (2.35:1) letterboxed. Dolby Digital Mono. $24.95. Keepcase. *LANG:* English. *SUB:* English; Spanish; Portuguese; Chinese; Korean; Thai. *FEATURES:* 28 chapter links ▪ "Making of" featurette ▪ Theatrical trailer ▪ Cast and crew thumbnail biographies.
1971 (PG) 183m/C Michael Jayston, Janet Suzman, Tom Baker, Laurence Olivier, Michael Redgrave, Harry Andrews, Jack Hawkins, Alexander Knox, Curt Jurgens; *D:* Franklin J. Schaffner; *W:* James Goldman; *C:* Frederick A. (Freddie) Young; *M:* Richard Rodney Bennett. *AWARDS:* Academy Awards '71: Best Art Direction/Set Decoration, Best Costume Design; *NOM:* Academy Awards '71: Best Actress (Suzman), Best Cinematography, Best Picture, Best Original Dramatic Score.

Nick of Time

Real-time thriller begins at noon in Los Angeles' Union Station where two threatening figures, Mr. Smith (Walker) and Ms. Jones (Maffia), are looking for a victim. When they spot accountant Gene Watson (Depp) and his young daughter Lynn (Chase), they know they've found their mark. They take the little girl and force Gene into a choice. They give him a revolver and a photograph of a woman (Mason) who will be coming to a nearby hotel. If he doesn't shoot her by 1:30, they'll kill his little girl. The clock is ticking and they're watching.

Movie: 🎵🎵🎵 **DVD:** NYR
Paramount Home Video (Cat #330417). Dolby Digital 5.1 Surround Stereo. $29.99.
1995 (R) 98m/C Johnny Depp, Christopher Walken, Charles S. Dutton, Peter Strauss, Roma Maffia, Gloria Reuben, Marsha Mason, Courtney Chase, Bill Smitrovich, G.D. Spradlin; *D:* John Badham; *W:* Patrick Duncan; *C:* Roy Wagner; *M:* Arthur B. Rubinstein.

Nico Icon

Documentary probes the life of Velvet Underground sensation and Warhol superstar Nico. It's a pastiche showing V.U. concert footage and movie clips from Nico's most famous film appearances: Fellini's *La Dolce Vita* and Warhol's *The Chelsea Girls.* Also features interviews from Warhol's Factory inhabitants, band members, and Nico's grown son Ari. As visually interesting as the subject herself, the film manages to bring the viewer closer to the untouchable Teutonic figure without being sensational or overly flashy. Director Paul Morrissey and musician Jackson Browne make appearances. Naturally the quality of the preprint material goes all over the place, and there's not much the DVD transfer can do to make up for some of it. But since there is some footage that looks just great, and since the DVD is superior to the VHS release, let's assume that any problems with the image are the fault of the original source material. The disc seems an accurate representation of the theatrical version and doesn't add much extra grain or artifacts. Colors are good and blacks fairly true. Contrast and brightness vary a touch but are comfortable for the most part. The sound is only mono but even that is very good at times. —*JO*

Movie: 🎵🎵🎵 **DVD:** 🎵🎵🎵
Fox/Lorber Home Video (Cat #FLV5012, UPC #720917050126). Full frame. Mono. $29.95. Keepcase. *LANG:* English. *FEATURES:* 9 chapter links ▪ Theatrical trailer ▪ Production notes.
1995 (R) 75m/C *GE* *D:* Susanne Ofteringer; *W:* Susanne Ofteringer; *C:* Judith Kaufmann.

A Night at the Roxbury

The Butabi brothers, like so many Saturday Night Live veterans before them, make the move to feature film and find that they're still not ready for prime time. Steve (Ferrell) and Doug (Kattan) continue their fruitless quest to gain entry to the hallowed Roxbury night club. Their lives change when they have a fender-bender with Richard Grieco (playing himself). The rise to celebrity status, or something sort of like it, provides scattershot laughs. The DVD captures the garish lighting, violently clashing colors, and patterns with unfortunate precision. The same applies to the disco soundtrack. —*MM*

Movie: 🎵▶ **DVD:** 🎵🎵🎵
Paramount Home Video (Cat #335947, UPC #097363359470). Widescreen letter-

boxed. Dolby Digital Surround Stereo; Dolby Digital 5.1 Surround Stereo. $29.98. English. *LANG:* English; French. *FEATURES:* 19 chapter links • Theatrical trailer. **1998 (PG-13) 83m/C** Will Ferrell, Chris Kattan, Molly Shannon, Dan Hedaya, Loni Anderson, Richard Grieco, Elisa Donovan, Lochlyn Munro, Dwayne Hickman, Mark McKinney; *D:* John Fortenberry; *W:* Steve Koren, Will Ferrell, Chris Kattan; *C:* Francis Kenny; *M:* David Kitay.

Night Caller from Outer Space

This British sf horror almost manages to live up to its inspired title. The titular creature arrives in London and proceeds to kidnap nubile young women! It's a rough variation on Roger Corman's oft-filmed *Not of This Earth,* but prolific director John Gilling, known best for his work with Hammer Films, handles things with a slightly lighter touch. On DVD, the film probably looks better than it did in its first theatrical run. The black-and-white photography is absolutely superb and even in mono, the period soundtrack is totally groovy. The presentation of the menu, borrowing elements from the film, sets precisely the right tone. To some tastes, this one may look like an escapee from *Mystery Science Theater 3000,* but to anyone who appreciates low-budget '60s movies, it's a keeper. —*MM AKA:* Blood Beast from Outer Space; The Night Caller.
Movie: 🐾🐾🐾 *DVD:* 🐾🐾🐾
Image Entertainment (Cat #ID5374FWDVD, UPC #014381534720). Full frame. Dolby Digital Mono. $24.99. Snapper. *LANG:* English. *FEATURES:* 16 chapter links • Filmographies for John Saxon and John Gilling.
1966 84m/B *GB* John Saxon, Maurice Denham, Patricia Haines, Alfred Burke, Jack Watson, Aubrey Morris; *D:* John Gilling; *W:* James O'Connolly; *C:* Stephen Dade; *M:* Johnny Gregory.

Night Calls: The Movie

Silly tongue-in-cheek comedy is based on the Playboy channel's adult call-in show. However, on DVD it looks more like a game show with lots of flashing lights and fluorescent pinks, reds, and violets in the background. Exteriors tend to be very grainy. What plot there is concerns the two hosts, Juli Ashton and Doria, on a road trip to find some kind of loopy spiritual enlightenment. It ends with a brief nude synchronized swimming routine. —*MM*
Movie: 🐾🐾 *DVD:* 🐾🐾
Image Entertainment (Cat #ID5857PLDVD, UPC #014381585728). Full frame. Dolby Digital Stereo. $24.99. Snapper. *LANG:* English. *FEATURES:* 12 chapter links.
1998 85m/C Juli Ashton, Doria, Ceci Tailor, Daniel Mamath, Gina P. Everett, Rex Hooper; *D:* Bob (Robert) Kubilos; *W:* Eric Mittleman; *C:* Igor Meglic.

Night Calls: The Movie 2

Sequel finds TV hosts Juli Ashton and Doria going to a ranch for a treasure hunt. This one's even sillier than the first with fast-motion sequences and BOING sound effects. The DVD image is probably no better than VHS tape. —*MM*
Movie: 🐾🐾 *DVD:* 🐾🐾
Image Entertainment (Cat #ID5858PLDVD, UPC #014381585827). Full frame. $24.99. Snapper. *LANG:* English. *FEATURES:* 12 chapter links.
1999 91m/C Juli Ashton, Doria, Amber Newman, Nancy O'Brien, Maria Ford, Alan Stemm; *D:* Moctezuma Lobato; *W:* Eric Mittleman; *C:* Blain Brown, L.A. Roach.

Night Falls on Manhattan

One man's search for truth runs into serious problems in this adaptation of *Tainted Evidence* by Robert Daley. Former cop turned junior D.A. Sean Casey (Garcia) is chosen to lead the prosecution in a sensational NY trial involving a drug dealer/cop killer, who also seriously wounded Sean's longtime cop father, Liam (Holm). He wins, but allegations of police corruption dog the trial, thanks to liberal defense lawyer Vigoda (Dreyfuss). When Sean rather unexpectedly becomes the new district attorney, the issue becomes a full-blown scandal, leading the naive Sean very close to home. Veteran director Lumet knows this scandal-ridden territory very well and is aided by fine performances from his leads. The DVD's transfer is sharp and unhindered by grain or artifacts, whether the scene is light or dark. Colors are accurate and bleedless under all conditions. Blacks are true and the contrast is high enough that both picture detail and color shadings are defined even in the dim sequences. The 5.1 sound makes use of the Surround mainly for ambience and excellent fidelity and separation makes for clear dialogue and incidental music. —*JO*
Movie: 🐾🐾🐾 *DVD:* 🐾🐾🐾
Paramount Home Video (Cat #062927, UPC #097360629279). Widescreen (1.85:1) anamorphic. Dolby Digital 5.1; Dolby Surround. $29.99. Keepcase. *LANG:* English. *SUB:* Spanish. *CAP:* English. *FEATURES:* 48 chapter links • Theatrical trailer • Commentary: Lumet, Garcia, Leibman, Josh Kramer, Thom Mount.
1996 (R) 114m/C Andy Garcia, Ian Holm, Richard Dreyfuss, Lena Olin, James Gandolfini, Ron Leibman, Colm Feore, Shiek Mahmud-Bey, Paul Guilfoyle; *D:* Sidney Lumet; *W:* Sidney Lumet; *C:* David Watkin; *M:* Mark Isham.

Night Fire

Barry (Laughlin) is hoping to jumpstart his marriage to Lydia (Tweed) with a weekend at their luxurious ranch. As luck would have it, they are joined by Cal (Hewitt) and Gwen (Swanson), a couple of sexual adventurers. Could Barry have set it up? Judged as an erotic video premiere, this one's not much better or worse than most. The main problem is that the big house seems to have been lit by a single 25-watt bulb. The DVD is generally dark and hard to watch. The indefatigable Ms. Tweed treats it more seriously than it needs. The disc is made from the unrated version. —*MM*
Movie: 🐾🐾 *DVD:* 🐾🐾
Image Entertainment (Cat #ID5612FMDVD, UPC #014381561227). Full frame. Dolby Digital Surround Stereo. $19.99. Snapper. *LANG:* English. *FEATURES:* 16 chapter links.
1994 93m/C Shannon Tweed, John Laughlin, Martin Hewitt, Rochelle Swanson; *D:* Mike Sedan; *W:* Catherine Tavel, Helen Haxton; *C:* Zoran Hochstatter; *M:* Miriam Cutler.

Night of the Hunted

One of Rollin's better efforts was obviously made on a microscopic budget but it avoids many of the director's more excessive faults. Elisabeth (Lahaie) wanders onto a road and is picked up by a passing stranger. She's an amnesiac who has been held by an ominous group. The rest contains several fairly graphic sex scenes—many of the cast members came out of the world of porn—and some shots of shocking violence. As is so often the case with Rollin, the story is less important than the mood he summons up. Perhaps appropriately, the DVD image ranges between absolute clarity and scenes that are marked by snowy flecks. For the filmmaker's fans only. —*MM AKA:* La Nuit des Traquees.
Movie: 🐾🐾🐾 *DVD:* 🐾🐾🐾
Image Entertainment (Cat #ID5419SADVD, UPC #014381541922). Widescreen (1.66:1) letterboxed. Dolby Digital Mono. $24.99. Snapper. *LANG:* French. *SUB:* English. *FEATURES:* 10 chapter links • Liner notes by Marc Morris.
1969 93m/C Brigitte Lahaie, Vincent Gardere, Dominique Journet, Bernard Papineau; *D:* Jean Rollin; *W:* Jean Rollin.

Night of the Warrior

Nightclub owner Miles Keane (Lamas) pays his disco bills by moonlighting as a fighter in an underground world of bare-knuckle martial arts. When he refuses to fight, the bad guy (Geary) kidnaps his girlfriend (Kinmont). The image on the DVD looks O.K., but the disc contains no index for chapter links. Essentially it's no different from the tape. —*MM*
Movie: 🐾 *DVD:* woof
Trimark Home Video (Cat #7051D, UPC #03139870433). Full frame. Stereo. $34.99. Keepcase. *LANG:* English. *FEATURES:* Theatrical trailer. Title is available for sale only as part of "Best of Action" 4-pack.
1991 (R) 96m/C Lorenzo Lamas, Anthony Geary, Kathleen Kinmont, Arlene Dahl; *D:*

Rafal Zielinski; *W:* Thomas Ian Griffith; *C:* Edward Pei; *M:* Ed Tomney.

Night Screams

The generic title is absolutely fitting for this connect-the-dots dead-teenager horror. It's about a group of kids having a house party while one's parents are away. Why do the lights keep going off? The DVD image is dark and intentionally dim in most of the important scenes. Actually, two things are a bit unusual. First, it appears to have been a local production, made in Wichita, KS. Second, non-hard-core scenes from a hard-core skin flick are included to spice things up. —*MM*
Movie: ♫ *DVD:* ♫
Image Entertainment (Cat #OVED6854 DVD, UPC #014381685428). Full frame. Dolby Digital Surround Stereo. $24.99. Snapper. *LANG:* English. *FEATURES:* 16 chapter links.
1987 85m/C Joe Manno, Ron Thomas, Randy Lundsford, Megan Wyss; *D:* Allen Plone.

Night Shift

Two New York city morgue attendants— straitlaced Chuck Lumley (Winkler) and manic Billy Blaze (Keaton)—decide to spice up their late-night shift by running a call-girl service on the side. In his film debut, Keaton makes an indelible impression. Winkler's more serious approach provides the film's sane center and familiar faces abound in background cameos. Ron Howard's comedy looks just fine on DVD with clear night exteriors and a noticeable lack of flashing in Venetian blinds. Sound is more than adequate. —*MM*
Movie: ♫♫♫ *DVD:* ♫♫♫
Warner Home Video, Inc. (Cat #20006, UPC #085392000623). Full frame; widescreen letterboxed. Dolby Digital Surround Stereo. $19.98. Snapper. *LANG:* English. *SUB:* English; French. *CAP:* English. *FEATURES:* 37 chapter links.
1982 (R) 106m/C Henry Winkler, Michael Keaton, Shelley Long, Kevin Costner, Pat Corley, Bobby DiCicco, Nita Talbot, Richard Belzer, Clint Howard, Joe Spinell, Shannen Doherty, Kevin Costner; *D:* Ron Howard; *W:* Babaloo Mandel, Lowell Ganz; *C:* James A. Crabe; *M:* Burt Bacharach; *V:* Vincent Schiavelli.

The Night Stalker

Double-sided DVD collects two complete made-for-TV movies on one disc. In *The Night Stalker*, reporter Carl Kolchak (McGavin) is on the trail of a vampire in glittering Las Vegas. In its first broadcast, the made-for-TV movie set ratings records, inspired a sequel and then a Kolchak TV series. In that sequel, *The Night Strangler*, the enterprising newsman goes up against a 120-year-old Jekyll-and-Hyde killer stalking Seattle's citizens. DVD packaging boasts that you will "see all the wrinkles in Kolchak's suit for the first time," and indeed the disc looks and sounds great

for a couple of old TV movies. Picky viewers will spot the digital compression artifacts visible in some of the darkest scenes, but they don't really distract. See the adventures of Carl Kolchak from their beginnings. They inspired producer Chris Carter to create TV's *The X-Files* two decades later. —*MB*
Movie: ♫♫♫ *DVD:* ♫♫▶
Anchor Bay (Cat #DV10501, UPC #013131050196). Full frame. Dolby Digital Mono. $29.98. Keepcase. *LANG:* English. *FEATURES:* 66 chapter links.
1971 73m/C Darren McGavin, Carol Lynley, Simon Oakland, Ralph Meeker, Claude Akins, Kent Smith, Larry Linville, Barry Atwater; *D:* John Llewellyn Moxey; *W:* Richard Matheson; *M:* Robert Cobert.

The Night Strangler

Please see review of *The Night Stalker*.
Movie: ♫♫▶
1972 90m/C Darren McGavin, Richard Anderson, Simon Oakland, Wally Cox, Margaret Hamilton, John Carradine, Al Lewis; *D:* Dan Curtis; *W:* Richard Matheson; *M:* Robert Cobert.

The Night That Never Happened

A bachelor party gets out of control the night before the wedding. The bride sends her trusted friend Tori (McDermott) along as a chaperone for the boys. Oops, seems she gets caught up in the fun as well. This misadventure sets the stage for lots of sex and undulating bodies, with a loose plot involving strippers, kidnapping, stolen money, blackmail, and sexual domination. The picture here is consistent but average. Colors are a bit underplayed and drab. The sound is passable but muddles frequently in segueing from scene to scene. —*AB*
Movie: ♫♫ *DVD:* ♫♫▶
Image Entertainment (Cat #ID5841PLDVD, UPC #1438158412). Widescreen. Dolby Digital Stereo. Snapper. *LANG:* English. *SUB:* English. *FEATURES:* 16 chapter links.
1997 (R) 95m/C James Wellington, Lisa Boyle, Colleen McDermott; *D:* James Winner; *W:* Sahara Riley; *C:* Ben Kufrin; *M:* Carl Schurtz.

Night Tide

Dennis Hopper chose a typically (for him) offbeat role for his first starring effort. He's Johnny Drake, a lonely sailor who falls for Mora (Lawson), a sideshow mermaid. In their commentary track, Hopper and writer-director Harrington talk about the story's debt to Val Lewton's *Cat People*, but the film works just as well as a period piece. It's a beautifully photographed black-and-white snapshot of Southern California in 1960. Though the DVD image is marred by a few flaws, it is extremely sharp. The mono sound is fine, too. Hopper and Harrington sound a bit uncomfortable at first, but they warm to their task and go into interesting details of

the production, the film's checkered history and spotty distribution. —*MM*
Movie: ♫♫♫ *DVD:* ♫♫♫
Image Entertainment (Cat #ID5928MLSD-VD, UPC #014381592825). Widescreen (1.85:1) letterboxed. Dolby Digital Mono. $29.99. Snapper. *LANG:* English. *FEATURES:* 14 chapter links • Theatrical trailer • Commentary: Hopper and Harrington • Liner notes by Richard Valley.
1963 84m/B Dennis Hopper, Gavin Muir, Linda Lawson, Luana Anders, Marjorie Eaton, Tom Dillon, Bruno VeSota; *D:* Curtis Harrington; *W:* Curtis Harrington; *C:* Vilis Lapenieks; *M:* David Raksin.

A Night to Remember

This gripping tale of the fateful voyage of the doomed Titanic is more drama than melodrama because each episode of courage amid despair is based upon the true accounts by Titanic survivors. A large cast is effectively used in this British production, considered by many the best Titanic movie prior to 1997's *Titanic* by director James Cameron. Some say it's still the best, adapted by Eric Ambler from the book by Walter Lord. The transfer looks generally good on this dual-layer disc, and the mono soundtrack is fine, considering the movie's vintage. Scratches and other blemishes are visible but do not distract. The commentary track and documentary are first-class additions aboard this disc. —*MB*
Movie: ♫♫♫▶ *DVD:* ♫♫♫
Criterion Collection (Cat #CC1517D, UPC #715515009058). Widescreen (1.66:1) letterboxed. Dolby Digital 1.0. $39.95. Keepcase. *LANG:* English. *FEATURES:* 42 chapter links • Commentary: Titanic experts Don Lynch and Ken Marshall • Theatrical trailer • 60-minute documentary.
1958 119m/B Kenneth More, David McCallum, Anthony Bushell, Honor Blackman, Michael Goodliffe, George Rose, Laurence Naismith, Frank Lawton, Alec McCowen, Jill Dixon, John Cairney, Joseph Tomelty, Jack Watling, Richard Clarke, Ralph Michael, Kenneth Griffith; *D:* Roy Ward Baker; *W:* Eric Ambler; *C:* Geoffrey Unsworth. *AWARDS:* Golden Globe Awards '59: Best Foreign Film.

Night Train to Terror

Strange things happen on a train where a rock band makes its last appearance and God and Satan argue philosophy. Clips from other horror movies were pieced together to make this film that's so bad it's almost good. The operative word there is "almost." The original footage is poorly focused and dark and the clips may have been taken from second or third generation duplicates. —*MM AKA:* Shiver.
Movie: woof *DVD:* woof
Simitar Entertainment (Cat #7596, UPC #082551759620). Full frame. Dolby Digital Stereo. $14.98. Keepcase. *LANG:* English. *FEATURES:* 8 links • Production factoids • Cameron Mitchell factoids.

1984 **(R)** **98m/C** John Phillip Law, Cameron Mitchell, Marc Lawrence, Charles Moll, Ferdinand "Ferdy" Mayne; **D:** Jay Schlossberg-Cohen; **W:** Philip Yordan.

Nighthawks

New York city cops DaSilva (Stallone) and Fox (Williams) scour Manhattan to track down international terrorist Wulfgar (Hauer), who's threatening to continue the series of bombings that he began in England. They race from nightclubs to subway to the Roosevelt Island aerial tramway. In visual terms, the DVD is nothing special, but the shaggy, filmed-on-location look of the film is appropriate, both for its age and for its intentions. It's not supposed to be slick. Given the predominance of disco in those days, the monaural soundtrack is a blessing. —*MM*

Movie: 🎬🎬🎬 ***DVD:*** 🎬🎬
Goodtimes Entertainment (Cat #05-81055, UPC #018713810557). Full frame. Dolby Digital Mono. $19.98. Snapper. *LANG:* English. *SUB:* French; Spanish. *CAP:* English. *FEATURES:* 18 chapter links • Theatrical trailer • Production notes.
1981 **(R)** **100m/C** Sylvester Stallone, Billy Dee Williams, Rutger Hauer, Lindsay Wagner, Nigel Davenport, Persis Khambatta, Catherine Mary Stewart, Joe Spinell; **D:** Bruce Malmuth; **W:** David Shaber; **C:** James A. Contner; **M:** Keith Emerson.

Nightmare at Noon

Sf thriller is set in a small desert town where spooky guys led by spooky Brion James conduct a mind-control experiment. Only the sheriff (Kennedy), a tourist couple (Hauser and Beck), and a stranger (Hopkins) are able to fight back. The DVD looks fine, though there's nothing particularly special. This one's a lively B-movie and looks it. —*MM*

Movie: 🎬🎬▶ ***DVD:*** 🎬🎬▶
Simitar Entertainment (Cat #7613, UPC #082551761326). Full frame. Dolby Digital Stereo. $14.98. Keepcase. *LANG:* English. *FEATURES:* 8 chapter links • Production factoids • George Kennedy filmography.
1987 **(R)** **96m/C** Wings Hauser, George Kennedy, Bo Hopkins, Brion James, Kimberly Beck, Kimberly Ross; **D:** Nico Mastorakis.

The Nightmare before Christmas

Back when he was an animator trainee at Disney, Burton came up with this adventurous idea but couldn't get it made. Subsequent directorial success brought more clout. This animation relies on a painstaking stop-motion technique that took more than two years to film and is justifiably amazing. The story revolves around Jack Skellington, the Pumpkin King of the dangerously weird Halloweentown. Suffering from ennui, he accidentally discovers the wonders of Christmastown and decides to kidnap Santa and rule over this peaceable

holiday. Fast pace is maintained by the equally breathless score. Not cuddly, best appreciated by those with a feel for the macabre. This DVD is hard to top for overall image quality, and the sound keeps up equally well. The laserdisc box set is still great to have if only because it's the only way to get the Burton short "Vincent," but this DVD is superior in every way. —*JO*
AKA: Tim Burton's The Nightmare before Christmas.

Movie: 🎬🎬🎬▶ ***DVD:*** 🎬🎬🎬🎬
Buena Vista Home Entertainment (Cat #13080, UPC #717951000088). Widescreen (1.66:1) letterboxed. Dolby Digital 5.1; Dolby Surround. $29.99. Keepcase. *LANG:* English; French. *SUB:* Spanish. *CAP:* English. *FEATURES:* 20 chapter links • Theatrical trailer.
1993 **(PG)** **75m/C** **D:** Henry Selick; **W:** Caroline Thompson, Tim Burton, Michael McDowell; **C:** Pete Kozachik; **M:** Danny Elfman; **V:** Danny Elfman, Chris Sarandon, Catherine O'Hara, William Hickey, Ken Page, Ed Ivory, Paul (Pee-wee Herman) Reubens, Glenn Shadix. *AWARDS: NOM:* Academy Awards '93: Best Visual Effects; Golden Globe Awards '94: Best Score.

A Nightmare on Elm Street

One of the most influential of modern horror films gets the full treatment on DVD, and though I have never been a true fan of the series, I must admit that this is a worthy effort. On the commentary track, the filmmakers (with the notable absence of star Robert Englund) do an excellent job of describing what they were trying to do and how they did it. The self-congratulation that is so often the point of commentary tracks is kept to a minimum. Instead, the participants are more technical, focusing on the problems involved in difficult shots or effects. They're also very funny at times, particularly toward the end, and they never try to make more of the film than it is. The remastered transfer looks superb, better than the original theatrical release, if memory serves. Since this film and its sequels have been so popular, the DVD comes with a full array of extras (listed below). It is also available as part of a set containing all of the *Elm Street* films to date. —*MM*

Movie: 🎬🎬▶ ***DVD:*** 🎬🎬🎬▶
New Line Home Video (Cat #N4664, UPC #794043466427). Full frame; widescreen letterboxed. Dolby Digital Mono; Dolby Digital 5.1 Surround Stereo. $24.98. Snapper. *LANG:* English. *SUB:* English. *FEATURES:* 25 chapter links with animated menus • Jump to Nightmare links • Commentary: Craven, Haitkin, Langenkamp, and Saxon • Press kit biographies of cast and crew • Original theatrical trailer. DVD-ROM includes screenplay, trivia game, information on cast and crew.
1984 **(R)** **92m/C** John Saxon, Heather Langenkamp, Ronee Blakley, Robert Englund, Amanda Wyss, Nick Corri, Johnny Depp, Charles Fleischer; **D:** Wes Craven;

W: Wes Craven; **C:** Jacques Haitkin; **M:** Charles Bernstein.

A Nightmare on Elm Street 2: Freddy's Revenge

Fans of this series have long held that the even-numbered entries are the worst, and 2 certainly bears them out. Some of the sillier effects involve flying tennis balls, exploding hotdogs, and a possessed parakeet, not to mention the boy who talks with his mouth full. Everything about this one from the opening dream sequence to the slaughtered teens to the cliched ending strictly follows the formula. The unintentional humor is a relief from the numbing routine. It has developed a following as the most overtly "homoerotic" of the *Elm Street* horrors. —*MM*

Movie: 🎬 ***DVD:*** 🎬🎬🎬
New Line Home Video (Cat #N4820, UPC #794043478826). Widescreen (1.85:1) letterboxed. Dolby Digital 5.1 Surround Stereo; Mono. $24.98. Snapper. *LANG:* English. *SUB:* English. *FEATURES:* 26 chapter links • "Jump to a Nightmare" screen navigation • Cast and crew thumbnail biographies • DVD-ROM features. Also available as part of "The Nightmare on Elm Street Collection" boxed set ($129.98), catalog #N4788.
1985 **(R)** **87m/C** Mark Patton, Hope Lange, Clu Gulager, Robert Englund, Kim Myers, Robert Rusler, Marshall Bell, Sydney Walsh; **D:** Jack Sholder; **W:** David Chaskin; **C:** Jacques Haitkin.

A Nightmare on Elm Street 3: Dream Warriors

Sheer inventiveness alone does not make a good horror movie. Neither do special effects involving tongues, and this is the virtual *Gone with the Wind* of tongue-effect movies. Other than those, it's more of the same as the ubiquitous Freddy (Englund) shows up everywhere, even on *The Dick Cavett Show*, and preys on institutionalized kids including the then almost–famous Patricia Arquette and Laurence (then Larry) Fishburne, whose resume already included *Apocalypse Now* and the TV soap *One Life to Live*. Original heroine Heather Langenkamp returns. Throughout, the pace is quick and director Charles Russell *(The Mask)* never seems to take this silly stuff seriously. Many fans rate this among the best of the series. Perhaps the participation of Frank Darabont *(Shawshank Redemption)* on the script has something to do with that. DVD makes the most of the visual effects, and it also does justice to Angelo Badalamenti's fine score. —*MM*

Movie: 🎬🎬 ***DVD:*** 🎬🎬🎬▶
New Line Home Video (Cat #N4821, UPC #794043478826). Widescreen (1.85:1) letterboxed. Dolby Digital 5.1 Surround Stereo; Mono. $24.98. Snapper. *LANG:* English. *SUB:* English. *FEATURES:* 31 chap-

ter links • "Jump to a Nightmare" scene navigation • Cast and crew thumbnail biographies • DVD-ROM extras. Also available as part of "The Nightmare on Elm Street Collection" boxed set ($129.98), catalog #N4788.
1987 (R) 96m/C Patricia Arquette, Robert Englund, Heather Langenkamp, Craig Wasson, Laurence "Larry" Fishburne, Priscilla Pointer, John Saxon, Brooke Bundy, Jennifer Rubin, Rodney Eastman, Nan Martin, Dick Cavett, Zsa Zsa Gabor; *D:* Chuck Russell; *W:* Chuck Russell, Bruce Wagner, Wes Craven, Frank Darabont; *C:* Roy Wagner; *M:* Angelo Badalamenti.

A Nightmare on Elm Street 4: Dream Master

Since, as the subtitle indicates, the movie is essentially a dream from the first shot, it contains no real scares—just shocks and surprises on some remarkable sets. As you ought to expect from any sequel with a *4* in the title, the plot is familiar. The main characters are blandly, generically attractive. Harlin shows off with flashy overdirection whenever he can. He gives the production such a high gloss that it's the most glittering piece of eye-candy in the series. Because the big effects scenes look so good, DVD heightens the shortcomings of other, more pedestrian moments. Some conventional interiors lack sharp focus. Sound is fine. —*MM*
Movie: 🐾🐾 **DVD:** 🐾🐾🐾
New Line Home Video (Cat #N4822, UPC #794043478826). Widescreen (1.85:1) letterboxed. Dolby Digital 5.1 Surround Stereo; Stereo. $24.98. Snapper. *LANG:* English. *SUB:* English. *FEATURES:* 27 chapter links • Cast and crew thumbnail biographies • "Jump to a Nightmare" screen navigation • DVD-ROM extras. Also available as part of "The Nightmare on Elm Street Collection" boxed set ($129.98), catalog #N4788.
1988 (R) 99m/C Robert Englund, Rodney Eastman, Danny Hassel, Andras Jones, Tuesday Knight, Lisa Wilcox, Ken Sagoes, Toy Newkirk, Brooke Theiss, Brooke Bundy; *D:* Renny Harlin; *W:* Brian Helgeland, Scott Pierce; *C:* Steven Fierberg; *M:* Craig Safan.

A Nightmare on Elm Street 5: Dream Child

Freddy (Englund) attacks Alice's (Wilcox) unborn fetus. (No, the film has nothing to add to the abortion debate.) Again, the dream structure eliminates real scares, so the filmmakers concentrate on imaginative effects. Also, since so much of the horror is based on pregnancy, childbirth, and monster infants, women may react to the story on a more fundamental level. Credit writer Leslie Bohem. The DVD looks very good, particularly in the opening Bedlam sequence and in the big finish where the

many black areas are clearly defined. Sound is good. —*MM*
Movie: 🐾🐾 **DVD:** 🐾🐾🐾
New Line Home Video (Cat #N4823, UPC #794043478826). Widescreen (1.85:1) anamorphic. Dolby Digital 5.1 Surround Stereo; Stereo. $24.98. Snapper. *LANG:* English. *SUB:* English. *FEATURES:* 23 chapter links • Cast and crew thumbnail biographies • "Jump to a Nightmare" scene navigation • DVD-ROM extras. Also available as part of "The Nightmare on Elm Street Collection" boxed set ($129.98), catalog #N4788.
1989 (R) 90m/C Robert Englund, Lisa Wilcox, Kelly Jo Minter, Danny Hassel, Erika Anderson, Nicholas Mele, Beatrice Boepple; *D:* Stephen Hopkins; *W:* Leslie Bohem; *C:* Peter Levy; *M:* Jay Ferguson. *AWARDS:* Golden Raspberry Awards '89: Worst Song ("Bring Your Daughter to the Slaughter").

The "Nightmare on Elm Street" Collection

This eight-disc boxed set contains everything that even the most devoted fan could ever want to know about the series. Of course, all seven films are included (see reviews) along with *The Nightmare Series Encyclopedia*, (cat. # N4838), a collection of interviews with the various creative people who have worked behind the cameras and in front of them. Rachael Talalay, director of *6 calls 2* "shockingly homoerotic." Surprisingly, many of the comments are more honest and critical than viewers might expect, though they are still aimed at the target audience of fans. If such treatment seems like overkill, it's hard to imagine any other series (horror or mainstream) deserving consideration as a distinct body of work. Many critics and reviewers, including me, have found fault with the series, but the filmmakers have maintained respectable production values, and a consistent vision of what they were trying to accomplish. —*MM*
Movie: 🐾🐾🐾 **DVD:** 🐾🐾🐾🐾
New Line Home Video (Cat #N4788, UPC #794043478826). Widescreen letterboxed. Dolby Digital 5.1 Surround Stereo; Stereo; Mono. $129.98. Snapper. *LANG:* English. *CAP:* English.
1999 m/C

Nightmares

So-so anthology benefits from the presence of stars on the verge of fame. In the first story, Lisa (Raines) goes out for smokes while a homicidal maniac is on the loose. JJ (Estevez) plays a video game for very high stakes. Suffering a crisis of faith, desert priest Father Frank (Henriksen) battles a four-wheel-drive devil in the best episode. Finally, Stephen (Masur) and Claire's (Cartwright) house is attacked by giant supernatural polter-rats. Veteran film and TV director Sargent handles things briskly. Some grain appears in the dark scenes, particularly in the final

episode where the dated optical effects are involved. But what should anyone really expect of a film that was made for television and then released to theatres because it was too violent? —*MM*
Movie: 🐾🐾 **DVD:** 🐾🐾🐾
Anchor Bay (Cat #DV10869, UPC #0131311086997). Full frame. Dolby Digital Mono. $24.98. Keepcase. *LANG:* English. *FEATURES:* 26 chapter links • Theatrical trailer.
1983 (PG) 99m/C Christina Raines, Emilio Estevez, Moon Zappa, Lance Henriksen, Richard Masur, Veronica Cartwright; *D:* Joseph Sargent; *W:* Christopher Crowe, Jeffrey Bloom; *C:* Mario DiLeo, Gerald Perry Finnerman; *M:* Craig Safan.

Nights of Cabiria

It's impossible to watch Fellini's early international hit and not fall in love with star Giulietta Masina, at least a little. She's Cabiria, the original prostitute with a heart of gold who survives a series of amorous misadventures. The Criterion DVD is based on the 1998 restoration that played theatrically. If the clips featured in the restoration demonstration are at all accurate, the changes in image and sound are dramatic. The new black-and-white images have been transformed from muddy, grainy ghosts into sharp clarity emphasizing the lighter shades. In a few scenes the work is less than perfect with some flashing of patterns but that's a quibble. The subtitles are based on a new, more colloquial translation, and they're easy to read. The disc contains an assortment of unusual extras including the famous "man with a sack" scene deleted by producer Dino De Laurentiis, who explains why in a separate interview. The primary attraction is still the film and its star. —*MM AKA:* Le Notti de Cabiria; Cabiria.
Movie: 🐾🐾🐾🐾 **DVD:** 🐾🐾🐾🐾
Criterion Collection (Cat #NIG040). Full frame. Dolby Mono. $29.95. Keepcase. *LANG:* Italian; English. *SUB:* English. *FEATURES:* 24 chapter links • Liner notes by Fellini (from *I Fellini*, by Charlotte Chandler) • Original theatrical trailer • Re-release trailer • David D'Arcy NPR interview with producer De Laurentiis • Filmed interview with Dominique Delouche, Fellini's assistant • Restoration demonstration • Scenes from *The White Sheik*.
1957 117m/B *IT* Giulietta Masina, Amedeo Nazzari, Francois Perier, Franca Marzi, Dorian Gray, Aldo Silvani, Ennio Girolami; *D:* Federico Fellini; *W:* Federico Fellini, Tullio Pinelli, Ennio Flaiano; *C:* Aldo Tonti; *M:* Nino Rota. *AWARDS:* Academy Awards '57: Best Foreign Film; Cannes Film Festival '57: Best Actress (Masina).

Nikki, the Wild Dog of the North

In 1899 Canada, trader Andre Dupas (Coutu) is travelling down river with his Malumute pup Nikki when they find an

orphaned bear cub, Neewa. It's your basic guy-meets-dog/guy-loses-dog/guy-gets-dog-back story, adapted from James Oliver Curwood's novel *Nomads of the North*. The action is a bit too scenic and slow-moving for some younger viewers; others will be happy with all of the cute fuzzy animal scenes. On DVD, the Disney film is sharply detailed with undimmed colors that are brighter than many much younger films that have not been so carefully preserved. Sound is adequate. —*MM*
Movie: 𝄞𝄞▶ **DVD:** 𝄞𝄞▶
Image Entertainment (Cat #DV10992, UPC #013131099294). Full frame. Dolby Digital Mono. $24.98. Keepcase. *LANG:* English. *FEATURES:* 20 chapter links • 4.5" x 7" poster suitable for decorating an extremely small room.
1961 (G) 73m/C *CA* Jean Coutu, Emile Genest, Uriel Luft, Robert Rivard; *D:* Jack Couffer, Don Haldane, Ralph Wright; *W:* Winston Hibler, Ralph Wright; *C:* Lloyd Beebe; *M:* Oliver Wallace.

9 1/2 Weeks

Chance meeting between a Wall Street exec (Rourke) and an art gallery employee (Basinger) evolves into an experimental sexual relationship bordering on sado-masochism. Video version is more explicit than the theatrical release, but not by much. Strong characterizations by both actors prevent this from being strictly pornography. It's well-written, with strength of male and female personalities nicely balanced; intriguing, but not for all tastes. The DVD is nowhere near as slick-looking as the MGM laserdisc release, and at times the picture is soft and somewhat grainy. However, colors are very good—vibrant and accurate with very little bleed, and almost make up for some of the lack of sharpness. Blacks are true and both contrast and brightness levels are consistently very good. The sound seems a little muffled when compared to the VHS and laserdisc editions, but doesn't detract that much. —*JO*
Movie: 𝄞𝄞▶ **DVD:** 𝄞𝄞▶
MGM Home Entertainment (Cat #907028, UPC #027616702821). Widescreen (1.85:1) letterboxed. Dolby Surround. $24.98. Keepcase. *LANG:* English; French. *SUB:* English; Spanish; French. *CAP:* English. *FEATURES:* 28 chapter links • Theatrical trailer • Additional explicit footage • 8-page booklet.
1986 (R) 114m/C Mickey Rourke, Kim Basinger, Margaret Whitton, Karen Young, David Margulies, Christine Baranski, Roderick Cook, Dwight Weist; *D:* Adrian Lyne; *W:* Patricia Louisianna Knop, Zalman King; *C:* Peter Biziou; *M:* Jack Nitzsche.

1941

Proved to be the most expensive comedy of all time with a budget exceeding $35 million. The depiction of Los Angeles in the chaotic days after the bombing of Pearl Harbor combines elements of fantasy and black humor, as a Japanese submarine (commanded by Mifune) attempts to invade mainland U.S.A. Hated by critics but loved by a lot of fans. This is the longer 145-minute director's cut, which actually slows down the intensity of the film a bit, although some of the added scenes are well worth it. Half of *1941* was shot in some sort of fog, and the DVD appears to have some problem with it. The picture is not as sharp as the laserdisc; the DVD has grain not apparent on the LD as well. Colors are more vibrant than on the LD, but there is some bleed. Blacks range from true to grayish with a touch of grain. Contrast and brightness are O.K. The sound is far from spectacular, sounding muffled at times and struggling with the mix, which intensely focuses mainly on effects and music and seems to have a little too much mid-range. —*JO*
Movie: 𝄞𝄞𝄞▶ **DVD:** 𝄞𝄞▶
Universal Studios Home Video (Cat #20550, UPC #025192055027). Widescreen (2.35:1) letterboxed. Dolby Digital 5.1. $34.98. Keepcase. *LANG:* English. *SUB:* Spanish; French. *CAP:* English. *FEATURES:* 60 chapter links: movie • 19 chapter links: "making of" featurette • Theatrical trailers • Deleted scenes • Production notes • Cast and filmmaker bios • Stills • Comic relief • Marketing • Dual-layered RSDL.
1979 (PG) 145m/C John Belushi, Dan Aykroyd, Patti LuPone, Ned Beatty, Slim Pickens, Murray Hamilton, Christopher Lee, Tim Matheson, Toshiro Mifune, Warren Oates, Robert Stack, Nancy Allen, Elisha Cook Jr., Lorraine Gary, Treat Williams, Mickey Rourke, John Candy, Wendie Jo Sperber, Lucille Benson, Eddie Deezen, Bobby DiCicco, Dianne Kay, Perry Lang, Frank McRae, Lionel Stander, Dub Taylor, Joe Flaherty, David Lander, Michael McKean, Samuel Fuller, Audrey Landers, John Landis, Walter Olkewicz, Donovan Scott, Penny Marshall; *D:* Steven Spielberg; *W:* Robert Zemeckis, Bob Gale, John Milius; *C:* William A. Fraker; *M:* John Williams. *AWARDS: NOM:* Academy Awards '79: Best Cinematography, Best Sound.

90 Degrees South: With Scott to the Antarctic

This is the film record of Capt. Robert Scott's ill-fated 1910 journey to the South Pole, "the uttermost end of the Earth," as producer-photographer-narrator Herbert Ponting puts it. Scott was racing Norwegian explorer Roald Amundsen, and though Ponting wasn't able to go all the way to the pole, the footage he shot in Antarctica is still spectacular. The film was released in various versions, beginning in 1911. Narration and music were added in 1933. Today's nature documentaries may be more sophisticated in their observations of animal behavior, but they lack the sense of wonder, excitement, and real adventure that Ponting brings across so vividly. My only reservation is one reference to a black cat named "Nigger." In the context of the film and the times, it's meant to be playful and innocent. Today, it will bring viewers up short. The DVD is equal in image and sound clarity to the Lumivision laserdisc edition, a bit scratchy and snowy but overall exceptionally sharp. —*MM*
Movie: 𝄞𝄞𝄞 **DVD:** 𝄞𝄞𝄞
Image Entertainment (Cat #ID5919MLSD-VD, UPC #014381591927). Full frame. Dolby Digital Mono. $24.99. Snapper. *LANG:* English. *FEATURES:* 14 chapter links.
1933 72m/B *D:* Herbert Ponting; *C:* Herbert Ponting; *Nar:* Herbert Ponting.

Ninja Scroll

Ninja Jubei is caught between warring supernatural forces in an animated feature that is so absurdly complicated and bizarre that it takes several screens of dense single-spaced type in the supplementals section of this DVD to create a synopsis. Both image and sound are very good. The sharply defined colors are fine, but the stiff, slow physical action doesn't test the limits of the medium. Even so, the imaginative horror and sheer unpredictability of the story give this one a kick. —*MM* *AKA:* Wicked City 3.
Movie: 𝄞𝄞𝄞 **DVD:** 𝄞𝄞𝄞
Rykodisc USA (Cat #47611). Full frame. Dolby Digital 5.1 Surround Stereo. $29.95. Keepcase. *LANG:* Japanese. *SUB:* English. *FEATURES:* 24 chapter links • Synopsis • Character guide.
1993 94m/C *JP D:* Yoshiaki Kawajiri; *W:* Yoshiaki Kawajiri.

Ninth Street

Period drama set in the 1960s.
Movie: NYR **DVD:** NYR
Ideal Enterprises/Video (Cat #80522). Full frame. $14.98. Slipcase.
1998 (R) 98m/B Kevin Willmott, Don Washington, Nadine Griffith, Byron Myrick, Isaac Hayes, Kaycee Moore, Martin Sheen, Queen Bey; *D:* Kevin Willmott, Tim Rebman; *W:* Kevin Willmott; *C:* Troy Paddock; *M:* Wayne Hawkins.

Nixon

Stone again "interprets" historical events of the '60s and '70s with a sprawling, bold bio of Richard Nixon. Covering all the highlights of Nixon's public life, and speculating on his private one, Hopkins convincingly portrays "Tricky Dick" as an embattled, lonely political genius. Gigantic all-star cast is led by Oscar-caliber performance of Joan Allen as Pat Nixon. Even at over three hours, there isn't nearly enough time to explore the significance of all the events covered here. As usual, Stone has taken some creative license, which lead to the Nixon daughters publicly trashing the film, and Walt Disney's daughter expressing "shame" at being affiliated with it. The DVD has not been given the royal treatment that the laserdisc was (supplemental-wise), but has an improved image with better sharpness and more intense colors. Grain and artifacts never enter the picture. Blacks are excellent and at times blend into the black bars of the letterboxing. Contrast and brightness levels are consistent and comfortable throughout. The sound is also improved with much deeper bass and better energy in the mids and highs. —*JO*

Movie: 🎞🎞🎞 **DVD:** 🎞🎞🎞▸

Buena Vista Home Entertainment (Cat #17246, UPC #717951002396). Widescreen (2.35:1) letterboxed. Dolby Digital 5.1. $29.99. Keepcase. *LANG:* English. *CAP:* English. *FEATURES:* 31 chapter links.

1995 (R) 192m/C Anthony Hopkins, Joan Allen, Ed Harris, Bob Hoskins, David Paymer, Paul Sorvino, J.T. Walsh, James Woods, Madeline Kahn, Brian Bedford, Mary Steenburgen, Powers Boothe, E.G. Marshall, David Hyde Pierce, Kevin Dunn, Annabeth Gish, Tony Goldwyn, Larry Hagman, Edward Herrmann, Saul Rubinek, Tony LoBianco; *D:* Oliver Stone; *W:* Christopher Wilkinson, Stephen J. Rivele, Oliver Stone; *C:* Robert Richardson; *M:* John Williams. *AWARDS:* Los Angeles Film Critics Association Awards '95: Best Supporting Actress (Allen); National Society of Film Critics Awards '95: Best Supporting Actress (Allen); *NOM:* Academy Awards '95: Best Actor (Hopkins), Best Original Screenplay, Best Supporting Actress (Allen), Best Original Dramatic Score; British Academy Awards '95: Best Supporting Actress (Allen); Golden Globe Awards '96: Best Actor—Drama (Hopkins); Screen Actors Guild Award '95: Best Actor (Hopkins), Best Actress (Allen), Cast.

No Escape

In 2022, Captain Robbins (Liotta) has been banished to a prison colony island inhabited by the most dangerous criminals. With no walls and no guards, the prisoners are left to kill each other. Then Robbins discovers a relatively peaceful community of prisoners who help each other. But this group is soon bedeviled by the evil nasties on the other side of the island. Attempts at escape define the plot, so the film is filled with superhuman feats of sheer courage, determination, and guts. The DVD transfer is overall very good with the most impressive feature being the full-bodied 5.1 sound, with plenty of bass and super crisp highs, and excellent Surround that is non-stop active, filled with musical and environmental ambience, and plenty of crash-bang effects. The picture is also very good, sharp with little grain or artifacts. Colors are both accurate and vibrant and blacks are true. Contrast is punchy and brightness is comfortable. —*JO*

Movie: 🎞🎞▸ **DVD:** 🎞🎞🎞▸

HBO Home Video (Cat #91562, UPC #026359098222). Widescreen (1.85:1) letterboxed. Dolby Digital 5.1; Dolby Surround. $24.98. Snapper. *LANG:* English (DD5.1); Spanish (DS); French (DS). *SUB:* English; Spanish; French. *CAP:* English.

FEATURES: 35 chapter links • Cast and filmmaker bios.

1994 (R) 118m/C Ray Liotta, Lance Henriksen, Stuart Wilson, Kevin Dillon, Kevin J. O'Connor, Michael Lerner, Ernie Hudson, Ian McNeice, Jack Shepherd; *D:* Martin Campbell; *W:* Joel Gross; *C:* Phil Meheux; *M:* Graeme Revell.

No Mercy

A Chicago cop (Gere) plunges into the Cajun bayou to avenge the murder of his partner. He falls for a beautiful girl enslaved by the killer, but that doesn't stop him from using her to flush out the powerful swamp-inhabiting crime lord. Absurd story without much plot. The picture is plenty sharp on this DVD, and the colors are strong and accurate. What stands out the most are the deep true blacks, which are so dark that until you get used to it, you may think the image is in need of brightness. The Dolby Surround is fairly dead and at times sounds a little muted. —*JO*

Movie: 🎞🎞 **DVD:** 🎞🎞🎞

Trimark Home Video (Cat #83759, UPC #043396837591). Widescreen (1.85:1) letterboxed; full frame. Dolby Surround. $29.95. Keepcase. *LANG:* English; French; Spanish. *SUB:* English; French; Spanish. *CAP:* English. *FEATURES:* 28 chapter links • Theatrical trailer.

1986 (R) 108m/C Richard Gere, Kim Basinger, Jeroen Krabbe, George Dzundza, William Atherton, Ray Sharkey, Bruce McGill; *D:* Richard Pearce; *W:* Jim Carabatsos; *C:* Michel Brault; *M:* Alan Silvestri.

No Strings Attached

Mark Demetrius (Spano) is a reporter working on a story about women's sexual fantasies. To the distress of his fiancee, he enters a relationship with a mysterious woman he knows only through telephone conversations. To nobody's surprise, murder ensues. Image and sound are no different from VHS tape on this bare-bones disc. —*MM*

Movie: 🎞🎞 **DVD:** 🎞🎞

Sunland Studios (Cat #PM 359-D, UPC #757449335933). Full frame. Stereo. $24.99. Keepcase. *LANG:* English.

1998 (R) 97m/C Vincent Spano, Cheryl Pollak, Traci Lind, David Packer, Michael McKean; *D:* Josef Rusnak; *W:* Nicholas Bogner, Michael Holden; *C:* Wedigo von Schultzendorff; *M:* Eric Lundmark.

Noah's Ark

Made-for-TV epic of the Old Testament story doesn't exactly stay close to its biblical roots. It's eccentric, special effects–laden and bordering on the irreverent. Noah (Voight) builds his ark, gathers the animals (and his family), watches as the world is destroyed, and survives the 40 days and nights of flooding.

Movie: 🎞🎞 **DVD:** NYR

Hallmark Home Entertainment (Cat #70073). Full frame. Dolby Digital Stereo. $19.98. Keepcase. *FEATURES:* Production notes • Trailer • Cast and crew thumbnail bios.

1999 178m/C Jon Voight, Mary Steenburgen, F. Murray Abraham, Carol Kane, James Coburn, Jonathan Cake, Alexis Denisof, Emily Mortimer, Sydney Poitier, Sonya Walger; *D:* John Irvin; *W:* Peter Barnes; *C:* Mike Molloy; *M:* Paul Grabowsky.

The North Avenue Irregulars

Slapstick Disney comedy along the lines of their earlier live-action work involves a preacher (Herrmann) and members of the local ladies' club who try to bust a crime syndicate. The solid cast handles the flimsy material with pure professionalism, though seeing Karen Valentine dolled up as a faux hooker is about as uncomfortable as you'd expect in a 1970s Disney comedy. (The studio would have to wait a decade or so to strike gold with that notion in *Pretty Woman*.) With the exception of some streaks in one spot from a flaw on the original print or negative, the image is fine, but the overall production values are on a made-for-TV level. —*MM*

Movie: 🎞🎞▸ **DVD:** 🎞🎞▸

Anchor Bay (Cat #DV10829, UPC #01313108299). Full frame; widescreen (1.66:1). Dolby Digital. $24.98. Keepcase. *FEATURES:* 17 chapter links.

1979 (G) 99m/C Edward Herrmann, Barbara Harris, Susan Clark, Karen Valentine, Michael Constantine, Cloris Leachman, Melora Hardin, Alan Hale Jr., Ruth Buzzi, Patsy Kelly, Virginia Capers; *D:* Bruce Bilson; *W:* Don Tait; *C:* Leonard J. South; *M:* Robert F. Brunner.

Nosferatu

The first film adaptation of Bram Stoker's *Dracula* remains one of the creepiest and most atmospheric versions. Murnau knew how to add just the right touches (not to mention shadows) to make this one of the best vampire films ever made. All it lacks is the name of Dracula, which was changed due to copyright problems with Stoker's widow. Filmed in Bavaria. Remade by Werner Herzog in 1979. Unfortunately, the original source material of this silent masterpiece has quite a bit of damage. However, the DVD transfer presents the best version yet on home video, and overall does a good job in taking away the distractions the scratches, splices, and such cause. For a film this old, the picture is fairly sharp and the contrast is good. Ghosting along high-contrast lines is minimal. The stereo organ soundtrack sounds full and adds much in the way of atmosphere. —*JO* *AKA:* Nosferatu, Eine Symphonie des Grauens; Nosferatu, A Symphony of Terror; Nosferatu, A Symphony of Horror; Nosferatu, the Vampire; Terror of Dracula; Die Zwolfte Stunde.

Movie: 🎞🎞🎞🎞 **DVD:** 🎞🎞🎞

Image Entertainment (Cat #ID4098DSDVD, UPC #014381409826). Full frame. Stereo. $29.95. Snapper. *LANG:* Silent. *SUB:* English intertitles. *FEATURES:* 10 chapter links • Audio essay: Lokke Heiss.
1922 63m/B *GE* Max Schreck, Alexander Granach, Gustav von Wagenheim, Greta Schroder, John Gottowt, Ruth Landshoff, G.H. Schnell; *D:* F.W. Murnau; *W:* Henrik Galeen; *C:* Fritz Arno Wagner, Gunther Krampf.

Nosferatu the Vampyre

Herzog's tribute to fellow countryman's F.W. Murnau's 1922 silent film interpretation of Bram Stoker's *Dracula* story features Kinski as the disgustingly rodent-like Count, with Ganz as Jonathan Harker, and Adjani as Harker's wife and the beautiful object of the Count's lust. The DVD contains two separate versions of the film: the 107-minute German language version, and the 96-minute English-language version. Both are valid since the English language one was truly filmed, for the most part, in English, and has not just been dubbed. There are quite a few differences between the two, some of which may be the result of the varying degrees of comfort actors feel while speaking a language other than their native tongue. Some of the performances are quite varied, and some scenes are played out with an entirely different feel. The image quality is about the same on both versions. The picture is sharp, but becomes grainy when the lights go down. Colors also suffer from different lighting conditions and in the dark, the deeper colors bleed. The 5.1 sound is pretty straightforward, with very little Surround or even right/left imaging. Herzog loves to talk and is a natural promoter. His commentary is personable and informative, with loads of film facts as well as some juicy anecdotes about Kinski. —JO
Movie: ♫♫ *DVD:* ♫♫➤
Anchor Bay (Cat #DV10677, UPC #013131067798). Widescreen (1.85:1) letterboxed. Dolby Digital 5.1; Mono. $34.95. Keepcase. *LANG:* German; English. *SUB:* English. *FEATURES:* 2 theatrical cuts • Original German-language version • English-language version • Audio commentary • 2 U.S. theatrical trailers • Spanish theatrical trailer • Behind-the-scenes featurette.
1979 107m/C *FR GE* Klaus Kinski, Isabelle Adjani, Bruno Ganz, Roland Topor, Walter Ladengast; *D:* Werner Herzog; *W:* Werner Herzog; *C:* Jorge Schmidt-Reitwein; *M:* Popul Vuh, Florian Fricke.

Nostalghia

Russian academic Jankowsky comes to Tuscany to research the life of an 18th-century composer and meets the mysterious Josephson, who's convinced the end of the world is near. And soon the homesick Russian is in a search for himself. Tarkovsky's first film outside his native Russia is filled with Christian iconography and some extraordinary images. Tarkovsky's rich color texturings and excellent sense of scene composition come through without a hitch on this DVD, which is sharper than their own VHS release. The subtitles have been improved from the laserdisc to highly visible yellow. In some darker scenes the digital grain factor kicks up, and there are quite a few scenes where artifacts are noticeable. —JO
Movie: ♫♫ *DVD:* ♫♫➤
Fox/Lorber Home Video (Cat #FLV5041, UPC #720917504124). Widescreen (1.66:1) letterboxed. Mono. $29.98. Keepcase. *LANG:* Russian; Italian. *SUB:* English. *FEATURES:* 8 chapter links • Theatrical trailer.
1983 126m/C *IT* Oleg Jankowsky, Erland Josephson, Domiziana Giordano, Delia Boccardo; *D:* Andrei Tarkovsky; *W:* Andrei Tarkovsky, Tonino Guerra; *C:* Giuseppe Lanci.

Nothing but Trouble

This is one weird flick. Yuppie couple out for weekend drive find themselves smoldering in small town hell thanks to a traffic ticket. Sets are entertaining but some of the horror and humor mix like oil and water in Aykroyd's debut as director. This full-frame transfer is not great to look at. Darker scenes incur a lot of grain and picture sharpness itself varies. Colors are a bit better and are generally vibrant enough to accent the film's unique color design. Blacks are deep enough but pick up some grain in dim light. Contrast is O.K., but at times the brightness level seems too high. The sound mix is as offbeat as the set design, and the Dolby Surround carries it nicely with good dynamics and a fairly extreme use of all channels. —JO
Movie: ♫♫ *DVD:* ♫♫➤
Warner Home Video, Inc. (Cat #16376, UPC #085391637622). Full frame. Dolby Surround. $19.98. Snapper. *LANG:* English. *CAP:* English. *FEATURES:* 29 chapter links.
1991 (PG-13) 93m/C Dan Aykroyd, Demi Moore, Chevy Chase, John Candy, Taylor Negron, Bertila Demas, Valri Bromfield; *D:* Dan Aykroyd; *W:* Dan Aykroyd, Peter Aykroyd; *C:* Dean Cundey. *AWARDS:* Golden Raspberry Awards '91: Worst Supporting Actor (Aykroyd).

Nothing Sacred

Slick, overzealous reporter (March) takes advantage of a small-town girl's (Lombard) situation. As a publicity stunt, his newspaper brings her to the Big Apple to distract her from her supposedly imminent death (and to boost circulation figures). Innocent young Lombard, however, is far from death's door and deftly exploits her exploitation. Scathing indictment of mass media and bovine mentality of the masses is both hysterically funny and bitterly cynical. The film boasts Lombard's finest performance. The DVD version includes home movie footage of a Lombard-Gable hunting trip and two Mack Sennett shorts, "Campus Vamp" and "Matchmaking Mama." This early color film emphasizes reds and blacks, giving much of the image a faded look. Many other flaws come from the original material though one scene vibrates in an odd out-of-focus way. Sound is scratchy throughout. —MM
Movie: ♫♫♫ *DVD:* ♫♫
Lumivision Corp. (Cat #1497). Full frame. Dolby Digital Mono. $24.95. Keepcase. *LANG:* English. *FEATURES:* Trailer • Home movies • Mack Sennett comedies • 20 chapter links. Title is also available from E-realbiz.com (cat. # 9824) for $19.99.
1937 75m/C Fredric March, Carole Lombard, Walter Connolly, Sig Rumann, Charles Winninger, Margaret Hamilton; *D:* William A. Wellman; *W:* Ben Hecht; *C:* William Howard Greene; *M:* Oscar Levant.

Nothing to Lose

Ad exec Nick Beam (Robbins) is having a very bad day. He loses his job, finds his wife is having an affair, then gets carjacked by streetwise but dim-witted thief T-Paul (Lawrence). T-Paul picked the wrong day to rob Nick, who takes T-Paul hostage. The unlikely pair find they have more in common than realized. Screwball buddy comedy shows its originality in casting, and not much else. Robbins and Lawrence are an inspired pair with great comedic potential but are trapped in a mundane story. Filming was delayed due, in part, to Lawrence's constant run-ins with the law. The action scenes get pumped-up by the energetic 5.1 sound. While the image remains clean, the colors are solid and detailed with very good contrast. There are a couple of dark street shots where a little grain and minor artifacts appear, but they disappear as quickly as they come. —JO
Movie: ♫♫➤ *DVD:* ♫♫♫
Buena Vista Home Entertainment (Cat #14254, UPC #717951000354). Widescreen (1.85:1) letterboxed. Dolby Digital 5.1; Dolby Surround. $29.99. Keepcase. *LANG:* English; French. *SUB:* Spanish. *CAP:* English. *FEATURES:* 16 chapter links • Theatrical trailer.
1996 (R) 97m/C Tim Robbins, Martin Lawrence, John C. McGinley, Giancarlo Esposito, Kelly Preston, Michael McKean, Irma P. Hall, Susan Barnes, Rebecca Gayheart, Patrick Cranshaw; *D:* Steve Oedekerk; *W:* Steve Oedekerk; *C:* Donald E. Thorin; *M:* Robert Folk.

Notorious

In 1946, Alicia Huberman (Bergman), daughter of a convicted spy, is recruited by the roguishly handsome agent Devlin (Grant) to get close to escaped Nazi Alexander Sebastian (Rains) in Brazil. The scheme works better than anyone could have anticipated but the two spies fall in love. This is one of Hitchcock's most carefully wrought suspense stories. It's not as feverish as his later color work. DVD captures the full range of the superb black-

and-white cinematography (from director of photography Ted Tetzlaff). A purist might quibble that the black formal clothes lack details but they look as sharp as I remember them from theatrical viewings. Sound is fine, too, and since the film was not made for a wide screen, it really loses nothing on disc. For a no-extras disc, this is one of the best. —*MM*

Movie: ♪♪♪♪ **DVD:** ♪♪♪▶
Anchor Bay (Cat #DV10811, UPC #013131081190). Full frame. Dolby Digital Mono. $29.98. Keepcase. *LANG:* English. *FEATURES:* 18 chapter links.
1946 101m/B Cary Grant, Ingrid Bergman, Claude Rains, Louis Calhern, Madame Konstantin, Reinhold Schunzel, Moroni Olsen; **D:** Alfred Hitchcock; **W:** Ben Hecht; **C:** Ted Tetzlaff; **M:** Roy Webb. *AWARDS: NOM:* Academy Awards '46: Best Original Screenplay, Best Supporting Actor (Rains).

Notting Hill

Romantic comedy coasts by on charm and cast. Anna Scott (Roberts) is a famous, neurotic movie star who's making a film on location in London. She meets cute but shy bookstore owner William Thacker (Grant) and falls in love. Trouble begins when the paparazzi find out. William's face is splashed all over the tabloids and reporters camp out in his garden. Ifans is a scene-stealer as William's grubby and crazed housemate. The "Collector's Edition" DVD contains a wealth of extras, including a fine director-producer-writer commentary track filled with the kind of behind-the-scenes details fans want to hear. Image and sound are both excellent. —*MM*

Movie: ♪♪♪ **DVD:** ♪♪♪
Universal Studios Home Video (Cat #20640, UPC #025192064029). Widescreen (2.35:1) anamorphic. Dolby Digital 5.1 Surround Stereo; Dolby Digital Surround Stereo. $29.98. Keepcase. *LANG:* English; French. *SUB:* Spanish. *CAP:* English. *FEATURES:* 18 chapter links • "Hugh Grant's Movie Tips" featurette • Deleted scenes • Map and guide to the real Notting Hill • Commentary: Michell, Kenworthy, and Curtis • Cast and crew thumbnail biographies • Music highlights • Theatrical trailer • Production notes • DVD-ROM features.
1999 (PG-13) 123m/C Julia Roberts, Hugh Grant, Hugh Bonneville, Rhys Ifans, Tim McInnery, Gina McKee, James Dreyfus, Richard McCabe, Emma Chambers; **D:** Roger Michell; **W:** Richard Curtis; **C:** Michael Coulter; **M:** Trevor Jones. *AWARDS: NOM:* British Academy Awards '99: Best Film, Best Supporting Actor (Ifans); Golden Globe Awards '00: Best Actor—Musical/Comedy (Grant), Best Actress—Musical/Comedy (Roberts), Best Film—Musical/Comedy

Novel Desires

Perennial favorite on late-night cable (for a couple of well-staged love scenes) gains

nothing on DVD. The grainy image is identical to tape and the disc lacks even chapter links. What plot there is revolves around the scenarios that writer Brian Freedman (Gains) and his rival Vicky Chance (Monteith) dream up. —*MM*

Movie: ♪ **DVD:** ♪
Digital Versatile Disc Ltd. (Cat #DVD127, UPC #066479101273). Full frame. $24.95. Snapper. *LANG:* English.
1992 (R) 80m/C Tyler Gains, Caroline Monteith, Mitchell Clark, Lisa Hayland; **D:** Lawrence Unger.

Now and Then

Four women hold a reunion 25 years after their most eventful childhood summer to relive the good ol' days of childhood triumphs and tragedies. Flashbacks, which thankfully comprise about 85 percent of the film, explore first kisses, budding breasts, death, and divorce. Despite good intentions, this coming-of-ager for girls is a jumbled mass of borrowed formulas that can't shake the feeling of forced sentimentality. The young actresses are talented and charming, but their less convincing adult counterparts serve mostly as big names to draw crowds and studio support. On DVD, the colors are sharp, vibrant and consistent, and the sound excellent. —*AB*

Movie: ♪♪♪ **DVD:** ♪♪♪▶
New Line Home Video (Cat #N4926, UPC #9404349262). Full frame; widescreen (1.85:1) letterboxed. Dolby 5.1 Surround; Stereo Surround. $24.98. Keepcase. *LANG:* English. *SUB:* English. *FEATURES:* 24 chapter links • Theatrical trailer • Cast and crew filmographies.
1995 (PG-13) 97m/C Rosie O'Donnell, Melanie Griffith, Demi Moore, Rita Wilson, Christina Ricci, Thora Birch, Gaby Hoffman, Ashleigh Aston Moore, Cloris Leachman, Lolita (David) Davidovich, Bonnie Hunt, Brendan Fraser; **D:** Leslie Linka Glatter; **W:** I. Marlene King; **C:** Ueli Steiger; **M:** Cliff Eidelman.

Nowhere to Run

Kickboxer with heart seeks cross-over movie to establish real acting career. Unfortunately, even if such a movie existed, Van Damme wouldn't know what to do with it. Arquette plays the damsel in distress, facing eviction from the family farm with her two small children. Fortunately for Van Damme's escaped convict character, she is also a very lonely widow (nudge, nudge). He saves the day by abusing the daylights out of the big bad bankers, yet also finds time to play surrogate dad. Whatta guy. The DVD transfer looks pretty good, with a little above-average sharpness and fairly strong colors. The biggest problems develop during action sequences; these are more darkly lit and the picture seems to lose some sharpness during some minor artifacting. Since many of those scenes are among the most valid of the film, it is particularly aggravating.

The sound is no better than the VHS edition, and in fact may have less in the way of both imaging and Surround. —*JO*

Movie: ♪▶ **DVD:** ♪♪
Columbia Tristar Home Video (Cat #52379, UPC #043396523791). Widescreen (1.85:1) anamorphic; full frame. Dolby Surround. $28.95. Keepcase. *LANG:* English; French. *SUB:* English; French. *CAP:* English. *FEATURES:* 15 chapter links • Theatrical trailer.
1993 (R) 95m/C Jean-Claude Van Damme, Rosanna Arquette, Kieran Culkin, Tiffany Taubman, Joss Ackland, Ted Levine; **D:** Robert Harmon; **W:** Joe Eszterhas, Leslie Bohem, Randy Feldman; **C:** David Gribble, Doug Milsome, Michael A. Benson; **M:** Mark Isham.

Nude for Satan

According to Marc Morris's liner notes, this vintage Eurosleaze has been "lost" since its disastrous initial release. Given the excellent condition of the print that this DVD was made from, it's easy to believe that the film has seldom been shown. And after watching it, you'll understand why. Unintentional humor runs rampant in this story of two travelers (Calderoni and Harris) who, on a dark and stormy night, are trapped in an Italian castle that's caught in a time warp. Imagine a very poor rip-off of the TV series *Dark Shadows* with a fake giant spider, soft-core lesbian scenes, and a climactic scene of slow-motion nude interpretative dance. —*MM AKA:* Nuda per Satana.

Movie: ♪♪▶ **DVD:** ♪♪♪
Image Entertainment (Cat #ID4620SADVD, UPC #014381462029). Widescreen (2.35:1) letterboxed. Dolby Digital Mono. $24.99. Snapper. *LANG:* Italian. *SUB:* English. *FEATURES:* 13 chapter links • Theatrical trailers • Liner notes by Marc Morris.
1974 82m/C *IT* Rita Calderoni, James Harris, Renato Lupi, Iolanda Mascitti, Luigi Antonio Guerra, Barbara Lay, Augusto Boscardini; **D:** Luigi (Paolo Solvay) Batzella; **W:** Luigi (Paolo Solvay) Batzella; **C:** Antonio Maccoppi; **M:** Alberto Baldan Bembo.

No. 17

Humorous early thriller by the Master was made before *The 39 Steps.* Unsuspecting hobo Ben Tramp (Lion) accidentally discovers a jewel thief's cache. After various digressions—including a surprisingly realistic fist fight—a grand train-bus chase winds things up. Overall, the DVD image is acceptable, though it was made from a print that's been knocked around a bit. Sound is thick and often indistinct. The silent feature, *The Ring* (see review) is a second feature on the disc. —*MM*

Movie: ♪♪♪ **DVD:** ♪♪
Delta/Laserlight (Cat #82 031, UPC #018111997935). Full frame. $14.99. Keepcase. *LANG:* English. *SUB:* Spanish; Japanese; Chinese. *FEATURES:* 16 chapter

links ▪ Introduction by Tony Curtis ▪ Trailer for *I Confess*.
1932 64m/B *GB* Leon M. Lion, Anne Grey, John Stuart, Donald Calthrop; *D:* Alfred Hitchcock; *W:* Alfred Hitchcock; *C:* Jack Cox, Bryan Langley.

Nunsense

Taped performance of the long-running Broadway play is neither fish nor fowl on DVD. It was made for the A&E cable channel and on disc, the image is bright but lacks the depth and texture of film. The story has to do with a fictional revue put on to benefit the Little Sisters of Hoboken who have fallen victim to a terrible bout of food poisoning. The Reverend Mother Superior Sister Mary Regina (McClanahan) is in charge. The target audience is those who have had the benefit of a Catholic education. Many of the jokes and routines are lost on everyone else. —*MM*
Movie: 🐾🐾 *DVD:* 🐾🐾
Image Entertainment (Cat #ID4587DLDVD, UPC #014381458725). Full frame. Dolby Digital Stereo. $24.99. Snapper. *LANG:* English. *FEATURES:* 20 chapter links.
1993 112m/C Rue McClanahan, Christian Anderson, Semina De Laurentis, Christine Toy, Terri White; *D:* Dan Goggin; *W:* David Stern, Dan Goggin; *M:* Michael Rice.

The Nutt House

Identical twins—separated at birth—grow up to be a slimy politician and a nutcase (living up to the family name) with multiple personalities. Naturally, when the two are reunited, it makes for lots of outrageous complications. Original director Scott Spiegel is rumored to have been fired the first day on the set. The DVD is almost as big a waste as the film itself. The picture is never really sharp and there is very often noticeable color bleed. The colors themselves look pretty good, but the picture remains at times very near unwatchable. The sound has very poor separation but does have enough body and crispness. —*JO*
Movie: 🐾➤ *DVD:* 🐾➤
Image Entertainment (Cat #ID5613FMDVD, UPC #014381561326). Full frame. Dolby Surround. $24.95. Snapper. *LANG:* English. *FEATURES:* 11 chapter links.
1992 (PG-13) 90m/C Stephen Kearney, Traci Lords, Amy Yasbeck; *Cameos:* Stella Stevens, Robert Mandan, Catherine Bach; *D:* Adam Rifkin; *W:* Ron Zwang, Scott Spiegel, Sam Raimi; *C:* Bernd Heinl; *M:* Cameron Allan.

The Nutty Professor

Remake of the 1963 Jerry Lewis comedy stars Murphy as Professor Sherman Klump, a severely overweight but bright man whose heft gets in the way of his love life. He takes a swig of his own secret potion and is transformed into the slim and suave Buddy Love. Only the formula isn't perfect, and seems to wear off at the worst possible times. After a string of bad movies, Murphy may have stumbled upon his own formula for a comeback by relinquishing creative control and concentrating on the comedy. Reminiscent of *Coming to America*, Murphy plays eight different roles. The fat and fart jokes are plentiful and so are the laughs. Paramount's DVD is very good, surpassing both the laserdisc and VHS releases. The image is sharp and free of both artifacts and grain. Colors are accurate and extremely vibrant with practically no bleed. Contrast and brightness levels are similarly excellent and the picture at times really jumps off the screen. Blacks are true. The 5.1 sound is utilized to the fullest, with lots of Surround and excellent separation to go along with a deep clean bass that gives the subwoofer a good workout. —*JO*
Movie: 🐾🐾🐾 *DVD:* 🐾🐾🐾➤
Universal Studios Home Video (Cat #20148, UPC #025192014826). Widescreen (1.85:1) anamorphic. Dolby Digital 5.1; Dolby Surround. $24.98. Keepcase. *LANG:* English (DD5.1); French (DS). *SUB:* Spanish. *CAP:* English. *FEATURES:* 16 chapter links ▪ Theatrical trailer ▪ Cast and filmmaker bios ▪ Production notes.
1996 (PG-13) 96m/C Eddie Murphy, Jada Pinkett Smith, James Coburn, Dave Chappelle; *D:* Tom Shadyac; *W:* David Sheffield, Barry W. Blaustein, Steve Oedekerk, Tom Shadyac; *C:* Julio Macat; *M:* David Newman. *AWARDS:* Academy Awards '96: Best Makeup; National Society of Film Critics Awards '96: Best Actor (Murphy); *NOM:* Golden Globe Awards '97: Best Actor—Musical/Comedy (Murphy); MTV Movie Awards '97: Best Male Performance (Murphy), Best Comedic Performance (Murphy).

A Nymphoid Barbarian in Dinosaur Hell

Typically low-budget, unembarrassed schlock from Troma revolves around a post-apocalyptic babe in a fur bikini.
Movie: 🐾 *DVD:* NYR
Troma Team Video (Cat #10268). Dolby Digital Stereo. $24.95. Keepcase. *LANG:* English. *FEATURES:* Commentary: director Brett Piper ▪ Many Tromatic extras.
1994 90m/C Linda Corwin, Paul Guzzi; *D:* Bret Piper; *W:* Bret Piper.

The Object of Beauty

Two Americans (Malkovich and MacDowell) trapped in Europe by their love of pleasure and their lack of money, bicker over whether to sell their one object of value—a tiny Henry Moore sculpture. When it disappears, their relationship is challenged. Excellent acting and telling direction force an examination of one's own values.
Movie: 🐾🐾🐾 *DVD:* NYR
Pioneer Entertainment (Cat #DVD68948). Full frame. Dolby Digital Surround Stereo. $24.98. Keepcase. *FEATURES:* Trailer.
1991 (R) 105m/C Andie MacDowell, John Malkovich, Joss Ackland, Lolita (David) Davidovich, Peter Riegert, Bill Paterson, Rudi Davies, Ricci Harnett; *D:* Michael Lindsay-Hogg; *W:* Michael Lindsay-Hogg; *C:* David Watkin; *M:* Tom Bahler.

Object of Obsession

One wrong phone call propels divorcee Margaret (Anderson) into an affair with Brad (Valentine) that leads to kinky psycho/sexual games, a little kidnapping, bondage, etc. Video veteran Hippolyte handles the familiar subject matter with a bit more seriousness than usual. The full-frame, no-frills DVD is essentially identical to VHS tape with mostly dark interiors and unremarkable sound. —*MM*
Movie: 🐾➤ *DVD:* 🐾➤
Image Entertainment (Cat #ID4660APDVD, UPC #014381466027). Full frame. Dolby Digital Mono. $24.99. Snapper. *LANG:* English. *FEATURES:* 19 chapter links.
1995 (R) 91m/C Erika Anderson, Scott Valentine; *D:* Alexander Gregory (Gregory Dark) Hippolyte; *W:* Brad Marlowe; *C:* Wally Pfister.

An Occasional Hell

Ex-cop turned writer and college professor Ernest DeWalt (Berenger) investigates the murder of a colleague at the behest of the fetching widow Elizabeth (Golino) and then learns that the lady is the prime suspect. Atmospherically filmed in South Carolina and based on the novel by Silvis who wrote the screenplay. The DVD is graced with an unusually sharp image and sound, but, despite the claims of the box copy, it does not even contain chapter links. The interesting psychological thriller deserves better. —*MM*
Movie: 🐾🐾➤ *DVD:* 🐾🐾🐾
Trimark Home Video (Cat #7049D, UPC #03139870433). Full frame. Dolby Stereo. $34.99. Keepcase. *LANG:* English. *FEATURES:* Theatrical trailer. Title is available for sale only as part of "Best of Action" 4-pack.
1996 (R) 93m/C Tom Berenger, Valeria Golino, Kari Wuhrer, Robert Davi, Stephen Lang, Richard Edson, Geoffrey Lewis; *D:* Salome Breziner; *W:* Randall Silvis; *C:* Mauro Fiore; *M:* Anton Sanko.

October Sky

It would be pointless to list the flaws in this "based on a true story" exercise in nostalgia because in the end, it overcomes all of them. Suffice it to say that this is the finest film ever made about a science-fair project. It's the story of West Virginia high school student Homer Hickam Jr. (Gyllenhaal) who becomes fascinated with rocketry after the Soviets launch Sputnik in the fall of 1957. He and three friends conduct a series of experiments with homemade rockets. They do it despite Homer's father's (Cooper) strong objections and with the support of their teacher Miss Riley (Dern). The conflicts between young and old, coal miners and management, tradition and change are laid out in unambiguous terms, but somehow the conclusion

is emotionally honest and moving. The DVD contains all the right extras, beginning with the two screen ratios. The image transfer is flawless. The Surround soundtrack is put to full use in the rocket scenes. The film was only a modest success in its theatrical release. It will find an appreciative and much larger audience on disc and tape. —*MM*
Movie: ♪♪♪ **DVD:** ♪♪♪
Universal Studios Home Video (Cat #20557, UPC #025192055720). Full frame; widescreen (2.35:1) letterboxed. Dolby Digital 5.1 Surround Stereo; Dolby Surround Stereo. $29.98. Keepcase. *LANG:* English; French. *CAP:* English. *FEATURES:* 18 chapter links • "Making of" featurette • Production notes • Cast and crew thumbnail biographies • Theatrical trailer • Universal weblinks.
1999 (PG) 108m/C Jake Gyllenhaal, Chris Cooper, Laura Dern, Chris Owen, William Lee Scott, Chad Lindberg, Natalie Canerday, Scott Miles, Randy Stripling, Chris Ellis; *D:* Joe Johnston; *W:* Lewis Colick; *C:* Paul Murphy; *M:* Mark Isham. *AWARDS: NOM:* Writers Guild of America '99: Best Adapted Screenplay.

Odd Man Out

An Irish revolutionary (Mason) is injured during a robbery attempt. Suffering from gunshot wounds and closely pursued by the police, he must rely on the help of others who could betray him at any moment. A gripping tale of suspense and intrigue that will keep the proverbial seat's edge warm until the final credits. Adapted from F. L. Green's novel, previously filmed as *The Last Man*. The DVD transfer is absolutely pristine, with solid and crisp colors and well-defined blacks. The mono soundtrack is also crisp and clear, with no discernable lapses in dialogue or other sound effects (although some louder sounds tend to become a bit muddied). — *MJT* **AKA:** Gang War.
Movie: ♪♪♪▶ **DVD:** ♪♪♪
Image Entertainment (Cat #ID4539JFDVD, UPC #014381453928). Full frame. Dolby Digital Mono. $24.99. Snapper. *LANG:* English. *FEATURES:* 20 chapter links.
1947 111m/B *GB* James Mason, Robert Newton, Dan O'Herlihy, Kathleen Ryan, Cyril Cusack; *D:* Carol Reed; *W:* F.L. Green, R.C. Sherriff; *C:* Robert Krasker; *M:* William Alwyn. *AWARDS:* British Academy Awards '47: Best Film; *NOM:* Academy Awards '47: Best Film Editing.

The Odessa File

In 1963, German journalist Peter Miller (Voight) reads a Holocaust survivor's diary and discovers the existence of a conspiracy of SS officers, including the sadistic Capt. Roschmann (Schell). Following the lead of the source material, Frederick Forsyth's fact-based novel, veteran director Neame sacrifices high voltage action for a fairly somber tone. He treats the Holocaust seriously as a motivating element and does nothing to exploit it. Com-

pared to other '70s films, this one makes an unusually sharp transition to DVD. Though the picture was largely shot on location, it displays few visual flaws. The sound, including a score by Andrew Lloyd Webber, is very good. —*MM*
Movie: ♪♪♪ **DVD:** ♪♪♪
Columbia Tristar Home Video (Cat #03299, UPC #043396032996). Widescreen (2.35:1); full frame. Dolby Digital Mono. $24.95. Keepcase. *LANG:* English; Spanish. *SUB:* English; Spanish. *CAP:* English. *FEATURES:* 28 chapter links • Theatrical trailers • Cast and crew thumbnail biographies.
1974 (PG) 128m/C *GB GE* Jon Voight, Mary Tamm, Maximilian Schell, Maria Schell, Derek Jacobi, Peter Jeffrey, Klaus Lowitsch, Kurt Meisel, Hannes Meesember, Garfield Morgan, Shmuel Rodensku, Ernst Schroder, Noel Willman, Hans Canineberg, Towje Kleiner, Gunnar Moiler; *D:* Ronald Neame; *W:* Kenneth Ross, George Markstein; *C:* Oswald Morris; *M:* Andrew Lloyd Webber.

Of Mice and Men

Powerful adaptation of Steinbeck tragedy about the friendship between George (Meredith) and Lenny (Chaney), two itinerant ranch hands during the Great Depression. Chaney is fine as the mentally retarded giant, though he gets too overwrought in his "tell about the rabbits" scenes. In the more quiet role, Meredith is excellent, and so is cowboy star Bob Steele as the villainous Curley. On DVD, the image transfer is so clear that the shadows of the camera and cameraman are clearly visible in one early shot. Some might prefer a stereo remix for Aaron Copland's score, but this monoaural version sounds fine and it matches the understated black-and-white photography. Though this film, based on a stage play, is not as "cinematic" as Gary Sinise's 1992 version, it stands up well. —*MM*
Movie: ♪♪♪▶ **DVD:** ♪♪♪
Image Entertainment (Cat #ID4571CODVD, UPC #014381457124). Full frame. Uncompressed PCM. $24.98. Snapper. *LANG:* English. *FEATURES:* 28 chapter links.
1939 107m/C Lon Chaney Jr., Burgess Meredith, Betty Field, Bob Steele, Noah Beery Jr., Charles Bickford; *D:* Lewis Milestone; *W:* Eugene Solow; *C:* Norbert Brodine; *M:* Aaron Copland. *AWARDS: NOM:* Academy Awards '39: Best Picture, Best Sound, Best Original Score.

Office Space

Cartoon bigwig Mike Judge tries his hand at live action in a so-so satire of white collar corporate drudgery. Peter (Livingston) is a cubicle drone at a software company. His terminally laid-back bosses bug him because he can't seem to get the right coversheets on his TPS reports and a couple of consultants are about to downsize him when a hypnosis episode opens his eyes and he just doesn't care anymore. His no-work ethic is mistaken for "middle-

management potential," and so while his two pals Michael (Herman) and Samir (Naidu) are laid off, he's promoted. Root as the disgruntled and disturbed office nerd steals the film. Jennifer Aniston has such a tiny role that she barely makes an impression. This kind of comedy, with its roots in Judge's animated short films, really doesn't gain much on DVD. The image is bright and clear throughout; only the Dolby sound is superior to VHS tape and that's not really important, either. —*MM*
Movie: ♪♪▶ **DVD:** ♪♪▶
Twentieth Century Fox Home Entertainment (Cat #4111845, UPC #08616211 8456). Widescreen (1.85:1) letterboxed. Dolby 5.1 Surround; Dolby Surround Stereo. $29.98. Keepcase. *LANG:* English; French (DSS). *SUB:* English; Spanish. *FEATURES:* 28 chapter links • Theatrical trailer.
1998 (R) 89m/C Mike Judge, Ron Livingston, Jennifer Aniston, David Herman, Ajay Naidu, Gary Cole, Diedrich Bader, Stephen Root, Richard Riehle; *D:* Mike Judge; *W:* Mike Judge; *C:* Tim Suhrstedt; *M:* John Frizzell.

Oklahoma

Jones's film debut is a must-see for musical fans. A cowboy and country girl fall in love, but she is tormented by another unwelcomed suitor. At over two hours, cuteness wears thin for some. Actually filmed in Arizona. Adapted from Rodgers and Hammerstein's Broadway hit with original score; choreography by Agnes de Mille. The DVD is pretty sharp, with little grain, and nothing noticeable as far as artifacts. Colors are generally excellent with good fleshtones and sometimes very vibrant colors. Blacks are true and grainless. The contrast seems fine for the brighter colors, but lighter shades are a touch washed-out. Brightness levels are consistent. The 5.1 tracks sound good and have very good overall fidelity, though failing to make much use of the Surround. —*JO*
Movie: ♪♪♪▶ **DVD:** ♪♪♪
20th Century Fox (Cat #110865, UPC #086162108655). Widescreen (2.2:1) letterboxed. Dolby Digital 5.1; Stereo. $29.95. Keepcase. *LANG:* English. *SUB:* English; Spanish. *CAP:* English. *FEATURES:* 27 chapter links • Theatrical trailer.
1955 (G) 145m/C Gordon MacRae, Shirley Jones, Rod Steiger, Gloria Grahame, Eddie Albert, Charlotte Greenwood, James Whitmore, Gene Nelson, Barbara Lawrence, Jay C. Flippen; *D:* Fred Zinnemann; *W:* Sonya Levien, William Ludwig; *C:* Robert L. Surtees; *M:* Richard Rodgers, Oscar Hammerstein. *AWARDS:* Academy Awards '55: Best Sound, Scoring of a Musical; *NOM:* Academy Awards '55: Best Color Cinematography, Best Film Editing.

The Old Dark House

Atmospheric horror film, with more than a touch of comedy is well-directed by Whale. In an old haunted house live the bizarre Femm family: the 102-year-old patriarch,

an atheist son, a religious fanatic daughter, and a crazed pyromanic son, all watched over by the mute, scarred, and psychotic butler (Karloff's first starring role). Into this strange group wander five unsuspecting, stranded travelers who set all sorts of dastardly plots in motion. Based on the novel *Benighted* by J.B. Priestley. The DVD tries hard to make up for inadequacies in the film preprint, and though the image is far from perfect, it is very viewable. There is some ghosting around bright areas and overall the picture is not that sharp. Graytones are generally pretty good, and contrast and brightness give the film as much punch as most from the era. The mono sound is a little tinny and there is quite a bit of background noise but nothing extreme enough to warrant avoidance of this DVD. —*JO*
Movie: ♫♫♫ **DVD:** ♫♫♫
Image Entertainment (Cat #K113DVD, UPC #738329011321). Full frame. Mono. $29.99. Snapper. *LANG:* English. *FEATURES:* 22 chapter links ⚫ Commentary: Gloria Stuart ⚫ Commentary: James Curtis ⚫ Curtis Harrington interview ⚫ Stills gallery.
1932 71m/B Boris Karloff, Melvyn Douglas, Charles Laughton, Gloria Stuart, Ernest Thesiger, Raymond Massey, Lillian Bond, Eva Moore, Brember Wills, John Dudgeon; *D:* James Whale; *W:* Benn W. Levy, R.C. Sherriff; *C:* Arthur Edeson.

Oliver!

In a splendid big-budget musical adaptation of Dickens's *Oliver Twist*, an innocent young orphan is dragged into a life of crime when he is befriended by a gang of pickpockets. Like so many other musicals brought out on DVD, *Oliver* looks the best it ever has, benefitting from both a much sharper picture and far stronger colors, which are accurate as well. Despite the predominant earthtone color scheme, which sometimes results in grain and color bleed on a DVD, the picture remains crisp. The soundtrack has been given a new mix with more separation, better imaging, and a little more body. —*JO*
Movie: ♫♫♫▶ **DVD:** ♫♫♫▶
Columbia Tristar Home Video (Cat #02137, UPC #043396021372). Widescreen (2.35:1) anamorphic. Dolby Digital 5.1; Dolby Surround. NSL. Keepcase. *LANG:* English; French. *SUB:* English; French. *CAP:* English. *FEATURES:* 16 chapter links ⚫ "Making of" featurette ⚫ Photo gallery.
1968 (G) 145m/C *GB* Mark Lester, Jack Wild, Ron Moody, Shani Wallis, Oliver Reed, Hugh Griffith; *D:* Carol Reed; *W:* Vernon Harris; *C:* Oswald Morris; *M:* Lionel Bart. *AWARDS:* Academy Awards '68: Best Adapted Score, Best Art Direction/Set Decoration, Best Director (Reed), Best Picture, Best Sound; Golden Globe Awards '69: Best Actor—Musical/Comedy (Moody), Best Film—Musical/Comedy; *NOM:* Academy Awards '68: Best Actor (Moody), Best Adapted Screenplay, Best Cinematography, Best Costume Design, Best Film Editing, Best Supporting Actor (Wild).

Oliver Twist

David Lean's second adaptation of Dickens—the first is *Great Expectations* from 1946—is another gem. This time out though, Lean takes a more expressionistic approach to the material, in some ways similar to *The Third Man*, made a year later. As the title character, young John Howard Davies, eight at the time, is perhaps too angelic-looking for today's audiences, particularly when compared to the scruffy Artful Dodger (Newley). Though Alec Guinness's Fagin was criticized as anti-Semitic in 1948 (and caused 12 minutes of the film to be censored for U.S. audiences in 1951), he is really a sympathetic character and Guinness plays him beautifully. On DVD, Guy Green's black-and-white photography is re-created in its full depth and texture. From the opening storm to the busy streets of London to the grand finale on the rooftops, the images are clear, even in complex multi-layered night scenes created on John Bryan's sets. Though some might see the monaural sound as a problem, it's fine. Along with *Great Expectations*, these are the two best screen adaptations of arguably Dickens's two best novels. —*MM*
Movie: ♫♫♫▶ **DVD:** ♫♫♫♫
Criterion Collection (Cat #32, UPC #037429128121). Full frame. Dolby Digital Mono. $39.95. Keepcase. *LANG:* English. *CAP:* English. *FEATURES:* 28 chapters ⚫ Interactive menu ⚫ Theatrical trailer.
1948 116m/C *GB* Robert Newton, John Howard Davies, Alec Guinness, Francis L. Sullivan, Anthony Newley, Kay Walsh, Diana Dors, Henry Stephenson; *D:* David Lean; *W:* David Lean; *C:* Guy Green; *M:* Arnold Bax.

On Approval

Brilliant British comedy revolves around two wealthy women (Lillie and Withers) who take their boyfriends (Brook and Culver) to a remote Scottish island for a "trial" relationship. Nothing happens, of course, but the situation was considered scandalously shocking in the 1890 setting. The sprightly dialogue, from Frederick Lonsdale's play, rivals Noel Coward. Producer-director-screenwriter Brook handles all of his roles with impeccable style that's matched by Cecil Beaton's elegant costumes. The DVD is far from perfect with many surface scratches and an almost continuous hiss on the soundtrack, but those are minor flaws compared to the content here. This one's a delight. —*MM*
Movie: ♫♫♫▶ **DVD:** ♫♫
Image Entertainment (Cat #ID5663DSDVD, UPC #014381566321). Full frame. Dolby Digital Mono. $24.99. Snapper. *LANG:* English. *FEATURES:* 12 chapter links ⚫ Liner notes by E.V.H. Emmett.
1944 80m/B *GB* Clive Brook, Beatrice Lillie, Googie Withers, Roland Culver, O.B. Clarence, Lawrence Hanray, Elliot Mason, Hay Petrie, Marjorie Munks, Molly Munks; *D:* Clive Brook; *W:* Terence Young, Clive

Brook; *C:* Claude Friese-Greene; *M:* William Alwyn.

On Deadly Ground

Seagal nearly destroys Alaska in an effort to save it in this inane, preachy story of an oilrig roughneck out to protect the landscape from an evil oil company's drilling habits. Directorial debut for Seagal lumbers from scene to scene. Violence is expected, as is silly dialogue—just try to keep from laughing when stoney-faced Steven intones "What does it take to change the essence of man?" A better script, for one. This DVD is a good one, but really, who cares? The picture is super sharp and grainless whether extremely bright or very dark. Colors are accurate and as vibrant as they could be with very little bleed. Blacks are true, contrast is punchy, and the brightness is always up where it should be. The 5.1 sound has a lot of guts to it when called upon, and the Surround effects, though sparser than in some action films, come crashing in on many occasions. —*JO*
Movie: woof **DVD:** ♫♫♫▶
Warner Home Video, Inc. (Cat #13227, UPC #085391322726). Widescreen (1.85:1) letterboxed; full frame. Dolby Digital 5.1; Dolby Surround. $19.98. Snapper. *LANG:* English (DD5.1); French (DS). *SUB:* English; French. *CAP:* English. *FEATURES:* 34 chapter links.
1994 (R) 102m/C Steven Seagal, Michael Caine, Joan Chen, John C. McGinley, Billy Bob Thornton, R. Lee Ermey; *D:* Steven Seagal; *W:* Ed Horowitz; *C:* Ric Waite; *M:* Basil Poledouris. *AWARDS:* Golden Raspberry Awards '94: Worst Director (Seagal); *NOM:* Golden Raspberry Awards '94: Worst Picture.

On Golden Pond

Henry Fonda won his first (and long overdue) Oscar for his final screen appearance as the curmudgeonly patriarch of the Thayer family. He and his wife (Hepburn) have reluctantly agreed to look after a young boy while at their summer home in Maine. Through his gradually affectionate relationship with the boy, Fonda learns to allay his fears of mortality and comes to an understanding with his estranged daughter (Jane Fonda). As I remember it, the soft focus of the DVD comes from the original material. In both image and sound, the DVD re-creates the theatrical version faithfully. —*MM*
Movie: ♫♫♫▶ **DVD:** ♫♫♫
Artisan Entertainment (Cat #60479). Widescreen (1.85:1) letterboxed. Dolby Digital Stereo. $24.98. Snapper. *LANG:* English. *SUB:* Spanish. *CAP:* English. *FEATURES:* Trailer ⚫ Production notes ⚫ Commentary: Mark Rydell ⚫ Documentary "Loving Against Time" ⚫ Cast and crew thumbnail bios.
1981 (PG) 109m/C Henry Fonda, Jane Fonda, Katharine Hepburn, Dabney Coleman, Doug McKeon, William Lanteau; *D:* Mark Rydell; *W:* Ernest Thompson; *C:* Billy

Williams; *M:* Dave Grusin. *AWARDS:* Academy Awards '81: Best Actor (Fonda), Best Actress (Hepburn), Best Adapted Screenplay; British Academy Awards '82: Best Actress (Hepburn); Golden Globe Awards '82: Best Actor—Drama (Fonda), Best Film—Drama, Best Screenplay; National Board of Review Awards '81: Best Actor (Fonda); Writers Guild of America '81: Best Adapted Screenplay; *NOM:* Academy Awards '81: Best Cinematography, Best Director (Rydell), Best Film Editing, Best Picture, Best Sound, Best Supporting Actress (Fonda), Best Original Score.

On the Ropes

Filmmakers Burstein and Morgen attempt to do with boxing what the producers of *Hoop Dreams* did with basketball, but on a smaller scale. Their subject is trainer Harry Keitt, who runs the New Bud-Stuy Boxing Center, where he works with three young would-be fighters: George Walton, Noel Santiago, and a woman, Tyrene Manson. They face various problems and are working toward the 1997 Golden Gloves Tournament. Because the documentary was made on many grim locations, it has an intense naturalistic look that is not improved by DVD—and shouldn't be. The disc also contains a five-minute epilogue added since the film was a hit on the festival circuit. —*MM*
Movie: ♪♪♪✒ **DVD:** ♪♪♪
WinStar Home Entertainment (Cat #FLV5208, UPC #720917520827). Full frame. $24.98. Keepcase. *LANG:* English. *FEATURES:* 8 chapter links • Production credits • Theatrical trailer • Commentary: Burstein, Morgen, Shapiro • 5-minute epilogue • Cast and crew thumbnail biographies.
1999 90m/C Harry Keitt, Tyrene Manson, George Walton, Noel Santiago; *D:* Manette Burstein, Brett Morgen; *C:* Brett Morgen; *M:* Theodore Shapiro.

Once a Thief

A fun and action-packed TV movie finds adopted children Li Ann (Holt) and Mac (Sergei) being raised along with natural son Michael (Wong) by Hong Kong crime head Tang (Ito) and trained as daring professional thieves. A falling out finds Li Ann in Vancouver, involved with ex-cop Victor (Lea), and both of them working for a covert crime-fighting agency headed by a very tough director (Dale). Then Mac is forced to join the duo in an elaborate heist to bring down Michael and his family's criminal empire. This is one of the better-looking Tai Seng DVDs. The picture is sharp and grainless with the exception of long detailed shots. Colors are accurate, vibrant, and bleedless. Blacks, with the exception of a couple of darker sequences, are free of grain and true. Contrast is excellent and brightness levels are good but maybe a touch too bright. The 5.1 sound feels more like just stereo but has some body and dynamics to it. It

does have some high-end distortion, but nothing to worry about. —*JO*
Movie: ♪♪♪ **DVD:** ♪♪♪
Tai Seng Video Marketing (Cat #DVD020, UPC #601643191744). Full frame. Dolby Digital 5.1. $49.95. Keepcase. *LANG:* Mandarin; Chinese. *SUB:* English. *FEATURES:* 9 chapter links.
1996 (R) 101m/C Ivan Sergei, Sandrine Holt, Nicholas Lea, Michael Wong, Robert Ito, Jennifer Dale, Alan Scarfe; *D:* John Woo; *W:* Glenn Davis, William Laurin; *C:* Bill Wong; *M:* Amin Bhatia.

Once Upon a Time in China

Historical martial-arts epic is set during the formation of China as a nation. *AKA:* Wong Fei-hung.
Movie: ♪♪♪ **DVD:** NYR
Tai Seng Video Marketing (Cat #19614). $49.95. Keepcase. *LANG:* Cantonese. *SUB:* Bahasia (Malaysian); Cantonese; English; Japanese; Korean; Spanish. *FEATURES:* Trailer • Production notes.
1991 128m/C *HK* Jet Li, Yuen Biao, Jacky Cheung, Rosamund Kwan, Kent Cheng; *D:* Tsui Hark; *W:* Tsui Hark; *C:* Arthur Wong, David Chung; *M:* James Wong.

Once Upon a Time in China II

Jet Li returns as Wong Fey Hung, who's up against the White Lotus Society. The story is not as complex as the first, but the action scenes are strong. The second film in the series looks a little better on DVD than the first did, and has colors near theatrical accuracy and a fairly sharp image with little grain or artifacts. Contrast is a little low, but all in all this is far above the usual Tai Seng DVD release. —*JO AKA:* Wong Fei-hung Ji Yi: Naam Yi Dong Ji Keung.
Movie: ♪♪♪ **DVD:** ♪♪✒
Tai Seng Video Marketing (Cat #MS DVD02998, UPC #489501700299). Full frame. Dolby Digital 5.1. $49.95. Keepcase. *LANG:* Cantonese; Mandarin. *SUB:* English; Spanish; Japanese; Simplified Chinese; Bahasa; Korean. *FEATURES:* 9 chapter links • Theatrical trailer.
1992 (R) 118m/C *HK* Jet Li, Rosamund Kwan, Mok Siu Chung, Xiong Xin Xin, John Chiang, Zhang Tie Lin, Yen Chi Tan; *D:* Tsui Hark; *W:* Tsui Hark; *C:* Wong Ngok Tai; *M:* Richard Yuen.

Once Upon a Time in China III

The third installment of the popular series focuses on Chinese political history, but that doesn't mean that Jet Li doesn't shine in the martial arts scenes. This Tai Seng DVD release has the usual seemingly randomly placed chapter stops, but the image quality is actually very good. The picture is sharp and colors are more vibrant than any other Tai Seng release that I've seen. Contrast and brightness levels are consistent and comfortable.

The 5.1 sound is also the best so far from Tai Seng, and seems to have a more natural mix, which makes use of the Surround channels more often and realistically than their other releases. —*JO AKA:* Wong Fei-hung Tsi Sam: Siwong Tsangba.
Movie: ♪♪♪ **DVD:** ♪♪♪✒
Tai Seng Video Marketing (Cat #MD DVD03098, UPC #489501700305). Full frame. Dolby Digital 5.1. $49.95. Keepcase. *LANG:* Cantonese; Mandarin. *SUB:* English; Spanish; Japanese; Simplified Chinese; Bahasa; Korean. *FEATURES:* 9 chapter links • Theatrical trailer.
1993 (R) 105m/C *HK* Jet Li, Rosamund Kwan, Mok Siu Chung, Xiong Xin Xin, Shun Lau; *D:* Tsui Hark; *W:* Tsui Hark; *C:* Wai Keung Lau; *M:* Wai Lap Wu.

Once Upon a Time . . . When We Were Colored

Actor Reid makes a fine directorial debut with the story of a black youngster growing up parentless in '50s Mississippi. His family faces the usual troubles of the time, including poor wages and white bigotry, but manages to provide a positive and loving home life for him. The adaptation of Clifton Taulbert's autobiographical book is nostalgic, sensitive, and heartwarming.
Movie: ♪♪♪ **DVD:** NYR
Republic Pictures Home Video (Cat #39506). Widescreen (1.85:1) letterboxed. Dolby Digital Stereo. $24.98. Keepcase. *FEATURES:* Trailer.
1995 (PG) 112m/C Al Freeman Jr., Paula Kelly, Phylicia Rashad, Polly Bergen, Richard Roundtree, Charles Taylor, Willie Norwood Jr., Damon Hines, Leon; *D:* Tim Reid; *W:* Paul Cooper; *C:* Johnny Simmons; *M:* Steve Tyrell; *Nar:* Phill Lewis.

One Flew Over the Cuckoo's Nest

To my mind, this adaptation of Ken Kesey's brilliant novel is not as successful as *Cool Hand Luke*, which tells an essentially identical story with more originality. That little quibble aside, Jack Nicholson is superb as McMurtry, the small-time crook who thinks he's got it made in a mental hospital until he realizes that Nurse Ratchet (Fletcher) is really in charge of things. This has never been a particularly sharp film visually and the DVD reflects that, with an often grainy image and unflattering light. Sound is equally unspectacular. —*MM*
Movie: ♪♪♪✒ **DVD:** ♪♪♪
Warner Home Video, Inc. (Cat #36222). Widescreen (1.85:1) letterboxed; full frame. Dolby Digital Stereo. $24.98. Snapper. *LANG:* English; French. *SUB:* English; French; Spanish. *CAP:* English. *FEATURES:* 33 chapter links • Production notes.
1975 (R) 129m/C Jack Nicholson, Brad Dourif, Louise Fletcher, Will Sampson, William Redfield, Danny DeVito, Christopher Lloyd, Scatman Crothers, Vincent

Schiavelli, Michael Berryman, Peter Brocco, Louisa Moritz; **D:** Milos Forman; **W:** Ken Kesey, Bo Goldman; **C:** Haskell Wexler, Bill Butler, William A. Fraker; **M:** Jack Nitzsche. *AWARDS:* Academy Awards '75: Best Actor (Nicholson), Best Actress (Fletcher), Best Adapted Screenplay, Best Director (Forman), Best Picture; American Film Institute (AFI) '98: Top 100; British Academy Awards '76: Best Actor (Nicholson), Best Actress (Fletcher), Best Director (Forman), Best Film, Best Supporting Actor (Dourif); Directors Guild of America Awards '75: Best Director (Forman); Golden Globe Awards '76: Best Actor—Drama (Nicholson), Best Actress—Drama (Fletcher), Best Director (Forman), Best Film—Drama, Best Screenplay; National Board of Review Awards '75: Best Actor (Nicholson), National Film Registry '93; New York Film Critics Awards '75: Best Actor (Nicholson); National Society of Film Critics Awards '75: Best Actor (Nicholson); Writers Guild of America '75: Best Adapted Screenplay; *NOM:* Academy Awards '75: Best Cinematography, Best Film Editing, Best Supporting Actor (Dourif), Best Original Score.

101 Dalmatians

This crowd-pleaser is one of the highest grossing animated features in the history of Hollywood and it's easy to see why. The stylized animation is something of a departure from the familiar Disney style but it fits the fast-moving story perfectly and it captures animal movements accurately. The characters, both animal and human, have strong personalities, none more so than Cruella De Vil, one of the studio's most memorable villains. If there are any errors on the DVD, I couldn't spot them. The sound is superior. —MM
Movie: 🐾🐾🐾🖈 **DVD:** 🐾🐾🐾🖈
Buena Vista Home Entertainment (Cat #17973, UPC #717951003973). Full frame. THX Dolby Digital Surround Stereo. $39.99. Keepcase. *LANG:* English; French; Spanish. *CAP:* English. *FEATURES:* 17 chapter links.
1961 (G) 79m/C D: Clyde Geronimi, Wolfgang Reitherman, Hamilton Luske; **M:** George Bruns; **V:** Rod Taylor, Betty Lou Gerson, Lisa Davis, Ben Wright, Frederick Worlock, J. Pat O'Malley.

101 Dalmatians

The live-action version of the 1961 animated feature takes a relatively sophisticated approach to the same plot, and is surprisingly successful. First, casting Glenn Close as Cruella De Vil is a masterstroke. On DVD, her outrageous costumes and makeup get their full due. In general, the image is excellent in close-ups, less so in medium and long shots. It suffers more seriously in tracking shots that follow two Dalmatians dashing across a snowy field. Throughout, the sound is excellent and that's particularly important because, unlike their animated counterparts, these dogs (and other animals) can-

not speak. In the second half, much of the story is told visually and through natural sounds and music. (Cats will become nervous with all of the barking in some scenes.) The youngest videophiles may need help understanding what's going on, but most kids will be caught up in the puppies' fate. The VideoHound certainly was. —MM
Movie: 🐾🐾🐾 **DVD:** 🐾🐾🖈
Buena Vista Home Entertainment (Cat #14253, UPC #717951000347). Widescreen (2.35:1) letterboxed. Dolby Digital Stereo. $29.99. Keepcase. *LANG:* English; French; Spanish. *CAP:* English. *FEATURES:* 21 chapter links ▪ Theatrical trailer.
1996 (G) 103m/C Glenn Close, Jeff Daniels, Joely Richardson, Joan Plowright, Hugh Laurie, Mark Williams; **D:** Stephen Herek; **W:** John Hughes; **C:** Adrian Biddle; **M:** Michael Kamen. *AWARDS: NOM:* Golden Globe Awards '97: Best Actress—Musical/Comedy (Close).

One Hundred and One Nights

Simon Cinema (Piccoli) is a centenarian producer-director who sometimes believes that he's also the famous stars he worked with. Or did he just dream that he worked with them? To improve his memory, he hires young film student Camille Miralis (Gayet) to come to his house and talk to him and his Italian friend (Mastroianni) about his rich and imaginative past. That loose premise is an excuse for a long series of clips, re-enactments of famous moments, and cameo appearances, including a radiant and stunning Fanny Ardant. Fellini fans are the target audience here. The DVD image is very good, with no surface scratches and a generally pale image that appears to come from the original. Sound is fine. —MM *AKA:* Les Cent et Une Nuits de Simon Cinema.
Movie: 🐾🐾🐾 **DVD:** 🐾🐾🐾
WinStar Home Entertainment (Cat #FLV 5194, UPC #72091751925). Widescreen letterboxed. $29.98. Keepcase. *LANG:* French. *SUB:* English. *FEATURES:* 8 chapter links ▪ Filmographies and awards ▪ Production credits ▪ Trailers ▪ Weblink.
1994 101m/C Michel Piccoli, Julie Gayet, Henri Garcin, Mathieu Demy, Emmanuel Salinger, Anouk Aimee, Fanny Ardant, Jean-Paul Belmondo, Sandrine Bonnaire, Alain Delon, Catherine Deneuve, Robert De Niro, Gerard Depardieu, Harrison Ford, Gina Lollobrigida, Jeanne Moreau, Hanna Schygulla; **D:** Agnes Varda; **W:** Agnes Varda; **C:** Eric Gautier.

One Magic Christmas

All the elements are in place for a family Christmas classic in the tradition of *It's a Wonderful Life,* but despite the best of intentions, and a terrific cast, the magic of this Christmas miracle comes up just short. Writer Thomas Meehan, perhaps best known for his work with Mel Brooks on *Space Balls* and *To Be or Not to Be,* delivers an unrelenting and depressing

set-up—a family tossed from their home on the eve of Christmas; a father murdered in the heat of a bank hold-up; children drown in an icy river; and worst of all, Mary Steenburgen *(Melvin and Howard)* not willing to get into the Christmas spirit. Through the help and guidance of Gideon, the Christmas Angel, played by Harry Dean Stanton *(Alien),* all is set right by the final credits. Besides the consumer being given the choice of widescreen or full-frame versions for viewing, there is little else on hand to mark this as a DVD release versus the longstanding videocassette format. —RT
Movie: 🐾🐾🖈 **DVD:** 🐾🐾🖈
Anchor Bay (Cat #10928, UPC #013131092899). Widescreen; full frame. AC3 - 5.1 Dolby Surround; AC3 - 2 Channel. $24.98. Keepcase. *LANG:* English. *FEATURES:* 21 chapter links.
1985 (G) 88m/C Mary Steenburgen, Harry Dean Stanton, Gary Basaraba, Michelle Meyrink, Arthur Hill, Elisabeth Harnois, Robbie Magwood; **D:** Phillip Borsos; **W:** Thomas Meehan; **C:** Frank Tidy; **M:** Michael Conway Baker.

One Man's Justice

Army drill sergeant John North (Bosworth) heads for the streets of Venice, CA, to get the drug-dealing gun-running scum who killed his wife and daughter. Throw in a streetwise 10-year-old and all the usual suspects are in place.
Movie: 🐾🐾🖈 **DVD:** NYR
Artisan Entertainment (Cat #10515). $24.98.
1995 (R) 100m/C Brian Bosworth, Bruce Payne, Jeff Kober, DeJuan Guy, Hammer; **D:** Kurt Wimmer; **W:** Steven Selling; **C:** Jurgen Baum, John Huneck; **M:** Anthony Marinelli.

One Night Stand

Max (Snipes) is a commercial director in New York on business. While visiting his friend Charlie (Downey), a choreographer dying of AIDS, he meets willowy beauty Karen (Kinski). This chance meeting leads to, you guessed it, a one night stand. When Max returns home to L.A., he realizes how empty and stale his life is. One year later, he and wife Mimi (Wen) return to visit the quickly fading Charlie. They meet Charlie's brother Vernon (McLachlan) and his wife...Karen. Good performances (especially by Downey) and characterization make this more than a morality play about the ramifications of a sexual fling. Although paid for his original material, Joe Eszterhas didn't take any writing credit after Figgis totally rewrote the script. The soundtrack and picture on this disc are both quite exceptional. Both are crisp and clear. The 5.1 Dolby mix especially stands out. The Figgis commentary too, is also an enjoyable bonus. —MJT
Movie: 🐾🐾🐾 **DVD:** 🐾🐾🐾🖈
New Line Home Video (Cat #N4655, UPC #794043465529). Widescreen (1.85:1)

letterboxed; full frame. Dolby Digital 5.1 Surround Sound. $24.98. Snapper. *LANG:* English; French. *SUB:* English; French; Spanish. *FEATURES:* 18 chapter links • Commentary: director Mike Figgis • Isolated musical score • Cast filmographies and biographies • Theatrical trailer. **1997 (R) 103m/C** Mike Figgis, Wesley Snipes, Nastassia Kinski, Ming Na, Robert Downey Jr., Kyle MacLachlan, Glenn Plummer, Amanda Donohoe, Thomas Haden Church, Julian Sands, John Ratzenberger, Annabelle Gurwitch, Donovan Leitch, Zoe Nathenson, Vincent Ward, Susan Barnes; *Cameos:* Ione Skye, Xander Berkeley; *D:* Mike Figgis; *W:* Mike Figgis; *C:* Declan Quinn; *M:* Mike Figgis.

One True Thing

Archetypal tearjerker revolves around WASP-ish New York-Harvard family. Daughter Ellen (Zellweger) is an ambitious journalist; Dad's (Hurt) a tweedy professor; Mom (Streep) has an incurable disease. Director Franklin handles his high-powered cast well. The film plays fairly well on DVD, though such a low-keyed domestic story doesn't test the limits of the medium. The many dimly lit scenes are clear enough, and the realistic interiors have a believably lived-in look. Sound is acceptable. —*MM* *Movie:* ♫♫► *DVD:* ♫♫►
Universal Studios Home Video (Cat #20440, UPC #025192044021). Widescreen (1.85:1) letterboxed. Dolby Digital 5.1 Surround Stereo; Dolby Digital Surround Stereo. $24.98. Keepcase. *LANG:* English; French. *SUB:* Spanish. *CAP:* English. *FEATURES:* 30 chapter links • "Making of" featurette • Production notes • Cast and crew thumbnail biographies • Theatrical trailer • Universal web links. **1998 (PG-13) 128m/C** Meryl Streep, Renee Zellweger, William Hurt, Tom Everett Scott, Nicky Katt, Lauren Graham, James Eckhouse, Patrick Breen, Gerrit Graham; *D:* Carl Franklin; *W:* Karen Croner; *C:* Declan Quinn; *M:* Cliff Eidelman. *AWARDS:* *NOM:* Academy Awards '98: Best Actress (Streep); Golden Globe Awards '99: Best Actress—Drama (Streep); Screen Actors Guild Award '98: Best Actress (Streep).

Only You

According to her Ouija board, young Faith's (Tomei) true love is named Damon Bradley. But as the years pass, she's about to settle for a podiatrist—until an old school friend of her fiance calls from Venice, Italy, with best wishes. Guess what his name is? Faith and her pal Kate (Hunt) set off in search of Mr. Right. Then she meets shoe salesman Peter Wright (Downey) and wonders if the board got things wrong. If Jewison's comic touch doesn't deliver another *Moonstruck*, he and the attractive cast (and the Venetian locations) do very good work. A little grain shows up from time to time, but beyond that, the DVD is very good. —*MM* *AKA:* Him; Just in Time.
Movie: ♫♫► *DVD:* ♫♫►

Columbia Tristar Home Video (Cat #73269). Widescreen (1.85:1) letterboxed; full frame. Dolby Digital 5.1 Surround Stereo; Dolby Digital Surround Stereo. $29.95. Keepcase. *LANG:* English; French; Spanish. *SUB:* French; Spanish. *CAP:* English. *FEATURES:* Trailer.
1994 (PG) 108m/C Marisa Tomei, Robert Downey Jr., Bonnie Hunt, Fisher Stevens, Billy Zane, Joaquim de Almeida; *D:* Norman Jewison; *W:* Diane Drake; *C:* Sven Nykvist; *M:* Rachel Portman.

Open City

Rome, occupied by the Germans following Italy's capitulation in September of 1943, has been declared an "open city," but it is actually a place of brutality, where death can strike in an instant, and no one is exempt from retribution. Director Roberto Rossellini took to the streets of Rome immediately after the end of the war to shoot this gritty look at life in the city during the spring of 1944. While the film begins slowly, meandering unevenly through the lives of a number of the city's inhabitants, it builds to a startling climax, with visual images that are as disturbing today as they were powerful when the film was released in 1945/46. Rossellini's masterpiece is betrayed on DVD by a poor film transfer and a complete lack of supporting materials. *Open City* is a landmark film of the immediate post-war period in Europe and deserves more than what is delivered with this presentation. —*RT* *AKA:* Roma, Citta Aperta; Rome, Open City.
Movie: ♫♫♫ *DVD:* ♫♫
Image Entertainment (Cat #4102DS, UPC #014381410228). Full frame. AC3 - 1 Channel. $29.99. Snapper. *LANG:* Italian. *SUB:* English. *FEATURES:* 18 chapter links.
1945 103m/B *IT* Anna Magnani, Aldo Fabrizi, Marcel Pagliero, Maria Michi, Vito Annicchiarico, Nando Bruno, Harry Feist; *D:* Roberto Rossellini; *W:* Federico Fellini, Sergio Amidei; *C:* Ubaldo Arata; *M:* Renzo Rossellini. *AWARDS:* New York Film Critics Awards '46: Best Foreign Film; *NOM:* Academy Awards '46: Best Screenplay.

Opening Night

Very long study of an actress (Rowlands) and the play she's about to open on Broadway. Backstage turmoil increases her own insecurities and the bad luck persists when an adoring fan dies in an accident on opening night. Performances carry this neurotic epic along, including director Cassavettes as Rowland's costar and Blondell as the playwright.
Movie: ♫♫► *DVD:* NYR
Pioneer Entertainment (Cat #PSE-98-160). Full frame. Mono. $24.98. Keepcase.
1977 (PG-13) 144m/C Gena Rowlands, John Cassavetes, Joan Blondell, Ben Gazzara, Paul Stewart, Zohra Lampert, Laura Johnson; *D:* John Cassavetes; *W:* John Cassavetes; *C:* Frederick Elmes; *M:* Bo Harwood.

Operation Condor

Secret agent Jackie (Chan) is sent by the United Nations to retrieve tons of gold buried by the Nazis in the Moroccan desert during WWII. Naturally, he's not the only one after the treasure, but the plot is nothing more than a stage for some of the director-star's most ambitious stuntwork. The opening *Raiders of the Lost Ark* business involving a giant inflatable golf ball must be one of his loopiest. The image suffers a bit on DVD with noticeable artifacts in the night scenes and flashing lines in the extended fight scene at the end. —*MM*
Movie: ♫♫♫ *DVD:* ♫♫♫
Buena Vista Home Entertainment (Cat #17442, UPC #717951002921). Widescreen (2.35:1) letterboxed. Dolby Digital 5.1 Surround. $29.99. Keepcase. *LANG:* English. *CAP:* English. *FEATURES:* 17 chapter links.
1991 (PG-13) 92m/C Jackie Chan, Carol Cheng, Eva Cabo De Garcia, Ikeda Shoko; *D:* Jackie Chan; *W:* Edward Tang, Jackie Chan; *C:* Wong Ngok Tai; *M:* Stephen Endelman.

Operation Condor 2: The Armour of the Gods

Prequel to *Operation Condor* has Jackie as a treasure hunter who is asked by his exgirlfriend's (Kwan) new fiancé (Tam), who used to be his best friend, to rescue her from a cult and retrieve a set of medieval armor. Got that? The going's a bit slow in the first two thirds, but once Jackie rappels down a spectacular cliff to get to the cult's cave, the fights and stunts are firstrate. Overall, the widescreen image looks fine though it doesn't sparkle the way some of Jackie's more recent releases have. The sound is O.K., too, but the point here is the incredible stunt work which is capped by an astonishing bit of business involving a hot air balloon. And the concluding outtakes, of course. —*MM* *AKA:* Armour of God.
Movie: ♫♫♫ *DVD:* ♫♫♫
Buena Vista Home Entertainment (Cat #17443, UPC #717951002938). Widescreen (1.85:1) letterboxed. Dolby Digital Stereo. $29.99. Keepcase. *LANG:* English. *CAP:* English. *FEATURES:* 15 chapter links.
1986 (R) 88m/C *HK* Jackie Chan, Alan Tam, Rosamund Kwan, Lola Forner; *D:* Jackie Chan; *W:* Jackie Chan, Edward Tang.

Operation Delta Force 2: Mayday

Direct-to-video sequel is a by-the-numbers shoot-'em-up with iron-jawed guys in camo flexing their pecs as they lock-'n'-load their automatic weapons. The plot has to do with a terrorist using a Russian submarine to hold a luxury cruise liner hostage in exchange for $25 billion. But who cares about that? The gunfire is loud; the explosions are bright. There are no major visual flaws on the DVD even during the more kinetic action scenes. Followed by 3. — *MM*

Movie: 🎵🎵 **DVD:** 🎵🎵🎵
Image Entertainment (Cat #ID6280NGDVD, UPC #014381628029). Full frame. Dolby Digital Surround. $24.99. Snapper. *LANG:* English. *FEATURES:* 15 chapter links.
1997 (R) 98m/C Michael McGrady, J. Kenneth Campbell, Dale Dye, Simon Jones; *D:* Yossi Wein; *W:* David Sparling; *C:* Peter Belcher; *M:* Russell Stirling, Wessel Van Rensburg.

Operation Delta Force 3: Clear Target

Formula sequel made in South Africa sets the beefcake boys against Colombian drug lords and a stolen nuclear submarine (created by computer-generated effects). For a low-budget video premiere, the DVD looks pretty good with more clarity than VHS tape. Unfortunately, the acting, writing, and stunts are not quite so snappy. Strictly run-of-the-mill on any medium. —*MM*

Movie: 🎵▶ **DVD:** 🎵🎵
Image Entertainment (Cat #ID6303NGDVD, UPC #014381630329). Full frame. Dolby Digital Surround Stereo. $24.99. Snapper. *LANG:* English. *FEATURES:* 12 chapter links.
1998 (R) 96m/C Bryan Genesse, Danny Keogh, Jim Fitzpatrick, Greg Collins, Darcy La Pier; *D:* Mark Roper; *W:* David Sparling; *C:* John Scheepers; *M:* Serge Colbert.

Opposite of Sex

Teenaged terror Dedee (Ricci) wreaks havoc with the life of gay half-brother Bill (Donovan). She seduces his boyfriend Matt (Sergei), gets pregnant, steals his savings, and nearly costs him his high school teacher's job. Then she takes off for L.A., with Bill, his best friend Lucia (Kudrow), and sheriff Carl (Lovett) in pursuit. Quirky black comedy isn't shy, especially when Ricci's vamping across the screen, and features fine work by Kudrow (in a welcome departure from the dumb blonde roles) and Ricci (who can definitely remove the words "child actress" from her resume). Dedee's acerbic narration is another highlight. The DVD makes for enjoyable if not sensational viewing. Picture sharpness is above average and there is only slight grain. Artifacts are rare. Colors are accurate but not quite as vibrant as they were in the theatre. Contrast is good, as is the brightness. Blacks are true for most of the disc. The Dolby Surround has good fidelity and even a somewhat gutsy low end, but is lacking in the Surround department, which is used exclusively for ambience. —*JO*

Movie: 🎵🎵🎵 **DVD:** 🎵🎵▶
Columbia Tristar Home Video (Cat #01839, UPC #043396018396). Widescreen (1.85:1) anamorphic; full frame. Dolby Surround. NSL. Keepcase. *LANG:* English; French. *SUB:* English; French. *CAP:* English. *FEATURES:* 28 chapter links • Theatrical trailer • Commentary: Don Roos • Deleted scenes.

1998 (R) 105m/C Christina Ricci, Martin Donovan, Lisa Kudrow, Ivan Sergei, Lyle Lovett, Johnny Galecki, William Lee Scott, Colin Ferguson; *D:* Don Roos; *W:* Don Roos; *C:* Hubert Taczanowski; *M:* Mason Daring. *AWARDS:* Independent Spirit Awards '99: Best First Feature, Best Screenplay; National Board of Review Awards '98: Best Supporting Actress (Ricci); New York Film Critics Awards '98: Best Supporting Actress (Kudrow); *NOM:* Golden Globe Awards '99: Best Actress—Musical/Comedy (Ricci); Independent Spirit Awards '99: Best Actress (Ricci), Best Supporting Actress (Kudrow); Writers Guild of America '98: Best Screenplay.

Organized Crime & Triad Bureau

Comparisons between directors Kirk Wong and John Woo may not be completely fair, but the filmmakers do have a similar style and they both know how to spin entertaining yarns. Wong takes a more lyrical and somewhat less violent approach to crime stories. He can also create moments of intense beauty, many of them involving rain or water. (The best is chapter eight on this disc.) The good guys here are cops led by Inspector Lee (Lee) in relentless pursuit of gangster Tung (Wong, as good as always) and his mistress Cindy (Yip, equally fine). Tung has a highly placed informer in the ranks of the police and Lee's toothless superiors are no help. The film is structured as a chase, but Wong moves back and forth in time and despite the fast pace he takes time to develop the characters. On his commentary track, Wong sketches in some brief background and then talks about the film's genesis and its basis in reality. Though he sounds a bit uncertain and hesitant at first, he is informative. For those who do not speak Chinese but prefer the original dialogue, the subtitles are in easy-to-read English. Overall, the DVD image seems sharper than the tape. One of the best Hong Kong action films. —*MM AKA:* Chungon Satluk Linggei.

Movie: 🎵🎵🎵▶ **DVD:** 🎵🎵🎵🎵
Tai Seng Video Marketing (Cat #51364, UPC #601643513645). Widescreen. $49.95. Keepcase. *LANG:* English; Cantonese; Mandarin. *SUB:* English. *FEATURES:* 18 chapter links • Filmographies and biographies of actors and director • Trailers • Commentary: director.
1993 91m/C *HK* Danny Lee, Anthony Wong, Cecilia Yip, Roy Cheung, Elizabeth Lee; *D:* Kirk Wong; *W:* Winky Wong; *C:* Wing-hang Wong, Kwong-Hung Chan; *M:* Danny Chung, Ding-Yat Tsung.

Orlando

Based on Virginia Woolf's novel, the film begins in the England of 1600 where the young nobleman Orlando (Swinton) is a favorite of Queen Elizabeth and her court. For reasons that don't make much sense under close scrutiny but work fine in the film, Orlando decides never to grow old but

to remain young and beautiful in perpetuity. Orlando also has the odd habit of nodding off for long naps that last for days. After one of these, he wakes up to find that he's now a she. At that point she turns and addresses the camera and says, "Same person, no difference at all—just a different sex." Sure. If writer-director Sally Potter had persuasively accomplished her androgynous mission, that ridiculous oversimplification might generate some controversy. But the central failure of the work is that its protagonist/narrator is never the least bit convincing as a man, and the relative clarity of DVD only highlights her glowing beauty. It is more clearly detailed than the theatrical release I saw. Sound is very good. —*MM*

Movie: 🎵🎵▶ **DVD:** 🎵🎵🎵
Columbia Tristar Home Video (Cat #71549, UPC #043396715493). Widescreen (1.85:1) letterboxed. Dolby Digital Stereo. $27.95. Keepcase. *LANG:* English; Spanish. *SUB:* English; French; Spanish. *FEATURES:* 28 chapter links • Cast and crew thumbnail biographies • Theatrical trailer.
1992 (PG-13) 93m/C *GB* Tilda Swinton, Charlotte Valandrey, Billy Zane, Lothaire Bluteau, John Wood, Quentin Crisp, Heathcote Williams, Dudley Sutton, Thom Hoffman, Peter Eyre, Jimmy Somerville; *D:* Sally Potter; *W:* Sally Potter; *C:* Alexei Rodionov; *M:* Bob Last. *AWARDS: NOM:* Academy Awards '93: Best Art Direction/Set Decoration, Best Costume Design; Independent Spirit Awards '94: Best Foreign Film.

Orphans of the Storm

Two sisters (Dorothy and Lillian Gish) are separated and raised in opposite worlds— one by thieves, the other by aristocrats. The sisters' poignant search is hampered by the turbulent maelstrom preceding the French Revolution. Griffith's film is based on the French play *The Two Orphans*. The disc features a very crisp and well-done video transfer. The picture is vivid, except in some heavily tinted color scenes, but these instances are, for the most part, negligible. The remastered soundtrack is also excellent, replete with a superbly recorded orchestral score. —*MJT*

Movie: 🎵🎵🎵▶ **DVD:** 🎵🎵🎵
Image Entertainment (Cat #ID467DSDVD, UPC #014381467628). Full frame. Dolby Digital Stereo. $29.99. Snapper. *LANG:* Silent. *SUB:* English intertitles. *FEATURES:* 30 chapter links. Color tinted.
1921 150m/B Lillian Gish, Dorothy Gish, Monte Blue, Joseph Schildkraut; *D:* D.W. Griffith; *W:* D.W. Griffith; *C:* Billy (G.W.) Bitzer, Hendrik Sartov; *M:* Louis F. Gottschalk, William F. Peters.

Othello

William Shakespeare's classic tale of duplicity, jealously, and betrayal is delivered with style and a cinematic eye for detail by Orson Welles, its star, producer, and director. Filmed on locations throughout Italy and Morocco, this remains a powerful retelling of the intrigues and tragedy put upon Othello (Welles), a Moorish general in service to the Senate of Venice, and his young wife, Desdemona (Cloutier), by the double-dealings of his aide, Iago (MacLiammoir). The DVD presentation is from a film restoration (featurette details the efforts) that delivers a visual feast for all students of cinema in general and admirers of Welles, the master, in particular. The sound elements are still troubling, and the DVD cries out for subtitle/captioning, but the ability to view Welles's visual genius on a frame-by-frame basis more than offsets these failings. —*RT* *AKA:* Orson Welles's Othello; The Tragedy of Othello: The Moor of Venice.

Movie: 🎬🎬🎬 **DVD:** 🎬🎬🎬▸
Image Entertainment (Cat #5831, UPC #014381583120). Full frame. AC3 - 2 Channel. $24.99. Snapper. *LANG:* English. *FEATURES:* 12 chapters ▪ Featurette: "Restoring Othello" (22 min.) ▪ Orson Welles filmography.
1952 90m/B Orson Welles, Michael MacLiammoir, Suzanne Cloutier, Robert Coote, Hilton Edwards, Michael Lawrence, Nicholas Bruce, Fay Compton, Doris Dowling, Jean Davis, Joseph Cotten, Joan Fontaine; *D:* Orson Welles; *W:* Orson Welles; *C:* Anchise Brizzi, George Fanto, Alberto Fusi, Aldo (G.R. Aldo) Graziatti, Oberdan Troiani; *M:* Alberto Barberis, Angelo Francesco Lavagnino. *AWARDS:* Cannes Film Festival '52: Best Film.

The Other Sister

Mildly retarded but exuberant Carla (Lewis) is a member of the repressed Tate family. After leaving a "special school," she convinces her uptight parents (Keaton and Skerritt) to let her enroll in a vocational program. She falls for fellow retarded student Danny (Ribisi), much to her parents' dismay. Of course, love wins out in this typically sappy Hollywood dreck. On DVD, it is attractive dreck, with no serious flaws in image or sound. That, however, is still no excuse. —*MM*
Movie: 🎬 **DVD:** 🎬🎬🎬
Buena Vista Home Entertainment (Cat #17445, UPC #717951002952). Widescreen (2.35:1) letterboxed. Dolby Digital 5.1 Surround Stereo; Dolby Digital Surround Stereo. $29.99. Keepcase. *LANG:* English; French. *FEATURES:* 27 chapter links ▪ 2 music videos ▪ Theatrical trailer.
1998 (PG-13) 129m/C Juliette Lewis, Giovanni Ribisi, Diane Keaton, Tom Skerritt, Poppy Montgomery, Linda Thorson, Juliet Mills, Hector Elizondo, Sarah Paulson, Joe Flanigan; *D:* Garry Marshall; *W:* Garry Marshall, Bob Brunner; *C:* Dante Spinotti; *M:* Rachel Portman. *AWARDS:* NOM: Golden Raspberry Awards '99: Worst Supporting Actress (Lewis).

Our Daily Bread and Other Films of the Depression

Vidor's sequel to the 1928 The Crowd is about a young couple who inherit a farm during the Depression and succeed in managing the land while turning the place into a collective effort. Several sequences—including the famous irrigation scene—are highly influenced by directors Alexander Dovshenko and Sergei Eisenstein. On DVD, the film looks better than the 16mm print I saw in college and it comes with so many extras that it's an invaluable document of those painful years. First, in a 1983 "Prologue" Vidor explains how he came to make the film and the reaction to it. Two other short films, "California Election News #1 and #2" are propaganda for the conservative politics of the era. The disc also includes four short documentaries, "The Plow That Broke the Plains," "The River," "Power and the Land," and "The New Frontier." Image quality varies from excellent to good in those films. Required viewing for any serious student of American film. —*MM* *AKA:* Miracle of Life.

Movie: 🎬🎬🎬🎬 **DVD:** 🎬🎬🎬
Image Entertainment (Cat #ID4671DSDVD, UPC #014381467123). Full frame. Dolby Digital Mono. $24.99. Snapper. *LANG:* English. *FEATURES:* 37 chapter links.
1934 80m/B Karen Morley, Tom (George Duryea) Keene, John Qualen, Barbara Pepper, Addison Richards; *D:* King Vidor; *W:* King Vidor, Elizabeth Hill; *C:* Robert Planck.

Our Hospitality / Sherlock Junior

This superb disc belongs on the shelf next to The General in every videophile's Buster Keaton collection. The films are two of his best and they are superbly presented on DVD. In the first, Keaton plays a young man who returns to the South of the early 1800s to claim an inheritance but finds that he is still part of a feud. The best moments are scenes on an antique bicycle, a delightful train (a near-exact replica of the Stephenson Rocket), and a river chase in which Keaton was genuinely in danger. By the way, Keaton married his leading lady in real life. Though shorter, Sherlock Junior has some wonderful moments. Keaton plays a projectionist who falls asleep and dreams his way onto the screen. The pool table scene is a treat. The image is marked by a few scratches, but for films this old, the quality is astonishing. —*MM*

Movie: 🎬🎬🎬🎬 **DVD:** 🎬🎬🎬▸
Image Entertainment (Cat #K123DVD, UPC #738329012328). Full frame. $29.99. Snapper. *LANG:* English intertitles. *FEATURES:* 13 chapter links. Our Hospitality runs 74 minutes; Sherlock Junior, 44 minutes.
1923 74m/B Kathryn McGuire, Ward Crane, Buster Keaton, Natalie Talmadge, Joe Keaton, Buster Keaton Jr., Kitty Bradbury, Joe Roberts; *D:* John Blystone, Buster Keaton; *W:* Jean C. Havez, Joseph A. Mitchell, Clyde Bruckman; *C:* Elgin Lessley, Gordon Jennings, Byron Houck.

Out for Justice

A psycho Brooklyn hood goes on a murder spree, and homeboy turned lone-wolf cop Seagal races other police and the mob to get at him. Bloodthirsty and profane, it does try to depict N.Y.C.'s Italian-American community realistically—but 90 percent of them are dead by the end so what's the point? Better yet, why does it open with a quote from Arthur Miller? The DVD is as average as the film itself. Sharpness is O.K. with grain in the darker scenes. There are some minor artifacts when fast motion occurs in those scenes and backgrounds are sometimes obviously digitized. Colors are fairly accurate with only a little bleed. Blacks are true but have occasional bleed. Contrast is good and brightness levels are consistent and comfortable. The 5.1 sound is also nothing special, with limited Surround, but pretty gutsy bass to go along with crisp highs. —*JO*

Movie: 🎬 **DVD:** 🎬🎬▸
Warner Home Video, Inc. (Cat #12219, UPC #085391221920). Widescreen (1.85:1) letterboxed; full frame. Dolby Digital 5.1; Dolby Surround. $19.98. Snapper. *LANG:* English (DD5.1); French (DS). *SUB:* English; French. *CAP:* English. *FEATURES:* 26 chapter links.
1991 (R) 91m/C Steven Seagal, William Forsythe, Jerry Orbach, Julianna Margulies, Gina Gershon, John Leguizamo, Julie Strain; *D:* John Flynn; *W:* David Lee Henry; *C:* Ric Waite; *M:* David Michael Frank.

Out of Sight

Screen adaptation of Leonard's novel isn't quite Get Shorty, but it'll do. Bank robber Jack Foley (Clooney) busts out of jail and heads to Detroit, determined to pull one last job. Federal Marshall Karen Sisco (Lopez) is both hot on the trail and hot for Foley's bod. Climactic home robbery is staged with plenty of tension and humor. Steamy chemistry between Clooney and Lopez, along with zippy dialogue and unexpected twists, make this a winner. This DVD is close to flawless. The anamorphic transfer is sharp and free from grain. Colors are excellent (bleed is pretty much non-existent), as are the contrast and brightness levels. There are no artifacts, despite lots of motion (numerous snow-filled scenes) and dimly lit scenes. Excellent 5.1 and Dolby Surround tracks accent the cool jazzy score and numerous gunshots, as well as the dialogue. A pleasure to watch all the way through. Included in the deleted scenes is more of Clooney and Lopez's trunk flirtation. —*JO*

Movie: 🎬🎬🎬▸ **DVD:** 🎬🎬🎬▸
Universal Studios Home Video (Cat #20340, UPC #025192034022). Widescreen (1.85:1) anamorphic. Dolby Digital 5.1; Dolby Surround. $24.98. Keepcase. *LANG:* English (DD5.1, DS); Spanish (DS); French (DS). *SUB:* English; Spanish. *FEATURES:* 52 chapter links ▪ Theatrical trailer ▪ Deleted scenes ▪ Commentary: Steven Soderbergh and Scott Frank ▪

"Making of" documentary ● Music high-lights ● Dual-layered RSDL.

1998 (R) 122m/C George Clooney, Jennifer Lopez, Ving Rhames, Don Cheadle, Albert Brooks, Steve Zahn, Dennis Farina, Catherine Keener, Luis Guzman, Isaiah Washington, Keith Loneker, Nancy Allen; *Cameos:* Michael Keaton, Samuel L. Jackson; *D:* Steven Soderbergh; *W:* Scott Frank; *C:* Elliot Davis; *M:* Cliff Martinez. *AWARDS:* National Society of Film Critics Awards '98: Best Director (Soderbergh), Best Film, Best Screenplay; Writers Guild of America '98: Best Adapted Screenplay; *NOM:* Academy Awards '98: Best Adapted Screenplay, Best Film Editing; MTV Movie Awards '99: Best Female Performance (Lopez), Best Kiss (George Clooney/Jennifer Lopez).

Out of the Blue

When an imprisoned father's (Hopper) return fails to reunite this Woodstock-generation family, the troubled teenage daughter (Manz) takes matters into her own hands. *Easy Rider* star Hopper seems to have reconsidered the effects of the 1960s with this harsh, violent portrait of a shattered family. The film's DVD transfer is quite good, with nice clear colors. The audio, however, seems quite tinny in several sections. The audio commentary on the disc provides ample insight into the film's production and is the shining achievement of the disc, although director Hopper occasionally sounds as though he's not really interested. He's joined by executive producer Paul Lewis and distributor John Alan Simon. —*MJT*

Movie: 🎬🎬🎬 *DVD:* 🎬🎬🎬
Anchor Bay (Cat #DV10865, UPC #013131086591). Widescreen (1.85:1) letterboxed. Dolby Digital Mono. $29.90. Keepcase. *FEATURES:* 30 chapter links ● Commentary: Hopper, Lewis, and Simon ● Theatrical trailer ● Radio spot.
1980 (R) 94m/C Dennis Hopper, Linda Manz, Raymond Burr; *D:* Dennis Hopper; *W:* Gary Jules Jouvenat, Brenda Nielson, Leonard Yakir; *C:* Marc Champion; *M:* Tom Lavin.

Out of Time

Archeologist Jake Bonner (Fahey) discovers an artifact that may lead to the treasure of Alexander the Great, but a millionaire wants it. Any comparisons to Indiana Jones are out of place. This low-budget adventure is fuzzily focused, and the best moments have a pale, transparent look. Those may be acceptable at the drive-in, but not on DVD. —*MM AKA:* In Search of the Serpent of Death; The Serpent of Death.

Movie: 🎬🎬 *DVD:* 🎬▸
Simitar Entertainment (Cat #7300, UPC #082551730025). Full frame. PCM Stereo. $14.98. Keepcase. *LANG:* English. *FEATURES:* 8 chapter links ● Production factoids ● Jeff Fahey filmography.
1990 (R) 98m/C Jeff Fahey, Camilla More, Spiros Focas, Michael Gothard, Tuck Milligan; *D:* Anwar Kawadri; *W:* Jesse Graham; *C:* Fred Tammes; *M:* Alan Parker.

The Out-of-Towners

Nancy (Hawn) and Henry Clark (Martin) are empty-nesters headed for Henry's job interview in New York. Along the way they're thwarted by every traveler's nightmare imaginable, including rental-car woes and a snooty hotel manager (Cleese). Martin did the same things before (and with a lot more laughs) in *Planes, Trains, and Automobiles*. So did Neil Simon in the 1970 original. Uninspired and inconsistent with flashes of inspired physical comedy from the stars. On DVD, the image may be slightly better than VHS tape, but the focus is mushy throughout. Sound is better. —*MM*

Movie: 🎬🎬 *DVD:* 🎬🎬
Paramount Home Video (Cat #33448, UPC #097363344872). Widescreen anamorphic. Dolby Digital 5.1 Surround Stereo; Dolby Digital Surround Stereo. $29.99. Keepcase. *LANG:* English; French. *SUB:* English. *FEATURES:* 19 chapter links ● Theatrical trailer.
1999 (PG-13) 92m/C Mark McKinney, Goldie Hawn, Steve Martin, John Cleese, Oliver Hudson; *D:* Sam Weisman; *W:* Marc Lawrence; *C:* John Bailey; *M:* Marc Shaiman.

Outbreak

Smuggled African monkey spits on someone who kisses someone else who sneezes on a bunch of people, thus initiating the spread of a highly infectious mystery disease in a northern California 'burb. Hoffman leads a team of scientists in a search for the anti-serum, but it's a secret government plot to exterminate the victims that literally sends Hoffman and crew into action movie cliche overdrive (add "helicopter" to the list of chase scene vehicles). Not that that's so bad—if the beat-the-clock tempo doesn't grab you, paranoia certainly will. But Hoffman's hardly a threat to Arnold or Sylvester as the next action hero, and the talented Russo remains suspiciously ravishing even with festering pustules. Based on two books: Richard Preston's *The Hot Zone* and Laurie Garrett's *The Coming Plague*. Both picture and sound are outstanding on this DVD. The image is sharp and has virtually no visible grain or artifacts. Colors are dead accurate and both vibrant and free of bleed. Blacks are true and grainless. The picture is extremely punchy with excellent contrast and brightness that don't mess with colors or details. Finally, the sound is also superb with loads of Surround, plenty of that house-shaking bass we all love (even if the neighbors don't), and clean crisp highs. —*JO*

Movie: 🎬🎬🎬 *DVD:* 🎬🎬🎬🎬
Warner Home Video, Inc. (Cat #13632, UPC #085391363224). Widescreen (1.85:1) anamorphic; full frame. Dolby Digital 5.1; Dolby Surround. $24.98. Snapper. *LANG:* English (DD5.1); French (DS). *SUB:* English; Spanish; French. *CAP:* English. *FEATURES:* 5 chapter links ● Production notes.

1994 (R) 128m/C Dustin Hoffman, Rene Russo, Morgan Freeman, Donald Sutherland, Cuba Gooding Jr., Kevin Spacey, J.T. Walsh, Dale Dye; *D:* Wolfgang Petersen; *W:* Laurence Dworet, Robert Roy Pool; *C:* Michael Ballhaus; *M:* James Newton Howard. *AWARDS:* New York Film Critics Awards '95: Best Supporting Actor (Spacey).

Outland

On a volcanic moon of Jupiter, miners begin suffering from spells of insanity. A single federal marshal begins an investigation that threatens the colony's survival. No more or less than a western in space, and the science is rather poor. An acknowledged sci-fi remake of *High Noon* features a soundtrack that literally counts down to the showdown. The DVD has a lot of problems with this very dark film. The picture is sharp enough, but has a lot of grain and sometimes unbearable artifacts. At least the colors are accurate and at times vibrant, with very little bleed. Blacks are true and both the contrast and brightness levels are comfortable. The 5.1 sound is very detailed and has good low end on both music and effects. Mids and highs are also very distinct, giving power to all the dialogue. —*JO*

Movie: 🎬🎬🎬 *DVD:* 🎬🎬▸
Warner Home Video, Inc. (Cat #14982, UPC #085391498223). Widescreen (2.35:1) anamorphic; full frame. Dolby Digital 5.1; Mono. $24.98. Snapper. *LANG:* English; Spanish. *SUB:* English; Spanish; French. *CAP:* English. *FEATURES:* 31 chapter links ● Theatrical trailer ● Production notes.
1981 (R) 109m/C Sean Connery, Peter Boyle, Frances Sternhagen, James B. Sikking; *D:* Peter Hyams; *W:* Peter Hyams; *C:* Stephen Goldblatt; *M:* Jerry Goldsmith. *AWARDS: NOM:* Academy Awards '81: Best Sound.

The Outlaw Josey Wales

Eastwood plays a farmer with a motive for revenge—his family was killed and for years he was betrayed and hunted. His desire to play the lone killer is, however, tempered by his need for family and friends. He kills plenty, but in the end finds happiness. Considered one of the last great westerns, with many superb performances. Eastwood took over directorial chores during filming from Kaufman, who coscripted. Adapted from *Gone to Texas* by Forest Carter. The picture on the DVD is sharp and both grain and artifacts are minimal. Colors are accurate to the theatre and bleed is never a problem. Contrast and brightness are both excellent, and blacks are true. The 5.1 sound is harsh at times and the bass a little unnatural. Dialogue is clear, though, and there is excellent imaging and not-bad use of the Surround tracks for both effects and ambience. —*JO*

Movie: 🎬🎬🎬▸ *DVD:* 🎬🎬🎬

Warner Home Video, Inc. (Cat #12588, UPC #085391258827). Widescreen (1.85:1) anamorphic; full frame. Dolby Digital 5.1; Stereo. $19.98. Snapper. *LANG:* English. *SUB:* English; French. *CAP:* English. *FEATURES:* 35 chapter links • 13 theatrical trailers • Production notes.
1976 (PG) 135m/C Clint Eastwood, Chief Dan George, Sondra Locke, Matt Clark, John Vernon, Bill McKinney, Sam Bottoms, Will Sampson, Woodrow Parfrey, Royal Dano, John Quade, John Russell, John Mitchum, Kyle Eastwood; *D:* Clint Eastwood; *W:* Philip Kaufman; *C:* Bruce Surtees. *AWARDS:* National Film Registry '96; *NOM:* Academy Awards '76: Best Original Score.

Outlaw Justice

Aging gunslingers Nelson and Kristofferson meet up with their buddy Tritt to avenge the death of their old partner. Nothing new storywise but the cast is certainly comfortable with the material.
Movie: 🎵🎵▶ *DVD:* NYR
Sunland Studios (Cat #360). Full frame. $24.99. Keepcase.
1998 (R) 94m/C Kris Kristofferson, Willie Nelson, Sancho Garcia, Travis Tritt, Chad Willet; *D:* Bill Corcoran; *W:* Gene Quintano; *M:* Jay Gruska.

Outrage

Assigned to write about a traveling carnival, reporter Marco Vallez (Banderas) promptly falls for Anna (Neri), an equestrienne sharpshooter. Later, she is attacked and decides to take her own kind of revenge. Unfortunately, this serious film is marred by poor dubbing—the choice of subtitles would have been welcome—and an image that is exceptionally poor on DVD. Shapes lose their integrity during slow pans and many interiors are so dim and grainy that even facial expressions are difficult to make out. —*MM AKA:* Dispara.
Movie: 🎵🎵🎵 *DVD:* 🎵▶
Simitar Entertainment (Cat #7330, UPC #082551733026). Full frame. PCM Stereo. $14.98. Keepcase. *LANG:* English. *FEATURES:* 8 chapter links • Production factoids • Antonio Banderas thumbnail biography and filmography.
1993 (R) 108m/C *SP* Antonio Banderas, Francesca Neri, Eulalia Ramon, Walter Vidarte, Coque Malla; *D:* Carlos Saura; *W:* Carlos Saura; *C:* Javier Aguirresarobe; *M:* Alberto Iglesias.

Outrageous Fortune

Two would-be New York actresses—prim and proper Lynn (Long) and trampy Sandy (Midler)—chase after the same two timing boyfriend (Coyote) and get involved in a CIA plot. The hybrid road/comedy/female-buddy/thriller is far less than the sum of its parts. On DVD, the mediocre action looks and sounds every bit as good as it did in theatres. —*MM*
Movie: 🎵🎵 *DVD:* 🎵🎵
Buena Vista Home Entertainment (Cat #18532, UPC #717951005496). Wide-

screen (1.85:1) anamorphic. Dolby Digital Stereo. $29.99. Keepcase. *LANG:* English; French. *CAP:* English. *FEATURES:* 20 chapter links • Theatrical trailer.
1987 (R) 112m/C Shelley Long, Bette Midler, George Carlin, Peter Coyote; *D:* Arthur Hiller; *W:* Leslie Dixon; *C:* David M. Walsh; *M:* Alan Silvestri.

Outside Providence

In 1974, working class Rhode Island teen Tim Dunphy (Hatosy) is sent to a snotty prep school for his senior year by his dad (Baldwin) after he has a little run-in involving some pot and a crashed patrol car. Of course, he doesn't fit in, but after he meets Tina (Smart), he might not care. The story was written by the Farrelly brothers (*Something About Mary*) and it's gruff, profane, and somehow sweet-natured. Though the film never quite clicked in theatres, it ought to be an enduring hit on home video. DVD probably doesn't add much to the slightly soft-focus image with a bit of tinting to evoke nostalgia. The terrific oldies score is just as important. —*MM*
Movie: 🎵🎵🎵 *DVD:* 🎵🎵🎵
Miramax Pictures Home Video (Cat #18277, UPC #717951004673). Widescreen (1.85:1) anamorphic. Dolby Digital 5.1 Surround Stereo. $29.99. Keepcase. *LANG:* English; French. *CAP:* English. *FEATURES:* 15 chapter links.
1999 (R) 103m/C Shawn Hatosy, Alec Baldwin, George Wendt, Jonathan Brandis, Amy Smart, Gabriel Mann, Jon Abrahams, Adam LaVorgna; *D:* Michael Corrente; *W:* Peter Farrelly, Michael Corrente, Bobby Farrelly; *C:* Richard Crudo; *M:* Sheldon Mirowitz.

The Outsiders

Today, Francis Ford Coppola's adaptation of S.E. Hinton's popular young-adult novel is best known for the young and then-unknown cast of future stars. It's shamelessly melodramatic and overdone but with a nice sense of place and a good soundtrack. The DVD image is a step up from VHS tape, but on any medium, the cast is the key, not the visuals. —*MM*
Movie: 🎵🎵▶ *DVD:* 🎵🎵▶
Warner Home Video, Inc. (Cat #11310, UPC #085391131021). Widescreen letterboxed; full frame. Dolby Digital Surround Stereo. $19.98. Snapper. *LANG:* English. *SUB:* English; French. *FEATURES:* 12 chapter links • Theatrical trailer.
1983 (PG) 91m/C C. Thomas Howell, Matt Dillon, Ralph Macchio, Patrick Swayze, Diane Lane, Tom Cruise, Emilio Estevez, Rob Lowe, Tom Waits, Leif Garrett; *D:* Francis Ford Coppola; *W:* Kathleen Rowell; *C:* Stephen Burum; *M:* Carmine Coppola.

Over the Wire

Standard noirish "erotic thriller" from Playboy productions actually has an element of mystery. Telephone repairman Bruce

(Christensen) overhears one woman plotting to kill another. When he goes to the address, he finds two sisters (Hall and O'Brien) with similar voices. Who's up to what? The acting is laughable but that's not exactly the point. Ms. O'Brien is one of the sleekest actresses in the business. Surely it's a joke that the voice actor who plays "the phone sex guy" is Bob Dole. Now if it were Bill Clinton.... The disc emphasizes the film's flaws—soft focus, bare bones sets, less than perfect lighting—and so it's not that much different from the tape. —*MM*
Movie: 🎵🎵 *DVD:* 🎵🎵▶
Image Entertainment (Cat #ID5614FMDVD, UPC #014381561425). Full frame. Dolby Digital Stereo. $19.99. Snapper. *LANG:* English. *FEATURES:* 12 chapter links.
1995 90m/C David Christensen, Shauna O'Brien, Landon Hall, Tim Abell, John Lazar, Bob Dole; *D:* Fred Olen Ray; *W:* Pete Slate; *C:* Howard Wexler.

Overboard

Spoiled socialite Joanna Stayton (Hawn) falls off her yacht and gets amnesia. Carpenter Dean Proffitt (Russell) convinces her that she's his wife and the mother of his wild kids. Even though it's all been done before, you'll enjoy the screwy gags. On DVD, the luxurious sets are a mix of glowing reds and flashing mini-blinds. The high-contrast color is little better than tape. Sound is adequate. —*MM*
Movie: 🎵🎵 *DVD:* 🎵🎵
MGM Home Entertainment (Cat #906566, UPC #027616656629). Widescreen letterboxed. Dolby Digital Surround Stereo. $24.98. Keepcase. *LANG:* English. *SUB:* English; French. *FEATURES:* 32 chapter links • Theatrical trailer • 4-page booklet.
1987 (PG) 112m/C Goldie Hawn, Kurt Russell, Katherine Helmond, Roddy McDowall, Edward Herrmann; *D:* Garry Marshall; *W:* Leslie Dixon; *C:* John A. Alonzo; *M:* Alan Silvestri.

The Pajama Game

Sprightly musical is about the striking workers of a pajama factory and their plucky negotiator, who falls in love with the boss. The film is based on the hit Broadway musical, which was based on Richard Bissell's book *Seven and a Half Cents* and adapted for the screen by Bissell and Abbott. Bob Fosse choreographed the dance numbers. The DVD has a very sharp picture and basically no grain or artifacts. The colors are striking and have good punchy contrast. Blacks are deep and true. The Dolby Digital mono sound is very lively and has more bass than expected, as well as crisp, undistorted highs. —*JO*
Movie: 🎵🎵🎵▶ *DVD:* 🎵🎵🎵▶
Warner Home Video, Inc. (Cat #35085, UPC #08539350852). Widescreen (1.85:1) anamorphic; full frame. Dolby Digital Mono. $19.98. Snapper. *LANG:* English. *SUB:* English; French. *CAP:* English. *FEA-*

TURES: 29 chapter links ▪ Theatrical trailer ▪ Deleted song.
1957 101m/C Doris Day, John Raitt, Eddie Foy Jr., Reta Shaw, Carol Haney; *D:* Stanley Donen, George Abbott; *W:* George Abbott, Richard Bissell; *C:* Harry Stradling.

Pale Rider

A mysterious nameless stranger rides into a small California gold rush town to find himself in the middle of a feud between a mining syndicate and a group of independent prospectors. Christ-like Eastwood evokes comparisons to *Shane.* A classical western theme treated well and complemented by excellent cinematography and a rock-solid cast. Warner's widescreen laserdisc is preferable to this DVD transfer, which has problems with both sharpness and colors, with tints that are generally a bit off. The image also suffers from both grain and color bleed. Blacks try to be true but often pick up some grain themselves. The 5.1 sound is boisterously loud, delivering the expected nerve-shatteringly realistic gunshots. Music is harsh on the high end, but with plenty of bass power to drive things along. —*JO*
Movie: ♫♫♫ *DVD:* ♫▶
Warner Home Video, Inc. (Cat #11475, UPC #085391147527). Widescreen (2.35:1) anamorphic. Dolby Digital 5.1; Dolby Digital Mono. $24.98. Snapper. *LANG:* English (DD5.1); Spanish (DDM); French (DDM). *SUB:* English; Spanish; French. *CAP:* English. *FEATURES:* 28 chapter links ▪ Theatrical trailers ▪ Production notes.
1985 (R) 116m/C Clint Eastwood, Michael Moriarty, Carrie Snodgress, Sydney Penny, Richard Dysart, Richard Kiel, Christopher Penn, John Russell, Charles Hallahan, Douglas McGrath, Fran Ryan; *D:* Clint Eastwood; *W:* Michael Butler, Dennis Shryack; *C:* Bruce Surtees; *M:* Lennie Niehaus.

Palmetto

Bitter ex-con Harry (Harrelson) teams up with seductress Rhea (Shue) to stage a phony kidnapping of her stepdaughter Odette (Sevigny). Newly released from the joint after a frame-up, Harry is lured back to the steamy backwater that sent him up in the first place by ex-galfriend Nina (Gershon, in an unaccustomed good-girl role). Volker Schlondorff *(The Tin Drum)* helmed this adaptation of Rene Raymond's *(AKA James Hadley Chase)* novel *Just Another Sucker.* There is a little too much grain on the DVD and the picture is at times somewhat blurry, especially during the occasional artifacting. The blacks are close to true and the brightness good for the most part, but during some darker scenes there is too much contrast. As is often the case on a visually average DVD, the sound is very good. The 5.1 soundtrack is crisp and dynamic, with good highs and lows as well as nice Surround when called for. —*JO*
Movie: ♫♫▶ *DVD:* ♫♫

Warner Home Video, Inc. (Cat #C2533, UPC #053939253320). Widescreen (1.85:1) anamorphic; full frame. Dolby Digital 5.1. $24.98. Snapper. *LANG:* English. *SUB:* French. *CAP:* English. *FEATURES:* 29 chapter links ▪ 3 Theatrical trailers ▪ Cast and crew bios ▪ Production notes.
1998 (R) 114m/C Angela Featherstone, Woody Harrelson, Elisabeth Shue, Michael Rapaport, Gina Gershon, Chloe Sevigny, Rolf Hoppe, Tom Wright; *D:* Volker Schlondorff; *W:* E. Max Frye; *C:* Thomas Kloss; *M:* Klaus Doldinger.

Pancho Villa

Savalas has the lead in this fictional account of the famous Mexican revolutionary. He leads his men in a raid on an American fort after being hoodwinked in an arms deal. Connors tries to hold the fort against him. The finale, in which two trains crash head-on, is the most exciting event in the film.
Movie: ♫▶ *DVD:* NYR
Parade (Cat #55306). $17.98. *SUB:* Japanese. *FEATURES:* Cast and crew thumbnail bios ▪ Production notes.
1972 (PG) 92m/C *SP* Telly Savalas, Clint Walker, Anne Francis, Chuck Connors, Angel Del Pozo, Luis Davila; *D:* Eugenio (Gene) Martin; *W:* Julian Zimet; *C:* Alejandro Ulloa; *M:* Anton Abril.

The Pandora Project

Intelligence agent Bill Stenwick (Tyson) goes bad and steals a super secret weapon. John Lacy (Baldwin) has to find it before his impending marriage to Wendy Lane (Eleniak).
Movie: ♫▶ *DVD:* NYR
Pioneer Entertainment (Cat #10127). Full frame. Stereo. $19.98. Keepcase.
1998 (R) 89m/C Daniel Baldwin, Erika Eleniak, Richard Tyson, Tony Todd, Jeff Yagher, Bo Jackson, Robert Hegyes; *D:* John Terlesky; *W:* John Terlesky; *C:* Andrea V. Rossotto; *M:* Deddy Tzur.

Pandora's Box

This silent classic marked the end of the German Expressionist era and established Brooks as a major screen presence. She plays the tempestuous Lulu, who destroys everyone she comes in contact with, eventually sinking into prostitution and a fateful meeting with Jack the Ripper. Orchestral score. *AKA:* Die Buechse der Pandora; Lulu.
Movie: ♫♫♫♫ *DVD:* NYR
Home Vision Cinema (Cat #1264). Full frame. $39.95. *LANG:* Silent. *SUB:* English.
1928 110m/B *GE* Louise Brooks, Fritz Kortner, Francis Lederer, Carl Goetz, Alice Roberts, Gustav Diesl; *D:* G.W. Pabst; *W:* G.W. Pabst; *C:* Gunther Krampf.

Panther

Father and son Van Peebles's collaboration is an Oliver Stone fictionalization of

history. They portray the founders of the Black Panther party as idealistic and blameless Marxist revolutionaries. Bobby Seale (Vance) and Huey Newton (Chong) simply exercise their constitutional right to bear arms against the Oakland, CA, police department, which they see as an occupying army. In 1967, one of their first recruits is Judge (Hardison), a Vietnam vet. He's also signed up by police detective Brimmer (Baker) as an informer, and by Huey as a double agent against the cops. At the same time, FBI director J. Edgar Hoover (Dysart) declares the Panthers a threat to national security and launches the COINTELPRO operation against them. Brief passages from actual COINTELPRO documents are used to punctuate the film. Neither the real nor the imagined figures emerge as believable characters. The film never gets beneath the loud sloganeering rhetoric of the times to reveal genuine characters.
Movie: ♫♫ *DVD:* NYR
USA Home Entertainment (Cat #636309). Widescreen (1.85:1) letterboxed; full frame. $29.95. Keepcase. *FEATURES:* Cast and crew thumbnail bios ▪ Trailer.
1995 (R) 124m/C Kadeem Hardison, Marcus Chong, Courtney B. Vance, Bokeem Woodbine, Joe Don Baker, Anthony Griffith, Nefertiti, James Russo, Richard Dysart, M. Emmet Walsh, Mario Van Peebles; *D:* Mario Van Peebles; *W:* Melvin Van Peebles; *C:* Edward Pei; *M:* Stanley Clarke.

The Paper

Another crowd pleaser from director Howard follows a red letter day in the life of an editor at the tabloid New York *Sun* (modeled on the trashy *Post*). Fresh, fast-moving script by the Koepp brothers (who appear as reporters) offers a fairly accurate portrayal of the business of journalism (including the brisk language), with a few Hollywood exceptions. Pace suffers from cutaways to life outside, while script and direction sometimes coast past targets. Propelled by a fine cast, with cola-swigging Keaton the focus as he juggles his personal and professional lives. As a managing editor married to her work and ready to run over anyone in her way, Close is both funny and scary. Duvall contributes salt as the old newsroom horse. The 5.1 sound delivers the most audibly impressive printing press noises ever, and manages to keep that sort of energy going throughout the film whatever the set location. The Surround is immersing and bass high-end energy is good throughout. No complaints about the picture either, and sharpness is usually very good, with accurate colors as well. —*JO*
Movie: ♫♫♫ *DVD:* ♫♫♫▶
Universal Studios Home Video (Cat #20011, UPC #025192001123). Full frame. Dolby Digital 5.1; Dolby Surround. $24.95. Keepcase. *LANG:* English; French. *SUB:* Spanish. *CAP:* English. *FEATURES:* 16 chapter links ▪ Production notes ▪ Cast and filmmakers bios.

1994 (R) 112m/C Michael Keaton, Robert Duvall, Marisa Tomei, Glenn Close, Randy Quaid, Jason Robards Jr., Jason Alexander, Spalding Gray, Catherine O'Hara, Lynne Thigpen; **D:** Ron Howard; **W:** David Koepp, Steven Koepp; **C:** John Seale; **M:** Randy Newman. *AWARDS:* *NOM:* Academy Awards '94: Best Song ("Make Up Your Mind").

Papillon

McQueen is a criminal sent to Devil's Island in the 1930s. Hoffman is the swindler he befriends. A series of escapes and recaptures ensues. The sense of place and strong performances made this one a boxoffice winner, based on the autobiographical writings of French thief Henri Charriere. The DVD appears to have been made from a pristine original. It looks remarkably good for a film this old. Sound is fine. —*MM*
Movie: 🐾🐾🐾 *DVD:* 🐾🐾🐾
Warner Home Video, Inc. (Cat #832, UPC #012569083226). Widescreen letterboxed. Dolby Digital 5.1 Surround Stereo. $19.98. Snapper. *LANG:* English. *SUB:* English; French. *CAP:* English. *FEATURES:* 39 chapter links • Cast and crew thumbnail bios • Trailer • "Making of" featurette, "Magnificent Rebel."
1973 (PG) 150m/C Steve McQueen, Dustin Hoffman, Victor Jory, George Coulouris, Anthony Zerbe; **D:** Franklin J. Schaffner; **W:** Dalton Trumbo, Lorenzo Semple Jr.; **C:** Fred W. Koenekamp; **M:** Jerry Goldsmith. *AWARDS: NOM:* Academy Awards '73: Best Original Dramatic Score.

The Paradine Case

For many Hitchcock fans, this is the odd film they've somehow never managed to see, and that's easy to understand. It is perhaps the most windy and boring of all his work with a stuffy pace. Perhaps because producer David O. Selznick wrote the script, Hitch was reluctant to make the cuts and changes that might have made the courtroom drama more suspenseful. Gregory Peck plays a British lawyer who inexplicably falls for a client (Alida Valli) accused of bumping off her hubby. The DVD contains no serious visual flaws. It captures the superb black-and-white work of the director and cinematographer Lee Garmes, with intricate detail even in the blackest of cocktail dresses. The sound makes all of the dialogue completely clear. Overall, though, the no-extras disc is only slightly better than the excellent Anchor Bay tape. —*MM*
Movie: 🐾🐾 *DVD:* 🐾🐾🐾
Anchor Bay (Cat #DV10809, UPC #013131080995). Full frame. Dolby Digital Mono. $24.98. Keepcase. *LANG:* English. *FEATURES:* 18 chapter links.
1947 125m/B Gregory Peck, Alida Valli, Ann Todd, Louis Jourdan, Charles Laughton, Charles Coburn, Ethel Barrymore, Leo G. Carroll; **D:** Alfred Hitchcock; **W:** David O. Selznick; **C:** Lee Garmes; **M:** Franz Waxman. *AWARDS: NOM:* Academy

Awards '47: Best Supporting Actress (Barrymore).

The Parallax View

A reporter (Beatty) tries to disprove a report that states that a presidential candidate's assassination was not a conspiracy. As he digs deeper and deeper, he uncovers more than he bargained for and becomes a pawn in the conspirators' further plans. Beatty is excellent and the conspiracy is never less than believable. Lesser-known political thriller deserves to be more widely seen.
Movie: 🐾🐾🐾 *DVD:* NYR
Paramount Home Video (Cat #86707). Widescreen (2.35:1) letterboxed. Dolby Digital Mono. $29.99. Keepcase. *LANG:* English; French. *FEATURES:* Trailer.
1974 (R) 102m/C Warren Beatty, Hume Cronyn, William Daniels, Paula Prentiss, Kenneth Mars, Bill McKinney, Anthony Zerbe, Walter McGinn; **D:** Alan J. Pakula; **W:** David Giler, Lorenzo Semple Jr.; **C:** Gordon Willis; **M:** Michael Small. *AWARDS:* National Society of Film Critics Awards '74: Best Cinematography.

Paranoia

Psycho killer thriller in which an imprisoned killer uses a computer to harass the surviving member of the family he murdered.
Movie: 🐾🐾 *DVD:* NYR
Studio Home Entertainment (Cat #7155). Full frame. Stereo. $24.95. Keepcase. *LANG:* English. *SUB:* Spanish. *FEATURES:* Cast and crew thumbnail bios • Trailer.
1998 (R) 86m/C Larry Drake, Sally Kirkland, Scott Valentine, Brigitte Bako; **D:** Larry Brand; **W:** Larry Brand.

Parasite

An early appearance by an incredibly young Demi Moore and a blatant rip-off of the famous "chest-buster" moment from *Alien* are about all this slow-moving B-movie has to offer. Paul Dean (Robert Glaudini) is the post-apocalyptic scientist who has developed a species of parasitic critter and tries to destroy his work, but not before one of them gets inside him. Off he goes to a desert town to figure out how to kill it before it kills him. That's a fair premise but director Charles Band lets the action wander down some uninteresting sidetracks, and it's pretty slow throughout. He makes much quicker movies these days. Originally filmed in 3-D.
Movie: 🐾🐾 *DVD:* NYR
Full Moon Pictures (Cat #8008). $24.98. Jewel case. *FEATURES:* Trailer.
1982 (R) 90m/C Bob Glaudini, Demi Moore, Luca Bercovici, Cherie Currie, Gale Robbins, James Davidson, Al Fann, Cheryl "Rainbeaux" Smith, Vivian Blaine; **D:** Charles Band; **W:** Alan J. Adler, Frank Levering, Michael Shoob; **C:** Mac Ahlberg; **M:** Richard Band.

The Parent Trap

The updated remake of Disney's 1961 hit is certainly slicker than the original, but not an improvement. The tenuous premise is the same. Hallie and Annie (both played by Lohan) are identical twins separated as children when their parents divorced. Now dad (Quaid) is a Napa vintner while mom (Richardson) is a London fashion designer. The kids meet at summer camp and change places to bring the adults back together. Though she is undeniably cute as the Dickens, young Ms. Lohan is no Hayley Mills who, as an adolescent, had a huge impact on a generation of girls and young women. Both image and sound are very good on the DVD, though with such familiar material, it's probably not a significant improvement over VHS tape. —*MM*
Movie: 🐾🐾🐾 *DVD:* 🐾🐾🐾
Buena Vista Home Entertainment (Cat #15888, UPC #717951001092). Widescreen (1.85:1) letterboxed. Dolby Digital 5.1 Surround Stereo. $29.99. Keepcase. *LANG:* English; French. *CAP:* English. *FEATURES:* 20 chapter links • Theatrical trailer.
1998 (PG) 128m/C Dennis Quaid, Natasha Richardson, Lindsay Lohan, Polly Holliday, Elaine Hendrix, Joanna Barnes, Ronnie Stevens, Lisa Ann Walter, Simon Kunz, Maggie Wheeler; **D:** Nancy Meyers; **W:** Nancy Meyers, Charles Shyer; **C:** Dean Cundey; **M:** Alan Silvestri.

Parenthood

Four grown siblings and their parents struggle with various levels of parenthood. From the college drop-out, to the nervous single mother, to the yuppie couple raising an overachiever, every possibility is explored, including the perspective of the older generation, portrayed by Robards. It's genuinely funny with dramatic moments that work most of the time, with affecting performances from Martin and Wiest. Director Howard has four kids and was inspired to make this film when on a European jaunt with them. One of the better comedy-dramas about family life gets a so-so treatment on DVD. Though the colors are fine, the image is grainy. The Dolby Surround does have some nice imaging and separation and makes some use of the rear Surround. —*JO*
Movie: 🐾🐾🐾 *DVD:* 🐾🐾
Universal Studios Home Video (Cat #20174, UPC #025192017421). Full frame. Dolby Surround. $24.98. Keepcase. *LANG:* English; French. *SUB:* Spanish. *CAP:* English. *FEATURES:* 16 chapter links • Production notes • Cast and crew bios • Theatrical trailer.
1989 (PG-13) 124m/C Steve Martin, Mary Steenburgen, Dianne Wiest, Martha Plimpton, Keanu Reeves, Tom Hulce, Jason Robards Jr., Rick Moranis, Harley Jane Kozak, Joaquin Rafael (Leaf) Phoenix, Paul Linke, Dennis Dugan; **D:** Ron Howard; **W:** Ron Howard, Lowell Ganz, Babaloo Mandel; **C:** Donald McAlpine; **M:** Randy Newman. *AWARDS: NOM:* Academy

Awards '89: Best Song ("I Love to See You Smile"), Best Supporting Actress (Wiest).

Parents

Dark satire of middle-class suburban life in the '50s centers on a young boy who discovers that his parents aren't getting their meat from the local butcher. The film gives new meaning to leftovers and boasts a very disturbing barbeque scene. Balaban's debut is a strikingly visual and creative gorefest that has gained cult status. The eerie score is by Badalamenti, of *Twin Peaks* fame. Even if you're a carnivore, you've got to be a little disgusted by some of the shots of meat preparation and cooking in this film. Unfortunately, the gross-out experience is not as intense on the DVD, due to lack of sharpness and only moderately saturated colors, which tone down the disgusto-power of those scenes. The image is accompanied by a mono-sounding stereo soundtrack, which keeps the dialogue crisp enough, but does little to enhance the overall effect of the film. —*JO*

Movie: 🎬🎬🎬 **DVD:** 🎬▶
Pioneer Entertainment (Cat #DVD5278, UPC #013023023994). Full frame. Stereo. $24.98. Keepcase. *LANG:* English. *FEATURES:* 17 chapter links • Theatrical trailer • Cast and filmmakers bios.
1989 (R) 81m/C Randy Quaid, Mary Beth Hurt, Bryan Madorsky, Sandy Dennis, Kathryn Grody, Deborah Rush, Graham Jarvis, Juno Mills-Cockell; **D:** Bob Balaban; **W:** Christopher Hawthorne; **C:** Robin Vidgeon, Ernest Day; **M:** Angelo Badalamenti, Jonathan Elias, Sherman Foote.

Passion Fish

McDonnell plays May-Alice, a soap opera actress who is paralyzed after a taxi accident in New York. Confined to a wheelchair, the bitter woman moves back to her Louisiana home and alienates a number of live-in nurses until Chantelle (Woodard), who has her own problems, comes along. Blunt writing and directing by Sayles overcome the story's inherent sentimentality as do the spirited performances of the leads, including Curtis-Hall as the rogue romancing Chantelle and Strathairn as the Cajun badboy McDonnell once loved. When you talk about a Sayles film, the most commonly brought-up aspect is the intelligent and involving dialogue used to tell the story. But most also feature cinematography that consistently matches both the Quality and the mood of the story. *Passion Fish* is no exception and the lushness of the Louisiana locations are perfectly conveyed by the DVD's sharp picture and highly accurate colors. —*JO*
Movie: 🎬🎬🎬 **DVD:** 🎬🎬🎬▶
Columbia Tristar Home Video (Cat #53289, UPC #043396532892). Widescreen (1.85:1) letterboxed; full frame. Dolby Surround. $25.95. Keepcase. *LANG:* English; Spanish; French. *CAP:* English. *FEATURES:* 28 chapter links.

1992 (R) 136m/C Mary McDonnell, Alfre Woodard, David Strathairn, Vondie Curtis-Hall, Nora Dunn, Sheila Kelley, Angela Bassett, Maggie Renzi, Leo Burmester, Shauntisa Willis, John Henry, Michael Laskin; **D:** John Sayles; **W:** John Sayles; **C:** Roger Deakins; **M:** Mason Daring. *AWARDS:* Independent Spirit Awards '93: Best Supporting Actress (Woodard); *NOM:* Academy Awards '92: Best Actress (McDonnell), Best Original Screenplay.

Passion of Joan of Arc

An on-screen introduction states that this version of Dreyer's film, long thought lost, was made from a Danish copy that was discovered in 1981 in a closet at a Norwegian mental institution. That's oddly fitting for a silent meditation on mysticism. The stark clarity of the DVD is necessary to appreciate Dreyer's many extreme close-ups and his star Maria Falconetti's tortured performance. The disc also contains an adaptation of Richard Einhorn's oratorio, "Voices of Light," performed by the Anonymous Four with soloist Susan Narucki, and the Radio Netherlands Philharmonic and Choir. That music takes a similarly austere approach to the story of Joan's trial and execution. For those who prefer the original without accompaniment, the music is on a separate audio track. Both image and sound are first-rate, though this is such an unusual, almost experimental work that it is not recommended for everyone. —*MM*
Movie: 🎬🎬🎬 **DVD:** 🎬🎬🎬🎬
Criterion Collection (Cat #PAS050, UPC #037429139820). Full frame. Dolby Digital 5.1 Surround Stereo. $39.95. Keepcase. *LANG:* French intertitles. *SUB:* English. *FEATURES:* 24 chapter links • Separate audio track for "Voices of Light" • Audio essay by Dreyer scholar Casper Tybjerg • Notes on production design and other film versions of the story • Audio interview with Helene Falconetti, daughter of Maria Falconetti • Essay by Richard Einhorn on Joan of Arc and "Voices of Light" • Video essay on the music • "Voices of Light" libretto booklet with medieval texts and translations • Liner notes by Carl Theodor Dreyer.
1928 114m/B *FR* Renee (Marie) Falconetti, Eugena Sylvaw, Maurice Schultz, Antonin Artaud, Michel Simon; **D:** Carl Theodor Dreyer; **W:** Carl Theodor Dreyer, Joseph Delteil; **C:** Rudolph Mate.

Patch Adams (CE)

Unconventional med student "Patch" Adams (Williams) believes that laughter is a prime component in the healing process. The medical establishment is not ready for such a revolutionary idea. Standard based-on-a-true-story flick is fueled by yet another energetic performance from the star. On DVD, image and sound are fine for a Robin Williams movie. The extras, while numerous, are lacking. Director Tom Shadyac's commentary track is typically bland flattery to his cast and

crew, but the producers allowed the soundtrack to drown him out at times. The outtakes provide more of Williams's shtick and they prove that he's no Jackie Chan. —*MM*
Movie: 🎬🎬 **DVD:** 🎬🎬
Universal Studios Home Video (Cat #20546, UPC #025192054624). Widescreen (2.35:1) letterboxed. Dolby Digital 5.0 Surround Stereo. $34.98. Keepcase. *LANG:* English; French. *CAP:* English. *FEATURES:* 18 chapter links • "Making of" documentary • Commentary: director Tom Shadyac • Outtakes • Production notes • Cast and crew thumbnail biographies • Theatrical trailer • Universal web links. Also available in DTS Stereo sound (catalog #20629).
1998 (PG-13) 115m/C Robin Williams, Philip Seymour Hoffman, Monica Potter, Bob Gunton, Josef Sommer, Irma P. Hall, Daniel London, Frances Lee McCain, Harve Presnell, Peter Coyote, Michael Jeter, Harold Gould, Richard Kiley; **D:** Tom Shadyac; **W:** Steve Oedekerk; **C:** Phedon Papamichael; **M:** Marc Shaiman. *AWARDS:* *NOM:* Academy Awards '98: Best Original Musical/Comedy Score; Golden Globe Awards '99: Best Actor—Musical/Comedy (Williams), Best Film—Musical/Comedy.

Paths of Glory

Wrenching anti-war drama set in WWI France. A vain ambitious officer (Menjou) orders his own men to be fired upon, forcing them out of their trenches and into the slaughter that will further his career. When that fails, he demands that three soldiers be selected for execution as cowards. Douglas (who also produced) is properly heroic as the French officer who knows the truth and must defend the three. Based on a true story from Humphrey Cobb's novel of the same name. The screenplay was cowritten by director Kubrick. A slight bit of grain is the only problem with this DVD. The black-and-white film is presented with excellent contrast and brightness levels, as well as very good blacks and graytones. The film's mono soundtrack is unaltered, and though not re-mastered to 5.1 (as some seem to demand), delivers the dialogue, the sounds of battle, and the minimal score very well. —*JO*
Movie: 🎬🎬🎬🎬 **DVD:** 🎬🎬🎬▶
MGM Home Entertainment (Cat #907674, UPC #027616767424). Full frame. Dolby Digital Mono. $24.98. Keepcase. *LANG:* English; French. *SUB:* English; French. *FEATURES:* 32 chapter links • Theatrical trailer.
1957 86m/B Kirk Douglas, Adolphe Menjou, George Macready, Ralph Meeker, Richard Anderson, Wayne Morris, Timothy Carey, Susanne Christian, Bert Freed, Joe Turkel, Peter Capell; **D:** Stanley Kubrick; **W:** Stanley Kubrick, Calder Willingham, Jim Thompson; **C:** Georg Krause; **M:** Gerald Fried. *AWARDS:* National Film Registry '92.

The Patriot

Wesley McClaren (Seagal) is a former government immunologist who has become a rancher in Montana. His little mountain hamlet becomes a plague town when a neo-Nazi extremist group takes over and spreads a mysterious disease. As usual, the peace-loving doctor is forced to kick butt, though the overall level of violence is somewhat less egregious than it normally is when Seagal rips into stuntmen. The DVD also looks terrific in a Marlboro TV commercial kind of way. Director Semler and cinematographer Stephen F. Windon fill the widescreen with some spectacular landscapes and well-choreographed action scenes. The sound is very good, too. —MM

Movie: 🎬🎬 **DVD:** 🎬🎬🎬
Buena Vista Home Entertainment (Cat #17095, UPC #717951002099). Widescreen (1.85:1) letterboxed. Dolby Digital 5.1 Surround Stereo. $29.99. Keepcase. *LANG:* English. *CAP:* English. *FEATURES:* 22 chapter links.
1999 (R) 90m/C Steven Seagal, Gailard Sartain, L.Q. (Justus E. McQueen) Jones; *D:* Dean Semler; *C:* Stephen Windon; *M:* Steve Edwards.

Patriot Games

Jack Ryan, retired CIA analyst, takes his wife and daughter to England on a holiday and ends up saving a member of the Royal Family from assassination by IRA extremists. Ryan, who has killed one of the terrorists, then becomes the target of revenge by the dead man's brother. Good action sequences but otherwise predictable adaptation of the novel by Tom Clancy. Companion to *The Hunt for Red October,* with Ford taking over the role of Ryan from Alec Baldwin. A good DVD transfer with both a very sharp image and vibrant, accurate colors. Grain is minimal and there are only a couple of spots where artifacts intrude. Blacks are true. Contrast is punchy and brightness is both comfortable and consistent. The 5.1 sound features excellent imaging and fine use of the rear channels. There is also plenty of subwoofer activity giving the film a lot of energy. The mix is rounded out by crisp highs and clean, out-front dialogue. —JO

Movie: 🎬🎬🎬 **DVD:** 🎬🎬🎬▶
Paramount Home Video (Cat #325307, UPC #097363253075). Widescreen (2.35:1) letterboxed. Dolby Digital 5.1; Dolby Surround. $29.99. Keepcase. *LANG:* English; French. *SUB:* Spanish. *CAP:* English. *FEATURES:* 22 chapter links ▪ Theatrical trailer.
1992 (R) 117m/C Harrison Ford, Anne Archer, Patrick Bergin, Thora Birch, Sean Bean, Richard Harris, James Earl Jones, James Fox, Samuel L. Jackson, Polly Walker, Theodore (Ted) Raimi; *D:* Phillip Noyce; *W:* Donald Stewart, W. Peter Iliff; *C:* Donald McAlpine; *M:* James Horner.

Patriots

Alexis Shannon (Amendola), a young American woman with IRA sympathies, is brought into active involvement with the "Troubles" by Sean McGinniss (Newell), and learns that her ideas about right and wrong are far too simple for the situation. Frank Kerr's truth-based film tries to take an evenhanded look at the Irish conflict. On DVD, though, its serious purposes are partially undermined by a shabby image. Its high-contrast, overexposed look may be appropriate to the grim Belfast and Boston locations, but it's also so unforgiving that it does the unsympathetic characters no favors. —MM

Movie: 🎬🎬🎬 **DVD:** 🎬▶
Simitar Entertainment (Cat #7305, UPC #082551730520). Full frame. PCM Stereo. $14.98. Keepcase. *LANG:* English. *FEATURES:* 8 chapter links ▪ Production factoids.
1994 (R) 85m/C Linda Amendola, Mark Newell, Aidan Parkinson; *D:* Frank Kerr; *W:* Frank Kerr; *C:* Scott Williams.

Patton

One of Hollywood's finest biographies captures the life and times of the vain, temperamental American general who masterminded significant combat triumphs during WWII. Patton (Scott) produces victory after victory in Africa and Italy, but not without cost to his troops and to himself. Scott, who famously won an Oscar for his performance and refused it, is magnificent, capturing his subject's egomania, insecurity, and bravado. (He is so commanding a presence that it's easy to forget his last words, "All glory is fleeting.") Malden shines in the strong supporting role of Gen. Omar Bradley. The two-disc package contains the right extras, though the commentary track, an essay on the real Patton, has little to do with the film. The DVD image is better than VHS tape but only a small improvement over the widescreen edition. Sound is a solid advancement, particularly in the isolated Jerry Goldsmith score on the second disc. (It is accessed through your own audio control, not through the disc menu, as it appears to be.) The discs do justice to an enduring favorite. —MM *AKA:* Patton—Lust for Glory; Patton: A Salute to a Rebel.

Movie: 🎬🎬🎬🎬 **DVD:** 🎬🎬🎬▶
Twentieth Century Fox Home Entertainment (Cat #4112579, UPC #086162125 799). Widescreen letterboxed. Dolby Digital 5.1 Surround Stereo; Dolby Digital Surround Stereo; Mono. $29.98. Keepcase. *LANG:* English; French. *CAP:* English; Spanish. *FEATURES:* 37 chapter links on disc 1, the film itself ▪ 2 chapter links on disc 2, "making of" documentary and score ▪ Trailers ▪ Audio essay on the real Patton by Charles Province.
1970 (PG) 171m/C George C. Scott, Karl Malden, Stephen Young, Michael Strong, Frank Latimore, James Edwards, Lawrence (Larry) Dobkin, Michael Bates, Tim Considine, Edward Binns, John Doucette, Morgan Paull, Siegfried Rauch, Paul Stevens, Richard Muench; *D:* Franklin J. Schaffner; *W:* Francis Ford Coppola, Edmund H. North; *C:* Fred W. Koenekamp; *M:* Jerry Goldsmith. *AWARDS:* Academy Awards '70: Best Actor (Scott), Best Art Direction/Set Decoration, Best Director (Schaffner), Best Film Editing, Best Picture, Best Sound, Best Story & Screenplay; American Film Institute (AFI) '98: Top 100; Directors Guild of America Awards '70: Best Director (Schaffner); Golden Globe Awards '71: Best Actor—Drama (Scott); National Board of Review Awards '70: Best Actor (Scott); New York Film Critics Awards '70: Best Actor (Scott); National Society of Film Critics Awards '70: Best Actor (Scott); Writers Guild of America '70: Best Original Screenplay; *NOM:* Academy Awards '70: Best Cinematography, Best Original Score.

Paulie

Paulie (voice of Mohr) is a parrot who can talk and think. He tells his story to a janitor (Shalhoub). His goal is to return to Marie (Eisenberg), the little girl who raised him. The journey takes him through a series of owners played by a fine ensemble of character actors, led by Gena Rowlands. The action may be a little, er, talky for smaller kids, but the characters are so strong and the special effects so seamlessly integrated into the human action that the criticism is a quibble. The DVD looks fine, though it is probably not that much better than VHS tape. On either medium, this sleeper ought to find the audience on home video that it missed in theatres. —MM

Movie: 🎬🎬🎬▶ **DVD:** 🎬🎬🎬
DreamWorks Home Entertainment (Cat #84163, UPC #667068416329). Widescreen (1.85:1) letterboxed; full frame. Dolby Digital 5.1 Surround Stereo. $29.99. Keepcase. *LANG:* English; French; Spanish. *SUB:* Spanish. *CAP:* English. *FEATURES:* 16 chapter links ▪ Theatrical trailer ▪ Production notes ▪ Cast and crew thumbnail biographies.
1998 (PG) 91m/C Jay Mohr, Gena Rowlands, Tony Shalhoub, Richard "Cheech" Marin, Hallie Kate Eisenberg, Bruce Davison, Trini Alvarado, Buddy Hackett, Matt Craven, Bill Cobbs, Laura Harrington, Tia Texada; *D:* John Roberts; *W:* Laurie Craig; *C:* Tony Pierce-Roberts; *M:* John Debney; *V:* Jay Mohr.

Payback

The opening images of a bloody bullet dropped into a dirty glass of cheap whiskey sets a tone that this latter-day noir never really loses. A loose remake of 1969's *Point Blank,* the film sticks close to its fictional source material, *The Hunter,* by Richard Stark (AKA Donald Westlake). It's the violent, tricky story of Porter (Gibson), a thief who is betrayed by his wife (Unger) and friend Val (Henry). Thought dead, he returns to a grim unnamed Chicago to claim his share of the loot. A hooker (Bello) with a heart of gold (and a big dog), dapper mobsters, and crooked cops all come into play. The film's heavily textured design and stylized appearance push the limits of digital technology. The whole movie is tinted in shades of charcoal and black with red accents and otherwise muted colors. They are translated almost flawlessly to disc. It's brighter than the theatrical release and a scene-by-scene comparison to VHS tape reveals a noticeably higher degree of sharpness. The only flaw I could see—and I was looking for flaws—was some minimal flashing on a pinstripe shirt. Though the role is a little risky for a star of Gibson's magnitude, the film is a treat for fans who have seen too much sweetness and light. — *MM*

Movie: 🦴🦴🦴▶ **DVD:** 🦴🦴🦴🦴
Paramount Home Video (Cat #336327, UPC #097363363279). Widescreen anamorphic. Dolby Surround, 5.1 Surround (English); Dolby Surround Stereo (French). $29.98. Keepcase. *LANG:* English; French. *SUB:* English. *FEATURES:* 2 theatrical trailers ▪ 18 chapters ▪ "Making of" featurette.
1998 (R) 110m/C Mel Gibson, Gregg Henry, Maria Bello, David Paymer, Deborah Kara Unger, William Devane, Kris Kristofferson, Bill Duke, Jack Conley, John Glover, Lucy Alexis Liu, James Coburn; *D:* Brian Helgeland; *W:* Brian Helgeland, Terry Hayes; *C:* Ericson Core; *M:* Chris Boardman.

Peace Hotel

After an opening scene of a gangland massacre, Chow Yun-Fat founds a sanctuary for those fleeing various enemies. The violence is extreme and borrows much from the Italian westerns of Sergio Leone and Sergio Corbucci.
Movie: 🦴🦴▶ **DVD:** NYR
Tai Seng Video Marketing (Cat #41454). $49.95.
1995 ?m/C *HK* Chow Yun-Fat, Cecilia Yip, Lawrence Ng, Chin Ho; *D:* Kai-Fai Wai; *W:* Kai-Fai Wai; *C:* Wing-hang Wong; *M:* Cacine Wong, Healthy Poon.

The Peacekeeper

Maj. Frank Cross (Lundgren) is one unlucky officer. While guarding the president (Scheider) and carrying the briefcase with the nuclear launch codes, he is attacked by terrorists and the bag is snatched. Now psychos are blackmailing the United States. Actually, the offbeat casting of '60s star Sarrazin and TV personality Williams is more interesting than the generic plot of this Canadian thriller. On DVD, it is nothing special with a fairly grainy image that's not noticeably better than VHS tape. —*MM*
Movie: 🦴🦴 **DVD:** 🦴🦴
Image Entertainment (Cat #ID6313NGDVD, UPC #014381631326). Full frame. Dolby Digital Stereo. $24.99. Snapper. *LANG:* English. *FEATURES:* 14 chapter links ▪ Theatrical trailer.
1998 (R) 98m/C *CA* Dolph Lundgren, Roy Scheider, Michael Sarrazin, Montel Williams, Monika Schnarre; *D:* Frederic

Forestier; *W:* James H. Stewart, Robert Geoffrion; *C:* John Berrie; *M:* Francois Forestier.

The Peacemaker

Army Intelligence officer Thomas Devoe (Clooney) and White House nuclear weapons expert Dr. Julia Kelly (Kidman) work together to thwart terrorists who have stolen Russian warheads. Though the plot is familiar, the characters have some depth and they avoid the expected romantic entanglements. Also, the action sequences are handled particularly well by first-time feature director Leder. In that department, the DVD extras contain short but instructive examinations of the various pieces that go into the creation of one short car chase/crash sequence and a chase down a crowded city street. Both are excellent examples of the power of editing. Of course, the large special effects scenes lose power on the small screen. Otherwise, both image and sound are a bit better than the VHS tape. The disc is also available with DTS sound (catalog #84674). —*MM*
Movie: 🦴🦴▶ **DVD:** 🦴🦴🦴
DreamWorks Home Entertainment (Cat #84160, UPC #667068416022). Widescreen (2.35:1) letterboxed. Dolby Digital 5.1 Surround Stereo; Dolby Digital Surround Stereo. $29.99. Keepcase. *LANG:* English; French; Spanish. *SUB:* Spanish. *CAP:* English. *FEATURES:* 16 chapter links ▪ Deleted scenes ▪ Stunt footage of two action scenes ▪ Production notes ▪ Cast and crew thumbnail biographies ▪ Theatrical trailers ▪ Teaser.
1997 (R) 123m/C George Clooney, Nicole Kidman, Armin Mueller-Stahl, Marcel Iures, Alexander Baluyev, Randall Batinkoff, Jim Haynie, Michael Boatman, Gary Werntz, Holt McCallany, Joan Copeland, Carlos Gomez, Rene Medvesek, Alexander Strobele; *D:* Mimi Leder; *W:* Michael Schiffer; *C:* Dietrich Lohmann; *M:* Hans Zimmer.

Peach / A Bitter Song

Two short films star Lucy Lawless, from TV's *Xena*. In the first, she plays a sexy lesbian tow-truck driver. In "A Bitter Song," she's a nurse who helps a young girl in a hospital. The DVD also includes "Lavender Limelight," a documentary about lesbian filmmakers.
Movie: NYR **DVD:** NYR
First Run Features (Cat #FRF909099D, UPC #720229909099). Full frame. $29.95. Keepcase.
1995 95m/C Lucy Lawless, Tania Simon; *D:* Christine Parker; *W:* Christine Parker; *C:* Stuart Dryburgh.

The Pebble and the Penguin

Animated musical follows Hubie (Short), a shy romantic penguin who must present his lady love Marina (Golden) with a beautiful pebble to win her hand (or should that be wing?) before the villainous Drake

(Curry) can claim her. Hubie is helped by a cantankerous new friend (Belushi) he meets when stranded on a boat to Tahiti. Together the two race back to Antarctica fighting enemies and the elements along the way. The film is based on a true mating custom of the Adeli penguins and the story is satisfying for younger viewers but without the animation magic necessary for adult audiences. Beware of the sugary Manilow tunes.
Movie: 🦴🦴▶ **DVD:** NYR
MGM Home Entertainment (Cat #905403). Full frame. Dolby Digital 5.1 Surround Stereo. $24.98. Keepcase. *FEATURES:* Trailer.
1994 (G) 74m/C *D:* Don Bluth; *W:* Rachel Koretsky, Steve Whitestone; *M:* Barry Manilow, Bruce Sussman, Mark Watters; *V:* Martin Short, Annie Golden, Tim Curry, James Belushi; *Nar:* Shani Wallis.

Pecker

A kinder, gentler Waters? To be sure, he doesn't laugh at, but with, his working-class Baltimoreans. Still, you've got strippers (of both sexes), a "talking" statue of the Virgin Mary, and rats having sex, so this isn't a Disney film. Pecker (Furlong), who gets his name from pecking at his food, is a sweet teenager and amateur photog, who takes pictures of what's around him. His work catches the eye of New York art dealer Rorey Wheeler (Taylor), who wants to showcase the next hot trend, and Pecker becomes an overnight superstar in the fickle art world. But his celeb status has unexpected repercussions on his hometown friends and family. One of the most impressive features of the DVD is the commentary by Waters, who is able to relate both anecdotes and filmmaking technical aspects in an equally entertaining manner. The picture itself is sharp and the grain level is very low. Artifacts are also unobtrusive. Colors are accurate to the theatre even if they seem a little lackluster. Blacks are true. Contrast is good and brightness is excellent. Surround is limited on the 5.1 tracks (mainly just to scatter a little musical and environmental ambience) but it conveys dialogue and Waters's unique choice of music quite adequately. —*JO*
Movie: 🦴🦴🦴 **DVD:** 🦴🦴🦴🦴
New Line Home Video (Cat #N731, UPC #79043473128). Widescreen (1.85:1) anamorphic. Dolby Digital 5.1; Dolby Surround. $24.98. *LANG:* English. *SUB:* English. *CAP:* English. *FEATURES:* 20 chapter links ▪ Theatrical trailer ▪ Commentary: John Waters ▪ Cast and filmmaker bios ▪ Pecker's snapshot gallery ▪ Interview with Chuck Shacochis.
1998 (R) 87m/C Edward Furlong, Lili Taylor, Christina Ricci, Martha Plimpton, Mary Kay Place, Brendan Sexton III, Mark Joy, Mink Stole, Bess Armstrong, Patty Hearst, Mary Vivian Pearce, Lauren Hulsey, Jean Schertler; *D:* John Waters; *W:* John Waters; *C:* Robert Stevens; *M:* Stewart Copeland; *V:* John Waters. *AWARDS:*

National Board of Review Awards '98: Best Supporting Actress (Ricci).

Pee-wee's Big Adventure

Zany, endearing comedy follows the famous man-child's (Reubens) adventures attempting to recover his beloved stolen bicycle. It's chock-full of sequences that have become audience favorites, including the morning breakfast routine, a barroom encounter with several ornery bikers and a tour through the Alamo. The film's manic set design and clashing candy colors present no problems on disc. This one looks fine. There may have been some visual flaws, but I missed them because I was laughing at one of my favorite comedies. On their chummy commentary track, Reubens and director Burton don't try to upstage the outrageous action they created near the beginning of their careers. —MM

Movie: ♪♪♪➤ **DVD:** ♪♪♪➤
Warner Home Video, Inc. (Cat #17156). Widescreen letterboxed. Dolby Digital 5.1 Surround Stereo. $24.98. Snapper. LANG: English; French. SUB: English; French. FEATURES: 28 chapter links • Commentary: Paul Reubens and Tim Burton • Commentary: Danny Elfman with isolated score • Trailer • Cast and crew thumbnail bios • Deleted scenes • Production sketches and storyboards.
1985 (PG) 92m/C Paul (Pee-wee Herman) Reubens, Elizabeth (E.G.) Daily, Mark Holton, Diane Salinger, Judd Omen, Cassandra Peterson, James Brolin, Morgan Fairchild, Tony Bill, Jan Hooks, Phil Hartman, Jason Hervey, John Paragon; **D:** Tim Burton; **W:** Michael Varhol, Paul (Pee-wee Herman) Reubens, Phil Hartman; **C:** Victor Kemper; **M:** Danny Elfman.

Peeping Tom

In 1960, Michael Powell's other masterpiece (after *The Red Shoes*) was decades ahead of its time. But as the documentary included on this DVD makes clear, critics did not merely dislike the film, they loathed it. Their reaction was so strong that Powell's reputation was essentially ruined. He tells the story of Mark (Boehm), a twisted young film technician driven to murder women as he photographs them. He falls in love with Helen (Massey), but her blind mother (Audley) seems to know everything about him. The horror/thriller works on several levels. Voyeurism is writer Leo Marks's prime subject but it's also about the nature of film, from the perspective of both the creator and the viewer. Seen simply as a thriller, it's Hitchcockian in the very best sense of the term—complex, witty, suspenseful, unpredictable. The DVD was created from the Voyager laserdisc version. The print is as sharp as the technology of 1960 allowed, with overly bright colors and inherent graininess. Film theorist Laura Mulvey's commentary track may be too academic for some viewers but she

makes valid, perceptive points. As a landmark of modern horror, the film deserves to be ranked alongside *Psycho*, and this is the finest version available. —MM **AKA:** Face of Fear; The Fotographer of Panic.

Movie: ♪♪♪♪ **DVD:** ♪♪♪♪
Criterion Collection (Cat #PEE040, UPC #037429142929). Widescreen (1.66:1) letterboxed. Dolby Digital Mono. $39.95. Keepcase. LANG: English. SUB: English. FEATURES: 27 chapter links • "A Very British Psycho," a Channel 4 documentary • Theatrical trailer • Stills gallery • Commentary: film theorist Laura Mulvey.
1960 88m/C *GB* Karl-Heinz Boehm, Moira Shearer, Anna Massey, Maxine Audley, Esmond Knight, Shirley Anne Field, Brenda Bruce, Pamela Green, Jack Watson, Nigel Davenport, Susan Travers, Veronica Hurst, Martin Miller, Miles Malleson, Michael Powell; **D:** Michael Powell; **W:** Leo Marks; **C:** Otto Heller; **M:** Brian Easdale.

Peggy Sue Got Married

Uneven but entertaining comedy is about an unhappily married woman seemingly able to relive her life when she falls unconscious at a high school reunion and awakens to find herself back in school. Turner shines, but the film lags often, and Cage isn't around enough to elevate the entire work. O'Connor scores, though, as a sensitive biker. Look for musician Marshall Crenshaw as part of the reunion band. This is a fine transfer to DVD that is far sharper than any previous home video releases of the film. Colors are vibrant, with finely detailed shadings, and no bleed. The image is very sharp with no grain or artifacts. Seeing this film with this quality gives it new respect, and showcases Coppola's cinematic touches, which take it above the usual pabulum of this sort of sentimental journey. —JO

Movie: ♪♪➤ **DVD:** ♪♪♪➤
Columbia Tristar Home Video (Cat #81849, UPC #043396818491). Widescreen (1.85:1) anamorphic. Dolby Surround. NSL. Keepcase. LANG: English; Spanish; French. SUB: English; Spanish; French. CAP: English. FEATURES: 28 chapter links • Theatrical trailer.
1986 (PG-13) 103m/C Kathleen Turner, Nicolas Cage, Catherine Hicks, Maureen O'Sullivan, John Carradine, Helen Hunt, Lisa Jane Persky, Barbara Harris, Joan Allen, Kevin J. O'Connor, Barry Miller, Don Murray, Leon Ames, Sofia Coppola, Sachi Parker, Jim Carrey; **D:** Francis Ford Coppola; **W:** Jerry Leichtling, Arlene Sarner; **C:** Jordan Cronenweth; **M:** John Barry. AWARDS: National Board of Review Awards '86: Best Actress (Turner); NOM: Academy Awards '86: Best Actress (Turner), Best Cinematography, Best Costume Design.

Peking Opera Blues

There's adrenaline to spare in director Harks's exhilarating action comedy. The film follows three women in 1913 Beijing

as they buck traditions and find themselves neck-deep in intrigue. The pace is incredible; the action nonstop and stylized. It's great to see this fine action/comedy on DVD. The Tai Seng transfer is not great but is on par with most of their releases, and certainly very watchable. The picture is of average sharpness and has a few bouts with some rather nasty grain. Colors are a little faded and contrast is somewhat low. There are portions of the soundtrack where the dialogue would be hard to understand (even if you know Chinese) as a result of warbling and sudden loss of crispness. But no need to worry, thanks to Tai Seng's usual offering of multiple subtitles. —JO **AKA:** Dao Ma Dan.

Movie: ♪♪♪➤ **DVD:** ♪♪➤
Tai Seng Video Marketing (Cat #MS DVD03998, UPC #489501700381). Widescreen (1.85:1) letterboxed. Dolby Digital 5.1. $49.95. Keepcase. LANG: Cantonese; Mandarin. SUB: English; Spanish; Japanese; Simplified Chinese; Korean; Vietnamese; Bahasa; Thai. FEATURES: 9 chapter links • Theatrical trailer.
1986 104m/C *CH* Sally Yeh, Cherie Chung, Brigitte (Lin Ching-hsai) Lin; **D:** Tsui Hark; **W:** Kwok-wai To; **C:** Hang-Sang Poon; **M:** James Wong.

The Pelican Brief

Alan Pakula's adaptation of John Grisham's legal thriller about political assassination is long and slow-moving in stretches, but it's generally faithful to the source with an ending that's stronger than the original. The significant difference here is the casting of a black man (Washington) and a white woman (Roberts) in roles that are normally involved in a romantic relationship. It generates some unusual tension in the second half of the film. On DVD, the night scenes are acceptable, but some low-light interiors are overly dim. This is a two-sided disc that must be turned over. —MM

Movie: ♪♪➤ **DVD:** ♪♪➤
Warner Home Video, Inc. (Cat #12989, UPC #085391298922). Widescreen letterboxed. Dolby Digital 5.1 Surround; Dolby Surround Stereo. $24.98. Snapper. LANG: English; French; Spanish. SUB: English; French; Spanish. CAP: English. FEATURES: 32 chapter links • Cast and crew thumbnail biographies.
1993 (PG-13) 141m/C Julia Roberts, Denzel Washington, John Heard, Tony Goldwyn, Stanley Tucci, James B. Sikking, William Atherton, Robert Culp, John Lithgow, Sam Shepard, Hume Cronyn; **D:** Alan J. Pakula; **W:** Alan J. Pakula; **C:** Stephen Goldblatt; **M:** James Horner. AWARDS: NOM: MTV Movie Awards '94: Best Female Performance (Roberts), Most Desirable Male (Washington).

Penitentiary

Realistic story follows a black fighter (Kennedy) who survives his incarceration by winning bouts against other prisoners.

Unusually well made for a low-budget effort.
Movie: ♪♪▶ **DVD:** NYR
Xenon Entertainment (Cat #1035). $19.95.
1979 (R) 99m/C Leon Isaac Kennedy, Jamaa Fanaka, Badja Djola, Chuck "Porky" Mitchell; **D:** Jamaa Fanaka; **W:** Jamaa Fanaka; **C:** Marty Ollstein.

Penitentiary 2
Disappointing sequel finds a welterweight fighter going after the man who murdered his girlfriend. He is incarcerated at the same prison with Our Hero.
Movie: ♪ **DVD:** NYR
Xenon Entertainment (Cat #1036). $19.95.
1982 (R) 108m/C Leon Isaac Kennedy, Mr. T, Leif Erickson, Ernie Hudson, Glynn Turman; **D:** Jamaa Fanaka; **W:** Jamaa Fanaka; **C:** Stephen Posey; **M:** Jack Wheaton.

Penny Serenade
Newlyweds adopt a child, but tragedy awaits. Simplistic story nonetheless proves to be a moving experience. They don't make 'em like this anymore, and no one plays Grant better than Grant. Dunne is adequate.
Movie: ♪♪♪ **DVD:** NYR
Madacy Entertainment (Cat #99015). Full frame. Dolby Digital 5.1 Surround Stereo. $9.99. Keepcase. FEATURES: Cast and crew thumbnail bios.
1941 120m/B Cary Grant, Irene Dunne, Beulah Bondi, Edgar Buchanan, Ann Doran, Wallis Clark; **D:** George Stevens; **W:** Morrie Ryskind; **C:** Joseph Walker; **M:** W. Franke Harling. AWARDS: NOM: Academy Awards '41: Best Actor (Grant).

The People vs. Larry Flynt
Controversy surrounded director Forman's look at unrepentant pornographer and Hustler magazine publisher Larry Flynt (Harrelson). While feminists decried what they saw as a whitewash of Flynt's career, Forman insisted his movie was about Flynt's legal battles concerning the First Amendment and freedom of speech. If you can set aside your prejudices, you'll find a master storyteller at work and some great performances from Harrelson as Flynt, Love as his drug-addicted and ultimately tragic wife Althea, and Norton as Flynt's sometimes impatient attorney, Alan Isaacman, who does get his big moment before the U.S. Supreme Court (his speeches are taken from actual court transcripts). There's not a big improvement over the laserdisc release but this is not a bad DVD at all. The sharpness is nothing special but the colors are much more vibrant. The 5.1 sound is lacking in Surround effects but its dynamics allow all Harrelson's speechifyin' and Love's psycho-screaming to arrive at your home theatre totally intact, with far more guts than the sound on the LD. —JO
Movie: ♪♪♪ **DVD:** ♪♪♪

Columbia Tristar Home Video (Cat #82459, UPC #043396824591). Widescreen (2.35:1) anamorphic; full frame. Dolby Digital 5.1; Stereo. $29.95. Keepcase. LANG: English (DD5.1;DSl); French (DS); Spanish (DS). SUB: English; Spanish. CAP: English. FEATURES: 36 chapter links.
1996 (R) 130m/C Woody Harrelson, Courtney Love, Edward Norton, James Cromwell, Crispin Glover, Brett Harrelson, James Carville, Vincent Schiavelli, Richard Paul, Donna Hanover, Norm MacDonald, Miles Chapin, Jan Triska; **Cameos:** Larry Flynt; **D:** Milos Forman; **W:** Larry Karaszewski, Scott Alexander; **C:** Philippe Rousselot; **M:** Thomas Newman. AWARDS: Golden Globe Awards '97: Best Director (Forman), Best Screenplay; Los Angeles Film Critics Association Awards '96: Best Supporting Actor (Norton); National Board of Review Awards '96: Best Supporting Actor (Norton); New York Film Critics Awards '96: Best Supporting Actress (Love); NOM: Academy Awards '96: Best Actor (Harrelson), Best Director (Forman); Golden Globe Awards '97: Best Actor—Drama (Harrelson), Best Actress—Drama (Love), Best Film—Drama; MTV Movie Awards '97: Breakthrough Performance (Love); Screen Actors Guild Award '96: Best Actor (Harrelson).

A Perfect Murder
Steven Taylor (Douglas) is a rich commodities trader about to lose his fortune. He's married to young and also rich Emily (Paltrow), who's having an affair with boho artist David (Mortensen). Steven decides to solve his various problems by hiring David to kill Emily. Douglas, the aged yet sturdy centerpiece of the film, shines as the pompous rich dude devoid of morals and overpowers his youthful supporting cast. Inspired by Hitchcock's 1954 Dial M for Murder. The DVD makes the most of the film's highly polished production values, which are commented upon extensively in one of the two commentary tracks. Some of the large areas of black—noticeable mostly in the chi-chi clothes—are undifferentiated, but that's a minor imperfection. Sound is fine. The disc also includes alternate endings among the customary extras, including a second, more technical commentary track with producer Peter MacGregor-Scott, director of photography Dariusz Wolski, costume designer Ellen Mirojnick, set decorator Dera Schutt, and production designer Philip Rosenberg. —MM
Movie: ♪♪▶ **DVD:** ♪♪♪▶
Warner Home Video, Inc. (Cat #16643, UPC #085391664321). Full frame; widescreen letterboxed. Dolby Digital 5.1 Surround; Dolby Surround Stereo. $24.98. Snapper. LANG: English; French. SUB: English; French. CAP: English. FEATURES: Cast and crew thumbnail biographies • 32 chapter links • Commentary: Davis, Kelly, and Douglas • Technical commentary track • Alternate endings.
1998 (R) 105m/C Michael Douglas, Gwyneth Paltrow, Viggo Mortensen, David Suchet, Sarita Choudhury, Constance Tow-

ers, Novella Nelson; **D:** Andrew Davis; **W:** Patrick Smith Kelly; **C:** Darius Wolski; **M:** James Newton Howard.

Perfect Profile
Basketball drama with Nancy Lieberman.
Movie: NYR **DVD:** NYR
Digital Versatile Disc Ltd. (Cat #114). Full frame. $19.95. Keepcase.
1990 87m/C Nancy Lieberman, Tom Campitelli, Bruce Anderson, Nancy Buechler, Rocky Patterson, Rob Slyker; **D:** Jim Harris.

Permanent Midnight
Stiller stars as TV writer Jerry Stahl in this film version of his 1995 autobiography, which follows his plunge from a guy who has it all to a loser junkie who's as unlikable as this movie itself. At its real-life peak, Stahl's heroine habit reached $6,000 a week. There are some great flashes of dark humor—Jerry is obsessed with exercising and eating right even while pumping himself full of drugs—and some truly horrific sequences (at one low point, Stahl both scores and shoots up with his baby daughter by his side). The problem is that we don't care. Stiller's comic timing makes most of the bleak jokes work, and it's the only thing that makes the movie bearable; however, his brooding performance (possibly due to writer-director Veloz) lacks any charisma. Watch for Stahl himself as a pessimistic doctor at a methadone clinic. The DVD transfer is not bad, but it's also not great. The image is fairly sharp, but does have both grain and artifacts. Colors are close but a little pale, making fleshtones a touch off. Blacks are true with occasional grain. Contrast is a touch low but brightness levels seem fine. The 5.1 sound focuses on the dialogue and some ambience with a lot of midrange punch and fairly gutsy bass. —JO
Movie: ♪▶ **DVD:** ♪♪▶
Artisan Entertainment (Cat #60489, UPC #01236048909). Widescreen (1.85:1) anamorphic. Dolby Digital 5.1. $24.98. Keepcase. LANG: English. CAP: English. FEATURES: 36 chapter links • Theatrical trailer • Commentary: David Veloz • Deleted scenes • Cast and filmmaker bios • Production notes.
1998 (R) 85m/C Ben Stiller, Elizabeth Hurley, Maria Bello, Owen C. Wilson, Lourdes Benedicto, Peter Greene, Cheryl Ladd, Fred Willard, Charles Fleischer, Janeane Garofalo, Jerry Stahl; **D:** David Veloz; **W:** David Veloz; **C:** Robert Yeoman; **M:** Daniel Licht.

Peter Pan
This silent version of the famous play contains all the familiar characters and events. The special effects—including people in delightful costumes for Nana the dog and the Crocodile—are rudimentary, and the sentimentality of the entire production is equally dated. Anna May Wong

plays an Indian and the director of photography is the legendary James Wong Howe (*Sweet Smell of Success*). The film was thought lost for decades. This DVD, made from original nitrate elements, is still rough-looking compared to the best-preserved films of the era, most notably the Buster Keaton features. It would be unfair to expect anything more. Star Esther Ralston's reminiscences appears to be a home video shot at Christmas. —*MM*
Movie: ♫♫⯈ **DVD:** ♫♫⯈
Kino on Video (Cat #K140, UPC #73832901402). Full frame. $29.99. Keepcase. *LANG:* English intertitles. *FEATURES:* 9 chapter links • Essay by film historian Frederick C. Szebin • Photo gallery and original promotional material • Reminiscences by Esther Ralston • Orchestral score by Philip Carli.
1924 102m/B Betty Bronson, Ernest Torrence, Mary Brian, Virginia Brown Faire, Anna May Wong, Esther Ralston, Cyril Chadwick, Philippe De Lacey, Jack Murphy; **D:** Herbert Brenon; **W:** Willis Goldbeck; **C:** James Wong Howe; **M:** Philip Carli.

Peter Pan

Disney's interpretation of the story of a boy who refuses to grow up is still the best cinematic version. Animation and music are superb. The studio has always been so careful with the video presentation of its "classic" productions that, in visual and aural terms, the DVD is only marginally better than the excellent VHS tape. The real difference in the no-frills disc lies in scene accessibility and durability. Some kids will watch it over and over. —*MM*
Movie: ♫♫♫⯈ **DVD:** ♫♫♫⯈
Buena Vista Home Entertainment (Cat #18786, UPC #717951005854). Full frame. Dolby Digital Mono. $39.99. Keepcase. *LANG:* English; French. *CAP:* English. *FEATURES:* 31 chapter links.
1953 (G) 76m/C D: Hamilton Luske; **W:** Milt Banta, William Cottrell, Winston Hibler, Bill Peet, Erdman Penner, Joe Rinaldi, Ted Sears, Ralph Wright; **V:** Bobby Driscoll, Kathryn Beaumont, Hans Conried, Heather Angel, Candy Candido; **Nar:** Tom Conway.

Peter Pan

This TV classic is a taped performance of the 1954 Broadway musical adapted from the J.M. Barrie story. It features Mary Martin in one of her most famous roles as the eternally prepubescent Pan.
Movie: ♫♫♫⯈ **DVD:** NYR
Goodtimes Entertainment (Cat #18786). Full frame. Dolby Digital Stereo. $14.99. Keepcase. *LANG:* English. *SUB:* Spanish.
1960 100m/C Mary Martin, Cyril Ritchard, Sondra Lee, Heather Halliday, Luke Halpin; **D:** Vincent J. Donehue.

Petticoat Planet

Erotic sci-fi from prolific video auteur Dave DeCoteau.

Movie: ♫⯈ **DVD:** NYR
Full Moon Pictures (Cat #8020). Full frame. Dolby Digital Stereo. $24.95. Keepcase. *LANG:* English. *FEATURES:* Trailer.
1995 ?m/C Elizabeth Kaitan, Betsey Lynn George, Troy Vincent, Lesli Kay Sterling; **D:** David DeCoteau; **W:** Matthew Jason Walsh; **C:** Viorel Sergovici Jr.; **M:** Reg Powell.

Phantasm

The senseless plot concerns two parentless brothers who discover weird goings-on at the local funeral parlor, including the infamous airborne, brain-drilling chrome ball; malevolent hooded midgets in monk's robes; and the Tall Man (Scrimm). Creepy, unpredictable nightmare fashioned on a shoestring by young independent producer-writer-director Coscarelli contains enough imaginative twists and inventions for a dozen horror movies, but not enough logic for one. The plot and sensibility could have come straight from a Roadrunner cartoon, with about as much attention paid to the laws of physics. On DVD, this one looks much better than any low-budget 1979 production ought to. The other extras add to the film's wild-and-wooly reputation. —*MM* **AKA:** The Never Dead.
Movie: ♫♫♫ **DVD:** ♫♫♫⯈
MGM Home Entertainment (Cat #907793, UPC #027616779328). Widescreen (1.85:1) letterboxed. Dolby Digital 5.1 Surround Stereo; Mono. $24.98. Keepcase. *LANG:* English. *CAP:* English. *FEATURES:* Commentary: Coscarelli, Baldwin, Bannister, Thornbury • 1979 interview with Coscarelli and Scrimm • Deleted scenes • Trailer • TV and radio spots • Behind-the-scenes footage • Gallery of promotional material • Liner notes.
1979 (R) 90m/C Michael Baldwin, Bill Thornbury, Reggie Bannister, Kathy Lester, Terrie Kalbus, Ken Jones, Susan Harper, Lynn Eastman, David Arntzen, Angus Scrimm, Bill Cone; **D:** Don A. Coscarelli; **W:** Don A. Coscarelli; **M:** Fredric Myrow, Malcolm Seagrave.

The Phantom

Based on the Lee Falk comic strip created in 1936, this crowd-pleaser is faithful to the source material in look and spirit with a respectful nod to *Raiders of the Lost Ark*. Deep in the jungle on the island of Bengalla, The Ghost Who Walks (Zane) honors a 400-year-old legacy by fighting piracy, greed, and cruelty. With the help of beautiful newspaper heiress Diana Palmer (Swanson), he must keep evil American industrialist Xander Drax (Williams at his cheerful best) and a secret brotherhood from finding the three sacred skulls that will give them the power to rule the world. The swashbuckling story runs at a gallop, but it really succeeds on director Wincer's understanding of the material. The big scenes play remarkably well on DVD, though the computer-generated images are somewhat easier to spot than they were in theatres. Zane's letter-perfect performance is enhanced on the small

screen, too, and his neat costume looks even better. My only caveat: a commentary track with Wincer and writer Boam could have been instructive. —*MM*
Movie: ♫♫♫⯈ **DVD:** ♫♫♫⯈
Paramount Home Video (Cat #328507, UPC #097363285076). Widescreen letterboxed. Dolby Surround Stereo; Dolby 5.1 Surround Stereo. $29.98. Keepcase. *LANG:* English; French. *CAP:* English. *FEATURES:* 20 chapter links • Theatrical trailer.
1996 (PG) 100m/C Billy Zane, Kristy Swanson, Treat Williams, Catherine Zeta-Jones, James Remar, Jon Tenney, Patrick McGoohan, Samantha Eggar, Cary-Hiroyuki Tagawa, Robert Coleby, David Proval; **D:** Simon Wincer; **W:** Jeffrey Boam; **C:** David Burr; **M:** David Newman.

The Phantom of the Opera

Gaston LeRoux's tale is one of the most popular potboilers of all time—on stage, page, or screen. Chaney's version is the most famous and rightly so. The big scenes—the falling chandelier, the underground lake, the masked ball, the final chase, and, of course, the unmasking—are still terrific. Despite changes in dramatic style, this is one of Chaney's most impressive acting jobs. If you can take your eyes off his makeup, notice how expressively he uses his hands. The DVD version, taken from the 1990 laserdisc, re-creates the original tinting and has added a modern orchestral soundtrack. The print is only slightly scratchy. The darker scenes are as clear, in their way, as the rest, and the Bal Masque scene is done in an early Technicolor process emphasizing deep reds. The orchestral score is new and sounds fine. The disc was made from a master of the 1929 reissue that was projected at 20 frames per second. (Silent films were made to run at speeds ranging between 16 and 20 frames per second.) Michael F. Blake's extensive liner notes are exemplary. —*MM*
Movie: ♫♫♫♫ **DVD:** ♫♫♫⯈
Image Entertainment (Cat #ID4097DSDVD, UPC #014381409727). Full frame. Digital Stereo. $29.95. Snapper. *FEATURES:* 12 chapter links • Music performed by the I Musici de Montreal and Claudine Cote • Photos and artwork • Re-release trailer.
1925 101m/B Lon Chaney Sr., Norman Kerry, Mary Philbin, Gibson Gowland, Arthur Edmund Carewe, John St. Polis, Snitz Edwards, Virginia Pearson; **D:** Rupert Julian, Edward Sedgwick, Lon Chaney Sr.; **W:** Elliot J. Clawson, Raymond L. Schrock, Frank M. McCormack; **C:** Virgil Miller, Charles Van Enger, Milton Bridenbecker. *AWARDS:* National Film Registry '98.

The Phantom of the Opera

This version of the tragic tale of a disfigured mask-wearing opera lover emphasizes the *Beauty and the Beast* elements of the plot. Dance plays the phantom as a doomed romantic with Lancaster as his protective father (!) and Teri Polo as the ingenue Christine. The cast and director Tony Richardson handle the material seriously. Kopit adapted his stage play to a two-part mini-series and so the pace is slow. The producers elected to leave the two halves intact on DVD, rather than re-editing them into a single work. Since the production was always meant for the small screen, image and sound are fine, but they never reach the melodramatic heights of the original Chaney film. —MM

Movie: 🦴🦴▸ **DVD:** 🦴🦴🦴
Image Entertainment (Cat #ID5863SVDVD, UPC #014381586329). Full frame. Dolby Digital Stereo. $29.99. Snapper. *LANG:* English. *FEATURES:* 21 chapter links.
1990 200m/C *GB* Charles Dance, Burt Lancaster, Teri Polo, Ian Richardson, Andrea Ferreol, Adam Storke, Jean-Pierre Cassel; *D:* Tony Richardson; *W:* Arthur Kopit; *C:* Steve Yaconelli; *M:* John Addison.

The Phantom of the Opera

Dario Argento's remake is not as lively as his first pass at the story, *Terror at the Opera.* This version gives us a handsome Phantom (Sands) who was raised by rats. His lack of disfigurement is contrasted to such real horrors as child sexual abuse. That's a curious subplot considering the way Argento sexualizes his own daughter Asia in the role of Christine. The rest takes considerable liberties with the plot. On DVD, the film looks remarkably sharp. Some of the ornate opera house interiors lose definition during Argento's trademarked fast panning shots. The subterranean scenes hold up very well. The chandelier crash is good but not great. Sound is excellent. Argento's many fans will love all the extras on the disc, but they will have to admit that their man has done more ambitious work. Those not familiar with his brand of horror may find this to be a good introduction. The full-frame and widescreen versions are on opposite sides of the disc. —MM *AKA:* Dario Argento's Phantom of the Opera; Il Fantasma dell'Opera.
Movie: 🦴🦴▸ **DVD:** 🦴🦴🦴▸
A-PIX Entertainment Inc. (Cat #APX 27013DJ, UPC #783722701331). Full frame; widescreen anamorphic. Dolby Stereo; Dolby 5.1 Surround Stereo. $24.98. Keepcase. *LANG:* English. *SUB:* Spanish. *FEATURES:* 12 chapter links • Julian Sands interview • Filmographies for Dario Argento, Julian Sands, Asia Argento • Behind the scenes featurette • *Fangoria* magazine article • Photo gallery.
1998 100m/C *IT* Julian Sands, Asia Argento, Andrea Di Stefano, Nadia Rinaldi, Coralina Cataldi-Tassoni, Istvan Bubik, Zoltan Barabas; *D:* Dario Argento; *W:* Dario Argento, Gerard Brach; *C:* Ronnie Taylor; *M:* Ennio Morricone.

Phantoms

Novelist Dean Koontz does fine work with the familiar deserted town formula in an inventive sf thriller. When Dr. Jenny Pailey (Going) and her ne'er-do-well sister Lisa (McGowan) return to a little Colorado mountain resort, they find all the residents dead. They team up with sheriff Hammond (Affleck) and his deputy (Schrieber) to battle the evil force-thingie. Timothy Flyte (O'Toole, who's not quite as out of place as he might have been) appears as an expert on ancient plagues. Everyone involved treats the material with the right playfulness. Many of the big special effects scenes are carefully darkened and so they do not gain that much on the no-frills DVD, but the film still looks and sounds fine. Great fun for fans. —MM
Movie: 🦴🦴🦴 **DVD:** 🦴🦴🦴
Buena Vista Home Entertainment (Cat #14893, UPC #717951000590). Widescreen (1.85:1) letterboxed. Dolby Digital Stereo. $29.99. Keepcase. *LANG:* English. *CAP:* English. *FEATURES:* 15 chapter links.
1997 (R) 91m/C Peter O'Toole, Joanna Going, Rose McGowan, Ben Affleck, Liev Schreiber, Nicky Katt, Clifton Powell, Adam Nelson, John Hammil, John Scott Clough; *D:* Joe Chappelle; *W:* Dean Koontz; *C:* Richard Clabaugh; *M:* David Williams.

Phenomenon

Average small-town schmo George Malley (Travolta) is turned into a genius when he's struck by a bright light on his 37th birthday. This development brings him to the attention of the scientific community and, of course, the military. The locals scorn him, thus fulfilling the Hollywood stereotype of rural folks fearing anything they don't understand. Good-natured weeper plays the Gump card (but turns too paranoid) and wins as Travolta gets to be the nice guy, while attractive Sedgwick is fine as romantic interest Lace. A great DVD with excellent sharpness and warm colors. There is plenty of contrast and both image detail and color shadings are enhanced. The 5.1 sound has very little Surround but is near stunning with its crisp delivery of both music and dialogue. —JO
Movie: 🦴🦴▸ **DVD:** 🦴🦴🦴▸
Buena Vista Home Entertainment (Cat #13081, UPC #717951000095). Widescreen (2.35:1) letterboxed. Dolby Digital 5.1; Dolby Surround. $29.99. Keepcase. *LANG:* English; French. *SUB:* Spanish. *CAP:* English. *FEATURES:* 18 chapter links • Theatrical trailer.
1996 (PG) 123m/C John Travolta, Robert Duvall, Kyra Sedgwick, Forest Whitaker, Richard Kiley, Brent Spiner; *D:* Jon Turteltaub; *W:* Gerald DiPego; *C:* Phedon Papamichael; *M:* Thomas Newman. *AWARDS: NOM:* MTV Movie Awards '97: Best Male Performance (Travolta), Best Song ("Change the World"), Best Kiss (John Travolta/Kyra Sedgwick).

Philadelphia

Unfortunately, the best thing about Jonathan Demme's film is the Bruce Springsteen song that's played over the opening credits. (It sounds great on DVD.) The story—half courtroom drama, half social commentary—revolves around attorney Andrew Beckett (Hanks), who's fired from his prestigious firm after the bosses learn he has AIDS. Joe Miller (Washington) is the lawyer Beckett hires when he sues for damages. The performances are fine—Hanks won a well-deserved Oscar—but the rest is flawed by simplistic characters who are either pure good or evil. On one side are sensitive, intelligent, hard-working folk who accept everyone for who they are and support them unquestioningly. Beckett's extended family, led by Joanne Woodward, could have come straight from a Norman Rockwell *Saturday Evening Post* cover. On the other side are self-satisfied, rich, white, racist, homophobic heterosexual males who will do anything to keep their boy's club to themselves. Such comfortable stereotypes are fine for thrillers like Demme's *Silence of the Lambs,* but they ring false here. The no-frills DVD re-creates the theatrical release flawlessly in terms of image and sound, though such slow-moving material is hardly a challenge to the medium. —MM

Movie: 🦴🦴 **DVD:** 🦴🦴🦴
Columbia Tristar Home Video (Cat #52619, UPC #043396526198). Widescreen (1.85:1) letterboxed. Dolby Digital 5.1 Surround Stereo; Dolby Digital Surround Stereo. $24.95. Keepcase. *LANG:* English; Spanish; French. *SUB:* Spanish; Korean. *CAP:* English. *FEATURES:* 46 chapter links.
1993 (PG-13) 125m/C Tom Hanks, Denzel Washington, Antonio Banderas, Jason Robards Jr., Joanne Woodward, Mary Steenburgen, Ron Vawter, Robert Ridgely, Obba Babatunde, Robert Castle, Daniel Chapman, Roger Corman, John Bedford Lloyd, Roberta Maxwell, Warren Miller, Anna Deavere Smith, Kathryn Witt, Andre B. Blake, Ann Dowd, Bradley Whitford, Chandra Wilson, Charles Glenn, Peter Jacobs, Paul Lazar, Dan Olmstead, Joey Perillo, Lauren Roselli, Bill Rowe, Lisa Talerico, Daniel von Bargen, Tracey Walter; *Cameos:* Karen Finley, David Drake, Quentin Crisp; *D:* Jonathan Demme; *W:* Ron Nyswaner; *C:* Tak Fujimoto; *M:* Howard Shore. *AWARDS:* Academy Awards '93: Best Actor (Hanks), Best Song ("Streets of Philadelphia"); Berlin International Film Festival '94: Best Actor (Hanks); Golden Globe Awards '94: Best Actor—Drama (Hanks), Best Song ("Streets of Philadelphia"); MTV Movie Awards '94: Best Male Performance (Hanks); Blockbuster Entertainment Awards '95: Drama Actor, Video (Hanks); *NOM:* Academy Awards '93: Best Makeup, Best Original Screenplay, Best Song ("Philadelphia"); Golden Globe Awards '94: Best Screenplay; MTV Movie Awards '94: Best Film, Best On-Screen Duo (Tom Hanks/Denzel Washington), Best Song ("Streets of Philadelphia"); Writers Guild of America '93: Best Original Screenplay.

The Philadelphia Story

Hepburn plays a socialite whose plans to marry again go awry when her dashing ex-husband (Grant) returns to the scene. The plot spins into a complex, exhilarating whirlwind of comedy when Stewart shows up as a loopy reporter assigned to spy on the nuptials. It doesn't take him long to fall head over heels for the confused, blushing bride. This classic sophisticated comedy, with the lead acting triumvirate turning in delightfully memorable performances, is based on the Broadway hit by Philip Barry. It was remade as the musical *High Society* in 1956, but stick to the original. The DVD benefits from a spectacular B&W transfer, and the 60-year-old soundtrack is mono as expected. The trailer is a nice addition, but more extras would have been welcomed. —MB

Movie: ♫♫♫♫ **DVD:** ♫♫♫▶

MGM Home Entertainment (Cat #906613, UPC #027616661326). Full frame. Dolby Digital 1.0. Snapper. $24.98. *LANG:* English. *SUB:* English; French; Spanish. *CAP:* English. *FEATURES:* 30 chapter links • Theatrical trailer.

1940 112m/B Katharine Hepburn, Cary Grant, James Stewart, Ruth Hussey, Roland Young, John Howard, John Halliday, Virginia Weidler, Henry Daniell, Hillary Brooke, Mary Nash; *D:* George Cukor; *W:* Donald Ogden Stewart; *C:* Joseph Ruttenberg; *M:* Franz Waxman. *AWARDS:* Academy Awards '40: Best Actor (Stewart), Best Screenplay; American Film Institute (AFI) '98: Top 100, National Film Registry '95; New York Film Critics Awards '40: Best Actress (Hepburn); *NOM:* Academy Awards '40: Best Actress (Hepburn), Best Director (Cukor), Best Picture, Best Supporting Actress (Hussey).

Phoenix

First-rate cast is caught in second-rate neo-noir. Degenerate gambler cop Harry Collins (Liotta) resorts to robbery to pay off his gambling debts. His fellow cops (LaPaglia, Piven, Baldwin) are equally flawed. The influences of *Reservoir Dogs* and *The Usual Suspects* will be apparent to crime fans. On DVD, the image ranges between good and very good with minimal flashing of background Venetian blinds and other common problems. Sound isn't quite as strong. —MM

Movie: ♫♫▶ **DVD:** ♫♫▶

Trimark Home Video (Cat #VM6901D, UPC #031398690139). Widescreen. Dolby Digital Surround Stereo. $24.99. Keepcase. *LANG:* English. *SUB:* French; Spanish. *CAP:* English. *FEATURES:* 30 chapter links • Cast filmographies.

1998 (R) 104m/C Ray Liotta, Anthony LaPaglia, Daniel Baldwin, Jeremy Piven, Xander Berkeley, Giancarlo Esposito, Anjelica Huston, Tom Noonan, Kari Wuhrer, Brittany Murphy; *D:* Danny Cannon; *W:* Eddie Richey; *C:* James L. Carter; *M:* Graeme Revell.

Pi

Definitely a first—a religious/mathematical thriller about a man obsessed with decoding the real name of God. Max (Gullette) is a genius mathematician who believes everything can be understood in terms of numbers, so he works on his home-built supercomputer to unravel the stock market. Max begins to suffer hallucinations and blackouts just as his work draws the interest of both a high-powered Wall Street firm and a Hasidic cabalistic sect. A non-formula film that should be seen for its uniqueness alone. The transfer to DVD is pretty sharp and the grain of the original film doesn't seem to generate any additional digital grain. Artifacts are also minimal. Colors are accurate and have little bleed. Contrast is good and brightness remains consistent throughout. Blacks are mostly true but lean towards gray in a couple of scenes. The Dolby Surround isn't loaded with effects, but has good space and imaging, as well as decent low end and very good high end. The extensive supplemental section is hit and miss. —JO

Movie: ♫♫♫ **DVD:** ♫♫♫

Artisan Entertainment (Cat #60494, UPC #012236049401). Widescreen (1.66:1) letterboxed. Dolby Surround. $24.98. Keepcase. *LANG:* English. *FEATURES:* 36 chapter links • Theatrical trailer • Commentaries: Darren Aronofsky, cast • Behind-the-scenes montage • Lost scenes • Music video • Production notes • Cast and filmmaker bios.

1998 (R) 85m/B Sean Gullette, Mark Margolis, Ben Shenkman, Pamela Hart, Stephen Perlman, Samia Shoaib; *D:* Darren Aronofsky; *W:* Darren Aronofsky; *C:* Matthew Libatique; *M:* Clint Mansell. *AWARDS:* Independent Spirit Awards '99: First Screenplay; Sundance Film Festival '98: Best Director (Aronofsky); *NOM:* Independent Spirit Awards '99: Best First Feature.

The Piano

In the 1850s, Ada (Hunter), a mute Scottish widow with a young daughter, agrees to an arranged marriage with Stewart (Neill), a colonial landowner in New Zealand. The way she expresses her feelings is by playing her cherished piano, left behind on the beach by her new husband. Another settler, George (Keitel), buys it, arranges for lessons with Ada, and soon the duo begin a grand passion leading to a cruelly calculated revenge. Fiercely poetic and well acted (with Keitel in a notably romantic role), the film may be too dark and intense for some. Fine original score with Hunter doing her own piano playing. The picture on the DVD seems a little soft, and there is pretty much constant grain, an amplification of the grain on the original film, which was substantial. Colors are deep and accurate, complemented by dark true blacks and good contrast and brightness levels. The Dolby Surround sound is a little weak and occasionally muffled, with the result being that the beautiful score loses a lot of its power. —JO

Movie: ♫♫♫ **DVD:** ♫♫▶

Artisan Entertainment (Cat #60462, UPC #012236046202). Widescreen (1.85:1) letterboxed; full frame. Dolby Surround. $29.95. Snapper. *LANG:* English. *CAP:* English. *FEATURES:* 36 chapter links • Theatrical trailer • Cast and filmmaker bios • Production notes • Dual-layered RSDL.

1993 (R) 120m/C *AU* Holly Hunter, Harvey Keitel, Sam Neill, Anna Paquin, Kerry Walker, Genevieve Lemon; *D:* Jane Campion; *W:* Jane Campion; *C:* Stuart Dryburgh; *M:* Michael Nyman. *AWARDS:* Academy Awards '93: Best Actress (Hunter), Best Original Screenplay, Best Supporting Actress (Paquin); Australian Film Institute '93: Best Actor (Keitel), Best Actress (Hunter), Best Cinematography, Best Costume Design, Best Director (Campion), Best Film, Best Film Editing, Best Screenplay, Best Sound, Best Score; British Academy Awards '93: Best Actress (Hunter); Cannes Film Festival '93: Best Actress (Hunter), Best Film; Golden Globe Awards '94: Best Actress—Drama (Hunter); Independent Spirit Awards '94: Best Foreign Film; Los Angeles Film Critics Association Awards '93: Best Actress (Hunter), Best Cinematography, Best Director (Campion), Best Screenplay, Best Supporting Actress (Paquin); National Board of Review Awards '93: Best Actress (Hunter); New York Film Critics Awards '93: Best Actress (Hunter), Best Director (Campion), Best Screenplay; National Society of Film Critics Awards '93: Best Actress (Hunter), Best Screenplay; Writers Guild of America '93: Best Original Screenplay; *NOM:* Academy Awards '93: Best Cinematography, Best Costume Design, Best Director (Campion), Best Film Editing, Best Picture; British Academy Awards '94: Best Director (Campion), Best Film, Best Original Screenplay, Best Score; Directors Guild of America Awards '93: Best Director (Campion); Golden Globe Awards '94: Best Director (Campion), Best Film—Drama, Best Screenplay, Best Supporting Actress (Paquin), Best Score.

Picnic at Hanging Rock

A St. Valentine's Day outing for the girls at Mrs. Appleyard's school ends badly when three of them disappear at the ominous and forbidding Hanging Rock. Weir's eerie film is strong on atmosphere and properly short on specifics. On DVD, the brilliant work of Weir and his director of photography Russell Boyd looks about as good as you're ever going to see. The carefully diffuse, lyrical image, created from the original negative, is visually flawless. Sound is somewhat subdued, as it has always been. —MM

Movie: ♫♫♫▶ **DVD:** ♫♫♫▶

Criterion Collection (Cat #29, UPC #03742912625). Widescreen (1.66:1) letterboxed. Dolby Digital 5.1 Surround Stereo. $29.95. Keepcase. *LANG:* English. *SUB:* English. *FEATURES:* 33 chapter links • Liner notes by Vincent Canby.

1975 (PG) 110m/C *AU* Margaret Nelson, Rachel Roberts, Dominic Guard, Helen Morse, Jacki Weaver, Vivean Gray, Anne Louise Lambert; *D:* Peter Weir; *W:* Clifford Green; *C:* Russell Boyd; *M:* Bruce Smeaton.

Picture Perfect

Good-looking career-minded advertising exec Kate (Aniston) is angling to impress her new boss and land a big account. She thinks the boss wants her married so she attempts to pass off a stranger standing next to her in a photo as her fiance. The boss wants to meet her betrothed, so Kate hires the guy in the photo, Nick (Mohr), to play the part. Nick goes along with the deal for a while, until he falls in love with Kate (and who wouldn't). Misunderstandings abound in the cute, cliched plot. DVD colors, lighting, and sound here are vivid and consistent. However, at times the pop music soundtrack blasts away, virtually working its way into the story. It's hard to say if this is the fault of the DVD or the sound editors. —*AB*
Movie: 🎬🎬🎬 *DVD:* 🎬🎬🎬▸
Twentieth Century Fox Home Entertainment (Cat #2000028, UPC #2454300 028). Widescreen (1:85:1). Dolby Surround; Mono. $29.98. Keepcase. *LANG:* English (DS); French (Mono). *SUB:* English; Spanish. *FEATURES:* 22 chapter links ● Theatrical trailer.
1996 (PG-13) 100m/C Jennifer Aniston, Jay Mohr, Kevin Bacon, Illeana Douglas, Olympia Dukakis, Kevin Dunn, Faith Prince, Anne Twomey; *D:* Glenn Gordon Caron; *W:* Glenn Gordon Caron; *C:* Paul Sarossy; *M:* Carter Burwell.

Picture Windows

Three short cable movies are inspired by works of art. "Lightning," based on Frederic Remington sketches and a Zane Grey short story, finds western codger Keith striking gold with the help of his trusty mule. A David Hockney painting suggested "Armed Response," which features a confrontation between a wealthy lawyer (Loggia) and a burglar (Zahn). An anonymous 16th-century canvas, "Two Nudes Bathing," is given an imaginative history.
Movie: 🎬🎬 *DVD:* NYR
Pioneer Entertainment (Cat #DVD75163). Full frame. Dolby Digital Stereo. $24.98. Keepcase.
1995 (R) 95m/C Brian Keith, Robert Loggia, Steve Zahn, Charley Boorman; *D:* Joe Dante, Bob Rafelson, John Boorman.

Pierrot le Fou

A woman fleeing a gangster joins a man leaving his wife in this stunning, occasionally confusing classic from iconoclast Godard. A hallmark in 1960s improvisational filmmaking, with rugged Belmondo and always-photogenic Karina effortlessly excelling in leads. The Hound hopes that Fox/Lorber (WinStar) will someday remaster all of the fine films that they have put

out on average DVDs. *Pierrot* is about the same quality as most of their releases and has a moderately sharp picture that is usually much too grainy and has at least minor artifact problems. Colors are true and at times vibrant, but the disc does have occasional run-ins with bleed. In some dimmer scenes, the blacks pick up some grain. Contrast varies from above average to poor, and brightness levels are not any more consistent. The stereo sound is no better than most mono tracks when it comes to separation and imaging and nothing special as far as fidelity and dynamics. —*JO*
Movie: 🎬🎬🎬▸ *DVD:* 🎬🎬▸
Fox/Lorber Home Video (Cat #FLV5046, UPC #720917504629). Widescreen (1.66:1) letterboxed. Stereo. $29.98. Keepcase. *LANG:* French. *SUB:* English. *FEATURES:* 9 chapter links ● Production notes.
1965 110m/C *FR IT* Samuel Fuller, Jean-Pierre Leaud, Jean-Paul Belmondo, Anna Karina, Dirk Sanders; *D:* Jean-Luc Godard; *W:* Jean-Luc Godard; *C:* Raoul Coutard; *M:* Antoine Duhamel.

The Pillow Book

Greenaway's usual chilliness gives way to true erotic heat and intense sensuality that still keep to arcane violence and dazzling experiments. Japanese model Nagiko (Wu) longs for the childhood rituals enacted by her calligrapher father (Ogata) as he literally painted birthday greetings on her face with brush and ink. As an adult, Nagiko searches out calligraphers willing to use her body as paper but she is unsatisfied until she meets bisexual Englishman Jerome (McGregor), and he insists that she write on him. When Nagiko learns that Jerome's male lover is the publisher (Oida) who was once involved with her father, her jealousy triggers tragic consequences. The title refers to the 10th-century diary *The Pillow Book of Sei Shonagon*. Like all of Greenaway's work, this one is stylized and not meant to be judged by conventional narrative standards. The DVD seems to faithfully re-create his striking visuals with their overlapping images, varying screen ratios, and pictures within pictures. —*MM*
Movie: 🎬🎬▸ *DVD:* 🎬🎬🎬
Columbia Tristar Home Video (Cat #28709). Widescreen letterboxed; full frame. Dolby Digital Stereo. $29.95. Keepcase. *LANG:* English. *SUB:* English. *CAP:* English. *FEATURES:* Trailer ● 28 chapter links.
1995 (NC-17) 126m/C *NL FR GB* Vivian Wu, Ewan McGregor, Yoshi Oida, Ken Ogata, Hideko Yoshida, Judy Ongg, Ken Mitsuishi, Yutaka Honda, Ronald Guttman; *D:* Peter Greenaway; *W:* Peter Greenaway; *C:* Sacha Vierny.

Pillow Talk

The archetypal 1950s sex comedy revolves around an ambitious interior designer (Day) and a womanizing song

writer (Hudson) who must share a telephone line and detest each other. The two stars may never have been better—Doris Day received an Oscar nomination—and the material is much sharper than it's generally thought to be. On DVD, it looks very good with only a few minor surface flecks. Some of the shiny-bright stuff—kitchen appliances, department store windows—seem to glitter more than they should, and one red pillbox hat glows like a stoplight, but those are somehow appropriate to the era. Monaural sound is fine. —*MM*
Movie: 🎬🎬🎬▸ *DVD:* 🎬🎬🎬
Universal Studios Home Video (Cat #20532, UPC #025192053221). Widescreen (2.35:1) letterboxed. Dolby Digital Mono. $24.98. Keepcase. *LANG:* English. *SUB:* French. *CAP:* English. *FEATURES:* 19 chapter links ● Production notes ● Cast and crew thumbnail biographies ● Theatrical trailer.
1959 102m/C Rock Hudson, Doris Day, Tony Randall, Thelma Ritter, Nick Adams, Lee Patrick; *D:* Michael Gordon; *W:* Maurice Richlin, Stanley Shapiro; *C:* Arthur E. Arling; *M:* Frank DeVol. *AWARDS:* Academy Awards '59: Best Story & Screenplay; *NOM:* Academy Awards '59: Best Actress (Day), Best Art Direction/Set Decoration (Color), Best Supporting Actress (Ritter), Best Original Dramatic Score.

Pink Floyd: The Wall

Film version of Pink Floyd's 1979 album *The Wall* is an impressionistic combination of live-action and Gerald Scarfe's surreal animation. It's a long-form music video that works without conventional characters or plot. The concept is bombastic, overwrought, and self-pitying, but Geldof manages to remain believable as the burnt-out rock star. Many of the same or similar themes are handled with more anger and anarchy in *If...* Home video is really a better medium for the film than a conventional theatrical release, and disc is infinitely superior to tape. First, the sound is superb. Even without 5.1 Surround, the music is remarkable when heard through good headphones. The image has been preserved or restored to a level of clarity that few films of the early '80s can equal. The extras are well thought out. Recommended for fans and for the curious. —*MM*
Movie: 🎬🎬🎬 *DVD:* 🎬🎬🎬🎬
Sony Music Video Enterprises (Cat #CVD50198, UPC #074645019895). Widescreen letterboxed. Dolby Digital 5.1 Surround Stereo; PCM Stereo. $31.98. Keepcase. *LANG:* English. *SUB:* English. *FEATURES:* 27 chapter links ● Commentary: Roger Waters and Gerald Scarfe ● Music videos ● Lyrics subtitle track ● Deleted footage ● "Making of" documentary ● Trailer ● Stills ● Sound system set-up guide.
1982 (R) 95m/C *GB* Bob Geldof, Christine Hargreaves, Bob Hoskins, James Laurenson, Eleanor David, Kevin McKeon, David Bingham, Jenny Wright, Alex McAvoy, Nell Campbell, Joanne Whalley; *D:* Alan

Parker; *W:* Roger Waters; *C:* Peter Biziou; *M:* Michael Kamen, David Gilmour, Roger Waters.

The Pink Panther

A disaster-prone French inspector Clouseau (Sellers) invades a Swiss ski resort and becomes obsessed with capturing debonair jewel thief (Niven), who is out to lift the legendary "Pink Panther" diamond off of a sexy princess (Cardinale). Said thief is also the inspector's wife's (Capucine) lover, though the inspector doesn't know it. While more typical of one of Niven's caper films than what the series would become, the highlight is Sellers's first appearance as the bumbling Inspector Clouseau, who destroys everything in his path, while speaking in a funny French accent. Memorable score by Henry Mancini. Both the widescreen and full-frame transfers are fairly sharp with very good blacks and good contrast, even in the very bright snow scenes. The colors are sharp and vibrant. The sound, while mono and not spectacular, is better than average for a film of this age. —*JO*
Movie: ♪♪♪ **DVD:** ♪♪♪
MGM Home Entertainment (Cat #907041, UPC #027616704122). Widescreen (2.35:1) letterboxed; full frame. Dolby Digital Mono. $24.98. Keepcase. *LANG:* English (DD Mono). *SUB:* French. *CAP:* English. *FEATURES:* 32 chapter links • Theatrical trailer • 8-page booklet.
1964 113m/C *GB* Peter Sellers, David Niven, Robert Wagner, Claudia Cardinale, Capucine, Brenda de Banzie; *D:* Blake Edwards; *W:* Blake Edwards; *C:* Philip Lathrop; *M:* Henry Mancini. *AWARDS: NOM:* Academy Awards '64: Best Original Score.

The Pink Panther Strikes Again

Fifth in the series finds Clouseau's boss Inspector Dreyfus (Lom) completely mad and threatening to destroy the world via a doomsday machine. His only demand is the death of Clouseau (Sellers). Assassins from around the world answer the call but can't seem to overcome Clouseau's bumbling abilities. Features some of the best disguises and slapstick moments in the entire series. Both widescreen and full-frame transfers are somewhat grainy, particularly in the darker scenes, and the backgrounds are at times lacking detail. The blacks and contrast are good, but the colors are average and sometimes bleed a little. Overall the transfers seem a little flat, needing a boost in the brightness level. The sound is mono but crisp and clean. —*JO*
Movie: ♪♪♪ **DVD:** ♪♪
MGM Home Entertainment (Cat #908503, UPC #027616750327). Widescreen (2.35:1) letterboxed; full frame. Dolby Digital Mono. $24.98. Keepcase. *LANG:* English; French. *SUB:* English; French. *FEATURES:* 28 chapter links • Theatrical trailer • 8-page booklet.

1976 (PG) 103m/C *GB* Peter Sellers, Herbert Lom, Lesley-Anne Down, Colin Blakely, Leonard Rossiter, Burt Kwouk; *D:* Blake Edwards; *W:* Edwards Waldman, Frank Waldman; *C:* Harry Waxman; *M:* Henry Mancini. *AWARDS:* Writers Guild of America '76: Best Adapted Screenplay; *NOM:* Academy Awards '76: Best Song ("Come to Me").

Pinocchio

Disney's second animated film features the famous wooden puppet who wants to be a "real boy," kindly old Gepetto, Jiminy Cricket, and many other characters who have become instantly recognizable to generations of audiences. The DVD does them justice, particularly in the big scenes—Gepetto's cluttered shop, Pleasure Island, Monstro the whale. Throughout, image is superb with rich vivid colors. If the sound is not as spectacular in terms of today's technology, that's a quibble. This is one of the greats. —*MM*
Movie: ♪♪♪♪ **DVD:** ♪♪♪ ►
Buena Vista Home Entertainment (Cat #18665, UPC #717951005793). Full frame. Dolby Digital Mono. $39.99. Keepcase. *LANG:* English. *CAP:* English. *FEATURES:* 24 chapter links • Original 1940 theatrical trailer.
1940 (G) 87m/C *D:* Hamilton Luske, Ben Sharpsteen; *W:* Aurelius Battaglia, William Cottrell, Otto Englander, Erdman Penner, Joseph Sabo, Ted Sears, Webb Smith; *V:* Dick Jones, Cliff Edwards, Evelyn Venable, Walter Catlett, Frankie Darro, Charles Judels, Don Brodie, Christian Rub. *AWARDS:* Academy Awards '40: Best Song ("When You Wish Upon a Star"), Best Original Score, National Film Registry '94.

Piranha

A rural Texas resort area is plagued by attacks from ferocious man-eating fishies created by a scientist to be used as a secret weapon in the Vietnam War. Spoofy horror film—the title monsters are little more than bubbles and red dye in the water—follows the familiar quick-and-dirty Corman formula, and features director Dante's signature in-jokes in the background. One tiny stop-motion critter appears in an all-too-brief cameo. This was the first script by novelist/filmmaker John Sayles to be produced. He also appears as the Army sentry. Followed by a sequel (James Cameron's feature debut) in 1981, and remade but not improved upon in 1995. The DVD contains a newly remastered video transfer that is clean and crisp, making it hard to believe you are watching a 20 year-old low-budget movie. There are some obvious defects in the source print at times, mostly blips and small scratches, but these do not interfere with the viewing experience —*MM/ML*
Movie: ♪♪♪ **DVD:** ♪♪♪ ►
New Horizons Home Video (Cat #20189, UPC #736991458345). Full frame. Dolby Digital Stereo. $24.98. Keepcase. *LANG:* English. *FEATURES:* Outtakes and bloopers

• Commentary: Joe Dante and producer Jon Davison • "Making of" featurette • Cast and crew thumbnail bios.
1978 (R) 90m/C Bradford Dillman, Heather Menzies, Kevin McCarthy, Keenan Wynn, Barbara Steele, Dick Miller, Paul Bartel, John Sayles, Richard Deacon; *D:* Joe Dante; *W:* John Sayles; *C:* Jamie Anderson; *M:* Pino Donaggio.

Piranha

New version adds nothing to the early effort from director Joe Dante, writer John Sayles, and producer Roger Corman, who's also behind this one. In fact, it lacks that nice flourish of stop-motion animation and it may even reuse some of the silly little two-dimensional fish "monsters" from the original. The rest of the effects are accomplished, as they were before, with red dye and a bubble machine. Alexandra Paul and William Katt are the less-than-dynamic duo who must save the summer camp and the new lakefront development from the titular carnivorous fishies, created by the government as a secret weapon. If you have the choice, give this one a pass and find the real thing.
Movie: ♪ ► **DVD:** NYR
New Horizons Home Video (Cat #20583). Full frame. Dolby Digital Stereo. $24.98. Keepcase. *FEATURES:* Leonard Maltin interview with Roger Corman • Trailer.
1995 (R) 81m/C Alexandra Paul, William Katt, Soleil Moon Frye, Monte Markham, Darlene Carr, James Karen, Lincoln Kilpatrick; *D:* Scott Levy; *W:* Alex Simon; *C:* Christopher Baffa; *M:* Christopher Lennertz.

Plague of the Zombies

O.K., the title of this Hammer horror is a little silly and the plot does revolve around zombies in 19th-century Cornwall, England—not the usual setting—but that's not a problem. This is essentially a vampire story with a twist. Relative unknowns Andre Morell, as the Van Helsing character, and John Carson as the villainous Squire, are every bit as good as Cushing and Lee. Jacqueline Pearce and Diane Clare are demurely sexy Hammer heroines. The presence of familiar character actor Michael Ripper doesn't hurt either. The makeup is easily the equal of more recent living dead movies. And let's not overlook the political aspects of a story about the relationship between the upper class and workers. Zombies of the world, unite! You have nothing to lose but your shrouds! This film was late to arrive on home video and the DVD is made from the excellent restoration that was released on VHS tape. The image sparkles, with the red hunting jackets of the evil aristocrats glowing just as they should. —*MM*
Movie: ♪♪♪♪ **DVD:** ♪♪♪♪
Anchor Bay (Cat #DV10678, UPC #013131067897). Widescreen (1.85:1) letterboxed. Dolby Digital Mono. $29.98. Keepcase. *LANG:* English; French. *FEA-*

Theatrical trailers ◆ 27 chapter links ◆ *World of Hammer* episode "Mummies, Werewolves & Living Dead."
1966 90m/C *GB* Andre Morell, John Carson, Diane Clare, Alex Davion, Jacqueline Pearce, Brook Williams, Michael Ripper, Marcus Hammond, Roy Royston; *D:* John Gilling; *W:* Peter Bryan, John (Anthony Hinds) Elder; *C:* Arthur Grant; *M:* James Bernard.

Plan 9 from Outer Space

In his famous and sad final role, Bela Lugosi's screen time is less than two minutes. (The box copy admits as much with "almost starring BELA LUGOSI" right up front.) Wood's wife's chiropractor replaced the star and kept himself hidden behind cape and hat. The rest of Wood's alternative masterpiece—almost universally acknowledged to be the "worst" film ever made—is the stuff of Hollywood legend. Aliens in silk pajamas conspire to resurrect several slow-moving zombies from a cardboard graveyard and to conquer the Earth before we warlike humans destroy the rest of the universe with "solarite bombs." On DVD, the film looks even sharper than I remember it from that fateful night years ago in the dark ages before home video when I supervised dusk-to-dawn screenings, though, thankfully, my memory is hazy. The dual-layered disc also contains the two-hour documentary *Flying Saucers over Hollywood: The Plan 9 Companion.* For any fan, particularly younger ones, who have not been introduced to Wood's films, this is the place to start. —*MM* **AKA:** Grave Robbers from Outer Space.
Movie: 🎵🎵🎵 **DVD:** 🎵🎵🎵
Image Entertainment (Cat #ID8504CODVD, UPC #014381850420). Full frame. Dolby Digital Mono. $24.99. Snapper. *LANG:* English. *FEATURES:* 20 chapter links, *Plan 9* ◆ 24 chapter links, *Companion.*
1956 78m/B Bela Lugosi, Tor Johnson, Lyle Talbot, Vampira, Gregory Walcott, Tom (George Duryea) Keene, Dudley Manlove, Mona McKinnon, Duke Moore, Joanna Lee, Bunny Breckinridge, Criswell, Carl Anthony, Paul Marco, Norma McCarty, David DeMering, Bill Ash, Conrad Brooks, Tom Mason, Edward D. Wood Jr.; *D:* Edward D. Wood Jr.; *W:* Edward D. Wood Jr.; *C:* William C. Thompson; *M:* Trevor Duncan, Van Phillips, James Stevens.

Platoon

Stone's autobiographical Vietnam film is a grunt's view of the war in all its horrifying, inexplicable detail, though that does not deter the filmmaker from resorting to cheap sloganeering when it suits his political purposes. Young Chris Taylor (Sheen) is caught between the fire-breathing Sgt. Barnes (Berenger) and the more pacifistic Sgt. Elias (Dafoe). The jungle and combat sequences are some of the most realistic and frightening ever put on film. Even on DVD, they lose some detail—almost all

films set in a tropical jungle do—but that does not detract from the visceral power of the scenes, particularly those set at night. Dolby Surround Stereo is much more crisp and sharp than VHS tape. —*MM*
Movie: 🎵🎵🎵 **DVD:** 🎵🎵🎵
Artisan Entertainment (Cat #60454, UPC #012236045403). Widescreen (1.85:1) letterboxed. Dolby Digital 5.1 Surround Stereo; Dolby Digital Stereo. $29.95. Snapper. *LANG:* English. *CAP:* English. *FEATURES:* 44 chapter links (36 within film; 8 within documentary) ◆ "Making of" documentary ◆ Commentary: advisor Dale Dye and Stone.
1986 (R) 113m/C Charlie Sheen, Willem Dafoe, Tom Berenger, Francesco Quinn, Forest Whitaker, John C. McGinley, Kevin Dillon, Richard Edson, Reggie Johnson, Keith David, Johnny Depp, Dale Dye, Mark Moses, Chris Pederson, David Neidorf, Tony Todd, Ivan Kane, Paul Sanchez, Corey Glover, Oliver Stone; *D:* Oliver Stone; *W:* Oliver Stone; *C:* Robert Richardson; *M:* Georges Delerue. *AWARDS:* Academy Awards '86: Best Director (Stone), Best Film Editing, Best Picture, Best Sound; American Film Institute (AFI) '98: Top 100; British Academy Awards '87: Best Director (Stone); Directors Guild of America Awards '86: Best Director (Stone); Golden Globe Awards '87: Best Director (Stone), Best Film—Drama, Best Supporting Actor (Berenger); Independent Spirit Awards '87: Best Cinematography, Best Director (Stone), Best Film, Best Screenplay; *NOM:* Academy Awards '86: Best Cinematography, Best Original Screenplay, Best Supporting Actor (Berenger, Dafoe).

Play Time

The reigning *Emmanuelle* of soft-core video premieres is a classy production with realistic characters, glitzy sets, and a hot story of sexual experimentation between two married couples (Burton, Stepp, Parent, David). Eroticism, like beauty, is in the mind of the beholder, but writer Mary Ellen Hanover and director Dale Trevillion push all the right buttons. The film benefits from a smooth transfer to DVD. Some of the night scenes are grainy, but most of the well-photographed action belies a modest budget. —*MM*
Movie: 🎵🎵🎵 **DVD:** 🎵🎵🎵
Image Entertainment (Cat #ID5615FMDVD, UPC #014381561524). Full frame. Dolby Digital Stereo. $24.99. Snapper. *LANG:* English. *FEATURES:* 12 chapter links.
1994 90m/C Monique Parent, Craig Stepp, Jennifer Burton, Elliot David, Julie Strain, Tammy Parks, Ashlie Rhey; *D:* Dale Trevillion; *W:* Mary Ellen Hanover; *C:* Sven Kirsten; *M:* Joel Derouin.

The Player

In their commentary track, director Robert Altman and writer Michael Tolkin admit that this is "a pretty tame satire." Maybe so, but it's still hugely entertaining, and for fans who already know it well, the DVD (with their comments) is almost as enjoy-

able on a second viewing. In fact, this is one of those rare films that really benefits from the extras that DVD can utilize. (Those extras, by the way, are on the other side of the disc.) Robbins is letter-perfect as Griffin Mill, a young studio exec who's the chief suspect in a murder investigation. Throughout, the screen is packed with cameo appearances, and so the whole thing could turn into a huge inside joke if it weren't handled so deftly. Mill personifies Hollywood's cold ethics in a performance that's both calculating and vulnerable. On DVD, the film looks fine, though Altman is always more interested in emotion and character than in image and style. His explanation of the famous nine-minute opening shot is particularly illuminating. He has earned a reputation as a filmmaker who states his mind and that's certainly what he does here. The disc is loaded with extras and the film deserves every one of them. —*MM*
Movie: 🎵🎵🎵🎵 **DVD:** 🎵🎵🎵🎵
New Line Home Video (Cat #N4032, UPC #794043403224). Widescreen letterboxed. Dolby Surround 5.1 (English); Dolby Stereo (French). $24.98. Snapper. *LANG:* English; French. *SUB:* English; French; Spanish. *CAP:* English. *FEATURES:* 5 deleted scenes ◆ Commentary: Robert Altman and Michael Tolkin ◆ Robert Altman featurette ◆ Filmographies for actors in all speaking parts ◆ Theatrical trailer. Double-sided disc. The film itself and the commentary are on one side; extras on the other.
1992 (R) 123m/C Michael Tolkin, Louise Fletcher, Dennis Franz, Malcolm McDowell, Ray Walston, Rene Auberjonois, David Alan Grier, Jayne Meadows, Michael Bowen, Steve James, Brian Tochi, Tim Robbins, Greta Scacchi, Fred Ward, Whoopi Goldberg, Peter Gallagher, Brion James, Cynthia Stevenson, Vincent D'Onofrio, Dean Stockwell, Richard E. Grant, Dina Merrill, Sydney Pollack, Lyle Lovett, Randall Batinkoff, Gina Gershon, Burt Reynolds, Cher, Nick Nolte, Jack Lemmon, Lily Tomlin, Marlee Matlin, Julia Roberts, Bruce Willis, Anjelica Huston, Elliott Gould, Sally Kellerman, Steve Allen, Richard Anderson, Harry Belafonte, Shari Belafonte, Karen Black, Gary Busey, Robert Carradine, James Coburn, Cathy Lee Crosby, John Cusack, Brad Davis, Peter Falk, Teri Garr, Leeza Gibbons, Scott Glenn, Jeff Goldblum, Joel Grey, Buck Henry, Kathy Ireland, Sally Kirkland, Andie MacDowell, Martin Mull, Mimi Rogers, Jill St. John, Susan Sarandon, Rod Steiger, Joan Tewkesbury, Robert Wagner; *D:* Robert Altman; *W:* Michael Tolkin; *C:* Jean Lepine; *M:* Thomas Newman. *AWARDS:* British Academy Awards '92: Best Adapted Screenplay; Cannes Film Festival '92: Best Actor (Robbins), Best Director (Altman); Golden Globe Awards '93: Best Actor—Musical/Comedy (Robbins), Best Film—Musical/Comedy; Independent Spirit Awards '93: Best Film; New York Film Critics Awards '92: Best Cinematography, Best Director (Altman), Best Film; Writers Guild of America '92: Best Adapted Screenplay; *NOM:* Academy Awards '92:

Best Adapted Screenplay, Best Director (Altman), Best Film Editing.

The Players Club

Rapper/actor Ice Cube makes a surprisingly deft directorial debut with a comedy-drama about single mom Diana (LisaRaye) who's a college student by day, topless dancer by night. She works at a club owned by the bombastic Dollar Bill (Mac). Her cousin Ebony (Calhoun) joins her there and promptly succumbs to the temptations of that world. Blue (Foxx) is the DJ who falls for Diana. Ice Cube appears as a customer. For a low-budget film set in a shabby world, this one looks very good. (It's much better than most strip club exploitation flicks.) DVD heightens the ambitious visuals and audio techniques. Sound is excellent. In short, a genuine sleeper. —MM
Movie: ♫♫♫ **DVD:** ♫♫♫➤
New Line Home Video (Cat #N4684, UPC #794043468421). Widescreen (1.85:1) anamorphic; full frame. Dolby Digital 5.1 Surround Stereo; Dolby Surround Stereo. $24.98. Snapper. *LANG:* English. *SUB:* English. *FEATURES:* 21 chapter links ● 2 music videos ● Cast and crew thumbnail biographies ● Theatrical trailer.
1998 (R) 103m/C LisaRaye, Bernie Mac, Monica Calhoun, A.J. Johnson, Jamie Foxx, Ice Cube, Dick Anthony Williams, Tommy (Tiny) Lister, John Amos, Faizon Love, Alex Thomas, Chrystale Wilson, Adele Givens, Larry McCoy; **D:** Ice Cube; **W:** Ice Cube; **C:** Malik Hassan Sayeed; **M:** Hidden Faces.

Playgirls and the Vampire

This 1963 low-budget Italian effort was one of the first attempts to combine horror with explicit sex; well, semi-explicit sex. That side of the film is limited to a couple of kisses, several filmy negligees, and a naked female vampire who seldom steps far from the shadows. The story concerns a busload of showgirls who are stranded at the castle of Count Kernassy (Brandi). In terms of production values and overall quality this one can't be compared to the Hammer films of the same period, but director Piero Regnoli's dirty mind was headed in the right direction. He pointed the way for the thousands of exploitation flicks that have been made in the decades since. Today, its appeal is almost purely historical, limited to the most dedicated fans of cheap horror, who will also appreciate Tim Lucas's liner notes. On DVD, the black-and-white images range in quality from shot to shot, with extremely sharp focus in some scenes and virtually unwatchable muddiness in others. In this area, fans know what to expect. —MM
Movie: ♫♫➤ **DVD:** ♫♫➤
Image Entertainment (Cat #ID5827GODVD, UPC #014381582727). Full frame. Dolby Digital Mono. $19.99. Snapper. *LANG:* English. *FEATURES:* 14 chapter links ● Liner

notes by Tim Lucas, editor/publisher of *Video Watchdog.*
1963 70m/C *IT* Walter Brandi, Lyla Rocco, Alfredo Rizzo, Maria Giovannini; **D:** Piero Regnoli; **W:** Piero Regnoli; **M:** Aldo Piga.

Playing by Heart

This film is so overstuffed with characters and subplots it needs a 2.20:1 format and 43 chapters laid out on a set of valentine heart-decorated scene access screens. The story covers five couples representing various stages of emotional development including a mother-son dyad (Burstyn and Mohr), plus a wraparound of lonely guy in a bar (Quaid), in just over two hours. The critical favorite of these was the pairing of Rowlands and Connery as Paul and Hannah, who talk their way through an emotional impasse after 40 years of marriage. You may have to forcibly resist the tendency to pick a favorite plot thread a la *The Love Boat,* even though they are designed as puzzle pieces that fit together in the end. The script, though peppered with effective moments, could have benefitted from some cutting and refocusing. The disc offers almost perfect visual rendering and a soundtrack that, even with its periodic blasts of techno, never overpowers. With all the fine actors involved, the perpetually overcranked Miramax promotion machine, and the myriad ideas of its writer-director, this DVD's lack of extras is baffling. —JK **AKA:** Dancing about Architecture.
Movie: ♫♫ **DVD:** ♫♫♫➤
Miramax Pictures Home Video (Cat #17097, UPC #717951002112). Widescreen (2.20:1). Dolby Digital 5.1. $29.99. Keepcase. *LANG:* English. *CAP:* English. *FEATURES:* 43 chapter links ● Interactive menus.
1998 (R) 121m/C Sean Connery, Gena Rowlands, Ryan Phillippe, Angelina Jolie, Ellen Burstyn, Gillian Anderson, Dennis Quaid, Jay Mohr, Anthony Edwards, Madeleine Stowe, Jon Stewart, Patricia Clarkson, Nastassia Kinski, Jeremy Sisto; **D:** Willard Carroll; **W:** Willard Carroll; **C:** Vilmos Zsigmond; **M:** John Barry.

Playing God

Eugene Sands (Duchovny) is a doctor whose heroin habit hasn't yet spoiled his looks but has cost him his job. One night while scoring a hit at a bar, he saves a gangster's life with an impromptu operation. That brings him to the attention of crime boss Raymond (Hutton), who hires the bad doctor to be his own private emergency medical service. Raymond's hot-number girlfriend Claire (Jolie) spices things up a little more. The violence and medical scenes are played for all their gory thrills, and that's both the strength and weakness of the DVD. Throughout, this tawdry story is far too clear and crisp. When the image ought to be grim and gamey in trashy trailers, cheap bars, and

the brown California hills, it's crystalline. Still, the film moves right along and proves that Duchovny has more range than he has demonstrated on TV's *The X-Files* (or cable's *Red Shoes Diaries*). —MM
Movie: ♫♫♫ **DVD:** ♫♫♫
Buena Vista Home Entertainment (Cat #14371, UPC #717951000422). Widescreen (1.85:1) letterboxed. Dolby Digital Stereo. $29.99. Keepcase. *LANG:* English. *CAP:* English. *FEATURES:* 19 chapter links ● Theatrical trailer.
1996 (R) 94m/C David Duchovny, Timothy Hutton, Angelina Jolie, Michael Massee, Peter Stormare, Andrew Tiernan, John Hawkes, Gary Dourdan; **D:** Andy Wilson; **W:** Mark Haskell Smith; **C:** Anthony B. Richmond; **M:** Richard Hartley.

Pleasantville

Nerdy David (Maguire) and slut wanna-be Jennifer (Witherspoon) are sucked into the sterile and innocent world of Pleasantville, a 1950s B&W TV show in constant reruns, where they find themselves in the roles of Bud and Mary Sue, the blandly adorable children of George and Betty Parker (Macy and Allen). After Jennifer shows a classmate what lovers' lane is really for, the townspeople begin to lose their innocence; the black-and-white world becomes more colorful as each new human passion is realized. The performances are dead-on, particularly Allen as the sexually awakening mom. The transition from straight comedy to social commentary is adeptly handled. The great character actor J.T. Walsh gives his usual excellent (and sadly, last) performance as the stubborn head of the chamber of commerce bitterly fighting change. The DVD presents the shift from black-and-white to color well. The image is also very sharp and has very little grain, bleed, or artifacts. In both the black-and-white and the color sequences, the contrast and brightness levels are very good; details remain very clear. The 5.1 sound is great and features very good separation with good imaging, though little in the way of Surround "effects" are heard. Music is full and dialogue is crisp. —JO
Movie: ♫♫♫➤ **DVD:** ♫♫♫➤
New Line Home Video (Cat #N4728, UPC #794043472824). Widescreen (2.35:1) anamorphic. Dolby Digital 5.1; Dolby Surround. $24.98. Snapper. *LANG:* English. *SUB:* English. *FEATURES:* 37 chapter links ● Theatrical trailer ● "Making of" featurette ● Commentaries: Gary Ross, Steven Soderbergh, and Randy Newman ● Music video by Fiona Apple ● Script-to-screen with storyboards (DVD-ROM).
1998 (PG-13) 124m/C Tobey Maguire, Reese Witherspoon, William H. Macy, Joan Allen, Jeff Daniels, J.T. Walsh, Don Knotts, Paul Walker, Jane Kaczmarek, Marley Shelton; **D:** Gary Ross; **W:** Gary Ross; **C:** John Lindley; **M:** Randy Newman. *AWARDS:* Los Angeles Film Critics Association Awards '98: Best Supporting Actress (Allen); Broadcast Film Critics Association Awards

Plenty

Difficult but worthwhile film finds Streep in top form as a former member of the French Resistance. Upon returning to England, she finds life at home increasingly tedious and banal, and begins to fear that her finest hours may be behind her. Gielgud is flawless as the aging career diplomat. Adapting his play to the screen, David Hare presents an allegory of British decline.
Movie: ♪♪▶ *DVD:* NYR
Republic Pictures Home Video (Cat #11190). $24.98.
1985 (R) 119m/C Meryl Streep, Tracey Ullman, Sting, John Gielgud, Charles Dance, Ian McKellen, Sam Neill, Burt Kwouk; *D:* Fred Schepisi; *W:* David Hare; *C:* Ian Baker; *M:* Bruce Smeaton. *AWARDS:* Los Angeles Film Critics Association Awards '85: Best Supporting Actor (Gielgud); National Society of Film Critics Awards '85: Best Supporting Actor (Gielgud).

Plump Fiction

This movie proves that when you want to make fun of Quentin Tarantino, you should stick to his truly horrible acting. Instead, this spoof attacks his already over-the-top characters from *Pulp Fiction* and *Natural Born Killers*. Julius (Davenport) and Jimmy (Dinello) are the loser hit men. Mimi (Brown) is the gangster's wife who has a substance abuse problem, but it's not cocaine; it's food! She's fat, get it? Intersecting storylines feature Nicky (Glave) and Vallory (Segall, doing a dead-on Juliette Lewis) as *Natural Blonde Killers*. The only redeeming scene is that of Kane Picoy as "Christopher Walken character" doing an uncanny impersonation of the king of psychos.
Movie: ♪ *DVD:* NYR
Rhino Home Video (Cat #4467). Full frame. $24.95. Snapper. *FEATURES:* Commentary: Mark Roberts, Bob Koherr • Interviews with Julie Brown, Mark Roberts • Trailer.
1997 (R) 82m/C Tommy Davidson, Julie Brown, Sandra Bernhard, Paul Dinello, Dan Castellaneta, Colleen Camp, Pamela Segall, Kevin Meaney, Matthew Glave, Jennifer Rubin, Robert Costanzo, Phillipe Bergerone; *D:* Bob Koherr; *W:* Bob Koherr; *C:* Rex Nicholson; *M:* Michael Muhlfriedel.

Pocket Ninjas

Kids' martial arts adventure is a low-budget *Mortal Kombat*. Three young karate students (Bufanda, Sondi, Valencia) must battle the comic book villain Cobra Kahn (Z'Dar). Their teacher is Master Jack (Daniels). Unfortunately, both image and sound are fuzzy. The DVD is so poor that only the most devoted Gary Daniels fan will make it all the way through. —*MM*
Movie: ♪ *DVD:* woof

Simitar Entertainment (Cat #7486, UPC #082551748624). Full frame. Dolby Digital Mono. $14.98. Keepcase. *LANG:* English. *FEATURES:* 8 links • Production factoids.
1993 76m/C Robert Z'Dar, Richard Rabago, Brad Bufanda, Sondi, Joseph Valencia, Mel Novak, Rick Rabago, Gary Daniels; *D:* Dave Eddy; *C:* Dwight F. Lay.

Poetic Justice

The literal nature of the title is emblematic of director Singleton's heavy hand. Justice (Jackson in her movie debut, for better or worse) gives up college plans to follow a career in cosmetology after her boyfriend's murder. She copes with her loss by writing poetry (provided by Maya Angelou) and meets postal worker Lucky (Shakur) and goes on a road trip with their unpleasant friends.
Movie: ♪♪ *DVD:* NYR
Columbia Tristar Home Video (Cat #52399). Widescreen (1.85:1) anamorphic. Dolby Digital Stereo. $24.95. Keepcase.
1993 (R) 109m/C Janet Jackson, Tupac Shakur, Tyra Ferrell, Regina King, Joe Torry, Norma Donaldson; *D:* John Singleton; *W:* John Singleton; *C:* Peter Collister; *M:* Stanley Clarke. *AWARDS:* MTV Movie Awards '94: Best Female Performance (Jackson), Most Desirable Female (Jackson); Golden Raspberry Awards '93: Worst New Star (Jackson); *NOM:* Academy Awards '93: Best Song ("Again"); Golden Globe Awards '94: Best Song ("Again").

Point Blank

A bus full of Texas death-row convicts is ambushed and the bad guys take over a shopping mall. Cut-rate version of *Con Air* features similar bulging biceps—most obviously on beefed-up star Rourke whose skin has a deep orange hue in many scenes—and lots of gunplay. The stereo overemphasizes violent sound effects so that each punch is a loud SPLAT! Otherwise, the image is the same as VHS tape. —*MM*
Movie: ♪▶ *DVD:* ♪♪▶
Studio Home Entertainment (Cat #7105, UPC #658149710528). Full frame. Dolby Digital Stereo. $24.95. Keepcase. *LANG:* English. *CAP:* English. *FEATURES:* 18 chapter links • Production notes.
1998 (R) 90m/C Mickey Rourke, Danny Trejo, Kevin Gage, Michael Wright, Frederic Forrest, James Gammon; *D:* Matt Earl Beesley.

Point of No Return

Fonda is Maggie, a drugged-out loser condemned to death for her part in a murder spree, but if she agrees to work as a government assassin, she'll be given a reprieve. Fonda displays a certain perkiness as the assassin and is better in her early surly scenes; Keitel is creepy as another assassin. Flashy, exacting, but ultimately innocuous remake of the 1990

French thriller *La Femme Nikita*. Need more be said? Yes, the DVD is average and has image quality that is average at best, and at its worst points, very poor. Colors are lame as well, and the blacks gray out on numerous occasions. There aren't even any supplementals to make up for an average movie on an average DVD. The highpoint is the sound, which kicks up every now and then with a decent Surround effect, and is pretty energetic overall. —*JO*
Movie: ♪♪ *DVD:* ♪♪
Warner Home Video, Inc. (Cat #12819, UPC #085391281924). Widescreen (2.35:1) anamorphic; full frame. Dolby Digital 5.1; Dolby Surround; Mono. $24.98. Snapper. *LANG:* English (DD5.1; DS); French (DS); Spanish (mono). *SUB:* English; French; Spanish. *CAP:* English. *FEATURES:* 30 chapter links • Production notes • Theatrical trailer.
1993 (R) 108m/C Bridget Fonda, Gabriel Byrne, Dermot Mulroney, Miguel Ferrer, Anne Bancroft, Olivia D'Abo, Harvey Keitel, Richard Romanus, Lorraine Toussaint, Geoffrey Lewis, Calvin Levels; *D:* John Badham; *W:* Robert Getchell, Alexandra Seros; *C:* Michael Watkins; *M:* Hans Zimmer.

Poison Ivy

Barrymore solidified her reputation as a bad girl with her portrayal of a teen femme fatale in this trashy tale of a wayward high school student and her takeover of her best friend's family. Ivy quickly attaches herself to the lonely, neglected Sylvie (Gilbert), who must watch as the naughty blonde systematically seduces both her mother (Ladd) and father (Skerrit). Yes, it's glossy overdone pulp, but it is superior glossy overdone pulp. DVD heightens the cold blue look that director Katt Shea Ruben gives the proceedings. Like the other two entries in the series, the DVD contains both "R"- and unrated versions for the curious videophile to compare. Both image and sound are excellent for mid-level eroticism. —*MM*
Movie: ♪♪ *DVD:* ♪♪♪
New Line Home Video (Cat #N4846, UPC #794043484629). Widescreen (1.85:1) anamorphic; full frame. Dolby Digital 5.1 Surround Stereo; Dolby Digital Surround Stereo. $24.98. Snapper. *LANG:* English. *SUB:* English. *FEATURES:* 25 chapter links • Cast and crew thumbnail biographies • Theatrical trailer.
1992 (R) 91m/C Drew Barrymore, Sara Gilbert, Tom Skerritt, Cheryl Ladd; *D:* Katt Shea; *W:* Katt Shea, Andy Ruben; *C:* Phedon Papamichael; *M:* David Michael Frank.

Poison Ivy 2: Lily

Art student Lily (Milano) finds the provocative Ivy's diary and decides to take a walk on the wild side herself. This soft-core eroticism does not rise to the heights of director Goursaud's video premiere *Embrace of the Vampire* but it certainly accomplishes everything it sets out to do.

On DVD, both image and sound are consistent with the other entries in the series. Colors are muted; the focus is gauzy. Both the 106-minute "R"-rated version and the 108-minute unrated version are on the disc. —*MM*

Movie: 🐾🐾 *DVD:* 🐾🐾🐾
New Line Home Video (Cat #N4847, UPC #794043484728). Widescreen (1.85:1) anamorphic; full frame. Dolby Digital 5.1 Surround Stereo; Dolby Digital Surround Stereo. $24.98. Snapper. *LANG:* English. *SUB:* English. *FEATURES:* 21 chapter links ➛ Cast and crew thumbnail biographies.
1995 (R) 106m/C Alyssa Milano, Xander Berkeley, Johnathon Schaech, Belinda Bauer; *D:* Anne Goursaud; *W:* Chloe King; *C:* Suki Medencevic; *M:* Joseph Williams.

Poison Ivy 3: The New Seduction

Like the others in the series, this one's about a barely legal lower-class temptress Violet (Pressly), sister of the original Ivy, who insinuates her way into a wealthy but dysfunctional family and has her way with them. The familiar soapy plot is filled with jilted boyfriends, tennis, tuxedos, snobs, and, of course, oodles of extracurricular gamahuche, seasoned with a welcome dash of humor. Looking a lot like Traci Lords in the jailbait phase of her career, Jaime Pressly brings an exotic presence to the glossy production. Given the softly focused image, DVD is only a slight improvement over VHS tape. Sound is virtually identical. —*MM*

Movie: 🐾🐾 *DVD:* 🐾🐾
New Line Home Video (Cat #N4848, UPC #794043484827). Widescreen (1.85:1) anamorphic; full frame. Dolby Digital 5.1 Surround Stereo; Dolby Digital Surround Stereo. $24.98. Snapper. *LANG:* English. *SUB:* English. *FEATURES:* 19 chapter links ➛ Cast and crew thumbnail biographies.
1997 (R) 93m/C Jaime Pressly, Megan Edwards, Michael Des Barres, Greg Vaughan; *D:* Kurt Voss; *W:* Karen Kelly; *C:* Feliks Parnell; *M:* Reg Powell.

Police Academy

Hollywood's first comedy based on affirmative action is one of its funniest and most tasteless. True, the sequels have been pathetic rehashes but this one shines. Essentially, it re-creates the standard service comedy—misfits brought together and forged into a unit—in police blue. If memory serves, the DVD actually looks sharper and more focused than the theatrical release did, at least at first. The later scenes are grainier. Chapter 19, the podium scene, is a milestone of sexual humor. —*MM*

Movie: 🐾🐾🐾 *DVD:* 🐾🐾🐾
Warner Home Video, Inc. (Cat #20016, UPC #085392001620). Full frame. Dolby Digital Mono. $19.98. Snapper. *LANG:* English. *SUB:* English; Spanish; French. *CAP:* English. *FEATURES:* Cast and crew thumbnail biographies ➛ Production notes ➛

Theatrical trailers for all seven *Police Academy* films ➛ 31 chapter links.
1984 (R) 96m/C Steve Guttenberg, Kim Cattrall, Bubba Smith, George Gaynes, Michael Winslow, Leslie Easterbrook, Georgina Spelvin, Debralee Scott; *D:* Hugh Wilson; *W:* Hugh Wilson, Pat Proft, Neal Israel; *C:* Michael D. Margulies; *M:* Robert Folk.

Polish Wedding

Dreary, dreadful film has a message, and that message is: "catch a man anyway you can and have babies, as sadly this is your only purpose in life." Lena Olin (*The Unbearable Lightness of Being*) and Gabriel Byrne (*The Usual Suspects*) are Polish emigrants, living in Detroit in a two-story duplex. Their eldest son lives upstairs with his wife and new baby, while the other four boys and their only daughter (Danes) live downstairs. Byrne's a chain-smoking baker, his wife is a cleaning woman who is having an affair (with Serbedzija), and Danes is a high school dropout, who sleeps, eats, watches her brother's baby, and does as little as possible. She eventually sets her sites on her brother's friend and local policeman (Trese), gets pregnant, and the film mercifully comes to an end. An otherwise miserable film is blessed with an excellent DVD video presentation, adequate sound, and the curious inclusion of Spanish subtitles. —*RT*

Movie: 🐾 *DVD:* 🐾🐾🐾
Twentieth Century Fox Home Entertainment (Cat #4110380, UPC #086162103 803). Widescreen. AC3 - 2 Channel. $34.98. Keepcase. *LANG:* English. *SUB:* English; Spanish. *CAP:* English. *FEATURES:* 24 chapter links ➛ Theatrical trailer ➛ Actor filmographies.
1997 (PG-13) 107m/C Claire Danes, Lena Olin, Gabriel Byrne, Adam Trese, Rade Serbedzija, Mili Avital, Daniel Lapaine; *D:* Theresa Connelly; *W:* Theresa Connelly; *C:* Guy Dufaux; *M:* Luis Bacalov.

Poltergeist

Though Tobe Hooper directed this hugely popular horror hit, it was produced and cowritten by Steven Spielberg. In some ways, then, it can be seen as the dark side of *E.T.*, also released in the summer of 1982. The Freelings (Williams and Nelson) learn why they got such a good deal on their suburban tract house when it attacks them and their kids. Most of the scares are original and frightening, though the clarity of DVD heightens the shortcomings of many of the special effects. Heavy grain also shows up in exterior long shots. Structurally, the film is sound with careful preparation establishing place and mood. The main flaw is the conclusion, which ought to be more solidly connected to the earlier action. At the end, the characters simply need a better reason to spend more time in the place. Critics have floated many theories about the film's success—it's about the destruction of suburbia, Rea-

gan-era politics, etc—but it's simply a good, well-acted spooky movie. —*MM*

Movie: 🐾🐾🐾 *DVD:* 🐾🐾
MGM Home Entertainment (Cat #906039, UPC #027616603999). Widescreen letterboxed; full frame. Dolby Digital Surround Stereo. $24.98. Snapper. *LANG:* English; French; Spanish. *SUB:* English; French; Spanish. *CAP:* English; French; Spanish. *FEATURES:* 48 chapter links.
1982 (PG) 114m/C JoBeth Williams, Craig T. Nelson, Beatrice Straight, Heather O'Rourke, Zelda Rubinstein, Dominique Dunne, Oliver Robbins, Richard Lawson, James Karen, Michael McManus; *D:* Tobe Hooper; *W:* Steven Spielberg, Michael Grais, Mark Victor; *C:* Matthew F. Leonetti; *M:* Jerry Goldsmith. *AWARDS: NOM:* Academy Awards '82: Best Original Score.

Pom Pom Girls

High school seniors, intent on having one last fling before graduation, get involved in crazy antics, clumsy romances, and football rivalries.

Movie: 🐾🐾 *DVD:* NYR
Rhino Home Video (Cat #2053). Full frame. $19.95. Keepcase.
1976 (R) 90m/C Robert Carradine, Jennifer Ashley, Michael Mullins, Cheryl "Rainbeaux" Smith, Dianne Lee Hart, Lisa Reeves, Bill Adler; *D:* Joseph Ruben; *W:* Joseph Ruben; *C:* Stephen M. Katz; *M:* Michael Lloyd.

The Pompatus of Love

Remember the Steve Miller song, "The Joker"?—the one with the line about the "pompatus of love"—well, that's where the title comes from. The four protagonists (Cryer, Guinee, Pasdar, and Oliensis) of this ensemble drama don't understand it and the line comes to represent the mystery of women. They're bright and literate and they don't have a clue about love or how to grow up. Naturally, the women they know—or meet—are too smart for them.

Movie: 🐾🐾 *DVD:* NYR
WinStar Home Entertainment (Cat #5138). $24.98. Keepcase.
1995 (R) 99m/C Jon Cryer, Tim Guinee, Adrian Pasdar, Adam Oliensis, Kristin Wilson, Dana Wheeler-Nicholson, Paige Turco, Mia Sara, Kristin Scott Thomas, Arabella Field, Jennifer Tilly, Roscoe Lee Browne; *D:* Richard Schenkman; *W:* Jon Cryer, Adam Oliensis, Richard Schenkman; *C:* Russell Fine; *M:* John Hill.

Ponette

Four-year-old Ponette (Thivisol) is hard-pressed to understand what's happening to her family after her mother is killed in a car accident. Her father can't explain death properly so the little girl comes to her own acceptance with the help of school friends. The film drew some controversy when the very young Thivisol was given the best actress award at the Venice Film Festival. Since she was thought by some critics to be too young to "act," director Doillon was accused of manipulating the youngster to get the performance. Whatever the case, it is one of the most realistic portrayals of childhood ever put on-screen. Her fellow young actors are equally natural and their interaction is a carefully observed glimpse into the world of children. The DVD is bright with a near perfect image. The full-frame reproduction is fine because Doillon tells so much of the story through extreme close-ups of the characters. —MM

Movie: 🎬🎬🎬 **DVD:** 🎬🎬🎬▶
WinStar Home Entertainment (Cat #FLV5024, UPC #720917502427). Full frame. $29.99. Keepcase. *LANG:* English. *SUB:* French. *FEATURES:* 8 chapter links • Theatrical trailer • Production credits • Filmographies and awards for Doillon, Trintignant, Beauvois, Nebout.
1995 92m/C *FR* Victorie Thivisol, Marie Trintignant, Claire Nebout, Xavier Beauvois; *D:* Jacques Doillon; *W:* Jacques Doillon; *C:* Caroline Champetier; *M:* Philippe Sarde. *AWARDS:* New York Film Critics Awards '97: Best Foreign Film; Venice Film Festival '96: Best Actress (Thivisol).

Pork Chop Hill

Powerful account of the last hours of the Korean War is undercut somewhat by a mixed military-political message. But the body of the film, about the taking and holding of one ugly patch of dry ground, is some of the most visceral combat footage ever seen. Gregory Peck is excellent as Lt. Joe Clemons who has been ordered into action and then, through a series of miscommunications, is left out to dry. The real strength of the film, captured almost perfectly on DVD, is the striking black-and-white photography of director Milestone and cinematographer Sam Leavitt. It is among the most sharply detailed and evocative to come out of Hollywood and is still a marvel today. If the monaural sound is less explosive than we've come to expect of a war film, it is an accurate reproduction of the original. —MM

Movie: 🎬🎬🎬 **DVD:** 🎬🎬🎬▶
MGM Home Entertainment (Cat #907669, UPC #027616766922). Widescreen letterboxed; full frame. Dolby Digital Mono. $24.98. Keepcase. *LANG:* English; French. *SUB:* English; French. *FEATURES:* 36 chapter links.
1959 97m/B Gregory Peck, Harry Guardino, Rip Torn, George Peppard, James Edwards, Bob Steele, Woody Strode, Robert (Bobby) Blake, Martin Landau, Norman Fell, Bert Remsen, George Shibata, Biff Elliot, Barry Atwater, Martin Garth, Lew Gallo, Charles Aidman, Leonard Graves, Ken Lynch, Paul Comi, Cliff Ketchum, Abel Fernandez, Gavin MacLeod; *D:* Lewis Milestone; *W:* James R. Webb; *C:* Sam Leavitt; *M:* Leonard Rosenman.

Porky's

Investigation of teen horniness set in South Florida's Angel Beach High School during the fab '50s is an irreverent comedy that follows the misadventures of six youths who share a common interest: girls. Their main barrier to sexual success: the no-touch babes they lust after and the incredibly stupid adults who run the world. Fairly dumb and tasteless with occasional big laughs; earned mega bucks at the drive-in and created the perceived popular outcry for more Porky: *Porky's II: The Next Day* (1983) and *Porky's Revenge* (1985). This is not one of the better Fox DVDs. Since they're usually pretty good, it's most likely the result of the source material. The picture is far from sharp and has some grain most of the time, which increases in the darker scenes. Colors are weak and occasionally bleed. The contrast seems a little weak, but the blacks are generally O.K. The stereo soundtrack is pretty lame with only slight separation and average fidelity. —JO

Movie: 🎬🎬▶ **DVD:** 🎬🎬
20th Century Fox (Cat #4109069, UPC #086162090691). Widescreen (1.85:1) letterboxed. Stereo. $29.95. Keepcase. *LANG:* English; Spanish; French. *SUB:* English. *CAP:* English. *FEATURES:* 20 chapter links • Theatrical trailer.
1982 (R) 94m/C *CA* Dan Monahan, Wyatt Knight, Scott Colomby, Tony Ganios, Mark Herrier, Cyril O'Reilly, Roger Wilson, Alex Karras, Kim Cattrall, Kaki Hunter, Nancy Parsons, Boyd Gaines, Douglas McGrath, Susan Clark, Art Hindle, Wayne Maunder, Chuck "Porky" Mitchell, Eric Christmas, Bob (Benjamin) Clark; *D:* Bob (Benjamin) Clark; *W:* Bob (Benjamin) Clark; *C:* Reginald Morris; *M:* Paul Zaza, Carl Zittrer.

Portrait of a Lady

Adapted from the Henry James novel, *Portrait* paints the story of independent and newly wealthy American, Isabel Archer (Kidman). Abroad in Europe, she falls under the influence of the bitter, opportunistic Madame Merle (Hershey, in a strong portrayal), who manages to steer the innocent Isabel into a disastrous marriage with Gilbert Osmond (Malkovich). From there, the film deals with Isabel's efforts to flee the domineering Osmond and find herself again. Kidman plays her role with never-before-seen efficiency. Malkovich is suitably evil but plays his villain card a bit too early. Director Campion's voice carries the film through. This very rich-looking film, made in England and Italy, comes to DVD with a corresponding rich-looking transfer that delivers the beautiful cinematography with pin-point accuracy. The picture is detailed and sharp. Deep, vibrant colors are teamed with contrast and brightness levels that accent the finely varied shadings. Blacks are true. The music and environmental ambience added by the 5.1 sound's Surround tracks are never obviously intrusive and add to the fullness of the experience. —JO

Movie: 🎬🎬🎬 **DVD:** 🎬🎬🎬🎬
USA Home Entertainment (Cat #44004 37972, UPC #044004379724). Widescreen (2.35:1) letterboxed; full frame. Dolby Digital 5.1; Dolby Digital Mono. $29.95. Keepcase. *LANG:* English; French. *SUB:* Spanish. *FEATURES:* 31 chapter links • Cast and filmmakers bios.
1996 (PG-13) 142m/C *GB* Nicole Kidman, John Malkovich, Barbara Hershey, Martin Donovan, Christian Bale, Shelley Winters, Shelley Duvall, Mary-Louise Parker, Richard E. Grant, John Gielgud, Viggo Mortensen; *D:* Jane Campion; *W:* Laura Jones; *C:* Stuart Dryburgh; *M:* Wojciech Kilar. *AWARDS:* Los Angeles Film Critics Association Awards '96: Best Supporting Actress (Hershey); National Society of Film Critics Awards '96: Best Supporting Actor (Donovan), Best Supporting Actress (Hershey); *NOM:* Academy Awards '96: Best Costume Design, Best Supporting Actress (Hershey); Golden Globe Awards '97: Best Supporting Actress (Hershey).

Portrait of an Assassin

Unhappy with his marriage to a nagging wife (Arletty), Fabius (Brasseur) goes so far as to tell her that he killed a woman by mistake, thinking it was her. Can this marriage be saved? Before it's over, more infidelity and the inimitable von Stroheim have come into play. Unfortunately, the DVD image doesn't measure up to the unpredictable plot. The mediocre black-and-white photography is marred by near-continuous surface scratches. Sound is equally muddy. The yellow subtitles are easy to read. —MM

Movie: 🎬🎬 **DVD:** 🎬🎬
Image Entertainment (Cat #ID9067SIDVD, UPC #014381906721). Full frame. Dolby Digital Mono. $24.99. Snapper. *LANG:* French. *SUB:* English. *FEATURES:* 12 chapter links.
1949 86m/B Pierre Brasseur, Arletty, Maria Montez, Erich von Stroheim; *D:* Bernard Roland; *W:* Marcel Rivet; *C:* Roger Hubert; *M:* Maurice Hiriet.

The Poseidon Adventure

The cruise ship *Poseidon* is on its last voyage from New York to Athens on New Year's Eve when it is capsized by a tidal wave. The ten survivors struggle to escape the waterlogged tomb. Oscar-winning special effects, such as Shelley Winters floating in a boiler room, created an entirely new genre of filmmaking—the big-cast disaster flick. *The Poseidon Adventure* has never looked that good on home video. Even though the Fox widescreen laserdisc was O.K., it had weaker colors than this DVD. Besides the improved colors, the DVD is also very sharp and has more intense contrast. Blacks are deep and true. Even the mono sound on the DVD is very strong and features full-bodied fidelity with good bass and clarity. —JO

Movie: 🎬🎬▶ *DVD:* 🎬🎬🎬▶
20th Century Fox (Cat #4110422, UPC #086162104220). Widescreen (2.35:1) letterboxed. Dolby Digital Mono. $29.98. Keepcase. *LANG:* English; French. *SUB:* English; Spanish. *CAP:* English. *FEATURES:* 24 chapter links ▪ Theatrical trailer.
1972 (PG) 117m/C Gene Hackman, Ernest Borgnine, Shelley Winters, Red Buttons, Jack Albertson, Carol Lynley, Roddy McDowall; *D:* Ronald Neame; *W:* Wendell Mayes, Stirling Silliphant; *C:* Harold E. Stine; *M:* John Williams. *AWARDS:* Academy Awards '72: Best Song ("The Morning After"), Best Visual Effects; Golden Globe Awards '73: Best Supporting Actress (Winters); *NOM:* Academy Awards '72: Best Art Direction/Set Decoration, Best Cinematography, Best Costume Design, Best Film Editing, Best Sound, Best Supporting Actress (Winters), Best Original Dramatic Score.

Posse

Though it's carrying some racial and political baggage, Van Peebles's "black" western is a rip-roaring shoot-'em-up. It has no more to do with the historical "truth" of the Old West than Sergio Leone's operatic concoctions do. In fact, the film borrows heavily from Leone's work; a clip from *Once Upon a Time in the West* shows up in the closing credits. The story also lifts elements from *The Wild Bunch* and *The Magnificent Seven,* but the real inspiration is *Raiders of the Lost Ark,* with the exaggerated looks and pace of a music video, and appropriately shallow characters. Jessie Lee (Van Peebles) leads a group of Spanish American war veterans to Freemanville, a troubled community founded by former slaves.
Movie: 🎬🎬▶ *DVD:* NYR
USA Home Entertainment (Cat #88115). Widescreen (2.35:1) letterboxed; full frame. Dolby Digital Stereo. $29.95. Keepcase. *LANG:* English; French. *CAP:* English. *FEATURES:* Cast and crew thumbnail bios ▪ Trailer.
1993 (R) 113m/C Mario Van Peebles, Stephen Baldwin, Charles Lane, Tommy (Tiny) Lister, Big Daddy Kane, Billy Zane, Blair Underwood, Tone Loc, Salli Richardson, Reginald Hudlin, Richard Edson, Reginald Vel Johnson, Warrington Hudlin; *Cameos:* Melvin Van Peebles, Pam Grier, Isaac Hayes, Robert Hooks, Richard Jordan, Paul Bartel, Nipsey Russell, Woody Strode, Aaron Neville, Stephen J. Cannell; *D:* Mario Van Peebles; *W:* Sy Richardson, Dario Scardapane; *C:* Peter Menzies Jr.; *M:* Michel Colombier.

The Postman

In 1952, Mario (Troisi) is a shy villager who winds up being the personal postman of exiled Chilean poet Pablo Neruda (Noiret), who is living in the tiny Italian community of Isla Negra. The tongue-tied Mario has fallen in love with barmaid Beatrice (Cucinotta). He asks the poet's help in wooing the dark-eyed beauty, and strikes up an unlikely friendship with the worldly Neruda. Troisi, a beloved actor in his native Italy was gravely ill, needing a heart transplant, during the making of the film (all-too apparent from his gaunt appearance) and died the day after filming was completed. On his commentary track, director Radford talks at length about his star's dedication to the project, and the accommodations that were made to complete it. For the most part, he sticks close to the action on the screen and avoids excess sentimentality. If the action seems too dark in some of the interiors, Radford claims that he intended for the film to look that way. —*MM AKA: Il Postino.*
Movie: 🎬🎬🎬▶ *DVD:* 🎬🎬🎬▶
Miramax Pictures Home Video (Cat #15861, UPC #717951000965). Widescreen (1.66:1) letterboxed. Dolby Digital 2.0 Stereo. $39.99. Keepcase. *LANG:* French; Italian. *SUB:* English. *FEATURES:* 21 chapter links ▪ Commentary: Michael Radford ▪ *Poetry, Passion, "The Postman"—The Return of Pablo Neruda* ▪ Soundtrack featurette ▪ TV commercials ▪ Theatrical trailer.
1994 (PG) 115m/C *IT* Massimo Troisi, Philippe Noiret, Maria Grazia Cucinotta, Linda Moretti, Renato Scarpa, Anna Buonaiuto, Mariana Rigillo; *D:* Michael Radford; *W:* Massimo Troisi, Michael Radford, Furio Scarpelli, Anna Pavignano, Giacomo Scarpelli; *C:* Franco Di Giacomo; *M:* Luis Bacalov. *AWARDS:* Academy Awards '95: Best Original Dramatic Score; British Academy Awards '95: Best Director (Radford), Best Foreign Film, Best Score; Broadcast Film Critics Association Awards '95: Best Foreign Film; *NOM:* Academy Awards '95: Best Actor (Troisi), Best Adapted Screenplay, Best Director (Radford), Best Picture; British Academy Awards '95: Best Actor (Troisi), Best Adapted Screenplay; Cesar Awards '97: Best Foreign Film; Directors Guild of America Awards '95: Best Director (Radford); Screen Actors Guild Award '95: Best Actor (Troisi).

The Postman

It's post-apocalypse time (the year's 2013), with a nameless drifter (Costner) assuming the role of a postal carrier in order to bring hope to a devastated town terrorized by marauding hooligans, led by General Bethlehem (Patton). If you fancy deadpan dialogue and can swallow the image of a mail carrier as the symbol for patriotism, then this one's for you. Overall, Costner offers nothing new to the genre of the stranger offering hope, and soon the flick becomes a cornball exercise and extravagant waste of time for all involved. Costner's first directing effort since *Dances with Wolves.* No matter what you think of the movie, this DVD is excellent. The picture is incredibly sharp with virtually no grain or artifacts. Colors are superb, offering both vibrancy and accuracy. The blacks are dead-on and the contrast and brightness levels are punchy and consistent. The ambience injected by the 5.1 sound is both appealing and involving, and the Surround effects are of hit-you-in-the-face caliber. —*JO*

Warner Home Video, Inc. (Cat #15519, UPC #085391551928). Widescreen (2.35:1) anamorphic. Dolby Digital 5.1. $24.98. Snapper. *LANG:* English; French. *SUB:* English; Spanish; French. *CAP:* English. *FEATURES:* 44 chapter links ▪ Theatrical trailer ▪ Special effects documentary ▪ Production notes.
1997 (R) 170m/C Kevin Costner, Larenz Tate, Will Patton, Olivia Williams, James Russo, Tom Petty, Daniel von Bargen, Scott Bairstow, Giovanni Ribisi, Roberta Maxwell, Joe Santos, Peggy Lipton, Ron McLarty, Rex Linn, Todd Allen, Shawn Hatosy; *D:* Kevin Costner; *W:* Brian Helgeland, Eric Roth; *C:* Stephen Windon; *M:* James Newton Howard. *AWARDS:* Golden Raspberry Awards '97: Worst Picture, Worst Actor (Costner), Worst Director (Costner), Worst Screenplay, Worst Song (Entire Song Score).

The Postman Always Rings Twice

Mamet-Rafelson remake doesn't lay a glove on the original. Nicholson is Frank, the Depression-era drifter who lurches into an obsessive affair with Cora (Lange) and then plots with her to kill her husband (Colicos). This version is truer to James M. Cain's novel than the 1946 film in its brutal (and occasionally silly) sex scenes, but it's dreary and forgettable. For better or worse, the DVD is an accurate full-frame re-creation of the theatrical release with the brown-red tinting of interiors and misty focus. —*MM*
Movie: 🎬🎬 *DVD:* 🎬🎬▶
Warner Home Video, Inc. (Cat #673, UPC #012569067325). Full frame. Dolby Digital Stereo. $19.98. Keepcase. *LANG:* English. *SUB:* English; French; Spanish. *FEATURES:* 31 chapter links ▪ Cast and crew thumbnail biographies ▪ Trailers ▪ Production notes.
1981 (R) 123m/C Jack Nicholson, Jessica Lange, John Colicos, Anjelica Huston, Michael Lerner, John P. Ryan, Christopher Lloyd; *D:* Bob Rafelson; *W:* David Mamet; *C:* Sven Nykvist; *M:* Michael Small.

Postmortem

Sheen is an FBI serial killer profiler who leaves the job to become a novelist and find peace in a small town. But his quiet life is shattered by a murderer who writes the obituaries of his victims before he kills.
Movie: 🎬🎬 *DVD:* NYR
Studio Home Entertainment (Cat #7005). Full frame. Dolby Digital Stereo. $24.95. Keepcase. *FEATURES:* Cast and crew thumbnail bios ▪ Production notes.
1998 (R) 105m/C Charlie Sheen, Michael Halsey, Stephen McCole, Gary Lewis; *D:* Albert Pyun; *W:* John Lamb; *C:* George Mooradian; *M:* Tony Riparetti.

Pot o' Gold

Stewart plays a wealthy young man who signs on with a struggling band. He con-

vinces his uncle, who has a radio program, to let the band perform during a giveaway show he has concocted. Slight comedy. **AKA:** The Golden Hour.
Movie: 🎵🎵 **DVD:** NYR
Madacy Entertainment (Cat #99030). Full frame. Dolby Digital Mono. $9.99. Keepcase.
1941 87m/B Paulette Goddard, James Stewart, Charles Winninger, Horace Heidt, Art Carney; **D:** George Marshall; **W:** Walter DeLeon; **C:** Hal Mohr.

Powder

Fragments of a potentially excellent science-fiction film can be found within this one, but they're hard to spot. The pretentious orchestral score doesn't suit the simple story about an electromagnetic albino (Flanery), and the busy plot is filled with half-baked conflicts. The stars do their best, but TV's The X-Files treats similar material more effectively. Revelations of director Salva's criminal conviction for child molestation cast the film about teenaged characters in a disturbing light. It doesn't fare well on DVD either where venetian blinds and shiny objects—both of which feature prominently in key scenes—tend to flash, and any sharp diagonal line loses its edge. —MM
Movie: 🎵▶ **DVD:** 🎵🎵▶
Buena Vista Home Entertainment (Cat #17496, UPC #717951003140). Widescreen (1.85:1) letterboxed. Dolby 5.1 Surround (English); Dolby Surround (French). $29.99. Keepcase. **LANG:** English; French. **CAP:** English. **FEATURES:** 16 chapter links.
1995 (PG-13) 111m/C Sean Patrick Flanery, Mary Steenburgen, Lance Henriksen, Jeff Goldblum, Brandon Smith, Bradford Tatum, Susan Tyrrell, Missy Crider, Ray Wise, Esteban Louis Powell; **D:** Victor Salva; **W:** Victor Salva; **C:** Jerzy Zielinski; **M:** Jerry Goldsmith. **AWARDS: NOM:** MTV Movie Awards '96: Breakthrough Performance (Flanery).

The Power of One

Good cast is generally wasted in this liberal white look at apartheid South Africa in the 1940s. P.K. is a white orphan of British descent who is sent to a boarding school run by Afrikaaners (South Africans of German descent). Humiliated and bullied, particularly when England and Germany go to war, P.K. is befriended by a German pianist and a black boxing coach who teach him to box and stand up for his rights. It's preachy, filled with stereotypes, and based on the novel by Bryce Courtenay. The DVD fluctuates between an acceptably sharp image and one that is very poor. Most longshots with any amount of detail incur a lot of grain, and if those shots are in the least bit darker, artifacts join right in. The colors tend to remain fairly accurate and are occasionally vibrant. The Dolby Surround sound is one of the best non-5.1 mixes on any DVD, and has a live and energetic feel

with plenty of bass and makes excellent use of the back speakers. —JO
Movie: 🎵🎵 **DVD:** 🎵🎵
Warner Home Video, Inc. (Cat #12411, UPC #085391241126). Widescreen (1.85:1) letterboxed. Dolby Surround. $24.98. Snapper. **LANG:** English. **CAP:** English. **FEATURES:** 35 chapter links.
1992 (PG-13) 126m/C Stephen Dorff, Armin Mueller-Stahl, Morgan Freeman, John Gielgud, Fay Masterson, Marius Weyers, Tracy Brooks Swope, John Osborne, Daniel Craig, Dominic Walker, Alois Mayo, Ian Roberts, Maria Marais; **D:** John G. Avildsen; **W:** Robert Mark Kamen; **C:** Dean Semler; **M:** Hans Zimmer.

Practical Magic

Good cast, weak story. Gillian (Kidman) and Sally (Bullock) are modern-day witch sisters whose family suffers from an unfortunate 100-year-old curse. Any man they fall in love with is doomed to an early death. One more dead body, Gillian's abusive boyfriend Jimmy (Visnjic), brings out detective Gary Hallet (Quinn) and his charms prove mighty attractive to the frantic Sally. The most important aspect of this DVD is the way both soundtracks deliver the performances fully intact with excellent dynamics capturing the cast's expressive nuances. The Surround is not used much by either the 5.1 or the Dolby Surround. The image is pretty good, too; fairly sharp with cleanly detailed colors and true blacks. —JO
Movie: 🎵🎵▶ **DVD:** 🎵🎵🎵
Warner Home Video, Inc. (Cat #16322, UPC #085391632221). Widescreen (2.35:1) anamorphic. Dolby Digital 5.1; Dolby Surround. $24.98. Snapper. **LANG:** English; French. **SUB:** English; French. **CAP:** English. **FEATURES:** 31 chapter links ▪ Interactive game ▪ 2 documentaries ▪ Audio commentary ▪ Production notes ▪ 11 theatrical trailers and 3 TV spots.
1998 (PG-13) 105m/C Sandra Bullock, Nicole Kidman, Aidan Quinn, Stockard Channing, Dianne Wiest, Goran Visnjic; **D:** Griffin Dunne; **W:** Robin Swicord, Akiva Goldsman, Adam Brooks; **C:** Andrew Dunn; **M:** Alan Silvestri.

Pre-Code Hollywood: The Risque Years, Vol. 1

Three films made before the 1934 Production Code: Of Human Bondage (1934), Kept Husbands (1931), and Millie (1931).
Movie: NYR **DVD:** NYR
Roan Group (Cat #2004). Full frame. $39.95. Keepcase.
193? 249m/C

Pre-Code Hollywood: The Risque Years, Vol. 2

Two films made before the 1934 Production Code: Bird of Paradise (1932) and The Lady Refuses (1932).

Movie: NYR **DVD:** NYR
Roan Group (Cat #1027). Full frame. $29.95. Keepcase.
1932 150m/C

Predator

Schwarzenegger leads a team of CIA-hired mercenaries into the Central American jungles to rescue hostages. They encounter an alien force that begins to attack them one by one. Soon it's just Arnold and the Beast in this attention-grabbing, but sometimes silly, suspense film. Even though parts of the letterboxed laserdisc are sharper, overall, the DVD is far superior. The biggest difference is the color, which is much stronger, with better detail and shading. There is very little bleed, even when the dominant color in a scene is red. The DVD has some trouble with grain in the darker scenes, and that's where the laser has the real edge. The 5.1 sound improves upon the clarity and has a nice bass boost to beef up the action scenes. There is also a lot of edge added with crisp highs that never reach the point of being too harsh. —JO
Movie: 🎵🎵▶ **DVD:** 🎵🎵🎵
20th Century Fox (Cat #4109068, UPC #086162090684). Widescreen (1.85:1) letterboxed. Dolby Digital 5.1; Dolby Surround. $29.98. Keepcase. **LANG:** English (DD5.1; DS); French (stereo). **SUB:** English; Spanish. **CAP:** English. **FEATURES:** 35 chapter links ▪ Theatrical trailer.
1987 (R) 107m/C Arnold Schwarzenegger, Jesse Ventura, Sonny Landham, Bill Duke, Elpidia Carrillo, Carl Weathers, R.G. Armstrong, Richard Chaves, Shane Black, Kevin Peter Hall; **D:** John McTiernan; **W:** Jim Thomas, John Thomas; **C:** Donald McAlpine; **M:** Alan Silvestri.

Prehistoric Women

Half-baked rehash of She finds great white hunter Marchant (Latimer) captured by an African tribe that worships a white rhino. He escapes but is recaptured by the titular bikini-clad prehistoric babes where the brunettes, led by Queen Kari (Beswick), rule the blondes, and they're all desperately in search of acting lessons. Racist undertones are most evident in the "dance" routines. Though most of the action was filmed on cheap-looking sets, the DVD image is still bright and sharp. The feature is on one side of the two-sided disc; extras are on the flip side. —MM **AKA:** Slave Girls.
Movie: 🎵🎵 **DVD:** 🎵🎵🎵
Anchor Bay (Cat #DV10679, UPC #0131331067996). Widescreen (2.35:1) letterboxed. Dolby Digital Mono. $29.98. Keepcase. **LANG:** English. **FEATURES:** 25 chapter links ▪ Theatrical trailer ▪ TV spots ▪ World of Hammer episode "Lands Before Time."
1967 90m/C GB Michael Latimer, Martine Beswick, Edina Ronay, Carol White; **D:** Michael Carreras; **W:** Henry (Michael Carreras) Younger; **C:** Michael Reed; **M:** Carlo Martelli.

Presenting Felix the Cat: The Otto Mesmer Classics 1919–24

These early silent cartoons are so primitive that they're barely watchable. The images are high-contrast black and white. The stories are simple. The organ score is off-putting. Yes, they occupy an important place in the development of animation but even in their time, they were eclipsed by Mickey Mouse and others. The DVD is recommended to film historians only. —*MM*

Movie: 🐾🐾 **DVD:** 🐾▶
Image Entertainment (Cat #ID55328KDVD, UPC #014381553222). Full frame. Dolby Digital Stereo. $24.99. Snapper. *SUB:* English. *FEATURES:* 18 chapter links.
1996 ?m/B

Presumed Innocent

An assistant district attorney (Ford) is the prime suspect when a former lover turns up brutally murdered. Cover-ups surround him, the political climate changes, and friends and enemies switch sides. Slow-paced courtroom drama, skillfully adapted from the best-seller by Chicago attorney Scott Turow, boasts excellent performances from Ford, Julia, and Bedelia. The DVD is very sharp and has very little trouble with grain. While the blacks are true and nicely handled, the colors a little weak at times, particularly in the fleshtones and the earthtones of the courtroom scenes. A slight boost to the contrast might have made a lot of difference. Brightness levels are good. The Dolby Surround has some nice dynamics and fidelity, but not much use is made of the rear channel. Since the movie is dialogue driven, it's not really a problem and the dialogue is mixed up front with good presence. —*JO*

Movie: 🐾🐾🐾 **DVD:** 🐾🐾🐾
Warner Home Video, Inc. (Cat #12034, UPC #085391203421). Widescreen (1.85:1) letterboxed; full frame. Dolby Surround; Mono. $24.98. Snapper. *LANG:* English (DS); Spanish (mono); French (DS). *SUB:* English; Spanish; French. *CAP:* English. *FEATURES:* 35 chapter links • Theatrical trailer • Production notes.
1990 (R) 127m/C Harrison Ford, Brian Dennehy, Bonnie Bedelia, Greta Scacchi, Raul Julia, Paul Winfield, John Spencer, Joe Grifasi, Anna Maria Horsford, Sab Shimono, Christine Estabrook, Michael (Lawrence) Tolan, Tom Mardirosian; *D:* Alan J. Pakula; *W:* Frank Pierson, Alan J. Pakula; *C:* Gordon Willis; *M:* John Williams.

Pretty As a Picture: The Art of David Lynch

Though this generally praiseful documentary focuses mainly on Lynch's work with *Lost Highway*, it also provides a fair look at his background and childhood. Director Toby Keeler emphasizes the odder facets of his subject's career as an artist. Given the large number of people who appear to be so eager to talk about their association with Lynch, he seems to be a likeable enough fellow, and not nearly as removed from the mainstream as one might expect from the nature of his work. The best parts of the DVD focus on the nuts and bolts side of filmmaking; how he and his collaborators go about putting his unique ideas on-screen. The disc also includes about 15 minutes of interviews that could not be included on the tape version. Those who do not care for Lynch's work probably will not be converted by anything they see here, but his fans will love it. —*MM*

Movie: 🐾🐾🐾 **DVD:** 🐾🐾🐾
Image Entertainment (Cat #ID4810TKDVD, UPC #014381481020). Full frame. Dolby Digital Stereo. $24.99. Snapper. *LANG:* English. *FEATURES:* 22 chapter links • Photo montage.
1998 ?m/C Robert Loggia, David Lynch, Jack Nance, Bill Pullman; *D:* Toby Keeler.

Pretty Village, Pretty Flame

Powerful story of the Bosnian conflict is based on a true incident. The story flashes from the days of Yugoslavian unity under Marshal Tito to 1992, when members of a Serbian patrol are trapped (along with an American journalist) by Muslim militiamen in a tunnel connecting Zagreb and Belgrade with no hope for escape. *AKA:* Lepa Sela, Lepo Gore.

Movie: 🐾🐾🐾 **DVD:** NYR
WinStar Home Entertainment (Cat #5027). Widescreen (1.78:1) letterboxed. Dolby Digital Stereo. $29.98. Keepcase. *LANG:* Serbo-Croatian. *SUB:* English. *FEATURES:* Production notes • Trailer.
1996 125m/C Dragan Bjelogric, Nikola Kojo, Bata Zivojinovic, Dragan Maksimovic, Zoran Cvijanovic, Nikola Pejakovic, Lisa Moncure; *D:* Srdjan Dragojevic; *W:* Srdjan Dragojevic, Vanja Bulic, Nikola Pejakovic; *C:* Dusan Joksimovic; *M:* Lazar Ristovski.

Pretty Woman

An old story takes a fresh approach as a successful but stuffy business man hires a fun-loving, energetic young hooker to be his companion for a week. The film caused some controversy over its upbeat portrayal of prostitution, but its popularity at the boxoffice catapulted Roberts to stardom. This is the longer 124-minute director's cut of the film. Having only seen the movie once before, I could tell little difference, but I'm sure there were no added sex scenes. For such a "Hollywood" movie, the sound is really a bit dull and could have used some Surround embellishments. The picture is sharp enough, though, and deep colors warm the film nicely. Marshall's commentary is deceptively informative. —*JO*

Movie: 🐾🐾🐾 **DVD:** 🐾🐾🐾
Buena Vista Home Entertainment (Cat #14260, UPC #717951000415). Widescreen (1.85:1) letterboxed. Dolby Surround. $29.99. Keepcase. *LANG:* English. *FEATURES:* 20 chapter links • Commentary: Gary Marshall • 124-minute director's cut.
1990 (R) 124m/C Richard Gere, Julia Roberts, Ralph Bellamy, Jason Alexander, Laura San Giacomo, Hector Elizondo, Alex Hyde-White, Elinor Donahue, Larry Miller, Jane Morris; *D:* Garry Marshall; *W:* J.F. Lawton; *C:* Charles Minsky; *M:* James Newton Howard. *AWARDS:* Golden Globe Awards '91: Best Actress—Musical/Comedy (Roberts); *NOM:* Academy Awards '90: Best Actress (Roberts).

A Price above Rubies

Unsatisfied with her life as a stay-at-home mom in the New York Hasidic Jewish community, Sonia (Zellweger) works with her brother-in-law's (Eccleston) jewelry business. Their relationship is much more complicated and eventually it leads her to Ramon (Payne), a black artist. The real subject of the story, though, is the conflict between an independent woman and a patriarchal society. Writer-director Yakin deals with potentially exploitative material with the same seriousness that he brought to his first feature, the cult favorite *Fresh*. This kind of complex, character-based film really doesn't gain much on DVD. The no-extras disc exhibits no significant visual or aural flaws. A commentary track from Yakin might have been illuminating. —*MM*

Movie: 🐾🐾🐾 **DVD:** 🐾🐾▶
Miramax Pictures Home Video (Cat #17638, UPC #717951003485). Widescreen (1.85:1) letterboxed. Dolby Digital 5.1 Surround Stereo. $29.99. Keepcase. *LANG:* English. *CAP:* English. *FEATURES:* 25 chapter links • Theatrical trailer.
1997 (R) 117m/C Renee Zellweger, Christopher Eccleston, Glenn Fitzgerald, Allen Payne, Julianna Margulies, Kim Hunter, John Randolph, Kathleen Chalfant, Edie Falco, Tim Jerome, Phyllis Newman; *D:* Boaz Yakin; *W:* Boaz Yakin; *C:* Adam Holender; *M:* Lesley Barber.

The Price of Desire

Low-budget variation on *Indecent Proposal* revolves around a married couple's teasing games. Monica (Reed) flirts until hubby Mac (Frank) intervenes. But, an impoverished actor, he wants her to do more after she meets Joel (Justini), a casino owner. The DVD is marred by an unusual amount of pixelation and graininess, both in low-light scenes and in overly bright exteriors. Otherwise, performances are about average and production values are on a par with other Playboy productions. —*MM*

Movie: 🐾🐾▶ **DVD:** 🐾🐾
Image Entertainment (Cat #ID5970PLDVD, UPC #014381597028). Full frame. Dolby Digital Stereo. $24.99. Snapper. *LANG:* English. *FEATURES:* 14 chapter links.
1996 102m/C Moe Justini, Kira Reed, Dan Frank, Janine Lindemulder; *D:* Toby (Paul Thomas) Philips; *W:* Penny Antine; *C:* Stephan Schultze; *M:* Peter Carl Ganderup.

Pride and Prejudice

Lavish TV adaptation of the Jane Austen novel finds bright Elizabeth Bennet (Ehle) unwillingly smitten by the wealthy, mysterious, and arrogant Mr. Darcy (Firth). Her family, filled with unmarried daughters, is rather silly and, of course, Elizabeth should be looking to get married (or at least not hinder her sister's chances). This two-disc A&E mini-series was filmed on location in Derbyshire. The colors are quite good on this transfer, perfectly matching the diffused shades that go so well with an Austen adaptation. The audio transfer is equally solid, delivering a rich, clear soundtrack with no cracks or other intrusions. —*MJT*
Movie: ♪♪♪ *DVD:* ♪♪♪
Image Entertainment (Cat #ID4354ANDVD, UPC #014381435429). Full frame. Dolby Digital 2.0 Stereo. $69.95. Snapper. *LANG:* English. *FEATURES:* 34 chapter links.
1995 310m/C *GB* Jennifer Ehle, Colin Firth, Susannah Harker, Alison Steadman, Julia Sawalha, Benjamin Whitrow, Crispin Bonham Carter, Anna Chancellor, David Bamber, David Bark-Jones, Polly Maberly, Lucy Briers, Barbara Leigh-Hunt, Adrian Lukis; *D:* Simon Langton; *W:* Andrew Davies; *C:* John Kenway; *M:* Carl Davis.

The Pride of the Yankees

Everyone's favorite baseball movie is an excellent portrait of the great Lou Gehrig. Beginning as he joins the pinstripe boys in 1923, the film follows him through his moving farewell speech as his career was cut short by the disease that bears his name. Cooper is at his inspiring best in the title role. Inexplicably, this DVD was made from a "colorized" version of the film, and like all of those bastardized travesties, it simply looks wrong. Wait for the original black and white. —*MM*
Movie: ♪♪♪ *DVD:* ♪
HBO Home Video (Cat #91257). Full frame. $24.98. *LANG:* English. *SUB:* English; French; Spanish. *FEATURES:* 15 chapter links • Cast and crew thumbnail bios.
1942 128m/B Gary Cooper, Teresa Wright, Babe Ruth, Walter Brennan, Dan Duryea; *D:* Sam Wood; *W:* Herman J. Mankiewicz, Jo Swerling; *C:* Rudolph Maté; *M:* Leigh Harline. *AWARDS:* Academy Awards '42: Best Film Editing; *NOM:* Academy Awards '42: Best Actor (Cooper), Best Actress (Wright), Best Black-and-white Cinematography, Best Picture, Best Screenplay, Best Sound, Best Story, Best Original Dramatic Score.

Priest

The title character is Father Greg (Roache), a young, fairly conservative priest who comes to an inner-city parish in Liverpool. His colleague Father Matthew (Wilkinson) is something of a social firebrand who's prone to overstatement, strong drink, and other sins. Father Greg has to face two problems, a case of incest

he learns of in the confessional and his own homosexuality. Both cause him to question his faith and his calling. Can he remain silent while a child is being harmed? Is he meant to be celibate? When it's time to answer those questions, the film stacks the deck in favor of certain ideas—as did *On the Waterfront* and *Norma Rae* and *The Green Berets*. This is popular entertainment, not theology. Not all viewers will agree with the conclusions, but even the film's critics, who have been loud and vocal, will have to admit that it deals with spiritual issues in a serious manner, neither mocking nor making light of faith. The filmmakers also depict homosexuality in pretty much the same way that heterosexual relationships are shown in other "R"-rated films. That side of the film is said to have been re-edited considerably to meet the MPAA's curious sexual standards. DVD might have been the place to release a director's cut, but this is the theatrical version, without any deleted scenes or footage. Image and sound are fine throughout, though the film is never sharply focused or visually challenging. Character-driven stories aren't supposed to be. —*MM*
Movie: ♪♪♪♪ *DVD:* ♪♪♪
Miramax Pictures Home Video (Cat #17505, UPC #717951003232). Widescreen (1.66:1) letterboxed. Dolby Digital Surround Stereo. $29.99. Keepcase. *LANG:* English. *CAP:* English. *FEATURES:* 25 chapter links.
1994 (R) 98m/C *GB* Linus Roache, Tom Wilkinson, Cathy Tyson, Robert Carlyle, James Ellis, John Bennett, Rio Fanning, Jimmy Coleman, Lesley Sharp, Robert Pugh, Christine Tremarco; *D:* Antonia Bird; *W:* Jimmy McGovern; *C:* Fred Tammes; *M:* Andy Roberts. *AWARDS: NOM:* Australian Film Institute '95: Best Foreign Film.

Primal Fear

Chicago defense attorney Martin Vail (Gere) is torn between the fight for justice and the lure of fame. He seems to have found the spotlight when a gentle altar boy (newcomer Norton is a standout) is accused of savagely murdering an archbishop. This leads to some courtroom fireworks due, in part, to the fact that the prosecutor (Linney) is Vail's former lover. Gere turns in a satisfying performance, but except when he's with his client, can't keep the script afloat. Lame plot revelations and an obvious "shocker" ending don't help matters. Feature directorial debut of Hoblit, Emmy winner for TV's *Hill Street Blues, L.A. Law,* and *NYPD Blue.* This is one of the sharpest DVD releases from Paramount. The image has no problem with grain or color bleed, despite all the time spent in the courtroom, where lighting is lower level and the predominant colors are earthtones. What's more, the colors are accurate and, in the brighter scenes, very vibrant. The 5.1 mix is full-bodied and crisp, but rarely takes full advantage of the rear channels. —*JO*
Movie: ♪♪ *DVD:* ♪♪♪

Paramount Home Video (Cat #328327, UPC #097363283270). Widescreen (2.35:1) anamorphic. Dolby Digital 5.1; Dolby Surround. $29.99. Keepcase. *LANG:* English; French. *SUB:* Spanish. *CAP:* English. *FEATURES:* 26 chapter links • Theatrical trailer.
1996 (R) 130m/C Richard Gere, Laura Linney, Edward Norton, John Mahoney, Alfre Woodard, Frances McDormand, Terry O'Quinn, Andre Braugher, Steven Bauer, Joe Spano, Tony Plana, Stanley Anderson, Maura Tierney, Jon Seda; *D:* Gregory Hoblit; *W:* Steve Shagan, Ann Biderman; *C:* Michael Chapman; *M:* James Newton Howard. *AWARDS:* Golden Globe Awards '97: Best Supporting Actor (Norton); Los Angeles Film Critics Association Awards '96: Best Supporting Actor (Norton); National Board of Review Awards '96: Best Supporting Actor (Norton); *NOM:* Academy Awards '96: Best Supporting Actor (Norton); British Academy Awards '96: Best Supporting Actor (Norton); MTV Movie Awards '97: Best Villain (Norton).

Primary Colors

Mike Nichols's political comedy is a fun-fest for Clinton haters, but a mixed bag for everyone else. Based on Joe Klein's novel, it begins with broad humor, shifts to parody, and finally becomes something more serious. The central flaw is Travolta's performance as Jack Stanton. His insincerity is as phony as his Southern accent. The saving grace is Kathy Bates's Libby, the "Dust Buster," who's brought in to save Stanton's campaign from scandal. She overpowers everyone else on-screen with a bravura performance not far removed from her Oscar-winning portrayal of Annie Wilkes in *Misery.* Thornton is fine as the Carvillian advisor. The DVD looks exceptionally sharp with a crispness that is sometimes at odds with the unfocused, scattershot approach to the subject. —*MM*
Movie: ♪♪ *DVD:* ♪♪♪
Universal Studios Home Video (Cat #20283, UPC #025192028328). Widescreen (2.35:1) letterboxed. Dolby Digital 5.1 Surround Stereo. $24.98. Keepcase. *LANG:* English; French. *SUB:* Spanish. *CAP:* English. *FEATURES:* 40 chapter links • Production notes • Cast and crew thumbnail biographies • Theatrical trailer • Universal web links. Also available with DTS sound (catalog #20469).
1998 (R) 138m/C John Travolta, Emma Thompson, Adrian Lester, Kathy Bates, Billy Bob Thornton, Larry Hagman, Maura Tierney, Stacy Edwards, Diane Ladd, Gia Carides, Paul Guilfoyle, Tommy Hollis, Robert Klein, J.C. Quinn, Rob Reiner, Caroline Aaron, Allison Janney, Mykelti Williamson, Tony Shalhoub, John Vargas, Ben Jones, Bonnie Bartlett; *D:* Mike Nichols; *W:* Elaine May; *C:* Michael Ballhaus; *M:* Ry Cooder. *AWARDS:* British Academy Awards '98: Best Adapted Screenplay; Screen Actors Guild Award '98: Best Supporting Actress (Bates); Broadcast Film Critics Association Awards '98: Best Supporting Actress (Bates);

Prime Suspect

Producers Avnet and Tisch, each known for solid feature productions at one time or another, couldn't escape the bathetic TV "movie of the week" trajectory of forcing well-known small screen comedy performers to jump through sensationalistic plot hoops. It's supposed to be heart-tugging or heartwarming or heart something, but its unsavory subject matter can only be obliquely described as "child-related abductions" on the box cover. Terri Garr is the hair-trigger investigative reporter and Mike Farrell the average Joe whose life she threatens to ruin. There's no reason to get something on DVD that is best relegated to late-night showings on one of those "women only" cable or satellite channels. The much-hyped "film facts" section is a bare bones production credit list. As for technical quality, the film is held up and digitized well enough considering its origin and age. —JK
Movie: ♫♫♫ **DVD:** ♫♫♫
Simitar Entertainment (Cat #7584, UPC #082551758425). Full frame. Dolby Digital AC-3. $14.99. Keepcase. *LANG:* English. *FEATURES:* 8 chapter links • Interactive menus • Mike Farrell's bio and filmography • Production credits.
1982 100m/C Mike Farrell, Teri Garr, Veronica Cartwright, Lane Smith, Barry Corbin, James Sloyan, Charles Aidman; **D:** Noel Black; **C:** Reynaldo Villalobos; **M:** Charles Gross.

Prince of Darkness

One of John Carpenter's best and most underrated films works through intelligent dialogue, carefully measured special effects, and excellent performances from an ensemble cast. When a priest (Pleasence) learns that the last member of an odd order, the Brotherhood of Sleep, has died, he inspects the church that the brothers guarded. Why are street people so attracted to it, and what is that big jar of goop that looks like molten lime Jell-O in the basement? Theoretical physics and ultimate evil are involved. Fans will catch echoes of *Poltergeist* and Carpenter's own *Assault on Precinct 13*. DVD handles the dark scenes and special effects without any serious flaws. Sound is unspectacular but adequate. —MM
Movie: ♫♫♫ **DVD:** ♫♫♫
Image Entertainment (Cat #4275). Widescreen (2.35:1) letterboxed. Dolby Digital Stereo. $29.99. Snapper. *LANG:* English. *CAP:* English.
1987 (R) 102m/C Alice Cooper, Donald Pleasence, Lisa Blount, Victor Wong, Jame-

son Parker, Dennis Dun, Susan Blanchard, Anne Howard, Ken Wright, Dirk Blocker; **D:** John Carpenter; **W:** John Carpenter; **C:** Gary B. Kibbe; **M:** John Carpenter.

Prince of Egypt

DreamWorks' first animated feature is an ambitious undertaking that's comparable to Disney's more serious work. With a minimum of Hollywood streamlining, the film tells the story of Moses (Kilmer), first as a Prince of Egypt and then as the savior who leads his people out of bondage. On their commentary track, directors Chapman, Hickner, and Wells try to explain the basics of modern animation where one shot might "layer" different kinds of 3-D computer images with two-dimensional drawings and background paintings. They also talk about the changes that occur after the voice actors have made their contribution, and how other changes are incorporated as the story evolves. If the big Red Sea finish loses something on the small screen, it is still impressive. I could find no visual flaws. The extras are extensive. —MM
Movie: ♫♫♫► **DVD:** ♫♫♫►
DreamWorks Home Entertainment (Cat #84853, UPC #667068485325). Widescreen (1.85:1) letterboxed. Dolby Digital 5.1 Surround Stereo; Dolby Digital Surround Stereo. $34.99. Keepcase. *LANG:* English. *CAP:* English. *FEATURES:* 28 chapter links • Commentary: Brenda Chapman, Steve Hickner, and Simon Wells • "Making of" featurette • "When You Believe" multi-language presentation • "Chariot Race" animation • Stills gallery • 2 theatrical trailers • Cast and crew thumbnail biographies • Production notes • Previews of *The Road to El Dorado* and *Chicken Run*.
1998 (PG) 93m/C D: Simon Wells, Brenda Chapman, Steve Hickner; **M:** Hans Zimmer; **V:** Val Kilmer, Michelle Pfeiffer, Helen Mirren, Steve Martin, Martin Short, Ralph Fiennes, Sandra Bullock, Jeff Goldblum, Danny Glover, Patrick Stewart, Ofra Haza, James Avery, Eden Riegel. *AWARDS:* Academy Awards '98: Best Song ("When You Believe"); Broadcast Film Critics Association Awards '98: Best Song ("When You Believe"); VSDA DVD Festival '00: Best of Show—Children's DVD; *NOM:* Academy Awards '98: Best Original Musical/Comedy Score; Golden Globe Awards '99: Best Song ("When You Believe"), Best Score.

The Princess and the Pirate

Hope is at his craziest as a vaudevillian who falls for a beautiful princess while on the run from buccaneers on the Spanish Main. Look for Crosby in a closing cameo performance.
Movie: ♫♫♫ **DVD:** NYR
HBO Home Video (Cat #90666). Full frame. Stereo. $24.98. Snapper. *LANG:* English. *SUB:* Spanish.
1944 94m/C Bob Hope, Walter Slezak, Walter Brennan, Virginia Mayo, Victor

McLaglen; **Cameos:** Bing Crosby; **D:** David Butler; **W:** Everett Freeman, Don Hartman, Melville Shavelson; **C:** Victor Milner; **M:** David Rose. *AWARDS: NOM:* Academy Awards '44: Best Original Dramatic Score.

The Princess and the Pirate

Cute critter animation tells a story built on familiar archetypes. Sandokan the Tiger must regain his rightful throne from the evil Rajah. In the meantime, he has become a pirate in the South China Sea. Eventually he falls in love with the Rajah's beautiful niece, etc. The animation is simple with bright colors and minimal violence. The box copy suggests that it's meant for ages six and up (but not too much older). Without chapter links, the DVD is not much different from tape. —MM *AKA:* Sandokan the TV Movie.
Movie: ♫♫ **DVD:** ♫♫
Simitar Entertainment (Cat #7218, UPC #082551721825). Full frame. PCM uncompressed Stereo. $9.98. Keepcase. *LANG:* English.
1995 75m/C *AU* **D:** Claudio Biern Boyd; **W:** Dave Mallow, Doug Stone; **M:** Jordi Doncos.

The Princess Bride

Goldman's update of the basic fairy tale (as told by Peter Falk) is crammed with all the elements. The adventurously irreverent love story revolves around a beautiful maiden (Penn) and her young swain (Elwes) as they battle the evils of the mythical kingdom of Florin to be reunited with one another. Great dueling scenes and offbeat satire make this fun for adults as well as children.
Movie: ♫♫♫► **DVD:** NYR
USA Home Entertainment (Cat #636861). $29.95. Keepcase.
1987 (PG) 98m/C Cary Elwes, Mandy Patinkin, Robin Wright Penn, Wallace Shawn, Peter Falk, Andre the Giant, Chris Sarandon, Christopher Guest, Billy Crystal, Carol Kane, Fred Savage, Peter Cook, Mel Smith; **D:** Rob Reiner; **W:** William Goldman; **C:** Adrian Biddle; **M:** Mark Knopfler. *AWARDS: NOM:* Academy Awards '87: Best Song ("Storybook Love").

Princess Warrior

Amateurish ultra-low-budget sf scrapes the bottom. Transported to Earth from a distant place, good princess Ovule (Jones) battles her evil sister Curette (Fredsti) for the throne. The chapter titles tell it all: "Princess Escapes," "Wet T-shirt Contest 1," "Wet T-shirt Contest 2," "Spoon Up His Nose," "Tattoo," "Love Scene," "Cat Fight," "Happy ending." The whole thing is dark, grainy, and so badly written and acted that the visual flaws are a blessing. —MM
Movie: ♫ **DVD:** ♫
Simitar Entertainment (Cat #7308, UPC #082551730827). Full frame. PCM Stereo. $14.98. Keepcase. *LANG:* English.

FEATURES: 8 chapter links • Production factoids.
1990 85m/C Sharon Lee Jones, Dana Fredsti, Mark Pacific; **D:** Lindsay Norgard; **W:** John Riley; **C:** Robert Duffin.

Prison on Fire
A mobster sent to prison for murdering his wife becomes friends with an innocent prisoner who has been framed. Lam's direction is edgy more than stylized and, though this is more drama than action, the violence that does occur is gritty and violent. The Tai Seng DVD improves upon their VHS edition but still contains the slightly grainy picture they tend to deliver. Colors are a little washed-out and the soundtrack is undistorted but pretty bland. —JO
Movie: 🎬🎬▶ **DVD:** 🎬🎬▶
Tai Seng Video Marketing (Cat #5062, UPC #164306754000). Widescreen (2.35:1) anamorphic. Dolby Digital 5.1. $49.95. Keepcase. LANG: English; Cantonese. SUB: English; Japanese; Chinese; Korean; Vietnamese; Bahasa; Thai. CAP: English; Cantonese. FEATURES: 9 chapter links.
1987 98m/C HK Chow Yun-Fat, Tony Leung Ka-Fai; **D:** Ringo Lam; **W:** Yin Nam; **M:** Lowell Lo.

Prison on Fire 2
Many fans of Hong Kong action films believe that director Ringo Lam came into his own with this sequel, a prison drama that hinges on some complex moral choices. **AKA:** Tao Fan; Jian Yu Feng Yun Xu Ji.
Movie: 🎬🎬▶ **DVD:** NYR
Tai Seng Video Marketing (Cat #26704). $29.95.
1991 107m/C HK Chow Yun-Fat, Elvis Tsui, Kam-Kong Tsui, Yu Li; **D:** Ringo Lam.

Prisoner of Love
After bartender Tracy (Campbell) witnesses a shakedown gone wrong, low-level stooge Jonny (Thal) is told to get rid of her. But since he's fallen in lust with Tracy after flirting with her in a nightclub, Jonny kidnaps her and holds her prisoner in a warehouse until he can figure out how to keep them both alive. Not nearly as kinky as it sounds—in fact the sheer blandness makes this a miss.
Movie: 🎬▶ **DVD:** NYR
Studio Home Entertainment (Cat #7295). $24.95.
1999 (R) 100m/C Eric Thal, Naomi Campbell, Beau Starr, Carl Marotte; **D:** Steve DiMarco; **M:** Norman Orenstein.

Private Benjamin
Lighthearted fare about a pampered New York Jewish princess who impulsively enlists in the U.S. Army after her husband dies on their wedding night. Hawn, who also produced, creates a character loveable even at her worst moments and brings a surprising amount of depth to this otherwise frivolous look at high soci-

ety attitudes. Warner has improved the sharpness on this DVD release but the color tint is a little off, though the colors themselves are fairly strong. Grain occurs in darker scenes but overall the picture is pretty good. —JO
Movie: 🎬🎬▶ **DVD:** 🎬🎬🎬
Warner Home Video, Inc. (Cat #11075, UPC #085391107521). Full frame. Stereo. $24.98. Snapper. LANG: English; French. SUB: English; Spanish; French. FEATURES: 28 chapter links • Theatrical trailers • Production notes.
1980 (R) 110m/C Goldie Hawn, Eileen Brennan, Albert Brooks, Robert Webber, Armand Assante, Barbara Barrie, Mary Kay Place, Sally Kirkland, Craig T. Nelson, Harry Dean Stanton, Sam Wanamaker; **D:** Howard Zieff; **W:** Nancy Meyers, Charles Shyer, Harvey Miller; **C:** David M. Walsh; **M:** Bill Conti. AWARDS: Writers Guild of America '80: Best Original Screenplay; NOM: Academy Awards '80: Best Actress (Hawn), Best Original Screenplay, Best Supporting Actress (Brennan).

Private Obsession
Model Emmanuelle Griffith (Whirry) is kidnapped by obsessed fan Richard (Christian) and imprisoned in a bedroom of his house. After the usual soft-core action has transpired, the story becomes a question of who's controlling whom. Considering that drive-in cult director Lee Frost made almost the entire film in his own house, it looks acceptable on this frills-free DVD. The image may be slightly superior to VHS tape, but not much. So what? Ms. Whirry handles the misogynist material with more class than anyone could expect. —MM
Movie: 🎬🎬▶ **DVD:** 🎬🎬
Image Entertainment (Cat #ID5616FMDVD, UPC #014381561623). Full frame. Dolby Digital Stereo. $24.99. Snapper. LANG: English. FEATURES: 12 chapter links.
1994 (R) 93m/C Shannon Whirry, Michael Christian, Bo Svenson, Rip Taylor; **D:** Lee Frost; **W:** Lee Frost; **C:** William Boatman; **M:** Dean Andre.

Private Parts
Stern makes his movie debut as...himself! Self-effacing yet self-aggrandizing bio traces Stern's rise from gawky kid to gawky college student to awkward small-market DJ to New York madman to inauguration as self-proclaimed King of All Media. Funny and at times touching flick features good performances by the rookie actors in Stern's inner circle, as well as by the pros. Giamatti is exceptional as the young WNBC exec assigned to tame Howard. Script manages to show Stern's outrageousness and still make him likeable. While this is clearly a whitewash job, and under other circumstances Stern himself might make fun of its sentimentality, the pic should please everyone but the most rabid Stern-hater. If only the DVD were as sharp as the barb-slinging shock jock himself. Unfortunately, the image is usually grainy and never very sharp. Col-

ors are dull and off the mark. The 5.1 sound is at least worthwhile, with a lively mix and strong bass given to the band-oriented soundtrack, and an occasional unexpected effect thrown in to keep things interesting. —JO AKA: Howard Stern's Private Parts.
Movie: 🎬🎬▶ **DVD:** 🎬🎬
Paramount Home Video (Cat #332517, UPC #097363325178). Widescreen (1.85:1) letterboxed. Dolby Digital 5.1; Dolby Surround. $29.99. Keepcase. LANG: English (DD5.1; DS); French (DS). SUB: Spanish. CAP: English. FEATURES: 32 chapter links.
1996 (R) 109m/C Howard Stern, Robin Quivers, Mary McCormack, Paul Giamatti, Fred Norris, Gary Dell'Abate, Bobby Borriello, Michael Maccarone, Matthew Friedman, Jackie Martling, Carol Alt, Richard Portnow, Kelly Bishop, Henry Goodman, Jonathan Hadary, Paul Hecht, Allison Janney, Michael Murphy, James Murtaugh, Reni Santoni, Lee Wilkof, Theresa Lynn, Amber Smith; **D:** Betty Thomas; **W:** Len Blum, Michael Kalesniko; **C:** Walt Lloyd; **M:** Van Dyke Parks. AWARDS: NOM: Golden Raspberry Awards '97: Worst New Star (Stern).

Prizzi's Honor
Highly stylized black comedy revolves around an aging hit man (Nicholson) who falls in love with an upwardly mobile tax consultant (Turner) who's also a freelance hit woman, while a mob princess (Huston) is still carrying a torch for him. Skirting caricature in every frame, writers Richard Condon (author of the novel) and Janet Roach and director John Huston manage to maintain the right comedic balance throughout, making the film a critical and commercial hit. The excellent ensemble cast is the reason to watch this one, and the superb transfer lives up to their work. The disc lacks many of the extras that the medium is capable of, and so the four-bone technical rating is for the crystalline image and sound, in addition to the double presentation in widescreen and full frame. —MM
Movie: 🎬🎬🎬▶ **DVD:** 🎬🎬🎬🎬
Anchor Bay (Cat #DV10833, UPC #013131083392). Widescreen (1.85:1); full frame. Dolby Digital Stereo. $24.98. Keepcase. LANG: English. FEATURES: 16 chapter links • Huston and Condon trivia.
1985 (R) 130m/C Jack Nicholson, Kathleen Turner, Robert Loggia, John Randolph, Anjelica Huston, Lawrence Tierney, William Hickey, Lee Richardson, Michael Lombard, Joseph Ruskin, CCH Pounder; **D:** John Huston; **W:** Richard Condon, Janet Roach; **C:** Andrzej Bartkowiak; **M:** Alex North. AWARDS: Academy Awards '85: Best Supporting Actress (Huston); British Academy Awards '85: Best Adapted Screenplay; Golden Globe Awards '86: Best Actor—Musical/Comedy (Nicholson), Best Actress—Musical/Comedy (Turner), Best Director (Huston), Best Film—Musical/Comedy; Los Angeles Film Critics Association Awards '85: Best Supporting Actress (Huston); New York Film Critics

Awards '85: Best Actor (Nicholson), Best Director (Huston), Best Film, Best Supporting Actress (Huston); National Society of Film Critics Awards '85: Best Actor (Nicholson), Best Director (Huston), Best Supporting Actress (Huston); Writers Guild of America '85: Best Adapted Screenplay; *NOM:* Academy Awards '85: Best Actor (Nicholson), Best Adapted Screenplay, Best Costume Design, Best Director (Huston), Best Film Editing, Best Picture, Best Supporting Actor (Hickey).

The Prodigal Son

Small-town martial arts champ Biao learns all his fights were fixed by his wealthy father. Determined to prove himself fairly, Biao learns the true wisdom of kung fu from traveling entertainer Ying in typically over-the-top fight scenes.
Movie: 🐾🐾🐾 *DVD:* NYR
Tai Seng Video Marketing (Cat #6774). Dolby Digital 5.1 Surround Stereo. $34.95. Keepcase. *LANG:* Cantonese. *SUB:* Bahasa Indonesian & Malaysian; Chinese Simplified & Traditional; English; Japanese; Korean; Thai; Vietnamese.
1982 100m/C *HK* Yuen Biao, Lam Ching Ying, Sammo Hung; *D:* Sammo Hung; *W:* Jing Wong.

The Professional

Leon (Reno) is an eccentric French hit man, working New York's mean streets, when his 12-year-old neighbor Mathilda (Portman) comes knocking. Seems her family has been murdered by minions of crooked drug enforcement agent Stansfield (Oldman) and she'd like Leon to teach her how to be a "cleaner" so she can get revenge. And Leon obliges. The lovely young Portman (in her film debut) is a little too Lolita-ish for comfort as she manipulates the stolid Reno, with Oldman suitably extravagant in the role of sadistic psycho. Besson's stylized filmmaking is captured perfectly by the DVD's finely detailed image. Action scenes are alive with stunning colors and a power-packed 5.1 mix that throws in one Surround effect after another. The gunfire sounds more authentic than the real thing. The vibrant colors set the screen aglow yet still manage to retain the subtle details and shadings of Besson's composition. —*JO AKA:* Leon.
Movie: 🐾🐾 *DVD:* 🐾🐾🐾🐾
Columbia Tristar Home Video (Cat #74749, UPC #043396747494). Widescreen (2.35:1) letterboxed; full frame. Dolby Digital 5.1; Stereo. $29.95. Keepcase. *LANG:* English (DD5.1; Stereo); Spanish (Stereo); French (Stereo). *SUB:* English; Spanish; French. *CAP:* English. *FEATURES:* 28 chapter links ● Theatrical trailers.
1994 (R) 109m/C *FR* Jean Reno, Natalie Portman, Gary Oldman, Danny Aiello, Michael Badalucco, Ellen Greene; *D:* Luc Besson; *W:* Luc Besson; *C:* Thierry Arbogast; *M:* Eric Serra. *AWARDS: NOM:* Cesar Awards '94: Best Actor (Reno), Best Director (Besson), Best Film.

The Professionals

A terrific cast and fine direction make this one of Hollywood's best adventures. A Texas cattle baron (Bellamy) hires four specialists (Marvin, Lancaster, Strode, Ryan) to rescue his kidnapped young wife (Cardinale) from the Mexican bandit/revolutionary (Palance) who's holding her. The characters and turn-of-the-century setting—much of the film was made in Death Valley—are excellent. The Oscar nominations for Brooks's direction and screenplay, and for Hall's cinematography, are deserved. The widescreen is as sharp as I've seen on home video. If the sound lacks the richness of more recent action pictures, it's true to the source. Worth owning. —*MM*
Movie: 🐾🐾🐾🐾 *DVD:* 🐾🐾🐾
Columbia Tristar Home Video (Cat #03909, UPC #043396039094). Widescreen (2.35:1) letterboxed; full frame. Dolby Digital Mono. $24.95. Keepcase. *LANG:* English. *SUB:* Spanish; Portuguese; Chinese; Korean; Thai. *FEATURES:* 28 chapter links ● Theatrical trailer.
1966 (PG-13) 117m/C Burt Lancaster, Lee Marvin, Claudia Cardinale, Jack Palance, Robert Ryan, Woody Strode, Ralph Bellamy; *D:* Richard Brooks; *W:* Richard Brooks; *C:* Conrad Hall; *M:* Maurice Jarre. *AWARDS: NOM:* Academy Awards '66: Best Adapted Screenplay, Best Color Cinematography, Best Director (Brooks).

Progeny

Familiar horror boasts some scary creatures. Craig (Vosloo) and Sherry (McWhirter) are zapped by a bright light while in bed and don't remember what happened until a shrink (Crouse) and UFO investigator Clavell (Dourif) hypnotize them. Then Sherry remembers that she was abducted and impregnated by some slimy tentacled aliens and it's all just kind of predictably gross from there on out.
Movie: 🐾🐾 *DVD:* NYR
Studio Home Entertainment (Cat #7185). Widescreen (2.35:1) anamorphic. $29.95. Keepcase. *LANG:* English. *SUB:* Spanish. *FEATURES:* Storyboards ● Commentary: filmmakers and "actual alien abductees."
1998 100m/C Arnold Vosloo, Jillian McWhirter, Brad Dourif, Lindsay Crouse, Wilford Brimley; *D:* Brian Yuzna; *W:* Aubrey Solomon; *C:* James Hawkinson; *M:* Steven Morrell.

Project A-ko

Set in the near future, this Japanese animated feature concerns teenagers with strange powers, an alien spaceship, and lots of action. Seventeen-year-old A-ko possesses superhuman strength and a ditzy sidekick, C-ko. B-ko, the spoiled daughter of a rich business tycoon, decides to fight A-ko for C-ko's companionship. Meanwhile, the alien ship approacheth.
Movie: 🐾🐾 *DVD:* NYR
Image Entertainment (Cat #4640). Widescreen (1.85:1) letterboxed. Dolby Digital

Stereo. $24.99. Snapper. *LANG:* Japanese; English. *SUB:* English.
1986 86m/C *JP D:* Katsuhiko Nishijima; *W:* Tomoko Kawasaki.

Project: Eliminator

You know you're deep in B-movie territory when the boxed "special appearance by" credit goes to Vivian Schilling, previously known for her autobiographical one-two punch *Soultaker*, costarring Joe Estevez (yes, another Sheen progeny). The dramatic content boils down to some near futuristic fisticuffs by Special Forces vets Morrel and Slade (Carradine and Zagarino, featured prominently on the box cover). They've been hired to protect an anti-establishment scientist from government retribution, but—too late! Crypto-fascist FBI agents have kidnapped the doctor and his daughter! Now they'll just have to save The Entire Free World!! Actually, the DVD is a remarkable transfer of tightly budgeted, desert location shoots and a hyper-macho, clattering percussion score. The scene selector of stills in a counterclockwise array, is annoying because you have to go through them all one at a time to get to any other navigational button. —*JK*
Movie: 🐾🐾 *DVD:* 🐾🐾🐾🐾
Image Entertainment (Cat #ID5703PZDVD, UPC #014381570328). Full frame. Dolby Digital Stereo. $14.99. Snapper. *LANG:* English. *FEATURES:* 15 chapter links ● Scene access menu.
1991 (R) 89m/C David Carradine, Frank Zagarino, Drew Snyder, Hilary English, Vivian Schilling; *D:* H. Kaye Dyal; *W:* H. Kaye Dyal, Morris Asgar; *C:* Gerry Lively; *M:* John McCallum.

Project Moon Base

Fun in a retro-future sort of a way. Colonel Breiteis (pronounced Bright-Eyes), a female rocket pilot, and Major Moore, her copilot, are selected to orbit the Moon to survey a landing area for a future expedition, but a ruthless Russian spy-scientist aboard the ship causes it to land on the lunar surface, stranded and out of fuel. Dialogue isn't realistic, and there's plenty of male chauvinism in Robert Heinlein's script. But the visionary science-fiction author of *Stranger in a Strange Land* nonetheless provides a fascinating look at "the future" (as in 1970) of space travel. The film followed his first produced screenplay, *Destination Moon*, three years earlier. It's still an old B-movie and looks like it. There are blemishes in the original film element used for the video transfer, but by and large picture looks good with nice contrast in the B&W image. There are compression artifacts in the backgrounds of some scenes, however. Monaural soundtrack is what you expect, with clear, distinct sound and no distortion. No oomph, either. Menu design is simple, but is serviceable and looks nice. —*MB*
Movie: 🐾🐾 *DVD:* 🐾🐾
Image Entertainment (Cat #ID8688CODVD, UPC #014381868821). Full frame. Dolby

Digital 1.0. $24.99. Snapper. *LANG:* English. *FEATURES:* 12 chapter links.
1953 64m/B Donna Martell, Hayden Rourke, Ross Ford, Larry Johns, Herb Jacobs; *D:* Richard Talmadge; *W:* Robert Heinlein, Jack Seaman; *C:* William C. Thompson; *M:* Herschel Burke Gilbert.

Prom Night

Good acting and above-average production values are put in service of a plot that doesn't deviate a millimeter from the standard dead-teenager slasher/stalker formula. It borrows most blatantly from *Halloween* with the "six years before" prologue, and from *Carrie* in the second half. Jamie Lee Curtis and four of her high school friends are the prey of a killer out to avenge an earlier murder. But much more terrifying than that plot is the "Disco Madness" theme of the titular dance. Flashing lights, raised arms, pointing fingers, polyester—the horror, the horror. Given the film's often softish focus, the DVD is not a large improvement over VHS tape. —*MM*
Movie: ♫♫ *DVD:* ♫♫➧
Anchor Bay (Cat #DV10327, UPC #013131032796). Widescreen (1.85:1) letterboxed. Dolby Digital Mono. $24.99. Keepcase. *LANG:* English. *FEATURES:* 9 chapter links ▪ Theatrical trailer.
1980 91m/C CA Jamie Lee Curtis, Leslie Nielsen, Casey Stevens, Eddie Benton, Antoinette Bower, Michael Tough, Pita Oliver, David Mucci, Joy Thompson, Mary Beth Rubens; *D:* Paul Lynch; *W:* William Gray; *C:* Robert New; *M:* Paul Zaza.

The Prophecy

Enjoyable and surprisingly witty religious horror goes beyond the traditional structure of Good vs. Evil. Evil as represented by God and Satan. The key combatants are angels involved in an eons-long war with each other. These angels are not halo-topped sweetie-pies who float around performing the odd miracle here and there. To these creatures, humans are "talking monkeys" who have usurped their favored place in the presence of God. It's hard for Harry Dagget (Koteas), a priest-turned-cop, to know which side to take in the conflict. On one hand, Gabriel (Walken, at his deadpan creepiest) is willing to kill anyone who gets in his way. But since he can't drive, his mobility is limited. His opposite number Timothy (Stolz), seems to be looking for a soul to steal. They're after a young Arizona Indian girl whose only protection is her elementary school teacher (Madsen). First-time writer-director Widen gets excellent performances from his cast, and he gives the whole film a gritty, intense look that fits the subject. DVD captures those strong visuals, particularly the brown-gold tints that are used in the more ominous moments. The widescreen transfer replicates the theatrical image. Sound is fine. —*MM*
Movie: ♫♫♫➧ *DVD:* ♫♫♫

Buena Vista Home Entertainment (Cat #16454). Widescreen (2.35:1) letterboxed. Dolby Digital Stereo. $29.99. Keepcase. *LANG:* English. *CAP:* English. *FEATURES:* 17 chapter links.
1995 (R) 97m/C Christopher Walken, Eric Stoltz, Elias Koteas, Virginia Madsen, Amanda Plummer, Viggo Mortensen; *D:* Gregory Widen; *W:* Gregory Widen; *C:* Bruce Douglas Johnson, Richard Clabaugh; *M:* David Williams.

The Prophecy 2: Ashtown

Rare sequel is equal to the original, just as offbeat and even funnier. The first film establishes two warring factions of angels—those faithful to God and those who are jealous of humans, "talking monkeys," as they call us. They're heavenly Terminators and Gabriel (Walken) is the baddest bad boy of the human-hating bunch. He's after Valerie Rosales (Beals), a nurse who's been impregnated by his angelic enemy, Daniel (Wong). To find her, Gabriel must enlist the unwilling help of Izzy (Murphy), a suicidal young woman with a skewed sense of humor. For all his powers, Gabriel is a real klutz with commonplace earthly objects—cars, computers, telephones. Director Spence, also responsible for the surprise horror sleeper *Children of the Corn IV*, brings real wit and innovation to the story. Gabriel's entrance is a terrific set piece and the ending is even better. Some of the plotting is a tad too elaborate but that's not a real problem. Despite settings and action that are normally challenging to digital technology, the film looks fine on DVD. The dark scenes have no bothersome grain, even the aforementioned entrance set in a parking lot where hell literally opens up through the asphalt. —*MM*
Movie: ♫♫♫➧ *DVD:* ♫♫♫➧

Buena Vista Home Entertainment (Cat #17594, UPC #717951003317). Widescreen (1.85:1) letterboxed. Dolby Surround Stereo. $29.99. Keepcase. *LANG:* English. *FEATURES:* 12 chapter links.
1997 (R) 83m/C Christopher Walken, Russell Wong, Eric Roberts, Jennifer Beals, Bruce Abbott, Brittany Murphy, Steve Hytner, Glenn Danzig; *D:* Greg Spence; *W:* Greg Spence, Matt Greenberg; *C:* Richard Clabaugh; *M:* David Williams.

The Prophecy 3: The Ascent

Third time is definitely not the charm in the disappointing finale to the otherwise fine series. Danyael (Buzzotta), from the second film, has grown up and is being hunted by the angel Pyriel (Spano) while Gabriel (Walken) seems to have switched sides. The image has the same brown-gold tint of the others, but the video game–inspired violence is excessive and, in the final reel, ridiculous. Otherwise, Kiochi Sakamoto's stunt team does excellent work. The most unforgivable aspect of the DVD, though, is the inclusion of previews which the viewer

cannot avoid. You can't fast forward or skip past them. For that reason, the VHS tape is superior. —*MM*
Movie: ♫♫ *DVD:* ♫
Buena Vista Home Entertainment (Cat #18278, UPC #717951004680). Widescreen (1.85:1) anamorphic. Dolby Digital 5.1 Surround Stereo. $29.95. Keepcase. *LANG:* English. *FEATURES:* 25 chapter links.
1999 (R) 83m/C Christopher Walken, Vincent Spano, Brad Dourif, Dave Buzzotta, Steve Hytner, Scott Cleverdon, Kayren Ann Butler; *D:* Patrick Lussier; *W:* Joel Soisson, Carl DuPre; *C:* Nathan Hope.

Protector

Undercover cop Jack Valentine (Van Peebles) is supposed to be protecting a witness, who winds up being murdered. The cop is given 10 days to solve the crime or lose his badge. It's great that smaller companies have gotten into the DVD market this early. It's bad that they put out a product this inferior when the material they're working with is not that old. There are far worse DVDs than this one, but still, if it was the first DVD I purchased, I'd be tempted to return the player and stick with VHS. The image is average overall and has occasional problems with color bleed (and the color isn't that good to start) and artifacts. Same for the stereo sound, which is near low-fi and has very minimal separation and imaging. —*JO* *AKA:* Valentine's Day.
Movie: ♫♫ *DVD:* ♫♫
Studio Home Entertainment (Cat #7125, UPC #658149712522). Full frame. Stereo. $24.95. Keepcase. *LANG:* English. *SUB:* Spanish. *FEATURES:* 24 chapter links ▪ Trailer ▪ Production notes.
1997 (R) 97m/C Mario Van Peebles, Randy Quaid, Rae Dawn Chong, Ben Gazzara; *D:* Duane Clark.

Protocol

A series of not-so-comic accidents leads Washington cocktail waitress Sunny Davis (Hawn) into the State Department's employ as a protocol official. Once there, she is used as a pawn in an arms deal with a Middle Eastern country. The ending sinks to new lows, even for an unassuming, typical Hawn comedy. With a uniformly grainy image and few extras, the DVD is no better than the VHS tape, and why should it be? —*MM*
Movie: ♫➧ *DVD:* ♫♫
Warner Home Video, Inc. (Cat #11434, UPC #085391143420). Full frame. Dolby Surround Stereo. $14.98. Snapper. *LANG:* English. *SUB:* English. *CAP:* English. *FEATURES:* 26 chapter links.
1984 (PG) 100m/C Goldie Hawn, Chris Sarandon, Andre Gregory, Cliff DeYoung, Ed Begley Jr., Gail Strickland, Richard Romanus, Keith Szarabajka, James Staley, Kenneth Mars, Kenneth McMillan, Archie Hahn, Amanda Bearse; *D:* Herbert Ross; *W:* Nancy Meyers, Harvey Miller, Charles

Shyer, Buck Henry; **C:** William A. Fraker; **M:** Basil Poledouris.

Proud Rebel

Character study focuses on a stubborn widower (Ladd) who searches for a doctor to aid him in dealing with the problems of his mute son and the woman (de Havilland) who helps to tame the boy. Ladd's real-life son makes his acting debut.
Movie: 🎬🎬🎬 **DVD:** NYR
HBO Home Video (Cat #91174). Stereo; Mono. $24.98. Snapper. *LANG:* English; French; German; Italian; Spanish. *SUB:* French; Spanish. *CAP:* English. *FEATURES:* Cast and crew thumbnail bios.
1958 99m/C Alan Ladd, Olivia de Havilland, Dean Jagger, Harry Dean Stanton; **D:** Michael Curtiz; **W:** Lillie Hayward, Joseph Petracca; **C:** Ted D. McCord; **M:** Jerome Moross.

Psychic Killer

A wrongfully committed insane asylum inmate (Hutton) acquires psychic powers and uses them in deadly revenge against everyone who's ever done him wrong.
Movie: 🎬 **DVD:** NYR
Elite Entertainment, Inc. (Cat #7792). Mono. $24.95. Keepcase. *FEATURES:* Trailer.
1975 (PG) 89m/C Jim Hutton, Paul Burke, Julie Adams, Neville Brand, Aldo Ray, Rod Cameron, Della Reese; **D:** Ray Danton; **W:** Ray Danton, Mikel Angel, Greydon Clark; **C:** Herb Pearl; **M:** William Craft.

Psycho (CE)

Hitchcock broke all the rules in this story of violent murder, transvestism, and insanity, based on Robert Bloch's novel of actual serial killer Ed Gein. Leigh plays a fleeing thief who stops at the secluded Bates Motel where she meets her death in Hitchcock's classic shower scene. For creepiness, Perkins's gender-bending momma's boy portrayal of the killer is still unsurpassed. *Psycho* changed the Hollywood horror film forever. Followed by three theatrical sequels and a made-for-television movie, not to mention Gus Van Sant's pointless 1998 remake. There are still a few film scratches, and some of the backgrounds are a little grainy, but DVD is by far the best way to see this classic. The image is very sharp on close-ups and mid-shots and, if you concentrate on those, the backgrounds shouldn't be so aggravating. The graytones and contrast are very good, as is the brightness. Artifacts are not a problem. The soundtrack is mono and at times the music sounds a little tinny, but since the dialogue is usually fairly crisp, this is probably the best that could be done with the source material. *—JO*
Movie: 🎬🎬🎬🎬 **DVD:** 🎬🎬
Universal Studios Home Video (Cat #20251, UPC #025192025129). Widescreen (1.85:1) letterboxed. Mono. $34.98. Keepcase. *LANG:* English; French. *SUB:* Spanish. *CAP:* English. *FEATURES:*
Dual-layered RSDL • 26 chapter links • Theatrical and re-release trailers • Cast and filmmaker bios • Production notes and photographs • Lobby cards, posters, ads • Newsreel footage • Storyboards • Shower scene with and without music.
1960 109m/B Anthony Perkins, Janet Leigh, Vera Miles, John Gavin, John McIntire, Martin Balsam, Simon Oakland, Ted Knight, John Anderson, Frank Albertson, Patricia Hitchcock, Alfred Hitchcock; **D:** Alfred Hitchcock; **W:** Joseph Stefano; **C:** John L. Russell; **M:** Bernard Herrmann; **V:** Virginia Gregg, Jeanette Nolan. *AWARDS:* American Film Institute (AFI) '98: Top 100; Golden Globe Awards '61: Best Supporting Actress (Leigh), National Film Registry '92; *NOM:* Academy Awards '60: Best Art Direction/Set Decoration (B & W), Best Black-and-white Cinematography, Best Director (Hitchcock), Best Supporting Actress (Leigh).

Psycho

The central question about Gus Van Sant's remake has always been: Why? Despite repeated attempts at explanation by the director and several others in the supplemental material that comes with the DVD, the question remains unanswered. He admits that he was given the chance by Universal executives because *Good Will Hunting* was so successful. In the "Psycho Path" featurette, several critics wonder about the wisdom of a shot-for-shot remake, though Van Sant varies from the Hitchcock version in several significant scenes. The most obvious difference to even the most casual viewer is the change from black and white to color, and on disc the bright oranges and greens are even more virulent than they are on the theatre screen. The commentary track by Van Sant and costars Vaughn and Heche is even more fatuous than most and reveals that they really don't understand the original very well. It's all somehow appropriate for a film that is so deliberately unoriginal. *—MM*
Movie: 🎬 **DVD:** 🎬🎬
Universal Studios Home Video (Cat #20538, UPC #025192053825). Widescreen (1.85:1) letterboxed. Dolby Digital 5.1 Surround Stereo; Dolby Digital Surround Stereo. $34.98. Keepcase. *LANG:* English; French. *CAP:* English. *FEATURES:* 18 chapter links • "Making of" featurette • Commentary: Gus Van Sant, Vince Vaughn, and Anne Heche • Production notes • Cast and crew thumbnail biographies • Theatrical trailer • Universal web links • Screen savers.
1998 (R) 106m/C Vince Vaughn, Anne Heche, Julianne Moore, William H. Macy, Viggo Mortensen, Robert Forster, Philip Baker Hall, Anne Haney, Chad Everett, Rance Howard, Rita Wilson, James Remar, James LeGros; **D:** Gus Van Sant; **W:** Joseph Stefano; **C:** Christopher Doyle; **M:** Bernard Herrmann. *AWARDS:* Golden Raspberry Awards '98: Worst Remake/ Sequel, Worst Director (Van Sant); *NOM:*

Golden Raspberry Awards '98: Worst Remake/Sequel, Worst Actress (Heche).

Psycho 2

Sequel finds Norman Bates (Perkins) returning home after 22 years in an asylum and still haunted by "mother" and caught up in a series of murders. Compared to most horror sequels, this one's actually very good and entertaining, with both Perkins and Miles reprising their roles from the original.
Movie: 🎬🎬 **DVD:** NYR
Goodtimes Entertainment (Cat #81034). Full frame. Dolby Digital 5.1 Surround Stereo. $19.98. Snapper. *LANG:* English; French; Spanish. *SUB:* French; Spanish. *CAP:* English.
1983 (R) 113m/C Claudia Bryar, Anthony Perkins, Vera Miles, Meg Tilly, Robert Loggia, Dennis Franz; **D:** Richard Franklin; **W:** Tom Holland; **C:** Dean Cundey; **M:** Jerry Goldsmith.

Psycho 3

The second sequel finds Norman (Perkins, who also directed) drawn into his past by "mother" and the appearance of a woman (Scarwid) who reminds him of his original victim. Stretches the plausibility of the storyline to its limits but an element of parody makes this one entertaining for fans. The transfer is very good, without notable film artifacts. A few scenes exhibit some noise and film grain but for the most part, the transfer is stable and clean, and contains a high level of detail. Only in a few scenes where film grain is evident, the slightest pixelation artifacts are noticeable upon very close examination, but for the rest of the film, there are no compression artifacts visible at all, giving the movie a very pleasing and sharp appearance. The disc comes with an English Dolby Surround track that is well produced. It is never aggressive, but makes good use of the Surround for ambient effects, heightening the movie's atmosphere. *—GH*
Movie: 🎬🎬 **DVD:** 🎬🎬🎬
Goodtimes Entertainment (Cat #81045, UPC #018713810458). Widescreen (1.85:1) letterboxed. Dolby Digital Stereo. $14.99. Snapper. *LANG:* English. *SUB:* French; Spanish. *CAP:* English. *FEATURES:* 18 chapter links • Theatrical trailer.
1986 (R) 93m/C Anthony Perkins, Diana Scarwid, Jeff Fahey, Roberta Maxwell, Robert Alan Browne, Hugh Gillin, Lee Garlington; **D:** Anthony Perkins; **W:** Charles Edward Pogue; **C:** Bruce Surtees; **M:** Carter Burwell.

Public Access

Director Bryan Singer made quite a splash with his second film, *The Usual Suspects.* This, his first, contains some of the same inventiveness and flaws. In some ways, it's more interesting and more serious. But don't expect it to answer all the questions it raises. The film opens in the tran-

quil town of Brewster where the headline of the local paper reads "Crime and Unemployment Reach Record Low" and, clearly, things are about to go bad. The source is Whiley Pritcher (Marquette), an enigmatic man who walks into town and buys time on the local public access cable channel. He calls his show "Our Town." On-screen, he asks one question—"What's wrong with Brewster?"—and waits for his viewers to call in with answers. Like *The Usual Suspects,* the conflicts have to do with talk, with words. But here Singer and cowriter Christopher McQuarrie are also interested in the free-floating, often incoherent discontent that's so much a part of the American political landscape. Not surprisingly then, they don't come to a conventional ending. Unfortunately, the film gains little on DVD. The design of a bridge almost disintegrates in a tracking shot, and the dark scenes are exceptionally grainy. Overall, the image is somewhat superior to the tape, but this is not a strong visual film. Ditto sound. —*MM*
Movie: 🐾🐾🐾 **DVD:** 🐾🐾▶
Image Entertainment (Cat #ID5617FMDVD, UPC #014381561722). Widescreen (1.85:1) letterboxed. Dolby Surround Stereo. $24.99. Snapper. *LANG:* English. *FEATURES:* 12 chapter links.
1993 (R) 90m/C Ron Marquette, Dina Brooks, Burt Williams, Charles Kavanaugh, Larry Maxwell, Brandon Boyce; *D:* Bryan Singer; *W:* Bryan Singer, Christopher McQuarrie, Michael Feit Dougan; *C:* Bruce Douglas Johnson; *M:* John Ottman. *AWARDS:* Sundance Film Festival '93: Grand Jury Prize.

Pulp Fiction

Tarantino moves into the cinematic mainstream with his trademark violence and '70s pop culture mindset intact in this stylish crime trilogy. A day in the life of a criminal community unexpectedly shifts from outrageous, esoteric dialogue to violent mayhem with solid scripting that takes familiar stories to unexplored territory. Offbeat cast offers superb performances, led by Travolta in his best role to date as a hit man whose adventures with partner Jackson tie the seemingly unrelated stories together. The clever, almost gleeful look at everyday life on the fringes of mainstream society was inspired by *Black Mask* magazine. The DVD transfer is of average sharpness; both grain and artifacts are minor. Colors seem at times a little dull and at others very vibrant. In either case, bleed is very minor. Blacks are acceptable, though not perfect. Contrast and brightness levels are both very good. The Dolby Surround is pretty lively, with good ambient Surround and very good bass and treble. The low end comes in pretty good, even without the discreet subwoofer out of 5.1, especially during the numerous scenes of violence. —*JO*
Movie: 🐾🐾🐾🐾 **DVD:** 🐾🐾🐾
Buena Vista Home Entertainment (Cat #13850, UPC #717951000217). Wide-

screen (2.35:1) letterboxed. Stereo; Dolby Surround. $29.99. Keepcase. *LANG:* English (stereo); Spanish (DS). *CAP:* English. *FEATURES:* 27 chapter links.
1994 (R) 154m/C John Travolta, Samuel L. Jackson, Uma Thurman, Harvey Keitel, Tim Roth, Amanda Plummer, Maria De Medeiros, Ving Rhames, Eric Stoltz, Rosanna Arquette, Christopher Walken, Bruce Willis, Frank Whaley, Steve Buscemi, Peter Greene, David Arquette, Julia Sweeney, Quentin Tarantino, Dick Miller; *D:* Quentin Tarantino; *W:* Roger Roberts Avary, Quentin Tarantino; *C:* Andrzej Sekula; *M:* Karyn Rachtman. *AWARDS:* Academy Awards '94: Best Original Screenplay; American Film Institute (AFI) '98: Top 100; British Academy Awards '94: Best Original Screenplay, Best Supporting Actor (Jackson); Cannes Film Festival '94: Best Film; Golden Globe Awards '95: Best Screenplay; Independent Spirit Awards '95: Best Actor (Jackson), Best Director (Tarantino), Best Film, Best Screenplay; Los Angeles Film Critics Association Awards '94: Best Actor (Travolta), Best Director (Tarantino), Best Film, Best Screenplay; MTV Movie Awards '95: Best Film, Best Dance Sequence (John Travolta/Uma Thurman); National Board of Review Awards '94: Best Director (Tarantino), Best Film; New York Film Critics Awards '94: Best Director (Tarantino), Best Screenplay; National Society of Film Critics Awards '94: Best Director (Tarantino), Best Film, Best Screenplay; *NOM:* Academy Awards '94: Best Actor (Travolta), Best Director (Tarantino), Best Film Editing, Best Picture, Best Supporting Actor (Jackson), Best Supporting Actress (Thurman); Australian Film Institute '95: Best Foreign Film; Directors Guild of America Awards '94: Best Director (Tarantino); Golden Globe Awards '95: Best Actor—Drama (Travolta), Best Director (Tarantino), Best Film—Drama, Best Supporting Actor (Jackson), Best Supporting Actress (Thurman); Independent Spirit Awards '95: Best Supporting Actor (Stoltz); MTV Movie Awards '95: Best Male Performance (Travolta), Best Female Performance (Thurman), Best On-Screen Duo (John Travolta/Samuel L. Jackson), Best Song ("Girl, You'll Be a Woman Soon"); Screen Actors Guild Award '94: Best Actor (Travolta).

Pump Up the Volume

Though writer-director Allan Moyle wildly exaggerates the angst and loneliness of adolescence, he doesn't pander to his audience in this fierce comedy-drama. Recently arrived in Arizona, Mark Hunter (Slater) is a shy student during the day. At night, he turns his basement room into a pirate radio station and becomes Hard Harry, who vents all of his frustrations in free-form monologues about sex and alienation. The authorities are not amused. The DVD is remarkably free of the flaws that plague the medium. Background mini-blinds in Harry's suburban home, for example, do NOT flash, and his dim cluttered studio/bedroom is re-creat-

ed with the same depth of detail that was visible in the theatrical release. The stereo sound makes every syllable of Harry's rants distinct. —*MM*
Movie: 🐾🐾🐾▶ **DVD:** 🐾🐾🐾
New Line Home Video (Cat #N4894, UPC #794043489426). Widescreen (1.85:1) letterboxed; full frame. Dolby Digital 5.1 Surround Stereo; Dolby Digital Surround Stereo. $24.98. Snapper. *LANG:* English. *SUB:* English. *CAP:* English. *FEATURES:* 19 chapter links • Theatrical trailer • Cast and crew thumbnail biographies.
1990 (R) 105m/C Christian Slater, Scott Paulin, Ellen Greene, Samantha Mathis, Cheryl Pollak, Annie Ross, Andy Romano, Mimi Kennedy; *D:* Allan Moyle; *W:* Allan Moyle; *C:* Walt Lloyd; *M:* Cliff Martinez.

The Punisher

Lundgren portrays Frank Castle, the Marvel Comics anti-hero known as the Punisher. When his family is killed by the mob, Castle becomes obsessed with revenge and the bodies stack up mighty high. Fans have complained that he doesn't wear the "Punisher" uniform from the comic, but if you look close you'll see the "Punisher" skull formed by his beard as the film progresses, and the splattery violence comes from the same source. On the DVD the colorful credits look great, but the quality drops a couple notches when the film actually starts. What we end up with is a slightly better-than-average disc that is fairly sharp with grain rearing its ugly head mainly in smoke-filled explosions. The colors do remain good, although not as stunning as the credit sequence. Bleed is minimal. It would have been nice if the DVD were a little brighter, but the contrast levels are good, as are the blacks. Overall, the sound fidelity and dynamics are good, but the low end lacks a bit, and the Surround is only average. —*JO*
Movie: 🐾🐾▶ **DVD:** 🐾🐾▶
Artisan Entertainment (Cat #60490, UPC #012236049005). Widescreen (1.85:1) anamorphic. Dolby Surround. $24.98. Keepcase. *LANG:* English. *CAP:* English. *FEATURES:* 36 chapter links • Theatrical trailer • Production notes • Cast and crew bios.
1990 (R) 92m/C Dolph Lundgren, Louis Gossett Jr., Jeroen Krabbe, Kim Miyori; *D:* Mark Goldblatt; *W:* Boaz Yakin; *C:* Ian Baker; *M:* Dennis Dreith.

Puppet Films of Jiri Trnka

These stop-motion animation fairy tales contain some live-action scenes. They're probably a bit too stylized and slow-moving for young audiences, but older viewers—who, like me, may have a faint memory of seeing *The Emperor's Nightingale* on television decades ago—are likely to be more receptive. The films were made from the '40s to the '60s, and so the images have that burnished quality of old Technicolor. Also included: "Story of the Bass Cello" (1949, 15 min.), "Song of the Prairie"

(1949, 21 min.), "The Merry Circus" (1951, 11 min.), "A Drop Too Much" (1954, 14 min.), "The Hand" (1965, 18 min.), and "Jiri Trnka: Puppet Animation Master" (1999, 12 min.). —*MM*

Movie: ♫♫♫ **DVD:** ♫♫➤

Image Entertainment (Cat #ID9005ASDVD, UPC #014381900521). Full frame. Dolby Digital Mono. $29.99. Snapper. *LANG:* English. *FEATURES:* 18 chapter links.

19?? 156m/C D: Jiri Trnka; **W:** Phyllis McGinley; **M:** Vaclav Trojan.

Pure Country

An easygoing movie about a familiar subject is held together by the charm of Strait (in his movie debut) and the rest of the cast. Strait plays a country music superstar, tired of the career glitz, who decides to get out and go back to his home in Texas. He falls in love with the spunky Glasser and decides to run his career his own way. Warren is effective as his tough manager and old-time cowboy Calhoun is finely weathered as Glasser's gruff dad. Perhaps because I really don't like country music (no offense), I thought the music overwhelmed the dialogue in the 5.1 mix. The music did sound good, and there is a lot of energy throughout and a solid foot-stomping bass. There are even some pretty good Surround effects. The picture is also pretty good with vibrant defined colors and above-average sharpness. —*JO*

Movie: ♫♫➤ **DVD:** ♫♫♫

Warner Home Video, Inc. (Cat #12593, UPC #085391259329). Widescreen (1.85:1) anamorphic. Dolby Digital 5.1; Dolby Digital Mono; Dolby Surround. $24.98. Snapper. *LANG:* English; French. *SUB:* English; Spanish; French. *CAP:* English. *FEATURES:* 32 chapter links • Theatrical trailers • Production notes.

1992 (PG) 113m/C George Strait, Isabel Glasser, Lesley Ann Warren, Rory Calhoun, Kyle Chandler, John Doe, Molly McClure; **D:** Christopher Cain; **W:** Rex McGee; **C:** Rick Bota; **M:** Steve Dorff.

Purple Rain

Quasi-autobiographical video is a showcase for the pop-star Prince, in his struggle for love, attention, acceptance, and popular artistic recognition in Minneapolis. Not a bad film, for such a monumentally egotistical undertaking. The DVD made me appreciate just how well-done this movie is. The colors are superb and the image is grain-free and super sharp. Contrast and brightness levels are good whether in the concert hall or during the more sappy dramatic moments. The 5.1 sound seems souped up compared to the original CD, and there is tons more bass, but also much more distinctly crisp and sometimes screaming high end. —*JO*

Movie: ♫♫♫ **DVD:** ♫♫♫♫

Warner Home Video, Inc. (Cat #11398, UPC #085391139829). Full frame. Dolby Digital 5.1; Dolby Surround. $24.98. Snapper. *LANG:* English; French. *SUB:* English; Spanish; French. *CAP:* English. *FEATURES:*

28 chapter links • Theatrical trailers • Production notes.

1984 (R) 113m/C Prince, Apollonia, Morris Day, Olga Karlatos, Clarence Williams III; **D:** Albert Magnoli; **W:** William Blinn; **C:** Donald E. Thorin; **M:** Michel Colombier. *AWARDS:* Academy Awards '84: Original Song Score and/or Adaptation.

Pushing Hands

To anyone who's seen Ang Lee's *The Wedding Banquet* or *Eat, Drink, Man, Woman*, his first feature will be instantly familiar. It deals with the same themes and conflicts, and his star is the graceful gray-haired Sihung Lung, who was so effective in the other two films. He plays Mr. Chu, a retired tai chi master who moves from Beijing to his son Alex's (Wang) home in suburban New York. It's left to Alex's wife Martha (Snyder) to take care of the non-English-speaking Chu during the day while she's trying to work on her novel. The house is small and, in a deft introduction, Martha and Chu are presented as two people sharing the same physical space but who are, in all other respects, poles apart. Chu's presence does disrupt the family, but his own problems go deeper. The film was made on a limited budget, so it's not as polished as Lee's more recent work, including *Sense and Sensibility*. But Sihung Lung has a confident, crowd-pleasing charm not unlike Paul Newman, and his performance is the key to the film's success. Since this is a domestic story made on location, it doesn't gain much on DVD, though the occasional subtitles might be a little easier to read. The darker, busy scenes in a restaurant kitchen work well. In any form, this movie is one of the most enjoyable sleepers on video. —*MM*

Movie: ♫♫♫➤ **DVD:** ♫♫♫

Image Entertainment (Cat #ID5618FMDVD, UPC #014381561821). Full frame. Dolby Digital Mono. $24.99. Snapper. *LANG:* English; Chinese. *SUB:* English. *FEATURES:* 17 chapter links.

1992 100m/C Sihung Lung, Deb Snyder, Bo Z. Wang, Lai Wang; **D:** Ang Lee; **W:** Ang Lee; **C:** Jong Lin; **M:** Xiao-Song Qu.

Pushing Tin

Though based on a *New York Times* article, this tale of two air traffic controllers is really a retelling of Edgar Allan Poe's story "William Wilson." Nick Falzone (Cusack) is the reigning king of Long Island air traffic controllers until Russell Bell (Thornton) shows up. Where Nick is a fast-talking New Yorker who's always ready to fit another plane onto his screen, Russell is a Zen master whose cool is never ruffled. Nick is threatened, and the competition between the two finally involves their wives (Blanchett and Jolie), and brings out the worst in Nick. As long as the film sticks to the four main characters, it's funny ("Passenger safety is one of our highest priorities."), smart, and innovative.

But in the third act, the interesting women are pushed off-stage and the relationship between the men becomes more predictable. The image quality of the DVD is so good that the computer-generated aerial scenes have a noticeably different visual and audio quality. It's a small flaw since all of the important action takes place on the ground. Watch this one for the performances and the characters, not physical action. (By the way, a senior airline captain assures me that conditions inside the air traffic control center are grossly exaggerated.) —*MM*

Movie: ♫♫♫➤ **DVD:** ♫♫♫

Twentieth Century Fox Home Entertainment (Cat #4112306). Widescreen letterboxed. Dolby Digital Stereo. $34.98. Keepcase. *LANG:* English. *FEATURES:* 30 chapter links.

1999 (R) 124m/C John Cusack, Billy Bob Thornton, Cate Blanchett, Angelina Jolie, Matt Ross, Jerry Grayson, Michael Willis; **D:** Mike Newell; **W:** Glen Charles, Les Charles; **C:** Gale Tattersall; **M:** Anne Dudley.

Pyaar Kiya to Darna Kya

The title of this romantic variation on the "city mouse and country mouse" fable translates as "Love is in the air." Suraj (Salman Khan) is cocky and spoiled, dressed like the host of an MTV Beach Party. Muscan (Kajol) is the meek and overprotected village girl who wants to better herself by going to college. She arrives shadowed by her big brother, the suspicious Vishaal (Arbaaz Khan). When Vishaal takes Muscan back on the next bus, to pry her away from randy coeds, Suraj hitches a ride on top! The jaunty though not quite rollicking comedy is marred by unnecessary—at least by western standards—gunplay, broad caricatures, and a too-suddenly-neat ending. A handful of scenes contain fairly blatant product promotions for one soft drink maker. The denatured soundtrack feels like an American sitcom—you might even wonder what happened to the laugh track! Its middle-of-the-road pop score, however, plays well on all speakers. Visuals offer soft but not bleeding colors, and no serious problem with artifacts, but contrasting patterns often buzz and some fades pixelate. Worse, many scenes, including an entire musical number, take place in near darkness! The image is slightly letterboxed but still squared off, as if shot for television. English subtitles, white outlined in gray, are optional. The jazzy "making of" documentary looks widescreen, but that is probably the result of some post-production conceit, since the people appear squashed. Cuts are accompanied by white flashes likely to make your monitor flip. Interviews, mostly in English, openly admit that what we have on our hands is a simple lark. —*JK*

Movie: ♫♫ **DVD:** ♫♫

Video Sound (Cat #VSMD0200-DVD111, UPC #677565011194). Full frame. Dolby

Digital 5.1. $29.95. Keepcase. *LANG:* Hindi. *SUB:* English. *FEATURES:* 6 song links ▪ Interactive menu ▪ Full-color picture disc ▪ Behind-the-scenes documentary.
1998 162m/C IN Salman Khan, Dharmendra, Kajol, Arbaaz Khan; *D:* Sohail Khan; *W:* Sohail Khan; *C:* Rasool Ellore; *M:* Jatin-Lalit, Himesh Reshamiya.

Pyar to Hona Hi Tah

The cover blurb claims, "It could be your love story." Don't bet on it. A plot like this can only happen to Bollywood heartthrob Ajay Devgan. The opening credits are set to a music video as overblown (and overexposed looking) as anything Celine Dion and Elton John might produce together. The whole film is just as stagy, heavily key-lit, and unfocused looking. Clumsy, whiny Sanjana (Kajol) is afraid to fly. Shekhar (Devgan) is her grumpy seatmate on a plane bound from Paris to India. He stashes a hot necklace in her purse to avoid customs and she accuses him of being a bomb-smuggling terrorist! What else could they do after their first argument (not about bombs or terrorism; about his smoking in the non-smoker's section) but have a singalong (not about any of those things; about whether the plane will crash) right there in the tourist class cabin? Then, how else to follow all that, but to have him take her home to his village and meet the folks? Subplots involve Sanjana's ex-fiance Rahul (Anand) and Inspector Khan (Puri), who is sure that necklace must be in someone's luggage. The completely over-the-top ending is hampered by a couple of fairly long yet untranslated monologues. While some naturally lit exteriors are lovely, in general the blacks are unattractively wet-looking, and scenes fog up even when shot indoors! While the image hardly shows artifacts and does scan well, the sound mix and subtitling are often inconsistent. English subtitles, white outlined in gray, are optional. There is no scene access menu on the disc, only one for the songs. The title translates as "Love Will Blossom." *—JK*
Movie: 🐾🐾 *DVD:* 🐾▶
Video Sound (Cat #VSMD0200-DVD117, UPC #677565011798). Widescreen. Dolby Digital 5.1. $29.95. Keepcase. *LANG:* Hindi. *SUB:* English. *FEATURES:* 23 chapter stops ▪ "Select a song" feature with 6 links ▪ Interactive menus ▪ 2-color picture disc.
1998 165m/C IN Ajay Devgan, Om Puri, Kajol, Bijay Anand, Kashmira Shah; *D:* Anees Bazmee; *W:* Anees Bazmee; *C:* Nirmal Jani; *M:* Jatin-Lalit.

Q & A

Semi-taut thriller begins with NYPD Lt. Brennan (Nolte) trying to make his cold-blooded murder of a drug dealer look like self defense. Ex-cop turned DA Reilly (Hutton) is supposed to sweep the case under the rug, then he finds that drug dealer Tex-

ador (Assante) is also a witness. The raw language and location filming give the proceedings a fine feeling of place. The DVD image is as sharp and detailed as I remember the theatrical release, though not that much better than VHS tape. Sound is acceptable. *—MM*
Movie: 🐾🐾 *DVD:* 🐾🐾▶
HBO Home Video (Cat #90381, UPC #026359038129). Widescreen letterboxed. Dolby Digital 5.1 Surround Stereo; Dolby Digital Surround Stereo. $24.98. Snapper. *LANG:* English; French. *SUB:* English; French; Spanish. *FEATURES:* 16 chapter links.
1990 (R) 132m/C Nick Nolte, Timothy Hutton, Armand Assante, Patrick O'Neal, Lee Richardson, Luis Guzman, Charles S. Dutton, Jenny Lumet, Paul Calderon, Fyvush Finkel; *D:* Sidney Lumet; *W:* Sidney Lumet; *C:* Andrzej Bartkowiak; *M:* Ruben Blades.

Q: The Movie

Black teen throws a party while his parents are away.
Movie: NYR *DVD:* NYR
Xenon Entertainment (Cat #4072). Full frame. $19.95. Keepcase. *FEATURES:* Commentary: Barry Bowles and Brian Hooks ▪ Trailer.
1999 85m/C Brian Hooks, N.D. Brown; *D:* Barry Bowles.

Q (The Winged Serpent)

A cult of admirers surrounds this goony monster flick about dragonlike Aztec god Quetzlcoatl, summoned to modern Manhattan by gory human sacrifices, and hungry for rooftop sunbathers and construction teams. Direction and special effects are pretty ragged, but witty script helps the cast shine, especially Moriarty as a low-life crook who's found the beast's hidden nest. Anchor Bay's transfer tops the earlier home video versions. The image is sharp, and although perfect picture quality is not a prerequisite to enjoyment of this low-budget gem, the color is also very detailed and accurate. Blacks are very good and both contrasts and brightness levels remain consistently comfortable, whether in a dark scene or in a brightly lit sky. The stereo sound is nothing special but does its job. *—JO* **AKA:** Q; The Winged Serpent.
Movie: 🐾🐾🐾 *DVD:* 🐾🐾🐾
Anchor Bay (Cat #DV10485, UPC #013131048599). Widescreen (1.85:1) letterboxed. Stereo. $24.98. Keepcase. *LANG:* English. *FEATURES:* 12 chapter links.
1982 (R) 92m/C Michael Moriarty, Candy Clark, David Carradine, Richard Roundtree, Malachy McCourt, James Dixon, Eddie Jones, Bruce Carradine, Tony Page, Fred J. Scollay, Mary Louise Weller; *D:* Larry Cohen; *W:* Larry Cohen; *C:* Fred Murphy; *M:* Robert O. Ragland.

Quackser Fortune Has a Cousin in the Bronx

An Irish fertilizer salesman (Wilder) meets an exchange student (Kidder) from the U.S. who finds herself attracted to this unlearned but not unknowing man. An original love story with drama and appeal. **AKA:** Fun Loving.
Movie: 🐾🐾🐾 *DVD:* NYR
VCI Home Video (Cat #8216). Widescreen (1.66:1) letterboxed. Dolby Digital Mono. $24.99. Keepcase. *FEATURES:* Cast and crew thumbnail bios ▪ Trailer.
1970 (R) 88m/C IR Gene Wilder, Margot Kidder, Eileen Colgan, May Ollis, Seamus Ford, Danny Cummins, Liz Davis; *D:* Waris Hussein; *W:* Gabriel Walsh; *C:* Gilbert Taylor; *M:* Michael Dress.

Quantum Leap: The Pilot Episode

Disc presents the premiere movie-length episode of the sci-fi TV series that put Bakula on the prime-time map. In an attempt to defy the laws of time and space, futuristic scientist Sam Beckett (Bakula) awakens in the year 1956 and is inhabiting the body of Air Force pilot Tom Stratton. His only way out is to right a crucial error in the destiny of the man into whose life he has leapt. Soon enough, as the TV series unfolds, he will discover that he leaps from life to life and time to time, setting right what once went wrong. That is, until falling ratings and cancellation finally catches up to him. Both video and audio look and sound as good as the program did when it originally aired—a big improvement over the previous videotape release. *—MB*
Movie: 🐾🐾🐾 *DVD:* 🐾🐾🐾
Image Entertainment (Cat #ID4301USDVD, UPC #014381430127). Full frame. Dolby Digital Stereo. $24.98. Snapper. *LANG:* English. *FEATURES:* 19 chapter links.
1989 93m/C Scott Bakula, Dean Stockwell, Jennifer Runyon; *D:* David Hemmings; *W:* Donald P. Bellisario, Deborah Pratt; *C:* Roy Wagner; *M:* Mike Post.

The Quarrel

In 1948, writer Chaim Kovler (Thomson) meets his childhood friend Hersh (Rubinek) in a Montreal park. Fifteen years before, their relationship broke apart over Chaim's decision to give up the religious life for his writing. They immediately pick up their quarrel over faith and its value, particularly in light of the Holocaust. The two characters serve too much as careful ideologues to be compelling and the film never completely breaks free of its roots as a stage play. There is nothing special about either image or sound; both are essentially identical to VHS tape. *—MM*
Movie: 🐾🐾▶ *DVD:* 🐾🐾
WinStar Home Entertainment (Cat #FLV5177, UPC #720917517728). Full frame. Stereo. $24.98. Snapper. *LANG:* English. *FEATURES:* 12 chapter links ▪

Cast and crew filmographies • Production credits • Web link.
1993 88m/C *CA* Saul Rubinek, R.H. Thomson, Arthur Grosser; *D:* Eli Cohen; *W:* David Brandes; *M:* William Goldstein.

Quatermass and the Pit

The only flaws in this intelligent and consistently surprising British horror/sf are thin effects and a relatively weak conclusion to a strong story. Professor Quatermass (Kier) is a prickly scientist who counters military thick-headedness, in the person of Col. Breen (Glover), with skeptical humanism. Their point of contention is an object uncovered during the renovation of a London subway stop. Dr. Roney (Donald), an anthropologist, suspects it may be extraterrestrial. But what about the humanoid skeletons buried around it? Echoes of Nigel Kneale's script can be seen in *2001* and Stephen King's *The Tommyknockers*. Director Roy Ward Baker keeps the offbeat action on track throughout. Their commentary track, done from 35 years of memory, is so low-keyed that they sometimes need prompting to talk. They mention the limits that the budget placed on their special effects, but this is still a remarkably beautiful film that makes good use of color and light. The image is excellent on VHS tape; it sparkles on DVD. One of Hammer's best and that's very good, indeed. This is a two-sided disc with the feature on one side; extras on the flip. —*MM* **AKA:** Five Million Years to Earth.
Movie: 🎵🎵🎵 **DVD:** 🎵🎵🎵▸
Anchor Bay (Cat #DV10505, UPC #013131050592). Widescreen (1.66:1) letterboxed. Dolby Digital 5.1 Surround Stereo; Dolby Digital Stereo. $29.98. Keepcase. *LANG:* English. *FEATURES:* 10 chapter links • Commentary: writer Kneale and director Baker • Theatrical trailers • *World of Hammer* episode "Sci-Fi."
1967 97m/C *GB* James Donald, Andrew Keir, Barbara Shelley, Julian Glover, Duncan Lamont, Bryan Marshall; *D:* Roy Ward Baker; *W:* Nigel Kneale; *C:* Arthur Grant; *M:* Tristam Carey.

Queens Logic

Sleeper ensemble comedy is in the tradition of *The Big Chill* with the trials and episodic adventures of the "old neighborhood gang" who gather for a wedding. Most of the film centers on Olin and girlfriend Webb. Will he bolt before the ceremony?
Movie: 🎵🎵🎵 **DVD:** NYR
Pioneer Entertainment (Cat #DVD68923). Full frame. Dolby Digital Stereo. $24.98. Keepcase. *FEATURES:* Trailer.
1991 (R) 116m/C John Malkovich, Kevin Bacon, Jamie Lee Curtis, Linda Fiorentino, Joe Mantegna, Ken Olin, Tom Waits, Chloe Webb, Ed Marinaro, Kelly Bishop, Tony Spiridakis; *D:* Steve Rash; *W:* Tony Spiridakis; *C:* Amir M. Mokri; *M:* Joe Jackson.

The Quest

Jean-Claude Van Damme makes a credible directorial debut in this nicely staged if conventional martial arts movie. He also stars as Christopher DuBois, who takes it on the lam from New York gangsters, and immediately finds himself captured by gunrunners. Somewhere off the coast of China, he's "rescued" by the pirate Dobbs (Moore), then roped into the "ghangheng," a Tibetan martial arts Olympics with a solid gold dragon as the prize. The atmosphere is exotic with Oriental locales and a 1920s setting. The fight scenes are handled well and the violence is relatively restrained for the genre. The DVD image is generally equal to the theatrical release. The concluding fights are well lit with a golden saffron cast and the whole thing looks better than it needs to. —*MM*
Movie: 🎵🎵▸ **DVD:** 🎵🎵▸
Universal Studios Home Video (Cat #20258, UPC #025192025822). Widescreen (2.35:1) letterboxed. Dolby Digital 5.1 Surround Stereo; Dolby Digital Surround Stereo. $24.98. Keepcase. *LANG:* English; French. *SUB:* Spanish. *CAP:* English. *FEATURES:* 16 chapter links • Production notes • Cast and crew thumbnail biographies • Theatrical trailer.
1996 (PG-13) 95m/C Jean-Claude Van Damme, Roger Moore, Aki Aleong, James Remar, Jack McGee, Janet Gunn, Abdel Qissi, Louis Mandylor; *D:* Jean-Claude Van Damme; *W:* Stuart Klein, Paul Mones; *C:* David Gribble; *M:* Randy Edelman.

Quest for Camelot

Camelot's future lies in the hands of heroine Kayley, who sees an opportunity to win a spot at King Arthur's roundtable when Excalibur is stolen by evil knight Ruber (Oldman). On her quest to recover the sword, she meets blind hermit Garrett and two-headed dragon Devon and Cornwall (Idle and Rickles). With an all-star cast, this first full-length animated feature from Warner Bros. wants to be a contender for the Disney animation crown, but can't quite overcome its familiar story, one-dimensional villain, and forgettable songs. However, Kayley and Garrett are strong, non-stereotypical characters that children and adults will welcome. Based on the children's novel *The King's Damosel* by Vera Chapman. Story aside, for sheer animation thrills this DVD is as big a showpiece as any of the Disney DVD releases so far. The image stays extremely sharp throughout and there is never a hint of grain or artifacts. The colors are even more spectacular and are as vibrant as anything out there, with no bleed whatsoever. The 5.1 mix varies but is overall pretty good, with maybe too much emphasis on splashy sound effects and not enough attention given to ambience and even a more dimensional music breakdown. Included on the supplemental side is a step-by-step look at how some of the computer animation was put together. —*JO*
Movie: 🎵🎵▸ **DVD:** 🎵🎵🎵🎵

Warner Home Video, Inc. (Cat #16607, UPC #085391660729). Widescreen (1.85:1) letterboxed. Dolby Digital 5.1. $24.98. Snapper. *LANG:* English; French. *SUB:* English; French. *CAP:* English. *FEATURES:* 36 chapter links • Theatrical trailer • Documentary: "How It's Done" • Documentary: "The Voices" • 2 music videos • Isolated music and songs • Pencil sketches • Animation tests.
1998 (G) 85m/C *D:* Frederick Du Chan; *W:* Kirk De Micco, William Schifrin, David Seidler; *M:* Patrick Doyle; *V:* Jessalyn Gilsig, Cary Elwes, Gary Oldman, Eric Idle, Don Rickles, Jane Seymour, Pierce Brosnan, Gabriel Byrne, Bronson Pinchot, Jaleel White, John Gielgud. *AWARDS:* Golden Globe Awards '99: Best Song ("The Prayer"); *NOM:* Academy Awards '98: Best Song ("The Prayer"); Golden Globe Awards '99: Best Song ("The Magic Sword").

The Quick and the Dead

Stone is a tough gal gunslinger (a la a female Clint Eastwood) out to avenge the murder of her father. She arrives in the frontier town of Redemption where arch-villain Herod (Hackman) rules by means of violence and intimidation. Director Raimi is a master of using cliches in such a way that they seem fresh, thanks in part to Stone and gang playing things totally straight. The gunfights are wildly staged and extremely violent. Raimi's kinetic and stylized direction is captured perfectly on this DVD, which has no problems with either the rich comic book colors or the rapid and energetic camera moves. The image remains sharp and the excellent contrast and brightness retain details in fully lit or shadowy scenes. The usual Raim-ified and exaggerated sound effects liven things up even more and the 5.1 mix delivers it in an earth-shaking manner. —*JO*
Movie: 🎵🎵🎵 **DVD:** 🎵🎵🎵▸
Columbia Tristar Home Video (Cat #73519, UPC #043396735194). Widescreen (1.85:1) letterboxed; full frame. Dolby Digital 5.1; Dolby Digital 2.0. $29.95. Keepcase. *LANG:* English (DD5.1); French (DD2.0). *SUB:* English; French. *CAP:* English. *FEATURES:* 28 chapter links.
1994 (R) 105m/C Sharon Stone, Gene Hackman, Leonardo DiCaprio, Russell Crowe, Kevin Conway, Lance Henriksen, Roberts Blossom, Pat Hingle, Keith David, Michael Stone, Stacey Linn Ramsower; *Cameos:* Gary Sinise; *D:* Sam Raimi; *W:* Simon Moore; *C:* Dante Spinotti; *M:* Alan Silvestri.

The Quiet Man

The classic incarnation of Hollywood Irishness is one of Ford's best, and funniest films. Wayne is Sean Thornton, a weary American ex-boxer who returns to the Irish hamlet of his childhood and tries to take a spirited lass as his wife, despite the strenuous objections of her brawling brother (McLaglen). Thornton's aided by the leprechaun-like Fitzgerald and the local parish

priest, Bond. A high-spirited and memorable film filled with Irish stew, wonderful banter, and shots of the lush countryside. Unfortunately, the DVD for this beautifully photographed film isn't up to the task. The image is never very sharp and the gorgeous colors are pale, even compared to an old super 8mm film print I once saw. When a bright image is contrasted against a dark background, there is substantial ghosting. The sound is actually a little better than it's been on previous video releases, with a little more bass and overall crispness. It's possible that preprint caused most of the problems, but this gem would be worth restoring and remastering. Let's hope someone does it. —*JO*
Movie: ♫♫♫♫ **DVD:** ♫♪
Artisan Entertainment (Cat #53361, UPC #017153336122). Full frame. Dolby Digital Mono. $24.98. Keepcase. *LANG:* English. *CAP:* English. *FEATURES:* 36 chapter links • "Making of" featurette • Theatrical trailer.
1952 129m/C John Wayne, Maureen O'Hara, Barry Fitzgerald, Victor McLaglen, Arthur Shields, Jack MacGowran, Ward Bond, Mildred Natwick, Ken Curtis, Mae Marsh, Sean McClory, Francis Ford; *D:* John Ford; *W:* Frank Nugent; *C:* Archie Stout; *M:* Victor Young. *AWARDS:* Academy Awards '52: Best Color Cinematography, Best Director (Ford); Directors Guild of America Awards '52: Best Director (Ford); Venice Film Festival '52: Best Director (Ford); *NOM:* Academy Awards '52: Best Art Direction/Set Decoration (Color), Best Picture, Best Screenplay, Best Sound, Best Supporting Actor (McLaglen).

Quiz Show

Director Robert Redford's look at the 1958 scandal behind the prime-time game show *Twenty-One* is driven by an emotional coolness that's rare in American movies. John Turturro gets a bit wild as the contestant who's forced to make room for golden boy Charles Van Doren (Fiennes). Rob Morrow is the congressional investigator who uncovers the fix. It's an absorbing story until the end when it pins blame on the NBC president whose involvement has never been proved. Notable among the supporting cast is Oscar-nominee Scofield who turns in a powerful performance as the intellectual elder Van Doren. Directors Martin Scorsese and Barry Levinson appear as, respectively, the Sponsor and TV personality Dave Garroway. Redford and director of photography Michael Ballhaus add a slight sepia tone to the color, giving the sparkling sharp focus just a hint of nostalgia. But this is a tough-minded film that's finally about how easily people can be conned and how little we care when we find out that we've been conned. The DVD re-creates the film's evocative and imaginative visuals very well. One busy dress pattern vibrates annoyingly, and, as always, Venetian blinds flash, but the performances are the core of the film and the widescreen transfer captures the

tense characters and their cluttered world as well as the theatrical release. More historical background, possibly taken from the source material, Richard N. Goodwin's book *Remembering America: A Voice from the Sixties*, would have been welcome in the extras department. —*MM*
Movie: ♫♫♫♪ **DVD:** ♫♫♫♪
Buena Vista Home Entertainment (Cat #17639, UPC #717951003492). Widescreen (1.85:1) letterboxed. Dolby Surround. $29.99. Snapper. *LANG:* English; French. *CAP:* English. *FEATURES:* 30 chapter links • Theatrical trailer.
1994 (PG-13) 133m/C John Turturro, Rob Morrow, Ralph Fiennes, Paul Scofield, David Paymer, Hank Azaria, Christopher McDonald, Johann Carlo, Elizabeth Wilson, Mira Sorvino, Griffin Dunne, Martin Scorsese, Barry Levinson; *D:* Robert Redford; *W:* Paul Attanasio; *C:* Michael Ballhaus; *M:* Mark Isham. *AWARDS:* British Academy Awards '94: Best Adapted Screenplay; New York Film Critics Awards '94: Best Film; *NOM:* Academy Awards '94: Best Adapted Screenplay, Best Director (Redford), Best Picture, Best Supporting Actor (Scofield); Directors Guild of America Awards '94: Best Director (Redford); Golden Globe Awards '95: Best Director (Redford), Best Film—Drama, Best Screenplay, Best Supporting Actor (Turturro); Writers Guild of America '94: Best Adapted Screenplay.

Rabid Dogs

Complicated crime drama finds violent Doc (Poli), 32 (Montefiori), and Blade (Caponi) making their getaway by grabbing a woman hostage, Greta (Lander), and then commandeering a car driven by aged Riccardo (Cucciolla), who's travelling with a sick child. The criminals torment the hostages, people get killed, and there's a final twist to the whole bloody situation. At the time of this review, *Rabid Dogs* is a DVD exclusive. The film itself is in pretty bad shape, and the essay by Tim Lucas details the reasons (basically the footage was just recently dug up and put together after sitting on the shelf for years). There doesn't seem to be any digital distortion added to the presentation but the picture is soft focus and grainy, with weak colors as well. The soundtrack is in similar shape, but we should be grateful to have the Italian master's lost gem in any condition. —*JO* *AKA:* Semaforo Rosso; Cani Arribbiati.
Movie: ♫♫♫ **DVD:** ♫♫♫
Video Watchdog (Cat #LMDVD001, UPC #71875420091). Widescreen (1.66:1) letterboxed. Stereo. $39.95. Keepcase. *LANG:* Italian. *SUB:* English; German. *FEATURES:* Theatrical trailer • Filmographies • Essays: "Mario Bava" and "The Film's Reconstruction" by Tim Lucas • Photos gallery • Poster gallery.
1974 96m/C *IT* Riccardo Cucciolla, Maurice Poli, Luigi Montefiore, Lea Lander, Aldo Caponi, Erika Dario; *D:* Mario Bava; *W:* Alessandro Parenzo, Cesare Frugoni;

C: Mario Bava, Emilio Varriano; *M:* Stelvio Cipriano.

Rabid Grannies

What a title! Two aging sisters (Aymerie and Brockman) receive a surprise birthday present from their devil-worshipping nephew. The gift turns their party into a gorefest as they rip into various family members—literally. The bloody effects are laughably amateurish, but that's appropriate for this wicked (and sometimes too talky) satire. The good folks at Troma Team Video imported the schlock from Belgium. Recommended for fans of bad movies only. —*MM*
Movie: ♫♫♪ **DVD:** NYR
Troma Team Video (Cat #9970). Full frame. $24.95. Keepcase.
1989 (R) 89m/C *BE* Catherine Aymerie, Caroline Brackman, Danielle Daven, Raymond Lescot, Anne Marie Fox, Richard Cotica, Patricia Davie; *D:* Emmanuel Kervyn; *W:* Emmanuel Kervyn; *C:* Hugh Labye; *M:* Jean-Bruno Castelain, Pierre-Damien Castelain.

Race

Serious low-budget film attempts to take a serious look at practical politics on the local level. L.A. councilman Durman (Robertson) comes in third in the primary after redistricting. Tied for first are Lucinda Davis (Pounder), a black woman, and Gustavo Alvarez (Rodriguez), a Latino house painter. Their race touches all of the Southern California racial and ethnic hot buttons, and quickly turns nasty. Writer-director Musca necessarily simplifies the partisanship, but it's probably unfair to criticize any fiction for not living up to the unexpected extremes of today's politics. On DVD, the Los Angeles neighborhoods have a scrubbed clean look. Musca works through many tight close-ups that are handled with ease by the full-frame image. Sound is O.K. —*MM*
Movie: ♫♫♪ **DVD:** ♫♫♫
Image Entertainment (Cat #ID5900UM DVD, UPC #014381590029). Full frame. Dolby Digital Surround Stereo. $24.98. Snapper. *LANG:* English. *FEATURES:* 16 chapter links.
1999 (R) 103m/C Paul Rodriguez, CCH Pounder, Cliff Robertson, Annette Murphy; *D:* Tom Musca; *W:* Tom Musca, Mark Kemble; *C:* Arturo Smith; *M:* Stan Ridgway.

Rachel's Man

Biblical story of Jacob (Whiting) and Rachel (Bat-Adam) is told with more religious conviction than cinematic skill. The bare-bones Israeli production has an almost experimental look in the early scenes with characters in white-face and other non-realistic touches. It's all rather stiff and slow, and it fares poorly on DVD. The image is riddled with pixels throughout, completely lacking sharpness. That may be understandable in a film of its age, but it's still hard to take. —*MM*

Movie: 🎬🎬 **DVD:** 🎬
Simitar Entertainment (Cat #7249, UPC #082551724925). Full frame. PCM Stereo. $14.98. Keepcase. *LANG:* English. *FEATURES:* 8 chapter links ● Production factoids ● Mickey Rooney filmography.
1975 92m/C Mickey Rooney, Rita Tushingham, Leonard Whiting, Michal Bat-Adam; *D:* Moshe Mizrahi.

Radioland Murders

Would-be screwball comedy is an utter disaster that leaves a large cast stranded without a single giggle. Waves of pointless action are hurled across the screen at a hysterical pace. From the opening moments, it's all so frantic that there is no reason to care about the characters or to laugh at their situation. In Chicago, 1939, from its studio in a skyscraper, WBN is about to begin its first night of broadcasting without any finished scripts or clear direction. The station's owner (Beatty) has invited a bunch of potential affiliates while his main writer (Benben) and top executive (Masterson) are in the middle of a divorce. Curiously, on DVD, the comic misfire looks great. It was filmed completely on soundstages and so the polished production values shine through even the darkest scenes. —*MM*
Movie: woof **DVD:** 🎬🎬🎬
Image Entertainment (Cat #ID4224USDVD, UPC #014381422429). Widescreen (2.35:1) anamorphic. Dolby Digital Surround. $24.99. Snapper. *LANG:* English. *CAP:* English. *FEATURES:* 16 chapter links.
1994 (PG) 112m/C Brian Benben, Mary Stuart Masterson, Ned Beatty, George Burns, Brion James, Michael Lerner, Michael McKean, Jeffrey Tambor, Scott Michael Campbell, Anita Morris, Stephen Tobolowsky, Christopher Lloyd, Larry Miller, Corbin Bernsen; *Cameos:* Robert Klein, Harvey Korman, Peter MacNicol, Joey Lawrence, Bob(cat) Goldthwait; *D:* Mel Smith; *W:* Willard Huyck, Gloria Katz, Jeff Reno, Ron Osborn; *C:* David Tattersall; *M:* Joel McNeely.

Rage at Dawn

An outlaw gang is tracked by a special agent who must bend the rules a little to get the bad guys. Not surprisingly, he gets his girl as well. A solid standard of the genre with some clever plot twists. *AKA:* Seven Bad Men.
Movie: 🎬🎬▶ **DVD:** NYR
Roan Group (Cat #2015). $19.95. Keepcase. *FEATURES:* Trailer.
1955 87m/C Randolph Scott, Forrest Tucker, Mala Powers, J. Carrol Naish, Edgar Buchanan; *D:* Tim Whelan; *W:* Horace McCoy; *C:* Ray Rennahan; *M:* Paul Sawtell.

The Rage: Carrie 2

You don't need psychic powers to know that things aren't going to end well for the tormented teens in this slightly altered sequel. The heroine is Rachel (Bergl), a semi-Goth outcast who has a crush on good-guy jock Jesse (London). She also has the ability to rattle and explode things when she's upset. Sue (Irving), the only survivor of Carrie White's little tantrum years earlier, discovers that Rachel is related to the late telekinetic prom queen and tries to warn her. Lacks the character development and shock value of the first. The DVD features a highly detailed and stable video transfer. The picture is crystal clear, especially during the daytime exterior scenes, which appear incredibly crisp on the DVD. There is no artifacting present and no obvious flaws in the source material. The Surround sound is active throughout the film and is put to good use. During a storm, thunder reverberates from the speakers, and during the finale, we hear "They're all going to laugh at you" circling the room. —*ML* *AKA:* Carrie 2.
Movie: 🎬🎬 **DVD:** 🎬🎬🎬🎬
MGM Home Entertainment (Cat #907454, UPC #027616745422). Full frame; widescreen (1.85:1) anamorphic. Dolby Digital 5.1 Surround. $24.98. Keepcase. *LANG:* English; French. *SUB:* English; French. *CAP:* English. *FEATURES:* 40 chapter links ● Deleted scenes ● Alternative ending ● Commentary: director Katt Shea.
1999 (R) 97m/C Emily Bergl, Amy Irving, Jason London, J. Smith-Cameron, Zachery Ty Bryan, John Doe, Gordon Clapp, Rachel Blanchard, Mena Suvari, Eddie Kaye Thomas, Dylan Bruno, Charlotte Ayanna, Justin Urich, Elijah Craig; *D:* Katt Shea; *W:* Rafael Moreu; *C:* Donald M. Morgan; *M:* Danny P. Harvey.

Raging Bull

Scorsese's depressing but magnificent vision of the dying American Dream and suicidal macho codes in the form of the rise and fall of middleweight boxing champ Jake LaMotta, a brutish, dull-witted animal who can express himself only in the ring and through violence. A photographically expressive, brilliant drama, with easily the most intense and brutal boxing scenes ever filmed. De Niro provides a vintage performance, going from the young LaMotta to the aging has-been, and is ably accompanied by Moriarty as his girl and Pesci as his loyal, much beat-upon bro. This is a fine example of a DVD that improves on all prior home video editions including the excellent laserdisc issued as part of the Criterion Collection. When a black-and-white image is filmed and presented as accurately as on this DVD, it's an amazing thing to see. The image is packed full of incredibly sharp details and has an almost limitless feeling of depth. The Dolby Digital sound is also impressive in upping the brutality ante in the excruciating fight scenes. —*JO*
Movie: 🎬🎬🎬🎬 **DVD:** 🎬🎬🎬🎬
MGM Home Entertainment (Cat #906040, UPC #027616604095). Widescreen (1.85:1) letterboxed; full frame. Digital Surround; Mono. $24.98. Snapper. *LANG:* English (DS); French (mono); Spanish (mono). *SUB:* English; French; Spanish. *CAP:* Eng-lish. *FEATURES:* 30 chapter links ● Theatrical trailer.
1980 (R) 128m/B Robert De Niro, Cathy Moriarty, Joe Pesci, Frank Vincent, Nicholas Colasanto, Theresa Saldana; *D:* Martin Scorsese; *W:* Paul Schrader, Mardik Martin; *C:* Michael Chapman; *M:* Robbie Robertson. *AWARDS:* Academy Awards '80: Best Actor (De Niro), Best Film Editing; American Film Institute (AFI) '98: Top 100; Golden Globe Awards '81: Best Actor—Drama (De Niro); Los Angeles Film Critics Association Awards '80: Best Actor (De Niro), Best Film; National Board of Review Awards '80: Best Actor (De Niro), Best Supporting Actor (Pesci), National Film Registry '90; New York Film Critics Awards '80: Best Actor (De Niro), Best Actor (De Niro), Best Supporting Actor (Pesci); National Society of Film Critics Awards '80: Best Cinematography, Best Director (Scorsese), Best Supporting Actor (Pesci); *NOM:* Academy Awards '80: Best Cinematography, Best Director (Scorsese), Best Picture, Best Sound, Best Supporting Actor (Pesci), Best Supporting Actress (Moriarty).

Raid on Rommel

A British soldier (Burton) poses as a Nazi and tries to infiltrate Rommel's team with his rag-tag brigade of misfits. Predictable drivel; the best scenes are action footage from the 1967 film *Tobruck*. Another below average disc from Goodtimes. The film print itself is a part of the problem, as there are a lot of scratches and white flecks, particularly in the opening scenes. The picture ranges from average to poor and the grain is particularly bad in brightly lit outdoor sequences. The brightness is generally adequate, but most of the time the contrast is too high and the colors appear washed-out—if they weren't, there'd probably be more color bleed which is bothersome at times anyway. The blacks vary from near-true to grain-filled grays. You can't fault the DVD for the film's mono soundtrack, but occasional clipping is audible in the tinny track which seems to have no low end at all. —*JO*
Movie: 🎬🎬 **DVD:** 🎬▶
Goodtimes Entertainment (Cat #05-81012, UPC #018713810120). Widescreen (2.35:1) letterboxed. Mono. $19.95. Snapper. *LANG:* English. *SUB:* English; French; Spanish. *FEATURES:* 18 chapter links.
1971 (PG) 98m/C Richard Burton, John Colicos, Clinton Greyn, Wolfgang Preiss; *D:* Henry Hathaway; *W:* Richard M. Bluel; *C:* Earl Rath; *M:* Hal Mooney.

Rain

Director Lewis Milestone adapts Somerset Maugham's tale of a puritanical minister's attempt to reclaim a "lost woman" (Crawford) on the island of Pago Pago. Remake of the 1928 silent film *Miss Sadie Thompson* was remade again under that title in 1953.
Movie: 🎬🎬▶ **DVD:** NYR

Roan Group (Cat #2017). Full frame. Dolby Digital Mono. $19.95. Keepcase.

1932 92m/B Joan Crawford, Walter Huston, William Gargan, Guy Kibbee, Beulah Bondi, Walter Catlett; **D:** Lewis Milestone; **W:** Maxwell Anderson; **C:** Oliver Marsh; **M:** Alfred Newman.

Rain Man

When his father dies, ambitious and self-centered Charlie Babbit (Cruise) finds that he has an older autistic brother Raymond (Hoffman) who has been institutionalized for years. Needing him to claim an inheritance, Charlie takes Raymond on a road trip that leads to Vegas and redemption. Two brilliant performances are the power that drives this crowd-pleaser. It is not a particularly strong film in visual terms and that is reflected on the DVD with an image that is usually no better than good and only soars in the casino montage. The same is true of sound, but any imperfections in either come from the nature of the original, not the transfer to disc. —*MM*

Movie: 🐾🐾🐾▸ **DVD:** 🐾🐾🐾

MGM Home Entertainment (Cat #906041, UPC #027616604194). Widescreen letterboxed; full frame. Dolby Digital Surround Stereo. $24.98. Snapper. *LANG:* English; French; Spanish. *SUB:* English; French; Spanish. *CAP:* English; French; Spanish. *FEATURES:* 40 chapter links • Theatrical trailer.

1988 (R) 128m/C Dustin Hoffman, Tom Cruise, Valeria Golino, Jerry Molen, Jack Murdock, Michael D. Roberts, Ralph Seymour, Lucinda Jenney, Bonnie Hunt, Kim Robillard, Beth Grant; **D:** Barry Levinson; **W:** Ronald Bass, Barry Morrow; **C:** John Seale; **M:** Hans Zimmer. *AWARDS:* Academy Awards '88: Best Actor (Hoffman), Best Director (Levinson), Best Original Screenplay, Best Picture; Berlin International Film Festival '88: Golden Berlin Bear; Directors Guild of America Awards '88: Best Director (Levinson); Golden Globe Awards '89: Best Actor—Drama (Hoffman), Best Film—Drama; *NOM:* Academy Awards '88: Best Art Direction/Set Decoration, Best Cinematography, Best Film Editing, Best Original Score.

Rainbow Bridge

Hippies search for their consciousness in Hawaii. Concert footage from Jimi Hendrix's final performance is the high point.

Movie: 🐾 **DVD:** NYR

Rhino Home Video (Cat #4461). Full frame. Mono. $24.98. Snapper. *FEATURES:* Trailer.

1971 (R) 74m/C Chuck Wein, Herbie Fletcher, Pat Hartley; **D:** Chuck Wein; **C:** Vilis Lapenieks.

Raising Cain

Poor man's Hitchcock—about a child psychiatrist who just happens to be nuts—features Lithgow in five roles. Seems his supposedly dead Norwegian father has come to the United States and needs his son's help in stealing babies for a child

development experiment, so the son's alter ego, Cain, shows up to commit the nasty deed. Unfortunately, Lithgow also catches his wife with another man, and that's when the bodies start piling up. Director DePalma parodies himself in several scenes and supplies several jumps. Watching this DVD reveals many details that may go unnoticed when watching the VHS tape, making the film even more enjoyable. The image is crisp and colors are true and finely detailed, allowing full appreciation of the lush cinematography and frame composition. A great Dolby Surround mix adds to the atmosphere and suspense. —*JO*

Movie: 🐾🐾🐾 **DVD:** 🐾🐾🐾▸

Universal Studios Home Video (Cat #20386, UPC #025192038624). Widescreen (1.85:1) anamorphic. Dolby Surround. $24.98. Keepcase. *LANG:* English; French; Spanish. *SUB:* Spanish. *CAP:* English. *FEATURES:* 16 chapter links • Theatrical trailer • Cast and filmmakers bios • Production notes • Film highlights.

1992 (R) 95m/C John Lithgow, Lolita (David) Davidovich, Steven Bauer, Frances Sternhagen, Cindy Girard, Tom Bower, Mel Harris, Gabrielle Carteris, Barton Heyman; **D:** Brian DePalma; **W:** Brian DePalma; **C:** Stephen Burum; **M:** Pino Donaggio.

Rambling Rose

Dern is Rose, a free-spirited, sexually liberated before her time young woman taken in by a Southern family in 1935. Rose immediately has an impact on the male members of the clan, father Duvall and son Haas, thanks to her insuppressible sexuality. This causes consternation with the straitlaced patriarch, who attempts to control his desire for the girl. Eventually Rose decides she must go back to one man, but this only causes further problems. Dern gives a fine performance in this excellent period piece, and solid support is offered from the rest of the cast, in particular Duvall and Dern's real-life mother Ladd. This is a superb DVD that both maintains the theatrical presentation of the film and offers an excellent supplemental section, including an alternate ending. Director Coolidge's commentary offers as many insights into filmmaking as any other thus far. The film has a soft feel with very warm colors. The DVD makes no alterations, and at the same time does not have the detail and grain problems that similarly photographed films have. The stereo sound is full and has excellent imaging, at times sounding very much like there is a Surround channel also at work. Don't pass this one up. —*JO*

Movie: 🐾🐾🐾▸ **DVD:** 🐾🐾🐾🐾

Pioneer Entertainment (Cat #DVD 69000WS, UPC #013023014398). Widescreen (1.85:1) letterboxed. Stereo. $24.98. Keepcase. *LANG:* English. *CAP:* English. *FEATURES:* 32 chapter links • Commentary: Martha Coolidge • Interview with Martha Coolidge • Deleted scenes • Alternate ending.

1991 (R) 115m/C Laura Dern, Diane Ladd, Robert Duvall, Lukas Haas, John Heard, Kevin Conway, Robert John Burke, Lisa Jakub, Evan Lockwood; **D:** Martha Coolidge; **W:** Calder Willingham; **C:** Johnny E. Jensen; **M:** Elmer Bernstein. *AWARDS:* Independent Spirit Awards '92: Best Director (Coolidge), Best Film, Best Supporting Actress (Ladd); *NOM:* Academy Awards '91: Best Actress (Dern), Best Supporting Actress (Ladd).

Rambo: First Blood, Part 2

If anyone can save Our Boys still held prisoner in Asia, it's John Rambo. Along the way he's tortured, flexes biceps, grunts, and then disposes of the bad guys by the dozen in one of filmdom's bigger dead-body parades. Mindless action best enjoyed by testosterone-driven fans of the genre. They really did a good job on the *Rambo* discs. Once again, Stallone finds himself surrounded by vibrant colors and taking on any and all minor artifacts that dare to tread upon his DVD's hallowed ground. Excess grain is also afraid to enter the digital battlefield, finding itself repulsed by the power of the mighty Dolby Surround, whose only weakness is slight under-use of the rear channel. In case that's too confusing, this is a very good DVD. —*JO*

Movie: 🐾🐾▸ **DVD:** 🐾🐾🐾▸

Artisan Entertainment (Cat #60466, UPC #012236046608). Widescreen (2.35:1) anamorphic. Dolby Surround. $24.98. Keepcase. *LANG:* English. *SUB:* Spanish. *CAP:* English. *FEATURES:* 36 chapter links • Commentary: director • Documentary • Theatrical trailer • Production notes • Cast and crew filmographies.

1985 (R) 93m/C Sylvester Stallone, Richard Crenna, Charles Napier, Steven Berkoff, Julia Nickson-Soul, Martin Kove; **D:** George P. Cosmatos; **W:** Sylvester Stallone, James Cameron; **C:** Jack Cardiff; **M:** Jerry Goldsmith. *AWARDS:* Golden Raspberry Awards '85: Worst Picture, Worst Actor (Stallone), Worst Screenplay, Worst Song ("Peace In Our Life").

Rambo 3

John Rambo, the famous Vietnam vet turned Buddhist monk, this time invades Afghanistan to rescue his mentor. Meets up with orphan and fights his way around the country. Typically exploitative "kill now, ask questions later" Rambo attack, lacking the sheer volume of no-brainer action of the first two *Rambos*. At the time, the most expensive film ever made, costing $58 million. Filmed in Israel. The excellent colors of the DVD help retain the cartoon-like feel of this last installment in the Rambo series. Add to that a very sharp picture with plenty of contrast, and there is no better way to watch scores of men being killed and things blown to bits. Even without a 5.1 remix, the Dolby Surround puts the viewer in the middle of whizzing bullets and showers of debris from exploding buildings, choppers, and bad guys. —JO

Movie: ♫♫ **DVD:** ♫♫♫►
Artisan Entertainment (Cat #60467, UPC #012236046707). Widescreen (2.35:1) anamorphic. Dolby Surround. $24.98. Keepcase. *LANG:* English. *SUB:* Spanish. *CAP:* English. *FEATURES:* Commentary: director • Featurette • Theatrical trailer • Production notes • Cast and crew info.

1988 (R) 102m/C Sylvester Stallone, Richard Crenna, Marc De Jonge, Kurtwood Smith, Spiros Focas; *D:* Peter McDonald; *W:* Sylvester Stallone; *C:* John Stanier; *M:* Jerry Goldsmith. *AWARDS:* Golden Raspberry Awards '88: Worst Actor (Stallone).

Ran

The culmination of Kurosawa's career stands as his masterpiece, a loose adaption of Shakespeare's *King Lear* with plot elements from *Macbeth*. He's fashioned an epic, heartbreaking statement about honor, ambition, and the futility of war. Aging medieval warlord Hidetora gives control of his empire to his oldest son, creating conflict with two other sons. Soon he's an outcast, as ambition and greed seize the two sons. Stunning battle scenes illuminate the full-blown tragedy of Kurosawa's vision. Superb acting with a scene-stealing Harada as the revenge-minded Lady Kaede. Any Kurosawa film deserves better than this DVD. *Ran*'s incredible use of color and finely detailed scene composition just don't come through on this DVD, with its weak colors and grainy image. That grain only increases in large areas of black. There are also problems dealing with long shots, which seem to cram more into the frame than the DVD can handle. Unfortunately, the letterboxed laserdisc, although sharper, also had very lackluster colors, making the VHS version possibly the best way to own this gorgeous film. —JO

Movie: ♫♫♫♫ **DVD:** ♫♫►
Fox/Lorber Home Video (Cat #FLV5034, UPC #720917503424). Widescreen (2.35:1) letterboxed. Stereo. $34.98. Keepcase. *LANG:* Japanese. *SUB:* English. *FEATURES:* Filmographies and awards • Trailer.

1985 (R) 160m/C *JP FR* Tatsuya Nakadai, Akira Terao, Jinpachi Nezu, Daisuke Ryu, Meiko Harada, Hisashi Igawa, Peter, Kazuo Kato, Takeshi Kato, Jun Tazaki, Toshiya Ito, Yoshiko Miyazaki, Masayuki Yui, Norio Matsui, Takashi Nomura; *D:* Akira Kurosawa; *W:* Akira Kurosawa, Hideo Oguni, Masato Ide; *C:* Asakazu Nakai, Takao Saito, Masaharu Ueda; *M:* Toru Takemitsu. *AWARDS:* Academy Awards '85: Best Costume Design; British Academy Awards '86: Best Foreign Film; Los Angeles Film Critics Association Awards '85: Best Foreign Film; National Board of Review Awards '85: Best Director (Kurosawa); New York Film Critics Awards '85: Best Foreign Film; National Society of Film Critics Awards '85: Best Cinematography, Best Film; *NOM:* Academy Awards

'85: Best Art Direction/Set Decoration, Best Cinematography, Best Director (Kurosawa).

Random Encounter

Romantic murder mystery.
Movie: NYR **DVD:** NYR
York Entertainment (Cat #1006). $24.98. Keepcase. *LANG:* English. *SUB:* Spanish. *FEATURES:* Trailer • Cast and crew thumbnail bios.

1998 100m/C *CA* Elizabeth Berkley, Joel Wyner, Frank Schorpion, Barry Flatman, Mark Walker, Ellen David, Susan Glover, Frank Fontaine; *D:* Douglas Jackson; *W:* Matt Dorff; *C:* Georges Archambault; *M:* Daniel Scott.

Ransom

Tight and crafty thriller proves millionaire airline magnate Tom Mullen (Gibson) is a force to be reckoned with when son Sean (Nolte, son of actor Nick) is kidnapped. A vigilante Donald Trump (only gorgeous and brave), Mullen treats this like a high-stakes business deal and decides to get his kid back by announcing on TV that the $2 million ransom demand will instead become a bounty on the kidnappers. Wife Kate (Russo) predictably flips out but Mullen, after a few encounters with the heinous abductors, has sized them up and is convinced he's done the right thing. Lindo is a by-the-book fed with bad dialogue and Sinise is a cop. Gibson's emergency appendectomy delayed filming but he was soon leaping over cars for director Howard's well-staged action scenes. Based on the 1956 flick starring Glenn Ford. Like *Scream*, the DVD for *Ransom* is not the longest cut of the film available on video. This one runs 121 minutes; the laserdisc runs 138 minutes. Who makes these insipid decisions? Other than that, the DVD looks pretty good with great colors and blacks so deep that they actually make overall film feel much darker. —JO

Movie: ♫♫♫ **DVD:** ♫♫♫
Buena Vista Home Entertainment (Cat #13075, UPC #717951000026). Widescreen (1.85:1) letterboxed. Dolby Digital 5.1. $29.99. Keepcase. *LANG:* English (DD5.1); French. *SUB:* Spanish. *CAP:* English. *FEATURES:* 23 chapter links • Theatrical trailer.

1996 (R) 121m/C Mel Gibson, Rene Russo, Gary Sinise, Delroy Lindo, Brawley Nolte, Lili Taylor, Liev Schreiber, Evan Handler, Dan Hedaya, Paul Guilfoyle, Jose Zuniga, Donnie Wahlberg, Michael Gaston, Nancy Ticotin; *Cameos:* Richard Price; *D:* Ron Howard; *W:* Richard Price, Alexander Ignon; *C:* Piotr Sobocinski; *M:* James Horner. *AWARDS:* *NOM:* Golden Globe Awards '97: Best Actor—Drama (Gibson).

Rasputin the Mad Monk

Hammer recycles both the principal sets and cast members from *Dracula, Prince of Darkness* for this grand melodrama. Natu-

rally, the key is Christopher Lee's energetic portrayal of the famous character. He interprets the monk as a charismatic combination of Jesus, Dracula, and Walt Whitman. Ignore the beard and wig. Listen to his rough loud voice, and notice the way he uses his hands. On the commentary track, Lee tells several stories about his odd connections with the character. When he was a child, he actually met Prince Yusupoff, one of the assassins. Beyond that, he has a fine story about the contradictory details surrounding Rasputin's death. In discussing the film he and his costars Barbara Shelley, Francis Matthews, and Suzan Farmer sound like old friends sitting around over drinks and watching home movies. Their camaraderie certainly seems genuine. On disc, the image is slightly better than the excellent VHS tape. —MM

Movie: ♫♫♫ **DVD:** ♫♫♫
Anchor Bay (Cat #DV10681, UPC #013131068191). Widescreen (2.10:1) letterboxed. Dolby Digital Mono. $29.98. Keepcase. *LANG:* English; French. *FEATURES:* 23 chapter links • Commentary: Lee, Shelley, Matthews, and Farmer • Theatrical trailer • TV spots • *World of Hammer* episode "Christopher Lee."

1966 90m/B *GB* Christopher Lee, Barbara Shelley, Richard Pasco, Francis Matthews, Suzan Farmer, Nicholas Pennell, Renee Asherson, Derek Francis; *D:* Don Sharp; *W:* John (Anthony Hinds) Elder; *C:* Michael Reed; *M:* Don Banks.

The Rat Pack

Cable biopic of Frank Sinatra (Liotta) and pals is quick to believe the most salacious stories about them. Dean Martin (Mantegna), Sammy David Jr. (Cheadle), Joey Bishop (Slayton), and Peter Lawford (McFadyen) get whatever they want in Hollywood and Las Vegas but they run into trouble when they try to cozy up to presidential candidate John F. Kennedy (Petersen). The film is lit and photographed to heighten the tinsel-tacky glamour of the settings, and that quality comes across just fine on DVD. In both image and sound, the disc is slightly better than the original broadcast, as I remember it. It's much better than the tape I made at the time. —MM

Movie: ♫♫♫ **DVD:** ♫♫♫
HBO Home Video (Cat #91551, UPC #026359155123). Full frame. Dolby Digital Surround Stereo. $24.98. Snapper. *LANG:* English; Spanish. *SUB:* English; French; Spanish. *FEATURES:* 13 chapter links • "Making of" featurette • Cast and crew thumbnail biographies.

1998 (R) 120m/C Ray Liotta, Don Cheadle, Angus Macfadyen, Joe Mantegna, Bobby Slayton, William L. Petersen, Zeljko Ivanek, Robert Miranda, Dan O'Herlihy, Deborah Kara Unger, Phyllis Lyons, Megan Dodds; *D:* Rob Cohen; *W:* Kario Salem; *C:* Shane Hurlbut; *M:* Mark Adler.

Raven

A covert mercenary team codenamed Raven is after a Soviet satellite decoder. They're double-crossed by renegade CIA agents, and their leader (Reynolds) decides to get his own brand of justice. Performances aren't great, but neither's the script. Visual noise is present in darker scenes, and framing suffers from pan-and-scan treatment. Soundtrack is OK, but the score is grating. Extras? Nope. —MB

Movie: 🐾 **DVD:** 🐾
Image Entertainment (Cat #ID4263LIDVD, UPC #014381426328). Full frame. Dolby Digital 2.0. $29.99. Snapper. *LANG:* English. *CAP:* English. *FEATURES:* 20 chapter links.
1997 (R) 93m/C Burt Reynolds, Krista Allen, Matt Battaglia, David Ackroyd, Richard Gant; *D:* Russell Solberg; *W:* Jacobsen Hart; *C:* John Dirlam; *M:* Harry Manfredini.

Ravenous

Off-kilter tale of cannibalism in the American West in 1847 (loosely based on the Donner Party) loses its way when it begins to use man-eating soldiers as a metaphor for American settlers carving up the land. When stringy, twitching Colqhoun (Carlyle) shows up starving and nearly frozen at an army fort in the Sierra Nevadas, he tells Captain John Boyd (Pearce) that he was with a party that resorted to eating their dead when stranded. When a team is sent to investigate, more than the facts are digested as Colqhoun is soon extolling the virtues of panfrying your pals to Boyd. The unusual subject and offbeat attempts at humor make this a recipe not for all tastes. The disc features an excellent video transfer that faithfully re-creates the film's foreboding cinematic look. Colors are crisp and blacks are solid. The soundtrack is fantastic, with clear dialogue and a killer musical score. The three audio commentary tracks enhance the technical worth of this disc. —MJT

Movie: 🐾🐾 **DVD:** 🐾🐾🐾
Twentieth Century Fox Home Entertainment (Cat #4111959, UPC #0861621195 90). Widescreen (2.35:1) letterboxed. Dolby Digital 5.1; Dolby Surround. $34.98. Keepcase. *LANG:* English. *SUB:* English; Spanish. *FEATURES:* 26 chapter links ▪ Theatrical trailer ▪ Commentary: director Antonia Bird and composer Damon Albarn ▪ Commentary: actor Robert Carlyle ▪ Commentary: writer Ted Griffin, actor Jeffrey Jones ▪ Deleted scenes, with commentary by director Antonia Bird ▪ Television spots ▪ Photo gallery ▪ Costume and set designs.
1999 (R) 100m/C John Spencer, Stephen Spinella, Neal McDonough, David Arquette, Guy Pearce, Robert Carlyle, Jeremy Davies, Jeffrey Jones; *D:* Antonia Bird; *W:* Ted Griffin; *C:* Anthony B. Richmond; *M:* Michael Nyman, Damon Albarn.

Raw Deal

Sadistic Rick Coyle (Burr) framed one-time associate Joe Sullivan (O'Keefe), who wound up in prison. Joe's moll Pat (Trevor) helps him escape and they take social worker Ann (Hunt), who's befriended Joe, as a hostage. They go after Coyle and Joe begins to fall for the demure dame who finds life on the wild side exciting. No good guys here, but it is fine film noir.

Movie: 🐾🐾🐾 **DVD:** NYR
Kino on Video (Cat #AED2002). Full frame. $39.95. Title is available on the two-disc set "The Film Noir of Anthony Mann" with *TMen* and *He Walked by Night*.
1948 79m/B Dennis O'Keefe, Claire Trevor, Raymond Burr, Marsha Hunt, John Ireland, Curt Conway, Whit Bissell; *D:* Anthony Mann; *W:* John C. Higgins, Leopold Atlas; *C:* John Alton; *M:* Paul Sawtell.

Raw Deal

Don't ever give Schwarzenegger a raw deal! FBI agent Schwarzie infiltrates the mob and shoots lots of people. Unlike later Arnold flicks, this one is played very straight and the violence is taken more seriously. Anchor Bay usually does a pretty good job on their DVDs. On this one, however, the color tints always seem quite a bit off. Blacks are also never precisely there and they pick up a bit of grain in the darker scenes. Picture sharpness is good though, and because of that the DVD is the best way to go on home video. —JO

Movie: 🐾 **DVD:** 🐾🐾
Anchor Bay (Cat #DV10337, UPC #013131033793). Widescreen (1.85:1) letterboxed. Stereo. $24.98. Keepcase. *LANG:* English. *FEATURES:* 27 chapter links.
1986 (R) 106m/C Arnold Schwarzenegger, Kathryn Harrold, Darren McGavin, Sam Wanamaker, Paul Shenar, Steven Hill; *D:* John Irvin; *W:* Patrick Edgeworth, Gary De Vore; *C:* Alex Thomson.

Rawhead Rex

An ancient demon released from his underground prison in Ireland by a plowing farmer begins to decapitate and maim at will. (That's the demon, not the farmer.) Adapted by Clive Barker from his own short story but, be warned, the author later disowned the film.

Movie: 🐾 **DVD:** NYR
Pioneer Entertainment (Cat #DVD5217). Full frame. Dolby Digital Stereo. $24.98. Keepcase.
1987 (R) 89m/C David Dukes, Kelly Piper, Niall Toibin, Niall O'Brien, Donal McCann, Gladys Sheehan, Cora Lunny, Heinrich von Schellendorf; *D:* George Pavlou; *W:* Clive Barker; *C:* John Metcalfe; *M:* Colin Towns.

Razor Blade Smile

Elements of *Dark Shadows*, *La Femme Nikita*, and *The Hunger* are whipped together with a rough Gothy-Grungy atmos-
phere to create this vampire/action exploitation. Lilith Silver (Daly) is an undead hitwoman who, over the decades, has found herself battling Sir Sethane Blake (Adamson). Sometimes amateurish acting and an overreliance on fake fangs and Hong Kong–inspired gun violence give the English import a tongue-in-cheek quality aimed squarely at horror fans. The DVD emphasizes the garish harsh qualities of the low-budget production, pretty much limiting its appeal to those who appreciate the genre. —MM

Movie: 🐾🐾 **DVD:** 🐾🐾
A-PIX Entertainment Inc. (Cat #APX27005, UPC #78372270053). Widescreen (1.85:1) letterboxed. Dolby Stereo 2.0. Keepcase. *LANG:* English. *FEATURES:* 26 chapter links ▪ Theatrical trailer and trailers for four other horror films ▪ *Femme Fatales* magazine article ▪ Stills gallery.
1998 (R) 101m/C GB Eileen Daley, Chris(topher) Adamson, Kevin Howarth, Jonathan Coote, Heidi James, David Warbeck; *D:* Jake West; *W:* Jake West; *C:* James Solan; *M:* Richard Wells.

Re-Animator

Based on an H.P Lovecraft story, this gruesome film is as funny as it is grizzly. Combs is over the top in both energy and camp as a medical student who re-animates the dead (and pieces of the dead). Things go haywire when his professor attempts to take credit for the discovery. Film's extremely dark humor quickly turned it into a cult classic. (On VHS tape, it is also available in an "R"-rated version that substitutes melodrama for gore and is missing the famous "head" joke.) This is the best this movie has ever looked; the DVD offers better color, though less sharpness, than the Elite laserdisc. The DVD sharpness is actually pretty good, but some digital grain in the background of many scenes makes it look soft at times. The blacks are good, and the contrast and brightness is again better than it ever has been on video. Although mono, the sound is full and dynamic (considering the source) and there is more low end than I remember in the theatre. Including the "R"-rated footage in the supplementals is kind of a waste, but the dream sequence is cool, as is the commentary. —JO

Movie: 🐾🐾🐾 **DVD:** 🐾🐾🐾
Elite Entertainment, Inc. (Cat #EE4324, UPC #790594432423). Widescreen (1.85:1) letterboxed. Dolby Digital Mono. $29.95. Keepcase. *LANG:* English. *FEATURES:* Theatrical trailer ▪ Television spots ▪ Commentary: director Stuart Gordon, producer Brian Yuzna, cast members ▪ 20 minutes of additional "R"-rated footage ▪ Dream sequence.
1984 86m/C Jeffrey Combs, Bruce Abbott, Barbara Crampton, David Gale, Robert Sampson, Gerry Black, Carolyn Purdy-Gordon; *D:* Stuart Gordon; *W:* Stuart Gordon, Dennis Paoli, William J. Norris; *C:* Mac Ahlberg; *M:* Richard Band.

Ready to Wear

Altman's take on the fashion business is an expanded version of "The Emperor's New Clothes"—literally. In typical Altman fashion, more than a dozen major and minor characters are caught up in the Paris whirl. His ensemble cast is a veritable who's-who of the movies. One of the best moments comes when Sophia Loren and Marcello Mastroianni re-create their *Yesterday, Today and Tomorrow* boudoir scene, but the big finish is stunning. Kim Basinger also stands out as Texas TV reporter. The whole thing is wonderfully funny (even at two hours-plus) for those who are tuned to Altman's wavelength and, admittedly, not everyone is. The DVD has trouble with the clashing colors and patterns in some outfits, but revealing the pervasive ugliness of the industry is part of the film's point. The stereo sound captures all of the overlapping dialogue. —MM **AKA:** Pret-a-Porter.
Movie: ♫♫♫ **DVD:** ♫♫➧
Miramax Pictures Home Video (Cat #17100). Widescreen (2.35:1) letterboxed. Dolby Digital Stereo. $29.99. Keepcase. *LANG:* English; French. *SUB:* English. *CAP:* English. *FEATURES:* 31 chapter links ➧ Theatrical trailer.
1994 (R) 132m/C Sophia Loren, Marcello Mastroianni, Julia Roberts, Tim Robbins, Kim Basinger, Stephen Rea, Anouk Aimee, Lauren Bacall, Lili Taylor, Sally Kellerman, Tracey Ullman, Linda Hunt, Rupert Everett, Forest Whitaker, Richard E. Grant, Danny Aiello, Teri Garr, Lyle Lovett, Jean Rochefort, Michel Blanc, Anne Canovos, Jean-Pierre Cassel, Francois Cluzet, Rossy de Palma, Kaisa Figura, Sam Robards, Cher, Harry Belafonte, Issey Miyake, Sonia Rykiel, Jean-Paul Gaultier, Thierry Mugler; **D:** Robert Altman; **W:** Barbara Shulgasser, Robert Altman; **C:** Jean Lepine, Pierre Mignot; **M:** Michel Legrand. *AWARDS: NOM:* Golden Globe Awards '95: Best Film—Musical/Comedy, Best Supporting Actress (Loren).

The Real Blonde

Entertaining ensemble piece daringly exposes the business side of show business through a disillusioned actor, his beleaguered girlfriend, and Bob (Caulfield), a successful soap star searching for a peroxide-free blonde in New York. The main focus is on feuding couple Joe and Mary (Modine and Keener), but that angle is undercut by the industry mania that surrounds them. Intelligent writing and caustic wit provide a few memorable scenes, such as the "Il Piano" debate in a crowded restaurant over a thinly veiled "acclaimed independent film" and Bob's resolution to his blonde quest. Modine also revs things up in an emotional improv. Thomas stands out from the crowd as a pretentious fashion photographer.
Movie: ♫♫➧ **DVD:** NYR
Paramount Home Video (Cat #334947). Dolby Digital 5.1 Surround Stereo. $29.99. Keepcase. *LANG:* English; French. *CAP:* English. *FEATURES:* Trailer.

1997 (R) 105m/C Matthew Modine, Catherine Keener, Daryl Hannah, Maxwell Caulfield, Elizabeth Berkley, Marlo Thomas, Buck Henry, Bridgette Wilson, Christopher Lloyd, Kathleen Turner, Denis Leary; **Cameos:** Steve Buscemi; **D:** Tom DiCillo; **W:** Tom DiCillo; **C:** Frank Prinzi; **M:** Jim Farmer.

The Real McCoy

Slow, simple caper movie is never believable on any level. Neither the technical details of the heist itself nor the characters—including Kim Basinger as the mom turned cat burglar—are remotely realistic. From the overly tricky introduction to the confusing finish, this one's a stinker. On DVD, it's a fairly attractive stinker with an image that's equal to the theatrical release in most scenes. Diagonal lines tend to break up, but that's a meaningless flaw in a negligible movie. —MM
Movie: woof **DVD:** ♫♫
Universal Studios Home Video (Cat #20397, UPC #025192039720). Widescreen (1.85:1) letterboxed. Dolby Digital 5.1 Surround Stereo; Dolby Digital Surround Stereo. $24.98. Keepcase. *LANG:* English; Spanish; French. *SUB:* Spanish. *CAP:* English. *FEATURES:* 16 chapter links ➧ Production notes ➧ Cast and crew thumbnail biographies ➧ Theatrical trailer ➧ Universal web links.
1993 (PG-13) 104m/C Kim Basinger, Val Kilmer, Terence Stamp, Zach English, Gailard Sartain; **D:** Russell Mulcahy; **W:** William Davies, William Osborne; **C:** Denis Crossan; **M:** Brad Fiedel.

Reality Bites

Humorous look at four recent college grads living, working, and slacking in Houston. Script by newcomer Childress is at its best when highlighting the trends: 7-Eleven Big Gulps, tacky '70s memorabilia, and games revolving around episodes of old TV shows like *Good Times,* to name a few. Definite appeal for those in their early 20s, but anyone over 25 may encounter a "Generation X-er" gap, a noticeable problem since *Reality* claims to speak for the entire twentysomething generation. Decent directorial debut for Stiller; good cast, particularly Garofalo, in her film debut. This film is dialogue driven and consequently, the 5.1 sound is a bit of a waste, especially since it is not even used to give a little more life to the music. Overall the DVD is pretty good though, with decent sharpness and bright colors, supported ably by smooth contrast and good brightness. —JO
Movie: ♫♫➧ **DVD:** ♫♫♫
Universal Studios Home Video (Cat #20234, UPC #025192023422). Widescreen (1.85:1) anamorphic. Dolby Digital 5.1; Dolby Surround. $24.98. Keepcase. *LANG:* English (DD5.1; DS); French (DS). *SUB:* Spanish. *CAP:* English. *FEATURES:* 16 chapter links.
1994 (PG-13) 99m/C Winona Ryder, Ethan Hawke, Ben Stiller, Janeane Garofa-

lo, Steve Zahn, Swoosie Kurtz, Joe Don Baker, John Mahoney; **Cameos:** David Pirner, Anne Meara, Jeanne Tripplehorn, Karen Duffy, Evan Dando; **D:** Ben Stiller; **W:** Helen Childress; **C:** Emmanuel Lubezki; **M:** Karl Wallinger. *AWARDS: NOM:* MTV Movie Awards '94: Best Kiss (Ethan Hawke/Winona Ryder).

Reap the Wild Wind

DeMille mini-epic focuses on salvagers off the Florida Keys in the 1840s. Wayne is the heroic captain; the villains are Massey and a giant squid. Good cast, lesser story; dated effects. On DVD, the Technicolor is exceptionally grainy. That comes from the original. The faint scratches and snow come from wear. —MM
Movie: ♫♫ **DVD:** ♫♫
MGM Home Entertainment (Cat #20437, UPC #025192043727). Full frame. Dolby Digital Mono. $24.98. Keepcase. *LANG:* English; Spanish. *SUB:* French; Spanish. *CAP:* English. *FEATURES:* 18 chapter links.
1942 123m/C Ray Milland, John Wayne, Paulette Goddard, Raymond Massey, Robert Preston, Lynne Overman, Susan Hayward, Charles Bickford, Walter Hampden, Louise Beavers, Martha O'Driscoll, Elisabeth Risdon, Hedda Hopper, Raymond Hatton, Barbara Britton; **D:** Cecil B. DeMille; **W:** Charles Bennett, Jesse Lasky Jr., Alan LeMay; **C:** Victor Milner; **M:** Victor Young. *AWARDS: NOM:* Academy Awards '42: Best Color Cinematography.

Rebecca

This is the only one of Hitch's films to win a Best Picture Academy Award, though the statue went to producer Selznick. (Hitchcock himself never won an Oscar.) The film may be his most lavish black-and-white effort with memorable sets, a Franz Waxman score, and Oscar-winning photography by George Barnes. Olivier is suitably grim and haughty as Maxim deWinter, wealthy widower of the titular Rebecca, a *femme* so *fatale* she wore "underwear made by nuns." Joan Fontaine is mousily gorgeous as the nameless heroine who becomes Cinderella to Maxim's Prince not-so-Charming. Both of them are overshadowed by Judith Anderson's Mrs. Danvers, one of the screen's most memorable villains. The DVD does justice to their fine work, showing off the detailed and deeply shaded photography. And since the film was made for a conventional-sized screen, the image loses nothing in translation to video. Even without extras, the disc is one of the best. —MM
Movie: ♫♫♫♫ **DVD:** ♫♫♫
Anchor Bay (Cat #DV10808, UPC #013131 080896). Full frame. Dolby Digital Mono. $24.98. Keepcase. *LANG:* English. *FEATURES:* 19 chapter links.
1940 130m/B Joan Fontaine, Laurence Olivier, Judith Anderson, George Sanders, Nigel Bruce, Florence Bates, Gladys Cooper, Reginald Denny, Leo G. Carroll, Sir C. Aubrey Smith, Melville Cooper; **D:** Alfred Hitchcock; **W:** Joan Harrison, Robert Sher-

wood; **C:** George Barnes; **M:** Franz Waxman. *AWARDS:* Academy Awards '40: Best Black-and-white Cinematography, Best Picture; *NOM:* Academy Awards '40: Best Actor (Olivier), Best Actress (Fontaine), Best Director (Hitchcock), Best Film Editing, Best Screenplay, Best Supporting Actress (Anderson), Best Original Score.

Rebel Rousers

A motorcycle gang wreaks havoc in a small town where a drag race is being held. Dern's pregnant girlfriend is the prize. A young Nicholson in striped pants steals the show.
Movie: 🐾🐾 **DVD:** NYR
Victory Multimedia (Cat #2210). Full frame. $24.98. Keepcase.
1969 81m/C Jack Nicholson, Cameron Mitchell, Diane Ladd, Bruce Dern, Harry Dean Stanton; **D:** Martin B. Cohen; **W:** Martin B. Cohen, Abe Polsky, Michael Kars; **C:** Laszlo Kovacs, Glen R. Smith; **M:** William Loose.

Rebel without a Cause

James Dean's most memorable screen appearance is the second of his three films. He's Jim Stark, a troubled, alienated teen, new in town, who eventually befriends equally troubled and alienated Wood and Mineo. The key scenes have been parodied and ripped off so many times that the picture is almost a long cliche, but the performances save it. Certainly, the untimely ends met by the three have something to do with the film's enduring cult status. The DVD includes the California highway safety film that Dean made before his death in a car crash. The picture on this disc is practically picture-perfect and beautiful, especially considering the film's age. Without defects, the presentation boasts rich, fully saturated colors. Together with the deep blacks and natural fleshtones, watching the movie on this DVD is a sheer pleasure. No compression artifacts of any sort are evident in the transfer. The new 5.1 Surround remix is restrained, but the audio has a great, engulfing quality. The sound is never harsh or distorted, which is usually a sign of the film's age, making this an all-round perfect DVD. *—GH*
Movie: 🐾🐾🐾🐾 **DVD:** 🐾🐾🐾🐾
Warner Home Video, Inc. (Cat #14069, UPC #085391406921). Widescreen (2.35:1) anamorphic. Dolby Digital 5.1 Surround. $24.98. Snapper. *LANG:* English; French. *SUB:* French. *CAP:* English. *FEATURES:* 35 chapter links • 3 TV documentaries • "Rediscovering a Rebel" documentary • Biographies • Trailers • Production notes.
1955 111m/C James Dean, Natalie Wood, Sal Mineo, Jim Backus, Nick Adams, Dennis Hopper, Ann Doran, William Hopper, Rochelle Hudson, Corey Allen, Edward Platt; **D:** Nicholas Ray; **W:** Irving Shulman, Stewart Stern; **C:** Ernest Haller; **M:** Leonard Rosenman. *AWARDS:* American Film Institute (AFI) '98: Top 100, National Film Registry '90; *NOM:* Academy Awards '55: Best Story, Best Supporting Actor (Mineo), Best Supporting Actress (Wood).

Record of Lodoss War

Lodoss is a cursed island facing an awakening evil. Six warriors are drawn together, destined to become heroes in the forthcoming battle. Nothing innovative here, but still popular with anime fans who can't get enough. For an animated film, the DVD presentation is pretty weak. The picture is a little soft and the color is nowhere near as vibrant as on most other anime DVDs. There even seems to be a little bleed, and that's very rare with animation. A boost to the contrast might have helped a bit. The sound is also nothing special with O.K. dynamics, but fails to make much use of the stereo separation. *—JO*
Movie: 🐾🐾 **DVD:** 🐾
Central Park Media/U.S. Manga Corps (Cat #ID4411CTDVD, UPC #014381441123). Full frame. Stereo. $59.95. Snapper. *LANG:* English; Japanese. *SUB:* English. *FEATURES:* 59 chapter links • "Making of" documentary.
1990 ?m/C JP

Red Cherry

Story of the aftermath of the Chinese revolution in 1940 is based on truth. The orphaned Chuchu (Ke-Yu) and Luo (Xiaoli) are sent to a Russian school outside Moscow and settle into their new lives. But their precarious happiness is shattered when German troops invade during WWII. *AKA:* Hong Ying Tao.
Movie: 🐾🐾 **DVD:** NYR
WinStar Home Entertainment (Cat #5110). Full frame. Stereo. $29.98. Keepcase. *LANG:* Mandarin. *SUB:* English.
1995 (PG-13) 120m/C CH Guo Ke-Yu, Xu Xiaoli; **D:** Ye Ying.

Red Corner

Wrong-man scenario features American entertainment lawyer Jack Moore (Gere) being framed for the murder of a Chinese model he spent the night with in Beijing. As Jack's beautiful court-appointed attorney (Ling) explains the Chinese legal process: "If you plead not guilty, you will be shot within a week and the cost of the bullet will be charged to your family," but when she discovers inconsistencies in the case against him, she decides to help. The usual suspense cliches are balanced against a fine performance from Bai Ling and a good one from Gere. Director Avnet adds a political edge to his commentary track. The DVD image ranges between excellent and very good, reflecting the source material. Sound is fine. *—MM*
Movie: 🐾🐾 **DVD:** 🐾🐾🐾
MGM Home Entertainment (Cat #907023, UPC #027616702326). Widescreen anamorphic. Dolby Digital 5.1 Surround Stereo. $24.98. Keepcase. *LANG:* English; French. *SUB:* English; French; Spanish. *FEATURES:* 32 chapter links • Theatrical trailer.
1997 (R) 118m/C Richard Gere, Bai Ling, Byron Mann, Bradley Whitford, Peter Donat, Robert Stanton, Tsai Chin, James Hong, Tzi Ma, Richard Venture; **D:** Jon Avnet; **W:** Robert King; **C:** Karl Walter Lindenlaub; **M:** Thomas Newman.

Red Dawn

Russians, Cubans, and Nicaraguans overrun America. It's up to small-town teens to form a guerrilla band to drive the invaders out. Perhaps the most idiotic right-wing fantasy ever committed to film is a failure in every respect. The characters are poorly differentiated; interiors are overly dark. A talented young cast is left with little to do. Those are the most significant flaws of the original theatrical release. The image on the disc I attempted to watch (a rental copy) broke up into large pixels at regular intervals, though that might have been my machine's reaction to the film's overall ineptitude. *—MM*
Movie: woof **DVD:** 🐾
MGM Home Entertainment (Cat #906998, UPC #027616699824). Widescreen letterboxed; full frame. Dolby Digital Surround Stereo. $24.98. Keepcase. *LANG:* English; French. *SUB:* English; French; Spanish. *FEATURES:* 32 chapter links • Theatrical trailer • Production notes.
1984 (PG-13) 114m/C Patrick Swayze, C. Thomas Howell, Harry Dean Stanton, Powers Boothe, Lea Thompson, Charlie Sheen, Ben Johnson, Jennifer Grey, Ron O'Neal, William Smith; **D:** John Milius; **W:** John Milius, Kevin Reynolds; **C:** Ric Waite; **M:** Basil Poledouris.

The Red Desert

Antonioni's study of ennui, angst, and alienation is visually impressive—often in negative ways—and dramatically stultifying. Like so many European intellectual films of the 1960s, it contains almost no action. Instead, it's focused on a grim landscape and characters who cannot escape it. Do not attempt to adjust your DVD player during the out-of-focus opening credits. They're supposed to be that way. When cinematographer Carlo Di Palma gets his lenses sharpened up, viewers realize that they're trapped in a bleak Italian industrial wasteland where Monica Vitti and Richard Harris are having a passionless affair. Antonioni is often intentionally off-putting with dissonant sounds, clashing colors, and cramped compositions, all strikingly rendered on the disc. *—MM* *AKA:* Il Deserto Rosso.
Movie: 🐾🐾🐾 **DVD:** 🐾🐾🐾
Image Entertainment (Cat #ID4780SIDVD, UPC #014381478020). Widescreen (1.85:1) letterboxed. Dolby Digital Mono. $24.99. Snapper. *LANG:* Italian. *SUB:* English. *FEATURES:* 16 chapter links.
1964 120m/C IT Monica Vitti, Richard Harris, Carlos Chionetti; **D:** Michelangelo Antonioni; **W:** Michelangelo Antonioni, Tonino Guerra; **C:** Carlo Di Palma; **M:** Gio-

vanni Fusco. *AWARDS:* Venice Film Festival '64: Best Film.

Red Heat

Two cops—one from the Soviet Union (Schwarzenegger), one from Chicago (Belushi)—team up to catch the Eastern Bloc's biggest drug czar. Buddy-buddy stuff is familiar, but very few can direct action sequences like Hill. Film claims to be the first major U.S. production shot in Red Square, Moscow. The DVD's 5.1 sound is so intense it's scary. The film features almost nonstop action and your speakers will be rumbling and screaming all the way throughout, from the punches thrown in the opening Russian scene to the incredible bus chase. The image is sharp and clean with excellent colors and blacks. —JO

Movie: 🎵🎵 *DVD:* 🎵🎵🎵►
Artisan Entertainment (Cat #60445, UPC #012236044505). Widescreen (1.85:1) letterboxed; full frame. Dolby Digital 5.1; Dolby Surround; Mono. $24.98. Snapper. *LANG:* English (DD5.1); French (DS); Spanish (mono). *SUB:* English; French; Spanish. *CAP:* English. *FEATURES:* 52 chapter links • Theatrical trailer • Cast and crew bios • Production notes.
1988 (R) 106m/C Arnold Schwarzenegger, James Belushi, Peter Boyle, Ed O'Ross, Laurence "Larry" Fishburne, Gina Gershon, Richard Bright; *D:* Walter Hill; *W:* Walter Hill; *C:* Matthew F. Leonetti; *M:* James Horner.

The Red House

Robinson plays a crippled farmer who, after his daughter brings home a suitor, attempts to keep everyone away from a mysterious red house located on his property. Madness and murder prevail. Strange film noir based on George Agnew Chamberlain's novel revolves around tangled relationships and unsuccessful attempts to bury a horrid past. Initially, the soundtrack is filled with buzzy static but that clears up, to a degree. The image is scratched heavily in some scenes, more lightly in others. On average, it's about what you'd expect for a film of its age. —MM

Movie: 🎵🎵🎵 *DVD:* 🎵🎵
Madacy Entertainment (Cat #990573). Full frame. Dolby Digital Mono. $9.99. Keepcase. *LANG:* English. *FEATURES:* Cast and crew thumbnail bios • 8 chapter links • Edgar G. Robinson biography and filmography • Historical notes.
1947 100m/B Edward G. Robinson, Lon McCallister, Judith Anderson, Allene Roberts, Rory Calhoun, Ona Munson, Julie London, Harry Shannon, Arthur Space, Walter Sande, Pat Flaherty; *D:* Delmer Daves; *W:* Delmer Daves; *C:* Bert Glennon; *M:* Miklos Rozsa.

Red Line

Stock-car racer Jim (McQueen) loses his sponsorship, turns to petty crime to settle his debts, and winds up in trouble with the mob when he hooks up with a couple of hoods to steal some diamonds. "What do you think of those shocks?" one character asks another. The answer: "A little stiff." Yeah, well so's the acting, but some of the action sequences are fun. Video generally looks good, especially during the car chase early on. It's not widescreen, but that doesn't seem a problem. Disc sounds O.K., too. No extras; no need. —MB

Movie: 🎵► *DVD:* 🎵🎵►
Image Entertainment (Cat #ID5619FMDVD, UPC #014381561920). Full frame. Dolby Digital Stereo. $24.98. Snapper. *LANG:* English. *FEATURES:* 10 chapter links.
1996 (R) 102m/C Chad McQueen, Michael Madsen, Corey Feldman, Jan-Michael Vincent, Roxana Zal, Dom DeLuise, Julie Strain, Robert Z'Dar; *D:* John Sjogren; *W:* John Sjogren, Scott Ziehl, Rolfe Kanefsky; *C:* Kevin McKay; *M:* Craig Carothers, Junior Walker.

Red River

The classic Hawks epic about a grueling cattle drive and the battle of wills between father (Wayne) and son (Clift, in his first film). Generally regarded as one of the best westerns ever made, with Wayne's shining moment as a reprehensible, obsessive man. Large-scale action from gunfights to cattle stampede. This film holds up very well and the DVD's crisp black-and-white image is really invigorating. The transfer is so clean that any flaws can be blamed on the preprint material. Graytones and blacks are both excellent, and there's none of that overexposed ghosting one finds on a lot of older B&W films. The sound is a little dull, but for the most part is distortion-free. —JO

Movie: 🎵🎵🎵🎵 *DVD:* 🎵🎵🎵►
MGM Home Entertainment (Cat #906042, UPC #027616604224). Full frame. Mono. $24.98. Snapper. *LANG:* English. *SUB:* English; French; Spanish. *CAP:* English. *FEATURES:* 32 chapter links.
1948 133m/B John Wayne, Montgomery Clift, Walter Brennan, Joanne Dru, John Ireland, Noah Beery Jr., Paul Fix, Coleen Gray, Harry Carey Jr., Harry Carey Sr., Chief Yowlachie, Hank Worden; *D:* Howard Hawks; *W:* Borden Chase, Charles Schnee; *C:* Russell Harlan; *M:* Dimitri Tiomkin. *AWARDS:* National Film Registry '90; *NOM:* Academy Awards '48: Best Film Editing, Best Story.

Red Scorpion

A Soviet soldier (Lundgren) travels to Africa where he is to assassinate the leader of a rebel group. Will he succeed or will he switch sides? Poor acting and directing.
Movie: 🎵 *DVD:* NYR
Simitar Entertainment (Cat #7388). Full frame. Dolby Digital 5.1 Surround Stereo. $19.98. Keepcase. *FEATURES:* Cast and crew thumbnail bios • Production notes.
1989 (R) 102m/C Dolph Lundgren, M. Emmet Walsh, Al White, T.P. McKenna, Carmen Argenziano, Brion James, Regopstann; *D:* Joseph Zito; *W:* Arne Olsen, Jack Abramoff, Robert Abramoff; *C:* Joao Fernandes; *M:* Jay Chattaway.

The Red Shoes

The post-war British classic (inspired by a Hans Christian Andersen fairy tale) about a ballerina (Shearer) torn between love and career gets the full treatment on DVD. The image transfer—supervised by legendary cinematographer Jack Cardiff—maintains the voluptuous colors of the original 3-strip Technicolor process. Reds, of course, predominate and the more intense concentrations bleed a bit, though that is hardly a problem with a production that's often abstract and seldom aims for complete realism. Color is part of the narrative texture of the film and, like the rest, should not be taken literally. That's made clear in the complex commentary track, which has its own index, where film historian Ian Christie weaves in the ideas of the stars, Cardiff, composer Brian Easdale, and Martin Scorsese, who talks at length about the film's influence on his work. They all understand that *The Red Shoes* is one of those rare works that exists in a realm of its own and so conventional criticism is pointless. This lavish package ought to please even the most obsessive fan. —MM

Movie: 🎵🎵🎵🎵 *DVD:* 🎵🎵🎵🎵
Criterion Collection (Cat #44, UPC #037429128220). Full frame. Dolby Digital Mono. $39.95. Keepcase. *LANG:* English. *SUB:* English. *FEATURES:* Commentary: Christie, Goring, Shearer, Cardiff, Easdale, Scorsese • Excerpts from the novel *The Red Shoes,* read by Jeremy Irons • Scorsese's collection of memorabilia • "The Red Shoes Sketches," an animated film made from storyboards • Theatrical trailer • 36 chapter links • Powell and Pressburger filmography with clips and stills.
1948 136m/C *GB* Anton Walbrook, Moira Shearer, Marius Goring, Leonide Massine, Robert Helpmann, Albert Bassermann, Ludmila Tcherina, Esmond Knight; *D:* Emeric Pressburger, Michael Powell; *W:* Emeric Pressburger, Michael Powell; *C:* Jack Cardiff; *M:* Brian Easdale. *AWARDS:* Academy Awards '48: Best Art Direction/Set Decoration (Color), Best Original Dramatic Score; Golden Globe Awards '49: Best Score; *NOM:* Academy Awards '48: Best Film Editing, Best Picture, Best Story.

Red Surf

Action abounds in this surfer flick. A couple of hard-nosed wave-riders (pre-*ER* Clooney and Savant) become involved with big money drug gangs.
Movie: 🎵🎵 *DVD:* NYR
Tapeworm Video Distributors (Cat #303). Full frame. $19.95. Keepcase.
1990 (R) 104m/C George Clooney, Doug Savant, Dedee Pfeiffer, Gene Simmons, Rick Najera, Philip McKeon; *D:* H. Gordon

Boos; **W:** Vincent Robert; **C:** John Schwartzman; **M:** Sasha Matson.

The Red Violin

A 17th-century Italian Tarot card reading is the central event in this curiously constructed musical drama. It also concerns the violin that is made at the same time by master Bussotti (Cecchi). His pregnant wife (Grazioli) has the reading, and the violin is made to honor her. The rest of the film follows the instrument over the centuries as it passes from hand to hand, precipitating dramatic events wherever it appears, and finally arriving at a Montreal auction. The various episodes are of uneven quality but the complex plot machinations and the tremendous Oscar-winning score bind the film together nicely and carry it over the rough patches. The various languages are always subtitled in English. The DVD image is fine but unspectacular. Sound is much better. For those lacking a full home theatre stereo system, headphones are recommended. Director Girard also made the underrated and equally unusual *32 Short Films about Glenn Gould*. —MM **AKA:** Le Violon Rouge.
Movie: 🎻🎻🎻 **DVD:** 🎻🎻🎻
Universal Studios Home Video (Cat #20676, UPC #025192067624). Widescreen (1.85:1) anamorphic. Dolby Digital 5.1 Surround Stereo. $29.98. Keepcase. *LANG:* English; French; German; Chinese. *SUB:* English. *CAP:* English. *FEATURES:* 18 chapter links ☞ Production notes ☞ Cast and crew thumbnail biographies ☞ Trailer ☞ Isolated music track.
1998 (R) 131m/C CA Samuel L. Jackson, Don McKellar, Carlo Cecchi, Irene Grazioli, Jean-Luc Bideau, Jason Flemyng, Greta Scacchi, Christoph Koncz, Sylvia Chang, Colm Feore, Monique Mercure, Liu Zi Feng; **D:** Francois Girard; **W:** Don McKellar, Francois Girard; **C:** Alan Dostie; **M:** John Corigliano. *AWARDS:* Academy Awards '99: Best Original Score; Genie Awards '98: Best Art Direction/Set Decoration, Best Cinematography, Best Costume Design, Best Director (Girard), Best Film, Best Screenplay, Best Score; *NOM:* Genie Awards '98: Best Film Editing; Golden Globe Awards '00: Best Foreign Film.

Redline

Fair low-budget sf adventure revolves around "biosynthetic computer chips," a nasty-looking special effect that combines electronics with a pulsating little bit of tissue. The setting is Russia (actually Hungary) where smuggler John Wade (Hauer) is doublecrossed by his partner (Dacascos) who kills him. But he is reborn through one of the thingamabobs and sets off for revenge. On DVD, the image is sharp enough to clearly delineate the computer-generated effects from the "real" action, but that's not really a problem because some of those effects are pretty cool. The full-frame image is slightly better

than tape. The same goes for sound. —MM **AKA:** Deathline.
Movie: 🎻🎻 **DVD:** 🎻🎻
Image Entertainment (Cat #ID6314NGDVD, UPC #014381631425). Full frame. Dolby Digital Surround Stereo. $24.99. Snapper. *LANG:* English. *FEATURES:* 17 chapter links ☞ Theatrical trailer.
1997 (R) 96m/C Rutger Hauer, Mark Dacascos, Yvonne Scio, John Thompson; **D:** Tibor Takacs, Brian Irving; **W:** Tibor Takacs, Brian Irving; **C:** Zoltan David; **M:** Guy Zerafa.

Reefer Madness

Considered serious at the time of its release, this low-budget depiction of the horrors of marijuana has become an underground comedy favorite. Overwrought acting and an equally lurid script contribute to the fun. **AKA:** Tell Your Children; Dope Addict; Doped Youth; Love Madness; The Burning Question.
Movie: 🎻🎻 **DVD:** NYR
Madacy Entertainment (Cat #99026). Full frame. Dolby Digital Mono. $9.99. Keepcase. *FEATURES:* Cast and crew thumbnail bios.
1938 (PG) 67m/B Dave O'Brien, Dorothy Short, Warren McCollum, Lillian Miles, Thelma White, Carleton Young, Josef Forte, Harry Harvey Jr., Pat Royale; **D:** Louis Gasnier; **W:** Paul Franklin, Arthur Hoerl; **C:** Jack Greenhalgh; **M:** Abe Meyer.

Regina

Vaguely reminiscent of *Who's Afraid of Virginia Woolf?* this drama about a family with a dark secret slowly reveals itself over the dinner table. Gardner is a woman who controls all the activities of her ailing husband (Quinn, in a remarkable performance) and adult son (Sharkey). At age 36, her son is ready to leave home, but she refuses to let him go. Karina is the son's wife-to-be, who is bewildered by the goings-on in the home of her prospective in-laws. Strong performances all around make this a strange and disturbing film. In fact, you should buy this disc only to appreciate those performances, as this is a stinker of a DVD technically. The picture and sound are poor, resembling a home VHS recording more than a professionally mastered video on any format. There aren't even any chapter stops, much less niceties such as subtitles and alternate languages. —MB **AKA:** Regina Roma.
Movie: 🎻🎻 **DVD:** woof
Digital Versatile Disc Ltd. (Cat #DVD109, UPC #06647910109). Full frame. Dolby Digital Mono. $19.98. Keepcase. *LANG:* English. *SUB:* English. *CAP:* English.
1983 86m/C IT Anthony Quinn, Ava Gardner, Ray Sharkey, Anna Karina; **D:** Jean-Yves Prate.

Rehearsal for Murder

A year ago, playwright Alex Dennison's (Preston) fiancée Monica (Redgrave) committed suicide. It was the night of her

Broadway debut. He invites her castmates to a dark theatre for a read-through of his new play and it becomes clear that he thinks her death was murder. Very clever made-for-TV whodunnit comes from the creative team behind *Columbo*. It also features a first-rate cast. Unfortunately, it suffers on DVD. The image is unusually grainy, dim, and dark. This one cries out for a remake. —MM
Movie: 🎻🎻🎻 **DVD:** 🎻🎻
Simitar Entertainment (Cat #7529, UPC #082551752928). Full frame. Dolby Digital Stereo. $14.98. Keepcase. *LANG:* English. *FEATURES:* 8 chapter links ☞ Robert Preston filmography.
1982 96m/C Robert Preston, Lynn Redgrave, Patrick Macnee, Lawrence Pressman, Madolyn Smith, Jeff Goldblum, William Daniels; **D:** David Greene; **W:** Richard Levinson, William Link; **C:** Stevan Larner; **M:** Billy Goldenberg.

The Reincarnation of Isabel

This is a great Eurosleaze party flick that's light on plot but filled with nudity and gore (including a nasty impaling or two). The basic story revolves around a group of people who meet up at a castle, only to have the castle's past inhabitants sadistic ways wreak havoc upon them. Good campy fun and a fine addition to the library of any collector of the genre. As in several other Image releases of this ilk, colors are a little weak and there is quite a bit of preprint damage. The image is sharp enough, though, and the mono sound is good enough for a subtitled film. —JO **AKA:** Riti, Magie Nere e Segrete Orgel nel Trecento; Black Magic Rites: Reincarnations; The Ghastly Orgies of Count Dracula; The Horrible Orgies of Count Dracula; La Reincarnazione.
Movie: 🎻🎻 **DVD:** 🎻🎻
Image Entertainment (Cat #ID4610SA, UPC #014381461022!). Widescreen (1.66:1) letterboxed. Mono. $24.99. Snapper. *LANG:* Italian. *SUB:* English. *FEATURES:* 14 chapter links ☞ Theatrical trailer.
1972 ?m/C IT Mickey Hargitay, Consolata Moschera, William Darni, Max Dorian, Rita Calderoni, Raoul Traucher, Christa Barrymore, Marcello Bonini; **D:** Renato Polselli; **C:** Ugo Brunelli; **M:** Romolo Forlai, Gianfranco Reverberi.

The Relic

Following an exposition-packed South American introduction, the scene shifts to a Chicago natural history museum and the labyrinth of sewers and tunnels beneath it. That's where a mutant monster decapitates supporting characters and eats their hypothalamuses (hypothalami?). A tough cop (Sizemore) and a tough evolutionary biologist (Miller) set things right. The overqualified supporting cast members make the most of their tissue thin backup roles. Journeyman filmmaker Peter Hyams is an excellent director of photography and a so-so director. He creates an effective sense of place—overusing *The X-Files* device of flashlights cutting through gloomy darkness—and wisely keeps his monster under wraps until the third act when he reveals just enough of Stan Winston's beastie. Somehow, the whole thing is much more entertaining than it ought to be. On DVD, heavily shadowed blacks tend to swallow shapes, and much of the action takes place in the dark. Closely spaced lines flash. —*MM*

Movie: ♫♫♫ **DVD:** ♫♫♫
Paramount Home Video (Cat #331547, UPC #097363315476). Widescreen (1.66:1) anamorphic. Dolby Digital 5.1 Surround English; Dolby Surround Stereo. $29.99. Keepcase. *LANG:* English; French. *FEATURES:* 19 chapter links ▪ Theatrical trailer.
1996 (R) 110m/C Penelope Ann Miller, Tom Sizemore, Linda Hunt, James Whitmore, Clayton Rohner, Thomas Ryan, Lewis Van Bergen, Chi Muoi Lo, Robert Lesser; *D:* Peter Hyams; *W:* Amy Holden Jones, John Raffo, Rick Jaffa, Amanda Silver; *C:* Peter Hyams; *M:* John Debney.

Rent–A–Cop

Det. Tony Church (Reynolds) is bounced from the force after he survives a drug-bust massacre under suspicious circumstances. He becomes a security guard and continues to track down the still-at-large killer (Remar) with the help of call-girl Della Roberts (Minelli). Nothing but the minimal extras differentiate this pan-and-scan image from VHS tape. —*MM*

Movie: ♫♫ **DVD:** ♫♫
Trimark Home Video (Cat #7260D, UPC #031398726036). Full frame. Dolby Digital Stereo. $19.99. Keepcase. *LANG:* English. *FEATURES:* 21 chapter links ▪ Trailer ▪ Cast bios.
1988 (R) 95m/C Burt Reynolds, Liza Minnelli, James Remar, Richard Masur, Bernie Casey, John Stanton, John P. Ryan, Dionne Warwick, Robby Benson; *D:* Jerry London; *W:* Michael Blodgett; *C:* Giuseppe Rotunno; *M:* Jerry Goldsmith. *AWARDS:* Golden Raspberry Awards '88: Worst Actress (Minnelli).

The Replacement Killers

Hong Kong action star Chow Yun-Fat makes his American debut in this somewhat disappointing first feature from director Antoine Fuqua. Chow stars as John Lee, an assassin working for crime boss Mr. Wei (Tsang). When Lee decides not to carry out a hit on a cop's (Rooker) son, he becomes the target of the men sent to replace him. Needing a passport to get back to China, Lee goes to forger Meg Coburn (Sorvino). Before she can finish the papers, Wei's men begin the first of many high body-count gun battles. Fuqua, who was heavily influenced by John Woo (one of the film's exec producers), does a passable job of conveying the style of Chow and Woo's Hong Kong work, but he

doesn't leave much room for the substance. Chow's subtlety and charisma are crammed into a mechanical action plot, and only his talent saves the whole thing from imploding. The violence is very slick and usually takes place in scenes with darker hues accenting the stylized approach. The image on the DVD stays sharp and artifact-free under all conditions and there is nary a hint of grain. The Surround and subwoofer tracks really kick in during the numerous hail-of-bullets gun battles, yet the overall sound is dynamic enough to allow for whispers, footsteps on the pavement, and of course, the sensitive sound of an automatic chambering a bullet, over and over. —*JO*

Movie: ♫♫▶ **DVD:** ♫♫♫
Columbia Tristar Home Video (Cat #21629, UPC #043396216297). Widescreen (2.35:1) anamorphic; full frame. Dolby Digital 5.1; Stereo. $29.95. Keepcase. *LANG:* English; French; Spanish. *SUB:* English; French; Spanish. *CAP:* English. *FEATURES:* 28 chapter links ▪ Featurette.
1998 (R) 86m/C Chow Yun-Fat, Mira Sorvino, Michael Rooker, Kenneth Tsang, Juergen Prochnow, Danny Trejo, Til Schweiger, Clifton Gonzalez Gonzalez, Carlos Gomez, Frank Medrano; *D:* Antoine Fuqua; *W:* Ken Sanzel; *C:* Peter Collister; *M:* Harry Gregson-Williams.

The Reptile

Lesser-known Hammer entry follows the studio's proven formula with snake monsters filling in for the traditional vampires. Following the death of his brother Charles (Baron), Harry (Barrett) and Valerie (Daniel) move into the departed's English country cottage. They find sullen, frightened villagers, a disagreeable aristocrat (Willman), his beautiful daughter (Pearce), and secrets that are revealed at a tortuously languid pace. But Hammer films are about atmosphere and this one's got oodles. It also features perhaps the first use of a sitar in the score of an English film. The underlying message—the inability of rational white males to understand the larger world, much less to control it—is widely accepted as gospel now. The weakest part is the faintly ridiculous monster makeup. On DVD, the film is flawless, though it is not nearly as visually demanding as many of the studio's releases. —*MM*

Movie: ♫♫▶ **DVD:** ♫♫♫▶
Anchor Bay (Cat #DV10682, UPC #013131068290). Widescreen (1.85:1) letterboxed. Dolby Digital Mono. $29.98. Keepcase. *LANG:* English. *FEATURES:* 23 chapter links ▪ Theatrical trailer ▪ TV spots ▪ *World of Hammer* episode "Vamp."
1966 90m/C *GB* Jacqueline Pearce, Ray Barrett, Noel Willman, Jennifer Daniel, Michael Ripper, John Laurie, Marne Maitland, Charles Lloyd Pack, George Woodbridge, David Baron; *D:* John Gilling; *W:* John (Anthony Hinds) Elder; *C:* Arthur Grant; *M:* Don Banks.

Requiem for a Vampire

Jean Rollin's cheesy surreal horror film is virtually a perfect example of his early '70s work in the genre. It's a simple story of two girls (Castel and D'Argent) who escape from reform school and go to a castle where they find vampires who have funny little triangular fangs. The DVD looks much better than the various Rollin tapes that have been available on the "gray" video market for years. Some reds bleed and stripes flash and artifacts abound in the darkness, but Rollin is working with intentionally clashing primary colors so that criticism is irrelevant. For fans of the period only. —*MM* *AKA:* Caged Virgins; Dungeon of Terror; Virgins and Vampires.

Movie: ♫♫ **DVD:** ♫♫▶
Image Entertainment (Cat #ID5420SADVD, UPC #014381542028). Widescreen (1.66:1) letterboxed. Dolby Digital Mono. $24.99. Snapper. *LANG:* English; French. *SUB:* English. *FEATURES:* 16 chapter links ▪ English and French theatrical trailers ▪ Liner notes by Marc Morris ▪ Photo galleries.
1971 ?m/C *FR* Marie Pierre Castel, Mireille D'Argent, Philippe Gaste, Dominique, Paul Bisciglia; *D:* Jean Rollin; *W:* Jean Rollin; *C:* Renan Polles.

Reservoir Dogs

Ultraviolent tale of honor among thieves. Six professional criminals known by code names to protect their identities (Misters Pink, White, Orange, Blonde, Blue, and Brown) are assembled by Tierney to pull off a diamond heist. But two of the gang are killed in a police ambush. The survivors regroup in an empty warehouse and try to discover the informer in their midst. In probably the most stomach-churning scene (there is some competition here), a policeman is tortured just for the heck of it to the tune of the Stealers Wheel "Stuck in the Middle with You." Unrelenting; auspicious debut for Tarantino with strong ensemble cast anchored by Keitel as the very professional Mr. White. The tunes have never sounded better than they do in this 5.1 mix, which also energizes both the action and the dialogue. Everything about the DVD is top-notch, including sharpness, handling of the blacks and colors, and contrast and brightness levels. One would think that a film of this stature would warrant a decent supplemental section. Instead there are the usual bios and production notes of only minor interest. —*JO*

Movie: ♫♫♫▶ **DVD:** ♫♫♫▶
Artisan Entertainment (Cat #60442, UPC #012236044208). Widescreen (2.35:1) letterboxed; full frame. Dolby Digital 5.1. $24.98. Snapper. *LANG:* English. *SUB:* English; French; Spanish. *CAP:* English. *FEATURES:* 28 chapter links ▪ Production notes ▪ Cast and crew bios ▪ Theatrical trailer.
1992 (R) 100m/C Harvey Keitel, Tim Roth, Michael Madsen, Steve Buscemi, Christopher Penn, Lawrence Tierney, Kirk

Baltz, Quentin Tarantino, Eddie Bunker, Randy Brooks; **D:** Quentin Tarantino; **W:** Quentin Tarantino; **C:** Andrzej Sekula; **M:** Karyn Rachtman; **V:** Steven Wright. *AWARDS:* Independent Spirit Awards '93: Best Supporting Actor (Buscemi).

Restoration

Downey is irrepressible as 17th-century physician Robert Merivel, but he nonetheless loses his way when he abandons medicine for a life of debauchery and wretched excess. The setting is an elaborately realized London in the days after Charles II (Neill) is restored to the British throne, but the title just as well fits Merivel's journey and resulting spiritual and social restoration. After he uses all his medical prowess (and all his luck, too) to save the king's ailing spaniel, Merivel is invited to live among royalty. He mixes high living with low morality, turns his back on medicine, and falls in love with the monarch's mistress. It's surprising only to Merivel when the king ejects him from high society, but it's an important, character-building circumstance for the drunken playboy. Death, healing, love, and fatherhood join with the plague and London's great fire to help Merivel live up to his full potential. The exceptional costumes and art direction sell the period piece as reality, and an acceptable video transfer translates those details to the home screen. The audio disappoints, with no more than Dolby Surround to add to the ambience. The DVD extras are regrettably lacking, too, with only a ho-hum production featurette and the trailer. Better behind-the-scenes views of the sets and costume designs are missed opportunities. Adapted from Rose Tremain's 1989 novel. —*MB*
Movie: 🎜🎜🎜 **DVD:** 🎜🎜►
Miramax Pictures Home Video (Cat #17376, UPC #7179510028). Widescreen (1.85:1) letterboxed. Dolby Digital Surround Stereo. $29.98. Keepcase. *LANG:* English. *CAP:* English. *FEATURES:* Production featurette ▪ Theatrical trailer ▪ 21 chapter links.
1994 (R) 118m/C Robert Downey Jr., Meg Ryan, Sam Neill, Hugh Grant, David Thewlis, Polly Walker, Ian McKellen; **D:** Michael Hoffman; **W:** Rupert Walters; **C:** Oliver Stapleton; **M:** James Newton Howard. *AWARDS:* Academy Awards '95: Best Art Direction/Set Decoration, Best Costume Design.

Resurrection

Yet another serial killer prowls the streets. This time the scene is Chicago (actually Toronto, and not Louisiana, as the box copy states). Detectives Prudhomme (coproducer Lambert) and Hollinsworth (Orser) are on the case of a mutilating murder who is trying to re-create the body of Christ, or something to that effect. No serious flaws are visible on the DVD image. Sound is fine, too. Director Mulcahy's commentary track is low-keyed and

confident; sound is fine. Recommended for fans of apocalyptic thrillers. —*MM*
Movie: 🎜🎜 **DVD:** 🎜🎜🎜
Columbia Tristar Home Video (Cat #04492, UPC #043396044920). Widescreen (1.85:1) anamorphic; full frame. Dolby Digital 5.1 Surround Stereo; Dolby Digital Surround Stereo. $27.95. Keepcase. *LANG:* English; Spanish. *CAP:* English. *FEATURES:* 28 chapter links ▪ Cast and crew filmographies ▪ Theatrical trailer and TV spot.
1999 (R) 108m/C Christopher Lambert, Leland Orser, Robert Joy, Rick Fox, Barbara Tyson, James Kidnie, David Cronenberg; **D:** Russell Mulcahy; **W:** Brad Mirman; **C:** Jonathan Freeman; **M:** Jim McGrath.

Retrievers

A young man and a former CIA agent team up to expose the unsavory practices of the organization.
Movie: 🎜 **DVD:** NYR
Digital Versatile Disc Ltd. (Cat #111). Full frame. $19.95. Keepcase.
1982 90m/C Max Thayer, Roselyn Royce, Richard Anderson, Shawn Hoskins, Mary McCormick, Lenard Miller; **D:** Elliot Hong; **W:** Elliot Hong; **C:** Stephen Kim; **M:** Ted Ashford.

Retroactive

Scientist Brian (Whaley) has been experimenting with time reversal and finally manages to make his project work. Meanwhile, police psychologist Karen (Travis) has had car trouble and been given a ride by Frank (Belushi) and his wife Rayanne (Whirry). Karen soon realizes that Frank is a psycho and escapes to Brian's lab. But Brian's just reversed time and Karen winds up back in Frank's car.
Movie: 🎜🎜 **DVD:** NYR
MGM Home Entertainment (Cat #907788). Dolby Digital 5.1 Surround Stereo. $24.98. Keepcase. *LANG:* English; French. *SUB:* French. *CAP:* English. *FEATURES:* Trailer.
1997 (R) 91m/C James Belushi, Kylie Travis, Shannon Whirry, Frank Whaley, Jesse Borrego, M. Emmet Walsh, Guy Boyd; **D:** Louis Morneau; **W:** Robert Strauss, Phillip Badger; **C:** George Mooradian; **M:** Tim Truman.

The Return of Martin Guerre

In a strongly realized 16th-century France, a man claiming to be Martin Guerre (Depardieu) comes home to village and wife (Baye) after a long war. Eventually, a religious court must decide if he is the man he claims to be. It's a love story of second chances with Depardieu and Baye in rare form. The DVD is 12 minutes longer than the theatrical or tape versions. In many scenes, the image is slightly sharper too, though absolute clarity is less important than the bawdy, smoky, dirty look of the medieval world. Some graininess is visible in the darker interiors. (If memory serves, the same is true of both tape and film.) Sound is fine and the

light yellow subtitles are easy to read. —*MM AKA:* Le Retour de Martin Guerre.
Movie: 🎜🎜🎜► **DVD:** 🎜🎜🎜
WinStar Home Entertainment (Cat #FLV5008, UPC #720917050089). Widescreen (1.66:1) letterboxed. $29.99. Keepcase. *LANG:* French. *SUB:* English. *FEATURES:* 9 chapter links ▪ Production credits ▪ Filmographies of Depardieu, Baye, Vigne.
1983 123m/C *FR* Gerard Depardieu, Roger Planchon, Maurice Jacquemont, Barnard Pierre Donnadieu, Nathalie Baye; **D:** Daniel Vigne; **W:** Daniel Vigne, Jean-Claude Carriere; **C:** Andre Neau; **M:** Michel Portal. *AWARDS:* Cesar Awards '83: Best Writing, Best Score; National Society of Film Critics Awards '83: Best Actor (Depardieu); *NOM:* Academy Awards '83: Best Costume Design.

Return of the Blind Dead

De Ossorio's second *Blind Dead* effort is a strong sequel, much more tightly plotted than the original. Resurrected cannibalistic medieval knights have become something of a cottage industry in European horror. These Templars pop back up for the 500th anniversary of their execution, and, in *Night of the Living Dead* fashion, trap a diverse group of squabbling people in a building. The Knights themselves look like Klansmen in dirty sheets. But when they're riding their hooded horses in slow motion, they make a memorable impression. Both sound and image on the DVD are strong, but they are only a small improvement over the excellent Anchor Bay tape. —*MM AKA:* Return of the Evil Dead; El Ataque de los Muertos Sin Ojos.
Movie: 🎜🎜🎜 **DVD:** 🎜🎜🎜
Anchor Bay (Cat #DV10561, UPC #013131056198). Widescreen (1.66:1) letterboxed. Dolby Digital Mono. $29.98. Keepcase. *LANG:* Spanish. *SUB:* English. *FEATURES:* 10 chapter links. This is a double feature with *Tombs of the Blind Dead*.
1975 85m/C *SP PT* Tony Kendall, Esther Roy, Frank Blake, Fernando Sancho, Lone Fleming, Loreta Tovar, Jose Canalejas; **D:** Armando de Ossorio; **W:** Armando de Ossorio; **C:** Miguel Mila; **M:** Anton Abril.

Return of the Boogeyman

Despite the box copy, the title on the film is *Boogeyman 3* but a stinker is still a stinker no matter what you call it. This is standard, repetitious stalker stuff involving dreams and a broken mirror. It's boring and ugly with orange- and pink-tinted scenes and others that are ugly all on their own. The bargain-basement price tag and a complete lack of such basics as chapter links are completely fitting for this junk. —*MM AKA:* Boogeyman 3.
Movie: woof **DVD:** woof
Simitar Entertainment (Cat #7213, UPC #082551721320). Full frame. PCM Stereo. $7.98. Keepcase. *LANG:* English.

1994 76m/C Kelly Galindo, Suzanna Love, Richard Quick; **D:** Deland Nuse; **W:** Jack Smight; **C:** Ferdinand Krainer; **M:** Kyle Van Horne, David Porcinello.

Return of the Dragon

In Lee's last picture, he's a waiter at a Chinese restaurant in Rome. The place is menaced by gangsters who want to buy the property. On behalf of the owners, Lee fights an American karate champ in the Roman forum. Those scenes between Lee and Norris are great and make this one a must-see for martial arts fans. Though some exteriors have an overexposed look, the interiors are as clear as the other discs in this set. Some flecks mar the print; several of the many shades of red glow and bright diagonal lines break up. —MM

Movie: 🎬🎬▶ **DVD:** 🎬🎬▶
20th Century Fox (Cat #4112551). Widescreen letterboxed. Mono. $99.98. Box set. *LANG:* English. *FEATURES:* 14 chapter links. Title is available as part of "Bruce Lee: The Master Collection."
1973 (R) 91m/C CH Bruce Lee, Nora Miao, Chuck Norris; **D:** Bruce Lee; **W:** Bruce Lee; **C:** Ho Lang Shang; **M:** Joseph Koo.

Return to Oz

Picking up where *The Wizard of Oz* left off, Auntie Em deposits Dorothy (Balk) in a scary mental hospital to cure her of "delusions" of Oz. A storm once again aids her escape to the land of the yellow brick road, where magical creatures—both good and evil—battle for power. Based on a later L. Frank Baum book, the sequel has justifiably attracted a cult following. It's unforgettable and enjoyable for the whole family, though some scenes may frighten small children. Film's gloomy color scheme translates surprisingly well, and the creature and sound effects are stunning as ever. The disc also contains a thoughtful 10-minute interview with the now grown-up star, along with her short introduction. —JE

Movie: 🎬🎬🎬 **DVD:** 🎬🎬🎬
Anchor Bay (Cat #DV 10820, UPC #01313108209). Widescreen (1:85:1); full frame. Dolby Digital 5.1 Surround Stereo. $24.99. Snapper. *LANG:* English. *CAP:* English. *FEATURES:* 24 chapter links. Featurette, "Fairuza Balk Returns to Oz". Brief (10 sec.) film introduction by Balk.
1985 (PG) 109m/C Fairuza Balk, Piper Laurie, Matt Clark, Nicol Williamson, Jean Marsh; **D:** Walter Murch; **W:** Walter Murch, Gill Dennis; **C:** David Watkin; **M:** David Shire.

Return to Paradise

Sheriff (Vaughn) and Tony (Conrad), along with their new friend Lewis (Phoenix), take a vice-filled vacation in Malaysia. Done with the partying, the two New Yorkers return home while Lewis stays in Asia to

work with orangutans. Two years later, Lewis is in a Malaysian prison, facing execution for a brick of hashish, which Sheriff haphazardly tossed into the garbage. Enter Heche as lawyer Beth, who finds Sheriff and tells him that to save Lewis, he and Tony must return and take their share of the responsibility (and serve time in a squalid third-world prison). Loose retelling of the 1989 French film *Force Majeure* features a variety of lighting conditions, but is generally pretty dark. The DVD manages to stay pretty sharp with very little grain or artifacts. Colors are somber, but true to the theatrical release. Both contrast and brightness consistently keep up with the changing illumination. The 5.1 sound adds dimension and space via good use of the Surround channels and has excellent low-end that is both boisterous and clean. —JO **AKA:** All for One.

Movie: 🎬🎬🎬 **DVD:** 🎬🎬🎬▶
Polygram (Cat #0582712, UPC #044005827125). Widescreen (2.35:1) letterboxed; full frame. Dolby Digital 5.1; Stereo. $29.95. Keepcase. *LANG:* English; French. *SUB:* Spanish. *CAP:* English. *FEATURES:* 18 chapter links. Theatrical trailer. Cast and filmmakers bios. Filmographies.
1998 (R) 112m/C Vince Vaughn, Joaquin Rafael (Leaf) Phoenix, Anne Heche, David Conrad, Jada Pinkett Smith, Vera Farmiga, Nick Sandow; **D:** Joseph Ruben; **W:** Wesley Strick, Bruce Robinson; **C:** Reynaldo Villalobos; **M:** Mark Mancina.

Revenge

Retired pilot Costner makes the mistake of falling in love with another man's wife. Quinn gives a first-rate performance as the Mexican crime lord who punishes his spouse and her lover, beginning a cycle of vengeance. Sometimes contrived, but artfully photographed with tantalizing love scenes. The DVD made me appreciate the film far more than I had previously, because it delivered a much better representation of the lush and atmospheric cinematography. Even the widescreen laserdisc doesn't quite capture the film, but the DVD's exacting colors and detailed picture sharpness do the trick. It doesn't hurt that the Dolby Surround is also beefed up with a lot more bass, and makes very good use of its Surround track. —JO

Movie: 🎬🎬▶ **DVD:** 🎬🎬🎬▶
Columbia Tristar Home Video (Cat #50219, UPC #043396502192). Widescreen (1.85:1) letterboxed; full frame. Dolby Surround. $29.95. Keepcase. *LANG:* English; Spanish; French. *SUB:* English; Spanish; French. *CAP:* English. *FEATURES:* 28 chapter links. Theatrical trailer.
1990 (R) 123m/C Kevin Costner, Anthony Quinn, Madeleine Stowe, Sally Kirkland, Joe Santos, Miguel Ferrer, James Gammon, Tomas Milian; **D:** Tony Scott; **W:** Jim Harrison; **M:** Jack Nitzsche.

Revenge of the Pink Panther

Inspector Clouseau survives an assassination attempt, but allows the world to think that he is dead in order to pursue the drug lord Douvier (Webber), who is responsible for the crime. Clouseau follows Douvier to Hong Kong, where a $50 million heroin deal is about to go down. Tagging along with him is Douvier's former mistress (Cannon) and Clouseau's reinstated boss, Inspector Dreyfus (Lom). This is the last *Pink Panther* film before Sellers's death and, although it's not as funny as the others, it still has plenty of laughs. The widescreen and full-frame transfers are very good, probably the best of the *Pink Panther* series. The colors are crisp and have very little bleed. The blacks are true and the brightness and contrast levels are very good. A very clean transfer with no excessive grain or pixelation, even in the dark scenes. As with the other *Panthers*, the sound is mono but very good. —JO

Movie: 🎬🎬▶ **DVD:** 🎬🎬🎬
MGM Home Entertainment (Cat #907502, UPC #027616750228). Widescreen (2.35:1) letterboxed; full frame. Dolby Digital Mono. $24.98. Keepcase. *LANG:* English (DD Mono); French (DD Mono). *SUB:* English; French. *FEATURES:* 32 chapter links. Theatrical trailer. 8-page booklet.
1978 (PG) 99m/C Peter Sellers, Herbert Lom, Dyan Cannon, Robert Webber, Burt Kwouk, Robert Loggia; **D:** Blake Edwards; **W:** Frank Waldman, Blake Edwards, Ron Clark; **C:** Ernest Day; **M:** Henry Mancini.

Revolt of the Zombies

A mad scientist (Jagger) learns the secret of bringing the dead to life and musters the zombies into a unique and gruesome military unit during World War I. Strange early zombie flick looks silly by today's standards. This DVD was created from a heavily scratched original print. Faint static is constant in the background of the soundtrack; the score is thin and reedy. Chapters cannot be accessed from the menu. —MM

Movie: 🎬▶ **DVD:** 🎬▶
Roan Group (Cat #AED-2020, UPC #785604202028). Full frame. Dolby Digital Mono. $29.95. Keepcase. *LANG:* English. *FEATURES:* Cast credits. Film background. 17 chapter links. Title is available as half of a double feature with *King of the Zombies* and by itself from Madacy (cat. #990603) for $9.99.
1936 65m/B Dorothy Stone, Dean Jagger, Roy D'Arcy, Robert Noland, George Cleveland; **D:** Victor Halperin; **W:** Howard Higgin; **C:** Jockey A. Feindel, Arthur Martinelli.

Rich and Strange

Early Hitchcock movie is not in the same class as his later thrillers. A couple inherits a fortune and journeys around the world. Eventually the pair is shipwrecked.

The quality of the film print used for this DVD leaves a lot to be desired, but is par for the course for a minor work from 1932. It looks and sounds better than the bonus episode from the old *Alfred Hitchcock Presents* TV show, circa 1962 but not aired as part of the show's original network run. The episode is full of grain and marred by so many scratches it looks as though the film was threaded through a food processor. The soundtrack is so poor it's difficult to make out the dialogue. The included *Psycho* trailer is from a bad print, too, and is of lower quality than the same trailer on Universal's *Psycho* DVD. The video introduction by Tony Curtis is simply cheesy, a low-quality production. —MB **AKA:** East of Shanghai.
Movie: 🦴🦴▶ **DVD:** 🦴
Delta/Laserlight (Cat #82037, UPC #0181 11997331). Full frame. Dolby Digital Mono. $14.98. Keepcase. *LANG:* English; Spanish; Chinese; Japanese. *SUB:* Spanish; Chinese; Japanese. *FEATURES:* 34 chapter links • Intro by Tony Curtis • *Psycho* theatrical trailer.
1932 92m/B *GB* Henry Kendall, Joan Barry, Betty Amann, Percy Marmont, Elsie Randolph; **D:** Alfred Hitchcock; **W:** Alfred Hitchcock, Alma Reville; **C:** Jack Cox, Charles Martin.

Richard Pryor: Live in Concert

Someone had the bright idea of filming Richard Pryor live on stage in Long Beach, CA, back in 1979 and releasing the performance theatrically. It worked. This is Richard Pryor at the top of his form—raw, foul, raunchy, and very, very funny. He talks about his pets, about death, drugs, and family. He knows about such things and uses every banned-from-television word possible to convey his very personal experiences. In fact, he gets away with saying things that could easily start race riots, but somehow he doesn't and in the end it all works so very well. Not the best film-to-DVD transfer, but with Pryor as a one man show it really doesn't matter. The DVD-generated French and Spanish subtitles give new meaning to learning a foreign language. —RT
Movie: 🦴🦴▶ **DVD:** 🦴🦴
MPI Home Video (Cat #7084, UPC #030306708423). Full frame. AC3 - 2 Channel. $24.98. Keepcase. *LANG:* English. *SUB:* French; Spanish. *CAP:* English. *FEATURES:* 24 chapter markers • Richard Pryor biography & filmography.
1979 (R) 78m/C Richard Pryor; **D:** Jeff Margolis; **W:** Richard Pryor.

Richard Pryor: Live on the Sunset Strip

This one-man concert film captures some of Pryor's most perceptive and honest material. It was made soon after his drug-addiction had led to a near-fatal accident. That's the subject of the final chapters of the DVD. It's material that few comedians would have the courage to tackle. Pryor is

terrifyingly funny and unforgiving. The rest of his material is good, but he ends on such a strong note that even his fans may not recall his earlier comments on sex and "the N word." The full-frame DVD image has some rough moments—Pryor performs in a fire-engine red tux—but director Joe Layton's subtle camerawork gives the potentially static action a feeling of fluid energy. The sound captures every word and laugh. For fans, the many chapter breaks may be the most valuable feature. —MM
Movie: 🦴🦴🦴▶ **DVD:** 🦴🦴🦴
Columbia Tristar Home Video (Cat #40909, UPC #04339640909). Full frame. Dolby Digital Mono. $27.95. Keepcase. *LANG:* English. *SUB:* English; Spanish. *CAP:* English. *FEATURES:* 28 chapter links.
1982 (R) 96m/C Richard Pryor; **D:** Joe Layton; **W:** Richard Pryor; **M:** Harry Betts.

Ricochet

Rookie cop Washington causes a sensation when he single-handedly captures notorious psychopath Lithgow. But this particular criminal is a twisted genius, and from his prison cell he comes up with a plan to destroy the young cop. Teaming up with old friend Ice-T, the rookie tries to outwit his evil arch-nemesis. Genuinely scary, tense, and violent thriller. On the DVD there is a slight increase in grain in some of the dark sequences. Also, some of the long shots during the climax have a slight shimmering, most likely to enhance the detail. Otherwise the disc is pretty good; so's the soundtrack, with excellent bass and a good Surround mix. —JO
Movie: 🦴🦴🦴 **DVD:** 🦴🦴🦴
HBO Home Video (Cat #90683, UPC #026359068324). Widescreen (1.85:1) letterboxed. Dolby Digital 5.1; DS Stereo; Mono. $24.98. Snapper. *LANG:* English; French; Spanish. *SUB:* English; French; Spanish. *CAP:* English. *FEATURES:* 32 chapter links • Cast bios.
1991 (R) 104m/C Denzel Washington, John Lithgow, Ice-T, Jesse Ventura, Kevin Pollak, Lindsay Wagner, Mary Ellen Trainor, Josh Evans, Victoria Dillard, John Amos, John Cothran Jr.; **D:** Russell Mulcahy; **W:** Steven E. de Souza; **C:** Peter Levy; **M:** Alan Silvestri.

The Right Stuff

Rambunctious adaptation of Tom Wolfe's book about the development of the U.S. space program begins with Chuck Yeager's (Shepard) attempt to break the sound barrier and ends with John Glenn's (Harris) orbital flight. It tells that complex story with a well-chosen all-star cast and an ambitious script. To some tastes, though, it is overlong. The DVD captures the theatrical image without any serious problems that I could spot. The action scenes work well and the image is comfortable with both dark interiors and airplanes in flight. The two-sided disc must be turned over halfway through. —MM
Movie: 🦴🦴🦴 **DVD:** 🦴🦴🦴

Warner Home Video, Inc. (Cat #20027). Widescreen (1.85:1) letterboxed. Dolby Digital 5.1 Surround Stereo; Dolby Digital Stereo. $24.98. Snapper. *LANG:* English; French. *SUB:* English; French; Spanish. *CAP:* English. *FEATURES:* Cast and crew thumbnail bios • "Making of" featurette • Trailer • Production notes.
1983 (PG) 193m/C Ed Harris, Dennis Quaid, Sam Shepard, Scott Glenn, Fred Ward, Charles Frank, William Russ, Kathy Baker, Barbara Hershey, Levon Helm, David Clennon, Kim Stanley, Mary Jo Deschanel, Veronica Cartwright, Pamela Reed, Jeff Goldblum, Harry Shearer, Donald Moffat, Scott Paulin, Lance Henriksen, Scott Wilson, John P. Ryan, Royal Dano; **D:** Philip Kaufman; **W:** Philip Kaufman; **C:** Caleb Deschanel; **M:** Bill Conti. *AWARDS:* Academy Awards '83: Best Film Editing, Best Sound, Best Original Score; *NOM:* Academy Awards '83: Best Art Direction/Set Decoration, Best Cinematography, Best Picture, Best Supporting Actor (Shepard).

The Ring

Very early silent Hitchcock is about a boxer who marries a carnival girl, loses carnival girl, gets carnival girl back. It's a standard romantic yarn, interesting only as a measure of the young director's developing abilities. One opening bit is blatantly racist. The fuzzily focused image is barely watchable. (Title is available as a second feature on the *Number 17* DVD.) —MM
Movie: 🦴🦴▶ **DVD:** 🦴▶
Delta/Laserlight (Cat #82 031, UPC #01811997935). Full frame. $14.99. Keepcase. *LANG:* Silent. *SUB:* English intertitles. *FEATURES:* 16 chapter links • Introduction by Tony Curtis • Trailer for *I Confess*.
1927 82m/B *GB* Carl Brisson, Lillian Hall-Davis, Ian Hunter, Gordon Harker; **D:** Alfred Hitchcock; **W:** Alfred Hitchcock; **C:** Jack Cox.

Ringmaster

On the commentary track, director Neil Abramson admits that this movie was made quick and cheap to cash in on the TV host's moment of fame. The plot, such as it is, revolves around two families' appearance on the show. The subject: stepdads who are fooling around with their stepdaughters. The first shot is a trailer park. The rest is trashy, tacky, and unashamed. On DVD, the image looks terrific, but that's hardly the point, is it? Judging by the attitude Abramson takes, no one was taking this one very seriously. Viewers shouldn't either. —MM **AKA:** Jerry Springer's Ringmaster.
Movie: 🦴▶ **DVD:** 🦴🦴▶
Artisan Entertainment (Cat #60736, UPC #012236073604). Widescreen (1.85:1) letterboxed. Dolby Digital Surround Stereo. $29.98. Keepcase. *LANG:* English. *CAP:* English. *FEATURES:* 36 chapter links • Cast and crew thumbnail biographies • Production notes • Theatrical trailer.

1998 (R) 89m/C Jerry Springer, John Capodice, Jaime Pressly, Molly Hagan, Michael Dudikoff, Michael Jai White, William McNamara, Dawn Maxey, Wendy Raquel Robinson, Tangie Ambrose, Nicki Micheaux, Ashley Holbrook; **D:** Neil Abramson; **W:** Jon Bernstein; **C:** Russell Lyster; **M:** Kennard Ramsey. *AWARDS:* Golden Raspberry Awards '98: Worst New Star (Springer).

Rio Grande

In the last entry in Ford's cavalry trilogy—following *Fort Apache* and *She Wore a Yellow Ribbon*—a U.S. cavalry unit on the Mexican border conducts an unsuccessful campaign against marauding Indians. The commander (Wayne) faces an unhappy wife and is estranged from his son, a new recruit. Features an excellent Victor Young score and several songs by the Sons of the Pioneers. The picture on this DVD is great. Despite a little film damage here and there, it's super crisp with excellent contrast and graytones. As expected, the sound is nothing special but clear and fairly distortion-free. Having seen this film many times, the first thing I looked at on the DVD was the documentary, which is very anecdotal, providing lots of information in a very entertaining fashion. —*JO*
Movie: 🎜🎜🎜 **DVD:** 🎜🎜🎜
Republic Pictures Home Video (Cat #43456, UPC #017153345629). Full frame. Dolby Digital Mono. $24.98. Keepcase. *LANG:* English; French; Spanish. *SUB:* French; Spanish. *CAP:* English. *FEATURES:* 19 chapter links • "The Making of 'Rio Grande'" featurette • Theatrical trailer.
1950 105m/B John Wayne, Maureen O'Hara, Ben Johnson, Claude Jarman Jr., Harry Carey Jr., Victor McLaglen, Chill Wills, J. Carrol Naish; **D:** John Ford; **W:** James Kevin McGuinness; **C:** Bert Glennon; **M:** Victor Young.

Rising Sun

Fast-paced, noirish guilty pleasure is a sexy thriller. With Connery and Snipes in the leads, the film has star power to burn, and the supporting cast doesn't fade into the wallpaper either. At heart, the film is a straightforward murder mystery. Who killed a prostitute (Patitz) in the Los Angeles boardroom of the Nakamoto Corporation while a mammoth reception was going on downstairs? And why? LAPD detective Web Smith (Snipes) is called in by his boss (Keitel) but before he gets to the crime scene, he's told to pick up retired Captain John Connor (Connery). Things get twisty after that, and if the conclusion doesn't make complete sense, it feels right. The film works well on DVD with a very good image which, for the most part, is able to handle all the shades of black and charcoal that director Kaufman favors. Sound is fine. —*MM*
Movie: 🎜🎜🎜 **DVD:** 🎜🎜🎜
Twentieth Century Fox Home Entertainment (Cat #4112629). Widescreen letterboxed.

Dolby Digital 5.0 Surround Stereo; Dolby Digital Surround Stereo. $29.98. Keepcase. *LANG:* English; French. *SUB:* Spanish. *FEATURES:* 26 chapter links • Theatrical trailers.
1993 (R) 129m/C Sean Connery, Wesley Snipes, Tia Carrere, Harvey Keitel, Kevin Anderson, Stan Egi, Mako, Cary-Hiroyuki Tagawa, Ray Wise, Tatjana Patitz; **D:** Philip Kaufman; **W:** Michael Backes, Michael Crichton, Philip Kaufman; **C:** Michael Chapman; **M:** Toru Takemitsu.

Risky Business

With his parents out of town and awaiting word from the college boards, a teenager becomes involved in unexpected ways with a quick-thinking prostitute, her pimp, and assorted others. Cruise is likable, even when dancing in his underwear. Funny, well-paced, stylish prototypical '80s teen flick reintroduced Ray-Bans as the sunglasses for the wanna-be hip. What a party. The film remains one of the more stylized teen comedies with sensuous photography and an excellent Tangerine Dream soundtrack. The DVD brings the theatrical feel home with a good solid image that has only slight problems with some of the darker scenes (you'll only spot them if you're trying). The image is generally very sharp and colors are good. The stereo sound could be a little gutsier but overall does a good job in conveying the electronic score, the rock music, and the dialogue. —*JO*
Movie: 🎜🎜🎜 **DVD:** 🎜🎜🎜
Warner Home Video, Inc. (Cat #11323, UPC #085391132325). Widescreen (1.85:1) anamorphic. Dolby Surround; Dolby Digital Mono. $24.98. Snapper. *LANG:* English; Spanish; French. *SUB:* English; Spanish; French. *FEATURES:* 32 chapters • Theatrical trailer • Production notes.
1983 (R) 99m/C Tom Cruise, Rebecca DeMornay, Curtis Armstrong, Bronson Pinchot, Joe Pantoliano, Kevin Anderson, Richard Masur, Raphael Sbarge, Nicholas Pryor, Janet Carroll; **D:** Paul Brickman; **W:** Paul Brickman; **C:** Reynaldo Villalobos, Bruce Surtees; **M:** Tangerine Dream.

Rites of Passage

Before Victor Salva made the controversial *Powder*, he made the underrated video premiere *Nature of the Beast*. As he admits on the commentary track here, he is returning to those roots with this low-budget thriller. Set in the mountains outside L.A., it's about Del Farley (Stockwell), who tries to resolve several family problems with his son. They go to the remote cabin and find the younger son Campbell (Behr). Also on hand is that old genre favorite, the escaped convict (Remar) Dabbo, a psycho killer. On DVD, the film looks very good. Salva spent his budget wisely and so the film really doesn't attempt to do things that look cheap. The

image is absolutely sharp throughout. Sound is fine. —*MM*
Movie: 🎜🎜🎜 **DVD:** 🎜🎜🎜▶
Bell Canyon Entertainment Inc. (Cat #61012, UPC #97381160125). Widescreen. $24.98. *LANG:* English. *FEATURES:* 18 chapter links • Commentary: Victor Salva and Jason Behr • Photo gallery • Cast and crew thumbnail biographies • 4 deleted scenes with commentary.
1999 (R) 94m/C Dean Stockwell, James Remar, Jaimz Woolvett, Jason Behr, Robert Keith; **D:** Victor Salva; **W:** Victor Salva; **C:** Don E. Fauntleroy; **M:** Bennett Salvay.

The River

Farmers battle a river whose flood threatens their land. Spacek, as always, is strong and believable as the wife and mother, but Gibson falters. Beautiful photography is not enough to save the third in an onslaught of early '80s films dramatizing the plight of the small farmer. Both *Country* and *Places in the Heart* managed to convey important messages less cloyingly.
Movie: 🎜🎜 **DVD:** NYR
Universal Studios Home Video (Cat #20427). Widescreen (1.85:1) letterboxed. Dolby Digital 5.1 Surround Stereo. $26.98. Keepcase. *LANG:* English; French. *SUB:* Spanish. *CAP:* English. *FEATURES:* Cast and crew thumbnail bios • Trailer • Production notes.
1984 (PG) 124m/C Mel Gibson, Sissy Spacek, Scott Glenn, Billy Green Bush; **D:** Mark Rydell; **W:** Julian Barry, Robert Dillon; **C:** Vilmos Zsigmond; **M:** John Williams. *AWARDS:* NOM: Academy Awards '84: Best Actress (Spacek), Best Cinematography, Best Sound, Best Original Score.

A River Runs Through It

Contemplative exploration of family ties and coming-of-age is another well-crafted American tale from Redford (and Norman Maclean's book). In early 20th-century Montana, a Presbyterian minister (Skerritt) teaches his two sons, Paul (Pitt) and Norman (Sheffer), about life and religion via fly-fishing. The image is fine on this DVD; sound is not as sharp. Many natural sounds, such as the closing of a door, are amplified to ridiculous proportions, and Redford's commentary track from the laserdisc is not included. —*MM*
Movie: 🎜🎜🎜▶ **DVD:** 🎜🎜🎜
Columbia Tristar Home Video (Cat #3933). Widescreen (1.85:1) letterboxed; full frame. Dolby Digital Surround Stereo; Stereo; Mono. $24.95. Keepcase. *LANG:* English; French; Spanish. *SUB:* French; Spanish; Portuguese. *CAP:* English. *FEATURES:* 28 chapter links • Cast and crew thumbnail bios.
1992 (PG) 123m/C Craig Sheffer, Brad Pitt, Tom Skerritt, Brenda Blethyn, Emily Lloyd, Edie McClurg, Stephen Shellen, Susan Taylor; **D:** Robert Redford; **W:** Richard Friedenberg; **C:** Philippe Rous-

selot; *M:* Mark Isham. *AWARDS:* Academy Awards '92: Best Cinematography; *NOM:* Academy Awards '92: Best Adapted Screenplay, Best Original Score.

The River Wild

Dissatisfied wife Gail (Streep) plans a family white-water rafting vacation with 10-year-old son Roarke (Mazzello) and workaholic husband Tom (Strathairn). A former guide (and white-water expert) Gail comes to the aid of river novices Wade (boyishly menacing Bacon) and Terry (Reilly) who quickly turn out to be violent criminals needing help with their escape. Slow start leads to nonstop thrills with Streep an adept action heroine, though she's undercut by the flick's need to do something with Strathairn's thankless role. Beautiful Montana and Oregon settings. When I saw this film at the theatre I thought it was O.K., but seeing it again on DVD was a much more thrilling experience, thanks to the added intensity that the crisp picture and the 5.1 sound brought to it. Of course, this was particularly true of the white water sequences, where the soundtrack really takes over with incredible Surround tracks that really make you feel like you're riding the rapids yourself. The picture isn't bad either, and is always very sharp with excellent color. —*JO*
Movie: 🐾🐾🐾▶ *DVD:* 🐾🐾🐾▶
Universal Studios Home Video (Cat #20043, UPC #025192004322). Widescreen (2.35:1) anamorphic. Dolby Digital 5.1; Dolby Surround. $24.95. Keepcase. *LANG:* English; Spanish; French. *SUB:* Spanish. *CAP:* English; Spanish. *FEATURES:* 16 chapter links • Cast and filmmakers bios • Production notes • Film highlights.
1994 (PG-13) 111m/C Meryl Streep, David Strathairn, Joseph Mazzello, Kevin Bacon, John C. Reilly, Benjamin Bratt; *D:* Curtis Hanson; *W:* Raynold Gideon; *C:* Robert Elswit; *M:* Jerry Goldsmith. *AWARDS: NOM:* Golden Globe Awards '95: Best Actress—Drama (Streep), Best Supporting Actor (Bacon); Screen Actors Guild Award '94: Best Actress (Streep).

The Road to Morocco

Third installment in the series finds our boys stranded and broke in a Mediterranean shipwreck. To get dough, Buster (Crosby) sells Orville (Hope) into slavery to be Princess Shalimar's (Lamour) personal plaything. The punchline to that elaborate joke comes in chapter seven of the DVD, "Constantly." Set in the Princess's boudoir, it is one of the funniest moments in '40s movies. The DVD also captures the superb visuals that Hollywood could create in those years even on relatively modest budgets with black-and-white photography and studio soundstages. If the disc's sound lacks the full-frontal assault of today's multi-track systems, it's fine for Bing's effortless delivery, and for the banter among the stars. One of the funniest

and most enjoyable of the *Road* series. —*MM*
Movie: 🐾🐾🐾▶ *DVD:* 🐾🐾🐾
Image Entertainment (Cat #ID4281USDVD, UPC #014381428124). Full frame. Uncompressed PCM Mono. $24.99. Snapper. *LANG:* English. *CAP:* English. *FEATURES:* 16 chapter links.
1942 83m/C Bing Crosby, Bob Hope, Dorothy Lamour, Anthony Quinn, Dona Drake, Vladimir Sokoloff, Yvonne De Carlo; *D:* David Butler; *W:* Frank Butler, Don Hartman; *C:* William Mellor. *AWARDS:* National Film Registry '96; *NOM:* Academy Awards '42: Best Original Screenplay, Best Sound.

The Road to Utopia

Fourth of the *Road* films, wherein the boys wind up in Alaska posing as two famous escaped killers to locate a secret gold mine is one of the series' funniest and most spontaneous entries, abetted by Benchley's dry, upper-crust comments. It features many now standard tunes, including "Personality" and "Goodtime Charlie." This disc delivers solid blacks and the picture is as crisp and clear as it has ever been. The soundtrack, too, is exceptional, although it would benefit from a good remixing (thereby reducing some of the tinny aspects of the audio). —*MJT*
Movie: 🐾🐾🐾 *DVD:* 🐾🐾🐾
Image Entertainment (Cat #ID4291USDVD, UPC #014381429121). Full frame. Uncompressed PCM soundtrack. $29.99. Snapper. *LANG:* English. *FEATURES:* 16 chapter links.
1946 90m/B Bing Crosby, Bob Hope, Dorothy Lamour, Jack LaRue, Robert Benchley, Douglass Dumbrille, Hillary Brooke, Robert Barrat, Nestor Paiva; *D:* Hal Walker; *W:* Norman Panama, Melvin Frank; *C:* Lionel Lindon; *M:* Johnny Burke, Leigh Harline, James Van Heusen. *AWARDS: NOM:* Academy Awards '46: Best Original Screenplay.

The Road Warrior

The first sequel to *Mad Max* takes place after nuclear war has destroyed Australia. Max helps a colony of oil-drilling survivors defend themselves from the roving murderous outback gangs and escape to the coast. The climactic chase scene is among the most exciting ever filmed; this film virtually created the "action-adventure" picture of the 1980s. This DVD explodes into action, showing off its souped-up 5.1 sound (including the power-packed bass) right from the start. Engines revs and collisions are noisy and all involving as the Surround tracks kick in. The picture is great too, and the only real weakness of the disc is the grain that sneaks into some of the darker scenes. Despite that, this is a good disc to have around, both for entertainment and to show off your sound system. —*JO AKA:* Mad Max 2.
Movie: 🐾🐾🐾▶ *DVD:* 🐾🐾🐾▶
Warner Home Video, Inc. (Cat #11181, UPC #085391118121). Widescreen

(2.35:1) anamorphic; full frame. Dolby Digital 5.1; Dolby Surround. $24.98. Snapper. *LANG:* English; French. *SUB:* English; Spanish. *CAP:* English. *FEATURES:* 32 chapter links • Production notes • Theatrical trailer.
1982 (R) 95m/C *AU* Mel Gibson, Bruce Spence, Emil Minty, Vernon Wells, Virginia Hey, Max Phipps, Michael B. Preston, William Zappa; *D:* George Miller; *W:* George Miller, Terry Hayes; *C:* Dean Semler; *M:* Brian May. *AWARDS:* Los Angeles Film Critics Association Awards '82: Best Foreign Film.

Rob Roy

Kilt-raising though overlong tale of legendary Scot Robert Roy MacGregor mixes love and honor with bloodlust and revenge. Neeson's rugged clan leader fends off a band of dastardly nobles led by Cunningham (Roth), a foppish twit with an evil bent. Misty highland scenery and intense romantic interplay between Neeson and Lange as the spirited Mary MacGregor lend a passionate twist to an otherwise earthly, robust adventure of lore capped by one of the best sword fights in years. Roth's delightfully hammy performance as MacGregor's loathsome, bewigged nemesis delivers zip amid the high-minded speeches, plot lulls, and separated body parts. Visually stunning with on-location shooting in the Scottish Highlands. The best thing going for this DVD is the very good cinematography and excellent use of color. The DVD maintains a consistently sharp picture with vibrant colors. The blacks are deep and true and are supported by comfortable contrast and brightness levels throughout, under all lighting conditions. The 5.1 sound delivers a highly energized soundtrack with superb bass and crisp highs as well as well-mixed Surround tracks. —*JO*
Movie: 🐾🐾🐾 *DVD:* 🐾🐾🐾▶
MGM Home Entertainment (Cat #906260, UPC #027616626097). Widescreen (1.85:1) letterboxed. Dolby Digital 5.1. $24.98. Keepcase. *LANG:* English. *SUB:* English; Spanish; French. *CAP:* English. *FEATURES:* 32 chapter links • Theatrical trailer.
1995 (R) 144m/C Liam Neeson, Jessica Lange, Tim Roth, John Hurt, Eric Stoltz, Andrew Keir, Brian Cox, Brian McCardie, Gilbert Martin, Vicki Masson, David Hayman, Jason Flemyng, Shirley Henderson, Gilly Gilchrist, John Murtagh, Ewan Stewart; *D:* Michael Caton-Jones; *W:* Alan Sharp; *C:* Karl Walter Lindenlaub, Roger Deakins; *M:* Carter Burwell. *AWARDS:* British Academy Awards '95: Best Supporting Actor (Roth); *NOM:* Academy Awards '95: Best Supporting Actor (Roth); Golden Globe Awards '96: Best Supporting Actor (Roth).

Robbie Robertson: Going Home

Produced for the Disney Channel, this documentary about seminal rock musician

Robbie Robertson is a treat. It's essentially a history of popular music from the 1950s to the '90s. Robertson and colleagues tell his story through a combination of new interviews, which range from sparkling clarity to soft focus, and archival footage of varying quality. For the most part, these folks—who include producer Daniel Lanois, Martin Scorsese, Barry Levinson, Willie Dixon, Eric Clapton, and an incredibly young Bob Dylan—tell good stories. They're comfortable in front of the camera, and they don't dish dirt. The music is fine. There could have been much much more of it. Songs: "Mahk Jchi," "A Good Day to Die," "Go Back to Your Woods," "What About Now," "Raging Bull," "Jimmy Hollywood," "Skinwalker." —MM

Movie: 🎵🎵🎵 **DVD:** 🎵🎵🎵
Delta/Laserlight (Cat #82016, UPC #018111201636). Full frame. $14.99. Snapper. *LANG:* English. *FEATURES:* 27 chapter links • Brief explanation of production.
1998 70m/C Daniel Lanois, Martin Scorsese, Barry Levinson, Willie Dixon, Eric Clapton, Bob Dylan; *D:* Findlay Bunting; *W:* H.P. Newquist.

Robin Hood

Extravagant production casts Fairbanks as eponymous gymnastic swashbuckler who departs for Crusades as Earl of Huntington and returns as the hooded one to save King Richard's throne from the sinister Sheriff of Nottingham. Best-ever silent swashbuckling. Any time Kino puts out a classic on either VHS or DVD, my expectations are high and I usually assume that it's going to be the best possible version available. The only thing that disappointed in me in this DVD was the tinting of the picture, which may be the way the film was originally shown, but still tends to cover a lot of details. Turning the color down on your monitor doesn't help because everything is already buried. Still, this is a very nice transfer and the overall image is plenty sharp, and even with the tint, contrast and brightness levels are very good. The orchestral soundtrack is a little thin, which actually seems natural for a film of this age. —JO

Movie: 🎵🎵🎵 **DVD:** 🎵🎵🎵
Kino on Video (Cat #K116DVD, UPC #738329011628). Full frame. Stereo. $29.99. Snapper. *LANG:* Silent. *SUB:* English intertitles. *FEATURES:* 23 chapter links.
1922 110m/B Douglas Fairbanks Sr., Wallace Beery, Sam DeGrasse, Enid Bennett, Paul Dickey, William E. Lowery, Roy Coulson, Bill Bennett, Merrill McCormick, Wilson Benge, Willard Louis, Alan Hale, Maine Geary, Lloyd Talman; *D:* Allan Dwan; *W:* Douglas Fairbanks Sr.; *C:* Arthur Edeson.

The Robin Hood Gang

Brad (Taylor) and Frankie (Losak) are enterprising youngsters who collect empty soda cans to raise money to buy new bikes. But when they discover a suitcase full of cash in the attic of their apartment, they decide to share the wealth with their equally hard-up neighbors. When they learn that it's stolen bank loot, they must figure out how to catch the criminal and return the money. Nobody's going to mistake this modest kidvid for *Home Alone* but it's an acceptable time-waster for the short set. Given the modest production values, the DVD image and sound are probably not much better than VHS tape. —MM **AKA:** Angels in the Attic.

Movie: 🎵🎵 **DVD:** 🎵🎵
Image Entertainment (Cat #ID8800UM DVD, UPC #014381880021). Full frame. Dolby Digital Stereo. $24.99. Snapper. *LANG:* English. *FEATURES:* 12 chapter links.
1998 (PG) 86m/C Clayton Taylor, Steven Losak, Dalin Christlansen, Brenda Price, Scott Christopher; *D:* Eric Hendershot; *W:* Eric Hendershot; *C:* T.C. Christensen; *M:* Allen Williams.

Robin Hood: Prince of Thieves

Costner is the politically correct Rebel with a Cause, but a thinker, not a doer—and therein lies the problem. His quiet thoughtfulness doesn't add up to leadership and Rickman easily overpowers him as the wicked, crazed Sheriff of Nottingham. Freeman is excellent as a civilized Moor who finds England and its people inhospitable, dangerous, and not a little stupid. Mastrantonio, a last-minute choice, excels as the lovely Lady Marian. Great action sequences, a gritty and morbid picture of the Middle Ages, and some fun scenes with the Merry Men. Critics generally disapproved of the changes in the story and Costner's performance, though their comments about his lack of an English accent seem nitpicky in light of some basic plot problems. Still has lots of fun for lovers of action, romance, and fairy tales. Boasting a picture as lame as the star himself, this may not be a DVD to add to the collection. Colors are pretty good but the image is sometimes filled with grain, which increases in dark scenes, and is also present in the blacks. It's not that the DVD doesn't try; in fact, at times the contrast pushes color and detail beyond what is remembered from theatrical release. But, it comes down to the prerequisite that the image on a DVD be sharp and this one isn't. —JO

Movie: 🎵🎵 **DVD:** 🎵🎵
Warner Home Video, Inc. (Cat #14000, UPC #085391400028). Widescreen (2.35:1) letterboxed. Dolby Surround. $24.98. Snapper. *LANG:* English; French. *SUB:* English; French; Spanish. *CAP:* English. *FEATURES:* 17 chapter links • Production notes • Theatrical trailers.
1991 (PG-13) 144m/C Kevin Costner, Morgan Freeman, Mary Elizabeth Mastrantonio, Christian Slater, Alan Rickman, Geraldine McEwan, Michael McShane, Brian Blessed, Michael Wincott, Nick Brimble, Harold Innocent, Jack Wild; *Cameos:* Sean Connery; *D:* Kevin Reynolds; *W:* Pen Densham, John Watson; *C:* Billy Milton; *M:* Michael Kamen. *AWARDS:* British Academy Awards '91: Best Supporting Actor (Rickman); MTV Movie Awards '92: Best Song ("(Everything I Do) I Do for You"); Golden Raspberry Awards '91: Worst Actor (Costner); *NOM:* Academy Awards '91: Best Song ("(Everything I Do) I Do It for You").

RoboCop

A literally shot-to-pieces Detroit cop is used as the brain for a crime-fighting robot in this bleak vision of the future. Humor, satire, action, and violence keep the film moving in spite of its underlying sadness. Slick animation techniques from Phil Tippet. The Criterion Collection edition includes shots that director Verhoeven had to cut in order to receive an "R" rating. It's kind of silly because the "R"-rated version has violence-a-plenty and the added (and extended) shots, though more graphic, seem to tone down the violence a bit by making it more humorous and even more comic book–like. The DVD supplemental section is not huge but is nonetheless extremely interesting. The picture looks great and is both super sharp and colorful. The Dolby Surround has enough going on in the rear but overall the mix is a little thin, and distorted in the mids and highs. —JO

Movie: 🎵🎵🎵 **DVD:** 🎵🎵🎵
Criterion Collection (Cat #23, UPC #715515009324). Widescreen (1.66:1) letterboxed. Dolby Surround. $39.95. Keepcase. *LANG:* English. *FEATURES:* 27 chapter links • Audio commentary • Film-to-storyboard comparison • Illustrated essay • Theatrical trailers.
1987 (R) 103m/C Peter Weller, Nancy Allen, Ronny Cox, Kurtwood Smith, Ray Wise, Miguel Ferrer, Dan O'Herlihy, Robert DoQui, Felton Perry, Paul McCrane, Del Zamora; *D:* Paul Verhoeven; *W:* Michael Miner, Edward Neumeier; *C:* Jan De Bont; *M:* Basil Poledouris. *AWARDS: NOM:* Academy Awards '87: Best Film Editing, Best Sound.

RoboCop 2

Sequel to the fascinating look at the future, where police departments are run by corporations hungry for profit at any cost, is grimmer and more violent. A new and highly addictive drug has made Detroit more dangerous than ever. Robocop is replaced by a stronger cyborg with the brain of a brutal criminal. When the cyborg goes berserk, Robocop battles it and the drug lords for control of the city. Dark humor and graphic savagery, with little of the tenderness and emotion of the original. The DVD substantially improves upon both the laserdisc and VHS editions of the film. The picture is sharp and grain is minimal. It's the color that has benefited the most from the format, and it's very vibrant. The disc has stereo sound, and though that might be a disappointment to Surround fanatics, the tracks are full-bodied, undistorted, and have decent separation and imaging. —*JO*

Movie: 🎬🎬 **DVD:** 🎬🎬🎬
Orion Home Video (Cat #ID4072ORDVD, UPC #014381407228). Widescreen (1.85:1) letterboxed. Stereo. $29.90. Snapper. *LANG:* English. *CAP:* English. *FEATURES:* 19 chapter links.
1990 (R) 117m/C Peter Weller, Nancy Allen, Belinda Bauer, Dan O'Herlihy, Tom Noonan, Gabriel Damon, Galyn Gorg, Felton Perry, Patricia Charbonneau; *D:* Irvin Kershner; *W:* Walon Green; *C:* Mark Irwin; *M:* Leonard Rosenman.

RoboCop 3
Robocop's new Japanese owners plan to build a huge, new, ultra-modern city (in place of the decrepit 21st-century Detroit) but first must evict thousands of people in this third installment (which sat on the studio shelf before finally being released in 1993). There's an android Ninja warrior to do battle with Robo, who's gone over to the rebel underground, but the plot and action sequences are rehashed from better films. Watch the original. The DVD is comparable in quality to the first sequel's Orion release. Colors are in fact a little brighter (so is the film) and the contrast is given a boost. No Surround again, but good dynamics and left-to-right separation. —*JO*

Movie: 🎬▶ **DVD:** 🎬🎬🎬
Orion Home Video (Cat #ID4073ORDVD, UPC #014381407327). Widescreen (1.85:1) letterboxed. Dolby Surround. $29.99. Snapper. *LANG:* English. *CAP:* English. *FEATURES:* 20 chapter links.
1991 (PG-13) 104m/C Robert John Burke, Nancy Allen, John Castle, CCH Pounder, Bruce Locke, Rip Torn, Remi Ryan, Felton Perry; *D:* Fred Dekker; *W:* Frank Miller, Fred Dekker; *C:* Gary B. Kibbe; *M:* Basil Poledouris.

The Rock
Cage follows up his Oscar win with a big-budget action hero turn and great results. In an attempt to get benefits for the families of soldiers killed in various covert operations, a decorated general (Harris) and his commando squad occupy Alcatraz island, taking hostages and threatening to unleash a deadly gas bomb on San Francisco. Biochemical weapons expert Stanley Goodspeed (Cage) is called in to disarm the rockets, aided by John Patrick Mason (Connery), the only man to successfully escape from the island prison. Like most Simpson/Bruckheimer productions, credibility is stretched to the limit, but the action scenes and crisp pacing don't leave much time for pondering details, anyway. Connery, cool as ever, hasn't lost a step. Cage effectively plays up his character's inexperience at being the hero. Coproducer Don Simpson died of drug overdose during production. *The Rock* has looked pretty good on all the

previous video releases, with the Criterion Collection's laserdisc most accurately capturing the slick stylized look of the film. The DVD is even better, with a sharper image and super-vibrant colors combined with very dark blacks that bring the full theatrical representation to home video. The film's sound effects were also masterfully transferred to the 5.1 mix, where the rear channels are in constant use, as is the subwoofer. On a good system, this one really does look and sound as good as it did in the theatre. —*JO*

Movie: 🎬🎬🎬 **DVD:** 🎬🎬🎬🎬
Hollywood Pictures Home Video (Cat #13077, UPC #717951000040). Widescreen (2.35:1) letterboxed. Dolby Digital 5.1; Stereo. $29.99. Keepcase. *LANG:* English; French. *SUB:* Spanish. *CAP:* English. *FEATURES:* 22 chapter links • Theatrical trailer.
1996 (R) 136m/C Nicolas Cage, Sean Connery, Ed Harris, Michael Biehn, William Forsythe, David Morse, John Spencer, John C. McGinley, Tony Todd, Bokeem Woodbine, Danny Nucci, Vanessa Marcil, Claire Forlani, Gregory Sporleder; *D:* Michael Bay; *W:* Jonathan Hensleigh; *C:* John Schwartzman; *M:* Nick Glennie-Smith. *AWARDS:* MTV Movie Awards '97: Best On-Screen Duo (Sean Connery/Nicolas Cage); *NOM:* Academy Awards '96: Best Sound; MTV Movie Awards '97: Best Film, Best Action Sequence.

Rock-a-Doodle
Little Edmond is knocked out during a storm and has an Elvis-influenced vision. He sees Chanticleer, the sun-raising rooster, tricked into neglecting his duties by an evil barnyard owl. Humiliated and scorned, the earnest young bird leaves the farm and winds up in a Las Vegas–like city as an Elvis-impersonating singer (complete with pompadour) where he meets with success and all its trappings. It's all mildly amusing but bland by today's standards of animation with music that is certainly nothing to crow about.

Movie: 🎬🎬▶ **DVD:** NYR
HBO Home Video (Cat #90701). Full frame. Dolby Digital 5.1 Surround Stereo. $24.98. Keepcase. *LANG:* English. *SUB:* French; Spanish. *FEATURES:* Trailer.
1992 (G) 77m/C *D:* Don Bluth; *W:* David N. Weiss; *M:* Robert Folk; *V:* Glen Campbell, Christopher Plummer, Phil Harris, Sandy Duncan, Ellen Greene, Charles Nelson Reilly, Eddie Deezen, Toby Scott Granger, Sorrell Booke.

Rock 'n' Roll High School
The music of the Ramones highlights this non-stop high-energy cult classic about the students of Vince Lombardi High School who are out to thwart the principal (Woronov) at every turn. If it had been made in 1957, it would have been the ultimate rock 'n' roll teen movie. As it is, the '70s milieu works against the film, but the performances are perfect for the material

and the Ramones are great. The DVD was made from less-than-perfect original elements. The image is marred by scratches, both faint and serious, throughout and even some odd red snow that appears briefly. The soundtrack is scratchy and not as strong as it needs to be. —*MM*

Movie: 🎬🎬🎬 **DVD:** 🎬🎬
Lumivision Corp. (Cat #797, UPC #724117079796). Widescreen (1.85:1) letterboxed. Dolby Digital Mono. $19.99. Jewel case. *LANG:* English. *FEATURES:* Commentary: Arkush, Finnell, Whitley • Roger Corman interview with Leonard Maltin • Audio outtakes from Ramones concert • Isolated music track • Trailer • 29 chapter links in film; 10 links in extra material.
1979 (PG) 94m/C P.J. Soles, Vincent Van Patten, Clint Howard, Dey Young, Mary Woronov, Alix Elias, Dick Miller, Paul Bartel, Don Steele, Dee Dee Ramone, Joey Ramone, Johnny Ramone, Marky Ramone; *D:* Allan Arkush; *W:* Joe Dante, Russ Dvonch, Joseph McBride, Richard Whitley; *C:* Dean Cundey; *M:* The Ramones.

Rock 'n' Roll Invaders: The AM Radio DJs
This documentary, broadcast on the Bravo cable channel, is an affectionate look at the early days of rock. It begins with the valid point, often overlooked, that in the late 1940s, many people thought that the new medium of television was going to eclipse radio completely. Then the music changed and AM radio was reborn. Unlike so many of these nostalgia-intensive looks back, this one pays careful attention to the role that black radio stations and DJs played in the creation of this music, and it doesn't ignore the corrupt side of the business, either. Not surprisingly, the quality of the DVD image varies considerably with the historical footage. It never rises above its made-for-TV production values. The music is beyond criticism. —*MM*

Movie: 🎬🎬🎬 **DVD:** 🎬🎬🎬
WinStar Home Entertainment (Cat #WHE73031, UPC #720917303123). Full frame. $24.98. Keepcase. *LANG:* English. *FEATURES:* 8 chapter links • Thumbnail biographies of 13 early rock DJs.
199? 96m/C *D:* Paul Eichgrun; *W:* Paul Eichgrun; *Nar:* Ross Porter.

The Rock: The People's Champ
For anyone who, like me, has never seen professional wrestling, this DVD is fascinating. It's an unashamed piece of hero-worship for The Rock, a wrestler whose flair for theatricality is matched by genuine "presence," and a stuntman's ability to create believable, exciting physical action on-screen. The ongoing soap-opera that wrestling creates around itself is given some attention, but the focus stays squarely on the star who can create gonzo for the masses. Note this fractured greet-

ing delivered to an arena full of crazed fans: "Twenty thousand asses are standing on their feet with goosebumps running through their body, all chanting the Rock's name!" He often proclaims himself to be "the most electrifying man in sports entertainment." Remember to keep the emphasis on "entertainment." Visually, the fast-paced DVD is no better than the source material, almost all videotaped interviews and matches that are jazzed up with slow motion, jagged editing, and other simple tricks. Sound is fine. The disc is almost an hour longer than the VHS tape. —MM

Movie: ♫♫♫ **DVD:** ♫♫♫

World Wrestling Federation (Cat #WWF1004, UPC #651191100422). Full frame. Dolby Digital 5.1 Surround Stereo; Dolby Digital Surround Stereo. $24.95. Keepcase. *LANG:* English. *FEATURES:* 26 chapter links.
199? 143m/C

The Rocketeer

Cliff Secord (Campbell), a 1930s stunt flyer, finds an experimental jet backpack that's sought by Nazi spies, who are led by Hollywood star Sinclair (Dalton). Donning a mask that makes him looks like a vintage hood ornament, Cliff becomes a flying superhero. It's all breezy fun with stupendous special effects; even better if you know movie trivia. Sinclair is obviously based on Errol Flynn. Some of the art deco backgrounds aren't completely stable, but beyond that, the entire production is grade-A prime eye candy. The DVD image appears to be somewhat brighter than the tape, though the whole film is slightly overlit, giving the fantasy a luminescent quality. Admittedly, though, some of that might be due to Jennifer Connelly, who's an absolute knockout in her white satin evening dress. One of the most underrated of the comic-inspired adventure films of the '80s and '90s. —MM

Movie: ♫♫♫ **DVD:** ♫♫♫

Buena Vista Home Entertainment (Cat #17501, UPC #717951003195). Widescreen (2.35:1) letterboxed. Dolby Digital Surround. $29.99. Keepcase. *LANG:* English; French. *FEATURES:* 15 chapter links ● Theatrical trailer.
1991 (PG) 109m/C Bill Campbell, Jennifer Connelly, Alan Arkin, Timothy Dalton, Paul Sorvino, Melora Hardin, Tiny Ron, Terry O'Quinn, Ed Lauter, James Handy; **D:** Joe Johnston; **W:** Paul DeMeo, Danny Bilson; **C:** Hiro Narita; **M:** James Horner.

Rocky

Stallone plays Rocky, the underdog hoping to win fame and self-respect in a boxoffice smash and Oscar-winning rags-to-riches story about a young man from the slums of Philadelphia who dreams of becoming a boxing champion. Stallone delivered a knockout and the previously unknown actor became a boxoffice heavyweight. This intense portrayal of the American Dream loses some of its punch when weighted down by its numerous and inferi-

or sequels. Though the DVD image is marred by grain, the rough look has been with *Rocky* since its theatrical release. Still, the DVD suffers from damaged film elements used for the video transfer. Some restoration would be welcome for a future re-issue, as well as the anamorphic enhancement missing from the letterboxed side of this disc. The soundtrack is perhaps even more flawed, with distortion readily apparent and the dialogue muddy. Honored as Best Picture of its year, *Rocky* deserves better treatment on DVD, with many more hoped-for extras that aren't present here. —MB

Movie: ♫♫♫ **DVD:** ♫

MGM Home Entertainment (Cat #906043, UPC #027616604392). Widescreen (1.85:1) letterboxed; full frame. Dolby Digital 2.0. $24.98. Snapper. *LANG:* English; French; Spanish. *SUB:* English; French; Spanish. *CAP:* English. *FEATURES:* 25 chapter links ● Theatrical trailer.
1976 (PG) 125m/C Sylvester Stallone, Talia Shire, Burgess Meredith, Burt Young, Carl Weathers; **D:** John G. Avildsen; **W:** Sylvester Stallone; **C:** James A. Crabe; **M:** Bill Conti. *AWARDS:* Academy Awards '76: Best Director (Avildsen), Best Film Editing, Best Picture; American Film Institute (AFI) '98: Top 100; Directors Guild of America Awards '76: Best Director (Avildsen); Golden Globe Awards '77: Best Film—Drama; Los Angeles Film Critics Association Awards '76: Best Film; National Board of Review Awards '76: Best Supporting Actress (Shire); New York Film Critics Awards '76: Best Supporting Actress (Shire); *NOM:* Academy Awards '76: Best Actor (Stallone), Best Actress (Shire), Best Original Screenplay, Best Song ("Gonna Fly Now"), Best Sound, Best Supporting Actor (Meredith, Young).

Rocky 2

Unnecessary sequel finds Rocky (Stallone) frustrated by the commercialism that follows his championship fight from the first film. While wife Adrian (Shire) fights for life, he goes for a rematch. Image and sound are essentially identical to VHS tape. Considering the age of the original, that's to be expected. —MM

Movie: ♫♫ **DVD:** ♫♫

MGM Home Entertainment (Cat #906731, UPC #027616673121). Widescreen letterboxed; full frame. Dolby Digital Surround Stereo; Mono. $24.98. Snapper. *LANG:* English; French; Spanish. *SUB:* English; French; Spanish. *CAP:* English. *FEATURES:* 32 chapter links ● Theatrical trailer.
1979 (PG) 119m/C Sylvester Stallone, Talia Shire, Burt Young, Burgess Meredith, Carl Weathers; **D:** Sylvester Stallone; **W:** Sylvester Stallone; **C:** Bill Butler; **M:** Bill Conti.

Rocky 4

Rocky (Stallone) travels to Russia to fight the drug-enhanced Soviet champ Drago (Lundgren), who killed Apollo Creed (Weathers) in the ring. The flag-waving

patriotism is distasteful and craven. The DVD image looks fine. Sound is very good, too. So? —MM

Movie: ♫ **DVD:** ♫♫

MGM Home Entertainment (Cat #906732, UPC #027616673220). Widescreen letterboxed; full frame. Dolby Digital 5.1 Surround Stereo; Mono. $24.98. Snapper. *LANG:* English; French; Spanish. *SUB:* English; French; Spanish. *CAP:* English. *FEATURES:* 32 chapter links ● Theatrical trailer.
1985 (PG) 91m/C Sylvester Stallone, Talia Shire, Dolph Lundgren, Brigitte Nielsen, Michael Pataki, Burt Young, Carl Weathers; **D:** Sylvester Stallone; **W:** Sylvester Stallone; **C:** Bill Butler; **M:** Bill Conti, Vince Di Cola. *AWARDS:* Golden Raspberry Awards '85: Worst Actor (Stallone), Worst Supporting Actress (Nielsen), Worst Director (Stallone), Worst Screenplay, Worst New Star (Nielsen).

Rodgers and Hammerstein: The Sound of Movies

Shirley Jones hosts an affectionate tribute to the two acknowledged masters of the American musical. Though they're known best for their theatrical work, their films reached a larger audience and that's the focus. The clips from those films (two versions of *State Fair*, *Oklahoma*, *Carousel*, *The King and I*, *South Pacific*, *Flower Drum Song*, and *The Sound of Music*) are well chosen. Their quality varies depending on the state of the original, from early fuzzy gray television footage to sparkling widescreen technicolor. On DVD, both image and sound are noticeably superior to the VHS tape. Great stuff for fans. —MM

Movie: ♫♫♫ **DVD:** ♫♫♫

Image Entertainment (Cat #ID4512ANDVD, UPC #014381451221). Full frame with widescreen film clips. Uncompressed PCM Stereo. $24.99. Snapper. *LANG:* English. *FEATURES:* 12 chapter links.
1995 ?m/C D: Kevin Burns.

Rogue Trader

Truth-based film tells the story of banker Nick Leeson (McGregor) who stole millions from the British bank that employed him in Singapore. Since the script is based on Leeson's own account, it is not overly critical. He's presented as an ambitious young man with a pretty wife (Friel) who made a few mistakes and then realized how easy it would be to keep those little gaffes to himself with a secret account. Director Dearden tries to make the complexities comprehensible though it is sometimes difficult to understand the action since it is set in the Never-neverland of international finance where numbers and amounts of money have only an incidental relationship with physical realities. He captures the feeding frenzy of commodities trading well. A few fine lines and patterns vibrate but the DVD image is generally fine. McGregor's working-class accent is sometimes difficult to decipher. —MM

Movie: ♪♪♪ **DVD:** ♪♪▸
Miramax Pictures Home Video (Cat #18157, UPC #717951004369). Widescreen (1.85:1) anamorphic. Dolby Digital Stereo. $29.99. Keepcase. *LANG:* English. *CAP:* English. *FEATURES:* 21 chapter links.
1998 (R) 101m/C *GB* Ewan McGregor, John Standing, Anna Friel, Yves Beneyton, Tim McInnery, Betsy Brantley, Caroline Langrishe; *D:* James Dearden; *W:* James Dearden; *C:* Jean-Francois Robin; *M:* Richard Hartley.

Rollerball

In 2018, corporations have replaced governments and rollerball has replaced football as the public's favorite form of organized violence. Jonathan E. (Caan) is the sport's reigning star but the evil corporate boss (Houseman) wants to flatten individual heroes. Yes, Norman Jewison wears his politics on his sleeve, and he admits as much in his commentary/reminiscence recorded in 1997. DVD can do little to improve the roughness of the image, typical of mid-'70s films, and it should not. On disc, the film looks as good and as bad as it ever has. The newly recorded 5.1 Surround Stereo is a major step up, most notably in the final reel. A theatrical remake is in the works. *—MM*
Movie: ♪♪♪ **DVD:** ♪♪▸
MGM Home Entertainment (Cat #907015, UPC #027616701527). Widescreen letterboxed; full frame. Dolby Digital 5.1 Surround Stereo; Dolby Digital Surround Stereo. $24.98. Keepcase. *LANG:* English; French. *SUB:* English; French; Spanish. *FEATURES:* 30 chapter links ▪ Commentary: Norman Jewison ▪ "Making of" featurette ▪ Game.
1975 (R) 123m/C James Caan, John Houseman, Maud Adams, Moses Gunn, John Beck; *D:* Norman Jewison; *W:* William Harrison; *C:* Douglas Slocombe; *M:* Andre Previn.

Rollercoaster

A deranged extortionist threatens to sabotage an amusement park ride. Plucky Segal must stop him. Pop rockers Sparx are featured in a concert at the park. Video renters used to be spared the nauseating effects of film's original "Sensurround," but, maybe unfortunately, the DVD attempts to replicate it by giving a huge boost to the bass in the mono soundtrack. The bass does rock the subwoofer, but the film is more enjoyable if you cut it back a bit. The image transfer is great and both color and sharpness have been greatly improved over the older video versions. *—JO*
Movie: ♪♪ **DVD:** ♪♪♪
Universal Studios Home Video (Cat #20439, UPC #025192043925). Widescreen (2.35:1) letterboxed. Mono. $24.98. Keepcase. *LANG:* English; French. *SUB:* Spanish. *CAP:* English. *FEATURES:* 16 chapter links ▪ Production notes ▪ Cast and filmmaker bios ▪ Theatrical trailer ▪ Web links.

1977 (PG) 119m/C George Segal, Richard Widmark, Timothy Bottoms, Henry Fonda, Susan Strasberg, Harry Guardino; *D:* James Goldstone; *W:* William Link; *C:* David M. Walsh; *M:* Lalo Schifrin.

Romance

Catherine Breillat's ironically titled film successfully demystifies and de-eroticizes sex, though it goes far beyond conventional bounds of explicitness in its treatment of the subject. It's the story of Marie (Ducey), a mopey young woman who is in love with Paul (Stevenin), her handsome live-in boyfriend. He says that he cares for her, too, but refuses to sleep with her. Marie reacts with a series of affairs and one-night stands (including one with adult star Rocco Siffredi). To oversimplify, Marie and Paul reverse conventional sexual roles. Breillat's matter-of-fact style of filmmaking makes potentially shocking material mundane. (This is definitely not a guilty pleasure.) The film looks very good on DVD—much better than Breillat's *36 Fillet*—and makes the most of her unsubtle symbolic use of color. Sound is fine and the English language version is almost as expressive as the original French. As is so often the case, though, some of the dialogue sounds very strange to those accustomed to naturalistic speech: "That's the way it always is," Marie says in voice-over, "Women are the sacrificial victims on an altar of men's atonement." *—MM*
Movie: ♪♪♪ **DVD:** ♪♪♪
Trimark Home Video (Cat #VM7249D, UPC #031398724933). Widescreen letterboxed. $24.99. Keepcase. *LANG:* English; French; Spanish. *SUB:* English; French; Spanish. *CAP:* English. *FEATURES:* 24 chapter links ▪ Original promotional art.
1999 93m/C *FR* Caroline Ducey, Sagamore Stevenin, Francois Berleand, Rocco Siffredi; *D:* Catherine Breillat; *W:* Catherine Breillat; *C:* Yorgos Arvanitis; *M:* D.J. Valentin, Raphael Tidas.

Romeo and Juliet

Director Zeffirelli succeeds in casting relative novices Whiting and Hussey in the leads, and their overwrought emotional approach to the roles is legitimate, if a bit uncomfortable. (This is a story about teenagers, after all.) Overall, the film looks wonderful for a work of its age. Director of photography Pasqualino De Santis's work is handled particularly well, though Juliet's red gown bleeds a bit. Nino Rota's soaring score deserves something more than mono sound. Even so, this is an accessible if languidly paced adaptation. *—MM*
Movie: ♪♪♪▸ **DVD:** ♪♪♪▸
Paramount Home Video (Cat #06809, UPC #097360680973). Widescreen anamorphic. Dolby Digital Mono. $29.99. Keepcase. *LANG:* English. *SUB:* English. *FEATURES:* 18 chapter links ▪ Theatrical trailer.

1968 (PG) 138m/C *GB IT* Olivia Hussey, Leonard Whiting, Michael York, Milo O'Shea; *D:* Franco Zeffirelli; *W:* Franco Zeffirelli, Franco Brusati, Maestro D'Amico; *C:* Pasqualino De Santis; *M:* Nino Rota; *Nar:* Laurence Olivier. *AWARDS:* Academy Awards '68: Best Cinematography, Best Costume Design; Golden Globe Awards '69: Best Foreign Film; National Board of Review Awards '68: Best Director (Zeffirelli); *NOM:* Academy Awards '68: Best Director (Zeffirelli), Best Picture.

Romy and Michele's High School Reunion

This flick shares one unfortunate quality with most real-life high school reunions: It's not as much fun as you think it's going to be. Still, there are some entertaining moments as Sorvino and Kudrow play a pair of carefree party girls who reinvent themselves as wealthy and famous people for their 10-year high school reunion. When their stories prove preposterous (claims of inventing Post-It Notes, for example), their former classmates ridicule them. Yeah, Romy and Michelle are a pair of ditzes, but they're endearing ditzes in this comedy about individuality and the separation of classes. The girls may not have been among the popular set in high school, but they were ahead of bottom-feeder Heather (Garofalo). The music is good, and the goofy choreography of Romy and Michelle's dance floor moves is hilarious. Ultimately, however, the laughs are too few to warrant owning rather than renting this disc. Picture and sound are fine, but the included production featurette is a minimal bonus. *—MB*
Movie: ♪♪▸ **DVD:** ♪♪♪
Buena Vista Home Entertainment (Cat #17378, UPC #717951002822). Widescreen (1.85:1) letterboxed. Dolby Digital 5.1. $29.98. Keepcase. *LANG:* English; French. *CAP:* English. *FEATURES:* 17 chapter links ▪ Production featurette ▪ Theatrical trailer.
1997 (R) 91m/C Mira Sorvino, Lisa Kudrow, Janeane Garofalo, Alan Cumming, Julia Campbell, Elaine Hendrix, Jacob Vargas, Camryn Manheim; *D:* David Mirkin; *W:* Robin Schiff; *C:* Reynaldo Villalobos; *M:* Steve Bartek. *AWARDS: NOM:* MTV Movie Awards '98: Best Dance Sequence (Lisa Kudrow/Mira Sorvino/Alan Cumming).

Ronin

What a cast! What a director! What a disappointment! O.K., so it's not that bad—the scenery's spectacular (the action takes place between Paris and Nice) and there are some amazing car chases. But they go on much too long and the story's less than involving. Sam (De Niro) is a world-weary ex-spy (maybe) who gets involved with several international players (including Reno, Skarsgard, and Bean) to do a job for tough Irish lass Deirdre (McElhone). She's fronting (for the violent Pryce) a project to retrieve a mysterious suitcase from some

Russian bad guys. One of the best things the film's got going for it is the wary buddy relationship that builds between De Niro and Reno. This is an excellent DVD transfer that completely captures the theatrical presentation of the film. Although not vibrant, the dreary colors are extremely accurate. The DVD also contains one of the best 5.1 mixes out there, and its Surround effects can't be beat for both effects and totally immersing ambience. It seems like there is always something going on around you, whether the characters are talking in a restaurant or involved in a high-speed chase through city streets. The gunshots are very realistic sounding. The commentary is informative and full of details that may be of interest to real film fanatics. —JO

Movie: ♪♪♪ **DVD:** ♪♪♪♪
MGM Home Entertainment (Cat #907439, UPC #027616743923). Widescreen (2.35:1) anamorphic; full frame. Dolby 5.1. $24.98. Keepcase. *LANG:* English; French. *SUB:* English; French. *CAP:* English. *FEATURES:* 32 chapter links ● Audio commentary ● Alternate ending ● 8-page booklet.
1998 (R) 118m/C Robert De Niro, Jean Reno, Stellan Skarsgard, Natascha McElhone, Jonathan Pryce, Skipp Sudduth, Michael (Michel) Lonsdale, Sean Bean, Jan Triska, Feodor Atkine, Bernard Bloch, Katarina Witt; *D:* John Frankenheimer; *W:* David Mamet, J.D. Zeik; *C:* Robert Fraisse; *M:* Elia Cmiral. *AWARDS: NOM:* MTV Movie Awards '99: Best Action Sequence.

Rooster Cogburn

A Bible-thumping schoolmarm joins up with a hard-drinking, hard-fighting marshal to capture a gang of outlaws who killed her father. It's a tired sequel to *True Grit* but the chemistry between Wayne and Hepburn is right on target. This film is more enjoyable than ever thanks to the sharpness and detail on the DVD. The location filming is gorgeous and though the colors are a touch off, they are nonetheless vibrant, making even some of the duller scenes beautiful to look at. The Dolby Digital sound is full, with much better low-end than you find on older video releases, and the dialogue is a lot less harsh, without loss of overall crispness. —JO

Movie: ♪♪♪ **DVD:** ♪♪♪
Universal Studios Home Video (Cat #20170, UPC #025192017025). Widescreen (2.35:1) letterboxed. Dolby Digital Mono 2.0. $24.98. Keepcase. *LANG:* English; French; Spanish. *SUB:* Spanish. *CAP:* English. *FEATURES:* 16 chapter links ● Theatrical trailer ● Cast and filmmakers bios ● Production notes.
1975 (PG) 107m/C John Wayne, Katharine Hepburn, Richard Jordan, Anthony Zerbe, John McIntire, Strother Martin, Paul Koslo; *D:* Stuart Millar; *W:* Martin Julien; *C:* Harry Stradling Jr.; *M:* Laurence Rosenthal.

Rosewood

Based on the true story of the well-off African American community of Rosewood, FL, which was destroyed by a white mob in 1923. Rhames is Mr. Mann, a war vet, and Voight is a white shopkeeper. Together they try to save innocent people from the tragic massacre that begins when a woman falsely accuses a black man of rape. Voight's character is not overly romanticized as the great white hope. The real hero is the reticent Rhames, a fictitious blend of real-life characters and Hollywood machismo. Both performances are strong and film succeeds as a detailed visual reminder of country's tragic history. Real-life survivors of the bloodshed finally won reparation from the Florida legislature in 1993. This sad piece of history should have been accented by a supplemental documentary or at least essay, but unfortunately Warner stuck to some minor production notes and a rather boring commentary by director Singleton. On the plus side, the transfer is great and all the dark texturings of the film come to home video intact on the DVD, thanks to its excellent handling of mostly dimly lit film. The picture remains sharp throughout and the details of the color shadings are distinct. —JO

Movie: ♪♪♪ **DVD:** ♪♪♪▸
Warner Home Video, Inc. (Cat #14536, UPC #085391453628). Widescreen (2.35:1) anamorphic. Dolby Digital 5.1; Dolby Surround. $24.98. Snapper. *LANG:* English; Spanish. *SUB:* English; French; Spanish. *CAP:* English. *FEATURES:* 24 chapter links ● Production notes ● Theatrical trailer ● Commentary: director John Singleton.
1996 (R) 142m/C Ving Rhames, Jon Voight, Don Cheadle, Michael Rooker, Bruce McGill, Loren Dean, Esther Rolle, Elise Neal, Catherine Kellner, Akosua Busia, Paul Benjamin, Mark Boone Jr., Muse Watson, Badja Djola, Kathryn Meisle, Jaimz Woolvett; *D:* John Singleton; *W:* Gregory Poirier; *C:* Johnny E. Jensen; *M:* John Williams.

Rouge

Supernatural love story follows a spectral woman (Mui) who is finally reunited with the man of her dreams (Cheung). *AKA:* Yanzhi Kou.

Movie: ♪♪▸ **DVD:** NYR
Tai Seng Video Marketing (Cat #07194). $49.95.
1987 99m/C *HK* Anita Mui, Leslie Cheung, Alex Man, Emily Chu; *D:* Stanley Kwan; *W:* Lei Bik Wah, Chiu Tai An-Ping; *C:* Bill Wong; *M:* Michael Lai.

Rough Night in Jericho

Martin plays unredeemable scum in this cliched western. He's an ex-lawman trying to take over the town of Jericho and all that's left to own is the stagecoach line run by Simmons and McIntire. Coming to the rescue is Peppard as a former deputy marshal turned gambler.

Movie: ♪▸ **DVD:** NYR
Goodtimes Entertainment (Cat #81042). Widescreen (2.35:1) letterboxed. $14.99. Keepcase.
1967 104m/C Dean Martin, Jean Simmons, George Peppard, John McIntire, Slim Pickens, Don Galloway; *D:* Arnold Laven; *W:* Sydney Boehm, Marvin H. Albert; *C:* Russell Metty; *M:* Don Costa.

Roujin Z

Japanese animated film has an unusually sophisticated premise and enough innovative action for younger viewers. It's about the care of the elderly and the relative roles of government, health care organizations, and individuals. The Z-001 unit is a mobile machine that can do everything for the immobile, incontinent geriatric patient. Literally plugging into the user's brain, it's a super RoboNurse. But when the prototype is tested on an old man, his memories become part of the machine's circuitry. Who's in charge here? As anime fans expect, the action contains lots of explosions and radical transformations. But the film also has a more reflective and gentle side that's rare for the genre. If Katsuhiro Otomo's film isn't as visually powerful and ambitious as his masterpiece *Akira,* it's a solid story with well-written characters and a sometimes childish sense of humor. The film looks and sounds only slightly better on DVD than it does on VHS tape because this relatively simple style of animation is easily reproduced. —MM

Movie: ♪♪♪ **DVD:** ♪♪♪
Image Entertainment (Cat #ID4409CTDVD, UPC #01438144092). Widescreen (1.66:1) letterboxed. Dolby Digital Stereo. $24.99. Snapper. *LANG:* English. *SUB:* English; Japanese. *FEATURES:* 14 chapter links.
1995 (PG-13) 80m/C *D:* Katsuhiro Otomo.

Rounders

Damon plays Mike, a law student who used to be a poker hustler, but is now ready to leave the game and settle down with girlfriend Jo (Mol). His good intentions are undermined by his "friend" Worm (Norton), whose gambling debts are mounting. Mike's return to the table doesn't reduce the debt; instead, he loses money and his reputation. Knowing he must get the money himself, Mike sets up a final showdown with Teddy KGB (Malkovich)—a tense game of Texas Hold 'Em in which Malkovich's drawn-out accent provides the most fun of the movie. Damon holds his own, using some elaborate monologues reminiscent of *Good Will Hunting,* while Norton and Malkovich add a lot of spark. It's all style over substance, but that's what makes it (mostly) work. Since most major studio–released DVDs have pretty good colors, and bleed seems to be less and less a problem, it's worth mentioning that there is a problem in the reds on this disc. Other than that, the picture is sharp and clean with only slight grain added in the darker scenes, which dominate the film. The 5.1 sound is lacking in Surround effects but really kicks in with a fine music mix, while not obliterating the dialogue. —JO

Movie: 𝄞𝄞► **DVD:** 𝄞𝄞
Miramax Pictures Home Video (Cat #16449, UPC #717951001535). Widescreen (2.35:1) letterboxed. Dolby Digital 5.1. $29.99. Keepcase. *LANG:* English. *CAP:* English. *FEATURES:* 28 chapter links • Theatrical trailer.
1998 (R) 120m/C Matt Damon, Edward Norton, John Turturro, Gretchen Mol, Famke Janssen, John Malkovich, Martin Landau, Michael Rispoli, Melina Kanakaredes, Josh Mostel, Lenny Clarke, Tom Aldredge; **D:** John Dahl; **W:** David Levien, Brian Koppelman; **C:** Jean-Yves Escoffier; **M:** Christopher Young.

Route 9
Somewhat cliched story, reminiscent of *A Simple Plan*, has some decent performances and a sense of humor. Two small-town sheriff deputies (MacLachlan and Williams) discover a couple of dead bodies, drugs, and a stash of cash, which they decide to keep. But their boss (Coyote) is suspicious and then the feds come investigating. The full-frame image varies between good and very good. The same for sound. —MM
Movie: 𝄞𝄞► **DVD:** 𝄞𝄞►
Studio Home Entertainment (Cat #7195). Full frame. $24.95. Keepcase. *LANG:* English. *SUB:* Spanish. *CAP:* English. *FEATURES:* Commentary: MacLachlan and Mackay • Trailer • 23 chapter links.
1998 (R) 102m/C Kyle MacLachlan, Wade Williams, Peter Coyote, Roma Maffia, Amy Locane, Miguel Sandoval, Scott Coffey; **D:** David Mackay; **W:** Brendan Broderick, Rob Kerchner; **C:** Brian Sullivan; **M:** Don Davis.

Royal Hunt of the Sun
This curiously undernourished epic makes its home video debut on DVD and it's easy to see why it took so long. Though the scope and seriousness of the film invite comparisons to *Lawrence of Arabia* and other ambitious historical epics of the time, the film never really breaks free of Peter Shaffer's stage play upon which the script is based. The Peruvian and Spanish locations—rugged mountainscapes and deserts—are mostly empty and the limited budget shows through in every frame. That said, the performances by Robert Shaw, as the conquistador Pizarro, and Christopher Plummer, as the Inca king, are intense. The DVD image doesn't measure up. The first thing viewers will notice is the distracting bright blue letterbox. The disc was made from an imperfect print that's flecked, broken, and further marred by bad jumps between shots. The sound is tinny. The production factoids list the running time at 128 minutes. This version runs 88

minutes. Other sources list the running time at a little less than two hours. —MM
Movie: 𝄞𝄞 **DVD:** 𝄞►
Simitar Entertainment (Cat #7229, UPC #082551722921). Widescreen letterboxed. PCM Stereo. $14.98. Keepcase. *LANG:* English. *FEATURES:* 16 chapter links • Production factoids • Filmographies of Christopher Plummer and Robert Shaw.
1969 (G) 88m/C Christopher Plummer, Robert Shaw, Nigel Davenport, James Donald; **D:** Irving Lerner; **W:** Philip Yordan; **C:** Roger Barlow, Francisco Sempere; **M:** Marc Wilkinson.

Royal Tramp
Stephen Chow plays a clown who mugs his way through a slapstick historical action flick. The DVD lacks even the most elemental features—chapters, credit translations—and those it does have are substandard. The small pale white subtitles are impossible to read half the time. —MM
Movie: 𝄞 **DVD:** 𝄞
Tai Seng Video Marketing (Cat #DVD-124). Full frame. $49.95. Keepcase. *LANG:* Cantonese; Mandarin. *SUB:* Chinese; English.
1992 110m/C *HK* Stephen (Chiau) Chow, Cheung Man, Kong Yu, Wu Man Dat; **D:** Wong Jing.

Royal Tramp 2
Sequel costars Brigitte Lin.
Movie: NYR **DVD:** NYR
Tai Seng Video Marketing (Cat #30114). Dolby Digital 5.1 Surround Stereo. $49.95. *LANG:* Mandarin. *SUB:* English; Japanese; Thai; Vietnamese. *FEATURES:* Trailer.
1992 90m/C *HK* Stephen (Chiau) Chow, Brigitte Lin; **D:** Wong Jing.

Royal Wedding
Astaire and Powell play a brother-and-sister dance team who go to London during the royal wedding of Queen Elizabeth and find their own romances. The lightweight film is notable for the inspired songs and Astaire's incredible dancing on ceiling and walls (chapter 9), and his famous routine with a coatrack (chapter 4). The idea came from Adele Astaire's recent marriage to a British Lord. The lush Technicolor makes a rough transition to DVD. Reds and blacks both bleed; the focus is soft; clothing patterns flash and faint snow appears throughout. —MM *AKA:* Wedding Bells.
Movie: 𝄞𝄞𝄞 **DVD:** 𝄞𝄞
United American Video (Cat #40082, UPC #084296400829). Full frame. Dolby Digital Stereo. $9.99. Snapper. *LANG:* English. *FEATURES:* 9 chapter links. Title is also available from Madacy (cat. #99025) for $9.99.
1951 93m/C Fred Astaire, Jane Powell, Peter Lawford, Keenan Wynn, Sarah Churchill; **D:** Stanley Donen; **W:** Alan Jay Lerner; **C:** Robert Planck; **M:** Johnny Green, Burton Lane, Albert Sendry.

AWARDS: NOM: Academy Awards '51: Best Song ("Too Late Now").

Rude
Toronto pirate radio DJ Rude (Lewis) narrates three interwoven stories about contemporary urban life: window dresser Maxine (Crawford) deals with an abortion after her lover leaves her; frightened boxer Jordan (Chevolleau) faces his own homosexuality after participating with his friends in a bout of gay-bashing; and ex-con Luke (Wint) returns to his police officer wife and young son. Writer-director Virgo makes an impressive debut. DVD is a perfect medium for his stylized approach that uses non-realistic expressionistic sets and exaggerated colors with occasional solarized highlights. Sound is particularly important here, too, with Rude's intimate Jamaican-accented poetry acting as the connective tissue that holds the film together. Certainly not to all tastes, but festival fans should definitely give it a try. —MM
Movie: 𝄞𝄞𝄞 **DVD:** 𝄞𝄞𝄞
Simitar Entertainment (Cat #7294, UPC #082551729425). Full frame. PCM Stereo. $14.98. Keepcase. *LANG:* English. *FEATURES:* 8 chapter links • Production factoids.
1996 (R) 90m/C *CA* Sharon M. Lewis, Richard Chevolleau, Rachael Crawford, Maurice Dean Wint, Stephen Ellen, Clark Johnson, Melanie Nicholls-King, Stephen Shellen; **D:** Clement Virgo; **W:** Clement Virgo; **C:** Barry Stone; **M:** Aaron David.

Rudolph the Red–Nosed Reindeer: The Movie
Animated version of the famous song.
Movie: NYR **DVD:** NYR
Goodtimes Entertainment (Cat #81059). Widescreen (1.78:1) letterboxed. Dolby Digital Surround Stereo. $14.99. Snapper. *LANG:* English; French; Spanish. *SUB:* French; Spanish. *FEATURES:* Trailer.
1998 90m/C D: William R. Kowalchuk; **W:** Michael Aschner; **M:** Al Kasha, Michael Lloyd; **V:** John Goodman, Eric Idle, Bob Newhart, Debbie Reynolds, Richard Simmons, Whoopi Goldberg.

The Rugrats Movie
Precocious one-year-old Tommy is afraid he'll be forgotten by his parents with the arrival of baby brother Dil, so he and his pals decide to return the infant to the hospital. Boarding a talking wagon named Reptar (invented by Tommy's father), they embark on an adventure that takes them to a scary forest where they run into wolves, a "wizard," and a band of escaped circus monkeys that kidnap Dil in the film's most frightening sequence. While dishing out lessons about responsibility, bravery, friendship, and jealousy, film also contains parodies of (and homages to) several films, including *Raiders of the Lost Ark*. The humor

works on many levels, so this one is enjoyable for all ages. The first thing I noticed was that the 5.1 sound is slightly exaggerated and works nicely with this animated feature. It's one of the liveliest mixes out there, with Surround effects popping in and out all over the place. The picture is very sharp and the colors bright and contrasty, with no grain or artifacts. The bonus short is really an ad for *Catdog*. —JO

Movie: ♫♫♫ **DVD:** ♫♫♫♫
Paramount Home Video (Cat #333997, UPC #097363339977). Widescreen (1.85:1) letterboxed; full frame. Dolby Digital 5.1; Dolby Surround. $29.99. Keepcase. *LANG:* English (DD 5.1); French (DS). *FEATURES:* 19 chapter links • Theatrical trailer • Bonus short • Dual-layered RSDL.
1998 (G) 79m/C D: Norton Virgien, Igor Kovalyov; **W:** David N. Weiss, J. David Stem; **M:** Mark Mothersbaugh; **V:** Elizabeth (E.G.) Daily, Christine Cavanaugh, Tara Charendoff, Melanie Chartoff, Jack Riley, Joe Alaskey, Phil Proctor, Whoopi Goldberg, David Spade, Kath Soucie, Cheryl Case, Cree Summer, Michael Bell, Tress MacNeille, Busta Rhymes.

Rumble Fish

A young street punk (Dillon) worships his gang-leading older brother (Rourke), the only role model he's known. Crafted by Coppola into an important story of growing up on the wrong side of town, from the novel by S. E. Hinton (who has a cameo as a prostitute). The supporting cast is nothing short of amazing. It's ambitious, experimental, and beautifully photographed with an incredibly atmospheric music score by Stewart Copeland of the Police, which alone is worth the price of the DVD. Though some will complain that the soundtrack was not remastered to 5.1, the Dolby Surround is excellent and delivers the music in crisp highs and lows, features excellent dynamics, and still allows the dialogue to punch through. Coppola's scene composition can be fully appreciated thanks to accurate letterboxing. Very sharp black and white with very good graytones, excellent contrast and brightness levels, and minimal grain and artifacts. Some nasty film scratches near the beginning don't last long. —JO

Movie: ♫♫♫ **DVD:** ♫♫♫►
Universal Studios Home Video (Cat #20389, UPC #025192038921). Widescreen (1.85:1) letterboxed. Dolby Surround. $24.98. Keepcase. *LANG:* English. *SUB:* French; Spanish. *CAP:* English. *FEATURES:* 16 chapter links • Theatrical trailer • Cast and filmmaker bios • Production notes.
1983 (R) 94m/B Matt Dillon, Mickey Rourke, Dennis Hopper, Diane Lane, Vincent Spano, Nicolas Cage, Diana Scarwid, Christopher Penn, Tom Waits; **D:** Francis Ford Coppola; **W:** Francis Ford Coppola; **C:** Stephen Burum; **M:** Stewart Copeland.

Rumble in the Bronx

Chan is a Hong Kong cop who comes to the South Bronx (actually Vancouver in many scenes) to attend his uncle's wedding and winds up caught in a crime war between the mob and a motorcycle gang. As always, Chan choreographed and performed all of his own stunts and they are some of his better work, even the ones where he is hiding a broken foot. Though the film as a whole is not his finest vehicle, Chan's engaging personality is the key ingredient. Not surprisingly, it lacks the polish and clarity of his more recent (and more lavishly budgeted) American work and the DVD suffers somewhat in comparison to them. It also lacks extensive extras. —MM

Movie: ♫♫♫ **DVD:** ♫♫♫
New Line Home Video (Cat #N4410, UPC #794043441028). Full frame; widescreen (2.35:1). Dolby Digital 5.1 (English); Dolby Stereo (French). $24.98. Snapper. *LANG:* English; French. *SUB:* English; French. *FEATURES:* 22 chapter links • Brief Jackie Chan bio • Theatrical trailer.
1996 (R) 91m/C HK Jackie Chan, Anita Mui, Francoise Yip, Bill Tung, Morgan Lam, Marc Akerstream; **D:** Stanley Tong; **W:** Edward Tang, Fibe Ma; **C:** Jingle Ma; **M:** J. Peter Robinson.

Run Lola Run

Lola (Potente) has 20 minutes to get 100,000 marks ($60,000.00) to her desperate boyfriend Manni (Bleibtreu). That's the premise of Tom Tykwer's time-bending experimental thriller, but the simple idea is twisted into several cinematic permutations. It's a challenging idea but the filmmakers are careful always to engage the viewer and never to confuse, despite a breathless pace. On the commentary track, Tykwer and Potente explain how they worked out the unconventional plot lines and how they managed to make such an innovative film on a relatively small budget. On DVD, the Tykwer's combination of live action and animation, color and black and white, and 35mm and video looks fine. Many scenes are intentionally distressed. The only jarring flaw comes in the video sequence of chapter 21 where one panning shot briefly becomes an almost painful kaleidoscope. Many of the visual techniques that Tykwer uses have been seen recently in *The Matrix* and other sf films, but here they become integral parts of the narrative. The film's simply a stunner. If it loses anything in transition from large screen to small, the DVD adds accessibility and this is one that you need to see more than once to appreciate fully. —MM *AKA: Lola Rennt.*

Movie: ♫♫♫♫ **DVD:** ♫♫♫►
Columbia Tristar Home Video (Cat #4014). Widescreen (1.66:1) letterboxed; full frame. Dolby Digital Stereo; Dolby Digital 5.1 Surround Stereo. $28.95. Keepcase. *LANG:* German; English. *SUB:* English; French. *FEATURES:* 28 chapter links • Commentary: Tom Tykwer and Franka

Potente • Music video • Thumbnail talent biographies.
1998 (R) 81m/C GE Franka Potente, Moritz Bleibtreu, Joachim Krol, Herbert Knaup, Armin Rohde; **D:** Tom Tykwer; **W:** Tom Tykwer; **C:** Frank Griebe; **M:** Tom Tykwer. *AWARDS:* Independent Spirit Awards '00: Best Foreign Film; VSDA DVD Festival '00: Best use of Audio/Language Tracks (tie); *NOM:* British Academy Awards '99: Best Foreign Film.

Runaway Train

Tough jailbird Oscar Mannheim (Voight) and his sidekick Buck (Roberts) escape from a grim Alaskan maximum security prison, hijack a freight train, and set it careening across a snow-covered Canada. Harrowing existential drama (based on a screenplay by Akira Kurosawa) is no less frightening than Voight's rabid overacting. The DVD does an excellent job with difficult material. The dark action scenes are actually a bit sharper than I remember from the theatrical release and the sense of cold that director Konchalovsky is able to conjure up is strong. Sound is very good. —MM

Movie: ♫♫► **DVD:** ♫♫►
MGM Home Entertainment (Cat #907018, UPC #027616701824). Widescreen letterboxed; full frame. Dolby Digital Surround Stereo. $24.98. Keepcase. *LANG:* English; French. *SUB:* English; French; Spanish. *FEATURES:* 32 chapter links • Theatrical trailer.
1985 (R) 112m/C Jon Voight, Eric Roberts, Rebecca DeMornay, John P. Ryan, T.K. Carter, Kenneth McMillan, John Bloom; **D:** Andrei Konchalovsky; **W:** Andrei Konchalovsky, Djordje Milicevic, Edward Bunker; **C:** Alan Hume; **M:** Trevor Jones. *AWARDS:* Golden Globe Awards '86: Best Actor—Drama (Voight); *NOM:* Academy Awards '85: Best Actor (Voight), Best Film Editing, Best Supporting Actor (Roberts).

The Runner

Edward (Eldard) is a degenerate gambler who's desperate for money in Vegas. His uncle Rocco (Mantegna) hooks him up with bookie Deepthroat (Goodman) to work as a numbers runner. That, as Edward tells us in voice-over, is like hiring an alcoholic as a bartender. Even Edward's budding romance with waitress Katrina (Cox) can't keep him out of trouble. In the end, the thriller may not live up to the expectations engendered by its high-powered cast, but it's still a nice ride. On DVD, the full-frame image is slightly sharper than VHS tape, but it's not a striking difference. Director Moler is able to capture the visual side of a casino, but even with strong stereo sound, he doesn't get that incessant audio assault. —MM

Movie: ♫♫► **DVD:** ♫♫►
Image Entertainment (Cat #OVED8779DVD, UPC #014381877922). Full frame. Dolby Digital Surround Stereo. $24.99. Snapper. *LANG:* English. *FEATURES:* 12 chapter links • Theatrical trailer.

1999 (R) 95m/C Ron Eldard, John Goodman, Courteney Cox Arquette, Joe Mantegna, Bokeem Woodbine; **D:** Ron Moler; **W:** Anthony E. Zuiker, Dustin Lee Abraham; **C:** James Glennon; **M:** Anthony Marinelli, Anthony Marinelli.

The Running Man

Fast-moving sf action picture is one of Schwarzenegger's best. It's an adaptation of an early Stephen King novel about a futuristic game show where "stalkers" in full professional wrestling regalia chase convicts on live TV. Richard Dawson is excellent as the oily host and so is the star. The few-frills disc faithfully re-creates the neon strobe tackiness and energy that director Glaser created. More importantly, the film never tries to be anything more than entertaining popcorn with a sense of humor. —*MM*
Movie: 🎬🎬🎬 **DVD:** 🎬🎬🎬
Artisan Entertainment (Cat #60455, UPC #012236045502). Widescreen (1.85:1) letterboxed. Dolby Digital Surround Stereo. $24.98. Snapper. *LANG:* English. *CAP:* English. *FEATURES:* 24 chapter links • Theatrical trailer.
1987 (R) 101m/C Arnold Schwarzenegger, Richard Dawson, Maria Conchita Alonso, Yaphet Kotto, Mick Fleetwood, Dweezil Zappa, Jesse Ventura, Jim Brown; **D:** Paul Michael Glaser; **W:** Steven E. de Souza; **C:** Thomas Del Ruth; **M:** Harold Faltermeyer.

Running on Empty

Two 1960s radicals are still on the run in 1988 for a politically motivated Vietnam War–era crime. Though they have managed to stay one step ahead of the law, their son wants a "normal" life, even if it means never seeing his family again. Well-performed, quiet, plausible drama. In the hit-or-miss world of Warner's budget ($14.98) catalogue DVDs, this one is a winner with a very sharp digital transfer. Colors are accurate and even the blacks—often a problem in this line—are very good. The stereo sound is lively and full with decent separation that allows the soundtrack's different elements to all remain distinct. —*JO*
Movie: 🎬🎬🎬 **DVD:** 🎬🎬🎬
Warner Home Video, Inc. (Cat #11843, UPC #085391184324). Full frame. Stereo. $14.98. Snapper. *LANG:* English. *CAP:* English. *FEATURES:* 32 chapter links.
1988 (PG-13) 116m/C Christine Lahti, River Phoenix, Judd Hirsch, Martha Plimpton, Jonas Arby, Ed Crowley, L.M. Kit Carson, Steven Hill, Augusta Dabney, David Margulies, Sidney Lumet; **D:** Sidney Lumet; **W:** Naomi Foner; **C:** Gerry Fisher; **M:** Tony Mottola. *AWARDS:* Golden Globe Awards '89: Best Screenplay; Los Angeles Film Critics Association Awards '88: Best Actress (Lahti); National Board of Review Awards '88: Best Supporting Actor (Phoenix); *NOM:* Academy Awards '88: Best Original Screenplay, Best Supporting Actor (Phoenix).

Running Time

Noirish real-time black-and-white heist tale begins with Carl's (Campbell) release from prison. He's met at the gate by his old friend Patrick (Roberts), a screw-up with a bad haircut. They're minutes away from knocking over a money transfer, but in those few moments, everything goes wrong. Also involved are Donnie (Jennison), a junkie Patrick has chosen to drive the getaway car, and Janey (Barone), a hooker with a history. Becker uses quick cuts to black—with the camera passing through a deep shadow, for example—and the blurring of fast panning shots to disguise the transitions from one shot to another. It's a fairly pointless gimmick—Hitchcock tried it in *Rope*—and it works well enough, though Becker allows an unfortunate reflection in one car window. The swings between comedy and drama are uncertain and the plotting is forced. That said, the performances are convincing. Anita Barone is really effective. On DVD, the black-and-white photography is crisp with a slight tendency toward bright overexposure. Monaural sound is all right. The full-frame film was clearly made with the home video market in mind. —*MM*
Movie: 🎬🎬▶ **DVD:** 🎬🎬🎬
Anchor Bay (Cat #DV10989, UPC #013131098990). Full frame. Dolby Digital Mono. $24.98. Keepcase. *LANG:* English. *FEATURES:* 22 chapter links • Commentary: director Josh Becker and star Bruce Campbell • Theatrical trailer.
1997 70m/B Bruce Campbell, Jeremy Roberts, Anita Barone, Gordon Jennison, Stan Davis; **D:** Josh Becker; **W:** Josh Becker; **C:** Kurt Rauf.

Rush Hour

Though the script is little more than a collection of cop/buddy picture cliches, Brett Ratner directs with sure timing and he gets the most out of his costars, who have the comic chemistry of Abbott and Costello. Tucker plays a brash fast-talking L.A. cop who is partnered with Chan, his quiet Hong Kong counterpart after the 11-year-old daughter of a Chinese diplomat is kidnapped. The stereotyped FBI organization men want nothing to do with either. Tucker's clowning combined with Chan's gracefully choreographed athleticism made the film a theatrical smash hit. Meticulously transferred by Ratner and Mike Sowa, the DVD sparkles in every scene. The film has sharp colors dominated by blacks and reds, excellent stereo separation for sound effects, and a great Lalo Schifrin score. Ratner's commentary track is chatty and enthusiastic. Even without all the extras—and this one has a lot, even more for PCs—the DVD is one of the best to date. —*MM*
Movie: 🎬🎬🎬▶ **DVD:** 🎬🎬🎬🎬
New Line Home Video (Cat #N4717, UPC #794045717284). Widescreen (2.35:1). Dolby 5.1 Surround Stereo; Dolby Digital Surround Stereo. $24.98. Snapper. *SUB:* English. *FEATURES:* Commentary: director Brett Ratner • Isolated score with commentary by composer Lalo Schifrin • Deleted scenes • Cast and crew biographies and filmographies • Theatrical trailer • Short film, *Whatever Happened to Mason Reese,* with commentary • Music video, Dru Hill's "How Deep Is Your Love" • "Making of" featurette • 37 chapter links. PC DVD features: script to screen, access scene in film from script; print script pages; original interactive game; Web links; Chan info.
1998 (PG-13) 98m/C Jackie Chan, Chris Tucker, Tzi Ma, Julia Hsu, Philip Baker Hall, Rex Linn, Elizabeth Pena, Mark Rolston, Tom Wilkinson; **D:** Brett Ratner; **W:** Jim Kouf, Ross LaManna; **C:** Adam Greenberg; **M:** Lalo Schifrin. *AWARDS:* MTV Movie Awards '99: Best On-Screen Duo (Chris Tucker/Jackie Chan); *NOM:* MTV Movie Awards '99: Best Comedic Performance (Tucker), Best Song ("Can I Get A..."), Best Fight.

Rush Week

Halloween meets *Animal House.* Who's bumping off coeds while all the fraternity guys are getting drunk and disgusting? Could it be the evil dean (Thinnes)? About the best that can be said is that the cast is young and attractive, and the violence is restrained. Gregg Allman, of all people, has a bit part and the Dickies provide two songs. On DVD, the night scenes are well lit in blue, and the sound is O.K. —*MM*
Movie: 🎬🎬 **DVD:** 🎬🎬
Simitar Entertainment (Cat #7295, UPC #082551729524). Full frame. PCM Stereo. $14.98. Keepcase. *LANG:* English. *FEATURES:* 8 chapter links • Production factoids • Roy Thinnes filmography.
1988 (R) 93m/C Dean Hamilton, Gregg Allman, Kathleen Kinmont, Roy Thinnes, Pamela Ludwig; **D:** Bob Bravler; **W:** Michael W. Leighton, Russell V. Manzatt; **C:** Jeff Mart.

Rushmore

Fresh, original comedy from Wes Anderson (*Bottlerocket*) may be the best film that anyone has ever made about being a bright 15-year-old boy. Max Fischer (Schwartzman) is an underachieving but ambitious student at his beloved Rushmore Academy. He develops a hopeless crush on a teacher, Miss Cross (Williams), and enlists the help of wealthy alum Herman Blume (Murray) in his quest to impress her. They quickly become competitors for the young woman but that only hints at the dimensions of Anderson's plot. This coming-of-age story touches on almost every facet of Max's life. The Criterion Collection does its usual splendid job in bringing the film to DVD with flawless image and sound and a wealth of extras. Though the film's scope may appear to be modest, Anderson fills every frame with information and the apparently languid pace is actually very fast because the filmmakers have stripped away every unessential moment and gesture. After you've seen the film once, go back a sec-

ond time and listen to the commentary track to discover the autobiographical elements and to appreciate the low-keyed dry humor. —MM
Movie: 🎬🎬🎬🎬 **DVD:** 🎬🎬🎬🎬
Criterion Collection (Cat #65, UPC #715515010429). Widescreen (2.35:1) anamorphic. Dolby Digital 5.1 Surround Stereo. $39.99. Keepcase. *LANG:* English. *SUB:* English. *FEATURES:* 24 chapter links • "Making of" featurette • Film to storyboard comparisons • Storyboards • *Charlie Rose Show* episode with Anderson and Murray • Commentary: Anderson, Wilson, Schwartzman • Photo gallery • Auditions • 3 *Max Fischer Players* movie parodies for 1999 MTV Awards show • Map of Rushmore campus • Theatrical trailer.
1998 (R) 93m/C Bill Murray, Jason Schwartzman, Olivia Williams, Seymour Cassel, Brian Cox, Mason Gamble, Sara Tanaka, Connie Nielsen, Kim Terry, Stephen McCole, Ronnie McCawley, Keith McCawley; *D:* Wes Anderson; *W:* Wes Anderson, Owen C. Wilson; *C:* Robert Yeoman; *M:* Mark Mothersbaugh. *AWARDS:* Independent Spirit Awards '99: Best Director (54938), Best Supporting Actor (Murray); Los Angeles Film Critics Association Awards '98: Best Supporting Actor (Murray); New York Film Critics Awards '98: Best Supporting Actor (Murray); National Society of Film Critics Awards '98: Best Supporting Actor (Murray); *NOM:* Golden Globe Awards '99: Best Supporting Actor (Murray).

Russell Mulcahy's Tale of the Mummy

The "other" Mummy picture of 1999 made its debut on video and is really more closely akin to the original Universal series (and the Hammer versions) than the mainstream theatrical hit. It's been jazzed up with computer effects but the story of a reincarnated ancient priest covers well-trod ground. Sam (Lombard), daughter of the Egyptologist (Christopher Lee) who first discovers the tomb, is the heroine. Det. Riley (Jason Scott Lee) is the London cop trying to solve the series of inexplicable murders. At times, the bizarre humor is reminiscent of *Lair of the White Worm* and *Dr. Phibes Rises Again.* Director Mulcahy (*Highlander*) is just as interested in inventive stylish visuals as scares and laughs. The cast is made up of attractive if little-known newcomers and older character actors who handle the hokum with conviction. Even the big nocturnal finish looks fine on disc. The widescreen transfer makes the most of Bryce Walmsley's impressive sets and the effects from William Mesa, Robert Kurtzman, Gerg Nicotero, and Howard Berger. From beginning to end, this is a solid B-movie whose classy production values stand out on a no-frills DVD. —MM *AKA:* Tale of the Mummy; Talos the Mummy.
Movie: 🎬🎬 **DVD:** 🎬🎬🎬
Buena Vista Home Entertainment (Cat #18159, UPC #717951004376). Wide-

screen (2.35:1) letterboxed. Dolby Digital 5.1. $29.99. Keepcase. *LANG:* English. *FEATURES:* 30 chapter links.
1999 (R) 87m/C Jason Scott Lee, Louise Lombard, Sean Pertwee, Lysette Anthony, Michael Lerner, Jack Davenport, Honor Blackman, Christopher Lee, Shelley Duvall, Jon Polito; *D:* Russell Mulcahy; *W:* Russell Mulcahy, John Esposito; *C:* Gabriel Beristain.

Sabotage

Sabotage is a prewar suspense film centered on terrorist attack plans and an English-German couple (Sidney and Homolka) marked for suspicion. Its most famous scene is an excruciatingly long, painful sequence of a boy unknowingly carting a bomb around central London. That taught Hitchcock to avoid letting an audience down with such a thud ever again. This part of the double bill has only the barest hint of hiss and crackle on the soundtrack. The film unavoidably suffers slightly blooming highlights typical of old films, but the transfer shows brush-stroke aliasing. *The Lodger,* a silent with Ivor Novello as a stranger who may have murdered a series of women, was the director's first try at a thriller. It has a decent if pompous film score, but is riddled with blotches and specks on the film stock, fully complicated by quilted aliasing. The disc throughout has an upper half screen of a different contrast than the lower. There is also a slow, wide but noticeably constant ripple in the screen. The trailer is from another Hitch film entirely. Tony Curtis provides the wraparounds. —JK *AKA:* A Woman Alone; Hidden Power.
Movie: 🎬🎬🎬 **DVD:** 🎬🎬
Delta/Laserlight (Cat #82035, UPC #0181 11997539). Full frame. Dual-channel mono. $9.99. Keepcase. *LANG:* English; Spanish; Chinese; Japanese. *SUB:* Spanish; Chinese; Japanese. *FEATURES:* 19/20 chapter links • Interactive menus • Original, optional video introductions • Single-color picture disc • Theatrical trailers.
1936 81m/B Oscar Homolka, Sylvia Sidney, John Loder, Desmond Tester, Joyce Barbour, Matthew Boulton, S.J. Warmington, William Dewhurst, Austin Trevor, Torin Thatcher, Aubrey Mather, Peter Bull, Charles Hawtrey, Martita Hunt, Hal Walters, Frederick Piper; *D:* Alfred Hitchcock; *W:* Charles Bennett, Ian Hay, Alma Reville, E.V.H. Emmett, Helen Simpson; *C:* Bernard Knowles.

The Sadist

Three teachers on their way to Dodger Stadium are stranded at a roadside garage and terrorized by a sniveling lunatic (Hall). The story is serious, tense, and plausible. Beyond remarkably sharp restoration of the black-and-white image, the DVD boasts a commentary track by legendary cinematographer Vilmos Zsigmond. —MM *AKA:* The Profile of Terror.
Movie: 🎬🎬▶ **DVD:** 🎬🎬🎬

Elite Entertainment, Inc. (Cat #9708). Widescreen (1.66:1) letterboxed. Dolby Digital Mono. $24.99. Keepcase. *LANG:* English. *FEATURES:* Trailers • Production notes • Commentary: Vilmos Zsigmond.
1963 95m/B Arch Hall Jr., Helen Hovey, Richard Alden, Marilyn Manning; *D:* James Landis; *W:* James Landis; *C:* Vilmos Zsigmond.

Sagebrush Trail

Please see review of *Man from Utah.*
Movie: 🎬🎬🎬
1933 53m/B John Wayne, Yakima Canutt, Wally Wales; *D:* Armand Schaefer; *W:* Lindsley Parsons; *C:* Archie Stout.

The Saint

Gentleman thief and master of disguise Simon Templar (Kilmer) is hired by Russian strongman Tretiak (Serbedzija) to steal a formula for cold fusion from science babe Emma Russell (Shue). After more double-crosses and plot twists than *Mission: Impossible,* Templar and Emma are on the run from bunches of bad guys in Moscow and Oxford. The pace seldom slows enough for viewers to question the implausible logic of the plot. On DVD, the film looks fine, generally maintaining focus even in the fast tracking shots, and showing off the exotic locales. The most interesting feature, though, is director Noyce's commentary track. He mixes personal reminiscences with technical "how-we-did-this" stuff about the various locations, Russian culture, and the like. —MM
Movie: 🎬🎬▶ **DVD:** 🎬🎬🎬▶
Paramount Home Video (Cat #154967, UPC #097361549675). Widescreen anamorphic. Dolby Digital 5.1 Surround Stereo; Dolby Surround Stereo. $29.99. Keepcase. *LANG:* English; French. *SUB:* Spanish. *CAP:* English. *FEATURES:* 21 chapter links • Commentary: director Phillip Noyce • Theatrical trailer.
1997 (PG-13) 118m/C Val Kilmer, Elisabeth Shue, Rade Serbedzija, Valery Nikolaev, Henry Goodman, Alun Armstrong, Michael Byrne, Eugene Lazarev, Charlotte Cornwell, Irina Apeximova, Emily Mortimer; *D:* Phillip Noyce; *W:* Jonathan Hensleigh, Wesley Strick; *C:* Phil Meheux; *M:* Graeme Revell. *AWARDS: NOM:* Golden Raspberry Awards '97: Worst Actor (Kilmer).

Salem's Lot

This mini-series cut to feature length is rather abruptly edited at the beginning. Introductory material involving key characters is left on the cutting room floor, and the obvious commercial breaks are intrusive. The made-for-TV production values haven't improved with age, either, and those are even more apparent on DVD. The night scenes, even the interiors, are exceptionally black. That's simply the way '70s movies look, and the disc cannot change that. James Mason's dapper, effortless performance as the villainous Straker is still superb. Nobody else in the

cast comes close to him. The scares work fairly well, too, though the vampire effects have been eclipsed in several theatrical films that have been made since. The Barlow vampire makeup is based on the original *Nosferatu*. —*MM AKA:* Blood Thirst.
Movie: 🎬🎬▶ *DVD:* 🎬🎬▶
Warner Home Video, Inc. (Cat #12717, UPC #08539127172). Full frame. Dolby Digital Mono. $24.99. Snapper. *LANG:* English. *SUB:* English; French. *CAP:* English. *FEATURES:* 48 links.
1979 (PG) 112m/C David Soul, James Mason, Lance Kerwin, Bonnie Bedelia, Lew Ayres, Ed Flanders, Elisha Cook Jr., Reggie Nalder, Fred Willard, Kenneth McMillan, Marie Windsor; *D:* Tobe Hooper; *W:* Paul Monash; *C:* Jules Brenner; *M:* Harry Sukman.

Sally of the Sawdust
In Fields's first silent feature, he plays carnival barker Professor Eustace McGargle who's the guardian of orphaned Sally (Dempster). Then Sally's wealthy grandfather (Alderson), a stern judge, becomes determined to claim her from showbiz lowlifes. Fields gets to demonstrate his talent for juggling, conning customers, and car chasing. This interesting movie caught director Griffith on the decline and Fields on the verge of stardom. Remade as a talkie in 1936 entitled *Poppy*. Like many discs of silent films, the DVD features an extraordinarily good video transfer replete with crisp blacks and shadows that hold up remarkably well considering their age, and an above-average audio transfer to boot. —*MJT*
Movie: 🎬🎬▶ *DVD:* 🎬🎬🎬
Image Entertainment (Cat #ID4739DSDVD, UPC #014381473926). Full frame. Dolby Digital Stereo. $24.99. Snapper. *LANG:* Silent. *SUB:* English intertitles. *FEATURES:* 25 chapter links. Color tinted.
1925 113m/B W.C. Fields, Carol Dempster, Erville Alderson; *D:* D.W. Griffith; *W:* Forrest Halsey; *C:* Harry Fischbeck, H. Sintzenich.

Salo, or the 120 Days of Sodom
Extremely graphic film follows 16 children (eight boys and eight girls) who are kidnapped by a group of men in Fascist Italy. On reaching a secluded villa in the woods, the children are told to follow strict rules and then are subjected to incredible acts of sadomasochism, rape, violence, and mutilation. This last film of Pasolini's was taken from a novel by the Marquis de Sade. Viewers are strongly recommended to use their utmost discretion when watching this controversial film. Though the DVD is not spectacular, it is a better transfer than both the Water Bearer Films VHS release and even Criterion's own laserdisc. The picture is of average sharpness, at best, most likely because of the preprint. Colors are much improved, as are the brightness and the contrast, which are still high but a little smoother. The

sound is fuller, with a little more on the low end, but still retains the crisp and mildly distorted highs that only enhance the pseudo-documentary feel of some scenes. —*JO*
Movie: 🎬🎬🎬 *DVD:* 🎬🎬🎬
Criterion Collection (Cat #CC1539D, UPC #71551509225). Widescreen (1.85:1) letterboxed. Dolby Digital Mono. $29.95. Snapper. *LANG:* Italian. *SUB:* English. *FEATURES:* 29 chapter links.
1975 117m/C *IT* Giorgio Cataldi, Umberto P. Quinavalle, Paolo Bonacelli; *D:* Pier Paolo Pasolini; *W:* Sergio Citti; *C:* Tonino Delli Colli; *M:* Ennio Morricone.

Salome / The Forbidden
Two of author-director Clive Barker's early forays into filmmaking are presented on this DVD. Both seem experimental in nature and "The Forbidden" features some skinning sequences that Barker would later expand upon in the *Hellraiser* series. Doug Bradley, who went on to portray "Pinhead," is featured. Both films are blurry and a little hard to watch—the source material was 8mm film, which offers only very low resolution. There is no synch sound to the films although there is an electronic music score. An interview with Barker and pals is also included. —*JO AKA:* Clive Barker's Salome and The Forbidden.
Movie: 🎬🎬▶ *DVD:* 🎬🎬
Image Entertainment (Cat #ID4606SADVD, UPC #014381460629). Full frame. Mono. $24.95. Snapper. *LANG:* English. *FEATURES:* 12 chapter links • Interview with Clive Barker and others.
1973 78m/C Doug Bradley, Clive Barker, Peter Atkins, Anne Taylor; *D:* Clive Barker; *M:* Adrian Carson.

Salome's Last Dance
Surreal, theatrical adaptation of the Wilde play is typically flamboyant Russell.
Movie: 🎬🎬 *DVD:* NYR
Pioneer Entertainment (Cat #DVD6029). $29.98. Keepcase. *FEATURES:* Commentary: Ken Russell • Trailer.
1988 (R) 113m/C Glenda Jackson, Stratford Johns, Nickolas Grace, Douglas Hodge, Imogen Millais Scott; *D:* Ken Russell; *W:* Ken Russell; *C:* Harvey Harrison.

Salt of the Earth
Finally available in America after being suppressed for years, this controversial film was made by a group of blacklisted filmmakers during the McCarthy era when it was deemed anti-American communist propaganda. The story deals with the anti-Hispanic racial strife that occurs in a New Mexico zinc mine where union workers organize a strike.
Movie: 🎬🎬🎬▶ *DVD:* NYR
Pioneer Entertainment (Cat #DVD1005). $24.98. Keepcase. *FEATURES:* Cast and

crew thumbnail bios • Production notes • Trailer.
1954 94m/B Rosaura Revueltas, Will Geer, David Wolfe; *D:* Herbert Biberman; *W:* Michael Wilson; *C:* Stanley Meredith, Leonard Stark; *M:* Sol Kaplan. *AWARDS:* National Film Registry '92.

Samurai 1: Musashi Miyamoto
The first installment in the film version of Musashi Miyamoto's life shows him leaving his 17th-century village as a warrior in a local civil war. In the second, he wanders the disheveled landscape looking for glory and love, while in the third he confronts his lifelong enemy in a climactic battle. Taken as a whole, this epic depicts Miyamoto's spiritual awakening and realization that love and hatred exist in all of us. The DVDs are all very similar in quality and therefore, this review covers all three. There is some preprint damage and the image is only average as far as sharpness; the Criterion laserdiscs are a little sharper. Colors are about the same as they are on the laserdisc and seem a bit faded. Contrast is a little low, and there are occasions where some digital grain appears. The mono sound is a little thin and at times muffled. —*JO*
Movie: 🎬🎬🎬▶ *DVD:* 🎬🎬▶
Criterion Collection (Cat #SAM100, UPC #037429125427). Full frame. Dolby Digital Mono. $29.95. Keepcase. *LANG:* Japanese. *SUB:* English. *FEATURES:* 34 chapter links • Theatrical trailer.
1955 92m/C *JP* Toshiro Mifune, Kaoru Yachigusa, Rentaro Mikuni, Eiko Miyoshi; *D:* Hiroshi Inagaki; *W:* Hiroshi Inagaki, Tikuhei Wakao; *C:* Jun Yasumoto; *M:* Ikuma Dan. *AWARDS:* Academy Awards '55: Best Foreign Film.

Samurai 2: Duel at Ichijoji Temple
See review of *Samurai 1*. —*JO*
Movie: 🎬🎬🎬▶ *DVD:* 🎬🎬▶
Criterion Collection (Cat #SAM110, UPC #037429125526). Full frame. Dolby Digital Mono. $29.95. Keepcase. *LANG:* Japanese. *SUB:* English. *FEATURES:* 35 chapter links • Theatrical trailer.
1955 102m/C *JP* Toshiro Mifune, Akihiko Hirata, Daisuke Kato, Mariko Okada, Sachio Sakai, Kaoru Yachigusa; *D:* Hiroshi Inagaki; *W:* Hiroshi Inagaki; *C:* Jun Yasumoto; *M:* Ikuma Dan.

Samurai 3: Duel at Ganryu Island
See *Samurai 1* review. —*JO*
Movie: 🎬🎬🎬▶ *DVD:* 🎬🎬▶
Criterion Collection (Cat #SAM120, UPC #037429125625). Full frame. Dolby Digital Mono. $29.95. Keepcase. *LANG:* Japanese. *SUB:* English. *FEATURES:* 38 chapter links • Theatrical trailer.

1956 102m/C *JP* Toshiro Mifune, Koji Tsurata, Kaoru Yachigusa, Mariko Okada; *D:* Hiroshi Inagaki; *W:* Hiroshi Inagaki, Tikuhei Wakao; *C:* Kazuo Yamada; *M:* Ikuma Dan.

Sanctuary

A former government agent, Luke Connolly has completely changed his life by becoming a clergyman. However, when his old agency discovers his whereabouts, the deadly skills he's renounced may be all that can save him. This DVD manages to find a way to look bad in almost all lighting conditions, with the worst scenes being the dark ones, where the typical problem with grain comes into play. There is also some grain in the brighter scenes where there is too much detail, and there are occasional artifacts under both conditions. Colors are never great and are usually either a shade off or bleed. However, the sound is usually fairly good. —*JO*
Movie: 🎵🎵 *DVD:* 🎵▶
Studio Home Entertainment (Cat #7055, UPC #658149705524). Full frame. Stereo. $24.95. Keepcase. *LANG:* English. *SUB:* Spanish. *FEATURES:* 18 chapter links ▪ Theatrical trailer ▪ Production notes.
1998 (R) 110m/C Mark Dacascos, Kylie Travis, Jaimz Woolvett, Alan Scarfe; *D:* Tibor Takacs; *W:* Michael Stokes; *M:* Norman Orenstein.

Sands of Iwo Jima

John Wayne cemented his status as an archetypal American hero with his portrayal of Sgt. Stryker, and he won his first Oscar nomination. The film is also one of his most entertaining, a rousing piece of propaganda. In his "making of" featurette on the disc, writer-producer Leonard Maltin alludes to the political maneuvering between Hollywood and the Marine Corps that led to the film's production. He spends more time on the technical side of the filming. With the increased clarity of DVD, the intercutting between the actual footage of Marines fighting in the Pacific and the battles that were re-created at Camp Pendleton is more obvious than it is on VHS tape. It's a fairly minor flaw, one that's shared by virtually every war film of the period. The black-and-white work of director of photography Reggie Lanning and director Allan Dwan hasn't looked this crisp and sharp since the first print rolled out of the lab. The sound is not as strong. —*MM*
Movie: 🎵🎵🎵▶ *DVD:* 🎵🎵🎵▶
Republic Pictures Home Video (Cat #45570, UPC #017153557022). Full frame. Dolby Digital Mono. $24.98. Keepcase. *LANG:* English; Spanish. *SUB:* French; Spanish. *CAP:* English. *FEATURES:* 26 chapter links ▪ "Making of" featurette ▪ Theatrical trailer.
1949 109m/B John Wayne, Forrest Tucker, John Agar, Richard Jaeckel, Adele Mara, Wally Cassell, James Brown, Richard Webb, Arthur Franz, Julie Bishop, William Murphy, George Tyne, Hal Baylor, John McGuire, Martin Milner, William Self, Peter Coe, I. Stanford Jolley, Col. D.M. Shoup, Lt. Col. H.P. Crowe, Capt. Harold G. Shrier, Rene A. Gagnon, Ira H. Hayes, John H. Bradley; *D:* Allan Dwan; *W:* Harry Brown, James Edward Grant; *C:* Reggie Lanning; *M:* Victor Young. *AWARDS: NOM:* Academy Awards '49: Best Actor (Wayne), Best Film Editing, Best Sound, Best Story.

Sanjuro

Kurosawa's companion piece to *Yojimbo* is less serious in tone, but retains its focus on the grizzled samurai (Mifune). His scratching, swaggering performance is one of his best and that's about as good as you'll ever see. His task is to help a group of younger, naive warriors who are trying to remove evil clan leaders. Overall, the transfer of the black-and-white photography is good, but the DVD is hampered by an unusually large number of flashing patterns in kimonos and even in wood grains. Sound is fine. —*MM AKA:* Tsubaki Sanjuro.
Movie: 🎵🎵🎵 *DVD:* 🎵🎵🎵
Criterion Collection (Cat #53, UPC #0374 29141526). Widescreen (2.35:1) letterboxed. Dolby Digital Mono. $29.95. Keepcase. *LANG:* Japanese. *SUB:* English. *FEATURES:* 24 chapter links ▪ Theatrical trailer ▪ Liner notes by Michael Sragow.
1962 96m/B *JP* Toshiro Mifune, Tatsuya Nakadai, Keiju Kobayashi, Yuzo Kayama; *D:* Akira Kurosawa; *W:* Akira Kurosawa, Ryuzo Kikushima, Hideo Oguni; *C:* Fukuzo Koizumi, Takao Saito; *M:* Masaru Sato.

The Santa Clause

If you like Allen, you'll enjoy this lightweight holiday comedy about divorced workaholic dad Scott Calvin and eight-year-old son Charlie (Lloyd). Seems Santa injures himself falling off the Calvin roof and dad winds up in Santa's suit. But as it turns out when you put on Santa's suit, you become Santa, including a noticeable weight gain, a fluffy beard, and all those reindeer and elves to deal with (but where's Mrs. Claus?). Super picture quality with enjoyably bright colors is enhanced by the DVD's ability to handle any and all lighting conditions. The sound mix is unimaginative but full-bodied. —*JO*
Movie: 🎵🎵▶ *DVD:* 🎵🎵🎵▶
Buena Vista Home Entertainment (Cat #14898, UPC #717951000637). Widescreen (1.85:1) letterboxed. Dolby Digital 5.1; Dolby Surround. $29.99. Keepcase. *LANG:* English; French. *FEATURES:* 17 chapter links ▪ Theatrical trailer.
1994 (PG) 97m/C Tim Allen, Eric Lloyd, Judge Reinhold, Wendy Crewson, David Krumholtz, Mary Gross; *D:* John Pasquin; *W:* Leo Benvenuti, Steve Rudnick; *C:* Walt Lloyd; *M:* Michael Convertino. *AWARDS:* Blockbuster Entertainment Awards '95: Male Newcomer, Theatrical (Allen); *NOM:* MTV Movie Awards '95: Breakthrough Performance (Allen), Best Comedic Performance (Allen).

Santa Fe

Muddled romantic drama has an appealing cast and timely subject. It's taken cop Paul Thomas (Cole) eight months to recover from bullet wounds suffered in a disastrous shoot-out with a local cult. His wife Leah (Kelley) distances herself from the marriage and urges Paul to group counseling with New-Age guru Eleanor (Davidovich). Despite his mistrust, the two are drawn together. On DVD, solid lighting and photography elevate the film above the B-status to which it might otherwise be relegated. Acting is believable throughout. Sound is acceptable. —*MM*
Movie: 🎵🎵▶ *DVD:* 🎵🎵🎵
Image Entertainment (Cat #ID6319NGDVD, UPC #014381631920). Full frame. Dolby Digital Surround Stereo. $24.99. Snapper. *LANG:* English. *FEATURES:* 16 chapter links.
1997 (R) 97m/C Gary Cole, Lolita (David) Davidovich, Sheila Kelley, Tina Majorino, Jere Burns, Pamela Reed, Phyllis Frelich, Mark Medoff, Tony Plana, Jeffrey Jones; *D:* Andrew Shea; *W:* Andrew Shea, Mark Medoff; *C:* Paul Elliott; *M:* Mark Governor.

Santa Fe Trail

Historically inaccurate but entertaining tale about the pre–Civil War fight for "bloody Kansas" depicts future generals J.E.B. Stuart (Flynn) and George Armstrong Custer (Reagan) as they begin their military careers. (Custer was really just a youth at this time.) Good action scenes are backed up with a typically energetic Max Steiner score. The image ranges between good and very good with only minor print damage, and a light hiss on the soundtrack. The chapters cannot be accessed through the menu. —*MM*
Movie: 🎵🎵🎵 *DVD:* 🎵🎵
Roan Group (Cat #2029, UPC #78560420 2929). Full frame. Dolby Digital Mono. $19.95. Keepcase. *LANG:* English. *FEATURES:* Cast and credits ▪ Film background ▪ 16 chapter links. Title is also available from Parade (cat. #55216) for $17.98.
1940 110m/B Errol Flynn, Olivia de Havilland, Ronald Reagan, Van Heflin, Raymond Massey, Alan Hale; *D:* Michael Curtiz; *C:* Sol Polito; *M:* Max Steiner.

Santo Bugito 1

Included on this disc are five episodes of the bizarre yet thoroughly enjoyable show that describes the goings-on in a small desert town in the middle of nowhere. The catch is that the town is home to all types of bugs. They are a crazy group of characters who get into a slew of hilarious adventures (one right after the other) with a Tex-Mex flair. The image quality of this disc is absolutely stunning; colors are vibrant and really stand out. The audio transfer is also exceptional, with crisp dialogue and a wall-of-sound musical score/effects track that really delivers. —*MJT*
Movie: 🎵🎵🎵 *DVD:* 🎵🎵🎵

Image Entertainment (Cat #ID8503KCDVD, UPC #014381850321). Full frame. Dolby Digital Stereo. $19.99. Snapper. *LANG:* English; Spanish. *FEATURES:* 25 chapter links. **1999 116m/C**

The Saphead

Keaton's first portrayal of a rich playboy is the role that made him a star. He's Bertie Van Alstyne, the none-too-bright, none-too-ambitious son of a Wall Street mogul. Though this is not his best film, by any means, it does show flashes of his comic potential. The DVD is marred by a few fine vertical scratches and snowy flecks but, like most of the Keaton works on disc, the image is very good. The dark interiors are true to the original. Overall, the film is not as sharp as Keaton's later features; it never has been. The two shorter films on the disc—*The High Sign* and *One Week*—are more prop-based comedy. They're fast and funny, and they contain a few added sound effects. —*MM*
Movie: 𝄢𝄢𝄢 **DVD:** 𝄢𝄢🕨
Kino on Video (Cat #K134DVD, UPC #738329013424). Full frame. $29.99. Snapper. *LANG:* Silent. *SUB:* English intertitles. *FEATURES:* 23 chapter links. *The Saphead* runs 78 minutes; *The High Sign,* 21 minutes; *One Week,* 12 minutes.
1921 118m/B Al "Fuzzy" St. John, Sybil Sealey, William H. Crane, Buster Keaton, Carol Holloway, Edward Connelly, Irving Cummings; *D:* Herbert Blache, Edward F. (Eddie) Cline, Buster Keaton; *W:* June Mathis, Edward F. (Eddie) Cline, Buster Keaton; *C:* Harold Wenstrom, Elgin Lessley.

Sarah, Plain and Tall

New England school teacher (Close) travels to Kansas, circa 1910, to care for the family of a widowed farmer (Walken) who has advertised for a wife. Fine writing, off-beat casting in the case of Walken, and genuine chemistry between the stars make this one of the finest films ever made for television. The nostalgic, sepia-toned image looks very good on DVD with no serious flaws. Sound is equally good. The title is available for sale in a two-disc, three-film set with limited but well-chosen extras. (See reviews of *Skylark* and *Sarah, Plain and Tall: Winter's End.)* —*MM*
Movie: 𝄢𝄢𝄢 **DVD:** 𝄢𝄢𝄢
Hallmark Home Entertainment (Cat #102 00, UPC #707729102007). Full frame. Dolby Digital Stereo. Keepcase. *LANG:* English. *CAP:* English. *FEATURES:* 312 chapter links • Cast and crew thumbnail biographies • Production notes.
1991 (G) 98m/C Glenn Close, Christopher Walken, Lexi Randall, Margaret Sophie Stein, Jon DeVries, Christopher Bell; *D:* Glenn Jordan; *W:* Carol Sobieski; *C:* Mike Fash; *M:* David Shire.

Sarah, Plain and Tall: Winter's End

In the final volume of the *Sarah* trilogy, Jacob's father (Palance) returns to recon-

cile with his grown son. As in the first two films, high production values and inspired casting save the story from the heartwarming sappiness that so many made-for-TV productions of this ilk are prone to. And like the others, this one looks and sounds fine on DVD. (See separate reviews of *Sarah, Plain and Tall* and *Skylark*.) —*MM* **AKA:** *Winter's End.*
Movie: 𝄢𝄢𝄢 **DVD:** 𝄢𝄢𝄢
Hallmark Home Entertainment (Cat #102 00, UPC #707729102007). Full frame. Dolby Digital Stereo. Keepcase. *LANG:* English. *CAP:* English. *FEATURES:* 30 chapter links • Cast and crew thumbnail biographies • Production notes • Q&A with producer-star Glenn Close • "Making of" featurette. Available only as part of a two-disc, three-film boxed set that includes *Sarah, Plain and Tall* and *Skylark* for $34.98.
1999 (G) 99m/C Glenn Close, Christopher Walken, Jack Palance, Lexi Randall, Christopher Bell; *D:* Glenn Jordan; *C:* Ralf Bode; *M:* David Shire.

Sarfarosh

The story of a proxy war that Pakistan is waging against India, *Sarfarosh* focuses on an honest young man, Ajay (Khan), whose life is never the same after an encounter with terrorists. This episode leaves Ajay with a dead brother and a paraplegic father. Despite the odds, he finds a reason to live. The video transfer is very good, with rich color and solid blacks. During some scenes, however, I did notice an overall decline in clarity (but that may be more the fault of the negative than the disc). The audio transfer is also decent enough, with clear dialogue and no distortion during the numerous action sequences. —*MJT*
Movie: 𝄢𝄢🕨 **DVD:** 𝄢𝄢𝄢
Eros International (Cat #DVDE237). Widescreen (1.85:1) letterboxed. Dolby Digital 5.1. $19.99. Keepcase. *LANG:* Indian. *SUB:* English. *FEATURES:* 22 chapter links • Song selection • Film recommendations.
1998 155m/C *IN* Mukesh Rishi, Aamir Khan, Sonali Bendre, Naseeruddin Shah; *D:* John Mathew Martin; *W:* John Mathew Martin; *C:* Vikas Sivaraman.

The Satanic Rites of Dracula

Hammer films always fare better with a period setting. This ludicrously plotted, disjointed effort concerns a coven of witches, vampirism, espionage, Nobel Prize winners and finally, Armageddon. Lee and Cushing manage to bring their usual strength to the familiar roles of the Count and Van Helsing, but the rest is so much claptrap, poorly written, and over-directed with too many extreme camera angles. The DVD was made from the same original elements as the VHS tape, so the image is excellent. The main difference is in the extras, which are on the flip side of the double-sided disc. —*MM* **AKA:** *Count*

Dracula and His Vampire Bride; Dracula Is Dead and Well and Living in London.
Movie: 𝄢🕨 **DVD:** 𝄢𝄢🕨
Anchor Bay (Cat #DV10503, UPC #013131050394). Widescreen (1.85:1) letterboxed. Dolby Digital Mono. $29.98. Keepcase. *LANG:* English. *FEATURES:* 12 chapter links • Theatrical trailers • *World of Hammer* episode "Dracula and the Undead."
1973 88m/C *GB* Christopher Lee, Peter Cushing, Michael Coles, William Franklyn, Freddie Jones, Joanna Lumley, Richard Vernon, Patrick Barr, Barbara Yu Ling; *D:* Alan Gibson; *W:* Don Houghton; *C:* Brian Probyn; *M:* John Cacavas.

Saturn 3

Scientists Adam (Douglas) and Alex (Fawcett) have created a futuristic Garden of Eden until the psychotic Capt. James (Keitel) arrives with his robot Hector. It's almost impossible to believe that Stanley Donen directed this loopy stuff, but he did, from a script by novelist Martin Amis. In their defense, the film is very much a product of its time. The extremely high color contrasts come from the original, not the transfer to DVD. The same goes for the often muffled sound dubbing. Overall, not significantly different from VHS tape. —*MM*
Movie: 𝄢🕨 **DVD:** 𝄢𝄢
Artisan Entertainment (Cat #DVD69903, UPC #013023029293). Full frame. Dolby Digital Mono. $24.98. Keepcase. *LANG:* English. *FEATURES:* 18 chapter links • Theatrical trailer.
1980 (R) 88m/C *GB* Farrah Fawcett, Kirk Douglas, Harvey Keitel, Ed Bishop; *D:* Stanley Donen; *W:* Martin Amis; *C:* Billy Williams; *M:* Elmer Bernstein.

Saving Private Ryan

DVD heightens both the breathtaking achievement of Steven Spielberg's epic World War II "unit picture" and its flaws. Repeated viewings reveal the weakness of the last reels, but digital technology delivers a re-creation of the film that's about as close to the theatrical experience as home video can deliver. The story is simple. After a lengthy introduction—chapter one, which can easily be skipped—the scene shifts to a Higgins boat off the coast of France on D-Day. What follows is one of the most accurate and frightening depictions of combat ever put on film. (For the immediate future, all realistic war films will be judged against it.) Three days after the invasion, Capt. Miller (Hanks) and a small squad of soldiers head off to find Pvt. Ryan (Damon), somewhere near the German lines. Why? All of his brothers were killed and the Army brass is determined that he won't join them. If the fact-based premise becomes a bit cliched before the end, the performances remain excellent. Pay particular attention to the quiet scene between Hanks and Tom Sizemore, as his protective sergeant, at night in a church. The first thing that viewers will notice about the disc is the remarkable sound field created in the opening scenes. It complements the use of desaturated colors, recalling the black-and-white of earlier "serious" war films, and inventive camerawork and editing, which immediately involve you in the action. Even when seen on less-than-perfect video and audio equipment, the film looks and sounds very much as it did in theatres. If the extras are not extensive, they are appropriate. —MM

Movie: 🐾🐾🐾➤ **DVD:** 🐾🐾🐾➤
DreamWorks Home Entertainment (Cat #84433, UPC #667068443325). Widescreen (1.85:1) anamorphic. Dolby Digital 5.1 Surround Stereo. $34.99. Keepcase. *LANG:* English. *CAP:* English. *FEATURES:* 20 chapter links ● "Into the Breach" historical documentary on the D-Day invasion ● Message from Steven Spielberg on the D-Day museum ● Theatrical trailers ● Production notes ● Cast and crew thumbnail bios.
1998 (R) 175m/C Tom Hanks, Edward Burns, Tom Sizemore, Jeremy Davies, Giovanni Ribisi, Adam Goldberg, Barry Pepper, Vin Diesel, Matt Damon, Ted Danson, Dale Dye, Dennis Farina, Harve Presnell, Paul Giamatti, Bryan Cranston, David Wohl, Leland Orser, Joerg Stadler, Maximillian Martini, Amanda Boxer, Harrison Young; *D:* Steven Spielberg; *W:* Robert Rodat, Frank Darabont; *C:* Janusz Kaminski; *M:* John Williams. *AWARDS:* Academy Awards '98: Best Cinematography, Best Director (Spielberg), Best Film Editing, Best Sound, Best Sound Effects Editing; British Academy Awards '98: Best Sound; Directors Guild of America Awards '98. Best Director (Spielberg); Golden Globe Awards '99: Best Director (Spielberg), Best Film—Drama; Los Angeles Film Critics Association Awards '98: Best Cinematography, Best Director (Spielberg), Best Film; New York Film Critics Awards '98: Best Film; Broadcast Film Critics Association Awards '98: Best Director (Spielberg), Best Film, Best Score; VSDA DVD Festival '00: Best Overall Transfer, Best Overall Audio Presentation; *NOM:* Academy Awards '98: Best Actor (Hanks), Best Art Direction/Set Decoration, Best Makeup, Best Original Screenplay, Best Picture, Best Original Dramatic Score; British Academy Awards '98: Best Actor (Hanks), Best Cinematography, Best Director (Spielberg), Best Film, Best Film Editing, Best Score; Golden Globe Awards '99: Best Actor—Drama (Hanks), Best Screenplay, Best Score; MTV Movie Awards '99: Best Film, Best Male Performance (Hanks), Best Action Sequence; Screen Actors Guild Award '98: Best Actor (Hanks), Cast; Writers Guild of America '98: Best Screenplay.

Savior

Right up front on his commentary track, director Antonijevic admits that he wanted to begin this story of ethnic hatred and revenge in Bosnia without the obligatory opening which establishes Joshua Rose's (Quaid) motivation for becoming a mercenary for the Serbs. The conflict between

an attempt to combine a serious topical story and Hollywood conventions continues throughout. At a prisoner exchange, Rose meets Vera (Ninkovic), a Serbian woman pregnant by a Muslim rapist. Quaid is excellent but the film never really finds its proper level. On DVD, the image is perfectly clear and crisp, more than it needs to be, really, for such a haunted tale. Sound is very good, too. —MM

Movie: 🐾🐾🐾 **DVD:** 🐾🐾🐾
Columbia Tristar Home Video (Cat #03107, UPC #043396031074). Widescreen (2.35:1) letterboxed; full frame. Dolby Digital 5.1 Surround Stereo; Dolby Digital Surround Stereo. $29.95. Keepcase. *LANG:* English; Spanish. *SUB:* English; Spanish. *FEATURES:* 28 chapter links ● Theatrical trailer ● Production notes ● Commentary: Peter Antonijevic.
1998 (R) 104m/C Dennis Quaid, Natasa Ninkovic, Sergej Trifunovic, Stellan Skarsgard, Nastassia Kinski; *D:* Pedrag (Peter) Antonijevic; *W:* Robert Orr; *C:* Ian Wilson; *M:* David Robbins.

Saviour of the Soul

Bounty Hunters Ching, Siu Chuen, and Yiu May-kwan stand against killer Silver Fox. Silver Fox kills Siu Chuen, and Yiu May-kwan disappears after being injured. Ching begins a search for Yiu May-kwan that brings him back to Silver Fox. The transfer on this DVD contains some dust and scratch marks, but they are never distracting. The transfer is very detailed but appears soft at times with slightly bleeding edges. Overall, however, the transfer is pleasing and warm. Colors are powerful, nicely reproducing the hues of the superbly photographed film. The disc features a full Surround mix in Mandarin, but Surround usage is limited to a few ambient effects for the most part, and a few effectively placed sound effects. The audio is well produced with a rather natural-sounding quality. —GH

Movie: 🐾🐾🐾➤ **DVD:** 🐾🐾🐾
Tai Seng Video Marketing (UPC #6016437 57346). Widescreen (1.85:1) letterboxed. Dolby Digital 5.1 Surround; Dolby Digital Mono. $24.95. Keepcase. *LANG:* Cantonese; Mandarin. *SUB:* English; Chinese. *FEATURES:* Trailers ● Filmographies.
1992 94m/C *CH* Anita Mui, Andy Lau, Kenny Bee; *D:* Corey Yuen.

Scarface

Al Pacino is a Cuban refugee who becomes powerful in the drug trade until the life gets the better of him. Loose remake of the 1932 classic gangster film—although the first film has more plot—is extremely violent, often unpleasant, but not easily forgotten. The DVD picture is not as sharp as one would like and colors are generally a tad off. Both contrast and brightness levels are a little low. It's too bad, because DePalma's stylized films are always, at the very least, beautiful to look at, and a lot of his composition is lost in the dark. But the DVD still looks

pretty good and has an excellent supplemental section, particularly the informative documentary which deals with DePalma's style, his war with the ratings board, and many other interesting and anecdotal subjects. —JO

Movie: 🐾🐾🐾 **DVD:** 🐾🐾🐾
Universal Studios Home Video (Cat #20175, UPC #025192017520). Widescreen (2.35:1) letterboxed. Dolby Surround. $34.98. Keepcase. *LANG:* English. *SUB:* Spanish; French. *CAP:* English. *FEATURES:* 35 chapter links ● Theatrical trailer ● Photo gallery ● "Making of" documentary ● Dual-layered RSDL.
1983 (R) 170m/C Al Pacino, Steven Bauer, Michelle Pfeiffer, Robert Loggia, F. Murray Abraham, Mary Elizabeth Mastrantonio, Harris Yulin, Paul Shenar, Oliver Stone; *D:* Brian DePalma; *W:* Oliver Stone; *C:* John A. Alonzo; *M:* Giorgio Moroder.

The Scarlet Pimpernel

The title character, supposedly a dandy of the English court, assumes a dual identity to outwit the French Republicans and aid innocent aristocrats during the French Revolution. Fine adaptation of Baroness Orczy's novel is full of daring exploits, period costumes, intrigue, etc.

Movie: 🐾🐾🐾➤ **DVD:** NYR
Madacy Entertainment (Cat #99023). Full frame. Dolby Digital Mono. $9.99. Keepcase. *FEATURES:* Credits ● Cast and crew thumbnail bios.
1934 95m/B *GB* Leslie Howard, Joan Gardner, Merle Oberon, Raymond Massey, Anthony Bushell, Nigel Bruce, Bramwell Fletcher, Walter Rilla, O.B. Clarence, Ernest Milton, Edmund Breon, Melville Cooper, Gibb McLaughlin, Morland Graham, Allan Jeayes; *D:* Harold Young; *W:* Robert Sherwood, Arthur Wimperis, Lajos Biro; *C:* Harold Rosson; *M:* Arthur Benjamin.

Scarred City

Thoroughly cliched and predictable actioner is graced with an excellent cast. Trigger-happy cop John Trace (Baldwin) is forced to join Lt. Laine Devon's (Palminteri) elite crime unit, the Scar Squad, which uses any means necessary to get the job done. When Trace saves hooker Candy (Carrere) from a mob hit, the outlaw cops turn on him. Many, many bullets fly. On DVD, the full-frame image is so clear that it reveals set design that's really too neat for an allegedly tough urban setting. Even dimly lit interiors are completely clear. Sound is acceptable. —MM

Movie: 🐾🐾🐾 **DVD:** 🐾🐾
Image Entertainment (Cat #ID6321NGDVD, UPC #014381632125). Full frame. Dolby Digital Surround Stereo. $24.99. Snapper. *LANG:* English. *FEATURES:* 18 chapter links ● Theatrical trailer.
1998 (R) 95m/C Chazz Palminteri, Stephen Baldwin, Tia Carrere, Gary Dourdan, Michael Rispoli, Steve Flynn; *D:* Ken

Sanzel; **W:** Ken Sanzel; **C:** Michael Slovis; **M:** Anthony Marinelli.

Scent of a Woman

Pacino is a powerhouse (verging on caricature) in a story that, with anyone else in the lead, would be your run-of-the-mill, overly sentimental coming-of-age/redemption flick. Blind, bitter, and semi-alcoholic Pacino is a retired army colonel under the care of his married niece. He's home alone over Thanksgiving, under the watchful eye of local prep school student Charlie (O'Donnell). Pacino's abrasive (though wonderfully intuitive and romantic) colonel makes an impact on viewers that lingers like a woman's scent long after the last tango. O'Donnell is competently understated in key supporting role, while the tango lesson between Pacino and Anwar dances to the tune of "classic." Boxoffice winner is a remake of 1975 Italian film *Profumo di Donna*. The colors on the DVD are very weak but the image is actually pretty sharp. One wonders if the picture would not be as sharp if the composer of the DVD had boosted the color level to where it should be (you can't necessarily tell just by turning up the color on your monitor). The Dolby Surround is fine for the dialogue and does an admiral job of delivering the score with dynamics and fidelity intact. —*JO*
Movie: 🎬🎬🎬 **DVD:** 🎬🎬▶
Universal Studios Home Video (Cat #202 60, UPC #025192026027). Widescreen (1.85:1) anamorphic. Dolby Surround. $26.98. Keepcase. *LANG:* English; French. *SUB:* Spanish. *CAP:* English. *FEATURES:* 16 chapter links • Cast and filmmaker bios • Production notes • Dual-layered RSDL.
1992 (R) 157m/C Al Pacino, Chris O'Donnell, James Rebhorn, Gabrielle Anwar, Philip Seymour Hoffman, Richard Venture, Bradley Whitford, Rochelle Oliver, Margaret Eginton, Tom Riis Farrell, Frances Conroy, Ron Eldard; **D:** Martin Brest; **W:** Bo Goldman; **C:** Donald E. Thorin; **M:** Thomas Newman. *AWARDS:* Academy Awards '92: Best Actor (Pacino); Golden Globe Awards '93: Best Actor—Drama (Pacino), Best Film—Drama, Best Screenplay; *NOM:* Academy Awards '92: Best Adapted Screenplay, Best Director (Brest), Best Picture; British Academy Awards '93: Best Adapted Screenplay.

School Ties

David Greene (Fraser) is a talented 1950s quarterback who gets a scholarship to the elite St. Matthew prep school. To conform to the close-mindedness of the McCarthy era, both his father and coach suggest that he hide his Jewish religion. His compliance results in Big-Man-on-Campus status until his rival (Damon) and new girlfriend (Locane) discover the truth. What could have been just another teen hunk flick looks at much more than all the pretty faces in a successful treatment of anti-Semitism. On DVD, the close shots are fine, but long and medium shots tend to

be imperfectly focused. The usual problems with bright diagonals show up, too, but they're not serious. —*MM*
Movie: 🎬🎬🎬 **DVD:** 🎬🎬▶
Paramount Home Video (Cat #322907, UPC #097363229070). Widescreen anamorphic. Dolby Digital 5.1 Surround Stereo; Dolby Digital Surround Stereo. $29.99. Keepcase. *LANG:* English; French. *CAP:* English. *FEATURES:* 17 chapter links.
1992 (PG-13) 110m/C Brendan Fraser, Matt Damon, Chris O'Donnell, Randall Batinkoff, Andrew Lowery, Cole Hauser, Ben Affleck, Anthony Rapp, Amy Locane, Peter Donat, Zeljko Ivanek, Kevin Tighe, Michael Higgins, Ed Lauter; **D:** Robert Mandel; **W:** Darryl Ponicsan, Dick Wolf; **C:** Freddie Francis; **M:** Maurice Jarre.

The Sci-Fi Files

This disc is a four-volume history of science-fiction on-screen (and the printed page) that was produced by The Learning Channel. Most of the visuals come from film clips, trailers, newsreels, and interviews with writers and others in the field. Mark Hamill provides the narration. The quality of the archival material varies widely, but generally the images are all right. Initially, the producers overstate the importance of sf in popular culture, but that's a fan's prerogative and the body of the documentary takes an intelligent look at the field. —*MM*
Movie: 🎬🎬🎬 **DVD:** 🎬🎬▶
WinStar Home Entertainment (Cat #WHE 73014, UPC #720917301426). Full frame. $34.98. Keepcase. *LANG:* English. *FEATURES:* 8 chapter links • Mark Hamill filmography.
1997 200m/C D: Peter Swain, Chris Lethbridge; **Nar:** Mark Hamill.

Sci-Fighters

Renegade cop Cameron Grayson (Piper) is tracking rapist Adrian Dunn (Drago) in 2009 Boston and discovers that Dunn has been exposed to a deadly, mutating virus. It's actually changing the bad guy into an alien methane-breathing life form that, of course, wants to inhabit the Earth. He is infecting his victims with the virus, with horrible consequences for them. The alien makeup is appropriately gross and some of the effects are decent. The cropping of the DVD's pan-and-scan presentation is claustrophobic in some shots, and the video quality is not a tremendous improvement over earlier formats. No extras, and no riveting audio. —*MB*
Movie: 🎬🎬▶ **DVD:** 🎬🎬
Image Entertainment (Cat #ID5620FMDVD, UPC #015381562026). Full frame. Dolby Digital 2.0. $24.98. Snapper. *LANG:* English. *FEATURES:* 20 chapter links.
1996 (R) 94m/C Roddy Piper, Billy Drago, Jayne Heitmeyer; **D:** Peter Svatek; **W:** Mark Sevi; **C:** Barry Gravelle; **M:** Milan Kymlicka.

Score

Back in 1972, when this soft-core romp was released theatrically, *Time Out NY* called it a cross between *Who's Afraid of Virginia Woolf* and the TV show *Love, American Style* and, nutty as it may sound, that's absolutely accurate. It's about a swinging married couple (Wilbur and Culver) who decide to seduce two newlyweds (Lowry and Grant). The various pairings-off cross conventional lines between homo- and heterosexuality. Director Metzger always took pains to make his skin flicks look good and this DVD benefits from his efforts. The images are sparklingly clear with only a little pixelation on the surface of a lake and other negligible effects. —*MM*
Movie: 🎬🎬▶ **DVD:** 🎬🎬🎬
Image Entertainment (Cat #ID5544FFDVD, UPC #014381554427). Widescreen (1.85:1) letterboxed. Dolby Digital Mono. $24.99. Snapper. *LANG:* English. *FEATURES:* Theatrical trailer • 12 chapter links.
1972 89m/C Calvin Culver, Claire Wilbur, Lynn Lowry, Gerald Grant, Carl Parker; **D:** Radley Metzger; **W:** Jerry Douglas; **C:** Franco Vodopivec.

Scorned 2

It's never a good idea for a college professor (O'Brien) to fool around with a pretty coed (Schumacher), particularly when there's a strong possibility that his wife (McClure) is a psycho killer. Actually this erotic thriller is a cut above the genre, both in the inventiveness of the plot and its appearance on DVD. Director Rodney MacDonald worked well within his budget, and so the image is particularly clear with subtle lighting and photography. Sound is adequate. —*MM*
Movie: 🎬🎬 **DVD:** 🎬🎬▶
Simitar Entertainment (Cat #7459, UPC #082551745920). Full frame. Dolby Digital Stereo. $14.98. Keepcase. *LANG:* English. *FEATURES:* 8 chapter links • Production factoids • Andrew Stevens filmography.
1996 (R) 105m/C Tane McClure, Wendy Schumacher, Myles O'Brien, John McCook, Andrew Stevens, Seth Jaffe; **D:** Rodney McDonald; **W:** Sean McGinley; **C:** Gary Graver; **M:** Patrick Seymour.

The Scorpio Factor

Murder and mayhem follow a microchip heist.
Movie: 🎬🎬 **DVD:** NYR
Digital Versatile Disc Ltd. (Cat #116). Full frame. $19.95. Keepcase.
1990 87m/C Attila Bertalan, David Nerman, Wendy Dawn Wilson.

Scream (CS)

Director Craven playfully tweaks the cliches of teen slasher pics with this tongue-in-cheek thriller. Yep, where there's a mad slasher on the loose, there must be a group of teenagers "just out for a good

time." The difference is both the killer and the victims have been raised on '80s splatter movies and, therefore, know all the rules. Sexual activity and/or substance abuse? Start picking out the coffins. The stalker uses his cellular phone to terrorize his victims. He also uses it to ask his prey trivia questions or offer critiques of low-grade horror movies. More fun than a bucket full of Karo Syrup laced with #3 red dye. This "Collector's Series" edition of *Scream* is the same "R"-rated theatrical version that appears on both the regular DVD and VHS versions. Why the slightly longer and gorier director's cut of the film (that was released on laserdisc) was not used is anybody's guess, but it sure seems like a collector's edition would have the most complete cut. Instead, there are added supplemental materials, including a couple of featurettes and some interviews. The actual film transfer appears to be the same as the regular edition and is pretty good with deep colors and heavy contrast. The film is very dark but the picture holds up well. —JO *AKA:* Scary Movie.
Movie: 🐾🐾🐾▸ *DVD:* 🐾🐾🐾
Buena Vista Home Entertainment (Cat #15638, UPC #717951000835). Widescreen (2.35:1) letterboxed. Dolby Digital 5.1. $39.99. Keepcase. *LANG:* English. *CAP:* English. *FEATURES:* 16 chapter links ▪ Theatrical trailer ▪ TV spots ▪ Commentary: Wes Craven, Kevin Williamson ▪ "Making of" featurette ▪ Behind-the-scenes featurette ▪ Special effects gallery ▪ Cast and filmmakers bio ▪ Cast and crew Q&A.
1996 (R) 111m/C Drew Barrymore, Neve Campbell, Courteney Cox Arquette, David Arquette, Skeet Ulrich, Rose McGowan, Henry Winkler, Liev Schreiber, W. Earl Brown, Jamie Kennedy, Lawrence Hecht; *Cameos:* Wes Craven, Linda Blair; *D:* Wes Craven; *W:* Kevin Williamson; *C:* Mark Irwin; *M:* Marco Beltrami. *AWARDS:* MTV Movie Awards '97: Best Film; *NOM:* MTV Movie Awards '97: Best Female Performance (Campbell).

Scream 2

Sidney (Campbell) trades psychotherapy for college, only to be harassed by a lunatic willing to duplicate her nightmares from the original. All the cast that survived the first pic are back (and some new faces, with O'Connell as Sidney's new boyfriend) including TV tabloider Gale Weathers (Cox), who has turned a best-seller about the murders into a movie called *Stab*; lovable, huggable sheriff Dewey (Arquette); and horror film fanatic Randy (Kennedy). Director Craven and writer Williamson add more of the satirical spark that propelled its predecessor into boxoffice success. By following the rules of sequels, they increase the suspense (everyone is a suspect) and gore to tantalizing fun, making this entry to the popular franchise a hard one to top. There are a couple of legitimate jumps in the film and, thanks to the DVD's boisterous sound-

track, they have an effect even upon repeated viewing. The DVD handles the dark scenes extremely well and there is neither grain nor artifacts added to the picture. Colors are outstanding with plenty of contrast, which combines with consistent brightness levels to ensure every gory detail remains intact, no matter how dark the murder scene. —JO *AKA:* Scream Again.
Movie: 🐾🐾🐾 *DVD:* 🐾🐾🐾▸
Buena Vista Home Entertainment (Cat #14377, UPC #717951000484). Widescreen (2.35:1) letterboxed. Dolby Digital 5.1. $29.99. Keepcase. *LANG:* English. *CAP:* English. *FEATURES:* 21 chapter links ▪ Theatrical trailer.
1997 (R) 120m/C Courteney Cox Arquette, Neve Campbell, Jerry O'Connell, David Arquette, Jada Pinkett Smith, Jamie Kennedy, Liev Schreiber, Sarah Michelle Gellar, Laurie Metcalf, Elise Neal, Lewis Arquette, Duane Martin, Omar Epps, David Warner, Timothy Olyphant, Rebecca Gayheart, Portia de Rossi; *Cameos:* Tori Spelling, Heather Graham; *D:* Wes Craven; *W:* Kevin Williamson; *C:* Peter Deming; *M:* Marco Beltrami. *AWARDS:* MTV Movie Awards '98: Best Female Performance (Campbell).

Screamers

In their first incarnation, Screamers are little mechanical buzzsaw beasties that rip through the sand the way Bugs Bunny burrows his way to the Carrot Festival at Pismo Beach. But these critters shred the human inhabitants of Sirius 6B in 2078. Why? It has to do with a war that has burned out Commander Joe Hendriksen (Weller). Director Duguay draws out the plot at a methodical pace, the better to appreciate the frozen Canadian landscapes, grim industrial interiors, and the above-average effects. Jennifer Rubin is fine as the tough Hawksian heroine. She and Weller handle the naturalistic dialogue more comfortably than their costars. Horror fans will catch references to *Alien* and Cronenberg's *The Brood*. The DVD image, particularly the widescreen version, is a distinct step up from videotape. Where the disc really gets high marks, though, is in the sound, which becomes an even more important element. —MM
Movie: 🐾🐾▸ *DVD:* 🐾🐾🐾▸
Columbia Tristar Home Video (Cat #11869, UPC #043396118690). Widescreen (1.85:1) letterboxed; full frame. Dolby Digital 5.1 Surround Stereo; Dolby Digital Surround Stereo. $29.95. Keepcase. *LANG:* English; French; Spanish. *SUB:* English; French; Spanish. *FEATURES:* 28 chapter links ▪ Theatrical trailer.
1996 (R) 107m/C Peter Weller, Jennifer Rubin, Andrew Lauer, Charles Powell, Ron White, Michael Caloz; *D:* Christian Duguay; *W:* Dan O'Bannon, Miguel Tejada-Flores; *C:* Rodney Gibbons; *M:* Normand Corbeil. *AWARDS:* *NOM:* Genie Awards '96: Best Art Direction/Set Decoration, Best Supporting Actor (White), Best Score.

Scrooged

Somewhat disjointed version of the Dickens's classic revolves around a callous TV executive (Murray) staging *A Christmas Carol* who is visited by the three ghosts (among them a terrific Kane) and sees the light. Heavy-handed but funny.
Movie: 🐾🐾 *DVD:* NYR
Paramount Home Video (Cat #320547). Widescreen (1.85:1) anamorphic. Dolby Digital 5.1 Surround Stereo; Dolby Digital Surround Stereo. $29.99. Keepcase. *LANG:* English; French. *CAP:* English.
1988 (PG-13) 101m/C Bill Murray, Carol Kane, John Forsythe, David Johansen, Bob(cat) Goldthwait, Karen Allen, Michael J. Pollard, Brian Doyle-Murray, Alfre Woodard, John Glover, Robert Mitchum, Buddy Hackett, Robert Goulet, Jamie Farr, Mary Lou Retton, Lee Majors; *D:* Richard Donner; *W:* Mitch Glazer, Michael O'Donoghue; *C:* Michael Chapman; *M:* Danny Elfman.

Sea of Love

Tough, tightly wound thriller follows an alcoholic cop (Pacino) in a mid-life crisis. While he and his partner (Goodman) are following the track of a serial killer, he embarks on a torrid relationship with the prime suspect (Barkin). The familiar stuff is handled very well, but the full-frame DVD image is little better than VHS tape. —MM
Movie: 🐾🐾🐾▸ *DVD:* 🐾🐾▸
Universal Studios Home Video (Cat #20226). Full frame. Dolby Digital 5.1 Surround Stereo. $24.98. Keepcase. *LANG:* English; French. *SUB:* Spanish. *CAP:* English. *FEATURES:* Cast and crew thumbnail bios ▪ Production notes ▪ Trailer.
1989 (R) 113m/C Al Pacino, Ellen Barkin, John Goodman, Michael Rooker, William Hickey, Richard Jenkins; *D:* Harold Becker; *W:* Richard Price; *C:* Ronnie Taylor; *M:* Trevor Jones.

Sea Wolves

These true wartime exploits were hidden until the 1978 British Official Secrets Act lifted security restrictions. In 1943, a German merchant vessels of neutral Goa (a Portuguese colony on India's western coast) transmits information about Allied ships to a predatory U-boat. Unable to launch a raid in neutral waters, the British draft some "unofficial" commandoes. The transfer on this DVD is clean without defects, but the compression on the disc varies quite a bit. While the anamorphic transfer is mostly free of distracting compression artifacts, the full-frame version is riddled with pixelation and ringing. The audio is well balanced and always understandable, but sounds a bit harsh at times without the natural bass roll-off that would make it more pleasant. The 3.5 technical bone rating is for the widescreen version. —GH
Movie: 🐾🐾▸ *DVD:* 🐾🐾🐾▸
Warner Home Video, Inc. (Cat #709, UPC #012569070929). Widescreen (1.85:1)

anamorphic; full frame. Dolby Stereo. $19.98. Snapper. *LANG:* English. *SUB:* English; French. *CAP:* English. *FEATURES:* 43 chapter links.
1981 (PG) 120m/C *GB* Gregory Peck, Roger Moore, David Niven, Trevor Howard, Patrick Macnee; *D:* Andrew V. McLaglen; *W:* Reginald Rose.

Search and Destroy

Sci-fi action flick revolves around the capture of a secret biological warfare research station. Lots of action at the expense of plot.
Movie: 🐾 *DVD:* NYR
Simitar Entertainment (Cat #7573). Full frame. Dolby Digital Stereo. $14.98. Keepcase. *FEATURES:* Production notes.
1988 (R) 87m/C Stuart Garrison Day, Dan Kuchuck, Peggy Jacobsen; *D:* J. Christian Ingvordsen; *W:* J. Christian Ingvordsen; *C:* Steven Kaman; *M:* Chris Burke.

The Searchers

John Wayne is the hard-hearted frontiersman who spends years doggedly pursuing his niece, who was kidnapped by Indians. A simple western structure supports Ford's most moving, mysterious, complex film. Many feel this is the best western of all time, and features one of Wayne's finest, and at times meanest, portrayals. It's certainly one of Ford's most beautiful films and this great DVD makes it more enjoyable to watch than ever. The colors are excellent—deep with good detail and contrast. The image is also very sharp. If there is a weakness to the disc, it's the sound, which is limited by the film's age and is a little scratchy and thin at times. —*JO*
Movie: 🐾🐾🐾🐾 *DVD:* 🐾🐾🐾▶
Warner Home Video, Inc. (Cat #14651, UPC #085391465126). Widescreen (1.85:1) letterboxed. Dolby Digital Mono. $19.98. Snapper. *LANG:* English; French; Spanish. *SUB:* English; French; Spanish. *CAP:* English. *FEATURES:* 44 chapter links • Theatrical trailer • Documentary shorts • Production notes.
1956 119m/C John Wayne, Jeffrey Hunter, Vera Miles, Natalie Wood, Ward Bond, John Qualen, Harry Carey Jr., Olive Carey, Antonio Moreno, Henry (Kleinbach) Brandon, Hank Worden, Lana Wood, Dorothy Jordan, Patrick Wayne; *D:* John Ford; *W:* Frank Nugent; *C:* Winton C. Hoch; *M:* Max Steiner. *AWARDS:* American Film Institute (AFI) '98: Top 100, National Film Registry '89.

The Secret Adventures of Tom Thumb

Avant-garde British fantasy combines 3-D animation with pixelation to tell an unsettling saga of a tiny child, kidnapped from his poor parents. Tom is taken to a sinister laboratory, where he befriends the equally teeny Jack the Giant Killer, is subjected to bizarre experiments, and strives

to destroy the full-sized villains. Not intended for children. This often-requested rental title comes to DVD paired with the creative and weird short, "The Saint Inspector." The image is pretty sharp. Grain and artifacts are rare. The colors appear a little washed-out, but after comparison to the VHS release, this may be a preprint problem. —*JO*
Movie: 🐾🐾🐾▶ *DVD:* 🐾🐾🐾
Polygram (Cat #8006355872, UPC #7800 63558723). Full frame. Stereo. $29.95. Keepcase. *LANG:* English. *SUB:* English. *FEATURES:* 8 chapter links • Theatrical trailer • Bonus short • Bolex Brothers bio.
1994 60m/C *GB D:* Dave Borthwick; *W:* Dave Borthwick; *C:* Dave Borthwick, Frank Passingham; *M:* John Paul Jones.

The Secret Agent

Presumed dead, a British intelligence agent (Gielgud) reappears and receives a new assignment—the elimination of an enemy agent in Switzerland. Strange Hitchcockian melange of comedy and intrigue; atypical but worth watching, particularly by those who are familiar only with his later work. Despite the box copy credit to Daphne Du Maurier, the film is based on Somerset Maugham's episodic novel, *Ashenden.* A young Peter Lorre appears as the curly-locked "Hairless Mexican." On DVD, the 1936 film is in better shape than many of its age, but the black-and-white photography is often murky, and the British production lacks that Hollywood sheen. —*MM*
Movie: 🐾🐾🐾 *DVD:* 🐾🐾▶
Delta/Laserlight (Cat #82029, UPC #018111998130). Full frame. $14.99. Keepcase. *LANG:* English; Spanish; Chinese; Japanese. *SUB:* Spanish; Chinese; Japanese. *FEATURES:* Introduction by Tony Curtis • Promo feature with Jimmy Stewart for *Man Who Knew Too Much* • 19 chapter links.
1936 83m/B *GB* Madeleine Carroll, Peter Lorre, Robert Young, John Gielgud, Lilli Palmer, Percy Marmont, Charles Carson, Florence Kahn; *D:* Alfred Hitchcock; *W:* Charles Bennett; *C:* Bernard Knowles; *M:* Louis Levy.

Secret Games

An unhappily married woman (Brin) searches for relief from her restrictive but wealthy marriage. She becomes a member of the "Afternoon Demitasse," an exclusive brothel where society dames tart themselves up and fulfill their fantasies. Then one of her customers (Hewitt) turns out to be a psycho. Don't you just hate when that happens! Director Hippolyte understands this kind of classy soft-core stuff perfectly and handles it well.
Movie: 🐾🐾▶ *DVD:* NYR
Studio Home Entertainment (Cat #4040). Full frame. Stereo. $24.95. Keepcase. *FEATURES:* Cast and crew thumbnail bios • Trailer.

1992 (R) 90m/C Martin Hewitt, Michele Brin, Delia Sheppard, Billy Drago; *D:* Alexander Gregory (Gregory Dark) Hippolyte; *W:* Georges des Esseintes; *C:* Wally Pfister, Thomas Denove; *M:* Joseph Smith.

Secret Games 3

When her doctor hubby spends too much time at work, leaving her alone in their new house, what is Diana (Rochelle Swanson) to do but go to work part-time at an upscale suburban bordello? Overall, the image of this "erotic thriller" ranges from fair to good on DVD, though this is the "R"-rated version with abruptly shortened love scenes. —*MM*
Movie: 🐾🐾 *DVD:* 🐾🐾
Simitar Entertainment (Cat #7364, UPC #082551736423). Full frame. PCM Stereo. $14.98. Keepcase. *LANG:* English. *FEATURES:* 8 chapter links • Production factoids.
1994 (R) 82m/C Woody Brown, Brenda Swanson, Rochelle Swanson; *D:* Alexander Gregory (Gregory Dark) Hippolyte; *C:* Wally Pfister.

The Secret Garden

Rekindled interest in Frances Hodgon Burnett's classic tale has prompted a Broadway musical, two TV movies, and this feature. Mary Lennox is an orphan sent to live in her reclusive uncle's forbidding mansion filled with secrets, including a crippled cousin she didn't know she had. She discovers a secret neglected garden and becomes determined to bring it back to life. Befitting director Holland's reputation, this version is beautiful but dark, with children prey to very adult anxieties. The DVD appears a little dark but is accurate to the theatrical presentation of the beautiful cinematography. Part of the reason is that the blacks are exceptionally deep and, as a result, the overall picture seems darker. The image is very crisp, as is the Dolby Surround sound, which is extremely lively and full-bodied. —*JO*
Movie: 🐾🐾🐾 *DVD:* 🐾🐾🐾
Warner Home Video, Inc. (Cat #19000, UPC #085391900023). Widescreen (1.77:1) anamorphic; full frame. Dolby Surround. $19.98. Snapper. *LANG:* English; Spanish; French. *SUB:* English; Spanish; French. *CAP:* English. *FEATURES:* 30 chapter links • 3 theatrical trailers • Production notes.
1993 (G) 102m/C Kate Maberly, Maggie Smith, Haydon Prowse, Andrew Knott, John Lynch; *D:* Agnieszka Holland; *W:* Caroline Thompson; *C:* Roger Deakins; *M:* Zbigniew Preisner. *AWARDS:* Los Angeles Film Critics Association Awards '93: Best Score; *NOM:* British Academy Awards '93: Best Supporting Actress (Smith).

The Secret Life of Walter Mitty

An entertaining adaptation of the James Thurber short story about a meek man

(Kaye) who lives an unusual secret fantasy life. Henpecked by his fiancee and mother, oppressed at his job, he imagines himself in the midst of various heroic fantasies. While Thurber always professed to hate Kaye's characterization and the movie, it scored at the boxoffice and today stands as a comedic romp for Kaye. A superb DVD. This film has never looked this good either on home video or on cable. The colors are astounding and the image is very sharp. The only real problem is some minor artifacting, which occurred in only a few scenes. The mono soundtrack seems a little more natural than the stereo mix, where only the music makes any use of the separation. —JO

Movie: 🦴🦴🦴 **DVD:** 🦴🦴🦴

HBO Home Video (Cat #9065, UPC #02635906522). Full frame. Mono; Stereo. $24.98. Snapper. *LANG:* English; French; Italian. *CAP:* English. *FEATURES:* 22 chapter links • Theatrical trailer • Cast and filmmaker bios.

1947 110m/C Danny Kaye, Virginia Mayo, Boris Karloff, Ann Rutherford, Fay Bainter, Florence Bates; *D:* Norman Z. McLeod; *W:* Everett Freeman, Ken Englund, Philip Rapp; *C:* Lee Garmes; *M:* Sylvia Fine, David Raksin.

The Secret of Anastasia

Animated version of the oft-filmed story of the lost Russian princess.

Movie: NYR **DVD:** NYR

Universal Studios Home Video (Cat #20412). Full frame. $24.98. Snapper. *LANG:* English. *CAP:* English. Title is also available from United American Video (cat. #40089) for $9.99.

1997 ?m/C

The Secret of My Success

Country bumpkin Fox goes to the Big Apple to make his mark. He becomes the corporate mailboy who rises meteorically to the top of his company (by impersonating an executive) to win the love of an icy woman executive. He spends his days running frantically between his real job in the mailroom and his fantasy position, with various sexual shenanigans with the boss's wife thrown in to keep the viewer alert. Fox is charismatic while working with a cliche-ridden script that ties up everything very neatly at the end. There are no major problems at all with this DVD; the worst aspect is the Dolby Surround, which is both a little thin and at the same time lacking crispness on the high end. Picture sharpness is good and colors warm and accurate. —JO

Movie: 🦴🦴 **DVD:** 🦴🦴🦴

Universal Studios Home Video (Cat #20412, UPC #025192041228). Widescreen (1.85:1) letterboxed. Dolby Surround. $24.98. Keepcase. *LANG:* English; Spanish; French. *SUB:* Spanish. *CAP:* English. *FEATURES:* 20 chapter links • 2 the-

atrical trailers • Cast and filmmaker bios • Production notes • Film highlights.

1987 (PG-13) 110m/C Michael J. Fox, Helen Slater, Richard Jordan, Margaret Whitton, Fred Gwynne; *D:* Herbert Ross; *W:* Jim Cash, Jack Epps Jr., A.J. Carothers; *C:* Carlo Di Palma; *M:* David Foster.

Seduction of Mimi

Comic farce of politics and seduction follows a Sicilian laborer's escapades with the Communists and the local Mafia. Giannini is wonderful as the stubborn immigrant in the big city who finds himself in trouble. Contains one of the funniest love scenes ever filmed. **AKA:** Mimi Metallurgico Ferito Nell'Onore.

Movie: 🦴🦴🦴 **DVD:** NYR

WinStar Home Entertainment (Cat #5020). $29.98. Keepcase. *LANG:* Italian. *SUB:* English. *FEATURES:* Cast and crew thumbnail bios.

1972 (R) 92m/C IT Giancarlo Giannini, Mariangela Melato, Turi Ferro, Agostina Belli, Elena Fiore; *D:* Lina Wertmuller; *W:* Lina Wertmuller; *C:* Dario Di Palma; *M:* Piero Piccioni.

Selena

Lopez is appealing in the title role of the 23-year-old Tejano superstar singer who was just breaking into international prominence when she was murdered by the president of her fan club in 1995. Flashbacks show dad Abraham's (Olmos) dashed musical aspirations and he serves as a stage father to his children, recognizing his daughter's exceptional voice. Film covers her marriage to guitarist Chris Perez (Seda) and her building success until the final tragedy (which isn't shown). Film concludes with concert footage of the real Selena. You gotta think that Warner could have made this DVD sound better. The 5.1 mix is not nearly lively enough and could have sent a lot more signal to both the subwoofer and Surround outputs. Maybe all the money was spent on the picture, which is quite sharp and features true colors and blacks. The image quality would have made for a much higher overall rating on most films, but since so much of this movie is music-related, it had to be dropped a bone or so. —JO

Movie: 🦴🦴🦴 **DVD:** 🦴🦴

Warner Home Video, Inc. (Cat #14909, UPC #085391490910). Widescreen (2.35:1) anamorphic. Dolby Digital 5.1. $24.98. Snapper. *LANG:* English; Spanish; French. *SUB:* English; Spanish; French. *CAP:* English. *FEATURES:* 37 chapter links • Production notes.

1996 (PG) 127m/C Jennifer Lopez, Edward James Olmos, Jon Seda, Constance Marie, Jacob Vargas, Lupe Ontiveros, Jackie Guerra, Sal Lopez, Rebecca Lee Mezza; *D:* Gregory Nava; *W:* Gregory Nava; *C:* Edward Lachman; *M:* Dave Grusin. *AWARDS:* NOM: Golden Globe Awards '98: Best Actress—Musical/Comedy (Lopez); MTV Movie Awards '98: Breakthrough Performance (Lopez).

Sense and Sensibility

Thanks to the machinations of greedy relatives, the impecunious Dashwood family is forced to move to a country cottage when father dies. Sensible Elinor (Thompson) looks after the household while overly romantic Marianne (Winslet) pines for passion—ignoring the noble attentions of middle-aged neighbor Brandon (Rickman) for the more dashing Willoughby (Wise). Elinor has her own hopes for marriage with boyishly ineffectual Edward (Grant), but all three men have secrets that could crush romantic dreams (at least temporarily). Somewhat slow-paced but witty adaptation (by Thompson) of Jane Austen's first novel is well acted and beautifully photographed. The image quality of the anamorphic transfer is breathtakingly sharp and colorful. Highly detailed and with rich hues, this transfer brings out the best of the film's stylish photography. No distracting artifacts are visible and the picture has a very warm and balanced feel throughout. The soundtracks are well balanced and create a good sense of ambience for the film. Dialogue is always understandable, although due to the heavy English accents, the subtitles came in very handy on this release. —GH

Movie: 🦴🦴🦴 **DVD:** 🦴🦴🦴🦴

Columbia Tristar Home Video (Cat #11599, UPC #043396115996). Widescreen (1.85:1) anamorphic. Dolby Digital Stereo. $27.95. Keepcase. *LANG:* English; Portuguese; Spanish. *SUB:* Korean; Portuguese; Spanish; Thai. *FEATURES:* 28 chapter links • Deleted scenes • Commentary: Thompson, Doran • Commentary: Lee, Schamus • Trailers • Thompson's Golden Globes acceptance speech.

1995 (PG) 135m/C GB Emma Thompson, Kate Winslet, Hugh Grant, Alan Rickman, Greg Wise, Robert Hardy, Elizabeth Spriggs, Emile Francois, Gemma Jones, James Fleet, Harriet Walter, Imogen Stubbs, Imelda Staunton, Hugh Laurie, Richard Lumsden; *D:* Ang Lee; *W:* Emma Thompson; *C:* Michael Coulter; *M:* Patrick Doyle. *AWARDS:* Academy Awards '95: Best Adapted Screenplay; British Academy Awards '95: Best Actress (Thompson), Best Film, Best Supporting Actress (Winslet); Golden Globe Awards '96: Best Film—Drama, Best Screenplay; Los Angeles Film Critics Association Awards '95: Best Screenplay; National Board of Review Awards '95: Best Actress (Thompson), Best Director (Lee), Best Film; New York Film Critics Awards '95: Best Director (Lee); Screen Actors Guild Award '95: Best Supporting Actress (Winslet); Writers Guild of America '95: Best Adapted Screenplay; Broadcast Film Critics Association Awards '95: Best Film, Best Screenplay; NOM: Academy Awards '95: Best Actress (Thompson), Best Cinematography, Best Costume Design, Best Picture, Best Supporting Actress (Winslet), Best Original Dramatic Score; British Academy Awards '95: Best Adapted Screenplay, Best Cinematography, Best Director (Lee), Best Supporting Actor (Rickman), Best Supporting Actress (Spriggs), Best Score;

Directors Guild of America Awards '95: Best Director (Lee); Golden Globe Awards '96: Best Actress—Drama (Thompson), Best Director (Lee), Best Supporting Actress (Winslet), Best Score; Screen Actors Guild Award '95: Best Actress (Thompson), Cast.

Senseless

Hard-working but impoverished college student Darryl (Wayans) competes with his smarmy classmate Scott (Spade, who looks about ten years late for his Econ class) for a high-powered Wall Street job. Then Darryl agrees to be the subject of a medical experiment that heightens his senses one by one. As each is amplified, the others are dampened. The film certainly has its funny moments, but many more are simply embarrassing. The two stars are fine in roles that are slight variations on characters that they have played often. On DVD, both image and sound are more than adequate for the formulaic material. No visible or aural flaws on the bare-bones disc. —MM
Movie: 🐾🐾 **DVD:** 🐾🐾🐾
Buena Vista Home Entertainment (Cat #17635, UPC #717951003454). Widescreen (1.85:1) letterboxed. Dolby Digital 5.1 Surround Stereo. $29.99. Keepcase. *LANG:* English. *CAP:* English. *FEATURES:* 11 chapter links.
1998 (R) 93m/C Marlon Wayans, David Spade, Matthew Lillard, Rip Torn, Tamara Taylor, Brad Dourif, Ken Lerner, Ernie Lively, Richard McGonagle, Esther Scott, Kenya Moore; *D:* Penelope Spheeris; *W:* Greg Erb, Craig Mazin; *C:* Daryn Okada; *M:* Yello.

The Sentinel

Big-budget horror borrows freely from *Rosemary's Baby* and *The Exorcist*—too freely, really—but it's still entertaining in a mainstream vein with a few solid scares. Supermodel Alison Parker (Raines) is going through serious personal problems which are revealed in ham-fisted flashback when she moves into a new Brooklyn brownstone and meets her "very strange" neighbors. For openers, they may be ghosts, but cops Eli Wallach and Christopher Walken suspect that all may not be kosher with Alison and her fiance Michael (Sarandon). The apartment building's sense of reality helps considerably. The big spooky finish directly quotes Tod Browning's *Freaks*.
Movie: 🐾🐾🐾 **DVD:** NYR
Goodtimes Entertainment (Cat #81044). Full frame. $14.99. Snapper.
1976 (R) 92m/C Chris Sarandon, Christina Raines, Ava Gardner, Jose Ferrer, Sylvia Miles, John Carradine, Burgess Meredith, Tom Berenger, Beverly D'Angelo, Jeff Goldblum, Arthur Kennedy, Deborah Raffin, Eli Wallach, Christopher Walken; *D:* Michael Winner; *W:* Michael Winner, Jeffrey Konvitz; *C:* Richard Kratina; *M:* Gil Melle.

Sgt. Bilko

Popular '50s sitcom doesn't march so much as limp to the big screen with Martin leading the troops as the wise-cracking title character, crafted so brilliantly by Phil Silvers on the small screen. Martin films and flams with frenetic energy as he tries to save his base from Washington cutbacks and the film from utter disaster. Enter Major Thorn (Hartman), Bilko's old adversary, who's plotting revenge on the con artist sergeant. Aykroyd's Col. Hall, Bilko's naive boss, but has little to do. Director Lynn finds his usual comic flair on leave this time around—too few laughs, spread too thin. Sentimental stroke has Catherine Silvers, Phil's daughter, playing Lt. Monday. The DVD is only average and doesn't seem to add anything to this lackluster film. In fact, the Dolby Digital 5.0 sound is a little weaker than the sound on the laserdisc release. —JO
Movie: 🐾🐾 **DVD:** 🐾🐾🐾
Universal Studios Home Video (Cat #20279, UPC #025192027925). Widescreen (2.35:1) anamorphic. Dolby Digital 5.0. $24.98. Keepcase. *LANG:* English; French. *SUB:* Spanish. *CAP:* English. *FEATURES:* 16 chapter links • Theatrical trailer • Production notes • Cast and filmmakers bios • Film highlights.
1995 (PG) 95m/C Steve Martin, Dan Aykroyd, Phil Hartman, Glenne Headly, Darryl (Chill) Mitchell, Max Casella, Brian Leckner, Pamela Segall, Eric Edwards, Dan Ferro, John Marshall Jones, Brian Ortiz, Dale Dye; *D:* Jonathan Lynn; *W:* Andy Breckman; *C:* Peter Sova; *M:* Alan Silvestri.

Sgt. Kabukiman N.Y.P.D.

Sgt. Harry Griswold (Gianisi) is magically transformed into the spoofy superhero Kabukiman, with makeup and costume based on a character in the traditional Japanese theatre. The whys and wherefores of Harry's elevation are not completely clear, but they do involve eating worms. His antagonist is a billionaire who has hatched an astrological plan to rule the world. Kabukiman's weapons are flying chopsticks, full-contact sushi, and his slam bang parasol. Unfortunately, Harry doesn't know how to use all of his new Kabuki powers and his Japanese girlfriend (Byun) provides little help. Troma founders and codirectors Lloyd Kaufman and Michael Herz keep the action fast and silly, and they don't let their strong liberal social commentary get in the way. This DVD was one of the studio's first efforts and it's not without problems. The image is rough and grainy, and an insert explains that the chapter menu is not fully functioning. You can't go directly to chapter eight, which has the sex scene—how UnTromatic!—and other chapters take you to the previous selection. The two-sided disc contains the film on one side and the extras on the other. —MM
Movie: 🐾🐾🐾 **DVD:** 🐾🐾

Troma Team Video (Cat #DVD9600, UPC #790357960033). Full frame. $24.95. Keepcase. *LANG:* English. *FEATURES:* 10 chapter links (see review) • 6 short Troma promotional featurettes • Commentary: codirector Lloyd Kaufman.
1994 104m/C Rick Gianisi, Susan Byun, Brick Bronsky, Bill Weeden, Thomas Crnkovich, Larry Robinson, Noble Lee Lester; *D:* Lloyd (Samuel Weil) Kaufman, Michael Herz; *W:* Lloyd (Samuel Weil) Kaufman, Andrew Osborn; *C:* Bob Williams; *M:* Bob Mithoff.

Serial Bomber

A would-be bomber (London) in Seattle targets his ex-girlfriend but his plan is foiled by FBI agent Sara Davis (Petty). So he shifts targets. This video premiere is a genuine sleeper with fine action scenes and an inventive plot. As the protagonist, Lori Petty brings real energy to the role. On DVD, the image is remarkably sharp. It's a dark film, done in blacks and charcoal grays that can lose definition on disc, but these are fine. Japanese dialogue is clearly subtitled in yellow. —MM
Movie: 🐾🐾🐾 **DVD:** 🐾🐾🐾
Simitar Entertainment (Cat #7299, UPC #082551729920). Full frame. Dolby Digital Stereo; Dolby Digital 5.1 Surround Stereo. $14.98. Keepcase. *LANG:* English; Japanese. *SUB:* English. *FEATURES:* 8 chapter links • Production factoids • Lori Petty filmography.
1996 (R) 89m/C Jason London, Lori Petty, James LeGros, Yuki Amami; *D:* Keoni Waxman.

Serial Mom

June Cleaver–like housewife Beverly Sutphin (Turner) is nearly perfect, unless someone disrupts her orderly life. Didn't rewind your videotape? Wear white shoes after Labor Day? Watch out. Stardom reigns after she's caught and the murderer-as-celebrity phenomenon is exploited to the fullest. This darkly funny Waters satire tends toward the mainstream and isn't as shocking as his earlier efforts but still maintains an edge (vital organs are good for an appearance or two). Turner's chameleonic performance as the perfect mom/crazed killer is right on target, recalling *The War of the Roses*. Waterston, Lake, and Lillard are terrific as her generic suburban family. The DVD image is very clear and without noticeable defects. As with most of Waters's films, there is an interesting color palette and it is displayed well here, although the picture is a bit dark at times. The Dolby Digital 2-channel soundtrack is quite good and very active throughout the film. —ML
Movie: 🐾🐾🐾 **DVD:** 🐾🐾🐾
HBO Home Video (Cat #90980, UPC #026359098029). Widescreen (1.66:1) letterboxed. Dolby Digital 5.1; Dolby Surround; Dolby Digital Stereo. $24.98. Snapper. *LANG:* English; French. *SUB:* French; Spanish. *CAP:* English. *FEATURES:* 31 chapter links • Trailers and TV spots •

Commentary: John Waters • Featurette • Biographies.
1994 (R) 93m/C Kathleen Turner, Sam Waterston, Ricki Lake, Matthew Lillard, Mink Stole, Traci Lords, Suzanne Somers, Joan Rivers, Patty Hearst, Mary Jo Catlett, Justin Whalin, Susan Lowe, Alan J. Wendl, Mary Vivian Pearce; **D:** John Waters; **W:** John Waters; **C:** Robert Stevens; **M:** Basil Poledouris; **V:** John Waters.

The Serpent and the Rainbow

Ambitious Craven effort is far from his best. It's a handsome production—too handsome in ways and the DVD makes the most of the strong visuals and Haitian locations. Out in the Amazon jungle, a shaman gives credulous Harvard don Dennis Allan (Pullman) some magic mushroom juice. He has visions and seven years later, he pops down to Haiti to investigate "zombification" drugs. The rest of the story wanders through grotesque horror, gauzy romanticism, political terror, and hallucinations. The acting is mannered, and though some of the shocks are really jolting, the whole unfocused thing takes itself far too seriously. Zakes Mokae steals the film as the Ton Ton Macute villain. The credits claim "based on a true story" and it might have been interesting for Craven and/or Wade Davis, author of that true story, to have explained that dubious claim on a commentary track. —MM
Movie: 🎬🎬 **DVD:** 🎬🎬🎬➤
Image Entertainment (Cat #ID4625USDVD, UPC #014381462524). Widescreen (1.85:1) letterboxed. Dolby Digital Surround. $24.99. Snapper. *LANG:* English. *FEATURES:* Wes Craven filmography • 20 chapter links.
1987 (R) 98m/C Bill Pullman, Cathy Tyson, Zakes Mokae, Paul Winfield, Conrad Roberts, Badja Djola, Theresa Merritt, Brent Jennings, Michael Gough; **D:** Wes Craven; **W:** Richard Maxwell, A.R. Simoun; **C:** John Lindley; **M:** Brad Fiedel.

Set It Off

Explosive *Waiting to Exhale* finds four female friends in Los Angeles pushed over the edge and taking up bank robbery. Their aims: escape poverty and strike a blow against "the man." The felonious divas of crime include Stony (Pinkett, who seems to be having fun with her role) and Latifah as Cleo, in a powerhouse performance. The action sequences are the most entertaining. Melodramatic subplots, including Stony's romance with Keith (Underwood) drag. The score is terrific and the sound is excellent. Like the original, the sharpness of the DVD varies with the economic ranking of the setting. The image is crisp in wealthy downtown L.A., less so in the gritty environs of the projects. —MM
Movie: 🎬🎬 **DVD:** 🎬🎬🎬
New Line Home Video (Cat #N4787, UPC #794043478727). Widescreen (1.78:1)

anamorphic; full frame. Dolby Digital 5.1 Surround Stereo; Dolby Digital Surround Stereo. $24.98. Snapper. *LANG:* English. *CAP:* English. *FEATURES:* 26 chapter links • Theatrical trailer • Cast and crew thumbnail biography • "Let It Go" music video with Ray J.
1996 (R) 121m/C Jada Pinkett Smith, Queen Latifah, Vivica A. Fox, Kimberly Elise, Blair Underwood, John C. McGinley, Anna Maria Horsford, Ella Joyce, Charles Robinson, Chaz Lamas Shepard, Vincent Baum, Van Baum, Tom Byrd, Samantha MacLachlan; **D:** F. Gary Gray; **W:** Kate Lanier, Takashi Bufford; **C:** Marc Reshovsky; **M:** Christopher Young. *AWARDS: NOM:* Independent Spirit Awards '97: Best Supporting Actress (Queen Latifah).

Seven

If this grim thriller can't make you jump, you're dead, and you won't be the only one. Arrogant, ignorant detective David Mills (Pitt) is newly partnered with erudite old-timer William Somerset (Freeman), and they're stuck with the bizarre case of a morbidly obese man who was forced to eat himself to death. The weary Somerset is certain it's just the beginning and he's right—the non-buddies are on the trail of a serial killer who uses the seven deadly sins (gluttony, greed, sloth, pride, lust, envy, and wrath) as his modus operandi. Since most of the film is shot in dark, grimy, and unrelentingly rainy circumstances, much of the grotesqueness of the murders is left to the viewer's imagination—which will be in overdrive. This film is incredibly dark both in subject matter and in lighting conditions. This DVD looks almost as good as the transfer used for the Criterion Collection Box Set, which was done from the original nitrate of the film. Almost every scene is incredibly dark and yet details are excellent with very little grain. The image is crisp and smooth all the way, with super contrast and very consistent brightness levels. The 5.1 mix appears to be the same one as on the laserdisc and is very robust with excellent imaging and knock-out Surround. —JO *AKA:* Se7en.
Movie: 🎬🎬🎬 **DVD:** 🎬🎬🎬🎬
New Line Home Video (Cat #N4381, UPC #794043438127). Widescreen (2.35:1) letterboxed. Dolby Digital 5.1. $24.98. Snapper. *LANG:* English (DD 5.1); French (stereo). *SUB:* English; French; Spanish. *CAP:* English. *FEATURES:* 38 chapter links • Cast and crew bios.
1995 (R) 127m/C Brad Pitt, Morgan Freeman, Gwyneth Paltrow, Kevin Spacey, R. Lee Ermey, Richard Roundtree, John C. McGinley, Julie Araskog, Reg E. Cathey, Peter Crombie; **D:** David Fincher; **W:** Andrew Kevin Walker; **C:** Darius Khondji; **M:** Howard Shore. *AWARDS:* MTV Movie Awards '96: Best Film, Most Desirable Male (Pitt), Best Villain (Spacey); National Board of Review Awards '95: Best Supporting Actor (Spacey); New York Film Critics Awards '95: Best Supporting Actor

(Spacey); Broadcast Film Critics Association Awards '95: Best Supporting Actor (Spacey); *NOM:* Academy Awards '95: Best Film Editing; British Academy Awards '95: Best Original Screenplay; MTV Movie Awards '96: Best On-Screen Duo (Brad Pitt/Morgan Freeman).

Seven Beauties

Very dark war comedy about a small-time Italian crook in Naples with seven ugly sisters to support. He survives a German prison camp and much else; unforgettably, he seduces the ugly commandant of his camp to save his own life. Good acting and tight direction. *Seven Beauties* is the film that first brought director Wertmuller critical acclaim. This more recent Fox/Lorber release offers the promise that they may have finally gotten their DVD act together. The picture is pretty sharp and their "trademark" grain is practically gone. Colors are also better, in fact accurate and as vibrant as the original film source. Pretty good blacks too! The stereo mix sounds more mono but is fairly full-bodied and free of distortion. —JO *AKA:* Pasqualino Settebellezze; Pasqualino: Seven Beauties.
Movie: 🎬🎬🎬🎬 **DVD:** 🎬🎬🎬
Fox/Lorber Home Video (Cat #FLV5040, UPC #720918750025). Widescreen (1.85:1) letterboxed. Stereo. $29.98. Keepcase. *LANG:* English; Italian. *SUB:* English. *FEATURES:* 9 chapter links • Filmographies.
1976 116m/C *IT* Giancarlo Giannini, Fernando Rey, Shirley Stoler, Elena Fiore, Enzo Vitale; **D:** Lina Wertmuller; **W:** Lina Wertmuller; **C:** Tonino Delli Colli. *AWARDS: NOM:* Academy Awards '76: Best Actor (Giannini), Best Director (Wertmuller), Best Foreign Film, Best Original Screenplay.

Seven Brides for Seven Brothers

The eldest of seven fur-trapping brothers in the Oregon Territory brings home a wife. She begins to civilize the other six, who realize the merits of women and begin to look for romances of their own. Thrilling choreography by Michael Kidd—don't miss "The Barn Raising." Charming performances by Powell and Keel, both in lovely voice. Based on Stephen Vincent Benet's story. Thrills, chills, singin', dancin'—a classic Hollywood good time. MGM seems to know just how to treat their colorful musicals when transferring them to DVD. Colors are almost always dead-on and super vibrant, and this DVD is no exception. The disc is also very sharp and has great contrast. The improvement over the former video editions is immediately obvious, and it's much easier to lose yourself in this wonderful escapist entertainment. The sound is also improved and has very good dynamics and fidelity, but sounds basically like a stereo mix. —JO
Movie: 🎬🎬🎬➤ **DVD:** 🎬🎬🎬➤

MGM Home Entertainment (Cat #906567, UPC #027616656728). Widescreen (1.85:1) letterboxed. Dolby Digital 5.1. $24.98. Keepcase. *LANG:* English. *SUB:* English; French. *CAP:* English. *FEATURES:* 38 chapter links ➣ Theatrical trailer ➣ "Making of" featurette ➣ 8-page booklet. **1954 103m/C** Howard Keel, Jane Powell, Russ Tamblyn, Julie Newmar, Jeff Richards, Tommy Rall, Virginia Gibson; *D:* Stanley Donen; *W:* Albert Hackett, Frances Goodrich, Dorothy Kingsley; *C:* George J. Folsey. *AWARDS:* Academy Awards '54: Scoring of a Musical; *NOM:* Academy Awards '54: Best Color Cinematography, Best Film Editing, Best Picture, Best Screenplay.

Seven Chances

Keaton almost did not make this seminal comedy, thinking that it should go to Harold Lloyd. He plays lawyer Jimmie Shannon, who must marry by 7:00 that night if he is to inherit $7 million. Of course, his true sweetie (Dwyer) would be happy to oblige, but a series of misunderstandings leads him to think that he must find another. The grand climax has him being chased by hundreds of potential brides and boulders. The DVD image is an exceptionally clear sepia. The two shorter films on the disc—*Neighbors* and *The Balloonatic*—are not quite as sharp but still quite watchable. *(Seven Chances* was remade as *The Bachelor.)* —MM
Movie: 🎵🎵🎵➣ *DVD:* 🎵🎵🎵
Kino on Video (Cat #K125DVD, UPC #738329012526). Full frame. $29.99. Snapper. *LANG:* Silent. *SUB:* English intertitles. *FEATURES:* 21 chapter links. *Seven Chances* (1925) runs 56 minutes; *Neighbors* (1920), 18 minutes; and *The Balloonatic* (1923), 22 minutes.
1925 96m/B Virginia Fox, Phyllis Haver, Buster Keaton, T. Roy Barnes, Snitz Edwards, Ruth Dwyer, Frankie Raymond; *D:* Edward F. (Eddie) Cline, Buster Keaton; *W:* Clyde Bruckman, Jean C. Havez, Joseph A. Mitchell, Edward F. (Eddie) Cline; *C:* Byron Houck, Elgin Lessley; *M:* Robert Israel, John Muri.

The Seven-Per-Cent Solution

Dr. Watson (Duvall) persuades Sherlock Holmes (Williamson) to meet with Sigmund Freud (Arkin) to cure his cocaine addiction. Holmes and Freud then find themselves teaming up to solve a supposed kidnapping. Nicholas Meyer adapted the script from his own novel. This is one of the more charming Holmes films; well-cast, intriguing blend of mystery, drama, and fun. The disc features an adequate video transfer, though the brownish tint utilized throughout the film doesn't lend itself to any great degree of crispness. The soundtrack is as good a mono soundtrack as I've heard, with easily understandable speech and discernable sound effects. —MJT
Movie: 🎵🎵🎵 *DVD:* 🎵🎵➣

Image Entertainment (Cat #ID4269USDVD, UPC #014381426922). Full frame. Dolby Digital Mono. $29.95. Snapper. *FEATURES:* 16 chapter links.
1976 (PG) 113m/C Alan Arkin, Nicol Williamson, Laurence Olivier, Robert Duvall, Vanessa Redgrave, Joel Grey, Samantha Eggar, Jeremy Kemp, Charles Gray, Regine; *D:* Herbert Ross; *W:* Nicholas Meyer; *C:* Oswald Morris; *M:* John Addison. *AWARDS: NOM:* Academy Awards '76: Best Adapted Screenplay, Best Costume Design.

Seven Samurai

Kurosawa's masterpiece, set in 16th-century Japan. A small farming village, beset by marauding bandits, hires seven professional soldiers to rid itself of the scourge. Wanna watch a samurai movie? This is the one. Sweeping, complex human drama with all the ingredients: action, suspense, comedy. It's been available in several versions of varying length, all long—and all too short. The DVD contains the full version of the film and is nothing short of spectacular. The picture is super sharp with great contrasts and graytones that fully convey Kurosawa's mastery of scene composition. Overall the DVD seems even a little sharper than Criterion's own laserdisc edition. The Dolby Digital Mono track is very clean, and packs a little more power than previous releases, giving much fuller tone to the score. —JO *AKA:* Shichinin No Samurai; The Magnificent Seven.
Movie: 🎵🎵🎵🎵 *DVD:* 🎵🎵🎵➣
Criterion Collection (Cat #SEV040, UPC #037429121726). Full frame. Dolby Digital Mono. $39.95. Keepcase. *LANG:* Japanese. *SUB:* English. *FEATURES:* 30 chapter links ➣ Audio commentary ➣ Theatrical trailer.
1954 204m/B *JP* Toshiro Mifune, Takashi Shimura, Yoshio Inaba, Kuninori Kodo, Isao (Ko) Kimura, Seiji Miyaguchi, Minoru Chiaki, Daisuke Kato, Bokuzen Hidari, Kamatari Fujiwara, Yoshio Kosugi, Yoshio Tsuchiya, Jun Tatara, Sojin, Kichijiro Ueda, Jun Tazaki, Keiji Sakakida, Keiko Tsushima, Gen Shimizu; *D:* Akira Kurosawa; *W:* Akira Kurosawa, Shinobu Hashimoto, Hideo Oguni; *C:* Asakazu Nakai; *M:* Fumio Hayasaka. *AWARDS:* Venice Film Festival '54: Silver Prize; *NOM:* Academy Awards '56: Best Art Direction/Set Decoration (B & W), Best Costume Design (B & W).

Seven Years in Tibet

Austrian mountaineer Heinrich Harrer (Pitt) escapes from a British internment camp in India with fellow climber Peter Aufschnaiter (Thewlis). They travel to Tibet where Harrer becomes tutor to the young Dalai Lama (Wangchuk). Sweeping vistas and snow-capped (Andes) mountain scenery do little to aid the sluggish and unfocused narrative which tries to cover too many subplots and doesn't really get going until the halfway point. Pitt's screen presence is forceful; his Austrian accent is not. Though the DVD image is fine, this

is an archetypal big-screen movie that loses much of its power on anything smaller than a full-sized theatre with great sound. —MM
Movie: 🎵🎵➣ *DVD:* 🎵🎵🎵
Columbia Tristar Home Video (Cat #21819, UPC #043396218192). Widescreen (2.35:1) letterboxed; full frame. Dolby Digital 5.1 Surround Stereo; Dolby Digital Stereo. $29.95. Keepcase. *LANG:* English; French. *SUB:* English; French; Spanish. *FEATURES:* 28 chapter links.
1997 (PG-13) 131m/C Brad Pitt, David Thewlis, B.D. Wong, Jamyang Jamtsho Wangchuk, Mako, Victor Wong, Ingeborga Dapkounaite; *D:* Jean-Jacques Annaud; *W:* Becky Johnston; *C:* Robert Fraisse; *M:* John Williams. *AWARDS: NOM:* Golden Globe Awards '98: Best Score.

The Seventh Floor

Kate's (Shields) computer-controlled apartment becomes her prison when a psycho takes charge of the system. Surprisingly, Brooke Shields isn't bad in this inventive Australian thriller. On DVD, the image is generally good. Some wire grids don't hold steady in darker shots, but most scenes are well lit and photographed. Sound is acceptable. —MM
Movie: 🎵🎵 *DVD:* 🎵🎵➣
Simitar Entertainment (Cat #7319, UPC #082551731923). Full frame. PCM Stereo. $14.98. Keepcase. *LANG:* English. *FEATURES:* 8 chapter links ➣ Production factoids ➣ Brooke Shields filmography.
1993 (R) 99m/C *AU* Brooke Shields, Massaya Kato, Craig Pearce, Linda Cropper; *D:* Ian Barry.

The Seventh Seal

As the plague sweeps through Europe a weary knight convinces "death" to play one game of chess with him. If the knight wins, he and his wife will be spared. The game leads to a discussion of religion and the existence of God. Considered by some Bergman's masterpiece. Von Sydow is stunning as the knight. Criterion does it again with a great DVD transfer of this fine film. The image is extremely sharp with super contrasts and excellent graytones. The preprint used is pristine and there may be no better way to see this movie. The DVD features a filmography of Bergman's work and commentary by film historian Peter Cowie. —JO *AKA:* Det Sjunde Inseglet.
Movie: 🎵🎵🎵🎵 *DVD:* 🎵🎵🎵🎵
Criterion Collection (Cat #SEV100DVD, UPC #037429124529). Full frame. Stereo. $39.95. Keepcase. *LANG:* English; Swedish. *SUB:* English. *FEATURES:* 15 chapter links ➣ Theatrical trailer ➣ Commentary ➣ Bergman filmography.
1956 96m/B *SW* Gunnar Bjornstrand, Max von Sydow, Bibi Andersson, Bengt Ekerot, Nils Poppe, Gunnel Lindblom; *D:* Ingmar Bergman; *W:* Ingmar Bergman; *C:* Gunnar Fischer; *M:* Erik Nordgren. *AWARDS:* Cannes Film Festival '57: Grand Jury Prize.

The Seventh Sense

Just another soft-core, cable-ready erotic drama about a beautiful blind cellist. Frances (Jenner) is the musician whose sight might be restored by an experimental operation. But before then, she explores pleasures of the flesh with a jaded mentor (Hules). Like most Playboy productions, this one looks pretty good on DVD. the image ranges between excellent soft focus and medium heavy grain, much of it intentional. Sound is above average. So are the acting, writing, acting, and photography. —MM
Movie: 🎵🎵▶ **DVD:** 🎵🎵▶
Image Entertainment (Cat #ID5979PLDVD, UPC #014381597929). Full frame. Dolby Digital Stereo. $24.95. Snapper. *LANG:* English. *FEATURES:* 12 chapter links.
1999 98m/C Lucy Jenner, Endre Hules, Christian Malmin, Loridawn Messuri, Fayley Hogan; *D:* Lawrence Unger; *W:* Giorgio Serafini; *C:* Blain Brown; *M:* Nicholas Rivera.

The Seventh Sign

A pregnant woman realizes that the mysterious stranger boarding in her house and the bizarre events that accompany him are connected to Biblical prophesy and her unborn child. Tries hard, but it's difficult to get involved in the supernatural goings-on, although there are one or two good jumps. The DVD has a reasonably sharp picture and, though most scenes are dark, little grain and few artifacts. The image seems a little more contrasty and slightly brighter than in the theatre, but the color and blacks remain true. Better use of the Surround would have enhanced both the sinister atmosphere and the tension. —JO
Movie: 🎵🎵 **DVD:** 🎵🎵🎵
Columbia Tristar Home Video (Cat #70079, UPC #043396700796). Widescreen (2.35:1) anamorphic; full frame. Dolby Surround. NSL. Keepcase. *LANG:* English; French. *SUB:* English; French. *CAP:* English. *FEATURES:* 28 chapter links.
1988 (R) 105m/C Demi Moore, Juergen Prochnow, Michael Biehn, John Heard, Peter Friedman, Manny Jacobs, John Taylor, Lee Garlington, Akosua Busia; *D:* Carl Schultz; *W:* W.W. Wicket; *C:* Juan Ruiz-Anchia; *M:* Jack Nitzsche.

The Seventh Voyage of Sinbad

Ray Harryhausen's early stop motion masterpiece may look a little rough to younger audiences weaned on slick computer-generated effects, but they'll still be charmed by the personalities he could give his creations. Sinbad (Mathews) seeks to restore his Princess fiancee (Grant) from the midget size to which an evil sorcerer (Thatcher) has reduced her. Along the way, they encounter a giant cyclops/satyr, dragon, roc, and sword-wielding skeleton. Add in a terrific Bernard Herrmann score and you've got an ageless crowd-pleaser. DVD cannot disguise the film's heavy graini-

ness, particularly in the big effects scenes, but the film has been restored and so it looks (and sounds) as good as it ever has on home video. The dual-layer disc also contains abundant extras. In the Harryhausen canon, it is surpassed only by *Jason and the Argonauts.* —MM
Movie: 🎵🎵🎵▶ **DVD:** 🎵🎵🎵▶
Columbia Tristar Home Video (Cat #01149, UPC #043396011496). Widescreen (1.85:1) letterboxed. Dolby Digital Mono. $24.95. Keepcase. *LANG:* English; Spanish; Portuguese. *SUB:* English; Spanish; Portuguese; Korean; Thai. *FEATURES:* 28 chapter links ▪ Original poster ▪ Ray Harryhausen chronicles featurette ▪ "This Is Dynamation" featurette ▪ Interviews concerning *Voyage* and *Jason* ▪ Theatrical trailers ▪ Cast and crew thumbnail biographies.
1958 (G) 94m/C Kerwin Mathews, Kathryn Grant, Torin Thatcher, Richard Eyer, Alec Mango, Danny Green, Harold Kasket, Alfred Brown; *D:* Nathan (Hertz) Juran; *W:* Kenneth Kolb; *C:* Wilkie Cooper; *M:* Bernard Herrmann.

70 Years of Popeye

The producers of the *Cartoon Crazys* series turn their attention to the famous animated sailor. They have done admirable restoration work, as shown in the demonstration on the DVD, but these are still old-fashioned cartoons with glowing colors and heavy blacks. They're not going to go over well with kids who expect the diamond clarity of *Toy Story* and other computer-generated animation. These also contain a few flecks and marks, and their real value now is nostalgic. Each cartoon is introduced with optional credits and synopsis. Contents: Popeye for President, Assault and Flattery, Gopher Spinach, Fright to the Finish, Parlez Vou Woo, Bride and Gloom, Shuteye Popeye, Insect to Injury, Taxi Turvey, A Haul in One, Customers Wanted, Popeye the Sailor Meets Ali Baba and the Forty Thieves. —MM
Movie: 🎵🎵🎵 **DVD:** 🎵🎵🎵
WinStar Home Entertainment (Cat #WHE73077, UPC #720917307725). Full frame. Dolby Digital Stereo; Dolby Pro Logic Stereo. $19.98. Keepcase. *LANG:* English. *FEATURES:* 15 chapter links ▪ Restoration demonstration ▪ Production credits.
2000 100m/C *D:* Thomas R. Reich.

Sex and the Other Man

Q: What do you get when you combine a soft-core "erotic thriller" with an off-Broadway psychodrama about three people in a cluttered New York apartment? A: This curious festival hit. Bill (Ron Eldard) and Jessica (Kari Wuhrer) are having problems with their relationship. One night, she brings her boss Arthur (Stanley Tucci) home after work. Is it an assignation or a setup? The film looks fine on DVD because this kind of "carpet drama" makes so few visual demands. The light-

ing and sets are first-rate. So is the image. The real attraction is the acting, which is better than the sometimes off-target script. —MM **AKA:** Captive.
Movie: 🎵🎵🎵 **DVD:** 🎵🎵🎵
Simitar Entertainment (Cat #7456, UPC #082551745623). Full frame. Dolby Digital Stereo; Dolby Digital 5.1 Surround. $14.98. Keepcase. *LANG:* English. *FEATURES:* 8 links ▪ Production factoids ▪ Stanley Tucci filmography.
1995 (R) 89m/C Ron Eldard, Kari Wuhrer, Stanley Tucci; *D:* Karl Slovin; *W:* Karl Slovin; *C:* Frank Prinzi; *M:* Anton Sanko.

Sex and Zen

Famous soft-core Hong Kong import is based on the 17th-century novel *Prayer Mat for the Flesh* by Li Yu. Mei Yang (Ng) marries the beautiful Yuk Heung (Yip) but intends to commit adultery as often as possible. The rest is filled with bawdy bizarre sexual encounters, which include couples literally bouncing off the walls and swinging from the ceiling, and memorable calligraphy. Yuk ends up in a brothel while Mei finds that his decadent life is not quite as entertaining as he'd imagined. The DVD image ranges between softly focused, red/orange-tinted dreamlike scenes and more sharply detailed sequences. This version looks a bit better than VHS tape, but on any medium and judged by any standard, this is one of the truly great guilty pleasures. —MM
Movie: 🎵🎵🎵 **DVD:** 🎵🎵🎵
Tai Seng Video Marketing (Cat #67354). Widescreen letterboxed. Dolby Digital Mono. $49.95. Keepcase. *LANG:* Cantonese. *SUB:* Traditional & Simplified Chinese; English. *FEATURES:* 8 chapter links ▪ Cast thumbnail bios ▪ Trailer.
1993 99m/C HK Lawrence Ng, Amy Yip, Kent Cheng, Isabella Chow; *D:* Michael Mak; *W:* Lee Ying Kit; *C:* Peter Ngor; *M:* Chan Wing Leung.

Sex Crimes

Ersatz tough-guy mystery revolves around private eye and voice-over narrator Jake Handler (Lambie) who's hired by the wife of a dead entertainment executive to find the hooker who was with him when he was murdered. The DVD is substandard throughout with heavy pixelation even in ordinary daylight exteriors. It looks much worse than most VHS tapes. Considering the atrocious acting, perhaps the lack of sharpness is a blessing. No chapter links. —MM
Movie: 🎵 **DVD:** woof
Simitar Entertainment (Cat #7210, UPC #082551721023). Full frame. PCM Stereo. $7.98. Keepcase. *LANG:* English.
1992 ?m/C Samantha Phillips, Joe Lambie, Cindy Manella.

Sex Is . . .

In the early '90s AIDS awareness was competing for public attention with calls for media censorship and arts subsidy

cuts. Ten funds, seven grants, and over a hundred other supporters made this insistently rude documentary collage possible, down to the donated footage from and archival research by fellow independents like Barbara "The Names Project" Hammer. Very much a product of its time, the film opens with an illustrated dedication to Jessie Helms, shown trying and failing to pronounce the word "sadomasochism." Fifteen volunteers ranging from porn star to pastor, one of whom is the overbearingly confessional director, are interviewed in sterile, generically lit studio settings. Their revelations about early experiences and reflections on politics, religion, and death are jumbled together, then tattooed with file footage of demonstrations, performances, vintage porn, childhood photos, and segments of old mental hygiene films. Sound is consequently a mixed bag, but that neo-disco score is to die for! —JK
Movie: 🦴🦴🦴 **DVD:** 🦴🦴🦴
Water Bearer Films (Cat #WBF4001, UPC #759259140011). Full frame. LANG: English. FEATURES: 8 chapter links • Scene access menu • Full-color picture disc.
1993 80m/C D: Marc Huestis; **C:** Fawn Yacker.

sex, lies and videotape

Acclaimed independent film from first-timer Soderbergh details the complex relations among a married couple (MacDowell and Gallagher), her adulterous sister (Giacomo), and his mysterious college friend (Spader), who's obsessed with videotaping women as they talk about their sex lives. Even though strong visuals have never been the point with this film, it looks very good on DVD. Unfortunately, on the commentary track, Neil LaBute is so effusive in his praise of Soderbergh that it's virtually unlistenable. In that regard, at least, the laserdisc version is superior. —MM
Movie: 🦴🦴🦴 **DVD:** 🦴🦴🦴
Columbia Tristar Home Video (Cat #90489, UPC #043396904897). Widescreen (1.85:1) letterboxed; full frame. Dolby Digital Surround Stereo; Dolby Digital Stereo. $29.95. Keepcase. LANG: English; French; Spanish. SUB: English; French; Spanish. FEATURES: 28 chapter links • Theatrical trailer • Commentary: Neil LaBute and Steven Soderbergh.
1989 (R) 101m/C James Spader, Andie MacDowell, Peter Gallagher, Laura San Giacomo, Ron Vawter, Steven Brill; **D:** Steven Soderbergh; **W:** Steven Soderbergh; **C:** Walt Lloyd; **M:** Cliff Martinez. AWARDS: Cannes Film Festival '89: Best Actor (Spader), Best Film; Independent Spirit Awards '90: Best Actress (MacDowell), Best Director (Soderbergh), Best Film, Best Supporting Actress (San Giacomo); Los Angeles Film Critics Association Awards '89: Best Actress (MacDowell); Sundance Film Festival '89: Audience Award; NOM: Academy Awards '89: Best Original Screenplay.

The Sex Monster

Anyone who picks this title looking for a guilty pleasure will be disappointed. It's a Woody-Allen sort of story about Marty (writer-director Binder) who persuades his reluctant wife Laura (Hemingway) to involve another woman in their sex life. The not-particularly funny result is mostly talk and disappointment. Judged as a low-budget production, the DVD is acceptable but nothing more. Both image and sound are comparable to VHS tape. —MM
Movie: 🦴🦴 **DVD:** 🦴🦴
Trimark Home Video (Cat #VM7277D, UPC #031398727729). Full frame. Dolby Digital Stereo. $24.99. Keepcase. LANG: English. SUB: English; French; Spanish. CAP: English. FEATURES: 24 chapter links • Theatrical trailer.
1999 (R) 97m/C Mike Binder, Mariel Hemingway, Renee Humphrey, Taylor Nichols, Missy Crider, Stephen Baldwin; **D:** Mike Binder; **W:** Mike Binder; **C:** Keith L. Smith.

Sexual Malice

Erotic thriller finds bored Christine (Barton) falling for male stripper (Laughlin) who is more than he seems while her college professor hubby (Albert) remains clueless. The first half revolves around a woman's view of sexuality; the second reverts to conventional male fantasies. The glitzy sets lose a little of their luster on DVD. The image is not sharply focused. Bright reds are particularly fuzzy and the usual problems occur with Venetian blinds. Sound is adequate. —MM
Movie: 🦴🦴 **DVD:** 🦴🦴
Simitar Entertainment (Cat #7269, UPC #082551726929). Full frame. PCM Stereo. $14.98. Keepcase. LANG: English. FEATURES: 8 chapter links • Production factoids • Edward Albert filmography.
1993 (R) 96m/C Diana Barton, John Laughlin, Chad McQueen, Edward Albert, Don Swayze, Kathy Shower, Samantha Phillips; **D:** Jag Mundhra; **W:** Carl Austin; **C:** James Mathers.

Sexual Roulette

In a distaff and decidedly raunchier Indecent Proposal, Jed (Abell) and Sally (Hall) wind up in money trouble and get in deeper by trying to recoup their loses (and losing big-time) in a Vegas horse race. Then casino owner Sherry Lansing (McClure), who has some kinky preferences, makes Jed an offer he can't afford to refuse. The DVD is exceptionally rough and cheap-looking, even grainier than the VHS tape, if that's possible. —MM
Movie: 🦴▸ **DVD:** 🦴▸
Image Entertainment (Cat #ID5768UM DVD, UPC #014381576825). Full frame. Dolby Digital Stereo. $24.99. Snapper. LANG: English. FEATURES: 12 chapter links.

1996 (R) 90m/C Tane McClure, Tim Abell, Gabriella Hall, Richard Gabai, Myles O'Brien, G. Gordon Brer; **D:** Gary Graver; **W:** Sean McGinley; **C:** Gary Graver.

The Shadow

Lamont Cranston (Baldwin) is the Shadow, "who knows what evil lurks in the hearts of men." He also has the ability to "cloud men's minds" and thus is invisible to evil-doers in New York city. (He learned all this in Tibet.) He's doing just fine until Shiwan Khan (Lone) shows up and announces that he's going to conquer the world. (He can also cloud men's minds.) And then there's sexy newcomer Margo Lane (Miller). She can read Cranston's mind and he cannot cloud hers. Obviously, there are some problems to be worked out with this clouding business. The unclouded full-frame DVD is about the same as the VHS tape in terms of image and sound. —MM
Movie: 🦴🦴🦴 **DVD:** 🦴🦴▸
Universal Studios Home Video (Cat #200 12). Full frame. Dolby Digital Stereo; DTS Stereo. $24.98. Snapper. LANG: English; French. SUB: Spanish. CAP: English.
1994 (PG-13) 112m/C Alec Baldwin, John Lone, Penelope Ann Miller, Peter Boyle, Ian McKellen, Tim Curry, Jonathan Winters; **D:** Russell Mulcahy; **W:** David Koepp; **C:** Stephen Burum; **M:** Jerry Goldsmith.

The Shadow Riders

Two brothers who fought on opposite sides of the Civil War return home to find their brother's fiancee kidnapped by a renegade Confederate officer. He plans to use her as ransom in a prisoner exchange and they set out to rescue her. Made for television. AKA: Louis L'Amour's "The Shadow Riders."
Movie: 🦴🦴 **DVD:** NYR
Trimark Home Video (Cat #6906). Full frame. Stereo. $24.99. Keepcase. LANG: English. SUB: French; Spanish. CAP: English. FEATURES: Cast and crew thumbnail bios • Trailer.
1982 (PG) 96m/C Tom Selleck, Sam Elliott, Ben Johnson, Katharine Ross, Jeffery Osterhage, Gene Evans, R.G. Armstrong, Marshall Teague, Dominique Dunne, Jeanetta Arnette; **D:** Andrew V. McLaglen; **W:** Jim Byrnes; **C:** Jack Whitman; **M:** Jerrold Immel.

Shadowlands

Touching, tragic story of the late-in-life romance between celebrated author and Christian theologian C.S. Lewis (Hopkins) and brash New York divorcee Joy Gresham (Winger). Attenborough's direction is stately and sweeping but Winger is a little too young for her role. Hopkins is excellent as the repressed man who finds more emotions than he can handle. Bring a lot of Kleenex. Though not extremely sharp and with occasional but not unacceptable grain, the DVD does deliver the subtle color tones of the beautiful cinematography very well. Backgrounds with too much detail are a problem and artifacts become noticeable. The blacks are true and the contrast and brightness levels above average. The sound has very good imaging and ambience, particularly during any of the film's professorial lectures. —JO

Movie: 🎵🎵🎵 **DVD:** 🎵🎵

HBO Home Video (Cat #90968, UPC #026 359096822). Widescreen (2.35:1) letterboxed. Dolby Surround; Dolby Digital Stereo; Dolby Digital Mono. $24.98. Keepcase. *LANG:* English (DS); Spanish (DDM); French (DDS). *SUB:* English; Spanish; French. *FEATURES:* 25 chapter links • Theatrical trailer • TV spots • Behind-the-scenes featurettes • Cast and crew bios.

1993 (PG) 130m/C *GB* Anthony Hopkins, Debra Winger, Edward Hardwicke, Joseph Mazzello, Michael Denison, John Wood, Peter Firth, Peter Howell; *D:* Richard Attenborough; *W:* William Nicholson; *C:* Roger Pratt; *M:* George Fenton. *AWARDS:* British Academy Awards '93: Best Film; Los Angeles Film Critics Association Awards '93: Best Actor (Hopkins); National Board of Review Awards '93: Best Actor (Hopkins); *NOM:* Academy Awards '93: Best Actress (Winger), Best Adapted Screenplay; British Academy Awards '94: Best Actor (Hopkins), Best Actress (Winger), Best Adapted Screenplay, Best Director (Attenborough).

Shadrach

Ponderous, preachy Depression-era drama faces several hurdles. First, there's the matter of Andie MacDowell as a hardscrabble farm wife. Then there's the misty-eyed view of the past, but that is to be expected with daughter Susanna Styron directing an adaptation of her father William's short story. Shadrach (Sawyer) is an ex-slave who has walked from Alabama to Virginia in 1935 to die where he grew up. The frayed budget shows through in several scenes. Overall, the DVD image is fine, though in this case, the medium's clarity can be unforgiving. —MM

Movie: 🎵▶ **DVD:** 🎵🎵

Columbia Tristar Home Video (Cat #03106, UPC #043396031067). Widescreen (1.85:1) letterboxed; full frame. Dolby Digital Surround Stereo. $29.95. Keepcase. *LANG:* English; French. *SUB:* English; French; Spanish. *FEATURES:* 28 chapter links • Theatrical trailer.

1998 (PG-13) 88m/C Harvey Keitel, John Franklin Sawyer, Andie MacDowell, Scott Terra, Monica Bugajski, Darrell Larson, Deborah Hedwall, Daniel Treat; *D:* Susanna Styron; *W:* Susanna Styron, Bridget Terry; *C:* Hiro Narita; *M:* Van Dyke Parks.

Shaft

A black private eye (Roundtree) is hired to find a Harlem gangster's kidnapped daughter. Lots of violence, a little sex, and terrific New York locations. (This may be the finest evocation of the city in winter ever captured in a popular film.) The grain in the telephoto shots of street scenes has always been there. So has the less-than-perfect sound that's often muffled. But those qualities come from the original and to have cleaned them up would undermine the film's solid sense of the early '70s. My only criticism: a commentary track from director Parks could have been terrific. Remade much less successfully by John Singleton in 2000. —MM

Movie: 🎵🎵🎵 **DVD:** 🎵🎵🎵

Warner Home Video, Inc. (Cat #65051). Widescreen letterboxed; full frame. $24.98. Keepcase. *LANG:* English; French. *SUB:* English; French. *FEATURES:* 20 chapter links • "Making of" documentary • Awards • Trailer • Cast and crew thumbnail bios.

1971 (R) 98m/C Richard Roundtree, Moses Gunn, Charles Cioffi, Christopher St. John, Gwen Mitchell, Lawrence Pressman, Victor Arnold; *D:* Gordon Parks; *W:* John D.F. Black; *C:* Urs Furrer; *M:* Isaac Hayes. *AWARDS:* Academy Awards '71: Best Song ("Theme from Shaft"); Golden Globe Awards '72: Best Score; *NOM:* Academy Awards '71: Best Original Dramatic Score.

Shakedown

Power-packed action film from director Glickenhaus is so high on style that you won't mind the lack of logic and plot. An overworked attorney (Weller) and an undercover cop (Elliott) team up to stop crime on the streets and corruption in the NYPD. Sensational stunts and choreographed violence including a spectacular fight atop a roller coaster. This is one of the better Goodtimes DVDs, featuring very true blacks and good vibrant colors. Despite a few spots of grain, the sharpness is a little above average, save an occasional color bleed. Consistent brightness levels and good contrast combine to nicely showcase Glickenhaus's use of light and reflections. Dolby Surround is good overall with crisp highs and adequate lows. Separation and imaging up front is very good and the dialogue punches through even during action sequences. On a couple of explosions there was slight clipping from the Surround speakers, but only if you're listening for it. —JO

AKA: Blue Jean Cop.

Movie: 🎵🎵▶ **DVD:** 🎵🎵▶

Goodtimes Entertainment (Cat #0581018, UPC #018713810182). Full frame. Dolby Surround. $19.98. Snapper. *LANG:* English (DS). *SUB:* Spanish; French. *CAP:* English. *FEATURES:* 18 chapter links.

1988 (R) 96m/C Sam Elliott, Peter Weller, Patricia Charbonneau, Antonio Fargas, Blanche Baker, Richard Brooks, Jude Ciccolella, George Loros, Tom Waits, Shirley Stoler, Rockets Redglare, Kathryn Rossetter; *D:* James Glickenhaus; *W:* James Glickenhaus; *C:* John Lindley; *M:* Jonathan Elias.

Shakespeare in Love (CS)

Lively romantic comedy about a frustrated Elizabethan playwright suffering from writer's block who just happens to be William Shakespeare (Fiennes). Will owes a comedy to bankrupt theatre manager Henslowe (Rush) but he just can't come up with a suitable story. His creative (and other) juices are sparked by wealthy beauty Viola De Lesseps (Paltrow), who so loves the theatre that she disguises herself as a boy in order to act. (Women are forbidden to be seen on the stage.) But their affair is bittersweet since Viola is about to be married. Ah well, at least Will comes up with *Romeo and Juliet*. Terrific script, fine performances, spectacular costumes and cinematography, and you don't have to be a Shakespeare scholar to enjoy yourself. The audio and video transfers on this disc do not disappoint as both are excellent. The video features vibrant colors and crisp blacks, while the soundtrack is devoid of any crackling or distortion. The supplements are virtually a disc within the disc here. The two commentary tracks (one features almost every person who worked on or appeared in the film) are the crown jewels. The documentary, "Shakespeare in Love and on Film," is also quite entertaining and informative. A definite step up from the non-Collector's Series disc (also available). —MJT

Movie: 🎵🎵🎵🎵 **DVD:** 🎵🎵🎵🎵

Miramax Pictures Home Video (Cat #18528, UPC #717951005458). Widescreen (2.35:1) anamorphic. Dolby Digital 5.1. $39.99. Keepcase. *LANG:* English; French. *SUB:* English. *FEATURES:* 31 chapter links • "Shakespeare in Love and on Film" • TV spots • 1998 Academy Award–winning costumes • Commentary: John Madden • Commentary: cast and crew • Deleted scenes • Shakespeare facts • Theatrical trailer • Film recommendations. Also available as a non-Collector's Series disc devoid of any extras, cat. #17492, UPC #717951003102, for $29.99.

1998 (R) 122m/C Joseph Fiennes, Gwyneth Paltrow, Ben Affleck, Geoffrey Rush, Colin Firth, Judi Dench, Simon Callow, Tom Wilkinson, Imelda Staunton, Jim Carter, Rupert Everett, Martin Clunes, Anthony Sher, Joe Roberts; *D:* John Madden; *W:* Marc Norman, Tom Stoppard; *C:* Richard Greatrex; *M:* Stephen Warbeck. *AWARDS:* Academy Awards '98: Best Actress (Paltrow), Best Art Direction/Set Decoration, Best Costume Design, Best Original Screenplay, Best Picture, Best Supporting Actress (Dench), Best Original Musical/Comedy Score; British Academy Awards '98: Best Film, Best Film Editing, Best Supporting Actor (Rush), Best Supporting Actress (Dench); Golden Globe Awards '99: Best Actress—Musical/Comedy (Paltrow), Best Film—Musical/Comedy, Best Screenplay; MTV Movie Awards '99: Best Kiss (Joseph Fiennes/Gwyneth Paltrow); New York Film Critics Awards '98: Best Screenplay; National Society of Film Critics Awards '98: Best Supporting

Actress (Dench); Screen Actors Guild Award '98: Best Actress (Paltrow), Cast; Writers Guild of America '98: Best Original Screenplay; Broadcast Film Critics Association Awards '98: Best Original Screenplay; *NOM:* Academy Awards '98: Best Director (Madden), Best Film Editing, Best Makeup, Best Sound, Best Supporting Actor (Rush); British Academy Awards '98: Best Actor (Fiennes), Best Actress (Paltrow), Best Cinematography, Best Costume Design, Best Director (Madden), Best Original Screenplay, Best Sound, Best Supporting Actor (Wilkinson), Best Score; Directors Guild of America Awards '98: Best Director (Madden); Golden Globe Awards '99: Best Director (Madden), Best Supporting Actor (Rush), Best Supporting Actress (Dench); MTV Movie Awards '99: Best Film, Best Female Performance (Paltrow), Breakthrough Performance (Fiennes); Screen Actors Guild Award '98: Best Actor (Fiennes), Best Supporting Actor (Rush), Best Supporting Actress (Dench).

Shalako

Connery/Bardot paring promises something special but fails to deliver. European aristocrats on a hunting trip in New Mexico, circa 1880, are menaced by Apaches. U.S. Army scout (Connery) tries to save captured Countess (Bardot). The strange British attempt at a spaghetti western is poorly directed and pointless. The famous "bare back" scene in chapter 15, the subject of so many magazine photo spreads in the 1960s, is pretty tame stuff. The DVD image is as sharp as anyone could expect with only intermittent surface flecks, but the original material is harsh and grainy. Sound is more than adequate (particularly for the dated theme song). —*MM*
Movie: 🎬🎬 *DVD:* 🎬🎬📀
Anchor Bay (Cat #DV10621, UPC #01313 1062199). Widescreen letterboxed; full frame. Dolby Digital Mono. $24.98. Keepcase. *LANG:* English. *FEATURES:* 18 chapter links.
1968 113m/C Brigitte Bardot, Sean Connery, Stephen Boyd, Honor Blackman, Woody Strode, Alexander Knox; *D:* Edward Dmytryk; *W:* Scot (Scott) Finch, J.J. Griffith, Hal Hopper, Clarke Reynolds; *C:* Ted Moore; *M:* Robert Farnon.

Shallow Grave

Fiercely original exercise in suspense/comedy/horror is so consistently surprising that potential viewers should know as little as possible about the plot. In Glasgow, Scotland, narrator David (Eccleston) shares a large apartment with Alex (McGregor), a smart-alecky reporter, and Juliet (Fox), a doctor. The search for a fourth roommate leads them into uncharted psychological territory. Writer Hodge (a doctor by profession) and director Boyle take Hitchcockian delight in setting up audience expectations, then twisting them a few unsettling degrees and adding a strong dash of black humor. Judged by the

standards of most American films, the depiction of violence is so restrained as to be almost polite. But in a couple of significant moments, Boyle's approach is nauseatingly effective. Almost all of the action takes place within the apartment but the pace moves so quickly—the film is never dull—that it doesn't feel constrained. Though Boyle isn't above showing off with his camera, the tricks are always in service of the story and are usually employed to avoid slow spots. DVD captures all of his devices with ease, from the first dizzying race of the camera through city streets to the beautifully lit attic conclusion. Sound is fine. If only Hodge and Boyle could have been persuaded into a commentary track. —*MM*
Movie: 🎬🎬🎬🎬 *DVD:* 🎬🎬🎬📀
USA Home Entertainment (Cat #800 635 275-2, UPC #780063527521). Widescreen (1.85:1) letterboxed; full frame. Dolby Digital Stereo. $29.95. Keepcase. *LANG:* English. *SUB:* French. *CAP:* English. *FEATURES:* 19 chapter links • Cast and crew thumbnail biographies • Trailer.
1994 (R) 91m/C *GB* Kerry Fox, Christopher Eccleston, Ewan McGregor, Keith Allen, Ken Stott, Colin McCredie, John Hodge; *D:* Danny Boyle; *W:* John Hodge; *C:* Brian Tufano; *M:* Simon Boswell.

Shameless

Model Elizabeth Hurley is surprisingly effective as Antonia, the self-centered drugged-up daughter of aristocrat Harry Dyer (Treves). Her dealer Tony (Brett) is involved with Sandy (Delamere), daughter of corrupt narcotics cop Stringer (Ackland). Stringer discovers that the two girls know each other and irrationally blames Antonia for his daughter's heroine habit. Boyfriend Mike (Howell) plays with his long, poorly cut hair and tries to get Antonia off drugs. The pan-and-scan image is a scant improvement over VHS tape. It may be slightly clearer but closely spaced lines still flash. —*MM AKA:* Mad Dogs and Englishmen.
Movie: 🎬🎬🎬 *DVD:* 🎬🎬
WinStar Home Entertainment (Cat #FLV 5174, UPC #720917517421). Full frame. $24.98. Keepcase. *LANG:* English. *FEATURES:* 8 chapter links • Cast filmographies.
1994 (R) 99m/C *GB* Elizabeth Hurley, C. Thomas Howell, Joss Ackland, Jeremy Brett, Frederick Treves, Claire Bloom, Louise Delamere, Chris(topher) Adamson; *D:* Henry Cole; *W:* Tim Sewell; *C:* John Peters; *M:* Barrie Guard.

The Shanghai Gesture

Dated, stage-bound pre-war tale of decadence, lust, greed, and other deadly sins set almost entirely in the Shanghai gambling palace of Madame Gin Sling (Munson). Two magnificent set pieces (the gambling casino itself and the dining room on the fateful final evening), rather than the performances of his stellar cast, mark

famed director Josef von Sternberg's *(The Blue Angel, The Devil Is a Woman)* final film effort. We follow the decline and fall of Poppy (Tierney), a rebellious, privileged young woman who all-too-eagerly embraces the dark side of Shanghai night life. Helped along by Dr. Omar (Mature) and other minions of Gin Sling, Poppy's only hope for salvation lies in her cold-hearted financier father Sir Guy Charteris (Huston), a man with a mysterious China history of his own. Source material for the DVD shows its age. Visually, it's an often murky presentation, which lacks crisp black-and-white definition, and is checkered with a number of damaged passages. —*RT*
Movie: 🎬🎬 *DVD:* 🎬🎬
Image Entertainment (Cat #5375, UPC #014831537529). Full frame. Dolby Digital Surround Stereo. $24.99. Snapper. *LANG:* English. *FEATURES:* 10 chapters • Star biographies.
1942 97m/B Walter Huston, Gene Tierney, Victor Mature, Ona Munson, Albert Bassermann, Eric Blore, Maria Ouspenskaya, Phyllis Brooks, Mike Mazurki; *D:* Josef von Sternberg; *W:* Josef von Sternberg, Jules Furthman, Geza Herczeg, Karl Vollmoller; *C:* Paul Ivano; *M:* Richard Hageman. *AWARDS: NOM:* Academy Awards '42: Best Original Dramatic Score.

Shaolin Avengers

Monks from the Shaolin temple vow vengeance against the Ching dynasty after they've been attacked by the government. The action ranges between pure comedy and well-staged fight scenes with lots of spinning, running up walls, and the like. The DVD looks better than many Hong Kong imports. Like most movies of the genre, the dubbing is reminiscent of spaghetti westerns. The whole thing is lively, frivolous, and fun for fans. Others need not bother. —*MM*
Movie: 🎬🎬📀 *DVD:* 🎬🎬
Tai Seng Video Marketing (Cat #44514, UPC #601643445144). Full frame. $19.95. Keepcase. *LANG:* English. *FEATURES:* 6 chapter links.
1994 87m/C *HK* Jean Carlo, Mark Lim, Shirley Ng, Raymond Sun; *D:* Lee Chiu.

Shark Attack

South African import is one of those low-budget films that astonishes you with the brightness and clarity of the DVD image. After his friend mysteriously winds up in the belly of a shark, marine biologist Steven McKray (Van Dien) goes to Port Amanzi to find out what happened. Lawrence Rhodes (Hudson), the local land baron, may be up to something fishy. The plot moves along at a nice clip. Van Dien's impressive shelf of jaw is fine in the lead, but Hudson, reprising the cool Brit drawl that he introduced in *Congo*, steals the film from his human costars. The sharks are fine with some remarkable underwater photography that makes them look like they're going to jump right out of your TV. Stereo sound is excellent, too. —*MM*

Movie: 🎬🎬▶ **DVD:** 🎬🎬🎬
Trimark Home Video (Cat #VM7223D, UPC #031398722335). Full frame. Dolby Digital Stereo. $24.99. Keepcase. *LANG:* English. *SUB:* English; Spanish. *CAP:* English. *FEATURES:* 24 chapter links.
1999 (R) 95m/C *SA* Casper Van Dien, Ernie Hudson, Bentley Mitchum, Jenny McShane; *D:* Bob Misiorowski; *W:* Scott Devine, William Hooke; *C:* Lawrence Sher.

Sharky's Machine

A tough undercover cop (Reynolds, who also directed the film) is hot on the trail of a crooked crime czar. Meanwhile he falls for a high-priced hooker (Ward). Well-done but overdone action, with much violence. From the amount of preprint damage present in this film, it seems safe to say that *Sharky's Machine* has not been a part of the film preservation movement. The DVD also throws some grain and minor artifacts into the mix, resulting in a not-so-great image with weaker colors and fluctuating tints. The sound is pretty powerful, though; in fact, the music is as dynamic as in most 5.1 mixes. —*JO*

Movie: 🎬🎬▶ **DVD:** 🎬🎬▶
Warner Home Video, Inc. (Cat #22024, UPC #085392202423). Full frame. Dolby Surround. $14.98. Snapper. *LANG:* English. *CAP:* English. *FEATURES:* 36 chapter links.
1981 (R) 119m/C Burt Reynolds, Rachel Ward, Vittorio Gassman, Brian Keith, Charles Durning, Bernie Casey, Richard Libertini, Henry Silva, John Fiedler, Earl Holliman; *D:* Burt Reynolds; *W:* Gerald Di Pega; *C:* William A. Fraker.

Shattered Image

Jessie (Parillaud) is either a cold-blooded bad-hair hitwoman dreaming that she's a honeymooner or a newlywed dreaming that she's an assassin. Or both. On her way to Jamaica with her new husband (Baldwin), she nods off and is back in Seattle on her next job. Each "reality" features characters from the other, although (like Jessie) each has a different personality. Think *La Femme Nikita* meets *Julia and Julia*. Definitely not to all tastes despite Ruiz's homages to Welles and Hitchcock. On DVD, the full-frame image is really nothing special, despite the inventiveness of the plotting, the slickness of the dreamlike sets, and the authentic-looking Jamaican locations. Sound is acceptable. —*MM*

Movie: 🎬🎬 **DVD:** 🎬🎬
Universal Studios Home Video (Cat #207 27, UPC #025192072727). Full frame. Dolby Digital Surround Stereo. $24.98. Keepcase. *LANG:* English. *CAP:* English. *FEATURES:* 18 chapter links ▪ Theatrical trailer.
1998 102m/C Anne Parillaud, William Baldwin, Lisanne Falk, Graham Greene, Bulle Ogier, Billy Wilmott, O'Neil Peart, Leonie Forbes; *D:* Raul Ruiz; *W:* Duane Poole; *C:* Robby Muller; *M:* Jorge Arriagada.

The Shawshank Redemption

Convicted of the murder of his wife and her lover, banker Andy (Robbins) is sentenced to the "toughest prison in the Northeast." There he forms a friendship with lifer Red (Freeman, who narrates wonderfully), experiences the brutality of prison life, adapts, offers financial advice to the guards, and helps the warden (Gunton) cook the prison books all in a short 19 years. In his debut, director Darabont makes fine use of most of the genre cliches while Robbins's talent for playing ambiguous characters serves the story well. Freeman brings his usual grace to what could have been a stereotyped role. The DVD is equal to the theatrical release in image and sound, but why has this audience and critical favorite been released in such a bargain-basement package? A commentary track by Darabont and/or Stephen King, who wrote the short novel upon which the film is based, is the least that this one deserves. —*MM*

Movie: 🎬🎬🎬▶ **DVD:** 🎬🎬🎬▶
Warner Home Video, Inc. (Cat #C2583). Widescreen letterboxed. Dolby Digital Surround Stereo. $19.98. Snapper. *LANG:* English; French. *SUB:* English; French. *FEATURES:* 41 chapter links ▪ Awards ▪ Production stills ▪ Cast and crew thumbnail bios ▪ Trailer.
1994 (R) 142m/C Tim Robbins, Morgan Freeman, Bob Gunton, William Sadler, Clancy Brown, Mark Rolston, Gil Bellows, James Whitmore; *D:* Frank Darabont; *W:* Frank Darabont; *C:* Roger Deakins; *M:* Thomas Newman. *AWARDS: NOM:* Academy Awards '94: Best Actor (Freeman), Best Adapted Screenplay, Best Cinematography, Best Film Editing, Best Picture, Best Sound, Best Original Score; Directors Guild of America Awards '94: Best Director (Darabont); Golden Globe Awards '95: Best Actor—Drama (Freeman), Best Screenplay; Screen Actors Guild Award '94: Best Actor (Freeman), Best Actor (Robbins); Writers Guild of America '94: Best Adapted Screenplay.

She

First sound version of H. Rider Haggard's popular 1867 adventure tale shifts the location from Africa to the frozen Arctic. Explorers Vincey (Scott), Holly (Bruce), and Tanya (Mack) search for the fire that preserves life and does not destroy it. Captured by a mysterious tribe of aborigines who are prone to bad wigs and interpretative dance, they discover the living goddess—She-Who-Must-Be-Obeyed (Gahagan)—who regularly bathes in the aforementioned flame and so is immortal. The filmmakers are obviously trying to re-create the screen chemistry that had been so successful for them a couple of years earlier in *King Kong.* Some of the backdrops and art deco sets are impressive, but just as many (most obviously the saber-toothed tiger) are obvious shortcuts. Even so, the DVD looks terrific

for a film of its age with no noticeable flaws beyond the normal wear and tear. The Max Steiner score is still wonderful. —*MM*

Movie: 🎬🎬▶ **DVD:** 🎬🎬🎬
Kino on Video (Cat #K114DVD, UPC #738329011468). Full frame. $24.99. Snapper. *LANG:* English. *FEATURES:* 24 chapter links.
1935 95m/B Helen Gahagan, Randolph Scott, Nigel Bruce, Helen Mack, Gustav von Seyffertitz; *D:* Irving Pichel, Lansing C. Holden; *W:* Dudley Nichols, Ruth Rose; *C:* J. Roy Hunt; *M:* Max Steiner.

She Devils in Chains

Mid-'70s Filipino drive-in fare looks better on disc than it probably did in most ozoners, though the sound is not noticeably better than it was through the speaker that hung on the window. Even so, the soundtrack by Eddie Nova is a perfect example of the time and the genre. The wafer-thin story concerns three U.S. Olympic runners (Katon, Camp, and Anderson), who are kidnapped by gangsters during an appearance at Hong Kong games. The influence of TV's *Charlie's Angels* is evident throughout, and the action is certainly lively, but with a "PG" rating, the film isn't nearly as tawdry (or as much fun) as many of its contemporaries. Producer-director Cirio Santiago has made dozens of these exploitation pictures. This is one of his lesser efforts. —*MM* *AKA:* American Beauty Hostages; Ebony, Ivory, and Jade; Foxforce.

Movie: 🎬🎬 **DVD:** 🎬🎬
Anchor Bay (Cat #DV10821, UPC #013131082197). Full frame. $29.98. Keepcase. *FEATURES:* Chapter index.
1976 (PG) 82m/C Colleen Camp, Rosanne Katon, Sylvia Anderson, Ken Washington, Leo Martinez; *D:* Cirio H. Santiago; *M:* Eddie Nova.

Shelter

ATF agent Martin Roberts (Nelson) is set up by his commanding officer and has a bounty on his head. He takes refuge with a crime lord (Onorati), who's also on the bad-guy feds' hit list. They get even.

Movie: NYR **DVD:** NYR
Studio Home Entertainment (Cat #7015). Full frame. $24.95. Keepcase. *LANG:* English; Spanish. *FEATURES:* Cast and crew thumbnail bios ▪ Notes ▪ Trailer.
1998 (R) 92m/C John Allen Nelson, Peter Onorati, Brenda Bakke, Costas Mandylor, Charles Durning, Linden Ashby, Kurtwood Smith; *D:* Scott Paulin; *W:* Max Strom; *C:* Eric Goldstein; *M:* David Williams.

Sherlock Holmes Consulting Detective, Vol. 1

Somewhat shopworn thanks to its previous incarnations as a laserdisc and CD-ROM, this first of three volumes of interactive video whodunnits contains three mini-mysteries: "The Case of the Mummy's Curse," "The Case of the Tin Soldier," and "The Case of the Mystified Murderess." If you are old enough you might remember being frustrated by its interface in some other format, and that hasn't changed a bit! An eight-page instruction booklet and table of contents screen laid out as Holmes's own desktop offer scads of investigative options, each with its own pressable graphic, that's harder to navigate and activate with a remote than with a mouse. Because the game is mainly a set of animated puzzles, it seems unfair to judge any part as drama. The project's low-budget cast are all still unknowns, some clearly unprepared to produce consistent British accents. Just over an hour's worth of clue-laden inserts were shot on video in a studio, hence the high gain and hermetically sealed sound, augmented by a coy electronic score best described as, well, right out of a video game. Use of characters from the novels was arranged through Dame Jean Conan Doyle. A hint list and user forum are available at the official Web site, but the disc doesn't seem to allow direct online linking. —JK

Movie: ♪♪ **DVD:** ♪♪♪➤
DVD International (Cat #DVDI0725, UPC #647715072528). Full frame. Stereo. $24.99. Keepcase. *LANG:* English. *FEATURES:* 3 chapter links • Interactive menus • "Save current game" option.
1991 70m/C

She's All That

Updated *Pygmalion* with hip teens is no *Clueless*, though star Rachael Leigh Cook certainly is attractive. She's Laney Boggs, an artistic and allegedly geeky girl in glasses. Zack (Prinze) is the BMOC who's dumped by glam girl Taylor (O'Keefe). On a dare, he vows to turn ugly duckling Laney into a swan in time for the prom. Director Iscove gives the film an MTV look with bright candy colors in some scenes, acid hues in others, often washed over each other in zippy transitions. The DVD captures all of his visual flourishes easily. Stereo is fine, too, so in the end, the film looks and sounds better than it actually is. —MM

Movie: ♪♪ **DVD:** ♪♪➤
Miramax Pictures Home Video (Cat #17489, UPC #717951003072). Widescreen (1.85:1) letterboxed. Dolby Digital 5.1 Surround Stereo. $29.99. Keepcase. *LANG:* English. *CAP:* English. *FEATURES:* 24 chapter links • Music video.
1999 (PG-13) 97m/C Rachael Leigh Cook, Freddie Prinze Jr., Matthew Lillard, Paul Walker, Jodi Lyn O'Keefe, Kevin Pollak, Anna Paquin, Kieran Culkin, Elden Henson, Usher Raymond, Gabrielle Union, Dule Hill, Kimberly (Lil' Kim) Jones; *D:* Robert Iscove; *W:* R. Lee Fleming Jr.; *C:* Francis Kenny; *M:* Stewart Copeland. *AWARDS: NOM:* MTV Movie Awards '99: Breakthrough Performance (Cook), Best

On-Screen Duo (Freddie Prinze Jr./Rachel Leigh Cook).

Shine

The now–world famous, uniquely human odyssey of the life of mentally ill pianist David Helfgott (played by three performers including Geoffrey Rush) is controversially dramatized as a struggle between a sensitive boy and his haunted father. Technical elements are as electric as the film's style, subject, and performances. It looks virtually as good in scan mode as in play mode. The "multichannel" soundtrack makes as much impact with dead silence as with the likes of that punishing "Rach 3" concerto. The uncommonly elegantly laid out menus specify which features are segregated from the film, on the flip side. The director's interview is conveniently broken down into single-question sections, but suffers from the inclusion of a few sycophantic queries. Rush's awards speech is an odd inclusion. Perhaps it's a bit of nose-thumbing at those he mentions anonymously at the end, who had refused to back the film on grounds of his being cast as the adult lead! —JK

Movie: ♪♪♪➤ **DVD:** ♪♪♪♪
New Line Home Video (Cat #N4546, UPC #794043454622). Widescreen (1.85:1) anamorphic. Dolby Surround 5.1. $24.99. Snapper. *LANG:* English; French. *SUB:* English; French; Spanish. *CAP:* English. *FEATURES:* 32 chapter links • Interactive menus • Original theatrical trailer • Hybrid text/video interview with director • Embossed gatefold cover with photo montage and director's intro • Star bios and filmographies • Rush's Golden Globe acceptance speech from awards telecast.
1995 (PG-13) 105m/C *AU* Geoffrey Rush, Noah Taylor, Armin Mueller-Stahl, Lynn Redgrave, John Gielgud, Googie Withers, Chris Haywood, Sonia Todd, Alex Rafalowicz, Randall Berger; *D:* Scott Hicks; *W:* Jan Sardi; *C:* Geoffrey Simpson; *M:* David Hirschfelder. *AWARDS:* Academy Awards '96: Best Actor (Rush); Australian Film Institute '96: Best Actor (Rush), Best Cinematography, Best Director (Hicks), Best Film, Best Film Editing, Best Original Screenplay, Best Sound, Best Supporting Actor (Mueller-Stahl), Best Score; British Academy Awards '96: Best Actor (Rush); Golden Globe Awards '97: Best Actor—Drama (Rush); Los Angeles Film Critics Association Awards '96: Best Actor (Rush); National Board of Review Awards '96: Best Film; New York Film Critics Awards '96: Best Actor (Rush); Screen Actors Guild Award '96: Best Actor (Rush); Broadcast Film Critics Association Awards '96: Best Actor (Rush); *NOM:* Academy Awards '96: Best Director (Hicks), Best Film Editing, Best Original Screenplay, Best Picture, Best Supporting Actor (Mueller-Stahl), Best Original Dramatic Score; Australian Film Institute '96: Best Actor (Taylor); British Academy Awards '96: Best Director (Hicks), Best Film, Best Original Screenplay, Best Supporting Actor (Gielgud), Best Supporting Actress (Red-

grave); Directors Guild of America Awards '96: Best Director (Hicks); Golden Globe Awards '97: Best Director (Hicks), Best Film—Drama, Best Screenplay, Best Score; Screen Actors Guild Award '96: Best Supporting Actor (Taylor), Cast; Writers Guild of America '96: Best Original Screenplay.

The Shining

Very loose adaptation of the Stephen King horror novel about a writer and his family, snowbound in a huge hotel, who experience various hauntings caused by either the hotel itself or the writer's dementia. Technically stunning (plenty of Kubrick's incredible tracking shots), and pretty dang scary. Nicholson is excellent as the failed writer gone off the end. Kubrick films are generally pretty grainy, and this is no exception. The problem is that grainy films don't look quite right on DVD—the digital handling of the grain seems to exaggerate it with the end result being that this film looked a little better on laserdisc. That said, the disc is what you should expect. When you can see through the grain, the sharpness is above average and color bleed is minimal. Artifacts are not a problem. Blacks are good, as are the contrast and brightness levels. The sound is mono but very good and everything is very clear. Some complain about this release being full frame, but most Kubrick films, including this one, were shot very close to flat. Worth owning. —JO

Movie: ♪♪♪ **DVD:** ♪♪➤
Warner Home Video, Inc. (Cat #17369, UPC #085391736929). Full frame. Dolby Digital Mono. $24.98. Snapper. *LANG:* English. *SUB:* French. *CAP:* English. *FEATURES:* Dual-layered RSDL • 40 chapter links • Theatrical trailer • Behind-the-scenes documentary. Also available as part of the "Stanley Kubrick Collection" 7-DVD box set ($149.98).
1980 (R) 143m/C Jack Nicholson, Shelley Duvall, Danny Lloyd, Scatman Crothers, Joe Turkel, Barry Nelson, Philip Stone, Lia Beldam, Billie Gibson, Barry Dennan, David Baxt, Lisa Burns, Alison Coleridge, Kate Phelps, Anne Jackson, Tony Burton; *D:* Stanley Kubrick; *W:* Stanley Kubrick, Diane Johnson; *C:* John Alcott; *M:* Walter (Wendy) Carlos, Rachel Elkind.

The Shiver of the Vampires

Perhaps Rollin's most dreamlike horror film, this one opens in sepia and then drenches the screen in red. It's essentially a slow-moving fairy tale about a young married couple who drop by her ancestral castle on their honeymoon only to find that it's inhabited by vampires. But plot is relatively unimportant. It serves merely as an excuse for all of the female characters to disrobe and to engage in decorous sexual acts and offbeat violence. Today, they all appear more than a little silly, but such things were unheard of in horror films of 1970. The rock score is a near perfect

example of musical tastes of the era. In his liner notes, Marc Morris explains that the DVD was created from director Rollin's own 35mm inter-negatives. It probably looks better on disc than it did in its first theatrical run. Even the night scenes—many bathed in washes of red light—are clear. The monaural sound is fine. —MM
AKA: Le Frisson des Vampires; Sex and the Vampire; The Terror of the Vampires; Vampire Thrills; Thrill of the Vampires.
Movie: 🎬🎬▶ **DVD:** 🎬🎬🎬
Image Entertainment (Cat #ID5555SADVD, UPC #014381555523). Widescreen (1.66:1) letterboxed. Dolby Digital Mono. $24.99. Snapper. *LANG:* French. *SUB:* English. *FEATURES:* 19 chapter links • Photo gallery • Jean Rollin filmography • Liner notes by Marc Morris.
1970 96m/C Michel Delahaye, Dominique, Jean Durand, Sandra Julien, Nicole Nancel, Jacques Robiolles, Kuelan Herce, Marie Pierre Castel; **D:** Jean Rollin; **W:** Jean Rollin.

Shock Corridor

A reporter, dreaming of a Pulitzer Prize, fakes mental illness and is admitted to an asylum, where he hopes to investigate a murder. He is subjected to disturbing experiences, including shock therapy, and does manage to solve the crime—however, he suffers a mental breakdown in the process and is admitted for real. Disturbing and lurid. Everything is harsh about this DVD. The black-and-white picture is super sharp, and also very high contrast. The sound is middy and at times seems pushed to the very limit of volume distortion. Luckily it all works fine with Fuller's campy hit-you-in-the-face opus. —JO
Movie: 🎬🎬🎬 **DVD:** 🎬🎬🎬
Criterion Collection (Cat #SHO040, UPC #037429125922). Widescreen (1.85:1) letterboxed. Mono. $29.95. Keepcase. *LANG:* English. *FEATURES:* 25 chapter links • Theatrical trailer.
1963 101m/B Peter Breck, Constance Towers, Gene Evans, Hari Rhodes, James Best, Philip Ahn, Larry Tucker, Paul Dubov; **D:** Samuel Fuller; **W:** Samuel Fuller; **C:** Stanley Cortez; **M:** Paul Dunlap. *AWARDS:* National Film Registry '96.

Shocker

Another Craven gore-fest is practically a remake of his original *Nightmare on Elm Street.* A condemned serial killer is transformed into a menacing electrical force after being fried in the chair. Great special effects, a few enjoyable weird and sick moments. What's Dr. Timothy Leary doing here? *Shocker's* wild climactic video chase, where hero and bad guy chase each other through television channels, looks great and even edges toward believability on the TV screen. The DVD handles all the shifts in hues and even the jumping from color to black-and-white with no major glitches. In fact, the disc stays pretty sharp, and the colors stay true through the whole thing. The metal soundtrack is

delivered with crunch to spare by the Dolby Surround, which is otherwise nothing special. —JO
Movie: 🎬🎬🎬 **DVD:** 🎬🎬🎬
Universal Studios Home Video (Cat #20436, UPC #02519203628). Widescreen (1.85:1) anamorphic. Dolby Surround. $24.98. Keepcase. *LANG:* English, French. *SUB:* Spanish. *CAP:* English. *FEATURES:* 17 chapter links • Theatrical trailer • Cast and filmmaker bios • Production notes • Film highlights.
1989 (R) 111m/C Michael Murphy, Peter Berg, Camille (Cami) Cooper, Mitch Pileggi, Richard Price, Timothy Leary, Heather Langenkamp, Theodore (Ted) Raimi, Richard Brooks, Sam Scarber; **D:** Wes Craven; **W:** Wes Craven; **C:** Jacques Haitkin; **M:** William Goldstein.

Shoot Out

Gregory Peck portrays an aging outlaw. This transfer has been digitally restored to achieve the level of quality required for this release. Unfortunately, some restoration artifacts are evident in certain scenes, when parts of the image seem locked down in place for a number of frames and then suddenly jump or trail into their original position. While it is noticeable, it is for the most part not really problematic. The transfer has been well compressed for the DVD and the image is virtually free of artifacts, creating a picture that is bold with colors and detail. The soundtrack comes across clean and without noise, but seems a bit muffled and flat throughout—no doubt a result of the film's age. —GH **AKA:** Shootout.
Movie: 🎬🎬🎬 **DVD:** 🎬🎬
Goodtimes Entertainment (Cat #81037, UPC #018713810373). Full frame. Dolby Digital Mono. $19.98. Snapper. *LANG:* English. *SUB:* French; Spanish. *CAP:* English. *FEATURES:* 18 chapter links.
1971 94m/C Gregory Peck, Robert F. Lyons, Susan Tyrrell, Jeff Corey, James Gregory, Rita Gam, Pepe Serna, John Davis Chandler, Paul Fix, Arthur Hunnicutt, Nicolas Beauvy; **D:** Henry Hathaway; **W:** Marguerite Roberts; **C:** Earl Rath; **M:** Dave Grusin.

Shoot the Piano Player

Former concert pianist Charlie (Aznavour, splendidly cast) plays piano in a low-rent Paris cafe until a brother shows up, involving him with gangsters. The plot, based on David Goodis's pulp novel *Down There,* is an unpredictable mix of humor, drama, action, romance, and character development. On DVD, the film looks better than anyone could reasonably expect. Yes, the night exteriors are darker than younger videophiles are used to seeing, and even bright, snow-covered scenes have a rough look. But those are to be expected of any film of this age, budget, and origin. More importantly, the widescreen transfer is accomplished with a narrow black band at the top and a wider band at the bottom to

accommodate the clear subtitles. Even if the sound is not spectacular, it's fine for Georges Delerue's piano score. —MM
AKA: Tirez sur le Pianiste; Shoot the Pianist.
Movie: 🎬🎬🎬🎬 **DVD:** 🎬🎬🎬
WinStar Home Entertainment (Cat #FLV 5075, UPC #720917507521). Widescreen letterboxed. $29.99. Snapper. *LANG:* French. *SUB:* English. *FEATURES:* 6 chapter links • Filmographies and awards • Production credits • Theatrical trailers.
1962 92m/B FR Charles Aznavour, Marie DuBois, Nicole Berger, Michele Mercier, Albert Remy; **D:** Francois Truffaut; **W:** Marcel Moussey, Francois Truffaut; **C:** Raoul Coutard; **M:** Georges Delerue.

Shooting Fish

Georgie, a gamine British aristocrat who would have been played by Audrey Hepburn in the '50s, is Kate Beckinsale. She is rich in social position, but so cash-strapped to help her favorite cause. Can she melt the hearts of fast friends, Jez (Stuart Townsend) and Dylan (Dan Futterman), who scam unsuspecting businessmen for fun, profit, and a sense of revenge? Why, she does, and almost instantly, too! The film overall is as clever as its characters, perhaps to the point of annoyance. The look and poppy sound are both as quick and shimmery as a music video, despite running a gamut of lighting situation and shifts of dramatic pace and tone. —JK
Movie: 🎬🎬▶ **DVD:** 🎬🎬🎬🎬
20th Century Fox (Cat #4110397, UPC #086162103971). Widescreen (2.35:1) letterboxed. Dolby Digital Surround. $34.99. Keepcase. *LANG:* English. *SUB:* Spanish; English. *CAP:* English. *FEATURES:* 26 chapter links • Interactive menus • Original theatrical trailer • Full-color picture disc.
1998 (PG) 109m/C GB Dan Futterman, Stuart Townsend, Kate Beckinsale, Dominic Mafham, Claire Cox, Nickolas Grace, Peter Capaldi, Annette Crosbie, Jane Lapotaire; **D:** Stefan Schwartz; **W:** Stefan Schwartz, Richard Holmes; **C:** Henry Braham; **M:** Stanislas Syrewicz.

Short 1: Invention

This is the first release in the acclaimed DVD series originally titled *Short Cinema Journal.* The DVD starts off with the intense short film "Some Folks Call It a Sling Blade," starring Molly Ringwald, the late J.T. Walsh, and Billy Bob Thornton, who would later expand the concept into the full-length feature *Sling Blade.* Also included are: "Easter Sunday in NYC," Albert Watson's documentary portrait of punker/poet/artist Henry Rollins; "The Big Story," an Academy Award–nominated animated short; "Black Rider," an Academy Award–winning short that tackles racism with a twist; "Mr. Resistor," Mark Gustafson's energetic animated short; and finally, acclaimed director Michael

Apted talking about himself, filmmaking, and more. The DVD also includes excerpts from several other films. *Short Cinema Journal* came out early in the life of DVD and reassured videophiles that it would not just be big-budget mainstream pabulum that made it to DVD. The quality of the DVD is excellent and is only limited by the quality of the preprint material involved. The entire series is a must for any serious collector. —*JO*

Movie: 𝄢𝄢𝄢𝄢 **DVD:** 𝄢𝄢𝄢𝄢▸
Warner Home Video, Inc. (Cat #36845, UPC #085393684525). Full frame. Dolby Digital 5.1; Stereo. $14.98. Snapper. *LANG:* English. *FEATURES:* 6 chapter links.
19?? ?m/C

Short 2: Dreams

The second in the fine DVD series originally titled *Short Cinema Journal* includes the following short films: "La Jetee," Chris Marker's innovative film that formed the inspiration for *Twelve Monkeys,* composed of photographs; "Big Brass Ring," from a script by Orson Welles and recently turned in to a full-length feature staring William Hurt; "A Guy Walks into a Bar," the surrealistic wild western with Fred Savage of *The Wonder Years*; "Cafe Bar," an animated piece in which two people meet in a cafe and have radically different fantasies about each other; "Depth Solitude," featuring narration by Max von Sydow; and "Eye Like a Strange Balloon," from Canadian auteur Guy Maddin (*Tales from the Gimli Hospital*). The DVD is a fine transfer and everything on it is presented with the best quality that the source material allows. The picture is very sharp, and both color and black-and-white films have very good detail. As a bonus, the DVD also includes Mark Gustafson's "Bride of Resistor," his animated follow-up to "Mr. Resistor," which was featured on *Short 1*. —*JO*

Movie: 𝄢𝄢𝄢𝄢 **DVD:** 𝄢𝄢𝄢𝄢▸
Warner Home Video, Inc. (Cat #36846, UPC #085393684624). Full frame. Dolby Digital 5.1. $14.98. Snapper. *LANG:* English. *FEATURES:* 6 chapter links ▪ Animated short: "Bride of Resistor" ▪ Documentary: "Vincent the Junkie Chronicles."
19?? ?m/C

A Shot in the Dark

The second entry is easily the funniest of the "Pink Panther–Inspector Clouseau" comedy series. The bumbling Clouseau (Sellers at his best) investigates the case of a parlor maid (Sommer) accused of murdering her lover. Clouseau's libido convinces him that she's innocent, much to the displeasure of his boss (the long-suffering Lom). The gags are carefully established and hilarious. Not to be missed. The DVD contains a great transfer of the movie, although some scratches and dust are evident in the print. The colors in the presentation are nicely reproduced and give the movie a very natural-looking quali-

ty. Blacks are deep and accurate, giving the image depth. The compression is good and without distracting artifacts, putting this release a noticeable notch above the VHS releases in terms of quality. The mono audio track is clean and without noise or distortions, adding to the overall appeal of this disc. —*GH*

Movie: 𝄢𝄢𝄢▸ **DVD:** 𝄢𝄢𝄢▸
MGM Home Entertainment (Cat #907501, UPC #027616750129). Widescreen (2.35:1) anamorphic; full frame. Dolby Digital Mono. $24.98. Keepcase. *LANG:* English; French. *SUB:* English; French. *CAP:* English. *FEATURES:* 32 chapter links ▪ Trailer.
1964 101m/C Peter Sellers, Elke Sommer, Herbert Lom, George Sanders, Bryan Forbes; *D:* Blake Edwards; *W:* William Peter Blatty, Blake Edwards; *C:* Christopher Challis; *M:* Henry Mancini.

Show Boat

Third film version of the 1927 musical about the lives and loves of a Mississippi riverboat troupe boasts terrific musical numbers with dance routines from Champion who went on to great fame as a choreographer. Grayson is somewhat vapid but lovely to look at and hear. Gardner didn't want to do the part of Julie, although she eventually received fabulous reviews—her singing was dubbed Annette Warren. The 171-foot "Cotton Blossom" boat was built on the Tarzan lake set at the MGM back lot (at an astounding cost of $126,468). Warfield's film debut—his "Ol' Man River"—was recorded in one take.

Movie: 𝄢𝄢▸ **DVD:** NYR
Warner Home Video, Inc. (Cat #906614). Full frame. Dolby Digital Mono. $24.98. *LANG:* English. *SUB:* French; Spanish. *CAP:* English.
1951 115m/C Kathryn Grayson, Howard Keel, Ava Gardner, William Warfield, Joe E. Brown, Agnes Moorehead, Gower Champion; *D:* George Sidney; *W:* George Wells, Jack McGowan; *C:* Charles Rosher; *M:* Jerome Kern, Oscar Hammerstein. *AWARDS: NOM:* Academy Awards '51: Best Color Cinematography, Scoring of a Musical.

Showdown

Ken, the new kid in a particularly nasty high school, gets picked on by the martial-arts expert bully. After being beaten up a lot, Ken finds out that the janitor can turn him into a high-kicking fighter. Lots of fast-paced fight scenes, as the genre demands. *AKA:* Lookin' Italian.

Movie: 𝄢𝄢 **DVD:** NYR
MTI Home Video (Cat #222). Full frame. $24.95. Keepcase. *FEATURES:* Cast and crew thumbnail bios ▪ Commentary: Magar ▪ Trailer.
1994 (R) 90m/C Jay Acovone, Matt LeBlanc, Lou Rawls, John Lamotta, Stephanie Richards, Real Andrews; *D:* Guy Magar; *W:* Guy Magar; *C:* Gerry Lively; *M:* Jeff Beal.

Showdown in Little Tokyo

Lundgren stars as a martial arts master/L.A. cop who was raised in Japan, and has all the respect in the world for his "ancestors" and heritage. Brandon Lee (son of Bruce) is Lundgren's partner, and he's a bona fide American-made, pop-culture, mall junkie. Together, they go after a crack-smuggling gang of "yakuza" (Japanese thugs). Lots of high-kicking action and the unique angle on stereotypes make this a fun martial arts film. The film was pretty slick and stylized in the theatre, but most of that feel is lost on this DVD, where the picture is constantly grainy, and the colors dull. The overall image is in serious need of a boost to both contrast and brightness. —*JO*

Movie: 𝄢𝄢𝄢 **DVD:** 𝄢𝄢
Warner Home Video, Inc. (Cat #12311, UPC #085391231127). Full frame. Dolby Surround. $14.98. Snapper. *LANG:* English. *CAP:* English. *FEATURES:* 22 chapter links.
1991 (R) 78m/C Dolph Lundgren, Brandon Lee, Tia Carrere, Cary-Hiroyuki Tagawa; *D:* Mark L. Lester; *W:* Caliope Brattlestreet; *C:* Mark Irwin; *M:* David Michael Frank.

Sid & Nancy

The tragic, brutal, true love story of the Sex Pistols' Sid Vicious and American groupie Nancy Spungen, from the director of *Repo Man*. Remarkable lead performances in a very dark story that manages to be funny at times. The film is depressing but engrossing, with no appreciation of punk music or sympathy for the self-destructive way of life required. Oldman and Webb are superb. Music by Joe Strummer, the Pogues, and Pray for Rain. The DVD perfectly captures the theatrical presentation, neither detracting from or embellishing on the original look. Colors are accurate and image detail is superb. The movie is accompanied by an excellent supplemental section, which includes the very good behind-the-scenes documentary "England's Glory" and some fairly amazing interview footage and sounds. —*JO* *AKA:* Sid & Nancy: Love Kills.

Movie: 𝄢𝄢𝄢▸ **DVD:** 𝄢𝄢𝄢▸
Criterion Collection (Cat #CC1540D, UPC #715515009232). Widescreen (1.77:1) letterboxed. Stereo. $39.95. Keepcase. *LANG:* English. *FEATURES:* 25 chapter links ▪ Commentary ▪ Documentary: "England's Glory" ▪ 1976 Bill Gundy interview with the Sex Pistols ▪ Sid Vicious telephone interview ▪ Sid and Nancy interviews from *D.O.A.: A Right of Passage*.
1986 (R) 111m/C *GB* Gary Oldman, Chloe Webb, Debbie Bishop, David Hayman, Andrew Schofield, Tony London, Xander Berkeley, Biff Yeager, Courtney Love, Iggy Pop; *D:* Alex Cox; *W:* Alex Cox, Abbe Wool; *C:* Roger Deakins; *M:* The Pogues, Pray for Rain, Joe Strummer. *AWARDS:* National Society of Film Critics Awards '86: Best Actress (Webb).

The Siege

Big-budget political suspense thriller caused quite a ruckus for the wrong reasons when it was released theatrically. Arab-American groups protested negative stereotyping when the film actually attempts to deal with racial and cultural differences with intelligence and sympathy. First half centers on FBI honcho Hubbard (Washington) and his prominently Lebanese-American partner Haddad (Shalhoub) as they deal with terrorist bombings in New York. But eventually Brooklyn is placed under martial law and the semi-fascist Gen. Devereaux (Willis) rounds up and imprisons young Arab-Americans. CIA agent Elise Kraft (Bening) is in on things, too. Neither the conflicts nor the characters are as clearly defined as they need to be. On DVD, the film looks excellent. Subtitles and captions are easy to read in the lower portion of the letterbox. The clarity of the image makes director Zwick's aversion to the violence of his film seem coy at important moments. —*MM* **AKA:** Against All Enemies.

Movie: 🦴🦴📀 **DVD:** 🦴🦴🦴
Twentieth Century Fox Home Entertainment (Cat #4111053, UPC #086162001307). Widescreen (2.35:1) letterboxed. Dolby Digital Surround; Dolby Digital 5.1 Surround. $34.98. Keepcase. *LANG:* English; French. *SUB:* Spanish. *CAP:* English. *FEATURES:* 30 chapter links ▪ Theatrical trailer.
1998 (R) 116m/C Denzel Washington, Tony Shalhoub, Annette Bening, Bruce Willis, Sami Bouajila, David Proval, Jack Gwaltney, Chip Zien, Victor Slezak, Will Lyman, Dakin Matthews, John Rothman, E. Katherine Kerr, Jimmie Ray Weeks, Lance Reddick, Mark Valley, Liana Pai, Amro Salama; **D:** Edward Zwick; **W:** Edward Zwick, Menno Meyjes, Lawrence Wright; **C:** Roger Deakins; **M:** Graeme Revell. *AWARDS:* Golden Raspberry Awards '98: Worst Actor (Willis).

Silence of the Lambs

Foster is FBI cadet Clarice Starling, a woman with ambition, a cum laude degree in psychology, and a traumatic childhood. When a serial killer begins his ugly rounds, the FBI wants psychological profiles from other serial killers and she's sent to collect a profile from one who's exceptionally clever—psychiatrist Hannibal Lecter (Hopkins), a vicious killer prone to dining on his victims. Brilliant performances from Foster and Hopkins, finely detailed supporting characterizations, and elegant pacing from Demme balance some brutal visual effects. Excellent portrayals of women who refuse to be victims. Some would say that all the extras on the Criterion DVD and laserdisc make them the way to go. Unfortunately, the picture on the Criterion DVD just doesn't hold up when compared to the other home video editions. The image is of average sharpness and has occasional problems with grain, in the expected darker sequences. Artifacts are not a problem.

Colors are very close to accurate and there is not much bleed. Blacks are true. The brightness levels seem fine but a touch more contrast would have livened up the picture. The Dolby Surround is O.K., but features very little Surround. —*JO*
Movie: 🦴🦴🦴📀 **DVD:** 🦴🦴📀
Criterion Collection (Cat #CC1530DDV, UPC #715515009133). Widescreen (1.85:1) letterboxed. Dolby Surround. $39.98. Keepcase. *LANG:* English. *FEATURES:* 28 chapter links ▪ 7 deleted scenes ▪ Commentary: Demme, Foster, Hopkins, Ted Tally, John Douglas ▪ Storyboards ▪ Film-to-storyboard comparison ▪ FBI Crime Classification Manual ▪ Voices of Death (word-for-word statements of convicted serial killers) ▪ Dual-layered RSDL.
1991 (R) 118m/C Jodie Foster, Anthony Hopkins, Scott Glenn, Ted Levine, Brooke Smith, Charles Napier, Roger Corman, Anthony Heald, Diane Baker, Chris Isaak; **D:** Jonathan Demme; **W:** Ted Tally; **C:** Tak Fujimoto; **M:** Howard Shore. *AWARDS:* Academy Awards '91: Best Actor (Hopkins), Best Actress (Foster), Best Adapted Screenplay, Best Director (Demme), Best Picture; American Film Institute (AFI) '98: Top 100; British Academy Awards '91: Best Actor (Hopkins), Best Actress (Foster); Directors Guild of America Awards '91: Best Director (Demme); Golden Globe Awards '92: Best Actress—Drama (Foster); National Board of Review Awards '91: Best Director (Demme), Best Film, Best Supporting Actor (Hopkins); New York Film Critics Awards '91: Best Actor (Hopkins), Best Actress (Foster), Best Director (Demme), Best Film; Writers Guild of America '91: Best Adapted Screenplay; *NOM:* Academy Awards '91: Best Film Editing, Best Sound.

Silent Running

As the loner Freeman Lowell, Dern's job is to keep the plants alive aboard a giant "forest ship," a space station orbiting Saturn in a post-apocalyptic era in which all vegetation on Earth was destroyed in a nuclear inferno. When orders come to destroy the vegetation aboard his ship, Dern takes matters into his own hands. Speculative sci-fi painting a disturbing portrait of a future gone bad is Trumbull's directorial debut. (He created special effects for *2001* and *Close Encounters*.) Robot drones Huey, Dewey, and Louie foreshadow the droids of *Star Wars* six years later. Strange music enhances the alien atmosphere, but Joan Baez's tunes seem out of place. This pseudo-classic deserves better DVD treatment as the generally fair-to-poor picture points to low-quality videotape elements used for the DVD transfer. The sound is mono, and extras are altogether absent. —*MB*
Movie: 🦴🦴🦴 **DVD:** 🦴📀
Image Entertainment (Cat #ID4229USDVD, UPC #014381422924). Widescreen (1.85:1) letterboxed. Dolby Digital 1.0. $29.99. Snapper. *LANG:* English. *CAP:* English. *FEATURES:* 16 chapter links.

1971 (G) 90m/C Bruce Dern, Cliff Potts, Ron Rifkin; **D:** Douglas Trumbull; **W:** Michael Cimino, Deric Washburn, Steven Bochco; **C:** Charles F. Wheeler; **M:** Prof. Peter Schickele.

Silk 'n' Sabotage

Serious-minded Jamie (Skiru) comes up with a new program for a computer game that's stolen by a con artist. Actually more screen time is focused on the soft-core dalliances of her roommates, who run a lingerie business out of the apartment. Most scenes that do not take place in a shower or a bedroom are too dark or too light. —*MM* **AKA:** Wildchild 2.
Movie: 🦴📀 **DVD:** 🦴📀
Simitar Entertainment (Cat #7660, UPC #082551766024). Full frame. Dolby Digital 5.1 Surround Stereo. $14.98. Keepcase. *LANG:* English. *FEATURES:* 8 chapter links ▪ Production factoids.
1994 70m/C Cherilyn Shea, Stephanie Champlin, Julie Skiru; **D:** Joe Cauley.

Silkwood

This "based-on-a-true-story" film of Karen Silkwood (Streep), a nuclear power plant worker who died in a 1974 car crash under "mysterious circumstances," gets a curious New York/Hollywood treatment. Casting Streep and Cher as down-home good-old girls is questionable and so are the choices of cosmopolitan writers Ephron and Arlen and director Nichols. Admittedly, they treat the material seriously, but the subject comes with so much political baggage that it's never completely involving. On DVD, the image and sound are as clear as they need to be. The disc is without extras, and they're not really needed. Would commentary by Oscar-nominee Cher on the dangers of nuclear power have added anything? —*MM*
Movie: 🦴🦴📀 **DVD:** 🦴🦴🦴
Anchor Bay (Cat #DV10886, UPC #013131088694). Full frame; widescreen (1.85:1) letterboxed. Dolby Digital Stereo. $24.98. Keepcase. *FEATURES:* 26 chapter links.
1983 (R) 131m/C Meryl Streep, Kurt Russell, Cher, Diana Scarwid, Bruce McGill, Fred Ward, David Strathairn, Ron Silver, Josef Sommer, Craig T. Nelson; **D:** Mike Nichols; **W:** Nora Ephron, Alice Arlen; **C:** Miroslav Ondricek; **M:** Georges Delerue. *AWARDS:* Golden Globe Awards '84: Best Supporting Actress (Cher); *NOM:* Academy Awards '83: Best Actress (Streep), Best Director (Nichols), Best Film Editing, Best Original Screenplay, Best Supporting Actress (Cher).

Simon Birch

A film that begins with a character proclaiming his belief in God is taking a change, particularly when that character is played by Jim Carrey without a touch of irony or humor. That's indicative of director Johnson's bald approach to John Irving's novel *A Prayer for Owen Meany*. (At Irving's

demand, the credits state the film is "suggested by" the novel.) Young Simon Birch (Smith) believes that he is destined to be a hero despite his disability—dwarfism resulting from Morquoi's syndrome. In the mid 1960s, he and his friend Joe (Joseph Mazzello) try to find the identity and location of Joe's father. The two young actors are excellent, but Johnson's interpretation of the material is weak, particularly when compared to *The Cider House Rules*, which was made a couple of years later and handles similar material with more toughness. The pleasant DVD image reflects Johnson's sentimentality. It's a generally soft focus, almost misty, that's often bathed in yellow autumnal light. Sound is more than adequate. —*MM*
AKA: A Small Miracle.
Movie: ♫♫ **DVD:** ♫♫➤
Hollywood Pictures Home Video (Cat #17 241, UPC #717951002358). Widescreen (1.85:1) letterboxed. Dolby Digital 5.1 Surround Stereo. $29.99. Keepcase. *LANG:* English; French. *CAP:* English. *FEATURES:* 24 chapter links ➤ Theatrical trailer.
1998 (PG) 110m/C Ian Michael Smith, Joseph Mazzello, Ashley Judd, Oliver Platt, David Strathairn, Dana Ivey, Jan Hooks, Beatrice Winde, Ceciley Carroll, Sumela-Rose Keramidopulos, Sam Morton; *D:* Mark Steven Johnson; *W:* Mark Steven Johnson; *C:* Aaron Schneider; *M:* Marc Shaiman; *Nar:* Jim Carrey.

Simon Sez

Direct-to-video action flick casts basketball player Rodman as Simon, a motorcycle-riding Interpol agent hot on the trail of a computer disc that has something to do with the fate of the free world. The Bond wanna-be features lots of chases and shoot-outs on European locations and a fair sense of humor. Director Kevin Elders does all that anyone could ask to compensate for his star's lack of experience and talent. In visual terms, the DVD is a short step above VHS tape in its rendering of the first-rate stunt work. —*MM*
Movie: ♫ **DVD:** ♫♫➤
Columbia Tristar Home Video (Cat #04385, UPC #043396043855). Widescreen (1.78:1) letterboxed. Dolby Digital 5.1 Surround Stereo; Dolby Digital Surround Stereo. $19.95. Keepcase. *LANG:* English. *SUB:* English. *CAP:* English. *FEATURES:* 28 chapter links ➤ Dennis Rodman thumbnail biography ➤ Theatrical trailers ➤ "Making of" featurette.
1999 (PG-13) 85m/C Dennis Rodman, Dane Cook, Natalia Cigliuti, Filip Nicolic, John Pinette, Jerome Pradon, Ricky Harris; *D:* Kevin Elders; *W:* Andrew Miller, Andrew Lowery; *C:* Avi (Avraham) Karpik; *M:* Brian Tyler.

A Simple Plan

A chance encounter with a fox lures three Minnesotans—Hank (Pullman), his brother Jacob (Thornton), and their friend Lou (Briscoe)—into the snowy woods where they discover a crashed private plane with a dead pilot and $4 million in cash. They decide to keep the money and after that, everything goes wrong. Comparisons to *Fargo* are accurate only in the strong evocation of winter and place that the two films share. Writer Smith and director Raimi actually are working with more grimly Gothic material and they treat it brilliantly, with Elfman's dissonant score adding an effective undercurrent of weirdness. The DVD handles the snow-covered environment without noticeable flaws, beyond a few curious artifacts on the omnipresent crows. For Raimi, the film shows that he is capable of more serious material. A commentary track from him would have been welcome. —*MM*
Movie: ♫♫♫➤ **DVD:** ♫♫♫➤
Paramount Home Video (Cat #333767, UPC #097363337676). Widescreen anamorphic. Dolby Digital 5.1 Surround; Dolby Surround Stereo. $29.99. Keepcase. *LANG:* English. *FEATURES:* 14 chapter links ➤ Theatrical trailer.
1998 (R) 121m/C Bill Paxton, Billy Bob Thornton, Brent Briscoe, Bridget Fonda, Gary Cole, Becky Ann Baker, Chelcie Ross, Jack Walsh; *D:* Sam Raimi; *W:* Scott B. Smith; *C:* Alan Kivilo; *M:* Danny Elfman. *AWARDS:* Los Angeles Film Critics Association Awards '98: Best Supporting Actor (Thornton); Broadcast Film Critics Association Awards '98: Best Adapted Screenplay, Best Supporting Actor (Thornton); *NOM:* Academy Awards '98: Best Adapted Screenplay, Best Supporting Actor (Thornton); Golden Globe Awards '99: Best Supporting Actor (Thornton); Screen Actors Guild Award '98: Best Supporting Actor (Thornton); Writers Guild of America '98: Best Adapted Screenplay.

A Simple Wish

Equal employment opportunities now even extend to the fairy godmother realm. Anabel (Wilson) knows her dad (Pastorelli) wants to become a Broadway actor, so she wishes for a fairy godmother and gets stuck with Murray (Short), the first affirmative-action male practitioner, who's really not very good at spell-casting. Both Anabel and Murray have bigger problems—evil fairy godmother Claudia (Turner) is after all the fairy godmothers' magic wands so she can rule the world's wishes. Short's brand of comic energy plays right into the kid audience, and Wilson lights up every scene she's in. The DVD image is a faithful re-creation of a big budget Hollywood fantasy-comedy. It looks and sounds fine. —*MM*
Movie: ♫♫➤ **DVD:** ♫♫♫
Universal Studios Home Video (Cat #20271). Widescreen (1.85:1) anamorphic. Dolby Digital 5.1 Surround Stereo. $24.98. Keepcase. *LANG:* English; French; Spanish. *SUB:* Spanish. *FEATURES:* Cast and crew thumbnail bios ➤ Notes ➤ Trailer ➤ 16 chapter links.
1997 (PG) 95m/C Mara Wilson, Martin Short, Kathleen Turner, Robert Pastorelli, Amanda Plummer, Teri Garr, Francis Capra, Jonathan Hadary, Alan Campbell, Ruby

Dee; *D:* Michael Ritchie; *W:* Jeff Rothberg; *C:* Ralf Bode; *M:* Bruce Broughton.

Simply Irresistible

Whimsical, frothy romantic comedy stars Sarah Michelle Gellar, better known as Buffy from the television series *Buffy, the Vampire Slayer*, as a New York City restaurant owner whose cooking abilities make any fast food look gourmet. Through a bit of magic, her food takes on her feelings of the moment—sad, joyful, etc.—and she is transformed into a cooking sensation. Stir in a romantic interest, Sean Patrick Flanery, and a script that is a throw-back to 1950s, and you have a surprisingly enjoyable cinematic concoction. DVD presentation is quite good, complete with English and French audio tracks and a pristine transfer. —*RT*
Movie: ♫♫➤ **DVD:** ♫♫♫
Twentieth Century Fox Home Entertainment (Cat #4112005, UPC #0861621 20053). Widescreen. Dolby Digital 5.1 Surround Stereo; Dolby Surround Stereo. $34.98. Keepcase. *LANG:* English; French. *SUB:* English; Spanish. *CAP:* English. *FEATURES:* 18 chapter markers ➤ Theatrical trailer ➤ Cast biographies.
1999 (PG-13) 95m/C Sarah Michelle Gellar, Sean Patrick Flanery, Patricia Clarkson, Dylan Baker, Christopher Durang, Larry Gilliard Jr., Betty Buckley; *D:* Mark Tarlov; *W:* Judith Roberts; *C:* Robert Stevens; *M:* Gil Goldstein.

The Sinful Nuns of Saint Valentine

An engaging little mystery involving sex-hungry nuns and overzealous, politically corrupt heretic hunters during the Spanish Inquisition. The atmosphere is pretty good and there is enough nudity and fetishism to keep things interesting. Like the other releases in Image's "Redemption" line, the preprint used for this DVD is not in the best shape, but it's more than acceptable. The picture is reasonably sharp, but far from a showpiece. Colors are faded and contrast is low. The mono sound is also a little distorted, but, because Eurosleaze is so hot, this should be a very desirable disc. —*JO*
Movie: ♫♫♫ **DVD:** ♫♫➤
Image Entertainment (Cat #ID4618SADVD, UPC #01438146182). Widescreen (2.35:1) letterboxed. Mono. $24.99. Snapper. *LANG:* Italian. *SUB:* English. *FEATURES:* 13 chapter links ➤ Theatrical trailer.
1974 93m/C *IT D:* Sergio Grieco.

Singin' in the Rain

One of the all-time great movie musicals—an affectionate spoof of the turmoil that afflicted the motion picture industry in the late 1920s during the changeover from silent films to sound. Codirector Kelly and Hagen lead a glorious cast. The beautiful DVD transfers of MGM musicals could create a whole new audience. The DVD features colors that have been cleaned up and restored to their original glory, and even the mono sound feels more full-bodied than ever before on video. That MGM can bring such vibrant colors to DVD without sacrificing anything in the way of sharpness or detail is a marvel in itself. —JO

Movie: 🎵🎵🎵🎵 **DVD:** 🎵🎵🎵►
MGM Home Entertainment (Cat #906262, UPC #027616626295). Full frame. Mono. $24.98. Snapper. *LANG:* English; Spanish; French. *SUB:* English; Spanish; French. *CAP:* English. *FEATURES:* 60 chapter links • Theatrical trailer.
1952 103m/C Gene Kelly, Donald O'Connor, Jean Hagen, Debbie Reynolds, Rita Moreno, King Donovan, Millard Mitchell, Cyd Charisse, Douglas Fowley, Madge Blake, Joi Lansing; **D:** Gene Kelly, Stanley Donen; **W:** Adolph Green, Betty Comden; **C:** Harold Rosson; **M:** Nacio Herb Brown, Lennie Hayton. *AWARDS:* American Film Institute (AFI) '98: Top 100; Golden Globe Awards '53: Best Actor—Musical/Comedy (O'Connor), National Film Registry '89; *NOM:* Academy Awards '52: Best Supporting Actress (Hagen), Scoring of a Musical.

Single White Female

One of the best of the early '90s psycho-femme horrors casts Jennifer Jason Leigh as Hedra, the roommate from hell who takes over Allie's (Fonda) life. The motivation is a rent-controlled apartment and director Schroeder gives even the weirdest plot turn a sense of grim New York reality. The gradual revelation of Hedra's personality makes the story, based on John Lutz's novel, fascinating and frightening. Comparisons to Polansky's *Repulsion* and the cult hit *Apartment Zero* are in order. Fonda and Leigh turn in remarkable performances. Their strong, unbalanced relationship rings consistently true. Leigh has made her career on chancy roles, but this is about as close to the edge as she has ever worked. Though the image is fairly soft on this DVD, the sound is excellent. The disc captures the claustrophobic atmosphere and the two characters, which have always been the film's strongest points. —MM

Movie: 🎵🎵🎵 **DVD:** 🎵🎵🎵
Columbia Tristar Home Video (Cat #51439, UPC #043396514393). Widescreen (1.85: 1) letterboxed; full frame. Dolby Digital Surround Stereo. $29.95. Keepcase. *LANG:* English; French; Spanish. *SUB:* English; French; Spanish. *CAP:* English. *FEATURES:* 35 chapter links • Theatrical trailer.
1992 (R) 107m/C Bridget Fonda, Jennifer Jason Leigh, Steven Weber, Peter Friedman, Stephen Tobolowsky, Frances Bay, Renee Estevez, Kenneth Tobey; **D:** Barbet Schroeder; **W:** Don Roos; **C:** Luciano Tovoli; **M:** Howard Shore. *AWARDS:* MTV Movie Awards '93: Best Villain (Leigh).

Singles

Seattle's music scene is the background for this lighthearted look at single twentysomethings in the '90s. Hits dead-on

thanks to Crowe's tight script and a talented cast, and speaks straight to its intended audience—the "Generation X" crowd. Real life band Pearl Jam plays alternative band Citizen Dick and sets the tone for a great soundtrack, featuring the hot Seattle sounds of Alice in Chains, Soundgarden, and Mudhoney. The video contains six extra minutes of footage after the credits, which were thankfully edited out of the final cut. Look for Horton, Stoltz (as a mime), Skerritt, and Burton in cameos. Don't throw out your laserdisc copy if you've got one. The DVD not only has a softer image, it also needs some color correcting. The sound is at best as good as the laser and in fact feels like the Surround mix is a little weaker. —JO

Movie: 🎵🎵🎵 **DVD:** 🎵🎵►
Warner Home Video, Inc. (Cat #12410, UPC #085291241027). Widescreen (1.66: 1) letterboxed; full frame. Dolby Surround. $19.98. Snapper. *LANG:* English; French. *SUB:* English; French. *CAP:* English. *FEATURES:* 33 chapter links • Theatrical trailer • Deleted scenes.
1992 (PG-13) 100m/C Matt Dillon, Bridget Fonda, Campbell Scott, Kyra Sedgwick, Sheila Kelley, Jim True, Bill Pullman, James LeGros, Ally Walker, Devon Raymond, Camillo Gallardo, Jeremy Piven; **Cameos:** Peter Horton, Eric Stoltz, Tim Burton, Tom Skerritt; **D:** Cameron Crowe; **W:** Cameron Crowe; **C:** Ueli Steiger; **M:** Paul Westerberg.

Sink or Swim

TV writer-producer Brian (a suitably hang-dog Rea) is suffering from creative burnout that has left him virtually catatonic. His manic agent Danny (Arnold) has just landed him a new job writing an anthology TV series and he's dreading it. His poker buddies (and fellow writers) offer possible scenarios, amid their back-stabbing, but Brian may have reignited his creative spark after witnessing a romantic encounter between two silhouetted figures in a hotel window. He thinks that the woman may be Georgia (Douglas), and he wants her story. This often bitter and biting comedy arrives on DVD with a sharp image and often grotesque colors. For a full-frame video premiere, it looks and sounds very good. —MM *AKA:* Hacks.

Movie: 🎵🎵🎵 **DVD:** 🎵🎵🎵
Studio Home Entertainment (Cat #7115, UPC #658149711525). Full frame. Dolby Digital Stereo. $24.95. Keepcase. *LANG:* English. *SUB:* Spanish. *FEATURES:* 18 chapter links • Trailer • Cast and crew thumbnail biographies.
1997 (R) 93m/C Stephen Rea, Illeana Douglas, Tom Arnold, John Ritter, Dave Foley, Richard Kind, Ryan O'Neal, Ricky Jay, Jason Priestley, Olivia D'Abo; **D:** Gary Rosen; **W:** Gary Rosen; **C:** Ralf Bode; **M:** Anthony Marinelli.

Sirens

Staid minister takes Australian artist Norman Lindsay to task for submitting scan-

dalous works to public exhibitions. Noted by one reviewer as "Enchanted April with nipples," comedy of manners is witty but lacks plot and looks remarkably like a centerfold layout. Ample displays of nudity as the models (including supermodel Macpherson, in her acting debut) frolic in the buff. Grant is terrific as the seemingly enlightened but easily shocked minister, but Neill's Lindsay is thinly written and too often takes a back seat to the vamping models. Fictionalized account of a true incident from the 1930s; Lindsay's home and some of his artworks were used. Check out writer-director Duigan as a pompous village minister. The DVD is very impressive with a good sharp picture and sumptuous colors. There are no grain or artifacts even if you're looking for them and those great colors never bleed. Blacks are true. The contrast and brightness levels work well. The Dolby Surround is well mixed with a lot of ambient effects channeled to the rear, adding to the excellent imaging of the front speakers. Bass response is not as boisterous as the best 5.1 mixes, but is still very good, and the highs are crisp and clean. —JO

Movie: 🎵🎵► **DVD:** 🎵🎵🎵🎵
Buena Vista Home Entertainment (Cat #16795, UPC #717951001931). Widescreen (1.85:1) letterboxed. Dolby Surround. $29.99. Keepcase. *LANG:* English. *CAP:* English. *FEATURES:* 16 chapter links.
1994 (R) 96m/C *AU GB* Hugh Grant, Tara Fitzgerald, Sam Neill, Elle Macpherson, Kate Fischer, Portia de Rossi, Pamela Rabe, Ben Mendelsohn, John Polson, Mark Gerber, Julia Stone, Ellie MacCarthy, Vincent Ball; **Cameos:** John Duigan; **D:** John Duigan; **W:** John Duigan; **C:** Geoff Burton; **M:** Rachel Portman.

Sister Act 2: Back in the Habit

Shabby, slap-dash sequel embarrasses all concerned. Though a few of the musical numbers are lively and well-produced, the rest of the film is second-rate, notable only for the presence in small supporting roles of divas-in-training Lauryn Hill and Jennifer Love Hewitt. What story there is has to do with a San Francisco Catholic high school which is so poor with students who are so undisciplined that the only thing Sisters Mary Patrick (Najimy), Mary Lazarus (Wickes), and Mary Robert (Makkena), and Mother Superior (Smith) can do is go to Las Vegas and persuade Deloris Van Cartier (Goldberg) to give up her successful career and help them. She agrees, again becoming Sister Mary Clarence, and soon discovers that Mr. Crisp (Coburn), the evil administrator, wants to close the school and turn it into a parking lot. A couple of the music numbers take advantage of the superior DVD sound. Otherwise, the English-language version is little different from VHS tape. —MM

Movie: 🎵 **DVD:** 🎵🎵
Buena Vista Home Entertainment (Cat #17598, UPC #717951003355). Wide-

screen (1.85:1) letterboxed. Dolby Digital 5.1 Surround Stereo; Dolby Digital Surround Stereo. $29.99. Keepcase. *LANG:* English; French. *CAP:* English. *FEATURES:* 18 chapter links ➠ Theatrical trailer.

1993 (PG) 107m/C Whoopi Goldberg, Kathy Najimy, James Coburn, Maggie Smith, Wendy Makkena, Barnard Hughes, Mary Wickes, Sheryl Lee Ralph, Michael Jeter, Robert Pastorelli, Thomas Gottschalk, Lauryn Hill, Brad Sullivan, Jennifer Love Hewitt; *D:* Bill Duke; *W:* James Orr, Jim Cruickshank, Judi Ann Mason; *C:* Oliver Wood; *M:* Miles Goodman. *AWARDS:* Blockbuster Entertainment Awards '95: Comedy Actress, Video (Goldberg); *NOM:* MTV Movie Awards '94: Best Comedic Performance (Goldberg).

Sister My Sister

Any description or synopsis would make this psychological thriller sound like pure exploitation. In France, 1932, Christine (Richardson)—famous for her needlework—is maid to Madame Danzard (Walters) and her daughter Isabelle (Thursfield). At Christine's request, her sister Lea (May) is also brought into the household, but Lea is not nearly as quick or handy. Before long Madame's petty perfectionism becomes more hateful and the house becomes a claustrophobic prison. From the opening moments, the viewer knows that the story—also the basis for Genet's *The Maids*—is going to end in violence, but how does it come to that? On DVD, director Meckler's creation of tension through attention to small detail is even more evident. At times, the sisters' drab black uniforms lose definition, and the entire film is deliberately dim and textured, without sharp focus. That's appropriate for a story of inner conflicts. —*MM*
Movie: 🎬🎬🎬▶ **DVD:** 🎬🎬🎬
Image Entertainment (Cat #ID5769UM DVD, UPC #014381576924). Full frame. Dolby Digital Stereo. $24.99. Snapper. *LANG:* English. *FEATURES:* 24 chapter links.
1994 (R) 89m/C *GB* Julie Walters, Joely Richardson, Jodhi May, Sophie Thursfield; *D:* Nancy Meckler; *W:* Wendy Kellelman; *C:* Ashley Ropwe; *M:* Stephen Warbeck.

Six Days, Seven Nights

Brash magazine editor Robin Monroe (Heche) is on a tropical vacation with fiance Frank (Schwimmer) when a deadline crisis forces her to ask gruff pilot Quinn (Ford) for a lift to Tahiti. A sudden storm maroons them on a remote island where the two battling opposites learn to cooperate and, of course, fall in love, while fending off modern-day pirates. Meanwhile back at the resort, Frank is falling for Quinn's babe Angelica (Obradors). Nobody needs to have gone to film school to predict exactly how this (or virtually any other Reitman movie) is going to end. Perhaps because the image is so bright throughout, the aliasing in diagonal

lines is more noticeable on this disc than it normally is. Otherwise, the DVD is sharp and the sound is very good, particularly during the storm effects. —*MM*
Movie: 🎬🎬▶ **DVD:** 🎬🎬🎬
Buena Vista Home Entertainment (Cat #15641, UPC #71795100866). Widescreen (2.35:1) letterboxed. Dolby Digital 5.1 Surround Stereo. $29.99. Keepcase. *LANG:* English; French. *CAP:* English. *FEATURES:* 23 chapter links ➠ Theatrical trailer.
1998 (PG-13) 101m/C Harrison Ford, Anne Heche, David Schwimmer, Temuera Morrison, Jacqueline Obradors, Allison Janney, Danny Trejo; *D:* Ivan Reitman; *W:* Michael Browning; *C:* Michael Chapman; *M:* Randy Edelman.

Six Ways to Sunday

Weird mob drama about a killer and his oedipal relationship with his mom is based on the 1962 novel *Portrait of a Young Man Drowning* by Charles Perry. Passive, repressed teenager Harry Odum (Reedus) lives with his domineering mother Kate (Harry), who controls his life. That is, until Harry assists his hoodlum buddy Arnie (Brody) with a job and manages to impress Arnie's boss, Mr. Varga (Adler). Since Harry turns out to have a latent talent for violence, he's soon elevated to full hitman status—although mom's still a problem. The DVD is adequate, although some darker scenes do have a tendency to lose a little definition, but it's not an intolerable problem. The Dolby 5.1 soundtrack isn't all that fantastic. It only comes alive during a few sensory-overloaded scenes. —*MJT*
Movie: 🎬🎬 **DVD:** 🎬🎬🎬
A-PIX Entertainment Inc. (Cat #APX27003, UPC #7 83722700334). Widescreen (1.85:1) anamorphic. Dolby Digital 5.1; Dolby Stereo. $24.90. Keepcase. *FEATURES:* 17 chapter links ➠ Theatrical trailer.
1999 (R) 97m/C Norman Reedus, Deborah Harry, Adrien Brody, Jerry Adler, Peter Appel, Elina Lowensohn, Isaac Hayes, Anna Thompson; *D:* Adam Bernstein; *W:* Adam Bernstein, Marc Gerald; *C:* John Inwood; *M:* Theodore Shapiro.

Sixteen Candles

More than a decade after hitting the theatres, *Sixteen Candles* is still popular—reaching near cult status among generation X-ers. Hilarious comedy of errors features the pouty Ringwald as an awkward teen who's been dreaming of her 16th birthday. But the rush of her sister's wedding causes everyone to forget, turning her birthday into her worst nightmare. Hughes may not be critically acclaimed, but his movies are so popular they nearly take on a life of their own. Ringwald and Hall are especially charming as the angst-ridden teens, encountering one trauma after another. Great soundtrack includes the title song by The Stray Cats. This is

one of the best of Hughes's teen-angst films, and it deserves a much better DVD than this. The colors are pretty good but the image is never really sharp. With Hughes's usual excellent choice of music, it would also have been great to have a stereo remix, with at least the songs getting a little better treatment, although the mono track is certainly adequate. —*JO*
Movie: 🎬🎬🎬 **DVD:** 🎬🎬▶
Image Entertainment (Cat #ID4270USDVD, UPC #014381427028). Widescreen (1.85:1) letterboxed. Dolby Digital Mono. $24.99. Snapper. *LANG:* English. *CAP:* English. *FEATURES:* 16 chapter links.
1984 (PG) 93m/C Molly Ringwald, Justin Henry, Michael Schoeffling, Haviland Morris, Gedde Watanabe, Anthony Michael Hall, Paul Dooley, Carlin Glynn, Blanche Baker, Edward Andrews, Carole Cook, Max (Casey Adams) Showalter, Liane Curtis, John Cusack, Joan Cusack, Brian Doyle-Murray, Jami Gertz, Cinnamon Idles, Zelda Rubinstein, Billie Bird; *D:* John Hughes; *W:* John Hughes; *C:* Bobby Byrne; *M:* Ira Newborn.

The Sixth Sense

"I see dead people." With those simple words, writer-director Shyamalan creates one of the best and most successful supernatural suspense films. On the surface, it's about a troubled young boy, Cole Sear (Osment), and the doctor, Malcolm Crowe (Willis), who's trying to help him. Since the story does not depend on special effects, it is just as effective, if not more so, on home video as it is on the big screen. And the extensive extras on the DVD give it a clear edge over VHS tape. The producers made the unusual (but correct) choice to keep the extras separate from the film itself. Shyamalan's comments are limited to the extras and interviews, not a complementary audio track with the film. The disc exhibits a few problems with brick patterns and the like, but those are inconsequential. Sound is excellent, properly detailed even in the quieter moments. —*MM*
Movie: 🎬🎬🎬▶ **DVD:** 🎬🎬🎬▶
Hollywood Pictures Home Video (Cat #18307). Widescreen (1.85:1) anamorphic; full frame. Dolby Digital 5.1 Surround Stereo; Dolby Digital Surround Stereo. $29.99. Keepcase. *LANG:* English; French. *SUB:* Spanish. *CAP:* English. *FEATURES:* 19 chapter links ➠ Storyboard to film comparison scene ➠ "Cast" featurette ➠ "Music and Sound Design" featurette ➠ "Reaching the Audience" featurette ➠ Cast and crew thumbnail biographies ➠ "Rules and Clues" featurette ➠ 4 deleted scenes with introductions ➠ Conversation with M. Night Shyamalan ➠ "Night's first horror film" ➠ Theatrical trailers and TV spots.
1999 (PG-13) 107m/C Bruce Willis, Haley Joel Osment, Toni Collette, Olivia Williams, Donnie Wahlberg, Glenn Fitzgerald, Trevor Morgan, Mischa Barton, Bruce Norris; *D:* M. Night Shyamalan; *W:* M. Night Shyamalan; *C:* Tak Fujimoto; *M:* James Newton Howard. *AWARDS:* Broad-

cast Film Critics Association Awards '99: Breakthrough Performance (Osment); *NOM:* Academy Awards '99: Best Director (Shyamalan), Best Film, Best Film Editing, Best Original Screenplay, Best Supporting Actor (Osment), Best Supporting Actress (Collette); British Academy Awards '99: Best Director (Shyamalan), Best Film, Best Film Editing, Best Original Screenplay; Directors Guild of America Awards '99: Best Director (Shyamalan); Golden Globe Awards '00: Best Screenplay, Best Supporting Actor (Osment); MTV Movie Awards '00: Best Film, Best Male Performance (Willis), Breakthrough Performance (Osment), Best On-Screen Duo (Bruce Willis/Haley Joel Osment); Screen Actors Guild Award '99: Best Supporting Actor (Osment); Writers Guild of America '99: Best Original Screenplay.

The '60s

Three-hour mini-series follows the familiar two-families formula to hit the high spots of the titular decade. On one side are the Herlihys of Chicago; on another are the Taylors of Mississippi. Hippies, Black Panthers, Kennedys, the Summer of Love, drugs, rock 'n' roll. The soundtrack is probably the best thing about the double-sided disc. The image is about what you'd expect for a made-for-TV production. *—MM*

Movie: 🎬🎬 **DVD:** 🎬🎬▸
Trimark Home Video (Cat #VM7084D, UPC #031398708438). Full frame. Dolby Digital Stereo. $29.99. Keepcase. *LANG:* English. *SUB:* English; French; Spanish. *CAP:* English. *FEATURES:* 30 chapter links • Interview with executive producer Linda Obst • '60s quotes quiz.
1999 (PG-13) 171m/C Jerry O'Connell, Josh Hamilton, Julia Stiles, Bill Smitrovich, Annie Corley, Leonard Roberts, Charles S. Dutton, Jordana Brewster, David Alan Grier, Jeremy Sisto, Cliff Gorman, Donovan Leitch, Carnie Wilson, Rosanna Arquette; *D:* Mark Piznarski; *W:* Jeffrey Alladin Fiskin; *C:* Michael D. O'Shea.

Sizzle Beach U.S.A.

In a separate interview, producer Eric Louzil readily admits that this movie was filmed over the course of a year on weekends with no script and no budget. Essentially, everyone was having a good time and making it up as they went along. In that regard, it's no different from hundreds of other light hearted soft-core drive-in skin flicks. But this one is also the screen debut of a very young Kevin Costner and so it has achieved video immortality. This DVD, like the original and like the tape, is by turns dim and overexposed. As usual, the Troma folk have filled the disc with extras. *—MM AKA:* Malibu Hot Summer.
Movie: 🎬🎬 **DVD:** 🎬🎬▸
Troma Team Video (Cat #DVD9880, UPC #79035798802). Full frame. $24.95. Keepcase. *LANG:* English. *FEATURES:* 9 chapter links • Interview with producer Eric Louzil • Theatrical trailers to this and

other Troma films • Several short humorous vignettes.
1974 (R) 89m/C Terry Congie, Leslie Brander, Roselyn Royce, Kevin Costner; *D:* Richard Brander.

Skin Game

Two British families feud over land rights. Not thrilling; not characteristic of working with Hitchcock. Way too much talking in excruciating, drawn-out scenes adapted from the play of the same name. The image and sound quality are exactly what you would expect from a nearly 70-year-old movie, but it is a far cry from what you would expect from a DVD. The image transfer is especially bothersome (apparently a clean print of the film no longer exists). Likewise, the sound is sub par and at times even seems out of sync. Granted, the age of the film could be the cause of these problems, but the *Gone with the Wind* disc is far superior and a mere four years younger. *—MJT*
Movie: 🎬▸ **DVD:** 🎬🎬
Delta/Laserlight (Cat #82030, UPC #018111998031). Full frame. Dolby Digital Stereo. $10.09. Keepcase. *LANG:* English. *SUB:* Spanish; Chinese; Japanese. *FEATURES:* 21 chapter links • Introduction by Tony Curtis • Theatrical trailer for *Dial M for Murder.*
1931 87m/B *GB* Phyllis Konstam, Edmund Gwenn, Frank Lawton, C.V. France, Jill Esmond, Helen Haye; *D:* Alfred Hitchcock; *W:* Alfred Hitchcock; *C:* Jack Cox.

Skinner

Flawed examination of a repellant subject—serial murder and torture—has moments that approach *Henry: Portrait of a Serial Killer,* though they're not nearly as powerful or frightening. The quirky casting—Ricki Lake as an unsuspecting landlady, Ted Raimi (brother of Sam) as the killer, and particularly Traci Lords as a woman with several secrets and a mission—helps to counter an ultra-low budget. Director Ivan Nagy (a key participant in the infamous "Heidi Fleiss, Hollywood Madame" business) creates a Midwestern Gothic atmosphere of dread and horror, particularly at the beginning. When he gets more graphic, the story becomes bloody, sickening, and predictable. On DVD, the sound has a faint, distant quality. The image is acceptable, but in the third chapter, it briefly disintegrates into pixels and rolls. *—MM*
Movie: 🎬▸ **DVD:** woof
Simitar Entertainment (Cat #7342, UPC #082551734221). Full frame. PCM Stereo. $14.98. Keepcase. *LANG:* English. *FEATURES:* 8 chapter links • Production factoids • Ricki Lake and Traci Lords filmographies.
1993 (R) 89m/C Theodore (Ted) Raimi, Traci Lords, Ricki Lake; *D:* Ivan Nagy; *W:* Paul Hart-Wilden; *C:* Greg Littlewood.

Skylark

Second volume of the *Sarah* trilogy finds the unlikely bride and groom (Close and Walken) tiring of life in Kansas and thinking of returning to Maine. Then drought and fire threaten their farm. Close's "tough Yankee" thing gets a bit tiresome and the plot, as always, contains few surprises but the charm, nostalgia, and exceptionally high production values remain undiminished. On DVD, both image and sound are equal to the first film. The title is available on the two-disc, three film set, *Sarah, Plain and Tall: The DVD Collection.* (See reviews of that and *Sarah, Plain and Tall: Winter's End.*) *—MM*
Movie: 🎬🎬 **DVD:** 🎬🎬🎬
Hallmark Home Entertainment (Cat #102 00, UPC #707729102007). Full frame. Dolby Digital Stereo. $24.98. Keepcase. *LANG:* English. *CAP:* English. *FEATURES:* 32 chapter links • Cast and crew thumbnail biographies • Production notes.
1993 (G) 98m/C Glenn Close, Christopher Walken, Lexi Randall, Christopher Bell, Tresa Hughes, Lois Smith, Lee Richardson, Elizabeth Wilson, Margaret Sophie Stein, Jon DeVries, James Rebhorn, Woody Watson; *D:* Joseph Sargent; *W:* Patricia MacLachlan; *C:* Mike Fash; *M:* David Shire.

Slam

Documentarian Levin makes his feature film debut with this part-prison, part-ghetto drama. Street-smart, low-level drug dealer Ray (Williams) is living in gang-ridden D.C. when he's busted for possession and suspicion of murdering his supplier. Jail's just as rough as the streets, since two local inside gangs each want Ray's allegiance. Ray wants to keep to himself and work on his writing—the poetry he composes about what he sees in life. He manages to get bail and then has a lot of hard decisions to make. The image and audio transfers on this disc are awesome. The picture is crisp and the sound is never muddied or unimpressive. Of particular note are the many sensory-overloaded scenes wherein Ray is seen composing his poetry. Also of worth is the exquisite audio commentary track by director Marc Levin and cowriter Bonz Malone. *—MJT*
Movie: 🎬🎬▸ **DVD:** 🎬🎬🎬▸
Trimark Home Video (Cat #6973D, UPC #031398697336). Widescreen (1.85:1) letterboxed. Dolby Digital 5.1. $24.99. Keepcase. *LANG:* English. *SUB:* Spanish; English; French. *FEATURES:* 30 chapter links • Theatrical trailer • Commentary: director Marc Levin and cowriter Bonz Malone • Goodie Mob & Esthero music video, "The World I Know."
1998 (R) 100m/C Saul Williams, Sonja Sohn, Bonz Malone; *D:* Marc Levin; *W:* Marc Levin, Saul Williams, Sonja Sohn, Richard Stratton, Bonz Malone; *C:* Mark Benjamin. *AWARDS:* Sundance Film Festival '98: Grand Jury Prize; *NOM:* Independent Spirit Awards '99: Debut Performance (Sohn), Debut Performance (Williams).

Slap Shot

A profane satire of the world of professional hockey is charming in its own bone-crunching way. Over-the-hill player-coach Newman gathers an odd-ball mixture of has-beens and young players and reluctantly initiates them, using violence on the ice to make his team win. The strip-tease on ice needs to be seen to be believed. This DVD needs to be a lot more hit-you-in-the-face intense. The colors are paler than on both the VHS and laserdisc editions, although the DVD is a little sharper. It would also have been nice to have a little gutsier sound for all the on-ice action. —JO
Movie: 🎵🎵🎵 **DVD:** 🎵🎵
Universal Studios Home Video (Cat #20328, UPC #025192032820). Widescreen (1.85:1) anamorphic. Dolby Digital Mono. Keepcase. $24.98. *LANG:* English; Spanish; French. *SUB:* Spanish. *CAP:* English. *FEATURES:* 18 chapter links • Theatrical trailer • Production notes • Cast and filmmakers bios.
1977 (R) 123m/C Paul Newman, Michael Ontkean, Jennifer Warren, Lindsay Crouse, Jerry Houser, Melinda Dillon, Strother Martin, Andrew Duncan, M. Emmet Walsh, Nancy Dowd, Swoosie Kurtz; *D:* George Roy Hill; *W:* Nancy Dowd; *C:* Victor Kemper; *M:* Elmer Bernstein.

Slaughterhouse Five

Billy Pilgrim (Sacks) becomes "unstuck" in time and darts randomly among various points of his life—the suburban husband and optometrist, World War II prisoner of the Germans at Dresden, trapped on the planet Tralfamadore with his dog and starlet Montana Wildhack (Perrine). Director George Roy Hill and writer Stephen Geller capture the spirit of Kurt Vonnegut Jr.'s famous novel, but they cannot manage to re-create his offhand conversational tone and his ability to deal lightly with the most serious subjects. Still, the film is better than its tarnished reputation. On disc, it tends to look a little grainy, particularly in the extraterrestrial moments. The war scenes are by far the strongest and the most vivid. Glenn Gould's piano score is a fine accompaniment. —MM
Movie: 🎵🎵🎵► **DVD:** 🎵🎵►
Image Entertainment (Cat #ID4227USDVD, UPC #014381422726). Widescreen (1.85:1) letterboxed. Dolby Digital Mono. $29.99. Snapper. *LANG:* English. *FEATURES:* 16 chapter links.
1972 (R) 104m/C Michael Sacks, Valerie Perrine, Ron Leibman, Eugene Roche, Perry King; *D:* George Roy Hill; *W:* Stephen Geller; *C:* Miroslav Ondricek; *M:* Glenn Gould. *AWARDS:* Cannes Film Festival '72: Special Jury Prize.

Slave Girls from Beyond Infinity

Bikini-clad space babes escape prison ship only to crash on maniac's planet in sf remake of *The Most Dangerous Game*. This version is pure exploitation with the women's wardrobe consisting entirely of slinky dresses, lingerie, and underwear. Special effects range from fair to good, and the pace is brisk. Fun spoof of '50s movies takes nothing, including itself, seriously. Star Cayton also works as Elizabeth Kaitan. The no-frills full-frame image is indistinguishable from VHS tape. —MM
Movie: 🎵🎵🎵 **DVD:** 🎵🎵►
Full Moon Pictures (Cat #8013). Full frame. $24.98. Keepcase. *LANG:* English. *FEATURES:* 30 chapter links • Cast filmographies • Trailers.
1987 (R) 80m/C Elizabeth Cayton, Cindy Beal, Brinke Stevens, Don Scribner, Carl Horner, Kirk Graves, Randolph Roehbling, Bud Graves; *D:* Ken Dixon; *W:* Ken Dixon; *C:* Thomas Callaway, Kenneth Wiatrak; *M:* Carl Dante.

Slaves to the Underground

Love affair between Seattle bandmates Shelly (Gross) and Suzy (Ryan) runs into problems when Shelly's ex-boyfriend Jimmy (Bortz) re-enters the picture and old feelings are reignited. This slacker indie prod is mediocre but abrasive liberal feminist/lesbian agitprop. It may come across as funny or provocative to true believers but it's not going to convert (or entertain) anyone else. On DVD, the image is no better than the threadbare budget would allow. It's grainy and poorly lit, and the post–grunge rock soundtrack fares little better. —MM
Movie: 🎵► **DVD:** 🎵►
Image Entertainment (Cat #0VED6859 DVD, UPC #014381685923). Widescreen (1.85:1) letterboxed. Dolby Digital Surround Stereo. $24.99. Snapper. *LANG:* English. *FEATURES:* 15 chapter links • Previews for *The Stand-Ins* and *Alive and Kicking*.
1996 (R) 90m/C Jason Bortz, Molly Gross, Marisa Ryan; *D:* Kristine Peterson; *W:* Bill Cody; *C:* Zoran Hochstatter; *M:* Mike Martt.

SLC Punk!

Stevo (Lillard) is a punk rocker rebelling against "the establishment" in mid-'80s Salt Lake City, Utah, before it's time to head off to Harvard Law. He and his friends wander aimlessly from fights with rubes and hippies to trashy clubs to various girlfriends. Nothing really funny or particularly dramatic happens in the comedy-drama which seems like an exercise for director-writer Merendino to relive his carefree college years. On the "aren't we having fun" commentary track, he and his stars essentially admit as much. The relative clarity of DVD really does the film few favors. It looks and sounds sharper than it should. This material ought to be grungy and raw, but it's cold, clean, and self-absorbed. (The 2.5 technical bone rating is for those who appreciate the music.) —MM
Movie: 🎵🎵 **DVD:** 🎵🎵►

Columbia Tristar Home Video (Cat #04015, UPC #043396040151). Widescreen (2.35:1) letterboxed. Dolby Digital 5.1 Surround Stereo; Dolby Digital Surround Stereo. $27.95. Keepcase. *LANG:* English. *SUB:* English; French; Spanish. *FEATURES:* 28 chapter links • Comic book • Commentary: director and cast • Theatrical trailers • Isolated music track.
1999 (R) 97m/C Matthew Lillard, Michael Goorjian, Annabeth Gish, Jennifer Lien, Christopher McDonald, Devon Sawa, James Duval, Til Schweiger, Kevin Breznahan, Jason Segel, Summer Phoenix, Adam Pascal, Chiara Barzini; *D:* James Merendino; *W:* James Merendino; *C:* Greg Littlewood; *M:* Melanie Miller. *AWARDS:* NOM: Independent Spirit Awards '00: Best Screenplay.

Sleepers

Tense, gritty drama is based on Lorenzo Carcaterra's book. Four teenaged friends from Hell's Kitchen get into trouble and wind up being sent to a reform school, where they're brutalized by guards. John (Eldard) and Tommy (Crudup), who grow up to be hit men, recognize their chief abuser (Bacon) years later and kill him. Their trial is prosecuted by Michael (Pitt), another of the gang, who's now the assistant D.A. It's supposed to be a true story (the book is published as non-fiction) but doubt has been cast on Carcaterra's veracity (his character is the fourth member, journalist Lorenzo, played by Patric). De Niro and Hoffman excel in relatively minor, but pivotal, roles. The DVD increases the power of the film, with improvements to both sound and picture. The image is very sharp and the colors rich and detailed. The sound has more crispness and bass than earlier releases. —JO
Movie: 🎵🎵🎵 **DVD:** 🎵🎵🎵►
Warner Home Video, Inc. (Cat #14482, UPC #085391448228). Widescreen (2.35:1) anamorphic. Dolby Digital 5.1. $24.98. Snapper. *LANG:* English; French. *SUB:* English; Spanish; French. *CAP:* English. *FEATURES:* 43 chapter links • Theatrical trailer • Production notes.
1996 (R) 150m/C Brad Pitt, Jason Patric, Ron Eldard, Billy Crudup, Kevin Bacon, Robert De Niro, Dustin Hoffman, Vittorio Gassman, Minnie Driver, Terry Kinney, Brad Renfro, Jonathan Tucker, Joe Perrino, Geoff Wigdor, Bruno Kirby, Aida Turturro, Frank Medrano; *D:* Barry Levinson; *W:* Barry Levinson; *C:* Michael Ballhaus; *M:* John Williams. *AWARDS:* NOM: Academy Awards '96: Best Original Dramatic Score.

Sleepless in Seattle

An old-fashioned, sweet-natured comic love story is marred by one directorial slip which is repeated throughout the film. The premise—two strangers who are meant for each other—is as old as storytelling, but with a neatly updated twist. Recently widowed Sam Baldwin (Hanks) is tricked by his son into pouring out his heart on a nationwide radio call-in show. He's in Seattle. A continent away, just-engaged Annie Reed (Ryan) hears him and falls in love. Writer-director Ephron brings them slowly together in a clever plot. If only she hadn't chosen to hammer each emotional highpoint with music. They're fine pop standards, but her overreliance on them is a huge flaw. She might have addressed the issue on a commentary track, but this early DVD contains few extras beyond an overabundance of chapter links. The soft image actually gains little on disc. Obviously, the same goes for the score. —MM

Movie: 𝄞𝄞𝄞➤ **DVD:** 𝄞𝄞➤

Columbia Tristar Home Video (Cat #52419, UPC #043396524194). Widescreen (1.85: 1) letterboxed. Dolby Digital Surround Stereo. $29.95. Keepcase. *LANG:* English; French; Spanish. *SUB:* Spanish; Korean. *FEATURES:* 49 chapter links.

1993 (PG) 105m/C Tom Hanks, Meg Ryan, Bill Pullman, Ross Malinger, Rosie O'Donnell, Gaby Hoffman, Victor Garber, Rita Wilson, Barbara Garrick, Carey Lowell, Rob Reiner, Sarah Trigger; *D:* Nora Ephron; *W:* Jeffrey Arch, Larry Atlas, David S. Ward, Nora Ephron; *C:* Sven Nykvist; *M:* Marc Shaiman. *AWARDS: NOM:* Academy Awards '93: Best Original Screenplay, Best Song ("A Wink and a Smile"); British Academy Awards '93: Best Original Screenplay, Best Score; Golden Globe Awards '94: Best Actor—Musical/Comedy (Hanks), Best Actress—Musical/Comedy (Ryan), Best Film—Musical/Comedy; MTV Movie Awards '94: Best Female Performance (Ryan), Breakthrough Performance (Malinger), Best On-Screen Duo (Tom Hanks/Meg Ryan), Best Song ("When I Fall in Love"); Writers Guild of America '93: Best Original Screenplay.

Sleepy Hollow

In Tim Burton's version of the Washington Irving story, Ichabod Crane (Depp) is an 18th-century New York City constable who's sent upstate to investigate a series of decapitations. Katrina Van Tassel (Ricci) is the young woman he meets there. Christopher Walken has a virtual cameo as the Headless Hessian. In many ways, the film is a tribute to English horror movies, particularly those produced by the Hammer studio. The film was made in England and on his commentary track, Burton says that he was trying to make a "fairy tale" with a "silent movie quality." For my money, he succeeded brilliantly, and DVD re-creates his remarkable visuals (created with considerable help from production designer Rick Heinrichs) without flaws. The desaturated blues and skeletal blacks are sharply detailed. Sound is very good. The disc belongs in the library of every Burton fan. —MM

Movie: 𝄞𝄞𝄞➤ **DVD:** 𝄞𝄞𝄞➤

Paramount Home Video (Cat #32962, UPC #097363296270). Widescreen anamorphic. Dolby Digital 5.1 Surround Stereo; Dolby Digital Surround Stereo. $29.99. Keepcase. *LANG:* English; French. *SUB:* English. *FEATURES:* 19 chapter links •

Commentary: Tim Burton • Cast and crew interviews • Behind-the-scenes featurette • Photo gallery • Cast thumbnail bios.

1999 (R) 105m/C Johnny Depp, Christina Ricci, Miranda Richardson, Michael Gambon, Christopher Walken, Casper Van Dien, Jeffrey Jones, Richard Griffiths, Ian McDiarmid, Michael Gough, Christopher Lee, Marc Pickering, Lisa Marie, Steven Waddington, Claire Skinner, Alun Armstrong, Mark Spalding, Jessica Oyelowo; *Cameos:* Martin Landau; *D:* Tim Burton; *W:* Andrew Kevin Walker; *C:* Emmanuel Lubezki; *M:* Danny Elfman. *AWARDS:* Academy Awards '99: Best Art Direction/Set Decoration; British Academy Awards '99: Best Art Direction/Set Decoration, Best Costume Design; *NOM:* Academy Awards '99: Best Cinematography; British Academy Awards '99: Best Visual Effects; MTV Movie Awards '00: Best Villain (Walken).

Sleuth

A mystery novelist and his wife's lover face off in ever shifting, elaborate, and diabolical plots against each other, complete with red herrings, traps, and tricks. It's a playful, cerebral mystery thriller from top director Mankiewicz. Shaffer also scripted *Frenzy* for Hitchcock, from his play. There has never been a really good video version of this film and unfortunately, that trend continues with the DVD. The disc is a little sharper (but still has very weak colors), but that sharpness is wasted because intermittent scenes are distorted by artifacts. The sound is better than the old Media Home Entertainment VHS release and about the same as the laserdisc, which also distorted louder dialogue passages. —JO

Movie: 𝄞𝄞𝄞➤ **DVD:** 𝄞𝄞

Anchor Bay (Cat #DV10409, UPC #013131040999). Widescreen (1.66:1) letterboxed. Dolby Digital Mono. $24.95. Keepcase. *LANG:* English. *FEATURES:* 9 chapter links.

1972 (PG) 138m/C Laurence Olivier, Michael Caine; *D:* Joseph L. Mankiewicz; *W:* Anthony Shaffer; *C:* Oswald Morris; *M:* John Addison. *AWARDS:* New York Film Critics Awards '72: Best Actor (Olivier); *NOM:* Academy Awards '72: Best Actor (Caine), Best Actor (Olivier), Best Director (Mankiewicz), Best Original Dramatic Score.

Sliding Doors

First time writer-director Peter Howitt delivers a fresh and clever reworking of themes explored in Frank Capra's *It's a Wonderful Life* and Polish director Krzysztof Kieslowski's *The Double Life of Veronique*. Here, Helen (Paltrow) both catches and misses her ride on a London subway (hence: the sliding doors from which the title is derived), setting up parallel storylines. In one she catches her live-in boyfriend, Gerry (John Lynch), having an affair with Jeanne Tripplehorn. Helen moves out, sets up her own public relations business, and falls in love with

James (John Hannah). In the alternative universe, she arrives home after Tripplehorn has departed, stays with Gerry, has an unfulfilled life, and never meets James. At first it is confusing as to which story we are seeing, but as the film progresses Paltrow is able to define and deliver two separate personas of the same individual. The lack of a theatrical trailer, behind-the-scenes footage, and commentary from filmmaker Howitt spoil an otherwise excellent DVD presentation from pristine source material. —RT

Movie: 𝄞𝄞𝄞➤ **DVD:** 𝄞𝄞𝄞➤

Paramount Home Video (Cat #335767, UPC #097363357674). Widescreen. Dolby Digital Surround Stereo; Dolby Digital 5.1 Surround Stereo. $29.99. Keepcase. *LANG:* English. *SUB:* English; Spanish. *CAP:* English. *FEATURES:* 19 chapter links.

1997 (R) 98m/C Gwyneth Paltrow, John Lynch, John Hannah, Jeanne Tripplehorn, Virginia McKenna, Zara Turner, Douglas McFerran, Paul Brightwell, Nina Young; *D:* Peter Howitt; *W:* Peter Howitt; *C:* Remi Adefarasin; *M:* David Hirschfelder. *AWARDS: NOM:* British Academy Awards '98: Best Film.

Sling Blade

Mildly retarded killer Karl Childers (Thornton, making his feature directorial debut) is released from a mental hospital, where he was placed 25 years earlier, after killing his mother and her lover. Returning to his hometown, he befriends a boy (Black) with problems of his own. His mother is living with a mean, bullying drunkard (Yoakam, in a brilliant performance) who has no use for anyone, least of all mom's openly gay coworker (Ritter). Thornton's excellent script moves at the slow pace of its hero, providing the superb cast plenty of opportunity to explore the rich characterization and dialogue. Filmed in Thornton's home state of Arkansas. The DVD looks pretty good with deep accurate colors and true blacks. The biggest problem is that sharpness seems to vary. Overall, the stereo sound is a little flat but doesn't hinder delivery of the dialogue. —JO

Movie: 𝄞𝄞𝄞➤ **DVD:** 𝄞𝄞𝄞

Buena Vista Home Entertainment (Cat #13676, UPC #717951000118). Widescreen (1.85:1) letterboxed. Stereo. $29.99. Keepcase. *LANG:* English; French. *SUB:* Spanish. *CAP:* English. *FEATURES:* 25 chapter links.

1996 (R) 134m/C Billy Bob Thornton, Dwight Yoakam, John Ritter, Lucas Black, Natalie Canerday, James Hampton, Robert Duvall, J.T. Walsh, Rick Dial, Brent Briscoe, Christy Ward, Col. Bruce Hampton, Vic Chesnutt, Mickey Jones, Jim Jarmusch, Ian Moore; *D:* Billy Bob Thornton; *W:* Billy Bob Thornton; *C:* Barry Markowitz; *M:* Daniel Lanois. *AWARDS:* Academy Awards '96: Best Adapted Screenplay; Independent Spirit Awards '97: Best First Feature; Writers Guild of America '96: Best Adapted Screenplay; *NOM:* Academy Awards '96: Best Actor (Thornton); Screen Actors

Guild Award '96: Best Actor (Thornton), Cast.

The Slipper and the Rose

The Cinderella fairy tale told as a musical from a decidedly royalty-first/royalty-will-out point of view. The Prince (Richard Chamberlain—*Shogun*, *The Towering Inferno*) is duty-bound to follow through with a marriage of state despite falling in love with local maiden Cinderella (stage actress Gemma Craven). The traditional climatic moment of the story—where Cinderella fills the glass slipper and all live happily-ever-after—occurs about two-thirds of the way through the proceedings and leaves the viewer with the feeling that this fairy tale will never end. Indeed, there's something of a secret wish that the bucolic peasants will come to their senses and demand democratic elections and in the process throw these blue bloods out. A nicely rendered DVD presentation, complete with audio commentary by director Bryan Forbes, and a decent, if sometimes "wash-out," video transfer (seems very "pastel" throughout, which may have been what the cinematographer was going for in the first place), along with some nifty extras, including an interview with the Sherman brothers, Oscar winners for *Mary Poppins*. —RT

Movie: 🐾🐾 **DVD:** 🐾🐾🐾
Image Entertainment (Cat #ID6824CQ, UPC #014381682427). Widescreen. Dolby Digital 5.1 Surround. AC3 - 2 Channel. $24.99. Snapper. *LANG:* English. *FEATURES:* 30 chapter links • Commentary: director • "Making of" featurette • Interview with Sherman brothers (music composers).
1976 (G) 127m/C GB Richard Chamberlain, Gemma Craven, Annette Crosbie, Edith Evans, Christopher Gable, Michael Hordern, Margaret Lockwood, Kenneth More, Julian Orchard, Lally Bowers, Sherrie Hewson, Rosalind Ayres, John Turner, Keith Skinner, Polly Williams, Norman Bird, Roy Barraclough, Peter Graves; *Cameos:* Bryan Forbes; *D:* Bryan Forbes; *W:* Bryan Forbes, Robert B. Sherman, Richard M. Sherman; *C:* Tony Imi; *M:* Robert B. Sherman, Richard M. Sherman.

Slums of Beverly Hills

Every few months, Murray Abromowitz (Arkin) packs up daughter Vivian (Lyonne) and sons Ricky (Marienthal) and Ben (Krumholtz) to sneak out of their current dumpy apartment (without paying the rent) and move on to the next one, always within Beverly Hills so the kids can stay in a good school. When cousin Rita (Tomei) escapes from a rehab center, Murray takes her in. While Murray's main concern is the kids' education, Vivian is more obsessed with the size of her breasts and exploring her adolescent sexuality. Semi-autobiographical first film for Jenkins, who wrote the script while at the Sundance Institute, has lots of character and charm,

and just enough bite. Lyonne has no trouble being the center of attention and injects comedy into the many awkward social situations that a teenage girl must endure. The picture on this DVD is so sharp and the color shadings so detailed that the body double inserted for Tomei on the highway is even more obvious (not that it wasn't in the film itself). The soundtrack is one of the less-elaborately mixed, and seems to have practically no Surround at all. Still, there's nothing objectionable to it and this is nonetheless a pretty good DVD. —JO

Movie: 🐾🐾🐾 **DVD:** 🐾🐾🐾
20th Century Fox (Cat #4110379, UPC #086162103797). Widescreen (1.85:1) letterboxed. Dolby Digital 5.1; Stereo. $34.98. Keepcase. *LANG:* English; French. *SUB:* English; Spanish. *CAP:* English. *FEATURES:* 29 chapter links • Theatrical trailer.
1998 (R) 91m/C Natasha Lyonne, Alan Arkin, Marisa Tomei, Kevin Corrigan, David Krumholtz, Carl Reiner, Eli Marienthal, Jessica Walter, Rita Moreno; *D:* Tamara Jenkins; *W:* Tamara Jenkins; *C:* Tom Richmond; *M:* Rolfe Kent. *AWARDS: NOM:* Independent Spirit Awards '99: Best First Feature, First Screenplay.

Small Soldiers

Why do children get all the cool stuff? Toys designed to interact with kids are crossed with military machines due to a corporate merger, and the super-intelligent war toys hold a small Ohio town under siege. The leader of gung-ho commando action figures (voiced by Jones) mounts an assault on the gentle Gorgonites, led by the noble Archer (Langella), who enlist the help of teens Alan (Smith) and Christy (Dunst). Grownups will get a kick out of the vocal performances and send-up of both war movies and gadget-filled kiddie flicks. The skillful combination of computer animation, Stan Winston's animatronic puppets, and live action actually plays better on small screen. On DVD, both the overall image and sound quality are above average. A blandly unfunny blooper reel is included in the extensive extras, along with much good stuff. —JE

Movie: 🐾🐾🐾 **DVD:** 🐾🐾🐾
DreamWorks Home Entertainment (Cat #0-7832-3119-9, UPC #6706841612). Widescreen (2.35:1) anamorphic. Dolby Digital Surround Stereo; Dolby 5.1 Surround Stereo. $34.98. Snapper. *LANG:* English; Spanish; French. *SUB:* English; Spanish; French. *FEATURES:* 16 chapter links • Behind-the-scenes "making of" feature (11 min.) • 8 deleted scenes, including 2 deleted effects • Bloopers (5 min.) • Interactive game demo • Cast and filmmaker bios • Production notes • Theatrical trailers.
1998 (PG-13) 110m/C Gregory Edward Smith, Kirsten Dunst, Phil Hartman, Ann Magnuson, Jay Mohr, Denis Leary, Kevin Dunn, Wendy Schaal, Dick Miller, David Cross, Robert Picardo; *D:* Joe Dante; *W:* Gavin Scott, Adam Rifkin, Ted Elliott, Terry

Rossio; *C:* Jamie Anderson; *M:* Jerry Goldsmith; *V:* Tommy Lee Jones, Frank Langella, Ernest Borgnine, Jim Brown, Bruce Dern, George Kennedy, Clint Walker, Christopher Guest, Michael McKean, Harry Shearer, Sarah Michelle Gellar, Christina Ricci.

Smart Money

As soon as you open the package, you come face to face with a personal thank you note from the writer-director, with a little background on how he came to pull this shoestring action drama together. He was a stockbroker until the '89 crash led him to follow his dreams to Hollywood. After five years of trying to get others interested in this script, he decided to follow the example of *Mean Streets*. The behind-the-scenes featurette consists of Hennech expounding at a bit more length on the whole adventure. The movie, shot almost completely in L.A., has the feel of a TV cops-and-robbers production. The script shows ambition and some finesse, though, by hooking a familiar line of goons and gamblers into a novel concept of using dirty money to finance purchasing a seat on the NYSE! Jimmy (East) must choose between his bookie (Dobbins) and a girl named Rachel (Angel) and, as fate would have it, the life paths they represent. Not bad for something shot in two and a half weeks, including a real-time chase sequence that followed the sun along Manhattan's skyline. The Kodak 7287 film shows grain even with the best lighting, unfortunately, and the synth score competes openly with the dialogue at key dramatic high points. —JK

Movie: 🐾🐾 **DVD:** 🐾🐾
Image Entertainment (Cat #ID5961AHDVD, UPC #014381596120). Full frame. Dolby Stereo. $24.99. Keepcase. *LANG:* English. *CAP:* English. *FEATURES:* 26 chapter links • Interactive menus • Cast info • Production notes • Interview with director • Liner notes by director.
1997 90m/C Lira Angel, Santio East, Bobby Kaman, Sam Dobbins; *D:* Alex Hennech; *W:* Alex Hennech; *C:* John Tarver; *M:* Claude "Coffee" Cave.

Smashing Time

Abysmal British comedy was never widely released on this side of the Atlantic and it's easy to see why. The film follows two small-town girls—Brenda (Tushingham), who's mousy and bony, and Yvonne (Redgrave), who's loud and pushy—who come to London at the height of the swinging '60s. Unfortunately, they are two of the most unattractive comic heroines ever to hit the screen, and apparently that's a choice the filmmakers made deliberately. Moreover, their accents are difficult to understand and their voices could blister an elephant's hide. Much of the film was made on location, and so the DVD image is fairly rough. Sound is far too good. —MM

Movie: woof **DVD:** 🐾🐾

Anchor Bay (Cat #DV10946, UPC #013131094695). Widescreen (1.85:1) letterboxed. Dolby Digital Mono. $24.98. Keepcase. *LANG:* English. *FEATURES:* 13 chapter links.
1967 96m/C *GB* Rita Tushingham, Lynn Redgrave, Michael York, Anna Quayle, Irene Handl, Ian Carmichael; *D:* Desmond Davis; *W:* George Melly; *C:* Manny Wynn; *M:* John Addison.

Smoke Signals
Geeky, orphaned Thomas (Adams) lives on the Coeur d'Alene Indian Reservation, where he's looked after by stoic Victor (Beach), whose long-gone father Arnold (Farmer) saved Thomas from the fire that killed his parents. When they learn of Arnold's death in Phoenix, Thomas says he'll pay travel expenses if he can accompany Victor. In this sometimes comic, sometimes serious road movie, two foster brothers come to an understanding about each other and their common past. Based on stories from Alexie's book *The Lone Ranger and Tonto Fistfight in Heaven*. DVD has scant extras, but the widescreen transfer looks fine, with good contrast and brightness levels, particularly in the handsome outdoor scenes. —*JE*
Movie: 🎵🎵▶ **DVD:** 🎵🎵🎵
Miramax Pictures Home Video (Cat #17444, UPC #0788816152). Widescreen (1.85:1) letterboxed. Dolby Digital 5.1 Surround Stereo. $29.99. Keepcase. *LANG:* English. *CAP:* English. *FEATURES:* 22 chapter links ▪ Theatrical trailer.
1998 (PG-13) 88m/C Adam Beach, Evan Adams, Irene Bedard, Gary Farmer, Tantoo Cardinal, Michelle St. John, Robert Miano, Molly Cheek, Elaine Miles, Michael Greyeyes, Chief Leonard George, John Trudell, Tom Skerritt, Cody Lightning, Cynthia Geary, Simon Baker; *D:* Chris Eyre; *W:* Sherman Alexie; *C:* Brian Capener; *M:* B.C. Smith. *AWARDS:* Independent Spirit Awards '99: Debut Performance (Adams); Sundance Film Festival '98: Audience Award, Filmmakers Trophy; *NOM:* Independent Spirit Awards '99: Best Supporting Actor (Farmer), First Screenplay.

Smokey and the Bandit
One of the first and still the best of Reynolds's car movies, this one makes an astonishingly sharp transition to DVD. The focus is sharp and the road scenes have more clarity than many of that era. Reynolds and Reed are truckers running a load of Coors beer (which was then illegal west of Texas) to Atlanta. Jackie Gleason hams it up wonderfully as Sheriff Buford T. Justice. The monaural sound may not be too impressive on the more elaborate home theatre systems, but the whole film is still fresh, fun, and mindless. —*MM*
Movie: 🎵🎵▶ **DVD:** 🎵🎵🎵
Universal Studios Home Video (Cat #20411, UPC #025192041129). Widescreen (1.85:1) letterboxed. Dolby Digital Mono. $24.98. Keepcase. *LANG:* English;

French; Spanish. *SUB:* Spanish. *CAP:* English. *FEATURES:* 16 chapter links ▪ Production notes ▪ Cast and crew thumbnail biographies ▪ Theatrical trailer ▪ Universal web links.
1977 (PG) 96m/C Burt Reynolds, Sally Field, Jackie Gleason, Jerry Reed, Mike Henry, Paul Williams, Pat McCormick; *D:* Hal Needham; *W:* Charles Shyer; *C:* Bobby Byrne; *M:* Bill Justis, Jerry Reed. *AWARDS: NOM:* Academy Awards '77: Best Film Editing.

Snake Eyes
David Koepp's script involves a hurricane bearing down on Atlantic City, the assassination of the Secretary of Defense at a heavyweight championship fight, a high-rolling local cop (Cage), his friend a Navy security expert (Sinise), and assorted cameras. DePalma attempts to wrestle it all into submission with his typical (and overrated) show-off direction. Cage's hyperactive overacting matches his hideous clothes. Their sweaty exertions are really more than any DVD could handle. The garish colors are hard to watch closely and during DePalma's numerous fast whipping pans, the image becomes an unfocused blur. At least we are spared a commentary track. —*MM*
Movie: 🎵 **DVD:** 🎵🎵
Paramount Home Video (Cat #335417, UPC #097363354178). Widescreen letterboxed. Dolby Digital 5.1 Surround Stereo, Dolby Surround Stereo. $29.99. Keepcase. *LANG:* English; French. *CAP:* English. *FEATURES:* 12 chapter links ▪ Theatrical trailer.
1998 (R) 99m/C Nicolas Cage, Gary Sinise, Carla Gugino, John Heard, Stan Shaw, Kevin Dunn, Michael Rispoli, Joel Fabiani, Luis Guzman, Tamara Tunie; *D:* Brian DePalma; *W:* David Koepp; *C:* Stephen Burum; *M:* Ryuichi Sakamoto.

Sneakers
Competent thriller about five computer hackers with questionable pasts and an equally questionable government job. Of course, nothing is as it seems. Rather slow-going considering the talents and suspense involved, but includes enough turns to keep a viewer's interest. The DVD has a sharp-enough image with good, solid, true colors, but the harsh sound got on my nerves. Low-end response is weak; the highs seem to clip, and are at least consistently distorted. —*JO*
Movie: 🎵🎵▶ **DVD:** 🎵▶
Universal Studios Home Video (Cat #20178, UPC #025192017827). Widescreen (1.85:1) anamorphic. Dolby Surround. $24.98. Keepcase. *LANG:* English; Spanish; French. *SUB:* Spanish. *CAP:* English. *FEATURES:* 16 chapter links ▪ Theatrical trailer ▪ Production notes ▪ Cast and filmmakers bios.
1992 (PG-13) 125m/C Robert Redford, Sidney Poitier, River Phoenix, Dan Aykroyd, Ben Kingsley, David Strathairn, Mary McDonnell, Timothy Busfield, George

Hearn, Eddie Jones, James Earl Jones, Stephen Tobolowsky; *D:* Phil Alden Robinson; *W:* Lawrence Lasker, Walter F. Parkes, Phil Alden Robinson; *C:* John Lindley; *M:* James Horner, Branford Marsalis.

Snow White: A Tale of Terror
This one definitely puts the grim back in the Grimm Brothers version of the fairy tale. In medieval Austria, beautiful Claudia (Weaver) marries widowed Frederick who, unfortunately, has an even-more beautiful daughter, Lilli (Keena), who's put out by this rival for her father's affections. The stepmom/stepdaughter battle increases when Claudia's own long-awaited baby is still-born and the wrathful and unbalanced Claudia orders Lilli's death. Only she's rescued by seven outcasts (only one of whom is a dwarf) living in the forest. The witchy Claudia does still like to talk to her mirror, however. The DVD's image is fine during brighter scenes but softens when the lights go down, and they often do. Colors are saturated and bleed in those dimmer scenes. The soundtrack handles the dialogue clearly but the mix does nothing to enhance the feel of the film and seems more mono than stereo. —*JO* *AKA:* Snow White in the Black Forest; Grimm Brothers' Snow White.
Movie: 🎵🎵▶ **DVD:** 🎵▶
Polygram (Cat #0469072, UPC #044004690720). Widescreen (1.85:1) letterboxed. Stereo. $29.95. Snapper. *LANG:* English; French. *CAP:* English. *FEATURES:* 22 chapter links ▪ International theatrical trailer ▪ Filmographies ▪ Dual-layered RSDL.
1997 (R) 101m/C Sigourney Weaver, Sam Neill, Monica Keena, Gil Bellows, Taryn Davis; *D:* Michael Cohn; *W:* Thomas Szollosi, Deborah Serra; *C:* Mike Southon; *M:* John Ottman.

The Snows of Kilimanjaro
Called by Hemingway "The Snows of Zanuck," referring to the great producer, this film is actually an artful pastiche of several Hemingway short stories and novels. The title story acts as a framing device, in which the life of a successful writer (Peck) is seen through his fevered flashbacks as he and his rich wife (Hayward), while on safari, await a doctor to save his gangrenous leg.
Movie: 🎵🎵🎵 **DVD:** NYR
Madacy Entertainment (Cat #99027). Full frame. $9.99. Keepcase. *FEATURES:* Cast and crew thumbnail bios. Title is also available from United American Video (cat. #40105) for $9.99.
1952 117m/C Gregory Peck, Susan Hayward, Ava Gardner, Hildegarde Neff, Leo G. Carroll, Torin Thatcher, Ava Norring, Helene Stanley, Marcel Dalio, Vincente Gomez, Richard Allen, Leonard Carey; *D:* Henry King; *W:* Casey Robinson; *C:* Leon Shamroy; *M:* Bernard Herrmann. *AWARDS: NOM:* Academy Awards '52: Best Art

Direction/Set Decoration (Color), Best Color Cinematography.

So I Married an Axe Murderer

Romantic comedy revolves around a wed-lock-shy coffee house poet (Myers) who finally finds the perfect woman (Plummer). When it comes to love, Charlie Mackenzie has had his share of bad luck, and on top of that, he has a commitment problem. When Charlie meets Harriet Michaels everything changes; Harriet's not like the others. She's smart, sexy, and crazy about Charlie. This time Charlie is determined to overcome the fears that sabotaged his past relationships. This time, he's ready for some commitment. Sure, Harriet may have her shortcomings—but so what? After all those other women, what's the worst she could be? An axe murderer? For the most part, the picture on this DVD is very clear, but dark at times. The daylight scenes are fine, but the night shots are awash in shadow. Compression is well-done without noticeable artifacts or noise. The framing of the letterboxed picture is accurate and no bending is evident. The 2-channel soundtrack is lively, especially during the musical montages (of which there are many, featuring what we can assume are outtakes of Myers's playing around on the set). —ML

Movie: 🎬🎬▶ **DVD:** 🎬🎬🎬▶
Columbia Tristar Home Video (Cat #52429, UPC #043396524293). Widescreen (1.85:1) anamorphic; full frame. Dolby Surround. $27.95. Keepcase. *LANG:* English; Spanish; Portuguese. *SUB:* English; Spanish; Portuguese; Chinese; Korean; Thai. *CAP:* English. *FEATURES:* 28 chapter links • Trailer.
1993 (PG-13) 92m/C Mike Myers, Nancy Travis, Anthony LaPaglia, Amanda Plummer, Brenda Fricker, Matt Doherty; *Cameos:* Charles Grodin, Phil Hartman, Steven Wright, Alan Arkin, Michael Richards; *D:* Thomas Schlamme; *W:* Robbie Fox, Mike Myers; *M:* Bruce Broughton.

The Soft Skin

Author and lecturer Pierre Lachenay (Desailly) has an affair with Nicole (Dorleac), a flight attendant. After it ends, his wife confronts him with terrible results. Ignore the cliches of the plot; director Truffaut has the material firmly in control with superb performances and some of his finest black-and-white photography. Visually, the disc suffers from the usual breakup of moving diagonal lines and a flashing cobblestone pattern. Sound is fine, and the new subtitles by Laurent Bouzereau are exceptionally clear. —MM *AKA:* Le Peau Douce; Silken Skin.

Movie: 🎬🎬🎬 **DVD:** 🎬🎬▶
WinStar Home Entertainment (Cat #FLV5119, UPC #720917511924). Widescreen (1.66:1) letterboxed. $29.98. Keepcase. *LANG:* French. *SUB:* English. *FEATURES:* 6 chapter links • Production

credits • Filmographies and awards • Theatrical trailers.
1964 120m/B *FR* Jean Desailly, Nelly Benedetti, Francoise Dorleac, Daniel Ceccaldi; *D:* Francois Truffaut; *W:* Francois Truffaut, Jean-Louis Richard; *C:* Raoul Coutard; *M:* Georges Delerue.

Solar Crisis

Juvenile sf begins with the hyperbolic proclamation, "the cremation of the planet is at hand" as huge solar flares erupt. A space team is sent to divert them but could a saboteur be aboard? Director Richard Sarafian elected to use the Alan Smithee moniker for this stinker, but what did anyone reasonably expect from such a premise? The effects are dated and the DVD is no better than VHS tape in either image or sound. —MM

Movie: 🎬 **DVD:** 🎬
Trimark Home Video (Cat #7054D). Full frame. Dolby Digital Surround Stereo. $14.99. Keepcase. *LANG:* English. *FEATURES:* 11 chapter links.
1992 (PG-13) 111m/C Tim Matheson, Charlton Heston, Peter Boyle, Annabel Schofield, Jack Palance, Corin "Corky" Nemec; *D:* Richard Sarafian, Alan Smithee; *W:* Joe Gannon, Tedi Sarafian; *C:* Russell Carpenter; *M:* Maurice Jarre.

Solaris

With this film, the USSR tried to eclipse *2001: A Space Odyssey* in terms of cerebral sci-fi. Some critics thought they succeeded. You may disagree now that the lumbering effort is available on disc. Adapted from a Stanislaw Lem novel, it depicts a dilapidated space lab orbiting the planet Solaris, whose ocean, a vast fluid "brain," materializes the stir-crazy cosmonauts' obsessions—usually morose ex-girlfriends. Talk, talk, talk, minimal special effects. *AKA:* Solyaris.

Movie: 🎬🎬 **DVD:** NYR
Image Entertainment (Cat #45481). $29.99. Jewel case. *LANG:* Russian. *SUB:* English.
1972 167m/C *RU* Donatas Banionis, Natalya Bondarchuk, Juri Jarvet, Vladislav Dvorzhetsky, Nikolai Grinko, Anatoli Solonitzin, Sos Sarkisyan; *D:* Andrei Tarkovsky; *W:* Andrei Tarkovsky; *C:* Vadim Yusov; *M:* Eduard Artemyev. *AWARDS:* Cannes Film Festival '72: Grand Jury Prize.

Soldier

This one steals trite scenes from other post-apocalyptic sci-fi shoot-'em-ups just to prove that 47-year-old Kurt Russell had been working out. A genetically engineered soldier is discarded as obsolete on a garbage dump planet inhabited by a freedom-loving survivalist (Pertwee) and his band of human flotsam. When a force led by next-generation soldier Jason Scott Lee invades the planet, Russell helps save the skanky-looking group of squatters. Robbed of his Snake Plissken

smirk, Russell delivers a hollow character who is hard to like. The garbage planet set recycles props used in *Demolition Man, Executive Decision,* and *Event Horizon.* With all that said, this film is really entertaining—go figure. This film has a ton of dark scenes, which cause no problems for this excellent DVD. The picture is sharp and grain-free, and even when the motion is fast, or things are exploding, there are no artifacts. The color is also terrific—vibrant, with good detail and no bleed. Blacks are never a problem and the contrast is excellent. Brightness remains consistent in the light, the dark, or even in a futuristic haze. The 5.1 sound is superb, placing the action all around you and energizing the whole thing with as good a low end as you're likely to hear. —JO

Movie: 🎬🎬▶ **DVD:** 🎬🎬🎬🎬
Warner Home Video, Inc. (Cat #16958, UPC #085391695820). Widescreen (2.35:1) anamorphic; full frame. Dolby Digital 5.1. $19.98. Snapper. *LANG:* English; French. *SUB:* English; French. *CAP:* English. *FEATURES:* 31 chapter links • Theatrical trailer • Production notes.
1998 (R) 99m/C Kurt Russell, Jason Scott Lee, Gary Busey, Michael Chiklis, Sean Pertwee, Jason Isaacs, Connie Nielsen, Brenda Wehle, Mark Bringleson, K.K. Dodds; *D:* Paul Anderson; *W:* David Peoples; *C:* David Tattersall; *M:* Joel McNeely.

A Soldier's Tale

In Normandy, July 1944, Sgt. Saul Scorby (Byrne) leads a squad of British infantrymen against the Germans. He finds a farmhouse where beautiful young Isabelle (Basler) is living by herself. French resistance fighters accuse her of collaboration and demand that she come with them for punishment. For the basest of reasons, Saul protects her. Writer-director Larry Parr makes some good points about fear, innocence, and the realities of occupation and collaboration. The pace could be quicker though the French countryside is captured so lovingly that's not a serious problem. Byrne turns in his usual intense performance and Marianne Basler looks like a young Brigitte Bardot. Sound and the dark, grainy, full-frame image are identical to VHS tape for all practical purposes. —MM

Movie: 🎬🎬▶ **DVD:** 🎬🎬
Image Entertainment (Cat #OVED9033 DVD, UPC #014381903324). Full frame. Dolby Digital Mono. $24.99. Snapper. *LANG:* English. *FEATURES:* 17 chapter links.
1991 (R) 96m/C Gabriel Byrne, Marianne Basler, Judge Reinhold, Paul Wyett; *D:* Larry Parr; *W:* Larry Parr; *C:* Alun Bollinger; *M:* John Charles.

Solo

Solo (Van Peebles) is a robot soldier created by a secret Army research project. When he is field-tested against left-wing Central American guerrillas, he begins to

develop a conscience, refusing to harm non-combatants. When the stereotyped right-wing brass (led by Sadler) decide to eliminate him, Solo is caught in the middle. This combination of high-tech weaponry and effects with humanistic politics has never been a hit on the big screen or on the page, despite the high quality of Robert Mason's fine novels (*Weapon, Solo*). In most scenes, the DVD looks as good as the theatrical release, though some computer-generated effects are jarringly different from the "real" footage. The visual effects depicting the robot's point of view are better and Van Peebles is excellent throughout. —*MM*
Movie: 🦴🦴🦴 **DVD:** 🦴🦴🦴
Columbia Tristar Home Video (Cat #82589, UPC #043396825895). Widescreen (2.35:1) letterboxed; full frame. Dolby Digital 5.1 Surround Stereo; Dolby Digital Surround Stereo. $19.95. Keepcase. *LANG:* English. *CAP:* English. *FEATURES:* 28 chapter links • Production notes • "Making of" featurette • Cast and crew thumbnail biographies • Theatrical trailers.
1996 (PG-13) 106m/C Mario Van Peebles, William Sadler, Seidy Lopez, Barry Corbin, Adrien Brody, Abraham Verduzo, Jaime Gomez, Damian Bechir, Joaquin Garrido; *D:* Norberto Barba; *W:* David Corley; *C:* Chris Walling; *M:* Christopher Franke.

Somebody Has to Shoot the Picture

Photographer Scheider is hired by a convicted man to take a picture of his execution. Hours before the event, Scheider uncovers evidence that leads him to believe his subject is innocent. He then embarks on a race against time. Adapted for cable by Doug Magee from his book *Slow Coming Dark*.
Movie: 🦴🦴🦴 **DVD:** NYR
Goodtimes Entertainment (Cat #81038). Full frame. Dolby Digital Stereo. $19.98. Snapper. *LANG:* English. *SUB:* French; Spanish. *CAP:* English.
1990 (R) 104m/C Roy Scheider, Bonnie Bedelia, Robert Carradine, Andre Braugher, Arliss Howard; *D:* Frank Pierson; *W:* Doug Magee; *C:* Bojan Bazelli; *M:* James Newton Howard.

Someone to Watch Over Me

After witnessing the murder of a close friend, wealthy Manhattan socialite Claire Gregory (Rogers) must be protected from the killer. Det. Mike Keegan (Berenger) gets the job and is tempted away from his wife and son in Queens. In all of his films, director Scott is a superb visual stylist, and even if this one doesn't equal *Bladerunner*, it makes for a lovely DVD. Few films have depicted the world of ultra-wealth with such silky texture, captured beautifully on disc. Sound is very good. —*MM*
Movie: 🦴🦴🦴 **DVD:** 🦴🦴🦴
Columbia Tristar Home Video (Cat #08779, UPC #043396087798). Widescreen (1.85:1) letterboxed; full frame. Dolby Digi-

tal Surround Stereo. $25.95. Keepcase. *LANG:* English; Spanish. *SUB:* English; Spanish; Portuguese; Chinese; Korean; Thai. *FEATURES:* 28 chapter links • Theatrical trailer • Cast and crew thumbnail biographies.
1987 (R) 106m/C Tom Berenger, Mimi Rogers, Lorraine Bracco, Jerry Orbach, Andreas Katsulas, Tony DiBenedetto, James Moriarty, John Rubinstein; *D:* Ridley Scott; *W:* Howard Franklin; *C:* Steven Poster; *M:* Michael Kamen.

Something About Sex

Acerbic bachelor Art (Alexander under an abominable wig) broaches the subject of infidelity at a dinner party with three couples. The other six publicly denounce flings while privately flinging at the first temptation. In the opening sequence, Rifkin's camera restlessly and self-consciously circles the dinner table. As the action progresses, the characters do more talking than flinging. The frills-free DVD is no better than the pedestrian story. The image is grainy and most of the underlit sets have an odd greenish cast. Sound is unremarkable. —*MM AKA:* Denial.
Movie: 🦴🦴 **DVD:** 🦴🦴
Image Entertainment (Cat #ID5894UM DVD, UPC #014381589429). Full frame. Dolby Digital Mono. $24.99. Snapper. *LANG:* English. *FEATURES:* 12 chapter links.
1998 (R) 92m/C Patrick Dempsey, Jonathan Silverman, Christine Taylor, Amy Yasbeck, Jason Alexander, Leah Lail, Ryan Alosio; *Cameos:* Adam Rifkin; *D:* Adam Rifkin; *W:* Adam Rifkin; *C:* Francis Kenny.

Something Wicked This Way Comes

"First of all, it was October...." That's the way both Ray Bradbury's famous novel and his adaptation begin. It's a lyrical, unashamedly nostalgic horror film that remains strictly faithful to the magical tone of the fiction. Will Halloway (Peterson) and Jim Nightshade (Carson) are 12 years old and about to learn "the fearful needs of the human heart" when Dark's Pandemonium Carnival arrives in their small town. It's an evil, seductive entertainment where wishes are granted at a terrible price. Dark (Pryce) and the mute Dust Witch (Grier) know those wishes and are ready to accommodate them. Will's father (Robards), the town librarian, is the boys' guide. Director Clayton creates some truly frightening moments—particularly for those bothered by spiders—but he's more successful in evoking Bradbury's unique vision of youth and magic and things that cannot be explained. The DVD contains both the full-frame and widescreen versions on one side. The image is as sharp or sharper than I remember it from the initial theatrical release, certainly superior to tape. Pryce's fine performance is the basis for the series of luxury car ads he has appeared in, and it powers the

film. A commentary track by Bradbury would have been welcome. —*MM*
Movie: 🦴🦴🦴🦴 **DVD:** 🦴🦴🦴▸
Anchor Bay (Cat #DV10891, UPC #013131089196). Full frame; widescreen (1.66:1) letterboxed. Dolby Digital Surround. $24.98. Keepcase. *LANG:* English. *FEATURES:* 17 chapter links • Theatrical trailer.
1983 (PG) 94m/C Jason Robards Jr., Jonathan Pryce, Diane Ladd, Pam Grier, Richard Davalos, James Stacy, Royal Dano, Vidal Peterson, Shawn Carson; *D:* Jack Clayton; *W:* Ray Bradbury; *C:* Stephen Burum; *M:* James Horner.

Sometimes They Come Back

Jim Norman (Matheson) and his wife Sally (Adams) move back to the small town his parents left 27 years before. Jim finds that the horrors of his past haven't diminished and the ghosts are still there. Writers Lawrence Konner and Mark Rosenthal and director Tom McLoughlin effectively flesh out Stephen King's short story while retaining his weathered small-town atmosphere and his understanding of the enduring power of childhood bullies. Matheson's very good in a straight dramatic role. On video, the made-for-TV feature contains extra footage of violence and grotesque special effects. Inexplicably, this slender vehicle has become the basis for a moderately successful series.
Movie: 🦴🦴🦴 **DVD:** NYR
Trimark Home Video (Cat #7145). Full frame. $14.99. Keepcase.
1991 (R) 97m/C Tim Matheson, Brooke Adams, Robert Rusler, William Sanderson; *D:* Tom McLoughlin; *W:* Mark Rosenthal, Lawrence Conner; *C:* Bryan England; *M:* Terry Plumeri.

Sometimes They Come Back... Again

The plot to this sequel-remake is nothing special. It cannibalizes several other Stephen King works and tosses in a ton of witchcraft hokum. That said, the story of resurrected Satanic teen bullies who terrorize John Porter (Gross) and his daughter Michelle (Swank) is not without style and polish. A few of the effects are really striking. Alexis Arquette is very good as the lead bad guy, and so are Gross and Swank. On DVD, the title is available as a double feature with *Sometimes They Come Back*.
Movie: 🦴🦴▸ **DVD:** NYR
Trimark Home Video (Cat #6786). Dolby Digital Stereo. $34.98. Keepcase. *LANG:* English. *SUB:* French; Spanish. *FEATURES:* Cast and crew thumbnail bios • Trailer.
1996 (R) 98m/C Michael Gross, Hilary Swank, Alexis Arquette, Jennifer Elise Cox; *D:* Adam Grossman; *W:* Adam Grossman; *C:* Christopher Baffa; *M:* Peter Manning Robinson.

Sometimes They Come Back... For More

A nifty little haunted house mystery/thriller, set in an Antarctic research station, degenerates (about midway) into a silly tale about the opening of the gates of hell. Based (loosely...exceptionally loosely) on the characters developed in Stephen King's "Sometimes They Come Back," the film opens with military police Clayton Rohner (*The Relic, Bat 21*) and Chase Masterson being dropped into a remote Antarctic base where they find two survivors (Ford and Perlich) of some rather creepy goings-on. Rohner, as it turns out, is not what he seems—his partner is killed off—and a battle breaks out between him and one of the research scientists—his half-brother (Chapa) as it turns out—over the fate of the human race. Oh, please! DVD presentation rises above the material to deliver a nice film transfer and three different sets of captions—English, Spanish, and French. At least if the proceedings begin to take their toll on the viewer all is not lost, a bit of foreign language insight can be gained along the way. —RT
Movie: 🐾🐾 *DVD:* 🐾🐾➤
Trimark Home Video (Cat #VM 7184D, UPC #031398718437). Widescreen. AC3 - 2 Channel. $24.99. Keepcase. *LANG:* English. *SUB:* English; French; Spanish. *CAP:* English; French; Spanish. *FEATURES:* 24 chapter links • Trailer.
1999 (R) 89m/C Clayton Rohner, Chase Masterson, Faith Ford, Max Perlich, Damian Chapa; *D:* Daniel Berk.

Somewhere in Time

Playwright Reeve (in his first post–Clark Kent role) falls in love with a beautiful woman (Seymour) in an old portrait. Through self-hypnosis, he goes back in time to 1912 to discover what their relationship might have been. The film—a drippy rip-off of the brilliant novel *Time and Again* by Jack Finney—made a star of the Grand Hotel, located on Mackinac Island in Michigan, where it was shot. Reeve is adequate, but Seymour is underused. Far from a masterpiece but thoroughly enjoyable. The film's gorgeous settings and excellent cinematography are wasted on this DVD, where the picture is grainy and not at all sharp. Colors seem a little muted but are O.K., while blacks are not quite true. John Barry's beautiful reworking of Rachmaninov's theme is not treated right here either, as the mono soundtrack is lifeless. —JO
Movie: 🐾🐾➤ *DVD:* 🐾➤
Universal Studios Home Video (Cat #20294, UPC #02519202924). Widescreen (1.85:1) letterboxed. Dolby Digital 2.0 Mono. $24.98. Keepcase. *LANG:* English; Spanish; French. *SUB:* Spanish. *CAP:* English. *FEATURES:* 16 chapter links • Theatrical trailer • Cast and filmmaker bios • Production notes.

1980 (PG) 103m/C Christopher Reeve, Jane Seymour, Christopher Plummer, Teresa Wright; *D:* Jeannot Szwarc; *W:* Richard Matheson; *C:* Isidore Mankofsky; *M:* John Barry. *AWARDS: NOM:* Academy Awards '80: Best Costume Design.

Sommersby

Confederate veteran Jack Sommersby (Gere) returns to his western Virginia farm to find that his wife Laurel (Foster) is cool toward him. Has the war changed him that much, or is he a stranger impersonating her husband? Does she care? After all, he is cute, once she gets that nasty beard shaved off, and he's sensitive and racially enlightened. What's not to like? The loose remake of *The Return of Martin Guerre* doesn't play to the strengths of DVD. The muted colors of the Appalachian mountains are accurate, but director Amiel uses cloudy gray light throughout, and his softly lamp-lit nighttime interiors are exceedingly dim. Some woven patterns and tight lines flash, too. The stars are fine and they are the main selling points. —MM
Movie: 🐾🐾➤ *DVD:* 🐾🐾
Warner Home Video, Inc. (Cat #12649, UPC #085391264927). Full frame; widescreen letterboxed. Dolby Digital Surround Stereo. $19.98. Snapper. *LANG:* English; French. *SUB:* English; French. *CAP:* English. *FEATURES:* 30 chapter links.
1993 (PG-13) 114m/C Richard Gere, Jodie Foster, Bill Pullman, James Earl Jones, William Windom, Brett Kelley, Richard Hamilton, Maury Chaykin, Lanny Flaherty, Frankie Faison, Wendell Wellman, Clarice Taylor, R. Lee Ermey; *D:* Jon Amiel; *W:* Nicholas Meyer, Sarah Kernochan; *C:* Philippe Rousselot; *M:* Danny Elfman.

Son-in-Law

First, is it really a good thing to enhance a Pauly Shore movie? In this one, he plays Crawl, a professional L.A. college student who finds himself spending Thanksgiving in South Dakota. Result: standard city-boy-on-the-farm comedy involving chickens, combines, cow-pies, and the like. Some of those jokes work, but more of them fall flat, and all are familiar. Oddly for a Disney film, much of the humor has to do with sex; giggling, adolescent sex. Six writers get credit for the story and screenplay. Doubtless, all those fingerprints account for the film's patchwork quality. On DVD, the image is excellent, but again, is that worthwhile or necessary? —MM
Movie: 🐾 *DVD:* 🐾🐾🐾
Buena Vista Home Entertainment (Cat #17508, UPC #717951003263). Widescreen (1.85:1) letterboxed. Dolby Digital Stereo. $29.99. Keepcase. *LANG:* English; French. *CAP:* English. *FEATURES:* 19 chapter links • Theatrical trailer.
1993 (PG-13) 95m/C Pauly Shore, Carla Gugino, Lane Smith, Cindy Pickett, Mason Adams, Patrick Renna, Dennis Burkley, Dan Gauthier, Tiffani-Amber Thiessen; *D:* Steve Rash; *W:* Adam Small, Shawn

Schepps, Fax Bahr; *C:* Peter Deming; *M:* Richard Gibbs. *AWARDS: NOM:* MTV Movie Awards '94: Best Comedic Performance (Shore).

Sophie's Choice

William Styron's modern tragedy focuses on Sophie Zawistowska (Streep), a beautiful Polish Auschwitz survivor settled in Brooklyn after World War II. She has intense relationships with a schizophrenic genius (Kline) and an aspiring Southern writer (MacNicol). It's one of Hollywood's most successful interpretations of a serious novel with a commanding performance by the versatile Streep and adequate support from Kline and MacNicol, whose "Southern" accent still grates in voice-over. Both image and sound are very good, though one red roof dissolves into heavy grain and pixels. —MM
Movie: 🐾🐾🐾➤ *DVD:* 🐾🐾🐾
Artisan Entertainment (Cat #60487). Widescreen letterboxed. Dolby Digital Stereo. $14.98. Snapper. *LANG:* English. *SUB:* Spanish. *FEATURES:* Documentary, "Death Dreams of Mourning" • Theatrical trailer • Commentary: Pakula • Cast and crew thumbnail bios • Production notes • 36 chapter links (feature); 12 links (documentary).
1982 (R) 157m/C Meryl Streep, Kevin Kline, Peter MacNicol, Rita Karin, Stephen D. Newman, Josh Mostel; *D:* Alan J. Pakula; *W:* Alan J. Pakula; *C:* Nestor Almendros; *M:* Marvin Hamlisch. *AWARDS:* Academy Awards '82: Best Actress (Streep); Golden Globe Awards '83: Best Actress—Drama (Streep); Los Angeles Film Critics Association Awards '82: Best Actress (Streep); National Board of Review Awards '82: Best Actress (Streep); New York Film Critics Awards '82: Best Actress (Streep), Best Cinematography; National Society of Film Critics Awards '82: Best Actress (Streep); *NOM:* Academy Awards '82: Best Adapted Screenplay, Best Cinematography, Best Costume Design, Best Original Score.

Sorcerer

To put out an oil fire, four men on the run in South America agree to try to buy their freedom by driving trucks loaded with nitroglycerin over dangerous terrain—with many natural and man-made obstacles to get in their way. Remake of *The Wages of Fear* is nowhere as good as the classic original, but has exciting moments. Puzzlingly retitled, which may have contributed to the boxoffice failure and the near-demise of Friedkin's directing career. The main things going for this lame remake is Friedkin's stylized direction and the amazingly atmospheric score by Tangerine Dream. Unfortunately, neither is handled very well by this DVD. The image is very grainy and is consistently distorted by artifacts that hang in the air almost as long as a Peckinpah slow-motion blood burst. As for the sound, it is both listless and

dull. What a shame. —JO **AKA:** Wages of Fear.
Movie: 🎬🎬▶ **DVD:** 🎬▶
Universal Studios Home Video (Cat #20420, UPC #025192042027). Full frame. Dolby Surround. $24.98. Keepcase. *LANG:* English. *SUB:* Spanish; French. *CAP:* English. *FEATURES:* 18 chapter links • Theatrical trailer • Cast and filmmaker bios • Production notes • Film highlights.
1977 (PG) 121m/C Roy Scheider, Bruno Cremer, Francesco Rabal, Soudad Amidou, Ramon Bieri; *D:* William Friedkin; *W:* Walon Green; *C:* Dick Bush, John Stephens; *M:* Tangerine Dream. *AWARDS: NOM:* Academy Awards '77: Best Sound.

Sorceress

Wildly complicated, fast-paced, and cheesy soft-core horror flick is notable for a veteran cast and some not-so-special effects. It's about a couple of witches (Strain and Blair) competing over the career of a young executive (Poindexter). Producer Ray and director Wynorski grind out these video premieres like sausages. They know how to do a lot on a limited budget and don't try to do things they shouldn't. They don't exactly stretch the limits of the genre, either, and the mid-level production values show through in every frame. The heavy grain in the night scenes is even more apparent on DVD than it is on tape, so the disc is only a marginal improvement. —MM
Movie: 🎬🎬▶ **DVD:** 🎬🎬▶
Image Entertainment (Cat #ID5622FMDVD, UPC #014381652224). Full frame. Dolby Digital Stereo. $24.99. Snapper. *LANG:* English. *FEATURES:* 12 chapter links.
1994 (R) 93m/C Julie Strain, Larry Poindexter, Linda Blair, Edward Albert; *D:* Jim Wynorski; *W:* Mark Thomas McGee; *C:* Gary Graver; *M:* Chuck Cirino, Darryl Way.

Sore Losers

Sci-fi action flick.
Movie: NYR **DVD:** NYR
ETD (Cat #9964). Full frame. $24.99.
1997 89m/C Jack Oblivian, Kerine Elkins, Mike Maker, D'lana Tunnell, Hugh Brooks, Ghetty Chasun; *D:* John Michael McCarthy; *W:* John Michael McCarthy; *C:* Darin Ipema.

Sorority Babes in the Slimeball Bowl-A-Rama

An ancient gremlin-like creature is released into a bowling alley. Great-looking sorority babes have to battle it out at the mall with the help of a wacky crew of nerds. Horror spoof shows plenty of skin.
AKA: The Imp.
Movie: 🎬🎬 **DVD:** NYR
Full Moon Pictures (Cat #8021). Full frame. $24.95. Keepcase. *FEATURES:* Cast and crew thumbnail bios • Trailer.
1987 (R) 80m/C Linnea Quigley, Brinke Stevens, Andras Jones, John Wildman, Robin Rochelle, Michelle (McClellan)

Bauer, George "Buck" Flower; *D:* David DeCoteau; *W:* Sergei Hasenecz; *C:* Scott Ressler, Stephen Blake; *M:* Guy Moon; *V:* Michael Sonye.

Soul Food

Despite all the whining about Hollywood's dearth of family-centric films, this warm and positive portrayal of African-American home-life offers not one, two, or three but four strong roles for women, plus a handful of men who don't all "bust a cap" and get killed. It took hotshot music producer Kenneth "Babyface" Edmonds to put together the deal and bring on a raft of acts for the musical soundtrack. The expansive Irma P. Hall is no-nonsense matriarch Big Mama Joe, who keeps the kids coming back for her Sunday dinners until diabetes takes its toll. Her enforced retirement sets her three daughters into competition, leaving their men looking for someplace to hide! It's up to grandchild Sweet Pea (really Ahmad, played by newcomer Brandon Hammond, who also narrates) to patch things up. In the midst of life, death, marriage and divorce, unemployment, stupid moves and business launchings, laughs and bickering, come good eats. Neat cultural details (pinning money on the bride, cooking class, salon gossip) allow a vacation from gangsta flicks' hard-core rap. Can something like this be too soapy or sentimental with such a realistic, thoughtful ending? Relax, hon', a little cornpone and sweetener never hurt no one! Burnished color photography makes Chicago look like one big gingerbread house; only the brightest reds buzz a little if your set is out of whack. The grand, music-laced soundtrack is well-served. A lone quibble is the fairly useless cast list, one undated page of text. —JK
Movie: 🎬🎬🎬 **DVD:** 🎬🎬🎬🎬
20th Century Fox (Cat #4110434, UPC #086162104343). Widescreen (1.85:1) letterboxed. Dolby Surround 5.1. $29.99. Keepcase. *LANG:* English; French. *SUB:* English; Spanish. *CAP:* English. *FEATURES:* 31 chapter links • Cast list • Interactive menus • Promo featurette • Baby Face soundtrack music video "I Care for You" • Star bios and filmographies • Original theatrical trailer.
1997 (R) 114m/C Vanessa L(ynne) Williams, Vivica A. Fox, Nia Long, Michael Beach, Mekhi Phifer, Irma P. Hall, Jeffrey D. Sams, Gina Ravera, Brandon Hammond, Carl Wright, Mel Jackson, Morgan Michelle Smith, John M. Watson Sr.; *D:* George Tillman Jr.; *W:* George Tillman Jr.; *C:* Paul Elliott; *M:* Wendy Melvoin, Lisa Coleman. *AWARDS: NOM:* MTV Movie Awards '98: Best Female Performance (Fox), Best Song ("A Song for Mama").

Soultaker

Low-budget, overachieving regional production has become a solid cult hit. Made in Alabama and written by star Vivian Schilling, it's the story of four young people who are killed in a car wreck. Their

spirits are thrown clear and the title character (Estevez), a spooky guy with way too much mascara and a long black raincoat, is dispatched to take them to the other side, or wherever. Details and tricky special effects aren't too important here. The action has the senseless energy that makes B-movies so much fun. Example: the kids are running for all they're worth from the guy in black. They're burning up their Reeboks while he just keeps walking with an implacable, determined pace. And, of course, he catches them. Before it's over, the whole thing has become a sort of live-action Pepe LePew cartoon. Alas, the DVD magnifies the film's shortcomings. The image virtually disintegrates in fast panning and tracking shots and the night scenes, which take up most of the second half, are exceptionally grainy. Even so, for fans of low-budget horror, this one's a must-see. —MM
Movie: 🎬🎬🎬 **DVD:** 🎬🎬
Image Entertainment (Cat #ID5704PZDVD, UPC #014381570427). Full frame. Dolby Digital Stereo. $24.99. Snapper. *LANG:* English. *FEATURES:* 12 chapter links.
1990 (R) 94m/C Joe Estevez, Vivian Schilling, Gregg Thomsen, David Shark, Jean Reiner, Chuck Williams, Robert Z'Dar; *D:* Michael Rissi; *W:* Vivian Schilling; *C:* James Rosenthal; *M:* John McCallum.

South Pacific

A young American Navy nurse and a Frenchman fall in love during WWII. Expensive production included much location shooting in Hawaii. Based on Rodgers and Hammerstein's musical (not as good as the play, but still pretty darn good), which in turn was based on James Michener's *Tales of the South Pacific*, this is the film that made our favorite Martian, Ray Walston, a star. It's also another Fox musical hit DVD with stunning colors and immensely improved sound. Almost every color in the spectrum is used in this film, and the disc presents them all vibrantly with excellent contrasts and shading. The film print itself appears much cleaner than earlier video releases. The 5.1 sound gives more power to the music, making it more dynamic and with clearer highs and lows. A pleasure to watch. —JO
Movie: 🎬🎬🎬▶ **DVD:** 🎬🎬🎬🎬
20th Century Fox (Cat #4110864, UPC #086162108648). Widescreen (2.20:1) letterboxed. Dolby Digital Surround 5.1; Dolby Surround. $24.98. Keepcase. *LANG:* English. *SUB:* English; Spanish. *CAP:* English. *FEATURES:* 43 chapter links • Movietone news trailer.
1958 167m/C Mitzi Gaynor, Rossano Brazzi, Ray Walston, France Nuyen, John Kerr, Juanita Hall, Tom Laughlin; *D:* Joshua Logan; *W:* Paul Osborn; *C:* Leon Shamroy; *M:* Richard Rodgers, Oscar Hammerstein; *V:* Giorgio Tozzi. *AWARDS:* Academy Awards '58: Best Sound; *NOM:* Academy Awards '58: Best Color Cinematography, Scoring of a Musical.

The Southerner

A man used to working for others is given some land by an uncle and decides to pack up his family and try farming for himself. They find hardships as they struggle to support themselves in this superb naturalistic celebration of a family fight to survive amid the elements. Novelist William Faulkner had an uncredited hand in the adaptation of George Sessions Perry's story "Hold Autumn in Your Hand." Faulkner thought Renoir the best contemporary director and later said this film gave him more pleasure than any of his Hollywood work, though given Faulkner's overall opinion of the movie business, that's faint praise.
Movie: ♫♫♫♫ *DVD:* NYR
VCI Home Video (Cat #8211). Full frame. $19.99. Keepcase. *FEATURES:* Cast and crew thumbnail bios • Edgar Kennedy's comic short "Baby Daze."
1945 91m/B Zachary Scott, Betty Field, Beulah Bondi, Norman Lloyd, Bunny Sunshine, Jay Gilpin, Estelle Taylor, Blanche Yurka, Percy Kilbride, J. Carrol Naish; *D:* Jean Renoir; *W:* Jean Renoir, Hugo Butler, William Faulkner; *C:* Lucien N. Andriot; *M:* Werner Janssen. *AWARDS:* National Board of Review Awards '45: Best Director (Renoir); Venice Film Festival '46: Best Film; *NOM:* Academy Awards '45: Best Director (Renoir), Best Sound, Best Original Dramatic Score.

Southie

Danny Quinn (Wahlberg) comes back to his South Boston neighborhood to face a host of unsolved problems. His sister (McGowan) is living the wild life; the local boss (Tierney) is leaning on him; and what's to be done about his mother (Meara)? This shot-on-location production varies between autobiographical authenticity and the expected "mean streets" plot contrivances. On their commentary track, director Shea, writer-star Cummings, Wahlberg, and Meara go into considerable detail about the local roots of the film and the demands of low-budget moviemaking. The full-frame DVD image is exceptionally sharp for something that was made so quickly and cheaply. Sound is very good. All in all, this festival hit is an overachiever. —MM
Movie: ♫♫♫ *DVD:* ♫♫♫
Studio Home Entertainment (Cat #7275, UPC #658149727526). Full frame. Dolby Digital 5.1 Surround Stereo; Dolby Digital Surround Stereo. $24.95. Keepcase. *LANG:* English. *FEATURES:* 20 chapter links • Commentary: Shea, Cummings, Wahlberg, Meara • Trailer • Music spot • Cast and crew thumbnail biography.
1998 (R) 95m/C Donnie Wahlberg, Rose McGowan, Lawrence Tierney, James (Jimmy) Cummings, Anne Meara, Amanda Peet, John Shea; *D:* John Shea; *W:* James (Jimmy) Cummings, John Shea, Dave McLaughlin; *C:* Allen Baker; *M:* Wayne Sharp.

Space Jam

Big-budget, mindlessly enjoyable romp combines live action with animation—and basketball great Jordan with the Looney Tunes cast. Together, they are forced to play ball against evil intergalactic invaders who are out to capture Bugs Bunny and the rest of the cartoon all-stars. It's all fairly silly, but the kids will enjoy it. When DVD was a fledgling medium, *Space Jam* was an early release and a show-off disc. It still looks and sounds great, with a Surround sound effect almost every minute, but the pan-and-scan transfer will turn off the serious collector. Still, the colors are vibrant and the picture sharp as a tack.
—MB
Movie: ♫♫► *DVD:* ♫♫♫
Warner Home Video, Inc. (Cat #16400, UPC #085391640028). Full frame. Dolby Digital 5.1. $24.98. Snapper. *LANG:* English; French. *SUB:* English; French; Spanish. *CAP:* English. *FEATURES:* 38 chapter links • Production notes • Theatrical trailer.
1996 (PG) 87m/C Michael Jordan, Bill Murray, Wayne Knight, Theresa Randle; *D:* Joe Pytka; *C:* Michael Chapman; *M:* James Newton Howard; *V:* Danny DeVito. *AWARDS: NOM:* MTV Movie Awards '96: Best Song ("I Believe I Can Fly").

Space Truckers

Spoof about space hauler-truckers in the 21st century may be the finest sci-fi film made in Ireland to date. John Canyon (Hooper) accepts a dangerous assignment when he agrees to transport sealed containers to Earth—no questions asked. He, girlfriend Cindy (Mazar), and newbie driver Mike (Dorff) have their ship boarded by pirates led by Capt. Macaundo (Dance), who's part machine and wants to conquer the planet. Canyon and company must perform assorted heroics. Lots of campy bad taste, but, alas, not nearly as much bad taste as director Gordon's classic *Re-Animator*. On his commentary track, Gordon sticks close to the business at hand, talking about the differences in production in Ireland, his cast members, etc. No real surprises. The sharp clarity of the DVD image accentuates the tackiness of the props, sets, and special effects, which tend to flash and waver more than one would expect. Sound is adequate. —MM
Movie: ♫♫ *DVD:* ♫♫
Studio Home Entertainment (Cat #7205, UPC #658149720527). Widescreen letterboxed. Stereo. $24.95. Keepcase. *LANG:* English. *SUB:* Spanish. *FEATURES:* 18 chapter links • Storyboards • Commentary: Stuart Gordon • Theatrical trailer • Cast and crew thumbnail biographies • Trivia game.
1997 (PG-13) 97m/C *IR* Dennis Hopper, Stephen Dorff, Charles Dance, Debi Mazar, George Wendt, Shane Rimmer, Vernon Wells, Barbara Crampton; *D:* Stuart Gordon; *W:* Ted Mann; *C:* Mac Ahlberg; *M:* Colin Towns.

The Spanish Prisoner

Mamet goes Hitchcock in a thriller involving an elaborate con game. Naive inventor Joe Ross (Scott) develops an intricate formula for something called "The Process" and finds himself the victim of industrial espionage. Maybe. In a bit of stunt casting that works, Martin plays a sinister wealthy businessman who befriends and advises Joe about his corporate employers. The film's main flaw is Rebecca Pidgeon's approach to her role as the overly helpful and lippy secretary. Her line delivery is completely wrong in every important scene, though the blame for that should be placed on Mamet's shoulders. Even so, there are enough twists to keep you intrigued. Though the film is not particularly challenging, it makes an acceptable transition to DVD with rich colors and a nicely sharp image in the Caribbean scenes. When it moves back to New York, the image is more pedestrian. Sound is good. —MM
Movie: ♫♫♫► *DVD:* ♫♫♫►
Columbia Tristar Home Video (Cat #02608, UPC #043396026087). Widescreen (1.85:1) letterboxed; full frame. Dolby Digital Surround Stereo; Mono. $29.95. Keepcase. *LANG:* English; French; Spanish. *SUB:* English; French; Spanish. *FEATURES:* 28 chapter links • Theatrical trailer.
1997 (PG) 112m/C Campbell Scott, Steve Martin, Rebecca Pidgeon, Ben Gazzara, Ricky Jay, Felicity Huffman, Ed O'Neill; *D:* David Mamet; *W:* David Mamet; *C:* Gabriel Beristain; *M:* Carter Burwell. *AWARDS: NOM:* Independent Spirit Awards '99: Best Screenplay.

Sparrows

In this top-notch suspense melodrama, set in a cruel, Dickensian orphanage, a waif (a superb Pickford) protects a group of young orphans from kidnappers. There's a truly hair-raising chase scene through an alligator-infested swamp, plus engaging performances from the kids, and some innovative visual effects during the heroine's dream sequence. The black-and-white transfer is good, with sharp edges and subtle shadows, and the movie's expressionist scenic design is beautifully captured. Only the organ score sounds dated. —JE
Movie: ♫♫♫► *DVD:* ♫♫♫►
Image Entertainment (Cat #ID5958MLSD-VD, UPC #014381595823). Full frame. Dolby Digital Mono. $29.99. Snapper. *LANG:* Silent. *SUB:* English intertitles. *FEATURES:* 20 chapter links • Pickford's 1910 short "Wilful Peggy" • Pickford's 1912 short, "Mender of Nets."
1926 109m/B Mary Pickford, Gustav von Seyffertitz, Charlotte Mineau, Roy Stewart, Mary Louise Miller, "Spec" O'Donnell, Mary Frances McLean, Camilla Johnson, Seesel Ann Johnson; *D:* William Beaudine; *W:* C. Gardner Sullivan, Winifred Dunn; *C:* Charles Rosher, Karl Struss, Hal Mohr; *M:* William Perry.

Spartacus

In their second teaming (after *Paths of Glory*) director Kubrick and producer-star Douglas turn in one of Hollywood's better big-budget sword-and-sandal epics. The film's political ideas are honed to a fine edge, and it delivers the goods in the big battle scenes where the proverbial "cast of thousands" takes over. The more personal moments are just as good. Writer Dalton Trumbo gives the supporting players some fine moments. (Peter Ustinov, who won a Best Supporting Actor Oscar, greets the incoming freshmen at gladiator school by saying, "May fortune smile on most of you.") Douglas is excellent in the lead but the first act belongs to Woody Strode. The DVD is made from the Robert Harris and James Katz restoration, which returns the homosexual undercurrents in a bath scene with Olivier and Curtis. For a film of its age, this one looks very good. Graininess and less-than-perfect focus in a few shots can be traced to the original, not the transfer to disc. Some intricate tile patterns vibrate. As sharp as the image is, though, the panoramic battle scenes lose considerable power on anything smaller than a full-sized theatre screen. —*MM*

Movie: 🦴🦴🦴 **DVD:** 🦴🦴🦴
Universal Studios Home Video (Cat #20181, UPC #025192018121). Widescreen (2.35:1) letterboxed. Dolby Digital 5.1 Surround Stereo; Dolby Surround Stereo. $26.98. Keepcase. *LANG:* English; French. *SUB:* Spanish. *CAP:* English. *FEATURES:* 16 chapter links • Production notes • Cast and crew thumbnail biographies • Theatrical trailer • Universal web links.
1960 (PG-13) 196m/C Kirk Douglas, Laurence Olivier, Jean Simmons, Tony Curtis, Charles Laughton, Herbert Lom, Nina Foch, Woody Strode, Peter Ustinov, John Gavin, John Ireland, Charles McGraw, Joanna Barnes; **D:** Stanley Kubrick; **W:** Dalton Trumbo; **C:** Russell Metty; **M:** Alex North. *AWARDS:* Academy Awards '60: Best Art Direction/Set Decoration (Color), Best Color Cinematography, Best Costume Design (Color), Best Supporting Actor (Ustinov); Golden Globe Awards '61: Best Film—Drama; *NOM:* Academy Awards '60: Best Film Editing, Best Original Dramatic Score.

Spawn (SE)

Government agent Al Simmons (White) returns to Earth, six years after being murdered, in the form of Spawn, a hell-born creature with supernatural powers. He wants to avenge his death and also save his loved ones from the evil Violator (Leguizamo). With green eyes and a friendship with Satan, Spawn's more of a lethal weapon and way more sinister-looking than the villain. An unrecognizable Leguizamo and sleazy Sheen team up as adequate adversaries. Extravagant special effects, and a complex, dark story put a unique spin on the overexposed superhero premise, adapted from the best-selling comic book. (See also review for *Todd McFarlane's Spawn.*) This DVD features commentary that is both informative and entertaining, particularly from Todd McFarlane, the creator of the comic. The constant darkness of the film is no problem for the DVD and the image remains sharply detailed and rich, with cartoon-like color under all lighting conditions. The sound is given a boisterous 5.1 mix here, with as good bass as any DVD that's come through. —*JO*

Movie: 🦴🦴🦴 **DVD:** 🦴🦴🦴
New Line Home Video (Cat #N4610, UPC #794043461026). Widescreen (1.85:1) anamorphic. Dolby Digital 5.1; Stereo. $24.98. Snapper. *LANG:* English (Dolby Digital 5.1); French (stereo). *SUB:* English; Spanish; French. *CAP:* English. *FEATURES:* 24 chapter links • Theatrical trailer • Commentary: McFarlane, Dippe, Goldman, Williams • "Making of" featurette • Sketch gallery • 5 scene-to-storyboard comparisons • Cast and filmmaker bios • Todd McFarlane sketches • Filter & the Crystal Method music video • Preview of *Spawn: The Animated Series.*
1997 (PG-13) 97m/C Michael Jai White, John Leguizamo, Martin Sheen, Theresa Randle, D.B. Sweeney, Nicol Williamson, Melinda Clarke, Miko Hughes; **D:** Mark Dippe; **W:** Alan B. McElroy; **C:** Guillermo Navarro; **M:** Graeme Revell.

The Specialist

Buffed bods do not a movie make—at least not in this mechanical actioner featuring Stone as the revenge-minded May Munro. Seems May's parents were killed by Cuban gangsters, led by father/son thugs Joe (Steiger) and Tomas Leon (Roberts), and she decides ex-CIA bomb specialist Ray Quick (Stallone) is just the man she needs to settle the score. But Quick has his own reasons for accepting—his ex-partner is nutball Ned Trent (Woods), who's now working for the Leons. Things blow up a lot, the two leads show off their toned flesh (but not much acting), and Woods gets to steal the movie with his amusing scenery chewing. Both color and sharpness are improved over the other video formats. The 5.1 sound is loud and crunchy and just what you want when watching a rather lame action flick. —*JO*

Movie: 🦴 **DVD:** 🦴🦴🦴
Warner Home Video, Inc. (Cat #13574, UPC #085391357421). Widescreen (1.85:1) letterboxed. Dolby Digital 5.1; Dolby Surround. $24.98. Snapper. *LANG:* English; Spanish; French. *SUB:* English; Spanish; French. *CAP:* English. *FEATURES:* 34 chapter links • Theatrical trailer • Production notes.
1994 (R) 110m/C Sylvester Stallone, Sharon Stone, James Woods, Eric Roberts, Rod Steiger; **D:** Luis Llosa; **W:** Alexandra Seros; **C:** Jeffrey L. Kimball; **M:** John Barry. *AWARDS:* Golden Raspberry Awards '94: Worst Actress (Stone); *NOM:* MTV Movie Awards '95: Most Desirable Female (Stone); Golden Raspberry Awards '94: Worst Picture.

Specimen

Twenty-four years ago in the little town of Spruce Lake, aliens impregnated Carol Hillary and she gave birth to a son, Mark (Gosselaar). When they return to collect him, he does not understand his superhuman powers. So-so sf with *Terminator* ambitions. The DVD maintains a mostly clear image for both interiors and exteriors and captures Canadian autumn effectively. —*MM*

Movie: 🦴🦴 **DVD:** 🦴🦴
Simitar Entertainment (Cat #7460, UPC #082551746026). Full frame. Dolby Digital Stereo; Dolby Digital 5.1 Surround. $14.98. Keepcase. *LANG:* English. *FEATURES:* 8 chapter links • Production factoids • Mark Paul Gosselaar filmography.
1997 (R) 85m/C CA Mark Paul Gosselaar, Doug O'Keefe, Michelle Johnson, Andrew Jackson; **D:** John Bradshaw; **W:** Damian Lee, Sheldon Inkol; **C:** Gerald R. Goozie; **M:** Terence Gowan.

Speed

Excellent dude Reeves has grown up (and bulked up) as Los Angeles SWAT cop Jack Traven, pitted against bomb expert Howard Payne (Hopper, more maniacal than usual), who's after major ransom money. First it's a rigged elevator in a very tall building. Then it's a rigged bus—if it slows, it will blow; bad enough any day, but a nightmare in L.A. traffic—and that's still not the end. Terrific directorial debut for cinematographer De Bont, who certainly knows how to keep the adrenaline pumping. Fine support work by Daniels, Bullock, and Morton and enough wit in Yost's script to keep you chuckling. Great nonstop actioner from the *Die Hard* school. *Speed*'s action is even more pulse-pounding on this DVD than it was in the theatre. Many times that can be attributed to a beefed up soundtrack, but in this case the picture quality plays as big a part and actually seems sharper, with better contrast. The sound is super too; each slam-bang effect seems to get progressively louder and jarring while the Surround tracks answer in kind. One hell of a bass track, too. —*JO*

Movie: 🦴🦴🦴 **DVD:** 🦴🦴🦴🦴
20th Century Fox (Cat #4109164, UPC #086162091643). Widescreen (1.85:1) letterboxed. Dolby Digital 5.1. $29.98. Keepcase. *LANG:* English (DD 5.1); French; Spanish. *SUB:* English. *CAP:* English. *FEATURES:* 25 chapter links • Theatrical trailer.
1994 (R) 115m/C Keanu Reeves, Dennis Hopper, Sandra Bullock, Joe Morton, Jeff Daniels, Alan Ruck, Glenn Plummer, Richard Lineback, Beth Grant, Hawthorne James, David Kriegel, Carlos Carrasco, Natsuko Ohama, Daniel Villarreal; **D:** Jan De Bont; **W:** Graham Yost; **C:** Andrzej Bartkowiak; **M:** Mark Mancina. *AWARDS:* Academy Awards '94: Best Sound; MTV Movie Awards '95: Best Female Performance (Bullock), Most Desirable Female (Bullock), Best On-Screen Duo (Keanu Reeves/Sandra Bullock), Best Villain (Hop-

per), Best Action Sequence; Blockbuster Entertainment Awards '95: Movie, Video, Action Actress, Video (Bullock), Action Actress, Theatrical (Bullock); *NOM:* Academy Awards '94: Best Film Editing; MTV Movie Awards '95: Best Film, Best Male Performance (Reeves), Most Desirable Male (Reeves), Best Kiss (Keanu Reeves/Sandra Bullock).

Speed 2: Cruise Control

Bigger's certainly not better in this lame sequel. Annie's (Bullock) got a new beau, hot-headed cop Alex (Patric), and the two-some decide to go on a Caribbean cruise for a little romance. Annie's luck with transportation holds as the ship is taken over by villainous computer geek-with-a-grudge John Giger (a particularly wild-eyed Dafoe), who sends the liner on a collision course with an oil tanker. Since Alex is off performing heroics, there's not much togetherness and Annie's left to get taken hostage (again). De Bont spent $25 mil on the ship's endless crash into a Caribbean island, which still manages to look fake. Bullock's feisty but powerless to save the flick. This sea disaster crashes against the rocks of high expectations and poor execution. But wow! This DVD looks and sounds great. The movie still blows, and only a full fifth of tequila would really make things bearable, but with this DVD in the machine, the room is filled with splashes, crashes, and explosions, and the picture on your home theatre screen couldn't be better. Colors are super vibrant and blacks couldn't be blacker. The 5.1 sound makes nonstop use of the Surround channels and, almost as constantly, pummels you with its energetic bass. —*JO*
Movie: 🎧 *DVD:* 🎧🎧🎧🎧
20th Century Fox (Cat #4110400, UPC #086162104008). Widescreen (2.35:1) letterboxed. Dolby Digital 5.1; Dolby Surround. $24.95. Keepcase. *LANG:* English (DD5.1; DS); French (DS). *SUB:* English; Spanish. *CAP:* English. *FEATURES:* 28 chapter links • Theatrical trailer.
1997 (PG-13) 123m/C Sandra Bullock, Jason Patric, Willem Dafoe, Temuera Morrison, Brian McCardie, Glenn Plummer, Royale Watkins, Colleen Camp, Lois Chiles, Michael G. Hagerty, Kimmy Robertson, Christine Firkins, Bo Svenson, Patrika Darbo; *Cameos:* Tim Conway; *D:* Jan De Bont; *W:* Jan De Bont, Jeff Nathanson, Randall McCormick; *C:* Jack N. Green; *M:* Mark Mancina. *AWARDS:* Golden Raspberry Awards '97: Worst Remake/Sequel; *NOM:* Golden Raspberry Awards '97: Worst Picture, Worst Actress (Bullock), Worst Supporting Actor (Dafoe), Worst Director (De Bont), Worst Screenplay, Worst Song ("My Dream").

Spellbound

Ignore the breathless and totally illogical psychological underpinnings of Ben Hecht's script for this classic thriller. Appreciate instead the fun everyone is having with it. Gregory Peck and Ingrid Bergman, at her most stunning, are the lovers out to solve a baffling murder which he appears to have committed, if only he could remember it. The DVD captures the superb black-and-white cinematography with no noticeable flaws, and because the film was made before the advent of widescreen filmmaking, the image loses nothing on a conventional-sized monitor. —*MM*
Movie: 🎧🎧🎧 *DVD:* 🎧🎧🎧🎧►
Anchor Bay (Cat #DV10810, UPC #013131081091). Full frame. Dolby Digital Mono. $24.98. Keepcase. *LANG:* English. *FEATURES:* 16 chapter links.
1945 111m/B Ingrid Bergman, Gregory Peck, Leo G. Carroll, Michael Chekhov, Wallace Ford, Rhonda Fleming, Regis Toomey; *D:* Alfred Hitchcock; *W:* Ben Hecht; *C:* George Barnes; *M:* Miklos Rozsa. *AWARDS:* Academy Awards '45: Best Original Dramatic Score; New York Film Critics Awards '45: Best Actress (Bergman); *NOM:* Academy Awards '45: Best Black-and-white Cinematography, Best Director (Hitchcock), Best Picture, Best Supporting Actor (Chekhov).

Sphere

It must've looked good on paper, but bringing Michael Crichton's decade-old novel to the screen turned out to be a big mistake for all involved. Hoffman, Jackson, and Stone are a team of researchers sent underwater to investigate a mysterious 300-year-old space ship. After realizing the ship was American origins, they stumble across a huge liquid metal sphere that can make their deepest fears come true, in the form of huge squids and sea snakes. Despite three mega-stars and an A-list director, it's a hollow excursion low on thrills and originality, but there's plenty of existential ramblings about the power of the mind. The DVD is near stunning with excellent picture sharpness and low grain and artifact levels. Colors are dead-on and very vibrant with no bleed. Contrast is excellent and the brightness levels consistent and comfortable. Blacks are always true and handled nicely. The 5.1 sound seems a little blah and doesn't have enough environmental ambience for an underwater sci-fi would-be adventure. The high end could also have used a boost although the lows are fine and supply the only energy in the soundtrack. Though you might have a "who cares" attitude about this film (I do), it's worth giving the commentary a listen—in fact, the commentary is far more entertaining than the movie itself. —*JO*
Movie: 🎧► *DVD:* 🎧🎧🎧🎧
Warner Home Video, Inc. (Cat #15331, UPC #085391533122). Widescreen (2.35:1) anamorphic. Dolby Digital 5.1; Dolby Surround. $19.98. Snapper. *LANG:* English (DD5.1); French (DS). *SUB:* Spanish; French. *CAP:* English. *FEATURES:* 3 chapter links • Theatrical trailer • Commentary: Dustin Hoffman, Samuel L. Jackson • "Making of" featurette • Production notes • Dual-layered RSDL.

1997 (PG-13) 152m/C Dustin Hoffman, Sharon Stone, Samuel L. Jackson, Peter Coyote, Queen Latifah, Liev Schreiber; *D:* Barry Levinson; *W:* Paul Attanasio, Stephen Hauser; *C:* Adam Greenberg; *M:* Elliot Goldenthal.

Spice World: The Movie

Clear some space on the video rack next to *Cool As Ice*—the Spice Girls made a movie! Stretching their acting ability, the pop group plays a band of marginally talented singers who are inexplicably thrown to the top of the charts by a bitter twist of pop culture fate. What passes for the plot is stolen from the Beatles' *A Hard Day's Night*, depicting five days before a sellout concert at Albert Hall. The courageous champions of girl power do battle with the hassles of fame, bossy managers, and the media in their quest to get to the show. They find the time to visit a pregnant ex-Spice, change their clothes a kajillion times, and generally poke fun at themselves along the way. Unfortunately (at least for those over 13) they're not poked with anything really sharp. Loads of celebrity cameos (Elton John, Elvis Costello, Bob Hoskins), some of whom run off screen faster than if they were on fire. The best thing going for the film is its colors, which are exceptionally bright and give the film a near *Willy Wonka* look at times. The DVD presents them accurately and with seemingly better contrast than even in the theatre. The 5.1 sound does a great job with the concert scenes, making them sound both live and energetic. —*JO*
Movie: 🎧► *DVD:* 🎧🎧🎧
Columbia Tristar Home Video (Cat #01770, UPC #043396017702). Widescreen (1.85:1) letterboxed; full frame. Dolby Digital 5.1; Dolby Surround. $29.95. Keepcase. *LANG:* English (DD5.1; DS); Spanish (DS); French (DS). *SUB:* English; Spanish; French. *CAP:* English. *FEATURES:* 28 chapter links • Theatrical trailer • Music video.
1997 (PG) 92m/C *GB* Emma (Baby Spice) Bunton, Geri (Ginger Spice) Halliwell, Victoria (Posh Spice) Adams, Melanie (Sporty Spice) Chisholm, Melanie (Scary Spice) Brown, Richard E. Grant, Alan Cumming, George Wendt, Claire Rushbrook, Mark McKinney, Richard O'Brien, Roger Moore, Barry Humphries, Jason Flemyng, Meat Loaf Aday, Bill Paterson, Stephen Fry, Richard Briers, Michael Barrymore, Naoki Mori, Hugh Laurie, Jennifer Saunders; *Cameos:* Elvis Costello, Bob Geldof, Bob Hoskins, Elton John; *D:* Bob Spiers; *W:* Kim Fuller, Jamie Curtis; *C:* Clive Tickner; *M:* Paul Newcastle. *AWARDS:* Golden Raspberry Awards '98: Worst Actress (The Spice Girls); *NOM:* Golden Raspberry Awards '98: Worst Picture, Worst Supporting Actor (Moore), Worst Screenplay, Worst Song ("Too Much"), Worst New Star (The Spice Girls).

Spider Baby

The mad Merrye family lives in a remote decaying mansion somewhere between the *Little Shop of Horrors* and the Bates Motel. Chauffeur Lon Chaney Jr. protects the kids—Virginia (Banner), a Leatherface Lolita; Elizabeth (Washburn); and Ralph (Haig), their dog-like brother—from lawyers, greedy relatives, and other predators. The story is cut from the same cloth as *Little Shop* and *Bucket of Blood*, but it's more twisted than either. Veteran exploitation director Jack Hill cranked this comic quickie out in record time and talks about the production on a low-keyed commentary track. The DVD also contains an eight-minute "lost" scene that's mostly slow exposition. The image is fine if not exceptional black and white. The disc was made from the original "answer print" and so it looks much better than any tapes in distribution. —*MM AKA:* The Liver Eaters; Spider Baby, or the Maddest Story Ever Told; Cannibal Orgy, or the Maddest Story Ever Told.

Movie: 🎬🎬🎬 **DVD:** 🎬🎬🎬
Image Entertainment (Cat #ID5860JNDVD, UPC #014381586022). Full frame. Dolby Digital Mono. $19.99. Snapper. *LANG:* English. *FEATURES:* 16 chapter links • Director and cast filmographies • "Lost" eight-minute scene • Commentary: director Jack Hill • Liner notes by director Joe Dante.
1964 86m/B Lon Chaney Jr., Mantan Moreland, Carol Ohmart, Sid Haig, Beverly Washburn, Jill Banner, Quinn Redeker, Mary Mitchell; **D:** Jack Hill; **W:** Jack Hill; **C:** Alfred Taylor; **M:** Ronald Stein.

Spiders

One of the earliest surviving films by director Lang predates Indiana Jones by almost 60 years but works with the same narrative material. In these first two chapters ("The Golden Lake" and "The Diamond Ship") of an unfinished four-part thriller, millionaire sportsman Kay Hoog (de Vogt) tries to rescue a Harvard professor held prisoner by Incas in Peru and to find the mystically powerful diamond while, at the same time, battling the Spider cult. Anyone who thinks that graphic gun violence in movies is a recent development should take a look. The DVD is made from a scratchy 1979 restoration and like so many films of the era, this one was made in high-contrast black and white and then tinted. Clarity varies from shot to shot but is generally acceptable. —*MM*
Movie: 🎬🎬🎬 **DVD:** 🎬🎬🎬
Image Entertainment (Cat #ID4678DSDVD, UPC #014381467826). Full frame. Dolby Digital Mono. $29.99. Snapper. *LANG:* Silent. *FEATURES:* Lang filmography • 23 chapter links.
1918 137m/B *GE* Lil Dagover; **D:** Fritz Lang; **M:** Gaylord Carter.

Spies Like Us

Saturday Night Live alums aren't exactly Hope and Crosby in this latter-day "Road" picture, but that's the spirit that director Landis tries to evoke. Emmitt Fitzhume (Chase) and Austin Milbarge (Aykroyd) are government desk jockeys who are recruited by the CIA as decoys for a super secret mission. Many of Landis's fellow directors show up in cameos. On pan-and-scan DVD, the diverting little comedy looks clean and sharply focused. It's presented without frills. The best moment comes late when the guys impersonate giant lighted Christmas tree ornaments. —*MM*
Movie: 🎬🎬 **DVD:** 🎬🎬
Warner Home Video, Inc. (Cat #16885, UPC #085391688525). Full frame. Dolby Digital Surround Stereo. $14.98. Snapper. *LANG:* English. *SUB:* English. *CAP:* English.
1985 (PG) 103m/C Chevy Chase, Dan Aykroyd, Steve Forrest, Bruce Davison, William Prince, Bernie Casey, Tom Hatton, Donna Dixon, Frank Oz, Michael Apted, Constantin Costa-Gavras, Terry Gilliam, Ray Harryhausen, Joel Coen, Martin Brest, Bob Swaim; **D:** John Landis; **W:** Lowell Ganz, Babaloo Mandel, Dan Aykroyd; **C:** Robert Paynter; **M:** Elmer Bernstein.

Spirit of the Eagle

Mountain man Eli (Haggerty) and his young son move into a remote cabin and make friends with all the darling forest creatures and the local Indians until a scrofulous trapper (Smith) kidnaps the boy. On DVD, the image is acceptable, but there's little to be done to help this innocuous but insipid family fare. —*MM*
Movie: 🎬 **DVD:** 🎬🎬
Simitar Entertainment (Cat #7390, UPC #082551739028). Full frame. Dolby Digital Stereo. $14.98. Keepcase. *LANG:* English. *FEATURES:* 8 chapter links • Production factoids • Dan Haggerty filmography.
1990 (PG) 93m/C Dan Haggerty, Bill Smith, Don Shanks, Jeri Arredondo, Trever Yarrish; **D:** Boon Collins; **W:** Boon Collins; **C:** Lew V. Adams; **M:** Parmer Fuller.

Spirits of the Dead

Three Edgar Allen Poe stories are adapted and directed by three of Europe's finest, and at the time, most popular directors. Roger Vadim's *Metzengerstein* casts the Fondas as incestuous libertines; Louis Malle's *William Wilson* has Delon as a vicious army officer who attempts to cheat Bardot; in Fellini's *Toby Dammit* (AKA *Never Bet the Devil Your Head*), Stamp is an obnoxious British actor. In the *Barbarella* phase of her career, Jane Fonda was known as a "sex kitten," and her role in then-husband Vadim's section does nothing to contradict that image. The anthology is pretty hot stuff for the mid-'60s. It's well photographed with a clean transfer from film to disc. The autumnal fading is somehow appropriate in the first two films. Malle's entry eerily predates his *Au Revoir les Enfants* in some respects. Fellini's comedy has nothing to do with the other two in style or subject, save the nod to Poe. —*MM AKA:* Histoires Extraordinaires; Tre Passi nel Delirio; Tales of Mystery; Tales of Mystery and Imagination; Trois Histoires Extraordinaires d'Edgar Poe.
Movie: 🎬🎬🎬 **DVD:** 🎬🎬🎬
Image Entertainment (Cat #ID4420WB DVD, UPC #014381442021). Widescreen (1.75:1). Uncompressed PCM soundtrack. $24.99. Snapper. *LANG:* English; French. *SUB:* English. *FEATURES:* 16 chapter links.
1968 (R) 117m/C *IT FR* Jane Fonda, Peter Fonda, Carla Marlier, Francoise Prevost, James Robertson Justice, Brigitte Bardot, Alain Delon, Katia Christine, Terence Stamp, Salvo Randone; **D:** Roger Vadim, Louis Malle, Federico Fellini; **W:** Roger Vadim, Louis Malle, Federico Fellini, Daniel Boulanger, Barnardino Zapponi; **C:** Tonino Delli Colli, Claude Renoir, Giuseppe Rotunno; **M:** Nino Rota, Diego Masson; **Nar:** Vincent Price, Clement Biddle Wood.

Spiritual Kung Fu

Chan plays a mischievous pupil at the haunted Shaolin Temple. He's a leader in his class as he adopts a style of fighting taught by the spirits themselves. The picture is very soft, and the original film element used for the video transfer is loaded with nicks and scars. Audio is frequently distorted. The extra interview with Chan (same as on several other Chan DVDs) is revealing but production values are low. No subtitle option either. —*MB AKA:* Quan Jing.
Movie: 🎬 **DVD:** 🎬
Simitar Entertainment (Cat #7261, UPC #082551726127). Full frame. Dolby Digital 2.0. $14.98. Keepcase. *LANG:* English; Cantonese. *FEATURES:* 10 chapter links • Movie factoids • Biography/filmography • Interview with Chan.
1978 97m/C *HK* Jackie Chan; **D:** Lo Wei.

Splash

A beautiful mermaid (Hannah) ventures into New York City in search of a man (Hanks) she's rescued twice when he's fallen overboard. Charming performances by the then-young leads and sure direction by Howard give this love story just enough slapstick. Don't miss the lobster scene.
Movie: 🎬🎬🎬 **DVD:** NYR
Buena Vista Home Entertainment (Cat #16535). $29.99. Keepcase.
1984 (PG) 109m/C Tom Hanks, Daryl Hannah, Eugene Levy, John Candy, Dody Goodman, Shecky Greene, Richard B. Shull, Bobby DiCicco, Howard Morris; **D:** Ron Howard; **W:** Babaloo Mandel, Lowell Ganz; **C:** Don Peterman; **M:** Lee Holdridge.
AWARDS: National Society of Film Critics Awards '84: Best Screenplay; *NOM:* Academy Awards '84: Best Original Screenplay.

Splendor

A '90s screwball comedy about an unconventional sexual arrangement. Veronica (Robertson) is an aspiring L.A. actress who enjoys her sexual exploits and who falls for two men on the opposite ends of the romantic spectrum. Abel (Schaech) is a freelance music critic who's intelligent and handsome while punk rock drummer Zed (Keeslar) is dumb but really sexy. Veronica refuses to choose between the two, so both move in with her (and prove to be more immature than the lady herself). Then Veronica meets successful and wealthy TV director, Ernest (Mabius), and wonders if it's time for a real adult relationship. Surprisingly sweet and stylish fluff from Araki. *Movie:* 🎬🎬➤ *DVD:* NYR

Columbia Tristar Home Video (Cat #4384). Full frame (1.85:1) letterboxed. Dolby Digital 5.1 Surround Stereo. $27.95. Keepcase. *LANG:* English; Portuguese; Spanish. *SUB:* French; Portuguese; Spanish. *CAP:* English. *FEATURES:* Cast and crew thumbnail bios ➤ Trailer.
1999 (R) 93m/C Kathleen Robertson, Johnathon Schaech, Matt Keeslar, Eric Mabius, Kelly Macdonald; *D:* Gregg Araki; *W:* Gregg Araki; *C:* Jim Fealy; *M:* Daniel Licht.

Spoiler

Roger Mason (Daniels) wants to get home to see his daughter, but in this dystopian sf, he's a prisoner in time. After his first escape from prison, he's sentenced to "26 years of chemoligation." That is, he's put in suspended animation. At times, the restrictions of the budget show up in spare, darkened sets. The writing and the cast are better and the film has echoes of *Brazil* and *12 Monkeys*. In the lead, martial artist Daniels is given some substance to work with and he handles the dramatic work admirably. The DVD looks fine though it is not exceptional in image or sound. For fans of the star. —*MM*
Movie: 🎬🎬🎬 *DVD:* 🎬🎬

York Entertainment (Cat #VPD-1002, UPC #750723100227). Widescreen letterboxed. $24.98. Keepcase. *LANG:* English. *SUB:* Spanish. *FEATURES:* 16 chapter links ➤ Gary Daniels thumbnail biography.
1998 100m/C Gary Daniels, Meg Foster, Bryan Genesse, Jeffrey Combs, Arye Gross; *D:* Carmen Von Daacke; *W:* Michael Kalesniko; *C:* Philip Lee.

Spring Symphony

This fact-based story was filmed as *Fruhlingssinfonie* a year before but released in America a couple of years after the extraordinary success of *Amadeus*. The pivotal conflict pits composer Robert Schumann (Gronemeyer, of *Das Boot*) and his fiancee, piano prodigy Clara Wieck (Kinski), against her possessive stage father Friedrich (Hoppe). An intertwining of art and romance, swathed in a European travelogue of settings and 19th-century costumes, makes an irresistible combination for Masterpiece Theater fans with enough patience for subtitles. The visual transfer seems to have been handled decently, but fleshtones are sometimes noticeably inconsistent. The unimpeded classical sound, in mono, will probably not satisfy

purists. Subtitles are thankfully in yellow. —*JK AKA:* Fruhlingssinfonie.
Movie: 🎬🎬➤ *DVD:* 🎬🎬🎬
Image Entertainment (Cat #ID5751CHDVD, UPC #014381575125). Full frame. Dolby Digital Mono. $24.99. Snapper. *LANG:* German. *SUB:* English. *FEATURES:* 16 chapter links ➤ Interactive menu.
1986 (PG-13) 102m/C *GE* Nastassia Kinski, Rolf Hoppe, Herbert Gronemeyer; *D:* Peter Schamoni; *W:* Peter Schamoni; *C:* Gerard Vandenburg.

Sprung

Writer-director-star Rusty Cundieff's romantic comedy is about two very different black couples playing out variations on the old boy-meets-girl formula. The first half is quickly paced, inventive, and laugh-out-loud funny as the four meet each other on a Saturday night. Clyde (Torry) is a cocky conman who'll stoop to any trick to pick up a pretty girl. His pal Montel (Cundieff) is the shy guy who doesn't believe in games and has to be dragged along to a nightspot. Adina (Parker) is Clyde's opposite number—an unapologetic golddigger with dollar signs in her eyes and a wig for every occasion. Her pal Brandy (Tisha Campbell) is the shy girl who doesn't believe in games and has to be dragged along to a nightspot. As long as the focus stays on the costars, the film is terrific; when it shifts to the nice kids, it's too sweet and too familiar. The DVD handles potentially difficult visual material without problems. Differences in skin color—important to the story—are clearly defined. One loud stop sign–red suit glows warmly, just as it did in the theatrical release. —*MM*
Movie: 🎬🎬 *DVD:* 🎬🎬🎬
Trimark Home Video (Cat #VM6884D, UPC #031398688433). Widescreen letterboxed. Dolby Digital Surround Stereo. $19.99. Keepcase. *LANG:* English. *SUB:* French; Spanish. *CAP:* English. *FEATURES:* 24 chapter links ➤ "Making of" featurette ➤ Cast and crew thumbnail biographies ➤ Theatrical trailer.
1996 (R) 105m/C Tisha Campbell, Paula Jai Parker, Rusty Cundieff, Joe Torry, John Witherspoon, Clarence Williams III; *D:* Rusty Cundieff; *W:* Darin Scott, Rusty Cundieff; *C:* Joao Fernandes; *M:* Stanley Clarke.

Spy Hard

As movie spoofs go, this one has its moments but it's not as frantically funny or energetic as the *Naked Gun* series. Actually, it's a James Bond parody that owes a lot to the old *Get Smart* series, though it does find room to poke fun at *Speed*, *Home Alone*, *Pulp Fiction*, and even *Butch Cassidy and the Sundance Kid*. As Dick Steel, Agent WD-40, Leslie Nielsen is at ease with the physical comedy, and he gets some offbeat support from the supporting cast, including Andy Griffith as his nemesis General Rancor. First-time director Friedberg got his start in commercials

and rock videos. The DVD image is every bit as clear as the theatrical version. Sound is fine, too. —*MM*
Movie: 🎬🎬 *DVD:* 🎬🎬🎬
Hollywood Pictures Home Video (Cat #17248, UPC #717951002419). Widescreen (1.85:1) letterboxed. Dolby Digital 5.1 Surround Stereo. $29.99. Keepcase. *LANG:* English; French. *CAP:* English. *FEATURES:* 17 chapter links ➤ "Making of" featurette ➤ Theatrical trailer.
1996 (PG-13) 80m/C Leslie Nielsen, Nicolette Sheridan, Andy Griffith, Charles Durning, Marcia Gay Harden, Barry Bostwick; *D:* Rick Friedberg; *W:* Rick Friedberg, Dick Chudnow, Jason Friedberg, Aaron Seltzer; *C:* John R. Leonetti; *M:* Bill Conti.

The Spy Who Loved Me (SE)

James Bond teams up with female Russian Agent XXX to squash a villain's plan to use captured American and Russian atomic submarines in a plot to destroy the world. The villain's henchman, 7'2" Kiel, is the steel-toothed Jaws. Carly Simon sings the memorable Marvin Hamlisch theme song, "Nobody Does It Better." The film transfer itself looks pretty much the same as the earlier MGM DVD, which was already a big improvement over previous video versions. Colors are accurate and vibrant and the picture is sharp and grain-free. The sound is also given a big boost on the disc, with far more dynamics and a much gutsier bass track. The Special Edition has an expanded supplemental section and full-length commentary. —*JO*
Movie: 🎬🎬 *DVD:* 🎬🎬🎬➤
MGM Home Entertainment (Cat #908129, UPC #027616812926). Widescreen (2.35:1) anamorphic. Dolby Digital 5.1; Dolby Surround. $34.98. Keepcase. *LANG:* English (DD5.1); French (DS). *SUB:* English; French. *CAP:* English. *FEATURES:* 32 chapter links ➤ Commentary: Lewis Gilbert, cast, and crew members ➤ 2 original documentaries ➤ Still gallery ➤ TV ads and radio spots ➤ Theatrical trailer ➤ Dual-layered RSDL.
1977 (PG) 136m/C *GB* Roger Moore, Barbara Bach, Curt Jurgens, Richard Kiel, Caroline Munro, Walter Gotell, Geoffrey Keen, Valerie Leon, Bernard Lee, Lois Maxwell, Desmond Llewelyn; *D:* Lewis Gilbert; *W:* Christopher Wood, Richard Maibaum; *C:* Claude Renoir, Lamar Boren; *M:* Marvin Hamlisch, Paul Buckmaster. *AWARDS: NOM:* Academy Awards '77: Best Art Direction/Set Decoration, Best Song ("Nobody Does It Better"), Best Original Score.

Stagecoach

Varied group of characters with nothing in common are stuck together inside a coach besieged by bandits and Indians. Considered structurally perfect, with excellent direction by Ford, it's the film that made Wayne a star as the Ringo Kid, an outlaw looking to avenge the murder of his brother and father. The first pairing of Ford and

Wayne changed the course of the modern western. Stunning photography by Bert Glennon and Ray Binger captured the mythical air of Monument Valley, a site that Ford was often to revisit. Based on the story "Stage to Lordsburg" by Ernest Haycox, and remade miserably in 1966 and again—why?—as a TV movie in 1986. The DVD transfer is great and *Stagecoach* has never looked better. That's not to say that there aren't flaws in the image. The film has always been contrasty and that's how it is here. But the picture is very sharp and there are better graytones than the earlier video versions, resulting in much better depth and detail. There is some preprint damage, but hey, that just lets you know the vintage of the film. The sound is fuller than before, and despite some scratchiness, is a marked improvement. —*JO*
Movie: 𝄞𝄞𝄞𝄞 **DVD:** 𝄞𝄞𝄞▶
Warner Home Video, Inc. (Cat #35078, UPC #085393507824). Full frame. Stereo. $19.98. Snapper. *LANG:* English. *SUB:* English; Spanish; French. *CAP:* English. *FEATURES:* 24 chapter links ▪ 7 theatrical trailers ▪ Production notes.
1939 100m/B John Wayne, Claire Trevor, Thomas Mitchell, George Bancroft, John Carradine, Andy Devine, Donald Meek, Louise Platt, Berton Churchill, Tim Holt, Tom Tyler, Chris-Pin Martin, Francis Ford, Jack Pennick; *D:* John Ford; *W:* Dudley Nichols; *C:* Bert Glennon, Ray Binger. *AWARDS:* Academy Awards '39: Best Supporting Actor (Mitchell), Best Score; American Film Institute (AFI) '98: Top 100, National Film Registry '95; New York Film Critics Awards '39: Best Director (Ford); *NOM:* Academy Awards '39: Best Black-and-white Cinematography, Best Director (Ford), Best Film Editing, Best Picture.

Stalingrad

Group of German stormtroopers fall victim to the brutal war of attrition over Stalingrad in 1942 and 1943. Grimly realistic depiction of war is not for the fainthearted. Originally a TV miniseries and with the same production team as *Das Boot*. This is one hell of a bleak film and the DVD retains the necessarily dreary colors while delivering a sharp picture with very little grain. The stereo sound is very good with rich imaging throughout the film. —*JO*
Movie: 𝄞𝄞 **DVD:** 𝄞𝄞𝄞
Fox/Lorber Home Video (Cat #FLV5036, UPC #720917503622). Full frame. Stereo. $34.98. Keepcase. *LANG:* English; German. *SUB:* English. *FEATURES:* 9 chapter links ▪ Theatrical trailer ▪ Cast and filmmaker bios ▪ Production notes ▪ Dual-layered RSDL.
1994 150m/C GE Dominique Horwitz, Thomas Kretschmann, Jochen Nickel; *D:* Joseph Vilsmaier; *W:* Joseph Vilsmaier; *C:* Joseph Vilsmaier; *M:* Norbert J. Schneider.

Stand and Deliver

A tough teacher inspires students in an East L.A. barrio to take the Advanced Placement Test in calculus. A superb, inspirational true story, with a wonderful performance from Olmos. The DVD seems to have been done from a previous video transfer, with not much put into the authoring. The picture can never be called sharp and there is constant grain, which reaches totally unacceptable levels in the darker shots. The biggest aggravation, though, is the artifacts that seem to be in virtually every scene. The sound is O.K. and has more body than a lot of mono tracks. —*JO*
Movie: 𝄞𝄞𝄞 **DVD:** 𝄞
Warner Home Video, Inc. (Cat #16377, UPC #085391637721). Full frame. Mono. $14.98. Snapper. *LANG:* English. *CAP:* English. *FEATURES:* 30 chapter links.
1988 (PG) 105m/C Edward James Olmos, Lou Diamond Phillips, Rosana De Soto, Andy Garcia, Will Gotay, Ingrid Oliu, Virginia Paris, Mark Eliot, Eugene Glazer; *D:* Ramon Menendez; *W:* Ramon Menendez, Tom Musca; *C:* Tom Richmond; *M:* Craig Safan. *AWARDS:* Independent Spirit Awards '89: Best Actor (Olmos), Best Director (Menendez), Best Film, Best Screenplay, Best Supporting Actor (Phillips), Best Supporting Actress (De Soto); *NOM:* Academy Awards '88: Best Actor (Olmos).

Stand by Me

In a sentimental, observant adaptation of the Stephen King novella "The Body," four 12-year-olds trek into the Oregon wilderness to find the body of a missing boy, learning about death and personal courage. Told as a reminiscence by narrator "author" Dreyfuss with solid performances from all four child actors. Too much gratuitous obscenity, but a very good, gratifying film from can't-miss director Reiner. Most of the action takes place outside and the image is fairly bright overall. The DVD's colors reflect that and are generally pretty bright themselves. However, when a long shot is filled with a lot of detail (tree branches or such), some grain is added to the image. The mono sound is very good, though, with decent bass and overall undistorted clarity. —*JO*
Movie: 𝄞𝄞𝄞 **DVD:** 𝄞𝄞▶
Columbia Tristar Home Video (Cat #07369, UPC #043396073792). Widescreen (1.85:1) letterboxed. Dolby Surround. NSL. Keepcase. *LANG:* English; Spanish; French. *SUB:* Spanish; Korean. *CAP:* English. *FEATURES:* 40 chapter links.
1986 (R) 87m/C River Phoenix, Wil Wheaton, Jerry O'Connell, Corey Feldman, Kiefer Sutherland, Richard Dreyfuss, Casey Siemaszko, John Cusack; *D:* Rob Reiner; *W:* Raynold Gideon; *C:* Thomas Del Ruth; *M:* Jack Nitzsche. *AWARDS:* *NOM:* Academy Awards '86: Best Adapted Screenplay.

Stand-Ins

A half-dozen movie star "stand-ins" (a Harlow, a Garbo, a Hayworth, etc.) gather on a June night in 1937 at a local Hollywood watering hole to celebrate a birthday.

Drinking, drugs, and back-biting cat fights mark the evening, which is capped off by news of Jean Harlow's tragic death at 26 years of age, and the murder of one of the party-goers. The obvious transition from stage to film (play by Ed Kelleher) undercuts director Harvey Keith's *(Jezebel's Kiss, Mondo New York)* work with an all too claustrophobic feel. He fails to open the proceedings up—even at 89 minutes it seems over-long—with those infrequent trips outside the bar seemingly artificial and forced. DVD presentation is bare-bones, with no extras (a couple of cross-promotional trailers thrown in), but the video transfer is clean and the lengthy interior sequences are never dark or muddy. —*RT*
Movie: 𝄞𝄞 **DVD:** 𝄞𝄞▶
Image Entertainment (Cat #OVED6878, UPC #014381687828). Full frame. AC3 - 2 Channel. $24.99. Snapper. *LANG:* English. *FEATURES:* 12 chapter links ▪ Trailer ▪ Trailers for *Alive and Kicking, Slaves to the Underground.*
1997 89m/C Daphne Zuniga, Jordan Ladd, Sammi Davis, Missy Crider, Charlotte Chatton, Costas Mandylor, Katherine Heigl; *D:* Harvey Keith; *W:* Harvey Keith, Ed Kelleher; *C:* Andrzej Sekula; *M:* Bill Elliott.

Star 80

Based on the true-life tragedy of Playmate of the Year Dorothy Stratten and her manager-husband Paul Snider as they battle for control of her body, her mind, and her money, with gruesome results. Roberts is overpowering as the vile Snider, but the movie—Fosse's last—is generally un pleasant. This DVD is almost as grim as the film itself. It starts with a soft image and then adds colors that are both weak and have a little too much red. Grain is fairly abundant. Through almost the entire film, louder dialogue and music distorts, and the overall sound is thin. —*JO*
Movie: 𝄞𝄞▶ **DVD:** 𝄞▶
Warner Home Video, Inc. (Cat #20013, UPC #085392001323). Full frame. Stereo. $14.98. Snapper. *LANG:* English. *CAP:* English. *FEATURES:* 29 chapter links.
1983 (R) 104m/C Mariel Hemingway, Eric Roberts, Cliff Robertson, David Clennon, Josh Mostel, Roger Rees, Carroll Baker; *D:* Bob Fosse; *W:* Bob Fosse; *C:* Sven Nykvist; *M:* Ralph Burns.

A Star Is Born

The oft-remade story of an actress on her way up in love with an older actor on his way down was indeed original at this point, so the box cover's claim of it being "William Wellman's Classic Original" is not unjustified hyperbole. The first Esther Blodgett was Janet Gaynor. The first Norman Maine was Fredric March. Everyone and his brother must know the ending by now, of course. Just enjoy the two leads, aided by a solid cross-section of character actors, as they hurtle towards their fates. A five-item, one-shot costume test is the only extra on this DVD version. The Technicolor remastering was performed with an original 35mm nitrate print provided by the Selznick estate, and the sound is almost completely free of distortion. Unfortunately, the wavering color so typical of such ancient source material (from when Technicolor was a novelty) could not be corrected digitally. —*JK*

Movie: 🎬🎬🎬▶ **DVD:** 🎬🎬🎬
Kino on Video (Cat #ID4213SZDVD, UPC #014381421323). Full frame. Dolby Digital Mono. $29.99. Snapper. *LANG:* English. *FEATURES:* 26 chapter links ▪ Scene access menu ▪ Colorized gatefold cover with photo montage ▪ Costume test reel.
1937 111m/**C** Janet Gaynor, Fredric March, Adolphe Menjou, May Robson, Andy Devine, Lionel Stander, Franklin Pangborn; **D:** William A. Wellman; **W:** William A. Wellman, David O. Selznick, Dorothy Parker; **C:** William Howard Greene; **M:** Max Steiner. *AWARDS:* Academy Awards '37: Best Story; *NOM:* Academy Awards '37: Best Actor (March), Best Actress (Gaynor), Best Director (Wellman), Best Picture.

Star Trek 4: The Voyage Home

For those who can't keep up the numbers, this is the one with the whales, where the guys from the original series go back to San Francisco in a Klingon ship to save the world from future destruction. On DVD, it looks and sounds very good, though the contemporary ('80s) scenes have a rougher cast. The film's humor survives intact. The DVD also includes an interview with director-star Nimoy, previously available on VHS tape, as part of the studio's "director's series." Overall, one of the better entries in the long-running series. —*MM*

Movie: 🎬🎬🎬 **DVD:** 🎬🎬🎬
Paramount Home Video (Cat #01797, UPC #097360179774). Widescreen anamorphic. Dolby Digital 5.1 Surround Stereo; Dolby Digital Surround Stereo. $29.99. Keepcase. *LANG:* English; French. *SUB:* English. *FEATURES:* 17 chapter links ▪ Theatrical trailer ▪ Interview with Leonard Nimoy.
1986 (PG) 119m/**C** William Shatner, DeForest Kelley, Catherine Hicks, James Doohan, Nichelle Nichols, George Takei, Walter Koenig, Mark Lenard, Leonard Nimoy, Michael Berryman, Majel Barrett, Brock Peters, John Schuck, Jane Wyatt; **D:** Leonard Nimoy; **W:** Nicholas Meyer, Harve Bennett, Peter Krikes, Steve Meerson; **C:** Don Peterman; **M:** Leonard Rosenman. *AWARDS: NOM:* Academy Awards '86: Best Cinematography, Best Sound, Best Original Score.

Star Trek 5: The Final Frontier

A renegade Vulcan kidnaps the Enterprise and takes it on a journey to the mythic center of the universe. Shatner's big-action directorial debut (he also cowrote the script) is a poor follow-up to the Nimoy-directed fourth entry in the series. It's heavy-handed and pretentiously pseudo-do-theological. Although nice-looking, the transfer on this DVD does not measure up with some of the other installments in the *Star Trek* series. The colors are somewhat subdued and the image appears artificially sharpened. No compression artifacts are evident in the presentation however. The Surround sound on the DVD is very pleasing, creating an engaging experience that makes good use of the entire spectrum with deep basses. —*GH*

Movie: 🎬▶ **DVD:** 🎬🎬🎬
Paramount Home Video (Cat #320447, UPC #097363204473). Widescreen (2.35:1) letterboxed. Dolby Digital 5.1 Surround Stereo; Dolby Digital Surround Stereo. $29.99. Keepcase. *LANG:* English; French. *SUB:* Spanish. *CAP:* English. *FEATURES:* 15 chapter links ▪ Trailers.
1989 (PG) 107m/**C** William Shatner, Leonard Nimoy, DeForest Kelley, James Doohan, Laurence Luckinbill, Walter Koenig, George Takei, Nichelle Nichols, David Warner, Melanie Shatner, Harve Bennett; **D:** William Shatner; **W:** David Loughery, William Shatner; **C:** Andrew Laszlo; **M:** Jerry Goldsmith. *AWARDS:* Golden Raspberry Awards '89: Worst Picture, Worst Actor (Shatner), Worst Director (Shatner).

Star Trek 6: The Undiscovered Country

In the final episode starring only the original crew, the Federation and the Klingon Empire are preparing for a much-needed peace conference but Captain Kirk (Shatner) has doubts about the true intentions of his ancient enemies. When a Klingon ship is attacked, Kirk and company are accused of the misdeed and must find the real perpetrator. Despite the film's age, the visual effects are first-rate (though a bit familiar). The DVD presents an image that contains no significant flaws; certainly nothing to bother those who have always thought that *Star Trek* is more comfortable on the small screen, anyway. Sound is exemplary. —*MM*

Movie: 🎬🎬▶ **DVD:** 🎬🎬🎬
Paramount Home Video (Cat #323017, UPC #097363230175). Widescreen letterboxed. Dolby Digital 5.1 Surround Stereo; Dolby Digital Surround Stereo. $29.99. Keepcase. *LANG:* English; French. *CAP:* English. *FEATURES:* 15 chapter links ▪ Theatrical trailer ▪ Teaser.
1991 (PG) 110m/**C** William Shatner, Leonard Nimoy, DeForest Kelley, James Doohan, George Takei, Walter Koenig, Nichelle Nichols, Christopher Plummer, Kim Cattrall, Iman, David Warner, Mark Lenard, Grace Lee Whitney, Brock Peters, Kurtwood Smith, Rosana De Soto, John Schuck, Michael Dorn, Christian Slater; **D:** Nicholas Meyer; **W:** Nicholas Meyer, Denny Martin Flinn; **C:** Hiro Narita; **M:** Cliff Eidel-

man. *AWARDS: NOM:* Academy Awards '91: Best Makeup.

Star Trek: First Contact

The eighth big-screen Trek saga is firmly in the hands of the *Next Generation* cast as Picard and the Enterprise cross paths with the Borg and their sinister Queen. It's hard to tell whether the cry "Resistance Is Futile" is coming from the Borg, or the Trek franchise itself, as this installment may well bring in new "Trekkers" with its "less techno-babble, more action" approach and the fact that this crew can act. The Borg attempt to change history by travelling back in time (to 2063) to prevent scientist Cromwell from inventing warp drive. While the less-interesting members of the crew stay on Earth to help out with the launch, the battle for the Enterprise rages on up in space. Trademark effects, humor, and idealism are in abundant supply and should please the long-time fan as well as the neophyte. Paramount knows what an important franchise this is—there are fans who waited for the first *Star Trek* to get in to the format—and they have taken all the proper care to ensure that the *Trek* DVDs are done right. Most important, with a lot of the action taking place in deep space, is that the blacks are dead-on. The DVD has no problems with total darkness or blacks surrounding brightly colored explosive flashes. The picture is extremely sharp and the colors stand up to all scrutiny. The 5.1 mix is put to full use. —*JO*

Movie: 🎬🎬🎬 **DVD:** 🎬🎬🎬🎬▶
Paramount Home Video (Cat #15947, UPC #097361549477). Widescreen (2.35:1) letterboxed. Dolby Digital 5.1; Dolby Surround. $29.99. Keepcase. *LANG:* English (DD5.1; DS); French (DS). *SUB:* Spanish. *CAP:* English. *FEATURES:* 31 chapter links ▪ 2 theatrical trailers.
1996 (PG-13) 111m/**C** Patrick Stewart, Jonathon Frakes, Brent Spiner, LeVar Burton, Michael Dorn, Marina Sirtis, Gates McFadden, Alfre Woodard, James Cromwell, Alice Krige, Neal McDonough, Robert Picardo, Dwight Schultz; **D:** Jonathon Frakes; **W:** Brannon Braga, Ronald D. Moore; **C:** Matthew F. Leonetti; **M:** Jerry Goldsmith. *AWARDS: NOM:* Academy Awards '96: Best Makeup.

Star Trek: Generations

The sci-fi phenomenon continues with the first film spun off from the dearly departed *Star Trek: The Next Generation* TV series and the seventh following the adventures of the Enterprise crew. Captain Kirk is propelled into the future thanks to an explosion and manages to hook up with current starship captain, Picard. Of course, they're just in time to save the galaxy from the latest space loon, the villainous Dr. Soren (McDowell),

renegade Klingons, and your basic mysterious space entity. For comic relief, android Data gets an emotion chip. Terrific special effects (courtesy of Industrial Light and Magic) and yes, the heroic Kirk receives his mandatory grandiose death scene. Other original characters making a brief appearance are Scotty and Chekov. An entertaining romp through time and space. There isn't much to say other than this DVD is as superb as Paramount's other *Star Trek* discs. Image is sharp and colors excellent. As usual, the 5.1 sound packs plenty of power and totally immerses the viewer in everything from conversation to photon torpedo hits. —*JO*
Movie: ♫♫♫ **DVD:** ♫♫♫▶
Paramount Home Video (Cat #329887, UPC #097363298878). Widescreen (2.35:1) letterboxed. Dolby Digital 5.1; Dolby Surround. $29.99. Keepcase. *LANG:* English (DD5.1; DS); French (DS). *SUB:* Spanish. *CAP:* English. *FEATURES:* 16 chapter links.
1994 (PG) 117m/C William Shatner, Patrick Stewart, Malcolm McDowell, Whoopi Goldberg, Jonathon Frakes, Brent Spiner, LeVar Burton, Michael Dorn, Gates McFadden, Marina Sirtis, James Doohan, Walter Koenig, Alan Ruck; *D:* David Carson; *W:* Ronald D. Moore, Brannon Braga; *C:* John A. Alonzo; *M:* Dennis McCarthy; *V:* Majel Barrett.

Star Trek: Insurrection

In the ninth film, Captain Picard (Stewart) goes to Data's (Spiner) rescue when the android seemingly goes berserk while on a scientific mission to investigate the non-techno culture of the peaceful Ba'ku. What Picard discovers is a planet that's virtually a fountain of youth and a dastardly plan by the Federation and the evil Son'a, led by bitter Ru'afro (Abraham), to gain the secret even though it means destroying the planet to do so. More humor and romance than usual, done in the typical professional manner of the franchise. Another great DVD in the series with even more impressive sound than usual. Use this one to show off your system off; the Surround is nothing short of amazing and the bass is killer. The image is extremely sharp and colors are knock-out gorgeous. —*JO*
Movie: ♫♫▶ **DVD:** ♫♫♫♫
Paramount Home Video (Cat #335887, UPC #097363358879). Widescreen (2.35:1) letterboxed. Dolby Digital 5.1; Dolby Surround. $29.99. Keepcase. *LANG:* English (DD5.1; DS); French (DS). *CAP:* English. *FEATURES:* 24 chapter links • 2 theatrical trailers • Behind-the-scenes featurette.
1998 (PG) 100m/C Patrick Stewart, Brent Spiner, Donna Murphy, F. Murray Abraham, Jonathon Frakes, LeVar Burton, Michael Dorn, Anthony Zerbe, Gates McFadden, Marina Sirtis, Gregg Henry, Daniel Hugh-Kelly; *D:* Jonathon Frakes; *W:* Michael Piller; *C:* Matthew F. Leonetti; *M:* Jerry Goldsmith.

Stargate

U.S. military probe of a ring-shaped ancient Egyptian artifact (your tax dollars at work) sends he-man colonel Russell and geeky Egyptologist Spader into a parallel universe. There they meet the builders of the pyramids, who are enslaved by an evil despot (Davidson) posing as a sun god. Ambitious premise zapped from prepubescent imaginations gets an "A" for effort, but a silly plot that jumbles biblical epic panoramas and space odyssey special effects with otherworldly mysticism and needless emotional hang-ups trade shlock for style. Spader's shaggy scholar is neurotically fun, Russell's jarhead a bore, and Davidson's vampy villain an unintended hoot. This is the original theatrical release of the film, and not the extended special edition, which is also available on DVD. The disc is near flawless and the image sharpness would be hard to beat. The 5.1 mix really adds some gusto to all the action scenes and features a great rumbling bass as well as nonstop Surround effects. —*JO*
Movie: ♫♫ **DVD:** ♫♫♫♫
Artisan Entertainment (Cat #60440, UPC #01223604000). Widescreen (2.35:1) anamorphic. Dolby Digital 5.1; Stereo. $24.99. Snapper. *LANG:* English (DD5.1); French (stereo). *SUB:* English; Spanish; French. *CAP:* English. *FEATURES:* 38 chapter links • Theatrical trailer and teaser • Production notes • Cast and filmmakers bios • Dual-layered RSDL.
1994 (PG-13) 119m/C Kurt Russell, James Spader, Jaye Davidson, Viveca Lindfors, Alexis Cruz, Leon Rippy, John Diehl, Erik Avari, Mili Avital; *D:* Roland Emmerich; *W:* Dean Devlin, Roland Emmerich; *C:* Jeff Okun; *M:* David Arnold.

Starman

An alien from an advanced civilization lands in Wisconsin. He hides beneath the guise of a grieving young widow's recently deceased husband. He then makes her drive him across country to rendezvous with his spacecraft so he can return home. Well-acted, interesting twist on the "Stranger in a Strange Land" theme. Bridges is fun as the likeable starman; Allen is lovely and earthy in her worthy follow-up to *Raiders of the Lost Ark*. There's nothing really terrible about this DVD (not much grain or many artifacts), it just looks listless with average sharpness, and slightly dull colors in need of a little contrast. The sound does the job but does nothing to enhance the film. —*JO*
Movie: ♫♫♫ **DVD:** ♫♫▶
Columbia Tristar Home Video (Cat #04129, UPC #043396041295). Widescreen (2.35:1) letterboxed; full frame. Dolby Surround. NSL. Keepcase. *LANG:* English; Spanish; French. *SUB:* English; Spanish; French. *CAP:* English. *FEATURES:* 28 chapter links • Theatrical trailer.
1984 (PG) 115m/C Jeff Bridges, Karen Allen, Charles Martin Smith, Richard Jaeckel; *D:* John Carpenter; *W:* Bruce A. Evans, Raynold Gideon; *C:* Donald M. Mor-

gan; *M:* Jack Nitzsche. *AWARDS: NOM:* Academy Awards '84: Best Actor (Bridges).

Starship Troopers

Giant arachnids prove to be an invincible opponent with zero tolerance for things with less than four legs in director Verhoeven's comic-book styled, epic slaughter fest. The futuristic, fascist coed Mobile Infantry, led by renegade Commander Rasczak (Ironside), does battle with the sinister anthropods, usually resulting in much human bloodshed. The high body count includes many young actors, but unlike Verhoeven's *Showgirls,* their careers should remain unscathed. The acting is straight out of a Mattel toy factory, but the action and confrontations with the enemy insects are a thrill thanks to computer-animated special effects. Cheesy, bloody good fun based on the 1959 novel by Robert A. Heinlein. It's hard to find a flaw in this DVD. In every way the quality is excellent. You won't see any grain or artifacts. The colors are vibrant but not oversaturated, and there is no noticeable bleed anywhere on the disc. Perfect blacks, excellent contrast, and consistent brightness levels combine to give this DVD a visual punch not found on many others. The soundtrack is also excellent, with incredibly crisp highs, rock-the-house lows, and perfectly mastered Surround tracks. Loads of special features including commentary that's both informative and entertaining. Use this one to show off your system—unless the kiddies are around. —*JO*
Movie: ♫♫♫ **DVD:** ♫♫♫♫
Columbia Tristar Home Video (Cat #71719, UPC #043396717190). Widescreen (1.85:1) letterboxed. Dolby Digital 5.1; Dolby Surround. Keepcase. *LANG:* English (DD5.1; DS); French. *SUB:* English; Spanish; French. *FEATURES:* 28 chapter links • Theatrical trailer • Additional scenes • "Making of" documentary • Behind-the-scenes footage • Screen tests • Commentary.
1997 (R) 129m/C Casper Van Dien, Michael Ironside, Neil Patrick Harris, Clancy Brown, Denise Richards, Dina Meyer, Jake Busey, Patrick Muldoon, Seth Gilliam, Rue McClanahan, Marshall Bell, Eric Bruskotter, Blake Lindsley, Anthony Michael Ruivivar, Dean Norris, Dale Dye; *D:* Paul Verhoeven; *W:* Edward Neumeier; *C:* Jost Vacano; *M:* Basil Poledouris. *AWARDS: NOM:* Academy Awards '97: Best Visual Effects; MTV Movie Awards '98: Best Action Sequence.

State Fair

The second version of the glossy slice of Americana about a family at the Iowa State Fair features plenty of great songs by Rodgers and Hammerstein. Adapted from the 1933 screen version of Phil Stong's novel and remade again in 1962. Fox continues to put out gorgeous DVDs of their older musicals. The colors on this

1945 film are stunning and combined with some gutsy contrast, the image at times looks nearly 3-D. The blacks are as true as the color. The sound may seem like nothing special, but is quite pleasant and most likely a true representation of the original soundtrack. —JO **AKA:** It Happened One Summer.

Movie: 🐾🐾🐾 **DVD:** 🐾🐾🐾🐾
20th Century Fox (Cat #4110867, UPC #0861621086879). Full frame. Stereo. $24.98. Keepcase. *LANG:* English. *SUB:* English; Spanish. *CAP:* English. *FEATURES:* 28 chapter links • Theatrical trailer.
1945 100m/C Charles Winninger, Jeanne Crain, Dana Andrews, Vivian Blaine, Dick Haymes, Fay Bainter, Frank McHugh, Percy Kilbride, Donald Meek, William Marshall, Harry (Henry) Morgan; **D:** Walter Lang; **W:** Oscar Hammerstein; **C:** Leon Shamroy; **M:** Richard Rodgers, Oscar Hammerstein. *AWARDS:* Academy Awards '45: Best Song ("It Might as Well Be Spring"); *NOM:* Academy Awards '45: Scoring of a Musical.

Stay Awake

The ghost of an executed rapist-murderer returns to attack eight girls and their teacher in the remote St. Mary's School for Girls. The effects are bloody, dark, and non-frightening. Director John Bernard's relentless use of the stalking camera point of view quickly becomes tiresome. On DVD, the night scenes hold up well but that's not nearly enough to recommend this generic slasher horror. —MM
Movie: 🐾 **DVD:** 🐾🐾►
Image Entertainment (Cat #ID6323NGDVD, UPC #014381632323). Full frame. Dolby Digital Mono. $24.99. Snapper. *LANG:* English. *FEATURES:* 12 chapter links • Theatrical trailer.
1987 (R) 90m/C *SA* Shirley Jane Harris, Tanya Gordon, Jayne Hutton, Heath Porter; **D:** John Bernard.

Stealing Home

A washed-up baseball player (Harmon) learns that his former babysitter (Foster), who was also his first love and inspiration, has committed suicide. Their bittersweet relationship is told through flashbacks. Given the story's curious construction, the two stars never appear in the same scene.
Movie: 🐾🐾 **DVD:** NYR
Warner Home Video, Inc. (Cat #11818). Full frame. Dolby Digital Stereo. $19.98. Snapper. *LANG:* English; French. *SUB:* French. *CAP:* English.
1988 (PG-13) 98m/C Mark Harmon, Jodie Foster, William McNamara, Blair Brown, Harold Ramis, Jonathan Silverman, John Shea, Helen Hunt, Richard Jenkins, Ted Ross, Thatcher Goodwin, Yvette Croskey; **D:** Steven Kampmann, Will Aldis; **W:** Steven Kampmann, Will Aldis; **C:** Bobby Byrne; **M:** David Foster.

Steamboat Bill, Jr.

Bill Canfield Jr. (Keaton) returns to his father (Torrence) and is woefully unfit to take over the family riverboat. That doesn't stop him from falling for the daughter (Byron) of his dad's competitor (Lewis). The first half is fairly slowgoing but the film ends with a hurricane that inspires some of Keaton's most famous routines, including the incredible falling wall stunt. The DVD was made from a beautiful print and is virtually flawless. The disc also includes two shorter films, *Convict 13* (1920) and *Daydreams* (1922). One of the best Keaton DVDs. —MM
Movie: 🐾🐾🐾► **DVD:** 🐾🐾🐾►
Image Entertainment (Cat #K135DVD, UPC #738329013523). Full frame. $29.99. Snapper. *LANG:* Silent. *SUB:* English intertitles. *FEATURES:* 26 chapter links.
1928 111m/B Buster Keaton, Ernest Torrence, Marion Byron, Tom Lewis; **D:** Charles Reisner; **W:** Carl Harbaugh; **C:** Bert Haines, Devereaux Jennings.

Steele's Law

A loner cop (Williamson) is forced to take the law into his own hands to track down an insane international assassin.
Movie: 🐾🐾 **DVD:** NYR
Digital Versatile Disc Ltd. (Cat #115). Full frame. Mono. $19.95. Keepcase. *FEATURES:* Trailers.
1991 (R) 90m/C Fred Williamson, Bo Svenson, Doran Inghram, Phyllis Cicero; **D:** Fred Williamson; **W:** Charles Eric Johnson; **C:** David Blood; **M:** Mike Logan.

Stella Dallas

An uneducated woman lets go of the daughter she loves when she realizes that her ex-husband can give the girl more advantages. What could be sentimental turns out believable and worthwhile under Vidor's steady hand. Stanwyck never makes a wrong step. It's adapted from a novel by Olive Higgins Prouty and was remade in 1989 as *Stella* with Bette Midler.
Movie: 🐾🐾🐾 **DVD:** NYR
HBO Home Video (Cat #90760). Full frame. Dolby Digital Mono. $24.98. Snapper. *LANG:* English; French; German; Italian; Spanish. *SUB:* French; Spanish. *FEATURES:* Cast and crew thumbnail bios.
1937 106m/B Barbara Stanwyck, Anne Shirley, John Boles, Alan Hale, Marjorie Main; **D:** King Vidor; **W:** Sarah Y. Mason, Victor Heerman; **C:** Rudolph Mate; **M:** Alfred Newman. *AWARDS: NOM:* Academy Awards '37: Best Actress (Stanwyck), Best Supporting Actress (Shirley).

Stella Maris

Unity Blake (Pickford) is the plain-Jane orphan who works for the Risca household. She's in love with John Risca (Tearle), who's in love with brave, gorgeous, crippled Stella Maris (Pickford). Yes, the first diva of the silver screen does double duty in a typically overwrought melodrama. Despite a few nicks, the DVD image is very good. Made from excellent original materials, the film actually looks much better than some silents that were made much later. Sound is acceptable. —MM
Movie: 🐾🐾► **DVD:** 🐾🐾🐾
Image Entertainment (Cat #ID5930MLSD-VD, UPC #014381593020). Full frame. Dolby Digital Stereo. $29.99. Snapper. *LANG:* Silent. *SUB:* English intertitles. *FEATURES:* 13 chapter links • Home movies and newsreel clips.
1918 100m/B Mary Pickford, Conway Tearle, Camille Ankewich, Ida Waterman, Herbert Standing; **D:** Marshall Neilan; **W:** Frances Marion; **C:** Walter Stradling.

The Stepford Wives

Few films—and even fewer horror films—become part of the language, but "Stepford" is an all-purpose adjective for robotic mindlessness. It should be. Ira Levin's tale is one of the defining works of late–20th century American horror. His novel and William Goldman's screen adaptation are companion pieces to *Rosemary's Baby*, sharing the same respectable affluent villains and, more importantly, perfectly tuned paranoia. Director Forbes effectively creates menace out of the commonplace and ordinary. In the lead, Katherine Ross may be too restrained, but that's all right; the supporting cast (Prentiss, Newman, Louise) picks up the slack. Beyond the obvious feminist message, the film is really about the horror of bland comfortable suburban conformity. And in a way, the passage of time has proved the truth of Levin's central idea. Today, successful middle-aged corporate executives don't have "Stepford" wives; they have "trophy" wives. Is there a difference? The no-frills DVD makes only a marginal improvement in image and sound over the Anchor Bay tape. The excessive graininess comes from the original, not the transfer. —MM
Movie: 🐾🐾🐾► **DVD:** 🐾🐾
Anchor Bay (Cat #DV10326, UPC #013131032697). Widescreen (1.74:1) letterboxed. Dolby Digital Mono. $24.98. Keepcase. *LANG:* English. *FEATURES:* 9 chapter links.
1975 115m/C Katharine Ross, Paula Prentiss, Peter Masterson, Nanette Newman, Patrick O'Neal, Tina Louise, Dee Wallace Stone, William Prince, Mary Stuart Masterson, Carol Rossen; **D:** Bryan Forbes; **W:** William Goldman; **C:** Owen Roizman; **M:** Michael Small.

Stephen King's The Night Flier

You'd think that a vampire (Moss) who learns to fly a Cessna would update his wardrobe, but this one wears the full-length satin-lined cape. Though this made-for-cable feature is based on a King short story, it owes almost as much to *Kolchak, The Night Stalker*. Richard Dees (Ferrer) is a supermarket tabloid reporter who, after baring his burnt-out soul at length, goes on the trail of a bloodsucker who finds his victims at small airports. Dees's more enthusiastic competition is Katherine Blair

(Entwisle, who looks like a perky young Phoebe Cates). The effects are graphic enough to satisfy gore fans, particularly in the last reel, but some of the early physical action is stiffly choreographed. The film has a bright polish, clever structure, acting that's well above average, and a bang-up finish. It did so well on cable that it earned a theatrical release. The DVD looks fine, handling the dark scenes with ease, and all of the key scenes are very dark. A medium step up from VHS tape. —MM **AKA:** The Night Flier.
Movie: 🎬🎬🎬 **DVD:** 🎬🎬🎬
HBO Home Video (Cat #91466, UPC #026359146626). Widescreen letterboxed. Dolby Digital 5.1 Surround Stereo. $24.98. Snapper. *LANG:* English. *FEATURES:* 24 chapter links • Production factoids • Scene preview capability in scene selection • Theatrical trailer.
1996 (R) 97m/C Michael H. Moss, Miguel Ferrer, Julie Entwisle, Dan Monahan, John Bennes, Beverly Skinner, Rob Wilds, Richard Olsen, Elizabeth McCormick; **D:** Mark Pavia; **W:** Mark Pavia, Jack O'Donnell; **C:** David Connell; **M:** Brian Keane.

Stephen King's The Stand

Since King's huge novel has been a best-seller twice, everyone must be familiar with the story of an America decimated by "superflu" and turned into a battleground between Good and Evil. This adaptation, written by King and directed by Mick Garris, is faithful in tone and form to the fiction. Even at six hours, though, it still leaves out some material. Fans of the novel will also see where it cuts some corners in the big scenes, most notably those in the corn fields, and those are even more evident on DVD. Overall, the image is not that much better than VHS tape, but with a work of this length, the accessibility of the medium is important. For fans, the commentary track has all the stuff they already know and some that they don't. Sound is good. The entire work is on one double-sided, dual-layer disc. —MM **AKA:** The Stand.
Movie: 🎬🎬🎬▶ **DVD:** 🎬🎬🎬▶
Artisan Entertainment (Cat #10517, UPC #017153105179). Full frame. Dolby Digital 2.0 Surround Stereo. $39.98. Keepcase. *LANG:* English. *FEATURES:* 86 chapter links • Commentary: King, Garris, Lowe, Dee, Ferrer, Sheridan, Pat McMahon • Booklet.
1994 360m/C Jamey Sheridan, Ruby Dee, Gary Sinise, Molly Ringwald, Miguel Ferrer, Laura San Giacomo, Rob Lowe, Adam Storke, Matt Frewer, Corin "Corky" Nemec, Ray Walston, Bill Fagerbakke, Ossie Davis, Shawnee Smith, Rick Aviles, John (Joe Bob Briggs) Bloom, Michael Lookinland, Ed Harris, Kathy Bates, Kareem Abdul-Jabbar, Stephen King, Sam Raimi; **D:** Mick Garris; **W:** Stephen King; **C:** Edward Pei; **M:** W.G. Snuffy Walden.

Stephen King's The Storm of the Century

A small New England island town is cut off from civilization by a snowstorm. A mysterious figure emerges from the flurries to extend the offer of respite, but only if they let him name his price. He is Andre Linoge, played by Colm Feore. He's asked, "That's a French name, isn't it?" Soon enough, a series of murders ups the ante—and the suspense. In true Yankee tradition, the townsfolk will have to fend for themselves against the elements and the unknown. The sounds are authoritatively orchestrated and the sights are generally brilliant as ice sculpture. Jail cell shots, heavy on foreground lighting, were obviously difficult to transfer, but the partially flattened results actually look more spooky than unappealing. The dual-sided disc is heavily, even superfluously laden with extras. There are glossy stills on the menus, and the main screen is jazzed up with animated lightning and threatening boom-slosh-and-whish noises. A kangaroo logo leads you to an ad for the book of the same name. Second-channel comments by King and director Baxley tend towards the awkwardly prosaic. The writer, after introducing himself with "I wrote what you're looking at," is quick to disavow slapping his name on top of every adaptation of his works, in case anyone suspects him of vanity. He claims it's a marketing gimmick. The director keeps saying the story is "all about manipulation." Well, considering that all of King's material runs along those lines, duh. —JK **AKA:** Storm of the Century.
Movie: 🎬🎬▶ **DVD:** 🎬🎬🎬🎬
Trimark Home Video (Cat #7035D, UPC #031398703532). Full frame. Dolby Digital Surround 2.0. $29.99. Keepcase. *LANG:* English. *SUB:* Spanish; English. *CAP:* English. *FEATURES:* 30 chapter links (15 per side) • Animated interactive menus • Commentary: Stephen King and director Craig Baxley • Star filmographies.
1999 (PG-13) 247m/C Colm Feore, Timothy Daly, Debrah Farentino, Casey Siemaszko, Jeffrey DeMunn, Richard Blackburn; **D:** Craig R. Baxley; **W:** Stephen King; **C:** David Connell; **M:** Gary Chang.

Stephen King's The Tommyknockers

One of King's better evil-underground-monster tales translates well to video. Bobbie (Marg Helgenberger) uncovers something on her farm. It gives various inhabitants of Haven, ME, strange new creativity and intelligence, among other powers. Unfortunately, the best inventions of King's fiction don't make it to the screen. The double-sided DVD contains the full-length TV mini-series. It's longer than the VHS tape and looks marginally better, most noticeably in the big green-light finish. Sound is about the same. —MM **AKA:** The Tommyknockers.
Movie: 🎬🎬🎬 **DVD:** 🎬🎬▶
Trimark Home Video (Cat #VM6842D, UPC #031398684237). Full frame. Dolby Digi-

tal Surround Stereo. $24.98. Keepcase. *LANG:* English. *SUB:* French; Spanish. *CAP:* English. *FEATURES:* 30 chapter links • Trailer.
1993 (R) 120m/C Jimmy Smits, Marg Helgenberger, Joanna Cassidy, E.G. Marshall, Traci Lords, John Ashton, Allyce Beasley, Cliff DeYoung, Robert Carradine, Leon Woods, Paul McIver; **D:** John Power; **W:** Lawrence D. Cohen; **M:** Christopher Franke.

Stephen King's Thinner

Holland takes all the meat out of this supernatural horror by turning it into a formulaic pursuit-of-justice bore. Porcine lawyer Billy Halleck (Burke) accidentally hits a gypsy with his car and is cursed with a case of perpetual weight loss. Conveniently for Billy, the client he has just gotten an acquittal for is local mobster Richie "The Hammer" Ginelli (Mantegna), who is now determined to save him. Ponderous plot and lackluster-looking latex is redeemed by decent acting. King makes his requisite cameo as Dr. Bangor (get it, Maine?). Originally published in 1984 under King's pseudonym Richard Bachman. The DVD transfer wavers between good and bad. The image is sharp when bright but grainy, and consequently lacking sharpness, when the picture is dark. Colors are close to the original theatrical presentation, but they too have problems in the darker scenes and bleed a little. The sound is average with little separation and not enough drive to the low end. —JO **AKA:** Thinner.
Movie: 🎬🎬 **DVD:** 🎬🎬▶
Republic Pictures Home Video (Cat #46296, UPC #017153629620). Widescreen (1.85:1) letterboxed. Stereo. $24.98. Keepcase. *LANG:* English. *SUB:* French; Spanish. *CAP:* English. *FEATURES:* 33 chapter links • Featurette • Audio commentary.
1996 (R) 92m/C Robert John Burke, Joe Mantegna, Lucinda Jenney, Michael Constantine, Kari Wuhrer, John Horton, Sam Freed, Daniel von Bargen, Elizabeth Franz, Joy Lentz, Jeff Ware; **Cameos:** Stephen King; **D:** Tom Holland; **W:** Michael McDowell, Tom Holland; **C:** Kees Van Oostrum; **M:** Daniel Licht.

Stepmom

The opening scenes make it look like a comedic catfight-filled ride. Harris is a divorced dad with two kids, a supermom ex-wife (Sarandon), and a glamorous new girlfriend (Roberts), whose career seems more important than the kids. Jibes and glares are traded by the two women until mom is stricken with some form of untreatable terminal cancer. This changes the story from broad comedy to emotional drama as Sarandon must train the younger woman to be the new mom. Columbus seems comfortable with the shift, and manages to keep everything upbeat. The script, penned by five writers, becomes more cliched as the film goes on, but stays just this side of chick-flick. On the DVD the colors seem even warmer than in the theatre and the image is very sharp. Blacks are true and contrast is excellent. The movie is dialogue driven and with rare exception, the Surround is very limited, used mainly to enhance the music. —JO

Movie: ♫♫♫ **DVD:** ♫♫♫
Columbia Tristar Home Video (Cat #02852, UPC #043396028524). Widescreen (2.35:1) letterboxed; full frame. Dolby Digital 5.0; Dolby Surround. NSL. Keepcase. *LANG:* English. *SUB:* English. *CAP:* English. *FEATURES:* 29 chapter links ● Theatrical trailers ● Cast and filmmakers bios ● "Making of" featurette ● Behind-the-scenes footage ● Filmographies.
1998 (PG-13) 124m/C Julia Roberts, Susan Sarandon, Ed Harris, Jena Malone, Liam Aiken, Lynn Whitfield, Darrell Larson, Mary Louise Wilson; *D:* Chris Columbus; *W:* Jessie Nelson, Steven Rogers, Ronald Bass, Gigi Levangie, Karen Leigh Hopkins; *C:* Donald McAlpine; *M:* John Williams. *AWARDS:* National Board of Review Awards '98: Best Supporting Actor (Harris); *NOM:* Golden Globe Awards '99: Best Actress—Drama (Sarandon).

Stigmata

Gabriel Byrne, who played the devil in 1999's other end-of-the-world religious thriller, *End of Days*, plays a priest who's on the other side in this one. Frankie Paige (Arquette) is an atheistic good-time girl who receives the Stigmata, or wounds of Christ. Father Kiernan (Byrne), a Vatican investigator, must protect her from Cardinal Houseman (Pryce), who thinks that she has a secret which will destroy the church. Both image and sound are excellent, capturing the inventive special effects without any noticeable flaws. Director Wainwright's commentary track is nicely done. —MM

Movie: ♫♫♫ **DVD:** ♫♫♫▸
MGM Home Entertainment (Cat #907451). Widescreen (2.35:1) letterboxed. Dolby Digital 5.1 Surround Stereo. $24.98. Keepcase. *LANG:* English; French. *SUB:* French; Spanish. *CAP:* English. *FEATURES:* 28 chapter links ● Deleted scene ● Music video ● Commentary: Rupert Wainwright.
1999 (R) 103m/C Patricia Arquette, Gabriel Byrne, Jonathan Pryce, Portia de Rossi, Patrick Muldoon, Nia Long, Thomas Kopache, Rade Serbedzija, Enrico Colantoni, Dick Latessa, Ann Cusack; *D:* Rupert Wainwright; *W:* Rick Ramage, Tom Lazarus; *C:* Jeffrey L. Kimball; *M:* Elia Cmiral. *AWARDS:* *NOM:* Golden Raspberry Awards '99: Worst Supporting Actor (Byrne).

Still Twisted

Hosted by Bryan Brown *(FX, Breaker Morant)*, *Still Twisted* is a second volume of *Twisted* tales, an Australian version of *The Twilight Zone*, courtesy of the Nine Network Australia. Four stand-alone stories, each running approximately 20 minutes, unfold in the spirit of *The Twilight Zone*. In the first Nadine Garner learns a terrible lesson as a hit and run driver in "The Crossing," while Dee Smart seduces a hitman, Robert Mammone, into taking revenge in "Cold Revenge," and in the strongest of the four stories, Claudia Karvan is an escaped mental patient who meets her match in "One Way Ticket." A final stanza entitled "Dancing Partners" doesn't deliver the same biting edge as its companions. Attractive DVD presentation from original television broadcast material. Minimal chapter marker support and no biographical material, which would have been helpful considering the strictly Australian cast. —RT

Movie: ♫♫▸ **DVD:** ♫♫▸
Image Entertainment (Cat #5705PZ, UPC #014381570526). Full frame. Dolby Digital Stereo. $24.99. Snapper. *LANG:* English. *FEATURES:* 18 chapter links.
19?? 80m/C AU Nadine Garner, Dee Smart, Robert Mammone, Claudia Karvan.

The Sting

Newman and Redford together again in this sparkling story of a pair of con artists in 1930s Chicago. They set out to fleece a big-time racketeer, pitting brain against brawn and pistol. Very inventive, excellent acting, with Scott Joplin's wonderful ragtime music adapted by Marvin Hamlisch. The same directorial and acting team from *Butch Cassidy and the Sundance Kid* triumphs again. Joplin's life and music might have made a good documentary subject, but nothing has been done about it on this DVD. At least the mono sound has been updated to a much fuller Dolby Digital version and the music itself sounds very good. Image quality is also excellent with very good details, exacting colors, and true blacks. —JO

Movie: ♫♫♫▸ **DVD:** ♫♫♫▸
Universal Studios Home Video (Cat #20165, UPC #025192016523). Full frame. Dolby Digital 2.0 Mono. $24.98. Keepcase. *LANG:* English; Spanish; French. *SUB:* Spanish. *CAP:* English. *FEATURES:* 16 chapter links ● Cast and filmmaker bios ● Production notes.
1973 (PG) 129m/C Paul Newman, Robert Redford, Robert Shaw, Charles Durning, Eileen Brennan, Harold Gould, Ray Walston; *D:* George Roy Hill; *W:* David S. Ward; *C:* Robert L. Surtees; *M:* Marvin Hamlisch. *AWARDS:* Academy Awards '73: Best Art Direction/Set Decoration, Best Costume Design, Best Director (Hill), Best Film Editing, Best Picture, Best Story & Screenplay, Original Song Score and/or Adaptation; Directors Guild of America Awards '73: Best Director (Hill); *NOM:* Academy Awards '73: Best Actor (Redford), Best Cinematography, Best Sound.

Stir Crazy

Two down-on-their luck losers (Pryor and Wilder) find themselves convicted of a rob-

bery they didn't commit and sentenced to 120 years behind bars with a mean assortment of inmates. The stars' second teaming (after *Silver Streak*) isn't quite as successful but still provides plenty of laughs. This disc contains a nice 16x9 enhanced widescreen transfer that restores the film's original 1.85:1 aspect ratio, as well as a good-looking pan-and-scan transfer. The picture has a good level of detail with well-defined edges. The film's color scheme looks slightly dated but colors themselves are vibrant and vivid, creating a pleasing overall picture quality that is much better than the VHS version. The soundtrack is well produced giving it a natural quality. —GH

Movie: ♫♫▸ **DVD:** ♫♫♫▸
Columbia Tristar Home Video (Cat #3294, UPC #043396032941). Full frame; widescreen (1.85:1) anamorphic. Dolby Digital Mono. $29.98. Keepcase. *LANG:* English. *SUB:* Chinese; Korean; Portuguese; Spanish; Thai. *CAP:* English. *FEATURES:* 28 chapter links ● Cast and crew thumbnail bios ● Theatrical trailer.
1980 (R) 111m/C Richard Pryor, Gene Wilder, Nicolas Coster, Lee Purcell, Craig T. Nelson, JoBeth Williams; *D:* Sidney Poitier; *W:* Bruce Jay Friedman; *C:* Fred Schuler; *M:* Tom Scott, Michael Masser.

Stir of Echoes

At a party, Tom Witzky (Bacon) allows himself to be hypnotized by his sister-in-law Lisa (Douglas). The experience taps him into a supernatural world and he has visions of a murder that took place years before. Working from a fine Richard Matheson novel, first-time director David Koepp does excellent work. On DVD, the realistic, lived-in look that Koepp gives the action is re-created faithfully, giving the supernatural plot the same strong sense of "reality" that makes Matheson's fiction so memorable. It's similar to *Seven*, but not so affected. Sound is excellent. —MM

Movie: ♫♫♫ **DVD:** ♫♫♫
Artisan Entertainment (Cat #10197). Widescreen letterboxed. Dolby Digital 5.1 Surround Stereo. $29.98. Keepcase. *LANG:* English. *FEATURES:* 30 chapter links ● TV spots ● Trailer ● 2 featurettes ● Music video ● Commentary: David Koepp ● Production notes ● Cast and crew thumbnail bios.
1999 (R) 110m/C Kevin Bacon, Illeana Douglas, Kathryn Erbe, Liza Weil, Kevin Dunn, Conor O'Farrell, Zachary David Cope, Jenny Morrison, Eddie Bo Smith Jr.; *D:* David Koepp; *W:* David Koepp; *C:* Fred Murphy; *M:* James Newton Howard.

Stolen Kisses

The third in the Antoine Doinel series (following *400 Blows*) is perhaps Truffaut's most charming romantic film. *Stolen Kisses* picks up with Doinel leaving military prison and returning to his old ways and Paris neighborhood. He embarks on a series of ill-fated jobs, first as a hotel nightwatchman and finally as a private

detective. Doinel's awkward adventures with women continue as well, as he's torn between a serious-minded young violinist (Jade) and a glamorous, married older woman (Seyrig). Made during Truffaut's involvement in a political crisis involving the sack of Cinematique Francais director Henri Langlois. Truffaut dedicated the film to him and to the Cinematique. The DVD image is sharp yet warm, and the sound clear and sharp. The soundtrack comes through nicely. —AB **AKA:** Baisers Voles.
Movie: 🎬🎬🎬► **DVD:** 🎬🎬🎬►
WinStar Home Entertainment (Cat #FLV5118, UPC #2091751182). Full frame. $29.98. Keepcase. *LANG:* French. *SUB:* English. *FEATURES:* 6 chapter links ▪ Production credits ▪ Filmographies and awards ▪ 10 vintage Truffaut trailers ▪ Tribute to Jean-Pierre Leaud.
1968 90m/C *FR* Jean-Pierre Leaud, Delphine Seyrig, Michael (Michel) Lonsdale, Claude Jade; **D:** Francois Truffaut; **W:** Francois Truffaut, Claude de Givray; **C:** Denys Clerval; **M:** Antoine Duhamel. *AWARDS:* National Society of Film Critics Awards '69: Best Director (Truffaut); *NOM:* Academy Awards '68: Best Foreign Film.

Stonewall

Fictional account of the 1969 police raid on the Stonewall Inn (a Greenwich Village gay bar), which is considered to have launched the modern gay-rights movement. White-bread Midwestern activist Matty Dean (Weller) arrives in New York and gets thrown in jail for defending streetwise drag queen LaMiranda (Diaz) from harassing cops. They become lovers but Matty is also involved with conservative prepster Ethan (Corbalis), who thinks flamboyant queens give the gay movement a bad name. Meanwhile, the drag queens at the mob-backed Stonewall are getting fed up with police raids and brutal treatment. The film is adapted from Martin Duberman's social history. Director Finch died during the final editing stages.
Movie: 🎬🎬🎬 **DVD:** NYR
WinStar Home Entertainment (Cat #5136). Full frame. Dolby Digital Stereo. $29.98. Keepcase. *FEATURES:* Cast and crew thumbnail bios ▪ Production notes ▪ Trailer.
1995 (R) 93m/C Frederick Weller, Guillermo Diaz, Brendan Corbalis, Bruce MacVittie, Duane Boutle, Peter Ratray, Luis Guzman; **D:** Nigel Finch; **W:** Rikki Beadle Blair; **C:** Chris Seager; **M:** Michael Kamen.

Storm over Asia

This original story, made in the still newly Soviet Russia by State Film School graduates, is set in 1918 on the outer reaches of the Russian steppes. One Mongolian boy (Valeri Inkizhinov) comes into possession of a talisman that proclaims the lineage of Genghis Khan (hence the original Russian title of *Potomok Chingus-khana* or *The Heir of Genghis Khan*). British occupation troops discover the lad's find and exploit him as a puppet ruler to keep the

locals in line. He eventually rebels, becoming a true leader of his people. The film takes on a documentary feel by having been shot on location in the lead actor's hometown, with help from the young man's relatives. For the climactic uprise Pudovkin packs into one screen what Abel Gance only attempted with the help of three in *Napoleon*. The spirit of revolution appears by a trick of editing, as a nearly mythic band of Mongol warriors fade into view and roll across the landscape like windblown leaves. Amid frenetic, associative editing that predates music video quick-cuts by half a century, any serious defects in the print source (including sizeable nitrate bubbles and repair seams) only add to the sense of explosive destruction. The experience brings on a true thrill of propagandistic fervor, without trying to bludgeon the audience into submission, like action adventure films of today. The score is a new chamber orchestra performance. At 125 minutes the cut is promised to be a half-hour longer than any previous U.S. release. —JK **AKA:** The Heir to Genghis Khan.
Movie: 🎬🎬🎬🎬 **DVD:** 🎬🎬🎬►
Image Entertainment (Cat #ID4672DSDVD, UPC #014381467222). Full frame. Dolby Digital Stereo. $24.99. Snapper. *LANG:* Russian. *SUB:* English. *FEATURES:* 18 chapter links ▪ Scene access menu.
1928 70m/B *RU* I. Inkizhinov, Valeri Inkizhinov, A. Christiakov, A. Dedinstev, V. Tzoppi, Paulina Belinskaya; **D:** Vsevolod Pudovkin; **C:** Anatoli Golovnya.

The Story Lady

After she moves into a room in her daughter's suburban home, retiree Grace McQueen (Tandy) finds a new career reading children's stories on a public access cable channel. The show becomes so popular that greedy network executives try to exploit her. The star is at her grandmotherly best, but the entire film is saccharine. Production values are on a par with made-for-TV fare so the image gains little on DVD. —MM
Movie: 🎬🎬 **DVD:** 🎬🎬
Image Entertainment (Cat #ID5568BVDVD, UPC #014381556827). Full frame. Dolby Digital Stereo. $24.99. Snapper. *LANG:* English. *FEATURES:* 16 chapter links.
1993 120m/C Jessica Tandy, Lisa Jakub, Ed Begley Jr., Charles Durning, Stephanie Zimbalist; **D:** Larry Elikann; **M:** Leo Holdridge.

The Story of G.I. Joe

This late arrival to home video is one of the finest World War II films. It's based on the newspaper columns of Ernie Pyle (Meredith). The essentially plotless story follows him as he accompanies the men of C Company, 18th Infantry, through Tunisia, Sicily, and Italy. The other main characters are Lt. Bill Walker (Mitchum, who received his only Oscar nomination for this role) and Sgt. Warnicki (Steele).

Many members of the supporting cast are real soldiers who were playing themselves. Some of them, like the real Pyle, were killed in the Pacific before the film was released. The black-and-white cinematography is excellent and though the DVD is made from an original that's been nicked up a bit, it looks fine. In fact, the flaws add character to the world that these "mud-rain-frost-and-wind boys" inhabit. When the film was released, *Time* magazine called it "the least glamorous war picture ever made" and the record still stands. It's a low-key companion piece to Wellman's *Battleground,* still unavailable on disc. —MM
Movie: 🎬🎬🎬🎬 **DVD:** 🎬🎬🎬
Image Entertainment (Cat #ID9058VM DVD, UPC #014381905823). Full frame. Dolby Digital Mono. $24.99. Snapper. *LANG:* English. *FEATURES:* 18 chapter links ▪ Liner notes by James Tobin ▪ Archival footage of Pyle interviewing soldiers ▪ Gallery of Pyle columns.
1945 109m/B Burgess Meredith, Robert Mitchum, Wally Cassell, Billy (William) Benedict, William Murphy, Jimmy Lloyd, Fred Steele, William Self, Jack Reilly, Tito Renaldo, Hal Boyle, Chris Cunningham, Jack Foisie, George Lah, Bob Landry, Clete Roberts, Robert Rueben, Don Whitehead; **D:** William A. Wellman; **W:** Leopold Atlas, Guy Endore, Philip Stevenson, Ernie Pyle; **C:** Russell Metty; **M:** Louis Applebaum, Ann Ronell; ***Technical Advisor:*** Ernie Pyle.

The Story of Us

Director Reiner follows Ben (Willis) and Katie (Pfeiffer) through their long courtship, marriage, children, problems, breakups, etc. He uses flashbacks to crosscut through time, but the end result is slow and not as involving as it needs to be, despite both stars doing serious work—perhaps too serious. Domestic stories such as this translate well to the small screen and the DVD is essentially flawless, though not noticeably sharper than VHS tape. The stereo soundtrack is more than adequate for Eric Clapton's spare, minimalist score. The main difference is in Rob Reiner's commentary track. He's appropriately low-keyed and does not feel the need to fill every second with pearls of wisdom. Of course, he is thoroughly complimentary to everyone and, for the most part, sticks to matters of character and the business of filmmaking. —MM
Movie: 🎬🎬► **DVD:** 🎬🎬🎬
Universal Studios Home Video (Cat #20711, UPC #025192071126). Widescreen (1.85:1) letterboxed. Dolby Digital 5.1 Surround Stereo; Dolby Surround Stereo. $24.98. Keepcase. *LANG:* English; French. *CAP:* English. *FEATURES:* 18 chapter links ▪ "Making of" featurette ▪ Commentary: Rob Reiner ▪ Production notes ▪ Cast and crew thumbnail biographies ▪ Theatrical trailer. DVD-ROM contains other features.
1999 (R) 98m/C Bruce Willis, Michelle Pfeiffer, Rita Wilson, Paul Reiser, Rob Reiner, Tim Matheson, Julie Hagerty, Jayne

Meadows, Tom Poston, Betty White, Red Buttons; *D:* Rob Reiner; *W:* Alan Zweibel, Jessie Nelson; *C:* Michael Chapman; *M:* Eric Clapton, Marc Shaiman.

Strange Days

On anything smaller than a full-sized theatre screen, Kathryn Bigelow's ambitious sf action movie loses something. She creates a cluttered future (now past) where hustler Lenny Nero (Fiennes) deals in "wire-tripping" experiences in which his clients are able to share the ultimate vicarious thrills, reliving actual events by those who participated in them. The DVD re-creates the film with no bothersome flaws, but it's still not as impressive as the theatrical version. The choice of extras is less than completely successful. Beyond two deleted scenes, the main addition is the director's discussion of the opening "p.o.v." scene. It is important to the story and technically detailed, but she talks over the material that comes after it, so it is meant only to those already familiar with the film. Those flaws notwithstanding, this is a fine, intelligent film on any medium. Recommended. —*MM*
Movie: 🎬🎬🎬 *DVD:* 🎬🎬🎬
Twentieth Century Fox Home Entertainment (Cat #4110425, UPC #086162104 251). Widescreen (2.35:1) letterboxed. Dolby Digital 5.1 Surround Stereo; Dolby Digital Surround Stereo. $29.98. *LANG:* English; French. *SUB:* English; Spanish. *CAP:* English. *FEATURES:* 22 chapter links • Teaser • Trailer • 2 deleted scenes • Commentary: Kathryn Bigelow on opening scene.
1995 (R) 145m/C Ralph Fiennes, Angela Bassett, Juliette Lewis, Tom Sizemore, Michael Wincott, Brigitte Bako, Vincent D'Onofrio, William Fichtner, Richard Edson, Glenn Plummer, Josef Sommer; *D:* Kathryn Bigelow; *W:* James Cameron, Jay Cocks; *C:* Matthew F. Leonetti; *M:* Graeme Revell.

The Strange Love of Martha Ivers

Douglas is good in his screen debut as the wimpy spouse of unscrupulous Stanwyck. She shines as the woman who must stay with Douglas because of a crime she committed long ago. Tough, dark, melodramatic film noir.
Movie: 🎬🎬🎬 *DVD:* NYR
Parade (Cat #55246). Full frame. $17.98. Keepcase.
1946 117m/B Barbara Stanwyck, Van Heflin, Kirk Douglas, Lizabeth Scott, Judith Anderson; *D:* Lewis Milestone; *W:* Robert Rossen; *C:* Victor Milner; *M:* Miklos Rozsa. *AWARDS: NOM:* Academy Awards '46: Best Story.

The Stranger

Notably conventional feature for Welles is swell entertainment nonetheless. A war crimes tribunal sets Nazi thug Shayne free hoping he'll lead them to his superior, Welles. Robinson trails Shayne through Europe and South America to a small town in Connecticut. Tight suspense made on a tight budget saved Welles's directorial career. On disc, the black-and-white image is not the sharpest you've ever seen, but it has been exceptionally well preserved and, after all, this is Orson Welles. The blacks hold true and this one is almost as shadowy as *Lady from Shanghai* or *Touch of Evil.* —*MM*
Movie: 🎬🎬🎬▶ *DVD:* 🎬🎬🎬▶
Parade (Cat #55256). Full frame. Dolby Digital Mono. $17.98. *LANG:* English. *SUB:* Japanese. *FEATURES:* Cast and crew thumbnail bios • Critical comments • 11 chapter links.
1946 95m/B Edward G. Robinson, Loretta Young, Martha Wentworth, Konstantin Shayne, Richard Long, Orson Welles; *D:* Orson Welles; *W:* Victor Trivas; *C:* Russell Metty; *M:* Bronislau Kaper. *AWARDS: NOM:* Academy Awards '46: Best Story.

Stranger by Night

Detective Bobby Corcoran (Bauer) and his partner (Katt) are hunting a mutilating serial killer. Corcoran suffers from drunken black-outs and fits of rage so the evidence is pointing to him. And what about that ear in his freezer? The general look of the DVD is fine, even in the many dark scenes. The sound is only O.K. —*MM*
Movie: 🎬🎬 *DVD:* 🎬🎬🎬
Simitar Entertainment (Cat #7349, UPC #082551734924). Full frame. PCM Stereo. $14.98. Keepcase. *LANG:* English. *FEATURES:* 8 chapter links • Production factoids.
1994 (R) 96m/C Steven Bauer, William Katt, Jennifer Rubin, Michael Parks, Michele Greene, J.J. Johnston; *D:* Gregory (Gregory Dark) Brown; *W:* Daryl Haney; *C:* Wally Pfister; *M:* Ashley Irwin.

A Stranger in the Kingdom

In 1952, Rev. Walter Andrews (Hudson) is just about the first black man to occupy a position of importance in rural Kingdom County, Vermont. He becomes a suspect in a murder before the film is over, but director Craven is just as interested in local color and humor as he is in race relations and crime. The work is similar to his *Where the Rivers Flow North.* Though it was not made with a massive budget, it is as polished as any Hollywood production. The full-frame DVD image is a bit rough in the contrast department, but that's not really a flaw when so much of the action has a rustic setting. Sound is fine, too. Hudson, a busy but underappreciated character actor, turns in another excellent performance. —*MM*
Movie: 🎬🎬🎬 *DVD:* 🎬🎬🎬
Image Entertainment (Cat #ID5902UM DVD, UPC #014381590227). Full frame. Dolby Digital Stereo. $24.99. Snapper. *LANG:* English. *FEATURES:* 16 chapter links.
1998 (R) 111m/C Ernie Hudson, David Lansbury, Jean Louisa Kelly, Martin Sheen, Sean Nelson, Jordan Bayne, Bill Raymond, Henry Gibson, Larry Pine, Tom Aldredge, Carrie Snodgress; *D:* Jay Craven; *W:* Jay Craven, Don Bredos; *C:* Philip Holahan.

Stranger than Fiction

In the vein of *Very Bad Things* and *Best Laid Plans*, four friends—Emma (Meyer), Austin (Field), Violet (Wagner), and Jared (Astin)—in Salt Lake City begin an evening with a little not-so-innocent revenge, which leads to a car full of bodies. Nothing, of course, is what it first appears to be. The DVD image is very good. It holds true even when director Bross attempts some tricky visuals, solarized color, and the like. Sound is very good, too. Overall, this over-achieving little video premiere is an acceptable guilty pleasure. —*MM*
Movie: 🎬🎬🎬 *DVD:* 🎬🎬🎬
Image Entertainment (Cat #ID9357UM DVD, UPC #014381935721). Full frame. Dolby Digital Surround Stereo. $24.99. Snapper. *LANG:* English. *FEATURES:* 16 chapter links.
1999 (R) 100m/C MacKenzie Astin, Todd Field, Dina Meyer, Natasha Gregson Wagner; *D:* Eric Bross; *W:* Tim Garrick, Scott Russell; *C:* Horacio Marquinez; *M:* Larry Seymour.

Strangers on a Train

Long before there was *Throw Momma from the Train*, there was this Hitchcock super-thriller about two passengers who accidentally meet and plan to "trade" murders. Amoral Walker wants the exchange and the money he'll inherit by his father's death; Granger would love to end his stifling marriage and wed Roman, a senator's daughter, but finds the idea ultimately sickening. What happens is pure Hitchcock. The screenplay was cowritten by murder-mystery great Chandler from Patricia Highsmith's novel. Patricia Hitchcock, the director's only child, plays Roman's sister. The concluding "carousel" scene is a masterpiece. For film aficionados there are two versions of the film on the DVD—one on each side. The first is the 101-minute American release and the other is the two minute–longer British release. Both are similar in quality. The image is very sharp, which does make the preprint scratches and other damage more obvious. The picture is also a little contrasty, but graytones are good and the black-and-white cinematography's incredible details and depth is preserved. The sound could use some cleaning up, and the dialogue is hard to understand. —*JO*
Movie: 🎬🎬🎬🎬 *DVD:* 🎬🎬🎬
Warner Home Video, Inc. (Cat #15324, UPC #085391532422). Full frame. Mono. $19.98. Snapper. *LANG:* English; French. *SUB:* English; Spanish; French. *CAP:* English. *FEATURES:* 33 chapter links • Contains both the Hollywood and British versions • 5 Hitchcock trailers.

1951 101m/B Farley Granger, Robert Walker, Ruth Roman, Leo G. Carroll, Patricia Hitchcock, Marion Lorne; **D:** Alfred Hitchcock; **W:** Raymond Chandler; **C:** Robert Burks; **M:** Dimitri Tiomkin. *AWARDS: NOM:* Academy Awards '51: Best Black-and-white Cinematography.

Strangler of the Swamp

The ghost of an innocent man (Middleton) wrongly hanged for murder returns to terrorize the village where he was lynched. Future producer-director Edwards plays a potential victim; his recently returned sweetie (La Planche) vows to save him. Even with a fine transfer to DVD, this one looks and sounds like a 1940s B-movie. Nicks and breaks are visible on the print and the focus is often blurry. —*MM*
Movie: 🎬🎬 **DVD:** 🎬
Image Entertainment (Cat #ID5376FWDVD, UPC #014381537628). Full frame. Dolby Digital Mono. $19.99. Snapper. *LANG:* English. *FEATURES:* 10 chapter links.
1946 60m/B Rosemary La Planche, Blake Edwards, Charles Middleton, Robert Barrat; **D:** Frank Wisbar; **W:** Frank Wisbar; **C:** James S. Brown Jr.

Straw Dogs

An American mathematician, disturbed by the predominance of violence in American society, moves with his wife to an isolated Cornish village. He finds that primitive savagery exists beneath the most peaceful surface. After his wife is raped, Hoffman's character takes action. Hoffman is good, a little too wimpy at times. The violent, frightening film is a reaction to the violence of the 1960s. Anchor Bay has really improved on the earlier home video releases of this Peckinpah gem. The image is so much sharper that it'd be silly to compare it. Colors are for the most part vibrant and very accurate, although some sequences are weaker and may be attributed to preprint. Blacks are consistently true and the contrast and brightness levels have never been better. The sound mix sounds more mono than stereo but is crisp and clear. —*JO*
Movie: 🎬🎬🎬 **DVD:** 🎬🎬🎬
Anchor Bay (Cat #DV10607, UPC #013131060799). Widescreen (1.77:1) letterboxed. Stereo. $24.98. Keepcase. *LANG:* English. *FEATURES:* 13 chapter links.
1972 (R) 118m/C *GB* Dustin Hoffman, Susan George, Peter Vaughan, T.P. McKenna, David Warner; **D:** Sam Peckinpah; **W:** David Zelag Goodman; **C:** John Coquillon; **M:** Jerry Fielding. *AWARDS: NOM:* Academy Awards '71: Best Original Dramatic Score.

Street Fighter

Overachieving martial arts action flick has been jazzed up with smoke and mirrors and an unusually large ensemble cast. It's not the sort of thing that's going to win over any converts to the genre. Writer-director Steven de Souza's script, based on the video game "Street Fighter 2," leaves no cliche untouched. That gives a certain comfortable familiarity to this story of the megalomaniacal Asian warlord Bison (Julia), who's holding hostages and demanding a $20 billion ransom. He, of course, is out to conquer the world—that's what megalomaniacs are supposed to do—but he hasn't counted on the stalwart Col. Guile (Van Damme) and his Allied Nations commando force. On his commentary track, de Souza explains in some detail the film's roots in the game culture and his own attraction to it. He sounds intelligent and enthusiastic and he's more fun to listen to than most of the more serious filmmakers who gush fulsomely over their cast. The DVD image does justice to the inventive sets and costumes, especially Bison's Nazi-inspired leather ensemble. —*MM*
Movie: 🎬🎬🎬 **DVD:** 🎬🎬🎬
Universal Studios Home Video (Cat #20216, UPC #025192021626). Widescreen (2.35:1) letterboxed. Dolby Digital 5.1 Surround Stereo; Dolby Surround Stereo. $34.98. Keepcase. *LANG:* English; French. *SUB:* Spanish. *CAP:* English. *FEATURES:* 40 chapter links • "Making of" featurette • Commentary: writer-director Steven de Souza • Production notes • Cast and crew thumbnail biographies • Theatrical trailers.
1994 (PG-13) 101m/C Jean-Claude Van Damme, Raul Julia, Wes Studi, Ming Na, Damian Chapa, Simon Callow, Roshan Seth, Kylie Minogue, Byron Mann; **D:** Steven E. de Souza; **W:** Steven E. de Souza; **C:** William A. Fraker; **M:** Graeme Revell.

Street Law

Down-on-his-luck lawyer/kickboxer John Ryan (Wincott) finds help from his childhood friend Calderone (Prieto), but he must enter the world of illegal fighting. As far as the plot goes, this is the same old same old where bad guys have greasy pony tails, but on DVD the action actually looks pretty good with some sophisticated lighting. —*MM*
Movie: 🎬🎬 **DVD:** 🎬🎬🎬
Image Entertainment (Cat #ID5624FMDVD, UPC #014381561562). Full frame. Dolby Digital Stereo. $24.99. Snapper. *LANG:* English. *FEATURES:* 20 chapter links.
1995 (R) 98m/C Jeff Wincott, Paco Christian Prieto, Christina Cox; **D:** Damian Lee; **W:** Damian Lee; **C:** Gerald R. Goozie; **M:** Ronald J. Weiss.

Street Wars

A military cadet (Joseph) must take over a drug dealing operation when his older brother, a drug lord, is killed. This routine action entry presents some interesting moral dilemmas, as the young hero hopes to invest the drug trade's profits in a legitimate business—that is, if his brother's old cohorts don't stop him permanently.

From the director of the *Penitentiary,* a superior 1979 prison drama. Transfer is about average, with some dimly lit scenes. The sound quality—particularly in action sequences—is pretty good. —*JE*
Movie: 🎬🎬▶ **DVD:** 🎬🎬▶
Image Entertainment (Cat #ID5625SFMD-VD, UPC #014381562521). Full frame. Dolby Digital Mono. $19.99. Snapper. *LANG:* English. *FEATURES:* 20 chapter links.
1991 (R) 90m/C Alan Joseph, Bryan O'Dell, Clifford Shegog, Jean Pace, Vaughn Cromwell, Cardella Demilo; **D:** Jamaa Fanaka; **W:** Jamaa Fanaka; **C:** John L. Demps Jr.; **M:** Michael Dunlap, Yves Chicha.

A Streetcar Named Desire

Another superb film adaptation of a powerful Tennessee Williams play—this one about a neurotic Southern belle (Leigh) with a hidden past who comes to gritty-and-atmospheric New Orleans to visit her sister (Hunter) and is abused and driven mad by her brutal brother-in-law (Brando). There's not a sour apple in the cast, with deserved Oscars going to Malden, Leigh, and Hunter. Save the biggest kudos for Brando, however. Though he reportedly hated the role, he made a major impression. The pivotal scene in which he shouts out "Stella!" is justifiably famous and often imitated. The DVD image is generally good with plenty of contrast to pump vivid life into the black-and-white cinematography. But the picture suffers here and there from damaged film elements used for the transfer, proving *Streetcar* is in need of a restoration. It got one of sorts for recent video releases, which feature racy material removed prior to the original theatrical release. The original mono sound is more than adequate for cinephile purists who don't like artificial remixes for classic soundtracks. More extras would have been appreciated, but at least the production notes are something. —*MB*
Movie: 🎬🎬🎬🎬 **DVD:** 🎬🎬▶
Warner Home Video, Inc. (Cat #36041, UPC #085393604127). Full frame. Dolby Digital 1.0. $24.98. Snapper. *LANG:* English. *SUB:* English; French; Spanish. *CAP:* English. *FEATURES:* 28 chapter links • Production notes.
1951 (PG) 122m/B Vivien Leigh, Marlon Brando, Kim Hunter, Karl Malden; **D:** Elia Kazan; **W:** Tennessee Williams; **C:** Harry Stradling; **M:** Alex North. *AWARDS:* Academy Awards '51: Best Actress (Leigh), Best Art Direction/Set Decoration (B & W), Best Supporting Actor (Malden), Best Supporting Actress (Hunter); American Film Institute (AFI) '98: Top 100; British Academy Awards '52: Best Actress (Leigh); Golden Globe Awards '52: Best Supporting Actress (Hunter), National Film Registry '99; New York Film Critics Awards '51: Best Actress (Leigh), Best Director (Kazan), Best Film; *NOM:* Academy Awards '51: Best Actor (Brando), Best Black-and-white Cinematography, Best Costume

Streets of Fire

A soldier of fortune (Pare) rescues his ex-girlfriend (Lane), now a famous rock singer, after she's been kidnapped by a malicious motorcycle gang led by scene-stealing Dafoe. Violently energetic in its insistent barrage of imagery, director Hill's rock fable establishes a retro-futuristic feel and is beautifully photographed. Testosterone and style to spare. The soundtrack is so important to this one and the DVD is remastered to 5.1, making the film's action and music sequences more powerful than ever. At times the picture is a little soft, but mostly it's very sharp and the colors as lush as Hill intended them to be. There is only a little color bleed on some of the intense reds. Most scenes are pretty dark and the DVD handles it quite well. Blacks are excellent. Less grain than the laserdisc and very few artifacts (not to re-mention the incredible re-mastered soundtrack) make this DVD the only way to go. —JO

Movie: 🎬🎬🎬 **DVD:** 🎬🎬🎬
Universal Studios Home Video (Cat #20236, UPC #025192023620). Widescreen (1.77:1) letterboxed. Dolby Digital 5.1. $24.98. Keepcase. *LANG:* English (DD5.1); French (DS). *SUB:* Spanish. *CAP:* English. *FEATURES:* 16 chapter links ● Theatrical trailer ● Cast and filmmaker bios ● Production notes.
1984 93m/C Michael Pare, Diane Lane, Rick Moranis, Amy Madigan, Willem Dafoe, Deborah Van Valkenburgh, Richard Lawson, Rick Rossovich, Bill Paxton, Lee Ving, Stoney Jackson, Robert Townsend, Grand Bush, Mykelti Williamson, Elizabeth (E.G.) Daily, Lynne Thigpen, Marine Jahan, Ed Begley Jr., John Dennis Johnston, Olivia Brown; *D:* Walter Hill; *W:* Walter Hill, Larry Gross; *C:* Andrew Laszlo; *M:* Ry Cooder.

Striking Distance

Tom Hardy (Willis) is a hard-nosed fifth-generation Pittsburgh homicide cop whose police detective father (Mahoney) is killed, apparently by a serial killer. Hardy insists the perp was really a fellow cop and winds up on the River Rescue squad (at least his partner is the fetching Parker). When the serial killer starts striking at women with some connection to Hardy, he finds scant support from his fellow cops. High action quotient but the killer's identity won't be any surprise. The Dolby Surround is as lively as a lot of 5.1 mixes and there is a surprising amount of bass. Overall the DVD transfer is great and the image is sharp with good color and contrast. —JO

Movie: 🎬🎬▶ **DVD:** 🎬🎬🎬▶
Columbia Tristar Home Video (Cat #53689, UPC #043396066835). Widescreen (1.85:1) letterboxed; full frame. Dolby Surround. NSL. Keepcase. *LANG:* English; Spanish; French. *SUB:* English; Spanish;

French. *CAP:* English. *FEATURES:* 28 chapter links ● Theatrical trailer.
1993 (R) 101m/C Bruce Willis, Sarah Jessica Parker, Dennis Farina, Tom Sizemore, Brion James, Robert Pastorelli, Timothy Busfield, John Mahoney, Andre Braugher; *D:* Rowdy Herrington; *W:* Marty Kaplan, Rowdy Herrington; *C:* Mac Ahlberg; *M:* Brad Fiedel.

Striking Resemblance

Photographer Michael (Spirtas) and a model (O'Brien) are murdered after a night of videotaped sex. Police detective-babe Brody (Gian) is on the case when Michael's twin brother shows up. Does anyone need to know more about the plot of this Playboy production? It was made on a small budget and so the often grainy DVD image ranges between fair and good throughout. Sound is O.K. Overall, this one's no better than VHS tape. —MM

Movie: 🎬▶ **DVD:** 🎬▶
Image Entertainment (Cat #ID5843PLDVD, UPC #014381584325). Full frame. Dolby Digital Stereo. $19.99. Snapper. *LANG:* English. *FEATURES:* 16 chapter links.
1997 ?m/C Kevin Blair Spirtas, Nicole Gian; *D:* Kelley Cauthen.

Strip Search

Police detective Robby Durrel (Pare) lets his good-for-nothing brother Lawrence (Gray) lead him into trouble, but he's in way over his head when he falls for femme fatale Sela (Neron) and there's not much that his partner Jeanette (Grier) can do. The action sequences are pitifully weak imitations of John Woo. The rest of this Canadian production is overwrought but somehow entertaining. The DVD has a hint of grain in the continuous night scenes, which is not inappropriate for this kind of movie. The same goes for the bleeding reds and the shimmering vertical lines. Sound is substandard. —MM

Movie: 🎬🎬 **DVD:** 🎬🎬
Simitar Entertainment (Cat #7455, UPC #082551745524). Full frame. Dolby Digital 5.1 Surround Stereo. $14.98. Keepcase. *LANG:* English. *FEATURES:* 8 chapter links ● Production factoids ● Michael Pare and Pam Grier filmographies.
1997 (R) 90m/C *CA* Michael Pare, Pam Grier, Caroline Neron, Lucie Laurier, Maury Chaykin, Heidi von Palleske, MacKenzie Gray; *D:* Rod Hewitt.

Stripes

Feeling like losers and trying to straighten out their lives, two friends (Murray and Ramis) enlist in the Army under the mistaken impression that boot camp is something like summer camp for adults. The shaggy comedy became a boxoffice hit due to Murray's charm, his sparring with Oates, who's more memorable as the gruff sergeant, and fine support from the likes of Candy and other Second City players.
Movie: 🎬🎬🎬 **DVD:** NYR

Columbia Tristar Home Video (Cat #79169). $29.95. Keepcase. *LANG:* English. *SUB:* French.
1981 (R) 105m/C Bill Murray, Harold Ramis, P.J. Soles, Warren Oates, John Candy, John Larroquette, Judge Reinhold, Sean Young, Dave Thomas, Joe Flaherty; *D:* Ivan Reitman; *W:* Len Blum, Harold Ramis; *C:* Bill Butler; *M:* Elmer Bernstein.

Stripshow

Veteran Vegas stripper Raquel (McClure), on the run at the Amarcosa Hotel, tries to warn newcomer Kara (Parent) about the dangers of the business. Of course, several object lessons are included in this prime guilty pleasure. Curiously, though, on DVD, the eerie Death Valley landscapes are just as important. The film has a dry, dusty, 300-miles-from-anywhere atmosphere that's hard to define. The sound is not as good. —MM

Movie: 🎬🎬 **DVD:** 🎬🎬▶
Simitar Entertainment (Cat #7597, UPC #082551759729). Full frame. Dolby Digital Stereo. $14.98. Keepcase. *LANG:* English. *FEATURES:* 8 chapter links ● Production factoids ● Tane McClure filmography.
1995 (R) 96m/C Monique Parent, Tane McClure, Steven Tietsort; *D:* Gary Orona; *W:* Gary Orona.

Striptease

Carl Hiaasen's political/crime comedy is transformed into an inept star vehicle for Demi Moore, and her limitations have seldom been more apparent. She plays Erin Grant, a plucky mom whose no-good rotten ex-(Patrick) has won custody of their little daughter. To earn enough to pay her lawyer's fees, she is cruelly forced to be a dancer at the Eager Beaver strip joint. That's where Congressman Dilbeck (Reynolds) first sees her and falls in love. At the same time, he brains another patron with a champagne bottle and sets in motion a plot that attempts to combine pathos with slapstick, suspense, and stripping.
Movie: woof **DVD:** NYR
Warner Home Video, Inc. (Cat #2569). Widescreen letterboxed; full frame. Dolby Digital Surround Stereo. $19.98. Snapper. *LANG:* English. *SUB:* French. *CAP:* English.
1996 (R) 115m/C Demi Moore, Burt Reynolds, Ving Rhames, Armand Assante, Robert Patrick, Rumer Willis; *D:* Andrew Bergman; *W:* Andrew Bergman; *C:* Stephen Goldblatt; *M:* Howard Shore. *AWARDS:* Golden Raspberry Awards '96: Worst Picture, Worst Actress (Moore), Worst Director (Bergman), Worst Screenplay, Worst Song ("Pussy, Pussy, Pussy [Whose Kitty Cat Are You?]"); *NOM:* Golden Raspberry Awards '96: Worst Supporting Actor (Reynolds).

Stroker Ace

Flamboyant stock car driver tries to break an iron-clad promotional contract signed with a greedy fried-chicken magnate. Off duty, he ogles blondes as dopey as he is. One of the worst from Reynolds—and that's saying something. Unlike some of the Warner full-frame releases, the picture on this DVD is very good. Colors are strong and the image is sharp. Accompanied by a more than adequate mono soundtrack. —*JO*

Movie: woof **DVD:** 🎬🎬🎬
Warner Home Video, Inc. (Cat #11322, UPC #085391132226). Full frame. Dolby Digital Mono. $14.98. Snapper. *LANG:* English. *CAP:* English. *FEATURES:* 32 chapter links.
1983 (PG) 96m/C Burt Reynolds, Ned Beatty, Jim Nabors, Parker Stevenson, Loni Anderson, Bubba Smith; *D:* Hal Needham; *W:* Hal Needham, Hugh Wilson; *C:* Nick McLean; *M:* Al Capps. *AWARDS:* Golden Raspberry Awards '83: Worst Supporting Actor (Nabors).

Stuart Little

Crowd-pleasing boxoffice hit gets the royal treatment on DVD. E.B. White's famous story of a mouse who's adopted by the Little family works on a technical level with superb special effects, which are described on a separate track by John Dykstra and Jerome Chen, but it's just as successful with warm humor that's aimed at both kids and adults. Fine performances, too, from Laurie and Davis as the proud new parents, and from Fox, who gives voice to the rodent. The film's curious color scheme emphasizes reds and oranges, and they're a bit on the soft side, but that appears to be intentional. Such criticisms are fairly unimportant to younger viewers, who aren't likely to be interested in the extensive extras either. Those are mostly aimed at adults. —*MM*

Movie: 🎬🎬▶ **DVD:** 🎬🎬🎬▶
Columbia Tristar Home Video (Cat #4893). Widescreen letterboxed. Dolby Digital 5.1 Surround Stereo. $27.95. Keepcase. *LANG:* English. *SUB:* English. *FEATURES:* Game • Visual effects interactive featurette • Music videos • 28 chapter links • Artists' screen tests • Deleted scenes • Visual effects gag reel • Production gag reel • Boat race early concept reel • Isolated music score • Scrapbook • HBO special • Cast and crew thumbnail bios • Trailers • Commentary: director and animation supervisor • Commentary: visual effects supervisors.
1999 (PG) 92m/C Geena Davis, Hugh Laurie, Jonathan Lipnicki, Brian Doyle-Murray, Estelle Getty, Julia Sweeney, Dabney Coleman; *D:* Rob Minkoff; *W:* M. Night Shyamalan, Greg Booker; *C:* Guillermo Navarro; *M:* Alan Silvestri; *V:* Michael J. Fox, Nathan Lane, Chazz Palminteri, Steve Zahn, Bruno Kirby, Jennifer Tilly, David Alan Grier, Jim Doughan. *AWARDS:* NOM: Academy Awards '99: Best Visual Effects.

The Substitute

Berenger plays a Vietnam vet mercenary who poses as a substitute teacher to uncover a drug ring after his girlfriend (Venora) is roughed up by the gang. At one point, he displays his unique teaching style by throwing some unruly students out of the second floor window. Hmm....wonder if that was on the test. Being a concerned teacher, he decides to uncover the kingpin of the unruly drug gang. Being an unruly drug gang, they decide to shoot at him...a lot. Unless you're a fan of heavy weaponry, banal one liners, or yelling at the screen in frustration, substitute another movie for this one. As for the DVD, a lot of this film is either in the dark or in classrooms filled with earthtones. Both conditions are hard for some DVDs to handle, but this one has no problem and delivers a crisp, grain-free image with accurate colors and very good contrast. The 5.1 sound is not the best but has enough dynamic energy to carry the action scenes. —*JO*

Movie: 🎬 **DVD:** 🎬🎬🎬
Artisan Entertainment (Cat #60449, UPC #012236044901). Full frame. Dolby Digital 5.1; Dolby Surround. $24.98. Snapper. *LANG:* English (DD5.1); French (DS). *SUB:* English; Spanish; French. *CAP:* English. *FEATURES:* 47 chapter links • Theatrical trailer • Production notes • Cast and filmmakers bios.
1996 (R) 114m/C Tom Berenger, Ernie Hudson, Diane Venora, Marc Anthony, Glenn Plummer, Cliff DeYoung, William Forsythe, Raymond Cruz, Sharron Corley, Richard Brooks, Rodney A. Grant, Luis Guzman; *D:* Robert Mandel; *W:* Alan Ormsby, Roy Frumkes, Rocco Simonelli; *C:* Bruce Surtees; *M:* Gary Chang.

The Substitute 2: School's Out

Mercenary Carl Thompson (Williams) poses as a high school substitute teacher to hunt down the New York gang bangers who murdered his brother during a carjacking. But his plans for revenge put innocent schoolchildren at risk as well. This DVD is hard to judge because everything seems to fluctuate. The picture is sometimes sharp and the colors are sometimes vibrant. The fleshtones stay fairly good so the colors must be at least close to accurate. Blacks are generally good, except in the darker scenes where the image softens. The 5.1 sound is fairly energetic and has sporadic Surround effects. —*JO*

Movie: 🎬🎬 **DVD:** 🎬🎬
Artisan Entertainment (Cat #60481, UPC #012236048107). Widescreen (1.85:1) letterboxed. Dolby Digital 5.1. $29.98. Keepcase. *LANG:* English. *SUB:* Spanish. *CAP:* English. *FEATURES:* 36 chapter links • Theatrical trailer • Production notes • Cast and filmmaker's bios • Dual-layered RSDL.
1997 (R) 90m/C Treat Williams, B.D. Wong, Angel David, Michael Michele, Larry Gilliard Jr.; *D:* Steven Pearl; *W:* Roy Frumkes, Rocco Simonelli; *C:* Larry Banks; *M:* Joe Delia.

Subway

Surreal vision of life on the fringe of Paris society is heavily influenced by MTV. Lambert leads a band of French homeless punks who sport bad attitudes and worse haircuts. Plenty of angry attitude and way too much bad New Wave music. Director Besson has gone on to much better work. The full-frame DVD is virtually identical to VHS tape. —*MM*

Movie: 🎬▶ **DVD:** 🎬▶
Universal Studios Home Video (Cat #40097). Full frame. Dolby Digital Stereo. $19.99. Snapper. *LANG:* English. *SUB:* English. *FEATURES:* Trailer.
1985 (R) 103m/C *FR* Christopher Lambert, Isabelle Adjani, Jean-Hugues Anglade, Jean Reno; *D:* Luc Besson; *W:* Luc Besson; *C:* Carlo Varini; *M:* Eric Serra, Rickie Lee Jones. *AWARDS:* Cesar Awards '86: Best Actor (Lambert), Best Art Direction/Set Decoration, Best Sound; *NOM:* Cesar Awards '86: Best Supporting Actor (Anglade).

Succubus

Reynaud plays Lorna, first seen as a leather-clad, dominatrix stripper, whose act revolves around the simulated onstage torture and murders of her fellow actors. Soon, it's obvious that she's taking the act on the road, and the blood begins to flow for real. This Franco gem was originally rated "X" and even today contains enough over-the-top violence and nudity to still warrant an "R" rating. Psychedelic and surrealistic, with a great sleazy jazz score. If you've read any of the other reviews of the Anchor Bay Eurosleaze releases, you know that even poor sound and video quality doesn't detract much from the basic appeal of these films. This transfer is no worse than the rest and has only a moderately sharp picture with somewhat dull colors. Some of Franco's filming techniques give the DVD even more trouble and the grain increases. The stereo sound is a little thin and as a result things sound quite harsh, but even that matches the flavor of the film's campy and cool score. — *JO* *AKA:* Necronomicon; Necronomicon: Getraumte Sunden; Necronomicon: Dreamt Sin.

Movie: 🎬🎬🎬 **DVD:** 🎬🎬▶
Anchor Bay (Cat #DV10562, UPC #013131056297). Full frame. Stereo. $29.99. Keepcase. *LANG:* English. *FEATURES:* 10 chapter links • Theatrical trailer.
1969 91m/C *SP GE* Janine Reynaud, Jack Taylor, Howard Vernon, Michel Lemoine, Pier A. Caminnecci, Adrian Hoven; *D:* Jess (Jesus) Franco; *W:* Pier A. Caminnecci; *C:* Jorge Herrero, Franz X. Lederle.

Sucker the Vampire

Variation on *Buffy, the Vampire Slayer* is solid Troma, and fans know exactly what that means—bargain basement production values, acting that runs the gamut from pure ham to amateur ham, sophomoric humor brightened by flashes of real wit, enthusiastic appreciation of conventions of horror, oodles of T&A. Anthony (Yan Birch) is an effete vampire rocker, leader of the group Plasma. Reed (scene-stealing coproducer Erkiletian) is Anthony's roadie-Renfield. Vanessa Helsing (Baber) is the vampire hunter who's stalking Anthony. Director Rodionoff and Erkiletian use the commentary track to sketch in an overview of ultralow-budget filmmaking and to provide advice for those who would follow in their footsteps. Example: To attract a distributor, be sure to provide "nipplage in the first 20 minutes." Visually, the film does not gain much on DVD. It is as coarse and grainy as it is on tape. —*MM*

Movie: ♫♫ *DVD:* ♫♫➤
Troma Team Video (Cat #9920, UPC #790357992034). Full frame. $24.98. Keepcase. *LANG:* English. *FEATURES:* 9 chapter links ✺ Tour of Troma ✺ Commentary: Rodionoff and Erkiletian ✺ Preview of Troma comic books ✺ Troma Intelligence Test. DVD-ROM links to Troma website.
1998 91m/C Yan Birch, Alex Erkiletian, Monica Baber, P.K. Phillips, Colleen Moore, Greg Fawcett, Melissa Park, Gail Harris; *D:* Hans Rodionoff; *W:* Hans Rodionoff.

Sudden Fear

Successful playwright/heiress Myra Hudson (Crawford) has a whirlwind romance, leading to marriage, with oh-so-charming actor Lester Blaine (Palance). But Les is more interested in Myra's money and gets together with former flame Irene (always-the-bad-girl Grahame) to get rid of his new bride and inherit her fortune. But Myra finds out about the plot and puts her writing talent to work in coming up with a new scenario. Good suspenser with fine performances is adapted from the book by Edna Sherry. There are some problems with the DVD, but most seem attributable to the source material—it's mainly a matter of scratches, film grain, and maybe a little image softness from trying to cover those things up. The DVD does have a few problems with artifacts. The sound, though, has been cleaned up and has very few problems with scratchiness or other distortions. —*JO*

Movie: ♫♫♫ *DVD:* ♫♫➤
Image Entertainment (Cat #K115DVD, UPC #738329011529). Full frame. Dolby Digital Mono. $29.95. Snapper. *LANG:* English. *FEATURES:* 17 chapter links.
1952 111m/B Joan Crawford, Jack Palance, Gloria Grahame, Bruce (Herman Brix) Bennett, Virginia Huston, Mike Connors; *D:* David Miller; *W:* Lenore Coffee, Robert Smith; *C:* Charles B(ryant) Lang; *M:* Elmer Bernstein. *AWARDS: NOM:* Academy Awards '52: Best Actress (Crawford), Best Black-and-white Cinematography, Best Costume Design (B & W), Best Supporting Actor (Palance).

Suddenly

Crazed gunman Sinatra holds a family hostage in the backwater town of Suddenly, CA, while he waits to kill the President,

who's passing through on a train. Hayden is the sheriff. This tense but dated thriller is a good display for Sinatra's acting talent, though he forced United Artists to take it out of distribution after learning that Kennedy assassin Lee Harvey Oswald had watched the film only days before November 22, 1963. The original black-and-white photography is muddy, and little appears to have been done to clean it up on this bargain-basement disc. Even so, Sinatra's performance makes the film a curious companion piece to *The Manchurian Candidate*. —*MM*

Movie: ♫♫➤ *DVD:* ♫♫
Madacy Entertainment (Cat #DVD-9-9040, UPC #056775010591). Full frame. Dolby Digital Mono. $9.95. Keepcase. *FEATURES:* 9 chapter links ✺ Sinatra biography ✺ Trivia.
1954 75m/B Frank Sinatra, Sterling Hayden, James Gleason, Nancy Gates, Paul Frees, Willis Bouchey, Kim Charney, Christopher Dark; *D:* Lewis Allen; *W:* Richard Sale; *C:* Charles Clarke; *M:* David Raksin.

Suicide Kings

When the sister of one of four prep friends is kidnapped, the guys decide to take retired mobster Charlie Bartolucci (Walken) hostage so he'll help them. When Bartolucci suggests that one of the guys may be in on the kidnapping, the dynamics of the situation shift. If Walken overpowers his younger costars, it doesn't hurt the film. The plotting is less sure-footed. On their nuts-and-bolts commentary track, director O'Fallon and cowriter Rice focus the challenges of making such a film on a "thin" budget; how corners are cut and last-minute changes are dealt with. Virtually all of the action takes place in one house at night, so the visuals present no real problems for DVD. The disc is also filled with an unusually large number of extras. Recommended for *Usual Suspects* fans. —*MM*

Movie: ♫♫♫ *DVD:* ♫♫♫➤
Artisan Entertainment (Cat #60472, UPC #012236047209). Widescreen (1.85:1) letterboxed. Dolby Digital 5.1 Surround Stereo; Dolby Digital Surround Stereo. $14.98. Keepcase. *LANG:* English. *SUB:* Spanish. *CAP:* English. *FEATURES:* 36 chapter links ✺ Multiple angle scene ✺ Alternative endings ✺ Storyboards ✺ Theatrical trailers ✺ Commentary: Peter O'Fallon and Wayne Allan Rice ✺ Movie posters ✺ TV spot.
1997 (R) 106m/C Christopher Walken, Jay Mohr, Henry Thomas, Sean Patrick Flanery, Denis Leary, Jeremy Sisto, Johnny Galecki, Cliff DeYoung, Laura San Giacomo, Laura Harris; *D:* Peter O'Fallon; *W:* Josh McKinney, Gina Goldman, Wayne Rice; *C:* Christopher Baffa; *M:* Graeme Revell, Tim Simonec.

Suite 16

Though it's promoted as an "erotic thriller," this one's a Pinteresque psy-

chodrama that could be equally at home on the stage. Chris (Kamerling) is a young hustler who is trapped by his own greed with Glover (Postlethwaite), a millionaire, in a luxurious Monte Carlo hotel. They're a kinky odd couple whose proclivities and cravings come to feed off each other. Belgian director Deruddere creates a grainy sordid atmosphere that is re-created all too faithfully on DVD. The film is dark and indistinct. During the few moments that the characters do not speak English, their subtitles drop off the bottom of the screen. The disc may look marginally better than the tape, but that's all. —*MM*

Movie: ♫♫ *DVD:* ♫♫
Image Entertainment (Cat #ID5770UM DVD, UPC #014381577020). Full frame. Dolby Digital Stereo. $19.99. Snapper. *LANG:* English mostly. *SUB:* English but unreadable. *FEATURES:* 16 links.
1994 (R) 93m/C BE GB Pete Postlethwaite, Antoine Kamerling, Geraldine Pailhas, Tom Jansen; *D:* Dominique Deruddere; *W:* Charles Higson, Lise Mayer; *C:* Jean-Francois Robin; *M:* Walter Hus.

Summer

In the fifth (and perhaps the finest) of Eric Rohmer's "Comedies and Proverbs" series, young Parisienne Delphine (Riviere) finds her vacation plans disrupted by her friend's last-minute cancellation. She goes off to the beach by herself but cannot break free of her own lonely blues until she meets a spirited Swedish girl (Heredia). What happens after that is not what you expect. Rohmer has never made visually sophisticated films and this one is no exception. The image is seldom better than good and in the key concluding scenes, which appear to have been filmed with available light, heavy graininess, and pixels are abundant. In those same moments, though, Rohmer's use of available sounds gives the moment a feeling of authenticity and reality that no amount of polish could equal. Recommended on any medium—DVD or tape. —*MM AKA:* Le Rayon Vert; The Green Ray.

Movie: ♫♫♫➤ *DVD:* ♫♫
WinStar Home Entertainment (Cat #FLV5102, UPC #72091751022). Full frame. $29.98. Keepcase. *LANG:* French. *SUB:* English. *FEATURES:* 6 chapter links ✺ Production credits ✺ Filmographies and awards.
1986 (R) 98m/C FR Marie Riviere, Lisa Heredia, Beatrice Romand, Eric Hamm, Rosette, Isabelle Riviere; *D:* Eric Rohmer; *W:* Eric Rohmer; *C:* Sophie Maintigneux; *M:* Jean-Louis Valero.

Summer of Sam

Spike Lee's take on New York's summer of 1977 revolves around two couples—the compulsively unfaithful Vinny (Leguizamo) and his wife Diona (Sorvino), and punk rocker Ritchie (Brody) and Ruby (Esposito)—as the Son of Sam terrorizes the city with a series of murders. It's a garish world of acid colors, distorted images, indulgent drug use, music, baseball, and performance art. The DVD is an accurate re-creation of the deliberately unattractive theatrical release. The stereo soundtrack captures Lee's powerful integration of music into the story. Many critics unfavorably compared this one to *Do the Right Thing*. That's unfair. This is an ambitious, disturbing, and perceptive examination of urban individuals and groups told through harsh acid-etched images. —MM

Movie: 𝄞𝄞𝄞 **DVD:** 𝄞𝄞𝄞
Buena Vista Home Entertainment (Cat #18283, UPC #717951004734). Widescreen (1.85:1) letterboxed. Dolby Digital 5.1 Surround Stereo. $29.99. Keepcase. *LANG:* English. *CAP:* English. *FEATURES:* 22 chapter links • Theatrical trailer.
1999 (R) 142m/C Adrien Brody, John Leguizamo, Spike Lee, Mira Sorvino, Jennifer Esposito, Michael Badalucco, Anthony LaPaglia, Patti LuPone, Ben Gazzara, Bebe Neuwirth, John Savage, Roger Guenveur Smith, Michael Rispoli; *D:* Spike Lee; *W:* Spike Lee; *C:* Ellen Kuras; *M:* Terence Blanchard.

A Summer to Remember

A deaf boy (played by Gerlis, himself deaf since birth) develops a friendship with an orangutan through sign language. Bad guys abduct the friendly critter, but this is a nice family movie, so nothing too intense transpires. Actually, the clarity of the image on DVD makes a supporting character—a guy in a gorilla suit—even more blatant and non-frightening. Throughout, this one looks much better than other made-for-TV movies of its era. Just fine for kids. —MM

Movie: 𝄞𝄞▸ **DVD:** 𝄞𝄞▸
Simitar Entertainment (Cat #7277, UPC #082551727728). Full frame. PCM Stereo. $7.98. Keepcase. *LANG:* English. *FEATURES:* 8 chapter links • Production factoids • Tess Harper and James Farentino filmographies.
1984 (PG) 93m/C Tess Harper, James Farentino, Burt Young, Louise Fletcher, Sean Gerlis, Bridgette Andersen; *D:* Robert Lewis; *C:* Stephen W. Gray; *M:* Charles Fox.

Summertime

Spinster Hepburn vacations in Venice and falls in love with Brazzi. She is hurt when she learns that he's married, but her life has been so bleak that she is not about to end her one great romance. Moving, funny, richly photographed in a beautiful Old World city. Adapted from Arthur Laurents's play *The Time of the Cuckoo.* *AKA:* Summer Madness.

Movie: 𝄞𝄞𝄞▸ **DVD:** NYR
Home Vision Cinema (Cat #1307). Full frame. Dolby Digital Mono. $29.95. *LANG:* English. *CAP:* English. *FEATURES:* Trailer.
1955 98m/C Katharine Hepburn, Rossano Brazzi, Isa Miranda, Darren

McGavin, Mari Aldon, MacDonald Parke, Jeremy Spenser; *D:* David Lean; *W:* David Lean, H.E. Bates; *C:* Jack Hildyard; *M:* Alessandro Cicognini. *AWARDS:* New York Film Critics Awards '55: Best Director (Lean); *NOM:* Academy Awards '55: Best Actress (Hepburn), Best Director (Lean).

Sunday in the Park with George

This DVD is made from a taped theatrical performance of the Tony-, Grammy-, and Pulitzer Prize–winning musical play, which is based upon impressionist Georges Seurat's painting "A Sunday Afternoon on the Island of Grande Jatte." Features a celebrated musical score by Sondheim. The disc can boast a solid video transfer overall, though some subtle colors lack sharpness. The Digital Stereo soundtrack does a wonderful job of reproducing the theatre atmosphere. Also of note, for its enthusiastic nature, is the cast and crew commentary track. —MJT

Movie: 𝄞𝄞𝄞 **DVD:** 𝄞𝄞𝄞
Image Entertainment (Cat #ID4586MB DVD, UPC #014381458626). Full frame. Dolby Digital Stereo. $29.99. Snapper. *LANG:* English. *FEATURES:* 24 chapter links • Commentary: Sondheim, Lapine, Patinkin, and Peters.
1986 120m/C Mandy Patinkin, Bernadette Peters, Barbara Byrne, Charles Kimbrough; *D:* James Lapine; *M:* Stephen Sondheim.

Sunset

Director Edwards wanders through the range in this soft-centered farce about a couple of western legends out to solve a mystery. On the backlots of Hollywood, silent screen star Tom Mix (Willis) meets aging marshal Wyatt Earp (Garner) and participates in a time-warp western circa 1927. They encounter a series of misadventures while trying to finger a murderer. Garner ambles enjoyably, lifting himself a level above the rest of the cast. A fairly good-looking disc despite graininess in scenes with a lot of reddish browns. In dark scenes without those earthtones, it doesn't seem to be a problem. Blacks are good as are the brightness and contrast. The quality drops a little on the full-frame side. The Dolby Surround could be a little crisper and is overall just average. "More Bruce Willis" on the menu is the trailer for *Striking Distance.* —JO

Movie: 𝄞𝄞 **DVD:** 𝄞𝄞
Columbia Tristar Home Video (Cat #70099, UPC #043396700994). Widescreen (1.85:1) letterboxed; full frame. Dolby Surround. Keepcase. *LANG:* English (DS); Spanish; French. *SUB:* Spanish; French. *FEATURES:* 28 chapter links • *Striking Distance* trailer.
1988 (R) 101m/C Bruce Willis, James Garner, Mariel Hemingway, Darren McGavin, Jennifer Edwards, Malcolm McDowell, Kathleen Quinlan, M. Emmet Walsh, Patricia Hodge, Richard Bradford, Joe Dallesandro, Dermot Mulroney; *D:*

Blake Edwards; *W:* Blake Edwards, Rod Amateau; *C:* Anthony B. Richmond; *M:* Henry Mancini. *AWARDS:* Golden Raspberry Awards '88: Worst Director (Edwards); *NOM:* Academy Awards '88: Best Costume Design.

Super Speedway

This IMAX release is the DVD that most hardware vendors used over and over to sell customers on the up-and-coming DVD format. It's basically just cars, cars, cars (and their assorted very loud noises). There are a few places where an attempt is made to throw in some racing information, but who cares, let's get back to the race. The DVD is a showpiece. The image is super sharp and the sound is just incredible, making full use of even the most powerful sound system. Some shots of the cars whizzing by at 200 m.p.h. make your head spin, and some of the revs are ear shattering. —JO

Movie: 𝄞𝄞𝄞 **DVD:** 𝄞𝄞𝄞𝄞
Image Entertainment (Cat #ID46220W DVD, UPC #014381462227). Full frame. Dolby Digital 5.1. $24.99. Snapper. *LANG:* English; French Canadian; Mandarin; American Spanish. *FEATURES:* 49 chapter links • "Making of" featurette.
1997 ?m/C Mario Andretti, Michael Andretti; *D:* Stephen Low; *Nar:* Paul Newman.

Supercop

Super Hong Kong cop Kevin Chan (Chan) heads to China to assist the authorities in cracking an international drug ring. He's partnered with disciplined-but-beautiful Director Yang (Yeoh), who's also a terrific fighter, and the duo go undercover (as a married couple) to infiltrate the operation, which takes them to a Malaysian resort. Then Chan's girlfriend shows up, blowing their cover. Lots of action-packed fighting and wild chases. This domestic DVD release is shorter than the original Hong Kong edition (available for a few years as an import only). It shouldn't bother most fans, though, because all the action scenes are pretty much the same, and the main cuts were conversational. The DVD looks very good and sounds even better. The audio and the video are both vastly improved over the import tape. —JO *AKA:* Police Story 3: Supercop.

Movie: 𝄞𝄞▸ **DVD:** 𝄞𝄞𝄞▸
Buena Vista Home Entertainment (Cat #13852, UPC #717951000231). Widescreen (2.35:1) letterboxed. Stereo. $29.99. Keepcase. *LANG:* English. *SUB:* Spanish. *CAP:* English. *FEATURES:* 25 chapter links.
1992 (R) 93m/C *HK* Jackie Chan, Michelle Yeoh, Maggie Cheung, Kenneth Tsang, Yuen Wah; *D:* Stanley Tong; *W:* Edward Tang, Fibe Ma, Lee Wai Yee; *C:* Ardy Lam; *M:* Joel McNeely.

Supercop 2

Sequel focuses on Michelle Yeoh's Jessica Yang, high-kicking Hong Kong police Inspector who's called upon to stop a gang that's led by her ex-boyfriend. The plot is standard-issue for this kind of picture. The action sequences are well staged and inventively choreographed. Michelle Yeoh has the moves and the screen presence to hold her own with her male costars. (Jackie Chan makes a cameo appearance.) On DVD, the sound is fine and the image is exceptionally sharp for an import. Extras are minimal. —*MM*
AKA: Police Story 3, Part 2.
Movie: 🎬🎬▶ *DVD:* 🎬🎬🎬
Buena Vista Home Entertainment (Cat #18309, UPC #717951004949). Widescreen (1.85:1) letterboxed. Dolby Digital 5.1 Surround Stereo. $29.99. Keepcase. *LANG:* English. *CAP:* English. *FEATURES:* 18 chapter links.
1993 (R) 94m/C *HK* Michelle Yeoh, Yukari Oshima, Eric Tsang, Rongguang Yu, Athene Chu, Siu-wong Fan, Jackie Chan, Emile Chau, Chu Yan; *D:* Stanley Tong; *W:* Stanley Tong, Mok Tang Han, Sui Lai Kang.

The Superman Cartoons of Max & Dave Fleischer

A complete collection of the influential Superman cartoons (18 episodes) created by the Fleischers for Paramount in 1941. The video transfer is adequate, although it suffers from the condition of the source material. For the most part, the colors are well-defined, though darker colors tend to get lost. The soundtrack is clear albeit a bit on the tinny side. —*MJT*
Movie: 🎬🎬🎬 *DVD:* 🎬🎬▶
Image Entertainment (Cat #ID4388BRDVD, UPC #014381438826). Full frame. Mono PCM soundtrack. $34.99. Snapper. *LANG:* English. *FEATURES:* 18 chapter links.
1941 147m/C *D:* Max Fleischer, Dave Fleischer.

Superman, the Lost Episodes

These eight cartoons come from the 1940s and '50s. They'll probably strike younger viewers as hopelessly old-fashioned, but they certainly move quickly and the restoration work (illustrated in a short demo) gives them remarkable clarity. Just as important for fans, each cartoon comes with complete credits, history, and synopsis. For the serious collector of early animation, the disc is fine work. The same restoration team has worked on other cartoon collections for the distributor. See the *Cartoon Crazys* reviews. Contents: "Jap O Tears," "Showdown," "Eleventh Hour," "Destruction, Inc." "The Mummy Strikes," "Jungle Drums," "Underground World," "Secret Agent." —*MM*
Movie: 🎬🎬🎬 *DVD:* 🎬🎬🎬
WinStar Home Entertainment (Cat #WHE73029, UPC #72091730292). Full frame. Dolby Digital; Dolby Pro Logic;

Stereo. $19.98. Keepcase. *LANG:* English. *FEATURES:* 14 chapter links ▪ Production notes.
1999 100m/C

Supreme Sanction

Uninspired generic title is entirely adequate for this video premiere thriller. Government hit babe Jenna (Swanson) refuses to take out the journalist (Dukes) who wants to expose her organization. Her bosses (Madsen, Perlman) are not happy. Both image and sound are identical to VHS tape, or at best a hair sharper. —*MM*
Movie: 🎬🎬 *DVD:* 🎬🎬
Studio Home Entertainment (Cat #7305, UPC #658149730526). Widescreen (1.85:1) anamorphic. Dolby Digital Surround Stereo. $24.95. Keepcase. *LANG:* English. *FEATURES:* 20 chapter links ▪ Commentary: director John Terlesky ▪ Trailer ▪ Cast and crew thumbnail biographies.
1999 (R) 95m/C Michael Madsen, Kristy Swanson, David Dukes, Donald Adeosun Faison, Tommy (Tiny) Lister, Ron Perlman; *D:* John Terlesky; *W:* John Terlesky.

Surf Crazy

Bruce Brown will always be known best for his surf documentary *Endless Summer*. This film, his second, was made before that one. It's essentially a less-ambitious take on the same material. Brown follows surfers to beaches in Mexico, California, and Hawaii. Though that would hardly seem a compelling subject today, in 1959, the world of surfing was "the size of a BB," as Brown puts it. On the liner notes, he adds "Eisenhower was President. Hawaii had just become a state." The film is one short step up from home movies and the DVD was created from a print that has been nicked up a bit, but that somehow adds to the innocent charm of the film. —*MM*
Movie: 🎬🎬▶ *DVD:* 🎬🎬▶
Image Entertainment (Cat #ID7920TDVD, UPC #01438187923). Full frame. Dolby Digital Mono. $24.99. Snapper. *LANG:* English. *FEATURES:* 16 chapter links.
1959 71m/C *D:* Bruce Brown; *Nar:* Bruce Brown.

Surf Nazis Must Die (DC)

Camp variation on *A Clockwork Orange* revolves around a group of neo-Nazi surfers who take over California beaches in the wake of a devastating earthquake. Tongue-in-cheek, tasteless, cheap, and unashamed. This is vintage Troma, after all. The only value of the DVD over the VHS tape lies in the extensive Troma extras and the deleted scenes, mostly of Hawaiian surfers. —*MM*
Movie: 🎬🎬 *DVD:* 🎬
Troma Team Video (Cat #9820, UPC #790357982035). Full frame. Stereo. $24.95. Keepcase. *LANG:* English. *FEATURES:* 9 chapter links ▪ Troma tour, test,

and other cheesy stuff ▪ Interviews with director Peter George and producer Robert Tinnell ▪ Stills.
1987 83m/C Barry Brenner, Gail Neely, Michael Sonye, Dawn Wildsmith, Tom Shell, Bobbie Bresee; *D:* Peter George; *W:* John Ayre; *C:* Rolf Kestermann; *M:* John McCallum.

The Surgeon

Dr. Kildare meets *Re-Animator* in a dandy little medical horror/comedy with a first-rate ensemble cast. The title character (Haberle) is the proverbial mad scientist—actually he's a little madder than most—who's out to get everyone who has thwarted his research into "pituitary extract." Those include Malcolm McDowell and Charles Dance. Isabel Glasser and James Remar are the good doctors. Peter Boyle is the cop on the case. Director Carl Schenkel and special effects coordinator Steve Johnson have come up with some genuinely creepy moments, most of them infused with strong humor. It's difficult to maintain an effective ratio of laughs and scares, but they manage. The German-American production looks fine on DVD, even during the many flashlights-in-the-darkness scenes. —*MM AKA:* Exquisite Tenderness.
Movie: 🎬🎬🎬 *DVD:* 🎬🎬🎬
Simitar Entertainment (Cat #7343, UPC #08255173430). Full frame. PCM Stereo. $14.98. Keepcase. *LANG:* English. *FEATURES:* 8 chapter links ▪ Production factoids ▪ Peter Boyle and Malcolm McDowell filmographies.
1994 (R) 100m/C *GE* Isabel Glasser, James Remar, Sean Haberle, Charles Dance, Peter Boyle, Malcolm McDowell, Charles Bailey-Gates, Gregory West, Mother Love; *D:* Carl Schenkel; *W:* Patrick Cirillo; *C:* Thomas Burstyn; *M:* Christopher Franke.

Surviving the Game

Ernest Dickerson's version of *The Most Dangerous Game* is well-written, creatively cast, and directed with a real sense of excitement. Mason (Ice-T) is homeless and hopeless in Seattle until Cole (Dutton), a sympathetic social worker, offers him work. Cole's icy partner Burns (Hauer) tells him that they need help with a private hunt. Cinematographer turned director Dickerson shows that he's not limited to the gritty city stories he has told with Spike Lee. Some of his big outdoor action scenes are as good as the best, *Deliverance* or *First Blood*. He also got first-rate performances from his cast. In sound and image, the DVD is excellent, re-creating both rainy urban night exteriors and mountainscapes without visible flaws. Important sound effects come through clearly as does Stewart Copeland's score. A sleeper. —*MM*
Movie: 🎬🎬🎬 *DVD:* 🎬🎬🎬
New Line Home Video (Cat #N4895, UPC #794043489525). Widescreen (1.85:1)

letterboxed; full frame. Dolby Digital 5.1 Surround Stereo; Dolby Digital Surround Stereo. $24.98. Snapper. *LANG:* English. *CAP:* English. *FEATURES:* Theatrical trailer ⬝ 20 chapter links ⬝ Cast and crew thumbnail biographies.
1994 (R) 94m/C Rutger Hauer, Ice-T, F. Murray Abraham, Gary Busey, Charles S. Dutton, John C. McGinley, William McNamara, Jeff Corey; *D:* Ernest R. Dickerson; *W:* Eric Bernt; *C:* Bojan Bazelli; *M:* Stewart Copeland.

Suspicions

Six friends gather at a remote snowbound house on the anniversary of a seventh friend's death. As they are bumped off, the *Ten Little Indians* plot is reinterpreted. Surprisingly, this Pennsylvania production works through above-average performances from the unknown young cast, particularly Amy Tribbey. Director Sperrazza also creates a strong sense of place. On DVD, the image is seldom better than so-so, with several interiors poorly lit. Still, the film earns a solid recommendation to mystery fans. —*MM*
Movie: 🎵🎵🎵 *DVD:* 🎵🎵▸
Simitar Entertainment (Cat #7574, UPC #082551757428). Full frame. Dolby Digital Stereo. $14.98. Keepcase. *LANG:* English. *FEATURES:* 8 chapter links ⬝ Production factoids.
1995 83m/C Amy Tribbey, Eric Breien, Allison McDonell; *D:* Michael Sperrazza; *W:* Rick Ferguson; *C:* Ric Donovan.

Swashbuckler

Jaunty pirate returns from sea to find his friends held captive by dastardly dictator for their political views. He rescues them, and helps them overthrow the erstwhile despot. There are a few good moments, but overall the film feels very dated and older than it actually is. The transfer to DVD is pretty good. Colors are bright and the image is sharp. The mono sound lacks both energy and fidelity, and has very little bass. A "making of" documentary is thrown in, but even that is of little interest. —*JO* **AKA:** Scarlet Buccaneer.
Movie: 🎵 *DVD:* 🎵🎵▸
Universal Studios Home Video (Cat #20514, UPC #02519205125). Widescreen (2.35:1) anamorphic. Mono. $24.98. Keepcase. *LANG:* English; French. *SUB:* Spanish. *CAP:* English. *FEATURES:* 18 chapter links ⬝ Theatrical trailer ⬝ Cast and filmmaker bios ⬝ Production notes ⬝ "Making of" featurette.
1976 (PG) 101m/C Robert Shaw, James Earl Jones, Peter Boyle, Genevieve Bujold, Beau Bridges, Geoffrey Holder; *D:* James Goldstone; *W:* Jeffrey Bloom; *C:* Philip Lathrop; *M:* John Addison.

Sweepers

Land mine expert Christian Erickson (Lundgren) is called out of retirement after the death of his son to help Michelle Flynn (Stansfield) uncover a terrorist plot to plant mines in America. This African production is noticeably lackluster in the effects department. The many explosions are particularly unconvincing. In that regard, the relative clarity of the DVD image may be more hindrance than help. Sound is nothing special either. —*MM*
Movie: 🎵▸ *DVD:* 🎵🎵
Image Entertainment (Cat #ID6340NGDVD, UPC #014381634020). Full frame. Dolby Digital Stereo. $24.99. Snapper. *LANG:* English. *FEATURES:* 12 chapter links ⬝ Theatrical trailer.
1999 (R) 96m/C Dolph Lundgren, Claire Stansfield, Bruce Payne; *D:* Darby Black; *W:* Darby Black, Kevin Bernhardt; *C:* Yossi Wein.

Sweet Dreams

Biopic focuses on the stormy marriage between country star Patsy Cline (Lange) and Charlie Dick (Harris). Otherwise, it's pretty much the standard music biz story of quick success and early death by plane crash. The DVD image cannot improve on the limited production values. Sound is marginally better than VHS tape. —*MM*
Movie: 🎵🎵▸ *DVD:* 🎵🎵
HBO Home Video (Cat #93666, UPC #026359366628). Widescreen letterboxed. Dolby Digital Surround Stereo. $24.98. Snapper. *LANG:* English. *SUB:* English; French; Spanish. *FEATURES:* 14 chapter links ⬝ Trailer ⬝ Cast and crew thumbnail biographies.
1985 (PG-13) 115m/C Jessica Lange, Ed Harris, Ann Wedgeworth, David Clennon; *D:* Karel Reisz; *W:* Robert Getchell; *C:* Robbie Greenberg; *M:* Charles Gross. *AWARDS: NOM:* Academy Awards '85: Best Actress (Lange).

Sweet Evil

Following in the footsteps of the killer blondes in *Fatal Attraction* and *Hand That Rocks the Cradle*, Jenny (Wilson) is psycho-surrogate who agrees to help out Naomi (Matsuda) and Mike (Cohen). They learn too late that she's not the cutie-pie she appears. Save some pixelation in very dark backgrounds, the DVD looks and sounds fine. All in all, an acceptable little thriller. —*MM*
Movie: 🎵🎵 *DVD:* 🎵🎵▸
Simitar Entertainment (Cat #7421, UPC #082551742127). Full frame. Dolby Digital Stereo; Dolby Digital 5.1 Surround Stereo. $14.98. Keepcase. *LANG:* English. *FEATURES:* 8 chapter links ⬝ Production factoids ⬝ Peter Boyle filmography.
1995 (R) 92m/C Bridgette Wilson, Peter Boyle, Scott Cohen, Eiko Matsuda; *D:* Rene Eram.

The Sweet Hereafter

A schoolbus crash kills 14 children in the small town of Sam Dent, British Columbia. Big city lawyer Mitchell Stephens (Holm) arrives to persuade the townspeople to begin a class-action suit targeting city authorities and the bus manufacturer, while struggling to deal with his drug-addicted daughter Zoe (Banks). Paralyzed teenaged survivor Nicole Burnell (Polley) tries to cope with the aftermath of the tragedy as does widower Billy Ansell (Greenwood), whose two children died in the crash. But the case soon begins to tear the reeling town apart as everyone struggles with loss and fate. Egoyan's intimate, lyrical adaptation of the novel by Russell Banks is filled with wonderful performances, particularly by Polley. The DVD features one of the better supplemental sections available, including intelligent commentary and an excellent video discussion where novelist Banks and director Egoyan compare the book to the film in scene-specific manner. The film transfer itself is very sharp, with dead-on colors, and super blacks. The audio section is very powerful and serves to enhance the emotional impact of the near-perfect film. —*JO*
Movie: 🎵🎵🎵 *DVD:* 🎵🎵🎵🎵
New Line Home Video (Cat #N4654, UPC #794043465420). Widescreen (2.35:1) letterboxed. Dolby Digital 5.1. $24.98. Snapper. *LANG:* English (DD5.1); French (DD5.1). *SUB:* English; French; Spanish. *CAP:* English. *FEATURES:* 21 chapter links ⬝ Commentary: Atom Egoyan and Russell Banks ⬝ Video discussion of the book and film ⬝ Interviews with cast ⬝ *The Charlie Rose Show* interview with Atom Egoyan ⬝ Isolated music score ⬝ Theatrical trailers.
1996 (R) 110m/C *CA* Ian Holm, Sarah Polley, Bruce Greenwood, Tom McCamus, Arsinee Khanjian, Alberta Watson, Gabrielle Rose, Maury Chaykin, David Hemblen, Earl Pastko, Peter Donaldson, Caerthan Banks, Brook Johnson, Stephanie Morgenstern; *D:* Atom Egoyan; *W:* Atom Egoyan; *C:* Paul Sarossy; *M:* Mychael Danna. *AWARDS:* Cannes Film Festival '97: Grand Jury Prize; Genie Awards '97: Best Actor (Holm), Best Cinematography, Best Director (Egoyan), Best Film, Best Film Editing, Best Sound, Best Score; Independent Spirit Awards '98: Best Foreign Film; Toronto-City Award '97: Best Canadian Feature Film; *NOM:* Academy Awards '97: Best Adapted Screenplay, Best Director (Egoyan); Genie Awards '97: Best Actor (Greenwood), Best Actress (Polley, Rose), Best Screenplay.

Sweet Justice

When her sister is murdered, kickboxer Sunny Justice (Carter) turns butt-kicking avenger, assembling a band of female ex-commandos and exposing corruption in a small town. Routine martial arts action is enlivened, slightly, by distaff take on *The Magnificent Seven*. Nominally feminist flick still finds room for a lengthy sequence set in a strip club, as well as numerous gratuitous shots of the gals in workout gear. Film looks as though it was shot mainly at night, with inadequate lighting, and the DVD transfer is consequently dim, with poor black/blue contrasts, and occasionally muffled sound. Where's

Lance Henriksen when you really need him? —*JE*
Movie: 🐾🐾 **DVD:** 🐾🐾
Image Entertainment (Cat #ID 5626FMDVD, UPC #1438156262). Full frame. Dolby Digital Surround. $14.99. Snapper. *LANG:* English. *FEATURES:* Interactive menus ☞ 12 chapter links.
1992 (R) 92m/C Finn Carter, Kathleen Kinmont, Marc Singer, Frank Gorshin, Mickey Rooney; *D:* Allen Plone; *W:* Allen Plone, Jim Tabilio.

Sweet Talker
Following his release from prison, a charming con man (Brown) shows up in a coastal village, thinking that the townsfolk are ripe for the picking. What he doesn't know is that they can do some sweet talking of their own, and he soon finds himself caring for a pretty widow (Allen) and her son. Sleeper comedy works well thanks to the likeable leads.
Movie: 🐾🐾🐾 **DVD:** NYR
Pioneer Entertainment (Cat #DVD68918). Full frame. Dolby Digital Stereo. $24.98. Keepcase. *LANG:* English. *CAP:* English.
1991 (PG) 91m/C *AU* Bryan Brown, Karen Allen, Chris Haywood, Bill Kerr, Bruce Spence, Bruce Myles, Paul Chubb, Peter Hehir, Justin Rosniak; *D:* Michael Jenkins; *W:* Tony Morphett; *C:* Russell Boyd; *M:* Richard Thompson, Peter Filleul.

Swept Away . . .
A rich and beautiful Milanese woman is shipwrecked on a desolate island with a swarthy Sicilian deck hand, who also happens to be a dedicated communist. Isolated, the two switch roles, with the wealthy woman dominated by the crude proletarian. Sexy and provocative. Most of the film takes place in bright sunlight and the DVD's colors are consistently bright. The image is sharp and grain-free. The mono sound is O.K. with not-bad clarity and a little bit of body. —*JO* *AKA:* Swept Away . . . By an Unusual Destiny in the Blue Sea of August.
Movie: 🐾🐾🐾 **DVD:** 🐾🐾🐾🐾
Fox/Lorber Home Video (Cat #FLV5001, UPC #720917500126). Widescreen (1.85:1) letterboxed. Mono. $24.98. Keepcase. *LANG:* Italian. *SUB:* English. *FEATURES:* 9 chapter links ☞ Production notes ☞ Biographies.
1975 (R) 116m/C *IT* Giancarlo Giannini, Mariangela Melato; *D:* Lina Wertmuller; *W:* Lina Wertmuller; *C:* Julio Battiferri; *M:* Piero Piccioni.

Swept from the Sea
Shipwrecked foreigner Yanko (Perez) and ostracized servant girl Amy (Weisz) are star-crossed lovers in 19th-century Cornwall. In flashback, Dr. Kennedy (McKellen) tells the invalid Miss Swaffer (Bates) how he grew to understand the young man through chess, and how the young woman was suspected of having caused the storm that wrecked his ship. Defiantly

aimed at die-hard romantics, the film throws in all the melodrama it can muster and then some. The bucolic locations, filmed in the conventional misty focus, gain nothing on DVD. The stereo sound is more impressive in the big storm scenes. But none of the visuals can overpower the first-rate supporting cast. —*MM AKA:* Amy Foster.
Movie: 🐾🐾🐾 **DVD:** 🐾🐾🐾
Columbia Tristar Home Video (Cat #21649, UPC #04339621649). Widescreen (2.35:1) letterboxed; full frame. Dolby Digital 5.1 Surround Stereo; Dolby Digital Surround Stereo. $29.95. Keepcase. *LANG:* English; French; Spanish. *SUB:* English; French; Spanish. *FEATURES:* 28 chapter links ☞ Trailer.
1997 (PG-13) 115m/C *GB* Vincent Perez, Rachel Weisz, Kathy Bates, Ian McKellen, Joss Ackland, Tom Bell, Zoe Wanamaker, Tony Haygarth, Fiona Victory; *D:* Beeban Kidron; *W:* Tim Willocks; *C:* Dick Pope; *M:* John Barry.

Swimming with Sharks
Budding screenwriter Guy (Whaley) goes to work for notoriously insulting movie producer Buddy Ackerman (Spacey). Guy's girlfriend Dawn (Forbes) urges him to quit but he takes a different kind of revenge to even the score. Huang's Hollywood satire has more bite than *The Player* and a devious ending that will strike some viewers as wrong. Mostly, though, it's a showcase for Spacey, who turns in a breakthrough performance that presages the sharp work he would do in *The Usual Suspects* and *L.A. Confidential*. In fact, he's so good that the full-frame version of the DVD may be preferable to the widescreen. Beyond a few mild flashes in clothing patterns, the image is fine and the crisp sound captures all of Spacey's brilliant monologues. The snappy menu's pretty cool, too. —*MM AKA:* The Buddy Factor.
Movie: 🐾🐾🐾🐾 **DVD:** 🐾🐾🐾
Trimark Home Video (Cat #6837D, UPC #031398683735). Widescreen letterboxed; full frame. Dolby Digital Surround Stereo. $24.99. Keepcase. *LANG:* English. *SUB:* French; Spanish. *FEATURES:* Trailer ☞ Cast and crew thumbnail bios.
1994 (R) 93m/C Kevin Spacey, Frank Whaley, Michelle Forbes, Benicio Del Toro; *D:* George Huang; *W:* George Huang; *C:* Steven Firestone; *M:* Tom Heil. *AWARDS:* New York Film Critics Awards '95: Best Supporting Actor (Spacey); *NOM:* Independent Spirit Awards '96: Best Actor (Spacey).

Swimsuit
Adman Brian (Katt) aims to revitalize Katherine Allison's (Charisse) swimwear company by sponsoring a search for the perfect swimsuit model. Inoffensive made-for-TV fluff is absolutely average. Nothing is special about image or sound on the DVD. —*MM*
Movie: 🐾🐾 **DVD:** 🐾🐾

Simitar Entertainment (Cat #7271, UPC #082551727124). Full frame. PCM Stereo. $7.98. Keepcase. *LANG:* English. *FEATURES:* 8 chapter links ☞ Production factoids ☞ Cyd Charisse and William Katt filmographies.
1989 100m/C William Katt, Catherine Oxenberg, Cyd Charisse, Nia Peeples, Tom Villard, Cheryl Pollak, Billy Warlock, Jack Wagner; *D:* Chris Thomson; *W:* Robert Schiff; *C:* Laszlo George; *M:* John D'Andrea.

Swingers
Hip, hilarious, and highly entertaining low-budget comedy features five young show-biz wanna-bes on the prowl for career breaks and beautiful "babies" in the Hollywood retro club scene. Mike (screenwriter Favreau) is a struggling actor-comedian from New York who's having trouble getting over his ex. His slick, handsome friend Trent (Vaughn, in a star-making turn) and the rest of his neo–Rat Pack buddies try to get him back in the game with nightly parties and lounge-hopping. Witty script and clever camera work make this one "money, baby, money!" One of the film's strong points is its easy-listening swing soundtrack, and the DVD would be more enjoyable had the Dolby Surround been hopped up a bit. It's not terrible, but needs a little more ambient Surround and a definite bass boost. The image is good and sharp, with very pleasing colors that are both accurate and true. —*JO*
Movie: 🐾🐾🐾 **DVD:** 🐾🐾🐾
Buena Vista Home Entertainment (Cat #14378, UPC #717951000491). Widescreen (1.85:1) letterboxed. Dolby Surround. $29.99. Keepcase. *LANG:* English. *SUB:* Spanish. *CAP:* English. *FEATURES:* 13 chapter links ☞ Theatrical trailer.
1996 (R) 96m/C Jon Favreau, Vince Vaughn, Ron Livingston, Patrick Van Horn, Alex Desert, Brooke Langton, Heather Graham, Deena Martin, Katherine Kendall, Blake Lindsley; *D:* Doug Liman; *W:* Jon Favreau; *C:* Doug Liman; *M:* Justin Reinhardt. *AWARDS:* MTV Movie Awards '97: Best New Filmmaker Award (Liman).

The Swinging Cheerleaders
Kate (Johnston), a reporter for the Mesa University campus newspaper, goes undercover to find out what really goes on within the cheerleading squad. In the post-Watergate world of 1974, conspiracies and conflicts between the jocks and the radicals loom large, but the real focus is on three of the pleated-skirt crew (Camp, Katon, and Smith). Though racy in its day, the film has a sweet, almost innocent quality now. The image transfer is good; in fact, the interiors look better now than they did in the initial theatrical release, as I remember that particular drive-in. On the commentary track, director Hill and interviewer Johnny Legend do not try to make the film any more important than it was, though they are careful to give it a prominent

place in the mid'70s cheerleader/ pom-pom girl exploitation mini-wave. They also talk about the constraints of the time in the depiction of sexual material, and at one point, Hill manages—in good fun—to compare himself to Ingmar Bergman. —MM

Movie: 𝄞𝄞𝄞 **DVD:** 𝄞𝄞𝄞

Anchor Bay (Cat #DV10826, UPC #01313 1082692). Widescreen (1.66:1). Dolby Digital Mono. $24.98. Keepcase. FEATURES: TV spots • Commentary: Jack Hill and film historian Johnny Legend • 25 chapter links.

1974 (PG) 90m/C Cheryl "Rainbeaux" Smith, Colleen Camp, Rosanne Katon, Jo Johnston, Mae Mercer, Bob Minor, George D. Wallace; **D:** Jack Hill; **W:** Betty Conklin; **C:** Alfred Taylor; **M:** William Allen Castleman, William Loose.

Swiss Conspiracy

Ex-government investigator David Christopher (Janssen) tries to stop a blackmailer preying on the numbered bank account set. An all-star cast is cast adrift in this confusing suspense flick. The DVD is simply abominable. It appears to have been made from a worn print. The image is unfocused; most colors are slightly off and the sound is even worse. —MM

Movie: 𝄞➤ **DVD:** woof

Simitar Entertainment (Cat #7251, UPC #082551725120). Full frame. PCM Stereo. $14.98. Keepcase. LANG: English. FEATURES: 8 chapter links • Production factoids • David Janssen, Senta Berger filmographies.

1977 (PG) 92m/C GE David Janssen, Senta Berger, John Saxon, Ray Milland, Elke Sommer; **D:** Jack Arnold; **W:** Norman Klenman, Philip Saltzman, Michael Stanley; **M:** Klaus Doldinger.

Switchback

FBI agent LaCross (Quaid) pursues a serial killer who kidnapped his son. Against the backdrop of a Texas sheriff's (Ermey) election and a Colorado snowstorm, the killer who may be either former rail worker Goodhall (Glover) or the hitchhiking ex-doctor (Leto) he picked up leads LaCrosse on a convoluted cat-and-mouse game with no apparent logic or motive. First-time director Stuart, responsible for the Die Hard and Fugitive scripts, wrote this one in film school and it shows. Ermey is impressive as the put-upon small town lawman. The stunt work is well-done and the Colorado countryside looks great. The DVD handles the challenging material without glaring flaws. Even the helicopter, snow, and night scenes look fine. If only the contents equaled the packaging. —MM AKA: Going West in America.

Movie: 𝄞𝄞 **DVD:** 𝄞𝄞𝄞➤

Paramount Home Video (Cat #331207, UPC #097363312079). Widescreen letterboxed. Dolby Digital 5.1 Surround Stereo; Dolby Surround Stereo. $29.99. Keepcase. LANG: English; French. SUB: Spanish. CAP:

English. FEATURES: 34 chapter links • Theatrical trailer.

1997 (R) 120m/C Dennis Quaid, Danny Glover, Jared Leto, R. Lee Ermey, William Fichtner, Ted Levine, Leo Burmester, Merele Kennedy, Julio Mechoso; **D:** Jeb Stuart; **W:** Jeb Stuart; **C:** Oliver Wood; **M:** Basil Poledouris.

Sworn Enemies

This action sleeper is powered by a quirky sense of humor and equally strange characters. The town drunk Pershing Green (Pare) is filling in for the sheriff on the weekend that his old partner Clifton Santier (Greene) tries to pull off a drug deal that turns violent very quickly. The Canadian production looks exceptionally good from beginning to end. The no-frills DVD is fine in terms of sound and image. This one is much better than its generic title and box art would lead one to expect. —MM

Movie: 𝄞𝄞𝄞 **DVD:** 𝄞𝄞𝄞

Simitar Entertainment (Cat #7452, UPC #082551745227). Full frame. PCM Stereo. $14.98. Keepcase. LANG: English. FEATURES: 8 chapter links • Production factoids • Michael Pare filmography.

1996 (R) 101m/C CA Peter Greene, Michael Pare, Macha Grenon; **D:** Shimon Dotan; **W:** Rod Hewitt; **C:** Sylvain Brault; **M:** Walter Christian Rothe, Richard Anthony Boast.

T-Men

Treasury Department agents Dennis O'Brien (O'Keefe) and Tony Genaro (Ryder) infiltrate a mob counterfeiting gang. Filmed in a semi-documentary style, the exciting tale also serves as an effective commentary on the similarities between the agents and those they pursue. Mann and cinematographer Alton do especially fine work.

Movie: 𝄞𝄞𝄞 **DVD:** NYR

Kino on Video (Cat #AED2002). Full frame. $39.95. Available as part of triple feature 2-disc set "The Film Noir of Anthony Mann" with Raw Deal and He Walked by Night.

1947 96m/B Alfred Ryder, Dennis O'Keefe, June Lockhart, Mary Meade, Wallace Ford, Charles McGraw; **D:** Anthony Mann; **W:** John C. Higgins; **C:** John Alton; **M:** Paul Sawtell. AWARDS: NOM: Academy Awards '47: Best Sound.

Tactical Assault

Think Top Gun with a psychotic villain for this Hungarian production. Pilots Lee Banning (Patrick) and John "Doc" Holiday (Hauer) are serving together in Bosnia, but their history goes back to the Gulf War where they were involved in an incident with an Iraqi airliner. The primary focus is on military hardware, and the DVD handles the aerial footage competently. The story, which begins realistically enough but steadily becomes more and more foolish, is another matter. The disc is only slightly

sharper than VHS tape in image and sound. The generic title is apt. —MM

Movie: 𝄞𝄞 **DVD:** 𝄞𝄞

Trimark Home Video (Cat #7191D, UPC #031398719137). Full frame. Dolby Digital Surround Stereo. $24.99. Keepcase. LANG: English. SUB: English; French; Spanish. CAP: English. FEATURES: 24 chapter links • Trailer.

1999 (R) 89m/C Rutger Hauer, Robert Patrick, Isabel Glasser, Ken Howard; **D:** Mark Griffiths.

Tail Lights Fade

In the tradition of Truth or Consequences, N.M. and Best Laid Plans, this crime flick involves a cast of attractive young actors who all try to look fairly scuzzy, a twisty plot, realistic locations, and junky-but-cool old Detroit land yachts. A jailbird sets up a pot deal, but is double-crossed by Eve (Berkley). His sister (Allen), her boyfriend (Meyer), and a sexy blonde (Richards) find themselves heading for Vancouver. Each has different and often conflicting aims, which tend to change with circumstances. For a modestly budgeted road movie, this one looks O.K. on DVD, though it's not significantly sharper than VHS tape. No serious visual flaws; fine sound. —MM

Movie: 𝄞𝄞 **DVD:** 𝄞𝄞

Trimark Home Video (Cat #VM7280D, UPC #031398728023). Widescreen letterboxed. Dolby Digital Stereo. $24.99. Keepcase. LANG: English. SUB: English; French; Spanish. FEATURES: 24 chapter links • Theatrical trailer.

1999 (R) 87m/C CA Tanya Allen, Breckin Meyer, Jake Busey, Denise Richards, Lisa Marie, Elizabeth Berkley, Jaimz Woolvett; **D:** Malcolm Ingram; **W:** Matthew Gissing; **C:** Brian Pearson.

Take the Money and Run

Allen's directorial debut—he also stars and cowrote—is a "mockumentary" that follows timid would-be felon Virgil Starkwell, who can't get his career off the ground and keeps landing in jail. Little plot, but so what? The one-liners, slapstick, and sight gags are some of Allen's early best, particularly the long bank robbery scene. Overall, the DVD image and sound match the quality of this modest, overachieving effort, though the nominal letterboxing makes the difference between the full-frame and widescreen presentations negligible. It's easy to spot the beginnings of themes and jokes that Allen would develop in his next comedies—Bananas, Sleeper, Everything You Always Wanted to Know about Sex.... Commentary by the director or a knowledgeable critic would be welcome. —MM

Movie: 𝄞𝄞𝄞➤ **DVD:** 𝄞𝄞𝄞

Anchor Bay (Cat #DV10835, UPC #013131083590). Full frame; widescreen (1.66:1) letterboxed. Dolby Digital Mono. $24.98. Keepcase. FEATURES: 20 chapter links.

1969 (PG) 85m/C Woody Allen, Janet Margolin, Marcel Hillaire, Louise Lasser, Jacquelyn Hyde, Lonny (Loni) Chapman, Jan Merlin, James Anderson, Jackson Beck, Howard Storm; **D:** Woody Allen; **W:** Mickey Rose, Woody Allen; **C:** Lester Shorr; **M:** Marvin Hamlisch.

A Tale of Two Kitties

Simple animated musical teaches lessons about friendship and maturity. Spunky and Chester, two farm cats, don't know what to do when it rains. Then Aunt Lucy and her kitten Timmy come to visit. The animation and the songs are so simple that they present no challenges to DVD technology. The story is aimed at very young children. Box copy suggests ages 2–7. Parents will probably know within the first five minutes if the kids are going to be entertained. The film was produced in Poland and imported through Canada. —*MM*
Movie: 🐾🐾 **DVD:** 🐾🐾
Simitar Entertainment (Cat #7201, UPC #082551720125). Full frame. PCM Uncompressed Stereo. $7.98. Keepcase. *LANG:* English. *FEATURES:* Links to songs.
1996 65m/C D: Ireneusz Czesny, Ryszard Szynczak.

Tale of Two Sisters

The relationship between two sisters (Breiman and Christian) is explored through the poetry of Charlie Sheen. (Charlie Sheen?) It's a non-linear tale told through Felliniesque images and extra narration from Charlie Sheen. (Charlie Sheen?) On DVD, the image is very poor. Diagonal lines break up; tile patterns vibrate, black clothes are ink blots, and then there's the banal apparently improvised dialogue. Overall, one of the most inexcusable mistakes ever perpetrated on film. Charlie Sheen? —*MM*
Movie: woof **DVD:** woof
Simitar Entertainment (Cat #7493, UPC #082551749324). Full frame. Dolby Digital Mono. $14.98. Keepcase. *LANG:* English. *FEATURES:* 8 chapter links • Production factoids • Claudia Christian filmography.
1989 90m/C Valerie Breiman, Claudia Christian, Sydney Lassick, Jeff Conaway, Peter Berg; **D:** Adam Rifkin; **W:** Charlie Sheen; **Nar:** Charlie Sheen.

Tales from the Crypt Presents Bordello of Blood

Detective Rafe Guttman (Miller) is on the case of a Bible thumper's (Eleniak) missing brother (Feldman). The trail leads him to a unique establishment, a brothel presided over by vampire queen Lilith (Everhart), whose clients all wind up dead (but probably with smiles on their faces), and the strange Reverend Current (Sarandon, who made a fine vampire himself in *Fright Night*). Crypt Keeper's second big screen outing showcases Miller's slant on the leading man gig and serves up campy fun with the blood. Image's DVD transfer is pretty good and the sound is much improved over the VHS and laserdisc versions. There is some low-level grain that remains throughout most of the film, which is generally darkly lit. —*JO* **AKA:** Bordello of Blood.
Movie: 🐾🐾 **DVD:** 🐾🐾🐾
Image Entertainment (Cat #ID4225USDVD, UPC #014381422528). Widescreen (1.85:1) letterboxed. Dolby Digital 5.1. $29.95. Snapper. *LANG:* English. *FEATURES:* 34 chapter links.
1996 (R) 87m/C Dennis Miller, Angie Everhart, Chris Sarandon, Corey Feldman, Erika Eleniak; **D:** Gilbert Adler; **W:** Gilbert Adler, A.L. Katz; **C:** Tom Priestley; **M:** Chris Boardman.

Tales from the Crypt Presents Demon Knight

Gruesomely garish big-screen version of the TV series that was inspired by the lurid 1950s E.C. comics. Horrormeister Crypt Keeper offers his usual pun-filled introduction to a tale set in a seedy boardinghouse. Brayker (Sadler) is the guardian of an ancient key that keeps the forces of darkness from overwhelming mankind, a key desired by the charismatic Collector (Zane), who unleashes a disgusting mix of demons against the house's inhabitants. Curious hybrid of spoof/splatter pic that doesn't quite work in either genre. The picture quality on *Demon Knight* is comparable to *Bordello of Blood,* but the sound is a little inferior, due in part to the Dolby Surround lacking the bass of the other's 5.1 mix. —*JO* **AKA:** Demon Knight; Demon Keeper.
Movie: 🐾🐾 **DVD:** 🐾🐾
Image Entertainment (Cat #ID4233USDVD, UPC #014381423327). Widescreen (1.85:1) letterboxed. Dolby Surround. $29.95. Snapper. *LANG:* English. *CAP:* English. *FEATURES:* 16 chapter links.
1994 (R) 93m/C Billy Zane, William Sadler, Jada Pinkett Smith, Brenda Bakke, CCH Pounder, Dick Miller, Thomas Haden Church, John Schuck, Gary Farmer, Charles Fleischer; **D:** Ernest R. Dickerson; **W:** Ethan Reiff, Cyrus Voris, Mark Bishop; **C:** Rick Bota; **M:** Ed Shearmur; **V:** John Kassir.

Tales from the Hood

Horror anthology with that urban twist. Three young thugs search for lost drugs inside a funeral parlor run by creepy Mr. Simms (Williams III) and instead walk into a world of four chilling and funny stories of fright dealing with racism and black-on-black crime. Tales aren't very original and are often too preachy for true enjoyment, but it's nice to see someone attempt to breathe life into an old and familiar genre. Williams III, with his pop-eyed stares and Don King coif, is fitting as the eerie storyteller. The picture sharpness during most of the brighter sequences is unfortunately less common than the softer, grain-filled image during the film's more-numerous darker scenes. Colors are O.K., though. The Dolby Surround is pretty good, and definitely more energetic than a lot of low-budget releases. —*JO*
Movie: 🐾🐾 **DVD:** 🐾🐾
HBO Home Video (Cat #91217, UPC #026359121722). Full frame. Dolby Surround; Dolby Digital Mono. $24.98. Snapper. *LANG:* English (DS); Spanish (DDM). *CAP:* English. *FEATURES:* 22 chapter links • Cast bios.
1995 (R) 97m/C Clarence Williams III, Corbin Bernsen, David Alan Grier, Wings Hauser, Rosalind Cash, Rusty Cundieff, Joe Torry, Anthony Griffith; **D:** Rusty Cundieff; **W:** Rusty Cundieff, Darin Scott; **C:** Anthony B. Richmond; **M:** Christopher Young.

Tales of Ordinary Madness

Gazzara stars as a poet who drinks and sleeps with assorted women. Based on the stories of Charles Bukowski, the film is pretentious and dull, but possessing a cult following. Don't run out and buy this DVD; it offers little improvement over the older VHS version (Image concurrently released a VHS edition), except for a cleaner soundtrack. The picture remains somewhat soft and the preprint material is far from perfect. At least the DVD hasn't added any grain or artifacts. —*JO*
Movie: 🐾 **DVD:** 🐾
Image Entertainment (Cat #ID47822SIDVD, UPC #014381478228). Widescreen (1.77:1) letterboxed. Dolby Digital Mono. $24.95. Snapper. *LANG:* English. *FEATURES:* 12 chapter links.
1983 107m/C Ben Gazzara, Ornella Muti, Susan Tyrrell, Tanya Lopert, Roy Brocksmith, Katya Berger; **D:** Marco Ferreri; **W:** Marco Ferreri, Sergio Amidei, Anthony Foutz; **C:** Tonino Delli Colli; **M:** Philippe Sarde.

Tampopo

A hilarious, sensuous, and episodic Japanese comedy. A widowed noodle shop owner is coached by a ten-gallon-hatted stranger in how to make the perfect noodle. The popular, freeform hit that established Itami in the West is not a great DVD, but a pretty good one. The colors are a little faded compared to the laserdisc release, and that fact alone scaled down the sensuousness of the food sex scenes, and the overall stylized spaghetti-western feel of the film. Picture sharpness is O.K., and there is relatively little grain. The stereo sound is scratchy at times and lacks body. —*JO* **AKA:** Dandelion.
Movie: 🐾🐾🐾 **DVD:** 🐾🐾
Fox/Lorber Home Video (Cat #FLV5045, UPC #720917504520). Widescreen (1.77:1) letterboxed. Stereo. $29.98. Keepcase. *LANG:* Japanese. *SUB:* English. *FEATURES:* 30 chapter links • Filmographies.
1986 114m/C *JP* Ken Watanabe, Tsutomu Yamazaki, Nobuko Miyamoto, Koji Yakusho, Rikiya Yasuoka, Kinzo Sakura,

Shoji Otake; **D:** Juzo Itami; **W:** Juzo Itami; **C:** Masaki Tamura; **M:** Kunihiko Murai.

Tango and Cash

Stallone and Russell are L.A. cops with something in common: they both think they are the best in the city. Forced to work together to beat drug lord Palance, they flex their muscles a lot. Directing completed by Albert Magnoli, after Andrei Konchalovsky left in a huff. The movie's still stupid, but the DVD looks and sounds great. Though the earlier VHS and laserdisc version had trouble presenting all the dark scenes accurately (and there are a lot of them—style no doubt), this DVD handles them with no problem. The picture is as sharp and the colors as vibrant as on most brightly lit films. Contrast level are excellent and the image has consistently good definition of details and hues. The sound is also energized with loads of bass and nicely imaged Surround. —JO
Movie: 🎬➤ **DVD:** 🎬🎬🎬➤
Warner Home Video, Inc. (Cat #11951, UPC #085391195122). Widescreen (2.35:1) anamorphic. Dolby Digital 5.1; Dolby Surround. $24.98. Snapper. *LANG:* English (DD5.1); French (DS). *SUB:* English; Spanish; French. *FEATURES:* 31 chapter links • Theatrical trailers • Production notes.
1989 (R) 104m/C Sylvester Stallone, Kurt Russell, Jack Palance, Brion James, Teri Hatcher, Michael J. Pollard, James Hong, Marc Alaimo, Robert Z'Dar; **D:** Andrei Konchalovsky; **W:** Randy Feldman; **C:** Donald E. Thorin; **M:** Harold Faltermeyer.

Tank

Retired Army officer Garner's son is thrown into jail on a trumped up charge by a small-town sheriff. Dad comes to the rescue in his restored Sherman tank. The trite and unrealistic portrayal of good vs. evil is made palatable by Garner's performance.
Movie: 🎬➤ **DVD:** NYR
Goodtimes Entertainment (Cat #81019). Full frame. Dolby Digital Mono. $19.98. Snapper. *LANG:* English; French. *SUB:* English; French; Spanish.
1983 (PG) 113m/C James Garner, Shirley Jones, C. Thomas Howell, Mark Herrier, Sandy Ward, Jenilee Harrison, Dorian Harewood, G.D. Spradlin; **D:** Marvin J. Chomsky; **W:** Dan Gordon; **C:** Donald Birnkrant; **M:** Lalo Schifrin.

Tarantella

Given the original promotional image, of the star in an off-the-shoulder peasant blouse and erotically tousled hair, this barely released film was likely written off as another romantic "coming-of-age" story. It is really about identity and female family relationships. Sorvino plays Diana Di Sorella, who must piece together some understanding of her immigrant mother after learning too late of her death. She

gets practical help and emotional support from her grandmother's friend (Gregorio). The most unusual and compelling sections are symbolic interludes staged with Sandy Spieler marionettes in In the Heart of the Beast Puppet and Mask Theatre. These are not just flights of fancy; they hold the key to the plot. We can at least thank the label for back-pedaling on sensationalism for this edition. Too bad the low-budget design is so unappealing, with its diffuse-looking box cover and precious yet slapped-together menus. The visual quality of the movie tends towards reddish interiors and washed-out exteriors. Even the greens bleed. The sound fares better, considering its "seat of the pants" recording situations on neighborhood front porches, in cars, and on the beach. —JK
Movie: 🎬🎬➤ **DVD:** 🎬🎬➤
BWE (Bonneville Worldwide Entertainment) Video (Cat #ID5569BVDVD, UPC #014381 556926). Full frame. Dolby Digital Mono. $24.99. Snapper. *LANG:* English. *FEATURES:* 12 chapter links • Interactive menus.
1995 84m/C Mira Sorvino, Rose Gregorio, Stephen Spinella, Matthew Lillard, Antonia Rey, Frank Pellegrino; **D:** Helen DeMichiel; **W:** Helen DeMichiel, Richard Hoblock; **C:** Teodoro Maniaci; **M:** Norman Moll.

Tarzan

Disney's streamlined version of Edgar Rice Burroughs's perennially popular tale is one of the best screen adaptations, live action or animation. The introduction sets a zippy pace and establishes the characters without wasting a frame. Tarzan (voice of Goldwyn) is adopted by gorilla mom Kala (Close) after her own baby is killed, but the boy is never accepted by the leader Kerchak (Henriksen, whose voice has seldom been used more dramatically). Lessons about acceptance are kept to a minimum. Jane (Driver) and Terk (O'Donnell) add needed humor. Clayton (Blessed) is another testosterone-enhanced Disney villain. The DVD re creates the theatrical image flawlessly. True, the vertiginous arboreal chases lose some intensity. Phil Collins's Oscar-winning score sounds just as good. For kids, the access to favorite scenes and the music videos may prove to be the most popular extras. All in all, the disc is one of the studio's modern best along with *Little Mermaid* and *Beauty and the Beast*.—MM
Movie: 🎬🎬🎬 **DVD:** 🎬🎬🎬
Buena Vista Home Entertainment (Cat #18150, UPC #717951004291). Widescreen (1.66:1) letterboxed. Dolby Digital 5.0 Surround Stereo. $39.99. Keepcase. *LANG:* English; French; Spanish. *SUB:* Spanish. *CAP:* English. *FEATURES:* 2 music videos • Interactive read-along • Trivia game • Preview of *Dinosaur* • Theatrical trailer • DVD-ROM extras.
1999 (G) 88m/C D: Kevin Lima, Chris Buck; **W:** Tab Murphy, Bob Tzudiker, Noni White; **M:** Phil Collins; **V:** Tony Goldwyn, Minnie Driver, Rosie O'Donnell, Glenn

Close, Lance Henriksen, Wayne Knight, Brian Blessed, Nigel Hawthorne, Alex D. Linz. *AWARDS:* Academy Awards '99: Best Song ("You'll Be In My Heart"); Golden Globe Awards '00: Best Song ("You'll Be In My Heart").

Tarzan and the Lost City

Gorgeous South African locations are a decided plus in this routine hero/adventure story. Lord Greystoke, AKA Tarzan (Van Dien), returns to Africa from England to save his home from mercenaries hunting the Lost City of Opar. Spunky fiancee Jane (March) heads to the jungle after her Ape Man and get into (and out of) trouble with bad guy Nigel Ravens (Waddington). The effects aren't much but Van Dien looks good in a loincloth and the action moves well. *AKA:* Tarzan and Jane; Greystoke 2: Tarzan and Jane.
Movie: 🎬🎬 **DVD:** NYR
Warner Home Video, Inc. (Cat #16647). $14.98. Snapper. *LANG:* English; French. *CAP:* English.
1998 (PG) 84m/C Casper Van Dien, Jane March, Steven Waddington, Winston Ntshona, Rapulana Seiphemo, Ian Roberts; **D:** Carl Schenkel; **W:** Bayard Johnson, J. Anderson Black; **C:** Paul Gilpin; **M:** Christopher Franke.

Tarzan in Manhattan

This made-for-TV foolishness is certainly in the running for the worst *Tarzan* movie ever. In this one, the ape man (Lara) flies to the Big Apple to rescue the kidnapped Cheetah and to find the guy who shot his ape mother. (Really.) He meets a friendly cabbie named, you guessed it, Jane (Crosby). The DVD looks pretty bad with heavy pixelation in the background vegetation. The night scenes are a little better, but not much. Tarzan's best line: "Why is that man dressed like a banana?" —MM
Movie: 🎬🎬 **DVD:** 🎬🎬
Simitar Entertainment (Cat #7273, UPC #082551727322). Full frame. PCM Stereo. $14.98. Keepcase. *LANG:* English. *FEATURES:* 8 chapter links • Production factoids • Tony Curtis filmography.
1989 (PG) 94m/C Joe Lara, Kim Crosby, Tony Curtis, Jan-Michael Vincent; **D:** Michael A. Schultz.

The Taste of Cherry

A prize-winner at Cannes, this Iranian import is aimed at the serious festival crowd. The story of Mr. Badii (Ershadi), who drives around the outskirts of Tehran and contemplates suicide owes more to such European filmmakers as Bresson and Bergman than to Hollywood. Though the DVD lacks extras, this is not the kind of film that calls for them. The image captures the dusty sienna light that director Kiarostami uses to paint his landscape. It also fits his stark tone and methodical pace. The Dolby Mono is fine for the naturalistic soundtrack. In the end, this one is

certainly not for everyone. The right audiences will love it. —*MM* **AKA:** Ta'm e Guilass; Taste of Cherries.
Movie: 🐾🐾🐾➤ **DVD:** 🐾🐾🐾🐾
Criterion Collection (Cat #TAS020, UPC #037429137222). Widescreen (1.66:1) letterboxed. Dolby Digital Mono. $29.95. Keepcase. *LANG:* Farsi. *SUB:* English. *FEATURES:* Theatrical trailer • Interview with Kiarostami by Iranian film scholar Dr. Jamsheed Akrami • Kiarostami filmography • 14 chapter links.
1996 95m/C Homayon Ershadi, Abdolrahma Bagheri, Afshin Bakhtiari; *D:* Abbas Kiarostami; *W:* Abbas Kiarostami; *C:* Homayun Payvar. *AWARDS:* Cannes Film Festival '97: Best Film; National Society of Film Critics Awards '98: Best Foreign Film.

Taxi Driver (CE)

Many critics and viewers have tried to turn Travis Bickle (De Niro) into either a hero or a villain. He's neither. He's a sympathetic monster, "God's lonely man," he calls himself, who's driven deeper and deeper into madness by the surreal nightmare city surrounding him. Writer Paul Schrader, director Martin Scorsese, and composer Bernard Herrmann make that world indelibly real. Though the film isn't often considered a work of horror, it's told through the conventions of the genre. Bickle's slow transformation from stoic loner to insane assassin, and his essentially accidental redemption, are deeply frightening. With remastered sound and image, the DVD is infinitely superior to VHS tape—particularly those older ones that have been rented hundreds of times at the video store. That said, the film is supposed to be dark, grim, and hellish, and the disc does not attempt to change that. It's still brighter and sharper than the theatrical release, as I remember it. With the extensive extras, a commentary track might have been nice, but the film speaks for itself. The disc belongs in the collection of any serious fan. —*MM*
Movie: 🐾🐾🐾🐾 **DVD:** 🐾🐾🐾🐾
Columbia Tristar Home Video (Cat #03481, UPC #043396034815). Widescreen (1.85:1) anamorphic. Dolby Digital Surround Stereo. $25.95. Keepcase. *LANG:* English. *SUB:* English; Spanish; Portuguese; Chinese; Korean; Thai. *FEATURES:* 28 chapter links • Screenplay-to-scene navigation • Trailers • "Making of" featurette • Storyboard sequence • Advertising materials • Filmographies • Liner notes.
1976 (R) 112m/C Robert De Niro, Jodie Foster, Harvey Keitel, Cybill Shepherd, Peter Boyle, Albert Brooks, Leonard Harris, Joe Spinell, Martin Scorsese; *D:* Martin Scorsese; *W:* Paul Schrader; *C:* Michael Chapman; *M:* Bernard Herrmann. *AWARDS:* American Film Institute (AFI) '98: Top 100; British Academy Awards '76: Best Supporting Actress (Foster); Cannes Film Festival '76: Best Film; Los Angeles Film Critics Association Awards '76: Best Actor (De Niro), National Film Registry '94; New York Film Critics Awards '76: Best Actor (De Niro); National Society

of Film Critics Awards '76: Best Actor (De Niro), Best Director (Scorsese), Best Supporting Actress (Foster); *NOM:* Academy Awards '76: Best Actor (De Niro), Best Picture, Best Supporting Actress (Foster), Best Original Score.

A Taxing Woman

Satiric Japanese comedy is about a woman tax collector in pursuit of a crafty millionaire tax cheater. Director Itami is a master at reflecting cultural and social problems in a humorous fashion. Followed by the much grimmer, but still funny *A Taxing Woman Returns*. Both the DVD and the preprint used as the source material are flawed, but the disc is still enjoyable. The picture is a little soft and colors are faded. The DVD adds a small amount of grain, and during a few scenes there are some artifacts. The soundtrack lacks energy and sounds more mono than stereo. Some preprint noise is also evident. —*JO* **AKA:** Marusa No Onna.
Movie: 🐾🐾🐾➤ **DVD:** 🐾🐾➤
Fox/Lorber Home Video (Cat #FLV5042, UPC #720917504223). Full frame. Stereo. $29.98. Keepcase. *LANG:* Japanese. *SUB:* English. *FEATURES:* 8 chapter links • Theatrical trailer • Filmographies.
1987 127m/C *JP* Nobuko Miyamoto, Tsutomu Yamazaki, Hideo Murota, Shuji Otaki; *D:* Juzo Itami; *W:* Juzo Itami; *C:* Yonezo Maeda; *M:* Toshiyuki Honda.

Tea with Mussolini

Which name does not belong on this list: Dame Judi Dench, Joan Plowright, Maggie Smith, Cher? Therein lies the central problem with this otherwise pleasant bit of nostalgia. In prewar Florence, a group of eccentric Englishwomen—including Mary (Plowright), Hester (Smith), and Annabella (Dench)—are upset by the arrival of wealthy, crass (and Jewish) American Elsa (Cher). Then there's the matter of the fascists. After the outbreak of war, their situation deteriorates. Actually, She of the Tattooed Tush doesn't embarrass herself too badly, but only because she's reinforced by Lily Tomlin, and that name belongs on any list. With its intentionally soft focus, Zeffirelli's film is not much better on DVD than it is on VHS tape. For fans of the locales, only a full-size theatre screen is acceptable. For fans of the cast, even tape is O.K. —*MM*
Movie: 🐾🐾 **DVD:** 🐾🐾🐾
MGM Home Entertainment (Cat #907918, UPC #027616791825). Widescreen anamorphic; full frame. Dolby 5.1 Surround Stereo; Dolby Digital Surround Stereo. $24.98. Keepcase. *LANG:* English; French. *SUB:* English; French. *FEATURES:* 32 chapter links • Theatrical trailer.
1999 (PG) 116m/C *IT GB* Joan Plowright, Maggie Smith, Judi Dench, Cher, Baird Wallace, Charlie Lucas, Lily Tomlin, Paolo Seganti, Massimo Ghini, Claudio Spadaro; *D:* Franco Zeffirelli; *W:* Franco Zeffirelli, John Mortimer; *C:* David Watkin; *M:* Alessio Vlad, Stefano Arnaldi. *AWARDS:*

British Academy Awards '99: Best Supporting Actress (Smith); *NOM:* British Academy Awards '99: Best Costume Design.

Teaching Mrs. Tingle

Bright high school student Leigh (Holmes) and her pals Jo Lynn (Coughlin) and Luke (Watson) are forced to take desperate measures after the tyrannical Mrs. Tingle (Mirren) attempts to ruin Leigh's chances for a college scholarship. Trying to turn a premise involving kidnapping and murder into a comedy is more than Kevin Williamson (writer of *Scream*) can handle in his directorial debut. On DVD, both image and sound are average. —*MM* **AKA:** Killing Mrs. Tingle.
Movie: 🐾🐾 **DVD:** 🐾🐾
Buena Vista Home Entertainment (Cat #18267, UPC #717951004604). Widescreen (1.85:1) letterboxed. DTS 5.1 Surround Stereo; Dolby Digital Surround Stereo. $29.99. Keepcase. *LANG:* English. *CAP:* English. *FEATURES:* 18 chapter links • Theatrical trailer.
1999 (PG-13) 96m/C Katie Holmes, Helen Mirren, Liz Stauber, Barry Watson, Jeffrey Tambor, Vivica A. Fox, Marisa Coughlan, Molly Ringwald, Michael McKean; *D:* Kevin Williamson; *W:* Kevin Williamson; *C:* Jerzy Zielinski; *M:* John Frizzell.

Teenage Mutant Ninja Turtles: The Movie

When an inexplicable wave of petty theft strikes the Big Apple, it's up to four sewer-dwelling hardshell heroes to save the day. Aided by their ninja master, Splinter, and a feisty TV reporter (Hoag), the four Italo-American-Amphibians must face the warlord Shredder. Having been exposed to toxic radiation, they have grown to human size but have the intelligence and maturity of teenagers. The humor and action scenes stay strictly within the limits of the "PG" rating, and so the film is fine for all ages, but cinematic martial arts have grown much more sophisticated, fast-paced, and complex. On disc, some of the night scenes are heavily grained, and from beginning to end, the image lacks the sharp sparkle of more recent comic book-inspired movies. Still, kids old enough to handle a DVD remote will probably be entertained by the breezy story and the extras. —*MM*
Movie: 🐾🐾➤ **DVD:** 🐾🐾➤
New Line Home Video (Cat #N4121, UPC #794043412127). Full frame; widescreen letterboxed. Dolby Digital 5.1; Mono. $24.98. Snapper. *LANG:* English; French. *SUB:* English; French; Spanish. *CAP:* English. *FEATURES:* "Sewer Maze" interactive game • Fairly extensive character biographies • Original theatrical trailer • New Line previews • Interactive menus • 20 chapter links.
1990 (PG) 95m/C Judith Hoag, Elias Koteas; *D:* Steven Barron; *W:* Todd W. Lan-

gen; **C:** John Fenner; **M:** John Du Prez; **V:** Robbie Rist, Corey Feldman, Brian Tochi, Kevin Clash, David McCharen.

Telling Lies in America

Semi-autobiographical tale from writer Eszterhas is set in early-'60 Cleveland. That's where teenager Karchy Jones (Renfro) falls under the spell of slick, sleazy DJ Billy Magic (Bacon). After winning a contest, the boy becomes his idol's go-fer. The twisted rock 'n' roll mentor shows him a highly cynical version of the American Dream which, naturally, leads to trouble. The performances are letter-perfect, including Calista Flockhart, as the girl of Karchy's dreams. Despite a few cliches, this sleeper is a solid hit that works beautifully on DVD. It presents that distant world of the last century with a properly misty golden glow which does not make for a sharply focused image. The disc is only a marginal improvement over VHS tape. —MM
Movie: 🎜🎜🎜 **DVD:** 🎜🎜🎜
WinStar Home Entertainment (Cat #FLV 5175, UPC #720917517520). Full frame. $24.98. Keepcase. *LANG:* English. *FEATURES:* 8 chapter links • Trailer • Filmographies • Production credits • Weblink.
1996 (PG-13) 101m/C Kevin Bacon, Brad Renfro, Maximilian Schell, Calista Flockhart, Paul Dooley, Jonathan Rhys Meyers, Luke Wilson; **D:** Guy Ferland; **W:** Joe Eszterhas; **C:** Reynaldo Villalobos; **M:** Nicholas Pike.

Temptation of a Monk

Costume drama about China's 7th-century Tang Dynasty finds General Shi (Hsin-kuo) duped into an assassination plot against the crown prince. After a massacre, the General flees and finds sanctuary with a group of Buddhist monks at a remote temple. Also involved are the General's sometime-lover and a mystery woman (both played by Chen). Sometimes slow-moving and confusing but with exotic visuals. The picture on this Fox/Lorber DVD is pretty sharp and relatively grain-free. Unfortunately, the VHS tape seems to have more vibrant colors. The stereo sound is a fairly lifeless mix, but does have ample body and clarity. —IO
Movie: 🎜🎜 **DVD:** 🎜🎜🎜
Fox/Lorber Home Video (Cat #FLV5014, UPC #72091705014O). Full frame. Stereo. $29.98. Keepcase. *LANG:* Mandarin. *SUB:* English. *FEATURES:* 9 chapter links • Production notes • Cast and filmmakers bios • Trailer.
1994 118m/C *CH* Wu Hsin-kuo, Joan Chen, Zhang Fengyi, Michael Lee; **D:** Clara Law; **W:** Eddie L.C. Fong; **C:** Andrew Lesnie; **M:** Tats Lau.

The Temptations

Miniseries bio follows the Motown group from its high school beginnings in 1958 (under various names) through a meeting with Motown founder Berry Gordy (Babatunde) and major successes in the '60s. It's told from the viewpoint of the last original Temp, Otis Williams (Whitfield), as he and his buddies Melvin Franklin (Woodside) and Paul Williams (Payton) hook up with first lead singer Eddie Kendricks (Brooks). When Kendricks goes solo, it's the turn of David Ruffin (Leon) but the group suffers various ego traumas and tragedies. Naturally, the music's the real highlight.
Movie: 🎜🎜🎜 **DVD:** NYR
Hallmark Home Entertainment (Cat #99032). Full frame. Stereo. $19.98. Keepcase. *LANG:* English. *CAP:* English.
1998 150m/C Charles Malik Whitfield, DB Woodside, Terron Brooks, Christian Payton, Leon, Alan Rosenberg, Obba Babatunde, Charles Ley, Tina Lifford, Gina Ravera, Vanessa Bell Calloway, Chaz Lamar Shepherd; **D:** Allan Arkush; **W:** Kevin Arkadie, Robert P. Johnson; **C:** Jamie Anderson.

10

Caught up in his mid-life crisis, successful songwriter George Webber (Moore) falls in lust with a bride (Derek) he sees in a passing car. At laborious length, he learns who she is and pursues her to Mexico where she's on her honeymoon. As the long-suffering girlfriend, Julie Andrews steals the film. Her performance has aged well. On DVD, the night scenes are rough and grainy and any large area of black is absolutely solid, without detail. Those are a reflection of filmmaking techniques of the time, not the digital transfer. —MM
Movie: 🎜🎜🎜 **DVD:** 🎜🎜🎜
Warner Home Video, Inc. (Cat #2002, UPC #012569200227). Full frame; widescreen letterboxed. Dolby Digital Mono. $19.98. Snapper. *LANG:* English; French. *SUB:* English; French; Spanish. *CAP:* English. *FEATURES:* 35 chapter links • Cast and crew thumbnail biographies • "Making of" featurette • Theatrical trailer.
1979 (R) 121m/C Dudley Moore, Julie Andrews, Bo Derek, Dee Wallace Stone, Brian Dennehy, Robert Webber; **D:** Blake Edwards; **W:** Blake Edwards; **C:** Frank Stanley; **M:** Henry Mancini. *AWARDS: NOM:* Academy Awards '79: Best Song ("Song from 10 (It's Easy to Say)"), Best Original Score.

Ten Benny

Frustrated New Jersey shoe salesman Ray (Brody) borrows $10,000 from a local wiseguy to stake himself at the track and set himself up in business. Bad idea. As his luck continues its downward spiral, he abuses his wife (Temchen) into the arms of his buddy (Gallagher) and becomes more desperate to climb out of the hole he has dug for himself. First-time director Bross has obviously studied at the Scorsese school of filmmaking, but he must have skipped the classes on originality and characterization. There's not much going here that hasn't been done (better)

somewhere else, but Brody turns in a fine performance. *AKA:* Nothing to Lose.
Movie: 🎜🎜 **DVD:** NYR
WinStar Home Entertainment (Cat #5137). Widescreen (1.66:1) letterboxed. Stereo. $29.98. Keepcase. *FEATURES:* Cast and crew thumbnail bios • Trailer • Production notes.
1998 (R) 98m/C Adrien Brody, Sybil Temchen, Michael Gallagher, Tony Gillan, James Moriarty, Frank Vincent; **D:** Eric Bross; **W:** Eric Bross, Tom Cudworth; **C:** Horacio Marquinez; **M:** Chris Hajian.

The Ten Commandments

DeMille's remake of his 1923 silent classic (and his last film) is a lavish biblical epic that tells the story of Moses, who turned his back on a privileged life to lead his people to freedom outside of Egypt. Exceptional cast, with Fraser Heston (son of Charlton) as the baby Moses. Parting of Red Sea rivals any modern special effects. *The Ten Commandments* has never looked so good. The colors are stunning and fleshtones are accurate. Bleed is close to nonexistent. Blacks are also true and the contrast is far punchier than in any earlier home video release. The picture is also very sharp and grain is minimal, with the exception of a couple of long, detailed shots. The 5.1 sound is another definite improvement and the orchestral score sounds great. There is not a lot in the way of Surround effects, but a lot of very nice ambience has been added to the mix. —JO
Movie: 🎜🎜🎜 **DVD:** 🎜🎜🎜
Paramount Home Video (Cat #155087, UPC #097361550879). Widescreen (1.85:1) anamorphic. Dolby Digital 5.1; Dolby Surround; Mono. $34.99. Keepcase. *LANG:* English; French. *FEATURES:* 48 chapter links • 3 theatrical trailers • Dual-layered RSDL.
1956 (G) 219m/C Charlton Heston, Yul Brynner, Anne Baxter, Yvonne De Carlo, Nina Foch, John Derek, H.B. Warner, Henry Wilcoxon, Judith Anderson, John Carradine, Douglass Dumbrille, Cedric Hardwicke, Martha Scott, Vincent Price, Debra Paget; **D:** Cecil B. DeMille; **W:** Aeneas MacKenzie, Jesse Lasky Jr., Frederic M. Frank, Jack Gariss; **C:** Loyal Griggs; **M:** Elmer Bernstein. *AWARDS:* National Film Registry '99; *NOM:* Academy Awards '56: Best Art Direction/Set Decoration (Color), Best Color Cinematography, Best Costume Design (Color), Best Film Editing, Best Picture, Best Sound.

Ten Days That Shook the World

Eisenstein's silent masterpiece (with some sound effects and the 1948 Shostakovich score) is loosely based on American John Reed's book. Commissioned by the Soviet government on the tenth anniversary of the glorious Bolshevik Revolution of 1917, the film is an ambitious effort. The director was later forced to cut his portrayal of Leon Trotsky when the revolutionary became an enemy of the state. The film includes rare footage of the Czar's Winter Palace in Petrograd (later Leningrad). Along with *Battleship Potemkin,* this is Eisenstein's most striking work, even for those who do not share his politics. The restored DVD contains some unbelievably clear scenes. Many of the best moments look better than comparable scenes in films half as old. The revised title cards are easy to read, particularly the ones that are done in VERY LARGE LETTERS FOR EMPHASIS. The liner notes provide excellent if brief historical background, making the disc a fine resource for film students. —*MM* **AKA:** October; Oktyabr.

Movie: ♪♪♪ **DVD:** *♪♪♪*
Image Entertainment (Cat #ID4576CODVD, UPC #014381457629). Full frame. Dolby Digital Mono. $24.99. Snapper. *SUB:* English. *FEATURES:* 12 chapter links • Liner notes by Rob Edelman.
1927 104m/B *RU* Nikandrov, N. Popov, Boris Livanov; *D:* Sergei Eisenstein, Grigori Alexandrov; *W:* Sergei Eisenstein, Grigori Alexandrov; *C:* Vladimir Popov, Eduard Tisse; *M:* Dimitri Shostakovich, Edmund Meisel.

Ten Things I Hate about You

William Shakespeare is once again adapted for teens in this update of his very un-PC comedy *The Taming of the Shrew.* Obstetrician and single dad Walter (Miller) has seen enough teen pregnancies to fear all adolescent boys who show up with flowers. He decrees that his ultra-popular daughter Bianca (Oleynik) cannot date before her man-hating sister Kat (Stiles) does. Two lovesick suitors, vain Joey (Keegan) and sensitive guy Cameron (Gordon-Levitt), bribe new-kid-in-town Patrick (Ledger) to make advances on Kat in order to play "jumpeth the maiden" with Bianca. Kat and Patrick then engage in a duel of verbal thrusts and parries, gradually falling for each other. The film incorporates some of Shakespeare's dialogue, but glosses over the more chauvinistic elements of his play. The video is quite good with vibrant, rich colors and only a minimal loss of definition with some blacks. The soundtrack is more impressive with crisp dialogue and an energetic musical score. —*MJT*
Movie: ♪♪♪ **DVD:** *♪♪♪*
Buena Vista Home Entertainment (Cat #18142, UPC #717951004208). Widescreen (1.85:1) letterboxed. Dolby Digital 5.1. $29.99. Keepcase. *LANG:* English; French. *SUB:* English. *FEATURES:* 22 chapter links • Theatrical trailer • Film recommendations.
1999 (PG-13) 97m/C Julia Stiles, Heath Ledger, Larisa Oleynik, Joseph Gordon-Levitt, Andrew Keegan, David Krumholtz, Larry Miller, Susan May Pratt, Darryl (Chill) Mitchell, Allison Janney, David Leisure, Gabrielle Union; *D:* Gil Junger; *W:* Karen McCullah Lutz, Kirsten Smith; *C:* Mark Irwin; *M:* Richard Gibbs. *AWARDS:* NOM:

MTV Movie Awards '00: Breakthrough Performance (Stiles).

Tenchi the Movie: Tenchi Myuo in Love

This is the first movie based on the Japanese TV series featuring Tenchi and pals. Merciless Kain escapes from sub-space where he has been captive. After destroying the headquarters of the Galactic Police, he next targets Earth. Back on the planet, Tenchi's house has suddenly disappeared. What's even worse is that Tenchi's body is disappearing too. Apparently, something must have happened in the past to Tenchi's mother, Achika, so the gang journeys back in time to 1970 to right what must have gone wrong. The sharp, colorful video shows off to great effect the breathtaking, multilayered animation that looks like a graphic novel come to life. The soundtrack is top-quality, too, and features music composed by Christopher Franke *(Babylon 5)*. Menu design is clever, lively, and very functional. Non-standard packaging is a bummer. —*MB*
Movie: ♪♪♪ **DVD:** *♪♪♪*
Pioneer Entertainment (Cat #PIDA-1390V, UPC #013023000391). Widescreen (1.85:1) letterboxed. Dolby Digital 5.1. $29.99. Jewel case. *LANG:* English; Japanese. *SUB:* English; Japanese. *CAP:* English. *FEATURES:* 35 chapter links • Interactive menus in English and Japanese • Production notes with director's comments • Interview with composer Christopher Franke • Theatrical trailers • TV spot.
1996 95m/C *JP D:* Hiroshi Negishi; *M:* Christopher Franke.

Tender Loving Care

Allison (Caldare) refuses to accept the death of a child. Her husband (Esposito) turns to Dr. Turner (Hurt), who installs Kathryn (Tegarden) as a live-in nurse. Serious headgames ensue. The DVD is an interactive experience. At key moments in the story, the action stops and the viewer must make certain choices and assumptions about the characters and their actions. You must also take multiple-choice psychological "tests" which then determine the course of the story. That makes for slowgoing and if you stop the disc, you must record your results and rekey them to return to the proper place later. To my taste, the slow-moving story wasn't worth the effort, but those who are more involved with game- and role-playing might well disagree. The images are clear enough, though the computer-generated maps and 3-D environments might have come from a first-generation rock video. In 1999, the DVD won the Technical Achievement Award at the DVD Pro Conference and the Most Creative Use of DVD Technology at the European DVD Summit. —*MM*
Movie: ♪♪ **DVD:** *♪♪*
DVD International (Cat #DVDI 0719, UPC #647715071927). Full frame. Dolby Digital Stereo. Keepcase. *LANG:* English. *FEA-*

TURES: Full interactivity • Alternate scenes • Multiple endings • Personality analysis • 3-D environments • Supplemental material.
1999 ?m/C Michael Esposito, Beth Tegarden, Marie Caldare, John Hurt, Brandy Carson, Holly Weber; *D:* David Wheeler, Calvin Kennedy; *W:* David Wheeler; *M:* John Welsman.

Tender Mercies

A down-and-out country singer (Duvall) finds his life redeemed by the love of a good woman (Harper). Aided by Horton Foote's script, Duvall, Harper and Barkin keep this material from being simplistic and sentimental. Duvall wrote and performed the songs in his Oscar-winning performance.
Movie: ♪♪♪ **DVD:** NYR
Republic Pictures Home Video (Cat #39003). Widescreen (1.85:1) letterboxed. $24.98. Keepcase.
1983 (PG) 88m/C Robert Duvall, Tess Harper, Betty Buckley, Ellen Barkin, Wilford Brimley; *D:* Bruce Beresford; *W:* Horton Foote; *C:* Russell Boyd; *M:* George Dreyfus. *AWARDS:* Academy Awards '83: Best Actor (Duvall), Best Original Screenplay; Golden Globe Awards '83: Best Actor— Drama (Duvall); Los Angeles Film Critics Association Awards '83: Best Actor (Duvall); New York Film Critics Awards '83: Best Actor (Duvall); Writers Guild of America '83: Best Original Screenplay; NOM: Academy Awards '83: Best Director (Beresford), Best Picture, Best Song ("Over You").

Tequila Sunrise

Towne's twisting film about two lifelong friends and a beautiful woman. Gibson is a (supposedly) retired drug dealer afraid of losing custody of his son to his nagging ex-wife. Russell is the cop and old friend who's trying to get the lowdown on a drug shipment coming in from Mexico. Pfeiffer runs the poshest restaurant on the coast and is actively pursued by both men. Questions cloud the plot and confuse the viewer in a film loaded with double-crosses, intrigue, and surprises around every corner. Still, the photogenic leads are pleasant to watch. The image on the DVD is fairly sharp with few artifacts, but some occurrences of grain. Colors are mostly true but seem to shimmer and wash out a touch on brighter images. Blacks are mostly true with solid contrast and brightness levels. The sound is fairly dynamic, and there is plenty of bass for a Dolby Surround mix, but little use is made of the Surround. The commentary is one of the most boring I've heard, even of the ones that do nothing but give the play-by-play. — *JO*
Movie: ♪♪ **DVD:** *♪♪*
Warner Home Video, Inc. (Cat #11821, UPC #085391182122). Widescreen (1.85:1) anamorphic; full frame. Dolby Surround; Mono. $24.98. Snapper. *LANG:* English; French; Spanish. *SUB:* English; Span-

ish; French. *CAP:* English. *FEATURES:* 31 chapter links • Theatrical trailer • Production notes • Commentary: Thom Mount.

1988 (R) 116m/C Mel Gibson, Kurt Russell, Michelle Pfeiffer, Raul Julia, Arliss Howard, Arye Gross, J.T. Walsh, Ann Magnuson; *D:* Robert Towne; *W:* Robert Towne; *C:* Conrad Hall; *M:* Dave Grusin. *AWARDS: NOM:* Academy Awards '88: Best Cinematography.

Terminal Rush

No, this is not the story Grand Central Station at 5:00 pm. It's about terrorists (led by Piper) threatening to blow up Hoover Dam. Former Army Ranger, now deputy sheriff Johnny Price (Wilson) is the only one who can stop them. Even though Piper plays his role with the same psychotic bravado he brought to pro wrestling, the fights involving him and Wilson are not his best work. Overall, the DVD looks so good that it belies an obviously low budget. The action in the dam interiors is well-lit and well-staged, though nothing new. —*MM*

Movie: ♪ *DVD:* ♪♪▶
Image Entertainment (Cat #ID4762DRDVD, UPC #014381476224). Full frame. Dolby Digital Stereo. $24.99. Snapper. *LANG:* English. *FEATURES:* 12 chapter links.
1996 (R) 94m/C Don "The Dragon" Wilson, Roddy Piper; *D:* Damian Lee.

Terminal Velocity

Silly live-action cartoon has all the right moves and none of the right chemistry. Skydiving instructor Ditch Brodie (Sheen) loses novice pupil Chris Morrow (Kinski) on her first jump. SPLAT! But is she dead? Of course not. Not when there are Russian bad guys around. The plot makes no sense. Neither do the stunts. The unpersuasive effects gain nothing on DVD. —*MM*

Movie: ♪ *DVD:* ♪
Hollywood Pictures Home Video (Cat #16319, UPC #717951001382). Widescreen (2.35:1) letterboxed. Dolby Digital 5.1 Surround Stereo; Dolby Digital Surround Stereo. $29.99. Keepcase. *LANG:* English; French. *CAP:* English. *FEATURES:* 20 chapter links • Theatrical trailer.
1994 (PG-13) 132m/C Charlie Sheen, Nastassia Kinski, James Gandolfini, Christopher McDonald, Melvin Van Peebles; *D:* Deran Sarafian; *W:* David N. Twohy; *C:* Oliver Wood; *M:* Joel McNeely.

The Terminator

The mother of the modern sf action thriller arrives on DVD without many of the bells and whistles. Instead, it is a virtual re-creation of the original theatrical release that does not attempt to update the flaws that time has created. The story revolves around a cyborg (Schwarzenegger) who arrives from the future to kill Sarah Connor (Hamilton), who will be the mother of humanity's savior, if she survives. Against him is Reese (Biehn), a soldier from the

future who tumbles, like his antagonist, naked and unarmed into the present. Cameron's script is a solid combination of inspired action sequences, plot revelations, and character development. The film is also a showcase for character actors and stars who would become famous. (Yes, that's Bill Paxton as the leader of the punks.) Overall the image and mono sound are fine, though some sharpness is lost in fine lines and grids, including a door that has some strange patterns. More obvious are the future scenes created with models and the stop-motion animation shots. Technological changes—many created by the success of this film—have made them look a little primitive, but why dwell on them? This overachieving B-movie made stars of Schwarzenegger and Cameron. It might have been interesting to hear their reactions to it now on a commentary track, along with the thoughts of special effects magician Stan Winston. —*MM*

Movie: ♪♪♪♪ *DVD:* ♪♪♪▶
Image Entertainment (Cat #ID3949NSBD-VD, UPC #014381394924). Widescreen (1.85:1) letterboxed. Dolby Digital Mono. $29.99. Keepcase. *LANG:* English. *FEATURES:* 32 chapter links.
1984 (R) 108m/C Arnold Schwarzenegger, Michael Biehn, Linda Hamilton, Paul Winfield, Lance Henriksen, Bill Paxton, Rick Rossovich, Dick Miller, Earl Boen; *D:* James Cameron; *W:* James Cameron; *M:* Brad Fiedel.

Terminator 2: Judgment Day

He said he'd be back, and he wasn't lying. Along with Schwarzenegger, costar Hamilton and director Cameron also came back to create this thrill-ride sequel to *The Terminator* that cost ten times as much to make and delivers twice the excitement. Jaw-dropping special effects are responsible for a new style of shape-shifting Terminator that keeps on terminating, but credit a frightening dream sequence depicting a nuclear holocaust for being the most frightening component of *T2*. Patrick is the next-generation terminator sent back in time to kill the boy who will become mankind's leader in the post-nuke war against the machines. The tables are turned by Schwarzenegger playing an "old-style" terminator sent back to save the child. As the song says, he's bad to the bone. A beefed-up Hamilton teams up with the T-man to save her son. The first-ever DVD to employ dual-layer technology without interrupting the movie, the disc's incredibly sharp image and rich sound benefit from all the extra room for data. Other DVDs have eclipsed this one in the extras count, but *T2* remains a showpiece title. To really show off a home theatre sound system, crank the volume up and wait for the robot foot to crush the human skull in the opening battle sequence set in a harrowing future. Warning: You'll risk eviction if you do this in an apartment building. (Note: This DVD is the theatrical

release, not the director's cut currently available only on laserdisc.) —*MB*
Movie: ♪♪♪▶ *DVD:* ♪♪♪♪
Artisan Entertainment (Cat #60441, UPC #012236044109). Widescreen (2.35:1) letterboxed. Dolby Digital 5.1. $34.98. Snapper. *LANG:* English; French; Spanish. *SUB:* English; French; Spanish. *CAP:* English. *FEATURES:* 73 chapter links • Production notes • Cast and crew biographies • Theatrical trailer • Descriptive Video Service for the visually impaired.
1991 (R) 139m/C Arnold Schwarzenegger, Linda Hamilton, Edward Furlong, Robert Patrick, Earl Boen, Joe Morton; *D:* James Cameron; *W:* James Cameron; *C:* Adam Greenberg; *M:* Brad Fiedel. *AWARDS:* Academy Awards '91: Best Makeup, Best Sound, Best Sound Effects Editing, Best Visual Effects; MTV Movie Awards '92: Best Film, Best Male Performance (Schwarzenegger), Best Female Performance (Hamilton), Breakthrough Performance (Furlong), Most Desirable Female (Hamilton), Best Action Sequence; *NOM:* Academy Awards '91: Best Cinematography, Best Film Editing.

Terrified

This quirky suspenser defies easy categorization. It's a guessing game. We know that Olive (Graham) is a troubled young woman. With good reason. But when she claims that she is being stalked by a stranger and is attacked in her apartment, is she fantasizing or telling the truth? Are director Merendino and cowriter Heath taking *Repulsion* as their model, or is it *Psycho*? Or are they up to something else entirely? Balancing that elliptical uncertainty, much of the dialogue seems absolutely authentic. Despite some narrative lapses and a conclusion that won't sit well with all viewers, this one still earns a strong recommendation for fans of psychological puzzles. On DVD, the film also comes across as an overachiever. Despite its obviously skimpy budget, the money was well spent, first on a young cast that was almost famous when it was made, and then on good lighting that heightens the unusual mood. The disc contains virtually no visual flaws. —*MM*
Movie: ♪♪♪ *DVD:* ♪♪♪
Image Entertainment (Cat #ID4659APDVD, UPC #014381465921). Full frame. Dolby Digital Surround Stereo. $24.99. Snapper. *LANG:* English. *FEATURES:* 24 chapter links.
1994 (R) 90m/C Heather Graham, Lisa Zane, Rustam Branaman, Tom Breznahan, Max Perlich, Balthazar Getty, Richard Lynch, Don Calfa; *D:* James Merendino; *W:* James Merendino, Megan Heath.

The Terror

Legendary Roger Corman production boasts no less than five directors. Corman has written that he began the film hoping to crank out another Poe-inspired Gothic quickie. As various complications ensued, he had young Francis Ford Coppo-

la shoot some footage in Big Sur; and cowriter Jack Hill also took a shot. So did Monte Hellman and finally star Jack Nicholson got behind the camera. Why not? He was then married to his pregnant costar Sandra Knight. This serial collaboration begins as a hallucination with a delirious Napoleonic officer (Nicholson) riding down a beach. Then it becomes a turgid period piece when he reaches Boris Karloff's castle, and finally the oft-revised plot virtually disintegrates. In the end, it's mostly about characters wandering down dark hallways and paths for no discernible reason. On DVD, the image ranges between grainy softness in some castle interiors and sharp focus exteriors. It probably is an improvement over VHS tape, but who cares? —MM **AKA:** Lady of the Shadows.
Movie: ♪ **DVD:** ♪♪
Parade (Cat #5531). Full frame. Dolby Digital Surround Stereo. $17.98. Keepcase. LANG: English. SUB: Japanese. FEATURES: Cast and crew thumbnail bios • 10 chapter links. Title is also available from United American Video (cat. #40092) for $9.99; Parade (#55316) for $17.99; and Essex (#1004) for $10.97.
1963 81m/C Boris Karloff, Jack Nicholson, Sandra Knight, Dick Miller, Dorothy Neumann, Jonathan Haze; **D:** Roger Corman, Jack Hill, Francis Ford Coppola, Monte Hellman, Dennis Jacob, Jack Nicholson; **W:** Roger Corman, Leo Gordon, Jack Hill; **C:** John M. Nickolaus Jr.; **M:** Ronald Stein.

Terror Is a Man

A mad scientist attempts to turn a panther into a man on a secluded island. Early Filipino horror film inspired by H.G. Wells's The Island of Doctor Moreau was gritty for its time. The soundtrack is a little scratchy in places, and there is some film damage, but overall the DVD looks pretty amazing when you consider the source of the original material. The black-and-white picture is actually pretty sharp and has good contrast and brightness. This is the best home video version of this film, and should only disappoint those who won't buy any DVD that doesn't have 5.1 sound. —JO **AKA:** Blood Creature.
Movie: ♪♪▸ **DVD:** ♪♪▸
Image Entertainment (Cat #ID554811DVD, UPC #014381554823). Full frame. Dolby Digital Mono. $24.95. Snapper. LANG: English. FEATURES: 12 chapter links.
1959 89m/B PH Francis Lederer, Greta Thyssen, Richard Derr, Oscar Keesee; **D:** Gerardo (Gerry) De Leon; **W:** Harry Paul Harber; **C:** Emmanuel I. Rojas; **M:** Ariston Aulelino.

Terror of Frankenstein

Low-keyed, faithful adaptation of Mary Shelley's novel should probably be ranked second only to the James Whale/Boris Karloff film. It's certainly superior to the excesses of Kenneth Branagh and I'd put

it ahead of the Hammer versions. Writer-director Floyd focuses on the relationship between Victor (Vitali) and the Monster (Oscarsson). He makes fine use of Irish locations to give the film a lonely, haunted feeling. The DVD image is very good, actually excellent for a film of this age. It's somewhat pale at times and some nocturnal interiors are intentionally dark. But the disc was made from a pristine original and so it is free of surface marks and scratches. Sound is acceptable. —MM **AKA:** Victor Frankenstein.
Movie: ♪♪♪ **DVD:** ♪♪♪
Image Entertainment (Cat #ID5549IIDVD, UPC #014381554922). Full frame. Dolby Digital Mono. $24.99. Snapper. LANG: English. FEATURES: 12 chapter links.
1975 91m/C SW IR Leon Vitali, Per Oscarsson, Nicholas Clay, Stacey Dorning, Jan Ohlsson; **D:** Calvin Floyd; **W:** Calvin Floyd, Yvonne Floyd; **C:** Tony Forsberg; **M:** Gerard Victory.

Terror of Mechagodzilla

Aliens build a 400-foot robot called Mechagodzilla and match him up against the original fire-breather in their quest to conquer planet Earth. And then there's Titanasaurus, the amphibious dinosaur who's controlled by the professor's psychic daughter! Actually, the Elvisian hair styles on the humans are more frightening than the creatures. After this entry, the series went into hibernation for seven years. The DVD image is filled with artifacts and heavily grained dark scenes, but the action is so bland and repetitious that the low level of the picture quality is the least of the film's problems. The lack of extras (compared to the other discs in the series) is appropriate. —MM **AKA:** Monsters from the Unknown Planet; The Escape of Megagodzilla; Mekagojira No Gyakushu.
Movie: ♪♪ **DVD:** ♪▸
Simitar Entertainment (Cat #7476, UPC #082551747627). Full frame. Dolby Digital Mono; Dolby Digital 5.1 Surround Stereo. $19.98. Keepcase. LANG: English. FEATURES: 8 chapter links • Trivia.
1978 (G) 79m/C JP Katsuhiko Sasakai, Tomoko Ai; **D:** Inoshiro Honda; **W:** Yukiko Takayama; **C:** Mototaka Tomioka; **M:** Akira Ifukube.

Tess of the Storm Country

Pickford's remake of her 1914 film is one of the silent screen's great melodramas. Tess is the feisty daughter of a "squatter," a village of kindly fishermen who live at the foot of the hill beneath Elias Graves's mansion. He'll do anything to get rid of them. Of course, his son falls for Tess. On DVD, the image clarity is about as sharp as anyone could expect from a 1922 film with the usual dings, and intermittent stretches that are faded or bleached, almost to pure whiteout in the worst instances. The real attraction, though, is the star, and the film proves that Mary

Pickford's appeal is timeless. In fact, her combination of high spirits and youthful beauty has been re-created (or attempted by lesser actresses) over and over in the generations that have followed. The newly recorded symphonic score is fine accompaniment. —MM
Movie: ♪♪♪ **DVD:** ♪♪
Image Entertainment (Cat #ID5932MLSD-VD, UPC #014381593228). Full frame. Dolby Digital Stereo. $29.99. Snapper. LANG: Silent. SUB: English intertitles. FEATURES: 15 chapter links • Mary Pickford filmography.
1922 120m/B Mary Pickford, Lloyd Hughes, David Torrence, Gloria Hope, Jean Hersholt; **D:** John S. Robertson; **W:** Elmer Harris; **C:** Charles Rosher, Paul Eagler; **M:** Jeffrey Mark Silverman.

Tetsuo: The Iron Man

In a weird live-action science-fiction cartoon, a white-collar Japanese worker finds himself being gradually transformed into a walking metal collection of cables, drills, wires, and gears. The newly formed metal creature then faces off with an equally bizarre metal fetishist (played by the director). What a pleasure it was to get this DVD. There were a few artifacts here and there, but overall the black-and-white picture is substantially improved over the VHS and laserdisc editions. The director's energetic style and imaginative use of stop-motion animation as well as severe lighting conditions provide a real test for the DVD, but prove no problem. The sound will most likely never be great on any edition of this film, but even the Dolby Digital mono used here seems a little dull. —JO **AKA:** The Ironman.
Movie: ♪♪ **DVD:** ♪♪♪
Image Entertainment (Cat #ID4266FLDVD, UPC #014381426625). Full frame. Dolby Digital Mono. $29.99. Snapper. LANG: Japanese. SUB: English. FEATURES: 10 chapter links.
1992 67m/B JP Tomoroh Taguchi, Kei Fujiwara, Shinya Tsukamoto; **D:** Shinya Tsukamoto; **W:** Shinya Tsukamoto; **C:** Shinya Tsukamoto; **M:** Chu Ishikawa.

Tetsuo 2: Body Hammer

Taniguchi (Yaguchi) strikes back at the cyborgs who kidnapped and killed his young son by transforming himself into a killer robotic machine man. Tsukamato delivers another fascinatingly grotesque and kinetically directed mechanized horror film that feels just a little less off the wall than the Tetsuo: The Iron Man. This one's in color and the DVD substantially improves upon the VHS release. There are still lots of excessively quick movements and varied lighting conditions, but the DVD handles them with great response and very little grain or artifacts. The sound is better than it is in the original and has much more body, as well as a stereo mix with at least a few separation effects. —JO
Movie: ♪♪ **DVD:** ♪♪♪

Rykodisc USA (Cat #4023, UPC #660202002327). Full frame. Stereo. $29.95. Keepcase. *LANG:* English. *FEATURES:* 12 chapter links • Director bio.
1997 83m/C *JP* Tomoroh Taguchi; **D:** Shinya Tsukamoto; **W:** Shinya Tsukamoto; **C:** Shinya Tsukamoto.

Tex

S.E. Hinton's coming-of-age story receives respectful but slow-moving treatment. Teenaged Tex McCormick (Dillon) can't understand the things that his older brother Mason (Metzler) has to do to hold onto their place while their wayward dad is off on the rodeo circuit. The performances are fine, particularly Dillon's. The Oklahoma locations are a plus, too. The film treats the characters and their situation with genuine seriousness. Like most of the Anchor Bay restorations of Disney films, this one looks fine with a negligible amount of flecks and scratches. The sound is O.K. The two-sided disc has the full-frame version on one side, widescreen on the other. —MM
Movie: ♪♪♪ **DVD:** ♪♪♪
Anchor Bay (Cat #DV10936, UPC #013131093698). Widescreen (1.85:1) letterboxed; full frame. Dolby Digital Mono. $24.98. Keepcase. *LANG:* English. *FEATURES:* 22 chapter links.
1982 (PG) 103m/C Matt Dillon, Jim Metzler, Meg Tilly, Bill McKinney, Frances Lee McCain, Ben Johnson, Emilio Estevez; **D:** Tim Hunter; **W:** Tim Hunter, Charles Haas; **C:** Ric Waite; **M:** Pino Donaggio.

The Texas Chainsaw Massacre

The movie that put the "power" in power tools. An idyllic summer afternoon drive becomes a nightmare for a group of young people pursued by a chainsaw-wielding maniac. Made with tongue firmly in cheek, this is nevertheless a mesmerizing saga of gore, flesh, mayhem, and violence, although most of the actual cut-'em-ups are off camera. Usually remembered as far more gory than it is. This DVD is loaded with extras and they're well worth watching and listening to. The movie has always been grainy, with fairly weak colors, and the DVD seems to be a good representation of the theatrical release. There is no added grain and the picture is relatively sharp. Colors are accurate (though an unfamiliar viewer might think they are a little washed-out), and bleed is minimal. Blacks are basically clear with a few incidents of grain. The disc also retains the film's contrast, newsreel feel, and the brightness levels follow along. The Dolby Surround is a re-channeled synthesized mix of the original mono, and though it livens things up, I prefer the original track, which works well with the feel of the film. —JO
Movie: ♪♪♪ **DVD:** ♪♪♪
Pioneer Entertainment (Cat #DVD0123, UPC #01302300939). Widescreen (1.85:1) letterboxed. Dolby Surround;

Mono. $29.98. Keepcase. *LANG:* English. *FEATURES:* 17 chapter links • Theatrical trailer • TV spots • Commentary: Tobe Hooper, Daniel Pearl, Gunnar Hansen • Deleted scenes and alternate footage • Blooper reel • Photo stills • Posters and collectibles.
1974 (R) 86m/C Marilyn Burns, Allen Danziger, Paul A. Partain, William Vail, Teri McMinn, Edwin Neal, Jim Siedow, Gunnar Hansen, John Dugan, Jerry Lorenz; **D:** Tobe Hooper; **W:** Tobe Hooper, Kim Henkel; **C:** Daniel Pearl; **M:** Tobe Hooper, Wayne Bell; **Nar:** John Larroquette.

The Texas Chainsaw Massacre 4: The Next Generation

Four promgoers—including Jennie (Zellweger)—who are so obnoxious that they deserve anything that happens to them, wander out into the boonies where they're attacked by the familiar family of maniacs led by Vilmer (McConaughey), who has a mechanical leg. The plot is essentially a slightly comic parody of the original. The production values are the highest of the four films, but so what? Curiosity value from the pre-fame presence of the two stars is all the derivative material has to offer. **AKA:** Return of the Texas Chainsaw Massacre.
Movie: ♪ **DVD:** NYR
Columbia Tristar Home Video (Cat #3741). Full frame; widescreen (1.85:1) letterboxed. $19.95. Keepcase. *LANG:* English; Spanish. *SUB:* Chinese; Korean; Spanish; Thai. *CAP:* English. *FEATURES:* Production notes • Trailer.
1995 (R) 94m/C Renee Zellweger, Matthew McConaughey, Tony Perenski, Robert Jacks, Lisa Marie Newmyer; **D:** Kim Henkel; **W:** Kim Henkel; **C:** Levie Isaacks; **M:** Wayne Bell.

Thakshak

Ishaan (Devgan) is lost in a concrete jungle until he finds Suman, an idealistic young lady. Suman is played by Tabu, whose sari always seems to float behind her even when she's sitting still. She is a writer of surprisingly hypnotic verse (courtesy of poet Suryablanu Gupt), but her recitations clash with the film's electropop nightclub numbers and Ishaan's drippy serenades. There's even a *Showgirls*-inspired, waterfall-and-volcano lounge act among the Vegas-style musical interludes. The underworld conspires against the lovers when Ishaan tries to break his oath of loyalty and leave the family business. It is quickly made clear that his freedom will not be had without bloodshed. The image is strangely framed in widescreen, with two bands of black outlining two bands of green. Visual quality actually improves when the DVD is run in scan mode. Otherwise, colors are often blobby, buzzy, and sharp in the same shot! Allowances can be made, considering how the overcast exteriors and violently shifting light qualities in the Steadicam sequences were

probably difficult to render even on the original Eastmancolor film. English subtitles, white outlined in gray, are optional. There is no scene access menu on the disc, but an illustrated, printed insert outlines all chapter stops. The main menu consists of a music video clip that recycles itself. The bilingual "making of" featurette is untranslated, with unsubtitled film clips. Only Ajay's comments in that section are spoken in English. Whenever you reload anything, you have to sit through an ad for an online shopping site featuring Indian gear. —JK
Movie: ♪♪♪ **DVD:** ♪♪♪
Video Sound (Cat #VSMD1199-DVD206, UPC #677565020691). Widescreen. Dolby Digital 5.1. $29.95. Keepcase. *LANG:* Hindi. *SUB:* English. *FEATURES:* 26 chapter stops plus intermission • "Select a song" feature with 7 links • Interactive menu • Full-color picture disc • Behind-the-scenes documentary.
1999 171m/C *IN* Ajay Devgan, Tabu; **D:** Govind Nihalani; **W:** Kamlesh Pandey; **C:** Govind Nihalani; **M:** A.R. Rahman.

That Old Feeling

Bette Midler and Dennis Farina may not be Katherine Hepburn and Spencer Tracy but they manage to make sparks fly in a bawdy comedy about Lilly and Dan, a happily divorced couple who are brought back together by the marriage of their daughter (Marshall). It's old-fashioned material nicely handled by director Carl Reiner. The New York–Toronto locations look all right, but the image lacks the bright sparkle of the best DVDs. Tuxedos and other black clothes tend to solidify; Ms. Midler's red outfits glow. Some dark scenes, most noticeably the interior of a van, are too dim. The sound is fine but not exceptional. —MM
Movie: ♪♪♪ **DVD:** ♪♪♪
Universal Studios Home Video (Cat #20259, UPC #025192025921). Widescreen (1.85:1) letterboxed. Dolby Digital 5.1 Surround Stereo; Dolby Surround Stereo. $24.98. Keepcase. *LANG:* English; French; Spanish. *SUB:* Spanish. *CAP:* English. *FEATURES:* 16 chapter links • Production notes • Theatrical trailer • Cast and crew thumbnail biographies.
1996 (PG-13) 105m/C Bette Midler, Dennis Farina, Danny Nucci, Paula Marshall, Gail O'Grady, David Rasche, Jayne Eastwood; **D:** Carl Reiner; **W:** Leslie Dixon; **C:** Steve Mason; **M:** Patrick Williams.

That Uncertain Feeling

A couple's (Oberon and Douglas) marital problems increase when she develops the hiccups and embarks on a relationship with a grouchy concert pianist (Meredith). The famous Lubitsch touch is evident throughout in this light comedy. The film looks and sounds good for a work of its age, though large dark areas tend to become solid black. —MM
Movie: ♪♪♪ **DVD:** ♪♪♪

Roan Group (Cat #AED-2030, UPC #78604203025). Full frame. Dolby Digital Mono. $19.95. Keepcase. *LANG:* English. *FEATURES:* Cast list ☞ Lubitsch thumbnail biography ☞ 12 chapter links.
1941 86m/B Merle Oberon, Melvyn Douglas, Burgess Meredith, Alan Mowbray, Eve Arden, Sig Rumann, Harry Davenport; *D:* Ernst Lubitsch; *W:* Donald Ogden Stewart, Walter Reisch; *C:* George Barnes; *M:* Werner R. Heymann. *AWARDS: NOM:* Academy Awards '41: Best Original Dramatic Score.

Thelma & Louise
Davis is the ditzy Thelma, a housewife rebelling against her dominating, unfaithful, abusive husband (who, rather than being disturbing, provides some of the best comic relief in the film). Sarandon is Louise, a hardened and world-weary waitress in the midst of an unsatisfactory relationship. They hit the road for a respite from their mundane lives, only to find violence and a part of themselves they never knew existed. Outstanding performances from Davis and especially Sarandon, with Pitt notable as the stud who gets Davis's motor revved. Director Scott has a fine eye for set details, and they are presented intact on this very good DVD. The picture is sharp and there is very little grain. Artifacts are rare. The colors are great, with bright hues and subtle texturing, which are clearly defined in both light and dark scenes. Excellent contrast and brightness levels keep the picture punchy throughout. Blacks are deep and true. The 5.1 sounds great with good clean bass and energized highs. There is, however, far less Surround than expected. —*JO*
Movie: 🎬🎬🎬 **DVD:** 🎬🎬🎬▶
MGM Home Entertainment (Cat #906727, UPC #027616672728). Widescreen (1.85:1) letterboxed; full frame. Dolby Digital 5.1; Dolby Surround. $24.98. Snapper. *LANG:* English (DD5.1); Spanish (DS); French (DS). *SUB:* English; Spanish; French. *CAP:* English. *FEATURES:* 36 chapter links ☞ Theatrical trailer ☞ Commentary: Ridley Scott ☞ Alternative ending.
1991 (R) 130m/C Susan Sarandon, Geena Davis, Harvey Keitel, Christopher McDonald, Michael Madsen, Brad Pitt, Timothy Carhart, Stephen Tobolowsky, Lucinda Jenney; *D:* Ridley Scott; *W:* Callie Khouri; *C:* Adrian Biddle; *M:* Hans Zimmer. *AWARDS:* Academy Awards '91: Best Original Screenplay; National Board of Review Awards '91: Best Actress (Sarandon), Best Actress (Davis); National Society of Film Critics Awards '91: Best Supporting Actor (Keitel); Writers Guild of America '91: Best Original Screenplay; *NOM:* Academy Awards '91: Best Actress (Davis), Best Actress (Sarandon), Best Cinematography, Best Director (Scott), Best Film Editing.

There's Something about Mary
Outrageously lowbrow comedy that's one third slapstick genius, one third nauseating gross-out, and one third dull-as-dirt filler. Prologue introduces high school dweeb Ted (Stiller), who scores a prom date with the class knockout Mary (Diaz) by sticking up for her retarded brother Warren (Brown). But Ted's dream night is not to be: a tuxedo zipper snags his privates. Thirteen years later, Ted hires Pat (Dillon), a sleazy detective, to find her. Like everyone else, though, Pat's dazzled by the title character. For the true Farrelly fan, this DVD offers several quease-inducing extras, including a blooper reel with even more lingering shots of Ted's wounded area and his memorably messed-up ear. Though the movie wasn't especially handsome to begin with, the disc looks good, with decent contrasts in its tropical-fruit color scheme. —*JE*
Movie: 🎬🎬▶ **DVD:** 🎬🎬🎬
Twentieth Century Fox Home Entertainment (Cat #4111457, UPC #086162114 571). Widescreen (1.85:1) letterboxed. Dolby Digital 5.1 Surround Stereo; Dolby Surround Stereo. $34.98. Keepcase. *LANG:* English; French. *SUB:* English; Spanish. *FEATURES:* 30 chapter links ☞ Commentary: the Farrelly brothers ☞ 5-minute blooper reel ☞ "Build Me Up Buttercup" music video ☞ Karaoke video of same ☞ Cast and director bios.
1998 (R) 118m/C Ben Stiller, Matt Dillon, Cameron Diaz, Chris Elliott, Lee Evans, Lin Shaye, Jeffrey Tambor, Markie Post, Keith David, Jonathan Richman, W. Earl Brown; *D:* Bobby Farrelly, Peter Farrelly; *W:* Bobby Farrelly, Peter Farrelly, Edward Decter, John J. Strauss; *C:* Mark Irwin; *M:* Jonathan Richman. *AWARDS:* MTV Movie Awards '99: Best Film, Best Female Performance (Diaz), Best Villain (Dillon), Best Fight; New York Film Critics Awards '98: Best Actress (Diaz); *NOM:* Golden Globe Awards '99: Best Actress—Musical/Comedy (Diaz), Best Film—Musical/Comedy; MTV Movie Awards '99: Best Comedic Performance (Diaz), Best Comedic Performance (Stiller), Best Original Screenplay, Best Kiss (Ben Stiller/Cameron Diaz).

Therese & Isabelle
Based on Violette Leduc's novel, this is a story told from memory about two French schoolgirls who have a brief experimental affair. Therese (Persson, a dead ringer for Sandra Bernhard) is a respectable matron who stops by her old school. She wanders around the empty buildings and remembers her friendship with the blonde Isabelle (Gael). The pace is appropriately languid with flashbacks within flashbacks until the last reel when the action heats up considerably. Again, what's actually shown isn't that explicit. The unashamed purple voice-over narration, however, is unbelievably florid. Metzger's muted black-and-white cinematography doesn't gain much on DVD, and some patterns on school uniforms and stained glass windows quiver annoyingly. —*MM*
Movie: 🎬🎬▶ **DVD:** 🎬🎬▶
Image Entertainment (Cat #ID5545FFDVD, UPC #014381554526). Widescreen (2.35:1) letterboxed. Dolby Digital Mono. $24.99. Snapper. *LANG:* English. *FEATURES:* 12 chapter links.
1967 118m/B Essy Persson, Anna Gael, Barbara Laage, Anne Vernon; *D:* Radley Metzger; *W:* Jesse Vogel; *C:* Hans Jura; *M:* Georges Auric.

Thesis
Superb Spanish thriller is more suspenseful and engaging than most American films that deal with similar subjects. Angela (Torrent) is a graduate student working on a thesis on "audiovisual violence." She discovers a snuff film made on campus and comes to believe that she is an intended victim. Who can she trust? The geekish Chema (Martinez), who is perhaps too involved with pornographic violence, or the seductively handsome Bosco (Noriega)? Even her professors could be involved. Both image and sound have a coarseness that's largely been polished out of most American studio releases. On DVD, this one is reminiscent of a '70s film with well-chosen locations and a heavy emphasis on natural sounds. Director Amenabar also uses large bright splashes of primary colors to add an unsettling nightmarish quality to the realistic setting. Those elements give the film a believability and reality that's too often lacking in the genre. Add in a series of terrific endings and you've got a solid, thoughtful sleeper. —*MM AKA:* Tesis; Snuff.
Movie: 🎬🎬🎬 **DVD:** 🎬🎬▶
Vanguard International Cinema, Inc. (Cat #TF1001, UPC #681116100237). Widescreen (1.66:1) letterboxed. $29.95. Keepcase. *LANG:* Spanish. *SUB:* English. *FEATURES:* 20 chapter links.
1996 (R) 121m/C *SP* Ana Torrent, Fele Martinez, Eduardo Noriega; *D:* Alejandro Amenabar; *W:* Alejandro Amenabar, Mateo Gil; *C:* Hans Burman; *M:* Alejandro Amenabar, Mariano Marin.

They Came from Within
The occupants of a high-rise building go on a sex and violence spree when stricken by an aphrodisiac parasite who enters unknowing victims in very private orifices. There is a lot of the queasy, sleazy, weird stuff to make you squirm. First major film by Cronenberg. A lot of horror fans were waiting for a good version of this film to street. Unfortunately, this DVD doesn't quite fill the need. The picture is very grainy and the transfer rate is fairly low, resulting in some very nasty artifacts that totally distort the image. Backgrounds are also so digitized that the sharper foreground images appear 3-D against them. The mono sound is pretty lame, but is most likely a result of the original tracks. —*JO AKA:* Shivers; The Parasite Murders; Frissons.
Movie: 🎬🎬▶ **DVD:** 🎬▶
Image Entertainment (Cat #ID4602AVDVD, UPC #0138160223). Full frame. Mono.

$24.99. Snapper. *LANG:* English. *FEA-TURES:* 18 chapter links ● Theatrical trailer ● David Cronenberg interview ● Unrated director's cut.

1975 110m/C *CA* Paul Hampton, Joe Silver, Lynn Lowry, Barbara Steele, Susan Petrie, Allan Migicovsky, Ronald Mlodzik; *D:* David Cronenberg; *W:* David Cronenberg; *C:* Robert Saad; *M:* Ivan Reitman.

They Got Me Covered

Two WWII-era journalists become involved with a comic web of murder, kidnapping, and romance. Hope is very funny and carries the rest of the cast. Look for Doris Day in a bit part and listen for Bing Crosby singing whenever Hope opens his cigarette case.
Movie: ♫♫ *DVD:* NYR
HBO Home Video (Cat #91255). Full frame. Stereo. $24.98. *LANG:* English. *SUB:* Spanish.
1943 95m/B Bob Hope, Dorothy Lamour, Otto Preminger, Eduardo Ciannelli, Donald Meek, Walter Catlett; *D:* David Butler; *W:* Harry Kurnitz; *C:* Rudolph Mate; *M:* Leigh Harline.

They Live

A semi-serious science-fiction spoof about a drifter (Piper) who discovers an alien conspiracy. They're taking over the country under the guise of Reaganism, capitalism, and yuppiedom. Screenplay was written by Carpenter under a pseudonym. Starts out fun, deteriorates into cliches and bad special effects makeup. A ten-minute one-on-one exaggerated slugfest is a definite highlight. The DVD is very sharp and neither grain nor artifacts are excessive. Colors are excellent; accurate, and vibrantly delivered with very little bleed. The contrast accents those colors, and brightness levels are very good. Blacks are true. The soundtrack is crisp and has a decent amount of bass but is lacking in Surround effects or ambience to the real channel. —*JO* *AKA:* Creepers.
Movie: ♫♫► *DVD:* ♫♫♫
Image Entertainment (Cat #ID4234USDVD, UPC #014381423426). Widescreen (2.35:1) letterboxed. Dolby Surround. $29.99. Snapper. *LANG:* English. *CAP:* English. *FEATURES:* 20 chapter links.
1988 (R) 88m/C Roddy Piper, Keith David, Meg Foster, George "Buck" Flower, Peter Jason, Raymond St. Jacques, John Lawrence, Sy Richardson, Jason Robards III, Larry Franco, Wendy Brainard, Dana Bratton; *D:* John Carpenter; *W:* John Carpenter, Frank Armitage; *C:* Gary B. Kibbe; *M:* John Carpenter, Alan Howarth.

They Might Be Giants

Watch this one twice; first to discover (or rediscover) a sleeper that has been unjustly overlooked for decades. Justin Fairplay (Scott) is a judge who has suffered a breakdown and now believes that he is Sherlock Holmes. Mildred Watson (Woodward) is a psychiatrist who has been brought in by a scheming brother to get Fairplay committed. But Holmes has found his Dr. Watson and the game is afoot! They're off to locate Prof. Moriarty on the streets of New York. Both stars are at their best; Scott had just made *Patton* and his Holmes is a companion performance to the Scrooge he created in *A Christmas Carol.* On your second watching, turn on the commentary track by film archivist Robert Harris and director Anthony Harvey. Their comfortable talk is a wide-ranging conversation that touches upon the film's re-cutting by the studio, Harvey's work as editor on *Dr. Strangelove* with Stanley Kubrick, his long association with composer John Barry, and the many problems that beset a low-budget production, which was made entirely on location in the middle of the coldest winter New York had experienced in decades. Most commentary tracks are meant only for the most serious students; this one is for anyone who loves movies. —*MM*
Movie: ♫♫♫♫ *DVD:* ♫♫♫♫
Anchor Bay (Cat #DV10986, UPC #013131098693). Widescreen (1.85:1) anamorphic. Dolby Digital Mono. $29.98. Keepcase. *LANG:* English. *FEATURES:* 19 chapter links ● Commentary: Harvey and Robert Harris ● 2 deleted scenes ● Theatrical trailer ● Cast and crew thumbnail biographies.
1971 (G) 98m/C George C. Scott, Joanne Woodward, Jack Gilford, Eugene Roche, Kitty Winn, F. Murray Abraham, M. Emmet Walsh; *D:* Anthony Harvey; *W:* James Goldman; *C:* Victor Kemper; *M:* John Barry.

They Shoot Horses, Don't They?

In Depression-era California, a dance marathon becomes a brutal endurance contest as one by one, hour by hour, couples weaken and fail. Director Sidney Pollack does nothing to soft pedal the unsubtle political overtones of Horace McCoy's novel. As the cynical protagonist Gloria, Jane Fonda is fairly persuasive, but some of her posturing seems forced. The same is not true for Gig Young's Rocky, the loquacious crooked promoter. He won a well-deserved Oscar for his work. The DVD is an accurate re-creation of the theatrical release, sacrificing polish for a more realistic approach. The dance hall has the tatty glamour and tinhorn sound that the story requires. —*MM*
Movie: ♫♫♫► *DVD:* ♫♫♫►
Anchor Bay (Cat #DV10924, UPC #013131092493). Widescreen (2.35:1) letterboxed; full frame. Dolby Digital Mono. $24.99. Snapper. *LANG:* English. *FEATURES:* 17 chapter links ● Theatrical trailer ● "Making of" featurette.
1969 (R) 121m/C Jane Fonda, Michael Sarrazin, Susannah York, Gig Young, Red Buttons, Bonnie Bedelia, Bruce Dern, Allyn Ann McLerie, Chaing I, Al Lewis, Michael Conrad; *D:* Sydney Pollack; *W:* James Poe; *C:* Philip Lathrop; *M:* Johnny Green. *AWARDS:* Academy Awards '69: Best Supporting Actor (Young); British Academy Awards '70: Best Supporting Actress (York); Golden Globe Awards '70: Best Supporting Actor (Young); New York Film Critics Awards '69: Best Actress (Fonda); *NOM:* Academy Awards '69: Best Actress (Fonda), Best Adapted Screenplay, Best Art Direction/Set Decoration, Best Costume Design, Best Director (Pollack), Best Film Editing, Best Supporting Actress (York), Scoring of a Musical.

They Were Expendable

One of Ford's best (and most underrated) films concerns the Navy in the first days of World War II. As American forces evacuate the Philippines, PT boats under the command of Rusty Ryan (Wayne) and John Brickley (Montgomery, who also directed some scenes) try to buy time for the retreating troops. The black-and-white photography is superb; the air-sea combat scenes are some of the very best of the era. At the beginning, Ford ostentatiously wraps himself in patriotism and religion, but by the end, he comes around to a simple statement about duty. The DVD image is only slightly better than the excellent VHS tapes that are in distribution. Any war movie fan looking for a terrific double feature ought to run this one with *Bataan.* —*MM*
Movie: ♫♫♫► *DVD:* ♫♫♫►
MGM Home Entertainment (Cat #907661, UPC #027616766120). Full frame. Dolby Digital Mono. $24.98. Keepcase. *LANG:* English. *SUB:* English; French. *FEATURES:* 44 chapter links ● Booklet ● Trailer.
1945 135m/B Robert Montgomery, John Wayne, Donna Reed, Jack Holt, Ward Bond, Cameron Mitchell, Leon Ames, Marshall Thompson, Paul Langton, Donald Curtis, Jeff York, Murray Alper, Jack Pennick, Alex Havier, Charles Trowbridge, Robert Barrat, Bruce Kellogg, Louis Jean Heydt, Russell Simpson, Philip Ahn, Betty Blythe, William B. Davidson, Pedro de Cordoba, Arthur Walsh, Harry Tenbrook, Tim Murdock, Vernon Steele; *D:* John Ford; *W:* Frank Wead; *C:* Joseph August; *M:* Herbert Stothart, Eric Zeisl. *AWARDS: NOM:* Academy Awards '45: Best Sound.

Thief

A big-time professional thief (Caan) loves to work solo but is coerced to sign up with the mob to make one last big score and retire. Turns out the gangster types just can't be trusted and Caan is forced to go after his new "business" partners. Taut and atmospheric thriller is director Mann's feature film debut. Watch for a pudgy Dennis Farina *(Crime Story)* as a piece of mob muscle. Mann's films are always very stylized, making good use of colors and sound. *Thief* is no exception. The opening safe-cracking scene has some artifacts, but after that they don't detract. The colors are very vibrant and even red neon reflecting off of wet streets doesn't produce any bleed. The picture is also sharp;

grain is near non-existent. Blacks are amazingly true, even in extremely high-contrast scenes. Brightness and contrast are very good. The 5.1 Surround delivers the all important Tangerine Dream score with as much (or more) clarity and dynamics as the versions on CD, yet doesn't impair the dialogue or the climatic gunfire. —*JO* **AKA:** Violent Streets.

Movie: ♫♫♫ **DVD:** ♫♫♫
MGM Home Entertainment (Cat #907024, UPC #027616702425). Widescreen letterboxed. Dolby Digital 5.1. $24.98. Keepcase. *LANG:* English. *SUB:* French; Spanish. *CAP:* English. *FEATURES:* 32 chapter links • Theatrical trailer • Commentary: director Michael Mann and James Caan • 8-page booklet.
1981 (R) 124m/C James Caan, Tuesday Weld, Willie Nelson, James Belushi, Elizabeth Pena, Robert Prosky, Dennis Farina; *D:* Michael Mann; *W:* Michael Mann; *C:* Donald E. Thorin; *M:* Tangerine Dream.

A Thin Line Between Love and Hate
Writer-director-star Lawrence shows that there's no line between a crude, foul-mouthed ego trip and an unfunny, unsuspenseful film. Darnell Wright is a smooth talker constantly on the lookout for women to conquer and discard. Eventually, he meets the wrong woman, Brandi (Whitfield), who is introduced as a normal woman but, when the script calls for it, is inexplicably transformed into *Fatal Attraction* psycho. This tangle of genres looks very good on DVD with superb image and sound. Go figure. —*MM*

Movie: ♫ **DVD:** ♫♫♫
New Line Home Video (Cat #N4851, UPC #794043485121). Widescreen (2.35:1) letterboxed; full frame. Dolby Digital 5.1 Surround Stereo; Dolby Digital Surround Stereo. $24.98. Snapper. *LANG:* English. *FEATURES:* 21 chapter links • Cast and crew thumbnail biographies • Theatrical trailer • Commentary: producer George Jackson.
1996 (R) 106m/C Martin Lawrence, Lynn Whitfield, Regina King, Bobby Brown, Della Reese, Roger E. Mosley, Malinda Williams, Darryl (Chill) Mitchell, Simbi Khali; *D:* Martin Lawrence; *W:* Martin Lawrence, Bentley Kyle Evans, Kenny Buford, Kim Bass; *C:* Francis Kenny; *M:* Roger Troutman.

The Thin Red Line
The first adaptation of James Jones's autobiographical novel focuses on the relationship between Sgt. Welsh (Warden) and Pvt. Doll (Dullea). As battle experiences on Guadalcanal harden Doll, the mutual hatred the two share changes to a grudging respect. The film effectively portrays the dehumanizing psychological effects of war. Unfortunately, the pan-and-scan DVD is no better than VHS tape, and it appears to have been made from a damaged print. —*MM*
Movie: ♫♫➤ **DVD:** ♫♫

Simitar Entertainment (Cat #7231). Full frame. PCM Stereo. $14.98. Keepcase. *LANG:* English. *FEATURES:* Newsreel footage.
1964 99m/B Keir Dullea, Jack Warden, James Philbrook, Kieron Moore, Ray Daley, Merlyn Yordan, Bob Kanter, Stephen Levy; *D:* Andrew Marton; *W:* Bernard Gordon; *C:* Manuel Berenguer; *M:* Malcolm Arnold.

The Thin Red Line
After a long absence, director Malick returns with this unsatisfactory WWII saga about a rifle company fighting on Guadalcanal. Visually stunning, particularly on DVD, but woozily focused on the thoughts, inner feelings, and philosophical ramblings of the soldiers, the film sacrifices plot and intensity to worry over questions of Man vs. Nature and the Origin of Evil. Plot difficulties are highlighted by the physical similarities of many of the cast members. But it is difficult to blame the cast of pretty boys for the lack of their characters' depth. Malick shuffles them on and off stage so quickly and without introduction that they leave no impression. They're just a bunch of guys with heavy five-o'clock shadows, soulful expressions, and steel helmets. On disc, Malick's visual touches are even more striking than they were in theatres. Even scenes of highly contrasted dark and light are clear with well defined textures, and the use of natural sounds is equally heightened. But those are particularly useful to a supposedly tense war movie. This one is considerably less than the sum of its parts. A longer version is rumored to exist, but to date, it has not appeared on any form of home video. —*MM*

Movie: ♫♫ **DVD:** ♫♫♫➤
Twentieth Century Fox Home Entertainment (Cat #4111850). Widescreen letterboxed. Dolby Digital Surround Stereo; Dolby Digital 5.1 Surround Stereo. $34.98. Keepcase. *LANG:* English. *SUB:* Spanish. *CAP:* English. *FEATURES:* 31 chapter links • 11 Melanesian songs on a separate track.
1998 (R) 170m/C James Caviezel, Adrien Brody, Sean Penn, Nick Nolte, John Cusack, George Clooney, Woody Harrelson, Ben Chaplin, Elias Koteas, Jared Leto, John Travolta, Tim Blake Nelson, John C. Reilly, John Savage, Arie Verveen, David Harrod, Thomas Jane, Paul Gleason, Penelope Allen, Don Harvey, Shawn Hatosy, Donal Logue, Dash Mihok, Larry Romano; *D:* Terrence Malick; *W:* Terrence Malick; *C:* John Toll; *M:* Hans Zimmer; *Technical Advisor:* Mike Stokey. *AWARDS:* New York Film Critics Awards '98: Best Director (Malick); National Society of Film Critics Awards '98: Best Cinematography; *NOM:* Academy Awards '98: Best Adapted Screenplay, Best Cinematography, Best Director (Malick), Best Film Editing, Best Picture, Best Sound; Australian Film Institute '99: Best Foreign Film; Directors Guild of America Awards '98: Best Director (Malick).

The Thing
A team of scientists at a remote Antarctic outpost discover a buried spaceship with an unwelcome alien survivor still alive. Bombastic special effects overwhelm the suspense and the solid cast. Less a remake of the 1951 science-fiction classic than a more faithful version of John Campbell's short story "Who Goes There?," since the seeds/spores take on human shapes. Overall the DVD looks pretty good. Even if it didn't, it would be worth the purchase price just to pick up the "making of" documentary, which contains loads of information, including how Bottin accomplished the amazing non-CGI special effects. Carpenter and Russell deliver a lively commentary. —*JO*

Movie: ♫♫♫ **DVD:** ♫♫♫
Universal Studios Home Video (Cat #20329, UPC #025192032929). Widescreen (2.35:1) letterboxed. Dolby Digital 5.1; Dolby Surround. $34.98. Keepcase. *LANG:* English (DD5.1); French (DS). *SUB:* Spanish. *CAP:* English. *FEATURES:* 37 chapter links • Commentary: John Carpenter and Kurt Russell • Documentary • Theatrical trailer • Outtakes • Photo gallery.
1982 (R) 109m/C Kurt Russell, Wilford Brimley, T.K. Carter, Richard Masur, Keith David, Richard Dysart, David Clennon, Donald Moffat, Thomas G. Waites, Charles Hallahan; *D:* John Carpenter; *W:* Bill Lancaster; *C:* Dean Cundey; *M:* Ennio Morricone.

Things to Do in Denver When You're Dead
Jimmy the Saint (Garcia) is an ex-mobster gone straight (in a slyly funny new occupation) who is called upon by his former boss, the Man with the Plan (Walken), to do one last easy-money job. Jimmy rounds up his old gang, a colorfully offbeat group including Pieces (Lloyd), a porn movie projectionist, and Critical Bill (Williams), a hair-trigger psycho who works in a funeral parlor. Eventually they become targets of hitman Mr. Shhh (Buscemi). Hipster dialogue, edgy names, crime-gone-wrong formula, and cast all suggest warmed-over Tarantino. But the performances and the stylish direction make it worthwhile. The DVD captures Fleder's moody lighting and careful staging. (Note Walken's entrance.) The sound is very good too. For those who missed this one in its brief theatrical release, DVD is the best home video medium. —*MM*

Movie: ♫♫♫ **DVD:** ♫♫♫
Miramax Pictures Home Video (Cat #17094, UPC #717951002082). Widescreen (1.85:1) letterboxed. Dolby Digital 5.1 Surround Stereo. $29.99. Keepcase. *LANG:* English. *CAP:* English. *FEATURES:* 20 chapter links • Theatrical trailer • "Making of" featurette.
1995 (R) 115m/C Andy Garcia, Christopher Lloyd, William Forsythe, Bill Nunn, Treat Williams, Jack Warden, Steve Busce-

mi, Fairuza Balk, Gabrielle Anwar, Christopher Walken, Glenn Plummer, Don Cheadle, Bill Cobbs, Josh Charles, Michael Nicolosi, Marshall Bell, Sarah Trigger, Jenny McCarthy, Tommy (Tiny) Lister; **D:** Gary Fleder; **W:** Scott Rosenberg; **C:** Elliot Davis; **M:** Michael Convertino.

The Third Man

"We had no desire to move people's political emotions; we wanted to entertain them, to frighten them a little, to make them laugh." That's how Graham Greene described this multilayered post-war thriller, about the shadowy Harry Lime (Welles) and Holley Martins (Cotten), the archetypal innocent American abroad. This DVD was made from the 1999 50th anniversary theatrical restoration and re-release. It's the European version with director Carol Reed's voice-over introduction. (The Joseph Cotten voice-over used in the original American theatrical release is included as an extra.) The image is near perfect with no visual flaws even in the inkiest depths of the Vienna sewer. The monaural sound is fine; any enhancement of Anton Karas's zither score would have been gilding the lily. The extras are well chosen. Simply one of the best. —*MM*
Movie: 𝄇𝄇𝄇𝄇 **DVD:** 𝄇𝄇𝄇𝄇
Criterion Collection (Cat #THI060, UPC #037429135228). Full frame. Dolby Digital Mono. $39.95. Keepcase. *LANG:* English. *SUB:* English. *FEATURES:* 24 chapter links ▪ Introduction by Peter Bogdanovich ▪ Separate audio track of Richard Clark reading the first draft treatment ▪ Production notes and stills ▪ "Ticket to Tangiers" episode of *The Third Man* on radio ▪ Lux Radio Theatre adaptation of *The Third Man* ▪ Joseph Cotten's voice-over introduction ▪ Newsreel short of Anton Karas playing zither ▪ Newsreel footage of Vienna sewer police ▪ 2 theatrical trailers ▪ Graham Greene's written 1950 preface to *The Third Man* ▪ Restoration demonstration.
1949 104m/B **GB** Joseph Cotten, Orson Welles, Alida Valli, Trevor Howard, Bernard Lee, Wilfrid Hyde-White, Ernst Deutsch, Erich Ponto, Siegfried Breuer, Hedwig Bleibtreu, Paul Hoerbiger, Herbert Halbik, Frederick Schreicker, Jenny Werner, Nelly Arno, Alexis Chesnakov, Leo Bieber, Paul Hardtmuth, Geoffrey Keen, Annie Rosar; **D:** Carol Reed; **W:** Graham Greene; **C:** Robert Krasker; **M:** Anton Karas. *AWARDS:* Academy Awards '50: Best Black-and-white Cinematography; American Film Institute (AFI) '98: Top 100; British Academy Awards '49: Best Film; Cannes Film Festival '49: Best Film; Directors Guild of America Awards '49: Best Director (Reed); *NOM:* Academy Awards '50: Best Director (Reed), Best Film Editing.

The Thirteenth Floor

An investigation into the murder of a tycoon (Mueller-Stahl) leads to the discovery that he lived in parallel worlds, one of the 1990s, one of 1937. His colleagues Hall (Bierko) and Whitney (D'Onofrio) may

have something to do with the death. Femme fatale Jane Fuller (Mol) claims to be his daughter. Comparisons to *The Matrix* are not out of place. DVD captures some adventurous special effects with no problem. On the commentary track, director Rusnak and production designer Kurt Petrocelli mostly limit their discussion to matters at hand, and so that audio option is recommended to special effects fans. Sound is very good. —*MM*
Movie: 𝄇𝄇𝄇 **DVD:** 𝄇𝄇𝄇▶
Columbia Tristar Home Video (Cat #02848, UPC #043396028487). Widescreen (2.35:1) letterboxed; full frame. Dolby Digital 5.1 Surround Stereo; Dolby Digital Surround Stereo. $24.95. Keepcase. *LANG:* English. *SUB:* English. *FEATURES:* 28 chapter links ▪ Music video ▪ Conceptual art gallery ▪ Sfx gallery ▪ Trailers ▪ Cast and crew thumbnail biographies ▪ Commentary: director Rusnak and production designer Petrocelli.
1999 (R) 100m/C Craig Bierko, Vincent D'Onofrio, Armin Mueller-Stahl, Gretchen Mol, Dennis Haysbert, Steven Schub, Jeremy Roberts; **D:** Josef Rusnak; **W:** Josef Rusnak; **C:** Wedigo von Schultzendorff; **M:** Harold Kloser.

The 13th Warrior

Despite its checkered theatrical release pattern—the film sat on a shelf for a time before it was greeted by a mediocre commercial reception—this medieval adventure is thoroughly enjoyable on home video. Based on Michael Crichton's novel *Eaters of the Dead* (itself a retelling of *Beowulf*), it's about emissary Ibn Fahdlan (Banderas), who is drafted by a band of Norsemen to help them battle ferocious creatures who are attacking their homeland. What follows is a straight-ahead adventure tale filled with fairly graphic violence. For the most part, both image and sound range between good and very good, handling such potentially difficult props as chain mail with no disruption of the visuals. In the last reels though, when the action moves underground, the darkness and pale colors seem to come from the original. Forget the reputation; any fan of *The Vikings* or *Conan, the Barbarian* will enjoy this one. —*MM* *AKA:* Eaters of the Dead.
Movie: 𝄇𝄇𝄇 **DVD:** 𝄇𝄇𝄇
Buena Vista Home Entertainment (Cat #18273, UPC #717951004659). Widescreen (2.35:1) anamorphic. Dolby Digital 5.1 Surround Stereo. $29.99. Keepcase. *LANG:* English; French. *CAP:* English. *FEATURES:* 17 chapter links.
1999 (R) 103m/C Antonio Banderas, Vladimir Kulich, Clive Russell, Omar Sharif, Diane Venora, Sven Wollter, Dennis Storhoi, Anders T. Anderson, Richard Bremmer, Neil Maffin, Tony Curran, Mischa Hausserman, Asbjorn Riis, Daniel Southern, Oliver Sveinall, Albie Woodington; **D:** Michael Crichton, John McTiernan; **W:** Michael Crichton; **C:** Peter Menzies Jr.; **M:** Jerry Goldsmith.

36 Fillete

Fourteen-year-old Lili (Zentout) is literally bursting out of her dress—the title refers to the largest size of a child's garment—when she decides to seduce an older man. But her mercurial behavior reflects her precarious status as a child in a woman's body. Director Breillat handles the potentially exploitative material with a deft touch, never romanticizing these essentially unlikable but intriguing characters. Unfortunately, the image is so dark and grainy that the disc is difficult to watch. The first half of the film looks like it was made in black and ochre, and the dark shapes are absolutely solid and without detail. The harshness probably comes from the original. —*MM*
Movie: 𝄇𝄇▶ **DVD:** 𝄇𝄇
WinStar Home Entertainment (Cat #FLV5 115, UPC #720917511528). Full frame. $29.98. Keepcase. *LANG:* French. *SUB:* English. *FEATURES:* 6 chapter links ▪ Filmographies and awards ▪ Trailer.
1988 88m/C **FR** Delphine Zentout, Etienne Chicot, Oliver Parniere, Jean-Pierre Leaud; **D:** Catherine Breillat; **W:** Catherine Breillat, Roger Salloch; **C:** Laurent Dailland.

The 39 Steps

The prototypical Hitchcock mistaken-man-caught-in-intrigue thriller features some of the most copied set-pieces and the surest visual flair of his pre-war British period. It's a fast-moving chase story with Donat as Richard Hannay on the run from the authorities, the bad guys, and everyone else. Though the film is rough-looking compared to his later work, this few-frills DVD reproduction boasts a crisp black-and-white image and sometimes thin sound. Tony Curtis's introduction probably won't tell fans anything they don't already know, but for newcomers to the Master's work, this is a fine version of one of his seminal works. —*MM*
Movie: 𝄇𝄇𝄇𝄇 **DVD:** 𝄇𝄇𝄇
Delta/Laserlight (Cat #82022, UPC #018111202237). Full frame. Stereo. $14.99. Keepcase. *LANG:* English. *SUB:* Spanish; Chinese; Japanese. *FEATURES:* Scene access ▪ Trailer for *North by Northwest* ▪ Tony Curtis introduction.
1935 81m/B **GB** Robert Donat, Madeleine Carroll, Godfrey Tearle, Lucie Mannheim, Peggy Ashcroft, John Laurie, Wylie Watson, Helen Haye, Frank Cellier, Gus McNaughton, Jerry Verno, Peggy Simpson, Hilda Trevelyan, John Turnbull, Elizabeth Inglis, Wilfrid Brambell; **D:** Alfred Hitchcock; **W:** Charles Bennett, Alma Reville, Ian Hay; **C:** Bernard Knowles; **M:** Louis Levy.

The 39 Steps (Criterion)

The Criterion Collection edition of Hitchcock's early thriller looks a bit better than the less-expensive LaserLight disc, and it contains many more extras. The most

unusual of those is the 1935 Press Book. For the master's fans, those extras are the real difference between the two. Visually, both are fine. —*MM*
Movie: 🐾🐾🐾🐾 **DVD:** 🐾🐾🐾▶
Criterion Collection (Cat #THI120, UPC #037429135228). Full frame. Dolby Digital Mono. $39.95. Keepcase. *LANG:* English. *SUB:* English. *FEATURES:* Commentary: Hitchcock scholar Marian Keene ▪ 12 chapter links ▪ 1937 Lux Radio Theater adaptation with Robert Montgomery and Ida Lupino ▪ Janus Films documentary on early British phase of Hitchcock's career ▪ 1935 press book ▪ Production design drawings.
1935 81m/B

This Is My Father

Teacher Kieran Johnson (Caan) decides to research his Irish roots after discovering a photo of his mother with a mystery man who may have been his father. Told in flashback, the story details the class differences in rural Ireland in the '30s and the doomed romance between wealthy teenaged Fiona Flynn (Farrelly) and Kieran O'Dea (Quinn), a poor tenant farmer who works for the Flynn family. It's an affecting role and personal for Aidan Quinn, who worked with brothers Paul and Declan. The script is based on a story Theresa Quinn told her children. Director Paul Quinn uses an exaggerated color scheme and the DVD reflects it with glowing blues and emerald greens, and some reds that are saturated almost to black. Sound is very good, too. —*MM*
Movie: 🐾🐾 **DVD:** 🐾🐾🐾
Columbia Tristar Home Video (Cat #4059). Widescreen (1.78:1) letterboxed. Dolby Digital Stereo. $27.95. Keepcase. *LANG:* English. *SUB:* French; Spanish. *CAP:* English. *FEATURES:* Production notes ▪ Trailer ▪ Commentary: Paul and Aidan Quinn.
1999 (R) 120m/C Aidan Quinn, James Caan, Stephen Rea, Moya Farrelly, John Cusack, Jacob Tierney, Colm Meaney, Donal Donnelly, Brendan Gleeson; **D:** Paul Quinn; **W:** Paul Quinn; **C:** Declan Quinn; **M:** Donal Lunny.

This Is Spinal Tap

Pseudo-rockumentary about heavy-metal band Spinal Tap profiles their career from "England's loudest band" to an entry in the "where are they now" file. Hilarious satire features music performed by Guest, McKean, Shearer, and others. Great cameos, particularly David Letterman's Paul Shaffer as a record promoter and Billy Crystal as a surly mime. Followed by *The Return of Spinal Tap.* This out-of-print DVD has been one of the most sought-after items on internet auction sites. It is chock-full of supplemental material, which, in many cases, is as funny as the film itself. Of most interest is a full hour of unused footage, about half of which is hilarious. There are also fake commercials, trailers, music videos, and more. The image itself is as good as the Criteri-

on laserdisc (also out of print) and is far superior to the earlier VHS and laserdisc editions. (A new edition is on the way.) — *JO* **AKA:** Spinal Tap.
Movie: 🐾🐾🐾▶ **DVD:** 🐾🐾🐾▶
Criterion Collection (Cat #CC1529D, UPC #715515009126). Widescreen (1.70:1) letterboxed. Stereo. $39.95. Keepcase. *LANG:* English. *FEATURES:* 32 chapter links ▪ Commentary: Reiner, Guest, McKean, Shearer ▪ Deleted scenes ▪ Promotional films ▪ Theatrical trailers.
1984 (R) 82m/C Michael McKean, Christopher Guest, Harry Shearer, Tony Hendra, Bruno Kirby, Rob Reiner, June Chadwick, Howard Hesseman, Billy Crystal, Dana Carvey, Ed Begley Jr., Patrick Macnee, Fran Drescher, Paul Shaffer, Anjelica Huston, Fred Willard, Paul Benedict, Archie Hahn; **D:** Rob Reiner; **W:** Michael McKean, Christopher Guest, Harry Shearer, Rob Reiner; **C:** Peter Smokler; **M:** Michael McKean, Christopher Guest, Harry Shearer, Rob Reiner.

This Sporting Life

Director Anderson's first dramatic feature marks the end of the Angry Young Man period in British cinema; a knuckle-cracking story of a young coal miner (Harris) trying to kick his way out of Yorkshire as a rugby player. British critics and audiences, by then warming up to colorful romps like *Tom Jones,* found it far too tough and not sexy at all. It does have a look and feel comparable to *Raging Bull.* Certainly the scenes of violence and their aftermath are quite toe-curling. Glenda Jackson debuted in a supporting role. The full sound and sparkling black-and-white imagery come courtesy of a Janus print. Liner notes by a British journalist dishes all the dirt on the production's financing, fighting, and bad press. —*JK*
Movie: 🐾🐾🐾🐾 **DVD:** 🐾🐾🐾🐾
Image Entertainment (Cat #ID4538JFDVD, UPC #014381453829). Widescreen (1.66:1). Dolby Digital Mono. $24.99. Snapper. *LANG:* English. *FEATURES:* 20 chapter links ▪ Scene access menu ▪ Cover essay by Adrian Turner.
1963 134m/B *GB* Richard Harris, Rachel Roberts, Alan Badel, William Hartnell, Colin Blakely, Vanda Godsell, Arthur Lowe; **D:** Lindsay Anderson; **W:** David Storey; **C:** Denys Coop; **M:** Roberto Gerhard. *AWARDS:* British Academy Awards '63: Best Actress (Roberts); Cannes Film Festival '63: Best Actor (Harris); *NOM:* Academy Awards '63: Best Actor (Harris), Best Actress (Roberts).

The Thomas Crown Affair

Updated adaptation of the 1968 Steve McQueen/Faye Dunaway caper is slick, lavish, and loose. Thomas Crown (Brosnan) is a self-made New York billionaire, who just can't resist pulling off the perfect crime by stealing a Monet from the Metropolitan Museum of Art. Catherine Banning (Russo) is the gorgeous insurance investigator on

his trail, who can't help falling for the very charming criminal. The fortysomething duo sizzle (how fantastic to see two age-appropriate lovers for a change) and if the ending has a tacked-on feel, it doesn't really matter. Dunaway makes a cameo appearance as Crown's therapist. The DVD looks slick and glossy, just as the film did in the theatre, and the 5.1 sound is excellent, with super bass on the energetic music score. The Surround speakers never rest, supplying both great ambience and plenty of action effects. —*JO*
Movie: 🐾🐾🐾 **DVD:** 🐾🐾🐾▶
MGM Home Entertainment (Cat #907452, UPC #027616745224). Widescreen (2.35:1) anamorphic; full frame. Dolby Digital 5.1. $24.98. Keepcase. *LANG:* English; French. *SUB:* English; French. *CAP:* English. *FEATURES:* 36 chapter links ▪ Audio commentary ▪ 2 theatrical trailers ▪ Collectible booklet.
1999 (R) 111m/C Pierce Brosnan, Rene Russo, Denis Leary, Frankie Faison, Ben Gazzara, Fritz Weaver, Charles Keating, Mark Margolis, Faye Dunaway, Esther Canadas; **D:** John McTiernan; **W:** Leslie Dixon, Kurt Wimmer; **C:** Tom Priestley; **M:** Bill Conti.

Those Bedroom Eyes

Despondent Harvard professor William Tauber (Matheson) is saved from suicide by an extemporaneous sexual encounter with Ali Broussard (Rogers). Could such a caring woman also be the dominatrix who is bumping off upper-class Bostonians? The hot-and-heavy action is only hinted at in this made-for-TV thriller. On DVD, the image is slightly overexposed, giving the film a bright look even in the night scenes. Stars and supporting cast are better than the slight material. —*MM* **AKA:** A Kiss to Die For.
Movie: 🐾🐾 **DVD:** 🐾🐾
Simitar Entertainment (Cat #7583, UPC #082551758320). Full frame. Dolby Digital Stereo. $14.98. Keepcase. *LANG:* English. *FEATURES:* 8 chapter links ▪ Production factoids ▪ Tim Matheson filmography.
1992 93m/C Tim Matheson, Mimi Rogers, Carlos Gomez, Carroll Baker, William Forsythe; **D:** Leon Ichaso; **W:** Deborah Dalton.

A Thousand Acres

The plot is *King Lear* on an Iowa farm; the source is Jane Smiley's Pulitzer Prize–winning novel. Sisters Rose (Pfeiffer), Ginny (Lange), and Caroline (Leigh) learn that their father (Robards) has decided to divide the family's farm among the three of them. When an old beau (Firth) returns to town, they're further divided by romantic entanglements. It's all melodramatic and contrived with every hot-button women's issue thrown into the mix. Director Moorhouse purportedly considered removing her name, but she's responsible for the self-absorbed star turns that her leads indulge in and the slow pace. Despite the plot problems and the atrocious acting,

the film looks terrific on DVD. Tak Fujimoto's superb rural landscapes and interiors are reproduced flawlessly. —*MM*
Movie: 🎬🎬 **DVD:** 🎬🎬🎬
Buena Vista Home Entertainment (Cat #14252, UPC #717951000330). Widescreen (1.85:1) letterboxed. Dolby Digital Stereo. $29.99. Keepcase. *LANG:* English. *CAP:* English. *FEATURES:* 17 chapter links ▪ Theatrical trailer.
1997 (R) 105m/C Jessica Lange, Michelle Pfeiffer, Jennifer Jason Leigh, Colin Firth, Jason Robards Jr., Keith Carradine, Pat Hingle, Kevin Anderson, John Carroll Lynch, Anne Pitoniak, Vyto Ruginis, Michelle Williams, Elissabeth Moss; *D:* Jocelyn Moorhouse; *W:* Laura Jones; *C:* Tak Fujimoto; *M:* Richard Hartley. *AWARDS: NOM:* Golden Globe Awards '98: Best Actress—Drama (Lange).

Three Ages
Keaton's first feature is a parody of D.W. Griffith's *Intolerance*. It's much shorter and much funnier, with three interlaced tales of romance in the Stone Age, Ancient Rome, and the Jazz Era. Even though it is far from the comic's best, kids will probably be more receptive to it than to his other work. The reason is the Stone Age sequence which predates *The Flintstones* with goofy dinosaur models, mammoths, and such. But one of the shorter films on the disc, "The Goat" is the sleeper. It's an extended chase that contains some wonderfully funny gags. As a group, these three early films are not as detailed or as clearly focused as the films Keaton would make just a few years later and there is nothing that DVD can do to improve the originals. Image and sound are more than acceptable for works of this age. —*MM* *AKA:* The Goat; My Wife's Relations.
Movie: 🎬🎬🎬 **DVD:** 🎬🎬🎬
Kino on Video (Cat #K136DVD, UPC #738329013622). Full frame. $29.99. Snapper. *LANG:* Silent. *SUB:* English intertitles. *FEATURES:* 15 chapter links.
1923 59m/B Virginia Fox, Kate Price, Wallace Beery, Oliver Hardy, Buster Keaton; *D:* Buster Keaton, Edward F. (Eddie) Cline; *W:* Malcolm St. Clair, Buster Keaton, Edward F. (Eddie) Cline; *M:* Robert Israel.

Three Amigos
Three unemployed silent screen stars (Martin, Short, Chase) are asked to defend a Mexican town from bandits; they think it's a public appearance. Spoof of the Three Stooges and Mexican bandito movies falls short at times, given the enormous amount of comedic talent involved. Still, it's generally enjoyable with some very funny scenes.
Movie: 🎬🎬 **DVD:** NYR
HBO Home Video (Cat #90007). $24.98. Snapper. *LANG:* English. *SUB:* French; Spanish. *CAP:* English. *FEATURES:* Cast and crew thumbnail bios.
1986 (PG) 105m/C Chevy Chase, Steve Martin, Martin Short, Joe Mantegna,

Patrice Martinez, Jon Lovitz, Phil Hartman, Randy Newman, Alfonso Arau; *D:* John Landis; *W:* Lorne Michaels, Steve Martin, Randy Newman; *C:* Ronald W. Browne; *M:* Elmer Bernstein.

Three Days of the Condor
CIA researcher Joseph Turner (Redford) goes on the run from unknown killers when he is left the sole survivor of the mass murder of his New York office staff. Good performances by Dunaway as the photographer who shelters him, and by von Sydow whose role is harder to define. All in all, a fine, tightly constructed suspense film. The fight in the apartment is comparable to the similar scene in *The Manchurian Candidate*. The DVD captures the rough on-location look of the best '70s films. That calls for considerable graininess. Sound is fine. —*MM*
Movie: 🎬🎬🎬 **DVD:** 🎬🎬🎬
Paramount Home Video (Cat #088037, UPC #097360880373). Widescreen anamorphic. Dolby Digital Surround Stereo; Dolby Digital 5.1 Surround Stereo. $29.99. Keepcase. *LANG:* English; French. *SUB:* English. *FEATURES:* 16 chapter links ▪ Theatrical trailer.
1975 (R) 118m/C Robert Redford, Faye Dunaway, Cliff Robertson, Max von Sydow, John Houseman; *D:* Sydney Pollack; *W:* David Rayfiel; *C:* Owen Roizman; *M:* Dave Grusin. *AWARDS: NOM:* Academy Awards '75: Best Film Editing.

Three Kings
In the waning days of the Gulf War, four American soldiers (Clooney, Wahlberg, Ice Cube, Jonze) take off on their own to liberate Kuwaiti gold that had been stolen by Iraqi soldiers. In the process, they become more personally involved in the conflict. A foreword to the DVD explains that director Russell chose to use several inventive visual distortions to tell this story. In a separate interview, director of photography Sigel explains what was done—desaturated colors, tricky bits of slow- and fast-motion, the use of unusual film stock—and what those techniques were meant to accomplish in thematic and narrative terms. Sigel gives it a good shot, but the directorial gimmicks are still more offputting than they're intended to be and this otherwise fine film would have been much better if auteur Russell had simply told the story. Even so, the film is worth seeing. Because the visuals are so strange, it really works better on home video than it did on theatre screens. —*MM*
Movie: 🎬🎬🎬 **DVD:** 🎬🎬🎬▪
Warner Home Video, Inc. (Cat #17862). Widescreen letterboxed. Dolby Digital 5.1 Surround Stereo. $24.98. Snapper. *LANG:* English. *SUB:* English; French. *FEATURES:* 32 chapter links ▪ Cast and crew thumbnail bios ▪ Commentary: director David O. Russell ▪ Commentary: producers Charles Roven and Ed McDonnell ▪

Behind-the-scenes documentary ▪ Tour of Iraqi Village set ▪ Russell's video journal ▪ Deleted scenes ▪ Interview with director of photography Newton Thomas Sigel ▪ Interview with Ice Cube ▪ Photographs by Spike Jonze ▪ Trailer.
1999 (R) 115m/C George Clooney, Mark Wahlberg, Ice Cube, Spike Jonze, Nora Dunn, Jamie Kennedy, Mykelti Williamson, Clifford Curtis, Said Taghmaoui, Judy Greer, Liz Stauber, Holt McCallany; *D:* David O. Russell; *W:* David O. Russell; *C:* Newton Thomas (Tom) Sigel; *M:* Carter Burwell. *AWARDS:* Broadcast Film Critics Association Awards '99: Breakthrough Performance (Jonze); *NOM:* Writers Guild of America '99: Best Original Screenplay.

The Three Musketeers
D'Artagnan (producer Fairbanks) swashbuckles silently amid stylish sets, scores of extras, and exquisite costumes. The plot follows the now-familiar tale of the Cardinal's (de Brulier) schemes to discredit the Queen (MacLaren) and the Musketeers' attempts to foil him. The sword fights are energetic, but a bit tame (and sometimes unintentionally funny) by today's standards. The DVD image is a generally pale gray with light to moderate scratching throughout. The 1921 score sounds all right though it too is difficult for contemporary audiences to appreciate. —*MM*
Movie: 🎬🎬 **DVD:** 🎬🎬▪
Kino on Video (Cat #K117DVD, UPC #738329011727). Full frame. $29.99. Snapper. *LANG:* Silent. *SUB:* English intertitles. *FEATURES:* 24 chapter links.
1921 120m/B Douglas Fairbanks Sr., Leon Bary, George Siegmann, Eugene Pallette, Boyd Irwin, Thomas Holding, Sidney Franklin, Charles Stevens, Nigel de Brulier, Willis Robards, Mary MacLaren; *D:* Fred Niblo; *W:* Lotta Woods, Douglas Fairbanks Sr.; *C:* Arthur Edeson; *M:* Louis F. Gottschalk.

The Three Musketeers
Extravagant and extremely funny version of the Dumas novel is the best film adaptation. The three swashbucklers (Chamberlain, Reed, and Finlay) are joined by young D'Artagnan (York) as they set out to save the honor of the queen (Chaplin) from the plottings of the Cardinal (Heston, in one of his best roles). Screenwriter George MacDonald Fraser, author of the *Flashman* novels, and director Lester never let the film's slapstick energy get in the way of their sharp political points. The physical action is brilliantly choreographed by fight arranger William Hobbs (he plays the assassin who fights Frank Finlay in the country courtyard). The opening title sequence alone is worth the price of the disc. The nominal letterboxing occasionally misses action on the edge of the frame, though otherwise the image and sound are fine, highlighting Michael Legrand's excellent score. Followed by *The Four Mus-*

keteers and *The Return of the Musketeers*, not yet available on DVD. —*MM*
Movie: 🎬🎬🎬🎬 **DVD:** 🎬🎬🎬🎬
WinStar Home Entertainment (Cat #FLV 5029, UPC #720917502922). Widescreen letterboxed. $29.98. Keepcase. *LANG:* English. *FEATURES:* 12 chapter links ⦁ Production credits ⦁ Filmographies.
1974 (PG) 105m/C Richard Chamberlain, Oliver Reed, Michael York, Raquel Welch, Frank Finlay, Christopher Lee, Faye Dunaway, Charlton Heston, Geraldine Chaplin, Simon Ward, Jean-Pierre Cassel, William Hobbs; *D:* Richard Lester; *W:* George MacDonald Fraser; *C:* David Watkin; *M:* Michel Legrand. *AWARDS:* Golden Globe Awards '75: Best Actress—Musical/Comedy (Welch).

Three Musketeers

Anglo-Italian animation gives the familiar story of D'Artagnan and the guys the Saturday morning treatment, with cute animals thrown in for sidekicks, exaggerated stereotypes, and a fairly catchy theme that's repeated ad nauseum. The DVD has an unusually scratchy look, particularly at first. Throughout the artwork is a little stodgy and slow-moving. Since this low-cost disc lacks chapter links, it's not really different from a tape. —*MM*
Movie: 🎬🎬 **DVD:** 🎬🎬
Simitar Entertainment (Cat #7216, UPC #082551721627). Full frame. Uncompressed PCM Stereo. $9.98. Keepcase. *LANG:* English.
1988 74m/C *D:* John Halas; *W:* Howard Clewes, Paolo Di Girolano; *M:* Michel Polaroff.

The Three Musketeers

This "lite" take on the venerable swashbuckler might have been called "D'Artagnan's Excellent Adventure." On his first day in Paris, D'Artagnan (O'Donnell), looking like the only teenager at a party for grown-ups) manages to insult and instigate duels with the title characters: Aramis (Sheen), Athos (Sutherland), and Porthos (Platt). He then joins them in their valiant efforts to save France from the evil machinations of Cardinal Richelieu (Curry) and his minions Milady De Winter (DeMornay) and Rochefort (Wincott). The rest is so-so swordfights, chases, narrow escapes, intrigue, damsels in distress, and the like. On DVD, the action fares poorly. The overemphasized "schwing" sound effects are even sillier, and moving sword blades are seldom in hard focus. The 1974 Richard Lester film remains the definitive version of the story. —*MM*
Movie: 🎬🎬▶ **DVD:** 🎬🎬▶
Buena Vista Home Entertainment (Cat #17502, UPC #717951003201). Widescreen (2.35:1) letterboxed. Dolby Digital 5.1 Surround Stereo; Dolby Digital Surround Stereo. $29.99. Keepcase. *LANG:* English; French. *FEATURES:* 19 chapter links ⦁ "Making of" featurette ⦁ "All for Love" music video.

1993 (PG) 105m/C Kiefer Sutherland, Charlie Sheen, Chris O'Donnell, Oliver Platt, Rebecca DeMornay, Tim Curry, Gabrielle Anwar, Julie Delpy, Michael Wincott; *D:* Stephen Herek; *W:* David Loughery; *C:* Dean Semler; *M:* Michael Kamen. *AWARDS:* NOM: MTV Movie Awards '94: Best Song ("All for Love").

Thumbelina

Ornery little girl named Mia is magically sucked into the pages of the storybook she's reading and finds all sorts of adventures. Loose adaptation of Hans Christian Andersen's "Thumbelina" by Bluth is lackluster with acceptable songs. It's not up to the level of the best Disney animated features, but pleasant enough for the kids. *AKA:* Hans Christian Andersen's Thumbelina.
Movie: 🎬🎬▶ **DVD:** NYR
Warner Home Video, Inc. (Cat #24000). Widescreen (1.85:1) letterboxed; full frame. Dolby Digital Stereo. $19.98. Snapper. *LANG:* English; French. *SUB:* French. *CAP:* English. *FEATURES:* Trailer.
1994 (G) 86m/C *D:* Don Bluth, Gary Goldman; *W:* Don Bluth; *M:* William Ross, Barry Manilow, Barry Manilow, Jack Feldman, Bruce Sussman; *V:* Jodi Benson, Gary Imhoff, Charo, Gilbert Gottfried, Carol Channing, John Hurt, Will Ryan, June Foray, Kenneth Mars. *AWARDS:* Golden Raspberry Awards '94: Worst Song ("Marry the Mole").

Thunderball

The fourth installment in the Bond films finds 007 (Connery) on a mission to thwart SPECTRE, which has threatened to blow up Miami with a stolen atomic bomb. After the success of *Goldfinger*, a bloated quality crept into the series, and this is not one of the best. The DVD looks about as good as a mid-'60s picture could be expected to look; the stereo sounds better than the original, enhancing one of John Barry's better scores. The disc comes with all the expected bells and whistles. —*MM*
Movie: 🎬🎬▶ **DVD:** 🎬🎬🎬▶
MGM Home Entertainment (Cat #907857, UPC #027616785725). Widescreen anamorphic. Dolby Digital 5.1 Surround Stereo; Mono. $34.98. Keepcase. *LANG:* English; French. *FEATURES:* 3 documentary featurettes ⦁ 3 trailers ⦁ 5 TV spots ⦁ 10 radio spots ⦁ 52 chapter links.
1965 (PG) 125m/C *GB* Sean Connery, Claudine Auger, Adolfo Celi, Luciana Paluzzi, Rik von Nutter, Martine Beswick, Molly Peters, Guy Doleman, Bernard Lee, Lois Maxwell, Desmond Llewelyn; *D:* Terence Young; *W:* John Hopkins, Richard Maibaum; *C:* Ted Moore; *M:* John Barry. *AWARDS:* Academy Awards '65: Best Visual Effects.

Thunderheart

Ray (Kilmer), a young FBI agent, is sent to an Oglala Sioux reservation to investigate

a murder. He is part Sioux but resents being chosen for the assignment because of it. He's aided by a veteran partner (Shepard) and a shrewd local tribal police officer (Greene in top form). Set in the late 1970s and filmed (beautifully by cinematographer Roger Deakins) on the Pine Ridge Reservation in South Dakota, the film is loosely based on director Apted's documentary about Leonard Peltier, *Incident at Oglala*.
Movie: 🎬🎬▶ **DVD:** NYR
Columbia Tristar Home Video Widescreen (1.85:1) letterboxed; full frame. Dolby Digital Stereo. $29.95. Keepcase. *LANG:* English; French. *SUB:* French. *CAP:* English. *FEATURES:* Trailer.
1992 (R) 118m/C Val Kilmer, Sam Shepard, Graham Greene, Fred Ward, Fred Dalton Thompson, Sheila Tousey, Chief Ted Thin Elk, John Trudell, Dennis Banks, David Crosby; *D:* Michael Apted; *W:* John Fusco; *C:* Roger Deakins; *M:* James Horner.

Ticket to Heaven

Dealing with the painful breakup of a love affair, David (Mancuso) falls under the spell of a cultish religious order. His friends (including Rubinek) and family, worried about the group's influence, have him kidnapped for deprogramming. Though the story has become fairly familiar over the years, the cast is excellent. The dark scenes are intentionally dim and so they're grainy on disc. Otherwise, the image is acceptable, but nothing more. Overall, the film looks as good as a low-budget effort of its age could be expected to look. —*MM*
Movie: 🎬🎬 **DVD:** 🎬🎬
Simitar Entertainment (Cat #7306, UPC #082551730629). Full frame. PCM Stereo. $14.98. Keepcase. *LANG:* English. *FEATURES:* 8 chapter links ⦁ Production factoids ⦁ Nick Mancuso filmography.
1981 (PG) 109m/C *CA* Nick Mancuso, Meg Foster, Kim Cattrall, Saul Rubinek, R.H. Thomson, Jennifer Dale, Guy Boyd, Paul Soles; *D:* Ralph L. (R.L.) Thomas; *W:* Anne Cameron; *C:* Richard Leiterman; *M:* Micky Erbe. *AWARDS:* Genie Awards '82: Best Actor (Mancuso), Best Film, Best Supporting Actor (Rubinek).

Tiger Bay

Korchinsky (Buchholz), a Polish sailor on leave in Cardiff, murders his unfaithful girlfriend. Ten-year-old Gillie (Hayley Mills) sees him do it. Confronted by Superintendent Graham (John Mills, her real father), she lies, and a delicate relationship develops between the smart kid and the killer. Her performance is remarkably good, and she was only 13 when the film was made! Director J. Lee Thompson (*The Guns of Navarone*) builds suspense beautifully. The disc looks very good, though the black-and-white photography is not as richly detailed as the best studio work. Many darker areas simply solidify. Laurie Johnson's lush '50s score is a delight. —*MM*

Movie: ♪♪♪ **DVD:** ♪♪♪
Image Entertainment (Cat #ID4536JFDVD, UPC #014381453621). Full frame. Dolby Digital Mono. $24.99. Snapper. *LANG:* English. *FEATURES:* 27 chapter links.
1959 107m/B *GB* John Mills, Horst Buchholz, Hayley Mills, Yvonne Mitchell, Megs Jenkins, Anthony Dawson, Kenneth Griffith, Michael Anderson Jr.; **D:** J. Lee Thompson; **W:** John Hawkesworth; **C:** John Hawkesworth; **M:** Laurie Johnson.

Till the Clouds Roll By

In typical Hollywood fashion, all-star high-gloss biography of song-writer Jerome Kern bears little resemblance to the composer's real life. But it is filled with wonderful songs from his Broadway hit.
Movie: ♪♪♪ **DVD:** NYR
Madacy Entertainment (Cat #99008). Full frame. $9.99. Keepcase. *FEATURES:* Cast and crew thumbnail bios. Title is also available from Parade (cat. #55276), for $17.98.
1946 137m/C Robert Walker, Van Heflin, Judy Garland, Frank Sinatra, Lucille Bremer, Kathryn Grayson, June Allyson, Dinah Shore, Lena Horne, Virginia O'Brien, Tony Martin; **D:** Richard Whorf; **W:** Myles Connolly, Jean Holloway; **C:** Harry Stradling; **M:** Conrad Salinger, Roger Edens, Lennie Hayton.

Tillie's Punctured Romance

Charlie Chaplin's first feature-length film (1914 and directed by Mack Sennett) delivers all that one has grown to expect from this master of visual comedy. Chaplin is teamed with Mabel Normand as con artists, with the core of the story built around Chaplin bilking matronly farm girl Marie Dressler out of her father's money, dumping her, and then discovering that she is heir to her uncle's fortune. Much slapstick, pratfalls, and general silliness follow as Dressler and the Keystone Cops pursue Chaplin around Los Angeles and other vintage points of interest. Dreadful DVD presentation from substandard source material. This is probably an overly harsh reaction considering that the film was made in 1914, but a major opportunity was missed in that an audio commentary (historical and/or critical) would have easily overcome the damaged source material presented here. A bonus short, "Mabel's Married Life," featuring Charlie Chaplin and Mabel Normand, softens the blow a bit. —*RT*
Movie: ♪♪♪ **DVD:** ♪♪
Image Entertainment (Cat #4670DS, UPC #014381467024). Full frame. AC3 - 2 Channel. $24.99. Snapper. *LANG:* Silent. *FEATURES:* 24 chapter links • Bonus short subject—"Mabel's Married Life" • Chaplin filmography.
1914 73m/B Charlie Chaplin, Marie Dressler, Mabel Normand, Mack Swain, Chester Conklin; **D:** Mack Sennett; **W:** Hampton Del Ruth; **C:** Frank D. Williams.

Tim

Film follows the relationship between a handsome mentally retarded young man (Gibson) and an attractive older businesswoman (Laurie). Sappy storyline is redeemed by Gibson's fine performance. Based on Colleen McCullough's first novel.
Movie: ♪♪♪ **DVD:** NYR
Essex (Cat #1000). Full frame. $10.97. Keepcase.
1979 94m/C *AU* Mel Gibson, Piper Laurie, Peter Gwynne, Alwyn Kurts, Pat Evison; **D:** Michael Pate; **W:** Michael Pate; **C:** Paul Onorato; **M:** Eric Jupp. *AWARDS:* Australian Film Institute '79: Best Actor (Gibson).

Time Bandits

A group of dwarves help a young boy to travel through time and space with the likes of Robin Hood, Napoleon, Agamemnon, and other time-warp playmates. Epic fantasy from Monty Python alumni. This Criterion DVD features a slightly better transfer than the Anchor Bay release, with the main difference being that the Anchor Bay release has a few artifacts during darker sequences while the Criterion does not. The picture is fairly sharp and during brightly lit scenes the colors are vibrant. There is not much bleed and blacks are mostly true. The Dolby Surround is adequate but not spectacular. As with the other commentaries done by members of the Python gang, the comments are often hilarious. —*JO*
Movie: ♪♪♪ **DVD:** ♪♪♪♪
Criterion Collection (Cat #CC1551D, UPC #715515010123). Widescreen (1.85:1) letterboxed. Dolby Surround. $39.95. Keepcase. *LANG:* English. *CAP:* English. *FEATURES:* 23 chapter links • Commentary: Gilliam, Palin, Cleese, David Warner, and Craig Warnock • Film scrapbook • Theatrical trailer.
1981 (PG) 110m/C *GB* John Cleese, Sean Connery, Shelley Duvall, Katherine Helmond, Ian Holm, Michael Palin, Ralph Richardson, Kenny Baker, Peter Vaughan, David Warner, Craig Warnock; **D:** Terry Gilliam; **W:** Terry Gilliam, Michael Palin; **C:** Peter Biziou; **M:** Mike Moran, George Harrison.

Time Masters

Director Laloux's animated feature is a companion piece to his *Fantastic Planet.* In terms of plot and artistic style, the two are very similar. This one's about a young boy named Piel who's been marooned on the planet Perdide. Jaffar, a friend of the kid's father, comes to the rescue. Readers of *Heavy Metal* magazine will be familiar with the designs and ideas of cocreator Moebius, but the content here is much tamer. On DVD, the simple colors and limited movement are easily handled, but still, the image is grainy with pixels noticeable in the darker areas. Sound is nothing special. —*MM* *AKA:* Les Maitres du Temps.

Movie: ♪♪♪ **DVD:** ♪♪♪
Image Entertainment (Cat #ID9061SIDVD, UPC #014381906127). Full frame. Dolby Digital Mono. $24.99. Snapper. *LANG:* French. *SUB:* English. *FEATURES:* 10 chapter links.
1982 79m/C *FR* **D:** Rene Laloux; **W:** Rene Laloux, Moebius; **M:** Pierre Tardy, Christian Zanesi; **V:** Jean Valmont, Michel Elias, Sady Rebbot, Alain Cuny, Yves Brainville, Francois Chaumette.

A Time to Kill

Powerful story of revenge, racism, and the question of justice in the "new south." John Grisham had a lot of clout when he finally sold his first and favorite novel to the movies, including veto power over the leading man—director Schumacher was for Woody Harrelson, Grisham was opposed but both finally agreed on newcomer McConaughey. He's outstanding as idealistic small-town Mississippi lawyer Jake Brigance, called to defend anguished father Carl Lee Hailey (Jackson), who's accused of killing the rednecks who raped his young daughter. Jake's assisted by former mentor Lucien Wilbanks (Sutherland) and ambitious northern law student Ellen Roark (Bullock) against ruthless prosecutor Rufus Buckley (Spacey). Is it emotionally manipulative? You betcha. But Grisham's done well on-screen and Schumacher (who also did *The Client*) knows how to get the most from his cast and script. The image on the DVD is exceptional with excellent contrast and brightness levels. The color conveys all the subtle shadings of the cinematography, and bleed is pretty much nonexistent. The 5.1 sound is a perfect mix of ambience and scattered Surround effects supported by powerful dynamics and excellent fidelity. —*JO*
Movie: ♪♪♪♪ **DVD:** ♪♪♪♪
Warner Home Video, Inc. (Cat #Snapper, UPC #085391431725). Widescreen (2.35:1) anamorphic. Dolby Digital 5.1. $24.98. Snapper. *LANG:* English; French. *SUB:* English; French; Spanish. *CAP:* English. *FEATURES:* 23 chapter links • Theatrical trailer • Production notes.
1996 (R) 150m/C Matthew McConaughey, Samuel L. Jackson, Sandra Bullock, Kevin Spacey, Donald Sutherland, Brenda Fricker, Oliver Platt, Charles S. Dutton, Kiefer Sutherland, Chris Cooper, Ashley Judd, Patrick McGoohan, Rae'ven Kelly, John Diehl, Tonea Stewart, M. Emmet Walsh, Anthony Heald, Kurtwood Smith; **D:** Joel Schumacher; **W:** Akiva Goldsman; **C:** Peter Menzies Jr.; **M:** Elliot Goldenthal. *AWARDS:* MTV Movie Awards '97: Breakthrough Performance (McConaughey); *NOM:* Golden Globe Awards '97: Best Supporting Actor (Jackson); MTV Movie Awards '97: Best Female Performance (Bullock), Best Villain (Sutherland).

Timecop

Terminator rip-off is fodder for Van Damme followers with lots of action and special effects. 2004 policeman Max Walker (Van Damme) must travel back in time to prevent corrupt politician McComb (Silver) from altering history for personal gain. It's also Walker's chance to alter his personal history since his wife (Sara) was killed in an explosion he can now prevent. Based on a Dark Horse comic.

Movie: ♫♫☞ **DVD:** NYR
Universal Studios Home Video (Cat #20147). Full frame. Dolby Digital 5.1 Surround Stereo. $24.98. Keepcase. *FEATURES:* Cast and crew thumbnail bios • Production notes • Trailer.
1994 (R) 98m/C Jean-Claude Van Damme, Ron Silver, Mia Sara, Bruce McGill, Scott Lawrence, Kenneth Welsh, Gabrielle Rose, Duncan Fraser, Ian Tracey, Gloria Reuben, Scott Bellis, Jason Schombing, Kevin McNulty, Sean O'Byrne, Malcolm Stewart, Alfonso Quijada, Glen Roald, Theodore Thomas; **D:** Peter Hyams; **W:** Mark Verheiden, Gary De Vore; **C:** Peter Hyams; **M:** Mark Isham.

Timelock

In the 23rd century, asteroid Alpha 4 serves as a maximum security prison for the most dangerous criminals. However, the inmates have now gained control, and it's up to the reluctant heroics of a petty thief and a shuttle pilot to get the bad guys back in their cages.

Movie: ♫♫ **DVD:** NYR
MTI Home Video (Cat #1053). Full frame. $24.95. Keepcase. *FEATURES:* Cast and crew thumbnail bios.
1999 100m/C Maryam D'Abo, Arye Gross, Jeff Speakman, Jeffrey Meek, Martin Kove; **D:** Robert Munic; **W:** Joseph John Barmettler Jr.

Tin Cup

You've got your romantic triangle; you've got your sports; you've got Costner reteamed with Shelton—*Bull Durham* on a golf course. Can lightening strike twice? Ron "Tin Cup" McAvoy (Costner) is a West Texas golf hustler who has the ability but not the steadiness to be on the pro tour. When McAvoy decides on a last-ditch effort to qualify for the U.S. Open, he turns to psychologist Dr. Molly Griswold (Russo) to get his game together. And the fact that Molly is the girlfriend of McAvoy's longtime rival—and successful PGA player—Don Simms (Johnson)...well, Tin Cup isn't averse to playing for the lady's affections, either. The U.S. Open scenes were filmed at Houston's Kingwood Country Club and the actors do hit their own shots. Golf courses are naturally pretty and the DVD makes them look even better. The colors are lush and the picture stays sharp, even on the course where the large amounts of image detail might have thrown some transfers off. The 5.1 has limited Surround but is well driven by a boosted bass track and dynamically pleasing music mix. —*JO*
Movie: ♫♫♫ **DVD:** ♫♫♫

Warner Home Video, Inc. (Cat #14318, UPC #085391431824). Widescreen (1.85:1) anamorphic; full frame. Dolby Digital 5.1; Dolby Surround. $24.98. Snapper. *LANG:* English; French. *SUB:* English; French; Spanish. *CAP:* English. *FEATURES:* 36 chapter links • Production notes.
1996 (R) 133m/C Kevin Costner, Don Johnson, Rene Russo, Richard "Cheech" Marin, Linda Hart, Dennis Burkley, Rex Linn, Lou Myers, Richard Lineback, Mickey Jones; **D:** Ron Shelton; **W:** Ron Shelton, John Norville; **C:** Russell Boyd; **M:** William Ross. *AWARDS: NOM:* Golden Globe Awards '97: Best Actor—Musical/Comedy (Costner).

Tin Drum

German child in the 1920s wills himself to stop growing in response to the increasing Nazi presence in Germany. He communicates his anger and fear by pounding on a tin drum. Memorable scenes, excellent cast. Adapted from the novel by Gunter Grass. The film was banned in Oklahoma for a brief period when some fanatics decided it was "kiddie porn," but soon restored to the shelves as the masterpiece it is. The DVD transfer is excellent with a sharp picture mostly free of grain or artifacts. The colors are very accurate and reflect the unique color composition of the film. Contrast and brightness are consistently very good, and blacks are true with rare exception. Bright yellow subtitles are easy to read. The soundtrack has very good dynamics and very little distortion. —*JO* *AKA:* Die Blechtrommel.

Movie: ♫♫♫♫ **DVD:** ♫♫♫☞
Image Entertainment (Cat #K104, UPC #738329010423). Widescreen (1.85:1) letterboxed. Stereo. $39.99. Snapper. *LANG:* German. *SUB:* English. *FEATURES:* 18 chapter links • Commentary: Volker Schlondorff • Video essay • Maurice Jarre's score isolated on alternate audio channel.
1979 (R) 141m/C *GE* David Bennent, Mario Adorf, Angela Winkler, Daniel Olbrychski, Katharina Thalbach, Heinz Bennent, Andrea Ferreol, Charles Aznavour; **D:** Volker Schlondorff; **W:** Jean-Claude Carriere, Volker Schlondorff; **C:** Igor Luther; **M:** Maurice Jarre. *AWARDS:* Academy Awards '79: Best Foreign Film; Cannes Film Festival '79: Best Film; Los Angeles Film Critics Association Awards '80: Best Foreign Film.

The Tingler

Producer-director Castle's on-screen introductory warning about the "tingling sensation" that some viewers may experience refers to the famous gimmick he'd planned for the film's theatrical release. Some theatre seats were to be wired to give audience members a mild shock in key scenes. The Tingler is an insect-like creature created in the spine by "the force of fear." It's all as hokey and silly as it sounds. Vincent Price's conversational, understated performance as a curious

coroner with a faithless frau (Lincoln) is one of his best. Beyond the loopy horror aspects, which are a ton of fun, the film's subtext of male-female sexual and economic competition in the 1950s is fascinating. The DVD includes a re-creation of the famous "scream for your lives" scene set in a drive-in. The black-and-white photography is fine. The heavy graininess in the "red" scenes comes from the original, not the transfer. —*MM*

Movie: ♫♫♫ **DVD:** ♫♫♫
Columbia Tristar Home Video (Cat #07779, UPC #043396077799). Widescreen (1.85:1) anamorphic. Dolby Digital Mono. $19.95. Keepcase. *LANG:* English; Spanish. *SUB:* English; Spanish; Portuguese; Chinese; Korean; Thai. *FEATURES:* 26 chapter links • "Scream for your lives" featurette • Drive-in "scream" scene with narration by Castle • Original "scream" scene • Trailers • Cast and crew thumbnail biographies.
1959 82m/B Vincent Price, Darryl Hickman, Judith Evelyn, Philip Coolidge, Patricia Cutts, Pamela Lincoln; **D:** William Castle; **W:** Robb White; **C:** Wilfred M. Kline; **M:** Von Dexter.

Titanic

James Cameron's masterpiece of popular entertainment arrives on DVD without many of the extras that some discs boast. (Most notable among them is the rumored "director's cut," which according to studio sources does not exist.) Instead—flaws and all—it is a pristine translation of the theatrical version to home video. A shot-by-shot comparison to the widescreen VHS tape reveals how much better a careful DVD transfer can look and sound. In the image, both clarity and brightness are much stronger. The soundtrack has added crispness and detail. Moments that typically give digital technology trouble play well here, particularly in the big scenes: the arrival at Southampton, the poker game, the entrance into the first-class dining room, the party below decks, and flying on the bow of the ship. The only places where the film's limitations show are in the sinking. There, the shots focused on figures silhouetted against the starry sky reveal the matte lines more noticeably than the tape, because the characters are more clearly defined. That enhanced definition also helps the two young leads. In close-up they're even more striking, though Kate Winslet's hennaed hair calls attention to itself. Leonardo DiCaprio's performance somehow gets better with repeated viewings. He may not be a great actor, but he certainly is a great movie star. For the Academy Awards to have snubbed him without a nomination is still inexplicable. Finally, on DVD, Cameron's transitions between past and present become even more fluid and moving. Despite all the advances in special effects, the film is still an old-fashioned, epic potboiler, and this DVD is the finest home version available. —*MM*
Movie: ♫♫♫☞ **DVD:** ♫♫♫☞

Paramount Home Video (Cat #15522, UPC #09736155227). Widescreen letterboxed. Dolby Digital Surround Stereo; Dolby Digital 5.1 Surround Stereo. $29.99. Keepcase. *LANG:* English; French. *SUB:* English; French; Spanish. *FEATURES:* 30 chapter links ▪ Theatrical trailer.

1997 (PG-13) 197m/C Kate Winslet, Leonardo DiCaprio, Billy Zane, Kathy Bates, Frances Fisher, Gloria Stuart, Jonathan Hyde, Danny Nucci, David Warner, Bill Paxton, Bernard Hill, Victor Garber, Suzy Amis, Bernard Fox; *D:* James Cameron; *W:* James Cameron; *C:* Russell Carpenter; *M:* James Horner. *AWARDS:* Academy Awards '97: Best Art Direction/ Set Decoration, Best Cinematography, Best Costume Design, Best Director (Cameron), Best Film Editing, Best Picture, Best Song ("My Heart Will Go On"), Best Sound, Best Sound Effects Editing, Best Visual Effects, Best Original Score; Directors Guild of America Awards '97: Best Director (Cameron); Golden Globe Awards '98: Best Director (Cameron), Best Film—Drama, Best Song ("My Heart Will Go On"), Best Score; MTV Movie Awards '98: Best Film, Best Male Performance (DiCaprio); Screen Actors Guild Award '97: Best Supporting Actress (Stuart); Broadcast Film Critics Association Awards '97: Best Director (Cameron); *NOM:* Academy Awards '97: Best Actress (Winslet), Best Makeup, Best Supporting Actress (Stuart); British Academy Awards '97: Best Cinematography, Best Costume Design, Best Director (Cameron), Best Film, Best Film Editing, Best Sound, Best Score; Golden Globe Awards '98: Best Actor—Drama (DiCaprio), Best Actress—Drama (Winslet), Best Screenplay, Best Supporting Actress (Stuart); MTV Movie Awards '98: Best Female Performance (Winslet), Best On-Screen Duo (Kate Winslet/Leonardo DiCaprio), Best Villain (Zane), Best Song ("My Heart Will Go On"), Best Kiss (Kate Winslet/Leonardo DiCaprio), Best Action Sequence; Screen Actors Guild Award '97: Best Actress (Winslet), Cast; Writers Guild of America '97: Best Original Screenplay.

Titanica

Documentary narrated by Leonard Nimoy follows the historic real-life collaboration of a joint Russian-American science expedition as they examine the sunken ocean liner Titanic using three-man submarines. The DVD's picture quality is stunning. In fact, viewers who have already seen the laserdisc release (which was also very good) might want to re-rent the title on DVD, just to see how many more details are revealed in the underwater footage. This IMAX release also features an excellent 5.1 mix with great fidelity and Surround. —*JO*
Movie: 🦴🦴🦴 *DVD:* 🦴🦴🦴▶
Buena Vista Home Entertainment (Cat #14892, UPC #717951000583). Full frame. Dolby Digital 5.1. $29.99. Keepcase. *LANG:* English. *FEATURES:* 13 chapter links.
1998 75m/C *Nar:* Leonard Nimoy.

T.N.T.

Gruner's managed to extricate himself from a covert fighting force but they're threatening his family unless he does what he's told.
Movie: 🦴🦴 *DVD:* NYR
Monarch Home Video (Cat #7529). Full frame. Dolby Digital Surround Stereo. $19.95. Keepcase. *LANG:* English. *SUB:* Spanish.
1998 (R) 87m/C Olivier Gruner, Eric Roberts, Randy Travis, Sam Jones, Rebecca Staab; *D:* Robert Radler; *C:* Bryan Duggan; *M:* Steve Edwards.

To Catch a Killer

A chilling performance by Dennehy highlights this true crime tale of serial killer John Wayne Gacy, who preyed on young men and hid the bodies in his home. Though this made-for-TV movie had no outstanding production values to start with, it is a taut, unforgettable thriller. The full-frame transfer looks about as good as the VHS version, but it runs nearly twice as long. —*IF*
Movie: 🦴🦴🦴 *DVD:* 🦴▶
Image Entertainment (Cat #5864, UPC #1438158642). Full frame. Dolby Digital Stereo. $29.99. Snapper. *LANG:* English. *FEATURES:* 17 chapter links ▪ Promotional trailer.
1992 189m/C Brian Dennehy, Michael Riley, Margot Kidder, Meg Foster; *D:* Eric Till; *W:* Judson Kinberg; *C:* Rene Ohashi; *M:* Paul Zaza.

To Cross the Rubicon

Slight romantic comedy finds Kendall (Royce, who also wrote and coproduced) being dumped by her longtime boyfriend David (Souther), who then reconnects with old flame Claire (Devon). Meanwhile Kendall enjoys James (Burke), a young rocker. She also becomes buddies with Claire. The action is far too talky and the disc mirrors that problem with an exceptionally grainy image and muddy sound. The many night scenes lack detail. —*MM*
Movie: 🦴🦴▶ *DVD:* 🦴▶
Simitar Entertainment (Cat #7262, UPC #082551727226). Full frame. Dolby Digital Stereo. $7.98. Keepcase. *LANG:* English. *FEATURES:* 8 chapter links ▪ Production factoids.
1991 120m/C Patricia Royce, J.D. Souther, Lorraine Devon, Billy Burke; *D:* Barry Caillier; *W:* Patricia Royce, Lorraine Devon; *C:* Christopher Tufty; *M:* Paul Speer, David Lanz.

To Die For

In Little Hope, NH, manipulative Suzanne Stone (Kidman) wants to be somebody—preferably a big TV personality—and lets nothing stop her. She recruits a scruffy trio to help her dispose of sweet-but-inconvenient hubby Larry (Dillon), even if it means seducing aimless teenager Jimmy (Phoenix). The black comedy is loosely based on the Pamela Smart murder case, adapted from Joyce Maynard's novel. It takes on our media-obsessed culture with a wicked grin. Van Sant retains his fresh and hip storytelling in his first film for a major studio. Backed by Henry's zesty script, all the actors shine—with standout performances from Kidman playing a creature of pure ambition, and Phoenix. This DVD boasts a superb image and terrific sound that highlights Danny Elfman's devilish score, but the truth is, this is such a smart comedy that it's difficult to pay much attention to the technical stuff. On any medium, watch and enjoy. —*MM*
Movie: 🦴🦴🦴 *DVD:* 🦴🦴🦴▶
Columbia Tristar Home Video (Cat #73439). Widescreen (1.85:1) letterboxed; full frame. Dolby Digital 5.1 Surround Stereo; Dolby Digital Surround Stereo. $29.95. Keepcase. *LANG:* English; French. *SUB:* French. *CAP:* English. *FEATURES:* Trailers ▪ 28 chapter links.
1995 (R) 103m/C Nicole Kidman, Matt Dillon, Joaquin Rafael (Leaf) Phoenix, Casey Affleck, Alison Folland, Illeana Douglas, Dan Hedaya, Wayne Knight, Kurtwood Smith, Holland Taylor, Maria Tucci, Susan Traylor; *Cameos:* George Segal, Buck Henry; *D:* Gus Van Sant; *W:* Buck Henry, Johnny Burne; *C:* Eric Alan Edwards; *M:* Danny Elfman. *AWARDS:* Golden Globe Awards '96: Best Actress—Musical/Comedy (Kidman); Broadcast Film Critics Association Awards '95: Best Actress (Kidman); *NOM:* British Academy Awards '95: Best Actress (Kidman); MTV Movie Awards '96: Most Desirable Female (Kidman).

To Kill a Mockingbird

Faithful adaptation of powerful Harper Lee novel is both an evocative portrayal of childhood innocence and a denunciation of bigotry. Peck's performance as southern lawyer defending a black man accused of raping a white woman is flawless. Duvall debuted as the dim-witted Boo Radley. Lee based her characterization of "Dill" on Truman Capote, a childhood friend. The "making of" documentary on the DVD is better than most. The film itself is presented splendidly, with very good sharpness, deep dark blacks, and no digital interference. The Dolby Digital mono tracks are full-bodied and powerful, and sound far cleaner than on the last version I viewed (most likely a laserdisc). —*JO*
Movie: 🦴🦴🦴🦴 *DVD:* 🦴🦴🦴▶
Universal Studios Home Video (Cat #20252, UPC #02519205228). Widescreen (1.85:1) letterboxed. Dolby Digital Mono. $34.98. Keepcase. *LANG:* English; French. *SUB:* Spanish. *CAP:* English. *FEATURES:* 39 chapter links ▪ "Making of" documentary ▪ Theatrical trailer ▪ Cast and filmmakers bios ▪ Production notes ▪ Film highlights.
1962 129m/B Gregory Peck, Brock Peters, Phillip Alford, Mary Badham, Robert Duvall, Rosemary Murphy, William Windom, Alice Ghostley, John Megna, Frank Overton, Paul Fix, Collin Wilcox-Paxton; *D:* Robert Mulligan; *W:* Horton Foote; *C:* Russell Harlan; *M:* Elmer Bernstein;

Nar: Kim Stanley. *AWARDS:* Academy Awards '62: Best Actor (Peck), Best Adapted Screenplay, Best Art Direction/Set Decoration (B & W); American Film Institute (AFI) '98: Top 100; Golden Globe Awards '63: Best Actor—Drama (Peck), Best Score, National Film Registry '95; *NOM:* Academy Awards '62: Best Black-and-white Cinematography, Best Director (Mulligan), Best Picture, Best Supporting Actress (Badham), Best Original Score.

To Kill with Intrigue

Chan as Siao Lei intends to get even after his entire family is slaughtered by a gang. Ding, the gang's leader, spares Siao because she loves him, but she knows he will never reciprocate. She redeems herself by passing on her skills to Siao. Cramped pan-and-scan picture isn't any better than previous low-quality VHS releases. Audio isn't good either, distorting horribly on occasion. No subtitle option. —*MB* **AKA:** Jian Hua Yan Yu Jiang Nan.
Movie: 🐾🐾▶ **DVD:** 🐾
Simitar Entertainment (Cat #7239, UPC #082551723928). Full frame. Dolby Digital 2.0. $14.98. Keepcase. *LANG:* English; Cantonese. *FEATURES:* 10 chapter links ▪ Movie factoids ▪ Biography/filmography ▪ Interview with Chan.
1985 107m/C *HK* Jackie Chan; **D:** Lo Wei.

To Play or To Die

Krom, the director and cowriter, started under Paul Verhoeven. He seems to share that filmmaker's taste in violent suspense and overheated sexual tension. This film, about barely teenage boys and hardly an hour long, ends with a hallucinatory sequence that recalls Polanski's baffling *The Tenant*! Kees (Hunaerts) is the new kid in an all-boys school, placed at the bottom of its pecking order by fearfully attractive class bully Charel (Gerritsma). So begins a power struggle the two rivals play out after school, once Kees's parents are away and his house is empty. Typical of its period, the photography has a dusty, muted look that just cannot digitize well. Bright details like strands of hair or wrinkled skin do pop up, but only momentarily. The visuals are herky-jerky in scan mode, and freeze frames waver uncontrollably. The skeletal music and effects tracks are given full stereo treatment, though overall the DVD intentionally sounds as claustrophobic as it looks. Subtitles, though white, are in readably heavy typeface. —*JK*
Movie: 🐾🐾 **DVD:** 🐾🐾
Water Bearer Films (Cat #WBF4002, UPC #759259140028). Widescreen. Stereo. $29.95. Keepcase. *LANG:* Dutch. *SUB:* English. *FEATURES:* 9 chapter links ▪ Interactive menus ▪ Full-color picture disc.
1991 150m/C *NL* Geert Hunaerts, Tjebbo Gerritsma; **D:** Frank Krom; **W:** Anne Van De Putte, Frank Krom; **C:** Nils Post; **M:** Kim Hayworth, Ferdinand Bakker.

Todd McFarlane's Spawn

The animated cable-TV version of McFarlane's comic book creation is far more entertaining than the live-action film. Hellspawn was once human CIA assassin Al Simmons, murdered in the line of duty, who sold his soul to see his wife one last time. When he comes back from the grave with superhuman powers, it's again as a killer with attitude, who leaves a high body count. This DVD is made up of the first six episodes done for HBO. As with most animation, details are limited and the disc's image is incredibly sharp with stunning color. Though the Dolby Surround seems more like a stereo mix, it packs plenty of energy and sounds great. —*JO* **AKA:** Spawn.
Movie: 🐾🐾🐾▶ **DVD:** 🐾🐾🐾▶
HBO Home Video (Cat #91425, UPC #026359122529). Full frame. Dolby Surround; Mono. $24.98. Snapper. *LANG:* English (DS); Spanish (Mono). *CAP:* English. *FEATURES:* 32 chapter links ▪ Storyboards ▪ Todd McFarlane interview.
1997 147m/C D: Eric Rademski; **W:** Alan B. McElroy, Gary Hardwick; **V:** Keith David, Richard Dysart, Ronny Cox.

Todd McFarlane's Spawn 2

This DVD presents this animated combination of six HBO episodes with incredible intensity. The image remains sharp throughout and colors are saturated with absolutely no bleed, despite all the reds inherent in something this gory. The picture is very dark most of the way through, but both the image and colors remain very detailed thanks to excellent contrast and brightness levels. The soundtrack features some gimmicky Surround effects that work fine with an animated subject, and is overall loud and full-bodied. —*JO* **AKA:** Spawn 2.
Movie: 🐾🐾🐾 **DVD:** 🐾🐾🐾▶
HBO Home Video (Cat #91487, UPC #026359148729). Full frame. Dolby Surround. $24.98. Snapper. *LANG:* English; Spanish. *CAP:* English. *FEATURES:* 19 chapter links ▪ Cast bios ▪ Collector's trading card.
1998 109m/C

Tokyo Decadence

Fascinating but grim film examines the life of a prostitute. Ai (Miho Nikaido) caters to the sadistic sexual proclivities of upscale clients. She's superstitious, none-too-bright and, despite her profession, naive. Murakami based the screenplay on his own novel and directed the film. It's slowly paced and Felliniesque at times, but throughout, he manages to tell a story about the most serious kinds of exploitation without ever being exploitative. He presents this young woman without making value judgments. Once the shock value of her profession has worn off, she's really uninteresting and banal. The DVD

image reflects that transition. In the opening scenes, it is sharply focused and bright. The later scenes are grainier, reflecting Ai's emotional decline. —*MM*
Movie: 🐾🐾▶ **DVD:** 🐾🐾🐾
Image Entertainment (Cat #ID5627FMDVD, UPC #014381562729). Full frame. Dolby Digital Mono. $29.99. Keepcase. *LANG:* Japanese; English. *SUB:* English. *CAP:* English. *FEATURES:* 14 chapter links.
1991 (NC-17) 92m/C *JP* Miho Nikaido, Tenmei Kano, Yayoi Kusama, Sayoko Amano; **D:** Ryu Murakami; **W:** Ryu Murakami; **C:** Tadashi Aoki; **M:** Ryuichi Sakamoto.

Tokyo Drifter

Tokyo Drifter is a Yakuza epic that follows reformed killer Tetsu (Tetsuya) as he tries to remain loyal to his boss and to himself, while a rival unreformed gangster tries to steal his boss's building. Tetsu does his best to go straight, but if he is pushed more than twice, he can't stop himself from throwing a few punches, doing a lot of shooting, or breaking into song. Director Suzuki stages a final shootout with choreography that would look great in most MGM musicals—except for all that shooting and falling bodies. Once you get past the opening black-and-white sequence (which is very harsh and grainy), this DVD is above average. However, like the other Criterion Suzuki DVD *(Branded to Kill)*, the laserdisc is a touch better. Picture is average and there is a lot of grain in long shots that feature movement. Suzuki's excellent use of colors are conveyed vibrantly by the DVD, but colors bleed nastily at times. The brightness, contrast, and handling of blacks are all very good. The mono soundtrack is nothing special, but it's an accurate representation of the film itself and doesn't detract. All in all, a slightly above-average DVD that is comfortable to watch. —*JO* **AKA:** Tokyo Nagaremono.
Movie: 🐾🐾🐾 **DVD:** 🐾🐾▶
Criterion Collection (Cat #39, UPC #037429136126). Widescreen (2.35:1) letterboxed. Dolby Digital Mono. $29.95. Keepcase. *LANG:* Japanese. *SUB:* English. *FEATURES:* 29 chapter links ▪ Interview with director Seijun Suzuki.
1966 83m/C *JP* Eiji Go, Chieko Matsubara, Tetsuya Watari; **D:** Seijun Suzuki.

Tokyo Fist

In his third film, Tsukamoto continues his theme of transformation, although this time he stays completely human. The director plays an insurance salesman whose fiancée has been stolen by a pro-boxer. The boxer is a real slimeball, and unfortunately, the salesman is a total wimp. To win his lover back—thinking the only way to do that is in the ring—our hero is forced to embark on a torturous regimen that makes Rocky Balboa look like a sissy. Director Tsukamoto's over-the-top kinetic style is handled very well by this DVD. The picture is very sharp and there is almost no grain (other than what was in the original film). The brightness and contrast levels remain consistent no matter how harshly or subtly lit the scene is. Although the color is at times very minimal, the DVD is vibrant when it needs to be. Blacks are also very good. The crunching soundtrack hits you in the face with its bone crushing, full-range dynamics, proving once again that you don't need 5.1 Surround to feel a film (and in this case, the punches). —JO

Movie: 🎬🎬🎬➤ **DVD:** 🎬🎬🎬
Rykodisc USA (Cat #6020040222/ WR01, UPC #660200402228). Widescreen (1.85:1) letterboxed. Dolby Surround. $29.95. Keepcase. *LANG:* Japanese. *SUB:* English. *FEATURES:* 14 chapter links • Director bio and filmography • Anti-drug trailer • Manga commercial • Manga trailer.
1996 87m/C Shinya Tsukamoto, Naoto Takenaka, Tomoroh Taguchi, Chu Ishikawa, Kahori Fujii, Naomasa Musaka; *D:* Shinya Tsukamoto; *W:* Shinya Tsukamoto.

Tol'able David

David (Barthelmess) is a Midwestern boy in the quasi-mythic Greenstream. He gets a chance to show his mettle when the postal delivery driver is too inebriated to continue his run. Antiques don't get any more cob-webbed than this! The box is colored like a sampler of gourmet chocolates. Its gatefold essay (so long the package is twice as heavy as average) is elegiac: concerned with long dead or nearly unheard of film folk, and dedicated to a deceased movie historian. The writer might overstate his case that this particular David is like the biblical hero, but in his own American land of milk and honey. Yet, if you're not willing to go along with that sort of florid sentiment then you will likely not enjoy the film. The film is rescued as it can be from its nitrate originals (two different release prints and a negative dupe were used). The gimmicky soundtrack is performed by a small orchestra that attempts to re-create a live accompaniment circa 1921. Unfortunately, it tends to blare a shade too theatrically during suspense sequences. The last four chapters are a 16-minute, 1977 video interview with the director done on university equipment at Claremont in California by the DVD's producer, David Shepard. —JK
Movie: 🎬🎬 **DVD:** 🎬🎬🎬➤
Image Entertainment (Cat #ID4729DSDVD, UPC #014381472929). Full frame. Dolby Digital Stereo. $24.99. Snapper. *LANG:* English. *FEATURES:* 18 chapter links • Scene access menu • Liner notes by Walter Coppedge • Henry King interview.
1921 91m/B Richard Barthelmess, Gladys Hulette, Ernest Torrence; *D:* Henry King; *W:* Henry King, Edmund Goulding; *C:* Henry Cronjager.

The Toll Gate

Early western star William S. Hart plays a train robber who interrupts his outlaw journey to save a young boy's life—and befriend the boy's lonely mother. Hart's status as filmdom's top tough guy may be long gone, but western fans will admire the lean storytelling and action sequences. Different scenes are tinted blue, green, and red from the original black and white, a special effect that works eerily well. The picture quality and sound are very good, considering the film's vintage. —JE
Movie: 🎬🎬🎬 **DVD:** 🎬🎬🎬
Image Entertainment (Cat #ID4748DSDVD, UPC #014381472820). Full frame. Dolby Digital Stereo. $24.99. Snapper. *LANG:* English. *FEATURES:* Hart's 1916 short "His Bitter Pill," a Mack Sennet parody • 16 chapter links.
1920 73m/B William S. Hart, Anna Q. Nilsson, Jack Richardson, Joseph Singleton; *D:* Lambert Hillyer; *W:* Lambert Hillyer; *C:* Joseph August.

Tom Clancy's Netforce

In 2005, technology has become so advanced that a special unit of the FBI, known as Netforce, has been established to police the Internet. Alex Michaels (Bakula) heads the unit after the murder of predecessor Steve Day (Kristofferson), leading Michaels to believe that criminals are trying to cause a global computer crash. Michael's two prime suspects are computer mogul Will Stiles (Reinhold) and crime boss Leong Cheng (Tagawa). This adaptation of Tom Clancy's techno-thriller is presented in a very good full-frame presentation. The image is very clear and highly detailed without any noise or distracting film artifacts. The color balance on this release is very fine with good contrast and color reproduction. Blacks are solid and highlights are well balanced throughout. No compression artifacts are evident in the release. —GH *AKA:* Netforce.
Movie: 🎬🎬➤ **DVD:** 🎬🎬🎬➤
Trimark Home Video (Cat #7087, UPC #031398708735). Full frame. Dolby Digital Stereo. $29.99. Keepcase. *LANG:* English; French; Spanish. *SUB:* English. *FEATURES:* 30 chapter links • Commentary: Robert Lieberman.
1998 (R) 90m/C Scott Bakula, Joanna Going, Brian Dennehy, Kris Kristofferson, Judge Reinhold, Cary-Hiroyuki Tagawa, CCH Pounder, Paul Hewitt, Chelsea Field, Frank Vincent; *D:* Robert Lieberman; *W:* Lionel Chetwynd; *C:* David Hennings; *M:* Jeff Rona.

Tom Jones

Bawdy comedy based on Henry Fielding's novel about a rustic playboy's wild life in 18th-century England is hilarious and clever with a grand performance by Finney. One of the sexiest eating scenes ever. The DVD features the 121-minute "director's cut" of the film, which seems to move much more quickly than the original cut. The image on the disc has both film grain (from the preprint) and digital grain, and the combination at times nearly ruins the picture. The source material is pretty ragged and there is a lot of film damage. Colors have a weird tint on the DVD, but that is probably also from the original film. A stereo soundtrack is listed, but separation is so limited that it still feels like mono. —JO
Movie: 🎬🎬🎬🎬 **DVD:** 🎬🎬
HBO Home Video (Cat #90664, UPC #026359066429). Widescreen (1.66:1) letterboxed. Stereo. Mono. $24.98. Snapper. *LANG:* English; French; Spanish. *CAP:* English. *FEATURES:* 29 chapter links.
1963 121m/C *GB* Albert Finney, Susannah York, Hugh Griffith, Edith Evans, Joan Greenwood, Diane Cilento, George Devine, David Tomlinson, Joyce Redman, Lynn Redgrave, Julian Glover, Peter Bull, David Warner; *D:* Tony Richardson; *W:* John Osborne; *C:* Walter Lassally; *M:* John Addison. *AWARDS:* Academy Awards '63: Best Adapted Screenplay, Best Director (Richardson), Best Picture, Best Original Score; British Academy Awards '63: Best Film, Best Screenplay; Directors Guild of America Awards '63: Best Director (Richardson); Golden Globe Awards '64: Best Film—Musical/Comedy, Best Foreign Film; National Board of Review Awards '63: Best Director (Richardson); New York Film Critics Awards '63: Best Actor (Finney), Best Director (Richardson), Best Film; *NOM:* Academy Awards '63: Best Actor (Finney), Best Art Direction/Set Decoration (Color), Best Supporting Actor (Griffith), Best Supporting Actress (Cilento, Evans, Redman).

Tom Sawyer

Animated version of the oft-filmed novel casts cute furry critters in Twain's famous characters. Country music stars provide most of the voices. The level of animation is a step above Saturday morning cartoons, several steps below the best theatrical releases. The main advantage DVD has over VHS tape is in excellent stereo sound, not image. —MM
Movie: 🎬🎬 **DVD:** 🎬🎬➤
MGM Home Entertainment (Cat #908393, UPC #027616839329). Full frame. Dolby Digital 5.1 Surround Stereo. $19.98. Keepcase. *LANG:* English. *SUB:* French; Spanish. *FEATURES:* 24 chapter links.
1999 89m/C *D:* Paul Sabella, Phil Mendez; *W:* Patricia Jones, Donald Reiker; *M:* Mark Watters; *V:* Rhett Akins, Mark Wills, Lee Ann Womack, Hank Williams Jr., Waylon Jennings, Don Knotts, Betty White.

Tombs of the Blind Dead

Amando de Ossorio's first use of the resurrected Knights Templar is one of the most influential horrors of the early 1970s. Though the film is clumsily plotted, it sets the stage for several sequels and the more general trend, particularly in European films, of mixing sex (exploitative and otherwise) and graphic horror. Ossorio's Templars are 13th-century Portuguese knights who torture young women

and drink their blood to gain immortality. They're executed and blinded by crows that peck out their eyes, but rise up out of their graves centuries later whenever young women are nearby. Though they cannot see, they locate their victims by sound and, like American "living dead," eat them. (Later films would correct the illogical nature of the Templars' condition by changing the backstory to have them blinded before they're executed.) Questions of sexual politics aside (and the film does raise many issues in that area), the Templars are memorable, nightmarish figures. On DVD, image and sound are only marginally better than the excellent Anchor Bay tape. —*MM* **AKA:** The Blind Dead; La Noche dell Terror Ciego; La Noche de la Muerta Ciega; Crypt of the Blind Dead; Night of the Blind Dead.
Movie: 🎬🎬🎬 **DVD:** 🎬🎬🎬
Anchor Bay (Cat #DV10561, UPC #013131056198). Widescreen (1.66:1) letterboxed. Dolby Digital Mono. $29.98. Keepcase. *LANG:* Spanish. *SUB:* English. *FEATURES:* 12 chapter links. This is a double feature with *Return of the Blind Dead*.
1972 (PG) 102m/C *SP PT* Caesar Burner, Lone Fleming, Helen Harp, Joseph Thelman, Rufino Ingles, Maria Silva; **D:** Armando de Ossorio; **W:** Armando de Ossorio; **C:** Pablo Ripoll; **M:** Anton Abril.

Tombstone

Saga of Wyatt Earp and his band of law-enforcing big mustaches. Legendary lawman Earp (Russell) moves to Tombstone, AZ, aiming to start a new life with his brothers, but alas, that's not to be. The infamous gunfight at the OK Corral is here, and so is best buddy Doc Holiday, gunslinger and philosopher, the perfect role for Kilmer. Russell spends a lot of time looking troubled by the violence while adding to the body count. High energy level thanks to despicable villains Lang, Biehn, and Boothe. The sound on this DVD is excellent: the brass on the orchestral score really punches through; you can feel the sub-woofer when those old west hand cannons go off; the separation on the Surround is pretty much the best that a non-5.1 soundtrack can be. The image is sharper than the laserdisc and handles the colors much better (only a little bleed on the reds). Dark scenes are handled almost as well as the bright ones with true blacks, and very good contrast and brightness levels. —*JO*
Movie: 🎬🎬🎬 **DVD:** 🎬🎬🎬
Hollywood Pictures Home Video (Cat #13078, UPC #717951000065). Widescreen (2.35:1) letterboxed. Dolby Surround. $29.99. Keepcase. *LANG:* English (DS); Spanish (DS); French (DS). *SUB:* English; Spanish. *FEATURES:* 25 chapter links • Theatrical trailer • Theatrical teaser.
1993 (R) 130m/C Kurt Russell, Val Kilmer, Michael Biehn, Sam Elliott, Dana Delany, Bill Paxton, Powers Boothe, Stephen Lang, Jason Priestley, Dana Wheeler-Nicholson, Billy Zane, Thomas Haden Church, Joanna Pacula, Michael

Rooker, Harry Carey Jr., Billy Bob Thornton, Charlton Heston, Robert John Burke, John Corbett, Buck Taylor, Terry O'Quinn, Pedro Armendariz Jr., Chris Mitchum, Jon Tenney; **D:** George P. Cosmatos; **W:** Kevin Jarre; **C:** William A. Fraker; **M:** Bruce Broughton; **Nar:** Robert Mitchum. *AWARDS: NOM:* MTV Movie Awards '94: Best Male Performance (Kilmer), Most Desirable Male (Kilmer).

Tommy and the Computoys

This computer animation is strictly for kids with a bland animated character called Tommy, who has some very two-dimensional adventures meeting other computer-generated objects. Very young viewers may be diverted by the bright colors and jaunty music, but there's no story to speak of and the CG effects pale in comparison to similar films made just a year or two later. —*JE*
Movie: 🎬► **DVD:** 🎬🎬►
Image Entertainment (Cat #ID5561M3 DVD, UPC #014381556124). Full frame. Dolby Digital Stereo. $14.98. Snapper. *LANG:* English. *FEATURES:* 23 chapter links • Web access.
1995 ?m/C

Tommy Boy

Not-too-bright rich kid Tommy (Farley) teams up with snide officious accountant Richard (Spade) to save the family auto parts business after dad (Dennehy) shuffles off this mortal coil. They must deal with a conniving stepmom (Derek) and stepbrother (Lowe), a ruthless rival (Aykroyd), and a road trip from hell to drum up new business. Not as bad as it sounds but inconsistent direction and too-familiar characters offset the chemistry between the two leads.
Movie: 🎬🎬 **DVD:** NYR
Paramount Home Video (Cat #331317). Widescreen (1.85:1) anamorphic. Dolby Digital 5.1 Surround Stereo. $29.99. Keepcase. *LANG:* English; French. *CAP:* English. *FEATURES:* Trailer.
1995 (PG-13) 98m/C Chris Farley, David Spade, Brian Dennehy, Bo Derek, Dan Aykroyd, Julie Warner, Rob Lowe; **D:** Peter Segal; **W:** Bonnie Turner, Terry Turner; **C:** Victor Kemper; **M:** David Newman. *AWARDS:* MTV Movie Awards '96: Best On-Screen Duo (Chris Farley/David Spade); *NOM:* MTV Movie Awards '96: Best Comedic Performance (Farley).

Tomorrow Never Dies (SE)

The 18th installment of the James Bond series is all style and little else packaged in a tedious action adventure. Our villain is a media mogul (Pryce) who plans to increase his newspaper revenues by causing World War III. (Rupert Murdoch, start your lawyers!) In between the blatant product placements (from Heineken to Visa), our secret agent Bond (Brosnan, who

seems bored with the role in his second appearance) sets out to foil the nutty plans. He gets help from Hong Kong action queen Yeoh as a Chinese agent, and a bevy of toys from the antiquated Q, including a BMW controlled by remote. Direction and flow is on autopilot after the opening scene and despite Yeoh's energetic high-kicks and the sleek techno toys, it can't revitalize what has become a third-class imitator of its predecessors. The Bond special editions always seem to utilize the same transfer as in the earlier editions, but that doesn't really matter because they have always looked good. The image on the DVD is sharp and the vibrant colors stand up to the original theatrical presentation. Blacks are dead-on, and you really couldn't ask for a punchier picture. The sound is very dynamic and the music is great. The Surround mix sends a lot to the rear channel and both the rears and the subwoofer signals are boosted during action scenes. —*JO*
Movie: 🎬🎬 **DVD:** 🎬🎬🎬►
MGM Home Entertainment (Cat #906756, UPC #027616675620). Widescreen (2.35:1) anamorphic. Dolby Digital 5.1; Dolby Surround. $34.98. Keepcase. *LANG:* English (DD5.1); French (DS). *SUB:* English; French; Spanish. *CAP:* English. *FEATURES:* 28 chapter links • 2 commentary tracks • Storyboards • 45-minute "Secrets of 007" featurette • Music video • Digital effects reel • Isolated music score • Theatrical trailer and teaser.
1997 (PG-13) 119m/C Pierce Brosnan, Jonathan Pryce, Michelle Yeoh, Teri Hatcher, Judi Dench, Colin Salmon, Samantha Bond, Desmond Llewelyn, Joe Don Baker, Ricky Jay, Vincent Schiavelli, Geoffrey Palmer; **D:** Roger Spottiswoode; **W:** Bruce Feirstein; **C:** Robert Elswit; **M:** David Arnold. *AWARDS: NOM:* Golden Globe Awards '98: Best Song ("Tomorrow Never Dies"); MTV Movie Awards '98: Best Action Sequence, Best Fight (Michelle Yeoh/bad guys).

Top Dog

Another cop-and-dog-team-up-to-get-the-bad-guys flick. This one, however, is meant to appeal to kids who liked *Sidekicks*. Jake Wilder (Norris), a beer swillin' karate-choppin' loner cop, teams up with canine Reno, whose ex-partner was killed by neo-Nazi terrorists. Weak script and erratic storyline can't find a comfortable balance between the too-cute pooch scenes and the toned-down violence. Reno steals his scenes.
Movie: 🎬► **DVD:** NYR
Artisan Entertainment (Cat #11278). Widescreen (1.85:1) anamorphic. $19.98. Keepcase. *FEATURES:* Trailer.
1995 (PG-13) 93m/C Chuck Norris, Clyde Kusatsu, Michele Lamar Richards, Carmine Caridi, Peter Savard Moore, Erik von Detten, Herta Ware, Kai Wulff, Francesco Quinn, Timothy Bottoms; **D:** Aaron Norris; **W:** Ron Swanson; **C:** Joao Fernandes.

Top Gun

Buffed-up young Navy pilots compete against each other in the air and on the volleyball court at the elite Fighter Weapons School. Cruise is all testosterone and sneer as Maverick who comes of age in Ray Bans, but Edwards shines as his buddy Goose. DVD emphasizes the high-volume soundtrack and aerial footage shot on and around carriers. It can do nothing about the preposterous excuse for a plot. —*MM*

Movie: ♪♪ *DVD:* ♪♪♪
Paramount Home Video (Cat #016927, UPC #097360169270). Widescreen letterboxed; full frame. Dolby Digital 5.1 Surround Stereo; Dolby Digital Surround Stereo. $29.99. Keepcase. *LANG:* English; French. *SUB:* Spanish. *CAP:* English. *FEATURES:* 30 chapter links.
1986 (PG) 109m/C Tom Cruise, Kelly McGillis, Val Kilmer, Tom Skerritt, Anthony Edwards, Meg Ryan, Rick Rossovich, Michael Ironside, Barry Tubb, Whip Hubley, John Stockwell, Tim Robbins, Adrian Pasdar; *D:* Tony Scott; *W:* Jim Cash, Jack Epps Jr.; *C:* Jeffrey L. Kimball; *M:* Harold Faltermeyer. *AWARDS:* Academy Awards '86: Best Song ("Take My Breath Away"); Golden Globe Awards '87: Best Song ("Take My Breath Away"); *NOM:* Academy Awards '86: Best Film Editing, Best Sound.

Top of the World

Pallid thriller involves the ridiculous heist of a Vegas casino. Ex-cop/ex-con Mercer (Weller) is caught in the middle when his wife (Carrere) stops by the place right after his release. Hopper and Pantoliano sleepwalk through their roles as nasty casino managers. The rest of the cast and veteran director Furie handle their work with the same nonchalance. The thin material looks just fine on DVD. Even night scenes on the Vegas strip, on a roller coaster, and at Hoover dam are properly lit so that they're completely clear. Sound is nothing special. —*MM*

Movie: ♪♪ *DVD:* ♪♪➤
Image Entertainment (Cat #ID6341NGDVD, UPC #014381634129). Full frame. Dolby Digital Stereo. $24.99. Snapper. *LANG:* English. *FEATURES:* 16 chapter links ➤ Theatrical trailer.
1997 (R) 98m/C Peter Weller, Tia Carrere, Dennis Hopper, Joe Pantoliano, Martin Kove, Peter Coyote, David Alan Grier, Cary-Hiroyuki Tagawa; *D:* Sidney J. Furie; *W:* Bart Madison; *C:* Alan Caso; *M:* Robert O. Ragland.

Tora! Tora! Tora!

The story of the events leading up to the attack on Pearl Harbor is told by three directors from both Japanese and American viewpoints. This was one of the last of Hollywood's "epic" re-creations of real WWII engagements and it's one of the best. In place of the conventional "all-star cast," an ensemble of familiar and talented character actors handles the action.

They and the writers manage to find a surprising amount of tension in a story that everyone thinks they know. The DVD is at its best in the most visual moments; the attack itself, of course, but other moments are just as impressive. The best of them is in chapter 19, when the Japanese planes take off into a predawn sky. It's an unusually emotional and beautiful moment. Aliasing is noticeable in some scenes when the diagonal edge of a wing or an awning may lose its true shape. Otherwise, sound and image are excellent. —*MM*

Movie: ♪♪♪ *DVD:* ♪♪♪➤
Twentieth Century Fox Home Entertainment Widescreen letterboxed. Dolby Digital 4.1 Surround Stereo; Dolby Surround Stereo; Mono. $29.98. Keepcase. *LANG:* English; French. *SUB:* English; Spanish. *FEATURES:* 31 chapter links ➤ Theatrical trailers.
1970 (G) 144m/C Martin Balsam, So Yamamura, Joseph Cotten, E.G. Marshall, Tatsuya Mihashi, Wesley Addy, Jason Robards Jr., James Whitmore, Leon Ames, George Macready, Takahiro Tamura, Eijiro Tono, Shogo Shimada, Koreya Senda, Jun Usami, Richard Anderson, Kazuo Kitamura, Keith Andes, Edward Andrews, Neville Brand, Leora Dana, Walter Brooke, Norman Alden, Ron Masak, Edmon Ryan, Asao Uchida, Frank Aletter, Jerry Fogel; *D:* Richard Fleischer, Toshio Masuda, Kinji Fukasaku; *W:* Ryuzo Kikushima, Hideo Oguni, Larry Forrester; *C:* Sinsaku Himeda, Charles F. Wheeler, Osamu Furuya; *M:* Jerry Goldsmith. *AWARDS:* Academy Awards '70: Best Visual Effects; *NOM:* Academy Awards '70: Best Art Direction/Set Decoration, Best Cinematography, Best Film Editing, Best Sound.

Tornado Run

Blue-light special adventure flick has little to offer. It's about arms dealers vs. government agents (led by Bruneau and Rector). The alleged plot is padded with several exploding cars. On DVD, the image is pale and poorly focused. All the usual flaws show up—flashing patterns, broken diagonal lines, graininess—making this one tough to watch. It lacks any extras, including chapter links. —*MM*

Movie: ♪ *DVD:* woof
Simitar Entertainment (Cat #7206, UPC #082551720620). Full frame. PCM Stereo. $7.98. Keepcase. *LANG:* English.
1995 ?m/C Sharon Bruneau, Jeff Rector; *D:* Barry Hickey.

Torso

Influential "giallo" horror was one of the first slasher films to mix sex and violence so blatantly. The story concerns a psycho killer who's after four young college students, including model Suzy Kendall. According to the box copy, much of the most graphic material was cut for American release. Those scenes contain no English dialogue and so are presented in Italian with subtitles. This version looks

as sharp as any early-'70s import could be expected to look. (It's certainly sharper than the print I saw at a drive-in eons ago.) The digital monaural soundtrack heightens the artificiality of the dubbing. —*MM AKA:* I Corpi Presentano Tracce Di Violenza Carnale; Bodres Bear Traces of Carnal Violence.

Movie: ♪♪ *DVD:* ♪♪
Anchor Bay (Cat #DV11073, UPC #013131 107395). Widescreen (1.85:1) anamorphic. Dolby Digital Mono. $29.98. Keepcase. *LANG:* English; Italian. *SUB:* English. *FEATURES:* 24 chapter links ➤ 2 theatrical trailers.
1973 (R) 91m/C *IT* Suzy Kendall, Tina Aumont, John Richardson; *D:* Sergio Martino; *W:* Ernesto Gastaldi, Sergio Martino; *C:* Giancarlo Ferrando; *M:* Guido de Angelis, Maurizio de Angelis.

Torture Chamber of Baron Blood

Young American Peter Kleist (Cantafora) goes to Austria to discover his family roots. He's the ancestor of a particularly vicious Baron and ignorantly resurrects the guy. Most of the action is set in a castle where director Bava makes full use of the towers, dungeons, and secret passageways, and revisits some of the images he first used in *Black Sunday*. The highpoint is a long strikingly lit night chase. In that scene, the graininess that pervades the DVD is actually an asset. Overall, the film looks about as good as a mid-budget horror of its age could be expected. The main visual flaw is a distracting distortion of patterns on a couple of horse-blanket sportscoats. —*MM AKA:* Baron Blood; Gli Orrori del Castello di Norimberga; The Blood Baron; Chamber of Tortures; The Thirst of Baron Blood.

Movie: ♪♪➤ *DVD:* ♪♪
Image Entertainment (Cat #ID5939AODVD, UPC #014381593921). Widescreen (1.85:1) letterboxed. Dolby Digital Mono. $24.99. Keepcase. *LANG:* English. *FEATURES:* 16 chapter links ➤ Cast and crew thumbnail biographies ➤ Theatrical trailer ➤ Photo and poster gallery ➤ Liner notes by *Video Watchdog* publisher Tim Lucas.
1972 (PG) 90m/C *IT* Joseph Cotten, Elke Sommer, Massimo Girotti, Rada Rassimov, Antonio Cantafora; *D:* Mario Bava; *W:* Vincent Fotre, William Bairn; *M:* Les Baxter.

Total Eclipse

Director Holland is more interested in the mutually destructive passions of 19th-century French poets Paul Verlaine (Thewlis) and Arthur Rimbaud (DiCaprio) than in their work. Rimbaud was a 16-year-old Parisian sensation for his iconoclastic work. DiCaprio plays him as a charismatic, boorish egomaniac, and seems to be having a whale of a time doing it. Thewlis's Verlaine is more complex and dissolute. To my tastes, two stars doing fine work redeems the film from its innate sordidness. And even harsh critics will have to agree that the DVD is flawless with a sharp, smoky image and adequate sound. —MM

Movie: ♫♫ **DVD:** ♫♫♫
New Line Home Video (Cat #N4850, UPC #794043485022). Widescreen (1.85:1) letterboxed; full frame. Dolby Digital 5.1 Surround Stereo; Dolby Digital Surround Stereo. $24.98. Snapper. *LANG:* English. *SUB:* English. *FEATURES:* 23 chapter links.
1995 (R) 111m/C Leonardo DiCaprio, David Thewlis, Romane Bohringer, Dominique Blanc; **D:** Agnieszka Holland; **W:** Christopher Hampton; **C:** Yorgos Arvanitis; **M:** Jan A.P. Kaczmarek.

Total Reality

Time-tripping sf borrows heavily from *The Terminator*. Rand (Bradley) leads a group of criminals from the future back to the present to prevent the destruction of the human race, etc. etc. Lots of things explode and many large weapons are fired. On DVD, it's a dark film with an icy blue look throughout. The computer-generated effects are acceptable. It was filmed in Portland, Oregon. —MM

Movie: ♫♫ **DVD:** ♫♫▶
York Entertainment (Cat #YPD-1016, UPC #750723101620). Full frame. $24.98. Keepcase. *LANG:* English. *SUB:* Spanish. *CAP:* English. *FEATURES:* 25 chapter links ▪ Filmographies of Ely Pouget and David Bradley ▪ Theatrical trailer.
1997 (R) 97m/C David Bradley, Thomas Kretschmann, Ely Pouget, Bill Shaw, Misa Koprova; **D:** Phillip J. Roth; **W:** Phillip J. Roth, Robert Tossberg; **C:** Andres Garreton.

Total Recall

Construction worker Quaid (Schwarzenegger) dreams every night about the colonization of Mars, so he decides to visit a travel service that specializes in implanting vacation memories into its clients' brains—a memory trip to the planet. Only during the implant, Quaid discovers his memories have been artificially altered and he must find out just what's real and what's not. Intriguing plot and spectacular special effects are laced with graphic violence. For the most part the DVD looks pretty good, but there are instances where grain becomes a problem. Colors are excellent and overall the picture is intense. The 5.1 sound is tremendous, giving equal attention to both the dialogue and effects and a superb, ambient mix to the excellent score. —JO

Movie: ♫♫♫ **DVD:** ♫♫♫▶
Artisan Entertainment (Cat #60439, UPC #012236043904). Widescreen (1.85:1) letterboxed; full frame. Dolby Digital 5.1; Dolby Surround 2.0. $24.98. Snapper. *LANG:* English (DDS5.1); French (DS). *SUB:* English; French; Spanish. *CAP:* English. *FEATURES:* 41 chapter links ▪ Production notes ▪ Cast and crew bios ▪ Theatrical teaser and trailer.
1990 (R) 113m/C Arnold Schwarzenegger, Rachel Ticotin, Sharon Stone, Michael Ironside, Ronny Cox, Roy Brocksmith, Marshall Bell, Mel Johnson Jr.; **D:** Paul Verho-

even; **W:** Gary Goldman, Dan O'Bannon; **C:** Jan De Bont; **M:** Jerry Goldsmith. *AWARDS:* Academy Awards '90: Best Visual Effects; *NOM:* Academy Awards '90: Best Sound.

Total Recall 2070: Machine Dreams

Sequel in theme and title only is set in a near crimeless future. Cop David Hume (Easton) does not have much to do until a trio of cyborgs turn murderous. The special effects have a made-for-cable-TV quality. They're good enough but limited in scope. The same could be said of the DVD. Director Azzopardi uses moody lighting to give the film a grubby *Seven* look with derivative references to *Blade Runner*. Recommended to the most dedicated sf fans only. —MM

Movie: ♫♫ **DVD:** ♫♫▶
Buena Vista Home Entertainment (Cat #18294, UPC #717951004802). Full frame. Dolby Digital Surround Stereo. $29.99. Keepcase. *LANG:* English; French. *CAP:* English. *FEATURES:* 25 chapter links.
1999 (R) 83m/C Michael Easton, Karl Pruner, Cyndy Preston, Judith Krant, Nick Mancuso; **D:** Mario Azzopardi; **C:** Peter Wunstorf.

Tower of Evil

Prosaic dialogue and plot developments make up this film's strongest and weakest points by turns. It's a creaky creepfest with a soundtrack that moans like Jacob Marley, featuring an unintimidating rubber-masked baddie. See, there's this island, with a tower on it, right? And, like, people who go there get scared by the evil! Sure, they're supposed to be anthropologists, but they all seem dressed for a night at the disco. The sound quality is as good as you can expect from something recorded on cardboard and papier mache sets. Admirably rendered doom and gloom effects include fog and flames. Yet even they are topped by a particularly challenging, flash-filled, quasi-psychedelic hypnosis sequence. The hippie chic costumes are a pageant unto themselves; one more tribute to the gifts of this disc's engineers. —JK *AKA:* Horror on Snape Island; Beyond the Fog.

Movie: woof **DVD:** ♫♫♫♫
Elite Entertainment, Inc. (Cat #EE8693, UPC #790594869328). Widescreen (1.85:1). Dual-channel Mono. $24.99. Keepcase. *LANG:* English. *FEATURES:* 16 chapter links ▪ Interactive menus ▪ 2-color picture disc ▪ Theatrical trailer.
1972 (R) 86m/C *GB* Bryant Halliday, Jill Haworth, Jack Watson, Mark Edwards, George Coulouris; **D:** James O'Connolly; **W:** James O'Connolly; **C:** Desmond Dickinson.

The Towering Inferno

Raging blaze engulfs the world's tallest skyscraper on the night of its glamorous dedication ceremonies. Performances

overcome the flaws in the script. Allen had invented the disaster du jour genre two years earlier with *The Poseidon Adventure*. The DVD looks great and is much improved over even the letterboxed Fox laserdisc. The picture is sharp and both grain and artifacts have to be looked for to be seen. Colors are vibrant and accurate with very little bleed. The true blacks are enhanced by the overall excellent and consistent contrast and brightness levels. The 5.1 sound gives the film far more power than the earlier home video editions, and has gutsy bass and crisp highs. Dynamics are very good, as is the imaging on the front tracks. Surround is minimal. —JO

Movie: ♫♫ **DVD:** ♫♫♫▶
20th Century Fox (Cat #4110429, UPC #086162104299). Widescreen (2.35:1) letterboxed. Dolby Digital 5.1; Dolby Surround. $29.98. Keepcase. *LANG:* English. *SUB:* English; Spanish. *CAP:* English. *FEATURES:* 26 chapter links ▪ Theatrical trailer.
1974 (PG) 165m/C Steve McQueen, Paul Newman, William Holden, Faye Dunaway, Fred Astaire, Jennifer Jones, Richard Chamberlain, Susan Blakely, O.J. Simpson, Robert Vaughn, Robert Wagner; **D:** John Guillermin, Irwin Allen; **W:** Stirling Silliphant; **C:** Joseph Biroc, Fred W. Koenekamp; **M:** John Williams. *AWARDS:* Academy Awards '74: Best Cinematography, Best Film Editing, Best Song ("We May Never Love Like This Again"); British Academy Awards '75: Best Supporting Actor (Astaire); Golden Globe Awards '75: Best Supporting Actor (Astaire); *NOM:* Academy Awards '74: Best Art Direction/Set Decoration, Best Picture, Best Sound, Best Supporting Actor (Astaire), Best Original Dramatic Score.

The Toxic Avenger (DC)

Made on a miniscule budget on location in New Jersey, Troma's alternative superhero is a *Mad* magazine/Three Stooges horror comedy. It rises to new levels of bad taste in this "unrated director's cut," with box copy proudly boasting that it contains "the full 'head crushing' scene." Toxie, the monstrous avenger, is created when bullies dump the nebbish Melvin (Torgl) into a vat of toxic waste and he emerges as a rough cross between Arnold Schwarzenegger and Mr. Potato-Head. He fights injustice wherever he finds it and has gone on to star in two sequels to date and an animated TV series. The DVD contains all the Troma extras, and despite director Lloyd Kaufman's honestly earned reputation for working with ultra-low budgets, the image looks fine. Of course the night scenes are grainy but overall, the disc is a solid step up from VHS tape. —MM

Movie: ♫♫♫ **DVD:** ♫♫♫▶
Troma Team Video (Cat #DVD9000, UPC #790357900039). Full frame. $24.95. Keepcase. *LANG:* English. *FEATURES:* 9 chapter links ▪ 5 deleted scenes ▪ Tour of Troma studios and other studio releases

- Interview with Toxie • Commentary: Lloyd Kaufman • Interview with Mark Torgl • Theatrical trailer • Stills.
1986 90m/C Mitchell Cohen, Andree Maranda, Jennifer Baptist, Robert Prichard, Cindy Manion, Mark Torgl, David Weiss; **D:** Michael Herz, Lloyd (Samuel Weil) Kaufman; **W:** Joe Ritter; **C:** James London.

The Toxic Avenger, Part 2

Sequel finds the disfigured superhero (Fazio) fighting international corporations and others who dump toxic waste in Tromaville, New Jersey. Our hero must go to Japan to find his long-lost father and save his accordion-playing blind girlfriend (Legere). The disc comes with all the Troma bells and whistles—including uncommonly perceptive commentary tracks—and though some might think that nothing is to be gained by presenting a Troma production in its most pristine form, the film delivers with a crisp digitally mastered image, bargain-basement production values, and attitude to burn. (Jokes about tattooed black midget bodybuilders are only the beginning.) Troma makes the best low-budget movies in the business and this is one of the studio's finest moments. —MM
Movie: 🎬🎬🎬 **DVD:** 🎬🎬🎬
Troma Team Video (Cat #DVD9810, UPC #790357981038). Full frame. $24.95. Keepcase. *LANG:* English. *FEATURES:* Intro and commentary by codirector and Troma president Lloyd Kaufman • Interactive tour of Troma • Troma Intelligence Test • Comments by Mike Mayo • Comments by star Lisa Gay • Links to Troma website • 9 chapter links. The DVD contains many other extras.
1989 (R) 90m/C Ron Fazio, Phoebe Legere, Rick Collins, John Altamura, Rikiya Yasuoka, Lisa Gaye, Mayako Katsuragi; **D:** Michael Herz, Lloyd (Samuel Weil) Kaufman; **W:** Lloyd (Samuel Weil) Kaufman, Gay Partington Terry; **C:** James London; **M:** Barrie Guard.

Trader Hornee

Legendary exploitation comedy is still best remembered for its inspired title. The sexual content is now well within the limits of an "R" rating. It's very silly, frivolous stuff about an impromptu safari to the deepest African jungle (actually, the California countryside) to find a missing heiress and a white gorilla, etc. On his commentary track, producer David Friedman remembers the filming fondly. (The pseudonymous director was his neighbor.) The DVD image is generally good, with no serious imperfections that cannot be traced to the quality of the original. The sound is thin. —MM
Movie: 🎬🎬 **DVD:** 🎬🎬
Something Weird Video (Cat #ID6099SWDVD, UPC #014381609929). Widescreen (1.66:1) letterboxed. Dolby Digital Mono. $24.99. Snapper. *LANG:* Eng-

lish. *FEATURES:* 15 chapter links • Commentary: David Friedman and Mike Vraney • Original theatrical trailer • Gallery of exploitation ad materials.
1970 84m/C Buddy Pantsari, Elizabeth Monica, John Alderman, Christine Murray, Deek Sills; **D:** Dan (Jonathan Lucas) Tsanusdi; **W:** David Friedman; **C:** Paul Hipp; **M:** Billy Allen, William Loose.

The Train

In August 1944, as Paris is about to fall to the Allies, Nazi Col. Von Waldheim (Scofield) steals a huge collection of French paintings and prepares to ship them back to the Fatherland on a train. Railway inspector and Resistance leader Labiche (Lancaster) learns of the looting but is reluctant to risk men for art. Events quickly hurtle out of control and the result is a brilliant Hitchcockian thriller. On DVD, make sure to catch the incredible action in chapters 7 and 8 when an entire railroad yard is destroyed. After you've watched the film once, give the disc another spin and listen to Frankenheimer's concise commentary. His admiration for Lancaster, who did all of his own stunts, is immense. Critical viewers will notice a few inconsequential visual flaws but this overlooked masterpiece of suspense ought to find an appreciative audience on disc. One of the best. —MM *AKA:* Le Train; Il Treno.
Movie: 🎬🎬🎬🎬 **DVD:** 🎬🎬🎬🎬
MGM Home Entertainment (Cat #907539, UPC #027616753922). Widescreen letterboxed. Dolby Digital Mono. $24.98. Keepcase. *LANG:* English. *SUB:* English; French. *FEATURES:* 32 chapter links • Commentary: director John Frankenheimer • Isolated track for Maurice Jarre's score • 8-page booklet • Trailer.
1965 133m/C *FR IT* Burt Lancaster, Paul Scofield, Jeanne Moreau, Michel Simon, Suzanne Flon, Wolfgang Preiss, Albert Remy, Charles Millot, Jacques Marin, Donald O'Brien, Jean-Pierre Zola, Arthur Brauss, Howard Vernon, Richard Munch, Paul Bonifas, Jean-Claude Bercq; **D:** John Frankenheimer; **W:** Frank Davis, Walter Bernstein, Franklin Coen; **C:** Jean Tournier, Walter Wottitz; **M:** Maurice Jarre. *AWARDS: NOM:* Academy Awards '65: Best Story & Screenplay.

Train Ride to Hollywood

This curiosity never received wide theatrical release and it's easy to see why. Made in the mid-'70s, it's a throwback to big-band musical comedy/revues. The lively but poorly named R&B group, the Bloodstones, play themselves as four guys who go back in a dream where they board a train and meet impersonators of Bogie, W.C. Fields, Nelson Eddy and Jeanette MacDonald, Scarlett and Rhett, Bela Lugosi, and the Godfather. Of course, they sing a lot, too. Director Rondeau is a television veteran and it shows. The grainy

image is typical of films of its time. The sound is fine but not exceptional. —MM
Movie: 🎬🎬 **DVD:** 🎬🎬
Anchor Bay (Cat #DV10941, UPC #013131094190). Widescreen (1.66:1) letterboxed. Dolby Digital Stereo. $24.98. Keepcase. *LANG:* English. *FEATURES:* 20 chapter links • Theatrical trailer • Commentary: Braunstein, Draffin, Williams, McCormick, Love • Cast thumbnail biographies.
1975 89m/C Willis Draffin, Harry Williams, Charles McCormick, Charles Love, Phyllis E. Davis, Guy Marks, Jay Lawrence, Tracy Reed; **D:** Charles R. Rondeau; **W:** Dan Gordon; **C:** Al Francis; **M:** Pip Williams.

Trainspotting

From the same team who brought us the violently comedic *Shallow Grave*, comes an equally destructive look at a group of Edinburgh junkies and losers. Heroin-user Mark Renton (McGregor) once again decides to get off junk, but to do so he has to get away from his friends: knife-wielding psycho Begbie (Carlyle), Sick Boy (Miller), Spud (Bremner), and Tommy (McKidd). He heads for a semi-respectable life in London but Begbie and Spud wind up involving him in a serious-money drug deal that spells trouble. Strong fantasy visuals depict drug highs and lows, while heavy Scottish accents (and humor) may prove difficult. Based on the 1993 cult novel by Irvine Welsh, the film drew much controversy for its supposedly pro-heroin stance, but the junkie's life is hardly portrayed as attractive. Somehow, re-watching this darkly comic film on DVD increased the squirm factor of many scenes. The picture is very sharp and the colors seem more vibrant than remembered, although the tint seems a little different. The 5.1 sound is powerful with excellent clarity, making the heavy dialect easier to understand. —JO
Movie: 🎬🎬🎬 **DVD:** 🎬🎬🎬
Miramax Pictures Home Video (Cat #13851, UPC #717951000224). Widescreen (1.85:1) letterboxed. Dolby Digital 5.1. $29.99. Keepcase. *LANG:* English. *FEATURES:* 25 chapter links.
1995 (R) 94m/C *GB* Ewan McGregor, Ewen Bremner, Jonny Lee Miller, Robert Carlyle, Kevin McKidd, Kelly Macdonald, Shirley Henderson, Pauline Lynch; **D:** Danny Boyle; **W:** John Hodge; **C:** Brian Tufano. *AWARDS:* British Academy Awards '95: Best Adapted Screenplay; *NOM:* Academy Awards '96: Best Adapted Screenplay; Australian Film Institute '96: Best Foreign Film; British Academy Awards '95: Best Film; Independent Spirit Awards '97: Best Foreign Film; MTV Movie Awards '97: Breakthrough Performance (McGregor); Writers Guild of America '96: Best Adapted Screenplay.

Trapper County War

Two Jersey boys (Estes and Blake) get lost in the North Carolina mountains and run

afoul of the powerful Liedigger clan when one of them falls for the pretty daughter (Russell). The redneck revenge plot really cranks up when a Vietnam vet (Hudson) appears to aid our stalwart heroes. Though this kind of material is really more at home on the drive-in screen than on DVD, the image is excellent throughout, even in the night scenes, shot on location. —MM
Movie: 🎞️🎞️▶ **DVD:** 🎞️🎞️
Simitar Entertainment (Cat #7291, UPC #082551729128). Full frame. PCM Stereo. $14.98. Keepcase. *LANG:* English. *FEATURES:* 8 chapter links • Production factoids • Rob Estes filmography.
1989 (R) 98m/C Robert Estes, Bo Hopkins, Ernie Hudson, Betsy Russell, Don Swayze, Noah Blake; **D:** Worth Keeter; **W:** Russell V. Manzatt; **C:** Irl Dixon; **M:** Shuki Levy.

Trash

Andy Warhol gives us a profile of a depraved couple (Warhol-veteran Dallesandro and female impersonator Woodlawn) living in a lower east side basement and scouting the streets for food and drugs. Not for those easily offended by nymphomaniacs, junkies, lice, and the like; a must for fans of underground film and the cinema verite style. Similar in quality to *Flesh* and *Heat*, and the DVD probably does the best it can with the original source material. —JO▶
Movie: 🎞️🎞️ **DVD:** 🎞️🎞️▶
Image Entertainment (Cat #ID4732PYDVD, UPC #014381473223). Full frame. Dolby Digital Mono. $24.95. Snapper. *LANG:* English. *FEATURES:* 12 chapter links.
1970 110m/C Joe Dallesandro, Holly Woodlawn, Jane Forth, Michael Sklar, Geri Miller, Bruce Pecheur, Andrea Feldman; **D:** Paul Morrissey; **W:** Paul Morrissey; **C:** Paul Morrissey.

Treasure Island

Stevenson's familiar adventure is recast with cute furry animals in this animated version made for British TV. (Jim's a dog; Long John Silver's a peg-legged fox.) The art work is acceptable and it's carried off with enough energy to occupy some kids, but those who demand a really fast pace or the depth of detail found in the best cartoons will probably become bored. The action provides no real challenge to DVD. Sound and image are fine. —MM
Movie: 🎞️🎞️▶ **DVD:** 🎞️🎞️▶
Image Entertainment (Cat #ID5706PZDVD, UPC #014381570625). Full frame. Dolby Digital Stereo. $14.99. Snapper. *LANG:* English. *FEATURES:* 16 chapter links.
1997 (G) 86m/C *GB* **D:** Dino Anthanassiou; **M:** Barrington Pheloung; **V:** Dawn French, Juliet Stevenson, Chris Barrie, Richard E. Grant, Hugh Laurie, Robert Powell.

Treehouse Hostage

Notorious storyteller Timmy Taylor (Zimmerman) is overdue with his current

events project, but then he and his pals manage to capture escaped convict Carl Banks (Varney). If they can keep the cops from finding Carl, they'll use him as the project. But before that happens, various bumbling adults must be outfoxed. A little bathroom humor might make this one unacceptable for the youngest kids, but it's fine for Varney's fans. Remarkably, the DVD image sparkles. The film looks better than many that cost twice as much to make. —MM
Movie: 🎞️🎞️▶ **DVD:** 🎞️🎞️▶
Trimark Home Video (Cat #VM7105D, UPC #031398710530). Full frame. Dolby Digital Stereo. $14.99. Keepcase. *LANG:* English; Spanish. *SUB:* English. *CAP:* English. *FEATURES:* 30 chapter links.
1999 (PG) 90m/C Jim Varney, Joey Zimmerman, Richard Kline; **D:** Sean McNamara.

Trees Lounge

First-time director-writer Buscemi takes a look at the downward spiraling life of Tommy Basilio (Buscemi), a working-class misfit who loses his job and then spends most of his time hanging out at the dreary local bar. He finally winds up driving an ice cream truck, only leading to more trouble when his teenaged helper, Debbie (Sevigny), develops a crush on him—a situation her hot-headed father Jerry (Baldwin) takes exception to. The irresponsible Tommy is finally forced to realize that his ill-concerned actions have consequences. The first thing I noticed on the DVD is that the commentary by Buscemi didn't hold my attention. I have talked to others who love it, and thought that it went well with the film, but I guess his on-screen personality led me to expect more. Give it a shot, though. The DVD is grainier than the laserdisc release, but overall the image is a little sharper, with better color, and slightly preferable. —JO
Movie: 🎞️🎞️▶ **DVD:** 🎞️🎞️▶
Pioneer Entertainment (Cat #DVD60291-WS, UPC #013023013995). Widescreen (1.85:1) letterboxed. Stereo. $24.98. Keepcase. *LANG:* English. *CAP:* English. *FEATURES:* 14 chapter link • Theatrical trailer • Commentary: Steve Buscemi • Music video.
1996 (R) 94m/C Steve Buscemi, Chloe Sevigny, Daniel Baldwin, Elizabeth Bracco, Anthony LaPaglia, Debi Mazar, Carol Kane, Seymour Cassel, Mark Boone Jr., Eszter Balint, Mimi Rogers, Kevin Corrigan, Samuel L. Jackson; **D:** Steve Buscemi; **W:** Steve Buscemi; **C:** Lisa Rinzler; **M:** Evan Lurie. *AWARDS: NOM:* Independent Spirit Awards '97: Best First Feature, First Screenplay.

Tremors

A tiny desert town is attacked by giant man-eating worm-creatures. Bacon and Ward are the handymen trying to save the town. Great campy fun has plenty of humor, thrills, and good special effects. The supplementals found on the Universal Signature laserdisc are included on the

DVD, and the "making of" documentary is well worth looking at, even if it's just to see the original ending of the film. *Tremors* itself is given a fine transfer that is crystal clear and features strong detailed colors. The Dolby Surround mix from the LD is retained and it's a good one with forceful dynamics and an excellent Surround track that is used primarily for effects. —JO
Movie: 🎞️🎞️🎞️ **DVD:** 🎞️🎞️🎞️▶
Universal Studios Home Video (Cat #202 18, UPC #025192021824). Widescreen (1.85:1) letterboxed. Dolby Surround. $34.98. Keepcase. *LANG:* English; French; Spanish. *SUB:* Spanish. *CAP:* English. *FEATURES:* 39 chapter links • "Making of" documentary • Outtakes • Theatrical trailers • Photo gallery.
1989 (PG-13) 96m/C Kevin Bacon, Fred Ward, Finn Carter, Michael Gross, Reba McEntire, Bibi Besch, Bobby Jacoby, Charlotte Stewart, Victor Wong, Tony Genaros, Ariana Richards; **D:** Ron Underwood; **W:** S.S. Wilson, Brent Maddock; **C:** Alexander Grusynski; **M:** Ernest Troost.

Tremors 2: Aftershocks

Above-average sequel re-creates the original's sense of humor and builds on the inventive special effects that were so much fun before. Ward and Gross reprise their roles as cowboy and survivalist. Writer-director S.S. Wilson cowrote the first film, so this one retains its offbeat sensibility. Monster earthworms, called "Graboids," have returned to the oilfields of Chiapis, Mexico. Since Earl Bassett (Ward) has frittered away the wealth and fame that came from his earlier triumph over the monsters, he accepts an offer from the Mexican government to hunt down this infestation. Off he goes with new sidekick Grady (Gartin). This one isn't as lively or as explosive as the first film— sequels almost never are—but it's still enjoyable because the characters are treated seriously, and the violence isn't excessive. The improved detail of DVD can be a detriment to some mid-level films, but these special effects lose nothing. They're just as effective as they were on tape and the image is sharper. —MM
Movie: 🎞️🎞️▶ **DVD:** 🎞️🎞️🎞️
Universal Studios Home Video (Cat #202 96, UPC #025192029622). Widescreen (1.85:1) letterboxed. Dolby Digital Surround Stereo. $24.98. Keepcase. *LANG:* English; French; Spanish. *SUB:* Spanish. *CAP:* English. *FEATURES:* 16 chapter links • Production notes • Cast and crew thumbnail biographies.
1996 (PG-13) 100m/C Fred Ward, Michael Gross, Helen Shaver, Christopher Gartin, Marcelo Tubert; **D:** S.S. Wilson; **W:** S.S. Wilson, Brent Maddock; **C:** Virgil Harper; **M:** Jay Ferguson.

Trespass

Violent crime tale set in East St. Louis, IL. Two redneck firemen learn about stolen

gold artifacts supposedly hidden in an abandoned building and go on a treasure hunt. When they witness a murder they also get involved in a battle between two crime lords—who want these interlopers dead. What follows is a deadly game of cat-and-mouse. Lots of action but it's all fairly routine. The DVD has many problems with the darker sequences, which make up most of the film. The picture is grainy and in this case, it almost seems like cutting back the color might have helped. Blacks tend to grain up even further. Since this is basically an action flick, a beefier soundtrack with more use of the Surround would have been welcome. —JO **AKA:** Looters.
Movie: 🎬🎬 **DVD:** 🎬🎬
Goodtimes Entertainment (Cat #0581006, UPC #018713810069). Widescreen (1.78:1) anamorphic. Dolby Digital Surround. $19.95. Snapper. *LANG:* English. *SUB:* French; Spanish. *CAP:* English. *FEATURES:* 18 chapter links.
1992 (R) 104m/C Ice Cube, Ice-T, William Sadler, Bill Paxton, Art Evans; **D:** Walter Hill; **W:** Robert Zemeckis, Bob Gale; **C:** Lloyd Ahern; **M:** Ry Cooder.

The Trial

Orson Welles's take on the famous Franz Kafka novel is arch and expressionistic. Young clerk Josef K. (Perkins) is arrested and placed on trial in an unnamed bureaucratic country. Much of the film was made in an abandoned Paris railway station and some of those dark panoramic scenes have the hallucinatory power of a dream. The image is somewhat marred by light to moderate visual static. Sound is unimpressive with poor dubbing and some echoes that may be intentional. Actually, the DVD is in exceptionally good shape considering the difficulties that Welles's productions faced at that low ebb in his career. The disc includes an alternative opening that was made for American television. —MM **AKA:** Le Proces; Der Prozess; Il Processo.
Movie: 🎬🎬🎬 **DVD:** 🎬🎬🎬
Image Entertainment (Cat #ID5933MLSD-VD, UPC #014381593327). Widescreen (1.66:1) letterboxed. Dolby Digital Mono. $29.99. Snapper. *LANG:* English. *FEATURES:* 16 chapter links • Theatrical trailer • Alternate opening.
1963 118m/B *FR* Anthony Perkins, Jeanne Moreau, Orson Welles, Romy Schneider, Akim Tamiroff, Elsa Martinelli; **D:** Orson Welles; **W:** Orson Welles; **C:** Edmond Richard; **M:** Jean Ledrut.

The Trial

MacLachlan is the nearly anonymous Josef K. Shaken out of bed by self-identified investigators on the morning of his 13th birthday, he spends what becomes endless days fighting authorities over unnamed charges. Even this early '90s version of the famed novel looks stuck in the '40s. The vocally cryptic Pinter adapting the dramatically cryptic Kafka results in something likely twice too abbreviated

for some. The typically pasty, almost sepia-toned BBC photography holds together under most circumstances, but skin tones are sometimes mottled and mid-range grays look unstable. The image becomes distorted in scan mode. The soundtrack is more tightly controlled. —JK
Movie: 🎬🎬 **DVD:** 🎬🎬
Fox/Lorber Home Video (Cat #ID4265FLDVD, UPC #014381426526). Full frame. Dolby Digital 5.0. $29.99. Snapper. *LANG:* English. *FEATURES:* 20 chapter links • Scene access menus.
1993 120m/C Kyle MacLachlan, Anthony Hopkins, Jason Robards Jr., Polly Walker, Juliet Stevenson, Alfred Molina; **D:** David Hugh Jones; **W:** Harold Pinter; **C:** Phil Meheux; **M:** Carl Davis.

Trial & Error

Satire based on John Mortimer's play finds hapless lawyer Margenhall (Sellers) thinking he's finally got his big chance when he defends wife murderer Fowle (Attenborough). Fowle wants to plead guilty but Morgenhall dreams of being a star and insists on pleading his client innocent. Disaster awaits. All of the DVD's charm lies in the cast with Sellers playing his character at different ages. Both image and sound are average; not much better than on VHS tape. —MM **AKA:** The Dock Brief.
Movie: 🎬🎬 **DVD:** 🎬🎬
WinStar Home Entertainment (Cat #FLV5057, UPC #72091750572). Full frame. $29.98. Keepcase. *LANG:* English. *FEATURES:* 6 chapter links • Production notes • Filmographies.
1962 78m/B *GB* Peter Sellers, Richard Attenborough, Beryl Reid, David Lodge, Frank Pettingell, Eric Woodburn; **D:** James Hill; **W:** Pierre Rouve; **C:** Edward Scaife; **M:** Ron Grainer.

Trial and Error

Jonathan Lynn's legal comedy is a companion piece to *My Cousin Vinny.* Both are about an inept big city lawyer (Daniels) in small town trials. Both feature strong, attractive women characters. Both are really enjoyable. This one's actually a more effective combination of comedy and drama, making full use of star Michael Richards's comic talents, and it ends on a surprisingly strong note. Rip Torn's wonderful "Pumpkin Boy" speech is a small masterpiece. The film belongs to Michael Richards, who makes a smooth transition from a supporting role on TV's *Seinfeld* to big-screen leading man. His creative physical comedy is the equal of Jim Carrey's, and his dramatic range is much broader. Most viewers probably expect him to be funny with slapstick, and he certainly is, but he's just as good in the quieter, more serious moments. That's particularly evident in his scenes with Jessica Steen. The look and sound of the DVD are everything you'd expect from a big-budget studio romantic comedy. The dramatic loca-

tions (Independence, CA) are particularly impressive. —MM
Movie: 🎬🎬🎬 **DVD:** 🎬🎬🎬
New Line Home Video (Cat #N4857, UPC #794043485725). Widescreen (2:1) letterboxed; full frame. Dolby Digital 5.1 Surround Stereo; Dolby Digital Surround Stereo. $24.98. Snapper. *LANG:* English. *SUB:* English. *FEATURES:* 23 chapter links • Theatrical trailer • Cast and crew thumbnail biographies.
1996 (PG-13) 98m/C Michael Richards, Jeff Daniels, Rip Torn, Charlize Theron, Jessica Steen, Austin Pendleton, Alexandra Wentworth, Lawrence Pressman, Dale Dye, Max Casella, Jennifer Coolidge; **D:** Jonathan Lynn; **W:** Sarah Bernstein, Gregory Bernstein; **C:** Gabriel Beristain; **M:** Phil Marshall.

Trick

Gay romantic comedy-drama finds would-be playwright Gabe (Campbell) and Mark (Pitoc), who meet on the subway, trying to find a place to spend the night together. Gabe's pal Katherine (Spelling), an aspiring and untalented actress (insert your own joke here), complicates things. Given the unpolished production values of this shot-on-location material, it's not much better-looking on DVD than it is on VHS tape. And given the gaudy choices of costume, hair color, and makeup, that's probably not a bad thing. —MM
Movie: 🎬🎬 **DVD:** 🎬🎬
New Line Home Video (Cat #N4929). Widescreen (1.66:1) letterboxed. Dolby Digital 5.1 Surround Stereo; Dolby Digital Surround Stereo. $24.98. Snapper. *LANG:* English. *SUB:* English. *FEATURES:* 15 chapter links • Theatrical trailer • Cast and crew thumbnail biographies.
1999 (R) 90m/C Christian Campbell, John Paul (J.P.) Pitoc, Tori Spelling, Brad Beyer, Clinton Leupp, Lorri Bagley, Steve Hayes; **D:** Jim Fall; **W:** Jason Schafer; **C:** Terry Stacey; **M:** David Friedman.

The Trigger Effect

Nightmare in yuppiedom when a suspicious electromagnetic pulse knocks out all electrical power, telephone, and broadcast signals for hundreds of miles around a tranquil southern California community, which becomes increasingly unsettled. Matt (MacLachlan), wife Annie (Shue), and friend Joe (Mulroney) hang out together during the mystery power outage with lots of mounting tension both within and without. Film, however dread-producing, doesn't really make that much sense. As expected, the majority of the movie is in the dark and the DVD is up to the task of delivering a bright picture without grain or artifacts. Colors are excellent and remain accurate along with the blacks. Bleed is never a problem. The 5.1 sound delivers quite a bit to the rear channels and is energy packed, with punchy bass and clean crisp highs. —JO
Movie: 🎬 **DVD:** 🎬🎬🎬

Universal Studios Home Video (Cat #20061, UPC #025192006128). Widescreen (1.85:1) anamorphic. Dolby Digital 5.1; Dolby Surround. $24.98. Keepcase. *LANG:* English (DD5.1); French (DS). *CAP:* English. *FEATURES:* 23 chapter links • Theatrical trailer • Cast and filmmaker bios • Production notes • Film highlights.
1996 (R) 103m/C Kyle MacLachlan, Elisabeth Shue, Dermot Mulroney, Michael Rooker, Richard T. Jones, Bill Smitrovich, William Lucking, Molly Morgan, Richard Schiff; *D:* David Koepp; *W:* David Koepp; *C:* Newton Thomas (Tom) Sigel; *M:* James Newton Howard.

Trilogy of Terror
Anyone who's wondered about the source of the band name "The Voluptuous Horror of Karen Black" hasn't seen this made-for-TV masterpiece. She stars in three Richard Matheson stories directed by Dan Curtis of *Dark Shadows* fame. "Julie" is a nice reversal on an adolescent male fantasy. "Millicent and Therese" is a transparent sisters story. The capper is "Amelia." It's an adaptation of Matheson's famous "Prey" (featuring the Zuni fetish doll), and is simply one of the scariest mini-monster yarns ever written—perfectly constructed with a final image that comes straight from a nightmare. In a liner-notes interview with Scott Michael Bosco, Karen Black claims that she invented the central effect in the shot. Horror fans who have been able to see only older tapes will appreciate the clarity of the disc. Both image and sound are clean. The DVD lacks other extras. —MM
Movie: ♫♫♫ *DVD:* ♫♫♫
Anchor Bay (Cat #DV10862, UPC #013131086294). Full frame. Dolby Digital Mono. $24.98. Keepcase. *LANG:* English. *FEATURES:* 14 chapter links.
1975 78m/C Karen Black, Robert Burton, John Karlen, Gregory Harrison, George Gaynes, James Storm, Kathryn Reynolds, Tracy Curtis; *D:* Dan Curtis; *W:* Richard Matheson; *C:* Paul Lohmann; *M:* Robert Cobert.

Trinity and Beyond: The Atomic Bomb Movie
Peter Kuran's documentary follows the development of America's nuclear weapons beginning with the Manhattan Project. Though he admits in his commentary track that the genesis of the idea came when he visited Hiroshima as a youth, the film is not an anti-nuclear polemic. Instead, he lets footage of the explosions make his point: that these devices are unimaginably destructive. We have become so used to fake explosions in movies—Kuran himself works in special effects—that we become blase to reality. This collection of real bomb tests is enough to bring back the mushroom cloud nightmares so common to those of us who grew up in the 1950s and '60s.

Though the quality of the images, most taken from government sources, varies, they are mostly very clear and Kuran has edited his material skillfully. The disc is genuinely frightening. —MM
Movie: ♫♫♫▶ *DVD:* ♫♫♫▶
Goldhil Home Media (Cat #GH1232, UPC #743457123228). Full frame. Dolby Digital 5.1 Surround Stereo. Keepcase. *LANG:* English. *FEATURES:* 6 chapter links • Director's commentary • 3-D section (glasses included) • Unedited March 17, 1953, detonation • Filmmaker and subject thumbnail bios • DVD-ROM listing of all U.S. nuclear detonations • Photo gallery • Production notes.
1999 120m/C *D:* Peter Kuran; *M:* William T. Stromberg; *Nar:* William Shatner.

Troma's War (DC)
Codirector and studio honcho Lloyd Kaufman calls this "the most Troma of Tromovies." Whether that is still true or not, the film is also a personal favorite of his and he explains his reasons briefly in the box copy—it was made in answer to Reagan and Rambo—and on a full length commentary track. As for the film, it's the sexy, violent story of plane crash survivors on a Caribbean island filled with terrorists engaged in a civil war. The DVD contains the full-length cut along with interviews with just about anyone connected with the film (including the caterer!) who could be persuaded in front of a camera. If half of what they say is to be believed, then the making of a Troma movie is everything fans had dreamed of and dreaded. Image and sound are raw and rough. So are the violence and sex. That's the point. —MM
Movie: ♫♫♫ *DVD:* ♫♫♫
Troma Team Video (Cat #DVD9870, UPC #790357987030). Full frame. $24.95. Keepcase. *LANG:* English. *FEATURES:* 9 chapter links • Commentary: director • Interviews with cast and crew • Several humorous featurettes.
1988 (R) 90m/C Carolyn Beauchamp, Sean Bowen, Michael Ryder, Jessica Dublin, Steven Crossley, Lorayn Lane DeLuca, Charles Kay Hune, Ara Romanoff, Alex Cserhart, Aleida Harris; *D:* Michael Herz, Lloyd (Samuel Weil) Kaufman; *W:* Lloyd (Samuel Weil) Kaufman, Mitchell Dana, Eric Hattler, Thomas Martinek; *C:* James London; *M:* Christopher De Marco.

Tromeo & Juliet
One of Troma's most ambitious and Tromatic releases, this is a contemporary version of the Bard's tragic romance that's told with flagrant poor taste. Any videophile who cannot find something to be offended by here really isn't trying. Excessive body piercing, child abuse, bizarre transformations, sexual perversions of every stripe—all are part of the story of Romeo Que (Keenan) and Juliet Capulet (Jensen), a couple of New York teens whose fathers hate each other. Why? It has to do with a film studio scam and other betrayals hidden deep in the

past. Likewise, the rest takes Shakespeare as a starting point and soars off in other directions. Writer-director-studio head Kaufman means to be funny and provocative and he succeeds. On disc, his commentary tells you all you want to know about the making of the film, including details of the penis-monster effects and his own views on vegetarianism. DVD producer Mark Waldrop fills the disc with extras (listed below), the funniest of which is the PSA. The clarity of the image heightens the film's often harsh lighting and equally hard-edged humor. —MM
Movie: ♫♫♫ *DVD:* ♫♫♫▶
Troma Team Video (Cat #DVD9400, UPC #790357940035). Full frame. $24.95. Keepcase. *LANG:* English. *FEATURES:* 6 deleted scenes • Stills • Director's commentary throughout • Cast commentaries featurette • Troma studio tour • Painproof rubber girls featurette • Original theatrical trailer for this and other Troma films • Troma Intelligence Test • Troma public service announcement • 9 chapter links. Unrated director's cut.
1995 (R) 95m/C Will Keenan, Jane Jensen, Debbie Rochon, Lemmy, Valentine Miele, Sean Gunn; *D:* Lloyd (Samuel Weil) Kaufman; *W:* James Gunn; *C:* Brendan Flynt; *M:* Willie Wisely.

Tron
A video game designer enters into his computer, where he battles the computer games he created and seeks revenge on other designers who have stolen his creations. Sounds better than it plays. The old-style computer-created graphics and terrific special effects come alive with the excellent colors on this DVD. There are a lot of dark colors and blacks in this film and they're all delivered accurately. The picture is also very sharp and contrast is better than ever. The 5.1 mix very rarely uses the rear Surround channels, but the overall sound is more power packed than ever. —JO
Movie: ♫♫ *DVD:* ♫♫♫▶
Buena Vista Home Entertainment (Cat #14256, UPC #717951000378). Widescreen (2.2:1) letterboxed. Dolby Digital 5.1; Dolby Surround. $29.99. Keepcase. *LANG:* English (DD5.1); Spanish (DS); French (DS). *CAP:* English. *FEATURES:* 28 chapters • Theatrical trailer.
1982 (PG) 96m/C Jeff Bridges, Bruce Boxleitner, David Warner, Cindy Morgan, Barnard Hughes, Dan Shor, Peter Jurasik, Tony Stephano; *D:* Steven Lisberger; *W:* Steven Lisberger; *C:* Bruce Logan; *M:* Walter (Wendy) Carlos. *AWARDS: NOM:* Academy Awards '82: Best Costume Design, Best Sound.

Troublemakers
What a curious title for a Christmas western. This one's a throwback to the early days of spaghetti westerns—the stars have been in the business since the 1960s—but without the graphic violence and killings. Instead, the action is old-fash-

ioned fist fights, shooting guns out of hands, and such. The light humor will remind older viewers of Jerry Lewis and Dean Martin. Hill (who directed) and Spencer play feuding brothers whose Mom (fellow '60s survivor Ruth Buzzi) wants them to come home for Christmas. The complications involve comic outlaws, a pretty veterinarian, and a bear. The whole thing goes on a little too long but the New Mexico locations look terrific, particularly on DVD. Throughout the image is astonishingly bright, sharp, and detailed. The disc is a definite sleeper, strongly recommended for fans of early westerns. —*MM*
Movie: 🎵🎵 ***DVD:*** 🎵🎵🎵
Image Entertainment (Cat #ID5628FMDVD, UPC #014381562828). Full frame. Dolby Digital Stereo. $24.99. Snapper. *LANG:* English. *FEATURES:* 14 chapter links.
1994 (PG) 98m/C Terence Hill, Bud Spencer, Anne Kasprik, Ruth Buzzi, Ron Carey; ***D:*** Terence Hill; ***W:*** Jess Hill; ***C:*** Carlo Tafani; ***M:*** Pino Donaggio.

Trucks

Remake of Stephen King's *Maximum Overdrive* shifts the scene to Area 51 where locals and visitors are terrorized by driverless trucks—from semis to toys—that attack and kill. The image is acceptable, but the sound, which could have been an important component of the monstrous vehicles' power, is only so-so. This one's recommended to King completists only. —*MM*
Movie: 🎵🎵 ***DVD:*** 🎵🎵
Trimark Home Video (Cat #VM6876D, UPC #3139868763). Widescreen (4:3) letterboxed. Dolby Digital Surround Stereo. $19.99. Keepcase. *LANG:* English. *SUB:* French; Spanish. *CAP:* English. *FEATURES:* 24 chapter links ● Trailer.
1997 (R) 99m/C Timothy Busfield, Brenda Bakke, Brendan Fletcher, Jay Brazeau, Amy Stewart; ***D:*** Chris Thomson; ***W:*** Brian Taggert; ***C:*** Rob Draper, Keith Holland; ***M:*** Michael Richard Plowman.

True Crime

Mary Giordino (Silverstone), daughter of a slain policeman, is fascinated by her father's work. She pores over articles she reads and re-reads in copies of *True Crime* magazine. When a classmate at her Catholic high school is brutally murdered, she suspects a serial killer. Police cadet Tony Campbell (Dillon) thinks she's right. Neither of them can do anything officially, but that doesn't stop them. As their "investigation" progresses, she comes to believe that Tony might not be all he seems. All that is familiar stuff and nothing really new or innovative is done with it. But the performances by the two leads are remarkably good. The DVD is somewhat sharper than VHS tape, but the difference in sound and image is minimal. —*MM*
AKA: Dangerous Kiss.
Movie: 🎵🎵▶ ***DVD:*** 🎵🎵▶
Trimark Home Video (Cat #VM7015D, UPC #031398701538). Full frame. Dolby Digi-

tal Stereo. $24.99. Keepcase. *LANG:* English. *SUB:* English; French; Spanish. *CAP:* English. *FEATURES:* 30 chapter links.
1995 (R) 94m/C Alicia Silverstone, Kevin Dillon, Bill Nunn, Michael Bowen; ***D:*** Pat Verducci; ***W:*** Pat Verducci; ***C:*** Chris Squires; ***M:*** Blake Leyh.

True Friends

Low-budget independent production is made with more spirit and enthusiasm than style and polish. In 1980, young JJ (Botero) moves to the Bronx with his mother and becomes friends with two other 12-year-olds, Joey (Quattrochi) and Louie (Mauro). In the years that follow they grow up and share episodic adventures. Think of wistful Scorsese with Woody Allen narration. Most of the film belies its modest resources. On DVD one brick pattern dissolves into heavy pixels but artful lighting, that tints some scenes amber, helps to make the film look more expensive. Overall, the image is stronger than the sound. —*MM*
Movie: 🎵🎵▶ ***DVD:*** 🎵🎵▶
MTI Home Video (Cat #3054, UPC #039414030549). Full frame. $24.95. Keepcase. *LANG:* English. *FEATURES:* 20 chapter links ● Cast and crew thumbnail biographies.
1998 (R) 98m/C James Quattrochi, Loreto Mauro, Rodrigo Botero, Dan Lauria, MacKenzie Phillips, John Capodice, Peter Onorati, Bertilla Damas, Leo Rossi; ***D:*** James Quattrochi; ***W:*** James Quattrochi, Rodrigo Botero; ***C:*** Jeff Baustert; ***M:*** Charles Dayton.

True Lies

Brain candy with a bang offers eye-popping special effects and a large dose of unbelievability. Sort of like a big screen *Scarecrow and Mrs. King* as supposed computer salesman Ah-nuld keeps his spy work secret from mousy, neglected wife Curtis, who has a few secrets of her own and inadvertently ends up right in the thick of things. It's raunchy and extremely sexist, but not without charm; the stupidity is part of the fun. Perfectly cast sidekick Arnold holds his own as a pig, but Heston is wasted as the head honcho. Tons of special effects culminate in a smashing finish. Another superb Fox DVD release of one of their catalogue titles. The picture is as sharp as can be, with neither grain nor artifacts to get in the way. Colors are so vibrant they want to jump off the screen, yet are completely accurate to the theatre. There is no bleed. Blacks are excellent, contrast is punchy, and the brightness levels are consistent and comfortable throughout. The 5.1 sound is superb as explosions rock you with soundwaves from your subwoofer and the Surround engulfs you in all of the action. The dialogue is always crisp and out front and the music delivered with great fidelity and expressive dynamics. —*JO*
Movie: 🎵🎵▶ ***DVD:*** 🎵🎵🎵🎵

20th Century Fox (Cat #4111054, UPC #086162110542). Widescreen (2.35:1) letterboxed. Dolby Digital 5.1; Dolby Surround. $29.98. Keepcase. *LANG:* English (DD5.1; DS); French (DS). *SUB:* English; Spanish. *CAP:* English. *FEATURES:* 44 chapter links ● Theatrical trailer.
1994 (R) 114m/C Arnold Schwarzenegger, Jamie Lee Curtis, Tom Arnold, Bill Paxton, Tia Carrere, Art Malik, Eliza Dushku, Charlton Heston, Grant Heslov; ***D:*** James Cameron; ***W:*** James Cameron; ***C:*** Russell Carpenter; ***M:*** Brad Fiedel. *AWARDS:* Golden Globe Awards '95: Best Actress—Musical/Comedy (Curtis); Blockbuster Entertainment Awards '96: Action Actress, Video (Curtis); *NOM:* Academy Awards '94: Best Visual Effects; MTV Movie Awards '95: Best Female Performance (Curtis), Best Comedic Performance (Arnold), Best Kiss (Arnold Schwarzenegger/Jamie Lee Curtis), Best Action Sequence, Best Dance Sequence (Arnold Schwarzenegger/Tia Carrere).

True Romance

Geeky Clarence (Slater) and wide-eyed whore Alabama (Arquette) meet and fall instantly in love. The inept duo skip town after an accidental murder and hit the road with the mob in pursuit. Gem performances include Walken's debonair mafioso who's not adverse to torture; Pitt's space-case druggie; and Clarence's dad (Hopper), who runs afoul of Walken. Horrific violence mixed with very black humor (courtesy of a script by Quentin Tarantino and director Scott). The DVD is the unrated director's cut only, as is the laserdisc. Overall, the widescreen side of the DVD looks very good, with extremely sharp foreground images and occasional moderate grain in some of the backgrounds. The blacks are very good and the colors really stand out, with no bleed, even in the early-on sequences where Slater and Arquette are brightly lit against dark backdrops with splashes of neon and colored lighting. On the full-frame side, the image quality drops a little as some grain and artifacts appear—on the plus side the foregrounds and backgrounds are closer in clarity than the widescreen. The Dolby Surround is very good, with crisp highs and clear rumbling lows. —*JO*
Movie: 🎵🎵🎵 ***DVD:*** 🎵🎵🎵🎵
Warner Home Video, Inc. (Cat #13158, UPC #085391315827). Widescreen (2.35:1) letterboxed; full frame. Dolby Surround. $24.98. Snapper. *LANG:* English. *SUB:* Spanish; French. *CAP:* English. *FEATURES:* 34 chapter links ● Theatrical trailer ● Production notes ● Cast and crew bios.
1993 (R) 116m/C Christian Slater, Patricia Arquette, Gary Oldman, Brad Pitt, Val Kilmer, Dennis Hopper, Christopher Walken, Samuel L. Jackson, Christopher Penn, Bronson Pinchot, Michael Rapaport, Saul Rubinek, Conchata Ferrell, James Gandolfini, Tom Sizemore, Ed Lauter; ***D:*** Tony Scott; ***W:*** Quentin Tarantino; ***C:*** Jeffrey L. Kimball; ***M:*** Hans Zimmer, Mark Mancina. *AWARDS: NOM:* MTV Movie

Awards '94: Best Kiss (Christian Slater/Patricia Arquette).

True Stories

Quirky, amusing look at the eccentric denizens of a fictional, off-center Texas town celebrating its 50th anniversary. Notable are Kurtz, the Laziest Woman in America, and Goodman as a blushing suitor who tries everything (including advertising) to find a bride. Directorial debut of Byrne is loosely based on filler newspaper articles about real-life eccentrics. Worth a look. DVD belongs to the Warner Bros. budget line—the price is right but not much effort is put into extras or even preserving the original aspect ratio. This one is presented pan and scan. The disc is average at best with grain, color bleed, and some artifacts. Color and contrast is also average, as is the handling of the blacks. At least the sound is good and the numerous musical sequences liven up the presentation. Byrne's film deserves better. —JO

Movie: 🎵🎵🎵 **DVD:** 🎵
Warner Home Video, Inc. (Cat #11654, UPC #085391165422). Full frame. Dolby Digital Surround Stereo. $14.98. Snapper. *LANG:* English. *CAP:* English. *FEATURES:* 29 chapter links.
1986 (PG) 89m/C David Byrne, John Goodman, Swoosie Kurtz, Spalding Gray, Annie McEnroe, Pops Staples, Tito Larriva, Alix Elias, Scott Valentine, Jo Harvey Allen; *D:* David Byrne; *W:* Beth Henley, Stephen Tobolowsky, David Byrne; *C:* Edward Lachman; *M:* David Byrne.

The Truman Show

Starring elastic-faced Carrey, director Weir's dark satire about a young man who doesn't realize he's been the subject of a TV show since the day he was born is an imaginative production that's both entertaining and provocative. It also is a perfect showcase for an unusually and appropriately restrained performance by Carrey. Harris is Christof, the mastermind producer who has created a virtual world populated with actors, props, and scenery. Nothing is real except Truman, the good-natured innocent who lives in what he thinks is a small seaside town. He goes to work every day and has a wife and a nice home. What he doesn't know—and only begins to suspect when a piece of television equipment falls from the "sky"—is that his every move is viewed by millions, and the show within the movie reaches its peak ratings when Truman begins to suspect his environs and plot his escape. The film has a point to make, but credit Weir for preventing the satirical theme from becoming heavy-handed. The DVD video quality is generally very good, but widescreen TV owners will be majorly disappointed the letterboxed image has not been enhanced for their sets. Extras are minimal, but there are two trailers. —MB
Movie: 🎵🎵🎵🎵 **DVD:** 🎵🎵🎵

Paramount Home Video (Cat #331127, UPC #09736331127). Widescreen (1.85:1) letterboxed. Dolby Digital 5.1. $29.98. Keepcase. *LANG:* English; French. *SUB:* English. *CAP:* English. *FEATURES:* 24 chapter links • Theatrical trailers.
1998 (PG) 102m/C Jim Carrey, Ed Harris, Laura Linney, Noah Emmerich, Natascha McElhone, Holland Taylor, Paul Giamatti, Philip Baker Hall, Brian Delate, Una Damon; *D:* Peter Weir; *W:* Andrew Niccol; *C:* Peter Biziou; *M:* Philip Glass, Burkhard Dallwitz. *AWARDS:* British Academy Awards '98: Best Director (Weir), Best Original Screenplay; Golden Globe Awards '99: Best Actor—Drama (Carrey), Best Supporting Actor (Harris), Best Score; MTV Movie Awards '99: Best Male Performance (Carrey); National Board of Review Awards '98: Best Supporting Actor (Harris); *NOM:* Academy Awards '98: Best Director (Weir), Best Original Screenplay, Best Supporting Actor (Harris); Australian Film Institute '99: Best Foreign Film; British Academy Awards '98: Best Cinematography, Best Film, Best Supporting Actor (Harris); Directors Guild of America Awards '98: Best Director (Weir); Golden Globe Awards '98: Best Film—Drama; Golden Globe Awards '99: Best Director (Weir), Best Screenplay; MTV Movie Awards '99: Best Film; Writers Guild of America '98: Best Screenplay.

Truth or Consequences, N.M.

Sutherland makes a competent but seriously flawed directorial debut. The main problems in his Tarantinian crime tale—complete with the obligatory cheap clothes, bad hair, and banal conversation—are lack of originality, a predictable conclusion, and unsympathetic characters. Ex-con Raymond (Gallo) engineers an inside job on a drug dealer (McGinley). It goes wrong when Curtis (Sutherland) gets trigger-happy. They take it on the lam with Marcus (Williamson) and Raymond's girlfriend Addie (Dickens), and quickly kidnap Gordon (Pollak) and Donna (Phillips), who are so blase and unresponsive to their situation that it pretty well destroys any suspense on that plotline. The characters are such repellent jerks that viewers will hope that they get what's coming to them ASAP. Unfortunately, it takes almost two hours, unless you can keep your hand away from the fast-forward button. The rough images and low-rent desert locations look no better on DVD than they do on VHS tape. —MM
Movie: 🎵🎵 **DVD:** 🎵🎵
Columbia Tristar Home Video (Cat #82699, UPC #04339682699). Widescreen (1.85:1) letterboxed; full frame. Dolby Digital 5.1 Surround Stereo; Dolby Digital Surround Stereo. $29.95. Keepcase. *LANG:* English; Spanish. *SUB:* English; French; Spanish. *FEATURES:* 28 chapter links • Theatrical trailers.
1997 (R) 106m/C Vincent Gallo, Kim Dickens, Kiefer Sutherland, Mykelti Williamson, Grace Phillips, Kevin Pollak, Martin Sheen, Rod Steiger, Rick Rosso-

vich, John C. McGinley, Max Perlich; *D:* Kiefer Sutherland; *W:* Brad Mirman; *C:* Ric Waite; *M:* Jude Cole.

Truth or Dare

A quasi-concert-documentary—here is music superstar Madonna tarted up in fact, fiction, and fantasy—exhibitionism to the nth power. It's tacky, self-conscious, and ultimately, if you are a Madonna fan, moving. On camera Madonna stings ex-boyfriend Warren Beatty, disses admirer Kevin Costner, quarrels with her father, reminisces, and does sexy things with a bottle. Oh yes, she occasionally sings and dances. Both those who worship and dislike the Material Girl will find much to pick apart here. The anamorphic transfer is extremely sharp, both in the black-and-white and color sequences. Neither one seems to add any digital video grain and artifacts are rare. The colors are both vibrant and true with little or no bleed. The contrast and brightness levels are consistent and punchy on both films stocks and the black and white has excellent graytones and a great sense of detail and depth. Blacks are true throughout. As it should be, the 5.1 sound is excellent. There is plenty of deep clean bass to drive the musical sequences and overall the fidelity and dynamics are superb. The Surround tracks are mainly ambient, which works well with this documentary. —JO
AKA: In Bed with Madonna; Madonna Truth or Dare.
Movie: 🎵🎵 **DVD:** 🎵🎵🎵
Artisan Entertainment (Cat #60448, UPC #012236044802). Widescreen (1.85:1) anamorphic; full frame. Dolby Digital 5.1. $24.99. Snapper. *LANG:* English. *SUB:* English; French; Spanish. *CAP:* English. *FEATURES:* 27 chapter links • Production notes • Cast and crew bios • Theatrical trailer.
1991 (R) 118m/C Madonna; *D:* Alek Keshishian.

The Tune

Three thousand ink and watercolor drawings make up Plympton's first full-length animated feature. It's a gem that tells the story of Del (Neiden), a failed songwriter who gets a fresh start when he makes a wrong turn on the freeway and winds up in Flooby Nooby. The strange inhabitants of this town teach Del to throw out his rhyming dictionary and write about his experiences. The DVD's video quality is actually quite good, with solid blacks and crisp colors although Plympton's extensive use of pastels does not make this all too evident. Certain scenes really pop off the screen with plenty of vibrant colors. The soundtrack, too, is exceptional (as far as stereo soundtracks go). —MJT
Movie: 🎵🎵 **DVD:** 🎵🎵🎵
Image Entertainment (Cat #ID4188OCDVD, UPC #014381418828). Full frame. Dolby Digital Stereo. $29.99. Snapper. *FEATURES:* 17 chapter links.
1992 80m/C *D:* Bill Plympton; *W:* Maureen McElheron, Bill Plympton, P.C. Vey; *C:*

John Donnelly; **M:** Maureen McElheron; **V:** Daniel Neiden, Maureen McElheron, Marty Nelson, Emily Bindiger, Chris Hoffman.

Turbulence

When you fly, it's usually the turbulence that makes you throw up. Well, this movie isn't that bad, but you may experience a touch of nausea. Flight attendant Teri (Holly) is pushing the drink cart on a strangely vacant New York–to–L.A. Christmas Eve run. Among the passengers are convicted felons Ryan (Liotta) and Stubbs (Gleeson), who are either on their way to a more secure prison or fulfilling the "consumption of airline food" portion of their sentence. The prisoners seize a gun from the marshals and accidentally rub out the cockpit crew. With all the passengers locked away, Teri must battle the serial rapist/killer Ryan as well as learn to fly the plane through a horrible storm. Passengers on the left of the screen may look out and see *Passenger 57*, while those on the right can see the ancient monument of *Airport 75*. Another dumb movie given a super transfer to DVD. The image is so sharp and the colors so vibrant that I almost made it through the entire film. The sound is also pretty mind blowing so this could be a good movie to use scan mode on. —*JO*
Movie: ♪⊳ **DVD:** ♪♪♪⊳
HBO Home Video (Cat #91387, UPC #026359138720). Widescreen (1.85:1) letterboxed. Dolby Digital 5.1; Dolby Surround. $24.99. Snapper. *LANG:* English; French. *CAP:* English. *FEATURES:* 42 chapter links • Cast and filmmakers bios.
1996 (R) 103m/C Ray Liotta, Lauren Holly, Hector Elizondo, Brendan Gleeson, Ben Cross, Rachel Ticotin, Jeffrey DeMunn, John Finn, Catherine Hicks; **D:** Robert Butler; **W:** Jonathan Brett; **C:** Lloyd Ahern; **M:** Shirley Walker. *AWARDS: NOM:* Golden Raspberry Awards '97: Worst Actress (Holly).

The Turning

Cliff Harnish (Dolan) returns home after a four-year absence to shock his family with strident neo-Nazi beliefs. The film's main claim to fame is the presence of a pre-*X-Files* Anderson in a dark kitchen sex scene with brief nudity. Based on a play by Ceraso. *AKA:* Home Fires Burning.
Movie: ♪⊳ **DVD:** NYR
MTI Home Video (Cat #216). Full frame. Dolby Digital Stereo. $24.95. Keepcase. *FEATURES:* Cast and crew thumbnail bios • Trailer • Production notes.
1992 92m/C Michael Dolan, Raymond J. Barry, Karen Allen, Tess Harper, Gillian Anderson; **D:** L.A. Puopolo; **W:** L.A. Puopolo, Chris Ceraso; **C:** J. Michael McClary.

The Twelve Chairs

A madcap treasure hunt, Mel Brooks style. When a rich matron admits on her deathbed that she has hidden her jewels in the upholstery of one of 12 chairs that are no longer in her home, the hunt

begins. This take-off on Russian folktale was first filmed in Yugoslavia in 1927. There's nothing spectacular about the monaural soundtrack, of course, but at least the dialogue is easy to understand. Unfortunately, digital compression artifacts are all too visible to those who scrutinize the backgrounds of many scenes. Keep your eyes on the characters, and you may not be bothered. The theatrical trailer is at the 16th chapter stop of the simple but effective menu. —*MB*
Movie: ♪♪♪ **DVD:** ♪♪
Image Entertainment (Cat #ID9174CUDVD, UPC #014381917420). Widescreen (1.85:1) letterboxed. Dolby Digital 1.0. $24.99. Snapper. *LANG:* English. *CAP:* English. *FEATURES:* 16 chapter links • Theatrical trailer.
1970 (PG) 94m/C Mel Brooks, Dom DeLuise, Frank Langella, Ron Moody, Bridget Brice; **D:** Mel Brooks; **W:** Mel Brooks; **C:** Djordje Nikolic; **M:** Mel Brooks, John Morris.

12 Monkeys

Forty years after a plague wipes out 99 percent of the human population and sends the survivors underground, scientists send prisoner James Cole (Willis) to the 1990s to investigate the connection between the virus and seriously deranged fanatic Jeffrey Goines (Pitt), whose father happens to be a renowned virologist. Director Gilliam's demented vision is a bit tougher and less capricious than usual, and the convoluted plot and accumulated detail require a keen attention span, but as each piece of the puzzle falls into place the story becomes a fascinating sci-fi spectacle. Pitt drops the pretty-boy image with a nutzoid performance that'll make revelers stop swooning in a heartbeat. Inspired by the 1962 French short *La Jetee*. The excellent DVD transfer has blacks so deep and true that everything seems darker. It's really just a more accurate representation of the film itself than usually found on home video. The picture is very sharp, and colors are vibrant and retain shading details even in the difficult lighting conditions. The 5.1 sound gives the film a kick with good separation and imaging as well as a pumped-up bass track to keep things moving. —*JO*
Movie: ♪♪♪ **DVD:** ♪♪♪⊳
Universal Studios Home Video (Cat #20186, UPC #025192018626). Widescreen (1.85:1) anamorphic. Dolby Digital 5.1. $34.98. Keepcase. *LANG:* English; French. *SUB:* French; Spanish. *CAP:* English. *FEATURES:* 44 chapter links • Documentary • Cast and filmmakers bios • Production notes • Film highlights.
1995 (R) 131m/C Bruce Willis, Madeleine Stowe, Brad Pitt, Christopher Plummer, David Morse, Frank Gorshin, Jon Seda; **D:** Terry Gilliam; **W:** David Peoples, Janet Peoples; **C:** Roger Pratt; **M:** Paul Buckmaster. *AWARDS:* Golden Globe Awards '96: Best Supporting Actor (Pitt), *NOM:* Academy Awards '95: Best Costume Design, Best Supporting Actor (Pitt); MTV

Movie Awards '96: Best Male Performance (Pitt).

20,000 Leagues under the Sea

Outstanding silent adaptation of Jules Verne's *20,000 Leagues under the Sea* and *The Mysterious Island* was filmed with a then-revolutionary underwater camera. The effects, including an octopus, are fun. The DVD was made from the David Shepard–Dean Duncan restoration, and it is remarkably clear and undamaged compared to others of its age. The tinted image is simply superb. One of the best early silent films. —*MM*
Movie: ♪♪♪ **DVD:** ♪♪♪
Image Entertainment (Cat #ID4666DSDVD, UPC #014381466621). Full frame. Dolby Digital Stereo. $24.99. Snapper. *LANG:* Silent. *FEATURES:* 16 chapter links.
1916 105m/B Matt Moore, Allen Holubar, June Gail, William Welsh, Chris Benton, Dan Hamlon; **D:** Stuart Paton; **W:** Stuart Paton; **C:** Eugene Gaudio.

Twice upon a Yesterday

Variation on the *Sliding Doors* idea of second chances is an offbeat love story with an attractive cast. Self-centered actor Victor (Henshall) is desperate to win back his longtime girlfriend Sylvia (Headey), who left him after he admitted an affair. She's about to marry someone else when Victor is sent back in time by two unlikely magicians. Will he make the same mistakes again, or will the sudden appearance of the lovely Louise (Cruz) change everything? This sort of character-based story really doesn't gain much on DVD, but the no-frills disc looks fine with no flaws worth noting. The same goes for the sound. —*MM*
Movie: ♪♪⊳ **DVD:** ♪♪♪
Trimark Home Video (Cat #VM7207D, UPC #031398720737). Widescreen letterboxed. Dolby Digital Surround Stereo. $24.99. Keepcase. *LANG:* English. *SUB:* English; French; Spanish. *CAP:* English. *FEATURES:* 25 chapter links • Theatrical trailer.
1998 (R) 94m/C *GB* Douglas Henshall, Lena Headey, Mark Strong, Penelope Cruz, Elizabeth McGovern, Eusebio Lazaro, Charlotte Coleman, Gustavo Salmeron, Neil Stuke; **D:** Maria Ripoli; **W:** Rafa Russo; **C:** Javier Salmones.

Twilight

It's a pleasure to see pros at work, even if the story is a familiar one. In the noir world of L.A., ex-cop, ex-drunk, ex-PI. Harry Ross (Newman) is living above the garage at the estate of movie star marrieds Jack (Hackman) and Catherine (Sarandon) Ames, for whom Harry has done several jobs. The cancer-stricken Jack asks Harry to handle a blackmail payoff, which seems to resurrect the circumstances of femme fatale Catherine's first husband's alleged suicide.

Also involved is Harry's colleague Raymond Hope (Garner) and Harry's ex-flame, Verna (Channing), a cop investigating a murder with ties to the entire ugly situation. A super DVD. The image is so crystal clear, there are times it feels like looking through glass. There is no grain or artifacts. Colors are exceptionally bright and accurate with no bleed. Blacks are never off and both the contrast and brightness settings are perfect. The 5.1 sound is top-notch, with superb highs and deep clean bass making the music very full and the dialogue very crisp. The Surround is used sparingly and mainly for ambience, as it was in the theatre. —JO *AKA:* The Magic Hour.

Movie: 𝄞𝄞𝄞 **DVD:** 𝄞𝄞𝄞𝄞
Paramount Home Video (Cat #334957, UPC #097363349570). Widescreen (1.85:1) letterboxed. Dolby Digital 5.1; Dolby Surround. $29.99. Keepcase. *LANG:* English (DD5.1; DS); French (DS). *SUB:* Spanish. *CAP:* English. *FEATURES:* 23 chapter links • Theatrical trailer.
1998 (R) 94m/C Paul Newman, Susan Sarandon, Gene Hackman, James Garner, Stockard Channing, Reese Witherspoon, Giancarlo Esposito, Liev Schreiber, Margo Martindale, John Spencer, M. Emmet Walsh; *D:* Robert Benton; *W:* Robert Benton, Richard Russo; *C:* Piotr Sobocinski; *M:* Elmer Bernstein.

The Twilight of the Golds

The upper-class Jewish Gold family seems conventional if fretful: there's doctor dad Walter (Marshall), concerned mom Phyllis (Dunaway), married daughter Suzanne (Beals), and aspiring theatrical producer son David (Fraser), who's gay. It seems everyone has dealt with David's homosexuality until Suzanne's geneticist husband Rob (Tenney) informs his pregnant wife that tests on their unborn son show genes statistically link him to being gay. (The theory is unproved.) Suzanne considers abortion and David is understandably upset when no one tries to talk her out of it, beginning a family estrangement. The visuals don't stand out here, and appear lifeless in spots. While consistent, the lighting and color have look of a made-for-cable outing. The sound, too, is consistent if unspectacular. —AB

Movie: 𝄞𝄞▶ **DVD:** 𝄞𝄞𝄞
Fox/Lorber Home Video (Cat #FLV5154, UPC #2091751542). Full frame. Keepcase. *LANG:* English. *SUB:* English. *FEATURES:* Eight chapter links • Production credits • Filmographies and awards • Trailer.
1997 (PG-13) 90m/C Garry Marshall, Faye Dunaway, Jennifer Beals, Brendan Fraser, Jon Tenney, Jack Klugman, Sean O'Bryan, Rosie O'Donnell; *D:* Ross Kagen Marks; *W:* Jonathan Tolins, Seth Bass; *C:* Tom Richmond; *M:* Lee Holdridge.

Twin Dragons

The venerable twins-separated-at-birth plot is dusted off and retooled as a vehi-cle for Jackie Chan. He plays John Ma, internationally famous American orchestra conductor, and Boomer, Hong Kong auto mechanic and martial arts expert. A comic sidekick (Teddy Robin), confused girlfriends (Maggie Cheung and Nina Li Chi), and a gaggle of gangsters provide all of the expected complications. The best moments are a variation on the famous Marx brothers mirror routine played out in a bathtub and the grand finale in an auto-testing facility. The rest is fair Hong Kong action on the light side. Look for cameos from directors Tsui Hark, Ringo Lam, and John Woo. The DVD looks fine all the way through with crisp visuals in even the fastest scenes, many of which make full use of the widescreen. Sound ranges from good to fair. Perhaps because the film was made in 1992 and re-edited years later for American release, it lacks outtakes in the closing credits. —MM
AKA: Shuang Long Hui.

Movie: 𝄞𝄞𝄞 **DVD:** 𝄞𝄞𝄞
Buena Vista Home Entertainment (Cat #17760, UPC #717951003607). Widescreen (2.35:1) letterboxed. Dolby Digital 5.1 Surround. $29.99. Snapper. *LANG:* English. *CAP:* English. *FEATURES:* 25 chapter links.
1992 (PG-13) 89m/C *HK* Jackie Chan, Maggie Cheung, Anthony Chan, Philip Chan, Nina Li Chi, Sylvia Chang, James Wong, Kirk Wong, Ringo Lam, John Woo, Tsui Hark, Teddy Robin; *D:* Ringo Lam, Tsui Hark; *W:* Barry Wong, Tsui Hark; *C:* Wong Wing Hang, Wong Ngor Tai; *M:* Michael Wandmacher, Phe Loung.

Twins

A genetics experiment gone awry produces twins rather than a single child. One is a genetically engineered superman, the other a short, lecherous petty criminal. Schwarzenegger learns he has a brother, and becomes determined to find him, despite their having been raised separately. The two meet and are immediately involved in a contraband scandal. Amusing pairing of Schwarzenegger and DeVito, but don't even think about buying this DVD. The picture has almost as much grain as the worst of the early Goodtimes DVDs, and this is a Universal release. The grain is so bad that nothing else about the disc really matters. —JO

Movie: 𝄞𝄞▶ **DVD:** 𝄞
Universal Studios Home Video (Cat #20266, UPC #025192026621). Full frame. Dolby Surround. $24.98. Keepcase. *LANG:* English; Spanish; French. *SUB:* Spanish. *CAP:* English. *FEATURES:* 26 chapter links.
1988 (PG) 107m/C Arnold Schwarzenegger, Danny DeVito, Kelly Preston, Hugh O'Brian, Chloe Webb, Bonnie Bartlett, Marshall Bell, Trey Wilson, Nehemiah Persoff; *D:* Ivan Reitman; *W:* William Davies, William Osborne, Timothy Harris, Herschel Weingrod; *C:* Andrzej Bartkowiak; *M:* Georges Delerue, Randy Edelman.

Twisted

Hosted by Bryan Brown (*FX, Breaker Morant*), *Twisted* is an Australian version of *The Twilight Zone,* courtesy of the Nine Network Australia. Presented here are four separate stories, each running approximately 20 minutes, and very much in the tradition and spirit of Serling series. "Bonus Mileage" has Geoffrey Rush (*Shakespeare in Love*) as an obsessed airline passenger caught up in an "identity" crisis; Rachel Ward stars in "Third Party" and Bryan Brown turns up in an episode entitled "Confident Man." Finally, there's "Directly from My Heart to You," featuring Kimberly Davies as an attractive, if somewhat "mechanical" assassin. The DVD presentation is clear and crisp, with adequate sound (considering its source as television programming) and only a bare-bones selection menu. —RT

Movie: 𝄞𝄞▶ **DVD:** 𝄞𝄞▶
Image Entertainment (Cat #5707PZ, UPC #014381570724). Full frame. AC3 - 2 Channel. $24.99. Snapper. *LANG:* English. *FEATURES:* 15 chapter links.
1996 (PG-13) 86m/C *AU* Geoffrey Rush, Rachel Ward, Bryan Brown, Kimberly Davies, Shane Briant; *D:* Samantha Lang, Christopher Robbin Collins, Gregor Jordan, Catherine Millar; *C:* James Bartle; *M:* Nerida Tyson-Chew; *Nar:* Bryan Brown.

Twister

Director De Bont's sophomore directorial effort is another non-stop adrenaline drive, but instead of a mad bomber, nature is the bad guy. Hunt leads a collegiate team of storm-chasing scientists through Oklahoma in hopes of placing a robotic mechanism inside a tornado, which, in turn, will help them predict and prepare for future funnel forces. There's also the matter of Hunt's soon-to-be ex-husband Paxton, and a competitor (Elwes) who's in charge of a slick group of rival scientists. There's a lot of things flying around, including trucks, houses, cows, and the plausibility of the plot. Some nice chemistry between Hunt and Paxton, apparently the only people who can still look attractive in high winds and blowing debris. This early Warner DVD release should have been their showcase DVD, but boy did they blow it. The picture is fine until something moves, and then the artifacts start in and ruin any sharpness there was. Colors are pretty good and the sound mix is great, but the disc is near unwatchable. —JO

Movie: 𝄞𝄞▶ **DVD:** 𝄞
Warner Home Video, Inc. (Cat #18321, UPC #085391832126). Widescreen (2.35:1) anamorphic. Dolby Digital 5.1; DTS. $24.98. Snapper. *LANG:* English; French. *SUB:* English; Spanish; French. *CAP:* English. *FEATURES:* 34 chapter links • Theatrical trailer • Production notes • Commentary: Jan De Bont and Stefen Fangmeier • "Making of" documentary • Van Halen music video.
1996 (PG-13) 105m/C Bill Paxton, Helen Hunt, Cary Elwes, Jami Gertz, Alan Ruck,

Lois Smith, Sean Whalen, Gregory Sporleder, Abraham Benrubi, Jake Busey, Joey Slotnick, Philip Seymour Hoffman, Jeremy Davies, Zach Grenier; *D:* Jan De Bont; *W:* Michael Crichton, Anne-Marie Martin; *C:* Jack N. Green; *M:* Mark Mancina. *AWARDS:* MTV Movie Awards '97: Best Action Sequence; *NOM:* Academy Awards '96: Best Sound, Best Visual Effects; MTV Movie Awards '97: Best Female Performance (Hunt); Golden Raspberry Awards '96: Worst Supporting Actress (Gertz).

Twitch of the Death Nerve

Typically confused giallo horror from the prolific Mario Bava concerns murders that take place near a bay that is scheduled to be developed. *AKA:* Bay of Blood; Last House on the Left, Part 2; Carnage.
Movie: 🐶🐶🐶 *DVD:* NYR
Simitar Entertainment (Cat #7654). Dolby Digital 5.1 Surround Stereo. $14.98. Keepcase.
1971 (R) 87m/C *IT* Claudine Auger, Chris Avran, Isa Miranda, Laura Betti, Luigi Pistilli, Sergio Canvari, Anna M. Rosati; *D:* Mario Bava; *W:* Mario Bava, Filippo Ottoni, Joseph McLee, Gene Luotto; *C:* Mario Bava; *M:* Stelvio Cipriano.

Two English Girls

This wispy period romance, adapted from a novel, unfolds to the music of harp and flute. Young French Claude (Leaud) becomes caught up with two English sisters after he takes a room in their mother's house. He courts Muriel (Tendeter) at the behest of Anne (Markham), but when the families separate Muriel and Claude for a trial period, emotional complications arise. The DVD was mastered from a fully restored Janus print. The color is generally creamy, though a climactic love scene is beset with mottling; what a shame. The new subtitles are white but outlined to ease eyestrain. The mono-sourced sound leans on the center speaker. A bonus *Vintage Truffaut Trailer Collection* is ten theatrical reels, not arranged in any order but playable either individually or as one long sequence. —*JK* *AKA:* Les Deux Anglaises et le Continent; Anne and Muriel.
Movie: 🐶🐶🐶▶ *DVD:* 🐶🐶🐶
WinStar Home Entertainment (Cat #FLV5 076, UPC #720917507620). Widescreen. Dual-channel Mono. $29.99. Keepcase. *LANG:* French. *SUB:* English. *FEATURES:* 6 chapter links • Interactive menus • Grayscale picture disc • Awards and filmographies • Coming attractions trailers.
1972 (R) 130m/C *FR* Jean-Pierre Leaud, Kika Markham, Stacey Tendeter, Sylvia Marriott, Marie Mansert, Philippe Leotard; *D:* Francois Truffaut; *W:* Francois Truffaut; *C:* Nestor Almendros; *M:* Georges Delerue.

200 Cigarettes

Directorial debut from former casting director Garcia follows the adventures of various self-absorbed hipsters on New Year's Eve, 1981, in New York. The excellent ensemble cast is given spotty material. The primary goal of these unlikable jerks is to find someone (or anyone) to sleep with before the night is over. They all hook up in this ode to the high life of pre-AIDS promiscuity, but you don't care about them. Chapelle, as the philosophy-spouting disco cabbie, is the best of the weak lot. On DVD, the funky, trashy, shiny, silly look of the too-bright colors gets full play. The whole thing looks so sharp that it's often painful to watch if you're not of that generation and share that generation's eclectic tastes. —*MM*
Movie: 🐶🐶 *DVD:* 🐶🐶🐶
Paramount Home Video (Cat #33493, UPC #097363349372). Widescreen anamorphic. Dolby Digital Surround Stereo; Dolby Digital 5.1 Surround Stereo. $29.99. Keepcase. *LANG:* English; French. *SUB:* English. *FEATURES:* 18 chapter links.
1998 (R) 101m/C Ben Affleck, Casey Affleck, Jay Mohr, Dave Chappelle, Gaby Hoffman, Courtney Love, Christina Ricci, Paul Rudd, Catherine Kellner, Martha Plimpton, Janeane Garofalo, Guillermo Diaz, Angela Featherstone, Brian McCardie, Nicole Parker, Kate Hudson, Elvis Costello; *D:* Risa Bramon Garcia; *W:* Shana Larsen; *C:* Frank Prinzi; *M:* Mark Mothersbaugh, Bob Mothersbaugh.

The Two Jakes

Ten years have passed and Jake Gittes (Nicholson) is still a private investigator in this sequel to *Chinatown*. When a murder occurs while he's digging up dirt on an affair between the wife of a real estate executive and the man's partner, Jake has to return to his past for answers. Despite solid performances, it's unreasonably difficult to follow, and Nicholson's lethargic voice-over narration is little help. DVD is kind to Vilmos Zsigmond's outstanding photography that captures the atmosphere of post-WWII Los Angeles with real grace. Sound is very good. —*MM*
Movie: 🐶🐶 *DVD:* 🐶🐶🐶
Paramount Home Video (Cat #01854, UPC #097360185478). Widescreen anamorphic. Dolby Digital 5.1 Surround Stereo; Dolby Digital Surround Stereo. $29.99. Keepcase. *LANG:* English; French. *SUB:* English. *FEATURES:* 14 chapter links • Theatrical trailer.
1990 (R) 137m/C Jack Nicholson, Harvey Keitel, Meg Tilly, Madeleine Stowe, Eli Wallach, Ruben Blades, Frederic Forrest, David Keith, Richard Farnsworth, Tracey Walter; *D:* Jack Nicholson; *W:* Robert Towne; *C:* Vilmos Zsigmond; *M:* Van Dyke Parks.

Two Lane Blacktop

One of the first things that director Monte Hellman and producer Gary Kurtz discuss on their commentary track is the reason that it took this famous "lost" film 28 years to appear on home video. The answer is music rights. Much of the rest of their talk tends toward the technical, concerning both the original production (which presented a host of problems because it was a travelling location shoot, filmed in sequence) and the transfer to video. The loosely plotted story revolves around a coast-to-coast race between GTO (Oates) and The Driver (Taylor), who's accompanied by The Mechanic (Wilson) and The Girl (Bird). Seen again, the film is definitely a mixed bag. Warren Oates may never have been better than he is here, but it is no accident that his costars have not made another movie. (Ms. Bird did appear in two other films.) Though the picture was never meant to be a conventionally polished Hollywood production, on disc it looks remarkably good, capturing the time and landscape with powerful nostalgia. Many of the night scenes were filmed with existing light and they are well detailed. Hellman and Kurtz give credit to Greg Sandor, who is credited as visual consultant but actually did most of the photography. The film has never been the masterpiece that some have claimed but it is a terrific road movie, well worth another look all these years later. —*MM*
Movie: 🐶🐶🐶 *DVD:* 🐶🐶🐶
Anchor Bay (Cat #DV10937, UPC #013131 093797). Widescreen (2.35:1) letterboxed. Dolby Digital 5.1 Surround Stereo; Dolby Digital Surround Stereo. $29.98. Keepcase. *LANG:* English. *FEATURES:* 24 chapter links • Commentary: director Monte Hellman and producer Gary Kurtz • Monte Hellman documentary by George Hickenlooper • Cast and crew thumbnail biographies • Theatrical trailer.
1971 103m/C James Taylor, Dennis Wilson, Warren Oates, Laurie Bird, Harry Dean Stanton; *D:* Monte Hellman; *W:* Rudy Wurlitzer, Will Corry; *C:* Jackson Deerson.

Two Lost Worlds

Alternative wonder finds Capt. Kirk Hamilton (James Arness, listed in the credits as Jim Aurness) a 19th-century seafarer who battles semi-monstrous dinosaurs, pirates, and more when he and his shipmates are shipwrecked on an uncharted island. Don't miss the footage from *Captain Fury*, *One Million B.C.*, and *Captain Caution*. The loony narration adds an extra dimension of silliness to the already silly proceedings. The DVD image heightens the shortcomings of the effects, sets, and backdrops. Wonderful entertainment for the right audience. —*MM*
Movie: 🐶🐶 *DVD:* 🐶🐶▶
Image Entertainment (Cat #ID5377FWDVD, UPC #014381537727). Full frame. $24.99. Snapper. *LANG:* English. *FEATURES:* 10 chapter links • James Arness filmography.
1950 63m/B James Arness, Laura Elliott, Bill Kennedy, Bill Kennedy; *D:* Norman Dawn; *W:* Tom Hubbard; *C:* Harry Neumann.

Two Minute Warning

A sniper plans to take out the president of the United States at an NFL playoff game in this boring, pointless disaster film that goes on forever. Features all the ready-made characters inherent in the genre, but, until it's too late, precious little of the mayhem. To get caught watching the TV version, which features more characters and an additional subplot, would be truly disastrous. This Universal catalog release has a much sharper picture than some, and very little grain. Colors are pretty accurate and actually seem a little brighter than they were in the theatre (or on TV). The Dolby Digital mono track is both thin and muffled at the same time. —JO

Movie: 🐾🐾 **DVD:** 🐾🐾▶

Universal Studios Home Video (Cat #20425h, UPC #025192042522). Widescreen (2.35:1) letterboxed. Dolby Digital Mono. $24.98. Keepcase. *LANG:* English (DDM); Spanish (DDM); French (DDM). *SUB:* Spanish. *CAP:* English. *FEATURES:* 16 chapter links • Production notes • Cast and filmmakers bios • Theatrical trailer • Web links.

1976 (R) 116m/C Charlton Heston, John Cassavetes, Martin Balsam, Beau Bridges, Marilyn Hassett, David Janssen, Jack Klugman, Walter Pidgeon, Gena Rowlands; *D:* Larry Peerce; *W:* Ed Hume; *C:* Gerald Hirschfeld; *M:* Charles Fox. *AWARDS: NOM:* Academy Awards '76: Best Film Editing.

2000 Maniacs

To contemporary audiences, accustomed to hyper-realistic violent effects, Herschell Gordon Lewis's pioneering effort in gore is almost pure comedy. The giggling red-necks of Pleasant Valley, GA (actually St. Cloud, FL), trick vacationing Yankees into their small town, planning to make the visitors the guests of honor at the centennial barbecue. The hayseed humor and the soundtrack of folk music and cheap electric organ make it resemble an episode of *Hee-Haw* that's given in to the dark side of the force. The DVD is much sharper in image and sound than VHS tape, particularly those older ones back in the cult section of your video store, which have been rented dozens, if not hundreds, of times. It's really remarkable for a film of its age and budget. On their commentary track, Friedman and Lewis are their usual hearty selves. —MM

Movie: 🐾🐾 **DVD:** 🐾🐾▶

Something Weird Video (Cat #ID5998SW DVD, UPC #014381599824). Full frame. Dolby Digital Mono. $24.99. Snapper. *LANG:* English; French. *FEATURES:* 12 chapter links • Theatrical trailer • Outtakes • Gallery of exploitation ad material • Commentary: Friedman, Lewis, Mike Vraney.

1964 75m/C Thomas Wood, Connie Mason, Jeffrey Allen, Ben Moore, Gary Bakeman, Jerome Eden, Shelby Livingston, Michael Korb, Yvonne Gilbert, Mark Douglas, Linda Cochran, Vincent Santo, Andy Wilson; *D:* Herschell Gordon Lewis; *W:* Herschell Gordon Lewis; *C:* Her-

schell Gordon Lewis; *M:* Herschell Gordon Lewis, Larry Wellington.

2001: A Space Odyssey

Space voyage to Jupiter turns chaotic when a computer, HAL 9000, takes over. Seen by some as a mirror of man's historical use of machinery and by others as a grim vision of the future, the special effects and music are still stunning. Critically acclaimed by some, confusing to others. From the Arthur C. Clarke short story "The Sentinel" and followed by a sequel, *2010: The Year We Make Contact.* The DVD has some problems with distortion along the high-contrast lines of the outer space scenes, but on the whole is above average with good sharpness and only a little grain. Colors are very good and the only bleed appears in a couple red-lit spaceship interiors. Brightness is excellent. The remastered Dolby Digital 5.1 tracks are superb. The music alone will blow you away with its crisp highs and clear low end, and the dialogue is always up front. The layer change is placed at the beginning of the intermission and does not disturb the film. A beautiful disc to watch and listen to. —JO

Movie: 🐾🐾🐾 **DVD:** 🐾🐾▶

Warner Home Video, Inc. (Cat #65000, UPC #012569500020). Widescreen (2.35:1) letterboxed. Dolby Digital 5.1; Mono. $24.98. Snapper. *LANG:* English (DD5.1); French (Mono). *SUB:* French; Spanish. *CAP:* English. *FEATURES:* Dual-layered RSDL • 32 chapter links • Theatrical trailers • Interview with Arthur C. Clarke. Also available as part of the "Stanley Kubrick Collection" 7-DVD box set ($149.98).

1968 139m/C *GB* Keir Dullea, Gary Lockwood, William Sylvester, Dan Richter, Leonard Rossiter, Margaret Tyzack, Robert Beatty, Vivian Kubrick; *D:* Stanley Kubrick; *W:* Stanley Kubrick, Arthur C. Clarke; *C:* Geoffrey Unsworth, John Alcott; *V:* Douglas Rain. *AWARDS:* Academy Awards '68: Best Visual Effects; American Film Institute (AFI) '98: Top 100, National Film Registry '91; *NOM:* Academy Awards '68: Best Art Direction/Set Decoration, Best Director (Kubrick), Best Story & Screenplay.

2001: A Space Odyssey (MGM)

A basic plot synopsis for Kubrick's science-fiction opus might simply state: Astronauts and a homicidal computer investigate an alien presence. But *2001* is about so much more than that. In fact, decades after it wowed audiences with "the ultimate trip," cinephiles and sci-fi aficionados are still debating the film's meaning. At casual glance, the story is about a space trip to Jupiter that turns chaotic when the HAL 9000 talking computer kills most of the crew. Deeper inspection reveals Kubrick (aided by legendary science-fiction author Clarke) made a movie that spans millennia with a

theme that delves into the very nature of humanity, intelligence, technology, and perhaps religion. Epic in scope and beautiful in execution, the film nonetheless is as confounding to some as it is appreciated by others. Its ground-breaking special effects remain absolutely convincing. *2001* has never looked better on home video. That said, however, it's an unforgivable shame MGM failed to issue this great film as a special-edition DVD right out of the gate. Extras are minimal, though the included trailers for *2001* and the less-regarded sequel, *2010*, are welcome. The interview with Clarke is neither new nor particularly revealing. The generous bonuses of the out-of-print Criterion Collection laserdisc are nowhere to be found. What this widescreen epic cries out for above all else is a new, anamorphic transfer that would give the picture crispness even on large, widescreen monitors. The new Dolby Digital 5.1 sound mix is OK, but the soundtrack lacks the fidelity of more contemporary motion pictures. Still, Kubrick's choices in classical music remain influential. Too bad the production notes are relegated to a lackluster, printed booklet. *2001* has yet to receive the definitive DVD treatment. —MB

Movie: 🐾🐾🐾🐾 **DVD:** 🐾🐾▶

MGM Home Entertainment (Cat #906309, UPC #027616630926). Widescreen (2.2:1) letterboxed. Dolby Digital 5.1. $24.98. Keepcase. *LANG:* English; French. *SUB:* French; Spanish. *CAP:* English. *FEATURES:* 32 chapter links • Interview with Arthur C. Clarke • Theatrical trailers for *2001* and *2010* • 8-page booklet with trivia and production notes.

1968 139m/C

2010: The Year We Make Contact

Americans and Russians unite to investigate the abandoned starship *Discovery*'s decaying orbit around Jupiter and try to determine why the HAL 9000 computer sabotaged its mission years before, while signs of cosmic change are detected on and around the giant planet. The surprisingly enjoyable film is based on work of Arthur C. Clarke, his sequel to *2001: A Space Odyssey.* The Surround tracks are not used much on this DVD, but overall the 5.1 mix is pretty exhilarating, especially during the music passages. The picture is very sharp and grain either nonexistent or unnoticeable. Deep space is deep black and remains true throughout. The colors are very vibrant and the effects, particularly the climactic ignition, are stunning. —JO

Movie: 🐾🐾🐾 **DVD:** 🐾🐾🐾▶

MGM Home Entertainment (Cat #907046, UPC #027616704627). Widescreen (2.35:1) letterboxed. Dolby Digital 5.1; Dolby Surround. $24.98. Keepcase. *LANG:* English (DD5.1); French (DS). *SUB:* English; French; Spanish. *CAP:* English. *FEATURES:* 32 chapter links • Behind-the-scenes featurette.

1984 (PG) 116m/C Roy Scheider, John Lithgow, Helen Mirren, Bob Balaban, Keir Dullea, Madolyn Smith, Mary Jo Deschanel; **D:** Peter Hyams; **W:** Peter Hyams, Arthur C. Clarke; **C:** Peter Hyams; **M:** David Shire; **V:** Douglas Rain, Candice Bergen. AWARDS: NOM: Academy Awards '84: Best Art Direction/Set Decoration, Best Costume Design, Best Makeup, Best Sound.

Two Undercover Angels

Spoofy '60s exploitation isn't as misogynistic as many of director Franco's later works. It's about two sexy comic book private eyes (Reynauld and Yanni) in pursuit of various madmen, including Morpho the dog-faced boy, across a series of garish European locations and sets with fashion models, cat burglars, and kidnappings all part of the mix. Producer Hoven is the bad guy with the eye patch and Franco shows up in a comic interrogation scene. Like the acting, the voice dubbing is wonderfully bad, which is 90% of the charm of this particular kind of alternative fare. The tacky, orangish tint of many scenes is also appropriate. On DVD, the film looks and sounds about as good as it possibly could, though those are not necessarily virtues. —MM **AKA:** Sadisterotica; El Caso de las Dos Bellezas; Rote Lippen.
Movie: ♪♪▶ **DVD:** ♪♪▶
Anchor Bay (Cat #DV10822, UPC #013131 082296). Full frame. Dolby Digital. $24.98. Keepcase. LANG: English. FEATURES: Theatrical trailer ▪ 12 chapter links.
1968 ?m/C GE Janine Reynaud, Rossana Yanni, Adrian Hoven, Chris Howland, Michel Lemoine, Marta Reeves, Jess (Jesus) Franco; **D:** Jess (Jesus) Franco; **W:** Jess (Jesus) Franco; **C:** Jorge Herrero; **M:** Fernando Garcia Morcillo.

Two Women

A mother (Loren) and her 13-year-old daughter travel during war-torn Italy during WWII and must survive starvation, crazed monks, and brutal soldiers. It's tragic, moving, and well-directed. Loren deserves the Academy Award she received. Unfortunately, this is one of the worst DVDs ever burned, a total rip-off even with the cut-rate price tag. It appears to have been made from a third-generation VHS copy on a machine with a dirty recording head. The ghostly image is unwatchable; the sound is unbearable. —MM **AKA:** La Ciociara.
Movie: ♪♪♪♪ **DVD:** woof
Madacy Entertainment (Cat #99020, UPC #056775005696). Full frame. Dolby Digital Mono. $9.99. Keepcase. LANG: Italian. SUB: English. FEATURES: Sophia Loren thumbnail biography ▪ 9 chapter links.
1961 99m/B IT Sophia Loren, Raf Vallone, Eleonora Brown, Jean-Paul Belmondo; **D:** Vittorio De Sica; **W:** Cesare Zavattini, Vittorio De Sica; **C:** Gabor Pogany; **M:** Armando Trovajoli. AWARDS: Academy Awards '61: Best Actress (Loren); British Academy Awards '61: Best Actress

(Loren); Cannes Film Festival '61: Best Actress (Loren); Golden Globe Awards '62: Best Foreign Film; New York Film Critics Awards '61: Best Actress (Loren).

U-Turn

Bobby (Penn) is a two-bit gambler on his way to pay off the balance of a debt in Las Vegas (the down payment was two of his fingers) when he is stranded in the town of Superior, AZ. He becomes mixed up with a married couple (Nolte and Lopez), each of whom want Bobby to kill the other. Adding to the fun in this Mayberry-on-mescaline are the walking grease pit of a mechanic (Thornton) and a local tough guy named TNT (Phoenix), who thinks Bobby is making a play for his nymphet girlfriend (Danes). Also appearing is the stock issue Oliver Stone wise old Indian who dispenses wisdom, or something like it. The characters meet for the predestined showdown in the desert, with predictable results. Stone has a good time taking stereotypical noir characters and putting his unique twist on them, although you may not have as much fun watching them. The colors on this DVD are superb and they may be the key to the excellent delivery of Stone's kinetic images. The picture remains sharp, with punchy contrasts and comfortable brightness throughout. Also key to any Oliver Stone film is the merging of visuals with his high-energy sound montages. The 5.1 sound delivers it in fine form with thundering bass and super crisp highs, all rolled into a great mix that utilizes the rear channels almost nonstop. — JO **AKA:** Stray Dogs.
Movie: ♪♪▶ **DVD:** ♪♪♪▶
Columbia Tristar Home Video (Cat #32529, UPC #043396325296). Widescreen (1.85:1) anamorphic; full frame. Dolby Digital 5.1; Dolby Surround. $29.95. Keepcase. LANG: English; French; Spanish. SUB: English; French; Spanish. CAP: English. FEATURES: 28 chapter links ▪ Theatrical trailer.
1997 (R) 125m/C Sean Penn, Jennifer Lopez, Claire Danes, Nick Nolte, Joaquin Rafael (Leaf) Phoenix, Powers Boothe, Billy Bob Thornton, Jon Voight, Abraham Benrubi, Julie Hagerty, Bo Hopkins, Valery Nikolaev, Aida Linares, Laurie Metcalf, Liv Tyler; **D:** Oliver Stone; **W:** John Ridley; **C:** Robert Richardson; **M:** Ennio Morricone. AWARDS: NOM: Golden Raspberry Awards '97: Worst Supporting Actor (Voight), Worst Director (Stone).

UFOs Above and Beyond

Star Trek's Scotty, James Doohan, hosts this cheesy, 48-minute documentary that purports to show never-before-seen video footage of UFO water landings, alien probes, Area 51, and other UFO sightings. Doohan introduces UFO researchers, and tells viewers, "The evidence is overwhelming." Video and audio are acceptable, although most of the "authentic UFO

footage" is fuzzy and grainy as expected. —MB
Movie: woof **DVD:** ♪♪
Image Entertainment (Cat #ID5872UFDVD, UPC #014381587227). Full frame. Dolby Digital 1.0. $19.98. Snapper. LANG: English. FEATURES: 10 chapter links ▪ 52-min. interview with former government scientist Bob Lazar.
1997 48m/C Nar: James Doohan.

The Ugly

Give the New Zealand filmmakers credit for truth in titling. This is one visually repellent film, filled with clashing colors, grotesque sets, unattractive characters, and sordid crimes. Confessed serial killer Simon (Rotondo) has celebrity shrink Karen Schumaker (Hobbs) evaluate him to determine if he's fit to stand trial. Their relationship is told through fantasies and flashbacks, all bloody and stylized. It's difficult to judge the quality of the DVD since its purpose is to display repugnant material repugnantly. In that regard, it is all too successful. —MM
Movie: ♪♪ **DVD:** ♪♪
Trimark Home Video (Cat #VM6894D, UPC #031398689430). Widescreen letterboxed. Dolby Digital Surround Stereo. $19.99. Keepcase. LANG: English. SUB: French; Spanish. CAP: English. FEATURES: 24 chapter links ▪ Trailer.
1996 93m/C NZ Paolo Rotondo, Rebecca Hobbs, Jennifer Ward-Lealand, Roy Ward, Vanessa Byrnes; **D:** Scott Reynolds; **W:** Scott Reynolds; **C:** Simon Raby; **M:** Victoria Kelly.

Ulzana's Raid

An aging scout (Lancaster) and an idealistic Cavalry lieutenant (Davison) lock horns as they track down a vicious Apache chieftain. As they close in, each side escalates the violence, forcing the lieutenant to re-evaluate his values. A brutal, gritty western that enjoyed critical reevaluation years after its first release. This DVD has so many artifacts and such bad resolution that it is almost uncomfortable to watch. The only time the picture quality is bearable is during a close-up, and even then, any movement at all ruins the image (blinking included). The sound is very flat, the music clips, and there are some portions of the mono track in which the dialogue is hard to distinguish. This is another case where the VHS tape is the better investment. —JO
Movie: ♪♪♪ **DVD:** ♪
Goodtimes Entertainment (Cat #0581035, UPC #018713810359). Full frame. Mono. $19.98. Snapper. LANG: English. SUB: Spanish; French. CAP: English. FEATURES: 18 chapter links.
1972 (R) 103m/C Burt Lancaster, Bruce Davison, Richard Jaeckel, Lloyd Bochner, Jorge Luke; **D:** Robert Aldrich; **W:** Alan Sharp; **C:** Joseph Biroc; **M:** Frank DeVol.

Umbrellas of Cherbourg

Bittersweet operetta has no spoken dialogue. Deneuve is the teenaged daughter of a widow who owns an umbrella shop. She and her equally young boyfriend (Castelnuovo) are separated by his military duty in Algeria. Finding she is pregnant, she marries a wealthy man. When her beau returns, he too marries someone else. But then they meet again. The DVD was made from the 1996 restoration and so all of the glistening reds, greens, and pinks look terrific, though the film has always had a strong anachronistic quality that defies conventional comparisons. The sound is very good, but not terrific, reflecting the technology of the early 1960s. —MM **AKA:** Les Parapluies de Cherbourg; Die Regenschirme von Cherbourg.

Movie: 🎬🎬🎬▶ **DVD:** 🎬🎬🎬▶
WinStar Home Entertainment (Cat #FLV 5003, UPC #72091750032). Widescreen (1.66:1) letterboxed. Dolby Digital Surround Stereo. $29.98. Keepcase. LANG: French. SUB: English. FEATURES: 9 chapter links ▪ Notes on restoration ▪ Trailer ▪ Credits ▪ Filmographies.
1964 90m/C FR Catherine Deneuve, Nino Castelnuovo, Anne Vernon, Ellen Farner, Marc Michel, Mireille Perrey, Jean Champion, Alfred Wolff, Dorothee Blanck; **D:** Jacques Demy; **W:** Jacques Demy; **C:** Jean Rabier; **M:** Michel Legrand. AWARDS: Cannes Film Festival '64: Best Film; NOM: Academy Awards '65: Best Foreign Film, Best Song ("I Will Wait for You"), Best Story & Screenplay, Best Original Score.

Un Air de Famille

French comedy about the now-familiar dysfunctional family bears a slight resemblance to *Big Night*. This group gets together once a week for dinner at Sleepy Dad's Cafe. It's son Phillipe's (Yordanoff) wife Yolande's (Frot) birthday. The place is run by his brother Henri (Bacri), whose wife calls to say she's left him while their tactless mother (Maurier) frets that sister Betty (Jaoui) is 30 and single. Nobody knows that Betty is seeing bartender Dennis (Darroussin), the only one who really knows what's going on. Unlike so many French imports, this one looks terrific on DVD with a crisply photographed image and very good sound. —MM **AKA:** Respectable Families; Family Resemblances.

Movie: 🎬🎬 **DVD:** 🎬🎬🎬
WinStar Home Entertainment (Cat #FLV 5077, UPC #720917507729). Widescreen. $29.98. Keepcase. LANG: French. SUB: English. FEATURES: 6 chapter links ▪ Production credits ▪ Filmographies and awards.
1996 107m/C FR Jean-Pierre Bacri, Agnes Jaoui, Jean-Pierre Darroussin, Catherine Frot, Claire Maurier, Wladimir Yordanoff; **D:** Cedric Klapisch; **W:** Jean-Pierre Bacri, Agnes Jaoui, Cedric Klapisch; **C:** Benoit Delhomme. AWARDS: Cesar Awards '97: Best Supporting Actor (Dar-

roussin), Best Supporting Actress (Frot), Best Writing; NOM: Cesar Awards '97: Best Director (Klapisch), Best Film.

The Unbearable Lightness of Being

Tomas (Day-Lewis), a young Czech doctor in the late 1960s, leads a sexually and emotionally carefree existence with a number of women, including his mistress Sabina (Olin), a lusty artist. When he marries the fragile Tereza (Binoche), he may be falling in love for the first time. On the eve of the Russian invasion of 1968, the two flee to Switzerland, but Tereza cannot reconcile herself to exile. With extraordinary length and realism, the complex personal and political relationships are resolved. Some will think that this intellectual story (based on Milan Kundera's novel) is too long and slow. Others will be more appreciative of director Kaufman's blend of bawdy eroticism and serious emotion. The DVD certainly receives top drawer treatment, with a transfer to disc that equals the theatrical release in clarity and sound. Kaufman's commentary is dry, smart, and remote, much like his movies. —MM

Movie: 🎬🎬🎬 **DVD:** 🎬🎬🎬
Criterion Collection (Cat #UNB010, UPC #037429140222). Widescreen (1.85:1) letterboxed. Dolby Digital Surround. $39.95. Keepcase. LANG: English. SUB: English. FEATURES: 43 chapter links ▪ Commentary: Kaufman, Jean-Claude Carriere, Walter Murch, Lena Olin.
1988 (R) 172m/C Daniel Day-Lewis, Juliette Binoche, Lena Olin, Derek De Lint, Erland Josephson, Pavel Landovsky, Donald Moffat, Daniel Olbrychski, Stellan Skarsgard, Tormek Bork, Bruce Myers, Pavel Slaby, Pascale Kalensky, Jacques Ciron, Anne Lonnberg, Laszlo Szabo, Vladimir Valenta, Clovis Cornillac, Leon Lissek, Consuelo de Haviland; **D:** Philip Kaufman; **W:** Jean-Claude Carriere, Philip Kaufman; **C:** Sven Nykvist; **M:** Mark Adler, Ernie Fosselius, Leos Janacek. AWARDS: British Academy Awards '88: Best Adapted Screenplay; Independent Spirit Awards '89: Best Cinematography; National Society of Film Critics Awards '88: Best Director (Kaufman), Best Film; NOM: Academy Awards '88: Best Adapted Screenplay, Best Cinematography.

Uncle Buck

When Mom and Dad have to go away suddenly, the only babysitter they can find is good ol' Uncle Buck, a lovable lout who spends much of his time smoking cigars, trying to make up with his girlfriend, and enforcing the teenage daughter's chastity. More intelligent than the average slob/teen comedy with a heart, due in large part to Candy's dandy performance. Memorable pancake scene. This Universal catalog release is pretty good, and features a sharp and colorful image that markedly improves upon VHS and laserdisc releases. The Dolby Surround is

also very good and even the rear Surround gets a bit of a workout. —JO
Movie: 🎬🎬🎬 **DVD:** 🎬🎬🎬
Universal Studios Home Video (Cat #20317, UPC #025192031724). Widescreen (1.85:1) anamorphic. Dolby Surround. $24.95. Keepcase. LANG: English; Spanish; French. SUB: Spanish. CAP: English. FEATURES: 16 chapter links ▪ Production notes ▪ Cast and filmmakers bios ▪ Film highlights.
1989 (PG) 100m/C John Candy, Amy Madigan, Jean Kelly, Macaulay Culkin, Jay Underwood, Gaby Hoffman, Laurie Metcalf, Elaine Bromka, Garrett M. Brown; **D:** John Hughes; **W:** John Hughes; **C:** Ralf Bode; **M:** Ira Newborn.

Uncle Sam

The box art is cool but this is basically a video horror. Desert Storm hero Sam Harper (Fralick) returns home—in a coffin. Only he doesn't stay dead and decides to liven up his small town's Fourth of July celebration by dressing up as Uncle Sam and going on a killing spree. This DVD is worth picking up just for the commentary by Lustig and Hayes. Lustig always comes across as the ultimate movie fan who loves what he does, and loves to talk about it. Enthusiastic and informative—what more can you ask for? The DVD delivers the film with suitable color intensity and is very sharp. The 5.1 mix has tons of bass, energetic highs, and a great Surround mix, all rare in the low-budget horror genre. —JO
Movie: 🎬 **DVD:** 🎬🎬🎬▶
Elite Entertainment, Inc. (Cat #EE7262, UPC #790594726225). Widescreen (2.35:1) letterboxed. Dolby Digital 5.1; Dolby Surround. $29.95. Keepcase. LANG: English. FEATURES: 21 chapter links ▪ Theatrical trailer ▪ Commentary: William Lustig and Isaac Hayes.
1996 (R) 91m/C David Fralick, Timothy Bottoms, Robert Forster, Isaac Hayes, Bo Hopkins; **D:** William Lustig; **W:** Larry Cohen; **C:** James Lebovitz; **M:** Mark Governor.

Uncle Tom's Cabin

Even though this silent Universal film was considered enlightened in its time, it's difficult to watch today. The treatment of black characters and the prevalence of racial stereotypes are so blatant that many viewers will cringe. But to leave it at that is unfair. The film tells a story that was familiar to many of its first viewers and it means well. The famous conclusion on the ice floe is masterfully staged (and no more ridiculous in its way than the end of *Titanic*). The film varies in quality from scene to scene. Overall, the DVD image is excellent with comparatively few flaws marring the print. The extras contain material from two deleted scenes. —MM
Movie: 🎬🎬🎬 **DVD:** 🎬🎬🎬
Kino on Video (Cat #K141, UPC #738329014124). Full frame. $29.99. Keepcase. LANG: Silent. SUB: English

intertitles. *FEATURES:* 12 chapter links • Stills from 2 deleted scenes • Photo gallery and original promotional material • Essay on the film's production by historian David Pierce • Original score by Erno Rapee.

1927 112m/B James B. Lowe, Margarita Fischer, George Siegmann, Virginia Grey; *D:* Harry Pollard; *W:* Harry Pollard, Harvey Thew; *C:* Charles Stumar, Jacob Kull; *M:* Erno Rapee.

Under Siege

The *USS Missouri* becomes the battleground for good-guy-with-a-secret-past Seagal. He's up against the deranged Jones, as an ex–Special Forces leader, and Busey, a corrupt naval officer looking to steal the battleship's nuclear arsenal. May be predictable (especially the graphic violence) but the action is fast, the villains swaggering, and Seagal efficient at dispatching the enemy. Work for *Die Hard 3* was reportedly scrapped after Warner announced this film because DH's John McClane was supposed to save the passengers of a boat from terrorists. Sound familiar? A fine action DVD with crisp image and colors backed by a great and sometimes pulverizing 5.1 mix. —*JO*

Movie: 𝕵𝕵 *DVD:* 𝕵𝕵𝕵▸
Warner Home Video, Inc. (Cat #12420, UPC #085391242024). Widescreen (1.85:1) anamorphic. Dolby Digital 5.1; Dolby Surround. $24.98. Snapper. *LANG:* English; Spanish; French. *SUB:* English; Spanish; French. *CAP:* English. *FEATURES:* 29 chapter links • Theatrical trailer • Production notes.

1992 (R) 100m/C Steven Seagal, Tommy Lee Jones, Gary Busey, Patrick O'Neal, Erika Eleniak, Dale Dye, Richard Jones; *D:* Andrew Davis; *W:* J.F. Lawton; *C:* Frank Tidy; *M:* Gary Chang. *AWARDS: NOM:* Academy Awards '92: Best Sound, Best Sound Effects Editing.

Under Siege 2

Kicking terrorists' butts and slinging hash have worn out ex–Navy SEAL and gourmet chef Casey Ryback (Seagal), so he takes a little vacation to the Rocky Mountains. By coincidence, the train he boards is command central for psychotic computer expert Dane's (Bogosian) scheme to control the world's deadliest satellite. Pretty familiar territory for Seagal, who's acting technique consists of "look mad and hurt people." Bigger budget means bigger and more frequent, explosions. Bogosian takes over the Jones/Busey role of evil villain—talented actor. Ridiculous and exaggerated, but fun. The image is sharp and has only slight grain in some of the darker sequences, as well as a few spots of minor artifacting. Colors are pretty punchy and accurate with very little bleed. Blacks are deep and true with good support from the consistent contrast and brightness levels. The rear channels are used enough to keep the viewer in the action, and the overall sound is fairly live with good ambi-

ence, good crunch to the low end, and undistorted crisp highs. —*JO*

Movie: 𝕵𝕵𝕵 *DVD:* 𝕵𝕵𝕵▸
Warner Home Video, Inc. (Cat #13665, UPC #085391366522). Widescreen (1.85:1) anamorphic; full frame. Dolby Digital 5.1. $24.98. Snapper. *LANG:* English; French. *SUB:* English; Spanish; French. *CAP:* English. *FEATURES:* 31 chapter links • 8 theatrical trailers • Production notes.

1995 (R) 100m/C Steven Seagal, Eric Bogosian, Katherine Heigl, Morris Chestnut, Everett McGill, Andy Romano, Nick Mancuso, Brenda Bakke, Dale Dye; *D:* Geoff Murphy; *W:* Richard Hatem; *C:* Robbie Greenberg; *M:* Basil Poledouris.

Under the Gun

Debt-ridden club owner Frank Torrance (Norton) is in trouble with everyone he knows. But he can't clear his debts just by quitting the business, so he decides to fight back. The image is soft, but audio is clean enough to hear the poorly delivered dialogue. No extras, but are they necessary in this case? —*MB*

Movie: 𝕵▸ *DVD:* 𝕵▸
Image Entertainment (Cat #ID5629FMDVD, UPC #014381562927). Full frame. Dolby Digital 2.0. $24.98. Snapper. *LANG:* English. *FEATURES:* 12 chapter links.

1995 (R) 90m/C Jane Badler, Peter Lindsey, Richard Norton, Kathy Long; *D:* Matthew George; *W:* Matthew George; *C:* Dan Burstall; *M:* Frank Strangio.

Undercover

Hot policebabe Cindy Hanen (Massey) goes undercover in an upscale bordello to solve the murder of a prostitute. It's all an excuse for interesting undies and hanky-panky from veteran erotic-thriller director Hippolyte. The DVD captures his polished production values, but the disc is made from the "R"-rated version of the film, not the unrated, and so its editing is abrupt. —*MM*

Movie: 𝕵𝕵▸ *DVD:* 𝕵𝕵▸
Simitar Entertainment (Cat #7363, UPC #082551736324). Full frame. PCM Stereo. $14.98. Keepcase. *LANG:* English. *FEATURES:* 8 chapter links • Production factoids.

1994 (R) 93m/C Athena Massey, Tom Tayback, Anthony Guidera, Rena Riffel, Jeffrey Dean Morgan, Meg Foster; *D:* Alexander Gregory (Gregory Dark) Hippolyte; *W:* Oola Bloome, Lalo Wolf; *C:* Philip Hurn; *M:* Ashley Irwin.

Undercurrent

Action drama with Caribbean setting.
Movie: NYR *DVD:* NYR
Avalanche Entertainment (Cat #13921). Full frame. $24.95. Keepcase. *FEATURES:* Cast and crew thumbnail bios • Trailer • Production notes.

1999 (R) 99m/C Lorenzo Lamas, Frank Vincent, Brenda Strong; *D:* Frank Kerr; *C:* Carlos Gaviria; *M:* Christopher Lennertz.

Underground

Fresh off the farm, young Allison (Carr) is easy prey for the slimy guys who run a Hollywood strip club that's also a front for a white slavery ring. Will the brave DJ Rudy (von Franckenstein) be able to save her? This unrelievedly grubby little cheapie looks terrible. Dark and padded with boring strip scenes, it gains nothing on DVD where its many flaws are even more flagrant. —*MM*

Movie: 𝕵 *DVD:* 𝕵
Simitar Entertainment (Cat #7310, UPC #082551731022). Full frame. PCM Stereo. $14.98. Keepcase. *LANG:* English. *FEATURES:* 8 chapter links • Production factoids.

1990 87m/C Clement von Franckenstein, Rachel Carr, Sean Rankin, Jack Savage, Fred Gartner; *D:* Bret Carr; *W:* P.B. Florenz, J.D. Hall.

The Underneath

Recovering gambling addict Michael Chambers (Gallagher) returns home after skipping out on his debts and his wife Rachel (sultry newcomer Elliott) several years before. Old passions ignite in more ways than one, and Michael's lust for his ex, now married to a hot-tempered hoodlum, leads him to risk it all for a final big score. Moody and tense study of the complexities of emotion is capped by smart lead performances but style wins out over substance and the finale definitely leaves more questions than answers. Remake of the 1949 film noir classic *Criss Cross*, based on Don Tracy's novel of the same name. Every nuance of Soderbergh's subtle and detailed scene composition is accurately transferred to the DVD. Sharpness, colors, and contrast are all excellent. The 5.1 sound is superb as well, with the emphasis on ambience and atmosphere rather than gimmicky effects. —*JO*

Movie: 𝕵𝕵𝕵▸ *DVD:* 𝕵𝕵𝕵▸
Universal Studios Home Video (Cat #20445, UPC #025192044526). Widescreen (2.35:1) letterboxed. Dolby Digital 5.1. $24.98. Keepcase. *LANG:* English. *SUB:* French; Spanish. *CAP:* English. *FEATURES:* 41 chapter links • Theatrical trailer • Cast and filmmakers bios • Production notes • Film highlights • Web links.

1995 (R) 99m/C Shelley Duvall, Richard Linklater, Dennis Hill, Peter Gallagher, Alison Elliott, William Fichtner, Elisabeth Shue, Adam Trese, Paul Dooley, Joe Don Baker, Anjanette Comer, Harry Goaz, Vincent Gaskins, Tony Perenski, Helen Cates, John Martin, David Jensen, Joseph Chrest; *D:* Steven Soderbergh; *W:* Daniel Fuchs, Sam Lowry; *C:* Elliot Davis; *M:* Cliff Martinez. *AWARDS: NOM:* Independent Spirit Awards '96: Best Cinematography.

Underworld

Considering the on-screen talent, this gangster comedy/thriller is a disappointment. Ex-wiseguy Johnny Crown (Leary) studied psychotherapy in the joint. When he is released, he decides to put his new-

found knowledge to work on bossman Frank Gavilan (Mantegna), who may have been behind the hit on Johnny's old man. Contrived dialogue and plot are the weakest parts of an otherwise sleek-looking production. Those inventive visual flourishes are heightened on DVD where the image ranges between good and very good. Sound is fair. —*MM*
Movie: 🎜🎜 **DVD:** 🎜🎜➤
Trimark Home Video (Cat #VM 7302D, UPC #03139873022). Full frame. Dolby Digital Stereo. $34.99. Keepcase. *LANG:* English. *FEATURES:* 8 chapter links ▪ Theatrical trailer ▪ "Making of" featurette. Title is available for sale only as part of the "Mob Hits" four-pack.
1996 (R) 95m/C Denis Leary, Joe Mantegna, Annabella Sciorra, Larry Bishop, Abe Vigoda, James Tolkan, Robert Costanzo; *D:* Roger Christian; *W:* Larry Bishop; *C:* Steven Bernstein; *M:* Anthony Marinelli.

Unforgiven

Will Munny (Eastwood) lives a quiet life with his stepchildren on his failing pig farm, but his desperado past catches up with him when the Schofield Kid invites him to a bounty hunt. Munny reluctantly agrees, mistakenly believing that once the killing is through he can take up his peaceful ways again. Enter sadistic sheriff Little Bill Daggett (Hackman), who doesn't want any gunmen messing up his town. Eastwood uses his own status as a screen legend to full advantage as the aging gunman who realizes too late that his past can never be forgotten. Director Eastwood is also in top form with his well-seasoned cast and myth-defying Old West realism. Surprising critical and boxoffice hit. The DVD has a little trouble with the dark hues and dim lighting of the film. The picture is only really sharp in the daylight and softens considerably elsewhere and the grain level increases. Colors are deep and accurate but bleed a little. The blacks also have some grain in them in the darker scenes. The 5.1 soundtrack is full-bodied on the music, crisp on the dialogue, and delivers incredibly jarring gunshots in a more than realistic manner. —*JO*
Movie: 🎜🎜🎜➤ **DVD:** 🎜🎜➤
Warner Home Video, Inc. (Cat #12531, UPC #085391253129). Widescreen (2.35:1) anamorphic; full frame. Dolby Digital 5.1; Dolby Surround. $24.98. Snapper. *LANG:* English; French. *SUB:* English; French; Spanish. *CAP:* English. *FEATURES:* 33 chapter links ▪ Production notes.
1992 (R) 131m/C Clint Eastwood, Gene Hackman, Morgan Freeman, Richard Harris, Jaimz Woolvett, Saul Rubinek, Frances Fisher, Anna Thomson, David Mucci, Rob Campbell, Anthony James; *D:* Clint Eastwood; *W:* David Peoples; *C:* Jack N. Green; *M:* Lennie Niehaus. *AWARDS:* Academy Awards '92: Best Director (Eastwood), Best Film Editing, Best Picture, Best Supporting Actor (Hackman); American Film Institute (AFI) '98: Top 100; British Academy Awards '92: Best Director (Eastwood), Best Film, Best Supporting Actor (Hackman); Directors Guild of America Awards '92: Best Director (Eastwood); Golden Globe Awards '93: Best Director (Eastwood), Best Supporting Actor (Hackman); Los Angeles Film Critics Association Awards '92: Best Actor (Eastwood), Best Director (Eastwood), Best Film, Best Screenplay, Best Supporting Actor (Hackman); New York Film Critics Awards '92: Best Supporting Actor (Hackman); National Society of Film Critics Awards '92: Best Director (Eastwood), Best Film, Best Screenplay, Best Supporting Actor (Hackman); *NOM:* Academy Awards '92: Best Actor (Eastwood), Best Art Direction/Set Decoration, Best Cinematography, Best Original Screenplay, Best Sound.

Unidentified Flying Oddball

Accidentally sent into space in an experimental faster-than-light ship, Tom Trimble (Dugan) and his robot double Hermes find themselves transported back in time to Arthurian England. Yes, it's another screwy variation on *A Connecticut Yankee in King Arthur's Court.* The special effects are so ordinary that only the youngest audiences won't be firing *Mystery Science Theater 3000* jokes at the screen. Even so, the film looks terrific on DVD, with brighter colors and fewer scratches than films half its age. Sound is so-so. The two-sided disc contains the full-frame version on one side and the widescreen on the other. —*MM*
Movie: 🎜🎜 **DVD:** 🎜🎜➤
Anchor Bay (Cat #DV10734, UPC #013307 3492). Widescreen (1.66:1) letterboxed; full frame. Dolby Digital Mono. $24.99. Keepcase. *LANG:* English. *FEATURES:* 16 chapter links.
1979 (G) 92m/C Dennis Dugan, Jim Dale, Ron Moody, Kenneth More, Rodney Bewes; *D:* Russ Mayberry; *W:* Don Tait; *C:* Paul Beeson; *M:* Ronald Goodwin.

Union City

In 1953, in downtown Union City, New Jersey, accountant Harlan (Lipscomb) and his wife Lillian (Harry) are so repressed that they are on the verge of emotional or physical eruption. The trigger is the thief in their apartment building who steals a little of Harlan's milk every morning. In his adaption of Cornell Woolrich's 1937 story, "The Corpse Next Door," writer-director Marcus Reichert aims for a slightly bilious David Lynch feel, accentuated by the presence of Everett McGill from *Twin Peaks.* The dim noirish retro look is deliberately off-putting and as important as the story. Though the DVD transfer captures the claustrophobic interiors, their moodiness works against the medium's strengths. In the opening credits, the strong reds tend to bleed, but that's less noticeable later. The performances are uniformly controlled but the film is still more successful as a mood piece than as conventional thriller. Think *Bound* without the excesses. —*MM*
Movie: 🎜🎜➤ **DVD:** 🎜🎜🎜

WinStar Home Entertainment (Cat #FLV5047, UPC #720917504728). Full frame. $29.98. Keepcase. *LANG:* English. *FEATURES:* Production credits ▪ Filmographies ▪ 9 chapter links ▪ Photo gallery.
1981 (R) 82m/C Deborah Harry, Everett McGill, Dennis Lipscomb, Pat Benatar, Irina Maleeva, Terina Lewis, Sam McMurray, Paul Andor, Tony Azito, CCH Pounder; *D:* Mark Reichert; *W:* Mark Reichert; *C:* Edward Lachman; *M:* Chris Stein.

Universal Soldier

Sci-fi shoot 'em-ups don't have to be too plausible, but they must contain at least a shred of common sense if they are to involve the audience. This one lacks even that shred. "Unisols," as they are called, are American soldiers who were killed in Vietnam and then revived by the government 25 years later to fight terrorists. Van Damme's the good one; Lundgren's the bad one; Ally Walker is the plucky reporter who might have been separated at birth from Meg Ryan. The fights are slow and the spectacular stuntwork staged at the Hoover Dam loses a lot on the small screen. The DVD is also marred by an unusually large number of flashing lines and patterns. Followed by a direct-to-video sequel. —*MM*
Movie: woof **DVD:** 🎜🎜
Artisan Entertainment (Cat #60474, UPC #012236047407). Widescreen (1.85:1) letterboxed. Dolby Digital 5.1 Surround Stereo. $24.98. Snapper. *LANG:* English. *SUB:* Spanish. *CAP:* English. *FEATURES:* 36 chapter links ▪ Teaser ▪ Theatrical trailer ▪ "Making of" featurette.
1992 (R) 98m/C Jean-Claude Van Damme, Dolph Lundgren, Ally Walker, Ed O'Ross, Jerry Orbach; *D:* Roland Emmerich; *W:* Dean Devlin, Christopher Leitch, Richard Rothstein; *C:* Karl Walter Lindenlaub; *M:* Christopher Franke.

Universal Soldier: The Return

Van Damme returns for a by-the-numbers sequel when a new "unisol," Seth (White) goes berserk and turns on his creators. Only the Bulgin' Belgian can save them. Lots of explosions, gunfire, chases; you know the drill. The rather stilted action scenes are filmed with a curious, shiny quality that gives the DVD image a plastic look. Otherwise, the carefully darkened interiors are fine. Same for sound. —*MM*
Movie: 🎜🎜 **DVD:** 🎜🎜
Columbia Tristar Home Video (Cat #03934, UPC #043396039346). Widescreen (1.85:1) letterboxed; full frame. Dolby Digital 5.1 Surround Stereo; Dolby Surround Stereo. $24.95. Keepcase. *LANG:* English. *CAP:* English. *FEATURES:* 28 chapter links ▪ Jean-Claude Van Damme featurette ▪ Michael Jai White featurette ▪ "Making of" featurette ▪ Cast and crew thumbnail biographies ▪ Liner notes.
1999 (R) 82m/C Jean-Claude Van Damme, Michael Jai White, Daniel von Bargen, Heidi Schanz, Xander Berkeley,

Justin Lazard; **D:** Mic Rodgers; **W:** John Fasano, William Malone; **C:** Michael A. Benson; **M:** Don Davis.

Unknown Island

Photographer Ted Osborne (Reed) and his fiancee Carol Lane (Grey) hire the thuggish Capt. Tarnowski's (MacLane) freighter to take them to an uncharted island in the South China Sea where they hope to find prehistoric creatures. Any resemblance to *King Kong* ends when they encounter their first dinosaurs. These plastic models wouldn't scare a five-year-old but that, after all, is part of the fun with a short but slow-moving flick like this. On DVD, the print is a little scratchy and the early "cinecolor" (a two-color process less expensive than Technicolor) has aged to a reddish tinge. —*MM*
Movie: 🎵🎵 **DVD:** 🎵🎵▶
Image Entertainment (Cat #ID5378FWDVD, UPC #014381537826). Full frame. Dolby Digital Mono. $19.99. Snapper. *LANG:* English. *FEATURES:* 14 chapter links.
1948 76m/C Virginia Grey, Philip Reed, Richard Denning, Barton MacLane; **D:** Jack Bernhard; **W:** Jack Harvey, Robert T. Shannon; **C:** Fred Jackman; **M:** Ralph Stanley.

The Unknown Marx Brothers

This documentary is so packed with funny clips, they keep interrupting the closing credits: sing along to the Schnitzel Bank theme song! Leslie Nielsen is the perfect choice to narrate the Marx Brothers' life histories. He's not only a proverbial barrel of monkeys himself, he also never seems to be just reading text but expressing genuine kinship with the brothers. Zuma Digital Design's interface takes unprecedented advantage of the material, though the coloring of their layout often obscures what's just been highlighted with the remote! The technical quality of the source materials, since they range all the way back to silent movies and turn-of-the-century photos, varies. The current day interviews were all decently rendered on film, though. Interviewees are well-informed, articulate, and never overindulgent. The lightning-quick, musical editing style is perfect foil for the comedy elements and swiftly moving narrative. Zoom-Links, a trademarked interactive feature, is explained on a nearly unreadable directions page, but no problem. It is introduced in the documentary itself at crucial points by a flashing button. When pressed, it jumps to one of the outtakes, then automatically returns to where it had left off in the documentary! The trivia game also automatically skips to a relevant section of the documentary whenever a correct answer is chosen. This is a perfect example of what can be done with a DVD without demanding too much of the viewer's patience. —*JK*
Movie: 🎵🎵🎵🎵 **DVD:** 🎵🎵🎵🎵

WinStar Home Entertainment (Cat #WHE73004, UPC #720917300429). Full frame. Dual-channel mono. $19.99. Keepcase. *LANG:* English. *FEATURES:* 8 chapter links • Interactive menus • Production notes • Marx Brothers' filmography and biography • 15 outtakes • Trivia game • ZoomLinks.
1993 126m/C D: David Leaf, John Scheinfeld; **W:** David Leaf, John Scheinfeld; **M:** Bill Marx; **Nar:** Leslie Nielsen.

Unlikely Angel

Brassy singer Ruby Diamond (Parton) dies suddenly in an accident but is having some trouble entering heaven. St. Peter (McDowall) thinks she's a likely prospect, but Ruby needs a few more good deeds before she can get her wings. So she's sent to help a frazzled widower (Kerwin) who is the father of two lonely preteens. The image isn't the sharpest but is quite acceptable, as is the stereo soundtrack. Parton gets to sing, of course. No need to look for extras. —*MB*
Movie: 🎵🎵 **DVD:** 🎵🎵▶
Image Entertainment (Cat #ID5570BVDVD, UPC #014381557022). Full frame. Dolby Digital 2.0. $24.99. Snapper. *LANG:* English. *FEATURES:* 20 chapter links.
1997 90m/C Dolly Parton, Roddy McDowall, Brian Kerwin; **D:** Michael Switzer.

The Untold Story

This infamous Hong Kong import is guaranteed to offend or gross out just about everyone. The plot, based on a true story, revolves around a mass murderer (Wong). The mildest element is cannibalism. The rest is so graphic, revolting, and grotesque—especially the demented rape scene—that it's almost impossible to watch. Even so, star Anthony Wong's award-winning portrayal of a murderous sociopath is every bit as authentic as Michael Rooker's in *Henry: Portrait of a Serial Killer* and Anthony Perkins's in *Psycho*. This film goes much farther than either of those, mixing horrific violence with broad humor in a way that's almost never seen in western films. The image in this DVD seems a bit brighter than the tape, despite the intentional ugliness of the production. Director Herman Yau uses harsh flourescent light in many scenes, and the night exteriors are just as grim. The disc also contains commentary tracks by Yau and Wong with Hong Kong film critic Miles Wood. Though the filmmakers' English is hesitant, they acquit themselves well enough. The film certainly deserves the special treatment, but it is still not for everyone. —*MM* **AKA:** The Untold Story: Human Meat Roast Pork Buns.
Movie: 🎵🎵🎵 **DVD:** 🎵🎵🎵▶
Tai Seng Video Marketing (Cat #45254, UPC #601643452548). Widescreen letterboxed. Dolby Digital Stereo. $29.99. Keepcase. *LANG:* Cantonese; Mandarin. *SUB:* English. *FEATURES:* 24 chapter links • Commentary: Herman Yau, Anthony Wong,

and Miles Wood • Filmographies for Anthony Wong, Danny Lee, and Herman Yau • Theatrical trailers.
1993 95m/C *HK* Anthony Wong, Danny Lee; **D:** Herman Yau.

Up Close and Personal

The short, sad life of Jessica Savitch got processed and repackaged into a connect-the-dots Hollywood romance, complete with Celine Dion theme song. A card dealer from Reno named Tally Atwater (Pfeiffer) gets her big break as a weather girl on a local TV station in Miami. Wizened media vet Warren Justice (Redford) quickly becomes her mentor, father figure and, predictably, the great love of her life. Their relationship becomes strained as her career takes off. The brightly colored menus are cute and the soundtrack bought with big studio money, but the actual video is riddled with blotchy skin tones that are more unforgiving with Redford than Pfeiffer. —*JK*
Movie: 🎵🎵🎵 **DVD:** 🎵🎵▶
Buena Vista Home Entertainment (Cat #17634, UPC #717951003447). Widescreen (1.85:1). Dolby Digital Stereo 5.1. $29.99. Keepcase. *LANG:* English; French. *CAP:* English. *FEATURES:* 27 chapter links • Interactive menus • Theatrical trailer.
1996 (PG-13) 124m/C Michelle Pfeiffer, Robert Redford, Kate Nelligan, Stockard Channing, Joe Mantegna, Glenn Plummer, James Rebhorn, Noble Willingham, Scott Bryce, Raymond Cruz, Dedee Pfeiffer, Miguel Sandoval, James Karen; **D:** Jon Avnet; **W:** Joan Didion, John Gregory Dunne; **C:** Karl Walter Lindenlaub; **M:** Thomas Newman. *AWARDS: NOM:* Academy Awards '96: Best Song ("Because You Loved Me"); Golden Globe Awards '97: Best Song ("Because You Loved Me").

Urban Legend

Scream-screen alumni litter the screen in this ode to modern tall tales that are passed along as truth by that friend of your cousin. Natalie (Witt) is the standard good girl who doesn't know why her friends are getting knocked off, even though her folklore prof (Englund) is the guy who played Freddy Krueger, and the gas station attendant (Dourif) is the voice of Chucky. The supporting characters are so irritating you'll be happy to see them kick the bucket. DVD has no problems with the dark-and-stormy-night visuals and audio; but then VHS tape doesn't either. —*MM*
Movie: 🎵 **DVD:** 🎵🎵🎵
Columbia Tristar Home Video (Cat #03091, UPC #043396030916). Widescreen (2.35: 1) letterboxed; full frame. Dolby Digital 5.1 Surround Stereo; Dolby Digital Surround Stereo. $24.95. Keepcase. *LANG:* English. *CAP:* English. *FEATURES:* 28 chapter links • Commentary: filmmakers • "Making of" featurette • Cast and crew filmographies and biographies • Theatrical trailer. Box copy states that the DVD has a French

language track and subtitles; my copy did not.

1998 (R) 100m/C Alicia Witt, Jared Leto, Rebecca Gayheart, Loretta Devine, Joshua Jackson, Tara Reid, John Neville, Robert Englund, Brad Dourif, Natasha Gregson Wagner, Danielle Harris, Michael Rosenbaum; **D:** Jamie Blanks; **W:** Silvio Horta; **C:** James Chressanthis; **M:** Christopher Young.

Urban Menace

Veteran video-premiere director Pyun creates a new genre with this feature-length (well, 73 minutes) action/horror/hip-hop music video. The whole story—about a preacher (Snoop Dogg) out to avenge the burning of his ghetto church—looks like a music video. It has a distressed fuzzy look, non-professional-level acting, and desaturated color. The entire work is done in shades of icy blue. The near constant use of the word "nigger" along with conventional profanity makes it completely distasteful to anyone not immersed in gangsta culture. —MM

Movie: 🎵 **DVD:** 🎵🎵
Studio Home Entertainment (Cat #7335, UPC #658149733527). Widescreen letterboxed. Dolby Digital 5.1 Surround Stereo; Dolby Digital Surround Stereo. $28.97. Keepcase. LANG: English. SUB: Spanish. FEATURES: 24 chapter links • Isolated music track • Commentary: director Albert Pyun • Commentary: T.J. Storm and Tahitia • Theatrical trailers • Thumbnail biographies and filmographies • "Making of" featurette • Photo gallery.
1999 (R) 73m/C Snoop Doggy Dogg, Big Pun, Ice-T, Fat Joe, T.J. Storm, Vincent Klyn, Romany Malco, Tahitia, Karen Dyer, Ernie Hudson; **D:** Albert Pyun; **W:** Tim Story; **C:** Philip Alan Waters.

Urotsukidoji: Perfect Collection

The most well-known Japanese erotic-horror anime is a grotesque phantasmagoria of sexual violence and blood-drenched gore involving humans, angelic beings, and huge Lovecraftian monsters. The plot revolves around scenes that attempt to recreate the hellish nightmares of Hieronymous Bosch, and often succeed in stomach-churning fashion. Director Hideki Takayama and creator Toshio Maeda spin it all out with the fast pace and raw energy of an early Godzilla film. If the whole thing didn't go so far beyond the bounds of good taste, it could be dismissed as misogynist porn. But this is Grand Guignol on an epic scale, intentionally offensive and provocative. The umbrella title "Urotsukidoji" refers to a long-running series and the various installments and compilations exist in several versions. The mildest of those are definitely not meant for children and this, the most explicit version, crosses over into hard-core animation. The two-disc DVD set is perhaps a bit more sharply focused than the five-volume tape set, but the main difference between

the two lies in the optional subtitles. —MM
Movie: 🎵🎵🎵 **DVD:** 🎵🎵🎵
Central Park Media/U.S. Manga Corps (Cat #A18D1833D). Full frame. $59.99. Keepcase. LANG: Japanese. SUB: English. FEATURES: Trailers • Toshio Maeda thumbnail biography • 20 chapter links. DVD-ROM supplements.
1989 250m/C JP **D:** Hideki Takayama.

Urusei Yatsura Movie 2: Beautiful Dreamer

An alien princess with supernatural powers is married to the loutish Lum. They and their classmates at Tomobiki High School find themselves reliving one day over and over. Actually, this animated feature is not another Groundhog Day. Instead, it's more like a slightly raunchy Archie comic book with dreamlike sf overtones and the occasional metaphysical sidetrip into the nature of time and human consciousness. The animation is good but not spectacular, about on a par with most Japanese imports. The main difference between the DVD and the tape is the choice of languages and subtitles, and the heightened quality of realistic sounds. Aimed at teen viewers who might well give it a higher rating. —MM
Movie: 🎵🎵 **DVD:** 🎵🎵🎵
Central Park Media/U.S. Manga Corps (Cat #USMD1728, UPC #719987172821). Full frame. Dolby Digital Stereo. $29.95. Keepcase. LANG: English; Japanese. SUB: English; Japanese. FEATURES: 30 chapter links • 11 character references.
1984 90m/C JP **D:** Oshii Mamoru.

U.S. Marshals

Jones reprises his Oscar-winning role from The Fugitive as the hound dog U.S. Marshal Sam Gerard in this lackluster sequel. He tracks down Sheridan (Snipes), who is framed for the double homicide of two federal agents. Gerard's probing reveals that Sheridan really isn't the average Joe he seems, and the presence of shifty agent Downey Jr. further confirms Gerard's suspicions of a government cover-up. Jones remains solid in a popular role, supported well by his sidekick Cosmo (Pantoliano). The stunts equal if not better its predecessor, yet a poorly developed Sheridan, compounded by Snipes's lack of intensity, drag this chase movie down to a slow crawl. Image and sound are both very good on this DVD transfer. The picture is sharp, with no grain or artifacts to get in the way of details. Colors are strongly presented with good accuracy and very little bleed. Blacks are true. Contrast is very punchy and combines with excellent brightness for a very enjoyable presentation. The 5.1 sound is slam-bang energetic; the plane crash and other action sequences pack in plenty of Surround effects. The bass track is a gut shaker, and highs are edgy without being painful. —JO
Movie: 🎵🎵 **DVD:** 🎵🎵🎵▶

Warner Home Video, Inc. (Cat #15625, UPC #085391562528). Widescreen (1.85:1) anamorphic. Dolby Digital 5.1; Dolby Surround. $19.98. Snapper. LANG: English (DD5.1); French (DS). SUB: English; Spanish; French. CAP: English. FEATURES: 40 chapter links • 2 theatrical trailers and 2 TV spots • Commentary: Stuart Baird • Behind-the-scenes featurette • Historical documentary "Justice under the Star" • Production notes.
1998 (PG-13) 133m/C Tommy Lee Jones, Robert Downey Jr., Wesley Snipes, Joe Pantoliano, Kate Nelligan, Irene Jacob, Daniel Roebuck, Tom Wood, Latanya Richardson, Michael Paul Chan; **D:** Stuart Baird; **W:** John Pogue; **C:** Andrzej Bartkowiak; **M:** Jerry Goldsmith.

The Usual Suspects

Several crooks, a $91 million heist, and mysterious crime lord Keyser Soze are twisted together in this noir-thriller. Customs agent Kujan (Palminteri) tries to get a straight story out of small-time con man "Verbal" Kint (Spacey) about a burning tanker in the San Pedro harbor, 27 dead bodies, and the other four temperamental criminals involved: ex-cop-turned thief Keaton (Byrne), explosives expert Hockney (Pollak), and hot-headed partners McManus (Baldwin) and Fenster (Del Toro). Nothing is as it seems, and the ending keeps everyone guessing, right up to the final credits. Terrific performances from all complement the intelligent, humorous script. And yes, the title does come from the famous line in Casablanca. The DVD is the only way to view this dark and stylized noir. The image is consistently crisp and the colors are dead-on accurate. Cinematic details punch through the dark lighting conditions that make up most of the film, and both contrast and brightness levels remain strong and comfortable. The Dolby Surround is as energized as most 5.1 tracks and delivers the bass almost as strongly. —JO
Movie: 🎵🎵🎵▶ **DVD:** 🎵🎵🎵▶
Polygram (Cat #8006302272, UPC #780063022729). Widescreen (2.35:1) letterboxed; full frame. Dolby Surround. $24.95. Expanded jewel case. LANG: English. SUB: English; French; Spanish. CAP: English. FEATURES: 19 chapter links • Cast and crew bios.
1995 (R) 105m/C Kevin Spacey, Gabriel Byrne, Chazz Palminteri, Kevin Pollak, Stephen Baldwin, Benicio Del Toro, Giancarlo Esposito, Pete Postlethwaite, Dan Hedaya, Suzy Amis, Paul Bartel, Peter Greene; **D:** Bryan Singer; **W:** Christopher McQuarrie; **C:** Newton Thomas (Tom) Sigel; **M:** John Ottman. AWARDS: Academy Awards '95: Best Original Screenplay, Best Supporting Actor (Spacey); British Academy Awards '95: Best Original Screenplay, Best Supporting Actor (Spacey); Independent Spirit Awards '96: Best Screenplay, Best Supporting Actor (Del Toro); National Board of Review Awards '95: Best Supporting Actor (Spacey); New York Film Critics Awards '95: Best Sup-

porting Actor (Spacey); Broadcast Film Critics Association Awards '95: Best Supporting Actor (Spacey); *NOM:* British Academy Awards '95: Best Film; Golden Globe Awards '96: Best Supporting Actor (Spacey); Independent Spirit Awards '96: Best Cinematography; Screen Actors Guild Award '95: Best Supporting Actor (Spacey).

Utopia

Laurel and Hardy inherit a paradisiacal island but their peace is disturbed when uranium is discovered. Final screen appearance of the team is diminished by poor direction and script. *AKA:* Atoll K; Robinson Crusoeland; Escapade.
Movie: 🎜🎜 *DVD:* NYR
Digital Disc Entertainment (Cat #585). Full frame. $9.99. *LANG:* English. *CAP:* English. Also available as a double feature with *The Flying Deuces* from Madacy (cat. #99113) for $12.98.
1951 82m/B *FR* Stan Laurel, Oliver Hardy, Suzy Delair, Max Elloy; *D:* Leo Joannon; *W:* Rene Wheeler, Piero Tellini; *C:* Louis Nee, Armand Thirard; *M:* Paul Misraki.

Vampire Journals

Revenge-minded Zachary (Gunn) vows to destroy Ash (Morris), the ancient vampire who created him centuries before, especially when they both become interested in the same mortal woman, Sofia (Cerre). Noting exceptional plot-wise but excellent atmosphere. Shot on location in Transylvania. The DVD is an improvement over the VHS release and the picture is fairly sharp. There is some grain that may be intentional or film-stock related. Artifacts exist but are minimal. Colors are subdued but appear accurate, and despite the dim lighting throughout most of the film, subtle shadings are detailed, and blacks mostly true, with only a couple instances of grain. Contrast is good and brightness consistent. The music and dialogue are delivered nicely with good fidelity and decent dynamics, and there is good imaging and space between the stereo tracks. —*JO*
Movie: 🎜🎜▶ *DVD:* 🎜🎜▶
Full Moon Pictures (Cat #8001, UPC #728096800167). Full frame. Stereo. $24.95. Keepcase. *LANG:* English. *FEATURES:* 18 chapter links.
1996 (R) 82m/C David Gunn, Jonathan Morris, Kirsten Cerre, Starr Andreeff; *D:* Ted Nicolaou; *W:* Ted Nicolaou; *C:* Adolfo Bartoli; *M:* Richard Kosinski.

Vampyr

Carl Dreyer's seminal horror film admits that it's a dream in the opening scenes and never pretends to have a formal "realistic" narrative plot structure or a reliable protagonist. David Grey (West) may well hallucinate the whole slow-moving tale for all the logical sense it makes. Barely connected images of death, sickness, and burial hint at a vampire story, and all of the key moments have been copied count-

less times since, most recently in the work of David Lynch. By today's standards of sound and image, the film is rough. The bright restored DVD images look much better than many of the older tapes that are on the market, but even here the image jitters slightly, and scratches and nicks are apparent throughout. The score sounds new. —*MM AKA:* Vampyr, Ou l'Etrange Aventure de David Gray; Vampyr, Der Traum des David Gray; Not against the Flesh; Castle of Doom; The Strange Adventure of David Gray; The Vampire.
Movie: 🎜🎜🎜🎜 *DVD:* 🎜🎜🎜
Image Entertainment (Cat #ID4308DSDVD, UPC #014381430820). Full frame. Dolby Digital Mono. $24.99. Snapper. *LANG:* German. *SUB:* English. *FEATURES:* 19 chapter links ● Ladislas Starewicz's 1934 short stop-motion animated film "The Mascot."
1931 75m/B *GE FR* Julian West, Sybille Schmitz, Henriette Gerard, Maurice Schutz, Rena Mandel, Jan Hieronimko, Albert Bras; *D:* Carl Theodor Dreyer; *W:* Carl Theodor Dreyer, Christen Jul; *C:* Rudolph Mate, Louis Nee; *M:* Wolfgang Zeller.

The Van

A recent high school graduate passes on college so he can spend more time picking up girls in his van. Typical early '70s drive-in teen sex comedy. *AKA:* Chevy Van.
Movie: 🎜🎜▶ *DVD:* NYR
Rhino Home Video (Cat #5736). $14.95. Snapper.
1977 (R) 92m/C Stuart Getz, Deborah White, Danny DeVito, Harry Moses, Maurice Barkin; *D:* Sam Grossman; *W:* Robert J. Rosenthal, Celia Susan Cotelo; *C:* Irv Goodnoff; *M:* Steve Eaton.

The Vanishing

A young couple, Rex (Bervoets) and Saskia (Ter Steege), are on their way to a vacation in France. After a curious quarrel, she disappears. Also involved is a middle-class family man, Raymond Lemorne (Donnadieu). That's all anyone should know about the plot. Director Sluizer lets events unfold at their own pace, using completely ordinary settings and situations to study the nature of evil. Though his film shares some thematic similarities with *Silence of the Lambs*, it's working on an entirely different, more subtle and frightening level. Without showing a single drop of blood or overt physical violence, this one will scare you in a way that movies almost never attempt, much less succeed at. It's an unsettling experience that you'll find yourself remembering at odd moments. And when you do, you'll feel a deep chill. Sluizer remade the film in English in 1993. On DVD, the only noticeable flaw is a slight graininess in the night scenes, but when those occur, the full dimensions of Sluizer's horror are just being revealed and it's unimportant. One of the best. —*MM AKA:* Spoorloos.
Movie: 🎜🎜🎜▶ *DVD:* 🎜🎜🎜

Image Entertainment (Cat #ID4264FLDVD, UPC #014381426427). Full frame. Dolby Digital Mono. $24.99. Snapper. *LANG:* French; Dutch. *SUB:* English. *FEATURES:* 15 chapter links.
1988 107m/C *NL FR* Barnard Pierre Donnadieu, Johanna Ter Steege, Gene Bervoets, Gwen Eckhaus, Bernadette Le Sache, Tania Latarjet, Lucille Glenn, Roger Souza; *D:* George Sluizer; *W:* George Sluizer, Tim Krabbe; *C:* Toni Kuhn; *M:* Henny Vrienten.

Varsity Blues

After star quarterback Lance (Walker) goes down with an injury, uncertain backup Mox (Van Der Beek) learns the perks of stardom in the small football-obsessed town of West Canaan, TX. It's not all free six-packs and groupies with whipped cream bikinis, however. He butts heads with blood-and-guts coach Kilmer (Voight, at his nasty best), whose win-at-all-costs philosophy is hurting his players. Mox leads a players' rebellion. At its best, the film zips along at a music video pace with the same stylized look—it was partially produced by MTV—but that will put off as many viewers as it attracts. On DVD, both image and sound are fine, though nothing really special. —*MM*
Movie: 🎜🎜▶ *DVD:* 🎜🎜🎜
Paramount Home Video (Cat #336437, UPC #097363364375). Widescreen anamorphic. Dolby Digital 5.1 Surround Stereo; Dolby Surround Stereo. $29.99. Keepcase. *LANG:* English; French. *FEATURES:* Theatrical trailer ● 20 chapter links.
1998 (R) 103m/C James Van Der Beek, Jon Voight, Paul Walker, Ron Lester, Scott Caan, Richard Lineback, Amy Smart, Thomas F. Duffy, Tony Perenski, Tiffany C. Love, Eliel Swinton, Jill Parker Jones, Joe Pichler, Ali Larter; *D:* Brian Robbins; *W:* W. Peter Iliff; *C:* Charles Cohen; *M:* Mark Isham. *AWARDS:* MTV Movie Awards '99: Breakthrough Performance (Van Der Beek); *NOM:* MTV Movie Awards '99: Best Song ("Nice Guys Finish Last").

Vegas Vacation

It may not have come out under the "National Lampoon" banner but you'll recognize both the characters and the situations. The innocent Griswold clan head from their Chicago home to the bright lights and gambling temptations of Las Vegas. Clark (Chase) blows all their money, Ellen (D'Angelo) reveals a hidden passion for Wayne Newton, daughter Audrey (Nichols) decides to become a go-go dancer, and son Rusty (Embry) turns into a high roller who draws the attention of the mob. Oh yeah, dimwit cousin Eddie (Quaid) also tries to supply a few yucks. On the DVD the neon colors of the film bleed a little against dark backgrounds but are overall vibrant and accurate. The image is a little soft, a symptom of many full-frame DVD transfers. The blacks look good when they have something bright to play off of, but become grainy and a little gray-green in an overall dark scene. It would have been nice had the 5.1 mix delivered a little more ambience, especially in the casino scenes, but the sound is overall energetic and crisp. —JO

Movie: 🎬 **DVD:** 🎬🎬▶
Warner Home Video, Inc. (Cat #14906, UPC #085391490623). Full frame. Dolby Digital 5.1. $24.98. Snapper. *LANG:* English; French. *SUB:* English; French; Spanish. *CAP:* English. *FEATURES:* 32 chapter links • Theatrical trailer.
1996 (PG) 98m/C Chevy Chase, Beverly D'Angelo, Randy Quaid, Ethan (Randall) Embry, Miriam Flynn, Marisol Nichols, Shae D'Lyn, Wallace Shawn, Wayne Newton; *Cameos:* Sid Caesar, Julia Sweeney, Christie Brinkley; *D:* Stephen Kessler; *W:* Elisa Bell; *C:* William A. Fraker; *M:* Joel McNeely.

Velvet Goldmine

Director Haynes takes on the excesses of the '70s British glam-rock with cinematic techniques from the '60s. In 1984 journalist Arthur Stuart (Bale) is assigned to write a "whatever happened to" article on the ten-year disappearance of allegedly assassinated superstar Brian Slade (Rhys Myers doing a fine David Bowie). He is led to Slade's viperish ex-wife (Collette) and ex-manager (Izzard). The key, though, is the relationship between Slade and fellow pop idol Curt Wild (McGregor channelling Iggy Pop). The story might be average but the visuals are spectacular and the DVD captures them flawlessly. The experimental techniques are re-created in eye-popping colors and inventive cutting. Beyond the score, the sound is excellent. Use headphones if possible and crank up the volume. —MM

Movie: 🎬🎬▶ **DVD:** 🎬🎬🎬
Miramax Pictures Home Video (Cat #17096, UPC #717951002105). Widescreen (1.85:1) letterboxed. Dolby Digital 5.1 Surround Stereo. $29.99. Keepcase. *LANG:* English. *CAP:* English. *FEATURES:* 30 chapter links • Theatrical trailer.
1998 (R) 120m/C *GB* Ewan McGregor, Jonathan Rhys Meyers, Christian Bale, Toni Collette, Eddie Izzard, Emily Woof, Michael Feast; *D:* Todd Haynes; *W:* Todd Haynes; *C:* Maryse Alberti; *M:* Carter Burwell. *AWARDS:* British Academy Awards '98: Best Costume Design; Independent Spirit Awards '99: Best Cinematography; *NOM:* Academy Awards '98: Best Costume Design; Independent Spirit Awards '99: Best Director (Haynes), Best Film.

The Vengeance of She

The main attraction of this sequel is the star's uncanny resemblance to Ursula Andress, who played the same role in the original. Both in looks and the near-complete blankness of expression, Olinka Berova is a dead ringer for the more famous sex symbol. The film itself is a rather modest undertaking about a young woman who is being psychically drawn

from her home in Europe to the African desert by a priest (Godfrey) of an ancient sect that worships "She Who Must Be Obeyed." Despite a '60s setting and a script by Peter O'Donnell, creator of *Modesty Blaise*, this one is slow, stilted, and too obviously trying to make the most of a tiny budget. Even so, it looks terrific. On DVD, the image has the crystalline clarity that Anchor Bay gives to all of the Hammer productions. The film itself is on one side of the disc; the extras are on the other. Best line of dialogue: "Eternal life is not a fate I desire. It is a burden I will humbly accept as my duty to all mankind." —MM *AKA:* The Return of She.

Movie: 🎬🎬 **DVD:** 🎬🎬🎬
Anchor Bay (Cat #DV10687, UPC #013131068795). Widescreen (1.66:1) letterboxed. Dolby Digital Mono. $29.98. Keepcase. *LANG:* English. *FEATURES:* 25 chapter links • Theatrical trailer • TV spots • *World of Hammer* episode "Lands Before Time."
1968 101m/C *GB* Olinka (Schoberova) Berova, John Richardson, Derek Godfrey, Edward Judd, Colin Blakely; *D:* Cliff Owen; *W:* Peter O'Donnell; *C:* Peter Suschitzsky; *M:* Mario Nascimbene.

Vengeance Valley

Lancaster and Walker are foster brothers with Walker being an envious weasel who always expects Lancaster to get him out of scrapes. Lancaster is even accused of a crime committed by Walker and must clear himself. Good cast is let down by uneven direction.

Movie: 🎬🎬 **DVD:** NYR
Roan Group (Cat #2016). Full frame. $19.95. Keepcase.
1951 83m/C Burt Lancaster, Joanne Dru, Robert Walker, Sally Forrest, John Ireland, Hugh O'Brian; *D:* Richard Thorpe; *W:* Irving Ravetch; *C:* George J. Folsey; *M:* Rudolph Kopp.

The Venus Wars

The story of war between human colonists on the planet Venus borrows from some of the juvenile work of famous sci-fi writer Robert Heinlein. The telling owes just as much to video games with frequent futuristic motorcycle races and chases. The characters are familiar—Hiro, the hotshot rider; Susan, the plucky reporter from Earth; Gen. Donner, the dictator. The animation makes Venus strongly reminiscent of Iraq and so the brown, earthy colors have a muted look. The action scenes are not as detailed or as kinetic as the best anime, *Akira* for example, but nobody's going to get bored. The character profiles are scenes from the film, not additions or background information. —MM

Movie: 🎬🎬▶ **DVD:** 🎬🎬🎬
Central Park Media/U.S. Manga Corps (Cat #USMD 1743, UPC #719987174320). Widescreen (1.85:1) letterboxed. Dolby Digital Stereo. $29.95. Keepcase. *LANG:* English; Japanese. *SUB:* English. *FEATURES:* 28 chapter links • Previews.

1989 104m/C *JP D:* Yoshikazu Yasuhiko; *W:* Yoshikazu Yasuhiko, Yuichi Sasamoto; *C:* Yoshiyuki Tamagawa.

Vertigo (CE)

Hitchcock's romantic story of obsession, manipulation, and fear. Stewart plays a detective forced to retire after his fear of heights causes the death of a policeman and, perhaps, the death of a woman he'd been hired to follow. The appearance of her double (Novak), whom he compulsively transforms into the dead girl's image, leads to a mesmerizing cycle of madness and lies. With the opening credits printed over swirling color animations and the red-tinted close-up of Novak's eye, this DVD is put to an immediate test and passes it very nicely: no artifacts, crisp colors with very little bleed, and no noticeable grain. Once into the film, the picture appears a little sharper than the remastered laserdisc and the feeling of depth given to almost every scene by Hitch's composure is retained throughout. It's great to hear the 5.1 soundtrack with the dynamic range and imaging, allowing Hermann's magnificent score to affect the film more than ever. Both the audio commentary and the included documentary *Obsessed with Vertigo* give new insight into the film-restoration process, as well as its necessity. —JO

Movie: 🎬🎬🎬🎬 **DVD:** 🎬🎬🎬▶
Universal Studios Home Video (Cat #20183, UPC #025192025129). Widescreen (1.85:1) letterboxed. Dolby Digital 5.1; Mono. $34.98. Keepcase. *LANG:* English (DD5.1); French; Spanish. *SUB:* French; Spanish. *CAP:* English. *FEATURES:* Dual-layered RSDL • 35 chapter links • Theatrical trailer • Documentary • Commentary: Herbert Coleman, Robert A. Harris, James C. Katz • Cast and filmmaker bios • Production notes • Film highlights.
1958 (PG) 126m/C James Stewart, Kim Novak, Barbara Bel Geddes, Tom Helmore, Ellen Corby, Henry Jones, Raymond Bailey, Lee Patrick; *D:* Alfred Hitchcock; *W:* Sam Taylor; *C:* Robert Burks; *M:* Bernard Herrmann. *AWARDS:* American Film Institute (AFI) '98: Top 100, National Film Registry '89; *NOM:* Academy Awards '58: Best Art Direction/Set Decoration, Best Sound.

Very Bad Things

A drug- and booze-fueled Las Vegas bachelor party goes seriously wrong and becomes a murderous blood bath. Kyle (Favreau), the groom-to-be, has flown the coop from his control-freak fiancee (Diaz), and turns things over to his unscrupulous friend Boyd (Slater) after disaster strikes. As the guys and their pals try to cover up their crimes, each step leads to a nastier complication. The result is a guilty pleasure, which I am genuinely ashamed to admit that I enjoyed. (But I did.) On DVD, the image is even sharper than it was in theatres, and the craziness of Berg's story is somehow even more wicked on the small screen. Sound is fine. Of the two ver-

sions, the full-frame is recommended for fans of the cast, who will want the sweaty close-ups as large as possible. —*MM*
Movie: 🎵🎵🎵 **DVD:** 🎵🎵🎵
USA Home Entertainment (Cat #440 058 277-2, UPC #044005827729). Widescreen (1.85:1) anamorphic; full frame. Dolby Digital 5.1 Surround Stereo; Dolby Digital Surround Stereo. $19.95. Keepcase. *LANG:* English; French. *CAP:* English. *FEATURES:* 18 chapter links ▪ Theatrical trailer ▪ Cast and crew thumbnail biographies.
1998 (R) 100m/C Jon Favreau, Christian Slater, Cameron Diaz, Jeremy Piven, Daniel Stern, Leland Orser, Jeanne Tripplehorn, Joey Zimmerman; *D:* Peter Berg; *W:* Peter Berg; *C:* David Hennings; *M:* Stewart Copeland.

A Very Natural Thing

For once, a 25th anniversary edition DVD actually marks an important date! A true first of its kind in American commercial film distribution, this touching and funny story is by and about uncloseted gay men experiencing sincere, nurturing relationships. Its dialogue is part manifesto, part demographics study, and part pillow talk. Mark (Gareth) and Jason (White) lock eyes across the proverbial crowded room at a New York party. Then they groove on the dance floor like proverbial suburban nerds! No good old-fashioned romance is complete without firelight, plaintive string music (by Barber, Telemann, and Orff), and philosophical strolls in the park. Mark is bisexual, though, and not monogamous, so Jason must gather his thoughts during that year's Gay Pride Parade. The grainy image on the box cover reproduces the final pre-credit freeze frame in the film. That gives you an idea of what's in store, possibly a 16mm source, or 16 blown up to 35mm. The image often looks as if projected onto a sheet of fabric, especially dim sequences, though some well-lit surfaces stand out nicely. Mono sound, often done on location with hand-held mikes, relegates itself to the center speaker. New, computer-generated text buzzes, but the Technicolor film is not like that at all. Scene entry points have cute names like "Wrestling Before Marriage" and "Say Cheese, I Love You." —*JK*
Movie: 🎵🎵🎵 **DVD:** 🎵🎵🎵
Water Bearer Films (Cat #WBF4000, UPC #759259140004). Full frame. Mono. $29.95. Keepcase. *LANG:* English. *FEATURES:* 9 chapter links ▪ Interactive menus ▪ 4-color picture disc.
1973 85m/C Robert Joel, Curt Gareth, Bo White; *D:* Christopher Larkin; *W:* Christopher Larkin, Joseph Coencas; *C:* C.H. Douglass; *M:* Gordon Gottlieb, Bert Lucarelli.

The Very Thought of You

"I want to talk about love, friendship, and deceit." That's what Laurence (Fiennes) tells his psychiatrist neighbor to explain how his life has been turned upside down

in three days. That's the space of time since Martha (Potter) arrived in London and Laurence and his two childhood friends Frank (Sewell) and Daniel (Hollander) all fell in love with her. It's obvious from the opening frame that the filmmakers were aiming at the effervescence of *Four Weddings and a Funeral* but they didn't quite get it. One reason is the absolutely uncanny Julia Roberts impersonation that Ms. Potter carries off. The DVD is first-rate in image and sound with no flaws worth mentioning. No extras either. —*MM* **AKA:** *Martha, Meet Frank, Daniel and Laurence.*
Movie: 🎵🎵 **DVD:** 🎵🎵🎵
Miramax Pictures Home Video (Cat #18328, UPC #717951005144). Widescreen (1.85:1) anamorphic. Dolby Digital Stereo. $29.99. Keepcase. *LANG:* English. *FEATURES:* 12 chapter links.
1998 (PG-13) 88m/C *GB* Monica Potter, Rufus Sewell, Joseph Fiennes, Tom Hollander, Ray Winstone; *D:* Nick Hamm; *W:* Peter Morgan; *C:* David Johnson; *M:* Ed Shearmur.

Victim of Love

A therapist doesn't know what to believe when she learns that she and one of her more neurotic patients are sharing the same boyfriend. Only the patient claims the man murdered his wife-to-be with his lover. Who will be the next victim? Made for television.
Movie: 🎵🎵 **DVD:** NYR
Studio Home Entertainment (Cat #4015). $24.95. Keepcase. *FEATURES:* Cast and crew thumbnail bios ▪ Trailer.
1991 (PG-13) 92m/C Pierce Brosnan, JoBeth Williams, Virginia Madsen, Georgia Brown; *D:* Jerry London, James Desmarais; *C:* Billy Dickson; *M:* Richard Stone.

Victory

Soccer match between WWII American prisoners of war and a German team is set up so that the players can escape through the sewer tunnels of Paris. Of course, they want to finish the game first. Not particularly believable as either a soccer flick (even with Pele and other soccer stars) or a great escape, but watchable. The image on the DVD is very sharp, with very little grain or artifacts. Colors are excellent, with good detail, and are accurate to the theatre. There is a little very minor bleed on some of the earthtones. Blacks are mostly true. Contrast and brightness remain consistent and comfortable. The Dolby Surround is unspectacular, but does the job; in fact, the music sounds quite good and the dialogue is crisp. —*JO*
Movie: 🎵🎵 **DVD:** 🎵🎵🎵
Warner Home Video, Inc. (Cat #708, UPC #012569070820). Widescreen (2.35:1). Dolby Surround; Mono. $24.98. Snapper. *LANG:* English (DS); French (mono). *SUB:* English; Spanish; French. *CAP:* English.

FEATURES: 31 chapter links ▪ Theatrical trailer ▪ Production notes.
1981 (PG) 116m/C Sylvester Stallone, Michael Caine, Max von Sydow, Pele, Carole Laure, Bobby Moore, Daniel Massey; *D:* John Huston; *W:* Jeff Maguire, Djordje Milicevic; *C:* Gerry Fisher; *M:* Bill Conti.

Videodrome

Woods is a cable TV programmer with a secret yen for sex and violence, which he satisfies by watching a pirated TV show. *Videodrome* appears to show actual torture and murder, and also seems to control the thoughts of its viewers—turning them into human VCRs. The film's hallucinatory feel has been much imitated since. Cronenberg would not direct another one of his original concepts until *eXistenZ* 17 years later. All hail the special effects by Rick Baker. The DVD finally gives *Videodrome* the treatment it deserves. Sharpness is very good and the grain found on earlier releases (including the laserdisc) is all but gone. Colors are accurate and the powerful ending aboard the rusted ship has never looked better, or felt so emotionally draining. The sound is also markedly improved but still lacks fidelity, with the most likely culprit being the source material. Still, it's great to see. Long live the new flesh! —*JO*
Movie: 🎵🎵🎵 **DVD:** 🎵🎵🎵
Universal Studios Home Video (Cat #20387, UPC #025192038723). Widescreen (1.85:1) letterboxed. Dolby Digital Mono. $24.98. Keepcase. *LANG:* English; French. *SUB:* French; Spanish. *CAP:* English. *FFATURES:* 16 chapter links ▪ Theatrical trailer ▪ Cast and filmmakers bios ▪ Production notes ▪ Film highlights.
1983 87m/C *CA* James Woods, Deborah Harry, Sonja Smits, Peter Dvorsky; *D:* David Cronenberg; *W:* David Cronenberg; *C:* Mark Irwin; *M:* Howard Shore. *AWARDS:* Genie Awards '84: Best Director (Cronenberg).

Vigilante

Heavy-handed urban revenge flick is based on the *Death Wish* formula, but is cut from the same low-budget cloth as *Exterminator*, made a few years before. Forster is the blue-collar householder who, after his wife is attacked by psychotic thugs, joins Williamson in cleaning up the mean streets of New York. There's not much DVD can do to smooth the rough edges of this shot-on-location work. Image is exceptionally grainy and the echoing natural sounds lack crispness and definition. The disc's best feature is the commentary track featuring the director and cast members. —*MM* **AKA:** *Street Gang.*
Movie: 🎵🎵 **DVD:** 🎵🎵
Anchor Bay (Cat #DV10493, UPC #013131 049398). Widescreen (2.35:1) letterboxed. Dolby Digital 5.1 Surround Stereo; Dolby Digital Surround Stereo. $24.98. Keepcase. *LANG:* English; French. *FEATURES:* 11 chapter links ▪ 4 theatrical trailers ▪

TV commercials ▪ Stills gallery ▪ Commentary: Lustig, Forster, Williamson, Pesce. **1983 91m/C** Robert Forster, Fred Williamson, Carol Lynley, Rutanya Alda, Richard Bright, Woody Strode, Donald Blakely, Joseph Carberry, Joe Spinell, Frank Pesce; **D:** William Lustig; **W:** Richard Vetere; **C:** James Lemmo; **M:** Jay Chattaway.

The Viking Queen

Lively historical hokum manages to overcome a less-than-lavish budget. In Roman-ruled Britain Salina (Carita), a Druid, takes over after her father dies, and falls for Justinian (Murray), the humane representative of Rome. But the evil Octavian (Kier) has a plan to take over and mass rebellion ensues with raping, pillaging, and tree worship. It's not exactly *Spartacus* or *Braveheart* but the intention is the same with a cast of hundreds, not thousands. The DVD looks fine, even in the "big" battle scenes, though the production lacks the polish of the best Hammer films. The film is on one side of the two-sided disc; the extras are on the other. —*MM*
Movie: 🦴🦴▸ **DVD:** 🦴🦴🦴
Anchor Bay (Cat #DV10688, UPC #013131068894). Widescreen (1.85:1) letterboxed. Dolby Digital Mono. $29.98. Keepcase. *LANG:* English. *FEATURES:* 20 chapter links ▪ Theatrical trailer ▪ *World of Hammer* episode "Lands Before Time."
1967 91m/C *GB* Carita, Don Murray, Andrew Keir, Donald Houston, Adrienne Corri, Niall MacGinnis, Nicola Pagett, Patrick Troughton; **D:** Don Chaffey; **W:** Clarke Reynolds; **C:** Stephen Dade; **M:** Gary Hughes.

Village of Dreams

Middle-aged twin brothers Yukihiko and Seizo (Keigo and Shogo Matsuyama) remember their pastoral childhood in a village in the Kochi Prefecture, 1948. As mischievous eight-year-olds, the two spend their time playing pranks, spying on neighbors, painting, and entertaining themselves in the woods and streams. Based on the memoir *The Village of My Paintings* by Seizo Tashima, the film is similar to Fellini's *Amarcord* in its nostalgic treatment of the subject. Since the picture was made largely on location, the DVD lacks sharp focus. Stories told from memory don't need it, anyway. The sound is excellent, particularly in its treatment of the excellent score by the Catherina Early Music Consort. —*MM*
Movie: 🦴🦴▸ **DVD:** 🦴🦴▸
Image Entertainment (Cat #ID5934MLSD-VD, UPC #014381593426). Widescreen (1.85:1) letterboxed. Dolby Digital Stereo. $24.99. Snapper. *LANG:* Japanese. *SUB:* English. *FEATURES:* 22 chapter links.
1997 112m/C *JP* Keigo Matsuyama, Shogo Matsuyama; **D:** Yoichi Higashi; **W:** Takehiro Nakajima, Yoichi Higashi; **C:** Yoshio Shimizu.

Village of the Damned

The plot—long familiar to sf fans—involves the isolated village of Midwich, located here on the scenic California coast. An unexplained force causes all of the inhabitants to pass out for several hours. When they awaken, several of the women are pregnant. Neither the local doctor (Reeve) nor the government scientist (Alley) who drops by knows what to make of the phenomenon. Years later, the babies grow to be little kids with silvery wigs and psychic powers. In this telling, the characters have no personalities, the dialogue is sloppy and stilted, the plot comes to a slapdash conclusion, and the effects are pedestrian. Curiously, though, the DVD image is clear and crisp. The sound is equally good, but that is not a recommendation. —*MM*
Movie: 🦴 **DVD:** 🦴🦴▸
Universal Studios Home Video (Cat #20444, UPC #025192044427). Widescreen (2.35:1) letterboxed. Dolby Digital 5.1 Surround Stereo; Dolby Surround Stereo. $24.98. Keepcase. *LANG:* English; French. *SUB:* Spanish. *CAP:* English. *FEATURES:* 18 chapter links ▪ Production notes ▪ Cast and crew thumbnail biographies ▪ Theatrical trailer ▪ Universal web links.
1995 (R) 98m/C Christopher Reeve, Kirstie Alley, Linda Kozlowski, Mark Hamill, Meredith Salenger, Michael Pare, Peter Jason, Constance Forslund, Karen Kahn; **D:** John Carpenter; **W:** John Carpenter, David Himmelstein; **C:** Gary B. Kibbe; **M:** John Carpenter, Dave Davies.

Violent Zone

Mercenaries go on a supposed rescue mission in the wilderness.
Movie: 🦴 **DVD:** NYR
Digital Versatile Disc Ltd. (Cat #112). Full frame. $19.95. Keepcase. *FEATURES:* Trailer.
1989 92m/C John Douglas, Chad Hayward, Christopher Weeks; **D:** John Garwood; **W:** David Pritchard, John Bushelman.

Virasat

Thakur (Puri) and his son Shakti (Kapoor) are at odds now that the boy is an educated man. He has returned to his native village, with his coed girlfriend (Bartra) in tow. They have imagined marrying in the family temple, though it has been chained shut for years. Thakur has plans for Shakti to take his place in the family dynasty, quell village riots, and defend against a rival clan. Shakti can only see his hometown as backwards and uncivilized, but a tough choice must be made in the face of escalating violence. As in the best gangster genre films, the characters' blind personal convictions display a sort of warped, near-mythic heroism. The hit-spawning, hard-rocking score and award-winning choreography never throw the unexpectedly sophisticated drama out of sync, though bouts of sadistic humor sometimes do. Even the brooding, dark interiors come off well. The sometimes booming overdubs, required by the location shoots, never seem too hollow or muffled. —*JK* **AKA:** The Dynasty.
Movie: 🦴🦴🦴🦴 **DVD:** 🦴🦴🦴🦴
Video Sound (Cat #SDM98-DVD103). Widescreen. Dolby Digital AC-3 Surround Sound 5.1. $29.95. Keepcase. *LANG:* Hindi. *SUB:* English; Chinese; Japanese. *FEATURES:* 24 chapter links including 6 songs ▪ Animated interactive menus ▪ Autoqueue songs to play as an uninterrupted sequence ▪ Star bios and filmographies ▪ Coming attractions trailers. All regions coding.
1997 168m/C *IN* Anil Kapoor, Tabu, Pooja Bartra, Amrish Puri; **D:** Priyadarshan; **M:** Anu Malik.

Virtual Combat

In the near future, Las Vegas turns away from its "family friendly" image to promote full-body cybersex and cyberfighting martial arts matches, in which average men and women fulfill their various fantasies with the partners or enemies of their choice. Of course, a scientist (the venerable Turhan Bey!) takes the next step and brings the lovely Lana (Massey) and the nasty Dante (Michael Bernardo) from virtual reality to everyday reality. It's up to Gridrunner (groan) cop Quarry (Wilson) to bring them back. It's all every bit as derivative as it sounds. But director Andrew Stevens is a practiced hand at this material. Many of the effects are accomplished through colored lights and lasers, and they make the transition to DVD effectively. Overall, this video premiere looks much better on disc than many more expensive action flicks. —*MM*
Movie: 🦴🦴🦴 **DVD:** 🦴🦴🦴
Image Entertainment (Cat #ID5771UM DVD, UPC #014381577129). Full frame. Dolby Digital 4.0 Surround. $24.99. Snapper. *LANG:* English. *FEATURES:* 14 chapter links.
1995 (R) 97m/C Don "The Dragon" Wilson, Athena Massey, Loren Avedon, Kenneth McLeod, Turhan Bey, Stella Stevens, Michael Bernardo; **D:** Andrew Stevens; **W:** William Martell; **C:** David J. Miller; **M:** Claude Gaudette.

Virtual Desire

After his wife is murdered, Brad (Meyer) admits that he has been having a series of affairs initiated over the Internet. It's typical and undistinguished soft-core fluff. The substandard image is so rough and grainy that the no-frills DVD is virtually identical to VHS tape. —*MM*
Movie: 🦴 **DVD:** 🦴
Image Entertainment (Cat #ID5603FMDVD, UPC #014381563023). Full frame. Dolby Digital Stereo. $24.99. Keepcase. *LANG:* English. *FEATURES:* 12 chapter links.
1995 (R) 92m/C Michael Meyer, Julie Strain, Gail Harris; **D:** Noble Henri.

Virtuosity

Fast-paced, violent sf action flick is well acted with intelligence and dark humor laced throughout. Director Leonard builds on some of the same gimmicks he used in his first film, *Lawnmower Man*, to tell a much more interesting and well-constructed story. Stars Denzel Washington, as Peter Barnes, the cop with a tragic past and Russell Crowe, as Sid 6.7 the computer-generated killer who's responsible for said tragic past, are better than the excellent effects. The DVD image is fine but it's really only a slight improvement over VHS tape. —*MM*

Movie: 🎬🎬▸ **DVD:** 🎬🎬▸
Paramount Home Video (Cat #331447, UPC #097363314479). Widescreen anamorphic. Dolby Digital 5.1 Surround Stereo; Dolby Digital Surround Stereo. $29.99. Keepcase. *LANG:* English; French. *FEATURES:* 20 chapter links ▪ Theatrical trailer.
1995 (R) 105m/C Denzel Washington, Russell Crowe, Kelly Lynch, Stephen Spinella, William Forsythe, Louise Fletcher, William Fichtner, Costas Mandylor, Kevin J. O'Connor; *D:* Brett Leonard; *W:* Eric Bernt; *C:* Gale Tattersall; *M:* Christopher Young.

Virus

During a hurricane, the crew of a tugboat takes refuge on a Russian research ship only to find that the crew has been wiped out by an electric alien from outer space. This comic book–based story borrows elements from dozens of sci-fi/horror films, most obviously TV's *The X-Files* and *Alien*, but doesn't improve on the best of them. A veteran cast does acceptable work with the well-worn material, and the DVD looks fine, showing off the mechanical effects to their best advantage. On the commentary track, director John Bruno and cast member Marshall Bell talk mostly about technical problems, locations, sets, and staging. They're good-natured and do not try to make the film out to be anything more than it is. —*MM*

Movie: 🎬🎬 **DVD:** 🎬🎬🎬
Universal Studios Home Video (Cat #20431, UPC #025192043123). Widescreen (2.35:1) letterboxed. Dolby Digital 5.1 Surround Stereo; Dolby Surround Stereo. $29.98. Keepcase. *LANG:* English; French. *CAP:* English. *FEATURES:* 18 chapter links ▪ 2 "making of" featurettes ▪ 3 deleted scenes ▪ Commentary: director John Bruno and actor Marshall Bell ▪ Cast and crew thumbnail biographies ▪ Theatrical trailer ▪ Universal web links.
1998 (R) 100m/C Jamie Lee Curtis, William Baldwin, Donald Sutherland, Joanna Pacula, Sherman Augustus, Clifford Curtis, Marshall Bell, Julio Mechoso, Yuri Chervotkin, Keith Flippen; *D:* John Bruno; *W:* Chuck Pfarrer, Dennis Feldman; *C:* David Eggby; *M:* Joel McNeely.

Vision Quest

A high school student wants to win the Washington State wrestling championship and the affections of a beautiful older artist. He gives it his all as he trains for the meet and goes after his "visionquest." A winning performance by Modine raises this above the usual teen coming-of-age movie. Madonna sings "Crazy for You" in a nightclub. The DVD image is average with only moderate sharpness and colors that seem deep enough but so-so contrast and brightness levels prevent them from being called vibrant. Nothing special has been done to the Dolby Surround sound, but it delivers the soundtrack in a clear, if uninspired, manner. —*JO AKA:* Crazy for You.

Movie: 🎬🎬▸ **DVD:** 🎬🎬
Warner Home Video, Inc. (Cat #11459, UPC #085391145929). Full frame. Dolby Surround. $14.98. Snapper. *LANG:* English. *CAP:* English. *FEATURES:* 31 chapter links.
1985 (R) 107m/C Matthew Modine, Linda Fiorentino, Ronny Cox, Roberts Blossom, Daphne Zuniga, Charles Hallahan, Michael Schoeffling; *D:* Harold Becker; *W:* Darryl Ponicsan; *C:* Owen Roizman; *M:* Tangerine Dream; *Performed by:* Madonna.

Visions of Light: The Art of Cinematography

Excellent documentary examines the rarely discussed contribution of photographers to feature films. Scenes from 125 films—from *Birth of a Nation* to *GoodFellas*—are shown with commentary from a number of cinematographers including Gordon Willis, Ernest Dickerson, William A. Fraker, Conrad Hall, Vilmos Zsigmond, and Michael Chapman. They reveal how they achieved certain effects and their collaborative efforts with directors and actors. As a group, they're articulate and they can discuss their work much more effectively than many filmmakers who are household names. Of course, the quality of the image varies with the clips, but the general level is exceptionally high. Required viewing. —*MM*

Movie: 🎬🎬🎬🎬 **DVD:** 🎬🎬🎬▸
Image Entertainment (Cat #ID9175CUDVD, UPC #014381917529). Widescreen letterboxed; full frame. Dolby Digital Mono. $24.99. Keepcase. *LANG:* English. *FEATURES:* 30 chapter links.
1993 95m/C *D:* Arnold Glassman, Stuart Samuels, Todd McCarthy; *W:* Todd McCarthy; *C:* Nancy Schreiber. *AWARDS:* New York Film Critics Awards '93: Best Feature Documentary; National Society of Film Critics Awards '93: Best Feature Documentary.

Vive l'Amour

Yang Kuei-Mei and Chen Chao-Jung, an acting team popularized by the hit *Eat Drink Man Woman*, here play real estate agent May and Ah-jong, a street merchant. They meet up in a vacant Taipei apartment for trysts, but sometimes they are both there, each thinking he and she is alone! Another layer of complexity is added by an unnamed gay man (Lee Kang-Sheng), whose suicide attempt is interrupted by Ah-jong. Their extremely obtuse, hardly consummated menage-a-trois shows how secondary drama is to filmmaker Tsai Ming-Liang. The director-cowriter seems more absorbed by the intellectual appeal of traffic patterns and architectural space. People, no matter how erotic their activities, are often so dimly or back lit their faces are obscured. The minimalist sound means they spend more time eating (or just playing with their food) than talking. Even when they talk, it's generally on the phone. The film is not humorless but it is too often drearily slow or hesitant. The DVD's technical quality seems slipshod even while that may not be the result of carelessness. —*JK AKA:* Aiqing Wansui.

Movie: 🎬🎬 **DVD:** 🎬🎬
Fox/Lorber Home Video (Cat #FLV5016, UPC #720917501628). Widescreen. Dual-channel Mono. $29.99. Keepcase. *LANG:* Mandarin Chinese. *SUB:* English. *FEATURES:* 5 chapter links ▪ Interactive menus ▪ Filmographies ▪ Production credits.
1994 118m/C *TW* Yang Guimei, Chen Zhaorong, Li Kangsheng; *D:* Tsai Ming-Liang; *W:* Tsai Ming-Liang; *C:* Pen-jung Lioa, Ming-kuo Lin.

Volcano

L.A. has already had to deal with earthquakes, mudslides, raging fires, riots, and the acting career of Anna Nicole Smith. Now it's completely roasted by millions of gallons of molten lava. This overblown *Rescue 911* has Mike Roark (Jones), the standard take-charge guy, trying to avert total destruction while being assisted by the brainy-but-beautiful seismologist Dr. Amy Barnes (Heche). Many tongue-in-cheek jokes about the general state of chaos in L.A. even on the best of days; but aside from these, the dialogue is cheesy beyond belief. The special effects are very impressive, however. Wilshire Blvd. was actually re-created on a 17-acre set (believed to be the biggest ever) to meet its fiery doom. The DVD is spectacular in its delivery of both sound and visuals. When things start to erupt, the Surround puts you right in the center as hellfire rains down upon you. The 5.1 sound is also very full-bodied and the bass is energetically delivered with power to spare. High end is crisp and clear. The picture is very sharp, with nothing in the way of artifacts or grain, despite the fact that most scenes take place at night. The colors are also superb; very vibrant, and accurate. Blacks are dead-on and the contrast is consistently punchy while brightness levels remain comfortable. —*JO*

Movie: 🎬🎬 **DVD:** 🎬🎬🎬🎬
20th Century Fox (Cat #4110402, UPC #08616210022). Widescreen (1.85:1) letterboxed. Dolby Digital 5.1; Dolby Surround. $29.95. Keepcase. *LANG:* English (DD5.1; DS); French (DS). *SUB:* English;

Spanish; French. *CAP:* English. *FEATURES:* 23 chapter links ▪ Theatrical trailer.
1997 (PG-13) 120m/C Tommy Lee Jones, Anne Heche, Gaby Hoffman, Don Cheadle, Keith David, John Corbett, Michael Rispoli, John Carroll Lynch, Jacqueline Kim; *D:* Mick Jackson; *W:* Billy Ray, Jerome Armstrong; *C:* Theo van de Sande; *M:* Alan Silvestri.

Voltage Fighters! Gowcaizer: The Movie

In the near post-apocalyptic future, Tokyo has been destroyed by an earthquake. In its place, an island has arisen and Tron City has been built, but the world has not escaped. Teen heroes come to the rescue, sort of. This is mostly standard stuff for Japanese animation: powerful motorcycles, robots, weapons, and sexy babes with a little incest thrown in. The DVD image is a bit better than average for the genre, but not a substantial improvement over VHS tape. —*MM*
Movie: ♫♫ *DVD:* ♫♫
Image Entertainment (Cat #ID4408CTDVD, UPC #014381440829). Full frame. Dolby Digital Stereo. $24.99. Snapper. *LANG:* English; Japanese. *SUB:* English. *FEATURES:* 16 chapter links.
1998 90m/C *D:* Masami Ohbari; *W:* Kengo Asai.

Voodoo

When young Andy (Feldman) transfers to a new college, he decides to join a frat. He could've gone with the local party boys or the computer geeks, but no, Andy innocently opts for the fraternity of the walking dead. Zombie House! Bummer! The chapter prez (Edwards) has a scheme for eternal life. He needs just one more human sacrifice...er, pledge. Director Rene Eram creates a few good atmospheric scenes, but the pace drags too often. O.K. low-budget genre piece looks O.K. on disc. The added clarity of DVD reveals the bluish tint of Feldman's hair under some light. —*MM*
Movie: ♫♫ *DVD:* ♫♫
Simitar Entertainment (Cat #7327, UPC #082551732722). Full frame. PCM Stereo. $14.98. Keepcase. *LANG:* English. *FEATURES:* 8 chapter links ▪ Production factoids ▪ Corey Feldman filmography.
1995 (R) 91m/C Corey Feldman, Sarah Douglas, Jack Nance, Joel J. Edwards; *D:* Rene Eram; *W:* Brian DiMuccio, Dino Vindeni; *C:* Dan Gillham; *M:* Keith Bilderbeck.

Wag the Dog

Over-the-top Hollywood producer (Hoffman) is hired by White House officials to stage a military attack against the U.S. to divert media attention from accusations that the President fondled a Girl Scout. Show biz insiders say Hoffman's Motss resembles one-time studio head Robert Evans; Washington insiders won-

der if it's a documentary. In fact, the entire film is one big insider's joke. Luckily, it's smart enough, and short enough, to avoid becoming tiresome. Look for cameos by Woody Harrelson and Willie Nelson. Based on the Larry Beinhart's book *American Hero* about George Bush and the Gulf War and adapted by Hilary Henkin and David Mamet, the picture was made in a speedy 29 days on a $15 million budget. The film is dialogue driven, so it doesn't matter that much that the DVD totally wastes the Surround tracks in the 5.1 mix. The image is sharp enough and colors are accurate to the theatre. The commentary will be of interest to film fanatics and is chock-full of filmmaking and production information. —*JO*
Movie: ♫♫ *DVD:* ♫♫♫
New Line Home Video (Cat #N4658, UPC #794043465826). Widescreen (1.85:1) letterboxed; full frame. Dolby Digital 5.1. $24.98. Snapper. *LANG:* English; French. *SUB:* English; French. *CAP:* English. *FEATURES:* 22 chapter links ▪ Commentary: Barry Levinson and Dustin Hoffman ▪ "From Washington to Hollywood and Back" featurette ▪ Interviews ▪ "The Line Between Truth and Fiction" essay ▪ Theatrical trailer ▪ Cast and filmmakers bios.
1997 (R) 96m/C Dustin Hoffman, Robert De Niro, Anne Heche, Woody Harrelson, Denis Leary, Willie Nelson, Andrea Martin, Suzanne Cryer, John Michael Higgins, Suzy Plakson, Kirsten Dunst, William H. Macy, Michael Belson; *D:* Barry Levinson; *W:* Hilary Henkin, David Mamet; *C:* Robert Richardson; *M:* Mark Knopfler. *AWARDS:* National Board of Review Awards '97: Best Supporting Actress (Heche); *NOM:* Academy Awards '97: Best Actor (Hoffman), Best Adapted Screenplay; British Academy Awards '98: Best Adapted Screenplay; Golden Globe Awards '98: Best Actor—Musical/Comedy (Hoffman), Best Film—Musical/Comedy, Best Screenplay; Screen Actors Guild Award '97: Best Actor (Hoffman); Writers Guild of America '97: Best Adapted Screenplay.

Wages of Fear

In some ways, Clouzot's thriller is an updated *Treasure of the Sierra Madre,* a story of hard luck characters in a hard luck country who find one last chance. An American oil company offers $2,000 each to four men (Montand, Vanel, Van Eyck, Lulli) if they'll attempt a suicide drive across 300 miles of primitive mountain roads in two trucks loaded with nitroglycerine needed to put out a well fire. The first half sets up the characters and their desolate landscape—both moral and physical. The second is the tense drive. William Friedkin's ambitious 1977 remake, *Sorcerer,* suffers by comparison to Clouzot's suspenseful, harrowing journey. On DVD, Armand Thirard's black-and-white photography is carefully reproduced so that even moving strips of shadow look right. Even so, the original print was less than perfect with many nicks and one tear that was repaired with tape. In some harshly lit

exteriors and in the night driving scenes, blacks bleed and lose all definition. Given the quality of the story and the filmmaking, those criticisms should not be given too much weight. —*MM* *AKA:* Le Salaire de la Peur.
Movie: ♫♫♫ *DVD:* ♫♫♫
Criterion Collection (Cat #36, UPC #037429134924). Full frame (1.33:1). Dolby Digital Mono. $29.95. Keepcase. *LANG:* French; Spanish; Italian; English; German. *SUB:* English. *FEATURES:* 25 chapters ▪ Interactive menu.
1955 138m/B *FR* Yves Montand, Charles Vanel, Peter Van Eyck, Vera Clouzot, Folco Lulli, William Tubbs; *D:* Henri-Georges Clouzot; *W:* Henri-Georges Clouzot; *C:* Armand Thirard; *M:* Georges Auric. *AWARDS:* British Academy Awards '54: Best Film; Cannes Film Festival '53: Best Actor (Vanel), Best Film.

Waking Ned Devine

Old Ned Devine has the winning ticket for the Irish National Lottery—unfortunately, the shock of it has killed him. Jackie O'Shea (Bannen), his initially reluctant wife (Flanagan), and the rest of the inhabitants of Tulaigh Morh on the Isle of Man conspire to fool an innocent lottery official (Dempsey) into believing that Michael O'Sullivan (Kelly) is Devine. The villagers' personal problems further complicate the already tricky situation. As each obstacle to the payoff is dealt with, a larger hurdle appears and the comedy becomes more screwball. Warm and full of blarney, the film never becomes too sweet because a dark mordant streak runs throughout. If the DVD contains any serious flaws, they probably are most apparent during several comic chases, but those involve a naked Kelly on a motorcycle and they're so funny that few viewers are going to pay any attention to the background. The soundtrack highlights the superb music. Too bad a separate track for the score is not provided. Also, judging by the box art, at least one potentially important scene was left on the cutting room floor. No outtakes or deleted scenes are included on the disc. Play this one on a double feature with John Ford's *The Quiet Man.* —*MM*
Movie: ♫♫♫ *DVD:* ♫♫♫
Twentieth Century Fox Home Entertainment (Cat #4110385, UPC #086162103 858). Widescreen (2.35:1) letterboxed. Dolby Digital Surround. $34.98. Keepcase. *LANG:* English. *SUB:* English; Spanish. *CAP:* English. *FEATURES:* 24 chapter links ▪ Theatrical trailer.
1998 (PG) 91m/C Ian Bannen, David Kelly, Fionnula Flanagan, Susan Lynch, James Nesbitt, Maura O'Malley, Robert Hickey, Paddy Ward, James Ryland, Fintan McKeown, Matthew Devitt, Eileen Dromey, Dermot Kerrigan, Brendan F. Dempsey; *D:* Kirk Jones; *W:* Kirk Jones; *C:* Henry Braham; *M:* Shaun Davey. *AWARDS: NOM:* Screen Actors Guild Award '98: Best Supporting Actor (Kelly), Cast.

Waking Up Horton

What seems to have started out as a *Beetlejuice Meets the Old West,* has been transformed into *Nancy Drew Meets the Indian Imp,* with decidedly mixed results in this direct-to-video production. General cut-up and would-be comedian Raoul Trujillo plays the titular Horton, who is killed by a greedy gold prospector before he can complete the necessary rituals to become the tribe's Medicine Man. In the present day, the prospector's ancestor (Carrera) is making a movie in the forest of a nearby resort as a ruse to find the missing gold. Trujillo seeks the aid of the resort owner's (Benedict) daughter, Amelia (Peldon) to set things right. The DVD production is strictly bare-bones, with the title and key cover art having virtually nothing do to with the actual film presentation. —*RT* **AKA:** The Adventures of Young Brave.
Movie: 🎞🎞 *DVD:* 🎞🎞
Image Entertainment (Cat #5901, UPC #014381590128). Full frame. AC3 - 2 Channel. $19.99. Snapper. *LANG:* English. *FEATURES:* 14 chapter markers.
1999 (PG) 90m/C Dirk Benedict, Barbara Carrera, Raoul Trujillo, Ashley Peldon, Zachary Browne, Karen Moncrieff; *D:* Harry Bromley Davenport.

A Walk on the Moon

In the summer of 1969, the Kantrowitz family takes its vacation in the Catskills. Daughter Alison (Paquin) has become a teenager; mom Pearl (Lane) is restless; dad Marty (Schreiber) goes back to the city to work during the week. Enter hippie blouse salesman Walker (Mortensen). The attempt to integrate the family's problems with the momentous events of that time—Woodstock, the moon landing—are less than completely successful, and the too-neat ending is no better. Visually the no-frills disc is acceptable with some flashing in clothes patterns. Sound is equally good though the film overrelies on period music. —*MM*
Movie: 🎞🎞▶ *DVD:* 🎞🎞▶
Miramax Pictures Home Video (Cat #18146, UPC #717951004253). Widescreen (1.85:1) letterboxed. Dolby Digital 5.1 Surround Stereo. $29.99. Keepcase. *LANG:* English. *CAP:* English. *FEATURES:* 31 chapter links.
1999 (R) 107m/C Diane Lane, Liev Schreiber, Viggo Mortensen, Anna Paquin, Tovah Feldshuh, Bobby Boriello; *D:* Tony Goldwyn; *W:* Pamela Gray; *C:* Anthony B. Richmond; *M:* Mason Daring. *AWARDS:* NOM: Independent Spirit Awards '00: Best Actress (Lane).

Walkabout

Beautifully told and filmed story (by Roeg, in his debut), based on the novel by James Vance Marshall, follows a nameless young brother (John, Roeg's six-year-old son) and sister (Agutter), who are abandoned in the Australian outback when their father kills himself. The children wander, with little chance of survival, until a young aborigine (Gumpilil) finds them. He interrupts his own "walkabout," a rite of passage, to teach them to survive, leading to betrayal and tragedy. The beautifully photographed Australian countryside is a breathtaking backdrop, and the DVD video transfer nicely translates the stunning imagery to home video. John Barry's music score is an asset regrettably available only in mono. The printed Ebert essay is a nice touch, and the commentary track has been produced to Criterion's exacting production standards. —*MB*
Movie: 🎞🎞🎞▶ *DVD:* 🎞🎞🎞▶
Criterion Collection (Cat #WAL120, UPC #037429123225). Widescreen (1.77:1) letterboxed. Dolby Digital 1.0. $29.98. Keepcase. *LANG:* English. *SUB:* English. *FEATURES:* 28 chapter links • Commentary: Roeg and Agutter • Unrated director's cut • Theatrical trailers • Liner notes essay by critic Roger Ebert.
1971 (PG) 100m/C *AU* Jenny Agutter, Lucien John, David Gumpilil, John Meillon; *D:* Nicolas Roeg; *W:* Edward Bond; *C:* Nicolas Roeg; *M:* John Barry.

Walking Tall

Tennessee sheriff Buford Pusser (Baker) takes a hard stand against syndicate-run gambling, prostitution, and bootlegging. Buford is shot up and his wife is murdered, but the mob can't stop him and his big oak club. The violent crime saga wowed the public and spawned several sequels and a TV series. Based on the true story of folk-hero Pusser, admirably rendered by Baker. It doesn't look like much was put into the authoring of this DVD. Digital artifacts appear, particularly in the darker scenes, even when there is very little movement; during action sequences the image blurs and loses resolution. The sharpness is no better than a VHS tape and during scenes with a lot of red, the color bleed is very bad. Everything is audible on the mono soundtrack, but there is some clipping on the louder sections and very little dynamic range. —*JO*
Movie: 🎞🎞🎞 *DVD:* 🎞
Rhino Home Video (Cat #R24463, UPC #081227446321). Full frame. Mono. $24.99. Snapper. *LANG:* English. *FEATURES:* 31 chapter links.
1973 (R) 126m/C Joe Don Baker, Elizabeth Hartman, Noah Beery Jr., Gene Evans, Rosemary Murphy, Felton Perry; *D:* Phil Karlson; *W:* Mort Briskin; *C:* Jack Marta; *M:* Walter Scharf.

Wallace & Gromit: The First Three Adventures

Nick Park's brilliant stop-motion animation combines classic plotting with a particularly British sense of humor. In these short films, Gromit, a brainy dog, and Wallace, his putative master, become entangled with various contraptions. They go to the moon in "A Grand Day Out." "The Wrong Trousers," an Academy Award winner, is a heist thriller. "A Close Shave" revolves around romance and kidnapping. Park's comedy is fast-paced and surprising throughout. On DVD, the imperfections on his clay models are more obvious than they are on tape, but that's not really a flaw. The same criticism can be leveled at the original *King Kong.* The rough texture gives the characters complexity. The main attraction of the disc, though, lies in the easy accessibility of the short films and the extras, which give the viewer a peek inside the animation process. A welcome addition to any video library. —*MM*
Movie: 🎞🎞🎞▶ *DVD:* 🎞🎞🎞
20th Century Fox (Cat #4112596, UPC #086162125966). Full frame. Dolby Digital Surround Stereo. $34.98. Keepcase. *LANG:* English. *SUB:* Spanish. *CAP:* English. *FEATURES:* 32 chapter links • 4 of Park's early animation efforts • Excerpts from "Inside The Wrong Trousers" • BBC Christmas interstitials.
1999 85m/C *D:* Nick Park; *W:* Nick Park.

Waltz of the Toreadors

Retired general Sellers doesn't care for his wealthy, shrewish wife and tries to rekindle a 17-year-old romance with a French woman. It doesn't work out (seems his illegitimate son also has a soft spot for the lady), but the General decides to keep his eyes open for other possibilities. Interestingly cast adaptation of Jean Anouilh's play. Sellers is hilarious, as usual. The video transfer makes this 1962 movie look like, well, a 1962 movie. Although certain colors do stand out (such as bright reds and golds) with no bleeding, blacks do tend to be rather under-defined. I also noticed hairs flickering throughout the film, signifying a not-too-careful transfer. The mono soundtrack doesn't add anything either; speech is often muddied and sound effects come across a bit too tinny. —*MJT* **AKA:** The Amorous General.
Movie: 🎞🎞🎞 *DVD:* 🎞🎞▶
Image Entertainment (Cat #ID4535JFDVD, UPC #014381453522). Widescreen (1.66:1) letterboxed. Dolby Digital Mono. $24.99. Snapper. *FEATURES:* 16 chapter links.
1962 105m/C *GB* Peter Sellers, Dany Robin, Margaret Leighton, Cyril Cusack; *D:* John Guillermin; *W:* Wolf Mankowitz; *C:* John Wilcox; *M:* Richard Addinsell.

Wanted

Distraught over his hideous haircut, Johnny Scrico (Sutton) accidentally kills a high-level mobster and takes it on the lam. He hides out at a Catholic school for boys (run by Culp and Busfield), and learns several important lessons. The film has made-for-TV production values to go along with a fairly clumsy script, stiff direction, and poorly executed action sequences. The absolutely no-frills disc lacks a menu and chapter breaks. —*MM*
Movie: 🎞🎞 *DVD:* 🎞🎞
York Entertainment (Cat #YPD-1015, UPC #750723101521). Full frame. $24.98. Keepcase. *LANG:* English.

1998 100m/C Michael Sutton, Timothy Busfield, Robert Culp, Tracey Gold, James Quattrochi; **D:** Terence M. O'Keefe; **W:** Terence M. O'Keefe, Mark Evan Schwartz; **C:** Richard A. Jones.

The War

Post–Vietnam war drama, set in 1970 Mississippi, centers on a children's battle over a treehouse but becomes a sermon on love, death, family values, pacifism, and the physical and spiritual wounds of war. After helping son Stu (Wood) and daughter Lidia (Randall) build their treehouse, troubled Vietnam vet Stephen Simmons (Costner) tries to coax Stu to make peace with the bullies trying to take it over. Director Avnet allows a talented cast of kids to thoughtfully express a child's view of the world but gosh-darn-it, the cliched preachy tone can get downright annoying. Both the VHS and laserdisc editions of this film have their own problems and the DVD, though not perfect, is the preferred format. The biggest concern is the color, which on the DVD seems a little faded. Sharpness is about average and brightness and contrast levels are good. The soundtrack features a very lively 5.1 mix. —*JO*
Movie: 🦴🦴▶ **DVD:** 🦴🦴▶
Universal Studios Home Video (Cat #20533, UPC #025192053320). Widescreen (1.85:1) anamorphic. Dolby Digital 5.1. $26.98. Keepcase. *LANG:* English; French. *CAP:* English. *FEATURES:* 16 chapter links • Theatrical trailer • Production notes • Cast and filmmakers bios • Film highlights.
1994 (PG-13) 126m/C Elijah Wood, Kevin Costner, Lexi Randall, Mare Winningham, Christine Baranski, Bruce A. Young, Gary Basaraba, Raynor Scheine, Nick Searcy; **D:** Jon Avnet; **W:** Kathy McWorter; **C:** Geoffrey Simpson; **M:** Thomas Newman.

The War of the Worlds

H.G. Wells's seminal sf novel of the invasion of Earth by Martians is updated to 1950s California with spectacular special effects of destruction caused by the Martian war machines. It's still scary and tense (despite the shameless religiosity), and based as much on Orson Welles's radio broadcast as on the novel. Despite advances in computer-generated special effects, this stop-motion work remains impressive. It has been a perennial hit on home video and the DVD will doubtless continue to be. The image shows a slight amount of wear with flecks and scratches and blurring in a couple of shots, but the somewhat tinted colors are bright and the solidly constructed story is entertaining. Paul Frees's voice-over introduction sounds as commanding as ever and sets precisely the right tone. (He appears later as a radio announcer.) —*MM*
Movie: 🦴🦴🦴 **DVD:** 🦴🦴🦴▶
Paramount Home Video (Cat #053037, UPC #097360530377). Full frame. Dolby Digital Mono. $29.99. Keepcase. *LANG:*

English; French. *FEATURES:* Theatrical trailer • 13 chapter links.
1953 85m/C Gene Barry, Ann Robinson, Les Tremayne, Lewis Martin, Robert Cornthwaite, Sandro Giglio, George Pal, Jack Kruschen, Carolyn Jones, Alvy Moore, William Phipps, Paul Frees; **D:** Byron Haskin; **W:** Barre Lyndon; **C:** George Barnes; **M:** Leith Stevens; **V:** Cedric Hardwicke. *AWARDS: NOM:* Academy Awards '53: Best Film Editing, Best Sound.

The War Room

Eye-opening, sometimes disturbing documentary presents a behind-the-scenes peek at what really goes on during a Presidential campaign. When filming began in June '92, Bill Clinton was an unknown political quantity and advisors George Stephanopoulous and James Carville were masterminding his campaign. The "War Room" refers to the building in Little Rock where they struggled to organize a small army of volunteers into a winning team. Highlights include the Democratic National Convention, the North Carolina leg of Clinton's campaign bus tour, three Presidential debates, and the week leading up to election night. The picture quality isn't that important on this sort of documentary, especially since the picture varies from crisp and colorful to grainy and dull. The big problem is that the DVD actually seems to pick up the film grain and then the grain's images leave artifact trails. That alone is reason enough to watch the VHS. —*JO*
Movie: 🦴🦴🦴 **DVD:** 🦴
Trimark Home Video (Cat #VM6919D, UPC #031398691631). Full frame. Stereo. $14.99. Keepcase. *LANG:* English. *CAP:* English. *FEATURES:* 30 chapter links.
1993 (PG) 93m/C D: Chris Hegedus, D.A. Pennebaker; **C:** D.A. Pennebaker, Kevin Rafferty. *AWARDS:* National Board of Review Awards '93: Best Feature Documentary; *NOM:* Academy Awards '93: Best Feature Documentary.

The War Wagon

The Duke plans revenge on Cabot, the greedy mine owner who stole his gold claim and framed him for murder for which he spent years in prison. He assembles a gang to aid him, including a wise-cracking Indian (Keel) and the man sent by Cabot to kill him (Douglas). Wayne's plan is to steal the gold being shipped in Cabot's armor-plated stagecoach, the "war wagon." Well-written, good performances, lots of action. Based on the book *Badman* by Clair Huffaker. For some reason I've always liked this Wayne western and was really looking forward to the DVD release. When it arrived I was only a little disappointed. I was expecting image quality that probably isn't possible from the preprint. As it is, the DVD is fairly sharp but has a minor layer of some kind of haze. Colors are also less vibrant than expected. The last complaint is that the soundtrack, though stronger, still has noticeable mid-to high-end distortion. All in all, though,

the DVD is much improved over any prior version. —*JO*
Movie: 🦴🦴🦴 **DVD:** 🦴🦴🦴
Universal Studios Home Video (Cat #20298, UPC #025192029820). Widescreen (2.35:1) letterboxed. Dolby Digital Mono. $24.98. Keepcase. *LANG:* English; French; Spanish. *SUB:* Spanish. *CAP:* English. *FEATURES:* 16 chapter links • Theatrical trailer • Cast and filmmakers bios • Production notes • Film highlights.
1967 101m/C John Wayne, Kirk Douglas, Howard Keel, Robert Walker Jr., Keenan Wynn, Bruce Dern, Bruce Cabot, Joanna Barnes; **D:** Burt Kennedy; **W:** Clair Huffaker; **C:** William Clothier; **M:** Dimitri Tiomkin.

WarGames

A young computer whiz, thinking that he's sneaking an advance look at a new line of video games, breaks into the country's NORAD missile-defense system and challenges it to a game of Thermonuclear Warfare. The game just might turn out to be the real thing. Slick look at the possibilities of an accidental start to WWIII is entertaining and engrossing, but with a B-grade ending. On the DVD front, let's get the bad out of the way first. The picture sharpness is, at best, average with quite a bit of grain and artifacts in heavily detailed shots. Occasionally the backgrounds shimmer. Other than that, all the other specs are pretty good. The colors are vibrant and only the reds bleed (very infrequently). Blacks are true. Brightness stays consistent, as does the contrast. The 5.1 soundtrack almost makes up for the above flaws—some people have actually said that the sound is more important to them than the visuals. I disagree, but the soundtrack is better than it's been on any other video presentation of *War Games*. The music is full of dynamics, and is complemented by the great low end that also gives guts to the action sequences, and the Surround itself puts you right into the chaotic fray. —*JO*
Movie: 🦴🦴🦴 **DVD:** 🦴🦴▶
MGM Home Entertainment (Cat #907056, UPC #027616705624). Widescreen (1.85:1) letterboxed. Dolby Digital 5.1; Dolby Digital Mono. $24.98. Keepcase. *LANG:* English (DD5.1); French (DDM). *SUB:* French; Spanish. *CAP:* English. *FEATURES:* 32 chapter links • Theatrical trailer • Commentary: Badham, Lasker, and Parkes • Trivia and production notes • 8-page booklet.
1983 (PG) 110m/C Matthew Broderick, Dabney Coleman, John Wood, Ally Sheedy; **D:** John Badham; **W:** Walter F. Parkes, Lawrence Lasker; **C:** William A. Fraker; **M:** Arthur B. Rubinstein. *AWARDS: NOM:* Academy Awards '83: Best Cinematography, Best Original Screenplay, Best Sound.

Warlock

Passable little supernatural thriller mixes a comic book plot with unpersuasive special effects, above-average acting, and a strong sense of humor. Back in 1691, a

warlock (Sands) escapes execution by conjuring up some kind of timestorm. He and witchhunter Redfern (Grant) whisk forward 300 years to the living room of Kassandra (Singer), a plucky Los Angeles airhead. Before long, they're all hunting for the three parts of the *Grand Grimgroir*, a book that will bring about the "uncreation" of the universe. The pace is quick, the laughs intentional, and the plot avoids cliches. Followed by a sequel.
Movie: 🎬🎬▶ **DVD:** NYR
Trimark Home Video (Cat #6843). Full frame. Dolby Digital Stereo. $24.99. Keepcase. *LANG:* English. *SUB:* French; Spanish. *CAP:* English. *FEATURES:* Cast and crew thumbnail bios ▪ Trailer.
1991 (R) 103m/C Richard E. Grant, Julian Sands, Lori Singer, Mary Woronov, Richard Kuss, Kevin O'Brien, Anna Levine, Allan Miller, David Carpenter; *D:* Steve Miner; *W:* David N. Twohy; *C:* David Eggby; *M:* Jerry Goldsmith.

Warlock: The Armageddon

Sequel boasts better effects than the original and a plot that's just as nonsensical. The titular supernatural creature (Sands) tries to collect special runestones to bring his daddy Satan into the world, etc., etc. Small-town teens Kenny (Young) and Samantha (Marshall) must stop him. The inventive, graphic violence is leavened with equally bloody humor. Similar stuff is found in the 1995 *Prophecy* and *Buffy, the Vampire Slayer.*
Movie: 🎬🎬🎬 **DVD:** NYR
Trimark Home Video (Cat #7076). Dolby Digital Stereo. $24.99. Keepcase. *LANG:* English. *SUB:* French; Spanish. *CAP:* English. *FEATURES:* Cast and crew thumbnail bios ▪ Trailer.
1993 (R) 93m/C Julian Sands, Chris Young, Paula Marshall, Steve Kahan, Charles Hallahan, R.G. Armstrong, Bruce Glover, Zach Galligan, Dawn Ann Billings, Joanna Pacula; *D:* Anthony Hickox; *W:* Kevin Rock, Sam Bernard; *C:* Gerry Lively; *M:* Mark McKenzie.

Warlock 3: The End of Innocence

3 bears little resemblance to the first two installments in the series. It's a fairly standard kids-trapped-in-remote-house story that won't make anyone forget *Evil Dead.* College student Kris Miller (Laurence) inherits an old mansion. She and five friends go out to take a look. A handsome stranger (Payne) shows up and insinuates his way into the group. The scares and effects are O.K., making good use of sound. Like many horror films, this one is dark, but it works well enough on DVD. Both sets and costumes are done in cold gloomy grays and browns that are still well defined. The film was made in Ireland. —MM
Movie: 🎬🎬 **DVD:** 🎬🎬▶
Trimark Home Video (Cat #7203D, UPC #031398720331). Widescreen (1.66:1)

letterboxed. Dolby Digital Surround Stereo. $24.99. Keepcase. *LANG:* English. *SUB:* English; French; Spanish. *CAP:* English. *FEATURES:* 24 chapter links ▪ Trailer.
1998 (R) 94m/C Bruce Payne, Ashley Laurence, Angel Boris, Boti Ann Bliss, Paul Francis, Rick Hearst, Jan Schweiterman; *D:* Eric Freiser; *W:* Eric Freiser, Bruce David Eisen.

Warriors of Virtue

Teenaged Ryan Jefers (Yedidia) is transported to the land of Tao where he learns the five virtues (righteousness, benevolence, integrity, wisdom, and loyalty) from the kangaroo-like Warmblood warriors, who live in harmony with humans. Then he must use his knowledge to fight the evil Komodo (MacFadyen), who wishes to steal the energy from Tao to make himself immortal. Nice message for the kids, with enough action to keep them interested, but the Warmbloods are dorky-looking. One of Hong Kong's premiere directors makes his American film debut and MGM decides to issue a cropped, full-frame DVD? Maybe it was because they felt the film was mainly for kids (and it is, but action-packed enough for adults), and that the little darlings would be turned off by those black bar things. To add injury to insult, the picture is a little soft, with mild grain throughout and the colors seem washed-out when compared to even the VHS version. The sound is good, though, and adds a lot of energy to all the martial arts scenes. —JO
Movie: 🎬🎬🎬 **DVD:** 🎬▶
MGM Home Entertainment (Cat #907434, UPC #027616743428). Full frame. Dolby Digital 5.1; Dolby Surround. $24.98. Keepcase. *LANG:* English; French. *SUB:* English; French. *CAP:* English. *FEATURES:* 28 chapter links ▪ Theatrical trailer ▪ 4-page booklet.
1997 (PG) 101m/C Mario Yedidia, Angus Macfadyen, Marley Shelton, Chao-Li Chi; *D:* Ronny Yu; *W:* Michael Vickerman, Hugh Kelley; *C:* Peter Pau; *M:* Don Davis.

Watch Me

Photog Paul (Medford) is inspired by new neighbor Elise (Burns) and secretly snaps her through the window. Meanwhile, Elize is peering through her telescope at Paul's would-be gal Samantha (Burton), who's fooling around with her bud Alex (Sherwin). You do not need any more hints to figure out where this one is going. Unfortunately, the soft-core eroticism is undermined by substandard production values—heavily grained, dim interiors, lethargic pace—and a bony cast that appears to be seriously undernourished. Those are noticeable flaws on the VHS tape. On DVD, they are magnified immensely. —MM
Movie: 🎬 **DVD:** 🎬
Image Entertainment (Cat #ID5631FMDVD, UPC #014381563122). Full frame. Dolby Digital Stereo. $24.99. Snapper. *LANG:* English. *FEATURES:* 12 chapter links.

1996 (R) 90m/C Robert Medford, Kelly Burns, Jennifer Burton, Steven Sherwin; *D:* Lipo Ching; *W:* Beth Salmon; *C:* Andreas Kossak; *M:* Yoav Goren.

The Waterboy

Sandler's best film to date raises his loveable doofus character to a new level. He's Bobby Boucher who, at 31, still lives with his mom (Bates) on the bayou, wears Deputy Dawg pajamas, and loves his work—college football waterboy. It takes coach Klein (Winkler) of the South Central LSU Mud Dogs to discover Bobby's true talent—tackling—and a new star is born. Sandler's faux Cajun accent is wonderful. His mom's house is such an incredible clash of shapes, objects, and colors that it might cause some monitors to revert to a test pattern, but the DVD handles all of the action without a problem. Overall, both image and sound are much sharper and clearer than they have any reasonable need to be. —MM
Movie: 🎬🎬🎬 **DVD:** 🎬🎬🎬
Buena Vista Home Entertainment (Cat #16540, UPC #717951001665). Widescreen (1.85:1) letterboxed. Dolby Digital 5.1 Surround Stereo. $29.99. Keepcase. *LANG:* English; French. *CAP:* English. *FEATURES:* 25 chapter links ▪ "Making of" featurette ▪ Theatrical trailer.
1998 (PG-13) 90m/C Adam Sandler, Kathy Bates, Henry Winkler, Fairuza Balk, Jerry Reed, Larry Gilliard Jr., Blake Clark, Rob Schneider, Clint Howard, Allen Whiting, Robert Kokol; *D:* Frank Coraci; *W:* Tim Herlihy, Adam Sandler; *C:* Steven Bernstein; *M:* Alan Pasqua. *AWARDS: NOM:* MTV Movie Awards '99: Best Male Performance (Sandler), Best Comedic Performance (Sandler); Golden Raspberry Awards '98: Worst Actor (Sandler).

Waterworld

In the now-familiar post-apocalyptic future, the Earth is a seemingly endless ocean. The polar icecaps have melted; plain old dirt is the new gold standard; and "Dryland" is a possibly mythical paradise. Yes, it's *The Road Warrior* on water. The Mariner (Costner) is a "drifter" who sails around in an incredibly neat trimaran. He's your basic bad-attitude loner, Mad Max with webbed toes. He arrives at a settlement called the Atoll just in time for an attack by "Smokers," outlaws on jet skis who are led by Deacon (Hopper, at his villainous best). The best scenes are the ones that take place on the trimaran and they make a sharp transition to DVD, even though they contain elements that are often troublesome to the medium. Pixelation is notably absent in the shots of water and diagonal lines remain true even in fast panning shots. Overall, both image and sound are fine, and though the entire film is not the disaster some have claimed, it's not nearly as good as the Mel Gibson original, either. —MM
Movie: 🎬🎬🎬 **DVD:** 🎬🎬🎬

Universal Studios Home Video (Cat #20039, UPC #025192003929). Wide-screen (1.85:1) anamorphic. Dolby Digital 5.0 Surround Stereo. $26.98. Jewel case. *LANG:* English; French; Spanish. *SUB:* Spanish. *CAP:* English.
1995 (PG-13) 135m/C Kevin Costner, Dennis Hopper, Jeanne Tripplehorn, Tina Majorino, Michael Jeter, R.D. Call, Robert Joy; *D:* Kevin Reynolds; *W:* Peter Rader, Marc Norman, David N. Twohy; *C:* Dean Semler; *M:* James Newton Howard. *AWARDS:* Golden Raspberry Awards '95: Worst Supporting Actor (Hopper); *NOM:* Academy Awards '95: Best Sound; Golden Raspberry Awards '95: Worst Picture, Worst Actor (Costner).

Way Down East

The painstakingly opened-up film adaptation of a wildly popular stage play took a long time and cost Griffith's studio a great deal of money, but it yielded one of the most memorable scenes in cinema history. When Lillian Gish goes floating downstream on an ice floe with one hand dangling in icy water, she really is in danger of freezing! The shamelessly melodramatic plot involves a country bumpkin (Gish) being led into a sham marriage and suffering the oh-so-terrible consequences of being a woman wronged. David Shepard, who seems to have a lock on restoring silents, produced this DVD edition from a Blackhawk print, slightly letterboxed to preserve the original, squared-off celluloid format. Tinting the scenes apparently minimized the effect of any aliasing. The fetching, delicately colored box boasts a long gatefold essay excerpted from Richard Schickel's book-length Griffith biography and two index card-sized, sepia-toned production stills. The music, recorded in 1928 on the Vitaphone system, is low-fi mono. —*JK*
Movie: ♪♪♪ *DVD:* ♪♪♪♪
Image Entertainment Full frame. Dolby Digital Mono. $29.95. Snapper. *LANG:* English. *FEATURES:* 19 chapter links • Tinted scene access menus • Colorized cover • 2-color disc • Critical essay.
1920 107m/B Lillian Gish, Richard Barthelmess, Lowell Sherman, Creighton Hale, Burr McIntosh, Kate Bruce, Florence Short; *D:* D.W. Griffith; *W:* D.W. Griffith, Joseph R. Grismer; *C:* Billy (G.W.) Bitzer, Hendrik Sartov.

Web of Seduction

One couple (Acsell and Smith) is living in another couple's (Camus and Hays) guest house while their place is being worked on. Neither husband is attentive; both wives are dissatisfied; the maid (O'Brien) suggests that they get rid of the no-good rascals permanently. On DVD, this is one of Playboy's better productions. It's carefully lighted, with less grain than most of these mid-budget erotic thrillers contain. It's also very sexy. —*MM*
Movie: ♪♪► *DVD:* ♪♪►

Image Entertainment (Cat #ID5980PLDVD, UPC #014381598025). Full frame. Dolby Digital Stereo. $24.99. Snapper. *LANG:* English. *FEATURES:* 12 chapter links.
1999 (R) ?m/C Lauren Hays, Eric Acsell, Tracy N. Smith, Stephan Camus, Nancy O'Brien; *D:* Blain Brown.

The Wedding Singer

Despite almost nonexistent pacing and a script full of holes, *Singer* is an enjoyably goofy look at the mid '80s. Surprisingly toned-down and appealing Sandler is Robbie Hart, wedding singer, ultimate nice guy, and rock-star wanna-be, who's jilted at the altar. Waitress Barrymore is engaged to a skirt-chasing stock broker. It's clear that they belong together, and the rest of the movie is spent on them chasing each other through various contrived obstacles, to the obvious ending. Great cameos. Highlight is Sandler's rendition of the J. Geils Band's "Love Stinks." Above-average DVD has good sharpness and very little grain. The film is very colorful and the disc handles it very well with very little bleed. Contrast is excellent and the brightness is very consistent. The blacks are close to dead-on. Plenty of low end for the numerous rock songs on a very good, crisp soundtrack that features both French and English in Dolby Digital 5.1. Overall, the DVD is comfortable and fun to watch. The "karaoke bar" features five songs with or without vocals. —*JO*
Movie: ♪♪► *DVD:* ♪♪♪►
New Line Home Video (Cat #N4660, UPC #794043466021). Widescreen (1.85:1) letterboxed; full frame. Dolby Digital 5.1. $24.98. Snapper. *LANG:* English; French. *SUB:* Spanish; French. *CAP:* English. *FEATURES:* 24 chapter links • 5 karaoke songs • Trivia game • Cast biographies and filmographies • Photo gallery.
1997 (PG-13) 96m/C Adam Sandler, Drew Barrymore, Christine Taylor, Alan Covert, Matthew Glave, Ellen A. Dow, Angela Featherstone, Alexis Arquette, Christina Pickles, Jon Lovitz, Steve Buscemi, Kevin Nealon; *Cameos:* Billy Idol; *D:* Frank Coraci; *W:* Tim Herlihy; *C:* Tim Suhrstedt; *M:* Teddy Castellucci. *AWARDS:* MTV Movie Awards '98: Best Kiss (Adam Sandler/Drew Barrymore); *NOM:* MTV Movie Awards '98: Best On-Screen Duo (Adam Sandler/Drew Barrymore), Best Comedic Performance (Sandler).

Weekend at Bernie's

Two computer nerds discover embezzlement at their workplace after being invited to their boss's beach house for a weekend party. They find their host murdered. They endeavor to keep up appearances by (you guessed it) dressing and strategically posing the corpse during the party. Kiser as the dead man is memorable, and the two losers gamely keep the silliness flowing. Lots of fun. The DVD is sharp enough to please and both grain and artifact levels are very low. The main flaw with the DVD is the colors, which are very weak and

even off a shade. Both the VHS and laserdisc editions are preferable. —*JO*
AKA: Hot and Cold.
Movie: ♪♪► *DVD:* ♪♪►
Artisan Entertainment (Cat #60488, UPC #012236048800). Widescreen (1.85:1) letterboxed. Dolby Surround. $24.98. Keepcase. *LANG:* English. *SUB:* Spanish. *CAP:* English. *FEATURES:* 36 chapter links • Theatrical trailer • Cast and filmmakers bios • Production notes.
1989 (PG-13) 101m/C Andrew McCarthy, Jonathan Silverman, Catherine Mary Stewart, Terry Kiser, Don Calfa, Louis Giambalvo; *D:* Ted Kotcheff; *W:* Robert Klane; *C:* Francois Protat; *M:* Andy Summers.

Weird Science

Hall is appealing, and Hughes can write dialogue for teens with the best of them. However, many of the jokes are in poor taste (for this kind of film), and the movie seems to go on forever. Hall and his nerdy cohort Mitchell-Smith use a very special kind of software to create the ideal woman, who wreaks zany havoc in their lives from the outset. This Image DVD release of a Universal title looks super. The picture stays sharp and grain-free with no noticeable artifacts. Colors are vibrant, accurate, and bleed-free. Contrast and brightness levels are as high as can be without harming the image's accuracy. The Dolby stereo has minimal Surround effects but is overall very lively, and the music sounds terrific. It's always great to see a catalog release get the right treatment. —*JO*
Movie: ♪♪► *DVD:* ♪♪♪♪►
Image Entertainment (Cat #ID232USDVD, UPC #014381423228). Widescreen (1.85:1) letterboxed. Dolby Surround. $29.95. Snapper. *LANG:* English. *CAP:* English. *FEATURES:* 16 chapter links.
1985 (PG-13) 94m/C Kelly Le Brock, Anthony Michael Hall, Ilan Mitchell-Smith, Robert Downey Jr., Bill Paxton; *D:* John Hughes; *W:* John Hughes; *C:* Matthew F. Leonetti; *M:* Ira Newborn.

Welcome to the Dollhouse

Eleven years old and burdened with thick glasses, Dawn "Weinerdog" Weiner (Matarazzo) is the middle child of a middle-class family in her first year of junior high hell. She's bewildered by school, family, life in general, and where she fits in. Puberty sucks, and the cruelty of adolescence has seldom been shown with such painful and often funny honesty. This independent production has never had a particularly sharp image, and since it is exploring suburban tackiness in all its many forms, that relative lack of clarity is probably a blessing. The DVD is essentially the same as VHS tape in sound and image. —*MM*
Movie: ♪♪► *DVD:* ♪♪
Columbia Tristar Home Video (Cat #82569, UPC #043396825697). Widescreen

(1.85:1) letterboxed; full frame. Dolby Digital Stereo. $27.95. Keepcase. *LANG:* English. *SUB:* English; French; Spanish. *FEATURES:* 28 chapter links ▪ Trailer ▪ Cast and crew filmographies ▪ Production notes.

1995 (R) 87m/C Heather Matarazzo, Brendan Sexton III, Daria Kalinina, Matthew Faber, Angela Pietropinto, Eric Mabius; **D:** Todd Solondz; **W:** Todd Solondz; **C:** Randy Drummond; **M:** Jill Wisoff. *AWARDS:* Independent Spirit Awards '97: Debut Performance (Matarazzo); Sundance Film Festival '96: Grand Jury Prize; *NOM:* Independent Spirit Awards '97: Best Director (Solondz), Best Film, Best Supporting Actor (Faber), Debut Performance (Sexton).

Werewolf

This howler may well be the funniest of its kind since Michael Landon glued on the whiskers in *I Was a Teenage Werewolf.* Even for low-budget horror, it's bad in all the wrong ways—inept acting, cliched script, bargain-basement makeup. Though the setting is the Southwest, and some mention is made of American Indian "shapeshifters," nothing is really done with that angle. It's just a standard lycanthropy tale with little to recommend it, and its many flaws are magnified on DVD. The potentially sweeping landscapes are mediocre at best, and a little added clarity does nothing for the wolf masks. —*MM*
Movie: 🎞️ *DVD:* 🎞️
Simitar Entertainment (Cat #7293, UPC #082551729326). Full frame. PCM Stereo. $14.98. Keepcase. *LANG:* English. *FEATURES:* 8 chapter links ▪ Production factoids.
1995 (R) 99m/C George Rivero, Fred Cavalli, Adrianna Miles, Richard Lynch, Joe Estevez, R.C. Bates, Heidi Bjorn, Randall Oliver, Nena Belini, Tony Zarindast; **D:** Tony Zarindast; **W:** Tony Zarindast; **C:** Robert Hayes, Dan Gilman.

Werther

A superb film production of Jules Massanet's lyrical opera tells the story of Werther's intense passion for Charlotte and the tragedy that is destined to befall him. Shot on location in and around Prague. The video and audio transfers are both quite solid. The DVD boasts nicely defined colors and the audio has a full, rich soundtrack that breathes real life into the lushness of the opera being performed. —*MJT*
Movie: 🎞️🎞️ *DVD:* 🎞️🎞️
Image Entertainment (Cat #ID5657CLDVD, UPC #014381565720). Full frame. Dolby Digital Stereo. $24.99. Snapper. *LANG:* French. *SUB:* English. *FEATURES:* 13 chapter links.
1988 101m/C *GE CZ* Peter Dvorsky, Brigitte Fassbaender, Magdalena Vasary, Frantisek Zvarik, Hans Helm; **D:** Petr Weigl; **W:** Edourd Blau, Paul Milliet, George Hartmann.

Wes Craven's New Nightmare

The *Elm Street* series takes an unexpected intellectual turn at the end and becomes an entertaining exercise in horror. Most of the characters play themselves. They are the actors, filmmakers, and studio executives who are involved in a work in progress, *Wes Craven's New Nightmare.* Craven has not finished the script yet but Robert Englund is definitely interested in the project. So are producers Marianne Maddalena and Sara Risher and New Line Cinema chairman Robert Shaye. Star Heather Langenkamp needs to be persuaded. When she learns that her husband (Newsom) is secretly working on new special effects for Craven's project, she's really scared. Upon that premise, Craven builds an intricate construction about the act of storytelling and the power that some stories have. References to Hansel and Gretel are well taken. They bring up the responsibility of storytellers to their audience, particularly when children are involved. In the last reels, Craven returns to the simple, effective thrills of a good horror movie, from a harrowing freeway scene to the wild finale. On the DVD commentary track, he's intelligent and chatty, obviously aware that he's preaching to the choir. Only true fans are going to be listening to him and so he elaborates on the film's themes and comments on the details of the effects. Both image and sound are excellent. —*MM*
Movie: 🎞️🎞️🎞️ *DVD:* 🎞️🎞️🎞️🎞️
New Line Home Video (Cat #N4825, UPC #794043478826). Widescreen (1.85:1) letterboxed. Dolby Digital 5.1 Surround Stereo; Stereo. $24.98. Snapper. *LANG:* English. *SUB:* English. *FEATURES:* 29 chapter links ▪ Commentary: Wes Craven ▪ Cast and crew thumbnail biographies ▪ "Jump to Nightmare" screen navigation ▪ DVD-ROM extras. Also available as part of "The Nightmare on Elm Street Collection" boxed set ($129.98), catalog #N4788.
1994 (R) 112m/C Robert Englund, Heather Langenkamp, Miko Hughes, David Newsom, Tracy Middendorf, Fran Bennett, John Saxon, Wes Craven, Robert Shaye, Sara Risher, Marianne Maddalena; **D:** Wes Craven; **W:** Wes Craven; **C:** Mark Irwin; **M:** J. Peter Robinson. *AWARDS: NOM:* Independent Spirit Awards '95: Best Film.

West Side Story

Gang rivalry and ethnic tension on New York's West Side erupts in a ground-breaking musical. Loosely based on Shakespeare's *Romeo and Juliet,* the story follows the Jets and the Sharks as they fight for their turf while Tony and Maria fight for love. Features frenetic and brilliant choreography by codirector Robbins, who also directed the original Broadway show, and a high-caliber score by Bernstein and Sondheim. Wood's voice was dubbed by Marni Nixon and Jimmy Bryant dubbed Beymer's. There have been many video editions of

West Side Story and this DVD is by far the best. The colors are simply amazing and though saturated, are finely detailed with no bleed. And the picture's sharp too. The 5.1 track retains a basically stereo mix but is dynamic and full-bodied. —*JO*
Movie: 🎞️🎞️🎞️ *DVD:* 🎞️🎞️🎞️
MGM Home Entertainment (Cat #906733, UPC #027616673329). Widescreen (2.35:1) anamorphic. Dolby Digital 5.1. $24.98. Keepcase. *LANG:* English. *SUB:* English; French. *CAP:* English. *FEATURES:* 36 chapter links ▪ Theatrical trailer ▪ 8-page booklet.
1961 151m/C Natalie Wood, Richard Beymer, Russ Tamblyn, Rita Moreno, George Chakiris, Simon Oakland, Ned Glass; **D:** Robert Wise, Jerome Robbins; **W:** Ernest Lehman; **C:** Daniel F. Fapp; **M:** Leonard Bernstein, Stephen Sondheim. *AWARDS:* Academy Awards '61: Best Art Direction/Set Decoration (Color), Best Color Cinematography, Best Costume Design (Color), Best Director (Wise), Best Film Editing, Best Picture, Best Sound, Best Supporting Actor (Chakiris), Best Supporting Actress (Moreno), Scoring of a Musical; American Film Institute (AFI) '98: Top 100; Directors Guild of America Awards '61: Best Director (Wise), Best Director (Robbins); Golden Globe Awards '62: Best Film—Musical/Comedy, Best Supporting Actor (Chakiris), Best Supporting Actress (Moreno), National Film Registry '97; New York Film Critics Awards '61: Best Film; *NOM:* Academy Awards '61: Best Adapted Screenplay.

The Westerner

A sly, soft-spoken drifter champions Texas border homesteaders in a land war with the legendary Judge Roy Bean. "The Law West of the Pecos" sentences drifter Cooper to hang, but Cooper breaks out of jail. He falls for damsel Davenport and stays in the area, advocating the rights of homesteaders to Brennan. Brennan's Bean is unforgettable and steals the show from Cooper. Film debuts of actors Tucker and Andrews. Amazing cinematography; Brennan's Oscar was his third, making him the first performer to pull a hat trick. The DVD transfer looks like the best it can be using the original source material. The black-and-white image is sharp and contrasts and graytones are excellent. There are some scratches and both white and black flecks here and there, but with this vintage film you can put up with the preprint damage, and in fact, it sometimes enhances the feel of the film. The soundtrack has been remastered to Dolby Surround and is at least cleaner and slightly stronger than the original mono mix. —*JO*
Movie: 🎞️🎞️🎞️ *DVD:* 🎞️🎞️🎞️
HBO Home Video (Cat #90665, UPC #026359066528). Full frame. Dolby Surround; Mono. $24.98. Snapper. *LANG:* English; French; Italian; Spanish. *SUB:* English; French; Spanish. *CAP:* English. *FEATURES:* 20 chapter links ▪ Cast bios.

1940 100m/B Gary Cooper, Walter Brennan, Doris Davenport, Dana Andrews, Forrest Tucker, Charles Halton; **D:** William Wyler; **W:** Jo Swerling, Niven Busch; **C:** Gregg Toland; **M:** Dimitri Tiomkin. *AWARDS:* Academy Awards '40: Best Supporting Actor (Brennan); *NOM:* Academy Awards '40: Best Story.

Westworld

Crichton wrote and directed this story of an adult vacation resort of the future, which offers the opportunity to live in various fantasy worlds serviced by lifelike robots. Brolin and Benjamin are businessmen who choose a western fantasy world. When an electrical malfunction occurs, the robots go berserk. Brynner is perfect as a western gun-slinging robot whose skills are all too real. The DVD greatly improves the image quality over the letterboxed laserdisc and the full-frame VHS edition. Colors are fresh and the image is sharp. The sound is on par with the earlier releases and could use both more bass and a crisper high end. *—JO*
Movie: 🐾🐾🐾 **DVD:** 🐾🐾🐾
MGM Home Entertainment (Cat #907014, UPC #027616701428). Widescreen (2.35:1) anamorphic. Dolby Surround; Dolby Digital Mono. $24.98. Keepcase. *LANG:* English; French. *SUB:* English; French. *CAP:* English. *FEATURES:* 32 chapter links • Theatrical trailer • 8-page booklet.
1973 (PG) 90m/C Yul Brynner, Richard Benjamin, James Brolin, Dick Van Patten, Majel Barrett; **D:** Michael Crichton; **W:** Michael Crichton; **C:** Gene Polito; **M:** Fred Karlin.

What Dreams May Come

Romantic idea (loosely adapted from a Richard Matheson novel) and lushly colorful computer-generated imagery combine with sappy dialogue to turn surreal fantasy into average digital hocus-pocus. Dr. Chris Neilsen (Williams) and his artist-wife Annie (Sciorra) lose their two children in a traffic accident. Four years later, the doctor himself is killed in a freak accident. He finds that his heaven is much like a painting done by his wife (or Monet or Van Gogh) of their dream cottage. Unable to accept eternal separation, he sets off on an odyssey to find her. For the first half hour, Williams alternates between a *Patch Adams* rehearsal and over-emoting into the tear-filled eyes of Sciorra. DVD handles the overly bright clashing smushy-mushy colors with apparent ease. I did not see the theatrical release, but this one has almost surreal intensity, which appears deliberate. *—MM*
Movie: 🐾🐾 **DVD:** 🐾🐾🐾
USA Home Entertainment (Cat #440 058 275-2, UPC #044005827521). Widescreen anamorphic. Dolby Digital 5.1 Surround Stereo; Dolby Digital Stereo. $34.95. Keepcase. *LANG:* English. *SUB:* French; Spanish. *CAP:* English. *FEATURES:* Com-

mentary: Vincent Ward • "Making of" featurette • 19 chapter links • DVD-ROM features • Booklet with liner notes • Cast and crew thumbnail bios • Theatrical trailers • Alternate ending • Photo gallery.
1998 (PG-13) 113m/C Rosalind Chao, Robin Williams, Annabella Sciorra, Cuba Gooding Jr., Max von Sydow, Jessica Brooks Grant, Josh Paddock; **D:** Vincent Ward; **W:** Ronald Bass; **C:** Eduardo Serra; **M:** Michael Kamen. *AWARDS:* Academy Awards '98: Best Visual Effects; *NOM:* Academy Awards '98: Best Art Direction/Set Decoration.

What Ever Happened to Baby Jane?

Davis and Crawford portray aging sisters and former child stars living together in a decaying mansion. When the demented Jane (Davis) learns of her now-crippled sister's (Crawford) plan to institutionalize her, she tortures the wheelchair-bound sis. Davis plays her part to the hilt, unafraid of Aldrich's unsympathetic camera, and the viciousness of her character. She received her 10th Oscar nomination for the role. Another great black-and-white transfer to DVD with both picture and sound improved over the older home video editions. *—JO*
Movie: 🐾🐾🐾🐾 **DVD:** 🐾🐾🐾🐾
Warner Home Video, Inc. (Cat #11051, UPC #085391105121). Widescreen (1.85:1) letterboxed; full frame. Dolby Digital Surround. $19.98. Snapper. *LANG:* English; French. *SUB:* English; French; Spanish. *CAP:* English. *FEATURES:* 35 chapter links • Production note.
1962 132m/B Bette Davis, Joan Crawford, Victor Buono, Anna Lee, B.D. Merrill, Maidie Norman; **D:** Robert Aldrich; **W:** Lukas Heller; **C:** Ernest Haller; **M:** Frank DeVol. *AWARDS: NOM:* Academy Awards '62: Best Actress (Davis), Best Black-and-white Cinematography, Best Costume Design (B & W), Best Sound, Best Supporting Actor (Buono).

Whatever It Takes

Standard video-premiere action flick finds undercover cops De Marco (Wilson) and Menari (Clay) trying to break up Salerno's (Williamson) steroid ring in the world of professional wrestling and body-building. The formulaic material is well photographed with a sharp image throughout this no-frills DVD. *—MM*
Movie: 🐾🐾 **DVD:** 🐾🐾
Pioneer Entertainment (Cat #PEAD-003, UPC #013023017290). Widescreen letterboxed. $19.98. Keepcase. *LANG:* English. *FEATURES:* 36 chapter links • Theatrical trailer.
1997 (R) 89m/C Don "The Dragon" Wilson, Andrew Dice Clay, Fred Williamson; **D:** Brady MacKenzie.

What's Love Got to Do with It?

True or false, this rock bio-pic of Tina Turner (Bassett) is built on the stuff of good melodrama. The film doesn't show much about what it was like to be a black woman in the 1950s and '60s. Beyond the band's immediate concerns, it has little to say about one of the most vibrant and creative periods in the history of popular music. Instead, we learn a lot about Ike and Tina, more than some will want to know. Angela Bassett and Larry Fishburne do Oscar-caliber work. Both of them have that "presence" that turns actors into stars. But at the end of the movie, Tina emerges as pure as the wind-driven snow while Ike has been transformed into a monster straight from a Stephen King novel. If he'd been more human and she'd been more flawed, their conflict would have been more believable and more moving. The DVD is at its best during the performance scenes tinted with candy-colored light. The notable exception is one number when the back-up singers' black-and-white striped tops flash like crazy. Director Brian Gibson makes the most of Angela Bassett's physical presence and that's the film's real strength in any medium. *—MM*
Movie: 🐾🐾 **DVD:** 🐾🐾🐾🐾
Buena Vista Home Entertainment (Cat #17507, UPC #717551003256). Widescreen (1.85:1) letterboxed. Dolby Digital 5.1. $29.99. Keepcase. *LANG:* English; French. *FEATURES:* Theatrical trailer • 22 chapter links.
1993 (R) 118m/C Angela Bassett, Laurence "Larry" Fishburne, Vanessa Bell Calloway, Jenifer Lewis, Phyllis Stickney, Khandi Alexander, Pamela Tyson, Penny Johnson, Rae'ven Kelly, Robert Miranda, Chi McBride; **D:** Brian Gibson; **W:** Kate Lanier; **C:** Jamie Anderson; **M:** Stanley Clarke. *AWARDS:* Golden Globe Awards '94: Best Actress—Musical/Comedy (Bassett); Blockbuster Entertainment Awards '95: Female Newcomer, Video (Bassett); *NOM:* Academy Awards '93: Best Actor (Fishburne), Best Actress (Bassett); MTV Movie Awards '94: Best Female Performance (Bassett).

Wheels on Meals

A private eye (Hung) and a street food merchant (Chan) try to find an heiress (Forner) who has been kidnapped. *AKA:* Meals on Wheels; Million Dollar Heiress.
Movie: 🐾🐾 **DVD:** NYR
Tai Seng Video Marketing (Cat #56344). $29.95.
1984 ?m/C HK Jackie Chan, Yuen Biao, Lola Forner, Sammo Hung, Herb Edelman, Richard Ng; **D:** Sammo Hung; **W:** Edward Tong.

When a Man Loves a Woman

Alice Green (Ryan) is the mother of a perfect little family with a loving husband

(Garcia), two little girls, and satisfying career. She's also a closet alcoholic. The introductory scenes are cute to a fault. Alice's detox treatments and struggle back to sobriety are fertile ground for psycho-babble and 12-step cliches. The combination of smirky romantic humor with pathos is indigestible to anyone who's immune to the two stars' undeniable screen presence. On DVD, the film has the polished look and sound of a well-made, big-budget studio release. — *MM* *AKA:* To Have and to Hold; Significant Other.

Movie: 🎬🎬 *DVD:* 🎬🎬🎬
Buena Vista Home Entertainment (Cat #18529, UPC #717951005465). Widescreen (1.85:1) letterboxed. Dolby Digital Stereo. $29.99. Keepcase. *LANG:* English. *CAP:* English. *FEATURES:* 26 chapter links ▪ Theatrical trailer.
1994 (R) 126m/C Meg Ryan, Andy Garcia, Lauren Tom, Philip Seymour Hoffman, Tina Majorino, Mae Whitman, Ellen Burstyn, Eugene Roche, Latanya Richardson; *D:* Luis Mandoki; *W:* Ronald Bass, Al Franken; *C:* Lajos Koltai; *M:* Zbigniew Preisner. *AWARDS:* Blockbuster Entertainment Awards '95: Drama Actress, Video (Ryan); *NOM:* MTV Movie Awards '95: Best Female Performance (Ryan), Most Desirable Male (Garcia); Screen Actors Guild Award '94: Best Actress (Ryan).

When a Stranger Calls Back

It took the producers more than a decade to come up with this above-average sequel, and it's easy to see why. The first film is so curiously but well-constructed that it rules out standard follow-up stuff. The original villain is a fully realized individual, not a cliched movie psycho. The main characters grow during the film and the bad guy is definitely dead at the end. Still, the stalker-vs.-babysitter plot is repeated so often because it works, and writer-director Fred Walton handles it with real care. He treats the whole subject of violence against women seriously, and he comes up with an inventive (if not too believable) twist on the formula. It's also well acted with Jill Schoelen taking over as protagonist and Carol Kane and Charles Durning repeating their famous roles. The added clarity of DVD really adds little to the big finish with its camouflage gimmick. In visual terms, the disc is a slight improvement over VHS tape; sound is a bit better. —*MM*

Movie: 🎬🎬🎬 *DVD:* 🎬🎬🎬
Goodtimes Entertainment (Cat #05-81026, UPC #018713810267). Full frame. Dolby Digital Stereo. $19.98. Snapper. *LANG:* English. *SUB:* Spanish; French. *CAP:* English. *FEATURES:* 18 chapter links.
1993 (R) 94m/C Carol Kane, Charles Durning, Jill Schoelen, Gene Lythgow, Karen Austin; *D:* Fred Walton; *W:* Fred Walton; *C:* David Geddes; *M:* Dana Kaproff.

When Justice Fails

Vigilante goes after rapists.
Movie: NYR *DVD:* NYR
Sunland Studios (Cat #3362). Full frame. $24.95. Keepcase.
1998 (R) 90m/C Jeff Fahey, Marlee Matlin, Monique Mercure; *D:* Allan Goldstein; *W:* Tony Kayden; *C:* Barry Gravelle.

Where the Buffalo Roam

Bill Murray's impersonation of legendary "gonzo" journalist Hunter S. Thompson is pretty unsatisfying for fans of both, though Murray generally comes out better than the writer. The plot is loosely based—what else could it be—on two of Thompson's *Fear and Loathing* books. The film has never looked very good and DVD technology can do little to improve it. The image is seldom better than fair. Same for the mono sound. —*MM*

Movie: 🎬🎬 *DVD:* 🎬🎬
Anchor Bay (Cat #DV10943, UPC #013131094398). Widescreen (1.85:1) letterboxed. Dolby Digital Mono. $24.98. Keepcase. *LANG:* English. *FEATURES:* 18 chapter links ▪ Hunter S. Thompson thumbnail biography.
1980 (R) 98m/C Bill Murray, Peter Boyle, Susan Kellerman, Bruno Kirby, Rene Auberjonois, R.G. Armstrong, Rafael Campos, Craig T. Nelson; *D:* Art Linson; *W:* John Kaye; *C:* Tak Fujimoto; *M:* Neil Young.

Where the Red Fern Grows

A young boy in Dust Bowl–era Oklahoma learns maturity from his love and responsibility for two Redbone hounds. Family fare is well produced but a little hokey. Followed by a sequel nearly 20 years later.
Movie: 🎬🎬▸ *DVD:* NYR
United American Video (Cat #40083). Full frame. Dolby Digital Surround Stereo. $14.99. Snapper.
1974 (G) 97m/C James Whitmore, Beverly Garland, Jack Ging, Lonny (Loni) Chapman, Stewart Peterson; *D:* Norman Tokar; *W:* Douglas Day Stewart, Eleanor Lamb; *C:* Dean Cundey; *M:* Lex de Azevedo.

Where the Red Fern Grows: Part 2

Sequel to the popular family movie stars Brimley as Grandpa Coleman. It's a coming-of-age story set deep in the Louisiana woods.
Movie: 🎬🎬▸ *DVD:* NYR
United American Video (Cat #40093). Full frame. Dolby Digital Surround Stereo. $14.99. Keepcase. Title is also available from Universal Home Video (cat. #40093) for $19.99.
1992 (G) 105m/C Wilford Brimley, Doug McKeon, Lisa Whelchel, Chad McQueen; *D:* Jim McCullough; *W:* Samuel Bradford; *C:* Joseph M. Wilcots; *M:* Robert Sprayberry.

Where the Rivers Flow North

In 1927, crusty Vermonter Noel Lourdes (Torn) doesn't want to leave his forest land when he's forced to sell out to the power company. His wife/companion/ housekeeper Bangor (Cardinal) says it's time to take the money and move on. The story is adapted from Frank Mosher's novel and is reminiscent of early Ken Kesey. Strong performances from the two leads and a fine supporting cast are the best features. The DVD image is fine, though this kind of story, with its deep roots in a specific place and a distant time, is not particularly well suited to the digital medium. That said, this solid sleeper is still recommended. —*MM*

Movie: 🎬🎬🎬 *DVD:* 🎬🎬🎬
Simitar Entertainment (Cat #7318, UPC #082551731824). Full frame. PCM Stereo. $14.98. Keepcase. *LANG:* English. *FEATURES:* 8 chapter links ▪ Production factoids ▪ Rip Torn filmography.
1994 (PG-13) 104m/C Rip Torn, Tantoo Cardinal, Bill Raymond, Mark Margolis, John Griesemer, Amy Wright, Dennis Mientka, Jusef Bulos, Michael J. Fox, Treat Williams; *D:* Jay Craven; *W:* Jay Craven, Don Bredos; *C:* Paul Ryan.

While You Were Sleeping

Feel-good romantic comedy finds lonely Lucy Moderatz (Bullock) collecting tokens for the Chicago train system and admiring Yuppie lawyer Peter Callaghan (Gallagher) as he commutes to and fro. Fate conspires to throw them together when Lucy rescues Peter after a mugging. Trouble is, he's not conscious so Lucy goes to the hospital with him, where she's mistaken for his fiancee. She continues the charade and is warmly welcomed by the Callaghan family, with the exception of Peter's brother, Jack (Pullman), who smells a rat even as he falls under the token collector's spell. Meanwhile, Peter remains in a coma, allowing Jack and Lucy to supply romantic comedy. Gallagher brings a serenity to his role as the unconscious Peter, while Bullock and Pullman take the predictable plot and deliver performances that earn them another notch on the climb to stardom. This could have been a great DVD, but the colors are a shade off. Those colors are, however, very vibrant and without a trace of bleed. The image is also very sharp, and blacks are true. No grain or artifacts to interfere. The contrast and brightness levels are consistent and comfortable. The Dolby Surround also does a good job with nice imaging, plenty of Surround ambience, and a well-balanced equalization of dialogue and music. —*JO*

Movie: 🎬🎬🎬 *DVD:* 🎬🎬🎬
Buena Vista Home Entertainment (Cat #13680, UPC #/17951000156). Keepcase. Dolby Surround. $29.99. Keepcase. *LANG:* English; French. *SUB:* Spanish. *FEA-*

TURES: 21 chapter links • Theatrical trailer.
1995 (PG) 103m/C Sandra Bullock, Bill Pullman, Peter Gallagher, Jack Warden, Peter Boyle, Glynis Johns, Micole Mercurio, Jason Bernard, Michael Rispoli, Ally Walker, Monica Keena; *D:* Jon Turteltaub; *W:* Fred Lebow, Daniel G. Sullivan; *C:* Phedon Papamichael; *M:* Randy Edelman. *AWARDS:* Blockbuster Entertainment Awards '96: Comedy Actress, Video (Bullock), Comedy Actress, Theatrical (Bullock); *NOM:* Golden Globe Awards '96: Best Actress—Musical/Comedy (Bullock); MTV Movie Awards '96: Best Female Performance (Bullock), Most Desirable Female (Bullock).

Whisper Kill

When her partner is killed by "The Whisperer," reporter Liz Bartlett (Anderson) sets out to solve the case. When another investigative reporter (Penny) shows up, she becomes romantically involved. On DVD, this made-for-TV fare is nothing out of the ordinary. In every scene, the garish lighting seems keyed to Ms. Anderson's massive golden helmet of hair. —*MM*
Movie: ♪♪➤ *DVD:* ♪♪
Simitar Entertainment (Cat #758, UPC #082551758029). Full frame. Dolby Digital Stereo. $14.98. Keepcase. *LANG:* English. *FEATURES:* 8 chapter links • Production factoids • Loni Anderson filmography.
1988 93m/C Loni Anderson, Joe Penny, June Lockhart, James Sutorius, Jeremy Slate; *D:* Christian Nyby; *W:* John Robert Bensink; *M:* Charles Bernstein.

White Man's Burden

In a world where blacks have all the wealth and power, and whites comprise the struggling underclasses, Caucasian factory worker Travolta is fired by his bigoted black CEO (Belafonte) due to a misunderstanding. Driven by his poverty-level financial strain, Travolta kidnaps the boss to show him how the other half lives. Gimmicky premise is full of reverse stereotypes. Treads too lightly, and rehashes too many familiar stories to make any real impact. The biggest problem with this DVD is the unacceptable amount of digital grain. Other than that, it is very average in most ways, although the blacks are better than you'd expect on this disc. The sound is the other exception, crisp enough to convey the dialogue and dynamic enough for the music. The low end and Surround are above average. Another title that's as good or better on tape and superior on laserdisc. —*JO*
Movie: ♪♪➤ *DVD:* ♪♪
HBO Home Video (Cat #91289, UPC #026359128929). Full frame. Dolby Surround. $24.98. Snapper. *LANG:* English; French. *CAP:* English. *FEATURES:* 12 chapter links.
1995 (R) 89m/C John Travolta, Harry Belafonte, Kelly Lynch, Margaret Avery, Tom Bower, Carrie Snodgress, Sheryl Lee Ralph; *D:* Desmond Nakano; *W:* Desmond

Nakano; *C:* Willy Kurant; *M:* Howard Shore.

White Palace

Successful widowed Jewish lawyer Spader is attracted to older, less-educated hamburger waitress Sarandon. Ethnic/cultural strife ensues as does hot sex, which is certainly the high point of the film on any medium. The full-frame DVD image is only a very slight improvement over VHS tape. The steamy interiors are fine; daylight exteriors are grainy. —*MM*
Movie: ♪♪➤ *DVD:* ♪♪➤
Goodtimes Entertainment (Cat #05-81033). Full frame. $19.98. Snapper. *LANG:* English. *SUB:* English; French; Spanish. *FEATURES:* 18 chapter links.
1990 (R) 103m/C Susan Sarandon, James Spader, Jason Alexander, Eileen Brennan, Griffin Dunne, Kathy Bates, Steven Hill, Rachel Levin, Corey Parker, Spiros Focas, Renee Taylor, Kim Myers; *D:* Luis Mandoki; *W:* Alvin Sargent, Ted Tally; *C:* Lajos Koltai; *M:* George Fenton.

White Squall

Based on the 1960 true story of 13 young men who become students at Ocean Academy, a year-long adventure spent aboard the brigantine Albatross. Bridges plays the ship's captain and surrogate dad. The boys agonize over their various crises, making the first half of the movie into a veritable "Dead Poets Yachting Society." However, a sudden storm overtakes the ship in the Caribbean and several crew members are killed. There's a shift to a *Caine Mutiny*–type trial in which Bridges must prove the tragedy was not his fault while the survivors rally to his defense. Director Scott excels at showing the fury of nature in the prolonged storm scene, but takes his time getting there. Put the DVD in your player and skip directly to the climax of the film and you've got yourself a good action-packed short that manages to take advantage of all the DVD's capabilities. The sound during that sequence is tremendous, with near-nauseating intensity, as you're placed dead center in the action. It's actually scary, as things whirl around you and each wave crashes you back into your seat. Through the whole film the image is sharp and colors are excellent. That doesn't change during the climax, with extreme variations in the lighting. Great DVD, so-so movie. —*JO*
Movie: ♪➤ *DVD:* ♪♪♪➤
Buena Vista Home Entertainment (Cat #17247, UPC #717951002402). Widescreen (2.35:1) letterboxed. Dolby Digital 5.1; Stereo. $29.99. Keepcase. *LANG:* English; French. *CAP:* English. *FEATURES:* 21 chapter links • Theatrical trailer • "Making of" featurette.
1996 (PG-13) 128m/C Jeff Bridges, Scott Wolf, Caroline Goodall, Balthazar Getty, John Savage, Jeremy Sisto, Jason Marsden, David Selby, Zeljko Ivanek, Ryan Phillippe, David Lascher, Eric Michael

Cole, Julio Mechoso, Ethan (Randall) Embry; *D:* Ridley Scott; *W:* Todd Robinson; *C:* Hugh Johnson; *M:* Jeff Rona.

The White Zombie

Though it's terribly dated, Lugosi's follow-up to *Dracula* is still important as the first of its kind and the progenitor of today's *Living Dead* horrors. In a backlot Haiti, a rich lecher engages Lugosi to zombiefy the young bride for whom he lusts. The main flaws now are a florid acting style and Lugosi's silly makeup with its exaggerated widow's peak, caterpillar eyebrows and bald-chinned beard. —*MM*
Movie: ♪♪ *DVD:* NYR
Roan Group (Cat #2001). Full frame. $24.95.
1932 73m/B Bela Lugosi, Madge Bellamy, John Harron, Joseph Cawthorn, Robert Frazer, Brandon Hurst, George Burr Macannan, John Peters, Dan Crimmins, Clarence Muse; *D:* Victor Halperin; *W:* Garnett Weston; *C:* Arthur Martinelli; *M:* Xavier Cugat.

Who Framed Roger Rabbit

Technically dazzling combination of animation and live action is a detective story (based on Gary K. Wolf's novel *Who Censored Roger Rabbit?*) set in an alternative Hollywood of 1947 where 'toons are an abused minority working in the film business. Shamus Eddie Valiant (Hoskins) is hired to get the goods on sexy Jessica Rabbit so that her husband Roger will quit worrying about her and get back to work. The plot borrows bits from *Chinatown* and *Looney Tunes* with equal ease. Virtually all of the great cartoon characters from the past make cameo appearances. The DVD re-creates director Robert Zemeckis's richly detailed fantasy Tinseltown, and avoids many of the problems that plague the medium. Venetian blinds in an important early scene do not flash, but Dolores's (Cassidy) polka dot dress does. Jessica's torch song introduction (chapter 4, "Why Don't You Do Right?") is a still smoky show-stopper. Even without the frills that accompany most boxoffice hits, the disc is still one of the best. —*MM*
Movie: ♪♪♪➤ *DVD:* ♪♪♪➤
Buena Vista Home Entertainment (Cat #18140, UPC #717951004192). Widescreen (1.85:1) letterboxed. Dolby Digital 5.1. $29.99. Keepcase. *LANG:* English; French. *CAP:* English. *FEATURES:* 19 chapter links • Theatrical trailer.
1988 (PG) 104m/C Bob Hoskins, Christopher Lloyd, Joanna Cassidy, Alan Tilvern, Stubby Kaye; *D:* Robert Zemeckis; *W:* Jeffrey Price, Peter S. Seaman; *C:* Dean Cundey; *M:* Alan Silvestri; *V:* Charles Fleischer, Mae Questel, Kathleen Turner, Amy Irving, Mel Blanc, June Foray, Frank Sinatra. *AWARDS:* Academy Awards '88: Best Film Editing, Best Visual Effects; *NOM:* Academy Awards '88: Best Art Direction/Set Decoration, Best Cinematography, Best Sound.

Who Shot Pat?

Funny, nostalgic coming-of-age story is set in '50s Brooklyn. Bic Bickman (Knight) is the leader of a clean-living "gang" of seniors at the Brooklyn vocational school. Memorable vintage soundtrack features hits by legendary artists Chuck Berry and Bo Diddly. *AKA:* Who Shot Patakango?. **Movie:** 🎵🎵▶ **DVD:** NYR
Tapeworm Video Distributors (Cat #1636). Full frame. $19.95. Keepcase.
1992 (R) 102m/C David Knight, Sandra Bullock, Kevin Otto, Aaron Ingram, Brad Randall; **D:** Robert Brooks; **W:** Robert Brooks, Halle Brooks; **C:** Robert Brooks.

Who's Afraid of Virginia Woolf?

Nichols debuts as a director in this biting Edward Albee play. A teacher and his wife (Segal and Dennis) are invited to the home of a burned-out professor and his foul-mouthed, bitter, yet seductive wife (Burton and Taylor). The guests get more than dinner, as the evening deteriorates into brutal verbal battles between the hosts. Taylor and Dennis won Oscars; Burton's Oscar-nominated portrait of the tortured husband is magnificent. Richard and Liz's best film together. This is as good a black-and-white image as I've seen. The detail is incredible and the cinematography's depth is amazing. The Dolby Digital mono sound gives much more power to the performances. An excellent DVD. —*JO*
Movie: 🎵🎵🎵🎵 **DVD:** 🎵🎵🎵🎵
Warner Home Video, Inc. (Cat #12414, UPC #085391241423). Widescreen (1.85:1) letterboxed; full frame. Dolby Digital Mono. $19.98. Snapper. *LANG:* English. *SUB:* English; French; Spanish. *CAP:* English. *FEATURES:* 17 chapter links ● Production notes.
1966 (R) 127m/B Richard Burton, Elizabeth Taylor, George Segal, Sandy Dennis; **D:** Mike Nichols; **W:** Ernest Lehman; **C:** Haskell Wexler; **M:** Alex North. *AWARDS:* Academy Awards '66: Best Actress (Taylor), Best Art Direction/Set Decoration (B & W), Best Black-and-white Cinematography, Best Costume Design (B & W), Best Supporting Actress (Dennis); British Academy Awards '66: Best Actor (Burton), Best Actress (Taylor), Best Film; National Board of Review Awards '66: Best Actress (Taylor); New York Film Critics Awards '66: Best Actress (Taylor); *NOM:* Academy Awards '66: Best Actor (Burton), Best Adapted Screenplay, Best Director (Nichols), Best Film Editing, Best Picture, Best Sound, Best Supporting Actor (Segal), Best Original Score.

Why Do Fools Fall in Love?

Frankie Lymon was a teen do-wop singing sensation in the mid-'50s but a career slide led to heroin addiction and an OD death at the age of 25 in 1968. The other thing Frankie liked to do was marry—without bothering to get divorced. So there are three would-be widows battling for what's left of Lymon's estate: R&B singer Zola Taylor (Berry), goodtime girl and single mom Elizabeth Waters (Fox), and churchgoing schoolteacher Emira Eagle (Rochon). The ladies pull out all the stops but Lymon remains a mystery. The 5.1 sound delivers the goods during all of the music and is competent throughout. The image itself is crisp, with vibrant and accurate colors. The relaxed commentary is well worth listening to. —*JO*
Movie: 🎵🎵 **DVD:** 🎵🎵🎵▶
Warner Home Video, Inc. (Cat #16916, UPC #085391691624). Widescreen (1.85:1) letterboxed; full frame. Dolby Digital 5.1. $24.98. Snapper. *LANG:* English. *SUB:* English; French. *CAP:* English. *FEATURES:* 39 chapter links ● Theatrical trailer ● Commentary: Gregory Nava, Tina Andrews, and Paul Hall ● Production notes.
1998 (R) 115m/C Larenz Tate, Halle Berry, Lela Rochon, Vivica A. Fox, Paul Mazursky, Pamela Reed, Little Richard, Ben Vereen, Lane Smith, Alexis Cruz; **D:** Gregory Nava; **W:** Tina Andrews; **C:** Edward Lachman; **M:** Stephen James Taylor.

Why Has Bodhi-Darma Left for the East

Set in a remote monastery in the Korean mountains, Bae Yong-kyun's film follows an old Buddhist master, close to death, who must lead his disciples—a orphaned boy and a young monk—in their search for spiritual enlightenment and freedom. The film's title is a Zen *koan*—an unanswerable riddle that is both a challenge and an aid to spiritual transformation. The film looks very good on DVD, capturing textures particularly well—the surface of a stream, a gold gilt Buddha, a dusty frog. Even the mono sound is effective. Since stillness is one of the film's main points, it's certainly not for everyone, but the right audience will love it. —*MM*
Movie: 🎵🎵🎵 **DVD:** 🎵🎵🎵
Image Entertainment (Cat #ID5937MLSD-VD, UPC #014381593723). Widescreen (1.75:1) letterboxed. Dolby Digital Mono. $29.99. Snapper. *LANG:* Korean. *SUB:* English. *FEATURES:* 18 chapter links.
1989 135m/C Hae-Jin Huang, Su-Myong Ko, Yi Pan-Yong, Sin Won-Sop; **D:** Bae Young-kyun; **W:** Bae Young-kyun; **C:** Bae Young-kyun.

Wicked City

Humans are uneasily coexisting with Reptoids (creatures that can assume human shape) in this sci-fi tale based on a Japanese comic book. Then Hong Kong police discover a plot by the Reptoids to destroy mankind and rule the world (what else is new). Nifty special effects. This is a rare case where the live-action film is actually superior to the anime version. This Image DVD delivers a much better picture than would have been expected had Tai Seng or some other import-only specialist released it. The disc is sharp and colors are excellent. The only problems seem related to preprint. The mono sound is full and free of distortion. —*JO*
Movie: 🎵🎵🎵 **DVD:** 🎵🎵🎵
Image Entertainment (Cat #ID4664FLDVD, UPC #014381466423). Widescreen (1.66:1) letterboxed. Dolby Digital Mono. $24.95. Snapper. *LANG:* English; Cantonese. *FEATURES:* 12 chapter links.
1992 88m/C *HK* Jacky Cheung, Leon Lai, Michelle Li; **D:** Peter Mak; **W:** Tsui Hark, Roy Szeto; **C:** Andrew Lau, Joe Chan; **M:** Richard Yuen.

Wicked Ways

Stop me if you've heard this before: Matt (Rooker) is a traveling salesman. His wife Ruth (DeMornay) is extremely jealous and she's got reason. Matt has another wife in another town. From that admittedly familiar premise, Ron Senkowski spins out a deliriously inventive thriller. Rooker and DeMornay also served as executive producers, probably because they realized how well the material fit their particular gifts. Ms. DeMornay, in particular, takes her psycho-blonde femme fatale to a new level. This mid-budget production probably doesn't gain that much on DVD—VHS image is probably about the same—because the characters are so strong. Recommended on any medium. —*MM* *AKA:* A Table for One.
Movie: 🎵🎵🎵▶ **DVD:** 🎵🎵🎵
Image Entertainment (Cat #ID8811UM DVD, UPC #014381881127). Widescreen (1.78:1) anamorphic. Dolby Digital Stereo. $24.99. Snapper. *LANG:* English. *FEATURES:* 14 chapter links.
1999 (R) 110m/C Rebecca DeMornay, Michael Rooker, Lisa Zane, Mark Rolston, Peter Dobson; **D:** Ron Senkowski; **W:** Ron Senkowski; **C:** Chris Walling; **M:** Evan Evans.

The Wicked, Wicked West

Despite the titillating box copy and the title's similarity to *Wild Wild West*, this is a dreary look at the desolate lives of several prostitutes and their pragmatic madam Annie Ryan (Fricker) in a prairie bordello in the 1870s. The pale, undernourished DVD image is no better than VHS tape in any significant area. —*MM* *AKA:* Painted Angels.
Movie: 🎵 **DVD:** 🎵
Studio Home Entertainment (Cat #7035, UPC #658149703520). Full frame. $24.95. Keepcase. *LANG:* English. *FEATURES:* 18 chapter links ● Cast thumbnail biographies.
1997 (R) 108m/C Brenda Fricker, Kelly McGillis, Bronagh Gallagher, Meret Becker, Lisa Jakub; **D:** Jon Sanders; **W:** Jon Sanders; **C:** Gerald Packer.

The Wife

Therapists Jack and Rita (Noonan and Hagerty), who are also a married couple, host an impromptu dinner party with their client Cosmo (Shawn) and Arlie (Young), Cosmo's "wifey," when they should be focusing on their own problems. Tensions build throughout the night as they break off by twos in various combinations to unburden their souls, or at least kvetch. The proceedings are gently comic and compassionate, without pulling punches, compared to *Who's Afraid of Virginia Woolf?* or other more poisonous domestic barn-burners. The film deserves a point extra for giving Julie *Airplane* Hagerty a meaty serio-comic role, and for making Wallace Shawn the center of everyone's world instead of a throwaway bit player. Characters practically whisper in your ear and you can see the cold of the New England snow, but the film's moodily lit, analog charms could only have been a nightmare for the DVD producers. The bonus trailer is presented full frame. —*JK*
Movie: 🐾🐾🐾 **DVD:** 🐾🐾➤
Fox/Lorber Home Video (Cat #FLV5069, UPC #720917506920). Widescreen. Stereo. $29.99. Keepcase. *LANG:* English. *FEATURES:* 8 chapter links • Interactive menus • Full-color picture disc • Star filmographies • Production credits list • Trailer.
1995 (R) 101m/C Tom Noonan, Julie Hagerty, Karen Young, Wallace Shawn; *D:* Tom Noonan; *W:* Tom Noonan; *C:* Joe DeSalvo; *M:* Lodovico Sorret.

Wild America

Warner Bros. invades Disney's well-marked territory of family-friendly real-life adventures with this bio of famed nature documentarians Mark, Marty, and Marshall Stouffer. The story begins with their first footage of backyard wildlife, filmed with a used 16-mm. camera. They hit the road in the '60s to find more dangerous (and endangered) beasts to film. As expected, the scenery and critters are highlighted, and any realistic animal gore or violence is toned down, too. (The title is taken from Marty Stouffer's long-running PBS nature series.) On DVD, the image ranges from very good to good to fair in the more dramatic landscapes, which can be troublesome for the medium. Viewers who are more interested in the young stars will want to go with the full-frame version. —*MM*
Movie: 🐾🐾➤ **DVD:** 🐾🐾🐾
Warner Home Video, Inc. (Cat #1550). Widescreen (2.35:1) letterboxed; full frame. Dolby Digital 5.1 Surround Stereo. $24.98. Snapper. *LANG:* English; French. *SUB:* English; French; Spanish. *FEATURES:* 35 chapter links • Cast and crew thumbnail bios • Production notes • Trailer.
1997 (G) 105m/C Jonathan Taylor Thomas, Devon Sawa, Scott Bairstow, Jamey Sheridan, Frances Fisher, Tracey Walter, Don Stroud; *D:* William Dear; *W:*

David Michael Wieger; *C:* David Burr; *M:* Joel McNeely.

The Wild Bunch

Acclaimed western about a group of aging outlaws on their final rampage, realizing that time is passing them by. Features too many memorable characters to mention and unsurpassed action scenes. Highly influential in dialogue, montage editing, and lyrical slow-motion violence. Arguably the greatest western and one of the best American films of all time. This is Peckinpah's masterpiece, restored to its original glory (and running time) after being available in a cut version for over 20 years. The DVD also features "The Wild Bunch: An Album in Montage," the Academy Award–nominated documentary by Paul Seydor and Nick Redman. If Warner Bros. had done a shoddy job on this one, I probably would have trashed my DVD player. While the disc isn't perfect—there is a little too much grain—it is the best way to see this gem. There is a CAV laserdisc box set that's somewhat sharper but requires a side change every half-hour. The DVD's colors are good, as is the contrast and brightness. The blacks are very close to true and the grain doesn't increase in dark scenes. Artifacts are minimal. The sound has been mastered in 5.1 and sounded better to me than when I saw the restored film in the theatre. Jerry Fielding's excellent score has never sounded better, nor has the Wild Bunch's final shootout with Mapache's army. —*JO*
Movie: 🐾🐾🐾🐾 **DVD:** 🐾🐾🐾
Warner Home Video, Inc. (Cat #14034, UPC #085391403425). Widescreen (2.35:1) letterboxed. Dolby Digital 5.1; Dolby Surround. $24.98. Snapper. *LANG:* English (DD5.1, DS). *SUB:* Spanish; French. *CAP:* English. *FEATURES:* 46 movie chapter links • 10 documentary chapter links • Theatrical trailer • Documentary • Production notes.
1969 (R) 145m/C William Holden, Ernest Borgnine, Robert Ryan, Warren Oates, Strother Martin, L.Q. (Justus E. McQueen) Jones, Albert Dekker, Bo Hopkins, Edmond O'Brien, Ben Johnson, Jaime Sanchez, Emilio Fernandez, Dub Taylor; *D:* Sam Peckinpah; *W:* Walon Green, Sam Peckinpah; *C:* Lucien Ballard; *M:* Jerry Fielding. *AWARDS:* American Film Institute (AFI) '98: Top 100, National Film Registry '99; National Society of Film Critics Awards '69: Best Cinematography; *NOM:* Academy Awards '69: Best Story & Screenplay, Best Original Score.

The Wild One

In the original biker flick, two gangs descend upon a quiet town and each other. Johnny (Brando) is the leader of one, struggling against social prejudices and his pals' lawlessness to find love and a normal life. The depraved Chino (Marvin, who steals scenes if not the whole film from his more-famous costar) is in charge

of the other. The tribute to '50s rebelliousness—based vaguely, very vaguely, on a real incident—is now quaint, but still a touchstone of Brando's career. The clarity of DVD accentuates the film's flaws, most noticeably the abrupt pops and unfocused moments at edits. Monaural sound is nothing special. The flaws appear to come from a dinged-up original, not the transfer. —*MM*
Movie: 🐾🐾🐾 **DVD:** 🐾🐾➤
Columbia Tristar Home Video (Cat #06239, UPC #043396062399). Full frame. $29.95. Keepcase. *LANG:* English; French. *SUB:* English; French. *FEATURES:* 28 chapter links • Theatrical trailers.
1954 79m/B Marlon Brando, Lee Marvin, Mary Murphy, Robert Keith, Jerry Paris, Alvy Moore, Jay C. Flippen, Peggy Maley, Bruno VeSota; *D:* Laslo Benedek; *W:* John Paxton; *C:* Hal Mohr; *M:* Leith Stevens.

Wild Reeds

The Algerian war looms over southwest France in 1962. Three boys and a girl "explore the mysteries of the human heart," as the box cover puts it, in the video industry's shorthand for nascent homosexuality. They do the twist, attend Bergman films, flirt, copy homework, hear about deaths on the front lines, and go through sundry rites of passage set to a wistful, string-laden score. Folks who revel in bittersweet nostalgia may have already seen and liked this award-winner, but those who haven't felt any pressing need to see it yet will be asked to meet this DVD version more than halfway. The overall disc and package design is pedestrian. The subtitles are "enhanced" but white and still somewhat difficult to read. Interactivity is minimalist. The credits list is four pages long but promised "biographies" boil down to material about the director and no one else. The film has 27 chapter stops but only 9 are linked from the menu. The first link in skips the opening credits and initial scene. The image is thick with alias. That at least mimics impressionist brushwork, but still makes trying to watch a tough go. —*JK* *AKA:* Les Roseaux Sauvages.
Movie: 🐾🐾🐾 **DVD:** 🐾🐾🐾
WinStar Home Entertainment (Cat #FLV5006, UPC #720917050065). Widescreen (1.66:1) letterboxed. Stereo. $29.99. Keepcase. *LANG:* French. *SUB:* English (enhanced). *FEATURES:* 9 chapter links • Interactive menus • Production credits • Director bio and filmography • Theatrical trailer.
1994 110m/C *FR* Gael Morel, Stephane Rideau, Elodie Bouchez, Frederic Gorny, Michele Moretti; *D:* Andre Techine; *W:* Gilles Taurand, Olivier Massart, Andre Techine; *C:* Jeanne Lapoirie; *M:* Chubby Checker. *AWARDS:* Cesar Awards '95: Best Director (Techine), Best Film, Best Writing; Los Angeles Film Critics Association Awards '95: Best Foreign Film; National Society of Film Critics Awards '95: Best Foreign Film.

Wild Things

Titillating pulp friction can't decide between modern noir and swampy spoof. Miami guidance counselor and high school heartthrob fodder Sam Lombardo (Dillon) lectures on sex crimes and is accused of rape by two school girls: snotty rich Kelly (Richards) and trailer trash Suzie (Campbell). The seemingly upright investigator (Bacon) tries to figure out who's telling the truth. Murray pops up doing his best Bill Murray, but his hilarious presence doesn't play next to the oh-so-serious Dillon and gang. Even more out of place is Wagner's wooden cameo as Kelly's father. Speaking of wooden, the normally fine Russell is reduced to similar stereotype as Kelly's vampy, conniving mother. Endless exercise in audience manipulation has plot twists and turns relentlessly continue through the credits. This film has excellent cinematography to go along with the sleaze and the DVD's lush color makes the image even more appealing (not just the sex). The image is sharp all the way through, despite varying lighting conditions. Contrast and brightness levels are high and comfortable, but take nothing away from image definition or color shadings. The 5.1 sound matches the image in quality and has plenty of Surround information constantly fed to the rear channels. The commentary is lame, with even George Clinton not projecting his usual personality. —*JO*
Movie: 🐾🐾▸ *DVD:* 🐾🐾🐾▸
Columbia Tristar Home Video (Cat #02411, UPC #043396024113). Widescreen (2.35:1) letterboxed; full frame. Dolby Digital 5.1; Stereo. $29.95. Keepcase. *LANG:* English; French. *SUB:* English; French. *CAP:* English. *FEATURES:* 28 chapter links • Commentary: McNaughton, Clinton, Elena Maganini, Rodney Liber, et al • Deleted scenes • Theatrical trailers.
1998 (R) 108m/C Matt Dillon, Neve Campbell, Kevin Bacon, Denise Richards, Theresa Russell, Daphne Rubin-Vega, Bill Murray, Robert Wagner, Carrie Snodgress, Jeffery Perry, Marc Macaulay; *D:* John McNaughton; *W:* Steven Peters; *C:* Jeffrey L. Kimball; *M:* George S. Clinton. *AWARDS:* Los Angeles Film Critics Association Awards '98: Best Supporting Actor (Murray); *NOM:* MTV Movie Awards '99: Best Kiss (Matt Dillon/Neve Campbell/Denise Richards).

Wild Wild West

The best and the worst that can be said of this hit is that it is faithful to its source, the 1960s TV series. The plot is too silly for synopsis. The filmmakers take the cute gimmicks and thin characters from the original and attempt to overpower them with computer-generated effects that are as unimpressive on DVD as they were on theatre screens. Worse still, director Sonnenfeld and star Smith don't strike the same kind of escapist sparks that made *Men in Black* so much fun. Smith's Jim West is an intentionally stupid and not particularly likeable protagonist. The most

interesting thing on-screen here is villain Branagh's curious beard, which looks like Groucho's mustache on steroids. Kline isn't bad as sidekick Artemis Gordon. The rest of the capable supporting cast is wasted. On DVD, the big-budget gadgets and gizmos—even the huge mechanical spider—are clunky, and the whole thing lacks the bright, eye-popping snap of a really good digital transfer. It could be, though, that the substandard material has a lot to do with that judgment. —*MM*
Movie: woof *DVD:* 🐾🐾▸
Warner Home Video, Inc. (Cat #17175). Full frame; widescreen letterboxed. Dolby Digital 5.1 Surround; Dolby Digital Stereo. $24.98. Snapper. *LANG:* English. *SUB:* English. *FEATURES:* 31 chapter links • Commentary: director Barry Sonnenfeld • Cast and crew thumbnail biographies • HBO special • Explanation of gadgets, gizmos, and wardrobe.
1999 (PG-13) 105m/C Will Smith, Kevin Kline, Kenneth Branagh, Salma Hayek, M. Emmet Walsh, Ted Levine, Musetta Vander, Bai Ling, Rodney A. Grant, Frederique van der Wal, Garcelle Beauvais, Sofia Eng; *D:* Barry Sonnenfeld; *W:* Brent Maddock, S.S. Wilson, Jeffrey Price, Peter S. Seaman; *C:* Michael Ballhaus; *M:* Elmer Bernstein. *AWARDS:* Golden Raspberry Awards '99: Worst Picture, Worst Director (Sonnenfeld), Worst Screenplay, Worst Song ("Wild Wild West"); *NOM:* Golden Raspberry Awards '99: Worst Actor (Kline), Worst Supporting Actor (Branagh), Worst Supporting Actress (Hayek).

William Shakespeare's A Midsummer Night's Dream

Setting Shakespeare's fantasy in 19th-century Italy is a questionable choice. The largely American actors' fumbling attempts at the archaic language are much more troublesome. Only Kevin Kline pulls it off with any real style. Overall, neither the cast nor the director seems to understand the ephemeral nature of the material. That said, the DVD is visually gorgeous. Even the busiest scenes are well detailed, and the soundtrack makes every syllable understandable. That, however, is not always an asset. —*MM AKA:* A Midsummer Night's Dream.
Movie: 🐾🐾▸ *DVD:* 🐾🐾🐾
Twentieth Century Fox Home Entertainment (Cat #4112308, UPC #086162123085). Widescreen (2.35:1) letterboxed. Dolby Digital 5.1 Surround Stereo; Dolby Digital Surround Stereo. $34.98. Keepcase. *LANG:* English; Spanish. *SUB:* Spanish. *CAP:* English. *FEATURES:* 24 chapter links • Theatrical trailer.
1999 (PG-13) 115m/C Rupert Everett, Michelle Pfeiffer, Kevin Kline, Stanley Tucci, Calista Flockhart, Dominic West, Christian Bale, David Strathairn, Sophie Marceau, John Sessions, Anna Friel, Roger Rees, Max Wright, Gregory Jbara, Bill Irwin, Sam Rockwell, Bernard Hill; *D:* Michael

Hoffman; *W:* Michael Hoffman; *C:* Oliver Stapleton; *M:* Simon Boswell.

William Shakespeare's Romeo and Juliet

One wonders what the result might be if Shakespeare were hijacked by MTV. Australian director Baz Luhrmann (*Strictly Ballroom*) gives his vision of such an event, and the results are decidedly mixed. The classic William Shakespeare story of the tragic love affair between Romeo and Juliet gets a hip-hop update, with stilted dialogue delivered straight-faced by the protagonists, and .45 caliber pistols replacing swords of the original period. It is, in a word, silly. The star power of DiCaprio and Danes is largely wasted, with the only saving grace the ability of DVD to deliver subtitles to sort out the often incomprehensible prose. Outside of the inclusion of a theatrical trailer and subtitle options, this DVD release is pretty much a bare bones effort. The transfer is clean, and the sound is well-presented, but for such an odd theatrical outing, one might have expected more—music videos, behind the scenes and commentary by the director would have been appropriate. —*RT AKA:* Romeo and Juliet.
Movie: 🐾🐾 *DVD:* 🐾🐾▸
Twentieth Century Fox Home Entertainment (Cat #4110421, UPC #086162104213). Widescreen. Dolby Digital 5.1 Surround Stereo; Dolby Digital Surround Stereo. $29.98. Keepcase. *LANG:* English; French. *SUB:* English; Spanish. *CAP:* English; Spanish. *FEATURES:* 29 chapter markers • Theatrical trailer.
1996 (PG-13) 120m/C Leonardo DiCaprio, Claire Danes, John Leguizamo, Paul Sorvino, Brian Dennehy, Diane Venora, Pete Postlethwaite, Paul Rudd, Harold Perrineau Jr., Jesse Bradford, Miriam Margolyes, Vondie Curtis-Hall, Christina Pickles, M. Emmet Walsh; *D:* Baz Luhrmann; *W:* Baz Luhrmann, Craig Pearce; *C:* Donald McAlpine; *M:* Nellee Hooper. *AWARDS:* British Academy Awards '97: Best Adapted Screenplay, Best Art Direction/Set Decoration, Best Director (Luhrmann), Best Score; MTV Movie Awards '97: Best Female Performance (Danes); *NOM:* Academy Awards '96: Best Art Direction/Set Decoration; British Academy Awards '97: Best Cinematography, Best Film Editing, Best Sound; MTV Movie Awards '97: Best Film, Best Male Performance (DiCaprio), Best On-Screen Duo (Leonardo DiCaprio/Claire Danes), Best Song ("#1 Crush"), Best Kiss (Leonardo DiCaprio/Claire Danes).

Willy Wonka & the Chocolate Factory

When the last of five coveted "golden tickets" falls into the hands of sweet but very poor Charlie, he and his Grandpa Joe get a tour of the most wonderfully strange chocolate factory in the world. The owner

is the most curious hermit ever to hit the big screen. He leads the five young "winners" on a thrilling and often dangerous tour of his fabulous factory. Adapted from Roald Dahl's *Charlie and the Chocolate Factory.* Without a doubt one of the best "kid's" movies ever made; a family classic worth watching again and again. Once you've seen this movie on DVD you'll never watch it on any other format. The chocolate factory has never been so colorful. The colors are super bright with plenty of contrast, giving the picture even more of a candy-colored look than before. The image is also very sharp and there is no evidence of grain or artifacts. The blacks are excellent. The sound has been totally remastered to Dolby Digital 5.1, featuring some great Surround effects, and is packed with energy to match the picture. —*JO*
Movie: 🎜🎜🎜▶ **DVD:** 🎜🎜🎜▶
Warner Home Video, Inc. (Cat #14546, UPC #085391454625). Widescreen (1.85:1) anamorphic. Dolby Digital 5.1; Dolby Digital Mono; Dolby Surround. $24.98. Snapper. *LANG:* English (DD5.1); Spanish (DDM); French (DS). *SUB:* English; Spanish; French. *CAP:* English. *FEATURES:* 40 chapter links • Theatrical trailers • Production notes.
1971 (G) 100m/C Gene Wilder, Jack Albertson, Denise Nickerson, Peter Ostrum, Roy Kinnear, Aubrey Woods, Michael Bollner, Ursula Reit, Leonard Stone, Dodo Denney, Julie Dawn Cole, Gunter Meisner; *D:* Mel Stuart; *W:* Roald Dahl; *C:* Arthur Ibbetson; *M:* Leslie Bricusse, Anthony Newley, Walter Scharf. *AWARDS: NOM:* Academy Awards '71: Original Song Score and/or Adaptation.

The Wind

Best-selling novelist Sian Anderson (Foster) repairs to a Greek island to work on her next book, but finds a stalker instead. Hauser is his usual scene-stealing, menacing self. DVD doesn't offer much help to this low-budget thriller. Even the picturesque Greek scenery looks dull and underlit. Most of the important action takes place at night and those scenes are very hard to make out. On DVD, this one looks about the same as it did when it became something of a cult hit on tape. —*MM*
Movie: 🎜🎜 **DVD:** 🎜🎜
Simitar Entertainment (Cat #7623, UPC #082551762323). Full frame. Dolby Digital 5.1 Surround Stereo. $14.98. Keepcase. *LANG:* English. *FEATURES:* 8 chapter links • Production factoids • Meg Foster, Charles Morley filmographies.
1987 92m/C Meg Foster, Wings Hauser, Steve Railsback, David McCallum, Robert Morley; *D:* Nico Mastorakis; *W:* Nico Mastorakis, Fred C. Perry; *C:* Andreas Bellis; *M:* Stanley Myers, Hans Zimmer.

A Wind Named Amnesia

Imaginative apocalyptic anime opens two years after a wind sweeps across the planet and causes people everywhere to forget everything they know. Speech, technology, religion, family, civilization, culture—all gone. Humanity is ignorant, innocent, and brutal. One young man, Wataru (Japanese for "traveler"), has been re-educated through a curious plot device. He wanders a mostly deserted landscape searching for anyone else who has regained or retained intelligence. In San Francisco, he finds Sophia and a lethal robot (reminiscent of the Walkers in *Return of the Jedi*) that is driven to attack him. The well-constructed plot borrows from Stephen King. The animation and background art are fine though the simple colors and shapes don't really test the limits of the digital medium. Still, the image is strikingly clear. The character profiles are moments from the film, not explanations or additions. Though the film isn't as widely known as some Japanese imports, it's one of the best of its kind. —*MM*
Movie: 🎜🎜🎜 **DVD:** 🎜🎜🎜
Central Park Media/U.S. Manga Corps (Cat #USMD 1749, UPC #719987174924). Full frame. Dolby Digital. $29.99. Keepcase. *LANG:* English; Japanese. *SUB:* English; Japanese. *FEATURES:* 14 chapter links • Profiles of human and mechanical characters • Previews of Central Park Media releases.
1993 80m/C *JP D:* Kazuo Yamazaki; *W:* Hideyuki Kikuchi.

Winds of the Wasteland / The Lucky Texan

In the first film on this disc, Wayne and Chandler are Pony Express contractors who race rivals to land government work. In the second, Wayne is a tough Easterner who goes west and finds himself involved with miners and claim jumpers. These short B-movies helped to put the Duke on the Hollywood map.
Movie: 🎜🎜▶ **DVD:** NYR
Madacy Entertainment (Cat #990035). Full frame. Dolby Digital Mono. $9.99. Keepcase. *FEATURES:* Thumbnail bios.
1936 113m/B John Wayne, Phyllis Fraser, Lane Chandler, Yakima Canutt; *D:* Mack V. Wright; *W:* Joseph Poland; *C:* William Nobles.

Wing Commander

Unintentionally amusing sf action flick is essentially a World War II submarine flick in outer space. Hot-shot young pilots (Prinze Jr. and Lillard) battle an evil race of aliens who resemble a heavily armed road company of *Cats.* The real battle is with the heinous dialogue and silly techno-babble they're forced to spout. The film is adapted from a video game, but it lacks the depth of characterization and emotion found in the original. On DVD, the real stars—set decoration and special effects—look just great. Sound is acceptable. —*MM*
Movie: 🎜 **DVD:** 🎜🎜🎜

Twentieth Century Fox Home Entertainment (Cat #4112171, UPC #086162121715). Widescreen (2.35:1) letterboxed. Dolby Digital 5.1 Surround Stereo; Dolby Digital Surround Stereo. $34.98. Keepcase. *LANG:* English; French. *SUB:* English. *FEATURES:* 27 chapter links • Cast thumbnail biographies • TV spots • Theatrical trailer.
1999 (PG-13) 105m/C Freddie Prinze Jr., Matthew Lillard, Saffron Burrows, Tcheky Karyo, Juergen Prochnow, David Suchet, David Warner; *D:* Chris Roberts; *W:* Kevin Droney; *C:* Thierry Arbogast; *M:* Kevin Kiner.

The Wings of the Dove

Henry James's works are quintessentially novels in sheer heft as well as detail, but that hasn't stopped the film world from appropriating his works. From the oft-reinterpreted chestnut *The Turn of the Screw* or lesser favorite *The Golden Bowl,* to oddities like Jane Campion's stand-offish *Portrait of a Lady,* adapters have done everything from tinker with to improvise on his source material. This variation on his novel of the same name edges the time frame forward into the 20th century, and presents a franker sexuality than the Merchant-Ivory style of literary drama. The plot brings young Kate (Carter) out of poverty and into the society life she once only heard about from her mother, who had married in haste and repented in classic Victorian fashion. Kate's questionable suitor Merton (Roache), a yellow journalist, shadows her despite having been rebuffed. Meanwhile Kate falls in with an ailing heiress (Elliott), who inspires a neatly laid out but treacherous subterfuge, and seems willing to go along without a fight. The swirling strings and billowy period details blend into sumptuous audio-visual displays. Interviews with a Criterion staff historian and an English professor open up "Passion and Romance: The Wings of the Dove," a Miramax promotional featurette probably intended for cable. —*JK*
Movie: 🎜🎜🎜▶ **DVD:** 🎜🎜🎜🎜
Miramax Pictures Home Video (Cat #17245, UPC #717951002389). Widescreen (2.35:1). Dolby Digital Surround. $29.95. Keepcase. *LANG:* English. *CAP:* English. *FEATURES:* 15 chapter links • Interactive menus • Featurette • Theatrical trailer.
1997 (R) 101m/C *GB* Helena Bonham Carter, Linus Roache, Alison Elliott, Elizabeth McGovern, Charlotte Rampling, Alex Jennings, Michael Gambon; *D:* Iain Softley; *W:* Hossein Amini; *C:* Eduardo Serra; *M:* Gabriel Yared. *AWARDS:* British Academy Awards '97: Best Cinematography, Best Makeup; Los Angeles Film Critics Association Awards '97: Best Actress (Bonham Carter); National Board of Review Awards '97: Best Actress (Bonham Carter); Broadcast Film Critics Association Awards '97: Best Actress (Bonham Carter); *NOM:* Academy Awards '97: Best

Actress (Bonham Carter), Best Adapted Screenplay, Best Cinematography, Best Costume Design; British Academy Awards '97: Best Actress (Bonham Carter), Best Adapted Screenplay, Best Costume Design; Golden Globe Awards '98: Best Actress—Drama (Bonham Carter); Screen Actors Guild Award '97: Best Actress (Bonham Carter), Best Supporting Actress (Elliott); Writers Guild of America '97: Best Adapted Screenplay.

Winner Takes All
Buddy action picture.
Movie: NYR *DVD:* NYR
MTI Home Video (Cat #57001). Full frame. $24.95. Keepcase. *FEATURES:* Thumbnail bios.
1998 103m/C Alfred "Rubin" Thompson, Robert Hayes III, Joe Estevez; *D:* Daniel Zirilli; *W:* Daniel Zirilli, Robert Hayes III.

Winning
A race car driver (Newman) will let nothing, including his new wife (Woodward), keep him from winning the Indianapolis 500. Newman does his own driving. Thomas's film debut.
Movie: 𝄞𝄞𝄞 *DVD:* NYR
Universal Studios Home Video (Cat #205 26). $24.98. *LANG:* English. *SUB:* Spanish. *CAP:* English.
1969 (PG) 123m/C Paul Newman, Joanne Woodward, Robert Wagner, Richard Thomas, Clu Gulager; *D:* James Goldstone; *W:* Howard A. Rodman; *C:* Richard Moore; *M:* Dave Grusin.

Winstanley
In 17th-century England Gerard Winstanley (Halliwell) leads a religious sect called the Diggers to form a commune. The followers of Oliver Cromwell, recently put into power, take exception and try to get rid of their neighbors. In its attempt to create historical accuracy, the film is even more successful than *The Return of Martin Guerre.* (Many cast members are non-professional actors.) Its sense of time and place is astonishing. On DVD, a few moderate flecks and some vibrating cloth patterns are balanced against superb black-and-white photography. Many of the dimly lit interiors are purposefully inscrutable, but in this case, that accuracy is not a flaw. Sound is nothing special. The rarely seen film is remarkable. The disc also includes Eric Mival's documentary, "It Happened Here Again." —MM
Movie: 𝄞𝄞𝄞 *DVD:* 𝄞𝄞𝄞
Image Entertainment (Cat #ID5935MLSDVD, UPC #014381593525). Full frame. Dolby Digital Mono. $29.99. Snapper. *LANG:* English. *FEATURES:* 22 chapter links (15 in feature, 7 in documentary) ● "Making of" documentary.
1975 92m/B Miles Halliwell, Dawson France, Jerome Willis, Terry Higgins, Phil Oliver, David Bramley; *D:* Kevin Brownlow, Andrew Mollo; *W:* Kevin Brownlow, Andrew Mollo; *C:* Ernest Vincze.

Wishmaster
One of the first big effects shows a skeleton ripping itself out of a body and that's just the beginning. The story involves an ancient Persian demon-genie called a Djinn (Divoff) who's trapped in a jewel. Brought back to present day Los Angeles, he becomes psychically connected to gem appraiser Alex Amberson (Lauren) and does a Freddy Kreuger number on her and her friends. The effects rival those in the *Elm Street* series. Not surprising since first-time director Kurtzman comes to the job from a background in special effects. On the commentary track, he and writer Pete Atkins and 2nd unit director Greg Nicotero emphasize the technical aspects of their work. Their comments are aimed at horror fans. The DVD looks fine with no serious visual flaws. The familiar plot and overreliance on gore are more serious problems. The film is an exercise in bloody style over substance. (Also available on a disc with the sequel.) —MM
AKA: Wes Craven Presents Wishmaster.
Movie: 𝄞𝄞➤ *DVD:* 𝄞𝄞𝄞
Artisan Entertainment (Cat #60456, UPC #012236045601). Widescreen (1.85:1) letterboxed; full frame. Dolby Digital 5.1 Surround Stereo; Dolby Digital Surround Stereo. $29.98. Snapper. *LANG:* English. *CAP:* English. *FEATURES:* 24 chapter links ● Cast and crew thumbnail biographies ● Commentary: Kurtzman, Atkins, 2nd unit director Nicotero ● Trailer ● Teaser ● "Making of" featurette ● Production notes.
1997 (R) 90m/C Tammy Lauren, Andrew Divoff, Robert Englund, Chris Lemmon, Tony Crane, Wendy Benson, Jenny O'Hara, Tony Todd, Kane Hodder; *D:* Robert Kurtzman; *W:* Peter Atkins; *C:* Jacques Haitkin; *M:* Harry Manfredini.

Wishmaster 2: Evil Never Dies
Inexplicable direct-to-video sequel is available as second bill on double feature with the original. As expected, the effects, not that special to begin with, are rehashed. There are no noticeable flaws, but this is inconsequential stuff that does not need close scrutiny. —MM
Movie: 𝄞 *DVD:* 𝄞𝄞
Artisan Entertainment (Cat #10516). Widescreen (1.85:1) letterboxed. Dolby Digital 5.1 Surround Stereo. $29.98. Keepcase. *LANG:* English. *FEATURES:* 34 chapter links ● Trailer ● Production notes.
1998 (R) 96m/C Andrew Divoff, Paul Johansson, Holly Fields, Bokeem Woodbine, Tommy (Tiny) Lister; *D:* Jack Sholder; *W:* Jack Sholder; *C:* Carlos Gonzalez; *M:* David Williams.

Witchcraft
The first entry in an astonishingly popular series of video premieres borrows from *Rosemary's Baby, The Exorcist,* and *The Amityville Horror.* It lacks the grotesque special effects and overall nastiness so

prevalent in many theatrical horrors. The plot concerns a young woman's worries about her husband and creepy mother-in-law after the birth of her first child. A weird opening juxtaposes the LaMaze method with burning at the stake. Horror fans have seen better and much, much worse. DVD highlights the film's many shortcomings, beginning with the opening credits that note Jody Savin's "Orioginal" screenplay. The film is grainy and poorly focused throughout, even bright daylight scenes are filled with visible pixels. —MM
Movie: 𝄞𝄞 *DVD:* 𝄞
Simitar Entertainment (Cat #7263, UPC #082551726325). Full frame. PCM Stereo. $7.98. Keepcase. *LANG:* English. *FEATURES:* 8 chapter links ● Production factoids.
1988 (R) 90m/C Anat "Topol" Barzilai, Gary Sloan, Mary Shelley, Deborah Scott, Alexander Kirkwood, Lee Kisman, Edward Ross Newton; *D:* Robert Spera; *W:* Jody Savin; *C:* Jens Sturup; *M:* Randy Miller.

Witchcraft 2: The Temptress
Exploitative fluff is an odd mixture of the very good and the very bad. The small-town setting and characters are believably realistic. The erotic elements, concerning a witch's (Sheppard) attempt to seduce a teenager, produce unintentional laughs, and if overacting were a crime, most of the cast would be in jail. But it would be unfair to leave it at that; the film has some unsettling moments. On DVD, this one is maybe a hair better than the original VHS tape in terms of image quality but no more. —MM
Movie: 𝄞𝄞 *DVD:* 𝄞➤
Simitar Entertainment (Cat #7265, UPC #082551726523). Full frame. PCM Stereo. $14.98. Keepcase. *LANG:* English. *FEATURES:* 8 chapter links ● Production factoids.
1990 (R) 88m/C Charles Solomon, Mia Ruiz, Delia Sheppard; *D:* Mark Woods; *W:* Jim Hanson, Sal Manna; *C:* Jens Sturup; *M:* Miriam Cutler.

Witchcraft 9: Bitter Flesh
Seemingly endless erotic horror series continues with a hooker (Hall), who like Whoopi Goldberg in *Ghost,* can hear departed Will Spanner who wants her to stop a series of murders. The emphasis here is on the soft-core elements. The DVD itself is just as dim, grubby, and grainy as the others in the series. —MM
Movie: 𝄞𝄞 *DVD:* 𝄞➤
Simitar Entertainment (Cat #7266, UPC #082551726622). Full frame. PCM Stereo. $14.98. Keepcase. *LANG:* English. *FEATURES:* 8 chapter links ● Production factoids.
1996 (R) 90m/C Landon Hall, David Byrnes, Stephanie Beaton, Mikul Robins; *D:* Michael Paul Girard; *W:* Stephen J. Downing; *C:* Jeff Gateman; *M:* Michael Paul Girard.

Witchcraft 10: Mistress of the Craft

Tenth entry in the unbelievably long-lived supernatural series. Witch Celeste Sheridan has been hunting Raven and her band of vampires outside London. Meanwhile, LAPD detective Lucy Lutz arrives in London with an extradition order for Satanic serial killer, Hyde. But Raven and her vamps free Hyde to have him help in a ritual power-enhancing ceremony. After Celeste finds out, she teams up with Lucy and Interpol agent Chris Dixon to hunt down Raven and Hyde before they can finish their demonic work.
Movie: ♫ *DVD:* NYR
ETD (Cat #9926). Full frame. $29.95. Keepcase.
1998 90m/C Wendy Cooper, Eileen Daly, Stephanie Beaton, Kerry Knowlton, Sean Harry, Frank Scantori, Emily Bouffante, Lynn Michelle; *D:* Elisar Cabrera; *W:* Elisar Cabrera; *C:* Alvin Leong.

The Witches

On vacation, nine-year-old Luke (Fisher) finds himself in the midst of a witch convention and the prey of the Grand High Witch (Huston), who plans to turn all children into mice. With the help of his tough grandmother (Zetterling), he attempts to prevent the mass transmutation. Though the action is probably too frightening for smaller kids, this is superb fantasy from the book by Roald Dahl, director Nicolas Roeg, and executive producer Jim Henson. (It was Henson's final film project.) The pan-and-scan DVD delivers a finely detailed image with few glaring flaws, even in the special effects scenes. But whether she's in horror makeup or not, Anjelica Huston as "the most evil woman in creation" owns the film. Why no widescreen letterboxed option? —*MM*
Movie: ♫♫♫▶ *DVD:* ♫♫♫
Warner Home Video, Inc. (Cat #671, UPC #012569067127). Full frame. Dolby Digital Stereo. $14.98. Snapper. *LANG:* English; French. *CAP:* English. *FEATURES:* 30 chapter links.
1990 (PG) 92m/C Anjelica Huston, Mai Zetterling, Jasen Fisher, Rowan Atkinson, Charlie Potter, Bill Paterson, Brenda Blethyn, Jane Horrocks; *D:* Nicolas Roeg; *W:* Allan Scott; *C:* Harvey Harrison; *M:* Stanley Myers. *AWARDS:* Los Angeles Film Critics Association Awards '90: Best Actress (Huston); National Society of Film Critics Awards '90: Best Actress (Huston).

The Witches of Eastwick

Mad Max director Miller meets Hollywood in this unrestrained, vomit-filled treatment of John Updike's novel about three lonely small-town New England women and their sexual liberation. A strange, rich, over-weight, balding, but nonetheless charming man knows their deepest desires and makes them come true with decadent excess. Raunchy fun, with Nicholson over-acting wildly as the Mephisto. Miller lends a bombastic violent edge to the effort, sometimes at the expense of the story, filmed on location in Cohasset, Massachusetts. Wow, this DVD looks great. The film's intense and colorful picture is delivered crisply with super vibrant colors, and the image remains sharp throughout. Excellent contrasts give the film a fresh in-your-face look. The technical rating went down a notch for the 5.1 Surround, which is lively but has an artificial sound from the rear tracks. —*JO*
Movie: ♫♫▶ *DVD:* ♫♫♫▶
Warner Home Video, Inc. (Cat #11741, UPC #085391174127). Widescreen (2.35:1) anamorphic. Dolby Digital Surround 5.1; Dolby Surround. $24.98. Snapper. *LANG:* English (DD5.1); French (DS). *SUB:* English; Spanish; French. *CAP:* English. *FEATURES:* 32 chapter links • Theatrical trailer • Production notes.
1987 (R) 118m/C Jack Nicholson, Cher, Susan Sarandon, Michelle Pfeiffer, Veronica Cartwright, Richard Jenkins, Keith Joakum, Carel Struycken; *D:* George Miller; *W:* Michael Cristofer; *C:* Vilmos Zsigmond; *M:* John Williams. *AWARDS:* Los Angeles Film Critics Association Awards '87: Best Actor (Nicholson); New York Film Critics Awards '87: Best Actor (Nicholson); *NOM:* Academy Awards '87: Best Sound, Best Original Score.

Witchouse

Formulaic Full Moon Romanian production sends eight young people to a New England mansion on a dark and stormy night. Seance. Rituals. Tame sex. Monsters. Fans have seen it all before. The DVD may be slightly sharper than VHS tape, but you wouldn't want to try to make a living on the difference. Sound is O.K. —*MM*
Movie: ♫♫ *DVD:* ♫♫
Full Moon Pictures (Cat #8017, UPC #763843801769). Full frame. Dolby Digital Stereo. $24.95. Keepcase. *LANG:* English. *FEATURES:* 30 chapter links • Cast and crew filmographies • "Making of" featurette • Many Full Moon trailers.
1999 (R) 90m/C David Oren Ward, Ashley Mckinney, Matt Raftery, Monica Serene Garnich, Brooke Muller, Ariauna Albright, Marissa Tait, Dane Northcutt, Kimberly Pullis; *D:* Jack Reed; *W:* Matthew Jason Walsh; *C:* Viorel Sergovici Jr.

With Byrd at the South Pole: The Story of Little America

Little-seen historical film is a record of Admiral Byrd's 1928–30 flight over the South Pole that transformed Byrd and other expedition members into national heroes. The photography by Joseph Rucker and Willard Van der Veer is brilliant, and the restoration of the original 35mm print is astounding as well. The video transfer is very good with crisp blacks that refrain from bleeding. The soundtrack, however, did exhibit occasional cracks and other annoying forms of distortion. —*MJT*
Movie: ♫♫♫ *DVD:* ♫♫♫
Image Entertainment (Cat #ID5936MLSDVD, UPC #014381593624). Full frame. Dolby Digital Mono. $29.99. Snapper. *LANG:* Silent. *FEATURES:* 12 chapter links.
1930 82m/B C: Joseph Rucker, Willard Van der Veer. *AWARDS:* Academy Awards '30: Best Cinematography.

With Friends Like These

Ensemble horror comedy.
Movie: NYR *DVD:* NYR
Digital Versatile Disc Ltd. (Cat #145). Full frame. $19.95. Keepcase.
1990 85m/C Mark Ruel, Beth Lechance, Michael Burns, Norman Fell; *D:* Chris Malazdrewicz.

With Honors

Pesci is a bum who finds desperate Harvard student Fraser's Honors thesis, and, like any quick-witted bum with a yen for literature, holds it for ransom. Desperate to salvage his future gold card, Fraser and his roommates agree to fix Joe's homeless state. Self-involved students learn something about love and life while Madonna drones in the background. Fraser is believable as the ambitious student about to endure Pesci's enlightenment. Pesci is Pesci, doing his best to overcome numerous script difficulties. Average picture sharpness is marred by a consistently grainy image that often has artifacts as well. The sound is O.K. with decent body but marginal separation and imaging. —*JO*
Movie: ♫♫▶ *DVD:* ♫▶
Warner Home Video, Inc. (Cat #13079, UPC #085391307921). Full frame. Dolby Surround. $14.98. Snapper. *LANG:* English; French. *CAP:* English. *FEATURES:* 32 chapter links.
1994 (PG-13) 100m/C Joe Pesci, Brendan Fraser, Moira Kelly, Patrick Dempsey, Josh Hamilton, Gore Vidal; *D:* Alek Keshishian; *W:* William Mastrosimone; *C:* Sven Nykvist; *M:* Patrick Leonard. *AWARDS:* *NOM:* Golden Globe Awards '95: Best Song ("I'll Remember"); MTV Movie Awards '95: Best Song ("I'll Remember").

Within the Rock

Writer, director, and monster-maker Gary J. Tunnicliffe (makeup effects: *Blade, Candyman, Twin Falls Idaho,* etc.) serves up *Alien* meets *Armageddon* as a mining crew labors to dig tunnels and plant explosives on an Earthbound asteroid before time runs out. Complications set in when Ryan (Berkeley) and his crew uncover a killer alien buried two million years earlier and cast adrift in the eternal void of space. The low-budget, direct-to-video effort does contain an occasional effective moment, but the DVD presentation is on a par with that of VHS, nothing noteworthy, no extras, and only basic chapter links. —*RT*
Movie: ♫♫ *DVD:* ♫♫
Image Entertainment (Cat #5774, UPC #014381577426). Full frame. AC3 - 2

Channel. $24.99. Snapper. *LANG:* English. *FEATURES:* 16 chapter links.
1996 (R) 91m/C Xander Berkeley, Bradford Tatum, Brian Krause, Caroline Barclay, Calvin Levels, Earl Boen, Dale Dye; *D:* Gary J. Tunnicliffe; *W:* Gary J. Tunnicliffe; *C:* Adam Kane; *M:* Tony Fennell, Rod Gammons.

Without Air

In this gritty, realistic portrayal of a talented, but self-destructive Memphis singer living on the edge, Shay (Crook) lives with her slacker boyfriend, but is torn between singing and her part-time job as a stripper. It's a tough and uncompromising independent film, and the video transfer retains the grit that accompanies most low-budget independent black-and-white films. Unfortunately, that also means a loss of clarity in darkly lit scenes. The soundtrack is acceptable, with understandable dialogue, but it could have benefitted from some type of a remix. —*MJT*
Movie: 🎬🎬▶ *DVD:* 🎬🎬▶
Image Entertainment (Cat #ID8762SIDVD, UPC #014381876222). Widescreen (1.85:1) letterboxed. Dolby Digital Stereo. $24.99. Snapper. *LANG:* English. *FEATURES:* 12 chapter links.
1995 88m/B Lauri Crook, Pat Lawyer, Jack May, Leigh-Ann Taylor, Nokie Taylor; *D:* Neil Abramson; *W:* Neil Abramson; *C:* Neil Abramson; *M:* Kennard Ramsey.

Without Limits

Second biopic about '70s long distance runner Steve Prefontaine (after 1996's *Prefontaine*) focuses mainly on Prefontaine's (Crudup) relationship with his University of Oregon coach Bill Bowerman (Sutherland), who later was a cofounder of Nike. It also explores the heartbreak of the 1972 Olympics. Crudup does a fine job with the runner's playful arrogance, fearlessness, and iconoclasm (especially when dealing with the corrupt AAU). Sutherland, playing a three-dimensional character for the first time in a while, gives a fine performance. Kenny Moore, a close friend and fellow '72 Olympian, wrote the script with director Towne, with the full cooperation of Bowerman and Prefontaine's girlfriend. The film features fine cinematography and makes excellent use of the soundtrack. Both elements are delivered to near perfection on the DVD. The image is sharp, but most importantly the colors are strong and detailed enough to convey the subtle shadings. The 5.1 sound brings the film alive with its excellent fidelity. —*JO* AKA: Pre.
Movie: 🎬🎬🎬 *DVD:* 🎬🎬🎬▶
Warner Home Video, Inc. (Cat #14905, UPC #085391490524). Widescreen (2.35:1) letterboxed; full frame. Dolby Surround 5.1. $24.98. Snapper. *LANG:* English; French *SUB:* English; French. *CAP:* English. *FEATURES:* 33 chapter links • Theatrical trailer • Production notes.
1997 (PG-13) 117m/C Billy Crudup, Donald Sutherland, Monica Potter, Jeremy Sisto, Matthew Lillard, Billy Burke, Dean Norris, Gabriel Olds, Judith Ivey; *D:* Robert Towne; *W:* Robert Towne, Kenny Moore; *C:* Conrad Hall; *M:* Randy Miller. *AWARDS: NOM:* Golden Globe Awards '99: Best Supporting Actor (Sutherland).

Witness

A young Amish boy (Haas) travelling from his father's funeral witnesses a murder in a Philadelphia bus station men's room. Investigating detective John Book (Ford, in one of his best roles) soon discovers that the killing is part of a conspiracy within his own police department. He follows the child and his widowed mother (McGillis) to their rural Pennsylvania home. Their ensuing romance is set in a clash of cultures, and the thriller elements are never far from the surface. The DVD is partially successful in capturing the subtle sense of place created by director Weir and D.P. John Seale. The exteriors, particularly the beautiful fog-shrouded conclusion, are near perfect. But in several scenes, the dim country interiors are impenetrable, most noticeably when those rooms are filled with characters wearing solid black clothes. Then white faces appear to float in complete darkness. The rest of the film is so strong that those moments are far from fatal. Weir's short interview deals with the location work and the tough emotional dimensions of young Lucas Haas's work. —*MM*
Movie: 🎬🎬🎬▶ *DVD:* 🎬🎬🎬▶
Paramount Home Video (Cat #017367, UPC #097360173673). Widescreen anamorphic. Dolby Digital 5.1 Surround Stereo; Dolby Surround Stereo. $29.99. Keepcase. *LANG:* English; French. *FEATURES:* Theatrical trailer • 17 chapter links • Separate interview with director Peter Weir.
1985 (R) 112m/C Harrison Ford, Kelly McGillis, Alexander Godunov, Lukas Haas, Josef Sommer, Danny Glover, Patti LuPone; *D:* Peter Weir; *W:* William P. Kelley, Earl W. Wallace; *C:* John Seale; *M:* Maurice Jarre. *AWARDS:* Academy Awards '85: Best Film Editing, Best Original Screenplay; Writers Guild of America '85: Best Original Screenplay; *NOM:* Academy Awards '85: Best Actor (Ford), Best Art Direction/Set Decoration, Best Cinematography, Best Director (Weir), Best Picture, Best Original Score.

The Wiz

Black version of the long-time favorite *The Wizard of Oz* is based on the Broadway musical. Ross plays a Harlem schoolteacher who is whisked away to a fantasy version of New York City in a search for her identity. Some good character performances and musical numbers, but this is generally an overblown and garish effort with Ross too old for her role. Pryor is poorly cast, but Jackson is memorable as the Scarecrow. High budget ($24 million) production with a ton of name stars, lost $11 million, and cooled studios on black films. Horne's number as the Good Witch is the best reason to sit through this one. It looks like nobody cared enough about this film to keep the source material in decent shape. The colors are not bad but the picture is soft and there are occasions of substantial film damage. In the meager Dolby Surround mix, the rear is very rarely used and even up-front imaging and separation are poor. —*JO*
Movie: 🎬🎬 *DVD:* 🎬▶
Universal Studios Home Video (Cat #20534, UPC #025192053429). Widescreen (1.85:1) letterboxed. Dolby Surround. $26.98. Keepcase. *LANG:* English. *SUB:* French. *CAP:* English. *FEATURES:* 20 chapter links • Theatrical trailer • Production notes • Cast and filmmakers bios • Film highlights.
1978 (G) 133m/C Diana Ross, Michael Jackson, Nipsey Russell, Ted Ross, Mabel King, Thelma Carpenter, Richard Pryor, Lena Horne; *D:* Sidney Lumet; *W:* Joel Schumacher; *C:* Oswald Morris; *M:* Quincy Jones. *AWARDS: NOM:* Academy Awards '78: Best Art Direction/Set Decoration, Best Cinematography, Best Costume Design, Original Song Score and/or Adaptation.

The Wizard of Gore

Both the hammy overacting and the gore effects are slightly more sophisticated here than they were in the first two installments of Lewis's "gore" trilogy, but on DVD, the film is the weakest of the three. Colors are faded and red is so predominate that the image lacks sharpness. Sound is weak. The disposable story concerns Montag the Magnificent (Sager), whose bloody stage illusions are so real that TV host Sherry Carson (Cler) looks for the truth behind them. With Lewis's work, though, sophistication isn't really a virtue. This one's too slow, too talky, and lacking the hokey shock value of his first films. —*MM*
Movie: 🎬 *DVD:* 🎬▶
Something Weird Video (Cat #ID6102SW DVD, UPC #014381610222). Full frame. Dolby Digital Mono. $24.99. Snapper. *LANG:* English. *FEATURES:* 12 chapter links • Theatrical trailer • Commentary: Herschell Gordon Lewis and Mike Vraney • Gallery of exploitation art.
1970 (R) 96m/C Ray Sager, Judy Cler, Wayne Ratay, Phil Lauenson, Jim Rau, Don Alexander, Monika Blackwell, Corinne Kirkin, John Elliott; *D:* Herschell Gordon Lewis; *W:* Allen Kahn; *C:* Alex Ameri, Daniel Krogh; *M:* Larry Wellington.

The Wizard of Oz

In this adaptation of L. Frank Baum's fantasy, Kansas farm girl Dorothy Gale (Garland, in her immortal role) rides a tornado to a brightly colored world over the rainbow. It's a place full of talking scarecrows, munchkins, and a wizard who bears a strange resemblance to a Kansas fortuneteller (Morgan). She must outwit the Wicked Witch of the West (Hamilton) if she is ever to go home. Delightful performances from Lahr, Bolger, Haley, and

Hamilton; King Vidor is uncredited as codirector. Director Fleming originally wanted Deanna Durbin or Shirley Temple for the role of Dorothy, but settled for Garland, who made the song "Over the Rainbow" her own. She received a special Academy Award for her performance. The DVD contains the recently restored technicolor version of the film, and it's incredible. The earlier MGM boxed set was no slouch, but this one is improved at least a little in almost every way. The image is sharper and the colors much more vibrant and most likely as good as when the film was first released. The black-and-white sequence is more detailed than ever. There is also an excellent 5.1 remix, which takes full advantage of its capabilities by sending both ambience and effects to the rear and giving the film more low-end energy than would have been thought possible. At the same time, the music and vocals remain crisp, so no compromise was made. Plenty of supplementals have been added. —JO
Movie: 🎵🎵🎵🎵 **DVD:** 🎵🎵🎵🎵
Warner Home Video, Inc. (Cat #65123, UPC #012569512320). Full frame. Dolby Digital 5.1; Mono. $24.98. Snapper. *LANG:* English (DD5.1); French (mono). *SUB:* English; French. *CAP:* English. *FEATURES:* 55 chapter links (feature); 25 links (documentary) ● "Making of" documentary ● Period clips ● Trailers ● Deleted musical numbers ● Shooting script ● 1979 interviews with Hamilton, Bolger, and Haley ● Stills gallery ● Storyboards and makeup tests.
1939 101m/C Judy Garland, Margaret Hamilton, Ray Bolger, Jack Haley, Bert Lahr, Frank Morgan, Charley Grapewin, Clara Blandick, Mitchell Lewis, Billie Burke; *D:* Victor Fleming; *W:* Noel Langley; *C:* Harold Rosson; *M:* Herbert Stothart. *AWARDS:* Academy Awards '39: Best Song ("Over the Rainbow"), Best Original Score; American Film Institute (AFI) '98: Top 100, National Film Registry '89; *NOM:* Academy Awards '39: Best Color Cinematography, Best Picture.

Wolf

Judged strictly as an old-fashioned horror movie, *Wolf* is better than some of star Jack Nicholson's other work in the genre, particularly *The Shining*. With a solid script by novelist Jim Harrison and Wesley Strick, and equally capable direction from Mike Nichols, it's scary, smart, and funny. Nicholson is fine as a book editor who's bitten by a wolf on a snowy road. Costar Michelle Pfeiffer plays a curiously unsympathetic heroine. She and Nicholson never develop any screen "chemistry," but the last reel is terrific. The wolf makeup owes more to Lon Chaney's *The Wolf Man* than to recent work like *The Howling*. The DVD image is only marginally better than VHS because the transfer from big screen to tape was done with an "image enhancing technology" that improves the clarity of the image. The digital image is a slight improvement; sound is about the same. —MM
Movie: 🎵🎵🎵 **DVD:** 🎵🎵🎵

Columbia Tristar Home Video (Cat #71159, UPC #043396711594). Widescreen (1.85:1) letterboxed; full frame. Dolby Digital 5.1 Surround Stereo; Dolby Digital Surround Stereo. $24.95. Keepcase. *LANG:* English; French; Spanish. *SUB:* English; French; Korean. *FEATURES:* 61 chapter links.
1994 (R) 125m/C Jack Nicholson, Michelle Pfeiffer, James Spader, Kate Nelligan, Christopher Plummer, Richard Jenkins, Om Puri, Eileen Atkins, David Hyde Pierce, Ron Rifkin, Prunella Scales; *D:* Mike Nichols; *W:* Wesley Strick, Jim Harrison; *C:* Giuseppe Rotunno; *M:* Ennio Morricone.

The Wolf Man

Though he's usually ranked below the Frankenstein Monster and Dracula in Universal's roster of horror stars, the Wolf Man is one of the studio's most sympathetic creations, and he's always been popular with audiences. The key is the way the role of Lawrence Talbot plays to star Lon Chaney Jr.'s strengths as an actor. He combines physical power and vulnerability in both Talbot's guilt-ridden human side and his nocturnal, lunatic, bestial self. He shares that mixture of pathos and horror with Karloff's Monster. In one of his rare appearances in the genre, Claude Rains is excellent as the elder Talbot. To my mind, the poetic script and the lavish sets make the film much more successful and less dated than others of its time. It's a masterpiece that's been more often overlooked by critics than by fans. Universal goes a long way toward righting that lapse in this superb DVD. Though the image contains a few fine white flecks, it looks fine and this has always been one of the sharpest of the "classic" horrors. Both the *Monster by Moonlight* documentary and film historian Tom Weaver's commentary track are knowledgeable and gossipy in a good sense. Another must-own for horror fans. —MM
Movie: 🎵🎵🎵🎵 **DVD:** 🎵🎵🎵🎵
Universal Studios Home Video (Cat #20331, UPC #025192033124). Full frame. Dolby Digital Mono. $29.98. Keepcase. *LANG:* English. *SUB:* French. *CAP:* English. *FEATURES:* 18 chapter links ● *Monster by Moonlight* documentary ● Commentary: film historian Tom Weaver ● Stills and ads from *Wolf Man* archives ● Production notes ● Cast and crew thumbnail biographies ● Theatrical trailer ● Universal web links.
1941 70m/B Lon Chaney Jr., Claude Rains, Maria Ouspenskaya, Ralph Bellamy, Bela Lugosi, Warren William, Patric Knowles, Evelyn Ankers, Forrester Harvey, Fay Helm; *D:* George Waggner; *W:* Curt Siodmak; *C:* Joseph Valentine; *M:* Charles Previn, Hans J. Salter, Frank Skinner.

A Woman Is a Woman

Godard paved the way for *Umbrellas of Cherbourg* by collaborating with that famed French musical's composer Michel Legrand

on this twisted "Franscope" escapade. Angela (Karina) wants to be a stripper and a mom, but her lover (Brialy) foists fatherhood off onto his best friend Alfred (Belmondo), who is fond of Angela anyway. She stages her daily life as a series of jokey, abstract, would-be musical numbers. Her men collaborate when they're of a mind, after a stubbornly bizarre Godardian fashion. The transfer shows a regular pattern of artifacting that increases in scan mode. Viewers must recognize the difficulty the film presented with its vibrant primary colors set against hazardous backgrounds like corrugated metal and mottled plaster. The soundtrack is as bright as it is jaunty. The film's white subtitles are not below the letterbox margin and the visuals are uncomfortably compressed-looking. The DVD's interesting "animated palimpsest" menu design is hobbled at the scene access page, with its measly six entry points. —JK
AKA: Une Femme Est une Femme; La Donna E Donna.
Movie: 🎵🎵🎵 **DVD:** 🎵🎵🎵
Fox/Lorber Home Video (Cat #FLV5052, UPC #720917505220). Widescreen. Dualchannel Mono. $29.99. Keepcase. *LANG:* French. *SUB:* English. *FEATURES:* 6 chapter links ● Animated interactive menus ● 3-color disc ● Filmographies.
1960 88m/C *FR* Jean-Claude Brialy, Jean-Paul Belmondo, Anna Karina, Marie DuBois; *D:* Jean-Luc Godard; *W:* Jean-Luc Godard; *C:* Raoul Coutard; *M:* Michel Legrand.

The Woman Next Door

The domestic drama in one of Truffaut's last films involves a suburban husband (Depardieu) who resumes an affair with a tempestuous now-married woman (Ardant) after she moves in next door, with domestic complications all around. It's an insightful, humanistic paean to passion and fidelity. *AKA:* La Femme d'a Cote.
Movie: 🎵🎵🎵 **DVD:** NYR
WinStar Home Entertainment (Cat #5120). $29.98. *LANG:* French. *SUB:* English.
1981 (R) 106m/C *FR* Gerard Depardieu, Fanny Ardant, Michele Baumgarten, Veronique Silver, Roger Van Hool; *D:* Francois Truffaut; *W:* Suzanne Schiffman; *C:* William Lubtchansky; *M:* Georges Delerue.

Woman of the Year

Tracy and Hepburn—in their historical first on-screen pairing—are reporters on the same paper. She's the high-profile political columnist; he's the lowly sportswriter. Besides sharing a workplace in common, the terrible twosome also are husband and wife. Baseball scene with Hepburn at her first game is delightful. Hilarious, rich entertainment that tries to answer the question "What really matters in life?" Tracy and Hepburn began a close friendship that paralleled their quarter-century celluloid partnership. Factoid from the liner notes: Although Hepburn could have made

the film at any studio, she chose MGM so she could work with Tracy. Another: Clark Gable and Walter Pidgeon were her possible castmates before postponement of *The Yearling* paved the way for Tracy's availability. With another fine B&W video transfer, *Woman of the Year* has never looked better on home video. The soundtrack, presented as a monaural Dolby Digital track, shows its age with the occasional snap, crackle, and pop. DVD extras are minimal, but the trailer is appreciated, and the chapter stops and language choices are sufficiently plentiful. —*MB*
Movie: ♪♪♪♪ **DVD:** ♪♪♪
MGM Home Entertainment (Cat #906646, UPC #027616664624). Full frame. Dolby Digital 1.0. $24.98. Snapper. *LANG:* English; French; Spanish. *SUB:* English; French; Spanish. *CAP:* English. *FEATURES:* 32 chapter links ☛ Original theatrical trailer.
1942 114m/B Spencer Tracy, Katharine Hepburn, Fay Bainter, Dan Tobin, Reginald Owen, Roscoe Karns, William Bendix, Minor Watson; *D:* George Stevens; *W:* Ring Lardner Jr., Michael Kanin; *C:* Joseph Ruttenberg; *M:* Franz Waxman. *AWARDS:* Academy Awards '42: Best Original Screenplay, National Film Registry '99; *NOM:* Academy Awards '42: Best Actress (Hepburn).

The Woman Who Came Back

When a young woman returns to her isolated New England hometown, misfortune seems to follow her—leading her to believe that she suffers from a 300-year-old witch's curse. Routine chiller is undone by a weak windup. Understandably edgy heroine is played by Nancy Kelly, the beleaguered mom in *The Bad Seed*. The grainy transfer is helped a bit by the film's sharp black-and-white photography, which highlights ever spooky shadows. —*JE*
Movie: ♪♪ **DVD:** ♪☛
Image Entertainment (Cat #5379FW, UPC #1438153792). Full frame. Dolby Digital Mono. $19.99. Snapper. *LANG:* English. *FEATURES:* 12 chapter links.
1945 69m/B Nancy Kelly, Otto Kruger, John Loder, Ruth Ford, Jeanne Gail; *D:* Walter Colmes; *W:* Dennis J. Cooper, Lee Willis; *C:* Henry Sharp; *M:* Edward Plumb.

Women in Revolt

Three New York women are changed by their association with the politics of the women's movement but wind up being betrayed by a patriarchal society. Jackie (Curtis) and Holly (Woodlawn) are members of PIG (Politically Involved Girls), who raise money and attend rallies but backslide by getting involved in a series of sleazy guys. So does the new recruit, actress Candy (Darling). Men are scum. Music by John Cale. The Image DVD again delivers a Morrissey cult flick pretty much to the peak of the preprint materials limits, with no enhancements or detractions. The sound could be fuller but does the job. —*JO*

Movie: ♪♪ **DVD:** ♪♪☛
Image Entertainment (Cat ID4733PYDVD, UPC #014381473322). Full frame. Dolby Digital Mono. $24.95. Snapper. *LANG:* English. *FEATURES:* 16 chapter links.
1971 97m/C Jackie Curtis, Holly Woodlawn, Candy Darling, Sean O'Meara, Martin Kove, Michael Sklar, Johnny Kemper, Jonathan Kramer; *D:* Paul Morrissey; *W:* Paul Morrissey; *C:* Andy Warhol, Jed Johnson.

Women of Valor

During World War II, American nurses including Maggie Jessup (Sarandon) stationed in the Philippines are captured by the Japanese and must survive in a brutal prison camp. This made-for-TV feature is really too earnest and right-minded in presentation of fact-based events. The same or similar incidents have been brought to the screen much more forcefully in other films. On DVD, image and sound are unexceptional. Even tropical daylight exteriors look a little underexposed and that darkness is more pronounced in the interiors. —*MM*
Movie: ♪☛ **DVD:** ♪☛
Simitar Entertainment (Cat #7276, UPC #082551727629). Full frame. PCM Stereo. $7.98. Keepcase. *FEATURES:* 8 chapter links ☛ Production factoids ☛ Susan Sarandon, Kristy McNichol filmographies.
1986 95m/C Susan Sarandon, Kristy McNichol, Alberta Watson, Valerie Mahaffey, Suzanne Lederer, Pat Bishop, Terry O'Quinn, Neva Patterson; *D:* Buzz Kulik; *C:* Mike Fash; *M:* Georges Delerue.

Wonder Man

When a brash nightclub entertainer (Kaye) is killed by gangsters, his mild-mannered twin brother takes his place to smoke out the killers. One of Kaye's better early films is also the screen debut of Vera-Ellen and Cochran. Look for Mrs. Howell of *Gilligan's Island*.
Movie: ♪♪☛ **DVD:** NYR
HBO Home Video (Cat #90663). Full frame. Stereo; Mono. $24.98. *LANG:* English; French; Italian; Spanish. *SUB:* French; Spanish. *CAP:* English.
1945 98m/C Danny Kaye, Virginia Mayo, Vera-Ellen, Steve Cochran, S.Z. Sakall, Otto Kruger; *D:* H. Bruce Humberstone; *W:* Jack Jevne, Eddie Moran, Don Hartman, Melville Shavelson, Philip Rapp; *C:* Victor Milner; *M:* Ray Heindorf. *AWARDS:* *NOM:* Academy Awards '45: Best Song ("So in Love"), Best Sound, Scoring of a Musical.

The Wonderful, Horrible Life of Leni Riefenstahl

In this documentary portrait of Hitler's favorite filmmaker, Riefenstahl, then 91, tells of her start as an actress, her first directorial effort *The Blue Light* (1932), and the two infamous propaganda films,

Triumph of the Will (1935) and *Olympia* (1938), which still provoke. She discusses her relationship with Hitler and Joseph Goebbels and the accusations that have continued to haunt her life. Still active, Riefenstahl's most recent work is the underwater filming of rare aquatic life in the Seychelles Islands. The video transfer, although murky at times, is solid enough. It really shines when Riefenstahl's films are shown. The audio, too, is quite good although some low-end sounds do get lost from time to time. —*MJT* *AKA:* The Power of the Image: Leni Riefenstahl; Die Macht der Bilder: Leni Riefenstahl.
Movie: ♪♪♪ **DVD:** ♪♪♪
Image Entertainment (Cat #K107DVD, UPC #738329010720). Full frame. Dolby Digital 2.0 Stereo. $49.99. Snapper. *LANG:* German; English. *SUB:* English. *FEATURES:* 23 chapter links.
1993 180m/C GE *D:* Ray Muller; *C:* Michel Baudour.

Woodstock (DC)

Forty minutes of footage have been added to this "director's cut" of an already overlong documentary. Despite the filmmakers' reluctance to show anything but the good side of the famous "three days of peace, love, and music," the film's worth watching and listening to. The images on the DVD are no sharper than they have ever been, though crystalline clarity has never been the point with this material. The real value of the two-sided disc lies in its accessibility. For my money, the best moments are provided by Joan Baez singing "Joe Hill" (chapter 14), Sha-Na-Na (chapter 20), Sly and the Family Stone (chapter 12), and the entire Jimi Hendrix set (chapters 17–19). Others will disagree and they can skip to their own favorites. The new additions to this edition are from Canned Heat, Jefferson Airplane, Janis Joplin, Hendrix, and Crosby, Stills, and Nash. —*MM*
Movie: ♪♪♪ **DVD:** ♪♪♪
Warner Home Video, Inc. (Cat #13549, UPC #085391354925). Widescreen letterboxed. Dolby Digital 5.1 Surround Stereo. $24.98. Snapper. *LANG:* English. *SUB:* English; French; Spanish. *CAP:* English. *FEATURES:* 50 chapter links. Two-sided disc.
1970 (R) 180m/C *D:* Michael Wadleigh. *AWARDS:* Academy Awards '70: Best Feature Documentary, National Film Registry '96; *NOM:* Academy Awards '70: Best Film Editing, Best Sound.

Word of Mouth

Torri (Larranaga) is a high-caliber call girl who attracts the attention of a documentary filmmaker. She describes her encounters for the camera and then those are shown in guazily focused flashbacks. The interviews themselves are presented in clear hard focus, giving the film two distinct sides. It's also more serious than most Playboy productions. —*MM*
Movie: ♪♪☛ **DVD:** ♪♪☛

Image Entertainment (Cat #ID5977PLDVD, UPC #014381597721). Full frame. Dolby Digital Stereo. $24.99. Snapper. *LANG:* English. *FEATURES:* 19 chapter links.

1999 92m/C Catalina Larranaga, Loridawn Messuri, Robert Rand; *D:* Tom Lazarus; *W:* L.L. Thomaso; *C:* Bruce Finn; *M:* Nicholas Rivers.

The World's Greatest Animation

The 16 short cartoons on this DVD are uniformly wonderful. They're Academy Award nominees (and winners) from 1978–90, featuring work from people who have gone on to become household names in the world of animation, among them Nick Park, Bill Plympton, and Will Vinton. My own favorites are Park's "Creature Comforts" wherein zoo animals are interviewed about their views on captivity, and Frederic Back's "Crac!" a mini-epic that recalls the work of Marc Chagall. Like almost all animation, these fare well on DVD. The simplified colors, shapes, and movement are easily reproduced on the medium. More importantly, the scene access makes them easy to find and watch individually. Highly recommended. —MM

Movie: 🐾🐾🐾🐾 *DVD:* 🐾🐾🐾🐾➤
Image Entertainment (Cat #ID4530JFDVD, UPC #014381453027). Full frame. Dolby Digital Mono. $24.99. Snapper. *LANG:* English and silent. *FEATURES:* 16 chapter links.

1993 ?m/C

Wrongfully Accused

Yet another Nielsen spoof, with *The Fugitive* (along with several other movies) the target this time around. He's violinist Ryan Harrison, who has a tryst with socialite Lauren Goodhue (Le Brock) and then is convicted of her husband Hibbing's (York) murder. Harrison escapes, determined to find the actual killer—the one-armed, one-legged, and one-eyed man—while being hunted by Marshal Fergus Falls (Crenna). The genre has definitely had its day, with more clunkers than chuckles. This is one of the better Warner full-frame transfers and is pretty sharp, without any grain or artifacts to interfere. Colors are accurate and, more importantly, deep and vibrant with very little bleed. The 5.1 mix is suitably boisterous for this exaggerated comedy. —JO

Movie: 🐾➤ *DVD:* 🐾🐾🐾
Warner Home Video, Inc. (Cat #16129, UPC #085391612926). Full frame. Dolby Digital 5.1. $19.98. Snapper. *LANG:* English; French. *SUB:* English; French; Spanish. *FEATURES:* 20 chapter links ▪ Documentary ▪ Visual effects presentation ▪ Cast bios ▪ Theatrical trailers ▪ TV spots.

1998 (PG-13) 85m/C Leslie Nielsen, Richard Crenna, Kelly Le Brock, Melinda McGraw, Michael York, Sandra Bernhard; *D:* Pat Proft; *W:* Pat Proft; *C:* Glen MacPherson; *M:* Bill Conti.

Wuthering Heights

The first screen adaptation of Emily Bronte's romantic novel about the doomed love between Heathcliff and Cathy on the Yorkshire moors dynamically captures the madness and ferocity of the source, remaining possibly the greatest romance ever filmed. Excellent performances from Wyler's sure direction, particularly Olivier's, which made him a star, and Oberon in her finest hour as the exquisite but selfish Cathy. With rare exception, this is a fine black-and-white transfer to DVD. The contrasts are high but not edgy. Brightness is comfortable. And the all-important graytones are finely detailed, leading to that feeling of depth that comes from the beautifully staged cinematic compositions. The only time the image is off is when the transfer rate drops a touch and some artifacts appear, but this is rare. The mono sound is strong and has mainly some high-end distortion that is very livable. —JO

Movie: 🐾🐾🐾🐾 *DVD:* 🐾🐾🐾➤
HBO Home Video (Cat #90729, UPC #026359072925). Full frame. Mono. $24.98. Snapper. *LANG:* English. *FEATURES:* 24 chapter links ▪ Theatrical trailer ▪ Interview with Geraldine Fitzgerald.

1939 104m/B Laurence Olivier, Merle Oberon, David Niven, Geraldine Fitzgerald, Flora Robson, Donald Crisp, Cecil Kellaway, Leo G. Carroll, Miles Mander, Hugh Williams; *D:* William Wyler; *W:* Ben Hecht, Charles MacArthur; *C:* Gregg Toland; *M:* Alfred Newman. *AWARDS:* Academy Awards '39: Best Black-and-white Cinematography; American Film Institute (AFI) '98: Top 100; New York Film Critics Awards '39: Best Film; *NOM:* Academy Awards '39: Best Actor (Olivier), Best Director (Wyler), Best Picture, Best Screenplay, Best Supporting Actress (Fitzgerald), Best Original Score.

The X–Files

The TV series fifth-season cliffhanger continues in the big-screen adaptation, which supposedly has a plot clear enough for viewers unfamiliar with the show to follow. FBI agents Mulder (Duchovny) and Scully (Anderson) battle an intergalactic plot of seemingly limitless proportions. The bigger budget allows for some nice action sequences and special effects, and the leads comfortable relationship works well. The relative clarity of DVD is a mixed blessing in this case. The film looks very good, particularly when compared to a conventional episode of the show, but the widescreen image and enhanced sharpness seem somehow wrong for the characters and the coy interlocking conspiracies. Sound is excellent. —MM *AKA:* The X-Files: Fight the Future.

Movie: 🐾🐾➤ *DVD:* 🐾🐾🐾
20th Century Fox (Cat #4110394, UPC #086162103940). Widescreen (2.35:1) letterboxed. Dolby Digital 5.1 Surround Stereo; Dolby Digital Surround Stereo. $34.98. Keepcase. *LANG:* English; French. *SUB:* English; Spanish. *FEATURES:* 18

chapter links ▪ Commentary: Chris Carter and Rob Bowman ▪ "Making of" featurette ▪ Trailers ▪ Liner notes.

1998 (PG-13) 120m/C David Duchovny, Gillian Anderson, Martin Landau, William B. Davis, John Neville, Armin Mueller-Stahl, Blythe Danner, Mitch Pileggi, Terry O'Quinn, Jeffrey DeMunn, Lucas Black, Glenne Headly; *D:* Rob Bowman; *W:* Chris Carter; *C:* John Bartley; *M:* Mark Snow.

Xanadu

Dated relic of the late 1970s revels in the excesses of the era. The remake of 1947's *Down to Earth* casts Newton-John as a muse who comes to life and inspires a record-jacket artist (Beck). Gene Kelly's effortless presence is welcome but not nearly enough to offset his treacly costars. On DVD, the image quality varies as the story shifts from grainy "reality" to more polished "fantasy" sequences. The insipid pop score sounds O.K. —MM

Movie: 🐾 woof *DVD:* 🐾🐾
Universal Studios Home Video (Cat #20410, UPC #025192041020). Widescreen (1.85:1) letterboxed. Dolby Digital 4.0 Surround Stereo; Dolby Surround Stereo. $24.98. Keepcase. *LANG:* English; French. *CAP:* English. *FEATURES:* 18 chapter links ▪ Production notes ▪ Cast and crew thumbnail biographies ▪ Theatrical trailer ▪ Universal web links.

1980 (PG) 96m/C Olivia Newton-John, Michael Beck, Gene Kelly, Sandahl Bergman; *D:* Robert Greenwald; *W:* Richard Danus; *C:* Victor Kemper; *M:* Barry de Vorzon. *AWARDS:* Golden Raspberry Awards '80: Worst Director (Greenwald).

Xiu Xiu: The Sent Down Girl

Actress Joan Chen makes an impressive directorial debut with a story of the Cultural Revolution in China. Xiu Xiu (Lu Lu) is "sent down" to Tibet from her home in the city. Eventually, she comes to realize that she will never be allowed to return without the right political connections. She tries to make them using the only means she has: her body. The image ranges between fairly pale and harsh exteriors to carefully lit night scenes, but the focus here is on carefully drawn characters and excellent performances that cross cultural boundaries. —MM *AKA:* Tian Yu.

Movie: 🐾🐾🐾 *DVD:* 🐾🐾🐾
Image Entertainment (Cat #ID8755UM DVD, UPC #014381875522). Widescreen (1.66:1) anamorphic. Dolby Digital Surround Stereo. $24.99. Snapper. *LANG:* Mandarin. *SUB:* English. *FEATURES:* 12 chapter links.

1997 (R) 99m/C Lu Lu, Lopsang; *D:* Joan Chen; *W:* Joan Chen, Yan Geling; *C:* Lu Yue; *M:* Johnny Chen. *AWARDS:* *NOM:* Independent Spirit Awards '00: Best First Feature.

Xtro 3: Watch the Skies

Military unit arrives at a remote island where the government has covered up a UFO landing. However, the island is now inhabited by a pissed-off alien whose mate has been killed. The picture quality is so varied that it's hard to give an overall rating. A familiar problem to DVD, the bright scenes look great, and the dark scenes suck. On this disc, the grain is pretty much unbearable in the shadows or when the lights go down. The sound isn't much better and has both limited separation and way too much distortion. —*JO*
Movie: ♪♪ **DVD:** ♪
Image Entertainment (Cat #ID5632FMDVD, UPC #014381563221). Full frame. Stereo. $24.95. Snapper. *LANG:* English. *FEATURES:* 15 chapter links.
1995 (R) 90m/C Sal Landi, Jim Hanks, Robert Culp, Andrew Divoff, Karen Moncrieff; *D:* Harry Bromley Davenport; *W:* Daryl Haney.

The Year of Living Dangerously

First-rate political thriller features Gibson as Australian journalist Guy Hamilton, who's covering Indonesia in the mid-'60s when a coup against Sukarno is in the works. At the same time, he becomes involved with Jill Bryant (Weaver), a British attache. Novelist C.J. Koch collaborated with director Weir on the screenplay. Though the image is slightly soft throughout, the film looks fine on DVD. It's in remarkable shape for a work of its age, and the stereo sound is excellent, for both Linda Hunt's voice-over narration and Maurice Jarre's wonderful score. —*MM*
Movie: ♪♪♪ **DVD:** ♪♪♪
MGM Home Entertainment (Cat #906638, UPC #027616663825). Widescreen letterboxed. Dolby Digital Stereo; Mono. $24.98. Snapper. *LANG:* English; French; Spanish. *FEATURES:* 25 chapter links • Theatrical trailer.
1982 (PG) 114m/C *AU* Mel Gibson, Sigourney Weaver, Linda Hunt, Michael Murphy; *D:* Peter Weir; *W:* Peter Weir, David Williamson; *C:* Russell Boyd; *M:* Maurice Jarre. *AWARDS:* Academy Awards '83: Best Supporting Actress (Hunt); Los Angeles Film Critics Association Awards '83: Best Supporting Actress (Hunt); National Board of Review Awards '83: Best Supporting Actress (Hunt); New York Film Critics Awards '83: Best Supporting Actress (Hunt).

Yellow Pages

Comedy involving business and investigations.
Movie: NYR **DVD:** NYR
Simitar Entertainment (Cat #7651). Full frame. Dolby Digital 5.1 Surround Stereo. $14.98. Keepcase. *FEATURES:* Thumbnail bios • Production notes • Trailer.
1996 98m/C Sam Taft, Laura Kelly; *D:* Moe Schwartz.

Yellow Submarine

The acclaimed animated fantasy is based on a plethora of excellent mid- and late-career Beatles songs and the artistic influences of Rene Magritte, Marc Chagall, and Monty Python. The wide-eyed story, such as it is, finds the Fab Four battling the Blue Meanies for the sake of Sgt. Pepper, the Nowhere Man, Strawberry Fields, and Pepperland. The film features a host of talented cartoonists. Speaking voices are provided by John Clive (John), Geoff Hughes (Paul), Peter Batten (George), and Paul Angelis (Ringo). The Beatles sing for themselves and appear in a short scene at the end of the film. Their longtime collaborator George Martin is music director, and Erich Segal, of *Love Story* fame, cowrites. The DVD is loaded with extras, including a "music-only" track that eliminates dialogue. The image appears virtually flawless, though the black-and-white op art effects in the Sea of Holes sequence are almost painfully psychedelic. Otherwise, the large solid color masses and limited movement are bright with no visible artifacts. The sound, of course, is equally brilliant. Sure to be a popular DVD for showroom demonstrations. —*MM*
Movie: ♪♪♪► **DVD:** ♪♪♪♪
Twentieth Century Fox Home Entertainment (Cat #907508, UPC #027616750822). Widescreen letterboxed. Dolby Digital Mono; Dolby Digital 5.1 Surround Stereo. $22.98. Keepcase. *LANG:* English. *SUB:* English; French; Japanese; Spanish; Portuguese. *CAP:* English. *FEATURES:* 36 chapter links • Commentary: John Coates and Heinz Edelmann • "Making of" documentary: "The Beatles Mod Odyssey" • Isolated music track • Theatrical trailer • 3 storyboard sequences • Interviews with Angelis, Clive, Livesey, McMillan, Stokes, Segal • Pencil drawings • Behind-the-scenes photos.
1968 (G) 87m/C *GB* *D:* George Duning, Dick Emery; *W:* Erich Segal; *C:* John Williams; *M:* George Martin, George Harrison, John Lennon, Paul McCartney, Ringo Starr; *V:* John Clive, Geoff Hughes, Peter Batten, Paul Angelis, Dick Emery, Lance Percival, George Harrison, John Lennon, Paul McCartney, Ringo Starr. *AWARDS:* VSDA DVD Festival '00: Best Music DVD.

Yes Boss!

The story and character types, even the staging and color schemes of this high-key musical comedy are straight out of late '50s and early '60s Hollywood, despite its up-to-date references. Rahul (Khan) tries to succeed in business at an ad agency. Alas, his westernized boss (Pancholi) has turned him into more of a procurer than a gofer. The plot stops on a dime when the boss, a married man, points out a young model on a runway. She's the very girl Rahul himself has been eyeing! Rahul is ordered to play the stooge once more. Will his cover-up continue during their "working vacation" even after the boss's wife arrives unannounced? Carnivalesque numbers borrow so haphazardly from pop musical styles, they are as energetically

unrefined as rap music videos. The DVD transfer holds up admirably against their onslaught. —*JK*
Movie: ♪♪♪ **DVD:** ♪♪♪♪
Video Sound (Cat #SDM98-DVD102). Widescreen. Dolby Digital AC-3 Surround 5.1. $29.95. Keepcase. *LANG:* Hindi; English. *SUB:* English; Chinese; Japanese. *FEATURES:* 28 chapter links including 6 songs • Animated interactive menus • Auto-queue songs to play as an uninterrupted sequence • Star bios and filmographies • Coming attractions trailers. All regions coding.
1997 165m/C *IN* Shah Rukh Khan, Juhi Chawla, Aditya Pancholi; *D:* Aziz Mirza.

Young and Innocent

Alfred Hitchcock delivers an enjoyable installment of his classic "wrong man" theme as Derrick DeMarney is the first to spot a dead body in the surf and is quickly assumed to be the murderer. He escapes, recruits (reluctantly at first) the constable's daughter (Pilbeam), and together they go in search of a missing raincoat and a man with a twitch. The dated historical curiosity appeals mainly to film students and Hitchcock fans. Source material shows its age with an often dark, muddy transfer, complete with noticeable film splices, scratches, and numerous sound-pops. Teamed with a 1955 episode of *Alfred Hitchcock Presents,* "The Cheney Vase," featuring Darren McGavin as a greedy museum curator outsmarted in classic Hitchcock fashion. It's an adequate transfer considering the age and source of the film material. When compared to Anchor Bay's transfers of *The Paradine Case, Notorious,* etc., this one is clearly lacking. —*RT* *AKA:* The Girl Was Young; The Cheney Vase.
Movie: ♪♪ **DVD:** ♪
Delta/Laserlight (Cat #82034, UPC #01811199763). Full frame. AC3 - 2 Channel. $14.99. Keepcase. *LANG:* English. *SUB:* Spanish; Japanese; Chinese. *FEATURES:* 3-minute intro by Tony Curtis • Theatrical trailer for *Strangers on a Train* • 30 chapter links for *Young and Innocent* • 13 chapter links for "The Cheney Vase."
1937 80m/B *GB* Derrick DeMarney, Nova Pilbeam, Percy Marmont, Edward Rigby, Mary Clare, John Longden, George Curzon, Basil Radford, Pamela Carme, George Merritt, J.H. Roberts, Jerry Verno, H.F. Maltby, John Miller, Beatrice Varley, Syd Crossley, Frank Atkinson, Torin Thatcher; *D:* Alfred Hitchcock; *W:* Charles Bennett, Alma Reville, Gerald Savory, Antony Armstrong, Edwin Greenwood; *C:* Bernard Knowles; *M:* Louis Levy.

Young Frankenstein

Young Dr. Frankenstein (Wilder), a brain surgeon, inherits the family castle back in Transylvania. He's skittish about the family business, but when he learns his grandfather's secrets, he becomes obsessed with making his own monster. Wilder and monster Boyle make a memorable song-and-

dance team to Irving Berlin's "Puttin' on the Ritz," and Hackman's cameo as a blind man is inspired. Garr ("What knockers!" "Oh, sank you!") is adorable as a fraulein, and Leachman ("He's vass my—boyfriend!") is wonderfully scary. Wilder saves the creature with a switcheroo, in which the doctor ends up with a certain monster-sized body part. Viewing Brook's masterpiece on DVD really gives a sense of how much the original Universal *Frankenstein* films influenced the wonderful lighting and cinematography. The black-and-white image is rich in contrast and has excellent graytones, giving practically every frame the ability to stand on its own. Blacks are true. The sound is a little scratchy at times, but if anything that just enhances the feel of the film. The DVD includes plenty of supplementals, including an interesting documentary, a very entertaining commentary by Brooks, and a collection of—unfortunately—pretty lame bloopers. —*JO*
Movie: 𝄞𝄞𝄞𝄞 **DVD:** 𝄞𝄞𝄞▶
20th Century Fox (Cat #4109070, UPC #086162090707). Widescreen (1.85:1) letterboxed. Mono. $29.98. Keepcase. *LANG:* English (mono); French; Spanish. *SUB:* English. *CAP:* English. *FEATURES:* 28 chapter links • Documentary • Trailers and TV spots • Deleted scenes and outtakes • Commentary: Mel Brooks • Production stills.
1974 (PG) 108m/B Peter Boyle, Gene Wilder, Marty Feldman, Madeline Kahn, Cloris Leachman, Teri Garr, Kenneth Mars, Richard Haydn, Gene Hackman, Liam Dunn, Monte Landis; *D:* Mel Brooks; *W:* Mel Brooks, Gene Wilder; *C:* Gerald Hirschfeld; *M:* John Morris. *AWARDS: NOM:* Academy Awards '74: Best Adapted Screenplay, Best Sound.

Young Guns
Sophomoric Wild Bunch look-alike ends up resembling a western version of the Bowery Boys. It provides a portrait of Billy the Kid and his gang as they move from prairie trash to demi-legends and features several fine performances. The film uses some interesting color tinting to achieve an almost weathered look. The reddish earthtones are of the type that can cause both color bleed and grain, but neither is a problem on the DVD. In fact, the picture stays sharp throughout. The non-tinted sections have very vibrant colors and super contrast. The Dolby Surround is also very good and there is quite a bit of rear channel activity, combined with a good dynamic mix. —*JO*
Movie: 𝄞𝄞▶ **DVD:** 𝄞𝄞𝄞▶
Artisan Entertainment (Cat #60473, UPC #012236047308). Widescreen (1.66:1) letterboxed; full frame. Dolby Surround. $24.98. Snapper. *LANG:* English. *SUB:* Spanish. *CAP:* English. *FEATURES:* 36 chapter links • Theatrical trailer • Production notes • Cast and filmmakers bios.
1988 (R) 107m/C Emilio Estevez, Kiefer Sutherland, Lou Diamond Phillips, Charlie

Sheen, Casey Siemaszko, Dermot Mulroney, Terence Stamp, Terry O'Quinn, Jack Palance, Brian Keith, Patrick Wayne, Sharon Thomas; *D:* Christopher Cain; *W:* John Fusco; *C:* Dean Semler; *M:* Anthony Marinelli, Brian Backus, Brian Banks.

Your Friends & Neighbors
If these are your friends and neighbors, move and don't give out your forwarding address. Six characters lie, cheat, and deceive their way through LaBute's tale of modern immorality. Weasel Jerry (Stiller) sleeps with Mary (Brenneman), the supposedly happy wife of his old friend Barry (Eckhart). Meanwhile, his live-in girlfriend (Keener) is having a lesbian affair with Cheri (Kinski), and chilly misogynist Cary (Patrick) seduces and discards a string of women. On their commentary track, LaBute and producer Golin tacitly admit how removed from the material they are, barely even acknowledging the characters' names. The entire DVD is equally cool and distant. Like the image, the sound is adequate and uninspired. —*MM*
Movie: 𝄞𝄞 **DVD:** 𝄞𝄞
USA Home Entertainment (Cat #440 058 683-2, UPC #04400586326). Widescreen (2.35:1) anamorphic; full frame. Dolby Digital 5.1 Surround Stereo; Dolby Digital Stereo. $24.95. Keepcase. *LANG:* English. *SUB:* French. *FEATURES:* 25 chapter links • Theatrical trailer • Cast and crew thumbnail biographies.
1998 (R) 99m/C Jason Patric, Nastassia Kinski, Ben Stiller, Catherine Keener, Aaron Eckhart, Amy Brenneman; *D:* Neil LaBute; *W:* Neil LaBute; *C:* Nancy Schreiber.

You've Got Mail
Third remake of *The Shop Around the Corner* (*In the Good Old Summer Time* was number two) finds independent New York bookstore owner Ryan battling Hanks's chain operation to stay in business. How does this qualify as a romantic comedy? Because they're flirting with each other anonymously by email. The third teaming of the stars relies, almost too much, on their considerable chemistry. The soundtrack music was chosen for maximum onscreen and record store effect and so a "music only" option is available for those who want to watch the stars and the fresh-scrubbed Big Apple locations without all that bothersome plot to worry about. The softly focused image is just what this kind of fluff calls for. —*MM*
Movie: 𝄞𝄞▶ **DVD:** 𝄞𝄞𝄞
Warner Home Video, Inc. (Cat #16954, UPC #085391695424). Widescreen anamorphic. Dolby Digital 5.1 Surround Stereo. $24.98. Snapper. *LANG:* English. *SUB:* English; French. *CAP:* English. *FEATURES:* Commentary: Ephron and producer Lauren Shuler Donner • HBO featurette • Tour of Upper West Side movie locations • Trailers • 33 chapter links.
1998 (PG) 119m/C Meg Ryan, Tom Hanks, Parker Posey, Greg Kinnear, Jean

Stapleton, Steve Zahn, Dave Chappelle, Dabney Coleman, John Randolph, Michael Badalucco, Heather Burns, Hallee Hirsh; *D:* Nora Ephron; *W:* Nora Ephron; *C:* John Lindley; *M:* George Fenton. *AWARDS: NOM:* Golden Globe Awards '99: Best Actress—Musical/Comedy (Ryan).

Zachariah
Semi-comic rock western might have been a partial inspiration for the Eagles' "Desperado." Two young would-be gunfighters (Rubinstein and Johnson) pursue careers as band members and bad men. They separate and find curious, surreal adventures in a landscape littered with genre cliches. The spotty material was written by members of the Firesign Theater and features appearances by Country Joe and the Fish, the New York Rock Ensemble, and the James Gang. On DVD, the film is incredibly sharp. It was apparently made from pristine elements that have been well preserved. The image is much clearer than most films of the early '70s. Sound is only adequate. —*MM*
Movie: 𝄞𝄞 **DVD:** 𝄞𝄞▶
Anchor Bay (Cat #DV10945, UPC #013131094596). Widescreen (1.85:1) letterboxed. Dolby Digital Mono. $24.98. Keepcase. *LANG:* English. *FEATURES:* 22 chapter links.
1970 (PG) 93m/C Don Johnson, John Rubinstein, Pat Quinn, Dick Van Patten, William Challee, Country Joe McDonald, Elvin Jones, Doug Kershaw, Lawrence Kubik, Hank Worden; *D:* George Englund; *W:* Peter Bergman, Joe Massot, Phil Proctor, Philip Austin, David Ossman; *C:* Jorge Stahl Jr.; *M:* Jimmie Haskell.

A Zed & Two Noughts
Do not try to approach director Greenaway's second film as a conventional narrative. He uses a bizarre traffic accident to explore ideas of life, death, and decay. After their wives are killed, twin zoologists become obsessed with questions of mortality and sex. Greenaway uses both dialogue and a series of striking images to get his points across, and he is extraordinarily funny though his humor is difficult to define or describe. He's certainly not to all tastes. That said, those who are already familiar with *The Cook, the Thief, His Wife, and Her Lover* will appreciate what he's up to. In some ways, this film may be better on DVD than it is on a theatre screen. What's lost in the size of the image is gained with the pause and repeat functions which enable viewers to appreciate the way he works with tinted light and his sometimes shocking compositions. A commentary track could have been fascinating, but somehow, I doubt that the filmmaker would want to explain his work. —*MM*
Movie: 𝄞𝄞𝄞 **DVD:** 𝄞𝄞𝄞▶
WinStar Home Entertainment (Cat #FLV5195, UPC #720917519524). Widescreen (1.66:1) letterboxed. Mono. $29.98. Keepcase. *LANG:* English. *FEATURES:* 9 chapter links.

1988 115m/C *GB* Eric Deacon, Brian Deacon, Joss Ackland, Andrea Ferreol, Frances Barber; *D:* Peter Greenaway; *W:* Peter Greenaway; *C:* Sacha Vierny; *M:* Michael Nyman.

Zeder

A young novelist (Lavia) discovers fragments of curious documents on the ribbon of a used typewriter bought by his wife (Canovas). He comes to think that they suggest research into immortality. The rest of the film combines elements of suspense with horror in a fairly slow-moving, serious plot with references to Val Lewton's *Cat People*. On DVD, this Italian import is extremely rough. Even at its best moments, the image is grainy and difficult to watch. —*MM*
Movie: 🎬🎬 *DVD:* 🎬
Image Entertainment (Cat #ID4784SIDVD, UPC #014381478426). Full frame. Dolby Digital Mono. $24.99. Snapper. *LANG:* English. *FEATURES:* Theatrical trailer • 14 chapter links.
1983 98m/C *IT* Gabriele Lavia, Anne Canovas; *D:* Pupi Avati; *W:* Pupi Avati, Antonio Avati, Maurizio Costanzo.

Zeram

Zeram is a giant renegade space alien lured to Earth by a female bounty hunter. How does she expect to capture it? Why, with a warp machine, space bazooka, electric shield, and a computer named Bob, of course. Good action sequences combine with entertaining special effects. The colors on the DVD are more washed-out than on the VHS release and the picture varies but is generally fairly soft. There is occasional ghosting around brighter objects. The sound is lacking in both separation and body but seems comparable to the earlier edition. —*JO*
Movie: 🎬🎬 *DVD:* 🎬🎬
Image Entertainment (Cat #ID4665FLDVD, UPC #014381466522). Widescreen (1.77:1). Stereo. $24.95. Snapper. *LANG:* English. *FEATURES:* 10 chapter links.
1991 92m/C *JP* Yuko Moriyama, Yukihiro Hotaru, Kunihiko Ida; *D:* Keita Amemiya; *W:* Hajime Matsumoto; *C:* Hiroshi Kidokoro; *M:* Hirokazu Ohta.

Zero Boys

Teenage survivalists in the California wilderness are stalked by a murderous lunatic. Exploitative and mean-spirited.
Movie: WOOF *DVD:* NYR
Simitar Entertainment (Cat #7652). Full frame. Dolby Digital 5.1 Surround Stereo. $14.98. Keepcase. *FEATURES:* Thumbnail bios • Production notes • Trailer.
1986 (R) 89m/C Daniel Hirsch, Kelli Maroney, Nicole Rio, Joe Phelan; *D:* Nico Mastorakis; *W:* Nico Mastorakis, Fred C. Perry; *C:* Steve Shaw; *M:* Stanley Myers, Hans Zimmer.

Zero Effect

A cross between Howard Hughes and Sherlock Holmes, brilliant, eccentric detective Daryl Zero (Pullman), and his harried helper Steve Arlo (Stiller), take on the case of a blackmailed timber tycoon (O'Neal) in this comedic whodunit. The normally reclusive sleuth bites the bullet and agrees to trek to Oregon to personally investigate the particularly intriguing case, which also involves an attractive paramedic (Dickens). Pullman pulls off another quirky leading man performance with flair. Stiller is stellar as the exasperated assistant. Fresh idea and hip humor mark this debut for 22-year-old writer-director Kasdan, son of director Lawrence Kasdan. The DVD has a couple of spots where some grain appeared, but is overall very good. The picture is sharp, with excellent details. Colors are vibrant and both the contrast and brightness levels are very strong. The soundtrack doesn't really take advantage of the 5.1 capabilities, but does the basic job very well. —*JO*
Movie: 🎬🎬🎬 *DVD:* 🎬🎬🎬
Warner Home Video, Inc. (Cat #C2534, UPC #053939253429). Widescreen (1.85:1) anamorphic. Dolby Digital 5.1. $19.98. Snapper. *LANG:* English. *SUB:* English; French. *CAP:* English. *FEATURES:* 31 chapter links • Commentary: Jake Kasdan • 2 theatrical trailers • Production notes.
1997 (R) 150m/C Bill Pullman, Ben Stiller, Ryan O'Neal, Kim Dickens, Angela Featherstone; *D:* Jake Kasdan; *W:* Jake Kasdan; *C:* Bill Pope.

Zeus and Roxanne

Some Hollywood producer decided to combine *Flipper* with *Benji* and *The Parent Trap* for an insipid kid flick. Marine biologist and single mom Mary Beth (Quinlan) meets her unconventional (and conveniently widowed) new neighbor Terry (Guttenberg) and his dog Zeus. Cuteness ensues. Their kids try to get the adults together. Meanwhile Zeus and Roxanne, Mary Beth's dolphin, strike up a friendship of their own. Not much appeal for anyone over the age of nine. The sharp transfer is really much better than this idiotic material deserves. —*MM*
Movie: 🎬🎬 *DVD:* 🎬🎬🎬
HBO Home Video (Cat #91392, UPC #026359139222). Widescreen letter-boxed. $24.98. Snapper. *LANG:* English; French. *SUB:* Spanish. *CAP:* English. *FEATURES:* Thumbnail bios • Trailer • 9 chapter links.
1996 (PG) 98m/C Kathleen Quinlan, Steve Guttenberg, Arnold Vosloo, Miko Hughes, Dawn McMillan, Majandra Delfino; *D:* George Miller; *W:* Tom Benedek; *C:* David Connell; *M:* Bruce Rowland.

Zig Zag

Espionage drama set in Moscow.
Movie: NYR *DVD:* NYR
Tapeworm Video Distributors (Cat #3832). $24.95.

1999 87m/C Andrei Gradov, Hugh B. Holub, Anastasia Martino, Doug Mears, David Starzyk; *D:* Anatoly Niman; *W:* Robert J. Nowac; *C:* Eugene Shlugleit.

Ziggy Stardust and the Spiders from Mars

Aside from the buzzy, barely serviceable textual scene-access menu there are no extras, but the film itself is a sure cure for what ails kids who only hear "Watch That Man" on TV commercials. The '70s at their most extravagant tolled the death knell of David Bowie's most famous incarnation, Ziggy Stardust. His Hammersmith Odeon dressing room is the site of casual visits from the likes of Angie and Ringo, who banter with the resigned, philosophical David over the strains of Beethoven's Ninth. Ziggy's final concert with the Spiders has a genuinely personal feel of a homecoming that overcomes the kabuki-styled costumes and diffident posturing of glam rock. The film was remixed in '83 but the original was shot in '73, so the predictable "sound and vision" problems (thudding feedback on the drum track, swimming grain) are even more annoying on DVD yet clearly unavoidable. Crank this up for a great escape from today's canned promos, stadium tours, and lip-synched videos. —*JK*
Movie: 🎬🎬🎬 *DVD:* 🎬🎬
Image Entertainment (Cat #ID4704LYDVD, UPC #014381470420). Full frame. PCM Mono. $24.99. Snapper. *LANG:* English. *FEATURES:* 20 chapter links • Interactive menus.
1983 89m/C *GB* David Bowie, Angie Bowie, Mick Ronson, Trevor Bolder, Mick Woodmansy; *D:* D.A. Pennebaker.

Zigzag

Escaped convict melodrama.
Movie: NYR *DVD:* NYR
Digital Versatile Disc Ltd. (Cat #150). Full frame. Dolby Digital Surround Stereo. $19.95. Keepcase.
1997 87m/C Kim Kopf, Dan Reed, Nicol Zanzarella; *D:* Allen Nause; *W:* Dan Reed.

Zombie

One of Italian gore master Fulci's best. There are plenty of guts, heavily dwelled upon, but the atmosphere is the incredible thing here. The opening underwater zombie attack is a real treat and nobody can forget the long, agonizingly slow-moving splinter through the eye. The Hound hopes Anchor Bay will redo this DVD (they probably will, since the Anchor Bay people are real movie fans as well as businessmen). The film is almost constantly darkly lit and on this disc that means heavy grain and artifacts so bad that they've got better hang time than Michael Jordan. The color texturings remain but the disc is just hard to watch. The sound has been improved with a good bass boost that doesn't bury the highs, and adds a lot of energy. —*JO AKA:*

Zombie Flesh-Eaters; Island of the Living Dead; Zombi 2.
Movie: 🐾🐾🐾 **DVD:** 🐾
Anchor Bay (Cat #DV10500, UPC #013131050097). Widescreen (2.35:1) letterboxed. Dolby Digital 5.1. $29.98. Keepcase. *LANG:* English. *FEATURES:* 11 chapter links • Commentary: Tisa Farrow, Richard Johnson, and Ian McCulloch • Theatrical trailer • TV and radio spots.
1980 91m/C *IT* Tisa Farrow, Ian McCulloch, Richard Johnson, Al Cliver, Auretta Gay, Olga Karlatos, Stefania D'Amario,

Ugo Bologna, Monica Zanchi; **D:** Lucio Fulci; **W:** Elisa Briganti; **C:** Sergio Salvati; **M:** Fabio Frizzi, Giorgio Tucci.

Zu: Warriors of the Magic Mountain

The forces of evil are plotting to take over medieval China and a warrior endures the perils of the Zu Mountains to find the Twin Swords, the only weapons that can defeat the demons.

Movie: 🐾🐾 **DVD:** NYR
Tai Seng Video Marketing (Cat #25254). Dolby Digital 5.1 Surround Stereo. $49.95. Keepcase. *LANG:* Cantonese; Mandarin. *SUB:* Bahasa Indonesian & Malaysian; Cantonese; English; Japanese; Korean; Mandarin; Thai; Vietnamese.
1983 98m/C *HK* Adam Cheng, Yuen Biao, Brigitte Lin, Sammo Hung; **D:** Tsui Hark.

"DVD Connections" offers lists of DVD-related magazines and newsletters, websites (including retail and rental sources), books, and newsgroups to help you keep abreast of this fast-paced new technology.

Magazines/Newsletters

DVD Guide
NVI Publishing Group
10 Forest Ave.
Paramus, NJ 07652
(201)291-9444
888-735-6656
(201)291-9456 (fax)

Quarterly. $5.95/issue; $22.95/year in the U.S. ($26.95 in Canada).

DVD—Laser Disc Newsletter
Laser Disc Newsletter
PO Box 420
East Rockaway, NY 11518
800-551-4914
(516)594-9307 (fax)

Monthly. $35/year; $62.50/2 years in North America ($50/year; $95/2 years outside North America).

Laser Disc Gazette
Rad Bennett
Rd. 2, Box 654
Harpers Ferry, WV 25425
(304)725-0525
(304)725-0525 (fax)

Bimonthly. $11.95/year in U.S.; $19.95 elsewhere.

Schwann DVD Advance
Schwann Publications
1280 Santa Anita Ct.
Woodland, CA 95776
1-800-792-9447
www.schwann.com

Bimonthly. $29.95/year in U.S.; $7.95/issue.

Web Sites

Ace VCD DVD
www.acevcddvd.com

Sells Asian and Japanese movies, music, adult, and animation.

Active Buyer's Guide: DVDs
www.dvdplayers.activebuyersguide.com

Consumer guide to purchasing DVD players.

Active DVD
www.activewin.com/dvd

DVD news, tips, reveiws, and other related articles.

All DVD Links
www.alldvdlinks.com

DVD reviews, articles, and links.

All Star DVD
www.alldvdmovies.com

Mail-order distributor of video movies, CD-ROMS, laserdiscs, and books.

Anamorphic DVD Support Petition
www.schryver.org/curt/dvd/anamorphic.htm

Online petition and information in support of the anamorphic format.

Animania
www.animania-ent.com

Mail-order anime and manga.

Anime Castle
www.animecastle.com

DVD retail.

Anime on DVD
www.animeondvd.com

Anime articles and reviews.

Anti-DIVX
www.geocities.com/TelevisionCity/Studio/8884/divx.htm

Provides info on the extinct DIVX format.

Apollo Movie Guide
www.apolloguide.com/dvd.htm

Includes reviews of DVDs.

AsianXpress
www.asianxpress.net

Hong Kong DVD retailer.

Askew Reviews
www.askewreviews.com

DVD and movie reviews.

B1 Media
www.b1media.com

Provides DVD menu design.

Bargain Central
www.bargain-central.com

Provides links to DVD-specific purchases.

BargainFlix
www.bargainflix.com

Source for DVD bargains and coupons on the Internet.

Bay Distributors
www.baydistribution.com

DVD retail.

BestDVD
www.bestdvd.co.uk

DVD reviews.

Big Picture DVD Review Page
www.thebigpicturedvd.com/bigpicmain.shtml

DVD reviews and discussion, with emphasis on high-resolution display.

BigStar
www.bigstar.com

Retail DVD and VHS.

BinaryFlix
www.binaryflix.com

DVD discussion and menu details.

Black DVD Online
www.blackdvdonline.com

News, reviews, and discussion on African American–themed DVDs.

Blackstar
www.blackstar.co.uk

DVD retail for U.K. and international customers.

Blowout Video
www.blowoutvideo.com

Retail DVD and VHS.

BlueDVD.com
www.bluedvd.com

Adult DVD rental by mail.

Buy VcdDvd.com
www.buyvcddvd.com

Asian DVD and VCD retail.

C & L Internet Club
www.cnl.com

Canadian DVD retailer.

Cafe DVD
www.cafedvd.com

DVD rental.

Canadian DVD Users Group
www.canadiandvdgroup.com

DVD reviews and discussion for Canadians.

CD Playwright
www.cdplaywright.com

Sells products to protect CDs and DVDs.

Century DVD
www.centurydvd.com

DVD comparison shopping service.

Cinema Classics
www.cinemaclassics.com

DVD retail.

DC DVD
www.dc-dvd.co.uk

Retails Region 1 DVD in the U.K.

DealCatcher.com
www.dealcatcher.com

Dean's DVD Reviews
members.spree.com/sip/dvddean/

DVD reviews.

DesiFilms.com
www.desifilms.com

Indian DVD rental.

Digibuster
www.digibuster.com

DVD rental.

Digital Bits, The
www.thedigitalbits.com

DVD reviews and other articles.

Digital Entertainment, Inc.
www.indianfilmsdvd.com

Indian DVD retail.

Digital Eyes
www.digitaleyes.net

DVD retail.

Digital Ring
www.thedigitalring.com

Movie and DVD news and reviews.

Digital Video Depot
www.dv-depot.com

DVD retail.

DiscountFlix
www.discountflix.com

DVD comparison shopping service.

DVD Addiction
www.dvdaddiction.com

DVD reviews.

DVD Amigos
www.dvdamigos.com

DVD-related articles.

DVD Angle
www.dvdangle.com

DVD reviews.

DVD AniMania
www.ij.net/wildcoast/anime/

News and reviews on anime DVD.

DVD Answer Man
www.dvdanswerman.com

DVD info and reviews.

DVD Arena
www.dvdarena.com

Buys and sells used DVDs.

DVD Artist
www.dvdartist.com

DVD news.

DVD Authority
www.dvdauthority.com

DVD reviews.

DVD Bargain Update
www.dvdbargainupdate.com

Newsletter for DVD bargain hunters.

DVD Bid
www.dvd-bid.com

DVD auction.

DVD Box Office
www.dvdboxoffice.com

DVD retail.

DVD Buying Guide
www.dvdbuyingguide.com

DVD reviews and resources.

DVD Cache
www.dvdcache.com

DVD rental.

DVD Channel News
www.dvdchannelnews.com

DVD reviews and news.

DVD Cinema
www.dvdcinema.com

DVD retail.

DVD Corner Net
www.dvdcorner.net

DVD news and reviews.

DVD Coupon Post
www.dvdcouponpost.com

Information on DVD bargains.

DVD Cyber Center
www.dvdcc.com

DVD reviews and articles.

DVD Daily
www.dvd-daily.com

DVD magazine.

DVD Demystified
www.dvddemystified.com

DVD information, including an exhaustive DVD FAQ.

DVD Depot
www.dvddepot.co.uk

U.K. DVD retail.

DVD Digital Domain
www.dvddigital.com

DVD retail.

DVD Direct
www.dvd-uk.com

Retail DVD site.

DVD Dish
www.lightviews.com

DVD news, reviews, and previews.

DVD Dynamic
www.dvddynamic.com

DVD retail.

DVD Easter Eggs
www.dvdeastereggs.com

Provides info on DVD hidden features.

DVD Empire
www.dvdempire.com

DVD retailer.

DVD ESP
www.dvdesp.com

DVD shopping service.

DVD Express
www.dvdexpress.com

DVD retailer.

DVD File
www.dvdfile.com

DVD information.

DVD Freak
www.dvdfreak.com

DVD info and reviews.

DVD Insider
www.dvdinsider.com

DVD news and reviews.

DVD Journal
www.dvdjournal.com

DVD news, reviews, and commentary.

DVD King
www.dvdking.com

DVD retail.

DVD Mon
www.dvdmon.com

DVD news, reviews, and resources.

DVD Monthly
www.dvdmonthly.com

DVD movie and hardware reviews.

DVD Movie Review, The
www.dvdmoviereview.com

DVD Nightmare
www.dvdnightmare.com

News on horror DVDs.

DVD Overnight
www.dvdovernight.com

DVD rental.

DVD Palace
www.dvdpalace.com

DVD retail.

DVD pizza.com
www.dvdpizza.com

DVD retail.

DVD Planet
www.dvdplanet.com

DVD retail.

DVD Post
www.dvdpost.com

DVD reviews and links.

DVD Price Compare
www.dvdpricecompare.com

DVD bargain search service.

DVD Price Search
www.dvdpricesearch.com

Offers DVD price comparisons.

DVD Resource Page, The
www.dvdresource.com

DVD reviews, news, and features.

DVD Review
www.dvdreview.com

DVD reviews, news, interviews, links, and chat.

DVD Reviewer
www.dvd.reviewer.co.uk

DVD news, articles, and forums.

DVD Rumble
www.dvdrumble.co.uk

DVD Region 1 and Region 2 comparison reviews.

DVD Spin
www.dvd-spin.com

DVD news and reviews.

DVD Spotlight
www.dvdspotlight.net

DVD news and reviews.

DVD Store
www.dvd1.com

DVD retail.

DVD Street
www.dvdstreet.co.uk/

DVD retail.

DVD Superstore
www.dvdsuperstore.com

DVD retail.

DVD Talk
www.dvdtalk.com

DVD news, chats, and reviews.

DVD Time
www.dvdtime.co.uk

DVD news and info.

DVD Times
www.dvdtimes.co.uk

DVD news, reviews, and forums.

DVD TitleWaves
www.dvdtitlewaves.com

DVD retail.

DVD Tracker
www.dvdtracker.com
DVD purchase cataloging service.

DVD Verdict
www.dvdverdict.com
DVD movie and hardware reviews, forums, and news.

DVD Web
www.dvdweb.co.uk
DVD news, reviews, links, and competitions.

DVD Week
www.dvdforever.com
DVD news and links.

DVD.com
www.dvd.com
DVD news and info.

DVDden
www.dvdden.com
DVD news, reviews, schedules, and technical info.

DVDDirect.net
www.dvdirect.net
DVD retail.

dvdfuture.com
www.dvdfuture.com
DVD reviews, features, and forums.

DVDHunt.com
www.dvdhunt.com
Buys/sells/trades DVDs.

DVDLaser.com
www.DVDLaser.com
DVD reviews, info, commentary, links, and news.

DVDSpot
www.dvdspot.net
DVD news, reviews of movies and hardware, and links.

DVDTOWN.COM
www.dvdtown.com
DVD news and reviews.

Entertainment Warehouse
www.dvd-plus.com
Canadian DVD retail.

Guide to Current DVD
www.currentfilm.com
DVD reviews and other info.

HorrorDVDs
www.horrordvds.com
Horror DVD news, forums, reviews, contests, and links.

Incredible DVD
www.incredibledvd.com
DVD coupons, bargains, and freebies.

Indian DVD
www.desipadam.com
Hindi DVD rental.

Inside DVD
www.insidedvd.com
DVD news and reviews.

Ividea
www.ividea.com
DVD retail.

Jeff's Used LD/DVD Finder
www.rtr.com/~jeff/
Searches for used LDs and DVDs.

Ken Crane's
www.kencranes.com
DVD, laserdiscs, and DTS retail.

Kozmo
www.kozmo.com
DVD rental/retail.

Laser Discovery
www.laserdiscovery.com
DVD rental.

Laser Visions Direct
www.lvd.com
DVD retail.

Laserific
www.laserific.com
DVD rental/retail in Orlando, FL.

LaserQuest
members.home.net/laserquest/
DVD retail.

Laser's Edge
www.lasersedge.com
DVD retail.

Lasertown Video Discs, Inc.
www.lasertown.com
DVD retail.

Let's Get Digital
www.letsgetdigital.co.uk/
DVD news, articles, and links.

Lucy's DVDs
www.lucysdvds.com
DVD retail.

Movie Store, The
www.themovie-store.com
DVD retail.

Movietrak.com
www.movietrak.com
DVD rental in the U.K.

MyDVDsource.com
www.mydvdsource.com
DVD retail.

N2Video
www.n2video.com
DVD retail.

Netflix
www.netflix.com
DVD rental.

Pheran's DVD Review Index
trfn.clpgh.org/~ssnodgra/dvd/
DVD reviews.

Play247
www.play247.com
DVD retail.

Right Stuff International
www.rightstuf.com
Anime DVD retail.

Second Chance DVDs
www.scdvd.com
Buys and sells used DVDs.

SMR—Home Theatre DVD Review Archive
www.smr-home-theatre.org/dvd
Home theatre info.

Splatterhouse
www.splatterhouse.net
Reviews and other info on horror DVDs.

Starship Audio Industries
www.starlaser.com
DVD retail.

Thomas Video
www.thomasvideo.com
DVD, VHS, and LD retail.

Ultimate DVD Links
www.dvdlink.8m.com
Provides links to retailers, rentals, news and reviews, studios, coupons and deals, and bargain sites.

Undercover DVD
www.hewittco.com/bstreet/verification.tpl
Sells adult DVDs.

Video Ltd.
www.videoltd.com
DVD retail.

Video Zone
www.video-zone.com
DVD retail.

WebStation
www.replaydvd.com
DVD retail.

Widescreen Review Magazine
www.anamorphicDVD.com
DVD reviews.

Yanman's DVD Reviews
www.yanman.com
DVD reviews and discussion.

Books

Complete Guide to DVD
Andrew Yoder. 2000. Howard W. Sams & Co. $29.95 (paper).

Desktop Digital Video Production
Frederic Jones. 1998. Prentice Hall. $49.95 (paper).

The Dictionary of New Media: The New Digital World of Video, Audio, and Print
James Monaco. 1999. Harbor Electronic Publishing. $39.95; $19.95 (paper).

Digital Video for Dummies
Martin Doucette. 1999. IDG Books. $19.99 (paper).

Doug Pratt's DVD-Video Guide
Douglas Pratt. 1999. Harbor Electronic Publishing. $49.95; $19.95 (paper).

DVD Demystified: The Guidebook for DVD-Video and DVD-ROM
Jim Taylor. 1997. McGraw Hill. $42.95 (paper).

A Technical Introduction to Digital Video
Charles A. Poynton. 1996. John Wiley & Sons. $44.99.

Newsgroups

alt.video.dvd
alt.video.dvd.friends-of-joe
alt.video.laserdisc
aus.dvd
rec.video.dvd.advocacy
rec.video.dvd.marketplace
rec.video.dvd.misc.
rec.video.dvd.players
rec.video.dvd.tech
rec.video.dvd.titles
uk.media.dvd

No, we didn't forget to include *Animal House*. You can find the entry for this DVD in the Ns, because the real title is *National Lampoon's Animal House*. This and other mysteries can be solved by using this handy-dandy "Alternative Titles Index." Variant and translated titles for the DVDs reviewed in this book are provided below in alphabetical order followed by a cross-reference to the appropriate entry in the main review section. Please remember that English-language articles ("a," "an," and "the") are ignored in the sort, but non-English articles (such as "la" or "el" or "das") are NOT ignored. Enjoy.

Abbott and Costello in the Navy
 See In the Navy (1941)
Abraxas
 See Abraxas: Guardian of the Universe (1990)
Ace
 See The Great Santini (1980)
Ace Ventura Goes to Africa
 See Ace Ventura: When Nature Calls (1995)
The Actress
 See Center Stage (1991)
Addict
 See Born to Win (1971)
The Adventures of Chatran
 See The Adventures of Milo & Otis (1989)
The Adventures of Young Brave
 See Waking Up Horton (1999)
Aelita: The Revolt of the Robots
 See Aelita: Queen of Mars (1924)
AFO
 See Air Force One (1997)
Against All Enemies
 See The Siege (1998)
Ai No Borei
 See In the Realm of Passion (1980)
Ai No Corrida
 See In the Realm of the Senses (1976)
Aiqing Wansui
 See Vive l'Amour (1994)
Al-Ris-Alah
 See The Message (1977)
Al 33 di Via Orologio fa Sempre Freddo
 See Beyond the Door 2 (1979)
Alien 2
 See Aliens (SE) (1986)
All for One
 See Return to Paradise (1998)
The Alley of Miracles
 See Midaq Alley (1995)
Alone
 See Horton Foote's Alone (1997)
Alphaville, a Strange Case of Lemmy Caution
 See Alphaville (1965)
Alphaville, Une Etrange Aventure de Lemmy Caution
 See Alphaville (1965)
Amelia and the King of Plants
 See Bed of Roses (1995)
American Beauty Hostages
 See She Devils in Chains (1976)
American Nightmares
 See Combat Shock (1984)
The Amorous General
 See Waltz of the Toreadors (1962)
Amy Foster
 See Swept from the Sea (1997)
Andrews' Raiders
 See The Great Locomotive Chase (1956)

Andy Warhol's Flesh
 See Flesh (1968)
Andy Warhol's Heat
 See Heat (1972)
Andy Warhol's Young Dracula
 See Andy Warhol's Dracula (1974)
Angel of Vengeance
 See Ms. 45 (1981)
Angels in the Attic
 See The Robin Hood Gang (1998)
Animal House
 See National Lampoon's Animal House (1978)
Anne and Muriel
 See Two English Girls (1972)
Apres l'Amour
 See Love After Love (1994)
The Arena
 See Naked Warriors (1973)
Armour of God
 See Operation Condor 2: The Armour of the Gods (1986)
The Astral Factor
 See The Invisible Strangler (1976)
At First Sight
 See Entre-Nous (1983)
Atoll K
 See Utopia (1951)
Auch Zwerge Haben Klein Angefangen
 See Even Dwarfs Started Small (1969)
Austria 1700
 See Mark of the Devil (1969)
Avenging Godfather
 See Avenging Disco Godfather (1976)
A.W.O.L.
 See Lionheart (1990)
Babe, the Gallant Pig
 See Babe (1995)
Babes Ahoy
 See Going Overboard (1989)
Babes in Toyland
 See March of the Wooden Soldiers (1934)
Baisers Voles
 See Stolen Kisses (1968)
Bamboo Dolls House
 See The Big Doll House (1971)
Barbarella, Queen of the Galaxy
 See Barbarella (1968)
Baron Blood
 See Torture Chamber of Baron Blood (1972)
Battle of the Astros
 See Godzilla vs. Monster Zero (1968)
Bawang Bie Ji
 See Farewell My Concubine (1993)
Bay of Blood
 See Twitch of the Death Nerve (1971)
Besame Monstruo
 See Kiss Me Monster (1969)
Between Us
 See Entre-Nous (1983)

Beyond the Fog
 See Tower of Evil (1972)
The Big Boss
 See Fists of Fury (1973)
The Big Grab
 See Any Number Can Win (1963)
The Big Heart
 See Miracle on 34th Street (1947)
The Bird with the Glass Feathers
 See The Bird with the Crystal Plumage (1970)
Birds of a Feather
 See The Birdcage (1995)
The Black Buccaneer
 See The Black Pirate (1926)
Black Forest: Rage in Space
 See Hyper Space (1989)
Black Magic Rites: Reincarnations
 See The Reincarnation of Isabel (1972)
The Blind Dead
 See Tombs of the Blind Dead (1972)
The Blood Baron
 See Torture Chamber of Baron Blood (1972)
Blood Beast from Outer Space
 See Night Caller from Outer Space (1966)
Blood Castle
 See The Blood Spattered Bride (1972)
Blood Creature
 See Terror Is a Man (1959)
Blood for Dracula
 See Andy Warhol's Dracula (1974)
Blood on His Lips
 See Hideous Sun Demon (1959)
Blood Thirst
 See Salem's Lot (1979)
Bloodline
 See Hush (1998)
Bloody Fiance
 See The Blood Spattered Bride (1972)
The Bloody Scream of Dracula
 See Dracula, Prince of Darkness (1966)
Blue Jean Cop
 See Shakedown (1988)
Blue Vision
 See In Dreams (1998)
Blut an den Lippen
 See Daughters of Darkness (1971)
The Boat
 See Das Boot (DC) (1981)
Bodies Bear Traces of Carnal Violence
 See Torso (1973)
A Bold Affair
 See Interlocked (1998)
Boogeyman
 See Return of the Boogeyman (1994)
Bookworm
 See The Edge (1997)
Bordello of Blood
 See Tales from the Crypt Presents Bordello of Blood (1996)

Bowfinger's Big Thing
See Bowfinger (1999)
Braindead
See Dead Alive (1993)
Bram Stoker's Dracula
See Dracula (1992)
Brenn, Hexe, Brenn
See Mark of the Devil (1969)
Bride of the Atom
See Bride of the Monster (1955)
Bronenosets Potemkin
See The Battleship Potemkin (1925)
The Buddy Factor
See Swimming with Sharks (1994)
Burn, Witch, Burn
See Mark of the Devil (1969)
The Burning Question
See Reefer Madness (1938)
Cabiria
See Nights of Cabiria (1957)
Caged Virgins
See Requiem for a Vampire (1971)
California Hot Wax
See The Bikini Car Wash Company (1990)
California Man
See Encino Man (1992)
Call It Murder
See Midnight (1934)
Cani Arribbiati
See Rabid Dogs (1974)
Cannibal Orgy, or the Maddest Story Ever Told
See Spider Baby (1964)
Captive
See Sex and the Other Man (1995)
Carlo Collodi's Pinocchio
See The Adventures of Pinocchio (1996)
Carnage
See Twitch of the Death Nerve (1971)
Carne per Frankenstein
See Andy Warhol's Frankenstein (1974)
Carrie 2
See The Rage: Carrie 2 (1999)
The Case of Jonathan Drew
See The Lodger (1926)
Casey's Gift: For Love of a Child
See For Love of a Child (1990)
Castle of Doom
See Vampyr (1931)
Central Do Brasil
See Central Station (1998)
Chamber of Tortures
See Torture Chamber of Baron Blood (1972)
Cheeseburger Film Sandwich
See Amazon Women on the Moon (1987)
Chelovek s Kinoapparatom
See The Man with the Movie Camera (1929)
The Cheney Vase
See Young and Innocent (1937)
Cheun Gwong Tsa Sit
See Happy Together (1996)
Chevy Van
See The Van (1977)
Christmas Vacation
See National Lampoon's Christmas Vacation (1989)
Chungon Satluk Linggei
See Organized Crime & Triad Bureau (1993)
Ci Xi Mi Mi Sheng Huo
See Lover of the Last Empress (1995)
Citizen's Band
See FM (1978)
The Clairvoyant
See Killing Hour (1984)
The Clansman
See The Birth of a Nation (1915)
Class Reunion
See National Lampoon's Class Reunion (1982)
Clive Barker's Lord of Illusions
See Lord of Illusions (1995)
Clive Barker's Salome and The Forbidden
See Salome / The Forbidden (1973)
Coal
See Koyla (1998)
Communion
See Alice Sweet Alice (1976)
Como Agua para Chocolate
See Like Water for Chocolate (1993)
Como ser Mujer y No Morir en El
See How to Be a Woman and Not Die in the Attempt (1991)

Computer Killers
See Horror Hospital (1973)
The Con Man
See The Con Artists (1980)
Conqueror of the Desert
See The Conqueror (1956)
Cord
See Hide and Seek (2000)
Count Dracula and His Vampire Bride
See The Satanic Rites of Dracula (1973)
Coup de Foudre
See Entre-Nous (1983)
Courtesan
See Dangerous Beauty (1998)
Coyote Moon
See Desert Heat (1999)
Crazy for You
See Vision Quest (1985)
Created to Kill
See Embryo (1976)
Creatures of the Devil
See Dead Men Walk / The Monster Maker (1943)
Creepers
See They Live (1988)
Crypt of the Blind Dead
See Tombs of the Blind Dead (1972)
The Curse of Simba
See Curse of the Voodoo (1964)
Curse of the Living Dead
See Kill, Baby, Kill (1966)
Dairy Queens
See Drop Dead Gorgeous (1999)
Dancing about Architecture
See Playing by Heart (1998)
Dandelion
See Tampopo (1986)
Dangerous Kiss
See True Crime (1995)
Dao Ma Dan
See Peking Opera Blues (1986)
Dario Argento's Phantom of the Opera
See The Phantom of the Opera (1998)
Dark Empire
See Dark City (1997)
Dark World
See Dark City (1997)
Das Cabinet des Dr. Caligari
See The Cabinet of Dr. Caligari (1919)
Das Kabinett des Doktor Caligari
See The Cabinet of Dr. Caligari (1919)
Day of the Woman
See I Spit on Your Grave (1977)
De la Part des Copains
See Cold Sweat (1971)
Dead Man's Curve
See The Curve (1997)
The Deadly Three
See Enter the Dragon (SE) (1973)
Death Ride to Osaka
See Girls of the White Orchid (1985)
Death Trap
See Eaten Alive (1976)
Deathline
See Redline (1997)
Deep Red
See Deep Red: Hatchet Murders (1975)
Demon Keeper
See Tales from the Crypt Presents Demon Knight (1994)
Demon Knight
See Tales from the Crypt Presents Demon Knight (1994)
Demoni
See Demons (1986)
The Demon's Mask
See Black Sunday (1960)
Denial
See Something About Sex (1998)
Der Prozess
See The Trial (1963)
Det Sjunde Inseglet
See The Seventh Seal (1956)
The Devil and Dr. Frankenstein
See Andy Warhol's Frankenstein (1974)
The Devil and the Dead
See Lisa and the Devil / The House of Exorcism (1975)
The Devil in the House of Exorcism
See Lisa and the Devil / The House of Exorcism (1975)

The Devil Walks at Midnight
See The Devil's Nightmare (1971)
Dian Zhi Gong Fu Gan Chian Chan
See Half a Loaf of Kung Fu (1985)
Die Blechtrommel
See Tin Drum (1979)
Die Buechse der Pandora
See Pandora's Box (1928)
Die Hard 3
See Die Hard: With a Vengeance (1995)
Die Macht der Bilder: Leni Riefenstahl
See The Wonderful, Horrible Life of Leni Riefenstahl (1993)
Die Regenschirme von Cherbourg
See Umbrellas of Cherbourg (1964)
Die Xue Jie Tou
See A Bullet in the Head (1990)
Die Xue Shuang Xiong
See The Killer (1990)
Die Zwolfte Stunde
See Nosferatu (1922)
The Dirty Seven
See Emmanuelle: Queen of the Desert (1993)
Disciple of Dracula
See Dracula, Prince of Darkness (1966)
Disco Godfather
See Avenging Disco Godfather (1976)
Dispara
See Outrage (1993)
Django 2: Il Grande Ritorno
See Django Strikes Again (1987)
The Dock Brief
See Trial & Error (1962)
Doctor Blood Bath
See Horror Hospital (1973)
The Doctor from Seven Dials
See Corridors of Blood (1958)
Domicile Conjugal
See Bed and Board (1970)
Dope Addict
See Reefer Madness (1938)
Doped Youth
See Reefer Madness (1938)
Doppelganger
See Journey to the Far Side of the Sun (1969)
Dracula and the Seven Golden Vampires
See The Legend of the 7 Golden Vampires (1973)
Dracula Cerca Sangue di Vergine e…Mori de Sete
See Andy Warhol's Dracula (1974)
Dracula Is Dead and Well and Living in London
See The Satanic Rites of Dracula (1973)
Dracula Vuole Vivere: Cerca Sangue de Vergina
See Andy Warhol's Dracula (1974)
Dragon Forever
See Dragons Forever (1988)
Dripping Deep Red
See Deep Red: Hatchet Murders (1975)
Du Shen
See God of Gamblers (1989)
Dungeon of Terror
See Requiem for a Vampire (1971)
Duoluo Tianshi
See Fallen Angels (1995)
Dusting Cliff Seven
See The Last Assassins (1996)
The Dynasty
See Virasat (1997)
East Great Falls High
See American Pie (CE) (1999)
East of Shanghai
See Rich and Strange (1932)
Eaters of the Dead
See The 13th Warrior (1999)
Ebony, Ivory, and Jade
See She Devils in Chains (1976)
Eight Arms to Hold You
See Help! (1965)
El Ataque de los Muertos Sin Ojos
See Return of the Blind Dead (1975)
El Callejon de los Milagros
See Midaq Alley (1995)
El Caso de las Dos Bellezas
See Two Undercover Angels (1968)
El Diablo se Lleva a los Muertos
See Lisa and the Devil / The House of Exorcism (1975)

El la Nave Va
See And the Ship Sails On (1983)
El Mariachi 2
See Desperado (1995)
Elke
See Friend of the Family (1995)
Emmanuelle l'Antivierge
See Emmanuelle, the Joys of a Woman (1976)
Emmanuelle 2
See Emmanuelle, the Joys of a Woman (1976)
Emmanuelle's 7th Heaven
See Emmanuelle, the Joys of a Woman (1976)
Empire of Passion
See In the Realm of Passion (1980)
The Enforcer
See Jet Li's The Enforcer (1995)
Erzebeth
See Daughters of Darkness (1971)
Escapade
See Utopia (1951)
Escape from the Dark
See The Littlest Horse Thieves (1976)
The Escape of Megagodzilla
See Terror of Mechagodzilla (1978)
The Eternal
See The Eternal Kiss of the Mummy (1999)
Evil Dead 3
See Army of Darkness (1992)
Exquisite Tenderness
See The Surgeon (1994)
Face of Fear
See Peeping Tom (1960)
Falltime
See Fall Time (1994)
Family Resemblances
See Un Air de Famille (1996)
Fantastic Invasion of Planet Earth
See The Bubble (1967)
Farewell, Friend
See Honor Among Thieves (1968)
Father Goose
See Fly Away Home (1996)
Faust
See Jan Svankmajer's Faust (1994)
Fear 2
See The Fear: Halloween Night (1999)
Fear: Resurrection
See The Fear: Halloween Night (1999)
Feast of Flesh
See Blood Feast (SE) (1963)
Feng Yu Shuang Liu Xing
See The Killer Meteors (1987)
Film d'Amore et d'Anarchia
See Love and Anarchy (1973)
Finally, Sunday
See Confidentially Yours (1983)
The First Great Train Robbery
See The Great Train Robbery (1979)
First Strike
See Jackie Chan's First Strike (1996)
Fist of Fury
See Chinese Connection (1973)
Five Million Years to Earth
See Quatermass and the Pit (1967)
Flesh for Frankenstein
See Andy Warhol's Frankenstein (1974)
Flood
See Hard Rain (1997)
Flower of the Arabian Nights
See Arabian Nights (1974)
Flying Aces
See The Flying Deuces / Utopia (1939)
Flying Wild
See Fly Away Home (1996)
Fong Shi Yu
See Fong Sai Yuk (1993)
The Fortunes and Misfortunes of Moll Flanders
See Moll Flanders (1996)
47 Samurai
See The 47 Ronin, Parts 1 & 2 (1942)
The Fotographer of Panic
See Peeping Tom (1960)
Foxforce
See She Devils in Chains (1976)
Frankenstein
See Andy Warhol's Frankenstein (1974)
See Mary Shelley's Frankenstein (1994)
The Frankenstein Experiment
See Andy Warhol's Frankenstein (1974)

Frissons
See They Came from Within (1975)
Fruhlingssinfonie
See Spring Symphony (1986)
Fu Gui Lie Che
See The Millionaire's Express (1986)
Fun Loving
See Quackser Fortune Has a Cousin in the Bronx (1970)
Funeral Rites
See The Funeral (1984)
The Gallery Murders
See The Bird with the Crystal Plumage (1970)
Gang War
See Odd Man Out (1947)
Gangland Boss
See A Better Tomorrow, Part 1 (1986)
Gei Ba Ba de Xin
See Jet Li's The Enforcer (1995)
The Gentleman Tramp
See La Collectionneuse (1967)
The Ghastly Orgies of Count Dracula
See The Reincarnation of Isabel (1972)
Ghost Mom
See Bury Me in Niagara (1993)
The Girl Gets Moe
See Love to Kill (1997)
The Girl Was Young
See Young and Innocent (1937)
Giulietta Degli Spiriti
See Juliet of the Spirits (1965)
Glen or Glenda: The Confessions of Ed Wood
See Glen or Glenda? (1953)
Gli Orrori del Castello di Norimberga
See Torture Chamber of Baron Blood (1972)
The Goat
See Three Ages (1923)
Godzilla Fights the Giant Moth
See Godzilla vs. Mothra (1964)
Godzilla vs. the Giant Moth
See Godzilla vs. Mothra (1964)
Godzilla vs. the Thing
See Godzilla vs. Mothra (1964)
Going West in America
See Switchback (1997)
Gojira
See Godzilla, King of the Monsters (1956)
The Golden Hour
See Pot o' Gold (1941)
A Good Day for Fighting
See Custer of the West (1967)
A Good Marriage
See Le Beau Mariage (1982)
Gordon Il Pirata Nero
See The Black Pirate (1926)
Grandmother's House
See Grandma's House (1988)
Grave Robbers from Outer Space
See Plan 9 from Outer Space (1956)
The Great Monster War
See Godzilla vs. Monster Zero (1968)
The Green Ray
See Summer (1986)
Greystoke 2: Tarzan and Jane
See Tarzan and the Lost City (1998)
Grimm Brothers' Snow White
See Snow White: A Tale of Terror (1997)
The Grip of the Strangler
See The Haunted Strangler (1958)
Hacks
See Sink or Swim (1997)
Hak Gam
See Island of Greed (1997)
Hak Hap
See Black Mask (1996)
Hak Mau
See Black Cat (1991)
Halloween 7
See Halloween: H20 (1998)
Halloween: H20 (Twenty Years Later)
See Halloween: H20 (1998)
Hans Christian Andersen's Thumbelina
See Thumbelina (1994)
Harold Robbins' The Betsy
See The Betsy (1978)
The Hatchet Murders
See Deep Red: Hatchet Murders (1975)
The Haunted and the Hunted
See Dementia 13 (1963)

The Haunting of Hill House
See The Haunting (1999)
He or She
See Glen or Glenda? (1953)
The Heir to Genghis Khan
See Storm over Asia (1928)
Hellraiser 2
See Hellbound: Hellraiser 2 (1988)
Henry 2: Portrait of a Serial Killer
See Henry: Portrait of a Serial Killer 2: Mask of Sanity (1996)
Hexen bis aufs Blut Gequaelt
See Mark of the Devil (1969)
Hidden Face
See Jail Bait (1954)
Hidden Power
See Sabotage (1936)
Highlander 2: Renegade Version
See Highlander 2: The Quickening (1991)
Hill Number One
See James Dean Double Feature: Hill Number One / I Am a Fool (1951)
Him
See Only You (1994)
Histoires Extraordinaires
See Spirits of the Dead (1968)
Hit & Run
See Hot Blooded (1998)
Hokuto No Ken
See Fist of the North Star (1986)
The Hollywood Strangler
See Don't Answer the Phone (1980)
Holy Terror
See Alice Sweet Alice (1976)
Home Fires Burning
See The Turning (1992)
The Honest Courtesan
See Dangerous Beauty (1998)
Hong Ying Tao
See Red Cherry (1995)
The Horrible Orgies of Count Dracula
See The Reincarnation of Isabel (1972)
Horror Hotel Massacre
See Eaten Alive (1976)
Horror on Snape Island
See Tower of Evil (1972)
Hot and Cold
See Weekend at Bernie's (1989)
The Hounds of Zaroff
See The Most Dangerous Game (1932)
The House of Exorcism
See Lisa and the Devil / The House of Exorcism (1975)
House of Fright
See Black Sunday (1960)
The House of the Screaming Virgins
See Bloodsucking Freaks (1975)
How to Be a Player
See Def Jam's How to Be a Player (1997)
How to Be a Woman and Not Die Trying
See How to Be a Woman and Not Die in the Attempt (1991)
Howard Stern's Private Parts
See Private Parts (1996)
I Am a Fool
See James Dean Double Feature: Hill Number One / I Am a Fool (1951)
I Changed My Sex
See Glen or Glenda? (1953)
I Corpi Presentano Tracce Di Violenza Carnale
See Torso (1973)
I Led Two Lives
See Glen or Glenda? (1953)
I Love a Man in Uniform
See A Man in Uniform (1993)
I Racconti di Canterbury
See The Canterbury Tales (1971)
I Remember
See Amarcord (1974)
I Was a Teenage Teenager
See Clueless (1995)
Il Decameron
See The Decameron (1970)
Il Deserto Rosso
See The Red Desert (1964)
Il Diavolo e i Morti
See Lisa and the Devil / The House of Exorcism (1975)
Il Fantasma dell'Opera
See The Phantom of the Opera (1998)

Il Fiore delle Mille e Una Notte
See Arabian Nights (1974)
Il Marchio di Santana
See The Bloodsucker Leads the Dance (1975)
Il Monstro
See The Monster (1996)
Il Mostro e in Tavola...Barone Frankenstein
See Andy Warhol's Frankenstein (1974)
Il Postino
See The Postman (1994)
Il Processo
See The Trial (1963)
Il Treno
See The Train (1965)
Il Vangelo Secondo Matteo
See The Gospel According to St. Matthew (1964)
The Imp
See Sorority Babes in the Slimeball Bowl-A-Rama (1987)
In Bed with Madonna
See Truth or Dare (1991)
In Love
See Falling in Love Again (1980)
In Pursuit of Honor
See G.I. Jane (1997)
In Search of the Serpent of Death
See Out of Time (1990)
The Incredible Torture Show
See Bloodsucking Freaks (1975)
Indian Summer
See Alive and Kicking (1996)
Indiscretion
See Dangerous Beauty (1998)
Inferno
See Desert Heat (1999)
Inseminoid
See Horror Planet (1980)
Interlude
See Intermezzo (1936)
Invasion of Planet X
See Godzilla vs. Monster Zero (1968)
Invasion of the Astro-Monsters
See Godzilla vs. Monster Zero (1968)
Invasion of the Astros
See Godzilla vs. Monster Zero (1968)
The Iron Hand
See Chinese Connection (1973)
The Iron Kiss
See Naked Kiss (1964)
The Ironman
See Tetsuo: The Iron Man (1992)
Island of the Living Dead
See Zombie (1980)
It Ain't No Sin
See Belle of the Nineties (1934)
It Happened One Summer
See State Fair (1945)
It's My Life
See My Life to Live (1962)
Ivan Groznyi
See Ivan the Terrible, Part 1 (1944)
Ivan Groznyi 2
See Ivan the Terrible, Part 2 (1946)
Ivan the Terrible, Part 2: The Boyars' Plot
See Ivan the Terrible, Part 2 (1946)
Ja Cuba
See I Am Cuba (1964)
Jag, en Kvinna
See I, a Woman (1966)
Janacek: The Cunning Little Vixen
See The Cunning Little Vixen (1995)
Jealousy
See L'Enfer (1993)
Jerry Springer's Ringmaster
See Ringmaster (1998)
Jian Hua Yan Yu Jiang Nan
See To Kill with Intrigue (1985)
Jian Yu Feng Yun Xu Ji
See Prison on Fire 2 (1991)
Jiang-Hu: Between Love and Glory
See The Bride with White Hair (1993)
Jiang-Hu: Between Love and Glory 2
See The Bride with White Hair 2 (1993)
Jing Wu Men
See Chinese Connection (1973)
John Carpenter's Escape from L.A.
See Escape from L.A. (1996)

Juninatten
See June Night (1940)
Just in Time
See Only You (1994)
Kaiju Daisenso
See Godzilla vs. Monster Zero (1968)
Keep the Aspidistra Flying
See A Merry War (1997)
Killer Grizzly
See Grizzly (1976)
Killing Mrs. Tingle
See Teaching Mrs. Tingle (1999)
Kilronan
See Hush (1998)
Kiss of Evil
See Kiss of the Vampire (1962)
A Kiss to Die For
See Those Bedroom Eyes (1992)
Kondom des Grauens
See Killer Condom (1995)
Koneko Monogatari
See The Adventures of Milo & Otis (1989)
Koroshi no Rakuin
See Branded to Kill (1967)
Koukaku Kidoutai
See Ghost in the Shell (1995)
Kuroi Ame
See Black Rain (1988)
La Belle et la Bete
See Beauty and the Beast (1946)
La Casa Dell'Exorcismo
See Lisa and the Devil / The House of Exorcism (1975)
La Ciociara
See Two Women (1961)
La Cite des Enfants Perdus
See The City of Lost Children (1995)
La Desenchantee
See The Disenchanted (1990)
La Donna E Donna
See A Woman Is a Woman (1960)
La Femme d'a Cote
See The Woman Next Door (1981)
La Grande Illusion
See Grand Illusion (1937)
La Legge
See The Law (1959)
La Loi
See The Law (1959)
La Maschera del Demonio
See Black Sunday (1960)
La Morte Vivante
See The Living Dead Girl (1982)
La Motocyclette
See The Girl on a Motorcycle (1968)
La Noche de la Muerta Ciega
See Tombs of the Blind Dead (1972)
La Noche dell Terror Ciego
See Tombs of the Blind Dead (1972)
La Novia Esangrentada
See The Blood Spattered Bride (1972)
La Nuit des Traquees
See Night of the Hunted (1969)
La Nuit Fantastique
See The Fantastic Night (1942)
La Planete Sauvage
See Fantastic Planet (1973)
La Reincarnazione
See The Reincarnation of Isabel (1972)
La Sanguisuga Conduce la Danza
See The Bloodsucker Leads the Dance (1975)
La Vie de Jesus
See The Life of Jesus (1996)
La Vie Revee des Anges
See The Dreamlife of Angels (1998)
La Vita E Bella
See Life Is Beautiful (1998)
Ladri di Biciclette
See The Bicycle Thief (1948)
Lady of the Shadows
See The Terror (1963)
L'Ami de Mon Ami
See Boyfriends & Girlfriends (1988)
L'Amour d'apres-midi
See Chloe in the Afternoon (1972)
The Lane Frost Story
See 8 Seconds (1994)
L'Anee Derniere a Marienbad
See Last Year at Marienbad (1961)
Lashou Shentan
See Hard-Boiled (1992)

Last House on the Left, Part 2
See Twitch of the Death Nerve (1971)
Le Dernier Metro
See The Last Metro (1980)
Le Dernier Tango a Paris
See Last Tango in Paris (1973)
Le Frisson des Vampires
See The Shiver of the Vampires (1970)
Le Genou de Claire
See Claire's Knee (1971)
Le Monstre
See The Monster (1996)
Le Notti de Cabiria
See Nights of Cabiria (1957)
Le Peau Douce
See The Soft Skin (1964)
Le Proces
See The Trial (1963)
Le Rayon Vert
See Summer (1986)
Le Retour de Martin Guerre
See The Return of Martin Guerre (1983)
Le Rouge aux Levres
See Daughters of Darkness (1971)
Le Salaire de la Peur
See Wages of Fear (1955)
Le Train
See The Train (1965)
Le Violon Rouge
See The Red Violin (1998)
The Legend
See Fong Sai Yuk (1993)
The Legend of Fong Sai-Yuk
See Fong Sai Yuk (1993)
Legend of the Bayou
See Eaten Alive (1976)
Leon
See The Professional (1994)
Lepa Sela, Lepo Gore
See Pretty Village, Pretty Flame (1996)
L'Eredita Ferramonti
See The Inheritance (1976)
Les Boys
See The Boys (1997)
Les Cent et Une Nuits de Simon Cinema
See One Hundred and One Nights (1994)
Les Deux Anglaises et le Continent
See Two English Girls (1972)
Les Diabolique
See Diabolique (1955)
Les Feluettes
See Lilies (1996)
Les Maitres du Temps
See Time Masters (1982)
Les Nuits de la Pleine
See Full Moon in Paris (1984)
Les Parapluies de Cherbourg
See Umbrellas of Cherbourg (1964)
Les Quartre Cents Coups
See The 400 Blows (1959)
Les Roseaux Sauvages
See Wild Reeds (1994)
Letter to Daddy
See Jet Li's The Enforcer (1995)
L'Evangile Selon Saint-Matthieu
See The Gospel According to St. Matthew (1964)
Levres de Sang
See Lips of Blood (1975)
Life During Wartime
See The Alarmist (1998)
Life of Brian
See Monty Python's Life of Brian (1979)
Lifebreath
See Last Breath (1996)
Lightning
See Ed McBain's 87 Precinct (1996)
Lisa e il Diavolo
See Lisa and the Devil / The House of Exorcism (1975)
The Liver Eaters
See Spider Baby (1964)
Lo Squartatore de New York
See New York Ripper (1982)
Loaded Weapon 1
See National Lampoon's Loaded Weapon 1 (1993)
The Lodger: A Case of London Fog
See The Lodger (1926)
L'Oeuvre au Noir
See The Abyss (SE) (1989)

Quan Jing
See Spiritual Kung Fu (1978)

Quiet Killer
See Black Death (1991)

Rage of the Buccaneers
See The Black Pirate (1926)

The Rainmaker
See John Grisham's The Rainmaker (1997)

Re-Animator 2
See Bride of Re-Animator (1989)

Red Blooded American Girl 2
See Hot Blooded (1998)

The Red Lips
See Daughters of Darkness (1971)

Regina Roma
See Regina (1983)

Respectable Families
See Un Air de Famille (1996)

The Return of She
See The Vengeance of She (1968)

Return of the Evil Dead
See Return of the Blind Dead (1975)

Return of the Texas Chainsaw Massacre
See The Texas Chainsaw Massacre 4: The Next Generation (1995)

Revenant
See Modern Vampires (1998)

The Revenge of Al Capone
See Capone (1989)

Revenge of Dracula
See Dracula, Prince of Darkness (1966)

The Revenge of Milady
See The Four Musketeers (1975)

Revenge of the Living Dead
See Children Shouldn't Play with Dead Things (1972)

Revenge of the Vampire
See Black Sunday (1960)

The Ripper
See New York Ripper (1982)

Riti, Magie Nere e Segrete Orgel nel Trecento
See The Reincarnation of Isabel (1972)

Roaring Timber
See Come and Get It (1936)

Robinson Crusoeland
See Utopia (1951)

Roboforce
See I Love Maria (1988)

Rodgers & Hammerstein's Cinderella
See Cinderella (1997)

Roma, Citta Aperta
See Open City (1945)

Rome, Open City
See Open City (1945)

Romeo and Juliet
See William Shakespeare's Romeo and Juliet (1996)

Rookies
See Buck Privates (1941)

Rookies Come Home
See Buck Privates Come Home (1947)

Rote Lippen
See Two Undercover Angels (1968)

Ruan Ling-Yu
See Center Stage (1991)

The Sabre Tooth Tiger
See Deep Red: Hatchet Murders (1975)

Sadisterotica
See Two Undercover Angels (1968)

Sandokan the TV Movie
See The Princess and the Pirate (1995)

Satan
See Mark of the Devil (1969)

Satellite of Blood
See First Man into Space (1959)

The Savage Planet
See Fantastic Planet (1973)

The Scalper
See Just the Ticket (1998)

Scarlet Buccaneer
See Swashbuckler (1976)

Scary Movie
See Scream (CS) (1996)

Scream Again
See Scream 2 (1997)

Screwface
See Marked for Death (1990)

Scrooge
See A Christmas Carol (1951)

Semaforo Rosso
See Rabid Dogs (1974)

The Sentinel
See La Sentinelle (1992)

The Serpent of Death
See Out of Time (1990)

Se7en
See Seven (1995)

Seven Bad Men
See Rage at Dawn (1955)

The Seven Brothers Meet Dracula
See The Legend of the 7 Golden Vampires (1973)

Sex and the Vampire
See The Shiver of the Vampires (1970)

Shadowbuilder
See Bram Stoker's Shadowbuilder (1998)

Shanghai Express
See The Millionaire's Express (1986)

Shichinin No Samurai
See Seven Samurai (1954)

Ship of Fools
See The Imposters (1998)

Shiver
See Night Train to Terror (1984)

Shivers
See They Came from Within (1975)

Shock
See Beyond the Door 2 (1979)

Shock (Transfer Suspense Hypnos)
See Beyond the Door 2 (1979)

Shocked
See Mesmerized (1984)

Shockwave
See The Arrival (1996)

Shoot the Pianist
See Shoot the Piano Player (1962)

Shootout
See Shoot Out (1971)

Shuang Long Hui
See Twin Dragons (1992)

Shut Up and Dance
See Dance with Me (1998)

Sid & Nancy: Love Kills
See Sid & Nancy (1986)

Significant Other
See When a Man Loves a Woman (1994)

Silence
See Khamoshi the Musical (1996)

Silken Skin
See The Soft Skin (1964)

Siren's Kiss
See Body Strokes (1995)

Siunin Wong Fei-hung Tsi Titmalau
See Iron Monkey (1993)

Slave Girls
See Prehistoric Women (1967)

A Small Miracle
See Simon Birch (1998)

Snitch
See Monument Ave. (1998)

Snow White in the Black Forest
See Snow White: A Tale of Terror (1997)

Snuff
See Thesis (1996)

Solyaris
See Solaris (1972)

Something Is Out There
See Day of the Animals (1977)

Soy Cuba
See I Am Cuba (1964)

Spawn
See Todd McFarlane's Spawn (1997)

Spawn 2
See Todd McFarlane's Spawn 2 (1998)

Spider Baby, or the Maddest Story Ever Told
See Spider Baby (1964)

Spinal Tap
See This Is Spinal Tap (1984)

Spirit of the Dead
See The Asphyx (1972)

Spoorloos
See The Vanishing (1988)

Spring Break USA
See Lauderdale (1989)

Spring Fever USA
See Lauderdale (1989)

The Stand
See Stephen King's The Stand (1994)

Starlight Slaughter
See Eaten Alive (1976)

Steiner—Das Eiserne Kreuz
See Cross of Iron (1976)

Stepfather
See Beau Pere (1981)

Storm of the Century
See Stephen King's The Storm of the Century (1999)

Straight from the Heart
See Hum Dil De Chuke Sanam (1999)

The Strange Adventure of David Gray
See Vampyr (1931)

Strangeland
See Dee Snider's Strangeland (1998)

Stray Dogs
See U-Turn (1997)

Street Gang
See Vigilante (1983)

Subspecies 4
See Bloodstorm: Subspecies 4 (1998)

Subspecies 4: Bloodstorm—The Master's Revenge
See Bloodstorm: Subspecies 4 (1998)

Succubus
See The Devil's Nightmare (1971)

The Sullivans
See The Fighting Sullivans (1942)

Summer Madness
See Summertime (1955)

The Sun Demon
See Hideous Sun Demon (1959)

Suspense
See Beyond the Door 2 (1979)

Swept Away . . . By an Unusual Destiny in the Blue Sea of August
See Swept Away . . . (1975)

A Table for One
See Wicked Ways (1999)

Tale of the Mummy
See Russell Mulcahy's Tale of the Mummy (1999)

Tales of Mystery
See Spirits of the Dead (1968)

Tales of Mystery and Imagination
See Spirits of the Dead (1968)

Talos the Mummy
See Russell Mulcahy's Tale of the Mummy (1999)

Ta'm e Guilass
See The Taste of Cherry (1996)

Tang Shan da Xiong
See Fists of Fury (1973)

Tao Fan
See Prison on Fire 2 (1991)

Tarzan and Jane
See Tarzan and the Lost City (1998)

Taste of Cherries
See The Taste of Cherry (1996)

Tell Your Children
See Reefer Madness (1938)

Tengoku To Jigoku
See High & Low (1962)

Terror from the Sun
See Hideous Sun Demon (1959)

Terror of Dracula
See Nosferatu (1922)

The Terror of the Vampires
See The Shiver of the Vampires (1970)

Tesis
See Thesis (1996)

Texas Blood Money
See From Dusk Till Dawn 2: Texas Blood Money (1998)

Thinner
See Stephen King's Thinner (1996)

The Thirst of Baron Blood
See Torture Chamber of Baron Blood (1972)

A Thousand and One Nights
See Arabian Nights (1974)

Thrill of the Vampires
See The Shiver of the Vampires (1970)

Tian di xion xin
See Armageddon (1997)

Tian Yu
See Xiu Xiu: The Sent Down Girl (1997)

Till Death Us Do Part
See The Blood Spattered Bride (1972)

Tim Burton's The Nightmare before Christmas
See The Nightmare before Christmas (1993)

Tirez sur le Pianiste
See Shoot the Piano Player (1962)
To Have and to Hold
See When a Man Loves a Woman (1994)
Tokyo Nagaremono
See Tokyo Drifter (1966)
The Tommyknockers
See Stephen King's The Tommyknockers (1993)
Torment
See L'Enfer (1993)
Touche Pas a la Femme
See Don't Touch the White Woman! (1974)
The Tragedy of Othello: The Moor of Venice
See Othello (1952)
The Transvestite
See Glen or Glenda? (1953)
Travels with Anita
See Lovers and Liars (1981)
Tre Passi nel Delirio
See Spirits of the Dead (1968)
A Trip with Anita
See Lovers and Liars (1981)
Trois Histoires Extraordinaires d'Edgar Poe
See Spirits of the Dead (1968)
Tsubaki Sanjuro
See Sanjuro (1962)
Tunnels
See Criminal Act (1988)
Un, Deux, Trois, Quatre!
See Black Tights (1960)
Under Heaven
See In the Shadows (1998)
Une Femme Est une Femme
See A Woman Is a Woman (1960)
The Untold Story: Human Meat Roast Pork Buns
See The Untold Story (1993)
Up Frankenstein
See Andy Warhol's Frankenstein (1974)
Vacation
See National Lampoon's Vacation (1983)
The Valdez Horses
See Chino / Man with a Camera (1975)
Valdez the Half Breed
See Chino / Man with a Camera (1975)
Valentine's Day
See Protector (1997)
The Vampire
See Vampyr (1931)
Vampire Thrills
See The Shiver of the Vampires (1970)

Vampires
See John Carpenter's Vampires (1997)
Vampyr, Der Traum des David Gray
See Vampyr (1931)
Vampyr, Ou l'Etrange Aventure de David Gray
See Vampyr (1931)
Venice
See Dangerous Beauty (1998)
Victor Frankenstein
See Terror of Frankenstein (1975)
Vig
See Money Kings (1998)
Violent Streets
See Thief (1981)
Virgins and Vampires
See Requiem for a Vampire (1971)
Vivement Dimanche!
See Confidentially Yours (1983)
Vivre Sa Vie
See My Life to Live (1962)
Wages of Fear
See Sorcerer (1977)
Wang Jiao de Tian Kong
See Man Wanted (1994)
War of the Monsters
See Godzilla vs. Monster Zero (1968)
Watch That Man
See The Man Who Knew Too Little (1997)
Wedding Bells
See Royal Wedding (1951)
Welcome to Jericho
See Last Man Standing (1996)
The Well-Made Marriage
See Le Beau Mariage (1982)
Wes Craven Presents Carnival of Souls
See Carnival of Souls (1998)
Wes Craven Presents Wishmaster
See Wishmaster (1997)
Where the Hot Wind Blows
See The Law (1959)
Who Am I
See Jackie Chan's Who Am I (1998)
Who Shot Patakango?
See Who Shot Pat? (1992)
Wicked City 3
See Ninja Scroll (1993)
Wildchild 2
See Silk 'n' Sabotage (1994)
The Winged Serpent
See Q (The Winged Serpent) (1982)
Winter's End
See Sarah, Plain and Tall: Winter's End (1999)

A Woman Alone
See Sabotage (1936)
Women in Cages
See The Big Doll House (1971)
Women's Penitentiary 1
See The Big Doll House (1971)
Wong Fei-hung
See Once Upon a Time in China (1991)
Wong Fei-hung Ji Yi: Naam Yi Dong Ji Keung
See Once Upon a Time in China II (1992)
Wong Fei-hung Tsi Sam: Siwong Tsangba
See Once Upon a Time in China III (1993)
Wrong Bet
See Lionheart (1990)
The X-Files: Fight the Future
See The X-Files (1998)
Xin Buliao Qing
See C'est la Vie, Mon Cherie (1993)
Xin Ching-wu Men
See New Fist of Fury (1976)
Yanzhi Kou
See Rouge (1987)
Yatgo Ho Yan
See Mr. Nice Guy (1998)
Yeshou Xingjing
See Beast Cops (1998)
Ying Huang Boon Sik
See A Better Tomorrow, Part 1 (1986)
Yinghung Bunsik 2
See A Better Tomorrow, Part 2 (1988)
Young Dracula
See Andy Warhol's Dracula (1974)
Zhan Shen Chuan Shu
See The Moon Warriors (1992)
Zhong Hua Zhan Shi
See Magnificent Warriors (1987)
Zombi
See Dawn of the Dead (1978)
Zombi 2
See Zombie (1980)
Zombie
See Dawn of the Dead (1978)
Zombie Flesh-Eaters
See Zombie (1980)
Zombies
See Dawn of the Dead (1978)
Zorro
See The Mask of Zorro (1998)

The "Cast Index" provides a listing of cast members and the DVDs in which they appeared that are covered in this book. The listings for the actor names follow an alphabetical sort by last name (although the names appear in a first name, last name format). The videographies are listed chronologically, with the most recent appearance first. A (V) beside a movie title indicates voice-only work; an (N) indicates narration.

Caroline Aaron
Anywhere But Here '99
Primary Colors '98
Deconstructing Harry '97
Crimes & Misdemeanors '89

Tom Aaron
Body Puzzle '93

Bruce Abbott
The Prophecy 2: Ashtown '97
The Demolitionist '95
Bride of Re-Animator '89
Re-Animator '84

Bud Abbott
Jack & the Beanstalk '52
Abbott and Costello in the
  Foreign Legion '50
Buck Privates Come Home
  '47
Buck Privates '41
In the Navy '41

Kareem Abdul-Jabbar
BASEketball '98
Stephen King's The Stand
  '94
Fletch '85

Toru Abe
The Human Condition: No
  Greater Love '58

Alfred Abel
Metropolis '26

Walter Abel
Holiday Inn '42

Tim Abell
The Base '99
Sexual Roulette '96
Masseuse '95
Over the Wire '95

Ian Abercromble
Army of Darkness '92

Sivi Aberg
The Killing of Sister George
  '69

Michael Aberne
The Commitments '91

Christopher Abraham
Mischievous '99

F. Murray Abraham
Muppets from Space '99
Noah's Ark '99
Star Trek: Insurrection '98
Mimic '97
Mighty Aphrodite '95

Surviving the Game '94
Last Action Hero '93
National Lampoon's Loaded
  Weapon 1 '93
The Bonfire of the Vanities
  '90
Amadeus '84
Scarface '83
All the President's Men '76
They Might Be Giants '71

Jim Abrahams
Kentucky Fried Movie '77

Jon Abrahams
Outside Providence '99

Andrei Abrikosov
Alexander Nevsky '38

Victoria Abril
Kika '94
Comin' At Ya! '81

Frankie Acciarlo
Bad Lieutenant '92

Forrest J Ackerman
Innocent Blood '92
Amazon Women on the Moon
  '87
Kentucky Fried Movie '77

Joss Ackland
Swept from the Sea '97
Mother's Boys '94
Shameless '94
Nowhere to Run '93
The Mighty Ducks '92
The Object of Beauty '91
The Hunt for Red October '90
Lethal Weapon 2 '89
A Zed & Two Noughts '88

David Ackroyd
Raven '97

Jay Acovone
Showdown '94

Eric Acsell
Web of Seduction '99
Loveblind '98
Lolida 2000 '97

Eddie Acuff
The Flying Serpent '55

Amy Adams
Drop Dead Gorgeous '99

Brooke Adams
Sometimes They Come Back
  '91
Days of Heaven '78

Invasion of the Body Snatch-
  ers '78

Catlin Adams
The Jazz Singer '80
The Jerk '79

Don Adams
Inspector Gadget '99 (V)

Dorothy Adams
The Best Years of Our Lives
  '46

Elsie Adams
Minnie and Moskowitz '71

Evan Adams
Smoke Signals '98

Jane Adams
Mumford '99
Happiness '98

Jane Adams
The Brute Man '46

Joe Adams
The Manchurian Candidate
  '62

Joey Lauren Adams
Big Daddy '99
Mallrats '95
Dazed and Confused '93

Julie Adams
The Killer inside Me '76
Psychic Killer '75
Away All Boats '56

Mason Adams
From the Earth to the Moon
  '98
Son-in-Law '93

Maud Adams
Rollerball '75

Nick Adams
Godzilla vs. Monster Zero '68
Pillow Talk '59
Mister Roberts '55
Rebel without a Cause '55

Victoria (Posh Spice)
Adams
Spice World: The Movie '97

Chris(topher) Adamson
Razor Blade Smile '98
Shameless '94

Patrick Adamson
China O'Brien '88

Meat Loaf Aday
Fight Club '99
Black Dog '98
The Mighty '98
Spice World: The Movie '97

Dawn Addams
A King in New York / A
  Woman in Paris '57

Mark Addy
Jack Frost '98
The Full Monty '96

Wesley Addy
The Bostonians '84
Network '76
Tora! Tora! Tora! '70

Isabelle Adjani
Subway '85
Nosferatu the Vampyre '79

Bill Adler
Pom Pom Girls '76

Jay Adler
The Killing '56

Jerry Adler
Six Ways to Sunday '99
Manhattan Murder Mystery
  '93
Exclusive '82

Luther Adler
Absence of Malice '81
D.O.A. '49

Mario Adorf
Tin Drum '79
The Bird with the Crystal
  Plumage '70

Max Adrian
Henry V '44

Ben Affleck
Forces of Nature '99
Armageddon '98
Shakespeare in Love (CS)
  '98
200 Cigarettes '98
Good Will Hunting '97
Phantoms '97
Mallrats '95
Dazed and Confused '93
School Ties '92

Casey Affleck
Desert Blue '98
200 Cigarettes '98
Good Will Hunting '97
To Die For '95

John Agar
King Kong '76
Sands of Iwo Jima '49

Myc Agnew
The Fear: Halloween Night
  '99

Jenny Agutter
Child's Play 2 '90
Darkman '90
An American Werewolf in Lon-
  don '81
Logan's Run '76
Walkabout '71

Brian Aherne
Forever and a Day '43

Philip Ahn
Shock Corridor '63
Impact '49
They Were Expendable '45

Charles Aidman
Prime Suspect '82
Pork Chop Hill '59

Danny Aiello
The Last Don '97
City Hall '95
The Professional '94
Ready to Wear '94
Hudson Hawk '91
Mistress '91
Jacob's Ladder '90
Do the Right Thing '89
Moonstruck '87

Elaine Aiken
Caddyshack '80

Liam Aiken
Stepmom '98

Anouk Aimee
One Hundred and One Nights
  '94
Ready to Wear '94

Henry Ainley
As You Like It '36

Maria Aitken
A Fish Called Wanda '88

Spottiswoode Aitken
The Birth of a Nation '15

Franklin Ajaye
The Jazz Singer '80
Car Wash '76

Marc Akerstream
Rumble in the Bronx '96

Adewale Akinnuoye-Agbaje
Legionnaire '98

Claude Akins
Monster in the Closet '86
The Night Stalker '71
The Caine Mutiny '54

Rhett Akins
Tom Sawyer '99 (V)

Denis Akiyama
Johnny Mnemonic '95
Bury Me in Niagara '93

Tomoko Ai
Terror of Mechagodzilla '78

Marc Alaimo
The Fence '94
Tango and Cash '89

Joe Alaskey
The Rugrats Movie '98 (V)

Jessica Alba
Never Been Kissed '99

Eddie Albert
Brenda Starr '86
Dreamscape (SE) '84
Devil's Rain '75
The Heartbreak Kid '72
The Longest Day '62
Oklahoma '55

Edward Albert
Guarding Tess '94
Hard Drive '94
Sorceress '94
Sexual Malice '93

Giorgia Albertazzi
Last Year at Marienbad '61

Fritz Alberti
Metropolis '26

Frank Albertson
Psycho (CE) '60
It's a Wonderful Life '46

Jack Albertson
The Poseidon Adventure '72
Willy Wonka & the Chocolate Factory '71
Miracle on 34th Street '47

Karl Otto Alberty
The Great Escape '63

Ariauna Albright
Witchouse '99

Dan Albright
I Know What You Did Last Summer '97

Todd Alcott
Curtain Call '97

Alan Alda
Mad City '97
Murder at 1600 '97
Everyone Says I Love You '96
Flirting with Disaster '95
Manhattan Murder Mystery '93
Crimes & Misdemeanors '89

Robert Alda
Lisa and the Devil / The House of Exorcism '75

Rutanya Alda
The Dark Half '91
Vigilante '83
The Deer Hunter '78

Mary Alden
The Birth of a Nation '15

Norman Alden
Tora! Tora! Tora! '70

Richard Alden
The Sadist '63

John Alderman
Trader Hornee '70

Erville Alderson
Sally of the Sawdust '25
America '24

Mari Aldon
Summertime '55

Tom Aldredge
Message in a Bottle '98
Rounders '98
A Stranger in the Kingdom '98
Lawn Dogs '96
Into the Woods '90

Aki Aleong
The Quest '96

Frank Aletter
Tora! Tora! Tora! '70

Ben Alexander
All Quiet on the Western Front '30

Don Alexander
The Wizard of Gore '70

Jace Alexander
Love and a .45 '94
Mistress '91

Jane Alexander
Glory '89
The Betsy '78
All the President's Men '76

Jason Alexander
Something About Sex '98
Cinderella '97
The Paper '94
Jacob's Ladder '90
Pretty Woman '90
White Palace '90
Brighton Beach Memoirs '86

Khandi Alexander
Greedy '94
What's Love Got to Do with It? '93

Richard Alexander
All Quiet on the Western Front '30

Terry Alexander
Day of the Dead '85

Zoe Alexander
Little Witches '96

Constantin Alexandrov
Gorillas in the Mist '88

Grigori Alexandrov
The Battleship Potemkin '25

Dennis Alexio
Kickboxer '89

Lidia Alfonsi
Life Is Beautiful '98

Phillip Alford
To Kill a Mockingbird '62

Mary Alice
Down in the Delta '98

Elizabeth Allan
The Haunted Strangler '58

Peter Allas
Iron Maze '91

Landry Allbright
Con Air '97

Michael Alldredge
About Last Night . . . '86

Catherine Allegret
Last Tango in Paris '73

Christi Allen
Godmoney '99

Corey Allen
Rebel without a Cause '55

Gary Allen
Alice Sweet Alice '76

Ginger Lynn Allen
Bound and Gagged: A Love Story '93

Jeffrey Allen
2000 Maniacs '64

Jo Harvey Allen
True Stories '86

Joan Allen
Pleasantville '98
Face/Off '97
Mad Love '95
Nixon '95
In Country '89
Peggy Sue Got Married '86

Karen Allen
The Turning '92
Sweet Talker '91
Scrooged '88
Starman '84
National Lampoon's Animal House '78

Keith Allen
Shallow Grave '94

Krista Allen
Raven '97

Nancy Allen
Children of the Corn 666: Isaac's Return '99
Highway Hitcher '98
Out of Sight '98
The Last Assassins '96
RoboCop 3 '91
RoboCop 2 '90
RoboCop '87
1941 '79
The Last Detail '73

Penelope Allen
The Thin Red Line '98

Ray Allen
He Got Game '98

Richard Allen
The Snows of Kilimanjaro '52

Sage Allen
Mr. Saturday Night '92

Steve Allen
Casino '95
The Player '92
Amazon Women on the Moon '87

Tanya Allen
Tail Lights Fade '99

Tim Allen
For Richer or Poorer '97
The Santa Clause '94

Todd Allen
The Apostle '97
The Postman '97

Veronica Allen
Angel in Training '99

Woody Allen
Antz '98 (V)
The Imposters '98
Deconstructing Harry '97
Everyone Says I Love You '96
Mighty Aphrodite '95
Manhattan Murder Mystery '93
Crimes & Misdemeanors '89
Annie Hall '77
Take the Money and Run '69

Kirstie Alley
Drop Dead Gorgeous '99
Deconstructing Harry '97
For Richer or Poorer '97
The Last Don '97
Village of the Damned '95
Look Who's Talking '89

Bart Allison
It Happened Here '65

Gregg Allman
Rush Week '88

Christopher Allport
Jack Frost '97

Astrid Allwyn
Love Affair '39

June Allyson
Till the Clouds Roll By '46

Roy Alon
The Long Good Friday '80

Chelo Alonso
The Good, the Bad and the Ugly '67

Maria Conchita Alonso
The Running Man '87

Ryan Alosio
Something About Sex '98

Murray Alper
They Were Expendable '45

Carol Alt
Body Armor '96
Private Parts '96

John Altamura
The Toxic Avenger, Part 2 '89

Elena Altieri
The Bicycle Thief '48

Trini Alvarado
Paulie '98
The Frighteners '96
Little Women '94

Angel Alvarez
Django '68

George Alvarez
Interlocked '98

John Alvin
The Fighting Sullivans '42

Yuki Amami
Serial Bomber '96

Eisei Amamoto
Godzilla's Revenge '69

Tom Amandes
Brokedown Palace '99
The Long Kiss Goodnight '96

Betty Amann
Rich and Strange '32

Sayoko Amano
Tokyo Decadence '91

Yoshitaka Amano
New Rose Hotel '98

Caroline Ambrose
Allyson Is Watching '96

Lauren Ambrose
Can't Hardly Wait '98
In and Out '97

Tangie Ambrose
Ringmaster '98

Don Ameche
Corrina, Corrina '94
Coming to America '88

Linda Amendola
Patriots '94

Tony Amendola
The Mask of Zorro '98

Leon Ames
Peggy Sue Got Married '86
Tora! Tora! Tora! '70
They Were Expendable '45

Trudi Ames
Bye, Bye, Birdie '63

Soshana Ami
Drop Dead Rock '95

Madchen Amick
Dream Lover '93

Soudad Amidou
Sorcerer '77

Suzy Amis
Firestorm '97
Titanic '97
The Usual Suspects '95
Blown Away '94

John Amos
The Players Club '98
Ricochet '91
Die Hard 2: Die Harder '90
Lock Up '89
Coming to America '88

John Amplas
Creepshow '82

Bijay Anand
Pyar to Hona Hi Tah '98

Susan Anbeh
French Kiss '95

Luana Anders
Easy Rider '69
Dementia 13 '63
Night Tide '63

Bridgette Andersen
A Summer to Remember '84

Anders T. Anderson
The 13th Warrior '99

Angry Anderson
Mad Max: Beyond Thunderdome '85

Anthony Anderson
Life '99

"Broncho" Billy Anderson
Chaplin's Art of Comedy '66

Bruce Anderson
Perfect Profile '90

Carl Anderson
Jesus Christ, Superstar '73

Christian Anderson
Nunsense '93

Daniel Anderson
Body of Influence 2 '96

Eddie Anderson
Gone with the Wind '39
Jezebel '38

Erich Anderson
Bat 21 '88

Erika Anderson
Object of Obsession '95
A Nightmare on Elm Street 5: Dream Child '89

Gillian Anderson
The Mighty '98
Playing by Heart '98
The X-Files '98
The Turning '92

James Anderson
Take the Money and Run '69

Jeff Anderson
Clerks '94

Jo Anderson
From the Earth to the Moon '98
Daylight '96

John Anderson
Firehouse '87
Psycho (CE) '60

Judith Anderson
The Ten Commandments '56
The Red House '47

Fall Time '94
Pulp Fiction '94

Lewis Arquette
Scream 2 '97

Patricia Arquette
Goodbye, Lover '99
Stigmata '99
Infinity '96
Flirting with Disaster '95
True Romance '93
A Nightmare on Elm Street 3:
    Dream Warriors '87

Richmond Arquette
Love to Kill '97

Rosanna Arquette
The '60s '99
Hope Floats '98
I'm Losing You '98
Buffalo 66 '97
Crash '95
Pulp Fiction '94
Nowhere to Run '93
Amazon Women on the Moon
    '87

Jeri Arredondo
Spirit of the Eagle '90

Juan Jose Arreola
Fando and Lis '68

Simon Arriaga
Django '68

Nikolai Arsky
Alexander Nevsky '38

Antonin Artaud
Passion of Joan of Arc '28

Anna Arthur
The Alley Cats '65

Beatrice Arthur
History of the World: Part 1
    '81

Bill Ash
Plan 9 from Outer Space '56

Rochelle Ashana
Kickboxer '89

Stafford Ashani
Klash '95

Linden Ashby
Shelter '98

Peggy Ashcroft
The 39 Steps '35

Eve Brent Ashe
Fade to Black '80

Renee Asherson
Rasputin the Mad Monk '66
Henry V '44

Ron Asheton
Mosquito '95

Nick Ashford
New Jack City '91

Elizabeth Ashley
Happiness '98
Just the Ticket '98
Dragnet '87
Coma '78

Jennifer Ashley
Horror Planet '80
Pom Pom Girls '76

John Ashton
Instinct '99
Stephen King's The Tommy-
    knockers '93
Midnight Run '88

Juli Ashton
Night Calls: The Movie 2 '99
Night Calls: The Movie '98

Vali Ashton
Die Watching '93

Desmond Askew
Go '99

Luke Askew
Easy Rider '69
The Green Berets '68
Cool Hand Luke '67

Robin Askwith
Horror Hospital '73

Ed Asner
The Bachelor '99
Armistead Maupin's More
    Tales of the City '97
Hard Rain '97
JFK '91

Fred Asparagus
Just the Ticket '98

Chuck Aspegren
The Deer Hunter '78

Armand Assante
Striptease '96
Judge Dredd '95
Q & A '90
Private Benjamin '80

Pat Ast
Heat '72

Fred Astaire
Ghost Story '81
The Towering Inferno '74
Royal Wedding '51
Holiday Inn '42

Adriana Asti
Caligula '80

John Astin
The Frighteners '96

MacKenzie Astin
Stranger than Fiction '99
The Last Days of Disco '98
In Love and War '96

Sean Astin
Bulworth '98
Encino Man '92
Memphis Belle '90

Gertrude Astor
The Cat and the Canary '27

Mary Astor
The Hurricane '37
Dodsworth '36

Patti Astor
Assault of the Killer Bimbos
    '88

Annick Asty
Bed and Board '70

William Atherton
Mad City '97
Frank and Jesse '94
The Pelican Brief '93
Die Hard 2: Die Harder '90
Die Hard '88
No Mercy '86
Ghostbusters '84
The Hindenburg '75

Harvey Atkin
Critical Care '97
Meatballs '79

Feodor Atkine
Ronin '98
Le Beau Mariage '82

Christopher Atkins
Die Watching '93
The Blue Lagoon '80

Dave Atkins
Hellraiser '87

Eileen Atkins
The Avengers '98
Wolf '94

Peter Atkins
Salome / The Forbidden '73

Tom Atkins
Maniac Cop '88
Lethal Weapon '87
Halloween 3: Season of the
    Witch '82

Frank Atkinson
Young and Innocent '37

Jayne Atkinson
Free Willy '93
Capone '89

Rowan Atkinson
Bean '97
Four Weddings and a Funeral
    '94
The Witches '90

Teddy Atlas
Gloria '98

Yvan Attal
Love, etc. '96

Richard Attenborough
Elizabeth '98
The Great Escape '63
Trial & Error '62

Edward Atterton
The Man in the Iron Mask '98

Barry Atwater
The Night Stalker '71
Pork Chop Hill '59

Rene Auberjonois
Inspector Gadget '99
Batman Forever '95
The Player '92
Where the Buffalo Roam '80
King Kong '76

Diane Aubrey
The Haunted Strangler '58

Larry Aubrey
Fifth Day of Peace '72

Michel Auclair
Beauty and the Beast '46

Maxine Audley
Peeping Tom '60
A King in New York / A
    Woman in Paris '57

Stephane Audran
The Big Red One '80

Mischa Auer
And Then There Were None
    '45
My Man Godfrey '36

Patrick Auffay
The 400 Blows '59

Claudine Auger
Twitch of the Death Nerve
    '71
Thunderball '65

Robert August
The Endless Summer '66

Sherman Augustus
Virus '98

Marie Ault
The Lodger '26

Tina Aumont
Torso '73

Karen Austin
When a Stranger Calls Back
    '93
For Love of a Child '90
Assassin '86

Daniel Auteuil
La Separation '98
Ma Saison Preferee '93

Frankie Avalon
Casino '95

Stefan Avalos
The Last Broadcast '98

Erik Avari
The Mummy '99
Stargate '94

Loren Avedon
Virtual Combat '95

James Avery
The Colony '98
Prince of Egypt '98 (V)
Fletch '85

Margaret Avery
White Man's Burden '95
The Color Purple '85

Val Avery
Choices '81
Minnie and Moskowitz '71

Rick Aviles
Stephen King's The Stand
    '94

Chris Avran
Twitch of the Death Nerve
    '71

Chikage Awashima
The Human Condition: No
    Greater Love '58

Hoyt Axton
King Cobra '98
Gremlins '84

Charlotte Ayanna
The Rage: Carrie 2 '99

Sachiko Ayase
8 Man '92

Dan Aykroyd
Antz '98 (V)
The Blues Brothers 2000 '98
Grosse Pointe Blank '97
Feeling Minnesota '96
My Fellow Americans '96
Sgt. Bilko '95
Tommy Boy '95
Chaplin '92
Sneakers '92
My Girl '91
Nothing but Trouble '91
Driving Miss Daisy '89
Ghostbusters 2 '89
Caddyshack 2 '88
The Great Outdoors '88
My Stepmother Is an Alien
    '88
Dragnet '87
Spies Like Us '85
Ghostbusters '84
The Blues Brothers (CE) '80
1941 '79

Ethel Ayler
Eve's Bayou '97

Felix Aylmer
Henry V '44
As You Like It '36

John Aylward
Instinct '99

Catherine Aymerie
Rabid Grannies '89

Lew Ayres
Salem's Lot '79
All Quiet on the Western
    Front '30

Rosalind Ayres
Gods and Monsters '98
The Slipper and the Rose '76

Randle Ayrton
The Manxman '29

Hank Azaria
Bartok the Magnificent '99
    (V)
Mystery Men '99
Celebrity '98
Godzilla '98
Anastasia '97 (V)
Great Expectations '97
Grosse Pointe Blank '97
The Birdcage '95
Heat '95
Quiz Show '94

Tony Azito
Union City '81

Charles Aznavour
Tin Drum '79
Shoot the Piano Player '62

Obba Babatunde
Life '99
The Temptations '98
Multiplicity '96
Philadelphia '93

Barbara Babcock
Far and Away '92

Monica Baber
Sucker the Vampire '98

Lauren Bacall
The Mirror Has Two Faces '96
My Fellow Americans '96
Ready to Wear '94
The Big Sleep '46

Barbara Bach
The Spy Who Loved Me (SE)
    '77

Catherine Bach
The Nutt House '92
Criminal Act '88
Cannonball Run 2 '84

Dian Bachar
BASEketball '98

Burt Bacharach
Austin Powers 2: The Spy
    Who Shagged Me '99

Susan Backlinie
Day of the Animals '77

Jim Backus
Man of a Thousand Faces
    '57
Rebel without a Cause '55

Irving Bacon
Monsieur Verdoux '47

Kevin Bacon
Stir of Echoes '99
Digging to China '98
Wild Things '98
Picture Perfect '96
Sleepers '96
Telling Lies in America '96
Apollo 13 '95
The River Wild '94
A Few Good Men '92
JFK '91
Queens Logic '91
Flatliners '90
Tremors '89
Friday the 13th '80
National Lampoon's Animal
    House '78

Paul Bacon
The Asphyx '72

Jean-Pierre Bacri
Un Air de Famille '96
Entre-Nous '83

Michael Badalucco
Summer of Sam '99
You've Got Mail '98
The Professional '94

Hermione Baddeley
Mary Poppins '64

A Christmas Carol '51

Bolaji Badejo
Alien '79

Alan Badel
The Day of the Jackal '73
This Sporting Life '63

Sarah Badel
Mrs. Dalloway '97

Diedrich Bader
Office Space '98

Mary Badham
To Kill a Mockingbird '62

Annette Badland
Little Voice '98

Jane Badler
Under the Gun '95

Erykah Badu
The Blues Brothers 2000 '98
Deep Red: Hatchet Murders
'75

Buddy Baer
Jack & the Beanstalk '52

Parley Baer
Dave '93

Harold Baerow
The Alley Cats '65

Lynne Baggett
D.O.A. '49

Abdolrahma Bagheri
The Taste of Cherry '96

Lorri Bagley
Trick '99

Ross Bagley
The Little Rascals '94

Eion Bailey
Fight Club '99

G.W. Bailey
Burglar '87

Raymond Bailey
Vertigo (CE) '58

Charles Bailey-Gates
The Surgeon '94

Fay Bainter
The Secret Life of Walter
Mitty '47
State Fair '45
Dark Waters '44
Woman of the Year '42
Jezebel '38

Alecs Baird
Children Shouldn't Play with
Dead Things '72

Hugh Baird
America '24

Scott Bairstow
Black Circle Boys '97
The Postman '97
Wild America '97

Gary Bakeman
2000 Maniacs '64

Anita Baker
Corrina, Corrina '94

Art Baker
Impact '49

Becky Ann Baker
A Simple Plan '98

Betsy Baker
Evil Dead '83

Blanche Baker
Shakedown '88
Sixteen Candles '84

Carroll Baker
The Game '97

Those Bedroom Eyes '92
Kindergarten Cop '90
Star 80 '83
How the West Was Won '63

Diane Baker
Murder at 1600 '97
The Cable Guy '96
The Net '95
Silence of the Lambs '91
Baker's Hawk '76
Krakatoa East of Java '66

Don Baker
In the Name of the Father '93

Dylan Baker
Simply Irresistible '99
Celebrity '98
Happiness '98
Disclosure '94

Henry Judd Baker
Clean and Sober '88

Joe Don Baker
Tomorrow Never Dies (SE)
'97
Mars Attacks! '96
Congo '95
Goldeneye '95
Panther '95
The Underneath '95
Reality Bites '94
The Distinguished Gentleman
'92
Fletch '85
Final Justice '84
Walking Tall '73
Junior Bonner '72
Cool Hand Luke '67

Jolyon Baker
Final Analysis '92

Kathy Baker
Mad Dog and Glory '93
Clean and Sober '88
The Right Stuff '83

Kenny Baker
Amadeus '84
Time Bandits '81

Kirsten Baker
Friday the 13th, Part 2 '81

Lynn Baker
Billy Jack '71

Ray Baker
Anywhere But Here '99

Rick Baker
Kentucky Fried Movie '77
King Kong '76

Robert Baker
Chinese Connection '73

Ruth Baker
Marat/Sade '66

Simon Baker
Smoke Signals '98
L.A. Confidential '97
Most Wanted '97

Stanley Baker
The Guns of Navarone '61

Tom Baker
Nicholas and Alexandra '71

William "Billy" Bakewell
Gone with the Wind '39
All Quiet on the Western
Front '30

Afshin Bakhtiari
The Taste of Cherry '96

Brenda Bakke
Shelter '98
Trucks '97
Under Siege 2 '95
Tales from the Crypt Presents
Demon Knight '94

Brigitte Bako
Paranoia '98
Strange Days '95
A Man in Uniform '93

Scott Bakula
Tom Clancy's Netforce '98
Lord of Illusions '95
Color of Night '94
Quantum Leap: The Pilot
Episode '89

Bob Balaban
Jakob the Liar '99
Deconstructing Harry '97
Greedy '94
Dead Bang '89
2010: The Year We Make
Contact '84
Absence of Malice '81
Altered States '80
Midnight Cowboy '69

Adam Baldwin
Guilty by Suspicion '91
Next of Kin '89
Full Metal Jacket '87

Alec Baldwin
Outside Providence '99
The Confession '98
Mercury Rising '98
The Edge '97
The Juror '96
The Shadow '94
The Getaway '93
Malice '93
The Hunt for Red October '90
Beetlejuice '88

Daniel Baldwin
The Pandora Project '98
Phoenix '98
John Carpenter's Vampires
'97
Trees Lounge '96
Family of Cops '95
Born on the Fourth of July
'89

Dona Baldwin
Badlands '74

Michael Baldwin
Phantasm '79

Stephen Baldwin
The Sex Monster '99
Dean Koontz's Mr. Murder
'98
Scarred City '98
Half-Baked '97
Fled '96
The Usual Suspects '95
8 Seconds '94
Fall Time '94
Posse '93
Born on the Fourth of July
'89

Walter Baldwin
The Best Years of Our Lives
'46

William Baldwin
Shattered Image '98
Virus '98
Fair Game '95
Backdraft '91
Flatliners '90
Internal Affairs '90
Born on the Fourth of July
'89

Christian Bale
William Shakespeare's A Mid-
summer Night's Dream '99
Velvet Goldmine '98
Metroland '97
Portrait of a Lady '96
Little Women '94

Michael Balfour
The Canterbury Tales '71

Denise Balik
Humanoids from the Deep
'80

Eszter Balint
Trees Lounge '96

Fairuza Balk
American History X '98
The Waterboy '98
The Craft '96
The Island of Dr. Moreau '96
Things to Do in Denver When
You're Dead '95
Return to Oz '85

Angeline Ball
The General '98
The Commitments '91

Nicholas Ball
Lifeforce '85

Vincent Ball
Sirens '94
Breaker Morant '80

Carl Ballantine
Mr. Saturday Night '92

Timothy Balme
Dead Alive '93

Martin Balsam
All the President's Men '76
Two Minute Warning '76
Tora! Tora! Tora! '70
Breakfast at Tiffany's '61
Psycho (CE) '60

Kirk Baltz
Reservoir Dogs '92

Alexander Baluyev
Deep Impact '98
The Peacemaker '97

David Bamber
Pride and Prejudice '95

Gerry Bamman
Home Alone 2: Lost in New
York '92

Eric Bana
The Castle '97

Anne Bancroft
Antz '98 (V)
Critical Care '97
G.I. Jane '97
Great Expectations '97
How to Make an American
Quilt '95
Malice '93
Point of No Return '93
Honeymoon in Vegas '92
The Hindenburg '75

George Bancroft
Stagecoach '39

Antonio Banderas
The 13th Warrior '99
The Mask of Zorro '98
Evita '96
Assassins '95
Desperado '95
Four Rooms '95
Miami Rhapsody '95
Never Talk to Strangers '95
Interview with the Vampire
'94
Outrage '93
Philadelphia '93

Donatas Banionis
Solaris '72

Caerthan Banks
The Sweet Hereafter '96

Dennis Banks
Thunderheart '92

Jonathan Banks
Foolish '99
Body Shot '93
Boiling Point '93

Assassin '86

Leslie Banks
Henry V '44
Jamaica Inn '39
Fire Over England '37
The Man Who Knew Too
Much '34
The Most Dangerous Game
'32

Ian Bannen
Waking Ned Devine '98
Damage '92

Jill Banner
Spider Baby '64

Reggie Bannister
Phantasm '79

Li Bao-Tian
Ju Dou '90

Jennifer Baptist
The Toxic Avenger (DC) '86

Theda Bara
The Love Goddesses '65

Zoltan Barabas
The Phantom of the Opera
'98

Michael Barak
Cause of Death '90

Amiri Baraka
Bulworth '98

Vera Baranovskaya
Mother '26

Henryk Baranowski
The Decalogue '88

Christine Baranski
Bowfinger '99
Bulworth '98
Cruel Intentions '98
Neil Simon's The Odd Couple
2 '98
The Birdcage '95
New Jersey Drive '95
The War '94
9 1/2 Weeks '86

Adrienne Barbeau
Creepshow '82

Frances Barber
A Zed & Two Noughts '88

Gillian Barber
Double Jeopardy '99

Paul Barber
The Full Monty '96
The Long Good Friday '80

Urbano Barberini
Demons '86

Joyce Barbour
Sabotage '36

Artur Barcis
The Decalogue '88

Caroline Barclay
Within the Rock '96

Aleksander Bardini
The Decalogue '88

Brigitte Bardot
Shalako '68
Spirits of the Dead '68

Gillian Barge
Mesmer '94

Lynn Bari
The Bridge of San Luis Rey
'44

Anthony Barille
Hamburger Hill '87

Nora Baring
Murder '30

Natalie Barish
Lost and Found '99

David Bark-Jones
Pride and Prejudice '95

Bob Barker
Happy Gilmore '96

Clive Barker
Salome / The Forbidden '73

Lex Barker
Away All Boats '56

Ellen Barkin
Drop Dead Gorgeous '99
Fear and Loathing in Las
    Vegas '98
The Fan '96
Sea of Love '89
The Big Easy '87
Tender Mercies '83

Marcie Barkin
Fade to Black '80

Maurice Barkin
The Van '77

Peter Barkworth
The Littlest Horse Thieves
    '76

Ivor Barnard
Beat the Devil '53

Burke Barnes
The Land Before Time '88 (V)

Frank Barnes
The General '26

Isaiah Barnes
Don't Be a Menace to South
    Central While Drinking Your
    Juice in the Hood '95

Joanna Barnes
The Parent Trap '98
The War Wagon '67
Spartacus '60

Priscilla Barnes
The Killing Grounds '97
Mallrats '95
The Crossing Guard '94
License to Kill '89

Susan Barnes
One Night Stand '97
Nothing to Lose '96

T. Roy Barnes
Seven Chances '25

Theo Barnes
Brain Damage '88

David Baron
The Reptile '66

Sandy Baron
Leprechaun 2 '94

Elizabeth Barondes
Love to Kill '97

Anita Barone
Running Time '97

Carina Barone
The Living Dead Girl '82

Byron Barr
Double Indemnity '44

Patrick Barr
House of Whipcord '75
The Satanic Rites of Dracula
    '73

Roy Barraclough
The Slipper and the Rose '76

Robert Barrat
The Road to Utopia '46
Strangler of the Swamp '46
They Were Expendable '45

Jean-Louis Barrault
Chappaqua '66

The Longest Day '62

Marie-Christine Barrault
Chloe in the Afternoon '72
My Night at Maud's '69

Majel Barrett
Mommy '95
Star Trek: Generations '94
    (V)
Star Trek 4: The Voyage
    Home '86
Westworld '73

Ray Barrett
Don's Party '76
The Reptile '66

Tony Barrett
Impact '49

Barbara Barrie
Hercules '97 (V)
Private Benjamin '80

Chris Barrie
Treasure Island '97 (V)

Chuck Barris
Hugo Pool '97

Dana Barron
National Lampoon's Vacation
    '83

Diana Barrows
My Mom's a Werewolf '89

Gene Barry
The War of the Worlds '53

Jason Barry
Monument Ave. '98

Joan Barry
Rich and Strange '32

Raymond J. Barry
Flubber '97
The Chamber '96
Cool Runnings '93
Falling Down '93
The Turning '92
Born on the Fourth of July
    '89

Christa Barrymore
The Reincarnation of Isabel
    '72

Drew Barrymore
Never Been Kissed '99
Ever After: A Cinderella Story
    '98
Home Fries '98
The Wedding Singer '97
Everyone Says I Love You '96
Scream (CS) '96
Batman Forever '95
Mad Love '95
Boys on the Side '94
Poison Ivy '92
Firestarter '84
Altered States '80

Ethel Barrymore
The Paradine Case '47

John Barrymore
Dr. Jekyll and Mr. Hyde '20

Lionel Barrymore
Duel in the Sun '46
It's a Wonderful Life '46
The Bells / The Crazy Ray
    '26
America '24

Michael Barrymore
Spice World: The Movie '97

Judith Barsi
The Land Before Time '88 (V)
Jaws: The Revenge '87

Brett Barsky
Boys Life 2 '98

Vladimir Barsky
The Battleship Potemkin '25

Paul Bartel
Billy's Hollywood Screen Kiss
    '98
Armistead Maupin's More
    Tales of the City '97
The Usual Suspects '95
Posse '93
Amazon Women on the Moon
    '87
Rock 'n' Roll High School '79
Piranha '78
Eat My Dust '76

Richard Barthelmess
Tol'able David '21
Way Down East '20
Broken Blossoms '19

Bonnie Bartlett
Primary Colors '98
Dave '93
Twins '88

Robin Bartlett
City of Angels '98
Dangerous Minds '95
Lean on Me '89

Diana Barton
Sexual Malice '93

Mischa Barton
The Sixth Sense '99
Lawn Dogs '96

Peter Barton
Hell Night '81

Pooja Bartra
Virasat '97

Brad Bartram
Embrace the Darkness '98

Laurie Bartram
Friday the 13th '80

Billy Barty
The Naked Truth '92
The Bride of Frankenstein '35

Leon Bary
The Three Musketeers '21

Anat "Topol" Barzilai
Witchcraft '88

Chiara Barzini
SLC Punk! '99

Gary Basaraba
The War '94
Fried Green Tomatoes '91
One Magic Christmas '85

Richard Basehart
He Walked by Night '48

Count Basie
Blazing Saddles '74

Toni Basil
Easy Rider '69

Kim Basinger
L.A. Confidential '97
Ready to Wear '94
The Getaway '93
The Real McCoy '93
Final Analysis '92
Batman '89
My Stepmother Is an Alien
    '88
9 1/2 Weeks '86
No Mercy '86

Elya Baskin
Air Force One '97

Antoine Basler
Irma Vep '96

Marianne Basler
A Soldier's Tale '91

Alfie Bass
Help! '65

Albert Bassermann
The Red Shoes '48

The Shanghai Gesture '42

Angela Bassett
How Stella Got Her Groove
    Back '98
Contact '97
Strange Days '95
What's Love Got to Do with
    It? '93
Innocent Blood '92
Passion Fish '92
Boyz N the Hood '91

Peter Bassett
Desolation Angels '95

Steve Bassett
The Jackal (CE) '97

Tracy Bassett
Angel in Training '99

Alexandra Bastedo
The Blood Spattered Bride
    '72

Othon Bastos
Central Station '98

Michal Bat-Adam
The Impossible Spy '87
Rachel's Man '75

Nikolai Batalov
Mother '26
Aelita: Queen of Mars '24

Justine Bateman
The Fatal Image '90

Florence Bates
The Secret Life of Walter
    Mitty '47
Rebecca '40

Jeanne Bates
The Mask of Diijon '46

John Bates
Animal Instincts 3: The
    Seductress '95

Kathy Bates
Primary Colors '98
The Waterboy '98
Swept from the Sea '97
Titanic '97
Dolores Claiborne '94
Stephen King's The Stand
    '94
Fried Green Tomatoes '91
White Palace '90

Michael Bates
A Clockwork Orange '71
Patton '70

Paul Bates
Instinct '99
Coming to America '88

R.C. Bates
Werewolf '95

Randall Batinkoff
As Good As It Gets '97
The Curve '97
The Peacemaker '97
The Player '92
School Ties '92

Terrie Batson
Cyborg '89

Matt Battaglia
Raven '97

Peter Batten
Yellow Submarine '68 (V)

Patrick Bauchau
Creepers '85
Entre-Nous '83
La Collectionneuse '67

Belinda Bauer
Poison Ivy 2: Lily '95
RoboCop 2 '90

**Michelle (McClellan)
Bauer**
Sorority Babes in the Slime-
ball Bowl-A-Rama '87

Steven Bauer
Primal Fear '96
Stranger by Night '94
Raising Cain '92
Scarface '83

Van Baum
Set It Off '96

Vincent Baum
Set It Off '96

Michele Baumgartner
The Woman Next Door '81

David Baxt
The Shining '80

Anne Baxter
The Ten Commandments '56
The Blue Gardenia '53
All About Eve '50
The Fighting Sullivans '42

Meredith Baxter
All the President's Men '76

Frances Bay
Goodbye, Lover '99
Inspector Gadget '99
Changing Habits '96
Happy Gilmore '96
In the Mouth of Madness '95
Single White Female '92

Nathalie Baye
The Return of Martin Guerre
    '83
Beau Pere '81

Hal Baylor
A Boy and His Dog '75
Sands of Iwo Jima '49

Jordan Bayne
A Stranger in the Kingdom
    '98

Lawrence Bayne
Black Robe '91

Rene Bazinet
Alegria '98

Adam Beach
Smoke Signals '98

Michael Beach
Made Men '99
Soul Food '97
Internal Affairs '90
Lean on Me '89

Steven Beach
Cost of Living '97

Stephanie Beacham
Horror Planet '80

Cindy Beal
Slave Girls from Beyond Infin-
    ity '87

John Beal
The Firm '93

Aaron Beall
Habit '97

Jennifer Beals
The Last Days of Disco '98
The Prophecy 2: Ashtown '98
The Twilight of the Golds '97
Devil in a Blue Dress '95
Four Rooms '95

Orson Bean
Being John Malkovich '99

Sean Bean
Ronin '98
Goldeneye '95
Patriot Games '92
The Field '90

Krystal Benn
In Dreams '98

David Bennent
Tin Drum '79

Heinz Bennent
The Last Metro '80
Tin Drum '79

John Bennes
Stephen King's The Night
Flier '96

Bill Bennett
Robin Hood '22

**Bruce (Herman Brix)
Bennett**
Sudden Fear '52

Charles Bennett
America '24

Enid Bennett
Robin Hood '22

Fran Bennett
Wes Craven's New Nightmare
'94

Harve Bennett
Star Trek 5: The Final Frontier
'89

Jill Bennett
For Your Eyes Only (SE) '81

Joan Bennett
Father's Little Dividend '51

John Bennett
Priest '94

Joseph Bennett
Howard's End '92

June Marie Bennett
The Adventures of Priscilla,
Queen of the Desert '94

Zachary Bennett
Bury Me in Niagara '93

Abraham Benrubi
George of the Jungle '97
U-Turn '97
Twister '96

Jodi Benson
Thumbelina '94 (V)

Kelly Benson
The Fear: Halloween Night
'99

Lucille Benson
1941 '79

Martin Benson
The King and I '56

Robby Benson
Beauty and the Beast: The
Enchanted Christmas '97
(V)
Rent-A-Cop '88

Wendy Benson
Wishmaster '97

Chris Benton
20,000 Leagues under the
Sea '16

Eddie Benton
Prom Night '80

Susanne Benton
A Boy and His Dog '75

Femi Benussi
The Bloodsucker Leads the
Dance '75

Michael Benveniste
Flesh Gordon '72

Julie Benz
Darkdrive '98
Jawbreaker '98

Daniel Benzali
Murder at 1600 '97

George Beranger
The Birth of a Nation '15

Luca Bercovici
The Big Squeeze '96
Drop Zone '94
Clean and Sober '88
Parasite '82

Jean-Claude Bercq
The Train '65

Tom Berenger
A Murder of Crows '99
The Gingerbread Man '97
An Occasional Hell '96
The Substitute '96
The Field '90
Born on the Fourth of July
'89
Someone to Watch Over Me
'87
Platoon '86
The Big Chill '83
The Sentinel '76

Marisa Berenson
Barry Lyndon '75
Cabaret '72

Harry Beresford
Klondike Annie '36

Peter Berg
Cop Land '97
Across the Moon '94
Going Overboard '89
Shocker '89
Tale of Two Sisters '89

Candice Bergen
2010: The Year We Make
Contact '84 (V)

Polly Bergen
Once Upon a Time . . .
When We Were Colored '95
At War with the Army '50

Katya Berger
Tales of Ordinary Madness
'83

Nicole Berger
Shoot the Piano Player '62

Randall Berger
Shine '95

Senta Berger
Swiss Conspiracy '77
Cross of Iron '76

Sidney Berger
Carnival of Souls '98

William Berger
Django Strikes Again '87

Jacques Bergerac
Gigi '58

Phillipe Bergerone
Plump Fiction '97

Thommy Berggren
Elvira Madigan '67

Hiroko Berghauer
Bed and Board '70

Patrick Bergin
Patriot Games '92
Mountains of the Moon '90

Emily Bergl
The Rage: Carrie 2 '99

Erik "Bullen" Berglund
Intermezzo '36

Henry Bergman
Charles Chaplin—A First
National Collection
Modern Times '36
City Lights '31

Ingrid Bergman
Notorious '46
The Bells of St. Mary's '45
Spellbound '45
For Whom the Bell Tolls '43
Casablanca '42
June Night '40
Intermezzo '36

Sandahl Bergman
The Assault '97
Lipstick Camera '93
Conan the Barbarian '82
Xanadu '80

Elisabeth Bergner
As You Like It '36

Xander Berkeley
Universal Soldier: The Return
'99
Phoenix '98
Air Force One '97
One Night Stand '97
Barb Wire '96
Bulletproof '96
The Killing Jar '96
Within the Rock '96
Poison Ivy 2: Lily '95
Candyman '92
A Few Good Men '92
Sid & Nancy '86

Elizabeth Berkley
Tail Lights Fade '99
Random Encounter '98
The Real Blonde '97
The First Wives Club '96
Armitage 3: Polymatrix '94
(V)

Steven Berkoff
Legionnaire '98
Another 9 1/2 Weeks '96
Rambo: First Blood, Part 2
'85
A Clockwork Orange '71

Francois Berleand
Romance '99

Jeannie Berlin
The Heartbreak Kid '72

Charles Berling
Love, etc. '96

Peter Berling
Francesco '89

Warren Berlinger
Hero '92

Susan Berman
Curtain Call '97

Juan Manuel Bernal
Midaq Alley '95

Andre Bernard
The Crying Game '92

Jason Bernard
Liar Liar '97
While You Were Sleeping '95
All of Me '84

Nicolette Bernard
It Happened Here '65

Michael Bernardo
Virtual Combat '95

Joachim Bernhard
Das Boot (DC) '81

Sandra Bernhard
Wrongfully Accused '98
Plump Fiction '97
The Apocalypse '96
Hudson Hawk '91

Lionel Bernier
The Dirty Girls '64

Corbin Bernsen
An American Affair '99
The Dentist 2: Brace Yourself
'98

The Dentist '96
Tales from the Hood '95
Radioland Murders '94
Eat My Dust '76
King Kong '76

**Olinka (Schoberova)
Berova**
The Vengeance of She '68

Elizabeth Berridge
Five Corners '88
Amadeus '84
The Funhouse '81

Frank Berry
Dr. Strangelove, or: How I
Learned to Stop Worrying
and Love the Bomb '64

Halle Berry
Bulworth '98
Why Do Fools Fall in Love?
'98
Executive Decision '96
The Flintstones (CE) '94
Jungle Fever '91
The Last Boy Scout '91

Ken Berry
The Cat from Outer Space
'78

Sarah Berry
Evil Dead 2: Dead by Dawn
'87

Michael Berryman
Star Trek 4: The Voyage
Home '86
One Flew Over the Cuckoo's
Nest '75

Attila Bertalan
The Scorpio Factor '90

Roland Bertin
Diva '82

Angelo Bertolini
The Lady in White '88

Gene Bervoets
The Vanishing '88

Bibi Besch
Tremors '89

Aaron Bess
Moving Target '96

Ariel Besse
Beau Pere '81

Edna Best
The Man Who Knew Too
Much '34

James Best
Shock Corridor '63

Martine Beswick
Prehistoric Women '67
Thunderball '65
From Russia with Love '63

Anne Betancourt
Fools Rush In '97

Laura Betti
Lovers and Liars '81
The Canterbury Tales '71
Twitch of the Death Nerve
'71

Jack Betts
Gods and Monsters '98

Philippe Beuzen
The Eric Rohmer Collection:
The Moral Tales '62

Rodney Bewes
Unidentified Flying Oddball
'79

Nathan Bexton
Go '99

Queen Bey
Ninth Street '98

Turhan Bey
Virtual Combat '95

Brad Beyer
The General's Daughter '99
Trick '99

Richard Beymer
The Longest Day '62
West Side Story '61

Daniela Bianchi
From Russia with Love '63

Tino Bianchi
Black Sunday '60

Yuen Biao
Dragon from Shaolin '96
Deadful Melody '92
Once Upon a Time in China
'91
Miracles '89
Dragons Forever '88
Eastern Condors '87
The Millionaire's Express '86
My Lucky Stars '85
Wheels on Meals '84
Zu: Warriors of the Magic
Mountain '83
The Prodigal Son '82

Abner Biberman
His Girl Friday '40

Bruno Bichir
Midaq Alley '95

Charles Bickford
Brute Force '46
Duel in the Sun '46
Reap the Wild Wind '42
Of Mice and Men '39

Jean-Luc Bideau
The Red Violin '98

Leo Bieber
The Third Man '49

Michael Biehn
Asteroid '97
The Rock '96
Jade '95
Deadfall '93
Tombstone '93
Navy SEALS '90
The Abyss (SE) '89
The Seventh Sign '88
Aliens (SE) '86
The Terminator '84

Jessica Biel
I'll Be Home for Christmas
'98

Ramon Bieri
Sorcerer '77
Badlands '74
The Andromeda Strain '71

Craig Bierko
The Thirteenth Floor '99
Fear and Loathing in Las
Vegas '98
The Long Kiss Goodnight '96

Adam Biesk
Leprechaun 2 '94

Big Pun
Urban Menace '99

**Scott "Bam Bam"
Bigelow**
Major Payne '95

Jason Biggs
American Pie (CE) '99

Roxann Biggs-Dawson
Guilty by Suspicion '91

Theodore Bikel
My Fair Lady '64

Beatrice Boepple
A Nightmare on Elm Street 5: Dream Child '89

Dirk Bogarde
A Bridge Too Far '77

Humphrey Bogart
The Caine Mutiny '54
Beat the Devil '53
The Big Sleep '46
Casablanca '42
Dark Victory '39
Midnight '34

Peter Bogdanovich
Mr. Jealousy '98

Eric Bogosian
A Bright Shining Lie '98
Deconstructing Harry '97
Beavis and Butt-Head Do America '96 (V)
Under Siege 2 '95

Roman Bohnen
The Best Years of Our Lives '46

Richard Bohringer
Diva '82

Romane Bohringer
Total Eclipse '95

Samuel Boidin
The Life of Jesus '96

Curt Bois
Casablanca '42
The Hunchback of Notre Dame '39

Trevor Bolder
Ziggy Stardust and the Spiders from Mars '83

John Boles
Stella Dallas '37
Frankenstein '31

Ray Bolger
The Wizard of Oz '39

Florinda Bolkan
The Last Valley '71

Michael Bollner
Willy Wonka & the Chocolate Factory '71

Joseph Bologna
Big Daddy '99

Ugo Bologna
Zombie '80

David Bolt
The Killing Man '94

Emily Bolton
Moonraker (SE) '79

Lyn Bolton
Blood Feast (SE) '63

Jon Bon Jovi
The Leading Man '96

Paolo Bonacelli
Francesco '89
Caligula '80
Salo, or the 120 Days of Sodom '75

Danny Bonaduce
Baker's Hawk '76

Jacques Bonaffe
First Name: Carmen '83

Fortunio Bonanova
Double Indemnity '44
For Whom the Bell Tolls '43

Cynthia Bond
Def by Temptation '90

James Bond III
Def by Temptation '90

Lillian Bond
The Old Dark House '32

Samantha Bond
Tomorrow Never Dies (SE) '97
Goldeneye '95

Ward Bond
The Searchers '56
Mister Roberts '55
The Quiet Man '52
It's a Wonderful Life '46
They Were Expendable '45
The Fighting Sullivans '42
Gone with the Wind '39
It Happened One Night '34

Natalya Bondarchuk
Solaris '72

Beulah Bondi
It's a Wonderful Life '46
The Southerner '45
Penny Serenade '41
Rain '32

De'Aundre Bonds
Ill-Gotten Gains '97

Peter Bonerz
Man on the Moon '99

Lisa Bonet
Enemy of the State '98
Angel Heart '87

Crispin Bonham Carter
Pride and Prejudice '95

Helena Bonham Carter
Fight Club '99
Merlin '98
A Merry War '97
The Wings of the Dove '97
Mighty Aphrodite '95
Mary Shelley's Frankenstein '94
Howard's End '92
Francesco '89

Evan Bonifant
The Blues Brothers 2000 '98

Paul Bonifas
The Train '65

Marcello Bonini
The Reincarnation of Isabel '72

Sandrine Bonnaire
One Hundred and One Nights '94

Beverly Bonner
Brain Damage '88
Basket Case '82

Maria Bonnevie
Insomnia '97

Hugh Bonneville
Notting Hill '99

Celine Bonnier
The Assignment '97

Brian Bonsall
Mikey '92

Emilio Bonucci
In Love and War '96

Sorrell Booke
Rock-a-Doodle '92 (V)

Mark Boone Jr.
The General's Daughter '99
John Carpenter's Vampires '97
Rosewood '96
Trees Lounge '96

Richard Boone
Away All Boats '56
Beneath the 12-Mile Reef '53

Charley Boorman
Picture Windows '95

Excalibur '81
Deliverance '72

Imogen Boorman
Hellbound: Hellraiser 2 '88

Connie Booth
And Now for Something Completely Different '72

Powers Boothe
Joan of Arc '99
U-Turn '97
Nixon '95
Tombstone '93
Red Dawn '84

Caterina Boratto
Juliet of the Spirits '65

Mark Borchardt
American Movie '99

Ernest Borgnine
All Dogs Christmas Carol '98 (V)
BASEketball '98
Small Soldiers '98 (V)
Gattaca '97
Mistress '91
Laser Mission '90
The Black Hole '79
Devil's Rain '75
The Poseidon Adventure '72
The Wild Bunch '69
The Dirty Dozen '67

Bobby Boriello
A Walk on the Moon '99
Enemy of the State '98

Angel Boris
Warlock 3: The End of Innocence '98

Nicoletta Boris
Desperate Crimes '93

Tormek Bork
The Unbearable Lightness of Being '88

Gene Borkan
Bound '96

Jesse Borrego
Con Air '97
Retroactive '97

Bobby Borriello
Private Parts '96

Jason Bortz
Slaves to the Underground '96

Augusto Boscardini
Nude for Satan '74

Philip Bosco
Critical Care '97
Deconstructing Harry '97
My Best Friend's Wedding '97
The First Wives Club '96

Barbara Bosson
The Last Starfighter '84

Barry Bostwick
Spy Hard '96
Betrayed by Innocence '86

Brian Bosworth
One Man's Justice '95

Catherine Bosworth
The Horse Whisperer '97

Hobart Bosworth
My Best Girl '27

Rodrigo Botero
True Friends '98

Rob Bottin
Humanoids from the Deep '80

Joseph Bottoms
The Black Hole '79

Sam Bottoms
Apocalypse Now '79
The Outlaw Josey Wales '76

Timothy Bottoms
Diamondbacks '99
Uncle Sam '96
Top Dog '95
Invaders from Mars '86
Rollercoaster '77

Sami Bouajila
The Siege '98

Willis Bouchey
Suddenly '54

Elodie Bouchez
The Dreamlife of Angels '98
Wild Reeds '94

Emily Bouffante
Witchcraft 10: Mistress of the Craft '98

Jean Bouise
La Femme Nikita '91
I Am Cuba '64

Daniel Boulanger
Bed and Board '70

Matthew Boulton
Sabotage '36

Carole Bouquet
For Your Eyes Only (SE) '81
Blank Generation '79
Buffet Froid '79

Nathalie Boutefeu
Irma Vep '96

Dennis Boutsikaris
In Dreams '98
*batteries not included '87

Duane Boutte
Stonewall '95

Jean-Luc Boutte
La Sentinelle '92

Jean-Pierre Bouvier
Ma Saison Preferee '93

Julie Bovasso
Moonstruck '87

John Bowe
Cleopatra '99

Julie Bowen
An American Werewolf in Paris '97
Happy Gilmore '96
Multiplicity '96

Michael Bowen
Excess Baggage '96
True Crime '95
The Player '92

Sean Bowen
Troma's War (DC) '88

Antoinette Bower
Prom Night '80

David Bower
Four Weddings and a Funeral '94

Tom Bower
The Killing Jar '96
White Man's Burden '95
Raising Cain '92

Lally Bowers
The Slipper and the Rose '76

Angie Bowie
Ziggy Stardust and the Spiders from Mars '83

David Bowie
Labyrinth '86

Ziggy Stardust and the Spiders from Mars '83
The Man Who Fell to Earth '76

Trixxie Bowie
Fraternity Demon '92

Lee Bowman
Bataan '43
Buck Privates '41
Love Affair '39

Eddie Bowz
The Fear '94

Amanda Boxer
Saving Private Ryan '98

Bruce Boxleitner
Tron '82

Brandon Boyce
Public Access '93

Bob Boyd
Indomitable Teddy Roosevelt '83

Guy Boyd
Retroactive '97
Body Double '84
Ticket to Heaven '81

Patti Boyd
A Hard Day's Night '64

Stephen Boyd
Shalako '68

Charles Boyer
Barefoot in the Park '67
Love Affair '39

Sully Boyer
Car Wash '76

William Boyett
The Hidden '87

Brad Boyle
Hoosiers '86

Hal Boyle
The Story of G.I. Joe '45

Lara Flynn Boyle
Happiness '98
The Big Squeeze '96
Dead Poets Society '89

Lisa Boyle
Leaving Scars '97
The Night That Never Happened '97
Friend of the Family '95
I Like to Play Games '95

Peter Boyle
Dr. Dolittle '98
Milk and Money '97
Sweet Evil '95
While You Were Sleeping '95
The Shadow '94
The Surgeon '94
Honeymoon in Vegas '92
Solar Crisis '92
Red Heat '88
Conspiracy: The Trial of the Chicago Eight '87
Outland '81
Where the Buffalo Roam '80
Swashbuckler '76
Taxi Driver (CE) '76
Young Frankenstein '74
The Candidate '72

Jamie Bozian
Assault of the Killer Bimbos '88

Liu Bozizlo
Andy Warhol's Frankenstein '74

Marcel Bozonnet
The Disenchanted '90

Elizabeth Bracco
Analyze This '98

The Imposters '98
Trees Lounge '96

Lorraine Bracco
Hackers '95
The Basketball Diaries '94
Medicine Man '92
Goodfellas '90
Someone to Watch Over Me '87

Eddie Bracken
Home Alone 2: Lost in New York '92
National Lampoon's Vacation '83

Caroline Brackman
Rabid Grannies '89

Kitty Bradbury
Our Hospitality / Sherlock Junior '23

Dawn Bradfield
Dancing at Lughnasa '98

Jesse Bradford
William Shakespeare's Romeo and Juliet '96
Hackers '95

Richard Bradford
Just the Ticket '98
The Crossing Guard '94
Internal Affairs '90
Sunset '88

David Bradley
Total Reality '97

Doug Bradley
Hellbound: Hellraiser 2 '88
Hellraiser '87
Salome / The Forbidden '73

John H. Bradley
Sands of Iwo Jima '49

Leslie Bradley
The Conqueror '56

Carl Bradshaw
Klash '95

Alice Brady
My Man Godfrey '36

Janelle Brady
Class of Nuke 'Em High '86

John Brady
Mystery Science Theater 3000: The Movie '96

Scott Brady
Gremlins '84
The China Syndrome '79
Mohawk '56
He Walked by Night '48

Sonia Braga
From Dusk Till Dawn 3: The Hangman's Daughter '99

Wendy Brainard
They Live '88

Yves Brainville
Time Masters '82 (V)

Wilfrid Brambell
A Hard Day's Night '64
The 39 Steps '35

Marco Brambilla
Cool Runnings '93

David Bramley
Winstanley '75

Kenneth Branagh
Wild Wild West '99
Celebrity '98
The Gingerbread Man '97
Mary Shelley's Frankenstein '94
Much Ado about Nothing '93
Dead Again '91

Rustam Branaman
Love to Kill '97
Terrified '94

Lillo Brancato
Enemy of the State '98
Crimson Tide '95
A Bronx Tale '93

Armando Brancia
Amarcord '74

Neville Brand
Eaten Alive '76
Psychic Killer '75
Tora! Tora! Tora! '70
Mohawk '56
D.O.A. '49

Larry Brandenburg
The Mod Squad '99

Leslie Brander
Sizzle Beach U.S.A. '74

Walter Brandi
Playgirls and the Vampire '63

Jonathan Brandis
Outside Providence '99

Marlon Brando
The Island of Dr. Moreau '96
Don Juan DeMarco '94
The Freshman '90
Apocalypse Now '79
Last Tango in Paris '73
The Wild One '54
A Streetcar Named Desire '51

Henry (Kleinbach) Brandon
Assault on Precinct 13 '76
The Searchers '56
March of the Wooden Soldiers '34

Peter Brandon
Altered States '80

Scott Brandon
King Cobra '98

Brandy
I Still Know What You Did Last Summer '98

Marjorie Bransfield
Abraxas: Guardian of the Universe '90

Betsy Brantley
Rogue Trader '98
Havana '90

Willy Braque
The Demoniacs '74

Albert Bras
Vampyr '31

Nicoletta Braschi
Life Is Beautiful '98
The Monster '96

Melissa Brasselle
The Assault '97

Pierre Brasseur
The Law '59
Portrait of an Assassin '49

Benjamin Bratt
The River Wild '94
Demolition Man '93

Dana Bratton
They Live '88

Andre Braugher
City of Angels '98
Primal Fear '96
Striking Distance '93
Somebody Has to Shoot the Picture '90
Glory '89

Arthur Brauss
Cross of Iron '76

The Train '65

Robert Bray
The Caine Mutiny '54

Jay Brazeau
Better Than Chocolate '99
Double Jeopardy '99
Air Bud '97
Trucks '97

Edward Brazier
Dark Odyssey '57

Rossano Brazzi
Final Justice '84
Krakatoa East of Java '66
South Pacific '58
Summertime '55

Peter Breck
Benji '74
Shock Corridor '63

Bunny Breckinridge
Plan 9 from Outer Space '56

Patrick Breen
Just the Ticket '98
One True Thing '98

Edmund Breese
All Quiet on the Western Front '30

Mario Brega
The Good, the Bad and the Ugly '67

Eric Breien
Suspicions '95

Valerie Breiman
Tale of Two Sisters '89

Lucille Bremer
Till the Clouds Roll By '46

Richard Bremmer
The 13th Warrior '99

Ewen Bremner
Trainspotting '95

Brid Brennan
Felicia's Journey '99
Dancing at Lughnasa '98
Guinevere '99

Eileen Brennan
Boys Life 2 '98
Changing Habits '96
White Palace '90
Private Benjamin '80
FM '78
The Sting '73

Pat Brennan
Body of Influence 2 '96

Walter Brennan
How the West Was Won '63
Red River '48
The Princess and the Pirate '44
The Pride of the Yankees '42
Meet John Doe '41
The Westerner '40
Come and Get It '36
The Bride of Frankenstein '35

Amy Brenneman
Your Friends & Neighbors '98
Daylight '96
Fear '96
Heat '95

Barry Brenner
Surf Nazis Must Die (DC) '87

Dori Brenner
Infinity '96
Altered States '80

Eve Brent
The Green Mile '99

George Brent
Dark Victory '39
Jezebel '38

Gilbert Brenton
Class of Nuke 'Em High '86

Edmund Breon
The Scarlet Pimpernel '34

G. Gordon Brer
Sexual Roulette '96

Bobbie Bresee
Surf Nazis Must Die (DC) '87

Martin Brest
Spies Like Us '85

Richard Brestoff
Car Wash '76

Jeremy Brett
Shameless '94
My Fair Lady '64

Miroslav Breu
Mandragora '97

Jim Breuer
Half-Baked '97

Siegfried Breuer
The Third Man '49

Juliette Brewer
The Little Rascals '94

Kidd Brewer Jr.
The Abyss (SE) '89

Jordana Brewster
The '60s '99
The Faculty '98

Maia Brewton
Adventures in Babysitting '87

Kevin Breznahan
SLC Punk! '99

Tom Breznahan
Terrified '94

Jean-Claude Brialy
The Monster '96
Claire's Knee '71
A Woman Is a Woman '60
The 400 Blows '59

Mary Brian
Peter Pan '24

Shane Briant
Twisted '96

Bridget Brice
The Twelve Chairs '70

Beau Bridges
The Fabulous Baker Boys '89
Swashbuckler '76
Two Minute Warning '76

Jeff Bridges
Arlington Road '99
The Muse '99
The Big Lebowski '97
The Mirror Has Two Faces '96
White Squall '96
Blown Away '94
Fearless '93
The Fabulous Baker Boys '89
Starman '84
Tron '82
King Kong '76

Lloyd Bridges
Blown Away '94
High Noon '52

Ann Bridgewater
Full Contact '92

Lucy Briers
Pride and Prejudice '95

Richard Briers
Spice World: The Movie '97
Mary Shelley's Frankenstein '94
Much Ado about Nothing '93

Joe Bob Briggs
See John (Joe Bob Briggs) Bloom

Richard Bright
Beautiful Girls '96
Red Heat '88
Vigilante '83

Susie Bright
Bound '96

Paul Brightwell
Sliding Doors '97

Charlie Brill
Bloodstone '88

Eddie Brill
Drop Dead Rock '95

Nancy Brill
Demons 2 '87

Steven Brill
The Mighty Ducks '92
sex, lies and videotape '89

Nick Brimble
Robin Hood: Prince of Thieves '91

Wilford Brimley
Progeny '98
In and Out '97
My Fellow Americans '96
The Firm '93
Hard Target '93
Where the Red Fern Grows: Part 2 '92
Tender Mercies '83
The Thing '82
Absence of Malice '81
The China Syndrome '79
The Electric Horseman '79

Michele Brin
Secret Games '92

Mark Bringleson
Soldier '98
The Lawnmower Man '92

Christie Brinkley
Vegas Vacation '96
National Lampoon's Vacation '83

David Brinkley
Mallrats '95

David Brisbin
Goodbye, Lover '99
Leaving Las Vegas '95

Brent Briscoe
Another Day in Paradise '98
A Simple Plan '98
Sling Blade '96

Danielle Brisebois
As Good As It Gets '97

Carl Brisson
The Manxman '29
The Ring '27

Morgan Brittany
Body Armor '96
The Birds '63

Barbara Britton
Reap the Wild Wind '42

Pamela Britton
D.O.A. '49

Tony Britton
The Day of the Jackal '73

Herman Brix
See Bruce Bennett

Jim Broadbent
The Avengers '98
Little Voice '98
The Borrowers '97
Bullets over Broadway '94
The Crying Game '92

Kent Broadhurst
Boys Life 2 '98
The Dark Half '91

I. Brobov
The Battleship Potemkin '25

Peter Brocco
One Flew Over the Cuckoo's
Nest '75

Roy Brocksmith
Kull the Conqueror '97
Arachnophobia '90
Total Recall '90
Tales of Ordinary Madness
'83

Charlie Broderick
Leaving Scars '97

Erin Broderick
Black Dog '98

James Broderick
Dog Day Afternoon '75

Matthew Broderick
Election '99
Inspector Gadget '99
Godzilla '98
The Lion King: Simba's Pride
'98 (V)
Addicted to Love '96
The Cable Guy '96
Infinity '96
The Freshman '90
Glory '89
Ferris Bueller's Day Off '86
Ladyhawke '85
WarGames '83

Don Brodie
Eat My Dust '76

Helen Brodie
Monsoon '97

Steve Brodie
The Caine Mutiny '54

Adrien Brody
Six Ways to Sunday '99
Summer of Sam '99
Ten Benny '98
The Thin Red Line '98
Solo '96

James Brolin
Pee-wee's Big Adventure '85
Capricorn One '78
The Car '77
Westworld '73

Josh Brolin
Best Laid Plans '99
The Mod Squad '99
Mimic '97
Bed of Roses '95
Flirting with Disaster '95

Valri Bromfield
Nothing but Trouble '91

Elaine Bromka
Uncle Buck '89

Eleanor Bron
A Little Princess '95
Help! '65

Brick Bronsky
Sgt. Kabukiman N.Y.P.D. '94

Betty Bronson
Naked Kiss '64
Peter Pan '24

Charles Bronson
Family of Cops '95
Death Wish 5: The Face of
Death '94
Cabo Blanco / U.S. Marshal
'81
The Meanest Men in the
West '76
Chino / Man with a Camera
'75
Hard Times '75

Cold Sweat '71
Honor Among Thieves '68
The Dirty Dozen '67
The Great Escape '63
The Magnificent Seven '60

Claudio Brook
Devil's Rain '75

Clive Brook
On Approval '44

Jayne Brook
Gattaca '97
Kindergarten Cop '90

Hillary Brooke
Invaders from Mars '53
The Road to Utopia '46
The Philadelphia Story '40

Paul Brooke
The Lair of the White Worm
'88

Walter Brooke
Tora! Tora! Tora! '70

Michelle Brookhurst
Can't Hardly Wait '98

Albert Brooks
The Muse '99
Dr. Dolittle '98 (V)
Out of Sight '98
Critical Care '97
Broadcast News '87
Private Benjamin '80
Taxi Driver (CE) '76

Avery Brooks
American History X '98
The Big Hit '98

Conrad Brooks
Plan 9 from Outer Space '56
Bride of the Monster '55
Jail Bait '54
Glen or Glenda? '53

Dina Brooks
Public Access '93

Hadda Brooks
The Crossing Guard '94

Hugh Brooks
Sore Losers '97

Louise Brooks
Pandora's Box '28

Mel Brooks
History of the World: Part 1
'81
Blazing Saddles '74
The Twelve Chairs '70

Phyllis Brooks
The Shanghai Gesture '42

Rand Brooks
Gone with the Wind '39

Randi Brooks
The Man with Two Brains '83

Randy Brooks
Reservoir Dogs '92

Ray Brooks
House of Whipcord '75

Richard Brooks
The Crow 2: City of Angels
'96
The Substitute '96
Shocker '89
Shakedown '88
The Hidden '87

Terron Brooks
The Temptations '98

Edward Brophy
Last Hurrah '58

Kevin Brophy
Hell Night '81

Pierce Brosnan
The Thomas Crown Affair '99
Quest for Camelot '98 (V)
Dante's Peak '97
Tomorrow Never Dies (SE)
'97
Mars Attacks! '96
The Mirror Has Two Faces '96
Goldeneye '95
Mrs. Doubtfire '93
The Lawnmower Man '92
Mister Johnson '91
Victim of Love '91
Around the World in 80 Days
'89
The Long Good Friday '80

Dr. Joyce Brothers
National Lampoon's Loaded
Weapon 1 '93
The Lonely Guy '84
Embryo '76

Peter Brouwer
Friday the 13th '80

Alfred Brown
The Seventh Voyage of Sinbad '58

Barbara Brown
Jack & the Beanstalk '52
Born Yesterday '50
The Fighting Sullivans '42

Barry Brown
Flesh '68

Bille Brown
Fierce Creatures '96

Blair Brown
The Astronaut's Wife '99
Stealing Home '88
Altered States '80

Bobby Brown
A Thin Line Between Love
and Hate '96

Bruce Brown
The Endless Summer '66 (N)
Surf Crazy '59 (N)

Bryan Brown
Twisted '96 (N)
Sweet Talker '91
Gorillas in the Mist '88
Breaker Morant '80

Charisse Brown
Detention '98

Clancy Brown
Flubber '97
Starship Troopers '97
The Shawshank Redemption
'94
Highlander (DC) '86
Bad Boys '83

Dwier Brown
The Guardian '90

Eleonora Brown
Two Women '61

Garrett M. Brown
Uncle Buck '89

Georgia Brown
Victim of Love '91

James Brown
The Blues Brothers 2000 '98
The Blues Brothers (CE) '80

James Brown
Sands of Iwo Jima '49

Jim Brown
He Got Game '98
Small Soldiers '98 (V)
Mars Attacks! '96
The Running Man '87
The Dirty Dozen '67

Joe E. Brown
Show Boat '51

Johnny Mack Brown
Belle of the Nineties '34

Judy Brown
The Big Doll House '71

Julie Brown
Plump Fiction '97
Clueless '95
Fist of the North Star '95
Earth Girls Are Easy '89

Downtown Julie Brown
Bug Buster '99

L.P. Brown III
Fatal Pursuit '98

**Melanie (Scary Spice)
Brown**
Spice World: The Movie '97

Michael Brown
Jackie Chan: My Stunts '98
(N)

N.D. Brown
Q: The Movie '99

Olivia Brown
Streets of Fire '84

Ralph Brown
Alien3 '92
The Crying Game '92

Reb Brown
The Firing Line '91

Ron Brown
Charlie, the Lonesome
Cougar '67

Samantha Brown
New Jersey Drive '95

Tom Brown
Buck Privates Come Home
'47

Violet Brown
Firehouse '87

W. Earl Brown
There's Something about
Mary '98
Scream (CS) '96

Woody Brown
Secret Games 3 '94

Coral Browne
The Killing of Sister George
'69

Diana Browne
Basket Case '82

Robert Alan Browne
Psycho 3 '86

Roscoe Lee Browne
Babe: Pig in the City '98 (V)
Babe '95 (N)
The Pompatus of Love '95
Legal Eagles '86
Logan's Run '76
The Cowboys '72

Suzanne Browne
The Bikini Car Wash Company
'90

Zachary Browne
Waking Up Horton '99

Robert Broyles
Eat My Dust '76

Brenda Bruce
Peeping Tom '60

Ed Bruce
Fire Down Below '97

Kate Bruce
Way Down East '20

Nicholas Bruce
Othello '52

Nigel Bruce
Limelight '52
Rebecca '40
She '35
The Scarlet Pimpernel '34

Jane Brucker
Dirty Dancing '87
Dirty Dancing (CE) '87

Patrick Bruel
Lost and Found '99

Pamela Brull
The Guardian '90

Sharon Bruneau
Tornado Run '95

Genevieve Brunet
The City of Lost Children '95

Peter Bruni
Assault on Precinct 13 '76

Dylan Bruno
The Rage: Carrie 2 '99

Nando Bruno
Open City '45

Eric Bruskotter
Starship Troopers '97

Zachery Ty Bryan
The Rage: Carrie 2 '99

Virginia Bryant
Demons 2 '87

Claudia Bryar
Psycho 2 '83

Scott Bryce
Up Close and Personal '96
Exclusive '82

Larry Bryggman
Die Hard: With a Vengeance
'95

Andrew Bryniarski
Batman Returns '92

Yul Brynner
Westworld '73
The Magnificent Seven '60
The King and I '56
The Ten Commandments '56

Reine Brynolfsson
Les Miserables '97

Istvan Bubik
The Phantom of the Opera
'98

Colin Buchanan
Moll Flanders '96

Edgar Buchanan
McLintock! '63
Rage at Dawn '55
Penny Serenade '41

Horst Buchholz
Life Is Beautiful '98
The Magnificent Seven '60
Tiger Bay '59

Betty Buckley
Simply Irresistible '99
Frantic '88
Tender Mercies '83

Phil Buckman
An American Werewolf in
Paris '97

Helen Buday
Mad Max: Beyond Thunder-
dome '85

Nancy Buechler
Perfect Profile '90

Brad Bufanda
Pocket Ninjas '93

Jimmy Buffett
FM '78

The Man Who Would Be King
'75
Sleuth '72
The Last Valley '71
The Ipcress File '65

Shakira Caine
The Man Who Would Be King
'75

John Cairney
A Night to Remember '58

Jonathan Cake
Noah's Ark '99

Clara Calamai
Deep Red: Hatchet Murders
'75

Guiliana Calandra
Deep Red: Hatchet Murders
'75

Marie Caldare
Tender Loving Care '99

Todd Caldecott
Fear '96

Paul Calderon
Four Rooms '95
Lotto Land '95
Bad Lieutenant '92
Q & A '90

Rita Calderoni
Nude for Satan '74
The Reincarnation of Isabel
'72

Paula Cale
Milo '98

Don Calfa
Terrified '94
Weekend at Bernie's '89

Nicole Calfan
The Four Musketeers '75

Louis Calhern
Notorious '46
The Bridge of San Luis Rey
'44
Duck Soup '33

Monica Calhoun
The Best Man '99
The Players Club '98

Rory Calhoun
Pure Country '92
The Red House '47

R.D. Call
Last Man Standing '96
Waterworld '95

K. Callan
American Gigolo '79

Charlie Callas
Amazon Women on the Moon
'87
History of the World: Part 1
'81

Joseph Calleia
For Whom the Bell Tolls '43

Simon Callow
Shakespeare in Love (CS)
'98
Ace Ventura: When Nature
Calls '95
Four Weddings and a Funeral
'94
Street Fighter '94
Howard's End '92
Amadeus '84

Cab Calloway
The Blues Brothers (CE) '80

Vanessa Bell Calloway
The Temptations '98
Daylight '96
Crimson Tide '95

**What's Love Got to Do with
It?** '93
Coming to America '88

Michael Caloz
Screamers '96

Donald Calthrop
No. 17 '32

Toni Calvert
Blood Feast (SE) '63

James Cameron
The Muse '99
Last Action Hero '93

Kirk Cameron
The Best of Times '86

Rod Cameron
Psychic Killer '75

Pier A. Caminnecci
Succubus '69

Colleen Camp
Election '99
Plump Fiction '97
Speed 2: Cruise Control '97
Die Hard: With a Vengeance
'95
Greedy '94
Apocalypse Now '79
She Devils in Chains '76
The Swinging Cheerleaders
'74

Alan Campbell
A Simple Wish '97

Bill Campbell
Armistead Maupin's More
Tales of the City '97
Dracula '92
The Rocketeer '91

Bruce Campbell
From Dusk Till Dawn 2: Texas
Blood Money '98
Running Time '97
Escape from L.A. '96
The Hudsucker Proxy '93
Army of Darkness '92
Maniac Cop '88
Evil Dead 2: Dead by Dawn
'87
Evil Dead '83

Cheryl Campbell
Chariots of Fire '81

Christian Campbell
Trick '99
I've Been Waiting for You '98

Donald Campbell
Army of Darkness '92

Eric Campbell
The Chaplin Mutuals, Vol. 1
'90s
The Chaplin Mutuals, Vol. 2
'90s
The Chaplin Mutuals, Vol. 3
'90s

Glen Campbell
Rock-a-Doodle '92 (V)

J. Kenneth Campbell
Operation Delta Force 2: Mayday '97

Jessica Campbell
Election '99

John Campbell
The Fighting Sullivans '42

Julia Campbell
Diary of a Serial Killer '97
Romy and Michele's High
School Reunion '97

Ken Campbell
The Big Red One '80

Naomi Campbell
Prisoner of Love '99

Miami Rhapsody '95

Nell Campbell
Great Expectations '97
Pink Floyd: The Wall '82

Neve Campbell
54 '98
The Lion King: Simba's Pride
'98 (V)
Wild Things '98
Scream 2 '97
The Craft '96
Scream (CS) '96

Nicholas Campbell
The Boys Club '96
Dancing in the Dark '95
A Bridge Too Far '77

Paul Campbell
Klash '95

Rob Campbell
Boys Don't Cry '99
Unforgiven '92

Scott Michael Campbell
Radioland Murders '94

Tisha Campbell
Sprung '96
Little Shop of Horrors '86

William Campbell
Dementia 13 '63

Tom Campitelli
Perfect Profile '90

Rafael Campos
Where the Buffalo Roam '80

Stephan Camus
Web of Seduction '99

Esther Canadas
The Thomas Crown Affair '99

Jose Canalejas
Return of the Blind Dead '75

John Candy
Cool Runnings '93
Career Opportunities '91
JFK '91
Nothing but Trouble '91
Home Alone '90
Uncle Buck '89
The Great Outdoors '88
Little Shop of Horrors '86
Brewster's Millions '85
Splash '84
National Lampoon's Vacation
'83
Heavy Metal '81 (V)
Stripes '81
The Blues Brothers (CE) '80
1941 '79

Natalie Canerday
October Sky '99
Sling Blade '96

Hans Canineberg
The Odessa File '74

Bobby Cannavale
The Bone Collector '99

Stephen J. Cannell
Posse '93

Dyan Cannon
Caddyshack 2 '88
Deathtrap '82
Heaven Can Wait '78
Revenge of the Pink Panther
'78

J.D. Cannon
Cool Hand Luke '67

Anne Canovos
Ready to Wear '94
Zeder '83

Antonio Cantafora
Torture Chamber of Baron
Blood '72

Giorgio Cantarini
Life Is Beautiful '98

Eric Cantona
Elizabeth '98

Yakima Canutt
For Whom the Bell Tolls '43
Gone with the Wind '39
Lucky Texan '34
Sagebrush Trail '33

Sergio Canvari
Twitch of the Death Nerve
'71

Peter Capaldi
Shooting Fish '98
Bean '98
Dangerous Liaisons '88
The Lair of the White Worm
'88

Peter Capell
Paths of Glory '57

Virginia Capers
Ferris Bueller's Day Off '86
The North Avenue Irregulars
'79

John Capodice
Enemy of the State '98
Ringmaster '98
True Friends '98
Honeymoon in Vegas '92
The Hard Way '91

Aldo Caponi
Rabid Dogs '74

Patrizia Capparelli
The Decameron '70

Francis Capra
A Simple Wish '97
A Bronx Tale '93

Ahna Capri
Enter the Dragon (SE) '73

Kate Capshaw
The Love Letter '99
The Alarmist '98
How to Make an American
Quilt '95
Just Cause '94
Black Rain '89
Dreamscape (SE) '84

Capucine
The Con Artists '80
The Pink Panther '64

Paul Carafotes
Choices '81

Tyke Caravelli
Crackdown '88

Joseph Carberry
Vigilante '83

Linda Cardellini
Dee Snider's Strangeland '98

Lori Cardille
Day of the Dead '85

Tantoo Cardinal
Smoke Signals '98
Legends of the Fall '94
Where the Rivers Flow North
'94
Black Robe '91
Dances with Wolves '90

Claudia Cardinale
Fitzcarraldo '82
The Professionals '66
The Pink Panther '64

Nathalie Cardone
L'Enfer '94

James B. Cardwell
The Fighting Sullivans '42

Lianella Carell
The Bicycle Thief '48

Julien Carette
Grand Illusion '37

Arthur Edmund Carewe
The Cat and the Canary '27
The Phantom of the Opera
'25

Harry Carey Sr.
Red River '48
Angel and the Badman '47
Duel in the Sun '46

Harry Carey Jr.
Tombstone '93
Mask '85
Alvarez Kelly '66
The Searchers '56
Mister Roberts '55
Rio Grande '50
Red River '48

Julius J. Carey III
Avenging Disco Godfather '76

Leonard Carey
The Snows of Kilimanjaro '52

Mariah Carey
The Bachelor '99

Olive Carey
The Searchers '56

Phil Carey
Mister Roberts '55

Ron Carey
Lucky Luke '94
Troublemakers '94
History of the World: Part 1
'81

Timothy Carey
Minnie and Moskowitz '71
Paths of Glory '57
The Killing '56

Patrick Cargill
Help! '65

Timothy Carhart
Thelma & Louise '91
Ghostbusters '84

Gia Carides
Austin Powers 2: The Spy
Who Shagged Me '99
Primary Colors '98
Last Breath '96

Carmine Caridi
Top Dog '95

Len Cariou
Executive Decision '96
Never Talk to Strangers '95
The Lady in White '88

Carita
The Viking Queen '67

Deborah Carlin
Fraternity Demon '92

George Carlin
Outrageous Fortune '87
Car Wash '76

Mary Carlisle
Dead Men Walk / The Mon-
ster Maker '43

Jean Carlo
Shaolin Avengers '94

Johann Carlo
Fair Game '95
Quiz Show '94

Karen Carlson
The Candidate '72

Richard Carlson
The Little Foxes '41

Ing-mari Carlsson
My Life As a Dog '85

Mark Carlton
Angel's Dance '99

Reg E. Cathey
Ill-Gotten Gains '97
Seven '95

Mary Jo Catlett
Serial Mom '94

Walter Catlett
They Got Me Covered '43
Rain '32

Michael Caton
The Castle '97

Kim Cattrall
Baby Geniuses '98
Modern Vampires '98
Star Trek 6: The Undiscovered Country '91
The Bonfire of the Vanities '90
Police Academy '84
Porky's '82
Ticket to Heaven '81

Maxwell Caulfield
The Real Blonde '97
Animal Instincts '92

Fred Cavalli
Werewolf '95

Valeria Cavalli
Double Team '97

Megan Cavanagh
For Richer or Poorer '97
A League of Their Own '92

Christine Cavanaugh
The Rugrats Movie '98 (V)
Babe '95 (V)

Lumi Cavazos
Bottle Rocket '95
Like Water for Chocolate '93

Marc Cavell
Cool Hand Luke '67

Glen Cavender
The General '26

Nicola Cavendish
Air Bud '97

Dick Cavett
Beetlejuice '88
A Nightmare on Elm Street 3: Dream Warriors '87
Annie Hall '77

James Caviezel
The Thin Red Line '98
G.I. Jane '97

Joseph Cawthorn
The White Zombie '32

Elizabeth Cayton
Slave Girls from Beyond Infinity '87

John Cazale
The Deer Hunter '78
Dog Day Afternoon '75

Daniel Ceccaldi
Chloe in the Afternoon '72
Bed and Board '70
The Soft Skin '64

Carlo Cecchi
The Red Violin '98

Jon Cedar
Day of the Animals '77

Pina Cei
La Traviata '82

Henry Cele
The Ghost and the Darkness '96

Maria Celedonio
How to Make an American Quilt '95

Adriano Celentano
The Con Artists '80

Adolfo Celi
Thunderball '65

Ara Celi
From Dusk Till Dawn 3: The Hangman's Daughter '99
Looking for Lola '98

Frank Cellier
The 39 Steps '35

Peter Cellier
And the Ship Sails On '83

Petr Cepek
Jan Svankmajer's Faust '94 (V)

John Dayton (J.D.) Cerna
Boys Life 2 '98

Kirsten Cerre
Vampire Journals '96

Claude Cerval
Any Number Can Win '63

Jeff Cesario
Jack Frost '98

Peter Cester
Naked Warriors '73

Kader Chaatouf
The Life of Jesus '96

Lacey Chabert
Lost in Space '98

The Lady Chablis
Midnight in the Garden of Good and Evil (SE) '97

Cyril Chadwick
Peter Pan '24

June Chadwick
This Is Spinal Tap '84

Sarah Chadwick
The Adventures of Priscilla, Queen of the Desert '94

George Chakiris
West Side Story '61

Kathleen Chalfant
A Price above Rubies '97

Feodor Chaliapin Jr.
Moonstruck '87

Sarah Chalke
I've Been Waiting for You '98

William Challee
Zachariah '70

Georges Chamarat
Diabolique '55

Howland Chamberlain
The Best Years of Our Lives '46

Richard Chamberlain
The Slipper and the Rose '76
The Four Musketeers '75
The Three Musketeers '74
The Towering Inferno '74

Wilt Chamberlain
Conan the Destroyer '84

Emma Chambers
Notting Hill '99

Wheaton Chambers
The Flying Serpent '55

Gower Champion
Show Boat '51

Jean Champion
Umbrellas of Cherbourg '64

Stephanie Champlin
Silk 'n' Sabotage '94

Anthony Chan
Twin Dragons '92

Dennis Chan
Kickboxer '89

Ellen Chan
Inspector Wears Skirts '88

Jackie Chan
Jackie Chan: My Stunts '98
Jackie Chan's Who Am I '98
Mr. Nice Guy '98
Rush Hour '98
Jackie Chan's First Strike '96
Rumble in the Bronx '96
Supercop 2 '93
City Hunter '92
Supercop '92
Twin Dragons '92
Operation Condor '91
Miracles '89
Dragons Forever '88
The Killer Meteors '87
Operation Condor 2: The Armour of the Gods '86
Half a Loaf of Kung Fu '85
Heart of Dragon '85
My Lucky Stars '85
To Kill with Intrigue '85
Cannonball Run 2 '84
Wheels on Meals '84
Fearless Hyena: Part 2 '83
The Dragon Fist '80
Fearless Hyena '79
Spiritual Kung Fu '78
New Fist of Fury '76
Enter the Dragon (SE) '73

Jordan Chan
Hot War '98
Big Bullet '96

Kelly Chan
Hot War '98

Kim Chan
The Corruptor '99

King Chan
Long Arm of the Law '84

Michael Paul Chan
The Insider '99
U.S. Marshals '98
Falling Down '93

Philip Chan
Hard-Boiled '92
Twin Dragons '92

Anna Chancellor
The Man Who Knew Too Little '97
Pride and Prejudice '95

Betty Chandler
Don't Look in the Basement '73

Helen Chandler
Dracula '31

Jeff Chandler
Away All Boats '56

John Davis Chandler
Shoot Out '71

Kyle Chandler
Angel's Dance '99
Pure Country '92

Lane Chandler
Winds of the Wasteland / The Lucky Texan '36

Simon Chandler
Incognito '97
The Man Who Knew Too Little '97

Lon Chaney Sr.
The Phantom of the Opera '25

Lon Chaney Jr.
Spider Baby '64
The Indestructible Man / The Amazing Transparent Man '56

High Noon '52
The Wolf Man '41
Of Mice and Men '39

David Chang
The Legend of the 7 Golden Vampires '73

Sylvia Chang
The Red Violin '98
C'est la Vie, Mon Cherie '93
Twin Dragons '92
All About Ah Long '89

Carol Channing
Thumbelina '94 (V)

Stockard Channing
Practical Magic '98
Twilight '98
The First Wives Club '96
Up Close and Personal '96

Rosalind Chao
What Dreams May Come '98

Winston Chao
Island of Greed '97

Damian Chapa
Sometimes They Come Back ... For More '99
Street Fighter '94

Miles Chapin
The People vs. Larry Flynt '96
The Funhouse '81

Ben Chaplin
The Thin Red Line '98

Carmen Chaplin
Ma Saison Preferee '93

Charlie Chaplin
Charles Chaplin—A First National Collection
The Chaplin Mutuals, Vol. 1 '90s
The Chaplin Mutuals, Vol. 2 '90s
The Chaplin Mutuals, Vol. 3 '90s
Chaplin's Essanay Comedies, Vol. 1 '90s
Chaplin's Essanay Comedies, Vol. 2 '90s
Chaplin's Essanay Comedies, Vol. 3 '90s
Chaplin's Art of Comedy '66
A King in New York / A Woman in Paris '57
Limelight '52
Monsieur Verdoux '47
The Great Dictator '40
Modern Times '36
City Lights '31
The Gold Rush '25
The Kid / A Dog's Life '21
The Circus '19
Tillie's Punctured Romance '14

Geraldine Chaplin
Cousin Bette '97
Chaplin '92
The Four Musketeers '75
The Three Musketeers '74

Josephine Chaplin
The Canterbury Tales '71

Michael Chaplin
A King in New York / A Woman in Paris '57

Sydney Chaplin
Limelight '52

Alexander Chapman
Lilies '96

Daniel Chapman
Philadelphia '93

Graham Chapman
Monty Python's The Meaning of Life '83

Monty Python's Life of Brian '79
And Now for Something Completely Different '72

Judith Chapman
Fire on the Amazon '93

Lonny (Loni) Chapman
Where the Red Fern Grows '74
Take the Money and Run '69
The Birds '63

Marguerite Chapman
The Amazing Transparent Man '60

Sean Chapman
Hellbound: Hellraiser 2 '88
Hellraiser '87

Dave Chappelle
200 Cigarettes '99
You've Got Mail '98
Con Air '97
Half-Baked '97
The Nutty Professor '96

Patricia Charbonneau
RoboCop 2 '90
Shakedown '88

Tara Charendoff
The Rugrats Movie '98 (V)

Cyd Charisse
Swimsuit '89
Black Tights '60
Brigadoon '54
Singin' in the Rain '52

Josh Charles
Muppets from Space '99
Crossworlds '96
Things to Do in Denver When You're Dead '95
Dead Poets Society '89

Ray Charles
The Blues Brothers (CE) '80

Ian Charleson
Chariots of Fire '81

Kim Charney
Suddenly '54

Stu Charno
Friday the 13th, Part 2 '81

Charo
Thumbelina '94 (V)

Christian Charriere
The Eric Rohmer Collection: The Moral Tales '62

Spencer Charters
The Bat Whispers '30

Melanie Chartoff
The Rugrats Movie '98 (V)

Charley Chase
Laurel and Hardy and Friends '90s
The Lost Films of Laurel and Hardy, Vol. 3 '90s

Chevy Chase
Dirty Work '97
Vegas Vacation '96
Last Action Hero '93
Hero '92
Nothing but Trouble '91
National Lampoon's Christmas Vacation '89
Caddyshack 2 '88
Funny Farm '88
Three Amigos '86
Fletch '85
Spies Like Us '85
National Lampoon's Vacation '83
Caddyshack '80

Courtney Chase
Nick of Time '95

Rony Clanton
Def by Temptation '90

Stefan Clapczynski
Funny Games '97

Gordon Clapp
The Rage: Carrie 2 '99

Eric Clapton
Robbie Robertson: Going Home '98

Diane Clare
Plague of the Zombies '66

Mary Clare
Young and Innocent '37

O.B. Clarence
Great Expectations '46
On Approval '44
The Scarlet Pimpernel '34

Al Clark
The Adventures of Priscilla, Queen of the Desert '94

Blake Clark
The Waterboy '98

Bob (Benjamin) Clark
Porky's '82

Candy Clark
Q (The Winged Serpent) '82
The Man Who Fell to Earth '76
American Graffiti '73

Gemma Clark
Damage '92

Joseph Clark
The Big Red One '80

Madison Clark
Embrace the Darkness '98

Matt Clark
Return to Oz '85
The Outlaw Josey Wales '76

Mitchell Clark
Novel Desires '92

Mystro Clark
Chairman of the Board '97

Spencer Treat Clark
Arlington Road '99
Double Jeopardy '99

Susan Clark
Porky's '82
The North Avenue Irregulars '79
Airport '75 '75
Madigan '68

Tom Clark
Emmanuelle, the Joys of a Woman '76

Wallis Clark
Penny Serenade '41

Bernardette L. Clarke
Love Jones '96

Caitlin Clarke
Cost of Living '97

Downing Clarke
America '24

Graham Clarke
Laser Mission '90

Joe Clarke
Basket Case '82

Lenny Clarke
Rounders '98

Mae Clarke
Frankenstein '31

Melinda Clarke
Spawn (SE) '97

Richard Clarke
A Night to Remember '58

Robert Clarke
Hideous Sun Demon '59

Robin Clarke
Horror Planet '80

Warren Clarke
A Clockwork Orange '71

D. A. Clarke-Smith
The Man Who Knew Too Much '34

Patricia Clarkson
The Green Mile '99
Simply Irresistible '99
Playing by Heart '98

Kevin Clash
The Adventures of Elmo in Grouchland '99 (V)

Andrew Dice Clay
Foolish '99
Whatever It Takes '97
Casual Sex? '88
Amazon Women on the Moon '87

Nicholas Clay
Merlin '98
The Hound of the Baskervilles '83
Excalibur '81
Terror of Frankenstein '75

Jill Clayburgh
Fools Rush In '97

Cynthia Cleese
Fierce Creatures '96

John Cleese
The Out-of-Towners '99
George of the Jungle '97 (V)
Fierce Creatures '96
Mary Shelley's Frankenstein '94
A Fish Called Wanda '88
Monty Python's The Meaning of Life '83
Time Bandits '81
Monty Python's Life of Brian '79
And Now for Something Completely Different '72

Christian Clemenson
Lost and Found '99
Hero '92

Pierre Clementi
Hideous Kinky '99

Lorenzo Clemons
The Fence '94

David Clennon
Light Sleeper '92
Matinee '92
Conspiracy: The Trial of the Chicago Eight '87
Legal Eagles '86
Sweet Dreams '85
The Right Stuff '83
Star 80 '83
The Thing '82

Judy Cler
The Wizard of Gore '70

Corinne Clery
The Con Artists '80
Moonraker (SE) '79

Carol Cleveland
Monty Python's The Meaning of Life '83
Monty Python's Life of Brian '79
And Now for Something Completely Different '72

George Cleveland
Revolt of the Zombies '36

Scott Cleverdon
The Prophecy 3: The Ascent '99

Richard Clifford
Much Ado about Nothing '93

Montgomery Clift
Red River '48

Elmer Clifton
Intolerance '16
The Birth of a Nation '15

Emily Cline
In the Company of Men '96

Mildred Clinton
Alice Sweet Alice '76

Colin Clive
The Bride of Frankenstein '35
Frankenstein '31

E.E. Clive
The Bride of Frankenstein '35

John Clive
A Clockwork Orange '71
Yellow Submarine '68 (V)

Al Cliver
Zombie '80

George Clooney
Three Kings '99
Out of Sight '98
The Thin Red Line '98
Batman and Robin '97
The Peacemaker '97
From Dusk Till Dawn '95
Red Surf '90

Del Close
Mommy 2: Mommy's Day '97
Ferris Bueller's Day Off '86

Glenn Close
Cookie's Fortune '99
Sarah, Plain and Tall: Winter's End '99
Tarzan '99 (V)
Air Force One '97
Mars Attacks! '96
101 Dalmatians '96
The Paper '94
Skylark '93
Sarah, Plain and Tall '91
Dangerous Liaisons '88
The Big Chill '83

John Scott Clough
Phantoms '97

Suzanne Cloutier
Othello '52

Vera Clouzot
Diabolique '55
Wages of Fear '55

H. M. Clugston
The Navigator '24

Martin Clunes
Shakespeare in Love (CS) '98

Francois Cluzet
French Kiss '95
Ready to Wear '94
L'Enfer '93

Kim Coates
Innocent Blood '92

Lee J. Cobb
The Meanest Men in the West '76
The Exorcist (SE) '73
How the West Was Won '63

Randall "Tex" Cobb
Liar Liar '96
The Golden Child '86

Bill Cobbs
Hope Floats '98
I Still Know What You Did Last Summer '98

Paulie '98
Air Bud '97
Things to Do in Denver When You're Dead '95
The Hudsucker Proxy '93
The Bodyguard '92
Carolina Skeletons '92

Giancarlo Cobelli
Barbarella '68

Charles Coburn
Impact '49
The Paradine Case '47
Made for Each Other '39

James Coburn
Noah's Ark '99
Dean Koontz's Mr. Murder '98
Payback '98
Affliction '97
Eraser '96
Keys to Tulsa '96
The Nutty Professor '96
Maverick '94
Deadfall '93
Sister Act 2: Back in the Habit '93
The Player '92
Hudson Hawk '91
Cross of Iron '76
Midway '76
Hard Times '75
Charade '63
The Great Escape '63
The Magnificent Seven '60

Imogene Coca
National Lampoon's Vacation '83

Linda Cochran
2000 Maniacs '64

Steve Cochran
The Best Years of Our Lives '46
Wonder Man '45

Michael Cochrane
Incognito '97

Rory Cochrane
The Last Don '97
Love and a .45 '94
Dazed and Confused '93

Arlene Cockburn
The Governess '98

Gary Cockrell
Lolita '62

Camille Coduri
King Ralph '91

George Coe
Bustin' Loose '81

Peter Coe
Sands of Iwo Jima '49

Joel Coen
Spies Like Us '85

Joelle Coeur
The Demoniacs '74

Paul Coeur
Cool Runnings '93

Scott Coffey
Route 9 '98
Dream Lover '93

Frederick Coffin
The Base '99
Hard to Kill '89

Theo Cohan
Class of Nuke 'Em High '86

Jessica Lynn Cohen
George Balanchine's The Nutcracker '93

Lynn Cohen
Manhattan Murder Mystery '93

Mitchell Cohen
The Toxic Avenger (DC) '86

Scott Cohen
Sweet Evil '95

Enrico Colantoni
Stigmata '99

Nicholas Colasanto
Raging Bull '80

Claudette Colbert
The Love Goddesses '65
It Happened One Night '34

Maurice Colbourne
The Littlest Horse Thieves '76

Tim Colceri
Full Metal Jacket '87

Dallas Cole
Glitch! '88

Eric Michael Cole
White Squall '96

Gary Cole
I'll Be Home for Christmas '98
Office Space '98
A Simple Plan '98
Santa Fe '97
In the Line of Fire '93

George Cole
A Christmas Carol '51

Julie Dawn Cole
Willy Wonka & the Chocolate Factory '71

Michael Cole
The Bubble '67

Nat King Cole
The Blue Gardenia '53

Robert Coleby
The Phantom '96

Charlotte Coleman
Twice upon a Yesterday '98
Four Weddings and a Funeral '94

Dabney Coleman
Inspector Gadget '99
Stuart Little '99
You've Got Mail '98
Dragnet '87
WarGames '83
On Golden Pond '81
Melvin and Howard '80

Gary Coleman
Dirty Work '97

Jack Coleman
The Landlady '98

Jimmy Coleman
Priest '94

Layne Coleman
Abraxas: Guardian of the Universe '90

Ornette Coleman
Chappaqua '66

Patricia Coleman
Habit '97

Renee Coleman
A League of Their Own '92

Alison Coleridge
The Shining '80

Charles "Honi" Coles
Dirty Dancing '87
Dirty Dancing (CE) '87

Roger Corman
Philadelphia '93
Silence of the Lambs '91

Michael Cornelison
Mommy 2: Mommy's Day '96
Mommy '95

Ellie Cornell
Halloween 4: The Return of
Michael Myers '88

Clovis Cornillac
The Unbearable Lightness of
Being '88

Robert Cornthwaite
Matinee '92
The War of the Worlds '53

Aurora Cornu
Claire's Knee '71

Anne Cornwall
College '27

Charlotte Cornwell
The Saint '97

Georges Corraface
Escape from L.A. '96

Mady Correll
Monsieur Verdoux '47

Adrienne Corri
A Clockwork Orange '71
The Viking Queen '67
Corridors of Blood '58

Nick Corri
A Nightmare on Elm Street
'84

Sergio Corrieri
I Am Cuba '64

Kevin Corrigan
Lulu on the Bridge '98
Slums of Beverly Hills '98
Buffalo 66 '97
Trees Lounge '96

Lloyd Corrigan
The Manchurian Candidate
'62

Shirley Corrigan
The Devil's Nightmare '71

Bud Cort
Heat '95
Invaders from Mars '86

Joe Cortese
American History X '98
Exclusive '82

Valentina Cortese
The Adventures of Baron
Munchausen '89
Juliet of the Spirits '65

Julia Cortez
The Adventures of Priscilla,
Queen of the Desert '94

Ricardo Cortez
Last Hurrah '58

Linda Corwin
A Nymphoid Barbarian in
Dinosaur Hell '94

James Cosmo
Babe: Pig in the City '98 (V)
Emma '96

Pierre Cosso
An American Werewolf in
Paris '97

James Costa
Joe the King '99

**Constantin Costa-
Gavras**
Spies Like Us '85

Suzanne Costallos
Lotto Land '95

Robert Costanzo
Plump Fiction '97
Underworld '96
Honeymoon in Vegas '92
Die Hard 2: Die Harder '90

Bob Costas
BASEketball '98

Deirdre Costello
The Full Monty '96

Elvis Costello
Austin Powers 2: The Spy
Who Shagged Me '99
200 Cigarettes '98
Spice World: The Movie '97

Lou Costello
Jack & the Beanstalk '52
Abbott and Costello in the
Foreign Legion '50
Buck Privates Come Home
'47
Buck Privates '41
In the Navy '41

Nicolas Coster
Stir Crazy '80
The Electric Horseman '79

Kevin Costner
Message in a Bottle '98
The Postman '97
Tin Cup '96
Waterworld '95
The War '94
The Bodyguard '92
JFK '91
Robin Hood: Prince of
Thieves '91
Dances with Wolves '90
Revenge '90
Bull Durham '88
Night Shift '82
Sizzle Beach U.S.A. '74

Tina Cote
Mean Guns '97

John Cothran Jr.
Ricochet '91

Richard Cotica
Rabid Grannies '89

Joseph Cotten
Torture Chamber of Baron
Blood '72
Tora! Tora! Tora! '70
Othello '52
The Third Man '49
Duel in the Sun '46

James Cotton
After Dark, My Sweet '90

Genevieve Cottreel
The Life of Jesus '96

Marjorie Cottreel
The Life of Jesus '96

Marisa Coughlan
Teaching Mrs. Tingle '99

George Coulouris
The Long Good Friday '80
Papillon '73
Tower of Evil '72
For Whom the Bell Tolls '43

Roy Coulson
Robin Hood '22

Mary Count
Naked Warriors '73

Gene Courtier
Blood Feast (SE) '63

Del Courtney
Hideous Sun Demon '59

Jean Coutu
Nikki, the Wild Dog of the
North '61

Alan Covert
The Wedding Singer '97
Bulletproof '96
Happy Gilmore '96

John Cowley
The Field '90

Alan Cox
Mrs. Dalloway '97

Brian Cox
The Corruptor '99
Desperate Measures '98
Rushmore '98
The Boxer '97
Kiss the Girls '97
The Glimmer Man '96
The Long Kiss Goodnight '96
Rob Roy '95

Christina Cox
Better Than Chocolate '99
Street Law '95

Claire Cox
Shooting Fish '98

Jennifer Elise Cox
Sometimes They Come Back
... Again '96

Julie Cox
Alegria '98

Ronny Cox
Forces of Nature '99
From the Earth to the Moon
'98
Murder at 1600 '97
Todd McFarlane's Spawn '97
(V)
Total Recall '90
RoboCop '87
Vision Quest '85
The Car '77
Deliverance '72

Wally Cox
The Night Strangler '72

Courteney Cox Arquette
The Runner '99
Scream 2 '97
Scream (CS) '96
Ace Ventura: Pet Detective
'93

Peter Coyote
Patch Adams (CE) '98
Route 9 '98
Sphere '97
Top of the World '97
Kika '94
Outrageous Fortune '87

Cylk Cozart
Conspiracy Theory '97

Paolo Cozza
Demons '86

Scott Craft
Closer and Closer '96

Charles Crafts
Glen or Glenda? '53

Carolyn Craig
House on Haunted Hill '58

Daniel Craig
Elizabeth '98
Moll Flanders '96
The Power of One '92

Elijah Craig
The Rage: Carrie 2 '99

Jeanne Crain
State Fair '45

Barbara Crampton
Cold Harvest '97
Space Truckers '97
Castle Freak '95
Body Double '84
Re-Animator '84

Fred Crane
Gone with the Wind '39

Norma Crane
Fiddler on the Roof '71

Tony Crane
Wishmaster '97

Ward Crane
Our Hospitality / Sherlock
Junior '23

William H. Crane
The Saphead '21

Kenneth Cranham
The Boxer '97
Hellbound: Hellraiser 2 '88

Lorcan Cranitch
Dancing at Lughnasa '98

Patrick Cranshaw
Nothing to Lose '96
The Amazing Transparent
Man '60

Bryan Cranston
From the Earth to the Moon
'98
Saving Private Ryan '98

Rich Crater
Carnal Crimes '91

Gemma Craven
The Slipper and the Rose '76

Matt Craven
Paulie '98
The Juror '96
Crimson Tide '95
A Few Good Men '92
Jacob's Ladder '90

Mimi Craven
Mikey '92

Wes Craven
Scream (CS) '96
The Fear '94
Wes Craven's New Nightmare
'94

Broderick Crawford
Born Yesterday '50

Cindy Crawford
Fair Game '95

David Crawford
Dawn of the Dead '78

Joan Crawford
I Saw What You Did '65
What Ever Happened to Baby
Jane? '62
Sudden Fear '52
Rain '32

Michael Crawford
Condorman '81

Rachael Crawford
Rude '96

Sophia Crawford
Beauty Investigator '93

Jack Creley
Dr. Strangelove, or: How I
Learned to Stop Worrying
and Love the Bomb '64

Bruno Cremer
Sorcerer '77

Richard Crenna
Wrongfully Accused '98
Jade '95
Leviathan '89
Rambo 3 '88
Rambo: First Blood, Part 2
'85
The Flamingo Kid '84
First Blood '82
Body Heat '81

Marshall Crenshaw
La Bamba '87

Laura Hope Crews
Gone with the Wind '39

Wendy Crewson
Better Than Chocolate '99
Air Force One '97
Corrina, Corrina '94
The Santa Clause '94

Mik Cribben
Beware! Children at Play '95

Missy Crider
The Sex Monster '99
Stand-Ins '97
Powder '95

Dan Crimmins
The White Zombie '32

Donald Crisp
Last Hurrah '58
National Velvet '44
Wuthering Heights '39
Jezebel '38
The Black Pirate '26
Broken Blossoms '19
The Birth of a Nation '15

Quentin Crisp
Philadelphia '93
Orlando '92

Peter Criss
Detroit Rock City '99

Criswell
Plan 9 from Outer Space '56

Thomas Crnkovich
Sgt. Kabukiman N.Y.P.D. '94

Peter Crombie
Seven '95

James Cromwell
The Bachelor '99
The General's Daughter '99
The Green Mile '99
Babe: Pig in the City '98
Deep Impact '98
L.A. Confidential '97
Eraser '96
The People vs. Larry Flynt '96
Star Trek: First Contact '96
Babe '95
The Man with Two Brains '83

Vaughn Cromwell
Street Wars '91

Gail Cronauer
The Newton Boys '97

David Cronenberg
Resurrection '99
Last Night '98

Laurel Cronin
Beethoven '92

Paul Cronin
Children Shouldn't Play with
Dead Things '72

Hume Cronyn
Horton Foote's Alone '97
Marvin's Room '96
The Pelican Brief '93
*batteries not included '87
Brewster's Millions '85
Impulse '84
The Parallax View '74
Brute Force '46

Lauri Crook
Without Air '95

Peter Crook
Chaplin '92

Linda Cropper
The Seventh Floor '93

Annette Crosbie
Shooting Fish '98
The Slipper and the Rose '76

Double Dragon '94

Frances Dade
Dracula '31

Willem Dafoe
eXistenZ '99
Lulu on the Bridge '98
New Rose Hotel '98
Affliction '97
Speed 2: Cruise Control '97
The English Patient '96
Clear and Present Danger '94
Light Sleeper '92
Born on the Fourth of July '89
Mississippi Burning '88
Platoon '86
Streets of Fire '84

Jensen Daggett
Asteroid '97

Laila Dagher
Angel in Training '99

Lil Dagover
The Cabinet of Dr. Caligari '19
Spiders '18

Arlene Dahl
Night of the Warrior '91

Elizabeth (E.G.) Daily
Babe: Pig in the City '98 (V)
The Rugrats Movie '98 (V)
Pee-wee's Big Adventure '85
Streets of Fire '84

Robert Dalban
Diabolique '55

Jennifer Dale
Once a Thief '96
Ticket to Heaven '81

Jim Dale
Unidentified Flying Oddball '79

Virginia Dale
Holiday Inn '42

Eileen Daley
Razor Blade Smile '98

Ray Daley
The Thin Red Line '64

Fabienne Dali
Kill, Baby, Kill '66

Tracy Dali
American Streetfighter '96

Marcel Dalio
The Snows of Kilimanjaro '52
Casablanca '42
Grand Illusion '37

Charlene Dallas
Criminal Act '88

Joe Dallesandro
The Limey '99
Bad Love '95
Sunset '88
Andy Warhol's Dracula '74
Andy Warhol's Frankenstein '74
Heat '72
Trash '70
Flesh '68

Abby Dalton
Cyber-Tracker '93

Timothy Dalton
Cleopatra '99
Made Men '99
Last Action Hero '93
The Rocketeer '91
License to Kill '89
Brenda Starr '86
Flash Gordon '80

Roger Daltrey
Like It Is '98

Eileen Daly
Witchcraft 10: Mistress of the Craft '98

Jane Daly
Children Shouldn't Play with Dead Things '72

Timothy Daly
Stephen King's The Storm of the Century '99
From the Earth to the Moon '98
The Associate '96

Tyne Daly
Money Kings '98

Stefania D'Amario
Zombie '80

Bertilla Damas
True Friends '98

Paul D'Amato
The Deer Hunter '78

Leo Damian
Hard Drive '94

Marcus D'Amico
Full Metal Jacket '87

Gabriel Damon
Iron Maze '91
RoboCop 2 '90
The Land Before Time '88 (V)

Matt Damon
Rounders '98
Saving Private Ryan '98
Good Will Hunting '97
John Grisham's The Rainmaker '97
Geronimo: An American Legend '93
School Ties '92

Una Damon
The Truman Show '98

Leora Dana
Tora! Tora! Tora! '70

Malcolm Danare
Godzilla '98

Charles Dance
Hilary and Jackie '98
The Blood Oranges '97
Space Truckers '97
Michael Collins '96
The Surgeon '94
Last Action Hero '93
Alien3 '92
The Phantom of the Opera '90
The Golden Child '86
Plenty '85
For Your Eyes Only (SE) '81

Evan Dando
Reality Bites '94

Lawrence Dane
Bride of Chucky '98

Claire Danes
Brokedown Palace '99
The Mod Squad '99
I Love You, I Love You Not '97
John Grisham's The Rainmaker '97
Les Miserables '97
Polish Wedding '97
U-Turn '97
William Shakespeare's Romeo and Juliet '96
How to Make an American Quilt '95
Little Women '94

Beverly D'Angelo
American History X '98
Vegas Vacation '96

National Lampoon's Christmas Vacation '89
Aria '88
National Lampoon's Vacation '83
Hair '79
Annie Hall '77
The Sentinel '76

Rodney Dangerfield
Meet Wally Sparks '97
Caddyshack '80

Carmel Daniel
The Amazing Transparent Man '60

Jennifer Daniel
The Reptile '66
Kiss of the Vampire '62

Henry Daniell
The Great Dictator '40
The Philadelphia Story '40

Alex Daniels
Cyborg '89

Bebe Daniels
Male and Female '19

Gary Daniels
Cold Harvest '98
Spoiler '98
American Streetfighter 2: The Full Impact '97
American Streetfighter '96
Fist of the North Star '95
Pocket Ninjas '93
City Hunter '92

Jeff Daniels
My Favorite Martian '98
Pleasantville '98
Fly Away Home '96
101 Dalmatians '96
Trial and Error '96
Dumb & Dumber '94
Speed '94
Arachnophobia '90

Marty Daniels
Lady of the Lake '98

Phil Daniels
Meantime '81

William Daniels
Her Alibi '88
Rehearsal for Murder '82
The Blue Lagoon '80
The Parallax View '74

Lisa Daniely
Curse of the Voodoo '64

Alexandra Danilova
Alexander Nevsky '38

Blythe Danner
Forces of Nature '99
The Love Letter '99
The X-Files '98
Mad City '97
Brighton Beach Memoirs '86
The Great Santini '80

Sybil Danning
Amazon Women on the Moon '87

Royal Dano
The Dark Half '91
The Right Stuff '83
Something Wicked This Way Comes '83
The Killer inside Me '76
The Outlaw Josey Wales '76
Big Bad Mama '74

Rami Danon
The Impossible Spy '87

Cesare Danova
National Lampoon's Animal House '78
Mean Streets '73

Joshua Danowsky
A Brother's Kiss '97

Ted Danson
Mumford '99
Saving Private Ryan '98
Made in America '93
Creepshow '82
Body Heat '81

Michael Dante
Naked Kiss '64

Helmut Dantine
The Killer Elite '75
Casablanca '42

Ray Danton
The Longest Day '62

Tony Danza
Love to Kill '97
Last Action Hero '93

Glenn Danzig
The Prophecy 2: Ashtown '97

Allen Danzinger
The Texas Chainsaw Massacre '74

Ingeborga Dapkounaite
Seven Years in Tibet '97

John D'Aquino
The Babysitter's Seduction '96

Patti D'Arbanville
Celebrity '98
The Fan '96
Father's Day '96
Flesh '68

Patrika Darbo
Speed 2: Cruise Control '97

Roy D'Arcy
Revolt of the Zombies '36

Ruth Dardick
Don't Go in the House '80

Dominique Darel
Andy Warhol's Dracula '74

Mireille D'Argent
Requiem for a Vampire '71

Alan Dargin
The Adventures of Priscilla, Queen of the Desert '94

Erika Dario
Rabid Dogs '74

Christopher Dark
Suddenly '54

Jennie Dark
Maniac / Narcotic '34

Candy Darling
Women in Revolt '71
Flesh '68

Jean Darling
March of the Wooden Soldiers '34

Gerard Darmon
Diva '82

Robert Darnell
Christine '84

William Darni
The Reincarnation of Isabel '72

James Darren
The Guns of Navarone '61

Frankie Darro
Forbidden Planet '56

Al Darrouch
Fraternity Demon '92

Jean-Pierre Darroussin
Un Air de Famille '96

Tony Darrow
Analyze This '98
Goodfellas '90

Danny Darst
Cookie's Fortune '99

Jane Darwell
Last Hurrah '58
Gone with the Wind '39

Stacey Dash
Clueless '95

Jean Daste
Grand Illusion '37

Wu Man Dat
Royal Tramp '92

Richard Davalos
Something Wicked This Way Comes '83
Cool Hand Luke '67

Danielle Daven
Rabid Grannies '89

Doris Davenport
The Westerner '40

Harry Davenport
That Uncertain Feeling '41
Gone with the Wind '39
The Hunchback of Notre Dame '39

Jack Davenport
Russell Mulcahy's Tale of the Mummy '99

Milla Davenport
Daddy Long Legs '19

Nigel Davenport
A Christmas Carol '84
Chariots of Fire '81
Nighthawks '81
The Last Valley '71
Royal Hunt of the Sun '69
Peeping Tom '60

Robert Davi
An Occasional Hell '96
License to Kill '89
Die Hard '88

Angel David
The Substitute 2: School's Out '97
The Crow '93

Eleanor David
Pink Floyd: The Wall '82

Ellen David
Random Encounter '98

Elliot David
Play Time '94

Keith David
Armageddon '98
There's Something about Mary '98
Todd McFarlane's Spawn '97 (V)
Volcano '97
Clockers '95
Dead Presidents '95
The Quick and the Dead '94
Final Analysis '92
Marked for Death '90
Always '89
They Live '88
Platoon '86
The Thing '82

Thayer David
The Eiger Sanction '75

Lolita (David) Davidovich
Gods and Monsters '98
Santa Fe '97
Now and Then '95
Boiling Point '93
Raising Cain '92
JFK '91

Keith Diamond
Dr. Giggles '92

Neil Diamond
The Jazz Singer '80

Reed Edward Diamond
Memphis Belle '90

Selma Diamond
All of Me '84

Cameron Diaz
Being John Malkovich '99
Fear and Loathing in Las
 Vegas '98
There's Something about
 Mary '98
Very Bad Things '98
A Life Less Ordinary '97
My Best Friend's Wedding '97
Feeling Minnesota '96
Keys to Tulsa '96
The Mask '94

Guillermo Diaz
200 Cigarettes '98
Half-Baked '97
Stonewall '95

Maria Diaz
Extramarital '98

Tony DiBenedetto
Gloria '98
Someone to Watch Over Me
 '87
Exterminator '80

Leonardo DiCaprio
Celebrity '98
The Man in the Iron Mask '98
Titanic '97
Marvin's Room '96
William Shakespeare's
 Romeo and Juliet '96
Total Eclipse '95
The Basketball Diaries '94
The Quick and the Dead '94

George DiCenzo
About Last Night . . . '86

Bobby DiCicco
Splash '84
Night Shift '82
The Big Red One '80
1941 '79

Andy Dick
Inspector Gadget '99
The Lion King: Simba's Pride
 '98 (V)
The Cable Guy '96

Kim Dickens
Mercury Rising '98
Great Expectations '97
Truth or Consequences, N.M.
 '97
Zero Effect '97

George Dickerson
After Dark, My Sweet '90

James Dickey
Deliverance '72

Paul Dickey
Robin Hood '22

Olga Dickie
Kiss of the Vampire '62

Angie Dickinson
Big Bad Mama '74

John Diehl
Anywhere But Here '99
Monument Ave. '98
A Time to Kill '96
Stargate '94
Falling Down '93
Mikey '92
National Lampoon's Vacation
 '83

Vin Diesel
Iron Giant '99 (V)

Saving Private Ryan '98

Gustav Diesl
Pandora's Box '28

Bo Dietle
The Curve '97

Daniel Dietrich
Dawn of the Dead '78

Marlene Dietrich
The Love Goddesses '65

Max Dietze
Metropolis '26

Anton Diffring
Little Mother '71
Fahrenheit 451 '66

Uschi Digart
Kentucky Fried Movie '77

Taye Diggs
The Best Man '99
Go '99
House on Haunted Hill '99
How Stella Got Her Groove
 Back '98

Arthur Dignam
Gods and Monsters '98

Frank DiLeo
Goodfellas '90

Mimi Dillard
The Manchurian Candidate
 '62

Victoria Dillard
The Best Man '99
Deep Cover '92
Ricochet '91

Phyllis Diller
A Bug's Life (CE) '98 (V)

Bradford Dillman
Piranha '78

Brandan Dillon
The Killing of Sister George
 '69

Kevin Dillon
True Crime '95
No Escape '94
The Doors '91
Platoon '86

Matt Dillon
There's Something about
 Mary '98
Wild Things '98
In and Out '97
Albino Alligator '96
Beautiful Girls '96
Grace of My Heart (CE) '96
To Die For '95
Mr. Wonderful '93
Singles '92
Drugstore Cowboy '89
The Flamingo Kid '84
The Outsiders '83
Rumble Fish '83
Tex '82

Melinda Dillon
How to Make an American
 Quilt '95
A Christmas Story '83
Absence of Malice '81
Slap Shot '77

Paul Dillon
Austin Powers: International
 Man of Mystery '97

Tom Dillon
Night Tide '63

Paul Dinello
Plump Fiction '97

Charles Dingle
The Little Foxes '41

Mihai Dinvale
Bloodstorm: Subspecies 4
 '98

Silvia Dionisio
Andy Warhol's Dracula '74

Bob Dishy
Don Juan DeMarco '94
Brighton Beach Memoirs '86

Teresa Dispina
The Big Squeeze '96

Andrew Divoff
Wishmaster 2: Evil Never
 Dies '98
Wishmaster '97
Xtro 3: Watch the Skies '95
Interceptor '92

Robert Dix
Forbidden Planet '56

Jason Dixie
In the Company of Men '96

Madhuri Dixit
Koyla '98

Donna Dixon
Spies Like Us '85

Ivan Dixon
Car Wash '76

James Dixon
Q (The Winged Serpent) '82

Jill Dixon
A Night to Remember '58

MacIntyre Dixon
Funny Farm '88

Steve Dixon
Mosquito '95

Willie Dixon
Robbie Robertson: Going
 Home '98

Omid Djalili
The Mummy '99

Badja Djola
Rosewood '96
Mississippi Burning '88
The Serpent and the Rainbow
 '87
Penitentiary '79

Michal Dlouhy
Lady Macbeth of Mtsensk
 '92

Shae D'Lyn
Vegas Vacation '96
Bury Me in Niagara '93

DMX
Belly '98

Wayne Doba
The Funhouse '81

Sam Dobbins
Smart Money '97

Lawrence (Larry) Dobkin
Patton '70

Kevin Dobson
Midway '76

Kevin J. Dobson
For Love of a Child '90

Peter Dobson
Wicked Ways '99
The Dig Squeeze '96
The Frighteners '96

Tamara Dobson
Cleopatra Jones '73

Vernon Dobtcheff
Hilary and Jackie '98

K.K. Dodds
Soldier '98
A Life Less Ordinary '97

Megan Dodds
Ever After: A Cinderella Story
 '98
The Rat Pack '98

Jack Dodson
The Getaway '72

John Doe
Brokedown Palace '99
Forces of Nature '99
The Rage: Carrie 2 '99
Highway Hitcher '98
Black Circle Boys '97
Boogie Nights '97
Georgia '95
Pure Country '92

Darrick Doerner
In God's Hands '98

Matt Doherty
So I Married an Axe Murderer
 '93
The Mighty Ducks '92

Shannen Doherty
Mallrats '95
Heathers '89
Night Shift '82

Michael Dolan
The Turning '92
Hamburger Hill '87

Bob Dole
Over the Wire '95

Guy Doleman
The Ipcress File '65
Thunderball '65

Jessica Dollarhide
Castle Freak '95

Arielle Dombasle
Around the World in 80 Days
 '89
Le Beau Mariage '82

Richard Domeier
Evil Dead 2: Dead by Dawn
 '87

Placido Domingo
La Traviata '82

Arturo Dominici
Black Sunday '60

Germana Dominici
Black Sunday '60

Dominique
Requiem for a Vampire '71
The Shiver of the Vampires
 '70

Elinor Donahue
Freddy's Dead: The Final
 Nightmare '91
Pretty Woman '90

Heather Donahue
The Blair Witch Project (SE)
 '99

Troy Donahue
American Rampage '89

James Donald
Royal Hunt of the Sun '69
Quatermass and the Pit '67
The Great Escape '63

Arthur Donaldson
America '24

Norma Donaldson
Poetic Justice '93

Peter Donaldson
The Sweet Hereafter '96

Peter Donat
The Game '97
Red Corner '97
School Ties '92
The China Syndrome '79

Robert Donat
The 39 Steps '35

Michael Donavan
America '24

Len Doncheff
Moving Target '96

Jason Done
Merlin '98

Chad E. Donella
Disturbing Behavior '98

Brian Donlevy
Big Combo '55
Impact '49

Mike Donlin
The General '26

Steve Donmyer
Glitch! '88

**Barnard Pierre
Donnadieu**
The Vanishing '88
The Return of Martin Guerre
 '83

Donal Donnelly
This Is My Father '99
Mesmer '94

Robert Donner
Cool Hand Luke '67

Eddy Donno
The Green Berets '68

Joseph D'Onofrio
A Bronx Tale '93
Goodfellas '90

Vincent D'Onofrio
The Thirteenth Floor '99
Boys Life 2 '98
The Newton Boys '97
Feeling Minnesota '96
Good Luck '96
Strange Days '95
Mr. Wonderful '93
The Player '92
JFK '91
Adventures in Babysitting '87
Full Metal Jacket '87

Amanda Donohoe
I'm Losing You '98
One Night Stand '97
Liar Liar '96
The Lair of the White Worm
 '88

Elisa Donovan
A Night at the Roxbury '98
Clueless '95

King Donovan
Invasion of the Body Snatch-
 ers '56
Singin' in the Rain '52

Martin Donovan
Heaven '99
Living Out Loud '98
Opposite of Sex '98
Portrait of a Lady '96

Robert Donovan
Curse of the Puppet Master:
 The Human Experiment '98

Tate Donovan
Hercules '97 (V)
Murder at 1600 '97
Memphis Belle '90
Dead Bang '89
Clean and Sober '88

Terence Donovan
Breaker Morant '80

James Doohan
Bug Buster '99
UFOs Above and Beyond '97
 (N)
Star Trek: Generations '94

National Lampoon's Loaded
 Weapon 1 '93
Star Trek 6: The Undiscov-
 ered Country '91
Star Trek 5: The Final Frontier
 '89
Star Trek 4: The Voyage
 Home '86

Paul Dooley
Guinevere '99
Happy, Texas '99
Telling Lies in America '96
The Underneath '95
Evolver '94
Monster in the Closet '86
Sixteen Candles '84

John Doolittle
The Clan of the Cave Bear
 '86

Robert DoQui
RoboCop '87

Allen Doraine
Boys Life 2 '98

Ann Doran
Rebel without a Cause '55
Meet John Doe '41
Penny Serenade '41

Bruce Doran
Black Eagle '88

Matt Doran
The Matrix '99

Stephen Dorff
Earthly Possessions '99
Blade '98
Space Truckers '97
Judgment Night '93
The Power of One '92

Doria
Night Calls: The Movie 2 '99
Night Calls: The Movie '98

Max Dorian
The Reincarnation of Isabel
 '72

Patrick Shane Dorian
In God's Hands '98

Francoise Dorleac
The Soft Skin '64

Michael Dorn
Star Trek: Insurrection '98
Star Trek: First Contact '96
Star Trek: Generations '94
Star Trek 6: The Undiscov-
 ered Country '91

Stacey Dorning
Terror of Frankenstein '75

Therese Dorny
Diabolique '55

Diana Dors
Oliver Twist '48

Joe Dorsey
Bat 21 '88

Julian Roy Doster
Menace II Society '93

Karen Dotrice
Mary Poppins '64

Roy Dotrice
Amadeus '84

Els Dottermans
Antonia's Line '95

Paul Doucet
America '24

John Doucette
Patton '70

David Douche
The Life of Jesus '96

Doug E. Doug
Cool Runnings '93

Jim Doughan
Stuart Little '99 (V)

Illeana Douglas
Happy, Texas '99
Stir of Echoes '99
Message in a Bottle '98
Sink or Swim '97
Grace of My Heart (CE) '96
Picture Perfect '96
To Die For '95
Goodfellas '90

John Douglas
Violent Zone '89

Kirk Douglas
Greedy '94
Saturn 3 '80
The War Wagon '67
Spartacus '60
Paths of Glory '57
The Strange Love of Martha
 Ivers '46

Mark Douglas
2000 Maniacs '64

Melvyn Douglas
Ghost Story '81
The Candidate '72
That Uncertain Feeling '41
The Old Dark House '32

Michael Douglas
A Perfect Murder '98
The Game '97
The Ghost and the Darkness
 '96
The American President '95
Disclosure '94
Falling Down '93
Basic Instinct '92
Black Rain '89
The China Syndrome '79
Coma '78
Napoleon and Samantha '72

Sarah Douglas
The Demolitionist '95
Voodoo '95
Conan the Destroyer '84

Shirley Douglas
Barney's Great Adventure '98
Dead Ringers '88
Lolita '62

Suzanne Douglas
How Stella Got Her Groove
 Back '98

Robyn Douglass
The Lonely Guy '84

Brenda Doumani
Bug Buster '99
Follow Your Heart '98

Lorenzo Doumani
Misery Brothers Y2K '95

Gary Dourdan
Scarred City '98
Playing God '96

Brad Dourif
The Prophecy 3: The Ascent
 '99
Bride of Chucky '98 (V)
Progeny '98
Senseless '98
Urban Legend '98
Color of Night '94
Jungle Fever '91
Child's Play 2 '90 (V)
Child's Play '88
Mississippi Burning '88
Dune '84
One Flew Over the Cuckoo's
 Nest '75

Alain Doutey
The Big Red One '80

Billie Dove
The Black Pirate '26

Ellen A. Dow
54 '98
The Wedding Singer '97

Graham Dow
Gallipoli '81

Tony Dow
Kentucky Fried Movie '77

Ann Dowd
Apt Pupil '97
Philadelphia '93

Nancy Dowd
Slap Shot '77

Barbara Dowling
Dementia 13 '63

Doris Dowling
Othello '52

Lesley-Anne Down
Family of Cops '95
Death Wish 5: The Face of
 Death '94
The Great Train Robbery '79
The Betsy '78
The Pink Panther Strikes
 Again '76

Robert Downey
Boogie Nights '97

Robert Downey Jr.
Bowfinger '99
In Dreams '98
U.S. Marshals '98
The Gingerbread Man '97
Hugo Pool '97
One Night Stand '97
Only You '94
Restoration '94
Heart and Souls '93
Chaplin '92
Air America '90
Chances Are '89
Weird Science '85

Johnny Downs
March of the Wooden Sol-
 diers '34

Robin Downs
Leaving Scars '97

Jacqueline Doyen
Entre-Nous '83

Maria Doyle Kennedy
The General '98
The Matchmaker '97
The Commitments '91

Brian Doyle-Murray
Stuart Little '99
As Good As It Gets '97
Multiplicity '96
Groundhog Day '93
JFK '91
Ghostbusters 2 '89
National Lampoon's Christ-
 mas Vacation '89
Scrooged '88
Sixteen Candles '84
National Lampoon's Vacation
 '83
Caddyshack '80

Robert Dracup
Don't Look in the Basement
 '73

Willis Draffin
Train Ride to Hollywood '75

Billy Drago
Convict 762 '98
Sci-Fighters '96
Secret Games '92

Jessica Dragonette
Gulliver's Travels '39 (V)

David Drake
Philadelphia '93

Dona Drake
The Road to Morocco '42

Larry Drake
Desert Heat '99
Paranoia '98
Bean '97
Darkman 2: The Return of
 Durant '94
Dr. Giggles '92
Darkman '90

Tom Drake
The Great Rupert '50

Beau Dremann
My Science Project '85

Fran Drescher
This Is Spinal Tap '84

Marie Dressler
Tillie's Punctured Romance
 '14

Valerie Dreville
La Sentinelle '92

Griffin Drew
Friend of the Family '95
Masseuse '95

James Dreyfus
Notting Hill '99

Jean Claude Dreyfus
The City of Lost Children '95

Richard Dreyfuss
Night Falls on Manhattan '96
The American President '95
The Last Word '95
Mr. Holland's Opus '95
Always '89
Stand by Me '86
American Graffiti '73

Burkhard Driest
Cross of Iron '76

Brian Drillinger
Brighton Beach Memoirs '86

Bobby Driscoll
The Fighting Sullivans '42

Delaney Driscoll
Election '99

Robert Drivas
Cool Hand Luke '67

Ian Driver
Moll Flanders '96

Minnie Driver
An Ideal Husband '99
Tarzan '99 (V)
The Governess '98
Good Will Hunting '97
Grosse Pointe Blank '97
Hard Rain '98
Sleepers '96
Big Night '95
Goldeneye '95
Circle of Friends '94

Eileen Dromey
Waking Ned Devine '98

Joanne Dru
Vengeance Valley '51
Red River '48

Alice Drummond
The Love Letter '99

James Drury
The Meanest Men in the
 West '76

Jeanie Drynan
Don's Party '76

Hayley Du Mond
Hunter's Moon '97

Denise DuBarry
Monster in the Closet '86

Jessica Dublin
Troma's War (DC) '88

Marie DuBois
Shoot the Piano Player '62
A Woman Is a Woman '60

Paulette Dubost
The Last Metro '80

Paul Dubov
Shock Corridor '63
Atomic Submarine '59

Kristie Ducati
The Bikini Car Wash Company
 '90

Caroline Ducey
Romance '99

David Duchovny
The X-Files '98
Playing God '96
Kalifornia '93
Beethoven '92
Chaplin '92

Rick Ducommun
Encino Man '92
The 'Burbs '89
Die Hard '88

John Dudgeon
The Old Dark House '32

Michael Dudikoff
Freedom Strike '98
Ringmaster '98
Moving Target '96

Carl Duering
A Clockwork Orange '71

Denice Duff
Bloodstorm: Subspecies 4
 '98

Howard Duff
Monster in the Closet '86
The Naked City '48
Brute Force '46

Nicola Duffett
Howard's End '92

Shay Duffin
Leprechaun '93

Karen Duffy
Dumb & Dumber '94
Reality Bites '94

Thomas F. Duffy
Varsity Blues '99

Dennis Dugan
Happy Gilmore '96
Parenthood '89
Unidentified Flying Oddball
 '79

John Dugan
The Texas Chainsaw Mas-
 sacre '74

Tom Dugan
I've Been Waiting for You '98
Bataan '43

Andrew Duggan
The Bears & I '74

Claire Duhamel
Bed and Board '70

John Duigan
Sirens '94

Olympia Dukakis
Joan of Arc '99
Armistead Maupin's More
 Tales of the City '97
Milk and Money '97
Picture Perfect '97
Mighty Aphrodite '95
Mr. Holland's Opus '95

Stephen Eckholdt
Message in a Bottle '98

James Eckhouse
One True Thing '98
Junior '94

Helen Jerome Eddy
Klondike Annie '36

Herb Edelman
The Naked Truth '92
Wheels on Meals '84

Jerome Eden
Color Me Blood Red '64
2000 Maniacs '64
Blood Feast (SE) '63

Peter Edmund
Full Metal Jacket '87

Beatie Edney
In the Name of the Father '93
Mister Johnson '91
Highlander (DC) '86

Nekohachi Edoya
The Funeral '84

Richard Edson
Lulu on the Bridge '98
An Occasional Hell '96
Bad Love '95
Strange Days '95
Posse '93
Jungle Fever '91
Do the Right Thing '89
Ferris Bueller's Day Off '86
Platoon '86

Annie-Joe Edwards
Bullets over Broadway '94

Anthony Edwards
Playing by Heart '98
The Client '94
Top Gun '86

Bill Edwards
First Man into Space '59

Blake Edwards
Strangler of the Swamp '46

Cliff Edwards
His Girl Friday '40
Gone with the Wind '39

Danny Edwards
Heaven '99

Don Edwards
The Horse Whisperer '97

Eric Edwards
Sgt. Bilko '95

Hilton Edwards
Othello '52

James Edwards
Patton '70
The Manchurian Candidate '62
Pork Chop Hill '59
Men in War '57
The Killing '56

Jennifer Edwards
Sunset '88

Joel J. Edwards
Voodoo '95

Luke Edwards
Mother's Boys '94
Guilty by Suspicion '91

Mark Edwards
Tower of Evil '72

Megan Edwards
Poison Ivy 3: The New Seduction '97

Ronnie Clair Edwards
8 Seconds '94

Snitz Edwards
Battling Butler '26

The Phantom of the Opera '25
Seven Chances '25

Stacy Edwards
The Bachelor '99
Primary Colors '98
In the Company of Men '96

Ted Edwards
Maniac / Narcotic '34

Vince Edwards
The Fear '94
The Killing '56

Joseph Eero
Igor & the Lunatics '85

Aeryk Egan
Flatliners '90

Peter Egan
Bean '97

Susan Egan
Hercules '97 (V)

Will Egan
Glitch! '88

Julie Ege
The Legend of the 7 Golden Vampires '73

Samantha Eggar
The Astronaut's Wife '99
Hercules '97 (V)
The Phantom '96
Exterminator '80
The Seven-Per-Cent Solution '76

Konstantin Eggert
Aelita: Queen of Mars '24

Nicole Eggert
The Demolitionist '95

Deven Eggleston
New Jersey Drive '95

Stan Egi
Rising Sun '93

Margaret Eginton
Scent of a Woman '92

Jennifer Ehle
Pride and Prejudice '95

Lisa Eichhorn
Goodbye, Lover '99

Christopher Eigeman
The Last Days of Disco '98
Mr. Jealousy '98

Jill Eikenberry
Arthur '81

Lisa Eilbacher
Leviathan '89

Hallie Kate Eisenberg
The Insider '99
Paulie '98

Ned Eisenberg
Last Man Standing '96

Sergei Eisenstein
The Battleship Potemkin '25

Anthony Eisley
Naked Kiss '64

Carmen Ejogo
The Avengers '98
Metro '96

Bengt Ekerot
The Seventh Seal '56

Gosta Ekman
The Inside Man '84

Gosta Ekman
Intermezzo '36

Hasse (Hans) Ekman
Intermezzo '36

Jack Elam
Cannonball Run 2 '84

Dana Elcar
All of Me '84
Condorman '81

Ron Eldard
The Runner '99
Deep Impact '98
Bastard out of Carolina '96
Sleepers '96
Sex and the Other Man '95
Scent of a Woman '92

Carmen Electra
The Chosen One: Legend of the Raven '98

Erika Eleniak
The Pandora Project '98
Tales from the Crypt Presents Bordello of Blood '96
Under Siege '92

John Elerick
Embryo '76

Danny Elfman
The Nightmare before Christmas '93 (V)

Jenna Elfman
EDtv '99
Can't Hardly Wait '98

Alix Elias
True Stories '86
Rock 'n' Roll High School '79

Michel Elias
Time Masters '82 (V)

Mark Eliot
Stand and Deliver '88

Christine Elise
Boiling Point '93
Child's Play 2 '90

Kimberly Elise
Beloved '98
Set It Off '96

Shannon Elizabeth
American Pie (CE) '99

Hector Elizondo
The Other Sister '98
Turbulence '96
Pretty Woman '90
Leviathan '89
The Flamingo Kid '84
American Gigolo '79
Born to Win '71

Kerine Elkins
Sore Losers '97

Stephen Ellen
Rude '96

Yvonne Elliman
Jesus Christ, Superstar '73

Biff Elliot
Pork Chop Hill '59

Alison Elliott
The Eternal Kiss of the Mummy '99
The Wings of the Dove '97
The Underneath '95

Chris Elliott
There's Something about Mary '98
Kingpin '96
Groundhog Day '93
The Abyss (SE) '89

Denholm Elliott
The Hound of the Baskervilles '83
A Bridge Too Far '77

John Elliott
The Wizard of Gore '70

Laura Elliott
Two Lost Worlds '50

Ross Elliott
The Indestructible Man / The Amazing Transparent Man '56

Sam Elliott
The Big Lebowski '97
Tombstone '93
Shakedown '88
Mask '85
The Shadow Riders '82
Butch Cassidy and the Sundance Kid '69

Stephen Elliott
Arthur '81

Tom Elliott
American Rampage '89

Chris Ellis
October Sky '99
Home Fries '98

James Ellis
Priest '94

Tracey Ellis
The Crow 2: City of Angels '96

Max Elloy
Utopia '51

Nicoletta Elmi
Demons '86
Deep Red: Hatchet Murders '75
Andy Warhol's Frankenstein '74

Kareem Elseify
Bikini Hotel '97

Isobel Elsom
Monsieur Verdoux '47

Ben Elton
Much Ado about Nothing '93

Cary Elwes
From the Earth to the Moon '98
Quest for Camelot '98 (V)
Kiss the Girls '97
Liar Liar '96
Twister '96
Dracula '92
Days of Thunder '90
Glory '89
The Princess Bride '87

Kelly Emberg
Dumb Luck in Vegas '97

Ethan (Randall) Embry
Can't Hardly Wait '98
Dancer, Texas—Pop. 81 '98
Disturbing Behavior '98
Vegas Vacation '96
White Squall '96
Evolver '94

Hope Emerson
Adam's Rib '50

Roy Emerton
Henry V '44

Dick Emery
Yellow Submarine '68 (V)

David Emge
Dawn of the Dead '78

Daniel Emilfork
The City of Lost Children '95
The Devil's Nightmare '71

Colette Emmanuelle
The Devil's Nightmare '71

Noah Emmerich
Life '99
Monument Ave. '98
The Truman Show '98
Cop Land '97

Beautiful Girls '96

Fern Emmett
Dead Men Walk / The Monster Maker '43

Sofia Eng
Wild Wild West '99

Roy Engelman
Children Shouldn't Play with Dead Things '72

Audie England
Free Enterprise '98

Bradford English
Capone '89

Hilary English
Project: Eliminator '91

Jessica English
Caress of the Vampire (CE) '96

Zach English
The Real McCoy '93

Robert Englund
Dee Snider's Strangeland '98
Urban Legend '98
Wishmaster '97
Wes Craven's New Nightmare '94
Freddy's Dead: The Final Nightmare '91
A Nightmare on Elm Street 5: Dream Child '89
A Nightmare on Elm Street 4: Dream Master '88
A Nightmare on Elm Street 3: Dream Warriors '87
A Nightmare on Elm Street 2: Freddy's Revenge '85
A Nightmare on Elm Street '84
Eaten Alive '76

Julie Entwisle
Stephen King's The Night Flier '96

Nora Ephron
Crimes & Misdemeanors '89

Omar Epps
In Too Deep '99
The Mod Squad '99
Scream 2 '97

Kathryn Erbe
Stir of Echoes '99

Ethan Erickson
Jawbreaker '98

Leif Erickson
Penitentiary 2 '82
I Saw What You Did '65
Invaders from Mars '53
James Dean Double Feature: Hill Number One / I Am a Fool '51

Alex Erkiletian
Sucker the Vampire '98

R. Lee Ermey
Life '99
Switchback '97
The Frighteners '96
Leaving Las Vegas '95
Seven '95
On Deadly Ground '94
Body Snatchers '93
Sommersby '93
Mississippi Burning '88
Full Metal Jacket '87
Apocalypse Now '79

Homayon Ershadi
The Taste of Cherry '96

Eileen Erskine
Great Expectations '46

Bill Erwin
Chairman of the Board '97

Jill Esmond
Skin Game '31

Bella Esperance
Lady Dragon '92

Roque Espiritu
Bataan '43

Giancarlo Esposito
Big City Blues '99
Phoenix '98
Twilight '98
Nothing to Lose '96
Klash '95
The Usual Suspects '95
Do the Right Thing '89

Jennifer Esposito
The Bachelor '99
Summer of Sam '99
I Still Know What You Did
   Last Summer '98

Michael Esposito
Tender Loving Care '99

Paul Esser
Daughters of Darkness '71

Christine Estabrook
Presumed Innocent '90

Robert Estes
Trapper County War '89

Emilio Estevez
Mission: Impossible '96
Judgment Night '93
National Lampoon's Loaded
   Weapon 1 '93
The Mighty Ducks '92
Young Guns '88
The Breakfast Club '85
Nightmares '83
The Outsiders '83
Tex '82

Joe Estevez
Winner Takes All '98
Werewolf '95
Expert Weapon '93
Soultaker '90

Renee Estevez
Single White Female '92
Heathers '89

Erik Estrada
National Lampoon's Loaded
   Weapon 1 '93
The Naked Truth '92
Alien Seed '89

Art Evans
Metro '96
Trespass '92
Die Hard 2: Die Harder '90

Auriol Evans
Hilary and Jackie '98

Clifford Evans
Kiss of the Vampire '62

Edith Evans
The Slipper and the Rose '76
Tom Jones '63

Evans Evans
Dead Bang '89
Bonnie & Clyde '67

Gene Evans
The Shadow Riders '82
Walking Tall '73
Shock Corridor '63

Josh Evans
The Doors '91
Ricochet '91
Born on the Fourth of July
   '89

Lee Evans
There's Something about
   Mary '98
The Fifth Element '97
Mouse Hunt '97

Maurice Evans
The Jerk '79

Robert Evans
Man of a Thousand Faces
   '57

Troy Evans
The Frighteners '96
The Lawnmower Man '92

Trevor Eve
Dracula '79

Judith Evelyn
The Tingler '59

Chad Everett
Psycho '98

Gina P. Everett
Night Calls: The Movie '98

Rupert Everett
An Ideal Husband '99
Inspector Gadget '99
William Shakespeare's A Mid-
   summer Night's Dream '99
Shakespeare in Love (CS)
   '98
My Best Friend's Wedding '97
Ready to Wear '94

Tom Everett
Air Force One '97
My Fellow Americans '96

Angie Everhart
Another 9 1/2 Weeks '96
Tales from the Crypt Presents
   Bordello of Blood '96
Jade '95

Jason Evers
The Green Berets '68

Pat Evison
Tim '79

Tom Ewell
Adam's Rib '50

Blake Ewing
The Little Rascals '94

Richard Eyer
The Seventh Voyage of Sinbad '58

Peter Eyre
Dangerous Beauty '98
Orlando '92

Maynard Eziashi
Ace Ventura: When Nature
   Calls '95
Mister Johnson '91

Jacques Fabbri
Diva '82

Matthew Faber
Welcome to the Dollhouse
   '95

Fabian
The Longest Day '62

Francoise Fabian
My Night at Maud's '69

Joel Fabiani
Snake Eyes '98

Pierre Fabre
Bed and Board '70

Aldo Fabrizi
Open City '45

Peter Facinelli
Can't Hardly Wait '98
Dancer, Texas—Pop. 81 '98

Bill Fagerbakke
Stephen King's The Stand
   '94

Jeff Fahey
Johnny 2.0 '99
Extramarital '98

When Justice Fails '98
The Lawnmower Man '92
Iron Maze '91
Out of Time '90
Psycho 3 '86

Douglas Fairbanks Sr.
The Black Pirate '26
Robin Hood '22
The Three Musketeers '21
Mark of Zorro '20

Douglas Fairbanks Jr.
Ghost Story '81

Craig Fairbrass
Cliffhanger '93

Morgan Fairchild
Holy Man '98
Pee-wee's Big Adventure '85

Virginia Brown Faire
Peter Pan '24

Michael Fairman
Forces of Nature '99

Donald Adeosun Faison
Supreme Sanction '99
Clueless '95
New Jersey Drive '95

Frankie Faison
The Thomas Crown Affair '99
Sommersby '93
Do the Right Thing '89
Coming to America '88
Mississippi Burning '88

Marianne Faithfull
The Girl on a Motorcycle '68

Eduardo Fajardo
Lisa and the Devil / The
   House of Exorcism '75
Django '68

Edie Falco
Cop Land '97
Cost of Living '97
A Price above Rubies '97

Gerard Falconetti
Claire's Knee '71

**Renee (Marie)
Falconetti**
Passion of Joan of Arc '28

Lisanne Falk
Shattered Image '98
Heathers '89

Peter Falk
Money Kings '98
The Player '92
The Princess Bride '87

Kasey Fallo
King Cobra '98

Siobhan Fallon
The Negotiator '98

Siu-wong Fan
Supercop 2 '93

Terry Fan
Dragons of the Orient '88

Jamaa Fanaka
Penitentiary '79

Al Fann
Parasite '82

Rio Fanning
Priest '94

Stephanie Faracy
The Great Outdoors '88

Daniel Faraldo
Above the Law '88

Debrah Farentino
Stephen King's The Storm of
   the Century '99
Bugsy '91
Capone '89

James Farentino
Bulletproof '96
Her Alibi '88
A Summer to Remember '84

Antonio Fargas
Milo '98
Shakedown '88
Firestarter '84
Car Wash '76

Dennis Farina
The Mod Squad '99
Out of Sight '98
Saving Private Ryan '98
Eddie '96
That Old Feeling '96
Get Shorty '95
Striking Distance '93
Midnight Run '88
Thief '81

Chris Farley
Dirty Work '97
Beverly Hills Ninja '96
Tommy Boy '95
Billy Madison '94

Jim Farley
The General '26

Bill Farmer
An Extremely Goofy Movie
   '99 (V)

Frances Farmer
Come and Get It '36

Gary Farmer
Smoke Signals '98
Tales from the Crypt Presents
   Demon Knight '94

Mimsy Farmer
Autopsy '78

Suzan Farmer
Dracula, Prince of Darkness
   '66
Rasputin the Mad Monk '66

Vera Farmiga
Return to Paradise '98

Ellen Farner
Umbrellas of Cherbourg '64

Richard Farnsworth
Havana '90
The Two Jakes '90

William Farnum
Jack & the Beanstalk '52

Jamie Farr
Scrooged '88
Cannonball Run 2 '84

Mike Farrell
Prime Suspect '82

Nicholas Farrell
Legionnaire '98

Timothy Farrell
Jail Bait '54
Glen or Glenda? '53

Tom Rils Farrell
Scent of a Woman '92

Moya Farrelly
This Is My Father '99

Patrick Farrelly
Exterminator '80

Mia Farrow
Miami Rhapsody '95
Crimes & Misdemeanors '89

Tisa Farrow
Zombie '80

Brigitte Fassbaender
Werther '88

Fat Joe
Urban Menace '99

Dan Fauci
Bloodsucking Freaks '75

Edward Faulkner
The Green Berets '68

James Faulkner
A Kid in Aladdin's Palace '97
Guinevere '93

Jon Favreau
Deep Impact '98
Very Bad Things '98
Swingers '96
Batman Forever '95

Farrah Fawcett
The Apostle '97
Saturn 3 '80
Logan's Run '76

Greg Fawcett
Sucker the Vampire '98

Frank Faylen
It's a Wonderful Life '46
Gone with the Wind '39

Ron Fazio
The Toxic Avenger, Part 2 '89

Hugh Feagin
Don't Look in the Basement
   '73

Michael Feast
Velvet Goldmine '98

Susan Featherly
Awakening of Gabriella '99

Angela Featherstone
Palmetto '98
200 Cigarettes '98
Con Air '97
The Wedding Singer '97
Zero Effect '97
Family of Cops '95

Jan Fedder
Das Boot (DC) '81

Melinda Fee
Fade to Black '80

Friedrich Feher
The Cabinet of Dr. Caligari
   '19

Oded Fehr
The Mummy '99

Harry Feist
Open City '45

Fritz Feld
History of the World: Part 1
   '81

Eric Feldary
For Whom the Bell Tolls '43

Clarence Felder
The Hidden '87

Andrea Feldman
Heat '72
Trash '70

Corey Feldman
Red Line '96
Tales from the Crypt Presents
   Bordello of Blood '96
Voodoo '95
Lipstick Camera '93
National Lampoon's Loaded
   Weapon 1 '93
The 'Burbs '89
The Lost Boys '87
Stand by Me '86
Gremlins '84

Marty Feldman
Young Frankenstein '74

Tovah Feldshuh
The Corruptor '99
A Walk on the Moon '99
Brewster's Millions '85

Jose Feliciano
Fargo '96

Norman Fell
The Naked Truth '92
With Friends Like These '90
Bullitt '68
Pork Chop Hill '59

Julian Fellowes
Damage '92

Rockliffe Fellowes
Monkey Business '31

Tom Felton
The Borrowers '97

Liu Zi Feng
The Red Violin '98

Zhang Fengyi
Temptation of a Monk '94
Farewell My Concubine '93

Lev Fenin
Alexander Nevsky '38

Tanya Fenmore
My Stepmother Is an Alien '88

Sherilyn Fenn
Just Write '97

Lance Fenton
Heathers '89

Simon Fenton
Matinee '92

Colm Feore
The Insider '99
Stephen King's The Storm of the Century '99
City of Angels '98
The Red Violin '98
Critical Care '97
Face/Off '97
Night Falls on Manhattan '96

Colin Ferguson
Opposite of Sex '98
Armistead Maupin's More Tales of the City '97

Matthew Ferguson
Lilies '96

Sandra Ferguson
Interlocked '98

Colin Fernandes
An American Werewolf in London '81

Abel Fernandez
Pork Chop Hill '59

Emilio Fernandez
The Wild Bunch '69

Juan Fernandez
Fire on the Amazon '93

Wilhelmenia Wiggins Fernandez
Diva '82

Abel Ferrara
Ms. 45 '81
Driller Killer '74

Rebecca Ferratti
Hard Vice '94

Michelle Ferre
Jackie Chan's Who Am I '98

Conchata Ferrell
My Fellow Americans '96
True Romance '93

Tyra Ferrell
Poetic Justice '93
Boyz N the Hood '91
Jungle Fever '91

Will Ferrell
Austin Powers 2: The Spy Who Shagged Me '99

A Night at the Roxbury '98
Austin Powers: International Man of Mystery '97

Andrea Ferreol
The Phantom of the Opera '90
Francesco '89
A Zed & Two Noughts '88
The Last Metro '80
Tin Drum '79

Jose Ferrer
Dune '84
The Sentinel '76
The Caine Mutiny '54

Leilani Sarelle Ferrer
Basic Instinct '92

Mel Ferrer
Eaten Alive '76
The Longest Day '62

Miguel Ferrer
Mulan '98 (V)
Mr. Magoo '97
Stephen King's The Night Flier '96
Stephen King's The Stand '94
Point of No Return '93
The Guardian '90
Revenge '90
RoboCop '87

Marco Ferreri
Don't Touch the White Woman! '74

Martin Ferrero
Gods and Monsters '98

Claudia Ferri
The Assignment '97

Babette Ferrier
Chloe in the Afternoon '72

Lou Ferrigno
The Naked Truth '92

Pam Ferris
Matilda '96
Meantime '81

Dan Ferro
Sgt. Bilko '95

Turi Ferro
Seduction of Mimi '72

Larry Fessenden
Habit '97

Mark Feuerstein
The Muse '99

Peggy Feury
All of Me '84

William Fichtner
Go '99
Armageddon '98
Contact '97
Switchback '97
Albino Alligator '96
Heat '95
Strange Days '95
The Underneath '95
Virtuosity '95

John Fiedler
Sharky's Machine '81

Arabella Field
Godzilla '98
Dante's Peak '97
The Pompatus of Love '95

Betty Field
The Southerner '45
Of Mice and Men '39

Bobby Field
Godmoney '99

Chelsea Field
Tom Clancy's Netforce '98
Extreme Justice '93

The Dark Half '91
The Last Boy Scout '91

Karen Field
The Alley Cats '65

Sally Field
Mrs. Doubtfire '93
Absence of Malice '81
Hooper '78
Smokey and the Bandit '77

Shirley Anne Field
Peeping Tom '60

Todd Field
Eyes Wide Shut '99
The Haunting '99
Stranger than Fiction '99

Christopher John Fields
Alien3 '92

Holly Fields
Wishmaster 2: Evil Never Dies '98

Suzanne Fields
Flesh Gordon '72

Tony Fields
Across the Moon '94

W.C. Fields
Sally of the Sawdust '25

Joseph Fiennes
Elizabeth '98
Shakespeare in Love (CS) '98
The Very Thought of You '98

Ralph Fiennes
The Avengers '98
Prince of Egypt '98 (V)
The English Patient '96
Strange Days '95
Quiz Show '94

Harvey Fierstein
Mulan '98 (V)
Kull the Conqueror '97
Independence Day '96
Bullets over Broadway '94
Mrs. Doubtfire '93

Mike Figgis
One Night Stand '97

Jean-Luke Figueroa
Gloria '98

Marc Figueroa
Capone '89

Kaisa Figura
Ready to Wear '94

Dennis Fimple
King Kong '76

Peter Finch
Network '76

Fyvush Finkel
Q & A '90

Frank Finlay
Lifeforce '85
A Christmas Carol '84
The Four Musketeers '75
The Three Musketeers '74

James Finlayson
The Flying Deuces / Utopia '39

Cameron Finley
Hope Floats '98
Leave It to Beaver '97

Karen Finley
Philadelphia '93

William Finley
The Funhouse '81
Eaten Alive '76

Frank Finn
Avenging Disco Godfather '76

John Finn
Atomic Train '99
Turbulence '96
Glory '89

Dave Finnegan
The Commitments '91

Warren Finnerty
Easy Rider '69
Cool Hand Luke '67

Albert Finney
Tom Jones '63

Allen Finzat
For the Love of Benji '77

Elena Fiore
Seven Beauties '76
Seduction of Mimi '72

Linda Fiorentino
Jade '95
Queens Logic '91
Vision Quest '85

Christine Firkins
Speed 2: Cruise Control '97

Colin Firth
My Life So Far '98
Shakespeare in Love (CS) '98
A Thousand Acres '97
The English Patient '96
Pride and Prejudice '95
Circle of Friends '94

Peter Firth
Mighty Joe Young '98
Shadowlands '93
The Hunt for Red October '90
Lifeforce '85

Kate Fischer
Sirens '94

Margarita Fischer
Uncle Tom's Cabin '27

Nancy Fish
Death Becomes Her '92

Laurence "Larry" Fishburne
The Matrix '99
Event Horizon '97
Fled '96
Just Cause '94
What's Love Got to Do with It? '93
Deep Cover '92
Boyz N the Hood '91
Red Heat '88
A Nightmare on Elm Street 3: Dream Warriors '87
Apocalypse Now '79

Carrie Fisher
Austin Powers: International Man of Mystery '97
The 'Burbs '89
Amazon Women on the Moon '87
The Blues Brothers (CE) '80

Eddie Fisher
All About Eve '50

Frances Fisher
Titanic '97
Wild America '97
Unforgiven '92

Jasen Fisher
The Witches '90

Jodie Fisher
Body of Influence 2 '96

Joely Fisher
Inspector Gadget '99

Lewis Fitz-Gerald
Breaker Morant '80

Marsha Fitzalan
An Ideal Husband '99

Barry Fitzgerald
The Quiet Man '52
The Naked City '48
And Then There Were None '45
Going My Way / Holiday Inn '44

Ciaran Fitzgerald
The General '98
The Boxer '97

Geraldine Fitzgerald
Arthur '81
Dark Victory '39
Wuthering Heights '39

Gerry Fitzgerald
Baby Geniuses '98

Glenn Fitzgerald
The Sixth Sense '99
A Price above Rubies '97
Flirting with Disaster '95

Leo Fitzgerald
Baby Geniuses '98

Myles Fitzgerald
Baby Geniuses '98

Tara Fitzgerald
New World Disorder '99
Brassed Off '96
The Englishman Who Went up a Hill But Came down a Mountain '95
Sirens '94

Charles Fitzpatrick
Badlands '74

Gabrielle Fitzpatrick
Desert Heat '99
Mr. Nice Guy '98

Jim Fitzpatrick
Operation Delta Force 3: Clear Target '98

Leo Fitzpatrick
Kids '95

Paul Fix
Shoot Out '71
To Kill a Mockingbird '62
Red River '48

Joe Flaherty
Happy Gilmore '96
Heavy Metal '81 (V)
Stripes '81
1941 '79

Lanny Flaherty
Home Fries '98
Sommersby '93

Pat Flaherty
The Red House '47

Georges Flament
The 400 Blows '59

Fionnula Flanagan
Waking Ned Devine '98

Ed Flanders
Salem's Lot '79

Keeley Flanders
Hilary and Jackie '98

Sean Patrick Flanery
Simply Irresistible '99
Eden '98
Suicide Kings '97
Powder '95
Guinevere '93

Joe Flanigan
The Other Sister '98

Barry Flatman
Random Encounter '98

Flea
Fear and Loathing in Las Vegas '98
The Big Lebowski '97

Sidney Fox
Midnight '34

Virginia Fox
College '27
Seven Chances '25
Three Ages '23

Vivica A. Fox
Teaching Mrs. Tingle '99
Why Do Fools Fall in Love? '98
Batman and Robin '97
Soul Food '97
Booty Call '96
Independence Day '96
Set It Off '96
Born on the Fourth of July '89

Robert Foxworth
The Invisible Strangler '76

Jamie Foxx
The Players Club '98
Booty Call '96

Eddie Foy Jr.
The Pajama Game '57

Tracy Fraim
Fear '96

James Frain
Elizabeth '98
Hilary and Jackie '98

Jonathon Frakes
Star Trek: Insurrection '98
Star Trek: First Contact '96
Star Trek: Generations '94

David Fralick
Uncle Sam '96

C.V. France
Skin Game '31

Dawson France
Winstanley '75

Richard France
Dawn of the Dead '78

Tan Hung Francione
Full Metal Jacket '87

Anthony (Tony) Franciosa
City Hall '95

Anne Francis
Pancho Villa '72
Forbidden Planet '56

Derek Francis
Rasputin the Mad Monk '66

Kay Francis
The Cocoanuts '29

Linda Francis
Naked Kiss '64

Paul Francis
Warlock 3: The End of Innocence '98

Robert Francis
The Caine Mutiny '54

Don Francks
Heavy Metal '81 (V)

Jess (Jesus) Franco
Two Undercover Angels '68

Larry Franco
They Live '88

Emile Francois
Sense and Sensibility '95

Ben Frank
Don't Answer the Phone '80

Charles Frank
The Right Stuff '83

Dan Frank
The Price of Desire '96

Diana Frank
Eye of the Serpent '92

Jerry Frank
The Big Doll House '71

Al Franken
From the Earth to the Moon '98

Aretha Franklin
The Blues Brothers 2000 '98
The Blues Brothers (CE) '80

Don Franklin
Asteroid '97

John Franklin
Children of the Corn 666: Isaac's Return '99

Sidney Franklin
The Three Musketeers '21

William Franklyn
The Satanic Rites of Dracula '73

Chloe Franks
The Littlest Horse Thieves '76

Arthur Franz
Atomic Submarine '59
The Caine Mutiny '54
Invaders from Mars '53
Sands of Iwo Jima '49

Dennis Franz
City of Angels '98
Dr. Dolittle '98 (V)
The Player '92
Die Hard 2: Die Harder '90
Kiss Shot '89
Body Double '84
Psycho 2 '83

Elizabeth Franz
Stephen King's Thinner '96

Brendan Fraser
Dudley Do-Right '99
The Mummy '99
Blast from the Past '98
Gods and Monsters '98
George of the Jungle '97
The Twilight of the Golds '97
Now and Then '95
With Honors '94
Encino Man '92
School Ties '92

Curtis Fraser
Black Cat '91

Duncan Fraser
Timecop '94

Hugh Fraser
The Draughtsman's Contract '82

Phyllis Fraser
Winds of the Wasteland / The Lucky Texan '36

Ronald Fraser
The Killing of Sister George '69

William Frawley
Miracle on 34th Street '47
Monsieur Verdoux '47

Robert Frazer
The White Zombie '32

Joe Frazier
Just the Ticket '98

Dana Fredsti
Princess Warrior '90

Bert Freed
Billy Jack '71
Paths of Glory '57

Sam Freed
Stephen King's Thinner '96

Jill Freedman
Mother's Boys '94

Al Freeman Jr.
Down in the Delta '98
Once Upon a Time . . . When We Were Colored '95

Bill Freeman
Basket Case '82

J.E. Freeman
Go '99
Mother's Boys '94

K. Todd Freeman
Grosse Pointe Blank '97

Kathleen Freeman
The Blues Brothers 2000 '98
Dragnet '87
The Blues Brothers (CE) '80

Mike Freeman
The Killing of Sister George '69

Morgan Freeman
Deep Impact '98
Amistad '97
Hard Rain '97
Kiss the Girls '97
Seven '95
Outbreak '94
The Shawshank Redemption '94
The Power of One '92
Unforgiven '92
Robin Hood: Prince of Thieves '91
The Bonfire of the Vanities '90
Driving Miss Daisy '89
Glory '89
Lean on Me '89
Clean and Sober '88

Paul Freeman
Double Team '97
The Long Good Friday '80

Paul Frees
Suddenly '54
The War of the Worlds '53

Ace Frehley
Detroit Rock City '99

Robert Freitag
The Great Escape '63

Phyllis Frelich
Santa Fe '97

Dawn French
Treasure Island '97 (V)

Leigh French
Aloha, Bobby and Rose '74

Victor French
Choices '81

Pierre Fresnay
Grand Illusion '37
The Man Who Knew Too Much '34

Bernard Fresson
Honor Among Thieves '68

Matt Frewer
Hercules '97 (V)
Stephen King's The Stand '94
Monty Python's The Meaning of Life '83

Glenn Frey
Jerry Maguire '96

Leonard Frey
Fiddler on the Roof '71

Brenda Fricker
The Wicked, Wicked West '97
A Time to Kill '96
So I Married an Axe Murderer '93

Home Alone 2: Lost in New York '92
The Field '90
My Left Foot '89

Gavin Friday
Creepers '85

David Friedman
Blood Feast (SE) '63

Matthew Friedman
Private Parts '96

Peter Friedman
Single White Female '92
The Seventh Sign '88

John Friedrich
The Boy in the Plastic Bubble '76

Anna Friel
William Shakespeare's A Midsummer Night's Dream '99
Rogue Trader '98

Colin Friels
Dark City '97
Darkman '90

Arno Frisch
Funny Games '97

Roger Fritz
Cross of Iron '76

Gert Frobe
Chitty Chitty Bang Bang '68
Goldfinger '64
The Longest Day '62

Gustav Froehlich
Metropolis '26

Sadie Frost
Dracula '92

Terry Frost
The Flying Serpent '55
The Monster Maker '44

Catherine Frot
Un Air de Famille '96

Toby Froud
Labyrinth '86

Stephen Fry
Spice World: The Movie '97

Taylor Fry
A Little Princess '95

Dwight Frye
Dead Men Walk / The Monster Maker '43
The Bride of Frankenstein '35
Dracula '31
Frankenstein '31

Soleil Moon Frye
I've Been Waiting for You '98
Motel Blue '98
Piranha '95

Steve Frye
The Horse Whisperer '97

Bonnie Fu
Full Contact '92

Gaby Fuchs
Mark of the Devil '69

Miguel Angel Fuentes
Fitzcarraldo '82

Tatsuya Fuji
In the Realm of Passion '80
In the Realm of the Senses '76

Kahori Fujii
Tokyo Fist '96

Yu Fujiki
Godzilla vs. Mothra '64

Hiroshi Fujioka
In the Line of Duty 3 '88

Susumu Fujita
The Human Condition: Road to Eternity '59

Kamatari Fujiwara
Seven Samurai '54

Kei Fujiwara
Tetsuo: The Iron Man '92

Christopher Fulford
Moll Flanders '96

Dolores Fuller
Bride of the Monster '55
Jail Bait '54
Glen or Glenda? '53

Jonathan Fuller
Castle Freak '95

Penny Fuller
Cat on a Hot Tin Roof '84
All the President's Men '76

Robert Fuller
Maverick '94

Samuel Fuller
1941 '79
Pierrot le Fou '65

Christina Fulton
Hard Drive '94

Jessie Lee Fulton
Don't Look in the Basement '73

Bo-Bo Fung
C'est la Vie, Mon Cherie '93

John Furey
Friday the 13th, Part 2 '81

Edward Furlong
Detroit Rock City '99
American History X '98
Pecker '98
Last Action Hero '93
Terminator 2: Judgment Day '91

Stephen Furst
National Lampoon's Animal House '78

George Furth
Goodbye, Lover '99
The Man with Two Brains '83
Butch Cassidy and the Sundance Kid '69

Dan Futterman
Shooting Fish '98
The Birdcage '95

Herbert Fux
Mark of the Devil '69

Jim Fyfe
The Frighteners '96

Richard Gabai
Sexual Roulette '96

Martin Gabel
James Dean Story '57 (N)

Jean Gabin
Any Number Can Win '63
Grand Illusion '37

Christopher Gable
The Lair of the White Worm '88
The Slipper and the Rose '76

Clark Gable
Gone with the Wind '39
It Happened One Night '34

June Gable
Brenda Starr '86

Eva Gabor
Gigi '58
The Last Time I Saw Paris '54

George Gaynes
Police Academy '84
Trilogy of Terror '75

Janet Gaynor
A Star Is Born '37

Mitzi Gaynor
South Pacific '58

Eunice Gayson
From Russia with Love '63
Dr. No (SE) '62

Wendy Gazelle
The Net '95

Ben Gazzara
Summer of Sam '99
The Thomas Crown Affair '99
Happiness '98
The Big Lebowski '97
Buffalo 66 '97
Protector '97
The Spanish Prisoner '97
Tales of Ordinary Madness '83
Opening Night '77

Anthony Geary
Night of the Warrior '91

Bud Geary
Bataan '43

Cynthia Geary
Smoke Signals '98
The Killing Grounds '97
8 Seconds '94

Karl Geary
The Eternal Kiss of the Mummy '99

Maine Geary
Robin Hood '22

Jason Gedrick
The Last Don '97
Backdraft '91

Ellen Geer
Neil Simon's The Odd Couple 2 '98

Will Geer
Jeremiah Johnson '72
Napoleon and Samantha '72
Salt of the Earth '54

Judy Geeson
Horror Planet '80

Martha Gehman
Father of the Bride '91
The Flamingo Kid '84

Bob Geldof
Spice World: The Movie '97
Pink Floyd: The Wall '82

Sarah Michelle Gellar
Simply Irresistible '99
Cruel Intentions '98
Small Soldiers '98 (V)
I Know What You Did Last Summer '97
Scream 2 '97

Laura Gemser
Emmanuelle: Queen of the Desert '93
Emmanuelle, the Joys of a Woman '76

Tony Genaros
Tremors '89

Denise Gence
Buffet Froid '79

Francois-Eric Gendron
Boyfriends & Girlfriends '88

Bryan Genesse
Cold Harvest '98
Operation Delta Force 3: Clear Target '98
Spoiler '98

Emile Genest
Nikki, the Wild Dog of the North '61

Li Geng
Frozen '98

Leo Genn
The Longest Day '62
Henry V '44

Minnie Gentry
Def by Temptation '90

Race Gentry
Men in War '57

Paul Geoffrey
Excalibur '81

Betsey Lynn George
Petticoat Planet '95

Chief Dan George
The Outlaw Josey Wales '76
The Bears & I '74

Christopher George
Exterminator '80
Day of the Animals '77
Grizzly '76
Midway '76

Gladys George
The Best Years of Our Lives '46

Heinrich George
Metropolis '26

Chief Leonard George
Smoke Signals '98

Lynda Day George
Day of the Animals '77

Matt George
In God's Hands '98

Melissa George
The Limey '99
Dark City '97

Susan George
Straw Dogs '72

Olga Georges-Picot
The Day of the Jackal '73
Honor Among Thieves '68

Tom Georgeson
A Fish Called Wanda '88

Carmelita Geraghty
My Best Girl '27

Marita Geraghty
Groundhog Day '93

Henriette Gerard
Vampyr '31

Mark Gerber
Sirens '94

Richard Gere
The Jackal (CE) '97
Red Corner '97
Primal Fear '96
First Knight '95
Sommersby '93
Final Analysis '92
Internal Affairs '90
Pretty Woman '90
No Mercy '86
American Gigolo '79
Days of Heaven '78

Sean Gerlis
A Summer to Remember '84

Nane Germon
Beauty and the Beast '46

Flo Gerrish
Don't Answer the Phone '80

Tjebbo Gerritsma
To Play or To Die '91

Gina Gershon
Guinevere '99

The Insider '99
I'm Losing You '98
Lulu on the Bridge '98
Palmetto '98
Face/Off '97
Bound '96
The Player '92
Out for Justice '91
Red Heat '88

Valeska Gert
Juliet of the Spirits '65

Jami Gertz
Twister '96
The Lost Boys '87
Sixteen Candles '84

Balthazar Getty
Big City Blues '99
Habitat '97
White Squall '96
Don't Do It '94
Terrified '94

Estelle Getty
Stuart Little '99
Mask '85

John Getz
Born on the Fourth of July '89

Stan Getz
Exterminator '80

Stuart Getz
The Van '77

Marilyn Ghigliotti
Clerks '94

Massimo Ghini
Tea with Mussolini '99

Alice Ghostley
Neil Simon's The Odd Couple 2 '98
To Kill a Mockingbird '62

Salim Ghouse
Koyla '98

Paul Giamatti
Man on the Moon '99
The Negotiator '98
Saving Private Ryan '98
The Truman Show '98
My Best Friend's Wedding '97
Private Parts '96

Louis Giambalvo
Weekend at Bernie's '89

Nicole Gian
Striking Resemblance '97

Rick Gianisi
Sgt. Kabukiman N.Y.P.D. '94

Giancarlo Giannini
Mimic '97
Lovers and Liars '81
Seven Beauties '76
Swept Away . . . '75
Love and Anarchy '73
Seduction of Mimi '72

Leeza Gibbons
The Player '92

Courtney Gibbs
The Naked Truth '92

Marla Gibbs
Foolish '99
Lost and Found '99

Billie Gibson
The Shining '80

Henry Gibson
A Stranger in the Kingdom '98
Around the World in 80 Days '89
Brenda Starr '86
Monster in the Closet '86
The Blues Brothers (CE) '80

Kentucky Fried Movie '77

Mel Gibson
Lethal Weapon 4 '98
Payback '98
Conspiracy Theory '97
Ransom '96
Maverick '94
Forever Young '92
Lethal Weapon 3 '92
Air America '90
Bird on a Wire '90
Lethal Weapon 2 '89
Tequila Sunrise '88
Lethal Weapon '87
The Lost Boys '87
Mad Max: Beyond Thunderdome '85
The River '84
The Road Warrior '82
The Year of Living Dangerously '82
Gallipoli '81
Mad Max '80
Tim '79

Thomas Gibson
Eyes Wide Shut '99
Armistead Maupin's More Tales of the City '97
Far and Away '92

Virginia Gibson
Seven Brides for Seven Brothers '54

Pamela Gidley
Bad Love '95

John Gielgud
Elizabeth '98
Merlin '98
Quest for Camelot '98 (V)
Dragonheart (SE) '96 (V)
Portrait of a Lady '96
First Knight '95
Shine '95
The Power of One '92
Plenty '85
Arthur '81
Chariots of Fire '81
Lion of the Desert '81
Caligula '80
The Secret Agent '36

Stefan Gierasch
Dave '93
High Plains Drifter '73

Frank Giering
Funny Games '97

Kathie Lee Gifford
Dudley Do-Right '99

Sandro Giglio
The War of the Worlds '53

Vincent Gil
Mad Max '80

Darrel Gilbeau
Lauderdale '89

Billy Gilbert
The Great Dictator '40
His Girl Friday '40

Colin Gilbert
The Big Red One '80

Marcus Gilbert
Army of Darkness '92

Sara Gilbert
Desert Blue '98
Poison Ivy '92

Yvonne Gilbert
2000 Maniacs '64

Steven Gilborn
Dr. Dolittle '98

Gilly Gilchrist
Rob Roy '95

Gwynne Gilford
Fade to Black '80

Jack Gilford
They Might Be Giants '71

Tony Gillan
Ten Benny '98

Aidan Gillen
Circle of Friends '94

Jeff Gillen
Children Shouldn't Play with Dead Things '72

Dana Gillespie
Gustav Mahler: To Live, I Will Die '87
Lost Continent '68

Aden Gillett
The Borrowers '97

Anita Gillette
Boys on the Side '94
Moonstruck '87

Warrington Gillette
Friday the 13th, Part 2 '81

Burton Gilliam
Blazing Saddles '74

Seth Gilliam
Starship Troopers '97

Terry Gilliam
Spies Like Us '85
Monty Python's The Meaning of Life '83
Monty Python's Life of Brian '79
And Now for Something Completely Different '72

Larry Gilliard Jr.
Simply Irresistible '99
The Waterboy '98
The Substitute 2: School's Out '97
Lotto Land '95

Hugh Gillin
Psycho 3 '86

Larry Gilman
Cool Runnings '93

Danny Gilmore
Lilies '96

Jack Gilpin
Last Breath '96
Funny Farm '88

Jay Gilpin
The Southerner '45

Jessalyn Gilsig
Quest for Camelot '98 (V)

Daniel Gimenez Cacho
Midaq Alley '95

Erica Gimpel
The Fence '94

Jack Ging
Where the Red Fern Grows '74
High Plains Drifter '73

Hermione Gingold
Munster, Go Home! '66
The Music Man '62
Bell, Book and Candle '58
Gigi '58

Allen Ginsberg
Chappaqua '66

Robert Ginty
Lady Dragon '92
Exterminator '80

Rocky Giordani
Cop and a Half '93
After Dark, My Sweet '90

Domiziana Giordano
Interview with the Vampire '94
Nostalghia '83

Thatcher Goodwin
Stealing Home '88

Michael Goorjian
SLC Punk! '99
Hard Rain '97

Allen Goorwitz
See Allen (Goorwitz) Garfield

Alicia (Lecy) Goranson
Boys Don't Cry '99
How to Make an American
Quilt '95

Bernard Gorcey
The Great Dictator '40

Barbara Gordon
Dead Ringers '88

Don Gordon
Bullitt '68

Dorothy Gordon
The Haunted Strangler '58

Eve Gordon
I'll Be Home for Christmas
'98

Gale Gordon
The 'Burbs '89

Gavin Gordon
The Bat '59
The Bride of Frankenstein '35

Hannah Taylor Gordon
Jakob the Liar '99

Keith Gordon
Christine '84

Serena Gordon
Goldeneye '95

Tanya Gordon
Stay Awake '87

Joseph Gordon-Levitt
Ten Things I Hate about You
'99
Halloween: H20 '98
The Juror '96

Charles Gordone
Angel Heart '87

Galyn Gorg
RoboCop 2 '90

Marius Goring
The Red Shoes '48

Cliff Gorman
The '60s '99

Robert Gorman
Leprechaun '93

Felim Gormley
The Commitments '91

Peggy Gormley
Bad Lieutenant '92

Karen Gorney
The Hard Way '91

Walt Gorney
Friday the 13th, Part 2 '81
Friday the 13th '80

Frederic Gorny
Wild Reeds '94

Frank Gorshin
12 Monkeys '95
Sweet Justice '92

Marjoe Gortner
Earthquake '74

Mark Paul Gosselaar
Dead Man on Campus '97
Specimen '99

Louis Gossett Jr.
Iron Eagle 4 '95
Flashfire '94
Carolina Skeletons '92

The Punisher '90
The Deep '77

Robert Gossett
Arlington Road '99

Will Gotay
Stand and Deliver '88

Walter Gotell
For Your Eyes Only (SE) '81
Moonraker (SE) '79
The Spy Who Loved Me (SE)
'77
From Russia with Love '63
The Guns of Navarone '61

Michael Gothard
Out of Time '90
Lifeforce '85
For Your Eyes Only (SE) '81

Heinrich Gotho
Metropolis '26

Gilbert Gottfried
Dr. Dolittle '98 (V)
Def Jam's How to Be a Player
'97
Thumbelina '94 (V)

John Gottowt
Nosferatu '22

Thomas Gottschalk
Sister Act 2: Back in the
Habit '93

Michael Gough
Sleepy Hollow '99
Batman and Robin '97
Batman Forever '95
Batman Returns '92
Batman '89
The Serpent and the Rainbow
'87
Horror Hospital '73
Anna Karenina '48

Elliott Gould
American History X '98
The Big Hit '98
The Player '92
Bugsy '91
Conspiracy: The Trial of the
Chicago Eight '87
Falling in Love Again '80
The Last Flight of Noah's Ark
'80
Capricorn One '78
A Bridge Too Far '77

Harold Gould
My Giant '98
Patch Adams (CE) '98
Killer: A Journal of Murder
'95
The Sting '73

Robert Goulet
Beetlejuice '88
Scrooged '88

Arun Govil
Lav Kush '97

Peter Gowen
Dancing at Lughnasa '98

Gibson Gowland
The Phantom of the Opera
'25

Betty Grable
The Love Goddesses '65

Nickolas Grace
Shooting Fish '98
Salome's Last Dance '88

Andrei Gradov
Zig Zag '99

Robert Graf
The Great Escape '63

Todd Graff
The Abyss (SE) '89
Five Corners '88

Aimee Graham
Brokedown Palace '99

Bill Graham
Bugsy '91
The Doors '91

Gerrit Graham
One True Thing '98
Child's Play 2 '90
National Lampoon's Class
Reunion '82

Heather Graham
Austin Powers 2: The Spy
Who Shagged Me '99
Bowfinger '99
Lost in Space '98
Boogie Nights '97
Scream 2 '97
Swingers '96
Don't Do It '94
Terrified '94
Drugstore Cowboy '89

John Michael Graham
Halloween '78

Lauren Graham
One True Thing '98

Marcus Graham
Animal Instincts 3: The
Seductress '95

Morland Graham
The Scarlet Pimpernel '34

Ronny Graham
Gallipoli '81

Sheilah Graham
Impact '49

Stuart Graham
Michael Collins '96

Gloria Grahame
Oklahoma '55
Sudden Fear '52
It's a Wonderful Life '46

Gawn Grainger
Love and Death on Long
Island '97

Kelsey Grammer
Bartok the Magnificent '99
(V)
Mickey's Once upon a Christ-
mas '99 (V)
Anastasia '97 (V)

Alexander Granach
For Whom the Bell Tolls '43
Nosferatu '22

Farley Granger
Hans Christian Andersen '52
Strangers on a Train '51

Toby Scott Granger
Rock-a-Doodle '92 (V)

Beth Grant
Dance with Me '98
Lawn Dogs '96
Speed '94
The Dark Half '91
Rain Man '88

Cary Grant
Charade '63
The Bishop's Wife '47
Notorious '46
Penny Serenade '41
His Girl Friday '40
The Philadelphia Story '40
I'm No Angel '33

David Marshall Grant
The Chamber '96
Forever Young '92
Air America '90
Bat 21 '88

Donald Grant
Monster in the Closet '86

Gerald Grant
Score '72

Hugh Grant
Notting Hill '99
The Englishman Who Went up
a Hill But Came down a
Mountain '95
Sense and Sensibility '95
Four Weddings and a Funeral
'94
Restoration '94
Sirens '94
The Lair of the White Worm
'88

Jessica Brooks Grant
What Dreams May Come '98

Kathryn Grant
The Seventh Voyage of Sinbad '58

Richard E. Grant
A Merry War '97
Spice World: The Movie '97
Treasure Island '97 (V)
Portrait of a Lady '96
Ready to Wear '94
Dracula '92
The Player '92
Hudson Hawk '91
L.A. Story '91
Warlock '91
Henry & June '90
Mountains of the Moon '90

Rodney A. Grant
The Jack Bull '99
Wild Wild West '99
The Killing Grounds '97
The Substitute '96
Geronimo: An American Leg-
end '93
Dances with Wolves '90

Stacy Grant
The Fear: Halloween Night
'99

Charley Grapewin
The Wizard of Oz '39

Floriella Grappini
Bloodstorm: Subspecies 4
'98

Janice Graser
Cyborg '89

Bud Graves
Slave Girls from Beyond Infinity '87

Kirk Graves
Slave Girls from Beyond Infinity '87

Leonard Graves
Pork Chop Hill '59

Peter Graves
The Slipper and the Rose '76
Beneath the 12-Mile Reef '53

Rupert Graves
Cleopatra '99
Mrs. Dalloway '97
Damage '92

Fernand Gravet
The Fantastic Night '42

Charles Gray
The Seven-Per-Cent Solution
'76

Christopher Gray
Fear '96

Coleen Gray
The Killing '56
Red River '48

David Barry Gray
Lawn Dogs '96

Dorian Gray
Nights of Cabiria '57

MacKenzie Gray
Strip Search '97

Pamela Gray
The Devil's Advocate '97

Spalding Gray
Drunks '96
Gray's Anatomy '96
The Paper '94
True Stories '86

Vivean Gray
Picnic at Hanging Rock '75

Jerry Grayson
Pushing Tin '99

Kathryn Grayson
Show Boat '51
Till the Clouds Roll By '46

Irene Grazioli
The Red Violin '98

Calvin Green
Exotica '94

Danny Green
The Seventh Voyage of Sinbad '58

D.L. Green
Dear Santa '98

Harry Green
A King in New York / A
Woman in Paris '57

Marika Green
Emmanuelle '74

Nigel Green
The Ipcress File '65
Jason and the Argonauts '63
Corridors of Blood '58

Pamela Green
Peeping Tom '60

Seth Green
Austin Powers 2: The Spy
Who Shagged Me '99
Can't Hardly Wait '98
Enemy of the State '98
Austin Powers: International
Man of Mystery '97
My Stepmother Is an Alien
'88

Stan Green
Gallipoli '81

Shon Greenblatt
Freddy's Dead: The Final
Nightmare '91

Bill Greene
Lolita '62

Ellen Greene
Killer: A Journal of Murder
'95
The Professional '94
Rock-a-Doodle '92 (V)
Pump Up the Volume '90
Little Shop of Horrors '86

Graham Greene
The Green Mile '99
Shattered Image '98
Die Hard: With a Vengeance
'95
Maverick '94
Thunderheart '92
Dances with Wolves '90

Lorne Greene
Battlestar Galactica '78
Earthquake '74

Michele Greene
Stranger by Night '94

Peter Greene
Black Cat Run '98
Permanent Midnight '98
Sworn Enemies '96
The Usual Suspects '95
The Mask '94

Pulp Fiction '94
Judgment Night '93

Shecky Greene
Splash '84

Jeff Greenman
Lauderdale '89

Sydney Greenstreet
Casablanca '42

Tom Greenway
Impact '49

Bruce Greenwood
Hide and Seek '00
Double Jeopardy '99
Disturbing Behavior '98
Father's Day '96
The Sweet Hereafter '96
Exotica '94

Charlotte Greenwood
Oklahoma '55

Joan Greenwood
Tom Jones '63

Dabbs Greer
The Green Mile '99

Jane Greer
Man of a Thousand Faces
'57

Judy Greer
Three Kings '99
Jawbreaker '98
Kissing a Fool '98

Everley Gregg
Great Expectations '46

Virginia Gregg
Psycho (CE) '60 (V)

Pascal Greggory
Le Beau Mariage '82

Rose Gregorio
Tarantella '95
Five Corners '88

Andre Gregory
Goodbye, Lover '99
Celebrity '98
The Bonfire of the Vanities
'90
Protocol '84
My Dinner with Andre '81

James Gregory
Shoot Out '71
The Manchurian Candidate
'62

Robert Greig
Animal Crackers '30

Kim Greist
Homeward Bound: The
Incredible Journey '93
Brazil '85
Brazil (Criterion SE) '85

Becket Gremmels
The Newton Boys '97

Zach Grenier
Donnie Brasco '96
Twister '96

Aidan Grennell
In the Name of the Father '93

Macha Gronon
Sworn Enemies '96

Anne Grey
No. 17 '32

Jennifer Grey
Dirty Dancing '87
Dirty Dancing (CE) '87
Ferris Bueller's Day Off '86
Red Dawn '84

Joel Grey
The Player '92

The Seven-Per-Cent Solution
'76
Cabaret '72

Virginia Grey
Naked Kiss '64
Unknown Island '48
Uncle Tom's Cabin '27

Michael Greyeyes
Smoke Signals '98
Firestorm '97

Clinton Greyn
Raid on Rommel '71

Richard Grieco
A Night at the Roxbury '98
The Demolitionist '95

David Alan Grier
The '60s '99
Stuart Little '99 (V)
Top of the World '97
Jumanji (CS) '95
Tales from the Hood '95
The Player '92

Pam Grier
In Too Deep '99
Jawbreaker '98
Strip Search '97
Escape from L.A. '96
Mars Attacks! '96
Posse '93
Above the Law '88
Something Wicked This Way
Comes '83
Naked Warriors '73
The Big Doll House '71

John Griesemer
Where the Rivers Flow North
'94

Joe Grifasi
Batman Forever '95
Money Train '95
Presumed Innocent '90
Chances Are '89
The Deer Hunter '78

Simone Griffeth
Death Race 2000 '75

Ethel Griffies
The Birds '63

Anthony Griffin
The Curve '97

Eddie Griffin
Foolish '99

Kathy Griffin
Muppets from Space '99

Merv Griffin
The Lonely Guy '84
The Man with Two Brains '83

Rhonda Griffin
The Creeps '97

Andy Griffith
Spy Hard '96

Anthony Griffith
Panther '95
Tales from the Hood '95

Hugh Griffith
The Canterbury Tales '71
Oliver! '68
Tom Jones '63

James Griffith
The Amazing Transparent
Man '60

Kenneth Griffith
The Englishman Who Went up
a Hill But Came down a
Mountain '95
Four Weddings and a Funeral
'94
Tiger Bay '59
A Night to Remember '58

Melanie Griffith
Another Day in Paradise '98
Celebrity '98
Now and Then '95
The Bonfire of the Vanities
'90
Body Double '84

Nadine Griffith
Ninth Street '98

Raymond Griffith
All Quiet on the Western
Front '30

Thomas Ian Griffith
John Carpenter's Vampires
'97
Kull the Conqueror '97

Derek Griffiths
Fierce Creatures '96

Rachel Griffiths
Hilary and Jackie '98
My Best Friend's Wedding '97
My Son the Fanatic '97

Richard Griffiths
Sleepy Hollow '99
Guarding Tess '94

Dan Grimaldi
Don't Go in the House '80

Roger Grimsby
Exterminator '80

Nikolai Grinko
Solaris '72
Andrei Rublev '66

Stephen Grives
Horror Planet '80

Charles Grodin
Beethoven's 2nd '93
Dave '93
Heart and Souls '93
So I Married an Axe Murderer
'93
Beethoven '92
Midnight Run '88
The Lonely Guy '84
Heaven Can Wait '78
King Kong '76
The Meanest Men in the
West '76
The Heartbreak Kid '72

Kathryn Grody
Limbo '99
Parents '89

Herbert Gronemeyer
Spring Symphony '86
Das Boot (DC) '81

Arye Gross
Big City Blues '99
Timelock '99
Spoiler '98
Tequila Sunrise '88

Frances B. Gross
Faces of Death '78 (N)

Mary Gross
The Santa Clause '94
Casual Sex? '88

Michael Gross
Ground Control '98
Sometimes They Come Back
... Again '96
Tremors 2: Aftershocks '96
Tremors '89

Molly Gross
Slaves to the Underground
'96

Arthur Grosser
The Quarrel '93

Richard Grove
Army of Darkness '92

Gulsham Grover
Monsoon '97

Robert Grubb
Mad Max: Beyond Thunder-
dome '85
Gallipoli '81

Gustav Grundgens
M '31

Olivier Gruner
T.N.T. '98
Nemesis '93

Ilka Gruning
Casablanca '42

Nicky Guadagni
Cube '98

Dominic Guard
Picnic at Hanging Rock '75

Harry Guardino
Rollercoaster '77
Dirty Harry '71
Madigan '68
Pork Chop Hill '59

Michael Guerin
Curse of the Puppet Master:
The Human Experiment '98

Camille Guerini
Diabolique '55

Jackie Guerra
Selena '96

Luigi Antonio Guerra
Nude for Satan '74

Fausto Guerzoni
Black Orpheus '58
The Bicycle Thief '48

Christopher Guest
Small Soldiers '98 (V)
A Few Good Men '92
The Princess Bride '87
Little Shop of Horrors '86
This Is Spinal Tap '84

Lance Guest
Jaws: The Revenge '87
The Last Starfighter '84
Halloween 2: The Nightmare
Isn't Over! '81

Nicholas Guest
Nemesis '93
National Lampoon's Christ-
mas Vacation '89
Criminal Act '88

Georges Guetary
An American in Paris '51

Carla Gugino
Snake Eyes '98
Miami Rhapsody '95
Son-in-Law '93

Anthony Guidera
Undercover '94

Ann Guilbert
Grumpier Old Men '95

Paul Guilfoyle
In Dreams '98
The Negotiator '98
Primary Colors '98
Air Force One '97
L.A. Confidential '97
Night Falls on Manhattan '96
Ransom '96
Mother's Boys '94
Final Analysis '92

Robert Guillaume
The Lion King: Simba's Pride
'98 (V)
Lean on Me '89

Yang Guimei
Vive l'Amour '94

Francis Guinan
Guinevere '99

Tim Guinee
Blade '98
John Carpenter's Vampires
'97
How to Make an American
Quilt '95
The Pompatus of Love '95

Alec Guinness
Lovesick '83
Oliver Twist '48
Great Expectations '46

Clu Gulager
The Hidden '87
A Nightmare on Elm Street 2:
Freddy's Revenge '85
Winning '69

Sean Gullette
Pi '98

David Gumpilil
Walkabout '71

Anna Gunn
Enemy of the State '98

David Gunn
Vampire Journals '96

Janet Gunn
The Quest '96

Moses Gunn
Firestarter '84
Rollerball '75
Shaft '71

Peter Gunn
Blue Juice '95

Sean Gunn
Tromeo & Juliet '95

Charles Gunning
The Newton Boys '97

Bob Gunton
Patch Adams (CE) '98
Changing Habits '96
The Glimmer Man '96
Ace Ventura: When Nature
Calls '95
Broken Arrow '95
The Shawshank Redemption
'94
Demolition Man '93
Glory '89

Isha Gupta
Lav Kush '97

Alizia Gur
From Russia with Love '63

Eric Gurry
Bad Boys '83

Annabelle Gurwitch
One Night Stand '97

Louis Guss
Moonstruck '87

Steve Guttenberg
Zeus and Roxanne '96
Amazon Women on the Moon
'87
Police Academy '84

Lucy Gutteridge
A Christmas Carol '84

Ronald Guttman
Just the Ticket '98
The Pillow Book '95

DeJuan Guy
One Man's Justice '95
Candyman '92

Jasmine Guy
Guinevere '99
Klash '95

Deryck Guyler
A Hard Day's Night '64

Luis Guzman
The Bone Collector '99
The Limey '99
Out of Sight '98
Snake Eyes '98
Boogie Nights '97
The Substitute '96
Lotto Land '95
Stonewall '95
Carlito's Way '93
Mr. Wonderful '93
The Hard Way '91
Q & A '90

Paul Guzzi
A Nymphoid Barbarian in
    Dinosaur Hell '94

Jack Gwaltney
The Siege '98

Edmund Gwenn
Life with Father '47
Miracle on 34th Street '47
Forever and a Day '43
Skin Game '31

David Gwillim
The Island at the Top of the
    World '74

Jack Gwillim
Jason and the Argonauts '63

Michael Gwynn
Jason and the Argonauts '63

Fred Gwynne
The Secret of My Success
    '87
Munster, Go Home! '66

Peter Gwynne
Tim '79

Jake Gyllenhaal
October Sky '99

Deanna Haas
Devonsville Terror '83

Lukas Haas
Everyone Says I Love You '96
Mars Attacks! '96
Rambling Rose '91
The Lady in White '88
Witness '85

Sean Haberle
The Surgeon '94

Buddy Hackett
Paulie '98
Scrooged '88
The Music Man '62

Gene Hackman
Antz '98 (V)
Enemy of the State '98
Twilight '98
Absolute Power '97
The Chamber '96
The Birdcage '95
Crimson Tide '95
Get Shorty '95
The Quick and the Dead '94
The Firm '93
Geronimo: An American Leg-
    end '93
Unforgiven '92
Bat 21 '88
Mississippi Burning '88
Hoosiers '86
A Bridge Too Far '77
Young Frankenstein '74
The Poseidon Adventure '72
Bonnie & Clyde '67

Jonathan Hadary
A Simple Wish '97
Private Parts '96

Julie Ann Haddock
The Great Santini '80

Dayle Haddon
Cyborg '89

Sara Haden
The Great Rupert '50
Mr. Ace '46

Mary Ann Haenel
The Deer Hunter '78

Molly Hagan
Election '99
Ringmaster '98

Richard Hageman
New Orleans '47

Jean Hagen
Singin' in the Rain '52
Adam's Rib '50

Julie Hagerty
The Story of Us '99
Boys Will Be Boys '97
U-Turn '97
The Wife '95

Michael G. Hagerty
Best Laid Plans '99
Inspector Gadget '99
Speed 2: Cruise Control '97

Dan Haggerty
Spirit of the Eagle '90

Britt Hagman
Intermezzo '36

Larry Hagman
Primary Colors '98
Nixon '95

Archie Hahn
Amazon Women on the Moon
    '87
Protocol '84
This Is Spinal Tap '84

Charles Haid
Capone '89
Altered States '80

Jack Haig
The Ghost Goes Gear '66

Sid Haig
The Big Doll House '71
Spider Baby '64

Corey Haim
The Lost Boys '87

Patricia Haines
Night Caller from Outer
    Space '66

Herbert Halbik
The Third Man '49

Alan Hale
Santa Fe Trail '40
Stella Dallas '37
It Happened One Night '34
Robin Hood '22

Alan Hale Jr.
The North Avenue Irregulars
    '79

Barbara Hale
Airport '70

Creighton Hale
The Cat and the Canary '27
Way Down East '20

Georgia Hale
The Gold Rush '25

Georgina Hale
Mahler '74

Michael Hale
The Devil Bat's Daughter '46

Jack Haley
The Wizard of Oz '39

Bryant Haliday
Curse of the Voodoo '64

Alaina Reed Hall
Death Becomes Her '92

Albert Hall
Beloved '98
Devil in a Blue Dress '95
Major Payne '95
Apocalypse Now '79

Anthony Michael Hall
The Killing Grounds '97
The Breakfast Club '85
Weird Science '85
Sixteen Candles '84
National Lampoon's Vacation
    '83

Arch Hall Jr.
The Sadist '63

Arsenio Hall
Coming to America '88
Amazon Women on the Moon
    '87

Brad Hall
The Guardian '90

Brian Hall
The Long Good Friday '80

Bug Hall
The Little Rascals '94

Delores Hall
Lethal Weapon 3 '92

Gabriella Hall
Lolida 2000 '97
Sexual Roulette '96

Henry Hall
The Flying Serpent '55

Irma P. Hall
Beloved '98
Patch Adams (CE) '98
Midnight in the Garden of
    Good and Evil (SE) '97
Soul Food '97
Nothing to Lose '96

Jerry Hall
Batman '89

John Hall
Detention '98

Jon Hall
The Hurricane '37

Juanita Hall
South Pacific '58

Kevin Peter Hall
Predator '87

Landon Hall
Witchcraft 9: Bitter Flesh '96
Over the Wire '95

Lois Hall
Kalifornia '93
Dead Again '91

Philip Baker Hall
The Insider '99
Enemy of the State '98
Psycho '98
Rush Hour '98
The Truman Show '98
Air Force One '97
Boogie Nights '97

Porter Hall
Miracle on 34th Street '47
Double Indemnity '44
Going My Way / Holiday Inn
    '44
His Girl Friday '40

Ruth Hall
Monkey Business '31

Scott H. Hall
Color Me Blood Red '64
Blood Feast (SE) '63

Lillian Hall-Davis
The Farmer's Wife '28

The Ring '27

Charles Hallahan
Dante's Peak '97
Warlock: The Armageddon
    '93
Pale Rider '85
Vision Quest '85
The Thing '82

John Hallam
Lifeforce '85

Jane Hallaren
Body Heat '81

Bryant Halliday
Tower of Evil '72

Heather Halliday
Peter Pan '60

John Halliday
The Philadelphia Story '40

**Geri (Ginger Spice)
Halliwell**
Spice World: The Movie '97

Miles Halliwell
Winstanley '75

Luke Halpin
Matinee '92
Peter Pan '60

Brett Halsey
Atomic Submarine '59

Michael Halsey
Postmortem '98
Mean Guns '97

Charles Halton
The Best Years of Our Lives
    '46
It's a Wonderful Life '46
The Westerner '40
Come and Get It '36
Dodsworth '36

Mark Hamill
Laserhawk '99
The Sci-Fi Files '97 (N)
Village of the Damned '95
The Big Red One '80

Pete Hamill
The Insider '99

Ashley Hamilton
Beethoven's 2nd '93

Dean Hamilton
Rush Week '88

George Hamilton
Doc Hollywood '91

Guy Hamilton
Barry Lyndon '75

Josh Hamilton
The '60s '99
The House of Yes '97
With Honors '94

Linda Hamilton
Dante's Peak '97
Terminator 2: Judgment Day
    '91
The Terminator '84

Lisa Gay Hamilton
Beloved '98
Drunks '96
Last Breath '96

Mahlon Hamilton
Daddy Long Legs '19

Margaret Hamilton
The Night Stranger '72
The Wizard of Oz '39
Nothing Sacred '37

Murray Hamilton
1941 '79

Neil Hamilton
America '24

Richard Hamilton
Message in a Bottle '98
Sommersby '93
In Country '89

Ellen Hamilton-Latzen
Boys Life 2 '98

Dan Hamlon
20,000 Leagues under the
    Sea '16

Eric Hamm
Summer '86

Hammer
One Man's Justice '95
Last Action Hero '93

John Hammil
Phantoms '97

Jennifer Leigh Hammon
Allyson Is Watching '96

Brandon Hammond
Soul Food '97

Darrell Hammond
The King and I '99 (V)
The Blues Brothers 2000 '98

Marcus Hammond
Plague of the Zombies '66

Walter Hampden
Reap the Wild Wind '42
The Hunchback of Notre
    Dame '39

Col. Bruce Hampton
Sling Blade '96

James Hampton
Sling Blade '96
Condorman '81
The China Syndrome '79

Paul Hampton
They Came from Within '75

Maggie Han
The Last Emperor '87

Lou Hancock
Evil Dead 2: Dead by Dawn
    '87

Sheila Hancock
Love and Death on Long
    Island '97

Irene Handl
Smashing Time '67

Evan Handler
Ransom '96

Tres Handley
Grim '95

James Handy
The Rocketeer '91
Arachnophobia '90
K-9 '89
Burglar '87

Anne Haney
Psycho '98
Midnight in the Garden of
    Good and Evil (SE) '97
Changing Habits '96
Liar Liar '96

Carol Haney
The Pajama Game '57

Larry Hankin
Billy Madison '94

Jim Hanks
Xtro 3: Watch the Skies '95

Tom Hanks
The Green Mile '99
Saving Private Ryan '98
You've Got Mail '98
Apollo 13 '95
Philadelphia '93
Sleepless in Seattle '93
A League of Their Own '92

The Bonfire of the Vanities '90
The 'Burbs '89
Big '88
Dragnet '87
Splash '84

Jimmy Hanley
Lost Continent '68

Adam Hann-Byrd
Halloween: H20 '98
Jumanji (CS) '95

Daryl Hannah
Hide and Seek '00
My Favorite Martian '98
The Gingerbread Man '97
The Last Don '97
The Real Blonde '97
Grumpier Old Men '95
The Little Rascals '94
Grumpy Old Men '93
Crimes & Misdemeanors '89
The Clan of the Cave Bear '86
Legal Eagles '86
Splash '84
Blade Runner (DC) '82

John Hannah
The Mummy '99
Sliding Doors '97
Four Weddings and a Funeral '94

Alyson Hannigan
American Pie (CE) '99
Dead Man on Campus '97
My Stepmother Is an Alien '88

Taimi Hannum
Awakening of Gabriella '99

Donna Hanover
Just the Ticket '98
The People vs. Larry Flynt '96

Lawrence Hanray
On Approval '44

Glen Hansard
The Commitments '91

Gale Hansen
Dead Poets Society '89

Gunnar Hansen
Mosquito '95
The Texas Chainsaw Massacre '74

Richard Hanson
Boston Kickout '95

Setsuko Hara
Chushingura '62

Meiko Harada
Ran '85

Yoshio Harada
The Hunted '94

Marcia Gay Harden
Desperate Measures '98
Meet Joe Black '98
Curtain Call '97
Flubber '97
The First Wives Club '96
Spy Hard '96

Jerry Hardin
The Firm '93
The Hot Spot '90

Melora Hardin
Absolute Power '97
The Rocketeer '91
Dead Poets Society '89
The North Avenue Irregulars '79

Ty Hardin
Custer of the West '67

Kadeem Hardison
Drive '96

Panther '95
Def by Temptation '90

Paul Hardtmuth
The Third Man '49

Cedric Hardwicke
The Ten Commandments '56
The War of the Worlds '53 (V)
The Hunchback of Notre Dame '39

Edward Hardwicke
Elizabeth '98
Shadowlands '93

Oliver Hardy
Laurel and Hardy and Friends '90s
The Lost Films of Laurel and Hardy, Vol. 1 '90s
The Lost Films of Laurel and Hardy, Vol. 2 '90s
The Lost Films of Laurel and Hardy, Vol. 3 '90s
The Lost Films of Laurel and Hardy, Vol. 5 '99
The Lost Films of Laurel and Hardy, Vol. 6 '99
Utopia '51
The Flying Deuces / Utopia '39
March of the Wooden Soldiers '34
Three Ages '23

Robert Hardy
Mrs. Dalloway '97
Sense and Sensibility '95
Mary Shelley's Frankenstein '94

Mark Harelik
Election '99

Dorian Harewood
Kiss Shot '89
Full Metal Jacket '87
The Falcon and the Snowman '85
Tank '83
An American Christmas Carol '79

Mariska Hargitay
Lake Placid '99
Leaving Las Vegas '95

Mickey Hargitay
The Reincarnation of Isabel '72

Christine Hargreaves
Pink Floyd: The Wall '82

John Hargreaves
Cry Freedom '87
Don's Party '76

Tsui Hark
Twin Dragons '92
I Love Maria '88

Gordon Harker
The Farmer's Wife '28
The Ring '27

Susannah Harker
Pride and Prejudice '95

John Harkins
Absence of Malice '81

Dan Harlan
Blood, Guts, Bullets and Octane '99

Jean Harlow
The Love Goddesses '65
City Lights '31

Shalom Harlow
In and Out '97

Mark Harmon
Fear and Loathing in Las Vegas '98
From the Earth to the Moon '98

Stealing Home '88

Ricci Harnett
The Object of Beauty '91

Elisabeth Harnois
One Magic Christmas '85

Ralf Harolde
I'm No Angel '33

Helen Harp
Tombs of the Blind Dead '72

Frank Harper
Lock, Stock and 2 Smoking Barrels '98
In the Name of the Father '93

Hill Harper
In Too Deep '99
He Got Game '98

Robert Harper
Final Analysis '92

Susan Harper
Phantasm '79

Tess Harper
The Jackal (CE) '97
The Turning '92
Her Alibi '88
A Summer to Remember '84
Tender Mercies '83

Michele Harrell
Exterminator '80

Brett Harrelson
Dee Snider's Strangeland '98
From Dusk Till Dawn 2: Texas Blood Money '98
The People vs. Larry Flynt '96

Woody Harrelson
Austin Powers 2: The Spy Who Shagged Me '99
EDtv '99
Palmetto '98
The Thin Red Line '98
Wag the Dog '97
Kingpin '96
The People vs. Larry Flynt '96
Money Train '95
The Cowboy Way '94
Doc Hollywood '91

Laura Harrington
Paulie '98
The Devil's Advocate '97

Aleida Harris
Troma's War (DC) '88

Barbara Harris
Grosse Pointe Blank '97
Dirty Rotten Scoundrels '88
Peggy Sue Got Married '86
The North Avenue Irregulars '79

Baxter Harris
Home Alone 3 '97

Cassandra Harris
For Your Eyes Only (SE) '81

Danielle Harris
Urban Legend '98
Daylight '96
The Last Boy Scout '91
Marked for Death '90
Halloween 4: The Return of Michael Myers '88

Ed Harris
Stepmom '98
The Truman Show '98
Absolute Power '97
The Rock '96
Apollo 13 '95
Nixon '95
Just Cause '94
Stephen King's The Stand '94
The Firm '93
Needful Things '93
The Abyss (SE) '89

Sweet Dreams '85
The Right Stuff '83
Creepshow '82
Coma '78

Estelle Harris
Lost and Found '99
Chairman of the Board '97

Gail Harris
Sucker the Vampire '98
Virtual Desire '95

Heath Harris
Gallipoli '81

James Harris
Nude for Satan '74

Jared Harris
The Eternal Kiss of the Mummy '99
Happiness '98
Lost in Space '98
Father's Day '96

Jo Ann Harris
The Beguiled '70

Jonathan Harris
A Bug's Life (CE) '98 (V)

Julie Harris
The Dark Half '91
Gorillas in the Mist '88

Julius W. Harris
Live and Let Die '73

Lara Harris
Habitat '97

Laura Harris
The Faculty '98
Just the Ticket '98
Suicide Kings '97

Leonard Harris
Taxi Driver (CE) '76

Mel Harris
Raising Cain '92
K-9 '89

Neil Patrick Harris
Joan of Arc '99
Starship Troopers '97
Animal Room '95

Phil Harris
Rock-a-Doodle '92 (V)

Richard Harris
Patriot Games '92
Unforgiven '92
The Field '90
The Cassandra Crossing '76
Camelot '67
The Red Desert '64
This Sporting Life '63
The Guns of Navarone '61

Ricky Harris
Simon Sez '99

Rosalind Harris
Fiddler on the Roof '71

Rosemary Harris
My Life So Far '98

Shirley Jane Harris
Stay Awake '87

Steve Harris
The Mod Squad '99

Zelda Harris
He Got Game '98
Crooklyn '94

Andrew Harrison
The Littlest Horse Thieves '76

Emily Harrison
Curse of the Puppet Master: The Human Experiment '98

George Harrison
The Beatles: The First U.S. Visit '91
Monty Python's Life of Brian '79
Yellow Submarine '68 (V)
Magical Mystery Tour '67
Help! '65
A Hard Day's Night '64

Gregory Harrison
Trilogy of Terror '75

Jenilee Harrison
Tank '83

John Harrison
Lolita '62

Kathleen Harrison
A Christmas Carol '51

Rex Harrison
My Fair Lady '64

Schae Harrison
Interlocked '98

David Harrod
The Thin Red Line '98

Kathryn Harrold
Raw Deal '86

John Harron
The White Zombie '32

Robert "Bobbie" Harron
The Birth of a Nation '15

Deborah Harry
Six Ways to Sunday '99
Cop Land '97
Drop Dead Rock '95
Videodrome '83
Union City '81

Sean Harry
Witchcraft 10: Mistress of the Craft '98

Ray Harryhausen
Mighty Joe Young '98
Spies Like Us '85

Dianne Lee Hart
Pom Pom Girls '76

Dorothy Hart
The Naked City '48

Henry Hart
D.O.A. '49

Ian Hart
Monument Ave. '98
Michael Collins '96
The Englishman Who Went up a Hill But Came down a Mountain '95

Linda Hart
Tin Cup '96

Pamela Hart
Pi '98

Roxanne Hart
Horton Foote's Alone '97
Highlander (DC) '86

Sunshine Hart
My Best Girl '27

William S. Hart
The Toll Gate '20

Mariette Hartley
Encino Man '92

Nina Hartley
Boogie Nights '97

Pat Hartley
Rainbow Bridge '71

David Hartman
The Island at the Top of the World '74

Elizabeth Hartman
Walking Tall '73

The Beguiled '70

Phil Hartman
Small Soldiers '98
Jingle All the Way '96
Sgt. Bilko '95
Greedy '94
National Lampoon's Loaded
   Weapon 1 '93
So I Married an Axe Murderer
   '93
Amazon Women on the Moon
   '87
Three Amigos '86
Pee-wee's Big Adventure '85

William Hartnell
This Sporting Life '63

Josh Hartnett
The Faculty '98
Halloween: H20 '98

Alex Harvey
Fire Down Below '97

Don Harvey
The Thin Red Line '98
Die Hard 2: Die Harder '90

Forrester Harvey
The Wolf Man '41

Harry Harvey Jr.
Reefer Madness '38

Laurence Harvey
The Manchurian Candidate
   '62

Michael Harvey
Don't Look in the Basement
   '73

Rodney Harvey
Five Corners '88

Tom Harvey
Moving Target '96

Keisha Harvin
Detention '98

David Haskell
Body Double '84

Kam Haskin
Blackjack '97

Danny Hassel
A Nightmare on Elm Street 5:
   Dream Child '89
A Nightmare on Elm Street 4:
   Dream Master '88

David Hasselhoff
Baywatch: Nightmare Bay /
   River of No Return '94

Kulani Hassen
Down in the Delta '98

Marilyn Hassett
Two Minute Warning '76

Richard Hatch
Battlestar Galactica '78

Riley Hatch
America '24

Teri Hatcher
Tomorrow Never Dies (SE)
   '97
Tango and Cash '89

Hurd Hatfield
Her Alibi '88

Shawn Hatosy
Anywhere But Here '99
Outside Providence '99
The Thin Red Line '98
In and Out '97
The Postman '97

Raymond Hatton
Reap the Wild Wind '42
Male and Female '19

Rondo Hatton
The Brute Man '46

Tom Hatton
Spies Like Us '85

Sabine Haudepin
The Last Metro '80

Rutger Hauer
New World Disorder '99
Tactical Assault '99
Merlin '98
Redline '97
Crossworlds '96
Surviving the Game '94
Ladyhawke '85
Blade Runner (DC) '82
Nighthawks '81

Cole Hauser
Good Will Hunting '97
Dazed and Confused '93
School Ties '92

Wings Hauser
The Insider '99
Tales from the Hood '95
Nightmare at Noon '87
The Wind '87

Mischa Hausserman
The 13th Warrior '99

Phyllis Haver
Seven Chances '25

Nigel Havers
Chariots of Fire '81

Alex Havier
They Were Expendable '45
Bataan '43

June Havoc
Gentleman's Agreement '47

Keeley Hawes
The Avengers '98

Ethan Hawke
Joe the King '99
Gattaca '97
Great Expectations '97
The Newton Boys '97
Before Sunrise '94
Floundering '94
Reality Bites '94
Dead Poets Society '89

John Hawkes
I Still Know What You Did
   Last Summer '98
Playing God '96

Terri Hawkes
The Killing Man '94

Jack Hawkins
Nicholas and Alexandra '71

Goldie Hawn
The Out-of-Towners '99
Everyone Says I Love You '96
The First Wives Club '96
Death Becomes Her '92
Bird on a Wire '90
Overboard '87
Protocol '84
Lovers and Liars '81
Private Benjamin '80

Jill Haworth
Tower of Evil '72

James H. Hawthorne
Avenging Disco Godfather '76

Nigel Hawthorne
The Big Brass Ring '99
Tarzan '99 (V)
Amistad '97
Demolition Man '93

Charles Hawtrey
Sabotage '36

Sterling Hayden
Dr. Strangelove, or: How I
   Learned to Stop Worrying
   and Love the Bomb '64
The Killing '56
Suddenly '54

Richard Haydn
Young Frankenstein '74

Helen Haye
The 39 Steps '35
Skin Game '31

Salma Hayek
Wild Wild West '99
The Faculty '98
54 '98
Fools Rush In '97
Fled '96
Desperado '95
Fair Game '95
Four Rooms '95
From Dusk Till Dawn '95
Midaq Alley '95

Chris Hayes
In the Company of Men '96

George "Gabby" Hayes
Great Expectations '46
Lucky Texan '34
Man from Utah / Sagebrush
   Trail '34

Helen Hayes
Candleshoe '78
Airport '70

Ira H. Hayes
Sands of Iwo Jima '49

Isaac Hayes
Six Ways to Sunday '99
Ninth Street '98
Uncle Sam '96
Posse '93
Betrayed by Innocence '86

Patricia Hayes
A Fish Called Wanda '88

Robert Hayes III
Winner Takes All '98

Sean P. Hayes
Billy's Hollywood Screen Kiss
   '98

Steve Hayes
Trick '99

Tony Haygarth
Swept from the Sea '97
Dracula '79

Lisa Hayland
Novel Desires '92

Grace Hayle
The Great Dictator '40

David Hayman
The Jackal (CE) '97
Rob Roy '95
Sid & Nancy '86

Dick Haymes
State Fair '45

Tommy Haynes
Glen or Glenda? '53

Jim Haynie
The Peacemaker '97
The Bridges of Madison
   County '95

Lauren Hays
Web of Seduction '99
Life of a Gigolo '98

Robert Hays
Homeward Bound: The
   Incredible Journey '93

Dennis Haysbert
The Thirteenth Floor '99
Absolute Power '97
Heat '95

Mr. Baseball '92
Navy SEALS '90

Chad Hayward
Violent Zone '89

Leland Hayward
The Fear '94

Louis Hayward
And Then There Were None
   '45

Rachel Hayward
The Fear: Halloween Night
   '99

Susan Hayward
The Conqueror '56
The Snows of Kilimanjaro '52
Reap the Wild Wind '42

Chris Haywood
Shine '95
Sweet Talker '91
Breaker Morant '80

Rita Hayworth
The Love Goddesses '65

Ofra Haza
Prince of Egypt '98 (V)

Jonathan Haze
The Terror '63

Ruby Head
The Long Good Friday '80

Lena Headey
Merlin '98
Twice upon a Yesterday '98
Mrs. Dalloway '97

Shari Headley
Coming to America '88

Glenne Headly
Babe: Pig in the City '98 (V)
The X-Files '98
Bastard out of Carolina '96
Mr. Holland's Opus '95
Sgt. Bilko '95
Mortal Thoughts '91
Dirty Rotten Scoundrels '88

Anthony Heald
Deep Rising '98
8mm '98
A Time to Kill '96
The Client '94
Silence of the Lambs '91

Darin Heames
The Fear '94

John Heard
Desert Blue '98
Snake Eyes '98
Men '97
My Fellow Americans '96
The Pelican Brief '93
Home Alone 2: Lost in New
   York '92
Rambling Rose '91
Awakenings '90
Home Alone '90
Big '88
The Seventh Sign '88
Cat People '82

George Hearn
Barney's Great Adventure '98
The Devil's Own '96
Sneakers '92

Patty Hearst
Pecker '98
Serial Mom '94

Rick Hearst
Warlock 3: The End of Innocence '98

Charlie Heath
Leprechaun 2 '94

Darrell Heath
Don't Be a Menace to South
   Central While Drinking Your
   Juice in the Hood '95

Jean Heather
Double Indemnity '44

Patricia Heaton
Beethoven '92

Anne Heche
Psycho '98
Return to Paradise '98
Six Days, Seven Nights '98
I Know What You Did Last
   Summer '97
Volcano '97
Wag the Dog '97
Donnie Brasco '96
The Juror '96

Lawrence Hecht
Scream (CS) '96

Paul Hecht
Private Parts '96

Eileen Heckart
The First Wives Club '96

Dan Hedaya
A Night at the Roxbury '98
A Life Less Ordinary '97
Daylight '96
The First Wives Club '96
Marvin's Room '96
Ransom '96
Clueless '95
To Die For '95
The Usual Suspects '95
Maverick '94
Boiling Point '93
Mr. Wonderful '93
Commando '85

David Hedison
License to Kill '89
Live and Let Die '73

Jack Hedley
New York Ripper '82
For Your Eyes Only (SE) '81

Tippi Hedren
The Break Up '98
The Birds '63

Deborah Hedwall
Shadrach '98

Van Heflin
Airport '70
The Strange Love of Martha
   Ivers '46
Till the Clouds Roll By '46
Santa Fe Trail '40

Hugh Hefner
History of the World: Part 1
   '81

O.P. Heggie
The Bride of Frankenstein '35
Midnight '34

Robert Hegyes
The Pandora Project '98

Peter Hehir
Sweet Talker '91

Horace Heidt
Pot o' Gold '41

Katherine Heigl
Bug Buster '99
Bride of Chucky '98
Stand-Ins '97
Under Siege 2 '95

Amelia Heinle
The Limey '99
Black Cat Run '98

Jayne Heitmeyer
An American Affair '99
Dead End '98
Face the Evil '97

Sci-Fighters '96

Helen
Khamoshi the Musical '96

Marg Helgenberger
Fire Down Below '97
Bad Boys '95
The Cowboy Way '94
Stephen King's The Tommy-knockers '93
Always '89

Richard Hell
Blank Generation '79

William Hellfire
Caress of the Vampire 2:
Teenage Girl a Go-Go '96

Brigitte Helm
Metropolis '26

Fay Helm
The Wolf Man '41

Hans Helm
Werther '88

Levon Helm
Fire Down Below '97
Feeling Minnesota '96
The Right Stuff '83

Katherine Helmond
Fear and Loathing in Las Vegas '98
The Lady in White '88
Overboard '87
Brazil '85
Brazil (Criterion SE) '85
Time Bandits '81

Tom Helmore
Vertigo (CE) '58

Robert Helpmann
The Red Shoes '48
Henry V '44

David Hemblen
Booty Call '96
The Sweet Hereafter '96
Exotica '94
Mesmer '94
A Man in Uniform '93

Margaux Hemingway
Bad Love '95

Mariel Hemingway
The Sex Monster '99
Deconstructing Harry '97
Sunset '88
Creator '85
Star 80 '83

Martin Hemme
Das Boot (DC) '81

David Hemmings
Deep Red: Hatchet Murders '75
Barbarella '68
Camelot '67

Sherman Hemsley
Misery Brothers Y2K '95

Joseph Henabery
The Birth of a Nation '15

Frederique Hender
The Devil's Nightmare '71

Dell Henderson
Love Affair '39

Don Henderson
The Adventures of Baron Munchausen '89

Douglas Henderson
The Manchurian Candidate '62

Sarah Henderson
Kids '95

Shirley Henderson
Rob Roy '95
Trainspotting '95

Tony Hendra
This Is Spinal Tap '84

Elaine Hendrix
The Parent Trap '98
Romy and Michele's High School Reunion '97

Gloria Hendry
Live and Let Die '73

Ian Hendry
Journey to the Far Side of the Sun '69

Barry (Shabaka) Henley
Life '99
How Stella Got Her Groove Back '98

Carrie Henn
Aliens (SE) '86

Marilu Henner
Man on the Moon '99
L.A. Story '91
Cannonball Run 2 '84

Jill Hennessy
Most Wanted '97

Sam Hennings
Drop Zone '94

Paul Henreid
Casablanca '42

Lance Henriksen
Tarzan '99 (V)
Face the Evil '97
The Last Assassins '96
Powder '95
Color of Night '94
No Escape '94
The Quick and the Dead '94
Hard Target '93
Alien3 '92
Aliens (SE) '86
The Terminator '84
Nightmares '83
The Right Stuff '83
Dog Day Afternoon '75

Anders Henrikson
Intermezzo '36

Buck Henry
I'm Losing You '98
Curtain Call '97
The Real Blonde '97
To Die For '95
Grumpy Old Men '93
The Player '92
Aria '88
Heaven Can Wait '78
The Man Who Fell to Earth '76

Charlotte Henry
March of the Wooden Soldiers '34

Gregg Henry
The Big Brass Ring '99
Payback '98
Star Trek: Insurrection '98
Body Double '84

John Henry
Passion Fish '92

Justin Henry
Sixteen Candles '84

Mike Henry
Smokey and the Bandit '77
The Green Berets '68

William Henry
Mister Roberts '55

Douglas Henshall
Twice upon a Yesterday '98
Kull the Conqueror '97

Elden Henson
She's All That '99
The Mighty '98

Jim Henson
The Dark Crystal '82 (V)

Audrey Hepburn
Always '89
My Fair Lady '64
Charade '63
Breakfast at Tiffany's '61

Katharine Hepburn
On Golden Pond '81
Rooster Cogburn '75
Guess Who's Coming to Dinner '67
Summertime '55
Adam's Rib '50
Woman of the Year '42
The Philadelphia Story '40

Hans Herbert
Impact '49

Percy Herbert
The Guns of Navarone '61

Rick Herbst
Brain Damage '88

Kuelan Herce
The Shiver of the Vampires '70

Kenneth Herdigein
The Johnsons '92

Lisa Heredia
Summer '86

David Herman
Office Space '98

Jimmy Herman
Dances with Wolves '90

Woody Herman
New Orleans '47

Patricia Hermenier
The Demoniacs '74

Sammy Hernandez
Cop and a Half '93

Mark Herrier
Tank '83
Porky's '82

Edward Herrmann
Atomic Train '99
Critical Care '97
Nixon '95
The Lost Boys '87
Overboard '87
The North Avenue Irregulars '79
The Betsy '78

Barbara Hershey
Portrait of a Lady '96
Falling Down '93
Hoosiers '86
The Right Stuff '83

Jean Hersholt
Tess of the Storm Country '22

Whitby Hertford
Mikey '92

Jason Hervey
Pee-wee's Big Adventure '85

Grant Heslov
Dante's Peak '97
Congo '95
True Lies '94

Sandra Hess
Mortal Kombat 2: Annihilation '97

Howard Hesseman
Gridlock'd '96
Black Death '91

Amazon Women on the Moon '87
This Is Spinal Tap '84
Billy Jack '71

Charlton Heston
Hercules '97 (N)
In the Mouth of Madness '95
True Lies '94
Tombstone '93
Solar Crisis '92
Midway '76
Two Minute Warning '76
Airport '75 '75
The Four Musketeers '75
Earthquake '74
The Three Musketeers '74
Call of the Wild '72
The Ten Commandments '56

Charles Heung
God of Gamblers '89

Jennifer Love Hewitt
Can't Hardly Wait '98
I Still Know What You Did Last Summer '98
I Know What You Did Last Summer '97
Sister Act 2: Back in the Habit '93

Martin Hewitt
Night Fire '94
Secret Games '92
Carnal Crimes '91

Paul Hewitt
Tom Clancy's Netforce '98

David Hewlett
Cube '98
Black Death '91

Sherrie Hewson
The Slipper and the Rose '76

Virginia Hey
The Road Warrior '82

Louis Jean Heydt
The Big Sleep '46
They Were Expendable '45

Barton Heyman
Raising Cain '92
The Exorcist (SE) '73

John Benjamin Hickey
The Bone Collector '99
The General's Daughter '99
Finding North '97
Eddie '96

Paul Hickey
The Matchmaker '97

Robert Hickey
Waking Ned Devine '98

William Hickey
Mouse Hunt '97
Major Payne '95
The Nightmare before Christmas '93 (V)
My Blue Heaven '90
National Lampoon's Christmas Vacation '89
Sea of Love '89
Prizzi's Honor '85

Chaz Hickman
The Alley Cats '65

Darryl Hickman
The Tingler '59

Dwayne Hickman
A Night at the Roxbury '98

Howard Hickman
Gone with the Wind '39

Catherine Hicks
Turbulence '96
Animal Room '95
Child's Play '88
Peggy Sue Got Married '86

Star Trek 4: The Voyage Home '86

Charles Hicks
Cool Hand Luke '67

Dan Hicks
Evil Dead 2: Dead by Dawn '87

Taral Hicks
Belly '98
A Bronx Tale '93

Bokuzen Hidari
Seven Samurai '54

Jan Hieronimko
Vampyr '31

Anthony Higgins
Alive and Kicking '96
The Draughtsman's Contract '82

Clare Higgins
Hellbound: Hellraiser 2 '88
Hellraiser '87

John Michael Higgins
Wag the Dog '97

Michael Higgins
School Ties '92
Dead Bang '89
Angel Heart '87

Terry Higgins
Winstanley '75

Torri Higginson
Jungleground '95

Angelia High
Embrace the Darkness '98

Arthur Hill
One Magic Christmas '85
A Bridge Too Far '77
The Killer Elite '75
The Andromeda Strain '71

Benny Hill
Chitty Chitty Bang Bang '68

Bernard Hill
William Shakespeare's A Midsummer Night's Dream '99
Titanic '97
The Ghost and the Darkness '96
Mountains of the Moon '90

Dennis Hill
The Underneath '95

Dule Hill
She's All That '99

Lauryn Hill
Sister Act 2: Back in the Habit '93

Marianna Hill
The Invisible Strangler '76
High Plains Drifter '73
The Baby '72

Ross Hill
Iron Eagle 4 '95

Steven Hill
The Firm '93
White Palace '90
Running on Empty '88
Legal Eagles '86
Raw Deal '86

Terence Hill
Lucky Luke '94
Troublemakers '94

Marcel Hillaire
Take the Money and Run '69

Colette Hiller
Aliens (SE) '86

John Hillerman
Around the World in 80 Days '89

History of the World: Part 1
'81
Blazing Saddles '74
Chinatown '74

Richard Hillman
Men '97

Ty Hillman
The Horse Whisperer '97

Art Hindle
Porky's '82
Invasion of the Body Snatch-
ers '78

Samuel S. Hinds
It's a Wonderful Life '46

Damon Hines
Once Upon a Time . . .
When We Were Colored '95
Lethal Weapon '87

Gregory Hines
Good Luck '96
History of the World: Part 1
'81

Robert Hines
Hellraiser '87

Pat Hingle
Muppets from Space '99
Batman and Robin '97
Hunter's Moon '97
A Thousand Acres '97
Batman Forever '95
The Quick and the Dead '94
Batman Returns '92
The Grifters '90
Batman '89
The Land Before Time '88 (V)
Brewster's Millions '85
The Falcon and the Snowman
'85
The Gauntlet '77
Hang 'Em High '67

Kristin Hinojosa
Dazed and Confused '93

Paul Hipp
Another Day in Paradise '98
Midnight in the Garden of
Good and Evil (SE) '97

Keith Cooke Hirabayashi
Beverly Hills Ninja '96

Akihiko Hirata
Godzilla, King of the Mon-
sters '56
Samurai 2: Duel at Ichijoji
Temple '55

Daniel Hirsch
Zero Boys '86

Judd Hirsch
Man on the Moon '99
Independence Day '96
Running on Empty '88

Hallee Hirsh
You've Got Mail '98

Christianne Hirt
Firestorm '97

Alfred Hitchcock
The Birds '63
Psycho (CE) '60
The Lady Vanishes '38
The Lodger '26

Michael Hitchcock
Happy, Texas '99

Patricia Hitchcock
Psycho (CE) '60
Strangers on a Train '51

Paul Hittscher
Fitzcarraldo '82

Chin Ho
Peace Hotel '95

Don Ho
Joe's Apartment '96

Judith Hoag
Teenage Mutant Ninja Tur-
tles: The Movie '90

Florence Hoath
The Governess '98

Rebecca Hobbs
The Ugly '96

William Hobbs
The Three Musketeers '74

Valerie Hobson
Great Expectations '46
The Bride of Frankenstein '35

Emil Hoch
America '24

Corrine Hochwarter
Gustav Mahler: To Live, I Will
Die '87

Kane Hodder
Wishmaster '97

Douglas Hodge
Salome's Last Dance '88

John Hodge
Shallow Grave '94

Patricia Hodge
The Leading Man '96
Sunset '88

Paul Hoerbiger
The Third Man '49

Abbie Hoffman
Born on the Fourth of July
'89

Dustin Hoffman
Mad City '97
Sphere '98
Wag the Dog '97
Sleepers '96
Outbreak '94
Hero '92
Rain Man '88
All the President's Men '76
Papillon '73
Straw Dogs '72
Midnight Cowboy '69

Elizabeth Hoffman
Dante's Peak '97

Gaby Hoffman
200 Cigarettes '98
Volcano '97
Everyone Says I Love You '96
Now and Then '95
Sleepless in Seattle '93
Uncle Buck '89

Howard Hoffman
House on Haunted Hill '58

Isabella Hoffman
The Colony '98

Linda Hoffman
The Dentist 2: Brace Yourself
'98
The Dentist '96
Jane Street '96

Philip Seymour Hoffman
Happiness '98
Patch Adams (CE) '98
The Big Lebowski '97
Boogie Nights '97
Twister '96
When a Man Loves a Woman
'94
Scent of a Woman '92

Thom Hoffman
Orlando '92

Susanna Hoffs
The Allnighter '87

Charlie Hofheimer
Father's Day '96

Marco Hofschneider
The Island of Dr. Moreau '96

Bosco Hogan
In the Name of the Father '93

Fayley Hogan
The Seventh Sense '99

Ashley Holbrook
Ringmaster '98

Hal Holbrook
The Bachelor '99
Hush '98
Hercules '97 (V)
The Firm '93
Creepshow '82
Capricorn One '78
All the President's Men '76
Midway '76

Sarah Holcomb
Caddyshack '80
National Lampoon's Animal
House '78

Alexandra Holden
In and Out '97

Jennifer Holden
Jailhouse Rock '57

Marjean Holden
Mortal Kombat 2: Annihilation '97

William Holden
Network '76
The Towering Inferno '74
The Wild Bunch '69
Alvarez Kelly '66
Born Yesterday '50

Geoffrey Holder
Swashbuckler '76
Live and Let Die '73

Thomas Holden
The Three Musketeers '21

Billie Holiday
New Orleans '47

Brenda Holiday
Fraternity Demon '92

Edwin Holland
America '24

Adam Hollander
Halloween '78

Tom Hollander
The Very Thought of You '98

Steve Hollar
Hoosiers '86

Judy Holliday
Adam's Rib '50
Born Yesterday '50

Polly Holliday
The Parent Trap '98
Gremlins '84

Earl Holliman
Sharky's Machine '81
Forbidden Planet '56
Big Combo '55

Tommy Hollis
Primary Colors '98

Laurel Holloman
Boogie Nights '97

Carol Holloway
The Saphead '21

Stanley Holloway
My Fair Lady '64

Lauren Holly
Money Kings '98
Beautiful Girls '96
Turbulence '96

Dumb & Dumber '94
Dragon: The Bruce Lee Story
'93

Celeste Holm
All About Eve '50
Gentleman's Agreement '47

Ian Holm
eXistenZ '99
The Fifth Element '97
A Life Less Ordinary '97
Night Falls on Manhattan '96
The Sweet Hereafter '96
Big Night '95
Mary Shelley's Frankenstein
'94
Brazil '85
Brazil (Criterion SE) '85
Chariots of Fire '81
Time Bandits '81
Alien '79

Brittany Ashton Holmes
The Little Rascals '94

Katie Holmes
Go '99
Teaching Mrs. Tingle '99
Disturbing Behavior '98

Mark Holmes
The Adventures of Priscilla,
Queen of the Desert '94

**Prudence Wright
Holmes**
In Dreams '98

Wendell Holmes
Lotto Land '95

Rosie Holotik
Don't Look in the Basement
'73

Jack Holt
They Were Expendable '45

Sandrine Holt
Once a Thief '96
Black Robe '91

Tim Holt
Stagecoach '39

Mark Holton
Leprechaun '93
A League of Their Own '92
Pee-wee's Big Adventure '85

Hugh B. Holub
Zig Zag '99

Allen Holubar
20,000 Leagues under the
Sea '16

Oscar Homolka
Ball of Fire '41
Sabotage '36

Yutaka Honda
The Pillow Book '95

Ruby Honeycat
Caress of the Vampire 2:
Teenage Girl a Go-Go '96

Allen D. Hong
The King and I '99 (V)

James Hong
Mulan '98 (V)
Red Corner '97
Tango and Cash '89
The Golden Child '86

Leanne Hong
Full Metal Jacket '87

Shin Hong
Center Stage '91

Yu Lan Hong
Girls Unbuttoned '93

Jia Hongshen
Frozen '98

Heinz Honig
Das Boot (DC) '81

Darla Hood
The Bat '59

Don Hood
Dean Koontz's Mr. Murder
'98
Absence of Malice '81

John Lee Hooker
The Blues Brothers (CE) '80

Brian Hooks
Q: The Movie '99

David Hooks
Dark Odyssey '57

Jan Hooks
Simon Birch '98
Batman Returns '92
Pee-wee's Big Adventure '85

Robert Hooks
Posse '93

Rex Hooper
Night Calls: The Movie '98

Bob Hope
The Road to Utopia '46
The Princess and the Pirate
'44
They Got Me Covered '43
The Road to Morocco '42

Gloria Hope
Tess of the Storm Country
'22

Leslie Hope
Bram Stoker's Shadowbuilder
'98

Wayne Hope
The Castle '97

William Hope
Hellbound: Hellraiser 2 '88
Aliens (SE) '86

Anthony Hopkins
Instinct '99
The Mask of Zorro '98
Meet Joe Black '98
Amistad '97
The Edge '97
Nixon '95
Legends of the Fall '94
Shadowlands '93
The Trial '93
Chaplin '92
Dracula '92
Howard's End '92
Silence of the Lambs '91
A Bridge Too Far '77

Barrett Hopkins
Firehouse '87

Bo Hopkins
From Dusk Till Dawn 2: Texas
Blood Money '98
U-Turn '97
Uncle Sam '96
Trapper County War '89
Nightmare at Noon '87
Midnight Express '78
The Killer Elite '75
American Graffiti '73
The Getaway '72
The Wild Bunch '69

Harold Hopkins
Gallipoli '81

Jermaine Hopkins
Def Jam's How to Be a Player
'97

Paul Hopkins
Armistead Maupin's More
Tales of the City '97

Rolf Hoppe
Palmetto '98
Spring Symphony '86

Dennis Hopper
EDtv '99
Space Truckers '97
Top of the World '97
Waterworld '95
Speed '94
Boiling Point '93
True Romance '93
Hoosiers '86
My Science Project '85
The Inside Man '84
Rumble Fish '83
Out of the Blue '80
Apocalypse Now '79
Easy Rider '69
Cool Hand Luke '67
Night Tide '63
Rebel without a Cause '55

Hedda Hopper
Reap the Wild Wind '42

William Hopper
Rebel without a Cause '55

Russell Hopton
I'm No Angel '33

Gerard Horan
Much Ado about Nothing '93

James Horan
Allyson Is Watching '96

Michael Hordern
The Slipper and the Rose '76
A Christmas Carol '51

Gen Horiuchi
George Balanchine's The Nutcracker '93

Amy Horne
Cost of Living '97

Lena Horne
The Wiz '78
Till the Clouds Roll By '46

Carl Horner
Slave Girls from Beyond Infinity '87

Jane Horrocks
Little Voice '98
Memphis Belle '90
The Witches '90

Anna Maria Horsford
Set It Off '96
Presumed Innocent '90

Edward Everett Horton
Forever and a Day '43
Lost Horizon '37

Helen Horton
Alien '79 (V)

John Horton
Stephen King's Thinner '96

Peter Horton
Singles '92
Amazon Women on the Moon
'87

Dominique Horwitz
Stalingrad '94

Yuriko Hoshi
Godzilla vs. Mothra '64

Bob Hoskins
Felicia's Journey '99
Cousin Bette '97
Spice World: The Movie '97
Michael '96
Nixon '95
Who Framed Roger Rabbit
'88
Brazil '85
Brazil (Criterion SE) '85
Pink Floyd: The Wall '82
The Long Good Friday '80

Shawn Hoskins
Retrievers '82

Yukihiro Hotaru
Zeram '91

Paul Houde
The Boys '97

Katharine Houghton
Guess Who's Coming to Dinner '67

Djimon Hounsou
Deep Rising '98
Amistad '97
Ill-Gotten Gains '97

John Houseman
Ghost Story '81
Rollerball '75
Three Days of the Condor '75

Jerry Houser
Slap Shot '77

Candice Houston
The Land Before Time '88 (V)

Donald Houston
The Viking Queen '67

Whitney Houston
Cinderella '97
The Bodyguard '92

Anders Hove
Bloodstorm: Subspecies 4
'98

Adrian Hoven
Kiss Me Monster '69
Mark of the Devil '69
Succubus '69
Two Undercover Angels '68

Helen Hovey
The Sadist '63

Natasha Hovey
Demons '86

Anne Howard
Prince of Darkness '87

Arliss Howard
Somebody Has to Shoot the
Picture '90
Tequila Sunrise '88
Full Metal Jacket '87

Arthur Howard
The Ghost Goes Gear '66

Clint Howard
Austin Powers 2: The Spy
Who Shagged Me '99
EDtv '99
The Waterboy '98
Barb Wire '96
Body Armor '96
Leprechaun 2 '94
Far and Away '92
Backdraft '91
Night Shift '82
Rock 'n' Roll High School '79
Eat My Dust '76

Esther Howard
Klondike Annie '36

Gertrude Howard
I'm No Angel '33

Jean Speegle Howard
Apollo 13 '95

John Howard
The Philadelphia Story '40
Lost Horizon '37

Ken Howard
Tactical Assault '99
At First Sight '98
The Net '95

Kevyn Major Howard
Full Metal Jacket '87

Kyle Howard
Baby Geniuses '98

Leslie Howard
Gone with the Wind '39
The Scarlet Pimpernel '34

Rance Howard
Psycho '98
Far and Away '92
Eat My Dust '76
Cool Hand Luke '67

Ron Howard
Eat My Dust '76
American Graffiti '73
The Music Man '62

Shemp Howard
Buck Privates '41

**Terrence DaShon
Howard**
The Best Man '99

Traylor Howard
Dirty Work '97

Trevor Howard
Sea Wolves '81
The Third Man '49

Kevin Howarth
Razor Blade Smile '98

Clark Howat
Billy Jack '71

C. Thomas Howell
Shameless '94
Red Dawn '84
The Outsiders '83
Tank '83

Hoke Howell
Humanoids from the Deep
'80

Peter Howell
Shadowlands '93

Sally Ann Howes
Chitty Chitty Bang Bang '68
Anna Karenina '48

Chris Howland
Kiss Me Monster '69
Two Undercover Angels '68

Rodolfo Hoyos
The Brave One '56

Carol Hoyt
Midnight Confessions '95

John Hoyt
Flesh Gordon '72
The Conqueror '56

Marketa Hrubesova
Lady Macbeth of Mtsensk
'92

Wong Tsu Hsien
A Chinese Ghost Story '87

Wu Hsin-kuo
Temptation of a Monk '94

Julia Hsu
Rush Hour '98

Sibelle Hu
Crystal Hunt '92
Inspector Wears Skirts '88
My Lucky Stars '85

Hae-Jin Huang
Why Has Bodhi-Darma Left
for the East '89

Patrick Huard
The Boys '97

Harold Huber
Klondike Annie '36

Whip Hubley
Armistead Maupin's More
Tales of the City '97
Executive Decision '96
Top Gun '86

Cooper Huckabee
The Funhouse '81

David Huddleston
The Big Lebowski '97
Frantic '88
Blazing Saddles '74

Joseph Hudgins
Flesh Gordon '72

Reginald Hudlin
Joe's Apartment '96 (V)
Posse '93

Warrington Hudlin
Posse '93

Ernie Hudson
Shark Attack '99
Urban Menace '99
A Stranger in the Kingdom
'98
Mr. Magoo '97
The Substitute '96
Congo '95
The Basketball Diaries '94
The Cowboy Way '94
No Escape '94
The Crow '93
The Hand that Rocks the Cra-
dle '92
Ghostbusters 2 '89
Leviathan '89
Trapper County War '89
Ghostbusters '84
Penitentiary 2 '82
The Jazz Singer '80

Kate Hudson
Desert Blue '98
200 Cigarettes '98

Oliver Hudson
The Out-of-Towners '99

Rochelle Hudson
Rebel without a Cause '55

Rock Hudson
Embryo '76
Pillow Talk '59

Kevin Huff
The Curve '97

Felicity Huffman
The Spanish Prisoner '97

Daniel Hugh-Kelly
From the Earth to the Moon
'98
Star Trek: Insurrection '98

Barnard Hughes
Neil Simon's The Odd Couple
2 '98
Sister Act 2: Back in the
Habit '93
Doc Hollywood '91
The Lost Boys '87
Tron '82
Midnight Cowboy '69

Carol Hughes
Love Affair '39

Frank John Hughes
Angel's Dance '99

Geoff Hughes
Yellow Submarine '68 (V)

Lloyd Hughes
The Lost World '25
Tess of the Storm Country
'22

Miko Hughes
Mercury Rising '98
Spawn (SE) '98
Zeus and Roxanne '96
Apollo 13 '95
Wes Craven's New Nightmare
'94

Tresa Hughes
Skylark '93

D.L. Hughley
Inspector Gadget '99 (V)

Kara Hui
Inspector Wears Skirts '88

Michael Hui
Chinese Box '97

Ricky Hui
Mr. Vampire '86

Steve Huison
The Full Monty '96

Tom Hulce
Mary Shelley's Frankenstein
'94
Fearless '93
Parenthood '89
Amadeus '84
National Lampoon's Animal
House '78

Endre Hules
The Seventh Sense '99

Gladys Hulette
Tol'able David '21

Dianne Hull
Aloha, Bobby and Rose '74

Henry Hull
Midnight '34

Lauren Hulsey
Pecker '98

Renee Humphrey
The Sex Monster '99
French Kiss '95
Mallrats '95

Barry Humphries
Spice World: The Movie '97
The Leading Man '96

Geert Hunaerts
To Play or To Die '91

Charles Kay Hune
Troma's War (DC) '88

Hui Siu Hung
Expect the Unexpected '98

Sammo Hung
Mr. Nice Guy '98
Dragons Forever '88
Eastern Condors '87
The Millionaire's Express '86
Heart of Dragon '85
My Lucky Stars '85
Wheels on Meals '84
Zu: Warriors of the Magic
Mountain '83
The Prodigal Son '82

Wai Ying Hung
Legend of the Drunken Tiger
'92

Arthur Hunnicutt
Shoot Out '71

Bonnie Hunt
The Green Mile '99
A Bug's Life (CE) '98 (V)
Kissing a Fool '98
Jerry Maguire '96
Jumanji (CS) '95
Now and Then '95
Only You '94
Beethoven's 2nd '93
Dave '93
Beethoven '92
Rain Man '88

Brad Hunt
Fire Down Below '97

Helen Hunt
As Good As It Gets '97
Twister '96
Mr. Saturday Night '92
Next of Kin '89
Stealing Home '88
Peggy Sue Got Married '86

Jimmy Hunt
Invaders from Mars '53

Linda Hunt
Eat Your Heart Out '96
The Relic '96
Ready to Wear '94
Kindergarten Cop '90
The Bostonians '84
Dune '84
The Year of Living Dangerously '82

Marsha Hunt
Raw Deal '48

Martita Hunt
Anna Karenina '48
Great Expectations '46
Sabotage '36

Bill Hunter
Moby Dick '98
The Adventures of Priscilla,
   Queen of the Desert '94

Harold Hunter
Kids '95

Holly Hunter
Living Out Loud '98
A Life Less Ordinary '97
Copycat '95
Crash '95
The Firm '93
The Piano '93
Always '89
Broadcast News '87

Ian Hunter
The Ring '27

Jeffrey Hunter
Custer of the West '67
The Longest Day '62
Last Hurrah '58
The Great Locomotive Chase '56
The Searchers '56

Kaki Hunter
Porky's '82

Kim Hunter
Midnight in the Garden of
   Good and Evil (SE) '97
A Price above Rubies '97
A Streetcar Named Desire '51

Rachel Hunter
Just a Little Harmless Sex '99

Shedric Hunter Jr.
Caught Up '98

Sam Huntington
Detroit Rock City '99

Howard Huntsberry
La Bamba '87

Isabelle Huppert
La Separation '98
Love After Love '94
Entre-Nous '83

Elizabeth Hurley
Austin Powers 2: The Spy
   Who Shagged Me '99
EDtv '99
My Favorite Martian '98
Permanent Midnight '98
Austin Powers: International
   Man of Mystery '97
Dangerous Ground '96
Shameless '94

Brandon Hurst
The White Zombie '32
Dr. Jekyll and Mr. Hyde '20

Paul Hurst
Gone with the Wind '39

Veronica Hurst
Peeping Tom '60

Ian Hurt
Enemy of the State '98

John Hurt
Tender Loving Care '99
The Climb '97
Contact '97
Love and Death on Long
   Island '98
Rob Roy '95
Thumbelina '94 (V)
King Ralph '91
The Field '90
Aria '88
History of the World: Part 1 '81
Alien '79
Midnight Express '78

Mary Beth Hurt
Boys Life 2 '98
Affliction '97
From the Journals of Jean
   Seberg '95
Light Sleeper '92
Parents '89

William Hurt
The Big Brass Ring '99
Lost in Space '98
One True Thing '98
Dark City '97
Michael '96
Mr. Wonderful '93
Broadcast News '87
The Big Chill '83
Body Heat '81
Altered States '80

Olivia Hussey
Romeo and Juliet '68

Ruth Hussey
James Dean Double Feature:
   Hill Number One / I Am a
   Fool '51
The Philadelphia Story '40

Anjelica Huston
Ever After: A Cinderella Story '98
Phoenix '98
Buffalo 66 '97
The Crossing Guard '94
Manhattan Murder Mystery '93
The Player '92
The Grifters '90
The Witches '90
Crimes & Misdemeanors '89
Prizzi's Honor '85
This Is Spinal Tap '84
The Postman Always Rings
   Twice '81

John Huston
Lovesick '83
Chinatown '74

Virginia Huston
Sudden Fear '52

Walter Huston
Duel in the Sun '46
And Then There Were None '45
The Shanghai Gesture '42
Dodsworth '36
Rain '32

Will Hutchins
Maverick '94

Doug Hutchison
The Green Mile '99

Ken Hutchison
Ladyhawke '85

Jayne Hutton
Stay Awake '87

Jim Hutton
Psychic Killer '75
The Green Berets '68
Hellfighters '68

Lauren Hutton
Just a Little Harmless Sex '99
54 '98
American Gigolo '79

Timothy Hutton
The General's Daughter '99
Money Kings '98
Beautiful Girls '96
Playing God '96
French Kiss '95
The Last Word '95
The Dark Half '91
Q & A '90
The Falcon and the Snowman '85

Jacquelyn Hyde
Take the Money and Run '69

Jonathan Hyde
Joan of Arc '99
The Mummy '99
Titanic '97
Anaconda '96
Jumanji (CS) '95

Alex Hyde-White
Pretty Woman '90

Wilfrid Hyde-White
My Fair Lady '64
The Third Man '49
The Man Who Knew Too
   Much '34

Diana Hyland
The Boy in the Plastic Bubble '76

Scott Hylands
Earthquake '74

Mike Hynson
The Endless Summer '66

Steve Hytner
Forces of Nature '99
The Prophecy 3: The Ascent '99
The Prophecy 2: Ashtown '97

Chaing I
They Shoot Horses, Don't
   They? '69

Yuen Shun I
Buddhist Fist '80

Ice Cube
Three Kings '99
The Players Club '98
Anaconda '96
Dangerous Ground '96
Friday '95
Trespass '92
Boyz N the Hood '91

Ice-T
Urban Menace '99
Crazy Six '98
Mean Guns '97
Johnny Mnemonic '95
Surviving the Game '94
Trespass '92
New Jack City '91
Ricochet '91

Etsuko Ichihara
Black Rain '88

Chusha Ichikawa
Chushingura '62

Utaemon Ichikawa
The 47 Ronin, Parts 1 & 2 '42

Kunihiko Ida
Zeram '91

Eric Idle
Dudley Do-Right '99
Quest for Camelot '98 (V)
Rudolph the Red-Nosed Rein-
   deer: The Movie '98 (V)

**The Adventures of Baron
Munchausen** '89
Around the World in 80 Days '89
Monty Python's The Meaning
   of Life '83
Monty Python's Life of Brian '79
And Now for Something Com-
   pletely Different '72

Cinnamon Idles
Sixteen Candles '84

Billy Idol
The Wedding Singer '97
The Doors '91

Rhys Ifans
Notting Hill '99
Dancing at Lughnasa '98

Hisashi Igawa
Ran '85

Togo Igawa
Incognito '97

Igor Ilinski
Aelita: Queen of Mars '24

Iman
L.A. Story '91
Star Trek 6: The Undiscov-
   ered Country '91

Gary Imhoff
Angel in Training '99
Thumbelina '94 (V)

Michael Imperioli
Last Man Standing '96
The Basketball Diaries '94
Goodfellas '90

Celia Imrie
Hilary and Jackie '98
The Borrowers '97
Mary Shelley's Frankenstein '94

Yoshio Inaba
Seven Samurai '54

Angelo Infanti
Emmanuelle: Queen of the
   Desert '93

Randi Ingerman
Desperate Crimes '93

Doran Inghram
Steele's Law '91

Rufino Ingles
Tombs of the Blind Dead '72

Elizabeth Inglis
The 39 Steps '35

Aaron Ingram
Who Shot Pat? '92

Joan Ingram
The Ghost Goes Gear '66

Rex Ingram
Dark Waters '44

Frankie Ingrassia
Election '99

I. Inkizhinov
Storm over Asia '28

Valeri Inkizhinov
Storm over Asia '28

Neil Innes
Monty Python's Life of Brian '79
Magical Mystery Tour '67

Harold Innocent
Robin Hood: Prince of
   Thieves '91

Antonella Interlenghi
New York Ripper '82

Aharon Ipale
The Mummy '99
A Kid in Aladdin's Palace '97

Marie Irakane
Bed and Board '70

Enrique Irazoqui
The Gospel According to St.
   Matthew '64

Jill Ireland
Chino / Man with a Camera '75
Hard Times '75
Cold Sweat '71

John Ireland
Farewell, My Lovely '75
I Saw What You Did '65
Spartacus '60
Vengeance Valley '51
Raw Deal '48
Red River '48

Kathy Ireland
National Lampoon's Loaded
   Weapon 1 '93
The Player '92

Jeremy Irons
The Man in the Iron Mask '98
Chinese Box '97
Die Hard: With a Vengeance '95
Damage '92
Dead Ringers '88

Michael Ironside
Johnny 2.0 '99
Starship Troopers '97
The Killing Man '94
Highlander 2: The Quickening '91
Total Recall '90
Top Gun '86
The Falcon and the Snowman '85

Amy Irving
The Rage: Carrie 2 '99
The Confession '98
Deconstructing Harry '97

Margaret Irving
Animal Crackers '30

Penny Irving
House of Whipcord '75

Bill Irwin
William Shakespeare's A Mid-
   summer Night's Dream '99
Just the Ticket '98
My Blue Heaven '90

Boyd Irwin
The Three Musketeers '21

Jason Isaacs
Armageddon '98
Soldier '98
Event Horizon '97
Dragonheart (SE) '96

Chris Isaak
From the Earth to the Moon '98
Grace of My Heart (CE) '96
Little Buddha '93
Silence of the Lambs '91

Ryo Ishibashi
The Crossing Guard '94

Keisuke Ishida
Black Rain '88

Akira Ishihama
The Human Condition: No
   Greater Love '58

Chu Ishikawa
Tokyo Fist '96

Sylvain Itkine
Grand Illusion '37

Emi Ito
Godzilla vs. Mothra '64

Robert Ito
Once a Thief '96

Toshiya Ito
Ran '85

Yumi Ito
Godzilla vs. Mothra '64

Marcel Iures
The Peacemaker '97

Zeljko Ivanek
A Civil Action '98
The Rat Pack '98
Donnie Brasco '96
Infinity '96
White Squall '96
School Ties '92

Vera Ivasheva
Alexander Nevsky '38

Burl Ives
Baker's Hawk '76

Dana Ivey
Mumford '99
The Imposters '98
Simon Birch '98
Home Alone 2: Lost in New York '92
Dirty Rotten Scoundrels '88

Judith Ivey
The Devil's Advocate '97
A Life Less Ordinary '97
Without Limits '97
In Country '89
Brighton Beach Memoirs '86
The Lonely Guy '84

Ed Ivory
The Nightmare before Christmas '93 (V)

Victor Izay
Billy Jack '71

Eddie Izzard
Mystery Men '99
The Avengers '98
Velvet Goldmine '98

Kary J
American Rampage '89

Michael Jace
Boogie Nights '97

James Jackel
Color Me Blood Red '64

Ian Jacklin
American Streetfighter '96
Expert Weapon '93

Robert Jacks
The Texas Chainsaw Massacre 4: The Next Generation '95

Andrew Jackson
Bram Stoker's Shadowbuilder '98
Specimen '97

Anne Jackson
The Shining '80

Bo Jackson
The Pandora Project '98
The Chamber '96

Freda Jackson
Great Expectations '46
Henry V '44

Glenda Jackson
Salome's Last Dance '88
Marat/Sade '66

Gordon Jackson
The Great Escape '63

Janet Jackson
Poetic Justice '93

Jeanine Jackson
Election '99

John M. Jackson
Career Opportunities '91

Jonathan Jackson
The Deep End of the Ocean '98

Joshua Jackson
Cruel Intentions '98
Urban Legend '98
Apt Pupil '97
The Mighty Ducks '92

Kate Jackson
Black Death '91

Mel Jackson
Soul Food '97

Michael Jackson
The Wiz '78

Philip Jackson
Little Voice '98
Brassed Off '96

Reggie Jackson
BASEketball '98

Robert Jason Jackson
New Jersey Drive '95

Rose Jackson
Dead Presidents '95

Samuel L. Jackson
Deep Blue Sea '99
The Negotiator '98
Out of Sight '98
The Red Violin '98
Eve's Bayou '97
Sphere '97
The Long Kiss Goodnight '96
A Time to Kill '96
Trees Lounge '96
Die Hard: With a Vengeance '95
Pulp Fiction '94
Menace II Society '93
National Lampoon's Loaded Weapon 1 '93
True Romance '93
Patriot Games '92
Jungle Fever '91
Def by Temptation '90
Goodfellas '90
Coming to America '88

Selmer Jackson
The Fighting Sullivans '42

Stoney Jackson
Streets of Fire '84

Victoria Jackson
Casual Sex? '88

Irene Jacob
The Big Brass Ring '99
My Life So Far '98
U.S. Marshals '98
Incognito '97

Joelle Jacob
The Lady in White '88

Derek Jacobi
Dead Again '91
The Odessa File '74
The Day of the Jackal '73

Lou Jacobi
Amazon Women on the Moon '87
Arthur '81

Herb Jacobs
Project Moon Base '53

Manny Jacobs
The Seventh Sign '88

Mike Jacobs Jr.
Die Watching '93

Peter Jacobs
Philadelphia '93

Peggy Jacobsen
Search and Destroy '88

Andy Jacobson
The Firing Line '91

Bobby Jacoby
Tremors '89

Carlos Jacott
Mr. Jealousy '98

Maurice Jacquemont
The Return of Martin Guerre '83

Hattie Jacques
A Christmas Carol '51

Anna Jacyszyn
The First 9 1/2 Weeks '98

Claude Jade
Bed and Board '70
Stolen Kisses '68

Richard Jaeckel
Starman '84
Day of the Animals '77
Grizzly '76
Ulzana's Raid '72
The Dirty Dozen '67
Sands of Iwo Jima '49

Sam Jaffe
Lost Horizon '37

Seth Jaffe
Scorned 2 '96

Saeed Jaffrey
The Man Who Would Be King '75

Dean Jagger
Proud Rebel '58
Revolt of the Zombies '36

Marine Jahan
Streets of Fire '84

Lisa Jakub
The Wicked, Wicked West '97
The Story Lady '93
Matinee '92
Rambling Rose '91

Anthony James
Unforgiven '92

Art James
Mallrats '95

Brion James
In God's Hands '98
The Fifth Element '97
Hunter's Moon '97
American Strays '96
The Killing Jar '96
Radioland Murders '94
Striking Distance '93
The Player '92
Another 48 Hrs. '90
Red Scorpion '89
Tango and Cash '89
Nightmare at Noon '87
Blade Runner (DC) '82

Clifton James
Carolina Skeletons '92
The Bonfire of the Vanities '90
The Last Detail '73
Live and Let Die '73
Cool Hand Luke '67
David and Lisa '62

Don James
Hamburger Hill '87

Gennie James
Broadcast News '87

Geraldine James
The Man Who Knew Too Little '97

Hawthorne James
Speed '94

Heidi James
Razor Blade Smile '98

Jesse James Jr.
Message in a Bottle '98
The Gingerbread Man '97

John James
The Devil Bat's Daughter '46

Lennie James
Lost in Space '98

Rick James
Life '99

Ron James
The Boogey Man '80

Steve James
The Player '92
Exterminator '80

Walter James
Battling Butler '26

Georges Jamin
Daughters of Darkness '71

Krystyna Janda
The Decalogue '88

Thomas Jane
Deep Blue Sea '99
The Thin Red Line '98
Boogie Nights '97
The Crow 2: City of Angels '96

Conrad Janis
Mr. Saturday Night '92
The Buddy Holly Story '78

Oleg Jankowsky
Nostalghia '83

Allison Janney
Drop Dead Gorgeous '99
Ten Things I Hate about You '99
Celebrity '98
The Imposters '98
Primary Colors '98
Six Days, Seven Nights '98
Private Parts '96
Big Night '95

Tom Jansen
Suite 16 '94

David Janssen
Swiss Conspiracy '77
Two Minute Warning '76
The Green Berets '68

Famke Janssen
House on Haunted Hill '99
Celebrity '98
Deep Rising '98
The Faculty '98
Monument Ave. '98
Rounders '98
The Gingerbread Man '97
Goldeneye '95
Lord of Illusions '95

Samantha Janus
Breeders '97

Agnes Jaoui
Un Air de Famille '96

Claude Jarman Jr.
Rio Grande '50

Jim Jarmusch
Sling Blade '96

Jerry Jarret
Killer's Kiss '55

Juri Jarvet
Solaris '72

Graham Jarvis
Parents '89

Neville Jason
The Message '77

Peter Jason
The Demolitionist '95
In the Mouth of Madness '95
Village of the Damned '95
Arachnophobia '90
They Live '88

Jose Jaspe
Horror Express '72

Mark Jax
Merlin '98

Ricky Jay
Mystery Men '99
Boogie Nights '97
Sink or Swim '97
The Spanish Prisoner '97
Tomorrow Never Dies (SE) '97

Jayapradha
Lav Kush '97

Michael Jayston
Nicholas and Alexandra '71

Gregory Jbara
William Shakespeare's A Midsummer Night's Dream '99
In and Out '97

Marianne Jean-Baptiste
A Murder of Crows '99
Mr. Jealousy '98

Zizi Jeanmarie
Black Tights '60
Hans Christian Andersen '52

Isabel Jeans
Gigi '58

Allan Jeayes
The Scarlet Pimpernel '34

Kieron Jecchinis
Full Metal Jacket '87

Jeetendra
Lav Kush '97

Meghan Jeffers
Altered States '80

Doug Jeffery
Monsoon '97
Mischievous '98

Barbara Jefford
And the Ship Sails On '83

Myles Jeffrey
Babe: Pig in the City '98 (V)

Peter Jeffrey
The Adventures of Baron Munchausen '89
The Odessa File '74

Lionel Jeffries
Chitty Chitty Bang Bang '68
Camelot '67

Richard Jeni
The Mask '94

Jackie "Butch" Jenkins
National Velvet '44

Ken Jenkins
Last Man Standing '96

Larry "Flash" Jenkins
Ferris Bueller's Day Off '86
Fletch '85

Megs Jenkins
Tiger Bay '59

Noam Jenkins
Moving Target '96

Richard Jenkins
The Mod Squad '99
The Imposters '98
Eddie '96
Flirting with Disaster '95
Wolf '94
Sea of Love '89
Stealing Home '88

The Witches of Eastwick '87

Frank Jenks
His Girl Friday '40

Bruce Jenner
Grambling's White Tiger '81

Lucy Jenner
The Seventh Sense '99

Lucinda Jenney
Desert Blue '98
G.I. Jane '97
Stephen King's Thinner '96
Leaving Las Vegas '95
Matinee '92
Thelma & Louise '91
Rain Man '88

Alex Jennings
The Wings of the Dove '97

Brent Jennings
Life '99
The Serpent and the Rainbow '87

DeWitt Jennings
The Bat Whispers '30

Waylon Jennings
Tom Sawyer '99 (V)
Maverick '94

Gordon Jennison
Running Time '97

Salome Jens
I'm Losing You '98

Cleo Jensen
Elvira Madigan '67

David Jensen
The Underneath '95

Jane Jensen
Tromeo & Juliet '95

Maren Jensen
Battlestar Galactica '78

Sasha Jensen
Dazed and Confused '93

Todd Jensen
Breeders '97
Alien Chaser '96

Roy Jenson
The Car '77

Sasha Jenson
Halloween 4: The Return of Michael Myers '88

Tim Jerome
A Price above Rubies '97

Jeanne Jerrems
Dark Odyssey '57

James Jeter
Cool Hand Luke '67

Michael Jeter
The Green Mile '99
Jakob the Liar '99
Fear and Loathing in Las Vegas '98
Patch Adams (CE) '98
Air Bud '97
Mouse Hunt '97
Waterworld '95
Drop Zone '94
Sister Act 2: Back in the Habit '93
Dead Bang '89

Isabel Jewell
Gone with the Wind '39
Lost Horizon '37

Zheng Jian
Ju Dou '90

Xiu Jim Jiang
Long Arm of the Law II '87

Penn Jillette
Fear and Loathing in Las Vegas '98
Hackers '95

Ann Jillian
Girls of the White Orchid '85

Soledad Jiminez
For Whom the Bell Tolls '43

Keith Joakum
The Witches of Eastwick '87

Robert Joel
A Very Natural Thing '73

Zita Johan
The Mummy '32

David Johansen
Scrooged '88

Paul Johansson
Carnival of Souls '98
Wishmaster 2: Evil Never Dies '98

Scarlett Johansson
Home Alone 3 '97
The Horse Whisperer '97

Elton John
Spice World: The Movie '97

Georg John
M '31

Gottfried John
Goldeneye '95

Lucien John
Walkabout '71

Glynis Johns
While You Were Sleeping '95
Mary Poppins '64
Court Jester '56

Larry Johns
Project Moon Base '53

Mervyn Johns
A Christmas Carol '51

Stratford Johns
The Lair of the White Worm '88
Salome's Last Dance '88

Tracy C. Johns
New Jack City '91

A.J. Johnson
The Players Club '98
Def Jam's How to Be a Player '97

Anne-Marie Johnson
Down in the Delta '98
Asteroid '97

Ariyan Johnson
Bulworth '98

Ashley Johnson
Dancer, Texas—Pop. 81 '98

Ben Johnson
Red Dawn '84
The Shadow Riders '82
Tex '82
The Getaway '72
Junior Bonner '72
The Wild Bunch '69
Rio Grande '50

Beverly Johnson
Def Jam's How to Be a Player '97

Brad Johnson
Always '89

Brook Johnson
The Sweet Hereafter '96

Camilla Johnson
Sparrows '26

Clark Johnson
Junior's Groove '97

Rude '96

Corey Johnson
The Mummy '99

Don Johnson
Goodbye, Lover '99
Tin Cup '96
The Hot Spot '90
Dead Bang '89
A Boy and His Dog '75
Zachariah '70

Hassan Johnson
Belly '98

Jack Johnson
Lost in Space '98

Julie Johnson
Barney's Great Adventure '98 (V)

Laura Johnson
Judge & Jury '96
Opening Night '77

Linda Johnson
Impact '49

Lynn-Holly Johnson
Hyper Space '89
For Your Eyes Only (SE) '81

Mel Johnson Jr.
Total Recall '90

Michael Johnson
Bride of Chucky '98

Michelle Johnson
Specimen '97
The Glimmer Man '96
Moving Target '96
Body Shot '93
Death Becomes Her '92
Far and Away '92

Noble Johnson
The Most Dangerous Game '32
The Mummy '32
The Navigator '24

Penny Johnson
What's Love Got to Do with It? '93

Reggie Johnson
Platoon '86

Richard Johnson
Zombie '80
Fifth Day of Peace '72

Sandy Johnson
Halloween '78

Seesel Ann Johnson
Sparrows '26

Tor Johnson
Carousel '56
Plan 9 from Outer Space '56
Bride of the Monster '55
Abbott and Costello in the Foreign Legion '50

Van Johnson
Brigadoon '54
The Caine Mutiny '54
The Last Time I Saw Paris '54

Victoria (Vicki) Johnson
Grizzly '76

Bobby Johnston
Loveblind '98
Body Strokes '95

Darrell Johnston
Dancing at Lughnasa '98

J.J. Johnston
Stranger by Night '94
Mad Dog and Glory '93

Jo Johnston
The Swinging Cheerleaders '74

John Dennis Johnston
Streets of Fire '84

Kristen Johnston
Austin Powers 2: The Spy Who Shagged Me '99

Oliver Johnston
A King in New York / A Woman in Paris '57

Marilyn Joi
Kentucky Fried Movie '77

Angelina Jolie
The Bone Collector '99
Pushing Tin '99
Playing by Heart '98
Playing God '96
Hackers '95

I. Stanford Jolley
Sands of Iwo Jima '49

Andras Jones
The Demolitionist '95
A Nightmare on Elm Street 4: Dream Master '88
Sorority Babes in the Slime-ball Bowl-A-Rama '87

Ben Jones
Primary Colors '98

Carolyn Jones
Eaten Alive '76
How the West Was Won '63
Invasion of the Body Snatchers '56
The War of the Worlds '53

Cherry Jones
The Horse Whisperer '97

Claude Earl Jones
Bride of Re-Animator '89
Impulse '84

Dean Jones
Clear and Present Danger '94
Beethoven '92
Jailhouse Rock '57

Eddie Jones
Sneakers '92
Q (The Winged Serpent) '82

Elvin Jones
Zachariah '70

Freddie Jones
Dune '84
Firestarter '84
And the Ship Sails On '83
The Satanic Rites of Dracula '73

Gemma Jones
Sense and Sensibility '95

Gordon Jones
McLintock! '63

Grace Jones
Conan the Destroyer '84

Griffith Jones
Henry V '44

Henry Jones
Arachnophobia '90
The Grifters '90
Deathtrap '82
Napoleon and Samantha '72
Butch Cassidy and the Sundance Kid '69
Vertigo (CE) '58

James Earl Jones
The Lion King: Simba's Pride '98 (V)
Merlin '98 (V)
Horton Foote's Alone '97
Good Luck '96

Clear and Present Danger '94
Sommersby '93
Patriot Games '92
Sneakers '92
The Hunt for Red October '90
Coming to America '88
Conan the Barbarian '82
Swashbuckler '76
Dr. Strangelove, or: How I Learned to Stop Worrying and Love the Bomb '64

Janet Jones
The Flamingo Kid '84

Jeffrey Jones
Ravenous '99
Sleepy Hollow '99
The Devil's Advocate '97
Santa Fe '97
The Hunt for Red October '90
Beetlejuice '88
Ferris Bueller's Day Off '86
Amadeus '84

Jennifer Jones
The Towering Inferno '74
Beat the Devil '53
Duel in the Sun '46

Jeny Jones
Avenging Disco Godfather '76

Jerry Jones
Dolemite '75

Jill Parker Jones
Varsity Blues '98

John Marshall Jones
Sgt. Bilko '95

Ken Jones
Phantasm '79

Kimberly (Lil' Kim) Jones
She's All That '99

L.Q. (Justus E. McQueen) Jones
The Jack Bull '99
The Patriot '99
The Mask of Zorro '98
The Edge '97
Casino '95
A Boy and His Dog '75
The Wild Bunch '69
Men in War '57

Marie Jones
In the Name of the Father '93

Mickey Jones
Sling Blade '96
Tin Cup '96
Drop Zone '94
National Lampoon's Vacation '83

Quincy Jones
A Great Day in Harlem / The Spitball Story '94 (N)

Richard Jones
The Newton Boys '97
Under Siege '92

Richard T. Jones
Event Horizon '97
Kiss the Girls '97
The Trigger Effect '96

Sam Jones
T.N.T. '98
American Strays '96
Hard Vice '94
Expert Weapon '93
Flash Gordon '80

Sharon Lee Jones
Princess Warrior '90

Shirley Jones
Tank '83
The Music Man '62
Carousel '56

Andreas Katsulas
The Fugitive '93
Next of Kin '89
Someone to Watch Over Me '87

Kokinji Katsura
The Human Condition: Road to Eternity '59

Mayako Katsuragi
The Toxic Avenger, Part 2 '89

Nicky Katt
The Limey '99
One True Thing '98
Phantoms '97

William Katt
Jawbreaker '98
Piranha '95
Stranger by Night '94
Swimsuit '89

Chris Kattan
House on Haunted Hill '99
A Night at the Roxbury '98

David Katz
Henry: Portrait of a Serial Killer '90

Omri Katz
Matinee '92

Cristen Kauffman
Betrayed by Innocence '86

Caroline Kava
Born on the Fourth of July '89

Charles Kavanaugh
Public Access '93

Julie Kavner
Dr. Dolittle '98 (V)
Deconstructing Harry '97
Awakenings '90

Chojuro Kawarazaki
The 47 Ronin, Parts 1 & 2 '42

Kunitaro Kawarazaki
The 47 Ronin, Parts 1 & 2 '42

Yusuke Kawazu
The Human Condition: Road to Eternity '59

Dianne Kay
1941 '79

Yuzo Kayama
Chushingura '62
Sanjuro '62

Danny Kaye
Court Jester '56
Hans Christian Andersen '52
The Secret Life of Walter Mitty '47
Wonder Man '45

Lila Kaye
An American Werewolf in London '81

Stubby Kaye
Who Framed Roger Rabbit '88

Lainie Kazan
The Big Hit '98

Guo Ke-Yu
Red Cherry '95

James Keach
National Lampoon's Vacation '83

Stacy Keach
Children of the Corn 666: Isaac's Return '99
American History X '98
Escape from L.A. '96
The Killer inside Me '76

Staci Keanan
For Love of a Child '90

James Keane
Apocalypse Now '79

William Keane
The First 9 1/2 Weeks '98

Stephen Kearney
The Nutt House '92

Billy Kearns
Bed and Board '70

Charles Keating
The Thomas Crown Affair '99
The Bodyguard '92

Buster Keaton
Limelight '52
Forever and a Day '43
Steamboat Bill, Jr. '28
College '27
Battling Butler '26
The General '26
Seven Chances '25
The Navigator '24
Our Hospitality / Sherlock Junior '23
Three Ages '23
The Saphead '21

Buster Keaton Jr.
Our Hospitality / Sherlock Junior '23

Camille Keaton
I Spit on Your Grave '77

Diane Keaton
The Other Sister '98
The First Wives Club '96
Marvin's Room '96
Manhattan Murder Mystery '93
Father of the Bride '91
Annie Hall '77

Joe Keaton
The General '26
Our Hospitality / Sherlock Junior '23

Michael Keaton
Desperate Measures '98
Jack Frost '98
Out of Sight '98
Multiplicity '96
The Paper '94
Much Ado about Nothing '93
Batman Returns '92
Batman '89
Beetlejuice '88
Clean and Sober '88
Night Shift '82

Ele Keats
Lipstick Camera '93

Brian L. Keaulana
In God's Hands '98

Hugh Keays-Byrne
Moby Dick '98
Mad Max '80

Andrew Keegan
Ten Things I Hate about You '99

Howard Keel
The War Wagon '67
Seven Brides for Seven Brothers '54
Show Boat '51

Geoffrey Keen
For Your Eyes Only (SE) '81
Moonraker (SE) '79
The Spy Who Loved Me (SE) '77
The Third Man '49

Malcolm Keen
The Manxman '29
The Lodger '26

Monica Keena
Snow White: A Tale of Terror '97
While You Were Sleeping '95

Will Keenan
Tromeo & Juliet '95

Tom (George Duryea) Keene
Plan 9 from Outer Space '56
Our Daily Bread and Other Films of the Depression '34

Catherine Keener
Being John Malkovich '99
Out of Sight '98
Your Friends & Neighbors '98
The Real Blonde '97
Box of Moonlight '96

Eliott Keener
Hard Target '93
Angel Heart '87

Oscar Keesee
Terror Is a Man '59

Matt Keeslar
Splendor '99
The Last Days of Disco '98
Mr. Magoo '97

Jack Kehler
Austin Powers 2: The Spy Who Shagged Me '99
Dudley Do-Right '99
My Fellow Americans '96
Bloodstone '88

Jack Kehoe
Falling Down '93

Andrew Keir
Rob Roy '95
Quatermass and the Pit '67
The Viking Queen '67
Dracula, Prince of Darkness '66

Harvey Keitel
Finding Graceland '98
Lulu on the Bridge '98
Shadrach '98
Cop Land '97
Clockers '95
From Dusk Till Dawn '95
Get Shorty '95
Pulp Fiction '94
The Piano '93
Point of No Return '93
Rising Sun '93
Bad Lieutenant '92
Reservoir Dogs '92
Bugsy '91
Mortal Thoughts '91
Thelma & Louise '91
The Two Jakes '90
Saturn 3 '80
Blue Collar '78
Taxi Driver (CE) '76
Mean Streets '73

Stella Keitel
Bad Lieutenant '92

Brian Keith
Follow Your Heart '98
Picture Windows '95
Young Guns '88
Sharky's Machine '81
Hooper '78
Krakatoa East of Java '66

David Keith
Hot Blooded '98
Judge & Jury '96
The Two Jakes '90
Firestarter '84
The Great Santini '80

Robert Keith
Rites of Passage '99

Robert Keith
Men in War '57

The Wild One '54

Harry Keitt
On the Ropes '99

Cecil Kellaway
Guess Who's Coming to Dinner '67
Wuthering Heights '39

David Henry Keller
Mob War '88

Sally Kellerman
Ready to Wear '94
The Player '92

Susan Kellerman
Where the Buffalo Roam '80

Barry Kelley
The Manchurian Candidate '62

Brett Kelley
Sommersby '93

DeForest Kelley
Star Trek 6: The Undiscovered Country '91
Star Trek 5: The Final Frontier '89
Star Trek 4: The Voyage Home '86

Kimberly Kelley
Hard Bounty '94

Sheila Kelley
Santa Fe '97
Passion Fish '92
Singles '92

Walter Kelley
Men in War '57

Mike Kellin
At War with the Army '50

Catherine Kellner
200 Cigarettes '98
Rosewood '96

Bruce Kellogg
They Were Expendable '45

David Kelly
Waking Ned Devine '98

David Patrick Kelly
In Too Deep '99
Last Man Standing '96
Flirting with Disaster '95
Crooklyn '94
The Crow '93
Commando '85
Dreamscape (SE) '84

D.K. Kelly
Jane Street '96

Gene Kelly
Xanadu '80
Brigadoon '54
Singin' in the Rain '52
An American in Paris '51

Grace Kelly
High Noon '52

Ian Kelly
In Love and War '96

Jack Kelly
Forbidden Planet '56

Jean Kelly
Uncle Buck '89

Jean Louisa Kelly
A Stranger in the Kingdom '98
Mr. Holland's Opus '95

Jim Kelly
Enter the Dragon (SE) '73

Kevin Kelly
The Amazing Transparent Man '60

Laura Kelly
Yellow Pages '96

Moira Kelly
Dangerous Beauty '98
Changing Habits '96
With Honors '94
Chaplin '92

Nancy Kelly
The Woman Who Came Back '45

Patsy Kelly
The North Avenue Irregulars '79
Naked Kiss '64

Paula Kelly
Once Upon a Time . . . When We Were Colored '95
The Andromeda Strain '71

Rae'ven Kelly
Milo '98
A Time to Kill '96
What's Love Got to Do with It? '93

Roz Kelly
American Pop '81 (V)

Teresa Kelly
Billy Jack '71

Linda Kelsey
The Babysitter's Seduction '96

Pert Kelton
The Music Man '62

Paul Kember
An American Werewolf in London '81

Violet Kemble-Cooper
Gone with the Wind '39

Warren Kemmerling
Eat My Dust '76

Elizabeth Kemp
Killing Hour '84

Gary Kemp
The Bodyguard '92

Jeremy Kemp
Four Weddings and a Funeral '94
The Seven-Per-Cent Solution '76

Martin Kemp
Embrace of the Vampire '95

Michelle Kemp
Lauderdale '89

Paul Kemp
M '31

Johnny Kemper
Women in Revolt '71

Brenda Kempner
Marat/Sade '66

Breanda Kendall
Dead Alive '93

Henry Kendall
Rich and Strange '32

Katherine Kendall
Swingers '96

Suzy Kendall
Torso '73
The Bird with the Crystal Plumage '70

Tony Kendall
Return of the Blind Dead '75

Adam Kennedy
Men in War '57

Arthur Kennedy
The Sentinel '76

Bill Kennedy
Two Lost Worlds '50

Douglas Kennedy
The Amazing Transparent
Man '60

Edgar Kennedy
Duck Soup '33

George Kennedy
Small Soldiers '98 (V)
Nightmare at Noon '87
Airport '75 '75
The Eiger Sanction '75
Earthquake '74
Airport '70
Cool Hand Luke '67
The Dirty Dozen '67
Charade '63

Graham Kennedy
Don's Party '76

Jamie Kennedy
Bowfinger '99
Three Kings '99
Enemy of the State '98
Highway Hitcher '98
Scream 2 '97
Scream (CS) '96

Jihmi Kennedy
Glory '89

Leon Isaac Kennedy
Penitentiary 2 '82
Penitentiary '79

Merele Kennedy
Switchback '97
Nemesis '93

Merna Kennedy
The Circus '19

Mimi Kennedy
Death Becomes Her '92
Pump Up the Volume '90

Sarah Kennedy
Jack Be Nimble '94

Tom Kennedy
Monkey Business '31

Doug Kenney
Heavy Metal '81 (V)
National Lampoon's Animal
House '78

Patsy Kensit
Grace of My Heart (CE) '96
Lethal Weapon 2 '89

Jean Kent
The Haunted Strangler '58

Regina Kent
Legacy of Rage '86

Danny Keogh
Operation Delta Force 3:
Clear Target '98

Jimmy Keogh
The Matchmaker '97

**Sumela-Rose
Keramidopulos**
Simon Birch '98

Steven Kerby
China O'Brien '88

Bill Kerr
Sweet Talker '91
Gallipoli '81

Deborah Kerr
The King and I '56

E. Katherine Kerr
The Siege '98

Frederick Kerr
Frankenstein '31

John Kerr
South Pacific '58

Linda Kerridge
Fade to Black '80

Mary Kerridge
Curse of the Voodoo '64

Dermot Kerrigan
Waking Ned Devine '98

Norman Kerry
The Phantom of the Opera
'25
Amarilly of Clothesline Alley
'18

Doug Kershaw
Zachariah '70

Brian Kerwin
Mr. Jealousy '98
Unlikely Angel '97

Lance Kerwin
Salem's Lot '79

Boyd Kestner
The General's Daughter '99

Cliff Ketchum
Pork Chop Hill '59

Wong She Key
The Fruit Is Swelling '97

Evelyn Keyes
Gone with the Wind '39

Irwin Keyes
The Flintstones (CE) '94

Simbi Khali
A Thin Line Between Love
and Hate '96

Persis Khambatta
Nighthawks '81

Aamir Khan
Sarfarosh '98

Arbaaz Khan
Pyaar Kiya to Darna Kya '98

Chaka Khan
The Blues Brothers (CE) '80

Cynthia Khan
In the Line of Duty 5 '90
In the Line of Duty 4 '89
In the Line of Duty 3 '88

Salman Khan
Hum Dil De Chuke Sanam
'99
Pyaar Kiya to Darna Kya '98
Khamoshi the Musical '96

Shah Rukh Khan
Koyla '98
Yes Boss! '97

Arsinee Khanjian
Felicia's Journey '99
Irma Vep '96
The Sweet Hereafter '96
Exotica '94

Kiatenai
Detention '98

Guy Kibbee
Rain '32

Margot Kidder
Junior's Groove '97
To Catch a Killer '92
Mob Story '90
Quackser Fortune Has a
Cousin in the Bronx '70

Nicole Kidman
Eyes Wide Shut '99
Practical Magic '98
The Peacemaker '97
The Leading Man '96
Portrait of a Lady '96
Batman Forever '95
To Die For '95
Malice '93
Far and Away '92

Days of Thunder '90
Dead Calm '89

James Kidnie
Resurrection '99

Richard Kiel
Happy Gilmore '96
Pale Rider '85
Moonraker (SE) '79
The Spy Who Loved Me (SE)
'77

Shih Kien
Enter the Dragon (SE) '73

Udo Kier
End of Days '99
Blade '98
Modern Vampires '98
The Adventures of Pinocchio
'96
Barb Wire '96
Johnny Mnemonic '95
Andy Warhol's Dracula '74
Andy Warhol's Frankenstein
'74
Mark of the Devil '69

Rya Kihlstedt
Home Alone 3 '97

Percy Kilbride
The Southerner '45
State Fair '45

Terence Kilburn
Lolita '62
National Velvet '44

Richard Kiley
Patch Adams (CE) '98
Phenomenon '96

Val Kilmer
Joe the King '99
At First Sight '98
Prince of Egypt '98 (V)
The Saint '97
The Ghost and the Darkness
'96
The Island of Dr. Moreau '96
Batman Forever '95
Heat '95
The Real McCoy '93
Tombstone '93
True Romance '93
Thunderheart '92
The Doors '91
Top Gun '86

Kevin Kilner
Home Alone 3 '97

Lincoln Kilpatrick
Piranha '95

Jacqueline Kim
Brokedown Palace '99
Volcano '97

Charles Kimbrough
Sunday in the Park with
George '86

Isao (Ko) Kimura
Seven Samurai '54

Richard Kind
A Bug's Life (CE) '98 (V)
Sink or Swim '97

Adrienne King
Friday the 13th, Part 2 '81
Friday the 13th '80

Alan King
Casino '95
The Bonfire of the Vanities
'90

B.B. King
The Blues Brothers 2000 '98
Amazon Women on the Moon
'87

Cammie King
Gone with the Wind '39

Carl King
The Love Goddesses '65 (N)

Dave King
The Long Good Friday '80

Erik King
Atomic Train '99

Kenneth King
Jade '95

Larry King
Dave '93

Loretta King
Bride of the Monster '55

Mabel King
The Jerk '79
The Wiz '78

Meegan King
Humanoids from the Deep
'80

Perry King
Killing Hour '84
Slaughterhouse Five '72

Regina King
Enemy of the State '98
How Stella Got Her Groove
Back '98
Mighty Joe Young '98
Jerry Maguire '96
A Thin Line Between Love
and Hate '96
Friday '95
Poetic Justice '93

Stephen King
Stephen King's Thinner '96
Stephen King's The Stand
'94
Creepshow '82

Ben Kingsley
Alice in Wonderland '99
The Confession '98
The Assignment '97
Dave '93
Sneakers '92
Bugsy '91

Alex Kingston
Moll Flanders '96

Kathleen Kinmont
Sweet Justice '92
Night of the Warrior '91
Bride of Re-Animator '89
Halloween 4: The Return of
Michael Myers '88
Rush Week '88

Melinda Kinnaman
My Life As a Dog '85

Greg Kinnear
Mystery Men '99
You've Got Mail '98
As Good As It Gets '97

Roy Kinnear
The Four Musketeers '75
Willy Wonka & the Chocolate
Factory '71
Help! '65

Terry Kinney
Fly Away Home '96
Sleepers '96
Devil in a Blue Dress '95
Body Snatchers '93
The Firm '93

Leonid Kinskey
Casablanca '42
Duck Soup '33

Klaus Kinski
Fitzcarraldo '82
Nosferatu the Vampyre '79
For a Few Dollars More '65

Nastassia Kinski
Playing by Heart '98
Savior '98

Your Friends & Neighbors '98
One Night Stand '97
Father's Day '96
Terminal Velocity '94
Spring Symphony '86
Cat People '82

Bruce Kirby
Interlocked '98

Bruno Kirby
Stuart Little '99 (V)
Donnie Brasco '96
Sleepers '96
The Basketball Diaries '94
The Freshman '90
This Is Spinal Tap '84
Where the Buffalo Roam '80

Jessie Kirby
Don't Look in the Basement
'73

George Robert Kirk
The Abyss (SE) '89

James Kirk
National Lampoon's Golf
Punks '99

Joe Kirk
Impact '49

Corinne Kirkin
The Wizard of Gore '70

Sally Kirkland
EDtv '99
Paranoia '98
Excess Baggage '96
The Player '92
JFK '91
Revenge '90
Private Benjamin '80
Big Bad Mama '74

Jess Kirkpatrick
D.O.A. '49

Alexander Kirkwood
Witchcraft '88

Gene Kirkwood
The Crossing Guard '94

Mia Kirshner
Mad City '97
The Crow 2: City of Angels
'96
Exotica '94

Terry Kiser
Weekend at Bernie's '89

Lee Kisman
Witchcraft '88

Charles Kissinger
Grizzly '76

Darci Kistler
George Balanchine's The Nutcracker '93

Nam Kit-Ying
The Bride with White Hair '93

Kazuo Kitamura
Black Rain '88
Tora! Tora! Tora! '70

Takeshi "Beat" Kitano
Johnny Mnemonic '95

Michael Kitchen
Mrs. Dalloway '97
Goldeneye '95

Sam Kitchin
Holy Man '98

Eartha Kitt
Ill-Gotten Gains '97 (V)

John Kitzmiller
Dr. No (SE) '62

Barry Kivel
Bound '96

Gunter Kleeman
I Spit on Your Grave '77

Chris Klein
American Pie (CE) '99
Election '99

Gerard Klein
Frantic '88

Jean-Pierre Klein
The Last Metro '80

Robert Klein
Primary Colors '98
Radioland Murders '94
Hooper '78

Rudolf Klein-Rogge
Metropolis '26
The Cabinet of Dr. Caligari '19

Henry Kleinbach
See Henry (Kleinbach) Brandon

Towje Kleiner
The Odessa File '74

Brandon Kleyla
Gods and Monsters '98

Kevin Kline
Wild Wild West '99
William Shakespeare's A Midsummer Night's Dream '99
In and Out '97
Fierce Creatures '96
French Kiss '95
Dave '93
Chaplin '92
A Fish Called Wanda '88
Cry Freedom '87
The Big Chill '83
Sophie's Choice '82

Richard Kline
Treehouse Hostage '99

Heidi Kling
The Mighty Ducks '92

Jack Klugman
The Twilight of the Golds '97
Around the World in 80 Days '89
Two Minute Warning '76

Vincent Klyn
Urban Menace '99
Nemesis '93
Cyborg '89

Joseph Knafelmacher
Kids '95

Herbert Knaup
Run Lola Run '98

Hildegarde Knef
Lost Continent '68

David Knight
Who Shot Pat? '92
Demons 2 '87

Esmond Knight
Peeping Tom '60
The Red Shoes '48
Henry V '44

Felix Knight
March of the Wooden Soldiers '34

Sandra Knight
The Terror '63

Shirley Knight
As Good As It Gets '97
Color of Night '94

Ted Knight
Caddyshack '80
Psycho (CE) '60

Tuesday Knight
A Nightmare on Elm Street 4: Dream Master '88

Wayne Knight
Tarzan '99 (V)
For Richer or Poorer '97
Space Jam '96
To Die For '95
Basic Instinct '92
Dead Again '91
JFK '91

Wyatt Knight
Porky's '82

Kristen Knittle
Body Strokes '95

Pierre Knoessen
Laser Mission '90

Andrew Knott
The Secret Garden '93

Don Knotts
Tom Sawyer '99 (V)
Pleasantville '98
Cannonball Run 2 '84

Christopher Knowings
Crooklyn '94

Patric Knowles
The Wolf Man '41

Kerry Knowlton
Witchcraft 10: Mistress of the Craft '98

Alexander Knox
Nicholas and Alexandra '71
Shalako '68
The Longest Day '62

Peggy Knudsen
The Big Sleep '46

Su-Myong Ko
Why Has Bodhi-Darma Left for the East '89

Mpho Koaho
Down in the Delta '98

Keiju Kobayashi
Sanjuro '62

Jeff Kober
The Colony '98
One Man's Justice '95

Marta Kober
Friday the 13th, Part 2 '81

Marianne Koch
A Fistful of Dollars '64

Sabrina Koch
The Alley Cats '65

Momoko Kochi
Godzilla, King of the Monsters '56

Kuninori Kodo
Seven Samurai '54

Walter Koenig
Star Trek: Generations '94
Star Trek 6: The Undiscovered Country '91
Star Trek 5: The Final Frontier '89
Star Trek 4: The Voyage Home '86

Manisha Koirala
Khamoshi the Musical '96

Hiroshi Koizumi
Godzilla vs. Mothra '64

Nikola Kojo
Pretty Village, Pretty Flame '96

Robert Kokol
The Waterboy '98

Erik Kol
Lawyer Lawyer '97

Clarence Kolb
Impact '49

His Girl Friday '40

Scott Kolk
All Quiet on the Western Front '30

Rich Komenich
Henry: Portrait of a Serial Killer 2: Mask of Sanity '96

Liliana Komorowska
The Assignment '97

Maja Komorowska
The Decalogue '88

Christoph Koncz
The Red Violin '98

Chu Kong
Fong Sai Yuk '93
The Killer '90

Phyllis Konstam
Skin Game '31
Murder '30

Madame Konstantin
Notorious '46

Thomas Kopache
Stigmata '99

Bernie Kopell
Bug Buster '99
Follow Your Heart '98

Kim Kopf
Zigzag '97

Karen Kopins
Creator '85

Misa Koprova
Total Reality '97

Michael Korb
2000 Maniacs '64

Harvey Korman
Jingle All the Way '96
The Flintstones (CE) '94 (V)
Radioland Murders '94
History of the World: Part 1 '81
Blazing Saddles '74

Korobei
The Battleship Potemkin '25

Alix Koromzay
Children of the Corn 666: Isaac's Return '99
The Haunting '99

Charlie Korsmo
Can't Hardly Wait '98

Fritz Kortner
Pandora's Box '28

Sylva Koscina
Lisa and the Devil / The House of Exorcism '75
Juliet of the Spirits '65

Paul Koslo
Judge & Jury '96
Rooster Cogburn '75
Joe Kidd '72

Sho Kosugi
Black Eagle '88

Yoshio Kosugi
The Human Condition: No Greater Love '58
Seven Samurai '54

Elias Koteas
Living Out Loud '98
The Thin Red Line '98
Apt Pupil '97
Fallen '97
Gattaca '97
Crash '95
The Prophecy '95
Exotica '94
Teenage Mutant Ninja Turtles: The Movie '90

Yaphet Kotto
Extreme Justice '93
Freddy's Dead: The Final Nightmare '91
Midnight Run '88
The Running Man '87
Alien '79
Blue Collar '78
Live and Let Die '73

Nancy Kovack
Jason and the Argonauts '63

Ernie Kovacs
Bell, Book and Candle '58

Martin Kove
Timelock '99
Top of the World '97
Judge & Jury '96
Rambo: First Blood, Part 2 '85
Death Race 2000 '75
Women in Revolt '71

Ron Kovic
Born on the Fourth of July '89

Shigeru Koyama
Black Rain '89

Harley Jane Kozak
Dark Planet '97
Arachnophobia '90
Parenthood '89

Linda Kozlowski
Village of the Damned '95

Jeroen Krabbe
An Ideal Husband '99
Dangerous Beauty '98
Ever After: A Cinderella Story '98
The Fugitive '93
The Punisher '90
No Mercy '86

Jane Krakowski
Go '99
Dance with Me '98
National Lampoon's Vacation '83

Eric Allen Kramer
The Colony '98

Hope Kramer
The Flying Serpent '55

Jeffrey Kramer
Halloween 2: The Nightmare Isn't Over! '81

Jonathan Kramer
Women in Revolt '71

Stephanie Kramer
Beyond Suspicion '94
The Man with Two Brains '83

Judith Krant
Total Recall 2070: Machine Dreams '99

Brian Krause
Within the Rock '96

Jamie Krause
Beware! Children at Play '95

Werner Krauss
The Cabinet of Dr. Caligari '19

John Kreng
Glitch! '88

Nathan Kress
Babe: Pig in the City '98 (V)

Thomas Kretschmann
Total Recall '97
Stalingrad '94

David Kriegel
Speed '94

Anneline Kriel
Kill and Kill Again '81

Alice Krige
Habitat '97
Star Trek: First Contact '96
Chariots of Fire '81
Ghost Story '81

Viju Krim
Bloodsucking Freaks '75

Sylvia Kristel
Emmanuelle, the Joys of a Woman '76
Emmanuelle '74

Marta Kristen
Lost in Space '98

Jason Kristofer
The Crossing Guard '94

Kris Kristofferson
Limbo '99
Blade '98
Dance with Me '98
Outlaw Justice '98
Payback '98
Tom Clancy's Netforce '98
Fire Down Below '97
Millennium '89

Joachim Krol
Run Lola Run '98

Christiane Kruger
Little Mother '71

Hardy Kruger
The Inside Man '84
A Bridge Too Far '77
Barry Lyndon '75

Otto Kruger
High Noon '52
The Woman Who Came Back '45
Wonder Man '45

David Krumholtz
Ten Things I Hate about You '99
Slums of Beverly Hills '98
The Santa Clause '94

Gene Krupa
Ball of Fire '41

Olek Krupa
Home Alone 3 '97

Jack Kruschen
McLintock! '63
The War of the Worlds '53

Alex Kubik
Carnal Crimes '91

Lawrence Kubik
Zachariah '70

Akira Kubo
Godzilla vs. Monster Zero '68

Tak Kubota
The Hunted '94

Vivian Kubrick
2001: A Space Odyssey '68

Dan Kuchuck
Search and Destroy '88

Lisa Kudrow
Analyze This '98
Opposite of Sex '98
Romy and Michele's High School Reunion '97

Valentina Kuindzi
Aelita: Queen of Mars '24

Vladimir Kulich
The 13th Warrior '99
Firestorm '97

William Kunstler
The Doors '91

A Nightmare on Elm Street '84

A.J. Langer
Escape from L.A. '96

Caroline Langrishe
Cleopatra '99
Rogue Trader '98

Brooke Langton
Swingers '96

Paul Langton
They Were Expendable '45

Daniel Lanois
Robbie Robertson: Going Home '98

Angela Lansbury
Anastasia '97 (V)
Beauty and the Beast: The Enchanted Christmas '97 (V)
The Manchurian Candidate '62
Court Jester '56
National Velvet '44

David Lansbury
A Stranger in the Kingdom '98

Joi Lansing
Atomic Submarine '59
The Brave One '56
Singin' in the Rain '52

Robert Lansing
The 4D Man '59

Leonard Lansink
Killer Condom '95

William Lanteau
On Golden Pond '81

Fabio Lanzoni
Death Becomes Her '92

Anthony LaPaglia
Summer of Sam '99
Phoenix '98
Trees Lounge '96
The Client '94
So I Married an Axe Murderer '93
Innocent Blood '92

Daniel Lapaine
Brokedown Palace '99
Dangerous Beauty '98
Polish Wedding '97

Ivan Lapikov
Andrei Rublev '66

Jane Lapotaire
Shooting Fish '98
The Asphyx '72

Joe Lara
Armstrong '99
Tarzan in Manhatten '89

John Larch
Dirty Harry '71

Bryan Larkin
Born on the Fourth of July '89

Scott LaRose
Booty Call '96

Catalina Larranaga
Word of Mouth '99
Loveblind '98

Tito Larriva
Just a Little Harmless Sex '99
True Stories '86

John Larroquette
Cat People '82
Stripes '81
Altered States '80

The Texas Chainsaw Massacre '74 (N)

Darrell Larson
Shadrach '98
Stepmom '98
Hero '92

Ali Larter
House on Haunted Hill '99
Varsity Blues '98

Jack LaRue
The Road to Utopia '46

David Lascher
White Squall '96

Michael Laskin
Limbo '99
Passion Fish '92

Louise Lasser
Mystery Men '99
Happiness '98
Take the Money and Run '69

Sydney Lassick
Deep Cover '92
Tale of Two Sisters '89

Tania Latarjet
The Vanishing '88

Dick Latessa
Stigmata '99

Philip Latham
Dracula, Prince of Darkness '66

Sanaa Lathan
The Best Man '99
Blade '98

Michael Latimer
Prehistoric Women '67

Frank Latimore
Patton '70

Joseph Latimore
Lord of Illusions '95

Ryan Latshaw
Jack-O '95

Andy Lau
The Conman '98
Armageddon '97
Full Throttle '96
The Moon Warriors '92
Saviour of the Soul '92
Lee Rock '91

Carina Lau
Center Stage '91

Damian Lau
Jet Li's The Enforcer '95

Shun Lau
Once Upon a Time in China III '93

Philippe Laudenbach
Confidentially Yours '83

Phil Lauenson
The Wizard of Gore '70

Andrew Lauer
I'll Be Home for Christmas '98
Screamers '96

Justin Lauer
The Creeps '97

John Laughlin
Night Fire '94
Sexual Malice '93
The Lawnmower Man '92
Crimes of Passion '84

Tom Laughlin
Billy Jack '71
South Pacific '58

Charles Laughton
Spartacus '60

The Paradine Case '47
Forever and a Day '43
The Hunchback of Notre Dame '39
Jamaica Inn '39
The Old Dark House '32

Charles Laulette
Fraternity Demon '92

Mitchell Laurance
The Hand that Rocks the Cradle '92

Carole Laure
Victory '81

Stan Laurel
Laurel and Hardy and Friends '90s
The Lost Films of Laurel and Hardy, Vol. 1 '90s
The Lost Films of Laurel and Hardy, Vol. 2 '90s
The Lost Films of Laurel and Hardy, Vol. 3 '90s
The Lost Films of Laurel and Hardy, Vol. 5 '99
The Lost Films of Laurel and Hardy, Vol. 6 '99
Utopia '51
The Flying Deuces / Utopia '39
March of the Wooden Soldiers '34

Greg Lauren
Boys Life '94

Tammy Lauren
Wishmaster '97
The Last Flight of Noah's Ark '80

Veronica Lauren
Homeward Bound: The Incredible Journey '93

Ashley Laurence
Warlock 3: The End of Innocence '98
Mikey '92
Hellbound: Hellraiser 2 '88
Hellraiser '87

Caroline Laurence
Emmanuelle, the Joys of a Woman '76

James Laurenson
Pink Floyd: The Wall '82

Dan Lauria
Dean Koontz's Mr. Murder '98
From the Earth to the Moon '98
True Friends '98

Hugh Laurie
Stuart Little '99
The Man in the Iron Mask '98
The Borrowers '97
Cousin Bette '97
Spice World: The Movie '97
Treasure Island '97 (V)
101 Dalmatians '96
Sense and Sensibility '95

John Laurie
The Reptile '66
Henry V '44
The 39 Steps '35

Piper Laurie
The Faculty '98
Horton Foote's Alone '97
The Crossing Guard '94
Return to Oz '85
Tim '79

Lucie Laurier
Strip Search '97

Ed Lauter
A Bright Shining Lie '98
Leaving Las Vegas '95

Extreme Justice '93
True Romance '93
School Ties '92
The Rocketeer '91
King Kong '76

Dominque Lavanant
The Monster '96

Gabriele Lavia
Zeder '83
Deep Red: Hatchet Murders '75

Marc Lavoine
L'Enfer '93

Adam LaVorgna
Outside Providence '99
I'll Be Home for Christmas '98

Desiree Law
Mah Jong Dragon '97

John Phillip Law
Night Train to Terror '84
The Cassandra Crossing '76
Barbarella '68

Jude Law
eXistenZ '99
Gattaca '97
I Love You, I Love You Not '97
Midnight in the Garden of Good and Evil (SE) '97

Phyllida Law
Emma '96
Much Ado about Nothing '93

Christopher Lawford
The Confession '98

Peter Lawford
The Longest Day '62
Royal Wedding '51

Lucy Lawless
Peach / A Bitter Song '95

Andy Lawrence
Jack Frost '98

Barbara Lawrence
Oklahoma '55

Bruno Lawrence
Jack Be Nimble '94

Gail Lawrence
Maniac '80
Bye Bye Monkey '77

Jay Lawrence
Train Ride to Hollywood '75

Joey Lawrence
Radioland Murders '94

John Lawrence
They Live '88
The Asphyx '72
The Manchurian Candidate '62

Marc Lawrence
The Big Easy '87
Night Train to Terror '84
Abbott and Costello in the Foreign Legion '50

Martin Lawrence
Life '99
Nothing to Lose '96
A Thin Line Between Love and Hate '96
Bad Boys '95

Michael Lawrence
Othello '52

Scott Lawrence
Timecop '94

Sid Lawrence
Naked Warriors '73

Steve Lawrence
The Blues Brothers 2000 '98

The Lonely Guy '84
The Blues Brothers (CE) '80

Linda Lawson
Night Tide '63

Richard Lawson
How Stella Got Her Groove Back '98
Streets of Fire '84
Poltergeist '82

Frank Lawton
A Night to Remember '58
Skin Game '31

Pat Lawyer
Without Air '95

Barbara Lay
Nude for Satan '74

John Lazar
Over the Wire '95

Paul Lazar
Philadelphia '93

Justin Lazard
Universal Soldier: The Return '99

Eugene Lazarev
The Saint '97

Eusebio Lazaro
Twice upon a Yesterday '98

George Lazenby
Kentucky Fried Movie '77

Ngoc Le
Full Metal Jacket '87

Maiwenn Le Besco
The Fifth Element '97

Kelly Le Brock
Wrongfully Accused '98
Hard Bounty '94
Hard to Kill '89
Weird Science '85

Renee Madeleine Le Guerrier
Barney's Great Adventure '98

Brent Le Page
Halloween '78

Madeleine Le Roux
Cry Uncle '71

Bernadette Le Sache
The Vanishing '88

Nicholas Lea
Once a Thief '96

Cloris Leachman
Iron Giant '99 (V)
Beavis and Butt-Head Do America '96 (V)
Now and Then '95
History of the World: Part 1 '81
The North Avenue Irregulars '79
Death Sentence '74
Young Frankenstein '74
Butch Cassidy and the Sundance Kid '69

Damien Leake
Apocalypse Now '79

Michael Learned
Dragon: The Bruce Lee Story '93

Denis Leary
The Thomas Crown Affair '99
A Bug's Life (CE) '98 (V)
Monument Ave. '98
Small Soldiers '98
The Matchmaker '97
The Real Blonde '97
Suicide Kings '97
Wag the Dog '97
Underworld '96

Bethel Leslie
Message in a Bottle '98

Joan Leslie
Love Affair '39

Len Lesser
Grandma's House '88

Robert Lesser
The Relic '96

Adrian Lester
Primary Colors '98

Kathy Lester
Phantasm '79

Mark Lester
Oliver! '68
Fahrenheit 451 '66

Noble Lee Lester
Sgt. Kabukiman N.Y.P.D. '94

Ron Lester
Varsity Blues '98

Jared Leto
Fight Club '99
The Thin Red Line '98
Urban Legend '98
Switchback '97
How to Make an American Quilt '95

Matt Letscher
The Mask of Zorro '98

Al Lettieri
The Getaway '72

Rudolf Lettinger
The Cabinet of Dr. Caligari '19

Chan Chi Leung
Full Contact '92

Fiona Leung
A Hero Never Dies '98

Gigi Leung
First Option '96
Full Throttle '96

Jade Leung
Black Cat '91

Tony Leung Chiu-Wai
Happy Together '96
Lover of the Last Empress '95
Hard-Boiled '92
The Longest Nite '92
Center Stage '91
A Chinese Ghost Story III '91
A Bullet in the Head '90
I Love Maria '88

Tony Leung Ka-Fai
Prison on Fire '87

Clinton Leupp
Trick '99

Oscar Levant
An American in Paris '51

Levchenko
The Battleship Potemkin '25

Calvin Levels
Within the Rock '96
Point of No Return '93
Adventures in Babysitting '87

Marcel Levesque
The Fantastic Night '42

Rachel Levin
White Palace '90

Anna Levine
Warlock '91

Jerry Levine
Born on the Fourth of July '89
Casual Sex? '88

Ted Levine
Wild Wild West '99
From the Earth to the Moon '98
Moby Dick '98
Flubber '97
Mad City '97
Switchback '97
Georgia '95
Heat '95
Nowhere to Run '93
Silence of the Lambs '91

Barry Levinson
Robbie Robertson: Going Home '98
Quiz Show '94
History of the World: Part 1 '81

Carri Levinson
Henry: Portrait of a Serial Killer 2: Mask of Sanity '96

Uta Levka
Carmen, Baby '66
The Alley Cats '65

Alexandr Levshin
The Battleship Potemkin '25

Adam Levy
The Governess '98

Eugene Levy
American Pie (CE) '99
Multiplicity '96
Father of the Bride '91
Splash '84
National Lampoon's Vacation '83
Heavy Metal '81 (V)

Stephen Levy
The Thin Red Line '64

James Lew
High Voltage '98

Margaret LeWars
Dr. No (SE) '62

Jose Lewgoy
Fitzcarraldo '82

Al Lewis
The Night Strangler '72
They Shoot Horses, Don't They? '69
Munster, Go Home! '66

Charlotte Lewis
Embrace of the Vampire '95
The Golden Child '86

David Lewis
Lake Placid '99

Gary Lewis
Postmortem '98

Geoffrey Lewis
Midnight in the Garden of Good and Evil (SE) '97
An Occasional Hell '96
Maverick '94
Point of No Return '93
The Lawnmower Man '92

Gilbert Lewis
Candyman '92

Jenifer Lewis
The Mighty '98
Corrina, Corrina '94
What's Love Got to Do with It? '93

Jerry Lewis
Mr. Saturday Night '92
At War with the Army '50

Juliette Lewis
The Other Sister '98
From Dusk Till Dawn '95
Strange Days '95
The Basketball Diaries '94
Kalifornia '93

National Lampoon's Christmas Vacation '89
My Stepmother Is an Alien '88

Mitchell Lewis
The Wizard of Oz '39

Phill Lewis
Once Upon a Time . . . When We Were Colored '95 (N)

Ralph Lewis
The Flying Serpent '55
The Birth of a Nation '15

Rawle Lewis
Cool Runnings '93

Richard Lewis
Hugo Pool '97
Drunks '96
Leaving Las Vegas '95

Robert Lewis
Monsieur Verdoux '47

Russell Scott Lewis
Boys Life '94

Sharon M. Lewis
Rude '95

Terina Lewis
Union City '81

Tom Lewis
Steamboat Bill, Jr. '28

Vicki Lewis
Godzilla '98
Mouse Hunt '97

Charles Ley
The Temptations '98

John Leyton
Krakatoa East of Java '66
The Great Escape '63

Thierry Lhermitte
An American Werewolf in Paris '97

Gong Li
Chinese Box '97
The Great Conqueror's Concubine '94
The Great Conqueror's Concubine, Part 2 '94
Farewell My Concubine '93
Ju Dou '90

Jet Li
Hitman '98
Lethal Weapon 4 '98
Black Mask '96
High Risk '95
Jet Li's The Enforcer '95
Fist of Legend '94
Fong Sai Yuk '93
Once Upon a Time in China III '93
The Master '92
Once Upon a Time in China II '92
Once Upon a Time in China '91
Dragons of the Orient '88

Michelle Li
Wicked City '92

Nina Li
Fractured Follies '88

Yu Li
Prison on Fire 2 '91

Nina Li Chi
Twin Dragons '92

Richard Libertini
The Bonfire of the Vanities '90
Fletch '85
All of Me '84
Sharky's Machine '81

Richard Liberty
Day of the Dead '85

Anki Liden
My Life As a Dog '85

Nancy Lieberman
Perfect Profile '90

Jennifer Lien
SLC Punk! '99
American History X '98

Tina Lifford
The Temptations '98

Cody Lightning
Smoke Signals '98

Marilyn Lightstone
Abraxas: Guardian of the Universe '90

Max Ligosh
Joe the King '99

Matthew Lillard
She's All That '99
SLC Punk! '99
Wing Commander '99
Senseless '98
The Curve '97
Without Limits '97
Animal Room '95
Hackers '95
Tarantella '95
Serial Mom '94

Beatrice Lillie
On Approval '44

Kay Tong Lim
Dragon: The Bruce Lee Story '93

Mark Lim
Shaolin Avengers '94

Andrew Lin
God.com '99

Brigitte (Ching Hsia) Lin
The Bride with White Hair '93
The Bride with White Hair 2 '93
Deadful Melody '92
Royal Tramp 2 '92
Dream Lovers '86
Peking Opera Blues '86
Zu: Warriors of the Magic Mountain '83

Robert Lin
Kundun '97

Terence Lin
Hot War '98

Zhang Tie Lin
Once Upon a Time in China II '92

Aida Linares
U-Turn '97
Clueless '95

Andrew Lincoln
Boston Kickout '95

Pamela Lincoln
The Tingler '59

Traci Lind
No Strings Attached '98

Boguslaw Linda
The Decalogue '88

Chad Lindberg
October Sky '99
Black Circle Boys '97

Gunnel Lindblom
The Seventh Seal '56

Janine Lindemulder
The Price of Desire '96

Eric Linden
Gone with the Wind '39

Cec Linder
Goldfinger '64
Lolita '62

Viveca Lindfors
Stargate '94
Creepshow '82

Natasha Lindinger
Double Team '97

Audra Lindley
The Heartbreak Kid '72

Delroy Lindo
The Devil's Advocate '97
A Life Less Ordinary '97
Feeling Minnesota '96
Ransom '96
Broken Arrow '95
Clockers '95
Get Shorty '95
Crooklyn '94
Mountains of the Moon '90

Margaret Lindsay
Jezebel '38

Robert Lindsay
Fierce Creatures '96

Elizabeth Lindsey
The Corruptor '99

Joseph Lindsey
Caught Up '98

Peter Lindsey
Under the Gun '95

Blake Lindsley
Starship Troopers '97
Swingers '96

Helga Line
Horror Express '72

Richard Lineback
Varsity Blues '98
The Jackal (CE) '97
Tin Cup '96
Speed '94

Rosaleen Linehan
The Matchmaker '97

Bai Ling
Wild Wild West '99
Red Corner '97
The Crow '94

Kung Ka Ling
Erotic Ghost Story: Perfect Match '97

Theo Lingen
M '31

Paul Linke
Parenthood '89

Richard Linklater
Beavis and Butt-Head Do America '96 (V)
The Underneath '95

Rex Linn
Neil Simon's The Odd Couple 2 '98
Rush Hour '98
The Postman '97
Tin Cup '96
Drop Zone '94
Cliffhanger '93

Laura Linney
The Truman Show '98
Absolute Power '97
Armistead Maupin's More Tales of the City '97
Primal Fear '96
Congo '95
Dave '93

Larry Linville
Earth Girls Are Easy '89
The Night Stalker '71

Alex D. Linz
Tarzan '99 (V)

Anaconda '96
Selena '96
Money Train '95

Kamala Lopez
Born in East L.A. '87

Perry Lopez
Chinatown '74
McLintock! '63
Mister Roberts '55

Sal Lopez
Selena '96
Full Metal Jacket '87

Seidy Lopez
Solo '96

Trini Lopez
The Dirty Dozen '67

Lopsang
Xiu Xiu: The Sent Down Girl
'97

Jack Lord
Dr. No (SE) '62

Traci Lords
Me & Will '99
Blade '98
Extramarital '98
Serial Mom '94
Desperate Crimes '93
Skinner '93
Stephen King's The Tommy-
knockers '93
Laser Moon '92
The Nutt House '92

Sophia Loren
Grumpier Old Men '95
Ready to Wear '94
The Cassandra Crossing '76
The Love Goddesses '65
Two Women '61
The Millionairess '60

Jerry Lorenz
The Texas Chainsaw Mas-
sacre '74

Livio Lorenzon
The Good, the Bad and the
Ugly '67

Lynn Loring
Journey to the Far Side of the
Sun '69

Marion Lorne
Strangers on a Train '51

George Loros
Shakedown '88

Peter Lorre
Beat the Devil '53
Casablanca '42
The Secret Agent '36
The Man Who Knew Too
Much '34
M '31

Steven Losak
The Robin Hood Gang '98

Susanne Lothar
Funny Games '97

Eb Lottimer
Diamondbacks '99

Jackson Lou
Jackie Chan's First Strike '96

Dorothy Loudon
Midnight in the Garden of
Good and Evil (SE) '97

Willard Louis
Robin Hood '22

Julia Louis-Dreyfus
A Bug's Life (CE) '98 (V)
Deconstructing Harry '97
Father's Day '96
National Lampoon's Christ-
mas Vacation '89

Marie Louise
Naked Warriors '73

Tina Louise
The Stepford Wives '75

Todd Louiso
Jerry Maguire '96

Heath Lourwood
Black Circle Boys '97

Bessie Love
The Lost World '25
Intolerance '16

Charles Love
Train Ride to Hollywood '75

Courtney Love
Man on the Moon '99
200 Cigarettes '98
Feeling Minnesota '96
The People vs. Larry Flynt '96
Sid & Nancy '86

Darlene Love
Lethal Weapon 4 '98
Lethal Weapon 3 '92
Lethal Weapon 2 '89
Lethal Weapon '87

Faizon Love
The Players Club '98

Lucretia Love
Naked Warriors '73

Mother Love
The Surgeon '94

Patti Love
The Long Good Friday '80

Suzanna Love
Return of the Boogeyman '94
Devonsville Terror '83
The Boogey Man '80
Blank Generation '79

Tiffany C. Love
Varsity Blues '98

Tim Loveface
Mosquito '95

Jacqueline Lovell
Key to Sex '98
Lolida 2000 '97
Femalien '96

Ray Lovelock
Autopsy '78
Fiddler on the Roof '71

Lyle Lovett
Cookie's Fortune '99
Fear and Loathing in Las
Vegas '98
Opposite of Sex '98
Bastard out of Carolina '96
Ready to Wear '94
The Player '92

Jon Lovitz
Lost and Found '99
Happiness '98
The Wedding Singer '97
National Lampoon's Loaded
Weapon 1 '93
A League of Their Own '92
Big '88
My Stepmother Is an Alien
'88
Three Amigos '86

Chuck Low
Goodfellas '90

Arthur Lowe
This Sporting Life '63

James B. Lowe
Uncle Tom's Cabin '27

Rob Lowe
Atomic Train '99
Austin Powers 2: The Spy
Who Shagged Me '99
Crazy Six '98

For Hire '98
Contact '97
Tommy Boy '95
Frank and Jesse '94
Stephen King's The Stand
'94
About Last Night . . . '86
The Outsiders '83

Susan Lowe
Serial Mom '94

Carey Lowell
Fierce Creatures '96
Leaving Las Vegas '95
Sleepless in Seattle '93
The Guardian '90
License to Kill '89

Tom Lowell
The Manchurian Candidate
'62

Elina Lowensohn
Six Ways to Sunday '99
Jane Doe '96

Andrew Lowery
Cost of Living '97
Color of Night '94
School Ties '92

William E. Lowery
Robin Hood '22

Klaus Lowitsch
Cross of Iron '76
The Odessa File '74

Jane Lowry
Alice Sweet Alice '76

Jennifer Lowry
Brain Damage '88

Lynn Lowry
They Came from Within '75
Score '72

T.J. Lowther
Mad Love '95

Myrna Loy
Airport '75 '75
The Best Years of Our Lives
'46

Lu Lu
Xiu Xiu: The Sent Down Girl
'97

Charlie Lucas
Tea with Mussolini '99

Angela Luce
The Decameron '70

Fabrice Luchini
Full Moon in Paris '84

Joseph Lucien
The City of Lost Children '95

Laurence Luckinbill
Star Trek 5: The Final Frontier
'89
Death Sentence '74

William Lucking
The Trigger Effect '96

Arnold Lucy
All Quiet on the Western
Front '30

Charles Ludlam
The Big Easy '87

Pamela Ludwig
Rush Week '88

Laurette Luez
D.O.A. '49

Uriel Luft
Nikki, the Wild Dog of the
North '61

Bela Lugosi
Plan 9 from Outer Space '56
Bride of the Monster '55

Glen or Glenda? '53
The Wolf Man '41
The White Zombie '32
Dracula '31

Elaine Lui
The Bride with White Hair '93

James Luisi
Fade to Black '80

Paul Lukas
The Lady Vanishes '38
Dodsworth '36

Jorge Luke
Ulzana's Raid '72

Keye Luke
Gremlins '84

Adrian Lukis
Pride and Prejudice '95

Folco Lulli
Wages of Fear '55

Jenny Lumet
Q & A '90

Sidney Lumet
Running on Empty '88

Joanna Lumley
The Satanic Rites of Dracula
'73

Richard Lumsden
Sense and Sensibility '95

Dolph Lundgren
Sweepers '99
The Peacekeeper '98
Blackjack '97
Johnny Mnemonic '95
Universal Soldier '92
Showdown in Little Tokyo '91
The Punisher '90
Red Scorpion '89
Rocky 4 '85

Randy Lundsford
Night Screams '87

Jessica Lundy
Just a Little Harmless Sex
'99
Caddyshack 2 '88

Sihung Lung
Pushing Hands '92

Ti Lung
City War '89
A Better Tomorrow, Part 1 '86

Cherie Lunghi
Mary Shelley's Frankenstein
'94
Excalibur '81

Cora Lunny
Rawhead Rex '87

Renato Lupi
Nude for Satan '74

Ida Lupino
Devil's Rain '75
Junior Bonner '72
Forever and a Day '43

Patti LuPone
Summer of Sam '99
Driving Miss Daisy '89
Witness '85
1941 '79

John Lurie
New Rose Hotel '98

Robert Luster
Cool Hand Luke '67

William Lustig
Army of Darkness '92
Maniac '80

Jimmy Lydon
Life with Father '47

Leslie Lyles
My Teacher's Wife '95

Will Lyman
The Siege '98

David Lynch
Pretty As a Picture: The Art of
David Lynch '98

Jimmy Lynch
Avenging Disco Godfather '76

John Lynch
Sliding Doors '97
In the Name of the Father '93
The Secret Garden '93

John Carroll Lynch
Face/Off '97
A Thousand Acres '97
Volcano '97
Fargo '96

Kate Lynch
Meatballs '79

Kelly Lynch
Mr. Magoo '97
Virtuosity '95
White Man's Burden '95
Drugstore Cowboy '89

Ken Lynch
Pork Chop Hill '59

Pauline Lynch
Trainspotting '95

Richard Lynch
Armstrong '99
Midnight Confessions '95
Werewolf '95
Terrified '94

Susan Lynch
Waking Ned Devine '98

Paul Lynde
Bye, Bye, Birdie '63

Amy Lyndon
Big City Blues '99

Carol Lynley
Vigilante '83
The Poseidon Adventure '72
The Night Stalker '71

Jonathan Lynn
Greedy '94

Meredith Scott Lynn
Forces of Nature '99
Billy's Hollywood Screen Kiss
'98

Theresa Lynn
Private Parts '96

Melanie Lynskey
Ever After: A Cinderella Story
'98

Sue Lyon
The Invisible Strangler '76
Lolita '62

Natasha Lyonne
American Pie (CE) '99
Detroit Rock City '99
Modern Vampires '98
Slums of Beverly Hills '98
Everyone Says I Love You '96

Phyllis Lyons
The Rat Pack '98

Robert F. Lyons
Shoot Out '71

Gene Lythgow
When a Stranger Calls Back
'93

Tzi Ma
Rush Hour '98
Dante's Peak '97
Red Corner '97

Art Malik
Cleopatra '99
Booty Call '96
True Lies '94

Eddie Malin
A Hard Day's Night '64

Joshua Malina
Bulworth '98

Ross Malinger
Sleepless in Seattle '93

John Malkovich
Being John Malkovich '99
The Man in the Iron Mask '98
Rounders '98
Con Air '97
Portrait of a Lady '96
In the Line of Fire '93
The Object of Beauty '91
Queens Logic '91
Dangerous Liaisons '88

Coque Malla
Outrage '93

Miles Malleson
Peeping Tom '60
A Christmas Carol '51

Odile Mallet
The City of Lost Children '95

Tania Mallet
Goldfinger '64

James Mallon
Mystery Science Theater 3000: The Movie '96

Matt Malloy
Cookie's Fortune '99
Drop Dead Gorgeous '99
Election '99
In the Company of Men '96

Lennart Malmer
Elvira Madigan '67

Christian Malmin
The Seventh Sense '99

Bonz Malone
Slam '98

Clancy Malone
Jail Bait '54

Dorothy Malone
Basic Instinct '92
Man of a Thousand Faces '57
The Big Sleep '46

Jena Malone
Stepmom '98
Contact '97
Bastard out of Carolina '96

H.F. Maltby
Young and Innocent '37

Peter Mamakos
The Conqueror '56

Daniel Mamath
Night Calls: The Movie '98

Valerie Mamches
Children Shouldn't Play with Dead Things '72

Robert Mammone
Still Twisted

Alex Man
Long Arm of the Law II '87
Rouge '87
Hong Kong 1941 '84

Cheung Man
God of Gambler's Return '94
King of Beggars '92
Royal Tramp '92
Lee Rock '91
God of Gamblers '89

Fok Siu Man
Dragon from Shaolin '96

Al Mancini
The Dirty Dozen '67

Carla Mancini
Andy Warhol's Frankenstein '74

Nick Mancuso
Total Recall 2070: Machine Dreams '99
Under Siege 2 '95
Ticket to Heaven '81

Robert Mandan
The Nutt House '92

Howie Mandel
Gremlins '84 (V)

Rena Mandel
Vampyr '31

Miles Mander
Wuthering Heights '39
Murder '30

Costas Mandylor
Shelter '98
Just Write '97
Stand-Ins '97
Fist of the North Star '95
Virtuosity '95
The Doors '91

Louis Mandylor
Champions '96
The Quest '96

Cindy Manella
Sex Crimes '92

Silvana Mangano
Dune '84
The Decameron '70

Alec Mango
The Seventh Voyage of Sinbad '58

Camryn Manheim
Happiness '98
Romy and Michele's High School Reunion '97

Cindy Manion
The Toxic Avenger (DC) '86

Blu Mankuma
Atomic Train '99

Dudley Manlove
Plan 9 from Outer Space '56

Byron Mann
The Corruptor '99
Red Corner '97
Street Fighter '94

Danny Mann
Babe: Pig in the City '98 (V)
Babe '95 (V)

Gabriel Mann
Outside Providence '99

Hank Mann
City Lights '31

Leslie Mann
Big Daddy '99
George of the Jungle '97
The Cable Guy '96
Last Man Standing '96

Paul Mann
Fiddler on the Roof '71

Wesley Mann
My Stepmother Is an Alien '88

Monique Mannen
The Fear '94

David Manners
The Mummy '32
Dracula '31

Lucie Mannheim
The 39 Steps '35

Marilyn Manning
The Sadist '63

Patricia Manning
Hideous Sun Demon '59

Joe Manno
Night Screams '87

Dinah Manoff
Child's Play '88

Marie Mansert
Two English Girls '72

Martha Mansfield
Dr. Jekyll and Mr. Hyde '20

Tyrene Manson
On the Ropes '99

Joe Mantegna
The Runner '99
Celebrity '98
For Hire '98
The Rat Pack '98
The Last Don '97
Albino Alligator '96
Stephen King's Thinner '96
Underworld '96
Up Close and Personal '96
Bugsy '91
Queens Logic '91
Three Amigos '86

Joe Mantell
The Birds '63

Linda Manz
Out of the Blue '80
Days of Heaven '78

David Manzy
The Baby '72

Angela Mao
Enter the Dragon (SE) '73

Marla Maples
Happiness '98

Adele Mara
Sands of Iwo Jima '49

Mary Mara
Bound '96
Mr. Saturday Night '92

Jean Marais
Beauty and the Beast '46

Marla Marais
The Power of One '92

Andree Maranda
The Toxic Avenger (DC) '86

Marcel Marceau
Barbarella '68

Sophie Marceau
Lost and Found '99
William Shakespeare's A Midsummer Night's Dream '99

Fredric March
The Best Years of Our Lives '46
Nothing Sacred '37
A Star Is Born '37

Jane March
Tarzan and the Lost City '98
Color of Night '94

Guy Marchand
Entre-Nous '83

Nancy Marchand
The Bostonians '84

David Marciano
The Last Don '97
Kiss Shot '89

Vanessa Marcil
The Rock '96

Paul Marco
Plan 9 from Outer Space '56
Bride of the Monster '55

James Marcus
A Clockwork Orange '71

Stephen Marcus
Lock, Stock and 2 Smoking Barrels '98

Jordan Marder
American History X '98
Lord of Illusions '95

Tom Mardirosian
The Dark Half '91
Presumed Innocent '90

Ivano Marescotti
The Monster '96

Margo
Lost Horizon '37

Janet Margolin
Ghostbusters 2 '89
Annie Hall '77
Take the Money and Run '69
David and Lisa '62

Stuart Margolin
Guilty by Suspicion '91
Days of Heaven '78

Mark Margolis
Jakob the Liar '99
The Thomas Crown Affair '99
Pi '98
Where the Rivers Flow North '94

Miriam Margolyes
End of Days '99
Mulan '98 (V)
William Shakespeare's Romeo and Juliet '96
Babe '95 (V)

David Margulies
Last Breath '96
Ghostbusters 2 '89
Running on Empty '88
9 1/2 Weeks '86
Ghostbusters '84

Julianna Margulies
The Newton Boys '97
A Price above Rubies '97
Out for Justice '91

Constance Marie
Selena '96

Kathlena Marie
The Firing Line '91

Lisa Marie
Sleepy Hollow '99
Tail Lights Fade '99
Mars Attacks! '96

Eli Marienthal
Iron Giant '99 (V)
Jack Frost '98
Slums of Beverly Hills '98

Jacques Marin
The Island at the Top of the World '74
The Train '65

Richard "Cheech" Marin
Paulie '98
Tin Cup '96
Desperado '95
From Dusk Till Dawn '95
Ghostbusters 2 '89
Born in East L.A. '87

Ed Marinaro
Queens Logic '91

Dan Marino
Ace Ventura: Pet Detective '93

Barbara Markham
House of Whipcord '75

Kika Markham
Two English Girls '72

Monte Markham
Piranha '95

Margaret Markov
Naked Warriors '73

Guy Marks
Train Ride to Hollywood '75

Jack Marks
Friday the 13th, Part 2 '81

Ben Marley
From the Earth to the Moon '98

Cedella Marley
Klash '95

John Marley
Hooper '78
The Car '77

Carla Marlier
Spirits of the Dead '68
Any Number Can Win '63

Hugh Marlowe
All About Eve '50

Scott Marlowe
Men in War '57

Percy Marmont
Young and Innocent '37
The Secret Agent '36
Rich and Strange '32

Kelli Maroney
Zero Boys '86

Carl Marotte
Prisoner of Love '99

Serge Marquand
The Big Red One '80
Barbarella '68

Peter Marquardt
El Mariachi '93

Ron Marquette
Public Access '93

Sylvia Marriott
Two English Girls '72

Hyla Marrow
Maniac '80

Kenneth Mars
Thumbelina '94 (V)
Fletch '85
Protocol '84
The Parallax View '74
Young Frankenstein '74
Butch Cassidy and the Sundance Kid '69

Maurice Marsac
The Big Red One '80

James Marsden
Disturbing Behavior '98

Jason Marsden
An Extremely Goofy Movie '99 (V)
The Lion King: Simba's Pride '98 (V)
White Squall '96

Carol Marsh
A Christmas Carol '51

David Marsh
Assault of the Killer Bimbos '88

Jamie Marsh
Best Laid Plans '99

Jean Marsh
Return to Oz '85

Mae Marsh
The Quiet Man '52
Impact '49
The Fighting Sullivans '42

Yusaku Matsuda
Black Rain '89

Norio Matsui
Ran '85

Koshiro Matsumoto
Chushingura '62

Keigo Matsuyama
Village of Dreams '97

Shogo Matsuyama
Village of Dreams '97

Kathy Mattea
Maverick '94

Walter Matthau
Neil Simon's The Odd Couple
2 '98
Grumpier Old Men '95
Grumpy Old Men '93
JFK '91
Earthquake '74
The Front Page '74
Charade '63

James Matthew
Animal Instincts 3: The
Seductress '95

Al Matthews
Aliens (SE) '86

Dakin Matthews
The Muse '99
From the Earth to the Moon
'98
The Siege '98
Bean '97

Francis Matthews
Dracula, Prince of Darkness
'66
Rasputin the Mad Monk '66
Corridors of Blood '58

Jessie Matthews
Forever and a Day '43

Liesl Matthews
Air Force One '97
A Little Princess '95

Walter Matthews
Naked Kiss '64

Victor Mature
The Shanghai Gesture '42

Wayne Maunder
Porky's '82

Carmen Maura
How to Be a Woman and Not
Die in the Attempt '91

Glauco Mauri
Deep Red: Hatchet Murders
'75

Claire Maurier
Un Air de Famille '96
The 400 Blows '59

Loreto Mauro
True Friends '98

Reinhard Mauser
Gustav Mahler: To Live, I Will
Die '87

Dawn Maxey
Ringmaster '98

Larry Maxwell
Public Access '93

Lois Maxwell
Eternal Evil '87
For Your Eyes Only (SE) '81
Moonraker (SE) '79
The Spy Who Loved Me (SE)
'77
Live and Let Die '73
Thunderball '65
Goldfinger '64
From Russia with Love '63
Dr. No (SE) '62

Lolita '62
Firestorm '97

Roberta Maxwell
Last Night '98
The Postman '97
Philadelphia '93
Psycho 3 '86

Jack May
Without Air '95

Jodhi May
Sister My Sister '94

Martin May
Das Boot (DC) '81

Mathilda May
The Jackal (CE) '97
Lifeforce '85

Rik Mayall
An American Werewolf in London '81

Chip Mayer
Liar Liar '96

Ian Maynard
Drop Dead Rock '95

**Ferdinand "Ferdy"
Mayne**
Night Train to Terror '84

Alois Mayo
The Power of One '92

Virginia Mayo
The Secret Life of Walter
Mitty '47
The Best Years of Our Lives
'46
Wonder Man '45
The Princess and the Pirate
'44

Whitman Mayo
Boyz N the Hood '91

Melanie Mayron
My Blue Heaven '90
Car Wash '76

Jefferson Mays
The Big Brass Ring '99

Debi Mazar
The Insider '99
Hush '98
Meet Wally Sparks '97
Space Truckers '97
Trees Lounge '96
Bad Love '95
Batman Forever '95
Beethoven's 2nd '93
Goodfellas '90

Mike Mazurki
The Shanghai Gesture '42

Paul Mazursky
Antz '98 (V)
Why Do Fools Fall in Love?
'98
Miami Rhapsody '95
History of the World: Part 1
'81

Joseph Mazzarino
The Adventures of Elmo in
Grouchland '99 (V)

Joseph Mazzello
Simon Birch '98
The River Wild '94
Shadowlands '93

Ray McAnally
My Left Foot '89

Alex McArthur
Devil in the Flesh '98
Kiss the Girls '97
Ed McBain's 87 Precinct '96

Alex McAvoy
Pink Floyd: The Wall '82

Tom McBeath
Firestorm '97

Daron McBee
Mortal Kombat 2: Annihilation '97

Chi McBride
Mercury Rising '98
The Frighteners '96
What's Love Got to Do with
It? '93

Donald McBride
The Brute Man '46

Simon McBurney
Mesmer '94

Richard McCabe
Notting Hill '99

Ruth McCabe
My Left Foot '89

Frances Lee McCain
Patch Adams (CE) '98
Gremlins '84
Tex '82

Holt McCallany
Three Kings '99
The Peacemaker '97
Alien3 '92

Lon McCallister
The Red House '47

David McCallum
The Wind '87
The Great Escape '63
A Night to Remember '58

Neil McCallum
Lost Continent '68

Macon McCalman
Doc Hollywood '91

Mercedes McCambridge
The Exorcist (SE) '73 (V)

Tom McCamus
The Sweet Hereafter '96
A Man in Uniform '93

Donal McCann
Rawhead Rex '87

Sean McCann
Affliction '97
Iron Eagle 4 '95

Brian McCardle
200 Cigarettes '98
Speed 2: Cruise Control '97
The Ghost and the Darkness
'96
Rob Roy '95

Brooke McCarter
The Lost Boys '87

Andrew McCarthy
New World Disorder '99
I'm Losing You '98
Weekend at Bernie's '89

Frank McCarthy
The Man with Two Brains '83

Jenny McCarthy
BASEketball '98
Things to Do in Denver When
You're Dead '95

Kevin McCarthy
Just Cause '94
The Distinguished Gentleman
'92
Matinee '92
Invasion of the Body Snatch-
ers '78
Piranha '78
Invasion of the Body Snatch-
ers '56

Molly McCarthy
The Flamingo Kid '84

Sheila McCarthy
Armistead Maupin's More
Tales of the City '97
Die Hard 2: Die Harder '90

Paul McCartney
The Beatles: The First U.S.
Visit '91
Yellow Submarine '68 (V)
Magical Mystery Tour '67
Help! '65
A Hard Day's Night '64

Mary McCarty
The Fighting Sullivans '42

Norma McCarty
Plan 9 from Outer Space '56

Keith McCawley
Rushmore '98

Ronnie McCawley
Rushmore '98

Rue McClanahan
Starship Troopers '97
Nunsense '93

Kevin McClatchy
Boys Life '94

Danny McClaughlin
Beware! Children at Play '95

Michelle McClellan
See Michelle Bauer

Belinda McClory
The Matrix '99

Sean McClory
The Quiet Man '52

Leigh McCloskey
Inferno '80

Doug McClure
Maverick '94
Humanoids from the Deep
'80

Molly McClure
Finding North '97
Pure Country '92

Tane McClure
Scorned 2 '96
Sexual Roulette '96
Lap Dancing '95
Stripshow '95

Edie McClurg
A Bug's Life (CE) '98 (V)
Flubber '97
A River Runs Through It '92
Ferris Bueller's Day Off '86

Ken McCluskey
The Commitments '91

Stephen McCole
Postmortem '98
Rushmore '98

Warren McCollum
Reefer Madness '38

Matt McColm
Body Armor '96

Lorissa McComas
Lap Dancing '95

Heather McComb
Apt Pupil '97

Matthew McConaughey
EDtv '99
Amistad '97
Contact '97
The Newton Boys '97
A Time to Kill '96
The Texas Chainsaw Mas-
sacre 4: The Next Genera-
tion '95
Boys on the Side '94
Dazed and Confused '93

Marilyn McCoo
My Mom's a Werewolf '89

John McCook
Scorned 2 '96

Catherine McCormack
Dancing at Lughnasa '98
Dangerous Beauty '98

Eric McCormack
Free Enterprise '98
Holy Man '98

Mary McCormack
The Alarmist '98
Deep Impact '98
Private Parts '96

Patty McCormack
Mommy 2: Mommy's Day '96
Mommy '95

Charles McCormick
Train Ride to Hollywood '75

Elizabeth McCormick
Stephen King's The Night
Flier '96

Mary McCormick
Retrievers '82

Merrill McCormick
Robin Hood '22

Pat McCormick
Smokey and the Bandit '77

Grayson McCouch
Armageddon '98

Emer McCourt
Boston Kickout '95

Malachy McCourt
Q (The Winged Serpent) '82

Alec McCowen
Cry Freedom '87
A Night to Remember '58

Larry McCoy
The Players Club '98
Bulletproof '96

Matt McCoy
The Assault '97
L.A. Confidential '97
Monsoon '97
The Apocalypse '96
Hard Bounty '94
Hard Drive '94
The Hand that Rocks the Cra-
dle '92

Steve McCoy
I Was a Teenage Zombie '87

Tony McCoy
Bride of the Monster '55

Mark McCracken
Matinee '92

Paul McCrane
RoboCop '87

Joel McCrea
Come and Get It '36
The Most Dangerous Game
'32

Colin McCredie
Shallow Grave '94

Ian McCulloch
Zombie '80

Suli McCullough
Don't Be a Menace to South
Central While Drinking Your
Juice in the Hood '95

Hattie McDaniel
Gone with the Wind '39
I'm No Angel '33

Colleen McDermott
Embrace the Darkness '98

Allyn Ann McLerie
They Shoot Horses, Don't
They? '69

John McLiam
Cool Hand Luke '67

Marshall McLuhan
Annie Hall '77

Karen McLymont
Mr. Nice Guy '98

Ed McMahon
Just Write '97

Michael McManus
Poltergeist '82

John McMartin
Legal Eagles '86

Niles McMaster
Alice Sweet Alice '76
Bloodsucking Freaks '75

Dawn McMillan
Zeus and Roxanne '96

Kenneth McMillan
Runaway Train '85
Dune '84
Killing Hour '84
Protocol '84
Salem's Lot '79

Richard McMillan
Bram Stoker's Shadowbuilder
'98

Teri McMinn
The Texas Chainsaw Mas-
sacre '74

Sam McMurray
Drop Dead Gorgeous '99
The Mod Squad '99
L.A. Story '91
Union City '81

Kevin McNally
Cry Freedom '87

Brian McNamara
Arachnophobia '90

William McNamara
Ringmaster '98
Copycat '95
Surviving the Game '94
Stealing Home '88

Gus McNaughton
The 39 Steps '35

Ian McNeice
A Life Less Ordinary '97
Ace Ventura: When Nature
Calls '95
The Englishman Who Went up
a Hill But Came down a
Mountain '95
No Escape '94

Kristy McNichol
Women of Valor '86

Kevin McNulty
Timecop '94

Graham McPherson
A Man in Uniform '93

Butterfly McQueen
Duel in the Sun '46
Gone with the Wind '39

Chad McQueen
Red Line '96
Sexual Malice '93
Where the Red Fern Grows:
Part 2 '92

Steve McQueen
The Towering Inferno '74
Papillon '73
The Getaway '72
Junior Bonner '72
Bullitt '68
The Great Escape '63

The Magnificent Seven '60

Frank McRae
Last Action Hero '93
License to Kill '89
Lock Up '89
*batteries not included '87
National Lampoon's Vacation
'83
1941 '79

Jenny McShane
Shark Attack '99
Monsoon '97

Michael McShane
Drop Dead Gorgeous '99
A Bug's Life (CE) '98 (V)
Robin Hood: Prince of
Thieves '91

Gerard McSorley
Felicia's Journey '99
The Boxer '97
Michael Collins '96
In the Name of the Father '93

Mark McTague
Family Reunion '79

Jillian McWhirter
The Dentist 2: Brace Yourself
'98
Progeny '98

Courtland Mead
The Little Rascals '94

Mary Meade
T-Men '47

Jayne Meadows
The Story of Us '99
Casino '95
The Player '92

Ray Meagher
Breaker Morant '80

Colm Meaney
This Is My Father '99
Monument Ave. '98
Con Air '97
The Englishman Who Went up
a Hill But Came down a
Mountain '95
Far and Away '92
The Commitments '91
Die Hard 2: Die Harder '90

Kevin Meaney
Plump Fiction '97

Russell Means
Black Cat Run '98

Anne Meara
Southie '98
Reality Bites '94
Awakenings '90

Doug Mears
Zig Zag '99

Julio Mechoso
Virus '98
Switchback '97
White Squall '96

Robert Medford
Watch Me '96

Patricia Medina
The Killing of Sister George
'69
Abbott and Costello in the
Foreign Legion '50

Mark Medoff
Santa Fe '97

Frank Medrano
Kissing a Fool '98
The Replacement Killers '98
Sleepers '96

Rene Medvesek
The Peacemaker '97

Heather Medway
The Fear '94

Olga Meediz
Evita '96

Donald Meek
State Fair '45
They Got Me Covered '43
Stagecoach '39

Jeffrey Meek
Timelock '99

Ralph Meeker
The Night Stalker '71
The Dirty Dozen '67
Paths of Glory '57

Conrad Meertin Jr.
New Jersey Drive '95

Hannes Meesember
The Odessa File '74

John Megna
To Kill a Mockingbird '62

Thomas Meighan
Male and Female '19

John Meillon
Walkabout '71

Kurt Meisel
The Odessa File '74

Kathryn Meisle
Rosewood '96

Gunter Meisner
Willy Wonka & the Chocolate
Factory '71

Mariangela Melato
Swept Away . . . '75
Love and Anarchy '73
Seduction of Mimi '72

Wendel Meldrum
Hush Little Baby '93

Nicholas Mele
Capone '89
A Nightmare on Elm Street 5:
Dream Child '89

Anna Melita
Naked Warriors '73

Randle Mell
Cookie's Fortune '99

Breno Mello
Black Orpheus '58

Mace Melonas
A Kid Called Danger '99

Christopher Meloni
Bound '96

George Memmoli
Mean Streets '73

Ben Mendelsohn
Sirens '94

Antonio Mendoza
Easy Rider '69

Adolphe Menjou
Paths of Glory '57
A Star Is Born '37

Ernest Menzer
Bed and Board '70

Heather Menzies
Piranha '78

Patrick Mercado
The Dreamlife of Angels '98

Beryl Mercer
All Quiet on the Western
Front '30

Mae Mercer
The Swinging Cheerleaders
'74

Michele Mercier
Call of the Wild '72
Shoot the Piano Player '62

Melina Mercouri
The Law '59

Monique Mercure
The Red Violin '98
When Justice Fails '98

Micole Mercurio
While You Were Sleeping '95

Paul Mercurio
The First 9 1/2 Weeks '98
Dark Planet '97

Burgess Meredith
Grumpier Old Men '95
Across the Moon '94
Grumpy Old Men '93
Rocky 2 '79
Rocky '76
The Sentinel '76
The Hindenburg '75
The Story of G.I. Joe '45
That Uncertain Feeling '41
Of Mice and Men '39

Ifan Meredith
Metroland '97

Macha Meril
Beau Pere '81
Deep Red: Hatchet Murders
'75

Lee Meriwether
The 4D Man '59

Una Merkel
The Bat Whispers '30

Franco Merli
Arabian Nights '74

Jan Merlin
Take the Money and Run '69

Joanna Merlin
City of Angels '98

B.D. Merrill
What Ever Happened to Baby
Jane? '62

Dina Merrill
The Player '92
Caddyshack 2 '88

Gary Merrill
Another Man's Poison '52
All About Eve '50

Ryan Merriman
The Deep End of the Ocean
'98

Clive Merrison
The English Patient '96

George Merritt
Young and Innocent '37

Theresa Merritt
Billy Madison '94
The Serpent and the Rainbow
'87

Franco Mescolini
The Monster '96

Jason Meshover-Iorg
Lethal Weapon 3 '92

Hannes Messemer
The Great Escape '63

Marc Messier
The Boys '97

Loridawn Messuri
The Seventh Sense '99
Word of Mouth '99

Edward Metcalf
Animal Crackers '30

Laurie Metcalf
Bulworth '98

Scream 2 '97
U-Turn '97
Leaving Las Vegas '95
JFK '91
Mistress '91
Internal Affairs '90
Uncle Buck '89

Mark Metcalf
National Lampoon's Animal
House '78

Asher Metchik
Milo '98

Method Man
Belly '98

Art Metrano
The Heartbreak Kid '72

Jim Metzler
Tex '82

Paul Meurisse
Diabolique '55

Anne-Laure Meury
Boyfriends & Girlfriends '88

Jason Mewes
Mallrats '95
Clerks '94

Breckin Meyer
Go '99
Tail Lights Fade '99
Dancer, Texas—Pop. 81 '98
54 '98
Clueless '95

Dina Meyer
Stranger than Fiction '99
Starship Troopers '97
Dragonheart (SE) '96
Johnny Mnemonic '95

Michael Meyer
Virtual Desire '95

Russ Meyer
Amazon Women on the Moon
'87

Bruce Meyers
The Governess '98

Michelle Meyrink
One Magic Christmas '85

Rebecca Lee Mezza
Selena '96

Clipper Miano
Alegria '98

Robert Miano
Smoke Signals '98
Donnie Brasco '96

Nora Miao
The Dragon Fist '80
Return of the Dragon '73

Gertrude Michael
I'm No Angel '33

Ralph Michael
A Night to Remember '58

Al Michaels
BASEketball '98

Bret Michaels
In God's Hands '98

T.J. Michaels
Igor & the Lunatics '85

Nicki Micheaux
Ringmaster '98

Marc Michel
Umbrellas of Cherbourg '64

Michael Michele
The Substitute 2: School's
Out '97
New Jack City '91

Anne Michelle
House of Whipcord '75

Yoshiko Miyazaki
Ran '85

Eric Miyeni
Dangerous Ground '96

Kim Miyori
Metro '96
Body Shot '93
The Punisher '90

Eiko Miyoshi
Samurai 1: Musashi Miyamoto '55

Isaac Mizrahi
Celebrity '98

Kumi Mizuno
Godzilla vs. Monster Zero '68

Ronald Mlodzik
They Came from Within '75

Genevieve Mnich
Beau Pere '81

Teresa Mo
Hard-Boiled '92

Tony Mockus Sr.
Backdraft '91

Matthew Modine
The Real Blonde '97
Cutthroat Island '95
Memphis Belle '90
Full Metal Jacket '87
Vision Quest '85

Gaston Modot
Grand Illusion '37

Joe Moeller
Caress of the Vampire (CE) '96

Monica Moench
Clay Pigeons '98

Donald Moffat
Cookie's Fortune '99
Clear and Present Danger '94
The Bonfire of the Vanities '90
The Unbearable Lightness of Being '88
The Best of Times '86
The Right Stuff '83
The Thing '82

D.W. Moffett
Falling Down '93

Gerald Mohr
Love Affair '39

Jay Mohr
Go '99
Paulie '98 (V)
Playing by Heart '98
Small Soldiers '98
200 Cigarettes '98
Suicide Kings '97
Jerry Maguire '96
Picture Perfect '96

Gunnar Moller
The Odessa File '74

Karen Mok
Lawyer Lawyer '97
Black Mask '96
God of Cookery '96
Fallen Angels '95
Chinese Odyssey, Part One: Pandora's Box '94
Chinese Odyssey, Part Two: Cinderalla '94

Zakes Mokae
Cry Freedom '87
The Serpent and the Rainbow '87

Gretchen Mol
The Thirteenth Floor '99
Celebrity '98

Finding Graceland '98
New Rose Hotel '98
Rounders '98

Jerry Molen
Rain Man '88

Alfred Molina
Dudley Do-Right '99
The Imposters '98
Boogie Nights '97
The Man Who Knew Too Little '97
Maverick '94
The Trial '93
Ladyhawke '85
Meantime '81

Antonio Molina
For Whom the Bell Tolls '43

Charles Moll
Night Train to Terror '84

Richard Moll
The Flintstones (CE) '94
National Lampoon's Loaded Weapon 1 '93
Gargoyles '72

Clifford Mollison
A Christmas Carol '51

Marjorie Monaghan
Nemesis '93

Dan Monahan
Stephen King's The Night Flier '96
Porky's '82

Debi Monahan
Laser Mission '90

Karen Moncrieff
Waking Up Horton '99
Xtro 3: Watch the Skies '95

Lisa Moncure
Pretty Village, Pretty Flame '96

Paulina Monet
Caress of the Vampire (CE) '96

Yoyo Mong
A Hero Never Dies '98

Elizabeth Monica
Trader Hornee '70

Alan Monk
La Traviata '82

Debra Monk
The Devil's Advocate '97
Bed of Roses '95

Lawrence Monoson
Mask '85

Lochlan Monroe
High Voltage '98

Marilyn Monroe
The Love Goddesses '65
All About Eve '50

Jacques Monseau
The Devil's Nightmare '71

Lee Montague
Mahler '74

Paolo Montalban
Cinderella '97

Ricardo Montalban
Cannonball Run 2 '84

Yves Montand
The Law '59
Wages of Fear '55

Luigi Montefiore
Rabid Dogs '74

Elias Monteiro da Silva
Medicine Man '92

Caroline Monteith
Novel Desires '92

Fernanda Montenegro
Central Station '98

Maria Montez
Portrait of an Assassin '49

Belinda J. Montgomery
For Love of a Child '90

Lee Montgomery
Baker's Hawk '76

Poppy Montgomery
Life '99
The Other Sister '98
Dead Man on Campus '97

Robert Montgomery
They Were Expendable '45

Rita Montone
Maniac '80

Muriel Montosse
Fascination '79

Michael Monty
The Firing Line '91

Elizabeth Moody
Dead Alive '93

Jim Moody
Bad Boys '83

Ron Moody
Unidentified Flying Oddball '79
The Twelve Chairs '70
Oliver! '68

Alvy Moore
A Boy and His Dog '75
The Wild One '54
The War of the Worlds '53

Andre Moore
New Jersey Drive '95

Ashleigh Aston Moore
Now and Then '95

Ben Moore
2000 Maniacs '64

Bobby Moore
Victory '81

Colleen Moore
Sucker the Vampire '98

Deborah Maria (Barrymore) Moore
Chaplin '92

Demi Moore
Deconstructing Harry '97
G.I. Jane '97
Beavis and Butt-Head Do America '96 (V)
The Juror '96
Striptease '96
Now and Then '95
Disclosure '94
A Few Good Men '92
Mortal Thoughts '91
Nothing but Trouble '91
The Seventh Sign '88
About Last Night . . . '86
Parasite '82
Choices '81

Dudley Moore
Lovesick '83
Arthur '81
10 '79

Duke Moore
Plan 9 from Outer Space '56

Eva Moore
The Old Dark House '32

Ian Moore
Sling Blade '96

Julianne Moore
Cookie's Fortune '99

An Ideal Husband '99
Psycho '98
The Big Lebowski '97
Boogie Nights '97
Assassins '95
The Fugitive '93
The Hand that Rocks the Cradle '92

Katie Moore
For Richer or Poorer '97

Kaycee Moore
Ninth Street '98

Kenya Moore
Senseless '98

Kieron Moore
The Thin Red Line '64
Anna Karenina '48

Mary Moore
Murder at 1600 '97

Mary Tyler Moore
Keys to Tulsa '96
Flirting with Disaster '95

Matt Moore
20,000 Leagues under the Sea '16

Michael Moore
The Insider '99

Peter Savard Moore
Top Dog '95

Roger Moore
Spice World: The Movie '97
The Quest '96
For Your Eyes Only (SE) '81
Sea Wolves '81
Moonraker (SE) '79
The Spy Who Loved Me (SE) '77
Live and Let Die '73
The Last Time I Saw Paris '54

Rudy Ray Moore
Avenging Disco Godfather '76
Dolemite '75

Terry Moore
Beneath the 12-Mile Reef '53
The Great Rupert '50

Agnes Moorehead
How the West Was Won '63
The Bat '59
The Conqueror '56
Show Boat '51

Tiriel Mora
The Castle '97

Esai Morales
Atomic Train '99
Don't Do It '94
La Bamba '87
Bad Boys '83

Nick Moran
Lock, Stock and 2 Smoking Barrels '98

Polly Moran
Adam's Rib '50

Rick Moranis
The Flintstones (CE) '94
My Blue Heaven '90
Ghostbusters 2 '89
Parenthood '89
Little Shop of Horrors '86
Brewster's Millions '85
Ghostbusters '84
Streets of Fire '84

Richard Morant
Mahler '74

Marcello Morante
The Gospel According to St. Matthew '64

Camilla More
Out of Time '90

Kenneth More
Unidentified Flying Oddball '79
The Slipper and the Rose '76
The Longest Day '62
A Night to Remember '58

Jeanne Moreau
Ever After: A Cinderella Story '98
I Love You, I Love You Not '97
One Hundred and One Nights '94
La Femme Nikita '91
The Train '65
The Trial '63
The 400 Blows '59

Elizabeth Morehead
Interceptor '92

Gael Morel
Wild Reeds '94

Mantan Moreland
Spider Baby '64
King of the Zombies '41

Andre Morell
Plague of the Zombies '66

Antonio Moreno
The Searchers '56

Lea Moreno
Jungle Boy '96

Rita Moreno
Slums of Beverly Hills '98
West Side Story '61
The King and I '56
Singin' in the Rain '52

Linda Moretti
The Postman '94

Michele Moretti
Wild Reeds '94

Cindy Morgan
Tron '82
Caddyshack '80

Debbi Morgan
Eve's Bayou '97

Frank Morgan
The Wizard of Oz '39

Garfield Morgan
The Odessa File '74

Harry (Henry) Morgan
Dragnet '87
The Cat from Outer Space '78
How the West Was Won '63
High Noon '52
State Fair '45

Jeffrey Dean Morgan
Undercover '94

Michele Morgan
Bulworth '98

Molly Morgan
The Trigger Effect '96

Nancy Morgan
Lucky Luke '94

Ralph Morgan
The Monster Maker '44

Red Morgan
The Amazing Transparent Man '60

Robbi Morgan
Friday the 13th '80

Trevor Morgan
The Sixth Sense '99
Barney's Great Adventure '98

Stephanie Morgenstern
The Sweet Hereafter '96

Naoki Mori
Spice World: The Movie '97

Cathy Moriarty
Digging to China '98
Gloria '98
A Brother's Kiss '97
Cop Land '97
Hugo Pool '97
Matinee '92
Kindergarten Cop '90
Raging Bull '80

James Moriarty
Ten Benny '98
Someone to Watch Over Me '87

Michael Moriarty
Pale Rider '85
Q (The Winged Serpent) '82
The Last Detail '73

P. H. Moriarty
Lock, Stock and 2 Smoking Barrels '98
The Long Good Friday '80

Philippe Morier-Genoud
Confidentially Yours '83

Noriyuki "Pat" Morita
Desert Heat '99
King Cobra '98
Mulan '98 (V)
Misery Brothers Y2K '95
Honeymoon in Vegas '92

Louisa Moritz
Death Race 2000 '75
One Flew Over the Cuckoo's Nest '75

Yuko Moriyama
Zeram '91

Karen Morley
Our Daily Bread and Other Films of the Depression '34

Robert Morley
Around the World in 80 Days '89
The Wind '87
Beat the Devil '53

Sechaba Morojele
Dangerous Ground '96

Anita Morris
Radioland Murders '94
Aria '88

Aubrey Morris
Lifeforce '85
A Clockwork Orange '71
Night Caller from Outer Space '66

Chester Morris
The Bat Whispers '30

Dorothy Morris
Bataan '43

Edna Morris
Another Man's Poison '52

Haviland Morris
Home Alone 3 '97
Sixteen Candles '84

Howard Morris
Splash '84
History of the World: Part 1 '81

Jane Morris
Pretty Woman '90

Jeff Morris
The Crossing Guard '94

Jonathan Morris
Bloodstorm: Subspecies 4 '98
Vampire Journals '96

Phil Morris
Clay Pigeons '98
Devil in the Flesh '98

Wayne Morris
Paths of Glory '57

Jenny Morrison
Stir of Echoes '99

Temuera Morrison
From Dusk Till Dawn 3: The Hangman's Daughter '99
Six Days, Seven Nights '98
Speed 2: Cruise Control '97
Barb Wire '96
The Island of Dr. Moreau '96

David Morrissey
Hilary and Jackie '98

Bruce Morrow
Dirty Dancing '87
Dirty Dancing (CE) '87

Mari Morrow
Dead Man on Campus '97
Def Jam's How to Be a Player '97

Rob Morrow
Quiz Show '94

Vic Morrow
Humanoids from the Deep '80
Men in War '57

David Morse
The Green Mile '99
The Negotiator '98
Contact '97
The Long Kiss Goodnight '96
The Rock '96
12 Monkeys '95
The Crossing Guard '94
The Getaway '93

Helen Morse
Picnic at Hanging Rock '75

Glenn Morshower
The Jack Bull '99

Viggo Mortensen
A Walk on the Moon '99
A Perfect Murder '98
Psycho '98
G.I. Jane '97
Albino Alligator '96
Daylight '96
Portrait of a Lady '96
Crimson Tide '95
The Prophecy '95
Boiling Point '93
Carlito's Way '93

Emily Mortimer
Noah's Ark '99
Elizabeth '98
The Saint '97
The Ghost and the Darkness '96

Joe Morton
The Astronaut's Wife '99
The Blues Brothers 2000 '98
Apt Pupil '97
Executive Decision '96
Speed '94
Forever Young '92
Terminator 2: Judgment Day '91

Sam Morton
Simon Birch '98

Consolata Moschera
The Reincarnation of Isabel '72

Maurice Moscovich
The Great Dictator '40
Love Affair '39

David Moscow
Big '88

Harry Moses
The Van '77

Mark Moses
Platoon '86

Roger E. Mosley
A Thin Line Between Love and Hate '96

Carrie-Anne Moss
The Matrix '99

Elissabeth Moss
Earthly Possessions '99
Mumford '99
A Thousand Acres '97

Michael H. Moss
Stephen King's The Night Flier '96

Mireille Mosse
The City of Lost Children '95

Josh Mostel
Big Daddy '99
Rounders '98
Great Expectations '97
The Basketball Diaries '94
Billy Madison '94
Star 80 '83
Sophie's Choice '82
Jesus Christ, Superstar '73

Erika Mottl
Gustav Mahler: To Live, I Will Die '87

Greg Mottola
Celebrity '98

Alan Mowbray
The King and I '56
That Uncertain Feeling '41
My Man Godfrey '36

Bill Moynihan
The Creeps '97

David Mucci
Unforgiven '92
Prom Night '80

Leonard Mudie
The Mummy '32

Armin Mueller-Stahl
Jakob the Liar '99
The Thirteenth Floor '99
The X-Files '98
The Game '97
The Peacemaker '97
Shine '95
The Power of One '92

Richard Muench
Patton '70

Thierry Mugler
Ready to Wear '94

Minister Benjamin F. Muhammed
Belly '98

Ulrich Muhe
Funny Games '97

Anita Mui
Rumble in the Bronx '96
Jet Li's The Enforcer '95
The Executioners '93
The Heroic Trio '93
The Moon Warriors '92
Saviour of the Soul '92
Miracles '89
Rouge '87

Gavin Muir
Night Tide '63

Patrick Muldoon
Stigmata '99
Black Cat Run '98
Starship Troopers '97

Chris Mulkey
Bound and Gagged: A Love Story '93

The Hidden '87

Martin Mull
Jingle All the Way '96
The Player '92
FM '78

Carrie Mullan
Hideous Kinky '99

Kathryn Mullen
The Dark Crystal '82 (V)

Marie Mullen
Dancing at Lughnasa '98

Brooke Muller
Witchouse '99

Paul Muller
Naked Warriors '73

Rod Mullinar
Dead Calm '89
Breaker Morant '80

Michael Mullins
Pom Pom Girls '76

Dermot Mulroney
Goodbye, Lover '99
My Best Friend's Wedding '97
Bastard out of Carolina '96
Box of Moonlight '96
The Trigger Effect '96
Copycat '95
How to Make an American Quilt '95
Point of No Return '93
Career Opportunities '91
Sunset '88
Young Guns '88

Kieran Mulroney
Career Opportunities '91

Richard Munch
The Train '65

Kevin Mundy
Better Than Chocolate '99

Marjorie Munks
On Approval '44

Molly Munks
On Approval '44

Caroline Munro
Maniac '80
The Spy Who Loved Me (SE) '77

Lochlyn Munro
A Night at the Roxbury '98
Dead Man on Campus '97

Ona Munson
The Red House '47
The Shanghai Gesture '42
Gone with the Wind '39

Fuyuki Murakami
Godzilla vs. Monster Zero '68
Godzilla, King of the Monsters '56

Hiroaki Murakami
Iron Maze '91

George Murcell
Cutthroat Island '95

Jack Murdock
Rain Man '88
Altered States '80

Tim Murdock
They Were Expendable '45

Gheorghe Muresan
My Giant '98

Peter Murnik
Hard Rain '97

Hideo Murota
A Taxing Woman '87

Annette Murphy
Race '99

Brittany Murphy
Phoenix '98
The Prophecy 2: Ashtown '97
Drive '96
Clueless '95

Donna Murphy
The Astronaut's Wife '99
Star Trek: Insurrection '98

Eddie Murphy
Bowfinger '99
Life '99
Dr. Dolittle '98
Holy Man '98
Mulan '98 (V)
Metro '96
The Nutty Professor '96
The Distinguished Gentleman '92
Another 48 Hrs. '90
Coming to America '88
The Golden Child '86

George Murphy
Bataan '43

Jack Murphy
Peter Pan '24

Johnny Murphy
The Commitments '91

Kevin Murphy
Mystery Science Theater 3000: The Movie '96

Mary Murphy
The Wild One '54

Michael Murphy
Private Parts '96
Batman Returns '92
Shocker '89
Mesmerized '84
The Year of Living Dangerously '82

Padraigin Murphy
Blackjack '97

Reilly Murphy
Body Snatchers '93

Rosemary Murphy
Message in a Bottle '98
Walking Tall '73
To Kill a Mockingbird '62

Shannon Murphy
Firehouse '87

William Murphy
Sands of Iwo Jima '49
The Story of G.I. Joe '45

Barbara Murray
Another Man's Poison '52

Bill Murray
Rushmore '98
Wild Things '98
The Man Who Knew Too Little '97
Kingpin '96
Space Jam '96
Groundhog Day '93
Mad Dog and Glory '93
Ghostbusters 2 '89
Scrooged '88
Little Shop of Horrors '86
Ghostbusters '84
Stripes '81
Caddyshack '80
Where the Buffalo Roam '80
Meatballs '79

Christine Murray
Trader Hornee '70

Don Murray
Peggy Sue Got Married '86
The Viking Queen '67

Pauline Murray
It Happened Here '65

Tom Murray
The Gold Rush '25

John Murtagh
Rob Roy '95

James Murtaugh
Private Parts '96

Naomasa Musaka
Tokyo Fist '96

Tony Musante
The Bird with the Crystal Plumage '70

Mike Muscat
Assault of the Killer Bimbos '88

Clarence Muse
The Black Stallion '79
The White Zombie '32

Robert Musgrave
Bottle Rocket '95

Louis Mustillo
Dudley Do-Right '99
Just the Ticket '98

Ornella Muti
Tales of Ordinary Madness '83
Flash Gordon '80

Roger Mutton
The Girl on a Motorcycle '68

Bruce Myers
The Unbearable Lightness of Being '88

Dwight Errington Myers
New Jersey Drive '95

Harrison Myers
Dear Santa '98

Harry Myers
City Lights '31

Kim Myers
White Palace '90
A Nightmare on Elm Street 2: Freddy's Revenge '85

Lou Myers
Tin Cup '96

Mike Myers
Austin Powers 2: The Spy Who Shagged Me '99
54 '98
Austin Powers: International Man of Mystery '97
So I Married an Axe Murderer '93

Bruce Myles
Sweet Talker '91

John Mylong
For Whom the Bell Tolls '43

Byron Myrick
Ninth Street '98

Jim Nabors
Cannonball Run 2 '84
Stroker Ace '83

George Nader
Away All Boats '56

Lycia Naff
Lethal Weapon '87

Yasushi Nagata
The Human Condition: No Greater Love '58

Don Nagel
Bride of the Monster '55

Ajay Naidu
Office Space '98

Jimmy Nail
Evita '96

J. Carrol Naish
Rage at Dawn '55
Beneath the 12-Mile Reef '53
Rio Grande '50

The Southerner '45
The Monster Maker '44

Laurence Naismith
Jason and the Argonauts '63
A Night to Remember '58

Rick Najera
Red Surf '90

Kathy Najimy
Bride of Chucky '98
Hope Floats '98
Sister Act 2: Back in the Habit '93

Machiko Naka
Godzilla's Revenge '69

Tatsuya Nakadai
Ran '85
High & Low '62
Sanjuro '62
The Human Condition: Road to Eternity '59
The Human Condition: No Greater Love '58

Aio Nakajima
In the Realm of the Senses '76

Reggie Nalder
Salem's Lot '79
The Bird with the Crystal Plumage '70
Mark of the Devil '69

Nita Naldi
Dr. Jekyll and Mr. Hyde '20

Koji Nambara
Branded to Kill '67

Shinji Nambara
The Human Condition: No Greater Love '58

Jack Nance
Pretty As a Picture: The Art of David Lynch '98
Little Witches '96
The Demolitionist '95
Voodoo '95
Across the Moon '94
The Hot Spot '90
Dune '84

Nicole Nancel
The Shiver of the Vampires '70

Neriah Napaul
The Bikini Car Wash Company '90

Charles Napier
Austin Powers 2: The Spy Who Shagged Me '99
Fatal Pursuit '98
Austin Powers: International Man of Mystery '97
Hunter's Moon '97
The Cable Guy '96
Body Shot '93
Silence of the Lambs '91
The Grifters '90
Rambo: First Blood, Part 2 '85
The Blues Brothers (CE) '80

Tony Nappo
Better Than Chocolate '99

Kathrine Narducci
A Bronx Tale '93

Brian Narelle
Dark Star '74

Nas
Belly '98

Arthur J. Nascarelli
Cop Land '97

Marilyn Nash
Monsieur Verdoux '47

Mary Nash
The Philadelphia Story '40

Niecy Nash
Cookie's Fortune '99

Nick Nasta
Combat Shock '84

Anthony Natale
Mr. Holland's Opus '95

Zoe Nathenson
One Night Stand '97

Mari Natsuki
The Hunted '94

Yosuke Natsuki
Chushingura '62

Mildred Natwick
Dangerous Liaisons '88
Barefoot in the Park '67
Court Jester '56
The Quiet Man '52

David Naughton
An American Werewolf in London '81

James Naughton
The First Wives Club '96

Alla Nazimova
The Bridge of San Luis Rey '44

Amedeo Nazzari
Nights of Cabiria '57

Anna Neagle
Forever and a Day '43

Billie Neal
Mortal Thoughts '91

Edwin Neal
The Texas Chainsaw Massacre '74

Elise Neal
Def Jam's How to Be a Player '97
Scream 2 '97
Rosewood '96

Patricia Neal
Cookie's Fortune '99
Ghost Story '81
Breakfast at Tiffany's '61

Tom Neal
The Brute Man '46

Kevin Nealon
The Wedding Singer '97
Happy Gilmore '96

Christopher Neame
Bloodstone '88

Holly Near
Minnie and Moskowitz '71

Claire Nebout
Ponette '95

Ted Neeley
Jesus Christ, Superstar '73

Gail Neely
Surf Nazis Must Die (DC) '87

Liam Neeson
The Haunting '99
Les Miserables '97
Michael Collins '96
Rob Roy '95
Darkman '90
Next of Kin '89
Excalibur '81

Nefertiti
Panther '95

Hildegarde Neff
The Snows of Kilimanjaro '52

Taylor Negron
A Kid in Aladdin's Palace '97
The Last Boy Scout '91

Nothing but Trouble '91

David Neidorf
Hoosiers '86
Platoon '86

Marshall Neilan
Daddy Long Legs '19

Sam Neill
Merlin '98
Event Horizon '97
The Horse Whisperer '97
Snow White: A Tale of Terror '97
In the Mouth of Madness '95
Restoration '94
Sirens '94
The Piano '93
The Hunt for Red October '90
Dead Calm '89
Plenty '85

Stacey Nelkin
Halloween 3: Season of the Witch '82

Krista Nell
The Bloodsucker Leads the Dance '75

Kate Nelligan
U.S. Marshals '98
Up Close and Personal '96
How to Make an American Quilt '95
Wolf '94
Dracula '79

Adam Nelson
Phantoms '97
The Abyss (SE) '89

Ann Nelson
My Girl '91

Barry Nelson
The Shining '80
Airport '70
Bataan '43

Craig T. Nelson
The Devil's Advocate '97
Action Jackson '88
Silkwood '83
Poltergeist '82
Private Benjamin '80
Stir Crazy '80
Where the Buffalo Roam '80
Flesh Gordon '72 (V)

Ed Nelson
Jackie Chan's Who Am I '98
Brenda Starr '86
For the Love of Benji '77
Airport '75 '75

Gene Nelson
Oklahoma '55

John Allen Nelson
Shelter '98

Judd Nelson
New Jack City '91
The Breakfast Club '85

Lori Nelson
Mohawk '56

Margaret Nelson
Picnic at Hanging Rock '75

Mark Nelson
Friday the 13th '80

Michael J. Nelson
Mystery Science Theater 3000: The Movie '96

Novella Nelson
A Perfect Murder '98

Patriece Nelson
Crooklyn '94

Sean Nelson
A Stranger in the Kingdom '98

Shannon Nelson
Drop Dead Gorgeous '99

Tim Blake Nelson
The Thin Red Line '98

Willie Nelson
Austin Powers 2: The Spy Who Shagged Me '99
Outlaw Justice '98
Half-Baked '97
Wag the Dog '97
Thief '81
The Electric Horseman '79

Corin "Corky" Nemec
Drop Zone '94
Stephen King's The Stand '94
Solar Crisis '92

Christiane Nere
The Fantastic Night '42

Francesca Neri
Outrage '93

Rosalba (Sara Bay) Neri
Naked Warriors '73

David Nerman
The Scorpio Factor '90

Franco Nero
Die Hard 2: Die Harder '90
Django Strikes Again '87
Fifth Day of Peace '72
Django '68
Camelot '67

Caroline Neron
Strip Search '97

James Nesbitt
Waking Ned Devine '98

Ruth Neuman
Basket Case '82

Dorothy Neumann
The Terror '63

Jenny Neumann
Hell Night '81

Bebe Neuwirth
An Extremely Goofy Movie '99 (V)
Summer of Sam '99
All Dogs Christmas Carol '98 (V)
Celebrity '98
The Faculty '98
The Adventures of Pinocchio '96
The Associate '96
Jumanji (CS) '95
Malice '93
Bugsy '91

Aaron Neville
Posse '93

John Neville
Goodbye, Lover '99
Urban Legend '98
The X-Files '98
The Fifth Element '97
Dangerous Minds '95
Little Women '94
The Adventures of Baron Munchausen '89

Shearan Neville
The Last Game '95

Robyn Nevin
The Castle '97

George Newbern
Father of the Bride '91
Adventures in Babysitting '87

Flora Newbigin
The Borrowers '97

Mark Newell
Patriots '94**

Don Novello
Just the Ticket '98

Ivor Novello
The Lodger '26

Tom Novembre
An American Werewolf in Paris '97

Vasili Novikov
Alexander Nevsky '38

Wanda Nowicki
Armitage 3: Polymatrix '94 (V)

Michael Nowka
Cross of Iron '76

Winston Ntshona
Tarzan and the Lost City '98

Danny Nucci
Titanic '97
The Big Squeeze '96
Eraser '96
The Rock '96
That Old Feeling '96
Crimson Tide '95

Miguel Nunez
Life '99
For Richer or Poorer '97

Bill Nunn
Foolish '99
He Got Game '98
Kiss the Girls '97
Mad City '97
Bulletproof '96
Things to Do in Denver When You're Dead '95
True Crime '95
New Jack City '91
Def by Temptation '90
Do the Right Thing '89

Loredana Nusciak
Django '68

France Nuyen
South Pacific '58

Carrie Nye
Creepshow '82

Carroll Nye
Gone with the Wind '39

Jack Oakie
The Great Dictator '40

Simon Oakland
The Night Strangler '72
The Night Stalker '71
Bullitt '68
West Side Story '61
Psycho (CE) '60

Cicely Oates
The Man Who Knew Too Much '34

Warren Oates
Stripes '81
1941 '79
Badlands '74
Two Lane Blacktop '71
The Wild Bunch '69

Dan O'Bannon
Dark Star '74

Charles Oberly
Flirting with Disaster '95

Merle Oberon
Dark Waters '44
Forever and a Day '43
That Uncertain Feeling '41
Wuthering Heights '39
The Scarlet Pimpernel '34

Jack Oblivian
Sore Losers '97

Jacqueline Obradors
Six Days, Seven Nights '98

Claudio Obregon
Midaq Alley '95

Rodrigo Obregon
Django Strikes Again '87

Hugh O'Brian
Twins '88
Vengeance Valley '51

Seamus O'Brian
Bloodsucking Freaks '75

Austin O'Brien
Last Action Hero '93

Clay O'Brien
The Cowboys '72

Dave O'Brien
Reefer Madness '38

Donald O'Brien
The Train '65

Edmond O'Brien
The Wild Bunch '69
The Longest Day '62
D.O.A. '49
The Hunchback of Notre Dame '39

Kevin O'Brien
Warlock '91

Mary O'Brien
Battling Butler '26

Myles O'Brien
Scorned 2 '96
Sexual Roulette '96

Nancy O'Brien
Night Calls: The Movie 2 '99
Web of Seduction '99

Niall O'Brien
Rawhead Rex '87

Pat O'Brien
Last Hurrah '58

Richard O'Brien
Dark City '97
Spice World: The Movie '97

Shauna O'Brien
Body Armor '96
Friend of the Family 2 '96
Friend of the Family '95
Over the Wire '95

Tom O'Brien
The Big Easy '87

Virginia O'Brien
Till the Clouds Roll By '46

Erin O'Brien-Moore
Destination Moon '50

Sean O'Bryan
I'll Be Home for Christmas '98
The Twilight of the Golds '97

Sean O'Byrne
Timecop '94

Andrea Occhipinti
New York Ripper '82

Uwe Ochsenknecht
Das Boot (DC) '81

Arthur O'Connell
The Last Valley '71

Deirdre O'Connell
Fearless '93

Jerry O'Connell
The '60s '99
Can't Hardly Wait '98
Scream 2 '97
Jerry Maguire '96
Joe's Apartment '96
Stand by Me '86

Raoul O'Connell
Boys Life '94

Derrick O'Connor
End of Days '99
Deep Rising '98
How to Make an American Quilt '95
Lethal Weapon 2 '89

Donald O'Connor
Singin' in the Rain '52

Glynnis O'Connor
The Boy in the Plastic Bubble '76

Kevin J. O'Connor
The Mummy '99
Black Cat Run '98
Deep Rising '98
Gods and Monsters '98
Lord of Illusions '95
Virtuosity '95
Color of Night '94
No Escape '94
Hero '92
Peggy Sue Got Married '86

Renee O'Connor
Darkman 2: The Return of Durant '94

Una O'Connor
The Bride of Frankenstein '35

Hugh O'Conor
My Left Foot '89

Bryan O'Dell
Street Wars '91

Fritz Odemar
M '31

Christophe Odent
First Name: Carmen '83

Cathy O'Donnell
The Best Years of Our Lives '46

Chris O'Donnell
The Bachelor '99
Cookie's Fortune '99
Batman and Robin '97
The Chamber '96
In Love and War '96
Batman Forever '95
Mad Love '95
Circle of Friends '94
The Three Musketeers '93
Scent of a Woman '92
School Ties '92
Fried Green Tomatoes '91

Rosie O'Donnell
Tarzan '99 (V)
The Twilight of the Golds '97
Beautiful Girls '96
Now and Then '95
The Flintstones (CE) '94
Sleepless in Seattle '93
A League of Their Own '92

"Spec" O'Donnell
Sparrows '26

Martha O'Driscoll
Reap the Wild Wind '42

Conor O'Farrell
Stir of Echoes '99

George Offerman Jr.
The Fighting Sullivans '42

Ken Ogata
The Pillow Book '95

Bulle Ogier
Shattered Image '98
Irma Vep '96

Pascale Ogier
Full Moon in Paris '84

Ian Ogilvy
Death Becomes Her '92

Gail O'Grady
That Old Feeling '96

Sandra Oh
Guinevere '99
Last Night '98
Bean '97

Soon-Teck Oh
Mulan '98 (V)
Beverly Hills Ninja '96

Brian O'Halloran
Mallrats '95
Clerks '94

Jack O'Halloran
Dragnet '87
King Kong '76
Farewell, My Lovely '75

Natsuko Ohama
Speed '94

Catherine O'Hara
Bartok the Magnificent '99 (V)
Home Fries '98
The Paper '94
The Nightmare before Christmas '93 (V)
Home Alone 2: Lost in New York '92
Home Alone '90
Beetlejuice '88

David O'Hara
The Matchmaker '97

Jenny O'Hara
Wishmaster '97
Career Opportunities '91

Maureen O'Hara
McLintock! '63
The Quiet Man '52
Rio Grande '50
Miracle on 34th Street '47
The Hunchback of Notre Dame '39
Jamaica Inn '39

Paige O'Hara
Beauty and the Beast: The Enchanted Christmas '97 (V)

Dan O'Herlihy
The Rat Pack '98
RoboCop 2 '90
RoboCop '87
The Last Starfighter '84
Halloween 3: Season of the Witch '82
Odd Man Out '47

Jan Ohlsson
Terror of Frankenstein '75

Carol Ohmart
Spider Baby '64
House on Haunted Hill '58

Yoshi Oida
The Pillow Book '95

Mariko Okada
Samurai 3: Duel at Ganryu Island '56
Samurai 2: Duel at Ichijoji Temple '55

Dennis O'Keefe
Raw Deal '48
T-Men '47

Doug O'Keefe
Specimen '97

Jodi Lyn O'Keefe
She's All That '99
Halloween: H20 '98

Michael O'Keefe
Caddyshack '80
The Great Santini '80

Miles O'Keeffe
Diamondbacks '99
Cartel '90

Nikolai P. Okhlopkov
Alexander Nevsky '38

Sophie Okonedo
Ace Ventura: When Nature Calls '95

Yuji Okumoto
Mean Guns '97
Nemesis '93

Ken Olandt
Darkdrive '98
Leprechaun '93

Daniel Olbrychski
The Decalogue '88
The Unbearable Lightness of Being '88
Tin Drum '79

Gary Oldman
Lost in Space '98
Quest for Camelot '98 (V)
Air Force One '97
The Fifth Element '97
The Professional '94
True Romance '93
Dracula '92
JFK '91
Sid & Nancy '86
Meantime '81

Gabriel Olds
Without Limits '97
Animal Room '95

Larisa Oleynik
Ten Things I Hate about You '99

Adam Oliensis
The Pompatus of Love '95

Ken Olin
Queens Logic '91

Lena Olin
Mystery Men '99
Polish Wedding '97
Night Falls on Manhattan '96
Havana '90
The Unbearable Lightness of Being '88

Ingrid Oliu
Stand and Deliver '88

Christian Oliver
Eat Your Heart Out '96

David Oliver
The Chosen One: Legend of the Raven '98

Larry Oliver
Born Yesterday '50

Phil Oliver
Winstanley '75

Pita Oliver
Prom Night '80

Randall Oliver
Werewolf '95

Rochelle Oliver
Scent of a Woman '92

Enrico Oliveri
Black Sunday '60

Laurence Olivier
The Jazz Singer '80
Dracula '79
The Betsy '78
A Bridge Too Far '77
The Seven-Per-Cent Solution '76
Sleuth '72
Nicholas and Alexandra '71
Romeo and Juliet '68 (N)
Spartacus '60
Henry V '44
Rebecca '40
Wuthering Heights '39
Fire Over England '37
As You Like It '36

Debra Paget
The Ten Commandments '56

Nicola Pagett
The Viking Queen '67

Marcel Pagliero
Open City '45

Eros Pagni
Deep Red: Hatchet Murders
'75

Dre Pahich
Dark Star '74

Liana Pai
The Siege '98

Maggie Paige
The Killing of Sister George
'69

Geraldine Pailhas
Don Juan DeMarco '94
Suite 16 '94

Heidi Paine
Alien Seed '89

Nestor Paiva
The Road to Utopia '46

Maria Pakulnis
The Decalogue '88

George Pal
The War of the Worlds '53

Riccardo Palacio
Comin' At Ya! '81

Holly Palance
The Best of Times '86

Jack Palance
Sarah, Plain and Tall: Winter's
End '99
Solar Crisis '92
Batman '89
Tango and Cash '89
Young Guns '88
The Professionals '66
Sudden Fear '52

Michael Palin
Fierce Creatures '96
A Fish Called Wanda '88
Brazil '85
Brazil (Criterion SE) '85
Monty Python's The Meaning
of Life '83
Time Bandits '81
Monty Python's Life of Brian
'79
And Now for Something Com-
pletely Different '72

Anna Palk
Fahrenheit 451 '66

Erik Palladino
Can't Hardly Wait '98

Laura Pallas
Evita '96

Aubert Pallascio
Lilies '96

Anita Pallenberg
Barbarella '68

Eugene Pallette
My Man Godfrey '36
The Three Musketeers '21
Intolerance '16
The Birth of a Nation '15

Betsy Palmer
The Fear: Halloween Night
'99
Friday the 13th, Part 2 '81
Friday the 13th '80
Mister Roberts '55

Geoffrey Palmer
Mrs. Brown '97
Tomorrow Never Dies (SE)
'97

A Fish Called Wanda '88

Lilli Palmer
The Secret Agent '36

Chazz Palminteri
Stuart Little '99 (V)
Analyze This '98
Scarred City '98
Jade '95
The Last Word '95
The Usual Suspects '95
Bullets over Broadway '94
A Bronx Tale '93
Innocent Blood '92

J.C. Palmore
Hamburger Hill '87

Carlos Palomino
Die Watching '93
Geronimo: An American Leg-
end '93

Gwyneth Paltrow
Hush '98
A Perfect Murder '98
Shakespeare in Love (CS)
'98
Great Expectations '97
Sliding Doors '97
Emma '96
Seven '95

Luciana Paluzzi
Thunderball '65

Yi Pan-Yong
Why Has Bodhi-Darma Left
for the East '89

Aditya Pancholi
Yes Boss! '97

Andrew Pang
The Corruptor '99

Diana Pang
Erotic Ghost Story: Perfect
Match '97

Franklin Pangborn
A Star Is Born '37
My Man Godfrey '36

Stuart Pankin
Arachnophobia '90

John Pankow
Mortal Thoughts '91

Irina Pantaeva
Mortal Kombat 2: Annihilation '97

Joe Pantoliano
The Matrix '99
U.S. Marshals '98
Top of the World '97
Bound '96
Bad Boys '95
The Last Word '95
The Fugitive '93
Midnight Run '88
La Bamba '87
Risky Business '83

Buddy Pantsari
Trader Hornee '70

Irene Papas
Lion of the Desert '81
The Message '77
The Guns of Navarone '61

Bernard Papineau
Night of the Hunted '69

Anna Paquin
She's All That '99
A Walk on the Moon '99
Amistad '97
Fly Away Home '96
The Piano '93

John Paragon
Pee-wee's Big Adventure '85

Michael Pare
Hope Floats '98
Strip Search '97
Sworn Enemies '96
Village of the Damned '95
Streets of Fire '84

Marisa Paredes
Life Is Beautiful '98

Mila Parely
Beauty and the Beast '46

Monique Parent
Key to Sex '98
Dark Secrets '95
Masseuse '95
Midnight Confessions '95
Stripshow '95
Play Time '94

Judy Parfitt
Ever After: A Cinderella Story
'98
Dolores Claiborne '94

Woodrow Parfrey
The Outlaw Josey Wales '76

Anne Parillaud
The Man in the Iron Mask '98
Shattered Image '98
Innocent Blood '92
La Femme Nikita '91

Jerry Paris
The Caine Mutiny '54
The Wild One '54

Virginia Paris
Stand and Deliver '88

Diane Parish
Alive and Kicking '96

Kim Park
New Jack City '91

Kris Park
I Love You, I Love You Not '97

Melissa Park
Sucker the Vampire '98

Steve Park
Fargo '96

MacDonald Parke
Summertime '55

Alan Parker
Evita '96

Anthony Ray Parker
The Matrix '99

Carl Parker
Score '72

Cecil Parker
Court Jester '56
The Lady Vanishes '38

Corey Parker
White Palace '90

F. William Parker
Jack Frost '97

Fess Parker
The Great Locomotive Chase
'56

Jameson Parker
Prince of Darkness '87

Jean Parker
The Flying Deuces / Utopia
'39

Mary-Louise Parker
Goodbye, Lover '99
Portrait of a Lady '96
Boys on the Side '94
Bullets over Broadway '94
The Client '94
Mr. Wonderful '93
Fried Green Tomatoes '91

Molly Parker
In the Shadows '98

Nathaniel Parker
Beverly Hills Ninja '96

Nicole Parker
200 Cigarettes '98
Boogie Nights '97

Norman Parker
Killing Hour '84

Paula Jai Parker
Sprung '96

Sachi Parker
Peggy Sue Got Married '86

Sarah Jessica Parker
Dudley Do-Right '99
The First Wives Club '96
Mars Attacks! '96
Miami Rhapsody '95
Striking Distance '93
Honeymoon in Vegas '92
L.A. Story '91

Trey Parker
BASEketball '98

Aidan Parkinson
Patriots '94

Bert Parks
The Freshman '90

Michael Parks
From Dusk Till Dawn 3: The
Hangman's Daughter '99
From Dusk Till Dawn '95
Death Wish 5: The Face of
Death '94
Stranger by Night '94

Tammy Parks
Play Time '94

Dita Parlo
Grand Illusion '37

Oliver Parniere
36 Fillete '88

Leslie Parrish
The Invisible Strangler '76
The Manchurian Candidate
'62

Nicholas Parson
The Ghost Goes Gear '66

Estelle Parsons
Bonnie & Clyde '67

Fern Parsons
Hoosiers '86

Karyn Parsons
Major Payne '95

Nancy Parsons
Porky's '82

Paul A. Partain
The Texas Chainsaw Mas-
sacre '74

Peter Parten
The Dirty Girls '64

Dolly Parton
Unlikely Angel '97

Adam Pascal
SLC Punk! '99

Richard Pasco
Mrs. Brown '97
Rasputin the Mad Monk '66

Adrian Pasdar
A Brother's Kiss '97
The Pompatus of Love '95
Carlito's Way '93
Top Gun '86

Pier Paolo Pasolini
The Canterbury Tales '71
The Decameron '70

Susanna Pasolini
The Gospel According to St.
Matthew '64

Franck Pasquier
The Last Metro '80

Earl Pastko
The Sweet Hereafter '96

Robert Pastorelli
Modern Vampires '98
A Simple Wish '97
Eraser '96
Michael '96
Sister Act 2: Back in the
Habit '93
Striking Distance '93
Dances with Wolves '90

Michael Pataki
Halloween 4: The Return of
Michael Myers '88
Rocky 4 '85
The Baby '72

Michael Pate
McLintock! '63

Nana Patekar
Khamoshi the Musical '96

Bill Paterson
Hilary and Jackie '98
Spice World: The Movie '97
Chaplin '92
The Object of Beauty '91
The Witches '90
The Adventures of Baron
Munchausen '89

Mandy Patinkin
The Adventures of Elmo in
Grouchland '99
Lulu on the Bridge '98
The Princess Bride '87
Sunday in the Park with
George '86

Tatjana Patitz
Rising Sun '93

Angela Paton
Groundhog Day '93

Jason Patric
Your Friends & Neighbors '98
Incognito '97
Speed 2: Cruise Control '97
Sleepers '96
Geronimo: An American Leg-
end '93
After Dark, My Sweet '90
The Lost Boys '87

Butch Patrick
Munster, Go Home! '66

Dennis Patrick
Choices '81

Dorothy Patrick
New Orleans '47

Gail Patrick
My Man Godfrey '36

Lee Patrick
Pillow Talk '59
Vertigo (CE) '58

Robert Patrick
Forgotten City '99
Tactical Assault '99
The Faculty '98
From Dusk Till Dawn 2: Texas
Blood Money '98
Cop Land '97
Striptease '96
Double Dragon '94
Body Shot '93
Last Action Hero '93
Terminator 2: Judgment Day
'91
Die Hard 2: Die Harder '90

Neva Patterson
Women of Valor '86
David and Lisa '62

Rocky Patterson
Perfect Profile '90

Lethal Weapon 3 '92
JFK '91
Goodfellas '90
Home Alone '90
Lethal Weapon 2 '89
Raging Bull '80

Danielle Pessis
Angel in Training '99

Peter
Ran '85

Bernadette Peters
Anastasia '97 (V)
Beauty and the Beast: The Enchanted Christmas '97 (V)
Cinderella '97
Into the Woods '90
Sunday in the Park with George '86
The Jerk '79

Brock Peters
Star Trek 6: The Undiscovered Country '91
Star Trek 4: The Voyage Home '86
To Kill a Mockingbird '62

John Peters
The White Zombie '32

Molly Peters
Thunderball '65

Scott Peters
Girl Hunters '63

Werner Peters
The Bird with the Crystal Plumage '70

Amy Petersen
Foolish '99

Paul Petersen
Mommy 2: Mommy's Day '96

William L. Petersen
The Rat Pack '98
Fear '96

Cassandra Peterson
Pee-wee's Big Adventure '85

Clifford Peterson
Charlie, the Lonesome Cougar '67

Dorothy Peterson
I'm No Angel '33

Nan Peterson
Hideous Sun Demon '59

Stewart Peterson
Where the Red Fern Grows '74

Vidal Peterson
Something Wicked This Way Comes '83

Roland Petit
Black Tights '60

Robert Petkoff
Milk and Money '97

Ian Petrella
A Christmas Story '83

Hay Petrie
Great Expectations '46
On Approval '44

Susan Petrie
They Came from Within '75

Jouri (Yuri) Petrov
Jackie Chan's First Strike '96

Sonia Petrovna
The Fatal Image '90

Frank Pettingell
Trial & Error '62

Lori Petty
Serial Bomber '96
Free Willy '93
A League of Their Own '92

Tom Petty
The Postman '97

Dedee Pfeiffer
Up Close and Personal '96
Falling Down '93
Red Surf '90

Michelle Pfeiffer
The Story of Us '99
William Shakespeare's A Midsummer Night's Dream '99
The Deep End of the Ocean '98
Prince of Egypt '98 (V)
A Thousand Acres '97
Up Close and Personal '96
Dangerous Minds '95
Wolf '94
Batman Returns '92
The Fabulous Baker Boys '89
Dangerous Liaisons '88
Tequila Sunrise '88
Amazon Women on the Moon '87
The Witches of Eastwick '87
Ladyhawke '85
Scarface '83
Falling in Love Again '80

Robert Phalen
Halloween '78

Joe Phelan
Zero Boys '86

Kate Phelps
The Shining '80

Mekhi Phifer
I Still Know What You Did Last Summer '98
Soul Food '97
Clockers '95

Mary Philbin
The Phantom of the Opera '25

Regis Philbin
Dudley Do-Right '99

James Philbrook
The Thin Red Line '64

Dominic Philie
For Hire '98
The Boys '97

Robert Philip
Children Shouldn't Play with Dead Things '72

Jean-Loup Philippe
Lips of Blood '75

Ryan Phillippe
Cruel Intentions '98
54 '98
Playing by Heart '98
I Know What You Did Last Summer '98
White Squall '96

Bobbie Phillips
Carnival of Souls '98

Chynna Phillips
Caddyshack 2 '88

Ethan Phillips
Glory '89
Lean on Me '89

Grace Phillips
Truth or Consequences, N.M. '97

Leslie Phillips
Mountains of the Moon '90

Lou Diamond Phillips
Brokedown Palace '99
Another Day in Paradise '98

The Big Hit '98
Extreme Justice '93
Stand and Deliver '88
Young Guns '88
La Bamba '87

MacKenzie Phillips
True Friends '98
American Graffiti '73

Pam Phillips
Family Reunion '79

P.K. Phillips
Sucker the Vampire '98

Robert Phillips
The Dirty Dozen '67

Sam Phillips
Die Hard: With a Vengeance '95

Samantha Phillips
Sexual Malice '93
Sex Crimes '92

Sian Phillips
Dune '84

Sydney Coale Phillips
Cause of Death '90

Vincent Phillips
Boston Kickout '95

Wendy Phillips
Bugsy '91
Midnight Run '88

Max Phipps
The Road Warrior '82

William Phipps
The War of the Worlds '53

Joaquin Rafael (Leaf) Phoenix
Clay Pigeons '98
8mm '98
Return to Paradise '98
U-Turn '97
To Die For '95
Parenthood '89

River Phoenix
Sneakers '92
Running on Empty '88
Stand by Me '86

Summer Phoenix
SLC Punk! '99

Ben Piazza
Guilty by Suspicion '91
Clean and Sober '88

Robert Picardo
Small Soldiers '98
Star Trek: First Contact '96
Matinee '92

Michel Piccoli
One Hundred and One Nights '94
Don't Touch the White Woman! '74

Joe Pichler
Varsity Blues '98

Raymond Pickard
The Borrowers '97

James Pickens Jr.
Gridlock'd '96

Slim Pickens
1941 '79
Blazing Saddles '74
The Cowboys '72
The Getaway '72
Rough Night in Jericho '67
Dr. Strangelove, or: How I Learned to Stop Worrying and Love the Bomb '64

Marc Pickering
Sleepy Hollow '99

Cindy Pickett
Evolver '94
Son-in-Law '93
Ferris Bueller's Day Off '86

Mary Pickford
My Best Girl '27
Sparrows '26
Tess of the Storm Country '22
Daddy Long Legs '19
Amarilly of Clothesline Alley '18
Stella Maris '18

Christina Pickles
The Wedding Singer '97
William Shakespeare's Romeo and Juliet '96

Vivian Pickles
Candleshoe '78

Molly Picon
Cannonball Run 2 '84
Fiddler on the Roof '71

Rebecca Pidgeon
The Spanish Prisoner '97

Walter Pidgeon
Two Minute Warning '76
Big Red '62
Forbidden Planet '56
The Last Time I Saw Paris '54

Guy Pierauld
Bed and Board '70

Bradley Michael Pierce
The Borrowers '97
Jumanji (CS) '95
For Love of a Child '90

David Hyde Pierce
A Bug's Life (CE) '98 (V)
Nixon '95
Wolf '94

Jill Pierce
Darkroom '90

Justin Pierce
A Brother's Kiss '97
Kids '95

Richard Pierce
Basket Case '82

Wendell Pierce
Bulworth '98
Hackers '95

Antonio Pierfederici
Black Sunday '60

Eric Pierpont
Little Witches '96

Marina Pierro
The Living Dead Girl '82

Frank Pietrangolare
A Bronx Tale '93

Angela Pietropinto
Finding North '97
Welcome to the Dollhouse '95
Honeymoon in Vegas '92
Goodfellas '90

Christopher Piggins
Lady of the Lake '98

Luciano Pigozzi
The Bloodsucker Leads the Dance '75

Marianne Piketi
Bed and Board '70

Joe Pilato
Day of the Dead '85

Nova Pilbeam
Young and Innocent '37
The Man Who Knew Too Much '34

Mitch Pileggi
The X-Files '98
Shocker '89

Bronson Pinchot
Quest for Camelot '98 (V)
The First Wives Club '96
True Romance '93
The Flamingo Kid '84
Risky Business '83

Jackson "Rock" Pinckney
Cyborg '89

Larry Pine
A Stranger in the Kingdom '98

Phillip Pine
Men in War '57

Robert Pine
The Best Revenge '96
Munster, Go Home! '66

John Pinette
Simon Sez '99

Jada Pinkett Smith
Return to Paradise '98
Scream 2 '97
The Nutty Professor '96
Set It Off '96
Tales from the Crypt Presents Demon Knight '94
Menace II Society '93

Dominique Pinon
The City of Lost Children '95
Diva '82

Frederick Piper
Sabotage '36

Kelly Piper
Rawhead Rex '87
Maniac '80

Roddy Piper
Sci-Fighters '96
Terminal Rush '96
Jungleground '95
Immortal Combat '94
They Live '88

David Pirner
Reality Bites '94

Salvatore Paul Piro
Desecration '99

Joe Piscopo
King Kong '76

Luigi Pistilli
Twitch of the Death Nerve '71
The Good, the Bad and the Ugly '67

Mario Pisu
Juliet of the Spirits '65

Maria Pitillo
Godzilla '98

John Paul (J.P.) Pitoc
Trick '99

Sacha Pitoeff
Inferno '80
Last Year at Marienbad '61

Anne Pitoniak
A Thousand Acres '97

Brad Pitt
Fight Club '99
Meet Joe Black '98
Seven Years in Tibet '97
The Devil's Own '96
Sleepers '96
Seven '95
12 Monkeys '95
Interview with the Vampire '94
Legends of the Fall '94
Kalifornia '93

Susan May Pratt
Ten Things I Hate about You '99

Wolfgang Preiss
A Bridge Too Far '77
Raid on Rommel '71
The Train '65

Albert Prejean
The Bells / The Crazy Ray '26
The Crazy Ray '22

Karen Prell
Labyrinth '86

Otto Preminger
They Got Me Covered '43

Paula Prentiss
The Stepford Wives '75
The Parallax View '74
Born to Win '71

Micheline Presle
The Fantastic Night '42

Elvis Presley
Jailhouse Rock '57

Harve Presnell
A Bright Shining Lie '98
Patch Adams (CE) '98
Saving Private Ryan '98
Face/Off '97
Fargo '96

Jaime Pressly
Ringmaster '98
Poison Ivy 3: The New Seduction '97

Lawrence Pressman
American Pie (CE) '99
Mighty Joe Young '98
Trial and Error '96
Rehearsal for Murder '82
Shaft '71

Jason Presson
The Lady in White '88

Jo Prestia
The Dreamlife of Angels '98

Cyndy Preston
Total Recall 2070: Machine Dreams '99

J.A. Preston
A Few Good Men '92
Body Heat '81

Kelly Preston
Holy Man '98
Jack Frost '98
Addicted to Love '96
Jerry Maguire '96
Nothing to Lose '96
From Dusk Till Dawn '95
Twins '88
Amazon Women on the Moon '87
Christine '84

Michael B. Preston
The Road Warrior '82

Robert Preston
The Last Starfighter '84
Rehearsal for Murder '82
Junior Bonner '72
How the West Was Won '63
The Music Man '62
Reap the Wild Wind '42

Jan Preucil
The Dandelion Crown '93

Francoise Prevost
Spirits of the Dead '68

Brenda Price
The Robin Hood Gang '98

Darien Price
Caress of the Vampire (CE) '96

Dennis Price
Horror Hospital '73
Curse of the Voodoo '64
The Millionairess '60

Kate Price
Three Ages '23
Amarilly of Clothesline Alley '18

Lonny Price
Dirty Dancing '87
Dirty Dancing (CE) '87

Richard Price
Shocker '89

Vincent Price
Spirits of the Dead '68 (N)
The Bat '59
The Tingler '59
House on Haunted Hill '58
The Ten Commandments '56

Robert Prichard
Class of Nuke 'Em High '86
The Toxic Avenger (DC) '86

Jason Priestley
Love and Death on Long Island '97
Sink or Swim '97
Tombstone '93

Paco Christian Prieto
Street Law '95

Barry Primus
Guilty by Suspicion '91
Absence of Malice '81
Autopsy '78

Prince
Purple Rain '84

Faith Prince
Picture Perfect '96
Dave '93

William Prince
Spies Like Us '85
The Stepford Wives '75

Victoria Principal
Dancing in the Dark '95
Earthquake '74

Andrew Prine
Grizzly '76

Freddie Prinze Jr.
She's All That '99
Wing Commander '99
I Still Know What You Did Last Summer '98
Money Kings '98
The House of Yes '97
I Know What You Did Last Summer '97

Juergen Prochnow
Wing Commander '99
The Replacement Killers '98
Air Force One '97
The English Patient '96
In the Mouth of Madness '95
Judge Dredd '95
Interceptor '92
The Seventh Sign '88
Dune '84
Das Boot (DC) '81

Emily Procter
Guinevere '99

Phil Proctor
The Rugrats Movie '98 (V)

Robert Prosky
Dudley Do-Right '99
Mad City '97
The Chamber '96
Last Action Hero '93
Mrs. Doubtfire '93
Far and Away '92
Broadcast News '87
Christine '84
Thief '81

David Proval
The Siege '98
Dumb Luck in Vegas '97
The Phantom '96
Four Rooms '95
Innocent Blood '92
Mean Streets '73

David Prowse
A Clockwork Orange '71

Haydon Prowse
The Secret Garden '93

Harrison Pruett
Embrace of the Vampire '95

Karl Pruner
Total Recall 2070: Machine Dreams '99

Jonathan Pryce
Stigmata '99
Ronin '98
Tomorrow Never Dies (SE) '97
Evita '96
The Adventures of Baron Munchausen '89
Brazil '85
Brazil (Criterion SE) '85
Something Wicked This Way Comes '83

Nicholas Pryor
The Falcon and the Snowman '85
Risky Business '83

Richard Pryor
Brewster's Millions '85
Richard Pryor: Live on the Sunset Strip '82
Bustin' Loose '81
Stir Crazy '80
Richard Pryor: Live in Concert '79
Blue Collar '78
The Wiz '78
Car Wash '76

Roger Pryor
Belle of the Nineties '34

Robert Pugh
Priest '94

Willard Pugh
The Color Purple '85

Frank Puglia
For Whom the Bell Tolls '43
Casablanca '42

Michele Pulaski
The Last Broadcast '98

Benjamin Pullen
An Ideal Husband '99

Kimberly Pullis
Witchouse '99

Bill Pullman
Brokedown Palace '99
Lake Placid '99
Pretty As a Picture: The Art of David Lynch '98
Zero Effect '97
Independence Day '96
While You Were Sleeping '95
Malice '93
Sleepless in Seattle '93
Sommersby '93
A League of Their Own '92
Singles '92
The Serpent and the Rainbow '87

Maylin Pultar
In God's Hands '98

Dick Purcell
King of the Zombies '41

Lee Purcell
Betrayed by Innocence '86
Stir Crazy '80

Carolyn Purdy-Gordon
Re-Animator '84

Amrish Puri
Koyla '98
Virasat '97

Om Puri
Pyar to Hona Hi Tah '98
My Son the Fanatic '97
The Ghost and the Darkness '96
Wolf '94

Linda Purl
Mighty Joe Young '98

Edna Purviance
Charles Chaplin—A First National Collection
The Chaplin Mutuals, Vol. 1 '90s
The Chaplin Mutuals, Vol. 2 '90s
The Chaplin Mutuals, Vol. 3 '90s
Chaplin's Essanay Comedies, Vol. 1 '90s
Chaplin's Essanay Comedies, Vol. 2 '90s
Chaplin's Essanay Comedies, Vol. 3 '90s
Chaplin's Art of Comedy '66
The Kid / A Dog's Life '21

Jack Purvis
The Adventures of Baron Munchausen '89

Jeff Pustil
The Killing Man '94

Denver Pyle
Maverick '94
Bonnie & Clyde '67

John Pyper-Ferguson
For Richer or Poorer '97
Drive '96

Lu Qi
Farewell My Concubine '93

Xu Qing
The Emperor's Shadow '96

Abdel Qissi
The Quest '96

John Quade
The Outlaw Josey Wales '76

Dennis Quaid
The Parent Trap '98
Playing by Heart '98
Savior '98
Switchback '97
Dragonheart (SE) '96
The Big Easy '87
Dreamscape (SE) '84
The Right Stuff '83

Randy Quaid
Bug Buster '99
Hard Rain '97
Protector '97
Ed McBain's 87 Precinct '96
Independence Day '96
Kingpin '96
Vegas Vacation '96
The Paper '94
Days of Thunder '90
National Lampoon's Christmas Vacation '89
Parents '89
Caddyshack 2 '88
National Lampoon's Vacation '83
Midnight Express '78
The Last Detail '73

John Qualen
The Searchers '56
Dark Waters '44
Casablanca '42
His Girl Friday '40

Our Daily Bread and Other Films of the Depression '34

Van Quattro
Desperate Crimes '93

James Quattrochi
True Friends '98
Wanted '98

Anna Quayle
Chitty Chitty Bang Bang '68
Smashing Time '67
A Hard Day's Night '64

Anthony Quayle
The Guns of Navarone '61

Queen Latifah
The Bone Collector '99
Living Out Loud '98
Sphere '97
Set It Off '96

Valerie Quennessen
Conan the Barbarian '82

John Quern
Assault of the Killer Bimbos '88

Mae Questel
National Lampoon's Christmas Vacation '89

Diana Quick
The Leading Man '96

Richard Quick
Return of the Boogeyman '94

Linnea Quigley
Jack-O '95
Innocent Blood '92
Sorority Babes in the Slimeball Bowl-A-Rama '87

Alfonso Quijada
Timecop '94

Tim Quill
Army of Darkness '92
Hamburger Hill '87

Denis Quilley
Mister Johnson '91

Umberto P. Quinavalle
Salo, or the 120 Days of Sodom '75

Kathleen Quinlan
A Civil Action '98
My Giant '98
Event Horizon '97
Lawn Dogs '96
Zeus and Roxanne '96
Apollo 13 '95
The Doors '91
Sunset '88
American Graffiti '73

Aidan Quinn
This Is My Father '99
In Dreams '98
Practical Magic '98
The Assignment '97
Michael Collins '96
Legends of the Fall '94
Mary Shelley's Frankenstein '94

Anthony Quinn
Last Action Hero '93
Jungle Fever '91
Revenge '90
Regina '83
Lion of the Desert '81
The Con Artists '80
The Message '77
The Inheritance '76
The Guns of Navarone '61
The Road to Morocco '42

Bill Quinn
Bustin' Loose '81

Lance Reddick
The Siege '98

Brian Reddy
Dante's Peak '97

Helen Reddy
Airport '75 '75

Quinn Redeker
Spider Baby '64

Tara Redepenning
Drop Dead Gorgeous '99

William Redfield
One Flew Over the Cuckoo's
Nest '75

Robert Redford
The Horse Whisperer '97
Up Close and Personal '96
Sneakers '92
Havana '90
Legal Eagles '86
The Electric Horseman '79
A Bridge Too Far '77
All the President's Men '76
Three Days of the Condor '75
The Sting '73
The Candidate '72
Jeremiah Johnson '72
Butch Cassidy and the Sun-
dance Kid '69
Barefoot in the Park '67

Rockets Redglare
Shakedown '88

Corin Redgrave
Four Weddings and a Funeral
'94
In the Name of the Father '93
Excalibur '81

Jemma Redgrave
Howard's End '92

Lynn Redgrave
Gods and Monsters '98
Shine '95
Rehearsal for Murder '82
Smashing Time '67
Tom Jones '63

Michael Redgrave
Nicholas and Alexandra '71
The Lady Vanishes '38

Vanessa Redgrave
Deep Impact '98
Lulu on the Bridge '98
Mrs. Dalloway '97
Mission: Impossible '96
Mother's Boys '94
Howard's End '92
The Bostonians '84
The Seven-Per-Cent Solution
'76
Camelot '67

Nick Reding
Mister Johnson '91

Joyce Redman
Tom Jones '63

Kathryn Reece
Animal Crackers '30

Dan Reed
Zigzag '97

Donna Reed
The Last Time I Saw Paris
'54
It's a Wonderful Life '46
They Were Expendable '45

Jerry Reed
The Waterboy '98
Bat 21 '88
Smokey and the Bandit '77

Kira Reed
The Price of Desire '96

Oliver Reed
The Adventures of Baron
Munchausen '89
Condorman '81
Lion of the Desert '81
The Four Musketeers '75
The Three Musketeers '74
Oliver! '68

Pamela Reed
Why Do Fools Fall in Love?
'98
Bean '97
Santa Fe '97
Junior '94
Kindergarten Cop '90
The Best of Times '86
The Clan of the Cave Bear
'86
The Right Stuff '83
Melvin and Howard '80

Philip Reed
Unknown Island '48
Klondike Annie '36

Robert Reed
The Boy in the Plastic Bubble
'76

Tracy Reed
Train Ride to Hollywood '75
Dr. Strangelove, or: How I
Learned to Stop Worrying
and Love the Bomb '64

Lady Reeds
Avenging Disco Godfather '76
Dolemite '75

Norman Reedus
Six Ways to Sunday '99

Jorgen Reenberg
I, a Woman '66

Roger Rees
William Shakespeare's A Mid-
summer Night's Dream '99
Mountains of the Moon '90
A Christmas Carol '84
Star 80 '83

Della Reese
A Thin Line Between Love
and Hate '96
Psychic Killer '75

Christopher Reeve
Village of the Damned '95
The Bostonians '84
Deathtrap '82
Somewhere in Time '80

George Reeves
The Blue Gardenia '53
Gone with the Wind '39

Keanu Reeves
The Matrix '99
The Devil's Advocate '97
Feeling Minnesota '96
Johnny Mnemonic '95
Speed '94
Little Buddha '93
Much Ado about Nothing '93
Dracula '92
Parenthood '89
Dangerous Liaisons '88

Lisa Reeves
Pom Pom Girls '76

Marta Reeves
Two Undercover Angels '68

Phil Reeves
Election '99

Steve Reeves
Jail Bait '54

Steve Reevis
Fargo '96

Serge Reggiani
Don't Touch the White
Woman! '74

Nadja Regin
Goldfinger '64
From Russia with Love '63

Regine
The Seven-Per-Cent Solution
'76

Natacha Regnier
The Dreamlife of Angels '98

Regopstann
Red Scorpion '89

Hans Leo Reich
Metropolis '26

Mimi Reichmeister
Little Witches '96

Beryl Reid
The Killing of Sister George
'69
Trial & Error '62

Kate Reid
The Andromeda Strain '71

Michael Earl Reid
Army of Darkness '92

Tara Reid
American Pie (CE) '99
Urban Legend '98
The Big Lebowski '97

Tim Reid
Dead Bang '89

Wallace Reid
The Birth of a Nation '15

Charles Nelson Reilly
All Dogs Christmas Carol '98
(V)
Boys Will Be Boys '97
Rock-a-Doodle '92 (V)
Cannonball Run 2 '84

Jack Reilly
The Story of G.I. Joe '45

John C. Reilly
Never Been Kissed '99
The Thin Red Line '98
Boogie Nights '97
Georgia '95
Dolores Claiborne '94
The River Wild '94
Days of Thunder '90

Carl Reiner
Slums of Beverly Hills '98
The Jerk '79

Jean Reiner
Soultaker '90

Rob Reiner
EDtv '99
The Muse '99
The Story of Us '99
Primary Colors '98
The First Wives Club '96
Bullets over Broadway '94
Sleepless in Seattle '93
This Is Spinal Tap '84
The Jerk '79

Tracy Reiner
Apollo 13 '95
A League of Their Own '92

Judge Reinhold
Tom Clancy's Netforce '98
The Santa Clause '94
A Soldier's Tale '91
Gremlins '84
Stripes '81

Scott H. Reiniger
Dawn of the Dead '78

Michelle Reis
Armageddon '97
Fallen Angels '95
Fong Sai Yuk '93
A Chinese Ghost Story II '90

Hans Reiser
The Great Escape '63

Paul Reiser
The Story of Us '99
Aliens (SE) '86

Ursula Reit
Willy Wonka & the Chocolate
Factory '71

Ivan Reitman
Legal Eagles '86

Joseph D. Reitman
Clay Pigeons '98

Winston Rekert
Eternal Evil '87

Devi Rekha
Kama Sutra: A Tale of Love
'96

James Remar
Rites of Passage '99
Psycho '98
Mortal Kombat 2: Annihila-
tion '97
The Phantom '96
The Quest '96
Across the Moon '94
Boys on the Side '94
The Surgeon '94
Drugstore Cowboy '89
Rent-A-Cop '88
The Clan of the Cave Bear
'86

Erika Remberg
The Lickerish Quartet '70

Lee Remick
Around the World in 80 Days
'89

Leah Remini
Follow Your Heart '98

Bert Remsen
Maverick '94
Pork Chop Hill '59

Albert Remy
The Train '65
Shoot the Piano Player '62
The 400 Blows '59

Duncan Renaldo
For Whom the Bell Tolls '43

Tito Renaldo
The Story of G.I. Joe '45
For Whom the Bell Tolls '43

Brad Renfro
Apt Pupil '97
Sleepers '96
Telling Lies in America '96
The Client '94

Patrick Renna
Son-in-Law '93

Deborah Rennard
Lionheart '90

Callum Keith Rennie
eXistenZ '99
Last Night '98

Jean Reno
Godzilla '98
Ronin '98
Mission: Impossible '96
French Kiss '95
The Professional '94
La Femme Nikita '91
Subway '85

Kelly Reno
The Black Stallion '79

Sophie Renoir
Boyfriends & Girlfriends '88
Le Beau Mariage '82

Renoly
Con Air '97

Eva Renzi
The Bird with the Crystal
Plumage '70

Maggie Renzi
Passion Fish '92

Repnikova
The Battleship Potemkin '25

**Francisco Tsirene Tsere
Rereme**
Medicine Man '92

Dan Resin
Caddyshack '80

Antonio Resines
How to Be a Woman and Not
Die in the Attempt '91

Mary Lou Retton
Scrooged '88

Gloria Reuben
Nick of Time '95
Timecop '94

**Paul (Pee-wee Herman)
Reubens**
Mystery Men '99
Dr. Dolittle '98 (V)
Beauty and the Beast: The
Enchanted Christmas '97
(V)
Matilda '96
The Nightmare before Christ-
mas '93 (V)
Batman Returns '92
Pee-wee's Big Adventure '85
The Blues Brothers (CE) '80

Anne Revere
Gentleman's Agreement '47
National Velvet '44

Rosaura Revueltas
Salt of the Earth '54

Antonia Rey
Tarantella '95

Fernando Rey
Cabo Blanco / U.S. Marshal
'81
Seven Beauties '76
Cold Eyes of Fear '70

Ivelka Reyes
Crooklyn '94

Tiasha Reyes
Crooklyn '94

Janine Reynaud
Kiss Me Monster '69
Succubus '69
Two Undercover Angels '68

Burt Reynolds
Big City Blues '99
Crazy Six '98
Bean '97
Boogie Nights '97
Hunter's Moon '97
Meet Wally Sparks '97
Raven '97
Striptease '96
Cop and a Half '93
The Player '92
Rent-A-Cop '88
Cannonball Run 2 '84
Stroker Ace '83
Sharky's Machine '81
Hooper '78
Smokey and the Bandit '77
Deliverance '72

Debbie Reynolds
Rudolph the Red-Nosed Rein-
deer: The Movie '98 (V)
In and Out '97
The Bodyguard '92
How the West Was Won '63
Singin' in the Rain '52

Kathryn Reynolds
Trilogy of Terror '75

Austin Powers 2: The Spy Who Shagged Me '99
Nothing to Lose '96
Ready to Wear '94
The Shawshank Redemption '94
The Hudsucker Proxy '93
The Player '92
Jungle Fever '91
Jacob's Ladder '90
Bull Durham '88
Five Corners '88
Top Gun '86

Chuck Roberson
The Green Berets '68

Alice Roberts
Pandora's Box '28

Allene Roberts
The Hoodlum '51
The Red House '47

Clete Roberts
The Story of G.I. Joe '45

Conrad Roberts
The Serpent and the Rainbow '87

Doris Roberts
My Giant '98
National Lampoon's Christmas Vacation '89

Eliza Roberts
Dead End '98

Eric Roberts
Dead End '98
T.N.T. '98
Most Wanted '97
The Prophecy 2: Ashtown '97
American Strays '96
The Specialist '94
Final Analysis '92
Runaway Train '85
Star 80 '83

Ian Roberts
Tarzan and the Lost City '98
The Power of One '92

Jeremy Roberts
The Thirteenth Floor '99
Running Time '97
Jungle Boy '96

J.H. Roberts
Young and Innocent '37

Joe Roberts
Shakespeare in Love (CS) '98
College '27
Our Hospitality / Sherlock Junior '23

Julia Roberts
Notting Hill '99
Stepmom '98
Conspiracy Theory '97
My Best Friend's Wedding '97
Everyone Says I Love You '96
Michael Collins '96
I Love Trouble '94
Ready to Wear '94
The Pelican Brief '93
The Player '92
Flatliners '90
Pretty Woman '90
Firehouse '87

Leona Roberts
Gone with the Wind '39

Leonard Roberts
The '60s '99
Love Jones '96

Mark Roberts
Bulletproof '96

Michael D. Roberts
Rain Man '88

Pernell Roberts
Around the World in 80 Days '89

Rachel Roberts
Picnic at Hanging Rock '75
This Sporting Life '63

Roy Roberts
He Walked by Night '48
The Fighting Sullivans '42

Tony Roberts
Annie Hall '77

Cliff Robertson
Race '99
Escape from L.A. '96
Dreams of Gold: The Mel Fisher Story '86
Brainstorm '83
Star 80 '83
Midway '76
Three Days of the Condor '75

Francoise Robertson
Armistead Maupin's More Tales of the City '97

Jenny Robertson
Bull Durham '88

Kathleen Robertson
Splendor '99

Kimmy Robertson
Speed 2: Cruise Control '97
Leprechaun 2 '94

Robbie Robertson
The Crossing Guard '94

George Robey
Henry V '44

Kim Robillard
Home Fries '98
Rain Man '88

Dany Robin
Waltz of the Toreadors '62

Teddy Robin
Twin Dragons '92

Laila Robins
The Blood Oranges '97

Mikul Robins
Witchcraft 9: Bitter Flesh '96

Amy Robinson
Mean Streets '73

Andrew (Andy) Robinson
Hellraiser '87
Cobra '86
Mask '85
Dirty Harry '71

Ann Robinson
The War of the Worlds '53

Betty Robinson
Naked Kiss '64

Charles Robinson
Set It Off '96

Edward G. Robinson
The Red House '47
The Stranger '46
Double Indemnity '44

Larry Robinson
Sgt. Kabukiman N.Y.P.D. '94

Michael Robinson
Beware! Children at Play '95

Nancy June Robinson
The Fighting Sullivans '42

Norman Robinson
Kill and Kill Again '81

Paul Michael Robinson
Friend of the Family 2 '96

Wendy Raquel Robinson
Ringmaster '98

Jacques Robiolles
Bed and Board '70
The Shiver of the Vampires '70

Rafael H. Robledo
Darkman '90

Flora Robson
Wuthering Heights '39
Fire Over England '37

May Robson
A Star Is Born '37

Wayne Robson
Cube '98
Affliction '97

Luigina Rocchi
Arabian Nights '74

Alex Rocco
Dudley Do-Right '99
Goodbye, Lover '99
A Bug's Life (CE) '98 (V)
Just Write '97
The Lady in White '88

Lyla Rocco
Playgirls and the Vampire '63

Eugene Roche
When a Man Loves a Woman '94
Slaughterhouse Five '72
They Might Be Giants '71

Sebastien Roche
Merlin '98

Jean Rochefort
Ready to Wear '94

Robin Rochelle
Sorority Babes in the Slimeball Bowl-A-Rama '87

Spencer Rochfort
Motel Blue '98

Debbie Rochon
Tromeo & Juliet '95

Lela Rochon
The Big Hit '98
Knock Off '98
Why Do Fools Fall in Love? '98
The Chamber '96

Chris Rock
Dr. Dolittle '98 (V)
Lethal Weapon 4 '98
Beverly Hills Ninja '96
New Jack City '91

Charles Rocket
The Killing Grounds '97
Father's Day '96
Dumb & Dumber '94
Dances with Wolves '90
Earth Girls Are Easy '89

Sam Rockwell
The Green Mile '99
William Shakespeare's A Midsummer Night's Dream '99
Box of Moonlight '96
Lawn Dogs '96

Allison Roddan
Monsieur Verdoux '47

Shmuel Rodensku
The Odessa File '74

Anton Rodgers
Dirty Rotten Scoundrels '88

Walter Rodgers
All Quiet on the Western Front '30

Dennis Rodman
Simon Sez '99
Double Team '97

Rick Rodney
Godmoney '99

Michael Rodrick
Desolation Angels '95

Madeleine Rodrigue
The Bells / The Crazy Ray '26
The Crazy Ray '22

Agustin Rodriguez
Final Analysis '92

Celia Rodriguez
I Am Cuba '64

Freddy Rodriguez
Dead Presidents '95

Marco Rodriguez
The Crow '93
Internal Affairs '90

Paul Rodriguez
Race '99
Made in America '93
Born in East L.A. '87

Rosa Ma Rodriguez
The Blood Spattered Bride '72

Valente Rodriguez
The Big Squeeze '96

Paul Roebling
Carolina Skeletons '92

Daniel Roebuck
U.S. Marshals '98
The Fugitive '93

Randolph Roehbling
Slave Girls from Beyond Infinity '87

Charles "Buddy" Rogers
My Best Girl '27

Ingrid Rogers
Carlito's Way '93

Mimi Rogers
Lost in Space '98
Austin Powers: International Man of Mystery '97
The Mirror Has Two Faces '96
Trees Lounge '96
The Player '92
Those Bedroom Eyes '92
The Doors '91
Someone to Watch Over Me '87

Wayne Rogers
Cool Hand Luke '67

Naum Rogozhin
Alexander Nevsky '38

Reine Rohan
The Dirty Girls '64

Armin Rohde
Run Lola Run '98

Clayton Rohner
Sometimes They Come Back ... For More '99
The Relic '96
Bat 21 '88

Maria Rojo
Midaq Alley '95

Roxie Roker
Amazon Women on the Moon '87

Denise Roland
The Dirty Girls '64

Gilbert Roland
Cabo Blanco / U.S. Marshal '81
Beneath the 12-Mile Reef '53

Charlotte Roldan
Jawbreaker '98

Henri Rollan
The Bells / The Crazy Ray '26
The Crazy Ray '22

Esther Rolle
Down in the Delta '98
My Fellow Americans '96
Rosewood '96
How to Make an American Quilt '95
Driving Miss Daisy '89

Henry Rollins
Jack Frost '98
Heat '95
Johnny Mnemonic '95

Howard E. Rollins Jr.
Drunks '96

Mark Rolston
Wicked Ways '99
From the Earth to the Moon '98
Rush Hour '98
Hard Rain '97
Daylight '96
Eraser '96
The Shawshank Redemption '94
Aliens (SE) '86

Freddie Roman
Finding North '97

Ruth Roman
Day of the Animals '77
The Baby '72
Strangers on a Train '51

Viviane Romance
Any Number Can Win '63

Beatrice Romand
Summer '86
Le Beau Mariage '82
Claire's Knee '71

Andy Romano
Eraser '96
Under Siege 2 '95
Drop Zone '94
Pump Up the Volume '90

Larry Romano
The Thin Red Line '98

Renato Romano
The Bird with the Crystal Plumage '70

Ara Romanoff
Troma's War (DC) '88

Richard Romanus
Point of No Return '93
Protocol '84
Heavy Metal '81 (V)
Mean Streets '73

George A. Romero
Dawn of the Dead '78

Rebecca Romijn-Stamos
Austin Powers 2: The Spy Who Shagged Me '99

Tiny Ron
The Rocketeer '91

Paul Ronan
The Devil's Own '96

Edina Ronay
Prehistoric Women '67

Maurice Ronet
Beau Pere '81

Mick Ronson
Ziggy Stardust and the Spiders from Mars '83

Linda Ronstadt
FM '78

Michael Rooker
The Bone Collector '99
Wicked Ways '99

Bram Stoker's Shadowbuilder
   '98
The Replacement Killers '98
Bastard out of Carolina '96
Keys to Tulsa '96
Rosewood '96
The Trigger Effect '96
Mallrats '95
Cliffhanger '93
Tombstone '93
The Dark Half '91
JFK '91
Days of Thunder '90
Henry: Portrait of a Serial
   Killer '90
Sea of Love '89
Above the Law '88
Mississippi Burning '88

Conrad Rooks
Chappaqua '66

Jonah Rooney
Boys Life 2 '98

Mickey Rooney
Babe: Pig in the City '98
Boys Will Be Boys '97
Sweet Justice '92
The Black Stallion '79
Rachel's Man '75
Breakfast at Tiffany's '61
National Velvet '44

Stephen Root
From the Earth to the Moon
   '98
Office Space '98

Tom Rosales
John Carpenter's Vampires
   '97

Annie Rosar
The Third Man '49

Anna M. Rosati
Twitch of the Death Nerve
   '71

Clifford Rose
Marat/Sade '66

Gabrielle Rose
The Sweet Hereafter '96
Timecop '94

George Rose
A Night to Remember '58

Ian Rose
Like It Is '98

Sherrie Rose
Me & Will '99
Devil in the Flesh '98

Roseanne
Freddy's Dead: The Final
   Nightmare '91

John Roselius
Con Air '97

Lauren Roselli
Philadelphia '93

Ed Roseman
America '24

Michael Rosenbaum
Urban Legend '98

Alan Rosenberg
The Temptations '98
Capone '89

Zachary Rosencrantz
Hard to Kill '89

Rosette
Summer '86

Justin Rosniak
Sweet Talker '91

Annie Ross
Pump Up the Volume '90

Chelcie Ross
A Simple Plan '98
Basic Instinct '92
The Last Boy Scout '91
Above the Law '88

Diana Ross
The Wiz '78

Gaylen Ross
Dawn of the Dead '78

Gene Ross
Halloween 4: The Return of
   Michael Myers '88
Don't Look in the Basement
   '73

**Howard (Renato
Rossini) Ross**
New York Ripper '82

Katharine Ross
The Shadow Riders '82
The Betsy '78
The Stepford Wives '75
Butch Cassidy and the Sun-
   dance Kid '69
Hellfighters '68

Kimberly Ross
Nightmare at Noon '87
The Last Starfighter '84

Lanny Ross
Gulliver's Travels '39 (V)

Lee Ross
Metroland '97

Mary Ella Ross
Bound and Gagged: A Love
   Story '93

Matt Ross
Pushing Tin '99
Face/Off '97

Michael Ross
D.O.A. '49

Ricco Ross
Aliens (SE) '86

Stanley Ralph Ross
Babe: Pig in the City '98 (V)

Ted Ross
Stealing Home '88
Arthur '81
The Wiz '78

Isabella Rossellini
The Imposters '98
Merlin '98
Big Night '95
Fearless '93
Death Becomes Her '92

Carol Rossen
The Stepford Wives '75

Kathryn Rossetter
Shakedown '88

Leo Rossi
Analyze This '98
True Friends '98
The Assault '97
Misery Brothers Y2K '95

Eleanora Rossi-Drago
Camille 2000 '69

**Giacomo "Jack" Rossi-
Stuart**
The Bloodsucker Leads the
   Dance '75
Kill, Baby, Kill '66

Norman Rossington
A Hard Day's Night '64

Leonard Rossiter
The Pink Panther Strikes
   Again '76
2001: A Space Odyssey '68

Angelo Rossitto
Mad Max: Beyond Thunder-
   dome '85

Eddie Rosson
Cool Hand Luke '67

Rick Rossovich
Truth or Consequences, N.M.
   '97
Navy SEALS '90
Top Gun '86
Streets of Fire '84
The Terminator '84

Andrea Roth
Crossworlds '96

Lillian Roth
Alice Sweet Alice '76
Animal Crackers '30

Tim Roth
Everyone Says I Love You '96
Gridlock'd '96
Four Rooms '95
Rob Roy '95
Pulp Fiction '94
Reservoir Dogs '92
Meantime '81

John Rothman
The Siege '98
Copycat '95

Cynthia Rothrock
Lady Dragon '92
China O'Brien '88
Inspector Wears Skirts '88
The Millionaire's Express '86

Paolo Rotondo
The Ugly '96

Richard Roundtree
George of the Jungle '97
Once Upon a Time . . .
   When We Were Colored '95
Seven '95
Maniac Cop '88
Q (The Winged Serpent) '82
Earthquake '74
Shaft '71

Robert Rounseville
Carousel '56

Hayden Rourke
Project Moon Base '53

Mickey Rourke
Point Blank '98
Buffalo 66 '97
Double Team '97
John Grisham's The Rainmak-
   er '97
Another 9 1/2 Weeks '96
Fall Time '94
Francesco '89
Angel Heart '87
9 1/2 Weeks '86
Rumble Fish '83
Body Heat '81
Fade to Black '80
1941 '79

Myriem Roussel
First Name: Carmen '83

Kelly Rowan
Exclusive '82

Bill Rowe
Philadelphia '93

Brad Rowe
Billy's Hollywood Screen Kiss
   '98

Victoria Rowell
Barb Wire '96
Dumb & Dumber '94
The Distinguished Gentleman
   '92

David Rowlands
Minnie and Moskowitz '71

Gena Rowlands
Hope Floats '98
The Mighty '98
Paulie '98
Playing by Heart '98
Opening Night '77
Two Minute Warning '76
Minnie and Moskowitz '71

**Mary Allen "Lady"
Rowlands**
Minnie and Moskowitz '71

Esther Roy
Return of the Blind Dead '75

Pat Royale
Reefer Madness '38

Patricia Royce
To Cross the Rubicon '91

Roselyn Royce
Retrievers '82
Sizzle Beach U.S.A. '74

Selena Royle
The Fighting Sullivans '42

Roy Royston
Plague of the Zombies '66

Gregory Rozakis
Five Corners '88

Mary Beth Rubens
Prom Night '80

Jan Rubes
Mesmer '94

Jennifer Rubin
Plump Fiction '97
Little Witches '96
Screamers '96
Stranger by Night '94
A Nightmare on Elm Street 3:
   Dream Warriors '87

Michael Rubin
I Was a Teenage Zombie '87

Daphne Rubin-Vega
Wild Things '98

Saul Rubinek
Blackjack '97
Nixon '95
I Love Trouble '94
The Quarrel '93
True Romance '93
Unforgiven '92
The Bonfire of the Vanities
   '90
Ticket to Heaven '81

John Rubinstein
Someone to Watch Over Me
   '87
The Car '77
Zachariah '70

Zelda Rubinstein
Little Witches '96
Sixteen Candles '84
Poltergeist '82

Alan Ruok
Twister '96
Speed '94
Star Trek: Generations '94
Ferris Bueller's Day Off '86

Paul Rudd
200 Cigarettes '98
William Shakespeare's
   Romeo and Juliet '96
Clueless '95

Claude-Oliver Rudolph
Das Boot (DC) '81

Ken Rudolph
Blood, Guts, Bullets and
   Octane '98

Joshua Rudoy
Flatliners '90

Kristin Rudrud
Fargo '96

Johan Ruebeck
Evil Ed '96

Robert Rueben
The Story of G.I. Joe '45

Mercedes Ruehl
Last Action Hero '93
Big '88

Mark Ruel
With Friends Like These '90

Rufus
Metroland '97

Wesley Ruggles
Chaplin's Art of Comedy '66

Vyto Ruginis
The Devil's Advocate '97
A Thousand Acres '97

Barbara Ruick
Carousel '56

**Anthony Michael
Ruivivar**
Starship Troopers '97

Mia Ruiz
Witchcraft 2: The Temptress
   '90

Janice Rule
Alvarez Kelly '66

Sig Rumann
That Uncertain Feeling '41
Nothing Sacred '37

Jenny Runacre
The Canterbury Tales '71

Kicki Rundgren
My Life As a Dog '85

Jennifer Runyon
Quantum Leap: The Pilot
   Episode '89
Dreams of Gold: The Mel
   Fisher Story '86
The Falcon and the Snowman
   '85

Ying Ruocheng
Little Buddha '93
The Last Emperor '87

Deborah Rush
In and Out '97
Parents '89

Geoffrey Rush
House on Haunted Hill '99
Mystery Men '99
Elizabeth '98
Shakespeare in Love (CS)
   '98
Les Miserables '97
Twisted '96
Shine '95

Claire Rushbrook
Spice World: The Movie '97

Jared Rushton
Big '88
The Lady in White '88

Joseph Ruskin
King Cobra '98
Cyber-Tracker '93
Prizzi's Honor '85

Robert Rusler
Sometimes They Come Back
   '91
A Nightmare on Elm Street 2:
   Freddy's Revenge '85

William Russ
American History X '98
The Right Stuff '83

Betsy Russell
Trapper County War '89

Brian Russell
Charlie, the Lonesome
Cougar '67

Clive Russell
The 13th Warrior '99

Evelyn Russell
Eat My Dust '76

Gail Russell
Angel and the Badman '47

Harold Russell
The Best Years of Our Lives
'46

John Russell
Pale Rider '85
The Outlaw Josey Wales '76

Keri Russell
The Curve '97
The Babysitter's Seduction
'96

Kurt Russell
Soldier '98
Escape from L.A. '96
Executive Decision '96
Stargate '94
Tombstone '93
Backdraft '91
Tango and Cash '89
Tequila Sunrise '88
Overboard '87
The Best of Times '86
Silkwood '83
The Thing '82

Nipsey Russell
Posse '93
The Wiz '78

Rebel Russell
The Adventures of Priscilla,
Queen of the Desert '94

Rosalind Russell
His Girl Friday '40

Theresa Russell
Wild Things '98
Aria '88

James Russo
Love to Kill '97
The Postman '97
American Strays '96
Donnie Brasco '96
Panther '95

Rene Russo
The Thomas Crown Affair '99
Lethal Weapon 4 '98
Ransom '96
Tin Cup '96
Get Shorty '95
Outbreak '94
In the Line of Fire '93
Lethal Weapon 3 '92

Leon Russom
The Big Lebowski '97

Babe Ruth
The Pride of the Yankees '42

Ann Rutherford
The Secret Life of Walter
Mitty '47
Gone with the Wind '39

Erik Rutherford
Lady of the Lake '98

Susan Ruttan
Chances Are '89

Basil Ruysdael
The Cocoanuts '29

Amanda Ryan
Metroland '97

Eddie Ryan
The Fighting Sullivans '42

Edmon Ryan
Tora! Tora! Tora! '70

Eileen Ryan
Anywhere But Here '99
The Crossing Guard '94

Fran Ryan
Chances Are '89
Pale Rider '85

James Ryan
Kill and Kill Again '81

John P. Ryan
Bound '96
Rent-A-Cop '88
Runaway Train '85
The Right Stuff '83
The Postman Always Rings
Twice '81

Kathleen Ryan
Odd Man Out '47

Marisa Ryan
Slaves to the Underground
'96

Meg Ryan
City of Angels '98
You've Got Mail '98
Anastasia '97 (V)
Addicted to Love '96
French Kiss '95
Restoration '94
When a Man Loves a Woman
'94
Sleepless in Seattle '93
The Doors '91
Top Gun '86

Michael Ryan
The Crossing Guard '94

Mitchell Ryan
Grosse Pointe Blank '97
The Devil's Own '96
Liar Liar '96
Lethal Weapon '87
High Plains Drifter '73

Paddy Ryan
An American Werewolf in London '81

Remi Ryan
RoboCop 3 '91

R.L. Ryan
Class of Nuke 'Em High '86

Robert Ryan
The Wild Bunch '69
The Dirty Dozen '67
The Professionals '66
The Longest Day '62
Men in War '57

Thomas Ryan
The Relic '96

Will Ryan
Thumbelina '94 (V)
The Land Before Time '88 (V)

Bobby Rydell
Bye, Bye, Birdie '63

Christopher Rydell
Blood and Sand '89

Mark Rydell
Havana '90

Alfred Ryder
T-Men '47

Michael Ryder
Troma's War (DC) '88

Winona Ryder
Celebrity '98
How to Make an American
Quilt '95
Little Women '94
Reality Bites '94
Dracula '92
Heathers '89
Beetlejuice '88

Sonia Rykiel
Ready to Wear '94

James Ryland
Waking Ned Devine '98

Daisuke Ryu
Ran '85

Antonio Sabato
High Voltage '98

Antonio Sabato Jr.
The Big Hit '98
High Voltage '98

Ernie Sabella
The Lion King: Simba's Pride
'98 (V)

Kyle Sabihy
Analyze This '98

Marcel Sabourin
Lilies '96

Michael Sacks
Slaughterhouse Five '72

Keiji Sada
The Human Condition: Road
to Eternity '59
The Human Condition: No
Greater Love '58

William Sadler
The Green Mile '99
Disturbing Behavior '98
Solo '96
The Shawshank Redemption
'94
Tales from the Crypt Presents
Demon Knight '94
Trespass '92
Die Hard 2: Die Harder '90
The Hot Spot '90
Hard to Kill '89

William Sage
Cost of Living '97

Ray Sager
The Wizard of Gore '70

Ken Sagoes
A Nightmare on Elm Street 4:
Dream Master '88

Katie Sagona
In Dreams '98

Kenji Sahara
Godzilla's Revenge '69
Godzilla vs. Mothra '64

Ed Sahely
Bury Me in Niagara '93

Yam Sai-kun
Iron Monkey '93

Raymond St. Jacques
Glory '89
They Live '88
The Green Berets '68

Al "Fuzzy" St. John
Dead Men Walk / The Mon-
ster Maker '43
The Saphead '21

Betta St. John
Corridors of Blood '58

Christopher St. John
Shaft '71

Howard St. John
Born Yesterday '50

Jill St. John
The Player '92
Around the World in 80 Days
'89

Michelle St. John
Smoke Signals '98

Irma St. Paule
Desecration '99

Lucille Saint Peter
Brain Damage '88

John St. Polis
The Phantom of the Opera
'25

Sachio Sakai
Godzilla's Revenge '69
Godzilla, King of the Mon-
sters '56
Samurai 2: Duel at Ichijoji
Temple '55

Keiji Sakakida
Seven Samurai '54

S.Z. Sakall
Wonder Man '45
Casablanca '42
Ball of Fire '41

Ryuichi Sakamoto
New Rose Hotel '98
The Last Emperor '87

Amy Sakasitz
Mad Love '95

Harold Sakata
Goldfinger '64

Gene Saks
Deconstructing Harry '97

Kinzo Sakura
Tampopo '86

Amro Salama
The Siege '98

Richard Salamanca
Boys Life '94

Theresa Saldana
Raging Bull '80

Damon Saleem
Caught Up '98

Meredith Salenger
Bug Buster '99
Lake Placid '99
Village of the Damned '95

Enrico Maria Salerno
The Bird with the Crystal
Plumage '70

Nicola Salerno
Beyond the Door 2 '79

Sam Saletta
The Little Rascals '94

Diane Salinger
Pee-wee's Big Adventure '85

Emmanuel Salinger
One Hundred and One Nights
'94
La Sentinelle '92

John Salley
Eddie '96
Bad Boys '95

Gustavo Salmeron
Twice upon a Yesterday '98

Albert Salmi
The Meanest Men in the
West '76

Colin Salmon
Tomorrow Never Dies (SE)
'97

Lea Salonga
Mulan '98 (V)

Clare Salstrom
The Colony '98

Jennifer Salt
Gargoyles '72

Gino Saltamerenda
The Bicycle Thief '48

Elizabeth Saltarelli
Bound and Gagged: A Love
Story '93

Ivor Salter
House of Whipcord '75

James Salter
Blood, Guts, Bullets and
Octane '99

Candy Samples
Flesh Gordon '72

Robert Sampson
Re-Animator '84

Will Sampson
The Outlaw Josey Wales '76
One Flew Over the Cuckoo's
Nest '75

Jeffrey D. Sams
Just Write '97
Soul Food '97

Joanne Samuel
Mad Max '80

Laura San Giacomo
Suicide Kings '97
The Apocalypse '96
Eat Your Heart Out '96
Stephen King's The Stand
'94
Pretty Woman '90
sex, lies and videotape '89

Jaime Sanchez
The Wild Bunch '69

Paul Sanchez
Navy SEALS '90
Platoon '86

Fernando Sancho
Return of the Blind Dead '75

Shauna Sand
The Chosen One: Legend of
the Raven '98

Dominique Sanda
Cabo Blanco / U.S. Marshal
'81
The Inheritance '76

Walter Sande
The Red House '47

John Sanderford
Leprechaun '93

Dirk Sanders
Pierrot le Fou '65
Black Tights '60

George Sanders
A Shot in the Dark '64
All About Eve '50
Rebecca '40

Jay O. Sanders
Earthly Possessions '99
The Jack Bull '99
The Confession '98
Neil Simon's The Odd Couple
2 '98
For Richer or Poorer '97
Kiss the Girls '97
The Matchmaker '97
Daylight '96
JFK '91
Glory '89
Assault of the Killer Bimbos
'88

Marlene Sanders
Mumia: A Case for Reason-
able Doubt? '96 (N)

William Sanderson
Last Man Standing '96
Sometimes They Come Back
'91
Fletch '85
Blade Runner (DC) '82

Paul Schrader
American Gigolo '79

Bitty Schram
Kissing a Fool '98
A League of Their Own '92

Max Schreck
Nosferatu '22

Liev Schreiber
Jakob the Liar '99
A Walk on the Moon '99
Twilight '98
Phantoms '97
Scream 2 '97
Sphere '97
Ransom '96
Scream (CS) '96

Frederick Schreicker
The Third Man '49

Ernst Schroder
The Odessa File '74

Greta Schroder
Nosferatu '22

Rick Schroder
Crimson Tide '95
The Last Flight of Noah's Ark '80

Steven Schub
The Thirteenth Floor '99

Karin Schubert
Cold Eyes of Fear '70

John Schuck
Tales from the Crypt Presents Demon Knight '94
Star Trek 6: The Undiscovered Country '91
My Mom's a Werewolf '89
Star Trek 4: The Voyage Home '86

Matt Schue
Femalien '96

Rebecca Schull
Analyze This '98
Neil Simon's The Odd Couple 2 '98

Dwight Schultz
Star Trek: First Contact '96

Harry Schultz
Driller Killer '74

Maurice Schultz
Passion of Joan of Arc '28

Tom Schultz
Eye of the Serpent '92

Paul Schulzie
Hand Gun '93

Wendy Schumacher
Scorned 2 '96
Animal Instincts 3: The Seductress '95

Reinhold Schunzel
Notorious '46

Maurice Schutz
Vampyr '31

Lonnie Schuyler
Cybernator '91

Jason Schwartzman
Rushmore '98

Arnold Schwarzenegger
End of Days '99
Batman and Robin '97
Eraser '96
Jingle All the Way '96
Junior '94
True Lies '94
Dave '93
Last Action Hero '93
Terminator 2: Judgment Day '91

Kindergarten Cop '90
Total Recall '90
Red Heat '88
Twins '88
Predator '87
The Running Man '87
Raw Deal '86
Commando '85
Conan the Destroyer '84
The Terminator '84
Conan the Barbarian '82

Til Schweiger
SLC Punk! '99
The Replacement Killers '98

Jan Schweiterman
Warlock 3: The End of Innocence '98

David Schwimmer
Kissing a Fool '98
Six Days, Seven Nights '98
Apt Pupil '97

Rusty Schwimmer
A Little Princess '95

Hanna Schygulla
One Hundred and One Nights '94
Dead Again '91

Yvonne Scio
Redline '97

Annabella Sciorra
Mr. Jealousy '98
New Rose Hotel '98
What Dreams May Come '98
Asteroid '97
Cop Land '97
Underworld '96
Mr. Wonderful '93
The Hand that Rocks the Cradle '92
The Hard Way '91
Jungle Fever '91
Internal Affairs '90

Dean Scofield
The Last Assassins '96

Paul Scofield
Quiz Show '94
The Train '65

Peter Scolari
From the Earth to the Moon '98

Fred J. Scollay
Q (The Winged Serpent) '82

Catherine Scorsese
Goodfellas '90

Martin Scorsese
The Muse '99
Robbie Robertson: Going Home '98
Quiz Show '94
Guilty by Suspicion '91
Taxi Driver (CE) '76

Izabela Scorupco
Goldeneye '95

Alex Scott
The Asphyx '72
Fahrenheit 451 '66

Campbell Scott
The Imposters '98
The Spanish Prisoner '97
Big Night '95
Singles '92
Dead Again '91

Deborah Scott
Witchcraft '88

Debralee Scott
Police Academy '84

Donovan Scott
1941 '79

Dougray Scott
Deep Impact '98
Ever After: A Cinderella Story '98
Another 9 1/2 Weeks '96

Esther Scott
Senseless '98

George C. Scott
Gloria '98
Malice '93
A Christmas Carol '84
Firestarter '84
The Hindenburg '75
They Might Be Giants '71
Patton '70
Dr. Strangelove, or: How I Learned to Stop Worrying and Love the Bomb '64

Imogen Millais Scott
Salome's Last Dance '88

Keith Scott
George of the Jungle '97 (N)

Kimberly Scott
Batman Forever '95
Flatliners '90
The Abyss (SE) '89

Lizabeth Scott
The Strange Love of Martha Ivers '46

Martha Scott
The Ten Commandments '56

Randolph Scott
Rage at Dawn '55
She '35

Seann W. Scott
American Pie (CE) '99

Kristin Scott Thomas
The Horse Whisperer '97
The English Patient '96
The Pompatus of Love '95
Four Weddings and a Funeral '94

Timothy Scott
Fried Green Tomatoes '91

Tom Everett Scott
The Love Letter '99
One True Thing '98
An American Werewolf in Paris '97
Dead Man on Campus '97

William Scott
Amarilly of Clothesline Alley '18

William Lee Scott
October Sky '99
Opposite of Sex '98

Zachary Scott
The Southerner '45

Ivan Scratuglia
Django '68

Don Scribner
Slave Girls from Beyond Infinity '87

Angus Scrimm
Phantasm '79

Terry Scully
The Asphyx '72

Steven Seagal
The Patriot '99
My Giant '98
Fire Down Below '97
Executive Decision '96
The Glimmer Man '96
Under Siege 2 '95
On Deadly Ground '94
Under Siege '92
Out for Justice '91
Marked for Death '90
Hard to Kill '89

Above the Law '88

Jenny Seagrove
The Guardian '90

Sybil Sealey
The Saphead '21

Ed Seamon
Boys Life 2 '98

Nick Searcy
From the Earth to the Moon '98
The War '94

Jean Seberg
Airport '70

Kyle Secor
Drop Zone '94

Jon Seda
Primal Fear '96
Selena '96
12 Monkeys '95

Kyra Sedgwick
Critical Care '97
Phenomenon '96
Heart and Souls '93
Singles '92
Born on the Fourth of July '89

Catherine See
The Eric Rohmer Collection: The Moral Tales '62

Alison Seebohm
A Hard Day's Night '64

George Segal
The Cable Guy '96
The Mirror Has Two Faces '96
Flirting with Disaster '95
To Die For '95
Look Who's Talking '89
Rollercoaster '77
Born to Win '71
Who's Afraid of Virginia Woolf? '66

Pamela Segall
Plump Fiction '97
Eat Your Heart Out '96
Bed of Roses '95
Sgt. Bilko '96

Paolo Seganti
Tea with Mussolini '99
L.A. Confidential '97

Jason Segel
SLC Punk! '99

Mii Seghers
Antonia's Line '95

Pierre Segui
The Deer Hunter '78

Seib Seibl
Crackdown '88

Emmanuelle Seigner
Frantic '88

Rapulana Seiphemo
Tarzan and the Lost City '98

John Seitz
Five Corners '88

Johnny Sekka
The Message '77

David Selby
Horton Foote's Alone '97
White Squall '96

Marian Seldes
The Haunting '99
Digging to China '98
Affliction '97
Home Alone 3 '97

William Self
Sands of Iwo Jima '49
The Story of G.I. Joe '45

Tom Selleck
The Love Letter '99
In and Out '97
Mr. Baseball '92
Her Alibi '88
The Shadow Riders '82
Coma '78
Midway '76

Peter Sellers
Revenge of the Pink Panther '78
The Pink Panther Strikes Again '76
Dr. Strangelove, or: How I Learned to Stop Worrying and Love the Bomb '64
The Pink Panther '64
A Shot in the Dark '64
Lolita '62
Trial & Error '62
Waltz of the Toreadors '62
The Millionairess '60

Dean Selmier
The Blood Spattered Bride '72

Udo Semel
Killer Condom '95

Harry Semels
America '24

Martin Semmelrogge
Das Boot (DC) '81

Koreya Senda
Tora! Tora! Tora! '70

Noriko Sengoku
Godzilla vs. Monster Zero '68

Susan Sennett
Big Bad Mama '74

Rade Serbedzija
Eyes Wide Shut '99
Stigmata '99
Mighty Joe Young '98
Polish Wedding '97
The Saint '97

Ivan Sergei
Opposite of Sex '98
Once a Thief '96

Nikolai Sergeyev
Andrei Rublev '66

Meika Seri
In the Realm of the Senses '76

Assumpta Serna
The Craft '96

Pepe Serna
The Jerk '79
Shoot Out '71

Nestor Serrano
The Insider '99
The Negotiator '98
City Hall '95
Brenda Starr '86

Michel Serrault
Buffet Froid '79
Diabolique '55

Christopher Serrone
Goodfellas '90

Jean Servais
The Devil's Nightmare '71

John Sessions
William Shakespeare's A Midsummer Night's Dream '99
Cousin Bette '97

Asif Mohammed Seth
Jungle Boy '96

Roshan Seth
Street Fighter '94
Mountains of the Moon '90

Brian Setzer
La Bamba '87

Joan Severance
Lethal Weapon '87

Chloe Sevigny
Boys Don't Cry '99
The Last Days of Disco '98
Palmetto '98
Trees Lounge '96
Kids '95

Rufus Sewell
Dangerous Beauty '98
The Very Thought of You '98
Dark City '97

Brendan Sexton III
Boys Don't Cry '99
Desert Blue '98
Pecker '98
Welcome to the Dollhouse '95

Carolyn Seymour
Girls of the White Orchid '85

Jane Seymour
Quest for Camelot '98 (V)
Hollywood Christmas '96 (N)
Somewhere in Time '80
Battlestar Galactica '78
Live and Let Die '73

Ralph Seymour
Rain Man '88
Fletch '85

Delphine Seyrig
Daughters of Darkness '71
Stolen Kisses '68
Last Year at Marienbad '61

Glenn Shadix
Chairman of the Board '97
Demolition Man '93
The Nightmare before Christmas '93 (V)
Heathers '89
Beetlejuice '88

Dirk Shafer
Man of the Year '95

Paul Shaffer
Hercules '97 (V)
This Is Spinal Tap '84

Kashmira Shah
Pyar to Hona Hi Tah '98

Naseeruddin Shah
Sarfarosh '98

Tupac Shakur
Gridlock'd '96
Poetic Justice '93

Tony Shalhoub
A Civil Action '98
The Imposters '98
Paulie '98
Primary Colors '98
The Siege '98
Gattaca '97
A Life Less Ordinary '97
Big Night '98
Honeymoon in Vegas '92

Garry Shandling
Dr. Dolittle '98 (V)

Ravi Shankar
Chappaqua '66

Don Shanks
Spirit of the Eagle '90

Harry Shannon
The Red House '47

Molly Shannon
Never Been Kissed '99
Analyze This '98
A Night at the Roxbury '98

Omar Sharif
The 13th Warrior '99

The Last Valley '71

David Shark
Soultaker '90

Ray Sharkey
Cop and a Half '93
Capone '89
No Mercy '86
Regina '83

Lesley Sharp
The Full Monty '96
Priest '94

Melanie Shatner
Star Trek 5: The Final Frontier '89

William Shatner
Trinity and Beyond: The Atomic Bomb Movie '99 (N)
Free Enterprise '98
Star Trek: Generations '94
National Lampoon's Loaded Weapon 1 '93
Star Trek 6: The Undiscovered Country '91
Star Trek 5: The Final Frontier '89
Star Trek 4: The Voyage Home '86
Devil's Rain '75
Big Bad Mama '74

Grant Shaud
The Distinguished Gentleman '92

Mickey Shaughnessy
Jailhouse Rock '57

Billy Joe Shaver
The Apostle '97

Helen Shaver
The Craft '96
Tremors 2: Aftershocks '96
The Land Before Time '88 (V)
The Color of Money '86

Bill Shaw
Total Reality '97

Crystal Shaw
Laser Moon '92

Fiona Shaw
The Avengers '98
Mountains of the Moon '90
My Left Foot '89

Martin Shaw
The Hound of the Baskervilles '83

Oscar Shaw
The Cocoanuts '29

Reta Shaw
The Pajama Game '57

Robert Shaw
The Deep '77
Swashbuckler '76
The Sting '73
Royal Hunt of the Sun '69
Custer of the West '67
From Russia with Love '63

Sebastian Shaw
It Happened Here '65

Stan Shaw
Snake Eyes '98
Daylight '96
Cutthroat Island '95
Fried Green Tomatoes '91

Vanessa Shaw
Horror Hospital '73

Victoria Shaw
Alvarez Kelly '66

Vinessa Shaw
Eyes Wide Shut '99

Joan Shawlee
Buck Privates Come Home '47

Wallace Shawn
An Extremely Goofy Movie '99 (V)
My Favorite Martian '98
Critical Care '97
Just Write '97
Vegas Vacation '96
Clueless '95
The Wife '95
The Princess Bride '87
The Bostonians '84
My Dinner with Andre '81

Michele Shay
He Got Game '98

Lin Shaye
Detroit Rock City '99
There's Something about Mary '98

Robert Shaye
Wes Craven's New Nightmare '94

Konstantin Shayne
The Stranger '46

Robert Shayne
The Indestructible Man / The Amazing Transparent Man '56

Cherilyn Shea
Silk 'n' Sabotage '94

John Shea
Southie '98
Stealing Home '88
The Impossible Spy '87

Harry Shearer
Godzilla '98
Small Soldiers '98 (V)
A League of Their Own '92 (V)
This Is Spinal Tap '84
The Right Stuff '83

Moira Shearer
Black Tights '60
Peeping Tom '60
The Red Shoes '48

Ally Sheedy
The Breakfast Club '85
Bad Boys '83
WarGames '83

Gladys Sheehan
Rawhead Rex '87

Charlie Sheen
Being John Malkovich '99
Postmortem '98
The Arrival '96
Terminal Velocity '94
Deadfall '93
National Lampoon's Loaded Weapon 1 '93
The Three Musketeers '93
Navy SEALS '90
Tale of Two Sisters '89 (N)
Young Guns '88
Ferris Bueller's Day Off '86
Platoon '86
Red Dawn '84

Martin Sheen
Lost and Found '99
Monument Ave. '98
Ninth Street '98
A Stranger in the Kingdom '98
Spawn (SE) '97
Truth or Consequences, N.M. '97
The American President '95
Conspiracy: The Trial of the Chicago Eight '87
Firestarter '84
Apocalypse Now '79
The Cassandra Crossing '76

Badlands '74

Craig Sheffer
Fire on the Amazon '93
A River Runs Through It '92

Jeremy Sheffield
Merlin '98

Clifford Shegog
Street Wars '91

Tom Shell
Surf Nazis Must Die (DC) '87

Stephen Shellen
Rude '96
A River Runs Through It '92
Casual Sex? '88

Barbara Shelley
Quatermass and the Pit '67
Dracula, Prince of Darkness '66
Rasputin the Mad Monk '66

Carol Shelley
Hercules '97 (V)

Mary Shelley
Witchcraft '88

Deborah Shelton
Body Double '84

Marley Shelton
The Bachelor '99
Never Been Kissed '99
Pleasantville '98
Warriors of Virtue '97

Huang Chin Shen
The Descendant of Wing Chun '78

Paul Shenar
Raw Deal '86
Scarface '83

Ben Shenkman
Pi '98

Chaz Lamas Shepard
Set It Off '96

Sam Shepard
Curtain Call '97
The Pelican Brief '93
Thunderheart '92
The Right Stuff '83
Frances '82
Days of Heaven '78

Chaz Lamar Shepherd
The Temptations '98

Cybill Shepherd
The Last Word '95
Chances Are '89
Moonlighting '85
Taxi Driver (CE) '76
The Heartbreak Kid '72

Jack Shepherd
No Escape '94

Michael Shepley
Henry V '44

Della Sheppard
Animal Instincts '92
Secret Games '92
Witchcraft 2: The Temptress '90

Mark Sheppard
In the Name of the Father '93

Paula Sheppard
Alice Sweet Alice '76

Anthony Sher
Shakespeare in Love (CS) '98
Mrs. Brown '97
Alive and Kicking '96

Travis Sher
Boys Life 2 '98

Jamey Sheridan
Wild America '97
Stephen King's The Stand '94

Nicolette Sheridan
Beverly Hills Ninja '96
Spy Hard '96

Barry Sherman
Lord of Illusions '95

Editta Sherman
Ms. 45 '81

Lowell Sherman
Way Down East '20

Marlene Sherter
The Dirty Girls '64

Steven Sherwin
Watch Me '96

Anthony Sherwood
Closer and Closer '96

Siu Sheung
Center Stage '91

George Shibata
Pork Chop Hill '59

Arthur Shields
The Quiet Man '52

Brooke Shields
The Bachelor '99
The Seventh Floor '93
Brenda Starr '86
The Blue Lagoon '80
Alice Sweet Alice '76

James Shigeta
Mulan '98 (V)
Drive '96
Die Hard '88

Shogo Shimada
Tora! Tora! Tora! '70

Yoko Shimada
The Hunted '94

Armin Shimerman
Looking for Lola '98

Gen Shimizu
Seven Samurai '54

Sab Shimono
The Big Hit '98
Presumed Innocent '90

Takashi Shimura
Godzilla, King of the Monsters '56
Seven Samurai '54

Sofia Shinas
The Crow '93

Ful-On Shing
The Killer '90
God of Gamblers '89

Toshi Shioya
Mr. Baseball '92

Talia Shire
The Landlady '98
Rocky 4 '85
Rocky 2 '79
Rocky '76

Anne Shirley
Stella Dallas '37

Joe Shishido
Branded to Kill '67

Kai Shishido
8 Man '92

Samia Shoaib
Pi '98

William Shockley
Dream Lover '93

Ikeda Shoko
Operation Condor '91

Dan Shor
Mesmerized '84
Tron '82

Dinah Shore
Till the Clouds Roll By '46

Pauly Shore
An Extremely Goofy Movie
'99 (V)
Son-in-Law '93
Encino Man '92

Dorothy Short
Reefer Madness '38

Florence Short
Way Down East '20

Martin Short
Alice in Wonderland '99
Mumford '99
Merlin '98
Prince of Egypt '98 (V)
A Simple Wish '97
Mars Attacks! '96
The Pebble and the Penguin
'94 (V)
Father of the Bride '91
Three Amigos '86

Robin Shou
Mortal Kombat 2: Annihila-
tion '97
Beverly Hills Ninja '96

Col. D.M. Shoup
Sands of Iwo Jima '49

**Max (Casey Adams)
Showalter**
Sixteen Candles '84
The Indestructible Man / The
Amazing Transparent Man
'56

Kathy Shower
Sexual Malice '93

Capt. Harold G. Shrier
Sands of Iwo Jima '49

Jimmy Shubert
Go '99

Andrew Shue
John Grisham's The Rainmaker '97

Elisabeth Shue
Palmetto '98
Cousin Bette '97
Deconstructing Harry '97
The Saint '97
The Trigger Effect '96
Leaving Las Vegas '95
The Underneath '95
Heart and Souls '93
Adventures in Babysitting '87

Richard B. Shull
Splash '84

John Shum
I Love Maria '88

Josephine Siao
Mah Jong Dragon '97
Fong Sai Yuk '93

Sicily
How Stella Got Her Groove
Back '98

Sylvia Sidney
Mars Attacks! '96
Beetlejuice '88
Mr. Ace '46
Blood on the Sun '45
Sabotage '36

Jim Siedow
The Texas Chainsaw Mas-
sacre '74

Donald Siegel
Invasion of the Body Snatchers '78

Invasion of the Body Snatchers '56

George Siegmann
Uncle Tom's Cabin '27
The Three Musketeers '21
The Birth of a Nation '15

Casey Siemaszko
Limbo '99
Stephen King's The Storm of
the Century '99
Young Guns '88
Stand by Me '86

Nina Siemaszko
Goodbye, Lover '99
Jakob the Liar '99
Armistead Maupin's More
Tales of the City '97
The American President '95

Gregory Sierra
Deep Cover '92

Rocco Siffredi
Romance '99

Tom Signorelli
Alice Sweet Alice '76
Big Bad Mama '74

Simone Signoret
Diabolique '55

Caroline Sihol
Confidentially Yours '83

James B. Sikking
The Pelican Brief '93
Around the World in 80 Days
'89
Outland '81
The Electric Horseman '79

Deek Sills
Trader Hornee '70

Henry Silva
Above the Law '88
Cannonball Run 2 '84
Sharky's Machine '81
The Manchurian Candidate
'62

Maria Silva
Tombs of the Blind Dead '72

Rebeca Silva
Enemy of the State '98

Trinidad Silva
The Jerk '79

Aldo Silvani
Nights of Cabiria '57

Joe Silver
They Came from Within '75

Robert Silver
Devil in the Flesh '98

Ron Silver
The Arrival '96
Timecop '94
Mr. Saturday Night '92
Lovesick '83
Silkwood '83

Veronique Silver
The Woman Next Door '81

Frank Silvera
Killer's Kiss '55

David Michael Silverman
Metro '96
Copycat '95

Jonathan Silverman
Just a Little Harmless Sex
'99
Neil Simon's The Odd Couple
2 '98
Something About Sex '98
Death Becomes Her '92
Weekend at Bernie's '89
Caddyshack 2 '88
Stealing Home '88

Brighton Beach Memoirs '86

Laura Silverman
Half-Baked '97

Candace Silvers
My Science Project '85

Alicia Silverstone
Blast from the Past '98
Batman and Robin '97
Excess Baggage '96
Clueless '95
True Crime '95

Alastair Sim
The Littlest Horse Thieves
'76
The Millionairess '60
A Christmas Carol '51

Jon Simanton
The Creeps '97

Anthony Simcoe
The Castle '97

Peter Similuk
Hideous Sun Demon '59

John Simm
Boston Kickout '95

Beverly Simmons
Buck Privates Come Home
'47

Gene Simmons
Detroit Rock City '99
Red Surf '90

Jaason Simmons
Highway Hitcher '98

Jean Simmons
How to Make an American
Quilt '95
Rough Night in Jericho '67
Spartacus '60
Great Expectations '46

J.K. Simmons
The Jackal (CE) '97

Kadamba Simmons
Breeders '97

Pat Simmons
My Science Project '85

Richard Simmons
Rudolph the Red-Nosed Reindeer: The Movie '98 (V)

Michel Simon
The Train '65
Passion of Joan of Arc '28

Paul Simon
Annie Hall '77

Tania Simon
Peach / A Bitter Song '95

Martine Simonet
The Last Metro '80

Freddie Simpson
A League of Their Own '92

O.J. Simpson
Capricorn One '78
The Cassandra Crossing '76
The Towering Inferno '74

Peggy Simpson
The 39 Steps '35

Russell Simpson
They Were Expendable '45

Adam Sims
Lost in Space '98

Ammie Sin
Booty Call '96

Frank Sinatra
Cannonball Run 2 '84
The First Deadly Sin '80
The Manchurian Candidate
'62

Suddenly '54
Till the Clouds Roll By '46

Sinbad
Jingle All the Way '96

Madge Sinclair
Coming to America '88

Donald Sinden
The Island at the Top of the
World '74

Ngai Sing
Jet Li's The Enforcer '95

Lori Singer
Warlock '91
The Falcon and the Snowman
'85

Marc Singer
Sweet Justice '92

Richard Singer
American Pop '81 (V)

Steve Singer
Ms. 45 '81

Susie Singer
The Landlady '98

Dara Singh
Lav Kush '97

Joseph Singleton
The Toll Gate '20

Gary Sinise
The Green Mile '99
Snake Eyes '98
Albino Alligator '96
Ransom '96
Apollo 13 '95
The Quick and the Dead '94
Stephen King's The Stand
'94

Albert Sinkys
Ms. 45 '81

Joseph Siravo
Carlito's Way '93

Marina Sirtis
Star Trek: Insurrection '98
Star Trek: First Contact '96
Star Trek: Generations '94

Jeremy Sisto
The '60s '99
Playing by Heart '98
Suicide Kings '97
Without Limits '97
White Squall '96
Clueless '95

Rocco Sisto
Innocent Blood '92

Errol Sitahal
A Little Princess '95

Maggie Siu
The Longest Nite '92

Frank Sivero
Foolish '99
Dumb Luck in Vegas '97
Cop and a Half '93
Goodfellas '90

Tom Sizemore
Enemy of the State '98
Saving Private Ryan '98
The Relic '96
Bad Love '95
Devil in a Blue Dress '95
Heat '95
Strange Days '95
Heart and Souls '93
Striking Distance '93
True Romance '93
Born on the Fourth of July
'89

Gunnar Sjoberg
June Night '40

Stellan Skarsgard
Deep Blue Sea '99
Ronin '98
Savior '98
Amistad '97
Good Will Hunting '97
Insomnia '97
My Son the Fanatic '97
The Unbearable Lightness of
Being '88

Tom Skerritt
The Other Sister '98
Smoke Signals '98
Contact '97
Poison Ivy '92
A River Runs Through It '92
Singles '92
Top Gun '86
Alien '79
Devil's Rain '75
Big Bad Mama '74

Beverly Skinner
Stephen King's The Night
Flier '96

Claire Skinner
Sleepy Hollow '99

Keith Skinner
The Slipper and the Rose '76

Julie Skiru
Silk 'n' Sabotage '94

Michael Sklar
Women in Revolt '71
Trash '70

Seth Sklarey
Children Shouldn't Play with
Dead Things '72

Pavel Skripaz
Mandragora '97

Ione Skye
One Night Stand '97
Four Rooms '95

Pavel Slaby
The Unbearable Lightness of
Being '88

Max Elliott Slade
Apollo 13 '95

Jeremy Slate
The Lawnmower Man '92
Whisper Kill '88

Christian Slater
Very Bad Things '98
Hard Rain '97
Bed of Roses '95
Broken Arrow '95
Interview with the Vampire
'94
True Romance '93
Robin Hood: Prince of
Thieves '91
Star Trek 6: The Undiscov-
ered Country '91
Pump Up the Volume '90
Heathers '89

Helen Slater
The Secret of My Success
'87

Jonathon Slater
Leaving Scars '97

John Slattery
From the Earth to the Moon
'98

Jonathan Slavin
Free Enterprise '98

Bobby Slayton
The Rat Pack '98

Carrie Slaza
I Love You, I Love You Not '97

Victor Slezak
The Siege '98

The Bridges of Madison
County '95

Walter Slezak
Abbott and Costello in the
Foreign Legion '50
The Princess and the Pirate
'44

Gary Sloan
Witchcraft '88

Joey Slotnick
Blast from the Past '98
Twister '96
A League of Their Own '92

James Sloyan
Prime Suspect '82

Rob Slyker
Perfect Profile '90

Marya Small
American Pop '81 (V)

Neva Small
Fiddler on the Roof '71

Robert Small
Holy Man '98

Amy Smart
Outside Providence '99
Dee Snider's Strangeland '98
High Voltage '98
Varsity Blues '98

Dee Smart
Still Twisted

Jean Smart
Guinevere '99
Neil Simon's The Odd Couple
2 '98
Homeward Bound: The
Incredible Journey '93
Mistress '91

Ron Smerczak
Jackie Chan's Who Am I '98

Robert Smigel
Happy Gilmore '96

Amber Smith
Def Jam's How to Be a Player
'97
L.A. Confidential '97
Private Parts '96

Anna Deavere Smith
The American President '95
Dave '93
Philadelphia '93

Bill Smith
Spirit of the Eagle '90

Brandon Smith
Powder '95

Britta Smith
In the Name of the Father '93

Brooke Smith
Silence of the Lambs '91

Bubba Smith
The Naked Truth '92
Police Academy '84
Stroker Ace '83

Sir C. Aubrey Smith
And Then There Were None
'45
Forever and a Day '43
Rebecca '40
The Hurricane '37

Charles Smith
The General '26

Charles Martin Smith
Deep Impact '98
Deep Cover '92
The Hot Spot '90
Starman '84
The Buddy Holly Story '78
American Graffiti '73

**Cheryl "Rainbeaux"
Smith**
Parasite '82
Melvin and Howard '80
Laserblast '78
Pom Pom Girls '76
Farewell, My Lovely '75
The Swinging Cheerleaders
'74

Cotter Smith
K-9 '89

Cynthia Smith
For the Love of Benji '77
Benji '74

Ebbe Roe Smith
The Big Easy '87

Eddie Bo Smith Jr.
Stir of Echoes '99

Geraldine Smith
Flesh '68

Gregory Smith
The Climb '98

Gregory Edward Smith
Small Soldiers '98

Hillary Bailey Smith
Last Breath '96

Howard K. Smith
Dawn of the Dead '78

Ian Michael Smith
Simon Birch '98

Jaime Renee Smith
Dante's Peak '97

Jamie Smith
Killer's Kiss '55

Joe Smith
The Creeps '97

Kent Smith
The Night Stalker '71

Kevin Smith
Mallrats '95
Clerks '94

Kurtwood Smith
A Bright Shining Lie '98
Shelter '98
A Time to Kill '96
To Die For '95
Star Trek 6: The Undiscov-
ered Country '91
Dead Poets Society '89
Rambo 3 '88
RoboCop '87

Lane Smith
From the Earth to the Moon
'98
Why Do Fools Fall in Love?
'98
Son-in-Law '93
The Distinguished Gentleman
'92
The Mighty Ducks '92
Air America '90
Frances '82
Prime Suspect '82
Blue Collar '78

Liz Smith
A Merry War '97

Lois Smith
The Eternal Kiss of the
Mummy '99
Twister '96
How to Make an American
Quilt '95
Falling Down '93
Skylark '93
Fried Green Tomatoes '91

Madeleine Smith
Live and Let Die '73

Madolyn Smith
Funny Farm '88
All of Me '84
2010: The Year We Make
Contact '84
Rehearsal for Murder '82

Maggie Smith
Tea with Mussolini '99
Curtain Call '97
The First Wives Club '96
The Secret Garden '93
Sister Act 2: Back in the
Habit '93

Martha Smith
National Lampoon's Animal
House '78

Mel Smith
The Princess Bride '87

Morgan Michelle Smith
Soul Food '97

Norman Smith
The Amazing Transparent
Man '60

Oliver Smith
Hellbound: Hellraiser 2 '88
Hellraiser '87

Paul Smith
Maverick '94
Dune '84
Midnight Express '78

Queenie Smith
The Great Rupert '50

Roger Smith
Man of a Thousand Faces
'57

Roger Guenveur Smith
Summer of Sam '99
Deep Cover '92

Sean Smith
Atomic Train '99
The King and I '99 (V)

Seth Smith
The Climb '97
Home Alone 3 '97

Shawnee Smith
Carnival of Souls '98
Stephen King's The Stand
'94

Shelley Smith
National Lampoon's Class
Reunion '82

Terri Susan Smith
Basket Case '82

Tracy N. Smith
Web of Seduction '99

Will Smith
Wild Wild West '99
Enemy of the State '98
Independence Day '96
Bad Boys '95
Made in America '93

William Smith
Cybernator '91
Cartel '90
Maniac Cop '88
Red Dawn '84
Conan the Barbarian '82

Yeardley Smith
As Good As It Gets '97
Just Write '97

J. Smith-Cameron
The Rage: Carrie 2 '99
In and Out '97

Bill Smitrovich
The '60s '99
Dean Koontz's Mr. Murder
'98
Futuresport '98

Air Force One '97
The Trigger Effect '96
Nick of Time '95

Jimmy Smits
The Last Word '95
Stephen King's The Tommy-
knockers '93

Sonja Smits
Videodrome '83

Jake Smollett
Eve's Bayou '97

Jurnee Smollett
Eve's Bayou '97

Dick Smothers
Casino '95

Meredith Snaider
Habit '97

William Snape
The Full Monty '96

Dee Snider
Dee Snider's Strangeland '98

Wesley Snipes
Blade '98
Down in the Delta '98
Futuresport '98
U.S. Marshals '98
Murder at 1600 '97
One Night Stand '97
The Fan '96
Money Train '95
Drop Zone '94
Boiling Point '93
Demolition Man '93
Rising Sun '93
Jungle Fever '91
New Jack City '91

Carrie Snodgress
A Stranger in the Kingdom
'98
Wild Things '98
White Man's Burden '95
8 Seconds '94
Pale Rider '85

Snoop Doggy Dogg
Urban Menace '99
Caught Up '98
Half-Baked '97

Arlen Dean Snyder
Mommy 2: Mommy's Day '96
Marked for Death '90

Deb Snyder
Pushing Hands '92

Drew Snyder
Project: Eliminator '91
Firestarter '84

Susan Marie Snyder
Betrayed by Innocence '86

Michele (Michael) Soavi
Demons '86
Creepers '85

Barry Sobel
Doc Hollywood '91

Leelee Sobieski
Eyes Wide Shut '99
Joan of Arc '99
Never Been Kissed '99
Deep Impact '98

Mario Socrate
The Gospel According to St.
Matthew '64

Camilla Soeberg
Mouse Hunt '97

Sonja Sohn
Slam '98

Sojin
Seven Samurai '54

Vladimir Sokoloff
For Whom the Bell Tolls '43
The Road to Morocco '42

Paul Soles
Ticket to Heaven '81

P.J. Soles
Jawbreaker '98
Stripes '81
Rock 'n' Roll High School '79
Halloween '78
The Boy in the Plastic Bubble
'76

Yulia Solntseva
Aelita: Queen of Mars '24

Bruce Solomon
Children Shouldn't Play with
Dead Things '72

Charles Solomon
Witchcraft 2: The Temptress
'90

Todd Solondz
As Good As It Gets '97

Anatoli Solonitzin
Solaris '72
Andrei Rublev '66

Suzanne Somers
Serial Mom '94
Exclusive '82
American Graffiti '73

Jimmy Somerville
Orlando '93

Elke Sommer
Swiss Conspiracy '77
The Invisible Strangler '76
Lisa and the Devil / The
House of Exorcism '75
Torture Chamber of Baron
Blood '72
A Shot in the Dark '64
Daniella by Night '61

Josef Sommer
Patch Adams (CE) '98
Strange Days '95
Malice '93
The Mighty Ducks '92
Chances Are '89
Witness '85
Silkwood '83
Absence of Malice '81

Sondi
Pocket Ninjas '93

Michael Sonye
Sorority Babes in the Slime-
ball Bowl-A-Rama '87 (V)
Surf Nazis Must Die (DC) '87

Jack Soo
The Green Berets '68

Kevin Sorbo
Kull the Conqueror '97

Louis Sorin
Animal Crackers '30

Mira Sorvino
Summer of Sam '99
At First Sight '98
Lulu on the Bridge '98
The Replacement Killers '98
Mimic '97
Romy and Michele's High
School Reunion '97
Beautiful Girls '96
Mighty Aphrodite '95
Tarantella '95
Quiz Show '94

Paul Sorvino
Bulworth '98
Knock Off '98
Most Wanted '97
William Shakespeare's
Romeo and Juliet '96
Nixon '95

The Firm '93
The Rocketeer '91
Goodfellas '90
Betrayed by Innocence '86
Cry Uncle '71

Ann Sothern
The Blue Gardenia '53

Talisa Soto
Mortal Kombat 2: Annihilation '97
Mortal Kombat 1: The Movie '95
Don Juan DeMarco '94
License to Kill '89

Claudine Soubrier
The Eric Rohmer Collection: The Moral Tales '62

Kath Soucie
The Rugrats Movie '98 (V)

David Soul
Salem's Lot '79

J.D. Souther
To Cross the Rubicon '91

Daniel Southern
The 13th Warrior '99

Roger Souza
The Vanishing '88

Tammara Souza
Assault of the Killer Bimbos '88

Arthur Space
The Red House '47

Sissy Spacek
Blast from the Past '98
Affliction '97
JFK '91
The River '84
The Man with Two Brains '83 (V)
Badlands '74

Kevin Spacey
A Bug's Life (CE) '98 (V)
The Negotiator '98
L.A. Confidential '97
Midnight in the Garden of Good and Evil (SE) '97
A Time to Kill '96
Seven '95
The Usual Suspects '95
Outbreak '94
Swimming with Sharks '94
Henry & June '90

Claudio Spadaro
Tea with Mussolini '99

David Spade
Lost and Found '99
The Rugrats Movie '98 (V)
Senseless '98
Tommy Boy '95

James Spader
Critical Care '97
Curtain Call '97
Keys to Tulsa '96
Crash '95
Stargate '94
Wolf '94
Dream Lover '93
White Palace '90
sex, lies and videotape '89

Mark Spalding
Sleepy Hollow '99

Laurette Spang
Battlestar Galactica '78

Joe Spano
From the Earth to the Moon '98
Primal Fear '96
American Graffiti '73

Vincent Spano
The Prophecy 3: The Ascent '99
No Strings Attached '98
Creator '85
Rumble Fish '83

Adrian Sparks
My Stepmother Is an Alien '88

George Spartels
Mad Max: Beyond Thunderdome '85

Dan Speaker
Glitch! '88

Jeff Speakman
Timelock '99

Phil Spector
Easy Rider '69

Carol Speed
Avenging Disco Godfather '76

Hugo Speer
The Full Monty '96

Tori Spelling
Trick '99
The House of Yes '97
Scream 2 '97
Last Action Hero '93

Peter Spellos
Bound '96

Georgina Spelvin
Police Academy '84

Bruce Spence
Moby Dick '98
Dark City '97
Sweet Talker '91
Mad Max: Beyond Thunderdome '85
The Road Warrior '82

Sebastian Spence
Firestorm '97
Family of Cops '95

Bud Spencer
Troublemakers '94

Chris Spencer
Don't Be a Menace to South Central While Drinking Your Juice in the Hood '95

John Spencer
Ravenous '99
The Negotiator '98
Twilight '98
Cop Land '97
Albino Alligator '96
The Rock '96
Presumed Innocent '90
Black Rain '89

Kenneth Spencer
Bataan '43

Spencer Davis Group
The Ghost Goes Gear '66

Jeremy Spenser
Summertime '55

Wendie Jo Sperber
1941 '79

Shirley Speril
Glen or Glenda? '53

Scott Spiegel
Evil Dead '83

David Spielberg
Christine '84

Steven Spielberg
The Blues Brothers (CE) '80

Laurent Spielvogel
The Monster '96
French Kiss '95

Mickey Spillane
Mommy 2: Mommy's Day '96
Mommy '95
Girl Hunters '63

Joe Spinell
Vigilante '83
Night Shift '82
Nighthawks '81
Maniac '80
Taxi Driver (CE) '76

Stephen Spinella
Ravenous '99
Great Expectations '97
The Jackal (CE) '97
Tarantula '95
Virtuosity '95

Brent Spiner
Star Trek: Insurrection '98
Independence Day '96
Phenomenon '96
Star Trek: First Contact '96
Star Trek: Generations '94

Victor Spinetti
Magical Mystery Tour '67
Help! '65
A Hard Day's Night '64

Carroll Spinney
The Adventures of Elmo in Grouchland '99 (V)

Tony Spiridakis
Queens Logic '91

Kevin Blair Spirtas
Embrace the Darkness '98
Striking Resemblance '97

Madame Spivy
The Manchurian Candidate '62

Lisa Spoonhauer
Clerks '94

Gregory Sporleder
Clay Pigeons '98
The Rock '96
Twister '96
A League of Their Own '92

G.D. Spradlin
The Long Kiss Goodnight '96
Nick of Time '95
Carolina Skeletons '92
Tank '83
Apocalypse Now '79

Elizabeth Spriggs
Sense and Sensibility '95

Jerry Springer
Austin Powers 2: The Spy Who Shagged Me '99
Ringmaster '98

Pamela Springsteen
My Science Project '85

Cole Sprouse
Big Daddy '99

Dylan Sprouse
Big Daddy '99

Rebecca Staab
T.N.T. '98

Nick Stabile
Bride of Chucky '98

Robert Stack
Mumford '99
BASEketball '98
Beavis and Butt-Head Do America '96 (V)
Caddyshack 2 '88
1941 '79

James Stacy
Something Wicked This Way Comes '83

Lewis J. Stadlen
The Imposters '98

In and Out '97

Joerg Stadler
Saving Private Ryan '98

Michael Stadvec
The Chosen One: Legend of the Raven '98
The Dentist '96

Jon Stafford
Full Metal Jacket '87

Jerry Stahl
Permanent Midnight '98

Nick Stahl
Disturbing Behavior '98

Ernest Stahl-Nachbaur
M '31

Enzo Staiola
The Bicycle Thief '48

James Staley
Protocol '84

Frank Stallone
Hudson Hawk '91

Sage Stallone
Daylight '96

Sylvester Stallone
Antz '98 (V)
Cop Land '97
Daylight '96
Assassins '95
Judge Dredd '95
The Specialist '94
Cliffhanger '93
Demolition Man '93
Lock Up '89
Tango and Cash '89
Rambo 3 '88
Cobra '86
Rambo: First Blood, Part 2 '85
Rocky 4 '85
First Blood '82
Nighthawks '81
Victory '81
Rocky 2 '79
Rocky '76
Death Race 2000 '75
Farewell, My Lovely '75

Terence Stamp
Bowfinger '99
The Limey '99
The Adventures of Priscilla, Queen of the Desert '94
The Real McCoy '93
Young Guns '88
Legal Eagles '86
Spirits of the Dead '68

Sira Stampe
Hideous Kinky '99

Lionel Stander
1941 '79
The Cassandra Crossing '76
A Star Is Born '37

Herbert Standing
Stella Maris '18

John Standing
Rogue Trader '98
The Man Who Knew Too Little '97
Mrs. Dalloway '97
Chaplin '92

Florence Stanley
Neil Simon's The Odd Couple 2 '98

Helene Stanley
The Snows of Kilimanjaro '52

Kim Stanley
Cat on a Hot Tin Roof '84
The Right Stuff '83
Frances '82
To Kill a Mockingbird '62 (N)

Maxfield Stanley
The Birth of a Nation '15

Paul Stanley
Detroit Rock City '99

Rebecca Stanley
Body Double '84

Claire Stansfield
Sweepers '99
Darkdrive '98
Drop Zone '94

Harry Dean Stanton
The Green Mile '99
Fear and Loathing in Las Vegas '98
The Mighty '98
Fire Down Below '97
Never Talk to Strangers '95
One Magic Christmas '85
Christine '84
Red Dawn '84
Private Benjamin '80
Alien '79
Farewell, My Lovely '75
Two Lane Blacktop '71
Rebel Rousers '69
Cool Hand Luke '67
Proud Rebel '58

John Stanton
Rent-A-Cop '88

Robert Stanton
Mercury Rising '98
Red Corner '97

Barbara Stanwyck
The Strange Love of Martha Ivers '46
Double Indemnity '44
Ball of Fire '41
Meet John Doe '41
Stella Dallas '37

Pops Staples
True Stories '86

Jean Stapleton
Dr. Dolittle '98 (V)
You've Got Mail '98
Michael '96
Bury Me in Niagara '93

Maureen Stapleton
Addicted to Love '96
Airport '70
Bye, Bye, Birdie '63

Beau Starr
Prisoner of Love '99
Never Talk to Strangers '95
Goodfellas '90
Halloween 4: The Return of Michael Myers '88
Fletch '85

Mike Starr
Gloria '98
Dumb & Dumber '94
Mad Dog and Glory '93
The Bodyguard '92
Goodfellas '90

Ringo Starr
The Beatles: The First U.S. Visit '91
Yellow Submarine '68 (V)
Magical Mystery Tour '67
Help! '65
A Hard Day's Night '64

Jack Starrett
First Blood '82

David Starzyk
Zig Zag '99

Jason Statham
Lock, Stock and 2 Smoking Barrels '98

Liz Stauber
Teaching Mrs. Tingle '99
Three Kings '99

Imelda Staunton
Shakespeare in Love (CS) '98
Sense and Sensibility '95
Much Ado about Nothing '93

Alison Steadman
Pride and Prejudice '95
The Adventures of Baron Munchausen '89

John Steadman
Fade to Black '80

Ken Steadman
I Like to Play Games '95

Amy Steel
Friday the 13th, Part 2 '81

Anthony Steel
Another Man's Poison '52

Barbara Steele
Piranha '78
They Came from Within '75
Black Sunday '60

Bob Steele
Atomic Submarine '59
Pork Chop Hill '59
The Big Sleep '46
Of Mice and Men '39

Don Steele
Rock 'n' Roll High School '79
Death Race 2000 '75

Fred Steele
The Story of G.I. Joe '45

Rob Steele
Breaker Morant '80

Tommy Steele
The Happiest Millionaire '67

Vernon Steele
They Were Expendable '45

Jan Steen
Antonia's Line '95

Jessica Steen
Armageddon '98
Trial and Error '96

Mary Steenburgen
Noah's Ark '99
Nixon '95
Powder '95
Philadelphia '93
Parenthood '89
One Magic Christmas '85
Melvin and Howard '80

Burr Steers
The Last Days of Disco '98

Leslie Stefanson
The General's Daughter '99

Yvette Stefens
Carnal Crimes '91

Rod Steiger
End of Days '99
Modern Vampires '98
Incognito '97
Truth or Consequences, N.M. '97
Mars Attacks! '96
The Specialist '94
The Player '92
Lion of the Desert '81
The Longest Day '62
Oklahoma '55

Ben Stein
Miami Rhapsody '95
The Mask '94
Dave '93
Honeymoon in Vegas '92
Ghostbusters 2 '89
Ferris Bueller's Day Off '86

Franz Stein
M '31

Margaret Sophie Stein
Skylark '93
Sarah, Plain and Tall '91

Mary Stein
Babe: Pig in the City '98

Saul Stein
New Jersey Drive '95

Margot Steinberg
In Love and War '96

John Steiner
Caligula '80
Beyond the Door 2 '79

Alan Stemm
Night Calls: The Movie 2 '99

Miriam Stepanova
The Dandelion Crown '93

Tony Stephano
Tron '82

Nancy Stephens
Halloween: H20 '98
Halloween '78

Robert Stephens
Chaplin '92
The Bonfire of the Vanities '90
The Asphyx '72

Toby Stephens
Cousin Bette '97

Henry Stephenson
Oliver Twist '48

Pamela Stephenson
History of the World: Part 1 '81

Craig Stepp
Play Time '94

Lesli Kay Sterling
Petticoat Planet '95

Mindy Sterling
Austin Powers 2: The Spy Who Shagged Me '99
Drop Dead Gorgeous '99
Austin Powers: International Man of Mystery '97

Philip Sterling
My Giant '98

Tisha Sterling
The Killer inside Me '76

Daniel Stern
Very Bad Things '98
Home Alone 2: Lost in New York '92
Home Alone '90
My Blue Heaven '90
Leviathan '89
Born in East L.A. '87

Howard Stern
Private Parts '96

Frances Sternhagen
Curtain Call '97
Raising Cain '92
Doc Hollywood '91
Outland '81

Sagamore Stevenin
Romance '99

Andrew Stevens
Scorned 2 '96
Day of the Animals '77

Brinke Stevens
Mommy 2: Mommy's Day '96
Jack-O '95
Masseuse '95
Mommy '95
Grandma's House '88
Slave Girls from Beyond Infinity '87
Sorority Babes in the Slimeball Bowl-A-Rama '87

Carrie Stevens
Jane Street '96

Casey Stevens
Prom Night '80

Charles Stevens
The Three Musketeers '21

Fisher Stevens
Hackers '95
Only You '94
My Science Project '85
The Flamingo Kid '84

Inger Stevens
Madigan '68
Hang 'Em High '67

Paul Stevens
Patton '70

Rise Stevens
Going My Way / Holiday Inn '44

Ronnie Stevens
The Parent Trap '98

Stella Stevens
Bikini Hotel '97
Virtual Combat '95
Hard Drive '94
The Nutt House '92
Monster in the Closet '86

Warren Stevens
Forbidden Planet '56

Cynthia Stevenson
Happiness '98
The Player '92

Juliet Stevenson
Treasure Island '97 (V)
Emma '96
The Trial '93

McLean Stevenson
The Cat from Outer Space '78

Parker Stevenson
Stroker Ace '83

Amy Stewart
Trucks '97

Byron Stewart
Grambling's White Tiger '81

Catherine Mary Stewart
Weekend at Bernie's '89
The Last Starfighter '84
Nighthawks '81

Charlotte Stewart
Tremors '89

Ewan Stewart
The Big Brass Ring '99
Rob Roy '95

James Stewart
How the West Was Won '63
Bell, Book and Candle '58
Vertigo (CE) '58
It's a Wonderful Life '46
Pot o' Gold '41
The Philadelphia Story '40
Made for Each Other '39

Jon Stewart
Big Daddy '99
The Faculty '98
Playing by Heart '98
Half-Baked '97

Kate McGregor Stewart
Father of the Bride '91

Malcolm Stewart
Timecop '94

Mel Stewart
Bride of Re-Animator '89

Patrick Stewart
Moby Dick '98
Prince of Egypt '98 (V)

Star Trek: Insurrection '98
Conspiracy Theory '97
Star Trek: First Contact '96
Star Trek: Generations '94
L.A. Story '91
Lifeforce '85
Dune '84
Excalibur '81

Paul Stewart
Opening Night '77

Robert Stewart
Motel Blue '98

Robin Stewart
The Legend of the 7 Golden Vampires '73

Roy Stewart
Sparrows '26

Sara Stewart
Drop Dead Gorgeous '99

Tonea Stewart
A Time to Kill '96

Phyllis Stickney
What's Love Got to Do with It? '93

David Ogden Stiers
Beauty and the Beast: The Enchanted Christmas '97 (V)
Meet Wally Sparks '97
Everyone Says I Love You '96
Mighty Aphrodite '95
Doc Hollywood '91
Creator '85

Julia Stiles
The '60s '99
Ten Things I Hate about You '99

Ben Stiller
Mystery Men '99
Permanent Midnight '98
There's Something about Mary '98
Your Friends & Neighbors '98
Zero Effect '97
Happy Gilmore '96
Flirting with Disaster '95
Reality Bites '94
Next of Kin '89

Fred Stillkrauth
Cross of Iron '76

Brett Stimely
Bloodstone '88

Sting
Lock, Stock and 2 Smoking Barrels '98
The Adventures of Baron Munchausen '89
Plenty '85
Dune '84

Colin Stinton
In Love and War '96

Nigel Stock
Lost Continent '68
The Great Escape '63

Dean Stockwell
Rites of Passage '99
Air Force One '97
John Grisham's The Rainmaker '97
The Player '92
Quantum Leap: The Pilot Episode '89
Dune '84
Gentleman's Agreement '47

John Stockwell
Top Gun '86
My Science Project '85
Christine '84

Austin Stoker
Assault on Precinct 13 '76

Mink Stole
Pecker '98
Serial Mom '94

Shirley Stoler
Shakedown '88
The Deer Hunter '78
Seven Beauties '76

Fred Stoller
Chairman of the Board '97

Eric Stoltz
A Murder of Crows '99
Mr. Jealousy '98
Anaconda '96
Grace of My Heart (CE) '96
Jerry Maguire '96
Keys to Tulsa '96
The Prophecy '95
Rob Roy '95
Little Women '94
Pulp Fiction '94
Singles '92
Memphis Belle '90
Mask '85

Dorothy Stone
Revolt of the Zombies '36

Julia Stone
Sirens '94

Leonard Stone
Willy Wonka & the Chocolate Factory '71

Lewis Stone
The Lost World '25

Marianne Stone
Lolita '62

Matt Stone
BASEketball '98

Michael Stone
The Quick and the Dead '94

Oliver Stone
Dave '93
Born on the Fourth of July '89
Platoon '86
Scarface '83
Midnight Express '78

Philip Stone
The Shining '80

Sean Stone
JFK '91

Sharon Stone
The Muse '99
Antz '98 (V)
Gloria '98
The Mighty '98
Sphere '97
Casino '95
The Quick and the Dead '94
The Specialist '94
Last Action Hero '93
Basic Instinct '92
Total Recall '90
Blood and Sand '89
Above the Law '88
Action Jackson '88

Stuart Stone
The Boys Club '96

Sherri Stoner
Impulse '84

Paolo Stoppa
The Law '59

Larry Storch
Airport '75 '75

Dennis Storhol
The 13th Warrior '99

Veronica Stork
Combat Shock '84

Adam Storke
Stephen King's The Stand '94
Death Becomes Her '92
The Phantom of the Opera '90

Howard Storm
Take the Money and Run '69

James Storm
Trilogy of Terror '75

Olaf Storm
Metropolis '26

T.J. Storm
Urban Menace '99

Peter Stormare
Armageddon '98
8mm '98
Mercury Rising '98
The Big Lebowski '97
Fargo '96
Playing God '96
Damage '92

Ludwig Stossel
Casablanca '42

Ken Stott
The Boxer '97
Shallow Grave '94

Jerry Stovin
Lolita '62

Madeleine Stowe
The General's Daughter '99
Playing by Heart '98
12 Monkeys '95
Revenge '90
The Two Jakes '90

Henry Stozier
The Curve '97

Beatrice Straight
Poltergeist '82
Network '76

Julie Strain
Red Line '96
Dark Secrets '95
Midnight Confessions '95
Virtual Desire '95
Play Time '94
Sorceress '94
Out for Justice '91

George Strait
Pure Country '92

Ralph Strait
Halloween 3: Season of the Witch '82

Harry Strang
The Fighting Sullivans '42

Glenn Strange
Jailhouse Rock '57

Robert Strange
Dead Men Walk / The Monster Maker '43

Lee Strasberg
The Cassandra Crossing '76

Susan Strasberg
Rollercoaster '77

Teresa Stratas
La Traviata '82

David Strathairn
Limbo '99
William Shakespeare's A Midsummer Night's Dream '99
Simon Birch '98
The Climb '97
L.A. Confidential '97
Dolores Claiborne '94
The River Wild '94
The Firm '93
A League of Their Own '92
Passion Fish '92

Sneakers '92
Memphis Belle '90
Silkwood '83

Peter Strauss
Joan of Arc '99
Keys to Tulsa '96
Nick of Time '95

Robert Strauss
The 4D Man '59

Meryl Streep
Dancing at Lughnasa '98
One True Thing '98
Marvin's Room '96
The Bridges of Madison County '95
The River Wild '94
Death Becomes Her '92
Plenty '85
Silkwood '83
Sophie's Choice '82
The Deer Hunter '78

Barbra Streisand
The Mirror Has Two Faces '96

David Strickland
Forces of Nature '99

Gail Strickland
Protocol '84

Sherry Stringfield
54 '98

Randy Stripling
October Sky '99

Oliver Stritzel
Das Boot (DC) '81

Joe Strnad
The Deer Hunter '78

Preston Strobel
Cookie's Fortune '99

Alexander Strobele
The Peacemaker '97

Woody Strode
Posse '93
Vigilante '83
Shalako '68
The Professionals '66
Spartacus '60
Pork Chop Hill '59

Andrew Strong
The Commitments '91

Brenda Strong
Undercurrent '99
Black Dog '98
The Deep End of the Ocean '98

John Strong
The Glimmer Man '96

Mark Strong
Twice upon a Yesterday '98

Michael Strong
Patton '70

Randi-Lynn Strong
A Kid Called Danger '99

Rider Strong
My Giant '98

Dorothy Strongin
Basket Case '82

Don Stroud
Wild America '97
Cartel '90
Hyper Space '89
The Buddy Holly Story '78
The Killer inside Me '76
Joe Kidd '72
Madigan '68

Sally Struthers
The Getaway '72

Carel Struycken
The Witches of Eastwick '87

Amy Stryker
Impulse '84

Gloria Stuart
The Love Letter '99
Titanic '97
The Old Dark House '32

John Stuart
No. 17 '32

Imogen Stubbs
Sense and Sensibility '95

Levi Stubbs Jr.
Little Shop of Horrors '86 (V)

Wes Studi
Mystery Men '99
Deep Rising '98
The Killing Jar '96
Heat '95
Street Fighter '94
Geronimo: An American Legend '93
The Doors '91
Dances with Wolves '90

Jerzy Stuhr
The Decalogue '88

Neil Stuke
Twice upon a Yesterday '98

Johnny Stumper
Mob War '88

Shannon Sturges
Convict 762 '98

Darlene Stuto
Ms. 45 '81

Tara Subkoff
The Last Days of Disco '98
As Good As It Gets '97
Black Circle Boys '97

David Suchet
Wing Commander '99
A Perfect Murder '98
Executive Decision '96
The Falcon and the Snowman '85

Skipp Sudduth
54 '98
Ronin '98

Kin Sugai
The Funeral '84

Barbara Sukowa
Johnny Mnemonic '95

Barry Sullivan
Earthquake '74

Brad Sullivan
Sister Act 2: Back in the Habit '93
Guilty by Suspicion '91
Funny Farm '88

Ed Sullivan
The Beatles: The First U.S. Visit '91
Bye, Bye, Birdie '63

Francis L. Sullivan
Oliver Twist '48
Great Expectations '46

Susan Sullivan
My Best Friend's Wedding '97

Cree Summer
The Rugrats Movie '98 (V)

Slim Summerville
All Quiet on the Western Front '30

Paulyn Sun
Island of Greed '97

Raymond Sun
Shaolin Avengers '94

Bunny Sunshine
The Southerner '45

Ethan Suplee
American History X '98
Desert Blue '98

Nicolas Surovy
Forever Young '92

Victoria Sus
Evita '96

Claudette Sutherland
Man of the Year '95

Donald Sutherland
Instinct '99
Virus '98
The Assignment '97
Fallen '97
Without Limits '97
A Time to Kill '96
Disclosure '94
Outbreak '94
Backdraft '91
JFK '91
Lock Up '89
The Great Train Robbery '79
Invasion of the Body Snatchers '78
National Lampoon's Animal House '78
Kentucky Fried Movie '77
The Dirty Dozen '67

Joan Sutherland
Maria Stuarda '88 (V)

Kiefer Sutherland
The Break Up '98
Ground Control '98
Dark City '97
Truth or Consequences, N.M. '97
A Time to Kill '96
Armitage 3: Polymatrix '94 (V)
The Cowboy Way '94
The Three Musketeers '93
A Few Good Men '92
Flatliners '90
Young Guns '88
The Lost Boys '87
Stand by Me '86

James Sutorius
Whisper Kill '88

Dudley Sutton
Orlando '92

John Sutton
The Bat '59

Michael Sutton
Wanted '98

Mena Suvari
American Pie (CE) '99
Atomic Train '99
The Rage: Carrie 2 '99

Janet Suzman
And the Ship Sails On '83
The Draughtsman's Contract '82
Nicholas and Alexandra '71

David Svec
Mandragora '97

Oliver Sveinall
The 13th Warrior '99

Bo Svenson
Speed 2: Cruise Control '97
Private Obsession '94
Steele's Law '91

Bob Swaim
Spies Like Us '85

Dominique Swain
Face/Off '97

Mack Swain
The Gold Rush '25

Tillie's Punctured Romance '14

Hilary Swank
Boys Don't Cry '99
Sometimes They Come Back ... Again '96

Brenda Swanson
Secret Games 3 '94

Gary Swanson
The Guardian '90

Gloria Swanson
Airport '75 '75
The Love Goddesses '65
Male and Female '19

Jackie Swanson
Lethal Weapon '87

Kristy Swanson
Big Daddy '99
Supreme Sanction '99
Ground Control '98
The Phantom '96
Ferris Bueller's Day Off '86

Rochelle Swanson
Hard Bounty '94
Night Fire '94
Secret Games 3 '94

Don Swayze
Sexual Malice '93
Trapper County War '89

Patrick Swayze
Black Dog '98
Next of Kin '89
Dirty Dancing '87
Dirty Dancing (CE) '87
Red Dawn '84
The Outsiders '83

Birdy Sweeney
The Crying Game '92

D.B. Sweeney
Spawn (SE) '97
Memphis Belle '90

Julia Sweeney
Stuart Little '99
Vegas Vacation '96
Pulp Fiction '94

Steve Sweeney
Lock, Stock and 2 Smoking Barrels '98

Vonte Sweet
American Strays '96
Menace II Society '93

Jeep Swenson
Batman and Robin '97
Bulletproof '96

Tommy Swerdlow
Child's Play '88
Hamburger Hill '87

Joel Swetow
Lord of Illusions '95

Francie Swift
Last Breath '96

Eliel Swinton
Varsity Blues '98

Tilda Swinton
Orlando '92

Loretta Swit
Dreams of Gold: The Mel Fisher Story '86

Tracy Brooks Swope
The Power of One '92

Brenda Sykes
Cleopatra Jones '73

Eugena Sylvaw
Passion of Joan of Arc '28

William Sylvester
2001: A Space Odyssey '68

Benj Thall
Homeward Bound: The
Incredible Journey '93

Torin Thatcher
The Seventh Voyage of Sin-
bad '58
The Snows of Kilimanjaro '52
Great Expectations '46
Young and Innocent '37
Sabotage '36

John Thaw
Chaplin '92
Cry Freedom '87

Max Thayer
Retrievers '82

Brooke Theiss
A Nightmare on Elm Street 4:
Dream Master '88

Joseph Thelman
Tombs of the Blind Dead '72

Brother Theodore
The 'Burbs '89

Serge Theriault
The Boys '97

Charlize Theron
The Astronaut's Wife '99
Celebrity '98
Mighty Joe Young '98
The Devil's Advocate '97
Trial and Error '96

Ernest Thesiger
A Christmas Carol '51
Henry V '44
The Bride of Frankenstein '35
The Old Dark House '32

David Thewlis
Besieged '98
The Big Lebowski '97
Seven Years in Tibet '97
Dragonheart (SE) '96
The Island of Dr. Moreau '96
Total Eclipse '95
Restoration '94

Jack Thibeau
Lethal Weapon '87
Ms. 45 '81
Apocalypse Now '79

Rose Thiery
Beau Pere '81

Joe Thiesman
Good Luck '96

Tiffani-Amber Thiessen
From Dusk Till Dawn 2: Texas
Blood Money '98
Son-in-Law '93

Lynne Thigpen
The Insider '99
Just Cause '94
The Paper '94
Lean on Me '89
Streets of Fire '84

Chief Ted Thin Elk
Thunderheart '92

Roy Thinnes
Rush Week '88
Airport '75 '75
The Hindenburg '75
Journey to the Far Side of the
Sun '69

Victorie Thivisol
Ponette '95

Alex Thomas
The Players Club '98

Damien Thomas
The Message '77

Dave Thomas
Stripes '81

Doug Thomas
Hangmen '87

Eddie Kaye Thomas
American Pie (CE) '99
The Rage: Carrie 2 '99

Harry Thomas
Glen or Glenda? '53

Heather Thomas
My Giant '98

Henry Thomas
Moby Dick '98
Suicide Kings '97
Legends of the Fall '94

Jameson Thomas
The Farmer's Wife '28

Jay Thomas
Mr. Holland's Opus '95

Jennifer Thomas
Desolation Angels '95

Jonathan Taylor Thomas
I'll Be Home for Christmas
'98
Wild America '97
The Adventures of Pinocchio
'96

Koran C. Thomas
New Jersey Drive '95

Leonard Thomas
Bad Lieutenant '92

Marlo Thomas
The Real Blonde '97

Michelle Rene Thomas
The Last Don '97

Richard Thomas
Winning '69

Robin Thomas
About Last Night . . . '86

Ron Thomas
Night Screams '87

Rufus Thomas
Cookie's Fortune '99

Sean Patrick Thomas
Cruel Intentions '98

Sharon Thomas
Young Guns '88

Tamara Craig Thomas
The Curve '97

Theodore Thomas
Timecop '94

Tim Thomerson
Fear and Loathing in Las
Vegas '98
Die Watching '93
Nemesis '93
Air America '90
Fade to Black '80

Vendela Thommessen
Batman and Robin '97

**Alfred "Rubin"
Thompson**
Winner Takes All '98

Anna Thompson
Six Ways to Sunday '99

Brian Thompson
Mortal Kombat 2: Annihila-
tion '97
Dragonheart (SE) '96
The Naked Truth '92
Lionheart '90

Derek Thompson
The Long Good Friday '80

Elizabeth Thompson
The Car '77

Emma Thompson
Primary Colors '98
Sense and Sensibility '95
Junior '94
In the Name of the Father '93
Much Ado about Nothing '93
Howard's End '92
Dead Again '91

Fred Dalton Thompson
In the Line of Fire '93
Thunderheart '92
Days of Thunder '90
Die Hard 2: Die Harder '90
The Hunt for Red October '90

Hal Thompson
Animal Crackers '30

Jack Thompson
Midnight in the Garden of
Good and Evil (SE) '97
Excess Baggage '96
Breaker Morant '80

John Thompson
Redline '97

Joy Thompson
Prom Night '80

Lea Thompson
Casual Sex? '88
Red Dawn '84

Marshall Thompson
First Man into Space '59
They Were Expendable '45

Rex Thompson
The King and I '56

Ron Thompson
American Pop '81 (V)

Scott Thompson
Armistead Maupin's More
Tales of the City '97

Shaun Thompson
In God's Hands '98

Shawn Thompson
Bram Stoker's Shadowbuilder
'98

Shelley Thompson
Labyrinth '86

Sophie Thompson
Dancing at Lughnasa '98
Emma '96
Four Weddings and a Funeral
'94

William C. Thompson
Glen or Glenda? '53

Gregg Thomsen
Soultaker '90

Anna Thomson
Drunks '96
The Crow '93
Unforgiven '92

R.H. Thomson
The Quarrel '93
Ticket to Heaven '81

Frankie Thorn
Bad Lieutenant '92

Bill Thornbury
Phantasm '79

Russell Thorndike
Henry V '44

Courtney Thorne-Smith
Chairman of the Board '97

Billy Bob Thornton
Pushing Tin '99
Armageddon '98
Primary Colors '98
A Simple Plan '98
The Apostle '97
U-Turn '97
Sling Blade '96

Floundering '94
On Deadly Ground '94
Tombstone '93

David Thornton
Hush '98
The Last Days of Disco '98
Home Alone 3 '97

Sven-Ole Thorsen
Foolish '99
Kull the Conqueror '97
Dragon: The Bruce Lee Story
'93
Abraxas: Guardian of the Uni-
verse '90

Linda Thorson
The Other Sister '98

Frank Thring Jr.
Mad Max: Beyond Thunder-
dome '85

Ingrid Thulin
The Cassandra Crossing '76

Theodora Thurman
Jail Bait '54

Uma Thurman
The Avengers '98
Batman and Robin '97
Gattaca '97
Les Miserables '97
Beautiful Girls '96
Pulp Fiction '94
Mad Dog and Glory '93
Final Analysis '92
Henry & June '90
The Adventures of Baron
Munchausen '89
Dangerous Liaisons '88

Sophie Thursfield
Sister My Sister '94

Greta Thyssen
Terror Is a Man '59

Nancy Ticotin
Ransom '96

Rachel Ticotin
Con Air '97
Turbulence '96
Don Juan DeMarco '94
Falling Down '93
Total Recall '90

Inga Tidblad
Intermezzo '36

James Tien
Half a Loaf of Kung Fu '85
The Dragon Fist '80
Chinese Connection '73

Andrew Tiernan
Playing God '96

Brigid Tierney
Affliction '97

Edward Tierney
The Hoodlum '51

Gene Tierney
The Shanghai Gesture '42

Jacob Tierney
This Is My Father '99
Dead End '98

Lawrence Tierney
Southie '98
Reservoir Dogs '92
Prizzi's Honor '85
Custer of the West '67
The Hoodlum '51

Maura Tierney
Forces of Nature '99
Instinct '99
Primary Colors '98
Liar Liar '96
Primal Fear '96

Steven Tietsort
Stripshow '95

Kevin Tighe
Mumford '99
Geronimo: An American Leg-
end '93
A Man in Uniform '93
School Ties '92
Another 48 Hrs. '90
K-9 '89

Ramon Tikaram
Kama Sutra: A Tale of Love
'96

Robert Tiller
China O'Brien '88

Jennifer Tilly
Hide and Seek '00
Bartok the Magnificent '99
(V)
The Muse '99
Stuart Little '99 (V)
Bride of Chucky '98
American Strays '96
Bound '96
Liar Liar '96
Embrace of the Vampire '95
The Pompatus of Love '95
Bullets over Broadway '94
The Getaway '93
Made in America '93
The Fabulous Baker Boys '89

Meg Tilly
Body Snatchers '93
The Two Jakes '90
Impulse '84
The Big Chill '83
Psycho 2 '83
Tex '82

Alan Tilvern
Who Framed Roger Rabbit
'88

Charles Tingwell
The Castle '97
Breaker Morant '80
Dracula, Prince of Darkness
'66

Gabriele Tinti
Emmanuelle: Queen of the
Desert '79
Lisa and the Devil / The
House of Exorcism '75

Jamie Tirelli
Lotto Land '95

Alex To
Inspector Wears Skirts '88

Kenneth Tobey
Body Shot '93
Single White Female '92
The Great Locomotive Chase
'56

George Tobias
The Hunchback of Notre
Dame '39

Oliver Tobias
Breeders '97

Dan Tobin
Woman of the Year '42

Stephen Tobolowsky
The Insider '99
Black Dog '98
Boys Life 2 '98
Mr. Magoo '97
The Glimmer Man '96
Radioland Murders '94
Groundhog Day '93
Basic Instinct '92
Hero '92
Single White Female '92
Sneakers '92
Thelma & Louise '91
Bird on a Wire '90
Mississippi Burning '88

Brian Tochi
The Player '92

Ann Todd
The Paradine Case '47

Antonio Todd
The Fear '94

Beverly Todd
Lean on Me '89

Richard Todd
The Longest Day '62

Sonia Todd
Shine '95

Thelma Todd
Laurel and Hardy and Friends
  '90s
Horse Feathers '32
Monkey Business '31

Tony Todd
Bram Stoker's Shadowbuilder
  '98
Caught Up '98
The Pandora Project '98
Wishmaster '97
The Rock '96
The Crow '93
Candyman '92
Platoon '86

Bruno Todeschini
La Sentinelle '92

Chotaro Togin
Godzilla's Revenge '69

Ugo Tognazzi
Don't Touch the White
  Woman! '74
Barbarella '68

Niall Toibin
Rawhead Rex '87

**Michael (Lawrence)
Tolan**
Presumed Innocent '90

Fabiola Toledo
Demons '86

James Tolkan
Underworld '96
Boiling Point '93

Michael Tolkin
The Player '92

Lauren Tom
When a Man Loves a Woman
  '94

Nicholle Tom
Beethoven's 2nd '93
Beethoven '92

Concetta Tomei
The Muse '99

Marisa Tomei
Slums of Beverly Hills '98
A Brother's Kiss '97
Four Rooms '95
Only You '94
The Paper '94
Chaplin '92

Frances Tomelty
The Field '90

Joseph Tomelty
A Night to Remember '58

Tamlyn Tomita
The Killing Jar '96
Four Rooms '95

Lily Tomlin
Tea with Mussolini '99
Flirting with Disaster '95
The Player '92
All of Me '84

David Tomlinson
Mary Poppins '64

Tom Jones '63

Stephen Tompkinson
Brassed Off '96

Jerry S. Tondo
Mulan '98 (V)

Franchot Tone
Dark Waters '44

Tone Loc
Freedom Strike '98
Heat '95
Ace Ventura: Pet Detective
  '93
Posse '93

Eric Tonken
Beware! Children at Play '95

Eijiro Tono
Tora! Tora! Tora! '70
The Human Condition: No
  Greater Love '58

Regis Toomey
The Bishop's Wife '47
The Big Sleep '46
Spellbound '45
Meet John Doe '41

Lisa Toothman
Eye of the Serpent '94

Gordon Tootoosis
Legends of the Fall '94

Chaim Topol
For Your Eyes Only (SE) '81
Flash Gordon '80
Fiddler on the Roof '71

Roland Topor
Nosferatu the Vampyre '79

Mark Torgl
The Toxic Avenger (DC) '86

Rip Torn
The Insider '99
Senseless '98
Hercules '97 (V)
Trial and Error '96
How to Make an American
  Quilt '95
Where the Rivers Flow North
  '94
RoboCop 3 '91
Cat on a Hot Tin Roof '84
Coma '78
The Man Who Fell to Earth
  '76
Pork Chop Hill '59

Hengko Tornando
Lady Dragon '92

Regina Torne
Like Water for Chocolate '93

David Torrence
Tess of the Storm Country
  '22

Ernest Torrence
Steamboat Bill, Jr. '28
Peter Pan '24
Tol'able David '21

Pip Torrens
Incognito '97

Ana Torrent
Thesis '96
Blood and Sand '89

Raquel Torres
Duck Soup '33

Guy Torry
Life '99
American History X '98

Joe Torry
Sprung '96
Tales from the Hood '95
Poetic Justice '93

Sylvia Tortosa
Horror Express '72

Michael Tough
Prom Night '80

Huguette Tourangeau
Maria Stuarda '88 (V)

Sheila Tousey
Thunderheart '92

Lorraine Toussaint
Dangerous Minds '95
Mother's Boys '94
Point of No Return '93

Loreta Tovar
Return of the Blind Dead '75

Luis Felipe Tovar
Midaq Alley '95

Constance Towers
A Perfect Murder '98
Naked Kiss '64
Shock Corridor '63

Tom Towles
Gridlock'd '96
Mad Dog and Glory '93
Henry: Portrait of a Serial
  Killer '90

Robert Townsend
Streets of Fire '84

Stuart Townsend
Shooting Fish '98

Christine Toy
Nunsense '93

Giorgio Tozzi
South Pacific '58 (V)

Ian Tracey
Timecop '94

Margaret Tracey
George Balanchine's The Nutcracker '93

Jeff Trachta
Interlocked '98

Michelle Trachtenberg
Inspector Gadget '99

Spencer Tracy
Guess Who's Coming to Din-
  ner '67
How the West Was Won '63
Last Hurrah '58
Father's Little Dividend '51
Adam's Rib '50
Woman of the Year '42

Mary Ellen Trainor
Ricochet '91
Lethal Weapon 2 '89
Die Hard '88
Lethal Weapon '87

Thuy Trang
The Crow 2: City of Angels
  '96

Raoul Traucher
The Reincarnation of Isabel
  '72

Daniel J. Travanti
Just Cause '94
Millennium '89

Henry Travers
It's a Wonderful Life '46
The Bells of St. Mary's '45
Ball of Fire '41
Dark Victory '39

Linden Travers
The Lady Vanishes '38

Susan Travers
Peeping Tom '60

Kylie Travis
Sanctuary '98
Retroactive '97

Nancy Travis
Greedy '94
So I Married an Axe Murderer
  '93
Chaplin '92
Air America '90
Internal Affairs '90

Randy Travis
Black Dog '98
T.N.T. '98
Boys Will Be Boys '97
Fire Down Below '97
John Grisham's The Rainmak-
  er '97
Frank and Jesse '94

Joey Travolta
Dumb Luck in Vegas '97
The Last Game '95
Amazon Women on the Moon
  '87

John Travolta
The General's Daughter '99
A Civil Action '98
Primary Colors '98
The Thin Red Line '98
Face/Off '97
Mad City '97
Michael '96
Phenomenon '96
Broken Arrow '95
Get Shorty '95
White Man's Burden '95
Pulp Fiction '94
Look Who's Talking '89
The Boy in the Plastic Bubble
  '76
Devil's Rain '75

Susan Traylor
Bastard out of Carolina '96
To Die For '95

Arthur Treacher
National Velvet '44

Daniel Treat
Shadrach '98

Mary Treen
It's a Wonderful Life '46

Peter Tregloan
Grim '95

Danny Trejo
Desert Heat '99
From Dusk Till Dawn 3: The
  Hangman's Daughter '99
From Dusk Till Dawn 2: Texas
  Blood Money '98
Point Blank '98
The Replacement Killers '98
Six Days, Seven Nights '98
Con Air '97
Anaconda '96
Champions '96
From Dusk Till Dawn '95

Christine Tremarco
Priest '94

Les Tremayne
Forbidden Planet '56 (N)
The War of the Worlds '53

Adam Trese
Polish Wedding '97
The Underneath '95

N. Tretyakova
Aelita: Queen of Mars '24

Hilda Trevelyan
The 39 Steps '35

Frederick Treves
Shameless '94

Vic Trevino
Born in East L.A. '87

Austin Trevor
Sabotage '36

Claire Trevor
Raw Deal '48
Stagecoach '39

Amy Tribbey
Suspicions '95

Paula Trickey
The Base '99
Carnal Crimes '91

Ivan Triesault
The Amazing Transparent
  Man '60

Sergej Trifunovic
Savior '98

Sarah Trigger
Good Luck '96
Things to Do in Denver When
  You're Dead '95
Don't Do It '94
Deadfall '93
Sleepless in Seattle '93

Jerry Trimble
The Master '92

Susie Trinh
The Corruptor '99

Jean-Louis Trintignant
The City of Lost Children '95
  (V)
Confidentially Yours '83
My Night at Maud's '69

Marie Trintignant
Ponette '95

Jeanne Tripplehorn
Monument Ave. '98
Very Bad Things '98
Sliding Doors '97
Waterworld '95
Reality Bites '94
The Firm '93
Basic Instinct '92

Jan Triska
Ronin '98
Apt Pupil '97
The People vs. Larry Flynt '96

Travis Tritt
Outlaw Justice '98
The Cowboy Way '94

Massimo Troisi
The Postman '94

Patrick Troughton
The Viking Queen '67

Charles Trowbridge
They Were Expendable '45

Verne Troyer
Austin Powers 2: The Spy
  Who Shagged Me '99

Michael Trubshawe
The Guns of Navarone '61

John Trudell
Smoke Signals '98
Thunderheart '92

Jim True
Affliction '97
The Hudsucker Proxy '93
Singles '92

Rachel True
Half-Baked '97
The Craft '96
Embrace of the Vampire '95

Ernest Truex
His Girl Friday '40

Francois Truffaut
The 400 Blows '59

Sally Truitt
Angel in Training '99

Raoul Trujillo
Waking Up Horton '99

Ralph Truman
Henry V '44

Karen Trumbo
Jessica: A Love Story '92

Donald Trump
Celebrity '98
Home Alone 2: Lost in New
York '92

Kirk Trutner
Dante's Peak '97

Tom Tryon
The Longest Day '62

Eric Tsang
Hitman '98
Supercop 2 '93

Kenneth Tsang
The Replacement Killers '98
Supercop '92
The Killer '90

Tanzin Thuthob Tsarong
Kundun '97

Ludmila Tselikovskaya
Ivan the Terrible, Part 2 '46
Ivan the Terrible, Part 1 '44

Nikolai Tseretelli
Aelita: Queen of Mars '24

Irene Tsu
The Green Berets '68

Yoshio Tsuchiya
Godzilla vs. Monster Zero '68
Seven Samurai '54

Elvis Tsui
Erotic Ghost Story: Perfect
Match '97
The Fruit Is Swelling '97
Prison on Fire 2 '91

Kam-Kong Tsui
Deadful Melody '92
Prison on Fire 2 '91

Shinya Tsukamoto
Tokyo Fist '96
Tetsuo: The Iron Man '92

Yoko Tsukasa
Chushingura '62

Koji Tsurata
Samurai 3: Duel at Ganryu
Island '56

Keiko Tsushima
Seven Samurai '54

Barry Tubb
Guilty by Suspicion '91
Top Gun '86
Mask '85

William Tubbs
Wages of Fear '55

Marcelo Tubert
Tremors 2: Aftershocks '96

Maria Tucci
To Die For '95

Stanley Tucci
In Too Deep '99
William Shakespeare's A Mid-
summer Night's Dream '99
The Alarmist '98
The Imposters '98
Deconstructing Harry '97
A Life Less Ordinary '97
Big Night '95
Sex and the Other Man '95
The Pelican Brief '93
Beethoven '92

Jessica Tuck
Batman Forever '95

Chris Tucker
Rush Hour '98
The Fifth Element '97
Dead Presidents '95
Friday '95

Forrest Tucker
Rage at Dawn '55
Sands of Iwo Jima '49
The Westerner '40

Jonathan Tucker
Sleepers '96

Larry Tucker
Shock Corridor '63

Michael Tucker
For Love of a Child '90

Richard Tucker
The Bat Whispers '30

Dick Tufeld
Lost in Space '98 (V)

Marco Tulli
Beat the Devil '53

Tom Tully
The Caine Mutiny '54

Bill Tung
Jackie Chan's First Strike '96
Rumble in the Bronx '96

Tamara Tunie
Snake Eyes '98
The Devil's Advocate '97
Eve's Bayou '97 (N)

D'lana Tunnell
Sore Losers '97

Robin Tunney
End of Days '99
The Craft '96
Encino Man '92

Paige Turco
The Pompatus of Love '95

Paolo Turco
The Lickerish Quartet '70

Ann Turkel
The Fear '94
Humanoids from the Deep
'80
The Cassandra Crossing '76

Joe Turkel
Blade Runner (DC) '82
The Shining '80
Paths of Glory '57
The Killing '56

Glynn Turman
Deep Cover '92
Gremlins '84
Penitentiary 2 '82

John Turnbull
The 39 Steps '35

Janine Turner
Leave It to Beaver '97
Cliffhanger '93

Jim Turner
Joe's Apartment '96

John Turner
The Slipper and the Rose '76

Kathleen Turner
Baby Geniuses '98
The Real Blonde '97
A Simple Wish '97
Serial Mom '94
Peggy Sue Got Married '86
Prizzi's Honor '85
Crimes of Passion '84
The Man with Two Brains '83
Body Heat '81

Timothy Turner
The Haunted Strangler '58

Tina Turner
Mad Max: Beyond Thunder-
dome '85

Tyrin Turner
Belly '98
Menace II Society '93

Zara Turner
Sliding Doors '97

Ben Turpin
Chaplin's Essanay Comedies,
Vol. 1 '90s
Chaplin's Essanay Comedies,
Vol. 2 '90s
Chaplin's Essanay Comedies,
Vol. 3 '90s
Chaplin's Art of Comedy '66

Aida Turturro
Deep Blue Sea '99
Celebrity '98
Sleepers '96
Junior '94

John Turturro
He Got Game '98
Rounders '98
The Big Lebowski '97
Box of Moonlight '96
Grace of My Heart (CE) '96
Clockers '95
Quiz Show '94
Fearless '93
Jungle Fever '91
Do the Right Thing '89
Five Corners '88
The Color of Money '86

Nicholas Turturro
Excess Baggage '96

Rita Tushingham
Rachel's Man '75
Smashing Time '67

Dorothy Tutin
Alive and Kicking '96

Shannon Tweed
Face the Evil '97
Hard Vice '94
Night Fire '94
The Naked Truth '92
The Firing Line '91

Twiggy
The Blues Brothers (CE) '80

Billy Two Rivers
Black Robe '91

Anne Twomey
The Confession '98
Picture Perfect '96

Ian Tyler
Full Metal Jacket '87

Judy Tyler
Jailhouse Rock '57

Liv Tyler
Cookie's Fortune '99
Armageddon '98
U-Turn '97

Tom Tyler
Stagecoach '39

George Tyne
Sands of Iwo Jima '49

Charles Tyner
Cool Hand Luke '67

Susan Tyrrell
The Demolitionist '95
Powder '95
Tales of Ordinary Madness
'83
The Killer inside Me '76
Shoot Out '71

Barbara Tyson
Resurrection '99

Cathy Tyson
Priest '94
The Serpent and the Rainbow
'87

Cicely Tyson
Life '99
Fried Green Tomatoes '91
Bustin' Loose '81

Pamela Tyson
What's Love Got to Do with
It? '93

Richard Tyson
The Pandora Project '98
Monsoon '97
Kindergarten Cop '90

Margaret Tyzack
Mrs. Dalloway '97
2001: A Space Odyssey '68

V. Tzoppi
Storm over Asia '28

Asao Uchida
Tora! Tora! Tora! '70

Ryohei Uchida
The Human Condition: Road
to Eternity '59

Fabiana Udenio
Austin Powers: International
Man of Mystery '97
Bride of Re-Animator '89

Kichijiro Ueda
Seven Samurai '54

Kenjiro Uemura
The Human Condition: Road
to Eternity '59

Tracey Ullman
Bullets over Broadway '94
Ready to Wear '94
Plenty '85

Liv Ullmann
The Long Shadow '92
A Bridge Too Far '77
Cold Sweat '71

Skeet Ulrich
As Good As It Gets '97
The Newton Boys '97
Albino Alligator '96
The Craft '96
Scream (CS) '96

Marianne O. Ulrichsen
Insomnia '97

Edward Underdown
Beat the Devil '53

Blair Underwood
Deep Impact '98
Set It Off '96
Just Cause '94
Posse '93

Jay Underwood
Uncle Buck '89

Deborah Kara Unger
Payback '98
The Rat Pack '98
The Game '97
Keys to Tulsa '96
Crash '95

Gabrielle Union
She's All That '99
Ten Things I Hate about You
'99

Mary Ure
Custer of the West '67

Justin Urich
The Rage: Carrie 2 '99
Boys Life 2 '98

**Benny "The Jet"
Urquidez**
Grosse Pointe Blank '97

Jun Usami
Tora! Tora! Tora! '70

Peter Ustinov
Alice in Wonderland '99
The Bachelor '99
Around the World in 80 Days
'89
Logan's Run '76
Spartacus '60
Lola Montes '55

Brenda Vaccaro
The Mirror Has Two Faces '96
The First Deadly Sin '80
Capricorn One '78
Midnight Cowboy '69

David Vadim
Air Force One '97

William Vail
The Texas Chainsaw Mas-
sacre '74

Charlotte Valandrey
Orlando '92

**Armando Valdes-
Kennedy**
Billy's Hollywood Screen Kiss
'98

Jerry Vale
Casino '95
Goodfellas '90

Joseph Valencia
Pocket Ninjas '93

Vladimir Valenta
The Unbearable Lightness of
Being '88

Nathan Valente
Boston Kickout '95

Barbara Valentin
Carmen, Baby '66

Karen Valentine
The North Avenue Irregulars
'79

Kim Valentine
Grandma's House '88

Scott Valentine
Paranoia '98
Object of Obsession '95
True Stories '86

Rosa Valetti
M '31

Marcel Vallee
The Crazy Ray '22

Mark Valley
The Siege '98

Alida Valli
The Cassandra Crossing '76
Lisa and the Devil / The
House of Exorcism '75
The Third Man '49
The Paradine Case '47

Raf Vallone
Lion of the Desert '81
Two Women '61

Jean Valmont
Time Masters '82 (V)

Vampira
Plan 9 from Outer Space '56

Willeke Van Ammelrooy
Antonia's Line '95

Lewis Van Bergen
The Relic '96
Bugsy '91

Tomas Van Bromssen
My Life As a Dog '85

Lee Van Cleef
Bad Man's River '72
The Good, the Bad and the
Ugly '67
For a Few Dollars More '65
The Conqueror '56
Big Combo '55
High Noon '52

Jean-Claude Van Damme
Desert Heat '99
Universal Soldier: The Return
'99
Knock Off '98
Legionnaire '98
Double Team '97
The Quest '96
Street Fighter '94
Timecop '94
Hard Target '93

John Grisham's The Rainmaker '97
Most Wanted '97
U-Turn '97
Anaconda '96
Mission: Impossible '96
Rosewood '96
Heat '95
Runaway Train '85
The Odessa File '74
Deliverance '72
Midnight Cowboy '69

John Voldstad
Leprechaun '93

Gian Marie Volonte
For a Few Dollars More '65
A Fistful of Dollars '64

Daniel von Bargen
The General's Daughter '99
Universal Soldier: The Return '99
The Postman '97
Stephen King's Thinner '96
Lord of Illusions '95
Philadelphia '93

Erik von Detten
Leave It to Beaver '97
Top Dog '95

Lenny Von Dohlen
Home Alone 3 '97

Clement von Franckenstein
Underground '90

Loni von Friedl
Journey to the Far Side of the Sun '69

Wilhelm von Homburg
Ghostbusters 2 '89

Rik von Nutter
Thunderball '65

Heidi von Palleske
Strip Search '97
Dead Ringers '88

Heinrich von Schellendorf
Rawhead Rex '87

Gustav von Seyffertitz
She '35
The Bells / The Crazy Ray '26
Sparrows '26

Erich von Stroheim
Portrait of an Assassin '49
The Mask of Diijon '46
Grand Illusion '37
Intolerance '16
The Birth of a Nation '15

Max von Sydow
What Dreams May Come '98
Judge Dredd '95
Needful Things '93
Awakenings '90
Dreamscape (SE) '84
Dune '84
Conan the Barbarian '82
Victory '81
Flash Gordon '80
Three Days of the Condor '75
The Exorcist (SE) '73
The Seventh Seal '56

Hans von Twardowski
The Cabinet of Dr. Caligari '19

Gustav von Wagenheim
Nosferatu '22

Hertha von Walther
M '31

Danielle von Zerneck
La Bamba '87
My Science Project '85

Lark Voorhies
Def Jam's How to Be a Player '97

Arnold Vosloo
The Mummy '99
Progeny '98
Diary of a Serial Killer '97
Zeus and Roxanne '96
Darkman 2: The Return of Durant '94
Hard Target '93

Frank Vosper
The Man Who Knew Too Much '34

Yorgo Voyagis
Frantic '88

Vlasta Vrana
The Assignment '97

Frederick Vroom
The General '26
The Navigator '24

Olivera Vuco
Mark of the Devil '69

Milena Vukotic
Andy Warhol's Dracula '74

Waigwa Wachira
Gorillas in the Mist '88

Steven Waddington
Sleepy Hollow '99
Tarzan and the Lost City '98

Sara Lee Wade
Darkroom '90

Julian Wadham
A Merry War '97
The English Patient '96

Anthony Wager
Great Expectations '46

Jack Wagner
Swimsuit '89

Kristina Malandro Wagner
Double Dragon '94

Lindsay Wagner
Ricochet '91
Nighthawks '81

Natasha Gregson Wagner
Stranger than Fiction '99
Another Day in Paradise '98
Modern Vampires '98
Urban Legend '98

Robert Wagner
Austin Powers 2: The Spy Who Shagged Me '99
Wild Things '98
Austin Powers: International Man of Mystery '97
Dragon: The Bruce Lee Story '93
The Player '92
Around the World in 80 Days '89
Midway '76
The Towering Inferno '74
Winning '69
The Pink Panther '64
The Longest Day '62
Beneath the 12-Mile Reef '53

Yuen Wah
The Master '92
Supercop '92
Dragons Forever '88

Donnie Wahlberg
The Sixth Sense '99
Southie '98
Black Circle Boys '97
Ransom '96

Mark Wahlberg
The Corruptor '99

Three Kings '99
The Big Hit '98
Boogie Nights '97
Fear '96
The Basketball Diaries '94

Lam Wai
Long Arm of the Law '84

Shum Wai
Long Arm of the Law '84

James Wainwright
Joe Kidd '72

Ralph Waite
Cliffhanger '93
The Bodyguard '92
Cool Hand Luke '67

Thomas G. Waites
The Clan of the Cave Bear '86
The Thing '82

Tom Waits
Mystery Men '99
Dracula '92
Queens Logic '91
Shakedown '88
The Outsiders '83
Rumble Fish '83

Hugh Wakefield
The Man Who Knew Too Much '34

Anton Walbrook
Lola Montes '55
The Red Shoes '48

Gregory Walcott
Joe Kidd '72
Plan 9 from Outer Space '56

Mary Walden
Devonsville Terror '83

Shawna Waldron
The American President '95

Wally Wales
Sagebrush Trail '33

Sonya Walger
Noah's Ark '99

Christopher Walken
The Eternal Kiss of the Mummy '99
The Prophecy 3: The Ascent '99
Sarah, Plain and Tall: Winter's End '99
Sleepy Hollow '99
Antz '98 (V)
Blast from the Past '98
New Rose Hotel '98
Mouse Hunt '97
The Prophecy 2: Ashtown '97
Suicide Kings '97
Excess Baggage '96
Last Man Standing '96
Nick of Time '95
The Prophecy '95
Things to Do in Denver When You're Dead '95
Pulp Fiction '94
Skylark '93
True Romance '93
Batman Returns '92
Mistress '91
Sarah, Plain and Tall '91
Brainstorm '83
The Deer Hunter '78
Annie Hall '77
The Sentinel '76

Ally Walker
Happy, Texas '99
Bed of Roses '96
While You Were Sleeping '95
Singles '92
Universal Soldier '92

Clint Walker
Small Soldiers '98 (V)

Baker's Hawk '76
Pancho Villa '72
The Dirty Dozen '67

Dominic Walker
The Power of One '92

Fiona Walker
The Asphyx '72

Helen Walker
Big Combo '55
Impact '49

Jonathan Walker
Finding North '97 (V)

Kerry Walker
The Piano '93

Kim Walker
Heathers '89

Mark Walker
Random Encounter '98

Paul Walker
She's All That '99
Pleasantville '98
Varsity Blues '98

Polly Walker
Curtain Call '97
Emma '96
Restoration '94
The Trial '93
Patriot Games '92

Robert Walker
Strangers on a Train '51
Vengeance Valley '51
Till the Clouds Roll By '46
Bataan '43

Robert Walker Jr.
Devonsville Terror '83
Easy Rider '69
The War Wagon '67

Bob Wall
Enter the Dragon (SE) '73

Baird Wallace
Tea with Mussolini '99

Basil Wallace
Caught Up '98
Marked for Death '90

George Wallace
Batman Forever '95

George D. Wallace
Forces of Nature '99
The Swinging Cheerleaders '74
Forbidden Planet '56

Jean Wallace
Big Combo '55

Linda Wallace
Charlie, the Lonesome Cougar '67

Marcia Wallace
My Mom's a Werewolf '89

Dee Wallace Stone
Black Circle Boys '97
The Frighteners '96
10 '79
The Stepford Wives '75

Eli Wallach
The Associate '96
Mistress '91
The Two Jakes '90
The Impossible Spy '87
The Deep '77
The Sentinel '76
The Good, the Bad and the Ugly '67
How the West Was Won '63
The Magnificent Seven '60

Anthony Waller
An American Werewolf in Paris '97

Deborah Walley
Benji '74
The Bubble '67

Jacqueline Wallis
Kiss of the Vampire '62

Shani Wallis
The Pebble and the Penguin '94 (N)
Oliver! '68

Arthur Walsh
They Were Expendable '45

Dylan Walsh
Eden '98
Men '97
Changing Habits '96
Congo '95

Frank Walsh
America '24

Jack Walsh
A Simple Plan '98

Joey Walsh
Hans Christian Andersen '52

J.T. Walsh
The Negotiator '98
Pleasantville '98
Executive Decision '96
Sling Blade '96
Nixon '95
The Client '94
Outbreak '94
National Lampoon's Loaded Weapon 1 '93
Needful Things '93
A Few Good Men '92
Backdraft '91
Iron Maze '91
The Grifters '90
Tequila Sunrise '88

Katherine Walsh
Henry: Portrait of a Serial Killer 2: Mask of Sanity '96

Kay Walsh
Oliver Twist '48

M. Emmet Walsh
Iron Giant '99 (V)
Me & Will '99
Wild Wild West '99
Twilight '98
Chairman of the Board '97
My Best Friend's Wedding '97
Retroactive '97
Albino Alligator '96
The Killing Jar '96
A Time to Kill '96
William Shakespeare's Romeo and Juliet '96
Panther '95
The Naked Truth '92
Red Scorpion '89
Clean and Sober '88
Sunset '88
The Best of Times '86
Fletch '85
Blade Runner (DC) '82
The Jerk '79
Slap Shot '77
They Might Be Giants '71

Raoul Walsh
The Birth of a Nation '15

Sydney Walsh
A Nightmare on Elm Street 2: Freddy's Revenge '85

Ray Walston
My Favorite Martian '98
Stephen King's The Stand '94
The Player '92
The Sting '73
South Pacific '58

Harriet Walter
The Governess '98
A Merry War '97

Lucky Texan '34
Sagebrush Trail '33

Naunton Wayne
The Lady Vanishes '38

Patrick Wayne
Her Alibi '88
Young Guns '88
The Bears & I '74
The Green Berets '68
McLintock! '63
The Searchers '56
Mister Roberts '55

Michael Weatherly
The Colony '98
The Last Days of Disco '98

Carl Weathers
Happy Gilmore '96
Action Jackson '88
Predator '87
Rocky 4 '85
Rocky 2 '79
Rocky '76

Fritz Weaver
The Thomas Crown Affair '99
Creepshow '82

Jacki Weaver
Picnic at Hanging Rock '75

Sigourney Weaver
Snow White: A Tale of Terror
'97
Copycat '95
Dave '93
Alien3 '92
Ghostbusters 2 '89
Gorillas in the Mist '88
Aliens (SE) '86
Ghostbusters '84
The Year of Living Dangerous-
ly '82
Alien '79

Hugo Weaving
The Matrix '99
Babe '95 (V)
The Adventures of Priscilla,
Queen of the Desert '94

Alan Webb
The Great Train Robbery '79

Chloe Webb
The Newton Boys '97
Queens Logic '91
Twins '88
Sid & Nancy '86

Danny Webb
Alien3 '92

Jack Webb
He Walked by Night '48

Julie Webb
Billy Jack '71

Richard Webb
Sands of Iwo Jima '49

Veronica Webb
In Too Deep '99
Jungle Fever '91

Robert Webber
Assassin '86
Private Benjamin '80
10 '79
Revenge of the Pink Panther
'78
The Dirty Dozen '67

Catherine Weber
Body Strokes '95

Holly Weber
Tender Loving Care '99

Jake Weber
Dangerous Beauty '98
Meet Joe Black '98

Steven Weber
All Dogs Christmas Carol '98
(V)
At First Sight '98
The Break Up '98
Leaving Las Vegas '95
Single White Female '92
Hamburger Hill '87

Patrizia Webley
The Bloodsucker Leads the
Dance '75

Ann Wedgeworth
Hunter's Moon '97
Love and a .45 '94
My Science Project '85
Sweet Dreams '85

Bill Weeden
Sgt. Kabukiman N.Y.P.D. '94

Christopher Weeks
Violent Zone '89

Jimmie Ray Weeks
Analyze This '98
The Siege '98
The Abyss (SE) '89
Frantic '88

Michelle Weeks
Little Shop of Horrors '86

Brenda Wehle
Soldier '98

Li Wei
Ju Dou '90

Virginia Weidler
The Philadelphia Story '40

Paul Weigel
The Great Dictator '40

Rafer Weigel
Free Enterprise '98

Teri Weigel
Marked for Death '90
Glitch! '88

Liza Weil
Stir of Echoes '99

Lance Weiler
The Last Broadcast '98

Chuck Wein
Rainbow Bridge '71

Josh Weinstein
Boys Life '94

Cindy Weintraub
Humanoids from the Deep
'80

Peter Weireter
The General's Daughter '99

David Weiss
The Toxic Avenger (DC) '86

Erick Weiss
The Fear '94

George Weiss
Glen or Glenda? '53

Shaun Weiss
The Mighty Ducks '92

Dwight Weist
9 1/2 Weeks '86

Rachel Weisz
The Mummy '99
Swept from the Sea '97

Bruce Weitz
The Landlady '98

Raquel Welch
Chairman of the Board '97
The Four Musketeers '75
The Three Musketeers '74

Tahnee Welch
Johnny 2.0 '99

Tuesday Weld
Feeling Minnesota '96
Falling Down '93
Mistress '91
Thief '81

Frank Welker
Mulan '98 (V)

Frederick Weller
Stonewall '95

Mary Louise Weller
Q (The Winged Serpent) '82
National Lampoon's Animal
House '78

Peter Weller
Top of the World '97
Screamers '96
Mighty Aphrodite '95
RoboCop 2 '90
Leviathan '89
Shakedown '88
RoboCop '87

Gwen Welles
Boys Life '94

Orson Welles
The Trial '63
Othello '52
The Third Man '49
The Stranger '46

James Wellington
The Night That Never Hap-
pened '97

Thomas Wellington
The Creeps '97

Wendell Wellman
Sommersby '93

Vernon Wells
Space Truckers '97
Commando '85
The Road Warrior '82

Kenneth Welsh
Habitat '97
Death Wish 5: The Face of
Death '94
Legends of the Fall '94
Timecop '94

William Welsh
20,000 Leagues under the
Sea '16

Jiang Wen
The Emperor's Shadow '96

Alan J. Wendl
Serial Mom '94

George Wendt
Alice in Wonderland '99
Outside Providence '99
Space Truckers '97
Spice World: The Movie '97
Forever Young '92
Guilty by Suspicion '91
Fletch '85
Dreamscape (SE) '84

Klaus Wennemann
Das Boot (DC) '81

Alexandra Wentworth
Trial and Error '96

Martha Wentworth
The Stranger '46

Barbara Werle
Krakatoa East of Java '66

Doug Werner
The Big Red One '80

Jenny Werner
The Third Man '49

Oskar Werner
Fahrenheit 451 '66
Lola Montes '55

Otto Wernicke
M '31

Gary Werntz
The Peacemaker '97

Kassie Wesley
Evil Dead 2: Dead by Dawn
'87

Dick Wesson
Destination Moon '50

Adam West
Drop Dead Gorgeous '99
Hooper '78

Billy West
Joe's Apartment '96 (V)

Bob West
Barney's Great Adventure '98

Dominic West
William Shakespeare's A Midsummer Night's Dream '99

Gregory West
The Surgeon '94

Julian West
Vampyr '31

Mae West
The Love Goddesses '65
Klondike Annie '36
Belle of the Nineties '34
I'm No Angel '33

Martin West
Assault on Precinct 13 '76

Norma West
And the Ship Sails On '83

Red West
John Grisham's The Rainmaker '97

Samuel West
Howard's End '92

Tegan West
Hamburger Hill '87

Timothy West
Ever After: A Cinderella Story
'98
Cry Freedom '87

**Floyd "Red Crow"
Westerman**
The Last Assassins '96
Dances with Wolves '90

David Westhead
Mrs. Brown '97

James Westmoreland
Don't Answer the Phone '80

Celia Weston
Flirting with Disaster '95

Jack Weston
Dirty Dancing '87
Dirty Dancing (CE) '87

Patricia Wettig
Dancer, Texas—Pop. 81 '98
Guilty by Suspicion '91

Marius Weyers
The Power of One '92

Sean Whalen
Never Been Kissed '99
Twister '96

Frank Whaley
Curtain Call '97
Retroactive '97
Broken Arrow '95
Pulp Fiction '94
Swimming with Sharks '94
Career Opportunities '91
The Doors '91
JFK '91
The Freshman '90
Born on the Fourth of July
'89

Justin Whalin
Serial Mom '94

Joanne Whalley
The Man Who Knew Too Little
'97
Mother's Boys '94
Navy SEALS '90
Pink Floyd: The Wall '82

Darryl Wharton
Detention '98

Kevin Whately
The English Patient '96

Wil Wheaton
Flubber '97
Stand by Me '86
The Last Starfighter '84

Maggie Wheeler
The Parent Trap '98

Dana Wheeler-Nicholson
The Pompatus of Love '95
Tombstone '93
Fletch '85

Alison Whelan
My Left Foot '89

Wendy Whelan
George Balanchine's The Nutcracker '93

Lisa Whelchel
Where the Red Fern Grows:
Part 2 '92

Shannon Whirry
Fatal Pursuit '98
Retroactive '97
Private Obsession '94
Animal Instincts '92

Christina Whitaker
Assault of the Killer Bimbos
'88

Duane Whitaker
From Dusk Till Dawn 2: Texas
Blood Money '98

Forest Whitaker
Phenomenon '96
Blown Away '94
Ready to Wear '94
Body Snatchers '93
The Crying Game '92
The Color of Money '86
Platoon '86

Johnny Whitaker
Napoleon and Samantha '72

Elizabeth Whitcraft
Angel Heart '87

Al White
Red Scorpion '89

Bernie White
Killing Obsession '94

Betty White
Lake Placid '99
The Story of Us '99
Tom Sawyer '99 (V)
Hard Rain '97

Bo White
A Very Natural Thing '73

Carol White
Prehistoric Women '67

Deborah White
The Van '77

De'voreaux White
Die Hard '88

Jaleel White
Quest for Camelot '98 (V)

Jesse White
Matinee '92
Monster in the Closet '86

Die Hard: With a Vengeance
'95
Four Rooms '95
12 Monkeys '95
Color of Night '94
Pulp Fiction '94
Striking Distance '93
Death Becomes Her '92
The Player '92
Hudson Hawk '91
The Last Boy Scout '91
Mortal Thoughts '91
The Bonfire of the Vanities
'90
Die Hard 2: Die Harder '90
In Country '89
Die Hard '88
Sunset '88
Moonlighting '85

Jerome Willis
Winstanley '75

Michael Willis
Pushing Tin '99

Rumer Willis
Striptease '96

Shauntisa Willis
Passion Fish '92

Noel Willman
The Odessa File '74
The Reptile '66
Kiss of the Vampire '62

Kevin Willmott
Ninth Street '98

Rudolph Willrich
Alice Sweet Alice '76

Brember Wills
The Old Dark House '32

Chill Wills
McLintock! '63
Rio Grande '50

Mark Wills
Tom Sawyer '99 (V)

Douglas Wilmer
Jason and the Argonauts '63

Billy Wilmott
Shattered Image '98

Andre Wilms
L'Enfer '93

Andrew Wilson
Bottle Rocket '95

Andy Wilson
2000 Maniacs '64

Bridgette Wilson
House on Haunted Hill '99
I Know What You Did Last
Summer '97
The Real Blonde '97
Mortal Kombat 1: The Movie
'95
Sweet Evil '96
Billy Madison '94
Last Action Hero '93

Carnie Wilson
The '60s '99

Chandra Wilson
Philadelphia '93

Chrystale Wilson
The Players Club '98

David Wilson
The Inside Man '84

Dennis Wilson
Two Lane Blacktop '71

**Don "The Dragon"
Wilson**
Whatever It Takes '97
Terminal Rush '96
Batman Forever '95
Virtual Combat '95

Cyber-Tracker '93
Born on the Fourth of July
'89

Dooley Wilson
Casablanca '42

Elizabeth Wilson
Quiz Show '94
Skylark '93

Jim Wilson
Charlie, the Lonesome
Cougar '67

Kristen Wilson
Bulletproof '96
The Pompatus of Love '95

Lambert Wilson
The Leading Man '96

Luke Wilson
Home Fries '98
Telling Lies in America '96
Bottle Rocket '95

Mara Wilson
A Simple Wish '97
Matilda '96
Mrs. Doubtfire '93

Marie Wilson
March of the Wooden Sol-
diers '34

Mary Louise Wilson
Stepmom '98

Owen C. Wilson
The Haunting '99
Armageddon '98
Permanent Midnight '98
Anaconda '96
Bottle Rocket '95

Paul Wilson
Devonsville Terror '83

Richard Wilson
The Man Who Knew Too Little
'97

Rita Wilson
The Story of Us '99
From the Earth to the Moon
'98
Psycho '98
Jingle All the Way '96
Now and Then '95
Sleepless in Seattle '93

Rod Wilson
Darkman 2: The Return of
Durant '94

Roger Wilson
Porky's '82

Ruby Wilson
Cookie's Fortune '99

Scott Wilson
The Jack Bull '99
Clay Pigeons '98
G.I. Jane '97
The Right Stuff '83

Stuart Wilson
Enemy of the State '98
The Mask of Zorro '98
Crossworlds '96
No Escape '94
Lethal Weapon 3 '92

Teddy Wilson
Kiss Shot '89

Tom Wilson
Battling Butler '26

Trey Wilson
Bull Durham '88
Twins '88

Wendy Dawn Wilson
The Scorpio Factor '90

Penelope Wilton
Cry Freedom '87

Walter Wilz
Carmen, Baby '66

Brian Wimmer
Lipstick Camera '93

Jeff Wincott
Street Law '95
The Killing Man '94

Michael Wincott
Metro '96
Strange Days '95
The Crow '93
The Three Musketeers '93
The Doors '91
Robin Hood: Prince of
Thieves '91

Beatrice Winde
Simon Birch '98

William Windom
Sommersby '93
To Kill a Mockingbird '62

Marie Windsor
Salem's Lot '79
The Killing '56

Paul Winfield
Mars Attacks! '96
Cliffhanger '93
Presumed Innocent '90
The Serpent and the Rainbow
'87
The Terminator '84

Oprah Winfrey
Beloved '98
The Color Purple '85

Debra Winger
Shadowlands '93
Legal Eagles '86

Drew Winget
Boys Will Be Boys '97

Angela Winkler
Tin Drum '79

Henry Winkler
Ground Control '98
The Waterboy '98
Scream (CS) '96
Night Shift '82
An American Christmas Carol
'79

Mel Winkler
City Hall '95
Devil in a Blue Dress '95

Kitty Winn
The Exorcist (SE) '73
They Might Be Giants '71

Charles Winninger
State Fair '45
Pot o' Gold '41
Nothing Sacred '37

Mare Winningham
Georgia '95
The War '94

Kate Winslet
Hideous Kinky '99
Titanic '97
Sense and Sensibility '95

Michael Winslow
Police Academy '84

Helen Winston
A Boy and His Dog '75

Ray Winstone
The Very Thought of You '98

Maurice Dean Wint
Cube '98
Rude '96

Alex Winter
The Lost Boys '87

Jonathan Winters
The Flintstones (CE) '94

The Shadow '94

Kristoffer Ryan Winters
Hot Blooded '98

Shelley Winters
Portrait of a Lady '96
Cleopatra Jones '73
The Poseidon Adventure '72
Lolita '62

Steve Winwood
The Ghost Goes Gear '66

Billy Wirth
Me & Will '99
The Fence '94
Body Snatchers '93
The Lost Boys '87

Robert Wisden
Excess Baggage '96

Greg Wise
Sense and Sensibility '95

Ray Wise
Powder '95
Body Shot '93
Rising Sun '93
RoboCop '87

Joseph Wiseman
Dr. No (SE) '62

Googie Withers
Shine '95
On Approval '44
The Lady Vanishes '38

Jimmy Witherspoon
Georgia '95

John Witherspoon
Sprung '96
Friday '95

Reese Witherspoon
Best Laid Plans '99
Election '99
Cruel Intentions '98
Pleasantville '98
Twilight '98
Fear '96

Alicia Witt
Urban Legend '98
Four Rooms '95
Mr. Holland's Opus '95

Katarina Witt
Ronin '98

Kathryn Witt
Philadelphia '93

Damian Woetzel
George Balanchine's The Nutcracker '93

David Wohl
Saving Private Ryan '98

Hillary Wolf
Home Alone 2: Lost in New
York '92

Scott Wolf
Go '99
White Squall '96
Double Dragon '94

David Wolfe
Salt of the Earth '54

Frank Wolfe
Cold Eyes of Fear '70

Traci Wolfe
Lethal Weapon 3 '92
Lethal Weapon 2 '89
Lethal Weapon '87

Alfred Wolff
Umbrellas of Cherbourg '64

Frank Wolff
The Lickerish Quartet '70

Wolfman Jack
American Graffiti '73

Louis Wolheim
All Quiet on the Western
Front '30
America '24
Dr. Jekyll and Mr. Hyde '20

Sven Wollter
The 13th Warrior '99

Illya Woloshyn
Hush Little Baby '93

John Womack Jr.
Badlands '74

Lee Ann Womack
Tom Sawyer '99 (V)

Sin Won-Sop
Why Has Bodhi-Darma Left
for the East '89

Anna May Wong
Impact '49
Peter Pan '24

Anthony Wong
Beast Cops '98
Armageddon '97
The Heroic Trio '93
Organized Crime & Triad
Bureau '93
The Untold Story '93
Full Contact '92
Hard-Boiled '92

B.D. Wong
Mulan '98 (V)
Seven Years in Tibet '97
The Substitute 2: School's
Out '97
Executive Decision '96
Father of the Bride '91
The Freshman '90

James Wong
Twin Dragons '92
Fractured Follies '88

Joey Wong
A Chinese Ghost Story III '91
A Chinese Ghost Story II '90
A Chinese Ghost Story '87

Keen Wong
Long Arm of the Law '84

Kirk Wong
Twin Dragons '92

Michael Wong
Beast Cops '98
Knock Off '98
First Option '96
Once a Thief '96
In the Line of Duty 4 '89
Legacy of Rage '86

Pauline Wong
Long Arm of the Law II '87
Mr. Vampire '86

Raymond Wong
Expect the Unexpected '98

Ruby Wong
Expect the Unexpected '98

Russell Wong
The Prophecy 2: Ashtown '97
New Jack City '91

Tsing-ying Wong
Iron Monkey '93

Victor Wong
Seven Years in Tibet '97
Tremors '89
The Last Emperor '87
Prince of Darkness '87
The Golden Child '86

Wyman Wong
Knock Off '98

Yo Yo Wong
Expect the Unexpected '98

John Woo
Hard-Boiled '92

Kim Yates
Loveblind '98

Chingmy Yau
Lawyer Lawyer '97
High Risk '95
Lover of the Last Empress '95
City Hunter '92

Tomonori Yazaki
Godzilla's Revenge '69

Wei Ye
Frozen '98

Biff Yeager
Sid & Nancy '86

Mario Yedidia
Warriors of Virtue '97

Derek Yee
Magnificent Warriors '87

Sally Yeh
The Killer '90
I Love Maria '88
Peking Opera Blues '86

Peter Yellen
Ms. 45 '81
Driller Killer '74

Donnie Yen
Iron Monkey '93
Crystal Hunt '92
In the Line of Duty 4 '89

Michelle Yeoh
Tomorrow Never Dies (SE) '97
The Executioners '93
The Heroic Trio '93
Supercop 2 '93
Supercop '92
Magnificent Warriors '87

Vladimir Yershov
Alexander Nevsky '38

Don Yesso
Hero '92

Bolo Yeung
Legacy of Rage '86

Cher Yeung
Dream Lovers '86

Pauline Yeung
Dragons Forever '88

Vanessa Yeung
Hot War '98

Maria Yi
Fists of Fury '73

Shang Feng Yi
The Great Conqueror's Concubine '94

Zhang Yi
The Great Conqueror's Concubine, Part 2 '94
Ju Dou '90

Kong Yan Yin
In the Line of Duty 5 '90

Lam Ching Ying
Mr. Vampire '86
The Prodigal Son '82

Amy Yip
Sex and Zen '93
Erotic Ghost Story '90

Cecilia Yip
Peace Hotel '95
Organized Crime & Triad Bureau '93
Hong Kong 1941 '84

Francoise Yip
Futuresport '98
Black Mask '96
Rumble in the Bronx '96

Barbara Yo Ling
The Satanic Rites of Dracula '73

Dwight Yoakam
The Newton Boys '97
Sling Blade '96

Malik Yoba
Cop Land '97
Cool Runnings '93

Charlie Yoeh
High Risk '95

Erica Yohn
Corrina, Corrina '94

Merlyn Yordan
The Thin Red Line '64

Wladimir Yordanoff
Un Air de Famille '96

Jeff York
They Were Expendable '45

John J. York
Closer and Closer '96

Kathleen York
Dream Lover '93

Michael York
Austin Powers 2: The Spy Who Shagged Me '99
54 '98
Wrongfully Accused '98
Austin Powers: International Man of Mystery '97
Dark Planet '97
The Long Shadow '92
Logan's Run '76
The Four Musketeers '75
The Three Musketeers '74
Cabaret '72
Romeo and Juliet '68
Smashing Time '67

Sarah York
Evil Dead '83

Susannah York
A Christmas Carol '84
Falling in Love Again '80
The Killing of Sister George '69
They Shoot Horses, Don't They? '69
Tom Jones '63

Hideko Yoshida
The Pillow Book '95

Kazuko Yoshiyuki
In the Realm of Passion '80

Ge You
The Emperor's Shadow '96
Farewell My Concubine '93

Aden Young
In the Shadows '98
Cousin Bette '97
Black Robe '91

Alan Young
Baker's Hawk '76

Bruce A. Young
The War '94
Basic Instinct '92

Burt Young
Hot Blooded '98
Going Overboard '89
Rocky 4 '85
A Summer to Remember '84
Rocky 2 '79
Rocky '76
The Killer Elite '75
Chinatown '74

Carleton Young
Reefer Madness '38

Charlie Young
Fallen Angels '95

Chris Young
Warlock: The Armageddon '93
The Great Outdoors '88

Dey Young
Rock 'n' Roll High School '79

Gig Young
The Hindenburg '75
The Killer Elite '75
They Shoot Horses, Don't They? '69

Harrison Young
Saving Private Ryan '98

Karen Young
Joe the King '99
Daylight '96
The Wife '95
Jaws: The Revenge '87
9 1/2 Weeks '86

Loretta Young
The Bishop's Wife '47
The Stranger '46

Nedrick Young
Dead Men Walk / The Monster Maker '43

Nina Young
Sliding Doors '97

Otis Young
The Last Detail '73

Polly Ann Young
Man from Utah / Sagebrush Trail '34

Ric Young
The Corruptor '99
Dragon: The Bruce Lee Story '93
The Last Emperor '87

Richard Young
Assassin '86

Robert Young
The Secret Agent '36

Roland Young
And Then There Were None '45
Forever and a Day '43
The Philadelphia Story '40

Sean Young
Motel Blue '98
Men '97
Ace Ventura: Pet Detective '93
Dune '84
Blade Runner (DC) '82
Stripes '81

Stephen Young
Patton '70

Henny Youngman
Goodfellas '90
Amazon Women on the Moon '87
History of the World: Part 1 '81

Chief Yowlachie
Red River '48

Bai Yu
Frozen '98

Kong Yu
Royal Tramp '92

Rongguang Yu
Jet Li's The Enforcer '95
Man Wanted '94
Iron Monkey '93
Supercop 2 '93

Sun Yueh
City on Fire '87

Anita Yuen
C'est la Vie, Mon Cherie '93

Masayuki Yui
Ran '85

Jimmy Yuill
Much Ado about Nothing '93

Harris Yulin
Bean '97
Murder at 1600 '97
Multiplicity '96
Cutthroat Island '95
Clear and Present Danger '94
Final Analysis '92
Ghostbusters 2 '89
Scarface '83

Chow Yun-Fat
The Corruptor '99
The Replacement Killers '98
Peace Hotel '95
God of Gambler's Return '94
Full Contact '92
Hard-Boiled '92
Prison on Fire 2 '91
The Killer '90
All About Ah Long '89
City War '89
God of Gamblers '89
A Better Tomorrow, Part 2 '88
Fractured Follies '88
City on Fire '87
Prison on Fire '87
A Better Tomorrow, Part 1 '86
Dream Lovers '86
Hong Kong 1941 '84

Victor Sen Yung
Men in War '57

Charles Yunupingu
Gallipoli '81

Blanche Yurka
The Southerner '45
The Bridge of San Luis Rey '44

William Zabka
High Voltage '98

Grace Zabriskie
Me & Will '99
Bastard out of Carolina '96
Drop Zone '94
Fried Green Tomatoes '91
Child's Play 2 '90
Drugstore Cowboy '89
The Big Easy '87

John Zacherle
Brain Damage '88 (V)

Frank Zagarino
Armstrong '99
Convict 762 '98
Alien Chaser '96
The Apocalypse '96
Project: Eliminator '91

Steve Zahn
Forces of Nature '99
Happy, Texas '99
Stuart Little '99 (V)
Out of Sight '98
You've Got Mail '98
Crimson Tide '95
Picture Windows '95
Reality Bites '94

Ichiro Zaitsu
The Funeral '84

Jerry Zaks
Crimes & Misdemeanors '89

Roxana Zal
Big City Blues '99
Red Line '96

Zbigniew Zamachowski
The Decalogue '88

Del Zamora
RoboCop '87

Dominic Zamprogna
The Boys Club '96

Monica Zanchi
Zombie '80

Billy Zane
Cleopatra '99
Titanic '97
The Phantom '96
Flashfire '94
Only You '94
Tales from the Crypt Presents Demon Knight '94
Posse '93
Tombstone '93
Orlando '92
Memphis Belle '90
Dead Calm '89
Going Overboard '89

Lisa Zane
Wicked Ways '99
Floundering '94
Terrified '94
Freddy's Dead: The Final Nightmare '91

Bruno Zanin
Amarcord '74

Nicol Zanzarella
Zigzag '97

Ahmet Zappa
Jack Frost '98

Dweezil Zappa
Jack Frost '98
The Running Man '87

Moon Zappa
Nightmares '83

William Zappa
The Road Warrior '82

Tony Zarindast
Werewolf '95

Yuri Zavadsky
Aelita: Queen of Mars '24

Robert Z'Dar
Fatal Pursuit '98
Red Line '96
Pocket Ninjas '93
Soultaker '90
Tango and Cash '89
Maniac Cop '88

Kevin Zegers
Bram Stoker's Shadowbuilder '98
Air Bud '97

Srdjan Zelenovic
Andy Warhol's Frankenstein '74

Renee Zellweger
The Bachelor '99
One True Thing '98
A Price above Rubies '97
Jerry Maguire '96
The Texas Chainsaw Massacre 4: The Next Generation '95
Love and a .45 '94

Suzanne Zenor
The Baby '72

Delphine Zentout
36 Fillete '88

Anthony Zerbe
Star Trek: Insurrection '98
Asteroid '97
License to Kill '89
Farewell, My Lovely '75
Rooster Cogburn '75
The Parallax View '74
Papillon '73
Cool Hand Luke '67

Catherine Zeta-Jones
Entrapment '99
The Haunting '99
The Mask of Zorro '98
The Phantom '96

Blue Juice '95

Mai Zetterling
The Witches '90

Ken Zhuo Zhao
Mah Jong Dragon '97

Chen Zhaorong
Vive l'Amour '94

Henry Zhou
The Dragon Fist '80

Howard Zieff
Flesh Gordon '72

Chip Zien
The Siege '98
Black Death '91
Into the Woods '90

Madeline Zima
The Hand that Rocks the Cradle '92

Yvonne Zima
The Long Kiss Goodnight '96

Efrem Zimbalist Jr.
Airport '75 '75

Stephanie Zimbalist
The Story Lady '93

Ben Zimet
The Demoniacs '74

Kim Zimmer
Body Heat '81

Laurie Zimmer
Assault on Precinct 13 '76

Joey Zimmerman
Treehouse Hostage '99
Very Bad Things '98
Mother's Boys '94

Karl Zinny
Demons '86

Hanns Zischler
Francesco '89

Bata Zivojinovic
Pretty Village, Pretty Flame '96

Moses Znaimer
Abraxas: Guardian of the Universe '90

Jean-Pierre Zola
The Train '65

Adam Zolotin
Leave It to Beaver '97

Zouzou
Chloe in the Afternoon '72

Rod Zuanic
Mad Max: Beyond Thunderdome '85

George Zucco
The Flying Serpent '55
Dead Men Walk / The Monster Maker '43
The Hunchback of Notre Dame '39

David Zucker
Kentucky Fried Movie '77

Jerry Zucker
Kentucky Fried Movie '77

Jessica Zucman
The Last Metro '80

Daphne Zuniga
Stand-Ins '97
Vision Quest '85

Jose Zuniga
Con Air '97
Ransom '96
Crooklyn '94

Anne Zupa
Boys Life '94

Frantisek Zvarik
Werther '88

Darrell Zwerling
Chinatown '74

Elsa Zylberstein
Metroland '97

The "Director Index" provides a listing for all directors of movies reviewed in this book. The listings for the director names follow an alphabetical sort by last name (although the names appear in a first name, last name format). The videographies are listed chronologically, from most recent film to the oldest. If a director helmed more than one film in the same year, these movies are listed alphabetically within the year.

Paris Barclay
Don't Be a Menace to South Central While Drinking Your Juice in the Hood '95

Clive Barker
Lord of Illusions '95
Hellraiser '87
Salome / The Forbidden '73

Mike Barker
Best Laid Plans '99

Steven Barron
Merlin '98
The Adventures of Pinocchio '96
Teenage Mutant Ninja Turtles: The Movie '90

Ian Barry
Crime Broker '94
The Seventh Floor '93

Paul Bartel
Death Race 2000 '75

Charles T. Barton
Buck Privates Come Home '47

Luigi (Paolo Solvay) Batzella
Nude for Satan '74

Noah Baumbach
Mr. Jealousy '98

Lamberto Bava
Body Puzzle '93
Demons 2 '87
Demons '86

Mario Bava
Beyond the Door 2 '79
Lisa and the Devil / The House of Exorcism '75
Rabid Dogs '74
Torture Chamber of Baron Blood '72
Twitch of the Death Nerve '71
Kill, Baby, Kill '66
Black Sunday '60

Craig R. Baxley
Stephen King's The Storm of the Century '99
Action Jackson '88

Michael Bay
Armageddon '98
The Rock '96
Bad Boys '95

Anees Bazmee
Pyar to Hona Hi Tah '98

Warren Beatty
Bulworth '98
Heaven Can Wait '78

William Beaudine
Sparrows '26

Harold Becker
Mercury Rising '98
City Hall '95
Malice '93
Sea of Love '89
Vision Quest '85

Josh Becker
Running Time '97

James Becket
The Best Revenge '96

Matt Earl Beesley
Point Blank '98

Melissa Behr
Me & Will '99

Jean-Jacques Beineix
Diva '82

Ana Belen
How to Be a Woman and Not Die in the Attempt '91

Earl Bellamy
Munster, Go Home! '66

Laslo Benedek
The Wild One '54

Roberto Benigni
Life Is Beautiful '98
The Monster '96

Richard Benjamin
Made in America '93
My Stepmother Is an Alien '88

Spencer Gordon Bennet
Atomic Submarine '59

Robert Benton
Twilight '98

Michael Benveniste
Flesh Gordon '72

Luca Bercovici
Convict 762 '98

Bruce Beresford
Double Jeopardy '99
Black Robe '91
Mister Johnson '91
Driving Miss Daisy '89
Aria '88
Her Alibi '88
Tender Mercies '83
Breaker Morant '80
Don's Party '76

Peter Berg
Very Bad Things '98

Andrew Bergman
Striptease '96
Honeymoon in Vegas '92
The Freshman '90

Ingmar Bergman
The Seventh Seal '56

Michael Bergmann
Milk and Money '97

Daniel Berk
Sometimes They Come Back ... For More '99

John Bernard
Stay Awake '87

Jack Bernhard
Unknown Island '48

Adam Bernstein
Six Ways to Sunday '99

Bernardo Bertolucci
Besieged '98
Little Buddha '93
The Last Emperor '87
Last Tango in Paris '73

Luc Besson
The Fifth Element '97
The Professional '94
La Femme Nikita '91
Subway '85

Jonathan Betuel
My Science Project '85

Sanjay Leela Bhansali
Hum Dil De Chuke Sanam '99
Khamoshi the Musical '96

Herbert Biberman
Salt of the Earth '54

Robert Bierman
A Merry War '97

Kathryn Bigelow
Strange Days '95

Tony Bill
Five Corners '88

Bruce Bilson
The North Avenue Irregulars '79

Mike Binder
The Sex Monster '99

Antonia Bird
Ravenous '99
Mad Love '95
Priest '94

Brad Bird
Iron Giant '99

Herbert Blache
The Saphead '21

Darby Black
Sweepers '99

Noel Black
Prime Suspect '82

Jamie Blanks
Urban Legend '98

Milan Blazekovic
The Elm-Chanted Forest '97

Bertrand Blier
Beau Pere '81
Buffet Froid '79

Don Bluth
Bartok the Magnificent '99
Anastasia '97
The Pebble and the Penguin '94
Thumbelina '94
Rock-a-Doodle '92
The Land Before Time '88

John Blystone
Our Hospitality / Sherlock Junior '23

David Blyth
Hot Blooded '98

Peter Bogdanovich
Mask '85

Mauro Bolognini
The Inheritance '76

James Bond III
Def by Temptation '90

Mike Bonifer
Lipstick Camera '93

Thomas Bontross
Hideous Sun Demon '59

John Boorman
The General '98
Picture Windows '95
Excalibur '81
Deliverance '72
Hell in the Pacific '69

H. Gordon Boos
Forgotten City '99
Red Surf '90

Robert Boris
Frank and Jesse '94

Phillip Borsos
One Magic Christmas '85

Dave Borthwick
The Secret Adventures of Tom Thumb '94

John Bowen
Dark Secrets '95

Barry Bowles
Q: The Movie '99

Rob Bowman
The X-Files '98

Claudio Biern Boyd
The Princess and the Pirate '95

Danny Boyle
A Life Less Ordinary '97
Trainspotting '95

Shallow Grave '94

Robert North Bradbury
Lucky Texan '34
Man from Utah / Sagebrush Trail '34

John Bradshaw
Specimen '97

Marco Brambilla
Excess Baggage '96
Demolition Man '93

Risa Bramon Garcia
200 Cigarettes '98

Kenneth Branagh
Mary Shelley's Frankenstein '94
Much Ado about Nothing '93
Dead Again '91

Larry Brand
Paranoia '98

Richard Brander
Sizzle Beach U.S.A. '74

Tinto Brass
Caligula '80

Bob Bravier
Rush Week '88

Catherine Breillat
Romance '99
36 Fillete '88

Valerie Breiman
Going Overboard '89

Herbert Brenon
Peter Pan '24

Martin Brest
Meet Joe Black '98
Scent of a Woman '92
Midnight Run '88

Salome Breziner
An Occasional Hell '96

Marshall Brickman
Lovesick '83

Paul Brickman
Risky Business '83

James Bridges
The China Syndrome '79

Jean Brismee
The Devil's Nightmare '71

Matthew Broderick
Infinity '96

Clive Brook
On Approval '44

Peter Brook
Marat/Sade '66

Albert Brooks
The Muse '99

James L. Brooks
As Good As It Gets '97
Broadcast News '87

Mel Brooks
History of the World: Part 1 '81
Blazing Saddles '74
Young Frankenstein '74
The Twelve Chairs '70

Richard Brooks
The Professionals '66
The Last Time I Saw Paris '54

Robert Brooks
Who Shot Pat? '92

Nick Broomfield
Fetishes '96

Eric Bross
Stranger than Fiction '99
Ten Benny '98

Blain Brown
Web of Seduction '99

Bruce Brown
The Endless Summer '66
Surf Crazy '59

Clarence Brown
National Velvet '44

Georg Stanford Brown
Grambling's White Tiger '81

Gregory (Gregory Dark) Brown
Stranger by Night '94

Tod Browning
Dracula '31

Kevin Brownlow
Winstanley '75
It Happened Here '65

S.F. Brownrigg
Don't Look in the Basement '73

James Bruce
Love to Kill '97

Clyde Bruckman
The General '26

John Bruno
Virus '98

Bill Bryden
Aria '88

Chris Buck
Tarzan '99

Judas Bullhorn
GWAR: Phallus in Wonderland '92

Vicangelo Bulluck
Jane Street '96

Peter Gathings Bunche
Champions '96

Findlay Bunting
Robbie Robertson: Going Home '97

Robert Meyer Burnett
Free Enterprise '98

Kevin Burns
Hollywood Christmas '96
Rodgers and Hammerstein: The Sound of Movies '95

Manette Burstein
On the Ropes '99

Tim Burton
Sleepy Hollow '99
Mars Attacks! '96
Batman Returns '92
Batman '89
Beetlejuice '88
Pee-wee's Big Adventure '85

Steve Buscemi
Trees Lounge '96

David Butler
The Princess and the Pirate '44
They Got Me Covered '43
The Road to Morocco '42

Robert Butler
Turbulence '96
Moonlighting '85

Mark Byers
Criminal Act '88

David Byrne
True Stories '86

Elisar Cabrera
Witchcraft 10: Mistress of the Craft '98

Barry Caillier
To Cross the Rubicon '91

The Serpent and the Rainbow '87
A Nightmare on Elm Street '84

Mik Cribben
Beware! Children at Play '95

Charles Crichton
A Fish Called Wanda '88

Michael Crichton
The 13th Warrior '99
The Great Train Robbery '79
Coma '78
Westworld '73

Donald Crisp
The Navigator '24

Armando Crispino
Autopsy '78

John Cromwell
Made for Each Other '39

David Cronenberg
eXistenZ '99
Crash '95
Dead Ringers '88
Videodrome '83
They Came from Within '75

Evan Crooke
The Killing Jar '96

Cameron Crowe
Jerry Maguire '96
Singles '92

Billy Crystal
Mr. Saturday Night '92

Alfonso Cuaron
Great Expectations '97
A Little Princess '95

George Cukor
My Fair Lady '64
Adam's Rib '50
Born Yesterday '50
The Philadelphia Story '40

Rusty Cundieff
Sprung '96
Tales from the Hood '95

Sean S. Cunningham
Friday the 13th '80

Dan Curtis
Trilogy of Terror '75
The Night Strangler '72

Vondie Curtis-Hall
Gridlock'd '96

Michael Curtiz
Proud Rebel '58
Life with Father '47
Casablanca '42
Santa Fe Trail '40

Ireneusz Czesny
A Tale of Two Kitties '96

Paul Czinner
As You Like It '36

Renee Daalder
Habitat '97

Morton DaCosta
The Music Man '62

John Dahl
Rounders '98

Bob Dahlin
Monster in the Closet '86

Rod Daniel
Beethoven's 2nd '93
K-9 '89

Joe Dante
Small Soldiers '98
Picture Windows '95
Matinee '92
The 'Burbs '89

Amazon Women on the Moon '87
Gremlins '84
Piranha '78

Ray Danton
Psychic Killer '75

Frank Darabont
The Green Mile '99
The Shawshank Redemption '94

Jonathan Darby
Hush '98

Eric Darnell
Antz '98

Jules Dassin
The Law '59
The Naked City '48
Brute Force '46

Harry Bromley Davenport
Waking Up Horton '99
Xtro 3: Watch the Skies '95

Delmer Daves
The Red House '47

Boaz Davidson
Looking for Lola '98

Andrew Davis
A Perfect Murder '98
The Fugitive '93
Under Siege '92
Above the Law '88

Beau Davis
Laser Mission '90

Charles Davis
Die Watching '93

Desmond Davis
Smashing Time '67

Tamra Davis
Half-Baked '97
Billy Madison '94

Norman Dawn
Two Lost Worlds '50

Anthony (Antonio Margheriti) Dawson
Andy Warhol's Dracula '74

Robert Day
First Man into Space '59
Corridors of Blood '58
The Haunted Strangler '58

Lyman Dayton
Baker's Hawk '76

Jan De Bont
The Haunting '99
Speed 2: Cruise Control '97
Twister '96
Speed '94

Hubert de la Bouillerie
The Apocalypse '96

Gerardo (Gerry) De Leon
Terror Is a Man '59

Marcus de Leon
The Big Squeeze '96

Robert De Niro
A Bronx Tale '93

Armando de Ossorio
Return of the Blind Dead '75
Tombs of the Blind Dead '72

Vittorio De Sica
Two Women '61
The Bicycle Thief '48

Tom De Simone
Hell Night '81

Steven E. de Souza
Street Fighter '94

Andre de Toth
Dark Waters '44

William Dear
Wild America '97

James Dearden
Rogue Trader '98

Tom DeCerchio
Boys Life 2 '98

David DeCoteau
Curse of the Puppet Master: The Human Experiment '98
Petticoat Planet '95
American Rampage '89
Sorority Babes in the Slimeball Bowl-A-Rama '87

Fred Dekker
RoboCop 3 '91

Guillermo del Toro
Mimic '97

Dom DeLuise
Boys Will Be Boys '97

Helen DeMichiel
Tarantella '95

Cecil B. DeMille
The Ten Commandments '56
Reap the Wild Wind '42
Male and Female '19

Jonathan Demme
Beloved '98
Philadelphia '93
Silence of the Lambs '91
Melvin and Howard '80

Ted Demme
Life '99
Monument Ave. '98
Beautiful Girls '96

Jacques Demy
Umbrellas of Cherbourg '64

Brian DePalma
Snake Eyes '98
Mission: Impossible '96
Carlito's Way '93
Raising Cain '92
The Bonfire of the Vanities '90
Body Double '84
Scarface '83

Dominique Deruddere
Suite 16 '94

James Desmarais
Victim of Love '91

Arnaud Desplechin
La Sentinelle '92

Howard Deutch
Neil Simon's The Odd Couple 2 '98
Grumpier Old Men '95
The Great Outdoors '88

Maurice Devereaux
Lady of the Lake '98

Danny DeVito
Matilda '96

Tom DiCillo
The Real Blonde '97
Box of Moonlight '96

Ernest R. Dickerson
Futuresport '98
Bulletproof '96
Surviving the Game '94
Tales from the Crypt Presents Demon Knight '94

William Dieterle
The Hunchback of Notre Dame '39

Steve DiMarco
Prisoner of Love '99

Dennis Dimster
Mikey '92

Mark Dippe
Spawn (SE) '97

Mark DiSalle
Kickboxer '89

Jamie Dixon
Bram Stoker's Shadowbuilder '98

Ken Dixon
Slave Girls from Beyond Infinity '87

Edward Dmytryk
Shalako '68
Alvarez Kelly '66
The Caine Mutiny '54

Darren Doane
Godmoney '99

David Dobkin
Clay Pigeons '98

Kevin J. Dobson
For Love of a Child '90

Jacques Doillon
Ponette '95

Roger Donaldson
Dante's Peak '97
The Getaway '93

Vincent J. Donehue
Peter Pan '60

Stanley Donen
Saturn 3 '80
Charade '63
The Pajama Game '57
Seven Brides for Seven Brothers '54
Singin' in the Rain '52
Royal Wedding '51

Clive Donner
A Christmas Carol '84

Richard Donner
Lethal Weapon 4 '98
Conspiracy Theory '97
Assassins '95
Maverick '94
Lethal Weapon 3 '92
Lethal Weapon 2 '89
Scrooged '88
Lethal Weapon '87
Ladyhawke '85

Shimon Dotan
Sworn Enemies '96

Lorenzo Doumani
Bug Buster '99
Follow Your Heart '98
Misery Brothers Y2K '95

Robert Downey
Hugo Pool '97

Srdjan Dragojevic
Pretty Village, Pretty Flame '96

Franco Dragone
Alegria '98

Carl Theodor Dreyer
Vampyr '31
Passion of Joan of Arc '28

Frederick Du Chan
Quest for Camelot '98

Adam Dubin
Drop Dead Rock '95

Dennis Dugan
Big Daddy '99
Beverly Hills Ninja '96
Happy Gilmore '96

Christian Duguay
Joan of Arc '99
The Assignment '97

Screamers '96

John Duigan
Lawn Dogs '96
The Leading Man '96
Sirens '94

Bill Duke
Sister Act 2: Back in the Habit '93
Deep Cover '92

Bruno Dumont
The Life of Jesus '96

Duwayne Dunham
Homeward Bound: The Incredible Journey '93

George Duning
Yellow Submarine '68

Griffin Dunne
Practical Magic '98
Addicted to Love '96

Evan Dunsky
The Alarmist '98

Robert Duvall
The Apostle '97

Julien Duvivier
Anna Karenina '48

Allan Dwan
Sands of Iwo Jima '49
Robin Hood '22

H. Kaye Dyal
Project: Eliminator '91

Clint Eastwood
Absolute Power '97
Midnight in the Garden of Good and Evil (SE) '97
The Bridges of Madison County '95
Unforgiven '92
Pale Rider '85
The Gauntlet '77
The Outlaw Josey Wales '76
The Eiger Sanction '75
High Plains Drifter '73

Dave Eddy
Pocket Ninjas '93

John Edginton
Mumia: A Case for Reasonable Doubt? '96

Blake Edwards
Sunset '88
10 '79
Revenge of the Pink Panther '78
The Pink Panther Strikes Again '76
The Pink Panther '64
A Shot in the Dark '64
Breakfast at Tiffany's '61

Atom Egoyan
Felicia's Journey '99
The Sweet Hereafter '96
Exotica '94

Paul Eichgrun
Rock 'n' Roll Invaders: The AM Radio DJs '90s

Sergei Eisenstein
Ivan the Terrible, Part 2 '46
Ivan the Terrible, Part 1 '44
Alexander Nevsky '38
Ten Days That Shook the World '27
The Battleship Potemkin '25

Kevin Elders
Simon Sez '98

Richard Elfman
Modern Vampires '98

Harry Elfont
Can't Hardly Wait '98

Larry Elikann
The Story Lady '93

Doug Ellin
Kissing a Fool '98

Stephan Elliott
The Adventures of Priscilla,
  Queen of the Desert '94

Joseph Ellison
Don't Go in the House '80

Javier Elorrieta
Blood and Sand '89

Dick Emery
Yellow Submarine '68

Roland Emmerich
Godzilla '98
Independence Day '96
Stargate '94
Universal Soldier '92

Harrison Engle
Indomitable Teddy Roosevelt
  '83

George Englund
Zachariah '70

Nora Ephron
You've Got Mail '98
Michael '96
Sleepless in Seattle '93

Rene Eram
Sweet Evil '95
Voodoo '95

John Erman
Carolina Skeletons '92

Chester Erskine
Midnight '34

Dwain Esper
Maniac / Narcotic '34

Gary Evans
The Challenge of Flight: Disc
  One

Osmond Evans
The Complete Uncensored
  Private Snafu '46

Chris Eyre
Smoke Signals '98

John Eyres
Judge & Jury '96

Jim Fall
Trick '99

Jamaa Fanaka
Street Wars '91
Penitentiary 2 '82
Penitentiary '79

Bobby Farrelly
There's Something about
  Mary '98
Kingpin '96

Peter Farrelly
There's Something about
  Mary '98
Kingpin '96
Dumb & Dumber '94

John Fawcett
The Boys Club '96

Neill Fearnley
Johnny 2.0 '99

Federico Fellini
And the Ship Sails On '83
Amarcord '74
Spirits of the Dead '68
Juliet of the Spirits '65
Nights of Cabiria '57

Guy Ferland
Telling Lies in America '96

Abel Ferrara
New Rose Hotel '98

Body Snatchers '93
Bad Lieutenant '92
Ms. 45 '81
Driller Killer '74

Marco Ferreri
Tales of Ordinary Madness
  '83
Bye Bye Monkey '77
Don't Touch the White
  Woman! '74

Larry Fessenden
Habit '97

Sally Field
From the Earth to the Moon
  '98

Mike Figgis
One Night Stand '97
Leaving Las Vegas '95
Internal Affairs '90

Nigel Finch
Stonewall '95

David Fincher
Fight Club '99
The Game '97
Seven '95
Alien3 '92

John P. Finegan
Girls School Screamers '86

Sam Firstenberg
Motel Blue '98

Michael Fischa
My Mom's a Werewolf '89

Terence Fisher
Dracula, Prince of Darkness
  '66

Gary Fleder
From the Earth to the Moon
  '98
Kiss the Girls '97
Things to Do in Denver When
  You're Dead '95

Dave Fleischer
The Superman Cartoons of
  Max & Dave Fleischer '41
Gulliver's Travels '39

Max Fleischer
The Superman Cartoons of
  Max & Dave Fleischer '41

Richard Fleischer
Conan the Destroyer '84
The Jazz Singer '80
Tora! Tora! Tora! '70

Andrew Fleming
The Craft '96

Victor Fleming
Gone with the Wind '39
The Wizard of Oz '39

Rodman Flender
Leprechaun 2 '94

Clive Fleury
Big City Blues '99

John Florea
The Invisible Strangler '76

Isaac Florentine
Cold Harvest '98
High Voltage '98

Robert Florey
The Cocoanuts '29

Calvin Floyd
In Search of Dracula '76
Terror of Frankenstein '75

John Flynn
Out for Justice '91
Lock Up '89

James Foley
The Corruptor '99

The Chamber '96
Fear '96
After Dark, My Sweet '90

Jorge Fons
Midaq Alley '95

**Bruno (Roger Fontaine)
Fontana**
Emmanuelle: Queen of the
  Desert '93

Bryan Forbes
The Slipper and the Rose '76
The Stepford Wives '75

John Ford
How the West Was Won '63
Last Hurrah '58
The Searchers '56
Mister Roberts '55
The Quiet Man '52
Rio Grande '50
They Were Expendable '45
Stagecoach '39
The Hurricane '37

Frederic Forestier
The Peacekeeper '98

Milos Forman
Man on the Moon '99
The People vs. Larry Flynt '96
Amadeus '84
Hair '79
One Flew Over the Cuckoo's
  Nest '75

John Fortenberry
A Night at the Roxbury '98

Bob Fosse
Star 80 '83
Cabaret '72

Jonathon Frakes
Star Trek: Insurrection '98
Star Trek: First Contact '96

Pascal Franchot
Milo '98

Jess (Jesus) Franco
Kiss Me Monster '69
Succubus '69
Two Undercover Angels '68

Melvin Frank
Court Jester '56

David Frankel
From the Earth to the Moon
  '98
Miami Rhapsody '95

John Frankenheimer
Ronin '98
The Island of Dr. Moreau '96
Dead Bang '89
The Train '65
The Manchurian Candidate
  '62

Carl Franklin
One True Thing '98
Devil in a Blue Dress '95

Richard Franklin
Psycho 2 '83

Stephen Frears
Hero '92
The Grifters '90
Dangerous Liaisons '88

Morgan J. Freeman
Desert Blue '98

Eric Freiser
Warlock 3: The End of Innocence '98

Isadore "Friz" Freleng
The Complete Uncensored
  Private Snafu '46

Karl Freund
The Mummy '32

Jeff Frey
Bikini Hotel '97

Ron Fricke
Baraka '93
Chronos '85

Rick Friedberg
Spy Hard '96

William Friedkin
Jade '95
The Guardian '90
Sorcerer '77
The Exorcist (SE) '73

Harvey Frost
National Lampoon's Golf
  Punks '99

Lee Frost
Private Obsession '94

Robert Fuest
Devil's Rain '75

Kinji Fukasaku
Tora! Tora! Tora! '70

Lucio Fulci
New York Ripper '82
Zombie '80

Samuel Fuller
The Big Red One '80
The Meanest Men in the
  West '76
Naked Kiss '64
Shock Corridor '63

Antoine Fuqua
The Replacement Killers '98

Sidney J. Furie
Hide and Seek '00
Top of the World '97
Iron Eagle 4 '95
The Ipcress File '65

John Gale
The Firing Line '91

Ricardo Jacques Gale
Eye of the Serpent '92

Andrew Gallerani
Just Write '97

Vincent Gallo
Buffalo 66 '97

Pierre Gang
Armistead Maupin's More
  Tales of the City '97

Tay Garnett
Bataan '43

Mick Garris
Stephen King's The Stand
  '94

John Garwood
Violent Zone '89
Crackdown '88

Louis Gasnier
Reefer Madness '38

Peter Geiger
The Colony '98

George W. George
James Dean Story '57

Matthew George
Under the Gun '95

Peter George
Surf Nazis Must Die (DC) '87

Terry George
A Bright Shining Lie '98

Fred Gerber
Closer and Closer '96

Clyde Geronimi
101 Dalmatians '61

Francis Giacobetti
Emmanuelle, the Joys of a
  Woman '76

Alan Gibson
The Satanic Rites of Dracula
  '73

Brian Gibson
The Juror '96
What's Love Got to Do with
  It? '93

Lewis Gilbert
Moonraker (SE) '79
The Spy Who Loved Me (SE)
  '77

Jack Gill
Body Armor '96

Jim Gillespie
I Know What You Did Last
  Summer '97

Terry Gilliam
Fear and Loathing in Las
  Vegas '98
12 Monkeys '95
The Adventures of Baron
  Munchausen '89
Brazil '85
Brazil (Criterion SE) '85
Monty Python's The Meaning
  of Life '83
Time Bandits '81
And Now for Something Com-
  pletely Different '72

John Gilling
Night Caller from Outer
  Space '66
Plague of the Zombies '66
The Reptile '66

Buddy Giovinazzo
Combat Shock '84

Francois Girard
The Red Violin '98

Michael Paul Girard
Witchcraft 9: Bitter Flesh '96

William Girdler
Day of the Animals '77
Grizzly '76

Hugh Gladwish
The Ghost Goes Gear '66

Paul Michael Glaser
The Running Man '87

Arnold Glassman
Visions of Light: The Art of
  Cinematography '93

Leslie Linka Glatter
Now and Then '95

John Glen
License to Kill '89
For Your Eyes Only (SE) '81

James Glickenhaus
Shakedown '88
Exterminator '80

Arne Glimcher
Just Cause '94

Jean-Luc Godard
Aria '88
First Name: Carmen '83
Alphaville '65
Pierrot le Fou '65
My Life to Live '62
A Woman Is a Woman '60

Jim Goddard
The Impossible Spy '87

Dan Goggin
Nunsense '93

Menahem Golan
Armstrong '99

Sandra Goldbacher
The Governess '98

Howard Goldberg
Eden '98

Mark Goldblatt
The Punisher '90

Michael Goldenberg
Bed of Roses '95

Gary Goldman
Bartok the Magnificent '99
Anastasia '97
Thumbelina '94

Jill Goldman
Bad Love '95

Allan Goldstein
When Justice Fails '98
Jungle Boy '96
Death Wish 5: The Face of
    Death '94

James Goldstone
Dreams of Gold: The Mel
    Fisher Story '86
Rollercoaster '77
Swashbuckler '76
Winning '69

Tony Goldwyn
A Walk on the Moon '99

Steve Gomer
Barney's Great Adventure '98

Nick Gomez
New Jersey Drive '95

Bryan Gordon
Career Opportunities '91

George Gordon
The Complete Uncensored
    Private Snafu '46

Michael Gordon
Pillow Talk '59

Steve Gordon
Arthur '81

Stuart Gordon
Space Truckers '97
Castle Freak '95
Re-Animator '84

Marleen Gorris
Mrs. Dalloway '97
Antonia's Line '95

Raja Gosnell
Never Been Kissed '99
Home Alone 3 '97

Ernst Gossner
Jan Svankmajer's Faust '94

Carl Gottlieb
Amazon Women on the Moon
    '87

Lisa Gottlieb
Across the Moon '94

Edmund Goulding
Forever and a Day '43
Dark Victory '39

Anne Goursaud
Another 9 1/2 Weeks '96
Embrace of the Vampire '95
Poison Ivy 2: Lily '95

James Edward Grant
Angel and the Badman '47

Gary Graver
Angel in Training '99
Sexual Roulette '96

F. Gary Gray
The Negotiator '98
Set It Off '96
Friday '95

John Gray
The Glimmer Man '96

Peter Greenaway
The Pillow Book '95
A Zed & Two Noughts '88
The Draughtsman's Contract
    '82

David Greene
Rehearsal for Murder '82

Robert Greenwald
Xanadu '80

Leslie Greif
Keys to Tulsa '96

John Greyson
Lilies '96

Sergio Grieco
The Sinful Nuns of Saint
    Valentine '74

Charles B. Griffith
Eat My Dust '76

D.W. Griffith
Sally of the Sawdust '25
America '24
Orphans of the Storm '21
Way Down East '20
Broken Blossoms '19
Intolerance '16
The Birth of a Nation '15

Mark Griffiths
Tactical Assault '99

Douglas K. Grimm
Laser Moon '92

Wiktor Grodecki
Mandragora '97

Ulu Grosbard
The Deep End of the Ocean
    '98
Georgia '95

Adam Grossman
Carnival of Souls '98
Sometimes They Come Back
    ... Again '96

Sam Grossman
The Van '77

John Guillermin
King Kong '76
The Towering Inferno '74
Waltz of the Toreadors '62

Wang Ha
The Descendant of Wing
    Chun '78

Philip Haas
The Blood Oranges '97

Taylor Hackford
The Devil's Advocate '97
Dolores Claiborne '94

Randa Haines
Dance with Me '98

Richard W. Haines
Class of Nuke 'Em High '86

John Halas
Three Musketeers '88

Don Haldane
Nikki, the Wild Dog of the
    North '61

Ivan Hall
Kill and Kill Again '81

Peter Hall
Never Talk to Strangers '95

Lasse Hallstrom
My Life As a Dog '85

Victor Halperin
Revolt of the Zombies '36
The White Zombie '32

Gary Halvorson
The Adventures of Elmo in
    Grouchland '99

Guy Hamilton
Live and Let Die '73
Goldfinger '64

Nick Hamm
The Very Thought of You '98

Robert Hammer
Don't Answer the Phone '80

David Hand
Animaland '48

Michael Haneke
Funny Games '97

Tom Hanks
From the Earth to the Moon
    '98

Ed Hansen
The Bikini Car Wash Company
    '90

Curtis Hanson
L.A. Confidential '97
The River Wild '94
The Hand that Rocks the Cra-
    dle '92

C.B. Harding
Loveblind '98

Cedric Hardwicke
Forever and a Day '43

David Hare
The Designated Mourner '97

Tsui Hark
Knock Off '98
Double Team '97
Once Upon a Time in China III
    '93
The Master '92
Once Upon a Time in China II
    '92
Twin Dragons '92
Once Upon a Time in China
    '91
Peking Opera Blues '86
Zu: Warriors of the Magic
    Mountain '83

Renny Harlin
Deep Blue Sea '99
The Long Kiss Goodnight '96
Cutthroat Island '95
Cliffhanger '93
Die Hard 2: Die Harder '90
A Nightmare on Elm Street 4:
    Dream Master '88

Robert Harmon
Nowhere to Run '93

Curtis Harrington
Night Tide '63

James B. Harris
Boiling Point '93

Jim Harris
Perfect Profile '90

George Harrison
Magical Mystery Tour '67

Anthony Harvey
They Might Be Giants '71

Byron Haskin
The War of the Worlds '53

Masanori Hata
The Adventures of Milo &
    Otis '89

Henry Hathaway
Raid on Rommel '71
Shoot Out '71
How the West Was Won '63

Michael Hawes
Family Reunion '79

Howard Hawks
Red River '48
The Big Sleep '46
Ball of Fire '41

His Girl Friday '40
Come and Get It '36

Todd Haynes
Velvet Goldmine '98

Amy Heckerling
Clueless '95
Look Who's Talking '89

Victor Heerman
Animal Crackers '30

Chris Hegedus
The War Room '93

Brian Helgeland
Payback '98

Monte Hellman
Two Lane Blacktop '71
The Terror '63

David Hemmings
Quantum Leap: The Pilot
    Episode '89

Eric Hendershot
A Kid Called Danger '99
The Robin Hood Gang '98

Frank Henenlotter
Brain Damage '88
Basket Case '82

Kim Henkel
The Texas Chainsaw Mas-
    sacre 4: The Next Genera-
    tion '95

Alex Hennech
Smart Money '97

Noble Henri
Virtual Desire '95

Buck Henry
Heaven Can Wait '78

Jim Henson
Labyrinth '86
The Dark Crystal '82

Stephen Herek
Holy Man '98
101 Dalmatians '96
Mr. Holland's Opus '95
The Three Musketeers '93
The Mighty Ducks '92

Jean Herman
Honor Among Thieves '68

Mark Herman
Little Voice '98
Brassed Off '96

Rowdy Herrington
A Murder of Crows '99
Striking Distance '93

Marshall Herskovitz
Dangerous Beauty '98

Michael Herz
Sgt. Kabukiman N.Y.P.D. '94
The Toxic Avenger, Part 2 '89
Troma's War (DC) '88
The Toxic Avenger (DC) '86

Werner Herzog
Fitzcarraldo '82
Nosferatu the Vampyre '79
Even Dwarfs Started Small
    '69

Eugene Hess
Don't Do It '94

Fraser Heston
Needful Things '93

Peter Hewitt
The Borrowers '97

Rod Hewitt
Strip Search '97

Winston Hibler
Charlie, the Lonesome
    Cougar '67

George Hickenlooper
The Big Brass Ring '99

Barry Hickey
Tornado Run '95

Steve Hickner
Prince of Egypt '98

Anthony Hickox
Warlock: The Armageddon
    '93

Douglas Hickox
The Hound of the
    Baskervilles '83

Scott Hicks
Shine '95

Yoichi Higashi
Village of Dreams '97

George Roy Hill
Funny Farm '88
Slap Shot '77
The Sting '73
Slaughterhouse Five '72
Butch Cassidy and the Sun-
    dance Kid '69

Jack Hill
The Swinging Cheerleaders
    '74
The Big Doll House '71
Spider Baby '64
The Terror '63

James Hill
Trial & Error '62

Terence Hill
Lucky Luke '94
Troublemakers '94

Timothy Hill
Muppets from Space '99

Walter Hill
Last Man Standing '96
Geronimo: An American Leg-
    end '93
Trespass '92
Another 48 Hrs. '90
Red Heat '88
Brewster's Millions '85
Streets of Fire '84
Hard Times '75

David Hillenbrand
King Cobra '98

Scott Hillenbrand
King Cobra '98

Arthur Hiller
Outrageous Fortune '87
The Lonely Guy '84

Paul Hills
Boston Kickout '95

Lambert Hillyer
The Toll Gate '20

Ha Sau Hin
Dragon from Shaolin '96

**Alexander Gregory
(Gregory Dark)
Hippolyte**
Animal Instincts 3: The
    Seductress '95
Object of Obsession '95
Secret Games 3 '94
Undercover '94
Animal Instincts '92
Secret Games '92
Carnal Crimes '91

Alfred Hitchcock
The Birds '63
Psycho (CE) '60
Vertigo (CE) '58
Strangers on a Train '51
The Paradine Case '47
Notorious '46
Spellbound '45
Rebecca '40

Steven Kampmann
Stealing Home '88

Deborah Kaplan
Can't Hardly Wait '98

Jonathan Kaplan
Brokedown Palace '99
Girls of the White Orchid '85

Shekhar Kapur
Elizabeth '98

Wong Kar-Wai
Happy Together '96
Fallen Angels '95

Phil Karlson
Walking Tall '73

Eric Karson
Black Eagle '88

Jake Kasdan
Zero Effect '97

Lawrence Kasdan
Mumford '99
French Kiss '95
The Big Chill '83
Body Heat '81

Peter Kassovitz
Jakob the Liar '99

Lloyd (Samuel Weil) Kaufman
Tromeo & Juliet '95
Sgt. Kabukiman N.Y.P.D. '94
The Toxic Avenger, Part 2 '89
Troma's War (DC) '88
Class of Nuke 'Em High '86
The Toxic Avenger (DC) '86

Philip Kaufman
Rising Sun '93
Henry & June '90
The Unbearable Lightness of Being '88
The Right Stuff '83
Invasion of the Body Snatchers '78

Anwar Kawadri
Out of Time '90

Yoshiaki Kawajiri
Demon City Shinjuku '93
Ninja Scroll '93

Tony Kaye
American History X '98

Elia Kazan
A Streetcar Named Desire '51
Gentleman's Agreement '47

Nicholas Kazan
Dream Lover '93

Buster Keaton
College '27
Battling Butler '26
The General '26
Seven Chances '25
The Navigator '24
Our Hospitality / Sherlock Junior '23
Three Ages '23
The Saphead '21

Toby Keeler
Pretty As a Picture: The Art of David Lynch '98

Worth Keeter
Trapper County War '89

Harvey Keith
Stand-Ins '97

David Kellogg
Inspector Gadget '99

Gene Kelly
Singin' in the Rain '52

Burt Kennedy
The Killer inside Me '76

Calvin Kennedy
Tender Loving Care '99

Frank Kerr
Undercurrent '99
Patriots '94

Irvin Kershner
RoboCop 2 '90

Emmanuel Kervyn
Rabid Grannies '89

Alek Keshishian
With Honors '94
Truth or Dare '91

Stephen Kessler
Vegas Vacation '96

Sohail Khan
Pyaar Kiya to Darna Kya '98

Abbas Kiarostami
The Taste of Cherry '96

Beeban Kidron
Swept from the Sea '97

Krzysztof Kieslowski
The Decalogue '88

Henry King
Carousel '56
The Snows of Kilimanjaro '52
Tol'able David '21

Robert Lee King
Boys Life '94

Zalman King
In God's Hands '98

Cedric Klapisch
Un Air de Famille '96

Randal Kleiser
The Blue Lagoon '80
The Boy in the Plastic Bubble '76

Steven Kloves
The Fabulous Baker Boys '89

Philip Ko
Killer's Romance '90

Masaki Kobayashi
The Human Condition: Road to Eternity '59
The Human Condition: No Greater Love '58

David Koepp
Stir of Echoes '99
The Trigger Effect '96

Bob Koherr
Plump Fiction '97

Andrei Konchalovsky
Tango and Cash '89
Runaway Train '85

Henry Koster
The Bishop's Wife '47

Ted Kotcheff
Family of Cops '95
Weekend at Bernie's '89
First Blood '82

Igor Kovalyov
The Rugrats Movie '98

William R. Kowalchuk
Rudolph the Red-Nosed Reindeer: The Movie '98

Bernard L. Kowalski
Krakatoa East of Java '66

Stanley Kramer
Guess Who's Coming to Dinner '67

Frank Krom
To Play or To Die '91

Bob (Robert) Kubilos
Night Calls: The Movie '98
Allyson Is Watching '96

Stanley Kubrick
Eyes Wide Shut '99
Full Metal Jacket '87
The Shining '80
Barry Lyndon '75
A Clockwork Orange '71
2001: A Space Odyssey '68
Dr. Strangelove, or: How I Learned to Stop Worrying and Love the Bomb '64
Lolita '62
Spartacus '60
Paths of Glory '57
The Killing '56
Killer's Kiss '55

Buzz Kulik
Around the World in 80 Days '89
Women of Valor '86

Roger Kumble
Cruel Intentions '98

Harry Kumel
Daughters of Darkness '71

Peter Kuran
Trinity and Beyond: The Atomic Bomb Movie '99

Akira Kurosawa
Ran '85
High & Low '62
Sanjuro '62
Seven Samurai '54

Robert Kurtzman
Wishmaster '97
The Demolitionist '95

Diane Kurys
Love After Love '94
Entre-Nous '83

Stanley Kwan
Center Stage '91
Rouge '87

Richard Kwietniowski
Love and Death on Long Island '97

William Kyriakis
Dark Odyssey '57

Gregory La Cava
My Man Godfrey '36

Richard LaBrie
Good Luck '96

Neil LaBute
Your Friends & Neighbors '98
In the Company of Men '96

Susan Lacy
Leonard Bernstein: Reaching for the Note '98

Rob LaDuca
The Lion King: Simba's Pride '98

John Lafia
Child's Play 2 '90

Richard LaGravenese
Living Out Loud '98

David (Dai Wei) Lai
Mah Jong Dragon '97

Ivan Lai
God.com '99

Frank Laloggia
The Lady in White '88

Rene Laloux
Time Masters '82
Fantastic Planet '73

Ngai Kai Lam
Erotic Ghost Story '90

Ringo Lam
Full Contact '92
Twin Dragons '92
Prison on Fire 2 '91
City on Fire '87
Prison on Fire '87

Tsui Pak Lam
Crystal Hunt '92

Charles Lamont
Abbott and Costello in the Foreign Legion '50

Lew (Louis Friedlander) Landers
The Mask of Diijon '46

James Landis
The Sadist '63

John Landis
The Blues Brothers 2000 '98
Innocent Blood '92
Coming to America '88
Amazon Women on the Moon '87
Three Amigos '86
Spies Like Us '85
An American Werewolf in London '81
The Blues Brothers (CE) '80
National Lampoon's Animal House '78
Kentucky Fried Movie '77

Fritz Lang
The Blue Gardenia '53
M '31
Metropolis '26
Spiders '18

Samantha Lang
Twisted '96

Walter Lang
The King and I '56
State Fair '45

Simon Langton
Pride and Prejudice '95

Lawrence Lanoff
The Chosen One: Legend of the Raven '98

James Lapine
Earthly Possessions '99
Into the Woods '91
Sunday in the Park with George '86

Christopher Larkin
A Very Natural Thing '73

Sheldon Larry
Black Death '91

John Lasseter
A Bug's Life (CE) '98

Steve Latshaw
Jack-O '95

David Michael Latt
Killers '97

Jeff Lau
Chinese Odyssey, Part One: Pandora's Box '94
Chinese Odyssey, Part Two: Cinderalla '94

Larry Lau
Lee Rock '91

Ricky Lau
Mr. Vampire '86

Wai Keung Lau
Lover of the Last Empress '95

Michael Laughlin
Mesmerized '84

Tom Laughlin
Billy Jack '71

Arnold Laven
Rough Night in Jericho '67

Clara Law
Temptation of a Monk '94

Rocky Law
Dragons of the Orient '88

Martin Lawrence
A Thin Line Between Love and Hate '96

Jonathan Lawton
The Hunted '94

Joe Layton
Richard Pryor: Live on the Sunset Strip '82

Tom Lazarus
Word of Mouth '99

David Leaf
The Unknown Marx Brothers '93

David Lean
Summertime '55
Oliver Twist '48
Great Expectations '46

Conan LeClaire
Faces of Death '78

Bruce Leddy
My Teacher's Wife '95

Mimi Leder
Deep Impact '98
The Peacemaker '97

Paul Leder
Killing Obsession '94

Ang Lee
Sense and Sensibility '95
Pushing Hands '92

Bruce Lee
Return of the Dragon '73

Damian Lee
Moving Target '96
Terminal Rush '96
Street Law '95
Abraxas: Guardian of the Universe '90

Malcolm Lee
The Best Man '99

Rowland V. Lee
The Bridge of San Luis Rey '44

Spike Lee
Summer of Sam '99
He Got Game '98
Clockers '95
Crooklyn '94
Jungle Fever '91
Do the Right Thing '89

Michael Lehmann
My Giant '98
Hudson Hawk '91
Heathers '89

Mike Leigh
Meantime '81

Christopher Leitch
I've Been Waiting for You '98

Kasi Lemmons
Eve's Bayou '97

Paul Leni
The Cat and the Canary '27

John Lennon
Magical Mystery Tour '67

Brett Leonard
Virtuosity '95
The Lawnmower Man '92

Sergio Leone
The Good, the Bad and the Ugly '67

For a Few Dollars More '65
A Fistful of Dollars '64

John R. Leonetti
Mortal Kombat 2: Annihilation '97

Irving Lerner
Royal Hunt of the Sun '69

Mervyn LeRoy
Mister Roberts '55

Wolfgang Lesowsky
Gustav Mahler: To Live, I Will Die '87

Mark L. Lester
The Base '99
Extreme Justice '93
Showdown in Little Tokyo '91
Commando '85
Firestarter '84

Richard Lester
The Four Musketeers '75
The Three Musketeers '74
Help! '65
A Hard Day's Night '64

Chris Lethbridge
The Sci-Fi Files '97

Sheldon Lettich
Lionheart '90

Clarence Fok Yiu Leung
Naked Killer '92

Po-Chi Leung
Hong Kong 1941 '84

Brian Levant
Jingle All the Way '96
The Flintstones (CE) '94
Beethoven '92

Jeremy Leven
Don Juan DeMarco '94

Marc Levin
Slam '98

Barry Levinson
Sphere '97
Wag the Dog '97
Sleepers '96
Disclosure '94
Bugsy '91
Rain Man '88

Robert L. Levy
A Kid in Aladdin's Palace '97

Scott Levy
Piranha '95

Herschell Gordon Lewis
The Wizard of Gore '70
Color Me Blood Red '64
2000 Maniacs '64
Blood Feast (SE) '63

Joseph H. Lewis
Big Combo '55

Robert Lewis
A Summer to Remember '84

Marcel L'Herbier
The Fantastic Night '42

Robert Lieberman
Tom Clancy's Netforce '98

Kevin Lima
Tarzan '99

Doug Liman
Go '99
Swingers '96

Per Lindberg
June Night '40

Michael Lindsay-Hogg
Horton Foote's Alone '97
The Object of Beauty '91

Richard Linklater
The Newton Boys '97

Before Sunrise '94
Dazed and Confused '93

Art Linson
Where the Buffalo Roam '80

Steven Lisberger
Tron '82

Dwight Little
Murder at 1600 '97
Marked for Death '90
Bloodstone '88
Halloween 4: The Return of Michael Myers '88

Luis Llosa
Anaconda '96
The Specialist '94
Fire on the Amazon '93

Frank Lloyd
Blood on the Sun '45
Forever and a Day '43

Moctezuma Lobato
Night Calls: The Movie 2 '99
I Like to Play Games '95

Joshua Logan
Camelot '67
South Pacific '58

Dimitri Logothetis
Body Shot '93

Ulli Lommel
Devonsville Terror '83
The Boogey Man '80
Blank Generation '79

Jerry London
Victim of Love '91
Kiss Shot '89
Rent-A-Cop '88

Robert Longo
Johnny Mnemonic '95

Eric Louzil
Fatal Pursuit '98

Stephen Low
Super Speedway '97

Dick Lowry
Atomic Train '99
Dean Koontz's Mr. Murder '98

Richard Lowry
Jessica: A Love Story '92

Arthur Lubin
Impact '49
New Orleans '47
Buck Privates '41
In the Navy '41

Ernst Lubitsch
That Uncertain Feeling '41

George Lucas
American Graffiti '73

Baz Luhrmann
William Shakespeare's Romeo and Juliet '96

Sidney Lumet
Gloria '98
Critical Care '97
Night Falls on Manhattan '96
Q & A '90
Running on Empty '88
Deathtrap '82
The Wiz '78
Network '76
Dog Day Afternoon '75

Hamilton Luske
101 Dalmatians '61
Lady and the Tramp '55
Peter Pan '53
Pinocchio '40

Patrick Lussier
The Prophecy 3: The Ascent '99

William Lustig
Uncle Sam '96
Maniac Cop '88
Vigilante '83
Maniac '80

David Lynch
Dune '84

Paul Lynch
Face the Evil '97
Prom Night '80

Adrian Lyne
Jacob's Ladder '90
9 1/2 Weeks '86

Jonathan Lynn
Trial and Error '96
Sgt. Bilko '95
Greedy '94
The Distinguished Gentleman '92

Francis D. Lyon
The Great Locomotive Chase '56

Jingle Ma
Hot War '98

Joe Ma
Lawyer Lawyer '97

Peter Macdonald
Legionnaire '98

Carl Macek
8 Man '92
Megazone 23 Part 1 '85

David Mackay
Route 9 '98

Brady MacKenzie
Whatever It Takes '97

John MacKenzie
The Long Good Friday '80

Gilles Mackinnon
Hideous Kinky '99

John Madden
Shakespeare in Love (CS) '98
Mrs. Brown '97

Guy Magar
Showdown '94

Albert Magnoli
Dark Planet '97
Purple Rain '84

Johnnie Mak
Long Arm of the Law '84

Michael Mak
Island of Greed '97
Sex and Zen '93
Long Arm of the Law II '87

Peter Mak
Wicked City '92

Dusan Makavejev
Montenegro '81

Chris Malazdrewicz
With Friends Like These '90

Rob Malenfant
The Landlady '98

Terrence Malick
The Thin Red Line '98
Days of Heaven '78
Badlands '74

Louis Malle
Damage '92
My Dinner with Andre '81
Spirits of the Dead '68

David Mallet
Cats '98

James Mallon
Mystery Science Theater 3000: The Movie '96

Bruce Malmuth
Hard to Kill '89
Nighthawks '81

William Malone
House on Haunted Hill '99

David Mamet
The Spanish Prisoner '97

Oshii Mamoru
Urusei Yatsura Movie 2: Beautiful Dreamer '84

Robert Mandel
The Substitute '96
School Ties '92

Luis Mandoki
Message in a Bottle '98
When a Man Loves a Woman '94
White Palace '90

James Mangold
Cop Land '97

Joseph L. Mankiewicz
Sleuth '72
All About Eve '50

Tom Mankiewicz
Dragnet '87

Anthony Mann
Men in War '57
He Walked by Night '48
Raw Deal '48
T-Men '47

Michael Mann
The Insider '99
Heat '95
Thief '81

Paul Marcus
The Break Up '98

Andreas Marfori
Desperate Crimes '93

Jeff Margolis
Richard Pryor: Live in Concert '79

Edwin L. Marin
Mr. Ace '46

Richard "Cheech" Marin
Born in East L.A. '87

Gabriel Markiw
Mob Story '90

Jancarlo Markiw
Mob Story '90

Peter Markle
Bat 21 '88

Ross Kagen Marks
The Twilight of the Golds '97

Joel B. Marsden
Ill-Gotten Gains '97

Frank Marshall
From the Earth to the Moon '98
Congo '95
Arachnophobia '90

Garry Marshall
The Other Sister '98
Pretty Woman '90
Overboard '87
The Flamingo Kid '84

George Marshall
How the West Was Won '63
Pot o' Gold '41

Penny Marshall
A League of Their Own '92
Awakenings '90
Big '88

D'Urville Martin
Dolemite '75

Eugenio (Gene) Martin
Bad Man's River '72
Horror Express '72
Pancho Villa '72

John Mathew Martin
Sarfarosh '98

Lionel C. Martin
Def Jam's How to Be a Player '97

Raymond Martino
Dumb Luck in Vegas '97

Sergio Martino
Torso '73

Andrew Marton
The Thin Red Line '64
The Longest Day '62

Nico Mastorakis
The Naked Truth '92
Glitch! '88
Nightmare at Noon '87
The Wind '87
Zero Boys '86

Armand Mastroianni
Killing Hour '84

Toshio Masuda
Tora! Tora! Tora! '70

Shoichi Masuo
Crimson Wolf '94

Rudolph Mate
D.O.A. '49

Paul Matthews
Breeders '97
Grim '95

Garth Maxwell
Jack Be Nimble '94

Bradford May
Asteroid '97
Darkman 2: The Return of Durant '94

Elaine May
The Heartbreak Kid '72

Russ Mayberry
Unidentified Flying Oddball '79

Les Mayfield
Flubber '97
Encino Man '92

Albert Maysles
The Beatles: The First U.S. Visit '91

David Maysles
The Beatles: The First U.S. Visit '91

Des McAnuff
Cousin Bette '97

Jim McBride
The Big Easy '87

Tim McCanlies
Dancer, Texas—Pop. 81 '98

Tim McCann
Desolation Angels '95

Leo McCarey
The Bells of St. Mary's '45
Going My Way / Holiday Inn '44
Love Affair '39
Belle of the Nineties '34
Duck Soup '33

Douglas McCarthy
An Extremely Goofy Movie '99

John Michael McCarthy
Sore Losers '97

Peter McCarthy
Floundering '94

Todd McCarthy
Visions of Light: The Art of Cinematography '93

Paul McCartney
Magical Mystery Tour '67

Jim McCullough
Where the Red Fern Grows: Part 2 '92

Peter McDonald
Rambo 3 '88

Rodney McDonald
Scorned 2 '96

Bernard McEveety
The Bears & I '74
Napoleon and Samantha '72

Douglas McGrath
Emma '96

Don McKellar
Last Night '98

Andrew V. McLaglen
The Shadow Riders '82
Sea Wolves '81
Hellfighters '68
McLintock! '63

Norman Z. McLeod
The Secret Life of Walter Mitty '47
Horse Feathers '32
Monkey Business '31

Tom McLoughlin
Sometimes They Come Back '91

Sean McNamara
Treehouse Hostage '99

Ian McNaughton
And Now for Something Completely Different '72

John McNaughton
Wild Things '98
Mad Dog and Glory '93
Henry: Portrait of a Serial Killer '90

Carlton McRae
Awakening of Gabriella '99

John McTiernan
The 13th Warrior '99
The Thomas Crown Affair '99
Die Hard: With a Vengeance '95
Last Action Hero '93
Medicine Man '92
The Hunt for Red October '90
Die Hard '88
Predator '87

Nancy Meckler
Alive and Kicking '96
Sister My Sister '94

Don Medford
James Dean Double Feature: Hill Number One / I Am a Fool '51

Gus Meins
March of the Wooden Soldiers '34

Phil Mendez
Tom Sawyer '99

Ramon Menendez
Stand and Deliver '88

William Cameron Menzies
Invaders from Mars '53

James Merendino
SLC Punk! '99
Hard Drive '94
Terrified '94

Marc Messenger
American Streetfighter 2: The Full Impact '97

Tim Metcalfe
Killer: A Journal of Murder '95

Alan Metzger
Exclusive '82

Radley Metzger
Score '72
Little Mother '71
The Lickerish Quartet '70
Camille 2000 '69
Therese & Isabelle '67
Carmen, Baby '66
The Alley Cats '65
The Dirty Girls '64
Dark Odyssey '57

Nicholas Meyer
Star Trek 6: The Undiscovered Country '91

Dave Meyers
Foolish '99

Nancy Meyers
The Parent Trap '98

John E. Michalakis
I Was a Teenage Zombie '87

Roger Michell
Notting Hill '99

George Mihalka
Eternal Evil '87

Lewis Milestone
Pork Chop Hill '59
The Strange Love of Martha Ivers '46
Of Mice and Men '39
Rain '32
All Quiet on the Western Front '30

John Milius
Red Dawn '84
Conan the Barbarian '82

Catherine Millar
Twisted '96

Stuart Millar
Rooster Cogburn '75

David Miller
Sudden Fear '52

George Miller
Zeus and Roxanne '96

George Miller
Babe: Pig in the City '98
The Witches of Eastwick '87
Mad Max: Beyond Thunderdome '85
The Road Warrior '82
Mad Max '80

Michael Miller
National Lampoon's Class Reunion '82

Robert Ellis Miller
Brenda Starr '86

Troy Miller
Jack Frost '98

Bill Milling
Lauderdale '89

Steve Miner
Lake Placid '99
Halloween: H20 '98
Forever Young '92
Warlock '91
Friday the 13th, Part 2 '81

Wu Ming
Frozen '98

Tsai Ming-Liang
Vive l'Amour '94

Anthony Minghella
The English Patient '96
Mr. Wonderful '93

Rob Minkoff
Stuart Little '99

Vincente Minnelli
Gigi '58
Brigadoon '54
An American in Paris '51
Father's Little Dividend '51

David Mirkin
Romy and Michele's High School Reunion '97

Aziz Mirza
Yes Boss! '97

Bob Misiorowski
Shark Attack '99

David Mitchell
The Killing Man '94

Kenji Mizoguchi
The 47 Ronin, Parts 1 & 2 '42

Moshe Mizrahi
Rachel's Man '75

Gustaf Molander
Intermezzo '36

Ron Moler
The Runner '99

William H. Molina
The Last Assassins '96

Andrew Mollo
Winstanley '75
It Happened Here '65

Christopher Monger
The Englishman Who Went up a Hill But Came down a Mountain '95

Mario Monicelli
Lovers and Liars '81

Guiliano Montaldo
Fifth Day of Peace '72

Jorge Montesi
Hush Little Baby '93

Jocelyn Moorhouse
A Thousand Acres '97
How to Make an American Quilt '95

Brett Morgen
On the Ropes '99

Louis Morneau
Made Men '99
Retroactive '97

David Burton Morris
The Babysitter's Seduction '96

Paul Morrissey
Andy Warhol's Dracula '74
Andy Warhol's Frankenstein '74
Heat '72
Women in Revolt '71
Trash '70
Flesh '68

Terry Morse
Godzilla, King of the Monsters '56

Jonathan Mostow
From the Earth to the Moon '98

John Llewellyn Moxey
The Night Stalker '71

Allan Moyle
Pump Up the Volume '90

Robert Mugge
Kuma Hula: Keepers of the Culture '89
Hawaiian Rainbow '87

Russell Mulcahy
Resurrection '99
Russell Mulcahy's Tale of the Mummy '99
The Shadow '94
The Real McCoy '93
Highlander 2: The Quickening '91
Ricochet '91
Highlander (DC) '86

Ray Muller
The Wonderful, Horrible Life of Leni Riefenstahl '93

Robert Mulligan
To Kill a Mockingbird '62

Danny Mulroon
Desert Heat '99

Jag Mundhra
Monsoon '97
Sexual Malice '93

Robert Munic
Timelock '99

Ryu Murakami
Tokyo Decadence '91

Walter Murch
Return to Oz '85

F.W. Murnau
Nosferatu '22

Geoff Murphy
Under Siege 2 '95

Tom Musca
Race '99

John Musker
Hercules '97
The Little Mermaid '89

Floyd Mutrux
Aloha, Bobby and Rose '74

Daniel Myrick
The Blair Witch Project (SE) '99

Ivan Nagy
Skinner '93

Mira Nair
Kama Sutra: A Tale of Love '96

Desmond Nakano
White Man's Burden '95

Lee Jua Nan
Beauty Investigator '93

Allen Nause
Zigzag '97

Gregory Nava
Why Do Fools Fall in Love? '98
Selena '96

Ronald Neame
The Odessa File '74
The Poseidon Adventure '72

Hal Needham
Cannonball Run 2 '84
Stroker Ace '83
Hooper '78
Smokey and the Bandit '77

Hiroshi Negishi
Tenchi the Movie: Tenchi Myuo in Love '96

Marshall Neilan
Daddy Long Legs '19
Amarilly of Clothesline Alley '18
Stella Maris '18

Daniel Neira
Immortal Combat '94

Gary Nelson
The Black Hole '79

Jessie Nelson
Corrina, Corrina '94

Ralph Nelson
Embryo '76

Kurt Neumann
Mohawk '56

Peter Newbrook
The Asphyx '72

Mike Newell
Pushing Tin '99
Donnie Brasco '96
Four Weddings and a Funeral '94

Sam Newfield
The Flying Serpent '55
The Monster Maker '44

Min Kun Ng
Deadful Melody '92

Fred Niblo
The Three Musketeers '21
Mark of Zorro '20

Andrew Niccol
Gattaca '97

Mike Nichols
Primary Colors '98
The Birdcage '95
Wolf '94
Silkwood '83
Who's Afraid of Virginia Woolf? '66

Jack Nicholson
The Two Jakes '90
The Terror '63

Ted Nicolaou
Bloodstorm: Subspecies 4 '98
Vampire Journals '96

John Nicolella
Kull the Conqueror '97

Govind Nihalani
Thakshak '99

Anatoly Niman
Zig Zag '99

Leonard Nimoy
Star Trek 4: The Voyage Home '86

Katsuhiko Nishijima
Project A-ko '86

Chris Noonan
Babe '95

Tom Noonan
The Wife '95

Lindsay Norgard
Princess Warrior '90

Stephen Norrington
Blade '98

Aaron Norris
Top Dog '95

Bill W.L. Norton
Gargoyles '72

Max Nosseck
The Hoodlum '51

Phillip Noyce
The Bone Collector '99
The Saint '97
Clear and Present Danger '94
Patriot Games '92
Dead Calm '89

Trevor Nunn
Cats '98

Deland Nuse
Return of the Boogeyman '94

David Nutter
Disturbing Behavior '98

Christian Nyby
Whisper Kill '88

Arch Oboler
The Bubble '67

Raoul O'Connell
Boys Life '94

James O'Connolly
Tower of Evil '72

Pat O'Connor
Dancing at Lughnasa '98
Circle of Friends '94

Steve Oedekerk
Nothing to Lose '96
Ace Ventura: When Nature
   Calls '95

Peter O'Fallon
Suicide Kings '97

Susanne Ofteringer
Nico Icon '95

George Ogilvie
Mad Max: Beyond Thunder-
   dome '85

Terrence O'Hara
Darkroom '90

Koichi Ohata
MD Geist (DC) '86

Tommy O'Haver
Billy's Hollywood Screen Kiss
   '98

Masami Ohbari
Voltage Fighters! Gowcaizer:
   The Movie '98

Terence M. O'Keefe
Wanted '98

Laurence Olivier
Henry V '44

Yasuo Ootsuka
Lupin III: The Mystery of
   Mamo '78

Max Ophuls
Lola Montes '55

Paul Oremland
Like It Is '98

Gary Orona
Stripshow '95

Mamoru Oshii
Ghost in the Shell '95

Nagisa Oshima
In the Realm of Passion '80
In the Realm of the Senses
   '76

Gerd Oswald
The Longest Day '62

Katsuhiro Otomo
Roujin Z '95

Cliff Owen
The Vengeance of She '68

Frank Oz
Bowfinger '99
In and Out '97
Dirty Rotten Scoundrels '88
Little Shop of Horrors '86
The Dark Crystal '82

G.W. Pabst
Pandora's Box '28

Alan J. Pakula
The Devil's Own '96
The Pelican Brief '93
Presumed Innocent '90
Sophie's Choice '82

All the President's Men '76
The Parallax View '74

Bruce Paltrow
Ed McBain's 87 Precinct '96

Norman Panama
Court Jester '56

Chuck Parello
Henry: Portrait of a Serial
   Killer 2: Mask of Sanity '96

Dean Parisot
Home Fries '98

Nick Park
Wallace & Gromit: The First
   Three Adventures '99

Alan Parker
Evita '96
The Commitments '91
Mississippi Burning '88
Angel Heart '87
Pink Floyd: The Wall '82
Midnight Express '78

Albert Parker
The Black Pirate '26

Bill Parker
Klash '95

Christine Parker
Peach / A Bitter Song '95

Oliver Parker
An Ideal Husband '99

Gordon Parks
Shaft '71

Billy Parolini
Igor & the Lunatics '85

Larry Parr
A Soldier's Tale '91

Robert Parrish
Journey to the Far Side of the
   Sun '69

Tom Parrish
The Last Game '95

Pier Paolo Pasolini
Salo, or the 120 Days of
   Sodom '75
Arabian Nights '74
The Canterbury Tales '71
The Decameron '70
The Gospel According to St.
   Matthew '64

John Pasquin
The Santa Clause '94

Ivan Passer
Creator '85
Born to Win '71

Michael Pate
Tim '79

Stuart Paton
20,000 Leagues under the
   Sea '16

Steven Paul
Falling in Love Again '80

Scott Paulin
Shelter '98

Mark Pavia
Stephen King's The Night
   Flier '96

George Pavlou
Rawhead Rex '87

Michael Paxton
Ayn Rand: A Sense of Life
   '98

Alexander Payne
Election '99

John Payson
Joe's Apartment '96

Richard Pearce
No Mercy '86

Steven Pearl
The Substitute 2: School's
   Out '97

Max Pecas
Daniella by Night '61

Sam Peckinpah
Cross of Iron '76
The Killer Elite '75
The Getaway '72
Junior Bonner '72
Straw Dogs '72
The Wild Bunch '69

Paul Peditto
Jane Doe '96

Larry Peerce
Two Minute Warning '76

Barbara Peeters
Humanoids from the Deep
   '80

Kimberly Peirce
Boys Don't Cry '99

Jean Pellerin
Laserhawk '99
For Hire '98

Mark Pellington
Arlington Road '99

Arthur Penn
Bonnie & Clyde '67

Sean Penn
The Crossing Guard '94

D.A. Pennebaker
The War Room '93
Ziggy Stardust and the Spi-
   ders from Mars '83

Richard Pepin
Cyber-Tracker '93

Anthony Perkins
Psycho 3 '86

Frank Perry
David and Lisa '62

Nickolas Perry
Boys Life 2 '98

P.J. Pesce
From Dusk Till Dawn 3: The
   Hangman's Daughter '99

Daniel Peters
Masseuse '95

Wolfgang Petersen
Air Force One '97
Outbreak '94
In the Line of Fire '93
Das Boot (DC) '81

Kristine Peterson
Slaves to the Underground
   '96

Daniel Petrie
The Betsy '78

Donald Petrie
My Favorite Martian '98
The Associate '96
Grumpy Old Men '93

Joseph Pevney
Man of a Thousand Faces
   '57
Away All Boats '56

**Toby (Paul Thomas)
Philips**
The Price of Desire '96

Irving Pichel
Destination Moon '50
The Great Rupert '50
She '35
The Most Dangerous Game
   '32

John Pieplow
Dee Snider's Strangeland '98

Frank Pierson
Somebody Has to Shoot the
   Picture '90

Yuen Woo Ping
In the Line of Duty 4 '89
Buddhist Fist '80

Bret Piper
A Nymphoid Barbarian in
   Dinosaur Hell '94

Peter Pistor
The Fence '94

Mark Piznarski
The '60s '99

Allen Plone
Sweet Justice '92
Night Screams '87

Bill Plympton
The Tune '92

Sidney Poitier
Stir Crazy '80

Roman Polanski
Frantic '88
Chinatown '74

Jeff Pollack
Lost and Found '99
Booty Call '96

Sydney Pollack
The Firm '93
Havana '90
Absence of Malice '81
The Electric Horseman '79
Three Days of the Condor '75
Jeremiah Johnson '72
They Shoot Horses, Don't
   They? '69

Harry Pollard
Uncle Tom's Cabin '27

Jack Pollexfen
The Indestructible Man / The
   Amazing Transparent Man
   '56

Renato Polselli
The Reincarnation of Isabel
   '72

Herbert Ponting
90 Degrees South: With
   Scott to the Antarctic '33

Tim Pope
The Crow 2: City of Angels
   '96

P.J. Posner
Last Breath '96

Ted Post
The Baby '72
Hang 'Em High '67

Sally Potter
Orlando '92

Gerald Potterton
Heavy Metal '81

Dick Powell
The Conqueror '56

Michael Powell
Peeping Tom '60
The Red Shoes '48

John Power
Stephen King's The Tommy-
   knockers '93

Udayan Prasad
My Son the Fanatic '97

Jean-Yves Prate
Regina '82

Carl Prechezer
Blue Juice '95

Emeric Pressburger
The Red Shoes '48

Michael Pressman
Capone '89

Arthur Presson
James Dean Double Feature:
   Hill Number One / I Am a
   Fool '51

Leland Price
Life of a Gigolo '98

Barry Primus
Mistress '91

Priyadarshan
Virasat '97

Pat Proft
Wrongfully Accused '98

Yakov Protazanov
Aelita: Queen of Mars '24

Alex Proyas
Dark City '97
The Crow '93

Vsevolod Pudovkin
Storm over Asia '28
Mother '26

L.A. Puopolo
The Turning '92

Joe Pytka
Space Jam '96

Albert Pyun
Urban Menace '99
Crazy Six '98
Postmortem '98
Mean Guns '97
Nemesis '93
Cyborg '89

James Quattrochi
True Friends '98

Richard Quine
Bell, Book and Candle '58

John Quinn
Key to Sex '98

Paul Quinn
This Is My Father '99

Gene Quintano
National Lampoon's Loaded
   Weapon 1 '93

Eric Rademski
Todd McFarlane's Spawn '97

Peter Rader
Grandma's House '88

Michael Radford
The Postman '94

Robert Radler
T.N.T. '98

Michael Raeburn
Laserblast '78

Bob Rafelson
Picture Windows '95
Mountains of the Moon '90
The Postman Always Rings
   Twice '81

Sam Raimi
A Simple Plan '98
The Quick and the Dead '94
Army of Darkness '92
Darkman '90
Evil Dead 2: Dead by Dawn
   '87
Evil Dead '83

Peggy Rajski
Boys Life 2 '98

Harold Ramis
Analyze This '98
Multiplicity '96
Groundhog Day '93

National Lampoon's Vacation '83
Caddyshack '80

Tony Randel
Fist of the North Star '95
Hellbound: Hellraiser 2 '88

Whitney Ransick
Hand Gun '93

Krishna Rao
Crossworlds '96

V. Madhusudan Rao
Lav Kush '97

Mark Rappaport
From the Journals of Jean
Seberg '95

Irving Rapper
The Brave One '56
Another Man's Poison '52

Steve Rash
Eddie '96
Son-in-Law '93
Queens Logic '91
The Buddy Holly Story '78

Brett Ratner
Rush Hour '98

Rand Ravich
The Astronaut's Wife '99

Fred Olen Ray
Friend of the Family 2 '96
Over the Wire '95

Nicholas Ray
Rebel without a Cause '55

Tim Rebman
Ninth Street '98

Robert Redford
The Horse Whisperer '97
Quiz Show '94
A River Runs Through It '92

Carol Reed
Oliver! '68
The Third Man '49
Odd Man Out '47

Jack Reed
Witchouse '99

Joel M. Reed
Bloodsucking Freaks '75

Piero Regnoli
Playgirls and the Vampire '63

Thomas R. Reich
70 Years of Popeye '00

Mark Reichert
Union City '81

Tim Reid
Once Upon a Time . . .
When We Were Colored '95

Carl Reiner
That Old Feeling '96
All of Me '84
The Man with Two Brains '83
The Jerk '79

Rob Reiner
The Story of Us '99
The American President '95
A Few Good Men '92
The Princess Bride '87
Stand by Me '86
This Is Spinal Tap '84

Charles Reisner
Steamboat Bill, Jr. '28

Karel Reisz
Sweet Dreams '85

Wolfgang Reitherman
The Jungle Book '67
101 Dalmatians '61

Ivan Reitman
Six Days, Seven Nights '98
Father's Day '96
Junior '94
Dave '93
Kindergarten Cop '90
Ghostbusters 2 '89
Twins '88
Legal Eagles '86
Ghostbusters '84
Stripes '81
Meatballs '79

Jean Renoir
The Southerner '45
Grand Illusion '37

Alain Resnais
Last Year at Marienbad '61

Burt Reynolds
Sharky's Machine '81

Kevin Reynolds
Waterworld '95
Robin Hood: Prince of
Thieves '91

Michael Reynolds
The Brave Frog '87

Scott Reynolds
Heaven '99
The Ugly '96

Richard Rich
The King and I '99

Cybil Richards
Femalien '96

Dick Richards
Farewell, My Lovely '75

Sybil Richards
Lolida 2000 '97

Tony Richardson
The Phantom of the Opera
'90
Tom Jones '63

Meg Richman
In the Shadows '98

Adam Rifkin
Detroit Rock City '99
Something About Sex '98
The Nutt House '92
Tale of Two Sisters '89

Maria Ripoli
Twice upon a Yesterday '98

Michael Rissi
Soultaker '90

Guy Ritchie
Lock, Stock and 2 Smoking
Barrels '98

Michael Ritchie
A Simple Wish '97
The Golden Child '86
Fletch '85
Divine Madness '80
The Candidate '72

Alfredo Rizzo
The Bloodsucker Leads the
Dance '75

Jay Roach
Austin Powers 2: The Spy
Who Shagged Me '99
Austin Powers: International
Man of Mystery '97

Brian Robbins
Varsity Blues '98

Jerome Robbins
West Side Story '61

Matthew Robbins
*batteries not included '87

Genevieve Robert
Casual Sex? '88

Vincent Robert
The Fear '94

Chris Roberts
Wing Commander '99

John Roberts
Paulie '98

John S. Robertson
Tess of the Storm Country
'22
Dr. Jekyll and Mr. Hyde '20

Phil Alden Robinson
Sneakers '92

Mark Robson
Earthquake '74

Alexandre Rockwell
Four Rooms '95

Franc Roddam
Cleopatra '99
Moby Dick '98
Aria '88

Mic Rodgers
Universal Soldier: The Return
'99

Hans Rodionoff
Sucker the Vampire '98

Robert Rodriguez
The Faculty '98
Desperado '95
Four Rooms '95
From Dusk Till Dawn '95
El Mariachi '93

Nicolas Roeg
The Witches '90
Aria '88
The Man Who Fell to Earth
'76
Walkabout '71

Charles R. Rogers
March of the Wooden Sol-
diers '34

Eric Rohmer
Boyfriends & Girlfriends '88
Summer '86
Full Moon in Paris '84
Le Beau Mariage '82
Chloe in the Afternoon '72
Claire's Knee '71
My Night at Maud's '69
La Collectionneuse '67
The Eric Rohmer Collection:
The Moral Tales '62

Bernard Roland
Portrait of an Assassin '49

Jean Rollin
The Living Dead Girl '82
Fascination '79
Lips of Blood '75
The Demoniacs '74
Requiem for a Vampire '71
The Shiver of the Vampires
'70
Night of the Hunted '69

George A. Romero
The Dark Half '91
Day of the Dead '85
Creepshow '82
Dawn of the Dead '78

Charles R. Rondeau
Train Ride to Hollywood '75

Darrell Roodt
Dangerous Ground '96

Conrad Rooks
Chappaqua '66

Darrell Rooney
The Lion King: Simba's Pride
'98

Don Roos
Opposite of Sex '98

Mark Roper
Operation Delta Force 3:
Clear Target '98
Alien Chaser '96

Bernard Rose
Candyman '92

Sherrie Rose
Me & Will '99

Dan Rosen
The Curve '97

Gary Rosen
Sink or Swim '97

Anita Rosenberg
Assault of the Killer Bimbos
'88

Stuart Rosenberg
Cool Hand Luke '67

Seth Zvi Rosenfeld
A Brother's Kiss '97

Rick Rosenthal
Just a Little Harmless Sex
'99
Bad Boys '83
Halloween 2: The Nightmare
Isn't Over! '81

Rakesh Roshan
Koyla '98

Mark Rosman
Evolver '94

Gary Ross
Pleasantville '98

Herbert Ross
Boys on the Side '94
My Blue Heaven '90
The Secret of My Success
'87
Protocol '84
The Seven-Per-Cent Solution
'76

**Nello (Ted Archer)
Rossati**
Django Strikes Again '87

Roberto Rossellini
Open City '45

Lynn Roth
Changing Habits '96

Phillip J. Roth
Darkdrive '98
Total Reality '97

Roy Rowland
Girl Hunters '63

Joseph Ruben
Return to Paradise '98
Money Train '95
Dreamscape (SE) '84
Pom Pom Girls '76

C.B. Rubin
Fraternity Demon '92

John Rubino
Lotto Land '95

Alan Rudolph
Mortal Thoughts '91

Wesley Ruggles
I'm No Angel '33

Raul Ruiz
Shattered Image '98

Robert Rundle
Cybernator '98

Richard Rush
Color of Night '94

Josef Rusnak
The Thirteenth Floor '99
No Strings Attached '98

Yael Russcol
Extramarital '98

Chuck Russell
Eraser '96
The Mask '94
A Nightmare on Elm Street 3:
Dream Warriors '87

David O. Russell
Three Kings '99
Flirting with Disaster '95

Ken Russell
Aria '88
The Lair of the White Worm
'88
Salome's Last Dance '88
Crimes of Passion '84
Altered States '80
Mahler '74

Klaas Rusticus
The Dandelion Crown '93

Mark Rydell
The River '84
On Golden Pond '81
The Cowboys '72

Michael Rymer
In Too Deep '99

Paul Sabella
Tom Sawyer '99
All Dogs Christmas Carol '98

Bob Saget
Dirty Work '97

Louis Sala
The Boys '97

Malcolm St. Clair
College '27

Gene Saks
Brighton Beach Memoirs '86
Barefoot in the Park '67

Walter Salles
Central Station '98

Mikael Salomon
Hard Rain '97

Victor Salva
Rites of Passage '99
Powder '95

Bernard Salzman
Diamondbacks '99

Stuart Samuels
Visions of Light: The Art of
Cinematography '93

Eduardo Sanchez
The Blair Witch Project (SE)
'99

Jon Sanders
The Wicked, Wicked West '97

Mark Sandrich
Holiday Inn '42

Arlene Sanford
I'll Be Home for Christmas
'98

Cirio H. Santiago
She Devils in Chains '76

Joseph Santley
The Cocoanuts '29

Ken Sanzel
Scarred City '98

Deran Sarafian
Terminal Velocity '94

Richard Sarafian
Solar Crisis '92

Joseph Sargent
Skylark '93
Jaws: The Revenge '87
Nightmares '83

Takuya Sato
Armitage 3: Polymatrix '94

Carlos Saura
Outrage '93

Philip Saville
Metroland '97

Victor Saville
Forever and a Day '43

John Sayles
Limbo '99
Passion Fish '92

Armand Schaefer
Sagebrush Trail '33

Franklin J. Schaffner
Papillon '73
Nicholas and Alexandra '71
Patton '70

Peter Schamoni
Spring Symphony '86

John Scheinfeld
The Unknown Marx Brothers
'93

Carl Schenkel
Tarzan and the Lost City '98
The Surgeon '94

Richard Schenkman
The Pompatus of Love '95

Fred Schepisi
Fierce Creatures '96
Mr. Baseball '92
Plenty '85

Thomas Schlamme
So I Married an Axe Murderer
'93

John Schlesinger
The Falcon and the Snowman
'85
Midnight Cowboy '69

Volker Schlondorff
Palmetto '98
Tin Drum '79

Jay Schlossberg-Cohen
Night Train to Terror '84

Ernest B. Schoedsack
The Most Dangerous Game
'32

Michael Schoemann
The Magic Voyage '93

Stan Schofield
Cost of Living '97

Paul Schrader
Affliction '97
Light Sleeper '92
Cat People '82
American Gigolo '79
Blue Collar '78

Barbet Schroeder
Desperate Measures '98
Single White Female '92

Carl Schultz
The Seventh Sign '88

Michael A. Schultz
Tarzan in Manhattan '89
Car Wash '76

Joel Schumacher
8mm '98
Batman and Robin '97
A Time to Kill '96
Batman Forever '95
The Client '94
Falling Down '93
Flatliners '90
The Lost Boys '87

Moe Schwartz
Yellow Pages '96

Stefan Schwartz
Shooting Fish '98

Zack Schwartz
The Complete Uncensored
Private Snafu '46

Martin Scorsese
Kundun '97
Casino '95
Goodfellas '90
The Color of Money '86
Raging Bull '80
Taxi Driver (CE) '76
Mean Streets '73

Campbell Scott
Big Night '95

Darin Scott
Caught Up '98

Oz Scott
Bustin' Loose '81

Ridley Scott
G.I. Jane '97
White Squall '96
Thelma & Louise '91
Black Rain '94
Someone to Watch Over Me
'87
Blade Runner (DC) '82
Alien '79

Tony Scott
Enemy of the State '98
The Fan '96
Crimson Tide '95
True Romance '93
The Last Boy Scout '91
Days of Thunder '90
Revenge '90
Top Gun '86

Steven Seagal
On Deadly Ground '94

George Seaton
Airport '70
Miracle on 34th Street '47

Mike Sedan
Mischievous '96
Lap Dancing '95
Night Fire '94

Edward Sedgwick
The Phantom of the Opera
'25

Peter Segal
My Fellow Americans '96
Tommy Boy '95

Henry Selick
The Nightmare before Christmas '93

Dean Semler
The Patriot '99
Firestorm '97

Dominic Sena
Kalifornia '93

Ron Senkowski
Wicked Ways '99

Mack Sennett
Tillie's Punctured Romance
'14

Tom Shadyac
Patch Adams (CE) '98
Liar Liar '96
The Nutty Professor '96
Ace Ventura: Pet Detective
'93

Dirk Shafer
Man of the Year '95

Sebastian Shah
An American Affair '99

Don Sharp
Rasputin the Mad Monk '66
Kiss of the Vampire '62

Ben Sharpsteen
Pinocchio '40

William Shatner
Star Trek 5: The Final Frontier
'89

Andrew Shea
Santa Fe '97

John Shea
Southie '98

Katt Shea
The Rage: Carrie 2 '99
Poison Ivy '92

Ron Shelton
Tin Cup '96
Bull Durham '88

Jim Sheridan
The Boxer '97
In the Name of the Father '93
The Field '90
My Left Foot '89

Stephen Shin
The Great Conqueror's Concu-
bine '94
The Great Conqueror's Concu-
bine, Part 2 '94
Black Cat '91

Jack Sholder
Wishmaster 2: Evil Never
Dies '98
The Hidden '87
A Nightmare on Elm Street 2:
Freddy's Revenge '85

Lindsay Shonteff
Curse of the Voodoo '64

Allan Shustak
Midnight Confessions '95

M. Night Shyamalan
The Sixth Sense '99

Charles Shyer
I Love Trouble '94
Father of the Bride '91

George Sidney
Bye, Bye, Birdie '63
Show Boat '51

Donald Siegel
Escape from Alcatraz '79
Dirty Harry '71
The Beguiled '70
Madigan '68
Invasion of the Body Snatch-
ers '56

Brad Silberling
City of Angels '98

Scott Silver
The Mod Squad '99

Elliot Silverstein
Flashfire '94
Betrayed by Innocence '86
The Car '77

Yves Simoneau
Mother's Boys '94

Jane Simpson
Little Witches '96

Bryan Singer
Apt Pupil '97
The Usual Suspects '95
Public Access '93

Craig Singer
Animal Room '95

John Singleton
Rosewood '96
Poetic Justice '93
Boyz N the Hood '91

Gary Sinyor
The Bachelor '99

Robert Siodmak
Custer of the West '67

Andrew Sipes
Fair Game '95

Rob Sitch
The Castle '97

John Sjogren
Red Line '96

Erik Skjoldbjaerg
Insomnia '97

Keri Skogland
Children of the Corn 666:
Isaac's Return '99

Brian Sloan
Boys Life '94

Karl Slovin
Sex and the Other Man '95

George Sluizer
The Vanishing '88

Jack Smight
Midway '76
Airport '75 '75

Brian J. Smith
Body of Influence 2 '96

Charles Martin Smith
Air Bud '97

Chris Smith
American Movie '99

Gary Smith
AFI's 100 Years, 100 Movies
'98

John N. Smith
Dangerous Minds '95

Kent Smith
Forever and a Day '43

Kevin Smith
Mallrats '95
Clerks '94

Mel Smith
Bean '97
Radioland Murders '94

Richard Smith
The Dentist 2: Brace Yourself
'98

Alan Smithee
Solar Crisis '92

Steven Soderbergh
The Limey '99
Out of Sight '98
Gray's Anatomy '96
The Underneath '95
sex, lies and videotape '89

Iain Softley
The Wings of the Dove '97
Hackers '95

Russell Solberg
Raven '97

Alfred Sole
Alice Sweet Alice '76

Todd Solondz
Happiness '98
Welcome to the Dollhouse
'95

Stephen Sommers
The Mummy '99
Deep Rising '98

Barry Sonnenfeld
Wild Wild West '99
Get Shorty '95

Kevin Spacey
Albino Alligator '96

Greg Spence
The Prophecy 2: Ashtown '97

Richard Spence
New World Disorder '99

Robert Spera
Witchcraft '88

Michael Sperrazza
Suspicions '95

Penelope Spheeris
Senseless '98
The Little Rascals '94

Bryan Spicer
For Richer or Poorer '97

Scott Spiegel
From Dusk Till Dawn 2: Texas
Blood Money '98

Steven Spielberg
Saving Private Ryan '98
Amistad '97
Always '89
The Color Purple '85
1941 '79

Bob Spiers
Spice World: The Movie '97

Tony Spiridakis
The Last Word '95

Roger Spottiswoode
Tomorrow Never Dies (SE)
'97
Mesmer '94
Air America '90
The Best of Times '86

Sylvester Stallone
Rocky 4 '85
Rocky 2 '79

Andrew Stanton
A Bug's Life (CE) '98

Ringo Starr
Magical Mystery Tour '67

Jack Starrett
Cleopatra Jones '73

Darren Stein
Jawbreaker '98

Sandor Stern
Assassin '86

Andrew Stevens
Virtual Combat '95

George Stevens
Woman of the Year '42
Penny Serenade '41

Robert Stevenson
The Island at the Top of the
World '74
Mary Poppins '64
Forever and a Day '43

John Stewart
Cartel '90

Ben Stiller
The Cable Guy '96
Reality Bites '94

Whit Stillman
The Last Days of Disco '98

Oliver Stone
U-Turn '97
Nixon '95
The Doors '91
JFK '91
Born on the Fourth of July
'89
Platoon '86

Barbra Streisand
The Mirror Has Two Faces '96

Jeb Stuart
Switchback '97

Mel Stuart
Willy Wonka & the Chocolate
Factory '71

John Sturges
Chino / Man with a Camera
'75

Joe Kidd '72
The Great Escape '63
The Magnificent Seven '60

Charles Sturridge
Aria '88

Susanna Styron
Shadrach '98

Kevin Rodney Sullivan
How Stella Got Her Groove
Back '98

Edward Sutherland
The Flying Deuces / Utopia
'39

Kiefer Sutherland
Truth or Consequences, N.M.
'97

Seijun Suzuki
Branded to Kill '67
Tokyo Drifter '66

Jan Svankmajer
Jan Svankmajer's Faust '94

Peter Svatek
Sci-Fighters '96

E.W. Swackhamer
Death Sentence '74

Bob Swaim
The Climb '97

Peter Swain
The Sci-Fi Files '97

Michael Switzer
Unlikely Angel '97

Jeannot Szwarc
Somewhere in Time '80

Ryszard Szynczak
A Tale of Two Kitties '96

Robert Tai
Legend of the Drunken Tiger
'92

Tibor Takacs
Sanctuary '98
Redline '97

Hideki Takayama
Urotsukidoji: Perfect Collection '89

Rachel Talalay
Freddy's Dead: The Final
Nightmare '91

C.M. Talkington
Love and a .45 '94

Richard Talmadge
Project Moon Base '53

Lee Tamahori
The Edge '97

Quentin Tarantino
Four Rooms '95
Pulp Fiction '94
Reservoir Dogs '92

Andrei Tarkovsky
Nostalghia '83
Solaris '72
Andrei Rublev '66

Mark Tarlov
Simply Irresistible '99

Frank Tashlin
The Complete Uncensored
Private Snafu '46

Anna Maria Tato
Marcello Mastroianni: I
Remember '97

Jud Taylor
Guinevere '93

Sam Taylor
My Best Girl '27

Lewis Teague
Navy SEALS '90

Andre Techine
Wild Reeds '94
Ma Saison Preferee '93

Julien Temple
Earth Girls Are Easy '89
Aria '88

Andy Tennant
Ever After: A Cinderella Story
'98
Fools Rush In '97

John Terlesky
Supreme Sanction '99
The Pandora Project '98

Bela Ternovsky
Cat City '87

Frank Terranova
Caress of the Vampire (CE)
'96

Graham Theakston
Money Kings '98

Betty Thomas
Dr. Dolittle '98
Private Parts '96

David Thomas
Bury Me in Niagara '93

Ralph L. (R.L.) Thomas
Ticket to Heaven '81

J. Lee Thompson
Cabo Blanco / U.S. Marshal
'81
The Guns of Navarone '61
Tiger Bay '59

Chris Thomson
Trucks '97
Swimsuit '89

Billy Bob Thornton
Sling Blade '96

Richard Thorpe
Jailhouse Rock '57
Vengeance Valley '51

Eric Till
To Catch a Killer '92
An American Christmas Carol
'79

George Tillman Jr.
Soul Food '97

Johnny To
A Hero Never Dies '98
The Heroic Trio '93

Norman Tokar
Candleshoe '78
The Cat from Outer Space
'78
Where the Red Fern Grows
'74
The Happiest Millionaire '67
Big Red '62

Dante Tomaselli
Desecration '99

Stanley Tong
Mr. Magoo '97
Jackie Chan's First Strike '96
Rumble in the Bronx '96
Supercop 2 '93
Supercop '92

Roland Topor
Fantastic Planet '73

Robert Towne
Without Limits '97
Tequila Sunrise '88

Joey Travolta
Dumb Luck in Vegas '97
Hard Vice '94

Dale Trevillion
Play Time '94

Jiri Trnka
Puppet Films of Jiri Trnka

Francois Truffaut
Confidentially Yours '83
The Woman Next Door '81
The Last Metro '80
Two English Girls '72
Bed and Board '70
Stolen Kisses '68
Fahrenheit 451 '66
The Soft Skin '64
Shoot the Piano Player '62
The 400 Blows '59

Douglas Trumbull
Brainstorm '83
Silent Running '71

**Dan (Jonathan Lucas)
Tsanusdi**
Trader Hornee '70

Shinya Tsukamoto
Tetsuo 2: Body Hammer '97
Tokyo Fist '96
Tetsuo: The Iron Man '92

Stanley Tucci
The Imposters '98
Big Night '95

Anand Tucker
Hilary and Jackie '98

Ching Siu Tung
The Executioners '93
The Heroic Trio '93
A Chinese Ghost Story III '91
A Chinese Ghost Story II '90
A Chinese Ghost Story '87

Yee Tung-shing
Full Throttle '96
C'est la Vie, Mon Cherie '93

Gary J. Tunnicliffe
Within the Rock '96

Saul J. Turell
The Love Goddesses '65

Jon Turteltaub
Instinct '99
From the Earth to the Moon
'98
Phenomenon '96
While You Were Sleeping '95
Cool Runnings '93

David N. Twohy
The Arrival '96

Tom Tykwer
Run Lola Run '98

Edgar G. Ulmer
The Amazing Transparent
Man '60

Ron Underwood
Mighty Joe Young '98
Heart and Souls '93
Tremors '90

Lawrence Unger
The Seventh Sense '99
Novel Desires '92

Kinka Usher
Mystery Men '99

Roger Vadim
Barbarella '68
Spirits of the Dead '68

Luis Valdez
La Bamba '87

Jean-Claude Van Damme
The Quest '96

Rudolf Van Den Berg
The Johnsons '92

Mario Van Peebles
Panther '95

Posse '93
New Jack City '91

Gus Van Sant
Psycho '98
Good Will Hunting '97
To Die For '95
Drugstore Cowboy '89

Agnes Varda
One Hundred and One Nights
'94

David Veloz
Permanent Midnight '98

Gore Verbinski
Mouse Hunt '97

Pat Verducci
True Crime '95

Paul Verhoeven
Starship Troopers '97
Basic Instinct '92
Total Recall '90
RoboCop '87

Henri Verneuil
Any Number Can Win '63

Marion Vernoux
Love, etc. '96

Dziga Vertov
The Man with the Movie Camera '29

Charles Vidor
Hans Christian Andersen '52

King Vidor
Duel in the Sun '46
Stella Dallas '37
Our Daily Bread and Other
Films of the Depression
'34

Daniel Vigne
The Return of Martin Guerre
'83

Joseph Vilsmaier
Stalingrad '94

Christian Vincent
La Separation '98

Norton Virgien
The Rugrats Movie '98

Clement Virgo
Junior's Groove '97
Rude '96

Carmen Von Daacke
Spoiler '98

Josef von Sternberg
The Shanghai Gesture '42

Kurt Voss
Highway Hitcher '98
Poison Ivy 3: The New Seduc-
tion '97

Andy Wachowski
The Matrix '99
Bound '96

Larry Wachowski
The Matrix '99
Bound '96

Michael Wadleigh
Woodstock (DC) '70

George Waggner
The Wolf Man '41

Bruce Wagner
I'm Losing You '98

J. Robert Wagoner
Avenging Disco Godfather '76

Kai-Fai Wai
Peace Hotel '95

Rupert Wainwright
Stigmata '99

Hal Walker
At War with the Army '50
The Road to Utopia '46

Pete Walker
House of Whipcord '75

Randall Wallace
The Man in the Iron Mask '98

Tommy Lee Wallace
Halloween 3: Season of the
Witch '82

Anthony Waller
An American Werewolf in
Paris '97

Raoul Walsh
Klondike Annie '36

Fred Walton
When a Stranger Calls Back
'93

Martin Walz
Killer Condom '95

Steve Wang
Drive '96

Wayne Wang
Anywhere But Here '99
Chinese Box '97

David S. Ward
King Ralph '91

Vincent Ward
What Dreams May Come '98

Paul Warner
Fall Time '94

Norman J. Warren
Horror Planet '80

John Waters
Pecker '98
Serial Mom '94

Mark Waters
The House of Yes '97

Keoni Waxman
Serial Bomber '96

John Wayne
The Green Berets '68

Robert D. Webb
Beneath the 12-Mile Reef '53

Lo Wei
The Killer Meteors '87
To Kill with Intrigue '85
The Dragon Fist '80
Spiritual Kung Fu '78
New Fist of Fury '76
Chinese Connection '73
Fists of Fury '73

Petr Weigl
Lady Macbeth of Mtsensk
'92
Maria Stuarda '88
Werther '88

Lance Weiler
The Last Broadcast '98

Chuck Wein
Rainbow Bridge '71

Yossi Wein
Operation Delta Force 2: Mayday '97

Richard Weinman
Hunter's Moon '97

Peter Weir
The Truman Show '98
Fearless '93
Dead Poets Society '89
Witness '85
The Year of Living Dangerous-
ly '82
Gallipoli '81
Picnic at Hanging Rock '75

The "Screenwriter Index" lists all writers with at least one credit in the DVDs reviewed in this book. The listings for the writer names follow an alphabetical sort by last name (although the names appear in a first name, last name format). The videographies are listed chronologically, from most recent film to their first. If a writer wrote (or script doctored) more than one film in the same year, these movies are listed alphabetically within the year.

Paul Aaron
In Too Deep '99

Sidney Aaron
Altered States '80

George Abbott
The Pajama Game '57
All Quiet on the Western
Front '30

Simon Abbott
Beyond Suspicion '94

Dustin Lee Abraham
The Runner '99

Jim Abrahams
Kentucky Fried Movie '77

Jack Abramoff
Red Scorpion '89

Robert Abramoff
Red Scorpion '89

Jeffrey Abrams
Forever Young '92

J.J. Abrams
Armageddon '98

Neil Abramson
Without Air '95

Mikhaila Max Adams
Excess Baggage '96

Alan J. Adler
Parasite '82

Gilbert Adler
Tales from the Crypt Presents
Bordello of Blood '96

Felix Adlon
Eat Your Heart Out '96

Gilles Adrien
The City of Lost Children '95

Ben Affleck
Good Will Hunting '97

Yau Da Ah-Pin
Dream Lovers '86

Jeff Albert
The Base '99

Marvin H. Albert
Rough Night in Jericho '67

Todd Alcott
Antz '98
Curtain Call '97

Steve Alden
Fall Time '94

Will Aldis
Stealing Home '88

Scott Alexander
Man on the Moon '99
The People vs. Larry Flynt '96

Danielle Alexandra
G.I. Jane '97

Grigori Alexandrov
Ten Days That Shook the
World '27

Sherman Alexie
Smoke Signals '98

Ted Allan
Falling in Love Again '80

Curt Allen
Bloodstone '88

Janis Allen
Meatballs '79

Jay Presson Allen
Deathtrap '82
Cabaret '72

Peter Allen
Klash '95

Woody Allen
Celebrity '98
Deconstructing Harry '97
Everyone Says I Love You '96
Mighty Aphrodite '95
Bullets over Broadway '94
Manhattan Murder Mystery
'93
Crimes & Misdemeanors '89
Annie Hall '77
Take the Money and Run '69

Michael Allin
Enter the Dragon (SE) '73

Michael Almereyda
The Eternal Kiss of the
Mummy '99

Pedro Almodovar
Kika '94

Rami Alon
Choices '81

Mark Altman
Free Enterprise '98

Robert Altman
Ready to Wear '94

Aria '88

Rod Amateau
Sunset '88

Eric Ambler
A Night to Remember '58

Alejandro Amenabar
Thesis '96

Sergio Amidei
Tales of Ordinary Madness
'83
Open City '45

Hossein Amini
The Wings of the Dove '97

Martin Amis
Saturn 3 '80

Gee An
Mah Jong Dragon '97

Chiu Tai An-Ping
Rouge '87

Leo Anchoriz
Cold Eyes of Fear '70

Allison Anders
Grace of My Heart (CE) '96
Four Rooms '95

Gerry Anderson
Journey to the Far Side of the
Sun '69

Jane Anderson
How to Make an American
Quilt '95

Maxwell Anderson
Rain '32
All Quiet on the Western
Front '30

Paul Thomas Anderson
Boogie Nights '97

Wes Anderson
Rushmore '98
Bottle Rocket '95

William C. Anderson
Bat 21 '88

Del Andrews
All Quiet on the Western
Front '30

**Robert D. (Hardy)
Andrews**
Bataan '43

Tina Andrews
Why Do Fools Fall in Love?
'98

Mark Andrus
As Good As It Gets '97

Mikel Angel
Psychic Killer '75

Edward Anhalt
Jeremiah Johnson '72

Steve Antin
Gloria '98

Penny Antine
The Price of Desire '96

Michelangelo Antonioni
The Red Desert '64

Judd Apatow
The Cable Guy '96

Daniel Appleby
Bound and Gagged: A Love
Story '93

Gregg Araki
Splendor '99

Shimon Arama
Black Eagle '88

Vicente Aranda
The Blood Spattered Bride
'72

David Arata
Brokedown Palace '99

Jeffrey Arch
Sleepless in Seattle '93

Ted Archer
See Nello (Ted Archer) Rossati

Dario Argento
The Phantom of the Opera
'98
Demons 2 '87
Demons '86
Creepers '85
Inferno '80
Deep Red: Hatchet Murders
'75
The Bird with the Crystal
Plumage '70

Kevin Arkadie
The Temptations '98

Alice Arlen
Silkwood '83

Frank Armitage
They Live '88

Steve Armogida
Masseuse '95

Antony Armstrong
Young and Innocent '37

Jerome Armstrong
Volcano '97

Mike Armstrong
Monument Ave. '98

Elliott Arnold
Alvarez Kelly '66

Frank Arnold
Humanoids from the Deep
'80

David Arnott
Last Action Hero '93

Darren Aronofsky
Pi '98

Kengo Asai
Voltage Fighters! Gowcaizer:
The Movie '98

Michael Aschner
Rudolph the Red-Nosed Reindeer: The Movie '98

Morris Asgar
Project: Eliminator '91

Howard Ashman
Little Shop of Horrors '86

James Ashton
Devil's Rain '75

Olivier Assayas
Irma Vep '96

Eileen Atkins
Mrs. Dalloway '97

Peter Atkins
Wishmaster '97
Hellbound: Hellraiser 2 '88

Sean Atkins
Godmoney '99

Larry Atlas
Sleepless in Seattle '93

Leopold Atlas
Raw Deal '48
The Story of G.I. Joe '45

Paul Attanasio
Sphere '97
Donnie Brasco '96

Disclosure '94
Quiz Show '94

Remi Aubuchon
From the Earth to the Moon '98

Michel Audiard
Any Number Can Win '63

John August
Go '99

Jean Aurel
Confidentially Yours '83

Paul Auster
Lulu on the Bridge '98

Carl Austin
Sexual Malice '93

Philip Austin
Zachariah '70

Stefan Avalos
The Last Broadcast '98

Roger Roberts Avary
Pulp Fiction '94

Antonio Avati
Zeder '83

Pupi Avati
Zeder '83

Robert J. Avrech
Body Double '84

George Axelrod
The Manchurian Candidate '62
Breakfast at Tiffany's '61

Dan Aykroyd
The Blues Brothers 2000 '98
Nothing but Trouble '91
Ghostbusters 2 '89
Dragnet '87
Spies Like Us '85
Ghostbusters '84
The Blues Brothers (CE) '80

Peter Aykroyd
Nothing but Trouble '91

John Ayre
Surf Nazis Must Die (DC) '87

Rafael Azcona
Blood and Sand '89
Don't Touch the White Woman! '74

Jean Bach
A Great Day in Harlem / The Spitball Story '94

Michael Backes
Rising Sun '93

Jean-Pierre Bacri
Un Air de Famille '96

Phillip Badger
Retroactive '97

Jennifer Badham-Stewart
Diary of a Serial Killer '97

Alison Bagnall
Buffalo 66 '97

Fax Bahr
Son-in-Law '93

Steven Baigelman
Feeling Minnesota '96

Cameron Bailey
Junior's Groove '97

William Bairn
Torture Chamber of Baron Blood '72

Peter Bakalian
The King and I '99

Herbert Baker
The Jazz Singer '80

Antony Balch
Horror Hospital '73

John Lloyd Balderston
The Bride of Frankenstein '35
The Mummy '32
Frankenstein '31

Milt Banta
Peter Pan '53

Franco Barbieri
Beyond the Door 2 '79

Rudy Barcello
Alegria '98

Clive Barker
Lord of Illusions '95
Hellraiser '87
Rawhead Rex '87

Joseph John Barmettler Jr.
Timelock '99

Peter Barnes
Alice in Wonderland '99
Noah's Ark '99

Enrique Pineda Barnet
I Am Cuba '64

James Lee Barrett
The Green Berets '68

J.M. Barrie
As You Like It '36

Michael Barrie
Bad Boys '95
Amazon Women on the Moon '87

Steven Barron
The Adventures of Pinocchio '96

Julian Barry
The River '84

Peter Barsocchini
Drop Zone '94

Joel Basberg
Family of Cops '95

Harry Basil
Meet Wally Sparks '97

Kim Bass
A Thin Line Between Love and Hate '96

Ronald Bass
Entrapment '99
How Stella Got Her Groove Back '98
Stepmom '98
What Dreams May Come '98
My Best Friend's Wedding '97
Dangerous Minds '95
When a Man Loves a Woman '94
Rain Man '88

Seth Bass
The Twilight of the Golds '97

William Bast
The Betsy '78

Janet Scott Batchler
Batman Forever '95

Lee Batchler
Batman Forever '95

H.E. Bates
Summertime '55

Aurelius Battaglia
Pinocchio '40

Joe Batteer
Blown Away '94

Lloyd Battista
Comin' At Ya! '81

Lucio Battistrada
Autopsy '78

John Tucker Battle
Invaders from Mars '53

Luigi (Paolo Solvay) Batzella
Nude for Satan '74

Hans Bauer
Anaconda '96

Noah Baumbach
Mr. Jealousy '98

Lamberto Bava
Demons 2 '87
Demons '86
Beyond the Door 2 '79

Mario Bava
Lisa and the Devil / The House of Exorcism '75
Twitch of the Death Nerve '71
Kill, Baby, Kill '66
Black Sunday '60

Anees Bazmee
Pyar to Hona Hi Tah '98

Sergio Bazzini
The Inheritance '76

Wayne Beach
Murder at 1600 '97

Henry Bean
Desperate Measures '98
Deep Cover '92
Internal Affairs '90

Richard Beattie
Face the Evil '97

Warren Beatty
Bulworth '98
Heaven Can Wait '78

Simon Beaufoy
The Full Monty '96

Trace Beaulieu
Mystery Science Theater 3000: The Movie '96

Phil Beauman
Don't Be a Menace to South Central While Drinking Your Juice in the Hood '95

Josh Becker
Running Time '97

Dick Beebe
House on Haunted Hill '99

Marc Behm
Help! '65

Melissa Behr
Me & Will '99

Jean-Jacques Beineix
Diva '82

Elisa Bell
Vegas Vacation '96

Donald P. Bellisario
Quantum Leap: The Pilot Episode '89

Peter Bellwood
Highlander 2: The Quickening '91
Highlander (DC) '86

Jerry Belson
Always '89

Peter Benchley
The Deep '77

Barbara Benedek
The Big Chill '83

Tom Benedek
The Adventures of Pinocchio '96
Zeus and Roxanne '96

Roberto Benigni
Life Is Beautiful '98
The Monster '96

Charles Bennett
Forever and a Day '43
Reap the Wild Wind '42
Young and Innocent '37
Sabotage '36
The Secret Agent '36
The 39 Steps '35
The Man Who Knew Too Much '34

Harve Bennett
Star Trek 4: The Voyage Home '86

John Robert Bensink
Whisper Kill '88

Robert Benton
Twilight '98
Bonnie & Clyde '67

Michael Benveniste
Flesh Gordon '72

Leo Benvenuti
The Santa Clause '94

Clara Beranger
Dr. Jekyll and Mr. Hyde '20

Eric Bercovici
Hell in the Pacific '69

Leonardo Bercovici
High Noon '52
The Bishop's Wife '47

Bruce Beresford
Mister Johnson '91
Aria '88
Breaker Morant '80

Peter Berg
Very Bad Things '98

Robert Berger
Final Analysis '92

Per (Pelle) Berglund
My Life As a Dog '85

Andrew Bergman
Striptease '96
Honeymoon in Vegas '92
The Freshman '90
Fletch '85
Blazing Saddles '74

Ingmar Bergman
The Seventh Seal '56

Peter Bergman
Zachariah '70

Eric Bergren
Frances '82

Eleanor Bergstein
Dirty Dancing '87
Dirty Dancing (CE) '87

Sam Bernard
Warlock: The Armageddon '93

Kevin Bernhardt
Sweepers '99

Adam Bernstein
Six Ways to Sunday '99

Gregory Bernstein
Trial and Error '96

Jack Bernstein
Ace Ventura: Pet Detective '93

Jon Bernstein
Ringmaster '98

Marcos Bernstein
Central Station '98

Sarah Bernstein
Trial and Error '96

Walter Bernstein
The Betsy '78
The Train '65

Eric Bernt
Virtuosity '95
Surviving the Game '94

Christopher Bertolini
The General's Daughter '99

Bernardo Bertolucci
Besieged '98
The Last Emperor '87
Last Tango in Paris '73

Luc Besson
The Fifth Element '97
The Professional '94
La Femme Nikita '91
Subway '85

Jonathan Betuel
My Science Project '85
The Last Starfighter '84

A.I. Bezzerides
Beneath the 12-Mile Reef '53

Sanjay Leela Bhansali
Hum Dil De Chuke Sanam '99
Khamoshi the Musical '96

Ann Biderman
Primal Fear '96
Copycat '95

Andy Bienen
Boys Don't Cry '99

Andre Bijelic
Cube '98

Danny Bilson
The Rocketeer '91

Mike Binder
The Sex Monster '99

Brad Bird
*batteries not included '87

Lajos Biro
The Scarlet Pimpernel '34

John Bishop
Drop Zone '94

Larry Bishop
Underworld '96

Mark Bishop
Tales from the Crypt Presents Demon Knight '94

Richard Bissell
The Pajama Game '57

Rick Bitzelberger
Embrace the Darkness '98
Embrace the Vampire '95

Alan Black
Faces of Death '78

Darby Black
Sweepers '99

David Black
The Confession '98

J. Anderson Black
Tarzan and the Lost City '98

John D.F. Black
Shaft '71

Karen Black
Men '97

Shane Black
The Long Kiss Goodnight '96
Last Action Hero '93
The Last Boy Scout '91
Lethal Weapon '87

Rikki Beadle Blair
Stonewall '95

Michael Blake
Dances with Wolves '90

Jim Carabatsos
Hamburger Hill '87
No Mercy '86

Steven W. Carabatsos
The Last Flight of Noah's Ark '80

Alec Carlin
Darkdrive '98

Lewis John Carlino
The Great Santini '80

Hillary Carlip
An Extremely Goofy Movie '99

Joe Carnahan
Blood, Guts, Bullets and Octane '99

Matthew Carnahan
Black Circle Boys '97

Joao Emmanuel Carneiro
Central Station '98

Marc Caro
The City of Lost Children '95

Glenn Gordon Caron
Picture Perfect '96
Moonlighting '85
Condorman '81

A.J. Carothers
The Secret of My Success '87
The Happiest Millionaire '67

John Carpenter
John Carpenter's Vampires '97
Escape from L.A. '96
Village of the Damned '95
They Live '88
Prince of Darkness '87
Halloween 2: The Nightmare Isn't Over! '81
Halloween '78
Assault on Precinct 13 '76
Dark Star '74

Tito Carpi
Cold Eyes of Fear '70

Benjamin Carr
Curse of the Puppet Master: The Human Experiment '98
The Creeps '97

Michael Carreras Younger
See Henry (Michael Carreras) Younger

Jim Carrey
Ace Ventura: Pet Detective '93

Jean-Claude Carriere
Chinese Box '97
The Unbearable Lightness of Being '88
The Return of Martin Guerre '83
Tin Drum '79

Tod Carroll
Clean and Sober '88

Willard Carroll
Playing by Heart '98

Chris Carter
The X-Files '98

Jim Cash
Anaconda '96
The Secret of My Success '87
Legal Eagles '86
Top Gun '86

John Cassavetes
Opening Night '77
Minnie and Moskowitz '71

Sergio Casstner
Mark of the Devil '69

Enzo G. Castellari
Cold Eyes of Fear '70

Michael Castle
Don't Answer the Phone '80

Victor Andres Catena
A Fistful of Dollars '64

Liliana Cavani
Francesco '89

Frank Cavett
Going My Way / Holiday Inn '44

Vincenzo Cerami
Life Is Beautiful '98
The Monster '96

Chris Ceraso
The Turning '92

Jeff Cesario
Jack Frost '98

Claude Chabrol
L'Enfer '93

Kung-Yung Chai
Fong Sai Yuk '93

Ilene Chaiken
Barb Wire '96

Kitty Chalmers
Cyborg '89

Robert W. Chambers
America '24

Eric Champnella
Eddie '96

Benny Chan
Big Bullet '96

Gordon Chan
Beast Cops '98
Armageddon '97
First Option '96
King of Beggars '92
Dragons Forever '88

Jackie Chan
Jackie Chan's Who Am I '98
Jackie Chan: My Story '97
Operation Condor '91
Operation Condor 2: The Armour of the Gods '86
Fearless Hyena '79

Kin-Chung Chan
King of Beggars '92

Koon-Chung Chan
Hong Kong 1941 '84

Philip Chan
Long Arm of the Law II '87
Long Arm of the Law '84

Suk-Yin Chan
Big Bullet '96

Susan Chan
Jackie Chan's Who Am I '98

Susanne Chan
The Executioners '93

Robert Chandlee
The Killer inside Me '76

Elizabeth Chandler
A Little Princess '95

Raymond Chandler
Strangers on a Train '51
Double Indemnity '44

Tom Chaney
Mosquito '95

Jiang-Chung Change
Fong Sai Yuk '93

Charlie Chaplin
The Chaplin Mutuals, Vol. 1 '90s
The Chaplin Mutuals, Vol. 2 '90s
The Chaplin Mutuals, Vol. 3 '90s
Chaplin's Essanay Comedies, Vol. 1 '90s
Chaplin's Essanay Comedies, Vol. 2 '90s
Chaplin's Essanay Comedies, Vol. 3 '90s
A King in New York / A Woman in Paris '57
Limelight '52
Monsieur Verdoux '47
The Great Dictator '40
Modern Times '36
City Lights '31
The Gold Rush '25
The Kid / A Dog's Life '21
The Circus '19

Paul Chaplin
Mystery Science Theater 3000: The Movie '96

Graham Chapman
Monty Python's The Meaning of Life '83
Monty Python's Life of Brian '79
And Now for Something Completely Different '72

Matthew Chapman
Color of Night '94

Richard Chapman
My Fellow Americans '96

Dave Chappelle
Half-Baked '97

Glen Charles
Pushing Tin '99

Les Charles
Pushing Tin '99

Rebecca Charles
Nemesis '93

Borden Chase
Red River '48

Ilene Chase
The Brave Frog '87

David Chaskin
A Nightmare on Elm Street 2: Freddy's Revenge '85

Louis Chavance
The Fantastic Night '42

Paddy Chayefsky
Altered States '80
Network '76

Joan Chen
Xiu Xiu: The Sent Down Girl '97

Teddy Chen
Black Mask '96

Chung Kai Cheong
City War '89

Tsang Kan Cheong
Magnificent Warriors '87

Cy Chermack
The 4D Man '59

Lionel Chetwynd
Tom Clancy's Netforce '98

Helen Childress
Reality Bites '94

Stephen Chin
Another Day in Paradise '98

Wong Ching
Buddhist Fist '80

Chris Chisholm
Jane Street '96

Stephen (Chiau) Chow
God of Cookery '96

Taurus Chow
Expect the Unexpected '98

Mark Christopher
Boys Life 2 '98
54 '98

Dick Chudnow
Spy Hard '96

Janet Chun
A Bullet in the Head '90

John Cianetti
Judge & Jury '96

Cynthia Cidre
In Country '89

Santo Cilauro
The Castle '97

Michael Cimino
The Deer Hunter '78
Silent Running '71

Patrick Cirillo
The Surgeon '94

Sergio Citti
Salo, or the 120 Days of Sodom '75

Rene Clair
And Then There Were None '45

Bob (Benjamin) Clark
Baby Geniuses '98
A Christmas Story '83
Porky's '82
Children Shouldn't Play with Dead Things '72

Greydon Clark
Final Justice '84
Psychic Killer '75

Ron Clark
Revenge of the Pink Panther '78

Arthur C. Clarke
2010: The Year We Make Contact '84
2001: A Space Odyssey '68

Zoe Clarke-Williams
Men '97

James Clavell
The Last Valley '71
The Great Escape '63

Elliot J. Clawson
The Phantom of the Opera '25

John Cleese
Fierce Creatures '96
A Fish Called Wanda '88
Monty Python's The Meaning of Life '83
Monty Python's Life of Brian '79
And Now for Something Completely Different '72

Monica Clemens
Love to Kill '97

Dick Clement
Excess Baggage '96
The Commitments '91

Ron Clements
Hercules '97
The Little Mermaid '89

Gianfranco Clerici
New York Ripper '82

Howard Clewes
Three Musketeers '88

Edward F. (Eddie) Cline
College '27
Seven Chances '25
Three Ages '23
The Saphead '21

Robert Clouse
China O'Brien '88

Henri-Georges Clouzot
L'Enfer '93
Diabolique '55
Wages of Fear '55

Nicole Coady
Embrace of the Vampire '95

Marian Cockrell
Dark Waters '44

Jay Cocks
Strange Days '95

Jean Cocteau
Beauty and the Beast '46

Bill Cody
Slaves to the Underground '96

Ethan Coen
The Big Lebowski '97
Fargo '96
The Hudsucker Proxy '93

Franklin Coen
The Train '65

Joel Coen
The Big Lebowski '97
Fargo '96
The Hudsucker Proxy '93

Joseph Coencas
A Very Natural Thing '73

Lenore Coffee
Sudden Fear '52

Charlie Coffey
Earth Girls Are Easy '89

David Aaron Cohen
The Devil's Own '96

Joel Cohen
Goodbye, Lover '99

Larry Cohen
Uncle Sam '96
Maniac Cop '88
Q (The Winged Serpent) '82

Lawrence D. Cohen
Stephen King's The Tommyknockers '93
Ghost Story '81

Martin B. Cohen
Humanoids from the Deep '80
Rebel Rousers '69

Rob Cohen
Dragon: The Bruce Lee Story '93

Steve Cohen
The Bachelor '99

Alfred A. Cohn
The Cat and the Canary '27

Clifton Cole
Lee Rock '91

Lester Cole
Blood on the Sun '45

Lewis Colick
October Sky '99
Bulletproof '96
Judgment Night '93

Richard A. Colla
Battlestar Galactica '78

Michael Colleary
Face/Off '97

Boon Collins
Spirit of the Eagle '90

Pen Densham
Robin Hood: Prince of
Thieves '91

Alan Dent
Henry V '44

Brian DePalma
Raising Cain '92
Body Double '84

Georges des Esseintes
Animal Instincts '92
Secret Games '92

Helen Deutsch
National Velvet '44

Roger Deutsch
Blank Generation '79

Maurice Devereaux
Lady of the Lake '98

D.V. DeVincentis
Grosse Pointe Blank '97

Scott Devine
Shark Attack '99

Dean Devlin
Godzilla '98
Independence Day '96
Stargate '94
Universal Soldier '92

Lorraine Devon
To Cross the Rubicon '91

Christopher DeVore
Frances '82

Pete Dexter
Michael '96

Paolo Di Girolano
Three Musketeers '88

Gerald Di Pega
Instinct '99
Sharky's Machine '81

I.A.L. Diamond
The Front Page '74

Tom DiCillo
The Real Blonde '97
Box of Moonlight '96

James Dickey
Deliverance '72

Joan Didion
Up Close and Personal '96

Anton Diether
Cleopatra '99
Moby Dick '98

Frank Dietz
Cold Harvest '98

Richard Dilello
Bad Boys '83

Rich Dillon
Dumb Luck in Vegas '97

Robert Dillon
The River '84

Brian DiMuccio
Little Witches '96
The Demolitionist '95
Voodoo '95

Greg Dinner
The Matchmaker '97

Gerald DiPego
Message in a Bottle '98
Phenomenon '96

Mark DiSalle
Kickboxer '89

Ken Dixon
Slave Girls from Beyond Infinity '87

Leslie Dixon
The Thomas Crown Affair '99
That Old Feeling '96
Mrs. Doubtfire '93
Outrageous Fortune '87
Overboard '87

Darren Doane
Godmoney '99

Lem Dobbs
The Limey '99
Dark City '97
The Hard Way '91

Frances Doel
Big Bad Mama '74

Edward Doherty
The Fighting Sullivans '42

Jacques Doillon
Ponette '95

Bob Dolman
Far and Away '92

Richard Dominguez
Hyper Space '89

Jeannine Dominy
Dangerous Beauty '98

Simon Donald
My Life So Far '98

Sergio Donati
The Good, the Bad and the
Ugly '67

Martin Donovan
Death Becomes Her '92

Anita Doohan
Embryo '76

James Doran
The Ipcress File '65

Matt Dorff
Random Encounter '98
Closer and Closer '96

Michael Feit Dougan
Public Access '93

Jerry Douglas
Score '72

Lorenzo Doumani
Follow Your Heart '98
Misery Brothers Y2K '95

Nancy Dowd
Slap Shot '77

Allison Louise Downe
Blood Feast (SE) '63

Laura Downey
Hugo Pool '97

Stephen J. Downing
Witchcraft 9: Bitter Flesh '96

Roddy Doyle
The Commitments '91

Brian Doyle-Murray
Caddyshack '80

Srdjan Dragojevic
Pretty Village, Pretty Flame
'96

Diane Drake
Only You '94

Jay Dratler
Impact '49

Hal Dresner
The Eiger Sanction '75

Carl Theodor Dreyer
Vampyr '31
Passion of Joan of Arc '28

Robin Driscoll
Bean '97

Kevin Droney
Wing Commander '99

Mortal Kombat 1: The Movie
'95

Pierre Drouot
Daughters of Darkness '71

Mark Dubas
Boys Will Be Boys '97

Adam Dubin
Drop Dead Rock '95

Charles S. Dubin
The Meanest Men in the
West '76

John Duigan
The Leading Man '96
Sirens '94

Bruno Dumont
The Life of Jesus '96

Patrick Duncan
Nick of Time '95

Patrick Sheane Duncan
Mr. Holland's Opus '95

Ronald Duncan
The Girl on a Motorcycle '68

Winifred Dunn
Sparrows '26

John Gregory Dunne
Up Close and Personal '96

Evan Dunsky
The Alarmist '98

Roger Dunton
The Ghost Goes Gear '66

Carl DuPre
Detroit Rock City '99
The Prophecy 3: The Ascent
'99

Arnaud d'Usseau
Horror Express '72

Robert Duvall
The Apostle '97

Julien Duvivier
Anna Karenina '48

Russ Dvonch
Rock 'n' Roll High School '79

Laurence Dworet
Outbreak '94

H. Kaye Dyal
Project: Eliminator '91

Halle Eaton
Embrace of the Vampire '95

Janos Edelenyi
The Long Shadow '92

Patrick Edgeworth
Raw Deal '86

Blake Edwards
Sunset '88
10 '79
Revenge of the Pink Panther
'78
The Pink Panther '64
A Shot in the Dark '64

Atom Egoyan
Felicia's Journey '99
The Sweet Hereafter '96
Exotica '94

Kerry Ehrin
Inspector Gadget '99

Paul Eichgrun
Rock 'n' Roll Invaders: The
AM Radio DJs '90s

Bruce David Eisen
Warlock 3: The End of Innocence '98

Sergei Eisenstein
Ivan the Terrible, Part 2 '46

Ivan the Terrible, Part 1 '44
Alexander Nevsky '38
Ten Days That Shook the
World '27
The Battleship Potemkin '25

Philip Eisner
Event Horizon '97

**John (Anthony Hinds)
Elder**
Dracula, Prince of Darkness
'66
Plague of the Zombies '66
Rasputin the Mad Monk '66
The Reptile '66
Kiss of the Vampire '62

Lonnie Elder III
Bustin' Loose '81

Laurice Elehwany
My Girl '91

Harry Elfont
Can't Hardly Wait '98

Michael Elias
The Jerk '79

Joyce Eliason
The Last Don '97

Doug Ellin
Kissing a Fool '98

Stephan Elliott
The Adventures of Priscilla,
Queen of the Desert '94

Ted Elliott
The Mask of Zorro '98
Small Soldiers '98

Joseph Ellison
Don't Go in the House '80

Roland Emmerich
Godzilla '98
Independence Day '96
Stargate '94

E.V.H. Emmett
Sabotage '36

Guy Endore
The Story of G.I. Joe '45

Otto Englander
Pinocchio '40

Ken Englund
The Secret Life of Walter
Mitty '47

Delia Ephron
Michael '96

Henry Ephron
Carousel '56

Nora Ephron
You've Got Mail '98
Michael '96
Sleepless in Seattle '93
My Blue Heaven '90
Silkwood '83

Phoebe Ephron
Carousel '56

Jack Epps Jr.
Anaconda '96
The Secret of My Success
'87
Legal Eagles '86
Top Gun '86

Julius J. Epstein
Cross of Iron '76
The Last Time I Saw Paris
'54
Casablanca '42

Philip C. Epstein
The Last Time I Saw Paris
'54
Casablanca '42

Greg Erb
Senseless '98

Chester Erskine
Midnight '34

John Eskow
The Mask of Zorro '98

John Esposito
Russell Mulcahy's Tale of the
Mummy '99

Laura Esquivel
Like Water for Chocolate '93

Gabe Essoe
Devil's Rain '75

Howard Estabrook
The Bridge of San Luis Rey
'44

Joe Eszterhas
Telling Lies in America '96
Jade '95
Nowhere to Run '93
Basic Instinct '92

Bentley Kyle Evans
A Thin Line Between Love
and Hate '96

Bruce A. Evans
Starman '84

Gimel Everett
The Lawnmower Man '92

John Eyres
Judge & Jury '96

Wong Wing Fai
In the Line of Duty 4 '89

Douglas Fairbanks Sr.
The Black Pirate '26
Robin Hood '22
The Three Musketeers '21
Mark of Zorro '20

Marion Fairfax
The Lost World '25

Aleksey Fajko
Aelita: Queen of Mars '24

Jamaa Fanaka
Street Wars '91
Penitentiary 2 '82
Penitentiary '79

Hampton Fancher
Blade Runner (DC) '82

**Francis Edwards
Faragoh**
Frankenstein '31

Marty Farrell
AFI's 100 Years, 100 Movies
'98

Bobby Farrelly
Outside Providence '99
There's Something about
Mary '98
Kingpin '96
Dumb & Dumber '94

Peter Farrelly
Outside Providence '99
There's Something about
Mary '98
Dumb & Dumber '94

John Fasano
Universal Soldier: The Return
'99

Alvin L. Fast
Eaten Alive '76

William Faulkner
The Big Sleep '46
The Southerner '45

Jon Favreau
Swingers '96

Jacqueline Feather
The King and I '99
Dancing in the Dark '95

Peter Fedorenko
The Fence '94

F.X. Feeney
The Big Brass Ring '99

Bruce Feirstein
Tomorrow Never Dies (SE) '97

Mark Feldberg
Beverly Hills Ninja '96

Dennis Feldman
Virus '98
The Golden Child '86

Randy Feldman
Metro '96
Nowhere to Run '93
Tango and Cash '89
Hell Night '81

Federico Fellini
And the Ship Sails On '83
Amarcord '74
Spirits of the Dead '68
Juliet of the Spirits '65
Nights of Cabiria '57
Open City '45

Robert Fellows
Girl Hunters '63

Graeme Ferguson
The Love Goddesses '65

Larry Ferguson
The Hunt for Red October '90
Highlander (DC) '86

Rick Ferguson
Suspicions '95

Peter Fernandez
The Dirty Girls '64

Abel Ferrara
New Rose Hotel '98
Bad Lieutenant '92

Will Ferrell
A Night at the Roxbury '98

Marco Ferreri
Tales of Ordinary Madness '83

Franco Ferrini
Demons '86
Creepers '85

Michael Ferris
The Game '97
The Net '95

Jean Ferry
Daughters of Darkness '71

Larry Fessenden
Habit '97

Mike Figgis
One Night Stand '97
Leaving Las Vegas '95

Peter Filardi
The Craft '96
Flatliners '90

Charles Finch
The Dentist '96

Scot (Scott) Finch
Shalako '68

Morton S. Fine
Cabo Blanco / U.S. Marshal '81

John P. Finegan
Girls School Screamers '86

Harry Julian Fink
Dirty Harry '71

Rita M. Fink
Dirty Harry '71

Abem Finkel
Jezebel '38

Fred Finklehoffe
At War with the Army '50
Mr. Ace '46

Richard Fire
Henry: Portrait of a Serial Killer '90

Janice Fischer
The Lost Boys '87

Jeffrey Alladin Fiskin
The '60s '99
From the Earth to the Moon '98

Fannie Flagg
Fried Green Tomatoes '91

Ennio Flaiano
Juliet of the Spirits '65
Nights of Cabiria '57

Harvey Flaxman
Grizzly '76

Andrew Fleming
The Craft '96

R. Lee Fleming Jr.
She's All That '99

Charlie Fletcher
Fair Game '95

Clive Fleury
Big City Blues '99

P.B. Florenz
Underground '90

Robert Florey
Frankenstein '31

Calvin Floyd
Terror of Frankenstein '75

Yvonne Floyd
In Search of Dracula '76
Terror of Frankenstein '75

James Foley
After Dark, My Sweet '90

Peter Fonda
Easy Rider '69

Naomi Foner
Running on Empty '88

Eddie L.C. Fong
Temptation of a Monk '94

Bruno (Roger Fontaine) Fontana
Emmanuelle: Queen of the Desert '93

Horton Foote
Horton Foote's Alone '97
Tender Mercies '83
To Kill a Mockingbird '62

Bryan Forbes
Chaplin '92
The Slipper and the Rose '76

Ron Ford
The Fear '94

Carl Foreman
The Guns of Navarone '61
High Noon '52

Stephen H. Foreman
The Jazz Singer '80

Jean-Claude Forest
Barbarella '68

Larry Forrester
Tora! Tora! Tora! '70

Garrett Fort
Dracula '31
Frankenstein '31

Christian Forte
Albino Alligator '96

Bob Fosse
Star 80 '83

Robert Foster
Dead Bang '89

Vincent Fotre
Torture Chamber of Baron Blood '72

Christian Fournier
The Boys '97

Anthony Foutz
Tales of Ordinary Madness '83

Kevin Fox
The Negotiator '98

Robbie Fox
So I Married an Axe Murderer '93

Brian Foy
College '27

Michael France
Goldeneye '95
Cliffhanger '93

Dan Franck
La Separation '98

Jess (Jesus) Franco
Two Undercover Angels '68

Ricardo Franco
Blood and Sand '89

Bruno Frank
The Hunchback of Notre Dame '39

Frederic M. Frank
The Ten Commandments '56

Harriet Frank Jr.
The Cowboys '72

Hubert Frank
Call of the Wild '72

Melvin Frank
The Road to Utopia '46

Scott Frank
Out of Sight '98
Get Shorty '95
Malice '93
Dead Again '91

David Frankel
Miami Rhapsody '95

Al Franken
When a Man Loves a Woman '94

John Frankenheimer
The Manchurian Candidate '62

Carl Franklin
Devil in a Blue Dress '95

Howard Franklin
The Man Who Knew Too Little '97
Someone to Watch Over Me '87

Paul Franklin
Reefer Madness '38

Steve Franks
Big Daddy '99

David Franzoni
Amistad '97

George MacDonald Fraser
The Four Musketeers '75
The Three Musketeers '74

Robert Freedman
Cinderella '97

Everett Freeman
The Secret Life of Walter Mitty '47

The Princess and the Pirate '44

Gillian Freeman
The Girl on a Motorcycle '68

Leonard Freeman
Hang 'Em High '67

Morgan J. Freeman
Desert Blue '98

Eric Freiser
Warlock 3: The End of Innocence '98

James Frey
Kissing a Fool '98

Ron Fricke
Baraka '93

Jason Friedberg
Spy Hard '96

Rick Friedberg
Spy Hard '96

Richard Friedenberg
A River Runs Through It '92

William Friedkin
The Guardian '90

Brent Friedman
Mortal Kombat 2: Annihilation '97

Bruce Jay Friedman
Stir Crazy '80

David Friedman
Trader Hornee '70

Lewis Friedman
BASEketball '98

Nikolaj Frobenius
Insomnia '97

Lee Frost
Private Obsession '94

Cesare Frugoni
Rabid Dogs '74

Roy Frumkes
The Substitute 2: School's Out '97
The Substitute '96
The Johnsons '92

Rick Fry
Bride of Re-Animator '89

E. Max Frye
Palmetto '98

Thomas Fucci
Blood and Sand '89

Daniel Fuchs
The Underneath '95

Lucio Fulci
New York Ripper '82

Kim Fuller
Spice World: The Movie '97

Samuel Fuller
The Big Red One '80
Naked Kiss '64
Shock Corridor '63

Raymond Fung
Lee Rock '91

Jules Furthman
The Big Sleep '46
The Shanghai Gesture '42
Come and Get It '36

John Fusco
Thunderheart '92
Young Guns '88

Bob Gale
Trespass '92
1941 '70

John Gale
The Firing Line '91

Henrik Galeen
Nosferatu '22

Carlos Gallardo
El Mariachi '93

George Gallo
Midnight Run '88

Vincent Gallo
Buffalo 66 '97

Joe Gannon
Solar Crisis '92

Lowell Ganz
EDtv '99
Father's Day '96
Multiplicity '96
Greedy '94
A League of Their Own '92
Mr. Saturday Night '92
Parenthood '89
Spies Like Us '85
Splash '84
Night Shift '82

Fred Gardner
See Franco (Fred Gardner) Rossetti

Louis Garfinkle
The Deer Hunter '78

Jack Gariss
The Ten Commandments '56

Robert Garland
The Electric Horseman '79

Oliver H.P. Garrett
Duel in the Sun '46
The Hurricane '37

Tim Garrick
Stranger than Fiction '99

Romain Gary
The Longest Day '62

Ernesto Gastaldi
Torso '73

Tudor Gates
Barbarella '68

Joe Gayton
Bulletproof '96

Peter Geiger
The Colony '98

Yan Geling
Xiu Xiu: The Sent Down Girl '97

Stephen Geller
Slaughterhouse Five '72

Milton S. Gelman
Cabo Blanco / U.S. Marshal '81

Jonathan Gems
Mars Attacks! '96

Pierre Gendron
The Monster Maker '44

Robert Geoffrion
The Peacekeeper '98
Eternal Evil '87

Matt George
In God's Hands '98

Matthew George
Under the Gun '95

Peter George
Dr. Strangelove, or: How I Learned to Stop Worrying and Love the Bomb '64

Terry George
A Bright Shining Lie '98
The Boxer '97
In the Name of the Father '93

Maurice Geraghty
Mohawk '56

Marc Gerald
Six Ways to Sunday '99

Chris Gerolmo
Mississippi Burning '88

Jerome Geronimi
Diabolique '55

Robert Getchell
The Client '94
Point of No Return '93
Sweet Dreams '85

Francis Giacobetti
Emmanuelle, the Joys of a
Woman '76

Channing Gibson
Lethal Weapon 4 '98

William Gibson
Johnny Mnemonic '95

Nelson Gidding
The Hindenburg '75
The Andromeda Strain '71

Raynold Gideon
The River Wild '94
Stand by Me '86
Starman '84

Mateo Gil
Thesis '96

David Giler
The Parallax View '74

Jack Gill
Body Armor '96

Terry Gilliam
Fear and Loathing in Las
Vegas '98
The Adventures of Baron
Munchausen '89
Brazil '85
Brazil (Criterion SE) '85
Monty Python's The Meaning
of Life '83
Time Bandits '81
Monty Python's Life of Brian
'79
And Now for Something Com-
pletely Different '72

Sidney Gilliat
Jamaica Inn '39
The Lady Vanishes '38

Vince Gilligan
Home Fries '98

Tony Gilroy
The Devil's Advocate '97
Dolores Claiborne '94

Bryan Gindoff
Hard Times '75

Buddy Giovinazzo
Combat Shock '84

George Gipe
The Man with Two Brains '83

Francois Girard
The Red Violin '98

Francoise Giroud
The Law '59

Matthew Gissing
Tail Lights Fade '99

Robert Gittler
The Buddy Holly Story '78

Hugh Gladwish
The Ghost Goes Gear '66

Jonathan Glassner
Mikey '92

Mitch Glazer
Great Expectations '97
Scrooged '88

Tom Gleisner
The Castle '97

James Glickenhaus
Shakedown '88
Exterminator '80

Myron Goble
Down in the Delta '98

Jean-Luc Godard
Aria '88
Alphaville '65
Pierrot le Fou '65
My Life to Live '62
A Woman Is a Woman '60

Peter Godfrey
Forever and a Day '43

Carmen Rico Godoy
How to Be a Woman and Not
Die in the Attempt '91

Ivan Goff
Man of a Thousand Faces
'57

Dan Goggin
Nunsense '93

Menahem Golan
Armstrong '99

Sandra Goldbacher
The Governess '98

Willis Goldbeck
Peter Pan '24

Dan Goldberg
Heavy Metal '81

Harris Goldberg
I'll Be Home for Christmas
'98

Howard Goldberg
Eden '98

Mel Goldberg
Hang 'Em High '67

Michael Goldberg
Cool Runnings '93

Michael Goldenberg
Contact '97
Bed of Roses '95

Daniel Goldin
Darkman '90

Joshua Goldin
Darkman '90

Bo Goldman
Meet Joe Black '98
City Hall '95
Scent of a Woman '92
Melvin and Howard '80
One Flew Over the Cuckoo's
Nest '75

Gary Goldman
Navy SEALS '90
Total Recall '90

Gina Goldman
Suicide Kings '97

James Goldman
Nicholas and Alexandra '71
They Might Be Giants '71

William Goldman
The General's Daughter '99
Absolute Power '97
The Chamber '96
The Ghost and the Darkness
'96
Maverick '94
Chaplin '92
Casual Sex? '88
The Princess Bride '87
A Bridge Too Far '77
All the President's Men '76
The Stepford Wives '75
Butch Cassidy and the Sun-
dance Kid '69

Akiva Goldsman
Lost in Space '98

Practical Magic '98
Batman and Robin '97
A Time to Kill '96
Batman Forever '95
The Client '94

Allan Goldstein
Jungle Boy '96
Death Wish 5: The Face of
Death '94

Bryan Goluboff
The Basketball Diaries '94

Nick Gomez
New Jersey Drive '95

David Zelag Goodman
Logan's Run '76
Farewell, My Lovely '75
Straw Dogs '72

Frances Goodrich
Seven Brides for Seven
Brothers '54
Father's Little Dividend '51
It's a Wonderful Life '46

Scott Gorden
An Extremely Goofy Movie
'99

Alex Gordon
Bride of the Monster '55
Jail Bait '54

Bernard Gordon
Custer of the West '67
Krakatoa East of Java '66
The Thin Red Line '64

Dan Gordon
Tank '83
Train Ride to Hollywood '75
Gulliver's Travels '39

Don Gordon
The Assignment '97

Leo Gordon
The Terror '63

Robert Gordon
Addicted to Love '96

Ruth Gordon
Adam's Rib '50

Steve Gordon
Arthur '81

Stuart Gordon
The Dentist '96
Body Snatchers '93
Re-Animator '84

Marleen Gorris
Antonia's Line '95

Rene Goscinny
Lucky Luke '94

Carl Gottlieb
The Jerk '79

Clifford Gould
Krakatoa East of Java '66

Peter Gould
Double Dragon '94

Edmund Goulding
Tol'able David '21

David S. Goyer
Blade '98
Dark City '97
The Crow 2: City of Angels
'96

Bruce Graham
Anastasia '97

Jesse Graham
Out of Time '90

Michael Grais
Marked for Death '90
Poltergeist '82

James Edward Grant
McLintock! '63
Sands of Iwo Jima '49
Angel and the Badman '47

John Grant
Abbott and Costello in the
Foreign Legion '50
Buck Privates Come Home
'47
Buck Privates '41
In the Navy '41

Susannah Grant
Ever After: A Cinderella Story
'98

Robert Grasmere
Baby Geniuses '98

Jane Gray
Fire on the Amazon '93

Mike Gray
The China Syndrome '79

Pamela Gray
A Walk on the Moon '99

William Gray
Prom Night '80

Adolph Green
Singin' in the Rain '52

Bob Green
Baraka '93

Clarence Green
D.O.A. '49

Clifford Green
Picnic at Hanging Rock '75

F.L. Green
Odd Man Out '47

Lewis Green
Never Talk to Strangers '95

Walon Green
Eraser '96
RoboCop 2 '90
Sorcerer '77
The Wild Bunch '69

Peter Greenaway
The Pillow Book '95
A Zed & Two Noughts '88
The Draughtsman's Contract
'82

Dan Greenberg
The Guardian '90

Matt Greenberg
Halloween: H20 '98
The Prophecy 2: Ashtown '97

Graham Greene
The Third Man '49

Seth Greenland
My Teacher's Wife '95

Edwin Greenwood
Young and Innocent '37
The Man Who Knew Too
Much '34

Dan Greer
Baker's Hawk '76

Andre Gregory
My Dinner with Andre '81

Frederic Grendel
Diabolique '55

Grimes Grice
See Irene (Grimes Grice)
Kamp

Ted Griffin
Best Laid Plans '99
Ravenous '99

Charles B. Griffith
Eat My Dust '76
Death Race 2000 '75

D.W. Griffith
Orphans of the Storm '21
Way Down East '20
Broken Blossoms '19
Intolerance '16
The Birth of a Nation '15

J.J. Griffith
Shalako '68

Thomas Ian Griffith
Night of the Warrior '91

Nick Grinde
March of the Wooden Sol-
diers '34

John Grisham
The Gingerbread Man '97

Joseph R. Grismer
Way Down East '20

Tony Grisoni
Fear and Loathing in Las
Vegas '98

Wiktor Grodecki
Mandragora '97

Joel Gross
No Escape '94

Larry Gross
Chinese Box '97
Geronimo: An American Leg-
end '93
Streets of Fire '84

Adam Grossman
Carnival of Souls '98
Sometimes They Come Back
... Again '96

Jean-Claude Grumberg
The Last Metro '80

Susan Guathier
Anastasia '97

Paul Guay
Liar Liar '96
The Little Rascals '94

Tonino Guerra
And the Ship Sails On '83
Nostalghia '83
Amarcord '74
The Red Desert '64

Christopher Guest
This Is Spinal Tap '84

Val Guest
Another Man's Poison '52

Peer Guldbrandsen
I, a Woman '66

James Gunn
Tromeo & Juliet '95

Belinda Haas
The Blood Oranges '97

Charles Haas
Matinee '92
Tex '82

Philip Haas
The Blood Oranges '97

Albert Hackett
Seven Brides for Seven
Brothers '54
Father's Little Dividend '51
It's a Wonderful Life '46

Moshe Hadar
Cartel '90

Richard W. Haines
Class of Nuke 'Em High '86

Mary Hale
Multiplicity '96

Julian Halevy
Custer of the West '67

J.D. Hall
Underground '90

Kenneth J. Hall
Die Watching '93

Lasse Hallstrom
My Life As a Dog '85

Forrest Halsey
Sally of the Sawdust '25

James Hamilton
Cross of Iron '76

Sam Hamm
Batman '89

Robert Hammer
Don't Answer the Phone '80

Oscar Hammerstein
State Fair '45

Ellen Hammill
Don't Go in the House '80

Christopher Hampton
Total Eclipse '95
Dangerous Liaisons '88

Orville H. Hampton
Atomic Submarine '59

Mok Tang Han
Supercop 2 '93

John Lee Hancock
Midnight in the Garden of
Good and Evil (SE) '97

Michael Haneke
Funny Games '97

Daryl Haney
Xtro 3: Watch the Skies '95
Stranger by Night '94

Tom Hanks
From the Earth to the Moon
'98

Mary Ellen Hanover
Play Time '94

Erik Hansen
Heart and Souls '93

Gregory Hansen
Heart and Souls '93

Jim Hanson
Witchcraft 2: The Temptress
'90

Kenchiro Hara
The 47 Ronin, Parts 1 & 2
'42

Carl Harbaugh
Steamboat Bill, Jr. '28
College '27

Harry Paul Harber
Terror Is a Man '59

Gary Hardwick
Todd McFarlane's Spawn '97

Jonathon Hardy
Breaker Morant '80

Robert Hardy
See Robert D. (Hardy)
Andrews

David Hare
Damage '92
Plenty '85

Lance Z. Hargreaves
First Man into Space '59

Marion Hargrove
The Music Man '62

Tsui Hark
Black Mask '96
Iron Monkey '93
Once Upon a Time in China III
'93
Once Upon a Time in China II
'92
Twin Dragons '92
Wicked City '92

A Chinese Ghost Story III '91
Once Upon a Time in China
'91

Robert Harling
The First Wives Club '96

Robert Harrar
The Man Who Knew Too Little
'97

Stephen Harrigan
Cleopatra '99

Curtis Harrington
Night Tide '63

Daniel J. Harris
Bury Me in Niagara '93

Elmer Harris
Tess of the Storm Country
'22

James B. Harris
Boiling Point '93

Selwyn Harris
Animal Instincts 3: The
Seductress '95

Timothy Harris
Kindergarten Cop '90
My Stepmother Is an Alien
'88
Twins '88
Brewster's Millions '85

Vernon Harris
Oliver! '68

Hal Harrison Jr.
Baker's Hawk '76

Jim Harrison
Wolf '94
Revenge '90

Joan Harrison
Dark Waters '44
Rebecca '40
Jamaica Inn '39

William Harrison
Rollerball '75

Jacobsen Hart
Raven '97
Cyber-Tracker '93

Jim V. Hart
Dracula '92

Moss Hart
Hans Christian Andersen '52
Gentleman's Agreement '47

Paul Hart-Wilden
Skinner '93

Don Hartman
Wonder Man '45
The Princess and the Pirate
'44
The Road to Morocco '42

Phil Hartman
Pee-wee's Big Adventure '85

George Hartmann
Werther '88

Jack Harvey
Unknown Island '48

Johanna Harwood
From Russia with Love '63
Dr. No (SE) '62

Sergei Hasenecz
Sorority Babes in the Slimeball Bowl-A-Rama '87

Gustav Hasford
Full Metal Jacket '87

Shinobu Hashimoto
Seven Samurai '54

Richard Hatem
Under Siege 2 '95

Eric Hattler
Troma's War (DC) '88

Stephen Hauser
Sphere '97

Jean C. Havez
Seven Chances '25
The Navigator '24
Our Hospitality / Sherlock
Junior '23

Richard J. Havis
Jackie Chan: My Story '97

Michael Hawes
Family Reunion '79

John Hawkesworth
Tiger Bay '59

Richard Hawley
Mother's Boys '94

Christopher Hawthorne
Parents '89

Helen Haxton
Mischievous '96
Night Fire '94

Ian Hay
Sabotage '36
The 39 Steps '35

Al Hayes
The Gingerbread Man '97

Robert Hayes III
Winner Takes All '98

Steve Hayes
Fantastic Planet '73

Terry Hayes
Payback '98
Dead Calm '89
Mad Max: Beyond Thunder-
dome '85
The Road Warrior '82

Todd Haynes
Velvet Goldmine '98

Lillie Hayward
Proud Rebel '58

Ziao He
The Great Conqueror's Concubine '94
The Great Conqueror's Concubine, Part 2 '94

Matthew Healy
Clay Pigeons '98

Megan Heath
Terrified '94

Ben Hecht
Notorious '46
Spellbound '45
Wuthering Heights '39
Nothing Sacred '37

Amy Heckerling
Clueless '95
Look Who's Talking '89

Victor Heerman
Stella Dallas '37

Thomas Heggen
Mister Roberts '55

Robert Heinlein
Project Moon Base '53
Destination Moon '50

Brian Helgeland
Payback '98
Conspiracy Theory '97
L.A. Confidential '97
The Postman '97
Assassins '95
A Nightmare on Elm Street 4:
Dream Master '88

Lukas Heller
The Killing of Sister George
'69

The Dirty Dozen '67
What Ever Happened to Baby
Jane? '62

Lillian Hellman
The Little Foxes '41

Eric Hendershot
A Kid Called Danger '99
The Robin Hood Gang '98

Frank Henenlotter
Brain Damage '88
Basket Case '82

Liu Heng
The Great Conqueror's Concu-
bine '94
The Great Conqueror's Concu-
bine, Part 2 '94
Ju Dou '89

Kim Henkel
The Texas Chainsaw Massa-
cre 4: The Next Genera-
tion '95
Eaten Alive '76
The Texas Chainsaw Mas-
sacre '74

Hilary Henkin
Wag the Dog '97

Beth Henley
True Stories '86

Alex Hennech
Smart Money '97

Richard P. Henrick
Crimson Tide '95

Alain Henry
Entre-Nous '83

Buck Henry
To Die For '95
Protocol '84

David Lee Henry
Out for Justice '91

Jonathan Hensleigh
Armageddon '98
The Saint '97
The Rock '96
Die Hard: With a Vengeance
'95
Jumanji (CS) '95

Jim Henson
Labyrinth '86

Bruce Henstell
Hard Times '75

Geza Herczeg
The Shanghai Gesture '42

Tim Herlihy
Big Daddy '99
The Waterboy '98
The Wedding Singer '97
Happy Gilmore '96

Mark Herman
Little Voice '98
Brassed Off '96

Michael Herr
John Grisham's The Rainmak-
er '97
Full Metal Jacket '87
Apocalypse Now '79

Rowdy Herrington
A Murder of Crows '99
Striking Distance '93

Dodine Herry
Love, etc. '96

Nancy Hersage
The Babysitter's Seduction
'96

Marshall Herskovitz
Glory '89

Adam Herz
American Pie (CE) '99

Werner Herzog
Fitzcarraldo '82
Nosferatu the Vampyre '79
Even Dwarfs Started Small
'69

Eugene Hess
Don't Do It '94

Rod Hewitt
Sworn Enemies '96

Winston Hibler
Nikki, the Wild Dog of the
North '61
Peter Pan '53

George Hickenlooper
The Big Brass Ring '99

Yoichi Higashi
Village of Dreams '97

Howard Higgin
Revolt of the Zombies '36

John C. Higgins
He Walked by Night '48
Raw Deal '48
T-Men '47

Charles Higson
Suite 16 '94

Debra Hill
Escape from L.A. '96
Halloween 2: The Nightmare
Isn't Over! '81
Halloween '78

Elizabeth Hill
Our Daily Bread and Other
Films of the Depression
'34

Gladys Hill
The Man Who Would Be King
'75

Jack Hill
Spider Baby '64
The Terror '63

Jess Hill
Troublemakers '94

Robert F. "Bob" Hill
The Cat and the Canary '27

Walter Hill
Last Man Standing '96
The Getaway '93
Red Heat '88
Aliens (SE) '86
Streets of Fire '84
Hard Times '75
The Getaway '72

David Hillenbrand
King Cobra '98

Scott Hillenbrand
King Cobra '98

Paul Hills
Boston Kickout '95

Lambert Hillyer
The Toll Gate '20

David Himmelstein
Village of the Damned '95

Anthony Hinds
See John (Anthony Hinds)
Elder

Chan Hing-Kai
Beast Cops '98
First Option '96

Roger O. Hirson
A Christmas Carol '84

Michael Hirst
Elizabeth '98

Alfred Hitchcock
No. 17 '32
Rich and Strange '32
Skin Game '31
Murder '30
The Farmer's Wife '28
The Ring '27
The Lodger '26

Joel Hladecek
Hide and Seek '00

Doane R. Hoag
Hideous Sun Demon '59

Richard Hoblock
Tarantella '95

John Hodge
A Life Less Ordinary '97
Trainspotting '95
Shallow Grave '94

Steve Hodge
Mosquito '95

Adrian Hodges
Metroland '97

David Hodgin
Murder at 1600 '97

Jeno Hodi
Armstrong '99

Arthur Hoerl
Reefer Madness '38

Charles Hoffman
The Blue Gardenia '53

Michael Hoffman
William Shakespeare's A Midsummer Night's Dream '99

Tamar Simon Hoffs
The Allnighter '87

Michael Hogan
Forever and a Day '43

Brian Hohlfield
The Mighty Ducks '92

Yau Nai Hoi
Expect the Unexpected '98

Michael Holden
No Strings Attached '98

Tom Holland
Stephen King's Thinner '96
Child's Play '88
Psycho 2 '83

Don Holley
National Lampoon's Loaded
Weapon 1 '93

Jean Holloway
Till the Clouds Roll By '46

Richard Holmes
Shooting Fish '98

Lou Holtz Jr.
The Cable Guy '96

Edward Holzman
Friend of the Family '95

Szeto Cheuk Hon
My Lucky Stars '85

Inoshiro Honda
Godzilla, King of the Monsters '56

Elliot Hong
Retrievers '82

William Hooke
Shark Attack '99

Tobe Hooper
The Texas Chainsaw Mas-
sacre '74

John Hopkins
Thunderball '65

Karen Leigh Hopkins
Stepmom '98

Gerald Hopman
Devil's Rain '75

Dennis Hopper
Easy Rider '69

Hal Hopper
Shalako '68

Arthur T. Horman
Buck Privates '41
In the Navy '41

Ed Horowitz
On Deadly Ground '94

Silvio Horta
Urban Legend '98

Jason Horwitch
Finding Graceland '98

Hiroyuki Hoshiyama
Megazone 23 Part 1 '85

Don Houghton
The Legend of the 7 Golden
Vampires '73
The Satanic Rites of Dracula
'73

Adrian Hoven
Mark of the Devil '69

Ron Howard
Parenthood '89

Sidney Howard
Gone with the Wind '39
Dodsworth '36

Jana Howington
For Richer or Poorer '97

Peter Howitt
Sliding Doors '97

Perry Howze
Chances Are '89

Randy Howze
Chances Are '89

Rita Hsaio
Mulan '98

George Huang
Swimming with Sharks '94

Tom Hubbard
Two Lost Worlds '50

John Huff
Hunter's Moon '97

Clair Huffaker
Chino / Man with a Camera
'75
Hellfighters '68
The War Wagon '67

John Hughes
Flubber '97
Home Alone 3 '97
101 Dalmatians '96
Beethoven '92
Home Alone 2: Lost in New
York '92
Career Opportunities '91
Home Alone '90
National Lampoon's Christ-
mas Vacation '89
Uncle Buck '89
The Great Outdoors '88
Ferris Bueller's Day Off '86
The Breakfast Club '85
Weird Science '85
Sixteen Candles '84
National Lampoon's Vacation
'83
National Lampoon's Class
Reunion '82

Ken Hughes
Chitty Chitty Bang Bang '68

Cyril Hume
Forbidden Planet '56

Ed Hume
Two Minute Warning '76

Sammo Hung
The Millionaire's Express '86

Bob Hunt
The Hidden '87

Evan Hunter
The Birds '63
High & Low '62

Tim Hunter
Tex '82

William Hurlbut
The Bride of Frankenstein '35

John Huston
The Man Who Would Be King
'75
Beat the Devil '53
Jezebel '38

Ron Hutchinson
The Island of Dr. Moreau '96

Willard Huyck
Radioland Murders '94
American Graffiti '73

Peter Hyams
2010: The Year We Make
Contact '84
Outland '81
Capricorn One '78

Dick Irving Hyland
New Orleans '47

Ragnar Hylten-Cavalius
June Night '40

Jeremy Iacone
The Bone Collector '99

Ice Cube
The Players Club '98
Friday '95

Masato Ide
Ran '85

Eric Idle
Monty Python's The Meaning
of Life '83
Monty Python's Life of Brian
'79
And Now for Something Completely Different '72

Alexander Ignon
Ransom '96

W. Peter Iliff
Varsity Blues '98
Patriot Games '92

Mark Ilisley
Happy, Texas '99

Shohei Imamura
Black Rain '88

Hiroshi Inagaki
Samurai 3: Duel at Ganryu
Island '56
Samurai 1: Musashi Miyamo-
to '55
Samurai 2: Duel at Ichijoji
Temple '55

Agenore Incrocci
The Good, the Bad and the
Ugly '67

Don Ingalls
Airport '75 '75

J. Christian Ingvordsen
Mob War '88
Search and Destroy '88
Firehouse '87
Hangmen '87

Sheldon Inkol
Specimen '97

Kim Ip
In the Line of Duty 5 '90

Brian Irving
Redline '97

Christopher Isherwood
Forever and a Day '43

Toshiro Ishido
Black Rain '88

Neal Israel
Police Academy '84

Juzo Itami
A Taxing Woman '87
Tampopo '86
The Funeral '84

Peter Jackson
The Frighteners '96
Dead Alive '93

Alexander Jacobs
Hell in the Pacific '69

Jake Jacobs
Midnight Confessions '95

Anders Jacobsson
Evil Ed '96

Don Jacoby
John Carpenter's Vampires
'97

Benoit Jacquot
The Disenchanted '90

Rick Jaffa
The Relic '96

Don Jakoby
Double Team '97
Arachnophobia '90
Invaders from Mars '86
Lifeforce '85

Frederick James
Humanoids from the Deep
'80

Tom Jankiewicz
Grosse Pointe Blank '97

Steve Jankowski
The Assault '97

Hans Janowitz
The Cabinet of Dr. Caligari
'19

Karen Janszen
Digging to China '98
From the Earth to the Moon
'98
The Matchmaker '97

Agnes Jaoui
Un Air de Famille '96

Sebastien Japrisot
Honor Among Thieves '68

Derek Jarman
Aria '88

Kevin Jarre
The Devil's Own '96
Tombstone '93
Glory '89

Griffin Jay
The Devil Bat's Daughter '46
The Mask of Diijon '46

Tamara Jenkins
Slums of Beverly Hills '98

Jim Jennewein
The Flintstones (CE) '94

Peter C. Jensen
Grandma's House '88

James Jeremias
The Lost Boys '87

Jean-Pierre Jeunet
The City of Lost Children '95

Jack Jevne
Wonder Man '45

Ruth Prawer Jhabvala
Howard's End '92
The Bostonians '84

Neal Jimenez
Desperate Measures '98

Wong Jing
The Conman '98
High Risk '95
City Hunter '92

Alejandro Jodorowsky
Fando and Lis '68

Arrabal Jodorowsky
Fando and Lis '68

Bayard Johnson
Tarzan and the Lost City '98

Charles Eric Johnson
Steele's Law '91

David Johnson
DROP Squad '94

Demetria Johnson
Def Jam's How to Be a Player
'97

Diane Johnson
The Shining '80

J. Randall Johnson
The Doors '91

Marc Johnson
Leaving Scars '97

Mark Steven Johnson
Jack Frost '98
Simon Birch '98
Grumpier Old Men '95
Grumpy Old Men '93

Monica Johnson
The Muse '99

Nunnally Johnson
The Dirty Dozen '67

Randy Johnson
The Doors '91

Robert P. Johnson
The Temptations '98

Tom Johnson
The Challenge of Flight: Disc
One

**Agnes Christine
Johnston**
Daddy Long Legs '19

Becky Johnston
Seven Years in Tibet '97

Iain Johnstone
Fierce Creatures '96

Amy Holden Jones
The Relic '96
The Getaway '93
Beethoven '92

Bridget Jones
Mystery Science Theater
3000: The Movie '96

Gary Jones
Mosquito '95

James Jones
The Longest Day '62

Jerry Jones
Dolemite '75

Kirk Jones
Waking Ned Devine '98

Laura Jones
A Thousand Acres '97
Portrait of a Lady '96

Mike Krohn
Ed McBain's 87 Precinct '96

Frank Krom
To Play or To Die '91

Ehren Kruger
Arlington Road '99
New World Disorder '99

Stanley Kubrick
Eyes Wide Shut '99
Full Metal Jacket '87
The Shining '80
Barry Lyndon '75
A Clockwork Orange '71
2001: A Space Odyssey '68
Dr. Strangelove, or: How I
  Learned to Stop Worrying
  and Love the Bomb '64
Paths of Glory '57
The Killing '56
Killer's Kiss '55

Roger Kumble
Cruel Intentions '98

Harry Kumel
Daughters of Darkness '71

Hanif Kureishi
My Son the Fanatic '97

Harry Kurnitz
They Got Me Covered '43

Akira Kurosawa
Ran '85
High & Low '62
Sanjuro '62
Seven Samurai '54

Diane Kurys
Love After Love '94
Entre-Nous '83

Ron Kurz
Friday the 13th, Part 2 '81

Richard Kwietniowski
Love and Death on Long
  Island '97

William Kyriakis
Dark Odyssey '57

Gregory La Cava
My Man Godfrey '36

Neil LaBute
Your Friends & Neighbors '98
In the Company of Men '96

Antoine Lacomblez
Love After Love '94

Jay Lacopo
Bartok the Magnificent '99

Jose-Andre Lacour
L'Enfer '93

Susan Lacy
Leonard Bernstein: Reaching
  for the Note '98

Steph Lady
Mary Shelley's Frankenstein
  '94

John Lafia
Child's Play '88

Ian LaFrenais
Excess Baggage '96
The Commitments '91

Richard LaGravenese
Beloved '98
Living Out Loud '98
The Horse Whisperer '97
The Mirror Has Two Faces '96
The Bridges of Madison
  County '95
A Little Princess '95

Frank Laloggia
The Lady in White '88

Rene Laloux
Time Masters '82
Fantastic Planet '73

Kei To Lam
The Master '92

Wai-Lun Lam
Black Cat '91

Ross LaManna
Rush Hour '98

Eleanor Lamb
Where the Red Fern Grows
  '74

John Lamb
Postmortem '98

Mark Lamprell
Babe: Pig in the City '98

Bill Lancaster
The Thing '82

Peter Lance
Blackjack '97

James Landis
The Sadist '63

John Landis
The Blues Brothers 2000 '98
An American Werewolf in Lon-
  don '81
The Blues Brothers (CE) '80

Christopher Landon
Another Day in Paradise '98

Fritz Lang
M '31
Metropolis '26

Harry Langdon
The Flying Deuces / Utopia
  '39

Todd W. Langen
Teenage Mutant Ninja Tur-
  tles: The Movie '90

Noel Langley
A Christmas Carol '51
The Wizard of Oz '39

Kate Lanier
The Mod Squad '99
Set It Off '96
What's Love Got to Do with
  It? '93

James Lapine
Into the Woods '90

Ring Lardner Jr.
Woman of the Year '42

Christopher Larkin
A Very Natural Thing '73

Jeremy Larner
The Candidate '72

Shana Larsen
200 Cigarettes '98

Glen Larson
Battlestar Galactica '78

Lawrence Lasker
Sneakers '92
WarGames '83

Jesse Lasky Jr.
The Ten Commandments '56
Reap the Wild Wind '42

Greg Latter
Dangerous Ground '96

Tai-Muk Lau
Iron Monkey '93
The Master '92

Michael Laughlin
Mesmerized '84

Tom Laughlin
Billy Jack '71

Frank Launder
The Lady Vanishes '38

Dale Launer
Dirty Rotten Scoundrels '88

William Laurin
Once a Thief '96

Marc Lawrence
Forces of Nature '99
The Out-of-Towners '99

Martin Lawrence
A Thin Line Between Love
  and Hate '96

John Howard Lawson
Jungle Boy '96

J.F. Lawton
Under Siege '92
Mistress '91
Pretty Woman '90

Jonathan Lawton
The Hunted '94

Tom Lazarus
Stigmata '99

Philip LaZebnik
Mulan '98

David Leaf
The Unknown Marx Brothers
  '93

David Lean
Summertime '55
Oliver Twist '48
Great Expectations '46

Charles Leavitt
The Mighty '98

Fred Lebow
While You Were Sleeping '95

James Lecesne
Boys Life 2 '98

Charles Lecocq
The Devil's Nightmare '71

Bruce Leddy
My Teacher's Wife '95

Paul Leder
Killing Obsession '94

Charles Lederer
His Girl Friday '40

Ang Lee
Pushing Hands '92

Bruce Lee
Fists of Fury '73
Return of the Dragon '73

Cinque Lee
Crooklyn '94

Damian Lee
Specimen '97
Jungle Boy '96
Street Law '95
The Killing Man '94
Abraxas: Guardian of the Uni-
  verse '90

Joie Lee
Crooklyn '94

Lilian Lee
Farewell My Concubine '93

Malcolm Lee
The Best Man '99

S.O. Lee
Dark Planet '97

Spike Lee
Summer of Sam '99
He Got Game '98
Clockers '95
Jungle Fever '91
Do the Right Thing '89

Robert Lees
Buck Privates Come Home
  '47

Ernest Lehman
Who's Afraid of Virginia
  Woolf? '66
West Side Story '61
The King and I '56

Jerry Leichtling
Peggy Sue Got Married '86

Michael W. Leighton
Rush Week '88

Christopher Leitch
Universal Soldier '92

Alan LeMay
Reap the Wild Wind '42

Jonathan Lemkin
The Devil's Advocate '97

Kasi Lemmons
Eve's Bayou '97

Vicente Lenero
Midaq Alley '95

Peter M. Lenkov
Demolition Man '93

Gary Lennon
Drunks '96

Brett Leonard
The Lawnmower Man '92

Elmore Leonard
Joe Kidd '72

Alfred Leone
Lisa and the Devil / The
  House of Exorcism '75

Sergio Leone
The Good, the Bad and the
  Ugly '67
For a Few Dollars More '65
A Fistful of Dollars '64

Alan Jay Lerner
Camelot '67
My Fair Lady '64
Gigi '58
Brigadoon '54
An American in Paris '51
Royal Wedding '51

Sheldon Lettich
Legionnaire '98
Lionheart '90

Law Chi Leung
Full Throttle '96

Patrick Leung
A Bullet in the Head '90

Po-Chi Leung
Hot War '98

Gigi Levangie
Stepmom '98

Brian Levant
Leave It to Beaver '97

Jeremy Leven
Don Juan DeMarco '94
Creator '85

Frank Levering
Parasite '82

David Levien
Rounders '98

Sonya Levien
Oklahoma '55
The Hunchback of Notre
  Dame '39

Larry Levin
Dr. Dolittle '98

Marc Levin
Slam '98

Daniel Levine
Ed McBain's 87 Precinct '96

Barry Levinson
Sleepers '96

Richard Levinson
Rehearsal for Murder '82
The Hindenburg '75

Steve Levitt
At First Sight '98

Benn W. Levy
The Old Dark House '32

Herschell Gordon Lewis
Color Me Blood Red '64
2000 Maniacs '64

Dr. Jack Lewis
The Amazing Transparent
  Man '60

Warren Lewis
Black Rain '89

Marcel L'Herbier
The Fantastic Night '42

Michael Lindsay-Hogg
The Object of Beauty '91

Graham Linehan
The Matchmaker '97

William Link
Rehearsal for Murder '82
Rollercoaster '77
The Hindenburg '75

Richard Linklater
Before Sunrise '94
Dazed and Confused '93

Ken Lipper
City Hall '95

Steven Lisberger
Tron '82

Robert Locash
BASEketball '98

Gene Lockhart
Forever and a Day '43

Bey Logan
Jackie Chan: My Stunts '98
Jackie Chan: My Story '97

Joshua Logan
Mister Roberts '55

Ulli Lommel
Devonsville Terror '83
The Boogey Man '80
Blank Generation '79

Kenneth Lonergan
Analyze This '98

Dean Lorey
Major Payne '95

Hope Loring
My Best Girl '27

David Loucka
Eddie '96

David Loughery
Money Train '95
The Three Musketeers '93
Star Trek 5: The Final Frontier
  '89

Suzanna Love
The Boogey Man '80

Wolf Lowenthal
Comin' At Ya! '81

Andrew Lowery
Simon Sez '99

Richard Lowry
Jessica: A Love Story '92

Sam Lowry
The Underneath '95

Tung Lu
City War '89

Wei Lu
The Emperor's Shadow '96

George Lucas
American Graffiti '73

William Ludwig
Oklahoma '55

Kurt Luedtke
Absence of Malice '81

Baz Luhrmann
William Shakespeare's
  Romeo and Juliet '96

Steve Lukanic
For Richer or Poorer '97

Sidney Lumet
Night Falls on Manhattan '96
Q & A '90

Zoe Tamerlaine Lund
Bad Lieutenant '92

Chien Wen Lung
Jackie Chan: My Story '97

Gene Luotto
Twitch of the Death Nerve
  '71

Karen McCullah Lutz
Ten Things I Hate about You
  '99

David Lynch
Dune '84

Barre Lyndon
The War of the Worlds '53

Fibe Ma
Mr. Nice Guy '98
Rumble in the Bronx '96
Supercop '92

Joe Ma
Lawyer Lawyer '97

Charles MacArthur
Wuthering Heights '39

Aeneas MacKenzie
The Ten Commandments '56

Billy Mackinnon
Hideous Kinky '99

Patricia MacLachlan
Skylark '93

Don MacPherson
The Avengers '98

Jeanie Macpherson
Male and Female '19

Brent Maddock
Wild Wild West '99
Tremors 2: Aftershocks '96
Heart and Souls '93
Tremors '91
*batteries not included '87

Ben Maddow
Men in War '57

Bart Madison
Top of the World '97

David Madsen
Copycat '95

Jose Maesso
Django '68

Guy Magar
Showdown '94

Doug Magee
Somebody Has to Shoot the
  Picture '90

Maria Maggenti
The Love Letter '99

Mark Magidson
Baraka '93

Constantino Magnatta
Bury Me in Niagara '93

Jymn Magon
All Dogs Christmas Carol '98

Jeff Maguire
In the Line of Fire '93
Victory '81

Richard Maibaum
License to Kill '89
The Spy Who Loved Me (SE)
  '77
Thunderball '65
Goldfinger '64
From Russia with Love '63
Dr. No (SE) '62

Mike Mains
High Voltage '98

Daniel Mainwaring
Invasion of the Body Snatchers '56

Arduino Maiuri
Chino / Man with a Camera
  '75

Johnnie Mak
Island of Greed '97

Dusan Makavejev
Montenegro '81

Gloria Maley
Horror Planet '80

Nick Maley
Horror Planet '80

Terrence Malick
The Thin Red Line '98
Days of Heaven '78
Badlands '74

Louis Malle
Spirits of the Dead '68

James Mallon
Mystery Science Theater
  3000: The Movie '96

Dave Mallow
The Princess and the Pirate
  '95

Bonz Malone
Slam '98

William Malone
Universal Soldier: The Return
  '99

**Albert (John B. Sherry)
Maltz**
The Beguiled '70
The Naked City '48

David Mamet
Ronin '98
The Edge '97
The Spanish Prisoner '97
Wag the Dog '97
The Postman Always Rings
  Twice '81

Chow Siu Man
Hot War '98

Law Tai Man
In the Line of Duty 3 '88

Don Mancini
Bride of Chucky '98
Child's Play 2 '90
Child's Play '88

Babaloo Mandel
EDtv '99
Father's Day '96
Multiplicity '96
Greedy '94
A League of Their Own '92
Mr. Saturday Night '92
Parenthood '89
Spies Like Us '85
Splash '84
Night Shift '82

James Mangold
Cop Land '97

Herman J. Mankiewicz
The Pride of the Yankees '42

Joseph L. Mankiewicz
All About Eve '50

Tom Mankiewicz
Dragnet '87
Ladyhawke '85
The Cassandra Crossing '76
Live and Let Die '73

Wolf Mankowitz
Waltz of the Toreadors '62

Michael Mann
The Insider '99
Heat '95
Thief '81

Stanley Mann
Conan the Destroyer '84
Firestarter '84

Ted Mann
Space Truckers '97

Sal Manna
Witchcraft 2: The Temptress
  '90

Albert Mannheimer
Born Yesterday '50

Vincenzo Mannino
New York Ripper '82

Graeme Manson
Cube '98

Russell V. Manzatt
Trapper County War '89
Rush Week '88

David Marconi
Enemy of the State '98

Cindy Marcus
The Lion King: Simba's Pride
  '98

Frank Marcus
The Killing of Sister George
  '69

Andreas Marfori
Desperate Crimes '93

Richard "Cheech" Marin
Born in East L.A. '87

Frances Marion
Amarilly of Clothesline Alley
  '18
Stella Maris '18

Leo Marks
Peeping Tom '60

George Markstein
The Odessa File '74

Andrew Marlowe
End of Days '99
Air Force One '97

Brad Marlowe
Object of Obsession '95

Michel Marriott
New Jersey Drive '95

Joel B. Marsden
Ill-Gotten Gains '97

Garry Marshall
The Other Sister '98
The Flamingo Kid '84

Neil Marshall
The Flamingo Kid '84

William Martell
The Base '99
Virtual Combat '95

Anne-Marie Martin
Twister '96

Bruce Martin
Body Puzzle '93

John Mathew Martin
Sarfarosh '98

K.C. Martin
Lap Dancing '95

Mardik Martin
Raging Bull '80
Mean Streets '73

Steve Martin
Bowfinger '99
L.A. Story '91
Three Amigos '86
The Man with Two Brains '83
The Jerk '79

Denny Martin Flinn
Star Trek 6: The Undiscovered Country '91

Thomas Martinek
Troma's War (DC) '88

Sergio Martino
Torso '73

Rick Marx
Firehouse '87

Koichi Mashimo
Dominion Tank Police '89

Judi Ann Mason
Sister Act 2: Back in the
  Habit '93

Sarah Y. Mason
Stella Dallas '37

Olivier Massart
Wild Reeds '94

Rene Masson
Diabolique '55

Joe Massot
Zachariah '70

Master P
Foolish '99

Nico Mastorakis
The Naked Truth '92
Bloodstone '88
Glitch! '88
The Wind '87
Zero Boys '86

Armand Mastroianni
Killing Hour '84

William Mastrosimone
With Honors '94

Shoichi Masuo
Crimson Wolf '91

Berkely Mather
Dr. No (SE) '62

Richard Matheson
Somewhere in Time '80
Trilogy of Terror '75
The Night Strangler '72
The Night Stalker '71

June Mathis
The Saphead '21

Melissa Mathison
Kundun '97
The Black Stallion '79

Francisca Matos
Baby Geniuses '98

Hajime Matsumoto
Zeram '91

Zenzo Matsuyama
The Human Condition: Road
  to Eternity '59
The Human Condition: No
  Greater Love '58

Daryl Matthews
Dance with Me '98

Paul Matthews
Breeders '97
Grim '95

Tom Matthews
Mad City '97

Nat Mauldin
Dr. Dolittle '98

Garth Maxwell
Jack Be Nimble '94

Richard Maxwell
The Serpent and the Rainbow
  '87

Elaine May
Primary Colors '98
The Birdcage '95
Heaven Can Wait '78

Carl Mayer
The Cabinet of Dr. Caligari
  '19

Lise Mayer
Suite 16 '94

Paul Mayersberg
The Man Who Fell to Earth
  '76

Wendell Mayes
The Poseidon Adventure '72

Craig Mazin
Senseless '98

Steve Mazur
Liar Liar '96
The Little Rascals '94

Joseph Mazzarino
The Adventures of Elmo in
  Grouchland '99
Muppets from Space '99

Kevin Mcarthy
Moving Target '96

Joseph McBride
Rock 'n' Roll High School '79

Mary C. McCall
The Fighting Sullivans '42

Tim McCanlies
Iron Giant '99
Dancer, Texas—Pop. 81 '98

Tim McCann
Desolation Angels '95

Leo McCarey
Going My Way / Holiday Inn
  '44
Love Affair '39

John Michael McCarthy
Sore Losers '97

Peter McCarthy
Floundering '94

Todd McCarthy
Visions of Light: The Art of
  Cinematography '93

Frank M. McCormack
The Phantom of the Opera
  '25

Randall McCormick
Speed 2: Cruise Control '97

Horace McCoy
Rage at Dawn '55

Steve McCoy
I Was a Teenage Zombie '87

Michael McCullers
Austin Powers 2: The Spy
  Who Shagged Me '99

Michael McDowell
Stephen King's Thinner '96
The Nightmare before Christ-
  mas '93
Beetlejuice '88

Maureen McElheron
The Tune '92

Alan B. McElroy
Spawn (SE) '97
Todd McFarlane's Spawn '97
Halloween 4: The Return of
Michael Myers '88

Donald McEnery
A Bug's Life (CE) '98
Hercules '97

Mark Thomas McGee
Sorceress '94

Rex McGee
Pure Country '92

David McGillivray
House of Whipcord '75

Phyllis McGinley
Puppet Films of Jiri Trnka

Sean McGinley
Scorned 2 '96
Sexual Roulette '96

William McGivern
I Saw What You Did '65

Jimmy McGovern
Priest '94

Jack McGowan
Show Boat '51

Douglas McGrath
Emma '96
Bullets over Broadway '94

Frank McGuinness
Dancing at Lughnasa '98

**James Kevin
McGuinness**
Rio Grande '50

Steven McKay
Darkman 2: The Return of
Durant '94
Hard to Kill '89

Michael McKean
This Is Spinal Tap '84

Don McKellar
Last Night '98
The Red Violin '98

David McKenna
American History X '98

Charles McKeown
The Adventures of Baron
Munchausen '89
Brazil '85
Brazil (Criterion SE) '85

Vince McKewin
The Climb '97
Fly Away Home '96

Josh McKinney
Suicide Kings '97

Dave McLaughlin
Southie '98

Joseph McLee
Twitch of the Death Nerve
'71

Terry McMillan
How Stella Got Her Groove
Back '98

Terrance McNally
Earth Girls Are Easy '89

John McNaughton
Henry: Portrait of a Serial
Killer '90

Allen McNeil
My Best Girl '27

Scott McPherson
Marvin's Room '96

Christopher McQuarrie
The Usual Suspects '95
Public Access '93

Justus E. McQueen
See L.Q. (Justus E. McQueen)
Jones

Kathy McWorter
The War '94

Irene Mecchi
Hercules '97

Mark Medoff
Santa Fe '97

Thomas Meehan
One Magic Christmas '85

Marc Meeks
Lost and Found '99

Steve Meerson
Star Trek 4: The Voyage
Home '86

Frank Melford
Blood on the Sun '45

Greg Mellott
Jackie Chan's First Strike '96

George Melly
Smashing Time '67

Aaron Mendelsohn
Air Bud '97

Ric Menello
Drop Dead Rock '95

Ramon Menendez
Stand and Deliver '88

Jim Menza
The Last Assassins '96

Anne Meredith
Bastard out of Carolina '96

James Merendino
SLC Punk! '99
Hard Drive '94
Terrified '94

Monte Merrick
8 Seconds '94
Mr. Baseball '92
Memphis Belle '90

Tim Metcalfe
Killer: A Journal of Murder
'95
Kalifornia '93
Iron Maze '91

Radley Metzger
The Alley Cats '65
Dark Odyssey '57

Nicholas Meyer
Sommersby '93
Star Trek 6: The Undiscov-
ered Country '91
Star Trek 4: The Voyage
Home '86
The Seven-Per-Cent Solution
'76

Turi Meyer
Chairman of the Board '97
Leprechaun 2 '94

Nancy Meyers
The Parent Trap '98
Father of the Bride '91
Protocol '84
Private Benjamin '80

Menno Meyjes
The Siege '98
The Color Purple '85

Greg Michael
Baby Geniuses '98

Lorne Michaels
Three Amigos '86

William Mickelberry
Black Dog '98

Bette Midler
Divine Madness '80

Anne-Marie Mieville
First Name: Carmen '83

Djordje Milicevic
Runaway Train '85
Victory '81

John Milius
Clear and Present Danger
'94
Geronimo: An American Leg-
end '93
Red Dawn '84
Conan the Barbarian '82
Apocalypse Now '79
1941 '79
Jeremiah Johnson '72

Oscar Millard
The Conqueror '56

Andrew Miller
Simon Sez '99

Chris Miller
Multiplicity '96
National Lampoon's Animal
House '78

David Keith Miller
Allyson Is Watching '96
I Like to Play Games '95

Frank Miller
RoboCop 3 '91

George Miller
Babe '95
Mad Max: Beyond Thunder-
dome '85
The Road Warrior '82
Mad Max '80

Harvey Miller
Cannonball Run 2 '84
Protocol '84
Private Benjamin '80

Michael Miller
Joan of Arc '99

Roger Miller
Just a Little Harmless Sex
'99

Victor Miller
Friday the 13th '80

Paul Milliet
Werther '88

Bill Milling
Lauderdale '89

Sherry Mills
The Adventures of Pinocchio
'96

Paula Milne
Mad Love '95

David Scott Milton
Born to Win '71

Michael Miner
RoboCop '87

Lam Chi Ming
Buddhist Fist '80

Pang Ming
Frozen '98

Tsui Siu Ming
Buddhist Fist '80

Wu Ming
Frozen '98

Tsai Ming-Liang
Vive l'Amour '94

Anthony Minghella
The English Patient '96

Brad Mirman
Resurrection '99
Truth or Consequences, N.M.
'97

Craig Mitchell
Milo '98

David Mitchell
The Killing Man '94

Joseph A. Mitchell
Seven Chances '25
The Navigator '24
Our Hospitality / Sherlock
Junior '23

Keith Mitchell
Eddie '96

Eric Mittleman
Night Calls: The Movie 2 '99
Night Calls: The Movie '98

Moebius
Time Masters '82

Gustaf Molander
Intermezzo '36

William H. Molina
The Last Assassins '96

Andrew Mollo
Winstanley '75
It Happened Here '65

Paul Monash
Salem's Lot '79

Paul Mones
Double Team '97
The Quest '96

Christopher Monger
The Englishman Who Went up
a Hill But Came down a
Mountain '95

Mario Monicelli
Lovers and Liars '81

Martin Mooney
The Monster Maker '44

Brian Moore
Black Robe '91

Charles Philip Moore
The Last Assassins '96

Kenny Moore
Without Limits '97

Ronald D. Moore
Star Trek: First Contact '96
Star Trek: Generations '94

Simon Moore
The Quick and the Dead '94

Eddie Moran
Wonder Man '45

Patrick Moran
Jack-O '95

Rafael Moreu
The Rage: Carrie 2 '99
Hackers '95

Peter Morgan
The Very Thought of You '98

Tony Morphett
Crime Broker '94
Sweet Talker '91

Morris
Lucky Luke '94

Judy Morris
Babe: Pig in the City '98

Rebecca Morrison
Legionnaire '98

Paul Morrissey
Andy Warhol's Dracula '74
Andy Warhol's Frankenstein
'74
Heat '72

Women in Revolt '71
Trash '70
Flesh '68

Barry Morrow
Rain Man '88

John Mortimer
Tea with Mussolini '99

Bob Mosher
Munster, Go Home! '66

April Moskowitz
Body Strokes '95
Friend of the Family '95

Marcel Moussey
Shoot the Piano Player '62
The 400 Blows '59

Allan Moyle
Pump Up the Volume '90

Russell Mulcahy
Russell Mulcahy's Tale of the
Mummy '99

Jim Mulholland
Bad Boys '75
Amazon Women on the Moon
'87

Mark Mullin
The Killing Jar '96

Ryu Murakami
Tokyo Decadence '91

Takeo Murata
Godzilla, King of the Monsters '56

Walter Murch
Return to Oz '85

Jane Murfin
Come and Get It '36

Kevin Murphy
Mystery Science Theater
3000: The Movie '96

Tab Murphy
Tarzan '99

Warren B. Murphy
The Eiger Sanction '75

Tom Musca
Race '99
Stand and Deliver '88

John Musker
Hercules '97
The Little Mermaid '89

Floyd Mutrux
Aloha, Bobby and Rose '74

Mike Myers
Austin Powers 2: The Spy
Who Shagged Me '99
Austin Powers: International
Man of Mystery '97
So I Married an Axe Murderer
'93

Nancy Myers
I Love Trouble '94

Scott Myers
K-9 '89

Daniel Myrick
The Blair Witch Project (SE)
'99

Fred Myton
Dead Men Walk / The Mon-
ster Maker '43

Vladimir Nabokov
Lolita '62

Mira Nair
Kama Sutra: A Tale of Love
'96

Takehiro Nakajima
Village of Dreams '97

Desmond Nakano
White Man's Burden '95

Yin Nam
Prison on Fire '87

Nas
Belly '98

Michael Nash
Lost Continent '68

Vincenzo Natali
Cube '98

Mort Nathan
Kingpin '96

Jeff Nathanson
Speed 2: Cruise Control '97

Gregory Nava
Selena '96

Lex Neal
Battling Butler '26

L. Ford Neale
Hunter's Moon '97

Ronald Neame
Great Expectations '46

Hal Needham
Stroker Ace '83

Daniel Neira
Immortal Combat '94

B.J. Nelson
Alien Chaser '96

Jessie Nelson
The Story of Us '99
Stepmom '98
Corrina, Corrina '94

Michael J. Nelson
Mystery Science Theater
3000: The Movie '96

Sean Nelson
Godmoney '99

Joseph Nepp
Cat City '87

Edward Neumeier
Starship Troopers '97
RoboCop '87

John Thomas Neville
The Flying Serpent '55

David Newman
Bonnie & Clyde '67

Randy Newman
Three Amigos '86

H.P. Newquist
Robbie Robertson: Going
Home '98

Andrew Niccol
The Truman Show '98
Gattaca '97

Constantine Nicholas
Chronos '87

Genevieve Nicholas
Chronos '87

Dudley Nichols
And Then There Were None
'45
The Bells of St. Mary's '45
For Whom the Bell Tolls '43
Stagecoach '39
The Hurricane '37
She '35

William Nicholson
First Knight '95
Shadowlands '93

Ted Nicolaou
Bloodstorm: Subspecies 4
'98
Vampire Journals '96

Assault of the Killer Bimbos
'88

Brenda Nielson
Out of the Blue '80

Sergei Nolbandov
Fire Over England '37

Chris Noonan
Babe '95

Tom Noonan
The Wife '95

Marc Norman
Shakespeare in Love (CS)
'98
Cutthroat Island '95
Waterworld '95
Bat 21 '88
The Killer Elite '75

William J. Norris
Re-Animator '84

Edmund H. North
Patton '70

William W. Norton Sr.
Day of the Animals '77
Big Bad Mama '74

John Norville
Tin Cup '96

Robert J. Nowac
Zig Zag '99

Louis Nowra
The Matchmaker '97

Marti Noxon
Just a Little Harmless Sex
'99

Frank Nugent
Last Hurrah '58
The Searchers '56
Mister Roberts '55
The Quiet Man '52

Tom Nursall
I'll Be Home for Christmas
'98

Ron Nyswaner
Philadelphia '93

Dan O'Bannon
Screamers '96
Total Recall '90
Invaders from Mars '86
Lifeforce '85
Alien '79
Dark Star '74

Arch Oboler
The Bubble '67

Raoul O'Connell
Boys Life '91

James O'Connolly
Tower of Evil '72
Night Caller from Outer
Space '66

David Odell
The Dark Crystal '82
Cry Uncle '71

Jack O'Donnell
Stephen King's The Night
Flier '96

Peter O'Donnell
The Vengeance of She '68

Michael O'Donoghue
Scrooged '88

Steve Oedekerk
Patch Adams (CE) '98
Nothing to Lose '96
The Nutty Professor '96
Ace Ventura: When Nature
Calls '95

Susanne Ofteringer
Nico Icon '95

Tony O'Grady
Curse of the Voodoo '64

Hideo Oguni
Ran '85
Tora! Tora! Tora! '70
High & Low '62
Sanjuro '62
Seven Samurai '54

James O'Hanlon
Destination Moon '50

Tommy O'Haver
Billy's Hollywood Screen Kiss
'98

Kaori Okamura
Demon City Shinjuku '93

Terence M. O'Keefe
Wanted '98

Adam Ollensis
The Pompatus of Love '95

Deanna Oliver
My Favorite Martian '98

Laurence Olivier
Henry V '44

Arne Olsen
Cop and a Half '93
Red Scorpion '89

Dana Olsen
George of the Jungle '97
The 'Burbs '89

Yau Tai On-Ping
Center Stage '91

Max Ophuls
Lola Montes '55

**Anne Amanda
Opotowsky**
The Break Up '98

Timothy O'Rawe
Midnight Confessions '95

Alan Ormsby
The Substitute '96
Cat People '82
Children Shouldn't Play with
Dead Things '72

Gary Orona
Stripshow '95

Tom O'Rourke
Desert Heat '99

James Orr
Sister Act 2: Back in the
Habit '93

Robert Orr
Savior '98

Andrew Osborn
Sgt. Kabukiman N.Y.P.D. '94

Paul Osborn
South Pacific '58

Ron Osborn
Meet Joe Black '98
Radioland Murders '94

Jack O'Donnell
Stephen King's The Night
Flier '96

John Osborne
Tom Jones '63

William Osborne
The Real McCoy '93
Twins '88

Nagisa Oshima
In the Realm of Passion '80
In the Realm of the Senses
'76

David Ossman
Zachariah '70

Filippo Ottoni
Twitch of the Death Nerve
'71

Alun Owen
A Hard Day's Night '64

Fedor Ozep
Aelita: Queen of Mars '24

G.W. Pabst
Pandora's Box '28

Tang Pakee
The Dragon Fist '80

Alan J. Pakula
The Pelican Brief '93
Presumed Innocent '90
Sophie's Choice '82

Michael Palin
Monty Python's The Meaning
of Life '83
Time Bandits '81
Monty Python's Life of Brian
'79
And Now for Something Com-
pletely Different '72

Rospo Pallenberg
Excalibur '81

Chazz Palminteri
A Bronx Tale '93

Norman Panama
Court Jester '56
The Road to Utopia '46

Kamlesh Pandey
Thakshak '99

Dennis Paoli
The Dentist '96
Castle Freak '95
Body Snatchers '93
Re-Animator '84

Chuck Parello
Henry: Portrait of a Serial
Killer 2: Mask of Sanity '96

Alessandro Parenzo
Rabid Dogs '74

Nick Park
Wallace & Gromit: The First
Three Adventures '99

Alan Parker
Evita '96
Angel Heart '87

Bill Parker
Klash '95

Christine Parker
Peach / A Bitter Song '95

Dorothy Parker
A Star Is Born '37

Oliver Parker
An Ideal Husband '99

Ronald Parker
Joan of Arc '99

Tom S. Parker
The Flintstones (CE) '94

Walter F. Parkes
Sneakers '92
WarGames '83

Rick Parks
Ever After: A Cinderella Story
'98

Larry Parr
A Soldier's Tale '91

Lindsley Parsons
Sagebrush Trail '33

Michael Part
A Kid in Aladdin's Palace '97

Pier Paolo Pasolini
Arabian Nights '74
The Canterbury Tales '71
The Decameron '70
The Gospel According to St.
Matthew '64

Ivan Passer
Born to Win '71

Michael Pate
Tim '79

Stuart Paton
20,000 Leagues under the
Sea '16

Vincent Patrick
The Devil's Own '96

Elliot Paul
New Orleans '47

Steven Paul
Baby Geniuses '98

Mark Pavia
Stephen King's The Night
Flier '96

Anna Pavignano
The Postman '94

Pyotr Pavlenko
Alexander Nevsky '38

John Paxton
The Wild One '54

Michael Paxton
Ayn Rand: A Sense of Life
'98

Alexander Payne
Election '99

John Payson
Joe's Apartment '96

Craig Pearce
William Shakespeare's
Romeo and Juliet '96

Donn Pearce
Cool Hand Luke '67

Sam Peckinpah
The Wild Bunch '69
Invasion of the Body Snatch-
ers '56

Paul Peditto
Jane Doe '96

Susan Peehl
A Great Day in Harlem / The
Spitball Story '94

Ron Peer
Goodbye, Lover '99

Bill Peet
Peter Pan '53

Mary Jo Pehl
Mystery Science Theater
3000: The Movie '96

Kimberly Peirce
Boys Don't Cry '99

Nikola Pejakovic
Pretty Village, Pretty Flame
'96

Louis Pelletier
Big Red '62

Sean Penn
The Crossing Guard '94

Zak Penn
Inspector Gadget '99

Erdman Penner
Peter Pan '53
Pinocchio '40

Phil Penningroth
For Love of a Child '90

David Peoples
Soldier '98
12 Monkeys '95
Deadfall '93
Hero '92
Unforgiven '92
Leviathan '89
Blade Runner (DC) '82

Janet Peoples
12 Monkeys '95

Clare Peploe
Besieged '98

Mark Peploe
Little Buddha '93
The Last Emperor '87

S.J. Perelman
Horse Feathers '32
Monkey Business '31

Frank Ray Perilli
Laserblast '78

Nat Perrin
Duck Soup '33

Ross A. Perron
American Rampage '89

Eleanor Perry
David and Lisa '62

Fred C. Perry
The Wind '87
Zero Boys '86

Nickolas Perry
Boys Life 2 '98

Charlie Peters
Her Alibi '88

Steven Peters
Wild Things '98

Wolfgang Petersen
Das Boot (DC) '81

Denne Bart Petitclerc
Forgotten City '99

Joseph Petracca
Proud Rebel '58

Dan Petrie Jr.
The Big Easy '87

Harley Peyton
Keys to Tulsa '96

Chuck Pfarrer
Virus '98
The Jackal (CE) '97
Barb Wire '96
Darkman 2: The Return of
Durant '94
Hard Target '93
Darkman '90

Anna Hamilton Phelan
In Love and War '96
Gorillas in the Mist '88
Mask '85

Brian Phelan
Little Mother '71

Bill Phillips
Christine '84

Kenneth Phillips
Hum Dil De Chuke Sanam
'99

Arthur C. Pierce
The Invisible Strangler '76

Scott Pierce
A Nightmare on Elm Street 4:
Dream Master '88

Tedd Pierce
Gulliver's Travels '39

Frank Pierson
Presumed Innocent '90
In Country '89
Dog Day Afternoon '75
Cool Hand Luke '67

Krzysztof Piesiewicz
The Decalogue '88

Tseng Pik-Yin
The Bride with White Hair '93
Iron Monkey '93

Jeremy Pikser
Bulworth '98

Nicholas Pileggi
Casino '95
City Hall '95
Goodfellas '90

Michael Piller
Star Trek: Insurrection '98

Tullio Pinelli
Juliet of the Spirits '65
Nights of Cabiria '57

Lam Tam Ping
Black Cat '91

Shi Yang Ping
The Great Conqueror's Concubine '94
The Great Conqueror's Concubine, Part 2 '94

Steve Pink
Grosse Pointe Blank '97

Harold Pinter
The Trial '93

Bret Piper
A Nymphoid Barbarian in
Dinosaur Hell '94

Mark Pirro
My Mom's a Werewolf '89

Angelo Pizzo
Hoosiers '86

Alan Plater
A Merry War '97

Allen Plone
Sweet Justice '92

Bill Plympton
The Tune '92

James Poe
They Shoot Horses, Don't
They? '69

Charles Edward Pogue
Kull the Conqueror '97
Dragonheart (SE) '96
Psycho 3 '86
The Hound of the
Baskervilles '83

John Pogue
U.S. Marshals '98

Gregory Poirier
Rosewood '96

Joseph Poland
Winds of the Wasteland /
The Lucky Texan '36

Roman Polanski
Frantic '88

Harry Pollard
Uncle Tom's Cabin '27

Vicki Polon
Mr. Wonderful '93

Abraham Polonsky
Madigan '68

Abe Polsky
The Baby '72
Rebel Rousers '69

Darryl Ponicsan
School Ties '92
Vision Quest '85

DJ Pooh
Friday '95

Robert Roy Pool
Outbreak '94

Duane Poole
I've Been Waiting for You '98
Shattered Image '98

Calvin Poon
Hot War '98

Tim Pope
Don't Look in the Basement
'73

Tom Pope
Don't Look in the Basement
'73

Gregory Poppon
Boys Will Be Boys '97

Joel Posner
Last Breath '96

P.J. Posner
Last Breath '96

Dennis Potter
Mesmer '94

Sally Potter
Orlando '92

Michael Powell
The Red Shoes '48

Donna Powers
Deep Blue Sea '99

Kim Powers
Finding North '97

Wayne Powers
Deep Blue Sea '99

Deborah Pratt
Quantum Leap: The Pilot
Episode '89

Carl Prechezer
Blue Juice '95

Emeric Pressburger
The Red Shoes '48

Steven Pressfield
Above the Law '88

Jeffrey Price
Wild Wild West '99
Doc Hollywood '91
Who Framed Roger Rabbit
'88

Richard Price
Ransom '96
Clockers '95
Mad Dog and Glory '93
Sea of Love '89
The Color of Money '86

Barry Primus
Mistress '91

David Pritchard
Violent Zone '89

Phil Proctor
Zachariah '70

Pat Proft
Wrongfully Accused '98
Mr. Magoo '97
Police Academy '84

Alex Proyas
Dark City '97

Richard Pryor
Richard Pryor: Live on the
Sunset Strip '82
Bustin' Loose '81
Richard Pryor: Live in Concert
'79
Blazing Saddles '74

Robert Pucci
The Corruptor '99

L.A. Puopolo
The Turning '92

David Pursall
The Longest Day '62

Tony Puryear
Eraser '96

Mario Puzo
Earthquake '74

Ernie Pyle
The Story of G.I. Joe '45

Daniel Pyne
Doc Hollywood '91
The Hard Way '91

James Quattrochi
True Friends '98

John Quinn
Awakening of Gabriella '99

Paul Quinn
This Is My Father '99

Gene Quintano
Outlaw Justice '98
National Lampoon's Loaded
Weapon 1 '93

Peter Rader
Waterworld '95

Michael Radford
The Postman '94

Bob Rafelson
Mountains of the Moon '90

Stewart Raffill
Napoleon and Samantha '72

John Raffo
The Relic '96
Dragon: The Bruce Lee Story
'93

Martin Ragaway
Abbott and Costello in the
Foreign Legion '50

Ivan Raimi
Army of Darkness '92
Darkman '90

Sam Raimi
The Hudsucker Proxy '93
Army of Darkness '92
The Nutt House '92
Darkman '90
Evil Dead 2: Dead by Dawn
'87
Evil Dead '83

Rick Ramage
Stigmata '99

Harold Ramis
Analyze This '98
Multiplicity '96
Groundhog Day '93
Ghostbusters 2 '89
Caddyshack 2 '88
Ghostbusters '84
National Lampoon's Vacation
'83
Stripes '81
Caddyshack '80
Meatballs '79
National Lampoon's Animal
House '78

Ben Ramsey
The Big Hit '98

Robert Ramsey
Life '99

Tony Randel
Fist of the North Star '95

Joe Ranft
A Bug's Life (CE) '98

Whitney Ransick
Hand Gun '93

Krishna Rao
Crossworlds '96

Raman Rao
Crossworlds '96

Anne Rapp
Cookie's Fortune '99

Philip Rapp
The Secret Life of Walter
Mitty '47

Wonder Man '45

Fred A. Rappaport
AFI's 100 Years, 100 Movies
'98

I.C. Rappaport
Black Death '91

Mark Rappaport
From the Journals of Jean
Seberg '95

Sam Rappaport
The Chosen One: Legend of
the Raven '98

Judith Rascoe
Havana '90

Irving Ravetch
The Cowboys '72
Vengeance Valley '51

Rand Ravich
The Astronaut's Wife '99

A.H. Rawlinson
The Man Who Knew Too
Much '34

Billy Ray
Volcano '97
Color of Night '94

David Rayfiel
The Firm '93
Havana '90
Three Days of the Condor '75

Jan Read
Jason and the Argonauts '63
The Haunted Strangler '58

Katherine Reback
Fools Rush In '97

Robert Redlin
After Dark, My Sweet '90

Dan Reed
Zigzag '97

Joel M. Reed
Bloodsucking Freaks '75

Phil Reeves
Happy, Texas '99

Theodore Reeves
National Velvet '44

Piero Regnoli
Playgirls and the Vampire '63

Frank Rehwaldt
The Landlady '98

Mark Reichert
Union City '81

Dorothy Reid
Impact '49

J. Reifel
Convict 762 '98

Ethan Reiff
Tales from the Crypt Presents
Demon Knight '94

Donald Reiker
Tom Sawyer '99

William Reilly
Mortal Thoughts '91

Carl Reiner
The Man with Two Brains '83

Rob Reiner
This Is Spinal Tap '84

Al Reinert
From the Earth to the Moon
'98
Apollo 13 '95

Walter Reisch
That Uncertain Feeling '41

Robert Reneau
Demolition Man '93

Action Jackson '88

Jeff Reno
Meet Joe Black '98
Radioland Murders '94

Jean Renoir
The Southerner '45
Grand Illusion '37

Alain Resnais
Last Year at Marienbad '61

Paul (Pee-wee Herman) Reubens
Pee-wee's Big Adventure '85

Alma Reville
Young and Innocent '37
Sabotage '36
The 39 Steps '35
Rich and Strange '32

Bernard Revon
Bed and Board '70

Clarke Reynolds
Shalako '68
The Viking Queen '67

Jonathan Reynolds
My Stepmother Is an Alien '88

Kevin Reynolds
Red Dawn '84

Lee Reynolds
Jackie Chan's Who Am I '98

Scott Reynolds
Heaven '99
The Ugly '96

Patrice Rhomm
The Devil's Nightmare '71

Anne Rice
Interview with the Vampire '94

John Rice
Blown Away '94

Wayne Rice
Suicide Kings '97

Jean-Louis Richard
Emmanuelle '74
Fahrenheit 451 '66
The Soft Skin '64

Cybil Richards
Femalien '96

Kevin Richards
The Fear: Halloween Night '99

Doug Richardson
Money Train '95
Die Hard 2: Die Harder '90

Sy Richardson
Posse '93

Eddie Richey
Phoenix '98

Maurice Richlin
Pillow Talk '59

Meg Richman
In the Shadows '98

W.D. Richter
Needful Things '93
Dracula '79
Invasion of the Body Snatchers '78

Tom Rickman
Hooper '78

John Ridley
U-Turn '97

Dean Riesner
Dirty Harry '71

Adam Rifkin
Small Soldiers '98

Something About Sex '98
Mouse Hunt '97

John Riley
Princess Warrior '90

Sahara Riley
The Night That Never Happened '97

Joe Rinaldi
Peter Pan '53

Frederic Rinaldo
Buck Privates Come Home '47

Clements Ripley
Jezebel '38

Robert Riskin
Meet John Doe '41
Lost Horizon '37
It Happened One Night '34

Guy Ritchie
Lock, Stock and 2 Smoking Barrels '98

Joe Ritter
The Toxic Avenger (DC) '86

Rosemary Ritvo
Alice Sweet Alice '76

Thomas Ritz
The Killing Grounds '97

Stephen J. Rivele
Nixon '95

Marcel Rivet
Portrait of an Assassin '49

Alfredo Rizzo
The Bloodsucker Leads the Dance '75

Janet Roach
Prizzi's Honor '85

Alain Robbe-Grillet
Last Year at Marienbad '61

Matthew Robbins
Mimic '97
*batteries not included '87

Vincent Robert
Red Surf '90

Jonathan Roberts
Jack Frost '98

Judith Roberts
Simply Irresistible '99

Marguerite Roberts
Shoot Out '71

Stanley Roberts
The Caine Mutiny '54

William Roberts
The Magnificent Seven '60

Bruce Robinson
In Dreams '98
Return to Paradise '98

Butch Robinson
DROP Squad '94

Casey Robinson
The Snows of Kilimanjaro '52
Dark Victory '39

Phil Alden Robinson
The Chamber '96
Sneakers '92
All of Me '84

Todd Robinson
White Squall '96

Kevin Rock
Warlock: The Armageddon '93

Alexandre Rockwell
Four Rooms '95

Robert Rodat
Saving Private Ryan '98
Fly Away Home '96

Franc Roddam
Moby Dick '98
Aria '88

Hans Rodionoff
Sucker the Vampire '98

Howard A. Rodman
Winning '69

Robert Rodriguez
Desperado '95
Four Rooms '95
El Mariachi '93

Nicolas Roeg
Aria '88

Charles R. Rogers
The Flying Deuces / Utopia '39

Jean Scott Rogers
Corridors of Blood '58

Steven Rogers
Earthly Possessions '99
Hope Floats '98
Stepmom '98

Eric Rohmer
Boyfriends & Girlfriends '88
Summer '86
Full Moon in Paris '84
Le Beau Mariage '82
Chloe in the Afternoon '72
Claire's Knee '71
My Night at Maud's '69
La Collectionneuse '67
The Eric Rohmer Collection: The Moral Tales '62

Jean Rollin
The Living Dead Girl '82
Fascination '79
The Demoniacs '74
Requiem for a Vampire '71
The Shiver of the Vampires '70
Night of the Hunted '69

George A. Romero
The Dark Half '91
Day of the Dead '85
Dawn of the Dead '78

Brunello Rondi
Juliet of the Spirits '65

Darrell Roodt
Dangerous Ground '96

Conrad Rooks
Chappaqua '66

Don Roos
Opposite of Sex '98
Boys on the Side '94
Single White Female '92

Cliff Roquemore
Avenging Disco Godfather '76

Bernard Rose
Candyman '92

Mickey Rose
Take the Money and Run '69

Reginald Rose
Sea Wolves '81

Ruth Rose
She '35

Sherrie Rose
Me & Will '99

William Rose
Guess Who's Coming to Dinner '67

Jeb Rosebrook
Junior Bonner '72

Dan Rosen
The Curve '97

Gary Rosen
Sink or Swim '97
Major Payne '95

C.A. Rosenberg
Maniac '80

Jeanne Rosenberg
The Black Stallion '79

Scott Rosenberg
Disturbing Behavior '98
Con Air '97
Beautiful Girls '96
Things to Do in Denver When You're Dead '95

Seth Zvi Rosenfeld
A Brother's Kiss '97

Mark Rosenthal
Mercury Rising '98
Mighty Joe Young '98
Sometimes They Come Back '91

Robert J. Rosenthal
The Van '77

Mark Rosman
Evolver '94

Gary Ross
Pleasantville '98
Dave '93
Mr. Baseball '92
Big '88

Kenneth Ross
The Odessa File '74
The Day of the Jackal '73

Nello (Ted Archer) Rossati
Django Strikes Again '87

Robert Rossen
The Strange Love of Martha Ivers '46

Franco (Fred Gardner) Rossetti
Django '68

Terry Rossio
The Mask of Zorro '98
Small Soldiers '98

Eric Roth
The Insider '99
The Horse Whisperer '97
The Postman '97

Phillip J. Roth
Total Reality '97

Jeff Rothberg
A Simple Wish '97

Richard Rothstein
Universal Soldier '92

Russell Rouse
D.O.A. '49

Pierre Rouve
Trial & Error '62

Kathleen Rowell
The Outsiders '83

Roy Rowland
Girl Hunters '63

Patricia Royce
To Cross the Rubicon '91

Andy Ruben
Poison Ivy '92

Joseph Ruben
Pom Pom Girls '76

Bruce Joel Rubin
Deep Impact '98
Jacob's Ladder '90
Brainstorm '83

Daniel F. Rubin
Groundhog Day '93

Mann Rubin
The First Deadly Sin '80

John Rubino
Lotto Land '95

Harry Ruby
Duck Soup '33
Horse Feathers '32

David Rudkin
Fahrenheit 451 '66

Paul Rudnick
In and Out '97

Steve Rudnick
The Santa Clause '94

Mark Rudnitsky
Class of Nuke 'Em High '86

Jane Rusconi
Hush '98

Jordan Rush
Never Talk to Strangers '95

Richard Rush
Color of Night '94
Air America '90

Josef Rusnak
The Thirteenth Floor '99

Chuck Russell
A Nightmare on Elm Street 3: Dream Warriors '87
Dreamscape (SE) '84

David O. Russell
Three Kings '99
Flirting with Disaster '95

Ken Russell
Aria '88
The Lair of the White Worm '88
Salome's Last Dance '88
Mahler '74

Kurt Russell
Escape from L.A. '96

Scott Russell
Stranger than Fiction '99

Vy Russell
The Indestructible Man / The Amazing Transparent Man '56

Rafa Russo
Twice upon a Yesterday '98

Richard Russo
Twilight '98

Marti Rustam
Eaten Alive '76

Klaas Rusticus
The Dandelion Crown '93

Morrie Ryskind
Penny Serenade '41
My Man Godfrey '36
Animal Crackers '30
The Cocoanuts '29

Joseph Sabo
Pinocchio '40

Dardano Sacchetti
Demons '86
New York Ripper '82
Beyond the Door 2 '79

Ezra Sacks
FM '78

Malcolm St. Clair
College '27
Three Ages '23

Arthur St. Claire
The Mask of Diijon '46

Nicholas St. John
Body Snatchers '93
Ms. 45 '81
Driller Killer '74

Paul Salamon
The Long Shadow '92

Richard Sale
Suddenly '54

Kario Salem
The Rat Pack '98

Murray Salem
Kindergarten Cop '90

Roger Salloch
36 Fillete '88

Peter Salmi
Blue Juice '95

Beth Salmon
Watch Me '96

Waldo Salt
Midnight Cowboy '69

Mark Saltzman
The Adventures of Milo &
Otis '89

Philip Saltzman
Swiss Conspiracy '77

Victor Salva
Rites of Passage '99
Powder '95

Jon Robert Samsel
Animal Instincts '92
Carnal Crimes '91

Eduardo Sanchez
The Blair Witch Project (SE)
'99

Christopher Sanders
Mulan '98

Jon Sanders
The Wicked, Wicked West '97

Sonny Sanders
The Firing Line '91

Adam Sandler
Big Daddy '99
The Waterboy '98
Happy Gilmore '96
Billy Madison '94

Barry Sandler
Crimes of Passion '84

Donald S. Sanford
Midway '76

John Sansom
Dracula, Prince of Darkness
'66

Ken Sanzel
The Replacement Killers '98
Scarred City '98

Tedi Sarafian
Solar Crisis '92

Jan Sardi
Shine '95

Alvin Sargent
Anywhere But Here '99
White Palace '90

Arlene Sarner
Peggy Sue Got Married '86

Yuichi Sasamoto
The Venus Wars '89

George Saunders
The Landlady '98

Carlos Saura
Outrage '93

Jody Savin
Witchcraft '88

Gerald Savory
Young and Innocent '37

Johan Lindstroem Saxon
Elvira Madigan '67

John Sayles
Limbo '99
Mimic '97
Passion Fish '92
The Clan of the Cave Bear
'86
Piranha '78

Dario Scardapane
Posse '93

Furio Scarpelli
The Postman '94
The Good, the Bad and the
Ugly '67

Giacomo Scarpelli
The Postman '94

Franne Schacht
Laserblast '78

Jason Schafer
Trick '99

Peter Schamoni
Spring Symphony '86

Mimi Rothman Schapiro
Exclusive '82

John Scheinfeld
The Unknown Marx Brothers
'93

Richard Schenkman
The Pompatus of Love '95

Shawn Schepps
Son-in-Law '93
Encino Man '92

Jules Schermer
The Fighting Sullivans '42

Robert Schiff
Swimsuit '89

Robin Schiff
Romy and Michele's High
School Reunion '97

Stephen Schiff
The Deep End of the Ocean
'98

Michael Schiffer
The Peacemaker '97
Crimson Tide '95
Lean on Me '89

Karl Schiffman
Dead End '98

Suzanne Schiffman
Confidentially Yours '83
The Woman Next Door '81
The Last Metro '80

William Schifrin
Quest for Camelot '98

Alfred Schiller
The Flying Deuces / Utopia
'39

Vivian Schilling
Soultaker '90

Volker Schlondorff
Tin Drum '79

Ed Schmidt
Cost of Living '97

Stephen Schmidt
Cost of Living '97

Stephen Schneck
Across the Moon '94

Charles Schnee
Red River '48

Barry Schneider
Mother's Boys '94

G. Schock
A Fistful of Dollars '64

Amy Schor
Mr. Wonderful '93

David J. Schow
The Crow '93

Leonard Schrader
Blue Collar '78

Paul Schrader
Affliction '97
City Hall '95
Light Sleeper '92
Raging Bull '80
American Gigolo '79
Blue Collar '78
Taxi Driver (CE) '76

Raymond L. Schrock
The Phantom of the Opera
'25

Tom Schulman
Holy Man '98
Medicine Man '92
Dead Poets Society '89

Joel Schumacher
Batman and Robin '97
The Wiz '78
Car Wash '76

Mark Evan Schwartz
Wanted '98

Stefan Schwartz
Shooting Fish '98

Steven S. Schwartz
Critical Care '97

Martin Scorsese
Casino '95
Goodfellas '90
Mean Streets '73

Allan Scott
In Love and War '96
The Witches '90

Darin Scott
Caught Up '98
Sprung '96
Tales from the Hood '95

Gavin Scott
Small Soldiers '98
The Borrowers '97

Jack Seaman
Project Moon Base '53

Peter S. Seaman
Wild Wild West '99
Doc Hollywood '91
Who Framed Roger Rabbit
'88

Ted Sears
Peter Pan '53
Pinocchio '40

George Seaton
Airport '70
Miracle on 34th Street '47

Jack Seddon
The Longest Day '62

E. S. Seeley Jr.
Hideous Sun Demon '59

Erich Segal
Yellow Submarine '68

David Seidler
The King and I '99
Quest for Camelot '98
Dancing in the Dark '95

Matthew Seig
A Great Day in Harlem / The
Spitball Story '94

Shinichi Sekizawa
Godzilla's Revenge '69
Godzilla vs. Monster Zero '68

Godzilla vs. Mothra '64

David Self
The Haunting '99

Maurice Sellar
The Best of British Cinema:
Five Decades of Classic
British Films '88

Arthur Sellers
Forgotten City '99

Steven Selling
One Man's Justice '95

Aaron Seltzer
Spy Hard '96

David Seltzer
My Giant '98
Bird on a Wire '90

David O. Selznick
The Paradine Case '47
Duel in the Sun '46
A Star Is Born '37

George Seminara
I Was a Teenage Zombie '87

Lorenzo Semple Jr.
Flash Gordon '80
King Kong '76
The Parallax View '74
Papillon '73

Ron Senkowski
Wicked Ways '99

Al Septien
Chairman of the Board '97
Leprechaun 2 '94

Giorgio Serafini
The Seventh Sense '99
Loveblind '98

Mario Serandrei
Black Sunday '60

Alexandra Seros
The Specialist '94
Point of No Return '93

Deborah Serra
Snow White: A Tale of Terror
'97

Mark Sevi
Moving Target '96
Sci-Fighters '96

Edmond Seward
Gulliver's Travels '39

Tim Sewell
Shameless '94

David Shaber
Nighthawks '81

Sabi H. Shabtai
The Assignment '97

Tom Shadyac
The Nutty Professor '96
Ace Ventura: Pet Detective
'93

Dirk Shafer
Man of the Year '95

Anthony Shaffer
Sleuth '72

Peter Shaffer
Amadeus '84

Steve Shagan
Primal Fear '96

Tommy Sham
City on Fire '87

John Patrick Shanley
Congo '95
Five Corners '87
Moonstruck '87

Robert T. Shannon
Unknown Island '48

Stanley Shapiro
Dirty Rotten Scoundrels '88
Pillow Talk '59

Fred P. Sharkey
The Elm-Chanted Forest '97

Alan Sharp
Rob Roy '95
Ulzana's Raid '72

William Shatner
Star Trek 5: The Final Frontier
'89

Melville Shavelson
Wonder Man '45
The Princess and the Pirate
'44

Bob Shaw
A Bug's Life (CE) '98
Hercules '97

Sandy Shaw
The Heroic Trio '93

Wallace Shawn
The Designated Mourner '97
My Dinner with Andre '81

Andrew Shea
Santa Fe '97

John Shea
Southie '98

Katt Shea
Poison Ivy '92

Harry Shearer
This Is Spinal Tap '84

Arthur Sheekman
Duck Soup '33
Monkey Business '31

Charlie Sheen
Tale of Two Sisters '89

David Sheffield
The Nutty Professor '96
Coming to America '88

David Sheldon
Grizzly '76

Ron Shelton
Tin Cup '96
Bull Durham '88
The Best of Times '86

Jean Shepherd
A Christmas Story '83

Ted Sherdeman
Away All Boats '56

Jim Sheridan
The Boxer '97
In the Name of the Father '93
The Field '90
My Left Foot '89

Martin Sherman
Alive and Kicking '96

Richard M. Sherman
The Slipper and the Rose '76

Robert B. Sherman
The Slipper and the Rose '76

Sam M. Sherman
Chaplin's Art of Comedy '66

Tom Sherohman
Mr. Magoo '97

R.C. Sherriff
Odd Man Out '47
The Old Dark House '32

John B. Sherry
*See Albert (John B. Sherry)
Maltz*

Robert Sherwood
The Bishop's Wife '47
The Best Years of Our Lives
'46

Scarface '83
Conan the Barbarian '82
Midnight Express '78

Peter Stone
Charade '63

Robert Stone
Just Cause '94

Sherri Stoner
My Favorite Martian '98

Tom Stoppard
Shakespeare in Love (CS) '98
Brazil '85
Brazil (Criterion SE) '85

David Storey
This Sporting Life '63

Tim Story
Urban Menace '99

Richard Stratton
Slam '98

John J. Strauss
There's Something about Mary '98

Robert Strauss
Retroactive '97
Body Shot '93

Theodore Strauss
Indomitable Teddy Roosevelt '83

Wesley Strick
Return to Paradise '98
The Saint '97
Wolf '94
Final Analysis '92
Arachnophobia '90

Max Strom
Shelter '98

Stuart Strutin
Class of Nuke 'Em High '86

Jeb Stuart
Fire Down Below '97
Switchback '97
Just Cause '94
The Fugitive '93
Another 48 Hrs. '90
Leviathan '89
Lock Up '89
Die Hard '88

Charles Sturridge
Aria '88

Susanna Styron
Shadrach '98

C. Gardner Sullivan
Sparrows '26

Daniel G. Sullivan
While You Were Sleeping '95

Phoef Sutton
The Fan '96

Junko Suzuki
8 Man '92

Jan Svankmajer
Jan Svankmajer's Faust '94

David Svec
Mandragora '97

Ron Swanson
Top Dog '95

Tommy Swerdlow
Cool Runnings '93

Jo Swerling
It's a Wonderful Life '46
The Pride of the Yankees '42
The Westerner '40
Made for Each Other '39

Robin Swicord
Practical Magic '98

Matilda '96
Little Women '94

David Swift
Candleshoe '78

Roy Szeto
Wicked City '92
A Chinese Ghost Story III '91
Dragons Forever '88
Mr. Vampire '86

Thomas Szollosi
Snow White: A Tale of Terror '97

Jim Tabilio
Sweet Justice '92

Brian Taggert
Trucks '97

Cheng Chung Tai
All About Ah Long '89

Don Tait
The North Avenue Irregulars '79
Unidentified Flying Oddball '79

Tibor Takacs
Redline '97

Susumu Takahisa
Fist of the North Star '86

Yas Takata
Hide and Seek '00

Yukiko Takayama
Terror of Mechagodzilla '78

C.M. Talkington
Love and a .45 '94

Shirley Tallman
The Babysitter's Seduction '96

Ted Tally
The Juror '96
Silence of the Lambs '91
White Palace '90

Paul Tamasy
Air Bud '97

Cheung Tan
Iron Monkey '93

Edward Tang
Mr. Nice Guy '98
Rumble in the Bronx '96
Supercop '92
Operation Condor '91
Operation Condor 2: The Armour of the Gods '86

Pik-yin Tang
Iron Monkey '93

Daniel Taradash
Bell, Book and Candle '58

Quentin Tarantino
Four Rooms '95
From Dusk Till Dawn '95
Pulp Fiction '94
True Romance '93
Reservoir Dogs '92

Andrei Tarkovsky
Nostalghia '83
Solaris '72
Andrei Rublev '66

Susan Tarr
Cousin Bette '97

Gilles Taurand
Wild Reeds '94

Catherine Tavel
Night Fire '94

David Taylor
DROP Squad '94

Delores Taylor
Billy Jack '71

Jim Taylor
Election '99

Sam Taylor
Vertigo (CE) '58

Andre Techine
Wild Reeds '94
Ma Saison Preferee '93

Miguel Tejada-Flores
Screamers '96

Piero Tellini
Utopia '51

Julien Temple
Aria '88

Andy Tennant
Ever After: A Cinderella Story '98

John Terlesky
Supreme Sanction '99
The Pandora Project '98

Bridget Terry
Shadrach '98

Gay Partington Terry
The Toxic Avenger, Part 2 '89

Duccio Tessari
A Fistful of Dollars '64

Paul Theroux
Chinese Box '97

Harvey Thew
Uncle Tom's Cabin '27

Nick Thiel
The Associate '96

Robert Thom
Death Race 2000 '75

Jack W. Thomas
Embryo '76

Jim Thomas
Executive Decision '96
Predator '87

John Thomas
Executive Decision '96
Predator '87

Michael Thomas
Ladyhawke '85

Ralph Thomas
The Doors '91

L.L. Thomaso
Word of Mouth '99

Caroline Thompson
The Nightmare before Christmas '93
The Secret Garden '93

Carolyn Thompson
Homeward Bound: The Incredible Journey '93

Emma Thompson
Sense and Sensibility '95

Ernest Thompson
On Golden Pond '81

Jim Thompson
Paths of Glory '57
The Killing '56

Peggy Thompson
Better Than Chocolate '99

Rob Thompson
The Cowboy Way '94

Billy Bob Thornton
Sling Blade '96

George Tibbles
Munster, Go Home! '66

Ernest Tidyman
High Plains Drifter '73

George Tillman Jr.
Soul Food '97

Leung Wai Ting
City War '89

Kwok-wai To
Peking Opera Blues '86

James Toback
Bugsy '91

Stephen Tobolowsky
True Stories '86

Peter Tolan
Analyze This '98
My Fellow Americans '96

Jonathan Tolins
The Twilight of the Golds '97

Michael Tolkin
Deep Impact '98
Deep Cover '92
The Player '92

Stephen Tolkin
Dean Koontz's Mr. Murder '98

Judy Toll
Casual Sex? '88

Dante Tomaselli
Desecration '99

Edward Tong
Miracles '89
Wheels on Meals '84

Elliot Tong
Jackie Chan's First Strike '96

Stanley Tong
Jackie Chan's First Strike '96
Supercop 2 '93

Roland Topor
Fantastic Planet '73

Peter Torokvei
Guarding Tess '94
Caddyshack 2 '88

Robert Tossberg
Total Reality '97

Harry Alan Towers
Call of the Wild '72

Robert Towne
Without Limits '97
Mission: Impossible '96
The Firm '93
Days of Thunder '90
The Two Jakes '90
Tequila Sunrise '88
Chinatown '74
The Last Detail '73

Michael Traeger
Dead Man on Campus '97

Nick Tramontane
Jackie Chan's First Strike '96

Joey Travolta
Dumb Luck in Vegas '97
Hard Vice '94

Victor Trivas
The Stranger '46

Massimo Troisi
The Postman '94

Roberto Troni
Boston Kickout '95

Guy Troper
Jailhouse Rock '57

Joseph Tropiano
Big Night '95

Francois Truffaut
Confidentially Yours '83
The Last Metro '80
Two English Girls '72
Bed and Board '70
Stolen Kisses '68

Fahrenheit 451 '66
The Soft Skin '64
Shoot the Piano Player '62
The 400 Blows '59

Dalton Trumbo
Papillon '73
Spartacus '60
The Brave One '56

Alan R. Trustman
Bullitt '68

Kenneth Tsang
God of Cookery '96

Shinya Tsukamoto
Tetsuo 2: Body Hammer '97
Tokyo Fist '95
Tetsuo: The Iron Man '92

Stanley Tucci
The Imposters '98
Big Night '95

Richard Tuggle
Escape from Alcatraz '79

Yee Tung-shing
Full Throttle '96
C'est la Vie, Mon Cherie '93

Gary J. Tunnicliffe
Within the Rock '96

Saul J. Turell
The Love Goddesses '65

Barbara Turner
Georgia '95

Bonnie Turner
Tommy Boy '95

Terry Turner
Tommy Boy '95

David N. Twohy
G.I. Jane '97
The Arrival '96
Waterworld '95
Terminal Velocity '94
The Fugitive '93
Warlock '91

Tom Tykwer
Run Lola Run '98

Steve Tymon
Dark Secrets '95
Fraternity Demon '92

Nona Tyson
The Hot Spot '90

Bob Tzudiker
Tarzan '99
Anastasia '97

Alan Uger
Blazing Saddles '74

Jim Uhls
Fight Club '99

Alfred Uhry
Driving Miss Daisy '89

Roger Vadim
Barbarella '68
Spirits of the Dead '68

Laszlo Vadnay
The Great Rupert '50

Luis Valdez
La Bamba '87

Jean-Claude Van Damme
Lionheart '90
Kickboxer '89

Anne Van De Putte
To Play or To Die '91

Melvin Van Peebles
Panther '95

Rip Van Ronkel
Destination Moon '50

Gus Van Sant
Drugstore Cowboy '89

Leigh Vance
Curse of the Voodoo '64

Agnes Varda
One Hundred and One Nights
'94

Michael Varhol
Pee-wee's Big Adventure '85

John Varley
Millennium '89

Jean-Marc Vasseur
Emmanuelle, the Joys of a
Woman '76

David Veloz
Permanent Midnight '98

Chick Vennera
Angel in Training '99

Douglas Venturelli
Black Cat Run '98

Pat Verducci
True Crime '95

Mark Verheiden
Timecop '94

Henri Verneuil
Any Number Can Win '63

Marion Vernoux
Love, etc. '96

Dziga Vertov
The Man with the Movie Camera '29

Richard Vetere
Vigilante '83

P.C. Vey
The Tune '92

Michael Vickerman
Warriors of Virtue '97

Mark Victor
Marked for Death '90
Poltergeist '82

Gore Vidal
Caligula '80

King Vidor
Our Daily Bread and Other
Films of the Depression
'34

Daniel Vigne
The Return of Martin Guerre
'83

Dimitri Villard
In Love and War '96

Joseph Vilsmaier
Stalingrad '94

Christian Vincent
La Séparation '98

Luciano Vincenzoni
The Good, the Bad and the
Ugly '67
For a Few Dollars More '65

Dino Vindeni
Little Witches '96
The Demolitionist '95
Voodoo '95

Dan Vining
Black Dog '98

Jacques Viot
Black Orpheus '58

Clement Virgo
Junior's Groove '97
Rude '96

Piero Vivarelli
Django '68

Jesse Vogel
Therese & Isabelle '67
Carmen, Baby '66

Stephen Volk
The Guardian '90

Karl Vollmoller
The Shanghai Gesture '42

Thea von Harbou
M '31
Metropolis '26

Josef von Sternberg
The Shanghai Gesture '42

Cyrus Voris
Tales from the Crypt Presents
Demon Knight '94

Kurt Voss
Highway Hitcher '98

Andy Wachowski
The Matrix '99
Bound '96
Assassins '95

Larry Wachowski
The Matrix '99
Bound '96
Assassins '95

Kevin Wade
Meet Joe Black '98
Junior '94
Mr. Baseball '92

Bruce Wagner
I'm Losing You '98
A Nightmare on Elm Street 3:
Dream Warriors '87

J. Robert Wagoner
Avenging Disco Godfather '76

Lei Bik Wah
Rouge '87

Leung Hung Wah
In the Line of Duty 5 '90

Abe Kwong Man Wai
Inspector Wears Skirts '88

Kai-Fai Wai
Peace Hotel '95

Tikuhei Wakao
Samurai 3: Duel at Ganryu
Island '56
Samurai 1: Musashi Miyamo-
to '55

Edwards Waldman
The Pink Panther Strikes
Again '76

Frank Waldman
Revenge of the Pink Panther
'78
The Pink Panther Strikes
Again '76

Andrew Kevin Walker
Sleepy Hollow '99
8mm '98
Seven '95

Clark Lee Walker
The Newton Boys '97

Keith A. Walker
Free Willy '93

Earl W. Wallace
Witness '85

Naomi Wallace
Lawn Dogs '96

Randall Wallace
The Man in the Iron Mask '98

Tommy Lee Wallace
Halloween 3: Season of the
Witch '82

Anthony Waller
An American Werewolf in
Paris '97

Bill Walsh
Mary Poppins '64

Frances Walsh
The Frighteners '96
Dead Alive '93

Gabriel Walsh
Quackser Fortune Has a
Cousin in the Bronx '70

Matthew Jason Walsh
Witchouse '99
Petticoat Planet '95

Rupert Walters
Restoration '94

Fred Walton
When a Stranger Calls Back
'93

Martin Walz
Killer Condom '97

Wayne Wang
Chinese Box '97

David S. Ward
Sleepless in Seattle '93
King Ralph '91
The Sting '73

John Warren
Flashfire '94

Deric Washburn
The Deer Hunter '78
Silent Running '71

Daniel Waters
Demolition Man '93
Batman Returns '92
Hudson Hawk '91
Heathers '89

John Waters
Pecker '98
Serial Mom '94

Mark Waters
The House of Yes '97

Roger Waters
Pink Floyd: The Wall '82

Lawrence Edward Watkin
The Great Locomotive Chase
'56

Alan Watson
Horror Hospital '73

John Watson
Robin Hood: Prince of
Thieves '91

Damon Wayans
Major Payne '95

Keenen Ivory Wayans
Most Wanted '97

Marlon Wayans
Don't Be a Menace to South
Central While Drinking Your
Juice in the Hood '95

Shawn Wayans
Don't Be a Menace to South
Central While Drinking Your
Juice in the Hood '95

Frank Wead
They Were Expendable '45

James R. Webb
How the West Was Won '63
Pork Chop Hill '59

M. Coates Webster
The Brute Man '46

Lo Wei
New Fist of Fury '76
Chinese Connection '73

Fists of Fury '73

Lu Wei
Farewell My Concubine '93

Samuel Weil
*See Lloyd (Samuel Weil) Kauf-
man*

Lance Weiler
The Last Broadcast '98

John Weiner
Mob War '88

Herschel Weingrod
Kindergarten Cop '90
My Stepmother Is an Alien
'88
Twins '88
Brewster's Millions '85

Jerico Weingrod
See Jerico (Weingrod) Stone

Richard Weinman
Hunter's Moon '97

Peter Weir
The Year of Living Dangerous-
ly '82
Gallipoli '81

David Weisberg
Double Jeopardy '99

David N. Weiss
The Rugrats Movie '98
Rock-a-Doodle '92

Herman Weissman
The Bridge of San Luis Rey
'44

Chris Weitz
Antz '98

Paul Weitz
Antz '98

Colin Welland
Chariots of Fire '81

Michael Weller
Hair '79

Orson Welles
The Trial '63
Othello '52

David Wellington
A Man in Uniform '93

Peter Wellington
The Boys Club '96

William A. Wellman
A Star Is Born '37

Audrey Wells
Guinevere '99
George of the Jungle '97

Bill Wells
Exclusive '82

George Wells
Show Boat '51

Richard Wenk
Just the Ticket '98

Mike Werb
Face/Off '97
The Mask '94

Lina Wertmuller
Seven Beauties '76
Swept Away . . . '75
Love and Anarchy '73
Seduction of Mimi '72

Jake West
Razor Blade Smile '98

Mae West
Klondike Annie '36
Belle of the Nineties '34
I'm No Angel '33

Roland West
The Bat Whispers '30

Donald E. Westlake
The Grifters '90

Garnett Weston
The White Zombie '32

Frank Whaley
Joe the King '99

Darryl Wharton
Detention '98

John Whedon
The Bears & I '74
The Island at the Top of the
World '74

David Wheeler
Tender Loving Care '99

Rene Wheeler
Utopia '51

Tim Whelan
My Best Girl '27

Graeme Whifler
Dr. Giggles '92

Duane Whitaker
From Dusk Till Dawn 2: Texas
Blood Money '98

Rod Whitaker
The Eiger Sanction '75

Nat Whitcomb
Mean Guns '97

Mike White
Dead Man on Campus '97

Noni White
Tarzan '99
Anastasia '97

Robb White
The Tingler '59
House on Haunted Hill '58

Stephen White
Barney's Great Adventure '98

Tony White
Jackie Chan: My Story '97

Steve Whitestone
The Pebble and the Penguin
'94

Diane Whitley
Boston Kickout '95

Richard Whitley
Rock 'n' Roll High School '79

Preston A. Whitmore II
Fled '96

Stanford Whitmore
Dreams of Gold: The Mel
Fisher Story '86

Cormac Wibberly
Motel Blue '98

Marianne S. Wibberly
Motel Blue '98

W.W. Wicket
The Seventh Sign '88

Gregory Widen
The Prophecy '95
Backdraft '91
Highlander (DC) '86

Bo Widerberg
Elvira Madigan '67

David Michael Wieger
Wild America '97

Crane Wilbur
The Bat '59

Billy Wilder
The Front Page '74
Double Indemnity '44
Ball of Fire '41

Gene Wilder
Young Frankenstein '74

Christopher Wilkinson
Nixon '95

Charles Williams
The Hot Spot '90

Emlyn Williams
The Man Who Knew Too
Much '34

Hype Williams
Belly '98

Lona Williams
Drop Dead Gorgeous '99

Saul Williams
Slam '98

Tennessee Williams
Cat on a Hot Tin Roof '84
A Streetcar Named Desire
'51

Tyger Williams
Menace II Society '93

David Williamson
The Year of Living Dangerous-
ly '82
Gallipoli '81
Don's Party '76

Kevin Williamson
Teaching Mrs. Tingle '99
The Faculty '98
I Know What You Did Last
Summer '97
Scream 2 '97
Scream (CS) '96

Stan Williamson
Just Write '97

Calder Willingham
Rambling Rose '91
Paths of Glory '57

Lee Willis
The Woman Who Came Back
'45

Kevin Willmott
Ninth Street '98

Tim Willocks
Swept from the Sea '97

Hugh Wilson
Dudley Do-Right '99
Blast from the Past '98
Guarding Tess '94
Burglar '87
Police Academy '84
Stroker Ace '83

Michael Wilson
Salt of the Earth '54

Michael G. Wilson
License to Kill '89
For Your Eyes Only (SE) '81

Owen C. Wilson
Rushmore '98
Bottle Rocket '95

S.S. Wilson
Wild Wild West '99
Tremors 2: Aftershocks '96
Heart and Souls '93
Tremors '89

*batteries not included '87

Whip Wilson
Mary Poppins '64

Kurt Wimmer
The Thomas Crown Affair '99

Arthur Wimperis
The Scarlet Pimpernel '34

Shimon Wincelberg
Cold Sweat '71

Irwin Winkler
Guilty by Suspicion '91

Michael Winner
The Sentinel '76

Frank Wisbar
Strangler of the Swamp '46

William Wisher
Judge Dredd '95

Theodore Witcher
Love Jones '96

Andrew Witham
Mean Guns '97

William D. Wittliff
The Cowboy Way '94
Legends of the Fall '94
The Black Stallion '79

Dick Wolf
School Ties '92

Fred Wolf
Dirty Work '97

Lalo Wolf
Undercover '94

Robert Hewitt Wolfe
Futuresport '98

Andy Wolk
From the Earth to the Moon
'98

Michael Wolk
Innocent Blood '92

Barry Wong
Hard-Boiled '92
Twin Dragons '92
Heart of Dragon '85
My Lucky Stars '85

Jing Wong
Naked Killer '92
The Prodigal Son '82

Manfred Wong
Dream Lovers '86

Winky Wong
Organized Crime & Triad
Bureau '93

John Woo
Hard-Boiled '92
A Bullet in the Head '90
The Killer '90
A Better Tomorrow, Part 2 '88
A Better Tomorrow, Part 1 '86

Charles Wood
Help! '65

Christopher Wood
Moonraker (SE) '79

The Spy Who Loved Me (SE)
'77

Clement Biddle Wood
Barbarella '68

Edward D. Wood Jr.
Plan 9 from Outer Space '56
Bride of the Monster '55
Jail Bait '54
Glen or Glenda? '53

Frank E. Woods
The Birth of a Nation '15

Lotta Woods
The Three Musketeers '21

Abbe Wool
Sid & Nancy '86

Linda Woolverton
Homeward Bound: The
Incredible Journey '93

David Worth
Lady Dragon '92

Alexander Wright
The First 9 1/2 Weeks '98

Jeffrey Wright
BASEketball '98

Lawrence Wright
The Siege '98

Nicholas Wright
Armistead Maupin's More
Tales of the City '97

Ralph Wright
Nikki, the Wild Dog of the
North '61
Peter Pan '53

David Wu
The Bride with White Hair '93
The Bride with White Hair 2
'93

Rudy Wurlitzer
Little Buddha '93
Two Lane Blacktop '71

D. B. Wyndham-Lewis
The Man Who Knew Too
Much '34

Tracy Keenan Wynn
Carolina Skeletons '92
Capone '89
The Deep '77

Boaz Yakin
A Price above Rubies '97
The Punisher '90

Leonard Yakir
Out of the Blue '80

Atsushi Yamotoya
Lupin III: The Mystery of
Mamo '78

Yoshikazu Yasuhiko
The Venus Wars '89

Toshio Yasumi
Chushingura '62

Nai-Hoi Yau
A Hero Never Dies '98
The Longest Nite '92

Lee Wai Yee
Supercop '92

Bennett Yellin
Dumb & Dumber '94

Yevgeny Yevtushenko
I Am Cuba '64

Rafael Yglesias
Les Miserables '97
Fearless '93

Chan Kui Ying
In the Line of Duty 3 '88

Yoshikata Yoda
The 47 Ronin, Parts 1 & 2
'42

Philip Yordan
Night Train to Terror '84
Bad Man's River '72
Royal Hunt of the Sun '69
Men in War '57
Big Combo '55

Dan York
Flashfire '94

Soji Yoshikawa
Lupin III: The Mystery of
Mamo '78

Daniel Yost
Drugstore Cowboy '89

Graham Yost
From the Earth to the Moon
'98
Hard Rain '97
Broken Arrow '95
Speed '94

James Young
The Bells / The Crazy Ray
'26

Terence Young
On Approval '44

Bae Young-kyun
Why Has Bodhi-Darma Left
for the East '89

**Henry (Michael
Carreras) Younger**
Prehistoric Women '67

Ronny Yu
The Bride with White Hair '93

Patrick Yuen
In the Line of Duty 5 '90

Szeto Kam Yuen
Expect the Unexpected '98

Law Kai Yui
The Moon Warriors '92

Brian Yuzna
Bride of Re-Animator '89

Bruce Zabel
Mortal Kombat 2: Annihilation '97

Steve Zacharias
Eddie '96

Steven Zaillian
A Civil Action '98
Clear and Present Danger
'94
Awakenings '90

The Falcon and the Snowman
'85

Alex Zamm
Chairman of the Board '97

Chung Jie Zang
Beauty Investigator '93

Robert Zappia
Halloween: H20 '98

Barnardino Zapponi
Deep Red: Hatchet Murders
'75
Spirits of the Dead '68

Mier Zarchi
I Spit on Your Grave '77

Tony Zarindast
Werewolf '95

Cesare Zavattini
Two Women '61
The Bicycle Thief '48

Franco Zeffirelli
Tea with Mussolini '99
La Traviata '82
Romeo and Juliet '68

J.D. Zeik
Ronin '98

Robert Zemeckis
Trespass '92
1941 '79

Scott Ziehl
Red Line '96

Julian Zimet
Horror Express '72
Pancho Villa '72

Paul Zimmerman
Lovers and Liars '81

Vernon Zimmerman
Fade to Black '80

Daniel Zirilli
Winner Takes All '98

Chris Zois
New Rose Hotel '98

Erick Zonca
The Dreamlife of Angels '98

David Zucker
BASEketball '98
Kentucky Fried Movie '77

Jerry Zucker
Kentucky Fried Movie '77

Anthony E. Zuiker
The Runner '99

Ron Zwang
The Nutt House '92

Alan Zweibel
The Story of Us '99
Dragnet '87

Edward Zwick
The Siege '98

The "Cinematographer Index" lists all cinematographers, or Directors of Photography (D.P.), as they are also known, credited in at least one DVD reviewed in this book. The listings for the cinematographer names follow an alphabetical sort by last name (although the names appear in a first name, last name format). The videographies are listed chronologically, from most recent to oldest film. If a cinematographer lensed more than one film in the same year, these movies are listed alphabetically within the year.

Barry Abrams
Friday the 13th '80

Bernie Abramson
Baker's Hawk '76

Neil Abramson
Without Air '95

Thomas Ackerman
The Muse '99
My Favorite Martian '98
George of the Jungle '97
Jumanji (CS) '95
National Lampoon's Christ-
mas Vacation '89
Beetlejuice '88

Lance Acord
Being Inhn Malkovich '99
Buffalo 66 '97

Witold Adamek
The Decalogue '88

Lew V. Adams
Spirit of the Eagle '90

Steve Adcock
Boys Life 2 '98

Remi Adefarasin
Elizabeth '98
Sliding Doors '97

Javier Aguirresarobe
Outrage '93

Lloyd Ahern
Can't Hardly Wait '98
Last Man Standing '96
Turbulence '96
Geronimo: An American Leg-
end '93
Trespass '92
Miracle on 34th Street '47

Mac Ahlberg
Space Truckers '97
Striking Distance '93
Innocent Blood '92
Re-Animator '84
Parasite '82
Hell Night '81
I, a Woman '66

Robert Alazraki
Another 9 1/2 Weeks '96

Romano Albani
Creepers '85
Inferno '80

Arthur Albert
Dirty Work '97

Beverly Hills Ninja '96
Happy Gilmore '96

Maryse Alberti
Happiness '98
Velvet Goldmine '98
I Love You, I Love You Not '97
Crumb '94
Deadfall '93

Jose Luis Alcaine
Blast from the Past '98

John Alcott
The Shining '80
Barry Lyndon '75
A Clockwork Orange '71
2001: A Space Odyssey '68

G.R. Aldo
See Aldo (G.R. Aldo) Graziatti

Henri Alekan
Anna Karenina '48
Beauty and the Beast '46

Nestor Almendros
Confidentially Yours '83
Sophie's Choice '82
The Blue Lagoon '80
The Last Metro '80
Days of Heaven '78
Chloe in the Afternoon '72
Two English Girls '72
Claire's Knee '71
Bed and Board '70
My Night at Maud's '69
La Collectionneuse '67

Alan Almond
My Son the Fanatic '97

John A. Alonzo
Star Trek: Generations '94
The Guardian '90
Internal Affairs '90
Navy SEALS '90
Overboard '87
Scarface '83
Farewell, My Lovely '75
Chinatown '74

John Alton
Big Combo '55
An American in Paris '51
Father's Little Dividend '51
He Walked by Night '48
Raw Deal '48
T-Men '47

Alex Ameri
The Wizard of Gore '70

Juan Amoros
How to Be a Woman and Not
Die in the Attempt '91

Jack Anderson
Family Reunion '79

Jamie Anderson
Neil Simon's The Odd Couple
2 '98
Small Soldiers '98
The Temptations '98
Grosse Pointe Blank '97
The Juror '96
What's Love Got to Do with
It? '93
Piranha '78

Lucien N. Andriot
New Orleans '47
And Then There Were None
'45
The Southerner '45
The Fighting Sullivans '42

Tadashi Aoki
Tokyo Decadence '91

Ubaldo Arata
Open City '45

Thierry Arbogast
Wing Commander '99
The Fifth Element '97
The Professional '94
Ma Saison Preferee '93
La Femme Nikita '91

Georges Archambault
Dead End '98
Random Encounter '98

Simon Archer
The Bachelor '99

Arthur E. Arling
Pillow Talk '59

Arledge Armenaki
Avenging Disco Godfather '76

Chuck (Charles G.) Arnold
Assassin '86

John Aronson
In God's Hands '98

Fernando Arribas
Comin' At Ya! '81
The Blood Spattered Bride
'72

Yorgos Arvanitis
Romance '99

Total Eclipse '95

Monroe Askins
Napoleon and Samantha '72

Howard Atherton
Deep Rising '98
Bad Boys '95

Jimmy Au
In the Line of Duty 3 '88

Joseph August
They Were Expendable '45
The Hunchback of Notre
Dame '39
The Toll Gate '20

John G. Avildsen
Cry Uncle '71

Junichi Baba
8 Man '92

William W. Bacon III
Charlie, the Lonesome
Cougar '67

Hanania Baer
Bug Buster '99
Follow Your Heart '98
Choices '81

Christopher Baffa
Suicide Kings '97
Sometimes They Come Back
... Again '96
Piranha '95

King Baggot
Boiling Point '93
The Last Starfighter '84

John Bailey
The Out-of-Towners '99
Living Out Loud '98
As Good As It Gets '97
Groundhog Day '93
In the Line of Fire '93
My Blue Heaven '90
Brighton Beach Memoirs '86
The Big Chill '83
Cat People '82
American Gigolo '79

Allen Baker
Southie '98

Ian Baker
The Chamber '96
Fierce Creatures '96
Mr. Baseball '92
The Punisher '90
Plenty '85

Robert M. "Bob" Baldwin Jr.
Exterminator '80

Lucien Ballard
The Getaway '72
Junior Bonner '72
The Wild Bunch '69
The Killing '56

Antonio Ballesteros
Cold Eyes of Fear '70

Michael Ballhaus
Wild Wild West '99
Primary Colors '98
Air Force One '97
Sleepers '96
Outbreak '94
Quiz Show '94
Dracula '92
Guilty by Suspicion '91
Goodfellas '90
The Fabulous Baker Boys '89
Big '88
Dirty Rotten Scoundrels '88
Broadcast News '87
The Color of Money '86

Lionel Banes
The Haunted Strangler '58

Larry Banks
The Substitute 2: School's
Out '97

Charles L. Barbee
Free Enterprise '98

Bruno Barbey
The Eric Rohmer Collection:
The Moral Tales '62

Enzo Barboni
Django '68

Roger Barlow
Royal Hunt of the Sun '69

George Barnes
The War of the Worlds '53
The Bells of St. Mary's '45
Spellbound '45
Meet John Doe '41
That Uncertain Feeling '41
Rebecca '40

Boris Baromykin
Fantastic Planet '73

Michael Barrett
Finding North '97

Andrzej Bartkowiak
Lethal Weapon 4 '98

U.S. Marshals *'98*
Dante's Peak *'97*
The Devil's Advocate *'97*
The Mirror Has Two Faces *'96*
Jade *'95*
Speed *'94*
Falling Down *'93*
Q & A *'90*
Twins *'88*
Prizzi's Honor *'85*
Deathtrap *'82*

James Bartle
Twisted *'96*

John Bartley
Disturbing Behavior *'98*
The X-Files *'98*

Adolfo Bartoli
Bloodstorm: Subspecies 4 *'98*
The Creeps *'97*
Vampire Journals *'96*

Gianlorenzo Battaglia
Demons 2 *'87*
Demons *'86*

Julio Battiferri
Swept Away . . . *'75*

Michel Baudour
The Wonderful, Horrible Life of Leni Riefenstahl *'93*

Jurgen Baum
The Dentist 2: Brace Yourself *'98*
One Man's Justice *'95*

Jeff Baustert
True Friends *'98*

Mario Bava
Rabid Dogs *'74*
Twitch of the Death Nerve *'71*
Black Sunday *'60*

Bojan Bazelli
Dangerous Beauty *'98*
Surviving the Game *'94*
Body Snatchers *'93*
Kalifornia *'93*
Deep Cover *'92*
Somebody Has to Shoot the Picture *'90*

Alfonso Beato
The Big Easy *'87*

Maxwell J. Beck
Jack-O *'95*

Etienne Becker
Don't Touch the White Woman! *'74*

Lloyd Beebe
Charlie, the Lonesome Cougar *'67*
Nikki, the Wild Dog of the North *'61*

Paul Beeson
Unidentified Flying Oddball *'79*
Candleshoe *'78*
The Littlest Horse Thieves *'76*
Lost Continent *'68*

Peter Belcher
Operation Delta Force 2: Mayday *'97*

Andreas Bellis
The Naked Truth *'92*
The Wind *'87*

Mark Benjamin
Slam *'98*

Michael A. Benson
Universal Soldier: The Return *'99*
Nowhere to Run *'93*

Manuel Berenguer
The Thin Red Line *'64*

Gabriel Beristain
Russell Mulcahy's Tale of the Mummy *'99*
The Spanish Prisoner *'97*
Trial and Error *'96*
Dolores Claiborne *'94*
Greedy *'94*
The Distinguished Gentleman *'92*

Steven Bernstein
Mr. Jealousy *'98*
The Waterboy *'98*
Half-Baked *'97*
Murder at 1600 *'97*
Bulletproof *'96*
Underworld *'96*
Like Water for Chocolate *'93*

John Berrie
The Peacekeeper *'98*

Renato Berta
Full Moon in Paris *'84*

Thom Best
The Boys Club *'96*

Adrian Biddle
The Mummy *'99*
Holy Man *'98*
Event Horizon *'97*
Fierce Creatures *'96*
101 Dalmatians *'96*
Judge Dredd *'95*
Thelma & Louise *'91*
The Princess Bride *'87*
Aliens (SE) *'86*

Theo Bierkes
The Johnsons *'92*

Ray Binger
Stagecoach *'39*

Donald Birnkrant
Tank *'83*

Joseph Biroc
Blazing Saddles *'74*
The Towering Inferno *'74*
Ulzana's Raid *'72*
The Killing of Sister George *'69*
Bye, Bye, Birdie *'63*
The Bat *'59*
It's a Wonderful Life *'46*

Billy (G.W.) Bitzer
America *'24*
Orphans of the Storm *'21*
Way Down East *'20*
Broken Blossoms *'19*
Intolerance *'16*
The Birth of a Nation *'15*

Peter Biziou
The Truman Show *'98*
In the Name of the Father *'93*
Damage *'92*
Mississippi Burning *'88*
9 1/2 Weeks *'86*
Pink Floyd: The Wall *'82*
Time Bandits *'81*
Monty Python's Life of Brian *'79*

Stephen Blake
Sorority Babes in the Slimeball Bowl-A-Rama *'87*

Ken Blakey
Cyber-Tracker *'93*

Jacek Blawut
The Decalogue *'88*

John Blick
The Frighteners *'96*

David Blood
Steele's Law *'91*

Patrick Blossier
Mad City *'97*

William Boatman
Private Obsession *'94*

Ralf Bode
Sarah, Plain and Tall: Winter's End *'99*
A Simple Wish *'97*
Sink or Swim *'97*
Don Juan DeMarco *'94*
George Balanchine's The Nutcracker *'93*
Made in America *'93*
Uncle Buck *'89*

Oliver Bokelberg
Last Breath *'96*

Alun Bollinger
The Frighteners *'96*
A Soldier's Tale *'91*

Roger Bonnici
Boston Kickout *'95*

Lamar Boren
The Spy Who Loved Me (SE) *'77*

Dave Borthwick
The Secret Adventures of Tom Thumb *'94*

Jimmy Bosco
Lee Rock *'91*

Rick Bota
House on Haunted Hill *'99*
Barb Wire *'96*
The Glimmer Man *'96*
Tales from the Crypt Presents Demon Knight *'94*
Pure Country *'92*

Jean (Yves, Georges) Bourgoin
The Longest Day *'62*
Black Orpheus *'58*

Richard Bowen
Fair Game *'95*
Major Payne *'95*
The Little Rascals *'94*

Terry Bowen
Laserblast *'78*

Russell Boyd
Dr. Dolittle *'98*
Liar Liar *'96*
Tin Cup *'96*
Forever Young *'92*
Sweet Talker *'91*
In Country *'89*
Tender Mercies *'83*
The Year of Living Dangerously *'82*
Gallipoli *'81*
Picnic at Hanging Rock *'75*

Charles P. Boyle
The Great Locomotive Chase *'56*

John Boyle
The Bridge of San Luis Rey *'44*

Henry Braham
Shooting Fish *'98*
Waking Ned Devine *'98*

Russ Brandt
Don't Be a Menace to South Central While Drinking Your Juice in the Hood *'95*

Tinto Brass
Caligula *'80*

Michel Brault
No Mercy *'86*

Sylvain Brault
The Boys *'97*
Sworn Enemies *'96*

Brian J. Breheny
The Adventures of Priscilla, Queen of the Desert *'94*

Jochen Breitenstein
The Boogey Man *'80*

Jules Brenner
Salem's Lot *'79*

Milton Bridenbecker
The Phantom of the Opera *'25*

David Bridges
Big City Blues *'99*

Robert Brinkmann
The Cable Guy *'96*
Encino Man *'92*

Anchise Brizzi
Othello *'52*

Norbert Brodine
Of Mice and Men *'39*

Robert J. Bronner
Jailhouse Rock *'57*

Trevor Brooker
The Borrowers *'97*

Robert Brooks
Who Shot Pat? *'92*

Blain Brown
Night Calls: The Movie 2 *'99*
The Seventh Sense *'99*
Monsoon *'97*

James S. Brown Jr.
The Devil Bat's Daughter *'46*
Strangler of the Swamp *'46*

Karl Brown
Intolerance *'16*

Michael Brown
Just Write *'97*

Ronald W. Browne
Three Amigos *'86*

Kevin Brownlow
It Happened Here *'65*

Ugo Brunelli
The Reincarnation of Isabel *'72*

Bobby Bukowski
Arlington Road *'99*

Don Burgess
Contact *'97*

Robert Burks
The Birds *'63*
The Music Man *'62*
Vertigo (CE) *'58*
Strangers on a Train *'51*

Hans Burman
Thesis *'96*

David Burr
Wild America *'97*
The Phantom *'96*

Dan Burstall
Under the Gun *'95*
Crime Broker *'94*

Thomas Burstyn
The Surgeon *'94*

Geoff Burton
Sirens *'94*

Stephen Burum
Mystery Men *'99*
Snake Eyes *'98*
Father's Day *'96*
Mission: Impossible *'96*
The Shadow *'94*
Carlito's Way *'93*
Raising Cain *'92*
Body Double *'84*
The Outsiders *'83*
Rumble Fish *'83*
Something Wicked This Way Comes *'83*

Dick Bush
The Lair of the White Worm *'88*
Crimes of Passion *'84*
Sorcerer *'77*
Mahler *'74*

Bill Butler
Anaconda *'96*
Beethoven's 2nd *'93*
Cop and a Half *'93*
Child's Play *'88*
Rocky 4 *'85*
Stripes *'81*
Rocky 2 *'79*
Capricorn One *'78*
One Flew Over the Cuckoo's Nest *'75*

Bobby Byrne
Bull Durham *'88*
Stealing Home *'88*
Sixteen Candles *'84*
Blue Collar *'78*
Hooper *'78*
Smokey and the Bandit *'77*

John Cabrera
Call of the Wild *'72*

Sharon Calahan
A Bug's Life (CE) *'98*

Duke Callaghan
Conan the Barbarian *'82*
Jeremiah Johnson *'72*

Thomas Callaway
Caught Up *'98*
Cartel *'90*
Assault of the Killer Bimbos *'88*
Slave Girls from Beyond Infinity *'87*

Alistair Cameron
Like It Is *'98*

Brian Capener
Smoke Signals *'98*

Robert Caramico
Eaten Alive *'76*

Henri Carboni
Mischievous *'96*

Jack Cardiff
Rambo: First Blood, Part 2 *'85*
Conan the Destroyer *'84*
Ghost Story *'81*
The Girl on a Motorcycle *'68*
The Brave One *'56*
The Red Shoes *'48*
As You Like It *'36*

Carlo Carlini
Autopsy *'78*

Russell Carpenter
The Negotiator *'98*
Titanic *'97*
True Lies *'94*
Hard Target *'93*
The Lawnmower Man *'92*
Solar Crisis *'92*
The Lady in White *'88*

James L. Carter
Phoenix *'98*
Don't Answer the Phone *'80*

Walter Carvalho
Central Station *'98*

Alan Caso
The Adventures of Elmo in Grouchland *'99*
Muppets from Space *'99*
Top of the World *'97*

Jane Castle
Leprechaun 2 *'94*

Nino Celeste
Emmanuelle: Queen of the Desert *'93*

Mighty Aphrodite '95
Bullets over Broadway '94
Manhattan Murder Mystery
   '93
The Secret of My Success
   '87
The Red Desert '64

Dario Di Palma
Seduction of Mimi '72

Gianni Di Venanzo
Juliet of the Spirits '65

Ernest R. Dickerson
Jungle Fever '91
Def by Temptation '90
Do the Right Thing '89

Desmond Dickinson
Tower of Evil '72

Billy Dickson
Victim of Love '91

Mario DiLeo
Nightmares '83

Phillip W. Dingeldein
Mommy 2: Mommy's Day '96
Mommy '95

Andrew Dintenfass
Dancer, Texas—Pop. 81 '98
About Last Night . . . '86

John Dirlam
Raven '97

Irl Dixon
Trapper County War '89

Harris Done
Key to Sex '98

John Donnelly
The Tune '92

Ric Donovan
Suspicions '95

Alan Dostie
The Red Violin '98

C.H. Douglass
A Very Natural Thing '73

Christopher Doyle
Psycho '98
Happy Together '96
Fallen Angels '95

Rob Draper
Trucks '97
Dr. Giggles '92

Randy Drummond
Welcome to the Dollhouse
   '95

Stuart Dryburgh
Analyze This '98
Portrait of a Lady '96
Peach / A Bitter Song '95
The Piano '93

Guy Dufaux
Polish Wedding '97

Robert Duffin
Princess Warrior '90

Bryan Duggan
T.N.T. '98

Donald Duncan
Jack Be Nimble '94

Albert J. Dunk
Flashfire '94

Andrew Dunn
Ever After: A Cinderella Story
   '98
Hush '98
Practical Magic '98
Addicted to Love '96
The Bodyguard '92
L.A. Story '91

Elmer Dyer
The Flying Deuces / Utopia
   '39

Paul Eagler
The Hurricane '37
Tess of the Storm Country
   '22

Alric Edens
The Meanest Men in the
   West '76

Arthur Edeson
Casablanca '42
The Old Dark House '32
Frankenstein '31
All Quiet on the Western
   Front '30
The Lost World '25
Robin Hood '22
The Three Musketeers '21

Eric Alan Edwards
Another Day in Paradise '98
Clay Pigeons '98
Cop Land '97
Flirting with Disaster '95
Kids '95
To Die For '95

David Eggby
Virus '98
Daylight '96
Dragonheart (SE) '96
Dragon: The Bruce Lee Story
   '93
Warlock '91
Mad Max '80

Edgar Egger
Hot Blooded '98

Chuy Elizondo
Kiss Shot '89

Paul Elliott
Lost and Found '99
Santa Fe '97
Soul Food '97
My Girl '91

Rasool Ellore
Pyaar Kiya to Darna Kya '98

Frederick Elmes
Opening Night '77

Robert Elswit
8mm '98
Boogie Nights '97
Tomorrow Never Dies (SE)
   '97
The River Wild '94
The Hand that Rocks the Cra-
   dle '92

Susan Emerson
Men '97

Bryan England
Sometimes They Come Back
   '91
My Mom's a Werewolf '89

Jean-Yves Escoffier
Rounders '98
Good Will Hunting '97
The Crow 2: City of Angels
   '96
Excess Baggage '96
Grace of My Heart (CE) '96
Dream Lover '93

Ron Everslage
American Graffiti '73

Geoffrey Faithfull
First Man into Space '59
Corridors of Blood '58

George Fanto
Othello '52

Daniel F. Fapp
The Great Escape '63
West Side Story '61

Mike Fash
The Confession '98
Skylark '93
Sarah, Plain and Tall '91
Women of Valor '86

Don E. Fauntleroy
Rites of Passage '99

Jim Fealy
Splendor '99

Jockey A. Feindel
Revolt of the Zombies '36

Buzz Feitshans, IV
Black Dog '98
For Richer or Poorer '97

John Fenner
The Borrowers '97
Teenage Mutant Ninja Tur-
   tles: The Movie '90

Joao Fernandes
Sprung '96
Top Dog '95
Red Scorpion '89

Giancarlo Ferrando
Torso '73

Rick Fichter
Bride of Re-Animator '89

Steven Fierberg
Atomic Train '99
A Nightmare on Elm Street 4:
   Dream Master '88

Vilko Filac
Chinese Box '97

Russell Fine
The Pompatus of Love '95

Bruce Finn
Word of Mouth '99

Gerald Perry Finnerman
Nightmares '83

Mauro Fiore
An Occasional Hell '96

Steven Firestone
Swimming with Sharks '94

Harry Fischbeck
Sally of the Sawdust '25

Gunnar Fischer
The Seventh Seal '56

Gerry Fisher
Dead Bang '89
Running on Empty '88
Highlander (DC) '86
Lovesick '83
Victory '81

Pili Flores-Guerra
Fire on the Amazon '93

Brendan Flynt
Tromeo & Juliet '95

Stan Follis
Hideous Sun Demon '59

George J. Folsey
Forbidden Planet '56
Seven Brides for Seven
   Brothers '54
Vengeance Valley '51
Adam's Rib '50
Animal Crackers '30
The Cocoanuts '29

Larry Fong
Cost of Living '97

Roy Ford
The Legend of the 7 Golden
   Vampires '73

Tony Forsberg
Terror of Frankenstein '75

Joey Forsyte
Me & Will '99

The Curve '97

Ian Fox
Don't Do It '94

Robert Fraisse
Ronin '98
Seven Years in Tibet '97
Keys to Tulsa '96
Emmanuelle, the Joys of a
   Woman '76

William A. Fraker
The Island of Dr. Moreau '96
Vegas Vacation '96
Street Fighter '94
Tombstone '93
Honeymoon in Vegas '92
The Freshman '90
Chances Are '89
Burglar '87
Protocol '84
WarGames '83
Sharky's Machine '81
1941 '79
Heaven Can Wait '78
The Killer inside Me '76
One Flew Over the Cuckoo's
   Nest '75
Aloha, Bobby and Rose '74
Bullitt '68

Al Francis
Train Ride to Hollywood '75

Freddie Francis
School Ties '92
Glory '89
Her Alibi '88
Brenda Starr '86
Dune '84

David Franco
Earthly Possessions '99
The Assignment '97
A Man in Uniform '93

Robert Frank
Chappaqua '66

Tom Frazier
Midnight Confessions '95

Ellsworth Fredericks
Invasion of the Body Snatchers '56

Neal Fredericks
The Blair Witch Project (SE)
   '99

Jonathan Freeman
Resurrection '99
Junior's Groove '97

Karl Freund
Dracula '31
All Quiet on the Western
   Front '30
Metropolis '26

John Friberg
Alice Sweet Alice '76

Ron Fricke
Baraka '93
Chronos '87

Claude Friese-Greene
On Approval '44

Georges Fromentin
Fascination '79

Hideo Fujii
The Adventures of Milo &
   Otis '89

Tak Fujimoto
The Sixth Sense '99
Beloved '98
A Thousand Acres '97
Devil in a Blue Dress '95
Grumpier Old Men '95
Philadelphia '93
Silence of the Lambs '91
Ferris Bueller's Day Off '86
Melvin and Howard '80

Where the Buffalo Roam '80
Death Race 2000 '75
Badlands '74

Urs Furrer
Shaft '71

Osamu Furuya
Tora! Tora! Tora! '70

Alberto Fusi
Othello '52

Steve Gainer
Foolish '99

Rodrigo Garcia
Four Rooms '95

Greg Gardiner
Dean Koontz's Mr. Murder
   '98
The Apocalypse '96
Boys Life '94

Lee Garmes
The Paradine Case '47
The Secret Life of Walter
   Mitty '47
Forever and a Day '43

Andres Garreton
Darkdrive '98
Total Reality '97

Jeff Gateman
Witchcraft 9: Bitter Flesh '96

Eugene Gaudio
20,000 Leagues under the
   Sea '16

Eric Gautier
Irma Vep '96
Love, etc. '96
One Hundred and One Nights
   '94

Carlos Gaviria
Undercurrent '99

David Geddes
When a Stranger Calls Back
   '93

Lu Gengxin
The Emperor's Shadow '96

Laszlo George
Swimsuit '89

Andre Germain
Daniella by Night '61

Henry W. Gerrard
The Most Dangerous Game
   '32

Maury Gertsman
The Brute Man '46

Rodney Gibbons
Screamers '96

Gerald Gibbs
Curse of the Voodoo '64

Sue Gibson
Mrs. Dalloway '97

Pierre Gill
Joan of Arc '99

Dan Gillham
Voodoo '95

Dan Gilman
Werewolf '95

Paul Gilpin
Tarzan and the Lost City '98
Dangerous Ground '96

Michele Girardon
The Eric Rohmer Collection:
   The Moral Tales '62

Bert Glennon
Rio Grande '50
The Red House '47
Stagecoach '39
The Hurricane '37

Mister Johnson '91
Driving Miss Daisy '89

Nirmal Jani
Pyar to Hona Hi Tah '98

Andrzej Jaroszewicz
The Decalogue '88

Devereaux Jennings
Steamboat Bill, Jr. '28
Battling Butler '26
The General '26

Gordon Jennings
Our Hospitality / Sherlock
Junior '23

Johnny E. Jensen
Rosewood '96
Grumpy Old Men '93
Rambling Rose '91

Peter C. Jensen
Glitch! '88
Grandma's House '88

Peter Jessop
House of Whipcord '75

Thomas Jewett
Mikey '92

John A. Jimenez
Blood, Guts, Bullets and
Octane '99

Daniel Jobin
Lilies '96

Bruce Douglas Johnson
Happy, Texas '99
The Prophecy '95
Public Access '93

David Johnson
An Ideal Husband '99
Hilary and Jackie '98
The Very Thought of You '98

Hugh Johnson
G.I. Jane '97
White Squall '96

Jed Johnson
Women in Revolt '71

Dusan Joksimovic
Pretty Village, Pretty Flame
'96

Richard A. Jones
Wanted '98

Albert R. Jordan
Girls School Screamers '86

Ray June
Court Jester '56
Horse Feathers '32
The Bat Whispers '30

Jeffrey Jur
How Stella Got Her Groove
Back '98
Horton Foote's Alone '97
Dirty Dancing '87
Dirty Dancing (CE) '87

Hans Jura
Little Mother '71
The Lickerish Quartet '70
Therese & Isabelle '67
Carmen, Baby '66

Jurgen Jurges
Funny Games '97

Ernst W. Kalinke
Mark of the Devil '69

Steven Kaman
Mob War '88
Search and Destroy '88
Firehouse '87
Hangmen '87

Janusz Kaminski
Saving Private Ryan '98
Amistad '97

Jerry Maguire '96
How to Make an American
Quilt '95

Adam Kane
Within the Rock '96

Avi (Avraham) Karpik
Simon Sez '99

Stephen M. Katz
Baby Geniuses '98
Gods and Monsters '98
The Blues Brothers (CE) '80
Kentucky Fried Movie '77
Pom Pom Girls '76

Mikhail Kaufman
The Man with the Movie Camera '29

Judith Kaufmann
Nico Icon '95

Takashi Kawamata
Black Rain '88

Tony Kaye
American History X '98

David Keeson
My Best Girl '27

Ken Kelsch
The Imposters '98
New Rose Hotel '98
Big Night '95
Killer: A Journal of Murder
'95
DROP Squad '94
Bad Lieutenant '92
Driller Killer '74

Victor Kemper
Eddie '96
Jingle All the Way '96
Tommy Boy '95
Beethoven '92
Pee-wee's Big Adventure '85
The Lonely Guy '84
National Lampoon's Vacation
'83
Xanadu '80
The Jerk '79
Coma '78
Slap Shot '77
Dog Day Afternoon '75
The Candidate '72
They Might Be Giants '71

Francis Kenny
She's All That '99
A Night at the Roxbury '98
Something About Sex '98
Bean '97
A Thin Line Between Love
and Hate '96
New Jack City '91
Heathers '89

John Kenway
Pride and Prejudice '95

Rolf Kestermann
Casual Sex? '88
Surf Nazis Must Die (DC) '87

Cheng Siu Keung
A Hero Never Dies '98
In the Line of Duty 5 '90

Lee Kin Keung
Black Cat '91

Darius Khondji
In Dreams '98
Evita '96
The City of Lost Children '95
Seven '95

Gary B. Kibbe
John Carpenter's Vampires
'97
Escape from L.A. '96
In the Mouth of Madness '95
Village of the Damned '95
Double Dragon '94
RoboCop 3 '91

They Live '88
Prince of Darkness '87

Hiroshi Kidokoro
Zeram '91

Jan Kiesser
Georgia '95
Clean and Sober '88

Stephen Kim
Retrievers '82

Jeffrey L. Kimball
Stigmata '99
Wild Things '98
The Specialist '94
True Romance '93
Jacob's Ladder '90
Top Gun '86

Adam Kimmel
Monument Ave. '98
Beautiful Girls '96
Bed of Roses '95
New Jersey Drive '95

Sven Kirsten
Play Time '94
Mistress '91

Alan Kivilo
A Simple Plan '98

David Klein
Mallrats '95
Clerks '94

Benjamin (Ben H.) Kline
Munster, Go Home! '66

Richard H. Kline
Meet Wally Sparks '97
My Stepmother Is an Alien
'88
All of Me '84
Body Heat '81
King Kong '76
The Andromeda Strain '71
Camelot '67
Hang 'Em High '67

Wilfred M. Kline
The Tingler '59

Edward Klosinski
The Decalogue '88

Thomas Kloss
Palmetto '98
Fear '96

Douglas Knapp
Assault on Precinct 13 '76
Dark Star '74

Nicholas D. Knowland
Cats '98

Bernard Knowles
Young and Innocent '37
Sabotage '36
The Secret Agent '36
The 39 Steps '35

Chiu-lam Ko
The Longest Nite '92

Douglas Koch
Last Night '98

Fred W. Koenekamp
Embryo '76
The Towering Inferno '74
Papillon '73
Billy Jack '71
Patton '70

Michael Kohnhurst
Henry: Portrait of a Serial
Killer 2: Mask of Sanity '96

Fukuzo Koizumi
Sanjuro '62

Hajime Koizumi
Godzilla vs. Monster Zero '68
Godzilla vs. Mothra '64

Lajos Koltai
Just Cause '94
When a Man Loves a Woman
'94
White Palace '90

John Korty
The Candidate '72

Sergei Koslov
Merlin '98

Andreas Kossak
Watch Me '96

Laszlo Kovacs
Jack Frost '98
My Best Friend's Wedding '97
Multiplicity '96
Copycat '95
Legal Eagles '86
Mask '85
Ghostbusters '84
Frances '82
Easy Rider '69
Rebel Rousers '69

Pete Kozachik
The Nightmare before Christmas '93

Ferdinard Krainer
Return of the Boogeyman '94

Gunther Krampf
Pandora's Box '28
Nosferatu '22

Jon Kranhouse
Kickboxer '89

Robert Krasker
Another Man's Poison '52
The Third Man '49
Odd Man Out '47
Henry V '44

Milton Krasner
How the West Was Won '63
All About Eve '50
Buck Privates '41

Richard Kratina
The Sentinel '76

Lee Kraus
Body Puzzle '93

Georg Krause
Paths of Glory '57

Tai Krige
Kill and Kill Again '81

Daniel Krogh
The Wizard of Gore '70

Stanley Kubrick
Killer's Kiss '55

Dariusz Kuc
The Decalogue '88

Ben Kufrin
Ill-Gotten Gains '97
The Night That Never Hap-
pened '91

Toni Kuhn
The Vanishing '88

Jacob Kull
Uncle Tom's Cabin '27

Kwan Chi Kun
God.com '99

Willy Kurant
White Man's Burden '95

Ellen Kuras
The Mod Squad '99
Summer of Sam '99
Just the Ticket '98

Ben Kurfin
Loveblind '98

Toyomichi Kurita
Cookie's Fortune '99
Infinity '96

Luigi Kuveiller
New York Ripper '82
Deep Red: Hatchet Murders
'75
Andy Warhol's Dracula '74
Andy Warhol's Frankenstein
'74

Richard Labelle
Lady of the Lake '98

Hugh Labye
Rabid Grannies '89

Daniel Lacambre
Humanoids from the Deep
'80
Magical Mystery Tour '67
The Eric Rohmer Collection:
The Moral Tales '62

Edward Lachman
The Limey '99
Why Do Fools Fall in Love?
'98
Selena '96
Light Sleeper '92
True Stories '86
Union City '81

Serge Ladouceur
Armistead Maupin's More
Tales of the City '97

Ardy Lam
Supercop '92
A Bullet in the Head '90

Ko Chiu Lam
Expect the Unexpected '98

Raymond Lam
Mr. Nice Guy '98

Giuseppe Lanci
Francesco '89
Nostalghia '83

Ted D. Landon
The Bears & I '74

Charles B(ryant) Lang
Charade '63
How the West Was Won '63
The Magnificent Seven '60
Sudden Fear '52

Bryan Langley
No. 17 '32

Reggie Lanning
Sands of Iwo Jima '49

Roger Lanser
Much Ado about Nothing '93

Vilis Lapenieks
Rainbow Bridge '71
Night Tide '63
Hideous Sun Demon '59

Jeanne Lapoirie
Wild Reeds '94

Stevan Larner
Rehearsal for Murder '82
Caddyshack '80
The Buddy Holly Story '78
Badlands '74

Federico G. Larraya
A Fistful of Dollars '64

Joseph LaShelle
Barefoot in the Park '67
The Conqueror '56

Walter Lassally
The Bostonians '84
Tom Jones '63

Andrew Laszlo
Star Trek 5: The Final Frontier
'89
Streets of Fire '84
First Blood '82
The Funhouse '81

Ernest Laszlo
Logan's Run '76

Airport '70
D.O.A. '49
Impact '49

Peter Lathrop
The Killer Elite '75

Philip Lathrop
National Lampoon's Class
   Reunion '82
Swashbuckler '76
Airport '75 '75
Hard Times '75
Earthquake '74
They Shoot Horses, Don't
   They? '69
The Pink Panther '64

Andrew Lau
Wicked City '92
City on Fire '87

Moon-Tong Lau
A Chinese Ghost Story III '91

Tom Lau
The Heroic Trio '93

Wai Keung Lau
Once Upon a Time in China III
   '93

Dan Laustsen
Mimic '97

Charles Lawton Jr.
Last Hurrah '58

Dwight F. Lay
Pocket Ninjas '93

Vernon Layton
I Still Know What You Did
   Last Summer '98
The Englishman Who Went up
   a Hill But Came down a
   Mountain '95

Nickolai Lazarov
Armstrong '99

Jean-Yves Le Mener
The Fatal Image '90

Marcel Le Picard
America '24

Sam Leavitt
Guess Who's Coming to Din-
   ner '67
Pork Chop Hill '59

James Lebovitz
Uncle Sam '96

Franz X. Lederle
Succubus '69

Philip Lee
From Dusk Till Dawn 2: Texas
   Blood Money '98
Spoiler '98

Siu-Tin Lei
Miracles '89

Richard Leiterman
Ticket to Heaven '81

James (Momel) Lemmo
Vigilante '83
Ms. 45 '81

Denis Lenoir
La Separation '98

Dean Lent
Jack Frost '97
Bound and Gagged: A Love
   Story '93

John R. Leonetti
Detroit Rock City '99
Spy Hard '96
Mortal Kombat 1: The Movie
   '95
The Mask '94

Matthew F. Leonetti
Star Trek: Insurrection '98

Mortal Kombat 2: Annihila-
   tion '97
Fled '96
Star Trek: First Contact '96
Strange Days '95
Dead Again '91
Another 48 Hrs. '90
Hard to Kill '89
Action Jackson '88
Red Heat '88
Dragnet '87
Commando '85
Weird Science '85
Poltergeist '82

Alvin Leong
Witchcraft 10: Mistress of
   the Craft '98

Jean Lepine
Habitat '97
Ready to Wear '94
The Player '92

Andrew Lesnie
Babe: Pig in the City '98
Babe '95
Temptation of a Monk '94

Elgin Lessley
Seven Chances '25
The Navigator '24
Our Hospitality / Sherlock
   Junior '23
The Saphead '21

Pierre Letarte
Dangerous Minds '95

Cheung Tung Leung
Island of Greed '97
Black Mask '96

Pierre Levent
The Longest Day '62

Moshe Levin
Motel Blue '98

Peter Levy
Lost in Space '98
Broken Arrow '95
Cutthroat Island '95
Judgment Night '93
Ricochet '91
A Nightmare on Elm Street 5:
   Dream Child '89

David Lewis
Chairman of the Board '97

Herschell Gordon Lewis
Color Me Blood Red '64
2000 Maniacs '64
Blood Feast (SE) '63

Peter Lewnes
I Was a Teenage Zombie '87

Matthew Libatique
Pi '98

Charlie Lieberman
Henry: Portrait of a Serial
   Killer '90

Doug Liman
Go '99
Swingers '96

Jong Lin
Pushing Hands '92

Ming-kuo Lin
Vive l'Amour '94

Karl Walter Lindenlaub
The Jackal (CE) '97
Red Corner '97
Independence Day '96
Up Close and Personal '96
Rob Roy '95
Universal Soldier '92

John Lindley
Pleasantville '98
You've Got Mail '98
Michael '96
Money Train '95

I Love Trouble '94
Sneakers '92
Father of the Bride '91
Shakedown '88
The Serpent and the Rainbow
   '87
Girls of the White Orchid '85

Lionel Lindon
The Meanest Men in the
   West '76
The Manchurian Candidate
   '62
Destination Moon '50
The Great Rupert '50
The Road to Utopia '46
Going My Way / Holiday Inn
   '44

Robert Lindsay
Maniac '80

Rolf Lindstrom
My Life As a Dog '85

Pen-jung Lioa
Vive l'Amour '94

Greg Littlewood
SLC Punk! '99
Skinner '93

Gerry Lively
Friday '95
Showdown '94
Warlock: The Armageddon
   '93
Project: Eliminator '91

Art Lloyd
The Flying Deuces / Utopia
   '39
March of the Wooden Sol-
   diers '34

Walt Lloyd
Feeling Minnesota '96
Private Parts '96
Frank and Jesse '94
The Santa Clause '94
Pump Up the Volume '90
sex, lies and videotape '89

Bruce Logan
Tron '82
Big Bad Mama '74

Dietrich Lohmann
Deep Impact '98
The Peacemaker '97
Color of Night '94

Paul Lohmann
Trilogy of Terror '75

Ulli Lommel
Devonsville Terror '83

James London
The Toxic Avenger, Part 2 '89
Troma's War (DC) '88
The Toxic Avenger (DC) '86

Gordon C. Lonsdale
The Last Don '97

Emmanuel Lubezki
Sleepy Hollow '99
Meet Joe Black '98
Great Expectations '97
The Birdcage '95
A Little Princess '95
Reality Bites '94

William Lubtchansky
The Woman Next Door '81

Fabrizio Lucci
Forgotten City '99

Yang Lun
Ju Dou '90

Igor Luther
Tin Drum '79

Bernard Lutic
My Life So Far '98
Boyfriends & Girlfriends '88

Entre-Nous '83
Le Beau Mariage '82

Russell Lyster
Ringmaster '98

Jingle Ma
Island of Greed '97
Mr. Magoo '97
Jackie Chan's First Strike '96
Rumble in the Bronx '96
Fong Sai Yuk '93

Julio Macat
Home Alone 3 '97
My Fellow Americans '96
The Nutty Professor '96
Ace Ventura: Pet Detective
   '93
Home Alone 2: Lost in New
   York '92
Home Alone '90

William MacCollum
Dark Planet '97

Antonio Maccoppi
Nude for Satan '74

Joe MacDonald
Alvarez Kelly '66

Peter Macdonald
Hamburger Hill '87

Kenneth Macmillan
Dancing at Lughnasa '98
Circle of Friends '94
King Ralph '91

Glen MacPherson
Wrongfully Accused '98

Yonezo Maeda
A Taxing Woman '87
The Funeral '84

Ross A. Maehl
Desert Heat '99

Sophie Maintigneux
Summer '86

Denis Maloney
Highway Hitcher '98
Floundering '94

Svatopluk Maly
Jan Svankmajer's Faust '94

Chung Chi Man
Full Throttle '96

Wong Bo Man
In the Line of Duty 3 '88

Mel Mandl
GWAR: Phallus in Wonderland
   '92

Teodoro Maniaci
Tarantella '95

Isidore Mankofsky
The Jazz Singer '80
Somewhere in Time '80

Carlos Marcovich
Midaq Alley '95

Michael D. Margulies
Moonlighting '85
Police Academy '84
The Baby '72

Barry Markowitz
The Apostle '97
Sling Blade '96

J. Peverell Marley
Life with Father '47

Horacio Marquinez
Stranger than Fiction '99
Ten Benny '98

Oliver Marsh
Rain '32

Jeff Mart
Rush Week '88

Jack Marta
Walking Tall '73

Otello Martelli
The Law '59

Charles Martin
Rich and Strange '32

F. Smith Martin
Hard Vice '94

Arthur Martinelli
Revolt of the Zombies '36
The White Zombie '32

Miriana Marusic
The Castle '97

Steve Mason
BASEketball '98
That Old Feeling '96

Rudolph Mate
They Got Me Covered '43
The Pride of the Yankees '42
Love Affair '39
Stella Dallas '37
Come and Get It '36
Dodsworth '36
Vampyr '31
Passion of Joan of Arc '28

James Mathers
Sexual Malice '93

Christian Matras
Lola Montes '55
Grand Illusion '37

Thomas Mauch
Fitzcarraldo '82
Even Dwarfs Started Small
   '69

Tim Maurice-Jones
Lock, Stock and 2 Smoking
   Barrels '98

Bradford May
Darkman 2: The Return of
   Durant '94

Mike Mayers
Joe the King '99
Changing Habits '96

Alfredo Mayo
Kika '94

Donald McAlpine
Stepmom '98
The Edge '97
William Shakespeare's
   Romeo and Juliet '96
Clear and Present Danger
   '94
Mrs. Doubtfire '93
Medicine Man '92
Patriot Games '92
Career Opportunities '91
Parenthood '89
Predator '87
Breaker Morant '80
Don's Party '76

J. Michael McClary
The Turning '92

Gregory McClatchy
Blown Away '94

Lawrence McConkey
Hawaiian Rainbow '87

Ted D. McCord
Proud Rebel '58

David McDonald
Horror Hospital '73

William McGann
Mark of Zorro '20

Jack McGowan
Children Shouldn't Play with
   Dead Things '72

Kevin McKay
Red Line '96

Nick McLean
Cannonball Run 2 '84
Stroker Ace '83

Ronald W. McLeish
Monster in the Closet '86

Geary McLeod
Black Circle Boys '97

John McPherson
*batteries not included '87
Jaws: The Revenge '87

Suki Medencevic
Hunter's Moon '97
Embrace of the Vampire '95
Poison Ivy 2: Lily '95

Igor Meglic
Night Calls: The Movie '98
Allyson Is Watching '96

Phil Meheux
Entrapment '99
The Mask of Zorro '98
The Saint '97
Goldeneye '95
No Escape '94
The Trial '93
Highlander 2: The Quickening
    '91
The Long Good Friday '80

Anil Mehta
Hum Dil De Chuke Sanam
    '99
Khamoshi the Musical '96

William Mellor
The Road to Morocco '42

Chris Menges
The Boxer '97
Michael Collins '96

Peter Menzies Jr.
The General's Daughter '99
The 13th Warrior '99
Hard Rain '97
A Time to Kill '96
Die Hard: With a Vengeance
    '95
The Getaway '93
Posse '93

Stanley Meredith
Salt of the Earth '54

Mark Mervis
Billy's Hollywood Screen Kiss
    '98

John Mescall
Dark Waters '44
The Bride of Frankenstein '35

John Metcalfe
Rawhead Rex '87
Horror Planet '80

Russell Metty
Madigan '68
Rough Night in Jericho '67
Spartacus '60
Man of a Thousand Faces
    '57
The Stranger '46
The Story of G.I. Joe '45
Forever and a Day '43

Rexford Metz
The Gauntlet '77

Jean-Michel Meurice
The Eric Rohmer Collection:
    The Moral Tales '62

Terry Michos
Man on the Moon '99

Gregory Middleton
Better Than Chocolate '99

Pierre Mignot
Alegria '98
Ready to Wear '94

Miguel Mila
Return of the Blind Dead '75

Michael Mileham
Falling in Love Again '80

Arthur C. Miller
Gentleman's Agreement '47

David J. Miller
Virtual Combat '95

Virgil Miller
The Phantom of the Opera
    '25

Alec Mills
License to Kill '89

Charles Mills
Boyz N the Hood '91

Murray Milne
Dead Alive '93

Victor Milner
The Strange Love of Martha
    Ivers '46
Wonder Man '45
The Princess and the Pirate
    '44
Reap the Wild Wind '42

Doug Milsome
Legionnaire '98
Nowhere to Run '93
Full Metal Jacket '87

Billy Milton
Robin Hood: Prince of
    Thieves '91

Dan Mindel
Enemy of the State '98

Chan Hau Ming
Fractured Follies '88

Charles Minsky
Guinevere '99
Pretty Woman '90

Yoshio Miyajima
In the Realm of Passion '80
The Human Condition: Road
    to Eternity '59
The Human Condition: No
    Greater Love '58

Hal Mohr
The Wild One '54
Pot o' Gold '41
Sparrows '26

Amir M. Mokri
Queens Logic '91

William H. Molina
The Last Assassins '96

Mike Molloy
Noah's Ark '99

James Momel
    See James (Momel) Lemmo

Carlos Montaner
Lap Dancing '95

Joe Montgomery
Hugo Pool '97

Carlo Montuori
The Bicycle Thief '48

George Mooradian
Made Men '99
Postmortem '98
Mean Guns '97
Retroactive '97
Nemesis '93

Richard Moore
Winning '69

Ted Moore
Live and Let Die '73
Shalako '68
Thunderball '65
Goldfinger '64

From Russia with Love '63
Dr. No (SE) '62

Donald M. Morgan
The Rage: Carrie 2 '99
Christine '84
Starman '84

Ira Morgan
Modern Times '36

Brett Morgen
On the Ropes '99

Kramer Morgenthau
The Big Brass Ring '99

John Morrill
A Boy and His Dog '75
Hideous Sun Demon '59

John Morris
History of the World: Part 1
    '81

Oswald Morris
The Dark Crystal '82
The Wiz '78
The Seven-Per-Cent Solution
    '76
The Man Who Would Be King
    '75
The Odessa File '74
Sleuth '72
Fiddler on the Roof '71
Oliver! '68
Lolita '62
The Guns of Navarone '61
Beat the Devil '53

Reginald Morris
A Christmas Story '83
Porky's '82

Paul Morrissey
Heat '72
Trash '70
Flesh '68

Andrei Moskvin
Ivan the Terrible, Part 2 '46

Denis-Noel Mostert
Lady of the Lake '98

Sead Muhtarevic
Hard Drive '94

David Muir
And Now for Something Com-
    pletely Different '72

M. David Mullen
Lipstick Camera '93

Robby Muller
Shattered Image '98
Mad Dog and Glory '93

Maximo Munzi
Embrace the Darkness '98
Good Luck '96

Fred Murphy
Stir of Echoes '99
Dance with Me '98
Metro '96
Five Corners '88
Hoosiers '86
Q (The Winged Serpent) '82

Paul Murphy
October Sky '99

Nicholas Musuraca
The Blue Gardenia '53
Forever and a Day '43

Sead Mutarevic
American Strays '96

David Myers
FM '78

Asakazu Nakai
Ran '85
High & Low '62
Seven Samurai '54

Armando Nannuzzi
Chino / Man with a Camera
    '75

Hiro Narita
I'll Be Home for Christmas
    '98
Shadrach '98
The Arrival '96
The Rocketeer '91
Star Trek 6: The Undiscov-
    ered Country '91

Guillermo Navarro
Stuart Little '99
Spawn (SE) '97
The Long Kiss Goodnight '96
Desperado '95
Four Rooms '95
From Dusk Till Dawn '95

Andre Neau
The Return of Martin Guerre
    '83

Louis Nee
Utopia '51
Vampyr '31

Alex Nepomniaschy
Never Been Kissed '99
The Alarmist '98
The Associate '96

Harry Neumann
Two Lost Worlds '50

Robert New
The Chosen One: Legend of
    the Raven '98
Lionheart '90
Prom Night '80

John Newby
The Fence '94

Yuri Neyman
Milo '98

Peter Ngor
Sex and Zen '93
Mr. Vampire '86
My Lucky Stars '85

Wong Ngor Tai
Twin Dragons '92

Meredith Nicholson
The Amazing Transparent
    Man '60

Rex Nicholson
Plump Fiction '97

John M. Nickolaus Jr.
The Terror '63

Govind Nihalani
Thakshak '99

Djordje Nikolic
The Twelve Chairs '70

William Nobles
Winds of the Wasteland /
    The Lucky Texan '36

Eric Van Haren Noman
Dreams of Gold: The Mel
    Fisher Story '86

Danny Nowak
The Big Hit '98

Giles Nuttgens
Alice in Wonderland '99
A Merry War '97

Sven Nykvist
Celebrity '98
Curtain Call '97
Only You '94
With Honors '94
Sleepless in Seattle '93
Chaplin '92
Crimes & Misdemeanors '89
The Unbearable Lightness of
    Being '88
Star 80 '83

The Postman Always Rings
    Twice '81

L.W. O'Connell
The Bells / The Crazy Ray
    '26

Rene Ohashi
To Catch a Killer '92
Millennium '89

Azusa Ohno
Body of Influence 2 '96

Daryn Okada
Lake Placid '99
Halloween: H20 '98
Senseless '98

Jeff Okun
Stargate '94

Roger Olkowski
Hyper Space '89

Marty Ollstein
Penitentiary '79

Woody Omens
Coming to America '88
History of the World: Part 1
    '81

Miroslav Ondricek
A League of Their Own '92
Funny Farm '88
Amadeus '84
Silkwood '83
Hair '79
Slaughterhouse Five '72

Paul Onorato
Tim '79

Ronald Orieux
Booty Call '96
Black Death '91

Arthur Ornitz
Minnie and Moskowitz '71

Michael D. O'Shea
The '60s '99

Roy F. Overbaugh
Dr. Jekyll and Mr. Hyde '20

Gerald Packer
The Wicked, Wicked West '97

Troy Paddock
Ninth Street '98

Louis Page
Any Number Can Win '63

Theodore J. Pahle
The 4D Man '59

Krzysztof Pakulski
The Decalogue '88

Cecilio Paniagua
Lisa and the Devil / The
    House of Exorcism '75
Custer of the West '67

Bob Paone
Judge & Jury '96

Phedon Papamichael
Patch Adams (CE) '98
Mouse Hunt '97
Phenomenon '96
While You Were Sleeping '95
Cool Runnings '93
Poison Ivy '92

Bill Parker
Klash '95

Phil Parmet
Four Rooms '95

Feliks Parnell
Poison Ivy 3: The New Seduc-
    tion '97

Frank Passingham
The Secret Adventures of
    Tom Thumb '94

Ward Russell
The Last Boy Scout '91
Days of Thunder '90

Joseph Ruttenberg
Gigi '58
Brigadoon '54
The Last Time I Saw Paris '54
Woman of the Year '42
The Philadelphia Story '40

Giuseppe Ruzzolini
Firestarter '84
Arabian Nights '74

Ellery Ryan
In Too Deep '99
The Matchmaker '97

Paul Ryan
Box of Moonlight '96
Where the Rivers Flow North '94

Robert Saad
They Came from Within '75

Eric Saarinen
Eat My Dust '76

Morio Saegusa
Iron Maze '91

Takao Saito
Ran '85
High & Low '62
Sanjuro '62

Alik Sakharov
Ayn Rand: A Sense of Life '98
Lulu on the Bridge '98

Javier Salmones
Twice upon a Yesterday '98

Mikael Salomon
Far and Away '92
Backdraft '91
Arachnophobia '90
The Abyss (SE) '89
Always '89

Sergio Salvati
Zombie '80

Paul Sarossy
Felicia's Journey '99
Affliction '97
Picture Perfect '96
The Sweet Hereafter '96
Exotica '94

Hendrik Sartov
America '24
Orphans of the Storm '21
Way Down East '20

Harris Savides
The Game '97

Malik Hassan Sayeed
Belly '98
He Got Game '98
The Players Club '98
Clockers '95

Edward Scaife
The Dirty Dozen '67
Trial & Error '62

John Scheepers
Operation Delta Force 3: Clear Target '98

Jonathan Schell
Boys Life '94

Charles Schettler
Gulliver's Travels '39

Ronn Schmidt
Lord of Illusions '95

Jorge Schmidt-Reitwein
Nosferatu the Vampyre '79

Aaron Schneider
Simon Birch '98

Kiss the Girls '97

Emil Schoenemann
Aelita: Queen of Mars '24

Nancy Schreiber
Your Friends & Neighbors '98
Visions of Light: The Art of Cinematography '93

Barbet Schroeder
The Eric Rohmer Collection: The Moral Tales '62

Eugene Schufftan
Metropolis '26

Fred Schuler
Fletch '85
Arthur '81
Stir Crazy '80

Stephan Schultze
The Price of Desire '96

Philip D. Schwartz
High Voltage '98
King Cobra '99

John Schwartzman
EDtv '99
Armageddon '98
Conspiracy Theory '97
The Rock '96
Red Surf '90

Leonard Schway
Boys Will Be Boys '97

Chris Seager
Alive and Kicking '96
Stonewall '95

John Seale
At First Sight '98
City of Angels '98
The English Patient '96
The American President '95
The Paper '94
The Firm '93
Dead Poets Society '89
Gorillas in the Mist '88
Rain Man '88
Witness '85

John Seitz
Invaders from Mars '53
Double Indemnity '44

Andrzej Sekula
Cousin Bette '97
Stand-Ins '97
Four Rooms '95
Hackers '95
Across the Moon '94
Pulp Fiction '94
Reservoir Dogs '92

Dean Semler
The Bone Collector '99
Waterworld '95
The Cowboy Way '94
Last Action Hero '93
The Three Musketeers '93
The Power of One '92
Dances with Wolves '90
Dead Calm '89
K-9 '89
Young Guns '88
Mad Max: Beyond Thunderdome '85
The Road Warrior '82

Francisco Sempere
Royal Hunt of the Sun '69

Ben Seresin
Best Laid Plans '99

Michael Seresin
Mercury Rising '98
City Hall '95
Angel Heart '87
Midnight Express '78

Viorel Sergovici Jr.
Witchouse '99
Petticoat Planet '95

Eduardo Serra
What Dreams May Come '98
The Wings of the Dove '97

Leon Shamroy
South Pacific '58
The King and I '56
The Snows of Kilimanjaro '52
State Fair '45
Made for Each Other '39

Ho Lang Shang
Return of the Dragon '73

Henry Sharp
The Woman Who Came Back '45
Duck Soup '33
The Black Pirate '26

Steve Shaw
Zero Boys '86

Boots Shelton
Detention '98

Lawrence Sher
Shark Attack '99

Yoshio Shimizu
Village of Dreams '97

Law Wan Shing
I Love Maria '88
Magnificent Warriors '87

Eugene Shlugleit
Zig Zag '99

Lester Shorr
Take the Money and Run '69

Chen Yung Shu
Fearless Hyena '79

Yang Shu
Frozen '98

Newton Thomas (Tom) Sigel
Brokedown Palace '99
Three Kings '99
Apt Pupil '97
Fallen '97
The Trigger Effect '96
The Usual Suspects '95

Jami Silverstein
Boys Life 2 '98

Johnny Simmons
Once Upon a Time . . . When We Were Colored '95

Geoffrey Simpson
Life '99
Shine '95
Little Women '94
The War '94
Mr. Wonderful '93
Fried Green Tomatoes '91

Geza Sinkovics
Jane Street '96

H. Sintzenich
Sally of the Sawdust '25

Sandi Sissel
Barney's Great Adventure '98

Vikas Sivaraman
Sarfarosh '98

William V. Skall
Life with Father '47

Douglas Slocombe
Rollerball '75
Jesus Christ, Superstar '73

Michael Slovis
Scarred City '98

Arturo Smith
Race '99

Chris Smith
American Movie '99

Glen R. Smith
Rebel Rousers '69

Keith L. Smith
The Sex Monster '99
Diary of a Serial Killer '97
Love to Kill '97

Larry Smith
Eyes Wide Shut '99

Leonard Smith
National Velvet '44

Peter Smokler
This Is Spinal Tap '84

Reed Smoot
Homeward Bound: The Incredible Journey '93

William E. Snyder
The Conqueror '56

Piotr Sobocinski
Twilight '98
Marvin's Room '96
Ransom '96
The Decalogue '88

Witold Sobocinski
Frantic '88

Bing Sokolsky
Black Cat Run '98

James Solan
Razor Blade Smile '98

Chai Kittikum Som
A Bullet in the Head '90

Carl Sommers
The Firing Line '91

Jeri Sopanen
My Dinner with Andre '81

Robert Sorrentino
Day of the Animals '77

Leonard J. South
The North Avenue Irregulars '79
Hang 'Em High '67

Mike Southon
Air Bud '97
Snow White: A Tale of Terror '97

Peter Sova
Donnie Brasco '96
Sgt. Bilko '95

Alberto Spagnoli
Beyond the Door 2 '79

Theodor Sparkuhl
Blood on the Sun '45

David Sperling
The Boogey Man '80

Michael Spiller
Drop Dead Gorgeous '99
The House of Yes '97
Hand Gun '93

Dante Spinotti
Goodbye, Lover '99
The Insider '99
The Other Sister '98
L.A. Confidential '97
The Mirror Has Two Faces '96
Heat '95
The Quick and the Dead '94
Hudson Hawk '91

Chris Squires
True Crime '95

Terry Stacey
Trick '99

Jorge Stahl Jr.
Zachariah '70

Rufus Standefer
Lotto Land '95

John Stanier
Rambo 3 '88

Frank Stanley
10 '79
Car Wash '76
The Eiger Sanction '75

Oliver Stapleton
William Shakespeare's A Midsummer Night's Dream '99
The Designated Mourner '97
Restoration '94
Hero '92
The Grifters '90
Earth Girls Are Easy '89
Aria '88

Leonard Stark
Salt of the Earth '54

Willy Stassen
Antonia's Line '95

Robert Steadman
Above the Law '88

Ueli Steiger
Austin Powers 2: The Spy Who Shagged Me '99
Bowfinger '99
Godzilla '98
Now and Then '95
Singles '92
The Hot Spot '90

Peter Stein
Friday the 13th, Part 2 '81

Mack Stengler
King of the Zombies '41

Alan Stenvold
The Invisible Strangler '76

John Stephens
Sorcerer '77
Billy Jack '71

Robert Stevens
Simply Irresistible '99
Pecker '98
The Man Who Knew Too Little '97
Serial Mom '94
The 'Burbs '89

Rod Stewart
Alien Chaser '96

Harold E. Stine
The Poseidon Adventure '72

Barry Stone
Rude '96

Jeff Stonehouse
Mystery Science Theater 3000: The Movie '96

Vittorio Storaro
Bulworth '98
Little Buddha '93
The Last Emperor '87
Ladyhawke '85
Apocalypse Now '79
Last Tango in Paris '73
The Bird with the Crystal Plumage '70

Archie Stout
The Quiet Man '52
Angel and the Badman '47
Dark Waters '44
The Hurricane '37
Lucky Texan '34
Sagebrush Trail '33

Harry Stradling
My Fair Lady '64
The Pajama Game '57
Hans Christian Andersen '52
A Streetcar Named Desire '51
Till the Clouds Roll By '46
Jamaica Inn '39

Harry Stradling Jr.
Caddyshack 2 '88

Ric Waite
Truth or Consequences, N.M.
'97
On Deadly Ground '94
Out for Justice '91
Marked for Death '90
The Great Outdoors '88
Adventures in Babysitting '87
Cobra '86
Brewster's Millions '85
Red Dawn '84
Tex '82

Kent Wakeford
China O'Brien '88
Mean Streets '73

Joseph Walker
Born Yesterday '50
It's a Wonderful Life '46
Penny Serenade '41
His Girl Friday '40
Lost Horizon '37
It Happened One Night '34

Chris Walling
Wicked Ways '99
Crossworlds '96
Solo '96

Jack Wallner
Miami Rhapsody '95

David M. Walsh
Outrageous Fortune '87
My Science Project '85
Private Benjamin '80
Rollercoaster '77
Cleopatra Jones '73

Wing-Heng Wang
Hard-Boiled '92

Andy Warhol
Women in Revolt '71

Gilbert Warrenton
Atomic Submarine '59
The Cat and the Canary '27

Philip Alan Waters
Urban Menace '99
Cyborg '89

David Watkin
Tea with Mussolini '99
Gloria '98
Critical Care '97
Night Falls on Manhattan '96
The Object of Beauty '91
Memphis Belle '90
Moonstruck '87
Return to Oz '85
Chariots of Fire '81
The Four Musketeers '75
The Three Musketeers '74
Marat/Sade '66
Help! '65

Michael Watkins
Heart and Souls '93
Point of No Return '93

Harry Waxman
The Pink Panther Strikes
Again '76

Jesse Weathington
Interlocked '98

Lance Weiler
The Last Broadcast '98

Yossi Wein
Sweepers '99

Harold Wenstrom
The Saphead '21

Egon Werdin
An American Werewolf in
Paris '97

Tony Westman
Needful Things '93

Haskell Wexler
Limbo '99
One Flew Over the Cuckoo's
Nest '75
Who's Afraid of Virginia
Woolf? '66

Howard Wexler
Curse of the Puppet Master:
The Human Experiment '98
Over the Wire '95
Die Watching '93

Charles F. Wheeler
The Best of Times '86
Condorman '81
The Last Flight of Noah's Ark
'80
The Cat from Outer Space
'78
Silent Running '71
Tora! Tora! Tora! '70
The Bubble '67

Jack Whitman
The Shadow Riders '82

Kenneth Wiatrak
Slave Girls from Beyond Infinity '87

Joseph M. Wilcots
Where the Red Fern Grows:
Part 2 '92

John Wilcox
The Legend of the 7 Golden
Vampires '73
The Last Valley '71
Waltz of the Toreadors '62

Harry Wild
The Conqueror '56

Donald Wilder
Meatballs '79

Billy Williams
On Golden Pond '81
Saturn 3 '80
The Exorcist (SE) '73

Bob Williams
Sgt. Kabukiman N.Y.P.D. '94

Frank D. Williams
Tillie's Punctured Romance
'14

John Williams
Yellow Submarine '68

Scott Williams
Patriots '94

Gordon Willis
The Devil's Own '96
Malice '93
Presumed Innocent '90
Annie Hall '77
All the President's Men '76
The Parallax View '74

Ian Wilson
Savior '98
Emma '96
The Crying Game '92

Jack Wilson
The Gold Rush '25

Stephen Windon
Deep Blue Sea '99
The Patriot '99
Firestorm '97
The Postman '97

Peter Erik Winkler
Dark Odyssey '57

**Michael G.
Wojciechowski**
Angel's Dance '99
The Killing Jar '96

Darius Wolski
A Perfect Murder '98
Dark City '97
The Fan '96
Crimson Tide '95
The Crow '93

Arthur Wong
Knock Off '98
Iron Monkey '93
Once Upon a Time in China
'91
Heart of Dragon '85

Bill Wong
Blackjack '97
Once a Thief '96
Rouge '87
Dream Lovers '86

Horace Wong
Armageddon '97
First Option '96

Wing-hang Wong
Peace Hotel '95
Organized Crime & Triad
Bureau '93
Twin Dragons '92
A Bullet in the Head '90
The Killer '90
A Better Tomorrow, Part 1 '86

Oliver Wood
Mighty Joe Young '98
Face/Off '97
Switchback '97
Mr. Holland's Opus '95
Terminal Velocity '94
Sister Act 2: Back in the
Habit '93
Die Hard 2: Die Harder '90
Don't Go in the House '80

Ralph Woolsey
The Great Santini '80

Bruce Worrall
Beyond Suspicion '94

David Worth
Lady Dragon '92

Walter Wottitz
The Train '65
The Longest Day '62

Peter Wunstorf
Total Recall 2070: Machine
Dreams '99

Alvin Wyckoff
Male and Female '19

Manny Wynn
Smashing Time '67

Fawn Yacker
Sex Is . . . '93

Steve Yaconelli
The Phantom of the Opera
'90

Kazuo Yamada
Chushingura '62
Samurai 3: Duel at Ganryu
Island '56

Jun Yasumoto
Samurai 1: Musashi Miyamo-
to '55
Samurai 2: Duel at Ichijoji
Temple '55

Robert Yeoman
Permanent Midnight '98
Rushmore '98
Bottle Rocket '95
Drugstore Cowboy '89

William Yim
Naked Killer '92

Chan Chi Ying
Hot War '98

Lee Sun Yip
City War '89

**Frederick A. (Freddie)
Young**
The Asphyx '72
Nicholas and Alexandra '71

Bae Young-kyun
Why Has Bodhi-Darma Left
for the East '89

Lu Yue
Xiu Xiu: The Sent Down Girl
'97

Richard Yuricich
Brainstorm '83

Vadim Yusov
Solaris '72
Andrei Rublev '66

Wieslaw Zdort
The Decalogue '88

Yuri Zhelyabuzhsky
Aelita: Queen of Mars '24

Howard Ziehm
Flesh Gordon '72

Jerzy Zielinski
Teaching Mrs. Tingle '99
Home Fries '98
Powder '95

Bernard Zitzermann
The Blood Oranges '97
L'Enfer '93

Vilmos Zsigmond
Playing by Heart '98
The Ghost and the Darkness
'96
Assassins '95
The Crossing Guard '94
Maverick '94
The Bonfire of the Vanities
'90
The Two Jakes '90
The Witches of Eastwick '87
The River '84
The Deer Hunter '78
Deliverance '72
The Sadist '63

Kenneth Zunder
Ed McBain's 87 Precinct '96

The "Composer Index" provides a listing for all composers, arrangers, lyricists, and bands that have provided an original music score for any of the DVDs reviewed in this book. The listings for the composer names follow an alphabetical sort by last name (although the names appear in a first name, last name format). The videographies are listed chronologically, from most recent film to the first. If a composer provided music for more than one film in the same year, these movies are listed alphabetically within the year.

David Bell
Final Justice '84

Wayne Bell
The Texas Chainsaw Massacre 4: The Next Generation '95
Eaten Alive '76
The Texas Chainsaw Massacre '74

Roger Bellon
The Last Don '97

Marco Beltrami
The Faculty '98
Mimic '97
Scream 2 '97
Scream (CS) '96

Alberto Baldan Bembo
Nude for Satan '74

Arthur Benjamin
The Scarlet Pimpernel '34

Richard Rodney Bennett
Four Weddings and a Funeral '94
Nicholas and Alexandra '71

Efrem Bergman
Dark Secrets '95

Irving Berlin
The Cocoanuts '29

James Bernard
The Legend of the 7 Golden Vampires '73
Dracula, Prince of Darkness '66
Plague of the Zombies '66
Kiss of the Vampire '62

Charles Bernstein
Whisper Kill '88
The Allnighter '87
A Nightmare on Elm Street '84

Elmer Bernstein
Wild Wild West '99
The Deep End of the Ocean '98
Twilight '98
John Grisham's The Rainmaker '97
Bulletproof '96
Devil in a Blue Dress '95
Mad Dog and Glory '93
Rambling Rose '91
The Field '90
The Grifters '90
My Left Foot '89
Funny Farm '88
Legal Eagles '86
Three Amigos '86
Spies Like Us '85
Ghostbusters '84
An American Werewolf in London '81
Heavy Metal '81
Stripes '81
The Blues Brothers (CE) '80
The Great Santini '80
Saturn 3 '80
Meatballs '79
National Lampoon's Animal House '78
Slap Shot '77
The Great Escape '63
To Kill a Mockingbird '62
The Magnificent Seven '60
Men in War '57
The Ten Commandments '56
Sudden Fear '52

Leonard Bernstein
West Side Story '61

Peter Bernstein
Ed McBain's 87 Precinct '96
My Science Project '85
National Lampoon's Class Reunion '82

Harry Betts
Richard Pryor: Live on the Sunset Strip '82

Amin Bhatia
Once a Thief '96

Nick Bicat
A Christmas Carol '84

Keith Bilderbeck
Ill-Gotten Gains '97
Voodoo '95

Anjan Biswas
Hum Dil De Chuke Sanam '99

Ulf Bjorlin
Elvira Madigan '67

Wendy Blackstone
New Jersey Drive '95

Ruben Blades
Q & A '90

Howard Blake
My Life So Far '98
Flash Gordon '80

Terence Blanchard
Summer of Sam '99
Eve's Bayou '97
Clockers '95
Crooklyn '94
Jungle Fever '91

Chris Boardman
Payback '98
Tales from the Crypt Presents Bordello of Blood '96
The Color Purple '85

Richard Anthony Boast
Sworn Enemies '96

Michael Boddicker
The Adventures of Milo & Otis '89

Leland Bond
Just Write '97

Luis Bonfa
Black Orpheus '58

Marc Bonilla
Caught Up '98

Bono
In the Name of the Father '93

Simon Boswell
William Shakespeare's A Midsummer Night's Dream '99
Cousin Bette '97
Hackers '95
Lord of Illusions '95
Shallow Grave '94
Demons 2 '87
Creepers '85

Roger Bourland
New Jack City '91

David Bowie
Labyrinth '86

Euel Box
For the Love of Benji '77
Benji '74

Leslie Bricusse
Willy Wonka & the Chocolate Factory '71

Jeff Britting
Ayn Rand: A Sense of Life '98

David Broeckman
Frankenstein '31
All Quiet on the Western Front '30

Richard Bronskill
Body Strokes '95
Friend of the Family '95

Michael Brook
Affliction '97
Albino Alligator '96

Harvey Brooks
I'm No Angel '33

Mel Brooks
The Twelve Chairs '70

Bruce Broughton
Lost in Space '98
A Simple Wish '97
Infinity '96
Homeward Bound: The Incredible Journey '93
So I Married an Axe Murderer '93
Tombstone '93

Leo Brower
Like Water for Chocolate '93

Nacio Herb Brown
Singin' in the Rain '52

Paul Bruckmaster
Most Wanted '97

Anton Bruckner
It Happened Here '65

Robert F. Brunner
The North Avenue Irregulars '79

George Bruns
The Jungle Book '67
101 Dalmatians '61

Richie Buckley
The General '98

Paul Buckmaster
The Last Word '95
12 Monkeys '95
The Spy Who Loved Me (SE) '77

Geoffrey Burgon
Monty Python's Life of Brian '79

Chris Burke
Search and Destroy '88

Johnny Burke
The Road to Utopia '46
The Bells of St. Mary's '45

Martin Burke
Blood, Guts, Bullets and Octane '99

Sonny Burke
Lady and the Tramp '55

Ralph Burns
National Lampoon's Vacation '83
Star 80 '83
Cabaret '72

Carter Burwell
Being John Malkovich '99
The Corruptor '99
The General's Daughter '99
Three Kings '99
Gods and Monsters '98
Velvet Goldmine '98
The Big Lebowski '97
Conspiracy Theory '97
The Jackal (CE) '97
The Spanish Prisoner '97
The Chamber '96
Fargo '96
Fear '96
Picture Perfect '96
Rob Roy '95
The Hudsucker Proxy '93
Kalifornia '93
Doc Hollywood '91
Psycho 3 '86

Paul Bushnell
The Commitments '91

David Byrne
The Last Emperor '87

True Stories '86

John Cacavas
Airport '75 '75
The Satanic Rites of Dracula '73

Sammy Cahn
Court Jester '56

John Cale
Heat '72

Darrell Calker
The Amazing Transparent Man '60

Al Capps
Stroker Ace '83

Tristam Carey
Quatermass and the Pit '67

Philip Carli
Peter Pan '24

Robert Carli
Hide and Seek '00

Walter (Wendy) Carlos
Tron '82
The Shining '80
A Clockwork Orange '71

Ralph Carmichael
The 4D Man '59

Craig Carothers
Red Line '96

John Carpenter
Halloween: H20 '98
John Carpenter's Vampires '97
Escape from L.A. '96
In the Mouth of Madness '95
Village of the Damned '95
Halloween 4: The Return of Michael Myers '88
They Live '88
Prince of Darkness '87
Christine '84
Halloween 3: Season of the Witch '82
Halloween 2: The Nightmare Isn't Over! '81
Halloween '78
Assault on Precinct 13 '76
Dark Star '74

Adrian Carson
Salome / The Forbidden '73

Gaylord Carter
Spiders '18

Kristopher Carter
Boys Will Be Boys '97

Greco Casadeus
The Climb '97

Jean-Bruno Castelain
Rabid Grannies '89

Pierre-Damien Castelain
Rabid Grannies '89

Teddy Castellucci
Big Daddy '99
The Wedding Singer '97

Mario Castelnuovo-Tedesco
And Then There Were None '45

William Allen Castleman
The Swinging Cheerleaders '74

Daniel Catan
I'm Losing You '98

Claude "Coffee" Cave
Smart Money '97

Exene Cervenka
Across the Moon '94

Matthieu Chabrol
L'Enfer '93

Frankie Chan
Full Throttle '96
Fallen Angels '95

Stephen Chan
C'est la Vie, Mon Cherie '93

Gary Chang
Stephen King's The Storm of the Century '99
A Bright Shining Lie '98
Double Team '97
The Island of Dr. Moreau '96
The Substitute '96
Under Siege '92
Dead Bang '89
The Breakfast Club '85

Charlie Chaplin
Charles Chaplin—A First National Collection
A King in New York / A Woman in Paris '57
Limelight '52
Monsieur Verdoux '47
Modern Times '36
City Lights '31
The Gold Rush '25
The Circus '19

Graham Chapman
Monty Python's The Meaning of Life '83

John Charles
A Soldier's Tale '91

Jay Chattaway
Red Scorpion '89
Vigilante '83
Maniac '80

Chubby Checker
Wild Reeds '94

Johnny Chen
Xiu Xiu: The Sent Down Girl '97

Yves Chicha
Street Wars '91

Paul Chihara
Impulse '90
Death Race 2000 '75

Danny Chun
God.com '99

Danny Chung
Happy Together '96
Organized Crime & Triad Bureau '93
Black Cat '91

Alessandro Cicognini
Summertime '55
The Bicycle Thief '48

Stelvio Cipriano
Rabid Dogs '74
Twitch of the Death Nerve '71

Chuck Cirino
Sorceress '94

Eric Clapton
The Story of Us '99
Lethal Weapon 4 '98
Lethal Weapon 3 '92
Lethal Weapon 2 '89
Lethal Weapon '87

Stanley Clarke
The Best Man '99
Down in the Delta '98
Dangerous Ground '96
Eddie '96
Sprung '96
Panther '95
Poetic Justice '93
What's Love Got to Do with It? '93
Boyz N the Hood '91

Alf Clausen
Half-Baked '97

John Cleese
Monty Python's The Meaning of Life '83

Paul Clemente
Caligula '80

Nels Cline
Hard Drive '94

George S. Clinton
The Astronaut's Wife '99
Austin Powers 2: The Spy Who Shagged Me '99
Black Dog '98
Wild Things '98
Austin Powers: International Man of Mystery '97
Mortal Kombat 2: Annihilation '97
Beverly Hills Ninja '96
Mortal Kombat 1: The Movie '95
Mother's Boys '94

Elia Cmiral
Stigmata '99
Ronin '98

Robert Cobert
Trilogy of Terror '75
The Night Strangler '72
The Night Stalker '71

Barry Coffing
Love to Kill '97

Leonard Cohen
Love, etc. '96

Serge Colbert
Operation Delta Force 3: Clear Target '98

Ray Colcord
Devonsville Terror '83

Jude Cole
Truth or Consequences, N.M. '97

Cy Coleman
The Heartbreak Kid '72

Graeme Coleman
Better Than Chocolate '99

Lisa Coleman
Foolish '99
Soul Food '97

Anthony Collins
Forever and a Day '43

Phil Collins
Tarzan '99

Michel Colombier
How Stella Got Her Groove Back '98
Meet Wally Sparks '97
Barb Wire '96
Posse '93
Deep Cover '92
New Jack City '91
The Golden Child '86
Purple Rain '84

Combustible Edison
Four Rooms '95

Jean Constantin
The 400 Blows '59

Bill Conti
Desert Heat '99
The Thomas Crown Affair '99
Wrongfully Accused '98
Spy Hard '96
8 Seconds '94
Lean on Me '89
Lock Up '89
Broadcast News '87
Rocky 4 '85
Bad Boys '83
The Right Stuff '83

For Your Eyes Only (SE) '81
Victory '81
Private Benjamin '80
Rocky 2 '79
Rocky '76

Michael Convertino
Dance with Me '98
Critical Care '97
Bed of Roses '95
Things to Do in Denver When You're Dead '95
Guarding Tess '94
The Santa Clause '94
Bull Durham '88
The Hidden '87

Ry Cooder
Primary Colors '98
Last Man Standing '96
Geronimo: An American Legend '93
Trespass '92
Brewster's Millions '85
Streets of Fire '84

Stewart Copeland
Made Men '99
She's All That '99
Pecker '98
Very Bad Things '98
Gridlock'd '96
Surviving the Game '94
Highlander 2: The Quickening '91
Rumble Fish '83

Aaron Copland
Of Mice and Men '39

Carmine Coppola
The Outsiders '83
Apocalypse Now '79
The Black Stallion '79

Tony Cora
The Blair Witch Project (SE) '99

Normand Corbeil
Double Jeopardy '99
The Assignment '97
The Boys '97
Screamers '96

John Corigliano
The Red Violin '98
Altered States '80

Vladimir Cosma
Diva '82

Don Costa
Madigan '68
Rough Night in Jericho '67

Rick Cox
Bad Love '95
Corrina, Corrina '94

William Craft
Psychic Killer '75

Xavier Cugat
The White Zombie '32

Stephen Cullo
Belly '98

Phil Cunneen
Breaker Morant '80

Douglas J. Cuomo
Hand Gun '93

Miriam Cutler
Night Fire '94
Witchcraft 2: The Temptress '90

Richard Cuvillier
The Life of Jesus '96

Norman Dale
See Buddy (Norman Dale) Baker

Burkhard Dallwitz
The Truman Show '98

Ikuma Dan
Samurai 3: Duel at Ganryu Island '56
Samurai 1: Musashi Miyamoto '55
Samurai 2: Duel at Ichijoji Temple '55

John D'Andrea
Boiling Point '93
Swimsuit '89
Grambling's White Tiger '81

Hall Daniels
The Big Doll House '71

Mychael Danna
Felicia's Journey '99
The Confession '98
8mm '98
Kama Sutra: A Tale of Love '96
Lilies '96
The Sweet Hereafter '96
Exotica '94

Carl Dante
The Creeps '97
Slave Girls from Beyond Infinity '87

Ismail Darbar
Hum Dil De Chuke Sanam '99

Mason Daring
Limbo '99
A Walk on the Moon '99
Opposite of Sex '98
Passion Fish '92

Peter Dasent
Dead Alive '93

Shaun Davey
Waking Ned Devine '98

Aaron David
Rude '96

Dave Davies
Village of the Damned '95

Carl Davis
Pride and Prejudice '95
The Trial '93

Don Davis
House on Haunted Hill '99
The Matrix '99
Universal Soldier: The Return '99
Route 9 '98
Warriors of Virtue '97
Bound '96

Mark Davis
Bustin' Loose '81

Simon Davison
Blue Juice '95

Charles Dayton
True Friends '98

Guido de Angelis
Chino / Man with a Camera '75
Torso '73

Maurizio de Angelis
Chino / Man with a Camera '75
Torso '73

Lex de Azevedo
Baker's Hawk '76
Where the Red Fern Grows '74

Al De Lory
Devil's Rain '75

Waldo de los Rios
Bad Man's River '72

Christopher De Marco
Troma's War (DC) '88

Francesco De Masi
Naked Warriors '73
New York Ripper '82

Francois de Roubaix
Daughters of Darkness '71
Honor Among Thieves '68

Barry de Vorzon
Xanadu '80

John Debney
The Adventures of Elmo in Grouchland '99
End of Days '99
Inspector Gadget '99
Lost and Found '99
I'll Be Home for Christmas '98
My Favorite Martian '98
Paulie '98
I Know What You Did Last Summer '97
Liar Liar '96
The Relic '96
Cutthroat Island '95

Christopher Dedrick
Junior's Groove '97

Georges Delerue
Black Robe '91
Mister Johnson '91
Her Alibi '88
Twins '88
Platoon '86
Women of Valor '86
Mesmerized '84
Confidentially Yours '83
Silkwood '83
The Woman Next Door '81
The Last Metro '80
The Day of the Jackal '73
Two English Girls '72
The Soft Skin '64
Shoot the Piano Player '62

Joe Delia
The Substitute 2: School's Out '99
Drunks '96
Body Snatchers '93
Bad Lieutenant '92
Ms. 45 '81
Driller Killer '74

Gary DeMichele
The Imposters '98

Joel Derouin
Play Time '94

Simon des Innocents
Le Beau Mariage '82

Alexandre Desplat
Love, etc. '96

Frank DeVol
Ulzana's Raid '72
The Dirty Dozen '67
Guess Who's Coming to Dinner '67
Krakatoa East of Java '66
What Ever Happened to Baby Jane? '62
Pillow Talk '59

Barry DeVorzon
Hard Times '75

Von Dexter
The Tingler '59
House on Haunted Hill '58

Vince Di Cola
Rocky 4 '85

Paul Di Franco
Masseuse '95

Neil Diamond
The Jazz Singer '80

Romeo Diaz
Fong Sai Yuk '93
A Bullet in the Head '90

Andrew Dickson
Meantime '81

Roeland Dol
Frozen '98

Robert Emmett Dolan
The Bells of St. Mary's '45

Klaus Doldinger
Palmetto '98
Das Boot (DC) '81
Swiss Conspiracy '77

Pino Donaggio
Never Talk to Strangers '95
Troublemakers '92
Raising Cain '92
Body Double '84
Tex '82
Piranha '78

Jordi Doncos
The Princess and the Pirate '95

Steve Dorff
Dudley Do-Right '99
Blast from the Past '98
Dancer, Texas—Pop. 81 '98
Pure Country '92
Kiss Shot '89
Cannonball Run 2 '84

Patrick Doyle
Quest for Camelot '98
Great Expectations '97
Donnie Brasco '96
A Little Princess '95
Sense and Sensibility '95
Mary Shelley's Frankenstein '94
Carlito's Way '93
Much Ado about Nothing '93
Needful Things '93
Dead Again '91

Carmen Dragon
Invasion of the Body Snatchers '56

Dennis Dreith
The Punisher '90

Michael Dress
Quackser Fortune Has a Cousin in the Bronx '70

George Dreyfus
Tender Mercies '83

John Du Prez
Teenage Mutant Ninja Turtles: The Movie '90
A Fish Called Wanda '88
Monty Python's The Meaning of Life '83

Anne Dudley
Pushing Tin '99
American History X '98
The Full Monty '96
The Crying Game '92

Antoine Duhamel
Bed and Board '70
Stolen Kisses '68
Pierrot le Fou '65

Tan Dun
Fallen '97

Trevor Duncan
Plan 9 from Outer Space '56

George Duning
Bell, Book and Candle '58

Michael Dunlap
Street Wars '91

Paul Dunlap
Naked Kiss '64
Shock Corridor '63

Arie Dzierlatka
Chloe in the Afternoon '72

Brian Easdale
Peeping Tom '60
The Red Shoes '48

Steve Eaton
The Van '77

Randy Edelman
EDtv '99
Six Days, Seven Nights '98
For Richer or Poorer '97
Leave It to Beaver '97
Anaconda '96
Daylight '96
Dragonheart (SE) '96
The Quest '96
While You Were Sleeping '95
Billy Madison '94
Greedy '94
The Mask '94
Beethoven's 2nd '93
Dragon: The Bruce Lee Story '93
Beethoven '92
The Distinguished Gentleman '92
Kindergarten Cop '90
Ghostbusters 2 '89
Twins '88

Roger Edens
Till the Clouds Roll By '46

Bernard Edwards
Burglar '87

Steve Edwards
The Patriot '99
Cold Harvest '98
High Voltage '98
T.N.T. '98
Diary of a Serial Killer '97

Robert Een
Mr. Jealousy '98

Cliff Eidelman
One True Thing '98
Now and Then '95
Star Trek 6: The Undiscovered Country '91

Richard Einhorn
Don't Go in the House '80

Danny Elfman
Anywhere But Here '99
Instinct '99
Sleepy Hollow '99
A Civil Action '98
Modern Vampires '98
A Simple Plan '98
Flubber '97
Good Will Hunting '97
The Frighteners '96
Mars Attacks! '96
Mission: Impossible '96
Dead Presidents '95
To Die For '95
Dolores Claiborne '94
The Nightmare before Christmas '93
Sommersby '93
Army of Darkness '92
Batman Returns '92
Darkman '90
Batman '89
Beetlejuice '88
Midnight Run '88
Scrooged '88
Pee-wee's Big Adventure '85

Jonathan Elias
Leprechaun 2 '94
Parents '89
Shakedown '88

Rachel Elkind
The Shining '80

Bill Elliott
Stand-Ins '97

Jack Elliott
The Jerk '79

Marc Ellis
Assault of the Killer Bimbos '88

Keith Emerson
Nighthawks '81
Inferno '80

Stephen Endelman
Earthly Possessions '99
Finding Graceland '98
Keys to Tulsa '96
The Englishman Who Went up a Hill But Came down a Mountain '95
Flirting with Disaster '95
Operation Condor '91

Brian Eno
Dune '84

Micky Erbe
Blackjack '97
Dancing in the Dark '95
Ticket to Heaven '81

Leo Erdody
The Flying Serpent '55
Dead Men Walk / The Monster Maker '43

Esquivel
Four Rooms '95

Asher Ettinger
Joan of Arc '99

Evan Evans
Wicked Ways '99

Brian Fahey
Curse of the Voodoo '64

Harold Faltermeyer
Tango and Cash '89
The Running Man '87
Top Gun '86
Fletch '85

Carlos Farinas
I Am Cuba '64

Jim Farmer
The Real Blonde '97
Box of Moonlight '96

Robert Farnon
Shalako '68

Robert Farrar
Don't Look in the Basement '73

Barry Fasman
My Mom's a Werewolf '89

Lorraine Feather
All Dogs Christmas Carol '98

Louis Febre
Dean Koontz's Mr. Murder '98

Jack Feldman
Thumbelina '94

Eric Fenby
Jamaica Inn '39

Tony Fennell
Within the Rock '96

George Fenton
Dangerous Beauty '98
Ever After: A Cinderella Story '98
Living Out Loud '98
You've Got Mail '98
In Love and War '96
Multiplicity '96
Groundhog Day '93
Shadowlands '93
Final Analysis '92
Hero '92
Memphis Belle '90
White Palace '90
Dangerous Liaisons '88
Cry Freedom '87

Jay Ferguson
Tremors 2: Aftershocks '96
Double Dragon '94
A Nightmare on Elm Street 5: Dream Child '89

Ralph Ferraro
Flesh Gordon '72

Brad Fiedel
Eden '98
Johnny Mnemonic '95
True Lies '94
The Real McCoy '93
Striking Distance '93
Terminator 2: Judgment Day '91
The Big Easy '87
The Serpent and the Rainbow '87
Girls of the White Orchid '85
The Terminator '84

Jerry Fielding
Escape from Alcatraz '79
The Gauntlet '77
The Killer Elite '75
Junior Bonner '72
Straw Dogs '72
The Wild Bunch '69

Ernie Fields Jr.
Avenging Disco Godfather '76

Mike Figgis
One Night Stand '97
Leaving Las Vegas '95
Internal Affairs '90

Peter Filleul
Sweet Talker '91

Sylvia Fine
Court Jester '56
The Secret Life of Walter Mitty '47

William S. Fisher
Born to Win '71

Simon Fisher-Turner
The Eternal Kiss of the Mummy '99

Jeff Fishman
Carnal Crimes '91

Frank Fitzpatrick
Friday '95

Roberta Flack
Bustin' Loose '81

Stephen Flaherty
Bartok the Magnificent '99

Johnathon Flood
Judge & Jury '96

Darren Floyd
Def Jam's How to Be a Player '97

Robert Folk
Boys Life 2 '98
Booty Call '96
Nothing to Lose '96
Ace Ventura: When Nature Calls '95
National Lampoon's Loaded Weapon 1 '93
Rock-a-Doodle '92
Police Academy '84

Sherman Foote
Parents '89

Louis Forbes
The Bat '59
Made for Each Other '39

Francois Forestier
The Peacemaker '98

Romolo Forlai
The Reincarnation of Isabel '72

Keith Forsey
The Breakfast Club '85

Ernie Fosselius
The Unbearable Lightness of Being '88

David Foster
The Little Rascals '94
Stealing Home '88
The Secret of My Success '87

Charles Fox
Hard to Kill '89
A Summer to Remember '84
Two Minute Warning '76
Barbarella '68

Jim Fox
Deadfall '93

David Michael Frank
A Kid in Aladdin's Palace '97
Extreme Justice '93
Poison Ivy '92
Out for Justice '91
Showdown in Little Tokyo '91
Above the Law '88

Christopher Franke
Tarzan and the Lost City '98
Solo '96
Tenchi the Movie: Tenchi Myuo in Love '96
The Surgeon '94
Stephen King's The Tommyknockers '93
Universal Soldier '92

Florian Fricke
Nosferatu the Vampyre '79

Gavin Friday
The Boxer '97

Gerald Fried
The Baby '72
The Killing of Sister George '69
Paths of Glory '57
The Killing '56
Killer's Kiss '55

Hugo Friedhofer
The Bishop's Wife '47
The Best Years of Our Lives '46

David Friedman
Trick '99

John Frizzell
Teaching Mrs. Tingle '99
I Still Know What You Did Last Summer '98
Office Space '98
Dante's Peak '97
Beavis and Butt-Head Do America '96

Fabio Frizzi
Zombie '80

Dominic Frontiere
Color of Night '94
Hang 'Em High '67

Shiro Fukai
The 47 Ronin, Parts 1 & 2 '42

Parmer Fuller
Spirit of the Eagle '90

Michael Fung
Beauty Investigator '93

Giovanni Fusco
The Red Desert '64

Vincent Gallo
Buffalo 66 '98

Douglas Gamley
And Now for Something Completely Different '72

Rod Gammons
Within the Rock '96

Peter Carl Ganderup
The Price of Desire '96

Steven Ganji
The Dragon Fist '80

Roel A. Garcia
Full Throttle '96

Georges Garvarentz
Daniella by Night '61

Giorgio Gaslini
Deep Red: Hatchet Murders '75

Claude Gaudette
Virtual Combat '95

Martin Gauthier
Lady of the Lake '98

Roberto Gerhard
This Sporting Life '63

George Gershwin
An American in Paris '51

Ira Gershwin
An American in Paris '51

Michael Gibbs
Hard-Boiled '92

Richard Gibbs
Ten Things I Hate about You '99
Dr. Dolittle '98
Dirty Work '97
Son-in-Law '93

Herschel Burke Gilbert
Project Moon Base '53

Kevin Gilbert
My Teacher's Wife '95

David Gilmour
Pink Floyd: The Wall '82

Marcello Giombini
The Bloodsucker Leads the Dance '75

Ricky Giovinazzo
Combat Shock '84

Michael Paul Girard
Witchcraft 9: Bitter Flesh '96

Ronan Girre
Le Beau Mariage '82

Claudio Gizzi
Andy Warhol's Dracula '74
Andy Warhol's Frankenstein '74

Philip Glass
The Truman Show '98
Kundun '97
Candyman '92
Hamburger Hill '87

Albert Glasser
The Indestructible Man / The Amazing Transparent Man '56
The Monster Maker '44

Nick Glennie-Smith
The Man in the Iron Mask '98
Fire Down Below '97
Home Alone 3 '97
The Rock '96

Jesus Gluck
Blood and Sand '89

The Goblins
Dawn of the Dead '78
Deep Red: Hatchet Murders '75

Walter Goeher
Great Expectations '46

Cynthia Miller
Digging to China '98

Melanie Miller
SLC Punk! '99

Randy Miller
Without Limits '97
Darkman 2: The Return of Durant '94
Witchcraft '88

Sheldon Mirowitz
Outside Providence '99

Paul Misraki
Alphaville '65
Utopia '51

Bob Mithoff
Sgt. Kabukiman N.Y.P.D. '94

Kunio Miyauchi
Godzilla's Revenge '69

Cyril Mockridge
Miracle on 34th Street '47
The Fighting Sullivans '42

Charlie Mole
An Ideal Husband '99

Norman Moll
Tarantella '95

Francis Monkman
The Long Good Friday '80

Bill Montei
Cyber-Tracker '93

Michael Montes
Firehouse '87
Hangmen '87

Guy Moon
Sorority Babes in the Slimeball Bowl-A-Rama '87

Hal Mooney
The Meanest Men in the West '76
Raid on Rommel '71

Mike Moran
Time Bandits '81

Fernando Garcia Morcillo
Two Undercover Angels '68

Jaques Morelembaum
Central Station '98

Giorgio Moroder
Scarface '83
Cat People '82
American Gigolo '79
Midnight Express '78

Jerome Moross
Proud Rebel '58

Steven Morrell
Progeny '98

Ennio Morricone
Bulworth '98
The Phantom of the Opera '98
U-Turn '97
Disclosure '94
Wolf '94
In the Line of Fire '93
Bugsy '91
Frantic '88
The Thing '82
Lovers and Liars '81
Autopsy '78
Days of Heaven '78
The Inheritance '76
Salo, or the 120 Days of Sodom '75
Arabian Nights '74
The Canterbury Tales '71
The Bird with the Crystal Plumage '70
Cold Eyes of Fear '70
The Decameron '70

The Good, the Bad and the Ugly '67
For a Few Dollars More '65
A Fistful of Dollars '64

John Morris
Carolina Skeletons '92
Dirty Dancing '87
Dirty Dancing (CE) '87
Blazing Saddles '74
Young Frankenstein '74
The Twelve Chairs '70

Thomas Morse
The Big Brass Ring '99

Bob Mothersbaugh
200 Cigarettes '98

Mark Mothersbaugh
Drop Dead Gorgeous '99
The Rugrats Movie '98
Rushmore '98
200 Cigarettes '98
Dead Man on Campus '97
Men '97
The Big Squeeze '96
Happy Gilmore '96
The Birdcage '96
Bottle Rocket '95

Tony Mottola
Running on Empty '88

Michael Muhlfriedel
Plump Fiction '97

Kunihiko Murai
Tampopo '86

John Murl
College '27
Seven Chances '25

John Murphy
The Bachelor '99
Lock, Stock and 2 Smoking Barrels '98

William Murphy
Bound and Gagged: A Love Story '93

Stanley Myers
Iron Maze '91
The Witches '90
The Wind '87
Zero Boys '86
The Deer Hunter '78
House of Whipcord '75

Fredric Myrow
Phantasm '79

Vytas Nagisetty
Desert Blue '98

Mario Nascimbene
The Vengeance of She '68

Chris Neal
Jack Be Nimble '94

Kathryn Nelligan
The Brave Frog '87

Network Projects Music
The Challenge of Flight: Disc One

Ira Newborn
BASEketball '98
Mallrats '95
Ace Ventura: Pet Detective '93
Innocent Blood '92
My Blue Heaven '90
Uncle Buck '89
Caddyshack 2 '88
Amazon Women on the Moon '87
Dragnet '87
Ferris Bueller's Day Off '86
Weird Science '85
Sixteen Candles '84
The Blues Brothers (CE) '80

Paul Newcastle
Spice World: The Movie '97

Anthony Newley
Willy Wonka & the Chocolate Factory '71

Alfred Newman
Airport '70
All About Eve '50
Gentleman's Agreement '47
The Fighting Sullivans '42
Ball of Fire '41
The Hunchback of Notre Dame '39
Wuthering Heights '39
The Hurricane '37
Stella Dallas '37
Come and Get It '36
Dodsworth '36
Rain '32
City Lights '31

David Newman
Bowfinger '99
Brokedown Palace '99
Never Been Kissed '99
Anastasia '97
Jingle All the Way '96
Matilda '96
The Nutty Professor '96
The Phantom '96
Tommy Boy '95
Boys on the Side '94
The Cowboy Way '94
The Flintstones (CE) '94
I Love Trouble '94
Honeymoon in Vegas '92
The Mighty Ducks '92
The Freshman '90
Heathers '89

Randy Newman
A Bug's Life (CE) '98
Pleasantville '98
Michael '96
Maverick '94
The Paper '94
Awakenings '90
Parenthood '89

Thomas Newman
The Green Mile '99
Meet Joe Black '98
The Horse Whisperer '97
Mad City '97
Red Corner '97
The People vs. Larry Flynt '96
Phenomenon '96
Up Close and Personal '96
How to Make an American Quilt '95
Corrina, Corrina '94
Little Women '94
The Shawshank Redemption '94
The War '94
The Player '92
Scent of a Woman '92
Career Opportunities '91
Fried Green Tomatoes '91
The Great Outdoors '88
The Lost Boys '87

Lennie Niehaus
The Jack Bull '99
Absolute Power '97
Midnight in the Garden of Good and Evil (SE) '97
The Bridges of Madison County '95
Unforgiven '92
Pale Rider '85

Stefan Nilsson
The Inside Man '84

Jack Nitzsche
The Crossing Guard '94
The Hot Spot '90
Revenge '90
Next of Kin '89
The Seventh Sign '88
9 1/2 Weeks '86
Stand by Me '86
Starman '84
Blue Collar '78

One Flew Over the Cuckoo's Nest '75
The Exorcist (SE) '73

Erik Nordgren
The Seventh Seal '56

Alex North
Prizzi's Honor '85
Who's Afraid of Virginia Woolf? '66
Spartacus '60
A Streetcar Named Desire '51

Eddie Nova
She Devils in Chains '76

Michael Nyman
Ravenous '99
Gattaca '97
Mesmer '94
The Piano '93
A Zed & Two Noughts '88
The Draughtsman's Contract '82

Sinead O'Connor
In the Name of the Father '93

Hirokazu Ohta
Zeram '91

Alan Oldfield
The Invisible Strangler '76

Marc Olsen
In the Shadows '98

Norman Orenstein
Prisoner of Love '99
The First 9 1/2 Weeks '98
Sanctuary '98

Carl Orff
Badlands '74

Buxton Orr
First Man into Space '59
Corridors of Blood '58
The Haunted Strangler '58

John Ottman
Goodbye, Lover '99
Lake Placid '99
Halloween: H20 '98
Apt Pupil '97
Incognito '97
Snow White: A Tale of Terror '97
The Cable Guy '96
The Usual Suspects '95
Public Access '93

Vyacheslav Ovchinnikov
Andrei Rublev '66

Michael Palin
Monty Python's The Meaning of Life '83

Alan Parker
Out of Time '90

Jim Parker
Moll Flanders '96

Van Dyke Parks
Shadrach '98
Bastard out of Carolina '96
Private Parts '96
The Two Jakes '90
Casual Sex? '88

Stephen Parsons
Another 9 1/2 Weeks '96

Alan Pasqua
The Waterboy '98

Shawn Patterson
The Demolitionist '95

Alex Pauk
Last Night '98

Richard Peaslee
Marat/Sade '66

Michael Penn
Boogie Nights '97

Serge Perathone
Love After Love '94

Danilo Perez
Hugo Pool '97

William Perry
Sparrows '26

Alexander Peskanov
Killing Hour '84

William F. Peters
Orphans of the Storm '21

Barrington Pheloung
Hilary and Jackie '98
Treasure Island '97

John Phillips
The Man Who Fell to Earth '76

Stu Phillips
Battlestar Galactica '78

Van Phillips
Plan 9 from Outer Space '56

Piero Piccioni
Swept Away . . . '75
Seduction of Mimi '72

Aldo Piga
Playgirls and the Vampire '63

Nicholas Pike
Telling Lies in America '96

Antonio Pinto
Central Station '98

Nicola Piovani
Life Is Beautiful '98

Gianfranco Plenizio
Django Strikes Again '87
And the Ship Sails On '83

Michael Richard Plowman
Trucks '97

Edward Plumb
The Woman Who Came Back '45

Terry Plumeri
Death Wish 5: The Face of Death '94
Sometimes They Come Back '91
Black Eagle '88

The Pogues
Sid & Nancy '86

Michel Polareff
Three Musketeers '88

Basil Poledouris
Les Miserables '97
Starship Troopers '97
Switchback '97
Under Siege 2 '95
On Deadly Ground '94
Serial Mom '94
Free Willy '93
RoboCop 3 '91
The Hunt for Red October '90
RoboCop '87
Conan the Destroyer '84
Protocol '84
Red Dawn '84
Conan the Barbarian '82
The Blue Lagoon '80

Jocelyn Pook
Eyes Wide Shut '99

Healthy Poon
Peace Hotel '95

Lisa Popeil
Cyber-Tracker '93

Steve Porcaro
Metro '96

David Porcinello
Return of the Boogeyman '94

Michel Portal
The Return of Martin Guerre
'83

Rachel Portman
Beloved '98
Home Fries '98
The Other Sister '98
Beauty and the Beast: The
Enchanted Christmas '97
Addicted to Love '96
The Adventures of Pinocchio
'96
Emma '96
Marvin's Room '96
Only You '94
Sirens '94

Mike Post
Quantum Leap: The Pilot
Episode '89

Andrew Powell
Ladyhawke '85

John Powell
Forces of Nature '99
Antz '98
Face/Off '97

Reg Powell
Poison Ivy 3: The New Seduc-
tion '97
Petticoat Planet '95

Pray for Rain
Sid & Nancy '86

Zbigniew Preisner
When a Man Loves a Woman
'94
The Secret Garden '93
Damage '92
The Decalogue '88

Andre Previn
Rollerball '75
Jesus Christ, Superstar '73

Charles Previn
Buck Privates '41
The Wolf Man '41
My Man Godfrey '36

Prince
Batman '89

Robert Prince
Gargoyles '72

Mark Priolo
Blood, Guts, Bullets and
Octane '99

Sergei Prokofiev
Ivan the Terrible, Part 2 '46
Ivan the Terrible, Part 1 '44
Alexander Nevsky '38

Heinz Provost
Intermezzo '39

Xiao-Song Qu
Pushing Hands '92

Leonid Raab
He Walked by Night '48

Trevor Rabin
Deep Blue Sea '99
Armageddon '98
Enemy of the State '98
Jack Frost '98
Con Air '97
The Glimmer Man '96

Paul Rabjohns
The Colony '98

Karyn Rachtman
Pulp Fiction '94
Reservoir Dogs '92

Robert O. Ragland
Top of the World '97
Alien Chaser '96

The Fear '94
Q (The Winged Serpent) '82
Grizzly '76

A.R. Rahman
Thakshak '99

David Raksin
Night Tide '63
Big Combo '55
Suddenly '54
The Secret Life of Walter
Mitty '47

The Ramones
Rock 'n' Roll High School '79

Kennard Ramsey
Ringmaster '98
Without Air '95

Erno Rapee
Uncle Tom's Cabin '27

Roy J. Ravio
Fire on the Amazon '93

Jerry Reed
Smokey and the Bandit '77

Les Reed
The Girl on a Motorcycle '68

Alan Reeves
For Hire '98

Rob Reiner
This Is Spinal Tap '84

Justin Reinhardt
Swingers '96

Clutch Reiser
Brain Damage '88

Ivan Reitman
They Came from Within '75

Joe Renzetti
Child's Play '88
Exterminator '80
The Buddy Holly Story '78

Himesh Reshamiya
Pyaar Kiya to Darna Kya '98

Graeme Revell
The Insider '99
The Big Hit '98
Bride of Chucky '98
Lulu on the Bridge '98
The Negotiator '98
Phoenix '98
The Siege '98
Chinese Box '97
The Saint '97
Spawn (SE) '97
Suicide Kings '97
The Craft '96
The Crow 2: City of Angels '96
Fled '96
From Dusk Till Dawn '95
Killer: A Journal of Murder
'95
Strange Days '95
The Basketball Diaries '94
No Escape '94
Street Fighter '94
The Crow '93
Hard Target '93
The Hand that Rocks the Cra-
dle '92
Child's Play 2 '90
Dead Calm '89

Gianfranco Reverberi
The Reincarnation of Isabel
'72

John Reynders
Murder '30

Michael Rice
Nunsense '93

Tim Rice
Evita '96

Jonathan Richman
There's Something about
Mary '98

Nelson Riddle
Lolita '62

Stan Ridgway
Race '99

Tony Riparetti
Postmortem '98
Mean Guns '97

Lazar Ristovski
Pretty Village, Pretty Flame
'96

Nicholas Rivera
Godmoney '99
The Seventh Sense '99
Embrace the Darkness '98
Little Witches '96

Nicholas Rivers
Word of Mouth '99

David Robbins
Savior '98

Andy Roberts
Priest '94

Jonathan Roberts
I Was a Teenage Zombie '87

Eric N. Robertson
Millennium '89

Robbie Robertson
The Color of Money '86
Raging Bull '80

Teddy Robin
Black Mask '96

J. Peter Robinson
Detroit Rock City '99
Mr. Nice Guy '98
Firestorm '97
Jackie Chan's First Strike '96
Rumble in the Bronx '96
Wes Craven's New Nightmare
'94

Peter Manning Robinson
Sometimes They Come Back
... Again '96

Nile Rodgers
Earth Girls Are Easy '89
Coming to America '88

Richard Rodgers
Cinderella '97
South Pacific '58
Carousel '56
The King and I '56
Oklahoma '55
State Fair '45

Heinz Roemheld
Jack & the Beanstalk '52
Mr. Ace '46

Scott Roewe
Die Watching '93

Jeff Rona
Black Cat Run '98
Tom Clancy's Netforce '98
The House of Yes '97
White Squall '96
Lipstick Camera '93

Ann Ronell
The Story of G.I. Joe '45

Andrew Rose
Carnival of Souls '98

David Rose
The Princess and the Pirate
'44

Leonard Rosenman
RoboCop 2 '90
Star Trek 4: The Voyage
Home '86
The Jazz Singer '80

The Car '77
Hellfighters '68
Pork Chop Hill '59
Rebel without a Cause '55

Laurence Rosenthal
Rooster Cogburn '75
Death Sentence '74
Dark Odyssey '57

Matthew Ross
Carnal Crimes '91

William Ross
My Fellow Americans '96
Tin Cup '96
Thumbelina '94

Renzo Rossellini
Open City '45

Nino Rota
Amarcord '74
Love and Anarchy '73
Romeo and Juliet '68
Spirits of the Dead '68
Juliet of the Spirits '65
Nights of Cabiria '57

Walter Christian Rothe
Sworn Enemies '96

Bruce Rowland
Zeus and Roxanne '96

Miklos Rozsa
The Green Berets '68
Adam's Rib '50
The Naked City '48
The Red House '47
Brute Force '46
The Strange Love of Martha
Ivers '46
Blood on the Sun '45
Spellbound '45
Dark Waters '44
Double Indemnity '44

Xia Ru-jin
Ju Dou '90

Michael Rubini
Nemesis '93

Arthur B. Rubinstein
Nick of Time '95
The Hard Way '91
The Best of Times '86
WarGames '83

John Rubinstein
The Killer inside Me '76
The Candidate '72
Jeremiah Johnson '72

Harry Ruby
Duck Soup '33
Horse Feathers '32
Animal Crackers '30

Randall Rumage
The Brave Frog '87

Todd Rundgren
Dumb & Dumber '94

Gus Russo
Brain Damage '88
Basket Case '82

Carlo Rustichelli
Call of the Wild '72
Kill, Baby, Kill '66

Craig Safan
Major Payne '95
Capone '89
A Nightmare on Elm Street 4:
Dream Master '88
Stand and Deliver '88
The Last Starfighter '84
Nightmares '83
Fade to Black '80

Michael Sahl
Bloodsucking Freaks '75

Ryuichi Sakamoto
Snake Eyes '98

Little Buddha '93
Tokyo Decadence '91
The Last Emperor '87

Peter Salem
Alive and Kicking '96

Conrad Salinger
The Last Time I Saw Paris
'54
Till the Clouds Roll By '46

Hans J. Salter
The Brute Man '46
The Wolf Man '41

Bennett Salvay
Rites of Passage '99

Tomas San Miguel
Big City Blues '99

David Sanborn
Lethal Weapon 4 '98
Lethal Weapon 3 '92
Lethal Weapon 2 '89

Anton Sanko
Dee Snider's Strangeland '98
An Occasional Hell '96
Sex and the Other Man '95

Carlos Santana
La Bamba '87

Philippe Sarde
Ponette '95
Ma Saison Preferee '93
Lovesick '83
Tales of Ordinary Madness '83
Beau Pere '81
Ghost Story '81
Buffet Froid '79
Don't Touch the White
Woman! '74

Erik Satie
Badlands '74

Masaru Sato
High & Low '62
Sanjuro '62

Carlo Savina
Comin' At Ya! '81
Lisa and the Devil / The
House of Exorcism '75

Paul Sawtell
The Bubble '67
Rage at Dawn '51
Another Man's Poison '52
Raw Deal '48
T-Men '47

Mike Schank
American Movie '99

Walter Scharf
Walking Tall '73
Willy Wonka & the Chocolate
Factory '71

Amanda Scheer-Demme
Monument Ave. '98

Prof. Peter Schickele
Silent Running '71

Lalo Schifrin
Rush Hour '98
Tank '81
The Cat from Outer Space '78
Day of the Animals '77
Rollercoaster '77
Enter the Dragon (SE) '73
Joe Kidd '72
Dirty Harry '71
The Beguiled '70
Hell in the Pacific '69
Bullitt '68
Cool Hand Luke '67

Norbert J. Schneider
Stalingrad '94

Vic Schoen
Court Jester '56

Aaron Schroeder
Lucky Luke '94

Todd Schroeder
Lap Dancing '95

Walter Schumann
Buck Privates Come Home '47

Carl Schurtz
Loveblind '98
The Night That Never Happened '97

Daniel Scott
Random Encounter '98

John Scott
Lionheart '90
Horror Planet '80

Tom Scott
Stir Crazy '80

Malcolm Seagrave
Phantasm '79

Eckart Seeber
Bram Stoker's Shadowbuilder '98

John Seeley
Hideous Sun Demon '59

Craig Seeman
I Was a Teenage Zombie '87

Maurice Seezer
The Boxer '97

Bernardo Segall
Custer of the West '67

Ilona Sekacz
Mrs. Dalloway '97
Antonia's Line '95

Albert Sendry
Father's Little Dividend '51
Royal Wedding '51

Eric Serra
The Fifth Element '97
Goldeneye '95
The Professional '94
La Femme Nikita '91
Subway '85

Larry Seymour
Stranger than Fiction '99

Patrick Seymour
Scorned 2 '96
The Johnsons '92

Francis Seyrig
Last Year at Marienbad '61

Paul Shaffer
The Blues Brothers 2000 '98

Marc Shaiman
The Out-of-Towners '99
The Story of Us '99
My Giant '98
Patch Adams (CE) '98
Simon Birch '98
George of the Jungle '97
In and Out '97
The First Wives Club '96
The American President '95
Heart and Souls '93
Sleepless in Seattle '93
A Few Good Men '92
Mr. Saturday Night '92

Theodore Shapiro
On the Ropes '99
Six Ways to Sunday '99

Wayne Sharp
Southie '98

Allen Shawn
My Dinner with Andre '81

Harry Shearer
This Is Spinal Tap '84

Ed Shearmur
Jakob the Liar '99

Cruel Intentions '98
The Governess '98
The Very Thought of You '98
The Leading Man '96
Tales from the Crypt Presents Demon Knight '94

Bert Shefter
The Bubble '67

Garry Sherman
The Heartbreak Kid '72

Richard M. Sherman
The Slipper and the Rose '76
Chitty Chitty Bang Bang '68
The Happiest Millionaire '67
Mary Poppins '64
Big Red '62

Robert B. Sherman
The Slipper and the Rose '76
Chitty Chitty Bang Bang '68
The Happiest Millionaire '67
Mary Poppins '64
Big Red '62

David Shire
Sarah, Plain and Tall: Winter's End '99
Horton Foote's Alone '97
Skylark '93
Sarah, Plain and Tall '91
Return to Oz '85
2010: The Year We Make Contact '84
All the President's Men '76
Farewell, My Lovely '75
The Hindenburg '75

Howard Shore
eXistenZ '99
Fight Club '99
Analyze This '98
Gloria '98
Cop Land '97
The Game '97
Striptease '96
Crash '95
Seven '95
White Man's Burden '95
Mrs. Doubtfire '93
Philadelphia '93
Single White Female '92
Silence of the Lambs '91
Big '88
Dead Ringers '88
Videodrome '83

Dimitri Shostakovich
Ten Days That Shook the World '27
The Battleship Potemkin '25

Leo Shuken
The Flying Deuces / Utopia '39

Jeffrey Mark Silverman
Tess of the Storm Country '22

Alan Silvestri
Stuart Little '99
Holy Man '98
Neil Simon's The Odd Couple 2 '98
The Parent Trap '98
Practical Magic '98
Contact '97
Fools Rush In '97
Mouse Hunt '97
Volcano '97
Eraser '96
The Long Kiss Goodnight '96
Grumpier Old Men '95
Judge Dredd '95
Sgt. Bilko '95
Blown Away '94
The Quick and the Dead '94
Cop and a Half '93
Grumpy Old Men '93
Judgment Night '93
The Bodyguard '92
Death Becomes Her '92
Father of the Bride '91

Ricochet '91
The Abyss (SE) '89
My Stepmother Is an Alien '88
Who Framed Roger Rabbit '88
Outrageous Fortune '87
Overboard '87
Predator '87
The Clan of the Cave Bear '86
No Mercy '86

Marty Simon
Black Death '91

Yves Simon
Love After Love '94

Tim Simonec
Suicide Kings '97

Claudio Simonetti
Demons '86

Scott Singer
Midnight Confessions '95

Frank Skinner
Man of a Thousand Faces '57
The Wolf Man '41

Michael Small
Mountains of the Moon '90
Jaws: The Revenge '87
Brighton Beach Memoirs '86
The Postman Always Rings Twice '81
The Stepford Wives '75
The Parallax View '74

Bruce Smeaton
Plenty '85
Picnic at Hanging Rock '75

B.C. Smith
The Mod Squad '99
Smoke Signals '98

Joseph Smith
Animal Instincts '92
Secret Games '92

Paul J. Smith
The Great Locomotive Chase '56

Mark Snow
Disturbing Behavior '98
The X-Files '98
The Boy in the Plastic Bubble '76

Curt Sobel
The Flamingo Kid '84

Maribeth Solomon
Dancing in the Dark '95

Marc Oliver Sommer
La Sentinelle '92

Stephen Sondheim
Into the Woods '90
Sunday in the Park with George '86
West Side Story '61

Lodovico Sorret
The Wife '95

Paul Speer
To Cross the Rubicon '91

Herbert W. Spencer
Jesus Christ, Superstar '73

Scott Spock
Free Enterprise '98

Robert Sprayberry
Where the Red Fern Grows: Part 2 '92

Ralph Stanley
Unknown Island '48

Ringo Starr
Yellow Submarine '68
Magical Mystery Tour '67

Help! '65

Michael Stearns
Baraka '93

Chris Stein
Union City '81

Ronald Stein
Spider Baby '64
Dementia 13 '63
The Terror '63

Max Steiner
The Searchers '56
The Caine Mutiny '54
Life with Father '47
The Big Sleep '46
Casablanca '42
Santa Fe Trail '40
Dark Victory '39
Gone with the Wind '39
Jezebel '38
A Star Is Born '37
She '35
The Most Dangerous Game '32

Michael Sterns
Chronos '87

James Stevens
Plan 9 from Outer Space '56

Leith Stevens
James Dean Story '57
The Wild One '54
The War of the Worlds '53
Destination Moon '50

David A. Stewart
Cookie's Fortune '99
Beautiful Girls '96

Russell Stirling
Operation Delta Force 2: Mayday '97

Morris Stoloff
His Girl Friday '40

Christopher Stone
Fist of the North Star '95
Choices '81

Richard Stone
Victim of Love '91

David Storrs
Invaders from Mars '86

Herbert Stothart
They Were Expendable '45
National Velvet '44
The Wizard of Oz '39

Frank Stranglo
Under the Gun '95

John Strauss
Amadeus '84

Barbra Streisand
The Mirror Has Two Faces '96

William T. Stromberg
Trinity and Beyond: The Atomic Bomb Movie '99

Charles Strouse
Bonnie & Clyde '67

Joe Strummer
Grosse Pointe Blank '97
Sid & Nancy '86

Harry Sukman
Salem's Lot '79

Majrooh Sultanpuri
Khamoshi the Musical '96

Andy Summers
Weekend at Bernie's '89

Mark Suozzo
The Last Days of Disco '98

Ron Sures
Body of Influence 2 '96
A Man in Uniform '93

Bruce Sussman
The Pebble and the Penguin '94
Thumbelina '94

Matthew Sweet
Can't Hardly Wait '98

Jules Sylvain
June Night '40

Stanislas Syrewicz
Shooting Fish '98
The Lair of the White Worm '88

Taj
Hard Bounty '94

Toru Takemitsu
Rising Sun '93
Black Rain '88
Ran '85
In the Realm of Passion '80

Tangerine Dream
Vision Quest '85
Firestarter '84
Risky Business '83
Thief '81
Sorcerer '77

Pierre Tardy
Time Masters '82

Michael Tavera
Mr. Magoo '97

Stephen James Taylor
Why Do Fools Fall in Love? '98

Dennis Michael Tenney
Grim '95

Yann Thiersen
The Dreamlife of Angels '98

Maurice Thiriet
The Fantastic Night '42

Ian Thomas
Bury Me in Niagara '93

Linda Thompson
The Little Rascals '94

Richard Thompson
Sweet Talker '91

Ken Thorne
Help! '65

Raphael Tidas
Romance '99

Michael Timmins
The Boys Club '96

Dimitri Tiomkin
The War Wagon '67
The Guns of Navarone '61
High Noon '52
Strangers on a Train '51
D.O.A. '49
Red River '48
Duel in the Sun '46
It's a Wonderful Life '46
The Bridge of San Luis Rey '44
Meet John Doe '41
The Westerner '40
Lost Horizon '37

Tomandandy
Arlington Road '99

Ed Tomney
Night of the Warrior '91

Jannick Top
Love After Love '94

Colin Towns
Space Truckers '97
Rawhead Rex '87

Vaclav Trojan
Puppet Films of Jiri Trnka

Danny Troob
Boys Life 2 '98

Ernest Troost
Tremors '89

Roger Troutman
A Thin Line Between Love
  and Hate '96

Armando Trovajoli
Two Women '61

Tim Truman
Retroactive '97
Good Luck '96
Mikey '92

Ding-Yat Tsung
Organized Crime & Triad
  Bureau '93

Giorgio Tucci
Zombie '80

Jonathan Tunick
The Birdcage '95

Bhring Tupkari
Lav Kush '97

Tom Tykwer
Run Lola Run '98

Brian Tyler
Simon Sez '99

Christopher Tyng
The Associate '96
Across the Moon '94

Steve Tyrell
Once Upon a Time . . .
  When We Were Colored '95

Nerida Tyson-Chew
Twisted '96

Deddy Tzur
The Pandora Project '98

D.J. Valentin
Romance '99

Jean-Louis Valero
Boyfriends & Girlfriends '88
Summer '86

James Van Heusen
The Road to Utopia '46
The Bells of St. Mary's '45

Kyle Van Horne
Return of the Boogeyman '94

Georges Van Parys
Diabolique '55

Wessel Van Rensburg
Operation Delta Force 2: Mayday '97

Vangelis
Francesco '89
Blade Runner (DC) '82
Chariots of Fire '81

Varouje
Jungleground '95

Ben Vaughn
Black Mask '96

Giuseppe Verdi
La Traviata '82

Tom Verlaine
Love and a .45 '94

Gerard Victory
Terror of Frankenstein '75

Joseph Vitarelli
Kissing a Fool '98

Alessio Vlad
Tea with Mussolini '99
Besieged '98

Henny Vrienten
The Vanishing '88

Popul Vuh
Fitzcarraldo '82
Nosferatu the Vampyre '79

Rick Wakeman
Crimes of Passion '84

Dana Walden
Killing Obsession '94
My Mom's a Werewolf '89

W.G. Snuffy Walden
Stephen King's The Stand
  '94

Junior Walker
Red Line '96

Shirley Walker
Asteroid '97
Escape from L.A. '96
Turbulence '96

Oliver Wallace
Big Red '62
Nikki, the Wild Dog of the
  North '61

Karl Wallinger
Reality Bites '94

Jeff Walton
Jack-O '95

William Walton
Henry V '44
As You Like It '36

Gast Waltzing
New World Disorder '99

Michael Wandmacher
Modern Vampires '98
Twin Dragons '92

Fu-ling Wang
Chinese Connection '73
Fists of Fury '73

Nathan Wang
Jackie Chan's Who Am I '98

Stephen Warbeck
Mystery Men '99
Shakespeare in Love (CS)
  '98
Mrs. Brown '97
My Son the Fanatic '97
Sister My Sister '94

Roger Waters
Pink Floyd: The Wall '82

Mark Watters
Tom Sawyer '99
All Dogs Christmas Carol '98
The Pebble and the Penguin
  '94

Franz Waxman
Mister Roberts '55
The Paradine Case '47
Woman of the Year '42
The Philadelphia Story '40
Rebecca '40
The Bride of Frankenstein '35

Darryl Way
Sorceress '94

Roy Webb
Notorious '46
Love Affair '39

Andrew Lloyd Webber
Cats '98
Evita '96
The Odessa File '74
Jesus Christ, Superstar '73

Ronald J. Weiss
Street Law '95

Eric Weissburg
Deliverance '72

Larry Wellington
The Wizard of Gore '70
2000 Maniacs '64

Richard Wells
Razor Blade Smile '98

John Welsman
Tender Loving Care '99

Brahm Wenger
Air Bud '97

Jim West
Lady Dragon '92

Paul Westerberg
Singles '92

Nigel Westlake
Babe: Pig in the City '98
Babe '95

Robert Whaley
Joe the King '99

Jack Wheaton
Penitentiary 2 '82

Bill Whelan
Dancing at Lughnasa '98

Norman Whitfield
Car Wash '76

Matthew Wilder
Mulan '98

K. Alexander Wilkinson
Jane Street '96

Marc Wilkinson
Royal Hunt of the Sun '69

Allen Williams
The Robin Hood Gang '98

David Williams
Shelter '98
Wishmaster 2: Evil Never
  Dies '98
Phantoms '97
The Prophecy 2: Ashtown '97
The Killing Jar '96
The Prophecy '95

John Williams
Saving Private Ryan '98
Stepmom '98
Amistad '97
Seven Years in Tibet '97
Rosewood '97
Sleepers '96
Nixon '95
Far and Away '92
Home Alone 2: Lost in New
  York '92
JFK '91
Home Alone '90
Presumed Innocent '90
Always '89
Born on the Fourth of July
  '89
The Witches of Eastwick '87
The River '84
Dracula '79
1941 '79
The Deer Hunter '78
Midway '76
The Eiger Sanction '75
Earthquake '74
The Towering Inferno '74
The Cowboys '72
The Poseidon Adventure '72
Fiddler on the Roof '71

Joseph Williams
From Dusk Till Dawn 2: Texas
  Blood Money '98
Embrace of the Vampire '95
Poison Ivy 2: Lily '95

Ken Williams
In the Company of Men '96

Patrick Williams
That Old Feeling '96
All of Me '84

Paul Williams
The Boy in the Plastic Bubble
  '76

Pip Williams
Train Ride to Hollywood '75

Meredith Willson
The Music Man '62
The Little Foxes '41
The Great Dictator '40

Mortimer Wilson
The Black Pirate '26

Nancy Wilson
Jerry Maguire '96

Willie Wisely
Tromeo & Juliet '95

Jill Wisoff
Welcome to the Dollhouse
  '95

Cacine Wong
Peace Hotel '95
The Executioners '93

James Wong
Once Upon a Time in China
  '91
A Bullet in the Head '90
Peking Opera Blues '86

Ying-wah Wong
The Longest Nite '92

Frank Worth
Bride of the Monster '55

Arthur Wright
Dolemite '75

Wai Lap Wu
Once Upon a Time in China III
  '93

Alex Wurman
Eat Your Heart Out '96

David Wurst
The Last Assassins '96

Eric Wurst
The Last Assassins '96

Danny Wyman
The Lawnmower Man '92
Hoh Night '81

Motofumi Yamaguchi
The Hunted '95

Naozumi Yamamoto
Branded to Kill '67

Gabriel Yared
City of Angels '98
Message in a Bottle '98
The Wings of the Dove '97
The English Patient '96
Clean and Sober '88

Yello
Senseless '98

Chris Young
The Man Who Knew Too Little
  '97

Christopher Young
Entrapment '99
In Too Deep '99
Hush '98
Rounders '98
Urban Legend '98
Hard Rain '97
Murder at 1600 '97
Set It Off '96
Copycat '95
Tales from the Hood '95
Virtuosity '95
Dream Lover '93
The Dark Half '91
Bat 21 '88
Hellbound: Hellraiser 2 '88
Hellraiser '87
Invaders from Mars '86

Neil Young
Where the Buffalo Roam '80

Victor Young
The Brave One '56
The Conqueror '56
The Quiet Man '52
Rio Grande '50
Sands of Iwo Jima '49
For Whom the Bell Tolls '43
Reap the Wild Wind '42

Joji Yuasa
The Funeral '84

Richard Yuen
The Bride with White Hair '93
Once Upon a Time in China II
  '92
Wicked City '92

Lee Zahler
The Mask of Diijon '46

Christian Zanesi
Time Masters '82

Paul Zaza
The Base '99
Baby Geniuses '98
Hot Blooded '98
Face the Evil '97
Iron Eagle 4 '95
To Catch a Killer '92
A Christmas Story '83
Porky's '82
Prom Night '80

Eric Zeisl
They Were Expendable '45
Bataan '43

Wolfgang Zeller
Vampyr '31

Guy Zerafa
Redline '97

Jiping Zhao
The Emperor's Shadow '96
Ju Dou '90

Hans Zimmer
Prince of Egypt '98
The Thin Red Line '98
As Good As It Gets '97
The Peacemaker '97
The Fan '96
Broken Arrow '95
Crimson Tide '95
Drop Zone '94
Cool Runnings '93
Point of No Return '93
True Romance '93
A League of Their Own '92
The Power of One '92
Backdraft '91
Thelma & Louise '91
Bird on a Wire '90
Days of Thunder '90
Black Rain '89
Driving Miss Daisy '89
Rain Man '88
The Wind '87
Zero Boys '86

David Zippel
Mulan '98
Hercules '97

Carl Zittrer
A Christmas Story '83
Porky's '82
Children Shouldn't Play with
  Dead Things '72

The "Category Index" includes subject terms ranging from straight genre descriptions (Drama, Comedy, etc.) to more off-the-wall themes (Bodily Functions, Scared 'Chuteless). These terms can help you identify unifying themes (Baseball, Heists), characters (Dracula, Sherlock Holmes), settings (Period Pieces, Viva Las Vegas!), events (The Great Depression, World War II), occupations (Clowns, Cops, Serial Killers), ensembles (Monty Python, the Muppets), or suddenly animate objects (Killer Toys). You will also find categories for films produced outside the U.S. (See Foreign Films for cross references). Category terms are listed alphabetically; corresponding movie lists are also alphabetical.

Abbott & Costello

Abbott and Costello in the
  Foreign Legion
Buck Privates
Buck Privates Come Home
In the Navy
Jack & the Beanstalk

Action-Adventure

*See also: Adventure Drama;
Boom!; Comic Adventure; Disaster Flicks; Martial Arts;
Swashbucklers*
Armstrong
The Assault
Big Bullet
Buddhist Fist
City Hunter
Crackdown
Crystal Hunt
Desert Heat
Expect the Unexpected
First Option
Hitman
The Killer Meteors
Killer's Romance
Legend of the Drunken Tiger
Man Wanted
New World Disorder
Simon Sez
Tokyo Fist
Tornado Run

Action-Comedy

*See also: Action-Adventure;
Comedy*
High Risk
Royal Tramp
Rush Hour

Adaptations

*See: Bible Adaptations; Cartoon Adaptations; Comics
Adaptation; Fairy Tale Adaptations; Game Adaptations;
Opera Adaptations; Television
Adaptations*

Adolescence

*See: Coming of Age; Hell High
School; Teen Angst*

Adoption & Orphans

Anastasia
Batman Forever
Big Daddy
Big Red
The Blues Brothers 2000
Daddy Long Legs
Flirting with Disaster
Free Willy
Gloria
Great Expectations
The Kid / A Dog's Life
The Land Before Time
Mad Max: Beyond Thunderdome
Major Payne
Mercury Rising
Mighty Aphrodite
Mighty Joe Young
Napoleon and Samantha
Oliver!
Oliver Twist
Orphans of the Storm
Penny Serenade
The Quest
Red Cherry
Sally of the Sawdust
The Secret Garden
Shooting Fish
Stuart Little

Adventure Drama

*See also: Action-Adventure;
Boom!; Drama*
The Adventures of Milo &
  Otis
Air Force One
Alexander Nevsky
Aloha, Bobby and Rose
America
Apocalypse Now
Apollo 13
Around the World in 80 Days
Backdraft
Bataan
Beneath the 12-Mile Reef
Big Bad Mama
Blown Away
Call of the Wild
Clear and Present Danger
Con Air
Conspiracy Theory
The Corruptor
Crimson Tide
Dangerous Ground
Days of Thunder
Deliverance
Die Hard
Die Hard 2: Die Harder
Die Hard: With a Vengeance
Enemy of the State
Eraser
Executive Decision
For Whom the Bell Tolls
Free Willy
The Fugitive
The Ghost and the Darkness
The Great Escape
The Great Locomotive Chase
The Great Train Robbery
Hackers
Hell in the Pacific
Hellfighters
Homeward Bound: The
  Incredible Journey
The Hunt for Red October
Jamaica Inn
Johnny Mnemonic
The Killer
The Killer Elite
Lion of the Desert
The Man in the Iron Mask
The Mask of Zorro
Memphis Belle
Men in War
Midway
Moby Dick
Money Train
Ms. 45
The Negotiator
Out of Time
Outbreak
Papillon
Patriot Games
The Peacemaker
Peking Opera Blues
Penitentiary
Penitentiary 2
The Phantom
Platoon
Pork Chop Hill
Raid on Rommel
Ran
Reap the Wild Wind
The Replacement Killers
Revenge
The River Wild
Robin Hood: Prince of
  Thieves
RoboCop
Ronin
Runaway Train
The Saint
Sands of Iwo Jima
Sea Wolves
The Shadow
She
The Siege
Sorcerer
The Specialist
Speed
Spirit of the Eagle
Star Trek: Insurrection
Steele's Law
The Sting
Strange Days
Streets of Fire
Switchback
Tank
Tarzan in Manhattan
Thelma & Louise
They Were Expendable
The Three Musketeers
Top Gun
U.S. Marshals
White Squall
Winning
The Year of Living Dangerously

Advertising

*See also: Front Page; Mass
Media*
DROP Squad
Nothing to Lose
One Night Stand

African America

See also: New Black Cinema
Beloved
The Best Man
Blade
Blue Collar
Boyz N the Hood
Bulworth
Caught Up
Clockers
The Color Purple
Crooklyn
Dead Presidents
Detention
Devil in a Blue Dress
Do the Right Thing
Don't Be a Menace to South
  Central While Drinking Your
  Juice in the Hood
DROP Squad
Eve's Bayou
Firehouse
Foolish
Friday
Glory
The Golden Child
The Green Mile
Guess Who's Coming to Dinner
He Got Game
How Stella Got Her Groove
  Back
Ill-Gotten Gains
Junior's Groove
Lean on Me
Lotto Land
Love Jones
Menace II Society
Mississippi Burning
Mister Johnson
New Jack City
New Jersey Drive
Once Upon a Time . . .
  When We Were Colored
Panther
Penitentiary
Poetic Justice
Purple Rain
Richard Pryor: Live in Concert
Richard Pryor: Live on the
  Sunset Strip
Ricochet
Rosewood
Rude
Set It Off
Shaft
The '60s
Slam
Soul Food
Sprung
A Stranger in the Kingdom
Tales from the Hood
The Temptations
A Thin Line Between Love
  and Hate
A Time to Kill
What's Love Got to Do with
  It?
White Man's Burden
The Wiz

AIDS

*See also: Disease of the
Week*
Alive and Kicking
Boys on the Side
Kids
One Night Stand
Philadelphia
Playing by Heart
Sex Is . . .

Air Disasters

*See also: Airborne; Disaster
Flicks; Sea Disasters*
Air Force One
Airport
Airport '75
Apollo 13
Broken Arrow
The Buddy Holly Story
Con Air
Die Hard 2: Die Harder
Executive Decision
Fearless
Get Shorty
Ground Control
Hero
The Hindenburg
Turbulence
U.S. Marshals

Airborne

See also: Air Disasters

Air America
Air Force One
Airport
Airport '75
Always
Bulletproof
The Challenge of Flight: Disc One
Con Air
Die Hard 2: Die Harder
Dr. Strangelove, or: How I Learned to Stop Worrying and Love the Bomb
Drop Zone
Executive Decision
Fly Away Home
The Flying Deuces / Utopia
Freedom Strike
French Kiss
Independence Day
Interceptor
Iron Eagle 4
The Island at the Top of the World
La Bamba
Memphis Belle
Millennium
1941
October Sky
The Phantom
Pushing Tin
The Right Stuff
Six Days, Seven Nights
Stephen King's The Night Flier
Tactical Assault
Terminal Velocity
Top Gun
Turbulence

Airplanes

See: Air Disasters; Airborne

Alcoholism

See: On the Rocks

Alien Beings—Benign

See also: Alien Beings—Vicious; Aliens Are People, Too

The Abyss (SE)
*batteries not included
The Cat from Outer Space
Dark City
Earth Girls Are Easy
Femalien
Gremlins
The Hidden
Labyrinth
The Last Starfighter
The Man Who Fell to Earth
Muppets from Space
My Favorite Martian
My Stepmother Is an Alien
Star Trek 4: The Voyage Home
Star Trek: First Contact
Starman

Alien Beings—Vicious

See also: Alien Beings—Benign; Aliens Are People, Too

Alien
Alien Seed
Aliens (SE)
Alien3
The Arrival
Atomic Submarine
Battlestar Galactica
Body Snatchers
Breeders
The Colony
Crosswords
Dark Star
The Faculty
The Fifth Element
First Man into Space
Gremlins
The Hidden

Horror Planet
Independence Day
Invaders from Mars
Invasion of the Body Snatchers
Laserhawk
Leviathan
Lost in Space
Mars Attacks!
Night Caller from Outer Space
Plan 9 from Outer Space
Predator
Progeny
Sci-Fighters
Space Jam
Specimen
Star Trek: First Contact
Stargate
Stephen King's The Tommyknockers
Terror of Mechagodzilla
They Live
The Thing
Village of the Damned
Virus
The War of the Worlds
Wicked City
Within the Rock
The X-Files
Xtro 3: Watch the Skies
Zeram

Aliens Are People, Too

See also: Alien Beings—Benign; Alien Beings—Vicious

Alien
Aliens (SE)
Alien3
The Arrival
The Astronaut's Wife
Body Snatchers
The Hidden
Invaders from Mars
Invasion of the Body Snatchers
Mars Attacks!
My Favorite Martian
My Stepmother Is an Alien
Specimen
Starman
The Thing

American Indians

See: Native America

American South

See also: Southern Belles

Angel Heart
The Apostle
Bastard out of Carolina
The Beguiled
The Big Easy
Cat on a Hot Tin Roof
The Chamber
The Color Purple
Cookie's Fortune
Dancer, Texas—Pop. 81
Down in the Delta
Driving Miss Daisy
Eve's Bayou
Fled
Fried Green Tomatoes
The General's Daughter
The Gingerbread Man
Gone with the Wind
The Great Santini
The Green Mile
Hunter's Moon
Jezebel
John Grisham's The Rainmaker
Life
Midnight in the Garden of Good and Evil (SE)
Mississippi Burning
No Mercy
An Occasional Hell
Once Upon a Time . . . When We Were Colored
Passion Fish

Primary Colors
Rambling Rose
The Relic
Rosewood
Shadrach
Sling Blade
The Southerner
Sparrows
A Streetcar Named Desire
Tank
A Time to Kill
To Kill a Mockingbird
2000 Maniacs
Walking Tall
The War
The Waterboy
Wild Things

Amnesia

Armistead Maupin's More Tales of the City
Beyond the Door 2
Dead Again
The Great Dictator
Jackie Chan's Who Am I
The Killing Jar
The Long Kiss Goodnight
Overboard
Spellbound
Total Recall

Amusement Parks

See also: Carnivals, Circuses, Fairs & Expositions

Big
The Crying Game
Dr. Giggles
Mighty Joe Young
National Lampoon's Vacation
1941
Rollercoaster
Strangers on a Train
The Third Man

Angels

See also: Heaven Sent

Always
Angel in Training
The Bishop's Wife
City of Angels
Fallen
Heart and Souls
Heaven Can Wait
It's a Wonderful Life
A Life Less Ordinary
Michael
One Magic Christmas
The Prophecy
The Prophecy 2: Ashtown
The Prophecy 3: The Ascent
Soultaker
Unlikely Angel

Animals

See: Bears; Birds; Cats; Horses; Killer Apes & Monkeys; Killer Kats; King of Beasts (Dogs); Monkeyshines; Nice Mice; Pigs; Rabbits; Talking Animals; Wild Kingdom

Animated Musicals

See also: Animation & Cartoons; Musicals

American Pop
Anastasia
Art and Jazz in Animation
The Elm-Chanted Forest
Hercules
The Jungle Book
The King and I
Lady and the Tramp
The Little Mermaid
The Magic Voyage
Mulan
The Nightmare before Christmas
The Pebble and the Penguin
Pink Floyd: The Wall
Pinocchio
Prince of Egypt
Quest for Camelot

Rock-a-Doodle
A Tale of Two Kitties
Thumbelina
The Tune
Yellow Submarine

Animation & Cartoons

See also: Animated Musicals; Anime; Cartoon Adaptations; Live Action/Animated Combos

Aeon Flux
All Dogs Christmas Carol
Anastasia
Animaland
Animation Greats
Animation Legend: Winsor McCay
Antz
Bartok the Magnificent
Beauty and the Beast: The Enchanted Christmas
Beavis and Butt-Head Do America
The Best of Zagreb Film
The Brave Frog
A Bug's Life (CE)
Cartoon Crazys
Cartoon Crazys 2
Cartoon Crazys: And the Envelope, Please
Cartoon Crazys Christmas
Cartoon Crazys Goes to War
Cartoon Crazys: Kids All-Time Favorites
Cartoon Crazys Sci-Fi
Cat City
The Complete Uncensored Private Snafu
Darkside Blues
Dominion Tank Police
8 Man After: The Perfect Collection
An Extremely Goofy Movie
Fantastic Planet
Fist of the North Star
Ghost in the Shell
Gulliver's Travels
Heavy Metal
Hercules
The Hubley Collection: Everybody Rides the Carousel
The Hubley Collection, Vol. 1
The Hubley Collection, Vol. 2
Iron Giant
The Land Before Time
Masters of Russian Animation, Vol. 1
MD Geist (DC)
Mickey's Once upon a Christmas
The Nightmare before Christmas
101 Dalmatians
Peter Pan
Presenting Felix the Cat: The Otto Mesmer Classics 1919-24
The Princess and the Pirate
Project A-ko
Rudolph the Red-Nosed Reindeer: The Movie
The Rugrats Movie
Santo Bugito 1
The Secret Adventures of Tom Thumb
The Secret of Anastasia
70 Years of Popeye
The Superman Cartoons of Max & Dave Fleischer
Superman, the Lost Episodes
A Tale of Two Kitties
Tarzan
Tenchi the Movie: Tenchi Myuo in Love
Three Musketeers
Time Masters
Todd McFarlane's Spawn
Todd McFarlane's Spawn 2
Tom Sawyer
Tommy and the Computoys
Treasure Island

The Venus Wars
Voltage Fighters! Gowcaizer: The Movie
Wallace & Gromit: The First Three Adventures
The World's Greatest Animation

Anime

See also: Animation & Cartoons

Armitage 3: Polymatrix
Big Wars
Crimson Wolf
Darkside Blues
Demon City Shinjuku
Dominion Tank Police
Lupin III: The Mystery of Mamo
Megazone 23 Part 1
Ninja Scroll
Project A-ko
Record of Lodoss War
Roujin Z
Tenchi the Movie: Tenchi Myuo in Love
Urotsukidoji: Perfect Collection
Urusei Yatsura Movie 2: Beautiful Dreamer
The Venus Wars
Voltage Fighters! Gowcaizer: The Movie
A Wind Named Amnesia

Anthology

See also: Comedy Anthologies; Horror Anthologies

Art and Jazz in Animation
Boys Life
Boys Life 2
The Decameron
Four Rooms
Nightmares
Picture Windows
Pulp Fiction
Short 1: Invention
Short 2: Dreams
Twisted
With Friends Like These
The World's Greatest Animation

Anti-Heroes

See also: Rebel with a Cause

Belly
Billy Jack
Blade
Bonnie & Clyde
Butch Cassidy and the Sundance Kid
Casino
A Civil Action
Dirty Harry
Easy Rider
Hero
Last Man Standing
Lock, Stock and 2 Smoking Barrels
Playing God
Rebel without a Cause
Robin Hood: Prince of Thieves
Set It Off
Ten Benny
Thelma & Louise
Things to Do in Denver When You're Dead
12 Monkeys
U-Turn

Anti-War War Movies

See also: Satire & Parody

All Quiet on the Western Front
Apocalypse Now
Born on the Fourth of July
Dr. Strangelove, or: How I Learned to Stop Worrying and Love the Bomb
Gallipoli

Swimming with Sharks
To Die For
Trainspotting
Very Bad Things
The Witches of Eastwick

Black Gold
The Abyss (SE)
Hellfighters
On Deadly Ground

Blackmail
See also: Corporate Shenanigans; Crime & Criminals; Disorganized Crime; Organized Crime
The Big Brass Ring
Devil in the Flesh
Feeling Minnesota
The First Wives Club
Goodbye, Lover
An Ideal Husband
Keys to Tulsa
Opposite of Sex
A Perfect Murder
The Player
Twilight
Undercurrent
Zero Effect

Blindness
See also: Physical Problems
At First Sight
City Lights
Crimes & Misdemeanors
Good Luck
The Killer
Mask
Mr. Magoo
Return of the Blind Dead
Scent of a Woman
The Seventh Sense
Sneakers
The Toxic Avenger (DC)
Young Frankenstein

Bloody Messages
Die Hard
Seven
The Shining
Stephen King's The Night Flier

Boating
See: Sail Away

Bodily Functions
See: Flatulence; Hurling

Bodyguards
Absolute Power
Blackjack
The Bodyguard
Get Shorty
Guarding Tess
Half a Loaf of Kung Fu
In the Line of Fire

Books & Bookstores
See also: Libraries & Librarians; Writers
Better Than Chocolate
Fahrenheit 451
In the Mouth of Madness
The Love Letter
Notting Hill
You've Got Mail

Boom!
See also: Action-Adventure; Firemen & Fires
Airport
Arlington Road
Armageddon
Atomic Train
Black Dog
Blown Away
Broken Arrow
Casino
Clear and Present Danger
Con Air
Cutthroat Island

Dante's Peak
Daylight
Die Hard
Die Hard 2: Die Harder
Die Hard: With a Vengeance
Dr. Strangelove, or: How I Learned to Stop Worrying and Love the Bomb
Earthquake
Enemy of the State
The English Patient
Eraser
Face/Off
Fight Club
Fire Down Below
Firestorm
From Dusk Till Dawn
The Fugitive
Goldeneye
Grosse Pointe Blank
Independence Day
Lethal Weapon 3
Lethal Weapon 4
The Peacemaker
The Rock
Sabotage
Serial Bomber
The Siege
Simon Sez
The Specialist
Speed
Sweepers
The Terminator
Total Recall
True Lies
The Usual Suspects
The X-Files

Bounty Hunters
American Streetfighter 2: The Full Impact
Cold Harvest
A Fistful of Dollars
For a Few Dollars More
The Good, the Bad and the Ugly
Midnight Run
Most Wanted
Moving Target

Bowling
The Big Lebowski
Kingpin
Mr. Wonderful
Uncle Buck

Boxing
Battling Butler
Belle of the Nineties
The Boxer
Far and Away
Fight Club
Hard Times
Killer's Kiss
Like It Is
On the Ropes
Penitentiary
Penitentiary 2
The Power of One
Pulp Fiction
The Quest
The Quiet Man
Raging Bull
The Ring
Rocky
Rocky 2
Rocky 4
Rude
Snake Eyes

Brazilian (Production)
Black Orpheus
Central Station

Bridges
Bataan
The Bridge of San Luis Rey
The Bridges of Madison County
For Whom the Bell Tolls
George of the Jungle
The Ghost and the Darkness
Saving Private Ryan

Bringing Up Baby
See also: Parenthood; Pregnant Men; Pregnant Pauses
Baby Geniuses
Look Who's Talking
Penny Serenade
The Rugrats Movie
The Terminator
A Woman Is a Woman

British (Production)
The Adventures of Baron Munchausen
Alien
Alive and Kicking
An American Werewolf in London
And Now for Something Completely Different
Animaland
Anna Karenina
Another Man's Poison
Aria
As You Like It
The Asphyx
Bean
The Best of British Cinema: Five Decades of Classic British Films
Blue Juice
The Borrowers
Boston Kickout
The Boxer
Brassed Off
Brazil
Brazil (Criterion SE)
A Bridge Too Far
The Cassandra Crossing
Chaplin
Chariots of Fire
Chitty Chitty Bang Bang
A Christmas Carol
A Clockwork Orange
Corridors of Blood
Cross of Iron
Damage
Dancing at Lughnasa
The Designated Mourner
Dr. No (SE)
Dr. Strangelove, or: How I Learned to Stop Worrying and Love the Bomb
Dracula, Prince of Darkness
The Draughtsman's Contract
Earth Girls Are Easy
Elizabeth
The Englishman Who Went up a Hill But Came down a Mountain
Fahrenheit 451
Farewell, My Lovely
The Farmer's Wife
Felicia's Journey
The Field
Fire Over England
For Your Eyes Only (SE)
Four Weddings and a Funeral
From Russia with Love
The Full Monty
The General
The Ghost Goes Gear
The Girl on a Motorcycle
Goldfinger
Great Expectations
The Great Train Robbery
A Hard Day's Night
The Haunted Strangler
Hellbound: Hellraiser 2
Hellraiser
Help!
Henry V
Hideous Kinky
Hilary and Jackie
Horror Express
Horror Hospital
Horror Planet
The Hound of the Baskervilles
House of Whipcord
Howard's End
I Love You, I Love You Not

An Ideal Husband
The Impossible Spy
In the Name of the Father
The Ipcress File
It Happened Here
Jamaica Inn
Jan Svankmajer's Faust
Jason and the Argonauts
Journey to the Far Side of the Sun
A Kid in New York / A Woman in Paris
Kiss of the Vampire
The Lady Vanishes
The Lair of the White Worm
Lawn Dogs
The Leading Man
The Legend of the 7 Golden Vampires
License to Kill
Like It Is
Lion of the Desert
Little Voice
Live and Let Die
Lock, Stock and 2 Smoking Barrels
The Lodger
Lolita
The Long Good Friday
Love and Death on Long Island
Magical Mystery Tour
The Man Who Fell to Earth
The Man Who Knew Too Much
The Manxman
Marat/Sade
Mark of the Devil
Meantime
Mesmer
Mesmerized
The Message
Metroland
The Millionairess
Mrs. Brown
Mrs. Dalloway
Moll Flanders
Monty Python's Life of Brian
Monty Python's The Meaning of Life
Moonraker (SE)
Much Ado about Nothing
Murder
My Life So Far
My Son the Fanatic
Night Caller from Outer Space
No. 17
Odd Man Out
The Odessa File
Oliver!
Oliver Twist
On Approval
Orlando
Peeping Tom
The Phantom of the Opera
The Pillow Book
Pink Floyd: The Wall
The Pink Panther
The Pink Panther Strikes Again
Plague of the Zombies
Portrait of a Lady
Prehistoric Women
Pride and Prejudice
Priest
Quatermass and the Pit
Rasputin the Mad Monk
Razor Blade Smile
The Red Shoes
The Reptile
Rich and Strange
The Ring
Rogue Trader
Romeo and Juliet
The Satanic Rites of Dracula
Saturn 3
The Scarlet Pimpernel
Sea Wolves
The Secret Adventures of Tom Thumb

The Secret Agent
Sense and Sensibility
Shadowlands
Shallow Grave
Shameless
Shooting Fish
Sid & Nancy
Sirens
Sister My Sister
Skin Game
The Slipper and the Rose
Smashing Time
Spice World: The Movie
The Spy Who Loved Me (SE)
Straw Dogs
Suite 16
Swept from the Sea
Tea with Mussolini
The Third Man
The 39 Steps
This Sporting Life
Thunderball
Tiger Bay
Time Bandits
Tom Jones
Tower of Evil
Trainspotting
Treasure Island
Trial & Error
Twice upon a Yesterday
2001: A Space Odyssey
Velvet Goldmine
The Vengeance of She
The Very Thought of You
The Viking Queen
Waltz of the Toreadors
The Wings of the Dove
Yellow Submarine
Young and Innocent
A Zed & Two Noughts
Ziggy Stardust and the Spiders from Mars

Brothers & Sisters
American History X
American Streetfighter
Backdraft
Basket Case
Better Than Chocolate
Big Night
The Bodyguard
A Brother's Kiss
Carolina Skeletons
Cat People
Cookie's Fortune
Dancing at Lughnasa
Dangerous Ground
Dark Odyssey
Double Dragon
Duel in the Sun
EDtv
The Fabulous Baker Boys
Feeling Minnesota
The Fighting Sullivans
Final Analysis
Frank and Jesse
From Dusk Till Dawn
The Game
Georgia
Goodbye, Lover
Halloween: H20
Heart of Dragon
Hilary and Jackie
The Hoodlum
Howard's End
Jack Be Nimble
La Bamba
Labyrinth
Legends of the Fall
Limbo
Ma Saison Preferee
Meantime
Mr. Saturday Night
Mouse Hunt
The Newton Boys
A Night at the Roxbury
Opposite of Sex
Orphans of the Storm
Over the Wire
Practical Magic
The Quiet Man
Rain Man

Divine Madness
Richard Pryor: Live in Concert
Richard Pryor: Live on the
  Sunset Strip
Woodstock (DC)

Contemporary Noir

See also: Film Noir
After Dark, My Sweet
Albino Alligator
Angel Heart
Best Laid Plans
The Big Easy
Blade Runner (DC)
Body Double
Body Heat
Chinatown
Dark City
Devil in a Blue Dress
Goodbye, Lover
The Grifters
The Hot Spot
L.A. Confidential
The Limey
The Manchurian Candidate
9 1/2 Weeks
Palmetto
Payback
Pulp Fiction
Reservoir Dogs
sex, lies and videotape
Silence of the Lambs
The Spanish Prisoner
Taxi Driver (CE)
Tequila Sunrise
Things to Do in Denver When
  You're Dead
Twilight
The Two Jakes
U-Turn
The Underneath
Union City
The Usual Suspects
Wild Things

Cops

*See also: Buddy Cops; Detectives; Loner Cops; Women
Cops*
Abraxas: Guardian of the Universe
Action Jackson
Affliction
American Rampage
Animal Instincts
Assault on Precinct 13
Bad Boys
Bad Lieutenant
Beast Cops
Big Combo
The Big Easy
Black Mask
Black Rain
Blown Away
The Blues Brothers 2000
The Bone Collector
Bulletproof
Carmen, Baby
City Hall
Clockers
Cobra
Cop and a Half
Cop Land
Copycat
The Corruptor
The Crow
Dark City
Dead Bang
Dead End
Deep Cover
Demolition Man
The Designated Mourner
Devil in a Blue Dress
The Devil's Own
Die Hard
Die Hard 2: Die Harder
Die Hard: With a Vengeance
Dirty Harry
Diva
Dragnet
Drop Zone

Extreme Justice
Fair Game
Fallen
Family of Cops
Fargo
Feeling Minnesota
The First Deadly Sin
Flashfire
From Dusk Till Dawn 2: Texas
  Blood Money
The Gauntlet
The Glimmer Man
Go
Goodbye, Lover
Hard-Boiled
Hard Rain
Hard Vice
The Hard Way
He Walked by Night
Heart of Dragon
Heat
The Hidden
High & Low
In the Line of Duty 3
In the Line of Duty 4
In the Line of Duty 5
In Too Deep
Innocent Blood
Inspector Wears Skirts
Internal Affairs
Jet Li's The Enforcer
Judge Dredd
Jungleground
Just Cause
K-9
Killer Condom
L.A. Confidential
Laser Moon
Les Miserables
Lethal Weapon
Lethal Weapon 2
Lethal Weapon 3
Lethal Weapon 4
Mad Dog and Glory
Mad Max
Madigan
A Man in Uniform
Maniac Cop
Metro
The Mod Squad
Money Train
Murder at 1600
My Lucky Stars
The Naked City
National Lampoon's Loaded
  Weapon 1
The Negotiator
New Jack City
New Jersey Drive
New York Ripper
Next of Kin
Night Falls on Manhattan
Organized Crime & Triad
  Bureau
Phoenix
Police Academy
Practical Magic
The Prophecy
Protector
Q & A
Rent-A-Cop
The Replacement Killers
Resurrection
Ricochet
Rising Sun
RoboCop
Route 9
Rush Hour
Santa Fe
Scarred City
Sci-Fighters
Sgt. Kabukiman N.Y.P.D.
Seven
Shakedown
Shameless
Sharky's Machine
Snake Eyes
Speed
Speed 2: Cruise Control
Steele's Law
Stonewall

Strange Days
Stranger by Night
Striking Distance
Strip Search
Supercop
Supercop 2
The Thomas Crown Affair
Timecop
Top Dog
Total Recall 2070: Machine
  Dreams
True Romance
Truth or Consequences, N.M.
Undercover
The Untold Story
The Usual Suspects
Virtuosity
Whatever It Takes
Witness

Corporate Shenanigans

See also: Advertising
The Alarmist
The Associate
Baby Geniuses
BASEketball
The Bikini Car Wash Company
Boys Will Be Boys
Chairman of the Board
The China Syndrome
A Civil Action
The Devil's Advocate
Disclosure
Dr. Dolittle
Dodsworth
Fierce Creatures
Fire Down Below
The Flintstones (CE)
FM
Goodfellas
Hackers
Halloween 3: Season of the
  Witch
His Girl Friday
The Hudsucker Proxy
I Love Trouble
In the Company of Men
The Insider
John Grisham's The Rainmaker
Johnny Mnemonic
Meet Joe Black
Network
New Rose Hotel
Nowhere to Run
Office Space
Outland
The Pajama Game
The Paper
The Player
Private Parts
Rising Sun
RoboCop
RoboCop 2
RoboCop 3
Rogue Trader
Scrooged
The Secret of My Success
The Shawshank Redemption
The Spanish Prisoner
Swimming with Sharks
A Taxing Woman
Tommy Boy
Weekend at Bernie's
Wolf
You've Got Mail

Courtroom Drama

See: Order in the Court

Creepy Houses

An American Werewolf in
  Paris
The Bat Whispers
Beyond the Door 2
Castle Freak
The Craft
The Ghost Goes Gear
Girls School Screamers
Great Expectations
The Haunting
House on Haunted Hill

Malice
Mouse Hunt
Munster, Go Home!
The Old Dark House
Psycho (CE)
Psycho
Psycho 2
Psycho 3
Salem's Lot
The Shining
Warlock 3: The End of Innocence
Witchouse

Crime & Criminals

*See: Crime Drama; Crime
Sprees; Crimes of Passion;
Disorganized Crime; Fugitives;
Organized Crime; Serial
Killers; Urban Drama; Vigilantes*

Crime Drama

See also: Drama
Albino Alligator
Another Day in Paradise
Another Man's Poison
Assault on Precinct 13
Bad Boys
Bad Lieutenant
Beast Cops
Belly
Best Laid Plans
Black Rain
Blood, Guts, Bullets and
  Octane
Boiling Point
A Bronx Tale
Bugsy
Capone
Casino
Cop Land
Dead Presidents
Donnie Brasco
Entrapment
Fallen Angels
The General
Gloria
Goodfellas
Heat
High & Low
The Hoodlum
In Too Deep
Incognito
Internal Affairs
Kalifornia
Kiss the Girls
The Last Don
Last Man Standing
The Limey
The Long Good Friday
Love to Kill
M
Mean Streets
Menace II Society
Money Kings
Monument Ave.
New Jack City
Night Falls on Manhattan
Night of the Hunted
Out of Sight
Palmetto
Payback
Phoenix
Playing God
Pulp Fiction
Q & A
Rabid Dogs
Reservoir Dogs
Scarface
Seven
Showdown
A Simple Plan
Six Ways to Sunday
Sworn Enemies
Things to Do in Denver When
  You're Dead
Tom Clancy's Netforce
True Friends
The Underneath

Crime Sprees

*See also: Fugitives; Lovers on
the Lam*
Bonnie & Clyde
Heat
Love and a .45
Set It Off
Sworn Enemies
Virtuosity

Crimes of Passion

The Gingerbread Man
Jade
The Mask of Diijon
Single White Female
To Die For

Crop Dusters

The Bridges of Madison
  County
Days of Heaven
Doc Hollywood
The Field
Horton Foote's Alone
Nowhere to Run
Our Daily Bread and Other
  Films of the Depression
The River
Rock-a-Doodle
Sarah, Plain and Tall: Winter's
  End
Skylark
Sommersby
Son-in-Law
The Southerner
This Is My Father
A Thousand Acres

Cuban (Production)

I Am Cuba

Cults

See also: Occult; Satanism
Beware! Children at Play
Lord of Illusions
Ticket to Heaven

Culture Clash

Babe: Pig in the City
Black Robe
Cabaret
Deliverance
Down in the Delta
Encino Man
For Richer or Poorer
George of the Jungle
Gorillas in the Mist
Holy Man
Mister Johnson
Rush Hour
Splash
Starman
Swept from the Sea
Thunderheart
Witness

Cuttin' Heads

Born to Win
The Crying Game
Earth Girls Are Easy
Mississippi Burning
Poetic Justice
Stigmata

Cyberpunk

Blade Runner (DC)
The Crow 2: City of Angels
Cyborg
Demolition Man
Escape from L.A.
The Fifth Element
Hackers
Johnny Mnemonic
The Lawnmower Man
Mad Max
Mad Max: Beyond Thunderdome
Nemesis
The Road Warrior
RoboCop
RoboCop 2
RoboCop 3
The Terminator

Terminator 2: Judgment Day
Tetsuo: The Iron Man
Tetsuo 2: Body Hammer
Total Recall
Tron
Universal Soldier
Universal Soldier: The Return
Virtual Combat
Virtuosity

Czech (Production)
Jan Svankmajer's Faust
Mandragora
Werther

Dads

See also: Bad Dads; Moms;
Monster Moms; Parenthood
The Adventures of Pinocchio
Armageddon
Big Daddy
Billy Madison
The Birdcage
A Bronx Tale
Carousel
The Climb
Come and Get It
Desert Blue
Django Strikes Again
Father's Day
Fear
High & Low
In the Name of the Father
Jack Frost
Jet Li's The Enforcer
Jingle All the Way
Just Write
Liar Liar
Life Is Beautiful
Life with Father
The Limey
A Little Princess
The Mask of Zorro
Mulan
My Son the Fanatic
My Stepmother Is an Alien
National Lampoon's Christ-
mas Vacation
National Lampoon's Vacation
Nick of Time
Night Falls on Manhattan
The Pillow Book
Ponette
A River Runs Through It
The Santa Clause
A Simple Wish
Sleepless in Seattle
Slums of Beverly Hills
So I Married an Axe Murderer
Tank
A Time to Kill

Dance Fever

See also: Disco Musicals
Alive and Kicking
An American in Paris
Black Orpheus
Black Tights
Boogie Nights
Dance with Me
Dirty Dancing
Dirty Dancing (CE)
Everyone Says I Love You
George Balanchine's The Nut-
cracker
The Last Days of Disco
Limelight
Looking for Lola
Michael
The Red Shoes
Risky Business
Scent of a Woman
Seven Brides for Seven
Brothers
Singin' in the Rain
They Shoot Horses, Don't
They?

Dates from Hell

See also: Singles
Bride of Chucky
Reality Bites

Singles

A Day in the Life . . .

See also: Up All Night
Before Sunrise
The Breakfast Club
Groundhog Day
Last Night
Mrs. Dalloway

Deadly Implants
Drive
Escape from L.A.
Star Trek: First Contact
Total Recall

Deafness

See also: Physical Problems
Cop Land
In the Company of Men
Khamoshi the Musical
The Last Game
Mr. Holland's Opus
A Summer to Remember

Death & the Afterlife

See also: Angels; Funerals;
Ghosts, Ghouls & Goblins;
Great Death Scenes; Heaven
Sent; Occult; Suicide
Alive and Kicking
All of Me
Always
Angel Heart
The Asphyx
Beetlejuice
Boys on the Side
Carousel
The Cat and the Canary
Chances Are
A Christmas Carol
City of Angels
The Crow
The Crow 2: City of Angels
Dark Victory
Death Becomes Her
D.O.A.
Don't Go in the House
The English Patient
Faces of Death
Fearless
Flatliners
The Funeral
Heart and Souls
Heaven Can Wait
High Plains Drifter
I'm Losing You
The Indestructible Man / The
Amazing Transparent Man
Infinity
It's a Wonderful Life
Jacob's Ladder
Judge & Jury
The Lady in White
Marvin's Room
Meet Joe Black
Monty Python's The Meaning
of Life
Night Shift
Phantasm
Poltergeist
Ponette
The Prophecy
Scrooged
The Seventh Seal
The Sixth Sense
Sometimes They Come Back
Soultaker
Spawn (SE)
Stand by Me
Things to Do in Denver When
You're Dead
Weekend at Bernie's
What Dreams May Come
A Zed & Two Noughts

Death Row

See also: Men in Prison;
Women in Prison
The Chamber
The Green Mile
Killer: A Journal of Murder

Mommy 2: Mommy's Day
Mumia: A Case for Reason-
able Doubt?
The Seventh Sign

Dedicated Teachers

See also: Hell High School;
School Daze
Born Yesterday
Dangerous Minds
Dead Poets Society
Eden
Election
Kindergarten Cop
Lean on Me
Matilda
Mr. Holland's Opus
October Sky
Powder
Stand and Deliver
The Substitute

Deep Blue

See also: Go Fish; Sail Away;
Shipwrecked; Submarines
The Abyss (SE)
Crimson Tide
Deep Blue Sea
Free Willy
Moby Dick
Splash
The Spy Who Loved Me (SE)
Waterworld

Demons & Wizards

See also: Occult
Army of Darkness
Bram Stoker's Shadowbuilder
Conan the Barbarian
Conan the Destroyer
Demons
Evil Dead
Evil Dead 2: Dead by Dawn
Excalibur
Hellraiser
The Heroic Trio
Jack-O
The King and I
Ladyhawke
Rawhead Rex
Stay Awake
Tales from the Crypt Presents
Demon Knight
Warlock
Warlock: The Armageddon
Zu: Warriors of the Magic
Mountain

Dental Mayhem

See also: Doctors & Nurses;
Evil Doctors
Brazil
Brazil (Criterion SE)
The Dentist
The Dentist 2: Brace Yourself
Diabolique
Little Shop of Horrors
Serial Mom
12 Monkeys

**Desert War/Foreign
Legion**

See also: Deserts; Persian
Gulf War
Abbott and Costello in the
Foreign Legion
The Flying Deuces / Utopia
Lionheart
Three Kings

Deserts

See also: Desert War/Foreign
Legion
The Adventures of Priscilla,
Queen of the Desert
American Strays
Beavis and Butt-Head Do
America
Broken Arrow
Desert Blue
Desert Heat

Dune
The English Patient
Legionnaire
Mad Max
Mad Max: Beyond Thunder-
dome
The Mummy
The Mummy
Operation Condor
Patriot Games
The Road to Morocco
The Road Warrior
Stargate
Tremors
Tremors 2: Aftershocks

Detective Spoofs

See also: Detectives; Pink
Panther
Ace Ventura: Pet Detective
Ace Ventura: When Nature
Calls
Cry Uncle
Dragnet
Inspector Gadget
The Pink Panther
The Pink Panther Strikes
Again
Revenge of the Pink Panther
A Shot in the Dark
Zero Effect

Detectives

See also: Cops; Detective
Spoofs; Feds; Sherlock
Holmes
Above the Law
Ace Ventura: Pet Detective
Ace Ventura: When Nature
Calls
Alphaville
Angel Heart
The Big Sleep
Bullitt
Chinatown
City of Fire
City War
Cookie's Fortune
Cry Uncle
Dead Again
The Deep End of the Ocean
Devil in a Blue Dress
Dragnet
Ed McBain's 87 Precinct
Falling Down
Farewell, My Lovely
Fletch
Girl Hunters
Heat
The Hound of the
Baskervilles
Insomnia
K-9
Kiss the Girls
The Long Kiss Goodnight
Lord of Illusions
Manhattan Murder Mystery
Moonlighting
No. 17
The Pink Panther
The Pink Panther Strikes
Again
Revenge of the Pink Panther
Sea of Love
Seven
The Seven-Per-Cent Solution
Sherlock Holmes Consulting
Detective, Vol. 1
A Shot in the Dark
Someone to Watch Over Me
Stolen Kisses
Tales from the Crypt Presents
Bordello of Blood
There's Something about
Mary
They Might Be Giants
To Catch a Killer
Top Dog
Twilight
The Two Jakes
Two Undercover Angels

Vertigo (CE)
Who Framed Roger Rabbit
Wild Things
Witchcraft 10: Mistress of
the Craft
Witness
Zero Effect

Detroit

See also: Checkered Flag;
Motor Vehicle Dept.
Bird on a Wire
Detroit Rock City
Gridlock'd
Grosse Pointe Blank
The Last Word
Presumed Innocent
Private Parts
Ringmaster
RoboCop
RoboCop 2
RoboCop 3
True Romance

Devils
The Craft
The Devil's Advocate
End of Days
Jan Svankmajer's Faust
Needful Things
The Prophecy
Stephen King's The Stand
Tales from the Hood
The Witches of Eastwick

Dinosaurs
Barney's Great Adventure
The Land Before Time
The Lost World
Mass Extinctions
My Science Project
A Nymphoid Barbarian in
Dinosaur Hell
Two Lost Worlds
Unknown Island

Disaster Flicks

See also: Action-Adventure;
Air Disasters; Meltdown; Sea
Disasters
Airport
Airport '75
Armageddon
Asteroid
Atomic Train
The Cassandra Crossing
The China Syndrome
Dante's Peak
Daylight
Deep Impact
Earthquake
Firestorm
Hard Rain
The Hindenburg
The Hurricane
Independence Day
A Night to Remember
The Poseidon Adventure
Titanic
The Towering Inferno
Twister
Two Minute Warning
Volcano
White Squall

Disco Musicals

See also: Musicals
Car Wash
The Wiz
Xanadu

Disease of the Week

See also: AIDS; Emerging
Viruses
Black Death
The Boy in the Plastic Bubble
The Cassandra Crossing
Chinese Box
Cold Harvest
Down in the Delta
The First Deadly Sin
Hilary and Jackie

John Grisham's The Rainmaker
Last Breath
Marvin's Room
One True Thing
Philadelphia
The Pride of the Yankees
Shadowlands
Simon Birch
Stepmom

Disorganized Crime

See also: Crime & Criminals; Organized Crime
Albino Alligator
Bottle Rocket
Buffalo 66
Cop and a Half
Fargo
Get Shorty
Glitch!
Gridlock'd
Her Alibi
Home Alone
Home Alone 2: Lost in New York
Keys to Tulsa
Lock, Stock and 2 Smoking Barrels
Mad Dog and Glory
101 Dalmatians
Reservoir Dogs
Suicide Kings
Things to Do in Denver When You're Dead
Truth or Consequences, N.M.

Divorce

See also: Marriage; Singles
Celebrity
Falling Down
The First Wives Club
For Richer or Poorer
Hope Floats
Liar Liar
Living Out Loud
Mrs. Doubtfire
Mr. Wonderful
Now and Then
The Parent Trap
Peggy Sue Got Married
Stepmom
That Old Feeling
Twister

Doctors & Nurses

See also: AIDS; Dental Mayhem; Disease of the Week; Emerging Viruses; Evil Doctors; Sanity Check; Shrinks
Armistead Maupin's More Tales of the City
The Asphyx
At First Sight
Awakenings
Blade
City of Angels
Coma
Corridors of Blood
Crimes & Misdemeanors
Critical Care
Dark City
Dead Ringers
Death Becomes Her
Doc Hollywood
Dr. Dolittle
Don't Look in the Basement
The English Patient
Eyes Wide Shut
Flatliners
The Fugitive
Halloween 2: The Nightmare Isn't Over!
Horror Hospital
In Dreams
In Love and War
Junior
La Sentinelle
Malice
Marvin's Room
Mesmer

The Millionairess
Monty Python's The Meaning of Life
One Flew Over the Cuckoo's Nest
Outbreak
Patch Adams (CE)
The Patriot
Playing God
Restoration
The Surgeon
The Unbearable Lightness of Being
What Dreams May Come
Women of Valor

Docudrama

See also: Documentary
Conspiracy: The Trial of the Chicago Eight
Glen or Glenda?
Henry: Portrait of a Serial Killer
It Happened Here
Kids
The Naked City
Panther
Take the Money and Run
Ten Days That Shook the World
This Is Spinal Tap

Documentary

See also: Docudrama
American Movie
Ayn Rand: A Sense of Life
Battlecade: Extreme Fighting
Battlecade: Extreme Fighting 2
The Best of British Cinema: Five Decades of Classic British Films
Brother, Can You Spare a Dime?
Buena Vista Social Club
The Challenge of Flight: Disc One
Chronos
Crumb
Dario Argento's World of Horror
Dark Shadows (SE)
Dragons of the Orient
The Endless Summer
Faces of Death
Fetishes
Gray's Anatomy
A Great Day in Harlem / The Spitball Story
Gustav Mahler: To Live, I Will Die
Hawaiian Rainbow
Hollywood Christmas
In Search of Dracula
Indomitable Teddy Roosevelt
Jackie Chan: My Story
Jackie Chan: My Stunts
James Dean Story
Kuma Hula: Keepers of the Culture
Leonard Bernstein: Reaching for the Note
The Love Goddesses
The Man with the Movie Camera
Marcello Mastroianni: I Remember
Mass Extinctions
Mumia: A Case for Reasonable Doubt?
Nico Icon
90 Degrees South: With Scott to the Antarctic
On the Ropes
Pretty As a Picture: The Art of David Lynch
Rock 'n' Roll Invaders: The AM Radio DJs
Rodgers and Hammerstein: The Sound of Movies
The Sci-Fi Files

Sex Is . . .
Super Speedway
Trinity and Beyond: The Atomic Bomb Movie
Truth or Dare
UFOs Above and Beyond
The Unknown Marx Brothers
Visions of Light: The Art of Cinematography
The War Room
With Byrd at the South Pole: The Story of Little America
The Wonderful, Horrible Life of Leni Riefenstahl
Ziggy Stardust and the Spiders from Mars

Dogs

See: King of Beasts (Dogs)

Dolls That Kill

See: Killer Toys

Dracula

The Creeps
Dracula
Dracula
Dracula
Dracula, Prince of Darkness
The Legend of the 7 Golden Vampires
The Satanic Rites of Dracula

Dragons

See also: Medieval Romps
Dragonheart (SE)
Jason and the Argonauts
Mulan
Quest for Camelot
The Seventh Voyage of Sinbad

Drama

See: Adventure Drama; Comedy Drama; Crime Drama; Docudrama; Historical Drama; Musical Drama; Romantic Drama; Showbiz Drama; Sports Dramas; Tearjerkers; Tragedy

Drugs

See: Pill Poppin'

Dutch (Production)

Antonia's Line
The Johnsons
The Pillow Book
To Play or To Die
The Vanishing

Ears!

See also: Eyeballs!; Hearts!; Renegade Body Parts
Django
Feeling Minnesota
High Plains Drifter
Reservoir Dogs

Eat Me

When characters end up as food. See also: Cannibalism
Deep Blue Sea
Deep Rising
Event Horizon
Lake Placid
Little Shop of Horrors
Mimic
Ravenous
The Relic
Starship Troopers

Eco-Vengeance!

See also: Killer Bugs & Slugs
Anaconda
Arachnophobia
Body Snatchers
Day of the Animals
Grizzly
Habitat
Jaws: The Revenge
On Deadly Ground

Piranha
The Toxic Avenger (DC)

Edibles

See also: Cannibalism; Eat Me
The Big Hit
Big Night
Eat Your Heart Out
Felicia's Journey
God of Cookery
Goodfellas
Home Fries
Like Water for Chocolate
Men
Monty Python's The Meaning of Life
9 1/2 Weeks
Simply Irresistible
Soul Food
Tampopo
Tom Jones
The Untold Story
Willy Wonka & the Chocolate Factory

The Eighties

See: Period Piece: 1980s

Elevators

See also: Terror in Tall Buildings
Basic Instinct
The Client
Die Hard
In the Line of Fire
The Man with Two Brains
Nick of Time
Pretty Woman
The Secret of My Success
Silence of the Lambs
Sleepless in Seattle
Speed
Terminator 2: Judgment Day
The Towering Inferno
True Lies

Elvisfilm

Finding Graceland
Honeymoon in Vegas
Jailhouse Rock
Rock-a-Doodle
True Romance

Emerging Viruses

See also: Disease of the Week
The Andromeda Strain
Body Armor
Escape from L.A.
Mimic
Outbreak
The Patriot
Sci-Fighters
Stephen King's The Stand
12 Monkeys

The Empire State Building

King Kong
Love Affair
The Shadow
Sleepless in Seattle

Erotic Thrillers

See also: Sex & Sexuality
Allyson Is Watching
Animal Instincts 3: The Seductress
Basic Instinct
Body of Influence 2
Body Shot
Body Strokes
Color of Night
Dark Secrets
Die Watching
Disclosure
Embrace of the Vampire
Embrace the Darkness
Extramarital
Hard Drive
I Like to Play Games

Lipstick Camera
Midnight Confessions
Motel Blue
Night Fire
Notorious
Object of Obsession
Over the Wire
Poison Ivy 2: Lily
Poison Ivy 3: The New Seduction
Private Obsession
Scorned 2
Secret Games
Secret Games 3
Sexual Malice
Sexual Roulette
Suite 16
Terrified
Undercover
Virtual Desire

Escaped Cons

See also: Great Escapes; Men in Prison
Another Man's Poison
Black Cat Run
Con Air
Cool Hand Luke
Double Jeopardy
Escape from Alcatraz
Face/Off
Firestorm
Fled
From Dusk Till Dawn
The Fugitive
Great Expectations
Great Expectations
Happy, Texas
The Mighty
Out of Sight
Papillon
Point Blank
Prison on Fire 2
Rites of Passage
Runaway Train
Spoiler
Wrongfully Accused
Zigzag

Evil Doctors

See also: Doctors & Nurses; Mad Scientists
Baby Geniuses
Curse of the Puppet Master: The Human Experiment
Dead Ringers
The Dentist
Dr. Giggles
Dr. Jekyll and Mr. Hyde
Dr. No (SE)
Malice

Executing Revenge

Bad guys who come back for revenge after having been executed. See also: Death & the Afterlife; Death Row; Men in Prison; Revenge
Fallen
I Know What You Did Last Summer
The Indestructible Man / The Amazing Transparent Man
Judge & Jury
Shocker
Soldier

Exploitation

See also: Sexploitation
Def Jam's How to Be a Player
Faces of Death
Fascination
House of Whipcord
Reefer Madness
Ringmaster
The Shiver of the Vampires
Star 80
Suite 16
Two Undercover Angels

Explorers

Apollo 13

Congo
Forgotten City
The Magic Voyage
Mountains of the Moon
90 Degrees South: With
   Scott to the Antarctic
She
With Byrd at the South Pole:
   The Story of Little America

Eyeballs!

See also: Ears!; Hearts!;
*   Renegade Body Parts*
The Birds
A Clockwork Orange
Demolition Man
Die Hard 2: Die Harder
Evil Dead 2: Dead by Dawn
Halloween 2: The Nightmare
   Isn't Over!
Peeping Tom
The Phantom
Rocky
The Terminator
True Lies
Zombie

Fairs & Expositions

See also: Amusement Parks;
*   Carnivals, Circuses, Fairs &*
*   Expositions*

Fairy Tale Adaptations

The Adventures of Pinocchio
Beauty and the Beast
The Brave Frog
Cinderella
Ever After: A Cinderella Story
George Balanchine's The Nut-
   cracker
Hans Christian Andersen
Into the Woods
Jack & the Beanstalk
The Little Mermaid
March of the Wooden Sol-
   diers
Peter Pan
Pinocchio
The Princess Bride
Puppet Films of Jiri Trnka
The Slipper and the Rose
Snow White: A Tale of Terror
Thumbelina
The Witches

Family Ties

See also: Bad Dads; Brothers
*   & Sisters; Dads; The In-Laws;*
*   Incest; Moms; Monster*
*   Moms; Parenthood; Single*
*   Parents; Stepparents; Twins*
Air Force One
All About Ah Long
An American Christmas Carol
American Pop
Bastard out of Carolina
Beethoven
Beethoven's 2nd
The Betsy
Beyond the Door 2
Blue Collar
The Boxer
Buffalo 66
Candleshoe
The Castle
Castle Freak
Cat on a Hot Tin Roof
The Chamber
Chances Are
A Christmas Story
Cousin Bette
Crooklyn
Crumb
Dead End
Deadfall
Deep Impact
The Devil's Own
The Eternal Kiss of the
   Mummy
Everyone Says I Love You
Eve's Bayou
Excess Baggage

Family of Cops
Family Reunion
Father of the Bride
Father's Little Dividend
The Flintstones (CE)
Flirting with Disaster
Forever and a Day
Friend of the Family
The Funeral
The Great Outdoors
Greedy
Guess Who's Coming to Din-
   ner
Habitat
The Hand that Rocks the Cra-
   dle
Happiness
Hard Target
Heat
Homeward Bound: The
   Incredible Journey
The Horse Whisperer
Horton Foote's Alone
The House of Yes
How the West Was Won
Hugo Pool
I Love You, I Love You Not
I'm Losing You
In Country
It's a Wonderful Life
The Jazz Singer
Keys to Tulsa
The Last Assassins
The Last Don
Lawn Dogs
Leave It to Beaver
Lethal Weapon
Lethal Weapon 4
The Lickerish Quartet
Like Water for Chocolate
Little Buddha
Little Women
The Long Kiss Goodnight
The Lost Boys
Lost in Space
Lotto Land
Mad Max
Made in America
Marvin's Room
Maverick
Miami Rhapsody
Midnight
Miracle on 34th Street
The Mirror Has Two Faces
Mrs. Doubtfire
Monsieur Verdoux
Moonstruck
Mother
Mother's Boys
Multiplicity
My Best Girl
My Life So Far
National Lampoon's Christ-
   mas Vacation
Next of Kin
Noah's Ark
The Nutty Professor
The Old Dark House
On Golden Pond
Once Upon a Time . . .
   When We Were Colored
Only You
The Other Sister
Out of the Blue
Overboard
Pecker
Peggy Sue Got Married
Philadelphia
Poison Ivy
Polish Wedding
Pride and Prejudice
Prizzi's Honor
Pushing Hands
Quiz Show
Raging Bull
Ran
Ransom
Regina
The River Wild
Romeo and Juliet
Running on Empty

The Saphead
Sarah, Plain and Tall: Winter's
   End
Scent of a Woman
Selena
Shameless
The Shanghai Gesture
Showdown
A Simple Plan
Sixteen Candles
The '60s
Skin Game
Skylark
Smoke Signals
Sometimes They Come Back
   ... Again
Son-in-Law
Sorceress
The Southerner
Southie
Spider Baby
State Fair
Stella Dallas
Stir of Echoes
Striking Distance
Stuart Little
The Sweet Hereafter
Tarantella
Tex
This Is My Father
Ticket to Heaven
T.N.T.
Tommy Boy
Tromeo & Juliet
The Turning
The Twilight of the Golds
Un Air de Famille
Uncle Buck
Vegas Vacation
Village of Dreams
The War
Welcome to the Dollhouse
While You Were Sleeping
William Shakespeare's
   Romeo and Juliet
The Wings of the Dove

Fantasy

See also: Animation & Car-
*   toons; Musical Fantasy*
The Adventures of Baron
   Munchausen
The Adventures of Pinocchio
Alice in Wonderland
Babe
Babe: Pig in the City
Barbarella
Batman
Batman and Robin
Batman Forever
Batman Returns
*batteries not included
Big
The Bishop's Wife
The Cat from Outer Space
The City of Lost Children
The Clan of the Cave Bear
Conan the Barbarian
Conan the Destroyer
The Crazy Ray
Crossworlds
The Crow
The Crow 2: City of Angels
The Dark Crystal
Deadful Melody
Dragonheart (SE)
Dreamscape
Excalibur
Eye of the Serpent
Fando and Lis
The Fantastic Night
Guinevere
Gulliver's Travels
Heaven Can Wait
Heavy Metal
Highlander 2: The Quickening
It's a Wonderful Life
Jack Frost
Jan Svankmajer's Faust
Jason and the Argonauts
Jumanji (CS)

Jungle Boy
A Kid in Aladdin's Palace
King Kong
Kull the Conqueror
L.A. Story
Labyrinth
Ladyhawke
Leprechaun 2
The Lickerish Quartet
Logan's Run
Meet Joe Black
Merlin
Michael
Mighty Joe Young
Mortal Kombat 1: The Movie
Mortal Kombat 2: Annihila-
   tion
My Science Project
My Stepmother Is an Alien
Night Tide
The Nightmare before Christ-
   mas
One Magic Christmas
Peter Pan
Peter Pan
Pleasantville
Powder
Quantum Leap: The Pilot
   Episode
Record of Lodoss War
Return to Oz
Salome's Last Dance
Saviour of the Soul
The Secret Adventures of
   Tom Thumb
The Seventh Voyage of Sin-
   bad
A Simple Wish
Simply Irresistible
Slave Girls from Beyond Infin-
   ity
Snow White: A Tale of Terror
Something Wicked This Way
   Comes
Splash
Teenage Mutant Ninja Tur-
   tles: The Movie
Tenchi the Movie: Tenchi
   Myuo in Love
Time Bandits
Train Ride to Hollywood
The Tune
Twisted
Unidentified Flying Oddball
Warriors of Virtue
What Dreams May Come
William Shakespeare's A Mid-
   summer Night's Dream
Zu: Warriors of the Magic
   Mountain

Farming

See: Crop Dusters

Feds

See also: Detectives; Spies &
*   Espionage*
Absolute Power
Analyze This
The Assignment
Beavis and Butt-Head Do
   America
Black Dog
Blood, Guts, Bullets and
   Octane
Boiling Point
Capone
Clay Pigeons
Clear and Present Danger
The Client
Conspiracy Theory
Donnie Brasco
Double Team
The Eiger Sanction
Eraser
Exterminator
Face/Off
The Glimmer Man
Grosse Pointe Blank
Guarding Tess
In the Line of Fire

The Jackal (CE)
Knock Off
The Long Kiss Goodnight
Mercury Rising
Mission: Impossible
Mississippi Burning
Most Wanted
Murder at 1600
Nixon
Panther
Patriot Games
The Peacemaker
Ransom
Raw Deal
The Rock
Rush Hour
Serial Bomber
Silence of the Lambs
The Spanish Prisoner
Switchback
T-Men
Thunderheart
The X-Files

Feminism

See: Women; Wonder Women

Femme Fatale

See also: Wonder Women
All About Eve
Austin Powers: International
   Man of Mystery
Austin Powers 2: The Spy
   Who Shagged Me
Basic Instinct
Batman and Robin
Beverly Hills Ninja
The Blood Spattered Bride
Body Heat
Bound
Cleopatra
Cruel Intentions
Dangerous Ground
Dangerous Liaisons
Disclosure
Double Indemnity
Dream Lover
Final Analysis
First Name: Carmen
The Gingerbread Man
Girl Hunters
The Grifters
Impact
Jezebel
Lady and the Tramp
The Lair of the White Worm
Malice
Ms. 45
Night Tide
An Occasional Hell
Opposite of Sex
Palmetto
Playing God
Point of No Return
Poison Ivy
Poison Ivy 2: Lily
The Quick and the Dead
The Rage: Carrie 2
Ran
Sea of Love
A Thin Line Between Love
   and Hate
Truth or Dare
U-Turn
Who Framed Roger Rabbit
Wicked Ways
Wrongfully Accused

Fencing

See also: Swashbucklers
Court Jester
Dangerous Beauty
Rob Roy

The Fifties

See: Period Piece: 1950s

Filipino (Production)

Terror Is a Man

Film History

AFI's 100 Years, 100 Movies

Invasion of the Body Snatchers
The Ipcress File
It Happened One Night
It's a Wonderful Life
Ju Dou
Juliet of the Spirits
The King and I
L.A. Confidential
Lady and the Tramp
The Lady Vanishes
The Last Detail
The Last Emperor
Lisa and the Devil / The House of Exorcism
The Little Mermaid
Little Women
Lola Montes
Lolita
Lost Continent
Lost Horizon
M
The Magnificent Seven
Male and Female
The Man Who Would Be King
The Man with the Movie Camera
The Manchurian Candidate
Mean Streets
Midnight Cowboy
Modern Times
The Music Man
My Life As a Dog
My Life to Live
My Man Godfrey
National Velvet
Nights of Cabiria
Nosferatu
Notorious
Our Daily Bread and Other Films of the Depression
Our Hospitality / Sherlock Junior
Pandora's Box
Paths of Glory
Patton
Peeping Tom
The Phantom of the Opera
The Philadelphia Story
Pinocchio
Plague of the Zombies
The Player
The Professionals
Psycho (CE)
Pulp Fiction
The Quiet Man
Raging Bull
Ran
Rebecca
Rebel without a Cause
Red River
The Red Shoes
Run Lola Run
Rushmore
The Searchers
Seven Beauties
Seven Samurai
The Seventh Seal
Shakespeare in Love (CS)
Shallow Grave
Shoot the Piano Player
Short 1: Invention
Short 2: Dreams
Singin' in the Rain
Something Wicked This Way Comes
The Southerner
Stagecoach
Storm over Asia
The Story of G.I. Joe
Strangers on a Train
A Streetcar Named Desire
Taxi Driver (CE)
The Terminator
They Might Be Giants
The Third Man
The 39 Steps
The 39 Steps (Criterion)
The Three Musketeers
Tin Drum
To Kill a Mockingbird

Tom Jones
The Train
The Truman Show
2001: A Space Odyssey (MGM)
Two Women
The Unknown Marx Brothers
Vampyr
Vertigo (CE)
Virasat
Visions of Light: The Art of Cinematography
Who's Afraid of Virginia Woolf?
The Wild Bunch
The Wizard of Oz
The Wolf Man
Woman of the Year
The World's Greatest Animation
Wuthering Heights
Young Frankenstein

Frame-Ups
City Hall
Death Sentence
Family of Cops
The Fugitive
The Glimmer Man
Legacy of Rage
Most Wanted
Motel Blue
Moving Target
Murder
My Fellow Americans
Palmetto
Presumed Innocent
Prison on Fire
Red Corner
Shelter
Stir Crazy
Tank
U.S. Marshals
Wild Things

Frankenstein
Andy Warhol's Frankenstein
The Bride of Frankenstein
The Creeps
Frankenstein
Mary Shelley's Frankenstein
Nosferatu
Terror of Frankenstein
Young Frankenstein

Fraternities & Sororities
See also: Campus Capers
Hell Night
National Lampoon's Animal House
Scream 2
Sorority Babes in the Slimeball Bowl-A-Rama
Urban Legend

Front Page
See also: Mass Media; Shutterbugs
Absence of Malice
All the President's Men
Blank Generation
Brenda Starr
Chinese Box
Criminal Act
Cry Freedom
Dark Secrets
Deep Impact
Diary of a Serial Killer
Extramarital
Fletch
The Front Page
Gentleman's Agreement
Hero
His Girl Friday
The Hudsucker Proxy
I Love Trouble
In and Out
The Insider
L.A. Confidential
The Last Word
Meet John Doe
Message in a Bottle

Midnight in the Garden of Good and Evil (SE)
Mr. Nice Guy
Never Been Kissed
The Night Stalker
The Night Strangler
Nothing Sacred
Notting Hill
Novel Desires
The Odessa File
One True Thing
The Paper
The Pelican Brief
The Philadelphia Story
Scream 2
Shock Corridor
Snake Eyes
Spice World: The Movie
Stephen King's The Night Flier
The Story of G.I. Joe
They Got Me Covered
Three Kings
Velvet Goldmine
Where the Buffalo Roam
Whisper Kill
Woman of the Year
The Year of Living Dangerously

French (Production)
Alphaville
Andy Warhol's Dracula
Andy Warhol's Frankenstein
Any Number Can Win
Barbarella
Beau Pere
Beauty and the Beast
Bed and Board
Black Orpheus
Black Tights
Boyfriends & Girlfriends
Buffet Froid
Bye Bye Monkey
Chinese Box
Chloe in the Afternoon
The City of Lost Children
Claire's Knee
The Climb
Cold Sweat
Confidentially Yours
The Crazy Ray
Damage
Daniella by Night
Daughters of Darkness
The Decameron
Diabolique
The Disenchanted
Diva
Don't Touch the White Woman!
The Dreamlife of Angels
Emmanuelle
Emmanuelle, the Joys of a Woman
Entre-Nous
The Eric Rohmer Collection: The Moral Tales
Fahrenheit 451
The Fantastic Night
Fantastic Planet
Fascination
First Name: Carmen
The 400 Blows
Full Moon in Paris
Grand Illusion
Hideous Kinky
Honor Among Thieves
I Love You, I Love You Not
In the Realm of the Senses
Irma Vep
La Collectionneuse
La Femme Nikita
La Sentinelle
La Separation
The Last Metro
Last Tango in Paris
Last Year at Marienbad
The Law
Le Beau Mariage
L'Enfer
The Life of Jesus

Lips of Blood
The Living Dead Girl
Lola Montes
Love After Love
Love, etc.
Ma Saison Preferee
Metroland
My Life to Live
My Night at Maud's
Nosferatu the Vampyre
Passion of Joan of Arc
Pierrot le Fou
The Pillow Book
Ponette
The Professional
Ran
Requiem for a Vampire
The Return of Martin Guerre
Romance
Shoot the Piano Player
The Soft Skin
Spirits of the Dead
Stolen Kisses
Subway
Summer
36 Fillete
Time Masters
The Train
The Trial
Two English Girls
Umbrellas of Cherbourg
Un Air de Famille
Utopia
Vampyr
The Vanishing
Wages of Fear
Wild Reeds
A Woman Is a Woman
The Woman Next Door

Fugitives
See also: Lovers on the Lam
Ball of Fire
Boys on the Side
Butch Cassidy and the Sundance Kid
Desperate Measures
Fled
Frank and Jesse
The Fugitive
Gridlock'd
Klondike Annie
Posse
Three Days of the Condor
Truth or Consequences, N.M.
U.S. Marshals
Wrongfully Accused

Funerals
See also: Death & the Afterlife
The Big Chill
City Hall
Dangerous Ground
First Knight
Four Weddings and a Funeral
The Funeral
Heathers
Hope Floats
Mr. Saturday Night
My Girl
One Night Stand
Simon Birch
Sleepless in Seattle
The Wings of the Dove

Gambling
See also: Viva Las Vegas!
Any Number Can Win
Barry Lyndon
The Boys
Buffalo 66
Bugsy
Casino
The Color of Money
The Flamingo Kid
Four Rooms
Get Shorty
Havana
Heat
Heaven

Honeymoon in Vegas
Lock, Stock and 2 Smoking Barrels
Maverick
Money Kings
Money Train
Phoenix
Rain Man
Rounders
The Runner
Sgt. Bilko
The Shanghai Gesture
The Sting
Ten Benny
Uncle Buck
The Underneath
Vegas Vacation
Walking Tall
The Westerner

Game Adaptations
Double Dragon
Mortal Kombat 1: The Movie
Mortal Kombat 2: Annihilation
Street Fighter
Wing Commander

Game Shows
Mallrats
Quiz Show
The Running Man

Gangs
See also: Crime & Criminals; Organized Crime
Assault on Precinct 13
Belly
A Better Tomorrow, Part 1
A Better Tomorrow, Part 2
Big Bad Mama
Bonnie & Clyde
Boyz N the Hood
China O'Brien
The Corruptor
Dangerous Ground
Diva
Escape from L.A.
Exterminator
Foolish
Goodfellas
A Hero Never Dies
Jungleground
Last Man Standing
Menace II Society
Midnight
Mob Story
Mob War
One Man's Justice
The Outsiders
Pierrot le Fou
Return of the Dragon
Revenge
Rumble Fish
Rumble in the Bronx
Scarface
Shaft
Shoot the Piano Player
Slam
The Substitute
The Substitute 2: School's Out
West Side Story
The Wild One
Wonder Man

Gays
See also: Bisexuality; Gender Bending; Lesbians
Alive and Kicking
Arabian Nights
Armistead Maupin's More Tales of the City
As Good As It Gets
The Big Brass Ring
Billy's Hollywood Screen Kiss
The Birdcage
Blast from the Past
Boys Life
Boys Life 2
Cabaret
The Crying Game

Finding North
Four Weddings and a Funeral
Gods and Monsters
Happy Together
In and Out
Killer Condom
Like It Is
Lilies
Love and Death on Long
  Island
Man of the Year
Midnight Cowboy
Midnight in the Garden of
  Good and Evil (SE)
My Best Friend's Wedding
Opposite of Sex
Philadelphia
The Pillow Book
Priest
Ready to Wear
Rites of Passage
Rude
Stonewall
To Play or To Die
Total Eclipse
Trick
The Twilight of the Golds
A Very Natural Thing
Vive l'Amour
Wild Reeds

Gender Bending

See also: Gays; Lesbians;
Role Reversal
The Adventures of Priscilla,
  Queen of the Desert
At War with the Army
Better Than Chocolate
The Crying Game
Glen or Glenda?
Lilies
Mrs. Doubtfire
Psycho (CE)
Silence of the Lambs
Stonewall
Trash
Velvet Goldmine
The Year of Living Dangerous-
  ly

Generation X
Beautiful Girls
Before Sunrise
Blade
Bottle Rocket
Clerks
Don't Do It
Floundering
Half-Baked
Keys to Tulsa
Mallrats
Reality Bites
Singles

Genetics

See also: Mad Scientists;
Metamorphosis
Gattaca
The Island of Dr. Moreau
Mimic
Multiplicity
The Twilight of the Golds

Genies
A Kid in Aladdin's Palace
Wishmaster

Genre Spoofs

See also: Satire & Parody
Austin Powers: International
  Man of Mystery
Austin Powers 2: The Spy
  Who Shagged Me
Beverly Hills Ninja
Blazing Saddles
Don't Be a Menace to South
  Central While Drinking Your
  Juice in the Hood
Dragnet
Flesh Gordon
Hercules
Kentucky Fried Movie

Last Action Hero
The Man Who Knew Too Little
The Man with Two Brains
Mars Attacks!
Monster in the Closet
National Lampoon's Loaded
  Weapon 1
Plump Fiction
Scream (CS)
Space Truckers
Spy Hard
They Live
This Is Spinal Tap
Three Amigos
Trader Hornee
Tromeo & Juliet
Union City
Who Framed Roger Rabbit
Wrongfully Accused
Young Frankenstein

German (Production)
The Adventures of Baron
  Munchausen
Andy Warhol's Frankenstein
The Bird with the Crystal
  Plumage
The Cabinet of Dr. Caligari
Cross of Iron
Das Boot (DC)
Daughters of Darkness
The Decameron
Even Dwarfs Started Small
Fitzcarraldo
I Love You, I Love You Not
Killer Condom
M
Mark of the Devil
Metropolis
Nico Icon
Nosferatu
Nosferatu the Vampyre
The Odessa File
Pandora's Box
Run Lola Run
Spiders
Spring Symphony
Stalingrad
Succubus
The Surgeon
Swiss Conspiracy
Tin Drum
Two Undercover Angels
Vampyr
Werther
The Wonderful, Horrible Life
  of Leni Riefenstahl

**Ghosts, Ghouls &
Goblins**

See also: Death & the After-
life; Demons & Wizards;
Occult
An American Affair
An American Werewolf in
  Paris
Beetlejuice
Beloved
Bury Me in Niagara
Children Shouldn't Play with
  Dead Things
A Christmas Carol
Curtain Call
The Frighteners
Ghost Story
Ghostbusters
Ghostbusters 2
The Haunting
Heart and Souls
In the Realm of Passion
Jessica: A Love Story
Mr. Vampire
Phantoms
Poltergeist
Rouge
The Sixth Sense
Sleepy Hollow
Sometimes They Come Back
  ... Again
Soultaker
Stir of Echoes

Giants
Bride of the Monster
My Giant
The Nutty Professor
The Princess Bride
The Spy Who Loved Me (SE)
Teenage Mutant Ninja Tur-
  tles: The Movie
Tremors
Tremors 2: Aftershocks

Go Fish

See also: Deep Blue; Killer
Sea Critters
A Fish Called Wanda
Free Willy
Grumpier Old Men
Grumpy Old Men
Jaws: The Revenge
The Law
Limbo
Moby Dick
On Golden Pond
A River Runs Through It
Zeus and Roxanne

Godzilla and Friends
Godzilla
Godzilla, King of the Mon-
  sters
Godzilla vs. Monster Zero
Godzilla vs. Mothra
Godzilla's Revenge
Terror of Mechagodzilla

Going Native
Apocalypse Now
The Blue Lagoon
Congo
Dances with Wolves
George of the Jungle
Jeremiah Johnson

Golf
Caddyshack
Caddyshack 2
Enter the Dragon (SE)
Goldfinger
Happy Gilmore
National Lampoon's Golf
  Punks
Space Jam
Tin Cup

Governesses

See: Babysitting; The Help;
Female; Nannies & Gov-
ernesses

Grand Hotel

See also: No-Exit Motel
Billy Madison
Bugsy
Dirty Dancing
Dirty Dancing (CF)
Four Rooms
French Kiss
Holiday Inn
Home Alone 2: Lost in New
  York
New Rose Hotel
Nick of Time
The Out-of-Towners
Pretty Woman
Psycho (CE)
Psycho 2
Psycho 3
The Shining
Somewhere in Time
Suite 16

Great Death Scenes

See also: Death & the After-
life; Funerals
Bonnie & Clyde
Breaker Morant
Butch Cassidy and the Sun-
  dance Kid
Dangerous Liaisons
Dark Victory
Die Hard: With a Vengeance
Evita

Face/Off
From Dusk Till Dawn
Gallipoli
Glory
The Green Mile
Highlander (DC)
Joan of Arc
Johnny Mnemonic
Psycho (CE)
Shadowlands
Strangers on a Train
Things to Do in Denver When
  You're Dead
The Wizard of Oz

Great Depression

See also: Hard Knock Life;
Homeless
Big Bad Mama
Bonnie & Clyde
Chinatown
The Green Mile
Hard Times
Hunter's Moon
The Imposters
It Happened One Night
Last Man Standing
Life
Modern Times
Of Mice and Men
Our Daily Bread and Other
  Films of the Depression
The Postman Always Rings
  Twice
Radioland Murders
Rambling Rose
The Rocketeer
Shadrach
They Shoot Horses, Don't
  They?

Great Escapes

See also: Escaped Cons; Men
in Prison; POW/MIA; War, Gen-
eral; Women in Prison
Austin Powers: International
  Man of Mystery
The Big Doll House
Butch Cassidy and the Sun-
  dance Kid
Con Air
The Deer Hunter
Desperate Measures
Die Hard
Die Hard: With a Vengeance
Double Team
Escape from Alcatraz
Escape from L.A.
Face/Off
Feeling Minnesota
Fled
The Great Escape
The Great Train Robbery
Ladyhawke
Midnight Express
No Escape
Papillon
Raw Deal
Rob Roy
The Rock
Runaway Train
The Saint
The Seventh Floor
The Shining
Tequila Sunrise
Three Days of the Condor
Victory

Growing Older

See also: Death & the After-
life; Late Bloomin' Love
*batteries not included
The Best of Times
Buena Vista Social Club
Central Station
Driving Miss Daisy
The Field
Forever Young
Gods and Monsters
Greedy
Grumpier Old Men

Grumpy Old Men
Horton Foote's Alone
Light Sleeper
The Limey
Ma Saison Preferee
Meet Joe Black
Mrs. Dalloway
Mr. Saturday Night
Neil Simon's The Odd Couple
  2
On Golden Pond
The Out-of-Towners
Pushing Hands
Queens Logic
Rabid Grannies
Ran
Rooster Cogburn
Shoot Out
Star Trek: Insurrection
Twilight
Unforgiven
The Wild Bunch

Hackers

See also: Computers
Hackers
The Net
Sneakers
WarGames

Halloween
The Fear: Halloween Night
Halloween
Halloween 2: The Nightmare
  Isn't Over!
Halloween 3: Season of the
  Witch
Halloween 4: The Return of
  Michael Myers
Halloween: H20
I've Been Waiting for You
Jack-O
The Nightmare before Christ-
  mas

Hammer Films
Dracula, Prince of Darkness
Kiss of the Vampire
The Legend of the 7 Golden
  Vampires
Lost Continent
Plague of the Zombies
Prehistoric Women
Quatermass and the Pit
Rasputin the Mad Monk
The Reptile
The Satanic Rites of Dracula
The Vengeance of She
The Viking Queen

Hard Knock Life

See also: Great Depression;
Homeless
Broken Blossoms
Clockers
Dancing at Lughnasa
Dolores Claiborne
The Dreamlife of Angels
Foolish
The Full Monty
Gridlock'd
Hideous Kinky
Les Miserables
Little Women
Meantime
Moll Flanders
Monument Ave.
Restoration
Set It Off
Shadrach
Sparrows
Tess of the Storm Country
This Is My Father
White Man's Burden

Hearts!

See also: Ears!; Eyeballs!;
Renegade Body Parts
An American Werewolf in
  Paris
Angel Heart
Brainstorm

Dumb & Dumber
Legends of the Fall
Mary Shelley's Frankenstein
The Prophecy
The Prophecy 2: Ashtown
Pulp Fiction
Tales from the Crypt Presents
    Bordello of Blood
The Terminator

Heaven Sent

See also: Angels
All of Me
Always
The Bishop's Wife
Carousel
Chances Are
Heaven Can Wait
It's a Wonderful Life
One Magic Christmas
What Dreams May Come
Xanadu

Heists

*See also: Scams, Stings &
    Cons*
The Amazing Transparent
    Man
Any Number Can Win
Bad Boys
Belly
The Bicycle Thief
Bonnie & Clyde
Bottle Rocket
Bound
Casino
City on Fire
Crime Broker
Dead Presidents
Die Hard: With a Vengeance
Entrapment
French Kiss
The Getaway
The Getaway
The Great Train Robbery
Hand Gun
Happy, Texas
Hard Rain
Heat
The Hoodlum
Interceptor
The Killing
A Life Less Ordinary
Lock, Stock and 2 Smoking
    Barrels
Money Train
Once a Thief
Operation Condor 2: The
    Armour of the Gods
Out of Sight
The Pink Panther
The Real McCoy
Reservoir Dogs
Running Time
Set It Off
Smart Money
Sneakers
Thief
The Thomas Crown Affair
Three Kings
Truth or Consequences, N.M.
The Underneath
The Usual Suspects

Hell High School

*See also: Campus Capers;
    School Daze; Teen Angst*
Animal Room
Billy Madison
Black Circle Boys
Class of Nuke 'Em High
Clueless
The Craft
Creepers
Dazed and Confused
Detention
Disturbing Behavior
Fear
Ferris Bueller's Day Off
Halloween: H20
Heathers

Hoosiers
I Was a Teenage Zombie
Little Witches
Major Payne
Peggy Sue Got Married
Porky's
Prom Night
Pump Up the Volume
The Rage: Carrie 2
Rock 'n' Roll High School
School Ties
Sister Act 2: Back in the
    Habit
Sixteen Candles
Stay Awake
The Substitute
Teaching Mrs. Tingle
Urusei Yatsura Movie 2:
    Beautiful Dreamer
White Squall

The Help: Female

The Babysitter's Seduction
Gone with the Wind
Kama Sutra: A Tale of Love
The King and I
Rebecca
Sister My Sister

The Help: Male

Arthur
Batman
Batman and Robin
Batman Forever
Batman Returns
Candleshoe
Driving Miss Daisy
Mrs. Brown
My Man Godfrey

Hide the Dead Guy

Jawbreaker
Pulp Fiction
Shallow Grave
Very Bad Things
Waking Ned Devine

High School Reunions

See also: School Daze
Beautiful Girls
Grosse Pointe Blank
National Lampoon's Class
    Reunion
Peggy Sue Got Married
Romy and Michele's High
    School Reunion

**Highest Grossing Films
of All Time**

Batman
Ghostbusters
Gone with the Wind
Home Alone
Mrs. Doubtfire
Terminator 2: Judgment Day
Titanic

Hispanic America

Fools Rush In
Lotto Land
Miami Rhapsody
Selena
Stand and Deliver

Historical Drama

*See also: Medieval Romps;
    Period Piece*
Amadeus
Andrei Rublev
The Battleship Potemkin
The Big Red One
The Birth of a Nation
Black Robe
A Bridge Too Far
Dances with Wolves
Elizabeth
The Emperor's Shadow
Fire Over England
Forever and a Day
The 47 Ronin, Parts 1 & 2
Gallipoli
Geronimo: An American Leg-
    end

Glory
Guilty by Suspicion
Henry V
Ill-Gotten Gains
Ivan the Terrible, Part 1
Ivan the Terrible, Part 2
Jakob the Liar
James Dean Double Feature:
    Hill Number One / I Am a
    Fool
JFK
Joan of Arc
Kama Sutra: A Tale of Love
Kundun
The Last Emperor
The Last Valley
Mahler
Michael Collins
Mrs. Brown
Moll Flanders
Nicholas and Alexandra
Nixon
Orphans of the Storm
Passion of Joan of Arc
Portrait of a Lady
The Power of One
Restoration
The Right Stuff
Rosewood
Royal Hunt of the Sun
Royal Tramp
The Scarlet Pimpernel
Spartacus
The Ten Commandments
Ten Days That Shook the
    World
Winstanley

Hit Men

See also: Assassinations
Angel's Dance
Assassins
Big City Blues
The Big Hit
Blackjack
The Bodyguard
Bulworth
Desperado
Desperado / El Mariachi
Dumb & Dumber
El Mariachi
Fallen Angels
Goodbye, Lover
Grosse Pointe Blank
Hard-Boiled
The Jackal (CE)
The Killer
La Femme Nikita
Made Men
The Man Who Knew Too Little
The Manchurian Candidate
The Naked City
Over the Wire
Point of No Return
Prisoner of Love
Prizzi's Honor
The Professional
Pulp Fiction
Razor Blade Smile
The Replacement Killers
Sanctuary
Shattered Image
Six Ways to Sunday
Sleepers
The Specialist
Strangers on a Train
Suddenly
Things to Do in Denver When
    You're Dead
U-Turn

Hockey

The Boys
Happy Gilmore
Jack Frost
Lethal Weapon 3
The Mighty Ducks
Slap Shot

Holidays

*See Christmas; Halloween;
    New Year's Eve; Thanksgiving*

The Holocaust

*See also: Judaism; Nazis &
    Other Paramilitary Slugs;
    World War II*
The Architecture of Doom
I Love You, I Love You Not
Jakob the Liar
The Last Metro
Life Is Beautiful
Sophie's Choice

Home Alone

See also: Childhood Visions
Adventures in Babysitting
The Blue Lagoon
Boys Will Be Boys
Four Rooms
Home Alone
Home Alone 2: Lost in New
    York
Home Alone 3
Invaders from Mars
The Littlest Horse Thieves
Scream (CS)

**The Homefront:
U.S./Canada**

See also: World War II
A League of Their Own
1941

Homeless

*See also: Great Depression;
    Hard Knock Life; Yuppie Night-
    mares*
City Lights
The Kid / A Dog's Life
Midnight Cowboy
Oliver!
Oliver Twist
With Honors

Homosexuality

*See: Bisexuality; Gays; Les-
    bians*

Hong Kong (Production)

Angel Heart
Armageddon
Beast Cops
A Better Tomorrow, Part 1
A Better Tomorrow, Part 2
Black Cat
Black Mask
The Bride with White Hair
The Bride with White Hair 2
Buddhist Fist
A Bullet in the Head
Center Stage
C'est la Vie, Mon Cherie
Chinese Connection
A Chinese Ghost Story
A Chinese Ghost Story II
A Chinese Ghost Story III
Chinese Odyssey, Part One:
    Pandora's Box
City on Fire
Crystal Hunt
Eastern Condors
Erotic Ghost Story
The Executioners
Expect the Unexpected
Fallen Angels
Farewell My Concubine
First Option
Fist of Legend
Fong Sai Yuk
The Fruit Is Swelling
Full Contact
Full Throttle
Girls Unbuttoned
God.com
God of Cookery
God of Gamblers
God of Gambler's Return
The Great Conqueror's Concu-
    bine
The Great Conqueror's Concu-
    bine, Part 2
Half a Loaf of Kung Fu
Happy Together

Hard-Boiled
Heart of Dragon
A Hero Never Dies
The Heroic Trio
High Risk
Hitman
Hong Kong 1941
Hot War
I Love Maria
In the Line of Duty 3
In the Line of Duty 4
In the Line of Duty 5
Inspector Wears Skirts
Iron Monkey
Island of Greed
Jackie Chan's First Strike
Jackie Chan's Who Am I
Jet Li's The Enforcer
The Killer
The Killer Meteors
Killer's Romance
King of Beggars
Lawyer Lawyer
Lee Rock
Legacy of Rage
Long Arm of the Law
Long Arm of the Law II
The Longest Nite
Lover of the Last Empress
Magnificent Warriors
Mah Jong Dragon
Man Wanted
The Master
The Millionaire's Express
Miracles
Mr. Nice Guy
Mr. Vampire
The Moon Warriors
My Lucky Stars
Naked Killer
Once Upon a Time in China
Once Upon a Time in China II
Once Upon a Time in China III
Operation Condor 2: The
    Armour of the Gods
Organized Crime & Triad
    Bureau
Peace Hotel
Prison on Fire
Prison on Fire 2
The Prodigal Son
Rouge
Royal Tramp
Royal Tramp 2
Rumble in the Bronx
Sex and Zen
Shaolin Avengers
Spiritual Kung Fu
Supercop
Supercop 2
To Kill with Intrigue
Twin Dragons
The Untold Story
Wheels on Meals
Wicked City
Zu: Warriors of the Magic
    Mountain

Horror

*See: Classic Horror; Dracula;
    Frankenstein; Ghosts, Ghouls
    & Goblins; Horror Anthologies;
    Horror Comedy; Satanism;
    Supernatural Comedy; Super-
    natural Horror; Vampires;
    Witchcraft*

Horror Anthologies

Creepshow
Nightmares
Spirits of the Dead
Still Twisted
Tales from the Hood
Trilogy of Terror

Horror Comedy

An American Werewolf in
    Paris
Andy Warhol's Dracula
Andy Warhol's Frankenstein
Arachnophobia
Army of Darkness

Beetlejuice
Brain Damage
Bride of Chucky
Bride of Re-Animator
The Creeps
Erotic Ghost Story
The Frighteners
Gremlins
I Was a Teenage Zombie
Little Shop of Horrors
The Mask
Matinee
Mr. Vampire
Monster in the Closet
My Mom's a Werewolf
Nothing but Trouble
The Old Dark House
Piranha
Q (The Winged Serpent)
Rabid Grannies
Re-Animator
Sorority Babes in the Slime-
ball Bowl-A-Rama
Spider Baby
Tales from the Crypt Presents
Bordello of Blood
Tales from the Crypt Presents
Demon Knight
The Toxic Avenger (DC)
The Toxic Avenger, Part 2
Tremors
Tremors 2: Aftershocks

Horse Racing

See: Gambling; Horses

Horses

The Black Stallion
Chino / Man with a Camera
The Electric Horseman
The Flying Deuces / Utopia
Half-Baked
The Horse Whisperer
The Littlest Horse Thieves
Lucky Luke
Meet Wally Sparks
National Lampoon's Animal
House
National Velvet
The Quiet Man
Shooting Fish
Winds of the Wasteland /
The Lucky Texan

Hostage!

*See also: Kidnapped!; Miss-
ing Persons*
Air Force One
Albino Alligator
The Boys Club
Cold Sweat
Cube
Die Hard
Die Hard 2: Die Harder
Dog Day Afternoon
Face the Evil
Fall Time
Firestorm
Funny Games
Mad City
The Negotiator
Nick of Time
Nothing to Lose
Rabid Dogs
The Seventh Floor
Sex and the Other Man
Speed 2: Cruise Control
Suddenly
Truth or Consequences, N.M.
12 Monkeys

Hungarian (Production)

The Long Shadow

Hunted!

See also: Survival
Deliverance
Hard Target
The Hunted
Jungleground
The Most Dangerous Game
Solo

Surviving the Game

Hurling

Ace Ventura: When Nature
Calls
Anaconda
BASEketball
Car Wash
The Crying Game
The Exorcist (SE)
Fear and Loathing in Las
Vegas
Heathers
Kingpin
Monty Python's The Meaning
of Life
My Giant
National Lampoon's Animal
House
Parenthood
Sirens
Stand by Me
This Is Spinal Tap
The Witches of Eastwick

Immigration

Buck Privates Come Home
Coming to America
The Cowboy Way
Far and Away
A King in New York / A
Woman in Paris
Miami Rhapsody
Monkey Business
Tarantella

Impending Retirement

Lethal Weapon
Love to Kill
The Mask of Zorro
Seven

In-Laws

Hush
The Inheritance
Son-in-Law
Stir of Echoes

Incest

See also: Family Ties
Andy Warhol's Frankenstein
The Grifters
The House of Yes
Ringmaster
The Sweet Hereafter
A Thousand Acres
U-Turn

Indian (Production)

Hum Dil De Chuke Sanam
Kama Sutra: A Tale of Love
Khamoshi the Musical
Koyla
Lav Kush
Pyaar Kiya to Darna Kya
Pyar to Hona Hi Tah
Sarfarosh
Thakshak
Virasat
Yes Boss!

Insomnia

See also: Up All Night
Fight Club
The Haunting
Taxi Driver (CE)

Interracial Affairs

The Bodyguard
Broken Blossoms
Bulworth
Chinese Box
Corrina, Corrina
Driving Miss Daisy
Guess Who's Coming to Din-
ner
Jungle Fever
Made in America
Miami Rhapsody
One Night Stand
Othello

Inventors & Inventions

See also: Mad Scientists; Sci-

ence & Scientists
Chairman of the Board
Chitty Chitty Bang Bang
The Man Who Fell to Earth
The Spanish Prisoner

Invisibility

The Amazing Transparent
Man
The Invisible Strangler

Iranian (Production)

The Taste of Cherry

Irish (Production)

The Boxer
The Commitments
The Crying Game
Dancing at Lughnasa
The General
In the Name of the Father
My Left Foot
Quackser Fortune Has a
Cousin in the Bronx
Space Truckers
Terror of Frankenstein

Island Fare

See also: Sex on the Beach
The Blue Lagoon
Cutthroat Island
Hell in the Pacific
The Island of Dr. Moreau
The Last Flight of Noah's Ark
No Escape
The Postman
Rain
The Quest
Six Days, Seven Nights
Somewhere in Time
South Pacific
Speed 2: Cruise Control
Stephen King's The Storm of
the Century
Swept Away . . .
Tora! Tora! Tora!
Undercurrent
Utopia
Xtro 3: Watch the Skies
The Year of Living Dangerous-
ly

Israeli (Production)

The Long Shadow

Italian (Production)

Amarcord
And the Ship Sails On
Andy Warhol's Dracula
Andy Warhol's Frankenstein
Arabian Nights
Autopsy
Bad Man's River
Barbarella
Besieged
Beyond the Door 2
The Bicycle Thief
The Bird with the Crystal
Plumage
The Black Pirate
Black Sunday
The Bloodsucker Leads the
Dance
Body Puzzle
Bye Bye Monkey
Caligula
The Canterbury Tales
Chino / Man with a Camera
Cold Sweat
The Con Artists
Creepers
Daughters of Darkness
The Decameron
Deep Red: Hatchet Murders
Demons
Demons 2
The Devil's Nightmare
Fifth Day of Peace
A Fistful of Dollars
For a Few Dollars More
The Good, the Bad and the
Ugly

The Gospel According to St.
Matthew
Honor Among Thieves
Inferno
The Inheritance
Juliet of the Spirits
Kill, Baby, Kill
La Traviata
The Last Emperor
Last Tango in Paris
Last Year at Marienbad
The Law
Life Is Beautiful
Lisa and the Devil / The
House of Exorcism
Love and Anarchy
Lovers and Liars
Marcello Mastroianni: I
Remember
The Monster
New York Ripper
Nights of Cabiria
Nostalghia
Nude for Satan
Open City
The Phantom of the Opera
Pierrot le Fou
Playgirls and the Vampire
The Postman
Rabid Dogs
The Red Desert
Regina
The Reincarnation of Isabel
Romeo and Juliet
Salo, or the 120 Days of
Sodom
Seduction of Mimi
Seven Beauties
The Sinful Nuns of Saint
Valentine
Spirits of the Dead
Swept Away . . .
Tea with Mussolini
Torso
Torture Chamber of Baron
Blood
The Train
Twitch of the Death Nerve
Two Women
Zeder
Zombie

It's a Conspiracy, Man!

*See also: Capitol Capers;
Mystery & Suspense*
Absolute Power
All the President's Men
Armageddon
The Arrival
City Hall
Conspiracy Theory
Cop Land
Enemy of the State
Eraser
The Game
The Jackal (CE)
JFK
The Manchurian Candidate
The Matrix
Megazone 23 Part 1
Muppets from Space
Murder at 1600
Nixon
The Parallax View
Red Corner
Sneakers
They Live
Three Days of the Condor
Tom Clancy's Netforce
The X-Files

Jail

*See: Escaped Cons; Great
Escapes; Men in Prison;
Women in Prison*

James Bond

Dr. No (SE)
For Your Eyes Only (SE)
From Russia with Love
Goldeneye
Goldfinger

License to Kill
Live and Let Die
Moonraker (SE)
The Spy Who Loved Me (SE)
Thunderball
Tomorrow Never Dies (SE)

Japanese (Production)

The Adventures of Milo &
Otis
Armitage 3: Polymatrix
Big Wars
Black Rain
Branded to Kill
Chinese Box
Chushingura
Crimson Wolf
Demon City Shinjuku
Dominion Tank Police
8 Man
Fist of the North Star
The 47 Ronin, Parts 1 & 2
The Funeral
Ghost in the Shell
Godzilla, King of the Mon-
sters
Godzilla vs. Monster Zero
Godzilla vs. Mothra
Godzilla's Revenge
High & Low
The Human Condition: No
Greater Love
The Human Condition: Road
to Eternity
In the Realm of the Senses
Lupin III: The Mystery of
Mamo
MD Geist (DC)
Ninja Scroll
Project A-ko
Ran
Record of Lodoss War
Samurai 1: Musashi Miyamo-
to
Samurai 2: Duel at Ichijoji
Temple
Samurai 3: Duel at Ganryu
Island
Sanjuro
Seven Samurai
Tampopo
A Taxing Woman
Tenchi the Movie: Tenchi
Muyo in Love
Terror of Mechagodzilla
Tetsuo: The Iron Man
Tetsuo 2: Body Hammer
Tokyo Decadence
Tokyo Drifter
Urotsukidoji: Perfect Collec-
tion
Urusei Yatsura Movie 2:
Beautiful Dreamer
The Venus Wars
Village of Dreams
A Wind Named Amnesia
Zeram

Journalism

See: Front Page

Judaism

See also: The Holocaust
Deconstructing Harry
Fiddler on the Roof
Gentleman's Agreement
I Love You, I Love You Not
The Jazz Singer
The Last Metro
A Price above Rubies
The Quarrel
School Ties
The Twilight of the Golds

Jungle Stories

*See also: Monkeyshines; Trea-
sure Hunt*
Ace Ventura: When Nature
Calls
Anaconda
Bat 21
Brenda Starr

Congo
Fire on the Amazon
Fitzcarraldo
George of the Jungle
Gorillas in the Mist
Instinct
Jumanji (CS)
The Jungle Book
Jungle Boy
Medicine Man
The Phantom
Predator
Prehistoric Women
Solo
Tarzan
Tarzan and the Lost City
The Thin Red Line
Trader Hornee
Troma's War (DC)
Wages of Fear

Justice Prevails...?

See also: Order in the Court
Absence of Malice
The Chamber
A Civil Action
The Confession
Cyber-Tracker
In the Name of the Father
The Jack Bull
JFK
Judge Dredd
Just Cause
Night Falls on Manhattan
The Paper
Presumed Innocent
Sleepers
A Time to Kill
Trial & Error

Kidnapped!

See also: Hostage!; Missing Persons
Ace Ventura: Pet Detective
Beethoven's 2nd
Benji
The Big Hit
The Big Lebowski
Black Cat Run
Bound and Gagged: A Love Story
Buffalo 66
The City of Lost Children
Commando
The Crying Game
The Deep End of the Ocean
Django Strikes Again
Dumb & Dumber
Earthly Possessions
8 Man After: The Perfect Collection
Excess Baggage
Fargo
The Gingerbread Man
Guarding Tess
Hide and Seek
The Last Assassins
A Life Less Ordinary
The Mighty
Mystery Men
Nick of Time
The Nightmare before Christmas
101 Dalmatians
Operation Condor 2: The Armour of the Gods
Operation Delta Force 2: Mayday
Out of Sight
Private Obsession
The Quest
Ransom
The Real McCoy
Rush Hour
Street Fighter
Suicide Kings
Switchback
Teaching Mrs. Tingle

Killer Apes & Monkeys

See also: Monkeyshines

Congo
King Kong
Mighty Joe Young

Killer Brains

See also: Renegade Body Parts
Brain Damage

Killer Bugs & Slugs

Arachnophobia
Bug Buster
Creepers
Creepshow
Godzilla vs. Mothra
The Lair of the White Worm
Mosquito
Parasite
Starship Troopers
They Came from Within
Tremors
Tremors 2: Aftershocks

Killer Cars

See also: Motor Vehicle Dept.
Christine
Death Race 2000
Mad Max
Mad Max: Beyond Thunderdome
The Road Warrior

Killer Dreams

Freddy's Dead: The Final Nightmare
In Dreams
A Nightmare on Elm Street
A Nightmare on Elm Street 2: Freddy's Revenge
A Nightmare on Elm Street 3: Dream Warriors
A Nightmare on Elm Street 4: Dream Master
A Nightmare on Elm Street 5: Dream Child
Phantasm
Wes Craven's New Nightmare

Killer Kats

See also: Cats
Batman Returns
Cat People

Killer Plants

Body Snatchers
Invasion of the Body Snatchers
Little Shop of Horrors

Killer Reptiles

See also: Godzilla and Friends
The Flying Serpent
Godzilla, King of the Monsters
Godzilla vs. Monster Zero
Lake Placid
Q (The Winged Serpent)

Killer Rodents

The Bat

Killer Sea Critters

See also: Deep Blue; Go Fish
Baywatch: Nightmare Bay / River of No Return
Deep Blue Sea
Deep Rising
Godzilla vs. Mothra
Humanoids from the Deep
Jason and the Argonauts
Jaws: The Revenge
Lost Continent
Mean Streets
Memphis Belle
Piranha
Piranha
Reap the Wild Wind
Shark Attack
Sphere

Killer Toys

Bride of Chucky
Child's Play

Child's Play 2
Halloween 3: Season of the Witch
Poltergeist
Small Soldiers
Tales from the Hood
Trilogy of Terror

Kindness of Strangers

The Matchmaker
Powder
The Toll Gate

Stephen King

Apt Pupil
Christine
Creepshow
The Dark Half
Dolores Claiborne
Firestarter
The Green Mile
The Lawnmower Man
Needful Things
The Running Man
Salem's Lot
The Shawshank Redemption
The Shining
Sometimes They Come Back
Sometimes They Come Back ... Again
Stand by Me
Stephen King's The Night Flier
Stephen King's The Stand
Stephen King's The Storm of the Century
Stephen King's The Tommyknockers
Stephen King's Thinner
Trucks

King of Beasts (Dogs)

The Adventures of Milo & Otis
Air Bud
All Dogs Christmas Carol
As Good As It Gets
Babe: Pig in the City
Beethoven
Beethoven's 2nd
Benji
Big Red
A Boy and His Dog
Call of the Wild
Cool Hand Luke
Dumb & Dumber
An Extremely Goofy Movie
For the Love of Benji
Homeward Bound: The Incredible Journey
K-9
Lady and the Tramp
Lost and Found
The Mask
Michael
Nikki, the Wild Dog of the North
101 Dalmatians
There's Something about Mary
Top Dog
Where the Red Fern Grows
Where the Red Fern Grows: Part 2
The Wizard of Oz
Zeus and Roxanne

Kings

See: Royalty

Korean (Production)

Why Has Bodhi-Darma Left for the East

Korean War

The Manchurian Candidate
Men in War
Pork Chop Hill

Kung Fu

See: Martial Arts

Labor & Unions

See also: Miners & Mining
Blue Collar
The Pajama Game
Salt of the Earth
Silkwood

Las Vegas

See: Viva Las Vegas!

Late Bloomin' Love

See also: Growing Older
The Bridges of Madison County
Grumpy Old Men
Shadowlands
Summertime

Laurel & Hardy

The Flying Deuces / Utopia
Laurel and Hardy and Friends
The Lost Films of Laurel and Hardy, Vol. 1
The Lost Films of Laurel and Hardy, Vol. 2
The Lost Films of Laurel and Hardy, Vol. 3
The Lost Films of Laurel and Hardy, Vol. 5
The Lost Films of Laurel and Hardy, Vol. 6
Utopia

Law & Lawyers

See also: Order in the Court
Adam's Rib
Amistad
Big Daddy
The Candidate
Carlito's Way
The Chamber
A Civil Action
The Client
The Confession
Conspiracy Theory
Critical Care
The Devil's Advocate
Dragons Forever
Enemy of the State
Fair Game
Father's Day
Fear and Loathing in Las Vegas
A Few Good Men
The Firm
I'm No Angel
In the Name of the Father
The Island of Dr. Moreau
John Grisham's The Rainmaker
Judge Dredd
The Juror
Just Cause
Legal Eagles
Liar Liar
A Murder of Crows
Night Falls on Manhattan
Nixon
The Pelican Brief
The People vs. Larry Flynt
Philadelphia
Presumed Innocent
Primal Fear
Red Corner
Return to Paradise
Rounders
Sleepers
Stephen King's Thinner
A Stranger in the Kingdom
The Sweet Hereafter
A Time to Kill
To Kill a Mockingbird
The Trial
Trial & Error
Trial and Error
Wild Things

Lesbians

See also: Bisexuality; Gays; Gender Bending
The Alley Cats

Better Than Chocolate
The Blood Spattered Bride
Bound
Boys on the Side
Daughters of Darkness
Entre-Nous
The Killing of Sister George
Set It Off
Slaves to the Underground
Therese & Isabelle

Libraries & Librarians

See also: Books & Bookstores
Black Mask
The Breakfast Club
Ghostbusters
Hard-Boiled
It's a Wonderful Life
The Mummy
The Music Man
The Shawshank Redemption
Something Wicked This Way Comes
With Honors

Live Action/Animation Combos

Jan Svankmajer's Faust
Mary Poppins
Small Soldiers
Space Jam
Stuart Little
Tron
Who Framed Roger Rabbit
Xanadu

Loneliness

See: Only the Lonely

Loner Cops

See also: Cops
Above the Law
Action Jackson
Bad Lieutenant
Dead Bang
Die Hard
Die Hard 2: Die Harder
Die Hard: With a Vengeance
Dirty Harry
Heat
Judge Dredd
Rent-A-Cop
RoboCop
Sharky's Machine
Speed

Look Ma! I'm on TV!

See also: Mass Media
Eat Your Heart Out
Pleasantville
Sink or Swim
The Truman Show

Lost Worlds

See also: Parallel Universes
Brigadoon
Jumanji (CS)
Lost Horizon
The Lost World
Warriors of Virtue

Lovers on the Lam

See also: Fugitives
Badlands
Bonnie & Clyde
The Getaway
The Getaway
Kalifornia
Love and a .45
Mad Love
True Romance

Mad Scientists

See also: Inventors & Inventions; Science & Scientists
The Amazing Transparent Man
The Avengers
Bloodstorm: Subspecies 4
Body Armor
Brenda Starr

Tim

Metamorphosis

See also: Genetics; Werewolves

An American Werewolf in London
Boogie Nights
Cat People
Jack Frost
The Lair of the White Worm
The Nutty Professor
Stephen King's Thinner

Meteors, Asteroids & Comets

See also: Disaster Flicks

Armageddon
Creepshow
Deep Impact
The Killer Meteors
Lifeforce

Mexican (Production)

El Mariachi
Fando and Lis
Like Water for Chocolate
Midaq Alley

Military: Air Force

See also: Airborne

Memphis Belle
Tactical Assault

Military: Army

The Base
The Big Red One
The Dirty Dozen
The General's Daughter
Geronimo: An American Legend
Godzilla
The Green Berets
Independence Day
1941
Patton
The Peacemaker
Platoon
Private Benjamin
Ravenous
Saving Private Ryan
The Siege
Soldier
Starship Troopers
The Story of G.I. Joe
Stripes
The Thin Red Line
Three Kings

Military Comedy

See also: Comedy; War, General

Abbott and Costello in the Foreign Legion
At War with the Army
The Complete Uncensored Private Snafu
The Flying Deuces / Utopia
Major Payne
1941
Private Benjamin
Sgt. Bilko
Stripes

Military: Foreign

All Quiet on the Western Front
Breaker Morant
Das Boot (DC)
Gallipoli
The Hunt for Red October
Pretty Village, Pretty Flame
Savior
Stalingrad

Military: Marines

Bataan
A Few Good Men
Full Metal Jacket
Most Wanted
Platoon
Pork Chop Hill
The Rock

Sands of Iwo Jima

Military: Navy

See also: Sail Away

Crimson Tide
A Few Good Men
The Fighting Sullivans
Freedom Strike
G.I. Jane
The Hunt for Red October
The Last Detail
Mister Roberts
Navy SEALS
They Were Expendable
Top Gun
Under Siege

Miners & Mining

Brassed Off
Dudley Do-Right
Fire Down Below
Lucky Texan
October Sky
Pale Rider
Salt of the Earth
The War Wagon
Within the Rock

Missing Persons

See also: Hostage!; Kidnapped!

Frantic
Girl Hunters
In the Mouth of Madness
The Island at the Top of the World
The Lady Vanishes
Picnic at Hanging Rock
The Professionals
The Searchers
The Vanishing

Mistaken Identity

See also: Amnesia; Gender Bending; Not-So-True Identity; Role Reversal

As You Like It
The Assignment
The Big Lebowski
Body Snatchers
Charade
Court Jester
Dave
Don Juan DeMarco
El Mariachi
The Great Dictator
Hero
High & Low
The Imposters
Invasion of the Body Snatchers
Jade
Just Write
Made in America
The Man Who Knew Too Little
The Monster
My Man Godfrey
The Nutt House
Only You
Picture Perfect
The Player
The Return of Martin Guerre
The Santa Clause
The Secret of My Success
Sister Act 2: Back in the Habit
The 39 Steps
Twin Dragons
While You Were Sleeping

Model Citizens

Blackjack
Daniella by Night
In and Out
Ready to Wear

Modern Cowboys

See also: Western Comedy; Westerns; Westrogens

The Cowboy Way
8 Seconds
The Electric Horseman

The Horse Whisperer

Modern Shakespeare

Forbidden Planet
Ran
Ten Things I Hate about You
Tromeo & Juliet
West Side Story
William Shakespeare's Romeo and Juliet

Moms

See also: Bad Dads; Dads; Monster Moms; Parenthood

Antonia's Line
Anywhere But Here
Bastard out of Carolina
Beloved
Better Than Chocolate
Dangerous Beauty
The Deep End of the Ocean
Digging to China
Double Jeopardy
Down in the Delta
Drop Dead Gorgeous
Hope Floats
The Horse Whisperer
Junior's Groove
The Juror
Little Women
The Love Letter
Made in America
Mask
The Mighty
Nowhere to Run
One True Thing
Playing by Heart
Psycho
The Real McCoy
The River Wild
Simon Birch
So I Married an Axe Murderer
Stella Dallas
Striptease
Two Women
A Walk on the Moon
The Waterboy
When a Man Loves a Woman

Monkeyshines

See also: Jungle Stories; Killer Apes & Monkeys; Wild Kingdom

Babe: Pig in the City
Congo
George of the Jungle
Instinct
King Kong
Outbreak
Tarzan
Tarzan in Manhatten

Monster Moms

See also: Bad Dads; Dads; Moms; Parenthood

The Baby
Big Bad Mama
Dead Alive
Dolores Claiborne
Felicia's Journey
From Dusk Till Dawn 3: The Hangman's Daughter
The Grifters
Hush
Hush Little Baby
Invaders from Mars
Little Voice
The Manchurian Candidate
Mommy
Mommy 2: Mommy's Day
Mother's Boys
Parents
Psycho (CE)
Psycho 2
Psycho 3
Serial Mom
Six Ways to Sunday
The Ugly

Monsters, General

See: Dracula; Frankenstein; Ghosts, Ghouls & Goblins;

Giants; Killer Apes & Monkeys; Killer Brains; Killer Bugs & Slugs; Killer Dreams; Killer Kats; Killer Plants; Killer Reptiles; Killer Rodents; Killer Sea Critters; Killer Toys; Mad Scientists; Mummies; Robots & Androids; Vampires; Werewolves; Zombies

Monty Python

The Adventures of Baron Munchausen
And Now for Something Completely Different
Brazil
Brazil (Criterion SE)
A Fish Called Wanda
Monty Python's Life of Brian
Monty Python's The Meaning of Life
Time Bandits

Motor Vehicle Dept.

See also: Bikers; Buses; Cabbies; Checkered Flag; Killer Cars

Action Jackson
American Graffiti
The Betsy
Black Cat Run
Blood, Guts, Bullets and Octane
The Blues Brothers (CE)
The Car
Car Wash
Chitty Chitty Bang Bang
Crash
Dumb & Dumber
Ferris Bueller's Day Off
Jade
National Lampoon's Vacation
Silkwood
Stephen King's Thinner
Tail Lights Fade
Two Lane Blacktop
The Van

Mountaineering

Cliffhanger
The Eiger Sanction
Seven Years in Tibet

Mummies

See also: Zombies

The Creeps
The Mummy
The Mummy
Russell Mulcahy's Tale of the Mummy

The Muppets

The Adventures of Elmo in Grouchland
Labyrinth
Muppets from Space

Murderous Children

See also: Childhood Visions

Alice Sweet Alice
Milo
Village of the Damned

Museums

Ghostbusters 2
Mad City
The Relic
The Thomas Crown Affair

Musical Comedy

See also: Musicals

The Adventures of Priscilla, Queen of the Desert
The Blues Brothers (CE)
The Blues Brothers 2000
Bye, Bye, Birdie
The Cocoanuts
Court Jester
Everyone Says I Love You
Gigi
Going My Way / Holiday Inn
The Happiest Millionaire
Help!

Holiday Inn
In the Navy
Little Shop of Horrors
The Pajama Game
The Road to Morocco
The Road to Utopia
Rock 'n' Roll High School
Royal Wedding
Santo Bugito 1
Seven Brides for Seven Brothers
Singin' in the Rain
Spice World: The Movie
State Fair
Train Ride to Hollywood
A Woman Is a Woman
Wonder Man
Yes Boss!

Musical Drama

See also: Musicals

The Buddy Holly Story
Cabaret
Camelot
Evita
Fiddler on the Roof
George Balanchine's The Nutcracker
Jailhouse Rock
The Jazz Singer
Jesus Christ, Superstar
Khamoshi the Musical
The King and I
La Bamba
The Music Man
My Fair Lady
Oliver!
Purple Rain
The Red Shoes
Show Boat
Sunday in the Park with George
Sweet Dreams
Umbrellas of Cherbourg
West Side Story
What's Love Got to Do with It?

Musical Fantasy

See also: Musicals

Brigadoon
Carousel
Chitty Chitty Bang Bang
Cinderella
Labyrinth
Magical Mystery Tour
March of the Wooden Soldiers
Mary Poppins
Peter Pan
The Slipper and the Rose
Willy Wonka & the Chocolate Factory
The Wizard of Oz

Musicals

See also: Animated Musicals; Disco Musicals; Musical Comedy; Musical Drama; Musical Fantasy; Rodgers & Hammerstein

An American in Paris
Black Tights
Cats
Hair
Hans Christian Andersen
Into the Woods
Koyla
Nunsense
Oklahoma
Rodgers and Hammerstein: The Sound of Movies
South Pacific
Till the Clouds Roll By

Musician Biopics

Amadeus
Blank Generation
The Buddy Holly Story
The Doors
Hilary and Jackie
La Bamba

The Allnighter
American Gigolo
Armistead Maupin's More
   Tales of the City
Big City Blues
Boiling Point
Carmen, Baby
Casino
Celebrity
Crimes of Passion
Dangerous Beauty
Deconstructing Harry
Desperate Crimes
The Dirty Girls
Diva
Flesh
Gigi
Girls of the White Orchid
Hard Bounty
Hard Vice
He Got Game
Hot Blooded
Jade
John Carpenter's Vampires
L.A. Confidential
Leaving Las Vegas
Les Miserables
Lola Montes
The Man Who Knew Too Little
Mandragora
Midnight Cowboy
Moll Flanders
My Life to Live
My Son the Fanatic
Naked Kiss
Night Shift
Nights of Cabiria
Pandora's Box
The Players Club
Pretty Woman
Rain
Risky Business
Secret Games
Sharky's Machine
Taxi Driver (CE)
Things to Do in Denver When
   You're Dead
Tokyo Decadence
The Wicked, Wicked West
Word of Mouth

The Olympics

See also: Sports Dramas
Chariots of Fire
Cool Runnings
Without Limits

On the Rocks

See also: Pill Poppin'
Affliction
Arthur
The Big Lebowski
Casino
Cat on a Hot Tin Roof
The Chamber
Clean and Sober
The Crossing Guard
Dancer, Texas—Pop. 81
Drunks
The Electric Horseman
Frances
Georgia
Joe the King
Leaving Las Vegas
Little Voice
Pushing Tin
Scent of a Woman
Sling Blade
Tales of Ordinary Madness
Trees Lounge
When a Man Loves a Woman

Only the Lonely
Bed of Roses
Besieged
Central Station
Felicia's Journey
Full Moon in Paris
The Hunchback of Notre
   Dame
The Lonely Guy
Lulu on the Bridge

Minnie and Moskowitz
Pi
A Price above Rubies
The Red Desert
Samurai 2: Duel at Ichijoji
   Temple
Sleepless in Seattle
Summer
While You Were Sleeping

Opera

See also: Musicals
The Cunning Little Vixen
La Traviata
Lady Macbeth of Mtsensk
Maria Stuarda
The Phantom of the Opera
Werther

Opera Adaptations
Aria
Carmen, Baby
Farewell My Concubine
Fitzcarraldo
Jesus Christ, Superstar
The Phantom of the Opera

Order in the Court

See also: Justice Prevails...?;
   Law & Lawyers
Absence of Malice
Adam's Rib
Big Daddy
Breaker Morant
The Castle
The Chamber
A Civil Action
The Client
The Confession
Conspiracy: The Trial of the
   Chicago Eight
Crime Broker
Dangerous Beauty
Death Sentence
The Devil's Advocate
Disclosure
A Few Good Men
In the Name of the Father
Joan of Arc
John Grisham's The Rainmak-
   er
The Juror
Liar Liar
Midnight
Midnight in the Garden of
   Good and Evil (SE)
Murder
Night Falls on Manhattan
The Paradine Case
Passion of Joan of Arc
The People vs. Larry Flynt
Philadelphia
Presumed Innocent
Primal Fear
Red Corner
Return to Paradise
Sleepers
A Stranger in the Kingdom
A Time to Kill
To Kill a Mockingbird
The Trial
The Trial
Trial & Error
Trial and Error
White Squall
Why Do Fools Fall in Love?

Organized Crime

See also: Crime & Criminals;
   Disorganized Crime; Gangs;
   Yakuza
Absence of Malice
Analyze This
Angel's Dance
Avenging Disco Godfather
Ball of Fire
Big Combo
The Big Hit
Bound
The Boys
Branded to Kill
A Bronx Tale

Bugsy
Bullets over Broadway
Capone
Casino
City Hall
The Client
The Corruptor
Crazy Six
Death Wish 5: The Face of
   Death
Desperate Crimes
Donnie Brasco
Final Justice
The Firm
Fled
The Freshman
Gloria
Goldeneye
Goodfellas
Hard-Boiled
High Voltage
Innocent Blood
Island of Greed
The Juror
The Killer
The Killing Man
The Last Don
The Last Word
The Long Good Friday
Love to Kill
Mad Dog and Glory
Mean Streets
Money Kings
Moving Target
My Blue Heaven
Next of Kin
Once a Thief
Organized Crime & Triad
   Bureau
Out for Justice
Prizzi's Honor
Pulp Fiction
Raw Deal
Red Heat
Red Line
The Replacement Killers
The Runner
Showdown
Sleepers
Southie
Stephen King's Thinner
T-Men
Thief
To Die For
Tokyo Drifter
True Romance
Underworld
Wanted

Otherwise Engaged

See also: Romantic Triangles;
   Wedding Bells; Wedding Hell
Arthur
The Bachelor
The Birdcage
Coming to America
Everyone Says I Love You
Forces of Nature
Four Weddings and a Funeral
French Kiss
George of the Jungle
Gone with the Wind
His Girl Friday
The House of Yes
In and Out
Kissing a Fool
Love Affair
Miami Rhapsody
Moonstruck
My Best Friend's Wedding
My Best Girl
Only You
The Philadelphia Story
Picture Perfect
Pride and Prejudice
The Princess Bride
Robin Hood: Prince of
   Thieves
Shakespeare in Love (CS)
Shooting Fish
Six Days, Seven Nights

Sleepless in Seattle
Son-in-Law
Tarzan and the Lost City
That Old Feeling
Trial and Error
The Wedding Singer

Painting

See: Art & Artists

Parallel Universes

See also: Lost Worlds
Alice in Wonderland
Crossworlds
Dark City
Jumanji (CS)
Last Action Hero
The Little Mermaid
Logan's Run
Mortal Kombat 2: Annihila-
   tion
Splash
The Thirteenth Floor
Twisted
Who Framed Roger Rabbit

Parenthood

See also: Bad Dads; Bringing
   Up Baby; Dads; Moms; Mon-
   ster Moms; Single Parents;
   Stepparents
Aliens (SE)
Big Daddy
Crooklyn
The Deep End of the Ocean
Flirting with Disaster
Forbidden Planet
Hope Floats
Liar Liar
Matilda
My Mom's a Werewolf
On Golden Pond
The Parent Trap
Parenthood
Parents
Penny Serenade
The Red House
Red River
The Santa Clause
Stella Dallas
Tea with Mussolini
Tequila Sunrise

Party Hell
Hell Night
Meet Wally Sparks
Prom Night
Rabid Grannies
The Rage: Carrie 2

Patriotism & Paranoia

See also: Propaganda
Born on the Fourth of July
First Blood
Guilty by Suspicion
Ivan the Terrible, Part 1
Ivan the Terrible, Part 2
Nixon
Patton
Rambo: First Blood, Part 2
Rambo 3
Red Dawn
The Siege

Peculiar Partners

See also: Buddy Cops; Cops
Cop and a Half
The Glimmer Man
Gridlock'd
The Hard Way
The Hidden
Judge Dredd
K-9
Top Dog

Period Piece

See also: Historical Drama;
   Medieval Romps; Royalty
The Great Conqueror's Concu-
   bine
The Great Conqueror's Concu-
   bine, Part 2

Maria Stuarda
Rouge

Period Piece: 15th Century
Joan of Arc

Period Piece: 16th Century
Dangerous Beauty
Elizabeth
Henry V
Ivan the Terrible, Part 1
Ivan the Terrible, Part 2
Kama Sutra: A Tale of Love
Orlando
Seven Samurai
Shakespeare in Love (CS)

Period Piece: 17th Century
Black Robe
Ever After: A Cinderella Story
The Four Musketeers
The Man in the Iron Mask
Restoration
The Three Musketeers
The Three Musketeers
The Three Musketeers

Period Piece: 18th Century
Amadeus
Barry Lyndon
Dangerous Liaisons
Gulliver's Travels
Interview with the Vampire
Les Miserables
Mesmer
Moll Flanders
Orlando
Rob Roy
The Scarlet Pimpernel
Sleepy Hollow
Tom Jones

Period Piece: 19th Century
Anna Karenina
Belle of the Nineties
The Bostonians
A Christmas Carol
Cousin Bette
Dracula
Emma
Far and Away
Frankenstein
Geronimo: An American Leg-
   end
The Governess
Great Expectations
The Great Train Robbery
The Hound of the
   Baskervilles
Interview with the Vampire
The Jack Bull
Jamaica Inn
Jezebel
The King and I
The King and I
Life with Father
Little Women
Mesmerized
Mrs. Brown
Oliver!
Oliver Twist
Orlando
The Phantom of the Opera
The Phantom of the Opera
The Piano
Portrait of a Lady
Pride and Prejudice
Ravenous
The Secret Garden
Sense and Sensibility
Show Boat
Sommersby
Spring Symphony
Swept from the Sea
Total Eclipse
Wild Wild West

Period Piece: 20th Century
Interview with the Vampire
The Last Emperor
Legends of the Fall
Nicholas and Alexandra
Orlando
Rasputin the Mad Monk

Period Piece: 1900s
Fiddler on the Roof
Like Water for Chocolate
My Fair Lady
A River Runs Through It
William Shakespeare's A Midsummer Night's Dream

Period Piece: 1910s
The Englishman Who Went up a Hill But Came down a Mountain
From Dusk Till Dawn 3: The Hangman's Daughter
Howard's End
A Little Princess
Michael Collins
Peking Opera Blues
Sarah, Plain and Tall
Sarah, Plain and Tall: Winter's End
Skylark
The Wings of the Dove

Period Piece: 1920s
Bullets over Broadway
The Front Page
The Jazz Singer
Killer: A Journal of Murder
Legionnaire
Mrs. Dalloway
Mister Johnson
The Mummy
My Life So Far
The Newton Boys
The Quest
Rosewood
Where the Rivers Flow North

Period Piece: 1930s
The Field
The Hindenburg
A Merry War
Sirens
Tea with Mussolini
The Thirteenth Floor
This Is My Father

Period Piece: 1940s
Bugsy
Devil in a Blue Dress
Farewell, My Lovely
Hong Kong 1941
A League of Their Own
The Power of One
The Quarrel
Stand-Ins
The Two Jakes
Village of Dreams

Period Piece: 1950s
Badlands
Big Night
The Buddy Holly Story
Bye, Bye, Birdie
Circle of Friends
The Climb
Corrina, Corrina
Dead Poets Society
Dirty Dancing
Dirty Dancing (CE)
Fall Time
Guilty by Suspicion
The Hudsucker Proxy
A King in New York / A Woman in Paris
La Bamba
L.A. Confidential
Once Upon a Time . . . When We Were Colored
Parents
Peggy Sue Got Married
Pillow Talk
Porky's
Quiz Show

School Ties
Shadowlands
A Stranger in the Kingdom
The War of the Worlds
Who Shot Pat?
The Wild One

Period Piece: 1960s
American Graffiti
Austin Powers 2: The Spy Who Shagged Me
The Big Chill
Born on the Fourth of July
The Bridges of Madison County
A Bronx Tale
Children Shouldn't Play with Dead Things
Conspiracy: The Trial of the Chicago Eight
Dead Presidents
Digging to China
The Doors
Easy Rider
Five Corners
From the Earth to the Moon
Grace of My Heart (CE)
Hair
Hideous Kinky
Matinee
Metroland
Rainbow Bridge
The '60s
Telling Lies in America
A Walk on the Moon
Wild Reeds
Woodstock (DC)
Yellow Submarine

Period Piece: 1970s
Armistead Maupin's More Tales of the City
Boogie Nights
Casino
Crooklyn
Dazed and Confused
Detroit Rock City
Donnie Brasco
Drugstore Cowboy
Fear and Loathing in Las Vegas
54
From the Earth to the Moon
Hideous Kinky
Joe the King
Man on the Moon
Metroland
Slums of Beverly Hills
Summer of Sam
Velvet Goldmine
The War
Without Limits
Xiu Xiu: The Sent Down Girl

Period Piece: 1980s
Apt Pupil
The Assignment
The Last Days of Disco
Man on the Moon
SLC Punk!
200 Cigarettes
Velvet Goldmine
The Wedding Singer

Persian Gulf War
See also: Desert War/Foreign Legion
Tactical Assault

Philanthropy
See: Kindness of Strangers

Phobias!
Arachnophobia
Blackjack
Body Double
Copycat
Vertigo (CE)

Phone Terror
Don't Answer the Phone
I Saw What You Did
Scream (CS)

Scream 2
When a Stranger Calls Back

Photography
See: Shutterbugs

Physical Problems
See also: Blindness; Deafness; Mental Retardation
The Big Lebowski
The Bone Collector
Born on the Fourth of July
The Brute Man
Choices
Closer and Closer
Eden
Fallen Angels
Good Luck
Gray's Anatomy
Hugo Pool
The Hunchback of Notre Dame
Love Affair
Mask
My Left Foot
Passion Fish
The People vs. Larry Flynt
The Phantom of the Opera
Powder
Rumble in the Bronx
Scent of a Woman
Stella Maris
Suite 16
Things to Do in Denver When You're Dead
What Ever Happened to Baby Jane?
Wild Wild West

Pigs
Babe
Babe: Pig in the City
Doc Hollywood

Pill Poppin'
See also: On the Rocks
Above the Law
Air America
Altered States
Another Day in Paradise
Avenging Disco Godfather
Bad Boys
Bad Lieutenant
The Basketball Diaries
Belly
The Big Lebowski
Black Circle Boys
Boogie Nights
Born to Win
A Brother's Kiss
Carlito's Way
Cartel
Casino
Cause of Death
Chappaqua
Clean and Sober
Clockers
Corridors of Blood
Crackdown
The Crow 2: City of Angels
Dazed and Confused
Dead Presidents
Dead Ringers
Deep Cover
Desperado
Desperado / El Mariachi
Dr. Jekyll and Mr. Hyde
Down in the Delta
Drugstore Cowboy
Drunks
Easy Rider
Enter the Dragon (SE)
Fear and Loathing in Las Vegas
54
Flesh
Fletch
Frances
Friday
Georgia
Go
Godmoney

Goodfellas
Gridlock'd
Half-Baked
Heat
Hugo Pool
Jane Doe
Keys to Tulsa
Kids
La Bamba
Lethal Weapon
License to Kill
Light Sleeper
Live and Let Die
Marked for Death
Midnight Express
Mob War
The Mod Squad
New Jack City
Nico Icon
One Man's Justice
The People vs. Larry Flynt
Permanent Midnight
Point of No Return
Pulp Fiction
Red Heat
Red Surf
Reefer Madness
Return to Paradise
Rude
Scarface
The Seven-Per-Cent Solution
Shameless
Showdown in Little Tokyo
Sid & Nancy
The '60s
SLC Punk!
Strange Days
Street Wars
The Substitute
Suicide Kings
The Sweet Hereafter
The Temptations
Tequila Sunrise
The Third Man
The Tingler
Tombstone
Trainspotting
Trash
Trespass
True Romance
The Usual Suspects
Velvet Goldmine
Why Do Fools Fall in Love?
Woodstock (DC)

The Pink Panther
The Pink Panther
The Pink Panther Strikes Again
Revenge of the Pink Panther
A Shot in the Dark

Pirates
See also: Island Fare; Sail Away; Swashbucklers
The Black Pirate
Cutthroat Island
Peter Pan
The Phantom
The Princess and the Pirate
The Princess Bride
Six Days, Seven Nights
Space Truckers
Swashbuckler
Treasure Island

Poetry
Poetic Justice
The Postman
Tales of Ordinary Madness
Total Eclipse

Poisons
D.O.A.

Polish (Production)
The Decalogue

Politics
See also: Capitol Capers; Presidency
Absolute Power
The American President

Animal Instincts
The Big Brass Ring
The Birdcage
Bulworth
The Candidate
Casino
City Hall
Clear and Present Danger
Conspiracy: The Trial of the Chicago Eight
Dave
Devil in a Blue Dress
The Distinguished Gentleman
Don's Party
Elizabeth
Evita
G.I. Jane
Guilty by Suspicion
I Am Cuba
An Ideal Husband
In the Line of Fire
In the Name of the Father
JFK
Kundun
Les Miserables
Little Mother
The Manchurian Candidate
The Matchmaker
Meet Wally Sparks
Michael Collins
Nick of Time
Nixon
The Pelican Brief
Presumed Innocent
Primary Colors
Salt of the Earth
Striptease
Supreme Sanction
Temptation of a Monk
Timecop
Wag the Dog
The War Room
Wild Reeds

Pool
See also: Gambling
Albino Alligator
The Color of Money
Kiss Shot

Pornography
See also: Sex & Sexuality; Sexploitation
Body Double
Boogie Nights
The People vs. Larry Flynt

Portuguese (Production)
Black Orpheus
Return of the Blind Dead
Tombs of the Blind Dead

Post Apocalypse
See also: Negative Utopia; Technology—Rampant
A Boy and His Dog
Cold Harvest
Cyborg
Day of the Dead
Double Dragon
Fist of the North Star
Judge Dredd
Mad Max
Mad Max: Beyond Thunderdome
The Matrix
Nemesis
The Postman
The Road Warrior
RoboCop
Screamers
The Seventh Sign
Silent Running
Soldier
Stephen King's The Stand
Terminator 2: Judgment Day
12 Monkeys
Waterworld

Postwar
See also: Veterans
The Best Years of Our Lives

The Cowboy Way
8 Seconds
Junior Bonner
Man from Utah / Sagebrush
  Trail
Stir Crazy

Rodgers & Hammerstein
Carousel
The King and I
Oklahoma
South Pacific

Role Reversal
See also: Gender Bending
All of Me
Babe
Big
Billy Madison
Coming to America
Condorman
Dave
Dr. Jekyll and Mr. Hyde
Hero
Iron Maze
Junior
La Femme Nikita
The Lady Vanishes
Male and Female
My Blue Heaven
My Fair Lady
Overboard
Point of No Return
Psycho (CE)
Raid on Rommel
The Scarlet Pimpernel
Showdown in Little Tokyo
Sommersby
White Man's Burden
Wonder Man

Romance
*See: Late Bloomin' Love;
Lovers on the Lam;
May–December Romance;
Otherwise Engaged; Romantic
Comedy; Romantic Drama;
Romantic Triangles*

Romantic Comedy
About Last Night . . .
Adam's Rib
Addicted to Love
The Allnighter
Amarilly of Clothesline Alley
The American President
Annie Hall
Arthur
As Good As It Gets
Ball of Fire
Barefoot in the Park
Battling Butler
Better Than Chocolate
Billy's Hollywood Screen Kiss
Blast from the Past
Born Yesterday
Boyfriends & Girlfriends
Breakfast at Tiffany's
Bull Durham
Can't Hardly Wait
Career Opportunities
Chances Are
Changing Habits
Clueless
Coming to America
Court Jester
Creator
Curtain Call
Dance with Me
Dirty Rotten Scoundrels
Doc Hollywood
Don't Do It
Eat Your Heart Out
The Englishman Who Went up
  a Hill But Came down a
  Mountain
Fools Rush In
Four Weddings and a Funeral
French Kiss
Groundhog Day
Her Alibi
Home Fries

Honeymoon in Vegas
I Love Trouble
It Happened One Night
Jerry Maguire
Just a Little Harmless Sex
Just the Ticket
Just Write
King Ralph
Kiss Shot
Kissing a Fool
La Collectionneuse
L.A. Story
Le Beau Mariage
The Leading Man
Legal Eagles
The Lonely Guy
Look Who's Talking
Looking for Lola
Love Jones
Lovers and Liars
Made in America
Male and Female
The Matchmaker
Miami Rhapsody
Michael
Milk and Money
The Millionairess
Minnie and Moskowitz
The Mirror Has Two Faces
Mr. Jealousy
Mr. Wonderful
Moonstruck
Much Ado about Nothing
My Best Friend's Wedding
My Night at Maud's
My Stepmother Is an Alien
Never Been Kissed
Notting Hill
On Approval
Only You
The Other Sister
Outrageous Fortune
Overboard
Peggy Sue Got Married
Picture Perfect
Pillow Talk
The Pompatus of Love
Practical Magic
Pretty Woman
The Princess and the Pirate
Protocol
Pyaar Kiya to Darna Kya
Pyar to Hona Hi Tah
Quackser Fortune Has a
  Cousin in the Bronx
Queens Logic
The Quiet Man
Reality Bites
The Secret of My Success
The Sex Monster
Shakespeare in Love (CS)
She's All That
Simply Irresistible
Singles
Sixteen Candles
Sleepless in Seattle
Something About Sex
Splash
Splendor
Sprung
Stolen Kisses
The Story of Us
Sweet Talker
That Old Feeling
That Uncertain Feeling
There's Something about
  Mary
They Call Me Covered
Tillie's Punctured Romance
Tin Cup
To Cross the Rubicon
Tom Jones
Trick
Twice upon a Yesterday
The Very Thought of You
The Wedding Singer
While You Were Sleeping
William Shakespeare's A Mid-
  summer Night's Dream
Woman of the Year
You've Got Mail

Zeus and Roxanne

Romantic Drama
Alegria
Alive and Kicking
Always
Anna Karenina
At First Sight
Bad Love
Beauty and the Beast
Bed of Roses
Before Sunrise
Besieged
Blood and Sand
The Boxer
The Bridges of Madison
  County
Cabo Blanco / U.S. Marshal
Casablanca
Center Stage
C'est la Vie, Mon Cherie
Circle of Friends
Come and Get It
Corrina, Corrina
Daddy Long Legs
Damage
Dangerous Beauty
Dangerous Liaisons
Dark Odyssey
Don Juan DeMarco
8 Seconds
Emma
The English Patient
The Fantastic Night
Far and Away
First Knight
Full Moon in Paris
Gone with the Wind
The Governess
Guinevere
Havana
Hong Kong 1941
Hope Floats
The Horse Whisperer
In Love and War
In the Shadows
Infinity
Jane Doe
Jungle Fever
La Separation
La Traviata
The Last Time I Saw Paris
Legends of the Fall
Limbo
Love Affair
Love After Love
Lulu on the Bridge
Mad Love
Medicine Man
Men
Message in a Bottle
Of Mice and Men
The Phantom of the Opera
The Piano
Playing by Heart
Poetic Justice
Pride and Prejudice
Pure Country
Rachel's Man
The Return of Martin Guerre
The Ring
Rob Roy
Romeo and Juliet
Rouge
Santa Fe
Sarah, Plain and Tall
Sense and Sensibility
Shoot the Piano Player
The Soft Skin
A Soldier's Tale
Somewhere in Time
Sommersby
Summertime
Swept from the Sea
Tender Mercies
Tess of the Storm Country
Thakshak
36 Fillete
This Is My Father
Tim
True Romance
Two English Girls

The Unbearable Lightness of
  Being
Up Close and Personal
Virasat
Vive l'Amour
A Walk on the Moon
West Side Story
What Dreams May Come
White Palace
William Shakespeare's
  Romeo and Juliet
The Wings of the Dove
The Woman Next Door
Wuthering Heights

Romantic Triangles
See also: Otherwise Engaged
The Alley Cats
Body Heat
Broadcast News
Bull Durham
Casablanca
Casino
Damage
Dead Ringers
Emma
The English Patient
Everyone Says I Love You
First Knight
The First Wives Club
French Kiss
The Getaway
The Getaway
Goodbye, Lover
Henry & June
Hilary and Jackie
Hong Kong 1941
In the Shadows
Interlocked
Kissing a Fool
The Leading Man
Legends of the Fall
Love, etc.
Mr. Jealousy
Money Train
My Best Friend's Wedding
Once a Thief
One Night Stand
Only You
Opposite of Sex
Palmetto
The Philadelphia Story
Playing by Heart
Polish Wedding
A Price above Rubies
Pushing Tin
Reality Bites
Restoration
Revenge
Robin Hood: Prince of
  Thieves
Scorned 2
Sex and the Other Man
The Sex Monster
Slaves to the Underground
Sleepless in Seattle
Sliding Doors
Sommersby
Splendor
Stella Maris
Stonewall
Tequila Sunrise
There's Something about
  Mary
A Thin Line Between Love
  and Hate
Tin Cup
Twice upon a Yesterday
Twister
U-Turn
The Unbearable Lightness of
  Being
The Underneath
Vive l'Amour
A Walk on the Moon
While You Were Sleeping
Wild Things
The Wings of the Dove

Roommates from Hell
See also:

Psychotics/Sociopaths
Malice
Shallow Grave
Single White Female

Royalty
*See also: Historical Drama;
Medieval Romps; Period Piece*
Alexander Nevsky
Anastasia
Caligula
Chariots of Fire
Cinderella
Cleopatra
Coming to America
Court Jester
Dragonheart (SE)
Elizabeth
The Emperor's Shadow
Ever After: A Cinderella Story
Excalibur
First Knight
Guinevere
Henry V
Ivan the Terrible, Part 1
Ivan the Terrible, Part 2
Joan of Arc
Kama Sutra: A Tale of Love
A Kid in Aladdin's Palace
The King and I
The King and I
A King in New York / A
  Woman in Paris
King Ralph
The Last Emperor
Lav Kush
Lover of the Last Empress
The Man in the Iron Mask
The Man Who Would Be King
Maria Stuarda
Merlin
Mrs. Brown
Mulan
Nicholas and Alexandra
Orlando
Quest for Camelot
Rasputin the Mad Monk
Restoration
Return to Oz
Shakespeare in Love (CS)
Storm over Asia
The Three Musketeers

Russian (Production)
Aelita: Queen of Mars
Alexander Nevsky
Andrei Rublev
The Battleship Potemkin
I Am Cuba
Ivan the Terrible, Part 1
Ivan the Terrible, Part 2
The Man with the Movie Cam-
  era
Masters of Russian Anima-
  tion, Vol. 1
Mother
Solaris
Storm over Asia
Ten Days That Shook the
  World

Sail Away
*See also: Deep Blue; Go Fish;
Killer Sea Critters; Mutiny;
Scuba; Shipwrecked; Sub-
marines*
And the Ship Sails On
Away All Boats
The Battleship Potemkin
Beat the Devil
The Caine Mutiny
Crimson Tide
Das Boot (DC)
Dead Calm
The Deep
Deep Rising
Die Hard: With a Vengeance
The Fighting Sullivans
Going Overboard
The Hunt for Red October
The Imposters

Tetsuo 2: Body Hammer
The Thing
Time Masters
Timecop
Timelock
Total Recall
Total Recall 2070: Machine
Dreams
Tron
12 Monkeys
Two Lost Worlds
2001: A Space Odyssey
2010: The Year We Make
Contact
Urban Menace
The Venus Wars
Village of the Damned
Virtual Combat
Virtuosity
Virus
Voltage Fighters! Gowcaizer:
The Movie
The War of the Worlds
Waterworld
Weird Science
Westworld
Wicked City
A Wind Named Amnesia
Wing Commander
Within the Rock
The X-Files
Xtro 3: Watch the Skies
Zcram

Science & Scientists

See also: Genetics; Inventors
& Inventions; Mad Scientists
Altered States
The Andromeda Strain
Assassin
Contact
Dark Star
Darkman
Deep Blue Sea
The 4D Man
Gattaca
Habitat
Infinity
Junior
The Man with Two Brains
Medicine Man
Mimic
My Science Project
My Stepmother Is an Alien
October Sky
Outbreak
Senseless
The Thing
Titanica
Trinity and Beyond: The Atom-
ic Bomb Movie
Unknown Island
Virus

Screwball Comedy

See also: Comedy; Romantic
Comedy; Slapstick Comedy
As You Like It
The Chaplin Mutuals, Vol. 1
The Chaplin Mutuals, Vol. 2
The Chaplin Mutuals, Vol. 3
Chaplin's Art of Comedy
Chaplin's Essanay Comedies,
Vol. 1
Chaplin's Essanay Comedies,
Vol. 2
Chaplin's Essanay Comedies,
Vol. 3
The Circus
Forces of Nature
A Hard Day's Night
A Life Less Ordinary
Meatballs
My Man Godfrey
The Naked Truth
National Lampoon's Christ-
mas Vacation
National Lampoon's Vacation
Nothing Sacred
Stir Crazy
Stroker Ace

The Swinging Cheerleaders
Waltz of the Toreadors

Scuba

See also: Deep Blue
The Abyss (SE)
Beneath the 12-Mile Reef
The Deep
Leviathan
Navy SEALS
Thunderball

Sculptors

See also: Art & Artists
Fly Away Home
The Juror

Sea Disasters

See also: Air Disasters; Deep
Blue; Disaster Flicks; Ship-
wrecked
The Abyss (SE)
Das Boot (DC)
Deep Rising
Leviathan
A Night to Remember
The Poseidon Adventure
Waterworld

Serial Killers

See also: Crime & Criminals;
Crime Sprees
American Strays
American Streetfighter 2: The
Full Impact
The Bone Collector
Bride of Chucky
Clay Pigeons
Closer and Closer
Con Air
Copycat
Diary of a Serial Killer
Dirty Harry
Ed McBain's 87 Precinct
Fallen
The Fear: Halloween Night
Felicia's Journey
The Frighteners
The Glimmer Man
Henry: Portrait of a Serial
Killer
Henry: Portrait of a Serial
Killer 2: Mask of Sanity
In Dreams
The Invisible Strangler
Jack Frost
Kalifornia
Kiss the Girls
Laser Moon
M
Maniac Cop
The Monster
Never Talk to Strangers
Postmortem
Ravenous
Resurrection
Scream (CS)
Scream 2
Serial Mom
Seven
Silence of the Lambs
So I Married an Axe Murderer
Stranger by Night
Striking Distance
Summer of Sam
Switchback
To Catch a Killer
True Crime
Turbulence
The Ugly
Urban Menace
Witchcraft 10: Mistress of
the Craft

The Seventies

See: Period Piece: 1970s

Sex & Sexuality

See also: Crimes of Passion;
Erotic Thrillers; Pornography;
Sex on the Beach; Sexploita-

tion
The Alley Cats
The Allnighter
American Gigolo
American Pie (CE)
Animal Instincts
Animal Instincts 3: The
Seductress
Armistead Maupin's More
Tales of the City
Barbarella
Beau Pere
Before Sunrise
Belle of the Nineties
Better Than Chocolate
The Blood Oranges
The Blue Lagoon
Body Double
Body of Influence 2
Booty Call
A Boy and His Dog
Caligula
Camille 2000
The Canterbury Tales
Carmen, Baby
Carnal Crimes
Casual Sex?
Cat on a Hot Tin Roof
Cat People
Claire's Knee
Cleopatra
Color of Night
Cruel Intentions
Cry Uncle
Damage
Dangerous Liaisons
The Decameron
Def Jam's How to Be a Player
The Devil's Nightmare
Die Watching
The Dirty Girls
The Disenchanted
Dog Day Afternoon
Don's Party
Elizabeth
Embrace of the Vampire
Emmanuelle
Emmanuelle, the Joys of a
Woman
Exotica
Extramarital
Eyes Wide Shut
Femalien
54
Flesh
Flesh Gordon
Friend of the Family
Friend of the Family 2
The General's Daughter
The Girl on a Motorcycle
Glen or Glenda?
Goodbye, Lover
Habit
Happiness
Hard Drive
The Hot Spot
I, a Woman
I Like to Play Games
I'm No Angel
In the Realm of the Senses
Kids
Kika
Killer Condom
La Collectionneuse
Lap Dancing
Last Breath
Last Tango in Paris
The Law
The Lickerish Quartet
The Life of Jesus
Lifeforce
Like Water for Chocolate
Lipstick Camera
Little Mother
Lolida 2000
Lolita
Love After Love
The Love Goddesses
Masseuse
Metroland
Mischievous

Montenegro
Monty Python's The Meaning
of Life
Motel Blue
My Life to Live
My Teacher's Wife
Never Talk to Strangers
New Rose Hotel
Night Fire
Novel Desires
One Night Stand
Over the Wire
Peeping Tom
Play Time
Poison Ivy
Poison Ivy 2: Lily
Poison Ivy 3: The New Seduc-
tion
The Postman Always Rings
Twice
Pretty Woman
Rain
Raising Cain
Rambling Rose
The Red Violin
Romance
Score
Scorned 2
Sea of Love
Secret Games 3
The Seventh Sense
Sex and the Other Man
Sex and Zen
Sex Is . . .
Sexual Malice
Sexual Roulette
Silk 'n' Sabotage
Sirens
Something About Sex
Sprung
Star 80
Suite 16
Swingers
Tale of Two Sisters
Terrified
Therese & Isabelle
36 Fillete
Tokyo Decadence
Tom Jones
Trash
The Unbearable Lightness of
Being
Watch Me
Wild Things
The Witches of Eastwick
The Woman Next Door
Your Friends & Neighbors

Sex on the Beach

See also: Island Fare
The Blue Lagoon
The Firm
Swept Away . . .
Swept from the Sea

Sexcapades

Andy Warhol's Dracula
Andy Warhol's Frankenstein
Angel Heart
Another 9 1/2 Weeks
Bad Lieutenant
Crash
Crimes of Passion
The First 9 1/2 Weeks
Henry & June
Jade
Kama Sutra: A Tale of Love
9 1/2 Weeks
The Pillow Book
sex, lies and videotape

Sexploitation

See also: Erotic Thrillers;
Exploitation
Angel Heart
Awakening of Gabriella
The Big Doll House
The Bikini Car Wash Company
Carnal Crimes
Def Jam's How to Be a Player
Emmanuelle

Emmanuelle: Queen of the
Desert
Emmanuelle, the Joys of a
Woman
Erotic Ghost Story
Erotic Ghost Story: Perfect
Match
Firehouse
Flesh Gordon
The Fruit Is Swelling
Jane Street
Key to Sex
Life of a Gigolo
Lips of Blood
The Living Dead Girl
Loveblind
Naked Killer
Night Calls: The Movie
Night Calls: The Movie 2
Playgirls and the Vampire
The Price of Desire
Sex and Zen
She Devils in Chains
The Sinful Nuns of Saint
Valentine
Sorority Babes in the Slime-
ball Bowl-A-Rama
Striking Resemblance
Succubus
The Swinging Cheerleaders
Tokyo Decadence
Web of Seduction
Witchcraft 2: The Temptress
Word of Mouth

Sexual Abuse

See also: Incest; Rape;
Spousal Abuse
Mesmerized
Priest

Sexual Harrassment

Disclosure
G.I. Jane

William Shakespeare

See also: Modern Shake-
speare
As You Like It
Henry V
Much Ado about Nothing
Othello
Ran
Romeo and Juliet
Shakespeare in Love (CS)
Ten Things I Hate about You
Tromeo & Juliet
West Side Story
William Shakespeare's A Mid-
summer Night's Dream
William Shakespeare's
Romeo and Juliet

Sherlock Holmes

The Hound of the
Baskervilles
The Seven-Per-Cent Solution
Sherlock Holmes Consulting
Detective, Vol. 1
They Might Be Giants

Ships

See: Deep Blue; Mutiny; Sail
Away; Shipwrecked; Sub-
marines

Shipwrecked

See also: Sea Disasters
The Black Pirate
The Black Stallion
The Blue Lagoon
Male and Female
The Most Dangerous Game
Rich and Strange
Swept Away . . .
Swept from the Sea
Two Lost Worlds

Showbiz Comedies

Being John Malkovich
Blazing Saddles
Bowfinger

Mr. Baseball
Monty Python's The Meaning of Life
National Lampoon's Golf Punks
Slap Shot
Space Jam
Tin Cup
The Waterboy

Sports Dramas
Chariots of Fire
The Color of Money
Days of Thunder
8 Seconds
The Fan
Futuresport
Grambling's White Tiger
He Got Game
Hoosiers
The Pride of the Yankees
Raging Bull
Red Surf
Rocky
Rocky 2
Rocky 4
School Ties
This Sporting Life
Varsity Blues
Victory
Vision Quest
Without Limits

Spousal Abuse
See also: Sexual Abuse
The Break Up
Falling Down
Mesmerized
Mortal Thoughts
What's Love Got to Do with It?

Stagestruck
See also: Showbiz Comedies; Showbiz Dramas; Showbiz Thrillers
All About Eve
Bullets over Broadway
Interview with the Vampire
The Leading Man
Shakespeare in Love (CS)
William Shakespeare's A Midsummer Night's Dream

Stalked!
See also: Obsessive Love
Addicted to Love
The Cable Guy
Copycat
The Fan
The Gingerbread Man
Return of the Boogeyman
Taxi Driver (CE)

Star Gazing
The Arrival
My Stepmother Is an Alien

Stepparents
See also: Family Ties; Parenthood
Beau Pere
Ever After: A Cinderella Story
Everyone Says I Love You
Fear
Snow White: A Tale of Terror
Stepmom

Stewardesses
See also: Airborne
Executive Decision
Turbulence

Strained Suburbia
See also: Yuppie Nightmares
Arlington Road
Beavis and Butt-Head Do America
The 'Burbs
Home Alone
Home Alone 3
Hugo Pool

Marked for Death
My Blue Heaven
1941
Parents
Serial Mom
The Stepford Wives
The Stranger
The Trigger Effect
Your Friends & Neighbors

Strippers
Dangerous Ground
Exotica
From Dusk Till Dawn
The Full Monty
Heaven
Keys to Tulsa
Lap Dancing
The Last Word
Pecker
The Players Club
Strip Search
Stripshow
Striptease
Tin Cup
True Lies
Under Siege

Struggling Musicians
Gridlock'd
Jack Frost
Purple Rain
Streets of Fire
Sucker the Vampire
Tender Mercies
This Is Spinal Tap
Without Air

Stupid Is...
Bean
Beavis and Butt-Head Do America
Billy Madison
Caddyshack
Chairman of the Board
Dumb & Dumber
Half-Baked
Happy Gilmore
The Jerk
Lock, Stock and 2 Smoking Barrels
National Lampoon's Animal House
Pee-wee's Big Adventure
Romy and Michele's High School Reunion
Son-in-Law
Tommy Boy
The Waterboy

Submarines
See also: Deep Blue
The Abyss (SE)
Atomic Submarine
Crimson Tide
Das Boot (DC)
For Your Eyes Only (SE)
The Hunt for Red October
The Inside Man
Leviathan
1941
Operation Delta Force 2: Mayday
Operation Delta Force 3: Clear Target
The Spy Who Loved Me (SE)
20,000 Leagues under the Sea
Yellow Submarine

Subways
See also: Trains
Adventures in Babysitting
Carlito's Way
Die Hard: With a Vengeance
The Fugitive
Highlander 2: The Quickening
The Jackal (CE)
Lethal Weapon 3
Mimic
Money Train
Risky Business

Sliding Doors
Speed
Subway
Trick

Suicide
See also: Death & the Afterlife
Absence of Malice
Alien3
American Strays
Autopsy
The Big Chill
Cookie's Fortune
Crumb
The Curve
Dead Man on Campus
Dead Poets Society
Father's Day
The First Wives Club
Frozen
Heat
Heathers
The Hudsucker Proxy
It's a Wonderful Life
Last Tango in Paris
Leaving Las Vegas
Mrs. Dalloway
One Flew Over the Cuckoo's Nest
Peeping Tom
Primary Colors
Romeo and Juliet
Scent of a Woman
Stealing Home
Stella Maris
The Taste of Cherry
What Dreams May Come

Summer Camp
Deliverance
Evil Dead
Friday the 13th
Friday the 13th, Part 2
The Great Outdoors
Grizzly
Meatballs
The Parent Trap
The River Wild

Super Heroes
Batman
Batman and Robin
Batman Forever
Batman Returns
Black Mask
The Chosen One: Legend of the Raven
8 Man After: The Perfect Collection
Flash Gordon
The Mask
Mystery Men
The Phantom
The Punisher
Sgt. Kabukiman N.Y.P.D.
The Shadow
Spawn (SE)
The Superman Cartoons of Max & Dave Fleischer
Superman, the Lost Episodes
Todd McFarlane's Spawn
Todd McFarlane's Spawn 2
The Toxic Avenger, Part 2

Supernatural Comedies
See also: Comedy
Angel in Training
Beetlejuice
Bell, Book and Candle
The Craft
The Frighteners
Ghostbusters
Ghostbusters 2
Heart and Souls
Matilda
Michael

Supernatural Horror
See also: Classic Horror
Candyman
Christine

Curse of the Voodoo
Deep Red: Hatchet Murders
Def by Temptation
Demons
Demons 2
The Devil's Nightmare
Devil's Rain
Devonsville Terror
Embrace of the Vampire
Erotic Ghost Story: Perfect Match
The Exorcist (SE)
Fallen
Firestarter
From Dusk Till Dawn
Ghost Story
Hellbound: Hellraiser 2
Hellraiser
Horror Express
The Indestructible Man / The Amazing Transparent Man
Inferno
Kill, Baby, Kill
Lisa and the Devil / The House of Exorcism
Lord of Illusions
Maniac / Narcotic
Mark of the Devil
The Night Stalker
The Night Strangler
Phantasm
Phantoms
Poltergeist
The Prophecy
Rawhead Rex
The Relic
Revolt of the Zombies
Sorceress
Stephen King's The Storm of the Century
Stephen King's Thinner
Stir of Echoes
Witchcraft 10: Mistress of the Craft

Supernatural Martial Arts
The Crow
The Heroic Trio
The Legend of the 7 Golden Vampires
Sgt. Kabukiman N.Y.P.D.
Zu: Warriors of the Magic Mountain

Supernatural Westerns
John Carpenter's Vampires

Surfing
Blue Juice
Chairman of the Board
The Endless Summer
Escape from L.A.
In God's Hands
Lauderdale
Red Surf
Surf Crazy
Surf Nazis Must Die (DC)

Survival
See also: Hunted!; Negative Utopia; Post Apocalypse
Bat 21
Black Rain
Cliffhanger
The Colony
Cool Hand Luke
Das Boot (DC)
Daylight
Dead Calm
Deliverance
Fearless
High Noon
The Island at the Top of the World
Jeremiah Johnson
The Last Flight of Noah's Ark
Legionnaire
Limbo
Male and Female
The Most Dangerous Game
Nightmare at Noon

The Poseidon Adventure
Six Days, Seven Nights
Stagecoach
The Terror
Thief
Trucks
Two Women
Walkabout
Waterworld
Wild America

Suspended Animation
Aliens (SE)
Alien3
Austin Powers: International Man of Mystery
Chances Are
Coma
Encino Man
Forever Young

Suspense
See also: Mystery & Suspense
Arlington Road
The Best Revenge
The Devil's Advocate
Sphere
Suspicions
Zeder

Swashbucklers
See also: Action-Adventure; Fencing; Medieval Romps
The Black Pirate
Court Jester
Cutthroat Island
Don Juan DeMarco
The Four Musketeers
The Man in the Iron Mask
Mark of Zorro
The Mask of Zorro
Monty Python's The Meaning of Life
The Phantom
The Princess and the Pirate
The Princess Bride
The Scarlet Pimpernel
Swashbuckler
Three Amigos
The Three Musketeers
The Three Musketeers
Three Musketeers
The Three Musketeers
Treasure Island
Two Lost Worlds

Swedish (Production)
Elvira Madigan
Evil Ed
I, a Woman
The Inside Man
Intermezzo
June Night
Montenegro
My Life As a Dog
The Seventh Seal
Terror of Frankenstein

Swingers
9 1/2 Weeks
The Swinging Cheerleaders
Your Friends & Neighbors

Taiwanese (Production)
Vive l'Amour

Talking Animals
See also: Wild Kingdom
Babe
Babe: Pig in the City
Dr. Dolittle
George of the Jungle
Homeward Bound: The Incredible Journey
Paulie
Stuart Little

Tattoos
The Crow 2: City of Angels
Escape from L.A.
Son-in-Law
Waterworld

Mark of the Devil
Practical Magic
Return to Oz
Sleepy Hollow
Snow White: A Tale of Terror
Sorceress
Warlock
Warlock: The Armageddon
Warlock 3: The End of Inno-
cence
Witchcraft
Witchcraft 9: Bitter Flesh
Witchcraft 10: Mistress of
the Craft
The Witches
The Witches of Eastwick
Witchouse
The Wizard of Oz
The Woman Who Came Back

Witness Protection
Program

*See also: Organized Crime;
U.S. Marshals*
Eraser
Lethal Weapon 2
My Blue Heaven

Women

*See also: Femme Fatale;
Moms; Westrogens; Women
Cops; Women in Prison;
Women in War; Wonder
Women*
The Bostonians
Boys on the Side
The Color Purple
Deconstructing Harry
The Dreamlife of Angels
Eddie
Evita
The First Wives Club
Fried Green Tomatoes
From the Journals of Jean
Seberg
G.I. Jane
Grace of My Heart (CE)
The Heroic Trio
House of Whipcord
How to Be a Woman and Not
Die in the Attempt
How to Make an American
Quilt
Juliet of the Spirits
A League of Their Own
Little Mother
Little Women
Lola Montes
Love After Love
The Love Goddesses
Moll Flanders
Mortal Thoughts
Now and Then
One True Thing
Passion Fish
The Pillow Book
Poetic Justice
Portrait of a Lady
A Price above Rubies
Set It Off
What's Love Got to Do with
It?
Women in Revolt
The Wonderful, Horrible Life
of Leni Riefenstahl

Women Cops

See also: Cops
China O'Brien
Copycat
The Deep End of the Ocean

Fargo
The Mod Squad
Silence of the Lambs

Women in Prison

*See also: Exploitation; Men in
Prison; Sexploitation*
Alien3
The Big Doll House
Brokedown Palace
Emmanuelle: Queen of the
Desert
Midnight
Mommy 2: Mommy's Day

Women in War

*See also: Doctors & Nurses;
Korean War; Vietnam War;
Women; Wonder Women;
World War I; World War II*
The English Patient
G.I. Jane
In Love and War
South Pacific

Wonder Women

Alien
Aliens (SE)
Alien3
Angel's Dance
The Associate
Batman and Robin
Batman Returns
The Clan of the Cave Bear
Cleopatra Jones
Cutthroat Island
The Demolitionist
Evita
The Executioners
G.I. Jane
I Spit on Your Grave
Inspector Wears Skirts
La Femme Nikita
The Long Kiss Goodnight
Point of No Return
The Quick and the Dead
The River Wild
Silence of the Lambs
Speed 2: Cruise Control
Spice World: The Movie
Terminal Velocity

World War I

All Quiet on the Western
Front
Fifth Day of Peace
Gallipoli
Gods and Monsters
Grand Illusion
In Love and War
Legends of the Fall
Nicholas and Alexandra
Paths of Glory
Revolt of the Zombies

World War II

*See also: The Holocaust;
Postwar; POW/MIA; The
Resistance*
The Architecture of Doom
Away All Boats
Bataan
The Best Years of Our Lives
The Big Red One
Black Rain
Blood on the Sun
A Bridge Too Far
The Caine Mutiny
Casablanca
Cross of Iron
Das Boot (DC)
The Dirty Dozen

The English Patient
The Fighting Sullivans
Fist of Legend
The Great Escape
The Guns of Navarone
The Human Condition: No
Greater Love
The Human Condition: Road
to Eternity
Infinity
It Happened Here
The Last Metro
A League of Their Own
Life Is Beautiful
The Longest Day
Memphis Belle
Midway
Mister Roberts
1941
Open City
Patton
Raid on Rommel
Red Cherry
Salo, or the 120 Days of
Sodom
Sands of Iwo Jima
Saving Private Ryan
Sea Wolves
Seven Beauties
Seven Years in Tibet
A Soldier's Tale
South Pacific
Stalingrad
The Story of G.I. Joe
Tea with Mussolini
They Were Expendable
The Thin Red Line
Tin Drum
Tora! Tora! Tora!
The Train
Two Women
Victory
Women of Valor

Wrestling

Battlecade: Extreme Fighting
Battlecade: Extreme Fighting
2
The Rock: The People's
Champ
Vision Quest
Whatever It Takes

Writers

*See also: Books & Book-
stores; This Is Your Life*
Another Man's Poison
As Good As It Gets
The Basketball Diaries
The Best Man
Breakfast at Tiffany's
Celebrity
Closer and Closer
The Dark Half
Dean Koontz's Mr. Murder
Deathtrap
Deconstructing Harry
Father's Day
Fear and Loathing in Las
Vegas
For Hire
Henry & June
Her Alibi
In the Mouth of Madness
Jane Doe
Just Write
Kissing a Fool
Love and Death on Long
Island
A Merry War
Mr. Jealousy

A Murder of Crows
The Muse
The Pillow Book
Postmortem
Shadowlands
Shakespeare in Love (CS)
Sink or Swim
Slam
The Snows of Kilimanjaro
The Third Man
Zeder

The Wrong Man

*See also: Frame-Ups; Mistak-
en Identity*
Absolute Power
Body Heat
Cookie's Fortune
Dead End
Double Jeopardy
Fallen
The Fugitive
In the Name of the Father
Life
The Man Who Knew Too
Much
Most Wanted
The Negotiator
Presumed Innocent
Red Corner
Spoiler
A Stranger in the Kingdom
The 39 Steps
Three Days of the Condor
U.S. Marshals
Wrongfully Accused

Wrong Side of the
Tracks

See also: Rags to Riches
Amarilly of Clothesline Alley
Angel and the Badman
Dirty Dancing
Dirty Dancing (CE)
Far and Away
The Fence
The Flamingo Kid
Great Expectations
Hush
Iron Maze
It Happened One Night
Jungle Fever
King Ralph
La Traviata
My Man Godfrey
The Phantom of the Opera
The Rage: Carrie 2
Rocky
Rosewood
Rumble Fish
Set It Off
sex, lies and videotape
She's All That
This Sporting Life
White Palace

Yakuza

*See also: Crime & Criminals;
Organized Crime*
Black Rain
Girls of the White Orchid
Johnny Mnemonic
Organized Crime & Triad
Bureau
Showdown in Little Tokyo
Tokyo Drifter
Wicked City

You Lose, You Die

See also: Post Apocalypse
Death Race 2000

Futuresport
The Game
Mad Max: Beyond Thunder-
dome
Mean Guns
Naked Warriors
Rollerball
The Running Man
Tron

Yugoslavian
(Production)

The Best of Zagreb Film

Yuppie Nightmares

See also: Strained Suburbia
Beetlejuice
The Big Chill
The Bonfire of the Vanities
Clean and Sober
Coma
Dead Calm
The First Wives Club
The Game
The Guardian
The Hand that Rocks the Cra-
dle
Happiness
The Hard Way
In the Company of Men
Jungle Fever
L.A. Story
The Mighty Ducks
Mother's Boys
Nothing but Trouble
The Object of Beauty
Private Benjamin
The Secret of My Success
sex, lies and videotape
Straw Dogs
The Trigger Effect
Truth or Consequences, N.M.
Westworld
When a Man Loves a Woman
Wolf
Your Friends & Neighbors

Zombie Soldiers

See also: Zombies
Army of Darkness
Revolt of the Zombies

Zombies

*See also: Death & the After-
life; Ghosts, Ghouls & Gob-
lins; Zombie Soldiers*
Bride of Re-Animator
Children Shouldn't Play with
Dead Things
Dawn of the Dead
Day of the Dead
Dead Alive
Death Becomes Her
I Was a Teenage Zombie
King of the Zombies
The Legend of the 7 Golden
Vampires
The Mummy
The Mummy
Plague of the Zombies
Plan 9 from Outer Space
Re-Animator
Return of the Blind Dead
Revolt of the Zombies
Tombs of the Blind Dead
Torture Chamber of Baron
Blood
The White Zombie
Zombie

The "Distributor Index" provides contact information for the distributors indicated within the reviews, and the DVDs reviewed in this book which they offer. Beware: DVDs sometimes change hands frequently; we've tried to provide cross-references where applicable. Also, studio distributors do not usually sell to the public—they generally act as wholesalers, selling only to retail outlets. Many video stores provide an ordering service; check out the "DVD Connections" section on p. 511 for some websites to help you track down a title.

A-PIX ENTERTAINMENT INC.
200 Madison Ave., 24th Fl.
New York, NY 10016
(206)284-4700
800-245-6472
Fax: (206)286-4433
Jane Doe '96
The Phantom of the Opera '98
Razor Blade Smile '98
Six Ways to Sunday '99

ANCHOR BAY
1699 Stutz Dr.
Troy, MI 48084
(248)816-0909
800-786-8777
Fax: (248)816-3335
www.anchorbayentertainment.com
Alice Sweet Alice '76
The Allnighter '87
Aloha, Bobby and Rose '74
Autopsy '78
The Bears & I '74
Beyond the Door 2 '79
Big Red '62
The Black Hole '79
Blank Generation '79
The Blood Spattered Bride '72
Blue Collar '78
The Boogey Man '80
Brenda Starr '86
Candleshoe '78
The Car '77
The Cat from Outer Space '78
Charlie, the Lonesome Cougar '67
Condorman '81
Creepers '85
Crimes of Passion '84
Custer of the West '67
Daughters of Darkness '71
Dawn of the Dead '78
Day of the Dead '85
Deep Red: Hatchet Murders '75
Demons '86
Demons 2 '87
Devonsville Terror '83
Django '68
Django Strikes Again '87
Dracula, Prince of Darkness '66
Duel in the Sun '46
Even Dwarfs Started Small '69

Evil Dead 2: Dead by Dawn '87
Exterminator '80
Fade to Black '80
Fantastic Planet '73
Fitzcarraldo '82
The Flamingo Kid '84
FM '78
The Ghost Goes Gear '66
The Girl on a Motorcycle '68
The Great Locomotive Chase '56
The Guardian '90
Halloween '78
Halloween 4: The Return of Michael Myers '88
The Happiest Millionaire '67
The Heartbreak Kid '72
Heathers '89
Hell in the Pacific '69
Hell Night '81
Hellbound: Hellraiser 2 '88
Hellraiser '87
I Saw What You Did '65
Impulse '84
Inferno '80
Invaders from Mars '86
The Ipcress File '65
The Island at the Top of the World '74
Junior Bonner '72
Kentucky Fried Movie '77
Killing Hour '84
The Killing of Sister George '69
Kiss Me Monster '69
Krakatoa East of Java '66
The Last Flight of Noah's Ark '80
The Last Valley '71
The Legend of the 7 Golden Vampires '73
Lion of the Desert '81
The Littlest Horse Thieves '76
Lost Continent '68
Melvin and Howard '80
The Message '77
Minnie and Moskowitz '71
Moll Flanders '96
Monty Python's Life of Brian (Anchor Bay) '79
Moonlighting '85
My Science Project '85
Napoleon and Samantha '72
National Lampoon's Class Reunion '82
New York Ripper '82
The Night Stalker '71
Nightmares '83

The North Avenue Irregulars '79
Nosferatu the Vampyre '79
Notorious '46
One Magic Christmas '85
Out of the Blue '80
The Paradine Case '47
Plague of the Zombies '66
Prehistoric Women '67
Prizzi's Honor '85
Prom Night '80
Q (The Winged Serpent) '82
Quatermass and the Pit '67
Rasputin the Mad Monk '66
Raw Deal '86
Rebecca '40
The Reptile '66
Return of the Blind Dead '75
Return to Oz '85
Running Time '97
The Satanic Rites of Dracula '73
Shalako '68
She Devils in Chains '76
Silkwood '83
Sleuth '72
Smashing Time '67
Something Wicked This Way Comes '83
Spellbound '45
The Stepford Wives '75
Straw Dogs '72
Succubus '69
The Swinging Cheerleaders '74
Take the Money and Run '69
Tex '82
They Might Be Giants '71
They Shoot Horses, Don't They? '69
Tombs of the Blind Dead '72
Torso '73
Train Ride to Hollywood '75
Trilogy of Terror '75
Two Lane Blacktop '71
Two Undercover Angels '68
Unidentified Flying Oddball '79
The Vengeance of She '68
Vigilante '83
The Viking Queen '67
Where the Buffalo Roam '80
Zachariah '70
Zombie '80

ARTISAN ENTERTAINMENT
15400 Sherman Way
PO Box 10124
Van Nuys, CA 91410-0124

(818)988-5060
800-677-0789
Fax: (818)778-3259
www.artisanent.com
After Dark, My Sweet '90
Air America '90
Alice in Wonderland '99
An American Werewolf in London '81
Angel Heart '87
The Arrival '96
Bad Lieutenant '92
Basic Instinct '92
Belly '98
Black Mask '96
The Blair Witch Project (SE) '99
Buena Vista Social Club '99
Capricorn One '78
Caught Up '98
Chaplin '92
Critical Care '97
The Crying Game '92
Cutthroat Island '95
Dee Snider's Strangeland '98
Dirty Dancing '87
Dirty Dancing (CE) '87
The Doors '91
Drugstore Cowboy '89
Earth Girls Are Easy '89
The Fabulous Baker Boys '89
Felicia's Journey '99
First Blood '82
Foolish '99
Hamburger Hill '87
Jacob's Ladder '90
The Jazz Singer '80
Joan of Arc '99
Killer: A Journal of Murder '95
L.A. Story '91
The Last Emperor '87
The Limey '99
Lock Up '89
Merlin '98
Millennium '89
Moby Dick '98
On Golden Pond '81
One Man's Justice '95
Permanent Midnight '98
Pi '98
The Piano '93
Platoon '86
The Punisher '90
The Quiet Man '52
Rambo: First Blood, Part 2 '85
Rambo 3 '88
Red Heat '88
Reservoir Dogs '92

Ringmaster '98
The Running Man '87
Saturn 3 '80
Sophie's Choice '82
Stargate '94
Stephen King's The Stand '94
Stir of Echoes '99
The Substitute '96
The Substitute 2: School's Out '97
Suicide Kings '97
Terminator 2: Judgment Day '91
Top Dog '95
Total Recall '90
Truth or Dare '91
Universal Soldier '92
Weekend at Bernie's '89
Wishmaster '97
Wishmaster 2: Evil Never Dies '98
Young Guns '88

AVALANCHE ENTERTAINMENT
595 Burrard St., Ste. 3123
Bentall Three
Vancouver, BC, Canada V7X 1J1
(416)944-0104
Big City Blues '99
National Lampoon's Golf Punks '99
Undercurrent '99

BELL CANYON ENTERTAINMENT INC.
c/o Sue Procko Public Relations
101 S. Harper Ave.
Los Angeles, CA 90048
(232)653-5153
888 379 6769
Rites of Passage '99

BUENA VISTA HOME ENTERTAINMENT
500 S. Buena Vista St.
Burbank, CA 91521-1120
800-723-4763

Buena Vista is responsible for Touchstone, Disney Home Video, Walt Disney Home Video, Hollywood Pictures (see separate listing), Miramax Pictures (see separate listing), and other labels.
Adventures in Babysitting '87
Air Bud '97
Arachnophobia '90

Beautiful Girls '96
Beauty and the Beast: The
  Enchanted Christmas '97
Beloved '98
Blackjack '97
The Break Up '98
A Bug's Life (CE) '98
Celebrity '98
Children of the Corn 666:
  Isaac's Return '99
Cinderella '97
A Civil Action '98
The Color of Money '86
Con Air '97
Cool Runnings '93
Cop Land '97
Crimson Tide '95
Dead Poets Society '89
Dead Presidents '95
The Distinguished Gentleman
  '92
Don't Be a Menace to South
  Central While Drinking Your
  Juice in the Hood '95
Eddie '96
Emma '96
Enemy of the State '98
Evita '96
eXistenZ '99
An Extremely Goofy Movie
  '99
The Faculty '98
Farewell My Concubine '93
Father of the Bride '91
Fist of Legend '94
Flubber '97
Four Rooms '95
From Dusk Till Dawn '95
From Dusk Till Dawn 2: Texas
  Blood Money '99
From Dusk Till Dawn 3: The
  Hangman's Daughter '99
George of the Jungle '97
Georgia '95
Halloween: H2O '98
He Got Game '98
Hercules '97
Holy Man '98
Homeward Bound: The
  Incredible Journey '93
The Horse Whisperer '97
I Love Trouble '94
I'll Be Home for Christmas
  '98
In Too Deep '99
The Insider '99
Inspector Gadget '99
Instinct '99
Judge Dredd '95
The Jungle Book '67
Kundun '97
Lady and the Tramp '55
The Lion King: Simba's Pride
  '98
Little Buddha '93
The Little Mermaid '89
Mad Love '95
Mary Poppins '64
Medicine Man '92
Metro '97
Mickey's Once upon a Christ-
  mas '99
The Mighty Ducks '92
Mighty Joe Young '98
Mimic '97
Mr. Holland's Opus '95
Mr. Magoo '97
Mother's Boys '94
Mulan '98
Mumford '99
My Favorite Martian '98
The Nightmare before Christ-
  mas '93
Nixon '95
Nothing to Lose '96
101 Dalmatians '61
101 Dalmatians '96
Operation Condor '91
Operation Condor 2: The
  Armour of the Gods '86
The Other Sister '98

Outrageous Fortune '87
The Parent Trap '98
The Patriot '99
Peter Pan '53
Phantoms '97
Phenomenon '96
Pinocchio '40
Playing God '96
Powder '95
Pretty Woman '90
The Prophecy '95
The Prophecy 2: Ashtown '97
The Prophecy 3: The Ascent
  '99
Pulp Fiction '94
Quiz Show '94
Ransom '96
The Rocketeer '91
Romy and Michele's High
  School Reunion '97
Russell Mulcahy's Tale of the
  Mummy '99
The Santa Clause '94
Scream (CS) '96
Scream 2 '97
Senseless '98
Sirens '94
Sister Act 2: Back in the
  Habit '93
Six Days, Seven Nights '98
Sling Blade '96
Son-in-Law '93
Splash '84
Summer of Sam '99
Supercop '92
Supercop 2 '93
Swingers '96
Tarzan '99
Teaching Mrs. Tingle '99
Ten Things I Hate about You
  '99
The 13th Warrior '99
A Thousand Acres '97
The Three Musketeers '93
Titanica '92
Total Recall 2070: Machine
  Dreams '99
Tron '82
Twin Dragons '92
Up Close and Personal '96
The Waterboy '98
What's Love Got to Do with
  It? '93
When a Man Loves a Woman
  '94
While You Were Sleeping '95
White Squall '96
Who Framed Roger Rabbit
  '88

**BWE (BONNEVILLE
WORLDWIDE
ENTERTAINMENT)
VIDEO**
55 North 300 West, No. 315
Salt Lake City, UT 84110-
  1160
(801)575-3680
800-654-1686
Tarantella '95

**CENTRAL PARK
MEDIA/U.S. MANGA
CORPS**
250 W. 57th St., Ste. 317
New York, NY 10107
(212)977-7456
800-833-7456
Fax: (212)977-8709
Darkside Blues '99
Demon City Shinjuku '93
Dominion Tank Police '89
Record of Lodoss War '90
Urotsukidoji: Perfect Collec-
  tion '89
Urusei Yatsura Movie 2:
  Beautiful Dreamer '84
The Venus Wars '89
A Wind Named Amnesia '93

**COLUMBIA TRISTAR
HOME VIDEO**
Sony Pictures Plz.
10202 W. Washington Blvd.
Culver City, CA 90232
(310)280-5418
Fax: (310)280-2485
www.cthv.com
About Last Night . . . '86
Absence of Malice '81
The Adventures of Baron
  Munchausen '89
The Adventures of Elmo in
  Grouchland '99
The Adventures of Milo &
  Otis '89
Air Force One '97
The Alarmist '98
Alvarez Kelly '66
American Movie '99
American Pop '81
Anaconda '96
And Now for Something Com-
  pletely Different '72
Apt Pupil '97
Arlington Road '99
As Good As It Gets '97
The Assignment '97
Awakenings '90
Baby Geniuses '98
Bad Boys '95
Bell, Book and Candle '58
Beverly Hills Ninja '96
The Big Brass Ring '99
The Big Chill '83
Big Daddy '99
The Big Hit '98
Big Night '95
The Blue Lagoon '80
Body Double '84
Booty Call '96
Born Yesterday '50
Bottle Rocket '91
Boyz N the Hood '91
The Buddy Holly Story '78
Bugsy '91
Bye, Bye, Birdie '63
The Cable Guy '96
The Caine Mutiny '54
Candyman '92
Can't Hardly Wait '98
Central Station '98
Chances Are '89
The China Syndrome '79
Christine '84
The City of Lost Children '95
Cliffhanger '93
The Craft '96
Cruel Intentions '98
Crumb '94
Dance with Me '98
Dancer, Texas—Pop. 81 '98
Dancing at Lughnasa '98
The Dark Crystal '82
Das Boot (DC) '81
The Deep '77
The Deep End of the Ocean
  '98
Desert Blue '98
Desert Heat '99
Desperado '95
Desperado / El Mariachi '95
Desperate Measures '98
Devil in a Blue Dress '95
The Devil's Own '96
Dr. Strangelove, or: How I
  Learned to Stop Worrying
  and Love the Bomb '64
Donnie Brasco '96
Double Team '97
Dracula '92
The Dreamlife of Angels '98
Easy Rider '69
8mm '98
Excess Baggage '96
The Fan '96
A Few Good Men '92
The Fifth Element '97
Finding Graceland '98
First Knight '95
Flatliners '90

Fly Away Home '96
Fools Rush In '97
The Freshman '90
Futuresport '98
Gattaca '97
The General '98
Geronimo: An American Leg-
  end '93
Ghostbusters '84
Ghostbusters 2 '89
Gloria '98
Glory '89
Go '99
Godzilla '98
The Governess '98
Groundhog Day '93
Guarding Tess '94
Guess Who's Coming to Din-
  ner '67
The Guns of Navarone '61
Hard Times '75
Heavy Metal '81
Hero '92
Hideous Kinky '99
Howard's End '92
Hudson Hawk '91
Hush '98
I Know What You Did Last
  Summer '97
I Still Know What You Did
  Last Summer '98
In God's Hands '98
In the Company of Men '96
In the Line of Fire '93
It Happened One Night '34
Jackie Chan's Who Am I '98
Jakob the Liar '99
Jason and the Argonauts '63
Jawbreaker '98
Jerry Maguire '96
John Carpenter's Vampires
  '97
Johnny Mnemonic '95
Jumanji (CS) '95
The Juror '96
Knock Off '98
La Bamba '87
Labyrinth '86
Last Action Hero '93
The Last Detail '73
Last Hurrah '58
A League of Their Own '92
Legends of the Fall '94
Les Miserables '97
Limbo '99
Little Women '94
Look Who's Talking '89
Lost Horizon '37
Made Men '99
Manhattan Murder Mystery
  '93
Mary Shelley's Frankenstein
  '94
The Mask of Zorro '98
Matilda '96
Midnight Express '78
The Mirror Has Two Faces '96
Money Train '95
The Monster '96
Mortal Thoughts '91
Much Ado about Nothing '93
Multiplicity '96
Muppets from Space '99
My Best Friend's Wedding '97
My Girl '91
My Stepmother Is an Alien
  '88
The Net '95
Never Talk to Strangers '95
Nicholas and Alexandra '71
Nowhere to Run '93
The Odessa File '74
Oliver! '68
Only You '94
Opposite of Sex '98
Orlando '92
Passion Fish '92
Peggy Sue Got Married '86
The People vs. Larry Flynt '96
Philadelphia '93
The Pillow Book '95

Poetic Justice '93
The Professional '94
The Professionals '66
The Quick and the Dead '94
The Replacement Killers '98
Resurrection '99
Revenge '90
Richard Pryor: Live on the
  Sunset Strip '82
A River Runs Through It '92
Run Lola Run '98
Savior '98
Screamers '96
Sense and Sensibility '95
Seven Years in Tibet '97
The Seventh Sign '88
The Seventh Voyage of Sin-
  bad '58
sex, lies and videotape '89
Shadrach '98
Simon Sez '99
Single White Female '92
SLC Punk! '99
Sleepless in Seattle '93
So I Married an Axe Murderer
  '93
Solo '96
Someone to Watch Over Me
  '87
The Spanish Prisoner '97
Spice World: The Movie '97
Splendor '99
Stand by Me '86
Starman '84
Starship Troopers '97
Stepmom '98
Stir Crazy '80
Striking Distance '93
Stripes '81
Stuart Little '99
Sunset '88
Swept from the Sea '97
Taxi Driver (CE) '76
The Texas Chainsaw Mas-
  sacre 4: The Next Genera-
  tion '95
The Thirteenth Floor '99
This Is My Father '99
Thunderheart '92
The Tingler '59
To Die For '95
Truth or Consequences, N.M.
  '97
U-Turn '97
Universal Soldier: The Return
  '99
Urban Legend '98
Welcome to the Dollhouse
  '95
The Wild One '54
Wild Things '98
Wolf '94

**CRITERION
COLLECTION**
c/o The Voyager Co.
578 Broadway
New York, NY 10012
(212)431-5199
800-446-2001
www.criterionco.com
Alphaville '65
Amarcord '74
And the Ship Sails On '83
Andrei Rublev '66
Andy Warhol's Dracula '74
Andy Warhol's Frankenstein
  '74
Armageddon '98
Beauty and the Beast '46
Black Orpheus '58
Branded to Kill '67
Brazil (Criterion SE) '85
Charade '63
Dead Ringers '88
Diabolique '55
The 400 Blows '59
Grand Illusion '37
Great Expectations '46
Hard-Boiled '92
Henry V '44
High & Low '62

Insomnia '97
The Killer '90
The Long Good Friday '80
M '31
Monty Python's Life of Brian '79
The Most Dangerous Game '32
A Night to Remember '58
Nights of Cabiria '57
Oliver Twist '48
Passion of Joan of Arc '28
Peeping Tom '60
Picnic at Hanging Rock '75
The Red Shoes '48
RoboCop '87
Rushmore '98
Salo, or the 120 Days of Sodom '75
Samurai 1: Musashi Miyamoto '55
Samurai 2: Duel at Ichijoji Temple '55
Samurai 3: Duel at Ganryu Island '56
Sanjuro '62
Seven Samurai '54
The Seventh Seal '56
Shock Corridor '63
Sid & Nancy '86
Silence of the Lambs '91
The Taste of Cherry '96
The Third Man '49
The 39 Steps (Criterion) '35
This Is Spinal Tap '84
Time Bandits '81
Tokyo Drifter '66
The Unbearable Lightness of Being '87
Wages of Fear '55
Walkabout '71

CULT EPICS
PO Box 461556
Los Angeles, CA 90046
Driller Killer '74

CULT VIDEO
Full Moon Pictures
1645 N. Vine St.
Hollywood, CA 90028
(323)468-0599
Assault of the Killer Bimbos '88
Laserblast '78

DELTA/LASERLIGHT
1663 Sawtelle Blvd.
Los Angeles, CA 90025
(310)268-1205
Fax: (31)268-1279
Angel and the Badman '47
Cabo Blanco / U.S. Marshal '81
Chino / Man with a Camera '75
The Farmer's Wife '28
His Girl Friday '40
Jamaica Inn '39
James Dean Double Feature: Hill Number One / I Am a Fool '52
James Dean Story '57
The Lady Vanishes '38
Made for Each Other '39
The Man Who Knew Too Much '34
The Manxman '29
Murder '30
No. 17 '32
Rich and Strange '32
The Ring '27
Robbie Robertson: Going Home '98
Sabotage '36
The Secret Agent '36
Skin Game '31
The 39 Steps '35
Young and Innocent '37

DIAMOND ENTERTAINMENT CORPORATION
3961 E. Miraloma Ave.
Anaheim, CA 92807
(714)572-8622
800-966-3339
Fax: (714)693-3339
Laser Mission '90

DIGITAL DISC ENTERTAINMENT
PO Box 7304
North Hollywood, CA
At War with the Army '50
Jack & the Beanstalk '52
A Merry War '97
Utopia '51

DIGITAL VERSATILE DISC LTD.
15210 Keswick St.
Van Nuys, CA 91405
(818)994-2980
Fax: (818)994-1575
Criminal Act '88
Day of the Animals '77
Don't Go in the House '80
Final Justice '84
Grizzly '76
Kill and Kill Again '81
Midnight Confessions '95
Novel Desires '92
Perfect Profile '90
Regina '83
Retrievers '82
The Scorpio Factor '90
Steele's Law '91
Violent Zone '89
With Friends Like These '90
Zigzag '97

DMG ENTERTAINMENT
c/o Renegade Entertainment
1930 Village Center Cir. #3, Ste. 448
Las Vegas, NV 89134
Bug Buster '99
Follow Your Heart '98
Misery Brothers Y2K '95

DREAMWORKS HOME ENTERTAINMENT
100 Universal City Plz.
Universal City, CA 91608
Amistad '97
Antz '98
Forces of Nature '99
The Haunting '99
In Dreams '98
The Love Letter '99
Mouse Hunt '97
Paulie '98
The Peacemaker '97
Prince of Egypt '98
Saving Private Ryan '98
Small Soldiers '98

DVD INTERNATIONAL
PO Box 128
Mountain Lakes, NJ 07046

These titles are available through A-Pix.
Armistead Maupin's More Tales of the City '97
Sherlock Holmes Consulting Detective, Vol. 1 '91
Tender Loving Care '99

E-REALBIZ.COM
21333 Oxnard St.
Woodland Hills, CA 91367
(818)676-1000
Fax: (818)615-0811
The Impossible Spy '87

EI INDEPENDENT CINEMA
68 Forest St.
Montclair, NJ 07042
(201)509-1616
Fax: (201)746-6464
Caress of the Vampire (CE) '96

ELITE ENTERTAINMENT, INC.
PO Box 1177
Scarborough, ME 04070-1177
Rockaway, NJ 07886
(207)883-2000
Fax: (207)883-2579
The Asphyx '72
Curse of the Voodoo '64
Eaten Alive '76
Evil Dead '83
Horror Hospital '73
Horror Planet '80
I Spit on Your Grave '77
The Lady in White '88
Maniac '80
Maniac Cop '88
Psychic Killer '75
Re-Animator '84
The Sadist '63
Tower of Evil '72
Uncle Sam '96

EROS INTERNATIONAL
560 Sylvan Ave.
Englewood Cliffs, NJ 07632
(201)567-1196
Fax: (201)567-2773
www.erosentertainment.com
Sarfarosh '98

ESSEX
Address unknown
Born to Win '71
The Boy in the Plastic Bubble '76
Call of the Wild '72
Choices '81
Cold Sweat '71
Death Sentence '74
Honor Among Thieves '68
The Inside Man '84
Tim '79

ETD
13950 Senlac Dr., Ste. 300
Farmers Branch, TX 75234
(972)406-0866
800-541-1008
Sore Losers '97
Witchcraft 10: Mistress of the Craft '98

FACETS MULTIMEDIA, INC.
1517 W. Fullerton Ave.
Chicago, IL 60614
(773)281-9075
800-331-6197
Fax: (773)929-5437
The Decalogue '88

FANTOMA FILMS
660A Bryant St.
San Francisco, CA 94107
(415)348-8840
Fax: (415)348-8849
Fando and Lis '68

FIRST RUN FEATURES
153 Waverly Pl.
New York, NY 10014
(212)243-0600
800-229-8575
Fax: (212)989-7649
The Architecture of Doom '91
Daniella by Night '61
The Disenchanted '90
Like It Is '98
Peach / A Bitter Song '95

FOCUSFILM
PO Box 1177
Scarborough, ME 04070
The Challenge of Flight: Disc One

FOX/LORBER HOME VIDEO
419 Park Ave. S., 20th Fl.
New York, NY 10016
(212)686-6777
Fax: (212)685-2625

Fox/Lorber is now WinStar (see separate listing).
Buffet Froid '79
Chappaqua '66
David and Lisa '62
Diva '82
Don's Party '76
The Eric Rohmer Collection: The Moral Tales '62
Irma Vep '96
Last Year at Marienbad '61
Lola Montes '55
Love, etc. '96
The Man Who Fell to Earth '76
Marcello Mastroianni: I Remember '97
Meantime '81
The Millionairess '60
Mr. Jealousy '98
Montenegro '81
My Life As a Dog '85
Nico Icon '95
Nostalghia '83
Pierrot le Fou '65
Ran '85
Seven Beauties '76
Stalingrad '94
Swept Away . . . '75
Tampopo '86
A Taxing Woman '87
Temptation of a Monk '94
The Trial '93
The Twilight of the Golds '97
Vive l'Amour '94
The Wife '95
A Woman Is a Woman '60

FULL MOON PICTURES
1645 N. Vine St.
Hollywood, CA 90028
(323)468-0599
Bloodstorm: Subspecies 4 '98
Castle Freak '95
The Creeps '97
Curse of the Puppet Master: The Human Experiment '98
Femalien '96
Lolida 2000 '97
Parasite '82
Petticoat Planet '95
Slave Girls from Beyond Infinity '87
Sorority Babes in the Slimeball Bowl-A-Rama '87
Vampire Journals '96
Witchouse '99

GOLDHIL HOME MEDIA
137 E. Thousand Oaks Blvd., Ste. 207
Thousand Oaks, CA 91360
(805)495-0735
Fax: (805)373-1603
www.goldhil.com
Trinity and Beyond: The Atomic Bomb Movie '99

GOODTIMES ENTERTAINMENT
16 E. 40th St., 8th Fl.
New York, NY 10016-0113
(212)951-3000
Fax: (212)213-9319
www.goodtimes.com
Airport '70
Airport '75 '75
Away All Boats '56
Born in East L.A. '87
Brewster's Millions '85
Bustin' Loose '81
Car Wash '76
The Conqueror '56
Dr. Giggles '92
Double Dragon '94
Earthquake '74
The Front Page '74
The Funhouse '81
Halloween 2: The Nightmare Isn't Over! '81

Halloween 3: Season of the Witch '82
Jaws: The Revenge '87
Judgment Night '93
King Ralph '91
March of the Wooden Soldiers '34
McLintock! '63
The Meanest Men in the West '76
Mr. Baseball '92
Munster, Go Home! '66
New Jersey Drive '95
Nighthawks '81
Peter Pan '60
Psycho 2 '83
Psycho 3 '86
Raid on Rommel '71
Rough Night in Jericho '67
Rudolph the Red-Nosed Reindeer: The Movie '98
The Sentinel '76
Shakedown '88
Shoot Out '71
Somebody Has to Shoot the Picture '90
Tank '83
Trespass '92
Ulzana's Raid '72
When a Stranger Calls Back '93
White Palace '90

GORGON VIDEO
c/o MPI Home Video
16101 S. 108th Ave.
Orland Park, IL 60462
(708)460-0555
800-777-2223
Fax: (708)460-0175
www.gorgon-video.com
Faces of Death '78

HALLMARK HOME ENTERTAINMENT
6100 Wilshire Blvd., Ste. 1400
Los Angeles, CA 90048
(213)634-3000
Fax: (213)549-3760
Cleopatra '99
Noah's Ark '99
Sarah, Plain and Tall '91
Sarah, Plain and Tall: Winter's End '99
Skylark '93
The Temptations '98

HBO HOME VIDEO
1100 6th Ave.
New York, NY 10036
(212)512-7400
Fax: (212)512-7498
www.hbohomevideo.com
Ball of Fire '41
The Best Years of Our Lives '46
The Bishop's Wife '47
Black Cat Run '98
A Bright Shining Lie '98
A Bronx Tale '93
Circle of Friends '94
Come and Get It '36
Dodsworth '36
Earthly Possessions '99
From the Earth to the Moon '98
The Grifters '90
Hans Christian Andersen '52
The Hurricane '37
The Jack Bull '99
Kickboxer '89
The Little Foxes '41
Meatballs '79
My Left Foot '89
No Escape '94
The Pride of the Yankees '42
The Princess and the Pirate '44
Proud Rebel '58
Q & A '90
The Rat Pack '90

Ricochet '91
Rock-a-Doodle '92
The Secret Life of Walter Mitty '47
Serial Mom '94
Shadowlands '93
Stella Dallas '37
Stephen King's The Night Flier '96
Sweet Dreams '85
Tales from the Hood '95
They Got Me Covered '43
Three Amigos '86
Todd McFarlane's Spawn '97
Todd McFarlane's Spawn 2 '98
Tom Jones '63
Turbulence '96
The Westerner '40
White Man's Burden '95
Wonder Man '45
Wuthering Heights '39
Zeus and Roxanne '96

HEN'S TOOTH VIDEO
2805 E. State Blvd.
Fort Wayne, IN 46805
(219)471-4332
Fax: (219)471-4449
Cross of Iron '76
Flesh Gordon '72

HOLLYWOOD PICTURES HOME VIDEO
Fairmont Bldg. 526
500 S. Buena Vista St.
Burbank, CA 91505-9842
(818)562-3560
An American Werewolf in Paris '97
The Associate '96
Color of Night '94
Dangerous Minds '95
Deep Rising '98
Encino Man '92
G.I. Jane '97
Grosse Pointe Blank '97
The Hand that Rocks the Cradle '92
Miami Rhapsody '95
The Rock '96
Simon Birch '98
The Sixth Sense '99
Spy Hard '96
Terminal Velocity '94
Tombstone '93

HOME VISION CINEMA
5547 N. Ravenswood Ave.
Chicago, IL 60640-1199
(773)878-2600
800-826-3456
Fax: (773)878-8406
www.homevision.com
Naked Kiss '64
Pandora's Box '28
Summertime '55

IDEAL ENTERPRISES/VIDEO
16228 Main Ave. SE, No. 104
Prior Lake, MN 55372
(952)447-7406
Fax: (952)447-7409
www.ideal-video.com
Ninth Street '98

IMAGE ENTERTAINMENT
9333 Oso Ave.
Chatsworth, CA 91311
(818)407-9100
800-473-3475
Fax: (818)407-9111
www.image-entertainment.com
Abbott and Costello in the Foreign Legion '50
Across the Moon '94
Aelita: Queen of Mars '24
AFI's 100 Years, 100 Movies '98

Alegria '98
Alexander Nevsky '38
Alien Chaser '96
Alien Seed '89
Alive and Kicking '96
The Alley Cats '65
Allyson Is Watching '96
Amarilly of Clothesline Alley '18
Amazon Women on the Moon '87
America '24
An American Christmas Carol '79
The Andromeda Strain '71
Angel in Training '99
Animal Crackers '30
Animal Instincts 3: The Seductress '95
Animaland '48
Another Man's Poison '52
Any Number Can Win '63
Arabian Nights '74
Aria '88
Armstrong '99
Around the World in 80 Days '89
Art and Jazz in Animation '85
As You Like It '36
The Assault '97
Assault on Precinct 13 '76
Atomic Submarine '59
Awakening of Gabriella '99
Ayn Rand: A Sense of Life '98
The Baby '72
Bad Love '95
Basket Case '82
The Bat Whispers '30
Battlecade: Extreme Fighting '95
Battlecade: Extreme Fighting 2 '96
The Battleship Potemkin '25
Battling Butler '26
Belle of the Nineties '34
The Bells / The Crazy Ray '26
Beneath the 12-Mile Reef '53
Benji '74
The Best of British Cinema: Five Decades of Classic British Films '88
The Best of Zagreb Film
The Best Revenge '96
Beyond Suspicion '94
The Bicycle Thief '48
Big Combo '55
Big Wars '93
The Birth of a Nation '15
Black Circle Boys '97
Black Death '91
The Black Pirate '26
Black Sunday '60
The Bloodsucker Leads the Dance '75
The Blue Gardenia '53
Body Puzzle '93
Body Shot '93
Bound and Gagged: A Love Story '93
Boys Life '94
Boys Life 2 '98
Brain Damage '88
The Brave Frog '87
Bride of the Monster '55
The Bridge of San Luis Rey '44
Brighton Beach Memoirs '86
Broken Blossoms '19
Brother, Can You Spare a Dime? '75
Brute Force '46
The Brute Man '46
Buck Privates '41
Buck Privates Come Home '47
Bull Durham '88
Bye Bye Monkey '77
The Cabinet of Dr. Caligari '19

Caligula '80
Camille 2000 '69
The Canterbury Tales '71
Carmen, Baby '66
Carnal Crimes '91
Carolina Skeletons '92
Casual Sex? '88
The Cat and the Canary '27
Cat City '87
Cat on a Hot Tin Roof '84
Cat People '82
The Chaplin Mutuals, Vol. 1
The Chaplin Mutuals, Vol. 2
The Chaplin Mutuals, Vol. 3
Chaplin's Art of Comedy '66
Chaplin's Essanay Comedies, Vol. 1
Chaplin's Essanay Comedies, Vol. 2
Chaplin's Essanay Comedies, Vol. 3
Charles Chaplin—A First National Collection
Chushingura '62
The Circus '19
City Lights '31
The Cocoanuts '29
Cold Eyes of Fear '70
Cold Harvest '98
The Complete Uncensored Private Snafu '46
Corridors of Blood '58
Cost of Living '97
Crackdown '88
Crimes & Misdemeanors '89
Crimson Wolf '94
The Cunning Little Vixen '95
Curtain Call '97
Daddy Long Legs '19
Dances with Wolves '90
The Dandelion Crown '93
Dark Odyssey '57
Dark Waters '44
Dear Santa '98
The Decameron '70
The Demoniacs '74
Desecration '99
The Designated Mourner '97
Desperate Crimes '93
Destination Moon '50
The Devil Bat's Daughter '46
The Devil's Nightmare '71
Die Watching '93
The Dirty Girls '64
Dirty Rotten Scoundrels '88
D.O.A. '49
Dr. Jekyll and Mr. Hyde '20
Don't Do It '94
Don't Touch the White Woman! '74
Double Indemnity '44
Dracula '79
Dreamscape '84
Duck Soup '33
8 Man '92
8 Man After: The Perfect Collection '93
The Electric Horseman '79
The Elm-Chanted Forest '97
Embrace the Darkness '98
The Endless Summer '66
Evil Ed '96
Fahrenheit 451 '66
Fallen Angels '95
Family Reunion '79
The Fantastic Night '42
Fascination '79
Fatal Pursuit '98
The Fear: Halloween Night '99
The Fence '94
Firestarter '84
First Man into Space '59
Fist of the North Star '86
Flash Gordon '80
Flesh '68
The Flying Serpent '55
For the Love of Benji '77
Forever and a Day '43
The 47 Ronin, Parts 1 & 2 '42

The 4D Man '59
Friend of the Family '95
Friend of the Family 2 '96
From the Journals of Jean Seberg '95
The General '26
Ghost Story '81
Girl Hunters '63
Glen or Glenda? '53
Godmoney '99
The Gold Rush '25
The Gospel According to St. Matthew '64
A Great Day in Harlem / The Spitball Story '94
The Great Dictator '40
The Great Rupert '50
Grim '95
Gustav Mahler: To Live, I Will Die '87
Hand Gun '93
Hard Bounty '94
Hard Drive '94
The Haunted Strangler '58
Heat '72
Hideous Sun Demon '59
Hollywood Christmas '96
Horror Express (Image Entertainment) '84
Hot Blooded '98
The Hound of the Baskervilles '83
House of Whipcord '75
How to Be a Woman and Not Die in the Attempt '91
The Hubley Collection: Everybody Rides the Carousel
The Hubley Collection, Vol. 1 '92
The Hubley Collection, Vol. 2 '83
The Human Condition: No Greater Love '58
The Human Condition: Road to Eternity '59
I, a Woman '66
I Am Cuba '64
I Was a Teenage Zombie '87
Impact '49
In Search of Dracula '76
In the Navy '41
In the Realm of the Senses '76
In the Shadows '98
Indomitable Teddy Roosevelt '83
Into the Woods '90
Intolerance '16
Iron Maze '91
It Happened Here '65
Ivan the Terrible, Part 1 '44
Ivan the Terrible, Part 2 '46
Jack Be Nimble '94
Jack-O '95
Jail Bait '54
Jamaica Inn (Image) '39
Jan Svankmajer's Faust '94
Jane Street '96
The Johnsons '92
Journey to the Far Side of the Sun '69
Judge & Jury '96
Juliet of the Spirits '65
Jungleground '95
Junior's Groove '97
Key to Sex '98
The Kid / A Dog's Life '21
A Kid Called Danger '99
Kika '97
Killing Obsession '94
A King in New York / A Woman in Paris '57
Kiss of the Vampire '62
Klondike Annie '36
Lady Macbeth of Mtsensk '92
Landmarks of Early Film '94
Landmarks of Early Film, Vol. 2: The Magic of Melies '94
Lap Dancing '95
Laser Moon '92
Laurel and Hardy and Friends

The Law '59
Legal Eagles '86
The Lickerish Quartet '70
Life of a Gigolo '98
Limelight '52
Lips of Blood '75
Lipstick Camera '93
Lisa and the Devil / The House of Exorcism '75
Little Mother '71
Little Witches '96
The Living Dead Girl '82
Looking for Lola '96
The Lost Films of Laurel and Hardy, Vol. 1
The Lost Films of Laurel and Hardy, Vol. 2
The Lost Films of Laurel and Hardy, Vol. 3
The Lost Films of Laurel and Hardy, Vol. 5 '99
The Lost Films of Laurel and Hardy, Vol. 6 '99
The Love Goddesses '65
Loveblind '98
The Lumiere Brothers' First Films '97
Lupin III: The Mystery of Mamo '78
Mad Dog and Glory '93
Mad Max '80
The Magic Voyage '93
Mahler '74
Male and Female '19
Man of a Thousand Faces '57
The Man with the Movie Camera '29
Marat/Sade '66
Maria Stuarda '88
Mark of the Devil '69
Mark of Zorro '20
Mask '85
The Mask of Diijon '46
Masseuse '95
Masters of Russian Animation, Vol. 1 '97
Matinee '92
MD Geist (DC) '86
Megazone 23 Part 1 '85
Mesmer '94
Midnight Run '88
Midway '76
Milk and Money '97
Mischievous '96
Mississippi Burning '88
Mr. Ace '46
Modern Times '36
Monkey Business '31
Monsieur Verdoux '47
Monty Python's The Meaning of Life '83
Mosquito '95
Mother '26
Ms. 45 '81
My Best Girl '27
Mystery Science Theater 3000: The Movie '96
The Naked City '48
Navy SEALS '90
Night Caller from Outer Space '66
Night Calls: The Movie '98
Night Calls: The Movie 2 '99
Night Fire '94
Night of the Hunted '69
Night Screams '87
The Night That Never Happened '97
Night Tide '63
Nikki, the Wild Dog of the North '61
90 Degrees South: With Scott to the Antarctic '33
Nosferatu '22
Nude for Satan '74
Nunsense '93
The Nutt House '92
Object of Obsession '95
Odd Man Out '47
Of Mice and Men '39

Clerks '94
The Crossing Guard '94
The Crow '93
The Crow 2: City of Angels
'96
Down in the Delta '98
The English Patient '96
The Englishman Who Went up
a Hill But Came down a
Mountain '95
Everyone Says I Love You '96
Exotica '94
54 '98
Flirting with Disaster '95
Good Will Hunting '97
Guinevere '99
Happy, Texas '99
Heaven '99
The House of Yes '97
I Love You, I Love You Not '97
An Ideal Husband '99
Life Is Beautiful '98
Like Water for Chocolate '93
Little Voice '98
Marvin's Room '96
The Mighty '98
Mighty Aphrodite '95
Mrs. Brown '97
Monument Ave. '98
My Life So Far '98
My Son the Fanatic '97
Outside Providence '99
Playing by Heart '98
The Postman '94
A Price above Rubies '97
Priest '94
Ready to Wear '94
Restoration '94
Rogue Trader '98
Rounders '98
Shakespeare in Love (CS)
'98
She's All That '99
Smoke Signals '98
Things to Do in Denver When
You're Dead '95
Trainspotting '95
Velvet Goldmine '98
The Very Thought of You '98
A Walk on the Moon '99
The Wings of the Dove '97

MONARCH HOME VIDEO
2 Ingram Blvd.
La Vergne, TN 37086-7006
(615)287-4632
Fax: (615)287-4992
www.monarchvideo.com
Hunter's Moon '97
T.N.T. '98

MPI HOME VIDEO
16101 S. 108th Ave.
Orland Park, IL 60462
(708)460-0555
800-777-2223
Fax: (708)873-3177
www.mpimedia.com
Baraka '93
The Beatles: The First U.S.
Visit '91
Dark Shadows (SE) '99
A Hard Day's Night '64
Help! '65
Henry: Portrait of a Serial
Killer '90
Henry: Portrait of a Serial
Killer 2: Mask of Sanity '96
Image of an Assassination: A
New Look at the Zapruder
Film '98
Magical Mystery Tour '67
Richard Pryor: Live in Concert
'79

MTI HOME VIDEO
14216 SW 136th St.
Miami, FL 33186
(305)255-8684
Fax: (305)233-6943
www.mtivideo.com
Darkdrive '98

Detention '98
Killers '97
Lady of the Lake '98
Me & Will '99
Motel Blue '98
Showdown '94
Timelock '98
True Friends '98
The Turning '92
Winner Takes All '98

**MUSIC VIDEO
DISTRIBUTORS**
PO Box 280
Oaks, PA 19456
800-888-0486
www.musicvideodist.com
GWAR: Phallus in Wonderland
'92

**NEW HORIZONS HOME
VIDEO**
5885-D Live Oak Pkwy.
Norcross, GA 30093
(770)849-9910
800-854-3323
Fax: (770)849-9773
Big Bad Mama '74
The Big Doll House '71
Death Race 2000 '75
Eat My Dust '76
Fire on the Amazon '93
Humanoids from the Deep
'80
Naked Warriors '73
Piranha '78
Piranha '95

NEW LINE HOME VIDEO
116 N. Robertson Blvd.
Los Angeles, CA 90048
(310)967-6670
Fax: (310)854-0602
www.newline.com
The Adventures of Pinocchio
'96
American History X '98
The Astronaut's Wife '99
Austin Powers: International
Man of Mystery '97
Austin Powers 2: The Spy
Who Shagged Me '99
The Bachelor '99
Bed of Roses '95
Besieged '98
Blade '98
Blast from the Past '98
Boogie Nights '97
Corrina, Corrina '94
The Corruptor '99
Crash '95
Damage '92
Dangerous Ground '96
Dark City '97
Deconstructing Harry '97
Deep Cover '92
Detroit Rock City '99
Don Juan DeMarco '94
Drop Dead Gorgeous '99
Dumb & Dumber '94
8 Seconds '94
Embrace of the Vampire '95
Feeling Minnesota '96
Freddy's Dead: The Final
Nightmare '91
Friday '95
The Hidden '87
In Love and War '96
In the Mouth of Madness '95
The Island of Dr. Moreau '96
Jackie Chan's First Strike '96
Last Man Standing '96
The Lawnmower Man '92
Living Out Loud '98
The Long Kiss Goodnight '96
Lost in Space '98
Love Jones '96
The Mask '94
Menace II Society '93
Mr. Nice Guy '97
Mortal Kombat 1: The Movie
'95

Mortal Kombat 2: Annihila-
tion '97
Most Wanted '97
National Lampoon's Loaded
Weapon 1 '93
A Nightmare on Elm Street
'84
A Nightmare on Elm Street 2:
Freddy's Revenge '85
A Nightmare on Elm Street 3:
Dream Warriors '87
A Nightmare on Elm Street 4:
Dream Master '88
A Nightmare on Elm Street 5:
Dream Child '89
The "Nightmare on Elm
Street" Collection '99
Now and Then '95
One Night Stand '97
Pecker '98
The Player '92
The Players Club '98
Pleasantville '98
Poison Ivy '92
Poison Ivy 2: Lily '95
Poison Ivy 3: The New Seduc-
tion '97
Pump Up the Volume '90
Rumble in the Bronx '96
Rush Hour '98
Set It Off '96
Seven '95
Shine '95
Spawn (SE) '97
Surviving the Game '94
The Sweet Hereafter '96
Teenage Mutant Ninja Tur-
tles: The Movie '90
A Thin Line Between Love
and Hate '96
Total Eclipse '95
Trial and Error '96
Trick '99
Wag the Dog '97
The Wedding Singer '97
Wes Craven's New Nightmare
'94

NEW VIDEO GROUP
126 5th Ave.
New York, NY 10011
(212)210-1340
800-625-9000
Fax: (802)864-9846
The Avengers '67

ORION HOME VIDEO
MGM
2500 Broadway
Santa Monica, CA 90404-
6061
(310)449-3000
Fax: (310)449-3100
RoboCop 2 '90
RoboCop 3 '91

PARADE
Address unknown
*These titles are now availabe
through Mastertone Multime-
dia, Inc. (see separate listing).*
Bad Man's River '72
Blood on the Sun '45
Mohawk '56
Pancho Villa '72
The Strange Love of Martha
Ivers '46
The Stranger '46
The Terror '63

**PARAMOUNT HOME
VIDEO**
Bluhdorn Bldg.
5555 Melrose Ave.
Los Angeles, CA 90038
(213)956-3952
www.paramount.com
American Gigolo '79
Another 48 Hrs. '90
Apocalypse Now '79
Barbarella '68
Barefoot in the Park '67

Beavis and Butt-Head Do
America '96
Black Rain '89
Breakfast at Tiffany's '61
Chinatown '74
Clear and Present Danger
'94
Clueless '95
Coming to America '88
Congo '95
Court Jester '56
Days of Heaven '78
Days of Thunder '90
Dead Again '91
Dead Man on Campus '97
Deep Impact '98
Double Jeopardy '99
Drop Zone '94
Election '99
Escape from Alcatraz '79
Escape from L.A. '96
Event Horizon '97
Face/Off '97
Ferris Bueller's Day Off '86
The Firm '93
The First Wives Club '96
Friday the 13th '80
Friday the 13th, Part 2 '81
Gallipoli '81
The General's Daughter '99
The Ghost and the Darkness
'96
The Golden Child '86
Hard Rain '97
Heaven Can Wait '78
The Hunt for Red October '90
In and Out '97
Internal Affairs '90
Jade '95
John Grisham's The Rainmak-
er '97
King Kong '76
Kiss the Girls '97
Mission: Impossible '96
Neil Simon's The Odd Couple
2 '98
Nick of Time '95
A Night at the Roxbury '98
Night Falls on Manhattan '96
The Out-of-Towners '99
The Parallax View '74
Patriot Games '92
Payback '99
The Phantom '96
Primal Fear '96
Private Parts '96
The Real Blonde '97
The Relic '96
Romeo and Juliet '68
The Rugrats Movie '98
The Saint '97
School Ties '92
Scrooged '88
A Simple Plan '98
Sleepy Hollow '99
Sliding Doors '97
Snake Eyes '98
Star Trek 4: The Voyage
Home '86
Star Trek 5: The Final Frontier
'89
Star Trek 6: The Undiscov-
ered Country '91
Star Trek: First Contact '96
Star Trek: Generations '94
Star Trek: Insurrection '98
Switchback '97
The Ten Commandments '56
Three Days of the Condor '75
Titanic '97
Tommy Boy '95
Top Gun '86
The Truman Show '98
Twilight '98
200 Cigarettes '98
The Two Jakes '90
Varsity Blues '98
Virtuosity '95
The War of the Worlds '53
Witness '85

**PASSPORT
INTERNATIONAL
PRODUCTIONS**
10520 Magnolia Blvd.
North Hollywood, CA 91601
(818)505-0696
Embryo '76

**PIONEER
ENTERTAINMENT**
2265 E. 220th St.
Long Beach, CA 90810
(800)526-0363
www.pioneer-ent.com
Armitage 3: Polymatrix '94
Asteroid '97
Baywatch: Nightmare Bay /
River of No Return '94
Bride of Re-Animator '89
The Cassandra Crossing '76
Drop Dead Rock '95
Eat Your Heart Out '96
Fall Time '94
Farewell, My Lovely '75
The Field '90
For Hire '98
Free Enterprise '98
Ju Dou '90
The Lair of the White Worm
'88
Light Sleeper '92
Mistress '91
Mountains of the Moon '90
The Object of Beauty '91
Opening Night '77
The Pandora Project '98
Parents '89
Picture Windows '95
Queens Logic '91
Rambling Rose '91
Rawhead Rex '87
Salome's Last Dance '88
Salt of the Earth '54
Sweet Talker '91
Tenchi the Movie: Tenchi
Myuo in Love '96
The Texas Chainsaw Mas-
sacre '74
Trees Lounge '96
Whatever It Takes '97

POLYGRAM
*Most titles will be reissued
through MGM.*
The Basketball Diaries '94
Fargo '96
The Game '97
The Gingerbread Man '97
Gridlock'd '96
Kalifornia '93
The Last Days of Disco '98
Malice '93
Mr. Saturday Night '92
Return to Paradise '98
The Secret Adventures of
Tom Thumb '93
Snow White: A Tale of Terror
'97
The Usual Suspects '95

**REPUBLIC PICTURES
HOME VIDEO**
c/o Artisan Home Entertain-
ment
2700 Colorado Ave.
Santa Monica, CA 90404
(310)255-3700
Bad Boys '83
The Bells of St. Mary's '45
Bound '96
Frances '82
High Noon '52
Highlander (DC) '86
Highlander 2: The Quickening
'91
Invasion of the Body Snatch-
ers '56
It's a Wonderful Life '46
Once Upon a Time . . .
When We Were Colored '95
Plenty '85
Rio Grande '50

Sands of Iwo Jima '49
Stephen King's Thinner '96
Tender Mercies '83

RHINO HOME VIDEO
10635 Santa Monica Blvd., 2nd Fl.
Los Angeles, CA 90025-4900
(310)828-1980
800-843-3670
Fax: (310)453-5529
www.rhino.com/video/dvd.html
The Bostonians '84
The Bubble '67
Comin' At Ya! '81
Don't Answer the Phone '80
My Mom's a Werewolf '89
Plump Fiction '97
Pom Pom Girls '76
Rainbow Bridge '71
The Van '77
Walking Tall '73

ROAN GROUP
361 River Sound Village
Hayesville, NC 28904

These titles are now distributed by Troma Team Video (see separate listing).

The Bat '59
Dead Men Walk / The Monster Maker '43
The Fighting Sullivans '42
The Indestructible Man / The Amazing Transparent Man '56
King of the Zombies '41
Mommy '95
Mommy 2: Mommy's Day '96
Pre-Code Hollywood: The Risque Years, Vol. 1
Pre-Code Hollywood: The Risque Years, Vol. 2 '32
Rage at Dawn '55
Rain '32
Revolt of the Zombies '36
Santa Fe Trail '40
That Uncertain Feeling '41
Vengeance Valley '51
The White Zombie '32

RYKODISC USA
Shetland Park
27 Congress St.
Salem, MA 01970
(978)744-7678
Fax: (978)741-4506
Ghost in the Shell '95
Ninja Scroll '95
Tetsuo 2: Body Hammer '97
Tokyo Fist '96

ST. MULUS
Address unknown
Five Corners '88

SIMITAR ENTERTAINMENT
5555 Pioneer Creek
Maple Plain, MN 55359
(612)479-7000
800-486-TAPE
Fax: (612)479-7001
www.simitar.com
Abraxas: Guardian of the Universe '90
American Rampage '89
American Strays '96
American Streetfighter '96
American Streetfighter 2: The Full Impact '97
The Apocalypse '96
Assassin '86
The Babysitter's Seduction '96
Betrayed by Innocence '86
Bikini Hotel '97
Bloodstone '88
Body Armor '96
Body of Influence 2 '96
Body Strokes '95
The Boys Club '96

Boys Will Be Boys '97
Breeders '97
Bury Me in Niagara '93
Cartel '90
Cause of Death '90
Champions '96
Changing Habits '96
Chronos '87
Closer and Closer '96
The Con Artists '80
Conspiracy: The Trial of the Chicago Eight '87
Crime Broker '94
Cybernator '91
Dancing in the Dark '95
Dark Planet '97
Dark Secrets '95
Darkroom '90
Dead End '98
The Demolitionist '95
Devil in the Flesh '98
Diary of a Serial Killer '97
The Dragon Fist '80
Dreams of Gold: The Mel Fisher Story '86
Drive '96
Dumb Luck in Vegas '97
Ed McBain's 87th Precinct '96
Emmanuelle: Queen of the Desert '93
Eternal Evil '87
Exclusive '82
Expert Weapon '93
Eye of the Serpent '92
Face the Evil '97
Falling in Love Again '80
The Fatal Image '90
The Fear '94
Fearless Hyena '79
Fearless Hyena: Part 2 '83
Fetishes '96
Fifth Day of Peace '72
Firehouse '87
Floundering '94
For Love of a Child '90
Francesco '89
Fraternity Demon '92
Freedom Strike '98
Girls of the White Orchid '85
Glitch! '88
Godzilla, King of the Monsters '56
Godzilla vs. Monster Zero '68
Godzilla vs. Mothra '64
Godzilla's Revenge '69
Good Luck '96
Grambling's White Tiger '81
Grandma's House '88
Guinevere '94
Habitat '97
Half a Loaf of Kung Fu '85
Hangmen '87
Hard Vice '94
High Voltage '98
Horror Express '72
Hush Little Baby '93
Hyper Space '89
I Like to Play Games '95
Immortal Combat '94
The Inheritance '76
Interlocked '98
The Invisible Strangler '76
Jack Frost '97
Jessica: A Love Story '92
Jungle Boy '96
The Killer inside Me '76
The Killer Meteors '87
The Killing Grounds '97
The Killing Jar '96
The Killing Man '94
Krakatoa East of Java (Simitar) '66
The Last Assassins '96
Last Breath '96
The Last Game '95
Lauderdale '89
The Long Shadow '92
Love to Kill '97
Lucky Luke '94
A Man in Uniform '93
Mass Extinctions '93

Men '97
Mob Story '90
Mob War '88
Moving Target '96
The Naked Truth '92
New Fist of Fury '76
Night Train to Terror '84
Nightmare at Noon '87
Out of Time '88
Outrage '93
Patriots '94
Pocket Ninjas '93
Prime Suspect '82
The Princess and the Pirate '95
Princess Warrior '90
Rachel's Man '75
Red Scorpion '89
Rehearsal for Murder '82
Return of the Boogeyman '94
Royal Hunt of the Sun '69
Rude '96
Rush Week '88
Scorned 2 '96
Search and Destroy '88
Secret Games 3 '94
Serial Bomber '96
The Seventh Floor '93
Sex and the Other Man '95
Sex Crimes '93
Sexual Malice '93
Silk 'n' Sabotage '94
Skinner '93
Specimen '97
Spirit of the Eagle '90
Spiritual Kung Fu '78
Stranger by Night '94
Strip Search '97
Stripshow '95
A Summer to Remember '84
The Surgeon '94
Suspicions '95
Sweet Evil '77
Swimsuit '89
Swiss Conspiracy '77
Sworn Enemies '96
A Tale of Two Kitties '96
Tale of Two Sisters '89
Tarzan in Manhatten '89
Terror of Mechagodzilla '78
The Thin Red Line '64
Those Bedroom Eyes '92
Three Musketeers '88
Ticket to Heaven '81
To Cross the Rubicon '91
To Kill with Intrigue '85
Tornado Run '95
Trapper County War '89
Twitch of the Death Nerve '71
Undercover '94
Underground '90
Voodoo '95
Werewolf '95
Where the Rivers Flow North '94
Whisper Kill '88
The Wind '87
Witchcraft '88
Witchcraft 2: The Temptress '90
Witchcraft 9: Bitter Flesh '96
Women of Valor '86
Yellow Pages '96
Zero Boys '86

SLINGSHOT ENTERTAINMENT
15030 Ventura Blvd., No. 1776
Sherman Oaks, CA 91403
800-776-5864
www.slingshotdvd.com
Alaska: Spirit of the Wild '96
Antarctica '91
A Boy and His Dog '75
The Lost World '25

SOMETHING WEIRD VIDEO
PO Box 33664
Seattle, WA 98133

(206)361-3759
Fax: (206)364-7526
Blood Feast (SE) '63
Color Me Blood Red '64
Trader Hornee '70
2000 Maniacs '64
The Wizard of Gore '70

SONY MUSIC VIDEO ENTERPRISES
550 Madison Ave.
New York, NY 10022
(212)833-8000
www.sonymusicvideo.com
Aeon Flux '97
Pink Floyd: The Wall '82

STUDIO HOME ENTERTAINMENT
11846 Ventura Blvd., 3rd Fl.
Studio City, CA 91604
(818)762-0005
Fax: (818)762-0006
Animal Instincts '92
The Base '99
The Bikini Car Wash Company '90
Black Eagle '88
The Boys '97
Bram Stoker's Shadowbuilder '98
China O'Brien '88
The Confession '98
Crazy Six '98
Cyber-Tracker '93
The First 9 1/2 Weeks '98
I'm Losing You '98
Kiss Shot '89
Lady Dragon '92
Legionnaire '98
Mikey '92
Milo '98
Modern Vampires '98
Money Kings '98
A Murder of Crows '99
Nemesis '93
New Rose Hotel '98
Paranoia '98
Point Blank '98
Postmortem '98
Prisoner of Love '99
Progeny '98
Protector '97
Route 9 '98
Sanctuary '98
Secret Games '92
Shelter '98
Sink or Swim '97
Southie '98
Space Truckers '97
Supreme Sanction '99
Urban Menace '99
Victim of Love '91
The Wicked, Wicked West '97

SUNLAND STUDIOS
9450 Chivers Ave.
Sun Valley, CA 91352
(818)504-6332
800-934-2111
Fax: (818)504-6380
Extramarital '98
I've Been Waiting for You '98
Just a Little Harmless Sex '99
No Strings Attached '98
Outlaw Justice '98
When Justice Fails '98

SYNAPSE
PO Box 1860
Bloomington, IL 61701
(309)661-9201
Fax: (309)661-9140
www.synapse-films.com
Dario Argento's World of Horror '85

TAI SENG VIDEO MARKETING
170 S. Spruce Ave., Ste. 200
South San Francisco, CA 94080

(415)871-8118
800-888-3836
Fax: (415)871-2392
www.taiseng.com
All About Ah Long '89
Angel Heart '95
Armageddon '97
Beauty Investigator '93
A Better Tomorrow, Part 1 '86
A Better Tomorrow, Part 2 '88
Big Bullet '96
Black Cat '91
The Bride with White Hair '93
The Bride with White Hair 2 '93
Buddhist Fist '80
A Bullet in the Head '90
Center Stage '91
C'est la Vie, Mon Cherie '93
A Chinese Ghost Story '87
A Chinese Ghost Story II '90
A Chinese Ghost Story III '91
Chinese Odyssey, Part One: Pandora's Box '94
Chinese Odyssey, Part Two: Cinderalla '94
City Hunter '92
City on Fire '87
City War '89
The Conman '98
Crystal Hunt '92
Deadful Melody '92
The Descendant of Wing Chun '78
Dragon from Shaolin '96
Dragons Forever '88
Dragons of the Orient '88
Dream Lovers '86
Eastern Condors '87
Erotic Ghost Story '90
Erotic Ghost Story: Perfect Match '97
The Executioners '93
Expect the Unexpected '98
First Option '96
Fong Sai Yuk '93
Fractured Follies '88
The Fruit Is Swelling '97
Full Contact '92
Full Throttle '96
Girls Unbuttoned '93
God.com '99
God of Cookery '96
God of Gamblers '89
God of Gambler's Return '94
The Great Conqueror's Concubine '94
The Great Conqueror's Concubine, Part 2 '94
Heart of Dragon '85
A Hero Never Dies '98
The Heroic Trio '93
High Risk '95
Hitman '98
Hong Kong 1941 '84
Hot War '98
I Love Maria '88
In the Line of Duty 3 '88
In the Line of Duty 4 '89
In the Line of Duty 5 '90
Inspector Wears Skirts '88
Iron Monkey '93
Island of Greed '97
Jackie Chan: My Story '97
Jackie Chan: My Stunts '98
Jet Li's The Enforcer '95
Killer's Romance '90
King of Beggars '92
Lawyer Lawyer '97
Lee Rock '91
Legacy of Rage '86
Legend of the Drunken Tiger '92
Long Arm of the Law '84
Long Arm of the Law II '87
The Longest Nite '98
Lover of the Last Empress '95
Magnificent Warriors '87
Mah Jong Dragon '97
Man Wanted '94

The Master '92
The Millionaire's Express '86
Miracles '89
Mr. Vampire '86
The Moon Warriors '92
My Lucky Stars '85
Naked Killer '92
Once a Thief '96
Once Upon a Time in China '91
Once Upon a Time in China II '92
Once Upon a Time in China III '93
Organized Crime & Triad Bureau '93
Peace Hotel '95
Peking Opera Blues '86
Prison on Fire '87
Prison on Fire 2 '91
The Prodigal Son '82
Rouge '87
Royal Tramp '92
Royal Tramp 2 '92
Saviour of the Soul '92
Sex and Zen '93
Shaolin Avengers '94
The Untold Story '93
Wheels on Meals '84
Zu: Warriors of the Magic Mountain '83

TAPEWORM VIDEO DISTRIBUTORS
27833 Hopkins Ave., Unit 6
Valencia, CA 91355
(805)257-4904
Fax: (805)257-4820
www.tapeworm.com
The Firing Line '91
Lovers and Liars '81
Mesmerized '84
Monsoon '97
Red Surf '90
Who Shot Pat? '92
Zig Zag '99

TRIMARK HOME VIDEO
4553 Glencoe Ave.
Marina Del Rey, CA 94292
(310)314-2000
Fax: (310)392-0252
www.trimarkpictures.com
All of Me '84
Another Day in Paradise '98
Another 9 1/2 Weeks '96
Atomic Train '99
The Best of Times '86
Better Than Chocolate '99
The Big Easy '87
Billy's Hollywood Screen Kiss '98
Black Robe '91
Blood and Sand '89
The Blood Oranges '97
Blue Juice '95
Box of Moonlight '96
Capone '89
Carnival of Souls '98
Chairman of the Board '97
Chinese Box '97
The Colony '98
Creator '85
Crossworlds '96
Cube '98
The Curve '97
Dead Alive '93
Deadfall '93
Dean Koontz's Mr. Murder '98
Death Wish 5: The Face of Death '94
The Dentist '96
The Dentist 2: Brace Yourself '98
The Eternal '99
Eve's Bayou '97
Evolver '94
Extreme Justice '93
Family of Cops '95
Flashfire '94
Frank and Jesse '94

Going Overboard '89
Ground Control '98
Happiness '98
Hide and Seek '00
Interceptor '92
Iron Eagle 4 '95
Joe the King '99
Kama Sutra: A Tale of Love '96
A Kid in Aladdin's Palace '97
Kids '97
King Cobra '98
La Femme Nikita '91
The Landlady '98
The Last Don '97
The Last Word '95
Lawn Dogs '96
Leprechaun '93
Leprechaun 2 '94
Love and a.45 '94
Lulu on the Bridge '98
Mean Guns '97
Meet Wally Sparks '97
My Teacher's Wife '95
Night of the Warrior '91
No Mercy '86
An Occasional Hell '96
Phoenix '98
Rent-A-Cop '88
Romance '98
The Sex Monster '99
The Shadow Riders '82
Shark Attack '99
The '60s '99
Slam '98
Solar Crisis '92
Sometimes They Come Back '91
Sometimes They Come Back... Again '96
Sometimes They Come Back... For More '95
Sprung '96
Stephen King's The Storm of the Century '99
Stephen King's The Tommy-knockers '93
Swimming with Sharks '94
Tactical Assault '99
Tail Lights Fade '99
Tom Clancy's Netforce '98
Treehouse Hostage '99
Trucks '97
True Crime '95
Twice upon a Yesterday '98
The Ugly '96
Underworld '96
The War Room '93
Warlock '91
Warlock: The Armageddon '93
Warlock 3: The End of Innocence '98

TROMA TEAM VIDEO
733 9th Ave.
New York, NY 10019
(212)957-5678
800-83-TROMA
Fax: (212)957-4497
www.troma.com

Troma is also distributing titles found under the Roan Group (see separate listing).

Beware! Children at Play '85
Bloodsucking Freaks '75
The Chosen One: Legend of the Raven '98
Class of Nuke 'Em High '86
Combat Shock '84
Cry Uncle '71
Def by Temptation '90
Girls School Screamers '86
Igor & the Lunatics '85
Killer Condom '95
Monster in the Closet '86
A Nymphoid Barbarian in Dinosaur Hell '94
Rabid Grannies '89
Sgt. Kabukiman N.Y.P.D. '94
Sizzle Beach U.S.A. '74

Sucker the Vampire '98
Surf Nazis Must Die (DC) '87
The Toxic Avenger (DC) '86
The Toxic Avenger, Part 2 '89
Troma's War (DC) '88
Tromeo & Juliet '95

TWENTIETH CENTURY FOX HOME ENTERTAINMENT
PO Box 900
Beverly Hills, CA 90213
(310)369-3900
888-223-4FOX
Fax: (310)369-5811
www.foxhome.com/dvd
The Abyss (SE) '89
Alien '79
Aliens (SE) '86
Alien3 '92
All About Eve '50
Anastasia '97
Anywhere But Here '99
Bartok the Magnificent '99
Best Laid Plans '99
Big '88
Boys Don't Cry '99
Broadcast News '87
Brokedown Palace '99
Broken Arrow '95
Bulworth '98
Butch Cassidy and the Sundance Kid '69
Carousel '56
Chinese Connection '73
A Christmas Carol '84
Commando '85
The Commitments '91
Cousin Bette '97
Die Hard '88
Die Hard 2: Die Harder '90
Die Hard: With a Vengeance '95
Dr. Dolittle '98
The Edge '97
Entrapment '99
Ever After: A Cinderella Story '98
Fight Club '99
Firestorm '97
Fists of Fury '73
French Kiss '95
The Full Monty '96
Full Moon in Paris '84
Gentleman's Agreement '47
Great Expectations '97
History of the World: Part 1 '81
Home Alone '90
Home Alone 2: Lost in New York '92
Home Alone 3 '97
Hope Floats '98
How Stella Got Her Groove Back '98
How the West Was Won '63
The Imposters '98
Independence Day '96
Jingle All the Way '96
The King and I '56
Lake Placid '99
A Life Less Ordinary '97
The Longest Day '62
Marked for Death '90
Miracle on 34th Street '47
Mrs. Doubtfire '93
Never Been Kissed '99
The Newton Boys '97
Office Space '98
Oklahoma '55
Patton '70
Picture Perfect '96
Polish Wedding '97
Porky's '82
The Poseidon Adventure '72
Predator '87
Pushing Tin '99
Ravenous '99
Return of the Dragon '73
Rising Sun '93
Shooting Fish '98
The Siege '98

Simply Irresistible '99
Slums of Beverly Hills '98
Soul Food '97
South Pacific '58
Speed '94
Speed 2: Cruise Control '97
State Fair '45
Strange Days '95
There's Something about Mary '98
The Thin Red Line '98
Tora! Tora! Tora! '70
The Towering Inferno '74
True Lies '94
Volcano '97
Waking Ned Devine '98
Wallace & Gromit: The First Three Adventures '99
William Shakespeare's A Midsummer Night's Dream '99
William Shakespeare's Romeo and Juliet '96
Wing Commander '99
The X-Files '98
Yellow Submarine '68
Young Frankenstein '74

UAV ENTERTAINMENT
2200 Carolina Pl.
Fort Mill, SC 29708
(803)548-7300
800-486-6782
Fax: (803)548-3335
www.uavco.com
Baker's Hawk '76
Invaders from Mars '53
Royal Wedding '51
Where the Red Fern Grows '74
Where the Red Fern Grows: Part 2 '92

UNIVERSAL STUDIOS HOME VIDEO
100 Universal City Plz.
Universal City, CA 91608-9955
(818)777-1000
Fax: (818)866-1483
www.universalstudios.com
Affliction '97
All Quiet on the Western Front '30
Always '89
American Graffiti '73
American Pie (CE) '99
Apollo 13 '95
The Apostle '97
Army of Darkness '92
Babe '95
Babe: Pig in the City '98
Backdraft '91
BASEketball '98
*batteries not included '87
Battlestar Galactica '78
Beethoven '92
Beethoven's 2nd '93
The Beguiled '70
The Best Man '99
Billy Madison '94
Bird on a Wire '90
The Birds '63
Black Dog '98
Blood, Guts, Bullets and Octane '99
The Blues Brothers (CE) '80
The Blues Brothers 2000 '98
The Bone Collector '99
Born on the Fourth of July '89
Bowfinger '99
The Boxer '97
Brazil '85
The Breakfast Club '85
Bride of Chucky '98
The Bride of Frankenstein '35
Buffalo 66 '97
Bulletproof '96
The 'Burbs '89
Career Opportunities '91
Carlito's Way '93
Casino '95

The Chamber '96
Clockers '95
Conan the Barbarian '82
Conan the Destroyer '84
Cop and a Half '93
The Cowboy Way '94
Crooklyn '94
Cry Freedom '87
Dante's Peak '97
Darkman '90
Darkman 2: The Return of Durant '94
The Day of the Jackal '73
Daylight '96
Dazed and Confused '93
Death Becomes Her '92
The Deer Hunter '78
Do the Right Thing '89
Dragnet '87
Dragon: The Bruce Lee Story '93
Dragonheart (SE) '96
DROP Squad '94
Dudley Do-Right '99
Dune '84
EDtv '99
The Eiger Sanction '75
End of Days '99
Far and Away '92
Fear '96
Fear and Loathing in Las Vegas '98
Fierce Creatures '96
Fletch '85
The Flintstones (CE) '94
For Richer or Poorer '97
For Whom the Bell Tolls '43
Frankenstein '31
Fried Green Tomatoes '91
The Frighteners '96
The Getaway '93
Gods and Monsters '98
Going My Way / Holiday Inn '44
Gorillas in the Mist '88
Grace of My Heart (CE) '96
The Great Outdoors '88
Greedy '94
Half-Baked '97
Happy Gilmore '96
Hard Target '99
The Hard Way '91
Havana '90
Heart and Souls '93
Hellfighters '68
Henry & June '90
High Plains Drifter '73
The Hindenburg '75
Horse Feathers '32
How to Make an American Quilt '95
The Hunted '94
I'm No Angel '33
In the Name of the Father '93
The Jackal (CE) '97
The Jerk '79
Jesus Christ, Superstar '73
Joe Kidd '72
Jungle Fever '91
Junior '94
K-9 '89
Kindergarten Cop '90
Kissing a Fool '98
Kull the Conqueror '97
La Traviata '82
The Land Before Time '88
Last Night '98
The Last Starfighter '84
Leave It to Beaver '97
Liar Liar '96
Life '99
Lionheart '90
The Little Rascals '94
The Lonely Guy '84
Love and Death on Long Island '97
Madigan '68
Major Payne '95
Mallrats '95
Man on the Moon '99
Meet Joe Black '98

Mercury Rising '98
Metroland '97
Mister Johnson '91
The Mummy '32
The Mummy '99
Mystery Men '99
National Lampoon's Animal House '78
1941 '79
Notting Hill '99
The Nutty Professor '96
October Sky '99
One True Thing '98
Out of Sight '98
The Paper '94
Parenthood '89
Patch Adams (CE) '98
Pillow Talk '59
Primary Colors '98
Psycho (CE) '60
Psycho '98
The Quest '96
Raising Cain '92
The Real McCoy '93
Reality Bites '94
The Red Violin '98
The River '84
The River Wild '94
Rollercoaster '77
Rooster Cogburn '75
Rumble Fish '83
Scarface '83
Scent of a Woman '92
Sea of Love '89
The Secret of Anastasia '97
The Secret of My Success '87
Sgt. Bilko '95
The Shadow '94
Shattered Image '98
Shocker '89
A Simple Wish '97
Slap Shot '77
Smokey and the Bandit '77
Sneakers '92
Somewhere in Time '80
Sorcerer '77
Spartacus '60
The Sting '73
The Story of Us '99
Street Fighter '94
Streets of Fire '84
Subway '85
Swashbuckler '76
That Old Feeling '96
The Thing '82
Timecop '94
To Kill a Mockingbird '62
Tremors '89
Tremors 2: Aftershocks '96
The Trigger Effect '96
12 Monkeys '95
Twins '88
Two Minute Warning '76
Uncle Buck '89
The Underneath '95
Vertigo (CE) '58
Videodrome '83
Village of the Damned '95
Virus '98
The War '94
The War Wagon '67
Waterworld '95
Winning '69
The Wiz '78
The Wolf Man '41
Xanadu '80

USA HOME ENTERTAINMENT
1 W. Forest
Inglewood, NJ 07631
(201)871-1000
800-825-7781
The Adventures of Priscilla, Queen of the Desert '94
Barb Wire '96
Barney's Great Adventure '98
Bat 21 '88
Bean '97
Being John Malkovich '99
The Big Lebowski '97

The Borrowers '97
Cats '98
Clay Pigeons '98
Cookie's Fortune '99
Def Jam's How to Be a Player '97
Dream Lover '93
Elizabeth '98
Hilary and Jackie '98
Keys to Tulsa '96
Lock, Stock and 2 Smoking Barrels '98
The Matchmaker '97
The Muse '99
Needful Things '93
Panther '95
Portrait of a Lady '96
Posse '93
The Princess Bride '87
Shallow Grave '94
Very Bad Things '98
What Dreams May Come '98
Your Friends & Neighbors '98

VANGUARD INTERNATIONAL CINEMA, INC.
15061 Springdale St., Ste. 109
Huntington Beach, CA 92649
(714)901-9000
Fax: (714)901-9070
Animal Room '95
The Climb '97
Thesis '96

VCI HOME VIDEO
11333 E. 60th Pl.
Tulsa, OK 74146
(918)254-6337
800-331-4077
Fax: (918)254-6117
And Then There Were None '45
The Bird with the Crystal Plumage '70
Children Shouldn't Play with Dead Things '72
A Christmas Carol '51
Dark Star '74
Devil's Rain '75
Don't Look in the Basement '73
Gargoyles '72
Kill, Baby, Kill '66
Quackser Fortune Has a Cousin in the Bronx '70
The Southerner '45

VICTORY MULTIMEDIA
222 N. Sepulveda Blvd., Ste. 1306
El Segundo, CA 90245
(310)416-9140
Fax: (310)416-9839
Rebel Rousers '69

VIDEO SOUND
554 Bloomfield Ave., 2nd Fl.
Bloomfield, NJ 07003
(973)743-4701
Fax: (973)743-0763
Hum Dil De Chuke Sanam '99
Khamoshi the Musical '96
Koyla '94
Pyaar Kiya to Darna Kya '98
Pyar to Hona Hi Tah '98
Thakshak '99
Virasat '97
Yes Boss! '97

VIDEO WATCHDOG
PO Box 5283
Cincinnati, OH 45205-0283
(513)471-8989
800-275-8395
Fax: (513)471-8248
Rabid Dogs '74

VISTA STREET ENTERTAINMENT
9831 W. Pico Blvd., Ste. 4
Los Angeles, CA 90035

(310)556-3074
Fax: (310)556-8815
Leaving Scars '97

WARNER HOME VIDEO, INC.
5775 Linder Canyon Rd.
Westlake Village, CA 91362
(877)277-9272
www.dvdwb.com
Above the Law '88
Absolute Power '97
Ace Ventura: Pet Detective '93
Ace Ventura: When Nature Calls '95
Action Jackson '88
Addicted to Love '96
All the President's Men '76
Altered States '80
Amadeus '84
The American President '95
Analyze This '98
Arthur '81
Assassins '95
The Avengers '98
Badlands '74
Barry Lyndon '75
Batman '89
Batman and Robin '97
Batman Forever '95
Batman Returns '92
Beetlejuice '88
Before Sunrise '94
The Betsy '78
The Big Red One '80
The Big Sleep '46
Billy Jack '71
Blade Runner (DC) '82
Blazing Saddles '74
Body Heat '81
Body Snatchers '93
The Bodyguard '92
Boiling Point '93
The Bonfire of the Vanities '90
Bonnie & Clyde '67
Boys on the Side '94
Brainstorm '83
The Bridges of Madison County '95
Bullitt '68
Burglar '87
Cabaret '72
Caddyshack '80
Caddyshack 2 '88
Camelot '67
The Candidate '72
Cannonball Run 2 '84
Casablanca '42
Chariots of Fire '81
City Hall '96
City of Angels '98
The Clan of the Cave Bear '86
Clean and Sober '88
Cleopatra Jones '73
The Client '94
A Clockwork Orange '71
Cobra '86
The Color Purple '85
Coma '78
Conspiracy Theory '97
Contact '97
Cool Hand Luke '67
Copycat '95
The Cowboys '72
Creepshow '82
Dangerous Beauty '98
Dangerous Liaisons '88
Dave '93
Dead Bang '89
Dead Calm '89
Deathtrap '82
Deep Blue Sea '99
Deliverance '72
Demolition Man '93
The Devil's Advocate '97
Dirty Harry '71
Disclosure '94
Divine Madness '80
Doc Hollywood '91

Dog Day Afternoon '75
Dolores Claiborne '94
Driving Miss Daisy '89
Enter the Dragon (SE) '73
Eraser '96
Excalibur '81
Executive Decision '96
The Exorcist (SE) '73
Eyes Wide Shut '99
Fair Game '95
Fallen '97
Falling Down '93
Father's Day '96
Fearless '93
Final Analysis '92
Fire Down Below '97
The First Deadly Sin '80
Forever Young '92
Frantic '88
Free Willy '93
The Fugitive '93
Full Metal Jacket '87
Funny Farm '88
The Gauntlet '77
George Balanchine's The Nutcracker '93
The Getaway '72
The Glimmer Man '96
Goodbye, Lover '99
Goodfellas '90
The Great Santini '80
The Green Berets '68
The Green Mile '99
Gremlins '84
Grumpier Old Men '95
Grumpy Old Men '93
Guilty by Suspicion '91
Hard to Kill '89
Heat '95
Her Alibi '88
Home Fries '98
Hooper '78
House on Haunted Hill '58
House on Haunted Hill '99
The Hudsucker Proxy '93
The Hunchback of Notre Dame '39
In Country '89
Incognito '97
Innocent Blood '92
Interview with the Vampire '94
Iron Giant '99
Jack Frost '98
Jeremiah Johnson '72
JFK '91
Joe's Apartment '96
Just Cause '94
The King and I '99
L.A. Confidential '97
Ladyhawke '85
The Last Boy Scout '91
Lean on Me '89
Lethal Weapon '87
Lethal Weapon 2 '89
Lethal Weapon 3 '92
Lethal Weapon 4 '98
A Little Princess '95
Little Shop of Horrors '86
Lolita '62
Lost and Found '99
The Lost Boys '87
Lovesick '83
Mad City '97
Mad Max: Beyond Thunderdome '85
Made in America '93
The Man Who Knew Too Little '97
The Man Who Would Be King '75
The Man with Two Brains '83
Mars Attacks! '96
The Matrix '99
Maverick '94
Mean Streets '73
Memphis Belle '90
Message in a Bottle '98
Michael '96
Michael Collins '96

Midnight in the Garden of Good and Evil (SE) '97
Mister Roberts '55
Mr. Wonderful '93
Murder at 1600 '97
The Music Man '62
My Blue Heaven '90
My Fair Lady '64
My Fellow Americans '96
My Giant '98
National Lampoon's Christmas Vacation '89
National Lampoon's Vacation '83
The Negotiator '98
New Jack City '91
Next of Kin '89
Night Shift '82
Nothing but Trouble '91
On Deadly Ground '94
One Flew Over the Cuckoo's Nest '75
Out for Justice '91
Outbreak '94
Outland '81
The Outlaw Josey Wales '76
The Outsiders '83
The Pajama Game '57
Pale Rider '85
Palmetto '98
Papillon '73
Pee-wee's Big Adventure '85
The Pelican Brief '93
A Perfect Murder '98
Point of No Return '93
Police Academy '84
The Postman '97
The Postman Always Rings Twice '81
The Power of One '92
Practical Magic '98
Presumed Innocent '90
Private Benjamin '80
Protocol '84
Pure Country '92
Purple Rain '84
Quest for Camelot '98
Rebel without a Cause '55
The Right Stuff '83
Risky Business '83
The Road Warrior '82
Robin Hood: Prince of Thieves '91
Rosewood '96
Running on Empty '88
Salem's Lot '79
Sea Wolves '81
The Searchers '56
The Secret Garden '93
Selena '96
Shaft '71
Sharky's Machine '81
The Shawshank Redemption '94
The Shining '80
Short 1: Invention
Short 2: Dreams
Show Boat '51
Showdown in Little Tokyo '91
Singles '92
Sleepers '96
Soldier '98
Sommersby '93
Space Jam '96
The Specialist '94
Sphere '97
Spies Like Us '85
Stagecoach '39
Stand and Deliver '88
Star 80 '83
Stealing Home '88
Strangers on a Train '51
A Streetcar Named Desire '51
Striptease '96
Stroker Ace '83
Tango and Cash '89
Tarzan and the Lost City '98
10 '79
Tequila Sunrise '88
Three Kings '99

Thumbelina '94
A Time to Kill '96
Tin Cup '96
True Romance '93
True Stories '86
Twister '96
2001: A Space Odyssey '68
Under Siege '92
Under Siege 2 '95
Unforgiven '92
U.S. Marshals '98
Vegas Vacation '96
Victory '81
Vision Quest '85
What Ever Happened to Baby Jane? '62
Who's Afraid of Virginia Woolf? '66
Why Do Fools Fall in Love? '98
Wild America '97
The Wild Bunch '69
Wild Wild West '99
Willy Wonka & the Chocolate Factory '71
The Witches '90
The Witches of Eastwick '87
With Honors '94
Without Limits '97
The Wizard of Oz '39
Woodstock (DC) '70
Wrongfully Accused '98
You've Got Mail '98
Zero Effect '97

WATER BEARER FILMS
48 W. 21st St., No. 301
New York, NY 10010
(212)242-8686
800-551-8304
Fax: (212)242-4560
www.waterbearer.com
Mandragora '97
Sex Is . . . '93
To Play or To Die '91
A Very Natural Thing '73

WAVELENGTH RELEASING/VENTURA DISTRIBUTION
Address unknown
The Last Broadcast '98

WINSTAR HOME ENTERTAINMENT
419 Park Ave. S., 20th Fl.
New York, NY 10016
(212)686-6777
Fax: (212)686-0387
www.winstarhomevideo.com
Antonia's Line '95
Bastard out of Carolina '96
Beau Pere '81
Bed and Board '70
The Big Squeeze '96
Black Rain '88
Boston Kickout '95
Boyfriends & Girlfriends '88
Breaker Morant '80
A Brother's Kiss '97
Cartoon Crazys '97
Cartoon Crazys 2 '98
Cartoon Crazys: And the Envelope, Please '99
Cartoon Crazys Christmas '98
Cartoon Crazys Goes to War '98
Cartoon Crazys: Kids All-Time Favorites '99
Cartoon Crazys Sci-Fi '99
Chloe in the Afternoon '72
Claire's Knee '71
Confidentially Yours '83
Desolation Angels '95
Digging to China '98
The Draughtsman's Contract '82
Drunks '96
Eden '98
Elvira Madigan '67
Emmanuelle '74
Emmanuelle, the Joys of a Woman '76
The Emperor's Shadow '96

Entre-Nous '83
First Name: Carmen '83
Fist of the North Star '95
The 400 Blows (WinStar Edition) '59
The Four Musketeers '75
Frozen '98
The Funeral '84
Funny Games '97
Gray's Anatomy '96
Gulliver's Travels '39
Habit '97
Hawaiian Rainbow '87
Horton Foote's Alone '97
Hugo Pool '97
In the Realm of Passion '80
Infinity '96
Intermezzo '36
June Night '40
Just Write '97
Kuma Hula: Keepers of the Culture '89
La Collectionneuse '67
La Sentinelle '92
La Separation '98
The Last Metro '80
Le Beau Mariage '82
The Leading Man '96
L'Enfer '93
Leonard Bernstein: Reaching for the Note '98
The Life of Jesus '96
Lotto Land '95
Love After Love '94
Love and Anarchy '73
Lumiere and Company '96
Ma Saison Preferee '93
Man of the Year '95
Midaq Alley '95
Mrs. Dalloway '97
Mumia: A Case for Reasonable Doubt? '96
My Dinner with Andre '81
My Life to Live '62
My Night at Maud's '69
On the Ropes '99

One Hundred and One Nights '94
The Pompatus of Love '95
Ponette '95
Pretty Village, Pretty Flame '96
The Quarrel '93
Red Cherry '95
The Return of Martin Guerre '83
Rock 'n' Roll Invaders: The AM Radio DJs
The Sci-Fi Files '97
Seduction of Mimi '72
70 Years of Popeye '00
Shameless '94
Shoot the Piano Player '62
The Soft Skin '64
Stolen Kisses '68
Stonewall '95
Summer '86
Superman, the Lost Episodes '99
Telling Lies in America '96
Ten Benny '98
36 Fillete '88
The Three Musketeers '74
Trial & Error '62
Two English Girls '72
Umbrellas of Cherbourg '64
Un Air de Famille '96
Union City '81
The Unknown Marx Brothers '93
Wild Reeds '94
The Woman Next Door '81
A Zed & Two Noughts '88

WOLFE VIDEO
PO Box 64
New Almaden, CA 95042
(408)268-6782
800-438-9653
Fax: (408)268-9449
www.wolfevideo.com
Finding North '97
Lilies '96

WORLD WRESTLING FEDERATION
1241 E. Main St.
Stamford, CT 06902
(203)352-8600
The Rock: The People's Champ

XENON ENTERTAINMENT
1440 9th St.
Santa Monica, CA 90401
(310)451-5510
800-829-1913
Fax: (310)395-4058
www.xenonentertainment.com
Avenging Disco Godfather '76
Dolemite '75
Ill-Gotten Gains '97
Klash '95
Penitentiary '79
Penitentiary 2 '82
Q: The Movie '99

YORK ENTERTAINMENT
16133 Ventura Blvd., Ste. 1140
Encino, CA 91436
(818)788-4050
800-84-MOVIE
Fax: (818)788-4011
www.yorkentertainment.com
An American Affair '99
Angel's Dance '99
Convict 762 '98
Diamondbacks '99
Forgotten City '99
Highway Hitcher '98
Johnny 2.0 '99
Laserhawk '99
New World Disorder '99
Random Encounter '98
Spoiler '98
Total Reality '97
Wanted '98